Do you wonder what teaching will be like in the future?

ClassZone

www.mcdougallittell.com

Unlock the world of new ideas through ClassZone

ClassZone, McDougal Littell's companion website, is your classroom's online guide to *The Language of Literature*.

Access *The Language of Literature* ClassZone site to find:

- Links correlated to the textbook for relevant Internet exploration
- Self-scoring quizzes for students to check understanding of concepts
- Internet research tutorial to help students conduct research on the web
- Teacher center for classroom ideas (accessible to teachers only)

Log on to ClassZone at www.mcdougallittell.com

With the purchase of *The Language of Literature*, you have immediate access to ClassZone.

Teacher Key: MCDKLMLHLPIHU
The teacher key provides access to teacher-specific content.

Student Key: MCDB7CIJVTGHL
The student key provides access for students to build knowledge, practice skills and explore the Internet.

McDougal Littell
A HOUGHTON MIFFLIN COMPANY

www.mcdougallittell.com

McDougal Littell

THE LANGUAGE OF
LITERATURE

TEXAS TEACHER'S EDITION

Grade 7

McDougal Littell
A HOUGHTON MIFFLIN COMPANY
Evanston, Illinois • Boston • Dallas

TEXAS ADVISORS AND REVIEWERS

Texas Contributing Consultant

Sharon Sicinski-Skeans, *Ph. D.* Assistant Professor of Reading, University of Houston-Clear Lake

Texas Teacher Review Panel

The following educators provided ongoing review during the development of the tables of contents, lesson design, and key components of the program.

Gwen Ferguson, Assistant Principal, Northwood Middle School, North Forest Independent School District

Rebecca Hadavi, Parkland Middle School, Ysleta Independent School District

Patricia Jackson, Pearce Middle School, Austin Independent School District

Sandy Mattox, Coppell Middle School North, Coppell Independent School District

Adrienne C. Myers, Foster Middle School, Longview Independent School District

Pam Potts, Clute Intermediate School, Brazosport Independent School District

Frank Westermann, Jackson Middle School, North East Independent School District

Bessie B. Wilson, W. E. Greiner Middle School, Dallas Independent School District

Texas Program Reviewers

The following educators reviewed prototype lessons during the conceptualization of *The Language of Literature* program.

David Adcox, Trinity High School, Euless

Anita Arnold, Thomas Jefferson High School, San Antonio

Cassandra L. Asberry, Justin F. Kimball High School, Dallas

Jolene Auderer, Pine Tree High School, Longview

Rose Mary Bolden, Justin F. Kimball High School, Dallas

Angela Boyd, Andrews High School, Andrews

Hugh Delle Broadway, McCullough High School, The Woodlands

Ricardo Godoy, English Department Chairperson, Moody High School, Corpus Christi

Meredith Gunn, Secondary Language Arts Instructional Specialist, Katy

Linda Maxwell, MacArthur High School, Houston

Rebecca Miller, Taft High School, San Antonio

Cindy Rogers, MacArthur High School, Houston

Pauline Sahakian, English Department Chairperson, San Marcos High School, San Marcos

Jacqueline Y. Schmidt, Department Chairperson and Coordinator of English, San Marcos High School, San Marcos

Milinda Schwab, Judson High School, Converse

GayleAnn Turnage, Abilene High School, Abilene

ISBN 0-395-93192-4

3 4 5 6 7 8 9 – DWO – 06 05 04 03 02 01

Contents of the Texas Teacher's Edition

Using the Texas Teacher's Edition

This Texas Teacher's Edition provides the information you need to coordinate your teaching with Texas curriculum guidelines and assessments. Special Texas Resources will help you meet state requirements. Complete information about how *The Language of Literature* meets the requirements of Texas Essential Knowledge and Skills (TEKS) and Texas Assessment of Academic Skills (TAAS) will help you select materials to meet your teaching goals.

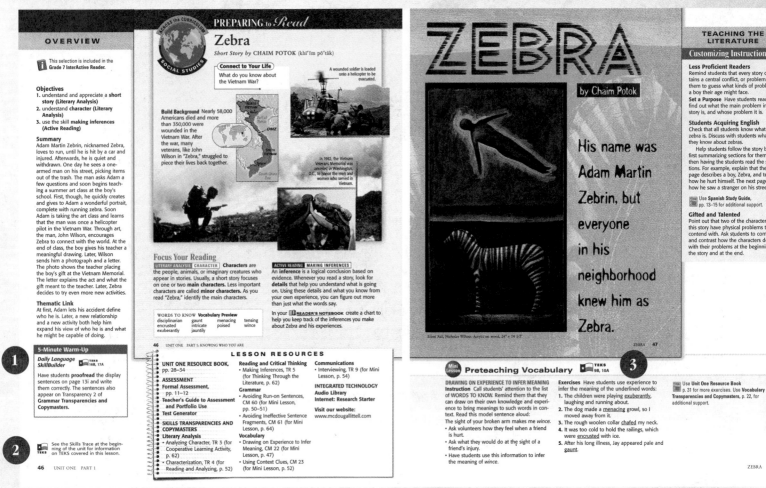

1 Each selection begins with a 5-minute warm-up activity that is based on one or more of the TEKS and/or TAAS objectives. These Daily Language SkillBuilders are also on transparencies in the *Grammar Transparencies and Copymasters* ancillary.

2 This reference will help you find the Skills Trace that lists the major TEKS and TAAS objectives met in this selection.

3 This reference lets you know which TEKS and/or TAAS objectives are met by this mini lesson. Other mini lessons include Grammar, Spelling, Speaking and Listening, Viewing and Representing, Standardized Test Practice, and Informal Assessment.

4 The *Spanish Study Guide* provides access for Spanish-speaking students with the following materials in Spanish: Selection Summary, Family and Community Involvement, Literary Analysis SkillBuilder, Active Reading SkillBuilder, SAE vocabulary activities and cultural information, and one selection per unit in Spanish.

UNIT ONE
PART 1 SKILLS TRACE

Features and Selections	Literary Analysis	TEKS	Reading and Critical Thinking	TEKS	Writing Opportunities	TEKS	Speaking and Listening Viewing and Representing	TEKS	Inquiry and Research
Learning from Experience Knowing Who You Are							Art Appreciation, 12	22A	
Learning the Language of Literature Fiction	Fiction, 15 TAAS READING OBJ. 2, 5	10H,12A, B, F, G							
The Active Reader Skills and Strategies			Reading Fiction, 19 TAAS READING OBJ. 4	10A, B, C, D, M, 11A					
SHORT STORY Seventh Grade Difficulty Level: *Easy*	Setting, 20, 22, 24, 26 Dialect, 26 TAAS READING OBJ. 2, 5	12G 14B, C	Connecting, 20, 22, 24, 26 Test Practice, 25 TAAS READING OBJ. 3, 4	10A, 11A, 14C 10G, K	Write a Letter, 27 Profile of Victor, 27 OBJ. 1	11B 11B, 10L, 15C	Magazine Ad, 27 Comedy Sketch, 27 Art Connection, 27	23D, 24A 5C, E, 11B, 15D 22A, 23A, B	Mexican Americans, 27
	Conflict, 29, 30, 32, 34	12G	Cause and Effect, Connect...			18A	Paired Activit... Film Re...		...Harlem, 35

The Skills Trace indicates major TEKS and TAAS objectives met in each selection and feature of *The Language of Literature.*

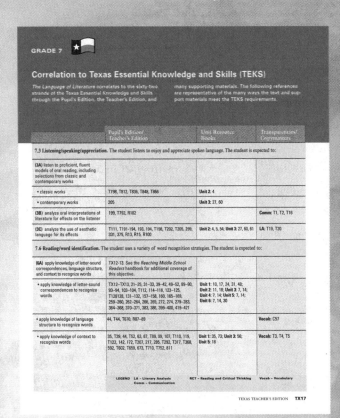

TEKS Correlations (pages TX17–TX29)

A 12-page chart provides a detailed correlation of *The Language of Literature* with Texas Essential Knowledge and Skills (TEKS) objectives. This correlation provides specific page references to the Pupil's Edition, Teacher's Edition, Unit Resource Books, and Skills Transparencies and Copymasters.

TAAS Correlation (pages TX14–TX16)

An easy-to-read chart provides a detailed correlation of the Texas Assessment of Academic Skills (TAAS) objectives with *The Language of Literature.* Specific page references are given to *The Language of Literature* where you will find lessons, activities, and mini lessons that will help students master the objective.

Professional Development and Appraisal System (pages TX30–TX32)

The Language of Literature supports teachers who participate in the Professional Development and Appraisal System. This chart shows how the program supports the domains and evaluation dimensions.

Additional Texas Teaching Resources

Professional Development and Planning Guide

This booklet will help you coordinate your teaching of *The Language of Literature* with Texas curriculum guidelines.

Contents include:

Lesson Plans

A detailed lesson plan is included for each major selection, Writing Workshop, and Communication Workshop in the Pupil's Edition. Each lesson plan includes:

- TEKS and TAAS objectives
- Suggestions for instruction, activities, and homework
- Teaching plans for both Regular and Block Scheduling
- Strategies for closure, assessment, and reteaching

Professional Development and Appraisal System

This section of the Planning Guide includes:

- Background information on the PDAS
- Description of the PDAS domains along with the levels of proficiency
- Chart showing features of *The Language of Literature* components that will help you address the different domains defined by PDAS
- Chart containing references to reading and writing instruction

Texas Test Preparation

A combination of student workbooks and copymasters provides skills practice and test practice to help you prepare students for Texas Assessment. **TAAS** practice is available for grades 6–8.

Each grade level includes:

- Student workbook for skills practice
- Copymasters for test practice
- Teacher's Edition with answer keys

Texas Test Generator

The Test Generator allows you to make up your own tests. You may choose questions from selection tests, part tests, and selection quizzes as well as from a bank of additional questions that were created specifically for the Test Generator. All questions are coded to specific TAAS and TEKS objectives.

Spanish Resources

The Language of Literature includes many resources for Spanish-speaking students who are acquiring English.

Spanish Study Guide

This guide includes the following pages in Spanish: Selection Summaries, Family and Community Involvement, Literary Analysis SkillBuilders, Active Reading SkillBuilders, SAE vocabulary activities, cultural information, and one selection per unit in Spanish.

Teacher's SourceBook for Language Development

Professional articles provide insights into language and language learners.

Audio Library (available on cassette or CD)

Professional readings of anthology selections make the literature accessible to more students, including students acquiring English.

LaserLinks with Spanish Track

This interactive treasury of full motion video, photographs, and fine art features both English and Spanish soundtracks.

Access for Students Acquiring English
Spanish Study Guide

McDougal Littell

THE LANGUAGE OF
LITERATURE

Family and Community Involvement
Summary and Vocabulary
Active Reading SkillBuilder
Literary Analysis SkillBuilder
Selection Translations
Answer Keys

McDougal Littell

AUDIO LIBRARY

A COLLECTION OF AUDIO CASSETTE TAPES
GRADE 7

THE LANGUAGE OF LITERATURE

McDougal Littell

LASERLINKS

GRADE 7
TEACHER'S SOURCEBOOK

THE LANGUAGE OF LITERATURE

THE LANGUAGE OF LITERATURE
Share Your Passion!

Reaching Middle School Readers

Effective Teaching Strategies

The Language of Literature provides an extensive instructional plan for grades 6 through 8, including systematic and direct instruction in the pupil's edition as well as comprehensive lessons in this teacher's edition. The instruction in *The Language of Literature* will enable the majority of your students to master the skills taught with each selection; however, from time to time you may need to enhance your teaching for students who need more direct instruction in specific skills. For these students, explicit instruction and reciprocal teaching prove highly effective.

Explicit Instruction

Explicit instruction is a three-part process for teaching strategies and skills. First, demonstrate the skill you're teaching for your students. Second, have students practice and apply the skill you just demonstrated. To conclude, offer feedback to students about their application of the skill.

An effective way to use explicit instruction in the classroom is to model the skill. When you model, you demonstrate a way of resolving questions about unfamiliar material by "thinking through" questions out loud, thereby modeling a thought process for your students. Here is an example of how you might model the skill of making inferences by using the passage below.

> *Then, a year ago, racing down Franklin Avenue, he had given himself that push and had begun to turn into an eagle, when a huge rushing shadow appeared in his line of vision, and crashed into him and plunged him into a darkness from which he emerged very, very slowly. . .*

Teacher: I'm not sure what happened to the boy, but I can make inferences by looking for clues in the sentences. Remember, when I make an inference I make a logical guess about something based on the text and my own knowledge or experience. This paragraph says that the boy had "begun to turn into an eagle." Because I read earlier that he is a fast runner, this must mean that he ran so fast it seemed he was flying like an eagle. A "huge rushing shadow" must mean something big, like a truck, was moving quickly. The phrase "appeared in his line of vision" probably means that he wasn't expecting to see it. The shadow "crashed into him and plunged him into a darkness," so perhaps he had an accident with a big truck, and it is taking him a long time to recover.

As the example shows, by modeling your thought process for students you provide a clear example of how they can learn and understand the skills they find most challenging.

Reciprocal Teaching

Reciprocal teaching is a technique in which the responsibility of asking comprehension questions is shared by you and your students. To use this technique, first teach students these four basic reciprocal teaching strategies:

•**question gathering** Students identify important information in the content, form questions about the content, and address their questions to peers.

•**summarizing** Students summarize the most important information in a specific passage.

•**clarifying** Students identify problems the passage presents, such as difficulty with vocabulary or comprehension.
•**predicting** Students rely on prior knowledge and information already presented to predict what the author will discuss in subsequent paragraphs.

Model for your students how good readers employ each strategy. Then appoint a student to share in the question-asking. Below is a sample paragraph followed by example dialogue in which you have selected Student 1 to ask questions.

> *More than 35,000 cowboys rode herd along the Texas cattle trails. Although folklore and picture postcards depicted the cowboy as an Anglo-American man, about 25 percent were African Americans and another 12 percent were Mexican vaqueros—cowboys who had worked in Texas since the days before Texas' independence. There were Native American cowboys, too, and a few women.*

Teacher: What questions do you have?

Student 1: Were all cowboys Anglo-American men?

Student 2: No, 25% were African-American.

Student 1: What about the rest?

Student 3: 12% were Mexican.

Student 4: Some were Native Americans and some were women.

Student 2: The rest were Anglo-American men.

Teacher: What is your summary of this passage?

Student 1: From the stories and pictures we see, many people think all cowboys were Anglo-American, but almost 40% were minorities.

Teacher: Does anything need to be clarified?

Student 1: We should clarify *vaqueros*.

Teacher: Is *vaqueros* defined here?

Student 5: Yes, vaqueros were Mexican cowboys who worked in Texas before it was independent.

Teacher: What do you predict the next paragraph will be about?

Student 6: I think the author will talk about Native Americans and women as cowboys and might tell us more about the vaqueros.

Support in *The Language of Literature*
Examples of direct instruction appear in the following program features:

Pupil's Edition
- •Learning the Language of Literature
- •The Active Reader
- •Focus Your Reading and Literary Analysis
- •Building Vocabulary
- •Vocabulary in Action
- •Grammar in Context
- •Real World Links

Teacher's Edition
- •Selection Lessons
- •Selection Mini Lessons
- •Learning the Language of Literature Lessons
- •The Active Reader Lessons
- •Real World Link Lessons

For more information about Effective Teaching Strategies, see the *Reaching Middle School Readers* handbook.

Reaching Middle School Readers

 ## Developing Fluent Readers

As a teacher you play an important role in helping students become fluent readers, readers who can read effortlessly and rapidly without experiencing word identification problems that interfere with comprehension. Readers faced with too many unfamiliar words or complicated sentence structures often put so much effort into figuring out individual words that they are unable to comprehend the text. However, with your guidance, students can select materials that are a good match for their reading abilities. And by reading materials that are accessible, students will increase their familiarity with written language and will gain confidence as readers.

Understanding Reading Levels

Every student reads at a specific level regardless of the grade in which he or she is placed. Reading level in this context involves the relationship between a specific selection or book and a student's reading ability. The reading level will change depending upon the material the student is reading. Listed below are common terms used to describe these levels.

• **independent level** The student reads material in which no more than 1 in 20 words is difficult. The material can be read without teacher involvement and is likely to be material the student would choose to read on his or her own.

• **instructional level** The student reads material in which no more than 2 in 20 words are difficult. The material is most likely found in school and is read with teacher involvement.

• **frustration level** The student reads material in which considerably more than 2 in 20 words are difficult. The student will get little out of reading the material and will require significant teacher involvement.

Identifying Reading Levels

Use the suggestions in the next column to help students find materials that will build fluency and improve reading skills. These suggestions are especially useful when students are looking for material suitable for independent reading.

1. Identify two or more sections of 20 words or more in a selection or book. Have the student read the material silently and then orally. As the student reads aloud, circle the words with which he or she has difficulty, and then use the criteria described above to determine the reading level:
   • 1 in 20 difficult words..................independent level
   • 2 in 20 difficult words..................instructional level
   • more than 2 in 20 words............. frustration level

2. As an alternative, have students do their own informal assessment. Follow the same process as above, but have students note words that are difficult or that interfere with comprehension, and then determine the correct reading level.

Administering an Informal Reading Inventory

Teachers often use an informal reading inventory to place students in the appropriate textbook. You can also use an IRI to help a student find the right books or articles for independent reading. To conduct an IRI, you need at least one 100-word passage from the material in question and 10 comprehension questions about the material. If you want to use several passages, select them randomly from the textbook. You can use the basic steps listed at the top of the next page to administer an informal reading inventory.

1. Have the student read the 100-word passage aloud.
2. As the student reads, note the number of errors he or she makes. Use these criteria for assessing reading levels after oral reading:
   - Fewer than 3 errors: the student can decode the text
   - Between 4 and 9 errors: the student is likely to have difficulty reading the text
   - More than 10 errors: the student is likely to have great difficulty and may need placement in a less demanding reading program
3. Have the student read the passage again, silently.
4. Ask the 10 comprehension questions.
5. Note the number of correct responses.
   - Eight or more: the student should be able to interpret all or most of the selections effectively
   - Five to seven: the student is likely to have difficulty
   - Fewer than five: the student requires individual help
6. Evaluate results from oral and silent reading to decide how good a match the material is for a student's independent or instructional level.

For more specific information about how to administer an informal reading inventory, refer to the *Reaching Middle School Readers* handbook.

Administering a Cloze Test

The cloze procedure is often used to place students in informational texts, but can also be used to match a student's reading level with classroom materials. Here are the basic steps for administering a cloze test:

1. Select a passage of 250–300 words that covers one topic, preferably from the beginning of an article or book.
2. Delete every 5th word in the passage, excluding the opening sentence.
3. Leave a blank for each word deleted. You should have approximately 50 blanks.
4. For each blank, have students generate an appropriate match for the word that has been deleted.
5. Use the following figures to determine reading level:
   - 29 of 50 correct answers...................independent level
   - 22 to 28 of 50 correct answers...........instructional level
   - 21 of 50 correct answers...................frustration level

Below is an example of a cloze test.

When Eleanor was born, her parents had wanted a boy. They were scarcely able _____ hide their disappointment. Later, _____ the arrival of two _____, Elliott and Hall, Eleanor _____ her mother hold the _____ on her lap and _____ stroke their hair, while _____ Eleanor there seemed only _____, distance.

Feeling unwanted, Eleanor _____ shy and withdrawn. She _____ developed many fears. She _____ afraid of the dark, _____ of animals, afraid of _____ children, afraid of being _____, afraid of strangers, afraid _____ people would not like _____. She was a frightened, _____ little girl.

Support in *The Language of Literature*

The Language of Literature provides the range of literature and the foundation of skills your students need to become fluent readers. Program reading materials include:
- a wide variety of literary selections recommended as Easy, Average, and Challenging
- On Your Own selections recommended specifically for independent reading
- Real World Link selections for real world reading
- comprehensive author biographies in program Author Studies
- Literature Connections for reading in extended works

Pupil's Edition
- Vocabulary in Action
- Building Vocabulary

Teacher's Edition
- Preteaching Vocabulary Mini Lessons
- Vocabulary Strategy Mini Lessons

For more information about Developing Fluent Readers, see the *Reaching Middle School Readers* handbook.

Reaching Middle School Readers

Teaching Decoding Strategies

By middle school, your students have had years of instruction in decoding strategies, primarily in phonics, structural analysis, and context clues. Readers are taught these strategies to help them determine the meanings of words unfamiliar in print but known as part of their speaking or receptive vocabulary.

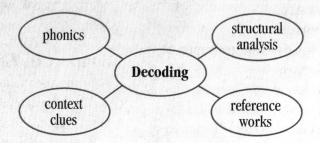

Phonics

Phonics is a system of teaching the basic sound-letter relationships in the English language. Many early-grade educators believe phonics lays the foundation for young readers to understand the relationship between spoken and written words. Instruction is usually coupled with decodable text so that students can apply skills to predictable reading and develop automaticity–the ability to recognize words in text automatically and effortlessly. Students who are good readers use phonics skills automatically in conjunction with other decoding strategies.

In the primary grades, phonics receives the main emphasis as a decoding strategy. As a result, many young students can decode the vast majority of phonetically regular words they read, words that make up about half of the words in the English language. In the intermediate grades and beyond the issue becomes how to decode irregular and multisyllabic words which appear increasingly in reading materials. Regardless of how well your students read, you can help them continue to develop their decoding strategies as they progress through the middle grades.

The chart below shows when phonics instruction occurs.

Phonics	Grade where taught
consonants (initial, medial, final)	through first half grade 2
consonant digrahs (/th/ th, etc.)	through first half grade 2
consonant clusters (*st, bl, br,* etc.)	through grade 2
short vowels	through grade 1
long vowels	through grade 2
r-controlled vowels (*er, ir, ar,* etc.)	through grade 2
diphthongs (*oi, oy,* etc.)	through grade 2
variant vowels (*ough, au, aw,* etc.)	through grade 2

Obviously, a majority of your students have mastered these phonics skills in the early grades; however, if you have students who need help with phonics, use the *Reaching Middle School Readers* handbook, which includes:

- lesson plans for direct instruction in phonics
- suggestions for ways to incorporate phonics instruction into classroom activities

Structural Analysis

Structural analysis is a strategy used to figure out the meaning of multisyllabic words. Students are taught to look for recognizable and meaningful parts, beginning with the root or base word and moving on to prefixes and suffixes. Using knowledge of these parts, the student determines a meaning and attempts to match clues with words already in his or her speaking or receptive vocabulary.

You can help your students use structural analysis as a decoding strategy by teaching the procedure outlined below the sample sentence.

His heart beat <u>thunderously.</u> There had been so many hope-filled moments before, all of them ending in bitter disappointment.

1. Find the root or base word and recall its meaning. (thunder)

2. Find the prefix and/or suffix and recall its meaning. (*-ous*: full of; *-ly*: in a way)

3. Use the knowledge clues to predict the word's meaning. (in a way full of thunder)

4. Check predicted meaning against the rest of the sentence. (His heart beat in a way full of thunder.)

5. Does the meaning make sense? (yes)

Context Clues

Using context clues means using the knowledge provided by surrounding words and phrases to figure out the meaning of words unfamiliar in print. Students are taught to look for clues such as restatements, examples, comparisons, contrasts, definitions, and general description. In addition to context clues, readers often use decoding strategies such as phonics and structural analysis.

You can help your students use context clues by teaching the procedure beneath the sample sentence.

In 1917 the United States entered World War I as an active <u>combatant.</u> Like many socially prominent women, Eleanor (Roosevelt) threw herself into the war effort.

1. Look at the surrounding context for a description of the word or other clues.
2. Look at the word and apply other decoding strategies.
3. Use these clues to predict the word's meaning.
4. Check predicted meaning against the rest of the sentence.
5. Does the meaning make sense?

Support in *The Language of Literature*
Pupil's Edition
- Vocabulary in Action
- Vocabulary and Spelling
- Building Vocabulary
- Spelling Handbook

Teacher's Edition
- Preteaching Vocabulary Mini Lessons
- Vocabulary Strategy Mini Lessons
- Spelling Mini Lessons
- Building Vocabulary Lessons
- Vocabulary in Action Lessons

For additional suggestions on Teaching Decoding Strategies, see the *Reaching Middle School Readers* handbook.

Correlation with the Texas Assessment of Academic Skills (TAAS)

The Language of Literature provides teachers with many opportunities to help students prepare for the Texas Assessment of Academic Skills (TAAS). The following list identifies some of these opportunities.

Under each TAAS skill description are the related reading and writing skills commonly emphasized in high school language arts and literature courses. Following

each skill description are references to pages in the Pupil's Edition that correlate to the TAAS skill and references to pages in the Teacher's Edition where you will find instruction, mini lessons, and assessment opportunities. Additional study materials for students and support for teachers may be found in the various ancillary components of the program.

Domain: Reading Comprehension

Objective 1: The student will determine the meaning of words in a variety of written texts.

Pupil's Edition Lessons and Activities
Context clues: 44, 67, 99, 119, 142, 217, 285, 373, 473, 499, 562, 673, 693, 811, R8
Meaning clues: 172, 285, 373, 468, 499, 531, 847
Spelling clues: 276, 547, 599, R86–R89
Prefixes, suffixes, and roots: 35, 44, 99, 119, 309, 738
Word origins: 233, 389, 745, 773
Synonyms/antonyms: 35, 297, 389, 547, 631, 691, 738
Denotation/connotation: 231, 572, R8, R9
Analogies: 398, 430, 615, 883
Using reference materials: 10, 20, 35, 44, 46, 65, 66, 87, 109, 171, 184, 185, 190, 201, 206, 219, 241, 327, 521, 522, 546, 590, 599, 617, 672, 737, 743, 767, 780–786, 828, 864, 887, R42, R43, R44–R45, R90, R91
Assessment Practice: 27, 162, 359, 456, 829

Teacher's Edition Instruction and Mini Lessons
Context clues: 21, 39, 52, 102, 207, 292, 317, 369
Meaning Clues: 279, 362, 452, 487, 719
Prefixes, suffixes, and roots: 158, 262, 422, 738
Word origins: 92, 168, 770
Synonyms/antonyms: 27, 289, 349, 526, 562, 597, 689
Denotation/connotation: 227
Analogies: 119, 213, 355, 538, 610, 664

Objective 2: The student will identify supporting ideas in a variety of written texts.

Pupil's Edition Lessons and Activities
46, 62, 86, 223, 230, 287, 305–308, 617–620, 732, 737, R106–R107

Teacher's Edition Instruction and Mini Lessons
25, 96, 104, 302, 325, 386, 393, 404, 428, 454, 468, 489, 507, 557, 628, 637, 688, 736, 760, 765

Objective 3: The student will summarize a variety of written texts.

Pupil's Edition Lessons and Activities
10, 86, 287, 297, 397, 620, 767, 772

Teacher's Edition Instruction and Mini Lessons
170, 297, 423, 468, 489, 529, 628, 678, 771, 841, 858, 863

Objective 4: The student will perceive relationships and recognize outcomes in a variety of written texts.

Pupil's Edition Lessons and Activities
16, 86, 87, 89, 98, 109, 118, 154, 161, 219–222, 247, 343–344, 358, 373, 381, 391, 395, 398, 430, 478, 491, 530, 615, 708, 709, 726, 883, R6, R7, R8, R20

Teacher's Edition Instruction and Mini Lessons
93, 115, 302, 325, 386, 507, 557, 637, 688, 852, 714, 724, 765, 845, 852, 874

Objective 5: The student will analyze information in a variety of written texts in order to make inferences and generalizations.

Pupil's Edition Lessons and Activities
Inferences: 46, 62, 201, 204, 347, 348, 551, 590, R12
Conclusions: 206, 216, 305, 307, 308, 590, 591, 598, R9
Generalizations: 305, 307, R12
Evaluations/judgments: 4–9, 19, 93, 94, 139–141, 195, 347, 414, 463, 467, 521, 590, 657, 731, R10
Strategies for reading: 4–9, 19, 86, 195, 249, 347, 414, 521, 590, 657, 708
Literary analysis
  plot: 16, 163, 171, 185, 216, 247, 343–346, 707, R15
  character: 17, 46, 118, 161, 247, 413, 586–589, R7
  theme: 14, 18, 81, 186, 187, 190, 244, 278, 284, 321, 332, 342, 409, 413, 492, 498, 513, 528, 585, 644, 645, 654, 705, 790, 791, R20
  setting: 18, 20, 26, 43, 413, 519, 520, 655–656, 658, 672, 679, 690, 707, 789, R18
  tone: 519–520, 522, 530, R20
  mood: 519–520, 522, 530, 643, R14

Teacher's Edition Instruction and Mini Lessons
Inferences: 205, 283, 356, 485, 870
Conclusions: 283, 870
Generalizations: 274, 611, 716, 725, 760, 803
Strategies for reading: 663
Evaluations/judgments: 270, 378, 466, 608, 723, 809, 819
Literary analysis
  plot: 16, 35, 247, 560, 825, 881
  character: 17, 57, 59, 247, 320, 589
  theme: 346
  setting: 18, 454, 655–656
  tone: 519–520
  mood: 519–520

Objective 6: The student will recognize points of view, propaganda, and/or statements of fact and opinion in a variety of written texts.

Pupil's Edition Lessons and Activities
Point of view: 24, 570, 601, 614, R14, R21
Author's purpose: 37, 101, 106, 388, 414, 415, 429, 520, R7
Author's perspective: 522, 530
Author's bias: 139, 141
Criteria for analyzing text and information: 65, 138, 219, 305, 396, 470, 549, 617, 675, 728, 784, R105–R106
Analyzing information: 82–86, 219–222, 305–308, 397, 470–471, 590, 617–620, 675–678, 708, 728–731
Fact and opinion: 86, 139–141, 467, 590, 657, 658, 672, R10
Persuasion: 24, 520, 522, 530, R105
Tone: 519–520, 522, 530, R20

Teacher's Edition Instruction and Mini Lessons
Point of view: 40, 427, 542
Author's purpose: 38, 42, 370, 542, 569
Author's perspective: 227
Analyzing information: 397
Fact and opinion: 668, 731

Domain: Written Communication

Objective 1: The student will respond appropriately in a written composition to the purpose/audience specified in a given topic.

Pupil's Edition Lessons and Activities
Writing Options: 276, 373, 562, 571, 630, 673, 811, 829
Comparing Literature: Assessment Practice: 323
Writing Workshops: 75–80, 324–329
Writing models: R49, R52

Teacher's Edition Instruction and Mini Lessons
Alternate ending: 276, 546
Dialogue: 322, 359, 547, 615, 727
Diary entry: 217, 231, 599
Letter to/from characters: 63, 107, 285, 322, 389, 531, 571
Newspaper article: 304, 373, 462
Summarizing: 863
Active/passive verb: 295, 298
Describing character: 320
Implied main idea: 529
Cause and effect: 557
Drawing conclusions: 596
Predicting: 874

Objective 2: The student will organize ideas in a written composition on a given topic.

Pupil's Edition Lessons and Activities
Writing Options: 27, 119, 231, 304, 389, 468, 562, 599, 615, 630, 691, 727, 865
Writing Workshops: 238–242, 403–408
Comparing Literature: Assessment Practice: 323

Teacher's Edition Instruction and Mini Lessons
Journal entry: 217, 231, 599
Letter to/from characters: 63, 107, 285, 322, 389, 531, 571
Understanding cause and effect: 852
Inferences and conclusions: 205

Action verbs: 277
Main idea: 393
Understanding cause and effect: 852
Supporting evidence: 784

Objective 3: The student will demonstrate control of the English language in a written composition on a given topic.

Pupil's Edition Lessons and Activities
Using different tenses: 286, 407, R68, R85
Writing Workshops: 178–183, 324–329, 506–511
Comparing Literature: Assessment Practice: 323

Teacher's Edition Instruction and Mini Lessons
137, 159, 162, 169, 172, 256, 276, 277, 286, 294, 295, 298, 329, 359, 360, 384, 390, 408, 423, 426, 437, 456, 457, 484, 510, 511, 541, 544, 547, 584, 599, 604, 630, 640, 666, 670, 674, 683, 684, 692, 712, 720, 722, 727, 738, 739, 754, 756, 763, 773, 787, 801, 804, 818, 821, 824, 838, 851, 860, 869, 872, 879, 889

Objective 4: The student will generate a written composition that develops/supports/elaborates the central idea stated in a given topic.

Pupil's Edition Lessons and Activities
Writing Options: 276, 323, 373, 395, 468, 615, 727, 865
Comparing Literature: Assessment Practice: 323
Writing Workshops: 699–704, 780–787, 830–835

Teacher's Edition Instruction and Mini Lessons
Alternate ending: 276, 546
Diary entry: 217, 231, 599
Letter to/from characters: 63, 107, 285, 322, 389, 531, 571
Newspaper article: 304, 373, 462
Parts of speech: 277, 360, 384, 390, 457, 532, 544, 548, 563, 584, 872
Time order: 484
Make generalizations: 725
Supporting evidence: 784

Objective 5: The student will recognize appropriate sentence construction within the context of a written passage.

Pupil's Edition Lessons and Activities
Sentences: 45, 64, 137, 172, 175, 674, 786, 834, R55, R59, R81, R82, R84
Subjects/predicates: 36, 108, R55, R81, R83, R84, R85
Subject-verb agreement: 242, R60–R63, R80
Parts of speech: 108, 218, 232, 328, R54, R72, R82, R85
Modifiers: 328, 360, 374, 390, 457, 469, R54, R70–R71, R80
Phrases: 548, 563, 616, R55, R80, R83
Clauses: 674, 692, 786, R72–R74, R80, R81
Conjunctions: 674, R54, R81
Parallelism: 182, 511
Tenses: 286, 407, R68, R85
Writing Workshops: 75–80, 178–183, 238–243, 324–329, 403–408, 506–511, 579–584, 636–641, 699–704, 780–785, 830–835, 884–889
Assessment Practice: 80, 183, 243, 329, 408, 511, 641, 704, 787, 835, 889
Reading and Writing for Assessment: 334, 646

Teacher's Edition Instruction and Mini Lessons

Sentences: 45, 50, 64, 137, 169, 172, 256, 541, 722, 838
Subjects/predicates: 28, 36, 162
Parts of speech: 100, 211
Modifiers: 90, 360, 450, 457, 527, 544, 584, 594, 641, 835, 872, 879
Phrases: 159, 630, 754
Clauses: 674, 692, 720, 727, 739, 754, 761, 824
Conjunctions: 33, 720
Tenses: 704
Analyzing character: 214

Teacher's Edition Daily Language SkillBuilders

13i–13k, 189i–189k, 341i–341k, 517i–517k, 653i–653k, 793e

Objective 6: The student will recognize appropriate English usage within the context of a written passage.

Pupil's Edition Lessons and Activities

Sentences: 45, 64, 137, 172, 175, 674, 786, 834, R55, R59, R81, R82, R84
Subjects/predicates: 36, 108, R55, R81, R83, R84, R85
Subject-verb agreement: 242, R60–R63, R80
Parts of speech: 108, 218, 232, 277, 328, R54, R72, R82, R85
Modifiers: 328, 360, 374, 390, 457, 469, R54, R70–R71, R80
Phrases: 548, 563, 616, R55, R80, R83
Clauses: 674, 692, 786, R72–R74, R80, R81
Pronouns: 120, 328, R54, R66, R67, R83
Parallelism: 182, 511
Tenses: 286, 407, R68, R85
Writing Workshops: 75–80, 178–183, 238–243, 324–329, 403–408, 506–511, 579–584, 636–641, 699–704, 780–785, 830–835, 884–889
Assessment Practice: 80, 183, 243, 329, 408, 511, 641, 704, 787, 835, 889
Comparing Literature: Assessment Practice: 323

Teacher's Edition Instruction and Mini Lessons

Sentences: 45, 50, 64, 137, 169, 172, 256, 541, 722, 838
Subjects/predicates: 28, 36, 162
Subject-verb agreement: 282, 286, 352
Pronouns: 114, 328, 329, 735, 787, 814
Parts of speech: 108, 211, 226, 232, 295, 384, 390, 426, 556, 571, 625, 662, 683, 804, 855
Modifiers: 90, 360, 450, 457, 527, 544, 584, 594, 641, 835, 872, 879
Appositives: 600
Phrases: 616, 754, 843
Clauses: 674, 720, 727, 739, 754, 761, 824
Parallelism: 511, 666, 742
Tenses: 408, 889
Transitions: 484, 488

Teacher's Edition Daily Language SkillBuilders

13i–13k, 189i–189k, 341i–341k, 517i–517k, 653i–653k, 793e

Objective 7: The student will proofread for spelling, capitalization, and punctuation errors within the context of a written passage.

Pupil's Edition Lessons and Activities

Capitalization: 888, R58, R72–R74
Punctuation: 45, 137, 773, R56–R57, R74–R79, R82
Contractions: R57, R81
Quotations: 773, R77–R78, R84
Sentences: 45, 64, 137, 172, 175, 674, 786, 834, R55, R59, R81, R82, R84
Parts of speech: 108, 218, 232, 277, 328, R54, R72, R82, R85
Modifiers: 328, 360, 374, 390, 457, 469, R54, R70–R71, R80
Pronouns: 120, 328, R54, R66, R67, R83
Writing Workshops: 75–80, 178–183, 403–408, 579–584, 636–641, 699–704
Assessment Practice: 80, 183, 243, 329, 408, 511, 641, 704, 787, 835, 889
Comparing Literature: Assessment Practice: 323

Teacher's Edition Instruction and Mini Lessons

Spelling: 22, 44, 49, 99, 112, 128, 276, 294, 359, 423, 437, 456, 547, 599, 670, 684, 712, 728, 754, 763, 801, 818, 821, 851, 860, 869
Capitalization: 24, 80
Punctuation: 41, 172, 329, 510, 640, 744, 773, 838
Sentences: 50, 64, 137, 169, 172, 256, 541, 722
Phrases: 159, 630, 754
Clauses: 674, 720, 727, 739, 754, 761, 824
Subjects/predicates: 28, 36, 162
Interrupters: 604

Teacher's Edition Daily Language SkillBuilders

13i–13k, 189i–189k, 341i–341k, 517i–517k, 653i–653k, 793e

Correlation to Texas Essential Knowledge and Skills (TEKS)

The Language of Literature correlates to the sixty-two strands of the Texas Essential Knowledge and Skills through the Pupil's Edition, the Teacher's Edition, and many supporting materials. The following references are representative of the many ways the text and support materials meet the TEKS requirements.

	Pupil's Edition/ Teacher's Edition	Unit Resource Books	Transparencies/ Copymasters
7.3 Listening/speaking/appreciation. The student listens to enjoy and appreciate spoken language. The student is expected to:			
(3A) listen to proficient, fluent models of oral reading, including selections from classic and contemporary works			
• classic works	T798, T812, T836, T848, T866	**Unit 2:** 4	
• contemporary works	205	**Unit 3:** 27, 60	
(3B) analyze oral interpretations of literature for effects on the listener	199, T198, T202, T792, R102		**Comm:** T1, T2, T16
(3C) analyze the use of aesthetic language for its effects	T111, T191-194, 193, 194, T198, T205, 299, 331, 375, R6, R11, R12, R13, R15, R17, R18, R21, R100	**Unit 2:** 4, 5, 54; **Unit 3:** 27, 60, 61	**LA:** T19, T20
7.6 Reading/word identification. The student uses a variety of word recognition strategies. The student is expected to:			
(6A) apply knowledge of letter-sound correspondences, language structure, and context to recognize words	TX12-13. See the *Reaching Middle School Readers* handbook for additional coverage of this objective.		
• apply knowledge of letter-sound correspondences to recognize words	TX12, 31–33, 39–42, 49–52, 89–90, 93–94, 103–104, T112, 114–116, T128, 131–132, 157–158, 160, 165–169, T217, 259–260, 262–264, 266, 269, 272, 274, 279–283, 364–368, 370–371, 383, 386, 399–400, 419–421, T547, T684, T869	**Unit 1:** 10, 17, 24, 31, 48; **Unit 2:** 11, 18; **Unit 3:** 7, 14; **Unit 4:** 7, 14; **Unit 5:** 7, 14; **Unit 6:** 7, 14, 30	
• apply knowledge of language structure to recognize words	TX13, 44, T44, T670, T719, R87–89		**Vocab:** C57
• apply knowledge of context to recognize words	TX13, 21, 35, T39, 44, T52, 63, 67, T89, 99, 107, T110, 119, T122, 142, 172, T207, 217, T279, 285, T292, T317, T369, T464, T495, T532, T554, 592, T602, T659, 673, T710, T752, 811	**Unit 1:** 35, 73; **Unit 3:** 56; **Unit 5:** 18	**Vocab:** T3, T4, T5

LEGEND   LA – Literary Analysis   RCT – Reading and Critical Thinking   Vocab – Vocabulary
Comm – Communication

	Pupil's Edition/ Teacher's Edition	Unit Resource Books	Transparencies/ Copymasters
7.6 Reading/word identification. *(continued from previous page)*			
(6B) use structural analysis to identify words, including knowledge of Greek and Latin roots and prefixes/suffixes	TX 12-13. See the *Reaching Middle School Readers* handbook for additional coverage of this objective.		
• use structural analysis to identify words	TX12–TX13, T158, T166, 233, T262, T294, 309, T422, T487, T719, T738, T752, T801, T860	**Unit 2:** 22, 55; **Unit 5:** 44	**Vocab:** T6, T7, T8, 25, C32, C34, C40, C51, C75
• use knowledge of Greek roots to identify words	T92, T716	**Unit 5:** 44	**Vocab:** T9
• use knowledge of Latin roots to identify words	T168, T763, T805	**Unit 5:** 44	**Vocab:** T9
• use knowledge of Greek prefixes/suffixes to identify words	T92, 389, 473, T651b, T716		
• use knowledge of Latin prefixes/suffixes to identify words	233, 309, 473, 745	**Unit 2:** 22, 55	
(6C) locate the meanings, pronunciations, and derivations of unfamiliar words using dictionaries, glossaries, and other sources			
• dictionaries	T27, T122, T130, T168, T251, T434, T437, T452, 473, T480, T523, 631, 693, 745, T770, 773, R92	**Unit 1:** 35, 69; **Unit 4:** 27, 55	**Vocab:** C26, C52
• glossaries	185, 331, 513, T622, 643, 789, R6-21		
• other sources	T102, T768, R90–91	**Unit 1:** 35; **Unit 4:** 27, 55; **Unit 5:** 18, 44	

7.7 Reading/fluency. The student reads with fluency and understanding in texts at appropriate difficulty levels. The student is expected to:

	Pupil's Edition/ Teacher's Edition	Unit Resource Books	Transparencies/ Copymasters
(7A) read regularly in independent-level materials (texts in which no more than approximately 1 in 20 words is difficult for the reader)	4–9, 10–11, 15–18, 19, 21–25, 30–33, 67, 68–74, 197–198, 224–228, 229, 234–237, 245–248, 249, 433–435, 460, 474–477, 501, 519–520, 521, 655–656, 657, 680–689, 694–698, 706–707, 708		
(7B) read regularly in instructional-level materials that are challenging but manageable (texts in which no more than approximately 1 in 10 words is difficult for the reader)	38–42, 47–61, 65–66, 88–96, 97, 102–104, 105, 207–215, 219–222, 251–274, 279–283, 300–302, 396–397, 416–428, 439–454, 464–466, 470–472, 592–596, 617–620, 622–628, 659–671, 675–678, 768–771, 800–803, 804–809, 814–819, 820–827		
(7C) adjust reading rate based on purposes for reading	TX10–TX11, T108, 219, 471, T620, 675, 678, T678, T847. See the *Reaching Middle School Readers* handbook for additional coverage of this objective.		**RCT:** T47
(7D) read aloud in selected texts in ways that both reflect understanding of the text and engage the listeners			
• reflect understanding	195, T195, 196, T198, 199, 205, T205, 249, T249, T260, T303, T377, 380, T380, 391, 458, T460, 462	**Unit 1:** 4; **Unit 3:** 27, 60	**Comm:** T11

	Pupil's Edition/ Teacher's Edition	Unit Resource Books	Transparencies/ Copymasters
7.7 Reading/fluency. *(continued from previous page)*			
• engage the listeners	205, T205, T377, 380, T460, 462, T462, T798	**Unit 1:** 4	**Comm:** T12
(7E) read silently with increasing ease for longer periods	68–74, T69, 143–149, T144, 234–237, T235, 249, T249, 399–402, T400, 573–578, T574, 632–635		

7.8 Reading/variety of texts. The student reads widely for different purposes in varied sources. The student is expected to:

	Pupil's Edition/ Teacher's Edition	Unit Resource Books	Transparencies/ Copymasters
(8A) read classic and contemporary works			
• read classic works	123–134, 251–274, 313–314, 565–569, 597, 800–803, 804–809, 814–819, 820–827, 838–841, 842–845, 850–852, 853–860, 861–863, 868–870		
• read contemporary works	4–9, 21–25, 30–33, 38–42, 47–61, 68–74, 88–96, T141, 143–149, 155–160, 164–170, 197–198, 279–283, 283, 288–295, 300–302, 317–320, 392–393, 399–402, 416–428, 433–435, 439–454, 534–545, 554–560, 573–578, 592–596, 602–613		
(8B) select varied sources such as plays, anthologies, novels, textbooks, poetry, newspapers, manuals, and electronic texts when reading for information or pleasure	4–9, 27, 35, 45, 64, 65–66, 68–74, 99, 100, 107, 231, 285, 304, T308, 322, 360, 374, 380, 389, 395, 396–397, 430, 437, 456, 462, 502, 514–515, 531, 731, 777, 778–779, 790–791, 810, 828, 846, 847, 864, T865, 882, 883, 891, R42, R90–91		
(8C) read for varied purposes such as to be informed, to be entertained, to appreciate the writer's craft, and to discover models for his/her own writing			
• read for varied purposes	10–11, 19, T19, 64, 100, T100, 108, 200, 277, 778–779, 847, T847, R18	**Unit 1:** 22, 53, 82; **Unit 2:** 57, 64; **Unit 3:** 40, 78	**RCT:** T13
• read to be informed	65–66, 150–153, 219–222, 298, 305–308, 374, 380, 474–477, 502, 531, 532, 547, 549–552, 617–620, 746–749, 774–775, 776, 794–797, 798–799, 812–813, 836–837, T847, 848–849, 866–867, R18	**Unit 1:** 22, 46, 53; **Unit 2:** 17, 48; **Unit 3:** 64; **Unit 4:** 49; **Unit 5:** 7, 36, 37, 47	
• read to be entertained	4–9, 68–74, 143–149, 234–237, 399–402, 462, 548, 727, R18	**Unit 1:** 22; **Unit 2:** 55; **Unit 4:** 20, 25, 26	
• read to appreciate the writer's craft	120, 175, 218, 232, 500–502, 504–505, T548, T596, 630, 744, T744, 776, 778–779	**Unit 1:** 82; **Unit 2:** 4, 5, 7, 55 **Unit 3:** 61, 72, 78; **Unit 4:** 25, 26, 36, 43; **Unit 5:** 47	
• read to discover models for his/her own writing	76-77, 175, 179-180, 325-326, 404-405, 502, 504-505, 507-508, 637-638, 700-701, R26-36		
(8D) read to take action such as to complete forms, make informed recommendations, and write a response	T27, 66, 75–80, T119, 141, T179, T217, T231, T285, 308, 548, T651a-T651b	**Unit 1:** 82; **Unit 2:** 57, 64; **Unit 3:** 63, 64, 72	

	Pupil's Edition/ Teacher's Edition	Unit Resource Books	Transparencies/ Copymasters
7.9 Reading/vocabulary development. The student acquires an extensive vocabulary through reading and systematic word study. The student is expected to:			
(9A) develop vocabulary by listening to selections read aloud	T69, T144, T235, T400, T633		**Vocab:** T13, T14, C22, C28, C30, C35, C50, C62, C65, C68, C71, C78
(9B) draw on experiences to bring meanings to words in context such as interpreting idioms, multiple-meaning words, and analogies	T47, 63, 67, T119, 142, T155, T207, T213, 276, 279, 285, T288, 297, T349, T355, T362, 373, T382, 398, T419, T434, T439, T452, 473, T480, 499, T526, 531, T534, T538, 547, T562, T597, 599, T610, 615, 631, T659, T664, T680, T689, 691, 693, T710, T733, 773, 829, 847, 865, 883, R6, R12	**Unit 1:** 35, 73; **Unit 3:** 29 **Unit 4:** 18	**Vocab:** T13, T14
(9C) use multiple reference aids, including a thesaurus, a synonym finder, a dictionary, and software, to clarify meaning and usage			
• use a thesaurus	T27, T31, T122, T175, T251, T480, 631, R91, R92	**Unit 4:** 55	
• use a synonym finder	T27, T31, T122, T175, T622		
• use a dictionary	T27, T122, T130, T168, T175, T251, T349, T434, 473, T480, T523, 631, 693, 745, R91, R92	**Unit 1:** 73; **Unit 3:** 69 **Unit 4:** 55; **Unit 5:** 18, 44	**Vocab:** C52
• use software	T175, R90–91		
(9D) determine meanings of derivatives by applying knowledge of the meanings of root words such as *like*, *pay*, or *happy* and affixes such as *dis-*, *pre-*, or *un-*			
• root words	T92, T166, T168, 233, T719, T752, T763, T805	**Unit 2:** 22; **Unit 3:** 69; **Unit 5:** 44	**Vocab:** T6, T9, C25, C34, C40, C75
• affixes	119, T158, T166, 233, T262, 309, T422, 473, T487, T719, T108, T860	**Unit 2:** 55; **Unit 3:** 69; **Unit 5:** 44	**Vocab:** T7, T8, T9, C32, C51
(9E) study word meanings systematically such as across curricular content areas and through current events	T339d, 470, T515b, 883		**Vocab:** T9
(9F) distinguish denotative and connotative meanings	T224, T227, 231, 349, T382, T562, 572, T689, R8, R9	**Unit 4:** 27	**Vocab:** T12, C37
(9G) use word origins as an aid to understanding historical influences on English word meanings	T130, T168, T437, T716, 745, T763, T770, 773, T844	**Unit 5:** 44	**Vocab:** C79
7.10 Reading/comprehension. The student uses a variety of strategies to comprehend a wide range of texts of increasing levels of difficulty. The student is expected to:			
(10A) use his/her own knowledge and experience to comprehend			

	Pupil's Edition/ Teacher's Edition	Unit Resource Books	Transparencies/ Copymasters
7.10 Reading/comprehension. *(continued from previous page)*			
• use knowledge to comprehend	20, T50, 278, 284, 347, T347, 521, T521, 530, 533, T542, 546, 590, T590, T608, T684, 708, T708, R9, R10	**Unit 1:** 29; **Unit 2:** 6, 9, 40 **Unit 3:** 5; **Unit 4:** 35, 42	**RCT:** T2, T5, T17, T33
• use experience to comprehend	4, T13, 19, T19, 20, 22, T22, T24, 26, T48, T50, 278, T280, T282, 284, 347, T347, T422, T524	**Unit 1:** 8, 29; **Unit 2:** 6, 9 **Unit 3:** 5; **Unit 4:** 12, 35, 42	**RCT:** T2, T5, T17, T33
(10B) establish and adjust purposes for reading such as reading to find out, to understand, to interpret, to enjoy, and to solve problems			
• establish purposes for reading	4, 19, T19, 312, T314, 315, 316, T318, T320, 321, R18	**Unit 2:** 57, 64	**RCT:** T13
• adjust purposes for reading	312, 470-472, 675-678, 750, R18, R107		**RCT:** T13, T48
(10C) monitor his/her own comprehension and make modifications when understanding breaks down such as by rereading a portion aloud, using reference aids, searching for clues, and asking questions			
• monitor comprehension	154, T156, T158, 160, 196, T198, 391, T392, 394, 414, T414, 458, T460, 461, 549, 729, 750, T752, T756, T760, 766, T775, R14	**Unit 1:** 75; **Unit 5:** 46	**RCT:** T1, T2, T7, T11, T12, T14, T19
• make modifications when understanding breaks down	154, 391, T392, 394, 458, 461, 750, T756, 766, R14	**Unit 1:** 75; **Unit 5:** 46	**RCT:** T1, T3, T11, T12, T16, T19, T20–23
(10D) describe mental images that text descriptions evoke	4, 19, T19, T40, T130, T132, T173, 195, T195, T224, 249, T249, 250, T252, 254, T258, 269, T272, 379, 428, T442, T448, T452, 478, T480, T482, T558, T560, 561, 679, T680, T684, T686, R21	**Unit 2:** 33; **Unit 3:** 18, 71 **Unit 4:** 19; **Unit 5:** 12	**RCT:** T10, T18
(10E) use the text's structure or progression of ideas such as cause and effect or chronology to locate and recall information			
• use the text's structure or progression of ideas to locate information	29, T30, T32, 34, 87, T88, 89, T92, T94, 98, 109, T110, T112, T114, T115, T116, 118, T302, 381, T490, 491, T494, T496, 621, T622, T624, T626, T838, T840, T842, T852, T856, R7, R8, R106–107		**LA:** T12, T23 **RCT:** T6, T8, T24
• use the text's structure or progression of ideas to recall information	T93, T115, T386, 388, T488, 491, 629, T688, 708, T708, T724, 726, T764, T852, T856, R7, R8, R106–107	**Unit 1:** 15, 46; **Unit 3:** 21 **Unit 5:** 29	**RCT:** T5, T6, T13
(10F) determine a text's main (or major) ideas and how those ideas are supported with details			
• determine a text's main (or major) ideas	18, T18, 86, T86, 96, T104, T158, T160, 223, 737, T824, T852, T856, R13, R103, R104		**LA:** T13 **RCT:** T25

	Pupil's Edition/ Teacher's Edition	Unit Resource Books	Transparencies/ Copymasters
7.10 Reading/comprehension. *(continued from previous page)*			
• determine how a text's main ideas are supported with details	18, 86, T96, T104, 223, T224, T226, T228, 230, T393, T428, T468, T489, 513, T529, T670, 732, T736, 737	**Unit 2:** 16; **Unit 5:** 36	**LA:** T13 **RCT:** T25
(10G) paraphrase and summarize text to recall, inform, or organize ideas			
• paraphrase text to recall, inform, or organize ideas	T714, 740, T742, 743, R15, R42, R103	**Unit 5:** 44	**RCT:** T16 **Writing:** T50, T52
• summarize text to recall, inform, or organize ideas	T25, 86, T86, T115, 287, T288, T290, T292, T294, 296, T297, 397, T714, 767, T768, T770, T771, 772, 777, T841, T863, R20, R42, R103	**Unit 2:** 47; **Unit 5:** 53	
(10H) draw inferences such as conclusions or generalizations and support them with text evidence and experience			
• draw inferences and support them with text evidence	46, T48, T50, T52, T54, T58, T92, T94, T134, T166, T283, 305, 308, 347, T347, 348, T350, T352, 355, T590, 591, 592, T592, T594, T596, 598, T606, T608, T844, T865, T870, T874, T876, R12, R15, R105	**Unit 1:** 29; **Unit 2:** 2, 9, 41; **Unit 3:** 5, 79; **Unit 4:** 42	
• draw inferences and support them with experience	46, T52, T60, 62, 201, 206, 216, T283, 347, T347, 348, T350, T356, 358, T485, 590, T590, 591, T596, 598, T606, T608, T610, T611, T696, T714, T723, T725, T741, T803, T804, T806, T808, T809, T819, T870, R12, R105	**Unit 1:** 29; **Unit 2:** 2, 9; **Unit 3:** 5; **Unit 4:** 42	**RCT:** T4, T5, T9, T14, T15, T17, T28
(10I) find similarities and differences across texts such as in treatment, scope, or organization			
• find similarities across texts	T50, 163, T798, T802, T812, T836, T848, T866, R8	**Unit 1:** 82; **Unit 2:** 57, 64f; **Unit 3:** 78	**RCT:** T2, T27
• find differences across texts	T50, 163, T798, T812, T836, T848, T866, R9	**Unit 1:** 82; **Unit 2:** 57, 64f; **Unit 3:** 78	**RCT:** T27
(10J) distinguish fact and opinion in various texts	86, T86, 467, T626, 657, T657, 658, T660, 662, T666, T668, 670, 672, T731, T744, T756, R10, R104	**Unit 5:** 6	**RCT:** T26
(10K) answer different types and levels of questions such as open-ended, literal, and interpretative as well as test-like questions such as multiple choice, true-false, and short answer			
• answer open-ended questions	26, 34, 43, 62, 98, 106, 118, 135, 161, 171, 199, 372, 379, 388, 394, 429, 436, 455, 461, 467, 491, 498, 530, 546, 561, 570, 598, 614, 629, 672, 690	**Unit 1:** 97; **Unit 2:** 80; **Unit 3:** 93; **Unit 4:** 65; **Unit 5:** 68; **Unit 6:** 54	
• answer literal questions	26, 34, 43, 62, 98, 106, 118, 135, 161, 171, 199, 204, 216, 230, 275, 284, 296, 303, 315, 321, 358, 372, 379, 388, 394, 429, 436, 455, 461, 467, 491, 498, 530, 546, 561, 570, 598, 614, 629, 672, 690	**Unit 1:** 13, 20, 27; **Unit 2:** 14, 21, 38, 45; **Unit 3:** 10, 17, 26, 45; **Unit 4:** 10, 17; **Unit 5:** 10, 17, 34; **Unit 6:** 10, 17	

	Pupil's Edition/ Teacher's Edition	Unit Resource Books	Transparencies/ Copymasters
7.10 Reading/comprehension. *(continued from previous page)*			
• answer interpretive questions	26, 34, 43, 62, 98, 106, 118, 135, 161, 171, 199, 372, 379, 388, 394, 429, 436, 455, 461, 467, 491, 498, 530, 546, 561, 570, 598, 614, 629, 672, 690, 726, 737, 743, 766, 722	**Unit 1:** 13, 20, 27; **Unit 2:** 14, 21, 38, 45; **Unit 3:** 10, 17, 26, 45; **Unit 4:** 10, 17; **Unit 5:** 10, 17, 34; **Unit 6:** 10, 17	
• answer multiple choice questions	T25, 27, T59, T96, 136, 162, T170, T214, T231, T274, T283, T297, T302, T356, T370, T378, T386, T542, T560, T569, T608, T611, T628, T663, T668, T688, T723, T724, T736, T741, T764, T771, T803	**Unit 1:** 13, 20, 27; **Unit 2:** 14, 21, 38, 45; **Unit 3:** 10, 17, 26, 45; **Unit 4:** 10, 17; **Unit 5:** 10, 17, 34; **Unit 6:** 10, 17	
• answer true-false questions	847		
• answer short answer questions	16–18, 26, 34, 43, 62, 65–66, 83–85, 98, 106, 118, 216, 219–222, 230, 245–248, 275, 284, 296, 303, 394, 396–397, 410–413, 429, 436, 455, 461, 467	**Unit 1:** 13, 20, 27; **Unit 2:** 14, 21, 38; **Unit 3:** 10, 17, 26, 45; **Unit 4:** 10, 17, 24; **Unit 5:** 10	
(10L) represent text information in different ways such as in outline, time line, or graphic organizer			
• outline	T119, T777	**Unit 2:** 16	**RCT:** T46 **Writing:** T49, T54
• time line	T92, T285, 298, T298, 380, 552	**Unit 1:** 46	**RCT:** T6, T19
• graphic organizer	10, 20, 27, 34, 35, T35, T51, 62, T64, T77, 99, T99, 199, 201, 204, T209, 216, T239, T270, 275, 276, 331, 358, 361, 372, T383, 388, T388, T404, 461, T701, 708, T708, 726, 737, 743, 767, T781, 789	**Unit 1:** 8, 15, 22; **Unit 2:** 4, 6, 9; **Unit 3:** 5, 21, 18, 27; **Unit 4:** 5, 12, 19; **Unit 5:** 6, 12,	**RCT:** T2, T3, T5, T6, T7, T8, T9, T10, T11, T12, T14, T15, T17, T18, T19, T25, T29, T30, T31, T32
(10M) use study strategies to learn and recall important ideas from texts such as preview, question, reread, and record	4, 10–11, 19, T19, T22, 34, 43, 62, T88, 98, 106, 204, 216, 230, T252, 275, 284, T288, 296, 299, 436, T440, 455, 461, 467, 471, T472, T480, 491	**Unit 1:** 75; **Unit 2:** 53; **Unit 3:** 60; **Unit 5:** 46	**RCT:** T1, T11, T12, T16, T46, T47, T48
7.11 Reading/literary response. The student expresses and supports responses to various types of texts. The student is expected to:			
(11A) offer observations, make connections, react, speculate, interpret, and raise questions in response to texts			
• offer observations in response to texts	T124, T198, T212, T254, T258, T264, T272, T280, T302, T318, T368, T450, T486, T536, T666, 668	**Unit 1:** 9, 22; **Unit 2:** 5; **Unit 3:** 40; **Unit 4:** 35; **Unit 6:** 13	
• make connections in response to texts	4, 19, T19, T132, T212, 347, T347, 492, T494, T496, 498, 521, T521, T524, T528, 533, T534, T684, T712, T722	**Unit 1:** 8; **Unit 2:** 40, 57; **Unit 3:** 22; **Unit 4:** 12, 35; **Unit 5:** 29 **Unit 6:** 35	**RCT:** T2, T3, T8
• react to texts	256, T280, 347, T347, T364, T368, T370, 379, T420, T426, 463, T464, T466, 467, 491, T500, T610, T612, 614, T666, 690, T760, T856, T868	**Unit 1:** 22, 53; **Unit 2:** 4, 33; **Unit 3:** 6, 12; **Unit 4:** 6, 19, 25, 26, 36; **Unit 5:** 12, 45	**RCT:** T14, T15, T17

	Pupil's Edition/ Teacher's Edition	Unit Resource Books	Transparencies/ Copymasters

7.11 Reading/literary response. *(continued from previous page)*

	Pupil's Edition/ Teacher's Edition	Unit Resource Books	Transparencies/ Copymasters
• speculate in response to texts	4, 19, T19, T22, T24, T32, T35, T70, T90, T112, 135, T145, T160, T166, T168, T170, 216, 230, 296, 297, T297, 322, 356, 361, T362, T364, T368, T440	**Unit 1:** 22, 29, 53, 67; **Unit 2:** 6 **Unit 3:** 12, 28, 40, 47, 54; **Unit 4:** 5, 6; **Unit 6:** 12	**RCT:** T7
• interpret texts	T60, 86, T86, 93, 94, T112, T114, T126, 130, T132, T258, T260, T262, T264, T266, T268, T270, T272, T378, 414, T414, T418, T420, T422, T424, T426	**Unit 1:** 61; **Unit 2:** 4, 6, 9, 40; **Unit 3:** 5, 22; **Unit 4:** 35, 43; **Unit 5:** 30, 44; **Unit 6:** 42	**RCT:** T16, T25, T28
• raise questions in response to texts	4, 19, T19, 130, T174, T263, 286, 299, T300, T302, 303, 353, 463, T554, T708, T756, T795, R16	**Unit 2:** 53; **Unit 3:** 22, 60, 63; **Unit 6:** 5	**RCT:** T12
(11B) interpret text ideas through such varied means as journal writing, discussion, enactment, and media			
• interpret text ideas through journal writing	T70, 119, T119, 217, T217, 231, T231, T575	**Unit 1:** 8, 15, 22; **Unit 2:** 4, 6; **Unit 3:** 5, 12, 18; **Unit 4:** 5, 12	
• interpret text ideas through discussion	26, 34, 43, 62, T69, T71, 99, T99, 106, T107, 118, T402, 429, 436, 455, T456, 461, 467, 491, 498, 598		
• interpret text ideas through enactment	27, T27, 35, T35, 63, 119, T119, 136, T136, 176, 437, T437, T448, 456, 462, 468, T497, 512, T512		
• interpret text ideas through media	107, 119, 136, T136, 200, T200, T236, 297, 359, 727, T727, 744, T744, T760, 776, T776, R97–99		
(11C) support responses by referring to relevant aspects of text and his/her own experiences			
• support responses by referring to relevant aspects of texts	62, T104, T144, T160, T173, T205, T277, T285, T297, T320, T322, 373, T373, 394, 467, 491, T497, T532, T602, T610, T612, 614, T725, T789, T802, T845	**Unit 1:** 29, 46; **Unit 2:** 6, 9, 33; **Unit 3:** 5, 12, 18; **Unit 4:** 5, 19; **Unit 5:** 12, 36	
• support responses by referring to his/her own experiences	T602, T604, T610, T612, 614, T725, T845	**Unit 1:** 8, 29; **Unit 2:** 6, 9, 40; **Unit 3:** 5; **Unit 4:** 12, 35, 42	
(11D) connect, compare, and contrast ideas, themes, and issues across text			
• connect ideas, themes, and issues across text	T65, 118, T138, T219, T305, 394, T396, 436, T470, T728, 744, T744, 778, T798, T802, T812, T818, T865, T866, T870, T880, R8	**Unit 1:** 82; **Unit 2:** 57, 64; **Unit 3:** 78	**LA:** T7, T32
• compare ideas, themes, and issues across text	34, 62, 64, 106, 120, T120, 163, T164, T170, 171, T352, 388, 390, T390, 436, 455, T457, 461, 532, T808, 811, T818, 829, T829, 847, 865, R8	**Unit 1:** 82; **Unit 2:** 57, 64; **Unit 3:** 78	**LA:** T7, T32
• contrast ideas, themes, and issues across text	62, 64, 98, 163, T170, 171, T173, 277, 388, 390, T390, T457, 461, T612, 614, 629, 726, T808, 811, 847, 865, R9	**Unit 1:** 82; **Unit 2:** 57, 64; **Unit 3:** 78	**LA:** T7, T32

	Pupil's Edition/ Teacher's Edition	Unit Resource Books	Transparencies/ Copymasters
7.12 Reading/text structures/literary concepts. The student analyzes the characteristics of various types of texts (genres). The student is expected to:			
(12A) identify the purposes of different types of texts such as to inform, influence, express, or entertain	15, T15, 82, T82, 84, T84, 191, T191, 245, T245, 310, 410, T410, 706, T706, R7, R106	**Unit 1:** 23, 47; **Unit 2:** 17, 48, 58, 65; **Unit 3:** 22, 41, 48, 55, 64; **Unit 4:** 20; **Unit 5:** 30, 37, 47, 54	**LA:** T16 **RCT:** T8
(12B) recognize the distinguishing features of genres, including biography, historical fiction, informational texts, and poetry			
• biography	83, T83, 87, T88, T90, T94, 98, 287, 296, T575, 732, T734, 737, R7	**Unit 1:** 23, 47; **Unit 2:** 48 **Unit 3:** 22; **Unit 5:** 37	**LA:** T10
• historical fiction	706–707, T706–707, 709, T710, T712, T718, T722, T724, 726, 789, R12	**Unit 5:** 30	**LA:** T1, T3, T4, T5, T6, T7, T8, T22
• informational texts	82–85, T82–85, 223, T224, T226, T228, 230, 381, T758, T760, T764, 766, 789, R15	**Unit 1:** 47; **Unit 2:** 17, 48; **Unit 3:** 64; **Unit 5:** 47	**LA:** T12, T13
• poetry	191–194, T191–194, 204, R11, R14, R16, R17	**Unit 2:** 5, 7, 54; **Unit 3:** 19, 28, 61; **Unit 4:** 26; **Unit 5:** 45	**LA:** T17, T19, T20, T21
(12C) compare communication in different forms such as contrasting a dramatic performance with a print version of the same story or comparing story variants	35, T35, 176, T176, T261, T266, T271, 277, 304, T304, 323, T323, T397, 503, T503, 673, T673, 829, T862	**Unit 2:** 58	
(12D) understand and identify literary terms such as playwright, theater, stage, act, dialogue, analogy, and scene across a variety of literary forms (texts)			
• playwright	R9		
• theater	R9		**LA:** T23
• stage	R9, R19	**Unit 1:** 34	**LA:** T23
• act	247, T247, R6		**LA:** T23
• dialogue	26, T30, T32, T52, T110, T112, 248, T248, T260, T262, T418, T424, T426, T442, T446, 502, 533, T534, T538, T544, 546, T556, 642, T768, R9	**Unit 1:** 34	**LA:** T23, T24
• analogy	615, R6	**Unit 3:** 29	**Vocab:** T14
• scene	247, T247, R18	**Unit 1:** 34	**LA:** T23
(12E) understand literary forms by recognizing and distinguishing among such types of texts as stories, poems, myths, fables, tall tales, limericks, plays, biographies, and autobiographies			

	Pupil's Edition/ Teacher's Edition	Unit Resource Books	Transparencies/ Copymasters
7.12 Reading/text structures/literary concepts. *(continued from previous page)*			
• stories	15–18, T15–18, R11	**Unit 1:** 9; **Unit 2:** 10; **Unit 3:** 13; **Unit 4:** 6; **Unit 5:** 13	
• poems	191–194, T191–194, T742, R11, R16	**Unit 2:** 5, 7, 54; **Unit 3:** 19, 28, 61; **Unit 4:** 26; **Unit 5:** 45	
• myths	796, T808, T840, T852, 890, R14		**LA:** T30
• fables	310, 312, T314, 315, 316, T318, T320, 321, 498, 796, T818, R10	**Unit 2:** 58, 65; **Unit 3:** 78	**LA:** T30
• tall tales	T797		**LA:** T30
• limericks	T192		
• plays	245–248, T245–248, 415, 429, R9	**Unit 2:** 34; **Unit 3:** 41; **Unit 4:** 20	
• biographies	83, T83, T88, T90, T94, 98, T575, R7	**Unit 1:** 47	**LA:** T10
• autobiographies	83, T83, 287, T288, T290, T292, T294, 296, T575, T622, T626, T628, 732, T734, 737, R7	**Unit 2:** 48	**LA:** T11
(12F) analyze characters, including their traits, motivations, conflicts, points of view, relationships, and changes they undergo			
• analyze characters' traits	17, T17, 46, T50, T54, T56, T90, T112, T116, T158, T166, T173, T214, T274, T282, T302, T454, T488, 587, T587, T806, T811, T822, 846, T856, T862, R7	**Unit 1:** 30; **Unit 2:** 10; **Unit 4:** 36, 43	**LA:** T2, T3
• analyze characters' motivations	T59, T173, T716, T811, T824, T878, R14	**Unit 6:** 6	**LA:** T3
• analyze characters' conflicts	T90, T96, 118, T292, T364, T366, T484, T488, T526, T680, T682, T684, T688, T734, T736, T754, T758, T762, T850, T856, R8	**Unit 1:** 16; **Unit 6:** 36	**LA:** T3, T8
• analyze characters' points of view	570, 591, T592, T594, T596, 598, 601, T602, T604, T606, T608, T612, 614, T686, T878, R16	**Unit 4:** 36, 43	**LA:** T3
• analyze characters' relationships	T50, T52, T54, T58, T130, T212, T320, T542, 587	**Unit 2:** 10	**LA:** T2, T3
• analyze changes characters undergo	T57, T58, T60, 62, T70, T114, 206, T208, T214, 216, T270, 275, 330, 345, 586, T589, 642, R7		**LA:** T2, T3
(12G) recognize and analyze story plot, setting, and problem resolution			
• recognize and analyze story plot	16, T16, 29, T30, T32, 34, T35, 109, T110, T116, T292, 343–346, T343–346, T384, T386, 388, T452, T868, T872, T874, T876, T880, T881, R8, R10, R15	**Unit 1:** 61, 76, 83; **Unit 3:** 72; **Unit 6:** 28, 43	**LA:** T5 **RCT:** T13
• recognize and analyze setting	18, T18, 20, T22, T24, 26, 43, T124, T126, T254, T354, T454, T528, 655–656, T655–656, 658, T660, 690, 707, T707, T710, T760, 789, T806, R18	**Unit 1:** 9; **Unit 5:** 7, 13	**LA:** T6

	Pupil's Edition/ Teacher's Edition	Unit Resource Books	Transparencies/ Copymasters
7.12 Reading/text structures/literary concepts. *(continued from previous page)*			
• recognize and analyze problem resolution	16, T16, 154, T156, T160, 161, 163, T164, T170, 171, 216, T274, 346, T346, T370, T454, T560, R37		**LA:** T5
(12H) describe how the author's perspective or point of view affects the text	37, T38, T40, T42, 43, 86, T86, 101, T102, T104 T382, T386, T397, 414, T414, 415, T422, 424, R20, R21, R106	**Unit 1:** 23, 54; **Unit 4:** 6	**LA:** T22
(12I) analyze ways authors organize and present ideas such as through cause/effect, compare/contrast, inductively, deductively, or chronologically	29, T30, T77, 86, T86, 87, T96, 98, T180, T239, T325, 381, 478, T557, 621, T637, T701, 708, T708, 709, T781, T832, R7, R8, R9, R12, R35–38, R105–R107	**Unit 1:** 54; **Unit 4:** 6	**LA:** T12 **RCT:** T24, T25
(12J) recognize and interpret literary devices such as flashback, foreshadowing, and symbolism			
• flashback	T262, 344, 690, R11	**Unit 1:** 76; **Unit 3:** 13	**LA:** T29
• foreshadowing	T145, T168, 344, 520, T542, T820, R11	**Unit 1:** 76; **Unit 3:** 13	**LA:** T28
• symbolism	T58, T236, T258, T268, 391, T392, 394, T482, R20	**Unit 3:** 28	
(12K) recognize how style, tone, and mood contribute to the effect of the text			
• style	175, 284, 303, T428, T466, T540, T544, R19	**Unit 4:** 25	**LA:** T9
• tone	T104, 519–520, T519–520, 522, T524, T526, T528, 530, R20–R21	**Unit 4:** 6	**LA:** T25
• mood	519–520, T519–520, 522, T524, T526, T528, 530	**Unit 4:** 6	**LA:** T26
7.13 Reading/inquiry/research. The student inquires and conducts research using a variety of sources. The student is expected to:			
(13A) form and revise questions for investigations, including questions arising from readings, assignments, and units of study			
• form questions for investigations	66, T107, T222, T380, T864, T880, R41	**Unit 5:** 59, 60	**Writing:** T1, T40
• revise questions for investigations	66, T222, T846, R41, T-R43	**Unit 5:** 59, 60	**Writing:** T1, T2, T3
• form and revise questions arising from readings	65, 286, T599, T630, T691, T811, R41	**Unit 2:** 53; **Unit 5:** 59, 60	**Writing:** T40
• form and revise questions arising from assignments	T308, T599, 828	**Unit 5:** 59, 60	**Writing:** T40
• form and revise questions arising from units of study	184–185, T187a-d, 330–331, T339a-d, 512–513, T515a-d, 642–643, 788–789, 890	**Unit 5:** 59, 60	**Writing:** T40

	Pupil's Edition/ Teacher's Edition	Unit Resource Books	Transparencies/ Copymasters
7.13 Reading/inquiry/research. *(continued from previous page)*			
(13B) use text organizers, including headings, graphic features, and tables of contents, to locate and organize information			
• use headings	219, T222, T374, T571, T620, R107		**RCT:** T46, T47 **Writing:** T43, T44
• use graphic features	219, 380, 471, 796–797, T865, R95–R96		**RCT:** T29, T30, T31, T32 **Writing:** T47–48
• use tables of contents	14, 81, 190, 244, 342, 409, 518, 581, 654, 705, R1, R20, T-R43		
• use other text organizers to locate and organize information	219, T620		**Writing:** T49, T54
(13C) use multiple sources, including electronic texts, experts, and print resources, to locate information relevant to research questions			
• use multiple sources	27, 322, T359, T380, 389, T468, T503, T552, 691		
• use electronic texts	T35, 45, T66, 99, 107, 136, T141, 176, T217, T222, T864, T882, T883, R90–91		
• use experts	T66, 107, 136, T141, 231, 322, 373, T373, 599, R102–R104, R104–105		
• use print resources	T35, 45, T66, 136, T141, 176, 231, 285, 304, T308, 864, T864, T865, T882, 883, T883, R42, R91		
(13D) interpret and use graphic sources of information such as maps, graphs, time lines, or tables to address research questions	87, 150–151, 474–475, T663, 746–747		**RCT:** T29, T30, T31, T32
(13E) summarize and organize information from multiple sources by taking notes, outlining ideas, and making charts			
• summarize by taking notes	617, 678, T791a, T791b, R42	**Unit 5:** 59, 60	**RCT:** T46, T48 **Writing:** T49, T51, T52
• summarize by outlining ideas	617, 620, T620, R43	**Unit 5:** 59, 60	**RCT:** T46, T48 **Writing:** T49, T51, T52
• summarize by making charts	T187b, T339b, T515b-d, R95–96	**Unit 5:** 59, 60	
• organize by taking notes	T552, 617-620, 784-785, T828, R43	**Unit 5:** 59, 60	**RCT:** T46 **Writing:** T49, T54
• organize by outlining ideas	617-620, 784-785, R42, R43	**Unit 5:** 59, 60	**RCT:** T46 **Writing:** T49
• organize by making charts	T176, 185, T222, 315, 828, T828, 864, R95–96	**Unit 5:** 59, 60	

	Pupil's Edition/ Teacher's Edition	Unit Resource Books	Transparencies/ Copymasters
7.13 Reading/inquiry/research. *(continued from previous page)*			
(13F) produce research projects and reports in effective formats for various audiences	35, 44, 99, 119, T215, 217, 276, T297, 298, T339a-d, T515a-d, T651b, 373, T738, 744, T758, T791a, 828, T828, 883, R24, R100	**Unit 5:** 61, 62, 63	**Writing:** T37
(13G) draw conclusions from information gathered from multiple sources	136, 430, 738, 777, 780-786, 884-888, R29–R31, R41-42	**Unit 5:** 61, 62, 63	
(13H) use compiled information and knowledge to raise additional, unanswered questions	470-472, 547, 675-678, 738, R41	**Unit 5:** 61, 62, 63	**Writing:** T2
(13I) present organized statements, reports, and speeches using visuals or media to support meaning			
• present organized statements	T119, 322, R95-R99	**Unit 6:** 48, 49, 50, 51, 52, 53	
• present organized reports	T136, T187a–187d, 205, T205, 231, T322, 468, T864, R35–38, R41–45, R95–99	**Unit 6:** 48, 49, 50, 51, 52, 53	
• present organized speeches	T35, T44, T54, T62, T99, T107, T108, R95–101	**Unit 6:** 48, 49, 50, 51, 52, 53	
7.14 Reading/culture. The student reads to increase knowledge of his/her own culture, the culture of others, and the common elements of cultures. The student is expected to:			
(14A) compare text events with his/her own and other readers' experiences			
• compare text events with his/her own experiences	19, T19, 22, T22, 26, 35, T35, 62, 98, 101, 106, 118, 218, 230, 274, 275, 278, T280, T282, 284, 296, 303, T722, 726, 737, 743, 766, 772, 788, T795, T852	**Unit 1:** 8, 97; **Unit 2:** 40; **Unit 4:** 12; **Unit 6:** 54	**RCT:** T2
• compare text events with other readers' experiences	22, T22, 26, 135, 184, 358, 512, 530, 788	**Unit 6:** 54	
(14B) determine distinctive and common characteristics of cultures through wide reading			
• determine distinctive characteristics of cultures	T254, T264, T269, T368, T525, T605, T718, T721, T806, T812, T815, T854, T873, T877, T878	**Unit 6:** 54	
• determine common characteristics of cultures	T61, T254, T264, T721, T794, T806, T812,T822, T836, 847, T847, T848, T854, T861, T866, T877, T878	**Unit 6:** 54	
(14C) articulate and discuss themes and connections that cross cultures	T385, T606, T802, T842, 847, T847, 890		**LA:** T32

Correlation with the Professional Development and Appraisal System (PDAS)

The Language of Literature supports teachers who participate in the Professional Development and Appraisal System. The following list identifies how the program supports teacher proficiencies.

Each domain and its evaluation dimensions are listed below. Following each evaluation dimension are references to examples of lessons, activities, or feature material in the Pupil's Edition or Teacher's Edition that will help teachers meet that evaluation dimension.

Domain I: *Active, Successful Student Participation in Learning Process*

a. Quantity and quality of student participation is evident.

For examples in the Pupil's Edition, see:
- Thinking Through the Literature questions and activities
- Group activities with Connect to Life and Literary Analysis
- Reader's Notebook activities
- Choices and Challenges activities
- Writing and Communication Workshops

b. Students are challenged by instruction and make connections to work and life applications, both within the discipline and with other disciplines.

For example, see:
- Prereading and postreading pages in the Pupil's Edition
- Real World Links
- Cross Cultural Link in the Pupil's Edition and Teacher's Edition
- Cross Curricular Link in the Teacher's Edition

Domain II: *Learner-Centered Instruction*

a. Instructional content is based on appropriate goals and instruction.

For examples, see:
- Objectives in the Teacher's Edition
- Skills Traces in the Teacher's Edition with correlations to TEKS and TAAS.

b. Instructional content includes basic knowledge and skills, as well as central themes and concepts, both within the discipline and with other disciplines.

For examples, see:
- Selections in the Pupil's Edition, including opening essays and instructional apparatus
- Objectives in the Teacher's Edition

- Skills Traces with correlations to TEKS and TAAS.
- Cross Cultural Link in the Pupil's Edition and Teacher's Edition
- Cross Curricular Link in the Teacher's Edition
- Fine Art Transparencies

c. Instructional strategies are aligned with learning objectives and activities, students needs, and work and life applications, both within the discipline and other disciplines.

For examples, see:
- Objectives and side notes in the Teacher's Edition
- Prereading and postreading pages in the Pupil's Edition
- Cross Cultural Link in the Pupil's Edition and Teacher's Edition
- Cross Curricular Link in the Teacher's Edition

d. Instructional strategies promote application of learning through critical thinking and problem solving.

For examples, see:
- Prereading pages in the Pupil's Edition: Literary Analysis, Active Reading, and corresponding Unit Resource Book pages
- Thinking Through the Literature in the Pupil's Edition: Think Abouts, What If, Different Perspectives, Critic's Corner, Extending Interpretations
- Comparing Literature and Literary Links in the Pupil's Edition
- Reading and Writing for Assessment in the Pupil's Edition
- Reading and Critical Thinking Transparencies/ Copymasters

e. The teacher uses appropriate motivational and instructional strategies which successfully and actively engage students in the learning process.

For examples, see:
- Prereading pages in the Pupil's Edition
- Side notes in the Teacher's Edition
- Literature in Performance videos

Domain III: *Evaluation and Feedback on Student Progress*

a. **The teacher aligns assessment and feedback with goals and objectives and instructional strategies.**

For examples, see:
- Comprehension Check questions in the Pupil's Edition
- Reflect and Assess self-assessment and goal setting in the Pupil's Edition
- Selection and part tests, test generator questions
- Standardized Test Practice and Informal Assessment Mini Lessons in the Teacher's Edition
- Integrated Assessment tests
- Guide to Assessment and Portfolio Use

b. **The teacher uses a variety of evaluation and feedback strategies which are appropriate to the varied characteristics of students.**

For examples, see:
- Comprehension Check questions in the Pupil's Edition
- Reflect and Assess self-assessment and goal setting
- Peer assessment, Rubrics in Writing Workshops, and Unit Resource Books
- Selection and part tests, test generator questions
- Standardized Test Practice and Informal Assessment Mini Lessons in the Teacher's Edition
- Integrated Assessment tests
- Guide to Assessment and Portfolio Use

Domain IV: *Management of Student Discipline, Instructional Strategies, Time, and Materials*

a. **Teacher effectively implements the discipline-management procedures approved by the district.**

Not Applicable

b. **Teacher establishes a classroom environment which promotes and encourages self-discipline and self-directed learning.**

For examples, see:
- Reader's Notebook activities in the Pupil's Edition
- Reflect and Assess self-assessment and goal setting in the Pupil's Edition
- Working Portfolio in the Pupil's Edition
- Reading and Writing for Assessment in the Pupil's Edition
- Choices and Challenges activities that encourage self-selection
- Unit Resource Book pages
- Guide to Assessment and Portfolio Use

c. **Teacher selects instructional materials which are equitable and acknowledge the varied characteristics of all students.**

For examples, see:
- Choices and Challenges in the Pupil's Edition
- Author Activity in the Pupil's Edition
- Customizing Instruction side notes in the Teacher's Edition
- Professional articles in the Professional Development and Planning Guide

d. **Teacher effectively and efficiently manages time and materials.**

For examples, see:
- Skill Traces in the Teacher's Edition
- Professional Development and Planning Guide
- Block Scheduling booklet

Domain V: *Professional Communication*

a. **Teacher uses appropriate and accurate written, verbal, and non-verbal modes of communication with students.**

For examples, see:
- Family and Community Involvement in the Unit Resource Books

b. **Teacher uses appropriate and accurate written, verbal, and non-verbal modes of communication with parents, staff, community members, and other professionals.**

For examples, see:
- Family and Community Involvement in the Unit Resource Books

c. **Teacher's interactions are supportive, courteous, respectful, and encouraging to students who are reluctant and having difficulty.**

For examples, see:
- Customizing Instruction sections in the Teacher's Edition
- Teacher's SourceBook for Language Development
- Professional articles in the Professional Development and Planning Guide

Domain VI: *Professional Development*

a. Teacher determines and participates in professional development goals and activities that are aligned with goals of the campus and goals of the district.

For examples, see:
- Professional articles in the Professional Development and Planning Guide

b. Teacher correlates professional development activities with assigned subject content and the varied needs of students.

For examples, see:
- Professional articles in the Professional Development Planning Guide

c. Teacher exhibits a willingness to collaborate with colleagues and other professionals for continuous growth and development.

For examples, see:
- Professional articles in the Professional Development and Planning Guide

d. Teacher correlates professional development activities with the prior performance appraisal.

Not Applicable

Domain VII: *Compliance with Policies, Operating Procedures and Requirements*

a. Teacher contributes to making the whole school safe and orderly, and a stimulating learning environment for children.

For examples, see:
- Pupil's Edition
- Teacher's Edition
- Audio-visual components
- Professional articles in the Professional Development and Planning Guide

b. Teacher respects the rights of students, parents, colleagues, and the community.

Not Applicable

Domain VIII: *Improvement of Academic Performance of all Students on the Campus*

a. Teacher diagnoses student needs and provides performance feedback to all appropriate TAAS-related objectives.

For examples, see:
- Skills Traces in the Teacher's Edition, which identify TAAS objectives
- Standardized Test Practice and Informal Assessment Mini Lessons in the Teacher's Edition
- Standardized Test Practice Booklets
- Standardized Test Practice in Formal Assessment

b. Teacher aligns planning and delivery of instruction to all appropriate TAAS-related objectives.

For examples, see:
- Skills Traces in the Teacher's Edition help teachers align instruction

c. Teacher collaborates with other faculty and administration to improve TAAS-related performance of all students on campus.

Not Applicable

d. Teacher identifies students who are at risk and develops appropriate strategies to assist these students.

For examples, see:
- Standardized Test Practice and Informal Assessment in the Teacher's Edition
- Customizing sections in the Teacher's Edition for instructional support

e. Teacher monitors the attendance of all students and intervenes to promote regular attendance.

Not Applicable

McDougal Littell

THE LANGUAGE OF
LITERATURE

TEACHER'S EDITION

Grade 7

McDougal Littell
A HOUGHTON MIFFLIN COMPANY
Evanston, Illinois • Boston • Dallas

Question

Visualize

Evaluate

Predict

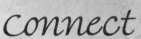

Connect

Clarify

A passion for reading and skills for success

Good readers are not born—they're made. ***The Language of Literature*** provides students with the tools they need to become thoughtful, active readers.

- **Active reading strategies** before, during, and after the selections teach students how to think as they read and to connect the printed word to their own experiences.
- **An engaging selection of literature,** including classic and contemporary fiction and nonfiction, motivates students to compare selections, authors, and cultures.
- **Comprehensive skills instruction** in reading, writing, critical thinking, and other skills naturally flows from the literature. Assessment instruction and practice prepare students to use those skills on standardized tests.

By teaching students the skills they need to become active readers, ***The Language of Literature*** helps them become successful students.

THE LANGUAGE OF LITERATURE

A passion for Reading
Skills for Success

Active Readers

Predict

Evaluate

Connect

Reading support from start to finish

The Language of Literature integrates literary skills and active reading skills at the beginning of every selection. When students finish reading, follow-up activities address those same skills.

PREPARING to *Read*

ACROSS the CURRICULUM
SOCIAL STUDIES

Eleanor Roosevelt

Biography by WILLIAM JAY JACOBS

Connect to Your Life
What women who have made significant social change do you know about?

Build Background Eleanor Roosevelt, wife of President Franklin Roosevelt, lived through a period of dramatic changes.

1939 Marian Anderson sings at the Lincoln Memorial. Roosevelt arranges the event after Anderson is not allowed to sing in a Washington concert hall because of her race.

1932 Franklin D. Roosevelt elected president. As first lady, Eleanor speaks out against economic and social injustice.

WIVES of WOMEN

1884 Eleanor Roosevelt is born into a wealthy, respected New York family which includes uncle Theodore Roosevelt.

1919 Congress passes the 19th Amendment, granting women the right to vote. The participation of women in politics grows.

1962 Eleanor Roosevelt dies.

NBC

1903 First airplane flight

1912 Titanic sinks

1914 WW I begins

1926 Great Depression begins

1939 *Grapes of Wrath* published

1941 U.S. enters WW II

1945 WW II ends; U.N. organized

1954 Supreme Court ends school segregation

1961 First American in space

Focus Your Reading
LITERARY ANALYSIS BIOGRAPHY A **biography** is the story of a person's life, written by another person. Biographers take information from many sources—letters, journals, interviews, documents—and bring it together to present accounts of their subjects' lives.

WORDS TO KNOW **Vocabulary Preview**
brooding migrant prominent
combatant priority

ACTIVE READING CHRONOLOGICAL ORDER
Chronological order is the order in which events happen in time. Signal words such as *before, during, after, first, next, while,* and *later* indicate the order of events. As you read, create a chart in your **READER'S NOTEBOOK** to keep track of the chronological order of important events in Eleanor Roosevelt's life.

LaserLink: Background for Reading Historical Connection

ELEANOR ROOSEVELT **87**

Thinking through the LITERATURE

Connect to the Literature

1. What Do You Think?
What words and phrases would you use to describe Eleanor Roosevelt?

Comprehension Check
• When did Roosevelt learn to be strong and think for herself?
• How did she help out during World War I?
• What was her role in the United Nations?

Think Critically

2. Which of Mrs. Roosevelt's accomplishments do you find most impressive? Why?

3. How do you think Eleanor's childhood experiences affected the choices she made later in life?

THINK ABOUT
• how she felt about herself
• her goals and values
• what she says in the excerpt from her autobiography on page 95

4. Adlai Stevenson said that Mrs. Roosevelt "would rather light a candle than curse the darkness." What do you think she meant? Explain.

5. **ACTIVE READING CHRONOLOGICAL ORDER** How well were you able to record the **chronological order** of the events of Mrs. Roosevelt's life in your **READER'S NOTEBOOK**? Compare your chart with a classmate's. Were there details that you missed? If so, add them to your chart in the chronologically correct places.

Extend Interpretations

6. **COMPARING TEXTS** Reread the excerpts from *The Autobiography of Eleanor Roosevelt* and *No Ordinary Time* on page 95. Do they give you an impression of Eleanor Roosevelt different from the one you got from William Jay Jacobs's biography? Why or why not?

7. **Connect to Life** If Eleanor Roosevelt were alive today, which national and world issues do you think would concern her? To what person living today would you compare her?

Literary Analysis

BIOGRAPHY A **biography** is the story of a person's life, told by someone else. In a good biography, the presentation of the subject's life is comprehensive and accurate. The **biographer** interviews the subject (if he or she can) and consults letters, journals, and other documents.

Biographers often focus on remarkable aspects of their subjects' lives, such as Eleanor Roosevelt's way of caring for others. Although they often present their subjects in a favorable light, biographers strive to balance their opinion of the person with the facts.

Paired Activity With a partner, go back through the selection and make a list of some of the signal words William Jay Jacobs uses to indicate the chronological order of the events of Eleanor Roosevelt's life. Discuss how these signal words help you understand the order in which events happened.

Signal Words
1. today
2. as
3. for a time
4. later
5.

98 UNIT ONE PART 2: MOMENTS OF DISCOVERY

THE LANGUAGE OF LITERATURE

THE *InterActive* READER

McDougal Littell

More reading support

The *InterActive Reader*™ is an interactive worktext that coaches students to become better readers. Students can underline, annotate, and mark up featured selections reprinted from *The Language of Literature.*

 *Question*  *Visualize*  *clarify*

comprehensive assessment
to help students succeed

The Language of Literature offers a full range of assessment options to meet your needs, including:
- standardized test practice
- reading skills assessment
- portfolio assessment

Assessment Resources

Teacher's Edition
Includes Formal and Informal Assessment Mini-Lessons and project assessments in the Speaking and Listening Projects.

Pupil's Edition
Features assessment practice in the Writing Workshops, Reading and Writing for Assessment, Vocabulary in Action: Assessment Practice, and Comparing Literature: Assessment Practice.

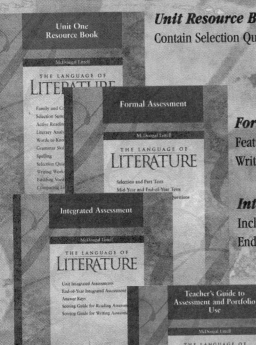

Unit Resource Books
Contain Selection Quizzes.

Formal Assessment
Features Selection Tests, Standardized Test Practice, Writing Prompts, and Scoring Rubrics.

Integrated Assessment
Includes Unit Integrated Assessments and an End-of-Year Integrated Assessment.

Teacher's Guide to Assessment and Portfolio Use
Contains portfolio assessment, writing rubrics, and other forms of open-ended assessment.

Test Generator CD-ROM
Provides over 1500 test items and the option to edit or create your own questions and tests.

Predict

Evaluate

Connect

There are three sides t
with The Lan

Skills to learn

questioning

researching

comparing

analyzing style

critical thinking

viewing and
representing

writing

evaluating

communicating

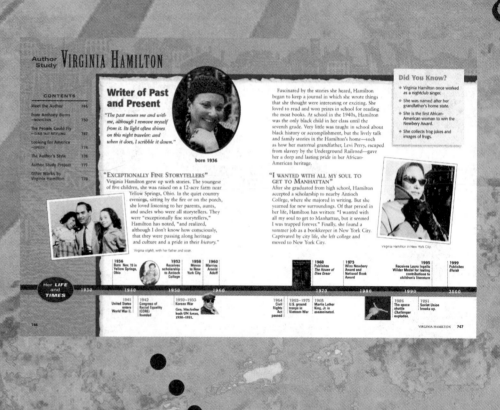

T6

 **Question**  **Visualize**  **Clarify**

very story
age of Literature!

LITERATURE IN PERFORMANCE

The Language of Literature connects print, audio/video, and computer resources to help students see the full picture of literature. Skills instruction and teaching resources work together to give students a passion for reading and skills for success!

Tools to teach

Literature in Performance Videos

NetActivities CD-ROM

ClassZone website

Audio Library cassettes and CDs

Transparencies and Copymasters

Formal Assessment

Informal Assessment

LaserLinks

The InterActive Reader™

THE LANGUAGE OF LITERATURE

A Passion for Reading

skills for success

 *Predict*

 *Evaluate*

 *Connect*

Resources that pu

When you spend your time hunting for teaching resources, you lose precious time for actual teaching. ***The Language of Literature*** gives you some important resources that help make preparing your lessons easier.

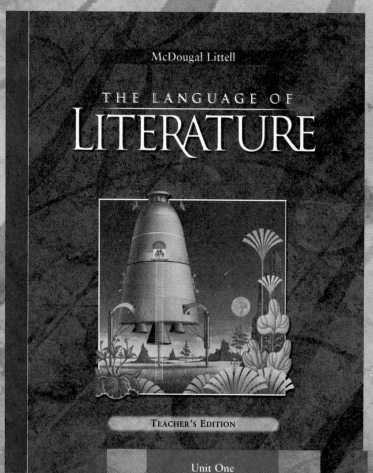

McDougal Littell

THE LANGUAGE OF LITERATURE

TEACHER'S EDITION

The ***Annotated Teacher's Edition*** is your complete reference manual for *The Language of Literature*. Each page contains teaching strategies, background information, references to ancillary materials, and a wealth of other information right at your fingertips.

The ***Unit Resource Books, Resource Management Guide*** and ***Lesson Plans*** offer teaching support in convenient, portable booklets. The Unit Resource Books, one per unit, provide additional skills work, activities, and exercises. The Resource Management Guide matches the appropriate ancillary materials for every selection. The Lesson Plans outline instructional opportunities from the student and teacher texts, with associated activities available in key ancillary components.

Unit One Resource Book

McDougal Littell

THE LANGUAGE OF LITERATURE

Family and Community Involvement
Selection Summary
Active Reading SkillBuilder
Literary Analysis SkillBuilder
Words to Know SkillBuilder
Grammar SkillBuilder
Spelling SkillBuilder
Selection Quiz
Building Vocabulary SkillBuilder
Writing Workshop
Rubric for Evaluation
Reflect and Assess
Answer Keys

Resource Management Guide

McDougal Littell

THE LANGUAGE OF LITERATURE

McDougal Littell
A HOUGHTON MIFFLIN COMPANY
Evanston, Illinois   Boston   Dallas

Question *visualize* *clarify*

eaching first

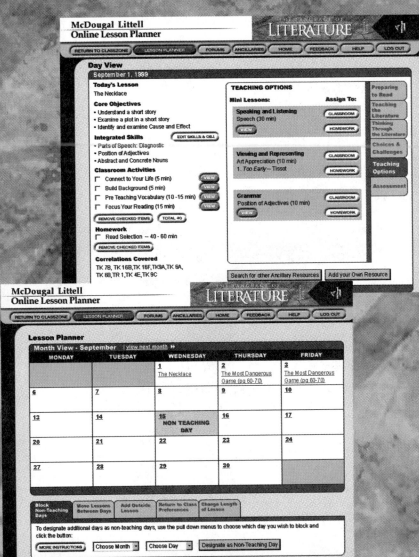

The **Electronic Teacher Tools** CD-ROM puts many of the teaching resources available for *The Language of Literature* on one convenient disc that you can use in class or from the comfort of your own home. Search for documents by resource, chapter, or keyword, and print them for use in your classroom.

The Internet-based **Online Lesson Planner** makes it easy to plan or check your lessons anytime, anywhere. Choose your ancillaries, your class times, and other options to customize your lesson plans to meet your needs.

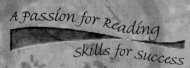

THE LANGUAGE OF LITERATURE

A Passion for Reading

skills for success

Complete Program Components

Core Components

Pupil's Edition
Teacher's Edition

Teaching Resources

Reaching Middle School Readers
Resource Management Guide
Organizational guide for each level that matches ancillary materials for each selection

Unit Resource Books
Complete resources for each selection, including reading, vocabulary, grammar, spelling, writing, and literature support plus annotated models and rubrics for evaluation

Lesson Planning Guides

Students Acquiring English
Teacher's Sourcebook for Language Development

Spanish Study Guide
Selection summaries in Spanish, ESL Strategies

Assessment
Teacher's Guide to Assessment and Portfolio Use
Portfolio Assessment, Writing Rubrics, and other open-ended forms of assessment

Formal Assessment
Selection Tests, Standardized Test Practice, Writing Prompts, Scoring Rubrics

Integrated Assessment

Skills Transparencies and Copymasters
- Writing
- Grammar
- Vocabulary (includes spelling practice)
- Communications (includes transparencies for Speaking, Listening, and for Viewing Fine Art)
- Literary Analysis
- Reading and Critical Thinking

The InterActive Reader™
An interactive worktext that builds reading comprehension

Technology Resources

Literature in Performance
Video Series
Help students compare written selections to adaptations of great literature.

Contents include:

- *Thank You, M'am,* adaptation of Hughes's story
- *Alias Jimmy Valentine,* adaptation of O. Henry's story
- *Casey at the Bat,* animated version
- *The Long Years,* adaptation of the story from Bradbury's *Martian Chronicles*
- *A Night to Remember,* a 15-minute excerpt from the 1958 film
- *Brother Coyote and Brother Cricket,* storytelling by Tim Tingle

Website: www.mcdougallittell.com
A treasury of online resources, including selection support, links, activities, and more

NetActivities (CD-ROM) Helps students extend learning and explore favorite authors in greater depth through interactive activities and links to the Internet

Audio Library (audio CD and cassette)

ClassZone (website)

LaserLinks (videodisc)

Writing Coach (CD-ROM)

Electronic Teacher Tools (CD-ROM)

Test Generator (CD-ROM)

Power Presentations (CD-ROM)

Online Lesson Planner (website)

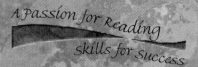

THE LANGUAGE OF LITERATURE

A Passion for Reading skills for success

McDougal Littell

THE LANGUAGE OF
LITERATURE

Senior Consultants

Arthur N. Applebee

Andrea B. Bermúdez

Sheridan Blau

Rebekah Caplan

Peter Elbow

Susan Hynds

Judith A. Langer

James Marshall

McDougal Littell
A HOUGHTON MIFFLIN COMPANY
Evanston, Illinois • Boston • Dallas

Acknowledgments

Unit One

Simon & Schuster: "A Day's Wait," from *The Short Stories of Ernest Hemingway* by Ernest Hemingway. Copyright © 1933 by Charles Scribner's Sons. Copyright renewed © 1961 by Mary Hemingway. Reprinted with permission of Simon & Schuster, Inc.

Harcourt Brace & Company: "Seventh Grade," from *Baseball in April and Other Stories* by Gary Soto. Copyright © 1990 by Gary Soto. Reprinted by permission of Harcourt Brace & Company.

Hill and Wang: "Thank You, M'am," from *Short Stories* by Langston Hughes. Copyright © 1996 by Ramona Bass and Arnold Rampersad. Reprinted by permission of Hill and Wang, a division of Farrar, Straus & Giroux, Inc.

Susan Bergholz Literary Services: "Names/Nombres" by Julia Alvarez, first published in *Nuestro*, March 1985. Copyright © 1985 by Julia Alvarez. Reprinted by permission of Susan Bergholz Literary Services, New York. All rights reserved.

Alfred A. Knopf: "Zebra," from *Zebra and Other Stories* by Chaim Potok. Copyright © 1998 by Chaim Potok. Reprinted by permission of Alfred A. Knopf, Inc.

Naomi Shihab Nye: "The Rider" by Naomi Shihab Nye, first published in *Invisible*. Reprinted by permission of the author.

Smithsonian Magazine: "Offerings at the Wall" by Don Moser, originally appeared in *Smithsonian*, May 1995. Reprinted with permission of the author.

Continued on page R129

ISBN 0-395-93170-3

Copyright © 2001 by McDougal Littell Inc. All rights reserved.

Printed in the United States of America.

2 3 4 5 6 7 8 9 DWO 05 04 03 02 01 00

Senior Consultants

The senior consultants guided the conceptual development for *The Language of Literature* series. They participated actively in shaping prototype materials for major components, and they reviewed completed prototypes and/or completed units to ensure consistency with current research and the philosophy of the series.

Arthur N. Applebee Professor of Education, State University of New York at Albany; Director, Center for the Learning and Teaching of Literature; Senior Fellow, Center for Writing and Literacy

Andrea B. Bermúdez Professor of Studies in Language and Culture; Director, Research Center for Language and Culture; Chair, Foundations and Professional Studies, University of Houston-Clear Lake

Sheridan Blau Senior Lecturer in English and Education and former Director of Composition, University of California at Santa Barbara; Director, South Coast Writing Project; Director, Literature Institute for Teachers; Vice President, National Council of Teachers of English

Rebekah Caplan High School and Middle Grades English/Language Arts Specialist for the New Standards Project, National Center on Education and the Economy, Washington, D.C.; served on the California State English Assessment Development Team for Language Arts

Peter Elbow Professor of English, University of Massachusetts at Amherst; Fellow, Bard Center for Writing and Thinking

Susan Hynds Professor and Director of English Education, Syracuse University, Syracuse, New York

Judith A. Langer Professor of Education, State University of New York at Albany; Co-director, Center for the Learning and Teaching of Literature; Senior Fellow, Center for Writing and Literacy

James Marshall Professor of English and English Education, University of Iowa, Iowa City

Contributing Consultants

Jeffrey N. Golub Assistant Professor of English Education, University of South Florida, Tampa

William L. McBride Reading and Curriculum Specialist; former middle and high school English instructor

Sharon Sicinski-Skeans, Ph.D. Assistant Professor of Reading, University of Houston-Clear Lake

Multicultural Advisory Board

The multicultural advisors reviewed literature selections for appropriate content and made suggestions for teaching lessons in a multicultural classroom.

Dr. Joyce M. Bell, Chairperson, English Department, Townview Magnet Center, Dallas, Texas

Dr. Eugenia W. Collier, author; lecturer; Chairperson, Department of English and Language Arts; teacher of Creative Writing and American Literature, Morgan State University, Maryland

Kathleen S. Fowler, President, Palm Beach County Council of Teachers of English, Boca Raton Middle School, Boca Raton, Florida

Noreen M. Rodriguez, Trainer for Hillsborough County School District's Staff Development Division, independent consultant, Gaither High School, Tampa, Florida

Michelle Dixon Thompson, Seabreeze High School, Daytona Beach, Florida

Teacher Review Panels

The following educators provided ongoing review during the development of the tables of contents, lesson design, and key components of the program.

TEXAS

Gloria Anderson, Language Arts Department Chairperson, Campbell Middle School, Cypress Fairbanks Independent School District

Gwen Ferguson, Assistant Principal, Northwood Middle School, North Forest Independent School District

Rebecca Hadavi, Parkland Middle School, Ysleta Independent School District

Patricia Jackson, Pearce Middle School, Austin Independent School District

continued on pages R142–R143

Manuscript Reviewers

The following educators reviewed prototype lessons and tables of contents during the development of *The Language of Literature* program

William A. Battaglia, Herman Intermediate School, San Jose, California

Hugh Delle Broadway, McCullough High School, The Woodlands, Texas

Robert M. Bucan, National Mine Middle School, Ishpeming, Michigan

Ann E. Clayton, Department Chair for Language Arts, Rockway Middle School, Miami, Florda

continued on page R143

Student Panel

LITERATURE REVIEWERS

The following students read and evaluated selections to assess their appeal
for the seventh grade.

Tommy Bartsch, Schimelpfenig Middle School, Plano, Texas

Tai-Ling Bloomfield, Mears Jr. High/Alyeska Central School, Anchorage, Alaska

Gabriel Bonilla, George Washington Carver Middle School, Coconut Grove, Florida

Christopher Bradrick, Theodore Schor Middle School, Piscataway, New Jersey

Eric de Armas, George Washington Carver Middle School, Coconut Grove, Florida

Christel Fowler, W. I. Stevenson Middle School, Houston, Texas

Ashley Barnett Green, Cooper Intermediate School, Fairfax County, Virginia

Stephanie Hicks, Grant Sawyer School, Las Vegas, Nevada

David C. Hsu, Foothill Middle School, Walnut Creek, California

Chrissy Kennedy, Foothill Middle School, Walnut Creek, California

Tony Liberati, Hampton Middle School, Allison Park, Pennsylvania

Danae Lowe, Kenilworth Jr. High School, Petaluma, California

Leslie Michelle Martinez, Sam Houston Jr. High School, Irving, Texas

Michael F. Regula, Old Trail School, Bath, Ohio

Scott Stanley Terrill, Swartz Creek Middle School, Swartz Creek, Michigan

ACTIVE READERS

The following students participated in
the development of The Active Reader:
Skills and Strategies pages in this book:

Anita Vasquez

Michael Reese

Matt Catanzano

Sophia Durbano

Elvia Lopes

Steve Mtunis

Leah Jaffe

Chase Abreu

Angeli Forber-Pratt

Rafael Moses

Erlin Guillen

Lindsay Sheah

STUDENT MODEL WRITERS

The following students wrote the
student models for Writing Workshop
pages that appear in this book:

Shoshannah Seed

Kristin Richardson

Sabrina Probasco

Steve Hernandez

J. Anderson

Rachel Lee Granzow

M. De los Santos

Andrea Martinez

Weston Sager

Stephen Shimshock

OVERVIEW

UNIT SIX Across Cultures: The Oral Tradition

STUDENT RESOURCE BANK

Glossary of Literary and Reading Terms

Writing Handbook

Grammar Handbook

Spelling Handbook

Communication Handbook

Literature Connections

Each of the books in the *Literature Connections* series combines a novel or play with related readings—poems, stories, plays, personal essays, articles—that add new perspectives on the theme or subject matter of the long work.

The Call of the Wild*
BY JACK LONDON

WITH THESE RELATED READINGS

Marie de France	**The Wolf and the Dog**
Elizabeth Marshall Thomas	*from* **The Hidden Life of Dogs**
A. G. Rochelle	**The Wolf Said to Francis**
Julius Lester	**The Man Who Was a Horse**
Sally Carrighar	**Unsentimental Mother**
Robert Murphy	**Long Duel**

Listed below are some of the most popular choices to accompany the Grade 7 anthology:

Across Five Aprils
BY IRENE HUNT

The Clay Marble
BY MINFONG HO

The Diary of Anne Frank
BY FRANCES GOODRICH AND ALBERT HACKETT

Dogsong
BY GARY PAULSEN

The Glory Field
BY WALTER DEAN MYERS

I, Juan de Pareja*
BY ELIZABETH BORTON DE TREVIÑO

Island of the Blue Dolphins
BY SCOTT O'DELL

Maniac Magee
BY JERRY SPINELLI

Roll of Thunder, Hear My Cry*
BY MILDRED D. TAYLOR

Taking Sides
BY GARY SOTO

A Wrinkle in Time
BY MADELEINE L'ENGLE

*A Spanish version is also available.

ACROSS CULTURES: THE ORAL TRADITION
For more stories related to the unit theme, see page 798.

Flights of Imagination

ACROSS CULTURES: THE ORAL TRADITION
For more stories related to the unit theme, see page 836.

Nothing Stays the Same

UNIT FIVE
PAGE 652

Personal Challenges

ACROSS CULTURES: THE ORAL TRADITION
For more stories related to the unit theme, see page 866.

UNIT SIX
PAGE 792

Across Cultures:
THE ORAL TRADITION

Student *Resource Bank*

Selections by Genre

Fiction

Fables

Nonfiction

Classical Myths

Oral Tradition

Parable

Special Features in This Book

Writing Workshops

Communication Workshops

Building Vocabulary

Assessment Pages

People
you'll
meet

Journeys
you'll
take

2

> *A* book is a gift you can open again and again.
>
> – Garrison Keillor
> *Writer*

Things you'll learn

Strategies
FOR
READING

Becoming an Active Reader involves more than just enjoying the power of storytelling. To understand and appreciate the literature in this book, you'll need to learn and apply the reading strategies listed here. As you begin to learn the strategies and how to use them, stop from time to time to **monitor** how well they are working for you. If it helps your reading, modify the strategies as necessary to suit your needs.

PREDICT Try to figure out what will happen next and how the selection might end. Read on to see how accurate your guesses were.

VISUALIZE Visualize characters, events, and setting to help you understand what's happening. When you read nonfiction, pay attention to the images that form in your mind as you read.

CONNECT Connect personally with what you're reading. Think of similarities between the descriptions in the selection and what you have personally experienced, heard about, and read about.

QUESTION Question what happens while you read. Searching for reasons behind events and characters' feelings can help you feel closer to what you are reading.

CLARIFY Stop occasionally to review what you understand, and expect to have your understanding change and develop as you read on. Use resources to help you clarify your understanding. Reread when necessary.

EVALUATE Form opinions about what you read, both while you're reading and after you've finished. Develop your own ideas about characters and events.

On the next page, you will see how two readers applied these strategies to the story "A Day's Wait."

Introducing the
READING MODEL

Alongside "A Day's Wait" are the comments of two seventh-grade students, **Anita Vasquez** and **Michael Reese**. Their comments reflect the kind of thinking that active readers do as they read. You'll notice that both Anita and Michael quite naturally used the reading strategies introduced on this page.

To get the most from this model, read the story first, jotting down your own responses on a piece of paper. (Cover up the side comments with a sheet of paper if you're tempted to peek.) Then read Anita's and Michael's responses and compare them with your own.

A Day's Wait

by Ernest Hemingway

He came into the room to shut the windows while we were still in bed and I saw he looked ill. He was shivering, his face was white, and he walked slowly as though it ached to move.

"What's the matter, Schatz?"

"I've got a headache."

"You better go back to bed."

"No. I'm all right."

"You go to bed. I'll see you when I'm dressed."

But when I came downstairs he was dressed, sitting by the fire, looking a very sick and miserable boy of nine years. When I put my hand on his forehead I knew he had a fever.

"You go up to bed," I said, "you're sick."

"I'm all right," he said.

When the doctor came he took the boy's temperature.

"What is it?" I asked him.

"One hundred and two."

Michael: "Schatz?" — I've never heard of anybody named that before. Maybe it's not a name. I wonder what it means?
QUESTIONING

Anita: The boy sounds really sick. Reminds me of when I had to stay home with the flu.
CLARIFYING, CONNECTING

Anita: "One hundred and two." — That's high. He really is sick.
CLARIFYING

Downstairs, the doctor left three different medicines in different-colored capsules with instructions for giving them. One was to bring down the fever, another a purgative, the third to overcome an acid condition. The germs of influenza can only exist in an acid condition, he explained. He seemed to know all about influenza and said there was nothing to worry about if the fever did not go above one hundred and four degrees. This was a light epidemic of flu and there was no danger if you avoided pneumonia.

Back in the room I wrote the boy's temperature down and made a note of the time to give the various capsules.

"Do you want me to read to you?"

"All right. If you want to," said the boy. His face was very white and there were dark areas under his eyes. He lay still in the bed and seemed very detached from what was going on.

I read aloud from Howard Pyle's *Book of Pirates;* but I could see he was not following what I was reading.

"How do you feel, Schatz?" I asked him.

"Just the same, so far," he said.

I sat at the foot of the bed and read to myself while I waited for it to be time to give another capsule. It would have been natural for him to go to sleep, but when I looked up he was looking at the foot of the bed, looking very strangely.

"Why don't you try to go to sleep? I'll wake you up for the medicine."

"I'd rather stay awake."

After a while he said to me, "You don't have to stay in here with me, Papa, if it bothers you."

"It doesn't bother me."

"No, I mean you don't have to stay if it's going to bother you."

I thought perhaps he was a little lightheaded and after giving him the prescribed capsules at eleven o'clock I went out for a while.

It was a bright, cold day, the ground covered with a sleet that had frozen so that it seemed as if all the bare trees, the bushes, the cut brush, and all the grass and the bare ground had been varnished with ice. I took the young Irish setter for a little walk

January's Shadows, Robert Frank.

up the road and along a frozen creek, but it was difficult to stand or walk on the glassy surface and the red dog slipped and slithered and I fell twice, hard, once dropping my gun and having it slide away over the ice.

We flushed a covey of quail under a high clay bank with overhanging brush and I killed two as they went out of sight over the top of the bank. Some of the covey lit in trees, but most of

Michael: *"We flushed a covey of quail" — That must be what they call a flock of quail. The father shoots a couple of them. The author didn't say that the man had a gun with him, and now the man's hunting.*
CLARIFYING

them scattered into brush piles and it was necessary to jump on the ice-coated mounds of brush several times before they would flush. Coming out while you were poised unsteadily on the icy, springy brush, they made difficult shooting and I killed two, missed five, and started back pleased to have found a covey close to the house and happy there were so many left to find on another day.

At the house they said the boy had refused to let anyone come into the room.

"You can't come in," he said. "You mustn't get what I have."

I went up to him and found him in exactly the position I had left him, white-faced, but with the tops of his cheeks flushed by the fever, staring still, as he had stared, at the foot of the bed.

I took his temperature.

"What is it?"

"Something like a hundred," I said. It was one hundred and two and four tenths.

"It was a hundred and two," he said.

"Who said so?"

"The doctor."

"Your temperature is all right," I said. "It's nothing to worry about."

"I don't worry," he said, "but I can't keep from thinking."

"Don't think," I said. "Just take it easy."

"I'm taking it easy," he said and looked straight ahead. He was evidently holding tight onto himself about something.

"Take this with water."

"Do you think it will do any good?"

"Of course it will."

I sat down and opened the *Pirate* book and commenced to read, but I could see he was not following, so I stopped.

"About what time do you think I'm going to die?" he asked.

"What?"

"About how long will it be before I die?"

"You aren't going to die. What's the matter with you?"

"Oh, yes, I am. I heard him say a hundred and two."

"People don't die with a fever of one hundred and two. That's a silly way to talk."

"I know they do. At school in France the boys told me you can't live with forty-four degrees. I've got a hundred and two."

He had been waiting to die all day, ever since nine o'clock in the morning.

Anita: If the boy's so worried about not giving anybody else what he's got, he must think it's really serious. But if it were so serious, I think the doctor would have said something to the boy's father. Something else is the matter here.
EVALUATING

Anita: He thinks he's going to die! That explains why he's behaving so strangely. But why would he think that?
EVALUATING, QUESTIONING

Michael: The author didn't say until now that the boy had been to school in France.
CLARIFYING

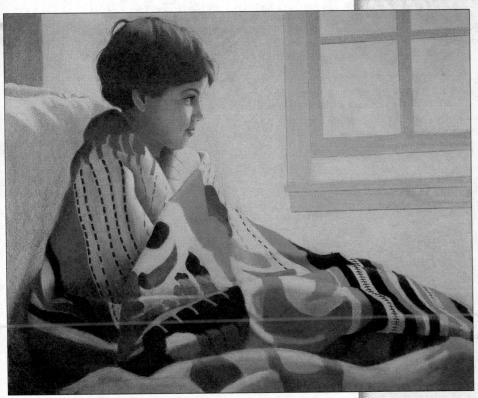

Mexican Morning (1942), Private Collection/GG Kopilak/Superstock.

"You poor Schatz," I said. "Poor old Schatz. It's like miles and kilometers. You aren't going to die. That's a different thermometer. On that thermometer thirty-seven is normal. On this kind it's ninety-eight."

"Are you sure?"

"Absolutely," I said. "It's like miles and kilometers. You know, like how many kilometers we make when we do seventy miles in the car?"

"Oh," he said.

But his gaze at the foot of the bed relaxed slowly. The hold over himself relaxed too, finally, and the next day it was very slack and he cried very easily at little things that were of no importance. ❖

Anita: *In France temperatures are measured in Celsius degrees, not Fahrenheit degrees. That's why he thought he was going to die. The temperature on the sign at the bank I pass on the way to school is given in both Celsius and Fahrenheit degrees, and the Celsius degrees are always much lower.*

CLARIFYING, CONNECTING

Creating a READER'S NOTEBOOK

Your Reader's Notebook

You can use almost any kind of notebook to help you interact with literature. Use a notebook of your choice to create your own Reader's Notebook. Then use your notebook to keep track of your thoughts as you read. Here are three ways to interact with the literature in this anthology.

1 Record Your Thoughts

In your 📖 **READER'S NOTEBOOK**, log in ideas, responses, connections, and questions **before**, **during**, and **after** you read a selection. (See "Strategies for Reading," page 4.) Summarize important passages, and include sketches and charts, too, if they will help. If you wish, compare your ideas with those of a classmate.

A Day's Wait
by Ernest Hemingway

Why is the boy so depressed? It's only the flu. It will go away in a couple days. Maybe there is something else bothering him.

- I could imagine what this boy would write in a letter to his old friends in France.
- It might be interesting to rewrite this story from the boy's perspective.

2 Collect Ideas for Writing

Be aware of interesting themes, passages, and thoughts of your own as you read or complete follow-up activities. In a special section of your 📖 **READER'S NOTEBOOK**, jot down anything that may later be a springboard to your own writing.

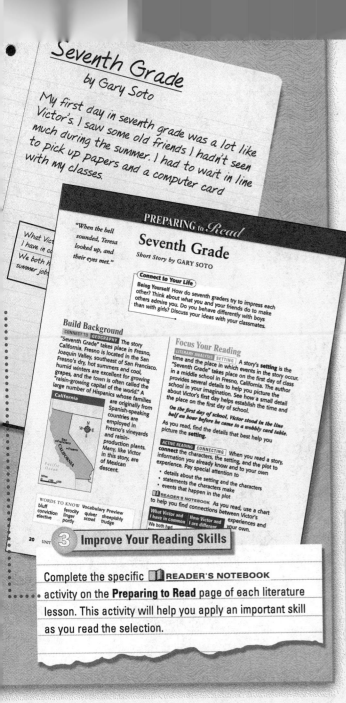

Seventh Grade
by Gary Soto

My first day in seventh grade was a lot like Victor's. I saw some old friends I hadn't seen much during the summer. I had to wait in line to pick up papers and a computer card with my classes.

What Vict[...]
I have in c[...]
We both [...]
summer job[...]

"When the bell sounded, Teresa looked up, and their eyes met."

PREPARING to *Read*

Seventh Grade
Short Story by GARY SOTO

Connect to Your Life

Being Yourself How do seventh graders try to impress each other? Think about what you and your friends do to make others admire you. Do you behave differently with boys than with girls? Discuss your ideas with your classmates.

Build Background

CONNECT TO GEOGRAPHY The story "Seventh Grade" takes place in Fresno, California. Fresno is located in the San Joaquin Valley, southeast of San Francisco. Fresno's dry, hot summers and cool, humid winters are excellent for growing grapes, and the town is often called the raisin-growing capital of the world." A large number of Hispanics whose families are originally from Spanish-speaking countries are employed in Fresno's vineyards and raisin-production plants. Many, like Victor in this story, are of Mexican descent.

California

Focus Your Reading

LITERARY ANALYSIS SETTING A story's **setting** is the time and the place in which events in the story occur. "Seventh Grade" takes place on the first day of class in a middle school in Fresno, California. The author provides several details to help you picture the school in your imagination. See how a small detail about Victor's first day helps establish the time and the place on the first day of school.

On the first day of school, Victor stood in the line half an hour before he came to a wobbly card table.

As you read, find the details that best help you picture the **setting**.

ACTIVE READING CONNECTING When you read a story, **connect** the characters, the setting, and the plot to information you already know and to your own experience. Pay special attention to
- details about the setting and the characters
- statements the characters make
- events that happen in the plot

READER'S NOTEBOOK As you read, use a chart to help you find connections between Victor's experiences and your own.

What Victor and I have in common	How Victor and I are different
We both had	

WORDS TO KNOW
bluff
conviction
elective
ferocity
linger
portly
quiver
scowl
Vocabulary Preview
sheepishly
trudge

20 UNIT

Improve Your Reading Skills

Complete the specific **READER'S NOTEBOOK** activity on the **Preparing to Read** page of each literature lesson. This activity will help you apply an important skill as you read the selection.

Your Working Portfolio

Artists and writers keep portfolios in which they store works in progress. Your portfolio can be a folder, a box, or a notebook. Add drafts of your writing experiments, summaries of your projects, and your goals and progress as a reader and writer.

Creating a Personal WORDList

Vocabulary As you read the selections in this book you will learn many new words. You can add these words to a special list called a **personal word list**—a list of words you want to use. Words for your list can come from:
- selections in this book
- stories and poems you write
- newspapers and magazines
- the Internet

Spelling There will be times when you misspell a word or need to write a word that you have not yet learned to spell. Add these words to a separate spelling list. To build your personal vocabulary and spelling lists, add a section for new words to your **READER'S NOTEBOOK** .

Go Beyond the Text

Your involvement doesn't stop with the last line of the text. Use these technology products to further your study and understanding:
- **Literature In Performance videos**
- **NetActivities CD-ROM**
- **Writing Coach CD-ROM**
- **McDougal Littell's companion Web site at www.mcdougallittell.com**

Learning from

Learning from Experience

In Unit One, students will read selections that show how people, young and old, can grow from their encounters with others and from their successes and failures. The unit is divided into two parts, "Knowing Who You Are" and "Moments of Discovery." Both parts complement the unit theme by exploring how ordinary and extraordinary people and events lead individuals to self-knowledge and an understanding of their place in the world.

———— Part 1 ————

Knowing Who You Are Selections in Part 1 examine the sometimes painful process that individuals must go through as they struggle to find their identities and reconcile their strengths and weaknesses. Roger in "Thank You, M'am" lets his desire for sneakers overwhelm his honesty before he finds out that there are better ways to reach his goals.

———— Part 2 ————

Moments of Discovery Revelations may be inspired by ordinary events or by crises, as the characters in the selections in Part 2 learn. The narrator in "The War of the Wall" learns that he is part of a larger community than his neighborhood and understands how much he has to learn about people after seeing the artist's finished mural. His view of himself and others around him is forever changed by the artist's vision.

12

  Viewing and Representing **TEKS 22A**

Illustration
by Brad Holland

ART APPRECIATION

Instruction Have students note that the detail of this illustration is primarily created by using shades of only two colors, blue and green. The variations in the shading draw the viewer's attention to the figure on the left, the opening of the jaws, and the palm trees. The illustrator has chosen those images to symbolically convey his meaning.

Ask: What do the elements of the illustration represent?

Possible Response: Responses will vary. The man appears to be reading a paper, unaware of the trap he is heading into. He might symbolize that people cannot always anticipate the future or may not learn from previous experience. The jaws represent intimidating or apparently negative experiences in life. The palm trees may indicate that even negative experiences can provide valuable lessons or that many experiences are neither totally good nor wholly bad.

Experience

"I think success has no rules, but you can learn a lot from failures."

Jean Kerr
American humorist
and dramatist

Painting. Copyright © 1999 Brad Holland. **13**

To help students explore the connections between the art, the quotation, and the unit theme, have them consider the following questions:

Ask: What are the kinds of lessons people might learn from experience?
Possible Responses: People might learn what they should and should not do in situations. They might learn what their strengths and weaknesses are. They might learn practical skills or grow in common sense. They might learn to be more careful or to take more risks. They might learn about others.

Ask: What does Jean Kerr mean when she says that "success has no rules, but you can learn a lot from failures"?
Possible Response: She might mean there is more than one way to achieve success or that the same formula for success may not work every time. However, every time a person fails, he or she knows what not to do next time.

Ask: Why is the man's location at the threshold of the mouth significant?
Possible Response: He still has time to turn back and reconsider his position or examine the situation he is about to enter.

Ask: What lessons have you learned from experience?
Responses will vary, although many students will cite experiences that have taught them to avoid potentially hazardous household situations.

Features and Selections	Literary Analysis	TEKS	Reading and Critical Thinking	TEKS	Writing Opportunities	TEKS
Learning from Experience **Knowing Who You Are**						
Learning the Language of Literature **Fiction**	Fiction, 15 TAAS READING OBJ. 2, 5	10H, 12A, B, F, G				
The Active Reader **Skills and Strategies**			Reading Fiction, 19 TAAS READING OBJ. 4	10A, B, C, D, M, 11A		
SHORT STORY **Seventh Grade** **Difficulty Level:** *Easy*	Setting, 20, 22, 24, 26 Dialect, 26 TAAS READING OBJ. 2, 5	12G 14B, C	Connecting, 20, 22, 24, 26 Standardized Test Practice, 25 TAAS READING OBJ. 3, 4	10A, 11A, 14C 10G, K	Write a Letter, 27 Profile of Victor, 27 TAAS READING OBJ. 1	11B 11B, 10L, 15C
SHORT STORY **Thank You, M'am** **Difficulty Level:** *Easy* Literary Link **If I Can Stop One Heart from Breaking**	Conflict, 29, 30, 32, 34 TAAS READING OBJ. 2, 5	1/G	Cause and Effect, 29, 30, 32, 34 Connect to Your Life, 29 Comparing Texts, 34 Informal Assessment, 35 TAAS READING OBJ. 2, 4, 5 TAAS WRITING OBJ. 1	12I 14C 10I, 11D 12G	Comparing Characters, 35	11B, 18A
PERSONAL ESSAY **Names/Nombres** **Difficulty Level:** *Challenging*	Personal Essay, 37, 38, 40, 42, 43 Review: Setting, 43 TAAS READING OBJ. 2, 5	12E 12G	Identifying Author's Purpose, 37, 38, 40, 42, 43 Connect to Your Life, 37 Informal Assessment, 42 TAAS READING OBJ. 6	10B, 12H 11B, 14C 12H	Personal Narrative, 44 Speech, 44	11B 11B
SHORT STORY **Zebra** **Difficulty Level:** *Challenging* Literary Link **The Rider**	Character, 46, 48, 50, 52, 54, 56, 60, 62 TAAS READING OBJ. 5	12F	Making Inferences, 46, 48, 50, 52, 54, 58, 60, 62 Comparing Texts, 62 Informal Assessment, 57 Standardized Test Practice, 59 TAAS READING OBJ. 2, 3, 4, 5	10H, F 11C, 11D 12F 10K, 12F	Personal Letter, 63 Road to Recovery Narrative, 63 TAAS READING OBJ. 1	11B, 15A 11B, 15A, C
Real World Link **Offerings at the Wall** **Building Vocabulary**			Forming and Revising Research Questions, 65	13A, 20A		
Writing Workshop: Response to Literature **Assessment Practice**			Analyzing a Student Model, 76 TAAS READING OBJ. 2, 3, 4, 6	10D, E, F, 12H, 14A, 19A	Writing Your Response to Literature, 78 Supporting Your Response with Quotations, 79 TAAS READING OBJ. 2, 3, 4,	11A, C, 14A, 15A, H, 19C 11C

LEGEND   DLS – Daily Language SkillBuilder   Green type – Teacher's Edition

Speaking and Listening Viewing and Representing	TEKS	Inquiry and Research	TEKS	Grammar, Usage, and Mechanics	TEKS	Vocabulary	TEKS
Art Appreciation, 12	22A						
Magazine Ad, 27 Comedy Sketch, 27 Art Connection, 27	23D, 24A 5C, E, 11B, 15D 22A, 23A, B	Mexican Americans, 27	13C	Subjects and Predicates, 28 DLS, 20 Capitalization and Punctuation of Simple Sentences, 24 Subject, Verb, and Predicate, 28 **TAAS WRITING OBJ. 3, 5, 6, 7**	17A 16B, D, 17F, G 17A 17A	Assessment Practice, 27 Using Context Clues, 21 Using the letters *dge*, 22 Antonyms, 27 **TAAS READING OBJ. 1**	10K 6A 16D 9C
Paired Activity, 34 Film Review, 35 Dramatic Dialogue, 35 Art Connection, 35 Art Appreciation, 30	10L, 11B 11B, 23B 5C, 11B 23A 22A	Life in Harlem, 35	11B, 13F	Compound Predicates, 36 DLS, 29 Coordinating Conjunctions, 33 Compound Subjects and Predicates, 36 **TAAS WRITING OBJ. 3, 5, 6, 7**	17A 17C, G 17B 17C	Synonyms, 35 Prefixes, 35 Synonyms, 31 **TAAS READING OBJ. 1** **TAAS WRITING OBJ. 3, 7**	6A 16C 9C
Cooperative Learning Activity, 43 Story Illustration, 44 Interview Questions, 44 Present a Report, 40 **TAAS READING OBJ. 4**	11A, B 11B, 24A 5A, B 4A, 5E	New Kid on the Block, 44 Dominican Heritage, 45	1D, 2A, 13F 11B	Combining Sentences, 45 DLS, 37 Commas after Introductory Elements, 41 Combining Sentences Using Introductory Elements, 45 **TAAS WRITING OBJ. 3, 5, 6, 7**	17A, B 16B, 17A 17A 17A	Context Clues, 44 Suffixes, 44 Using Context Clues, 39 Adverbs using *-ly*, 44 **TAAS READING OBJ. 1** **TAAS WRITING OBJ. 3, 7**	6A 16C 6A, 9B 16C
Cooperative Learning Activity, 62 Garbage People, 63 Story Mime, 63 Persuasive Speech, 63 Art Appreciation, 53, 60 Interview, 54 **TAAS READING OBJ. 4**	10L, 11A, B 11B, 24A 5C, 11B 5F, 11B 23A, B 13A, F, 20A, C	War Memorials, 63 Growing Up, 64 **TAAS READING OBJ. 4**	13I, 24A 11B, D	Sentence Fragments, 64 DLS, 46 Avoiding Run-On Sentences, 50 Avoiding Ineffective Sentence Fragments, 64 **TAAS WRITING OBJ. 3, 5, 7**	17A 16B, 17A 17A 17A	Word Meaning, 63 Drawing on Experience to Infer Meaning, 47 Suffixes: Silent *-e*, 49 Context Clues, 52 **TAAS READING OBJ. 1** **TAAS WRITING OBJ. 3, 7**	6C, 9B, C 9B, 10A 16C 6A
		Activity Link: "Zebra," 66 Inquiry & Research, 66	13A, F, 20A 13C			Understanding Context Clues, 67 **TAAS READING OBJ. 1**	6A, 9B
Picturing Text Structure, 77	10L			Correcting Run-On Sentences, 79 Revising and Editing, 80 Capitalization Errors, 80 **TAAS WRITING OBJ. 1–7**	17C, 18C, E 16B, 17A, F, 18E, H 17A		

LEGEND   DLS – Daily Language SkillBuilder   Green type – Teacher's Edition

Speaking and Listening Viewing and Representing	TEKS	Inquiry and Research	TEKS	Grammar, Usage, and Mechanics	TEKS	Vocabulary	TEKS
Paired Activity, 98 Time Line, 99 News Photograph, 94 **TAAS READING OBJ. 2, 4**	10E, 11B 10L, 11B, C, 24A 23C	Human Rights, 99 History for Today, 100	13A 11B	Predicate Adjectives, 100 DLS, 87 Vivid Adjectives, 90 Predicate Nouns, Adjectives, and Pronouns, 100 **TAAS WRITING OBJ. 3, 4, 5, 6, 7**	17A, D 17A, C 17D 17C	Context Clues, 99 -ant/-ent, 99 Using Context Clues, 89 Word Families, 92 Words Ending in -ance/-ant, 99 **TAAS READING OBJ. 1** **TAAS WRITING OBJ. 3, 7**	6A, 9B 16C 6A, 9B 9D 16C
Cooperative Learning Activity, 106 Drawing or Sculpture, 107 Interview, 107 Art Appreciation, 105 **TAAS READING OBJ. 4**	11A, B, C 11B, C, 24A 5B, 11B 23B	Helping the Homeless, 107 Something in Common, 108 **TAAS READING OBJ. 3**	13C, F 10G, 11B	Direct Objects, 108 DLS, 101 Direct and Indirect Objects, 108 **TAAS WRITING OBJ. 3, 5, 6, 7**	17A 16B, 17C 17C	Word Meanings, 107 Word Meanings, 102 **TAAS READING OBJ. 1**	6A, 9B 6C, 9C
Cooperative Learning Activity, 118 Plot Collage, 119 War of the Wall Rap, 119 Dedication Speech, 119 Art Appreciation, 116	11B, C 11B, 24A 5C, 11B, 15D 5C, 11B, 22A	Mural Subjects, 119 Growing Up in the City, 120 **TAAS READING OBJ. 4**	13A, F, 20A 4A, 11B, C, D	Clear Pronoun Antecedents, 120 DLS, 109 **TAAS WRITING OBJ. 3, 5, 6, 7**	17A 16B, D	Meaning Clues, 119 Suffixes, 119 Using Context Clues, 110 Analogies, 119 **TAAS READING OBJ. 1** **TAAS WRITING OBJ. 3, 7**	6A, 9B 16C 6A 9B
Cooperative Learning Activity, 135 Comic Book, 136 Radio Script, 136 Illustration, 132	11B, C 11B, 24A 5C, 11B, 22C	Just Like People?, 136 **TAAS READING OBJ. 5**	13C, G	Varying Sentence Length, 137 DLS, 121 Compound Sentences, 126 Sentence Variety, 137 **TAAS WRITING OBJ. 3, 5, 6, 7**	16B, 17A 17C 17A, B 17A	Assessment Practice, 136 Synonyms, 122 Learning and Remembering New Words, 130 **TAAS READING OBJ. 1**	6A, 9B, 10K 6A, C 9C, G
		Activity Link: "Rikki-tikki-tavi," 141 Inquiry & Research, 141 **TAAS READING OBJ. 5**	11C, 13G 11B, 13C			Informal Language: Idioms and Slang, 142 **TAAS READING OBJ. 1**	6A, C, 9B, C
Paired Activity, 161 Art Appreciation, 156	11B 22A			Unusual Order, 162 DLS, 154 Interrupting Phrases, 159 Subjects Not at the Beginning of the Sentence, 162 **TAAS WRITING OBJ. 3, 5, 6, 7**	17A, C 16B 16B, 17A 17A, C	Assessment Practice, 162 Antonyms, 155 Word Parts: Affixes, 158 **TAAS READING OBJ. 1** **TAAS WRITING OBJ. 3, 7**	10K 9B 6B, 9D
Cooperative Learning Activity, 171 Art Appreciation, 164	10L, 11B 22A, 23B			Kinds of Sentences, 172 DLS, 163 Four Kinds of Sentences, 169 Punctuating Sentences, 172 **TAAS WRITING OBJ. 3, 5, 6, 7**	16B, 17A 16B, 17A, F 16B, 17A 16B, 17A	Word Meaning, 172 Word Meaning, 166 Word Roots, 168 **TAAS READING OBJ. 1**	6A, 9B 6B, 9D 6B, C, 9G
Speaking and Listening, 175 Short Story and Video, 176 Creating a Scene, 176	2E, 4A 11B, 23B 5C, 11B, 15G	Back in Time, 176	13C				
Picturing Text Structure, 180 **TAAS READING OBJ. 2, 4**	10E, L, 12I			Parallelism, 182 Revising & Editing, 183 Run-On Sentences, 183 **TAAS WRITING OBJ. 1–7**	17C, 18E 16B, D, 17C, 18H 17A		
Discussing , 184	11B, 14A						

To introduce the theme of this unit, use Fine Art Transparencies T19–21 in the Communications Transparencies and Copymasters.

	Unit Resource Book	Assessment	Integrated Technology and Media	Additional Support — Literary Analysis Transparencies
Seventh Grade pp. 20–28	• Summary p. 7 • Active Reading p. 8 • Literary Analysis p. 9 • Words to Know p. 10 • Grammar p. 11 • Spelling p. 12 • Selection Quiz p. 13	• Selection Test, Formal Assessment pp. 5–6 Test Generator	Audio Library	• Setting T6
Thank You, M'am pp. 29–36	• Summary p. 14 • Active Reading p. 15 • Literary Analysis p. 16 • Words to Know p. 17 • Grammar p. 18 • Spelling p. 19 • Selection Quiz p. 20	• Selection Test, Formal Assessment pp. 7–8 Test Generator	Audio Library LaserLinks, Teacher's SourceBook p. 6 Video: Literature in Performance, Video Resource Book pp. 3–9	• Conflict T8
Names/Nombres pp. 37–45	• Summary p. 21 • Active Reading p. 22 • Literary Analysis p. 23 • Words to Know p. 24 • Grammar p. 25 • Spelling p. 26 • Selection Quiz p. 27	• Selection Test, Formal Assessment pp. 9–10 Test Generator	Audio Library Research Starter www.mcdougallittell.com	
Zebra pp. 46–64	• Summary p. 28 • Active Reading p. 29 • Literary Analysis p. 30 • Words to Know p. 31 • Grammar p. 32 • Spelling p. 33 • Selection Quiz p. 34	• Selection Test, Formal Assessment pp. 11–12 Test Generator	Audio Library Research Starter www.mcdougallittell.com	• Analyzing Character T3 • Characterization T4 • Dialogue T24

Writing Workshop: Response to Literature

		Unit Assessment	Unit Technology	
Unit One Resource Book • Prewriting p. 36 • Drafting and Elaboration p. 37 • Peer Response Guide pp. 38–39 • Revising, Editing, and Proofreading p. 40 • Student Models pp. 41–43 • Rubric for Evaluation p. 44	**Writing Coach** **Writing Transparencies** T1–4, T11, T26 **Grammar Transparencies and Copymasters** C122 **Teacher's Guide to Assessment and Portfolio Use**	• Unit One, Part 1 Test, Formal Assessment pp. 13–14 Test Generator • Unit One Integrated Test, Integrated Assessment pp. 1–6	ClassZone www.mcdougallittell.com Electronic Teacher Tools	

To introduce the theme of this unit, use Fine Art Transparencies T19–21 in the Communications Transparencies and Copymasters.

	Unit Resource Book	Assessment	Integrated Technology and Media	Additional Support — Literary Analysis Transparencies
Eleanor Roosevelt pp. 87–100	• Summary p. 45 • Active Reading p. 46 • Literary Analysis p. 47 • Words to Know p. 48 • Grammar p. 49 • Spelling p. 50 • Selection Quiz p. 51	• Selection Test, Formal Assessment pp. 15–16 Test Generator	Audio Library LaserLinks, Teacher's SourceBook p. 8 Research Starter www.mcdougallittell.com	• Biography T10
Homeless pp. 101–108	• Summary p. 52 • Active Reading p. 53 • Literary Analysis p. 54 • Words to Know p. 55 • Grammar p. 56 • Spelling p. 57 • Selection Quiz p. 58	• Selection Test, Formal Assessment pp. 17–18 Test Generator	Audio Library LaserLinks, Teacher's SourceBook p. 9	• Narrator and Point of View T22

Reading and Critical Thinking Transparencies	Grammar Transparencies and Copymasters	Vocabulary Transparencies and Copymasters	Writing Transparencies	Communications Transparencies and Copymasters
• Connecting T2	• Daily Language SkillBuilder T1 • Capitalization and Punctuation of Simple Sentences C121 • Subject, Verb, and Predicate C51	• Context Clues: Contrast Words C18 • Antonyms C19	• Point of View T23	• Impromptu Speaking: Dialogue, Role-Play T13
• Cause and Effect T3	• Daily Language SkillBuilder T1 • Coordinating Conjunctions C90 • Compound Subjects and Predicates C53	• Synonyms C20	• Structuring the Essay T6	• Evaluation Matrix: Film/Video T7
• Author's Purpose and Audience T4	• Daily Language SkillBuilder T2 • Commas After Introductory Elements C124 • Combining Sentences Using Introductory Elements C103	• Context Clues: General C21	• Achieving Unity T8	• Formal Presentations T10
• Making Inferences T5 • Vertical Category Chart T41	• Daily Language SkillBuilder T2 • Avoiding Run-On Sentences C60 • Avoiding Ineffective Sentence Fragments C61	• Drawing on Experience to Infer Meaning C22 • Context Clues: Definition and Restatement C23	• Comparison-and-Contrast Essay (by Subject) T28 • Comparison-and-Contrast Essay (by Feature) T29	• Interviewing T9 • Persuasive Techniques T3

STUDENTS ACQUIRING ENGLISH

The **Spanish Study Guide,** pp. 1–15, includes language support for the following pages:
• Family and Community Involvement (per unit)

• Selection Summaries and Vocabulary
• Active Reading
• Literary Analysis

Reading and Critical Thinking Transparencies	Grammar Transparencies and Copymasters	Vocabulary Transparencies and Copymasters	Writing Transparencies	Communications Transparencies and Copymasters
• Chronological Order T6	• Daily Language SkillBuilder T3 • Vivid Adjectives C78 • Predicate Nouns, Adjectives, and Pronouns C52	• Context Clues C24 • Word Families C25	• Locating Information Using the Internet T47–48	
• Author's Purpose and Audience T4	• Daily Language SkillBuilder T3 • Direct and Indirect Objects C56	• Locate Word Meanings and Pronunciations C26	• Topic Sentences and Thesis Statements T7 • How to Summarize T51	

	Unit Resource Book	Assessment	Integrated Technology and Media	Literary Analysis Transparencies
The War of the Wall *pp. 109–120*	• Summary p. 59 • Active Reading p. 60 • Literary Analysis p. 61 • Words to Know p. 62 • Grammar p. 63 • Spelling p. 64 • Selection Quiz p. 65	• Selection Test, Formal Assessment pp. 19–20 Test Generator	Audio Library LaserLinks, Teacher's SourceBook p. 10	• Plot T5
Rikki-tikki-tavi *pp. 121–137*	• Summary p. 66 • Active Reading p. 67 • Literary Analysis p. 68 • Words to Know p. 69 • Grammar p. 70 • Spelling p. 71 • Selection Quiz p. 72	• Selection Test, Formal Assessment pp. 21–22 Test Generator	Audio Library LaserLinks, Teacher's SourceBook p. 12	• Analyzing Character T3
After Twenty Years *pp. 154–162*	• Summary p. 74 • Active Reading p. 75 • Literary Analysis p. 76 • Words to Know p. 77 • Grammar p. 78 • Spelling p. 79 • Selection Quiz p. 80	• Selection Test, Formal Assessment pp. 23–24 Test Generator	Audio Library	• Irony T27 • Theme T7
A Retrieved Reformation *pp. 163–172*	• Summary p. 81 • Active Reading p. 82 • Literary Analysis p. 83 • Words to Know p. 84 • Grammar p. 85 • Spelling p. 86 • Selection Quiz p. 87	• Selection Test, Formal Assessment pp. 25–26 Test Generator	Audio Library LaserLinks, Teacher's SourceBook p. 13 Video: Literature in Performance, Video Resource Book pp. 11–16	• Plot T5

Writing Workshop: Personal Narative

		Unit Assessment	Unit Technology	
Unit One Resource Book • Prewriting p. 88 • Drafting and Elaboration p. 89 • Peer Response Guide pp. 90–91 • Revising, Editing, and Proofreading p. 92 • Student Models pp. 93–95 • Rubric for Evaluation p. 96	**Writing Coach** **Writing Transparencies** T1–4, T13, T16, T25 **Reading and Critical Thinking Transparencies and Copymasters** T39 **Grammar Transparencies and Copymasters** C183 **Teacher's Guide to Assessment and Portfolio Use**	• Unit One, Part 2 Test, Formal Assessment pp. 27–28 Test Generator • Unit One Integrated Test, Integrated Assessment pp. 1–6	ClassZone www.mcdougallittell.com Electronic Teacher Tools	

Reading and Critical Thinking Transparencies	Grammar Transparencies and Copymasters	Vocabulary Transparencies and Copymasters	Writing Transparencies	Communications Transparencies and Copymasters
• Cause and Effect T3 • Observation Chart T36	• Daily Language SkillBuilder T4 • Pronoun Subject-Verb Agreement C120	• Context Clues: General C27 • Analogies C28	• Organizing Your Writing T11	• Verbal Strategies T14 • Nonverbal Strategies T15
• Predicting T7	• Daily Language SkillBuilder T4 • Compound Sentences C104 • Sentence Variety C134	• Synonyms C29 • Learning and Remembering New Words C30	• Combining Sentences Using Conjunctions T19	• Impromptu Speaking: Dialogue, Role-Play T13
• Strategies for Reading T1 • Story Map T34	• Daily Language SkillBuilder T5 • Subjects Not at the Beginning of a Sentence C57 • Interrupting Phrases C133	• Antonyms C31 • Affixes: Word Parts C32	• Varying Sentence Openers and Closers T18	
• Compare and Contrast T8	• Daily Language SkillBuilder T5 • Four Kinds of Sentences C54 • Punctuating Four Types of Sentences C123	• Word Meaning C33 • Word Roots C34	• Revising Problem Sentences T20	• Evaluating Roles in Groups T8

STUDENTS ACQUIRING ENGLISH

The **Spanish Study Guide**, pp. 16–33, includes language support for the following pages:
• Family and Community Involvement (per unit)

• Selection Summaries and Vocabulary
• Active Reading
• Literary Analysis

Selection	SkillBuilder Sentences	Suggested Answers
Seventh Grade	1. Victor could of took Spanish, but he knew Teresa was in French class. 2. Michael thought a scowl made him look more old and attractiver to girl's, but Victor didn't agree.	1. Victor could **have taken** Spanish, but he knew Teresa was in French class. 2. Michael thought a scowl made him look **older** and **more attractive** to **girls**, but Victor didn't agree.
Thank You M'am	1. Roger did'nt expect Mrs. Jones' purse to be so heavy. 2. Roger might be thinking to hisself that stealing is wrong.	1. Roger did**n't** expect Mrs. Jone**s's** purse to be so heavy. 2. Roger might be thinking to **himself** that stealing is wrong.
Names/Nombres	1. She said "The Dominican Republic is in the Caribbean sea". 2. Julia's hobby writing poems and stories stayed with her for a long time.	1. She said, "The Dominican Republic is in the Caribbean **Sea."** 2. Julia's hobby, writing poems and stories, stayed with her for a long time.
Zebra	1. One of the characters in the story "zebra" had been in the Vietnam war. 2. Like a swift African zebra Adam ran down Franklin Avenue.	1. One of the characters in the story **"Zebra"** had been in the Vietnam **War**. 2. Like a swift African zebra, Adam ran down Franklin Avenue.

Selection	SkillBuilder Sentences	Suggested Answers
Eleanor Roosevelt	1. Fighting for social reforms were important to her.	1. Fighting for social reforms **was** important to her.
	2. Give me that book. So I can read more about her relief efforts.	2. Give me that **book so** I can read more about her relief efforts.
Homeless	1. Many people without homes lives in public buildings, such as the New York Port Authority Bus Terminal.	1. Many people without homes **live** in public buildings, such as the New York Port Authority Bus Terminal.
	2. The picture shown the woman's former home, which contained a couch, a stove, and curtains.	2. The picture show**ed** the woman's former home, which contained a couch, a stove, and curtains.
The War of the Wall	1. The narrator and Lou feel like saying to the women artist, Don't touch that wall.	1. The narrator and Lou feel like saying to the **woman** artist, **"**Don't touch that wall.**"**
	2. Their friend Jimmy Lyons never come back from Vietnam, so they carved his name into the wall.	2. Their friend Jimmy Lyons never **came** back from Vietnam, so they carved his name into the wall.
Rikki-tikki-tavi	1. "Why didn't you tell me about nagaina's eggs?" asked rikki-tikki.	1. "Why didn't you tell me about **N**againa's eggs?" asked **R**ikki-tikki.
	2. Rikki-tikki couldn't hardly take a breathe before there was another snake attack.	2. Rikki-tikki **could** hardly take a **breath** before there was another snake attack.

Selection	SkillBuilder Sentences	Suggested Answers
After Twenty Years	1. Twenty years ago, a mans friend had agreed to meet him here tonight. 2. A policemen stopped to talk while the man was waiting for his friend.	1. Twenty years ago, a man's friend had agreed to meet him here tonight. 2. A policeman stopped to talk while the man was waiting for his friend.
A Retrieved Reformation	1. Jimmy lived in the Hotel for a year after he arrived in elmore, Arkansas. 2. After falling in love with Annabel. Jimmy became a changed man.	1. Jimmy lived in the hotel for a year after he arrived in Elmore, Arkansas. 2. After falling in love with Annabel, Jimmy became a changed man.

	Unit One	Unit Two	Unit Three	Unit Four	Unit Five	Unit Six
Grammar Focus by Unit	The Sentence and Its Parts	Nouns, Pronouns, and Verbs	Modifiers	Phrases	Compound and Complex Sentences	Review

The Language of Literature offers several options for integrating grammar instruction and literature.

- Each unit has a specific grammar focus. The grammar focus for this unit is highlighted on the planning chart. Categories of grammar skills for this unit are shown in red.
- The Pupil's Edition includes instructive features entitled *Grammar in Context*. The instruction in these features arises from the selections and relates to the grammar focus for each unit.
- The Writing Workshops in the Pupil's Edition include grammar tips that help the students produce error-free drafts.
- Mini Lessons in the Teacher's Edition complement the instruction in the *Grammar in Context* features. Additional Mini Lessons relate to the grammar focus for each unit as well as to the literature.
- Daily Language SkillBuilders in the Teacher's Edition provide students with ongoing proofreading practice and reinforce punctuation, spelling, grammar and usage, and capitalization.
- Grammar Copymasters and Transparencies, which may be used independently or in conjunction with the Mini Lessons in the Teacher's Edition, present grammar in a traditional, systematic sequence.

PE instruction shown in black
TE Mini Lessons shown in green

Part 1

THE SENTENCE AND ITS PARTS
Subjects and Predicates
"Seventh Grade," p. 28
Subject, Verb, and Predicate
"Seventh Grade," p. 28
Compound Predicates
"Thank You, M'am," p. 36
Compound Subjects and Predicates
"Thank You, M'am," p. 36
Avoiding Run-On Sentences
"Zebra," p. 50
Sentence Fragments
"Zebra," p. 64
Avoiding Ineffective Sentence Fragments
"Zebra," p. 64
Correcting Run-on Sentences
Writing Workshop, p. 79

PREPOSITIONS, CONJUNCTIONS, AND INTERJECTIONS
Coordinating Conjunctions
"Thank You, M'am," p. 33

SENTENCE STRUCTURE
Combining Sentences Using Introductory Elements
"Names/Nombres," p. 45

CAPITALIZATION
Capitalization and Punctuation of Simple Sentences
"Seventh Grade," p. 24
Capitalization Errors
Writing Workshop, p. 80

PUNCTUATION
Commas After Introductory Elements
"Names/Nombres," p. 41

STYLE
Combining Sentences
"Names/Nombres," p. 45

Part 2

THE SENTENCE AND ITS PARTS
Predicate Nouns, Adjectives, and Pronouns
"Eleanor Roosevelt," p. 100
Direct Objects
"Homeless," p. 108
Direct and Indirect Objects
"Homeless," p. 108
Subjects Not at the Beginning of a Sentence
"After Twenty Years," p. 162
Subjects in Unusual Order
"After Twenty Years," p. 162
Four Kinds of Sentences
"A Retrieved Reformation," p. 169
Kinds of Sentences
"A Retrieved Reformation," p. 172
Run-On Sentences
Assessment Practice, p. 183

PRONOUNS
Clear Pronoun Antecedents
"The War of the Wall," p. 120

ADJECTIVES AND ADVERBS
Vivid Adjectives
"Eleanor Roosevelt," p. 90
Predicate Adjectives
"Eleanor Roosevelt," p. 100

SENTENCE STRUCTURE
Compound Sentences
"Rikki-tikki-tavi," p. 126

SUBJECT-VERB AGREEMENT
Pronoun Subject-Verb Agreement
"The War of the Wall," p. 120

PUNCTUATION
Interrupting Phrases
"After Twenty Years," p. 159
Punctuation of Four Types of Sentences
"A Retrieved Reformation," p. 172

STYLE
Varying Sentence Length
"Rikki-tikki-tavi," p. 137
Sentence Variety
"Rikki-tikki-tavi," p. 137
Parallelism
Writing Workshop, p. 182

Students work in small groups to produce a news program featuring characters from the unit who learned something new about themselves after an important experience. Students will collect characters' stories and compile them for a national evening newsmagazine broadcast.

Points at a glance The selections in Unit One feature characters who learn something new about themselves after an important experience. For this project, some students will assume the roles of characters in the stories and other students will interview them. Students will present the stories in a *60 Minutes*-type video newsmagazine format. Members will share responsibilities for researching the topic, writing the script, narrating, conducting interviews, and taping their segment. Each topic should be well thought out with a focus on a defining moment in the story, the events that led up to it, and the resulting self discovery. If your school has access to a video cameras, the program might be videotaped for presentation. If not, staging the program will work just as well.

SCHEDULING
Individual segments should take no more than ten minutes. The entire "program" should run about 60 minutes. You may want to schedule the presentation over the course of 2–3 class periods. This project can take place over the course of the unit or at the end, depending on your schedule.

PROJECT OBJECTIVES
- To demonstrate the speaking and listening skills in the activity
- To identify how key events in the stories taught characters something about themselves
- To conduct in-depth interviews with students playing character roles
- To write an original script synthesizing the events in a story
- To combine the story with those of other groups into a full-length program

SUGGESTED GROUP SIZE
4–5 students per group

 # Getting Started

Explain that students will be working in small groups to plan and produce a video newsmagazine similiar to *60 Minutes, Dateline,* or *20/20.* Each group will produce an interview segment with a character from a story in the unit. Characters will reveal what an important experience taught them.

Have students watch one of the shows mentioned above and note some key elements: background information, interviews, transitional statements made by the anchors, and introductory and concluding statements by the reporters.

If video equipment is available, have someone videotape each segment when it is ready.

Students who cannot videotape can present their findings as though on live television.

Interviews should be well rehearsed. If groups are using video equipment, arrange for interviewees to come to one taping at a specific time. Allow for extra time to complete the project.

Writing Workshop Connection

As a springboard, students may use the Writing Workshop assignment **Response to Literature,** p. 75, which they will complete in Part 1 of this unit.

 # Directing the Project

Preparing *(1 class period)* Divide students into groups of 4–5. Have students choose their favorite stories from the unit. List main characters from the stories and the experience that taught them something new. Ask groups to write a brief description of the character, the experience they are focusing on, and what the character learned as a result.

Assigning Roles
- Select two students to act as anchors.
- Assign one main character from a story, as well as minor characters for each group.
- Choose reporters to interview the main characters, and writers to help the reporters prepare questions.
- Assign a "tech team" to work the video camera, build sets or make cue cards.

▶ Have students brainstorm a list of interview questions for the main character. Meet with each group to refine the script, offer help, or make suggestions about the project as a whole. Group members should "prep" the main character by asking him or her about the events in the story. Have students review their notes. They'll feel more comfortable knowing they have more than enough material to present. Review with students the Speaking and Listening Skills listed on the next page.

Practicing *(2 class periods)* Allow time for students to coordinate their interview and to rehearse so that it flows smoothly when the actual presentation begins. Tell students that giving and receiving feedback during the rehearsal stage is crucial. Review the tips in the Feedback Center as students begin their rehearsals.

▶ Anchors should briefly meet with each group to write a script that can be used between the interviews. These students will need to "pre-screen" each interview so that they can also write an introduction and conclusion to the show as a whole.

Presenting *(2–3 class periods)* This project could culminate in a screening of the newsmagazine for the entire student body or just for your class.

▶ Have students take a few deep breaths and focus on what it is they want to communicate. Anchors should look directly into the camera during the introduction, transitional statements, and conclusions of each piece. They should appear natural, using gestures and facial expressions to fit the content. Characters should use appropriate verbal and nonverbal cues that reflect the tone of their stories. Reporters should appear interested but neutral.

Teaching the Speaking and Listening Skills

The student is expected to:

Demonstrate effective communication skills that reflect such demands as interviewing, reporting, requesting, and providing information

Teaching Suggestions: Have students review the interview guidelines on page R104–R105. Remind them that often an interviewer has to ask the same question in different ways to get the necessary information. Also tell students to take clear notes or tape the interview sessions to get a better idea of their subject's style and main points. Discuss the idea of the "objective reporter." In other words, reporters should present their findings in a balanced manner. They should also make sure that all main points should be supported with evidence and examples from the stories.

Use effective rate, volume, pitch, and tone for the audience and the setting

Teaching Suggestions: Tell students to rehearse their parts several times in front of the mirror. They should speak at a comfortable pitch, placing emphasis on important words. Coach them on making their delivery fit their message, audience, and setting.

Understand the major ideas and supporting evidence in spoken messages

Teaching Suggestions: Have the class reflect on the coherence of each piece. Did it make sense? Were major ideas supported by examples from the text? Were their conclusions logical? Were the characters convincing? To check for understanding, have audience members identify the challenge in the life of each featured character and summarize the lesson learned.

Feedback Center

Students can use the following guidelines when giving and receiving feedback during this project.

Giving Feedback

▶ Ask questions concerning content, delivery, purpose and point of view (for instance, is tone appropriate for the subject?).

▶ Provide feedback about the coherence and logic of the content, delivery, and overall impact on the listener.

▶ Comment on the verbal and nonverbal delivery (pitch, pace, volume, body language) and its impact on the listener.

▶ Respond to persuasive messages with questions, challenges, or affirmations.

▶ Question evidence to support the speaker's claims and conclusions.

Using Feedback

▶ Listen to constructive criticism with an open mind.

▶ Use audience feedback and modify presentation to clarify meaning or organization.

3 ▶ Assessing the Project

The following rubric can be used for group or individual assessment.

3 *Full Accomplishment*

The group produced a newsmagazine segment that shows what a character from a story learned as a result of a defining experience. Students worked effectively in a group and demonstrated all three of the Speaking and Listening Skills listed, including effective communication skills, appropriate delivery of information, and an understanding of the major ideas and supporting evidence.

2 *Substantial Accomplishment*

The students produced a newsmagazine segment, but it lacks some key information or clarity of subject matter. Students worked in a group with adequate communication in organizing and fulfilling individual roles. Students demonstrated two out of three of the Speaking and Listening Skills.

1 *Little Accomplishment*

The students' segment was incomplete or did not fulfill the requirements of the assignment. Students demonstrated only one of the Speaking and Listening Skills. Organization of the presentation was unclear and students didn't accurately carry out group roles.

Reflecting on the Theme Getting to know who you are is part of growing up and developing as an individual. Throughout history, people have regarded knowing who you are as the first step in learning about life. Literature can help you learn about both life and yourself. It provides the freedom to imagine yourself in different places or times. Often you recognize your own ideas and habits in a certain character and, therefore, you can see yourself more clearly. As you read these selections, judge how much you know about yourself.

ACTIVITY

Do people really know what you're about? As a class, play hangman or a game of charades in which you reveal a skill or an interest people may not know you have.

*F*iction

Great stories give us [images] which flash upon the mind the way lightning flashes upon the earth . . .
—Paula Fox

Where do stories come from? Some are whispered in the glow of a campfire. Others are discovered in a book. Wherever you find them, all stories begin in someone's imagination. Stories that come from a writer's imagination are called **fiction.** Two types of fiction are **short stories** and **novels.** Both contain the elements of **plot, character, setting,** and **theme.**

Sometimes a writer bases a fictional story on actual events or on real people, adding invented elements such as additional characters or dialogue. The purpose of fiction is to entertain, but it can also provide the reader with a deeper understanding of life.

Key Types of Fiction

short story
- usually revolves around a single idea
- is short enough to be read at one sitting

novel
- a longer work
- involves a more complicated plot

Objectives
- understand the following literary terms:

fiction	falling action
short stories	characters
plot	main character
conflict	minor character
exposition	setting
rising action	theme
climax	

- understand and appreciate fiction
- recognize the distinguishing features of fiction

Teaching the Lesson

This lesson introduces and analyzes the elements of fiction and demonstrates how each of these elements contributes to the work as a whole.

Introducing the Concepts
Have students think of a work of fiction they have recently read. Ask them to describe to the class the most memorable aspect of the work and explain their reasons.

Use **Literary Analysis Transparencies,** pp. 1–3, 5–7, for additional support.

 TEKS See the Skills Trace at the beginning of the unit for information on TEKS covered in this lesson.

15

Presenting the Concepts
Plot

Draw students' attention to the Plot at a Glance diagram. Discuss the diagram with them and be sure they have a clear understanding of each stage of plot development.

Then have students think about the plot of a story with which they are all familiar. Have them try to identify the elements of each stage of the story's plot. In doing this, students might want to sketch a plot diagram, like the one below, and write key details around the sketch.

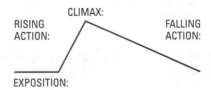

YOUR TURN
Possible Response: The conflict is between the two characters, one who thinks he is dying, the other who doesn't agree. The resolution could be that the sick boy gets better or that he dies.

Plot

The sequence of events in a story is called the **plot.** A plot is usually built around a **conflict**—a problem or struggle between opposing forces. Although the development of every plot is different, **most plots develop in four stages:**

- **Exposition** sets the stage for the story. Characters are introduced, and the setting is described.
- **Rising action** occurs as the story continues. The conflict begins to unfold as the plot becomes more complex and problems and complications arise. Suspense builds as the characters struggle to find solutions to the conflict.
- **Climax** is the turning point of the story. The action reaches a peak, and the outcome of the conflict is decided. The climax usually results in a change in the characters or a solution to the problem.
- **Falling action** (sometimes called **resolution**) occurs at the conclusion of the story. Loose ends are tied up, and the story ends.

YOUR TURN Read the passage above. What conflict is introduced? What do you think could happen to resolve the conflict?

PLOT

"About what time do you think I'm going to die?" he asked.

"What?"

"About how long will it be before I die?"

"You aren't going to die. What's the matter with you?"

"Oh, yes, I am. I heard him say a hundred and two."

"People don't die with a fever of one hundred and two. That's a silly way to talk."

"I know they do. At school in France the boys told me you can't live with forty-four degrees. I've got a hundred and two."

—Ernest Hemingway, "A Day's Wait"

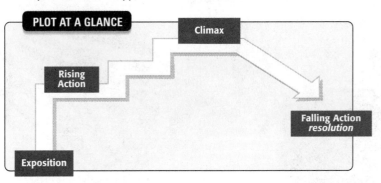

PLOT AT A GLANCE

Climax

Rising Action

Falling Action *resolution*

Exposition

Character

The **characters** in a story are the people, animals, or imaginary creatures who take part in the action. Usually a story focuses on the events surrounding one character—the **main character.** Other characters—**minor characters**—interact with the main character and help move the story along. Characters are revealed by their **traits,** or qualities.

YOUR TURN In the passage at the right, what words and details give you clues about what the boy is like?

The clerk was impressed by the clothes and the manner of Jimmy.
—O. Henry, "A Retrieved Reformation"

They shook hands *raza*-style and jerked their heads at one another in a *saludo de vato*.
—Gary Soto, "Seventh Grade"

CHARACTER

I went up to him and found him in exactly the position I had left him, white-faced, but with the tops of this cheeks flushed by the fever, staring still, as he had stared, at the foot of the bed.

I took his temperature.

"What is it?"

"Something like a hundred," I said. It was one hundred and two and four tenths.

"It was a hundred and two," he said.

"Who said so?"

"The doctor."

"Your temperature is all right," I said. "It's nothing to worry about."

"I don't worry," he said, "but I can't keep from thinking."

"Don't think," I said. "Just take it easy."

"I'm taking it easy," he said and looked straight ahead. He was evidently holding tight onto himself about something.

—Ernest Hemingway, "A Day's Wait"

"I don't worry," he said, "but I can't keep from thinking."
—Ernest Hemingway, "A Day's Wait"

Willie started to ask another question, but decided he would not get an answer.
—Avi, "What Do Fish Have to Do with Anything?"

Character

Write several letters of the alphabet on the board and invite students to brainstorm a fictional character for each letter. The characters can be drawn from films, books, and television. The letters can begin the character's first or last name. Have the students identify each character as a main character or a minor character. Then have students list two interesting traits of each character.

YOUR TURN

Possible Response: The author's description of the boy's physical appearance, the detail about his staring at the foot of the bed, and his comment about not being able to stop thinking are all clues about the character of the boy.

Setting

Ask students to sketch the following setting chart in their notebooks:

Story Title		
Time	Place	Importance of Setting

Then have them think about their favorite work of fiction and analyze the details of its setting. They can use the chart to record details that reveal the time and place of the story. In the chart they should also try to explain the importance of the setting to the story. For example, ask them how setting connects to or directly affects characters and events.

YOUR TURN

Possible Response: Some words and phrases that describe the setting are: *bright, cold day; the ground covered with sleet; bare trees varnished with ice; frozen creek; glassy surface.*

Theme

Ask students to name some stories they have read on their own and to explain the message about life that they discovered in each one. Encourage them to describe specific details that lead them to the theme. Then have them use the strategies listed on this page to uncover the theme in a story that everyone in the class has read.

Setting

The **setting** of a story is the time and place in which the action of the story happens. The time may be the past, present, or future; daytime or nighttime; or any season of the year. The events of the story may unfold in any place, real or imaginary. The writer's descriptions help readers picture the setting in their minds. Setting can help determine what happens to the characters and how they respond to problems.

YOUR TURN In the paragraph on the right, what words and phrases describe the setting of the story?

From "A Day's Wait"

SETTING

It was a bright, cold day, the ground covered with a sleet that had frozen so that it seemed as if all the bare trees, the bushes, the cut brush, and all the grass and the bare ground had been varnished with ice. I took the young Irish setter for a little walk up the road and along a frozen creek, but it was difficult to stand or walk on the glassy surface and the red dog slipped and slithered and I fell twice, hard, once dropping my gun and having it slide away over the ice.

—Ernest Hemingway, "A Day's Wait"

Theme

The **theme** of a story is the main message the writer wishes to share with the reader. This message might be a lesson about life or an insight into human nature. Most themes are not stated directly; the reader must infer them from the details and events of the story. Different readers may find different themes in the same story. Themes can be revealed by

- thinking about the meaning of the title of the story
- skimming the story for key phrases and sentences about big ideas such as courage, freedom, or honesty
- examining how the main character changes or noting what he or she learns about life

In this passage from "A Day's Wait," the statement, "You aren't going to die" is a clue to the theme of the story. This may be that a brush with death (whether it be real or imagined) can make us appreciate life.

THEME

"You poor Schatz," I said. ". . . You aren't going to die. That's a different thermometer. On that thermometer thirty-seven is normal. On this kind it's ninety-eight." . . .

"Oh," he said.

But his gaze at the foot of the bed relaxed slowly. The hold over himself relaxed too, finally, and the next day it was very slack and he cried very easily at little things that were of no importance.

—Ernest Hemingway, "A Day's Wait"

Great stories capture our imaginations. They create a world of interesting characters, faraway places, and exciting events. While many stories entertain, they may also inform us about ourselves and our circumstances. Try using the strategies explained here to get the most from a work of fiction.

Reading Fiction

How to Apply the Strategies

Preview the story and set a purpose for reading. Look at the title and illustrations. Then skim through the selection's pages. Can you tell what the story is about?

CONNECT Think about experiences and feelings that you share with the characters or the narrator. Can you connect any of their feelings, ideas, and values to your own?

QUESTION Ask questions about the story's events, characters, and ideas. As you read, look for the answers to your questions. Asking good questions is at the heart of good reading.

PREDICT Stop occasionally to predict what might happen next or how the story might end. To find out whether your predictions are correct, read on.

VISUALIZE Can you picture a similar setting in your mind? Is the action easy to imagine? Can you "see" the characters?

EVALUATE Do your feelings toward the characters and their actions change as you read? How well does the author tell the story?

CLARIFY Remember to pause now and then. Reread when necessary. It may also help to take notes or to discuss the story with a friend. Expect your thoughts to change as the story unfolds.

Here's how Matt uses the strategies:

"I like mysteries the best. When I read, it's almost like being a detective. I become involved in the story and **visualize** *how each character looks, where the story takes place, and how the events occur. I make* **connections** *to some parts of the story where I've had similar experiences. Above all I like to* **predict** *what will happen. My favorite books have twists in the plot. It keeps reading interesting."*

Need More Help?

Remember that active readers use the essential reading strategies explained on page 4: • visualize • predict • clarify • question • connect • evaluate • monitor.

THE ACTIVE READER **19**

Objectives
- understand fiction by analyzing its most basic elements
- learn to connect with a work of fiction
- focus on important details of a selection

Teaching the Lesson

The strategies on this page will help students interpret fiction by encouraging them to connect with what they read.

Presenting the Strategies
Tell students that this page can help them to get the most from a work of fiction. They should keep these strategies in mind as they read the selections in this unit and throughout the book.

PREVIEW
Give students time to preview a story in their book. Then ask them what they think the story is about. Have them identify the clues that helped them to guess the subject of the story.

CONNECT
Ask students to think about the excerpts from "A Day's Wait." With which incidents, settings, and characters did they particularly connect, and why? Ask them why finding common ground between themselves and characters might help them to better understand a work of fiction.

Possible Responses: Students might say that they too have thought about death. Some students may have walked in a cold winter setting or had the experience of falling on ice. They should understand that connecting with these experiences will make the story more real for them.

Use **Reading and Critical Thinking Transparencies,** p. 1, for additional support.

QUESTION
Remind students that, as they read, they should think about why characters behave the way they do and why certain events unfold.

PREDICT
As students ask themselves questions, they can try to predict the answers. Remind students that in order to make accurate predictions, they need to know their characters well.

VISUALIZE
Tell students that using details to create in their minds a picture of what is happening will make a story seem more realistic. Have students close their eyes and try to visualize the winter scene described in the passage from "A Day's Wait."

EVALUATE
Tell students that their opinion of a story will often be based on their own experiences and interests. They should feel free to use their own knowledge and experiences to evaluate a work.

CLARIFY
As students read a selection, you might ask them to talk about passages they had to reread for clarification.

This selection is included in the **Grade 7 InterActive Reader.**

Objectives
1. understand and appreciate a **short story** (Literary Analysis)
2. understand the role of **setting,** both **place** and **time,** in a short story (Literary Analysis)
3. use the active reading strategy of **connecting** to understand the setting of the story and motivation of the main character (**Active Reading**)

Summary
On the first day of seventh grade, Victor decides that he wants Teresa to be his girlfriend. He even signs up for French class because he knows she is taking it. When Teresa says hi to Victor in homeroom, he becomes flustered and blurts out a comment that sounds rude. He wonders why he couldn't think of something nice to say. In English class, Victor embarrasses himself when he gives Teresa's name as an example of a noun. Then in French class, he pretends he knows the French language in hopes of impressing Teresa. When the teacher asks him a question in French, he is forced to improvise with non-sense words. The teacher does not react or try to embarrass the boy. After class, Teresa praises Victor for his fluency. Victor ends the day with the feeling that he will like seventh grade and a resolve to really learn French.

Thematic Link
Victor begins his first day of seventh grade feeling awkward and foolish. By the end of the day, he feels hopeful and has new confidence in himself.

5-Minute Warm-Up

Daily Language SkillBuilder  **TEKS** 16B, 16D, 17F, 17G

Have students **proofread** the display sentences on page 13i and write them correctly. The sentences also appear on Transparency 1 of **Grammar Transparencies and Copymasters.**

 Mini Lesson **Preteaching Vocabulary**

If you would like to preteach the WORDS TO KNOW for this selection, use the Mini Lesson, p. 21.

"When the bell sounded, Teresa looked up, and their eyes met."

Seventh Grade
Short Story by GARY SOTO

 TEKS See the Skills Trace at the beginning of the unit for information on TEKS covered in this lesson.

(Connect to Your Life)

Being Yourself How do seventh graders try to impress each other? Think about what you and your friends do to make others admire you. Do you behave differently with boys than with girls? Discuss your ideas with your classmates.

Build Background

CONNECT TO GEOGRAPHY The story "Seventh Grade" takes place in Fresno, California. Fresno is located in the San Joaquin Valley, southeast of San Francisco. Fresno's dry, hot summers and cool, humid winters are excellent for growing grapes, and the town is often called the "raisin-growing capital of the world." A large number of Hispanics whose families are originally from Spanish-speaking countries are employed in Fresno's vineyards and raisin-production plants. Many, like Victor in this story, are of Mexican descent.

WORDS TO KNOW **Vocabulary Preview**

bluff	ferocity	quiver	sheepishly
conviction	linger	scowl	trudge
elective	portly		

Focus Your Reading

LITERARY ANALYSIS SETTING A story's **setting** is the time and the place in which events in the story occur. "Seventh Grade" takes place on the first day of class in a middle school in Fresno, California. The author provides several details to help you picture the school in your imagination. See how a small detail about Victor's first day helps establish the time and the place on the first day of school.

On the first day of school, Victor stood in the line half an hour before he came to a wobbly card table.

As you read, find the details that best help you picture the setting.

ACTIVE READING CONNECTING When you read a story, **connect** the characters, the setting, and the plot to information you already know and to your own experience. Pay special attention to

- details about the setting and the characters
- statements the characters make
- events that happen in the plot

READER'S NOTEBOOK As you read, use a chart to help you find connections between Victor's experiences and your own.

What Victor and I have in common	How Victor and I are different
We both had summer jobs.	Victor took French; I took Spanish.

LESSON RESOURCES

UNIT ONE RESOURCE BOOK, pp. 7–13

ASSESSMENT
Formal Assessment, pp. 5–6
Teacher's Guide to Assessment and Portfolio Use
Test Generator

SKILLS TRANSPARENCIES AND COPYMASTERS
Literary Analysis
- Setting, TR 6 (for Activity, p. 26)
Reading and Critical Thinking
- Connecting, TR 2 (for Thinking Through the Literature, p. 26)

Grammar
- Capitalization and Punctuation of Simple Sentences, CM 121 (for Mini Lesson, p. 24)
- Subject, Verb, and Predicate, CM 51 (for Mini Lesson, p. 28)
Vocabulary
- Context Clues: Contrast, CM 18 (for Mini Lesson, p. 21)
- Antonyms, CM 19 (for Mini Lesson, p. 27)

INTEGRATED TECHNOLOGY
Audio Library

Visit our website:
www.mcdougallittell.com

Seventh Grade

by Gary Soto

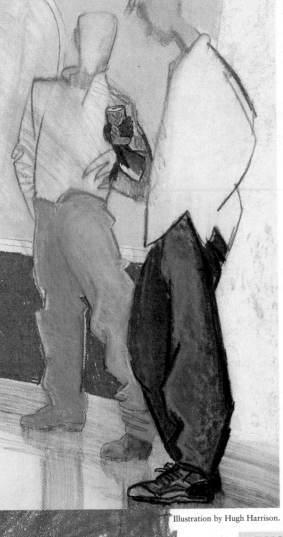

On the first day of school, Victor stood in line half an hour before he came to a wobbly card table. He was handed a packet of papers and a computer card on which he listed his one <u>elective</u>, French. He already spoke Spanish and English, but he thought some day he might travel to France, where it was cool; not like Fresno, where summer days reached 110 degrees in the shade. There were rivers in France, and huge churches, and fair-skinned people everywhere, the way there were brown people all around Victor.

Besides, Teresa, a girl he had liked since they were in catechism classes[1] at Saint Theresa's, was taking French, too. With any luck they would be in the same class. Teresa is going to be my girl this year, he promised himself as he left the gym full of students in their new fall clothes. She was cute. And good in math, too, Victor thought as he walked down the hall to his homeroom. He ran into his friend, Michael Torres, by the water fountain that never turned off.

---

1. **catechism classes** (kăt′ĭ-kĭz′əm): formal classes in religious instruction.

Illustration by Hugh Harrison.

WORDS
TO
KNOW   **elective** (ĭ-lĕk′tĭv) *n.* an optional academic course or subject

21

Mini Lesson **Preteaching Vocabulary**   **TEKS** 6A   **TAAS** Reading Obj. 1

CONTEXT CLUES: CONTRAST

Instruction Remind students that context clues can help them to understand unfamiliar words. A contrast between an unknown word and another part of a sentence, often indicated by *but, not,* or *on the other hand,* is a type of context clue. Give students the following sentence: French was an *elective,* but math and English had to be on Victor's schedule.

Have them use contrast to define *elective.* They should understand that an elective is an optional class.

Exercises Have students apply the strategy to figure out the meanings of the underlined WORDS TO KNOW.

1. The man was <u>portly</u>, not slender.
2. His scowl had <u>ferocity</u>, but his personality was gentle.
3. Most students dashed from the room, but Teresa <u>lingered</u>.

4. Victor thought, "I could try to <u>bluff</u>. On the other hand, I could stop pretending and be truthful."

Use **Unit One Resource Book,** p. 10, for more exercises. Use **Vocabulary Transparencies and Copymasters,** p. 18, for additional support.

TEACHING THE LITERATURE

Customizing Instruction

Less Proficient Readers
Help students to keep the events in the story in sequence by having them do a mock schedule of Victor's day. They should record what happens during homeroom, English, lunch, and French, and after school.

Set a Purpose Have students read to find out what new look Victor's friend Michael has and why.

Students Acquiring English

- Explain to students that this story follows Victor, the main character, as he goes through his first day of seventh grade. Discuss with students the concrete details that make the character of Victor and his school environment realistic.

- Tell students that the story contains some Spanish and French words. You might want to have students locate these words before they begin reading.

Use **Spanish Study Guide,** pp. 4–6, for additional support.

Gifted and Talented
Explain to students that a symbol is anything that stands for something beyond itself. For example, dark clouds can be a symbol of approaching danger. Ask students to offer their observations about the symbolism of the first day of a new school year.

Possible Responses: a beginning; a chance to start over

- As students read, have them consider how the first day of school setting influences the theme of Gary Soto's story.

To set up the story's premise, have students read the title and the opening line. Introduce the characters that they will encounter in their reading. Suggest to students that because Victor's French class is mentioned in the beginning of the story, it will be significant. Ask them to guess what they think might happen in French class.

Literary Analysis `SETTING`

Ask students to notice how the author indicates the passing of time in the story. Have them explain their observations.
Possible Responses: sound of the three-beat bell; ringing of the bell for first period; sequence of Victor's classes

 Use the **Unit One Resource Book,** p. 9, for more practice.

`ACTIVE READING`

A CONNECT Answers will vary. Thinking about their own friends will help students to relate to the characters in the story.

`ACTIVE READING`

B QUESTION Possible Responses: He is flustered; he can't think of anything clever to say.

Active Reading `CONNECTING`

C Ask students to explain how Victor feels after his comment to Teresa.
Possible Response: foolish
• Have students say what they might do in Victor's situation.
Possible Responses: try to talk to Teresa again as if nothing had happened; apologize; ignore the whole thing

 Use the **Unit One Resource Book,** p. 8, for more practice.

Illustration by Pamela Daly.

They shook hands, *raza*-style,[2] and jerked their heads at one another in a *saludo de vato*.[3] "How come you're making a face?" asked Victor.

`ACTIVE READING`

A CONNECT Do you and your friends have a special way of greeting each other? What is it?

"I ain't making a face, *ese*.[4] This *is* my face." Michael said his face had changed during the summer. He had read a *GQ* magazine that his older brother had borrowed from the Book Mobile and noticed that the male models all had the same look on their faces. They would stand, one arm around a beautiful woman, and _scowl_. They would sit at a pool, their rippled stomachs dark with shadow, and *scowl*. They would sit at dinner tables, cool drinks in their hands, and *scowl*.

"I think it works," Michael said. He scowled and let his upper lip quiver. His teeth showed along with the ferocity of his soul. "Belinda Reyes walked by a while ago and looked at me," he said.

Victor didn't say anything, though he thought his friend looked pretty strange. They talked about recent movies, baseball, their parents, and the horrors of picking grapes in order to buy their fall clothes. Picking grapes was like living in Siberia, except hot and more boring.

2. *raza*-**style** (rä'sä) *Spanish:* in the familiar manner that local Chicanos greet each other.
3. *saludo de vato* (sä-lōō'dō dĕ bä'tō) *Spanish:* greeting between Chicano buddies.
4. *ese* (ĕ'sĕ) *Spanish:* a slang term used when addressing someone, as in "Hey, man."

WORDS		
W O R D S	**scowl** (skoul) *v.* to look angry by drawing the eyebrows together and frowning	
T O	**quiver** (kwĭv'ər) *v.* to shake with a slight, rapid movement	
K N O W	**ferocity** (fə-rŏs'ĭ-tē) *n.* extreme fierceness; intensity	

22

Teaching Options

 Mini Lesson **Spelling** TEKS 16D / TAAS Writing Obj. 3, 7

USING THE LETTERS *DGE*
Instruction Explain to students that the letters *dge* are usually used in one-syllable words with short vowels. Because this letter combination is often followed by an *e*, the *g* has a soft sound.
Examples: *trudge, ledge, badge*

Exercises Have students read the following paragraph and correct any misspelled *dge* words. George was asked to judje his experience of learning to speak another language. He believes it was a good experience but one of the great

challenges of his life. In fact, he often could not buge from his desk for hours before a test in Spanish class. Today, George is glad he knows how to speak some Spanish. He believes language classes can form a bridje between cultures. Ask students to look for more words that fit this pattern, in their own writing and in things that they read, and to add these words to their personal word lists.

 Use **Unit One Resource Book,** p. 12, for more practice.

He felt himself blushing again.

"What classes are you taking?" Michael said, scowling.

"French. How 'bout you?"

"Spanish. I ain't so good at it, even if I'm Mexican."

"I'm not either, but I'm better at it than math, that's for sure."

A tinny, three-beat bell propelled students to their homerooms. The two friends socked each other in the arm and went their ways, Victor thinking, man, that's weird. Michael thinks making a face makes him handsome.

On the way to his homeroom, Victor tried a scowl. He felt foolish, until out of the corner of his eye he saw a girl looking at him. Umm, he thought, maybe it does work. He scowled with greater conviction.

In homeroom, roll was taken, emergency cards were passed out, and they were given a bulletin to take home to their parents. The principal, Mr. Belton, spoke over the crackling loudspeaker, welcoming the students to a new year, new experiences, and new friendships. The students squirmed in their chairs and ignored him. They were anxious to go to first period. Victor sat calmly, thinking of Teresa, who sat two rows away, reading a paperback novel. This would be his lucky year. She was in his homeroom, and would probably be in his English and math classes. And, of course, French.

The bell rang for first period, and the students herded noisily through the door. Only Teresa lingered, talking with the homeroom teacher.

"So you think I should talk to Mrs. Gaines?" she asked the teacher. "She would know about ballet?"

"She would be a good bet," the teacher said. Then added, "Or the gym teacher, Mrs. Garza."

Victor lingered, keeping his head down and staring at his desk. He wanted to leave when she did so he could bump into her and say something clever.

He watched her on the sly. As she turned to leave, he stood up and hurried to the door, where he managed to catch her eye. She smiled and said, "Hi, Victor."

He smiled back and said, "Yeah, that's me."

B His brown face blushed. Why hadn't he said, "Hi, Teresa," or "How was your summer?" or something nice?

As Teresa walked down the hall, Victor walked the other way, looking back, admiring how gracefully she walked, one foot in front of the other. So much for being in the same class, he thought. As he trudged to English, he practiced scowling.

In English they reviewed the parts of speech. Mr. Lucas, a portly man, waddled down the aisle, asking, "What is a noun?"

"A person, place, or thing," said the class in unison.

"Yes, now somebody give me an example of a person—you, Victor Rodriguez."

"Teresa," Victor said automatically. Some of the girls giggled. They knew he had a crush on Teresa. He felt himself blushing again.

"Correct," Mr. Lucas said. "Now provide me with a place."

Mr. Lucas called on a freckled kid who answered, "Teresa's house with a kitchen full of big brothers."

ACTIVE READING

QUESTION: Why do you think Victor answers Teresa so rudely?

B

C

3

WORDS TO KNOW
conviction (kən-vĭk'shən) *n.* a strong belief; assuredness
linger (lĭng'gər) *v.* to continue to stay; delay leaving
trudge (trŭj) *v.* to walk heavily; plod
portly (pôrt'lē) *adj.* stout or overweight

23

Customizing Instruction

Less Proficient Readers
Use the following questions to check students' recall and comprehension of the story.

1 What is Michael's new look and why does he have that look?
Possible Response: Michael's new look is a scowl, which he uses to impress girls.

2 What happens when Teresa says hi to Victor after homeroom?
Possible Response: Victor says something that he thinks sounds rude.

Set a Purpose Have students read to find out how the rest of Victor's day goes.

Students Acquiring English
Ask students to pick out words that are challenging, such as *squirmed* (moved restlessly), *herded* (walked as a group), and *waddled* (walked with side-to-side motion). Encourage them to use context clues to define unfamiliar words.

3 Make sure students understand how the word *automatically* affects the meaning of the sentence. Because Victor's mind is on Teresa, he says her name without thinking. Saying Teresa's name shows everyone that he likes her.

Multiple Learning Styles
Kinesthetic Learners
Have two students enact the conversation and actions of Michael and Victor before homeroom. Ask why Michael's scowl would grab the attention of other students.

BLOCK SCHEDULING: MANAGING TIME

If your schedule requires that you cover the lesson objectives in a shorter time, use . . .
• Preparing to Read, p. 20
• Thinking Through the Literature, p. 26
• Vocabulary in Action, p. 27
• Grammar in Context, p. 28

If you would like to take advantage of longer class time, use . . .
• TE Teaching Options: Preteaching Vocabulary, p. 21; Spelling, p. 22; Grammar, pp. 24, 28; Standardized Test Practice, p. 25; Vocabulary Strategy, p. 27
• Choices & Challenges, pp. 27–28

Reading and Analyzing

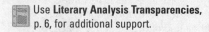 After English, Victor had math, his weakest subject. He sat in the back by the window, hoping he would not be called on. Victor understood most of the problems, but some of the stuff looked like the teacher made it up as she went along. It was confusing, like the inside of a watch.

After math he had a fifteen-minute break, then social studies, and, finally, lunch. He bought a tuna casserole with buttered rolls, some fruit cocktail, and milk. He sat with Michael, who practiced scowling between bites.

Girls walked by and looked at him.

"See what I mean, Vic?" Michael scowled. "They love it."

"Yeah, I guess so."

They ate slowly, Victor scanning the horizon for a glimpse of Teresa. He didn't see her. She must have brought lunch, he thought, and is eating outside. Victor scraped his plate and left Michael, who was busy scowling at a girl two tables away.

The small, triangle-shaped campus bustled with students talking about their new classes. Everyone was in a sunny mood. Victor hurried to the bag lunch area, where he sat down and opened his math book. He moved his lips as if he were reading, but his mind was somewhere else. He raised his eyes slowly and looked around. No Teresa.

He lowered his eyes, pretending to study, then looked slowly to the left. No Teresa. He turned a page in the book and stared at some math problems that scared him because he knew he would have to do them eventually. He looked to the right. Still no sign of her. He stretched out lazily in an attempt to disguise his snooping.

Then he saw her. She was sitting with a girlfriend under a plum tree. Victor moved to a table near her and daydreamed about taking her to a movie. When the bell sounded, Teresa looked up, and their eyes met. She smiled sweetly and gathered her books. Her next class was French, same as Victor's.

They were among the last students to arrive in class, so all the good desks in the back had already been taken. Victor was forced to sit near the front, a few desks away from Teresa, while Mr. Bueller wrote French words on the chalkboard. The bell rang, and Mr. Bueller wiped his hands, turned to the class, and said, *"Bonjour."*[5]

"Bonjour," braved a few students.

"Bonjour," Victor whispered. He wondered if Teresa heard him.

Mr. Bueller said that if the students studied hard, at the end of the year they could go to France and be understood by the populace.

One kid raised his hand and asked, "What's 'populace'?"

"The people, the people of France."

Mr. Bueller asked if anyone knew French. Victor raised his hand, wanting to impress Teresa. The teacher beamed and said, *"Très bien. Parlez-vous français?"*[6]

Victor didn't know what to say. The teacher wet his lips and asked something else in French. The room grew silent. Victor felt all eyes staring at him. He tried to <u>bluff</u> his way out by making noises that sounded French.

"La me vave me con le grandma," he said uncertainly.

Mr. Bueller, wrinkling his face in curiosity, asked him to speak up.

Great rosebushes of red bloomed on Victor's cheeks. A river of nervous sweat ran down his

---

5. *Bonjour* (bôn´zhoor) *French:* Good day.
6. *Très bien. Parlez-vous français?* (trĕ byăn pär´lā voō frän´sĕ) *French:* Very good. Do you speak French?

WORDS TO KNOW   **bluff** (blŭf) *v.* to mislead or deceive; to fake

24

Teaching Options

palms. He felt awful. Teresa sat a few desks away, no doubt thinking he was a fool. Without looking at Mr. Bueller, Victor mumbled, "Frenchie oh wewe gee in September."

Mr. Bueller asked Victor to repeat what he said.

"Frenchie oh wewe gee in September," Victor repeated.

ACTIVE READING

CONNECT: Have you ever done or said something to impress somebody that you later felt foolish about? What was it?

Mr. Bueller understood that the boy didn't know French and turned away. He walked to the blackboard and pointed to the words on the board with his steel-edged ruler.

"*Le bateau*," he sang.

"*Le bateau*," the students repeated.

"*Le bateau est sur l'eau*,"[7] he sang.

"*Le bateau est sur l'eau.*"

Victor was too weak from failure to join the class. He stared at the board and wished he had taken Spanish, not French. Better yet, he wished he could start his life over. He had never been so embarrassed. He bit his thumb until he tore off a sliver of skin.

The bell sounded for fifth period, and Victor shot out of the room, avoiding the stares of the other kids, but had to return for his math book. He looked sheepishly at the teacher, who was erasing the board, then widened his eyes in terror at Teresa who stood in front of him. "I didn't know you knew French," she said. "That was good."

Mr. Bueller looked at Victor, and Victor looked back. Oh please, don't say anything, Victor pleaded with his eyes. I'll wash your car, mow your lawn, walk your dog—anything! I'll be your best student, and I'll clean your erasers after school.

Mr. Bueller shuffled through the papers on his desk. He smiled and hummed as he sat down to work. He remembered his college years when he dated a girlfriend in borrowed cars. She thought he was rich because each time he picked her up he had a different car. It was fun until he had spent all his money on her and had to write home to his parents because he was broke.

Victor couldn't stand to look at Teresa. He was sweaty with shame. "Yeah, well, I picked up a few things from movies and books and stuff like that." They left the class together. Teresa asked him if he would help her with her French.

"Sure, anytime," Victor said.

"I won't be bothering you, will I?"

"Oh no, I like being bothered."

"*Bonjour,*" Teresa said, leaving him outside her next class. She smiled and pushed wisps of hair from her face.

"Yeah, right, *bonjour,*" Victor said. He turned and headed to his class. The rosebushes of shame on his face became bouquets of love. Teresa is a great girl, he thought. And Mr. Bueller is a good guy.

He raced to metal shop. After metal shop there was biology, and after biology a long sprint to the public library, where he checked out three French textbooks.

He was going to like seventh grade. ❖

7. *Le bateau est sur l'eau.* (lə bä´tō ĕ sür lō) *French:* The boat is on the water.

WORDS TO KNOW	**sheepishly** (shē´pĭsh-lē) *adv.* with a bashful or embarrassed look

25

Customizing Instruction

Less Proficient Readers
- Ask students to list signs that show Teresa might be interested in Victor.
  Possible Responses: She smiles at him outside; she tells him that his French is good and asks him if he will help her with her French; she smiles at him when she goes to her next class.
- How does Victor feel after his first day of seventh grade?
  Possible Response: He thinks he is going to like seventh grade.

Students Acquiring English
1 Be sure that students understand that Victor knows no French and is just mixing words together and saying them with a French accent. Spanish-speaking students may recognize words similar to Spanish words in his first sentence.
2 Discuss with students the choices that Mr. Bueller has when Teresa says that Victor speaks French well. Ask students why Mr. Bueller decides to say nothing.
Possible Response: He remembers what it was like trying to impress a girl.

Gifted and Talented
Challenge students to explain what they see as the theme of this story.
Possible Responses: Every day is a chance to be a better person; if someone thinks the best of us, we become the best; finding ourselves is a process of trial and error; we can learn from our mistakes and take each day as a chance to start over.

✓ **Assessment** **Standardized Test Practice**   **TEKS** 10G, 10K    **TAAS** Reading Obj. 3

CHOOSING THE BEST SUMMARY For some standardized tests, students will be asked to choose the best summary of a passage. To provide students with some help in choosing the best summary, read aloud or write on the board the following question: Which of the following statements best summarizes Victor's first day of school?
A. Victor embarrasses himself several times in his efforts to impress Teresa.
B. Victor realizes that seventh grade will be challenging academically and decides to study on his own.
C. Although Victor embarrasses himself in front of Teresa, he ends the day with a good feeling about seventh grade.

Lead students through the process of choosing the best summary. Consider each choice. Point out that while all of the statements contain accurate information about the story, the best summary should include the most important information. For that reason, *C* is the best choice.

Connect to the Literature

1. **Possible Responses:** Some students will feel that they would have done the same thing. Some will feel that Victor's actions were wrong and that he deserved to be embarrassed.

Comprehension Check
- Teresa was taking it.
- Mr. Bueller started talking to him in French.
- He goes to the library to borrow French textbooks so that he can learn French. He wants to be able to help Teresa and live up to her impression of him.

 Use Selection Quiz **Unit One Resource Book,** p. 13.

Think Critically

2. **Possible Responses:** He should feel proud because he accomplished his goal of impressing Teresa and now he will learn French. He should feel ashamed because he lied. He pretended to be someone he isn't.
3. **Responses will vary.** Encourage students to articulate why they can connect to specific experiences in the story.
4. **Possible Responses:** Mr. Bueller is sympathetic and understands the reason that Victor was faking; possibly he had done something similar. Also, he knows that Victor will have to live up to his bluff or risk losing Teresa's respect.
5. **Possible Responses:** Teresa seems like a friendly and nice girl. She speaks to Victor and smiles frequently at him. She must like Victor because she finds opportunities to say things to him.

 Use **Reading and Critical Thinking Transparencies,** p. 2, for additional support.

Literary Analysis

Setting Responses will vary. Students should include the details that create a realistic school setting such as the bells, the crackling loudspeaker, the specific details about Victor's school lunch.

Use **Literary Analysis Transparencies,** p. 6, for additional support.

Connect to the Literature

1. **What Do You Think?** What was your reaction to Victor's lie? Explain.

Comprehension Check
- What was the main reason that Victor wanted to take French?
- What happened when Victor told Mr. Bueller that he spoke French?
- Why does Victor go to the library? What is he going to do and why?

Think Critically

2. Do you feel Victor should feel proud of or ashamed of his actions? Why or why not?

 THINK ABOUT
- why he claimed to know French
- what happens, or might happen, as a result of his claim

3. **ACTIVE READING** **CONNECTING** Look at the chart that you made in your **READER'S NOTEBOOK.** In what ways did you connect to Victor's experience? Discuss this with a classmate.

4. The French teacher, Mr. Bueller, realizes that Victor is faking his knowledge of French. Why do you think he keeps the truth to himself?

5. It seems that Victor succeeds in impressing Teresa. What is your opinion of her? Support your answer with evidence from the story.

Extend Interpretations

6. **Different Perspectives** How do you think this story would be different if it were told from Teresa's perspective instead of Victor's?

7. **Connect to Life** Why do people feel the need to create false impressions of themselves? Has anyone ever tried to impress you by saying or doing something you knew was dishonest? What happened? Discuss your experiences with a classmate.

Literary Analysis

SETTING A story's **setting**—the time and the place of its action—may include the geographical location, the historical period, the time of day, and the beliefs, customs, and standards of a society. In some stories, such as "Seventh Grade," the setting is simple and straightforward—a school in Fresno, California in modern times.

Setting often plays an important role in what happens and why in a story. For example "*. . . he thought some day he might travel to France, where it was cool: not like Fresno, where summer days reached 110 degrees in the shade.*"

Activity Make a list of at least three details in "Seventh Grade" that are examples of setting.

Setting
Fresno
1st day of school
autumn

DIALECT A **dialect** is a form of language that is spoken in a certain place or by a certain group of people. In "Seventh Grade" the author makes his story more realistic and the setting and characters more vivid by including language used by Chicano young people.

"They shook hands, raza-style, and jerked their heads at one another in a saludo de vato."

Extend Interpretations

6. **Different Perspectives** Possible Responses: Teresa would be unaware of Victor's internal feelings of humiliation or his feelings that he has fallen short. Her feelings about Victor would be revealed instead of having to be inferred. He might appear more confident and less awkward if described from Teresa's perspective.

7. **Connect to Life** Possible Responses: Students might suggest that people feel inadequate and not good enough to impress others on their own merits; people are afraid of disappointing others; people don't like themselves; people admire characteristics of others and want to be like them.

After students have thought of examples in their own lives, they might consider whether there are good reasons for being dishonest or whether all dishonest attempts to impress someone should be considered wrong.

Choices & CHALLENGES

Writing Options

1. Write a Letter Draft a letter that Teresa might send to a good friend describing what happened in French class and her reaction to Victor. Place your draft in your **Working Portfolio.**

2. Profile of Victor Based on the evidence in the story, what do you know about Victor's character? Write a brief profile of him. A word web might help to get you started.

wants to speak French

Victor

Activities & Explorations

1. Magazine Ad Think about the reason Michael gave for scowling. Do you think that fashion magazines influence people to look or to act a certain way? With a small group, sketch or photograph an ad or an article that has influenced the way you look or would like to look. Post your completed work in the classroom. ~ **ART**

2. Comedy Sketch Watching someone try to impress someone else can sometimes be pretty funny. Write a short comedy sketch on this topic and perform it for your class. ~ **PERFORMING**

Art Connection

Look at Hugh Harrison's illustration on page 21. What does the posture of the boys tell you? Who do you think they are? What are they doing? Do you think this is a good illustration for "Seventh Grade"?

Inquiry & Research

Mexican Americans Mexican Americans make up a large part of the U.S. population. Consult history books, encyclopedias, and other resources to find out about Mexican Americans' contributions to the culture of the United States, or to an individual state, such as Texas or California.

Vocabulary in Action

EXERCISE: ASSESSMENT PRACTICE For each group of words below, write the letter of the word that is most nearly opposite in meaning to the boldfaced Word to Know.

1. elective:
(a) chosen (b) required (c) optional

2. scowl:
(a) frown (b) grimace (c) smile

3. quiver:
(a) tremble (b) vibrate (c) hold

4. ferocity:
(a) aggressiveness
(b) bravery
(c) gentleness

5. conviction:
(a) uncertainty (b) force (c) belief

6. linger:
(a) struggle (b) hasten (c) prolong

7. trudge:
(a) sprint (b) jump (c) amble

8. portly:
(a) fluid (b) overweight (c) lean

9. bluff:
(a) lie (b) admit (c) know

10. sheepishly:
(a) shyly (b) boldly (c) easily

Building Vocabulary
For an in-depth study of word relationships such as antonyms, see p. 631.

Mini Lesson Vocabulary Strategy

TEKS 9C **TAAS Reading Obj. 1**

ANTONYMS

Instruction Remind students that an antonym is a word that is opposite in meaning to another word. To choose the best antonym for a word, students must first know the meaning of the original word. Instruct students to use references such as a thesaurus or dictionary to clarify meaning. For example, *delicate* as it is used in the sentence, *The flower had delicate petals,* means fragile or easily damaged. A good antonym might be *tough* or *hardy.*

Application Have students work in pairs to think of the best antonyms for the following words.

1. mumbled *(shouted)*
2. embarrassed *(proud)*
3. boring *(exciting)*
4. gracefully *(clumsily)*
5. strange *(ordinary)*

Use **Vocabulary Transparencies and Copymasters,** p. 19.

Writing Options

1. Write a Letter To get students started on this assignment, have them reread this part of the story. Remind students to write from the first-person point of view. **Interpersonal learners** might record their letters on audiotape.

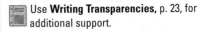 Use **Writing Transparencies,** p. 23, for additional support.

2. Profile of Victor Characteristics might include: likes Teresa; thinks on his feet; has to work to earn money for school clothes; knows Spanish and English. **Visual learners** might represent Victor's character by creating a collage that represents features of his personality.

Activities & Explorations

1. Magazine Ad To make this assignment easier, bring in recently discarded teen magazines and have students tear out the illustrations or ads that they feel influence them. **To make this assignment more challenging,** have students discuss whether the images they have collected are positive or negative influences on behavior or appearance.

2. Comedy Sketch To make this assignment easier, have students work in groups to brainstorm ideas and script out the actions and reactions of the characters. This assignment is well suited for **kinesthetic learners.**

Use **Communications Transparencies and Copymasters,** p. 13, for additional support.

Art Connection

Answers will vary. Students might say that the boys seem to be relaxed and friendly with each other.

Inquiry & Research

Mexican Americans To get students started on this assignment, list types of contributions such as political action, food, holiday traditions, vocabulary, and fashion. **To make this assignment easier,** allow students to work in pairs.

Vocabulary in Action

1. b	**4.** c	**7.** a	**10.** b
2. c	**5.** a	**8.** c	
3. c	**6.** b	**9.** b	

Grammar in Context

WRITING EXERCISE
Possible Responses:

1. Talking to Teresa **took** all of Victor's courage.
2. At lunch, Victor could not **find** Teresa.
3. The students **waited** for Victor to answer.
4. Mr. Bueller **listened** to Victor.

Gary Soto

Soto often writes about people and experiences familiar to him. In "Seventh Grade," Victor and Michael spent time during the summer picking grapes to earn money for school clothes. Soto also did this when he was a boy. In his book *Living Up the Street,* he describes this difficult experience: "The grapes rained into the pan, slowly filling like a belly, until I had my first tray and started my second. So it went all day, and the next, and all through the following week, so that by the end of thirteen days the foreman counted out . . . my pay of fifty-three dollars. . . . It wasn't until a few days before school that I let my fifty-three dollars slip quietly from my hands, buying a pair of pants, two shirts, and a maroon T-shirt."

Grammar in Context: Subjects and Predicates

Notice how Gary Soto uses a series of short sentences to create a feeling of Victor's anxiety.

> Victor **did**n't **know** what to say. The teacher **wet** his lips and **asked** something else in French. The room **grew** silent. Victor **felt** all eyes staring at him.

A sentence consists of a subject and a predicate. The **subject** tells whom or what the sentence is about. The **predicate** tells what the subject is or does. The predicate contains the **verb** and any helping verbs.

The **verb** expresses an action, a condition, or a state of being. Sometimes the verb is a complete predicate. In other cases the verb is part of a longer predicate.

WRITING EXERCISE Read these incomplete sentences. Write a predicate for each subject. Underline the verbs.

Example: *Original* **Mr. Bueller,** the French teacher,

Rewritten **Mr. Bueller,** the French teacher, **kept** Victor's secret.

1. **Talking** to Teresa
2. At lunch **Victor**
3. The **students**
4. **Mr. Bueller**

Connect to the Literature Imagine a study session during which Victor tutors Teresa. Write complete sentences for their dialogue. Circle your subjects and underline your verbs.

Grammar Handbook The Sentence and Its parts, p. R55

"I do get many of my ideas from remembering my own childhood in Fresno."

Gary Soto
born 1952

Mexican-American Roots Gary Soto grew up in a Mexican-American community in Fresno, California. His father worked for a raisin company, and his mother peeled potatoes at a food-processing company. At various times during his childhood, Soto wanted to be a priest, a hobo, and a paleontologist (a scientist who studies fossils).

Geography or Poetry? In college, Soto planned to study geography, until he discovered poetry. "I don't think I had any literary aspirations when I was a kid," says Soto. "In fact, we didn't have books, and no one encouraged us to read. So my wanting to write poetry was a sort of fluke."

Award-Winning Writer and Filmmaker Today Soto is a celebrated poet, essayist, novelist, and filmmaker. He taught English and ethnic studies at the University of California at Berkeley, and now devotes his time to writing for young people and working with students in the public schools. He has won numerous awards, including the American Book Award for *Living Up the Street* and the American Library Association's Andrew Carnegie Medal for excellence in filmmaking for his short film *The Pool Party.*

28 UNIT ONE   PART 1: KNOWING WHO YOU ARE

Mini Lesson **Grammar**   **TEKS** 17A   **TAAS** Writing Obj. 5, 7

SUBJECT, VERB, AND PREDICATE
Instruction Remind students that the subject is the part of a sentence that tells whom or what the sentence is about, and the simple subject is the noun or pronoun in the subject. The predicate is the part of a sentence that tells something about the subject, and it consists of a verb plus objects and modifiers. Tell them that the verb usually begins the complete predicate. Explain that a sentence is incomplete if it lacks a subject or a verb. Display the following sentence. The simple subject and verb are underlined.

Victor's <u>thoughts</u> about seventh grade/<u>are</u> hopeful.
Exercise Have students place a slash between the complete subject and complete predicate and underline the simple subject and the verb.

1. Mr. Bueller is a kind man. (*Mr. Bueller /is a kind man.*)
2. Teresa's sunny smile lifted Victor's spirits. (*Teresa's sunny <u>smile</u> /<u>lifted</u> Victor's spirits.*)
3. Michael scowls at every opportunity. (*Michael /<u>scowls</u> at every opportunity.*)

4. Some students understand more than one language. (*Some <u>students</u>/<u>understand</u> more than one language.*)

Use **Unit One Resource Book,** p. 11.
Use **Grammar Transparencies and Copymasters,** p. 51.

Use McDougal Littell's *Language Network,* Chapter 1, for more instruction and practice in subject, verb, and predicate.

Thank You, M'am

Short Story by LANGSTON HUGHES

 This selection appears in Spanish in the **Spanish Study Guide.**

I were young once and I wanted things I could not get.

Connect to Your Life

Good Neighbors An African proverb says, "It takes two parents to produce a child, but it takes an entire village to raise the child." What values do you associate with community spirit?

Community Spirit

caring

Build Background

CONNECT TO GEOGRAPHY The action of "Thank You, M'am" takes place in the late 1950s in Harlem, a section of New York City. In the early 1900s, Harlem attracted a community of African-American musicians, artists, and writers, including Langston Hughes. The vibrant and stimulating life of Harlem had a deep influence on the work of these creative people.

Manhattan Island

Historic photo of Harlem, showing 122nd Street between 7th and 8th Avenues. Copyright © Archive Photos.

 LaserLink: Background for Reading Cultural Connection

 See the Skills Trace at the beginning of the unit for information on TEKS covered in this lesson.

Focus Your Reading

LITERARY ANALYSIS CONFLICT The action of a plot is usually set in motion by a **central conflict,** or struggle between opposing forces. A character's struggle against an outside force—another character, a physical obstacle, nature, or society—is called an **external conflict.** A struggle within a character is an **internal conflict.** As you read "Thank You, M'am," look for examples of both types of conflict.

ACTIVE READING CAUSE AND EFFECT Events in stories are often related as **cause and effect**—that is, one event brings about another. Cause-and-effect relations are often signaled by words such as *because, since, thus, therefore, so,* and *as a result.* Sometimes an event will cause another event, which causes another, and so on until the end of the story. A series of events linked in this way is called a chain of causes and effects.

READER'S NOTEBOOK As you read this story, try to connect the major events in a chain of causes and effects. Make a diagram of the chain, including as many links as necessary.

WORDS TO KNOW
Vocabulary Preview

barren	presentable
frail	suede
mistrust	

THANK YOU, M'AM **29**

LESSON RESOURCES

UNIT ONE RESOURCE BOOK, pp. 14–20

ASSESSMENT
Formal Assessment, pp. 7–8
Teacher's Guide to Assessment and Portfolio Use
Test Generator

SKILLS TRANSPARENCIES AND COPYMASTERS
Literary Analysis
• Conflict, TR 8 (for Paired Activity, p. 34)

Reading and Critical Thinking
• Cause and Effect, TR 3 (for Thinking Through the Literature, p. 34)
Grammar
• Coordinating Conjunctions, CM 90 (for Mini Lesson, p. 33)
• Compound Subjects and Predicates, CM 53 (for Mini Lesson, p. 36)
Vocabulary
• Synonyms, CM 20 (for Mini Lesson, p. 31)

INTEGRATED TECHNOLOGY
Audio Library
LaserLinks
• Cultural Connection; Art Gallery. See **Teacher's SourceBook,** p. 6.
Video: Literature in Performance
• *Thank You, M'am.* See **Video Resource Book,** pp. 3–9.

Visit our website:
www.mcdougallittell.com

OVERVIEW

 This selection is included in the **Grade 7 InterActive Reader.**

This selection appears in Spanish in the **Spanish Study Guide.**

Objectives
1. understand and appreciate a **short story** (Literary Analysis)
2. understand the role of **conflict,** both **internal** and **external,** in plot (Literary Analysis)
3. use the reading skill **cause and effect** (Active Reading)

Summary
Late one night, as Mrs. Luella Bates Washington Jones is walking home from her job at a hotel beauty shop, a boy tries to steal her purse. He loses his balance, and Mrs. Jones grabs him, scolds him, and drags him to her room in a boarding house. Noticing that he has not been well cared for, she tells him to wash his face and then cooks a dinner and shares it with him. He explains that his motive for snatching her purse was to get money to buy a pair of blue suede shoes. Mrs. Jones tells him that when she was young, she too wanted things she could not get. Mrs. Jones gives Roger ten dollars to buy the shoes and urges him to stay out of trouble. The boy thanks her as she shuts the door, and they never see each other again.

Thematic Link
Roger, who thinks he can get easy money by snatching a woman's purse, learns a lesson about right and wrong and about himself. He realizes that he wants to be seen as someone who can be trusted.

5-Minute Warm-Up

Daily Language SkillBuilder **TEKS 17C, 17G**

Have students **proofread** the display sentences on page 13i and write them correctly. The sentences also appear on Transparency 1 of **Grammar Transparencies and Copymasters.**

 Mini Lesson **Preteaching Vocabulary**

If you would like to preteach the WORDS TO KNOW for this selection, use the Mini Lesson, p. 31.

THANK YOU, M'AM **29**

Literary Analysis `CONFLICT`

 Ask students to identify the conflict that begins the action of the story as internal or external.

Answer: external

• Tell students to look for other conflicts as they read and to identify them as internal or external.

Use **Unit One Resource Book,** p. 16 for more practice.

Active Reading

`CAUSE AND EFFECT`

Have students record the first event in their cause-and-effect chain. Remind them that this will lead to a series of effects. Ask students why the event's first effect is unexpected to the boy.

Possible Response: He is caught instead of getting away with the money.

Use **Unit One Resource Book,** p. 15 for more practice.

Literary Analysis: **DIALOGUE**

 Ask students why they think the author chose to have the woman say, "You a lie!" Encourage them to think about how dialogue enhances their understanding of the woman's character.

Possible Responses: The woman sees through the boy, stands up to him verbally as well as physically, and will not let him lie his way out of accepting the consequences of his actions.

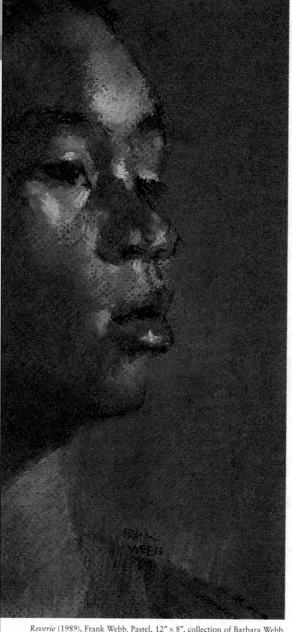

Reverie (1989), Frank Webb. Pastel, 12″ × 8″, collection of Barbara Webb.

30 UNIT ONE PART 1: KNOWING WHO YOU ARE

Thank You, M'am

BY LANGSTON HUGHES

She was a large woman with a large purse that had everything in it but hammer ▮1 and nails. It had a long strap, and she carried it slung across her shoulder. It was about eleven o'clock at night, and she was walking alone,

---

Teaching Options

 Mini Lesson **Viewing and Representing** TEKS 22A

Reverie
by Frank Webb

ART APPRECIATION *Reverie* was created in pastels by contemporary artist and teacher Frank Webb. Webb is known primarily as a watercolorist.
Instruction Webb enjoys using many colors in his paintings to convey specific moods. What colors does Webb use to convey the mood of this pastel?
Possible Responses: shades of green, brown, rust, yellow

Have students look at a side view of a partner and then the front view. Ask them to describe how the two perspectives differ.
Possible Response: Students might say that the profile offers an outline of the features. The front view fills in the details and gives a complete picture.
Application Ask students what Mrs. Jones realizes about the view she is getting of Roger when he tries to steal her purse.
Possible Responses: She realizes that there is more to him than this action shows; she is not seeing the total picture.

when a boy ran up behind her and tried to snatch her purse. The strap broke with the single tug the boy gave it from behind. But the boy's weight and the weight of the purse combined caused him to lose his balance so, instead of taking off full blast as he had hoped, the boy fell on his back on the sidewalk, and his legs flew up. The large woman simply turned around and kicked him right square in his blue-jeaned sitter. Then she reached down, picked the boy up by his shirt front, and shook him until his teeth rattled.

After that the woman said, "Pick up my pocketbook, boy, and give it here."

She still held him. But she bent down enough to permit him to stoop and pick up her purse. Then she said, "Now ain't you ashamed of yourself?"

Firmly gripped by his shirt front, the boy said, "Yes'm."

The woman said, "What did you want to do it for?"

The boy said, "I didn't aim to."

She said, "You a lie!"

By that time two or three people passed, stopped, turned to look, and some stood watching.

"If I turn you loose, will you run?" asked the woman.

"Yes'm," said the boy.

"Then I won't turn you loose," said the woman. She did not release him.

"I'm very sorry, lady, I'm sorry," whispered the boy.

"Um-hum! And your face is dirty. I got a great mind to wash your face for you. Ain't you got nobody home to tell you to wash your face?"

"No'm," said the boy.

"Then it will get washed this evening," said the large woman starting up the street, dragging the frightened boy behind her.

He looked as if he were fourteen or fifteen, <u>frail</u> and willow-wild, in tennis shoes and blue jeans.

The woman said, "You ought to be my son. I would teach you right from wrong. Least I can do right now is to wash your face. Are you hungry?"

"No'm," said the being-dragged boy. "I just want you to turn me loose."

"Was I bothering *you* when I turned that corner?" asked the woman.

"No'm."

"But you put yourself in contact with *me*," said the woman. "If you think that that contact is not going to last awhile, you got another thought coming. When I get through with you, sir, you are going to remember Mrs. Luella Bates Washington Jones."

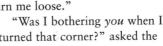

Sweat popped out on the boy's face and he began to struggle. Mrs. Jones stopped, jerked him around in front of her, put a half nelson[1] about his neck, and continued to drag him up the street. When she got to her door, she dragged the boy inside, down a hall, and into a large kitchenette-furnished room at the rear of the house. She switched on the light and left the door open.

---

1. **half nelson:** a wrestling hold with one arm under the opponent's arm from behind to the back of the neck.

WORDS TO KNOW   **frail** (frāl) *adj.* delicate; weak and fragile

31

Customizing Instruction

Less Proficient Readers
Use the following questions to involve students in the story:

- Why does the boy go with Mrs. Jones to her apartment?
  Possible Response: She is stronger than he is, and she drags him there.
- What does the location and type of apartment tell about the amount of money Mrs. Jones has?
  Possible Response: She does not have a lot of money.

Set a Purpose Have students read to find out what Mrs. Jones does with the boy.

Students Acquiring English
Introduce the story by telling students that *M'am* in the title is a contraction of the word *Madam* and is used as a form of polite address to an older woman. Ask students for similar titles used in their native languages.

Tell them that Hughes leaves out some words and uses dialect to make the dialogue of his characters sound realistic.

 Make sure students understand that *but* in this sentence means "except."

 Explain that the boy's reaction shows that he interprets her comment as a threat.

3 Point out the suffix *-ette* in *kitchenette* and elicit from students its meaning. (small)

Use **Spanish Study Guide**, pp. 7–9 for additional support.

Multiple Learning Styles
Kinesthetic Learners
Have partners take turns pantomiming the opening scene. Ask them to explain how each character's body language tells something about him or her.

Mini Lesson — Preteaching Vocabulary ★ TEKS 9C

SYNONYMS
Instruction Remind students that they can find synonyms for words by using a reference aid such as a thesaurus. Emphasize that not all synonyms will match the meaning of the word as it is used in a particular sentence. Tell students to determine the best synonym for the word by substituting each choice into the sentence to see if the meaning stays the same.
Exercise Have students choose the best synonym for each of the underlined WORDS TO KNOW by using the strategy described above.

1. He made himself <u>presentable</u> by combing his hair and washing his face. *(suitable, <u>tidy</u>, decent)*
2. The boy was <u>frail</u> and did not have the strength to pull away from Mrs. Jones. *(<u>weak</u>, brittle, short-lived)*
3. Her <u>barren</u> front steps gave the house a lonely look. *(<u>empty</u>, dull, unprofitable)*
4. Roger didn't want Mrs. Jones to <u>mistrust</u> him any longer. *(suspect, discredit, <u>doubt</u>)*

Use **Unit One Resource Book** p. 17 for more exercises. Use **Vocabulary Transparencies and Copymasters**, p. 20, for additional support.

Literary Analysis [CONFLICT]

A Ask students what types of conflict Roger is experiencing.

Possible Responses: an external conflict with Mrs. Jones; an internal conflict involving whether to run away or wash his face

How does he resolve his internal conflict?

Answer: He stays.

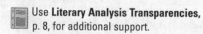 Use **Literary Analysis Transparencies,** p. 8, for additional support.

Literary Analysis: DIALOGUE

B Ask students what additional characteristics of Mrs. Jones are revealed by her words.

Possible Response: She is generous, understanding, and kind.

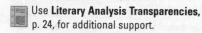 Use **Literary Analysis Transparencies,** p. 24, for additional support.

Active Reading
[CAUSE AND EFFECT]

C Ask students to explain why Roger sits so that Mrs. Jones can see him.

Possible Response: He doesn't want her to have a chance to mistrust him.

Use **Reading and Critical Thinking Transparencies,** p. 3, for additional support.

Reading Skills and Strategies: MAKING INFERENCES

D Ask students what else Roger might have wanted to say to Mrs. Jones.

Possible Responses: He might have wanted to tell her that she changed his life; that he would like to stay in touch with her; that she is a great woman.

The boy could hear other roomers laughing and talking in the large house. Some of their doors were open, too, so he knew he and the woman were not alone. The woman still had him by the neck in the middle of her room.

She said, "What is your name?"

"Roger," answered the boy.

"Then, Roger, you go to that sink and wash your face," said the woman, whereupon she turned him loose—at last. Roger looked at the door—looked at the woman—looked at the door—*and went to the sink.*

"Let the water run until it gets warm," she said. "Here's a clean towel."

"You gonna take me to jail?" asked the boy, bending over the sink.

"Not with that face, I would not take you nowhere," said the woman. "Here I am trying to get home to cook me a bite to eat and you snatch my pocketbook! Maybe you ain't been to your supper either, late as it be. Have you?"

"There's nobody home at my house," said the boy.

"Then we'll eat," said the woman. "I believe you're hungry—or been hungry—to try to snatch my pocketbook."

"I wanted a pair of blue suede shoes," said the boy.

"Well, you didn't have to snatch *my* pocketbook to get some suede shoes," said Mrs. Luella Bates Washington Jones. "You could of asked me."

"M'am?"

The water dripping from his face, the boy looked at her. There was a long pause. A very long pause. After he had dried his face and not knowing what else to do dried it again, the boy turned around, wondering what next. The door was open. He could make a dash for it down the hall. He could run, run, run, run, *run!*

The woman was sitting on the day-bed. After a while she said, "I were young once and I wanted things I could not get."

There was another long pause. The boy's mouth opened. Then he frowned, but not knowing he frowned.

The woman said, "Um-hum! You thought I was going to say *but,* didn't you? You thought I was going to say, *but I didn't snatch people's pocketbooks.* Well, I wasn't going to say that." Pause. Silence. "I have done things, too, which I would not tell you, son—neither tell God, if he didn't already know. So you set down while I fix us something to eat. You might run that comb through your hair so you will look presentable."

In another corner of the room behind a screen was a gas plate and an icebox. Mrs. Jones got up and went behind the screen. The woman did not watch the boy to see if he was going to run now, nor did she watch her purse which she left behind her on the day-bed. But the boy took care to sit on the far side of the room where he thought she could easily see him out of the corner of her eye, if she wanted to. He did not trust the woman *not* to trust him. And he did not want to be mistrusted now.

"Do you need somebody to go to the store," asked the boy, "maybe to get some milk or something?"

WORDS	**suede** (swād) *n.* leather with a soft, fuzzy surface
TO	**presentable** (prĭ-zĕn'tə-bəl) *adj.* fit to be seen by people
KNOW	**mistrust** (mĭs-trŭst') *v.* to have no confidence in

32

Teaching Options

BLOCK SCHEDULING: MANAGING TIME

If your schedule requires that you cover the lesson objectives in a shorter time, use . . .
- Preparing to Read, p. 29
- Thinking Through the Literature, p. 34
- Vocabulary and Spelling, p. 35
- Grammar in Context, p. 36

If you want to take advantage of longer class time, use . . .
- TE Teaching Options: Viewing and Representing, p. 30; Preteaching Vocabulary, p. 31; Grammar, pp. 33, 36; Informal Assessment, p. 35
- Choices & Challenges, pp. 35–36

"Don't believe I do," said the woman, "unless you just want sweet milk yourself. I was going to make cocoa out of this canned milk I got here."

"That will be fine," said the boy.

She heated some lima beans and ham she had in the icebox, made the cocoa, and set the table. The woman did not ask the boy anything about where he lived, or his folks, or anything else that would embarrass him. Instead, as they ate, she told him about her job in a hotel beauty-shop that stayed open late, what the work was like, and how all kinds of women came in and out, blondes, red-heads, and Spanish. Then she cut him a half of her ten-cent cake.

"Eat some more, son," she said.

When they were finished eating she got up and said, "Now, here, take this ten dollars and buy yourself some blue suede shoes. And next time, do not make the mistake of latching onto *my* pocketbook *nor nobody else's*—because shoes come by devilish like that will burn your feet. I got to get my rest now. But I wish you would behave yourself, son, from here on in."

She led him down the hall to the front door and opened it. "Goodnight! Behave yourself, boy!" she said, looking out into the street.

The boy wanted to say something else other than "Thank you, m'am" to Mrs. Luella Bates Washington Jones, but he couldn't do so as he turned at the <u>barren</u> stoop and looked back at the large woman in the door. He barely managed to say "Thank you" before she shut the door. And he never saw her again. ❖

[3]
[D]
[4]

LITERARY LINK

If I Can Stop One Heart from Breaking
by Emily Dickinson

If I can stop one Heart from breaking
I shall not live in vain
If I can ease one Life the Aching
Or cool one Pain

Or help one fainting Robin
Unto his Nest again
I shall not live in Vain.

WORDS TO KNOW   **barren** (băr'ən) *adj.* empty; deserted

33

Customizing Instruction

Students Acquiring English

[1] Tell students that blue suede shoes were fashionable in the 1950s.

[2] Explain that a gas plate is a small stove and an icebox is a simple refrigerator.

[3] Help students to understand that "shoes come by devilish like that will burn your feet" means that he would not enjoy wearing the shoes because they would make him feel guilty.

Less Proficient Readers

[4] What happens to Roger and Mrs. Jones at the end of the story?

Possible Response: After cleaning him up, feeding him, and giving him money for shoes, Mrs. Jones sends Roger on his way. They never see each other again.

LITERARY LINK

Use the following questions to help students analyze and understand the poem.

1. According to the speaker, what actions make a person's life worthwhile?
   Possible Response: reaching out to others and easing pain and discomfort

2. What connections do you see between the poem and the short story?
   Possible Response: The speaker wishes to do what Mrs. Jones did—make a difference in a person's life.

Emily Dickinson

Dickinson (1830–1886) wrote nearly eighteen hundred poems. Most of her poems are short, highly compressed lyrics that depart from conventional rhyme and meter. It was not until years after her death that Dickinson became one of America's most popular and influential poets.

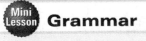 **Grammar** TEKS 17B

COORDINATING CONJUNCTIONS

Instruction Remind students that the coordinating conjunctions *and, but,* and *or* connect words or groups of words of equal importance. By using coordinating conjunctions, a writer can make his or her meaning clearer and streamline his or her writing. Point out the highlighted passage above and ask students to pick out the coordinating conjunctions.

Application Have each student write five original sentences about the story that contain coordinating conjunctions. Ask students to share their sentences with the class.

Example: Mrs. Jones was generous **and** shared with Roger.

 Use **Grammar Transparencies and Copymasters**, p. 90.

Use McDougal Littell's *Language Network*, Chapter 6, for more instruction and practice in coordinating conjunctions.

Thinking *through the* LITERATURE

Connect to the Literature

1. Possible Responses: Some students might be disappointed, thinking he would form a friendship. Others will say that Hughes shows the generosity of Mrs. Jones, who expected nothing in return.

Comprehension Check
- She drags him to her house.
- He wants blue suede shoes.
- She makes him wash, feeds him, talks to him, and gives him ten dollars.

 Use Selection Quiz **Unit One Resource Book,** p. 20.

Think Critically

2. **Possible Responses:** Some students may say that Mrs. Jones has learned the hard way that it is important to do what is right. Others may say that Mrs. Jones realizes that Roger has no one to look after him to see that he learns the difference between right and wrong.
3. **Possible Responses:** No, because he understood Mrs. Jones's lesson about living an honest life; yes, because even though Mrs. Jones scared him for a moment, he probably didn't learn his lesson.
4. **Possible Responses:** Roger grabs the purse; he is caught by Mrs. Jones; she drags him to her home and asks him questions; his answers lead to her inviting him for dinner; her kindness makes him want to be trusted by her; he stays even when he could leave; she gives him ten dollars; he feels gratitude.

 Use **Reading and Critical Thinking Transparencies,** p. 3, for additional support.

Literary Analysis

Conflict The way Mrs. Jones handles the conflict with Roger and the way he resolves his internal conflict and decides to stay reveal the most about the two characters. The conflicts that add the most excitement are those in which the outcome is unknown.

Use **Literary Analysis Transparencies,** p. 8, for additional support.

Connect to the Literature

1. **What Do You Think?** How did you feel about the last sentence in the story ("And he never saw her again")? Explain your reaction.

   Comprehension Check
   - What happens when Roger tries to steal Mrs. Jones's purse?
   - Why does Roger want to steal money from Mrs. Jones?
   - What happens when Mrs. Jones gets Roger to her house?

Think Critically

2. Why do you think Mrs. Jones treats Roger the way she does?

    THINK ABOUT
   - what she reveals about her past
   - what she seems to understand about Roger's life
   - how Roger answers her questions

3. Do you think Roger will steal again? Why or why not?

4. **ACTIVE READING** **CAUSE AND EFFECT** Compare the **cause-and-effect** diagram you made in your **READER'S NOTEBOOK** with a classmate's. How are the events and details in the two chains of causes and effects similar? How do they differ?

Extend Interpretations

5. **COMPARING TEXTS** Reread the poem on page 33. Which lines remind you of the way Mrs. Jones thinks?

6. **Connect to Life** In this story, Roger is willing to go to extreme lengths to get blue suede shoes. Most people would not approve of his actions. Can you think of other ways he could have tried to get the shoes? Discuss your ideas with a classmate.

Literary Analysis

CONFLICT A story's plot usually centers on a **conflict**—a struggle between opposing forces. An **external conflict** is a character's struggle against a force outside himself or herself. An **internal conflict** takes place inside a character. For example, a character may struggle against his or her fears or may experience a conflict between wanting something and knowing that taking it is wrong. Think about the external and internal conflicts that Roger and Mrs. Jones experience in this story.

Paired Activity Go through the story with a partner, looking for examples of conflict. Determine which are external and which are internal. Record your findings in a chart like the one shown here. After you finish, discuss these questions:

- Which conflicts convey important information about the characters?
- Which conflicts add the most excitement to the story?

Conflict	Internal	External
Roger tries to steal Mrs. Jones's purse.		✔
Mrs. Jones grabs Roger.		✔
Mrs. Jones must decide what to do with Roger.	✔	

Extend Interpretations

5. **Comparing Texts** Answers will vary. Students may cite the third and fifth lines as being particularly expressive of what Mrs. Jones does for Roger. **To make this question easier,** help the students to paraphrase the poem first.

6. **Connect to Life** Answers will vary. Students might suggest legitimate ways such as getting a part-time job; borrowing the money from someone; waiting for a shoe sale. **To make this question easier,** allow students to work in pairs.

To make this question more challenging, have students think about the symbolism of the shoes and what each method of obtaining them would represent.

Choices & CHALLENGES

Writing Options

Comparing Characters Write a short essay comparing Mrs. Jones with someone you know personally, such as a family member, a teacher, or a religious leader. Use a web diagram to jot down information about Mrs. Jones's character from the story before you start. Place your draft in your **Working Portfolio.**

Activities & Explorations

1. Film Review View the video version of "Thank You, M'am." Then, with classmates, discuss whether the video portrays the characters as you visualized them. ~ **VIEWING AND REPRESENTING**

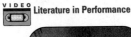 **V I D E O** Literature in Performance

2. Dramatic Dialogue Imagine that Roger and Mrs. Jones meet ten years after this story. With a partner, act out a conversation that they might have. ~ **SPEAKING AND LISTENING**

Art Connection

Look at Frank Webb's drawing *Reverie* on page 30. What are your impressions of the subject of the drawing?

Inquiry & Research

Life in Harlem With a group of classmates, research the history of Harlem. Present your findings in an oral report.

Vocabulary and Spelling

EXERCISE A: SYNONYMS On a sheet of paper, write the Word to Know that is most closely related in meaning to the italicized word or phrase in each sentence below.

1. Mrs. Jones wanted Roger to look more *pleasing* to people.
2. Shoes made of *soft, treated leather* usually cost more than shoes made of canvas.
3. When the students are gone, the school seems sad and *empty.*
4. Because Roger looked *delicate,* people often thought he was not very strong.
5. Roger didn't want Mrs. Jones to *suspect* or doubt him.

EXERCISE B: PREFIXES When a prefix is added to a root word, as in *mistrust,* do not drop a letter from either the prefix or the root word.

1. Write out the following words with prefixes.

   mis + trust = _____
   mis + spell = _____
   de + part = _____
   de + serve = _____
   ex + act   = _____
   ex + claim = _____

2. What three suffixes have been added to form the spelling words?

   _____ _____ _____

Spelling Handbook p. R86

WORDS TO KNOW	barren	mistrust	suede
	frail	presentable	

✓ **Assessment** **Informal Assessment** **TEKS 12G** **TAAS Reading Obj. 3** **TAAS Writing Obj. 1**

DESCRIBING PLOT You can informally assess students' understanding of the plot of the story by having them imagine that Roger's teacher gave his class the assignment to write a paragraph about an important incident that changed their lives. Students should write their paragraphs from Roger's point of view and narrate the events of the story and the change that he experienced.

RUBRIC

3 Full Accomplishment Paragraph includes the important events, maintains consistency of point of view, and explains change in character clearly.

2 Substantial Accomplishment Paragraph includes the majority of plot events in sequence, maintains point of view, and explains change in character.

1 Little or Partial Accomplishment Paragraph omits some significant events, has an inconsistent point of view, and does not show the change in character.

Writing Options

Comparing Characters After students complete the web of Mrs. Jones's character, have them think about people in their lives that bear a resemblance to her. Students should choose the person with the strongest similarities and may wish to organize the similarities between the two in a chart before writing the essay.

 Use **Writing Transparencies,** p. 6, for additional support.

Activities & Explorations

1. Film Review Discuss with students any changes that were made to the story in adapting it for film. **To make this assignment more challenging,** have students actually write a review of the film and read it to the class.

2. Dramatic Dialogue To get students started on this assignment, have them outline what they want to say in their dialogue and choose a setting for the meeting between the two. The path that Roger has taken through life and Mrs. Jones's influence on him should be revealed in the dialogue. Students should refer back to the story so that their speech is consistent with the speech of the characters. This activity is well suited to **interpersonal learners.**

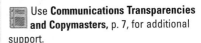 Use **Communications Transparencies and Copymasters,** p. 7, for additional support.

Art Connection

Responses will vary. Students might say that the subject appears to be in a state of serenity and seems to be thinking or looking inward or daydreaming.

Inquiry & Research

Life in Harlem To get students started on this assignment, discuss the references that they might use, such as history books, encyclopedias, or the Internet. Students should work in small groups and delegate the tasks of the assignment among members of the group.

Vocabulary in Action

Exercise A
1. presentable
2. suede
3. barren
4. frail
5. mistrust

Grammar in Context

Langston Hughes

After becoming a successful writer, Langston Hughes spent much of his free time talking to young, aspiring writers, encouraging them to continue their craft. He liked traveling and spent time in Mexico (where his father lived), Africa, and Europe. Widely celebrated, he became known as the poet laureate of Harlem.

Grammar in Context: Compound Predicates

Langston Hughes shows how quickly Mrs. Jones reacts when Roger tries to take her purse:

> **Mrs. Jones** stopped, jerked **him around in front of her,** put **a half nelson about his neck, and** continued **to drag him up the street.**

The words in green are all main verbs. They tell what the single subject, Mrs. Jones, does. When a sentence has two or more main verbs, it has a **compound predicate**.

Punctuation Tip: Use **commas** to separate each verb with its modifier:

> **She** reached down, picked the boy up by his shirt front, and shook him until his teeth rattled.

WRITING EXERCISE Streamline each pair of sentences by writing one complete sentence with a compound predicate.

Example: *Original* Roger, go to that sink. Wash your face at that sink.

Rewritten Roger, go to that sink and wash your face.

1. Roger ran up behind Mrs. Jones. Roger tried to snatch her purse.
2. Mrs. Jones switched on the light. She left the door open.
3. Take this ten dollars. Buy yourself some blue suede shoes.
4. She led him down the hall to the front door. She opened the front door.

Grammar Handbook The Sentence and Its Parts, p. R55

"Books began to happen to me, and I began to believe in nothing but books . . ."

Langston Hughes
1902–1967

Early Years Langston Hughes is one of the most renowned and influential of African-American writers. His poems have been widely translated and appear in poetry anthologies all over the world. Here's how he recalls his youth in Lawrence, Kansas: "Books began to happen to me, and I began to believe in nothing but books and the wonderful world in books—where if people suffered, they suffered in beautiful language, not in monosyllables, as we did in Kansas."

One of the First Hughes was one of the first African Americans to earn his living solely from writing. His first recognition came when, while working as a busboy, he left three of his poems at a table where the poet Vachel Lindsay was dining. Lindsay presented some of the young poet's works at one of his own poetry readings, and Hughes's career was launched.

Hughes went on to write novels, short stories, plays, song lyrics, and radio scripts as well as poetry. To portray the African-American experience, he often focused on the ordinary people whose vitality contributed to the special atmosphere of life in Harlem.

 LaserLink: Background for Reading
Art Gallery

Teaching Options

Mini Lesson **Grammar**   📋 **TEKS 17C**   ⭐ **TAAS Writing Obj. 6**

COMPOUND SUBJECTS AND PREDICATES
Instruction Explain that compound subjects joined with the conjunction *and* usually take a plural verb. Compound subjects joined with *or* must have a verb that agrees with the closest subject. If the predicate is compound, all parts of it must agree with the subject.

Display the following sentences to illustrate correct subject-verb agreement:

Lima beans and ham are requested often and have been popular for years.

Lima beans or a slice of ham does not make a complete meal and is not balanced nutritionally.

Exercise Have students choose the verb that agrees with the compound subject.

1. Her neighbors or Mrs. Jones (<u>sorts</u>, sort) and (<u>files</u>, file) the mail.
2. Wealthy customers and poor clients (visits, <u>visit</u>) Mrs. Jones's beauty shop.
3. Teenagers in Roger's day and teenagers now (wants, <u>want</u>) to fit in and (earns, <u>earn</u>) approval.
4. Her hairdresser or one of the others (<u>washes</u>, wash), (<u>cuts</u>, cut), and (<u>styles</u>, style) better than my hairdresser does.

Use **Unit One Resource Book,** p. 11.
Use **Grammar Transparencies and Copymasters,** p. 53.

Language Network Use McDougal Littell's *Language Network,* Chapter 1, for more instruction and practice in compound subjects and predicates.

Names/Nombres

Personal Essay by JULIA ALVAREZ

"Someday, the family predicted, my name would be well-known throughout the United States."

Connect to Your Life

Fitting In Think about a time when someone new joined your class. How did the newcomer try to fit in? If you were in a situation where you were a newcomer, how might you try to fit in? Discuss this with your class.

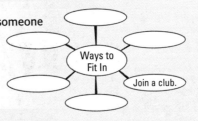

Ways to Fit In

Join a club.

Build Background

CONNECT TO **SOCIAL STUDIES** Like language and religion, names give important clues about a person's cultural background. In Spanish tradition, a child normally has two last names—the father's family name and the mother's maiden name. Often, a child's full name can include four generations of family names.

Although Julia Alvarez was born in New York City, she spent ten years of her childhood in the Dominican Republic, a country located on the island of Hispaniola in the Caribbean Sea.

WORDS TO KNOW **Vocabulary Preview**

chaotic   inevitably   merge
convoluted   initial   specify
ethnicity   ironically   usher
exotic

TEKS See the Skills Trace at the beginning of the unit for information on TEKS covered in this lesson.

Focus Your Reading

LITERARY ANALYSIS **PERSONAL ESSAY** "Names/Nombres" is a **personal essay,** a short form of nonfiction that expresses the author's thoughts and feelings about one subject. Often personal essays, like fiction, include elements of **character, setting,** and **plot.** Notice how Alvarez establishes setting and character in the very first sentence of this essay.

> *When we arrived in New York City, our names changed almost immediately. At Immigration, the officer asked my father,* Mister Elbures, *if he had anything to declare.*

ACTIVE READING **IDENTIFYING AUTHOR'S PURPOSE** An author can have various **purposes** in a single piece of writing. Usually these purposes include one or more of the following:

- to entertain
- to inform or to explain
- to express an opinion
- to persuade

As you read, think about the purpose or purposes that Julia Alvarez had for writing this essay.

READER'S NOTEBOOK As a writer, Julia Alvarez certainly wanted to write a good, entertaining essay. Still, as you read "Names/Nombres," think about what other purposes she may have had in mind, and jot them down.

NAMES/NOMBRES **37**

Reading and Analyzing

Literary Analysis | PERSONAL ESSAY

Remind students that an essay is a short work of nonfiction that deals with a single subject. A personal essay is one written from the personal experience of the writer. It may include story elements, such as characters, setting, and plot. As they read, have students identify the topic of Julia Alvarez's essay and what feelings it expresses.

Possible Responses: Julia Alvarez has written about her experiences as an immigrant in the United States, where being from a different culture and speaking a different language often cause confusion. She talks about how she feels out of place and sometimes wishes she could be like everyone else.

 Use **Unit One Resource Book**, p. 23, for more practice.

Active Reading
IDENTIFYING AUTHOR'S PURPOSE

A Discuss the writer's feelings about the way Americans pronounced her and her family's names. Did she think this was OK, or did she think the people should have tried harder to pronounce the names correctly? What does this tell you about her purpose in writing the story?

Possible Responses: Alvarez wants people to think about how other people might feel in similar circumstances. While her purpose is to entertain her readers, it is also to inform them about how others might feel, even if they meant no offense.

 Use **Unit One Resource Book**, p. 22, for more practice.

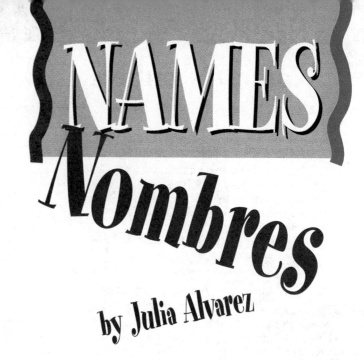

NAMES
Nombres

by Julia Alvarez

When we arrived in New York City, our names changed almost immediately.

At Immigration, the officer asked my father, *Mister Elbures*, if he had anything to declare. My father shook his head no, and we were waved through. I was too afraid we wouldn't be let in if I corrected the man's pronunciation, but I said our name to myself, opening my mouth wide for the organ blast of the *a*, trilling my tongue[1] for the drumroll of the *r*, *All-vah-rrr-es!* How could anyone get *Elbures* out of that orchestra of sound?

At the hotel my mother was *Missus Alburest*, and I was *little girl*, as in, "Hey, little girl, stop riding the elevator up and down. It's *not* a toy."

When we moved into our new apartment building, the super called my father *Mister Alberase*, and the neighbors who became mother's friends pronounced her name *Jew-lee-ah* instead of *Hoo-lee-ah*. I, her namesake, was known as *Hoo-lee-tah* at home. But at school I was *Judy* or *Judith*,

---

1. **trilling my tongue:** rapid vibration of the tongue against the roof of the mouth, as in pronouncing a Spanish *r*.

Teaching Options

BLOCK SCHEDULING: MANAGING TIME

If your schedule requires that you cover the lesson objectives in a shorter time, use . . .
- Preparing to Read, p. 37
- Thinking Through the Literature, p. 43
- Vocabulary in Action, p. 44
- Grammar in Context, p. 45

If you want to take advantage of longer class time, use . . .
- TE Teaching Options: Preteaching Vocabulary, p. 39; Speaking and Listening, p. 40; Grammar, pp. 41, 45; Informal Assessment, p. 42; Spelling, p. 44
- Choices & Challenges and Author Activity, pp. 44–45

Illustration by Rosanne Kaloustian.

and once an English teacher mistook me for *Juliet.*

It took a while to get used to my new names. I wondered if I shouldn't correct my teachers and new friends. But my mother argued that it didn't matter. "You know what your friend Shakespeare said, 'A rose by any other name would smell as sweet.'" My family had gotten into the habit of calling any literary figure "my friend" because I had begun to write poems and stories in English class.

By the time I was in high school, I was a popular kid, and it showed in my name. Friends called me *Jules* or *Hey Jude,* and once a group of troublemaking friends my mother forbade me to hang out with called me *Alcatraz.* I was *Hoo-lee-tah* only to Mami and

Papi and uncles and aunts who came over to eat *sancocho*[2] on Sunday afternoons—old world folk whom I would just as soon go back to where they came from and leave me to pursue whatever mischief I wanted to in America. JUDY ALCATRAZ: the name on the wanted poster would read. Who would ever trace her to me?

My older sister had the hardest time getting an American name for herself because *Mauricia* did not translate into English. <u>Ironically</u>, although she had the most foreign-sounding name, she and I were the Americans in the family. We had been born in New York

---

2. *sancocho* (säng-kō′chō) *Spanish:* traditional Caribbean stew of meat and vegetables.

WORDS TO KNOW	**ironically** (ī-rŏn′ ĭk-əl-lē) *adv.* in a way that is contrary to what is expected or intended

39

NAMES/NOMBRES **39**

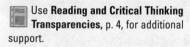

Reading and Analyzing

Literary Analysis PERSONAL ESSAY

Ask students to discuss some of the personal feelings Julia Alvarez writes about on these two pages.

Possible Response: She writes about her feelings about being different.

Active Reading

IDENTIFYING AUTHOR'S PURPOSE

 A Ask students to tell why they think the writer included the story about the woman who said, "Why'd ya give her an Irish name with so many pretty Spanish names to choose from?"

Possible Response: She probably wanted to show that it was silly to be ashamed of being different.

Use **Reading and Critical Thinking Transparencies,** p. 4, for additional support.

Reading Skills and Strategies: VISUALIZING

B Ask students to visualize the graduation scene. What words are especially helpful in evoking a mental image?

Possible Responses: *dark mourning dresses; full, droopy mustaches; rococo consonants*

Literary Analysis POINT OF VIEW

Remind students that the point of view is the perspective from which a story is told. A personal essay is told from the first person point of view and involves the reader in a very personal way. Ask how "Names/Nombres" would be different if it were told from the point of view of someone outside the family.

Possible Response: The story would include observations about the people, but it wouldn't be able to record their personal feelings in the same way.

Use **Literary Analysis Transparencies,** p. 22, for additional support.

Julia Altagracia María Teresa Álvarez Tavares

City when our parents had first tried immigration and then gone back "home," too homesick to stay. My mother often told the story of how she had almost changed my sister's name in the hospital.

 A After the delivery, Mami and some other new mothers were cooing over their new baby sons and daughters and exchanging names and weights and delivery stories. My mother was embarrassed among the Sallys and Janes and Georges and Johns to reveal the rich, noisy name of *Mauricia,* so when her turn came to brag, she gave her baby's name as *Maureen.*

"Why'd ya give her an Irish name with so many pretty Spanish names to choose from?" one of the women asked her.

My mother blushed and admitted her baby's real name to the group. Her mother-in-law had recently died, she apologized, and her husband had insisted that the first daughter be named after his mother, *Mauran.* My mother thought it the ugliest name she had ever heard, and she talked my father into what she believed was an improvement, a combination of *Mauran* and her own mother's name, *Felicia.*

"Her name is Mao-ree-shee-ah," my mother said to the group.

"Why, that's a beautiful name," the new mothers cried. *"Moor-ee-sha, Moor-ee-sha,"* they cooed into the pink blanket. *Moor-ee-sha* it was when we returned to the States eleven years later. Sometimes, American tongues found even that mispronunciation tough to say and called her *Maria* or *Marsha* or *Maudy* from her nickname *Maury.* I pitied her. What

an awful name to have to transport across borders!

My little sister, Ana, had the easiest time of all. She was plain *Anne*—that is, only her name was plain, for she turned out to be the pale, blond "American beauty" in the family. The only Hispanic-seeming thing about her was the affectionate nicknames her boyfriends sometimes gave her. *Anita,* or as one goofy guy used to sing to her to the tune of the banana advertisement, *Anita Banana.*

Later, during her college years in the late 60's, there was a push to pronounce Third World[3] names correctly. I remember calling her long distance at her group house and a roommate answering.

"Can I speak to Ana?" I asked, pronouncing her name the American way.

"Ana?" The man's voice hesitated. "Oh! You must mean *Ah-nah!*"

Our first few years in the States, though, ethnicity was not yet "in." Those were the blond, blue-eyed, bobby-sock years of junior high and high school before the 60's ushered in peasant blouses, hoop earrings, *sarapes.*[4] My initial desire to be known by my correct Dominican name faded. I just wanted to be Judy and merge with the Sallys and Janes in

---

3. **Third World:** the developing nations of Latin America, Africa, and Asia.

4. *sarapes* (sä-rä′pĕs) *Spanish:* a long, blanket-like shawl.

WORDS
TO
KNOW

ethnicity (ĕth-nĭs′ĭ-tē) *n.* a racial, national, or cultural heritage
usher (ŭsh′ər) *v.* to make known the presence or arrival of; to introduce
initial (ĭ-nĭsh′əl) *adj.* first
merge (mûrj) *v.* to blend together

40

Teaching Options

 Mini Lesson **Speaking and Listening** 🏴 **TEKS 4A, 5E**

PRESENT A REPORT

Prepare What's in a name? Discuss names and their origins. Encourage students to involve family members in researching the various names—both first names and surnames—in their families. Ask them to think about questions such as these:

• What do the names mean?
• Have any of the names been changed? If so, do they keep the same meaning?

Explain that some names are changed so that they are more like English words. Other names are translated. For example, a German Schneider may become an American Taylor. (Both names mean "tailor; one who makes clothes.")

Present Ask students to present their reports on names to the class. Remind them as they speak to use the rate, volume, and tone that is appropriate for their audience. Encourage

listeners to connect and compare their own information with that of the speakers.

Use **Communications Transparencies and Copymasters,** p. 10, for additional support.

BLOCK SCHEDULING This activity is particularly well suited for longer class periods.

my class. But, inevitably, my accent and coloring gave me away. "So where are you from, Judy?"

"New York," I told my classmates. After all, I had been born blocks away at Columbia Presbyterian Hospital.

"I mean, *originally*."

"From the Caribbean," I answered vaguely, for if I specified, no one was quite sure what continent our island was located on.

"Really? I've been to Bermuda. We went last April for spring vacation. I got the worst sunburn! So, are you from Portoriko?"

"No," I shook my head. "From the Dominican Republic."

"Where's that?"

"South of Bermuda."

They were just being curious, I knew, but I burned with shame whenever they singled me out as a "foreigner," a rare, exotic friend.

"Say your name in Spanish, oh, please say it!" I had made mouths drop one day by rattling off my full name, which, according to Dominican custom, included my middle names, Mother's and Father's surnames for four generations back.

"Julia Altagracia María Teresa Álvarez Tavares Perello Espaillat Julia Pérez Rochet González." I pronounced it slowly, a name as chaotic with sounds as a Middle Eastern bazaar or market day in a South American village.

I suffered most whenever my extended family attended school occasions. For my graduation, they all came, the whole noisy, foreign-looking lot of fat aunts in their dark mourning dresses and hair nets, uncles with full, droopy mustaches and baby-blue or salmon-colored suits and white pointy shoes and fedora hats,[5] the many little cousins who snuck in without tickets. They sat in the first row in order to better understand the Americans' fast-spoken English. But how could they listen when they were constantly speaking among themselves in florid-sounding[6] phrases, rococo[7] consonants, rich, rhyming vowels? Their loud voices carried.

Introducing them to my friends was a further trial to me. These relatives had such complicated names and there were so many of them, and their relationships to myself were so convoluted. There was my Tía[8] Josefina, who was not really an aunt but a much older cousin. And her daughter, Aída Margarita, who was adopted, *una hija de crianza*.[9] My uncle of affection, Tío José, brought my *madrina*[10] Tía Amelia and her *comadre*[11] Tía Pilar. My friends rarely had more than their

---

5. **fedora hats** (fĭ-dôr′ə): soft felt hats with low crowns.
6. **florid-sounding:** flowery; very ornate.
7. **rococo** (rə-kō′kō): elaborate; flamboyant.
8. **Tía/Tío** (tē′ä, tē′ō) *Spanish:* Aunt/Uncle.
9. *una hija de crianza* (ōō′nä ē′hä dě kryän′sä) *Spanish:* a child raised as if one's own.
10. *madrina* (mä-drē′nä) *Spanish:* godmother.
11. *comadre* (kō-mä′drě) *Spanish:* close friend.

WORDS
TO
KNOW

inevitably (ĭn-ěv′ĭ-tə-blē) *adv.* impossible to avoid or prevent
specify (spěs′ə-fī) *v.* to make known or identify
exotic (ĭg-zŏt′ĭk) *adj.* unusual or different
chaotic (kā-ŏt′ĭk) *adj.* confused; disordered
convoluted (kŏn′və-lōō′tĭd) *adj.* difficult to understand; complicated

41

Mini Lesson **Grammar** ▣ **TEKS** 17A 🏴 **TAAS** Writing Obj. 3, 7

COMMAS AFTER INTRODUCTORY ELEMENTS
Instruction Call students' attention to the highlighted passages on page 40. Explain that *After the delivery*, a prepositional phrase, and *Sometimes*, an adverb, are introductory elements. Each is followed by a comma. The pauses keep the parts of the sentence from running together. Tell students that most introductory elements, unless followed by very short pauses, are followed by commas.

Exercises Ask students to add a comma where it is needed in each of the following sentences.
1. In history class (,) I talked about my heritage.
2. When she says her name (,) she feels embarrassed.
3. Thoughtfully and quietly (,) she wrote her poem.
4. Among her friends (,) Julia gained nicknames.

📄 Use **Grammar Transparencies and Copymasters,** p. 124.

📕 Use McDougal Littell's *Language Network,* Chapter 11, for more instruction and practice in punctuation with introductory elements.

nuclear family[12] to introduce, youthful, glamorous-looking couples ("Mom and Dad") who skied and played tennis and took their kids for spring vacations to Bermuda.

After the commencement ceremony, my family waited outside in the parking lot while my friends and I signed yearbooks with nicknames which recalled our high school good times: "Beans" and "Pepperoni" and "Alcatraz." We hugged and cried and promised to keep in touch.

Sometimes if our goodbyes went on too long, I heard my father's voice calling out across the parking lot. *"Hoo-lee-tah! Vámonos!"*[13]

Back home, my tíos and tías and primas,[14] Mami and Papi, and *mis hermanas*[15] had a party for me with *sancocho* and a store-bought *pudín*,[16] inscribed with *Happy Graduation, Julie.* There were many gifts—that was a plus to a large family! I got several wallets and a suitcase with my initials and a graduation charm from my godmother and money from my uncles. The biggest gift was a portable typewriter from my parents for writing my stories and poems.

Someday, the family predicted, my name would be well-known throughout the United States. I laughed to myself, wondering which one I would go by. ❖

12. **nuclear family:** a family unit consisting of a mother and father and their children.
13. *Vámonos* (bä′mō-nōs) *Spanish:* Let's go.
14. *primas* (prē′mäs) *Spanish:* cousins.
15. *mis hermanas* (mēs ĕr-mä′näs) *Spanish:* my sisters.
16. *pudín* (pōō-thēn′) *Spanish:* pudding.

Cover Illustration by German Perez.

Courtesy of Algonquin Books of Chapel Hill.

Teaching Options

 Assessment **Informal Assessment**   TEKS 12H  TAAS Reading Obj. 6

AUTHOR'S POINT OF VIEW AND PURPOSE You can informally assess students' understanding of the selection by having them discuss why they think the author wrote "Names/Nombres." Discuss also the author's point of view about the way people from other countries might feel when Americans don't even attempt to pronounce their names correctly.

RUBRIC

3 Full Accomplishment Response shows full understanding of author's point of view and purpose.

2 Substantial Accomplishment Response shows correct but limited understanding of author's point of view and purpose.

1 Little or Partial Accomplishment Response shows little understanding of author's point of view and purpose.

Connect to the Literature

1. What Do You Think? If you were in Alvarez's position as a newcomer, do you think you might fit in as well as she did? Explain.

Comprehension Check
- Where is the Alvarez family from?
- Why did Mrs. Alvarez first tell the ladies at the hospital that her oldest daughter's name was Maureen?
- Why did Alvarez find it difficult to introduce her relatives to her friends?

Think Critically

2. **ACTIVE READING** **IDENTIFYING AUTHOR'S PURPOSE** Look at what you wrote in your 📖 **READER'S NOTEBOOK** about this writer's purpose. Besides wanting to tell an interesting story, what do you think Alvarez's purpose might be? Give evidence for your answer.

THINK ABOUT
- Alvarez's high-school days
- the experiences of her sisters
- her feelings toward her extended family

3. Why do you think some people permanently change their names when they come to the United States, while others don't?

4. How does the quotation from Shakespeare, "A rose by any other name would smell as sweet," apply to this essay?

5. How would you describe Mrs. Alvarez?

THINK ABOUT
- the scene in the hospital
- her quoting of Shakespeare
- what she calls her daughter

Extend Interpretations

6. The Writer's Style In this essay Alvarez uses humor to deal with otherwise serious topics. Why do you think she does that? How does humor help get her ideas across?

7. Connect to Life Alvarez says, "I just wanted to be Judy and merge with the Sallys and Janes in my class." What do you think she means by this? Do you agree? Why or why not?

Literary Analysis

 PERSONAL ESSAY One form of nonfiction is the **personal essay.** These essays are often **autobiographical,** focusing on a writer's own experiences. "Names/Nombres," like most personal essays, is centered around one main issue. In this essay, Alvarez shares her thoughts about her Dominican name and culture and the way they were interpreted by Americans when she and her family moved to the United States.

Cooperative Learning Activity Review Alvarez's essay. Then answer the following questions:
- What is the author's attitude toward her subject matter?
- What lessons did the author learn from her experiences?
- What is the author's purpose for writing this essay?

Compare your answers with those of some of your classmates.

 REVIEW **SETTING** The **setting** of a literary work is the time when the events described happen and the place where they happen. Julia Alvarez's essay is set in New York in the 1960s. Setting plays an important role in what happens and why. In this essay Alvarez writes of trying to bring into harmony aspects of her Dominican background and her new American home.

NAMES/NOMBRES **43**

Connect to the Literature

1. Responses will vary. Possible Response: Yes, I think I would, because I'm friendly and I like standing out in a crowd.

Comprehension Check
- They are from the Dominican Republic.
- She wanted to sound as American as possible, and she was embarrassed to be different.
- Her many relatives had complicated names, and their relationships to her were also complicated.

📋 Use Selection Quiz, **Unit One Resource Book,** p. 27.

Think Critically

2. Possible Responses: to show how upsetting it is for someone to feel different; to make people aware of some ways people differ.

3. Possible Response: Some people want to make their names easier to pronounce or just want to feel like they fit in. Others want to hold on to their heritage.

4. Possible Response: You are the same person, no matter what people call you.

5. Possible Response: She is a smart and creative woman with a good sense of humor, but she still feels uncomfortable being different.

📋 Use **Reading and Critical Thinking Transparencies,** p. 4, for additional support.

Literary Analysis

Personal Essay Responses will vary, but should include the author's attitude and purpose for writing, as well as what she learned from her experiences.

📋 Use **Literary Analysis Transparencies,** p. 11, for additional support.

Extend Interpretations

6. The Writer's Style Possible Response: Sometimes a sense of humor makes what a writer has to say less threatening for the reader. Rather than scolding Americans for their less-than-heartfelt attempts to make foreigners feel at home, she lets them know in a humorous way how these people might feel.

7. Connect to Life Possible Response: She means that she didn't want to stand out as different, but just blend in and be like everybody else. I know what she means, and I agree because I don't like to feel that I'm different from everybody else, either.

Writing Options

1. **Personal Narrative** Students' narratives should tell who and where they met, what their first impressions were, and how they have changed. To get students started on this assignment, have them recall their first meeting with a good friend or a favorite relative.

2. **Speech** Students' speeches should detail an experience that made them feel different. To get students started, have them recall speeches they have heard at graduations and other ceremonies.

Activities & Explorations

1. **Story Illustration** Illustrations should include some of the details Julia Alvarez describes on page 39. Remind students to use their visualization skills to plan their illustrations.

2. **Interview Questions** Students' introductions should include some pertinent information about Julia Alvarez. Questions should reflect their own curiosity about her life and possibly about other experiences she had as a newcomer.

Inquiry & Research

New Kid on the Block Suggest students work in pairs to create interview questions. To extend this activity, have students interview a second person and compare their experiences in adjusting to life in the United States.

Vocabulary in Action

Exercise A
1. exotic
2. ethnicity
3. initial
4. usher
5. chaotic

Exercise B
1. ironically   exotically
   chaotically   initially
   nationally   gradually
   inevitably   .   historically
   regrettably   capably
2. Answers will vary.

Writing Options

1. **Personal Narrative** Write a short narrative about a first-time meeting with someone you later got to know. Then tell whether or not your first impression was accurate.

Writing Handbook
See p. R33: Narrative Writing.

2. **Speech** Write your own graduation speech. Tell about a time where something about your culture or personal experiences has made you feel "different" from those around you. Place the speech in your **Working Portfolio.**

Activities & Explorations

1. **Story Illustration** Create a drawing or a painting that illustrates Alvarez's graduation, based on her description in the selection. ~ ART

2. **Interview Questions** Suppose you are a talk show host. You are interviewing writers who write about their childhood experiences. Julia Alvarez is one of your guests. How would you introduce her to your audience? What questions would you ask? ~ SPEAKING AND LISTENING

Inquiry & Research

New Kid on the Block The United States is a land of immigrants. Do you have a relative, a friend, or a neighbor who moved to the United States from another country? Ask about his or her adjustment to American life. Tape your conversation. Use your tape to create a short essay or oral report. ~ ART

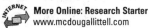 **More Online: Research Starter**
www.mcdougallittell.com

Vocabulary and Spelling

EXERCISE A: CONTEXT CLUES On a piece of paper, write the Word to Know that best completes each sentence.

1. Julia's friends were intrigued by her _____ looks and foreign-sounding name.

2. Julia wrote that, in the 1950s, _____ had not yet become popular in the United States, as it would be in the 1960s.

3. Julia's _____ desire was to be known by her Dominican name.

4. The 1960s were the decade that would _____ in a new era of openness.

5. A crowded, noisy marketplace can be described as _____.

EXERCISE B: SUFFIXES Add *-ly* to adjectives to form adverbs. When the suffix *-ly* is added to a word ending in *l,* as in *ironically,* both *l*'s are retained. Add *-ally* to adjectives that end in *-c,* as in *chaotically.* For words ending in *-ble,* just replace the *-e* with *-y,* as in *inevitably.*

1. Add the suffix *-ly* to the following words.

ironic	exotic
chaotic	initial
national	gradual
inevitable	historic
regrettable	capable

2. Use each of the spelling words in a complete sentence.

Spelling Handbook p. R86

WORDS TO KNOW	chaotic	ethnicity	inevitably	ironically	specify
	convoluted	exotic	initial	merge	usher

Teaching Options

Mini Lesson **Spelling** 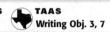 TEKS 16C TAAS Writing Obj. 3, 7

ADVERBS FORMED WITH *-LY*

Instruction Explain to students that the suffix *-ly* is often used to turn words into adverbs—words that describe how, when, where, and to what extent. In most cases, the suffix *-ly* does not change the spelling of the base word to which it is added. An exception to this rule is words ending in the suffix *-able.* Give students the following examples from the selection:

ironic + ly = ironically
initial + ly = initially
inevitable + ly = inevitably

Exercises Have students change the form of each of the following underlined words to make the sentences correct.

1. She handled the situation <u>admirable</u>. (admirably)

2. The interesting name suits her personality <u>beautiful</u>. (beautifully)

3. People listened <u>attentive</u> as she told her family's history. (attentively)

4. <u>Remarkable</u>, she adjusted. (remarkably)

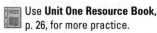 Use **Unit One Resource Book,** p. 26, for more practice.

Grammar in Context: Combining Sentences

In the compound sentence shown below, Julia Alvarez describes her family's experience with an immigration officer.

> **My father shook his head no**, and **we were waved through.**

When simple sentences are combined into one sentence, they become a **compound sentence**.

Here are three ways to join sentences.

1. Use *and, or,* or *but* preceded by a comma: **I was known as *Hoo-lee-tah* at home**, but **at school I was *Judy* or *Judith*.**

2. Use words like *however* or *therefore* preceded by a semicolon and followed by a comma: **I was known as *Hoo-lee-tah* at home**; **however, at school I was *Judy* or *Judith*.**

3. If there are no joining words, just use a semicolon: **I was known as *Hoo-lee-tah* at home**; **at school I was *Judy* or *Judith*.**

WRITING EXERCISE Combine each pair of sentences using one of the three methods above.

Example: ***Original*** I was afraid to correct the man's pronunciation. I said our name to myself.

Rewritten I was afraid to correct the man's pronunciation, <u>but</u> I said our name to myself.

1. Some friends called me *Jules* or *Hey Jude*. Other friends called me *Alcatraz*.

2. My friends had only their parents to introduce. My whole extended family attended school occasions.

3. I wanted to ask my new friends to say my name correctly. My mother said it didn't matter.

Grammar Handbook The Sentence and Its Parts, p. R55

"Mine was an American childhood."

Julia Alvarez
born 1950

New in New York Although Julia Alvarez was born in New York City, she lived in the Dominican Republic until she was ten. When Alvarez returned, she felt out of place—a foreigner with a different language, name, and way of life.

Young Writer Alvarez's first years back in New York were tough, but she soon found a way to cope. She started to write stories and poetry.

"I could save what I didn't want to lose—memories and smells and sounds, things too precious to put anywhere else." Alvarez's writings continue to draw on her early memories and immigrant experiences. Her best-selling novel, *How the Garcia Girls Lost Their Accents,* tells the story of an immigrant Dominican family and how they adjust to American life and become, like Alvarez, at home in two cultures.

AUTHOR ACTIVITY
Dominican Heritage Find out more about the Dominican Republic and the harsh government under which Alvarez and her family lived until returning to the United States in the early 1960s. Discuss your findings with your classmates.

Grammar in Context

WRITING EXERCISE
Possible Responses:
1. Some friends called me *Jules* or *Hey Jude;* other friends called me *Alcatraz.*
2. My friends had only their parents to introduce; however, my whole extended family attended school occasions.
3. I wanted to ask my new friends to say my name correctly, but my mother said it didn't matter.

Julia Alvarez

In her essay "Writing Matters," which appeared in *The Writer,* Julia Alvarez discusses what life is like for a writer. She believes that the writing process is all about hard work and that "there are no magic solutions to the hard work of writing." She also believes that an effective writer isn't a writer only when she sits at her desk. Alvarez says that her life is guided by the idea that she must pay close attention to the world around her at all times.

Author Activity

Tell students that they can find out about the history and current events of the Dominican Republic by looking at encyclopedias, books, maps, and online resources. You might encourage students to discuss how events in the country may have affected Alvarez's character and outlook on life.

 Grammar **TEKS 17A** 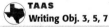 **TAAS Writing Obj. 3, 5, 7**

COMBINING SENTENCES BY USING INTRODUCTORY ELEMENTS

Instruction Remind students that good writers use a variety of sentence structures. One of the many ways to add variety is to combine two short sentences by turning one of the sentences into an introductory element—a word or phrase that gives details of where, how, or when. Tell students that introductory elements not only expand meaning in sentences but can also help writing to read more smoothly. Display the following example:

Julia Alvarez once had an accent. She had an accent when she first came to America.

Revised: When she first came to America, Julia Alvarez had an accent.

Exercises Ask students to combine each pair of sentences by turning one of the sentences in each pair into an introductory element.

1. We arrived. The man at immigration told us to get in line. *(When we arrived,)*

2. Julia's sister explained the history behind Julia's name. She explained it at the party. *(At the party,)*

3. Tia Pilar walked into the room. She was eager. *(Eagerly,)*

4. I visited New York City. People there stopped to ask if I was Julia's cousin. *(When I visited New York City,)*

Use **Unit One Resource Book,** p. 25.
Use **Grammar Transparencies and Copymasters,** p. 103.

 Use McDougal Littell's ***Language Network,*** Chapter 13, for more instruction in introductory elements.

OVERVIEW

This selection is included in the **Grade 7 InterActive Reader.**

Objectives
1. understand and appreciate a **short story** (Literary Analysis)
2. understand **character** (Literary Analysis)
3. use the skill **making inferences** (Active Reading)

Summary
Adam Martin Zebrin, nicknamed Zebra, loves to run, until he is hit by a car and injured. Afterwards, he is quiet and withdrawn. One day he sees a one-armed man on his street, picking items out of the trash. The man asks Adam a few questions and soon begins teaching a summer art class at the boy's school. First, though, he quickly creates and gives to Adam a wonderful portrait, complete with running zebra. Soon Adam is taking the art class and learns that the man was once a helicopter pilot in the Vietnam War. Through art, the man, John Wilson, encourages Zebra to connect with the world. At the end of class, the boy gives his teacher a meaningful drawing. Later, Wilson sends him a photograph and a letter. The photo shows the teacher placing the boy's gift at the Vietnam Memorial. The letter explains the act and what the gift meant to the teacher. Later, Zebra decides to try even more new activities.

Thematic Link
At first, Adam lets his accident define who he is. Later, a new relationship and a new activity both help him expand his view of who he is and what he might be capable of doing.

5-Minute Warm-Up

Daily Language SkillBuilder | **TEKS 16B, 17A**

Have students **proofread** the display sentences on page 13i and write them correctly. The sentences also appear on Transparency 2 of **Grammar Transparencies and Copymasters.**

See the Skills Trace at the beginning of the unit for information on TEKS covered in this lesson.

SOCIAL STUDIES

Zebra

Short Story by **CHAIM POTOK** (khī′ĭm pō′tăk)

Connect to Your Life

What do you know about the Vietnam War?

A wounded soldier is loaded onto a helicopter to be evacuated.

Build Background Approximately 58,000 Americans died and over 300,000 were wounded in the Vietnam War. After the war, many veterans, like John Wilson in "Zebra," struggled to piece their lives back together.

In 1982, the Vietnam Veterans Memorial was unveiled in Washington, D.C., to honor the men and, since 1993, the women who served in Vietnam.

Focus Your Reading

LITERARY ANALYSIS | **CHARACTER** **Characters** are the people, animals, or imaginary creatures who appear in stories. Usually, a short story focuses on one or two **main characters.** Less important characters are called **minor characters.** As you read "Zebra," identify the main characters.

ACTIVE READING | **MAKING INFERENCES** An **inference** is a logical conclusion based on evidence. Whenever you read a story, look for **details** that help you understand what is going on. Using these details and what you know from your own experience, you can figure out more than just what the words say.

In your 📖 **READER'S NOTEBOOK** create a chart to help you keep track of the inferences you make about Zebra and his experiences.

WORDS TO KNOW **Vocabulary Preview**

disciplinarian	gaunt	menacing	tensing
encrusted	intricate	poised	wince
exuberantly	jauntily		

LESSON RESOURCES

UNIT ONE RESOURCE BOOK, pp. 28–34

ASSESSMENT
Formal Assessment, pp. 11–12
Teacher's Guide to Assessment and Portfolio Use
Test Generator

SKILLS TRANSPARENCIES AND COPYMASTERS
Literary Analysis
• Analyzing Character, TR 3 (for Cooperative Learning Activity, p. 62)
• Characterization, TR 4 (for Reading and Analyzing, p. 52)

Reading and Critical Thinking
• Making Inferences, TR 5 (for Thinking Through the Literature, p. 62)
Grammar
• Avoiding Run-On Sentences, CM 60 (for Mini Lesson, pp. 50–51)
• Avoiding Ineffective Sentence Fragments, CM 61 (for Mini Lesson, p. 64)
Vocabulary
• Draw on Experience to Infer Meaning, CM 22 (for Mini Lesson, p. 47)

• Context Clues: Definition and Restatement, CM 23 (for Mini Lesson, p. 52)
Communications
• Interviewing, TR 9 (for Mini Lesson, p. 54)

INTEGRATED TECHNOLOGY
Audio Library
Internet: Research Starter

Visit our website:
www.mcdougallittell.com

ZEBRA

by Chaim Potok

Silent Fall, Nicholas Wilton. Acrylic on wood, 24" × 14 1/2"

His name was Adam Martin Zebrin, but everyone in his neighborhood knew him as Zebra.

Mini Lesson **Preteaching Vocabulary** **TEKS** 9B, 10A **TAAS** Reading Obj. 1

DRAW ON EXPERIENCE TO INFER MEANING
Instruction Call students' attention to the list of WORDS TO KNOW. Remind them that they can draw on their own knowledge and experience to bring meanings to such words in context. Read this model sentence aloud:
The sight of your broken arm makes me *wince*.
- Ask volunteers how they feel when a friend is hurt.
- Ask what they would do at the sight of a friend's injury.
- Have students use this information to infer the meaning of *wince*.

Exercises Have students use experience to infer the meanings of the underlined words:
1. The children were playing <u>exuberantly</u>, laughing and running about.
2. The dog made a <u>menacing</u> growl, so I moved away from it.
3. Examining the lace, Hector wondered how anyone could stitch something so <u>intricate</u>.
4. It was too cold to hold the railings, which were <u>encrusted</u> with ice.
5. After his long illness, Jay appeared pale and <u>gaunt</u>.

Use **Unit One Resource Book,** p. 31, for more exercises. Use **Vocabulary Transparencies and Copymasters**, p. 22, for additional support.

Literary Analysis CHARACTER

Remind students that stories have both main and minor characters. To help students understand and identify these literary terms, discuss how a story revolves around major characters, who often change. Minor characters just help move a story along. Ask students how they know that Zebra is a major character.
Possible Responses: the story's title; the narrator shows his thoughts and feelings; the first page is about him.

Use **Unit One Resource Book**, p. 30, for more practice. Use **Literary Analysis Transparencies**, p. 3, for additional support.

Active Reading MAKING INFERENCES

A Ask students to draw conclusions about what happened to Zebra and to support these conclusions with text evidence. Ask, "What happened to Zebra, and what clues help you know?"
Possible Response: A car or truck hit him. Clues include the huge rushing shadow that crashed into him, his mother's warning, and his injuries.

Use **Unit One Resource Book**, p. 29, for more practice. Use **Reading and Critical Thinking Transparencies**, p. 5, for additional support.

Reading Skills and Strategies: CONNECTING

B Ask students to draw conclusions about this man's actions and to support them from their own experience. Why is he fishing around in trash cans?
Possible Responses: He is homeless; he does not have money to buy items he wants or needs.

He couldn't remember when he began to be called by that name. Perhaps they started to call him Zebra when he first began running. Or maybe he began running when they started to call him Zebra.

He loved the name and he loved to run.

When he was very young, his parents took him to a zoo, where he saw zebras for the first time. They were odd-looking creatures, like stubby horses, short-legged, thick-necked, with dark and white stripes.

Then one day he went with his parents to a movie about Africa, and he saw zebras, hundreds of them, thundering across a grassy plain, dust rising in boiling brown clouds.

Was he already running before he saw that movie, or did he begin to run afterward? No one seemed able to remember.

He would go running through the neighborhood for the sheer joy of feeling the wind on his face. People said that when he ran he arched his head up and back, and his face kind of flattened out. One of his teachers told him it was clever to run that way, his balance was better. But the truth was he ran that way, his head thrown back, because he loved to feel the wind rushing across his neck.

Each time, after only a few minutes of running, his legs would begin to feel wondrously light. He would run past the school and the homes on the street beyond the church. All the neighbors knew him and would wave and call out, "Go, Zebra!" And sometimes one or two of their dogs would run with him awhile, barking.

He would imagine himself a zebra on the African plain. Running.

There was a hill on Franklin Avenue, a steep hill. By the time he reached that hill, he would feel his legs so light it was as if he had no legs at all and was flying. He would begin to descend the hill, certain as he ran that he needed only to give himself the slightest push

and off he would go, and instead of a zebra he would become the bird he had once seen in a movie about Alaska, he would swiftly change into an eagle, soaring higher and higher, as light as the gentlest breeze, the cool wind caressing his arms and legs and neck.

Then, a year ago, racing down Franklin Avenue, he had given himself that push and had begun to turn into an eagle, when a huge rushing shadow appeared in his line of vision and crashed into him and plunged him into a darkness from which he emerged very, very slowly. . . .

"Never, never, *never* run down that hill so fast that you can't stop at the corner," his mother had warned him again and again.

His schoolmates and friends kept calling him Zebra even after they all knew that the doctors had told him he would never be able to run like that again.

His leg would heal in time, the doctors said, and perhaps in a year or so the brace would come off. But they were not at all certain about his hand. From time to time his injured hand, which he still wore in a sling, would begin to hurt. The doctors said they could find no cause for the pain.

One morning, during Mr. Morgan's geography class, Zebra's hand began to hurt badly. He sat staring out the window at the sky. Mr. Morgan, a stiff-mannered person in his early fifties, given to smart suits and dapper[1] bow ties, called on him to respond to a question. Zebra stumbled about in vain for the answer. Mr. Morgan told him to pay attention to the geography inside the classroom and not to the geography outside.

"In this class, young man, you will concentrate your attention upon the earth, not upon the sky," Mr. Morgan said.

---

1. **dapper:** neatly dressed; stylish.

BLOCK SCHEDULING: MANAGING TIME

If your schedule requires that you cover the lesson objectives in a shorter time, use . . .
- Preparing to Read, p. 46
- Thinking Through the Literature, p. 62
- Vocabulary in Action, p. 63
- Grammar in Context, p. 64

If you would like to take advantage of longer class time, use . . .
- TE Teaching Options: Preteaching Vocabulary, p. 47; Spelling, p. 49; Grammar, pp. 50–51, 64; Vocabulary Strategy, p. 52; Viewing and Representing, pp. 53, 60; Speaking and Listening, p. 54; Cross-Curricular Links, pp. 56, 58; Informal Assessment, p. 57; Standardized Test Practice, p. 59; Multicultural Link, p. 61
- Choices & Challenges and Author Activity, pp. 63-64

Later, in the schoolyard during the midmorning recess, Zebra stood near the tall fence, looking out at the street and listening to the noises behind him.

His schoolmates were racing about, playing exuberantly, shouting and laughing with full voices. Their joyous sounds went ringing through the quiet street.

Most times Zebra would stand alongside the basketball court or behind the wire screen at home plate and watch the games. That day, because his hand hurt so badly, he stood alone behind the chain-link fence of the schoolyard.

That's how he happened to see the man. And that's how the man happened to see him.

One minute the side street on which the school stood was strangely empty, without people or traffic, without even any of the dogs that often roamed about the neighborhood—vacant and silent, as if it were already in the full heat of summer. The red-brick ranch house that belonged to Mr. Morgan, and the white clapboard two-story house in which Mrs. English lived, and the other homes on the street, with their columned front porches and their back patios, and the tall oaks—all stood curiously still in the warm golden light of the mid-morning sun.

Then a man emerged from wide and busy Franklin Avenue at the far end of the street.

Zebra saw the man stop at the corner and stand looking at a public trash can. He watched as the man poked his hand into the can and fished about but seemed to find nothing he wanted. He withdrew the hand and, raising it to shield his eyes from the sunlight, glanced at the street sign on the lamppost.

He started to walk up the street in the direction of the school.

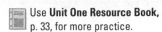

That's how he happened to see the man.

He was tall and wiry, and looked to be about forty years old. In his right hand he carried a bulging brown plastic bag. He wore a khaki army jacket, a blue denim shirt, blue jeans, and brown cowboy boots. His gaunt face and muscular neck were reddened by exposure to the sun. Long brown hair spilled out below his dark-blue farmer's cap. On the front of the cap, in large orange letters, were the words LAND ROVER.[2]

He walked with his eyes on the sidewalk and the curb, as if looking for something, and he went right past Zebra without noticing him.

Zebra's hand hurt very much. He was about to turn away when he saw the man stop and look around and peer up at the red-brick wall of the school. The man set down the bag and took off his cap and stuffed it into a pocket of his jacket. From one of his jeans pockets he removed a handkerchief, with which he then wiped his face. He shoved the handkerchief back into the pocket and put the cap back on his head.

Then he turned and saw Zebra.

He picked up the bag and started down the street to where Zebra was standing. When the man was about ten feet away, Zebra noticed that the left sleeve of his jacket was empty.

---

2. **Land Rover:** a type of sport utility vehicle.

WORDS TO KNOW
exuberantly (ĭg-zōō′bər-ənt-lē) *adv.* full of enthusiasm or joy
gaunt (gônt) *adj.* thin and bony

49

A The man came up to Zebra and said in a low, friendly, shy voice, "Hello."

Zebra answered with a cautious "Hello," trying not to look at the empty sleeve, which had been tucked into the man's jacket pocket.

The man asked, with a distinct Southern accent, "What's your name, son?"

Zebra said, "Adam."

"What kind of school is this here school, Adam?"

"It's a good school," Zebra answered.

"How long before you-all begin your summer vacation?"

"Three days," Zebra said.

"Anything special happen here during the summer?"

"During the summer? Nothing goes on here. There are no classes."

"What do you-all do during the summer?"

"Some of us go to camp. Some of us hang around. We find things to do."

1 Zebra's hand had begun to tingle and throb. Why was the man asking all those questions? Zebra thought maybe he shouldn't be talking to him at all. He seemed vaguely <u>menacing</u> in that army jacket, the dark-blue cap with the words LAND ROVER on it in orange letters, and the empty sleeve. Yet there was kindness in his gray eyes and ruddy features.

The man gazed past Zebra at the students playing in the yard. "Adam, do you think your school would be interested in having someone teach an art class during the summer?"

That took Zebra by surprise. "An *art* class?"

"Drawing, sculpting, things like that."

Zebra was trying *very hard* not to look at the man's empty sleeve. "I don't know. . . ."

"Where's the school office, Adam?"

"On Washington Avenue. Go to the end of the street and turn right."

"Thanks," the man said. He hesitated a moment. Then he asked, in a quiet voice, "What happened to you, Adam?"

"A car hit me," Zebra said. "It was my fault."

The man seemed to <u>wince</u>.

For a flash of a second, Zebra thought to ask the man what had happened to *him*. The words were on his tongue. But he kept himself from saying anything.

The man started back up the street, carrying the brown plastic bag.

Zebra suddenly called, "Hey, mister."

The man stopped and turned. "My name is John Wilson," he said softly.

"Mr. Wilson, when you go into the school office, you'll see signs on two doors. One says 'Dr. Winter,' and the other says 'Mrs. English.' Ask for Mrs. English."

Dr. Winter, the principal, was a <u>disciplinarian</u> and a grump. Mrs. English, the assistant principal, was generous and kind. Dr. Winter would probably tell the man to call his secretary for an appointment. Mrs. English might invite him into her office and offer him a cup of coffee and listen to what he had to say.

The man hesitated, looking at Zebra.

"Appreciate the advice," he said.

Zebra watched him walk to the corner.

Under the lamppost was a trash can. Zebra saw the man set down the plastic bag and stick his hand into the can and haul out a battered umbrella.

The man tried to open the umbrella, but its metal ribs were broken. The black fabric dangled flat and limp from the pole. He put the umbrella into the plastic bag and headed for the entrance to the school.

A moment later, Zebra heard the whistle

WORDS	**menacing** (mĕn´ĭs-ĭng) *adj.* threatening
TO	**wince** (wĭns) *v.* to shrink as in pain or distress
KNOW	**disciplinarian** (dĭs´ə-plə-nâr´ē-ən) *n.* someone who enforces strict discipline

50

 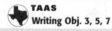 **Grammar**   TEKS 17A   TAAS Writing Obj. 3, 5, 7

hat signaled the end of recess. He followed his classmates at a distance, careful to avoid anyone's bumping against his hand.

He sat through his algebra class, copying the problems on the blackboard while holding down his notebook with his left elbow. The sling chafed[3] his neck and felt warm and clumsy on his bare arm. There were sharp pains now in the two curled fingers of his hand.

Right after the class he went downstairs to the office of Mrs. Walsh, a cheerful, gray-haired woman in a white nurse's uniform.

She said, "I'm sorry I can't do very much for you, Adam, except give you two Tylenols."

He swallowed the Tylenols down with water.

On his way back up to the second floor, he saw the man with the dark-blue cap emerge from the school office with Mrs. English. He stopped on the stairs and watched as the man and Mrs. English stood talking together. Mrs. English nodded and smiled and shook the man's hand.

The man walked down the corridor, carrying the plastic bag, and left the school building.

Zebra went slowly to his next class.

The class was taught by Mrs. English, who came hurrying into the room some minutes after the bell had rung.

"I apologize for being late," she said, sounding a little out of breath. "There was an important matter I had to attend to."

Mrs. English was a tall, gracious woman in her forties. It was common knowledge that early in her life she had been a journalist on a Chicago newspaper and had written short stories, which she could not get published. Soon after her marriage to a doctor, she had become a teacher.

This was the only class Mrs. English taught.

Ten students from the upper school—seventh and eighth grades—were chosen every year for this class. They met for an hour three times a week and told one another stories. Each story would be discussed and analyzed by Mrs. English and the class.

Mrs. English called it a class in the *imagination.* 3

Zebra was grateful he did not have to take notes in this class. He had only to listen to the stories.

That day, Andrea, the freckle-faced, redheaded girl with very thick glasses who sat next to Zebra, told about a woman scientist who discovered a method of healing trees that had been blasted apart by lightning.

Mark, who had something wrong with his upper lip, told in his quavery[4] voice about a selfish space cadet who stepped into a time machine and met his future self, who turned out to be a hateful person, and how the cadet then returned to the present and changed himself.

Kevin talked in blurred, high-pitched tones and often related parts of his stories with his hands. Mrs. English would quietly repeat many of his sentences. Today he told about an explorer who set out on a journey through a valley filled with yellow stones and surrounded by red mountains, where he encountered an army of green shadows that had been at war for hundreds of years with an army of purple shadows. The explorer showed them how to make peace.

When it was Zebra's turn, he told a story about a bird that one day crashed against a closed windowpane and broke a wing. A boy tried to heal the wing but couldn't. The bird died, and the boy buried it under a tree on his lawn. E

---

3. **chafed** (chāfd): irritated by rubbing.

4. **quavery** (kwā'vər-ē): quivering or trembling.

1. His name was Adam Zebrin, everyone called him Zebra. (*His name was Adam Zebrin, but everyone called him Zebra.*)

2. Adam saw real zebras in a movie about Africa. (*Correct*)

3. The leg would heal the brace would come off. (*The leg would heal, and the brace would come off.*)

4. Kids ran around the playground Zebra stood and watched. (*Kids ran around the playground. Zebra stood and watched.*)

5. The man stopped at the corner and looked at the trash can. (*Correct*)

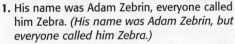 Use **Grammar Transparencies and Copymasters**, p. 60.

 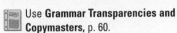 Use McDougal Littell's **Language Network**, Chapter 1, for more instruction and practice in avoiding run-on sentences.

Reading and Analyzing

Literary Analysis   `CHARACTER`

 A Remind students that they learn about characters in different ways. One way is by noting what other characters say about them. Discuss whether students agree with Andrea's assessment and why.

📑 Use **Literary Analysis Transparencies,** p. 4, for additional support.

Active Reading   `MAKING INFERENCES`

B Ask students to draw inferences about how hard or easy it is for the man to make this drawing. Have them support their answers with text evidence and experience.

Possible Response: It's not easy. Evidence includes the fact that he asks for help, he's sweating, and his tongue pushes against his cheek the way it does when someone is concentrating.

Literary Analysis: DIALOGUE

Discuss with students what they learn about the characters and about the plot from the dialogue on this page.

Possible Responses: Zebra tells sad stories; the man that he helped is grateful; he's giving art classes; Zebra doesn't want to take them; the man allows Zebra to say no.

📑 Use **Literary Analysis Transparencies,** p. 24, for additional support.

When he had finished, there was silence. Everyone in the class was looking at him.

"You always tell such sad stories," Andrea said.

The bell rang. Mrs. English dismissed the class.

 A In the hallway, Andrea said to Zebra, "You know, you are a very gloomy life form."

1 "Andrea, get off my case," Zebra said.

He went out to the schoolyard for the midafternoon recess. On the other side of the chain-link fence was the man in the dark-blue cap.

Zebra went over to him.

"Hello again, Adam," the man said. "I've been waiting for you."

"Hello," said Zebra.

"Thanks much for suggesting I talk to Mrs. English."

"You're welcome."

"Adam, you at all interested in art?"

"No."

"You ever try your hand at it?"

"I've made drawings for class. I don't like it."

"Well, just in case you change your mind, I'm giving an art class in your school during the summer."

"I'm going to camp in August," Zebra said.

"There's the big long month of July."

"I don't think so," Zebra said.

"Well, okay, suit yourself. I'd like to give you something, a little thank-you gift."

He reached into an inside pocket and drew out a small pad and a pen. He placed the pad against the fence.

2 "Adam, you want to help me out a little bit here? Put your fingers through the fence and grab hold of the pad."

Extending the fingers of his right hand, Zebra held the pad to the fence and watched

as the man began to work with the pen. He felt the pad move slightly.

"I need you to hold it real still," the man said.

He was standing bent over, very close to Zebra. The words LAND ROVER on his cap shone in the afternoon sunlight. As he worked, he glanced often at Zebra. His tongue kept pushing up against the insides of his cheeks, making tiny hills rise and fall on his face. Wrinkles formed <u>intricate</u> spidery webs in the skin below his gray eyes. On his smooth forehead, in the blue and purple shadows beneath the peak of his cap, lay glistening beads of sweat. And his hand—how dirty it was, the fingers and palm smudged with black ink and <u>encrusted</u> with colors.

Then Zebra glanced down and noticed the plastic bag near the man's feet. It lay partly open. Zebra was able to see a large pink armless doll, a dull metallic object that looked like a dented frying pan, old newspapers, strings of cord, crumpled pieces of red and blue cloth, and the broken umbrella.

"One more minute is all I need," the man said.

He stepped back, looked at the pad, and nodded slowly. He put the pen back into his pocket and tore the top page from the pad. He rolled up the page and pushed it through the fence. Then he took the pad from Zebra.

"See you around, Adam," the man said, picking up the plastic bag.

Zebra unrolled the sheet of paper and saw a line drawing, a perfect image of his face.

He was looking at himself as if in a mirror. His long straight nose and thin lips and sad eyes and gaunt face; his dark hair and smallish ears and the scar on his forehead where he had hurt himself years before while roller skating.

In the lower right-hand corner of the page

WORDS TO KNOW   **intricate** (ĭn′trĭ-kĭt) *adj.* arranged in a complex way
encrusted (ĕn-krŭst′əd) *adj.* covered with crusts

52

Teaching Options

Mini Lesson   Vocabulary Strategy   🏴 TEKS 6A   ⭐ TAAS Reading Obj. 1

CONTEXT CLUES: DEFINITION AND RESTATEMENT

Instruction Encourage students to use a variety of word recognition strategies as they read. Explain that writers sometimes help readers understand the meaning of a new term. The writer may define the word or restate it another way. By applying their knowledge of context, students can often determine a word's meaning. As an example, display this sentence on page 51:

Ten students from the upper school—seventh and eighth grades—were chosen every year for this class.

Exercises Ask students to determine the meanings of the underlined words below:

1. He walked down the street <u>jauntily</u>, as if he didn't have a care in the world.

2. Dr. Winter was a real <u>disciplinarian</u>. In other words, he always followed rules exactly.

3. The design was <u>intricate</u>, more complicated

than anything they had ever seen.

📑 Use **Vocabulary Transparencies and Copymasters,** p. 23, for additional support.

Jarvis (1996), Elizabeth Peyton. Oil on masonite, 11″ × 14″, courtesy Gavin Brown's enterprise, New York. Collection Susan & Michael Hort.

Mini Lesson — Viewing and Representing   TEKS 23A

Jarvis
by Elizabeth Peyton

ART APPRECIATION Ask students to study the painting, trying to interpret and evaluate the various ways the visual image maker represents meanings. Have them look at content, color, and placement.

Instruction Have students point out ways in which the artist focuses attention on the subject's eye and his vision.

Possible Responses: by placing it near the center of the picture; by placing it near the intersection of diagonal lines; by showing only one eye

• Have students evaluate how the boy's position or physical attitude affects the mood of the painting.

Possible Response: He looks disconnected from his physical surroundings, which makes the mood seem unreal and detached.

Application Ask students to describe ways in which the boy in the painting is like Zebra.

Possible Response: He is a watcher; he is inactive.

A To help students analyze characters, including their motivations and changes they undergo, ask students why Zebra tells the man his nickname.

Possible Responses: He is moved by the art; he wants to be friends.

Literary Analysis | CHARACTER

B After Zebra tells his nickname, the man changes his drawing. What does this action suggest about his character?

Possible Responses: He values Zebra's individuality; he is kind; he wants his gift to be meaningful.

Active Reading | MAKING INFERENCES

C Ask why Zebra wants to know about Vietnam.

Possible Response: He wants to know more about John Wilson.

Literary Analysis | CHARACTER

D What details about Mr. Morgan help you know his character?

Possible Responses: His clothing; his formal speech; his use of the pointer

---

the man had written: "To Adam, with thanks. John Wilson."

Zebra raised his eyes from the drawing. The man was walking away.

Zebra called out, "Mr. Wilson, all my friends call me Zebra."

The man turned, looking surprised.

A "From my last name," Adam said. "Zebrin. Adam Martin Zebrin. They call me Zebra."

"Is that right?" the man said, starting back toward the fence. "Well, in that case you want to give me back that piece of paper."

He took the pad and pen from his pocket, placed the page on the pad, and, with Zebra holding the pad to the fence, did something to the page and then handed it back.

"You take real good care of yourself, Zebra," the man said.

He went off toward Franklin Avenue.

Zebra looked at the drawing. The man had crossed out Adam and over it had drawn an animal with a stubby neck and short legs and **B** a striped body.

A zebra!

Its legs were in full gallop. It seemed as if it would gallop right off the page.

A strong breeze rippled across the drawing, causing it to flutter like a flag in Zebra's hand. He looked out at the street.

The man was walking slowly in the shadows of the tall oaks. Zebra had the odd sensation that all the houses on the street had turned toward the man and were watching him as he walked along. How strange that was: the windows and porches and columns and front doors following intently the slow walk of that tall, one-armed man—until he turned into Franklin Avenue and was gone.

The whistle blew, and Zebra went inside. Seated at his desk, he slipped the drawing carefully into one of his notebooks.

From time to time he glanced at it.

Just before the bell signaled the end of the school day, he looked at it again.

Now *that* was strange!

He thought he remembered that the zebra had been drawn directly over his name: the head over the A and the tail over the M. Didn't it seem now to have moved a little beyond the A?

Probably he was running a fever again. He would run mysterious fevers off and on for about three weeks after each operation on his hand. Fevers sometimes did that to him: excited his imagination.

He lived four blocks from the school. The school bus dropped him off at his corner. In his schoolbag he carried his books and the notebook with the drawing.

His mother offered him a snack, but he said he wasn't hungry. Up in his room, he looked again at the drawing and was astonished to discover that the zebra had reached the edge of his name and appeared poised to leap off.

It *had* to be a fever that was causing him to see the zebra that way. And sure enough, when his mother took his temperature, the thermometer registered 102.6 degrees.

She gave him his medicine, but it didn't seem to have much effect, because when he woke at night and switched on his desk light and peered at the drawing, he saw the little zebra galloping across the page, along the contours of his face, over the hills and valleys of his eyes and nose and mouth, and he heard the tiny clickings of its hooves as cloudlets of dust rose in its wake.

He knew he was asleep. He knew it was the fever working upon his imagination.

But it was so real.

The little zebra running . . .

When he woke in the morning the fever was

WORDS
TO
KNOW   **poised** (poizd) *adj.* balanced or held in suspension

54

Teaching Options

 Speaking and Listening 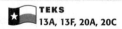 **TEKS** 13A, 13F, 20A, 20C

INTERVIEW

Prepare Allow students to work in small groups to find and interview a veteran of the Vietnam War. As a group, they need to decide how to locate veterans. Then they need to schedule an interview and create a list of 5–10 questions. Tell students that good interviewers frame questions to direct their research and do not ask factual questions that can be easily researched from printed sources. Point out that an interviewer should not ask questions that are easily answered by *yes* or *no*. Instead, they often begin with *who, what, where, when, why, how*. Students should record their interviews.

Present Encourage students to present their results in a variety of ways. These might include the following: written transcript; oral report; videotape presentation; or readers' theater. Students should discuss how individual interviews help them to understand the experience of the Vietnam veteran.

 Use **Communications Transparencies and Copymasters**, p. 9, for additional support.

BLOCK SCHEDULING This activity is particularly well suited for longer class periods.

gone, and the zebra was quietly in its place over ADAM.

Later, as he entered the school, he noticed a large sign on the bulletin board in the hallway:

SUMMER ART CLASS

The well-known American artist Mr. John Wilson will conduct an art class during the summer for students in 7th and 8th grades. For details, speak to Mrs. English. There will be no tuition fee for this class.

During the morning, between classes, Zebra ran into Mrs. English in the second-floor hallway.

"Mrs. English, about the summer art class . . . is it okay to ask where—um—where Mr. Wilson is from?"

"He is from a small town in Virginia. Are you thinking of signing up for his class?"

"I can't draw," Zebra said.

"Drawing is something you can learn."

"Mrs. English, is it okay to ask how did Mr. Wilson—um—get hurt?"

The school corridors were always crowded between classes. Zebra and Mrs. English formed a little island in the bustling, student-jammed hallway.

"Mr. Wilson was wounded in the war in Vietnam," Mrs. English said. "I would urge you to join his class. You will get to use your imagination."

For the next hour, Zebra sat impatiently through Mr. Morgan's geography class, and afterward he went up to the teacher.

"Mr. Morgan, could I—um—ask where is Vietnam?"

Mr. Morgan smoothed down the jacket of his beige summer suit, touched his bow tie,

But it was so real. The little zebra running...

rolled down a wall map, picked up his pointer, and cleared his throat.

"Vietnam is this long, narrow country in southeast Asia, bordered by China, Laos, and Cambodia. It is a land of valleys in the north, coastal plains in the center, and marshes in the south. There are barren mountains and tropical rain forests. Its chief crops are rice, rubber, fruits, and vegetables. The population numbers close to seventy million people. Between 1962 and 1973, America fought a terrible war there to prevent the south from falling into the hands of the communist north. We lost the war."

"Thank you."

"I am impressed by your suddenly awakened interest in geography, young man, though I must remind you that your class is studying the Mediterranean," said Mr. Morgan.

During the afternoon recess, Zebra was watching a heated basketball game, when he looked across the yard and saw John Wilson walk by, carrying a laden plastic bag. Some while later, he came back along the street, empty-handed.

Over supper that evening, Zebra told his parents he was thinking of taking a summer art class offered by the school.

His father said, "Well, I think that's a fine idea."

"Wait a minute. I'm not so sure," his mother said.

"It'll get him off the streets," his father said. "He'll become a Matisse[5] instead of a lawyer like his dad. Right, Adam?"

---

5. **Matisse** (mə-tēs′) (1869–1954): a French painter who was one of the most well-known artists of the 20th century.

"Just you be very careful," his mother said to Adam. "Don't do anything that might injure your hand."

"How can drawing hurt his left hand, for heaven's sake?" said his father.

That night, Zebra lay in bed looking at his hand. It was a dread and a mystery to him, his own hand. The fingers were all there, but like dead leaves that never fell, the ring and little fingers were rigid and curled, the others barely moved. The doctors said it would take time to bring them back to life. So many broken bones. So many torn muscles and tendons. So many injured nerves. The dark shadow had sprung upon him so suddenly. How stupid, stupid, *stupid* he had been!

He couldn't sleep. He went over to his desk and looked at John Wilson's drawing. The galloping little zebra stood very still over ADAM.

Early the following afternoon, on the last day of school, Zebra went to Mrs. English's office and signed up for John Wilson's summer art class.

"The class will meet every weekday from ten in the morning until one," said Mrs. English. "Starting Monday."

Zebra noticed the three plastic bags in a corner of the office.

"Mrs. English, is it okay to ask what Mr. Wilson—um—did in Vietnam?"

"He told me he was a helicopter pilot," Mrs. English said. "Oh, I neglected to mention that you are to bring an unlined notebook and a pencil to the class."

"That's all? A notebook and a pencil?"

He told me
he was a
helicopter
pilot...

Mrs. English smiled. "And your imagination."

When Zebra entered the art class the next Monday morning, he found about fifteen students there—including Andrea from his class with Mrs. English.

The walls of the room were bare. Everything had been removed for the summer. Zebra noticed two plastic bags on the floor beneath the blackboard.

He sat down at the desk next to Andrea's.

She wore blue jeans and a yellow summer blouse with blue stripes. Her long red hair was tied behind her head with a dark-blue ribbon. She gazed at Zebra through her thick glasses, leaned over, and said, "Are you going to make gloomy drawings, too?"

Just then John Wilson walked in, carrying a plastic bag, which he put down on the floor next to the two others.

He stood alongside the front desk, wearing a light-blue long-sleeved shirt and jeans. The left shirtsleeve had been folded back and pinned to the shirt. The dark-blue cap with the words LAND ROVER sat jauntily on his head.

"Good morning to you-all," he said, with a shy smile. "Mighty glad you're here. We're going to do two things this summer. We're going to make paper into faces and garbage into people. I can see by your expressions that you don't know what I'm talking about, right? Well, I'm about to show you."

He asked everyone to draw the face of someone sitting nearby.

| WORDS TO KNOW | **jauntily** (jôn′tĭ-lē) *adv.* in a light and carefree way |

Cross Curricular Link **American History**

THE VIETNAM WAR The Geneva Accords of 1954 divided Vietnam into Communist-controlled North Vietnam and non-Communist South Vietnam. When South Vietnamese Communists (the Vietcong) rebelled, both Presidents Eisenhower and Kennedy sent military advisers to Vietnam. In 1964, Congress passed the Tonkin Gulf Resolution, which granted President Johnson broad powers to extend American military involvement. Despite U.S. military escalation, the war became bogged down in a stalemate.

Back in the United States, the war spurred a growing antiwar movement that sharply divided the nation. The success of the Vietcong's Tet offensive in 1968 strengthened opposition to the war. In 1973 the United States signed a peace agreement and withdrew its forces from Vietnam. The war left many Americans with a more cautious outlook on foreign affairs and a more cynical attitude toward the government.

Zebra hesitated, looked around, then made a drawing of Andrea. Andrea carefully drew Zebra.

He showed Andrea his drawing.

"It's awful." She grimaced. "I look like a mouse."

Her drawing of him was good. But was his face really so sad?

John Wilson went from desk to desk, peering intently at the drawings. He paused a long moment over Zebra's drawing. Then he spent more than an hour demonstrating with chalk on the blackboard how they should not be thinking *eyes* or *lips* or *hands* while drawing, but should think only *lines* and *curves* and *shapes*; how they should be looking at where everything was situated in relation to the edge of the paper; and how they should not be looking *directly* at the edges of what they were drawing but at the space *outside* the edges.

Zebra stared in wonder at how fast John Wilson's hand raced across the blackboard, and at the empty sleeve rising and falling lightly against the shirt.

"You-all are going to learn how to *see* in a new way," John Wilson said.

They made another drawing of the same face.

"Now I look like a horse," Andrea said. "Are you going to add stripes?"

"You are one big pain, Andrea," Zebra said.

Shortly before noon, John Wilson laid out on his desk the contents of the plastic bags: a clutter of junked broken objects, including the doll and the umbrella.

Using strips of cloth, some lengths of string, crumpled newspaper, his pen, and his one hand, he swiftly transformed the battered doll into a red-nosed, umbrella-carrying clown, with baggy pants, a tattered coat, a derby hat, and a somber smile. Turning over the battered frying pan, he made it into a pedestal, on which he placed the clown.

"That's a sculpture," John Wilson said, with his shy smile. "Garbage into people."

The class burst into applause. The clown on the frying pan looked as if it might take a bow.

"You-all will be doing that, too, before we're done," John Wilson said. "Now I would like you to sign and date your drawings and give them to me."

When they returned the next morning the drawings were on a wall.

Gradually, in the days that followed, the walls began to fill with drawings. Sculptures made by the students were looked at with care, discussed by John Wilson and the class, and then placed on shelves along the walls: a miniature bicycle made of wire; a parrot made of an old sofa cushion; a cowboy made of rope and string; a fat lady made of a dented metal pitcher; a zebra made of glued-together scraps of cardboard.

"I like your zebra," Andrea said.

"Thanks," Zebra said. "I like your parrot."

One morning John Wilson asked the class members to make a contour drawing of their right or left hand. Zebra felt himself sweating and trembling as he worked.

"That's real nice," John Wilson said, when he saw Andrea's drawing.

He gazed at the drawing made by Zebra.

"You-all were looking at your hand," he said. "You ought to have been looking at the edge of your hand and at the space outside."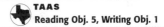

Zebra drew his hand again. Strange and ugly, the two fingers lay rigid and curled. But astonishingly, it looked like a hand this time.

One day, a few minutes before the end of class, John Wilson gave everyone an assignment: draw or make something at home, something very special that each person *felt deeply* about. And bring it to class.

Zebra remembered seeing a book titled *Incredible Cross-Sections* on a shelf in the

Less Proficient Readers

 Explain to students that this paragraph provides a condensed version of art instruction that is designed to help students see in new ways.

Set a Purpose Have students read to find out how this instruction affects Zebra and others in his class.

Students Acquiring English

2 Check that students can define *applaud.* You may wish to point out that the phrase *burst into applause* means "suddenly applauded." Students did this to show their delight in the teacher's creation.

3 You may wish to point out that *you-all* is a regional form of the word "you." It is used by some people in the southern part of the United States.

✔ **Assessment** **Informal Assessment** 🚩 **TEKS** 12F 🤠 **TAAS** Reading Obj. 5, Writing Obj. 1

UNDERSTANDING CHARACTER You can informally assess students' understanding of the character of Zebra by asking them to write a paragraph describing how Zebra's accident affects his character and then how he changes throughout the story.

RUBRIC

3 Full Accomplishment Response reflects an understanding that Zebra's accident damaged his self-image as well as his body.

2 Substantial Accomplishment Response shows that students understand that Zebra changed, but they may be unclear as to the reasons for the change.

1 Little or Partial Accomplishment Response shows little understanding of what the changes are or why they might have occurred.

A Ask students to infer why John Wilson might have reacted as he did to the helicopter.

Possible Responses: He was surprised that Zebra knew about it; he associated it with his injury.

Reading Skills and Strategies: CONTRASTING

B To help students analyze characters, including the changes they undergo, ask them what is different about Zebra here. What about him has changed?

Possible Responses: He is involved, not just watching; he uses his hand.

Reading Skills and Strategies: COMPARING

C In what way is the act of drawing similar for Zebra and for John Wilson?

Possible Responses: It takes effort; it involves them; they have to compensate for using only one hand.

Literary Analysis: SYMBOL

D Remind students that a symbol is a person or object that stands for something beyond itself. What do the zebra and the helicopter stand for? In what ways are they alike?

Possible Responses: They stand for Zebra and John; they are both capable of swift movement.

Reading Skills and Strategies: DRAWING CONCLUSIONS

E Ask students why John Wilson said that Leon "Would've been a much better artist than I'll ever be." Why won't he be?

Possible Response: He is dead.

---

family room at home. He found the book and took it into his room.

There was a color drawing of a rescue helicopter on one of the Contents pages. On pages 30 and 31, the helicopter was shown in pieces, its complicated insides displayed in detailed drawings. Rotor blades, control rods, electronics equipment, radar scanner, tail rotor, engine, lifeline, winch—all its many parts.

Zebra sat at his desk, gazing intently at the space outside the edges of the helicopter on the Contents page.

He made an outline drawing and brought it to class the next morning.

John Wilson looked at it. Was there a **A** stiffening of his muscular neck, a sudden <u>tensing</u> of the hand that held the drawing?

He took the drawing and tacked it to the wall.

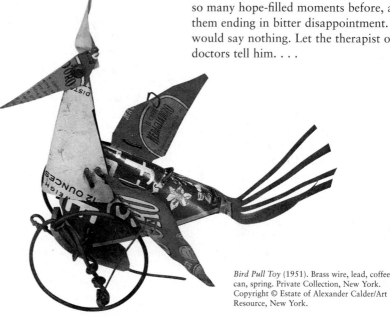

The next day he gave them all the same home assignment: draw or make something they *felt very deeply* about.

That afternoon, Zebra went rummaging through the trash bin in his kitchen and the garbage cans that stood near the back door of his home. He found some sardine cans, a broken eggbeater, pieces of cardboard, chipped buttons, bent bobby pins, and other odds and ends.

With the help of epoxy glue, he began to make of those bits of garbage a kind of helicopter. For support, he used his desktop, the floor, his knees, the elbow of his left arm, at one point even his chin. Struggling with the last piece—a button he wanted to position as a wheel—he realized that without thinking he had been using his left hand, and the two curled fingers had straightened slightly to his needs.

His heart beat thunderously. There had been so many hope-filled moments before, all of them ending in bitter disappointment. He would say nothing. Let the therapist or the doctors tell him. . . .

Bird Pull Toy (1951). Brass wire, lead, coffee can, spring. Private Collection, New York. Copyright © Estate of Alexander Calder/Art Resource, New York.

WORDS TO KNOW   **tensing** (tĕn′sĭng) *n.* a tightening or becoming taut **tense** *v.*

58

Teaching Options

Cross Curricular Link Art

ART THERAPY Besides being a means of expression, art is also considered therapeutic by many, and Art Therapy has been a recognized method of psychotherapy since the 1930s. Not only is art considered a clue to unconscious thoughts, feelings, and conflicts, but many people also believe that the creative act is restorative.

Therapists use different techniques. Some may ask clients to draw anything they want; others may direct them to use certain materials. Afterwards, the artwork and the feelings that surround it might be explored by both therapist and client. At other times, the very act of drawing, painting, or constructing helps people know and appreciate themselves better.

Many people believe that art therapy is especially effective with young people, allowing them to express feelings and memories that may be too difficult or too painful to put into words.

The following morning, he brought the helicopter to the class.

"Eeewwww, what is *that*?" Andrea grimaced.

"Something to eat you with," Zebra said.

"Get human, Zebra. Mr. Wilson will have a laughing fit over that."

But John Wilson didn't laugh. He held the helicopter in his hand a long moment, turning it this way and that, nodded at Zebra, and placed it on a windowsill, where it shimmered in the summer sunlight.

The next day, John Wilson informed everyone that three students would be leaving the class at the end of July. He asked each of those students to make a drawing for him that he would get to keep. Something to remember them by. All their other drawings and sculptures they could take home.

Zebra lay awake a long time that night, staring into the darkness of his room. He could think of nothing to draw for John Wilson.

In the morning, he sat gazing out the classroom window at the sky and at the helicopter on the sill.

"What are you going to draw for him?" Andrea asked.

Zebra shrugged and said he didn't know.

"Use your imagination," she said. Then she said, "Wait, what am I seeing here? Are you able to move those fingers?"

"I think so."

"You *think* so?"

"The doctors said there was some improvement."

Her eyes glistened behind the thick lenses. She seemed genuinely happy.

He sat looking out the window. Dark birds wheeled and soared. There was the sound of traffic. The helicopter sat on the windowsill,

its eggbeater rotor blades ready to move to full throttle.

Later that day, Zebra sat at his desk at home, working on a drawing. He held the large sheet of paper in place by pressing down on it with the palm and fingers of his left hand. He drew a landscape: hills and valleys, forests and flatlands, rivers and plateaus. Oddly, it all seemed to resemble a face.

Racing together over that landscape were a helicopter and a zebra.

It was all he could think to draw. It was not a very good drawing. He signed it: "To JOHN WILSON, with thanks. Zebra."

The next morning, John Wilson looked at the drawing and asked Zebra to write on top of the name "John Wilson" the name "Leon."

"He was an old buddy of mine, an artist. We were in Vietnam together. Would've been a much better artist than I'll ever be."

Zebra wrote in the new name.

"Thank you kindly," John Wilson said, taking the drawing. "Zebra, you have yourself a good time in camp and a good life. It was real nice knowing you."

He shook Zebra's hand. How strong his fingers felt!

"I think I'm going to miss you a little," Andrea said to Zebra after the class.

"I'll only be away a month."

"Can I help you carry some of those drawings?"

"Sure. I'll carry the helicopter."

Zebra went off to a camp in the Adirondack Mountains. He hiked and read and watched others playing ball. In the arts and crafts program he made some good drawings and even got to learn a little bit about watercolors. He put together clowns and airplanes and helicopters out of discarded cardboard and wood and clothing. From time to time his

Customizing Instruction

Less Proficient Readers

1 Help readers understand, if necessary, that Zebra is hoping that his hand is improving, but that he has been disappointed so many times before that he will not believe it until a physical therapist or doctor confirms it.

2 Ask students if the helicopter is really ready to move to full throttle, or if it just appears that way to Zebra's imagination.

Possible Response: It just seems that way.

Set a Purpose Ask students to read to find out what else Zebra creates using his imagination.

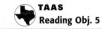

✓Assessment Standardized Test Practice TEKS 10K, 12F TAAS Reading Obj. 5

DESCRIBE CHARACTER In some standardized tests, students are asked to analyze characters, including their traits, motivations, conflicts, points of view, relationships, and changes they undergo, and to choose the answer that best describes the characters. Write the following question on the chalkboard or read it aloud:

How did Zebra feel when he made the helicopter out of trash for John Wilson?

A. scared
B. determined
C. angry
D. free

Lead students through the process of choosing the best answer. Help them recognize that no evidence supports answers A, C, or D. However, several details, including the description of his struggle with the button, suggest his determination. Therefore, the best answer is B.

Literary Analysis CHARACTER

A What has changed in Zebra's life?
Possible Responses: He participates in art classes; his fingers are improving; he doesn't need his brace.

Active Reading MAKING INFERENCES

B Ask students why Mrs. English might have touched her eyes.
Possible Response: She was moved to tears by the letter and the picture.

Reading Skills and Strategies: CLARIFYING

C Make sure that students understand that the names on the wall of the Vietnam Veterans Memorial are names of American soldiers who died in the war.

Reading Skills and Strategies: EVALUATING

D Ask students if they think John Wilson is worthy of a salute, and why.
Possible Responses: Yes. He overcame a physical disability; he helped Zebra; he shared his art; he remained a loyal friend.

Literary Analysis CHARACTER

E Explain that characters who change little in a story are called static characters, while those who change in some important way are called dynamic characters. Ask for ways in which Zebra has changed. Then ask if he is a static or dynamic character.
Possible Responses: He enjoys art; he is willing to try walking on Franklin Avenue; he is becoming "a pleasant life form"; he is dynamic.

 hand hurt, but the fingers seemed slowly to be coming back to life.

"Patience, young man," the doctors told him when he returned to the city. "You're getting there."

One or two additional operations were still necessary. But there was no urgency. And he no longer needed the leg brace.

On the first day of school, one of the secretaries found him in the hallway and told him to report to Mrs. English.

"Did you have a good summer?" Mrs. English asked.

"It was okay," Zebra said.

"This came for you in the mail."

She handed him a large brown envelope. It was addressed to Adam Zebrin, Eighth Grade, at the school. The sender was John Wilson, with a return address in Virginia.

"Adam, I admit I'm very curious to see what's inside," Mrs. English said.

She helped Zebra open the envelope.

Between two pieces of cardboard were a letter and a large color photograph.

The photograph showed John Wilson down on his right knee before a glistening dark wall. He wore his army jacket and blue jeans and boots, and the cap with the words LAND ROVER. Leaning against the wall to his right was Zebra's drawing of the helicopter and the zebra racing together across a facelike landscape. The drawing was enclosed in a narrow frame.

The wall behind John Wilson seemed to glitter with a strange black light.

Zebra read the letter and showed it to Mrs. English.

Man Walking (1958), Nathan Oliveira. Oil on canvas, 60 1/8″ × 48 1/8″, courtesy of Hirshhorn Museum and Sculpture Garden, Smithsonian Institution. Gift of Joseph H. Hirshhorn, 1966. Photo by Lee Stalsworth.

Mini Lesson Viewing and Representing   ★ TEKS 23B

Man Walking
by Nathan Oliveira

ART APPRECIATION Explain to students that artists use colors, forms, and light to express feelings, emotions, and events, just as writers use words.
Instruction Point out that color or lack of it can suggest feelings or emphasize body parts. Ask what the gray and white in this painting suggest.
Possible Responses: The dull gray color mirrors Zebra's feelings; the white arm draws attention to that arm.

Application Ask students if they think that this image is an effective illustration for the story. Why or why not?
Possible Responses: The figure appears to be a male, like Zebra or John Wilson; the left arm is different, just as John Wilson's is; unlike Zebra and John Wilson, who are lifelike, the man in the picture has no distinctive characteristics.

Dear Zebra,

One of the people whose names are on this wall was among my very closest friends. He was an artist named Leon Kellner. Each year I visit him and leave a gift—something very special that someone creates and gives me. I leave it near his name for a few hours, and then I take it to my studio in Virginia, where I keep a collection of those gifts. All year long I work in my studio, but come summer I go looking for another gift to give him.

Thank you for your gift.

Your friend,

John Wilson

P.S. I hope your hand is healing.

Mrs. English stood staring awhile at the letter. She turned away and touched her eyes. Then she went to a shelf on the wall behind her, took down a large book, leafed through it quickly, found what she was searching for, and held it out for Zebra to see.

Zebra found himself looking at the glistening black wall of the Vietnam Memorial in Washington, D.C. And at the names on it, the thousands of names. . . .

Later, in the schoolyard during recess, Zebra stood alone at the chain-link fence and gazed down the street toward Franklin Avenue. He thought how strange it was that all the houses on this street had seemed to turn toward John Wilson that day, the windows and porches and columns and doors, as if saluting him.

Had that been only his imagination?

Maybe, Zebra thought, just maybe he could go for a walk to Franklin Avenue on Saturday or Sunday. He had not walked along Franklin Avenue since the accident; had not gone down that steep hill. Yes, he would walk carefully down that hill to the corner and walk back up and past the school and then the four blocks home.

Andrea came over to him.

"We didn't get picked for the story class with Mrs. English," she said. "I won't have to listen to any more of your gloomy stories."

Zebra said nothing.

"You know, I think I'll walk home today instead of taking the school bus," Andrea said.

"Actually, I think I'll walk, too," Zebra said. "I was thinking maybe I could pick up some really neat stuff in the street."

"You are becoming a pleasant life form," Andrea said. ❖

E

LITERARY LINK

The Rider

by Naomi Shihab Nye

A boy told me
if he rollerskated fast enough
his loneliness couldn't catch up
   to him,

5   the best reason I ever heard
for trying to be a champion.

What I wonder tonight
pedaling hard down King William
   Street
10   is if it translates to bicycles.

A victory! To leave your loneliness
panting behind you on some
   street corner
while you float free into a cloud
15   of sudden azaleas,
luminous pink petals that have
   never felt loneliness,
no matter how slowly they fell.

Customizing Instruction

Less Proficient Readers

1 Help students recognize the amount of time that has passed here.

Multiple Learning Styles
Intrapersonal Learners

2 Invite students to recall particularly meaningful gifts that they have given or received. Ask if they think that Zebra gave or received more.

Possible Response: He received more, because meeting John Wilson changed his life.

LITERARY LINK

This piece reflects some of the ideas in the main selection and is suggested for students' independent reading. Optional discussion questions follow.

1. Why does the boy in this poem rollerskate?
   Answer: to escape his loneliness
2. What is the narrator doing and what is this person wondering?
   Possible Response: She or he is bike riding and wondering if it's possible to leave loneliness behind.
3. How do the narrator's views on bike riding compare with Zebra's feelings about running?
   Possible Response: They are similar; both feel as if they are floating.

Naomi Shihab Nye

Nye is a Palestinian-American poet, essayist, and songwriter. Her work has been influenced by her dual heritage and her experiences living in Jordan and in San Antonio, Texas. Nye is praised for her ability to use imagery to make the ordinary seem extraordinary.

 Multicultural Link   **Gifts**

The gift that Zebra gives to John Wilson is very important both to the character and to the story. Gifts are an important part of many cultures, and are shared in different situations:

- At the new year, many Cambodian children give gifts to their parents to show their respect and gratitude.
- In China, money inside red envelopes may be given to celebrate a wedding or the new year.
- Business meetings in Korea often begin with an exchange of carefully chosen gifts.
- In Vietnam, the family of a person who has recently died may pass out small gifts of candy.
- At Samoan weddings, food in boxes is given to guests. The food is meant as a gift to the families of the guests.

GUIDING STUDENT RESPONSE

Connect to the Literature

1. Responses will vary. Students should be able to explain what the letter reveals about John Wilson and how the letter makes them feel.

Comprehension Check
- He runs too fast down a steep hill and gets hit by a car.
- His arm was wounded in the war.
- He takes it to the Vietnam Memorial in Washington, D.C., and leaves it near the name of one of his good friends.

 Use Selection Quiz, **Unit One Resource Book**, p. 34.

Think Critically

2. He is sad and disappointed about the injury to his hand. He feels that his injury takes away some of his personality.

 Use **Reading and Critical Thinking Transparencies**, p. 5, for additional support.

3. Zebra is intrigued by John Wilson's presence and by the idea that he might be able to develop a new skill.

4. Possible Responses: In Zebra's discussion with his parents about the art class, readers learn that his father supports him and that his mother is worried about his injury. At the first art class, Zebra is impressed with John's skill and learns to see things in a new way. Zebra's helicopter appears to strike an emotional chord with John. This moment establishes the connection between the two. In the last conversation with Andrea, readers learn that art has truly affected Zebra's personality in a positive way.

5. Answers will vary. Students might say that John Wilson is a main character because his relationship with Zebra is the focus of the story and he is crucial to the plot and theme.

6. Answers will vary. Students should show a clear understanding of the character of Zebra.

Literary Analysis

Character Most information comes from what Zebra does and what others say about him. Students may offer such words as *fearful, healing,* or *growing*.

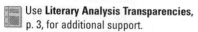 Use **Literary Analysis Transparencies**, p. 3, for additional support.

Connect to the Literature

1. **What Do You Think?** What was your reaction to the letter that John Wilson writes to Zebra?

   Comprehension Check
   - How does Zebra get hurt?
   - What is John Wilson's injury?
   - What does John Wilson do with Zebra's gift?

Think Critically

2. **ACTIVE READING MAKING INFERENCES** Why do you think Zebra spends a lot of time alone? Refer to the chart you made in your **READER'S NOTEBOOK**. Discuss with a classmate the **details** in the story that helped you make your **inferences.** How do your inferences compare with your partner's?

3. Why do you think Zebra chooses to take John Wilson's art class?

4. What role does art play in the story?

    THINK ABOUT
   - Zebra's discussion with his parents about taking an art class
   - Zebra's first class with John Wilson
   - John Wilson's reaction to Zebra's helicopter sculpture
   - Zebra's last conversation with Andrea

5. Would you describe John Wilson as a **main character** or a **minor character**? Give reasons for your answer.

6. Think about the characteristics of a zebra. Do you think Zebra is a good name for the main character? Why or why not?

Extend Interpretations

7. **COMPARING TEXTS** Consider the main character in "Zebra" and the boy in the poem "The Rider" on page 61. How are they alike and how do they differ? Support your answer with examples from the story and the poem.

8. **Connect to Life** In this story, John Wilson visits the Vietnam Veterans Memorial in Washington, D.C., as a way of healing. What are some other ways in which a person might attempt to heal emotional wounds?

Extend Interpretations

7. **Comparing Texts** Possible Response: Like Zebra, the boy in the poem is trying to grasp at something to ease his loneliness. Students might give examples of Zebra's interest in running or in learning how to create art.

8. **Connect to Life** Responses will vary but should reflect an understanding of healing.

Literary Analysis

CHARACTER Main characters are the most important characters in stories. The events of the stories' plots are based on what they think, feel, say, and do. A main character often grows or changes in some way, as Zebra does in this story. **Minor characters,** like Mrs. English, are less important. They usually do not grow or change.

All characters are revealed to the reader in three main ways: by what they do, by what they say, and by what other characters say about them.

Cooperative Learning Activity
Working with a partner, go back through the story, using a web like the one below to note what you learn about Zebra. When you are done, discuss the following questions with a larger group:

- Did you get most of your knowledge about Zebra from what he says, from what he does, or from what others say about him?
- If you could use only one word to describe Zebra, what would it be? Why?

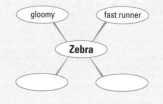

Choices & CHALLENGES

Writing Options

1. Personal Letter Imagining that you are Zebra, write a letter to John Wilson. You may want to write a response to the letter in the story, or you may want to write a letter in which Zebra shares his thoughts about what he learned in the art class. Place the letter in your **Working Portfolio.**

2. Road to Recovery Narrative Think of activities you love to do—participate in sports, draw, play a musical instrument, build things. Write a short narrative about what your life would be like if you suddenly couldn't do them anymore because of a serious injury or illness. Discuss what new activity you might take up to replace the ones you could no longer engage in.

Writing Handbook
See p. R35: Compare and Contrast.

Activities & Explorations

1. Garbage People The students in Mr. Wilson's class made "garbage into people." Create your own garbage person from discarded scraps and objects. ~ **ART**

2. Story Mime Select a scene in "Zebra" that you found emotionally powerful. In front of the class, silently act out the scene. Have the class try to identify the scene. ~ **PERFORMING**

3. Persuasive Speech Think of a class that you would like to attend in summer school. Present your idea to your classmates as if they were a panel deciding which classes to offer. Be sure to describe the class clearly and tell why you think you and other students would benefit from it. ~ **SPEAKING AND LISTENING**

Inquiry & Research

The Vietnam Veterans Memorial honors those who died in the Vietnam War. There are many other war memorials in the United States, especially in Washington, D.C. There may be a memorial in your hometown. Find out who designed it, when it was built, and what it memorializes. Create a brochure describing the memorial.

 Real World Link Read the magazine article on p. 65 to help you begin your research.

Vocabulary in Action

EXERCISE: WORD MEANING On a sheet of paper, write the letter of the word, or words, that is most different in meaning from the other words. Use a dictionary if you need help.

1. (a) joyously (b) glumly (c) enthusiastically (d) exuberantly
2. (a) thick (b) fat (c) gaunt (d) full
3. (a) dangerous (b) menacing (c) threatening (d) harmless
4. (a) recoil (b) flinch (c) approach (d) wince
5. (a) disciplinarian (b) weakling (c) drill sergeant (d) football coach
6. (a) elaborate (b) ornate (c) intricate (d) plain
7. (a) clean (b) dirt (c) grim (d) encrusted
8. (a) ready (b) poised (c) waiting (d) late
9. (a) jauntily (b) slowly (c) lively (d) sprightly
10. (a) easing (b) loosening (c) relaxing (d) tensing

Building Vocabulary
For an in-depth study of word relationships such as synonyms and antonyms, see p. 631.

Writing Options

1. Personal Letter Students' letters should exhibit an awareness of Zebra's interest in John Wilson or of what he learned from him. To get students started on this assignment, have them first decide which letter they will write. Have pairs of students brainstorm about what types of details their letters might contain.

2. Road to Recovery Narrative Before students write their narratives, have them first imagine the type of injury that would prevent them from continuing with their usual activities. Then have them consider what abilities they would be left with. Finally, ask them to imagine activities that require those abilities.

Activities & Explorations

1. **Garbage People** Encourage students to collect discarded items around the school. These might include bottle caps, boxes, scrap paper, packaging materials, or paper cups.
2. **Story Mime** Have students first decide if they want to work individually, in pairs, or in groups.
3. **Persuasive Speech** Encourage students to come up with several reasons why students would benefit from their class and to organize those reasons in order of importance.

Use **Communications Transparencies and Copymasters**, p. 3, for additional support.

Inquiry & Research

War Memorials To help students research local memorials, remind them that this country has fought in many wars. Some they might know of are the Revolutionary War, the Civil War, the two world wars, and the Vietnam War. Others, such as the War of 1812, are less well-known, yet might have memorials commemorating them.

Vocabulary in Action

1. b
2. c
3. d
4. c
5. b
6. d
7. a
8. d
9. b
10. d

Grammar in Context

WRITING EXERCISE
Possible Responses:

1. He imagined that he was running like a zebra.
2. In the world of his memories, Zebra could still run.
3. He had broken something that could never be repaired.
4. Zebra asked questions because he wanted to understand.
5. The buildings on the street seemed to salute him.

Author Activity

Growing Up Students may find it helpful to create Venn diagrams to help them organize their thoughts before writing.

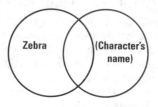

Use **Writing Transparencies,** pp. 28, 29, for additional support.

Grammar in Context: Sentence Fragments

Potok uses a series of fragments to reflect the intense feelings of the "broken" boy, Zebra, in this description.

> The doctors said it would take time to bring [his fingers] back to life. So many broken bones. So many torn muscles and tendons. So many injured nerves. . . . How stupid, stupid, *stupid* he had been!

A sentence expresses a complete thought. A **sentence fragment** is like a broken sentence. It is an incomplete thought because it is missing a subject, a verb, or both. Potok uses fragments to create a special effect, but writers usually avoid them because they are jarring and distracting to readers.

Apply to Your Writing Use sentence fragments as sparingly as possible.

WRITING EXERCISE Rewrite the following fragments as complete sentences. You may add or delete words.

Example: *Original* The darkness from which he emerged very slowly.

Rewritten He emerged very slowly from the darkness.

1. He imagined that he was a zebra. Running.
2. In the world of his memories.
3. Because he had broken something that could never be repaired.
4. Asking questions and wanting to understand.
5. Buildings on the street that seemed to salute him.

Grammar Handbook Writing Complete Sentences, p. R59

"Each of these characters . . . is really, I suppose, a different aspect of myself and a reflection of my fundamental interests."

Chaim Potok
born 1929

Early Days While growing up in the Bronx (a part of New York City), Chaim Potok lived the strict life of a Hasidic Jew. His parents, both Polish immigrants, wanted him to grow up to be a religious scholar. Potok himself wasn't so sure. By the time he was 16, he had started reading literature other than traditional Jewish texts. The more he read, the more he was struck by a contradiction between religious learning and the calling of a creative artist.

Coming to Terms Potok eventually left the Hasidic community for the Conservative movement of Judaism. He became a rabbi and served as a U.S. chaplain in Korea in the mid-1950s. Much of Potok's writing centers on characters who try to live both in the spiritual world and in the nonreligious world of everyday life. When asked whether his novels are autobiographical, Potok has said, "My characters tend to be loners. . . . They are extensions of my own being, because I grew up very much involved in the world of the mind, and in the worlds of art and literature."

AUTHOR ACTIVITY

Growing Up The short story you have read appears in Potok's book *Zebra and Other Stories.* All six stories in this collection feature young people facing challenges. Read one of the other stories in the book. Compare and contrast the main character with Zebra. Discuss your observations with your classmates.

64 UNIT ONE PART 1: KNOWING WHO YOU ARE

Teaching Options

AVOIDING INEFFECTIVE SENTENCE FRAGMENTS
Instruction Writers may use fragments on purpose, to make a point or to mimic the sounds of natural speech. For example, Zebra answers a question about when summer vacation begins by saying, "Three days." In this case, the fragment is effective, because readers can mentally supply missing words. Ineffective fragments, though, can confuse readers and should therefore be avoided. Readers should not need to ask, What is this about? or What happened?

(Mini Lesson) Grammar  **TEKS 17A** **TAAS Writing Obj. 3, 5, 7**

Exercise Rewrite the following passage, correcting any ineffective fragments.

"See you later!" said Andrea. Ran down the street and stopped at the corner. They turned at the same time. Saw each other staring. This time both of them. Waved and smiled.

*("See you later!" said Andrea. **She r**an down the street and stopped at the corner. They turned at the same time **and s**aw each other staring. This time both of them **w**aved and smiled.)*

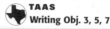 Use **Unit One Resource Book,** p 32.
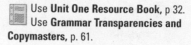 Use **Grammar Transparencies and Copymasters,** p. 61.

 Use McDougal Littell's *Language Network,* Chapter 1, for more instruction and practice in avoiding sentence fragments.

Offerings at The Wall

by Don Moser

"In the fall of 1982, a U.S. Navy officer walked up to the trench where the concrete for the foundation of The Wall was being poured. He stood over the trench for a moment, then tossed something into it and saluted. A workman asked him what he was doing. He said he was giving his dead brother's Purple Heart to The Wall. That was the first offering."

The story is told in a new book about the Vietnam Veterans Memorial, *Offerings at The Wall*, released by Turner Publishing Inc. The photographs in the book record some of the 30,000 objects and letters that have been placed at The Wall, as if at a shrine, by relatives and comrades of the men and women there memorialized.

These gifts of remembrance are collected each day by volunteers and preserved by the National Park Service in the Vietnam Veterans Memorial Collection, housed in a climate-controlled repository where the mementos lie

Reading for Information

In some classes you will be asked to write research reports after reading informative articles. Before you write such a report, you need to formulate a research question about a subject in the article that interests you.

FORMING AND REVISING RESEARCH QUESTIONS   To formulate a **research question,** find a subject that interests you in the article and turn it into a question. For example, if you are interested in the Purple Heart medal, you might ask, For what reasons were Purple Hearts awarded in Vietnam? This question is a guide for your research into the topic. The answer you give to your research question will become the **thesis statement** of your finished research report.

Real WORLD Link

Magazine Article

Objectives
- read to be informed
- raise questions in response to texts
- form and revise questions for investigations, including questions arising from readings
- evaluate his/her own research and frame new questions for further investigation

Connecting to the Literature

This magazine article presents a factual report about an important element in "Zebra": the gifts that are left at the Vietnam Veterans Memorial. Besides giving more information about the gifts themselves, the article also provides insight into a few of the reasons why soldiers leave them.

TEKS   See the Skills Trace at the beginning of the unit for information on TEKS covered in this lesson.

Reading for Information

As you go through the article with students, have them use the material in the left-hand column as a guide to formulating and revising research questions that are based on material in informative articles. The following are **possible responses** to the three questions and activities.

1 What is the origin of one particular collection in the Smithsonian Institution? Who decides what particular objects will be included in a collection?

2 Many students will answer that the question cannot be researched, because no one knows who left the cards.

3 The ideas might include any of the following: Are there any rules for leaving things? Can people read the poems? Who designed the memorial? How many people visit it? How many names are on it?

 Use **Writing Transparencies,** p. 40, for additional support.

Reading for Information continued

YOUR TURN *Use the questions and activities below to help you practice formulating and revising research questions.*

1 Be careful not to formulate a research question that is too broad. Remember the amount of time you have to complete your assignment. For example, you would have to do a lot of research to answer a research question like, "What is the origin of each of the collections in the Smithsonian Institution?" How might you revise that question to give it a narrower focus?

2 There are some topics for which research sources do not exist. Consider the question, "Why did someone leave a royal flush?" Do you think you would be able to research an answer to this question? Why or why not?

3 After you read the article, it may help to quickly brainstorm all the ideas that occur to you. Try brainstorming a list of ideas about the Vietnam Veterans Memorial.

Inquiry & Research

Activity Link: "Zebra," p. 63. Formulate your own research question about the Vietnam Veterans Memorial or another memorial. Write a short report about the memorial and share it with the class.

near such historic artifacts as the life mask of Abraham Lincoln. (Five hundred of the objects are on view in an exhibition at the Smithsonian's National Museum of American History.)

Some of the offerings were left with poems or letters (letters that were sealed will always remain so), but others bear meanings known only to those who offered them: a Bible, a fishing float, service ribbons, a sock for an amputee's stump, a popsicle stick, four mortarboard tassels, a foil wrapper from a chocolate candy. In his eloquent introduction to the book, Thomas B. Allen writes that The Wall "became a place for wishes, for futures that could not be. Tucked into a wreath are the things of an imagined life: new baby shoes for a baby who never would be, the pencils and crayons for a first day of kindergarten that never would be, champagne glasses to toast a wedding anniversary that never would be, ornaments for a Christmas tree that never would be." Someone left five cards, a royal flush for a poker game that never would be played. And a soldier left a photograph of a North Vietnamese man with a young girl, along with a note: "Dear Sir: For twenty-two years I have carried your picture in my wallet. I was only eighteen years old that day that we faced one another on that trail in Chu Lai, Vietnam. Why you did not take my life I'll never know. You stared at me for so long. . . . Forgive me for taking your life."

And the boots. So intimately shaped by those who wore them, yet so universal—the familiar black leather and tough green fabric, the lugged soles bearing the memory of the earth of the Delta or Con Thien—that they seem a symbol for the whole.

Mini Lesson Inquiry & Research 🚩 TEKS 13C

The Inquiry & Research activity on this page links to the Inquiry & Research activity of Choices & Challenges on page 63, following the story "Zebra."

Instruction Remind students to use multiple sources of information, including electronic texts, experts, and print resources to locate information relevant to their research questions. Encourage them to select sources that are appropriate to the war memorials they are researching. For example, a local veteran might be a good source of information about a local monument, while the Internet might be a better choice for a national memorial.

Practice Suggest that students work in pairs to identify and evaluate at least three possible sources of information for their reports. Then have them select two sources that they think would be most productive.

 Use **Writing Transparencies,** p. 50, for additional support.

Clues to Meaning

When you come across an unfamiliar word in your reading, you can figure out its meaning by looking at its **context**—the words and phrases around it. These words can provide clues to the word's meaning.

> But the boy took care to sit on the far side of the room where he thought she could easily see him out of the corner of her eye, if she wanted to. He did not trust the woman *not* to trust him. And he did not want to be mistrusted now.
>
> —Langston Hughes, "Thank You, M'am"

To figure out the meaning of mistrusted, look at the details that describe Roger's thoughts and actions.

Strategies for Building Vocabulary

In the example above, the context clues in the passage are known as **description clues.** The description of Roger's thoughts and actions shows that he does not want Mrs. Jones to doubt him. The word *mistrusted,* therefore, means "looked on without trust." Here are some other types of context clues.

❶ Definition and Restatement Clues Words that restate unfamiliar words' meanings are **definition clues** and **restatement clues.** In the second sentence of the following example, the meaning of the word *frail* is restated in simpler language:

> Roger looked as though he were frail. In other words, he looked weak and thin in his tennis shoes and jeans.

Restatement clues may be signaled by commas or by words like *as, or, that is, in other words,* and *also.*

❷ Example Clues An **example clue** illustrates another word's meaning by providing examples. Words like *including* and *such as* often signal example clues. In the following sentence, the examples after *such as* are clues to the meaning of *presentable:*

> Mrs. Jones wanted Roger to do things to make himself presentable for dinner, such as washing his face and running a comb through his hair.

❸ Comparison and Contrast Clues A **comparison clue** illustrates a word's meaning with a comparison to a more familiar word or idea.

> Mr. Lucas was as portly as a large bear.

A **contrast clue** involves a writer's pointing out differences between words or ideas. Contrast clues may be signaled by *although, but, however, yet,* and *in contrast.*

> Zebra at first thought the stranger seemed menacing, but Wilson turned out to be kind and friendly.

The contrast with "kind and friendly" shows that *menacing* means "possibly dangerous."

EXERCISE Use a context clue to define each underlined word. Then identify the kind of context clue that you used.

1. Roger wanted blue <u>suede</u> shoes. He thought about how the soft, fuzzy leather would feel on his feet.
2. Wilson was <u>gaunt</u>, a thin, bony shadow of a man.
3. Mrs. Jones's front stoop was as <u>barren</u> as the stoop of an abandoned home.
4. Several things reminded Julia of her <u>ethnicity</u>, including her long Spanish name.
5. The children played <u>exuberantly</u>. Zebra, on the other hand, stood sad and motionless.

BUILDING VOCABULARY   **67**

Objectives
• rely on context to determine the meanings of words

VOCABULARY EXERCISE
Possible Responses:
1. suede—soft, fuzzy leather; example clue
2. gaunt—thin, scrawny; definition and restatement clue
3. barren—deserted; comparison clue
4. ethnicity—example clue
5. exuberantly—happily, excitedly; contrast clue

Use **Unit One Resource Book,** p. 35, for more exercises. Use **Vocabulary Transparencies and Copymasters,** p. 3, for additional support.

A Crush

by Cynthia Rylant

Possible Objectives

You can use this selection to achieve one or more of the following objectives:

- enjoy silent sustained reading (Option One)
- read and analyze literature with a group (Option Two)
- use the Reader's Notebook to write in response to literature (Option Three)

Summary

One morning, the windows of Stan's Hardware begin filling with flowers that everyone assumes are meant for Dolores, the assistant manager. No one would leave flowers for Dick Wilcox, the married owner. Dolores has worked there for twenty years, and all the trades-people in town trust her. However, people are surprised that someone might have a crush on Dolores, because she has a tattoo, greasy hair, and "didn't fix herself up." People think she doesn't want love. Ernie, the man who sends the flowers, knows nothing about Dolores. He is developmentally disabled and lives in a group home. Before arriving there, he had accidentally received someone else's flower seeds in the mail. At the group home, Ernie watches Jack, a worker, grow a splendid vegetable garden. Jack takes Ernie out to breakfast across the street from Stan's Hardware, and Ernie sees Dolores and falls in love. He gives Jack his flower seeds, and when they grow into blooming plants, he picks the flowers, puts them in a jar, and secretly leaves them in front of Stan's. Every Wednesday he leaves more, and his gift has a positive effect on both Dolores and her boss. When summer is over and the outdoor flowers die, Jack brings Ernie some indoor lights and more seeds. "Violets," says Jack. Then he and his friend go out to get some dirt.

When the windows of Stan's Hardware started filling up with flowers, everyone in town knew something had happened. Excess flowers usually mean death, but since these were all real flowers bearing the aroma of nature instead of floral preservative, and since they stood bunched in clear Mason jars instead of impaled on Styrofoam crosses, everyone knew nobody had died. So they all figured somebody had a crush and kept quiet.

There wasn't really a Stan of Stan's Hardware. Dick Wilcox was the owner, and since he'd never liked his own name, he gave his store half the name of his childhood hero, Stan Laurel in the movies. Dick had been married for twenty-seven years. Once, his wife, Helen, had dropped a German chocolate cake on his head at a Lion's Club dance, so Dick and Helen were not likely candidates for the honest expression of the flowers in those clear Mason jars lining the windows of Stan's Hardware, and speculation had to move on to Dolores.

Dolores was the assistant manager at Stan's and had worked there for twenty years, since high school. She knew the store like a mother knows her baby, so Dick—who had trouble keeping up with things like prices and new brands of drywall compound—tried to keep himself busy in the back and give Dolores the run of the floor. This worked fine because the carpenters and plumbers and painters in town trusted Dolores and took her advice to heart. They also liked her tattoo.

Dolores was the only woman in town with a tattoo. On the days she went sleeveless, one could see it on the taut brown skin of her upper arm: "Howl at the Moon." The picture was of a baying coyote, which must have been a dark gray in its early days but which had faded to the color of the spackling paste Dolores stocked in the third aisle. Nobody had gotten out of Dolores the true story behind the tattoo. Some of the men who came in liked to show off their own, and they'd roll up their sleeves or pull open their shirts, exhibiting bald eagles and rattlesnakes and Confederate flags, and they'd try to coax out of Dolores the history of her coyote. All of the men had gotten their tattoos when they were in the service, drunk on weekend leave and full of the spitfire of young soldiers. Dolores had never been in the service, and she'd never seen weekend leave, and there wasn't a tattoo parlor anywhere near. They couldn't figure why or where any half-sober woman would have a howling coyote ground into the soft skin of her upper arm. But Dolores wasn't telling.

That the flowers in Stan's front window had anything to do with Dolores seemed completely improbable. As far as anyone knew, Dolores had never been in love, nor had anyone ever been in love with her. Some believed it was the tattoo, of course, or the fine dark hair coating Dolores's upper lip which kept suitors away. Some felt it was because Dolores was just more of a man than most of the men in town, and fellows couldn't figure out how to court someone who knew more about the carburetor of a car or the back side of a washing machine than they did. Others thought Dolores simply didn't want love. This was a popular theory among the women in town who sold Avon and Mary Kay cosmetics. Whenever one of them ran into the hardware for a package of light bulbs or some batteries, she would mentally pluck every one of the black hairs above Dolores's lip. Then she'd wash that grease out of Dolores's hair, give her a good blunt cut, dress her in a decent silk-blend blouse with a nice Liz Claiborne skirt from the Sports line, and, finally, tone down that swarthy, longshoreman look of Dolores's with a concealing beige foundation,[1] some frosted peach lipstick, and a good gray liner for the eyes.

Dolores simply didn't want love, the Avon lady would think as she walked back to her car carrying her little bag of batteries. If she did, she'd fix herself up.

The man who was in love with Dolores and who brought her zinnias and cornflowers and nasturtiums and marigolds and asters and four-o'clocks in clear Mason jars did not know any of this. He did not know that men showed Dolores their tattoos. He did not know that Dolores understood how to use and to sell a belt sander. He did not know that Dolores needed some concealing beige foundation so she could get someone to love her. The man who brought flowers to Dolores on Wednesdays when the hardware opened its doors at 7:00 A.M. didn't care who Dolores had ever been or what anyone had ever thought of her. He loved her, and he wanted to bring her flowers.

Ernie had lived in this town all of his life and had never before met Dolores. He was thirty-three years old, and for thirty-one of those years he had lived at home with his mother in a small dark house on the edge of town near Beckwith's Orchards. Ernie had been a beautiful baby, with a shock of shining black hair and large blue eyes and a round, wise face. But as he had grown, it had become clearer and clearer

> That the flowers in Stan's front window had anything to do with Dolores seemed completely improbable.

---

1. **concealing beige foundation:** a cosmetic that covers skin flaws.

Reading the Selections

Option One
Silent Sustained Reading

You might set aside time each week for independent reading. During this time, you and your students would read for enjoyment. "A Crush" will appeal to many students and can be read independently in 30 minutes or so. To encourage students to read for pleasure, consider making no assignments related to this selection. However, Options Two and Three below offer suggestions in case you do want to make assignments.

Option Two
Shared Reading Groups

You may assign students to groups or allow them to choose their own. Students can read the selection together, alternately reading sections aloud, or they can read independently and meet to cooperate on a project that portrays some element of the story.

Possible Projects

- Students can collaboratively discuss what might happen as a result of events so far. Will Ernie and Dolores ever meet, for example? Will anyone learn the secret of the tattoo?
- Students might enjoy dramatizing a televised news story about the mysterious appearance of flowers at Stan's Hardware. The story should include at least one reporter as well as interviews with such townspeople as the Avon lady or Dick Wilcox.
- Students can create posters for the story, similar to film posters, that contain art, a visual image, and a blurb.

Option Three
Reader's Notebook

Before students read, discuss the concept of a story's theme, explaining that it is a story's central idea or message about life or human nature. One way to figure out a story's theme is to think about what happens to the main characters and to generalize from that to a broad statement that applies to everyone.

Ask students as they read to pay attention to the main characters in this story and to notice how they change. Have them record notes about those changes in their Reader's Notebooks.

At the end of the story, have students consider what prompted or caused the changes that they noted. Have them jot their ideas in their Reader's Notebooks. Then have them use their notes to write a single statement about life or people that they think this story reveals. Point out, if necessary, that stories may contain several themes.

After Reading

Possible Activities
Independent Activities

• Ask gifted and talented students to think about the flowers and the different functions that they had for Dolores, Ernie, and Jack. Have them speculate about whether some other gift, such as candy, would have meant as much to all three characters. Ask them to jot down their ideas in their Reader's Notebooks.

• Have students write a diary entry that Dick or Helen Wilcox or Jack might write about the changes that he or she saw in the main characters or in other people. Encourage students to combine story details with what they imagine the characters' thoughts might be.

that though he was indeed a perfectly beautiful child, his mind had not developed with the same perfection. Ernie would not be able to speak in sentences until he was six years old. He would not be able to count the apples in a bowl until he was eight. By the time he was ten, he could sing a simple song. At age twelve, he understood what a joke was. And when he was twenty, something he saw on television made him cry.

Ernie's mother kept him in the house with her because it was easier, so Ernie knew nothing of the world except this house. They lived, the two of them, in tiny dark rooms always illuminated by the glow of a television set, Ernie's bags of Oreos and Nutter Butters littering the floor, his baseball cards scattered across the sofa, his heavy winter coat thrown over the arm of a chair so he could wear it whenever he wanted, and his box of Burpee seed packages sitting in the middle of the kitchen table.

These Ernie cherished. The seeds had been delivered to his home by mistake. One day a woman wearing a brown uniform had pulled up in a brown truck, walked quickly to the front porch of Ernie's house, set a box down, and with a couple of toots of her horn, driven off again. Ernie had watched her through the curtains and, when she was gone, had ventured onto the porch and shyly, cautiously, picked up the box. His mother checked it when he carried it inside. The box didn't have their name on it, but the brown truck was gone, so whatever was in the box was theirs to keep. Ernie pulled off the heavy tape, his fingers trembling, and found inside the box more little packages of seeds than he could count. He lifted them out, one by one, and examined the beautiful photographs of flowers on each. His mother was not interested, had returned to the television, but Ernie sat down at the kitchen table and quietly looked at each package for a long time, his fingers

running across the slick paper and outlining the shapes of zinnias and cornflowers and nasturtiums and marigolds and asters and four-o'clocks, his eyes drawing up their colors.

Two months later Ernie's mother died. A neighbor found her at the mailbox beside the road. People from the county courthouse came out to get Ernie, and as they ushered him from the home he would never see again, he picked up the box of seed packages from his kitchen table and passed through the doorway.

Eventually Ernie was moved to a large white house near the main street of town. This house was called a group home, because in it lived a group of people who, like Ernie, could not live on their own. There were six of them. Each had his own room. When Ernie was shown the room that would be his, he put the box of Burpee seeds—which he had kept with him since his mother's death—on the little table beside the bed, and then he sat down on the bed and cried.

Ernie cried every day for nearly a month. And then he stopped. He dried his tears, and he learned how to bake refrigerator biscuits and how to dust mop and what to do if the indoor plants looked brown.

Ernie loved watering the indoor plants, and it was this pleasure which finally drew him outside. One of the young men who worked at the group home—a college student named Jack—grew a large garden in the back of the house. It was full of tomato vines and the large yellow blossoms of healthy squash. During his first summer at the house, Ernie would stand at the kitchen window, watching Jack and sometimes a resident of the home move among the vegetables. Ernie was curious but too afraid to go into the garden.

Illustration by Patty Dryden. Copyright © Patty Dryden.

Discussion Activities

- Ask students if, based on this story, they think they would like the author, Cynthia Rylant, and why. What can they infer about her from this story?
- Discuss the contrast between how Ernie views Dolores and the way everyone else does. Is either view right or wrong? Why?

Assessment Opportunities

- You can assess students' comprehension by evaluating the theme statements that they wrote in their Reader's Notebooks.
- You can have students write an essay about the story's theme, using story details as supporting evidence.

Art

Encourage students to examine Patty Dryden's painting. Tell them that it has been said that the flowers in this piece tell us more about the man than his face would. To guide students as they think about this idea, give them the following questions for discussion:

- What adjectives might you use to describe the bouquet of flowers? What is particularly unique or eye-catching about them?
  Possible Responses: They are bright, large, and extravagant; the bouquet resembles a fire; the flowers seem to burst from the bouquet.
- What might this man be trying to do?
  Possible Responses: surprise someone he loves or admires with flowers; impress someone; draw attention to himself
- What might this bouquet of flowers say about the man?
  Possible Responses: He is romantic; he is creative; he is extravagant.

Then one day when Ernie was watching through the window, he noticed that Jack was ripping open several slick little packages and emptying them into the ground. Ernie panicked and ran to his room. But the box of Burpee seeds was still there on his table, untouched. He grabbed it, slid it under his bed, then went back through the house and out into the garden as if he had done this every day of his life.

He stood beside Jack, watching him empty seed packages into the soft black soil, and as the packages were emptied, Ernie asked for them, holding out his hand, his eyes on the photographs of red radishes and purple eggplant. Jack handed the empty packages over with a smile and with that gesture became Ernie's first friend.

Jack tried to explain to Ernie that the seeds would grow into vegetables, but Ernie could not believe this until he saw it come true. And when it did, he looked all the more intently at the packages of zinnias and cornflowers and the rest hidden beneath his bed. He thought more deeply about them, but he could not carry them to the garden. He could not let the garden have his seeds.

That was the first year in the large white house.

The second year, Ernie saw Dolores, and after that he thought of nothing else but her and of the photographs of flowers beneath his bed.

Jack had decided to take Ernie downtown for breakfast every Wednesday morning to ease him into the world outside that of the group home. They left very early, at 5:45 A.M., so there would be few people and almost no traffic to frighten Ernie and make him beg for his room. Jack and Ernie drove to the Big Boy restaurant which sat across the street from Stan's Hardware. There they ate eggs and bacon and French toast among those whose work demanded rising before the sun: bus drivers, policemen, nurses, mill workers. Their first time in the Big Boy, Ernie was too nervous to eat. The second time, he could eat, but he couldn't look up. The third time, he not only ate everything on his plate, but he lifted his head and he looked out the window of the Big Boy restaurant toward Stan's Hardware across the street. There he saw a dark-haired woman in jeans and a black T-shirt unlocking the front door of the building, and that was the moment Ernie started loving Dolores and thinking about giving up his seeds to the soft black soil of Jack's garden.

Love is such a mystery.

Love is such a mystery, and when it strikes the heart of one as mysterious as Ernie himself, it can hardly be spoken of. Ernie could not explain to Jack why he went directly to his room later that morning, pulled the box of Burpee seeds from under his bed, then grabbed Jack's hand in the kitchen and walked with him to the garden, where Ernie had come to believe things would grow. Ernie handed the packets of seeds one by one to Jack, who stood in silent admiration of the lovely photographs before asking Ernie several times, "Are you sure you want to plant these?" Ernie was sure. It didn't take him very long, and when the seeds all lay under the moist black earth, Ernie carried his empty packages inside the house and spent the rest of the day spreading them across his bed in different arrangements.

That was in June. For the next several Wednesdays at 7:00 A.M. Ernie watched every movement of the dark-haired woman behind the lighted windows of Stan's

Sweetpeas (1992), Julia Jordan. Acrylic on paper, private collection. Photo by James Hart.

Hardware. Jack watched Ernie watch Dolores and discreetly said nothing.

When Ernie's flowers began growing in July, Ernie spent most of his time in the garden. He would watch the garden for hours, as if he expected it suddenly to move or to impress him with a quick trick. The fragile green stems of his flowers stood uncertainly in the soil, like baby colts on their first legs, but the young plants performed no magic for Ernie's eyes. They saved their shows for the middle of the night and next day surprised Ernie with tender small blooms in all the colors the photographs had promised.

The flowers grew fast and hardy, and one early Wednesday morning when they looked as big and bright as their pictures on the empty packages, Ernie pulled a glass canning jar off a dusty shelf in the basement of his house. He washed the jar, half filled it with water, then carried it to the garden, where he placed in it one of every kind of flower he had grown. He met Jack at the car and rode off to the Big Boy with the jar of flowers held tight between his small hands. Jack told him it was a beautiful bouquet.

When they reached the door of the Big Boy, Ernie stopped and pulled at Jack's arm, pointing to the building across the street. "OK," Jack said, and he led Ernie to the front door of Stan's Hardware. It was 6:00 A.M., and the building was still dark. Ernie set the clear Mason jar full of flowers under the sign that read "Closed," then he smiled at Jack and followed him back across the street to get breakfast.

When Dolores arrived at seven and picked up the jar of zinnias and cornflowers and nasturtiums and marigolds and asters and four-o'clocks, Ernie and Jack were watching her from a booth in the Big Boy. Each had a wide smile on his face as Dolores put her nose to the flowers. Ernie giggled. They watched the lights of the hardware store come up and saw Dolores place the clear Mason jar on the ledge of the front window. They drove home still smiling.

All the rest of that summer Ernie left a jar of flowers every Wednesday morning at the front door of Stan's Hardware. Neither Dick Wilcox nor Dolores could figure out why the flowers kept coming, and each of them assumed somebody had a crush on the other. But the flowers had an effect on them anyway. Dick started spending more time out on the floor making conversation with the customers, while Dolores stopped wearing T-shirts to work and instead wore crisp white blouses with the sleeves rolled back off her wrists. Occasionally she put on a bracelet.

By summer's end Jack and Ernie had become very good friends, and when the flowers in the garden behind their house began to wither, and Ernie's face began to grow gray as he watched them, Jack brought home one bright day in late September a great long box. Ernie followed Jack as he carried it down to the basement and watched as Jack pulled a long glass tube from the box and attached this tube to the wall above a table. When Jack plugged in the tube's electric cord, a soft lavender light washed the room.

"Sunshine," said Jack.

Then he went back to his car for a smaller box. He carried this down to the basement, where Ernie still stood staring at the strange light. Jack handed Ernie the small box, and when Ernie opened it, he found more little packages of seeds than he could count, with new kinds of photographs on the slick paper.

"Violets," Jack said, pointing to one of them.

Then he and Ernie went outside to get some dirt. ❖

"It took me about seven years to feel like a writer."

Cynthia Rylant
born 1954

Inspiration In Kent, Ohio, where Cynthia Rylant lives, a strange man sometimes brings flowers to waitresses at a little diner. He became the inspiration for Ernie. Beside the diner is a hardware store. "That's where my imagination found Dolores," said Rylant, who claims that she enjoys taking "people who don't get any attention in the world and making them really valuable in my fiction—making them absolutely shine with their beauty."

Success Rylant has achieved success in many forms of writing. Her book *Missing May* (1992) was awarded the Newbery Medal in 1993.

 LaserLink: Background for Reading
Background Connection
Author Background
Art Gallery

CYNTHIA RYLANT
As the title of her first book, *When I Was Young in the Mountains,* suggests, Rylant did grow up in the mountains, in West Virginia. While her mother attended nursing school for four years, Rylant lived with her grandparents. Her grandfather was a coal miner, and the family lived in a small house with no plumbing. When Rylant's mother finished school, she found an apartment in which Rylant says she "felt rich" because "the whole place had running water and an indoor bathroom."

Writing Workshop

Response to Literature

Sharing thoughts about a story . . .

From Reading to Writing Stories touch people in different ways. Some readers might like "Seventh Grade" by Gary Soto because they recognize themselves in Victor. Others might like "Zebra" by Chaim Potok because they admire Zebra's strength. In a **response to literature,** you can share your thoughts and feelings about a piece of literature. You may include your feelings about a character, your impressions of the story, and any similarities and differences the story might have to your own life.

For Your Portfolio

Writing Prompt Write a personal response to a short story or poem.

Purpose: To share your thoughts and feelings about a piece of literature
Audience: Your classmates, teacher, friends, or family

Basics in a Box

Response to Literature at a Glance

Introduction
Introduces the title and author and a clear statement of your response

Body
Supports the response with evidence from the work

- Evidence
- examples from the story
- quotations
- connections to your own life

Conclusion
Summarizes the response

RUBRIC STANDARDS FOR WRITING

A successful response to literature should

- include an introduction that names the literary work and clearly states your overall response to it
- tell enough about the literature so that readers can understand your response
- contain clearly described, specific reactions and responses to the literary work
- support your statements with quotations and details from the story
- summarize the response in the conclusion

WRITING WORKSHOP **75**

LESSON RESOURCES

USING PRINT RESOURCES
Unit One Resource Book
- Prewriting, p. 36
- Drafting, p. 37
- Peer Response, pp. 38–39
- Revising, Editing, and Proofreading, p. 40
- Student Models, pp. 41–43
- Rubric, p. 44

LESSON SUPPORT
Writing Transparencies
- Writing Process Transparencies, TR 1–4
- Writing Structure Transparencies: Organizing Your Writing, TR 11
- Writing Template Transparencies: Response to Literature, TR 26

Grammar Transparencies and Copymasters
- Capitalization Errors, CM 122 (for Mini Lesson, p. 80)

INTEGRATED TECHNOLOGY
LaserLinks
Writing Springboards
See **Teacher's SourceBook,** p. 36, for bar codes.

Writing Coach CD-ROM
Visit our website:
www.mcdougallittell.com

Writing Workshop
Response to Literature

Objectives
- write a response to literature
- use a written text as a model for writing
- revise a draft to add supporting quotations
- identify and correct errors in capitalization of proper nouns

---

Introducing the Workshop

Response to Literature Ask volunteers to name some stories they have read and to tell whether they liked them or not. Elicit one reason for each answer. Then explain that most readers have some feelings about stories that they read: they may like them, dislike them, feel close to a character, or be totally confused. Each feeling is a response, and if students think, they can identify reasons for their responses.

Discuss what elements students like or dislike in stories. Then explain that writing a personal-response essay gives them a chance to record their thoughts and feelings about a story.

Basics in a Box
Using the Graphic Explain that a personal response identifies the work and gives readers a general idea of how the student feels about it. Then the essay provides specific reasons for this response, which may include story details or events from the student's life. A personal response ends with a summary or observation. Point out that the body of the essay—the reasons—forms the largest part.

Presenting the Rubric To help students better understand the assignment, review with them the Standards for Writing a Successful Response to Literature. You might also share with them the complete rubric, which describes several levels of proficiency.

See the Skills Trace at the beginning of the unit for information on TEKS covered in this lesson.

Use McDougal Littell's *Language Network,* Chapters 12–19, for more instruction in essential writing skills.

To engage students visually, use **Power Presentation** 1, Response to Literature.

Analyzing a Student Model

Personal Response to "Seventh Grade"

The student model is a response to a short story about a seventh-grade boy who has a crush on a girl in his class and makes a fool of himself trying to impress her. The student identified with this character and therefore liked the story.

After students have read the story, discuss the Rubric in Action with them. Point out the key words and phrases in the student model that correspond to the elements mentioned in the Rubric in Action.

1 Ask students why the author, the title, and the general idea are given right at the beginning.
   Possible Response: Readers may not have read the story and will need this information to understand the response.

2 The author of the essay actually gives two related responses. Ask students to tell what they are.
   Answer: She liked how well the story showed the real-life struggles; she identified with Victor, because she had once felt as he did.

3 Ask students why they think the writer chose to use this event to explain her feelings about the story and the character.
   Possible Responses: She liked it; she had done something like that.

4 Point out that the dialogue gives readers a better sense of the characters than a description alone might.

5 Ask students how they can tell that the writer has switched from the story to her own personal experience.
   Possible Response: She says "From my experience," and she uses the pronoun *I*.

Analyzing a Student Model

Shoshannah Seed
Edna Thomas Middle School

RUBRIC
IN ACTION

Personal Response to "Seventh Grade"

Life in seventh grade can be confusing. That's what Gary Soto shows us in the story "Seventh Grade." At the beginning of the story, Victor, the main character, starts seventh grade with a big crush on a girl named Teresa. This sets in motion a number of realistic scenes in which he struggles to get her attention. I liked how well the story shows the real-life struggles of searching for yourself in seventh grade. I was also surprised by how much I had in common with Victor. I, too, once had a crush and felt very unsure of myself.

In the story, Victor does many things to get Teresa's attention. It all starts with scowling, a trick he learns from his friend Michael. When Victor asks Michael why he is making a face, Michael answers, "I ain't making a face, *ese*. This *is* my face." Michael is imitating some scowling male models he saw in a magazine. He thinks they look really cool and that scowling is a good way to get girls to look at him. "Belinda Reyes walked by a while ago and looked at me," he tells Victor. I think Victor wonders if it would make Teresa look at him because later he tries scowling. When a girl notices him, he decides it works. In truth, the girl probably notices Michael and Victor because they look foolish, not handsome. From my experiences in seventh grade, I can say that everyone is trying to be noticed—to be seen as special in some way. However, not everyone knows how to handle it yet. Therefore, people go to drastic measures. I can relate to Victor and Michael because I, too, have tried doing something outrageous to get attention—wearing weird clothes or hairstyles.

In the story, Victor thinks of Teresa constantly and can't wait to see her in French class. One day at lunch, Victor wants to see if Teresa is around, but he doesn't want anyone to know he is looking for her. He acts like a spy. He pretends he is reading or stretching. I know just how Victor feels because I often find myself trying to hide my feelings by pretending in a similar way.

❶ Names title, author, and main character of the work in the introduction

❷ States a response to the story and the major reasons for the response

❸ Supports response with details from the story

❹ Includes dialogue to bring the story to life for readers

❺ Brings in personal experiences to support the response

Victor also tries to impress Teresa, but ends up really embarrassing himself. This is because he pretends to know something he doesn't. When Mr. Bueller, the French teacher, asks if anyone knows French, Victor raises his hand to impress Teresa. Mr. Bueller says to Victor in French, *"Très bien. Parlez-vous français?"* Victor doesn't know what that means because he only knows English and Spanish! A lot of people in seventh grade try to impress others. I think it is because they feel unsure of themselves and they don't think they're good enough as they are. In order to be liked and to feel secure, they try and make themselves into something they're not. Like Victor, I, too, have tried to be something different to impress someone I liked, only to find out the person thought I was okay just the way I was.

In conclusion, I really liked this story because I could relate to the struggles of the main character, Victor. I think the story's message is that everyone does embarrassing things when trying to impress others. In the end, though, you're better off being yourself. In my opinion, the story captures what really happens in the seventh grade. It describes the highs and lows, the stress of wanting so much for other people to like you, and the good feeling you get when they do.

❻ Writer uses a running style of organization. She alternates between telling about Victor and relating the story to her own life.

Other Option
• Describe the story first, then describe personal experiences.

❼ Ties up essay with a general observation about life in the seventh grade

Other Option
• States a lesson that was learned from the story that could be applied to life.

6 Point out that the writer of this essay used three main examples from the story. Have students identify each. Ask how the writer shows that she is switching from her own responses back to the story.

Possible Response: She writes "in the story" or uses the word *also*.

7 Ask what words or phrases the writer repeats from the introduction. Then ask what she adds to that.

Possible Response: She repeats that she likes the story because she could relate to the main character; she adds what she sees as the message; she gives her opinion that the story captures what happens in seventh grade.

 Viewing and Representing

PICTURING TEXT STRUCTURE

Instruction One way to structure a response to literature is to give an overall response, followed by examples that help explain the response. The writer of this student model paired each example from the story with a personal experience from her own life.

Activity Have students analyze the organization of the student model by constructing a diagram like the one shown to illustrate how the writer organized her personal response.

 Use **Writing Transparencies**, p. 11, for additional support.

TEKS 10L

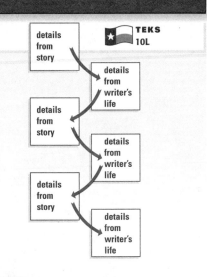

Prewriting

Choosing a Subject

If students are still having trouble selecting a story after reading the suggestions in the Idea Bank, suggest the following:

- Consider a story that you did not like at all, or one that contained a character you did not like. What didn't you like?
- Consider a story that you found very easy or hard to read. Think about what made it easy or hard.
- Consider a story that you think would make a good movie or television show. What elements would work well on film?

Planning Your Personal Response to Literature

1. Some students may find it helpful to imagine a conversation with a good friend who asks, "Should I read this story? Why?"
2. You may wish to encourage students to begin by listing descriptive words that come to mind, such as *happy, boring, realistic.* Then they can freewrite and focus their responses.
3. Students might make a response chart, listing story details in one column and their responses to them in another.

Drafting

Some students may find it easiest to begin by writing a brief summary or overview of the work. Others might find it easier to begin with their responses and the reasons for them. Their freewriting can help them recall story details that they want to include.

Ask Your Peer Reader

Asking peer readers to identify confusing passages is a good way to check whether enough reasons and story details are included.

IDEABank

1. Your Working Portfolio
Look for ideas in the **Writing Options** that you completed earlier in this unit.
- **Letter,** p. 27
- **Comparing Characters,** p. 35

2. Literary Journal
Keep a journal of your responses to literature that you read both in and out of school. Choose a piece to which you responded strongly.

3. Wishful Thinking
Find a story that is the kind of story that you wish you could write. Decide which part of the story you most admire and why.

Have a question?

See the **Writing Handbook,** Writing Introductions, p. R26

Writing Your Response to Literature

❶ Prewriting

Writing and reading decrease our sense of isolation.
—Anne Lamott, Contemporary American Writer

To select a short story for your response, **write down** your reactions to some of the short stories in this unit. Jot down the names of **characters** that most affected you. Think about whether you have had similar experiences to the ones described in the story. See the **Idea Bank** in the margin for more suggestions. After you have chosen a short story, follow the steps below.

Planning Your Response to Literature

▶ **1. Carefully reread the short story.** As you read, write down details that you notice.

▶ **2. Freewrite about your responses.** Spend five minutes writing down your thoughts and feelings about the story. Identify your reactions, such as sad, angry, excited, or curious.

▶ **3. Focus your response.** Decide whether you will respond to the entire story, to a character, to a particular event, or to the author's style. Think about the scene that most impressed you. Did it remind you of your own life? What did it make you think or feel?

▶ **4. Identify your audience.** How familiar is your audience with the story you are discussing? What will they need to know in order to understand your response?

❷ Drafting

Remember that there are no right or wrong answers in a response to literature. As long as you describe your **reactions** to the story and support your statements with **examples,** you'll be on the right track.

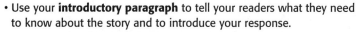

Ask Your Peer Reader

- What would make my essay more interesting to you?
- Why do you think I responded as I did?
- What feelings came through strongly in my writing?

- Use your **introductory paragraph** to tell your readers what they need to know about the story and to introduce your response.
- Give reasons for your response and examples in the **body** of your essay. Explain why you felt as you did.

- Include **quotations** and **descriptions** of scenes, among other things. Describe how these examples relate to your own life.
- **Summarize** your response in the conclusion of the essay.

❸ Revising

TARGET SKILL ▷ SUPPORTING YOUR RESPONSE WITH QUOTATIONS Using the actual words spoken by a character can help readers understand a character's personality and shows that you know the work well. Dialogue can also support your own thoughts about the story. Notice how the added quotations below give a glimpse of Michael's personality.

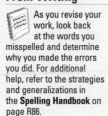

When Victor asks Michael why he is making a face, Michael *"I ain't making a face, ese. This is my face."* says ~~it happened over the summer.~~ Michael is imitating some scowling male models he saw in a magazine. He thinks they look really cool and that scowling is a good way to get girls to look at him. *He tells Victor, "Belinda Reyes walked by a while ago and looked at me."*

❹ Editing and Proofreading

TARGET SKILL ▷ CORRECTING RUN-ON SENTENCES A sentence expresses one complete thought. A run-on sentence is two or more sentences written as though they were one. Correct run-ons by rewriting long sentences as two separate sentences.

Life in the seventh grade can be confusing that's what Gary Soto shows us in the story "Seventh Grade."

❺ Reflecting

FOR YOUR WORKING PORTFOLIO How did writing about the short story help you to understand it? Did your feelings about the story change as you wrote your personal response essay? Attach your thoughts to your finished work. Save your personal response essay in your **Working Portfolio.**

Need revising help?

Review the **Rubric,** p. 75.

Consider **peer reader** comments.

Check **Revision Guidelines,** p. R23.

Puzzled about how to get nouns to behave properly?

See the **Grammar Handbook,** p. R63

Publishing
IDEAS

- Meet with a classmate who had a different response to the same story. Prepare a short debate for the class. Have class members discuss why they agree with one response or the other.
- Each month look back at the stories you have read and choose a "Story of the Month." Generate a class newsletter on the computer featuring that story.

More Online: Publishing Options www.mcdougallittell.com

Revising
SUPPORTING YOUR RESPONSE WITH QUOTATIONS
Encourage students to select quotations thoughtfully. They might begin by looking for passages that add details about the story, show an author's style, or reveal a character's personality.

Editing and Proofreading
CORRECTING RUN-ON SENTENCES
Remind students that run-on sentences create confusion for readers. As they proofread their writing, they might try reading aloud any long sentences that might be run-ons. They should ask themselves: Would the information in the sentence be easier to understand if the sentence were broken into two sentences? Does the sentence express two or more complete thoughts, rather than one complete thought?

Reflecting
Encourage students to be specific about the changes in their feelings. How did they first feel, for instance, and what changed these feelings? Students whose feelings did not change in the course of writing their response should be expected to describe those feelings and how they originated.

Option
Before students proofread, you may wish to review the punctuation of quotations and of story titles.

Demonstrate how students can eliminate incorrect choices for the first question.

A. This choice is incorrect, because a common noun, *school*, is capitalized, and part of the character's name, which is a proper noun, is not capitalized.

B. This choice is correct, because the character's entire name is capitalized.

C. This choice is incorrect, because the word *school* is a common noun, not a proper noun, and should not be capitalized.

D. This choice is incorrect, because the character's whole name is John Wilson but only part of his name is capitalized here.

Answers:
1. B; **2.** A; **3.** A; **4.** B; **5.** C; **6.** B

Assessment Practice Revising & Editing

Read this passage from the first draft of a personal response to a short story. The underlined sections may include the following types of errors.

- **run-on sentences**
- **capitalization errors**
- **spelling errors**
- **verb tense errors**

For each underlined section, choose the revision that most improves the writing.

> Zebra is the first person to see <u>john Wilson at the school.</u> He finds
> (1)
> out that Wilson is planning to teach an art class. <u>His Teacher, Mrs.</u>
> (2)
> <u>english,</u> urges Zebra to join the class. Zebra says, "I can't draw." Then
> the fact that Wilson has only one arm inspires him. Zebra decides to try.
> He <u>will learn</u> that his own <u>injurys</u> do not have to hold him back. He
> (3)   (4)
> helps Wilson when he gives him the drawing. Along the way he <u>helped</u>
> (5)
> himself. Ultimately, his hopes for his own life change. By the end of the
> story, his <u>freind</u> Andrea says, "You are becoming a pleasant life form."
> (6)

1. A. john Wilson at the School.
   B. John Wilson at the school.
   C. John Wilson at the School.
   D. Correct as is

2. A. His teacher, Mrs. English,
   B. His Teacher, Mrs. English,
   C. His teacher, mrs. English,
   D. Correct as is

3. A. learns
   B. will have learned
   C. learning
   D. Correct as is

4. A. injuiries
   B. injuries
   C. injuiryes
   D. Correct as is

5. A. will help
   B. had helped
   C. helps
   D. Correct as is

6. A. frend
   B. friend
   C. friende
   D. Correct as is

Need extra help?

See the **Grammar Handbook**

Quick Reference: Capitalization, p. R58

Quick Reference: Punctuation, p. R56

Run-on sentences, p. R59

 Mini Lesson **Grammar** **TEKS 17A** **TAAS Writing Obj. 7**

CAPITALIZATION ERRORS

Instruction Remind students that when they are proofreading their writing, they should always check for correct capitalization. Point out that proper nouns and proper adjectives name particular people, places, things, or ideas and should always be capitalized. A common noun names a whole class of persons, places, things, or ideas and is never capitalized. Display the following examples:

Proper Nouns: Victor, Puerto Rico
Proper Adjectives: English, Spanish
Common Nouns: boy, school

Exercises Have students identify words that need to be capitalized in the sentences below.

1. Did you know <u>julia</u> speaks two languages?

2. My brother will start seventh grade at <u>lincoln school.</u>

3. In that class we learned to speak <u>french.</u>

4. My teacher is quiet, but <u>ms. palo</u> is talkative.

 Use **Grammar Transparencies and Copymasters,** p. 122.

 Use McDougal Littell's **Language Network,** Chapter 10, for more instruction and practice in capitalization.

Reflecting on the Theme Not knowing what to expect can make new experiences frightening. At the same time, they are opportunities for discovery. The characters in Part 2 make discoveries about themselves, others, and the world around them.

LEARNING the Language of *Literature*

OVERVIEW

Objectives
- understand the following literary terms:
  - nonfiction
  - biography
  - biographer
  - autobiography
  - first-person point of view
  - essay
  - expository (formal) essay
  - personal (informal) essay
  - persuasive essay
  - informative nonfiction
  - informative article
  - interview
- understand and appreciate nonfiction
- understand literary forms by recognizing and distinguishing between biographies and autobiographies

Teaching the Lesson

This lesson defines nonfiction and analyzes five different types of nonfiction writing.

Introducing the Concepts
Have students think of a work of nonfiction they have recently read, such as a newspaper article or an article in a science magazine. Ask them to explain why they read it (e.g., to be entertained or to learn new facts) and to describe ways in which they can use the information in the article.

 Use **Literary Analysis Transparencies,** pp. 10–12, 16, for additional support.

 TEKS See the Skills Trace at the beginning of the unit for information on TEKS covered in this lesson.

Nonfiction

If I write about sharks or rattlesnakes, I want the reader to come away from my book with a greater appreciation of these remarkable living creatures. . . . If I write about frontier children, . . . I want to leave the reader with a . . . feeling of kinship with people of another era.

—Russell Freedman

When you read a movie review, a science textbook, or almost any article in a magazine like *Sports Illustrated for Kids,* you are reading nonfiction. **Nonfiction** is a type of writing that deals with real people, places, and events. A newspaper article, a set of instructions, and an encyclopedia article are also nonfiction. Nonfiction contains mostly factual information. The writer selects and organizes the information to suit his or her purpose.

Key Types of Nonfiction
- biography
- autobiography
- essay
- informative article
- interview

82

Biography

A **biography** is the story of a person's life as told by someone else. The writer, or **biographer,** gets information by interviewing the subject of the biography or people who knew the subject and by reading letters, diaries, and documents. Biographies contain some of the same elements as fiction, such as **character, setting,** and even **plot.**

YOUR TURN What details in the paragraph tell you about Eleanor Roosevelt's life and the setting around her?

BIOGRAPHY

Eleanor was born in a fine townhouse in Manhattan. Her family also owned an elegant mansion along the Hudson River, where they spent weekends and summers. As a child Eleanor went to fashionable parties. A servant took care of her and taught her to speak French. Her mother, the beautiful Anna Hall Roosevelt, wore magnificent jewels and fine clothing. Her father, Elliott Roosevelt, had his own hunting lodge and liked to sail and to play tennis and polo. Elliott, who loved Eleanor dearly, was the younger brother of Theodore Roosevelt, who in 1901 became president of the United States. The Roosevelt family, one of America's oldest, wealthiest families, was respected and admired.

—William Jay Jacobs, "Eleanor Roosevelt"

Autobiography

An **autobiography** is the story of a person's life told by that person. It is almost always written from the **first-person point of view,** using pronouns like *I* and *me.* An autobiography is usually book length because it covers a long period of the writer's life. Shorter forms of autobiographical writing include **journals, diaries, letters,** and **memoirs.**

YOUR TURN What details in the paragraph help you understand what Eleanor Roosevelt felt and experienced?

AUTOBIOGRAPHY

In the beginning, because I felt, as only a young girl can feel it, all the pain of being an ugly duckling, I was not only timid, I was afraid. Afraid of almost everything, I think: of mice, of the dark, of imaginary dangers, of my own inadequacy. My chief objective, as a girl, was to do my duty. This had been drilled into me as far back as I could remember. Not my duty as I saw it, but my duty as laid down for me by other people. It never occurred to me to revolt. Anyhow, my one overwhelming need in those days was to be approved, to be loved, and I did whatever was required of me, hoping it would bring me nearer to the approval and love I so much wanted.

—Eleanor Roosevelt,
The Autobiography of Eleanor Roosevelt

Presenting the Concepts
Biography

Have students think of a relative or a friend about whom they would like to write. Ask them to explain why this person interests them and what kind of information they would need in order to write a biography of this person.

YOUR TURN

Possible Response: Details such as her place of birth, her family background, details about the house where she lived, and details about her parents tell about Eleanor Roosevelt.

Autobiography

Explain to students that *auto* means "self," *bio* means "life," and *graphy* means "writing."

YOUR TURN

Possible Response: She explains that she felt she was ugly, which made her timid and afraid of almost everything. She also explains that she was very dutiful, hoping that by being good she would be loved and approved of.

Essay

An **essay** is a short piece of writing on a single subject. Essays are often found in newspapers and magazines. The writer might share an opinion, try to entertain or persuade the reader, or simply describe a topic or incident that has special meaning. Three common types of essays are expository (formal), personal (informal) and persuasive. Formal essays tend to have a scholarly tone while informal essays tend to have a conversational tone.

ESSAY

expository

- tightly structured
- impersonal style
- presents or explains information and ideas

The story of the *Titan* predicted exactly what would happen to the *Titanic* fourteen years later. It was an eerie prophecy of terrible things to come.

In 1907, nearly ten years after *The Wreck of the Titan* was written, two men began making plans to build a real titanic ship.

—Robert D. Ballard, *Exploring the* Titanic

personal

- looser structure
- more personal style
- expresses writer's thoughts and feelings

Sometimes I think we would be better off if we forgot about the broad strokes and concentrated on the details. Here is a woman without a bureau. There is a man with no mirror, no wall to hang it on. They are not the homeless. They are people who have no homes. No drawer that holds the spoons. No window to look out upon the world.

—Anna Quindlen, "Homeless"

persuasive

- presents arguments
- tries to convince readers to adopt a point of view

The only thing that can help [Native Americans] is genuine love. You must truly love us, be patient with us and share with us. And we must love you—with a genuine love that forgives and forgets. . . . This is brotherhood. . . . Anything less is not worthy of the name.

—Chief Dan George as told to Helmut Hirnschall, "I Am a Native of North America"

Informative Article

Informative articles provide facts about a subject. **Newspaper articles** and **feature stories** are examples of informative nonfiction. So are textbooks, pamphlets, history books, gardening books, and how-to books.

YOUR TURN What is the subject of this informative article?

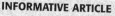

INFORMATIVE ARTICLE

Men, women, and children were packed into dark, foul-smelling compartments. They slept in narrow bunks stacked three high. They had no showers, no lounges, and no dining rooms. Food served from huge kettles was dished into dinner pails provided by the steamship company. Because steerage conditions were crowded and uncomfortable, passengers spent as much time as possible up on deck.

—Russell Freedman, *Immigrant Kids*

Interview

An **interview** is a conversation in which one person asks questions of another for the purpose of obtaining information. The interviewer takes notes on, tape-records, or films the conversation in order to keep an accurate record. Interviews with Ray Bradbury and Virginia Hamilton are included on pages 500 and 749.

YOUR TURN What information is the interviewer trying to obtain?

INTERVIEW

Q: I know you never have trouble coming up with ideas. Walk me through your daily inspiration and writing process.

A: I just wake up with ideas every morning from my subconscious percolating. At 7 in the morning I lie in bed and I watch all the fragments of ideas swarming around in my head and these voices talk to me. And when they get to a certain point, I jump out of bed and run to the typewriter. So I'm not in control. Two hours later I have a new short story or an essay or part of a play.

—"An Interview with Ray Bradbury," 1997

Informative Article
Ask students to think about a type of informative nonfiction that they might use in their daily lives or to help with schoolwork, with a hobby, or with a project.

YOUR TURN
Possible Response: The subject is living conditions for steerage passengers traveling to America.

Interview
Ask students to think about one living person they would like to interview. Have them discuss what specific questions they would like to ask that person.

YOUR TURN
Possible Response: The interviewer is trying to find out about Bradbury's writing process.

Objectives
- use a variety of strategies to read and appreciate nonfiction
- use main ideas and details and textual clues to understand nonfiction
- distinguish between fact and fiction

Teaching the Lesson

The strategies on this page will help students understand the nonfiction selections in this unit and other units.

Presenting the Strategies
Be sure students understand that the different strategies apply to different kinds of nonfiction. For example, because biography and autobiography are narrative forms, they require strategies similar to those for reading fiction. Essays, informative articles, and interviews call for strategies that involve analyzing and evaluating a writer's reasoning and purpose.

Preview Remind students that sections with headings can provide an outline of a piece's content. Words in boldface type often highlight the most important ideas presented in the article. Photographs, diagrams, and charts can also provide important information at a glance.

Clarify the Organization Tell students that they should try to figure out if a nonfiction piece is organized chronologically or by topic. Knowing how the piece is organized will help them to zero in on the information they need.

Nonfiction writing connects us to a world of information. **Autobiographies, biographies, essays, informative nonfiction,** and **interviews** teach us about real people, places, and events. The reading strategies explained below can help you to enjoy many types of nonfiction.

Reading Nonfiction

How to Apply the Strategies

Preview the selection. Look at the title, the pictures or diagrams, and any subtitles or terms in boldface or italic type. All of these will give you an idea of what the selection is about. As you read, stop now and then to **predict** what will come next.

Clarify the organization. If the work is a biography or an autobiography, the organization is probably **chronological**—events are presented in the order in which they happened. Other selections may be organized around ideas the author wants to discuss. As you read, look for dates and signal words that clarify the sequence of events, such as *before, during, after, first, next,* and *last*.

Summarize the main idea. Think about the main idea and details. Are there enough details to support the main points? Can you summarize them?

Separate facts and opinions. Facts are statements that can be proved. Opinions are statements that cannot be proved. They simply express a person's beliefs. Be aware that writers of nonfiction sometimes present opinions as if they were facts.

Evaluate what you read. Evaluating means forming opinions about people, events, and ideas. You can also evaluate the author's purpose. Did the author write this work to inform, influence, or to express an opinion or bias?

Here's how Sophia uses the strategies:

*"My hobby is ancient shipwrecks. When I read a ship's history, the events are told in **chronological order.** Knowing this helps me keep the facts straight. As I read, I think about the author's purpose and **evaluate** the information—to do this I need to know which of the writer's statements are facts and which are opinions. Then I come to my own conclusion."*

Need More Help?

Remember that active readers use the essential reading strategies explained on page 4: • **visualize** • **predict** • **clarify** • **question** • **connect** • **evaluate** • **monitor.**

Summarize the Main Idea Tell students that they should always look for the main idea of a selection and the facts that support it. They should be able to sift through the facts of a piece to find the most important ones.

Separate Facts and Opinions Explain that if students are learning about a subject from a source, it is crucial that they know the difference between facts and opinions. They should look for supporting details that prove any statements. They should also look for phrases such as "I think" and "In my opinion" that clearly indicate opinion.

Evaluate What You Read Explain to students that the foregoing strategies will help them to make judgments about what they read. Ask them to keep the following questions in mind: What did you like or dislike about the article? Was the explanation clear and factual? Do you need to seek other sources of information?

Eleanor Roosevelt

Biography by WILLIAM JAY JACOBS

SOCIAL STUDIES

TEKS See the Skills Trace at the beginning of the unit for information on TEKS covered in this lesson.

Connect to Your Life

What women who have made significant social change do you know about?

Build Background Eleanor Roosevelt, wife of President Franklin Roosevelt, lived through a period of dramatic changes.

1884 Eleanor Roosevelt is born into a wealthy, respected New York family which includes uncle Theodore Roosevelt.

1932 Franklin D. Roosevelt elected president. As first lady, Eleanor speaks out against economic and social injustice.

1939 Marian Anderson sings at the Lincoln Memorial. Roosevelt arranges the event after Anderson is not allowed to sing in a Washington concert hall because of her race.

1920 The 19th Amendment, granting women the right to vote, is ratified. The participation of women in politics grows.

1962 Eleanor Roosevelt dies.

| 1903 First airplane flight | 1912 *Titanic* sinks | 1914 WW I begins. | 1929 Great Depression begins | 1939 *Grapes of Wrath* published | 1941 U.S. enters WW II. | 1945 WW II ends; U.N. organized. | 1954 Supreme Court ends school segregation. | 1961 First American in space |

Focus Your Reading

LITERARY ANALYSIS **BIOGRAPHY** A **biography** is the story of a person's life, written by another person. Biographers take information from many sources—letters, journals, interviews, documents—and bring it together to present accounts of their subjects' lives.

WORDS TO KNOW **Vocabulary Preview**
brooding   migrant   prominent
combatant   priority

ACTIVE READING **CHRONOLOGICAL ORDER**
Chronological order is the order in which events happen in time. Signal words such as *before, during, after, first, next, while,* and *later* indicate the order of events. As you read, create a chart in your READER'S NOTEBOOK to keep track of the chronological order of important events in Eleanor Roosevelt's life.

LaserLink: Background for Reading
Historical Connection

LESSON RESOURCES

UNIT ONE RESOURCE BOOK, pp. 45–51

ASSESSMENT
Formal Assessment, pp. 15–16
Teacher's Guide to Assessment and Portfolio Use
Test Generator

SKILLS TRANSPARENCIES AND COPYMASTERS
Literary Analysis
• Biography, TR 10 (for Paired Activity, p. 98)
Reading and Critical Thinking
• Chronological Order, TR 6 (for Thinking Through the Literature, p. 98)

Grammar
• Vivid Adjectives, CM 78 (for Mini Lesson, p. 90)
• Predicate Nouns, Adjectives, and Pronouns, CM 52 (for Mini Lesson, p. 100)
Vocabulary
• Context Clues, CM 24 (for Mini Lesson, p. 89)
• Word Families, CM 25 (for Mini Lesson, p. 92)

INTEGRATED TECHNOLOGY
Audio Library
LaserLinks
• Historical Connection. See **Teacher's SourceBook,** p. 8
Internet: Research Starter

Visit our website:
www.mcdougallittell.com

OVERVIEW

 This selection is included in the **Grade 7 InterActive Reader.**

Objectives
1. understand and appreciate **biography (Literary Analysis)**
2. understand **internal conflict (Literary Analysis)**
3. use **chronological order (Active Reading)**

Summary
Eleanor Roosevelt, daughter of President Theodore Roosevelt's brother Elliot and Elliot's wife Anna, survived a difficult childhood to become a force for reform throughout the world. She married her distant cousin, Franklin Delano Roosevelt, helped him recover from polio, and supported his political career. Gradually, she lost her shyness and insecurity and began to speak up for her own beliefs. When her husband was elected president, she persuaded him to work for social reforms, and she led relief efforts during the Depression and World War II. After FDR died, Eleanor helped to found the United Nations. Until her death, she remained a tireless worker for human rights.

Editor's Note With the author's or copyright holder's permission, this selection has been edited slightly to delete material that may be considered objectionable.

Thematic Link
In order to make the kind of impact she did on the world, the shy, insecure Eleanor Roosevelt needed to make some very important discoveries about herself and her abilities.

5-Minute Warm-Up

Daily Language SkillBuilder TEKS 17A, 17C

Have students **proofread** the display sentences on page 13j and write them correctly. The sentences also appear on Transparency 3 of **Grammar Transparencies and Copymasters.**

 Mini Lesson **Preteaching Vocabulary**

If you would like to preteach the WORDS TO KNOW for this selection, use the Mini Lesson, p. 89.

Reading and Analyzing

PREVIEW

Encourage students to look ahead at the selection, noticing the photographs and the called-out quotations.

Literary Analysis | BIOGRAPHY |

Ask students what circumstances made Eleanor Roosevelt's childhood an unhappy one.

Possible Responses: She was made fun of because of her unattractive appearance; she had to wear a back brace; her parents were disappointed with her because they had wanted a boy.

 Use **Unit One Resource Book,** p. 47 for more practice.

Active Reading

| CHRONOLOGICAL ORDER |

Remind students that the events in a biography are usually presented in chronological order, but that sometimes authors include facts out of sequence. Have students determine where the first event of Eleanor's life is mentioned in this selection. Why, do they think, did the author choose to present other events first?

Possible Response: Eleanor's birth is mentioned in the fourth paragraph. By introducing the biography with the later accomplishments of her life, the author contrasts her adult self to the frightened child she once was.

 Use **Unit One Resource Book,** p. 46 for more practice.

| ACTIVE READING |

A CHRONOLOGICAL ORDER Possible Response: *then, next, the next year, a few months later*

Teaching Options

Eleanor Roosevelt
by William Jay Jacobs

President Franklin Delano Roosevelt and First Lady Eleanor Roosevelt. UPI/Bettmann.

88   UNIT ONE   PART 2: MOMENTS OF DISCOVERY

BLOCK SCHEDULING: MANAGING TIME

If your schedule requires that you cover the lesson objectives in a shorter time, use . . .
- Across the Curriculum, p. 87
- Thinking Through the Literature, p. 98
- Vocabulary and Spelling, p. 99
- Grammar in Context, p. 100

If you want to take advantage of longer class time, use . . .
- TE Teaching Options: Preteaching Vocabulary, p. 89; Grammar, pp. 90, 100; Vocabulary Strategy, p. 92; Informal Assessment, p. 93; Viewing and Representing, p. 94; Standardized Test Practice, p. 96; Cross-Curricular Link, p. 97, Spelling, p. 99
- Choices and Challenges, p. 99

Eleanor Roosevelt was the wife of President Franklin Delano Roosevelt. But Eleanor was much more than just a president's wife, an echo of her husband's career.

Sad and lonely as a child, Eleanor was called "Granny" by her mother because of her seriousness. People teased her about her looks and called her the "ugly duckling.". . .

Yet despite all of the disappointments, the bitterness, the misery she experienced, Eleanor Roosevelt refused to give up. Instead she turned her unhappiness and pain to strength. She devoted her life to helping others. Today she is remembered as one of America's greatest women.

Eleanor was born in a fine townhouse in Manhattan. Her family also owned an elegant mansion along the Hudson River, where they spent weekends and summers. As a child Eleanor went to fashionable parties. A servant took care of her and taught her to speak French. Her mother, the beautiful Anna Hall Roosevelt, wore magnificent jewels and fine clothing. Her father, Elliott Roosevelt, had his own hunting lodge and liked to sail and to play tennis and polo. Elliott, who loved Eleanor dearly, was the younger brother of Theodore Roosevelt, who in 1901 became president of the United States. The Roosevelt family, one of America's oldest, wealthiest families, was respected and admired.

To the outside world it might have seemed that Eleanor had everything that any child could want—everything that could make her happy. But she was not happy. Instead her childhood was very sad.

Almost from the day of her birth, October 11, 1884, people noticed that she was an unattractive child. As she grew older, she could not help but notice her mother's extraordinary beauty, as well as the beauty of her aunts and cousins. Eleanor was plain looking, ordinary, even, as some called her, homely. For a time she had to wear a bulky brace on her back to straighten her crooked spine.

When Eleanor was born, her parents had wanted a boy. They were scarcely able to hide their disappointment. Later, with the arrival of two boys, Elliott and Hall, Eleanor watched her mother hold the boys on her lap and lovingly stroke their hair, while for Eleanor there seemed only coolness, distance.

Feeling unwanted, Eleanor became shy and withdrawn. She also developed many fears. She was afraid of the dark, afraid of animals, afraid of other children, afraid of being scolded, afraid of strangers, afraid that people would not like her. She was a frightened, lonely little girl.

The one joy in the early years of her life was her father, who always seemed to care for her, love her. He used to dance with her, to pick her up and throw her into the air while she laughed and laughed. He called her "little golden hair" or "darling little Nell."

Then, when she was six, her father left. An alcoholic, he went to live in a sanitarium[1] in

ACTIVE READING

CHRONOLOGICAL ORDER What are some of the words the author uses here and in the next 4 paragraphs to indicate the order in which events happened?

---

1. **sanitarium** (săn´ĭ-târ´ē-əm): an institution for the care of people with a specific disease or other health problem.

TEKS 6A, 9B

TAAS Reading Obj. 1

Mini Lesson **Preteaching Vocabulary**

CONTEXT CLUES Call students' attention to the list of WORDS TO KNOW on page 87. Remind them that sometimes they can understand the meaning of an unfamiliar word by looking at the context in which it is used. Use the model sentences to demonstrate the strategy of using context clues that restate the meaning of a word.

Eleanor's family was <u>prominent</u>, or well-known.

She visited <u>migrant</u> farm workers— that is, workers who move from place to place.

Exercises Have students define the underlined WORDS TO KNOW in the following sentences.

1. We wondered about his <u>brooding</u>, or troubled, nature. *(sulking)*

2. My uncle George is a <u>prominent</u> citizen— that is, everyone in town knows who he is. *(well-known and respected)*

3. That is a <u>priority</u>. It must receive your attention first. *(something that is most important)*

4. The solder was an active <u>combatant</u>, or fighter. *(person who fights)*

Use **Unit One Resource Book,** p. 48, for more exercises. Use **Vocabulary Transparencies and Copymasters,** p. 24, for additional support.

Customizing Instruction

Less Proficient Readers
Engage students' interest in the subject of this biography by discussing the role of the president's wife (since all presidents heretofore have been men). Point out that Eleanor Roosevelt ushered in a new kind of role for First Ladies, and that in some ways, her childhood prepared her for this role.

Set a Purpose As they read, ask students to find out what Eleanor's childhood was like.

Students also may benefit from a review of the history of the United States during Eleanor Roosevelt's time as First Lady, focusing on the Depression and World War II and their effects on ordinary people.

Gifted and Talented
Have students brainstorm a list of other women whose accomplishments they rank with Eleanor's. Have students support their choices.

Students Acquiring English
1 Point out that the phrase "ugly duckling" refers to an unattractive child and comes from Hans Christian Andersen's tale about an ugly duckling that grows up to be a beautiful swan. Encourage interested students to find and read the story.

Use **Spanish Study Guide** for additional support, pp. 16–18.

Literary Analysis BIOGRAPHY

 A Ask students to explain why they think Jacobs included the detail about Eleanor holding her mother's head in her lap when she had headaches.

Possible Response: It shows that some of Eleanor's strengths were apparent even at an early age: her compassion and forgiveness.

Use **Literary Analysis Transparencies,** p. 10, for additional support.

Reading Skills and Strategies: CHARACTER TRAITS

Based on the information on this page, how would you describe Theodore Roosevelt?

Possible Response: He was playful, fun, outgoing, daring, and risk-taking, and he was kind to Eleanor.

Literary Analysis: INTERNAL CONFLICT

Remind students that conflict is a struggle between two opposing forces. Internal conflict is the struggle that occurs within a person or character. Ask what kinds of internal conflicts Eleanor faced.

Possible Response: Eleanor's internal conflicts include her struggles with her many fears—of the dark, of animals, and of other children.

Reading Skills and Strategies: SYNTHESIZING

Have students speculate why Eleanor was accepted by her schoolmates at Allenswood when she had never been accepted before.

Possible Responses: In the past, she was withdrawn, whereas at Allenswood she became a team player; her schoolmates respected her effort and determination.

Virginia in an attempt to deal with his drinking problem. Eleanor missed him greatly.

A Next her mother became ill with painful headaches. Sometimes for hours at a time Eleanor would sit holding her mother's head in her lap and stroking her forehead. Nothing else seemed to relieve the pain. At those times Eleanor often remembered how her mother had teased her about her looks and called her "Granny." But even at the age of seven Eleanor was glad to be helping someone, glad to be needed — and noticed.

The next year, when Eleanor was eight, her mother, the beautiful Anna, died. Afterward her brother Elliott suddenly caught diphtheria[2] and he, too, died. Eleanor and her baby brother, Hall, were taken to live with their grandmother in Manhattan.

A few months later another tragedy struck. Elliott Roosevelt, Eleanor's father, also died. Within eighteen months Eleanor had lost her mother, a brother, and her dear father.

For the rest of her life Eleanor carried with her the letters that her father had written to her from the sanitarium. In them he had told her to be brave, to become well educated, and to grow up into a woman he could be proud of, a woman who helped people who were suffering.

Only ten years old when her father died, Eleanor decided even then to live the kind of life he had described—a life that would have made him proud of her.

Few things in life came easily for Eleanor, but the first few years after her father's death proved exceptionally hard. Grandmother Hall's dark and gloomy townhouse had no place for children to play. The family ate meals in silence. Every morning Eleanor and Hall were expected to take cold baths for their health. Eleanor had to work at better posture by walking with her arms behind her back, clamped over a walking stick.

Instead of making new friends, Eleanor often sat alone in her room and read. For many months after her father's death she pretended that he was still alive. She made him the hero of stories she wrote for school. Sometimes, alone and unhappy, she just cried.

Some of her few moments of happiness came from visiting her uncle, Theodore Roosevelt, in Oyster Bay, Long Island. A visit with Uncle Ted meant playing games and romping outdoors with the many Roosevelt children.

Once Uncle Ted threw her into the water to teach her how to swim, but when she started to sink, he had to rescue her. Often he would read to the children old Norse tales and poetry. It was at Sagamore Hill, Uncle Ted's home, that Eleanor first learned how much fun it could be to read books aloud.

For most of the time Eleanor's life was grim. Although her parents had left plenty of money for her upbringing, she had only two dresses to wear to school. Once she spilled ink on one of them, and since the other was in the wash, she had to wear the dress with large ink stains on it to school the next day. It was not that Grandmother Hall was stingy. Rather, she was old and often confused.

The one joy in the early years of her life was her father, who always seemed to care for her, love her.

---

2. **diphtheria** (dĭf-thîr′ē-ə): a serious infectious disease.

Teaching Options

 Mini Lesson **Grammar** 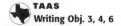 **TEKS 17D** **TAAS Writing Obj. 3, 4, 6**

VIVID ADJECTIVES Remind students that adjectives play an important role in describing a character. Good writers choose vivid and precise adjectives to describe people and things. This helps the reader to visualize the person or the scene more effectively.

Model Sentence:

Eleanor's mother had <u>bad</u> headaches.

Have students look for the sentence in which the general adjective *bad* is replaced by a more vivid adjective. What is it? *(painful)*

Discuss why this adjective is more vivid.

Exercises Have students replace the underlined adjective in each sentence with a more vivid or precise one.

1. Uncle Ted was <u>nice</u> to Eleanor.
2. Eleanor felt that she was <u>not pretty</u>.
3. Her early life was <u>sad</u>.

 Use **Grammar Transparencies and Copymasters,** p. 78.

 Use McDougal Littell's **Language Network,** Chapter 19, for more instruction and practice in using vivid adjectives.

Nor did she show much warmth or love for Eleanor and her brother. Usually she just neglected them.

Just before Eleanor turned fifteen, Grandmother Hall decided to send her to boarding school in England. The school she chose was Allenswood, a private academy for girls located on the outskirts of London.

It was at Allenswood that Eleanor, still thinking of herself as an "ugly duckling," first dared to believe that one day she might be able to become a swan.

At Allenswood she worked to toughen herself physically. Every day she did exercises in the morning and took a cold shower. Although she did not like competitive team sports, as a matter of self-discipline she tried out for field hockey. Not only did she make the team but, because she played so hard, also won the respect of her teammates.

They called her by her family nickname, "Totty," and showed their affection for her by putting books and flowers in her room, as was the custom at Allenswood. Never before had she experienced the pleasure of having schoolmates actually admire her rather than tease her.

At Allenswood, too, she began to look after her health. She finally broke the habit of chewing her fingernails. She learned to eat nutritious foods, to get plenty of sleep, and to take a brisk walk every morning, no matter

Elliott Roosevelt and his daughter, Eleanor, aged six. Eleanor adored her father, who called her "little golden hair" or "darling little Nell." UPI/Bettmann. **1**

how miserable the weather.

Under the guidance of the school's headmistress, Mademoiselle Souvestre (or "Sou"), **2** she learned to ask searching questions and think for herself instead of just giving back on tests what teachers had said.

She also learned to speak French fluently, a skill she polished by traveling in France, living for a time with a French family. Mademoiselle Souvestre arranged for her to have a new red dress. Wearing it, after all of the old, worn dresses Grandmother Hall had given her, made her feel very proud.

Eleanor was growing up, and the joy of young womanhood had begun to transform her personality.

In 1902, nearly eighteen years old, she left Allenswood, not returning for her fourth year there. Grandmother Hall insisted that, instead, she must be introduced to society as a debutante—to go to dances and parties and begin to take her place in the social world with other wealthy young women.

Away from Allenswood, Eleanor's old uncertainty about her looks came back again. She saw herself as too tall, too thin, too plain. She worried about her buckteeth, which she thought made her look horselike. The old teasing began again, especially on the part of Uncle Ted's daughter, "Princess" Alice Roosevelt, who seemed to take pleasure in making Eleanor feel uncomfortable.

Eleanor, as always, did as she was told. She went to all of the parties and dances. But she also began working with poor children at the Rivington Street Settlement House on New York's Lower East Side. She taught the girls gymnastic exercises. She took children to museums and to musical performances. She tried to get the parents interested in politics in order to get better schools and cleaner, safer streets.

Meanwhile Eleanor's life reached a turning point. She fell in love! The young man was her fifth cousin, Franklin Delano Roosevelt.

Eleanor and Franklin had known each other since childhood. Franklin recalled how once he had carried her piggyback in the nursery. When she was fourteen, he had danced with her at a party. Then, shortly after her return from Allenswood, they had met by chance on a train. They talked and almost at once realized how much they liked each other.

For a time they met secretly. Then they attended parties together. Franklin—tall, strong, handsome—saw her as a person he could trust. He knew that she would not try to dominate him.

 But did he really love her? Would he always? She wrote to him, quoting a poem she knew: "Unless you can swear, *'For life, for death!'* . . . Oh, never call it loving!"

Franklin promised that his love was indeed "for life," and Eleanor agreed to marry him. It was the autumn of 1903. He was twenty-one. She was nineteen.

On March 17, 1905, Eleanor and Franklin were married. "Uncle Ted," by then president of the United States, was there to "give the bride away." It was sometimes said that the dynamic, energetic Theodore Roosevelt had to be "the bride at every wedding and the corpse at every funeral." And it was certainly true that day. Wherever the president went, the guests followed at his heels.

Before long Eleanor and Franklin found themselves standing all alone, deserted. Franklin seemed annoyed, but Eleanor didn't mind. She had found the ceremony deeply moving. And she stood next to her husband in a glow of idealism—very serious, very grave, very much in love. In May 1906 the couple's first child was born. During the next nine years Eleanor gave birth to five more babies, one of whom died in infancy. Still timid, shy, afraid of making mistakes, she found herself so busy that there was little time to think of her own drawbacks.

Still, looking back later on the early years of her marriage, Eleanor knew that she should have been a stronger person, especially in the handling of Franklin's mother, or, as they both called her, "Mammá." Too often Mammá made the decisions about such things as where they would live, how their home would be furnished, how the children would be disciplined. Eleanor and Franklin let her pay for things they could not afford—extra servants, vacations, doctor bills, clothing. She offered, and they accepted.

Before long, trouble developed in the relationship between Eleanor and Franklin. Serious, shy, easily embarrassed, Eleanor could not share Franklin's interests in golf and tennis. He enjoyed light talk and flirting with women. She could not

> E leanor threw herself into the war effort. Sometimes she worked fifteen and sixteen hours a day.

Mini Lesson **Vocabulary Strategy** **TEKS** 9D   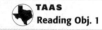 **TAAS** Reading Obj. 1

WORD FAMILIES
Instruction Discuss the meaning of *biography*. Point out that *bio* comes from a Greek word meaning "life" and *graph* comes from a Greek word meaning "writing." Tell students that when they know the meanings of word roots and parts, they will be able to understand the meanings of words that contain those parts. Other words based on the root *graph* include: *graphic, autograph, graphite,* and *telegraph.*

Application Have students work in pairs to find the meanings of these words: *graphic, autograph, graphite, telegraph.* Ask them to explain in their own words what each has to do with the original meaning ("to write"). Then ask them to use each word in a sentence.

 Use **Vocabulary Transparencies and Copymasters**, p. 25.

be lighthearted. So she stayed on the sidelines. Instead of losing her temper, she bottled up her anger and did not talk to him at all. As he used to say, she "clammed up." Her silence only made things worse, because it puzzled him. Faced with her coldness, her brooding silence, he only grew angrier and more distant.

Meanwhile Franklin's career in politics advanced rapidly. In 1910 he was elected to the New York State Senate. In 1913 President Wilson appointed him Assistant Secretary of the Navy—a powerful position in the national government, which required the Roosevelts to move to Washington, D.C.

In 1917 the United States entered World War I as an active combatant. Like many socially prominent women, Eleanor threw herself into the war effort. Sometimes she worked fifteen and sixteen hours a day. She made sandwiches for soldiers passing through the nation's capital. She knitted sweaters. She used Franklin's influence to get the Red Cross to build a recreation room for soldiers who had been shell-shocked in combat. . . .

In 1920 the Democratic Party chose Franklin as its candidate for vicepresident of the United States. Even though the Republicans won the election, Roosevelt became a well-known figure in national politics. All the time, Eleanor stood by his side, smiling, doing what was expected of her as a candidate's wife.

She did what was expected—and much more—in the summer of 1921 when disaster struck the Roosevelt family. While on vacation Franklin suddenly fell ill with infantile paralysis—polio—the horrible disease that each year used to kill or cripple thousands of children, and many adults as well. When Franklin became a victim of polio, nobody knew what caused the disease or how to cure it.

Franklin lived, but the lower part of his body remained paralyzed. For the rest of his life he never again had the use of his legs. He had to be lifted and carried from place to place. He had to wear heavy steel braces from his waist to the heels of his shoes.

His mother, as well as many of his advisers, urged him to give up politics, to live the life of a country gentleman on the Roosevelt estate at Hyde Park, New York. This time, Eleanor, calm and strong, stood up for her ideas. She argued that he should not be treated like a sick person, tucked away in the country, inactive, just waiting for death to come.

ACTIVE READING

EVALUATE What effect do you think Franklin's illness had in changing Eleanor's attitude toward her own role?

Franklin agreed. Slowly he recovered his health. His energy returned. In 1928 he was elected governor of New York. Then, just four years later, he was elected president of the United States.

Meanwhile Eleanor had changed. To keep Franklin in the public eye while he was recovering, she had gotten involved in politics herself. It was, she thought, her "duty." From childhood she had been taught "to do the thing that has to be done, the way it has to be done, when it has to be done."

With the help of Franklin's adviser Louis Howe, she made fund-raising speeches for the Democratic Party all around New York State. She helped in the work of the League of Women Voters, the Consumer's League, and the Foreign Policy Association. After becoming interested in the problems of working women, she gave time to the Women's Trade Union League (WTUL).

It was through the WTUL that she met a

WORDS	**brooding** (broo′dĭng) *adj.* full of worry; troubled **brood** *v.*	
TO	**combatant** (kəm-băt′nt) *n.* fighter	
KNOW	**prominent** (prŏm′ə-nənt) *adj.* well-known; widely recognized	

93

Customizing Instruction

Less Proficient Readers
Use these questions to highlight two major turning points in Eleanor's life: when she fell in love with and married Franklin and when Franklin was stricken by polio.
- What drew Eleanor and Franklin together?
  Possible Responses: They enjoyed talking with each other; Franklin felt Eleanor was someone he could trust.
- How did Eleanor change when Franklin was stricken by polio?
  Possible Responses: She stood up for her belief that he should not be treated like a sick person; she began to get involved in politics herself, traveling to places where he could not go and making speeches.

Students Acquiring English
1 Make sure students understand that to "give the bride away" is a custom wherein a relative from the bride's family presents her to the groom as a way of saying, "We trust you with our loved one." Also help them to understand that the quotation about Theodore Roosevelt—that he had to be "the bride at every wedding and the corpse at every funeral"—means that he had to be the center of attention, no matter what the occasion.

Multiple Learning Styles
Auditory Learners
Musical students might enjoy researching and sharing some of the songs from World War I and II that inspired patriotism and participation in the war efforts.

 Assessment Informal Assessment   **TEKS** 10E  **TAAS** Reading Obj. 2

ARRANGE DETAILS/EVENTS IN SEQUENTIAL ORDER
You can informally assess students' understanding of sequential order by asking them to list the events that have taken place in the selection so far in the order, or chronology, in which they occurred. Major events might be combined with some minor details.

RUBRIC
3 Full Accomplishment Response reflects an understanding of the sequential order of all the significant events and some details.

2 Substantial Accomplishment Response reflects an understanding of the sequential order of most of the significant events; a few events may be missing or out of order.

1 Little or Partial Accomplishment Response reflects little understanding of the sequential order of events or their importance.

group of remarkable women—women doing exciting work that made a difference in the world. They taught Eleanor about life in the slums. They awakened her hopes that something could be done to improve the condition of the poor. She dropped out of the "fashionable" society of her wealthy friends and joined the world of reform—social change.

For hours at a time Eleanor and her reformer friends talked with Franklin. They showed him the need for new laws: laws to get children out of the factories and into schools; laws to cut down the long hours that women worked; laws to get fair wages for all workers.

By the time that Franklin was sworn in as president, the nation was facing its deepest depression. One out of every four Americans was out of work, out of hope. At mealtimes people stood in lines in front of soup kitchens for something to eat. Mrs. Roosevelt herself knew of once-prosperous families who found themselves reduced to eating stale bread from thrift shops or traveling to parts of town where they were not known to beg for money from house to house.

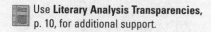

Eleanor worked in the charity kitchens, ladling out soup. She visited slums. She crisscrossed the country learning about the suffering of coal miners, shipyard workers, migrant farm workers, students, housewives—Americans caught up in the paralysis of the Great Depression. Since Franklin himself remained crippled, she became his eyes and ears, informing him of what the American people were really thinking and feeling.

Eleanor also was the president's conscience, personally urging on him some of the most compassionate, forward-looking laws of his presidency, including, for example, the National Youth Administration (NYA), which provided money to allow impoverished young people to stay in school.

She lectured widely, wrote a regularly syndicated[3] newspaper column, "My Day," and spoke frequently on the radio. She fought for equal pay for women in industry. Like no other First Lady up to that time, she became a link between the president and the American public.

Above all she fought against racial and religious prejudice. When Eleanor learned that the DAR (Daughters of the American Revolution)

would not allow the great black singer Marian Anderson to perform in their auditorium in Washington, D.C., she resigned from the organization. Then she arranged to have Miss Anderson sing in front of the Lincoln Memorial.

Similarly, when she entered a hall where, as often happened in those days, blacks and whites were seated in separate sections, she made it a point to sit with the blacks. Her example marked an important step in making the rights of blacks a matter of national priority.

On December 7, 1941, Japanese forces launched a surprise attack on the American naval base at Pearl Harbor, Hawaii, as well as on other American installations in the Pacific. The United States entered World War II, fighting not only against Japan but against the brutal dictators who then controlled Germany and Italy.

Eleanor helped the Red Cross raise money. She gave blood, sold war bonds. But she also did the unexpected. In 1943, for example, she visited barracks and hospitals on islands throughout the South Pacific. When she visited a hospital, she stopped at every bed. To each soldier she said

---

3. **syndicated:** sold to many newspapers for publication.

WORDS TO KNOW   **migrant** (mī′grənt) *adj.* moving from place to place
priority (prī-ôr′ĭ-tē) *n.* something that must receive attention first

94

N obody else had done so much to help raise the spirits of the men.

Eleanor Roosevelt talks animatedly as she has lunch with American soldiers in their mess hall, September 26, 1943. AP/Wide World Photos.

something special, something that a mother might say. Often, after she left, even battle-hardened men had tears in their eyes. Admiral Nimitz, who originally thought such visits would be a nuisance, became one of her strongest admirers. Nobody else, he said, had done so much to help raise the spirits of the men.

By spring 1945 the end of the war in Europe seemed near. Then, on April 12, a phone call brought Eleanor the news that Franklin Roosevelt, who had gone to Warm Springs, Georgia, for a rest, was dead.

As Eleanor later declared, "I think that sometimes I acted as his conscience. I urged him to take the harder path when he would have preferred the easier way. In that sense, I acted on occasion as a spur, even though the spurring was not always wanted or welcome.

"Of course," said Eleanor, "I loved him, and I miss him."

After Franklin's funeral, every day that Eleanor was home at Hyde Park, without fail, she placed flowers on his grave. Then she would stand very still beside him there.

With Franklin dead, Eleanor Roosevelt might have dropped out of the public eye, might have been remembered in the history books only as a footnote to the president's program of social reforms. Instead she found new strengths within herself, new ways to live a useful, interesting life—and to help others. Now, moreover, her successes were her own, not the result of being the president's wife.

In December 1945 President Harry S Truman invited her to be one of the American delegates going to London to begin the work of the United

D

Literary Analysis: INNER CONFLICT

A Why might Eleanor have hesitated when President Truman asked her to be a delegate to the soon-to-be-created United Nations?

Possible Response: Maybe she felt that, since she'd never held office, she should not be an official representative of the U.S. government.

Active Reading

CHRONOLOGICAL ORDER

B These paragraphs tell about Eleanor's life after her husband died. What words help students figure out the order in which the events took place?

Possible Responses: *Next, again, in December 1948, after*

LITERARY LINK

Doris Kearns Goodwin, born in 1943, has been a professor of government at Harvard University and served as a special consultant to President Johnson from 1969–1973. She has written several books on American politics. Goodwin won a 1995 Pulitzer Prize for *No Ordinary Time.* She is also an authority on baseball and a fan. Her 1997 book *Wait Till Next Year,* about the Brooklyn Dodgers, was a bestseller, and she served as a consultant for the popular PBS documentary *The History of Baseball.*

A Nations. Eleanor hesitated, but the president insisted. He said that the nation needed her; it was her duty. After that, Eleanor agreed.

In the beginning some of her fellow delegates from the United States considered her unqualified for the position, but after seeing her in action, they changed their minds.

It was Eleanor Roosevelt who, almost single-handedly, pushed through the United Nations General Assembly a resolution giving refugees from World War II the right *not* to return to their native lands if they did not wish to. The Russians angrily objected, but Eleanor's reasoning convinced wavering delegates. In a passionate speech defending the rights of the refugees she declared, "We [must] consider first the rights of man and what makes men more free— not governments, but man!"

B Next Mrs. Roosevelt helped draft the United Nations Declaration of Human Rights. The Soviets wanted the declaration to list the duties people owed to their countries. Again Eleanor insisted that the United Nations should stand for individual freedom—the rights of people to free speech, freedom of religion, and such human needs as health care and education. In December 1948, with the Soviet Union and its allies refusing to vote, the Declaration of Human Rights won approval of the UN General Assembly by a vote of forty-eight to zero.

Even after retiring from her post at the UN, Mrs. Roosevelt continued to travel. In places around the world she dined with presidents and kings. But she also visited tenement slums[4] in Bombay, India; factories in Yugoslavia; farms in Lebanon and Israel.

Everywhere she met people who were eager to greet her. Although as a child she had been

She would rather light a candle than curse the darkness.

brought up to be formal and distant, she had grown to feel at ease with people. They wanted to touch her, to hug her, to kiss her.

Eleanor's doctor had been telling her to slow down, but that was hard for her. She continued to write her newspaper column, "My Day," and to appear on television. She still began working at seven-thirty in the morning and often continued until well past midnight. Not only did she write and speak, she taught retarded children and raised money for health care of the poor.

As author Clare Boothe Luce put it, "Mrs. Roosevelt has done more good deeds on a bigger scale for a longer time than any woman who ever appeared on our public scene. No woman has ever so comforted the distressed or so distressed the comfortable."

Gradually, however, she was forced to withdraw from some of her activities, to spend more time at home.

On November 7, 1962, at the age of seventy-eight, Eleanor died in her sleep. She was buried in the rose garden at Hyde Park, alongside her husband.

Adlai Stevenson, the American ambassador to the United Nations, remembered her as "the First Lady of the World," as the person—male or female—most effective in working for the cause of human rights. As Stevenson declared, "She would rather light a candle than curse the darkness."

And perhaps, in sum, that is what the struggle for human rights is all about. ❖

---

4. **tenement slums:** parts of a city where poor people live in crowded, shabby buildings.

Teaching Options

✓ **Assessment Standardized Test Practice** TEKS 10F, K 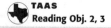 TAAS Reading Obj. 2, 3

RECALLING FACTS AND DETAILS THAT SUPPORT THE MAIN IDEA For some standardized tests, students will be asked to choose a fact or a detail that supports the main idea of a passage. To provide students with some help in choosing these facts and details, write the following on the chalkboard:

Which detail *best* supports the main idea of the passage on page 97, from *No Ordinary Time?*

A. Franklin didn't want to be bothered by Eleanor.
B. If Eleanor hadn't pressured him, Franklin would

not have done some of the things he did that made him a great president.
C. Franklin used to joke about how much Eleanor pressured him.
D. Franklin often dismissed Eleanor's ideas.

Instruct students to consider each choice, and point out that B is the best answer, because it tells *how* she went about making him a better president. The other answers provide information but do not support the main idea.

The Autobiography of Eleanor Roosevelt

from

by Eleanor Roosevelt

In the beginning, because I felt, as only a young girl can feel it, all the pain of being an ugly duckling, I was not only timid, I was afraid. Afraid of almost everything, I think: of mice, of the dark, of imaginary dangers, of my own inadequacy. My chief objective, as a girl, was to do my duty. This had been drilled into me as far back as I could remember. Not my duty as I saw it, but my duty as laid down for me by other people. It never occurred to me to revolt. Anyhow, my one overwhelming need in those days was to be approved, to be loved, and I did whatever was required of me, hoping it would bring me nearer to the approval and love I so much wanted.

As a young woman, my sense of duty remained as strict and rigid as it had been when I was a girl, but it had changed its focus. My husband and my children became the center of my life, and their needs were my new duty. I am afraid now that I approached this new obligation much as I had my childhood duties. I was still timid, still afraid of doing something wrong, of making mistakes, of not living up to the standards required by my mother-in-law, of failing to do what was expected of me.

As a result, I was so hidebound by duty that I became too critical, too much of a disciplinarian. I was so concerned with bringing up my children properly that I was not wise enough just to love them. Now, looking back, I think I would rather spoil a child a little and have more fun out of it.

No Ordinary Time

from

by Doris Kearns Goodwin

It was said jokingly in Washington during the war years that Roosevelt had a nightly prayer: "Dear God, please make Eleanor a little tired." But in the end, he often came around to her way of thinking. Labor adviser Anna Rosenberg had been one of those who criticized Eleanor's unceasing pressure on the president, but years later she changed her mind. "I remember him saying, 'We're not going to do that now. Tell Eleanor to keep away; I don't want to hear about that anymore.'

And then 2–3 weeks later he would say, 'Do you remember that thing Eleanor brought up? Better look into it, maybe there's something to it—I heard something to indicate that maybe she's right.' I'm not sure she would have had the opportunity to bring things to his attention unless she pressured him—I mean he was so involved and in retrospect it was never anything for herself. . . He would never have become the kind of president he was without her."

Cross Curricular Link **Social Studies**

WORLD WAR II: WOMEN ON THE HOME FRONT

During World War II, over a quarter of a million women served in the armed forces. But on the home front, the number of women involved in "war work" was much higher. More than 6 million women joined the 12 million already in the work force, but now many of them took on jobs that previously had been reserved for men. The men were off fighting the war, so somebody had to build the planes and work in the factories and run the farms. In fact, one of the enduring images of World War II is "Rosie the Riveter," the fictitious welder who showed that women were every bit as capable as men.

When the war ended and the men came home, many women left their jobs—but many didn't. Now that the world had seen what they could do, many continued to work in occupations where few women had worked before.

GUIDING STUDENT RESPONSE

Connect to the Literature

1. What Do You Think?
Possible Responses: *compassionate, strong, determined*

Comprehension Check
• She learned to be strong and to think for herself at Allenswood.
• She cooked and knitted for the soldiers and used her husband's influence to get them things they needed.
• She was an American delegate to the UN when it was just beginning.

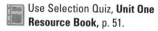 Use Selection Quiz, **Unit One Resource Book**, p. 51.

Think Critically

2. Possible Responses: her work for human rights and the UN; her bravery and outspokenness in the fight for racial equality; her work for women and the poor; her role as First Lady and political activist
3. Possible Response: She had been trained to do her duty as a child, so she chose to act dutifully later in life.
4. Possible Response: He meant that she would rather do something about a problem than just complain about it.
5. Students' charts should include the major events and some details from the selection.

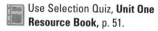 Use **Reading and Critical Thinking Transparencies**, p. 6, for additional support.

Literary Analysis

Paired Activity
Possible Responses: today; later; then; before; meanwhile.
Students might also recognize phrases that indicate chronological order such as "as a child," "When Eleanor was born," "in the early years of her life," and "when she was six" (all on page 89).

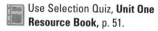 Use **Literary Analysis Transparencies**, p.10, for additional support.

Connect to the Literature

1. What Do You Think?
What words and phrases would you use to describe Eleanor Roosevelt?

Comprehension Check
• When did Roosevelt learn to be strong and think for herself?
• How did she help out during World War I?
• What was her role in the United Nations?

Think Critically

2. Which of Mrs. Roosevelt's accomplishments do you find most impressive? Why?

3. How do you think Eleanor's childhood experiences affected the choices she made later in life?

 THINK ABOUT
• how she felt about herself
• her goals and values
• what she says in the excerpt from her autobiography on page 97

4. Adlai Stevenson said that Mrs. Roosevelt "would rather light a candle than curse the darkness." What do you think he meant? Explain.

5. **ACTIVE READING** **CHRONOLOGICAL ORDER** How well were you able to record the **chronological order** of the events of Mrs. Roosevelt's life in your **READER'S NOTEBOOK**? Compare your chart with a classmate's. Were there details that you missed? If so, add them to your chart in the chronologically correct places.

Extend Interpretations

6. **COMPARING TEXTS** Reread the excerpts from *The Autobiography of Eleanor Roosevelt* and *No Ordinary Time* on page 97. Do they give you an impression of Eleanor Roosevelt different from the one you got from William Jay Jacobs's biography? Why or why not?

7. **Connect to Life** If Eleanor Roosevelt were alive today, which national and world issues do you think would concern her? To what person living today would you compare her?

Literary Analysis

BIOGRAPHY A **biography** is the story of a person's life told by someone else. In a good biography, the presentation of the subject's life is comprehensive and accurate. The **biographer** interviews the subject (if he or she can) and consults letters, journals, and other documents.

Biographers often focus on remarkable aspects of their subjects' lives, such as Eleanor Roosevelt's way of caring for others. Although they often present their subjects in a favorable light, biographers strive to balance their opinion of the person with the facts.

Paired Activity With a partner, go back through the selection and make a list of some of the signal words William Jay Jacobs uses to indicate the chronological order of the events of Eleanor Roosevelt's life. Discuss how these signal words help you understand the order in which events happened.

Signal Words
1. today
2. as
3. for a time
4. later
5.

Extend Interpretations

6. **Comparing Texts** Students may respond that the two excerpts support the impression of Eleanor Roosevelt they got from the Jacobs biography. In the autobiography, she discusses how shy and fearful she was, although she chides herself for being too dutiful. In the Goodwin excerpt, her legendary tirelessness and good sense are pointed out.

7. **Connect to Life** Students may respond that she would probably continue to work for human rights and oppose persecution, racism, hunger, and poverty throughout the world. Ask students to explain the basis of their comparisons.

Choices & CHALLENGES

Writing Options

Advice Column Eleanor Roosevelt wrote a regular advice column. Try your hand at giving some advice. Write a response to a teenager's question about how to build self-confidence. Place the response in your **Working Portfolio.**

Activities & Explorations

Time Line With a partner, make a list of important events in Mrs. Roosevelt's life. Then make a time line, including important details from the Across the Curriculum time line as well as details from your list. When you finish, discuss the following questions with a larger group:

- Which of Mrs. Roosevelt's challenges was the most difficult for her?
- Which event best reveals her character? How does it do so?
- Why do you think Jacobs chose to include the other events he presents?

Inquiry & Research

SOCIAL STUDIES **HUMAN RIGHTS**

Eleanor Roosevelt helped draft the first Universal Declaration of Human Rights. In 1968 the United Nations gave out its first awards in human rights to honor individuals who have taken a stand against oppression. Mrs. Roosevelt was among the first group of people chosen to receive the award. Identify another person who has received a human rights award. Look for information about the awards on the Internet, and then do some additional research to find out about that person.

 More Online: Research Starter www.mcdougallittell.com

Writing Options

Advice Column Student responses will vary but should include some of Eleanor's experiences that she felt worked for her, drawn from the selection. To get students started, bring in some advice columns from newspapers for them to use as models.

Activities & Explorations

Time Line Students' time lines should show a grasp of the most important details in the selection. Encourage them to present information in an informative, creative way. During discussions, students should show an understanding of Mrs. Roosevelt and the impact she had on the country.

Inquiry & Research

Students may wish to share their research in the form of an oral report on the award recipient or a poster or display showing the recipient and significant events of his or her life. They may also enjoy working in pairs to conduct a mock interview with the recipient.

 Use **Writing Transparencies,** pp. 47–48, for additional support.

Vocabulary and Spelling

EXERCISE: CONTEXT CLUES Write the Word to Know that best completes each sentence.

1. Because working for social justice was a _____ in Eleanor Roosevelt's life, she devoted a lot of time to it.
2. Eleanor Roosevelt was a _____ person, well known to the majority of Americans.
3. When the United States became an active _____ in World War I, Mrs. Roosevelt worked tirelessly for the war effort.
4. When Mrs. Roosevelt was troubled, her _____ silence made her seem difficult to be with.
5. Mrs. Roosevelt worked to better the lives of _____ farm workers, laborers who travel from place to place to find work.

EXERCISE B: -ANT/-ENT It is important to distinguish the spelling of the the suffixes *-ant* and *-ent.* They sound alike.

combat<u>ant</u>   effici<u>ent</u>
contest<u>ant</u>   defend<u>ant</u>
promin<u>ent</u>   suffici<u>ent</u>
adolesc<u>ent</u>   attend<u>ant</u>
inhabit<u>ant</u>   anci<u>ent</u>

1. Which prefix is added to complete words?
2. Which prefix is added to roots?
3. Which words have *ci* before *-ent*?
4. Write seven sentences, each of which uses one of the spelling words.

Spelling Handbook, p. R86

| WORDS TO KNOW | 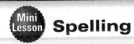 brooding | combatant | migrant | priority | prominent |

Vocabulary and Spelling

Exercise A	Exercise B
1. priority	1. ant-
2. prominent	2. ent-
3. combatant	3. ancient, efficient,
4. brooding	sufficient
5. migrant	4. Answers will vary.

Mini Lesson **Spelling** **TEKS** 16C   **TAAS** Writing Obj. 3, 7

WORDS ENDING IN -ANCE/-ANT

Instruction Explain to students that they should spell an adjective with *-ant* if they can trace it to a noun ending in *-ance.* Similarly, they should spell an adjective with *-ent* if they can trace it to a noun ending in *-ence.* Provide these examples.

Noun	Adjective
prominence	prominent
dominance	dominant
existence	existent

Exercise Have students complete this chart. Then have them look for more words with these endings to add to their personal word lists.

Noun	Adjective
	eminent
instance	
elegance	
permanence	
	fragrant

Answers
eminence
instant
elegant
permanent
fragrance

Use **Unit One Resource Book,** p. 50 for more practice.

Grammar in Context

WRITING EXERCISE
Possible Responses:

1. Eleanor Roosevelt seems courageous.
2. Eleanor's friends were proud of her.
3. During the depression, many families were very poor.

CONNECT TO THE LITERATURE
was grim; was stingy

William Jay Jacobs

In addition to being a writer, Jacobs has taught history and social studies in public schools in Darien, Connecticut. Before that, he taught at several colleges and universities.

Author Activity

Encourage each student to read the biography of someone whom they find to be particularly interesting or admirable. As they read, they should think about what special qualities of the person Jacobs has captured particularly well.

Grammar in Context: Predicate Adjectives

Jacobs states Eleanor Roosevelt's childhood fears through a series of **predicate adjectives.**

> Feeling unwanted, Eleanor **became** shy and withdrawn. She **was** afraid of the dark, afraid of animals, afraid of other children, afraid of being scolded, afraid of strangers, afraid that people would not like her.

A **predicate adjective** follows a **linking verb,** such as *be, seem, become,* or *feel,* and describes the subject.

Punctuation Tip: When you use a series of predicate adjectives, with or without a coordinating conjunction (*and, or, but*), separate them with commas: *Eleanor felt* **plain looking, ordinary,** *and* **homely.**

WRITING EXERCISE Complete each sentence with a linking verb and a predicate adjective. Underline the predicate adjective.

Example: *Original* As a child, Eleanor
Rewritten As a child, Eleanor felt <u>uncomfortable</u> about her appearance.

1. Eleanor Roosevelt
2. Eleanor's friends
3. During the depression, many families

Connect to the Literature Turn to page 90. Reread the paragraph beginning, "For most of the time Eleanor's life was grim." What linking verbs followed by predicate adjectives do you find in the paragraph?

<u>Grammar Handbook</u> The Sentence and Its Parts, p. R55

"I saw [Eleanor Roosevelt] as a woman of courage."

William Jay Jacobs
born 1933

Strong Role Model William Jay Jacobs admires Eleanor Roosevelt for her strength of character: "The more I learned about Eleanor Roosevelt, the more I saw her as a woman of courage. She turned her pain to strength." Jacobs believes that young people need role models like Eleanor Roosevelt—historical figures who faced tests and persisted. He says that by writing biographies he is "able to reach a very special audience: young people searching for models, trying to understand themselves."

Biography as Inspiration Jacobs has written many biographies for young people, including biographies of Hernando Cortés, Edgar Allan Poe, Abraham Lincoln, and Winston Churchill. Jacobs says that perhaps his primary task in writing biographies for young people "is to introduce them to that great reservoir of recorded history from which our civilization has drawn inspiration."

AUTHOR ACTIVITY
History for Today Read another biography by Jacobs, keeping in mind his claim that the lives of historical figures can inspire people today. Think about how the subject of the biography might serve as a role model to others. Share your ideas with classmates.

Teaching Options

 Grammar TEKS 17C TAAS Writing Obj. 6

PREDICATE NOUNS, ADJECTIVES, AND PRONOUNS The words that follow linking verbs and modify or describe the subject may be adjectives, nouns, or pronouns. (Predicate nouns, adjectives, and pronouns are also called complements.) Write the following sentences on the board and point out the predicate words:
Eleanor was <u>unhappy</u>. (adjective)
Eleanor was Franklin's <u>wife</u>. (noun)
A fine fellow is <u>he</u>. (pronoun)

Exercise Have students complete each of the following sentences with the type of predicate word indicated. (*Possible answers are given.*)

1. Franklin D. Roosevelt was _____. (noun; *president*)
2. When she was young, Eleanor was very _____. (adjective; *shy*)
3. The First Lady was _____. (pronoun; *she*)

4. The family thought Franklin was _____. (adjective; *important*)
5. Theodore Roosevelt was Eleanor's favorite _____. (noun; *uncle*)

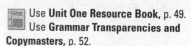 Use **Unit One Resource Book,** p. 49.
Use **Grammar Transparencies and Copymasters,** p. 52.

 Use McDougal Littell's *Language Network,* Chapters 1 and 3, for more instruction and practice in predicate nouns, adjectives, and pronouns.

". . . the thing that seems most wrong with the world to me right now is that there are so many people with no homes."

Homeless

Essay by ANNA QUINDLEN

 See the Skills Trace at the beginning of the unit for information on TEKS covered in this lesson.

Connect to Your Life

This selection tells you about homelessness in America. What do you know about homelessness? What do you want to know? With your classmates, make a chart like this one and fill in the first two columns. Complete the third after you read the selection.

What We Know About Homelessness	What We Want to Know	What We Learned

Build Background

CONNECT TO CURRENT EVENTS

Every night in cities across the United States, people without homes sleep on sidewalks, in bus stations, or in cardboard boxes or other temporary shelters. It is hard to get an exact count, but estimates of the nation's homeless population range from 250,000 to 3 million.

People become homeless for a variety of reasons. A commonly held image of the homeless is that they are bums—mainly older men with drinking problems who sleep in doorways. In the late 1990s, however, it was determined that about 40 percent of the people without homes were women, children, and families.

WORDS TO KNOW **Vocabulary Preview**
compassionate   enfeebled   rummage
crux   legacy

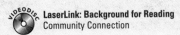 **LaserLink: Background for Reading** Community Connection

Focus Your Reading

LITERARY ANALYSIS FIRST-PERSON POINT OF VIEW A story or essay told from the **first-person point of view** is told with first-person pronouns: *I, me, we, us.* The narrator, or teller, of the story or essay is therefore also a participant in the action. Notice the first-person pronoun in this sentence from "Homeless":

> *I'm not simply talking about shelter from the elements, or three square meals a day. . . . I'm talking about a home.*

By using a first-person point of view in this personal essay, Quindlen shows her emotional closeness to the people and events she describes.

ACTIVE READING IDENTIFYING AUTHOR'S PURPOSE

Authors write for many reasons, including the following:
- to entertain
- to inform or explain
- to express an opinion
- to persuade

READER'S NOTEBOOK As you read this essay, jot down the purposes Quindlen may have had for writing it.

Detail	Purpose
Quindlen describes Ann, whom she met in the Port Authority Bus Terminal.	to inform
Quindlen says: "Home is where the heart is."	to express an opinion

---

Objectives
1. understand and appreciate a **personal essay (Literary Analysis)**
2. understand the role of **first-person point of view** in a personal essay **(Literary Analysis)**
3. identify the **author's purpose (Active Reading)**

Summary
Anna Quindlen, who loves her own home "with a ferocity totally out of proportion to its appearance or location," ponders the meaning of home and homelessness as she interviews Ann, a woman living in New York City's Port Authority Bus Terminal. Ann says that she is not homeless and shows Quindlen treasured photos of a house she once lived in. Quindlen realizes that a home provides not only shelter, but also privacy, security, and pride of ownership.

Thematic Link
Quindlen makes a discovery about the concept of home and about the people whom society calls "the homeless."

5-Minute Warm-Up

Daily Language SkillBuilder **TEKS** 16B, 17C

Have students **proofread** the display sentences on page 13j and write them correctly. The sentences also appear on Transparency 3 of **Grammar Transparencies and Copymasters.**

Mini Lesson Preteaching Vocabulary

If you would like to preteach the WORDS TO KNOW for this selection, use the Mini Lesson, p. 102.

Reading and Analyzing

Literary Analysis
FIRST-PERSON POINT OF VIEW

 A Have students search the first paragraph to locate the pronouns that refer to the narrator. Remind students that these pronouns show that the writer is using the first-person point of view. This point of view allows readers to know the writer's thoughts and feelings. Ask how this style differs from the way someone might write an encyclopedia article.

Possible Response: The pronouns include *we, I,* and *me.* Encyclopedia articles contain only facts and not the writers' feelings.

Use **Unit One Resource Book,** p. 54, for more practice.

Active Reading
IDENTIFYING AUTHOR'S PURPOSE

Ask students to identify facts in the first paragraph that answer the questions *who, where, when,* and *why.* Ask what other information they learned in the first two paragraphs. Discuss how the amount of factual information can give clues to an author's purpose.

Use **Unit One Resource Book,** p. 53, for more practice.

Literary Analysis: DESCRIPTION

 B Point out that Quindlen provided a clear description of Ann's house. Ask students what that description adds to their view of Ann.

Possible Responses: It shows that she once lived in an ordinary home, just like many other people. It shows a connection between Ann and other people that the students may know.

Teaching Options

by Anna Quindlen

Homeless

Woman in New York City.
Copyright © 1982 Christopher Morris/Black Star.

 Mini Lesson **Preteaching Vocabulary**   TEKS 6C, 9C   TAAS Reading Obj. 1

LOCATE WORD MEANINGS AND PRONUNCIATIONS
Instruction Call students' attention to the list of WORDS TO KNOW on page 101. Discuss why these words might be singled out as being words students should know.
Application Have students look through the selection to find the meaning of each word in the WORDS TO KNOW. Point out, if necessary, where the definitions appear.
• Ask volunteers to pronounce each word and read its definition.

• Ask a volunteer to find each word in the article and to read aloud the sentence that contains it.
• Have students take turns making up sentences that contain the words.
Have students discuss how the information in WORDS TO KNOW differs from that in the numbered footnotes.

Use **Unit One Resource Book,** p. 55, for more exercises. Use **Vocabulary Transparencies and Copymasters,** p. 26, for additional support.

Her name was Ann, and we met in the Port Authority Bus Terminal several Januarys ago. I was doing a story on homeless people. She said I was wasting my time talking to her; she was just passing through, although she'd been passing through for more than two weeks. To prove to me that this was true, she rummaged through a tote bag and a manila envelope and finally unfolded a sheet of typing paper and brought out her photographs.

They were not pictures of family, or friends, or even a dog or cat, its eyes brown-red in the flashbulb's light. They were pictures of a house. It was like a thousand houses in a hundred towns, not suburb, not city, but somewhere in between, with aluminum siding and a chainlink fence, a narrow driveway running up to a one-car garage and a patch of backyard. The house was yellow. I looked on the back for a date or a name, but neither was there. There was no need for discussion. I knew what she was trying to tell me, for it was something I had often felt. She was not adrift, alone, anonymous, although her bags and her raincoat with the grime shadowing its creases had made me believe she was. She had a house, or at least once upon a time had had one. Inside were curtains, a couch, a stove, potholders. You are where you live. She was somebody.

I've never been very good at looking at the big picture, taking the global view, and I've always been a person with an overactive sense of place, the legacy of an Irish grandfather. So it is natural that the thing that seems most wrong with the world to me right now is that there are so many people with no homes. I'm not simply talking about shelter from the elements, or three square meals a day or a mailing address to which the welfare[1] people can send the check—although I know that all these are important for survival. I'm talking about a home, about precisely those kinds of feelings that have wound up in cross-stitch and French knots on samplers[2] over the years.

Home is where the heart is. There's no place like it. I love my home with a ferocity totally out of proportion to its appearance or location. I love dumb things about it: the hot-water heater, the plastic rack you drain dishes in, the roof over my head, which occasionally leaks. And yet it is precisely those dumb things that make it what it is—a place of certainty, stability, predictability, privacy, for me and for my family. It is where I live. What more can you say about a place than that? That is everything.

Yet it is something that we have been edging away from gradually during my lifetime and the lifetimes of my parents and grandparents. There was a time when where you lived often was where you worked and where you grew the food you ate and even where you were buried. When that era passed, where you lived at least was where your parents had lived and where you would live with your children

She had a house, or at least once upon a time had had one.

---

1. **welfare:** program of financial aid provided to people in need by the government.

2. **in cross-stitch and French knots on samplers:** spelled out in fancy stitching on embroidered decorations.

WORDS TO KNOW
rummage (rŭm′ĭj) v. to search thoroughly by moving the contents about
legacy (lĕg′ə-sē) n. something handed down from an ancestor or from the past

Active Reading

IDENTIFYING AUTHOR'S PURPOSE

Ask students what information the author provides about what goes on inside a shelter.

Possible Responses: People may be locked in; there may be violence; they sleep on cots; they eat oatmeal; they are given special soap to kill bugs.

Use **Reading and Critical Thinking Transparencies,** p. 4, for additional support.

Literary Analysis: TONE

Remind students that authors have a tone, a way of speaking that reveals their attitude toward the subject. Have students discuss this author's tone towards people without homes. Encourage them to support their answers with details from the text.

Possible Responses: The tone is sympathetic. The author mentions the people's pain and what they lack.

Literary Analysis

FIRST-PERSON POINT OF VIEW

Ask students how the last two paragraphs differ from the two that came before. How does the first-person point of view affect the ending?

Possible Responses: The first two paragraphs focus on the homeless, while the last two focus on the thoughts, feelings, and ideas of the writer. The point of view allows readers to see those without homes in the same way that the narrator does.

Use **Literary Analysis Transparencies,** p. 22, for additional support.

---

when you became <u>enfeebled</u>. Then, suddenly, where you lived was where you lived for three years, until you could move on to something else and something else again.

And so we have come to something else again, to children who do not understand what it means to go to their rooms because they have never had a room, to men and women whose fantasy is a wall they can paint a color of their own choosing, to old people reduced to sitting on molded plastic chairs, their skin blue-white in the lights of a bus station, who pull pictures of houses out of their bags. Homes have stopped being homes. Now they are real estate.

People find it curious that those without homes would rather sleep sitting up on benches or huddled in doorways than go to shelters. Certainly some prefer to do so because they are emotionally ill, because they have been locked in before and they are damned if they will be locked in again. Others are afraid of the violence and trouble they may find there. But some seem to want something that is not available in shelters, and they will not compromise, not for a cot, or oatmeal, or a shower with special soap that

kills the bugs. "One room," a woman with a baby who was sleeping on her sister's floor, once told me, "painted blue." That was the <u>crux</u> of it; not size or location, but pride of ownership. Painted blue.

This is a difficult problem, and some wise and <u>compassionate</u> people are working hard at it. But in the main I think we work around it, just as we walk around it when it is lying on the sidewalk or sitting in the bus terminal—the problem, that is. It has been customary to take people's pain and lessen our own participation in it by turning it into an issue, not a collection of human beings. We turn an adjective into a noun: the poor, not poor people; the homeless, not Ann or the man who lives in the box or the woman who sleeps on the subway grate.

Sometimes I think we would be better off if we forgot about the broad strokes and concentrated on the details. Here is a woman without a bureau. There is a man with no mirror, no wall to hang it on. They are not the homeless. They are people who have no homes. No drawer that holds the spoons. No window to look out upon the world. My God. That is everything. ❖

They are not the homeless. They are people who have no homes.

WORDS
TO
KNOW

enfeebled (ĕn-fē'bəld) *adj.* deprived of strength; made weak **enfeeble** *v.*
crux (krŭks) *n.* the most important point or element
compassionate (kəm-păsh'ə-nĭt) *adj.* having sympathy for the sufferings of others

104

✓ **Assessment** **Informal Assessment**

 TEKS 10F, 11C   TAAS Reading Obj. 3   TAAS Writing

IDENTIFYING THE MAIN IDEA AND SUPPORTING DETAILS You can informally assess whether students can determine the text's main ideas and how those ideas are supported with details by having them summarize various paragraphs of the selection. Begin by asking volunteers to tell in a sentence or two what each section is about. Then have them locate details in each paragraph that prove, or support, their statements.

RUBRIC

3 Full Accomplishment Response reflects a full understanding of the main idea of each paragraph and how details support it.

2 Substantial Accomplishment Response shows that students generally understand the paragraph but are unable to restate the main idea concisely.

1 Little or Partial Accomplishment Response shows little distinction between important and trivial ideas.

BUMS IN THE ATTIC
from THE HOUSE ON MANGO STREET
by Sandra Cisneros

I want a house on a hill like the ones with the gardens where Papa works. We go on Sundays, Papa's day off. I used to go. I don't anymore. You don't like to go out with us, Papa says. Getting too old? Getting too stuck-up, says Nenny. I don't tell them I am ashamed—all of us staring out the window like the hungry. I am tired of looking at what we can't have. When we win the lottery . . . Mama begins, and then I stop listening.

People who live on hills sleep so close to the stars they forget those of us who live too much on earth. They don't look down at all except to be content to live on hills. They have nothing to do with last week's garbage or fear of rats. Night comes. Nothing wakes them but the wind.

One day I'll own my own house, but I won't forget who I am or where I came from. Passing bums will ask, Can I come in? I'll offer them the attic, ask them to stay,

because I know how it is to be without a house.

Some days after dinner, guests and I will sit in front of a fire. Floorboards will squeak upstairs. The attic grumble.

Rats? they'll ask.

Bums, I'll say, and I'll be happy.

River Under the Roof (1985), Friedensreich Hundertwasser. Japanese woodcut, work #763A. Copyright © 1995 Harel, Vienna, Austria.

This piece reflects some of the ideas in the main selection and is suggested for students' independent reading. Optional discussion questions follow.

1. What is the narrator's view of her or his situation?
   Possible Responses: tired of it, ashamed, embarrassed, resentful
2. What does the narrator believe his or her future will be like?
   Answer: She or he will own a house, help the homeless, and be happy.
3. How do the narrator's views on owning a home compare to Ann's?
   Possible Response: It is important to both of them; it gives them pride and pleasure.

Sandra Cisneros

For Sandra Cisneros, writing is a way to deal with the poverty, loneliness, and instability she faced as a child growing up in Chicago. In this book, she combined more than forty short narratives that she called "a cross between poetry and fiction." Today, she is a prolific writer who has created a unique style, blending her mother's working-class English and her father's gentle Spanish.

 Mini Lesson **Viewing and Representing** 📋 **TEKS 23B**

River Under the Roof
by Friedensreich Hundertwasser, 1955

ART APPRECIATION This complex woodcut, created in 17 different colors, is a modern version of a centuries-old art form.

Instruction To help students compare and contrast visual media with a written story, explain that artists show the importance or lack of importance of objects by placement, use of symbols, and size, among other things.

Application Ask students what the size and placement of the house suggests about its impor-

tance to the artist. Does the house have the same importance to the writer? Ask students how the visual artist and the writer both focused attention on the upper floor of the house.

Possible Response: Since the house in the picture is large and central, it is as important to the artist as it is to the writer. The artist used a rainbow to draw attention to the upper floor; the writer mentioned the attic in the title and several times in the piece.

Connect to the Literature

1. Responses will vary. Students may think beyond what was written. Encourage a variety of responses.

Comprehension Check
• Possible Responses: It makes her feel important, like "somebody"; it reminds her of a happier time; it helps her to set a goal about where she would like to be.
• It is a place where she is able to choose how she wants to live. It is everything.
• Some are afraid of being locked in or having harm done to them; others prefer to make their own homes with their own schedules.

 Use Selection Quiz, **Unit One Resource Book,** p. 58.

Think Critically

2. Possible Response: Students may say that they now realize that people without homes are individuals.

3. Possible Responses: to inform, to express an opinion

 Use **Reading and Critical Thinking Transparencies,** p. 4, for additional support.

4. Possible Response: By focusing on Ann's situation, Quindlen helped her readers understand that people who are homeless are like anybody else; therefore, she accomplished her purpose.

5. Possible Response: Students might agree with Quindlen and give examples.

Literary Analysis

First-Person Point of View Students' sentences should contain such first-person pronouns as *I, me, we,* and *my.*

 Use **Literary Analysis Transparencies,** p. 22, for additional support.

Connect to the Literature

1. **What Do You Think?** What is the main concern you had when you finished reading "Homeless"?

Comprehension Check
• What was Ann trying to tell Quindlen by showing her photographs of a house?
• What does Quindlen's home mean to her?
• Why do many homeless people prefer not to live in shelters?

Think Critically

2. Did reading this selection change any of your thoughts or opinions about homelessness? Explain your answer.

3. **ACTIVE READING** **AUTHOR'S PURPOSE** Look over the chart you made in your **READER'S NOTEBOOK.** What were Quindlen's purposes for writing this essay? Which do you think was her main purpose?

4. In your opinion, did Quindlen accomplish her main purpose for writing the essay? Why or why not?

THINK ABOUT
• why Quindlen focused on only one homeless person
• why she described her own home and her feelings about it
• the last sentence of the essay

5. What is your reaction to Quindlen's opinion that "home is where the heart is"? Explain your response.

Extend Interpretations

6. **COMPARING TEXTS** Reread Sandra Cisneros's anecdote on page 105. How do Cisneros's views on owning a home compare with Ann's?

7. **Connect to Life** Review the chart you created for Connect to Your Life on page 101. Do you have any questions the selection didn't answer? Discuss them with your classmates.

Literary Analysis

FIRST-PERSON POINT OF VIEW

"Homeless" is a personal essay told from a **first-person point of view**—that is, the author uses the first-person pronouns *I, me, we,* and *us* and is a participant in the events described. An essay told from a first-person point of view usually gives the reader a strong sense of the writer's personality and opinions. In "Homeless," the reader sees Ann through the the writer's eyes and learns the writer's opinions about the plight of Ann and other homeless people: "Homes have stopped being homes. Now they are real estate."

Cooperative Learning Activity
Working with a partner, go back through the essay and locate six sentences that contain first-person pronouns. Make a list of the sentences. When you are done, discuss the following questions with a larger group:
• Why did Anna Quindlen focus on only one homeless person?
• Did Quindlen change your mind about the homeless?
• What was the author's purpose for writing the essay?

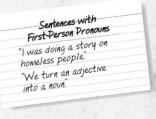

Sentences with First-Person Pronouns
"I was doing a story on homeless people."
"We turn an adjective into a noun."

Extend Interpretations

6. **Comparing Texts** Possible Responses: Both authors express the idea that having a nice home gives a person a sense of pride and identity; it's important for everyone to have his or her own home.

7. **Connect to Life** Responses may vary. If students don't have a sense of what is being done in support of the homeless, suggest that they contact their city or town hall and do some research.

Writing Options

1. Letter What is your response to this essay? Write Quindlen a letter in which you express your feelings and suggest solutions to the problem of homelessness. Place the letter in your **Working Portfolio**.

2. Definition One of the dictionary definitions of home is "a dwelling place." One of the ways Quindlen defines home is as a place "where the heart is." What does home mean to you? Write a paragraph explaining your definition.

Writing Handbook
See p. R35: Explanatory Writing.

Activities & Explorations

1. Drawing or Sculpture Quindlen lists three "dumb things" that she loves about her home. What dumb things do you love about your home? Make a drawing or sculpture of one of those things and explain why it is important to you. ~ **ART**

2. Interview Ask someone who works in a homeless shelter to tell you about the services available for homeless people in your area. Find out how many people use the shelter. Ask what is being done to help them find homes of their own. Share your findings with your classmates.
~ **SPEAKING AND LISTENING**

Inquiry & Research

Helping the Homeless In 1987 Congress passed the Homeless Assistance Act, providing almost a billion dollars for relief programs, including shelters, to help homeless people. Use reference materials, including the Internet, to find out more about what federal, state, or local governments are doing to help people without homes. Share your findings in an oral report to classmates.

Vocabulary in Action

EXERCISE A: WORD MEANING Substitute a Word to Know for each underlined word or phrase in the sentences below, or rewrite as necessary.

1. Many people see providing affordable housing as the <u>most significant part</u> of the battle against homelessness.

2. Food and clothing drives can help homeless people, who sometimes need to <u>search</u> through garbage cans for food and supplies.

3. Homeless people can become <u>weak</u> when they lack adequate clothing, food, housing, and medical attention.

4. Quindlen says that her parents and grandparents <u>handed down</u> many family traditions to her.

5. Many <u>kind and genuinely concerned</u> people treat homeless people with understanding and dignity.

EXERCISE B Present a speech about homeless people that contains at least three of the vocabulary words.

Building Vocabulary
For an in-depth study of learning and remembering new words, see p. 473.

WORDS TO KNOW	compassionate crux enfeebled legacy rummage

Writing Options

1. **Letter** Students' letters should contain both their responses to the piece or some aspect of it and their suggestions for solutions to the problem of homelessness. To get students started on this assignment, have them make two lists: one that identifies their feelings and another that lists possible solutions.

2. **Definition** Before students write their definitions, suggest that they start by completing the sentence, "Home is . . . ." This will keep them focused.

Use **Writing Transparencies**, p. 7, for additional support.

Activities and Explorations

1. **Drawing or Sculpture** First, have students discuss what Quindlen means by "dumb things." Then, after they have finished their artwork, allow time for them to share their drawings with the rest of the class.

2. **Interview** Before students conduct their interviews, have them prepare a written list of questions. Then have them decide how they will record the answers and what equipment they will need to take to the interview in order to do this.

Inquiry & Research

Helping the Homeless To extend this activity, have students combine the results of their research to create a booklet or brochure about available resources for people without homes. This publication could be available at community suppers, shelters, or similar sites.

 Use **Writing Transparencies**, p. 51, for additional support.

Vocabulary in Action

Exercise A
1. crux
2. rummage
3. enfeebled
4. Quindlen says that family traditions are her parents' and grandparents' legacy
5. compassionate

Exercise B
Speeches will differ, but should use three words from Words to Know.

Grammar in Context

WRITING EXERCISE
Possible Responses

1. I really <u>appreciate</u> my <u>home</u>.

2. The author <u>wrote</u> an important <u>story</u>.

3. Her tote bag <u>held</u> an <u>envelope</u>.

4. Her house <u>had</u> a narrow <u>driveway</u>.

Anna Quindlen

Anna Quindlen has received a great deal of attention for her columns in *The New York Times.* About her work as a journalist, she said, "I think of a column as having a conversation with a person that it just so happens I can't see."

Author Activity

Before students create summaries, encourage them to first skim the entire column and try to understand its general meaning. Then have them read the selection carefully, looking for its main ideas and supporting details. Have them take written notes, which they can refer to during their oral summaries.

 Use **Writing Transparencies,** p. 51, for additional support.

Grammar in Context: Direct Objects

Notice how the **direct objects** in these sentences from "Homeless" communicate important information about the subject of the sentence.

> She had a house, or at least once upon a time she had one. You are where you live. She was somebody. . . . Home is where the heart is. I love my home with a ferocity totally out of proportion to its appearance or location.

All sentences need a **subject** and a **verb.** Some sentences need a **direct object** after the verb in order to express a complete thought:

> She had a dream.

WRITING EXERCISE Read these incomplete sentences. Underline the verb once. Then complete each sentence by writing a logical direct object. Underline the direct object twice.
Example: *Original* Some homeless people fear
Rewritten Some homeless people <u>fear</u> <u>violence</u>.

1. I really appreciate
2. The author wrote
3. Her tote bag held
4. Her house had

Grammar Handbook The Sentence and Its Parts, p. R55

"Real life is in the dishes."

Anna Quindlen
born 1953

Cub Reporter After graduating from Barnard College in 1974, Anna Quindlen published her first story and started working as a newspaper reporter. In 1981 she was offered the "About New York" column in the *New York Times.* She has called writing that column her dream job, because she "got to write about anything": "I'd go to a cop's funeral or I'd go to Coney Island and talk to the homeless people. . . I developed a voice of my own. . . and I developed the ability to come up with column ideas."

Prize-Winning Columnist After the birth of her first child, Quindlen began writing a column

about her own family, called "Life in the 30s." In her next column, "Public & Private," she tackled public and political issues on the opinion-editorial page. In 1992 she won a Pulitzer Prize for commentary. Quindlen has also published a children's book and three novels about families. According to her, families mirror society. "Real life is in the dishes," she says.

AUTHOR ACTIVITY

Something in Common To readers of her newspaper columns and novels, Anna Quindlen is known for her personal concern about social issues. Find and read one of the columns in her collection *Thinking Out Loud* or *Living Out Loud.* Present an oral summary of the column to your classmates.

 LaserLink: Background for Reading
Social Studies Connection

Teaching Options

Mini Lesson Grammar TEKS 17C   TAAS Writing Obj. 6

DIRECT AND INDIRECT OBJECTS
Instruction Tell students that not all verbs have direct and indirect objects. A verb that has a direct object is called a *transitive verb.* A verb that has no object is called an *intransitive verb.* Sometimes, a verb is transitive in one sentence and intransitive in another.
Transitive: I <u>read</u> that book. (book is the direct object)
Intransitive: After dinner, I <u>read</u>.
Do not think that a verb is transitive only because another word follows it. That word

could be an adverb instead of an object. If the word tells how, where, when, or to what extent, it's an adverb. If it tells what or whom, it's a direct object.
Application Work with a partner to determine whether the verb in each sentence is transitive or intransitive. To do this, first decide whether the word in italics is a direct object or an adverb.

1. Quindlen loves her *home. (transitive)*
2. Some people feared *violence* in a shelter. *(transitive)*

3. One woman daydreamed *happily.* *(intransitive)*
4. No drawer holds her *clothes. (transitive)*
5. Quindlen writes *thoughtfully. (intransitive)*

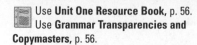 Use **Unit One Resource Book,** p. 56.
Use **Grammar Transparencies and Copymasters,** p. 56.

 Use McDougal Littell's *Language Network,* Chapter 4, for more instruction and practice in direct and indirect objects.

"And then we saw it. The wall."

The War of the Wall

Short Story by TONI CADE BAMBARA

Connect to Your Life

Hanging Out Is there a place in your neighborhood that seems to belong to young people? Perhaps it is a park or a schoolyard or a theater. What's special about the place? Why is it important to young people? Has it always been a hangout? What does the place mean to the rest of the community?

Build Background

CONNECT TO ART Murals are large pictures or scenes painted on or applied to a wall. Early artists drew on the walls of caves. In the 1990s, hundreds of paintings—believed to have been made about 30,000 years ago—were found on the walls of caves in southern France.

In the United States, during the hard times of the 1930s and the 1940s, a murals program was launched by the federal government. Artists in need were commissioned to paint murals in hundreds of new post offices. In Texas, for example, murals were completed in more than 60 post offices, bringing art directly to the people.

At the same time in Mexico, artists such as Diego Rivera, José Clemente Orozco, and David Siqueiros were representing Mexican life and history on the walls of public buildings.

In the 1960s, African-American artists began a "wall of respect" movement. These artists painted murals on walls in their communities as symbols of their respect for the neighborhoods.

WORDS TO KNOW Vocabulary Preview
beckon   drawl   inscription   liberation   scheme

LaserLinks: Background for Reading
Personal Connection

Focus Your Reading

LITERARY ANALYSIS CLIMAX The turning point in a plot, the moment of greatest intensity and interest, is called the **climax.** Usually, the climax of a story occurs near the end of the plot. It often involves an important event, decision, or discovery that affects the outcome of the story. As you read "The War of the Wall," look for the event, decision, or discovery that marks the climax of the story.

ACTIVE READING CAUSE AND EFFECT Two events have a **cause and effect** relationship when one event brings about the other. The event that happens first in time is the **cause;** the event that comes afterward is the **effect.** However, the effect may sometimes be *stated* before the cause.

READER'S NOTEBOOK As you read, jot down on a chart examples of causes and their effects.

Cause	Effect
A stranger was painting the wall.	Lou and the narrator were angry because they felt that the wall is *their* wall.

 See the Skills Trace at the beginning of the unit for information on TEKS covered in this lesson.

OVERVIEW

 This selection is included in the **Grade 7 InterActive Reader.**

Objectives
1. understand and appreciate a **short story (Literary Analysis)**
2. understand the role of **climax** in a short story **(Literary Analysis)**
3. use the active reading strategy of recognizing **cause and effect (Active Reading)**

Summary
When the narrator and Lou discover a stranger preparing to paint a mural on their neighborhood wall, they try a variety of tactics to stop her. The wall is special to the boys and to the neighborhood—the children have even honored a friend who died in Vietnam, Jimmy Lyons, by carving his name in the wall. Unable to discourage the artist, the boys later plot to deface the mural by spraying it with epoxy paint. As they approach the finished mural, they find the whole neighborhood admiring its depictions of African-American leaders and local adults and children, including Lou and the narrator. Jimmy Lyons's name appears in a painted rainbow, and the artist's inscription reveals that she is his cousin.

Thematic Link
The narrator and Lou make an important discovery when they see themselves in the mural that they had tried to sabotage. The mural shows the artist's understanding of the neighborhood and of the boys and links their lives to people who have gone before them.

5-Minute Warm-Up

Daily Language SkillBuilder **TEKS 16B, 16D**

Have students **proofread** the display sentences on page 13j and write them correctly. The sentences also appear on Transparency 4 of **Grammar Transparencies and Copymasters.**

Mini Lesson Preteaching Vocabulary

If you would like to preteach the WORDS TO KNOW for this selection, use the Mini Lesson, p. 110.

Reading Skills and Strategies: PREVIEW

Discuss the positive and negative symbolism of a wall.

Literary Analysis CLIMAX

Remind students that before the climax of a story can occur, conflict has to be developed. Ask students to identify the major conflict in the story.

Possible Response: Lou and the narrator don't want the woman to paint their wall.

Ask students what they think will happen to the conflict as the story progresses.

Possible Response: The antagonism of Lou and the narrator toward the painter will increase.

 Use **Unit One Resource Book,** p. 61, for more practice.

Active Reading CAUSE AND EFFECT

Ⓐ Even though Lou and the narrator are "at war" with the painter lady, Lou begins to admire her. Why?

Possible Response: because of her concentration and methods

What changes his reaction?

Possible Response: the narrator's reminders to see her as an enemy

 Use **Unit One Resource Book,** p. 60, for more practice.

Literary Analysis: DIALECT

Ⓑ Ask students why the author has her characters speak in dialect.

Possible Response: This style makes the characters and setting more realistic.

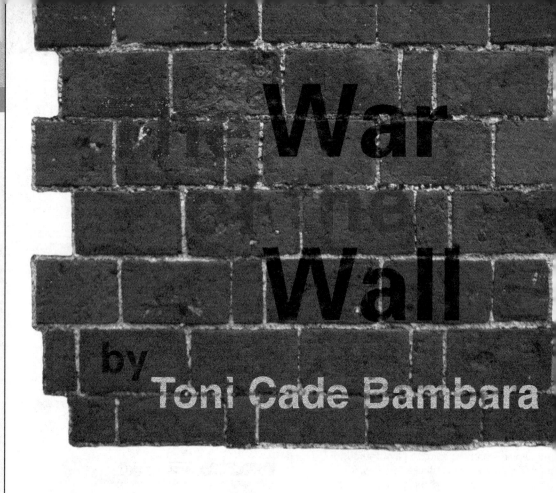

War the Wall
by Toni Cade Bambara

 Me and Lou had no time for courtesies. We were late for school. So we just flat out told the painter lady to quit messing with the wall. It was our wall, and she had no right coming into our neighborhood painting on it. Stirring in the paint bucket and not even looking at us, she mumbled something about Mr. Eubanks, the barber, giving her permission. That had nothing to do with it as far as we were concerned. We've been pitching pennies against that wall since we were little kids. Old folks have been dragging their chairs out to sit in the shade of the wall for years. Big kids have been playing handball against the wall since so-called integration[1] when the crazies 'cross town poured cement in our pool so we couldn't use it. I'd sprained my neck one time boosting my cousin Lou up to chisel Jimmy Lyons's name into the wall when we found out he was never coming home from the war in Vietnam to take us fishing.

"If you lean close," Lou said, leaning hipshot against her beat-up car, "you'll get a

---

1. **since so-called integration:** from the time in the 1960s when segregation, the separation of the races in public places, was outlawed. The narrator is being sarcastic, suggesting that integration has not been successful.

Teaching Options

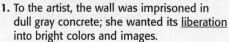 **Preteaching Vocabulary** TEKS 6A TAAS Reading Obj. 1

CONTEXT CLUES

Instruction Remind students that when they encounter an unfamiliar word, they should apply knowledge of the context in which the word is used to recognize its meaning. Display the sentence below to show how the meaning of *drawl* can be inferred to be "speak slowly." She uses a *drawl* instead of her usual fast speech when she wants to add emphasis.

Exercise Have students infer the meanings of the underlined WORDS TO KNOW in the following sentences.

1. To the artist, the wall was imprisoned in dull gray concrete; she wanted its <u>liberation</u> into bright colors and images.
2. The <u>inscription</u> at the bottom of the painting gave the information about the artist and the title of the work of art.
3. Neighbors <u>beckon</u> neighbors, waving them over to look at the wall.
4. They <u>schemed</u> quietly, hoping no one would catch on to their plan.

 Use **Unit One Resource Book,** p. 62, for more practice. Use **Vocabulary Transparencies and Copymasters,** p. 27, for additional support.

whiff of bubble gum and kids' sweat. And that'll tell you something—that this wall belongs to the kids of Taliaferro Street." I thought Lou sounded very convincing. But the painter lady paid us no mind. She just snapped the brim of her straw hat down and hauled her bucket up the ladder.

"You're not even from around here," I hollered up after her. The license plates on her old piece of car said "New York." Lou dragged me away because I was about to grab hold of that ladder and shake it. And then we'd really be late for school.

When we came from school, the wall was slick with white. The painter lady was running string across the wall and taping it here and there. Me and Lou leaned against the gumball machine outside the pool hall and watched. She had strings up and down and back and forth. Then she began chalking them with a hunk of blue chalk.

The Morris twins crossed the street, hanging back at the curb next to the beat-up car. The twin with the red ribbons was hugging a jug of cloudy lemonade. The one with yellow ribbons was holding a plate of dinner away from her dress. The painter lady began snapping the strings. The blue chalk dust measured off halves and quarters up and down and sideways too. Lou was about to say how hip it all was, but I dropped my book satchel on his toes to remind him we were at war.

Some good aromas were drifting our way from the plate leaking pot likker onto the Morris girl's white socks. I could tell from where I stood that under the tinfoil was baked ham, collard greens, and candied yams. And knowing Mrs. Morris, who sometimes bakes for my mama's restaurant, a slab of buttered cornbread was probably up under there too, sopping up some of the pot likker. Me and

Lou rolled our eyes, wishing somebody would send us some dinner. But the painter lady didn't even turn around. She was pulling the strings down and prying bits of tape loose.

Side Pocket came strolling out of the pool hall to see what Lou and me were studying so hard. He gave the painter lady the once-over, checking out her paint-spattered jeans, her chalky T-shirt, her floppy-brimmed straw hat. He hitched up his pants and glided over toward the painter lady, who kept right on with what she was doing.

"Whatcha got there, sweetheart?" he asked the twin with the plate.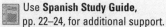

"Suppah," she said all soft and countrylike.

"For her," the one with the jug added, jerking her chin toward the painter lady's back.

Still she didn't turn around. She was rearing back on her heels, her hands jammed into her back pockets, her face squinched up like the masterpiece she had in mind was taking shape on the wall by magic. We could have been gophers crawled up into a rotten hollow for all

> She was rearing back on her heels, her hands jammed into her back pockets, her face squinched up like the masterpiece she had in mind was taking shape on the wall by magic.

she cared. She didn't even say hello to anybody. Lou was muttering something about how great her concentration was. I butt him with my hip, and his elbow slid off the gum machine.

"Good evening," Side Pocket said in his best ain't-I-fine voice. But the painter lady was moving from the milk crate to the step stool to the ladder, moving up and down fast, scribbling all over the wall like a crazy person. We looked at Side Pocket. He looked at the twins. The

Less Proficient Readers
Set a Purpose Have students read to find out how the other neighbors react to the painter lady.

Students Acquiring English
Tell students that the setting of the story is a neighborhood in the South. Encourage students to use context clues to figure out some of the unfamiliar dialect.

1 Point out that "Me and Lou" is technically ungrammatical. Standard English would be "Lou and I." Ask students what this usage suggests about the narrator.

2 Help students to practice using context to define "flat out" (bluntly, without preliminary comments).

3 Tell students that "pot likker" is liquid in which meat or vegetables have been cooked.

Use **Spanish Study Guide,** pp. 22–24, for additional support.

Gifted and Talented
Toni Cade Bambara once said that she wants "wholesomeness" in her writing. Ask students to consider what is wholesome about "The War of the Wall."

Multiple Learning Styles
Kinesthetic Learners
Lou and the narrator use sensory images to describe the wall, such as "if you lean close . . . you'll get a whiff of bubble gum and kids' sweat." Invite students to make a chart of the five senses—sound, touch, sight, taste, and smell—and fill in the sensations that describe the wall.

Use **Reading and Critical Thinking Transparencies,** p. 36, for additional support.

BLOCK SCHEDULING: MANAGING TIME

If your schedule requires that you cover the lesson objectives in a shorter time, use . . .
- Preparing to Read, p. 109
- Thinking Through the Literature, p. 118
- Vocabulary and Spelling, p. 119
- Grammar in Context, p. 120

If you want to take advantage of longer class time, use . . .
- TE Teaching Options: Preteaching Vocabulary, p. 110; Cross-Curricular Link, p. 113; Informal Assessment, p. 115; Viewing and Representing, p. 116; Vocabulary Strategy, p. 119; Grammar, p. 120
- Choices & Challenges and Author Activity, pp. 119–120

Reading and Analyzing

Literary Analysis: DIALECT

 A Ask students what the narrator means when he says the lady's eyes and mouth are "full of sky."
Possible Responses: a million miles away; unfocused or unthinking

Reading Skills and Strategies: CLARIFY

B Ask students what angers the narrator about this incident.
Possible Response: The artist shows no appreciation of the generosity and thoughtfulness of the twins' mother.

Literary Analysis: CHARACTER

Ask students to describe the impression of herself that the artist is creating.
Possible Responses: She doesn't seem to care about the feelings of the people in the neighborhood; she doesn't try to understand the way they do things; she appears unwilling to adapt to her environment.

Reading Skills and Strategies: PREDICT

C Ask students whether the artist will get a special meal and why or why not.
Possible Response: No, the artist won't get a special meal. Mama's language and attitude toward the woman indicate that she is not going to adjust or compromise.

Active Reading | CAUSE AND EFFECT |

D Why is Pop Johnson so happy?
Possible Response: He is getting extra helpings of rice.
Ask students what the reason is.
Possible Response: Mama is too irritated by the artist's questions to realize what she is doing.

---

twins looked at us. The painter lady was giving a show. It was like those old-timey music movies where the dancer taps on the tabletop and then starts jumping all over the furniture, kicking chairs over and not skipping a beat. She didn't even look where she was stepping. And for a minute there, hanging on the ladder to reach a far spot, she looked like she was going to tip right over.

"Ahh," Side Pocket cleared his throat and moved fast to catch the ladder. "These young ladies here have brought you some supper."

A "Ma'am?" The twins stepped forward. Finally the painter turned around, her eyes "full of sky," as my grandmama would say. Then she stepped down like she was in a trance. She wiped her hands on her jeans as the Morris twins offered up the plate and the jug. She rolled back the tinfoil, then wagged her head as though something terrible was on the plate.

"Thank your mother very much," she said, sounding like her mouth was full of sky too. "I've brought my own dinner along." And then, without even excusing herself, she went back up the ladder, drawing on the wall in a wild way. Side Pocket whistled one of those oh-brother breathy whistles and went back into the pool hall. The Morris twins shifted their weight from one foot to the other, then crossed the **B** street and went home. Lou had to drag me away, I was so mad. We couldn't wait to get to the firehouse to tell my daddy all about this rude woman who'd stolen our wall.

1 All the way back to the block to help my mama out at the restaurant, me and Lou kept asking my daddy for ways to run the painter lady out of town. But my daddy was busy talking about the trip to the country and telling Lou he could come too because Grandmama can always use an extra pair of hands on the farm.

Later that night, while me and Lou were in the back doing our chores, we found out that

the painter lady was a liar. She came into the restaurant and leaned against the glass of the steam table, talking about how starved she was. I was scrubbing pots and Lou was chopping onions, but we could hear her through the service window. She was asking Mama was that a ham hock in the greens, and was that a neck bone in the pole beans, and were there any vegetables cooked without meat, especially pork.

"I don't care who your spiritual leader is," Mama said in that way of hers. "If you eat in the community, sistuh, you gonna eat pig by-and-by, one way or t'other."

Me and Lou were cracking up in the kitchen, and several customers at the counter were clearing their throats, waiting for Mama to really fix her wagon for not speaking to the elders when she came in. The painter lady

All the way back to the block to help my mama out at the restaurant, me and Lou kept asking my daddy for ways to run the painter lady out of town.

took a stool at the counter and went right on with her questions. Was there cheese in the baked macaroni, she wanted to know? Were there eggs in the salad? Was it honey or sugar in the iced tea? Mama was fixing Pop Johnson's plate. And every time the painter lady asked a fool question, Mama would dump another spoonful of rice on the pile. She was tapping her foot and heating up in a dangerous way. But Pop Johnson was happy as he could be. Me and Lou peeked through the service window, wondering what planet the painter lady came from. Who ever heard of baked macaroni without cheese, or potato salad without eggs?

Teaching Options

Mini Lesson **Spelling** **TEKS** 16D   **TAAS** Writing Obj. 7

DIFFERENT *K* SOUNDS
Instruction Explain to students that the *k* sound has several different spellings. Usually, the letters *c, ck,* and *k*— as in the words *inscription, lock,* and *kid*— are used to spell the *k* sound. Sometimes, the letters *ch,* as in the word *scheme,* represent this sound. Write the following words on the board and ask students to identify the letters that spell the *k* sound:

1. attack (atta*ck*)
2. describe (des*c*ribe)

3. forecast (fore*c*ast)
4. bicker (bi*ck*er)
5. character (*ch*ara*c*ter)
6. school (s*ch*ool)

Ask students to look for more words that fit this pattern, in their own writing and in things that they read, and to add these words to their personal word lists.

Use **Unit One Resource Book,** p. 64, for more practice.

Sibling Rivals (1989), Phoebe Beasley. Collage, 32" × 40", courtesy of the artist.

Cross Curricular Link **Social Studies**

VIETNAM VETERANS MEMORIAL In 1980, over 1400 ideas were submitted in a contest to decide the design of the Vietnam Veterans Memorial. The winner was Maya Ying Lin of Athens, Ohio, who was studying architecture at Yale University at the time. Her design was inspired by her visit to the park where the memorial would be placed. She said that she wanted "something horizontal . . . that made you feel safe within the park." She created two walls of polished black granite, upon which are inscribed the names of all who died in the war in chronological order. Originally the wall had 57,939 names. Since then, more names have been added to bring the total to over 58,200 names. The Vietnam Veterans Memorial was dedicated in 1982. Over the years, millions of people have visited it. Some look for a particular name; others walk the length of the walls. Visitors often leave flowers, flags, military medals, letters, photographs, and other objects at the wall. These offerings are collected each day and are in a special exhibit at the Smithsonian Institution.

Literary Analysis: CHARACTER

A Ask students to analyze the change in Mama's attitude toward the painter lady.

Possible Response: She is more tolerant of her and sympathetic toward her. She says that it is hard to be an artist.

Reading Skills and Strategies: CLARIFY

B Ask students why the narrator and Lou slap five when they see the train covered with spray-painted drawings and writings.

Possible Response: Seeing the graffiti has given them an idea about what they will do to the wall to show their disdain for the painter lady's work.

Active Reading | CAUSE AND EFFECT

C What is the consequence of the narrator and Lou getting home later than usual?

Possible Response: They are too late to destroy the mural.

Reading Skills and Strategies: PREDICT

D Ask students to predict what they think might be on the wall.

Possible Responses: Answers will vary. They might include: famous people; the people of the neighborhood; a cityscape; a country scene; something religious; slogans

Reading Skills and Strategies: HYPOTHESIZING

E What does Mr. Eubanks's comment mean?

Possible Responses: She really did what she said she was going to do: she really painted a great mural.

"Do you have any bread made with unbleached flour?" the painter lady asked Mama. There was a long pause, as though everybody in the restaurant was holding their breath, wondering if Mama would dump the next spoonful on the painter lady's head. She didn't. But when she set Pop Johnson's plate down, it came down with a bang.

When Mama finally took her order, the starving lady all of a sudden couldn't make up her mind whether she wanted a vegetable plate or fish and a salad. She finally settled on the broiled trout and a tossed salad. But just when Mama reached for a plate to serve her, the painter lady leaned over the counter with her finger all up in the air.

"Excuse me," she said. "One more thing." Mama was holding the plate like a Frisbee, tapping that foot, one hand on her hip. "Can I get raw beets in that tossed salad?"

"You will get," Mama said, leaning her face close to the painter lady's, "whatever Lou back there tossed. Now sit down." And the painter lady sat back down on her stool and shut right up.

All the way to the country, me and Lou tried to get Mama to open fire on the painter lady. But Mama said that seeing as how she was from the North, you couldn't expect her to have any manners. Then Mama said she was sorry she'd been so impatient with the woman because she seemed like a decent person and was simply trying to stick to a very strict diet. Me and Lou didn't want to hear that. Who did that lady think she was, coming into our neighborhood and taking over our wall?

"Wellllll," Mama drawled, pulling into the filling station so Daddy could take the wheel,

"it's hard on an artist, ya know. They can't always get people to look at their work. So she's just doing her work in the open, that's all."

Me and Lou definitely did not want to hear that. Why couldn't she set up an easel downtown or draw on the sidewalk in her own

All weekend long me and Lou tried to scheme up ways to recapture our wall.

neighborhood? Mama told us to quit fussing so much; she was tired and wanted to rest. She climbed into the back seat and dropped down into the warm hollow Daddy had made in the pillow.

All weekend long, me and Lou tried to scheme up ways to recapture our wall. Daddy and Mama said they were sick of hearing about it. Grandmama turned up the TV to drown us out. On the late news was a story about the New York subways. When a train came roaring into the station all covered from top to bottom, windows too, with writings and drawings done with spray paint, me and Lou slapped five. Mama said it was too bad kids in New York had nothing better to do than spray paint all over the trains. Daddy said that in the cities, even grown-ups wrote all over the trains and buildings too. Daddy called it "graffiti." Grandmama called it a shame.

We couldn't wait to get out of school on Monday. We couldn't find any black spray paint anywhere. But in a junky hardware store downtown we found a can of white epoxy[2] paint, the kind you touch up old refrigerators with when they get splotchy and peely. We spent our whole allowance on it. And because it was

---

2. **epoxy** (ĭ-pŏk′sē): a plastic used in glues and paints.

WORDS
TO
KNOW

drawl (drôl) *v.* to speak slowly, stretching the vowel sound
scheme (skēm) *v.* to plot or plan in a secretive way

114

Teaching Options

too late to use our bus passes, we had to walk all the way home lugging our book satchels and gym shoes, and the bag with the epoxy.

When we reached the corner of Taliaferro and Fifth, it looked like a block party or something. Half the neighborhood was gathered on the sidewalk in front of the wall. I looked at Lou, he looked at me. We both looked at the bag with the epoxy and wondered how we were going to work our scheme. The painter lady's car was nowhere in sight. But there were too many people standing around to do anything. Side Pocket and his buddies were leaning on their cue sticks, hunching each other. Daddy was there with a lineman he catches a ride with on Mondays. Mrs. Morris had her arms flung around the shoulders of the twins on either side of her. Mama was talking with some of her customers, many of them with napkins still at the throat. Mr. Eubanks came out of the barbershop, followed by a man in a striped poncho, half his face shaved, the other half full of foam.

"She really did it, didn't she?" Mr. Eubanks huffed out his chest. Lots of folks answered right quick that she surely did when they saw the straight razor in his hand.

Mama <u>beckoned</u> us over. And then we saw it. The wall. Reds, greens, figures outlined in black. Swirls of purple and orange. Storms of blues and yellows. It was something. I recognized some of the faces right off. There was Martin Luther King, Jr. And there was a man with glasses on and his mouth open like he was laying down a heavy rap. Daddy came up alongside and reminded us that that was Minister Malcolm X. The serious woman with a rifle I knew was Harriet Tubman because my grandmama has pictures of her all over the house. And I knew Mrs. Fannie Lou Hamer 'cause a signed photograph of her hangs in the restaurant next to the calendar.

Then I let my eyes follow what looked like a vine. It trailed past a man with a horn, a woman with a big white flower in her hair, a handsome dude in a tuxedo seated at a piano, and a man with a goatee holding a book. When I looked more closely, I realized that what had looked like flowers were really faces. One face with yellow petals looked just like Frieda Morris. One with red petals looked just like Hattie Morris. I could hardly believe my eyes.

"Notice," Side Pocket said, stepping close to the wall with his cue stick like a classroom pointer. "These are the flags of <u>liberation</u>," he

I recognized some of the faces right off. There was Martin Luther King, Jr. And there was a man with glasses on and his mouth open like he was laying down a heavy rap.

said in a voice I'd never heard him use before. We all stepped closer while he pointed and spoke. "Red, black and green," he said, his pointer falling on the leaflike flags of the vine. "Our liberation flag. And here Ghana, there Tanzania. Guinea-Bissau, Angola, Mozambique." Side Pocket sounded very tall, as though he'd been waiting all his life to give this lesson.

Mama tapped us on the shoulder and pointed to a high section of the wall. There was a fierce-looking man with his arms crossed against his chest guarding a bunch of children. His muscles bulged, and he looked a lot like my daddy. One

WORDS TO KNOW
beckon (bĕk'ən) v. to summon or call, usually by a gesture or nod
liberation (lĭb'ə-rā'shən) n. a state of freedom reached after a struggle

115

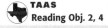

Customizing Instruction

Less Proficient Readers

1 Ask students what Lou and the narrator are going to do to win the war of the wall.

Possible Response: They are going to spray the wall with white paint.

2 Ask what the painter lady has done with the wall.

Possible Response: She has created a mural that depicts African-American heroes, the African-American flag and the flags of various African countries, and people who live in the neighborhood.

Set a Purpose Have students read to find out the reactions of the neighborhood and the narrator and Lou.

Students Acquiring English

3 Discuss with students how someone could sound tall. Point out that people who feel very proud often stand up straight and look taller.

Multiple Learning Styles
Visual Learners
Read the paragraphs about the mural aloud. Ask students to describe mental images that the text description evokes.

✓ **Assessment Informal Assessment**   ⬛ TEKS 10E   🏴 TAAS Reading Obj. 2, 4

UNDERSTANDING CAUSE AND EFFECT You can informally assess students' understanding of cause and effect relationships by asking them to explain how the events and the feelings of the narrator would have changed if the painter lady had revealed who she was and what she was planning to do from the beginning. Student responses should summarize the alternative events from the narrator's perspective.

RUBRIC

3 Full Accomplishment Response summarizes significant changes in plot and the feelings of the narrator in a style consistent with the narrator's perspective.

2 Substantial Accomplishment Response summarizes most of the changes in plot and feelings of the narrator from the narrator's perspective.

1 Little or Partial Accomplishment Response includes few of the changes in plot or feeling and does not maintain the narrator's perspective.

Reading and Analyzing

Literary Analysis: CHARACTER

A Ask students how the mural reveals the painter lady's character to be different from what the narrator and Lou saw in her.

Possible Response: The mural shows she understood the people and their relationships to each other and observed their important qualities.

Literary Analysis `CLIMAX`

B Tell students that the inscription is the climax of the story. However, finding Jimmy's name is a turning point for Lou and the narrator in their war against the painter. Why?

Possible Response: They realize that she preserved what they thought she would destroy.

C Ask students what Lou and the narrator discover about the painter and about themselves when they read the inscription.

Possible Responses: She was connected to the neighborhood in a very close way; they misjudged her because she was different; they almost destroyed something special because they didn't give her a chance.

Active Reading `CAUSE AND EFFECT`

Ask students why the painter lady came from the North to do this wall.

Possible Responses: to honor the memory of her cousin; as a gift to the people that her cousin loved

Another Times Voice Remembers My Passion's Humanity (1979), Calvin B. Jones and Mitchell Caton. Outdoor mural, 22′ × 48′, Elliott Donnelley Youth Center, Chicago. Restored in 1993 by Bernard Williams and Paige Hinson, Chicago Mural Project.

1 kid was looking at a row of books. Lou hunched me 'cause the kid looked like me. The one that looked like Lou was spinning a globe on the tip of his finger like a basketball. There were other kids there with microscopes and compasses. And the more I looked, the more it **A** looked like the fierce man was not so much guarding the kids as defending their right to do what they were doing.

Then Lou gasped and dropped the paint bag and ran forward, running his hands over a rainbow. He had to tiptoe and stretch to do it, it was so high. I couldn't breathe either. The painter lady had found the chisel marks and had painted Jimmy Lyons's name in a rainbow.

"Read the inscription, honey," Mrs. Morris said, urging little Frieda forward. She didn't have to urge much. Frieda marched right up, bent down, and in a loud voice that made everybody quit oohing and ahhing and listen, she read,

To the People of Taliaferro Street
I Dedicate This Wall of Respect
Painted in Memory of My Cousin **C**
Jimmy Lyons

> WORDS
> TO   **inscription** (ĭn-skrĭp′shən) *n.* something written, carved, or engraved on a surface
> KNOW

116

Teaching Options

 Mini Lesson **Viewing and Representing** `TEKS 22A`

Another Times Voice Remembers My Passion's Humanity
by Calvin B. Jones and Mitchell Caton

ART APPRECIATION

Instruction Tell students that this street mural was created in 1979 and restored in 1993. It was painted on the Elliott Donnelley Youth Center in Chicago. Mural artists rely on bright colors, the relationship of figures to each other, and large-scale images to convey their meaning. Have students note the way some of the figures look to the left, others to the right, and some face the front. What do these positions represent?

Possible Response: Left is the past; right is the future, and front is the present.

What is the artist saying about the past and the future?

Possible Response: They are connected by the present.

Application Ask students how the painter lady's mural connects past to present.

Possible Responses: She mingles people of the neighborhood with historical figures; she uses a vine.

from

Song of Myself

BY WALT WHITMAN

I exist as I am, that is enough,
If no other in the world be aware
    I sit content,
And if each and all be aware I sit
    content.

One world is aware and by far the
    largest to me, and that is myself,
And whether I come to my own
    today or in ten thousand or ten
    million years,
I can cheerfully take it now, or with
    equal cheerfulness I can wait.

Closed Windows, Hessam Abrishami. Giclee on paper.
Copyright © Collectors Editions.

SONG OF MYSELF **117**

GUIDING STUDENT RESPONSE

Connect to the Literature

1. Answers will vary. Some students may say they were surprised by the ending because the painter lady appeared to have no connection with the neighborhood. Others may say that they were not surprised, because they had guessed who the painter lady was.

Comprehension Check
- They resent her taking over the wall.
- She asks too many questions. She seems critical of the food in the restaurant and of the ways of the neighborhood.
- They are overcome with awe.

 Use **Selection Quiz, Unit One Resource Book,** p. 65.

Think Critically

2. Possible Responses: She is not sure what she is going to do; she is too absorbed in her work; she wants them to behave naturally so that she can see who they really are.
3. Possible Response: She connects the living neighborhood to the heroes of the past, to a personal hero (Jimmy Lyons), and to the wider world that includes nations of Africa.
4. Possible Responses: They are too late; there is a crowd in front of the mural; the mural is too wonderful to destroy.

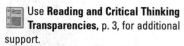 Use **Reading and Critical Thinking Transparencies,** p. 3, for additional support.

5. Possible Responses: Yes, the children will realize that there is a wide world beyond the neighborhood, filled with diverse people; they see that not everyone is just like they are; they will think of Jimmy Lyons each time they see the wall and will connect themselves with other African-American heroes; they will try to live up to the painter lady's impressions of them. No, the people don't need a mural to have self-respect.

Literary Analysis

Conflict Have students work in pairs to find the conflicts. Those that create the most excitement include the external: narrator and Lou versus the painter; Mama versus the painter. The conflicts experienced by the narrator reveal his character.

118 UNIT ONE PART 2

Connect to the Literature

1. **What Do You Think?** What do you think of the ending of the story?

Comprehension Check
- What do Lou and the narrator think of the painter lady at the beginning of the story?
- Why is Mama irritated by the painter lady?
- How do Lou and the narrator feel about the painter lady when they see her mural?

Think Critically

2. Why do you think the painter lady doesn't speak to the young people or tell them what her plans for the wall are?

3. What do you think the painter lady accomplishes by creating the mural?

4. 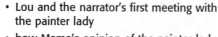 Look over the chart with examples of **cause and effect** that you made in your **READER'S NOTEBOOK.** Why didn't Lou and the narrator use the can of white epoxy paint?

5. Do you think the mural will make a difference in the lives of the neighborhood kids? Explain your answer.

THINK ABOUT
- Lou and the narrator's first meeting with the painter lady
- how Mama's opinion of the painter lady changes over time
- the people and the images depicted in the mural
- the last four lines of the story

Extend Interpretations

6. **COMPARING TEXTS** Would the narrator of "The War of the Wall" agree with the feelings expressed in the poem "Song of Myself" on page 117? Why or why not?

7. **Connect to Life** If an artist painted a mural in your neighborhood, what heroes do you think your neighbors would want represented? Explain.

118 UNIT ONE PART 2: MOMENTS OF DISCOVERY

Literary Analysis

CLIMAX A **climax,** or turning point of a story, is the moment when the plot has reached its greatest intensity, or force. The climax usually occurs near the end, after the reader understands the conflict and knows the characters. The climax of "The War of the Wall" occurs when the painter lady's inscription to Jimmy Lyons is unveiled.

REVIEW CONFLICT When struggle occurs between **characters** or between a character and another force, it is called **external conflict,** as in the struggle between the narrator and the painter lady. When the struggle occurs within a character, it is called **internal conflict,** such as Mama's conflicting feelings of irritation and respect for the painter lady.

Cooperative Learning Activity
Working with a partner, go back through the story and jot down examples of internal and external conflict. When you are done, discuss the following questions with a larger group.
- Which conflicts add the most excitement to the story?
- Which conflicts tell something important about one of the characters? Explain.
- What is the moment of highest tension, or **climax,** in the story?

Extend Interpretations

6. **Comparing Texts** Possible Responses: Yes, after he sees the mural, he would have an appreciation of the importance of individuality and of living up to one's own potential. No, he still wants others to agree with him and accept his point of view.

 Use **Literary Analysis Transparencies,** p. 5, for additional support.

7. **Connect to Life** Possible Responses: Encourage students to give specific names and explain why they would choose these heroes. Most heroes would be part of their common heritage so that neighborhood people would be inspired by them.

Writing Options

1. Newspaper Editorial Pretend you are a columnist for a local newspaper and write an editorial about the mural. Explain its creation, theme, and effect on the community.

2. Personal Narrative Write a short narrative about a conflict you have had with someone you know. Tell how you resolved the conflict. Share your writing with the class. Place your writing in your **Working Portfolio**.
Writing Handbook
See p. R33: Narrative Writing.

Activities & Explorations

1. Plot Collage Review the story "The War of the Wall." Then work with classmates to create a collage representing the key events. Exhibit your collage in class. ~ **VIEWING AND REPRESENTING**

2. War of the Wall Rap With a partner, create a rap using examples of conflict from the story and the climax of "The War of the Wall." Perform your rap for the class. ~ **PERFORMING**

3. Dedication Speech Write a speech that the painter lady might deliver to the community if she were to return for the dedication of the mural. Share your speech with the class. ~ **SPEAKING AND LISTENING**

Inquiry & Research

Mural Subjects Research the "wall of respect" movement or one of the four African-American heroes—Martin Luther King, Jr., Malcolm X, Harriet Tubman, Fannie Lou Hamer—that the narrator recognizes in the painter lady's mural. Prepare an oral report about the subject you researched.

Vocabulary and Spelling

EXERCISE A: MEANING CLUES On a sheet of paper, write the letter of the situation that best demonstrates the meaning of the Word to Know.

1. beckon
   a. you are hailing a taxicab
   b. you are passing a test
   c. you are eating lunch
2. inscription
   a. the end of a game
   b. the words on a tombstone
   c. the parts of a vehicle
3. drawl
   a. speak very slowly
   b. paddle a canoe
   c. make a sketch
4. scheme
   a. write a play
   b. go on a trip
   c. plan a surprise party
5. liberation
   a. end slavery
   b. go on a picnic
   c. attend a rally

EXERCISE B: SUFFIXES The word ending pronounced *shun* is usually spelled *-tion*. Many verbs ending in *-ate* can be changed to nouns by adding the suffix *-ion*, as in *liberate/liberation*. The hard *t* in *-ate* becomes the soft *t* in *-tion*.

1. Add the suffix *-ion* to the following verbs to make them nouns.

vacate	calculate
educate	graduate
celebrate	migrate
liberate	complicate
regulate	eliminate

2. Write a complete sentence using each of the spelling words.

Spelling Handbook p. R86

Writing Options

1. Newspaper Editorial Remind students to answer the questions *who, what, where, when,* and *how* in their editorial and to support opinions with facts. To get students started, have them read examples of editorials from the local newspaper.

 Use **Writing Transparencies**, p. 11, for additional support.

2. Personal Narrative To get students started, have them brainstorm important conflicts. They should outline the steps of resolving a conflict before writing their narrative. **Interpersonal learners** might role-play the conflict and resolution.

Activities & Explorations

1. Plot Collage To get students started, suggest they outline the key events. Remind students how the placement of images can suggest relationships and meaning.

2. War of the Wall Rap To get students started, have them write their lyrics first and then incorporate background music and movements. This activity is well suited to **auditory** and **linguistic** learners.

3. Dedication Speech Speeches should acknowledge the painter lady's relationship to the community through her cousin, Jimmy Lyons, and explain why she chose this way to commemorate him.

 Use **Communications Transparencies and Copymasters**, pp. 14, 15, for additional support.

Inquiry & Research

Mural Subjects Students may wish to incorporate visual aids into their presentations. **To make this assignment more challenging,** have students research the impact of the "wall of respect" movement on communities outside of the United States.

Vocabulary and Spelling

Exercise A	Exercise B
1. a	**1.** vacation, calculation, education, graduation, celebration, migration, liberation, complication, regulation, elimination
2. b	
3. a	
4. c	
5. a	**2.** Answers will vary.

(Mini Lesson) **Vocabulary Strategy** **TEKS 9B** **TAAS Reading Obj. 1**

ANALOGIES

Instruction Tell students that word analogies compare two pairs of words. The relationship between the words in each pair is the same. Types of relationships include: antonyms, synonyms, part of the whole, or cause and effect. Students are often asked to complete analogies by choosing a pair of words with the same relationship seen in the first pair. They should first determine the relationship and then state it in a sentence. For example, in the following analogy, a page is a part of the whole book. The pair of words that completes the analogy should show the same relationship.

page : book :: student : class

Exercise Have students state the relationship between the words in each of the following pairs.

1. war : destruction *(cause and effect)*
2. concentration : distraction *(antonyms)*
3. brick : wall *(part of the whole)*
4. courage : bravery *(synonyms)*
5. rude : polite *(antonyms)*

 Use **Vocabulary Transparencies and Copymasters**, p. 28.

Grammar in Context

Possible Responses:

1. The idea of the wall being painted made the boys angry, and they wanted the painter to stop painting.
2. The boys sparked Side Pocket's curiosity, so he came out of the pool hall to see what they were up to.
3. The Morris girls brought a covered plate with baked ham, greens, and yams, but the painter lady wouldn't eat the food.
4. The boys considered the wall theirs, and they wanted the painter lady to leave it alone.

Toni Cade Bambara

One of Toni Cade Bambara's strengths was her ability to create realistic dialogue. The writer Anne Tyler says about Bambara's characters, "Everything these people say, you feel, ordinary, real-life people are saying right now on any street corner. It's only that the rest of us didn't realize it was sheer poetry they were speaking."

Author Activity

Encourage students to compare the characters, theme, conflicts, and conclusion in the story they choose with those in "The War of the Wall." Students who choose the same story might present a panel discussion to the class.

Grammar in Context: Clear Pronoun Antecedents

In this description, Bambara captures the astonishment of the narrator when he first sees the mural the painter lady has created.

> And then we saw it. The wall. Reds, greens, figures outlined in black. Swirls of purple and orange. Storms of blues and yellows. It was something.

A **pronoun** is a word that replaces a noun. Using pronouns allows writers to avoid monotonous repetition of nouns, but for pronouns to be effective a reader needs to easily know exactly which noun they refer to, which is called the pronoun **antecedent**. In the first sentence of the passage, Bambara shows the narrator's amazement by leaving the antecedent of "it" momentarily unclear. What "it" refers to becomes clear in the next sentence. "It" is the wall.

WRITING EXERCISE Rewrite the sentences so they have no unclear pronoun antecedents.

Example: *Original* Although the boys were annoyed at first, <u>it</u> disappeared after they saw the mural.

Rewritten The annoyance the boys felt at first disappeared after they saw the mural.

1. The boys wanted the painter to stop painting the wall, <u>which</u> made them angry.
2. Side Pocket came out of the pool hall to see what the boys were up to. <u>It</u> had sparked his curiosity.
3. The Morris girls brought a covered plate with baked ham, greens, and yams, but the painter lady wouldn't eat <u>them</u>.
4. The boys considered the wall theirs. <u>It</u> is why they wanted the painter lady to leave it alone.

Grammar Handbook Using Nouns and Pronouns, p. R63

"I move toward the short story because I'm a sprinter . . ."

Toni Cade Bambara
1939–1995

City Life Toni Cade Bambara believed that writers "are everyday people who write stories that come out of their neighborhoods." "The War of the Wall" was inspired by her memories of growing up in New York City. As a child, she and her companions created a park in a vacant city lot. One day they found a large advertisement there. "We were incensed," she recalled. "We went to city hall and got the billboard removed."

A Variety of Interests After college, Bambara studied theater and mime in Europe and dance and film in the United States. She also worked in a welfare department, planned recreation for mentally ill patients, held community-action workshops, and taught college English and African-American studies. During her later years, Bambara led a writers' workshop and remained intensely involved in her community. Her writing won many major awards, including the American Book Award in 1981.

AUTHOR ACTIVITY

Growing Up in the City Bambara once said, "Temperamentally, I move toward the short story because I'm a sprinter rather than a long-distance runner. I cannot sustain characters over a long period of time." Many of her short stories are about young people facing the challenges of inner-city life. Read another short story by Bambara. Compare your choice to "The War of the Wall." Discuss your comparison with your classmates.

 LaserLinks: Background for Reading
Historical Connection
Art Gallery

Teaching Options

PRONOUN-VERB AGREEMENT

Instruction Remind students that if the subject is a singular personal or indefinite pronoun, the verb must be singular. The pronouns *I* and *you* take plural verbs as shown by the passage highlighted above. The indefinite pronouns *some, all, any, none,* and *most* can be singular or plural, depending upon whether they refer to one thing or many things. Display the following examples:

Mini Lesson **Grammar** **TEKS 17C** **TAAS Writing Obj. 6**

<u>Some</u> of the neighbors <u>are</u> polite to the artist.
<u>Some</u> of the wall <u>has</u> white paint on it.

Exercise Have students choose the correct verb.

1. All of the dinner choices (seems, <u>seem</u>) unappetizing to the artist.
2. Most of the class (<u>enjoys,</u> enjoy) reading her stories.
3. Most of the paint colors (was, <u>were</u>) gone.

4. She (<u>feels</u>, feel) sorry that she was impatient with the painter lady.

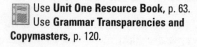 Use **Unit One Resource Book**, p. 63.
Use **Grammar Transparencies and Copymasters**, p. 120.

 Use McDougal Littell's ***Language Network,*** Chapter 9, for more instruction and practice in pronoun-verb agreement.

Rikki-tikki-tavi

Short Story by RUDYARD KIPLING

" . . . and that's a wild creature! I suppose he's so tame because we've been kind to him."

Connect to Your Life

Natural Enemies In nature some animals instinctually prey on other animals. Think about cats and birds. These animals are called natural enemies. What natural enemies in the animal kingdom can you name? Think of common enemies as well as exotic animals you may have heard about. With a partner, brainstorm a list of natural enemies. Share your list with your classmates.

Build Background

CONNECT TO **SOCIAL STUDIES**

If you lived in India, you certainly would know the mongoose and the cobra as a pair of natural enemies—a pair that will fight to the death. The mongoose, growing only to a length of 16 inches, seems hardly a match for the poisonous cobra, a snake that averages 6 feet in length and 6 inches around.

You will learn more about these animals in this story, which is set in India during the late 1800s. At that time, Great Britain ruled India. British families lived in open, airy houses called **bungalows**.

WORDS TO KNOW
Vocabulary Preview

| consolation | cunningly | scuttle |
| cower | revive | |

  LaserLinks:
Background for Reading
Cultural Connection

See the Skills Trace at the beginning of the unit for information on TEKS covered in this lesson.

Focus Your Reading

LITERARY CONCEPT **PERSONIFICATION** When a writer gives human qualities to an animal, object, or idea, the technique is called **personification.** Kipling uses personification in "Rikki-tikki-tavi," where he gives the animals human characteristics. Personification allows readers to imagine what the animals think, feel, and say about each other.

> *"Well," said Rikki-tikki, and his tail began to fluff up again, "marks or no marks, do you think it is right for you to eat fledgelings out of a nest?"*

As you read, look for examples of personification, especially in the character of Rikki-tikki-tavi and of his cobra enemies.

ACTIVE READING **PREDICTING** A **prediction** is an attempt to answer the question "What will happen next?" To make predictions, pay attention to the following:

- interesting details about character, **plot,** and setting
- unusual statements by the main characters

READER'S NOTEBOOK As you read this story, jot down at least three predictions, as well as a good reason for each guess. Record your predictions on a chart.

My Predictions		
Who?	**Why?**	**What Next?**
Rikki-tikki	Teddy's mother takes him home.	Rikki-tikki will live with Teddy's family.

 This selection is included in the **Grade 7 InterActive Reader.**

 This selection appears in Spanish in the **Spanish Study Guide.**

Objectives

1. understand and identify **personification (Literary Analysis)**
2. understand what constitutes a **classic story (Literary Analysis)**
3. understand **suspense** as an element of plot **(Literary Analysis)**
4. recognize and distinguish **major characters** and **minor characters** **(Literary Analysis)**
5. **predict outcomes (Active Reading)**

Summary

A mongoose, Rikki-tikki-tavi, becomes the house pet of an English family living in colonial India. On his first day, he meets Nag and Nagaina, two cobras, who try to bite him. Later, Rikki becomes the family hero when he kills a small poisonous snake and saves the boy Teddy. That night Rikki overhears the cobras plotting to kill the entire family. After Nag sneaks into the bathroom, Rikki-tikki attacks the snake. Teddy's father shoots the snake to death. The next morning, as the wife of Darzee the Tailorbird distracts Nagaina, Rikki-tikki begins destroying the cobra's eggs. Learning that Nagaina has gone to the house, Rikki follows and finds her on the veranda poised to strike Teddy. Rikki-tikki shows Nagaina her last egg, giving Teddy's father the chance to rescue his son. The cobra grabs her egg and carries it into her hole. Rikki-tikki follows and kills her.

Thematic Link

Rikki-tikki discovers that he is brave and strong enough to protect his human family.

5-Minute Warm-Up

Daily Language SkillBuilder   **TEKS 17C**

Have students **proofread** the display sentences on page 13j and write them correctly. The sentences also appear on Transparency 4 of **Grammar Transparencies and Copymasters.**

 Mini Lesson **Preteaching Vocabulary**

If you would like to preteach the WORDS TO KNOW for this selection, use the mini lesson, p. 122.

LESSON RESOURCES

UNIT ONE RESOURCE BOOK, pp. 66–72

ASSESSMENT
Formal Assessment, pp. 21, 22
Teacher's Guide to Assessment and Portfolio Use
Test Generator

SKILLS TRANSPARENCIES AND COPYMASTERS
Literary Analysis
- Analyzing Character, TR 3 (for Cooperative Learning Activity, p. 135)
Reading and Critical Thinking
- Predicting, TR 7 (for Thinking Through the Literature, p. 135)

Grammar
- Compound Sentences, CM 104 (for Mini Lesson, p. 126)
- Sentence Variety, CM 134 (for Mini Lesson, p. 137)
Vocabulary
- Synonyms, CM 29 (for Mini Lesson, p. 122)
- Learning and Remembering New Words, CM 30 (for Mini Lesson, p. 130)

INTEGRATED TECHNOLOGY
Audio Library
LaserLinks
- Cultural Connection; Science Connection. See **Teacher's SourceBook,** p. 12.

Visit our website:
www.mcdougallittell.com

Reading Skills and Strategies:
PREVIEW

Read the first three paragraphs of the story aloud to stimulate students' interest. Discuss Rikki's antagonist in the conflict, and have students look at the illustrations so that they can picture the characters of the mongoose and cobra.

Literary Analysis | PERSONIFICATION |

Ask students to explain how Kipling makes Rikki seem human in the first paragraph.

Possible Response: Kipling describes Rikki as he might a human soldier, as a fighter in a "great war."

Explore with students why Kipling would personify the mongoose in this story.

Possible Response: to help readers identify with the wild creature and become interested in his exploits.

Use **Unit One Resource Book,** p. 68 for more practice.

Active Reading | PREDICTING |

Remind students that making predictions involves them more fully in the story. Have students write down some of their predictions after they read the first part of the story. Students should revise their predictions as they continue reading so that they can take into account new information from the story.

Use **Unit One Resource Book,** p. 67 for more practice. Use **Reading and Critical Thinking Transparencies,** p. 7, for additional support.

 Preteaching Vocabulary **TEKS** 6A, 6C **TAAS** Reading Obj. 1

SYNONYMS

Instruction Tell students that a method of finding a synonym for an unfamiliar word is to determine how a word is used in context and think of another word that will convey the same meaning. Display the following sentence.

Being wrapped in cotton wool <u>revived</u> his energy and made him feel himself again.

Revived seems to mean bring back or restore.

Exercise Have students use the context clues to think of synonyms for the underlined words. Students should check their answers by using a thesaurus or dictionary.

1. He <u>cunningly</u> planned a surprise attack.
2. Teddy received <u>consolation</u> from his mother after his frightening experience.
3. The muskrat wasted no time as he <u>scuttled</u> into his hole.
4. Timid creatures <u>cowered</u> in fear when the cobras appeared.

Use **Unit One Resource Book** p. 69 for more practice. Use **Vocabulary Transparencies and Copymasters,** p. 29, for additional support.

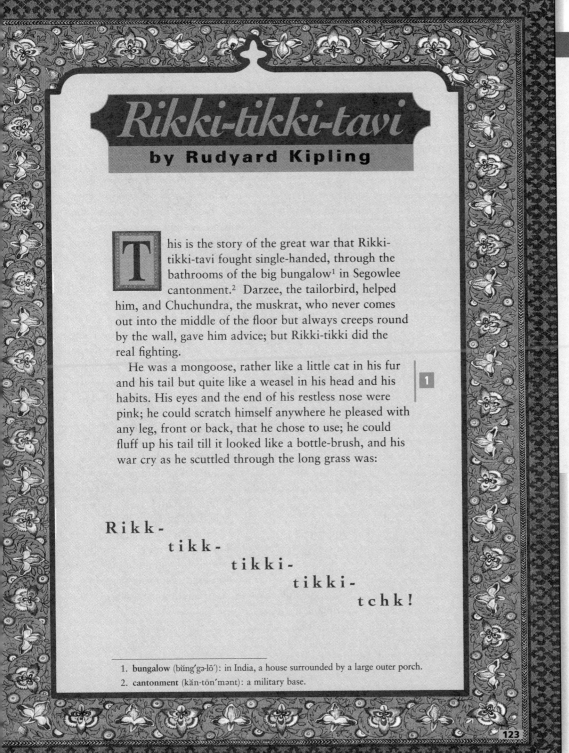

Rikki-tikki-tavi

by Rudyard Kipling

This is the story of the great war that Rikki-tikki-tavi fought single-handed, through the bathrooms of the big bungalow[1] in Segowlee cantonment.[2] Darzee, the tailorbird, helped him, and Chuchundra, the muskrat, who never comes out into the middle of the floor but always creeps round by the wall, gave him advice; but Rikki-tikki did the real fighting.

He was a mongoose, rather like a little cat in his fur and his tail but quite like a weasel in his head and his habits. His eyes and the end of his restless nose were pink; he could scratch himself anywhere he pleased with any leg, front or back, that he chose to use; he could fluff up his tail till it looked like a bottle-brush, and his war cry as he scuttled through the long grass was:

1

Rikk-
    tikk-
        tikki-
           tikki-
              tchk!

---

1. **bungalow** (bŭng′gə-lō′): in India, a house surrounded by a large outer porch.
2. **cantonment** (kăn-tōn′mənt): a military base.

123

A ne day, a high summer flood washed him out of the burrow where he lived with his father and mother and carried him, kicking and clucking, down a roadside ditch. He found a little wisp of grass floating there and clung to it till he lost his senses. When he <u>revived</u>, he was lying in the hot sun on the middle of a garden path, very draggled indeed, and a small boy was saying, "Here's a dead mongoose. Let's have a funeral."

"No," said his mother, "let's take him in and dry him. Perhaps he isn't really dead."

They took him into the house, and a big man picked him up between his finger and thumb and said he was not dead but half choked; so they wrapped him in cotton wool and warmed him over a little fire, and he opened his eyes and sneezed. "Now," said the big man (he was an Englishman who had just moved into the bungalow), "don't frighten him, and we'll see what he'll do."

B It is the hardest thing in the world to frighten a mongoose, because he is eaten up from nose to tail with curiosity. The motto of all the mongoose family is "Run and Find Out"; and Rikki-tikki was a true mongoose. He looked at the cotton wool, decided that it was not good to eat, ran all round the table, sat up and put his fur in order, scratched himself, and jumped on the small boy's shoulder.

"Don't be frightened, Teddy," said his father. "That's his way of making friends."

1 "Ouch! He's tickling under my chin," said Teddy.

Rikki-tikki looked down between the boy's collar and neck, snuffed at his ear, and climbed down to the floor, where he sat rubbing his nose.

2 "Good gracious," said Teddy's mother, "and that's a wild creature! I suppose he's so tame because we've been kind to him."

"All mongooses are like that," said her husband. "If Teddy doesn't pick him up by the tail or try to put him in a cage, he'll run in and out of the house all day long. Let's give him something to eat."

They gave him a little piece of raw meat. Rikki-tikki liked it immensely; and when it was finished, he went out into the veranda[3] and sat in the sunshine and fluffed up his fur to make it dry to the roots. Then he felt better.

"There are more things to find out about in this house," he said to himself, "than all my family could find out in all their lives. I shall certainly stay and find out."

He spent all that day roaming over the house. He nearly drowned himself in the bathtubs, put his nose into the ink on a writing table, and burnt it on the end of the big man's cigar, for he climbed up in the big man's lap to see how writing was done. At nightfall he ran into Teddy's nursery to watch how kerosene lamps were lighted, and when Teddy went to bed, Rikki-tikki climbed up too; but he was a restless companion, because he had to get up and attend to every noise all through the night and find out what made it. Teddy's mother and father came in, the last thing, to look at their boy, and Rikki-tikki was awake on the pillow.

"I don't like that," said Teddy's mother; "he may bite the child."

"He'll do no such thing," said the father. "Teddy is safer with that little beast than if he had a bloodhound to watch him. If a snake came into the nursery now—"

But Teddy's mother wouldn't think of anything so awful.

---

3. **veranda** (və-răn′də): a long open porch.

WORDS
TO
KNOW   **revive** (rĭ-vīv′) *v.* to become conscious; wake up

124

Early in the morning Rikki-tikki came to early breakfast in the veranda, riding on Teddy's shoulder, and they gave him banana and some boiled egg; and he sat on all their laps one after the other, because every well-brought-up mongoose always hopes to be a house mongoose some day and have rooms to run about in; and Rikki-tikki's mother (she used to live in the general's house at Segowlee) had carefully told Rikki what to do if ever he came across white men.

Then Rikki-tikki went out into the garden to see what was to be seen. It was a large garden, only half-cultivated,[4] with bushes, as big as summerhouses, of Marshal Niel roses, lime and orange trees, clumps of bamboos, and thickets of high grass. Rikki-tikki licked his lips. "This is a splendid hunting ground," he said, and his tail grew bottlebrushy at the thought of it; and he scuttled up and down the garden, snuffing here and there till he heard very sorrowful voices in a thorn bush. It was Darzee, the tailorbird, and his wife. They had made a beautiful nest by pulling two big leaves together and stitching them up the edges with fibers and had filled the hollow with cotton and downy fluff. The nest swayed to and fro, as they sat on the rim and cried.

"What is the matter?" asked Rikki-tikki.

"We are very miserable," said Darzee. "One of our babies fell out of the nest yesterday, and Nag ate him."

"H'm!" said Rikki-tikki, "that is very sad—but I am a stranger here. Who is Nag?"

Darzee and his wife only <u>cowered</u> down in the nest without answering, for from the thick grass at the foot of the bush there came a low hiss—a horrid, cold sound that made Rikki-tikki jump back two clear feet. Then inch by inch out of the grass rose up the head and spread hood of Nag, the big black cobra, and he was five feet long from tongue to tail. When he had lifted one-third of himself clear of the ground, he stayed, balancing to and fro exactly as a dandelion tuft balances in the wind; and he looked at Rikki-tikki with the wicked snake's eyes that never change their expression, whatever the snake may be thinking of.

"Who is Nag?" said he. "I am Nag. The great god Brahm[5] put his mark upon all our people when the first cobra spread his hood to keep the sun off Brahm as he slept. Look, and be afraid!"

---

4. **cultivated:** cleared for the growing of garden plants.

5. **Brahm:** another name for Brahma, creator of the universe in the Hindu religion.

WORDS TO KNOW

cower (kou′ər) v. to crouch or shrink down in fear

125

Cross Curricular Link History

BRITISH INDIA The British first became interested in India in the 1500s after the Portuguese had established a thriving spice trade. The British recognized the profitability of this trade and competed with the Portuguese traders. In 1599, a group of London merchants formed the East India Company. The next year, the company received a charter from the British government granting it exclusive trading rights in the East Indies and the power to maintain an army and a navy, declare war, and govern new territories.

When Indians rebelled against the East India Company in 1857, the British government stepped in and took direct control of India. India remained a British colony until 1947, when it gained its independence after a century-long struggle with the British government.

Literary Analysis: CONFLICT

A Ask students to identify the conflicts in this passage.

Possible Responses: Rikki faces an external conflict with Nag; both Rikki and Nag face internal struggles to overcome their fear as they prepare for battle.

Literary Analysis: SETTING

B Ask students to analyze the effect of setting on the plot.

Possible Response: In India there are deadly snakes; in the time of colonial India, there weren't as many ways to keep snakes away from the garden or house or effective cures for their venom.

ACTIVE READING

C **PREDICT** **Possible Response:** He probably plans to find a good place to bite the snake.

Reading Skills and Strategies: CLARIFYING

D Ask students to explain Rikki's amused reaction.

Possible Response: Rikki doesn't understand why the humans are praising him so much for doing what comes naturally.

Literary Analysis PERSONIFICATION

E Point out that Rikki refuses to eat or drink too much and is determined to stay fierce. Ask students what this behavior reveals about Rikki's character.

Possible Responses: Like a good soldier, Rikki does not let anything get in the way of duty; Rikki has the discipline needed for battle; he is already maturing.

He spread out his hood more than ever, and Rikki-tikki saw the spectacle mark on the back of it that looks exactly like the eye part of a hook-and-eye fastening. He was afraid for the minute, but it is impossible for a mongoose to stay frightened for any length of time; and though Rikki-tikki had never met a live cobra before, his mother had fed him on dead ones, and he knew that all a grown mongoose's business in life was to fight and eat snakes. Nag knew that too, and at the bottom of his cold heart, he was afraid.

"Well," said Rikki-tikki, and his tail began to fluff up again, "marks or no marks, do you think it is right for you to eat fledgelings out of a nest?"

Nag was thinking to himself and watching the least little movement in the grass behind Rikki-tikki. He knew that mongooses in the garden meant death sooner or later for him

and his family; but he wanted to get Rikki-tikki off his guard. So he dropped his head a little, and put it on one side.

"Let us talk," he said. "You eat eggs. Why should not I eat birds?"

"Behind you! Look behind you!" sang Darzee

Rikki-tikki knew better than to waste time in staring. He jumped up in the air as high as he could go, and just under him whizzed by the head of Nagaina, Nag's wicked wife. She had crept up behind him as he was talking, to make an end of him; and he heard her savage hiss as the stroke missed. He came down almost across her back, and if he had been an old mongoose, he would have known that there was the time to break her back with one bite; but he was afraid of the terrible lashing return stroke of the cobra. He bit, indeed, but did not bite long enough; and he jumped clear of the whisking tail, leaving Nagaina torn and angry.

"Wicked, wicked Darzee!" said Nag, lashing up as high as he could reach toward the nest in the thorn bush; but Darzee had built it out of reach of snakes, and it only swayed to and fro.

Rikki-tikki felt his eyes growing red and hot (when a mongoose's eyes grow red, he is angry), and he sat back on his tail and hind legs like a little kangaroo and looked all around him and chattered with rage. But Nag and Nagaina had disappeared into the grass. When a snake misses its stroke, it never says anything or gives any sign of what it means to do next. Rikki-tikki did not care to follow them, for he did not feel sure that he could manage two snakes at once. So he trotted off to the gravel path near the house and sat down to think. It was a serious matter for him.

If you read the old books of natural history, you will find they say that when the mongoose fights the snake and happens to get bitten, he runs off and eats some herb that cures him. That is not true. The victory is only a matter of quickness of eye and quickness of foot—

Teaching Options

COMPOUND SENTENCES

Instruction Remind students that compound sentences consist of two or more simple sentences that are joined by a comma and a conjunction or a semicolon. Point out the highlighted passage above. Ask students to identify the two simple sentences. Tell students that compound sentences without the comma and conjunction or semicolon become run-on sentences.

Mini Lesson **Grammar** **TEKS** 17A, 17B **TAAS** Writing Obj. 3, 5, 6, 7

Exercise Have students correctly rewrite the following sentences as compound sentences. (Possible answers are given.)

1. Nag enjoyed his control of the garden he was not about to give it up. *(; he)*
2. Rikki paralyzed Karait Teddy's father finished the snake off. *(, and Teddy's)*
3. Rikki's eyes grew red he controlled himself at the table. *(, but he)*

4. People had to watch out for snakes in India they would be bitten. *(, or they)*

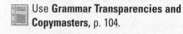 Use **Grammar Transparencies and Copymasters**, p. 104.

 Use McDougal Littell's **Language Network**, Chapter 8, for more instruction and practice in compound sentences.

snake's blow against mongoose's jump—and as no eye can follow the motion of a snake's head when it strikes, this makes things much more wonderful than any magic herb. Rikki-tikki knew he was a young mongoose, and it made him all the more pleased to think that he had managed to escape a blow from behind.

It gave him confidence in himself, and when Teddy came running down the path, Rikki-tikki was ready to be petted. But just as Teddy was stooping, something wriggled a little in the dust, and a tiny voice said, "Be careful. I am Death!" It was Karait, the dusty brown snakeling that lies for choice on the dusty earth; and his bite is as dangerous as the cobra's. But he is so small that nobody thinks of him, and so he does the more harm to people.

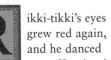

Rikki-tikki's eyes grew red again, and he danced up to Karait with the peculiar rocking, swaying motion that he had inherited from his family. It looks very funny, but it is so perfectly balanced a gait that you can fly off from it at any angle you please; and in dealing with snakes this is an advantage.

If Rikki-tikki had only known, he was doing a much more dangerous thing than fighting Nag; for Karait is so small and can turn so quickly, that unless Rikki bit him close to the back of the head, he would get the return stroke in his eye or his lip. But Rikki did not know: his eyes were all red, and he rocked back and forth, looking for a good place to hold. Karait struck out. Rikki jumped sideways and tried to run in, but the wicked little dusty gray head lashed within a fraction of his shoulder, and he had to jump over the body, and the head followed his heels close.

ACTIVE READING

PREDICT What do you think Rikki-tikki is planning to do next?

Teddy shouted to the house, "Oh, look here! Our mongoose is killing a snake"; and Rikki-tikki heard a scream from Teddy's mother. His father ran out with a stick, but by the time he came up, Karait had lunged out once too far, and Rikki-tikki had sprung, jumped on the snake's back, dropped his head far between his forelegs, bitten as high up the back as he could get hold, and rolled away.

That bite paralyzed Karait, and Rikki-tikki was just going to eat him up from the tail, after the custom of his family at dinner, when he remembered that a full meal makes a slow mongoose; and if he wanted all his strength and quickness ready, he must keep himself thin. He went away for a dust bath under the castor-oil bushes, while Teddy's father beat the dead Karait. "What is the use of that?" thought Rikki-tikki; "I have settled it all."

And then Teddy's mother picked him up from the dust and hugged him, crying that he had saved Teddy from death; and Teddy's father said that he was a providence,[6] and Teddy looked on with big scared eyes. Rikki-tikki was rather amused at all the fuss, which, of course, he did not understand. Teddy's mother might just as well have petted Teddy for playing in the dust. Rikki was thoroughly enjoying himself.

That night at dinner, walking to and fro among the wineglasses on the table, he might have stuffed himself three times over with nice things; but he remembered Nag and Nagaina,

D

E

6. **providence:** blessing; something good given by God.

Customizing Instruction

Less Proficient Readers
Check comprehension with the following questions.
- What does Nagaina try to do to Rikki?
  Answer: bite him
- Why does Rikki attack Karait?
  Possible Responses: They are natural enemies; to protect Teddy.
- How does the family treat Rikki after he kills Karait?
  Possible Responses: Like a hero; they praise and pamper him.

Set a Purpose Have students read to find out what Nag is planning and how Rikki will respond.

Multiple Learning Styles
Logical Learners
1 Ask students to think about ways that Rikki could defeat Nag and Nagaina with the least possible danger to himself. Have students present their plans to the class for a vote on the best plan.

Literary Analysis:
MINOR CHARACTERS

A Remind students that minor characters interact with the main characters and advance the plot. Ask students what Chuchundra's function is.
Possible Response: to warn Rikki about Nag

Literary Analysis PERSONIFICATION

B Ask students what Nag's words reveal about him and what effect his speech has.
Possible Response: His words show him as ruthless, and anticipation of what he is going to do adds suspense to the story.

Active Reading PREDICTING

C Have students predict whether Rikki will attack Nag now or later. Encourage them to base their predictions on what they already know about Rikki from the story.
Possible Responses: He will attack now because he is inexperienced; he will attack later because he is cautious and intelligent.

Literary Analysis: SUSPENSE

D Have students analyze this passage to discover how Kipling creates suspense.
Possible Response: Repeated words and phrases such as "still as death" and "muscle by muscle" help slow the action and build suspense.

and though it was very pleasant to be patted and petted by Teddy's mother and to sit on Teddy's shoulder, his eyes would get red from time to time, and he would go off into his long war cry of *"Rikk-tikk-tikki-tikki-tchk!"*

Teddy carried him off to bed and insisted on Rikki-tikki sleeping under his chin. Rikki-tikki was too well-bred to bite or scratch, but as soon as Teddy was asleep, he went off for his nightly walk around the house; and in the dark he ran up against Chuchundra, the muskrat, creeping around by the wall. Chuchundra is a brokenhearted little beast. He whimpers and cheeps all the night, trying to make up his mind to run into the middle of the room; but he never gets there.

"Don't kill me," said Chuchundra, almost weeping. "Rikki-tikki, don't kill me!"

"Do you think a snake killer kills muskrats?" said Rikki-tikki scornfully.

"Those who kill snakes get killed by snakes," said Chuchundra, more sorrowfully than ever. "And how am I to be sure that Nag won't mistake me for you some dark night?"

"There's not the least danger," said Rikki-tikki; "but Nag is in the garden, and I know you don't go there."

"My cousin Chua, the rat, told me—" said Chuchundra, and then he stopped.

"Told you what?"

"H'sh! Nag is everywhere, Rikki-tikki. You should have talked to Chua in the garden."

"I didn't—so you must tell me. Quick, Chuchundra, or I'll bite you!"

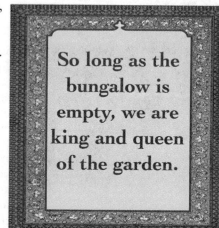

So long as the bungalow is empty, we are king and queen of the garden.

Chuchundra sat down and cried till the tears rolled off his whiskers. "I am a very poor man," he sobbed. "I never had spirit enough to run out into the middle of the room. H'sh! I mustn't tell you anything. Can't you *hear*, Rikki-tikki?"

Rikki-tikki listened. The house was as still as still, but he thought he could just catch the faintest *scratch-scratch* in the world—a noise as faint as that of a wasp walking on a windowpane—the dry scratch of a snake's scales on brickwork.

"That's Nag or Nagaina," he said to himself, "and he is crawling into the bathroom sluice.[7] You're right, Chuchundra; I should have talked to Chua."

He stole off to Teddy's bathroom, but there was nothing there, and then to Teddy's mother's bathroom. At the bottom of the smooth plaster wall, there was a brick pulled out to make a sluice for the bath water, and as Rikki-tikki stole in by the masonry curb where the bath is put, he heard Nag and Nagaina whispering together outside in the moonlight.

"When the house is emptied of people," said Nagaina to her husband, *"he* will have to go away, and then the garden will be our own again. Go in quietly, and remember that the big man who killed Karait is the first one to bite. Then come out and tell me, and we will hunt for Rikki-tikki together."

---

7. **bathroom sluice** (slōōs): a channel and opening in a wall through which the water in a bathtub can be drained outdoors.

128 UNIT ONE PART 2: MOMENTS OF DISCOVERY

Mini Lesson **Spelling** TEKS 16D   TAAS Writing Obj. 7

THE LETTERS *J, GE,* AND *DGE*

Instruction Explain to students that the sound *j* can be spelled *j, ge,* or *dge.* Tell them that familiarity with the following rules will help them improve their spelling.

- The letter *j* spells the *j* sound only at the beginning or in the middle of words: *just, enjoy.*
- The letters *ge* spell the *j* sound at the end of words: *cage*
- The letters *dge* appear at the end of one-syllable words with a short vowel: *edge.*

Exercise Have students write the following words as you read them aloud.

1. stranger
2. jealous
3. bridge
4. plunged
5. marriage
6. justice
7. advantage
8. pajamas
9. badge
10. dodge
11. fledgling
12. rejoice
13. danger
14. pledge
15. injury

Ask students to look for more words that fit this pattern and to add these words to their personal word lists.

 Use **Unit One Resource Book,** p. 71 for more practice.

"But are you sure that there is anything to be gained by killing the people?" said Nag.

"Everything. When there were no people in the bungalow, did we have any mongoose in the garden? So long as the bungalow is empty, we are king and queen of the garden; and remember that as soon as our eggs in the melon bed hatch (as they may tomorrow), our children will need room and quiet."

"I had not thought of that," said Nag. "I will go, but there is no need that we should hunt for Rikki-tikki afterward. I will kill the big man and his wife, and the child if I can, and come away quietly. Then the bungalow will be empty, and Rikki-tikki will go."

Rikki-tikki tingled all over with rage and hatred at this, and then Nag's head came through the sluice, and his five feet of cold body followed it. Angry as he was, Rikki-tikki was very frightened as he saw the size of the big cobra. Nag coiled himself up, raised his head, and looked into the bathroom in the dark, and Rikki could see his eyes glitter.

"Now, if I kill him here, Nagaina will know; and if I fight him on the open floor, the odds are in his favor. What am I to do?" said Rikki-tikki-tavi.

Nag waved to and fro, and then Rikki-tikki heard him drinking from the biggest water jar that was used to fill the bath. "That is good," said the snake. "Now, when Karait was killed, the big man had a stick. He may have that stick still, but when he comes in to bathe in the morning, he will not have a stick. I shall wait here till he comes. Nagaina— do you hear me?—I shall wait here in the cool till daytime."

There was no answer from outside, so Rikki-tikki knew Nagaina had gone away. Nag coiled himself down, coil by coil, around the bulge at the bottom of the water jar, and Rikki-tikki stayed still as death. After an hour he began to move, muscle by muscle, toward the jar. Nag was asleep, and Rikki-tikki looked at his big back, wondering which would be the best place for a good hold. "If I don't break his back at the first jump," said Rikki, "he can still fight; and if he fights—O Rikki!" He looked at the thickness of the neck below the hood, but that was too much for him; and a bite near the tail would only make Nag savage.

"It must be the head," he said at last; "the head above the hood. And, when I am once there, I must not let go."

Cross Curricular Link Science

COBRAS Cobras can be found in Africa, Australia, and Asia. Although all species form hoods by widening their neck ribs, the Indian cobra, which is about five and a half feet in length, has a distinctive spectacle mark on its hood. The venom of the cobra is enclosed in a groove in the short fangs at the front of the mouth. About ten percent of cobra bite victims die. The strength of the poison varies from species to species. The Indian cobra is not the largest or most poisonous of the species, but it kills several thousand people each year because of its habit of going into houses at dusk to catch rats.

Cobras feed mostly on small animals. Depending on the species, they either have live offspring or lay eggs. The female Indian cobra lays her eggs in a hollow tree or on the ground and guards them until they hatch.

Snake charmers often use cobras because their strikes are slow enough for the skillful charmer to avoid. The snakes sway in response to the charmer's movements, not his music.

A Ask students to pick out words and phrases that help them to see this battle in their minds.

Possible Responses: "as a rat is shaken by a dog"; "up and down, and round in great circles"; "body cart-whipped"; "upsetting the tin dipper and the soap dish"; "banged against the tin side"

ACTIVE READING

B **CLARIFY** **Possible Response:** Rikki attacked Nag, who began flinging Rikki back and forth. Teddy's father entered and shot and killed Nag.

ACTIVE READING

C **QUESTION** Point out Rikki's repeated question about Nagaina's location and ask students what danger Rikki still faces.

Possible Responses: He still faces Nagaina's anger, which will be even greater now that her husband is dead; he must get to Nagaina's eggs before they hatch.

Literary Analysis:
MINOR CHARACTERS

D Ask students how Darzee's wife affects the plot.

Possible Response: She draws Nagaina away from the eggs.

Active Reading PREDICTING

E Have students predict how Nagaina will react to the trick Darzee's wife uses.

Possible Responses: Nagaina is clever, so she will turn the tables and use her own trick on Rikki; Nagaina is blinded by arrogance and a desire for revenge, so she will fall for the trick and get mad.

Then he jumped. The head was lying a little clear of the water jar, under the curve of it; and, as his teeth met, Rikki braced his back against the bulge of the red earthenware to hold down the head. This gave him just one second's purchase,[8] and he made the most of it. Then he was battered to and fro as a rat is shaken by a dog—to and fro on the floor, up and down, and round in great circles; but his eyes were red, and he held on as the body cart-whipped over the floor, upsetting the tin dipper and the soap dish and the flesh brush, and banged against the tin side of the bath.

ACTIVE READING

CLARIFY What happened in the fight?

As he held, he closed his jaws tighter and tighter, for he made sure he would be banged to death; and, for the honor of his family, he preferred to be found with his teeth locked. He was dizzy, aching, and felt shaken to pieces when something went off like a thunderclap just behind him; a hot wind knocked him senseless, and red fire singed his fur. The big man had been awakened by the noise and had fired both barrels of a shotgun into Nag just behind the hood.

Rikki-tikki held on with his eyes shut, for now he was quite sure he was dead; but the head did not move, and the big man picked him up and said, "It's the mongoose again, Alice; the little chap has saved *our* lives now."

Then Teddy's mother came in with a very white face and saw what was left of Nag, and Rikki-tikki dragged himself to Teddy's bedroom and spent half the rest of the night shaking himself tenderly to find out whether he really was broken into forty pieces, as he fancied.

When morning came, he was very stiff but well pleased with his doings. "Now I have Nagaina to settle with, and she will be worse than five Nags, and there's no knowing when the eggs she spoke of will hatch. Goodness! I must go and see Darzee," he said.

 ithout waiting for breakfast, Rikki-tikki ran to the thorn bush where Darzee was singing a song of triumph at the top of his voice. The news of Nag's death was all over the garden, for the sweeper had thrown the body on the rubbish heap.

"Oh, you stupid tuft of feathers!" said Rikki-tikki angrily. "Is this the time to sing?"

"Nag is dead—is dead—is dead!" sang Darzee. "The valiant Rikki-tikki caught him by the head and held fast. The big man brought the bang stick, and Nag fell in two pieces! He will never eat my babies again."

"All that's true enough; but where's Nagaina?" said Rikki-tikki, looking carefully round him.

"Nagaina came to the bathroom sluice and called for Nag," Darzee went on; "and Nag came out on the end of a stick—the sweeper picked him up on the end of a stick and threw him upon the rubbish heap. Let us sing about the great, the red-eyed Rikki-tikki!" And Darzee filled his throat and sang.

ACTIVE READING

QUESTION What danger does Rikki still face?

"If I could get up to your nest, I'd roll your babies out!" said Rikki-tikki. "You don't know when to do the right thing at the right time. You're safe enough in your nest there, but it's war for me down here. Stop singing a minute, Darzee."

"For the great, the beautiful Rikki-tikki's sake I will stop," said Darzee. "What is it, O Killer of the terrible Nag?"

---

8. **purchase:** secure grasp or hold.

 Mini Lesson ## Vocabulary Strategy 🏴 TEKS 9C, 9G

LEARNING AND REMEMBERING NEW WORDS
Instruction Remind students that using a reference aid such as a dictionary will clarify the meaning of unfamiliar words. Because English is made up of words from many sources, finding out the origin, or etymology, of a new word can help students to recognize related words and remember the new word more easily. For example, *coil* is from French *"coillir,"* to collect or gather together. The meaning of *coil* is "to arrange in concentric rings." Help students to see that once they know the origin and meaning of *coil*, they can recognize

the word *uncoil* and infer its meaning.
Application Have students work in pairs to find words in the story that are unfamiliar to them. Students should look up the etymologies of these words and share their findings with the class. Discuss other words that are related to those they have defined, and encourage students to keep a notebook of words and their etymologies.

📋 Use **Vocabulary Transparencies and Copymasters**, p. 30.

"Where is Nagaina, for the third time?"

"On the rubbish heap by the stables, mourning for Nag. Great is Rikki-tikki with the white teeth."

"Bother my white teeth! Have you ever heard where she keeps her eggs?"

"In the melon bed, on the end nearest the wall, where the sun strikes nearly all day. She hid them there weeks ago."

"And you never thought it worthwhile to tell me? The end nearest the wall, you said?"

"Rikki-tikki, you are not going to eat her eggs?"

"Not eat exactly, no. Darzee, if you have a grain of sense, you will fly off to the stables and pretend that your wing is broken and let Nagaina chase you away to this bush. I must get to the melon bed, and if I went there now, she'd see me."

Darzee was a featherbrained little fellow who could never hold more than one idea at a time in his head; and just because he knew that Nagaina's children were born in eggs like his own, he didn't think at first that it was fair to kill them. But his wife was a sensible bird, and she knew that cobra's eggs meant young cobras later on; so she flew off from the nest and left Darzee to keep the babies warm and continue his song about the death of Nag. Darzee was very like a man in some ways.

She fluttered in front of Nagaina by the rubbish heap and cried out, "Oh, my wing is broken! The boy in the house threw a stone at me and broke it." Then she fluttered more desperately than ever.

Nagaina lifted up her head and hissed, "You warned Rikki-tikki when I would have killed him. Indeed and truly, you've chosen a bad place to be lame in." And she moved toward Darzee's wife, slipping along over the dust.

"The boy broke it with a stone!" shrieked Darzee's wife.

"Well! It may be some <u>consolation</u> to you when you're dead to know that I shall settle accounts with the boy. My husband lies on the rubbish heap this morning, but before night the boy in the house will lie very still. What is the use of running away? I am sure to catch you. Little fool, look at me!"

Darzee's wife knew better than to do *that,* for a bird who looks at a snake's eyes gets so frightened that she cannot move. Darzee's wife fluttered on, piping sorrowfully, and never leaving the ground, and Nagaina quickened her pace.

Rikki-tikki heard them going up the path from the stables, and he raced for the end of the melon patch near the wall. There, in the warm litter above the melons, very <u>cunningly</u> hidden, he found twenty-five eggs, about the size of a bantam's eggs[9] but with whitish skins instead of shells.

"I was not a day too soon," he said, for he could see the baby cobras curled up inside the

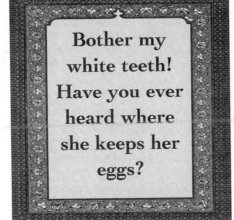

Bother my white teeth! Have you ever heard where she keeps her eggs?

---

9. **bantam's eggs:** the eggs of a small hen.

WORDS TO KNOW

consolation (kŏn′sə-lā′shən) *n.* something that comforts
cunningly (kŭn′ĭng-lē) *adv.* in a clever way that is meant to trick or deceive

Customizing Instruction

Less Proficient Readers
1 Ask students how the battle with Nag ends.
Possible Response: The man awakens and kills Nag with a gun.
Set a Purpose Have students read to find out what happens to Nagaina and her eggs.

Students Acquiring English
2 Encourage students to use their own experience to comprehend the way Rikki must feel after such a fierce battle. Discuss the phrase "forty pieces" as a metaphorical expression of how shaken up he is.
3 Remind students that the family in the story originally came from Great Britain and that the expression *bother* is British slang. It corresponds to the American English phrase *never mind.*

SYNTHESIZE

 Ask students why Rikki is speaking in this way to Nagaina, bragging of his deeds. Guide students to apply what they have already learned about Nagaina and Rikki.

Possible Response: He is drawing her attention away from the family and trying to provoke a fight so that he can finish her off.

EVALUATE

B Ask students what they think of Rikki's insistence on destroying Nagaina's children and of Nagaina's devotion to her eggs. Ask students if they feel any sympathy for Nagaina and her unborn children.

Possible Responses: Some might feel sympathy for Nagaina, because she is a living creature and protective of her children; some may not sympathize, because of her desire to kill the human family.

Reading Skills and Strategies: VISUALIZE

C Kipling creates vivid mental pictures of the action of the battle by including similes, comparisons using *like* or *as*. Ask students to identify similes that help them to see what is happening.

Possible Responses: "she gathered herself together like a watch spring"; "rustle of her tail...sounded like dry leaves"; "she...flew like an arrow"; "she goes like a whiplash flicked across a horse's neck"

skin, and he knew that the minute they were hatched they could each kill a man or a mongoose. He bit off the tops of the eggs as fast as he could, taking care to crush the young cobras, and turned over the litter from time to time to see whether he had missed any. At last there were only three eggs left, and Rikki-tikki began to chuckle to himself when he heard Darzee's wife screaming.

"Rikki-tikki, I led Nagaina toward the house, and she has gone into the veranda and—oh, come quickly—she means killing!"

Rikki-tikki smashed two eggs and tumbled backward down the melon bed with the third egg in his mouth and <u>scuttled</u> to the veranda as hard as he could put foot to the ground. Teddy and his mother and father were there at early breakfast; but Rikki-tikki saw that they were not eating anything. They sat stone still, and their faces were white. Nagaina was coiled up on the matting by Teddy's chair, within easy striking distance of Teddy's bare leg; and she was swaying to and fro, singing a song of triumph.

"Son of the big man that killed Nag," she hissed, "stay still. I am not ready yet. Wait a little. Keep very still, all you three! If you move, I strike, and if you do not move, I strike. Oh, foolish people who killed my Nag!"

Teddy's eyes were fixed on his father, and all his father could do was to whisper, "Sit still, Teddy. You mustn't move. Teddy, keep still."

Then Rikki-tikki came up and cried, "Turn round, Nagaina; turn and fight!"

"All in good time," said she, without moving her eyes. "I will settle my account with you presently. Look at your friends, Rikki-tikki. They are still and white. They are afraid. They dare not move, and if you come a step nearer, I strike."

"Look at your eggs," said Rikki-tikki, "in the melon bed near the wall. Go and look, Nagaina!"

The big snake turned half round and saw the egg on the veranda. "Ah-h! Give it to me," she said.

Rikki-tikki put his paws one on each side of the egg, and his eyes were blood-red. "What price for a snake's egg? For a young cobra? For a young king cobra? For the last—the very last of the brood? The ants are eating all the others down by the melon bed."

Nagaina spun clear round, forgetting everything for the sake of the one egg; and Rikki-tikki saw Teddy's father shoot out a big hand, catch Teddy by the shoulder, and drag him across the little table with the teacups, safe and out of reach of Nagaina.

"Tricked! Tricked! Tricked! *Rikk-tck-tck!*" chuckled Rikki-tikki. "The boy is safe, and it was I—I—I that caught Nag by the hood last night in the bathroom." Then he began to jump up and down, all four feet together, his head close to the floor. "He threw me to and fro, but he could not shake me off. He was dead before the big man blew him in two. I did it! *Rikki-tikki-tck-tck!* Come then, Nagaina. Come and fight with me. You shall not be a widow long."

Nagaina saw that she had lost her chance of killing Teddy, and the egg lay between Rikki-tikki's paws. "Give me the egg, Rikki-tikki. Give me the last of my eggs, and I will go away and never come back," she said, lowering her hood.

"Yes, you will go away, and you will never come back, for you will go to the rubbish heap with Nag. Fight, widow! The big man has gone for his gun! Fight!"

Rikki-tikki was bounding all round Nagaina, keeping just out of reach of her

WORDS TO KNOW   **scuttle** (skŭt'l) *v.* to run quickly, with hurried movements

132

Mini Lesson   **Viewing and Representing**   **TEKS 23A, B**

ILLUSTRATION

Instruction Explain that the illustration on page 133 is a composite of several photographic images. Ask students to examine the illustration and describe what it shows.

Possible Response: The illustration shows the confrontation of a mongoose and cobra.

Ask students what effect is created by showing a side view.

Possible Response: The attack poses of both the reptile and the mongoose are clearly shown. Both creatures are portrayed objectively with no favoritism revealed towards either. As a result, they appear evenly matched.

Application Ask students to compare this illustration with their mental images of Nagaina and Rikki-tikki and their battle.

Possible Responses: Similarities may include the red eyes of the mongoose, the stance of the cobra, the object that looks like an egg in the background, and the setting, which appears to be on a patio or veranda.

Customizing Instruction

Less Proficient Readers
• Why doesn't Rikki destroy the last egg?
  Possible Response: He is using it to distract Nagaina and draw her to him.

Set a Purpose Have students read to find out whether Rikki wins the battle with Nagaina.

Students Acquiring English
1 Tell students that the father hopes that Nagaina will not attack if Teddy doesn't move.

2 Explain that a widow is a woman whose husband has died. Tell students that a man whose wife has died is a widower.

Gifted and Talented
Explain that some critics have charged that Kipling's writing affirms his nationalistic views. Have students discuss whether they think Rikki's role as the family's bodyguard suggests the relationship between Britain and her colonies. Suggest that students read Kipling's poem "Gunga Din" and have them compare Rikki and Gunga Din.

stroke, his little eyes like hot coals. Nagaina gathered herself together and flung out at him. Rikki-tikki jumped up and backwards. Again and again and again she struck, and each time her head came with a whack on the matting of the veranda, and she gathered herself together like a watch spring. Then Rikki-tikki danced in a circle to get behind her, and Nagaina spun round to keep her head to his head, so that the rustle of her tail on the matting sounded like dry leaves blown along by the wind.

He had forgotten the egg. It still lay on the veranda, and Nagaina came nearer and nearer to it, till at last, while Rikki-tikki was drawing breath, she caught it in her mouth, turned to the veranda steps, and flew like an arrow down the path, with Rikki-tikki behind her. When the cobra runs for her life, she goes like a whiplash flicked across a horse's neck. Rikki-tikki knew that he must catch her, or all the trouble would begin again.

She headed straight for the long grass by the thorn bush, and as he was running, Rikki-tikki heard Darzee still singing his foolish little song of triumph. But Darzee's wife was wiser. She flew off her nest as Nagaina came along and flapped her wings about Nagaina's head. If Darzee had helped, they might have turned her; but Nagaina only lowered her hood and went on. Still, the instant's delay brought Rikki-tikki up to her, and as she plunged into the rat hole where she and Nag used to live, his little white teeth were clenched on her tail, and he went down with her—and very few mongooses, however wise and old they may be, care to follow a cobra into its hole.

A Ask students if they think Rikki's decision to follow Nagaina into the hole is wise. Have students support their judgments.

Possible Responses: It is unwise, because it traps Rikki in the dark and because the cobra can maneuver underground better than the mongoose; it is wise, because it is the only way to trap the cobra.

📖 Use **Reading and Critical Thinking Transparencies**, p. 15, for additional support.

Literary Analysis | PERSONIFICATION |

B Ask students to analyze the character of Rikki from what he says after the battle.

Possible Responses: Rikki is modest; he sees the killing of cobras as his duty.

C How is Rikki's character affected by his triumph?

Possible Response: He does not allow himself to get too proud or to relax his guard.

A It was dark in the hole; and Rikki-tikki never knew when it might open out and give Nagaina room to turn and strike at him. He held on savagely and stuck out his feet to act as brakes on the dark slope of the hot, moist earth.

Then the grass by the mouth of the hole stopped waving, and Darzee said, "It is all over with Rikki-tikki! We must sing his death song. Valiant Rikki-tikki is dead! For Nagaina will surely kill him underground."

So he sang a very mournful song that he made up on the spur of the minute; and just as he got to the most touching part, the grass quivered again, and Rikki-tikki, covered with dirt, dragged himself out of the hole leg by leg, licking his whiskers. Darzee stopped with a little shout. Rikki-tikki shook some of the dust out of his fur and **B** sneezed. "It is all over," he said. "The widow will never come out again." And the red ants that live between the grass stems heard him and began to troop down one after another to see if he had spoken the truth.

Rikki-tikki curled himself up in the grass and slept where he was—slept and slept till it was late in the afternoon, for he had done a hard day's work.

"Now," he said, when he awoke, "I will go back to the house. Tell the coppersmith, Darzee, and he will tell the garden that Nagaina is dead."

The coppersmith is a bird who makes a noise exactly like the beating of a little hammer on a copper pot; and the reason he is always making it is because he is the town crier to every Indian garden and tells all the news to everybody who cares to listen. As Rikki-tikki went up the path, he heard his "attention" notes like a tiny dinner gong, and then the steady "*Ding-dong-tock!* Nag is dead—*dong!* Nagaina is dead! *Ding-dong-tock!*" That set all the birds in the garden singing and the frogs croaking, for Nag and Nagaina used to eat frogs as well as little birds.

When Rikki got to the house, Teddy and Teddy's mother (she looked very white still, for she had been fainting) and Teddy's father came out and almost cried over him; and that night he ate all that was given him till he could eat no more and went to bed on Teddy's shoulder, where Teddy's mother saw him when she came to look late at night.

"He saved our lives and Teddy's life," she said to her husband. "Just think, he saved all our lives."

Rikki-tikki woke up with a jump, for the mongooses are light sleepers.

"Oh, it's you," said he. "What are you bothering for? All the cobras are dead; and if they weren't, I'm here."

Rikki-tikki had a right to be proud of himself; but he did not grow too proud, and he kept that garden as a mongoose should keep it, with tooth and jump and spring and bite, till never a cobra dared show its head inside the walls. ❖

> Very few mongooses, however wise and old they may be, care to follow a cobra into its hole.

Teaching Options

✓ Assessment **Informal Assessment** **TEKS** 10H, 11A 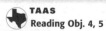 **TAAS** Reading Obj. 4, 5 **TAAS** Writi...

PREDICTING PROBABLE FUTURE ACTIONS AND OUTCOMES You can informally assess students' understanding of the selection by having them imagine a future conflict between Rikki and a cobra. Students should write the account as if Rikki is thinking to himself about what he should do. His plan should reflect what he learned from his battles with Nag and Nagaina.

RUBRIC

3 Full Accomplishment Response is a logical strategy that incorporates what Rikki has learned. Rikki's thoughts accurately represent his character as it is developed in the story.

2 Substantial Accomplishment Response is a good plan that includes much of what Rikki has learned. His thoughts reflect his character with some accuracy.

1 Little or Partial Accomplishment Response omits the lessons that Rikki has learned and is inconsistent with Rikki's character.

Thinking through the LITERATURE

Connect to the Literature

1. What Do You Think?
What did you think about Rikki-tikki by the end of the story?

> **Comprehension Check**
> - Why was Rikki-tikki grateful to Teddy's family?
> - Why did Rikki-tikki destroy Nagaina's eggs?
> - Why did Teddy's mother change her mind about Rikki-tikki?

Think Critically

2. What qualities or abilities enable Rikki-tikki to fight the cobras to the finish? Explain.

3. Which of Rikki-tikki's battles do you think takes the greatest courage? Explain your choice.

4. What do you think the use of personification adds to the story? Explain.

 THINK ABOUT
- Nagaina's threatened attack on the family at breakfast
- the battle with Nag in the bathroom
- Darzee's warnings to Rikki-tikki

5. **ACTIVE READING** **PREDICTING** Look back at the chart you made in your **READER'S NOTEBOOK.** How accurate were the **predictions** you made as you read the story? Discuss with a classmate the details in the story that either helped or misled you.

Extend Interpretations

6. Critic's Corner "Rikki-tikki-tavi" is considered by many to be a classic story—a story that has been enjoyed by many generations of readers. How would you explain what gives this story its lasting appeal?

7. Connect to Life Have you ever helped to take care of an unusual pet, or would you like to have one? Share your thoughts with a partner.

Literary Analysis

PERSONIFICATION When a writer gives human qualities to an animal, object, or idea, this is called **personification.** In "Rikki-tikki-tavi," the animals in the garden are personified, conversing as if they were human.

Cooperative Learning Activity
With a small group, make a list of animals in this story and brainstorm the "human" qualities that each shows. Rank the qualities on a scale from 1 to 10, with 10 being the most admirable. Then share your list with the rest of the class and give reasons for your rankings.

Animal	Rating	Qualities
Rikki-tikki-tavi	10	brave, loyal
Nag		

REVIEW **CLIMAX** The turning point in a plot, the moment of greatest intensity and highest interest, is called the **climax.** In "Rikki-tikki-tavi" the climax comes when Rikki-tikki emerges victorious from the cobra hole where he has killed Nagaina.

Extend Interpretations

6. Critic's Corner Possible Responses: The main character is heroic and admirable; the story is suspenseful and fast moving; the writing is brisk and colorful.

7. Connect to Life Responses will vary. Encourage students to find out something about the unusual pets that they mention. Discuss which have characteristics that would make them good pets.

Connect to the Literature

1. Responses will vary. Possible Response: Rikki is very brave and dutiful.

Comprehension Check
- They rescued him and revived him.
- They would hatch into more dangerous cobras.
- Rikki has saved her entire family.

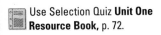 Use Selection Quiz **Unit One Resource Book,** p. 72.

Think Critically

2. Possible Responses: loyalty to his family and determination not to let them down; instinct, because the cobra is his natural enemy; courage to go down the snake hole when others would have turned back.

3. Possible Responses: Some say the fight with Karait takes the greatest courage because the snake is both elusive and lethal. Others may choose the battle with Nag because Rikki is inexperienced and vastly overpowered; others may mention the battle with Nagaina because Rikki is at a disadvantage in the dark rat hole.

4. Possible Responses: The characters of the animals are revealed clearly. Nagaina is seen as malevolent because of how she threatens the family; Nag is cold-blooded and intelligent as revealed through his plotting in the bathroom; the other animals emerge as individuals – some brave, some cowardly. Their personalities add suspense and interest to the story.

5. Responses will vary.

Use **Reading and Critical Thinking Transparencies,** p. 7, for additional support.

Literary Analysis

Personification Suggest that students select one person per group to share everyone's ideas and opinions, and one person to write the list and rankings.

Use **Literary Analysis Transparencies,** p. 3, for additional support.

Writing Options

1. **Song Lyrics** To get students started, have them reread the description of the battle before writing the lyrics. Suggest that a refrain be woven through the song and encourage students to set their words to a popular, familiar tune. The tune should have a rhythm and a melody that suit the mood of the words. This exercise is well suited for **auditory learners.**

Use **Writing Transparencies,** p. 17, for additional support.

2. **Different Perspectives** Remind students to base their paragraphs on the character of Nagaina as she is developed in the story. **To make this assignment easier,** direct students to the passage on page 132 in which she realizes that Rikki has her egg. Discuss what she would be feeling.

Activities & Explorations

1. **Comic Book** To get students started on this assignment, have them decide how many panels they will include and what each panel will show. Review some comic books with students for style tips.

2. **Radio Script** To get students started on this assignment, play a radio version or recording of another, similar story and discuss what was effective about the recording. Encourage them to create sound effects that echo the action in the story.

Use **Communications Transparencies and Copymasters,** p. 13, for additional support.

Inquiry & Research

Just Like People? To make the assignment easier, have students work in pairs to do their research or bring sources into the classroom for their use. Encourage students to support their opinions about the human qualities of animals with facts, examples, and incidents.

Visual learners may create a media display of the information they have discovered.

Vocabulary in Action

Assessment Practice

1. d   4. c
2. c   5. a
3. b

Writing Options

1. **Song Lyrics** In the story, Darzee sings a song about Rikki-tikki's killing of Nag. Write lyrics for this song, beginning with the words quoted in the story. Place the lyrics in your **Working Portfolio.**

2. **Different Perspectives** Most, but not all, of the characters in the story consider Rikki-tikki to be a hero. Write a paragraph or two of the story from Nagaina's perspective.

Writing Handbook
See p. R33: Narrative Writing.

Activities & Explorations

1. **Comic Book** Make a comic-book version of part of this story. Determine the important scenes you want to portray and what you want to include in the speech balloons. Illustrate the scenes and then share your comic book with younger audiences. ~ **ART**

2. **Radio Script** Stage a radio reading of a scene from the story. Assign students to perform the parts of the characters and the narrator, and have other students provide sound effects. Rehearse your performance, then tape-record it for other classes. ~ **PERFORMING**

Inquiry & Research

Just Like People? Skim the story for details about the mongoose. Then check an encyclopedia, other books, or a computer database for additional information about the animal's instincts and behavior. Many people think that animals don't have important human qualities—such as kindness and sympathy. The fictional character Rikki-tikki-tavi has these qualities in the story, but do real animals have them?

Real World Link
To begin your research, read "Primal Compassion" on p. 138.

Vocabulary in Action

EXERCISE: ASSESSMENT PRACTICE On a sheet of paper, write the letter of the word or phrase that is most similar in meaning to the underlined Word to Know in each sentence.

1. The warmth of the fire <u>revived</u> the wet little mongoose.
   a. warmed up   c. scared
   b. burned   d. woke up

2. When he saw the cobra, Darzee, the tailorbird, <u>cowered</u> in his nest.
   a. sang   c. cringed
   b. attacked   d. fluttered

3. It was a <u>consolation</u> to the family to have Rikki-tikki-tavi as a pet.
   a. duty   c. prize
   b. comfort   d. punishment

4. Rikki-tikki <u>cunningly</u> found the cobra eggs among the melons.
   a. quickly   c. cleverly
   b. carefully   d. bravely

5. The muskrat <u>scuttled</u> away when the cobra came near.
   a. hurried   c. strolled
   b. shuffled   d. sneaked

Grammar in Context: Varying Sentence Length

Notice how Rudyard Kipling sandwiches one long sentence between two shorter ones:

> Then Rikki-tikki went out into the garden to see what was to be seen. It was a large garden, only half-cultivated, with bushes, as big as summerhouses, of Marshal Niel roses, lime and orange trees, clumps of bamboos, and thickets of high grass. Rikki-tikki licked his lips.

Using sentences of different lengths adds variety to your writing. Using only short sentences can make your writing sound choppy.

Punctuation Tip: Notice how Kipling uses the **semicolon** to join three sentences:

> His eyes and the end of his restless nose were pink; he could scratch himself anywhere he pleased with any leg, front or back, that he chose to use; he could fluff up his tail till it looked like a bottlebrush. . . .

WRITING EXERCISE Choose two sentences from each group of three. Rewrite the two simple sentences as one longer sentence.

Example: ***Original*** Rikki-tikki's eyes grew red. He rocked back and forth. He looked for a good place to bite the snake.

Rewritten Rikki-tikki's eyes grew red. He rocked back and forth, looking for a good place to bite the snake.

1. Rikki-tikki ran all around the room. Rikki-tikki jumped up onto the table. Then he sneezed.
2. At night the mongoose slept with Teddy. The mongoose slept in the nursery. Rikki protected him.
3. No one liked cobras. Nag and Nagaina ate frogs for dinner. Nag and Nagaina ate small birds, too.

> *"I always prefer to believe the best of everybody—it saves so much trouble."*

Rudyard Kipling
1865–1936

Childhood in India Rudyard Kipling was born in Bombay, India, but educated in England. His father was an architect and artist, and his mother was devoted to the arts. As a child, Kipling loved to read and he wrote verse. After his schooling, he returned to India in 1882 and worked as a writer for a daily newspaper in Lahore. Kipling's stories about his Indian travels made him extremely popular in India. He returned to London in 1889, and wrote poems and new stories about India that made him famous.

Animal Storyteller When he had children of his own, Kipling turned to writing children's stories. Early collections, *The Jungle Book* and *The Second Jungle Book,* include animal stories set in India about an Indian boy raised by wolves.

Nobel Prize Kipling received numerous honors and awards. In 1907 he received the Nobel Prize in literature. He is buried in London in the Poets' Corner of Westminster Abbey.

 LaserLinks: Background for Reading
Science Connection

Grammar in Context

WRITING EXERCISE
Possible Responses

1. Rikki-tikki ran all around the room and jumped up onto the table. Then he sneezed.
2. At night the mongoose slept in the nursery with Teddy. Rikki protected him.
3. No one liked cobras. Nag and Nagaina ate frogs and small birds for dinner.

 Use **Writing Transparencies**, p. 19, for additional support.

Rudyard Kipling

Kipling believed it was the duty of the British Empire to spread its culture around the world, and much of his writing glorifies the British Empire. Although his popularity as a writer has faded somewhat over the years, he is generally regarded as a master of the short adventure story.

 Grammar **TEKS** 17A  **TAAS** Writing Obj. 3, 5, 7

SENTENCE VARIETY

Instruction Remind students that varying the length of the sentences that they use will help to keep their reader's attention. Compound and complex sentences can create a smoother flow in their writing; however, using short sentences for important ideas will help to draw attention to them. Display the following sentences:

Rikki-tikki clenched Nagaina's tail firmly in his teeth as he followed her into the rat hole. He was gone for a long time, but finally he emerged triumphant because Nagaina was dead. Although the sentences are grammatically correct, illustrate how the death of Nagaina stands out in this rewritten version:

REWRITTEN Rikki-tikki clenched Nagaina's tail firmly in his teeth as he followed her into the rat hole. He was gone for a long time, but finally he emerged triumphant. Nagaina was dead.

Application Have students write a paragraph of six simple sentences about the story. Then students should exchange papers with a part-ner and rewrite the paragraph with a variety of sentences, using simple sentences for emphasis. Students should take turns reading the first version and then the rewritten paragraph to each other so that they hear the difference.

 Use **Unit One Resource Book**, p. 70.
Use **Grammar Transparencies and Copymasters**, p. 134.

Use McDougal Littell's *Language Network,* Chapter 18, for more instruction and practice in sentence variety.

Objectives
- read to be informed
- raise questions in response to texts
- reinforce themes presented in the text

Connecting to the Literature
This magazine article is a fitting companion piece for "Rikki-Tikki-Tavi" because it is reflective of the relationship between the Rikki and his human family. Students will enjoy reading a piece about a real-life animal hero who seemed to reach out with compassion to a little boy. Like the story, the article raises questions about the possible relationships between humans and animals.

Primal Compassion ❶

By Charles Hirshberg and Robert Allison

It was gut-wrenching, seeing that little guy smack onto the concrete floor," says Robert Allison, who saw it, heard it and then started photographing it. He was there when Binti Jua (Swahili for "Daughter of Sunshine"), a western lowland gorilla in Illinois's Brookfield Zoo, came to the rescue of a three-year-old boy who had fallen 18 feet to the floor of her enclosure.

By now, thanks in no small part to Bob Allison, almost everyone knows of Binti, and it is common knowledge in Illinois that the boy—whose identity is being shielded by his parents—has made a complete recovery. Brookfield visitors can see that Binti has returned to the calm, dull life of a zoo animal, snacking on sweet potatoes and grooming Koola, her one-and-a-half-year-old baby. But there is much that remains unknown, as people around the world continue to ponder the lessons of the remarkable story. None ponder more deeply than the Allisons, a Bettendorf, Iowa, family changed forever by the emotional force of what they witnessed.

"We never made it to the aquarium"

It started when Bob, a 51-year-old carpenter, and his wife, Vicki, 50, a bookstore manager, decided to take a weekend in Chicago with their daughter-in-law Johnna, the 31-year-old wife of their son Randy, and the grandkids—Charli, 10, and Ryan, five. Also along for the adventure was Randy's brother, Eric, 31. The plan was to visit the zoo and the aquarium, but, says Bob wryly, "we never made it to the aquarium."

At Brookfield's Tropic World exhibit, Bob, who has been an animal lover since his Kentucky boyhood, was enthusiastically taking pictures of the gorillas with his point-and-shoot camera, even though the apes were having "a pretty boring day, staring at their feet." Eric was enjoying his niece and nephew almost as much as they were enjoying the animals. Little Ryan was having the time of his life, darting around in excitement.

Then, for reasons he can't explain, Eric

began watching a three-year-old boy as rambunctious as Ryan, climbing the rocks in front of a faux bamboo fence that surrounds the exhibit. "I know it sounds weird, but something kept telling me to look over there," Eric recalls. He watched the boy lifting himself toward the top of the fence and wondered with growing anxiety, "Is he going to go higher?" The boy's upper body teetered above the fence. And then, suddenly, his momentum carried him over.

Eric gasped as he watched the boy tumble wide-eyed through the air, caroming off a ledge that jutted from the cliff. A second later, Eric heard "a huge thud. Even people who had no idea what had happened knew it was something horrible."

Vicki began to tremble and reeled as though she might faint. Eric seized her and buried her face in his chest. "Don't look," he whispered. Five-year-old Ryan grew suddenly hysterical, springing into Johnna's arms wailing, "Don't let me fall! Don't let me fall!"

Bob, too, was upset, "but I also knew something incredible was about to happen." He moved along the rail, photographing the drama in the pit below. Though Eric, enraged, roared at him to stop, Bob went on shooting.

Binti had hopped off her perch without hesitation, and now she made her way toward the boy, little Koola still at her breast. "She moved with such deliberateness," says Bob,

still amazed several weeks later. When she reached the boy, "she lifted his arm as if she were looking for signs of life. She did that twice." To Eric, "it seemed like she was asking, 'Are you O.K.?'" Then, says Bob, "she lifted the boy and put him to her chest, just exactly the way she was holding her own baby."

"What's happening?" Vicki asked. "A gorilla's got him," Eric told her. It may seem like a strange thing to have said by way of comfort, but Eric swears that "you could tell, you could just feel she was going to help the boy."

At first Binti seemed to want to take him in the direction of the crowd, but, looking up, she appeared to sense panic from that direction. "You could definitely see her making decisions," Bob says. "You could see her look up and concentrate." Still carrying the child as though he were her own, she started off in the other direction. When Alpha, another female gorilla, much larger than Binti, approached, Binti stopped and challenged her with a guttural noise. "I don't think Alpha would have hurt the child," says Eric, "but that's the way a mom is."

Finally, to the amazement of everyone, Binti gently laid the boy by the door of the enclosure. Moments later, keepers came with fire hoses to hold the gorillas at bay while they collected the injured boy. The hoses bothered Eric. "She's gonna have a weird night tonight, trying to figure that out," he thought to himself. "She saves him, and then sees the hose."

Once the boy was removed, the Allisons spoke to authorities and left the zoo. At first, says Eric, "we could hardly look at each other." They returned to their motel room and, unable to sleep, began to open up. Though he admitted the event had been truly extraordinary, Eric was still angry that his father had taken pictures. "We came to a decision about the photographs as a family," says Bob. "If the boy didn't recover, we wouldn't show them."

Of course, the boy did recover. In a matter of days he was up and around and acting like a normal three-year-old, despite a broken hand and a vicious gash on the left side of his face. Doctors said he remembered nothing about what had happened.

In the wake of the good news about the boy, the Allisons began to pore over the pictures. "I can't begin to explain the thoughts, the feelings they've caused us to have," says Bob. He has read that some scientists have expressed skepticism about Binti's actions. ("Would Binti have acted any differently if it had been handling, say, a sack of flour?" a researcher asked in the *San Francisco Examiner*.) Bob agrees that "we can't know for sure what was going on in her mind." But there is not a glimmer of doubt in his mind about what her intentions were. And whenever he reexamines his pictures, he experiences a new sense of exhilaration. "I keep studying them, studying her face and her posture," he says. "I can't help but think there's a message in this. She didn't hesitate to help. If this animal that's supposed to be below us can be this way, why can't we?"

Reading for Information *continued*

3 An **opinion** is one possible interpretation of the facts. An opinion is a belief confidently held but not based on objective knowledge or proof. For example, your friend Mark gives you a present but won't tell you why. You then form an opinion about why he gave it to you. Look at the verbs the writers use to describe Binti Jua's actions. Are they expressing opinions or facts?

4 What are Bob and Eric's opinions of Binti Jua's rescue? What do they assume was going through the gorilla's mind?

5 What opposing opinion do the writers include? Which do you believe, the researcher's opinion or Bob Allison's? Explain your reasoning.

IDENTIFYING BIAS Do you think the writers lead you to believe that Binti Jua showed the human quality of compassion during the rescue? Support your opinion with evidence from the article. What is your evaluation of the information presented in the article?

Inquiry & Research

Activity Link: "Rikki-tikki-tavi," p. 136. After reading this article, do you think animals are able to show human qualities? Search for other articles on the subject, preferably ones that present opposing views. Then write a balanced paragraph explaining your opinion, using facts from your readings or personal observations to support your claim.

3 The writers express their opinions about what the gorillas might be thinking and feeling. There is no way they could know for sure if they are right.

4 **Possible Response:** They assume that the gorilla felt a compassionate connection to the boy.

5 **Possible Response:** Writers present the opposing opinion that Binti would have treated a sack of flour in the same way. Students should support their opinions with concrete reasons.

Use **Reading and Critical Thinking Transparencies,** p. 28, for additional support.

  Inquiry & Research TEKS 13C

The Inquiry & Research activity on this page links to the Inquiry & Research activity of Choices & Challenges on page 136, following the story "Rikki-Tikki-Tavi."

Instruction Students should use multiple sources of information, including electronic texts, experts, and print resources to locate information. Encourage them to contact people who work with animals, either at zoos, animal shelters, science labs, or nature centers. Opinions from these people should prove valuable.

Remind them to try to gather opinions from both sides. Before students interview a person, they should prepare a list of questions. They might also give people they are interviewing an overview of the story and the magazine article.

Practice Suggest that students work in pairs to identify and evaluate at least three possible sources of information for their paragraphs. Then have them select two sources that they think would be most productive.

Use **Writing Transparencies,** p. 53, for additional support.

Objectives

- expand vocabulary through wide reading
- rely on context to determine meanings of idioms and slang
- use reference materials such as a dictionary or thesaurus to determine word meanings

EXERCISE
Possible Responses:

1. stop fighting and make peace
2. relax with friends
3. discussed
4. money
5. changed their minds

 Use **Unit One Resource Book,** p. 73.
Use **Vocabulary Transparencies and Copymasters,** p. 5, for additional support.

Beyond the Meanings of Words

Most people use casual expressions when they are speaking in a relaxed atmosphere.

This expression has a definite meaning, but does not make sense when considered word by word. This is an example of an **idiom** — an expression that cannot be understood by simply putting together the meanings of the individual words. Many idioms are part of **informal English.**

> When Mama finally took her order, the starving lady all of a sudden couldn't **make up her mind** whether she wanted a vegetable plate or fish and a salad.
> —Toni Cade Bambara, "The War of the Wall"

This phrase means **"come to a definite decision"**

Strategies for Building Vocabulary

Informal English also includes **slang**—words and phrases that are specially made up or adapted for use in casual speech. The word *freaky* and the use of *cool* in the sentence "That's a cool car" are examples of slang. You can use the following strategies to help you understand unfamiliar slang and idioms.

❶ **Find Context Clues** English idioms and slang can sometimes be hard to understand, especially for people whose first language is not English. You can often figure out what an idiom or slang expression means by looking at its context—the surrounding words and phrases. Consider the following example:

> The rice, beans, and vegetables at the restaurant really **stick to the diners' ribs,** so they never leave hungry.

Here, *stick to the diners' ribs* means "are substantial or filling." You can understand the

idiom if you understand the situation: the diners are never hungry after eating the food.
The following passage contains slang:

> He gave the painter lady the once-over, **checking out** her paint-spattered jeans, her chalky T-shirt, her floppy-brimmed straw hat.
> —Toni Cade Bambara, "The War of the Wall"

Checking out means "examining." You can use the context to help you recognize that Side Pocket is examining the painter lady's clothes.

❷ **Use Reference Materials** Many dictionaries give the meanings of idioms and slang terms of the past and present. Look in a library or on the World Wide Web for dictionaries of slang terms and idioms.

EXERCISE Use context clues to define the underlined examples of informal language. Check your definitions in a dictionary.

1. After our fight, we decided to <u>bury the hatchet</u> and become friends.
2. I decided to <u>hang out</u> after school.
3. The boys <u>tossed around</u> a few ideas about how to save their wall from the painter.
4. The boys realized that they had only enough <u>dough</u> to buy one can of paint.
5. They <u>changed their tune</u> when they saw the amazing and wonderful mural.

142   UNIT ONE   PART 2: MOMENTS OF DISCOVERY

rk the Protector
by Gary Paulsen

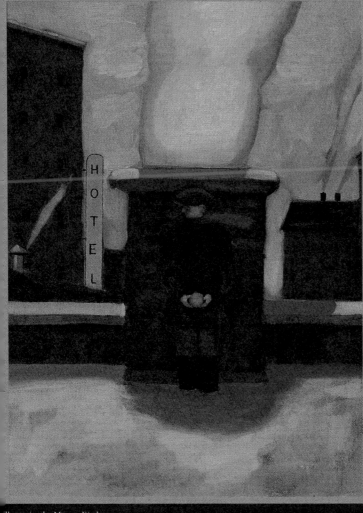

Illustration by Murray Kimber

Possible Objectives
You can use this selection to achieve one or more of the following objectives:
- enjoy silent sustained reading (Option One)
- read and analyze literature with a group (Option Two)
- use the Reader's Notebook to write in response to literature (Option Three)

Summary
Because of problems at home, the boy who narrates this story becomes a street kid, living in a basement. He earns money setting up pins at a bowling alley and selling newspapers. This puts him on the street late at night. There he becomes the target of a predatory group of boys who steal his money and beat him up. One night he leaves work by a new route, clutching a hamburger. Coming down a fire escape, he almost steps on a dog, which growls. The boy throws half the burger to the dog and escapes him but runs into the thugs, led by "Happy" Santun. The narrator hits Happy and the gang attacks him, but the beating suddenly stops. The narrator opens his eyes to see the dog with a piece of Happy's jeans in his mouth. Grateful, the boy gives the dog the rest of his hamburger. The animal follows him home and shares some food. The boy names his new companion Dirk after a character in a novel. The next day, Dirk again protects the boy from Happy. From then on, he is the boy's bodyguard.

That summer, the boy works on a farm, taking Dirk with him. Dirk feels at home and stays with Olaf, the farmer, when the boy returns to school. The next year, the boy visits and learns that Dirk now has a job—guarding Olaf's sheep from coyotes. Olaf and the boy agree that Dirk is indeed a good protector.

Option One
Silent Sustained Reading

Consider setting aside time each week for independent reading. During this time, you and your students would read for enjoyment. "Dirk the Protector" will appeal to many students and can be read independently in 30 minutes or so. If you want to encourage students to read for pleasure, you might forego assignments related to this selection. Options Two and Three offer suggestions should you choose to make assignments.

Option Two
Shared Reading Groups

You may assign students to groups or allow them to choose their own. Students can read the selection together, alternately reading sections aloud, or they can read independently and meet to cooperate in a project that portrays some element of the story.

Possible Projects

- Have students form two teams and debate whether Dirk would make a good pet or not. Remind students to support their positions with reasons and examples.
- Have students take a poll to decide whether the class thinks that the narrator really needs a protector or not.

For a time in my life I became a street kid. It would be nice to put it another way but what with the drinking at home and the difficulties it caused with my parents I couldn't live in the house.

I made a place for myself in the basement by the furnace and hunted and fished in the woods around the small town. But I had other needs as well—clothes, food, school supplies—and they required money.

I was not afraid of work and spent most of my summers working on farms for two, three and finally five dollars a day. This gave me enough for school clothes, though never for enough clothes or the right kind; I was never cool or in. But during the school year I couldn't leave town to work the farms. I looked for odd jobs but most of them were taken by the boys who stayed in town through the summer. All the conventional[1] jobs like working in the markets or at the drugstore were gone and all I could find was setting pins in the small bowling alley over the Four Clover Bar.

It had just six alleys and they were busy all the time—there were leagues each night from seven to eleven—but the pay for truly brutal work was only seven cents a line. There weren't many boys willing to do the work but with so few alleys, it was still very hard to earn much money. A dollar a night was not uncommon and three was outstanding.

To make up the difference I started selling newspapers in the bars at night. This kept me up and out late, and I often came home at midnight. But it added to my income so that I could stay above water.[2]

Unfortunately it also put me in the streets at a time when there was what might be called a rough element. There weren't gangs then, not exactly, but there were groups of boys who more or less hung out together and got into trouble. They were the forerunners of the gangs we have now, but with some singular differences. They did not have firearms—but many carried switchblade knives.

These groups were predatory,[3] and they hunted the streets at night.

I became their favorite target in this dark world. Had the town been larger I might have hidden from them, or found different routes. But there was only a small uptown section and it was impossible for me to avoid them. They would catch me walking a dark street and surround me and with threats and blows steal what money I had earned that night.

I tried fighting back but there were usually several of them. I couldn't win. Because I was from "the wrong side of the tracks" I didn't think I could go to the authorities. It all seemed hopeless.

And then I met Dirk.

The bowling alley was on a second floor and had a window in back of the pit area. When all the lanes were going, the heat from the pin lights made the temperature close to a hundred degrees. Outside the window a ladder led to the roof. One fall evening, instead of leaving work through the front door, I made my way out the window and up the ladder onto the roof. I hoped to find a new way home to escape the boys who waited for me. That night one of the league bowlers had bowled a perfect game—300—and in celebration had bought the pit boys hamburgers and Cokes. I had put the burger and Coke in a bag to take back to my basement. The bag had grease stains and smelled of toasted buns, and my mouth watered as I moved from the roof of the bowling alley to the flat roof over the hardware store, then down a fire escape that led to a dark alcove off an alley.

---

1. **conventional** (kən-vĕn′shə-nəl): usual, traditional.
2. **stay above water:** survive.
3. **predatory** (prĕd′ə-tôr′ē): stealing from or hurting others.

There was a black space beneath the stairs and as I reached the bottom and my foot hit the ground I heard a low growl. It was not loud, more a rumble that seemed to come from the earth and so full of menace that it stopped me cold, my foot frozen in midair.

I raised my foot and the growl stopped.

I lowered my foot and the growl came again. My foot went up and it stopped.

I stood there, trying to peer through the steps of the fire escape. For a time I couldn't see more than a dark shape crouched back in the gloom. There was a head and a back, and as my eyes became accustomed to the dark I could see that it had scraggly, scruffy hair and two eyes that glowed yellow.

We were at an impasse.[4] I didn't want to climb up the ladder again but if I stepped to the ground it seemed likely I would be bitten. I hung there for a full minute before I thought of the hamburger. I could use it as a decoy and get away.

The problem was the hamburger smelled so good and I was so hungry.

I decided to give the beast under the stairs half a burger. I opened the sack, unwrapped the tinfoil and threw half the sandwich under the steps, then jumped down and ran for the end of the alley. I was just getting my stride, legs and arms pumping, pulling air with a heaving chest, when I rounded the corner and ran smack into the latest group of boys who were terrorizing me.

There were four of them, led by a thug—he and two of the others would ultimately land in prison—named, absurdly, "Happy" Santun.

Happy was built like an upright freezer and had just about half the intelligence but this time it was easy. I'd run right into him.

"Well—lookit here. He came to us this time. . . ."

Over the months I had developed a policy of flee or die—run as fast as I could to avoid the pain, and to hang on to my hard-earned money. Sometimes it worked, but most often they caught me.

This time, they already had me. I could have handed over the money, taken a few hits and been done with it, but something in me snapped and I hit Happy in the face with every ounce of strength in my puny body.

He brushed off the blow easily and I went down in a welter of blows and kicks from all four of them. I curled into a ball to protect what I could. I'd done this before, many times, and knew that they would stop sometime—although I suspected that because I'd hit Happy it might take longer than usual for them to get bored hitting me.

Instead there was some commotion that I didn't understand and the kicks stopped coming. There was a snarling growl that seemed to come from the bowels of the earth, followed by the sound of ripping cloth, screams, and then the fading slap of footsteps running away.

For another minute I remained curled up, then opened my eyes to find that I was alone.

But when I rolled over I saw the dog.

It was the one that had been beneath the stairs. Brindled,[5] patches of hair gone, one ear folded over and the other standing straight and notched from fighting. He didn't seem to be any particular breed. Just big and rangy, right on the edge of ugly, though I would come to think of him as beautiful. He was Airedale crossed with hound crossed with alligator.

---

4. **impasse** (ĭm'păs'): a situation in which no progress can be made; a deadlock.

5. **brindled** (brĭn'dld): light brownish yellow or grayish with streaks or spots of a darker color.

Option Three
Reader's Notebook
Provide the following direction to students before they read:
Remind them that a story's title is often a clue to what is important in the story. Ask students to keep the title in mind as they read.

Ask students to read to the end of page 144 and to make a prediction about who or what Dirk might be. Have them record their predictions in their Reader's Notebooks. At the top of the second column of page 145, have them predict what is likely to happen and to record that prediction as well.

At the end of the story, ask students to reread their predictions and note whether either or both were correct and why they made them. Based on what they know from the story and title, ask if they should have been able to predict that Dirk would make a good guard dog for sheep. Have them note their answers to this question and their reasons.

Use **Reading and Critical Thinking Transparencies**, p. 7, for additional support.

After Reading

Possible Activities
Independent Activities

- Have students compose "lost dog" ads that Dirk's original owners might have written. How might they describe their dog?

- Have students think of people who might have good reasons to enjoy this story. Have students write personal letters to those people describing the story and explaining why they should read it.

Discussion Activities

- Have students hold a mock trial to determine if Dirk should be locked up as a vicious dog. Encourage them to formulate arguments both for and against locking him up.
- Have students predict, on the basis of what they know about the narrator, what is likely to happen to him. Have them identify clues, either in the story or in his character, that suggest this.

Assessment Opportunities

- You can assess students' comprehension by evaluating the predictions or final reasons that they wrote in their Reader's Notebooks.
- You can have students make a character web for either the narrator or for Dirk the Protector.

He was

Airedale

crossed with

hound

crossed with

alligator.

Dog (1955), Derrick Greaves. Oil on canvas. Arts Council Collection, Hayward Gallery, London, UK/Bridgeman Art Library, London/New York.

Alley dog. Big, tough, mean alley dog. As I watched he spit cloth—it looked like blue jeans—out of his mouth.

"You bit Happy, and sent them running?" I asked.

He growled, and I wasn't sure if it was with menace, but he didn't bare his teeth and didn't seem to want to attack me. Indeed, he had saved me.

"Why?" I asked. "What did I do to deserve . . . oh, the hamburger."

I swear, he pointedly looked at the bag with the second half of hamburger in it.

"You want more?"

He kept staring at the bag and I thought, Well, he sure as heck deserves it. I opened the sack and gave him the rest of it, which disappeared down his throat as if a hole had opened into the universe.

He looked at the bag.

"That's it," I said, brushing my hands together. "The whole thing."

A low growl.

"You can rip my head off—there still isn't any more hamburger." I removed the Coke and handed him the bag, which he took, held on the ground with one foot and deftly ripped open with his teeth.

"See? Nothing." I was up by this time and I started to walk away. "Thanks for the help . . ."

He followed me. Not close, perhaps eight feet back, but matching my speed. It was now nearly midnight and I was tired and sore from setting pins and from the kicks that had landed on my back and sides.

"I don't have anything to eat at home but crackers and peanut butter and jelly," I told him. I kept some food in the basement of the apartment building, where I slept near the furnace.

He kept following and, truth be known, I didn't mind. I was still half scared of him but the memory of him spitting out bits of Happy's pants and the sound of the boys running off made me smile. When I arrived at the apartment house I held the main door open and he walked right in. I opened the basement door and he followed me down the steps into the furnace room.

I turned the light on and could see that my earlier judgment had been correct. He was scarred from fighting, skinny and flat sided and with patches of hair gone. His nails were worn down from scratching concrete.

"Dirk," I said. "I'll call you Dirk." I had been trying to read a detective novel and there was a tough guy in it named Dirk. "You look like somebody named Dirk."

And so we sat that first night. I had two boxes of Ritz crackers I'd hustled somewhere, a jar of peanut butter and another one of grape jelly, and a knife from the kitchen upstairs. I would smear a cracker, hand it to him—he took each one with great care and gentleness—and then eat one myself. We did this, back and forth, until both boxes were empty and my stomach was bulging; then I fell asleep on the old outdoor lounge I used for furniture.

The next day was a school day. I woke up and found Dirk under the basement stairs, watching me. When I opened the door he trotted up the steps and outside—growling at me as he went past—and I started off to school.

He followed me at a distance, then stopped across the street when I went into the front of the school building. I thought I'd probably never see him again.

But he was waiting when I came out that afternoon, sitting across the street by a mailbox. I walked up to him.

He likes to guard things, doesn't he?

Dog in Field (1967), Richard Crozier. Courtesy of Tatistcheff Gallery, New York. Collection of Brooke L. Larson. Photo by Glenn Rudolph.

"Hi, Dirk." I thought of petting him but when I reached a hand out he growled. "All right—no touching."

I turned and made my way toward the bowling alley. It was Friday and sometimes on Friday afternoon there were people who wanted to bowl early and I could pick up a dollar or two setting pins.

Dirk followed about four feet back—closer than before—and as I made my way along Second Street and came around the corner by Ecker's Drugstore I ran into Happy. He had only two of his cohorts[6] with him and I don't think they had intended to do me harm, but I surprised them and Happy took a swing at me.

Dirk took him right in the middle. I mean bit him in the center of his stomach, hard, before Happy's fist could get to me. Happy screamed and doubled over and Dirk went around and ripped into his rear and kept tearing at it even as Happy and his two companions fled down the street.

It was absolutely great. Maybe one of the great moments in my life.

I had a bodyguard.

It was as close to having a live nuclear weapon as you can get. I cannot say we became friends. I touched him only once, when he wasn't looking—I petted him on the head and received a growl and a lifted lip for it. But we became constant companions. Dirk moved into the basement with me, and I gave him a hamburger every day and hustled up dog food for him and many nights we sat down there eating Ritz crackers and he watched me working on stick model airplanes.

---

6. **cohorts** (kō'hôrts'): companions or associates.

He followed me to school, waited for me, followed me to the bowling alley, waited for me. He was with me everywhere I went, always back three or four feet, always with a soft growl, and to my great satisfaction every time he saw Happy—every time—Dirk would try to remove some part of his body with as much violence as possible.

He caused Happy and his mob to change their habits. They not only stopped hunting me but went out of their way to avoid me, or more specifically, Dirk. In fact after that winter and spring they never bothered me again, even after Dirk was gone.

Dirk came to a wonderful end. I always thought of him as a street dog—surely nobody owned him—and in the summer when I was hired to work on a farm four miles east of town I took him with me. We walked all the way out to the farm, Dirk four feet in back of me, and he would trot along beside the tractor when I plowed, now and then chasing the hundreds of seagulls that came for the worms the plow turned up.

The farmer, whose name was Olaf, was a bachelor and did not have a dog. I looked over once to see Dirk sitting next to Olaf while we ate some sandwiches and when Olaf reached out to pet him Dirk actually—this was the first time I'd seen it—wagged his tail.

He'd found a home.

I worked the whole summer there and when it came time to leave, Dirk remained sitting in the yard as I walked down the driveway. The next summer I had bought an old Dodge for twenty-five dollars and I drove out to Olaf's to say hello and saw Dirk out in a field with perhaps two hundred sheep. He wasn't herding them, or chasing them, but was just standing there, watching the flock.

"You have him with the sheep?" I asked Olaf.

He nodded. "Last year I lost forty-three to coyotes," he said. "This year not a one. He likes to guard things, doesn't he?"

I thought of Dirk chasing Happy down the street, and later spitting out bits of his pants, and I smiled. "Yeah, he sure does." ❖

"I still read like . . . a wolf eats. I read myself to sleep every night."

Gary Paulsen
born 1939

Precious Gift Because Gary Paulsen's father was an army officer, his family moved frequently when he was a boy. "School was a nightmare because I was unbelievably shy, and terrible at sports," he recalls. One cold winter night when he was living in a small town in northern Minnesota, Paulsen went into a library to get warm. The librarian offered him a library card and the chance to take out books. Paulsen read the books he took out "as though I had been dying of thirst and the librarian had handed me a five gallon bucket of water."

Outdoor Adventures Besides being a writer, Paulsen has been, among other things, a soldier, a trapper, and a rancher. His experiences in the outdoors have been the inspiration for more than forty books, among them the Newbery Honor Books *Dogsong, Hatchet,* and *The Winter Room.*

GARY PAULSEN
According to Gary Paulsen, the librarian who gave him his first library card changed his life. He struggled with his school work, and one of his only activities outside of school was selling newspapers for extra money. Getting a library card and having access to books opened new doors for him. He says "It saved me, it really did."

Objectives
- appreciate the storytelling skill of a well-known American writer
- correlate events in O. Henry's life with the material in his fiction
- assess the place of O. Henry in American fiction

This Author Study gives students a chance to study an exciting author in depth. In this study, students will discover that good writers sometimes begin their careers in difficult or troubled circumstances.

Author Study O. HENRY

CONTENTS

O. Henry's uncle's drugstore

A Writer by Profession

"It was never intended that I should write novels. . . . I was designed, created, and set going to write short stories, and as long as I stick to that I will have my measure of success. . . ."

1862–1910

YOUNG READER

O. Henry is the pen name of William Sydney Porter, who was born in Greensboro, North Carolina. Will's mother died when he was three years old, leaving him to be raised by his aunt Lina, who ran a small private school. Under her guidance, Will developed a taste for literature and a talent for humorous drawing. He began by devouring dime novels but eventually moved on to one of his lifetime favorites, *The Arabian Nights,* as well as other classics.

Will left school at 15 and trained to be a pharmacist. The teenager spent many hours at his uncle's drugstore and gained a reputation as a

His LIFE and TIMES

1862
Born September 11 Greensboro, North Carolina

1865
Mother dies; family moves in with aunt and grandmother.

1877
Works in uncle's drugstore

1882
Moves to Texas

1860   1870   1880

1861–1865
Lincoln presidency; Civil War

1869
U.S. transcontinental railroad completed; joins East and West

1876
Alexander Graham Bell invents the telephone.

150

See the Skills Trace at the beginning of the unit for information on TEKS covered in this lesson.

150 UNIT ONE AUTHOR STUDY

prankster. Will would amuse the regular customers with his skillful caricature drawings of them or of the town elders.

A ROLLING STONE

By the age of 19, Porter was a licensed pharmacist, but a racking cough caused him concern. Both his mother and grandmother had died of tuberculosis, and Porter was terrified that he, too, might have the disease. In 1882, he moved to Texas—a state noted for its dry, healthy climate—where he lived on a cattle ranch. But Porter turned out to be an unusual cowboy, sometimes carrying a small dictionary in one pocket and a book of poems in the other.

Later, Porter moved to Austin. In his free time, he would stroll the sidewalks absorbing the atmosphere and noting the colorful characters he met. Many of the short stories he would later write contain vivid profiles of Texas Rangers, cattle rustlers, train robbers, and other Westerners.

In 1887 Porter married a local girl, Athol Estes, whose connections helped him find work as a bank teller in Austin. To earn extra money, he submitted sketches to newspapers and magazines. In 1894, while still working at the bank, he started *The Rolling Stone*, a humorous weekly newspaper.

While working in Austin, Texas, O. Henry started a weekly humor newspaper.

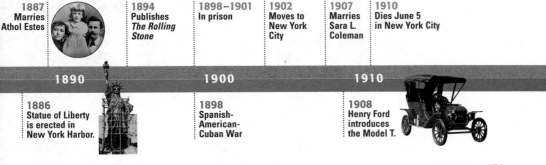

| 1887 Marries Athol Estes | 1894 Publishes *The Rolling Stone* | 1898–1901 In prison | 1902 Moves to New York City | 1907 Marries Sara L. Coleman | 1910 Dies June 5 in New York City |

| 1890 | 1900 | 1910 |

| 1886 Statue of Liberty is erected in New York Harbor. | 1898 Spanish-American-Cuban War | 1908 Henry Ford introduces the Model T. |

O. HENRY **151**

Parental Background

A Porter's mother, Mary Jane Virginia Swaim, delivered at her graduation from Greensboro Female College in 1850 an address with a topic that foreshadowed the life of her son: "The Influence of Misfortune on the Gifted." Porter's father, Dr. Algernon Sidney Porter, was regarded as "the best loved physician in Greensboro." After the death of Mary Jane in 1865, "Doctor Al," grieving and overwhelmed by the number of wounded soldiers—both Union and Confederate—who required his attention, withdrew from his practice. He spent his last years preoccupied with inventing a machine that would run on self-generated power.

Of Miss Lina's influence, Porter later remarked: "I did more reading between my thirteenth and nineteenth years than I have done in all the years since."

Literature

B The *Arabian Nights* is a set of tales based on stories from many sources. They include the stories of Aladdin, Sinbad, and Ali Baba and the Forty Thieves, all told by a young woman, Shaharazad.

Artistic Skill

C Porter's skill at lifelike drawing gave rise to the following story: A favored customer once asked to charge several items. Porter did not want to offend the man by admitting that he could not remember his name, so he merely listed the items on a slip and, after the customer had gone, added a sketch of his face. When the owner of the store returned, he had no trouble recognizing who the customer was and properly charging his account.

Character

D Porter went to Texas for a visit and wound up staying as a guest for years. His host was Richard Hall, who was managing a sheep ranch in La Salle County. Porter did little work on the ranch beyond a few errands. He later said, "I have never been a cowboy [or a] sheepherder. . . . But I lived 'on the ground' with cowboys for two years."

Letter

E When Porter was in prison, his daughter was not told the reason for his absence, so no reference to prison life appears in his letters to her. Instead, they are filled with light topics, gentle humor, and affection. At the close of one letter, for example, he adds: "I hope your watch runs all right. When you write again be sure and look at it and tell me what time it is, so I won't have to get up and look at the clock. With much love, Papa."

Prison

F Because of his experience as a pharmacist, Porter was able to secure a relatively easy position as night druggist in prison. He did not have to stay in a regular cell, but slept entirely outside the main cell block in the prison hospital. In time he became secretary to the prison steward and actually was able to walk the streets of the penitentiary town at will, living wholly outside the main prison. In his rounds as pharmacist, however, he saw the worst of prison life. In letters to his in-laws, he reported: "I never imagined human life was held as cheap as it is here. The men are regarded as animals without soul or feeling. . . . Consumption [tuberculosis] here is more common than bad colds at home. . . ." "We sometimes have a death every night for a week or so."

The paper lasted barely a year. Rumors were that Porter had used some of the money from the bank where he was working to finance his failing paper.

A NEW IDENTITY

In 1896, Porter was arrested and charged with stealing funds. He fled to Honduras, although his family and friends believed he was merely an innocent victim. Porter returned to Texas several months later to keep watch at the bedside of his wife, who was to die, at 29, of tuberculosis. **E**

It was while awaiting trial that Porter had his first short story published. In 1898 he was convicted and sentenced to five years in a federal prison. While serving his time, he supported his daughter, Margaret, by working as a pharmacist and writing stories about life **F** in Central America and the Southwest. On his early release after only three years, Porter left behind his shameful identity as a convict. **G** He changed his name to O. Henry, a name that soon would be known throughout America.

In 1902 O. Henry moved to New York City, where he was to live until his death writing weekly stories for newspapers and magazines. The vibrant city with its variety of inhabitants became the setting for O. Henry's most famous stories, including "After Twenty Years." (page 155) In 1904 O. Henry published his first book of stories, *Cabbages and Kings*. With his next collection, *The Four Million* (1906), O. Henry became famous worldwide.

In 1907 O. Henry remarried. Unhappily, his health was failing, and, as was true for most of his life, he had **H** no money. He continued to write at a furious pace, however, producing seven collections of short stories **I** in the last three years of his life. When he died in 1910, O. Henry steadfastly refused to admit to his birth name.

Portrait of O. Henry

FACT OR FICTION?

Because O. Henry guarded the secret of his past so carefully, biographers have drawn heavily on his stories to explain the author himself. Certainly, he lived as colorful a life as many of his characters, and his stories show a unique understanding of people on both sides of the law.

Most of O. Henry's famous "Westerns" were inspired by his years in Texas, and one of his most popular characters—Jimmy Valentine of "A Retrieved Reformation" (page 164)—was based on a safe-cracker he met while in prison. His tales are famous for their surprise endings, and the later stories are based on O. Henry's life in New York City.

More Online: Author Link
www.mcdougallittell.com

NetActivities: Author Exploration

THE TEXAS CATTLE BOOM

O. Henry lived on a cattle ranch in Texas in the 1880s. Cattle ranching had begun in Texas when settlers from Mexico arrived in the 1700s. After the Civil War, a new demand for beef turned ranching into big business. Cattle "kingdoms" spread over Texas.

The largest of these covered more then three million acres! Ranchers didn't fence their property but relied on cowboys to watch the cattle and drive them to market. Cowboys could be on a cattle drive for several months, depending on where they took the cattle.

More than 35,000 cowboys rode herd along the Texas cattle trails. Although folklore and picture postcards depicted the cowboy as Anglo-American, about 25 percent were African-American and another 12 percent were Mexican *vaqueros*—cowboys who had worked in Texas since the days before Texas's independence. There were Native American cowboys, too, and a few women. O. Henry did not actually stray far from the ranch where he lived, but the forty-or-so stories he set in Texas are rich in the details and characters of frontier life.

O. HENRY **153**

Pseudonym

G There are many theories about the origin of Porter's pseudonym. It may be based on any of the following and more: the name of a European chemist, O. Henry, common in a pharmacy catalog Porter must have seen; an African-American ranch hand Porter knew in Texas—an excellent storyteller named Old Henry; a cowboy song that asks "O Henry, what sentence have you got?"; a customer named Henry at the bank in Austin, who was constantly called back to the counter with the cry "Oh, Henry!"; a wharf master in Honduras to whom others often called, "Oh, Hennery!"; a captain of the prison guard whose name appeared as "O. Henry" in prison record books that Porter must have seen.

Marriage

H In 1907, Porter married Sara Lindsay Coleman, a woman he had known since his youth. Coleman, a writer herself, had long admired the work of "O. Henry." By chance, her mother discovered that the author her daughter so admired was really Will Porter, a boy she had played with many years earlier. Coleman wrote Porter and asked if he remembered the "small girl in a green-sprigged muslin dress." A two-year correspondence followed, and Porter proposed marriage on his 45th birthday. The marriage was strained by financial problems and Porter's declining health. Coleman was visiting her family in Asheville when Porter died on June 5, 1910.

Unfinished Work

I In addition to his published stories, Porter yearned to produce more serious work, but poor health prevented him from doing so. Porter planned but never wrote a series of stories contrasting the Old South with the New. He hoped to write a novel, and he hoped to dramatize some of his stories. He worked with Franklin Adams on composing the musical comedy *Lo!*, based on his story "He Also Serves." Porter sold the rights of his story, "A Retrieved Reformation" for $500. Dramatized by Paul Armstrong and retitled, the play became a hit in England, France, and Spain as well as America (see PE pages 173–174).

Objectives

1. understand the plot device of a **surprise ending** (Literary Analysis)
2. understand the role of the **setting** (Literary Analysis)
3. understand how to **monitor** as you read (Active Reading)

Summary

At 10 o'clock on a chilly night, a New York City police officer stops to speak with a man standing in a doorway. The man explains that he has come from the West and is waiting for a friend, Jimmy; they had agreed twenty years ago to meet here on this night. The man lights a cigar and reminisces about the friendship. The police officer asks a few questions and then passes on. Twenty minutes later, another man approaches, asking, "Is it you, Bob?" The waiting man acknowledges his name; they greet warmly and walk together toward a place to talk. The man from the West fills the other in on his life. Then they pass before a lighted store and see each other clearly. The man from the West realizes his companion is not Jimmy. The other man admits that he is a police officer and arrests Bob for crimes he committed in Chicago. He hands "Silky" Bob a note from Jimmy, the first officer, who writes that he had not wanted to arrest his old friend himself.

Thematic Link

This story is filled with unexpected discoveries. Jimmy discovers that his old friend has become a wanted criminal; Bob discovers that his companion is not his old friend; the reader and Bob discover together that the first policeman was Jimmy.

"But I know Jimmy will meet me here if he's alive, for he always was the truest, staunchest old chap in the world."

After Twenty Years

Short Story by O. HENRY

Me-Twenty Years From Now
• I will be 32 years old.

Connect to Your Life

Into the Future In this story, two friends meet again after twenty years. They discover that their lives have taken different paths. Have you ever wondered what your life might be like in twenty years? In a small group, describe how you see yourself twenty years from now. How will you be different? What choices might you have made in order to achieve your goals?

Build Background

CONNECT TO HISTORY The main character in "After Twenty Years" has just returned to New York from the West, where he made his fortune. After gold was discovered in California in 1848, adventure seekers poured into the American West hoping to get rich. In 1862 the federal government agreed to give western land to homesteaders.

Over the next fifty years, millions of people came west, some looking for quick riches and others settling the land. Gold and silver deposits were still being discovered as late as the 1890s, and the possibility of becoming millionaires overnight still lured scores of adventurers to the West from all over the world. The population of the West rose from just over a million in 1860 to nearly nine million in 1890. This dramatic rise in population, coupled with the growth of transcontinental railroads, changed the character of both the region and the nation.

> WORDS TO KNOW
> **Vocabulary Preview**
> dismally staunchest
> habitual vicinity
> simultaneously

Focus Your Reading

LITERARY ANALYSIS SURPRISE ENDING O. Henry is famous for the unexpected twists with which he ends his stories. These **surprise endings** may be a sudden turn in the action or a realization that gives a different look to the entire story. Usually there are clues in the story hinting at the ending. As you read "After Twenty Years," look for clues to how the story will end.

ACTIVE READING MONITORING When you read a story or other literary work, it helps to pause occasionally and **monitor,** or check, your understanding. Keep in mind the reading strategies you have learned and apply a different one if you are having difficulty. Stopping and rereading descriptive passages or dialogue will help you understand twists in the plot.

READER'S NOTEBOOK As you read "After Twenty Years," make notes of points in the story that help you monitor, or keep track of, how the main characters are described by the author and by other characters in the story.

LESSON RESOURCES

UNIT ONE RESOURCE BOOK, pp. 74–80

ASSESSMENT
Formal Assessment, pp. 23–24
Teacher's Guide to Assessment and Portfolio Use
Test Generator

SKILLS TRANSPARENCIES AND COPYMASTERS
Reading and Critical Thinking
• Strategies for Reading, TR 1 (for Thinking Through the Literature, p. 161)

Grammar
• Interrupting Phrases, CM 133 (for Mini Lesson, p. 159)
• Subjects Not at the Beginning of the Sentence, CM 57 (for Mini Lesson, p. 162)

Vocabulary
• Antonyms, CM 31 (for Mini Lesson, p. 155)
• Word Parts: Affixes, CM 32 (for Mini Lesson, p. 158)

INTEGRATED TECHNOLOGY
Audio Library

Visit our website:
www.mcdougallittell.com

AFTER TWENTY YEARS

by O. Henry

Illustration by
Stephen Peringer

155

TEACHING THE LITERATURE

Customizing Instruction

Less Proficient Readers
Have students keep track of these elements as they read:
- What is the setting?
- Who are the characters in this story?
- What events happened twenty years ago?
- What events happen "now"?

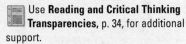 Use **Reading and Critical Thinking Transparencies**, p. 34, for additional support.

Students Acquiring English
Some of the vocabulary in this story is old-fashioned slang. Explain that *chum* and *partner* are synonyms for *friend*; *chap* is an informal, friendly synonym for *man*. Invite students to think of words that are contemporary slang for *friend* and *man*. Encourage students to use context clues to figure out any unfamiliar language.
Possible Responses: *bud(dy), guy*

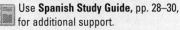 Use **Spanish Study Guide**, pp. 28–30, for additional support.

Gifted and Talented
Have students analyze O. Henry's use of irony, a contrast between what is expected and what actually happens. Ask students to identify examples of irony in the plot and to explain each example.
Possible Response:
The first police officer and the waiting man discuss what he will do if the friend is late. As it turns out, the friend was right on time.

 Use **Literary Analysis Transparencies**, p. 27, for additional support.

 Preteaching Vocabulary **TEKS** 9B **TAAS** Reading Obj. 1

ANTONYMS
Instruction Explain to students that, when a sentence presents a contrast between two ideas, recognizing and interpreting antonyms can help them to infer the meaning of an unfamiliar word.
Exercises Each of the following sentences contains one of the WORDS TO KNOW for this selection. Have students identify the word's antonym in the sentence. Then have them define the underlined word, using the antonym and a dictionary as necessary.

1. The evening walk was <u>habitual</u> exercise and not an unplanned activity. (antonym: *unplanned*)
2. She was the <u>staunchest</u> of employees and never unreliable. (antonym: *unreliable*)
3. The house was <u>dismally</u> quiet until the children returned, chattering cheerfully. (antonym: *cheerfully*)
4. The events happened <u>simultaneously</u>, not separately, as we had first thought. (antonym: *separately*)

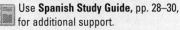 Use **Unit One Resource Book**, p. 77, for more exercises. Use **Vocabulary Transparencies and Copymasters**, p. 31, for additional support.

Reading and Analyzing

Literary Analysis SURPRISE ENDING

As students have already learned, this story is likely to have a surprise ending. Tell them to keep this in mind as they begin the story. Ask them to write down specific details that pique their interest or strike them as curious.

 Use the **Unit One Resource Book,** p. 76, for more practice.

Active Reading MONITORING

A Have students read the first two paragraphs. Then stop to monitor their understanding of setting and character. Use the words *question, clarify, connect, predict,* and *evaluate* to help students recognize the strategies they are using to make sense of the story. For example, *question* students: Why does the policeman "make a fine picture of a guardian of the peace"? Why is this image of him important?

Possible Response: He is impressive and watchful (connecting details). These are good qualities for a police officer (evaluating, connecting to experience). I wonder what a "swagger" is (questioning); I think it is a way of walking (clarifying). He's probably going to have to "guard the peace" (predicting).

Use the **Unit One Resource Book,** p. 75, for more practice.

Rainy Night (1929-30), Charles Ephraim Burchfield. Watercolor over pencil on paper, 30″ × 42″, San Diego Museum of Art. Gift of Anne R. and Amy Putnam.

156 UNIT ONE **AUTHOR STUDY**

Teaching Options

 Mini Lesson **Viewing and Representing** **TEKS 22A**

Rainy Night (1929–30)
by Charles Ephraim Burchfield

ART APPRECIATION Have students share their responses to and analyses of the painting.
Instruction Be sure students note the use and effects of light and shadow. Point out that light illuminates the people, such as the figure leaning in the storefront and the woman entering the cab, while other buildings and vehicles are in shadow. Ask students how the details convey setting and mood.

Possible Response: The scene is a city intersection in the age of trolleys, early automobiles, and early electricity. It is dark, probably late; the streets are wet and deserted. The figure seems to be alone, perhaps waiting.

Application Have students find lines in O. Henry's first three paragraphs that describe images that correspond to the scene depicted in the painting.

Possible Response: barely ten o'clock at night, chilly gusts of wind with a taste of rain in them, depeopled streets, pacific thoroughfare, occasional lights of a few stores, most businesses long since closed

The policeman on the beat moved up the avenue impressively. The impressiveness was <u>habitual</u> and not for show, for spectators were few. The time was barely ten o'clock at night, but chilly gusts of wind with a taste of rain in them had well nigh depeopled the streets.

Trying doors as he went, twirling his club with many intricate and artful movements, turning now and then to cast his watchful eye down the pacific[1] thoroughfare, the officer, with his stalwart form and slight swagger, made a fine picture of a guardian of the peace. The <u>vicinity</u> was one that kept early hours. Now and then you might see the lights of a cigar store or of an all-night lunch counter, but the majority of the doors belonged to business places that had long since been closed.

When about midway of a certain block, the policeman suddenly slowed his walk. In the doorway of a darkened hardware store a man leaned, with an unlighted cigar in his mouth. As the policeman walked up to him, the man spoke up quickly.

"It's all right, officer," he said reassuringly. "I'm just waiting for a friend. It's an appointment made twenty years ago. Sounds a little funny to you, doesn't it? Well, I'll explain if you'd like to make certain it's all straight. About that long ago there used to be a restaurant where this store stands—'Big Joe' Brady's restaurant."

"Until five years ago," said the policeman. "It was torn down then."

The man in the doorway struck a match and lit his cigar. The light showed a pale, square-jawed face with keen eyes and a little white

---

1. **pacific:** calm and peaceful.

WORDS
TO
KNOW

habitual (hə-bĭch′ō̄o-əl) *adj.* established by long use
vicinity (vĭ-sĭn′ĭ-tē) *n.* neighborhood

157

Customizing Instruction

Less Proficient Readers
Use these questions to monitor for understanding, helping students confirm by rereading as needed.
- What is the policeman like?
  Possible Response: responsible, watchful, friendly
- To whom does the policeman speak?
  Response: a man waiting in a doorway
- What is the man waiting for?
  Response: his friend to show up for an appointment they made twenty years ago

Students Acquiring English
Have students work in pairs to role-play the dialogue between the police officer and the waiting man. They may summarize lines if they wish.

Multiple Learning Styles
Kinesthetic Learners
Invite students to pantomime, in turn, the policeman and the waiting man, using gestures, posture, and facial expressions.

Visual Learners
Invite students to sketch the policeman and the waiting man, based on O. Henry's descriptions. They might caption their sketches with phrases of description taken from the text. Later, have them compare their sketches of the waiting man with the portrait on page 159.

BLOCK SCHEDULING: MANAGING TIME

If your schedule requires that you cover the lesson objectives in a shorter time, use . . .
- Preparing to Read, p. 154
- Thinking Through the Literature, p. 161
- Vocabulary in Action, p. 162
- Grammar in Context, p. 162

If you would like to take advantage of longer class time, use . . .
- TE Teaching Options: Preteaching Vocabulary, p. 155; Viewing and Representing, p.156; Vocabulary Strategy, p. 158; Grammar, pp. 159, 162; Informal Assessment, p. 160
- Choices & Challenges, p. 162

Ask students how they would describe the waiting man's character traits, based on what they have read so far.

Possible Response: He is loyal, having come 1000 miles to keep this appointment, yet a gambler, banking on his memories of his friend. He is also proud of himself, his wits, and his financial accomplishments, while being somewhat condescending about Jimmy's lack of ambition.

Literary Analysis: THEME

Ask students to describe the friendship between the waiting man and Jimmy.

Possible Response: They grew up as close as brothers; they promised to meet again in twenty years, but they haven't had any contact for nearly the whole twenty years. Still, the waiting man has faith in his friend.

Ask students to identify any ideas they see repeating in the story.

Possible Response: Jimmy was a true friend and a good man. The waiting man and his friend Jimmy went different ways twenty years ago.

Active Reading | MONITORING |

Ask students how they can find or confirm answers to questions about the theme. Have them reread to locate details supporting their assessments of the friendship between the waiting man and Jimmy.

Possible Responses: appointment made twenty years ago (p. 153); twenty years ago tonight (p. 158); my best chum and the finest chap in the world (p. 158)

---

scar near his right eyebrow. His scarf pin was a large diamond, oddly set.

"Twenty years ago tonight," said the man, "I dined here at 'Big Joe' Brady's with Jimmy Wells, my best chum and the finest chap in the world. He and I were raised here in New York, just like two brothers, together. I was eighteen and Jimmy was twenty. The next morning I was to start for the West to make my fortune. You couldn't have dragged Jimmy out of New York; he thought it was the only place on earth. Well, we agreed that night that we would meet here again exactly twenty years from that date and time, no matter what our conditions might be or from what distance we might have to come. We figured that in twenty years each of us ought to have our destiny² worked out and our fortunes made, whatever they were going to be."

"It sounds pretty interesting," said the policeman. "Rather a long time between meets, though, it seems to me. Haven't you heard from your friend since you left?"

"Well, yes, for a time we corresponded," said the other. "But after a year or two we lost track of each other. You see, the West is a pretty big proposition, and I kept hustling³ around over it pretty lively. But I know Jimmy will meet me here if he's alive, for he always was the truest, staunchest old chap in the world. He'll never forget. I came a thousand miles to stand in this door tonight, and it's worth it if my old partner turns up."

The waiting man pulled out a handsome watch, the lids of it set with small diamonds.

"Three minutes to ten," he announced.

"It was exactly ten o'clock when we parted here at the restaurant door."

"Did pretty well out West, didn't you?" asked the policeman.

"You bet! I hope Jimmy has done half as well. He was a kind of plodder, though, good fellow as he was. I've had to compete with some of the sharpest wits going to get my pile. A man gets in a groove⁴ in New York. It takes the West to put a razor edge on him."

The policeman twirled his club and took a step or two.

"I'll be on my way. Hope your friend comes around all right. Going to call time on him sharp?"

"I should say not!" said the other. "I'll give him half an hour at least. If Jimmy is alive on earth, he'll be here by that time. So long, officer."

"Good night, sir," said the policeman, passing on along his beat, trying doors as he went.

There was now a fine, cold drizzle falling, and the wind had risen from its uncertain puffs into a steady blow. The few foot passengers astir in that quarter hurried dismally and silently along with coat collars turned high and pocketed hands. And in the door of the hardware store the man who had come a thousand miles to fill an appointment, uncertain almost to absurdity, with the friend of his youth, smoked his cigar and waited.

---

2. **destiny:** the fate or outcome of a person's life.
3. **hustling** (hŭs′əl-ĭng): moving or working energetically and rapidly.
4. **groove:** a long funnel or narrow channel; slang for a settled routine.

WORDS TO KNOW	**staunchest** (stônch′əst) *adj.* strongest; most determined; most firm **dismally** (dĭz′məl-lē) *adv.* in a gloomy or depressed manner

158

WORD PARTS: AFFIXES

Instruction Remind students that they can use structural analysis to identify words by applying knowledge of root words and affixes, which include prefixes and suffixes. Prefixes are word parts added to the beginning of words; they change the words' meaning. Suffixes are parts added to the end of words; they usually change the words' part of speech. Help students to identify root words and affixes in the following WORDS TO KNOW and to determine how each affix changes the root word.

Mini Lesson **Vocabulary Strategy** **TEKS** 6B, 9D 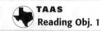 **TAAS** Reading Obj. 1

Exercises

habitual (*habit* + *-ual;* the suffix changes the form from noun to adjective)

staunchest (*staunch* + *-est;* the suffix changes the adjective to its superlative form)

dismally (*dismal* + *-ly;* the suffix changes the form from adjective to adverb)

absurdity (*absurd* + *-ity;* the suffix changes the form from adjective to noun)

egotism (*ego* + *-tism;* the suffix changes the noun from a thing to a quality)

 Use **Vocabulary Transparencies and Copymasters**, p. 32, for additional support.

Unfinished Portrait of Tadeusz Lempicki (about 1928), Tamara de Lempicka. Oil on canvas, 126 cm × 82 cm, Musée National d'Art Moderne, Centre National d'Art et de Culture Georges Pompidou, Paris. Copyright © 1999 Estate of Tamara de Lempicka/Artists Rights Society (ARS), New York.

Customizing Instruction

Less Proficient Readers

Ask students these questions to check and confirm understanding:

- What do you know about the waiting man?

  Possible Response: He is well-off (diamond pin and watch), uses big words, is loyal, on time, and has a scar.

- What happened twenty years ago?

  Response: The waiting man went West, and his friend stayed in New York, but they agreed to meet again tonight.

- What do you predict will happen next?

  Possible Response: The man's friend will show up.

Students Acquiring English

1 Have students use context and footnote to explain the slang term *groove*. Invite them to think of contemporary ways to use the term; for example, they might be in a "homework groove."

Gifted and Talented

Have students analyze how O. Henry uses speech to develop character. Suggest they create a two-column chart to record words and phrases that represent each character's speech.

Sample Response:

Police Officer	Waiting Man
"Rather a long time between meets"	"I dined here" "A man gets in a groove"

Multiple Learning Styles

Interpersonal Learners

Have students explain from Jimmy's point of view how he feels about meeting Bob again.

AFTER TWENTY YEARS **159**

 Mini Lesson **Grammar**   **TEKS** 16B, 17A 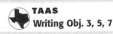 **TAAS** Writing Obj. 3, 5, 7

INTERRUPTING PHRASES

Instruction Tell students that commas are used before and after a word or phrase that interrupts the flow of a sentence. Note the following examples from page 158:

1. Rather a long time between meets, **though,** it seems to me.

2. And in the door of the hardware store the man who had come a thousand miles to fill an appointment, **uncertain almost to absurdity,** with the friend of his youth, smoked his cigar and waited.

Exercises Have students insert commas to set off interrupting words or phrases in the following sentences.

1. The waiting man (,) who is actually Bob (,) does not recognize his old friend.

2. Jimmy (,) though (,) does recognize Bob.

3. Perhaps Bob should have expected (,) since he knew his old friend so well (,) that Jimmy might become a police officer.

4. The fact remains (,) however (,) that Bob is taken totally by surprise.

5. Most readers (,) I expect (,) are also.

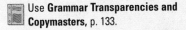 Use **Grammar Transparencies and Copymasters,** p. 133.

 Use McDougal Littell's *Language Network,* Chapter 11, for more instruction and practice with interrupting phrases.

Literary Analysis `SURPRISE ENDING`

 Take a poll: How many students were surprised by the ending? How many were not? Let the two groups explain their reactions.

Remind students that O. Henry is famous for ending his stories in unexpected ways—with a twist. Ask students to summarize the twist(s) in this story.

Possible Response: The first police officer turns out to be Jimmy, and he has his friend arrested because it turns out that "sharp," "successful," "Silky" Bob is actually a criminal.

Literary Analysis: THEME

Ask students to suggest clues and questions they can use to recognize theme in a story. Guide their responses.

Possible Responses:

• Title: How does it relate to the story?
• Main Characters: What are they like, and how do they change?
• Main Idea: What is the main idea of the story?
• Repeated Ideas: What ideas are mentioned again and again?

Have students use these ideas to identify a theme of "After Twenty Years." Remind them of the following guidelines:

• A theme is a generalized statement about life or human nature.
• A statement of theme *does not include story details* about characters, setting, or plot.
• Readers may identify different themes in a work.

Possible Response: Time can change friendships, even if the friends still care about each other.

Use **Literary Analysis Transparencies**, p. 7, for additional support.

About twenty minutes he waited, and then a tall man in a long overcoat, with collar turned up to his ears, hurried across from the opposite side of the street. He went directly to the waiting man.

"Is that you, Bob?" he asked, doubtfully.

"Is that you, Jimmy Wells?" cried the man in the door.

"Bless my heart!" exclaimed the new arrival, grasping both the other's hands with his own. "Yes Bob, sure as fate. I was certain I'd find you here if you were still in existence. Well, well, well!—twenty years is a long time. The old restaurant's gone, Bob; I wish it had lasted, so we could have had another dinner there. How has the West treated you, old man?"

"Bully;[5] it has given me everything I asked it for. You've changed lots, Jimmy. I never thought you were so tall by two or three inches."

"Oh, I grew a bit after I was twenty."

"Doing well in New York, Jimmy?"

"Moderately, I have a position in one of the city departments. Come on, Bob; we'll go around to a place I know of and have a good long talk about old times."

The two men started up the street, arm in arm. The man from the West, his egotism[6] enlarged by success, was beginning to outline the history of his character. The other, submerged in his overcoat, listened with interest.

At the corner stood a drugstore, brilliant with electric lights. When they came into this glare, each of them turned <u>simultaneously</u> to gaze upon the other's face.

The man from the West stopped suddenly and released his arm.

"You're not Jimmy Wells," he snapped. "Twenty years is a long time, but not long enough to change a man's nose from a Roman to a pug."[7]

"It sometimes changes a good man into a bad one," said the tall man. "You've been under arrest for ten minutes, 'Silky' Bob. Chicago thinks you may have dropped over our way and wires us she wants to have a chat with you. Going quietly, are you? That's sensible. Now, before we go to the station, here's a note I was asked to hand to you. You may read it here at the window. It's from Patrolman Wells."

The man from the West unfolded the little piece of paper handed him. His hand was steady when he began to read, but it trembled a little by the time he had finished. The note was rather short.

> Bob: I was at the appointed place on time. When you struck the match to light your cigar, I saw it was the face of the man wanted in Chicago. Somehow I couldn't do it myself, so I went around and got a plainclothes man to do the job.
>
> Jimmy

---

5. **bully:** excellent; great.

6. **egotism** (ēʹgə-tĭzʹəm): a sense of one's own great importance; conceit.

7. **"change a man's nose from a Roman to a pug":** a Roman nose has a high, prominent, bony ridge, whereas a pug nose is short and turned up at the end.

WORDS TO KNOW — **simultaneously** (sīʹməl-tāʹnē-əs-lē) *adv.* happening or done at the same time

160

Teaching Options

 ✓ **Assessment** **Informal Assessment**   **TEKS** 10H, 11C   **TAAS** Reading Obj. 4, 5

PREDICT PROBABLE FUTURE ACTIONS AND OUTCOMES Ask students to predict likely outcomes of this story, as follows:

1. Write three predictions:
   What will happen to Jimmy?
   What will happen to "Silky" Bob?
   What will happen to their friendship?
2. Support each prediction with at least two reasons that include information from the story. The information must support your predictions.

RUBRIC

3 Full Accomplishment Students write three predictions reflecting understanding of the story. They support each prediction with at least two reasons drawn from relevant story information.

2 Substantial Accomplishment Students write valid predictions but do not support each with at least two reasons drawn from the story.

1 Little or Partial Accomplishment Students cannot make reasonable predictions or support them with reasons drawn from the story.

Connect to the Literature

1. What Do You Think? What are your feelings about the ending of this story? Explain.

Comprehension Check
- How does "Silky" Bob describe his friend Jimmy to the policeman?
- How has "Silky" Bob made his fortune?
- Why doesn't Jimmy identify himself to "Silky" Bob right away?

Think Critically

2. Why do you think Jimmy turned his friend in?

THINK ABOUT
- the arrangement Jimmy made with "Silky" Bob twenty years earlier
- his loyalties as a police officer
- his loyalty as a friend

3. Jimmy and "Silky" Bob promise to meet after twenty years. What does that say about their friendship twenty years earlier?

4. **ACTIVE READING** **MONITORING** Review the notes you made in your ⬛**READER'S NOTEBOOK.** Compare the descriptions of the two main characters—Jimmy Wells and "Silky" Bob. How do they differ? How are they alike?

Extend Interpretations

5. Different Perspectives What if the story had been told from Jimmy Wells's perspective? Explain how the story would have been different.

6. Connect to Life What would you do if you were faced with the decision Jimmy had to make? Use details from the story when you respond.

Literary Analysis

SURPRISE ENDING A **surprise ending** is an unexpected outcome in the plot of a story. In "After Twenty Years," the moment when "Silky" Bob is arrested comes as a surprise.

The revelation that Jimmy Wells has become a police officer gives a new meaning to many details in the story. "Silky" Bob's description of Jimmy as the "truest, staunchest old chap," as a "kind of plodder," and as a "good fellow" are seen to mean something different from what "Silky" Bob meant when he first spoke the words.

Similarly, "Silky" Bob's statement that he has "had to compete with some of the sharpest wits going to get my pile" takes on a different meaning.

Paired Activity With a partner, go back through the story and look for hints that suggest the story's outcome. What clues were there to Jimmy Wells's character? to "Silky" Bob's?

REVIEW **CHARACTER** The people who appear in stories are called **characters.** The events in the story are based on what the **main characters** think, feel, say, and do. Less important characters are called **minor characters.** Who are the major and minor characters in "After Twenty Years"?

Extend Interpretations

5. Different Perspectives Possible Response: If Jimmy were telling the story, he might say that he hadn't seen Bob in twenty years, so, being a police officer, he waited for the man to identify himself. When Bob lit his cigar, Jimmy recognized his face as one on a wanted poster. He let his old friend tell his story, thinking how Bob had gone down the wrong path. Jimmy couldn't give away his own identity. He knew Bob should be arrested, and he didn't want to do it himself, so he enlisted the help of a fellow policeman. Then he sent Bob a note to let him know he hadn't forgotten the meeting.

6. Connect to Life Answers will vary. Possible Response: I would have arrested Bob myself, because I wouldn't have someone else pretend to be me so he could arrest my friend.

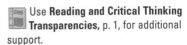

Grammar in Context

WRITING EXERCISE
Answers will vary. Students' letters should include four sentences and use three methods of placing a subject somewhere other than the beginning of the sentence. A sample response is given.

Here **are** my last **words** for you. Twenty years ago, **you and I were** best friends. I never thought you'd be the one to turn me in. In your betrayal **ends** our **friendship.**

Vocabulary in Action

1. c
2. d
3. c
4. d
5. a

Grammar in Context: Subjects in Unusual Order

O. Henry surprises the reader with twists and turns in plot in "After Twenty Years." Similarly, he writes sentences with **subjects** that do not always come at the beginning of the sentence.

> Twirling his club with many intricate and artful movements, the officer, with his stalwart form and slight swagger, made a fine picture of a guardian of the peace. . . . When about midway of a certain block, the policeman suddenly slowed his walk. In the doorway of a darkened hardware store, a man leaned with an unlighted cigar in his mouth.

Many sentences use the basic **subject-verb** pattern.

> I was eighteen. Jimmy was twenty. The officer spoke. The man stopped suddenly.

Placing the subject somewhere other than at the beginning of the sentence is one way to make your writing more interesting. Here are some suggestions:

1. Begin with an **introduction.**
   Twenty years ago, I dined here with Jimmy Wells.
   If Jimmy is alive on earth, he'll be here.

2. Another way to add variety to your writing is to invert the traditional **subject-verb** order.
   At the corner **stood** a **drug store.**

3. Sentences that start with **here** or **there** always invert the **subject-verb** order.
   Here **is** a **note.**
   There **were** two **strangers** by the hardware store.

WRITING EXERCISE "After Twenty Years" ends with a note from Jimmy to Bob. Compose a reply (four sentences) from Bob to Jimmy. Use two of the methods discussed above to add variety to your writing.

Grammar Handbook The Sentence and Its Parts, p. R55

Vocabulary in Action

EXERCISE: ASSESSMENT PRACTICE On a sheet of paper, write the letter of the word or phrase that is most clearly the opposite of the underlined Word to Know in each sentence.

1. Bob's clothing showed his wealth and habitual elegance.
   a. usual   **c.** irregular
   b. spontaneous   **d.** uncomfortable

2. Bob thought Jim the staunchest friend anybody could have.
   a. smartest   **c.** truest
   b. strongest   **d.** oldest

3. Bob stood waiting in the vicinity of a hardware store.
   a. doorway   **c.** block opposite
   b. shadow   **d.** neighborhood

4. The policeman simultaneously shook Bob's hand and snapped a pair of handcuffs on him.
   a. at first   **c.** finally
   b. at the same time   **d.** at a later time

5. Bob stood on the dark street, dismally reading Jim's letter.
   a. happily   **c.** gladly
   b. gloomily   **d.** quickly

Building Vocabulary
For an in-depth study of antonyms, see p. 631.

Teaching Options

 Mini Lesson **Grammar**  **TEKS** 17A, 17C **TAAS** Writing Obj. 3, 5, 6, 7

SUBJECTS NOT AT THE BEGINNING OF A SENTENCE

Instruction Direct students to the highlighted sentence on page 158; have them point to the subject. Ask a volunteer to identify the subject (*I*). Then have students find the subjects in the preceding sentence (*I* and *you*). Explain that in some sentences other information is given before the subject is named. Have students identify the information that precedes the subject in the highlighted sentence (*The next morning*).

Exercise: Have students find and jot down other sentences on page 158 in which the subjects are not at the beginning. Tell them to underline each subject.

Possible Responses:
- "Twenty years ago tonight . . . **I** dined here. . . ."
- "Well, yes, for a time **we** corresponded. . . ."
- "But after a year or two **we** lost track. . . ."
- "And in the door of the hardware store the **man** who had come a thousand miles . . . waited."

OPTION: Note the "understood" subject in "**(You)** Did pretty well out West, didn't you?"

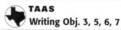 Use **Unit One Resource Book**, p. 78.
Use **Grammar Transparencies and Copymasters**, p. 57.

Language Network Use McDougal Littell's **Language Network,** Chapter 1, for more instruction and practice in identifying subjects not at the beginning of the sentence.

A Retrieved Reformation

Short Story by O. HENRY

"Get away from the door, all of you,' he commanded . . ."

⌐ **Connect to Your Life** ⌐

Making Friends In small groups, think up a list of characters in stories, books, and movies—or of people that you know—who change for the better or for the worse. How do you explain the reasons for the change in each of these characters? What do you think some of the most powerful motives for change are?

Build Background

CONNECT TO HISTORY Banks played an important role in the economy of small towns in the late 19th and early 20th centuries. The National Banking Act of 1863 helped establish a system of federally chartered banks. In the late 1800s, Will Porter, who would later take the pen name O. Henry, worked as a teller for the First National Bank in Austin, Texas.

Will Porter (O. Henry) working as a bank teller in Austin, Texas.

 LaserLinks: Background for Reading Historical Connection

Focus Your Reading

LITERARY ANALYSIS **FALLING ACTION** The plot of a story is usually set in motion by a **conflict** between opposing forces or characters. In "A Retrieved Reformation" the opposing characters are Jimmy Valentine and Ben Price. As the story moves ahead, the conflict increases until the moment of greatest intensity—the **climax**, or turning point, of the story. The climax usually involves an important event, decision, or discovery that affects the outcome of the story. After the climax, the central conflict of the story is usually resolved in a part of the plot called the **falling action.** As you read, note how the conflict in this story is resolved.

ACTIVE READING **COMPARING ACROSS TEXTS** Drawing connections between the different literary works you read will help you understand them better and enjoy them more. All of the important aspects of stories may be compared: plot, characters, setting, as well as others.

📖 **READER'S NOTEBOOK** As you read "A Retrieved Reformation," note similarities and differences between the main characters of the story and those of "After Twenty Years." Also think about the plots of the two stories. How are they similar? How do they differ?

WORDS TO KNOW	**Vocabulary Preview**			
assiduously	compulsory	eminent	retribution	unperceived
balk	elusive	rehabilitate	unobtrusively	virtuous

A RETRIEVED REFORMATION **163**

 See the Skills Trace at the beginning of the unit for information on TEKS covered in this lesson.

 This selection is included in the **Grade 7 InterActive Reader.**

Objectives
1. understand and appreciate a **short story (Literary Analysis)**
2. understand the significance of **falling action** in a **plot (Literary Analysis)**
3. use the reading skill of **compare across texts: note similarities and differences** with "After Twenty Years" **(Active Reading)**

Summary
Jimmy Valentine, an expert safecracker, receives a pardon and leaves prison. He resumes his career as a safecracker, burglarizing three banks. Then he arrives in Elmore and falls in love with Annabel Adams, the daughter of the local banker. Concealing his past, Jimmy changes his name to Ralph D. Spencer, opens a shoe business, and begins to live honestly. Annabel falls in love with him. Two weeks before they are to be married, detective Ben Price arrives in Elmore, pursuing Jimmy for the robberies he committed after leaving prison. As Price looks on, Annabel's young niece Agatha is accidentally locked inside a bank vault. Jimmy uses his safecracking tools to open the vault, freeing the child and revealing his identity. Price pretends not to know Jimmy and walks away, refusing to arrest him.

Thematic Link
Jimmy discovers that an honest life is possible; his identity is discovered and concealed by Price. After Jimmy falls in love and decides to reform, he opens the door to a new life; the door is held open by Price.

5-Minute Warm-Up

Daily Language SkillBuilder TEKS 16B, 17A, 17F

Have students **proofread** the display sentences on page 13k and write them correctly. The sentences also appear on Transparency 5 of **Grammar Transparencies and Copymasters.**

 Preteaching Vocabulary

If you would like to preteach the WORDS TO KNOW for this selection, use the Mini Lesson, page 166.

A RETRIEVED REFORMATION **163**

Literary Analysis `FALLING ACTION`

A Ask students to think about why O. Henry begins the story with the meeting between Jimmy and the warden. What might this meeting mean to the story as a whole?

Possible Response: This opening introduces Jimmy as a criminal, but the warden's comments make the reader wonder whether Jimmy might change.

Use the **Unit One Resource Book,** p. 83, for more practice. Use **Literary Analysis Transparencies,** p. 5, for additional support.

Active Reading

`COMPARING ACROSS TEXTS`

Have students identify similarities between the beginnings and the main characters of "A Retrieved Reformation" and "After Twenty Years."

Possible Responses: Each begins with an encounter between a law officer and the main character; the main characters are criminals.

Use the **Unit One Resource Book,** p. 82, for more practice. Use **Reading and Critical Thinking Transparencies,** p. 8, for additional support.

Portrait of Prince Eristoff (1925), Tamara de Lempicka. Private collection, New York. Copyright © 1996 Artists Rights Society (ARS), New York/SPADEM, Paris.

A Retrieved Reformation

by O. Henry

Teaching Options

 Mini Lesson **Viewing and Representing**   TEKS 22A, 23B

Portrait of Prince Eristoff
by Tamara de Lempicka

ART APPRECIATION The Polish-born Lempicka (1898–1980) was a leading artist of the art deco period (1920s). She painted into the 1960s.
Instruction Point out that the subject's physical presence is striking. The elongated limbs, immobile pose, contrasting tones, and lack of distracting background details help to achieve this effect. Ask students what details suggest that the subject of the painting is concerned about his appearance.

Possible Responses: lapel clip, handkerchief, trim mustache, disengaged attitude
Application Tell students that the character in this story is also concerned about appearances. After they read, ask students to compare O. Henry's descriptions of Jimmy with Lempicka's portrayal of Prince Eristoff.
Possible Responses: The author and artist pay attention to similar details; Jimmy and Prince Eristoff both dress well and affect attitudes; they both seem to enjoy fine things.

A guard came to the prison shoe shop, where Jimmy Valentine was <u>assiduously</u> stitching uppers, and escorted him to the front office. There the warden handed Jimmy his pardon, which had been signed that morning by the governor. Jimmy took it in a tired kind of way. He had served nearly ten months of a four-year sentence. He had expected to stay only about three months, at the longest. When a man with as many friends on the outside as Jimmy Valentine had is received in the "stir" it is hardly worthwhile to cut his hair.

"Now, Valentine," said the warden, "you'll go out in the morning. Brace up, and make a man of yourself. You're not a bad fellow at heart. Stop cracking safes, and live straight."

"Me?" said Jimmy, in surprise. "Why, I never cracked a safe in my life."

"Oh, no," laughed the warden. "Of course not. Let's see, now. How was it you happened to get sent up on that Springfield job? Was it because you wouldn't prove an alibi for fear of compromising somebody in extremely high-toned society? Or was it simply a case of a mean old jury that had it in for you? It's always one or the other with you innocent victims."

"Me?" said Jimmy, still blankly <u>virtuous</u>. "Why, warden, I never was in Springfield in my life!"

"Take him back, Cronin," smiled the warden, "and fix him up with outgoing clothes. Unlock him at seven in the morning, and let him come to the bull-pen. Better think over my advice, Valentine."

At a quarter past seven on the next morning Jimmy stood in the warden's outer office. He had on a suit of the villainously fitting, ready-made clothes and a pair of the stiff, squeaky shoes that the state furnishes to its discharged <u>compulsory</u> guests.

The clerk handed him a railroad ticket and the five-dollar bill with which the law expected him to <u>rehabilitate</u> himself into good citizenship and prosperity. The warden gave him a cigar, and shook hands. Valentine, 9762, was chronicled on the books "Pardoned by Governor," and Mr. James Valentine walked out into the sunshine.

Disregarding the song of the birds, the waving green trees, and the smell of the flowers, Jimmy headed straight for a restaurant. There he tasted the first sweet joys of liberty in the shape of a broiled chicken and a bottle of white wine—followed by a cigar a grade better than the one the warden had given him. From there he proceeded leisurely to the depot. He tossed a quarter into the hat of a blind man sitting by the door, and boarded his train. Three hours set him down in a little town near the state line. He went to the café of one Mike Dolan and shook hands with Mike, who was alone behind the bar.

"Sorry we couldn't make it sooner, Jimmy, me boy," said Mike. "But we had that protest from Springfield to buck against, and the governor nearly <u>balked</u>. Feeling all right?"

"Fine," said Jimmy. "Got my key?"

He got his key and went upstairs, unlocking the door of a room at the rear. Everything was just as he had left it. There on the floor was still Ben Price's collar-button that had been torn from that <u>eminent</u> detective's shirt-band when they had overpowered Jimmy to arrest him.

Pulling out from the wall a folding-bed, Jimmy slid back a panel in the wall and dragged out a dust-covered suitcase. He

WORDS
TO
KNOW

assiduously (ə-sĭj'ōō-əs-lē) *adv.* in a steady and hard-working way
virtuous (vûr'chōō-əs) *adj.* morally good; honorable
compulsory (kəm-pŭl'sə-rē) *adj.* that which must be done; required
rehabilitate (rē'hə-bĭl'ĭ-tāt') *v.* to restore to useful life, as through therapy and education
balk (bôk) *v.* to refuse to move or act
eminent (ĕm'ə-nənt) *adj.* better than most others; very famous

165

Reading Skills and Strategies: PREDICTING

A Have students predict what might happen in the plot based on Jimmy's actions in this paragraph.

Possible Response: Jimmy is taking out his carefully hidden burglary tools. His fond gaze and pride in them indicate that he is going to use them again. I predict that he hasn't changed and that he is going to return to a life of crime.

Literary Analysis: CHARACTERIZATION

B Note that short story writers must create and convey character efficiently. Ask students what this passage about the robberies suggests about Jimmy's and Ben's characters.

Possible Response: Jimmy is a confident, skillful thief who apparently feels no remorse for his thefts. Ben is smart and determined; others feel confidence in him.

Literary Analysis: PLOT

C Have students identify the event that causes Jimmy's reformation. Have them infer what happens in that moment.

Possible Response: He looks into the eyes of the young lady (Annabel) and becomes infatuated.

Reading Skills and Strategies: MAKING INFERENCES

D Ask students to explain why Jimmy chooses the shoe business.

Answer: He learned to make shoes in prison.

A

1

opened this and gazed fondly at the finest set of burglar's tools in the East. It was a complete set, made of specially tempered steel, the latest designs in drills, punches, braces and bits, jimmies, clamps, and augers, with two or three novelties invented by Jimmy himself, in which he took pride. Over nine hundred dollars they had cost him to have made at _____, a place where they make such things for the profession.

In half an hour Jimmy went downstairs and through the café. He was now dressed in tasteful and well-fitting clothes, and carried his dusted and cleaned suitcase in his hand.

"Got anything on?" asked Mike Dolan, genially.

"Me?" said Jimmy, in a puzzled tone. "I don't understand. I'm representing the New York Amalgamated Short Snap Biscuit Cracker and Frazzled Wheat Company."

This statement delighted Mike to such an extent that Jimmy had to take a seltzer-and-milk on the spot. He never touched "hard" drinks.

A week after the release of Valentine, 9762, there was a neat job of safe-burglary done in Richmond, Indiana, with no clue to the author. A scant eight hundred dollars was all that was secured. Two weeks after that a patented, improved, burglar-proof safe in Logansport was opened like a cheese to the tune of fifteen hundred dollars, currency; securities and silver untouched. That began to interest the rogue catchers. Then an old-fashioned bank safe in Jefferson City became active and threw out of its crater an eruption of banknotes amounting to five thousand dollars. The losses were now high enough to bring the matter up into Ben Price's class of work. By comparing notes, a remarkable similarity in the methods of the burglaries was noticed. Ben Price investigated the scenes of the robberies, and was heard to remark:

"That's Dandy Jim Valentine's autograph. He's resumed business. Look at that combination knob—jerked out as easy as pulling up a radish in wet weather. He's got the only clamps that can do it. And look how clean those tumblers were punched out! Jimmy never has to drill but one hole. Yes, I guess I want Mr. Valentine. He'll do his bit next time without any short-time or clemency foolishness."

Ben Price knew Jimmy's habits. He had learned them while working up the Springfield case. Long jumps, quick get-aways, no confederates,[1] and a taste for good society—these ways had helped Mr. Valentine to become noted as a successful dodger of <u>retribution</u>. It was given out that Ben Price had taken up the trail of the <u>elusive</u> cracksman, and other people with burglar-proof safes felt more at ease.

One afternoon Jimmy Valentine and his suitcase climbed out of the mailhack in Elmore, a little town five miles off the railroad down in the blackjack country of Arkansas. Jimmy, looking like an athletic young senior just home from college, went down the board sidewalk toward the hotel.

A young lady crossed the street, passed him at the corner, and entered a door over which

---

1. **confederates** (kən-fĕd′ər-ĭts): accomplices or associates in crime.

WORDS TO KNOW	**retribution** (rĕt′rə-byōō′shən) *n.* punishment for bad behavior **elusive** (ĭ-lōō′sĭv) *adj.* escaping from capture as by daring, cleverness, or skill

166

Teaching Options

 Mini Lesson ## Preteaching Vocabulary

WORD MEANING

Instruction Call students' attention to the list of WORDS TO KNOW. Remind them that sometimes they can use structural analysis to identify words by applying knowledge of the meanings of base words and prefixes or suffixes. Use the model below to demonstrate the strategy of separating a word into a base word and affixes. If necessary, a word's derivation and the meaning of its base word can be looked up in a dictionary.

Model: reformation = *re-* + *form* + *-ation*

Exercises

Have students identify the base word, its meaning, and any affixes for each word listed below. Some words may have no base word or no parts.

assiduously = *assiduous* (dilligent) + *-ly*

balk (no parts)

compulsory = (no base word)

elusive = (no base word)

eminent = (no base words)

rehabilitate = *re-* + *habilitate* (to enable)

retribution = *re-* + *tribute* (payment) + *-ion*

unobtrusively = *un-* + *obtrusive* (attracting attention) + *-ly*

unperceived = *un-* + *perceive* (to see) + *-ed*

virtuous = *virtue* (goodness) + *-ous*

Use **Unit One Resource Book**, p. 84, for more exercises. Use **Vocabulary Transparencies and Copymasters**, p. 33, for additional support.

was the sign "The Elmore Bank." Jimmy Valentine looked into her eyes, forgot what he was, and became another man. She lowered her eyes and colored slightly. Young men of Jimmy's style and looks were scarce in Elmore.

Jimmy collared a boy that was loafing on the steps of the bank as if he were one of the stockholders, and began to ask him questions about the town, feeding him dimes at intervals. By and by the young lady came out, looking royally unconscious of the young man with the suitcase, and went her way.

"Isn't that young lady Miss Polly Simpson?" asked Jimmy, with specious guile.[2]

"Naw," said the boy. "She's Annabel Adams. Her pa owns this bank. What'd you come to Elmore for? Is that a gold watch-chain? I'm going to get a bulldog. Got any more dimes?"

Jimmy went to the Planters' Hotel, registered as Ralph D. Spencer, and engaged a room. He leaned on the desk and declared his platform to the clerk. He said he had come to Elmore to look for a location to go into business. How was the shoe business, now, in the town? He had thought of the shoe business. Was there an opening?

The clerk was impressed by the clothes and manner of Jimmy. He, himself, was something of a pattern of fashion to the thinly gilded youth of Elmore, but he now perceived his shortcomings. While trying to figure out Jimmy's manner of tying his four-in-hand[3] he cordially gave information.

Yes, there ought to be a good opening in the shoe line. There wasn't an exclusive shoe store in the place. The dry-goods and general stores handled them. Business in all lines was fairly good. Hoped Mr. Spencer would decide to locate in Elmore. He would find it a pleasant town to live in, and the people very sociable.

Mr. Spencer thought he would stop over in the town a few days and look over the situation. No, the clerk needn't call the boy. He would carry up his suitcase, himself; it was rather heavy.

Mr. Ralph Spencer, the phoenix[4] that arose from Jimmy Valentine's ashes—ashes left by the flame of a sudden and alterative attack of love—remained in Elmore, and prospered. He opened a shoe store and secured a good run of trade.

Socially he was also a success and made many friends. And he accomplished the wish of his heart. He met Miss Annabel Adams, and became more and more captivated by her charms.

At the end of a year the situation of Mr. Ralph Spencer was this: he had won the respect of the community, his shoe store was flourishing, and he and Annabel were engaged to be married in two weeks. Mr. Adams, the typical, plodding, country banker, approved of Spencer. Annabel's pride in him almost equaled her affection. He was as much at home in the family of Mr. Adams and that of Annabel's married sister as if he were already a member.

One day Jimmy sat down in his room and wrote this letter, which he mailed to the safe address of one of his old friends in St. Louis:

DEAR OLD PAL:

I want you to be at Sullivan's place, in Little Rock, next Wednesday night, at nine o'clock. I want you to wind up some little matters for me. And, also, I want to make you a present

---

2. **specious guile** (spē'shəs gīl): innocent charm masking real slyness.

3. **four-in-hand:** a necktie tied in the usual way, that is, in a slipknot with the ends left hanging.

4. **phoenix** (fē'nĭks): a mythological bird that lived for over 500 years and then burned itself to death, only to rise out of its own ashes to live another long life. The phoenix is a symbol of immortality.

Customizing Instruction

Less Proficient Readers

1 Explain that this blank is used to suggest that the story is true and the author did not wish to provide the real name of the place.

2 Use the following questions to confirm students' understanding to this point:

- Who is Ben Price, and why is he following Jimmy?
  Answer: Price is a detective who wants to catch Jimmy and return him to jail.
- Who is Annabel Adams?
  Answer: the banker's daughter and the woman Jimmy falls in love with
- What is Jimmy's new name?
  Answer: Ralph D. Spencer
- Why does Jimmy change his name?
  Possible Response: to start a new life

Students Acquiring English

3 Students should be able to infer from the context that *naw* means "no." Model the correct pronunciation and intonation.

Explain that the idiom *stop over* means "to stay somewhere between two parts of a trip."

Gifted and Talented

Have students identify and explain examples of figurative language, such as "(a) safe in Logansport was *opened like a cheese*" (opened easily and cleanly).

Possible Responses: "(A) bank safe in Jefferson City *became active and threw out of its crater* an *eruption* of *banknotes*" (comparison to volcano); "Look at that combination knob—jerked out *as easy as pulling up a radish in wet weather*" (very easily).

Cross Curricular Link **History**

THE GILDED AGE This story is set in the last quarter of the 19th century, a period known as America's "Gilded Age." *Gilded* means "covered with gold," and the last decades of the 1800s were a time of fabulous industrial and economic growth, political corruption, and, for some people, wealth. Railroads finally crossed the country, opening up transportation. Entrepreneurs like Rockefeller, Carnegie, and Morgan made their fortunes in oil, steel, and banking. Philip Armour and Gustavus Swift started huge meat packing businesses. Thomas Edison invented the light bulb; Alexander Graham Bell invented the telephone. The public was eager for anything new. Few voices cautioned against the unrestrained growth and extravagance. Mark Twain and Charles Dudley Warner satirized the pell-mell mood and the decadence of the times in a novel called *The Gilded Age,* and the term became a title for the era.

Literary Analysis: POINT OF VIEW

Explain to students that the story is written from the third person point of view. Help them see the contrast between the first and third person points of view. Then ask students why the third person is a useful point of view for this short story.

Possible Response: Using the third person allows the narrator to tell what all characters are doing and thinking, wherever they are. The narrator is not limited to one character's point of view.

 Use **Literary Analysis Transparencies,** p. 22, for additional support.

Literary Analysis FALLING ACTION

A Explain that writers sometimes foreshadow, or provide hints about, events that will occur later in the plot. Have students speculate about what the details in this passage might foreshadow.

Possible Response: The children's delight in seeing the "shining metal and funny clock and knobs" suggests they will play with the safe and perhaps lock themselves in.

Reading Skills and Strategies: PREDICTING

Invite students to predict what they think will happen next, based on what they know about Jimmy.

Possible Responses: Jimmy will open the safe to save Agatha; he won't open the safe because doing that would give away his identity.

---

of my kit of tools. I know you'll be glad to get them—you couldn't duplicate the lot for a thousand dollars. Say, Billy, I've quit the old business—a year ago. I've got a nice store. I'm making an honest living, and I'm going to marry the finest girl on earth two weeks from now. It's the only life, Billy—the straight one. I wouldn't touch a dollar of another man's money now for a million. After I get married I'm going to sell out and go West, where there won't be so much danger of having old scores brought up against me. I tell you, Billy, she's an angel. She believes in me; and I wouldn't do another crooked thing for the whole world. Be sure to be at Sully's, for I must see you. I'll bring along the tools with me.

> **I wouldn't do another crooked thing for the whole world.**

Your old friend,
JIMMY

On the Monday night after Jimmy wrote this letter, Ben Price jogged <u>unobtrusively</u> into Elmore in a livery buggy. He lounged about town in his quiet way until he found out what he wanted to know. From the drugstore across the street from Spencer's shoe store he got a good look at Ralph D. Spencer.

"Going to marry the banker's daughter are you, Jimmy?" said Ben to himself, softly. "Well, I don't know!"

The next morning Jimmy took breakfast at the Adamses. He was going to Little Rock that day to order his wedding suit and buy something nice for Annabel. That would be the first time he had left town since he came to Elmore.

It had been more than a year now since those last professional "jobs," and he thought he could safely venture out.

After breakfast quite a family party went down together—Mr. Adams, Annabel, Jimmy, and Annabel's married sister with her two little girls, aged five and nine. They came by the hotel where Jimmy still boarded, and he ran up to his room and brought along his suitcase. Then they went on to the bank. There stood Jimmy's horse and buggy and Dolph Gibson, who was going to drive him over to the railroad station.

All went inside the high, carved oak railings into the banking room—Jimmy included, for Mr. Adams's future son-in-law was welcome anywhere. The clerks were pleased to be greeted by the good-looking, agreeable young man who was going to marry Miss Annabel. Jimmy set his suitcase down. Annabel, whose heart was bubbling with happiness and lively youth, put on Jimmy's hat and picked up the suitcase. "Wouldn't I make a nice drummer?" said Annabel. "My! Ralph, how heavy it is. Feels like it was full of gold bricks."

"Lot of nickel-plated shoehorns in there," said Jimmy, coolly, "that I'm going to return. Thought I'd save express charges by taking them up. I'm getting awfully economical."

The Elmore Bank had just put in a new safe and vault. Mr. Adams was very proud of it, and insisted on an inspection by everyone. The vault was a small one, but it had a new patented door. It fastened with three solid steel bolts thrown simultaneously with a single handle, and had a time lock. Mr. Adams beamingly

WORDS TO KNOW   **unobtrusively** (ŭn'əb-trōō'sĭv-lē) *adv.* in a way that attracts little or no attention

---

Teaching Options

 Mini Lesson  **Vocabulary Strategy** 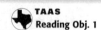 **TEKS** 6B, 6C, 9G **TAAS** Reading Obj. 1

WORD ROOTS

Instruction Remind students that many words in English have their roots in other languages, such as Greek and Latin. A complete dictionary will list the origins of most words. If a word's entry includes no information about origin, students should try looking up its base word. For example, to find the sources of *assiduously,* have students look up *assiduous.* The origin of that word should appear at the beginning or at the end of the dictionary entry:

[Latin *assiduus* <*assidēre,* to attend to: *ad-,* ad- + *sedēre,* to sit]

Point out that knowing the source *sedēre* helps in recognizing members of the same word family, such as *sedentary* and *sediment,* and in understanding how they are related in meaning.

Application Have students investigate the origins of the words *elusive* (Latin *ēlūsus* <*ē-,* out + *lūdere,* to pay), *retribution* (Latin *retribūtiō* <*re-,* back + *tributere,* to play), and *perceive* (Latin *percipere* <*per-,* completely + *capere,* to grasp). Ask students to list other words in the same families as these.

 Use **Vocabulary Transparencies and Copymasters,** p. 34, for additional support.

explained its workings to Mr. Spencer, who showed a courteous but not too intelligent interest. The two children, May and Agatha, were delighted by the shining metal and funny clock and knobs.

While they were thus engaged Ben Price sauntered in and leaned on his elbow, looking casually inside between the railings. He told the teller that he didn't want anything; he was just waiting for a man he knew.

Suddenly there was a scream or two from the women, and a commotion. Unperceived by the elders, May, the nine-year-old girl, in a spirit of play, had shut Agatha in the vault. She had then shot the bolts and turned the knob of the combination as she had seen Mr. Adams do.

The old banker sprang to the handle and tugged at it for a moment. "The door can't be opened," he groaned. "The clock hasn't been wound nor the combination set."

Agatha's mother screamed again, hysterically.

"Hush!" said Mr. Adams, raising his trembling hand. "All be quiet for a moment. Agatha!" he called as loudly as he could. "Listen to me." During the following silence they could just hear the faint sound of the child wildly shrieking in the dark vault in a panic of terror.

"My precious darling!" wailed the mother. "She will die of fright! Open the door! Oh, break it open! Can't you men do something?"

Copyright © Gary Kelley.

WORDS TO KNOW   **unperceived** (ŭn'pər-sēvd') *adj.* not seen

169

Customizing Instruction

Less Proficient Readers
Ask students the following questions to reinforce understanding:

• What details suggest that Jimmy has really changed?
Possible Responses: the letter to Billy, which says, "I wouldn't do another crooked thing for the whole world"; Jimmy's plan to send his burglary tools to Billy

• In what ways has Jimmy's life become more stable?
Possible Responses: He is settled in one town; he is to be married; he has an established, legitimate business.

When students finish the story, have them summarize the events that take place at the Elmore Bank.

Possible Response: Annabel's niece accidentally gets locked in a safe, and Jimmy uses his safecracking skills to get her out.

Ask the following questions to reinforce understanding.

• Who shouts "Ralph!" after Jimmy leaves the bank?
Answer: Annabel

• What does Ben do when Jimmy turns himself in?
Answer: Ben pretends that he doesn't know Jimmy.

 Grammar **TEKS** 16B, 17A   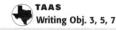**TAAS** Writing Obj. 3, 5, 7

FOUR KINDS OF SENTENCES
Instruction Help students recall the four kinds of sentences:
• Declarative sentences make statements.
• Interrogatory sentences ask questions.
• Exclamatory sentences express strong emotion.
• Imperative sentences give directions or orders.

Point out that imperative sentences sometimes identify the person being addressed, as in "Take him back, Cronin." Often, however, the person being addressed is not named: "Stop cracking safes." The unstated subject (you) is called an understood subject.

Explain that an exclamation such as "My precious darling!" is not a sentence (it has no verb).

Exercises Help students compare and identify these examples, highlighted in the text:
1. I tell you, Billy, she's an angel. *(declarative)*
2. Listen to me. *(imperative)*

3. Going to marry the banker's daughter are you, Jimmy? *(interrogatory)*
4. Well, I don't know! *(exclamatory)*

 Use **Grammar Transparencies and Copymasters**, p. 54.

 Use McDougal Littell's *Language Network*, Chapter 1, for more instruction and practice in identifying the four kinds of sentences.

Active Reading

| COMPARING ACROSS TEXTS |

Have students identify similarities and differences between "A Retrieved Reformation" and "After Twenty Years."

Possible Responses: Jimmy changes and leaves his life of crime; Bob does not. Ben Price pretends not to know Jimmy and allows him to remain free; Jimmy, the police officer in "After Twenty Years," keeps his own identity secret and has someone else arrest his one-time friend, Bob. Both law officers have integrity and compassion, though these qualities lead to different actions. Both stories have surprise endings.

Literary Analysis | FALLING ACTION |

A Have students identify the resolution of the story. How does the resolution "open doors" for Jimmy?

Answer: Ben Price pretends not to know Jimmy and so leaves him free to pursue his new life.

Reading Skills and Strategies: PREDICTING

Point out that the resolution leaves some unanswered questions. Discuss with students whether they think Annabel will still marry Jimmy.

Possible Responses: Yes, because Jimmy is no longer a criminal; no, because he lied about who he really was.

"There isn't a man nearer than Little Rock who can open that door," said Mr. Adams, in a shaky voice. "My God! Spencer, what shall we do? That child—she can't stand it long in there. There isn't enough air, and, besides, she'll go into convulsions from fright."

Agatha's mother, frantic now, beat the door of the vault with her hands. Somebody wildly suggested dynamite. Annabel turned to Jimmy, her large eyes full of anguish, but not yet despairing. To a woman nothing seems quite impossible to the powers of the man she worships.

"Can't you do something, Ralph—try, won't you?"

He looked at her with a queer, soft smile on his lips and in his keen eyes.

"Annabel," he said, "give me that rose you are wearing, will you?"

Hardly believing that she had heard him aright, she unpinned the bud from the bosom of her dress, and placed it in his hand. Jimmy stuffed it into his vest pocket, threw off his coat and pulled up his shirt sleeves. With that act Ralph D. Spencer passed away and Jimmy Valentine took his place.

"Get away from the door, all of you," he commanded, shortly.

He set his suitcase on the table, and opened it out flat. From that time on he seemed to be unconscious of the presence of anyone else. He laid out the shining, queer implements swiftly and orderly, whistling softly to himself as he always did when at work. In a deep silence and immovable, the others watched him as if under a spell.

In a minute Jimmy's pet drill was biting smoothly into the steel door. In ten minutes—breaking his own burglarious record—he threw back the bolts and opened the door.

Agatha, almost collapsed, but safe, was gathered into her mother's arms.

Jimmy Valentine put on his coat, and walked outside the railings toward the front door. As he went he thought he heard a faraway voice that he once knew call "Ralph!" But he never hesitated. At the door a big man stood somewhat in his way.

"Hello, Ben!" said Jimmy, still with his strange smile. "Got around at last, have you? Well, let's go. I don't know that it makes much difference, now."

And then Ben Price acted rather strangely.

"Guess you're mistaken, Mr. Spencer," he said. "Don't believe I recognize you. Your buggy's waiting for you, ain't it?"

And Ben Price turned and strolled down the street. ❖

Teaching Options

 Assessment **Standardized Test Practice** TEKS 10F, 10K  TAAS Reading Obj. 3

DESCRIBE PLOT In some standardized tests, students are asked to select the best plot description or summary statement for a passage they have read. Write the following question on the board or read it aloud:

Which statement best describes the plot of "A Retrieved Reformation"?

A. Jimmy Valentine moves to Elmore and changes his name to Mr. Ralph Spencer.

B. Ben Price trails Jimmy and then lets him stay free because he rescues Agatha.

C. Jimmy turns away from a life of crime and uses his safecracking skills to save a girl's life.

D. People who have been in jail can change their lives if they have the right motivation.

Guide students through the process of selecting the correct answer. A is not complete enough because it includes only rising action. B focuses on Ben Price, a secondary character. D is the theme, more general than a plot summary. C is the best answer because it includes the climax and summarizes rising and falling action.

Connect to the Literature

1. What Do You Think?
How did you react to Jimmy's decision to crack the safe? Explain.

Comprehension Check
- Why was Jimmy sent to prison?
- What successes does Jimmy have in Elmore?
- How does Ben Price react when Jimmy cracks the safe?

Think Critically

2. Why do you think Ben Price lets Jimmy go free?

3. What is your opinion of Jimmy Valentine?

 THINK ABOUT
- Jimmy's history and what the warden says about his character
- Jimmy's motives for changing
- what Jimmy risks in opening the vault

4. How do you think Jimmy will explain his actions to Annabel?

5. Both Jimmy Valentine and Ben Price make important decisions. Who showed more courage? Explain.

Extend Interpretations

6. **What If?** Suppose Agatha had not been locked in the safe. Do you think Jimmy ever would have confessed his past to Annabel?

7. **ACTIVE READING COMPARING ACROSS TEXTS** Review the notes you made in your **READER'S NOTEBOOK**. How would you describe the similarities and differences between the main characters in "A Retrieved Reformation" and "After Twenty Years"? Explain your response.

8. **Connect to Life** In both "After Twenty Years" and "A Retrieved Reformation," police officers have to make difficult decisions about turning someone in. If you were in the same situation as Ben Price, what would you do? Use details from the story to support your response.

Literary Analysis

FALLING ACTION The series of events that make up a story is its **plot.** The part of the plot in which the conflict intensifies is called the **rising action.** The point of highest tension is called the **climax,** or turning point. In "A Retrieved Reformation" the climax comes when Jimmy decides to crack the safe and free Agatha, thus making it inevitable that he will reveal his past to the people he most wanted to hide it from.

Jimmy's decision affects the resolution, or **falling action,** of the story. Because Jimmy has decided to sacrifice his own reputation to save Agatha, Ben makes the decision not to arrest Jimmy. In this way, the conflict that has moved the action of the story forward is resolved.

Cooperative Learning Activity
Working with a small group, go back through the story and create a pyramid plotting the events in "A Retrieved Reformation" that form the rising action, the climax, and the falling action.

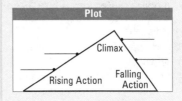

Plot
Climax / Rising Action / Falling Action

Extend Interpretations

6. **What If?** Possible Response: Jimmy might never have confessed his past, because he had made himself into a different person. Also he might have feared losing Annabel if he revealed his past without a reason.

7. **Comparing Across Texts** Possible Response: Both are criminals, both dress well and can be charming; Jimmy reforms and stays free; Bob doesn't change and is arrested.

Use **Reading and Critical Thinking Transparencies,** p. 8, for additional support.

8. **Connect to Life** Possible Response: I would let him go too, because I had seen that he had truly changed and wasn't going to go back to crime.

Connect to the Literature

1. What Do You Think?
Responses will vary. Students may have expected Jimmy to save Agatha because of his love for Annabel's family and because his new identity was one of integrity and selflessness. They may have been surprised, expecting Jimmy to resort to his old selfish ways and protect himself rather than save Agatha.

Comprehension Check
- He was a safecracker, or burglar.
- He opened a successful shoe store, made friends, and became engaged to Annabel.
- Ben Price pretends not to recognize Jimmy and so lets him stay free.

Use Selection Quiz **Unit One Resource Book,** p. 87.

Think Critically

2. Possible Response: Price believes Jimmy is reformed because Jimmy revealed himself to save Agatha. Also, he had not robbed anyone in a year.

3. Possible Response: Jimmy was changed by love and behaved admirably in being willing to give up his freedom to rescue Agatha.

4. Possible Response: Jimmy will tell her the truth about his past and the changes he has made.

5. Possible Response: Jimmy showed more courage because he risked going back to prison. There was little chance anyone would know what Price did.

Literary Analysis

Falling Action Students' charts should include **rising action** events (such as Jimmy's release, collecting of tools, robberies, arrival in Elmore, sight of Annabel, opening of store, proposal, letter to Billy; Price's pursuit), **climax** (Jimmy decides to crack the safe), and **falling action events** (Agatha is freed, Jimmy turns himself in, Price lets him go).

Use **Literary Analysis Transparencies,** p. 5, for additional support.

Grammar in Context

WRITING EXERCISE
Answers will vary. Student paragraphs must include one of each type of sentence. A sample response is given: What a terrifying experience! It was pitch black in the vault. Whenever I stopped screaming to listen, I heard my mother calling dimly— "Don't cry. Don't cry!" But how could I not cry?

CONNECT TO THE LITERATURE
Possible Responses:
Declarative: He had served nearly ten months of a four-year sentence.
Exclamatory: "Why, warden, I never was in Springfield in my life!"
Interrogatory: "How was it you happened to get sent up on that Springfield job?"
Imperative: "Brace up, and make a man of yourself."

Vocabulary in Action

1. True
2. False
3. True
4. False
5. False
6. False
7. True
8. False
9. True
10. False

Grammar in Context: Kinds of Sentences

Notice how O. Henry uses four types of sentences in "A Retrieved Reformation."

> "Did the mean old jury have it in for you?"
> The warden handed Jimmy his pardon.
> "Stop cracking safes, and live straight."
> "I never cracked a safe in my life!"

There are four types of sentences.

1. **Declarative sentences** make a statement. They end with a **period (.)**:
   The warden handed Jimmy his pardon.
2. **Exclamatory sentences** express strong emotion. They end with an **exclamation point (!)**:
   I never cracked a safe in my life!
3. **Interrogative sentences** ask a question. They are punctuated with a **question mark (?)**:
   Did the mean old jury have it in for you?
4. **Imperative sentences** issue a command. They end with a **period (.)**:
   Stop cracking safes, and live straight.

Vocabulary in Action

EXERCISE: WORD MEANING On your paper, write *True* if the statement is true. Write *False* if the statement is false.

1. A prison sentence is common **retribution** for a serious crime.
2. A police officer may refuse a **compulsory** assignment and not suffer any consequences.
3. A **virtuous** person shows concern for others.
4. An **unperceived** crime is one observed by several eyewitnesses.
5. Lazy people work **assiduously**.

Connect to the Literature Reread the last paragraph on page 169. The mother whose daughter is trapped in the bank vault speaks almost entirely in exclamatory sentences. This series of exclamations expresses her intense anxiety for her daughter's well-being.

Usage Tip Use exclamation points sparingly in your writing unless you want to convey intense emotion.

WRITING EXERCISE Remember when you were five years old. Imagine how you would feel if, like Agatha in the story, you had been trapped in a bank vault. Write a short paragraph about your imagined experience. Use each sentence type—declarative, exclamatory, interrogative, and imperative. Be careful to use end punctuation correctly.

Connect to the Literature Look at page 170 of "A Retrieved Reformation." Find an example of the four types of sentences.

Grammar Handbook The Sentence and Its Parts, p. R55

6. An **eminent** detective is likely to be new to the job.
7. To **rehabilitate** a criminal means to restore the person to honest ways.
8. You will attract much attention by entering a room **unobtrusively**.
9. Most thieves would not **balk** at stealing jewels.
10. An **elusive** criminal is easy to catch.

Building Vocabulary
For an in-depth study of learning and remembering new words, see p. 473.

Teaching Options

 Mini Lesson **Grammar** **TEKS** 16B, 17A 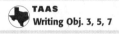 **TAAS** Writing Obj. 3, 5, 7

PUNCTUATING OF FOUR TYPES OF SENTENCES
Instruction Using these sentences from page 168, have students identify the punctuation used with each of the four types of sentences:
1. I tell you, Billy, she's an angel. *(declarative: period)*
2. Listen to me. *(imperative: period)*
3. "Going to marry the banker's daughter are you, Jimmy?" *(interrogatory: question mark)*
4. "Well, I don't know!" *(exclamatory: exclamation point)*

Point out that an imperative sentence can sometimes end with an exclamation point, and remind students that an exclamation such as "My!" is not a proper sentence.
Exercises Have students write each sentence, providing the correct punctuation.
Exclamatory: She will die of fright *(!)*
Interrogatory: Spencer, what shall we do *(?)*
Imperative: All be quiet for a moment *(.)*
Declarative: There isn't a man nearer than Little Rock who can open that door *(.)*

 Use **Unit One Resource Book**, p. 85.
Use **Grammar Transparencies and Copymasters**, p. 123.

Use McDougal Littell's *Language Network*, Chapter 11, for more instruction and practice in punctuating the four kinds of sentences.

O. HENRY

FROM SHORT STORY to the BIG SCREEN

Preparing to Read

Build Background

Not long after the motion picture's potential for visual storytelling was recognized, the first movies dealing with specific subject matters, or *genres,* began to appear.

Detective and gangster movies, westerns, adventure movies, science fiction and horror movies, dramatizations of literary classics, filmed versions of Shakespeare's plays, wacky comedies, and lavish musicals—all of these genres were introduced in the early years of filmmaking and remain popular with audiences today.

How many movies have you seen that fit into one of these genres?

Although O. Henry would not live to see a movie himself, his story "A Retrieved Reformation" (page 164) played an important part in launching a popular type of American film, the gangster movie. In 1909, the year before O. Henry's death, playwright Paul Armstrong dramatized O. Henry's story of the reformed bank robber and gave it the title *Alias Jimmy Valentine.* The play was one of the biggest hits on Broadway in the years before World War I. O. Henry was delighted with the play's early popularity, but died without ever suspecting how truly successful the play would become.

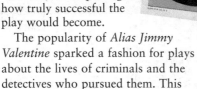

Poster for *Alias Jimmy Valentine* (1928).

The popularity of *Alias Jimmy Valentine* sparked a fashion for plays about the lives of criminals and the detectives who pursued them. This fashion occurred just as a new kind of artistic expression, motion pictures, was coming into being. In 1905 the first movie theater opened in the United States. Soon there were theaters across the nation.

By 1913 a number of studios producing motion pictures had established themselves in a suburb of Los Angeles, California, named Hollywood. Audiences were eager to see motion pictures, and Hollywood was on the lookout for screen plays to film. *Alias Jimmy Valentine* was filmed a total

TEACHING THE LITERATURE

Build Background

People began to experiment seriously with photographing motion in the 1800s. E. J. Marey, a French physiologist, is credited with making the first single- camera motion pictures in the 1880s. Later in that decade, Thomas Edison assigned an assistant named Dickson to create a movie-making device which they called a Kinetograph. In 1895 the Lumière brothers of France exhibited their cinematograph—the first documented device for photographing, printing, and projecting films. Early U.S. movie theaters came to be known as nickelodeons, after the name of a theater that was opened in 1905 in Pittsburgh, Pennsylvania.

Literary Analysis: CHARACTER

Tell students that people have said that Jimmy Valentine was one of the first American "Robin Hoods." For the first time in a movie, the public saw a criminal as more than just a "bad guy," but also as a human being with feelings. Ask students to explain this idea using examples from the story. Then, to help students analyze this character's influence on American film, have them compare Jimmy Valentine to other, similar film characters.

Possible Responses: Jimmy is flawed but clever; he has committed crimes, but he shows he can feel love and do right. Students might compare Jimmy to another villainous character who shows he or she has a sensitive, good side.

Reading Skills and Strategies: VISUALIZING

Invite students to visualize the story as a motion picture. Discuss with students what costumes, settings, music, and actors they can picture in the film.

A Ask students to imagine what it would be like to see a movie without sound. Encourage them to think about the sounds that typically fill a feature film, including dialogue, background noises, and music. What elements of a silent film would have to be emphasized to increase audience members' understanding?

Possible Response: Actors would have to use more dramatic movements and facial expressions.

Literary Analysis:
GENRE

B Point out to students that every story genre holds its own unique appeal. Ask students to name the specific characteristics of the detective/crime drama. Then have them explain why these kinds of stories are so popular in movie theaters.

Possible Response: Students might say a crime drama usually features villains and heroes, suspense, and mystery. These kinds of films give people excitement and challenge them to solve mysteries.

Thinking Through the Literature

1. **Possible Response:** O. Henry's story influenced popular culture in the early 1900s. He was a pioneer of the detective/gangster genre.

2. **Possible Response:** *Alias Jimmy Valentine* is easier to say. It gives audiences the impression that the story has elements of mystery and hidden identity. It also draws attention to the main character.

3. **Connect to Life** Responses will vary. Students might focus on how book and movie versions of the same stories differ and explain why

---

A of three times. In 1915 Maurice Touneur directed the first silent version. Audiences were fascinated with the reformed safe cracker and the detective who showed him mercy. Within five years, another silent version of the play was filmed. In 1927 the first "talkie," or movie with sound effects and dialogue, *The Jazz Singer*, was shown to the public. The next year *Alias Jimmy Valentine* made its third appearance, this time with spoken dialogue.

The demand for crime and detective films only grew during the "Roaring" Twenties and on into the 1930s, the years of the Great Depression. Certain actors, such as Edward G. Robinson, James Cagney, and Paul Muni became famous for their portrayal of "underworld" figures. Three of the most famous of these early films are *Little Caesar* (1930), *The Public Enemy* (1931), and *Scarface: The Shame of a Nation* (1932).

As popular as movies about gangsters were movies that told of the detectives who hunted the gangsters down. Two masterpieces of the detective movie are *The Maltese Falcon* (1941) and *Key Largo* (1948).

B The popularity of crime and detective films has not diminished since the time when *Alias Jimmy Valentine* made its first appearance as a silent film about a hundred years ago. This type of film remains a staple of the movie industry today. What movies have you seen that fit the crime and detective genre?

Poster for *"G"-Men* (1935)

Posters for two popular gangster films, *Key Largo* (1948) and *The Maltese Falcon* (1941).

Thinking Through the Literature

1. What insights into O. Henry did you gain from this article?

2. *Alias Jimmy Valentine* became very popular as a play and three films. Do you think that O. Henry's original title, "A Retrieved Reformation," would have had the same appeal? Why or why not?

3. **Connect to Life** Have you watched a movie or video version of a story you read first as a book? Or has a favorite movie or video sent you looking for the the book it was based on? Talk about your experiences with your classmates.

THE AUTHOR'S STYLE

O. Henry's Lively Description

O. Henry said he wrote his stories for the busy, ordinary people who wanted a quick, interesting story to distract them now and then. O. Henry's lively descriptions helped him accomplish his goal.

Key Style Points

Well-Chosen Modifiers O. Henry uses adjectives and adverbs to create vivid, interesting images in his writing. His colorful language enables readers to see, hear, and even feel the lives that he re-creates on paper. In the passage from "A Retrieved Reformation," look for the adjectives, adverbs, and the words they modify.

Simple Sentences O. Henry sometimes uses a series of simple sentences, one following the other, to give a feeling of rapid movement or urgency. Identify the simple sentences in this passage from "After Twenty Years."

Specific Details Part of O. Henry's talent for description lies in his use of specific details in his writing. What specific details stand out in the passage below from "After Twenty Years"?

Applications

1. **Active Reading** With a partner, look back at the stories. Find examples of each element of vivid description.

2. **Writing** Write a letter describing a typical day in summer. Use the three elements of O. Henry's style listed above. Underline vivid adjectives and adverbs, simple sentences, and specific details.

3. **Speaking and Listening** Choose one of the passages above that has plenty of vivid adjectives and adverbs. Rewrite it, substituting weak, less vivid adjectives and adverbs. Then, read it to a partner and discuss how the feeling of the passage has changed.

Well-Chosen Modifiers

. . . Jimmy stood in the warden's outer office. He had on a suit of the villainously fitting, ready-made clothes and a pair of the stiff, squeaky shoes that the state furnishes to its discharged compulsory guests.

—"A Retrieved Reformation"

Simple Sentences

"You bet! I hope Jimmy has done half as well. He was a kind of a plodder, though, good fellow as he was. I've had to compete with some of the sharpest wits going to get my pile. A man gets in a groove in New York. It takes the West to put a razor-edge on him."

—"After Twenty Years"

Specific Details

Trying doors as he went, twirling his club with many intricate and artful movements, turning now and then to cast his watchful eye down the pacific thoroughfare, the officer, with his stalwart form and slight swagger, made a fine picture . . .

—"After Twenty Years"

The Author's Style

Students will gain greater understanding of O. Henry's style by studying the Key Style Points listed on this page and examining the examples in the right margin.

Applications

1. **Active Reading** To encourage precise and careful reading, have students make a chart by dividing a piece of paper into three sections. In each section they should copy specific examples of each element of descriptive language, along with the number of the page on which the example occurs.

2. **Writing** As a prewriting exercise, have students list the many things that can happen on a summer day: cool dawn, warm morning, hot noon, the arrival of storm clouds with thunder and lightning, changed air after the storm, and warm evening. Then have them list adjectives appropriate to each event. Finally, have them use their lists to build a description of a summer day employing the three elements of O. Henry's style.

3. **Speaking and Listening** If students have trouble with the assignment, have them use multiple reference aids, including a thesaurus, a synonym finder, a dictionary, and software to clarify alternate word choices.

Writing Options

1. Supervisor's Report Explain to students that they are not actually writing a supervisor's report, but a report to their supervisor. Discuss with students what the best approach should be. Will they continue to pretend that they did not recognize Jimmy Valentine in the reformed criminal they saw in the bank? Or will they admit they found Valentine but try to argue that he should be left alone?

2. Book Cover Ask each student to skim through the story and identify the moment in the narrative that would make the most dramatic or interesting illustration. Remind them that the purpose of a book cover is to sell a book. Show them samples of the kind of writing typically found on the back covers of books.

Activities & Explorations

Short Story and Video Prompt students to compare literary elements such as character, setting, and dialogue. Students will want to discuss ways in which the video differs from the mental images they formed while reading the story. Ask them to be specific and to evaluate the effectiveness of the different treatments.

Inquiry & Research

Back in Time Extend the activity by having students prepare data sheets on New York at the turn of the century. Their data sheets could list facts for each of the items suggested in the activity, as well as for typical clothing, common occupations, transportation, well-known buildings, and similar matters of interest.

Author Study Project

CREATING A SCENE
Monitor the activity of the students to make sure that they follow the steps laid out in the activity.

MULTIMEDIA PROJECT
Students can use minimal props and alternative music to make their video depiction more striking and abstract.

Writing Options

1. Supervisor's Report Suppose you are Ben Price. Write a report to your supervisor explaining why you have closed the case on Jimmy Valentine. Save the report in your **Working Portfolio.**

2. Book Cover Design a book cover for one of the O. Henry stories you have read. The front cover should be an illustration (a work of art, drawing, collage, etc.) that relates in some way to the story. The back cover should include a brief plot summary and a note about the author.

Activities & Explorations

Short Story and Video View the video "Jimmy Valentine." How does the video differ from "The Retrieved Reformation" on which it was based?

~ VIEWING AND REPRESENTING

VIDEO Literature in Performance

Inquiry & Research

Back in Time Using nonfiction books, the Internet, and other media, find out what life was like in New York City at the beginning of the 20th century. Look for information about population, landmarks, social customs, and other aspects of life.

Author Study Project
Creating a Scene

Working with a small group, retell one of the stories, or parts of it, in dialogue form.

❶ **Choose a Dramatic Scene** With your group, decide which scene you will act out. Think about which scenes can best be adapted to dialogue; then narrow your choice to one.

❷ **Write a Script** Write the script for your scene. You may want to include dialogue from the story.

❸ **Rehearse the Skit** Once you have completed the script, have members of your group decide which of the roles they will play—the director, characters in the scene, members of the stage crew, and so on. Then read through the script, making any changes that members of your group feel are needed to improve it.

❹ **Assign a Publicity Crew** Assign classmates to make posters advertising your skit.

❺ **Perform the Skit** Performers should practice speaking clearly, making eye contact with the audience, and pacing the performance according to the dialogue of the script. Videotape the performance to share with other classes.

O. Henry is an acknowledged master of the surprise story ending. His stories remain popular today, however, not just for their plot twists, but because O. Henry was such a keen observer of ordinary human beings—rich and poor, winners and losers, con artists and cops. In his stories, O. Henry described in stark simplicity the tragedies, comedies, conflicts, and motives of ordinary men and women.

The Gift of the Magi

This story, O. Henry's most famous, tells the tale of a poor young husband and wife, each of whom sacrifices a treasured possession in order to buy a Christmas gift for the other. This beloved story has been dramatized for the stage and made into a movie and several television dramas.

The Ransom of Red Chief

Two dim-witted hoodlums carry out a kidnapping, planning to collect a large ransom from their victim's father. Hilariously, the boy they kidnap is so troublesome the two end up paying the boy's father to take his son off their hands.

One Thousand Dollars

A spendthrift nephew inherits a thousand dollars from a rich uncle. The inheritance is merely a small part of the uncle's great wealth, and it comes with a stipulation: the nephew must account for how he spends every cent of the inheritance. This story tells of the nephew's secret act of generosity.

You may find the three stories mentioned above, as well as many others, in various collections of the stories of O. Henry.

Objectives

- write a personal narrative
- use a written text as a model for writing
- revise a draft to add sensory details
- identify and correct errors in pronoun-referent agreement

Introducing the Workshop

Personal Narrative Ask students to recall important or meaningful events from their lives. Provide an example from your own life, contrasting, for instance, your first day of teaching with an ordinary day. Help students understand that everyone has moments that stand out in their minds for some reason or other. Personal narratives are a way of sharing those moments.

Have volunteers share interesting, scary, or amusing incidents. Encourage students to provide specific details as well as to discuss how the events affected the characters. Point out that personal narratives teach readers something about the characters as well as about the world.

Basics in a Box

Using the Graphic Explain that a personal narrative like a fictional story, has a beginning, a middle, and an end. Each part has a necessary job: to provide background that introduces the main incident; to describe the incident and explain its importance; and to tell what finally happened and how the writer felt about it.

Presenting the Rubric Review with students the standards for writing a successful personal narrative. Explain that these standards can help them understand the assignment. If necessary, explain that sensory details include what the writer saw, touched, smelled, heard, and tasted. Dialogue is what people said to each other.

You may also decide to share with them the complete rubric, which describes several levels of proficiency.

 Use McDougal Littell's **Language Network**, Chapters 12–19, for more instruction on essential writing skills.

 Power Presentation

To engage students visually, use **Power Presentation** 2, Personal Narrative.

Writing Workshop
Personal Narrative

Describing an important experience . . .

From Reading to Writing Many people love to tell stories about their lives. That may be why life stories are the subject of much great literature. For example, in "Names/Nombres," Julia Alvarez describes what it is like to move to a new place. In "Dirk the Protector" an unlikely companion helps the author through a difficult time in his life. Both of these selections describe events that taught people lessons about life. Writing a **personal narrative** is a chance to tell your own story. It is one way to explore what your experience has taught you.

For Your Portfolio

WRITING PROMPT Write a narrative about something that actually happened to you or to someone you know.

Purpose: To inform and entertain
Audience: Your classmates, family members, and friends

Basics in a Box

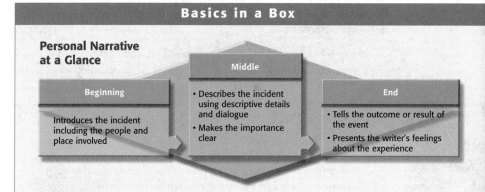

Personal Narrative at a Glance

Beginning
Introduces the incident including the people and place involved

Middle
- Describes the incident using descriptive details and dialogue
- Makes the importance clear

End
- Tells the outcome or result of the event
- Presents the writer's feelings about the experience

RUBRIC   STANDARDS FOR WRITING

A successful personal narrative should

- focus on one well-defined experience
- begin with an image or idea that makes readers want to find out more
- make the importance of the event clear
- show clearly the order in which events occurred
- use details that appeal to the senses to describe characters and setting
- use dialogue to develop characters
- provide a strong conclusion

 TEKS See the Skills Trace at the beginning of the unit for information on TEKS covered in this lesson.

LESSON RESOURCES

USING PRINT RESOURCES
Unit One Resource Book
- Prewriting, p. 88
- Drafting and Elaboration, p. 89
- Peer Response, pp. 90, 91
- Revising, Editing, and Proofreading, p. 92
- Student Models, pp. 93–95
- Rubric, p. 96

Writing Transparencies
- Writing Process Transparencies, pp. 1–4
- Writing Structure Transparency:

Elaboration, TR 13
- Writing Style Transparency: Sensory Word List, TR 16
- Writing Template Transparency: Personal Narrative, TR 25

Reading and Critical Thinking Transparencies and Copymasters
- Sequence Chain, TR 39 (for Mini Lesson, p. 180)

Grammar Transparencies and Copymasters
- Run-On Sentences, CM 58 (for Mini Lesson, p. 183)

INTEGRATED TECHNOLOGY
LaserLinks
Writing Springboards
See **Teacher's SourceBook,** p. 36, for bar codes.

Writing Coach CD-ROM
Visit our website:
www.mcdougallittell.com

Analyzing a Student Model

Kristin Richardson
Whipple Middle School

SPEAKING OPPORTUNITY
See the Communication Handbook, p. R100 for speaking and presenting tips.

"A View from the Outside"

"We're moving, but I'm not sure where," my father said one night at the dinner table. I sat there, staring at him. Then I dropped my fork.

"What did you say?" I managed.

"I'm taking a sabbatical."

"What's a sabbatical?" I looked at my mother.

She explained that this meant Dad would be taking a leave of absence from his job. It would last for one year. Then Dad said the family would be spending the year in Germany. Germany? I thought to myself. But what would happen to my spot on the volleyball team?

He explained that a friend of his from Marburg had invited us to spend a year there and live in his apartment. I had to really think twice about this. Since I had made such good friends last year, I did not want to leave. I also didn't want to leave because I would be starting the seventh grade. Still, I really did want to see Europe. How bad could it be? Little did I know there would be many more challenges than I had imagined.

Our trip started off badly. When we arrived in Germany, we were presented with a broken-down car, probably made in the early 1980s. It was so old that when we drove, exhaust would shoot out of the car! Next, the apartment we were to live in, which was very big and located in the center of the historic district, had electrical problems. Sometimes the lights would go out for no reason at all. But that was only the beginning.

I came to Germany not knowing a word of German. Because I was expected to go to a German school, I had to prepare myself before school started. I had a tutor for three months, and she came twice a week. But I only learned some of the basics, like "How are you?" and "Where is the bathroom?" I was unprepared on the first day of school. It seemed to last forever. No one spoke a word to me. In my old school I had been popular. Now I had to adjust to being on the outside of everything.

Eventually, one of my teachers introduced himself. His name was Herr Shauermann. He was the English teacher and was very nice to me. He brought me to meet my classmates. The kids in my grade were learning English, but they could hardly say much.

RUBRIC IN ACTION

❶ Introduces essay with a quote to capture readers' attention
Other Option:
• Begin with a question to the reader.

❷ Dialogue helps develop characters' personalities.

❸ Makes the order of events clear

❹ Vivid details create a sense of setting and help readers relate to the writer's feelings.

❺ Stays focused on one experience, adjusting to school in Germany

---

Teaching the Lesson

Analyzing a Student Model

"A View from the Outside"

This student model focuses on one student's experience as an outsider in a German school. The model concludes with a discussion about how this experience changed the narrator's attitudes and actions. After students read the model, discuss what makes it particularly interesting and meaningful to students like them.

Possible Response: The narrator is a student; many students feel like outsiders at one time or another.

Then discuss the Rubric in Action, pointing out key words and phrases in the student model that correspond to the elements mentioned in the Rubric in Action.

1 Ask how the opening statement creates suspense and makes readers want to read more.

   Possible Response: It contains an element of mystery: where are they going? It also signals a major change in the narrator's life.

2 Ask students what they learn about the characters from what they say.

   Possible Response: The father is impulsive; the speaker is curious.

3 Ask students what they learn in the first four paragraphs about the characters and the situation.

   Possible Responses: The father has made up his mind; the narrator is surprised and curious.

4 Have students identify specific details that help readers visualize the setting and the character's feelings.

   Possible Responses: the age of the car; the exhaust shooting out; the lights going out for no reason

5 Point out, if necessary, that this is where the main incident actually begins. Here is where readers learn about the narrator's lack of fluency and feelings of isolation.

6 Explain that transitions help readers understand when things happened and for how long. Ask students to give examples of different transitions that writers might use.

Possible Responses: Students might suggest *later*, *then*, *after a week*, *meanwhile*, or *last summer*.

7 Point out the frequent use of the word *I* in the conclusion. Ask students how that adds to the readers' feeling of personal involvement with the narrator.

Possible Response: It lets readers inside the narrator's head and heart.

<u>That first week</u> I stayed by myself during lunch. I tried hanging around with the other kids, hoping they would notice me. They never did. It made me think about kids who were outsiders at my old school. Did I ever invite them to play? Had I tried to include them or did I make them feel worse? Now I was in their shoes. Finally one day, I gathered my courage and walked up to some girls who were sitting on the steps, listening to music. I smiled at one of them. In broken English, she told me her name was Anja. She spoke English well enough because her father was American. She asked if I wanted to be shown around. We laughed and joked the whole day. We became the best of friends.

Though school continued to be challenging, everything else was marvelous. The town I lived in was very charming and had very pretty shops. On weekends and vacations, my family took trips to other nearby countries, and I enjoyed that a lot.

By the end of the year I had learned a little German. I was able to make my way around town by myself. But I rarely had to. Anja was with me often and together we shared many memories. Many days after school we'd sit in the park teaching each other our native languages. It was particularly fun trying to teach her English idioms like "It's raining cats and dogs" and "Play it by ear." Some things don't translate well into another language.

But friendship does.

Now I am home in the United States and am happy once again. Still, I haven't forgotten the lessons I learned in Germany. How could I? Anja and I keep our friendship alive by e-mailing almost every day. These days, when I see someone in school who looks as though he or she doesn't fit in, I go up and talk to that person because I know how it feels to be an outsider. I have even met some new friends this way. My experience in Germany taught me that everyone wants to fit in. Most people just need to be given a chance.

❻ Transitional words help establish chronological order.

❼ Conclusion explores the importance of the experience and tells the lessons that were learned.

Other Option:
• End with a recommendation or suggestion to readers.

 Mini Lesson ## Viewing and Representing   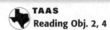 **TEKS** 10E, 10L   **TAAS** Reading Obj. 2, 4

PICTURING TEXT STRUCTURE

Instruction One way to structure a personal narrative is to relate events in chronological order, the order in which they actually happened. When the writer provides vivid details about all the events, readers get pulled into the story.

Activity Have students analyze the organization of the student model by constructing a diagram or other graphic organizer. The following event chain is an example. Discuss with students what details from the narrative might go in each section.

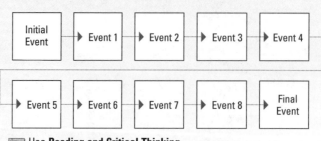

Use **Reading and Critical Thinking Transparencies**, p. 39, for additional support.

Writing Your Personal Narrative

❶ Prewriting

Stories sometimes begin with memory. . . .
> —Gary Soto, fiction writer, essayist, and poet

Brainstorming is a good way to begin working on your essay. Think about the recent past. What happened last summer? What experiences in your life have taught you a lesson? To get ideas, you might look in a box of souvenirs, or make a time line of your life. See the **Idea Bank** in the margin for other ways to get started. After you select an incident, follow the steps below.

Planning Your Personal Narrative

▶ **1. Freewrite about the incident.** Describe the emotions you felt. What sights, smells, and sounds do you remember? Who else was involved? Note when and where the events took place. If you can't remember every detail, try looking at family albums or talking to friends, family members, or neighbors.

▶ **2. Describe the importance of the event.** Think about why the incident was significant in your life. Did you learn an important lesson? Are you different than you were before the incident?

▶ **3. Make a time line.** List all the parts of the event in time order. Decide which parts to include and which parts are not necessary.

▶ **4. Tell your story aloud.** Try telling the incident to friends or family members. Use chronological order for this exercise. Which parts of your story make your audience react? Which parts seem confusing to them?

❷ Drafting

Begin exploring your ideas by writing them down. Try writing as if you are telling the story aloud. At this stage, don't worry about missing information, the flow of your ideas, or spelling and grammar. Just figure out what you really think and go wherever your draft takes you. Use dialogue and plenty of descriptive details.

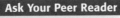

Ask Your Peer Reader

- Did you understand the order of events?
- Which details made you feel a part of my experience?
- What parts confused you?
- How did you feel after reading the piece? Why?

IDEABank

1. Your Working Portfolio
Look for ideas in the **Writing Options** that you completed earlier in this unit.
- **Speech,** p. 44
- **Personal Narrative,** p. 119

2. On Location
Use a web to brainstorm important places in your life, such as houses or apartments you've lived in, school or neighborhood playgrounds, etc. What important events have taken place there?

3. Good Neighbors
Talk to the neighbors who have known your family for a while and have seen you grow up. Ask them what they remember about your life. Write about one event that appeals to you.

Have a question?

See the **Writing Handbook**
Using Dialogue, p. R33
Presenting a Description, p. R31

Guiding Student Writing

Prewriting
Choosing a Subject
If students are still having trouble after reading the suggestions in the Idea Bank, suggest the following to them:
- Present or ask them to make a list of emotions, such as fear, joy, sadness, and pride. Have them recall one time when they felt each emotion.
- Have them recall a time when someone or some activity they know well surprised them.
- Tell them to think about the first time they tasted a food, smelled a scent, heard a special sound or noise, touched something new, or saw something out of the ordinary.

Planning Your Personal Narrative
1. Some students may find it helpful to create informal outlines that list notes about the key scenes in their narratives.
2. You may wish to show students how to make a sensory web or chart that will help them recall and record details.

Drafting
Encourage students to consider different ways they might begin their drafts: with the first event, with the most important event, with a description of the setting, with a question, with an interesting bit of dialogue. If students made lists or sensory webs, they might base their drafts on these. Once students begin, they should focus on telling everything that happened. As they write, they may recall events out of order. Have them include these as well; they can reorder them during revision.

Ask Your Peer Reader
Remind students that peer readers can help as well as criticize. When readers identify problems, writers could ask, "How could I fix that, do you think?" or "This is what I was trying to say. What would make it clear?"

Revising
USING SENSORY DETAILS

Explain to students the concept of "Show, don't tell." In other words, rather than telling readers that a room is large or a crowd happy, a writer might show this through such details as echoing footsteps or gleeful shouts. Have students offer suggestions for how writers might show such abstract concepts as fear, beauty, or fatigue.

Editing and Proofreading
PARALLELISM

Remind students that parallelism errors often occur in lists. For example:
In seventh grade Mark wanted to swim, play with the band, and student government. Ask students how they could correct this sentence.

Possible Response: In seventh grade Mark wanted to swim, play with the band, and join student government.

Reflecting

 After students identify what was hardest about writing their narratives, encourage them to consider what they might try the next time they write a personal narrative.

Option

Improving Dialogue

Before students revise, suggest that they try reading their dialogue aloud. Does it sound like natural speech? If not, they can improve it during revision.

Use **Writing Transparencies,** p. 24, for additional support.

Need revising help?

Review the **Rubric,** p. 178.

Consider **peer reader** comments.

Check **Revision Guidelines,** p. R23.

Puzzled about Parallelism?

See the **Grammar Handbook,** p. R77.

SPELLING
From Writing

As you revise your work, look back at the words you misspelled and determine why you made the errors you did. For additional help, refer to the strategies and generalizations in the **Spelling Handbook** on page R86.

Publishing
IDEAS

• To go along with your personal narrative, create a collage of images that symbolically tells your story and shows its importance.

• Separate the personal narratives written by your classmates into categories such as humorous or challenging. Have your classmates record their narratives in each category on audiotape. Use the taped versions to compare experiences that fall into the same category.

More Online:
Publishing Options
www.mcdougallittell.com

---

❸ Revising

TARGET SKILL ▶ USING SENSORY DETAILS Sensory details help your reader hear, see, and feel the experience you are writing about. For example, instead of writing, "I ran quickly," writer Gary Paulsen says, *"I was just getting my stride, legs and arms pumping, pulling air with a heaving chest, when I rounded the corner and ran smack into the latest group of boys who were terrorizing me."*

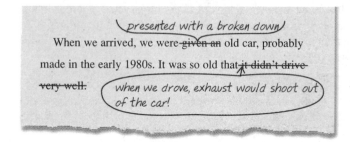

❹ Editing and Proofreading

TARGET SKILL ▶ PARALLELISM Keeping similar ideas parallel will help your writing flow more smoothly. Balance nouns with nouns, prepositional phrases with prepositional phrases, and so on.

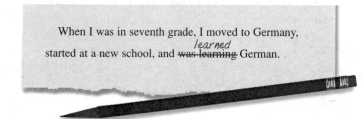

❺ Reflecting

FOR YOUR WORKING PORTFOLIO What was easiest about writing your narrative? What was hardest? What did you learn about the importance of the experience? Attach your reflections to your finished work. Save your personal narrative in your **Working Portfolio.**

Read this passage from the first draft of a personal narrative. The underlined sections may include the following kinds of errors:

- **lack of parallelism**
- **incorrect punctuation with coordinating conjunctions**
- **run-on sentences**
- **spelling errors**

For each underlined section, choose the revision that most improves the writing.

> My performance ended with a roar of laughter, <u>witch</u> filled the
> auditorium. My face <u>turned red and, hot tears</u> formed in my eyes. I
> ₍₁₎
> looked for <u>someone to rescue me but</u> only open mouths greeted my
> ₍₂₎
> stare. Every person in the audience was laughing, waving playbills, <u>and</u>
> ₍₃₎
> <u>talked.</u> Not even my older brothers could stop <u>themselfes</u> from laughing.
> ₍₄₎   ₍₅₎
> However, <u>one single glimmer of hope lit up the darkness perhaps I could</u>
> ₍₆₎
> <u>turn my talents to comedy.</u>

1. **A.** which
   B. whitch
   C. wich
   D. Correct as is

2. **A.** turned red, and, hot, tears
   B. turned red, and hot tears
   C. turned red; and hot tears
   D. Correct as is

3. **A.** someone to rescue me, but
   B. someone to rescue me but,
   C. someone to rescue me; but
   D. Correct as is

4. **A.** and they talked
   B. and talking.
   C. and would talk.
   D. Correct as is

5. **A.** themselfs
   B. themselves
   C. themselvs
   D. Correct as is

6. **A.** one single glimmer of hope lit up the darkness, perhaps I could turn my talents to comedy.
   B. one single glimmer of hope lit up the darkness. Perhaps I could turn my talents to comedy.
   C. one single glimmer of hope lit up the darkness; Perhaps I could turn my talents to comedy.
   D. Correct as is

Need extra help?

See the **Grammar Handbook**

Quick Reference: Capitalization, p. R58

Quick Reference: Punctuation, p. R56

Commas with Coordinating Conjunctions, p. R56

Run-on Sentences, p. R59

Assessment Practice
Demonstrate how students can eliminate incorrect choices for the first question.

A. This choice is correct, because the pronoun *which* is needed here.

B. This choice is incorrect, because it is an incorrect spelling of both *which* and *witch*.

C. This choice is incorrect, because it is also an incorrect spelling of both *which* and *witch*.

D. This choice is incorrect, because the noun *witch* makes no sense here.

Answers:
1. A; **2.** B; **3.** A; **4.** B; **5.** B; **6.** B

 Grammar TEKS 17A 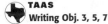 TAAS Writing Obj. 3, 5, 7

RUN-ON SENTENCES

Instruction Explain that a run-on sentence occurs when two or more sentences are incorrectly written as one sentence. The writer may have forgotten an end mark on the first sentence, or a comma may have been used incorrectly. To correct a run-on sentence, add the proper end mark to the first sentence and capitalize the first letter of the next sentence.

Exercises Have students explain how they

would revise each of the following run-on sentences. *(Possible answers are given.)*

1. I'm saving for a new bike mine is too small. *(bike. Mine)*
2. How could Tony get money he needed a job. *(money? He)*
3. Start a dog walking service lots of people around here have dogs. *(service. Lots)*
4. Mrs. Tsao has two dogs she probably needs help. *(dogs. She)*

5. Wait until summer people go on vacation then. *(summer. People)*

 Use **Grammar Transparencies and Copymasters**, p. 58.

 Use McDougal Littell's ***Language Network***, Chapter 1, for more instruction and practice in correcting run-on sentences.

Objectives

- reflect on unit themes
- draw inferences and support them with text evidence and experience
- review literary analysis skills used in the unit
- assess and build portfolios

Reflecting on the Theme

OPTION 1

A successful response will

- identify in the unit selections two discoveries that have significant value for young people
- explain concisely and clearly the importance of the discoveries
- demonstrate an awareness of the connections between the situations of characters in the selections and real life situations in which young people find themselves

OPTION 2

A successful response will

- illustrate through dialogue the discoveries of characters in the selection
- include word choice, diction, and usage appropriate to the characters, audience, purpose, and occasion

OPTION 3

Have students prepare for the discussion by meeting in pairs or groups of three or four to brainstorm discoveries relating to each of the various factors mentioned.

Self Assessment

Suggest to students that their charts should show "before" ideas in the left column and "after" ideas in the right column. As an example, tell students that they might list in the left column, "discoveries about oneself take place in a moment of surprise"; in the right column, "discoveries can take place over a long period of time and come into focus suddenly."

Learning from Experience

In this unit, new experiences lead characters to make discoveries about themselves, about other people, and about the world around them. Often the lessons they learn make them stronger. Did you recognize yourself in any of the characters? What did you learn from the characters? Explore these questions by completing some of the options in each of the following sections.

Painting Copyright © 1999 Brad Holland

Reflecting on the Theme

OPTION 1

Connecting Literature and Life The characters in this unit make many discoveries. Choose two of these discoveries that you think are especially important for young people to apply in their own lives. Explain your choices in a paragraph or two. Consider the parallels between the characters' situations and the situations of other young people.

OPTION 2

Creating Dialogue Select a character in Part 1 and a character in Part 2 who gain new insights from their experiences. With a partner, stage a dialogue between the characters, in which they comment on what they know about themselves and what they have learned.

OPTION 3

Discussing With a small group of classmates, discuss the different ways in which a person might learn that things are not as he or she believed them to be. Recall instances from your own experiences and from the selections. Think about the following factors:

friends	society	family
parents	human nature	the world

184 UNIT ONE   LEARNING FROM EXPERIENCE

Self ASSESSMENT

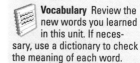 **READER'S NOTEBOOK**

Make a before-and-after chart. In it, show how one or more of your ideas about experience and discovery developed as you read the selections in this unit.

REVIEWING YOUR PERSONAL WORDList

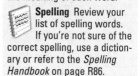 **Vocabulary** Review the new words you learned in this unit. If necessary, use a dictionary to check the meaning of each word.

Spelling Review your list of spelling words. If you're not sure of the correct spelling, use a dictionary or refer to the *Spelling Handbook* on page R86.

Reviewing Literary Concepts

OPTION 1

Comparing Characters A character may be classified as main or minor, depending on his or her importance to the plot of a story. Make a chart in which you list and classify the characters in the selections you have read. After you complete your chart, circle the name of the major character who you think changes the most. Explain your reasons for choosing that character.

Selection	Name of Character	Main or Minor?	Dynamic or Static?	Description of Change (If Dynamic)
"A Crush"	Ernie	Main	Dynamic	Overcomes his fear of getting involved

OPTION 2

Exploring Plot A plot is the sequence of events in a story. These events can usually be divided into rising and falling action. During the rising action, the conflicts in the story build in intensity until a climax, or turning point, is reached. The climax may involve an important revelation. The falling action follows the climax. In this part of the plot, the conflicts are resolved. With a partner, choose three stories from this unit and identify these elements of their plots. Discuss whether the stories could have turned out differently.

Building Your Portfolio

- **Writing Options** Several of the Writing Options in this unit asked you to expand upon situations in stories. Choose the response that you feel best captures the spirit of the story that it is based on. Write a note explaining the reasons for your choice. Place it in your **Presentation Portfolio.**

- **Writing Workshops** In this unit you wrote a personal response and about an autobiographical incident. Which do you think does a better job of communicating your personal perspective? Explain your choice on a cover page and place it in your **Presentation Portfolio.**

- **Additional Activities** Think about the assignments you completed for **Activities & Explorations** and **Inquiry & Research.** Keep a record in your portfolio of any assignments that you especially enjoyed, found helpful, or would like to explore further.

Self ASSESSMENT

READER'S NOTEBOOK

On a sheet of paper, copy the following literary terms introduced in this unit. Next to each term, jot down a brief definition. If you have trouble explaining a particular concept, refer to the **Glossary of Literary and Reading Terms** on p. R6.

setting	major characters
theme	autobiography
climax	external conflict
biography	point of view
essay	personification
internal conflict	surprise ending
personal essay	rising action
character	falling action
minor characters	

Self ASSESSMENT

At this point, you may just be beginning your **Presentation Portfolio.** Think about the pieces that you have selected to include in your portfolio. Do you think that you will keep these pieces as the year goes on?

Setting GOALS

Look back through your **READER'S NOTEBOOK.** What kinds of writing would you like to become more skilled at? What kinds of writing would you like to try for the first time?

Reviewing Literary Concepts

Option 1

Photocopy Unit One Resource Book, page 97, to provide students a chart for recording and analyzing character development.

Option 2

A successful response will
- identify rising action, climax, and falling action in three selections
- accurately analyze the turning point of each story
- sketch potential alternate endings or indicate why alternate endings are unlikely

Building Your Portfolio

Students should evaluate the items in their Working Portfolios and choose pieces that represent their highest-quality work for their Presentation Portfolios.

For more information on using portfolios, use *Teacher's Guide to Assessment and Portfolio Use,* beginning on page 53.

LITERATURE CONNECTIONS
Taking Sides

BY GARY SOTO

Lincoln Mendoza is a Mexican-American youth struggling to find himself. He has recently moved from the inner city to the suburbs. As Lincoln tries to adjust, he fears that he may lose an important part of himself—the barrio and its Mexican culture. His skills at basketball make him the star of his new school's team. As his new school plays his old one, Lincoln must decide where his loyalties lie.

These thematically related readings are provided along with *Taking Sides*:

Endless Search
BY ALONSO LOPEZ

from **Barrio Boy**
BY ERNESTO GALARZA

In the Inner City
BY LUCILLE CLIFTON

I Yearn
BY RICARDO SANCHEZ

Two Worlds
BY JIM YOSHIDA, WITH BILL HOSOKAWA

Granny Ed and the Lewisville Raiders
BY RAE RAINEY

A Game of Catch
BY RICHARD WILBUR

And Even *More* . . .

Holes

BY LOUIS SACHAR

In this tall tale, Stanley tries to escape a bad family tradition but ends up serving time at "Camp Green Lake." There, instead of "the largest lake in Texas," Stanley finds a dusty field of holes that he and other boys are sentenced to dig. His digging goes well below the surface as he uncovers the mysteries of his heritage.

Books
Song of the Buffalo Boy
BY SHERRY GARLAND
An teenager must decide whether to leave Vietnam to search for her father in America.

A Solitary Blue
BY CYNTHIA VOIGT
A boy discovers he has false impressions of family, friends, and even himself.

The Jungle Book
BY RUDYARD KIPLING
The tale of the boy raised by wolves has taught readers the laws of the jungle for more than a century.

The True Confessions of Charlotte Doyle

BY AVI

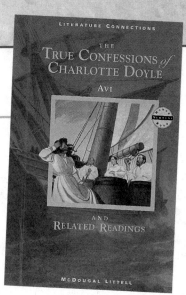

It is 1832. Thirteen-year-old Charlotte Doyle is booked on the Seahawk for a trans-Atlantic voyage, to join her family in America. From the beginning, things go wrong. During the dramatic two-month voyage, she learns more than she dreamed possible about seafaring, about command, and about herself.

These thematically related readings are provided along with *The True Confessions of Charlotte Doyle*:

Mary Patten *from* **Seafaring Women**
BY LINDA GRANT DE PAUW

from **Two Years Before the Mast**
BY RICHARD HENRY DANA

Walking the Trestle
BY JAY PARINI

The Princess and the Admiral
BY CHARLOTTE POMERANTZ

This Morning There Were Rainbows in the Sprinklers
BY LORNA DEE CERVANTES

Langston: a Play
BY OSSIE DAVIS
A biography in the form of a play, written by one of America's greatest storytellers.

Eleanor Roosevelt: A Life of Discovery
BY RUSSELL FREEDMAN
From childhood through old age, Eleanor influences a growing circle of friends.

Other Media
Rikki-tikki-tavi
Orson Welles narrates Kipling's

tale of an unlikely hero.
Chuck Jones Enterprises
(VIDEOCASSETTE)

Rikki-tikki-tavi
Illustrations and animation plus page-by-page discussion bring a classic to life.
Westwind
(CD-ROM)

The No-Guitar Blues
In this dramatization of a short story, Fausto Sanchez has a difficult decision.
Phoenix/BFA
(VIDEOCASSETTE)

Eleanor Roosevelt
Profile of the First Lady including her career after Franklin D. Roosevelt's death.
(VIDEOCASSETTE)

Conversations with Great Americans: Industrial Era and Modern
An interactive look at history through the eyes of Eleanor Roosevelt and others.
Focus Media
(CD-ROM)

Vietnam Veterans Memorial Design

OVERVIEW

The war in Vietnam divided the American people as few if any foreign military conflicts had before. Some believed that waging war in Vietnam was vital to American interests; if Communism could not be stopped in Vietnam, it could spread throughout Asia. Others felt that it was an unjust war, and that American soldiers were dying in a conflict that had nothing to do with the United States. The process of healing the wounds caused by the war is ongoing. The following project can complement a unit of study on the Vietnam War.

Research Questions

• How do Americans commemorate those who served in Vietnam?

• In what ways has some of the damage caused by the war been repaired?

Investigation Groups of four to six students design a memorial to those who served in the Vietnam War. The memorial should be designed for a location in their community. Each group will create a detailed illustration of their memorial design along with a written proposal. The proposal will express the need for such a memorial and explain why the group's design is appropriate.

Wrap-up Students can display their memorial designs in the school. Invite other students, parents, and community members to view the designs and proposals. The class may also wish to submit one or more of their proposals to a local planning board. You may wish to plan a field trip to a local memorial, or a visit by a Vietnam veteran or a member of a local historical society who can answer students' questions and discuss the project with them.

Links and Extended Reading
www.mcdougallittell.com
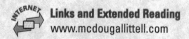

OBJECTIVES

❏ Research the impact of the war on the local community, and write a persuasive proposal for a war memorial.

❏ Design a Vietnam veterans memorial.

❏ Research the environmental effects of the war.

❏ Prepare a budget for a Vietnam veterans memorial.

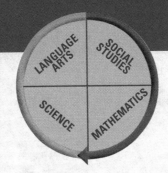

Team Teaching Assignments

CONNECT TO **LANGUAGE ARTS**   Maya Lin, the architect who designed "The Wall"—the National Vietnam Veterans Memorial in Washington, DC—was just 21 years old when her design was chosen in a national contest. Lin's design was controversial, but she defended her idea of how the memorial should express its message. Direct small groups of students to write a proposal, in the form of a persuasive pamphlet, for a memorial of their own design. The pamphlet should include: an introduction that summarizes the proposal, reasons for creating the memorial, a description of the memorial, fundraising ideas, and a call to action. To generate ideas, have students view the documentary film *Maya Lin: A Strong Clear Vision.* Also have them examine other war memorials. Students should consider if, and in what ways, the memorials are appropriate to the people and events they commemorate. Have students complete the interdisciplinary assignments below as they draft and revise their proposals. *(4 class periods)*

> **YOU WILL NEED:**
> - Web access (optional)
> - photographs of memorials
> - publishing software
> - video: *Maya Lin: A Strong Clear Vision*

CONNECT TO **SOCIAL STUDIES**   About 2.7 million American personnel served in Vietnam from 1964 to 1973. As the groups design their memorials, encourage them to consider the impact of the Vietnam War on their local community. Have groups divide up the following assignments:
- find out how many people from the local area served
- interview local community members with ties to Vietnam
- view and photograph existing public memorials in the area

Encourage students to look critically at existing memorials. A memorial may be anything from a garden to a sculpture to the dedication of a street or building. Have each group brainstorm ideas for an appropriate memorial, and then reach an agreement on one design. Direct them to illustrate their final design, with annotations that explain key features. *(4 class periods)*

> **YOU WILL NEED:**
> - reference books
> - tape recorder
> - camera (optional)
> - art materials

CONNECT TO **SCIENCE**   By the end of 1970, about 30 million acres of South Vietnam's forests and covered hills had been destroyed in the war. Ask students to investigate the causes of this destruction and how regeneration of the environment has occurred in Vietnam since the war. Have small groups create maps of Vietnam and use color coding and shading to show the geographical features of the country. Pose the following research prompts: How does ecological recovery take place? What, if any, human intervention is necessary? *(3–4 class periods)*

> **YOU WILL NEED:**
> - Web access (optional)
> - current reference books and articles on Vietnam
> - an atlas
> - graph or tracing paper
> - colored pencils

CONNECT TO **MATHEMATICS**   "The Wall" was built with approximately $9 million that was generated through fundraising. Once each group has decided on a design for their memorial, direct them to create a budget for the project. Decide on a maximum budget as a class. Then suggest that they itemize the costs involved in creating their memorial. For example, if a group intends their memorial to be made out of marble, have students estimate the amount of marble needed. They can consult catalogs or a teacher-created supply list to find out the price per unit and multiply to find the cost. Students should determine the cost of all other materials, and calculate the total cost of the project. If a group's proposal is too far over budget, their memorial may need to be redesigned. You may also have students consider how construction of the memorial would be funded. *(3–4 class periods)*

> **YOU WILL NEED:**
> - calculator
> - catalogs from building suppliers (could be created by teacher)

Women's History Newspaper

OVERVIEW

Between the time that Eleanor Roosevelt went away to school in 1900 and entered the White House in 1933, the lives of U.S. women changed significantly. They achieved suffrage, entered the workforce in unprecedented numbers, and made historical "firsts" in many fields.

Research Questions

- What do you know about U.S. women's lives at the beginning of this century?
- What achievements and changes for women occurred during Eleanor Roosevelt's lifetime?

Investigation The class will act as a team to produce a newspaper special edition about women in U.S. history from 1900 until World War II. Students will work together to generate articles, locate images, and lay out the final product. The newspaper will include biographies of famous women, information about the work of suffrage organizations, news about women's role in scientific progress, and data on women in the workforce. If possible, students should use a scanner and a word-processing program with a newspaper template. Otherwise, students may simply assemble and then photocopy the various components.

Wrap-up Enough copies should be made so that each student may have his or her own newspaper. In addition, students may wish to distribute newspapers to other classrooms. If possible, the class may visit a newspaper plant or newsroom, or have a professional journalist visit the classroom.

Links and Extended Reading
www.mcdougallittell.com

LaserLinks: Background Historical Connection

OBJECTIVES

❑ Research and write about the lives of famous women in American history.

❑ Learn about the significance of the woman suffrage movement.

❑ Describe scientific achievements made by women in the early 20th century.

❑ Represent the workforce participation and earning power of American women between 1900 and 1930.

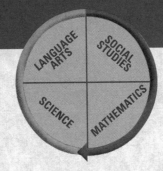

Team Teaching Assignments

CONNECT TO **LANGUAGE ARTS** Students should use reference books and the Internet to brainstorm names of women who made history in the United States between 1900 and World War II. Possibilities include Jeannette Rankin, the first woman elected to Congress; Amelia Earhart, who flew solo across the Atlantic; Zora Neale Hurston, the anthropologist and prominent writer of the Harlem Renaissance; or one of the suffrage leaders or scientists who will be studied in the activities below. Working in pairs, students should read what they can find about their subject. Next, they should write a one-page, present-tense feature article about the subject's "latest accomplishments," giving background on the subject's life and using quotes. Students may also wish to include images or lists of fun facts about their subjects' lives. *(3–4 class periods)*

YOU WILL NEED:
- Internet access (optional)
- reference books
- notebook

CONNECT TO **SOCIAL STUDIES** Women's struggle for the right to vote lasted more than seventy years. Working in small groups, students should research such organizations as The National American Woman Suffrage Association (NAWSA), The Women's Trade Union League (WTUL), and Alice Paul's National Woman's Party (NWP). Students should find out how these organizations fought for woman suffrage, and what their goals were after the 19th Amendment was ratified. Next, students should create full-page newspaper advertisements that commemorate the work of these organizations until 1920 and enumerate their goals afterward. *(3–4 class periods)*

YOU WILL NEED:
- Internet access (optional)
- reference books or periodical archives
- photocopier or scanner
- markers and drawing paper

CONNECT TO **SCIENCE** A surprising number of women were active in the sciences during the first decades of the 20th century. From physicist Lise Meitner to astronomers Annie Jump Cannon and Cecelia Payne-Gaposchkin, women at this time made scientific history. Less well known are the many women who spearheaded the once-powerful home economics movement, which sought to eliminate common illnesses, such as scurvy and rickets, that were caused by vitamin shortages. The Delany Sisters (Bessie and Sadie) are just two names associated with this important movement. Each student should choose a scientific discovery or concern with which women were associated and depict it in an illustrated news report. Captions should explain clearly the meaning and significance of the illustrations. *(2–3 class periods)*

YOU WILL NEED:
- reference books
- colored pens and pencils
- plain paper

CONNECT TO **MATHEMATICS** For the 1910s, 1920s, and 1930s, students should do research to answer the following questions: What percentage of women worked outside the home in this decade? What was the average weekly salary for a woman compared to the average weekly salary for a man? What could be purchased with this amount of money? Students can present their findings in a chart that includes bar graphs or pie charts. They may wish to illustrate items that could be purchased with an average weekly salary. *(2–3 class periods)*

YOU WILL NEED:
- reference books, especially almanacs and statistical abstracts
- graph paper or plain paper
- rulers and calculators

Relationships

In this unit, students will read selections that illustrate how people are interconnected and part of the larger world. The unit is divided into two parts, "Reaching Out" and "Facing Choices." Selections in both parts emphasize the importance of people connecting with one another.

———— Part 1 ————

Reaching Out In these selections, individuals expand their horizons and extend themselves to others to enrich their lives. To the speaker in "A Time to Talk," there is no doubt that friendly conversation is a more valuable way to spend time than continuing to work.

———— Part 2 ————

Facing Choices The selections in this part reinforce the idea that people are connected by showing how the decisions of individuals can have far-reaching effects. For example, Mr. Rickey in "The Noble Experiment" chooses to pursue his dream of equality in baseball for African Americans. As a result, the game of baseball is forever changed.

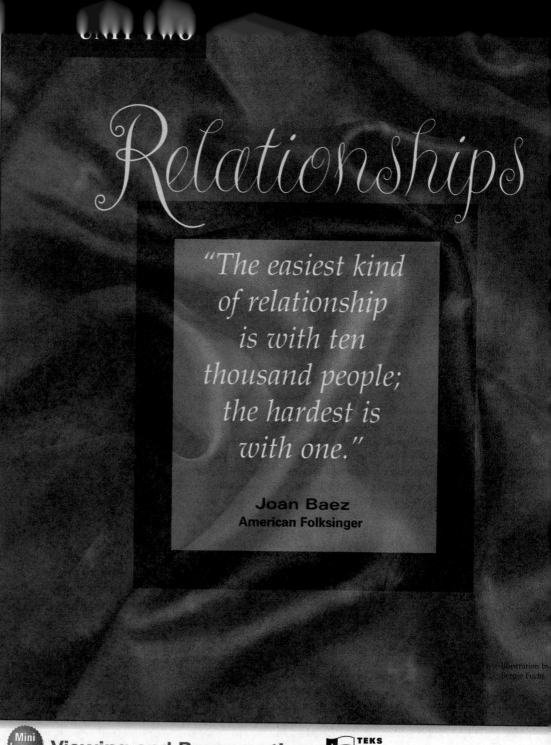

Relationships

"The easiest kind of relationship is with ten thousand people; the hardest is with one."

Joan Baez
American Folksinger

Illustration by
Bernie Fuchs

 Viewing and Representing **TEKS 22A**

Illustration
by Bernie Fuchs

ART APPRECIATION

Instruction The artist in this illustration has chosen to use the activity of dancing to convey a point about relationships. The dance that the two figures are participating in is a joyful dance. This is shown not only through the smiles on their faces, but also through their movements. Draw students' attention to the limbs of the figures. The woman's arms seem to be swinging while the little girl appears to have just clapped her hands. Their feet barely touch the ground.

Ask: In what ways is dancing with a partner like a relationship?

Possible Response: As in a relationship, dancing with a partner is most successful when each dancer is sensitive to what the other is doing and tries to complement his or her partner's movements. Sometimes, each partner dances on his or her own, but then comes back to the other. In a relationship, each person must have the freedom to be an individual as well as take a role in the relationship. In both situations, they must avoid stepping on each other's toes.

189

To help students explore the connections between the art, the quotation, and the unit theme, have them consider the following questions.

Ask: What are some important relationships that might be explored in this unit?
Possible Response: Family relationships; friendships; teacher-student; employer-employee; individual-group, etc.

Ask: How would you explain the quotation from Joan Baez?
Possible Response: A one-on-one relationship is more intense and emotionally demanding than a superficial, casual relationship with many people. A person has more responsibility in a relationship with one person.

Ask: After examining the illustration, how would you describe the relationship between the woman and the girl?
Possible Response: They are happy in each other's company and share the same emotions. They are close to each other. The woman looks out for the little girl, and the girl feels free to express herself.

Ask: What are some of the most significant relationships in your life? Why?
Possible Response: Responses will vary. Encourage students to give concrete reasons for their choices.

Features and Selections	Literary Analysis	TEKS	Reading and Critical Thinking	TEKS	Writing Opportunities	TEKS
Relationships **Reaching Out**						
Learning the Language of Literature **Poetry**	Poetry, 191 TAAS READING OBJ. 6	12A, B, E, J				
The Active Reader **Skills and Strategies**			Reading Poetry, 195 TAAS READING OBJ. 2, 3, 4, 5	10D, F, H, M, 12I, 14A		
POETRY **The Pasture** **A Time to Talk** Difficulty Level: *Average*	Rhyme, 196, 198, 199 TAAS READING OBJ.	12J	Read Aloud, 196, 198, 199 Connect to your Life, 196 Standardized Test Practice, 200 TAAS READING OBJ. 2, 5	7D, 10C, 11B 4A, 10L 10K, 12G	Creating a Recipe, 200	11B
POETRY **The World Is Not a Pleasant** **Place to Be** **To You** Difficulty Level: *Average*	Speaker, 201, 202, 204 Free Verse, 204 TAAS READING OBJ. 6	12H, J 12E, J	Making Inferences, 201, 202, 204 Connect to Your Life, 201 Informal Assessment, 205 TAAS READING OBJ. 5	4A, 10H, 11A, C 4A, 10L, 11B 10H	Personal Poem, 205	11B, 15D
SHORT STORY **What Do Fish Have to Do with** **Anything?** Difficulty Level: *Average*	Dynamic and Static Characters, 206, 208, 212, 214, 216 Review: Falling Action, 216 TAAS READING OBJ. 2, 5	12F 12G	Drawing Conclusions, 206, 208, 210, 216 Standardized Test Practice, 214 TAAS READING OBJ. 5	4A, 10A, H, 11B 10K, 12F	Willie's Journal, 217	11B, 15A
Real World Link **The Difference a City Year Makes**			Text Organizers, 219	10L, 22B		
INFORMATIVE NONFICTION *from* **Immigrant Kids** Difficulty Level: *Easy* Literary Link **The New Colossus** Building Vocabulary	Informative Nonfiction, 223, 224, 226, 230 TAAS READING OBJ. 6	12A, B, E	Main Idea and Details, 223, 224, 226, 228, 230 Standardized Test Practice, 231 TAAS READING OBJ. 2, 3	4A, 10F, 11B 10F, K	Journal Entry, 231 Pro-or-Con Statement, 231 TAAS WRITING OBJ. 1	11B, 15A 11C, 15A, B
Writing Workshop: Interpret a Poem Assessment Practice			Analyzing a Student Model, 239 Supporting Your Response with Examples, 242 TAAS READING OBJ. 2, 3, 4	10E, F, 12I, 11C, 19A, D 11C, 18D	Interpretive Essay, 240 TAAS WRITING OBJ. 2, 3, 4	15A,H, 18A,B, 19C

UNIT TWO
PART 2 SKILLS TRACE

Facing Choices						
Learning the Language of Literature **Drama**	Drama, 245 TAAS READING OBJ. 5, 6	12A, B, D, F, J				
The Active Reader: **Skills and Strategies**			Reading Drama, 249 TAAS READING OBJ. 2, 5	5C, 7E, 10C, 11B, 12F, G		

LEGEND   **DLS – Daily Language SkillBuilder**   **Green type – Teacher's Edition**

Speaking and Listening Viewing and Representing	TEKS	Inquiry and Research	TEKS	Grammar, Usage, and Mechanics	TEKS	Vocabulary	TEKS
Art Appreciation, 188	22A						
Paired Activity, 199 Illustrated Book, 200 Poetry Reading, 200 Oral Recitation of Poems, 198	11B, 10L 11B, 24A 8C, 11B, 5C 4A, 5C, E, 11B	The Vacation of a Lifetime!, 200 Poet for a Nation, 200	11B, 24A 8C, 11B	DLS, 196 **TAAS WRITING OBJ. 3, 7**	16B, D		
Cooperative Learning Activity, 204 Oral Report, 205 Poems on Tape, 205 Oral Recitation of Poems, 202	4A, 11B 3A, C 5D, 11B 4A, 5C, E, 11B	Times of Change, 205	24A	DLS, 201 **TAAS WRITING OBJ. 3, 5, 6, 7**	17A,G		
Paired Learning Activity, 216 Debate, 217 Art Connection, 217 Art Appreciation, 209 Oral Report on Safety, 215	10L, 11B 4A, 11B 22A 22A 1D, 2D, E, 5F	Homeless in America, 217 On Your Own, 218 **TAAS READING OBJ. 4, 5**	13F, G 8C, 11A	Choosing the Right Verb, 218 DLS, 206 Action Verbs, 211 Vivid, Precise Verbs, 218 **TAAS READING OBJ. 1, 6** **TAAS WRITING OBJ. 3, 4, 6, 7**	17C, D 16B, D 17C 9F	Context Clues, 217 Using Context Clues, 207 Analogies, 213 Hard and Soft c and g, 217 **TAAS READING OBJ. 1** **TAAS WRITING OBJ. 3 ,7**	6A 6A, 9B 9B 16F
		Activity Link: "What Do Fish Have to Do with Anything?", 222 Inquiry & Research, 222 **TAAS READING OBJ. 4**	11B, 10L 13B,18A, 20A				
Paired Activity, 230 Interview, 231 Family Tree, 231 Mock Interviews, 228	4A, 11B, C 5B 11B, 24A 5B, 11B	Ellis Island Before, 231 Photographs, 232	13C 8C, 11B	Abstract and Concrete Nouns, 232 DLS, 223 Identifying Nouns, 226 Identifying Abstract and Concrete Nouns, 232 **TAAS WRITING OBJ. 3, 6, 7**	17C 16F, 17C 17C 17C	Denotation, 231 Connotation, 231 Analyzing Word Parts, 233 Denotation, 224 Connotation, 227 **TAAS READING OBJ. 1, 6**	9F 9F 6B, 9D, G, 16G 9F 9F
Picturing Text Structure, 239 **TAAS READING OBJ. 2, 3, 4**	10E, F, L			Subject-Verb Agreement, 242 Revising and Editing, 243 Agreement of Subjects and Verbs, 242 Sentence Fragments, 243 **TAAS WRITING OBJ. 2–7**	17C, 18C, E 16B, F 17C 17A		

Features and Selections	Literary Analysis	TEKS	Reading and Critical Thinking	TEKS	Writing Opportunities	TEKS
DRAMA A Christmas Carol Difficulty Level: *Average*	Stage Directions, 250, 252, 256, 258, 260, 264, 266, 274, 275 Review: Character, 275 **TAAS READING OBJ. 5**	12D 12F	Visualizing, 250, 252, 258, 272, 275 Informal Assessment, 270 Standardized Test Practice, 274 **TAAS READING OBJ. 5**	10D, 11C 10L, 12F 10K, 12F	Last Will and Testament, 276 Dialogue, 276 Sequel, 276	11B, 15C 11B, 15G 15A
SHORT STORY The Scholarship Jacket Difficulty Level: *Average* **Literary Link** Graduation Morning	Theme, 278, 280, 284 **TAAS READING OBJ. 2, 3**	10F	Connecting, 278, 280, 282, 284 Standardized Test Practice, 283 **TAAS READING OBJ. 5**	10A, 11B, C, 14A 10H, K	Letter of Recommendation, 285	11B, 15A
AUTOBIOGRAPHY The Noble Experiment Difficulty Level: *Challenging*	Autobiography, 287, 288, 290, 292, 294, 296 **TAAS READING OBJ. 6**	12B, E, H	Summarizing, 287, 288, 290, 292, 294, 296 Standardized Test Practice, 297 **TAAS READING OBJ. 2, 3**	10F, G 10G, 10K	Letter, 297 Speech, 297 Definition, 297	11B, 15A 11B, C, 15A 15B
NARRATIVE POETRY Casey at the Bat Difficulty Level: *Average*	Sound Devices, 299, 300, 302, 303	12J	Questioning, 299, 300, 302, 303 Standardized Test Practice, 302 **TAAS READING OBJ. 2, 4**	10C, M 10E, K	Opinion Essay, 304 Newspaper Article, 304	11B, 15A, C, 18A 11B
Real World Link Out of the Ballpark **Building Vocabulary**			Making Generalizations & Drawing Conclusions, 305 **TAAS READING OBJ. 5**	10H		
Comparing Literature Fables	Fables, 310 **TAAS READING OBJ. 4**	10I, 11D, 12C, 14C	Points of Comparison 311 **TAAS READING OBJ. 4**	10I, L, 11D	Comparison-and-Contrast Essay, 311	15A, C
FABLE Ant and Grasshopper The Ant and the Grasshopper Difficulty Level: *Average*	Fable and Moral, 312, 314, 315	12E	Setting Purposes, 312, 314, 315	4A, 8C, 10B, 11B		
SHORT STORY The Richer, the Poorer Difficulty Level: *Challenging*	Modern Fable, 316, 318, 320, 321 Review: Theme, 321 **TAAS READING OBJ. 2, 3**	12E 10F	Setting Purposes, 316, 318, 320, 321 Informal Assessment, 320 **TAAS READING OBJ. 5** **TAAS WRITING OBJ. 1**	8C, 10B, 11C 11B, C, 12F		
Comparing Literature Assessment Practice			Reading the Prompt, 323	10C, 10K	Dialogue, 322 Letter to a Friend, 322 Speech, 322 Planning a Comparison-and-Contrast Essay, 323 Drafting Your Essay, 323 **TAAS WRITING OBJ. 2-4**	11B, 15G 11B, 15C 11B, C 18A 15H, 18B, D
Writing Workshop: **Character Sketch** **Assessment Practice**			Analyzing a Student Model, 325 **TAAS READING OBJ. 2, 3**	10D, F, 19A, D	Character Sketch, 326 **TAAS WRITING OBJ. 2, 4**	15A, 18A, B, 19C
Reflect and Assess	Rhyme and Rhythm, 331	12J, 10L	Visualizing Scenes, 331	10D, 11B, 12D	Making Connections, 330 Building Your Portfolio, 331	11C, 15C 19A, C

LEGEND   DLS – Daily Language SkillBuilder   **Green type – Teacher's Edition**

Speaking and Listening Viewing and Representing	TEKS	Inquiry and Research	TEKS	Grammar, Usage, and Mechanics	TEKS	Vocabulary	TEKS
View and Compare, 261, 271 Activity, 275 Radio Play, 276 You Be the Critic, 276 Dialogue, 260 Film/Drama, 266 Drama Performance, 272	23A 10L 5C, 11B 11B, 23B 3B, 5C 5D, 23B 5C, 11B	History of Carols, 276 From Novel to Play, 277 TAAS READING OBJ. 4	13F, I 8C, 10I, 11A, C, D	Action Verbs, 277 DLS, 250 Run-On Sentences, 256 Action Verbs in Effective Writing, 277 TAAS WRITING OBJ. 2–7	17C 16B, 17C 17A 15H	Synonyms and Antonyms, 276 Words Ending in a Silent e, 276 Synonyms/Antonyms, 251 Analyzing Word Parts, 262 Silent e, 276 TAAS READING OBJ. 1 TAAS WRITING OBJ. 3, 7	6A, 9B 16C 6C, 9C 6B, 9D 16C
Cooperative Learning Activity, 284 Population Map, 285 Art Connection, 285 Art Appreciation, 281	10L, 11B, C 13C, 22B, 24A 22A, 23B 22A, 23B	La Causa!, 285 Interview, 286	11B, 13I, 15C, 24A	Consistent Verb Tense, 286 DLS, 278 Subject-Verb Agreement, 282 Maintaining Consistent Verb Tenses, 286 TAAS WRITING OBJ. 3, 6, 7	17F 16B 17C 17F	Meaning Clues, 285 Using Meaning Clues, 279 TAAS READING OBJ. 1	6A 9B

Cooperative Learning Activity, 296
Interview, 297
Baseball Card, 297
Photograph, 288
Sportscasting, 293
	4A, 11B
	11B
	11B, 24A
	23A
	5A, C,
	11B
		Author Activity, 298
		Segregation, 297
		Time Line, 298
		
		TAAS READING OBJ. 5
			13G
			10L, 13F,
			I
				Active Voice and Passive
				  Voice, 298
				DLS, 287
				Identifying Active and Passive
				  Voice, 295
				Using Active and Passive
				  Verbs in Writing, 298
				TAAS WRITING OBJ. 1,
				3, 6, 7
					17C, F
					
					17B, C
					17C, 18E
					
					18E
						Synonyms, 297
						Synonyms, 289
						Using Context Clues, 292
						Spelling with Suffixes, 294
						
						TAAS READING OBJ. 1
						TAAS WRITING OBJ. 3, 7
							6A, 9B
							9B
							6A
							16C

Cooperative Learning Activity, 303 Film Review, 304 Art Appreciation, 301	11B 4A, 11B, 23B 22A	Record-Setters, 304 TAAS READING OBJ. 5	13C, G	DLS, 299 TAAS WRITING OBJ. 3, 7	16B, D		
		Activity Link: "Casey at the Bat," 308 Inquiry & Research, 308 TAAS READING OBJ. 5	10H, 11C, 15C 20A, C			Affixes, 309 TAAS READING OBJ. 1	6B, 9D
Paired Activity, 315	10L, 11B			DLS, 312 TAAS WRITING OBJ. 3, 6	17C, H		
Paired Activity, 321 Art Appreciation, 319	10L, 11B 22A			DLS, 316 TAAS WRITING OBJ. 3, 6, 7	16D, 17C	Using Context Clues, 317 TAAS READING OBJ. 1	6A
Dramatic Version, 322 Planning Options, 322	5C, 11B 10L, 13C, E	Insect Profiles, 322 TAAS READING OBJ. 5	10L, 13C, G, 24A	Quotations Within Quotations, 323 TAAS WRITING OBJ. 3, 7	16B		

Picturing Text Structure, 325
 	
TAAS READING OBJ. 2, 4
	10E, L			Vivid Verbs and Adjectives, 328
				
				Pronoun-Antecedent
				  Agreement, 328
				Revising and Editing, 329
				Possessive Pronoun-Referent
				  Agreement, 328
				Possessive Forms, 329
				TAAS WRITING OBJ. 2–7
					17D,
					18C, E
					17C, 18E
					
					16F,
					17A, C,
					F, G, 18H
					17C, G		

Discussing, 330 Role-Playing, 330 TAAS READING OBJ. 4	4A, 11A, B, C 4A, 11B, C						

	Unit Resource Book	Assessment	Integrated Technology and Media	Literary Analysis Transparencies
The Pasture A Time to Talk *pp. 196–200*	• Active Reading p. 4 • Literary Analysis p. 5	• Selection Test, Formal Assessment pp. 29–30 ◉ Test Generator	🎧 Audio Library 💿 LaserLinks, Teacher's SourceBook, p. 15	• Form in Poetry: Rhyme and Meter T17
The World Is Not a Pleasant Place to Be To You *pp. 201–205*	• Active Reading p. 6 • Literary Analysis p. 7	• Selection Test, Formal Assessment pp. 31–32 ◉ Test Generator	🎧 Audio Library 🌐 Research Starter www.mcdougallittell.com	• Poetry: Speaker T21
What Do Fish Have to Do with Anything? *pp. 206–218*	• Summary p. 8 • Active Reading p. 9 • Literary Analysis p. 10 • Words to Know p. 11 • Grammar p. 12 • Spelling p. 13 • Selection Quiz p. 14	• Selection Test, Formal Assessment pp. 33–34 ◉ Test Generator	🎧 Audio Library	• Static and Dynamic Characters T2
from **Immigrant Kids** *pp. 223–232*	• Summary p. 15 • Active Reading p. 16 • Literary Analysis p. 17 • Words to Know p. 18 • Grammar p. 19 • Spelling p. 20 • Selection Quiz p. 21	• Selection Test, Formal Assessment pp. 35–36 ◉ Test Generator	🎧 Audio Library 💿 LaserLinks, Teacher's SourceBook, p. 17 🌐 Research Starter www.mcdougallittell.com	• Primary/Secondary Source T14

Writing Workshop: Interpretive Essay

Unit Two Resource Book
• Prewriting p. 23
• Drafting and Elaboration p. 24
• Peer Response Guide pp. 25–26
• Revising, Editing, and Proofreading p. 27
• Student Models pp. 28–30
• Rubric for Evaluation p. 31

💿 **Writing Coach**

Writing Transparencies T1–4, T13, T31

Grammar Transparencies and Copymasters C61, C117

Teacher's Guide to Assessment and Portfolio Use

Unit Assessment
• Unit Two Part 1 Test, Formal Assessment pp. 37–38
◉ Test Generator
• Unit Two Integrated Test, Integrated Assessment pp. 7–12

Unit Technology
🌐 ClassZone www.mcdougallittell.com

Reading and Critical Thinking Transparencies	Grammar Transparencies and Copymasters	Vocabulary Transparencies and Copymasters	Writing Transparencies	Communications Transparencies and Copymasters
	• Daily Language SkillBuilder T6		• Locating Information Using the Internet T47–48	• Reading Aloud T11
• Making Inferences T5	• Daily Language SkillBuilder T6		• Interpretive Essay T31 • Poem T35 • Locating Material in the Library T41	• Formal Presentations T10 • Reading Aloud T11
• Drawing Conclusions T9	• Daily Language SkillBuilder T7 • Action Verbs C68 • Vivid, Precise Verbs C136	• Context Clues: Draw on Experience C35 • Analogies C36	• Elaboration T13 • Locating Information Using the Internet T47–48	• Persuasive Techniques T3 • Interviewing T9 • Formal Presentations T10
• Main Idea and Supporting Details T25	• Daily Language SkillBuilder T7 • Identifying Nouns C62 • Concrete and Abstract Nouns C63	• Denotation C37 • Connotation C38	• Opinion Statement T27 • Locating Information Using Print References T45 • Locating Information Using Technical Resources T46 • Locating Information Using the Internet T47–48	• Interviewing T9

STUDENTS ACQUIRING ENGLISH

The **Spanish Study Guide**, pp. 34–48, includes language support for the following pages:
• Family and Community Involvement (per unit)

• Selection Summaries and Vocabulary
• Active Reading
• Literary Analysis

PART 2

To introduce the theme of this unit, use Fine Art Transparencies T22–24 in the Communications Transparencies and Copymasters.

	Unit Resource Book	Assessment	Integrated Technology and Media	Literary Analysis Transparencies
A Christmas Carol *pp. 250–277*	• Summary p. 32 • Active Reading p. 33 • Literary Analysis p. 34 • Words to Know p. 35 • Grammar p. 36 • Spelling p. 37 • Selection Quiz p. 38	• Selection Test, Formal Assessment pp. 39–40 Test Generator	Audio Library LaserLinks, Teacher's SourceBook, p. 18	• Drama: Stage Directions T23
The Scholarship Jacket *pp. 278–286*	• Summary p. 39 • Active Reading p. 40 • Literary Analysis p. 41 • Words to Know p. 42 • Grammar p. 43 • Spelling p. 44 • Selection Quiz p. 45	• Selection Test, Formal Assessment pp. 41–42 Test Generator	Audio Library	• Theme T7
The Noble Experiment *pp. 287–298*	• Summary p. 46 • Active Reading p. 47 • Literary Analysis p. 48 • Words to Know p. 49 • Grammar p. 50 • Spelling p. 51 • Selection Quiz p. 52	• Selection Test, Formal Assessment pp. 43–44 Test Generator	Audio Library Research Starter www.mcdougallittell.com	• Autobiography T11
Casey at the Bat *pp. 299–304*	• Active Reading p. 53 • Literary Analysis p. 54	• Selection Test, Formal Assessment pp. 45–46 Test Generator	Audio Library LaserLinks, Teacher's SourceBook, p. 19 Video: Literature in Performance, Video Resource Book pp. 17–22	• Poetry: Sound Devices T20
Ant and Grasshopper **The Ant and the Grasshopper** *pp. 312–315*	• Summary p. 56 • Active Reading p. 57 • Literary Analysis p. 58 • Words to Know p. 59 • Grammar p. 60 • Spelling p. 61 • Selection Quiz p. 62	• Selection Test, Formal Assessment pp. 47–48 Test Generator	Audio Library	• Fables/Myths/Tall Tales T30
The Richer, the Poorer *pp. 316–322*	• Summary p. 63 • Active Reading p. 64 • Literary Analysis p. 65 • Words to Know p. 66 • Grammar p. 67 • Spelling p. 68 • Selection Quiz p. 69	• Selection Test, Formal Assessment pp. 49–50 Test Generator	Audio Library	• Fables/Myths/Tall Tales T30

Writing Workshop: Character Sketch

		Unit Assessment	Unit Technology	
Unit Two Resource Book • Prewriting p. 71 • Drafting and Elaboration p. 72 • Peer Response Guide pp. 73–74 • Revising, Editing, and Proofreading p. 75 • Student Models pp. 76–78 • Rubric for Evaluation p. 79	**Writing Coach** **Writing Transparencies** T1–4, T11, T15, T22, T30 **Reading and Critical Thinking Transparencies** T24 **Grammar Transparencies and Copymasters** C65 **Teacher's Guide to Assessment and Portfolio Use**	• Unit Two Part 2 Test, Formal Assessment pp. 51–52 Test Generator • Unit Two Integrated Test, Integrated Assessment pp. 7–12	ClassZone www.mcdougallittell.com	

Reading and Critical Thinking Transparencies	Grammar Transparencies and Copymasters	Vocabulary Transparencies and Copymasters	Writing Transparencies	Communications Transparencies and Copymasters
• Visualizing T10	• Daily Language SkillBuilder T8 • Run-On Sentences C59 • Action Verbs in Effective Writing C70	• Synonyms and Antonyms C39 • Analyzing Word Parts C40	• Dialogue T24 • Staging a Scene T38	• Evaluation Matrix: Film/Video T7 • Dramatic Reading T12 • Storyboard Templates C37, C38
• Connecting T2	• Daily Language SkillBuilder T8 • Subject-Verb Agreement C118 • Maintaining Consistent Verb Tenses C75	• Using Meaning Clues to Infer C41	• Elaboration T13	• Interviewing T9
• Summarizing T11	• Daily Language SkillBuilder T9 • Identifying Active and Passive Voice C140 • Using Active and Passive Verbs in Writing C141	• Synonyms C42 • Context Clues C43		• Interviewing T9
• Questioning T12	• Daily Language SkillBuilder T9			• Evaluation Matrix: Film/Video T7
• Setting a Purpose T13	• Daily Language SkillBuilder T10			
• Compare and Contrast T8 • Setting a Purpose T13	• Daily Language SkillBuilder T10 • Quotations Within Quotations C128	• Context Clues: General/Infer C44	• Organizing Your Writing T11 • Elaboration T13 • Using Periodical Indexes T44 • Using an Outline T54	• Dramatic Reading T12

STUDENTS ACQUIRING ENGLISH

The **Spanish Study Guide,** pp. 49–66, includes language support for the following pages:
• Family and Community Involvement (per unit)

• Selection Summaries and Vocabulary
• Active Reading
• Literary Analysis

Selection	SkillBuilder Sentences	Suggested Answers
The Pasture	1. I'm going to clean the leafs out of the pond in the pasture.	1. I'm going to clean the **leaves** out of the pond in the pasture.
A Time to Talk	2. When an old friend wants to talk, do you take time to listen.	2. When an old friend wants to talk, do you take time to listen**?**
The World Is Not a Pleasant Place to Be	1. Lifes' difficulties are easier to face when people have the support of family and friends.	1. Life**'s** difficulties are easier to face when people have the support of family and friends.
	2. The world is full of problems people can help each other solve them.	2. The world is full of problems**, but** people can help each other solve them.
What Do Fish Have to Do with Anything?	1. Willie's mother always asks "How was school?	1. Willie's mother always asks**,** "How was school**?"**
	2. No one accept Willie wanted to look at the homeless man.	2. No one **except** Willie wanted to look at the homeless man.
from Immigrant Kids	1. When the immigrants reached America they felt a mixture of fear and happy.	1. When the immigrants reached America**,** they felt a mixture of fear and **happiness**.
	2. Entire familys survived long, difficult journies at sea.	2. Entire **families** survived long, difficult **journeys** at sea.

Selection	SkillBuilder Sentences	Suggested Answers
A Christmas Carol	1. The novel A Christmas Carol was wrote by Charles Dickens to try to improve poor people's living conditions. 2. Even though the Cratchits do'nt have no money their house is filled with joy and love.	1. The novel **A Christmas Carol** was **written** by Charles Dickens to try to improve poor people's living conditions. 2. Even though the Cratchits **don't** have **any** money, their house is filled with joy and love.
The Scholarship Jacket	1. Martha overheard a conversation between Mr. Schmidt, her history teacher and Mr. Boone, her math teacher. 2. Where's Grandpa" she asked her Grandmother.	1. Martha overheard a conversation between Mr. Schmidt, her history teacher, and Mr. Boone, her math teacher. 2. "Where's Grandpa?" she asked her **g**randmother.
The Noble Experiment *from* I Never Had It Made	1. Jackie Robinson was nervous about his decision to play for Branch Rickey's team, and he joined anyway. 2. Branch Rickey prepared Jackie for the insults he faced when he plays for the Dodgers.	1. Jackie Robinson was nervous about his decision to play for Branch Rickey's team, **but** he joined anyway. 2. Branch Rickey prepared Jackie for the insults he faced when he **played** for the Dodgers.
Casey at the Bat	1. The game wasn't going good for the mudville team, and several fans decide to leave quick. 2. The appearance of the crowds favorite player lifts the fans spirits.	1. The game wasn't going **well** for the **M**udville team, and several fans decide**d** to leave **quickly.** 2. The appearance of the crowd**'s** favorite player lifts the fans**'** spirits.

Selection	SkillBuilder Sentences	Suggested Answers
Ant and Grasshopper	1. Gena has wrote a few fables of her own.	1. Gena has **written** a few fables of her own.
	2. Her and I read some Aesop's fables last week.	2. **She** and I read some Aesop's fables last week.
The Richer, the Poorer	1. Lottie and her sister Bess has lived completely different lives.	1. Lottie and her sister Bess **have** lived completely different lives.
	2. There sisters, so Lottie and Bess try to be their for each other.	2. **They're** sisters, so Lottie and Bess try to be **there** for each other.

The Language of Literature offers several options for integrating grammar instruction and literature.

- Each unit has a specific grammar focus. The grammar focus for this unit is highlighted on the planning chart. Categories of grammar skills for this unit are shown in red.

- The Pupil's Edition includes instructive features entitled *Grammar in Context*. The instruction in these features arises from the selections and relates to the grammar focus for each unit.

- The Writing Workshops in the Pupil's Edition include grammar tips that help the students produce error-free drafts.

- Mini Lessons in the Teacher's Edition complement the instruction in the *Grammar in Context* features. Additional Mini Lessons relate to the grammar focus for each unit as well as to the literature.

- Daily Language SkillBuilders in the Teacher's Edition provide students with ongoing proofreading practice and reinforce punctuation, spelling, grammar and usage, and capitalization.

- Grammar Copymasters and Transparencies, which may be used independently or in conjunction with the Mini Lessons in the Teacher's Edition, present grammar in a traditional, systematic sequence.

PE instruction shown in black
TE Mini Lessons shown in green

Part 1

THE SENTENCE AND ITS PARTS
Sentence Fragments
Assessment Practice, p. 243

NOUNS
Identifying Nouns
"Immigrant Kids," p. 226
Abstract and Concrete Nouns
"Immigrant Kids," p. 232
Identifying Abstract and Concrete Nouns
"Immigrant Kids," p. 232

VERBS
Action Verbs
"What Do Fish Have to Do with Anything?", p. 211

SUBJECT-VERB AGREEMENT
Subject-Verb Agreement
Writing Workshop, p. 242
Agreement of Subjects and Verbs
Writing Workshop, p. 242

STYLE
Choosing the Right Verb
"What Do Fish Have to Do with Anything?", p. 218
Vivid, Precise Verbs
"What Do Fish Have to Do with Anything?", p. 218

Part 2

THE SENTENCE AND ITS PARTS
Run-On Sentences
"A Christmas Carol," p. 256

PRONOUNS
Possessive Pronoun–Referent Agreement
Writing Workshop, p. 328
Possessive Pronoun–Referent Agreement
Writing Workshop, p. 328
Possessive Forms
Assessment Practice, p. 329

VERBS
Action Verbs
"A Christmas Carol," p. 277
Action Verbs in Effective Writing
"A Christmas Carol," p. 277
Consistent Verb Tense
"The Scholarship Jacket," p. 286
Maintaining Consistent Verb Tense
"The Scholarship Jacket," p. 286

SUBJECT-VERB AGREEMENT
Subject-Verb Agreement
"The Scholarship Jacket," p. 282

PUNCTUATION
Quotations Within Quotations
Assessment Practice, p. 323

STYLE
Identifying Active and Passive Voice
"The Noble Experiment," p. 295
Active and Passive Voice
"The Noble Experiment," p. 298
Using Active and Passive Verbs in Writing
"The Noble Experiment," p. 298

OVERVIEW

Students work in small groups to present a persuasive speech on community involvement.

Project at a glance The selections in Unit Two focus on community. For this project, each group of students will come up with an idea for community involvement and deliver a persuasive speech urging community members to get involved. Students will research their idea, gather evidence, and write a persuasive speech. Members of each group will share responsibilities for researching the topic, writing the speech, and conducting interviews. Each topic should be well thought out, with a focus on a workable community solution. Each student will present part of the speech so that everyone has a chance to speak. Students might present the speeches in a "Community Day."

SCHEDULING

Each group should take no more than ten minutes to present its persuasive speech. You may want to schedule the speeches over the course of 2–3 class periods. This project may take place over the course of the unit or at the end of the unit, depending on your scheduling purposes.

PROJECT OBJECTIVES

- To demonstrate the speaking and listening skills introduced in the activity
- To write a persuasive speech communicating the importance of community involvement
- To present a convincing and workable plan for community involvement
- To conduct in-depth research on their idea
- To effectively combine all parts of the speech into a coherent presentation

SUGGESTED GROUP SIZE

4–5 students per group

Persuasive Speech

1 Getting Started

Explain that students will be working in small groups to write and present a persuasive speech on community involvement. For ideas on community issues, see the Selections Overview for summaries of the stories in this unit.

Gather back copies of the op-ed section of local newspapers that deal with community issues. You might want to videotape a legislative session from a cable television channel so that students can get a flavor of the nature of persuasion. Also make sure students are familiar with persuasive speeches, page R101 of the Communication Handbook.

If you think students are ready to present their speeches before a real audience, you might create a Community Day. If students are giving their speeches in your classroom, there should be chairs available for audience members and, if possible, a lectern from which students can address the audience. A row of chairs for group members should be positioned next to the lectern. You might invite other classes, parents, or teachers to act as judges or audience members. For their convenience, schedule any adults well ahead of time.

Writing Workshop Connection

As a springboard, students may use the Writing Workshop assignments **Interpretive Essay,** p. 238, or **Character Sketch,** p. 324.

2 Directing the Project

Preparing *(1 class period)* As a class, have students discuss the community issues covered in this unit, as well as any other issues. Discuss the need for community involvement and the different forms it can take. Emphasize that researching and interviewing community members will add credibility to the speech.

▶ Divide students into groups of four to five. Each person will write and present a segment of the speech. Students can divide the speech into a five-paragraph essay format. For example, one student will do the introduction, another student will do a body paragraph, and so on.

Assigning Roles Roles might include writer, interviewer, researcher, and so on. You can choose one student to write and present an introduction and conclusion for the entire class presentation (or you could fill this position yourself).

▶ Meet with groups after they have chosen their ideas to make sure there are no duplications. Later, help students refine the speech, identify visual aids, or just make suggestions about the project as a whole.

▶ Well before the presentation, have students check to make sure that all of their main points are supported with facts and examples. Also review with students the Speaking and Listening Skills listed on the next page.

Practicing *(1 class period)* You should leave enough time for groups to rehearse. Group coordination is essential. The parts should have a similar feel and tone. Tell students that giving and receiving feedback during the rehearsal stage is crucial. Refer to the tips in the Feedback Center.

▶ Remind students that the point of a persuasive speech is to convince. They should appear enthusiastic yet natural and use gestures and facial expressions to fit the content. Their voices should be loud enough to be heard but not so loud that they are shouting. If students are using visual aids such as posters, these should be neat and visible to the audience.

Presenting *(1–3 class periods)* This project could culminate in a Community Day for the entire student body or just for your class.

▶ To begin, have students take a few deep breaths and focus on what they want to communicate. If they are using visual aids such as posters, these should be ready and on hand. Students should be seated in order of appearance next to the lectern so that they can quickly take the stage for their part.

Teaching the Speaking and Listening Skills

The student is expected to:

Clarify and support spoken ideas with evidence, elaborations, and examples

Teaching Suggestions: Remind students that they are trying to persuade people who either have no opinion or who disagree with their own opinion. Evidence, including facts and statistics, expert testimony, and details such as sensory details make your ideas more understandable and more convincing.

Set a purpose for listening

Teaching Suggestions: Discuss with students the purpose for listening to this speech. They might be listening to understand a different point of view, to learn something new, to solve a problem in their community, or to choose the best idea presented.

Eliminate barriers to effective listening

Teaching Suggestions: Tell students that barriers can prevent the listener from receiving the speaker's message. Review these strategies:

- Remove distracting noises
- Rein in your mind if it starts to wander
- List questions that occur to you as you listen
- Keep your eyes on the speaker
- Be aware of personal bias about the speaker or the message

Analyze a speaker's persuasive techniques and credibility

Teaching Suggestions: Remind the student audience that an important part of critical listening is recognizing persuasive devices. These often involve faulty reasoning and might include inaccurate generalizations, either/or, bandwagon, or snob appeal. (These can be found in the Communication Handbook, page R105–106.) Have students assess the credibility of the speaker. Does the speaker appear knowledgeable about the subject matter? Has he or she done the necessary research? Are the claims and ideas backed up with facts and evidence?

Feedback Center

Students can use the following guidelines when giving and receiving feedback during this project:

Giving Feedback

▶ Ask questions concerning content, delivery, purpose, and point of view (for instance, is tone appropriate to purpose?).

▶ Provide feedback about the coherence and logic of the content, delivery, and overall impact on the listener.

▶ Comment on the verbal and nonverbal delivery (pitch, pace, volume, body language) and its impact on the listener.

▶ Respond to persuasive messages with questions, challenges, or affirmations.

▶ Questions evidence to support the speaker's claims and conclusions.

Receiving Feedback

▶ Listen to constructive criticism with an open mind.

▶ Use audience feedback and modify the presentations to clarify meaning or organization.

 ## Assessing the Project

The following rubric can be used for group or individual assessment.

3 Full Accomplishment

The group presented a persuasive speech that included a convincing plan for community involvement. The ideas were well supported with evidence and clearly organized. Students worked effectively in a group and demonstrated all of the Speaking and Listening Skills listed, including effective communication skills, appropriate delivery of information, and logical presentation of the points.

2 Substantial Accomplishment

The group presented a persuasive speech, but it lacked focus or clarity of subject matter. There was some supporting evidence, but the speech lacked coherence. Two to three of the Speaking and Listening Skills were demonstrated.

1 Little Accomplishment

The group's segment was incomplete or did not fulfill the requirements of the assignment. The speech lacked a persuasive tone, the arguments were not supported, and only one of the Speaking and Listening Skills was demonstrated.

Reflecting on the Theme Sometimes it is hard to reach out to someone who is different from you. There are risks in letting someone into your life. Getting to know other people, however, can make your own life better in many ways. When you reach out to others, you open yourself up to new experiences, ideas, and emotions. As you read these selections, notice how the characters invite others into their lives.

ACTIVITY

Imagine that a student from another country will enter your class next week. With a small group, discuss what your class might do to help this student adjust to your school. If you could create a video guide for new students, what would you include? Use a word web for brainstorming.

190

Poetry

A man doesn't go in search of a poem—
the poem must come to him.
   —Yang Wan-Li, "Written on a Cold Evening"

Poems often come to us when we don't expect them.
They may occur to us when we see something beautiful,
like a blazing sunset or a flower after a rainstorm, or they
may find us in our dreams. A poem packs all kinds of
ideas, feelings, and sounds into a few carefully chosen
words. The words, the sounds, and even the shape of
a poem all work together to create a total effect.

Key Elements of Poetry

- form
- sound
- imagery
- figurative language
- speaker

Objectives

- understand the following literary terms:
   form
   lines
   stanzas
   sound
   rhyme
   rhythm
   meter
   repetition
   alliteration
   onomatopoeia
   imagery
   figurative language
   personification
   simile
   speaker
- understand and appreciate poetry
- recognize the distinguishing features
   of poetry

Teaching the Lesson

This lesson introduces the basic elements of poetry and demonstrates how
they work together in a poem to produce the desired effect.

Introducing the Concepts

Ask students to try to remember lines
from a poem or a nursery rhyme.
Discuss what makes these lines easy to
remember.

 Use **Literary Analysis Transparencies,**
pp. 17–21, for additional support.

 See the Skills Trace at the beginning of the unit for information
TEKS on TEKS covered in this lesson.

Form

Have students brainstorm about different forms a poem could take. Ask them to describe how they would make a poem about trees look on the page.

YOUR TURN

Possible Response: Both stanzas in this example have four lines, making the poem look structured and uniform on the page.

Limerick–Writing Contest

Students may have the impression that poetry deals only with serious and elevated topics. You may counter this by introducing students to a humorous verse form such as the limerick. A limerick is a five-line poem with a strong, loosely anapestic (dum-dum-DAH) rhythm. The first, second, and fifth lines (of three feet each) rhyme, while the third and fourth lines (each 2 feet) rhyme. Limericks frequently begin with the catch phrase, "There was a . . . " and end with the name of a person or place.

There was a young lady from Norway, **a**
Who casually sat in a doorway; **a**
   When the door squeezed her flat, **b**
   She exclaimed, "What of that?" **b**
This courageous young lady of Norway. **a**
—Edward Lear

Read several limericks, such as those found in Edward Lear's *A Book of Nonsense* (1846) and analyze the form. Then invite students to create their own limericks. You might encourage them to put on a limerick-writing contest. You may wish to encourage students to use local names in their first lines. A dictionary of rhyming words can be helpful.

Form

The way a poem looks on the page is called its **form.** The form of a poem can add to its meaning. Poems are written in **lines,** which may or may not be sentences. Poets choose the arrangement of lines and words deliberately to create the overall effect. In structured forms of poetry, the lines are grouped into **stanzas** in a regular, repeated pattern. Poems that have no regular pattern are called free verse poems. Read the examples of a structured form and of free verse below.

YOUR TURN How would you describe the form of this poem by Robert Frost? Refer to the number of lines and stanzas in your answer.

FORM

I'm going out to clean the pasture spring;
I'll only stop to rake the leaves away
(And wait to watch the water clear, I may):
I shan't be gone long. —You come too.

I'm going out to fetch the little calf
That's standing by the mother. It's so young
It totters when she licks it with her tongue.
I shan't be gone long. —You come too.

—Robert Frost, "The Pasture

STRUCTURED FORM

If I Can Stop One Heart from Breaking
by Emily Dickinson

If I can stop one Heart from breaking
I shall not live in vain
If I can ease one Life the Aching
Or cool one Pain

Or help one fainting Robin
Unto his Nest again
I shall not live in Vain.

FREE VERSE

The Rider
by Naomi Shihab Nye

A boy told me
if he rollerskated fast enough
his loneliness couldn't catch up
to him,

the best reason I ever heard
for trying to be a champion.

What I wonder tonight
pedaling hard down King William Street
is if it translates to bicycles.

A victory! To leave your loneliness
panting behind you on some
street corner
while you float free into a cloud
of sudden azaleas,
luminous pink petals that have
never felt loneliness,
no matter how slowly they fell.

Sound

Because most poems are meant to be read aloud, poets choose and arrange words to create **sounds** that appeal to the listener. Four techniques that poets use to create sound are **rhyme, rhythm, repetition,** and **onomatopoeia.**

- **Rhyme** is a similarity of sounds at the ends of words. Traditional or older forms of poetry contain rhyming words at the end of the lines. Free verse usually doesn't contain end rhymes, or rhyme that occurs at the end of lines.

- **Rhythm** is the pattern of stressed and unstressed syllables in the poem's lines. The stanza at the right shows the stressed syllables (ˊ) and the unstressed (˘) syllables. Some poems have a regular, repeated arrangement of stressed and unstressed syllables. This is called **meter.** Free verse poems do not have a regular repetition of stressed and unstressed syllables. Their rhythm is more like spoken language.

- **Repetition** of sounds, words, phrases, or whole lines in a poem is a device poets use to emphasize an idea or create a certain feeling. **Alliteration** is the repetition of consonant sounds at the beginning of words, such as in the line "And wait to watch the water clear, I may."

- **Onomatopoeia** is the use of words whose sounds suggest their meanings, such as *flashed, bang,* and *shattered.*

YOUR TURN Write a list of the rhyming words in these excerpts from "To You" and "Casey at the Bat." Where are they placed in the lines?

> ### RHYME
>
> To dream of vast horizons of the soul
> through dreams made whole,
> Unfettered free—help me!
>
> —Langston Hughes, "To You"

> ### RHYTHM
>
> There was ease in Casey's manner as he
> stepped into his place,
>
> There was pride in Casey's bearing and a
> smile on Casey's face;
>
> And when responding to the cheers, he
> lightly doffed his hat,
>
> No stranger in the crowd could doubt
> 'twas Casey at the bat.
>
> —Ernest Lawrence Thayer,
> "Casey at the Bat"

Invite students to explain how rhyme, rhythm, and repetition are used in their favorite popular song to create an effective composition.

- **Rhyme/Rhythm**
  Ask two volunteers to select a poem from this unit to read aloud. The first reader should use his or her voice to stress the rhyme; the second reader should tap out the rhythm.

- **Repetition**
  Ask students to think about a familiar nursery rhyme and to note the use of repetition. Discuss what effect repetition has in the nursery rhyme.

- **Onomatopoeia**
  Have students brainstorm a list of words whose sounds suggest their meanings.

YOUR TURN
Possible Response: In "To You," rhymed words are *soul* and *whole,* at the end of lines, and *free* and *me* within the last line. In "Casey at the Bat," rhymed words are *place* and *face* and *hat* and *bat,* all at the end of lines.

Imagery

Have students consider what images they would want to create if they were writing a poem about their daily life. Ask them to include examples of imagery for each of the five senses.

Figurative Language

Ask students to create examples of personification to describe aspects of their classroom. Start them off with an example such as "The old desks groaned and complained as they were moved once again."

YOUR TURN
Possible Response: The moose acts "goofy" and he looks and acts like a "walking house-frame." This comparison helps the reader see the moose because everyone knows what a house frame looks like. Therefore the moose is probably bony, large and awkward.

Speaker

Ask students if they can think of a poem or a song in which the poet or author creates a new voice. Have them explain what purpose this new voice might serve.

Imagery and Figurative Language

Imagery is language that appeals to the reader's five senses—sight, hearing, smell, taste, and touch. Writers often use imagery to draw readers into a scene. Think about the phrases "blistering sands" and "feather clouds." Do the images remind you of places you've been or experiences you've had?

Writers may use **figurative language** when they choose words and phrases that help readers picture ordinary things in new ways. There are three main types of figurative language.

- A **simile** is a comparison that uses the signal word *like* or *as.* An example is "her eyes shone like stars."

- A **metaphor** is a direct comparison, with no signal words. "Into the sea of death" is a metaphor that compares death to a sea.

- When a poet describes an animal or object as if it were human or had human qualities, that is called **personification.** "The warm smile of the sun" is one example of personification.

YOUR TURN What does the moose in the poem look and act like? How does that comparison help you "see" the moose?

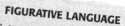

FIGURATIVE LANGUAGE

The goofy Moose, the walking house-frame
Is lost
In the forest. He bumps, he blunders,
he stands.

—Ted Hughes, "Moose

Speaker

The **speaker** of a poem is the **voice** that relates the story or ideas of the poem. The speaker may be the poet, speaking directly to the reader, or the speaker may be a character or voice created by the poet.

From "A Time to Talk"

Reading poetry can move us from laughter to tears. Why? Because many poems are written to express emotion. To understand the effect of a poem, pay attention to the elements of **form, sound, imagery, figurative language,** and **speaker**. To get the most from every poem, follow the reading strategies listed below.

Reading Poetry

How to Apply the Strategies

Preview the poem and read it aloud a few times. Notice the poem's form—what shape it has on the page, how long it is, how long the lines are, and whether or not it has stanzas. Look for end punctuation to help you find where each thought ends. As you read, listen for rhymes and rhythm and for the overall sound of the words.

Visualize the images. Create a mental picture of the images and comparisons you find in the poem. Do the images remind you of feelings or experiences you have had?

Clarify the words and phrases. Allow yourself to wonder about any phrases or words that seem to stand out. Think about what the choice of those words adds to the poem. Also think about the poem's speaker. What is his or her particular view of life? Look for clues that will help you make **inferences,** logical conclusions based on evidence about the speaker's experiences, attitudes, and personality.

Evaluate the poem's theme. Ask, what's the point of this poem? What message is the poet trying to send or help me to understand?

Let your understanding grow. Think about what the poem is saying to you. Does it relate to anything in your own life? Does it give you a new way of looking at something? Over time, your rereading of the poem, your discussions in class, and the other poetry you read

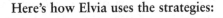

Here's how Elvia uses the strategies:

*"With some poems, you really know what the poet means. I like to read a poem aloud first, listening to how it sounds. I **visualize** the images and emotions. It's interesting to think about the speaker of the poem and look for details that describe his or her special way of looking at life."*

Need More Help?

Remember that active readers use the essential reading strategies explained on page 4: • **visualize** • **predict** • **clarify** • **question** • **connect** • **evaluate** • **monitor.**

THE ACTIVE READER **195**

Teaching the Lesson

The strategies on this page will help students apply skills for appreciating poetry.

Presenting the Strategies
When introducing these strategies, you might want to use a short poem as a model. Demonstrate how each strategy can be applied to the poem.

Use **Reading and Critical Thinking Transparencies,** p. 1, for additional support.

Preview
Remind students that most poems are meant to be read aloud. Reading a poem aloud can help them to get a feel for the language, rhyme, and rhythm of the poem.

Visualize the images
Tell students the best way to find meaning in poetry is to focus on the images. Details of a poem's imagery can bring them closer to a person, place, or emotion. If they stop to visualize images, they might find that they are reminded of something in their own experience.

Clarify the words and phrases
Remind students that language in poetry is carefully chosen. If they hear sounds repeated, or sounds that are especially soft or harsh, they should know that these sounds might be important elements of the poem. Tell students that reading aloud can help them to truly hear the language of a poem.

Objectives
• apply strategies that will help to understand poetry
• appreciate poetry by listening to sound devices

Evaluate the poem's theme
Tell students that each element of a poem can lead them to the theme. Tell them that often a poem's title also refers to a main idea in the selection. As students read selections in this book, they should try to figure out how individual selections are related to the themes of the units.

Let your understanding grow
Remind students to allow themselves to connect to poems. They should also listen to the opinions of others in class discussions.

This selection is included in the **Grade 7 InterActive Reader.**

Objectives

1. understand and appreciate two **lyric poems** (Literary Analysis)
2. examine **rhyme, end rhyme,** and **rhyme scheme** (Literary Analysis)
3. understand and appreciate **sensory imagery** (Literary Analysis)
4. practice reading poems **aloud** (Active Reading)

Summary

In "The Pasture," the speaker invites the reader to come along while the speaker cleans out the pasture spring and fetches in a young calf. Though the speaker "shan't be gone long," the reader senses these moments are special and will be pleasant to share.

In "A Time to Talk," a friend passing by on the road interrupts the speaker's field work. Rather than focusing on the work undone and simply calling "What is it?", the speaker lays aside his hoe and trudges up to the stone wall for a friendly chat.

Thematic Link

Robert Frost celebrates the simple but meaningful moments of his day by sharing them with a friend or neighbor.

5-Minute Warm-Up

Daily Language SkillBuilder   **TEKS** 16B, 16D

Have students **proofread** the display sentences on page 189i and write them correctly. The sentences also appear on Transparency 6 of **Grammar Transparencies and Copymasters.**

The Pasture   A Time to Talk

Poetry by ROBERT FROST

 TEKS   See the Skills Trace at the begining of the unit for information on TEKS covered in this lesson

Connect to Your Life

Slow Down! During a typical week, you probably have a lot to do after school and on weekends. Setting aside time for people who are important to you is essential to a healthy and happy life. Think of ways people benefit when they interrupt their busy lives to share time with friends, family, and neighbors. Share your ideas with your classmates.

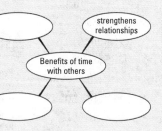

Build Background

CONNECT TO GEOGRAPHY   New England was shaped by a huge glacier, which covered the land during several ice ages. As the glacier moved forward, it dug out lakes and rivers and left huge mounds of soil and rocks scattered everywhere.

By the 1600s, when the first European immigrants arrived, New England was covered with thick forests. The immigrants established communities and turned this sometimes harsh environment into farmland.

Many of Robert Frost's poems are set on the rugged farms of New England, where he spent much of his adult life. His poems give the reader a vivid sense of the landscape with its rough-hewn character, changing seasons, farm animals, trees, and stone walls.

LaserLink: Background for Reading Geographical Connection

Focus Your Reading

LITERARY ANALYSIS   RHYME   **Rhyme** is a repetition of identical or similar sounds. The most common form is **end rhyme,** where the rhymes occur at the ends of lines. Notice the end rhymes in these lines from "The Pasture":

I'm going out to clean the pasture spring;
I'll only stop to rake the leaves away
(And wait to watch the water clear, I may):
I shan't be gone long. —You come too.

ACTIVE READING   READ ALOUD   **Reading a poem aloud** helps you enjoy the sound and understand the meaning. Before reading aloud, follow these steps:

- Read the poem to yourself to get a sense of the meaning.
- Try to picture the images or scenes that the poet creates.
- Try to imagine how the voice of the speaker might sound.

READER'S NOTEBOOK   Copy "The Pasture." Circle the punctuation that indicates where you should pause, draw an arrow at the end of lines where you should not pause, and draw a wavy line under words you want to emphasize.

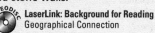

> I'm going out to clean the pasture spring.
>
> I'll only stop to rake the leaves away
>
> (And wait to watch the water clear, I may)
>
> I shan't be gone long. You come too.

LESSON RESOURCES

UNIT TWO RESOURCE BOOK, pp. 4–5

ASSESSMENT
Formal Assessment, pp. 29–30
Teacher's Guide to Assessment and Portfolio Use
Test Generator

SKILLS TRANSPARENCIES AND COPYMASTERS
Literary Analysis
- Form in Poetry: Rhyme and Meter, TR 17 (for Paired Activity, p. 199)

Communications
- Reading Aloud, TR 11 (for Mini Lesson, p. 198)

INTEGRATED TECHNOLOGY
Audio Library
LaserLinks
- Geographical Connection; Author Background; Art Gallery. See **Teacher's SourceBook,** p. 15.

Visit our website:
www.mcdougallittell.com

Silverstrim's Farm (1989),
David Bareford. Quester Gallery,
Stonington, Connecticut.

The Pasture

by Robert Frost

I'm going out to clean the pasture spring;
I'll only stop to rake the leaves away
(And wait to watch the water clear, I may):
I shan't be gone long.—You come too.

5 I'm going out to fetch the little calf
That's standing by the mother. It's so young
It totters when she licks it with her tongue.
I shan't be gone long.—You come too.

Thinking Through the Literature

1. Would you like to share the speaker's experiences? Why or why not?

2. Why might the speaker want a companion?

   THINK ABOUT { • what a companion might add to the experience
   • the tasks the speaker describes

3. How would you describe the speaker's attitude toward nature?

 Cross Curricular Link **Geography and Social Studies**

NEW HAMPSHIRE Much of Robert Frost's poetry draws upon and reflects experiences and insights gained during his years as a farmer in New Hampshire. From 1900 to 1909 he farmed in Derry, N.H. After living in England, he returned to New Hampshire in 1915 and settled on a farm in Franconia, though he spent a great part of the ensuing years traveling as a lecturer and professor. Like the rest of New England, New Hampshire is a rather difficult place to farm. The land is seldom level, the soil is often stony, and winters tend to be long and cold. Nonetheless, much of the land was farmed for generations. Frost's early poems tend to focus on the hardships of farming and the harsher aspects of nature; many of his later poems are more optimistic and charming. In New Hampshire, as in other places, farmland and farm life are steadily being swallowed up by urban and suburban development. Frost's poems preserve the memories, both harsh and idyllic, of a way of life that is fast disappearing.

TEACHING THE LITERATURE

Customizing Instruction

Less Proficient Readers
Have students keep the following questions in mind as they read:

• What tasks does the speaker do or try to do in the poems?
  Answer: In "The Pasture," the speaker intends to clean the spring and fetch the little calf. In "A Time to Talk," the speaker hoes the ground.

• Whom does the speaker invite to come along in "The Pasture"?
  Answer: the reader

• In "A Time to Talk," why does the speaker stop work to talk?
  Possible Response: Taking time to talk to a friend is at least as important as finishing a task.

Students Acquiring English
1 Point out the inverted word order in this line. Ask how the words would be ordered in speech.
Answer: I may wait to watch the water clear.
Ask students why the poet wrote the line this way.
Answer: to make it end in a rhyme

Use **Spanish Study Guide,** pp. 37–39 for additional support.

Gifted and Talented
Both pieces are about taking time to share experiences with others. Ask students to connect this theme to experiences in their own lives. Then have them write their own original lyric poems based on this theme.

Thinking Through the Literature

1. Answers will vary. Students' responses should reveal an understanding of the poem.
2. Answers will vary. The speaker might want companionship as he works.
3. The speaker appreciates nature.

Literary Analysis `RHYME`

Lyric poems often have clear rhyme patterns, as students will realize when they chart "The Pasture" and "A Time to Talk." Ask students how rhyme pattern contributes to the meaning of each poem.

Possible Response: The rhyme pattern in "The Pasture" emphasizes the rhythm of farm life and responsibilities. The lack of rhyme in each first line suggests that each experience is unique. The variations in the rhyme scheme of "A Time to Talk" match the speaker's willingness to interrupt his work and emphasize the difference between shouting "What is it?" and plodding up for a visit.

 Use **Unit Two Resource Book,** p. 5, for more practice.

Active Reading `READ ALOUD`

Ask students to listen as you read the poem aloud. Have them identify the words and phrases that appeal to the sense of hearing.

Possible Responses: "a friend calls," "slows his horse to a meaning walk," "shout," "thrust my hoe," "plod"

 Use **Unit Two Resource Book,** p. 4, for more practice.

Reading Skills and Strategies: CLARIFY

Ⓐ Have students read quietly aloud or listen to identify the line that defines the break between what the speaker doesn't do and what he does.

Answer: Line 6: "No, not as there is time to talk."

A Time to Talk

by Robert Frost

Galena (1988), Robert L. Barnum. Watercolor, private collection.

W̲hen a friend calls to me from the road
And slows his horse to a meaning walk,
I don't stand still and look around
On all the hills I haven't hoed,
Ⓐ 5 And shout from where I am, "What is it?"
No, not as there is a time to talk.
I thrust my hoe in the mellow ground,
Blade-end up and five feet tall,
And plod: I go up to the stone wall
10 For a friendly visit.

Teaching Options

 Mini Lesson **Speaking and Listening**  **TEKS** 4A, 5C, 5E, 11B

ORAL RECITATION OF POEMS

Instruction Explain to students that many poems are intended to be read aloud. Talk with students about qualities that help a speaker reach an audience—for example, rate, pitch, and tone.

Prepare: Have each student choose one of these poems to recite for the class, following the plan they have marked on the text of the poem. Tell them to plan and practice the rate, pitch, and tone of their speech, so that their delivery will be clear and will have the desired effect on an audience. Invite students to work in pairs on their readings, using two voices to highlight aspects of meaning,

rhythm, rhyme, or repetition. Remind them that alert posture, an engaged manner, and eye contact with the audience enhance recitation.

Perform Have students recite their poem for the class. Depending on students' comfort levels, you may wish to have listeners evaluate each reading against criteria established by the group to assess rate, pitch, tone, and other aspects of presentation.

BLOCK SCHEDULING This activity is particularly well suited for longer class periods.

Use **Communications Transparencies and Copymasters,** p. 11, for additional support.

Thinking through the LITERATURE

Connect to the Literature

1. What Do You Think?
What do you think about the speaker of "A Time to Talk"? What do you imagine he is like?

Comprehension Check
- What does the speaker mean by the phrase, "And slows his horse to a meaning walk"?
- According to the speaker, is it more important to get work done or to visit with a friend?

Think Critically

2. Why do you think the speaker in "A Time to Talk" chooses to stop and talk rather than to keep working?

 THINK ABOUT
- the solitary nature of farm work
- how a farmer decides when his work must be finished

3. What phrases or words in each poem provide you with images of life in the country?

4. How are the speakers of the two poems alike, and how are they different? How does each speaker "let others in"?

5. **ACTIVE READING** **READ ALOUD** Copy and mark up "A Time to Talk" in your ▨ **READER'S NOTEBOOK** as you did with "The Pasture." Then read both poems aloud. In your opinion, which poem sounds better when read aloud? Discuss your choices with the class.

Extend Interpretations

6. Critic's Corner Frost wrote that a poem should "begin in delight and end in wisdom." In your opinion, explain whether either of these poems fulfills Frost's goals of delight and wisdom for a poem.

7. The Writer's Style In both poems, Frost uses everyday language to write about ordinary experiences. What effect does this have as you read?

8. Connect to Life What advice might the speaker of these poems have for people living in today's fast-paced world?

Literary Analysis

RHYME **Rhyme** is a repetition of sounds at the end of words. Words rhyme when their accented vowels and all the letters that follow have identical sounds. For example, in "A Time to Talk," *road* and *hoed* rhyme, as do *walk* and *talk*. There are several other pairs of words that rhyme in this poem as well. Notice that the kind of rhyme in this poem is **end rhyme,** or rhyming that occurs at the end of lines. This end rhyme forms a pattern, or **rhyme scheme,** which can be charted.

Paired Activity Working with a partner, chart the rhyme schemes of "The Pasture" and "A Time to Talk." You can chart the pattern of the rhyme by assigning a letter of the alphabet to each line. Begin with the letter *a*, then *b*, and so forth. Lines that rhyme are given the same letter. The first four lines of "The Pasture" are done for you.

"The Pasture"		"A Time to Talk"
spring	a	
away	b	
may	b	
too	c	

Connect to the Literature

1. What Do You Think?
Responses will vary. Students may suggest physical characteristics (overalls, battered hat, sweat, age) or personality traits (hard-working; willing to break for a friend). Some may find the speaker wise to place a high value on friendship; others may think he should finish his work first and visit later.

Comprehension Check
- The friend slows his horse's pace to a walk, signaling that he wants to talk.
- Both are important; it's best to take a break from work to talk with a friend.

Think Critically

2. Possible Responses: The speaker has been working hard and alone; he is eager for a few moments of companionship; he is experienced enough to know that he will still get done what needs to be done. The title suggests he has "time to talk."

3. Possible Responses for "The Pasture": "clean the pasture spring," "fetch the little calf" that "totters" when the mother licks it. Possible responses for "A Time to Talk": "slows his horse," "hills I haven't hoed," "mellow ground," "stone wall."

4. Possible Response: Both speakers enjoy nature and want to share their experiences (let others in).

5. Accept all reasonable responses. Students may say "The Pasture" sounds better aloud because it is conversation rather than narrative, and its rhyme scheme and rhythm are more consistent.

Literary Analysis

Rhyme "The Pasture": *abbc deec*
"A Time to Talk": *abcadbceed*

▨ Use **Literary Analysis Transparencies,** p. 17, for additional support.

Extend Interpretations

6. Critic's Corner Accept all reasonable responses. Students may say that the beginnings of the poems aren't particularly delightful but that the poems leave one with the simple sort of wisdom one gains from life on a farm.

7. The Writer's Style Answers will vary. Sample response: The poems are generally easy to understand and convey an impression of useful, everyday wisdom.

8. Connect to Life Answers will vary. Sample response: The speaker would tell people today to slow down, feel the slower rhythms of nature, and spend time relaxing and talking with friends.

Writing Option

Creating a Recipe To help students get started, encourage them to visualize some of the best conversations they've had. Have them record characteristics of each of these conversations. Their recipes can emerge from these notes.

Activities & Explorations

1. **Illustrated Book** Students' illustrations may use a variety of art techniques. Lines from one of these poems should form the text under the illustrations.
2. **Poetry Reading** Students' presentations of poems should demonstrate strong recitation skills: effective use of rate, pitch, tone, posture, and eye contact.

Inquiry & Research

The Vacation of a Lifetime! Students might locate state tourist bureau websites or call travel agents for information and sample brochures.

 Use **Writing Transparencies,** pp. 47–48, for additional support.

Robert Frost

Throughout his early adulthood, Frost held a variety of jobs, including mill hand, teacher, and reporter. He credits these experiences with teaching him about different kinds of people and about life in New England.

Author Activity

Poet for a Nation Possible Response: Frost might have been marking one historic, transitional occasion (the inauguration) with reference to another: the colonists' decision to claim America.

Writing Option

Creating a Recipe Think about a person with whom you have really great talks. What qualities make it easy or interesting to talk to that person? Create a recipe that includes all the ingredients of a good conversation. Save your recipe in your **Working Portfolio.**

Recipe for a Good Conversation

3 cups good listener
a pinch humor

Activities & Explorations

1. **Illustrated Book** Create an illustrated book, using one of Frost's poems as the text. Base your illustrations on the rural images in the poem. Share the book with your class. ~ **ART**
2. **Poetry Reading** Read more of Robert Frost's poetry. With a small group of classmates, choose poems you think would make good oral interpretations. Practice and present a reading of them to the whole class. ~ **PERFORMING**

Inquiry & Research

The Vacation of a Lifetime! Frost is often called a regional writer because his poems focus on the landscape and people of New England, especially New Hampshire. Find out more about the region and the places people can visit to experience "Robert Frost's New England." Create a travel brochure to inspire people to visit the region.

"Something there is that doesn't love a wall, and wants it down."

Robert Frost
1874–1963

A Late Start The man who became one of America's most popular poets did not publish a book of poetry until he was 39 years old. By the end of Frost's life, his name had become known to most Americans.

A New Hampshire Farmer Frost spent his early years in San Francisco. At 11, he and his widowed mother moved East, where he attended Dartmouth College and Harvard University, married and raised a family, and began to write poetry.

An American Literary Hero Frost moved his family to England for a period, but ties to his native land eventually brought him back to New Hampshire. Frost won the Pulitzer Prize for poetry four times. Congress voted him a gold medal "in recognition of his poetry, which has enriched the culture of the United States and the philosophy of the world." In 1961 he recited one of his poems at the inauguration of President John F. Kennedy.

AUTHOR ACTIVITY

Poet for a Nation The poem Robert Frost recited at President Kennedy's inauguration was "The Gift Outright." Find a copy of this poem and read it. Then, with your classmates, discuss the reasons why Frost might have chosen this poem to read at the inauguration.

 LaserLinks: Background for Reading
Author Background
Art Gallery

Teaching Options

✓ **Assessment** **Standardized Test Practice** TEKS 10K, 12G 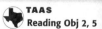 TAAS Reading Obj 2, 5

DESCRIBE SETTING In some standardized tests, students are asked to select the best setting description for a passage they have read. Write the following question on the board or read it aloud.

Which of the following statements best describes the setting of "A Time to Talk"?

A. The poem is a lyric about farm life and friendship.

B. It happens in a field bordered by a stone wall, in a time when people traveled by horseback.

C. The speaker decides that he can stop hoeing his fields for a while to visit with a friend.

D. Sometimes it's good to interrupt your work to talk with a friend.

Guide students through the process of selecting the correct answer. A is a description of genre. C summarizes the poem's events or plot. D is the theme, or message for the reader about life or human nature. B is the best answer because it describes place and time, the two components of setting.

The World Is Not a Pleasant Place to Be

Poetry by NIKKI GIOVANNI

To You

Poetry by LANGSTON HUGHES

Connect to Your Life

Alone or Together? People need time to be alone and time to be with others. With a partner, think about times when you or your friends like to be alone, as well as times when you like to be with friends or family members. Write down three examples of each. Discuss them with your partner.

Things I Like to Do Alone	Things I Like to Do with Others
1.	1.
2.	2.
3.	3.

Build Background

African-American Voices
Langston Hughes was a leading figure of the Harlem Renaissance, the period during the 1920s when many gifted African-American artists came to New York City. In his poetry Hughes celebrated the real life of black Americans. He wrote about ordinary people and their everyday struggles.

Nikki Giovanni began writing in the 1960s, a time of great social upheaval. Giovanni's bitter, sometimes violent, poems attracted wide audiences. In later years her poetry became more gentle. "The World Is Not a Pleasant Place to Be" comes from a book of poems entitled *My House*.

See the Skills Trace at the beginning of the unit for information on TEKS covered in this lesson.

Focus Your Reading

LITERARY ANALYSIS | **SPEAKER** In a poem, the **speaker** is the voice that "talks" to the reader. A speaker may be a distant observer, or he or she may be involved with the experiences and ideas expressed in the poem. A poem's speaker is not necessarily identical with the poet. The poet may have created the speaker with a distinct identity in order to achieve a particular effect. As you read these two poems, pay attention to the emotions and thoughts that the speakers express.

ACTIVE READING | **MAKING INFERENCES** An **inference** is a logical guess you make on the basis of evidence or your own knowledge. Making inferences is important when you read poetry. Because a poem usually does not tell a story directly, you must learn to "read between the lines" to decide who the speaker is and why he or she feels a certain way.

READER'S NOTEBOOK As you read "The World Is Not a Pleasant Place to Be" and "To You," try to **infer** what the speakers are like on the basis of what they say. In a chart like the one shown here, record the inferences you make about the speakers.

"The World Is Not ..."	"To You"
• The speaker seems to be lonely.	

THE WORLD IS NOT A PLEASANT PLACE TO BE / TO YOU **201**

Objectives

1. understand and appreciate two **lyric poems** (Literary Analysis)
2. understand what the **speaker** of the poem is (Literary Analysis)
3. use the active reading skill of **connect to your own experience** (Active Reading)

Summary

In "The World is Not a Pleasant Place to Be," the speaker compares people to elements of nature. Humans need to be embraced as a river needs to flow into something larger than itself. People need comfort and company as the ocean needs the clouds to "kiss her tears" so she can laugh. Without companionship, the world is not a pleasant place.

In "To You," the speaker invites fellow dreamers—those who sit and think and read and learn about the world beyond themselves—to help him dream of ways to remake the world.

Thematic Link

Both poems say that people need to reach out to help each other face or change a difficult world.

5-Minute Warm-Up

Daily Language SkillBuilder **TEKS 17A, 17G**

Have students **proofread** the display sentences on page 189i and write them correctly. The sentences also appear on Transparency 6 of **Grammar Transparencies and Copymasters.**

LESSON RESOURCES

UNIT TWO RESOURCE BOOK, pp. 6–7

ASSESSMENT
Formal Assessment, pp. 31–32
Teacher's Guide to Assessment and Portfolio Use
Test Generator

SKILLS TRANSPARENCIES AND COPYMASTERS
Literary Analysis
• Poetry: Speaker, TR 21 (for Cooperative Learning Activity, p. 204)
Reading and Critical Thinking
• Making Inferences, TR 5 (for Thinking Through the Literature, p. 204)

Communications
• Reading Aloud, TR 11 (for Mini Lesson, p. 202)

INTEGRATED TECHNOLOGY
Audio Library
Internet: Research Starter

Visit our website:
www.mcdougallittell.com

THE WORLD IS NOT A PLEASANT PLACE TO BE/TO YOU **201**

Reading and Analyzing

Literary Analysis `SPEAKER`

Invite students to consider the Build Background information provided on each poet. What similarities exist between each poet and speaker?

Possible Response: Giovanni began writing in a time of social upheaval; her speaker says "the world is not a pleasant place." Hughes was a leader of the Harlem Renaissance and celebrated the real life of black Americans; like his speaker, he dreamed of ways to improve society.

 Use **Unit Two Resource Book,** p. 7, for more practice.

Active Reading `MAKING INFERENCES`

Ask students what they can infer from the images in stanzas 2 and 3 about the speaker's state of mind.

Possible Response: They can infer that the speaker wants to connect with others, in the way that a river connects to a stream or clouds seem to connect with the ocean on the horizon.

 Use **Unit Two Resource Book,** p. 6, for more practice.

Thinking Through the Literature

1. Possible Responses: pain, loneliness, isolation
2. Possible Response: They are a contrast to what the speaker feels about himself.
3. Possible Response: The word describes something that is pleasing or that feels good. The speaker is lonely, and without someone to be with, the world is not a place that feels good.

Teaching Options

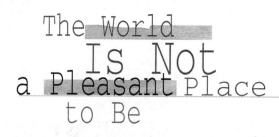

The World Is Not a Pleasant Place to Be

by Nikki Giovanni

the world is not a pleasant place
to be without
someone to hold and be held by

a river would stop
5   its flow if only
a stream were there
to receive it

an ocean would never laugh
if clouds weren't there
10 to kiss her tears

the world is not
a pleasant place to be without
someone

Thinking Through the Literature

1. How would you describe the feelings that the speaker expresses in the first stanza?
2. How do the examples from nature help you understand the speaker's feelings?
3. Why do you think the poet chose the word *pleasant* instead of another word?

Mini Lesson   ## Speaking and Listening    TEKS 4A, 5C,E, 11B

ORAL RECITATION OF POEMS

Instruction Note that free verse poems require careful interpretation. In some cases, meaning units correspond to line ends; in other cases, they do not. For example, in "To You," there should be no pause between lines 2 and 3. Giovanni's poem includes no punctuation, yet each verse contains a complete idea. The reader must determine how to interpret the poem to clearly communicate its ideas.

Prepare: Have each student choose one of these poems to recite. Tell them to plan and practice until they can clearly communicate the poem's ideas. Invite students to work in pairs on their

readings, using two voices to highlight aspects of meaning. Remind them that alert posture, engaged manner, and eye contact with the audience enhance recitation.

Perform Have students recite their poem for the class. Depending on students' confidence and comfort levels, you may wish to have listeners compare different interpretations.

BLOCK SCHEDULING This activity is particularly well suited for longer class periods.

 Use **Communications Transparencies and Copymasters,** p. 11, for additional support.

From *Harlem*, illustrated by Christopher Myers. Copyright © 1997 by Christopher Myers. Reprinted by permission of Scholastic Inc.

To You

by Langston Hughes

To sit and dream, to sit and read,
To sit and learn about the world
Outside our world of here and now—
    our problem world—
5   To dream of vast horizons of the soul
Through dreams made whole,
Unfettered free—help me!
All you who are dreamers, too,
Help me to make our world anew.
10 I reach out my dreams to you.

Cross Curricular Link Social Studies

THE HARLEM RENAISSANCE Langston Hughes was a major figure in the period of black American achievement called the Harlem Renaissance. In the early 1800s Harlem was as an elegant suburb of New York City. When Langston Hughes moved there in the early 1920s, as a student at Columbia University, Harlem was the nation's largest urban black community. It had become part of New York City and was populated by people migrating up from the South in search of good jobs, immigrants from the West Indies and Africa, and soldiers home from World War I. It was a city within a city, full of energy and black pride. People as different as Hughes, Duke Ellington, and W. E. B. Du Bois lived and worked in Harlem in the 1920s. During the Harlem Renaissance, blues and jazz became the musical rage in America and Europe. Black artists and writers gained widespread recognition.

On the political front, Harlem supported major offices of national organizations dedicated to advancing black rights. Harlem, like the rest of America, fell on hard times during the Great Depression of the 1930s, and it never regained the glory of the 1920s.

GUIDING STUDENT RESPONSE

Connect to the Literature

1. What Do You Think?
Responses will vary. Some students may feel positively about the speaker inviting them to dream with him about changing the world. Others may feel that the speaker is unrealistic.

Comprehension Check:
• Dreams help him reach beyond "our problem world" of "here and now" and imagine a new and better place.
• He wants the reader to help him "make the world anew."

Think Critically

2. Possible Response: "Our problem world" is the world we live in; the other world is the one the speaker imagines, a new and better place.

3. Possible Response: Dreaming is important because it frees us ("vast horizons of the soul"), allows us to imagine a new and better world, and brings us together in a common dream of building that new world.

4. Possible Response: The speaker of "The World" is lonely. He tells us twice that the world is not a pleasant place to be in without someone to be with. The speaker of "To You" is more upbeat. He thinks that we can "make our world anew."

 Use **Reading and Critical Thinking Transparencies,** p. 5, for additional support.

Literary Analysis

Speaker Review with students the speaker's convictions about making the world anew. In light of that conviction, note that the reader's help is crucially important if the speaker is to realize his dream. Ask students what emotion they hear in the lines quoted in boldface. Possible Responses: pleading, desperate, but hopeful

 Use **Literary Analysis Transparencies,** p. 21, for additional support.

Connect to the Literature

1. What Do You Think? How do you feel about the speaker of "To You"?

Comprehension Check
• What does the speaker say about dreaming?
• What help does the speaker want from the reader?

Think Critically

2. What do you think the speaker means by "our problem world"? Is there another kind of world for the speaker?

3. Why is dreaming important to the speaker?

 THINK ABOUT
• the phrase "vast horizons of the soul"
• the help that the speaker wants from other dreamers
• the last line

4. **ACTIVE READING** **MAKING INFERENCES**
Review the **inferences** you recorded in your **READER'S NOTEBOOK.** What did you infer about each speaker? What details or images helped you to make your inferences? Share your findings with a partner.

Extend Interpretations

5. Critic's Corner Look again at Robert Frost's comment that a poem should "begin in delight and end in wisdom" (page 199). In your opinion, do these poems do that? How would you describe the ways that they begin and end?

6. Connect to Life In "To You," the speaker asks dreamers for help. Do you think dreams are useful, or are they a waste of time? Explain your opinion.

Literary Analysis

SPEAKER A poem's **speaker** is the voice that "talks" to the reader. Some speakers show little or no emotion and seem detached from what they describe. Others express strong feelings about the ideas and experiences they present. Read these lines from "To You" aloud:

All you who are dreamers, too,
Help me to make our world
anew.

How would you describe the emotion in this speaker's voice?

Cooperative Learning Activity
Get together with a small group of classmates and choose one of the two poems. Compare your **READER'S NOTEBOOK** inferences about the speaker of that poem. Make a chart that includes the inferences of all the group members. Then, with a group that chose the other poem, discuss the similarities and differences between the two speakers.

FREE VERSE Poetry with no regular pattern of rhyme, rhythm, or line length is called **free verse.** Free verse often sounds like conversation. Read "The World Is Not a Pleasant Place to Be" aloud as naturally as you can. Do you think free verse is a good way of presenting the ideas in the poem? Explain.

Extend Interpretations

5. Critic's Corner Remind students of the definition of delight, something that pleases and makes you feel happy. Possible Responses: Students may feel that "The World" definitely does not begin by making you feel happy while "To You" does. Both poems provide "wisdom," a lesson about life, at the end. "The World" begins with the speaker saying that it is hard being alone in the world and emphasizes that idea by repeating it at the end. "To You" begins with the speaker sharing his dreams with us and ends by reminding us that dreaming helps us to be free.

6. Connect to Life Responses will vary. Students may say dreams are useful because they allow people to imagine possibilities and to think of ways to make things happen.

Writing Option

Personal Poem Try your hand at writing a poem about a thought or feeling you have had. The poem can be based on a happy experience or a sad one. It could be funny or surprising. Share your finished poem with classmates, then save it in your **Working Portfolio.**

Writing Handbook
See p. R22: Prewriting.

Activities & Explorations

1. Oral Report Find a recording of the "I Have a Dream" speech by Dr. Martin Luther King, Jr. As you listen to it, pay special attention to King's use of rhythm and repetition. Give a report to your class on King's speaking style, illustrating your ideas with excerpts from the recording. ~ **SPEAKING AND LISTENING**

2. Poems on Tape With a small group of classmates, listen to a recording of a poet reading his or her own work. Choose one poem you like, and find a printed version of it. Practice reading it aloud. Experiment with expression and timing. Then tape-record your reading and listen to it, along with the readings of the other members of the group. ~ **SPEAKING AND LISTENING**

Inquiry & Research

Times of Change Both Langston Hughes and Nikki Giovanni wrote during times of change for African Americans. Find out more about the Harlem Renaissance of the 1920s or about the Black Power movement of the 1960s. Look especially for books that have historic photographs. Then draw and paint a mural showing people from one of these time periods. Include captions in the mural.

 More Online: Research Starter
www.mcdougallittell.com

"I write out of my own experiences."

Nikki Giovanni
born 1943

Childhood Nikki Giovanni was born Yolande Cornelia Giovanni, Jr., in Knoxville, Tennessee. She spent her early years with her parents and sister in Cincinnati, Ohio. At 14, she went to live with her grandparents in Tennessee.

Early Success Giovanni graduated with honors from Fisk University and soon achieved national recognition for her poetry. An album of her readings, *Truth Is on Its Way*, was produced when she was 28 years old. It brought her huge popular success. She is the author of some 15 books of poetry and holds 14 honorary degrees. In addition to teaching, she lectures and reads her poetry all over the United States.

Poetry from Experience Many of Giovanni's poems reflect her childhood and her experience as an African-American woman. "I write," she says, "out of my own experiences—which also happen to be the experiences of my people. Human beings fascinate me. I just keep trying to dissect them poetically to see what's there."

Langston Hughes

See the biography on page 36.

 Assessment   Informal Assessment

 TEKS 10H   **TAAS** Reading Obj. 5   Writing Obj. 2

MAKE INFERENCES AND DRAW CONCLUSIONS
You can informally assess students' ability to make inferences and draw conclusions by having them write a profile of each speaker. Each profile should include the speaker's experience, attitude, and message. Each profile should be supported with text evidence.

RUBRIC

3 Full Accomplishment Students make inferences about each speaker's experience, draw conclusions about attitude and message, and provide text evidence.

2 Substantial Accomplishment Students offer reasonable inferences and conclusions but do not adequately support them.

1 Little or Partial Accomplishment Students do not offer reasonable inferences or conclusions, or do not provide evidence.

Writing Options

Personal Poem Students' poems should be free verse and focus on a thought or feeling. To get students started on this assignment, ask them to freewrite on several possible topics before deciding which will work best.

 Use **Writing Transparencies,** p. 35, for additional support.

Activities & Explorations

1. Oral Report Students should describe King's speaking style, including his use of rhythm and repetition. Their reports should incorporate excerpts from a recording of King's "I Have a Dream" speech to illustrate their points.

Use **Communications Transparencies and Copymasters,** p. 10, for additional support.

2. Poems on Tape Students' tape-recorded readings should reflect attention to expression and timing. Encourage them to mark a copy of the poem with symbols to aid their reading: slash marks where they want to pause, arrows where they should move on to the next line without pausing, and wavy lines under words or phrases they want to emphasize.

Inquiry & Research

Times of Change Some well-known names of the Harlem Renaissance include W. E. B. Du Bois (a founder of the NAACP), Alain LeRoy Locke, Marcus Garvey, Duke Ellington. Voices of the Black Power movement include Giovanni, Malcolm X, Eldridge Cleaver, James Meredith, and Stokely Carmichael.

Use **Writing Transparencies,** p. 41, for additional support.

Nikki Giovanni

In addition to her other achievements, Giovanni founded her own publishing company at the age of 27. Giovanni's fascinating life was the subject of the 1987 PBS documentary *Spirit to Spirit: The Poetry of Nikki Giovanni,* directed by Mirra Bank.

Objectives

1. understand and appreciate a **short story** (Literary Analysis)
2. understand the distinction between **static** and **dynamic** characters (Literary Analysis)
3. **draw conclusions** to understand characters (Active Reading)

Summary

Every day Mrs. Markham walks her son Willie home from school. Since the boy's father left, she seems sad and distant. One day they see a homeless man outside their building. The boy is curious, but the mother says to ignore the man; he's unhappy, she tells him. While his mother naps, Willie goes out and gives the man a nickel. Later, Mrs. Markham goes to work, leaving Willie at home alone. He feels as if he's in one of the caves he learned about in school; blind fish live in them. The next day Willie questions his mother about her unhappiness, the homeless man, his father, and the blind fish. She doesn't want to talk about any of it. Later, Willie speaks to the homeless man. The day after that they talk about many things, including making decisions for yourself, unhappiness, and the fish. On Friday, Willie gives the man some cake and learns from him the cure for unhappiness: "What a person needs is always more than they say." *They* means the experts. The next day, Willie tries to share this cure with his mother, but she becomes upset. He learns that she called the police to have the homeless man removed. Willie says that she is as blind as the fish in the cave.

Thematic Link

Willie is able to reach out to a homeless man and learn from him.

5-Minute Warm-Up

Daily Language SkillBuilder TEKS 16B, 16D

Have students **proofread** the display sentences on page 189i and write them correctly. The sentences also appear on Transparency 7 of **Grammar Transparencies and Copymasters.**

"What a person needs is always more than they say."

What Do Fish Have to Do with Anything?

Short Story by AVI

 See the Skills Trace at the beginning of the unit for information on TEKS covered in this lesson.

Connect to Your Life

Important Lessons Have you ever had an experience in which someone unexpected taught you an important lesson about life? Perhaps it was a person you knew well, like a sister, or a person you didn't know well but saw often, like a mail carrier. Perhaps it was someone you had never seen before. What was the lesson that you learned? Share your experience with your classmates.

Build Background

CONNECT TO CURRENT EVENTS In recent years, a growing number of children in the United States have had to take care of themselves while their parents were away at work. They have been called "latchkey" children because, every day when school gets out, they must get home on their own, let themselves into their houses, and try to stay safe. According to some estimates, there are over 12 million latchkey children in the United States today.

While parents try to prepare their children to be responsible and to know what to do in case of emergency, for many children being on their own brings loneliness and worry. In the following story Willie must stay home by himself while his mother works. As you read, think about whether this is the main cause of his unhappiness.

> **WORDS TO KNOW** **Vocabulary Preview**
> contemplated   interval   urgency
> intently   nuisance

Focus Your Reading

LITERARY ANALYSIS **DYNAMIC AND STATIC CHARACTERS**
Characters may be either of two types. **Static characters** are relatively simple characters who do not change throughout a story. **Dynamic characters** are more complex characters who undergo change as the result of events in a story's plot. As you read the story try to identify the static characters and the dynamic characters.

ACTIVE READING **DRAWING CONCLUSIONS** To understand a story, you need to **draw conclusions** about the **characters** based on information in the story and what you know from your own experience. You get to know characters from what they do, say, and think, and from what others say about them.

Mrs. Markham

Details	Conclusion
She gives Willie a glass of milk, a piece of cake she measures with her thumb, and a folded napkin every day.	She likes order and routine.
She cuts off Willie's questions about his father.	Willie's father is a painful subject for her.

📖 READER'S NOTEBOOK

As you read this story, choose a character and jot down details about him or her. Then write conclusions you can draw from the details.

LESSON RESOURCES

UNIT TWO RESOURCE BOOK, pp. 8–14

ASSESSMENT
Formal Assessment, pp. 33–34
Teacher's Guide to Assessment and Portfolio Use
Test Generator

SKILLS TRANSPARENCIES AND COPYMASTERS
Literary Analysis
• Static & Dynamic Characters, TR 2 (for Paired Activity, p. 216)
Reading and Critical Thinking
• Drawing Conclusions, TR 9 (for Thinking Through the Literature, p. 216)

Grammar
• Vivid, Precise Verbs, CM 136 (for Mini Lesson, p. 218)
• Action Verbs, CM 68–70 (for Mini Lesson, p. 211)
Vocabulary
• Context Clues: Draw on Experience, CM 35 (for Mini Lesson, p. 207)
• Analogies, CM 36 (for Mini Lesson, p. 213)

Communications
• Interviewing, TR 9 (for Mini Lesson, p. 215)
• Formal Presentations, TR 10 (for Mini Lesson, p. 215)

INTEGRATED TECHNOLOGY
Audio Library

Visit our website:
www.mcdougallittell.com

What Do Fish Have to Do with Anything?

by Avi

Every day at three o'clock Mrs. Markham waited for her son, Willie, to come out of school. They walked home together. If asked why she did it, Mrs. Markham would say, "Parents need to watch their children."

As they left the schoolyard, Mrs. Markham inevitably asked, "How was school?"

Willie would begin to talk, then stop. He was never sure his mother was listening. She seemed preoccupied with her own thoughts. She had been like that ever since his dad had abandoned them six months ago. No one knew where he'd gone. Willie had the feeling that his mother was lost too. It made him feel lonely.

One Monday afternoon, as they approached the apartment building where they lived, she suddenly tugged at him. "Don't look that way," she said.

"Where?"

"At that man over there."

Willie stole a look over his shoulder. A man, whom Willie had never seen before, was sitting on a red plastic milk crate near

Aquarium Green/Red (Two Small Scenes . . .) (1921), Paul Klee. Norton Simon Museum, Pasadena, CA, The Blue Four Galka Scheyer Collection, 1953.

 Preteaching Vocabulary   **TEKS** 6A, 9B   **TAAS** Reading Obj. 1

CONTEXT CLUES: DRAW ON EXPERIENCE

Instruction Tell students that they can draw on experiences to bring meanings to unfamiliar words in context. Call students' attention to the list of WORDS TO KNOW. Then read this model sentence aloud:

He stared *intently* at the knot, knowing how hard it would be to untie.

- Ask students how someone might stare at a knot that was hard to untie.
- Have students use this information to infer the meaning of *intently.*

Exercises Working in pairs, have students use context to infer the meaning of the underlined words:

1. Don't be a <u>nuisance</u>. Stop bothering me.
2. What was the <u>interval</u> between the alarm sounding and the fire truck arriving?
3. I knew it was a matter of some <u>urgency</u>, so I returned the call immediately.

 Use **Unit Two Resource Book** p. 11 for more exercises. Use **Vocabulary Transparencies and Copymasters,** p. 35, for additional support.

STATIC AND DYNAMIC CHARACTERS

 To help students analyze characters, including their relationships and the changes they undergo, introduce the concept of static and dynamic characters. Explain that static characters remain the same throughout a work of fiction; dynamic characters change. Ask students whether they can identify such characters at the beginning of a story. Have them give reasons.

Possible Response: No; when you first meet a character, you have no idea if that character will change.

Use **Unit Two Resource Book,** p. 10 for more practice.

Active Reading

DRAWING CONCLUSIONS

 To help students analyze characters' traits, ask why Mrs. Markham refuses to look at the man on the curb or give him anything.

Possible Responses: She doesn't want him to speak to her; she does not want to get close to him.

C From what students have read so far, have them draw conclusions about Mrs. Markham's character traits.

Possible Responses: She is rigid; she is sad; she values money.

Use **Unit Two Resource Book,** p. 9 for more practice.

A the curb. His matted, streaky gray hair hung like a ragged curtain over his dirty face. His shoes were torn. Rough hands lay upon his knees. One hand was palm up. No one seemed to pay him any mind. Willie was certain he had never seen a man so utterly alone. It was as if he were some spat-out piece of chewing gum on the pavement.

"What's the matter with him?" Willie asked his mother in a hushed voice.

Is unhappiness a sickness you can cure?

Keeping her eyes straight ahead, Mrs. Markham said, "He's sick." She pulled Willie around. "Don't stare. It's rude."

"What kind of sick?"

As Mrs. Markham searched for an answer, she began to walk faster. "He's unhappy," she said.

B "What's he doing?"

"Come on, Willie, you know perfectly well. He's begging."

"Do you think anyone gave him anything?"

"I don't know. Now, come on, don't look."

"Why don't you give him anything?"

"We have nothing to spare."

When they got home, Mrs. Markham removed a white cardboard box from the refrigerator. It contained pound cake. Using her thumb as a measure, she carefully cut a half-inch piece of cake and gave it to Willie on a clean plate. The plate lay on a plastic mat decorated with images of roses with diamondlike dewdrops. She also gave him a glass of milk and a folded napkin. She moved slowly.

Willie said, "Can I have a bigger piece of cake?"

Mrs. Markham picked up the cake box and ran a manicured pink fingernail along the nutrition information panel. "A half-inch piece is a portion, and a portion contains the following health requirements. Do you want to hear them?"

"No."

"It's on the box, so you can believe what it says. Scientists study people, then write these things. If you're smart enough you could become a scientist. Like this." Mrs. Markham tapped the box. "It pays well."

Willie ate his cake and drank the milk. When he was done he took care to wipe the crumbs off his face as well as to blot his milk mustache with the napkin. His mother liked him to be neat.

His mother said, "Now go on and do your homework. Carefully. You're in sixth grade. It's important."

Willie gathered up his books that lay on the empty third chair. At the kitchen entrance he paused and looked back at his mother. She was staring sadly at the cake box, but he didn't think she was seeing it. Her unhappiness made him think of the man on the street.

"What *kind* of unhappiness do you think he has?" he suddenly asked.

"Who's that?"

"That man."

Mrs. Markham looked puzzled.

"The begging man. The one on the street."

"Oh, could be anything," his mother said, vaguely. "A person can be unhappy for many reasons." She turned to stare out the window, as if an answer might be there.

"Is unhappiness a sickness you can cure?"

"I wish you wouldn't ask such questions."

"Why?"

After a moment she said, "Questions that have no answers shouldn't be asked."

"Can I go out?"

"Homework first."

Teaching Options

BLOCK SCHEDULING: MANAGING TIME

If your schedule requires that you cover the lesson objectives in a shorter time, use. . .
- Preparing to Read, p. 206
- Thinking Through the Literature, p. 216
- Vocabulary in Action, p. 217
- Grammar in Context, p. 218

If you would like to take advantage of longer class time, use. . .
- TE Teaching Options: Preteaching Vocabulary, p. 207; Viewing and Representing, pp. 209; Grammar, pp. 211, 218; Cross-Curricular Link, p. 212; Vocabulary strategy, p. 213; Standardized Test Practice, p. 214; Speaking and Listening, p. 215.
- Choices & Challenges and Author Activity, pp. 217-218
- Real World Link, pp. 219–222

Ada & Vincent (1967), Alex Katz. Oil on canvas, 94 1/2" x 71 1/2", © Alex Katz/ Licensed by VAGA, New York, NY/ Marlborough Gallery, NY.

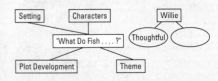

Customizing Instruction

Multiple Learning Styles
Visual Learners
Work with students to construct a web that they can fill in as they read. This will help them learn to represent text information in different ways.

Setting   Characters   Willie

"What Do Fish . . . . ?"   Thoughtful

Plot Development   Theme

Auditory Learners
Encourage students to "hear" dialogue as they read it. Have them practice by first reading a few lines aloud, using a different voice for each character. Then have them continue reading it silently.

Less Proficient Readers
To encourage students to paraphrase and summarize text, use the following questions:

• How many characters have you met so far and who are they?

• What are some of the questions that Willie asks?

Possible Responses: Three characters: Willie, his mother, and the begging man. Willie asks about the begging man and whether he can have more cake.

 Mini Lesson **Viewing and Representing** **TEKS 22A**

Ada & Vincent
by Alex Katz

ART APPRECIATION
Instruction To help students describe how an illustrator's choice of elements can help to represent or extend the text's meanings, point out that pictures, like stories, can have characters and settings. Like characters in stories, those in pictures may have certain traits and qualities. The artist can emphasize certain traits or qualities through size, placement, line, and color, among other methods. Ask what part of the face is emphasized here and which part is not.

Possible Response: The eyes are emphasized; the mouths are not; they are not even visible.

Application: Ask students to compare this picture with what they know from the text. What aspects of the story does it represent? What does it add to what they already know?

Possible Responses: It shows a boy and a woman who could be his mother; he looks worried or sad; she looks numb; the picture adds physical details, such as hair and eye color.

Reading and Analyzing

Active Reading
DRAWING CONCLUSIONS

A Ask students to draw conclusions about why Willie decided he would not get an answer and to support those conclusions with text evidence and experience.

Possible Responses: His mother told him not to ask such questions; she seldom gives satisfactory answers; people like her seldom change without a reason.

Reading Skills and Strategies:
INFER

B Why does Willie speak softly, do you think?

Possible Response: He doesn't want his mother to awaken and stop him.

C Why might Willie feel nervous?

Possible Responses: He fears the man; he knows his mother would disapprove.

Active Reading
DRAWING CONCLUSIONS

D Ask students to draw conclusions about why Willie's mother is quizzing and instructing him and to support those conclusions with text evidence and personal experience.

Possible Responses: She fears for his safety; she wants everything to be predictable.

Reading Skills and Strategies:
CONTRAST

E In what ways do Willie and his mother react differently to his father's absence?

Possible Responses: The mother hides and cries; the boy asks questions.

Teaching Options

Willie turned to go again.

1 "Money," Mrs. Markham suddenly said. "Money will cure a lot of unhappiness. That's why that man was begging. A salesman once said to me, 'Maybe you can't buy happiness, but you can rent a lot of it.' You should remember that."

"How much money do we have?"

"Not enough."

"Is that why you're unhappy?"

"Willie, do your homework."

A Willie started to ask another question, but decided he would not get an answer. He left the kitchen.

The apartment had three rooms. The walls were painted mint green. Willie walked down the hallway to his room, which was at the front of the building. By climbing up on the windowsill and pressing against the glass he could see the sidewalk five stories below. The man was still there.

It was almost five when he went to tell his mother he had finished his school assignments. He found her in her dim bedroom, sleeping. Since she had begun working the night shift at a convenience store—two weeks now—she took naps in the late afternoon.

For a while Willie stood on the threshold,[1] hoping his mother would wake up. When she didn't, he went to the front room and looked down on the street again. The begging man had not moved.

Willie returned to his mother's room.

B "I'm going out," he announced—softly.

Willie waited a decent <u>interval</u> for his mother to waken. When she did not, he made sure his keys were in his pocket. Then he left the apartment.

By standing just outside the building door, he could keep his eyes on the man. It appeared as if he had still not moved. Willie wondered

how anyone could go without moving for so long in the chill October air. Was staying still part of the man's sickness?

During the twenty minutes that Willie watched, no one who passed looked in the beggar's direction. Willie wondered if they even saw the man. Certainly no one put any money into his open hand.

A lady leading a dog by a leash went by. The dog strained in the direction of the man sitting on the crate. His tail wagged. The lady pulled the dog away. "Heel!" she commanded.

The dog—tail between his legs—scampered to the lady's side. Even so, the dog twisted around to look back at the beggar.

Willie grinned. The dog had done exactly what Willie had done when his mother told him not to stare.

Pressing deep into his pocket, Willie found a nickel. It was warm and slippery. He wondered how much happiness you could rent for a nickel.

Squeezing the nickel between his fingers, Willie walked slowly toward the man. When he came before him, he stopped, suddenly nervous. The man, who appeared to be looking at the ground, did not move his eyes. He smelled bad.

"Here." Willie stretched forward and dropped the coin into the man's open right hand.

"God bless you," the man said hoarsely as he folded his fingers over the coin. His eyes, like high beams on a car, flashed up at Willie, then dropped.

Willie waited for a moment, then went back up to his room. From his window he looked down on the street. He thought he saw the coin in the man's hand, but was not sure.

---

1. **threshold:** a doorway or entrance.

WORDS
TO
KNOW

interval (ĭn′tər-vəl) *n.* the amount of time between two events

210

After supper Mrs. Markham readied herself to go to work, then kissed Willie good night. As she did every night, she said, "If you have regular problems, call Mrs. Murphy downstairs. What's her number?"

"274-8676," Willie said.

"Extra bad problems, call Grandma."

"369-6754."

"Super special problems, you can call me."

"962-6743."

"Emergency, the police."

"911."

"Lay out your morning clothing."

"I will."

"Don't let anyone in the door."

"I won't."

"No television past nine."

"I know."

"But you can read late."

"You're the one who's going to be late," Willie reminded her.

"I'm leaving," Mrs. Markham said.

After she went, Willie stood for a long while in the hallway. The empty apartment felt like a cave that lay deep below the earth. That day in school Willie's teacher had told the class about a kind of fish that lived in caves. These fish could not see. They had no eyes. The teacher had said it was living in the dark cave that made them like that.

Willie had raised his hand and asked, "If they want to get out of the cave, can they?"

"I suppose."

"Would their eyes come back?"

"Good question," she said, but did not give an answer.

Before he went to bed, Willie took another look out the window. In the pool of light cast by the street lamp, Willie saw the man.

On Tuesday morning when Willie went to school, the man was gone. But when he came home from school with his mother, he was there again.

"*Please* don't look at him," his mother whispered with some urgency.

During his snack, Willie said, "Why shouldn't I look?"

"What are you talking about?"

"That man. On the street. Begging."

"I told you. He's sick. It's better to act as if you never saw him. When people are that way they don't wish to be looked at."

"Why not?"

Mrs. Markham pondered for a little while. "People are ashamed of being unhappy."

Willie looked thoughtfully at his mother. "Are you sure he's unhappy?"

"You don't have to ask if people are unhappy. They tell you all the time."

"How?"

"The way they look."

"Is that part of the sickness?"

"Oh, Willie, I don't know. It's just the way they are."

Willie contemplated the half-inch slice of cake his mother had just given him. A year ago his parents seemed to be perfectly happy. For Willie, the world seemed easy, full of light. Then his father lost his job. He tried to get another but could not. For long hours he sat in dark rooms. Sometimes he drank. His parents began to argue a lot. One day, his father was gone.

For two weeks his mother kept to the dark. And wept.

Willie looked at his mother. "You're unhappy," he said. "Are *you* ashamed?"

Mrs. Markham sighed and closed her eyes. "I wish you wouldn't ask that."

"Why?"

"It hurts me."

"But are you ashamed?" Willie persisted.

WORDS TO KNOW   **urgency** (ûr′jən-sē) *n.* insistence; a condition of pressing importance
contemplate (kŏn′təm-plāt′) *v.* to look at attentively and thoughtfully

211

Grammar 🚩TEKS 17C

ACTION VERBS Remind students that a verb expresses an action, states that something exists, or links the subject with a word that describes or renames it. An action verb says what the subject of a sentence does even if the action cannot be seen. Write these sentences on the board and read them aloud. Explain that each contains an action verb.
The woman *kissed* the child. She *loves* him.
Then write this sentence:
The woman *is* his mother.

Explain that the verb here is a linking verb. The verb is *is*. Ask what word the verb links to *woman*, the subject.
Answer: mother
Exercises: Ask students to complete each sentence below with an action verb. (*Possible responses are shown.*)
1. Many people ___ in cities. (*work*)
2. Willie ___ inside his apartment. (*stays*)
3. Mrs. Markham ___ her son. (*loves*)
4. That child ___ a lot. (*talks*)
5. The man and Willie ___ together. (*eat*)

📑 Use **Grammar Transparencies and Copymasters,** pp. 68–70, for additional support.

📖 Use McDougal Littell's *Language Network,* Chapter 4, for more instruction and practice in action verbs.

Reading Skills and Strategies:
CONNECT

A Ask students why the notion of not paying attention to something makes Willie think about the fish who live in caves. What is the connection?
Possible Responses: People may forget how to pay attention to what's inside if they stop doing it; like the fish, the people may become blind to what's happening.

Reading Skills and Strategies:
COMPARE AND CONTRAST

B How is the begging man's response like that of Willie's mother?
Possible Responses: She changes the subject; he doesn't want to answer.
C How is the man's response different from that of Willie's mother, and how does this affect Willie?
Possible Response: The man believes Willie, and Willie is surprised.

Literary Analysis

STATIC AND DYNAMIC CHARACTERS

D Ask students how they would describe the relationship between Willie and the man now.
Possible Responses: Willie doesn't pretend to ignore him; he talks to him every day.

He felt it was urgent that he know. So that he could do something.

She only shook her head.

Willie said, "Do you think Dad might come back?"

She hesitated before saying, "Yes, I think so."

Willie wondered if that was what she really thought.

"Do you think Dad is unhappy?" Willie asked.

"Where do you get such questions?"

"They're in my mind."

A "There's much in the mind that need not be paid attention to."

"Fish who live in caves have no eyes."

"What are you talking about?"

"My teacher said it's all that darkness. The fish forget how to see. So they lose their eyes."

"I doubt she said that."

"She did."

"Willie, you have too much imagination."

After his mother went to work, Willie gazed down onto the street. The man was there. Willie thought of going down, but he knew he was not supposed to leave the building when his mother worked at night. He decided to speak to the man the next day.

> ## Fish who live in caves have no eyes.

That afternoon—Wednesday—Willie stood before the man. "I don't have any money," Willie said. "Can I still talk to you?"

The man lifted his face. It was a dirty face with very tired eyes. He needed a shave.

"My mother," Willie began, "said you were unhappy. Is that true?"

"Could be," the man said.

"What are you unhappy about?"

The man's eyes narrowed as he studied Willie intently. He said, "How come you want to know?"

Willie shrugged.

"I think you should go home, kid."

"I am home." Willie gestured toward the apartment. "I live right here. Fifth floor. Where do you live?"

"Around."

"*Are* you unhappy?" Willie persisted.

The man ran a tongue over his lips. His Adam's apple bobbed. "A man has the right to remain silent," he said, and closed his eyes.

Willie remained standing on the pavement for a while before retreating back to his apartment. Once inside he looked down from the window. The man was still there. For a moment Willie was certain the man was looking at the apartment building and the floor where Willie lived.

The next day, Thursday—after dropping a nickel in the man's palm—Willie said, "I've never seen anyone look so unhappy as you do. So I figure you must know a lot about it."

The man took a deep breath. "Well, yeah, maybe."

Willie said, "And I need to find a cure for it."

"A *what*?"

"A cure for unhappiness."

The man pursed his cracked lips and blew a silent whistle. Then he said, "Why?"

"My mother is unhappy."

"Why's that?"

"My dad went away."

"How come?"

"I think because he was unhappy. Now my mother's unhappy too—all the time. So if I

Cross Curricular Link **Social Studies**

HOMELESSNESS The 1980s and '90s saw a rise in homelessness. Two of the factors partly responsible for the increase were a rise in poverty, especially extreme poverty, and a lack of affordable rental housing.

Not all homeless people are unemployed. In 2000, approximately one-fifth of the homeless held jobs but earned too little to cover their housing costs.

Not only have housing costs been rising, but the least expensive form of housing, single-room occupancy, has been disappearing as many cities demolish older residential hotels.

Idle Hands (1935), Will Barnett. Oil on canvas, 36" x 26". Licensed by VAGA, New York, NY.

Customizing Instruction

Less Proficient Readers

1 To help students monitor comprehension and make modifications when understanding breaks down, have them tell what has happened between the boy and the man during the past few days. If students have trouble answering, have them search for clues in the text.

Possible Response: The boy and the man began by saying little but now talk more. They talk every day.

Set a Purpose Have students read to find out what effect, if any, this relationship has on Willie and on the man.

Multiple Learning Styles

Interpersonal Learners

Ask students if the conversations between the man and the boy sound like ones that they have had themselves. What might each person be gaining from these talks?

Possible Responses: Most students will think the conversations sound real. The boy gains an audience, someone who listens to his questions and concerns; the man gains a real interaction with another person; someone treats him as if he has value.

found a cure for unhappiness, it would be a good thing, wouldn't it?"

"I suppose. Hey, you don't have anything to eat on you, do you?"

Willie shook his head, then said, "Would you like some cake?"

"What kind?"

"I don't know. Cake."

"Depends on the cake."

On Friday Willie said to the man, "I found out what kind of cake it is."

"Yeah?"

"Pound cake. But I don't know why it's called that."

"Long as it's cake it probably don't matter."

Neither spoke. Then Willie said, "In school my teacher said there are fish who live in caves and the caves are so dark the fish don't have eyes. What do you think? Do you believe that?"

"Sure."

"You do? How come?"

Mini Lesson ## Vocabulary Strategy   **TEKS 9B**   **TAAS Reading Obj. 1**

ANALOGIES

Instruction Explain to students that they can draw on experiences to bring meanings to words in analogies. Remind them that analogies ask them to think about how words are related. Show them this example:

Sleep is to *bedroom* as *cook* is to _____.

Ask students how *sleep* and *bedroom* are related. Tell them to answer with a sentence.

Possible Responses: People sleep in a bedroom; sleep takes place in a bedroom.

Instruction: Explain that the second pair of words will have the same relationship; they

could be substituted for *sleep* and *bedroom* in the sentence. Ask in what room people cook.

Answer: kitchen

Exercises Ask students to work in pairs to complete the following analogies:

1. RING : GOLD :: shoe : _____. *(leather)*
2. GOOD : BAD :: up : _____. *(down)*
3. DOG : ANIMAL :: tree : _____. *(plant)*
4. NURSE : HOSPITAL :: teacher : _____. *(school)*
5. TWIN : TWO :: triplet : _____. *(three)*

Use **Vocabulary Transparencies and Copymasters**, p. 36.

A Have students interpret what the man means when he says, "Not someone. You."

Possible Responses: Willie's ideas have value; the man trusts him.

Literary Analysis
STATIC AND DYNAMIC CHARACTERS

B Ask students why Willie is only now noticing things like the man's eye color, or the lines on his face.

Possible Response: For the first time, he is really looking at him.

Reading Skills and Strategies:
INFERRING

C Have students analyze Willie's motivation for giving the man another piece of cake.

Possible Response: He gives it because the man told him the cure for unhappiness.

D Have students analyze Mrs. Markham's reason for getting shrill.

Possible Responses: Willie has disobeyed her; she's losing control.

Literary Analysis
STATIC AND DYNAMIC CHARACTERS

E Have students look at the final paragraphs and analyze the changes that Willie has undergone.

Possible Responses: He argues with his mother; he knows how to keep from being unhappy.

A "Because you said so."

"You mean, just because someone *said* it you believe it?"

"Not someone. You."

Willie was puzzled. "But, well, maybe it *isn't* true."

The man grunted. "Hey, do you believe it?"

Willie nodded.

"Well, you're not just anyone. You got eyes. You see. You ain't no fish."

"Oh." Willie was pleased.

"What's your name?" the man asked.

"Willie."

"That's a boy's name. What's your grown-up name?"

"William."

"And that means another thing."

"What?"

"I'll take some of that cake."

Willie started. "You will?" he asked, surprised.

"Just said it, didn't I?"

Willie suddenly felt excited. It was as if the man had given him a gift. Willie wasn't sure what it was except that it was important and he was glad to have it. For a moment he just gazed at the man. He saw the lines on the man's face, the way his lips curved, the small **B** scar on the side of his chin, the shape of his eyes, which he now saw were blue.

"I'll get the cake," Willie cried and ran back to the apartment. He snatched the box from the refrigerator as well as a knife, then hurried back down to the street. "I'll cut you a piece," he said, and he opened the box.

"Hey, that don't look like a pound of cake," the man said.

Willie, alarmed, looked up.

"But like I told you, it don't matter."

Willie held his thumb against the cake to make sure the portion was the right size. With a poke of the knife he made a small mark for the proper width.

Just as he was about to cut, the man said, "Hold it!"

Willie looked up. "What?"

"What were you doing there with your thumb?"

"I was measuring the size. The right portion. A person is supposed to get only one portion."

"Where'd you learn that?"

"It says so on the box. You can see for yourself." He held out the box.

The man studied the box then handed it back to Willie. "That's just lies," he said.

"How do you know?"

"William, how can a box say how much a person needs?"

"But it does. The scientists say so. They measured, so they know. Then they put it there."

"Lies," the man repeated.

Willie began to feel that this man knew many things. "Well, then, how much should I cut?" he asked.

The man said, "You have to look at me, then at the cake, and then you're going to have to decide for yourself."

"Oh." Willie looked at the cake. The piece was about three inches wide. Willie looked up at the man. After a moment he cut the cake into two pieces, each an inch and a half wide. He gave one piece to the man and kept the other in the box.

"God bless you," the man said as he took the piece and laid it in his left hand. He began to break off pieces with his right hand and put them in his mouth one by one. Each piece was chewed thoughtfully. Willie watched him eat.

When the man was done, he licked the crumbs on his fingers.

"Now I'll give you something," the man said.

"What?" Willie said, surprised.

"The cure for unhappiness."

✓ **Assessment** **Standardized Test Practice** TEKS 10K, 12F TAAS Reading Obj. 5

ANALYZING CHARACTERS In some standardized tests, students are asked to analyze characters—including their traits, motivations, conflicts, points of view, and relationships, as well as changes they undergo—and to choose the answer that best describes the characters. Write the following question on the board or read it aloud:

The story suggests that Willie is—

A. rude

B. ashamed

C. curious

D. blind

Lead students through the process of choosing the best answer. Help them recognize that no evidence supports answers A, B, or D. However, several details, including the number of questions that he asks, suggest his curiosity. Therefore, the best answer is C.

"You know it?" Willie asked, eyes wide. The man nodded.

"What is it?"

"It's this: What a person needs is always more than they say."

"Who's *they*?" Willie asked.

The man pointed to the cake box. "The people on the box," he said.

In his mind Willie repeated what he had been told, then he gave the man the second piece of cake.

The man took it, saying, "Good man," and he ate it.

Willie grinned.

The next day was Saturday. Willie did not go to school. All morning he kept looking down from his window for the man, but it was raining and he did not appear. Willie wondered where he was, but could not imagine it.

Willie's mother woke about noon. Willie sat with her while she ate her breakfast. "I found the cure for unhappiness," he announced.

"Did you?" his mother said. She was reading a memo from the convenience store's owner.

"It's 'What a person needs is always more than they say.'"

His mother put her papers down. "That's nonsense. Where did you hear that?"

"That man."

"What man?"

"On the street. The one who was begging. You said he was unhappy. So I asked him."

"Willie, I told you I didn't want you to even look at that man."

"He's a nice man. . . ."

"How do you know?"

"I've talked to him."

"When? How much?"

Willie shrank down. "I did, that's all."

"Willie, I forbid you to talk to him. Do you understand me? Do you? Answer me!" She was shrill.

"Yes," Willie said, but he'd already decided he would talk to the man one more time. He needed to explain why he could not talk to him anymore.

On Sunday, however, the man was not there. Nor was he there on Monday.

"That man is gone," Willie said to his mother as they walked home from school.

"I saw. I'm not blind."

"Where do you think he went?"

"I couldn't care less. But you might as well know, I arranged for him to be gone."

Willie stopped short. "What do you mean?"

"I called the police. We don't need a <u>nuisance</u> like that around here. Pestering kids."

"He wasn't pestering me."

"Of course he was."

"How do you know?"

"Willie, I have eyes. I can see."

Willie glared at his mother. "No, you can't. You're a fish. You live in a cave." **3**

"Fish?" retorted Mrs. Markham. "What do fish have to do with anything? Willie, don't talk nonsense."

"My name isn't Willie. It's William. And I know how to keep from being unhappy. I do!" He was yelling now. "What a person needs is always more than they say! *Always!*"

He turned on his heel and walked back toward the school. At the corner he glanced back. His mother was following. He kept going. She kept following. ❖

Students Acquiring English

1 You may wish to point out that the idiom *Hold it* means "Wait a moment."

Gifted and Talented

2 Ask students if they agree or disagree with the statement that "What a person needs is always more than they say." Have them give reasons for their response. Instead of oral responses, you may wish to have students write personal essays on the topic.

Possible Responses: Students may say yes because many people think that they always need more than what they have. Some students may say no, because most people say what they really need.

Less Proficient Readers

3 Ask students why Mrs. Markham says she's not blind and she can see, while Willie says that she can't. Ask why Willie believes that she lives in a cave.

Possible Response: Mrs. Markham means that she literally can see things, but Willie is talking about her unwillingness to look at ideas or people that are unpleasant or challenging to her.

Mini Lesson Speaking and Listening   TEKS 1D, 2D,E, 5F

ORAL REPORT ON SAFETY

Prepare Ask students to interview a safety expert, such as a police or security officer, to gain information about safety rules that children should follow when they are alone in a home or apartment. Discuss how they can learn to listen by taking notes, organizing, and summarizing spoken ideas. Explain that each student will be expected to give an oral report on one safety tip and that students should be prepared to clarify and support spoken ideas with evidence, elaborations, and examples. Before students begin their interviews, they should meet as a group to discuss whom they might interview, what questions they might ask, and how they will record the answers.

Present Students can present their reports orally. Encourage students who are listening to monitor their own understanding of the spoken message and to seek clarification as needed.

BLOCK SCHEDULING This activity is particularly well suited for longer class periods.

Use **Communications Transparencies and Copymasters**, pp. 9–10, for additional support.

GUIDING STUDENT RESPONSE

Connect to the Literature

1. What Do You Think?
Possible Response: I felt angry because the homeless man wasn't doing any harm.

Comprehension Check:
- He's sick.
- She lives in a cave, i.e., she doesn't see important things.

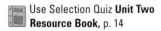 Use Selection Quiz **Unit Two Resource Book**, p. 14

Think Critically

2. Possible Response: Yes and no. She protects Willie by giving him a safe home, food, and clothing. She tries to but can't protect Willie from his curiosity about the homeless man and his parents' divorce.
3. Possible Response: The homeless man allows Willie to ask the questions he wants to, calls him by the "grown up" form of his name, and answers honestly Willie's question.
4. Possible Response: His mother is "in the dark" about many things—how much the homeless man means to Willie as well as what makes people happy or unhappy. Other references to "not seeing" include the woman who won't look at the homeless man while she is walking her dog.
5. Students may conclude that Willie is curious or rebellious. They may conclude that Mrs. Markham is upset about her husband's leaving because she doesn't want to talk about it.

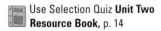 Use **Reading and Critical Thinking Transparencies**, p. 9, for additional support.

Literary Analysis

Dynamic and Static Characters Review the kinds of changes or lack of change that students observed. If no one chose to write about the homeless man, ask the students if they think he changed and point out that he changes from a silent to a speaking character.

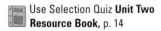 Use **Literary Analysis Transparencies**, p. 2, for additional support.

Connect to the Literature

1. What Do You Think?
How did you feel when you learned that Willie's mother had called the police about the homeless man?

Comprehension Check
- What does Willie's mother say is wrong with the homeless man?
- What does Willie say is wrong with his mother?

Think Critically

2. Willie's mother says, "Parents need to watch their children." Does she succeed in protecting Willie? Explain.

3. When the homeless man accepts Willie's offer of pound cake, Willie feels as if the man has given him a gift. What does he give Willie? Explain.

 THINK ABOUT
- Mrs. Markham's statement, "Questions that have no answers shouldn't be asked"
- the way the man who has no name calls Willie "William"
- "What a person needs is always more than they say"

4. At the end of the story Willie tells his mother, "You're a fish. You live in a cave." What does he mean? What other references to "not seeing" are in the story?

5. **ACTIVE READING** **DRAWING CONCLUSIONS** Find a classmate who took notes on the same character you did in his or her **READER'S NOTEBOOK**. Talk about how you reached your **conclusions.**

Extend Interpretations

6. **What If?** Imagine that Willie had explained to his mother how he felt about her calling the police instead of walking away from her. How would this have changed the meaning of the story for you?

7. **Connect to Life** Do you think that children sometimes have things to teach their parents? Describe a situation where this might happen.

Literary Analysis

DYNAMIC AND STATIC CHARACTERS
A **dynamic character** is one who changes as the result of events in the story. A character may think, act, even speak differently because he or she has come to understand something in a new way. Think how Willie's understanding changes over the course of the story. A **static character,** like Mrs. Markham, does not change or gain deeper understanding as the **plot** unfolds.

Paired Learning Activity Working with a partner, choose a dynamic or static character from the story and make a chart. Go back through the story together and record details that show change or lack of change in your character.

Willie		
Monday	Tuesday	Wednesday
asks mother questions about the homeless man	decides to talk to the homeless man	

REVIEW **FALLING ACTION**
The events that happen after the climax of a story are called the **falling action.** They show how the conflicts the main character has faced are resolved and the insight he or she has gained. The falling action in this story begins on Saturday as Willie waits for the homeless man to appear. What insight do you think Willie gains?

Extend Interpretations

6. **What If?** Possible Response: Willie might have helped his mother to "see" some important things about the homeless man, Willie's own relationship with his mother, and why people are unhappy. Students may have felt more positively about both characters if this had happened.

7. **Connect to Life** Responses will vary. Students might describe specific examples from their own lives.

Choices & CHALLENGES

Writing Options

Willie's Journal Suppose Willie had kept a journal to record his observations of the homeless man. How do the kinds of things Willie notices change as he gets to know the man better? How do the kinds of things Willie notices relate to his feelings about the man? Write some journal entries as you think Willie would have written them.

Monday I saw a man outside our building when I came home from school. He had dirty hair and dirty shoes. Mom told me not to talk to him because

Activities & Explorations

Debate Mrs. Markham quotes a salesman who said, "Maybe you can't buy happiness, but you can rent a lot of it." With a few classmates, form two teams and debate the truth of that statement. ~ **SPEAKING AND LISTENING**

Art Connection

Take another look at the painting on page 209. Do you think Alex Katz's *Ada & Vincent* captures the mood of "What Do Fish Have to Do with Anything?" What might the woman and boy be looking at?

Inquiry & Research

Homeless in America Go to your school or local library and do some research about homeless people or some other problem in your community. What is being done to help homeless people or others? Write up a report to present to the class.

 Real World Link Read "What a Difference a City Year Makes" on p. 219 to begin your research. Find out how young people can get involved in community service.

Vocabulary in Action

EXERCISE A: CONTEXT CLUES On your paper, fill in each blank with the Word to Know that best completes the sentence.

1. Willie waited a decent _____ before he went outside to talk to the man sitting on the sidewalk.

2. His mother tried, with some _____, to convince him to ignore the man.

3. Sometimes, Willie sat quietly for a long time and _____ the changes in his life since his father lost his job.

4. The man in the street stared _____ at Willie and wouldn't tell him anything at first.

5. Willie's mother thought the man was a _____, someone who bothered people, but Willie disagreed.

EXERCISE B Try having a partner guess each vocabulary word as you give one-word clues. You might want to include some physical action with the words.

Building Vocabulary
For an in-depth study of context clues, see p. 67.

WORDS TO KNOW	contemplated	intently	interval	nuisance	urgency

---

  Spelling TEKS 6A

HARD AND SOFT *C* AND *G*

Instruction Explain that when the letter *c* or *g* has a hard sound, it will be followed by the letter *a, o,* or *u.* Display the following examples: *code, game*

When *c* or *g* has a soft sound (pronounced like *s* and *j*), it will be followed by the letter *i, e,* or *y.* Display the following examples: *central, urgency.* A suffix that follows a soft *c* or *g* will always begin with an *i* or an *e,* such as *-ian, -ion, -ious,* or *-ence.*

Exercises For each of the following words, invite students to indicate if the *c* or *g* is soft or hard and then fill in the missing letters.

1. c_ncealed *(hard, o)*
2. trag_dy *(soft, e)*
3. innoc_nce *(soft, e)*
4. arg_ed. *(hard, u)*
5. org_nize *(hard, a)*
6. c_ntag_ous *(hard, o; soft, i)*

 Use **Unit Two Resource Book** p. 13 for more practice.

Writing Options

Willie's Journal Students' journals should exhibit an awareness of how Willie first noticed the man's dirtiness and smell, but later focused on more human details, such as eye color and voice. To get students started on this assignment, encourage them to reread the scenes in which both Willie and the man appear. After rereading each scene, they should write the entries for that scene.

Activities & Explorations

Debate Remind students that a good debate provides reasons that are supported with evidence, such as facts, anecdotes, quotations, or statistics. Provide time for preliminary research before the debate.

Use **Writing Transparencies**, p. 13, for additional support. Use **Communications Transparencies and Copymasters**, p. 3, for additional support.

Art Connection

Answers will vary.

Inquiry & Research

Homeless in America Two good sources of information are the National Coalition for the Homeless and the US Department of Health and Human Services. Students doing research online can search for the word *homeless* linked to the name of a state.

Use **Writing Transparencies**, p. 47–48, for additional support.

Vocabulary in Action

Exercise A
1. interval
2. urgency
3. contemplated
4. intently
5. nuisance

Grammar in Context: Choosing the Right Verb

Avi uses **vivid, precise verbs** to create strong and accurate descriptions.

> The dog strained in the direction of the man sitting on the crate. His tail wagged. The lady pulled the dog away. "Heel!" she commanded.
> The dog—tail between his legs—scampered to the lady's side. Even so, the dog twisted around to look back at the beggar.

Compare the same passage with overused general verbs: *The dog* pulled *in the direction of the man sitting on the crate. His tail* moved. *The lady pulled the dog away. "Heel!" she* said. *The dog—tail between his legs—*went *to the lady's side. Even so, the dog* turned *around to look back at the beggar.*

Apply to Your Writing Choosing a precise verb instead of an overused, more general one will strengthen your writing. If necessary, consult a dictionary or a thesaurus for ideas.

WRITING EXERCISE Replace the <u>overused, general verbs</u> in these sentences with vivid, precise verbs.

Example: ***Original*** Mrs. Markham <u>thought about</u> Willie's question.

Rewritten Mrs. Markham pondered Willie's question.

1. Willie <u>ran</u> toward the school.
2. He <u>put</u> his books down on his desk.
3. The man on the street <u>spoke</u> quietly.
4. From a distance, children <u>looked</u> at him.
5. Willie <u>walked</u> across the street with the pound cake.
6. The man <u>ate</u> the cake, even the crumbs.

Connect to the Literature Reread page 210. Find other examples of vivid, precise verbs. Explain your choices.

Grammar Handbook Parts of Speech, p. R54

"Ideas do not come to me whole; they are created slowly by looking at things and people and situations in terms of stories."

Avi
born 1937

School Years Avi Wortis was born in New York City and grew up in Brooklyn. His twin sister Emily gave him the name Avi when they were a year old, and that is the name he has used since. As a boy, he had trouble writing and spelling in school. He later discovered he had a learning disability called *dysgraphia* that affected his ability to write.

All Kinds of Jobs After graduating from the University of Wisconsin, Avi worked as a sign painter (sometimes making spelling mistakes), a carpenter, a theater coach, and a library clerk. He became a librarian because he loved books.

Writing and Rewriting Avi has published more than 35 novels, 2 of them Newbery Honor Books. He revises some books 40 to 50 times. He says the most important thing for a writer is to read deeply.

AUTHOR ACTIVITY

On Your Own Avi says, "Don't assume that because everyone believes a thing it is right or wrong. Reason things out for yourself. Work to get answers on your own. Understand why you believe things." Read one or more of Avi's works. Do his main characters do this? What does it take to get answers on your own?

Grammar in Context

WRITING EXERCISE
Possible Responses:

1. Willie <u>sprinted</u> toward the school.
2. He <u>slammed</u> his books down on his desk.
3. The man on the street <u>murmured</u> quietly.
4. From a distance, children <u>peeked</u> at him.
5. Willie <u>strutted</u> across the street with the pound cake.
6. The man <u>devoured</u> the cake, even the crumbs.

CONNECT TO THE LITERATURE
Possible Responses: *abandoned, approached, tugged, stole*

Avi

Avi believes that everyone has ideas; they just do different things with them. People can shape them into music, poems, or science. He shapes his into stories.

Author Activity

On Your Own You may wish to pair students with partners for this activity. Have both members of each pair read the same story and then answer the questions together. Remind them to answer the second question as well as the first.

Teaching Options

 Grammar **TEKS 9F** 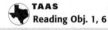 **TAAS Reading Obj. 1, 6**

VIVID, PRECISE VERBS
Instruction To help students distinguish denotative and connotative meanings of words, remind them that denotations are dictionary definitions, and connotations include the feelings associated with a word. As examples, point out the difference between *snitch* and *notify* and between *grin* and *sneer*.
Point out that when students replace general verbs with precise ones, they should consider the verbs' connotations as well as their denotations.

Exercise In the sentences below, have students replace each underlined verb with one that creates a more vivid picture. Tell them to select verbs that have positive connotations. *(Possible responses are shown.)*

1. The man <u>made</u> a birdhouse. *(constructed)*
2. A girl <u>played</u> her guitar. *(strummed)*
3. Leaves <u>moved</u> across the window. *(fluttered)*
4. An eagle <u>flew</u> overhead. *(soared)*
5. My teacher <u>mentioned</u> my report. *(praised)*

Use **Unit Two Resource Book**, p. 12.
Use **Grammar Transparencies and Copymasters**, p. 136.

 Use McDougal Littell's ***Language Network***, Chapter 19, for more instruction and practice in denotation and connotation.

① TEEN RAP

by Lauren Beckham

② The Difference a City Year Makes

W hat kind of person gets up at the break of dawn, spends all day tutoring teenagers, cleaning up former crack houses, or teaching kids to read and write—all in the name of community service?

The kind who joins City Year. Hundreds of young adults come together in Boston for CYZYGY, City Year's Annual Convention of Idealism, to show community leaders, business people and—most importantly—other young adults that community service, though difficult, is rewarding to both those who give and those who receive.

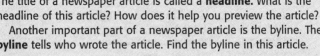

Reading for Information

Have you wondered how you could help your community? In this article you will find out how several teenagers answered that question.

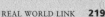 **TEXT ORGANIZERS** Newspaper articles often use **text organizers** such as headlines and photo captions to present information clearly. Skimming text organizers can help you preview an article.

YOUR TURN *Use the questions and activities below with the article to learn about text organizers.*

① "Teen Rap" is the name of a column. A **column** is a type of article that appears regularly in a newspaper and is usually written by the same writer, the columnist. What kind of topics would you infer a column called "Teen Rap" would deal with?

② The title of a newspaper article is called a **headline.** What is the headline of this article? How does it help you preview the article?

Another important part of a newspaper article is the byline. The **byline** tells who wrote the article. Find the byline in this article.

REAL WORLD LINK **219**

Real WORLD Link

Newspaper Article

Objectives
• read to be informed
• recognize the distinguishing features of genres, including informational texts
• use text organizers, including headings and graphic features, to locate and organize information
• collaborate with other writers to compose and organize various types of texts

Connecting to the Literature
The newspaper article "The Difference a City Year Makes" can help students to connect the story "What Do Fish Have to Do with Anything?" to the real world. Although the story is fiction, the plight of the homeless man and the various reactions to him are realistic. This article explains how young people in one community offer assistance to people in need, some of whom are homeless like the man in the story.

Reading for Information

Tell students that this article appeared in the *Boston Herald*, a daily newspaper. As you go through the article with students, have them use material in the right-hand column as a guide to gathering and interpreting information in the article. The following are *possible responses* to the questions.

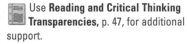 Use **Reading and Critical Thinking Transparencies,** p. 47, for additional support.

1 topics that affect teenagers
2 "The Difference a City Year Makes"; It lets the reader know that the article will be about making a difference. The byline reads "by Lauren Beckham."

City Year members participate in the Thomson Island Clean-Up.

3 Opening day for Young Heroes, City Year's program for middle school students, on Martin Luther King Day.

"Young people are coming together and giving back"

When Anthony Samuels of Dorchester graduated from Melrose High School last year, he had a specific plan.

"I was ready to give back to my community," Samuels, 19, said. "When I learned about City Year, I jumped right in."

Samuels spends his days at the Umana Barnes Middle School in East Boston, mentoring and tutoring at-risk boys in a remedial class.

"I could say that it was a challenge but that's what I needed," said the Dorchester teen. "And they needed me. I'm proud to be part of their accomplishments."

Samuels plans to attend Bunker Hill Community College next year and then pursue a bachelor's degree in child psychology. Meanwhile, he is looking forward to the CYZYGY conference.

"Hopefully in the next five years we'll have, instead of eight City Year sites, 15 to 20," he said. "CYZYGY will show Boston that young people are coming together and giving back."

"I kind of wish I had done it sooner"

Julie Xifaras' day is a little different than that of most 21-year-olds.

"I play a lot of kickball at recess," said the City Year volunteer from Marion, MA.

For the past 10 months, Xifaras has been volunteering as an education aide in the Chelsea Early Childhood Education Center with other members of Boston's City Year team.

"It's been awesome," she said. "I had never worked with kids, so I was a bit nervous at first. I have gained such an appreciation for children and in the process learned how to be a kid myself."

Xifaras took a break from her studies at Boston College last year after questioning

Members help out at the Special Olympics at the Massachusetts Institute of Technology.

She followed in her footsteps.

St. Jean and members of her City Year team run Young Heroes, a Saturday service corps for eighth graders. She also tutors Mission Pride children at the housing development's after-school program in Roxbury.

"It makes me feel real good to be with these kids," said St. Jean, 20. "Once I was in their shoes. I know what it feels like to live in the projects. I talk to them, I support them and tell them they can do anything they want to. That's what my sister told me."

St. Jean, who dropped out of high school in the 11th grade, is also working for her G.E.D. in City Year's education program.

"All we ever talk about is our diploma," she said. "Before I wasn't motivated enough. I got here and I got so much support, it makes me want to get it."

❹ "You get out of City Year what you put into it"

Attending college part-time and working full-time wasn't enough for 21-year-old Desiree Escajeda of San Jose, NM.

what she was doing with her life.

"I didn't think I was being productive. I had enjoyed BC, but I still needed to gain some focus," she said.

Xifaras suggested everybody take a year off after high school to volunteer because "it's a perfect time because you're in transition anyway."

"I've been exposed to so many different types of people and opportunities, anything from helping a kid tie a shoe to doing a presentation for corporate people," she said. "I have really grown. I kind of wish I had done it sooner."

"Every day you are helping someone"

Call it sibling rivalry.

Ludmia St. Jean of Boston was sick of listening to her older sister brag about how much fun she was having as a corps member of Boston's City Year. So she did what most sisters do.

Reading for Information *continued*

❸ Photographs often accompany informative articles in the newspaper. A photo **caption** can tell you a lot about the article to which it is attached. What information does this caption provide? How does it go with the article?

❹ Titles in boldface type within the article are called subheadings. **Subheadings** introduce the beginning of a new topic. What does the writer use as a subheading here?

3 The caption explains that City Year volunteers are preparing for Young Heroes, a program for middle school students. The photo and caption show volunteers working with school children, one important aspect of City Year.

4 "You get out of City Year what you put in it. " It introduces a section that will explain how and why volunteers participate.

5 Students might say it appeals to the emotions of the reader by telling what kids need. The quotation expresses an urgent need and seems to reach out directly to readers.

"I wasn't being challenged," she said. "I wasn't into school, I wasn't into work. I really wanted to make a difference."

She does—by working with third- through sixth-graders at the Santee Elementary School's vacation day camp in San Jose.

"I think you get out of City Year what you put into it," she said. "What I am doing turned out to be more than I ever expected. I have developed skills I never thought I could and discovered more of who I want to be."

Escajeda will attend West Valley Junior College in the fall and transfer to a four-year college within a year, which she admitted wasn't in her plans before she started volunteering.

"I feel like now I know where I want to go," she said. "I have more direction, more confidence and a better outlook on what I can do with my life."

And she's happy she was able to pass her positive attitude on to her students.

"City Year has given me a lot of opportunities to help kids," she said. "The fact that I can go into a school system and make kids feel good about themselves and their future is really amazing."

Reading for Information continued

5 Feature articles are special reports, unlike regular news stories that report the day's events. The subheadings in a feature article try to catch the readers' interest. How does this subheading catch your interest? How is it better than a one-line summary of the information contained in the section?

Inquiry & Research

Activity Link: "What Do Fish Have to Do with Anything?" p. 217. As a class, create a chart that records the different types of community service in your area. List the name of the service, such as a hospital or animal shelter, and include information about whom you should contact, what times they need help, and what type of work is involved. Use headings to present the information clearly.

Service	Contact	Times	Type of Work

5 "These kids need people to take the time to teach them"

Michael Ketcham wasn't out to change the world when he joined City Year.

The 20-year-old criminal-justice major simply wanted to work with his friend.

"I wasn't really ready for college when I graduated from high school," said the Columbia, S.C. native. "I stopped school and started a job. My friend was going to apply to City Year, so I figured we could do it together."

Ketcham works as a teacher's aide and tutor at Bradley Elementary School in Columbia.

"It's a challenge," Ketcham said. "But I really saw the difference I was making right from the start. These kids need people to take the time to teach them."

After he completes his year of service, Ketcham plans to spend the $4,725 City Year post-graduate award at Midland Technical College to continue his studies in criminal justice.

Ketcham said everyone should experience helping a child.

"When you see these kids walk away from you, knowing they learned something from you, the feeling is indescribable," he said. "One thing's for sure, I have a new respect for teachers."

Mini Lesson **Inquiry & Research** 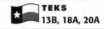 **TEKS** 13B, 18A, 20A

The Inquiry & Research activity on this page links to the Inquiry & Research activity of Choices & Challenges on page 217, following the story "What Do Fish Have to Do with Anything?"

Instruction Explain that thinking of potential headings and titles can help students find information as well as present it. Students should first identify areas that they want information about. Besides giving them ideas for possible chart headings, these areas can then suggest key words for finding information.

Practice Have students brainstorm the types of information that they want to present. This will help them focus their research. For example, if students are looking for the names of contacts at local hospitals or shelters, they might do an Internet search for *"[name of shelter]" +contact* or *"[name of shelter]" AND contact*.

PREPARING to *Read*

from Immigrant Kids
Informative Nonfiction by RUSSELL FREEDMAN

Connect to Your Life

What would it be like to move with your family to a different country?

A Nation of Immigrants The United States is called a nation of immigrants because most Americans' ancestors came from other countries.

Until the middle of the 20th century, the majority of immigrants came from Europe.

Today the majority of immigrants come not from Europe, but from Mexico, Central America, Asia, and the Caribbean.

Arrows indicate points of origin of immigrants to the United States.

Focus Your Reading

LITERARY ANALYSIS **INFORMATIVE NONFICTION**

Informative nonfiction provides factual information about real people, places, and events. Writers of informative works get their information from both primary and secondary sources. **Primary sources** are original, firsthand accounts or information. **Secondary sources** are descriptions based on primary sources.

WORDS TO KNOW **Vocabulary Preview**

| din | impoverished | teeming |
| fervent | indomitable | |

ACTIVE READING **MAIN IDEA AND DETAILS**

A **main idea** is a central idea that a writer tries to get across. It may be the central idea of an entire work or the thought expressed in the topic sentence of a paragraph. Nonfiction writers back up, or support, their main ideas with **details.** As you read, try to identify the main idea of this selection. Choose a paragraph in the selection and make a rough outline of it in your **READER'S NOTEBOOK.**

Laser Link: Background for Reading Historical Connection

LESSON RESOURCES

UNIT TWO RESOURCE BOOK, pp. 15–21

ASSESSMENT
Formal Assessment, pp. 35–36
Teacher's Guide to Assessment and Portfolio Use
Test Generator

SKILLS TRANSPARENCIES AND COPYMASTERS
Literary Analysis
• Primary and Secondary Sources, TR 14 (for Paired Activity, p. 230)

Reading and Critical Thinking
• Main Idea and Supporting Details, TR 25 (for Thinking Through the Literature, p. 230)
Grammar
• Identifying Nouns, CM 62 (for Mini Lesson, p. 226)
• Concrete and Abstract Nouns, CM 63 (for Mini Lesson, p. 232)
Vocabulary
• Denotation, CM 37 (for Mini Lesson, p. 224)
• Connotation, CM 38 (for Mini Lesson, p. 227)

Communications
• Interviewing, TR 9 (for Mini Lesson, p. 228)

INTEGRATED TECHNOLOGY
Audio Library
LaserLinks
• Historical Connection. See **Teacher's SourceBook,** p. 17.
Internet: Research Starter

Visit our website:
www.mcdougallittell.com

See the Skills Trace at the beginning of the unit for information on TEKS covered in this lesson.

Objectives
1. understand and appreciate **informative nonfiction (Literary Analysis)**
2. understand use of **primary and secondary sources (Literary Analysis)**
3. recognize **main idea and details (Active Reading)**

Summary
Russell Freedman describes the hardships that European immigrants faced while sailing to the United States between 1880 and 1920. He includes an excerpt from an autobiography by Edward Corsi, who immigrated to the United States in 1907, at age ten, and later became U.S. commissioner of immigration. Freedman explains how officials at Ellis Island interviewed and examined immigrants and how some immigrants were not allowed into the country. Angelo Pellegrini, who also immigrated to the United States as a child, recounts his family's experience at Ellis Island. Freedman points out that today, as in earlier times, immigrants must endure hardships as they seek to better their lives.

Thematic Link
At the turn of the century, many immigrants reached out to the United States for educational, social, and economic opportunities. Immigrants, in turn, have made significant contributions to the United States.

5-Minute Warm-Up

Daily Language SkillBuilder TEKS 16F, 17C

Have students **proofread** the display sentences on page 189i and write them correctly. The sentences also appear on Transparency 7 of **Grammar Transparencies and Copymasters.**

Mini Lesson **Preteaching Vocabulary**
If you would like to preteach the WORDS TO KNOW for this selection, use the Mini Lesson, p. 224.

Literary Analysis

`INFORMATIVE NONFICTION`

Remind students that much of the material that they read in newspapers and magazines is informative nonfiction. As students read the selection, have them keep a list of 5 pieces of factual information. For each fact on their list, have them identify the source of the fact as either primary or secondary.

 Use **Unit Two Resource Book**, p. 17 for more practice.

Active Reading

`MAIN IDEA AND DETAILS`

(A) Ask students to determine the main idea in the fourth paragraph. Then ask them to explain how this idea is supported with concrete details. Have students list specific details.

Possible Response: Main idea: Immigrants experienced poor living conditions on the steamship. Details: The compartments were dark and foul-smelling. There were no showers. Food was served from huge kettles into dinner pails.

 Use **Unit Two Resource Book**, p. 16 for more practice.

Reading Skills and Strategies: VISUALIZING

(B) Tell students that details can help them to visualize experiences described in the text. Ask students to think about the details Edward Corsi uses to describe arriving in America. Encourage them to close their eyes and visualize his experience.

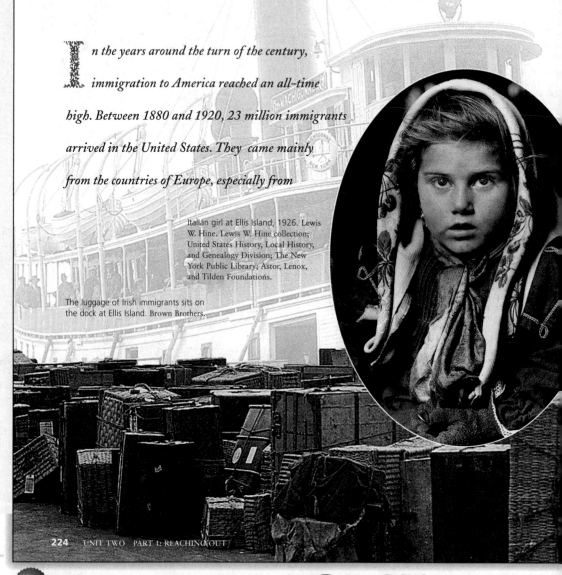

from IMMIGRANT KIDS

by Russell Freedman

*I*n the years around the turn of the century, immigration to America reached an all-time high. Between 1880 and 1920, 23 million immigrants arrived in the United States. They came mainly from the countries of Europe, especially from

Italian girl at Ellis Island, 1926. Lewis W. Hine. Lewis W. Hine collection; United States History, Local History, and Genealogy Division; The New York Public Library; Astor, Lenox, and Tilden Foundations.

The luggage of Irish immigrants sits on the dock at Ellis Island. Brown Brothers.

224   UNIT TWO   PART 1: REACHING OUT

Teaching Options

DENOTATION

Instruction Remind students that denotation refers to the literal meaning of a word. For example, the denotation of *fervent,* used in the following quotation from *Immigrant Kids,* is "having great warmth or depth of feeling": "The one thing they had in common was a *fervent* belief that in America, life would be better."

Tell students that they can figure out the denotation of a word by looking at language

Mini Lesson — Preteaching Vocabulary

TEKS 9F

TAAS Reading Obj. 1, 6

that surrounds the word in a sentence or paragraph. They can also consult a dictionary or thesaurus.

Exercise Have students give the denotations of the underlined WORDS TO KNOW.

1. They couldn't concentrate in the <u>din</u> of the crowded room. *(noisy confusion)*
2. Boats were <u>teeming</u> with immigrants. *(full)*
3. Many immigrants left <u>impoverished</u> areas in search of better lives. *(poor)*

4. The human spirit can be <u>indomitable</u> in the face of great difficulties. *(unconquerable)*

 Use **Unit Two Resource Book**, p. 18 for more practice. Use **Vocabulary Transparencies and Copymasters**, p. 37, for additional support.

impoverished towns and villages in southern and eastern Europe. The one thing they had in common was a fervent belief that in America, life would be better.

Most of these immigrants were poor. Somehow they managed to scrape together enough money to pay for their passage to America. Many immigrant families arrived penniless. Others had to make the journey in stages. Often the father came first, found work, and sent for his family later.

Immigrants usually crossed the Atlantic as steerage passengers. Reached by steep, slippery stairways, the steerage lay deep down in the hold of the ship. It was occupied by passengers paying the lowest fare.

Men, women, and children were packed into dark, foul-smelling compartments. They slept in narrow bunks stacked three high. They had no showers, no lounges, and no dining rooms. Food served from huge kettles was dished into dinner pails provided by the steamship company. Because steerage conditions were crowded and uncomfortable, passengers spent as much time as possible up on deck.

The voyage was an ordeal, but it was worth it. They were on their way to America.

The great majority of immigrants landed in New York City, at America's busiest port. They never forgot their first glimpse of the Statue of Liberty.

The voyage was an ordeal,

but it was worth it.

They were on their way to America.

Edward Corsi, who later became United States Commissioner of Immigration, was a ten-year-old Italian immigrant when he sailed into New York harbor in 1907:

> My first impressions of the New World will always remain etched in my memory, particularly that hazy October morning when I first saw Ellis Island. The steamer *Florida,* fourteen days out of Naples, filled to capacity

WORDS TO KNOW
impoverished (ĭm-pŏv′ər-ĭsht) *adj.* poor
fervent (fûr′vənt) *adj.* having or expressing great warmth or depth of feeling

225

Literary Analysis

INFORMATIVE NONFICTION

Point out the pictures that accompany this selection. Ask students where they think the pictures might have come from.

Possible Responses: They were taken by immigrants, or their families, by immigration officials, or by newspaper or magazine photographers.

Ask students to explain how pictures help their understanding of the selection and the immigrants' experiences.

Active Reading

MAIN IDEA AND DETAILS

A Ask students to explain the main idea of Freedman's first paragraph about Ellis Island. Ask them what he wants people to understand about the immigrants' experience there. As students read, they should note concrete details that support the main idea.

with 1,600 natives of Italy, had weathered one of the worst storms in our captain's memory; and glad we were, both children and grown-ups, to leave the open sea and come at last through the Narrows into the Bay.

My mother, my stepfather, my brother Giuseppe, and my two sisters, Liberta and Helvetia, all of us together, happy that we had come through the storm safely, clustered on the foredeck for fear of separation and looked with wonder on this miraculous land of our dreams.

Giuseppe and I held tightly to Stepfather's hands, while Liberta and Helvetia clung to Mother. Passengers all about us were crowding against the rail. Jabbered conversation, sharp cries, laughs and cheers—a steadily rising <u>din</u> filled the air. Mothers and fathers lifted up babies so that they too could see, off to the left, the Statue of Liberty. . . .

Finally the *Florida* veered to the left, turning northward into the Hudson River, and now the incredible buildings of lower Manhattan came very close to us.

A mother and her children arrive at Ellis Island. Brown Brothers.

WORDS TO KNOW

din (dĭn) *n.* a loud, confused mixture of noises

226

Teaching Options

 Grammar TEKS 17C  TAAS Writing Obj. 6

IDENTIFYING NOUNS

Instruction Remind students that a noun is a part of speech that names a person, place, thing, or idea.

Give the following examples of nouns:

person: child, teacher, Roberto, Grandma

place: New York, street, valley, United States

thing: car, paper, shoe, flag

idea: love, friendship, excitement, ambition

Application Help students to locate the following nouns in the highlighted passage on page 227: *anxiety, immigrants, Ellis Island, clothing.* Ask them to tell what each of these nouns names: a person, place, thing, or idea.

Answers: *anxiety,* idea; *immigrants,* persons; *Ellis Island,* place; *clothing,* thing

Invite them to find other examples of each type of noun in the rest of the selection.

 Use **Grammar Transparencies and Copymasters,** p. 62.

Use McDougal Littell's *Language Network,* Chapter 2, for more instruction and practice in identifying nouns.

Jewish war orphans arriving from eastern Europe, 1921. American Jewish Joint Distribution Committee, Inc., New York.

The officers of the ship . . . went striding up and down the decks shouting orders and directions and driving the immigrants before them. Scowling and gesturing, they pushed and pulled the passengers, herding us into separate groups as though we were animals. A few moments later we came to our dock, and the long journey was over.

Giuseppe and I held tightly to Stepfather's hands, while Liberta and Helvetia clung to Mother.

But the journey was not yet over. Before they could be admitted to the United States, immigrants had to pass through Ellis Island, which became the nation's chief immigrant processing center in 1892. There they would be questioned and examined. Those who could not pass all the exams would be detained; some would be sent back to Europe. And so their arrival in America was filled with great anxiety. Among the immigrants, Ellis Island was known as "Heartbreak Island."

When their ship docked at a Hudson River pier, the immigrants had numbered identity tags pinned to their clothing. Then they were herded onto special ferryboats that carried them to Ellis Island. Officials hurried them along, shouting "Quick! Run! Hurry!" in half a dozen languages.

Filing into an enormous inspection hall, the immigrants formed long lines separated by iron railings that made the hall look like a great maze.

Now the examinations began. First the immigrants were examined by two doctors of the United States Health Service. One doctor looked for physical and mental abnormalities. When a case aroused suspicion, the immigrant received a chalk mark on the right shoulder for further inspection: L for lameness, H for heart, X for mental defects, and so on.

A

1

2

IMMIGRANT KIDS   **227**

Customizing Instruction

Students Acquiring English

1 Help students understand that *anxiety* means "fear, distress, or worry." If the immigrants did not answer the questions satisfactorily, or if they failed the medical exams, they could have been sent back to Europe. Families could have become separated.

Less Proficient Readers

2 Ask students why doctors examined all immigrants. Have them list the chalk marks used by the doctors and tell what each represents.

Answer: They wanted immigrants to be in good physical and mental health. Chalk marks included L for lameness; H for heart; X for mental defects.

Multiple Learning Styles
Visual and Mathematical Learners

Have students locate Naples, Italy, on a map. Ask them to estimate the distance in miles from Naples to New York. Since Corsi's trip took 14 days, students can calculate how fast the ship traveled by dividing the number of miles by the number of days. They may then convert miles into knots to determine the ship's speed. (They should assume that the ship makes no stops at other ports.) Tell students that a knot is a unit of speed that is one nautical mile per hour. A nautical mile equals 1.15 statute miles.

Answer: Assume the distance to be 4,400 miles. Divide by 14 = 314 miles per day. Divide 314 by 24 = 13 miles per hour. 1 nautical mile equals 1.15 statute miles. Divide 13 by 1.15 = 11.3 knots.

 Mini Lesson Vocabulary Strategy **TEKS** 9F 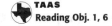**TAAS** Reading Obj. 1, 6

CONNOTATION

Instruction Remind students that connotation is a type of word meaning. While denotation refers to dictionary meaning, connotation refers to the feelings people associate with a word. For example, *slender* has a positive connotation. The word *skinny,* however, has a negative connotation. Although both words denote the same body type, each evokes a different feeling.

Exercise Revise the following sentences. Replace each underlined word with a word that has a similar denotation but either a more positive or a more negative connotation.

1. We went to the local store to hear the latest town gossip. (change to positive) *(news)*
2. That's our curious neighbor looking out the window at us. (change to negative) *(nosy)*
3. Because he is so thrifty, he always has plenty of money. (change to negative) *(cheap)*
4. His work is always perfect because he is so fussy. (change to positive) *(careful)*

Use **Vocabulary Transparencies and Copymasters**, p. 38.

A Ask students to identify the main idea of the last 2 paragraphs of the selection and to provide a supporting detail.

Possible Response: Main Idea: Immigrants continue to come to America for the same reasons as in the past. Detail: More than 8 million immigrants have come to America since the end of World War II.

Literary Analysis: PRIMARY SOURCES

Point out that Freedman could have used the writings of Corsi and Pellegrini as sources without including actual passages from the pieces. Have the students discuss the effect of Freedman's inclusion of these passages. Ask them why Freedman chose to include them.

Possible Responses: These firsthand accounts make the experience come alive for the reader. It is easier to identify with the feelings of immigrants when the reader is given the account in the words of real people who lived through the experience at Ellis Island.

The second doctor watched for contagious and infectious diseases. He looked especially for infections of the scalp and at the eyelids for symptoms of trachoma, a blinding disease. Since trachoma caused more than half of all medical detentions, this doctor was greatly feared. He stood directly in the immigrant's path. With a swift movement, he would grab the immigrant's eyelid, pull it up, and peer beneath it. If all was well, the immigrant was passed on.

Those who failed to get past both doctors had to undergo a more thorough medical exam. The others moved on to the registration clerk, who questioned them with the aid of an interpreter: What is your name? Your nationality? Your occupation? Can you read and write? Have you ever been in prison? How much money do you have with you? Where are you going?

Some immigrants were so flustered that they could not answer. They were allowed to sit and rest and try again.

About one immigrant out of every five or six was detained for additional examinations or questioning.

The writer Angelo Pellegrini has recalled his own family's detention at Ellis Island:

> We lived there for three days—Mother and we five children, the youngest of whom was three years old. Because of the rigorous physical examination that we had to submit to, particularly of the eyes, there was this terrible anxiety that one of us might be rejected. And if one of us was, what would the rest of the family do? My sister was indeed momentarily rejected; she had been so ill and had cried so much that her eyes were absolutely bloodshot, and Mother was told, "Well, we can't let her in." But fortunately, Mother was an indomitable spirit and finally made them understand that if her child had a few hours' rest and a little bite to eat she would be all right. In the end we did get through.

Most immigrants passed through Ellis Island in about one day. Carrying all their worldly possessions, they left the examination hall and waited on the dock for the ferry that would take them to Manhattan, a mile away. Some of them still faced long journeys overland before they reached their final destination. Others would head directly for the teeming immigrant neighborhoods of New York City. . . .

Immigrants still come to America. Since World War II, more than 8 million immigrants have entered the country. While this is a small number compared to the mass migrations at the turn of the century, the United States continues to admit more immigrants than any other nation.

Many of today's immigrants come from countries within the Western Hemisphere, and from Asia and Africa as well as Europe. When they reach the United States, they face many of the same problems and hardships that have always confronted newcomers. And they come here for the same reason that immigrants have always come: to seek a better life for themselves and their children. ❖

WORDS TO KNOW

indomitable (ĭn-dŏm′ĭ-tə-bəl) *adj.* unconquerable
teeming (tē′mĭng) *adj.* full of people or things **teem** *v.*

228

Teaching Options

 Mini Lesson **Speaking and Listening** **TEKS** 5B, 11B

MOCK INTERVIEWS Ask students to work in groups of four or five to conduct mock interviews with immigrants to the United States. One student should pose as the examiner, and the others should be the immigrants. Guide students to draw on their organizational and communication skills in role-playing these interviews.

Questions and answers should reflect knowledge gained in the reading of the selection. This activity will be especially helpful if students are asked to do the interview activity found on p. 231.

BLOCK SCHEDULING This activity is particularly well suited for longer class periods.

Use **Communications Transparencies and Copymasters**, p. 9, for additional support.

THE NEW COLOSSUS

by Emma Lazarus 1849–1887

Joseph Sohm/ChromoSohm Inc./Corbis.

Not like the brazen giant of Greek fame,[1]
With conquering limbs astride from land to land;
Here at our sea-washed, sunset gates shall stand
A mighty woman with a torch, whose flame
5 Is the imprisoned lightning, and her name
Mother of Exiles. From her beacon-hand
Glows world-wide welcome; her mild eyes command
The air-bridged harbor that twin cities frame.
"Keep, ancient lands, your storied pomp!"[2] cries she
10 With silent lips. "Give me your tired, your poor,
Your huddled masses yearning to breathe free,
The wretched refuse of your teeming shore.
Send these, the homeless, tempest-tost[3] to me,
I lift my lamp beside the golden door!"

---

1. **giant of Greek fame:** The original colossus was a huge Greek statue of the sun god Helios, considered to be one of the Seven Wonders of the World.
2. **storied pomp:** the splendor of your history.
3. **tempest-tost:** tossed by violent windstorms.

Customizing Instruction

Students Acquiring English
Some students might find the following words in the selection challenging.
- bunks *(n.):* narrow beds
- kettles *(n.):* metal pots
- etched *(v.):* impressed clearly
- jabbered *(adj.):* spoke unintelligibly

LITERARY LINK

Use the following questions to help students analyze and understand the poem.
1. Why does the speaker call the statue Mother of Exiles?
   Possible Response: It symbolizes immigration.
2. What is meaningful about the statue?
   Possible Response: It stands for freedom and a welcoming attitude.

Emma Lazarus

Lazarus died of cancer at the early age of 38, but her poem "The New Colossus" continues to inspire people as part of the Statue of Liberty. A Jewish-American native of New York City, Lazarus was always a good student with a strong interest in writing poetry. Her other interests included Jewish history and literature and politics.

Cross Curricular Link History

ELLIS ISLAND: THEN AND NOW Ellis Island is named after Samuel Ellis, a merchant and farmer who owned it in the 1700s. It became an immigration station in 1892 during the great wave of immigration that Freedman refers to in this selection. The station was closed in 1954 and underwent major restoration. The Ellis Island Immigration Museum containing old photographs and other exhibits is now open to the public. A wall of honor engraved with the names of more than 500,000 immigrants is also located there.

GUIDING STUDENT RESPONSE

Connect to the Literature

1. What Do You Think?

Students might comment on the difficulty of the immigrants' experiences on the ship as well as during the examinations at Ellis Island. Others might comment on the courage of the immigrants in leaving their homeland to seek a better life.

Comprehension Check

- The passengers paying the lowest fares ended up in steerage.
- Those immigrants who failed the examinations because of physical or mental abnormalities and those who had infectious diseases were not admitted.
- More than 8 million immigrants have come to the United States since World War II.

 Use Selection Quiz **Unit Two Resource Book,** p. 21.

Think Critically

2. Some students may say that the procedures at Ellis Island were most difficult because families had risked everything to come to the United States, and might have had to turn back if even one member was sick. Other students might suggest that the challenges the immigrants faced after they left Ellis Island were most difficult because they were living in a country where they did not speak the language or know the customs.

3. Some students might feel that the procedures were necessary since immigrants with diseases might infect other people. Other students might believe that Americans have a responsibility to help those who are less fortunate than themselves.

4. These lines suggest a positive and welcoming attitude toward immigrants coming to the United States at the time the poem was written.

5. Responses will vary. Students should support their opinions with concrete reasons.

 Use **Reading and Critical Thinking Transparencies,** p. 25, for additional support.

Connect to the Literature

1. What Do You Think?
What are your reactions to the immigrants' experiences?

Comprehension Check
- Which passengers traveled in the steerage part of the ship?
- Why were some immigrants not admitted into the country?
- How many immigrants have come to the United States since World War II?

Think Critically

2. Which of the hardships that the immigrants faced seem most difficult to you?

 THINK ABOUT
- the voyage across the sea
- the procedures at Ellis Island
- the challenges after leaving Ellis Island

3. Do you think all of the immigration procedures at Ellis Island were necessary? Why or why not?

4. The final lines of "The New Colossus" (page 229) are engraved on the base of the Statue of Liberty. Read this poem. What does it suggest about people's attitude toward immigrants at the time it was written?

5. **ACTIVE READING** **MAIN IDEA AND DETAILS** Look again at the outline you made in your **READER'S NOTEBOOK.** Compare your outline with a classmate's. Would you have outlined the paragraph that your classmate chose the way he or she did? Discuss your ideas with your classmate.

Extend Interpretations

6. **What If?** Imagine how the Pellegrini family felt when immigration officials said that Angelo's sister couldn't be let into the country. What decision do you think Mrs. Pellegrini would have made if the officials hadn't changed their minds?

7. **Connect to Life** Edward Corsi recorded the joy of immigrants arriving in New York Harbor: "Mothers and fathers lifted up babies so that they too could see . . . the Statue of Liberty. . . ." What does the Statue of Liberty mean to you?

Literary Analysis

INFORMATIVE NONFICTION

The type of nonfiction that provides factual information is called **informative nonfiction.** It is the type of nonfiction found in science and history books, encyclopedias, pamphlets, and many magazine and newspaper articles.

In this excerpt from *Immigrant Kids,* Russell Freedman describes how children and their parents journeyed to America at the beginning of the 20th century. He draws on **primary sources** and **secondary sources** to support his description. Among the primary sources are lively firsthand accounts from Edward Corsi and Angelo Pellegrini.

Paired Activity Think about Freedman's description of the challenges that faced children immigrating to the United States in the early 1900s. With a partner, discuss how the quotations from immigrants' own accounts added to the effectiveness of the selection. What did you learn from the primary sources that you wouldn't have learned any other way?

Literary Analysis

Informative Nonfiction Ask students whether they think the use of primary sources adds interest to the selection, and why or why not? Then ask them what they learned from the author that they could not have learned from primary sources alone.

 Use **Literary Analysis Transparencies,** p. 14, for additional support.

Extend Interpretations

6. **What If?** Recalling the fact that Ellis Island was known as "Heartbreak Island," students may suggest that the family would have been heartbroken. Mrs. Pellegrini would have returned to Italy rather than split up her family.

7. **Connect to Life** Students may feel that the Statue of Liberty represents opportunity and freedom. They may feel proud that America is a beacon of hope to millions of people around the world.

Writing Options

1. **Journal Entry** What kinds of thoughts would a long, uncomfortable voyage across the Atlantic inspire? Write a journal entry from the perspective of a young person on a ship bound for America in the early 1900s.

2. **Pro-or-Con Statement** Should anyone who wants to immigrate to the United States be allowed to do so? Write a pro-or-con statement on this question, including your reasons for answering it yes or no.

Activities & Explorations

1. **Interview** Interview someone who has immigrated to the United States. Ask questions such as the following: Why did you come to this country? Where did you come from? What were your expectations of the United States?
~ **SPEAKING AND LISTENING**

2. **Family Tree** Create a family tree showing your ancestry; or give an oral report about your ancestry, accompanied by a display of family pictures and heirlooms. ~ **ART**

Inquiry & Research

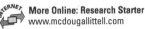

SOCIAL STUDIES
ELLIS ISLAND BEFORE

Samuel Ellis owned Ellis Island in the 18th century. Later it was named for him. Research the island's interesting past, especially how it came to be a major reception center for immigrants. Search a library for books and articles about Ellis Island, and look for helpful sites on the Internet.

 More Online: Research Starter
www.mcdougallittell.com

Vocabulary in Action

EXERCISE A: DENOTATION On your paper, match each vocabulary word in the left column with its dictionary meaning, or denotation, in the right column.

1. **din**   a. crowded
2. **fervent**   b. marked by intense emotion
3. **impoverished**   c. jumble of loud, conflicting sounds
4. **indomitable**   d. poor
5. **teeming**   e. unconquerable

EXERCISE B: CONNOTATION On your paper, write the letter of the phrase that best captures the connotation, or associated meaning, of each vocabulary word.

1. **din:** (a) steady rain falling on the roof (b) an orchestra playing loudly (c) the crowd during overtime at a basketball game, shouting encouragement for the teams

2. **fervent:** (a) the single-minded pursuit of a goal (b) the graduation of an older brother or sister (c) a lingering feeling of resentment

3. **impoverished:** (a) buying products with a credit card (b) leading a simple life with few possessions (c) lacking basic necessities of life

4. **indomitable:** (a) someone who overcomes great personal challenges through willpower (b) an especially talented athlete (c) a clever child who can talk his or her way out of any situation

5. **teeming:** (a) an overstuffed suitcase (b) thousands of tropical fish swimming around a coral reef (c) an apple tree with 20 ripe apples

Building Vocabulary
For an in-depth study of denotation and connotation, see p. 572.

 Assessment **Standardized Test Practice** TEKS 10F, K   TAAS Reading Obj. 3

MAIN IDEA AND DETAILS Some standardized tests ask students to recall information stated in a text. Pose these questions for students.

1. What were the peak years of immigration?
2. Where did most of the immigrants in these years come from?
3. What was the first step in the immigration process?
4. How often were immigrants detained for additional questioning?
5. What was most memorable as the immigrants first entered New York?

Answers
1. 1880–1920
2. Europe
3. Numbered identity tags were pinned to the immigrant's clothing.
4. 1 out of every 5 or 6
5. seeing the Statue of Liberty

Writing Options

1. **Journal Entry** A daily log of weather conditions might be included. Questions that you might use to prompt the students include: How well did the immigrant sleep and eat each day? Who is the immigrant planning to meet in America? Where will the immigrant live? How will the immigrant get an education or earn a living?

2. **Pro-or-Con Statement** Students who agree might reason that everyone should be given the same opportunities. Students who disagree might reason that some limits need to be in place since America's resources are limited.

Use **Writing Transparencies**, p. 27, for additional support.

Activities & Explorations

1. **Interview** Students can tape-record or videotape their interviews to create an oral history that can become part of a classroom exhibit. Students must explain to the subject how the material will be used.

Use **Communications Transparencies and Copymasters**, p. 9, for additional support.

2. **Family Tree** Students uncomfortable with this activity (such as foster and adopted children) can create a family crest instead. The crest should include items that represent the student's family, such as a baseball for athletic ability.

Inquiry & Research

Ellis Island Before In doing this assignment, students could be challenged to discover if any of their ancestors came through Ellis Island.

Use **Writing Transparencies**, pp. 45–48, for additional support.

Vocabulary in Action

EXERCISE A

1. c   4. e
2. b   5. a
3. d

EXERCISE B

1. c   4. a
2. a   5. b
3. c

Grammar in Context

WRITING EXERCISE
Possible Responses:

1. Many families nurtured a dream that America would be a land of promise.
2. Children and their parents showed remarkable bravery on the perilous journey.
3. The woman's courage was an example for her daughters and sons.
4. The immigrants felt tremendous joy on arriving at Ellis Island.
5. Doctors questioned the immigrants with the help of an interpreter.

CONNECT TO LITERATURE
Abstract nouns: abnormalities, suspicion, aid, detention, defects
Concrete nouns: doctors, eyelids, clerk, money, prison

Russell Freedman

Russell Freedman is one of the most highly respected writers of nonfiction for children. He has published more than 30 books, including *Lincoln: A Photobiography,* which was awarded the Newberry Medal in 1988.

Author Activity

Students may substitute a biographical work by a different author if this book is difficult to locate.

Grammar in Context: Abstract and Concrete Nouns

Russell Freedman uses both abstract and concrete nouns to describe modern-day immigrants to the United States.

> When they reach the United States, they face many of the same problems and hardships that have always confronted newcomers. And they come here for the same reason that immigrants have always come: to seek a better life for themselves and their children.

Abstract nouns name ideas, qualities, or feelings. **Concrete nouns** name persons, places, or things that can be perceived by the senses.

Apply to Your Writing While both abstract and concrete nouns are necessary, do not use an abstract noun when you can use a concrete one.

WRITING EXERCISE Provide an abstract and a concrete noun to complete each sentence.

Example: *Original* Their greatest _____ was that a family member might be rejected by one of the _____.

Rewritten Their greatest fear was that a family member might be rejected by one of the doctors.

1. Many families nurtured a _____ that _____ would be a land of promise.
2. _____ and their parents showed remarkable _____ on the perilous journey.
3. The woman's _____ was an example for her daughters and _____.
4. The immigrants felt tremendous _____ on arriving at _____.
5. Doctors questioned the _____ with the _____ of an interpreter.

Connect to the Literature Reread page 228. Find five abstract nouns and five concrete nouns.

". . . I always feel that I have a story to tell that is worth telling."

Russell Freedman
born 1929

Learning to Write Even as a young boy, Russell Freedman wanted to be a writer. His first job was as a reporter. "That's where I really learned to write," he says. "I learned to organize my thoughts, respect facts, and meet deadlines." A newspaper article about a 16-year-old blind boy who invented a Braille typewriter inspired his first book, *Teenagers Who Made History.* His career as a writer of nonfiction books had been launched.

Telling a Story In 1980, Freedman attended an exhibit featuring photos of children in 19th- and 20th-century America. He was deeply moved by the faces of the children, and he wrote *Immigrant Kids* to tell the story behind the pictures. "Like every writer," Freedman says, "a nonfiction writer is essentially a storyteller. Whatever my subject, I always feel that I have a story to tell that is worth telling."

AUTHOR ACTIVITY
Photographs Find out more about Freedman's storytelling by reading his book *Lincoln: A Photobiography.* Discuss with classmates how the many photographs in the book help Freedman to tell the story of Abraham Lincoln's life.

Teaching Options

 Mini Lesson **Grammar**  **TEKS 17C** **TAAS Writing Obj. 6**

IDENTIFYING ABSTRACT AND CONCRETE NOUNS
Instruction Remind students that concrete nouns name things you can see such as persons, places, and things. Abstract nouns name things you cannot see such as ideas, feelings, and characteristics. Examples: friend is concrete because it names a person; friendship is abstract because it names a feeling; map is concrete because it names a thing; cyberspace is abstract because it names an idea.

Exercise Write the following sentence on the board:
It was an honor for Gina to be selected editor of the newspaper at school.
Have students find the 5 nouns in the sentence. They should also identify each noun as either concrete or abstract and explain the reason for their choice.
Answers 1. honor, abstract, idea; 2. Gina, concrete, person; 3. editor, concrete, person; 4. newspaper, concrete, thing; 5. school, concrete, place.

Use **Unit Two Resource Book,** p. 18.
Use **Grammar Transparencies and Copymasters,** p. 63.

Use McDougal Littell's ***Language Network,*** Chapter 2, for more instruction and practice in abstract and concrete nouns.

Root Words and Word Families

Many of the words that you use every day belong to groups of related words called word families.

All members of a word family share the same root word.

Prefixes and suffixes can be added to the root words to form words with new meanings.

> She was staring sadly at the cake box, but he didn't think she was seeing it. Her **unhappiness** made him think of the man on the street. . . .
> "Oh, could be anything," his mother said, vaguely. "A person can be **unhappy** for many reasons."
>
> —Avi, "What Do Fish Have to Do with Anything?"

The **root word** can stand by itself.

Prefixes can be added to the **beginning** of root words and **suffixes** can be added to the **end** of root words.

Strategies for Building Vocabulary

In the example above, you can see how a single root word—*happy*—can be the source of more than one related word, or word family. Notice how the prefix and the suffix add to the root word's meaning.

❶ **Recognize Root Words** When you encounter a long word that is unfamiliar to you, see if you can recognize a root word in it. In the word *unhappiness,* for example, you probably recognized the root word *happy.* Identifying a root word can help you to figure out the meaning of a word in which other parts are added to it.

❷ **Recognize Other Word Parts** Once you have identified a root word, you can try to figure out the meanings of prefixes and suffixes attached to it. Think about how they change the root word's meaning. Look at the chart on this page to find the meanings of *un-* and *-ness.* Consider how they combine with the root word *happy* to produce the word *unhappiness,* meaning "a state of not being happy."

Root Word	Prefix or Suffix	Related Word
manage	*mis-* (wrong)	**mis**manage ("to manage badly")
	-ment (an act or state of)	manage**ment** ("an act of managing")
satisfy	*dis-* (the opposite of)	**dis**satisfy ("to do the opposite of satisfying")
	-ing (causing, engaged in)	satisfy**ing** ("causing to be satisfied")
safe	*un-* (not)	**un**safe ("not safe")
	-ly (in a certain way)	safe**ly** ("in a safe way")
perfect	*im-* (not)	**im**perfect ("not perfect")
	-ion (an act or state of)	perfect**ion** ("a state of being perfect")
build	*re-* (again)	**re**build ("to build again")
	-er (one who)	build**er** ("one who builds")
sad	*-ness* (a state of)	sad**ness** ("a state of being sad")
tolerate	*in-* (not)	**in**toler**able** ("not capable of being tolerated")
	-able (capable of being)	

EXERCISE Add prefixes and suffixes to these root words to make as many related words as you can.

1. contain   2. interpret   3. complain   4. polite   5. honor

Objectives
- apply meanings of root words in order to comprehend
- apply meanings of prefixes in order to comprehend
- apply meanings of suffixes in order to comprehend

EXERCISE
Possible Responses:
1. container, uncontainable, containment, containing
2. misinterpret, interpreter, interpreting
3. complainer, complaining, uncomplaining
4. impolite, politely
5. dishonor, honorable

Use **Unit Two Resource Book,** p. 22. Use **Vocabulary Transparencies and Copymasters,** pp. 7, 8, for additional support.

Possible Objectives

You can use this selection to achieve one or more of the following objectives:

- enjoy silent sustained reading (Option One)
- read and analyze literature with a group (Option Two)
- use the Reader's Notebook to write in response to literature (Option Three)

Summary

These two poems both explore close relationships between people. "Good Hot Dogs," by Sandra Cisneros, recalls (in English and in Spanish) a past time when two siblings or friends always ate lunch together at a store two blocks from school. The narrator describes how Kiki would always order and then both would sit down to eat. They always ate two good hot dogs, fries, and pop. The narrator would always swing her legs, while Kiki hummed. The other poem, "Scaffolding," by Seamus Heaney, is an extended metaphor, in which the scaffolding that surrounds new masonry is compared to the bridges—the human ties—between people. The speaker says that, even though the scaffolding may come apart, the solid wall behind the scaffolding remains.

GOOD HOT DOGS

by Sandra Cisneros

for Kiki

Fifty cents apiece
To eat our lunch
We'd run
Straight from school
5 Instead of home
Two blocks
Then the store
That smelled like steam
You ordered
10 Because you had the money
Two hot dogs and two pops for here
Everything on the hot dogs
Except pickle lily
Dash those hot dogs
15 Into buns and splash on
All that good stuff
Yellow mustard and onions
And french fries piled on top all
Rolled up in a piece of wax
20 Paper for us to hold hot
In our hands
Quarters on the counter
Sit down
Good hot dogs
25 We'd eat
Fast till there was nothing left
But salt and poppy seeds even
The little burnt tips
Of french fries
30 We'd eat
You humming
And me swinging my legs

234

para Kiki

BUENOS HOT DOGS

Translated from English
by Lori M. Carlson

Cincuenta centavos cada uno
Para comer nuestro lonche
Corríamos
Derecho desde la escuela
5 En vez de a casa
Dos cuadras
Después la tienda
Que olía a vapor
Tú pedías
10 Porque tenías el dinero
Dos hot dogs y dos refrescos para comer aquí
Los hot dogs con todo
Menos pepinos
Echa esos hot dogs
15 En sus panes y salpícalos
Con todas esas cosas buenas
Mostaza amarilla y cebollas
Y papas fritas amontonadas encima
Envueltos en papel de cera
20 Para llevarlos calientitos
En las manos
Monedas encima del mostrador
Siéntate
Buenos hot dogs
25 Comíamos
Rápido hasta que no quedaba nada
Menos sal y semillas de amapola hasta
Las puntitas quemadas
De las papas fritas
30 Comíamos
Tú canturreando
Y yo columpiando mis piernas

Option Three
Reader's Notebook

Provide the following direction to students before they read:

Discuss the concept of symbols, explaining that a symbol is a person, place, object, or activity that stands for something beyond itself. Symbols can often communicate many ideas quickly. In these two poems, for example, hot dogs mean more than just food, and solid walls are more than just stone structures.

Ask students as they read to think about what the symbols in each poem are and what they suggest. What words do students associate with each? What images do they visualize? Have them record notes about the symbols in their Reader's Notebooks.

After students have read both poems, have them choose the one whose symbol they find most appealing. Using their notes, have them write a sentence or two explaining why they chose the symbol that they did, and what they think the symbol suggests about the relationship between the characters.

After Reading

Possible Activities
Independent Activities

• Ask gifted and talented students to contrast the mood, or atmosphere, that each writer creates. Ask them to think about what words and phrases contribute to each mood. Have them jot down their ideas in their Reader's Notebook.

• Have students select one of the poems and then create an image that might illustrate it. Students might draw these images or create them from magazine illustrations or photographs. Encourage students to look beyond literal details to the feelings behind them.

SCAFFOLDING

Seamus Heaney

Masons when they start upon a building,
Are careful to test out the scaffolding;

Make sure that planks won't slip at busy points,
Secure all ladders, tighten bolted joints.

5 And yet all this comes down when the job's done
Showing off walls of sure and solid stone.

So if, my dear, there sometimes seem to be
Old bridges breaking between you and me

Never fear. We may let the scaffolds fall
10 Confident that we have built our wall.

236   UNIT TWO   PART 1: REACHING OUT

"I am the only daughter in a family of six sons. That explains everything."

Sandra Cisneros
born 1954

Moving Days Sandra Cisneros was born in Chicago, Illinois, and grew up as the only daughter in a family with seven children. Her father was Mexican, and her mother was Mexican American. The family moved frequently between Chicago and Mexico City. "I didn't like school because we moved so much, and I was always new and funny looking," she says.

Reading and Writing Despite her awkwardness in class, Cisneros read a great deal on her own. Reading led her to develop an interest in writing. While working for a master's degree, Cisneros began her novel *The House on Mango Street.* It is the story of Esperanza Cordero, a young girl who moves from house to house while growing up in Chicago.

Working with Youth After graduation, Cisneros completed her novel while teaching and counseling high school dropouts at Chicago's Latino Youth Alternative High School. The stories that her students told her about their lives influenced her writing. Later, she became a poet-in-residence at several schools.

Success as a Writer In 1986 Cisneros moved to San Antonio, Texas, where she currently lives. She continues to teach, and this once shy student has received numerous awards and other recognition for her writing.

"I think literature is there to open the spaces, not to erect tariff barriers."

Seamus Heaney
born 1939

Childhood Seamus Heaney's life, like his poetry, has been influenced by both the past and the present. Heaney loves the ancient Ireland of myth and legend, but he is also part of the modern Ireland of cities and factories. Born in Northern Ireland, he is the oldest of nine children. His parents owned a small farm, and his memories of working there appear in many of his poems.

Poetry When Heaney was 12, he won a scholarship to a boarding school 40 miles from home. At school he studied Latin and Irish, languages that opened new horizons for him and would later become important in his poetry. He went on to attend Queen's University in Belfast. There he met Marie Devlin, his future wife. Though Belfast was torn by the violence of civil conflict, it was during this time that Heaney began publishing poems expressing his love for his wife and memories of his boyhood.

Creativity Heaney's response to the growing violence in his native Northern Ireland was to encourage creativity and study. He began to translate ancient Irish myths. He also made translations of ancient Greek tragedies, which were performed by a theater company that he helped to found.

Recognition Today, Heaney lectures and conducts writing workshops in both Ireland and the United States. In 1995 he was awarded the Nobel Prize in literature.

Discussion Activities
- Ask students to try to visualize the speaker in each poem, the voice that talks to them. How are the speakers alike and how do they differ? How is the rhythm of their language alike and different? How is their word choice different?
- Discuss the goal of these two poets and how it differs from that of a nonfiction writer or a writer of short stories. Have students give examples of how other kinds of writers might have treated the theme of friendship. Encourage students to describe what other types of writers might do with this topic.

Assessment Opportunities
- You can assess students' comprehension by evaluating what they wrote about symbols in their Reader's Notebook.
- You can have students paraphrase each poem, either orally or in written form.
- You can have students compare and contrast the poems' themes, speakers, and form.

SANDRA CISNEROS
In her work, Cisneros makes frequent use of real details from her own life. Her family also figures in her art. She is particularly close to her brother Henry, who was nicknamed Kiki. Both he and his nickname appear often in her work. In one essay, she describes the relationship by saying, "We were co-conspirators. We were pals."

SEAMUS HEANEY
Another poet, Robert Lowell, called Heaney "the most important Irish poet since Yeats." His many and far-flung fans, called "Heaneyboppers," attest to the fact that his appeal reaches beyond the borders of his native country. The poets who influenced him include Robert Frost and William Wordsworth.

Writing Workshop
Interpretive Essay

Objectives
- write an Interpretive Essay
- use a written text as a model for writing
- revise a draft to include examples
- use verbs that agree with their subjects

Introducing the Workshop

Interpretive Essay Students may not readily recognize examples of interpretive writing. Help students to see that movie or book reviews often require the interpretation of symbols or action or character to arrive at an analysis of the film's meaning or the book's theme.

Basics in a Box

Using the Graphic The graphic emphasizes the importance of organizing the interpretive essay. Point out that the greatest portion of the interpretive essay is the evidence in support of the interpretation.

Presenting the Rubric To better understand the assignment, students can refer to the Standards for Writing a Successful Interpretive Essay. You may also want to share with them the complete rubric, which describes several levels of proficiency.

Use McDougal Littell's **Language Network,** Chapters 12–19, for more instruction on essential writing skills.

Power Presentation

To engage students visually, use **Power Presentation** 1, Interpretive Essay.

TEKS See the Skills Trace at the beginning of the unit for information on TEKS covered in this lesson.

Writing Workshop — Interpretive Essay

The meaning of a poem . . .

From Reading to Writing Some people say that reading a poem is like peeling an onion—with every layer you peel away, there is another underneath. At first, "The Pasture" by Robert Frost seems like a simple poem about chores on a farm. However, if you read it again, you may discover new meanings. Writing an **interpretive essay** means going beyond the surface to discover the deeper messages of a work. Great literature always reveals something new. Now is your chance to find it.

For Your Portfolio

WRITING PROMPT Write an essay exploring the meaning of a poem.

Purpose: To explain your interpretation
Audience: Your teacher, classmates, and anyone else familiar with the work

---

Basics in a Box

Interpretive Essay at a Glance

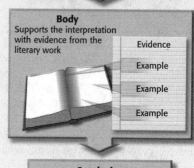

Introduction
Introduces the literary work and includes a clear thesis statement introducing the interpretation

Body
Supports the interpretation with evidence from the literary work

Evidence
Example
Example
Example

Conclusion
Summarizes the interpretation

RUBRIC STANDARDS FOR WRITING

A successful interpretive essay should
- identify the title and author of the work
- give a clearly stated interpretation of the work's message at or near the beginning of the essay
- present examples from the work to support the interpretation
- use transitions to guide the reader
- summarize the interpretation in the conclusion

LESSON RESOURCES

USING PRINT RESOURCES
Unit Two Resource Book
- Prewriting, p. 23
- Drafting, p. 24
- Peer Response, pp. 25–26
- Revising, Editing, and Proofreading, p. 27
- Student Models, pp. 28–30
- Rubric, p. 31

Writing Transparencies
- Writing Process Transparencies, TR 1–4
- Writing Structure Transparency: Elaboration, TR 13
- Writing Template Transparency: Interpretive Essay, TR 31

Grammar Transparencies and Copymasters
- Subject-Verb Agreement, CM 117 (for Mini Lesson, p. 242)

- Avoiding Ineffective Sentence Fragments, CM 61 (for Mini Lesson, p. 243)

INTEGRATED TECHNOLOGY
LaserLinks
Writing Springboards
See **Teacher's SourceBook,** p. 36, for bar codes.

Writing Coach CD-ROM
Visit our website:
www.mcdougallittell.com

Analyzing a Student Model

S P E A K I N G
See the
Communication
Handbook, p. R100,
for speaking and
presenting tips.
O P P O R T U N I T Y

Sabrina Probasco
Parkland Middle School

Interpretation of "The World Is Not a Pleasant Place to Be"

"The World Is Not a Pleasant Place to Be" by Nikki Giovanni is a poem that captures the many deep emotions of its author. Although the poem is built on the feeling of loneliness, it is actually hopeful and inspiring. Giovanni's message is that people need one another to be happy.

In the first stanza of the poem, Giovanni creates an atmosphere of loneliness. The line "the world is not a pleasant place/to be without/someone to hold and be held by" says a lot about her feelings. As I read this, I pictured the poet living in a big, empty apartment. She is alone in the world around her, and also in the world of feelings inside her. However, in the lines "without/someone to hold and be held by," she seems to be saying that there is hope. People don't need to feel this way. Each living creature can find comfort by feeling connected to others.

In the second stanza, Giovanni writes, "a river would stop/its flow if only/a stream were there/to receive it." The speaker is expressing the feeling of longing. She uses a metaphor from nature. The river is a symbol of a person with no direction or purpose in life. The river has no goals to follow or boundaries to hold it in. Without boundaries, it can flow on and on forever. In other words, a person without someone to care for, to hold, and to be held by may search forever in many different directions. I also think she is saying that the person who breaks away from his or her loved ones or tries to be free will find only loneliness. It seems to me that the thing that person is running from is the thing he or she is searching for—love and a connection to others. Like the river, the person will only stop running when another is there waiting. There is another meaning also. That is that people might stop searching so hard if they knew there was someone who was devoted to them.

The third stanza of the poem says that "an ocean would never laugh/if clouds weren't there/to kiss her tears." I think Giovanni's message here is that not only are all human beings connected but we also need each other to bring joy into our lives. Together, we can get past the pain, disappointments, and sorrows of life. Here,

---

Teaching the Lesson

Analyzing a Student Model

Interpretation of "The World Is Not a Pleasant Place to Be"
The student model is an interpretation of the poem "The World Is Not a Pleasant Place to Be" by Nikki Giovanni. The writer presents her view of the poem's message and then supports her interpretation with an analysis of the lines, metaphors, and symbols in each of the poem's four stanzas.

Have a volunteer read the model out loud, and discuss the Rubric in Action with students. Point out the key words that correspond to the elements mentioned in the Rubric in Action.

1. Ask students why it is important to include the statement of interpretation in the introduction.
   Possible Response: The statement helps to organize the essay and allows the reader to see how the details support the interpretation.
2. Ask students what the stanza-by-stanza method of organizing allows the writer to include in each paragraph.
   Possible Response: It allows the writer to include direct quotations, analysis of the lines, symbols, metaphors, and personal reactions to images.
3. Remind students that the reader of the essay may not have read the poem or have a copy available for reference. Including direct quotations gives the reader enough information about the poem to understand the interpretation and exposes the reader to the poet's style.

Mini Lesson **Viewing and Representing**

TEKS 10E, F, L   TAAS Reading Obj. 2, 3, 4

PICTURING TEXT STRUCTURE

Instruction Supporting main ideas with strong examples is important in an interpretive essay. The structure of the text or the way in which the supporting details are organized contributes to the effectiveness of the work.

Activity Have students analyze the organization of the student model by constructing a diagram or other graphic organizer. The following chart is an example.

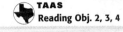

```
                    statement of interpretation
         ┌──────────────────┼──────────────────┐
  analysis of lines and   interpretation of literary devices   analysis of images
  images in stanza 1      and speaker's feelings in stanza 2   and lines in stanza 3

                    significance of poem's structure
                    importance of poem's meaning
```

4. Ask students what details the writer uses from the poem to support her interpretation.

Possible Response: The image of the ocean and clouds and the examination of the relationship that exists between them support the writer's interpretation of the stanza's meaning.

5. Have students notice that the writer shows the relevance of the theme of the poem for all readers and restates the main idea in different words. Ask students for other ways in which the writer could have ended her discussion.

Possible Response: The writer could have ended her discussion with a quote from the poet about why she wrote this poem, or an incident from the writer's life that reveals the truth of the theme she has drawn from the poem.

Guiding Student Writing

Prewriting
Choosing a Poem

If after reading the Idea Bank students have difficulty choosing a subject for their interpretive essays, suggest that they try the following:

- Find an unfamiliar poem by a familiar poet to interpret.
- Pick a subject like weather, friendship, or happiness and find as many poems as possible with that subject. Choose the one that you enjoy the most.
- Find a humorous poem and show the deeper meaning beneath the humor.

---

once again, the cycle of life is shown. The ocean is connected to the sky just as we are connected to each other. Ocean water evaporates into the clouds, which give off rain, filling the ocean again. I think the message here is that what we give comes back to us. All things come full circle.

The poem's final stanza, "the world is not/a pleasant place to be without/someone" repeats the first stanza. This gives the poem a feeling of completion. Once more, Giovanni presents her view of life. While many writers and poets try to entertain, Giovanni inspires us with her words. In my opinion, both the young and old will be able to relate to this poem. It is a short poem with a very big point: that all people are connected and need each other to be happy.

> ❹ Offers a clear statement of writer's interpretation of the meaning of the poem

> ❺ Conclusion summarizes and expands upon the writer's interpretation.

Writing Your Interpretive Essay

❶ Prewriting

> *To read a poem is to hear with our eyes; to hear it is to see it with our ears.*
>
> —Octavio Paz, poet

Go back to the poems in this unit and **read** each one aloud. Which sparked an idea or reminded you of something? Which has the most interesting sound devices or imagery? Also **list** the poems with unusual structures, powerful themes, or confusing lines. See the **Idea Bank** in the margin for more ideas. After you select a poem, follow the steps on the next page.

❷ Drafting

Now it is time to put your thoughts down on paper. Include all of the observations and examples you gathered that help make the poem effective. You can eliminate less important details later. For help, try filling in the blanks:

The main message of (name of poem) by (name of author) is _____.

Organize Your Essay. Use your **introductory** paragraph to identify the poem and the author and to briefly state your interpretation. For the **body** of your essay, decide which idea you want to present first. Then use examples to support your main points. **Conclude** with a summary of the meaning of the poem.

Ask Your Peer Reader

• What is my main point about the author's message or theme(s)?
• What examples best support my point?
• What do you disagree with or want to know more about?
• How could my conclusion be strengthened?

Planning Your Interpretive Essay

1. Have students take turns reading their poems to each other, or suggest that each student record his or her poem on audiotape and play it back, pausing often to reflect on the meaning.
2. Encourage students to focus on one element of the poem at a time. Have them write down the type of device or figurative language as well as the actual example of the device from the text.
3. Remind students to defend their reactions and views by citing evidence from the text.
4. Caution students against ignoring details to make their interpretation fit.

Drafting

Organize Your Essay Remind students that they might organize their analysis into a discussion either of the stanzas or of the poetic elements. If students find it difficult to include all details in their organizational structure, they may need to choose another method.

Ask Your Peer Reader
Remind students to use the peer reviewer's feedback when revising their drafts.

Revising

SUPPORTING YOUR RESPONSE WITH EXAMPLES

Discuss how the explanation of the metaphor adds to the effectiveness of the writer's point. To help students practice inserting examples, ask them to read paragraphs of their drafts to a partner and have the partner point out where examples should be included.

Editing and Proofreading

SUBJECT-VERB AGREEMENT

Remind students that in writing about literature, they use the present tense. Therefore, it is particularly important that they check for subject-verb agreement. Have students explain the changes in the sample. For more practice, see the Grammar Mini Lesson at the bottom of the page.

Reflecting

 Encourage students to analyze how writing an interpretive essay made them more aware of how the parts of a poem contribute to its meaning.

Option

Teaching Tip

Ask students to hand in a preliminary outline that shows how they are going to organize their essay and what will be included in each paragraph. Your quick review of these outlines will help eliminate organizational problems and lack of supporting details in the actual essay.

Need revising help?

Review the **Rubric,** p. 238.

Consider **peer reader** comments.

Check **Revision Guidelines,** p. R23.

Confused about complete sentences?

See the **Grammar Handbook,** p. R59.

SPELLING From Writing

As you revise your work, look back at the words you misspelled and determine why you made the errors you did. For additional help, refer to the strategies and generalizations in the **Spelling Handbook** on page R86.

Publishing IDEAS

• Create a poetry Web site and publish your interpretation as well as those of your classmates.

• Work with classmates who interpreted the same poem to prepare a lesson for the class.

More Online: Publishing Options www.mcdougallittell.com

---

❸ Revising

TARGET SKILL ▶ SUPPORTING YOUR RESPONSE WITH EXAMPLES In your interpretation, it is not enough to simply state your point. You must tell your reader how you reached that point. You can do this by supporting your point with direct quotes and other examples from the text itself. To help your readers understand, you might need to explain your thought process.

> The speaker is expressing the feeling of longing. She uses a metaphor from nature. *The river is a symbol of a person with no direction or purpose in life. The river has no goals to follow or boundaries to hold it in.*

❹ Editing and Proofreading

TARGET SKILL ▶ SUBJECT-VERB AGREEMENT Verbs should always agree with their subjects in number. A singular subject takes a singular verb. A plural subject takes a plural verb.

> The speaker ~~are~~ *is* expressing the feeling of longing. She use*s* a metaphor from nature. The river ~~are~~ *is* a symbol of a person with no direction or purpose in life. The river ~~have~~ *has* no goals to follow or boundaries to hold it in.

❺ Reflecting

FOR YOUR WORKING PORTFOLIO What did you learn about the poem as a result of writing this interpretation? Which step of the process gave you the most difficulty? What will you do differently the next time you write an interpretation? Attach your answers to your finished essay. Save your **interpretive essay** in your **Working Portfolio.**

Mini Lesson **Grammar** **TEKS 17C** **TAAS Writing Obj. 6**

SUBJECT-VERB AGREEMENT

For use with Editing and Proofreading, p. 242

Instructions Point out that compound subjects joined by *and* generally take a plural verb. However, when the parts of a compound subject are joined by *or* or *nor*, the verb agrees with the part of the subject nearer the verb. Remind students that they must also watch for interrupting phrases between the subject and verb. These phrases do not affect the choice of verb.

Exercises Have students determine whether the verb in each of these sentences agrees with the subject. Students should suggest corrections for those sentences that are wrong.

1. Henri, in addition to his friends, enjoy surfing. (*enjoys*)
2. Neither the teachers nor the principal was sure of the date. (*correct*)
3. Cats and dogs makes good pets. (*make*)
4. The trees behind the fence was scheduled to be cut down. (*were scheduled*)

5. The child and her parents walk to the park each day. (*correct*)

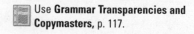 Use **Grammar Transparencies and Copymasters**, p. 117.

 Use McDougal Littell's *Language Network*, Chapter 9, for more instruction and practice in subject-verb agreement.

Read this passage from the first draft of a poem interpretation. The underlined sections may include the following kinds of errors:

- **subject-verb agreement**
- **sentence fragments**
- **spelling errors**
- **run-on sentences**

For each underlined section, choose the revision that most improves the writing.

"The Pasture" by Robert Frost is a poem <u>rich in imagery and meaning and the poet uses</u> sound devices and symbols to get across his
(1)
theme. The first task of the speaker <u>are to clear the spring,</u> and he
invites the listener to join him. He says, "I'll only stop to rake the leaves
(2)
away/(And wait to watch the water clear, I may)." <u>The symbol of water is
introduced in these lines, water</u> represents life. It is necessary for
(3)
existence. Later in the poem, <u>the young calf, to,</u> becomes a symbol of
(4)   (5)
rebirth. <u>Both symbols reinforces</u> the importance of nature.
(6)

---

1. A. rich in imagery and meaning, and the poet uses

    B. rich in imagery and meaning; and the poet uses

    C. rich in imagery and meaning. The poet uses

    D. Correct as is

2. A. were to clear the spring,

    B. is to clear the spring,

    C. are being to clear the spring,

    D. Correct as is

3. A. The symbol of water is introduced in these lines water

    B. The symbol of water is introduced in these lines. Water

    C. The symbol of water is introduced in these lines; and water

    D. Correct as is

4. A. existanse

    B. existense

    C. existince

    D. Correct as is

5. A. the young calf, too,

    B. the young calf, two,

    C. the young calf, tow,

    D. Correct as is

6. A. Both symbols reinforce

    B. Both symbols reinforcing

    C. Both symbols has reinforced

    D. Correct as is

Demonstrate how students can eliminate incorrect choices for the first question.

A. This choice is a compound sentence that incorrectly uses the conjunction *and*. *And* should not be used to connect two unrelated thoughts.

B. This choice incorrectly uses a semicolon with a conjunction.

C. This choice is correct because the run-on sentence needs to be two, separate, complete sentences.

D. This choice is incorrect because it is a run-on sentence.

Answers:
1. C; 2. B; 3. B; 4. D; 5. A; 6. A

Need extra help?

See the **Grammar Handbook**
Quick Reference:
Capitalization, p. R58

Quick Reference:
Punctuation, p. R56

Subject-Verb
Agreement, p. R60

WRITING WORKSHOP **243**

 Mini Lesson **Grammar** **TEKS 17C** **TAAS Writing Obj. 6**

AVOIDING INEFFECTIVE SENTENCE FRAGMENTS

Instruction Point out that leaving out the subject or leaving out the verb in a sentence can lead to a sentence fragment. Sometimes, both the subject and verb are missing. Students must read their sentences to make sure that they express complete ideas.

Practice Have students identify what is missing in each of the following fragments and suggest ways to rewrite it as a complete sentence. *(Answers will vary.)*

1. Rushed into the room and tripped over
2. We enjoying the writing activity
3. At the end of the class period
4. Rollerskating, running, and laughing the whole time
5. The dance before Thanksgiving vacation
6. After the disappointment of the loss
7. Growled and wrestled with each other in the middle of the carpet
8. The waiter with the towel over his arm and the spotless uniform
9. Asked us several questions about summer vacation
10. Jack and his twin sister Jodi

 Use **Grammar Transparencies and Copymasters**, p. 61.

 Use McDougal Littell's *Language Network*, Chapter 1, for more instruction and practice in correcting sentence fragments.

Reflecting on the Theme Some choices in a person's life are easy and not very important. Others are more difficult and involve risks. Some can even change the course of a person's life. As you read the selections, think about the obstacles and choices that the characters face. Picture yourself having to make similar choices and imagine how you would go about it. What do your choices say about you?

ACTIVITY

In newspapers or magazines, find articles about people facing difficult choices. Then, in a small group, take the roles of these people. Imagine you are on a TV talk show and discuss people who have made difficult choices. Afterwards, list the personal traits that all the guests have in common.

Shared Personal Traits
1.
2.
3.

Drama

All the world's a stage,
And all the men and women merely players . . .
—Shakespeare, As You Like It.

William Shakespeare was one of the great dramatists of all time. His scenes depict real-life struggles, sometimes through comedy and other times through tragedy. Although he lived and wrote 400 years ago, people are still performing and attending his plays. His work is proof that good drama is timeless.

A **drama** is a story that is intended to be performed for an audience, either on stage or before a camera. For this reason, dramas are written in a special form called a **script,** in which lines are written out for the characters to speak. You see drama on television, in movies, in videos, and on stage. Use the following passages to learn more about the elements of drama.

Key Elements of Drama
- stage direction
- plot
- characters
- dialogue

LEARNING THE LANGUAGE OF LITERATURE   **245**

Objectives
- understand and identify the following literary terms:
  - drama
  - script
  - exposition
  - conflict
  - rising action
  - stage directions
  - scenery
  - props
  - plot
  - climax
  - falling action
  - scenes
  - acts
  - main and minor characters
  - narrator
  - foils
  - dialogue
  - stage
  - theater
- understand and appreciate drama
- appreciate a writer's craft

Teaching the Lesson

This lesson introduces students to the terminology of drama and analyzes its key elements.

Introducing the Concepts
Ask students to discuss plays or musicals they may have seen or participated in on stage. Have them talk about how their experience was different from watching a movie or television program and how it felt to be a member of the audience or a member of the cast.

Use **Literary Analysis Transparencies,** pp. 2, 3, 5, 23, 24, for additional support.

 See the Skills Trace at the beginning of the unit for information
TEKS on TEKS covered in this lesson.

Presenting the Concepts

Stage Directions
Using the chart shown on this page, ask students to describe how they would arrange the scenery, props, and characters for a large party scene in a play. Have them describe what scenery they would use and what kinds of props they would need.

YOUR TURN
Possible Responses: a drum for the percussion, fake snowflakes, coal, a small bucket, a street scene with doorways and lampposts, an office scene with a desk and chair, coins

Stage Direction

A play's script includes instructions for the director, the actors, and the stage crew. These are called **stage directions.** They are often printed in italic type and enclosed in parentheses. In addition to telling the actors how to speak and move, the stage directions describe the **scenery**—the items that are on stage to help create the setting. Stage directions also describe the **props**, which are the objects the actors use during the play. Many scripts also include suggestions for lighting and sound.

YOUR TURN What scenery and props would be necessary to create the setting for this scene in the play *A Christmas Carol*, which is based on Charles Dickens's story?

STAGE DIRECTION

(The percussion thunders. Scrooge hurls himself through the descending snowflakes and sends the children scattering. They retreat, watching. Cratchit comes in. He takes some coal from the mound and puts it into a small bucket; as he carries it to a corner of the stage, the stage area is transformed from street to office. Scrooge's nephew Fred enters, talks with the children, gives them coins, and sends them away with a "Merry Christmas.")

—Charles Dickens, *A Christmas Carol*,
Dramatization by Frederick Gaines

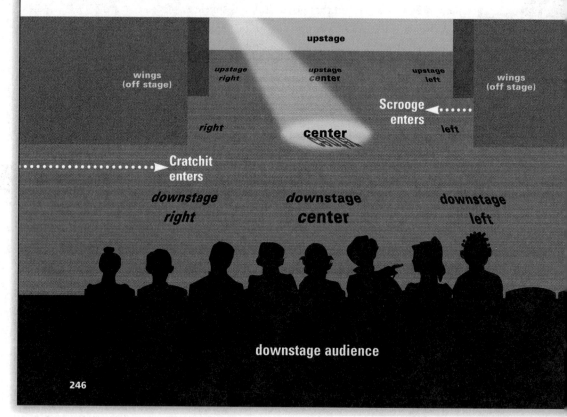

Plot

As in fiction, the **plot** of a drama is the sequence of related events that happen in the work. The plot begins with an **exposition,** which introduces the characters and setting and presents any necessary background. A **conflict,** or **complication,** starts the **rising action,** in which dramatic tension builds. The moment of highest tension is called the **climax.** After the climax comes the **falling action** (also called the **resolution**), in which all the loose ends of the plot are tied up. In drama, the action is often divided into **scenes.** The scene changes whenever the setting (the time and the place) changes. Sometimes two or more scenes are grouped into **acts.** (For more on plot, see pages 343–346)

Character

In a play the **main** and **minor characters** are often listed in the cast of characters at the beginning of the script. This list often includes a short description next to each character's name.

Occasionally one of the characters is a **narrator,** who sets the scene for the drama and may comment on what happens. Some characters, acting as **foils,** provide a sharp contrast to the qualities of the main characters. For instance, if the main character is lighthearted, the foil character might be serious.

YOUR TURN Read the dialogue between Scrooge and his nephew Fred in the beginning of Scene 1 of *A Christmas Carol.* How is Fred a foil for Scrooge?

From *A Christmas Carol*

> ### CHARACTER
>
> **Fred.** A Merry Christmas, Uncle! God save you!
>
> **Scrooge.** Bah! Humbug!
>
> **Fred.** Christmas a humbug, Uncle? I hope that's meant as a joke.
>
> **Scrooge.** Well, it's not. Come, come, what is it you want? Don't waste all the day, Nephew.
>
> **Fred.** I only want to wish you a Merry Christmas, Uncle. Don't be cross.
>
> **Scrooge.** What else can I be when I live in such a world of fools as this? Merry Christmas! Out with Merry Christmas!
>
> —Charles Dickens, *A Christmas Carol,* Dramatization by Frederick Gaines

Plot
Remind students that the plot of a play contains the same elements as the plot of a short story or novel. In a play, however, the divisions are usually scenes and acts rather than chapters.

Character
Ask students to think of the list of characters they would include if they wrote a play about their activities on an ordinary summer day. If they made themselves the main character, what qualities would they want to highlight? How would they use other characters to help highlight these qualities?

YOUR TURN
Possible Response: Fred's cheerfulness and holiday spirit provide a contrast to Scrooge's bad temper and lack of Christmas spirit, which makes Scrooge's characteristics seem more exaggerated.

Dialogue

Divide students into pairs. Have each pair create and write a dialogue, with stage directions, about the mysterious disappearance of the school's championship trophy from the display case. Ask volunteers to perform their dialogue for the rest of the class.

YOUR TURN

Possible Response: The hesitations and pauses in the play's dialogue help convey the message that the characters don't really believe what they are saying. The playwright's stage directions cue the actors to adjust the tone of their voices and their movements so that their nervousness and fake optimism is obvious to the audience.

Dialogue

A play is composed almost entirely **dialogue**, that is, conversation between the characters. Both the plot of the play and the characters' personalities are revealed through the dialogue. In the script, the dialogue appears in lines next to the characters' names.

YOUR TURN How does the playwright use dialogue and stage directions to reveal character and guide the actors in this excerpt from *The Monsters Are Due on Maple Street?*

From *The Monsters Are Due on Maple Street*

DIALOGUE

Steve. Go ahead, Tommy. We'll be right back. And you'll see. That wasn't any ship or anything like it. That was just a . . . meteor or something. Likely as not — (*He turns to the group, now t... ing very hard to sound more optimistic than . feels.*) No doubt it did have something to do wi... all this power failure and the rest of it. Meteors can do some crazy things. Like sunspots.

Don. (*picking up the cue*) Sure. That's the kin... of thing—like sunspots. They raise Cain with radio reception all over the world. And this thing being so close—why there's no telling the sort of stuff it can do. (*He wets his lips and smiles nervously.*) Go ahead, Charlie. You and Steve go into town and see if that isn't what's causing it all.

—Rod Serling
The Monsters Are Due on Maple Stree...

You can bring a drama to life just by reading the script—if you know how to visualize. Interesting **characters** and **dialogue**, powerful **themes**, **plots**, and detailed **stage directions** can all work together to produce an exciting dramatic story. To get the most from every play, follow the reading strategies suggested here.

$\mathcal{R}$eading Drama

How to Apply the Strategies

Read the play silently. Before you read the play aloud with others, read it to yourself. You should understand the entire plot and the characters before you perform.

Read the stage directions carefully. Stage directions tell you where and when each scene is happening. If you skip over them, you miss out on much of the play. Don't worry if you don't understand everything right away. You may have to reread the play a few times to figure out what is happening.

Get to know the characters. In drama, you get to know the characters through dialogue—the characters' own words. You can also **visualize** the characters as you read, picturing the set and props as the characters are moving about, speaking their lines.

Keep track of the plot. As in fiction, the plot of a drama centers on a main conflict that the characters try to resolve. Look for the conflict and let yourself become involved in the story. Watch for the action to build to a climax and then evaluate how that conflict is resolved.

Read the play aloud with others. When drama is performed, it becomes almost like real life. As you read the part of a character, you become an actor. Be ready with your character's lines and read only the words your character says. Do not read the stage directions aloud. You may enjoy playing someone totally different than you.

Here's how Steve uses the strategies:

*"I love being in plays. When I'm reading a script, I read all the stage directions and **visualize** how a character looks and acts. Sometimes I write down phrases that describe how my character might feel when he says his lines. I enjoy playing the part of someone who is different than me."*

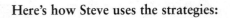

Need More Help?

Remember that active readers use the essential reading strategies explained on page 4: • **visualize** • **predict** • **clarify** • **question** • **connect** • **evaluate** • **monitor.**

THE ACTIVE READER **249**

Objectives
- notice the different elements that bring a drama to life
- understand how plot and character work in a drama

Teaching the Lesson

The strategies on this page will help students to appreciate the reading of drama.

Presenting the Strategies
To introduce the strategies, use as a model a play from the book or any play known by the students.

Read the Play Silently
Remind students that they can read the play as if it were a work of fiction.

Read the Stage Directions Carefully
Tell students that because the work is drama and not fiction, stage directions are often key to understanding a silent reading of a play. A drama is based on dialogue, so stage directions explain what characters are doing as they speak. The stage directions fill in the blanks where description would be in a work of fiction.

Get to Know the Characters
Tell students that dialogue is key to understanding characters. They should pay attention not only to what is being said, but how and when it is being said.

Keep Track of the Plot
Tell students that as they read, they might take notes about conflict. They should evaluate how characters respond in conflict.

Read the Play Aloud with Others
Drama is meant to be performed. Read the play aloud with a group of students to get the most from a dramatic work.

Objectives
1. understand and appreciate a **drama** (Literary Analysis)
2. understand and interpret **stage directions** (Literary Analysis)
3. practice **visualizing stage directions** (Active Reading)

Summary
It is Christmas Eve, but Bob Cratchit, an underpaid clerk, knows better than to expect any kindness from his employer, the mean and stingy Ebenezer Scrooge. That night, Scrooge is visited by four spirits: the ghost of Jacob Marley, his dead business partner; the Spirit of Christmas Past; the Spirit of Christmas Present; and the Spirit of Christmas Yet to Come. They show him the value of charity. They also reveal to him that Bob Cratchit's frail young son, Tiny Tim, will not live long without help. It becomes clear to Scrooge from what he sees with the Spirit of Christmas Yet to Come that if he does not change his ways, people will not be sorry when he dies. Scrooge awakens after the visits of the spirits to find it is Christmas morning. He changes his ways and provides a merry Christmas for the Cratchits and everyone else, including himself.

Thematic Link
Scrooge faces two choices, either to change and redeem his life or to continue in his stingy ways and live out his life miserably. When he chooses to embrace the Christmas spirit, he regains his humanity and realizes that real joy comes from doing good things for others.

5-Minute Warm-Up

Daily Language SkillBuilder

Have students **proofread** the display sentences on page 189j and write them correctly. The sentences also appear on Transparency 8 of **Grammar Transparencies and Copymasters.**

A Christmas Carol
Novel by CHARLES DICKENS
Dramatization by FREDERICK GAINES

"I only know one thing on Christmas: that one must be charitable."

(**Connect to Your Life**)

How people lead their lives depends partly on the choices they make. In a small group, discuss people you know and characters you've read about in this book. How do their choices affect them? How do their choices affect the people around them? Do any of their choices change their attitudes and behavior? Why or why not?

Build Background

CONNECT TO **HISTORY** Charles Dickens chose to write novels that criticized the attitudes of the greedy and exposed the abuses suffered by the poor. When he published *A Christmas Carol* in 1843, about one-third of the people in London, England, lived in poverty.

Factories had changed the face of London, with people flooding the city from rural areas. The city quickly became dirty and overcrowded. Wages were low and children were hungry. Jobs and housing were in short supply. The Poor Law of 1834 forced the homeless into workhouses that were little more than prisons for the poor and homeless.

By exposing the suffering of the poor in a vivid and sympathetic manner, Dickens convinced many readers that conditions had to be corrected.

WORDS TO KNOW **Vocabulary Preview**

abundance	emerge	mortal	solitude
anonymous	endeavor	odious	summon
charitable	finale	pledge	surplus
currency	incoherent	provision	transform
destitute	macabre	reassurance	welfare

LaserLink: Background for Reading
Historical Connection

Focus Your Reading

LITERARY ANALYSIS **STAGE DIRECTIONS** In adaptin Dickens's novel into a play, Frederick Gaines chose to depict some of the poor people and conditions of London in his stage directions. **Stage directions** are notes in the scripts of plays. These directions are frequently in italics, and guide actors and readers by explaining the settings of scenes, the movements of actors, the tones of voice of the dialogue, and the sound effects. When you read a play, don't skip the stage directions. They give you information that you won't get any other way.

ACTIVE READING **VISUALIZING** When you read the script of a play rather than see the play performed on a stage, use the stage directions to help you **visualize** the play's **setting, characters,** and **action.** Try to imagine what you would see if you were watching the play performed on a stage.

READER'S NOTEBOOK As you read the stage directions in this play, pause to visualize the scenes that are being described. Draw or sketch the scenes. Try to position the characters in the correct places on the stage.

TEKS See the Skills Trace at the beginning of the unit for information on TEKS covered in this lesson.

LESSON RESOURCES

UNIT TWO RESOURCE BOOK, pp. 32–38

ASSESSMENT
Formal Assessment, pp. 39–40
Teacher's Guide to Assessment and Portfolio Use
Test Generator

SKILLS TRANSPARENCIES AND COPYMASTERS
Literary Analysis
• Drama: Stage Directions, TR 23 (for Activity, p. 275)
Reading and Critical Thinking
• Visualizing, TR 10 (for Thinking Through the Literature, p. 275)

Grammar
• Action Verbs in Effective Writing, CM 70 (for Mini Lesson, p. 277)
• Run-on Sentences, CM 59 (for Mini Lesson, pp. 256–257)
Vocabulary
• Synonyms/Antonyms, CM 39 (for Mini Lesson, p. 251)
• Analyzing Word Parts, CM 40 (for Mini Lesson, pp. 262–263)
Writing
• Staging a Scene, TR 38 (for Mini Lesson, pp. 272–273)

Communications
• Dramatic Reading, TR 12 (for Mini Lessons, p. 260, pp. 272–273)
• Evaluation Matrix: Film/Video TR 7; Storyboard Templates, TR 37, TR 38 (for Mini Lesson p. 266)

INTEGRATED TECHNOLOGY
Audio Library
LaserLinks
• Historical Connection; Author Background. See **Teacher's SourceBook,** p. 18.

Visit our website:
www.mcdougallittell.com

A Christmas Carol

by Charles Dickens

Dramatized by Frederick Gaines

A CHRISTMAS CAROL **251**

Reading and Analyzing

Reading Skills and Strategies: PREVIEW

Discuss with students what they already know about *A Christmas Carol*. Have them look over the cast of characters and skim the play, noting the stage directions preceding some of the scenes. Direct their attention to the illustrations. Ask them to read to find out which experiences affect Scrooge the most.

Literary Analysis   `STAGE DIRECTIONS`

A Remind students that the stage directions not only give information about setting and sound effects, but also help to reveal characters' feelings and traits through their gestures, tone of voice, and other characters' reactions to them. Ask students what first impression of Scrooge is created by his description in the stage directions.
Possible Responses: He is in a hurry and has no time for children; he frightens children.
B Ask students how his nephew's character appears in contrast to Scrooge's.
Possible Responses: His nephew is kind and generous.

 Use **Unit Two Resource Book**, p. 34 for more practice.

Active Reading   `VISUALIZING`

Ask students to describe the mental images most vividly evoked by the stage directions.
Possible Responses: glowing coals against a dark night; driving snow; sound of Christmas carols in the background; groups of people walking up and down the streets.

 Use **Unit Two Resource Book**, p. 33 for more practice.

Characters

Carolers, Families, Dancers	Jacob Marley	Second Spirit (*the Spirit of Christmas Present*)
First Boy	Priest	
Second Boy	Leper	Poorhouse Children
Third Boy	First Spirit (*the Spirit of Christmas Past*)	Mrs. Cratchit
Girl with a doll		Several Cratchit Children
Ebenezer Scrooge	Jack Walton	Tiny Tim
Bob Cratchit, Scrooge's clerk	Ben Benjamin	Beggar Children, Hunger and Ignorance
Fred, Scrooge's nephew	Child Scrooge	
Gentleman Visitor	Fan, Scrooge's sister	Third Spirit (*the Spirit of Christmas Yet to Come*)
Warder and Residents of the Poorhouse	Fezziwig	
	Young Ebenezer	Peter, a Cratchit child
Sparsit, Scrooge's servant	Dick Wilkins	Boy
Cook	Sweetheart of Young Ebenezer	Butcher
Charwoman		Coachman

Prologue

The play begins amid a swirl of street life in Victorian London. Happy groups pass; brightly costumed carolers and families call out to one another and sing "Joy to the World." Three boys and a girl are grouped about a glowing mound of coal. As the carolers leave the stage, the lights dim and the focus shifts to the mound of coals, bright against the dark. Slowly, the children begin to respond to the warmth. A piano plays softly as the children talk.

Teaching Options

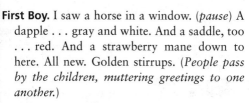

First Boy. I saw a horse in a window. (*pause*) A dapple . . . gray and white. And a saddle, too . . . red. And a strawberry mane down to here. All new. Golden stirrups. (*People pass by the children, muttering greetings to one another.*)

Second Boy. Christmas Eve.

Third Boy. Wish we could go.

First Boy. So do I.

Third Boy. I think I'd like it.

First Boy. Oh, wouldn't I . . . wouldn't I!

Second Boy. We're going up onto the roof. (*The boys look at him quizzically.*) My father has a glass. Telescope. A brass one. It opens up and it has twists on it and an eyepiece that you put up to look through. We can see all the way to the park with it.

Third Boy. Could I look through it?

Second Boy. Maybe . . . where would you look?

(*The third boy points straight up.*) Why there?

Third Boy. I'd like to see the moon. (*The boys stand and look upward as the girl sings to her doll. One of the boys makes a snow angel on the ground.*)

Girl (*singing*).

Christ the King came down one day,
Into this world of ours,
And crying from a manger bed,
Began the Christmas hour.

(*speaking*)

Christ the King, my pretty one,
Sleep softly on my breast,
Christ the King, my gentle one,
Show us the way to rest.

(*She begins to sing the first verse again. As snow starts to fall on the boy making the snow angel, he stands up and reaches out to catch a single flake.*)

Scene 1

SCROOGE IN HIS SHOP

A The percussion thunders. Scrooge *hurls himself through the descending snowflakes and sends the children scattering. They retreat, watching.* Cratchit *comes in. He takes some coal from the mound and puts it into a small bucket; as he carries it to a corner of the stage, the stage area is* transformed *from street to office.*

B Scrooge's *nephew* Fred *enters, talks with the children, gives them coins, and sends them away with a "Merry Christmas."*

Fred. A Merry Christmas, Uncle! God save you!

Scrooge. Bah! Humbug!

Fred. Christmas a humbug, Uncle? I hope that's meant as a joke.

Scrooge. Well, it's not. Come, come, what is it you want? Don't waste all the day, Nephew.

Fred. I only want to wish you a Merry Christmas, Uncle. Don't be cross.

Scrooge. What else can I be when I live in such a world of fools as this? Merry Christmas! Out with Merry Christmas! What's Christmas to you but a time for paying bills without money, a time for finding yourself a year

WORDS
TO
KNOW
transform (trăns-fôrm') *v.* To change the form or appearance of

253

Customizing Instruction

Multiple Learning Styles
Kinesthetic Learners

1 Invite volunteers to demonstrate how they would make a snow angel.

Students Acquiring English
Many students acquiring English come from non-Christian backgrounds, so you may want to provide background information on Christmas and the customs associated with it in the English-speaking world.

2 Say these two words aloud. Ask students what the words suggest about Scrooge's feelings toward Christmas.

Reading Skills and Strategies: EVALUATING

Ⓐ Ask students why Fred invited his uncle to dinner.

Possible Response: He is inspired by the spirit of Christmas and the belief that no one should be alone on Christmas.

Reading Skills and Strategies: CLARIFYING

Ⓑ Have students compare and contrast Fred's actions here with his earlier discussion with Scrooge to clarify why Fred hesitates.

Possible Response: Fred wished Scrooge a merry Christmas earlier and invited him to dinner. Scrooge rudely refused. The stage directions show that Scrooge has turned his back on Fred. Fred hesitates because he wants to say more, but he knows that Scrooge's response to whatever he says will be negative.

ACTIVE READING

Ⓒ **VISUALIZE** **Possible Responses:** Scrooge has his back turned to Fred; Fred leaves; a stranger approaches and comes in.

Literary Analysis: SETTING

Ⓓ Remind students that Dickens chose the Christmas setting deliberately. Ask students how Scrooge's attitude contrasts with the feelings and actions normally associated with Christmas.

Possible Response: Scrooge wants nothing to do with celebrating or sharing the holiday with loved ones or giving gifts to family or those who are less fortunate.

older and not an hour richer. If I could work my will, every idiot who goes about with "Merry Christmas" on his lips should be boiled with his own pudding and buried with a stake of holly through his heart.

Fred. Uncle!

Scrooge. Nephew, keep Christmas in your own way and let me keep it in mine.

Fred. But you don't keep it.

Scrooge. Let me leave it alone then. Much good may it do you. Much good it has ever done you.

Fred. There are many things from which I might have derived good by which I have not profited, I daresay, Christmas among the rest. And though it has never put a scrap of gold in my pocket, I believe it has done me good and will do me good, and I say, God bless it!

Scrooge. Bah!

Fred. Don't be angry, Uncle. Come! Dine with us tomorrow.

Scrooge. I'll dine alone, thank you.

Fred. But why?

Ⓐ **Scrooge.** Why? Why did you get married?

Fred. Why, because I fell in love with a wonderful girl.

Scrooge. And I with <u>solitude</u>. Good afternoon.

Fred. Nay, Uncle, but you never came to see me before I was married. Why give it as a reason for not coming now?

Scrooge. Good afternoon.

Fred. I am sorry with all my heart to find you so determined; but I have made the attempt in homage to[1] Christmas, and I'll keep that good spirit to the last. So, a Merry Christmas, Uncle.

Scrooge. Good afternoon!

Fred. And a Happy New Year!

Scrooge. Good afternoon! (*Fred hesitates as to say something more. He sees that Scroog has gone to get a volume down from the shel and so he starts to leave. As he leaves, th doorbell rings.*) Bells. Is necessary to always hav bells? (*The gentlema visitor enters, causing th doorbell to ring again* Cratchit!

ACTIVE READING

VISUALIZE Close your eyes and imagine the scene in Scrooge's shop. What do you see?

Cratchit. Yes, sir?

Scrooge. The bell, fool! See to it!

Cratchit. Yes, sir. (*He goes to the entrance.*)

Scrooge (*muttering*). Merry Christmas . . . Wolve howling and a Merry Christmas . . .

Cratchit. It's for you, sir.

Scrooge. Of course it's for me. You're ne receiving callers, are you? Show them in.

Cratchit. Right this way, sir. (*The gentlema visitor approaches Scrooge.*)

Scrooge. Yes, yes?

Gentleman Visitor. Scrooge and Marley's, believe. Have I the pleasure of addressing M Scrooge or Mr. Marley?

Scrooge. Marley's dead. Seven years tonigh What is it you want?

Gentleman Visitor. I have no doubt that h liberality[2] is well represented by his survivin partner. Here, sir, my card. (*He hand Scrooge his business card.*)

Scrooge. Liberality? No doubt of it? All righ all right, I can read. What is it you want? (*H returns to his work.*)

Gentleman Visitor. At this festive season of th year . . .

---

1. **in homage to** (hŏm′ĭj): in honor of.
2. **liberality** (lĭb′ə-răl′ĭ-tē): generousness.

WORDS
TO
KNOW   **solitude** (sŏl′ĭ-tōōd) *n.* the state of being alone

Multicultural Link ## New Year Celebrations

New Year's Day is celebrated on January 1, but it wasn't always so. During the Middle Ages, most European countries followed the Julian calendar. As a result, New Year's Day was celebrated on March 25. When the Gregorian calendar was introduced in the late 1500s, New Year's Day shifted to January 1 in most of Western Europe. Great Britain and the American colonies did not begin using that date until 1752.

However, in other cultures, New Year's Day occurs at times other than January 1. The Jewish New Year falls on the first and second days of the month of Tishri, usually around the end of September or the beginning of October. The Jewish New Year is called Rosh Hashanah. Traditionally, Chinese people celebrate the New Year somewhere between January 21 and February 19. The Vietnamese New Year, called Tet, lasts for three days. It falls at the same time as the Chinese New Year. Because no Native American tribe had a true calendar, the time of the beginning of the year varied among tribes. Some observed it in the spring, others in the fall.

Less Proficient Readers

Use the following questions to check students' comprehension.

- What is Scrooge's attitude toward his nephew?

  Possible Response: He has no time for him; Scrooge is unfriendly and rude.

- What is revealed about Fred's character from his reactions to his uncle?

  Possible Response: Fred is patient, kind, and forgiving.

Students Acquiring English

1 Explain that "liberality" means generosity and that the word is used ironically here, since it is already obvious to the audience that Scrooge is anything but generous.

A CHRISTMAS CAROL **255**

A **EVALUATE** Possible Responses: Scrooge's view of the poor is merciless and harsh; he is rude to his visitor and concerned only with himself. He doesn't know the meaning of charity.

Reading Skills and Strategies: CLARIFYING

B Ask students to explain why the scene in the workhouse is described.

Possible Responses: The description shows how gloomy the workhouse is and how uninterested Scrooge is in anything but his business.

Literary Analysis

STAGE DIRECTIONS

C Have students notice the contrast in the actions of Cratchit and Scrooge. Ask students what Cratchit's actions suggest about his character.

Possible Response: Cratchit is dancing, and Scrooge is working. Cratchit's dancing suggests that he is able to enjoy life's simple pleasures.

Reading Skills and Strategies: PREDICTING

D Have students predict what Scrooge's Christmas will be like by comparing Scrooge's attitude toward Christmas with Cratchit's.

Possible Responses: He will have a miserable, lonely holiday; he will be very happy all by himself, counting his money.

Scrooge. It's winter and cold. (*He continues his work and ignores the* gentleman visitor.)

Gentleman Visitor. Yes . . . yes, it is, and the more reason for my visit. At this time of the year it is more than usually desirable to make some slight <u>provision</u> for the poor and <u>destitute</u> who suffer greatly from the cold. Many thousands are in want of common necessaries; hundreds of thousands are in want of common comforts, sir.

Scrooge. Are there no prisons?

Gentleman Visitor. Many, sir.

Scrooge. And the workhouse?[3] Is it still in operation?

Gentleman Visitor. It is; still, I wish I could say it was not.

Scrooge. The poor law is still in full vigor then?

Gentleman Visitor. Yes, sir.

1 **Scrooge.** I'm glad to hear it. From what you said, I was afraid someone had stopped its operation.

Gentleman Visitor. Under the impression that they scarcely furnish Christian cheer of mind or body to the multitude, a few of us are <u>endeavoring</u> to raise a fund to buy the poor some meat and drink and means of warmth. We choose this time because it is the time, of all others, when want is keenly felt and <u>abundance</u> rejoices. May I put you down for something, sir?

Scrooge (*retreating into the darkness temporarily*). Nothing.

Gentleman Visitor. You wish to be <u>anonymous</u>?

Scrooge. I wish to be left alone. Since you ask me what I wish, sir, that is my answer. I don't make merry myself at Christmas, and I can't afford to make idle people merry. I help support the establishments I have mentioned

. . . they cost enough . . . and those who ar[e] poorly off must go there.

Gentleman Visitor. Many can't go there, an[d] many would rather die.

Scrooge. If they would rather die, they had bette[r] do it and decrease the <u>surplus</u> population. Tha[t] is not my affair. My business is. It occupies m[e] constantly. (*He talks bot[h] to the* gentleman visito[r] *and to himself while h[e] thumbs through h[is] books.*) Ask a man to giv[e] up life and means . . . fir[st] thing. What is it, I want to know[?] Charity? . . . (*His nose deep in his books, h[e] vaguely hears the dinner bell being rung in th[e] workhouse; he looks up as if he has heard [it] but never focuses on the actual scene. Th[e] warder of the poorhouse stands in a pool o[f] light at the far left, slowly ringing a bell.*)

A **EVALUATE** What do you think the author wants you to feel about Scrooge?

Warder. Dinner. All right. Line up. (*The poorl[y] clad, dirty residents of the poorhouse lin[e] up and file by to get their evening dish o[f] gruel,[4] wordlessly accepting it and going bac[k] to eat listlessly in the gloom. Scrooge return[s] to the business of his office. The processio[n] continues for a moment, then the image o[f] the poorhouse is obscured by darkness. Th[e] dejected gentleman visitor exits.*)

Scrooge. Latch the door, Cratchit. Firmly[,] firmly. Draft as cold as Christmas blowing i[n] here. Charity! (*Cratchit goes to the doo[r,] starts to close it, then sees the little girl wit[h] the doll. She seems to beckon to him; h[e]*

---

3. **workhouse:** prison where prisoners are required to work[.]
4. **gruel** (grōō′əl): a thin, watery food made by boiling ground grain in water or milk.

WORDS TO KNOW

provision (prə-vĭzh′ən) *n.* a supplying of needs
destitute (dĕs′tĭ-tōōt′) *n.* people lacking the necessities of life
endeavor (ĕn-dĕv′ər) *v.* to try
abundance (ə-bŭn′dəns) *n.* wealth
anonymous (ə-nŏn′ə-məs) *adj.* not having one's name known
surplus (sûr′pləs) *adj.* extra; more than needed

Teaching Options

  Grammar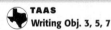

Mini Lesson · TEKS 17A · TAAS Writing Obj. 3, 5, 7

RUN-ON SENTENCES

Instruction Remind students that a run-on sentence occurs when two or more sentences are written as one. A run-on sentence combines ideas that should be separate. Normally, run-on sentences should not be used because they can lead to confusion for the reader. However, writers sometimes use them in dialogue to make their characters' speech sound natural or to convey emotion. In the highlighted run-on sentence above, Scrooge runs two complete sentences together. This reveals his strong feeling about

having to pay to support prisons and workhouses. Point out that to make this sentence grammatically correct, an exclamation point or period should be placed after *mentioned* instead of the ellipsis. *They* should be capitalized.

Exercises Have students correctly rewrite the following sentences as two or more complete sentences.

1. Scrooge's night passes in a flurry of activity he is taken on many journeys through time.
   (*Scrooge's night passes in a flurry of activity. He is taken on many journeys through time.*)

moves slowly toward her, and they dance together for a moment. Scrooge continues to work. Suddenly carolers appear on the platform, and a few phrases of their carol, "Angels We Have Heard on High," are heard. Scrooge looks up.) Cratchit! *(As soon as Scrooge shouts, the girl and the carolers vanish and Cratchit begins to close up the shop.)* Cratchit!

Cratchit. Yes, sir.

Scrooge. Well, to work then!

Cratchit. It's evening, sir.

Scrooge. Is it?

Cratchit. Christmas evening, sir.

Scrooge. Oh, you'll want all day tomorrow off, I suppose.

Cratchit. If it's quite convenient, sir.

Scrooge. It's not convenient, and it's not fair. If I was to deduct half a crown[5] from your salary for it, you'd think yourself ill-used, wouldn't you? Still you expect me to pay a day's wage for a day of no work.

Cratchit. It's only once a year, sir.

Scrooge. Be here all the earlier the next morning.

Cratchit. I will, sir.

Scrooge. Then off, off.

Cratchit. Yes, sir! Merry Christmas, sir!

Scrooge. Bah! *(As soon as Cratchit opens the door, the sounds of the street begin, very bright and loud. Cratchit is caught up in a swell of people hurrying through the street. Children pull him along to the top of an ice slide, and he runs and slides down it, disappearing in darkness as the stage suddenly is left almost empty. Scrooge goes around the room blowing out the candles, talking to himself.)* Christmas Eve. Carolers! Bah! There. Another day. *(He opens his door and peers out.)* Black, very black. Now where are they? *(The children are heard singing carols for a moment.)* Begging pennies for their songs, are they? Oh, boy! Here, boy! *(The little girl emerges from the shadows. Scrooge hands her a dark lantern, and she holds it while he lights it with an ember from the pile of coals.)*

---

5. **half a crown:** until 1971, an amount of British money equal to 2½ shillings or one-eighth of a pound.

Thinking Through the Literature

1. What was your response to the meeting between Ebenezer Scrooge and his nephew, Fred?

2. Skim the stage directions. How is the **mood**—the feeling conveyed to the reader—outside Scrooge's office different from the mood within the office?

WORDS
TO
KNOW

emerge (ĭ-mûrj′) v. to come into sight

257

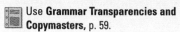

A Have students reread the passage on page 257 in which the young girl is dancing with Cratchit. Ask students to offer observations about who the young girl might be.

Possible Responses: the true spirit of Christmas; the joy of youth; an angel

Why does Scrooge refer to her as a boy?

Possible Responses: He is too self-absorbed to notice anyone else.

Reading Skills and Strategies:
EVALUATING

B Explain to students that it is customary to give servants a gift of extra money at holidays. Ask students what Scrooge's actions toward Cook and Sparsit reveal about his character.

Possible Responses: his extreme stinginess; his inability to enter into the Christmas spirit

Literary Analysis
STAGE DIRECTIONS

C Ask students what effect would be created by Marley's voice reverberating over a microphone.

Possible Response: The sound would be ghostly and unreal.

Active Reading VISUALIZING

D Ask students what mental images are evoked by this passage.

Possible Response: The chain that Marley carries is heavy; it is forged with locks and vaults and golden coins.

Literary Analysis: SYMBOL

E Have students interpret the symbolism of the funeral procession.

Possible Responses: Marley's death; Scrooge's death; the death of the Christmas spirit

Scene 2
SCROOGE GOES HOME

Scrooge (*talking to the little girl*). Hold it quiet! There. Off now. That's it. High. Black as pitch. Light the street, that's it. You're a bright lad! Good to see that. Earn your supper, boy. You'll not go hungry this night. Home. You know the way, do you? Yes, that's the way. The house of Ebenezer Scrooge. (*As the two find their way to Scrooge's house, the audience sees and hears a brief image of a cathedral interior with a living crèche and a large choir singing "Amen!"; the image ends in a blackout. The lights come up immediately, and Scrooge is at his door.*) Hold the light up, boy, up. (*The girl with the lantern disappears.*) Where did he go? Boy? No matter. There's a penny saved. Lantern's gone out. No matter. A candle saved. Yes, here's the key. (*He turns with the key toward the door, and Marley's face swims out of the darkness. Scrooge watches, unable to speak. He fumbles for a match, lights the lantern, and swings it toward the figure, which melts away. Pause. Scrooge fits the key in the lock and turns it as the door suddenly is opened from the inside by the porter, Sparsit. Scrooge is startled, then recovers.*) Sparsit?

Sparsit. Yes, sir?

Scrooge. Hurry, hurry. The door . . . close it.

Sparsit. Did you knock, sir?

Scrooge. Knock? What matter? Here, light me up the stairs.

Sparsit. Yes, sir. (*He leads Scrooge up the stairs. They pass the cook on the way. Scrooge brushes by her, stops, looks back, and she leans toward him.*)

Cook. Something to warm you, sir? Porridge?

Scrooge. Wha . . . ? No. No, nothing.

Cook (*waiting for her Christmas coin*). Merry Christmas, sir. (*Scrooge ignores the request and the cook disappears. Mumbling, Scrooge follows Sparsit.*)

Scrooge (*looking back after the cook is gone*). Fright a man nearly out of his life . . . Merry Christmas . . . bah!

Sparsit. Your room, sir.

Scrooge. Hmmm? Oh, yes, yes. And good night.

Sparsit (*extending his hand for his coin*). Merry Christmas, sir.

Scrooge. Yes, yes . . . (*He sees the outstretched hand; he knows what Sparsit wants and is infuriated.*) Out! Out! (*He closes the door after Sparsit, turns toward his chamber, and discovers the charwoman directly behind him.*)

Charwoman. Warm your bed for you, sir?

Scrooge. What? Out! Out!

Charwoman. Aye, sir. (*She starts for the door. Marley's voice is heard mumbling something unintelligible.*)

Scrooge. What's that?

Charwoman. Me, sir? Not a thing, sir.

Scrooge. Then, good night.

Charwoman. Good night. (*She exits, and Scrooge pantomimes shutting the door behind her. The voice of Marley over an offstage microphone whispers and reverberates: "Merry Christmas, Scrooge!" Silence. Scrooge hears the voice but cannot account for it. He climbs up to open a window and looks down. A cathedral choir singing "O Come, All Ye Faithful" is heard in the distance. Scrooge listens a moment, shuts the window, and prepares for bed. As soon as*

Teaching Options

Cross Curricular Link **Science**

GAS/ELECTRIC LIGHTING In 1843, when *A Christmas Carol* was published, not all streets were lit by lamps. Gas lamps had been placed on some streets as early as 1807, but in other areas pedestrians needed to carry their own lanterns to light their way.

Early lamps in homes used fuels such as vegetable oils or fish or whale oils. Kerosene became more popular after 1859. Coal gas, however, was the source of most street lighting, even though it was not considered to be as safe as other fuel sources.

The first incandescent light was patented in 1841, but electric lights were not commercially successful until 1879, when Thomas Alva Edison produced a carbon-filament lamp. Electric street lighting was soon afterward introduced in large cities in Europe and America.

he has shut the sound out of his room, figures appear; they seem to be coming down the main aisle of a church, bearing gifts to the living crèche. The orchestra plays "O Come, All Ye Faithful" as the procession files out. Scrooge, ready for bed, warms himself before the heap of coals. As he pulls his nightcap from a chair, a small hand-bell tumbles off onto the floor. Startled, he picks it up and rings it for <u>reassurance</u>; *an echo answers it. He turns and sees the little girl on the street; she is swinging her doll, which produces the echo of his bell. Scrooge escapes to his bed; the girl is swallowed up in the darkness. The bell sounds grow to a din,* <u>incoherent</u> *as in a dream, then suddenly fall silent. Scrooge sits up in bed, listens, and hears the chains of Marley coming up the stairs. Scrooge reaches for the bell pull to* <u>summon</u> *Sparsit. The bell responds with a gong, and Marley appears. He and Scrooge face one another.)*

Scrooge. What do you want with me?

Marley *(in a ghostly, unreal voice).* Much.

Scrooge. Who are you?

Marley. Ask who I was.

Scrooge. Who were you?

Marley. In life, I was your partner, Jacob Marley.

Scrooge. He's dead.

Marley. Seven years this night, Ebenezer Scrooge.

Scrooge. Why do you come here?

Marley. I must. It is commanded me. I must wander the world and see what I can no longer share, what I would not share when I walked where you do.

Scrooge. And must go thus?

Marley. The chain? Look at it, Ebenezer, study it.

Locks and vaults and golden coins. I forged it, each link, each day when I sat in these chairs, commanded these rooms. Greed, Ebenezer Scrooge, wealth. Feel them, know them. Yours was as heavy as this I wear seven years ago, and you have labored to build it since.

Scrooge. If you're here to lecture, I have no time for it. It is late; the night is cold. I want comfort now.

Marley. I have none to give. I know not how you see me this night. I did not ask it. I have sat invisible beside you many and many a day. I am commanded to bring you a chance, Ebenezer. Heed it!

Scrooge. Quickly then, quickly.

Marley. You will be haunted by three spirits.

Scrooge *(scoffing).* Is that the chance?

Marley. Mark it.

Scrooge. I do not choose to.

Marley *(ominously).* Then you will walk where I do, burdened by your riches, your greed.

Scrooge. Spirits mean nothing to me.

Marley *(slowly leaving).* Expect the first tomorrow, when the bell tolls one, the second on the next night at the same hour, the third upon the next night when the last stroke of twelve has ended. Look to see me no more. I must wander. Look that, for your own sake, you remember what has passed between us.

Scrooge. Jacob . . . Don't leave me! . . . Jacob! Jacob!

Marley. Adieu,[6] Ebenezer. *(At Marley's last words a funeral procession begins to move across the stage. A boy walks in front; a priest follows, swinging a censer;[7] sounds of*

------

6. **adieu** (ə-dyōō′): farewell.
7. **censer:** incense burner.

WORDS TO KNOW

reassurance (rē′ə-shŏŏr′əns) *n.* a restoring of confidence
incoherent (ĭn′kō-hîr′ənt) *adj.* without connection or harmony
summon (sŭm′ən) *v.* to call for or send for with authority or urgency; to order to come or appear

Customizing Instruction

Less Proficient Readers
• Ask students who Jacob Marley was in life.
  Answer: He was Scrooge's business partner.
• What is Marley's chain and why does he wear it?
  Possible Responses: Marley's chain represents the wealth he hoarded during his life; it is punishment for his greed.
• Why has Marley appeared?
  Possible Response: to warn Scrooge that he is destined for the same sad fate

Set a Purpose Have students read to find out what the Spirit of Christmas Past reveals.

Multiple Learning Styles
Auditory Learners
1 Invite students to select background music for this scene. Remind students to refer to the stage directions as well as to the dialogue to determine the scene's mood. Their music choices should reflect this mood.

Students Acquiring English
2 Point out that *adieu* is a French word for goodbye. Marley's use of it gives his leaving of Scrooge a very formal final feeling.

Reading Skills and Strategies: ANALYZING

A Have students think about what the little girl and the leper might represent.

Possible Responses: The little girl might represent hope; the leper, disease and death.

Literary Analysis   STAGE DIRECTIONS

B Have students read the stage directions carefully. Ask them what is revealed about Scrooge's frame of mind from his actions and words.

Possible Responses: He is disoriented, frightened, and confused. He doesn't know what to expect.

Reading Skills and Strategies: PREDICTING

C Guide students to combine the information from the stage directions and opening dialogue to predict what this spirit will reveal.

Possible Response: Scrooge's childhood and early years

---

mourning and the suggestion of church music are heard. Scrooge calls out, "Jacob, don't leave me!" as if talking in the midst of a bad dream. At the end of the procession is the little girl, swinging her doll and singing softly.)

Girl.

Hushabye, don't you cry,
Go to sleep, little baby.
When you wake, you shall have
All the pretty little horses,
Blacks and bays, dapples and grays,
All the pretty little horses.

A *(She stops singing and looks up at Scrooge; their eyes meet, and she solemnly rings the doll in greeting. Scrooge pulls shut the bed curtains, and the girl exits. The bell sounds are picked up by the bells of a leper[8] who enters, dragging himself along.)*

Leper *(calling out).* Leper! Leper! Stay the way! Leper! Leper! Keep away! *(He exits and the*

clock begins to chime, ringing the hours. Scrooge sits up in bed and begins to count the chimes.)

Scrooge. Eight . . . nine . . . ten . . . eleven . . . it can't be . . . twelve. Midnight? No. Not twelve. It can't be. I haven't slept the whole day through. Twelve? Yes, yes, twelve noon. *(He hurries to the window and looks out.)* Black. Twelve midnight. *(pause)* I must get up. A day wasted. I must get down to the office. *(Two small chimes are heard.)* Quarter past. But it just rang twelve. Fifteen minutes haven't gone past, not so quickly. *(Again two small chimes are heard.)* A quarter to one. The spirit . . . It's to come at one. *(He hurries to his bed as the chimes ring again.)* One.

---

8. **leper** (lĕp′ər): a person who has leprosy, a skin disease once believed to be highly contagious.

Scene 3

THE SPIRIT OF CHRISTMAS PAST

The hour is struck again by a large street clock, and the first spirit appears. It is a figure dressed to look like the little girl's doll.

Scrooge. Are you the spirit whose coming was foretold to me?

C **First Spirit.** I am.

Scrooge. Who and what are you?

First Spirit. I am the Ghost of Christmas Past.

Scrooge. Long past?

First Spirit. Your past.

Scrooge. Why are you here?

First Spirit. Your <u>welfare</u>. Rise. Walk with me.

Scrooge. I am <u>mortal</u> still. I cannot pass through air.

First Spirit. My hand. *(Scrooge grasps the spirit's hand tightly, and the doll's bell rings softly. Scrooge remembers a scene from his past in which two boys greet each other in the street.)*

First Voice. Halloo, Jack!

Second Voice. Ben! Merry Christmas, Ben!

Scrooge. Jack Walton. Young Jack Walton. Spirits . . . ?

First Voice. Have a good holiday, Jack.

Scrooge. Yes, yes, I remember him. Both of them. Little Ben Benjamin. He used to . . .

WORDS
TO
KNOW

welfare (wĕl′fâr′) *n.* well-being
mortal (môr′tl) *adj.* of the earth; not a spirit

260

Teaching Options

 Speaking and Listening   **TEKS 3B, 5C**

DIALOGUE

Prepare Explain to students that writers use dialogue, or a conversation between two or more characters, in stories, poems, and plays. Mention that plays and skits are made up almost entirely of dialogue. Tell the class that dialogue moves the action along, makes it more interesting, and helps readers understand the characters by providing clues about their thoughts and feelings. Look at some examples of dialogue from the play to show students that Scrooge's attitudes are suggested by what he says.

Present Have students reread the dialogue on pages 260–264 to find examples of how Scrooge becomes childlike when he recalls his early experiences. Then have students select passages of dialogue to read aloud, telling what each passage suggests about the thoughts and feelings of Scrooge or the other characters in the scene.

BLOCK SCHEDULING This activity is particularly well suited for longer class periods.

Use **Communications Transparencies and Copymasters**, p. 12, for additional support.

VIEW AND COMPARE

What does each of these interpretations of Scrooge tell you about his character? Which interpretation is closest to your own?

Frederic March in a televised musical version of *A Christmas Carol* (1954).

George C. Scott in a televised production of *A Christmas Carol* (1984).

Henry Winkler in an adaption called *An American Christmas Carol* (1979).

Bill Murray as Frank Cross, a character based on Ebenezer Scrooge, in an adaption called *Scrooged* (1988).

Customizing Instruction

Multiple Learning Styles
Kinesthetic Learners

1 Ask a volunteer to imitate Scrooge's actions in this scene to show how they reveal his panic and fear.

  View and Compare 🏴 TEKS 23A, B

Remind students that they are expected to analyze the significance of visual images.

Possible Responses: Proceeding counterclockwise, students may say that the first image suggests Scrooge's harshness and challenging attitude toward others who try to guide him. The second image shows a more vulnerable Scrooge; there is potential for reform in the sadness of the eyes. The third image presents the arrogance and wealth of Scrooge. He is seen as a man who cares only for himself and his comfort. The last image shows a defeated man, one who perhaps has recognized his wrongdoing and is bowed down by the burden of the past.

Students' responses will vary. Ask them to give specific reasons, based on the text, for their choices of the images that best match their interpretations.

Literary Analysis: DIALOGUE

A Ask students what they learn about Scrooge as a child from what he says and how he speaks.

Possible Responses: He loved to read and became involved with fictional characters. He had sympathy and imagination.

Literary Analysis: FLASHBACK

B Guide students to recognize the part of the plot that is out of chronological order and interpret its purpose.

Possible Responses: The events from Scrooge's past are out of order. Reliving the past allows Scrooge to learn from both pleasures and miseries, and the audience can compare Scrooge as a child with Scrooge as an old man.

Reading Skills and Strategies: EVALUATING

C Ask students what they think the Spirit is trying to teach Scrooge.

Possible Responses: The Spirit wants Scrooge to learn charity, sympathy, generosity, and enjoyment of life's offerings.

ACTIVE READING

D **QUESTION** **Possible Response:** The Spirit wants Scrooge to learn from his former master how to treat people and become a better master and person.

Reading Skills and Strategies: SPECULATING

E Ask students what they think Scrooge would like to say to Cratchit.

Possible Response: Scrooge would like to apologize to Cratchit for his unkindness or wish him "Merry Christmas."

First Voice. See you next term, Jack. Next . . . term . . .

Scrooge. They . . . they're off for the holidays and going home from school. It's Christmas time . . . all of the children off home now . . . No . . . no, not all . . . there was one . . . (*The spirit motions for* Scrooge *to turn, and he sees a young* boy *playing with a teddy bear and talking to it.*) Yes . . . reading . . . poor boy.

First Spirit. What, I wonder?

Scrooge. Reading? Oh, it was nothing. Fancy,[9] all fancy and make-believe and take-me-away. All of it. Yes, nonsense.

Child Scrooge. Ali Baba.[10]

Scrooge. Yes . . . that was it . . .

Child Scrooge. Yes, and remember . . . and remember . . . remember Robinson Crusoe?[11]

Scrooge. And the parrot!

Child Scrooge. Yes, the parrot! I love him best.

Scrooge (*imitating the parrot*). With his stripy green body and yellow tail drooping along and couldn't sing—awk—but could talk, and a thing like a lettuce growing out the top of his head . . . and he used to sit on the very top of the tree—up there.

Child Scrooge. And Robinson Crusoe sailed around the island, and he thought he had escaped the island, and the parrot said, the parrot said . . .

Scrooge (*imitating the parrot*). Robinson Crusoe, where you been? Awk! Robinson Crusoe, where you been?

Child Scrooge. And Robinson Crusoe looked up in the tree and saw the parrot and knew he hadn't escaped and he was still there, still all alone there.

Scrooge. Poor Robinson Crusoe.

Child Scrooge (*sadly replacing the teddy bear*). Poor Robinson Crusoe.

Scrooge. Poor child. Poor child.

First Spirit. Why poor?

Scrooge. Fancy . . . fancy . . . (*He tries to mas* *his feelings by being brusque.*) It's his way, child's way to . . . to lose being alone in . . . i dreams, dreams . . . Never matter if they ar all nonsense, yes, nonsense. But he'll be al right, grow out of it. Yes. Yes, he did outgrov it, the nonsense. Became a man and left there and he became, yes, he became a mar and . . . yes, successful . . . rich! (*The sadnes returns.*) Never matter . . . never matter. (*Far runs in and goes to* Child Scrooge.) Fan!

Fan. Brother, dear brother! (*She kisses Chil* Scrooge.)

Child Scrooge. Dear, dear Fan.

Fan. I've come to bring you home, home fo good and ever. Come with me, come now (*She takes his hand, and they start to run off but the* spirit *stops them and signals for th light on them to fade. They look at the* spirit aware of their role in the spirit's "education" of Scrooge.)

Scrooge. Let me watch them go? Let them b happy for a moment! (*The* spirit *says nothing* Scrooge *turns away from them, and the ligh goes out.*) A delicate, delicate child. A breath might have withered her.

First Spirit. She died a woman and had, as remember, children.

Scrooge. One child.

First Spirit. Your nephew.

Scrooge. Yes, yes, Fred, my nephew. (Scrooge *pauses, then tries to bluster through.*) Well Well, all of us have that, haven't we

---

9. **fancy:** illusion.

10. **Ali Baba** (ä′lē bä′bə): in the *Arabian Nights,* a poor woodcutter who discovers the treasure-filled cave of 40 thieves.

11. **Robinson Crusoe:** in the novel *Robinson Crusoe* by Daniel Defoe, a shipwrecked sailor who survives for years on a small island.

Teaching Options

Mini Lesson **Vocabulary Strategy** 🏴 **TEKS 6B, 9D** 🏴 **TAAS Reading Obj. 1**

ANALYZING WORD PARTS

Instruction Remind students that analyzing the parts of an unfamiliar word can help them to define the word. A prefix is a word part added to the beginning of a word. A suffix is a word part added to the end of a word. Tell students that knowing the meanings of some common prefixes and suffixes will help them to acquire a more extensive vocabulary. For example, the word *disbelief* has the prefix *dis-*, which means opposing. Therefore, disbelief is doubt, the opposite of belief.

Present the following prefixes and suffixes and their meanings to the students.

Prefix	Meaning
de-	down, out of
e-	away from, out
mis-	wrong, badly
non-	not
pro-	forward
re-	back, again
Suffix	**Meaning**
-able	able to, likely to

Childhoods? Sadnesses? But we grow and we become men, masters of ourselves. (*The spirit gestures for music to begin. It is heard first as from a great distance, then Scrooge becomes aware of it.*) I've no time for it, Spirit. Music and all of your Christmas folderol.[12] Yes, yes, I've learnt what you have to show me. (*Fezziwig, Young Ebenezer, and Dick appear, busily preparing for a party.*)

Fezziwig. Yo ho, there! Ebenezer! Dick!

Scrooge. Fezziwig! It's old Fezziwig that I 'prenticed[13] under.

First Spirit. Your master?

Scrooge. Oh, aye, and the best that any boy could have. There's Dick Wilkins! Bless me. He was very much attached to me was Dick. Poor Dick. Dear, dear.

Fezziwig. Yo ho, my boys! No more work tonight. Christmas Eve, Dick! Christmas, Ebenezer! Let's have the shutters up before a man can say Jack Robinson! (*The music continues. Chandeliers are pulled into position, and mistletoe, holly, and ivy are draped over everything by bustling servants. Dancers fill the stage for Fezziwig's wonderful Christmas party. In the midst of the dancing and the gaiety servants pass back and forth through the crowd with huge platters of food. At a pause in the music, Young Ebenezer, who is dancing, calls out.*)

Young Ebenezer. Mr. Fezziwig, sir, you're a wonderful master!

Scrooge and Young Ebenezer. A wonderful master!

Scrooge (*echoing the phrase*). A wonderful master! (*The music changes suddenly, and the dancers jerk into distorted postures and then begin to move in slow motion. The celebrants slowly exit, performing a <u>macabre</u> dance to discordant sounds.*)

First Spirit. Just because he gave a party? It was very small.

ACTIVE READING

QUESTION Why does the author show Scrooge's happy days with his first master?

Scrooge. Small!

First Spirit. He spent a few pounds[14] of your "mortal" money, three, four at the most. Is that so much that he deserves this praise?

Scrooge. But it wasn't the money. He had the power to make us happy, to make our service light or burdensome. The happiness he gives is quite as great as if it cost a fortune. That's what . . . a good master is.

First Spirit. Yes?

Scrooge. No, no, nothing.

First Spirit. Something, I think.

Scrooge. I should like to be able to say a word or two to my clerk just now, that's all.

First Spirit. But this is all past. Your clerk, Cratchit, couldn't be here.

Scrooge. No, no, of course not, an idle thought. Are we done?

First Spirit (*motioning for the waltz music to begin*). Nearly.

Scrooge (*hearing the waltz and remembering it*). Surely it's enough. Haven't you tormented me enough? (*Young Ebenezer is seen waltzing with his Sweetheart.*)

First Spirit. I only show the past, what it promised you. Look. Another promise.

Scrooge. Oh. Oh, yes. I had forgotten . . . her.

---

12. **folderol** (fŏl′də-rŏl′): foolishness, nonsense.

13. **'prenticed:** short for apprenticed, here meaning "learned a trade while working."

14. **pounds:** basic British units of money, each equal to 20 shillings.

WORDS TO KNOW **macabre** (mə-kä′brə) *adj.* suggesting the horror of death and decay

---

Customizing Instruction

Less Proficient Readers
Explore what the Spirit of Christmas Past reveals about Scrooge's childhood and early manhood.

- What was Scrooge like as a child?
  Possible Responses: lonely; he loved books and his sister
- According to Scrooge, why was Fezziwig a good master?
  Possible Response: He made his workers happy and their service light.

Set a Purpose Have students read to find out what lessons Scrooge learns from the Spirit of Christmas Present.

Students Acquiring English

1 Explain that holly, mistletoe, and ivy are readily available for decorating in England. Ask students to compare Christmas decorations in other cultures.

-ance	act, quality, state
-ity	act, quality, condition, state
-less	without
-ness	quality of being

Application Have students work in groups to define each of the following words. Students should first divide the word and then should use their knowledge of prefixes and suffixes to help them recognize the meaning. Ask students to share their definitions with the class.

1. provision
2. degrade
3. mistaken
4. generosity
5. charitable
6. evaporate
7. worthless
8. reassurance

Have students think of other words with the same prefixes or suffixes. Write them on the board and ask students to define them.

Use **Vocabulary Transparencies and Copymasters**, p. 40.

**Reading Skills and Strategies:
EVALUATING**

A Tell students that as an apprentice, Scrooge had no money of his own. Now that his apprenticeship is over, he has the chance to do well for himself. Ask why this circumstance leads to his sweetheart returning his ring.

Possible Response: Because she brings no dowry with her, Scrooge's sweetheart wants to release him from their original agreement so that he can find someone wealthier if he so desires.

Ask students what Scrooge's failure to pursue her indicates about his priorities.

Possible Response: He cares for money more than he cares for his sweetheart.

**Reading Skills and Strategies:
CLARIFYING**

B Ask students what the Spirit means by saying, "I am always with you."

Possible Response: The past can never be left behind; it remains with a person.

Literary Analysis STAGE DIRECTIONS

C Ask students what Scrooge's pause here means.

Possible Responses: He no longer feels the urge to talk to Bob; he doesn't know how to communicate with people.

**Reading Skills and Strategies:
MAKING JUDGMENTS**

D Ask students if "a world away" is an appropriate way to describe Cratchit's home. Have students explain their answers.

Possible Response: Symbolically, it is very far away because it represents a different social class and it has happiness.

Don't they dance beautifully? So young, so young. I would have married her if only . . .

Sweetheart. Can you love me, Ebenezer? I bring no dowry[15] to my marriage, only me, only love. It is no currency that you can buy and sell with, but we can live with it. Can you? (*She pauses, then returns the ring* Scrooge *gave her as his* pledge.) I release you, Ebenezer, for the love of the man you once were. Will that man win me again, now that he is free?

Scrooge (*trying to speak to her*). If only you had held me to it. You should not have let me go. I was young; I did love you.

Sweetheart (*speaking to* Young Ebenezer). We have never lied to one another. May you be happy in the life you have chosen. Good-bye. (*She runs out.* Young Ebenezer *slowly leaves.*)

Scrooge. No, no, it was not meant that way . . . !

First Spirit. You cannot change now what you would not change then. I am your mistakes, Ebenezer Scrooge, all of the things you could have done and did not.

Scrooge. Then leave me! I have done them. I shall live with them. As I have, as I do; as I will.

First Spirit. There is another Christmas, seven years ago, when Marley died.

Scrooge. No! I will not see it. I will not! He died. I could not prevent it. I did not choose for him to die on Christmas Day.

First Spirit. And when his day was chosen, what did you do then?

Scrooge. I looked after his affairs.

First Spirit. His business.

Scrooge. Yes! His business! Mine! It was all tha[t] I had, all that I could do in this world. I hav[e] nothing to do with the world to come after.

First Spirit. Then I will leave you.

Scrooge. Not yet! Don't leave me here! Tell m[e] what I must do! What of the other spirits?

First Spirit. They will come.

Scrooge. And you? What of you?

First Spirit. I am always with you. (*The little gir[l] appears with her doll; she takes* Scrooge'[s] *hand and gently leads him to bed. Numbe[d] he follows her. She leans against the foot o[f] the bed, ringing the doll and singing. The firs[t] spirit exits as she sings.*)

Girl.
When you wake, you shall have
All the pretty little horses,
Blacks and bays, dapples and grays,
All the pretty little horses.

(*She rings the doll, and the ringing become[s] the chiming of* Scrooge's *bell. The girl exit[s]* Scrooge *sits upright in bed as he hears th[e] chimes.*)

Scrooge. A minute until one. No one here. N[o] one's coming. (*A larger clock strikes on[e] o'clock.*)

---

15. **dowry:** the property a bride brings to her husband when they marry.

WORDS
TO
KNOW

currency (kûr′ən-sē) *n.* money
pledge (plĕj) *n.* something given to guarantee fulfillment of a promise

264

Teaching Options

Multicultural Link

Christmas Celebrations

Christmas in Latin America is swathed in rich tradition. In Puerto Rico, Venezuela, and some other Latin American countries, groups serenade outside friends' houses, a custom called *trulla* or *asalto.* The host rewards his friends with food and drink and joins the party. A Mexican tradition calls for children and adults to form a procession, or *posada,* to enact the attempt by Mary and Joseph to find a place to stay in Bethlehem on the night Jesus was born.

Epiphany is a special part of the Christmas cele-bration. In Puerto Rico, for instance, friends and family gather to sing and pray to the three kings at a celebration called *Vigilia de los Reyes.* At dawn, the vigil ends and the families have a feast, which often includes roasted pig, rice and pigeon peas, sausages, and banana croquettes. To prepare for the kings, children put shoeboxes lined with grass under their beds. The kings come during the night and leave toys for the children; their camels eat the grass!

Scene 4

THE SPIRIT OF CHRISTMAS PRESENT

A light comes on. Scrooge *becomes aware of it and goes slowly to it. He sees the* second spirit, *the Spirit of Christmas Present, who looks like Fezziwig.*

Scrooge. Fezziwig!

Second Spirit. Hello, Scrooge.

Scrooge. But you can't be . . . not Fezziwig.

Second Spirit. Do you see me as him?

Scrooge. I do.

Second Spirit. And hear me as him?

Scrooge. I do.

Second Spirit. I wish I were the gentleman, so as not to disappoint you.

Scrooge. But you're not . . . ?

Second Spirit. No, Mr. Scrooge. You have never seen the like of me before. I am the Ghost of Christmas Present.

Scrooge. But . . .

Second Spirit. You see what you will see, Scrooge, no more. Will you walk out with me this Christmas Eve?

Scrooge. But I am not yet dressed.

Second Spirit. Take my tails, dear boy, we're leaving.

Scrooge. Wait!

Second Spirit. What is it now?

Scrooge. Christmas Present, did you say?

Second Spirit. I did.

Scrooge. Then we are traveling here? In this town? London? Just down there?

Second Spirit. Yes, yes, of course.

Scrooge. Then we could walk? Your flying is . . . well, too sudden for an old man. Well?

Second Spirit. It's your Christmas, Scrooge; I am only the guide.

Scrooge (*puzzled*). Then we can walk? (*The* spirit *nods.*) Where are you guiding me to?

Second Spirit. Bob Cratchit's.

Scrooge. My clerk?

Second Spirit. You did want to talk to him? (Scrooge *pauses, uncertain how to answer.*) Don't worry, Scrooge, you won't have to.

Scrooge (*trying to change the subject, to cover his error*). Shouldn't be much of a trip. With fifteen bob[16] a week, how far off can it be?

Second Spirit. A world away, Scrooge, at least that far. (Scrooge *and the* spirit *start to step off a curb when a funeral procession enters with a child's coffin, followed by the* poorhouse children, *who are singing. Seated on top of the coffin is the little girl. She and* Scrooge *look at one another.*) That is the way to it, Scrooge. (*The procession follows the coffin offstage;* Scrooge *and the* spirit *exit after the procession. As they leave, the lights focus on* Mrs. Cratchit *and her* children. Mrs. Cratchit *sings as she puts* Tiny Tim *and the other* children *to bed, all in one bed. She pulls a dark blanket over them.*)

Mrs. Cratchit (*singing*).
When you wake, you shall have
All the pretty little horses,
Blacks and bays, dapples and grays,
All the pretty little horses.

---

16. **bob:** a British slang term for shilling.

Literary Analysis | STAGE DIRECTIONS

A Ask students what is significant about the Spirit and Scrooge entering the Cratchit home like a draft of cold air.

Possible Responses: They cannot be seen, but their presence is felt. Scrooge carries a chill with him as does the Spirit because he is supernatural.

Literary Analysis: THEME

B Ask students why they think Scrooge can't bear to hear the children sing. Guide students to relate this to the message about life the playwright presents.

Possible Responses: Scrooge understands the emotional poverty of his life; he finally sees how he has missed out on love and all human connection through his selfishness and greed.

Reading Skills and Strategies: EVALUATING

C Ask students why the Spirit says the first sentence.

Possible Response: The Spirit is reminding Scrooge of what he earlier said about the poor.

Why did the Spirit bring Scrooge to the Cratchit household?

Possible Responses: to learn that material possessions and selfishness do not bring happiness; to hear Mrs. Cratchit's honest opinion of him and to realize Bob Cratchit's loyalty to him

---

To sleep now, all of you. Christmas tomorrow. (*She kisses them and goes to* Bob Cratchit, *who is by the hearth.*) How did our little Tiny Tim behave?

Bob Cratchit. As good as gold and better. He told me, coming home, that he hoped the people saw him in church because he was a cripple and it might be pleasant to them to remember upon Christmas Day who made the lame to walk and the blind to see.

A **Mrs. Cratchit.** He's a good boy. (*The* second spirit *and* Scrooge *enter.* Mrs. Cratchit *feels a sudden draft.*) Oh, the wind. (*She gets up to shut the door.*)

Second Spirit. Hurry. (*He nudges* Scrooge *in before* Mrs. Cratchit *shuts the door.*)

Scrooge. Hardly hospitable is what I'd say.

1 **Second Spirit.** Oh, they'd say a great deal more, Scrooge, if they could see you.

Scrooge. Oh, they should, should they?

Second Spirit. Oh yes, I'd think they might.

Scrooge. Well, I might have a word for them . . .

Second Spirit. You're here to listen.

Scrooge. Oh. Oh yes, all right. By the fire?

Second Spirit. But not a word.

2 **Bob Cratchit** (*raising his glass*). My dear, to Mr. Scrooge. I give you Mr. Scrooge, the founder of the feast.

Mrs. Cratchit. The founder of the feast indeed! I wish I had him here! I'd give him a piece of my mind to feast upon, and I hope he'd have a good appetite for it.

Bob Cratchit. My dear, Christmas Eve.

Mrs. Cratchit. It should be Christmas Eve, I'm sure, when one drinks the health of such an <u>odious</u>, stingy, hard, unfeeling man as Mr. Scrooge. You know he is, Robert! Nobody knows it better than you do, poor dear.

Bob Cratchit. I only know one thing on Christmas: that one must be <u>charitable</u>.

Mrs. Cratchit. I'll drink to his health for your sake and the day's, not for his. Long life to him! A Merry Christmas and a Happy New Year. He'll be very merry and very happy, I have no doubt.

Bob Cratchit. If he cannot be, we must be happy for him. A song is what is needed. Tim!

Mrs. Cratchit. Shush! I've just gotten him down and he needs all the sleep he can get.

Bob Cratchit. If he's asleep on Christmas Eve, I'll be much mistaken. Tim! He must sing, dear, there is nothing else that might make him well.

Tiny Tim. Yes, Father?

Bob Cratchit. Are you awake?

Tiny Tim. Just a little.

Bob Cratchit. A song then! (*The* children *awaken and, led by* Tiny Tim, *sit up to sing "What Child Is This?" As they sing,* Scrooge *speaks.*)

Scrooge. (*He holds up his hand; all stop singing and look at him.*) I . . . I have seen enough. (*When the spirit signals to the children, they leave the stage, singing the carol quietly.* Tiny Tim *remains, covered completely by the dark blanket, disappearing against the black.*) Tiny Tim . . . will he live?

Second Spirit. He is very ill. Even song cannot keep him whole through a cold winter.

Scrooge. But you haven't told me!

Second Spirit (*imitating* Scrooge). If he be like to die, he had better do it and decrease the surplus population. (Scrooge *turns away.*) Erase, Scrooge, those words from your thoughts. You are not the judge. Do not judge, then. It may be that in the sight of heaven you are more worthless and less fit to live than millions like this poor man's child. Oh God! To hear an insect on a leaf pronouncing that there is too

WORDS TO KNOW

odious (ō'dē-əs) *adj.* causing or deserving strong dislike
charitable (chăr'ĭ-tə-bəl) *adj.* generous in giving

266

Teaching Options

 Mini Lesson **Speaking and Listening**

TEKS
5D, 5F, 23B, 24A

FILM/DRAMA

Prepare Show students one of the film versions of *A Christmas Carol*. As students view the film, they should be evaluating how closely it agrees with the way they envisioned the play. Then explain that filmmakers plan each scene with storyboards, or rough sketches, depicting plot, action, and characters. In groups, students should create their own storyboards of different scenes of the play, based on their interpretation and the film. Students should accompany their presentation of the storyboards with an explanation of which elements came from the written play and which

came from the film. They should clarify and support their ideas with elaborations and examples.

Present Each group should show their storyboards and present their explanations. The audience should generate criteria to evaluate the presentations and to assess whether the information enhances their understanding of the play.

BLOCK SCHEDULING This activity is particularly well suited for longer class periods.

Use **Communications Transparencies and Copymasters**, pp. 7, 37, 38, for additional support.

**Reading Skills and Strategies:
EVALUATING**

A Ask students to infer from details of Scrooge's character why he refuses to go to his nephew's house.

Possible Responses: Scrooge is too proud to go to Fred's house because he was so surly in refusing Fred's earlier gracious invitation. Scrooge is afraid of seeing more that will hurt him.

Literary Analysis: SYMBOL

B Have students interpret the significance of the children who represent Hunger and Ignorance. Ask why they are shown as children, and what the Spirit means by the last line here.

Possible Responses: Just as children grow, the problems of hunger and ignorance only get greater. If Scrooge ignores hunger and ignorance, they will get worse.

ACTIVE READING

C **VISUALIZE** **Possible Responses:** Responses will vary. Students may feel sorry for Scrooge or feel that he is getting what he deserves.

**Reading Skills and Strategies:
CLARIFYING**

D Ask students to explain why the servants are taking Scrooge's possessions.

Possible Response: He treated them so poorly when he was alive that they feel they can reward themselves now that he is dead.

**Reading Skills and Strategies:
HYPOTHESIZING**

E Ask students why Mrs. Cratchit's eyes are red and why she doesn't want her husband to see her reddened eyes.

Possible Responses: She has been crying. Someone has died or Bob Cratchit has lost his job or they are in need of money.

---

much life among his hungry brothers in the dust. Good-bye, Scrooge.

Scrooge. But is there no happiness in Christmas Present?

Second Spirit. There is.

Scrooge. Take me there.

Second Spirit. It is at the home of your nephew . . .

Scrooge. No!

Second Spirit (*disgusted with* Scrooge). Then there is none.

Scrooge. But that isn't enough . . . You must teach me!

Second Spirit. Would you have a teacher, Scrooge? Look at your own words.

Scrooge. But the first spirit gave me more . . . !

Second Spirit. He was Christmas Past. There was a lifetime he could choose from. I have only this day, one day, and you, Scrooge. I have nearly lived my fill of both. Christmas

Present must be gone at midnight. That ⬛ near now. (*He speaks to two* beggar childre *who pause shyly at the far side of the stage The* children *are thin and wan; they ar barefoot and wear filthy rags.*) Come. (*The go to him.*)

Scrooge. Is this the last spirit who is to come t⬛ me?

Second Spirit. They are no spirits. They ar⬛ real. Hunger, Ignorance. Not spirits, Scrooge passing dreams. They are real. They wal⬛ your streets, look to you for comfort. An⬛ you deny them. Deny them not too long Scrooge. They will grow and multiply, an⬛ they will not remain children.

Scrooge. Have they no refuge, no resource?

Second Spirit (*again imitating* Scrooge). Ar⬛ there no prisons? Are there no workhouses (*tenderly to the* children) Come. It's Christma Eve. (*He leads them offstage.*)

Scene 5

THE SPIRIT OF CHRISTMAS YET TO COME

Scrooge is entirely alone for a long moment. He is frightened by the darkness and feels it approaching him. Suddenly he stops, senses the presence of the third spirit, turns toward him, and sees him. The spirit is bent and cloaked. No physical features are distinguishable.

Scrooge. You are the third. (*The* spirit *says nothing.*) The Ghost of Christmas Yet to Come. (*The* spirit *says nothing.*) Speak to me. Tell me what is to happen—to me, to all of us. (*The* spirit *says nothing.*) Then show me what I must see. (*The* spirit *points. Light illumines the shadowy recesses of* Scrooge's *house.*) I know it. I know it too well, cold and cheerless. It is mine. (*The* cook *and the*

charwoman *are dimly visible in* Scrooge' *house.*) What is . . . ? There are . . . thieves There are thieves in my rooms! (*He starts forward to accost them, but the* spirit *beckons for him to stop.*) I cannot. You cannot tell m⬛ that I must watch them and do nothing. I wil⬛ not. It is mine still. (*He rushes into the house to claim his belongings and to protect them The two women do not notice his presence.*)

Teaching Options

Cross Curricular Link **Social Studies**

VICTORIAN ENGLAND *A Christmas Carol* was written during the Victorian Era (1837–1901), representing the reign of Queen Victoria. During this time, Britain was a great world power both on sea and on land. After Great Britain's victory in the Napoleonic Wars at the beginning of the century, the country became the world's greatest naval power, with control over most of the world's commerce. Furthermore, England was the world's leader in manufacturing.

Scrooge represents most industrialists' attitudes at this time. He voices the Social Darwinist

theory of "survival of the fittest." According to that doctrine, the poor are poor because of some fault on their part. This belief allows Scrooge to ignore the problems of the downtrodden.

By the 1840s, however, because of attention focused on conditions in industry, some reforms had been instituted. A Factory Act was passed in 1847. This limited the hours of work for children in textile factories to ten hours per day. Legislation was also passed to prohibit the employment of children under ten years old in the mines.

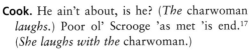

Cook. He ain't about, is he? (*The* charwoman *laughs.*) Poor ol' Scrooge 'as met 'is end.[17] (*She laughs with the* charwoman.)

Charwoman. An' time for it, too; ain't been alive in deed for half his life.

Cook. But the Sparsit's nowhere, is he . . . ?

Sparsit (*emerging from the blackness*). Lookin' for someone, ladies? (*The* cook *shrieks, but the* charwoman *treats the matter more practically, anticipating competition from* Sparsit.)

Charwoman. There ain't enough but for the two of us!

Sparsit. More 'an enough . . . if you know where to look.

Cook. Hardly decent is what I'd say, hardly decent, the poor old fella hardly cold and you're thievin' his wardrobe.

Sparsit. You're here out of love, are ya?

Charwoman. There's no time for that. (Sparsit *acknowledges* Scrooge *for the first time, gesturing toward him as if the living* Scrooge *were the corpse.* Scrooge *stands as if rooted to the spot, held there by the power of the* spirit.)

ACTIVE READING

VISUALIZE Close your eyes and imagine the scene. What do you see? How does what you see make you feel?

Sparsit. He ain't about to bother us, is he?

Charwoman. Ain't he a picture?

Cook. If he is, it ain't a happy one. (*They laugh.*)

Sparsit. Ladies, shall we start? (*The three of them grin and advance on* Scrooge.) Cook?

Cook (*snatching the cuff links from the shirt* Scrooge *wears*). They're gold, ain't they?

Sparsit. The purest, madam.

Charwoman. I always had a fancy for that nightcap of his. My old man could use it. (*She takes the nightcap from* Scrooge's *head.* Sparsit *playfully removes* Scrooge's *outer garment, the coat or cloak that he has worn in the previous scenes.*)

Sparsit. Bein' a man of more practical tastes, I'll go for the worsted[18] and hope the smell ain't permanent. (*The three laugh.*) Cook, we go round again.

Cook. Do you think that little bell he's always ringing at me is silver enough to sell? (*The three of them move toward the nightstand, and* Scrooge *cries out.*)

Scrooge. No more! No more! (*As the* spirit *directs* Scrooge's *attention to the tableau[19] of the three thieves standing poised over the silver bell,* Scrooge *bursts out of the house, clad only in his nightshirt.*) I cannot. I cannot. The room is . . . too like a cheerless place that is familiar. I won't see it. Let us go from here. Anywhere. (*The* spirit *directs his attention to the* Cratchit *house; the* children *are sitting together near* Mrs. Cratchit, *who is sewing a coat.* Peter *reads by the light of the coals.*)

Peter. "And he took a child and set him in the midst of them."

Mrs. Cratchit (*putting her hand to her face*). The light tires my eyes so. (*pause*) They're better now. It makes them tired to try to see by firelight, and I wouldn't show reddened eyes to your father when he comes home for the world. It must be near his time now.

Peter. Past it, I think, but he walks slower than he used to, these last few days, Mother.

Mrs. Cratchit. I have known him to walk with . . . I have known him to walk with Tiny Tim upon his shoulder very fast indeed. (*She catches herself, then hurries on.*) But he was

---

17. **'as met 'is end:** Cockney dialect for "has met his end." Cockneys (residents of the East End of London) drop the letter *h* when pronouncing words.

18. **worsted:** a smooth woolen fabric.

19. **tableau** (tăb′lō′): a portion of a play in which the actors momentarily freeze in their positions for dramatic effect.

Customizing Instruction

Less Proficient Readers

1 Discuss what Scrooge learns from the second Spirit.

• What do the Cratchits have that Scrooge doesn't?
Possible Responses: a loving family; a happy home; kind, charitable natures

• What does the second Spirit tell Scrooge about the needs of the poor?
Possible Responses: that the hunger and ignorance of the poor are real; that if he continues to ignore the needs of the poor, their needs will only increase

2 Ask students what the servants are doing with Scrooge's possessions.
Possible Response: Now that he is dead, they are dividing them up.

Set a Purpose As students read the rest of the play, have them see if Scrooge changes as a result of his experiences with the spirits.

Cross Curricular Link **Christmas Foods**

Christmas, like many holidays, is associated with traditional foods. In England, turkey or goose and plum pudding are often served. In America, people of Italian heritage often enjoy fish dinners on Christmas Eve and pasta as a first course on Christmas Day. On the Caribbean island of Barbados, people have a tangy red fruit drink called *sorrel* on Christmas morning.

Reading and Analyzing

Reading Skills and Strategies: HYPOTHESIZING

A Have students infer from the details in this passage what is going to happen on Sunday and where Bob Cratchit just came from.

Possible Responses: Sunday will be Tiny Tim's funeral; Bob just came from arranging the funeral.

Reading Skills and Strategies: EVALUATING

B Ask students what is revealed about the changes in Scrooge's character by his reaction to the news of Tiny Tim's death.

Possible Responses: He is able to sympathize with others; he feels guilt about not helping someone in need.

Thinking Through the Literature

1. **Possible Responses:** At first he may have felt angry. Then he may have felt sad that he had caused them to dislike him so greatly.

2. **Possible Responses:** Responses will vary. Some might say they were pleasantly surprised at Scrooge's reaction. Others might say that they had expected that kind of reaction.

3. **Possible Responses:** Scrooge feels guilty because he thinks he could have done something to help Tiny Tim live; Scrooge associates his own death with that of Tiny Tim and feels sorry for them both.

---

very light to carry and his father loved him, so that it was no trouble, no trouble. (*She hears* Bob Cratchit *approaching*.) Smiles, everyone, smiles.

Bob Cratchit (*entering*). My dear, Peter . . . (*He greets the other* children *by their real names*.) How is it coming?

Mrs. Cratchit (*handing him the coat*). Nearly done.

Bob Cratchit. Yes, good, I'm sure that it will be done long before Sunday.

Mrs. Cratchit. Sunday! You went today then, Robert?

Bob Cratchit. Yes. It's . . . it's all ready. Two o'clock. And a nice place. It would have done you good to see how green it is. But you'll see it often. I promised him that, that I would walk there on Sunday . . . often.

Mrs. Cratchit. We mustn't hurt ourselves for it, Robert.

Bob Cratchit. No. No, he wouldn't have wanted that. Come now. You won't guess who I've seen. Scrooge's nephew, Fred. And he asked after us and said he was heartily sorry and to

give his respect to my good wife. How h ever knew that, I don't know.

Mrs. Cratchit. Knew what, my dear?

Bob Cratchit. Why, that you were a good wife

Peter. Everybody knows that.

Bob Cratchit. I hope that they do. "Heartil sorry," he said, "for your good wife, and if can be of service to you in any way—" and h gave me his card—"that's where I live"—an Peter, I shouldn't be at all surprised if he go you a position.

Mrs. Cratchit. Only hear that, Peter!

Bob Cratchit. And then you'll be keeping company with some young girl and setting up for yourself.

Peter. Oh, go on.

Bob Cratchit. Well, it will happen, one day, bu remember, when that day does come—as i must—we must none of us forget poor Tiny Tim and this first parting in our family.

Scrooge. He died! No, no! (*He steps back and the scene disappears; he moves away from the spirit.*)

Thinking Through the Literature

1. What do you think Scrooge felt when he saw Sparsit, the charwoman, and the cook laughing over his corpse and dividing his belongings? Explain.

2. What thoughts came to mind when you read Scrooge's reaction to news of Tiny Tim's death?

3. Why do you think Tiny Tim's death affects Scrooge so deeply?

Teaching Options

✓ Assessment **Informal Assessment** TEKS 10L, 12F    TAAS Reading Obj. 5

BEFORE AND AFTER CHART You can informally assess how well your class understood the play by inviting them to create a before-and-after chart showing Scrooge's life, personality, and actions before and after the spirits' visits. Have students look through the play for specific examples, details, and quotations to include in their diagram.

RUBRIC

3 Full Accomplishment Students use specific details from the play to show Scrooge's

successful transformation from wretched miser to happy benefactor.

2 Substantial Accomplishment Students accurately describe the effect of the Spirits' visits on Scrooge's personality, but may include insufficient or inappropriate details from the play.

1 Little or Partial Accomplishment Students are unable to accurately show the change in Scrooge's personality as a result of his encounter with the three spirits.

Observe three of the spirits who visited Scrooge. Which has a more powerful impact on the viewer?

The Spirit of Christmas Present from *A Christmas Carol* (1938).

The ghost of Jacob Marley from *A Christmas Carol* (1938).

The Spirit of Christmas Yet to Come from *A Christmas Carol* (1938).

1 Explain to students that Bob Cratchit is describing the site of Tiny Tim's grave.

2 Tell students that his wife's comment might refer to the idea that they cannot dwell on Tiny Tim's death but must try to resume normal life.

3 Explain that "a position" is a job.

 View and Compare **TEKS** 23A, 23B

Direct students' attention to the photographs on this page. Have them analyze and critique the significance of each image to interpret the way filmmakers represent meanings.

Possible Responses: Jacob Marley is weighed down by his chains. His message is that wealth becomes a burden in the next world. Just as his appearance is ghastly, so is his message dreadful. The Spirit of Christmas Present appears jovial, happy, and friendly. His message matches his appearance; it is that Scrooge should fully live and experience the happiness in the world.

The Spirit of Christmas Yet to Come is not clearly seen. The future cannot be clearly seen either. Scrooge has the power to transform what will happen to him and others, which is why the Spirit's features are indistinguishable.

Students may say that the images match their interpretations or they may cite differences between the mental image that the text evokes and the image from the film. Ask them to give specific ways in which the film image differs from theirs.

A Have students summarize Scrooge's promises and evaluate his sincerity. Ask if students think that Scrooge has really changed this time and why or why not.

Possible Response: He is sincere, as shown by his selfless appeal for Tiny Tim's life: "Let the boy live."

**Reading Skills and Strategies:
VISUALIZING**

B Ask students to analyze the symbolism of the images that the text description evokes.

Possible Responses: The girl dressed in a cloak like that of the Virgin Mary suggests holiness; the dove symbolizes peace.

What do these images suggest about the sincerity of Scrooge's plea?

Possible Response: Scrooge has finally made peace with himself by embracing the sacredness of the Christmas spirit.

Literary Analysis: THEME

C Have students infer from Scrooge's actions and comments how he has changed. Guide students to make generalizations about the play's meaning, based on Scrooge's change of heart.

Possible Responses: The stingy miser has become generous. He cheerfully spends the money to make the Cratchits happy, and the prospect of making them happy makes him happy. This change of heart shows that joy comes from doing good things for others.

Scene 6

THE SPIRIT OF CHRISTMAS PRESENT

Scrooge. Because he would not . . . no! You cannot tell me that he has died, for that Christmas has not come! I will not let it come! I will be there . . . It was me. Yes, yes, and I knew it and couldn't look. I won't be able to help. I won't. (*pause*) Spirit, hear me. I am not the man I was. I will not be that man that I have been for so many years. Why show me all of this if I am past all hope? Assure me that I yet may change these shadows you have shown me. Let the boy live! I will honor Christmas in my heart and try to keep it all the year. I will live in the Past, the Present, and the Future. The spirits of all three shall strive within me. I will not shut out the lessons that they teach. Oh, tell me that I am not too late! (*A single light focuses on the little* girl, *dressed in a blue cloak like that of the Virgin Mary. She looks up, and from above a dove is slowly lowered in silence to her; she takes it and encloses it within her cloak, covering it. As soon as she does this, a large choir is heard singing "Gloria!" and the bells begin to ring. Blackout. When the lights come up again,* Scrooge *is in bed. The third spirit and the figures in the church have disappeared.* Scrooge *awakens and looks around his room.*) The curtains! They are mine and they are real. They are not sold. They are here. I am here; the shadows to come may be dispelled. They will be. I know they will be. (*He dresses himself hurriedly.*) I don't know what to do. I'm as light as a feather, merry as a boy again. Merry Christmas! Merry Christmas! A Happy New Year to all the world! Hello there! Whoop! Hallo! What day of the month is it? How long did the spirits keep me? Never mind. I don't care. (*He opens the window and calls to a boy in the street below.*) What's today?

Boy. Eh?

Scrooge. What's the day, my fine fellow?

Boy. Today? Why, Christmas Day!

Scrooge. It's Christmas Day! I haven't misse[d] it! The spirits have done it all in one nigh[t]. They can do anything they like. Of cours[e] they can. Of course they can save Tim. Hall[o] my fine fellow!

Boy. Hallo!

Scrooge. Do you know the poulterers[20] in th[e] next street at the corner?

Boy. I should hope I do.

Scrooge. An intelligent boy. A remarkable bo[y]. Do you know whether they've sold the priz[e] turkey that was hanging up there? Not th[e] little prize; the big one.

Boy. What, the one as big as me?

Scrooge. What a delightful boy! Yes, my bucke[t]

Boy. It's hanging there now.

Scrooge. It is? Go and buy it.

Boy. G'wan!

Scrooge. I'm in earnest! Go and buy it and te[ll] 'em to bring it here that I may give them th[e] direction where to take it. Come back wit[h] the butcher and I'll give you a shilling.[21] Come back in less than two minutes and I'[ll] give you half a crown!

Boy. Right, guv! (*He exits.*)

Scrooge. I'll send it to Bob Cratchit's. He shan'[t] know who sends it. It's twice the size of Tin[y] Tim and such a Christmas dinner it wi[ll] make. (Carolers *suddenly appear singing "Hark! The Herald Angels Sing."* Scrooge *leans out the window and joins them in the song.*) I must dress, I must. It's Christma[s]

---

20. **poulterers** (pōl'tər-ərz): people who sell poultry.

21. **shilling:** a British coin. Five shillings equal a crown.

Teaching Options

Mini Lesson **Speaking and Listening** TEKS 5C

DRAMA PERFORMANCE

Prepare Because of its form and content, *A Christmas Carol* is an ideal play for students to perform for families and for other classes. If you have not already done so, you may wish to show students a filmed version of the play to get a visual understanding of some of the elements of stagecraft. Then make a web like the one shown, listing each of the tasks involved in staging a play.

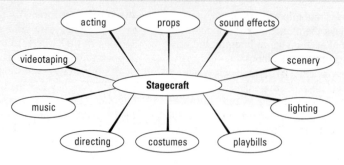

Less Proficient Readers

Ask students what changes can be seen in Scrooge as a result of his experiences with the spirits.

Possible Responses: He becomes kind, generous, and joyful.

Gifted and Talented

Explain that not all critics praise the play's characters and theme; some find Tiny Tim's death overly sentimental and Scrooge's conversion both hypocritical and improbable. Invite students to form two groups to debate these issues, with each group taking one side of the issue.

Present Assign each student a role in the production, according to his or her interests and learning style. Bodily-kinesthetic learners will enjoy performing the play, whereas interpersonal learners can be directors. Spatial learners can prepare scenery, lighting, costumes, and playbills; musical learners can create or find background music and sound effects. Assign logical-mathematical learners the task of designing the set and stage area; request that intrapersonal learners videotape rehearsals and the production. Then stage the play.

Use **Writing Transparencies,** p. 38, for additional support. Use **Communications Transparencies and Copymasters,** p. 12, for additional support.

A CONNECT Possible Responses: Responses will vary. Encourage students to give specific examples of how their celebrations are similar or different.

Literary Analysis STAGE DIRECTIONS

B Ask students what the parenthetical stage directions indicate about the Gentleman Visitor's reaction to being summoned by Scrooge.

Possible Responses: He is amazed at the kindness of the words and the warmth of the tone; he cannot believe it is the same man who was so rude to him the day before.

Literary Analysis: PLOT

C Remind students that the resolution is the part of the plot in which loose ends are tied up and the story is brought to a close. Ask students which significant conflicts are resolved in this scene.

Possible Responses: Scrooge's internal conflict with the values of the Christmas season is resolved; his neglect of the Cratchits is remedied with his generosity; he accepts his responsibility for the less fortunate of the world as shown by his gift to the Gentleman Visitor and his embracing of the little girl; he mends his relationship with his nephew Fred and allows himself to feel emotions.

Day! I must be all in my best for such a day. Where is my China silk shirt? (*The boy and the butcher run in with the turkey.*) What? Back already? And such a turkey. Why, you can't carry that all the way to Cratchit's. Here, boy, here is your half a crown and here an address in Camden Town. See that it gets there. Here, money for the cab, for the turkey, and for you, good man! (*The boy and the butcher, delighted, catch the money and run out. Scrooge sees the gentleman visitor walking by the window.*) Halloo, sir!

A CONNECT How is this holiday celebration like ones you have attended? How is it different?

Gentleman Visitor (*looking up sadly, less than festive*). Hello, sir.

Scrooge. My dear sir, how do you do? I hope you succeeded yesterday. It was very kind of you to stop by to see me.

B Gentleman Visitor (*in disbelief*). Mr. Scrooge?

Scrooge. Yes, that is my name, and I fear it may not be pleasant to you. Allow me to ask your pardon, and will you have the goodness to add this (*throwing him a purse*) to your good work!

Gentleman Visitor. Lord bless me! My dear Mr. Scrooge, are you serious?

Scrooge. If you please, not a penny less. A great many back payments are included in it, I assure you. Will you do me that favor?

Gentleman Visitor. My dear sir, I don't know what I can say to such generosity . . .

Scrooge. Say nothing! Accept it. Come and see me. Will you come and see me?

Gentleman Visitor. I will.

Scrooge. Thank 'ee. I am much obliged to you. I thank you fifty times. God bless you and Merry Christmas!

Gentleman Visitor. Merry Christmas to you, sir!

Scrooge (*running downstairs, out of his house and onto the street*). Now which is the way t[o] that nephew's house. Girl! Girl!

Girl (*appearing immediately*). Yes, sir?

Scrooge. Can you find me a taxi, miss?

Girl. I can, sir. (*She rings her doll, and [a] coachman appears.*)

Scrooge (*handing the coachman a card*). Ca[n] you show me the way to this home?

Coachman. I can, sir.

Scrooge. Good man. Come up, girl. (*The[y] mount to the top of the taxi. This action ma[y] be stylistically suggested.*) Would you be a[n] old man's guide to a Christmas dinner?

Girl. I would, sir, and God bless you!

Scrooge. Yes, God bless us every one! (*raising his voice almost in song*) Driver, t[o] Christmas! (*They exit, all three singing "Jo[y] to the World." Blackout. The lights come u[p] for the finale at Fred's house. The Cratchit[s] are there with Tiny Tim. All stop moving an[d] talking when they see Scrooge standing in th[e] center, embarrassed and humble.*) Well, I'[m] very glad to be here at my nephew's house[.] (*He starts to cry.*) Merry Christmas! Merr[y] Christmas!

All (*softly*). Merry Christmas. (*They sing "Deck the Halls," greeting one another an[d] exchanging gifts. Scrooge puts Tiny Tim o[n] his shoulders.*)

Tiny Tim (*shouting as the carol ends*). God bless us every one!

Scrooge (*to the audience*). Oh, yes! God bless us every one!

WORDS TO KNOW
finale (fə-năl′ē) *n.* the concluding part

Teaching Options

✓ Assessment **Standardized Test Practice** **TEKS** 10K, 12F  **TAAS** Reading Obj. 1

DESCRIBING CHARACTER For some standardized tests, students will be asked to choose the statement that best describes a character. To provide students with some help in choosing the best answer, read aloud or write on the board the following question:

Which of the following statements best describes the character of Ebenezer Scrooge as a young man?

A. He has the ability to enjoy life and to get pleasure from other people's company.

B. He is a pleasant young man who is ambitious and anxious to make his way in the world.

C. He is envious of people who have done well and wants to be successful himself.

Lead students through the process of choosing the best character description. Although A is true, it is not a complete view of Scrooge. The second part of C is true, but there is no support for the first part. Therefore, B would be the best choice. It includes all of the qualities of Scrooge as a young man that are revealed in the passage.

Connect to the Literature

1. What Do You Think?
If you had just seen this play on a stage, what is the first thing you would say to a friend about it?

Comprehension Check
- What kind of person is Scrooge in the first scene?
- What event most changed Scrooge during the visits of the three spirits?
- What does Scrooge do for Bob Cratchit's family at the end of the play?

Think Critically

2. **ACTIVE READING** **VISUALIZING** Review the sketches of scenes you made in your **READER'S NOTEBOOK.** What details in the stage directions most influenced your visualization of each scene?

3. Why do you think the Spirit of Christmas Present appeared to Scrooge as his old master Fezziwig?

THINK ABOUT
- how Fezziwig treated Scrooge
- Scrooge's feelings toward Fezziwig
- how Scrooge treated Bob Cratchit

4. Bob Cratchit and his wife differ on their attitudes toward Scrooge. What does this tell you about each character?

5. Which spirit do you think has the greatest influence in motivating Scrooge to change his life? Explain.

6. How did you react to Scrooge's change of heart in the final scene? Do you think it will be a lasting change? Why or why not?

Extend Interpretations

7. What If? Imagine that Scrooge had not had such a sad, lonely childhood. How do you think his story would have been different?

8. Connect to Life Charles Dickens wrote about many serious problems of his time. How would you compare the problems of poor people today with the problems of poor people in Dickens's time? Explain.

Literary Analysis

STAGE DIRECTIONS All plays have **stage directions**—instructions included in the script to help performers, directors, and stage crew put on the play, and to help readers visualize the action. Stage directions can suggest setting, lighting, music, sound effects, movement of actors, and how dialogue is spoken.

Activity Make a chart like the one below. Use it to record the major points you learned from the stage directions about aspects of the play, such as Scrooge's character, Scrooge's past, Scrooge's shop, Bob Cratchit's character, and the Cratchit family.

What I learned about . . .	Through stage directions
Scrooge's character	Scrooge hurls himself through the descending snowflakes and sends the children scattering.
Scrooge's past	

REVIEW **CHARACTER**
Characters may be described as static or dynamic. A **dynamic character** changes as a result of the events in the work. A **static character** remains unchanged. Which characters in *A Christmas Carol* would you describe as dynamic? Which are static?

Extend Interpretations

7. What If? Possible Response: Scrooge would have known how to show his feelings and share himself and his gifts with others if he had been exposed to more love in his own life. Friends might have been able to give him guidance and support to keep him from turning into the kind of man he became. Or, he may have become the same adult, regardless of his childhood experiences. He had positive influences in his life, such as his sister and Fezziwig, that did not seem to make a difference to his view of the world.

8. Connect to Life Possible Response: The problems are different today because poor people are not as desperate as they were in Dickens's time because of social welfare programs. However, the problems in many ways are the same because programs cannot help all poor people to attain adequate food, shelter, clothing, education, and health care.

Connect to the Literature

1. Responses will vary. Some students would enthusiastically recommend it; others might say that it was touching; others might find it improbable.

Comprehension Check
- He is bitter, miserable, and stingy.
- Seeing the future death of Tiny Tim most changed Scrooge.
- He sends them a huge turkey.

 Use Selection Quiz **Unit Two Resource Book**, p. 38.

Think Critically

2. Possible Responses: Students may offer the details that appeal to hearing, touch, or sight.

Use **Reading and Critical Thinking Transparencies**, p. 10, for additional support.

3. Possible Responses: Because of Scrooge's respect for Fezziwig, he might listen more carefully to what the Spirit has to say. Scrooge is reminded that Fezziwig was to Scrooge what Scrooge is to Cratchit. The difference in the way each treats his employee is startling and obvious and reinforces how wrong Scrooge is in his attitude toward others.

4. Possible Responses: Bob Cratchit is loyal to Scrooge and perhaps feels sorry for him because he knows what Scrooge is missing out on in life. Mrs. Cratchit is loyal to her husband, and she knows he deserves a better employer than Scrooge.

5. Possible Responses: Some students may mention the First Spirit because it shows Scrooge important experiences from his past. Other students may mention the Second Spirit because it shows Scrooge what he is missing in life. Still others may choose the Third Spirit because it is the most frightening and helps Scrooge see the kind of future he is creating.

6. Possible Responses: Some students will say that after seeing all that he did, Scrooge changed for the better.

Literary Analysis

Stage Directions After working through the stage directions chronologically, student charts should include several details about the characters and setting.

 Use **Literary Analysis Transparencies**, p. 23, for additional support.

Writing Options

1. **Last Will and Testament** Encourage students to use some legal words and phrases in drafting the will. Guide them to study the play's level of diction for guidelines in choosing other suitable words.

2. **Dialogue** Have students write their dialogue in the correct form. Each exchange should begin with the name of the character, followed by a period. The exact words of the character follow. Each exchange begins a new paragraph.

 Use **Writing Transparencies,** p. 24, for additional support.

3. **Sequel** To get students started on this assignment, have them brainstorm events that might happen. Remind students to arrange the events in chronological order and include conflicts, a climax, and a resolution.

Activities & Explorations

1. **Radio Play** To get students started on this assignment, have them assign specific roles to the students in their groups. Remind students that radio plays depend on effective communication of plot and characters through sound alone.

 Use **Communications Transparencies and Copymasters,** p. 12, for additional support.

2. **You Be the Critic** Suggest that students arrange their findings on a comparison/contrast chart or Venn diagram to make it easier for them to organize and remember key points.

Inquiry & Research

To make this assignment more challenging, have students find Victorian carols that are no longer popular.

Vocabulary and Spelling

EXERCISE A

1. S	6. S	11. S	16. S
2. S	7. A	12. A	17. A
3. A	8. S	13. S	18. A
4. A	9. S	14. S	19. A
5. S	10. A	15. A	20. S

EXERCISE B

1. reassurance   creative
   relation   amazing
   famous
2. Answers will vary.

Choices & CHALLENGES

Writing Options

1. Last Will and Testament Write a new will for Scrooge, explaining how he will share his wealth since his change of heart.

2. Dialogue Compose an imaginary dialogue in which two characters in this part of Unit Two discuss the choices they have made and the lessons they have learned from making those choices.

3. Sequel Has Scrooge been permanently changed by his experience? What will happen to the Cratchits? Write a plot summary for a sequel to this play, based on what you know about Scrooge and human nature.

Writing Handbook
See p. R33: Narrative Writing.

Activities & Explorations

1. Radio Play With some classmates, present *A Christmas Carol* as a radio play. Ask some students to read parts and others to provide sound effects. If possible, record your performance on audio-cassette so you can play it for another class. ~ **PERFORMING**

2. You Be the Critic With your classmates, watch a video of *A Christmas Carol.* Then get together in small groups to compare the video and the play versions. When you have finished, share your group's comparison with comments of other groups. ~ **SPEAKING AND LISTENING**

Inquiry & Research

Research the history of carols and caroling. Present your findings to the class in an oral report or speech. Try to include recordings or your own renditions of some of the carols mentioned in *A Christmas Carol.*

Vocabulary and Spelling

EXERCISE A: SYNONYMS/ANTONYMS On your paper, write *S* if the words are synonyms and *A* if they are antonyms.

1. **finale**—ending
2. **pledge**—promise
3. **surplus**—lack
4. **destitute**—wealthy
5. **transform**—change
6. **solitude**—isolation
7. **summon**—dismiss
8. **provision**—arrangement
9. **mortal**—human
10. **charitable**—stingy
11. **welfare**—well-being
12. **reassurance**—discouragement
13. **abundance**—plenty
14. **currency**—money
15. **emerge**—disappear
16. **endeavor**—try
17. **anonymous**—known
18. **incoherent**—understandable
19. **macabre**—pleasant
20. **odious**—hateful

EXERCISE B: WORDS ENDING IN A SILENT *e* When a suffix beginning with a vowel is added to a word ending in a silent *e*, the *e* is usually dropped, as in *reassurance.*

1. Add the suffixes to these words.
   reassure + ance = _____
   relate + ion = _____
   fame + ous = _____
   create + ive = _____
   amaze + ing = _____
2. Use each of the spelling words in a complete sentence.

Spelling Handbook p. R86

Teaching Options

 Mini Lesson **Spelling** **TEKS 16C** 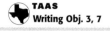 **TAAS Writing Obj. 3, 7**

SILENT *E*

Instruction Remind students that when a suffix beginning with a vowel is added to a word ending in a silent *e*, the *e* is usually dropped.
enrage + ed = enraged

Exercise Ask students to locate the misspelled words in the following paragraph and then rewrite each correctly.

We sat gazeing at the snow as it fell on busy shoppers. It was a holiday season, and people bustleed up and down ice-glazeed streets. Not being able to enjoy the cheerfulness of the surroundings was unimagineable. We were hopeful that everyone in town would enjoy a good holiday season.

Answers: *gazing, bustled, ice-glazed, unimaginable*

 Use **Unit Two Resource Book,** p. 37 for more practice.

Grammar in Context: Action Verbs

Playwright Frederick Gaines uses **action verbs** in his vivid adaption of Dickens's *A Christmas Carol:*

> The percussion thunders. Scrooge hurls himself through the descending snowflakes and sends the children scattering. They retreat, watching.

Compare these sentences: *The percussion sounds like thunder* and *The percussion thunders.* The second sentence, which uses an action verb, has fewer words and is more forceful than the first.

Apply to Your Writing Choosing action verbs to express your ideas will make your writing more concise and effective.

WRITING EXERCISE Rewrite each sentence using an action verb.

Example: ***Original*** In bed at night, Scrooge is afraid of the darkness.

Rewritten Afraid of the darkness, Scrooge trembled under the bed sheets.

1. Bob Cratchit was a devoted clerk.
2. Nevertheless, his family was poor.
3. At Christmas, many children are hungry.
4. This is the Spirit of Christmas Past.

Connect to the Literature Reread the accompanying stage directions at the beginning of Scene 2 on page 258. Starting with "As the two find . . . ," make a list of action verbs.

Grammar Handbook Using Verbs Correctly, p. R68

"Dickens's own childhood provided material for a number of his works."

Charles Dickens
1812–1870

Social Crusader Charles Dickens had intended to write a pamphlet called "An Appeal to the People of England, on Behalf of the Poor Man's Child," but instead he decided to get his idea across by using the form of a story. When *A Christmas Carol* came out in December 1843, about 6,000 copies were sold in just a few days. Since then, *A Christmas Carol* has become a classic holiday tradition.

Unhappy Childhood Dickens's own childhood provided material for a number of his works. When Dickens was 12, his father was imprisoned for debt, and Dickens had to leave

school and go to work in a rat-infested factory. The hopelessness and the shame he experienced there affected him deeply. One of his novels, *David Copperfield,* was based partly on his experiences in that factory. In such other novels as *Oliver Twist* and *Little Dorrit,* Dickens draws on childhood memories to depict the plight of the poor in a society that values wealth.

AUTHOR ACTIVITY

From Novel to Play You have read an adaptation of a novel by one of England's favorite authors. Read Dickens's novel *A Christmas Carol,* and then compare and contrast it with Frederick Gaines's dramatized version. What is lost in the dramatized version? What is gained? Which did you enjoy more?

 LaserLink: Background for Reading Author Background

A CHRISTMAS CAROL **277**

Grammar in Context
WRITING EXERCISE
Possible Responses

1. Bob Cratchit, a devoted clerk, often worked late.
2. Nevertheless, he struggled to support his poor family.
3. At Christmas, many hungry children begged for pennies.
4. The Spirit of Christmas Past took Scrooge on a journey.

CONNECT TO THE LITERATURE
Possible Responses: hold, light, earn, will go, know, find, sees, hears, ends, come, saved, swims, watches, fumbles, lights, swings, melts, fits, turns, hurry, did knock, leads, pass, brushes, leans

Charles Dickens

After the publication of *A Christmas Carol* in 1843, Dickens became so closely identified with the holiday that a child is said to have cried, upon hearing of his death, "Dickens dead! Then will Father Christmas die too?"

Author Activity

From Novel to Play Suggest that students organize their comparison in chart form and support their observations with evidence from both texts. **Auditory learners** might find it helpful to listen to *A Christmas Carol* on tape.

Mini Lesson **Grammar** **TEKS 15H** **TAAS** 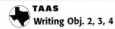 **Writing Obj. 2, 3, 4**

ACTION VERBS IN EFFECTIVE WRITING

Instruction Remind students that the goal of their writing is to communicate their ideas as clearly and precisely as possible. Using action verbs is a way to create a precise mental image in the mind of the reader. Action verbs also help to keep the reader's interest. Tell students that not all action verbs are equally effective in conveying meaning. Different verbs have different connotations or express varying degrees of the same action. For example, the sentence "Scrooge made a face at the carolers" does not create a precise image of what kind of face he

made. The action verb *scowled* or *frowned* would give a clearer picture.

Exercises Have students replace the underlined action verb and modifier with a more precise action verb.

1. The boy <u>went quickly</u> down the street. *(dashed, galloped, tore, raced)*
2. Bob Cratchit <u>walked quietly</u> past Tiny Tim. *(crept, tiptoed)*
3. Scrooge <u>called loudly</u> to the Gentleman Visitor. *(yelled, bellowed, screamed, shouted)*
4. Fezziwig <u>forcefully told</u> his employees to

enjoy themselves. *(urged, persuaded, encouraged)*
5. The lame man <u>went slowly</u> down the alley. *(limped, shuffled, hobbled)*

Use **Unit Two Resource Book**, p. 36.
Use **Grammar Transparencies and Copymasters**, p. 70.

 Use McDougal Littell's *Language Network*, Chapter 4, for more instruction and practice in action verbs.

A CHRISTMAS CAROL **277**

This selection appears in Spanish in the **Spanish Study Guide**.

Objectives

1. understand and appreciate a **short story** (Literary Analysis)
2. recognize the **theme** of a short story (Literary Analysis)
3. **connect** to your own experience (Active Reading)

Summary

Martha, who is being raised by her grandparents, has the best record of any eighth-grader and is entitled to win the school's highest academic honor—a scholarship jacket. Just before graduation, though, she overhears two teachers arguing. One, Mr. Schmidt, supports Martha's record and refuses to falsify grades. The other, Mr. Boone, points out that Joann's father is on the Board and owns the only store in town. He thinks the school could give the jacket to her and say it was a close tie. Mr. Schmidt threatens to quit and storms out. The next day, the principal tells Martha that she will have to pay $15 if she wants the jacket. Martha says that she will ask her grandfather. Although he can afford the money, he refuses on principle to pay. Martha tells the principal her grandfather's decision and blurts out that they will have to give the jacket to Joann. The principal thinks awhile and decides that Martha can have it after all. She goes home and finds her grandfather weeding. She joins him and tells him the good news.

Thematic Link

Martha learns a powerful lesson from her grandfather when he helps her choose between compromising her values to get something she wants very much and standing up for what is right and thereby possibly not getting what she wants.

5-Minute Warm-Up

Daily Language SkillBuilder

Have students **proofread** the display sentences on page 189j and write them correctly. The sentences also appear on Transparency 8 of **Grammar Transparencies and Copymasters**.

"He turned to me and asked quietly, 'What does a scholarship jacket mean?'"

The Scholarship Jacket

Short Story by MARTA SALINAS

Connect to Your Life

It's Not Right! Have you ever been treated unfairly? Have been the victim of prejudice? Have you ever had to stand up for your beliefs against someone more powerful than you? With two or three classmates, discuss an experience of prejudice you know about.

Build Background

CONNECT TO **SOCIAL STUDIES** Hispanic Americans are an important segment of the U.S. population. Many have family ties to Mexico, Puerto Rico, Cuba, or the Spanish-speaking countries of Central America. Others are members of families that have lived in what is now the United States for hundreds of years.

The more than 27 million Hispanic Americans have made many contributions to American history and culture, yet they often experience discrimination in jobs, housing, and education. "The Scholarship Jacket" is about a Mexican-American girl who lives in Texas. It tells how she and her grandfather deal with an instance of prejudice.

WORDS TO KNOW	Vocabulary Preview	
agile	falsify	resign
coincidence	fidget	valedictorian
despair	gaunt	vile
dismay	muster	

Focus Your Reading

LITERARY ANALYSIS **THEME** A story's **theme** is a message that the story expresses about human nature or life in general. Usually, a theme is not directly stated. The reader must figure it out by making logical inferences based on details in the story. A major theme of *A Christmas Carol*, for example, is the need for generosity and forgiveness. As you read the story, think about how the theme of "The Scholarship Jacket" is revealed through Martha's experiences.

ACTIVE READING **CONNECTING** When you use the strategy of **connecting** in reading a story, you look for elements that you can relate to your own knowledge and experience. While reading "The Scholarship Jacket," take note of things that you can connect with your own life. Do any of the **characters** resemble people you know? Which details, events, and emotions seem familiar? Which are unfamiliar?

READER'S NOTEBOOK As you read the story, jot down details that remind you of your own life, as well as details that seem unfamiliar.

Martha studied hard.

 See the Skills Trace at the beginning of the unit for information on TEKS covered in this lesson

LESSON RESOURCES

UNIT TWO RESOURCE BOOK, pp. 39–45

ASSESSMENT
Formal Assessment, pp. 41–42
Teacher's Guide to Assessment and Portfolio Use
Test Generator

SKILLS TRANSPARENCIES AND COPYMASTERS
Literary Analysis
• Theme, TR 7 (for Cooperative Learning Activity, p. 284)
Reading and Critical Thinking
• Connecting, TR 2 (for Thinking Through the Literature, p. 284)

Grammar
• Subject-Verb Agreement, CM 118 (for Mini Lesson, p. 282)
• Maintaining Consistent Verb Tense, CM 75 (for Mini Lesson, p. 286)
Vocabulary
• Meaning Clues, CM 41 (for Mini Lesson, p. 279)

INTEGRATED TECHNOLOGY
Audio Library

Visit our website:
www.mcdougallittell.com

The Scholarship Jacket

by Marta Salinas

The small Texas school that I went to had a tradition carried out every year during the eighth-grade graduation: a beautiful gold and green jacket (the school colors) was awarded to the class <u>valedictorian</u>, the student who had maintained the highest grades for eight years. The scholarship jacket had a big gold S on the left front side and your name written in gold letters on the pocket.

My oldest sister, Rosie, had won the jacket a few years back, and I fully expected to also. I was fourteen and in the eighth grade. I had been a straight A student since the first grade and this last year had looked forward very much to owning that jacket. My father was a farm laborer who couldn't earn enough money to feed eight children, so when I was six I was given to my grandparents to raise. We couldn't participate in sports at school because there were registration fees, uniform costs, and trips out of town; so, even though our family was quite <u>agile</u> and athletic there would never be a school sports jacket for us. This one, the scholarship jacket, was our only chance.

In May, close to graduation, spring fever had struck as usual with a vengeance.[1] No one paid any attention in class; instead we stared out the windows and at each other, wanting to speed up the last few weeks of school. I <u>despaired</u> every time I looked in the mirror. Pencil thin, not a curve anywhere. I was called "beanpole" and "string bean," and I knew that's what I looked like. A flat chest, no hips, and a brain; that's what I had. That really wasn't much for a fourteen-year-old to work with, I thought, as I absent-mindedly wandered from my history class to the gym. Another hour of sweating in basketball and displaying my toothpick legs was coming up. Then I remembered my P.E. shorts were still in a bag under my desk where I'd forgotten them. I had to walk all the way back and get them. Coach Thompson was a real bear if someone wasn't dressed for P.E. She had said I was a good forward and even tried to talk Grandma into letting me join the team once. Of course Grandma said no.

I was almost back at my classroom door when I heard voices raised in anger as if in some sort of argument. I stopped. I didn't mean to eavesdrop,[2] I just hesitated, not knowing

---

1. **with a vengeance** (věn′jəns): to an extreme degree.
2. **eavesdrop** (ēvz′drŏp′): to listen secretly to a private conversation of others.

WORDS	**valedictorian** (văl′ĭ-dĭk-tôr′ē-ən) *n.* student with highest academic rank in a class
TO	**agile** (ăj′əl) *adj.* quick and light in movement
KNOW	**despair** (dĭ-spâr′) *v.* to lose hope

279

 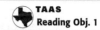
MEANING CLUES

Instruction Tell students that they can draw on their own experiences to infer the meanings of unfamiliar words in context. Readers sometimes must infer a word's meaning from what they know. Read this sentence as an example:

> What a <u>coincidence</u>! I was calling you at the same time you were calling me.

Discuss what students can infer about the meaning of *coincidence* from this sentence and what clues helped them determine this meaning.

Application Ask students to cover the WORDS TO KNOW at the bottom of page 279. Then have them find the first two underlined vocabulary words and independently read the passages around each word. Then have them discuss what they inferred about each word's meaning. After the discussion, students can check their inferences with the meanings at the bottom of the page.

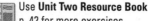 Use **Unit Two Resource Book** p. 42 for more exercises.

Use **Vocabulary Transparencies and Copymasters**, p. 41, for additional support.

TEACHING THE LITERATURE
Customizing Instruction

Students Acquiring English
Provide a brief summary of the story for students and link it to events with which they can identify. Have them use their own knowledge and experience to comprehend the main problem. Ask, for instance, how they would feel if they deserved and expected a prize and then learned that someone else might get it. As students read the story, encourage frequent predictions about what is likely to happen. Afterward, discuss with students what did happen and why.

 Use **Spanish Study Guide**, pp. 52–54 for additional support.

Less Proficient Readers
Students may have difficulty understanding the crucial scene in which Martha overhears the two teachers arguing. You may wish to have students read this scene with you.

Set a Purpose Have students read to find out what problem Martha faces and who helps her solve it.

Gifted and Talented
This story treats the issue of unfairness, which is particularly sensitive in a school setting. Invite students to identify the reason for the unfairness in this story. Then have them use this compiled information and knowledge to raise additional, unanswered questions about the topic. These questions might form the basis for a classwide discussion afterward.

Reading and Analyzing

Literary Analysis THEME

 A Remind students that one way to identify a story's theme is to think about what happens to a story's main character. From what students know about Martha so far, do they think she deserves the jacket or not? Why?

Possible Response: She deserves it because she is a straight A student and has worked hard for years.

Use the **Unit Two Resource Book,** p. 41 for more practice.

Active Reading CONNECTING

B Tell students that they can connect Martha's experiences and emotions to experiences and feelings that they've had. Doing this will draw them into the story and increase their understanding of the story's themes. Ask students to infer how Martha is feeling in this paragraph. Then have them think about a time when they've had similar feelings. As they read, students can use a chart like this to connect other details and emotions in the story to their own lives.

Martha's experience	My experience

Use **Unit Two Resource Book,** p. 40 for additional practice.

Reading Skills and Strategies: DRAWING CONCLUSIONS

C Ask students why the scholarship jacket isn't free this year.

Possible Response: Officials hope that only Joann will be able to afford it.

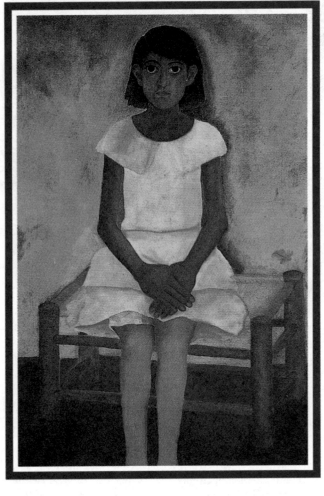

Retrato de muchacha [Portrait of a girl] (1929), Frida Kahlo. Oil on canvas, 46½″ × 31½″, collection of the Dolores Olmedo Patiño Foundation, Museo Frida Kahlo, Mexico City.

what to do. I needed those shorts and I was going to be late, but I didn't want to interrupt an argument between my teachers. I recognized the voices: Mr. Schmidt, my history teacher, and Mr. Boone, my math teacher. They seemed to be arguing about me. I couldn't believe it. I still remember the feeling of shock that rooted me flat against the wall as if I were trying to blend in with the graffiti written there.

"I refuse to do it! I don't care who her father is, her grades don't even begin to compare to Martha's. I won't lie or falsify records. Martha has a straight A-plus average and you know it." That was Mr. Schmidt and he sounded very angry. Mr. Boone's voice sounded calm and quiet.

"Look. Joann's father is not only on the Board, he owns the only store in town: we could say it was a close tie and—"

The pounding in my ears drowned out the rest of the words, only a word here and there filtered through. " . . . Martha is Mexican . . . resign . . . won't do it . . . . " Mr. Schmidt came

WORDS TO KNOW
falsify (fôl'sə-fī') *v.* to make false by adding to or changing
resign (rĭ-zīn') *v.* to give up (a job or an award, for instance)

280

Teaching Options

BLOCK SCHEDULING: MANAGING TIME

If your schedule requires that you cover the lesson objectives in a shorter time, use . . .
- Preparing to Read, p. 278
- Thinking Through the Literature, p. 284
- Vocabulary in Action, p. 285
- Grammar in Context, p. 286

If you would like to take advantage of longer class time, use . . .
- TE Teaching Options: Preteaching Vocabulary, p. 279; Viewing and Representing, p. 281; Grammar, pp. 282, 286; Standardized Test Practice, p. 283
- Choices & Challenges and Author Activity, pp. 285-286

rushing out and luckily for me went down the opposite way toward the auditorium, so he didn't see me. Shaking, I waited a few minutes and then went in and grabbed my bag and fled from the room. Mr. Boone looked up when I came in but didn't say anything. To this day I don't remember if I got in trouble in P.E. for being late or how I made it through the rest of the afternoon. I went home very sad and cried into my pillow that night so Grandmother wouldn't hear me. It seemed a cruel <u>coincidence</u> that I had overheard that conversation.

The next day when the principal called me into his office I knew what it would be about. He looked uncomfortable and unhappy. I decided I wasn't going to make it any easier for him, so I looked him straight in the eyes. He looked away and <u>fidgeted</u> with the papers on his desk.

"Martha," he said, "there's been a change in policy this year regarding the scholarship jacket. As you know, it has always been free." He cleared his throat and continued. "This year the Board has decided to charge fifteen dollars, which still won't cover the complete cost of the jacket."

I stared at him in shock, and a small sound of <u>dismay</u> escaped my throat. I hadn't expected this. He still avoided looking in my eyes.

"So if you are unable to pay the fifteen dollars for the jacket it will be given to the next one in line." I didn't need to ask who that was.

Standing with all the dignity I could <u>muster</u>, I said, "I'll speak to my grandfather about it, sir, and let you know tomorrow." I cried on the walk home from the bus stop. The dirt road was a quarter mile from the highway, so by the time I got home, my eyes were red and puffy.

"Where's Grandpa?" I asked Grandma, looking down at the floor so she wouldn't ask me why I'd been crying. She was sewing on a quilt as usual and didn't look up.

"I think he's out back working in the bean field."

I went outside and looked out at the fields. There he was. I could see him walking between the rows, his body bent over the little plants, hoe in hand. I walked slowly out to him, trying to think how I could best ask him for the money. There was a cool breeze blowing and a sweet smell of mesquite[3] fruit in the air, but I didn't appreciate it. I kicked at a dirt clod. I wanted that jacket so much. It was more than just being a valedictorian and giving a little thank you speech for the jacket on graduation night. It represented eight years of hard work and expectation. I knew I had to be honest with Grandpa; it was my only chance. He saw my shadow and looked up.

He waited for me to speak. I cleared my throat nervously and clasped my hands behind my back so he wouldn't see them shaking. "Grandpa, I have a big favor to ask you," I said in Spanish, the only language he knew. He still waited silently. I tried again. "Grandpa, this year the principal said the scholarship jacket is not going to be free. It's going to cost fifteen dollars, and I have to take the money in tomorrow, otherwise it'll be given to someone else." The last words came out in an eager rush. Grandpa straightened up tiredly and leaned his chin on the hoe handle. He looked out over the field that was filled with the tiny green bean plants. I waited, desperately hoping he'd say I could have the money.

He turned to me and asked quietly, "What does a scholarship jacket mean?"

---

3. **mesquite** (mě-skēt′): small spiny tree native to hot, dry regions of North America.

WORDS
TO
KNOW

coincidence (kō-ĭn′sĭ-dəns) *n.* accidental sequence of events that seems planned
fidget (fĭj′ĭt) *v.* to behave nervously or restlessly
dismay (dĭs-mā′) *n.* loss of courage in the face of trouble
muster (mŭs′tər) *v.* to call forth, to summon up

281

Customizing Instruction

Less Proficient Readers
☐1 Use the following questions to guide students to understand what the scholarship jacket is and what it means in this story.
• Why does Martha expect to win the scholarship jacket?
  Possible Response: She was a great student; she deserved it.
• Why might Martha not get the jacket?
  Possible Response: Another girl has a rich and powerful father; the school might give her the jacket.
• What change does the school suddenly make in how it awards the jacket? Why is this a problem for Martha?
  Possible Response: It now charges fifteen dollars for the jacket. Martha is poor.

Set a Purpose Have students read to find out what Martha's grandfather says when she asks for help.

Gifted and Talented
Invite students to debate which type of prize someone is likely to value and enjoy more: one won as the result of effort or one won as the result of luck. Have them give reasons for their choices.

Mini Lesson **Viewing and Representing** 🏴 TEKS 22A, 23B

Retrato de muchacha (Portrait of a Girl) (1929)
by Frida Kahlo

ART APPRECIATION Frida Kahlo (1907-1954) was one of Mexico's most talented and gifted painters.
Instruction Explain that an artist, like a writer, can reveal a subject's character by choosing what they will depict and how. Ask how the artist has managed to express that this subject has an inner life.
Possible Response: The girl's body is perfectly still; her eyes are open, as if she were thinking.

Application: Ask students to compare and contrast this picture with the written story. How do their impressions of this subject compare with their impressions of Martha?
Possible Responses: Like Martha, the girl is dignified; thoughtful; young; serious; alert. She displays few luxuries; she wears no jewelry, so perhaps she is poor.

Literary Analysis: SYMBOL

A What does this jacket symbolize, and how would paying for it change that?

Possible Responses: It symbolizes effort and academic work. Paying for it changes it into a financial transaction.

Reading Skills and Strategies: INTERPRETING

B Ask students to interpret the sentence that says, "Those were the days of belief and innocence." What did the narrator believe at the time and what innocence did she lose?

Possible Responses: She believed that the Board had really changed the rules; now she knows that the principal just made up that rule to keep her from getting the jacket.

Literary Analysis: CHARACTER

C When Martha says this, what does this reveal about her to the principal?

Possible Response: He knows that Martha knows that some people want Joann to win.

Active Reading CONNECTING

D Ask students what they do when they are very happy. Do they want to yell and jump like Martha did, or do they react in some other way?

Possible Responses: Some students may also react physically, while others may just smile or feel good inside.

Reading Skills and Strategies: INTERPRETING

E Ask students to interpret the sentence that says, "He didn't fool me." What did the narrator mean?

Possible Response: She knew that Grandpa was happy even though he did not say anything about the jacket.

I answered quickly; maybe there was a chance. "It means you've earned it by having the highest grades for eight years and that's why they're giving it to you." Too late I realized the significance of my words. Grandpa knew that I understood it was not a matter of money. It wasn't that. He went back to hoeing the weeds that sprang up between the delicate little bean plants. It was a time-consuming job; sometimes the small shoots were right next to each other. Finally he spoke again as I turned to leave, crying.

A "Then if you pay for it, Marta, it's not a scholarship jacket, is it? Tell your principal I will not pay the fifteen dollars."

I walked back to the house and locked myself in the bathroom for a long time. I was angry with Grandfather even though I knew he was right, and I was angry with the Board, whoever they were. Why did they have to change the rules just when it was my turn to **B** win the jacket? Those were the days of belief and innocence.

It was a very sad and withdrawn girl who dragged into the principal's office the next day. This time he did look me in the eyes.

"What did your grandfather say?"

I sat very straight in my chair.

"He said to tell you he won't pay the fifteen dollars."

The principal muttered something I couldn't understand under his breath and walked over to the window. He stood looking out at something outside. He looked bigger than usual when he stood up; he was a tall, gaunt man with gray hair, and I watched the back of his head while I waited for him to speak.

"Why?" he finally asked. "Your grandfather has the money. He owns a two-hundred-acre ranch."

I looked at him, forcing my eyes to stay dry. "I know, sir, but he said if I had to pay for it, then it wouldn't be a scholarship jacket." I stood up to leave. "I guess you'll just have to give it to Joann." I hadn't meant to say that, it had just slipped out. I was almost to the door when he stopped me.

"Martha—wait."

I turned and looked at him, waiting. What did he want now? I could feel my heart pounding loudly in my chest and see my blouse fluttering where my breasts should have been. Something bitter and <u>vile</u> tasting was coming up in my mouth; I was afraid I was going to be sick. I didn't need any sympathy speeches. He sighed loudly and went back to his big desk. He watched me, biting his lip.

"Okay. We'll make an exception in your case. I'll tell the Board, you'll get your jacket."

I could hardly believe my ears. I spoke in a trembling rush. "Oh, thank you, sir!" Suddenly I felt great. I didn't know about adrenalin in those days, but I knew something was pumping through me, making me feel as tall as the sky. I wanted to yell, jump, run the mile, do something. I ran out so I could cry in the hall where there was no one to see me.

At the end of the day, Mr. Schmidt winked at me and said, "I hear you're getting the scholarship jacket this year."

His face looked as happy and innocent as a baby's, but I knew better. Without answering I gave him a quick hug and ran to the bus. I cried on the walk home again, but this time because I was so happy. I couldn't wait to tell Grandpa and ran straight to the field. I joined him in the row where he was working, and without saying anything I crouched down and started pulling up the weeds with my hands. Grandpa worked alongside me for a few minutes, and he didn't ask what had

WORDS
TO
KNOW
   vile (vīl) *adj.* disgusting, unpleasant

  Grammar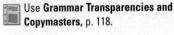

SUBJECT-VERB AGREEMENT Remind students that a verb must agree with its subject in number. A noun or pronoun that stands for one person, place, thing, or idea is singular. If a singular noun is the subject of a sentence, its verb must be singular. A noun that stands for more than one is plural. If a plural noun is the subject of a sentence, the verb must be plural. Point out the highlighted sentence and have students identify the subject and verb of

each clause. Ask which are singular and which are plural.

Answer: *It* and *was* are singular; *shoots* and *were* are plural.

Exercises Have students identify the subject and verb of each sentence and tell whether they are singular or plural.

1. Martha's <u>grandparents are</u> raising her. (*plural*)

2. The <u>girl works</u> hard at school. (*singular*)

3. The <u>teachers were</u> talking loudly. (*plural*)

4. <u>Martha hears</u> part of the discussion. (*singular*)

5. <u>She runs</u> home in tears. (*singular*)

 Use **Grammar Transparencies and Copymasters**, p. 118.

Use McDougal Littell's **Language Network,** Chapter 9, for more instruction and practice in subject-verb agreement.

happened. After I had a little pile of weeds between the rows, I stood up and faced him.

"The principal said he's making an exception for me, Grandpa, and I'm getting the jacket after all. That's after I told him what you said."

Grandpa didn't say anything; he just gave me a pat on the shoulder and a smile. He pulled out the crumpled red handkerchief that he always carried in his back pocket and wiped the sweat off his forehead.

"Better go see if your grandmother needs any help with supper."

I gave him a big grin. He didn't fool me. I skipped and ran back to the house whistling some silly tune. ❖

Customizing Instruction

Multiple Learning Styles
Kinesthetic Learners

Have students pantomime how Martha feels when she overhears the teachers' discussion, when her grandfather refuses to pay for the jacket, and when she learns that she will get the jacket.

LITERARY LINK

This piece reflects some of the ideas in the main selection and is suggested for students' independent reading. Optional discussion questions follow.

1. What is the relationship between the woman and the boy?
   Possible Responses: She is his parents' housekeeper; she loves him and he loves her.
2. Where is the woman on graduation morning? How does the boy find her?
   Answer: She is at his graduation. She is wearing black, while others are wearing sparkling clothes.
3. What feelings does the woman have at the end?
   Possible Response: happiness; sadness; love; pride

Pat Mora

Pat Mora (b. 1942) grew up in El Paso, Texas, where she was surrounded by both the Anglo and Mexican cultures. She knew firsthand the relationship between them, since one formed her culture at school and the other her culture at home. She writes, she says, because "I am fascinated by the pleasure and power of words."

LITERARY LINK

GRADUATION MORNING
by Pat Mora

for Anthony

She called him *Lucero*,[1] morning star,
snared him with sweet coffee, pennies,
Mexican milk candy, brown bony hugs.

Through the years she'd cross the Rio
5 Grande to clean his mother's home. "*Lucero,
mi*[2] *lucero,*" she'd cry, when she'd see him
running toward her in the morning,
when she pulled stubborn cactus thorns
from his small hands, when she found him
10 hiding in the creosote.[3]

Though she's small and thin,
black sweater, black scarf,
the boy in the white graduation robe
easily finds her at the back of the cathedral,
15 finds her amid the swirl of sparkling clothes,
finds her eyes.

Tears slide down her wrinkled cheeks.
Her eyes, *luceros*, stroke his face.

Copyright © The Stock Illustration Source, Inc.

1. lucero (lōō-sĕ'rō) *Spanish:* bright star.
2. mi (mē) *Spanish:* my.
3. creosote (krē'ə-sōt'): creosote bushes, shrubs found in Mexico and the southwestern United States.

THE SCHOLARSHIP JACKET   **283**

Assessment **Standardized Test Practice**   **TEKS** 10H, 10K  **TAAS** Reading Obj. 5

MAKE INFERENCES AND DRAW CONCLUSIONS In some standardized tests, students are asked to draw conclusions and support them with text evidence and experience. Write the following question on the chalkboard or read it aloud: Information in the story suggests that Mr. Schmidt is —
A. old
B. dishonest
C. honest
D. funny

Lead students through the process of choosing the best answer. Help them recognize that no evidence supports answers A, B, or D. However, several details suggest Mr. Schmidt's honesty: he refuses to falsify records; he is willing to resign. Therefore, the best answer is C.

Connect to the Literature

1. What Do You Think?
Possible Response: I felt glad that Martha got what she wanted and learned about not giving in to prejudice.
Identification with Martha's triumph may vary from student to student.

Comprehension Check
• They are arguing about not awarding the scholarship jacket to Martha and awarding it instead to another student, even though she is not qualified, because her father is rich.
• Because then the jacket wouldn't really be a scholarship jacket.
• He was surprised and annoyed.

 Use Selection Quiz
Unit Two Resource Book, p. 45.

Think Critically

2. Possible Response: Mr. Boone is a prejudiced man who is willing to falsify records to keep Martha from being awarded the scholarship jacket. Mr. Schmidt has strong principles and is willing to resign rather than give the jacket to a less qualified student. Mr. Boone only sees Martha as Mexican and therefore in his mind inferior; Mr. Schmidt sees Martha as a promising and deserving student.

3. Possible Response: The principal is a weak man who gave in to Mr. Boone too easily. Martha's grandfather's principles, as well as Martha's own courage, challenge him with an example of inner strength.

4. Possible Response: Martha has won the respect of the principal, the renewed confidence of Mr. Schmidt as well as a victory over the prejudice of Mr. Boone, and an awareness of her own strength in standing up for herself.

5. Possible Response: He teaches Martha to stand up for herself. He does this by asking the important question, what does a scholarship jacket really mean? By helping Martha to remind herself that the jacket is intended as a reward he can then help her to see that, if they paid for the jacket, they would be saying that Martha didn't really deserve the honor that the jacket represented.

6. Accept all reasonable responses.

 Use **Reading and Critical Thinking Transparencies**, p. 2, for additional support.

Connect to the Literature

1. What Do You Think?
How did you feel when you came to the end of the story? Did you feel like Martha?

Comprehension Check
• What are Mr. Boone and Mr. Schmidt arguing about?
• Why does Martha's grandfather refuse to pay for the jacket?
• How does the principal respond when Martha will not pay the 15 dollars?

Think Critically

2. How do Mr. Schmidt and Mr. Boone differ? What does Martha mean to each of them as a person?

3. Why do you think the principal changes his mind?

4. When at last Martha knows that she will get the jacket, what else has she won?

 THINK ABOUT
• Martha's conflicting feelings in the principal's office
• the ways different adults act toward her
• the amount of control she has over the decisions being made

5. Martha's grandfather says very little, but his words are very important. What does he teach Martha? How?

6. **ACTIVE READING CONNECTING** Look over the notes you took in your **READER'S NOTEBOOK** and compare them with a classmate's notes. Then discuss how the details in the story helped you relate to Martha's experience. Do you think a similar experience might happen to you? Discuss why or why not.

Extend Interpretations

7. The Writer's Style Consider the kinds of words and sentences Marta Salinas uses in this passage: "There was a cool breeze blowing and a sweet smell of mesquite fruit in the air, but I didn't appreciate it. I kicked at a dirt clod. I wanted that jacket so much." How does Salinas's style help you get to know her main character better?

8. Connect to Life In what settings can prejudice sometimes be found? Explain your response.

Literary Analysis

THEME A **theme** is a message about life or human nature that a literary work expresses. In most cases, readers must infer themes. (Remember, inferring consists of making logical guesses based on evidence.)

One way to infer a story's theme is to decide what general statement could be supported by the experiences of the main character. Look for clues to the theme of "The Scholarship Jacket" in key words and phrases, in dialogue, and in the ways that characters change as a result of the events in the story.

Cooperative Learning Activity
Working with a partner, identify an important theme in "The Scholarship Jacket." Look back at the text together, and jot down details of Martha's experiences that support the theme. Compare your ideas with those of another pair of classmates.

Diagram:
- "... Martha is Mexican ..."
- Cost of $15 is to prevent Martha from getting jacket she deserves.
- **Theme?**
- Principal looks uncomfortable when explaining cost to Martha.

Literary Analysis

Theme Invite students to share what Martha represented to them. Her experience and triumph illustrate important themes in the story, such as the importance of standing up for what you believe in or the importance of confronting prejudice. After students have worked through the Cooperative Learning Activity, invite them to share their findings with the class.

Use **Literary Analysis Transparencies**, p. 7, for additional support.

Extend Interpretations

7. The Writer's Style Invite students to imagine the kind of landscape that Salinas is describing and point out that she describes it by appealing to the reader's senses. There is a cool breeze and a sweet smell, so the landscape is a peaceful, pleasant place. The landscape is a contrast that help us to appreciate what Martha is feeling at that moment. She is so upset that she kicks at the dirt.

8. Connect to Life Accept all reasonable responses.

Writing Options

Letter of Recommendation Imagine you are the principal. Write a letter recommending Martha as a candidate for the statewide honor of "Eighth-Grade Graduate of the Year." What do you want to say about her? What has she, as a student, taught you? Save your letter in your **Working Portfolio.**

Martha's Positive Traits
smart
honest
stands up for what she
believes in

Activities & Explorations

Population Map Different Hispanic groups tend to live in different parts of the United States. Half of all Mexican Americans, for example, live in Texas and California. Using an almanac or encyclopedia, find out where different groups generally live. On an outline map of the United States, shade or color various areas to show what you have discovered. ~ **VIEWING AND REPRESENTING**

Inquiry & Research

La Causa! Cesar Chavez was a Mexican-American leader who worked to improve the lives of migrant workers. Find out about his life and about the United Farm Workers of America, the union that he helped to found. Then write a brief biography of Chavez, illustrating it with your own drawings or with copies of photographs. Share your biography with your classmates.

Art Connection

Look at Frida Kahlo's painting *Retrato de muchacha* on page 280. What are your impressions of the girl in the painting? How do they compare with your impressions of Martha in the story?

Vocabulary in Action

EXERCISE: MEANING CLUES On a separate sheet of paper, write the answer that best demonstrates the meaning of each vocabulary word.

1. **coincidence**
   a. setting a date for a party
   b. running into a friend far from home
   c. learning about a solar eclipse
2. **agile**
   a. learning a difficult song
   b. climbing a rock face easily
   c. finishing a job early
3. **despair**
   a. playing with the dog
   b. painting a brightly colored mural
   c. staring silently at a wall
4. **falsify**
   a. make a fake ID
   b. correct what someone else says
   c. speak in another language
5. **resign**
   a. put up a new sign
   b. change your mind
   c. quit a job or leave a position

Building Vocabulary
For an in-depth study of learning and remembering new words, see p. 473.

Writing Options

Letter of Recommendation Students' letters should be formatted correctly and contain all the elements of a standard business letter. Encourage students not only to describe Martha's accomplishments, but also to use examples from the story to support those descriptions.

Use **Writing Transparencies,** p. 13, for additional support.

Activities & Explorations

Population Map Statistics are compiled by the U.S. Census Bureau, so students may find information under the bureau's name as well as under *population*.

Inquiry & Research

La Causa! To make this assignment more challenging, invite students to create a timeline of the major events that took place during Chavez's life and afterwards.

Art Connection

To help students interpret and evaluate the various ways visual image makers, such as illustrators, represent meanings, ask them to consider what they can infer about the girl in the picture from her actions, her expression, and her clothing.

Vocabulary in Action

1. b
2. b
3. c
4. a
5. c

Grammar in Context

WRITING EXERCISE
Possible Responses:

1. I joined him, and without saying anything, I crouched down and started pulling up the weeds.
2. Grandpa worked alongside me for a few minutes, and he didn't ask what happened.
3. After I have a little pile of weeds between the rows, I stand up and face him.
4. Grandpa doesn't say anything; he just gives me a pat on the shoulder and a smile.
5. I skipped and ran back to the house, whistling some silly tune.

CONNECT TO THE LITERATURE
Responses will vary.

Marta Salinas

In *Nosotras: Latina Literature Today,* Salinas's story is one of thirty-five selections by well-known and lesser-known Hispanic writers. Like Salinas, each featured writer represents a major Latino community in the United States.

Author Activity

Interview Students might begin by making a chart like the one shown here.

What I want to know	What question I will ask to get this information

Use **Communications Transparencies and Copymasters,** p. 9, for additional support.

Grammar in Context: Consistent Verb Tense

In this excerpt Martha, the narrator of "The Scholarship Jacket," describes her meeting with the principal of her school about the jacket.

> The next day when the principal called me into his office I knew what it would be about. He looked uncomfortable and unhappy. I decided I wasn't going to make it any easier for him, so I looked him straight in the eyes. He looked away and fidgeted with the papers on his desk.

Because Martha is describing an incident from the past, she uses **verbs** in the past tense. The past tense is the basic time of the story. Martha uses other tenses only where they are logical, for example, when reporting the dialogue spoken by the characters. Otherwise, she uses the past tense consistently.

Apply to Your Writing Student writers sometimes shift tenses illogically without being aware of it. When you revise your writing, check to be sure that you have not made any illogical shifts in tense.

WRITING EXERCISE Rewrite the following sentences to make the verb tenses consistent.

Example: *Original* I couldn't wait to tell Grandpa, so I run straight to the field.

Rewritten I couldn't wait to tell Grandpa, so I ran straight to the field.

1. I joined him, and without saying anything, I crouch down and started pulling up the weeds.
2. Grandpa worked alongside me for a few minutes, and he doesn't ask what happened.
3. After I have a little pile of weeds between the rows, I stood up and face him.
4. Grandpa doesn't say anything; he just gave me a pat on the shoulder and a smile.
5. I skipped and run back to the house, whistling some silly tune.

Connect to the Literature Martha encountered prejudice. Recall a time when you believe that you were treated unfairly. Write five sentences about what you remember. Be careful to use past-tense verbs consistently.

Grammar Handbook Using Verbs Correctly, p. R68

Marta Salinas
born 1949

Young Author Born in Coalinga, California, Marta Salinas received an M.F.A. in creative writing from the University of California at Irvine. She has published several short stories in journals and anthologies. "The Scholarship Jacket" originally appeared in *Nosotras: Latina Literature Today.*

"What does a scholarship jacket mean?"

AUTHOR ACTIVITY
Interview Imagine that you are going to interview Marta Salinas about the story you have read. Make a list of questions you would like to ask her.

Teaching Options

MAINTAINING CONSISTENT VERB TENSE
Instruction Remind students that effective writers are careful not to shift tenses illogically in their writing. For example, if the basic time of the subject being narrated or described is the past, then all of the events that occurred at that time should be narrated or described in the past tense.

Write these sentences as examples:

> As we walked home, a big, ugly dog starts following us. When we sped up, it speeds up. When we slowed down, it slows down.

  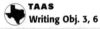

Grammar

Ask students to read the sentences, decide whether the basic tense should be past or present, and then make the tense of all verbs consistent.

Exercise Write the following paragraph on the board and have students make the tense of the underlined verbs consistent with the basic paragraph tense.

On Friday there <u>is</u> a match between our school and Lincoln Middle School, our biggest rival. Neither team <u>makes</u> a goal for the first 40 minutes, then a Lincoln striker <u>slams</u> one in. Finally our team made its first goal. The game <u>is</u> tied and <u>stays</u> that way for another 40 minutes. The goalkeepers for both teams <u>are</u> doing a great job; then, on a penalty kick, when everybody <u>is</u> really tired, our team <u>scores</u> again.

Answers: was, made, slammed, was, stayed, were, was, scored

Use **Unit Two Resource Book,** p. 43.
Use **Grammar Transparencies and Copymasters,** p. 75.

 Use McDougal Littell's *Language Network,* Chapter 4, for more instruction and practice in maintaining consistent verb tenses.

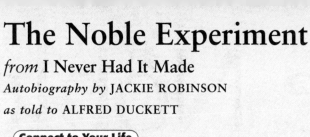

The Noble Experiment

from **I Never Had It Made**

Autobiography by JACKIE ROBINSON

as told to ALFRED DUCKETT

SOCIAL STUDIES

(Connect to Your Life)

What causes people to feel prejudice?

Build Background In the 1940s, African Americans faced many barriers created by prejudice. Segregation kept blacks from using schools, restaurants, and hospitals used by whites. In baseball, the Negro League was completely separate from the white league. Jackie Robinson would help change that.

The All Stars, in the Negro League, 1939.

Antidiscrimination poster, 1949.

SUNDAY GAMES IN JEOPARDY

Boston. City Councilman Isidore Muchneck has proposed a ban on Sunday ballgames at Fenway | attitude in baseball is that white business would suffer if blacks were hired. Most fans think baseball

Focus Your Reading

LITERARY ANALYSIS **AUTOBIOGRAPHY**

An **autobiography** is the story of a person's life, written by that person. In this excerpt, Jackie Robinson tells of Branch Rickey's plan to hire Robinson as a player.

ACTIVE READING **SUMMARIZING** When you **summarize**, you restate in your own words the **main ideas** and important **details** of something you've read. A summary should be shorter than the original work. Jot down important details in your 📖 READER'S NOTEBOOK. These will help you summarize the selection later on.

TEKS See the Skills Trace at the beginning of the unit for information on TEKS covered in this lesson.

WORDS TO KNOW	**Vocabulary Preview**		
cynical	insinuation	shrewdly	taunt
eloquence	integrated	speculating	ultimate
incredulous	retaliate		

LESSON RESOURCES

UNIT TWO RESOURCE BOOK, pp. 46–52

ASSESSMENT
Formal Assessment, pp. 43–44
Teacher's Guide to Assessment and Portfolio Use
Test Generator

SKILLS TRANSPARENCIES AND COPYMASTERS
Literary Analysis
• Autobiography, TR 11 (for Cooperative Learning Activity, p. 296)

Reading and Critical Thinking
• Summarizing, TR 11 (for Thinking Through the Literature, p. 296)
Grammar
• Identifying Active and Passive Voice, CM 140 (for Mini Lesson, p. 295)
• Using Active and Passive Verbs in Writing, CM 141 (for Mini Lesson, p. 298)
Vocabulary
• Synonyms, CM 42 (for Mini Lesson, p. 289)
• Context Clues, CM 43 (for Mini Lesson, p. 292)

INTEGRATED TECHNOLOGY
Audio Library
Internet: Research Starter

Visit our website:
www.mcdougallittell.com

ℹ️ This selection is included in the **Grade 7 InterActive Reader.**

Objectives
1. understand and appreciate **autobiography (Literary Analysis)**
2. use reading skill **summarize (Active Reading)**

Summary
Jackie Robinson recalls the events that led to his becoming the first African-American baseball player in the major leagues in the 20th century. Branch Rickey, president of the Brooklyn Dodgers, had always opposed segregation. In 1945, he convinced the team's board of directors to let him hire an African-American player. Working in secrecy, he chose Jackie Robinson not only for his skill, but for his character. The player would have to be able to endure other people's hatred and threats without fighting back. If the player fought back, race riots might erupt and it would then be a long time before any other African Americans would be allowed to enter the big leagues. Yet, the player also had to retain his dignity. At twenty-six, Robinson accepted the challenge.

Thematic Link
Jackie Robinson demonstrated great courage when he chose to fight for racial equality in baseball. By becoming the first African American to join a major league team, Jackie showed the world that prejudice had no place in sports.

5-Minute Warm-Up

Daily Language SkillBuilder **TEKS 17B, 17C**

Have students **proofread** the display sentences on page 189j and write them correctly. The sentences also appear on Transparency 9 of **Grammar Transparencies and Copymasters.**

Mini Lesson **Preteaching Vocabulary**

If you would like to preteach the WORDS TO KNOW for this selection, use the Mini Lesson, p. 289.

Reading and Analyzing

Reading Skills and Strategies:
PREVIEW

After you have discussed segregation with students, have them look through the story and examine the photographs. Ask students to imagine what it was like for Jackie Robinson to desegregate baseball. What challenges did he face?

Literary Analysis 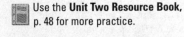 AUTOBIOGRAPHY

An autobiography is one type of informative nonfiction. It is the story of a person's life, written by that person. As they read, have students record details that show this selection is an autobiography. Students can organize their thoughts in a graphic organizer like the one below.

Excerpt	Autobiographical element

 Use the **Unit Two Resource Book,** p. 48 for more practice.

Active Reading SUMMARIZING

Ⓐ Have the students summarize what they have learned about Branch Rickey so far. Have them use their summaries to make predictions about what will happen next.

Use the **Unit Two Resource Book,** p. 47 for more practice.

The Noble

Jackie Robinson steals home during a Braves-Dodgers game at Ebbets Field in Brooklyn, August 22, 1948. UPI/Bettmann.

288   UNIT TWO   PART 2: FACING CHOICES

Teaching Options

 Viewing and Representing   TEKS 23A

Jackie Robinson steals home at Ebbets Field in Brooklyn, 1948.

Instruction During his career, Jackie Robinson stole 197 bases. He was among the few players brave enough to capture home plate. Point out the look of concentration on Jackie Robinson's face as he slides into home plate. What can you infer about Robinson from this photograph?

Possible Response Robinson appears to have worked hard to get to home plate. We can tell that he was a determined baseball player. Stealing a base, especially home plate, is a daring move; Robinson was a risk taker.

Application Based on this interpretation of the photograph, what connections might students make between the photo and the selection?

Possible Response: Just as Jackie Robinson had to work hard to get to home plate, he had to be determined to break through the color barriers in baseball.

from *I Never Had It Made*

Experiment

by Jackie Robinson as told to Alfred Duckett

In 1910 Branch Rickey was a coach for Ohio Wesleyan. The team went to South Bend, Indiana, for a game. The hotel management registered the coach and team but refused to assign a room to a black player named Charley Thomas. In those days college ball had a few black players. Mr. Rickey took the manager aside and said he would move the entire team to another hotel unless the black athlete was accepted. The threat was a bluff because he knew the other hotels also would have refused accommodations to a black man. While the hotel manager was thinking about the threat, Mr. Rickey came up with a compromise. He suggested a cot be put in his own room, which he would share with the unwanted guest. The hotel manager wasn't happy about the idea, but he gave in.

Years later Branch Rickey told the story of the misery of that black player to whom he had given a place to sleep. He remembered that Thomas couldn't sleep.

"He sat on that cot," Mr. Rickey said, "and was silent for a long time. Then he began to cry, tears he couldn't hold back. His whole body shook with emotion. I sat and watched him, not knowing what to do until he began tearing at one hand with the other—just as if he were trying to scratch the skin off his hands with his fingernails. I was alarmed. I asked him what he was trying to do to himself.

"'It's my hands,' he sobbed. 'They're black. If only they were white, I'd be as good as anybody then, wouldn't I, Mr. Rickey? If only they were white.'"

"Charley," Mr. Rickey said, "the day will come when they won't have to be white."

Thirty-five years later, while I was lying awake nights, frustrated, unable to see a future, Mr. Rickey, by now the president of the Dodgers, was also lying awake at night, trying to make up his mind about a new experiment.

He had never forgotten the agony of that black athlete. When he became a front-office executive in St. Louis, he had fought, behind the scenes, against the custom that consigned black spectators to the Jim Crow section of the Sportsman's Park, later to become Busch Memorial Stadium. His pleas to change the rules were in vain. Those in power argued that if blacks were allowed a free choice of seating, white business would suffer.

Branch Rickey lost that fight, but when he became the boss of the Brooklyn Dodgers in 1943, he felt the time for equality in baseball had come. He knew that achieving it would be

Customizing Instruction

Less Proficient Readers
To prepare students for the selection, ask them if they would enjoy being the first person ever to do something difficult. Have them explain why or why not.
Set a purpose Have students read to find out what the "Noble Experiment" was.

Students Acquiring English
Students from many cultures may be avid baseball fans. Invite volunteers to explain the baseball terms used in this selection, such as *coach, scout, farm club, box score,* and *shortstop.*
1 Help students understand the meaning of difficult phrases such as "The threat was a bluff." In this passage, *bluff* means "trick."

Use **Spanish Study Guide,** pp. 55–57 for additional support.

Gifted and Talented Students
Remind students that this is the story of Robinson's life, not Rickey's. As students read, have them explain why Robinson includes such an in-depth summary of Rickey's point of view.
Possible Responses: to show the difficulties that Robinson faced; to show Robinson's admiration for Rickey

 Preteaching Vocabulary **TEKS 9B** **TAAS Reading Obj. 1**

SYNONYMS
Instruction Remind students that different words can have similar or identical meanings. These words are called synonyms. Explain that they can use synonyms to convey thoughts or feelings without being repetitious.
Write the word *fast* in the middle of the board or chart paper.
Ask students to think of as many synonyms as they can for *fast.* Create a web with their words.

Application Have students review the list of WORDS TO KNOW and then try to locate each word in the selection. They should use sentence context to figure out the general meaning of each word. Then have students work in pairs to create synonym word webs for three of the words.

Use the **Unit One Resource Book,** p. 49 for more practice.
Use **Vocabulary Transparencies and Copymasters,** p. 42, for additional support.

Active Reading SUMMARIZING

Students should practice paraphrasing and summarizing text to organize ideas. Have students summarize the challenges Rickey and any black player he chose would face.

Possible Response: There would be public opposition, resentment among people in baseball, and violence. The player would face ridicule and rejection.

Literary Analysis AUTOBIOGRAPHY

A Have students read aloud sections of this paragraph that prove this story is an autobiography. What two clues tell readers that it is an autobiography?

Possible Responses: It is the story of the author's life; it is told using the first-person point of view; it is non-fiction.

terribly difficult. There would be deep resentment, determined opposition, and perhaps even racial violence. He was convinced he was morally right, and he <u>shrewdly</u> sensed that making the game a truly national one would have healthy financial results. He took his case before the startled directors of the club, and using persuasive <u>eloquence</u>, he won the first battle in what would be a long and bitter campaign. He was voted permission to make the Brooklyn club the pioneer in bringing blacks into baseball.

Winning his directors' approval was almost insignificant in contrast to the task which now lay ahead of the Dodger president. He made certain that word of his plans did not leak out, particularly to the press. Next, he had to find the ideal player for his project, which came to be called "Rickey's noble experiment." This player had to be one who could take abuse, name-calling, rejection by fans and sportswriters and by fellow players not only on opposing teams but on his own. He had to be able to stand up in the face of merciless persecution and not <u>retaliate</u>. On the other hand, he had to be a contradiction in human terms; he still had to have spirit. He could not be an "Uncle Tom."[1]

Jackie Robinson after he signed a contract with the Brooklyn Dodgers, April 10, 1947. AP/Wide World Photos.

His ability to turn the other cheek had to be predicated[2] on his determination to gain acceptance. Once having proven his ability as player, teammate, and man, he had to be able to cast off humbleness and stand up as a full-fledged participant whose triumph did not carry the poison of bitterness.

Unknown to most people and certainly to me, after launching a major scouting program, Branch Rickey had picked me as that player. The Rickey talent hunt went beyond national borders. Cuba, Mexico, Puerto Rico, Venezuela, and other countries where dark-skinned people lived had been checked out. Mr. Rickey had learned that there were a number of black players, war veterans mainly, who had gone to these countries, despairing of finding an opportunity in their own country. The manhunt had to be camouflaged. If it became known he was looking for a black recruit for the Dodgers, all hell would have broken loose. The gimmick he used as a cover-up was to make the world believe that he was about to establish a new Negro league. In the spring of 1945 he called a press conference and announced that the Dodgers were organizing the United States League, composed of all black teams. This, of course, made blacks and prointegration whites indignant. He was accused of trying to uphold the existing segregation and, at the same time, capitalize on black players. Cleverly, Mr. Rickey replied that his league would be better organized than the current ones. He said its main purpose, eventually, was to be absorbed

---

1. **Uncle Tom:** an offensive term for a black person who is regarded as trying overly hard to please white people; originally from the novel *Uncle Tom's Cabin*, written by Harriet Beecher Stowe in 1851.
2. **predicated** (prĕd′ĭ-kā′tĭd): based.

WORDS	shrewdly (shrōōd′lē) *adv.* wisely; in a clever way
TO	eloquence (ĕl′ə-kwəns) *n.* forceful, convincing speech
KNOW	retaliate (rĭ-tăl′ē-āt′) *v.* to get revenge; get even

Cross Curricular Link Negro League Baseball

The Negro Leagues were first formed in 1920. They arose in response to the segregation occurring in the major leagues. People believed that the African-American community had many talented and gifted athletes who deserved professional status in baseball in spite of the discrimination that existed.

Being a player in the Negro Leagues was challenging. Black team owners could schedule games when it only was convenient for the white stadium owners. That meant that players sometimes played as many as four games in one day. Athletes in the Negro Leagues moved at a grueling pace, traveling by bus. The players were faced with racism on a daily basis due to the Jim Crow laws. Players usually slept and ate on the bus because they were not allowed in many hotels and restaurants.

into the majors. It is ironic that by coming very close to telling the truth, he was able to conceal that truth from the enemies of integrated baseball. Most people assumed that when he spoke of some distant goal of integration, Mr. Rickey was being a hypocrite on this issue as so many of baseball's leaders had been.

Black players were familiar with this kind of hypocrisy. When I was with the Monarchs, shortly before I met Mr. Rickey, Wendell Smith, then sports editor of the black weekly Pittsburgh *Courier*, had arranged for me and two other players from the Negro league to go to a tryout with the Boston Red Sox. The tryout had been brought about because a Boston city councilman had frightened the Red Sox management. Councilman Isadore Muchneck threatened to push a bill through banning Sunday baseball unless the Red Sox hired black players. Sam Jethroe of the Cleveland Buckeyes, Marvin Williams of the Philadelphia Stars, and I had been grateful to Wendell for getting us a chance in the Red Sox tryout, and we put our best efforts into it. However, not for one minute did we believe the tryout was sincere. The Boston club officials praised our performance, let us fill out application cards, and said, "So long." We were fairly certain they wouldn't call us, and we had no intention of calling them.

Incidents like this made Wendell Smith as cynical as we were. He didn't accept Branch Rickey's new league as a genuine project, and he frankly told him so. During this conversation, the Dodger boss asked Wendell whether any of the three of us who had gone to Boston was really good major league material. Wendell said I was. I will be forever indebted to Wendell because, without his even knowing it, his recommendation was in the end partly responsible for my career. At the time, it started a thorough investigation of my background.

In August 1945, at Comiskey Park in Chicago, I was approached by Clyde Sukeforth, the Dodger scout. Blacks have had to learn to protect themselves by being cynical but not cynical enough to slam the door on potential

> Unknown to most people and certainly to me, after launching a major scouting program, Branch Rickey had picked me as that player.

opportunities. We go through life walking a tightrope to prevent too much disillusionment. I was out on the field when Sukeforth called my name and beckoned. He told me the Brown Dodgers were looking for top ballplayers, that Branch Rickey had heard about me and sent him to watch me throw from the hole.[3] He had come at an unfortunate time. I had hurt my shoulder a couple of days before that, and I wouldn't be doing any throwing for at least a week.

Sukeforth said he'd like to talk with me anyhow. He asked me to come to see him after the game at the Stevens Hotel.

Here we go again, I thought. Another time-wasting experience. But Sukeforth looked like a sincere person, and I thought I might as well listen. I agreed to meet him that night. When we met, Sukeforth got right to the point. Mr. Rickey wanted to talk to me about the

[3]

---

3. **throw from the hole:** to throw from deep in the infield to first base.

291

Customizing Instruction

Less Proficient Readers

1 To see if students understand the story so far, ask them to the explain what "the noble experiment" was.
Possible Response: Rickey's plan was to end segregation in baseball.

Set a Purpose Have students read to find out why Branch Rickey selected Jackie Robinson for the experiment. Use the following questions to guide students to understand Robinson's frustration about segregated baseball.

• Why had Robinson and two of his teammates been given the opportunity to try out for the Boston Red Sox?
Possible Response: A Boston city councilman threatened to create a bill banning Sunday baseball unless the Red Sox had African-American players on the team.

• How did Robinson know that he really wouldn't ever play for the Red Sox?
Possible Response: African-American players were familiar with this kind of proposition. Robinson and his teammates didn't expect to be called back.

Students Acquiring English

2 Point out that "It is ironic that . . ." introduces an idea opposite to what the reader expects. Here, readers expect that Rickey would give away his secret by telling so much of the truth, but actually he fools his enemies.

Multiple Learning Styles
Interpersonal Learners

3 Invite students to roleplay the encounter between Robinson and Sukeforth. They should use dialogue that captures each man's personality and feelings.

BLOCK SCHEDULING: MANAGING TIME

If your schedule requires that you cover the lesson objectives in a shorter time, use . . .
• Preparing to Read, p. 287
• Thinking Through the Literature, p. 296
• Vocabulary in Action, p. 297
• Grammar in Context, p. 298

If you want to take advantage of longer class time, use . . .
• TE Teaching Options: Viewing and Representing, p. 288; Preteaching Vocabulary, p. 289; Cross-Curricular Link, p. 290; Vocabulary Strategy, p. 292, Speaking and Listening, p. 293; Spelling, p. 294; Grammar, pp. 295, 298; Standardized Test Practice, p. 297
• Choices & Challenges and Author Activity, pp. 297–298

possibility of becoming a Brown Dodger. If I could get a few days off and go to Brooklyn, my fare and expenses would be paid. At first I said that I couldn't leave my team and go to Brooklyn just like that. Sukeforth wouldn't take no for an answer. He pointed out that I couldn't play for a few days anyhow because of my bum arm. Why should my team object?

I continued to hold out and demanded to know what would happen if the Monarchs fired me. The Dodger scout replied quietly that he didn't believe that would happen.

I shrugged and said I'd make the trip. I figured I had nothing to lose.

Branch Rickey was an impressive-looking man. He had a classic face, an air of command, a deep, booming voice, and a way of cutting through red tape and getting down to basics. He shook my hand vigorously and, after a brief conversation, sprang the first question.

"You got a girl?" he demanded.

It was a hell of a question. I had two reactions: why should he be concerned about my relationship with a girl; and, second, while I thought, hoped, and prayed I had a girl, the way things had been going, I was afraid she might have begun to consider me a hopeless case. I explained this to Mr. Rickey and Clyde.

Mr. Rickey wanted to know all about Rachel. I told him of our hopes and plans.

"You know, you *have* a girl," he said heartily. "When we get through today, you may want to call her up because there are times when a man needs a woman by his side."

My heart began racing a little faster again as I sat there <u>speculating</u>. First he asked me if I really understood why he had sent for me. I told him what Clyde Sukeforth had told me.

"That's what he was supposed to tell you," Mr. Rickey said. "The truth is you are not a

candidate for the Brooklyn Brown Dodgers. I've sent for you because I'm interested in you as a candidate for the Brooklyn National League Club. I think you can play in the major leagues. How do you feel about it?"

My reactions seemed like some kind of weird mixture churning in a blender. I was thrilled, scared, and excited. I was <u>incredulous</u>. Most of all, I was speechless.

"You think you can play for Montreal?" he demanded.

> Here was a guy questioning my courage. That virtually amounted to him asking me if I was a coward.

I got my tongue back. "Yes," I answered. Montreal was the Brooklyn Dodgers' top farm club. The players who went there and made it had an excellent chance at the big time.

I was busy reorganizing my thoughts while Mr. Rickey and Clyde Sukeforth discussed me briefly, almost as if I weren't there. Mr. Rickey was questioning Clyde. Could I make the grade?

Abruptly, Mr. Rickey swung his swivel chair in my direction. He was a man who conducted himself with great drama. He pointed a finger at me.

"I know you're a good ballplayer," he barked. "What I don't know is whether you have the guts."

I knew it was all too good to be true. Here was a guy questioning my courage. That virtually amounted to him asking me if I was a coward. Mr. Rickey or no Mr. Rickey, that was an <u>insinuation</u> hard to take. I felt the heat coming up into my cheeks.

> WORDS
> TO
> KNOW
>
> **speculating** (spĕk′yə-lā′-tĭng) *adj.* thinking about different possibilities; guessing what might happen **speculate** *v.*
> **incredulous** (ĭn-krĕj′ə-ləs) *adj.* unable or unwilling to believe something
> **insinuation** (ĭn-sĭn′yōō-ā′shən) *n.* a suggestion or hint intended to insult

292

Vocabulary Strategy   TEKS 6A   TAAS Reading Obj. 1

CONTEXT CLUES

Instruction Call students' attention to the list of WORDS TO KNOW. Remind them that sometimes they can understand the meaning of an unfamiliar word by examining the context in which the word is used. Use the model sentence to demonstrate the strategy of using context clues that provide inferences to word meaning.

Model Sentence:

If those students continue to *taunt* and tease the girls on the way to school, they will be asked to leave the bus.

Application Have students work in pairs to write sentences that reveal the meanings of each of the WORDS TO KNOW. Their sentences should show that they have a complete understanding of each word.

Use **Vocabulary Transparencies and Copymasters**, p. 43.

Before I could react to what he had said, he leaned forward in his chair and explained.

I wasn't just another athlete being hired by a ball club. We were playing for big stakes. This was the reason Branch Rickey's search had been so exhaustive. The search had spanned the globe and narrowed down to a few candidates, then finally to me. When it looked as though I might be the number-one choice, the investigation of my life, my habits, my reputation, and my character had become an intensified study.

"I've investigated you thoroughly, Robinson," Mr. Rickey said.

One of the results of this thorough screening were reports from California athletic circles that I had been a "racial agitator"[4] at UCLA. Mr. Rickey had not accepted these criticisms on face value. He had demanded and received more information and came to the conclusion that if I had been white, people would have said, "Here's a guy who's a contender, a competitor."

After that he had some grim words of warning. "We can't fight our way through this, Robinson. We've got no army. There's virtually nobody on our side. No owners, no umpires, very few newspapermen. And I'm afraid that many fans will be hostile. We'll be in a tough position. We can win only if we can convince the world that I'm doing this because you're a great ballplayer and a fine gentleman."

(From left) Gil Hodges, Gene Hermanski, Branch Rickey, and Jackie Robinson at Yankee Stadium during the World Series, October 4, 1949. The Bettmann Archive.

He had me transfixed as he spoke. I could feel his sincerity, and I began to get a sense of how much this major step meant to him. Because of his nature and his passion for justice, he had to do what he was doing. He continued. The rumbling voice, the theatrical gestures were gone. He was speaking from a deep, quiet strength.

---

4. **racial agitator** (ăj′ĭ-tā′tər): a negative term used for someone who tries to stir up trouble between the races.

 Mini Lesson **Speaking and Listening**   **TEKS** 5A, 5C, 11B

SPORTSCASTING

Prepare Invite students to name sportscasters. Discuss what makes their play-by-play so exciting: preparation, an alert attitude, and colorful words. Go over these sportscast guidelines with students:

• Be informed about the players and coaches. Find out the players' statistics, backgrounds, and controversies.
• Know the specialized sports vocabulary.
• Be enthusiastic.

Present Invite students to work in pairs or groups of three to write and present a play-by-play broadcast of Jackie Robinson's first day playing major-league baseball with the Brooklyn Dodgers. Guide students to return to the story to infer how the players and audience reacted to Robinson's debut. Students should study Jackie Robinson's remarks and personality to predict how he might react under stress.

BLOCK SCHEDULING This activity is particularly well suited for longer class periods.

Reading and Analyzing

Literary Analysis | AUTOBIOGRAPHY

A In this section of the autobiography, readers have a chance to learn what is most important to Robinson: his dignity. Based on your reading so far, why might Robinson place such importance on personal dignity?

Possible Response: As an African-American man, his dignity has probably been attacked often; he is a strong fighter.

Active Reading | SUMMARIZING

B Ask students to summarize the different ways in which Rickey tries to test Robinson to be sure he is strong enough.

Possible Response: He asks him difficult questions and pretends to be an angry white baseball player.

Reading Skills and Strategies:
AUTHOR'S PURPOSE

C Have students explain what the author's purpose for telling the story of Jackie Robinson might be.

Possible Response: His purpose might be to inspire a reader to be courageous and be the first person to try to change something that is unjust.

"So there's more than just playing," he said. "I wish it meant only hits, runs, and errors—only the things they put in the box score. Because you know—yes, you would know, Robinson, that a baseball box score is a democratic thing. It doesn't tell how big you are, what church you attend, what color you are, or how your father voted in the last election. It just tells what kind of baseball player you were on that particular day."

I interrupted. "But it's the box score that really counts—that and that alone, isn't it?"

"It's all that *ought* to count," he replied. "But it isn't. Maybe one of these days it *will* be all that counts. That is one of the reasons I've got you here, Robinson. If you're a good enough man, we can make this a start in the right direction. But let me tell you, it's going to take an awful lot of courage."

He was back to the crossroads question that made me start to get angry minutes earlier. He asked it slowly and with great care.

"Have you got the guts to play the game no matter what happens?"

"I think I can play the game, Mr. Rickey," I said.

The next few minutes were tough. Branch Rickey had to make absolutely sure that I knew what I would face. Beanballs[5] would be thrown at me. I would be called the kind of names which would hurt and infuriate any man. I would be physically attacked. Could I take all of this and control my temper, remain steadfastly loyal to our <u>ultimate</u> aim?

He knew I would have terrible problems and wanted me to know the extent of them before I agreed to the plan. I was twenty-six years old, and all my life—back to the age of eight when a little neighbor girl called me a nigger—I had believed in payback, retaliation.

> Beanballs would be thrown at me. I would be called the kind of names which would hurt and infuriate any man. I would be physically attacked.

The most luxurious possession, the richest treasure anybody has, is his personal dignity. I looked at Mr. Rickey guardedly, and in that second I was looking at him not as a partner in a great experiment, but as the enemy—a white man. I had a question, and it was the age-old one about whether or not you sell your birthright.

"Mr. Rickey," I asked, "are you looking for a Negro who is afraid to fight back?"

I never will forget the way he exploded.

"Robinson," he said, "I'm looking for a ballplayer with guts enough not to fight back."

After that, Mr. Rickey continued his lecture on the kind of thing I'd be facing.

He not only told me about it, but he acted out the part of a white player charging into me, blaming me for the "accident" and calling me all kinds of foul racial names. He talked about my race, my parents, in language that was almost unendurable.

"They'll <u>taunt</u> and goad you," Mr. Rickey said. "They'll do anything to make you react. They'll try to provoke a race riot in the ballpark. This is the way to prove to the public that a Negro should not be allowed in the major league. This is the way to frighten the fans and make them afraid to attend the games."

---

5. **beanballs:** pitches thrown purposefully at a batter's head.

WORDS TO KNOW

ultimate (ŭl´tə-mĭt) *adj.* final; most important
taunt (tônt) *v.* to make fun of; jeer

294

Teaching Options

Mini Lesson **Spelling** TEKS 16C  TAAS Writing Obj. 3, 7

SPELLING WITH SUFFIXES

Instruction Explain to students that when a suffix beginning with a vowel is added to a word ending in silent *e*, the *e* is usually dropped. Present the following examples from "The Noble Experiment."

base word	suffix	new word
speculate	-ing	speculating
integrate	-ed	integrated
insinuate	-ion	insinuation

Exercises Have students write each word using the suffix shown.

1. use + age
2. continue + ous
3. mature + ity
4. confuse + ion
5. refuse + al
6. create + ive
7. survive + al
8. believe + able

Encourage students to find five words ending with a silent *e* in the highlighted passage and add suffixes to them. (*courage, care, game, make, face, infuriate, take, ultimate, age*)

 Use **Unit Two Resource Book,** p. 51 for more practice.

If hundreds of black people wanted to come to the ballpark to watch me play and Mr. Rickey tried to discourage them, would I understand that he was doing it because the emotional enthusiasm of my people could harm the experiment? That kind of enthusiasm would be as bad as the emotional opposition of prejudiced white fans.

Suppose I was at shortstop. Another player comes down from first, stealing, flying in with spikes high, and cuts me on the leg. As I feel the blood running down my leg, the white player laughs in my face.

"How do you like that, nigger boy?" he sneers.

Could I turn the other cheek? I didn't know how I would do it. Yet I knew that I must. I had to do it for so many reasons. For black youth, for my mother, for Rae, for myself. I had already begun to feel I had to do it for Branch Rickey.

I was offered, and agreed to sign later, a contract with a $3,500 bonus and $600-a-month salary. I was officially a Montreal Royal. I must not tell anyone except Rae and my mother. ❖

The pennant-winning 1949 Brooklyn Dodgers team. Jackie Robinson is second from the right in the third row.
UPI/Bettmann.

Customizing Instruction

Students Acquiring English
1 Be sure that students understand that *nigger* is a racial epithet that is offensive and should never be used.

Less Proficient Readers
2 Ask students what Robinson is told could happen to him if he joins the team.
Possible Response: He could be attacked and insulted constantly.
3 Have students explore Robinson's reasons for taking part in the experiment.
Possible Response: He does it for the benefit of black youth, for his mother, his girlfriend, Rickey, and himself.

Multiple Learning Styles
Visual Learners
Have students design a monument to Jackie Robinson that might be displayed at a park or baseball field. The monument should reflect Robinson's importance to the game of baseball and to the African-American community. They should think about both the monument's design and what might be inscribed on it.

 Grammar **TEKS** 17C, 18E **TAAS** Writing Obj. 1, 3, 6

IDENTIFYING ACTIVE AND PASSIVE VOICE
Teach students that there are two kinds of verbs, active and passive. When the subject of the sentence performs the action, the verb is active. When the subject of the sentence receives the action, the verb is passive. Write the following sentences on the chalkboard:
Jackie hit the ball.
The ball was hit by Jackie.
Ask the students which sentence is passive and which is active.

Exercises Ask the students to identify the verbs in the following sentences and label them active or passive.
1. The sport of baseball was changed forever by Jackie Robinson. *(was changed, passive)*
2. The player heard the angry remarks from judgmental people. *(heard, active)*
3. He fought for his right to a career as an athlete. *(fought, active)*
4. People were taught a lesson about equality. *(were taught, passive)*

 Use **Grammar Transparencies and Copymasters,** p. 140.

Connect to the Literature

1. **What Do You Think?**
   Responses will vary.

Comprehension Check

• Rickey wanted to show the world that the time had come for equality in professional baseball. He intended for Jackie Robinson to become a pioneer in the professional sporting world. He knew that Robinson could change the face of baseball forever.

• Robinson would be confronted with racism and hatred every time he stepped out onto the baseball field. He would need to show his dignity and self-control by not fighting back and display his athletic talent to the world.

 Use Selection Quiz
Unit Two Resource Book, p. 52.

Think Critically

2. Answers will vary. Students' summaries should include Rickey's intentions when recruiting Robinson, how he went about looking for the right player for the experiment, and Robinson's feelings about being selected.

 Use **Reading and Critical Thinking Transparencies,** p. 11, for additional support.

3. Responses will vary. Make sure students include reasons to support their opinions.

4. Possible Response: He is trying to say that while African Americans try not to give up hope, they have been hurt before and fear it will happen again.

5. Possible Response: Rickey researched the reports and learned that Robinson was just a man who never gave up. This makes him a good competitor.

6. Most students will say that Robinson was more courageous. Evidence for this may include the following: Robinson is the one who had to fight so hard for his dreams; he was the one faced with the hatred on a daily basis.

Literary Analysis

Autobiography Encourage students to note specific details and moments from the book that illustrate each point.

 Use **Literary Analysis Transparencies,** p. 11, for additional support.

Connect to the Literature

1. **What Do You Think?**
   What is your impression of Jackie Robinson? What kind of a person was he?

   Comprehension Check
   • What was Rickey's intention when he recruited Jackie Robinson?
   • What challenges would Robinson face if he became a major-league player?

Think Critically

2. **ACTIVE READING SUMMARIZING** Review the notes you made in your **READER'S NOTEBOOK**. Then summarize Branch Rickey's plan to integrate major-league baseball.

3. What is your opinion of Rickey's plan?

    THINK ABOUT
   • his reasons for wanting to carry out the plan
   • how and why he kept it secret
   • the final results of the plan

4. What does Robinson mean when he says of African Americans, "We go through life walking a tightrope to prevent too much disillusionment"?

5. Rickey interpreted reports that Robinson had been a "racial agitator" at UCLA to mean that Robinson was "a contender, a competitor." What made him think that?

6. Consider the difficulties both Rickey and Robinson faced. Who showed the greater courage? Give reasons for your answer.

Extend Interpretations

7. **What If?** Imagine that Jackie Robinson had not been such a strong, self-controlled person or such an exceptional athlete. How might Rickey's plan have turned out differently?

8. **Connect to Life** Many saw Jackie Robinson as a role model for young people. Should we expect professional athletes to be role models, or should we judge them only on their athletic performance?

Literary Analysis

AUTOBIOGRAPHY

An **autobiography** is a form of **nonfiction** in which a person tells the story of his or her own life. An autobiography is usually written from the **first-person point of view.** The writer tells about past events from the perspective of being older and wiser. Therefore, autobiographies often provide revealing insights into the writer's attitudes toward the events that shaped and changed his or her life. Autobiographies also help the reader understand the society in which the writer lived.

Cooperative Learning Activity
With a small group, discuss one of the following two points. When you have finished, gather with a group that has chosen the other point and discuss how both points together contribute to the autobiography.

• Point 1: Robinson's attitude toward the important event in his life described in "The Noble Experiment"
• Point 2: The society in which Robinson's and Rickey's integration of major-league baseball took place

Discussion Results	
Our Group	Other Group

Extend Interpretations

7. **What if?** This question is well suited for **gifted students. If you wish to make this question easier,** you can have the class discuss the question as a group. You might want the students to brainstorm possible outcomes. Students may say that maybe fights would have broken out in the stands or that perhaps if Robinson hadn't worked out, African Americans wouldn't be playing professional sports today.

8. **Connect to Life** Students could respond to this question in a debate. Divide the class into two groups: those who believe that professional athletes have an obligation to serve as role models and those who believe they should just play their sport. Allow each team time to prepare for the debate and select a spokesperson. Then hold a debate in the classroom and allow each team time to speak and make their points. In the end, have the class summarize each team's point of view.

Choices & CHALLENGES

Writing Options

1. Letter What do you think Jackie Robinson would have said to Charley Thomas, the player whose suffering affected Branch Rickey? Write a letter that Robinson might have sent to Thomas after signing with the Dodgers.

2. Speech Using information from the selection, write a speech that Jackie Robinson might have given to a group of baseball officials about the effects of prejudice on baseball.

3. Definition Branch Rickey said that he was "looking for a ballplayer with guts enough not to fight back." Write a definition of courage you think Rickey would have agreed with. Save your definition in your **Working Portfolio.**

Activities & Explorations

1. Interview If you had an opportunity to interview Jackie Robinson and Branch Rickey, what questions would you ask them? Working with two other students, practice and then stage an interview with Robinson and Rickey for your class. ~ **SPEAKING & LISTENING**

2. Baseball Card Research Jackie Robinson's career as a baseball player. Design a baseball card that includes key details of his major-league record. Illustrate your card with a drawing of Robinson. ~ **ART**

Inquiry & Research

 **SOCIAL STUDIES** **SEGREGATION**

Jackie Robinson experienced prejudice and discrimination in breaking the "color barrier" in major-league baseball. Find out more about segregation policies, such as the Jim Crow laws, that existed during Robinson's lifetime. How did these policies affect African Americans? When and how were the laws changed?

More Online: Research Starter
www.mcdougallittell.com

Vocabulary in Action

EXERCISE: SYNONYMS On your paper, write the vocabulary word that is the best substitute for each italicized word or phrase below.

1. Branch Rickey *cleverly* devised a cover story for the press.
2. Robinson was *disbelieving* when Rickey said he wanted him to play for the Brooklyn National League Club.
3. The majority of newspapermen *guessing* about Rickey's plans had been wrong.
4. Many blacks felt very *mistrustful* of the sincerity of the promises made by whites.
5. Some ballplayers on other teams would *make fun of* Robinson and try to anger him.
6. Robinson was not allowed to *get even.*
7. The goal of the experiment was to have *desegregated* major leagues.
8. Sometimes a sportswriter would make a *suggestion* in his column intended to insult Robinson's character.
9. Several ministers spoke with *forceful verbal skill* about the evils of prejudice.
10. The *final* result of Rickey's "noble experiment" was highly successful.

Building Vocabulary
For an in-depth study of word relationships such as synonyms, see p. 631.

WORDS TO KNOW				
cynical	incredulous	integrated	shrewdly	taunt
eloquence	insinuation	retaliate	speculating	ultimate

CHOOSING THE BEST SUMMARY

For some standardized tests, students will be asked to choose the best summary of a passage. To provide students with some help in choosing the best summary, read aloud or write on the board the following question:

Which of the following statements best summarizes the first conversation between Branch Rickey and Jackie Robinson?

A. Rickey asks Robinson if he has a girl to stand by his side, because the job will be difficult.

B. Rickey explains to Robinson that he had thoroughly searched the world for a player like him.

C. Rickey questions Robinson and explains the challenges he will face as the first black player in the major leagues.

C is the best choice because it explains the intentions of Rickey and the feelings of Robinson. It contains the most important information.

Writing Options

1. Letter Student responses will vary but should include a description of Robinson's feelings and experiences. The letter should explain how Robinson met Branch Rickey and describe his mixed emotions.

2. Speech The speech should include information from the selection, such as that it is morally wrong to prohibit African Americans from playing baseball; that segregating baseball prevents it from becoming a true national sport; and that by keeping African-American players out of the sport, the major leagues were missing out on some great athletes.

3. Definition Definitions will vary, but should include the philosophy that Rickey preached: true courage is the self-control to not fight back.

Activities & Explorations

1. Interview Interview responses should be congruent with the thoughts expressed by Jackie Robinson in the autobiography.

Use **Communications Transparencies and Copymasters,** p. 9, for additional support.

2. Baseball Card Baseball cards should include some of these key details: 1945—plays for the Kansas City Monarchs in the Negro Leagues; 1947—signs with the Brooklyn Dodgers and wins the Rookie of the Year award; 1955—The Dodgers win the World Series; 1956—retires from baseball; 1962—is inducted into the Baseball Hall of Fame.

Inquiry & Research

Segregation After students complete their research, you might have them write a journal entry about what a society controlled by Jim Crow laws would be like. Students might work in groups to put together presentations on this subject.

Vocabulary in Action

1. shrewdly	6. retaliate
2. incredulous	7. integrated
3. speculating	8. insinuation
4. cynical	9. eloquence
5. taunt	10. ultimate

Grammar in Context: Active Voice and Passive Voice

Notice the use of verbs in the **active voice** to express Mr. Rickey's fear that the fans will harass Jackie Robinson.

> They'll taunt and goad you. . . . They'll do anything to make you react. They'll try to provoke a race riot in the ballpark.

Compare this sentence written in the **passive voice** with the original sentence above: *You will be taunted and goaded by them.* Verbs in the **active voice** emphasize the doer of the action. Verbs in the passive voice take emphasis away from the doer of an action and make sentences wordy.

Apply to Your Writing Generally use verbs in the active voice to make your writing stronger and more concise.

WRITING EXERCISE Rewrite each sentence, changing the verbs from the passive voice to the active voice.

Example: *Original* The Boston Red Sox were threatened by a councilman.

Rewritten A councilman threatened the Boston Red Sox.

1. A passion for justice was shown by Branch Rickey.
2. Robinson's performance was praised by Boston club officials.
3. Robinson was approached by Clyde Sukeforth the Dodger scout.
4. Many black athletes had been discouraged by years of lies and disappointments.

Grammar Handbook Using Verbs Correctly, p. R68

"I wasn't just another athlete being hired by a ball club. We were playing for big stakes."

—Jackie Robinson

Alfred Duckett
1917–1984

Fan and Writer It seems natural that Alfred Duckett would want to tell Jackie Robinson's story, since Duckett was born in Brooklyn, New York, and was a baseball fan as well as a journalist. Robinson and Duckett worked together to write *I Never Had It Made: An Autobiography.* Besides writing books, Duckett also wrote poetry, magazine articles, and speeches.

Full Life Duckett cofounded *Equal Opportunities* magazine and served as director of Associated Negro Press International. He appeared on national television programs and lectured in many schools, churches, and universities. He also cowrote some of the speeches of Dr. Martin Luther King, Jr. Until his death in 1984, Duckett ran a public relations firm in Chicago, Illinois.

AUTHOR ACTIVITY
Read the rest of Jackie Robinson's autobiography, *I Never Had It Made.* Create a time line of Robinson's accomplishments and give a report on his experiences in baseball and his other achievements.

Grammar in Context

WRITING EXERCISE
Possible Responses:
1. Since that time, Branch Rickey showed a passion for justice.
2. Boston club officials praised Robinson's performance.
3. Clyde Sukeforth, the Dodger scout, approached Robinson.
4. Years of lies and disappointments had discouraged many black athletes.

Alfred Duckett

Duckett's most famous speech, "I Have a Dream," was written with Dr. Martin Luther King, Jr., and delivered by King in front of the Lincoln Memorial in Washington, D.C., on August 28, 1963.

Author Activity

Timeline You might allow students to work in small groups. In their groups, students can work through the autobiography and then plan and create their timelines. To make this assignment more challenging, encourage them to add illustrations or quotations from the book to their timelines.

Teaching Options

Mini Lesson Grammar  **TEKS** 18E **TAAS** Writing Obj. 1, 3

USING ACTIVE AND PASSIVE VERBS IN WRITING
Explain to students that they can change the tone of their writing by choosing to use passive or active verbs. Active verbs work well in making writing more straightforward. Passive verbs can be used to shift emphasis subtly.

Exercise Ask students to identify the language of each sentence as active or passive. Then have them rewrite the sentences, changing either passive to active or active to passive.

1. Branch Rickey lost that fight . . . (*The fight was lost by Branch Rickey.*)
2. In August 1945 . . . I was approached by Clyde Sukeforth, the Dodger scout. (*In August 1945, Clyde Sukeforth, the Dodger scout, approached me.*)
3. Beanballs would be thrown at me . . . I would be physically attacked. (*Opponents would throw beanballs at me. They would physically attack me.*)
4. "They'll taunt you and goad you . . . They'll try to provoke a race riot . . ." (*"You'll be taunted and goaded. A race riot will be provoked."*)
5. I was offered . . . a contract with a $3,500 bonus. . . . (*Mr. Rickey offered me a contract with a $3,500 bonus.*)

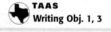 Use **Unit Two Resource Book,** p. 50.
 Use **Grammar Transparencies and Copymasters,** p. 141.

Casey at the Bat

 TEKS

See the Skills Trace at the beginning of the unit for information on TEKS covered in this lesson.

Poetry by ERNEST LAWRENCE THAYER

Connect to Your Life

Answer these questions, then discuss your answers with the class.
• My favorite athlete is _____.
• What I admire most about him or her is _____.
• When a game is "on the line," I expect him or her to _____.
• I was disappointed in him or her when _____.

Build Background

CONNECT TO **SOCIAL STUDIES** Baseball began in the United States in the mid-1800s. By the early 1900s the sport was so popular that people began calling it America's national pastime. Its popularity has prompted Jacques Barzun, a noted philosopher and educator, to state, "Whoever wants to know the heart and mind of America had better learn baseball."

In the light of the nation's continuing enthusiasm for baseball, it is small wonder that "mighty Casey" has remained a popular figure for more than 100 years. As you read this poem, think about what has changed in baseball since 1888, when the poem was written, and what has remained the same.

A cartoon showing baseball players and fans reacting to an umpire's call. Culver Pictures.

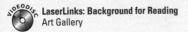 **LaserLinks: Background for Reading** Art Gallery

Focus Your Reading

LITERARY ANALYSIS **SOUND DEVICES** Poets often use **sound devices,** such as repetition, rhyme, and rhythm, in their poems.

• **Repetition** of a sound, word, phrase, or line can be used for emphasis.
• **Rhyme** is a repetition of sounds at the end of words.
• **Rhythm** is a pattern of stressed and unstressed syllables in the lines of a poem.

ACTIVE READING **QUESTIONING** Good readers ask questions both before they read a work and while they are reading it. "Casey at the Bat" is a **narrative poem**—poetry that tells a story. Before you read the poem, look at it to get an idea of what it's about. What is the **setting?** Who are the **characters?** What is the **conflict** that gets the **plot** moving?

READER'S NOTEBOOK As you read "Casey at the Bat," think about the setting, the conflict, and the characters. Jot down details that help you identify these elements. Also note any questions that occur to you.

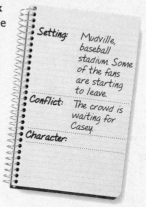

Setting: Mudville, baseball stadium. Some of the fans are starting to leave.

Conflict: The crowd is waiting for Casey.

Character:

Active Reading | QUESTIONING

A Have students list questions that they would ask to learn about the character of Casey.

Possible Responses: Who is Casey? What has Casey done in the past to earn the crowd's respect?

Use **Unit Two Resource Book**, p. 53 for more practice.

Literary Analysis: HYPERBOLE

B Explain to students that hyperbole is exaggeration. Ask students to identify the hyperbole in line 14 and its purpose.

Possible Response: "'tore the cover off the ball'"; to emphasize the force with which Blake hit the ball

Literary Analysis | SOUND DEVICES

C Remind students that rhyme contributes to the meaning. Ask students to identify the words that rhyme in the fifth stanza.

Answer: *yell, dell; flat, bat*
Ask what effect the rhyme has on the sound of the poem.

Possible Response: It adds drama to the poem because there is a pause at the end of each line that rhymes.
Have students tap out the rhythm of the fifth stanza. Ask them how the rhythm creates suspense.

Possible Response: The driving rhythm reinforces the idea that the crowd's excitement is rising.

Use **Unit Two Resource Book**, p. 54 for more practice.

---

by Ernest Lawrence Thayer

Casey at the Bat

It looked extremely rocky for the Mudville nine that day;
The score stood two to four, with but an inning left to play.
So, when Cooney died at second, and Burrows did the same,

1 | A pallor[1] wreathed the features of the patrons of the game.

5 A straggling few got up to go, leaving there the rest,
With that hope which springs eternal within the human breast.

A | For they thought: "If only Casey could get a whack at that,"
They'd put even money now, with Casey at the bat.

B | But Flynn preceded Casey, and likewise so did Blake,
10 | And the former was a pudd'n, and the latter was a fake.
So on that stricken multitude a deathlike silence sat;
For there seemed but little chance of Casey's getting to the bat.

But Flynn let drive a "single," to the wonderment of all.
And the much-despised Blakey "tore the cover off the ball."
15 And when the dust had lifted, and they saw what had occurred,

2 | There was Blakey safe at second, and Flynn a-huggin' third.

Then from the gladdened multitude went up a joyous yell—

C | It rumbled in the mountaintops, it rattled in the dell;[2]
It struck upon the hillside and rebounded on the flat;
20 | For Casey, mighty Casey, was advancing to the bat.

---

1. **pallor** (păl'ər): extreme paleness.
2. **dell**: valley.

Teaching Options

 Cross Curricular Link **Social Studies**

HISTORY OF BASEBALL Baseball has its origins in an English game called rounders. Rounders is very similar to the game that is now known in the United States as baseball, except the bat is shaped differently, and in rounders, a runner is out if he is hit with the thrown ball instead of tagged with the ball.

However, A. G. Spalding, a wealthy sporting-goods manufacturer, did not like the fact that America's national pastime descended from an English game. He formed a commission to investigate the history of baseball. Its 1908 report claimed that

Abner Doubleday, a Civil War general, invented baseball in 1839 at Cooperstown, New York. People accepted this history of baseball until it was proved false in 1939. By then, the National Baseball Hall of Fame and Museum had already been established at Cooperstown.

The rules of baseball were first officially formulated in 1845. The tagging rule led to the substitution of the hard ball for the softer ball used in rounders. As a result, two versions of the game were played until after the Civil War, when the hard-ball game won favor.

Baseball Scene of Batter, Catcher, and Umpire (1915), Joseph Christian Leyendecker. Photo courtesy of the Archives of the American Illustrators Gallery, New York. Copyright © 1995 ARTShows and Products of Holderness 03245.

Less Proficient Readers

Discuss the situation for the Mudville team before Casey gets up to bat.

Set a Purpose Have students read to find out what the crowd expects of Casey and whether or not these expectations are met.

Students Acquiring English

Encourage students to use context clues to help them define unfamiliar words.

1 Help students to understand the seriousness of the fans' feelings by paraphrasing this line. The fans' faces turn pale out of fear that Mudville will lose the game.

2 Point out that the prefix *a-* in *a-huggin'* is added to the verb to give it an informal, colloquial sound and to make it fit the rhythm of the poem. Have students find another verb that uses this prefix. (*a-watching*)

Use **Spanish Study Guide,** pp. 58–60 for additional support.

Gifted and Talented

Thayer uses some long and sometimes difficult words to refer to things that have common names, such as "spheroid" for the ball and "stricken multitude" for the anxious crowd. Ask students what purpose these words serve throughout the poem.

Possible Responses: They show how seriously the fans and Casey take the game; the author may be poking fun at how a game can become so serious; they give the poem a humorous tone.

Multiple Learning Styles
Visual Learners

Invite students to draw the infield of the ballpark, with the players in position as described in line 16. Remind students to include the dugout, where Casey may be waiting his turn at bat.

  ## Viewing and Representing   **TEKS 22A**

**Baseball Scene of Batter, Catcher, and Umpire
by Joseph Christian Leyendecker**

ART APPRECIATION This painting was done by the well-known illustrator J. C. Leyendecker in 1915. It demonstrates the artist's talent for accurately rendering the human form.

Instruction The artist conveys a mood through the details in his painting. Ask students what the mood of the work is and how the artist creates that mood.

Possible Responses: The mood is one of grim concentration or tension or expectancy. The expression on the batter's face and the poses of the catcher and umpire contribute to the mood. Ask students why the artist may have chosen not to sketch a background.

Possible Response: A background would have distracted from the focus on the figures.

Application Ask students to match this scene with a moment in the poem.

Possible Responses: Students might see this painting as illustrating the moment narrated in lines 43-46, when Casey faces the pitcher with a stern and cold demeanor.

Reading and Analyzing

Literary Analysis SOUND DEVICES

A Ask students how the repetition of Casey's name affects their impression of him.

Possible Response: It heightens the sense of his importance to the team and to the crowd.

Literary Analysis: CHARACTERIZATION

B Invite students to discuss what they can infer about Casey's character from lines 21-32.

Possible Responses: Casey is proud and self-assured; he is used to attention from the crowd.

Active Reading QUESTIONING

C Ask students what questions they would raise in response to this event.

Possible Responses: What is Casey thinking? What is he feeling? Why did he let a second ball go by without swinging?

Reading Skills and Strategies: VISUALIZING

D Ask students to identify the images that appeal to their senses in this stanza.

Possible Responses: "teeth are clenched," "pounds with cruel vengeance," "air is shattered by the force of Casey's blow"

A
There was ease in Casey's manner as he stepped into his place,
There was pride in Casey's bearing and a smile on Casey's face;
And when responding to the cheers he lightly doffed his hat,
No stranger in the crowd could doubt 'twas Casey at the bat.

25 Ten thousand eyes were on him as he rubbed his hands with dirt,
Five thousand tongues applauded when he wiped them on his shirt;
B
Then when the writhing[3] pitcher ground the ball into his hip,
Defiance glanced in Casey's eye, a sneer curled Casey's lip.

And now the leather-covered sphere came hurtling through the air,
30 And Casey stood a-watching it in haughty grandeur there.
Close by the sturdy batsman the ball unheeded sped;
"That ain't my style," said Casey. "Strike one," the umpire said.

From the benches, filled with people, there went up a muffled roar,
Like the beating of the storm waves on the stern and distant shore.
35 "Kill him! Kill the umpire!" shouted someone on the stand;
And it's likely they'd have killed him had not Casey raised his hand.

With a smile of honest charity great Casey's visage[4] shone;
He stilled the rising tumult,[5] he made the game go on;
He signaled to the pitcher, and once more the spheroid flew;
C
40 But Casey still ignored it, and the umpire said, "Strike two."

"Fraud!" cried the maddened thousands, and the echo answered "Fraud!"
But one scornful look from Casey and the audience was awed;
They saw his face grow stern and cold, they saw his muscles strain,
And they knew that Casey wouldn't let the ball go by again.

D
45 The sneer is gone from Casey's lips, his teeth are clenched in hate,
He pounds with cruel vengeance his bat upon the plate;
And now the pitcher holds the ball, and now he lets it go,
And now the air is shattered by the force of Casey's blow.

Oh, somewhere in this favored land the sun is shining bright,
50 The band is playing somewhere, and somewhere hearts are light;
And somewhere men are laughing, and somewhere children shout,
But there is no joy in Mudville: Mighty Casey has struck out.

---

3. **writhing** (rīth´ĭng): twisting, as in pain or embarrassment.
4. **visage** (vĭz´ĭj): face.
5. **tumult** (tōō´mŭlt´): a disorderly disturbance.

Teaching Options

✓ Assessment **Standardized Test Practice** TEKS 10E, K 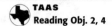 TAAS Reading Obj. 2, 4

ARRANGING DETAILS IN SEQUENTIAL ORDER In some standardized tests, students are asked to arrange details or events from a passage in chronological order. To provide students with some help in putting details in a logical sequence, ask them to arrange the following events from the poem in the order in which they occur.

A. Casey takes the first strike.
B. Fans lose heart, and several leave.
C. Flynn lands on third.
D. The crowd yells, "Kill him!"

E. Casey becomes stern and clenches his teeth.
F. Burrows dies at second.
G. Blake hits a double.
H. Casey takes a second strike.
I. Cooney only makes it to second.
J. Casey takes his cap off to the crowd.

Work with students to put the details in the following order: I, F, B, G, C, J, A, D, H, E.

Thinking through the LITERATURE

Connect to the Literature

1. What Do You Think? When you reached the end of the poem, how did you feel about Casey? How did you feel about the crowd?

Comprehension Check
- At the beginning of the poem, how many runs does the Mudville team have? What inning is it?
- How does Casey react to the first two pitches thrown to him?

Think Critically

2. What is your impression of Casey as he steps up to the plate? How might he have impressed the crowd?

3. How do you feel about Casey's response to his team's situation in the game?

THINK ABOUT
- his attitude as he steps up to the plate
- his "smile of honest charity" after the first strike is called
- his attitude after the second strike is called

4. **ACTIVE READING** **QUESTIONING** Look over the notes you took in your **READER'S NOTEBOOK**. With two other classmates, review the details and questions you wrote down. Answer any questions that are not answered in your notes.

Extend Interpretations

5. The Writer's Style A writer's use of exaggeration or overstatement for emphasis is called **hyperbole.** One example of hyperbole in this poem occurs in the description of the crowd's yell: "It rumbled in the mountaintops, it rattled in the dell." What does hyperbole add to "Casey at the Bat"?

6. Connect to Life Think of a real-life situation in which success or failure has depended upon the performance of a single person. What goes through a person's mind at a moment like that?

Literary Analysis

SOUND DEVICES Repetition, rhyme, and rhythm are three of the **sound devices** used in poetry. **Repetition** is a repeating of a sound, word, phrase, or line. **Rhyme** is a repetition of sounds at the end of words. (In many poems, lines end with rhyming words.) **Rhythm** is a pattern of stressed (´) and unstressed (�‿) syllables in a poem's lines.

These sound devices can intensify the emotional effect of a poem. All three can be heard in the following lines from "Casey at the Bat":

> *"Kill him! Kill the umpire!"*
>
> *shouted someone on the stand;*
>
> *And it's likely they'd have killed him*
>
> *had not Casey raised his hand.*

Cooperative Learning Activity Much of the energy and excitement of "Casey at the Bat" comes from the poet's use of repetition, rhyme, and rhythm. With a partner, copy the poem on a sheet of paper. On the copy, mark the rhythm, identify the rhyme scheme, and note any repetitions. Then, using your marked-up copy as a script, read the poem to your classmates.

CASEY AT THE BAT **303**

GUIDING STUDENT RESPONSE

Connect to the Literature

1. Responses will vary. Some students will say that they felt disappointment in Casey for letting the first two pitches go by. They may admire the loyalty of the crowd or feel that the crowd should have urged Casey to hit the second pitch.

Comprehension Check
- Mudville has two runs; it is the last inning.
- He refuses to swing at them, taking them for called strikes.

Think Critically

2. Possible Responses: Casey is arrogant and quite sure of himself. He wants to appear confident and relaxed.

3. Possible Responses: Casey is over-confident. He takes advantage of the admiration from the crowd and the position of his team to show his disdain for the pitcher and umpire.

4. Possible Responses: Encourage students to share details about setting, character, and conflict. Have students infer answers to their questions from the text.

Use **Reading and Critical Thinking Transparencies,** p. 12, for additional support.

Literary Analysis

Sound Devices Suggest that students read the poem aloud at a steady pace, clapping as they come to any stressed syllables. The predominant rhythm is created by the stressing of every other syllable, with some variations. The rhyme scheme is *aabb* and repetition occurs in stanzas 5, 6, 9, 12, and 13. Students may also note the poet's use of parallel structure, which adds to the dramatic effect. To help students understand the impact of the rhyme, rhythm, and repetition chosen by Thayer, have them rewrite a stanza and compare it with the original by reading it aloud.

Use **Literary Analysis Transparencies,** p. 20, for additional support.

Extend Interpretations

5. The Writer's Style Other examples of hyperbole include: "tore the cover off the ball"; "there went up a muffled roar, Like the beating of the storm waves on the stern and distant shore"; "Ten thousand eyes were on him . . . Five thousand tongues applauded." The poet's use of hyperbole increases the dramatic effect of the poem and emphasizes the seriousness of the game for the fans and the humor of the poem.

6. Connect to Life Responses will vary. Students may say that they imagine a person in that position would feel nervous or excited about the challenge. Students may suggest various ways to prepare, depending upon the situation. However, most will agree that at the time of the challenge, an individual should do his or her best.

Writing Options

1. **Opinion Essay** To get students started on this assignment, have them organize their brainstorming into paragraphs for the essay. Each paragraph should focus on one aspect of a team athlete's responsibility. Remind students to order the details in each paragraph from least to most important or in some other effective sequence. To adapt this assignment for **interpersonal learners,** have them debate the responsibilities of a team athlete.

2. **Newspaper Article** To get students started on this assignment, have them read some sports articles from the daily paper. Remind them to start their article with a catchy lead-in sentence.

Activities & Explorations

Film Review Before having students view the video, you might ask them to describe on paper their personal impressions of characters in the poem. They can then compare and contrast the details they recorded with details in the film.

Use **Communications Transparencies and Copymasters,** p. 7, for additional support.

Inquiry & Research

Record-Setters Some students might want to focus on record-setting athletes in sports other than baseball.

Ernest Lawrence Thayer

Although actor DeWolf Hopper made "Casey at the Bat" famous through his popular recitations in the late 1800s, for years he did not know who had written the poem. When he finally met Thayer, Hopper asked him to recite the poem. Hopper later said: "I have heard many another give 'Casey.' Fond mamas have brought their sons to me to hear their childish voices lisp the poem, but Thayer's was the worst of all."

Writing Options

1. **Opinion Essay** What makes a good team athlete? What is his or her responsibility to teammates? to fans? to the game? Does the athlete have a responsibility to live up to his or her own potential? Brainstorm answers to these questions with two or three classmates. Then, on your own, write an essay in which you express your personal opinions.

2. **Newspaper Article** Imagine that you are a reporter for the *Mudville Times.* Write a newspaper article describing the last inning of the game. If you want to include information that is not given in the poem, make it up. For example, you might invent names for the opposing team, the Mudville coach, the pitcher, and other players.

Activities & Explorations

Film Review View a clip from the film version of *Casey at the Bat.* Then with classmates, discuss whether the film portrays characters in the same way you visualized them. ~ **VIEWING AND REPRESENTING**

 Literature in Performance

Inquiry & Research

Record-Setters Consult a sports records book, almanac, or encyclopedia to find the names of baseball players whose accomplishments have made history. Choose one player to research in-depth. Whom did he play for? What do his fellow players say about him? What are his stats? Who previously held the record he broke?

 Real World Link Before you begin, read "Out of the Ballpark" on p. 305.

"I evolved 'Casey' from the situation I had seen so often in baseball . . ."

Ernest Lawrence Thayer
1863–1940

Early Years Although Ernest Lawrence Thayer wrote many poems for newspapers, he is remembered for just one: "Casey at the Bat." Thayer was educated at Harvard University, where he served as editor of its humor magazine, the *Lampoon.* After graduation, he joined the staff of the *San Francisco Examiner,* where in 1887 he began writing a poem for each Sunday issue. "Casey at the Bat" was first printed in the paper in 1888.

Origin of "Casey" Thayer said, "I evolved 'Casey' from the situation I had seen so often in baseball—a crack batsman coming to the bat with the bases filled, and then fallen down." Although he insisted that no particular person was the model for Casey, many ballplayers claimed to be the unfortunate hero of the poem. By the time of Thayer's death in 1940, "Casey at the Bat" had become an American favorite.

 LaserLinks: Background for Reading Art Gallery

Sports

Out of the Ballpark

SPECIAL REPORT

by Avery Foster

In the summer of 1998, Mark McGwire and Sammy Sosa raced to break the single season home run record set by Roger Maris in 1961. The two sluggers found themselves caught up in a surge of publicity. Thousands of cameras flashed each time they swung the bat. The nightly news never missed reporting a game. Suddenly, baseball was the subject everyone was talking about. Had one of them hit one out today? Did you hear that it smashed through a billboard? At times the media frenzy seemed to overwhelm Sosa and McGwire. Often, however, they coped with their success by drawing attention away from themselves. The skill it took to smash the ball out of the park day after day was extraordinary, but the ability to homer was not the most extraordinary thing about these two power hitters.

Fans surround Sosa and McGwire in Orlando.

Reading for Information

What motivates your favorite baseball players? What causes are they devoted to outside the ballpark?

MAKING GENERALIZATIONS & DRAWING CONCLUSIONS

When writers make broad general statements based on several individual pieces of information, they are **making generalizations.** "Elephants are large" and "Anita always gets up early" are examples of generalizations.

YOUR TURN *Use the questions below to learn more about making generalizations.*

❶ Words such as *everyone*, *no one*, *always*, and *never* often tell you that a statement is an **overgeneralization** based on too little information. In these two sentences, what words reveal that these statements are overgeneralizations?

REAL WORLD LINK   **305**

Objectives

• read and analyze news sources
• distinguish generalizations from overgeneralizations
• draw conclusions from a text and analyze the logic of a writer's conclusions
• read to be informed
• read in varied sources, such as newspapers

Connecting to the Literature

Although the character of Casey in the poem "Casey at the Bat" is revealed only through his performance during one baseball game, this newspaper article is a reminder that real-world sports heroes are scrutinized for their actions outside of sports. They face many choices about what they will do with their success. The portraits of Mark McGwire and Sammy Sosa in this article show that they are heroes both on and off the playing field.

Reading for Information

Tell students that this article appeared after the exciting 1998 baseball season. As you go through the article with students, have them use the material in the right-hand column as a guide to reading feature news articles. The following are **possible responses** to the five questions.

1 The writer uses phrases and words such as "At times" and "Often" to avoid making overgeneralizations.

Use **Reading and Critical Thinking Transparencies**, pp. 9, 14, 17, for additional support.

Better Than Babe Ruth

2 If McGwire wanted to brag about himself, he certainly could. In 1998, he towered over the rest of the league in both stats and stature. His powerful bat would have put him in the history books even if he hadn't surpassed Roger Maris's 61 home runs. For three seasons in a row he hit at least 50 homers (1996, 1997, and 1998), and his home run ratio was an astonishing one homer per 11.2 at bats. That means that if you chose to spend a beautiful summer afternoon watching McGwire at bat, you would have a better chance of seeing him smash one out than you would if you were watching any other player in history, including Babe Ruth.

3 When he signed with the Cardinals in the fall of 1997, McGwire was already making a name for himself away from the ballpark. At the televised press conference announcing the deal, he pledged to donate $1 million per year of his Cardinals salary to help abused children. More impressive than that pledge was what happened to the big guy when he tried to talk about his reasons for setting up the Mark McGwire Charitable Foundation. He couldn't. There was only silence. And then he started to cry. The sight instantly endeared him to the public. Here was a giant of a man who broke into tears when he thought about what was happening to defenseless children. It was a theme to which McGwire would return again and again throughout 1998. Breaking the record for the most home runs in a season was exhilarating, but the chance to help children affected McGwire more profoundly.

Right fielder Sammy Sosa trailed McGwire in total home runs for most of the season, but he too could rocket the ball out of the park. At 6'0" and 200 lbs., Sosa is not small by any means, but his performance in 1998 emphasized that smashing the ball out of the stadium also required excellent skill and timing. People were amazed when Sosa hit homer number 66 and pulled ahead of McGwire for only the second time during the season.

McGwire reacts to his 61st home run of the 1998 season.

McGwire follows through to hit a single against the Milwaukee Brewers.

Not only had the two sluggers battled to break the record of 61 home runs in a single season, they were continuing the battle.

Strength of Character

Besides a place in the record books, the home run race offered Sosa an opportunity to reveal his strength of character. Out of the batting box, he demonstrated the respect and humility that were the very model of sportsmanship. If he finished the season with the most home runs, Sammy said, he would be happy. If McGwire finished with more, he added, he still would be happy! It astonished everyone that Sosa and McGwire seemed to get along so well together. Again and again Sosa maintained that McGwire was a great player and he wished him the best. In an age when many sports superstars couldn't care less about being an example for others, the conduct of the Cubs right fielder was refreshing.

Reading for Information *continued*
When writers gather information from their research and combine it with logical ways to develop their own ideas on a topic, they are **drawing conclusions.** Readers draw conclusions by making inferences about the details in the works they read.

YOUR TURN *Use the questions below to learn more about drawing conclusions.*

❷ The writer begins this paragraph with a conclusion drawn from his research. What specific information does he provide in the rest of the paragraph to support the conclusion? Does the conclusion make sense?

❸ What conclusion can you draw about McGwire, based on the specific information in this paragraph?

2 The writer provides facts to support his conclusion. He tells about Mark McGwire's powerful batting ability. He includes the statistics that Mark McGwire hit at least 50 homers for three seasons in a row. His home-run ratio was one homer per 11.2 at bats. The writer also says that a spectator would stand a better chance of seeing him hit a homer than if he or she were watching any other player in history. All of the details in the paragraph support the conclusion drawn by the writer that Mark McGwire has a right to be proud of himself.

3 Mark McGwire is an outstanding person as well as a tremendous ballplayer. He believes that his success is a steppingstone to helping others, especially those unable to help themselves.

4 The conclusion of this paragraph is at the beginning. Despite Sammy Sosa's success, he has not forgotten the needy in his own country.

5 The three overgeneralizations are: "The entire nation," "There will never be another season like it," and "drew everyone into their success." The sentences might be rewritten in the following ways. "Most of the nation watched with excitement as two legendary players chased one of the most glorious records in baseball." "There will probably never be another season like it." "Sosa and McGwire, by reaching out to help others, drew many people into their success."

④ rowing up in the Dominican Republic, Sosa's first job as a kid was shining shoes, and he has never forgotten where he came from. By founding the Sammy Sosa Charitable Foundation, Sosa began helping his country, with the goal of providing aid for children's healthcare in his hometown of San Pedro. His country needed him most, however, when tragedy struck in September of 1998. Hurricane Georges swept quickly through the Caribbean, wreaking havoc on the Dominican Republic and leaving thousands homeless. Rising to the occasion, Sosa turned the constant publicity from the home run race into a daily opportunity for raising disaster relief funds. In the process, he sent three planeloads of food and medical supplies to the Dominican Republic and joined other Dominican baseball players in a pledge to help out any way possible.

Reading for Information *continued*

❹ Writers may state their conclusion as a topic sentence *before* the information that supports it or as a summing up *after* the information. Read this paragraph. Where is the conclusion? Restate it in your own words.

❺ There are three overgeneralizations in this paragraph. Rewrite them to make them valid generalizations.

Inquiry & Research

Activity Link: "Casey at the Bat," p. 304. Find out more about Roger Maris, a previous holder of the single season home run record. What characterized him as a player? What was he known for outside the ballpark? What controversy is associated with his record? Write a paragraph in which you make a generalization about Maris's accomplishments and draw a conclusion based on a group of facts.

Sosa takes a big swing.

⑤ Sosa may not have set the final home run record, but he proved himself an excellent ballplayer and an excellent human being. The entire nation watched with excitement as two legendary players chased one of the most glorious records in baseball. There will never be another season like it. Sosa and McGwire, by reaching out to help others, drew everyone into their success. With equal parts skill and heart, they propelled themselves into sports history. ∎

 Mini Lesson ## Inquiry & Research ⚑ **TEKS** 20A, 20C

The Inquiry & Research activity on this page links to the topic of the Inquiry & Research Activity of Choices & Challenges (page 304) following "Casey at the Bat."

As they do the Inquiry & Research activity, students will take notes from relevant and authoritative sources such as periodicals, reference books, and the Internet before presenting their conclusions in a strong paragraph.

Instruction Have students write down questions that they want to answer about Roger Maris in the course of their research. Asking older relatives and neighbors what they remember about the 1961 baseball season might give students possible subject headings to investigate.

Practice Although one source may provide answers to many of their questions, have students use at least two different sources to check the objectivity of the facts and to develop a detailed understanding of their subject before they draw a conclusion.

 Use **Writing Transparencies**, p. 49, for additional support.

Prefixes and Suffixes

The words *mistrust* and *excitable* each have an **affix**—a word part that can be attached to root words to make new words. Affixes added to the beginning of words are called **prefixes**; those added to the end are called **suffixes**.

mistrust

prefix *mis-* means "not" | root word: **trust**

excitable

root word: **excite** | suffix *-able* means "capable of being"

> The next day when the principal called me into his office I knew what it would be about. He looked uncomfortable and unhappy. I decided I wasn't going to make it any easier for him, so I looked him straight in the eyes. He looked away and fidgeted with the papers on his desk.
>
> —Marta Salinas, "The Scholarship Jacket"

Both words share the prefix *un-*, which means "not." Can you figure out their meaning?

Strategies for Building Vocabulary

Below are some common prefixes and suffixes used in forming English words.

❶ Recognize Common Affixes Knowing the meanings of some of the most common affixes can help you understand the meanings of unfamiliar words. Some of the most common prefixes and suffixes are listed in the charts below, along with their meanings.

❷ Analyze Words You can use your knowledge of prefixes, suffixes, and root words to analyze the meanings of words you don't know. Think about the word *resealable,* for example. The prefix *re-* means "again." The root word *seal* means "to close tightly." The suffix *-able* means "capable of." Therefore, *resealable* means "capable of being closed tightly again."

Prefix	Meaning	Examples
co-, com-, con-	with, together	costar, compress, conjunction
dis-	the absence of	disagree
e-, ex-	opposite of, out, away from	emigrate, exchange
em-, en-	to provide with, to cause to be	empower, enrich
im-, in-, il-, ir-	not	inoperable, imperfect, illogical, irresponsible
re-	again, back	recharge, review
trans-	across, change	transact, transcontinental
un-	not, opposite	unbearable, unhook, unnoticed

Suffix	Meaning	Examples
-able, -ible	likely to be, capable of being	adorable, flexible
-ance	an act or state of	appearance
-ate	characterized by, to cause to become	passionate, activate
-er, -or	one who	driver, visitor
-ion	an act or state of	creation, eruption
-ive	tending to, performing an act of	reflective, selective
-ous	full of, charcterized by	joyous, poisonous

EXERCISE Divide each word into a root word and a prefix or suffix. Then define the word.

1. transform   2. destitution   3. enable   4. inefficient   5. endurance

Objectives
- apply meanings of prefixes in order to comprehend
- apply meanings of suffixes in order to comprehend
- apply meanings of root words in order to comprehend

EXERCISE
Possible Responses:
1. trans- + form: "change"
2. destitute + -tion: "misery, poverty"
3. en- + able: "allow"
4. in- + efficient: "not productive or useful"
5. endure + -ance: "the act of being able to survive"

Use **Unit Two Resource Book,** p. 55.
Use **Vocabulary Transparencies and Copymasters,** pp. 7–8 for additional support.

OVERVIEW

This feature gives students an opportunity to compare, evaluate, and form opinions about traditional and modern fables. The focus is a comparison of character and moral in two fables.

Teaching Option

Because each fable is accompanied by its own introductory and response pages, you have the option of pairing the stories or teaching them individually. Used in conjunction with the Comparing Literature Assessment Practice on page 323, the selections may also be used to help students prepare for literature-based writing assignments.

Fables

You are about to read two versions of the **fable** "Ant and Grasshopper" by the ancient Greek storyteller Aesop. The fable teaches a simple lesson, or **moral,** about the importance of work. Then you will read "The Richer, the Poorer," a modern story based on Aesop's fable. The **characters** in "The Richer, the Poorer" have much in common with the ant and the grasshopper of the original fable, but the modern characters have a more complex view of the role of work in a happy life.

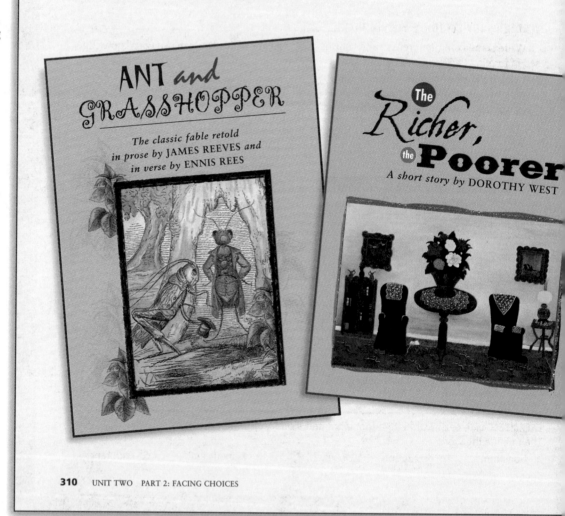

ANT *and* GRASSHOPPER

The classic fable retold in prose by JAMES REEVES *and in verse by* ENNIS REES

The Richer, *the* Poorer

A short story by DOROTHY WEST

310   UNIT TWO   PART 2: FACING CHOICES

TEKS

See the Skills Trace at the beginning of the unit for information on TEKS covered in this lesson.

Connect to Your Life

Hard Work and No Play

Why is work such an important part of life? How do you feel about your work? Do you put your best effort into it? Do you sometimes try to avoid it? What do you get in return for the work you do? Think about your attitudes toward work.

- How important is work for a happy life?

- Which is more important, work or play?

In a small group, discuss your views on the role of work in life.

POINTS OF COMPARISON

Fables are brief tales written in prose or verse that are told to illustrate a **moral**, or lesson. Traditional fables often have animal characters, and the moral appears in a statement at the end. **Modern fables** are often more subtle and complex. In the pages that follow you will compare and contrast a traditional and a modern fable. To help you note similarities and differences, keep these questions in mind as you read.

- ◆ When was the **fable** written?
- ◆ Who are the **characters**? What do they represent?
- ◆ What happens in the **fable**?
- ◆ What is the **moral**?

Use a diagram like the one at the right to take notes as you read.

	Ant and Grasshopper	The Richer, the Poorer
When was the fable written?		
Who are the characters? What do they represent?		
What happens in the fable?		
What is the moral?		

Assessment Option: Comparison-and-Contrast Essay

After you have finished reading both versions of "Ant and Grasshopper" and "The Richer, the Poorer," you will have the option of writing a comparison-and-contrast essay. Your notes will help you plan and write the essay.

Connect to Your Life

Have students consider the idea of work as it applies to schoolwork, chores at home, part-time jobs, and practice of musical instruments, sports, or some other activity. Ask students to think about what they would miss if they no longer had to "work" at something and what that reveals about the place of work in a happy life.

Possible Responses: satisfaction; sense of accomplishment; pride; self-respect; excitement; sense of challenge Students may say that a balance of work and play will contribute to a happy life.

Points of Comparison

Students will compare character, plot, and theme of both types of fable, creating and then filling in a diagram like that which follows each selection. Remind students to note other similarities or differences, such as their reactions to the characters or the overall effect of each fable.

Assessment Option: Comparison-and-Contrast Essay

Students should read both selections with attention to details that they will use to support their explanation of the similarities and differences between the traditional fable and the modern fable.

OVERVIEW

Objectives

1. understand and appreciate a classic **fable** (animal characters representing a concept, stated moral) **(Literary Analysis)**
2. **compare and contrast** two versions of a classic fable **(Literary Analysis)**
3. **set purposes for reading (Active Reading)**

Summary

In both versions of Aesop's fable, Ant has stored up grain to see her through a cold harsh winter. Grasshopper, who frittered the summer away, is starving in the winter and approaches Ant, hoping to share some of her food. In the prose account, the ant asks the grasshopper what he did all summer instead of planning for the months ahead. When he replies that he sang, she replies that he can dance all winter to keep warm. In the poem, Grasshopper ridicules Ant for working hard all summer. Then by winter, Grasshopper is hovering around Ant's house in an effort to scavenge some food.

Thematic Link

Ant and Grasshopper face important choices. Ant chooses to plan ahead; Grasshopper chooses to enjoy the present without thinking about the future.

5-Minute Warm-Up

Daily Language SkillBuilder **TEKS 17C, 17H**

Have students **proofread** the display sentences on page 189k and write them correctly. The sentences also appear on Transparency 10 of **Grammar Transparencies and Copymasters.**

Ant and Grasshopper

Aesop's fable retold in prose by JAMES REEVES

Aesop's fable retold in verse by ENNIS REES

Build Background

CONNECT TO BIOLOGY Both ants and grasshoppers are insects, but their habits are different. Ants live in organized communities called colonies, and are divided into queens, males, and workers. Most ants are workers, whose main job is to gather food. Ants eat both vegetable matter and other insects. Ants are also silent.

Grasshoppers, on the other hand, don't live in communities. Most grasshoppers eat vegetable matter, but some eat animal remains and other insects. Male grasshoppers can "sing" by rubbing their hind legs against their front wings. Grasshoppers can jump a distance of up to 20 times the length of their body. Grasshoppers spend most of their time searching for food and eating.

Focus Your Reading

LITERARY ANALYSIS **FABLE AND MORAL** A **fable** is a brief story that teaches a lesson that can be expressed in a short, clear statement, or **moral**. The **characters** in fables are often animals who represent ideas such as "patience" or "cleverness." As you read the two retellings of Aesop's "Ant and Grasshopper," notice that one is told in verse and the other in prose. However, the characters and the moral are the same in both versions. You should be able to restate the fable and its moral in your own words.

ACTIVE READING **SETTING PURPOSES** When you **set a purpose for reading,** you choose specific reasons for reading a work. Here you will read to compare and contrast two versions of the same fable. As you read, notice the difference between reading for fun and reading in order to prepare for writing an essay.

READER'S NOTEBOOK As you read, try to answer the Points of Comparison questions from page 311.

 TEKS See the Skills Trace at the beginning of the unit for information on TEKS covered in this lesson.

LESSON RESOURCES

UNIT TWO RESOURCE BOOK, pp. 56–62

ASSESSMENT
Formal Assessment, pp. 47–48
Teacher's Guide to Assessment and Portfolio Use
Test Generator

SKILLS TRANSPARENCIES AND COPYMASTERS
Literary Analysis
• Fables/Myths/Tall Tales, TR 30 (for Paired Learning Activity, p. 315)
Reading and Critical Thinking
• Setting a Purpose, TR 13 (for Thinking Through the Literature, p. 315)

INTEGRATED TECHNOLOGY
Audio Library

Visit our website:
www.mcdougallittell.com

ANT and GRASSHOPPER

Aesop's fable retold in prose by JAMES REEVES

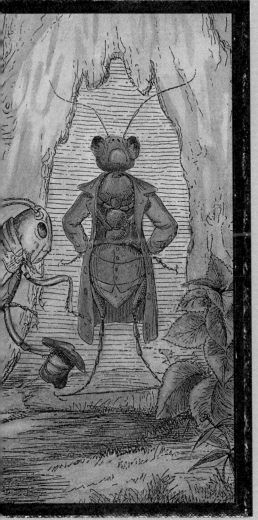

The Grasshopper and the Ant, Charles Henry Bennett (1828–1867).
Pen and ink drawing. The Granger Collection, New York.

All summer the ant had been working hard, gathering a store of corn for the winter. Grain by grain she had taken it from the fields and stowed it away in a hole in the bank, under a hawthorn bush.

One bright, frosty day in winter Grasshopper saw her. She was dragging out a grain of corn to dry it in the sun. The wind was keen, and poor Grasshopper was cold.

"Good morning, Ant," said he. "What a terrible winter it is! I'm half dead with hunger. Please give me just one of your corn grains to eat. I can find nothing, although I've hopped all over the farmyard. There isn't a seed to be found. Spare me a grain, I beg."

"Why haven't you saved anything up?" asked Ant. "I worked hard all through the summer, storing food for the winter. Very glad I am too, for as you say, it's bitterly cold."

"I wasn't idle last summer, either," said Grasshopper.

"And what did you do, pray?"

"Why, I spent the time singing," answered Grasshopper. "Every day from dawn till sunset I jumped about or sat in the sun, chirruping to my heart's content."

"Oh you did, did you?" replied Ant. "Well, since you've sung all summer to keep yourself cheerful, you may dance all winter to keep yourself warm. Not a grain will I give you!"

And she scuttled off into her hole in the bank, while Grasshopper was left cold and hungry.

IN GOOD TIMES PREPARE FOR WHEN THE
BAD TIMES COME.

ANT AND GRASSHOPPER **313**

Cross Curricular Link **History**

OTHER FABLES BY AESOP There are about two hundred fables credited to Aesop. The best-known have animal characters. One fable familiar to many is "The Hare and the Tortoise." The speedy hare challenges anyone to beat him in a race. When the tortoise accepts, the hare is so certain that he will achieve an easy victory that he stops to take a short nap in the middle of the race. As a result, he loses because the tortoise has reached the finish line by the time he wakes up. The moral is that "Slow and steady wins the race."

Some of Aesop's fables use humans to illustrate effective lessons. In one such fable, a Miser hides his gold in the ground, digging it up each week to gaze at it. When a robber steals it, the Miser cries so loudly that the neighbors rush to his aid. However, after hearing that the Miser never used his gold and only looked at it, one man suggests that he could just look at the hole in the ground instead, because "wealth unused might as well not exist."

The fables have endured for over 2500 years with morals that continue to be relevant.

Literary Analysis FABLE AND MORAL

 Ask students to discuss what each insect's character might represent.

Possible Responses: The ant might represent foresight, wisdom, organization, or diligence. The grasshopper might represent foolishness, carelessness, negligence, or frivolity.

Ask students to restate the moral of the prose version in their own words.

Possible Responses: Always be prepared. Don't put off until tomorrow what you can do today. Plan ahead.

B What words in the poem could serve as its moral?

Possible Response: "hard work / Isn't easy to beat."

Use the **Unit Two Resource Book**, p. 58 for more practice.

Active Reading SETTING PURPOSES

Remind students that they are noting similarities and differences as they read the two versions. Ask students to focus on the character of Grasshopper in the poem. In what ways does the characterization of the grasshopper in the poem differ from the prose version?

Possible Responses: Grasshopper in the poem is rude and outspoken. Grasshopper in the prose account is quite polite to the ant. He answers her questions without acting as if he is superior to her.

 Use **Unit Two Resource Book**, p. 57 for more practice.

The ANT and the GRASSHOPPER

Aesop's fable retold in verse by ENNIS REES

A mean grasshopper,
Green as a lime,
Noticed an ant
In the summertime
Climbing a plant,
Gathering food
To eat in the winter.
And since she was rude,
The grasshopper said:

A "To work in the summer
You must be dumber
Than almost anyone.
Don't you have any fun?
Even though you're an ant,
Surely you can't
Be quite so absurd!"

To this the ant
Didn't answer a word,
But she took the chance
To give her a glance

As sharp as a splinter,
Then worked right on
Getting ready for winter,
When there's little to light on **A**
And little to eat
And even less heat
Than that. And soon

Winter came. And the grasshopper,
Green as a lime,
Felt stiff and lame
In the wintertime.

"I'm old and I'm twice
As cold as lime ice,"
She said with a jerk.
And she started to lurk
Round the ant's house—to eat!
Which shows that hard work **B**
Isn't easy to beat.

ESOPO

"In good times prepare for when the bad times come."

Aesop
620–560 B.C.

A Mysterious Life Little is known about Aesop, the world's most famous creator of fables. Some historians think he may have been a slave who worked on Samos, an island off eastern Greece.

Fast Talker One account of Aesop's life is as eventful as one of his fables. According to this story, Aesop's second master granted him his freedom in appreciation of his wit. After telling stories throughout Greece and Egypt, Aesop was appointed ambassador by King Croesus. On diplomatic missions, Aesop told fables to advise, instruct, or win an argument. Most of the time, his skill with words enabled him to wriggle out of trouble. His luck, however, ran out in Delphi, where he was sent to distribute money to the citizens. Aesop found them so greedy that he returned the money to Croesus. As Aesop prepared to leave Delphi, someone hid a golden bowl in his baggage. He was arrested for theft, condemned by the court, and executed by being pushed off a cliff.

Connect to the Literature

1. What Do You Think? How did you feel about the ant's treatment of the grasshopper? Did you have the same reaction to both versions of the fable? Explain.

Comprehension Check
- How had the ant prepared for winter?
- What did the grasshopper want from the ant?
- How did the ant respond?

Think Critically

2. **ACTIVE READING** **SETTING PURPOSES** Review the notes you made in your **READER'S NOTEBOOK** while reading. With a partner, identify details both versions of "Ant and Grasshopper" share. Then discuss how looking for information changed the way you read the fables.

3. Connect to Life Think about how much time most Americans spend working. In a small group, discuss whether the ant or the grasshopper is the better symbol for Americans' attitudes toward work.

Literary Analysis

FABLE AND MORAL A **fable** is a short tale told to teach a lesson. The characters in fables are usually animals that represent ideas. In the fables you've just read, the ant represents "hard work" and the grasshopper represents "enjoying yourself when you should be preparing for the future." The lesson of the fable, called the **moral**, is sometimes directly stated at the end of the fable, as in James Reeves's retelling of "Ant and Grasshopper." Other times, as with Ennis Rees's version in verse, the reader must infer the moral from the characters' behavior. In either case, the same moral applies to both and can always be expressed in a simple statement.

POINTS OF COMPARISON

Paired Learning Activity With a partner, study both versions of the fable and answer the Points of Comparison questions from page 311. Together, complete the diagram you began earlier.

	Ant and Grasshopper	The Richer, the Poorer
When was the fable written?	in ancient Greece	
Who are the characters? What do they represent?	grasshopper = play ant = work	
What happens in the fable?		
What is the moral?		

POINTS OF COMPARISON

What happens in the fable? The ant stores up grain for the winter while the grasshopper spends the summer singing and enjoying himself. As a result, the ant has enough to eat during the winter, but the grasshopper is starving. He asks the ant for some grain. The ant refuses.

What is the moral? The moral is "In good times, prepare for when the bad times come" or "Hard work isn't easy to beat."

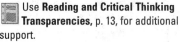

The Richer, the Poorer

Modern Fable by DOROTHY WEST

Summary

Lottie works hard because she wants the money to buy herself the best of everything. Soon, though, instead of spending her money, Lottie prefers to save it in the bank. As the years go by, she spends nothing on herself or her house until the day she is forced to retire from the restaurant where she has worked all her life. Then she receives the news that her sister's husband has died. Her sister Bess, who has lived a happy but itinerant life with her musician husband, has been left penniless and grief-stricken. Lottie sends her the money for her passage home and knows that she will have to take her sister in. In preparation for Bess's arrival, Lottie begins to fix up her house. As she redecorates, Lottie has more fun than she has ever had. Then she sees how dowdy she has become and treats herself to a day at the beauty salon. After Bess arrives, she tells Lottie stories about her life with her husband. Lottie sees that instead of feeling sorry for Bess, whose life is rich in memories, she should feel sorry for herself. Lottie is the one whose life has been poor. Bess tells her not to look back but to enjoy the time they both have left.

Thematic Link

Lottie chooses to save her money for the future instead of living her life in the present.

Build Background

CONNECT TO **SCIENCE** Have you wondered why some people are adventurous and outgoing risk takers while others are cautious and always worry about what the future might bring? Experts who study human behavior disagree about the factors that make people who they are. Some believe that it is nature—the genes inherited from a person's parents—that has the most important influence on personality. Others believe that nurture—the influence of other people and the environment on a person's life—has the most impact.

Focus Your Reading

LITERARY ANALYSIS **MODERN FABLE** **Modern fables** differ in some ways from traditional fables. The **characters** are not usually animals, and they are more complicated; they don't just represent an idea. The **moral** in a modern fable is seldom stated. The reader is left to infer it from what the characters do and say, and what is said about them. As you read, notice how the character Lottie changes.

ACTIVE READING **SETTING PURPOSES** When reading stories in order to **compare** and **contrast** them, your purpose is to find similarities and differences between them. As you read "The Richer, the Poorer," pay careful attention to the characters and the plot. Notice the lessons each character learns. Think about the title. Then think how these story elements relate to those in "Ant and Grasshopper."

 READER'S NOTEBOOK As you read, refer again to the Points of Comparison questions from page 311. Record your findings in your Reader's Notebook for later use in completing your Points of Comparison diagram.

WORDS TO KNOW **Vocabulary Preview**		
enhanced	self-denial	whim
frugally	sentimental	

 See the Skills Trace at the beginning of the unit for information on TEKS covered in this lesson.

5-Minute Warm-Up

Daily Language SkillBuilder **TEKS** 17C, 16D

Have students **proofread** the display sentences on page 189k and write them correctly. The sentences also appear on Transparency 10 of **Grammar Transparencies and Copymasters.**

LESSON RESOURCES

UNIT TWO RESOURCE BOOK, pp. 63–69

ASSESSMENT
Formal Assessment, pp. 49–50
Teacher's Guide to Assessment and Portfolio Use
Test Generator

SKILLS TRANSPARENCIES AND COPYMASTERS
Literary Analysis
• Fables/Myths/Tall Tales, TR 30 (for Paired Learning Activity, p. 321)

Reading and Critical Thinking
• Setting Purpose, TR 8, 13 (for Thinking Through the Literature, p. 321)
Grammar Transparencies and Copymasters
• Quotations within Quotations CM 128 (for Mini Lesson, p. 323)
Vocabulary
• Context Clues, CM 44 (for Mini Lesson, p. 317)

INTEGRATED TECHNOLOGY
Audio Library

Visit our website:
www.mcdougallittell.com

The Richer, the Poorer

by DOROTHY WEST

Victorian Parlor II (1945), Horace Pippin. Oil on canvas, 25 1/4" x 30". The Metropolitan Museum of Art, Arthur Hoppock Hearn Fund, 1958. (58.26)

Over the years Lottie had urged Bess to prepare for her old age. Over the years Bess had lived each day as if there were no other. Now they were both past sixty, the time for summing up. Lottie had a bank account that had never grown lean. Bess had the clothes on her back and the rest of her worldly possessions in a battered suitcase.

Lottie had hated being a child, hearing her parents' skimping and scraping. Bess had never seemed to notice. All she ever wanted was to go outside and play. She learned to skate on borrowed skates. She rode a borrowed bicycle. Lottie couldn't wait to grow up and buy herself the best of everything.

As soon as anyone would hire her, Lottie put herself to work. She minded babies; she ran errands for the old.

317

TEACHING THE LITERATURE

Customizing Instruction

Less Proficient Readers
Help students to see the contrast that the author immediately sets up between Lottie and Bess. Lottie has a serious outlook on life; Bess enjoys herself.

Set a Purpose Have students read to find out what happens in each sister's life.

Students Acquiring English
Explain to students that Lottie and Bess are in their sixties when the story begins. The author uses flashback to look at what has happened in both their lives.

1 Help students to understand that "summing up" means evaluating or measuring what they have accomplished.

2 Make sure that students know that the expression "skimping and scraping" means to try to save money in order to have enough to live on.

Use **Spanish Study Guide**, pp. 64–66, for additional support.

Gifted and Talented
Invite students to defend either Lottie's feelings about Bess's life before Bess returns, or Bess's lifestyle, which leaves her in the situation of having to return to Lottie.

Mini Lesson **Preteaching Vocabulary**   **TEKS** 6A   **TAAS** Reading Obj. 1

CONTEXT CLUES
Instruction Remind students that when they encounter an unfamiliar word, they should use knowledge of the context in which the word is used to infer the word's meaning. Display the sentence below to show how *sentimental* can be inferred to mean "showing tender emotions."

The man was so *sentimental* that he cried over sad movies before they even started.

Exercise Have students infer the meanings of the underlined WORDS TO KNOW in the following sentences.

1. Lottie practiced <u>self-denial</u> by refusing to buy herself new clothes even though she wanted them.
2. The thought of going to the beauty salon was a <u>whim</u> at first, but then it became a reality.
3. Her new image and the compliments that she received <u>enhanced</u> her feelings of happiness.
4. She kept track of every penny and tried to live as <u>frugally</u> as possible so that she could save more.

 Use **Unit Two Resource Book**, p. 66 for more exercises.
Use **Vocabulary Transparencies and Copymasters**, p. 44, for additional support.

Literary Analysis MODERN FABLE

A Remind students that the characters in a modern fable are more complex than those in a traditional fable. Ask students what happens to Lottie's desire to be able to buy herself the best of everything.

Possible Response: It is replaced by her desire to save as much money as she can.

B Ask students to analyze the differences in values between the two sisters.

Possible Responses: Lottie values security and stability. Bess values people and new experiences.

Use the **Unit Two Resource Book,** p. 65 for more practice.

Active Reading SETTING PURPOSES

C Remind students that because their purpose is to compare and contrast, they need to look at the events that affect the characters. Ask students what begins to change Lottie's outlook on life.

Possible Response: Lottie is forced to retire and has too much time on her hands to avoid thinking about her life. Bess's husband dies, and Lottie must take her in.

D Have students contrast Lottie's attitude as she redecorates with the way she previously approached life.

Possible Response: She is living in the present and enjoying her money instead of just saving it.

Have students pause to compare the characters of Lottie and Ant.

Possible Responses: Lottie is capable of changing and acquiring insight. Ant does not change.

Use the **Unit Two Resource Book,** p. 64 for more practice.

She never touched a penny of her money, though her child's mouth watered for ice cream and candy. But she could not bear to share with Bess, who never had anything to share with her. When the dimes began to add up to dollars, she lost her taste for sweets.

By the time she was twelve, she was clerking after school in a small variety store. Saturdays she worked as long as she was wanted. She decided to keep her money for clothes. When she entered high school, she would wear a wardrobe that neither she nor anyone else would be able to match.

But her freshman year found her unable to indulge so frivolous a <u>whim</u>, particularly when her admiring instructors advised her to think seriously of college. No one in her family had ever gone to college, and certainly Bess would never get there.

She would show them all what she could do, if she put her mind to it. She began to bank her money, and her bank became her most private and precious possession.

In her third year in high school, she found a job in a small but expanding restaurant, where she cashiered from the busy hour until closing. In her last year in high school, the business increased so rapidly that Lottie was faced with the choice of staying in school or working full time. She made her choice easily. A job in hand was worth two in the future.

Bess had a beau[1] in the school band, who had no other ambition except to play a horn. Lottie expected to be settled with a home and family while Bess was still waiting for Harry to earn enough to buy a marriage license.

That Bess married Harry straight out of high school was not surprising. That Lottie never married at all was not really surprising

> **To know how much there is to know is the beginning of learning to live.**

either. Two or three times she was halfway persuaded, but to give up a job that paid well for a homemaking job that paid nothing was a risk she was incapable of taking.

Bess's married life was nothing for Lottie to envy. She and Harry lived like gypsies, Harry playing in second-rate bands all over the country, even getting himself and Bess stranded in Europe. They were often in rags and never in riches.

Bess grieved because she had no child, not having sense enough to know she was better off without one. Lottie was certainly better off without nieces and nephews to feel sorry for. Very likely Bess would have dumped them on her doorstep.

That Lottie had a doorstep they might have been left on was only because her boss, having bought a second house, offered Lottie his first house at a price so low and terms so reasonable that it would have been like losing money to refuse.

She shut off the rooms she didn't use, letting them go to rack and ruin.[2] Since she ate her meals out, she had no food at home and did not encourage callers, who always expected a cup of tea.

Her way of life was mean and miserly, but she did not know it. She thought she lived <u>frugally</u> in her middle years so that she could live in comfort and ease when she most needed peace of mind.

The years, after forty, began to race. Suddenly Lottie was sixty and retired from her job by her boss's son, who had no <u>sentimental</u> feeling about keeping her on until she was ready to quit.

She made several attempts to find other

---

1. **beau:** boyfriend.
2. **go to rack and ruin:** become rundown; deteriorate.

WORDS TO KNOW	**whim** (hwĭm) *n.* a fanciful notion or impulse
	frugally (frōō′gə-lē) *adv.* in a thrifty way; economically
	sentimental (sĕn′tə-mĕn′tl) *adj.* showing or characterized by tender emotions

318

Cross Curricular Link History

DOROTHY WEST AND THE HARLEM RENAISSANCE
The black population of Harlem, a formerly upper-middle-class white section of New York City, grew from 14,000 in 1914 to 175,000 by 1925. Harlem had become a central meeting place for African Americans, West Indians, and Africans. From the stimulus of their cultural exchange grew the Harlem Renaissance. The Harlem Renaissance, which continued into the early 1930s, was a time of artistic, cultural, and social awakening among African Americans. This period was to have far-reaching implications on future artists and thinkers.

The exciting atmosphere of Harlem drew Dorothy West from Boston in 1926. She soon became friends with some of the notable figures from this period, including the writers Zora Neale Hurston and Langston Hughes, and her own writing flourished. She also turned her talents to acting. She had a role in the original stage production of *Porgy* and went with Langston Hughes to the Soviet Union in 1932 to make a film. She encouraged the literary efforts of African-American writers through the journals she edited and published in the '30s.

employment, but her dowdy³ appearance made her look old and inefficient. For the first time in her life Lottie would gladly have worked for nothing, to have some place to go, something to do with her day.

Harry died abroad, in a third-rate hotel, with Bess weeping as hard as if he had left her a fortune. He had left her nothing but his horn. There wasn't even money for her passage home.

Lottie, trapped by the blood tie, knew she would not only have to send for her sister but take her in when she returned. It didn't seem fair that Bess should reap the harvest of Lottie's lifetime of <u>self-denial</u>.

Carmen and Hilda (1941), Alice Neel. Watercolor on paper, 29″ x 22″. Schomburg Center for Research in Black Culture, Art & Artifacts Division, The New York Public Library, Astor, Lenox and Tilden Foundations. Copyright © The Estate of Alice Neel. Courtesy Robert Miller Gallery,

t took Lottie a week to get a bedroom ready, a week of hard work and hard cash. There was everything to do, everything to replace or paint. When she was through, the room looked so fresh and new that Lottie felt she deserved it more than Bess.

She would let Bess have her room, but the mattress was so lumpy, the carpet so worn, the curtains so threadbare that Lottie's conscience pricked her. She supposed she would have to redo that room, too, and went about doing it

with an eagerness that she mistook for haste. When she was through upstairs, she was shocked to see how dismal⁴ downstairs looked by comparison. She tried to ignore it, but with nowhere to go to escape it, the contrast grew more intolerable.

She worked her way from kitchen to parlor, persuading herself she was only putting the rooms to right to give herself something to do. At night she slept like a child after a long and happy day of playing house. She was having more fun than she had ever had in her life. She was living each hour for itself.

There was only a day now before Bess would arrive. Passing her gleaming mirrors, at first with vague awareness, then with painful clarity, Lottie saw herself as others saw her and could not stand the sight. She went on a spending spree from specialty shops to beauty salon, emerging transformed into a woman who believed in miracles.

She was in the kitchen basting a turkey when Bess rang the bell. Her heart raced, and she wondered if the heat from the oven was responsible. She went to the door, and Bess stood before her. Stiffly she suffered Bess's

_____

3. **dowdy:** dull and unfashionable.
4. **dismal:** dreary; gloomy.

WORDS TO KNOW   **self-denial** (sĕlf′dĭ-nī′əl) *n.* a giving up of one's own desires or interests

319

Less Proficient Readers
Ask students to summarize what has happened in Lottie's life.
Possible Response: Lottie has worked hard and has saved her money. She is forced to retire at sixty. She begins to enjoy spending her money when she redecorates the house in preparation for her sister's arrival.
What kind of life has Bess led?
Possible Response: Bess has led an exciting life. She and her husband have been poor but have traveled all over the world.

Set a Purpose Have students read to find out what Lottie realizes about the way she has lived her life.

Students Acquiring English
1 Acquaint students with the saying "A bird in the hand is worth two in the bush." Help students to see how the author has reworded the expression to convey the same idea. Both statements suggest that the actual possession of something is more valuable than the anticipated possession of something else.
2 Tell students that *mean* in this sentence is defined as ungenerous.
3 Explain to students that "reap the harvest" is used metaphorically. Lottie feels that Bess is the one being rewarded by Lottie's life of hard work.
4 Help students to appreciate the change in Lottie. A "spending spree" means that she was extravagant and did not count the cost.

Viewing and Representing TEKS 22A

Carmen and Hilda
by Alice Neel

ART APPRECIATION
Instruction In this watercolor, two girls are sitting close together on a chair. Ask students what might be inferred from their closeness.
Possible Response: They are sisters or good friends. Ask students to describe the expression on each girl's face.
Possible Response: The girl on the left looks serious while the girl on the right is not as rigid in posture and looks livelier.

Application Ask students whether they feel this painting represents Lottie and Bess. Why or why not?
Possible Response: Lottie and Bess never seemed to be good friends. However, Lottie resembles the girl on the left, who appears worried and solemn. The girl on the right might be Bess, who took life more lightly and may have been the younger of the two sisters.

embrace, her heart racing harder, her eyes suddenly smarting from the onrush of cold air.

"Oh, Lottie, it's good to see you," Bess said, but saying nothing about Lottie's splendid appearance. Upstairs, Bess, putting down her shabby suitcase, said, "I'll sleep like a rock tonight," without a word of praise for her lovely room. At the lavish table, top-heavy with turkey, Bess said, "I'll take light and dark both," with no marveling at the size of the bird or that there was turkey for two elderly women, one of them too poor to buy her own bread.

With the glow of good food in her stomach, Bess began to spin stories. They were rich with places and people, most of them lowly, all of them magnificent. Her face reflected her telling, the joys and sorrows of her remembering, and above all, the love she lived by that <u>enhanced</u> the poorest place, the humblest person.

Then it was that Lottie knew why Bess had made no mention of her finery, or the shining room, or the twelve-pound turkey. She had not even seen them. Tomorrow she would see the room as it really looked and Lottie as she really looked and the warmed-over turkey in its second-day glory. Tonight she saw only what she had come seeking, a place in her sister's home and heart.

She said, "That's enough about me. How have the years used you?"

"It was me who didn't use them," said Lottie wistfully. "I saved for them. I forgot the best of them would go without my ever spending a day or a dollar enjoying them. That's my life story in those few words, a life never lived. Now it's too near the end to try."

Bess said, "To know how much there is to know is the beginning of learning to live. Don't count the years that are left us. At our time of life it's the days that count. You've too much catching up to do to waste a minute of a waking hour feeling sorry for yourself."

Lottie grinned, a real wide-open grin, "Well, to tell the truth I felt sorry for you. Maybe, if I had any sense, I'd feel sorry for myself, after all. I know I'm too old to kick up my heels, but I'm going to let you show me how. If I land on my head, I guess it won't matter. I feel giddy[5] already, and I like it." ❖

---

5. **giddy:** lightheaded; frivolous.

"I knew I wanted to be a writer."

Dorothy West
1907–1998

Early Years Dorothy West was known to her fellow writers of the Harlem Renaissance—a literary movement of African-American artists during the 1920s—as the "kid," a name that fit because she started writing at age 7 and published her first article at 14. In the collections of stories and essays she called *The Richer, the Poorer,* West writes about the middle-class African-American family in which she grew up. "I knew I wanted to be a writer," West said. "Living with [my family] was like living inside a story." Later, friends such as Langston Hughes and Zora Neale Hurston became another family for her.

Unique Personal View West encouraged African-American writers. However, she also believed that "color is not important," that people should be understood as individuals influenced as much by class and values as by race. In this she disagreed with many activists of the 1960s. Today, West's work is well received. Her 1995 novel *The Wedding* became a bestseller and successful TV miniseries.

WORDS TO KNOW

enhance (ĕn-hăns') *v.* to increase the attractiveness of

320

Thinking *through the* LITERATURE

Connect to the Literature

1. What Do You Think? Did you think the ancient fable or the modern fable was more effective in getting across its moral? Explain.

Comprehension Check
- What was Lottie's main concern through most of her life?
- How did Bess spend her life?
- How did Lottie feel when she learned Bess was coming to stay with her?

Think Critically

2. ACTIVE READING SETTING PURPOSES Review the notes you made in your 📖 READER'S NOTEBOOK. How do they help you compare and contrast the two works?

3. What lessons do Lottie and Bess learn? How do they differ from those learned by Ant and Grasshopper?

4. Which sister has lived the more fulfilling life? Why? What do you think Lottie would do differently if she could live her life over again?

5. Connect to Life Think of a family member. In what ways are you similar to that person? How are you different? How can family members use their differences to help one another grow?

Literary Analysis

MODERN FABLE Unlike traditional fables, **modern fables** often contain complex characters. Instead of being character **types,** who represent single ideas Lottie and Bess represent several ideas. Also, Lottie changes to become more like Bess.

Modern fables do not have a stated **moral;** instead, they have a **theme,** or central message.

REVIEW THEME In a work of literature, the theme is the message about life or human nature that the writer presents to the reader. Sometimes the title of the work can give you an important clue to the theme. What does the title, "The Richer, the Poorer," suggest about the theme?

⬭ **POINTS OF COMPARISON** ⬭

Paired Learning Activity Now that you've read both traditional and modern versions of this fable, talk with a partner about the similarities and differences you found. Respond to the Points of Comparison questions from page 311. Use your discussion to help you complete your diagram.

	Ant and Grasshopper	The Richer, the Poorer
When was the fable written?	in ancient Greece	1920s
Who are the characters? What do they represent?	grasshopper = play ant = work	Bess = joy of living each day fully Lottie = at first the need to prepare for bad times; then, the wisdom of Bess's view
What happens in the fable?		
What is the moral?		

THE RICHER, THE POORER **321**

POINTS OF COMPARISON

What happens in the fable? Lottie works hard all her life and then is forced to retire. She begins to realize what she has missed by concentrating only on work and saving money. Bess lives a carefree existence and enjoys her life fully. After her husband dies, she returns to live with Lottie to help her get the most out of the time she has left. **What is the moral?** The moral is that money doesn't lead to happiness. It is important to provide for the future, but not if it costs the present.

GUIDING STUDENT RESPONSE

Connect to the Literature

1. Some students may say that the traditional fable was more direct in conveying the moral. Other students might say that the modern fable developed the characters more fully, which helped to bring out a theme more effectively.

Comprehension Check
- saving money
- She travels all over the world with her husband and has little money.
- Lottie feels bitter that Bess will get the advantage of Lottie's hard work.

Use Selection Quiz **Unit Two Resource Book,** p. 69.

Think Critically

2. Possible Responses: Responses will vary. Most students will agree that the details illustrate the complexity of a modern fable as compared to the simplicity of a traditional fable.

Use **Reading and Critical Thinking Transparencies,** p. 13, for additional support.

3. Possible Responses: Lottie learns that being totally concerned with the future can waste the present. She also learns that money and security aren't everything. Bess has learned that there is much more to life than wealth. Unlike Ant, Lottie realizes that security isn't enough to add up to a full life. Unlike Grasshopper, Bess has no regrets.

4. Possible Responses: Bess has lived a more fulfilling life because hers is full of memories and love. Lottie would probably save less and live more the next time around.

5. Connect to Life Possible Responses: Responses will vary. Students should see that learning from others can help them to develop more fully.

Literary Analysis

Modern Fable Possible Responses: The title suggests that having money is no guarantee of a rich life. Sometimes, the emphasis on gaining material wealth leads people to lose sight of what is truly important in life. Their lives are poor in comparison to the lives of those who have loved and who enjoy the beauty of the world.

 Use **Literary Analysis Transparencies,** p. 30, for additional support.

Writing Options

1. **Dialogue** To get students started on this assignment, have them brainstorm the ways in which Ant might change. To make this assignment easier, have students work in pairs, with each student taking a different role.

2. **Letter to a Friend** Encourage students to summarize each character's view of the world before choosing one. They should support their comparison with examples and reasons.

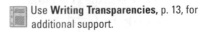 Use **Writing Transparencies,** p. 13, for additional support.

3. **Speech** Have students outline and organize the ideas they wish to include in their speech before writing it. Encourage students to practice their speeches in pairs.

Use **Writing Transparencies,** pp. 11, 54, for additional support.

Activities & Explorations

1. **Dramatic Version** To get students started, have them assign roles and responsibilities to each member of the group. To extend the assignment, videotape each production and discuss what each adds to the understanding of the fable.

Use **Communications Transparencies and Copymasters,** p. 12, for additional support.

2. **Planning Options** Students may wish to share their results before creating a graph or chart to give a broader interpretation.

Inquiry & Research

Insect Profiles Remind students to use indexes of magazines to help them locate information more easily. To illustrate the difference in personalities, students may wish to create a scenario which would provoke certain reactions from each insect.

To make this assignment more challenging, suggest that students create a slide show on the computer which explores the characteristics of each insect.

Use **Writing Transparencies,** p. 44, for additional support.

Writing Options

1. **Dialogue** Suppose Ant had learned the lesson Lottie gathers from Bess's life. Write the conversation Ant and Grasshopper might have had. Show ways in which they might act differently.

2. **Letter to a Friend** Imagine you are one of the characters from either "Ant and Grasshopper" or "The Richer, the Poorer." Think about your view of the world and of the other characters in your story. Then write a letter to a friend explaining your approach to work and contrasting it with the approach others take.

3. **Speech** Decide which fable's moral you most agree with. Write a speech you could give to younger students about the relative value of work and play. Use examples from the fables to support your position.

Activities & Explorations

1. **Dramatic Version** Stories with two characters can make interesting plays. Sets are limited, and costuming is simple. With a small group, create a stage version of one of the fables. Write a script and choose actors. Then design sets and costumes. Perform your play for classmates and other students. ~ **PERFORMING**

2. **Planning Options** People in real life prepare for bad times in many ways. Talk with adults, such as parents, teachers, or business owners. Find out what measures they take against a stormy day. Decide which are more common and which are less common. Create a chart or bar graph with your findings. ~ **ART/MATHEMATICS**

Inquiry & Research

Insect Profiles Using nature books and magazines, other resources, and direct observation, compare and contrast the way ants and grasshoppers behave. Do ants seem more focused on work? Do grasshoppers look like they don't work as hard? From what you learn, create a profile card for a typical ant and a typical grasshopper. Give your profiles specific personalities that fit the observations you made.

COMPARING LITERATURE

Assessment Practice

PART 1 ## Reading the Prompt

When you are asked to create a written response to a prompt like the one below, first read the entire prompt carefully. Then read it again, looking for key words that suggest the purpose of the essay.

> **Write a Comparison-and-Contrast Essay**
>
> Write a five- or six-paragraph essay <u>comparing and contrasting</u> the traditional **❶** fable "Ant and Grasshopper" and the modern fable "The Richer, the Poorer." <u>Show similarities and differences</u> between the **❷** characters and morals of the two fables. Support your ideas using <u>quotations and examples</u> from the fables. **❸**

STRATEGIES IN ACTION

❶ I have to **compare and contrast** a traditional and a modern fable.

❷ I have to show **similarities and differences** between the characters and the morals of the two versions.

❸ I need to use **quotations and examples** from the fables.

Reading the Prompt
Model the process of reading a prompt:
- Read through the prompt in its entirety.
- List key words of the assignment on the board. ("comparing and contrasting"; "Show similarities and differences"; "quotations and examples")
- Define each key word using the Strategies in Action to show how students can restate the prompts in their own words.

PART 2 ## Planning a Comparison-and-Contrast Essay

- Review the Points of Comparison diagram you began and completed.
- Create an outline with headings for "Introduction," "Body," and "Conclusion."

- Using your diagram, find examples of similarities and differences to use in the Body of your essay.

For more help in planning a comparison-and-contrast essay, see **Writing Workshop**, p. 636.

Introduction
Body
  I. The ancient and modern fables
     were written in different times.
  II.
  III.
Conclusion

Planning a Comparison-and-Contrast Essay

- Students can use the diagram that they have completed on the two fables.
- Suggest that students add a row to the diagram describing their reactions to each fable.
- Students might wish to fill in their outlines by listing similarities and then differences, or by listing points about each characteristic, or by recording details about one fable and then the other.

PART 3 ## Drafting Your Essay

Introduction Clearly state your essay's main purpose—to explain the similarities and differences you found when comparing a traditional and a modern fable. Briefly define the characteristics of a fable.

Body Decide the best way to organize your comparison-and-contrast essay. One way is to compare and contrast each important aspect of the ancient and modern fables one at a time. Use your Points of Comparison diagram for details and examples.

Conclusion End your essay with a strong statement about the most important difference between the traditional and modern fables. If you're having trouble identifying this difference, look again at your Points of Comparison chart.

Revising Make sure you always clearly indicate which fable you are discussing. Also, add signal words like *also* and *in contrast* to show the relationship you see between the fables.

Drafting Your Essay
Introduction Students should indicate in their introduction which characteristics are similar and which are different.
Body Remind students that another way to organize the information is to examine first the similarities of both fables and then the differences. A third way is to discuss all characteristics of one fable and then the other.
Conclusion Students may conclude that the most important difference between a traditional and modern fable is the development of character and plot in a modern fable, which lends itself to more interpretations of the moral.
Revising Have students check each paragraph of the body of their essay for strong topic sentences. A strong topic sentence will help them to maintain their organization and will make the order of comparison clear.

 Use **Unit Two Resource Book**, p. 70.

 Mini Lesson ## Grammar   **TEKS 16B**

QUOTATIONS WITHIN QUOTATIONS
Instruction Tell students that when passages that contain dialogue are quoted, double quotation marks are placed around the entire quotation. Single quotation marks are placed around the internal dialogue.
In this passage, readers see the tension between the ant and the grasshopper: "And since she was rude, / The grasshopper said: / 'To work in the summer / You must be dumber / than almost anyone.'"

Application Write the preceding lines of poetry on the board without the single and double quotation marks. Then ask students to rewrite them with proper punctuation.

 Use **Grammar Transparencies and Copymasters**, p. 128, for additional support.

 Use McDougal Littell's *Language Network*, Chapter 11, for more instruction and practice in punctuating quotations.

Objectives

- write a Character Sketch
- use a written text as a model for writing
- revise a draft to include vivid verbs and adjectives
- use pronouns that agree with their referents

Introducing the Workshop

Character Sketch Discuss with students character sketches they have read in magazines or the feature sections of newspapers. Have them think about what makes a character sketch memorable (vivid language, interesting quotations, focus on unusual characteristics). Although character sketches are often of famous or important people, anyone can be the subject of a profile.

Basics in a Box

Using the Graphic The graphic shows the facets of a person's character that, when put together, form a complete picture. Point out that the graphic suggests elements that students can include when they draft their sketches.

Presenting the Rubric To better understand the assignment, students can refer to the Standards for Writing a Successful Character Sketch. You may also want to share with them the complete rubric, which describes several levels of proficiency.

 Use McDougal Littell's *Language Network,* Chapters 12–19, for more instruction on essential writing skills.

 Power Presentation

To engage students visually, use **Power Presentation** 2, Character Sketch.

 See the Skills Trace at the beginning of the unit for information on TEKS covered in this lesson.

Writing Workshop
Character Sketch

Creating a portrait in words . . .

From Reading to Writing Drawing isn't the only way to create a portrait. You can also create a portrait using words—in a **character sketch.** For example, in *A Christmas Carol,* the reader forms an image of Scrooge's personality based on what he looks like, what he says, what he does, and how others behave toward him. Character sketches appear in many genres, from poetry to fiction to news stories. They can help your audience feel like they truly know your character.

For Your Portfolio

WRITING PROMPT Write a character sketch about someone who interests you.

Purpose: To reveal the key elements of an individual's personality
Audience: Anyone interested in your sketch

Basics in a Box

Character Sketch at a Glance

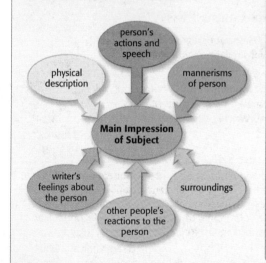

RUBRIC STANDARDS FOR WRITING

A successful character sketch should

- present a vivid picture of the personality and physical appearance of the person
- give a main impression of the person
- include dialogue, mannerisms, descriptions and other devices that show, rather than tell, what the character is like
- reveal the writer's response to the person
- place the person in natural surroundings to help readers understand him or her
- have a clear structure, a strong beginning, and a strong conclusion

LESSON RESOURCES

USING PRINT RESOURCES
Unit Two Resource Book
- Prewriting, p. 71
- Drafting, p. 72
- Peer Response, pp. 73–74
- Revising, Editing, and Proofreading, p. 75
- Student Models, pp. 76–78
- Rubric, p. 79

Writing Transparencies
- Writing Process Transparencies, TR 1–4
- Writing Style Transparency: Effective Language, TR 15

- Writing Template Transparency: Character Sketch, TR 30

Reading and Critical Thinking Transparencies
- Text Structure (Organization), TR 24

Grammar Transparencies and Copymasters
- Possessive Pronoun–Referent Agreement, CM 65 (for Mini Lesson, p. 328)
- Possessive Plurals, CM 64 (for Mini Lesson, p. 329)

INTEGRATED TECHNOLOGY
LaserLinks
Writing Springboards
See **Teacher's SourceBook,** p. 36, for bar codes.

Writing Coach CD-ROM

Visit our website:
www.mcdougallittell.com

Analyzing a Student Model

SPEAKING OPPORTUNITY

See the Communication Handbook, p. R100, for speaking and presenting tips.

Steve Hernandez
Parkland Middle School

Grandma Andrea

You could say I had three mothers, my real mom and my two grandmas, Rosa and Andrea. My grandmas took care of me because my mom needed a lot of help when I was little. Both of my grandmothers spoke Spanish, but only Grandma Andrea knew English, too. Because of this, we spent a good deal of time together. I thought there was something special about her because she was the only older lady I knew who could speak two languages. Ours was not a typical relationship between a boy and his grandma.

Grandma Andrea was not much taller than most of her grandchildren, but I looked up to her. She taught me things like discipline, manners, and respect. Whenever I was alone in the house with her, she'd speak to me in English and in Spanish. Once, I remember that she asked me in Spanish if I wanted a glass of milk and a snack. *"¿Te gustaría un vaso de leche y una merienda?"* I didn't answer her in Spanish, only in English. But she refused to give me my milk and snack until I answered her in Spanish. She didn't want me to be lazy about learning both English and Spanish.

Her brown eyes always looked gentle but I saw strength in them. She didn't give up when her husband died in 1979. Instead, she continued to work and raise ten kids, including my father, Raul Hernandez. No matter what her troubles were, she always made everyone feel at home. Every holiday was an excuse to celebrate and have family and friends together at her place. She was friendly with all her neighbors and was always ready to give a helping hand. When a neighbor was sick, she would bring food or medicine. She would also pray for them in church.

On Sundays, she dressed formally to go to church. She always wore her gray suit, and her curly dark hair framed her round face. I remember how she looked one Sunday morning. The front door had been left open to let the sun in. Activity filled the house. Everybody was talking, making breakfast, watching TV, or getting ready for church. Grandma Andrea stood in the doorway, and the sunlight acted like a spotlight. Her cheeks were flushed and she wore a proud smile as she looked out at her family. I'll

RUBRIC IN ACTION

❶ Introduction describes why the subject is important to the writer.
Other options:
- Begin with a strong visual image of the subject.
- Tell an anecdote or open with a quotation about or from the subject.

❷ Dialogue shows what the character is like.

❸ Background information helps to establish a main impression of the person as strong and compassionate.

❹ Concrete details create a physical portrait of the subject.

❺ The writer places the person in her natural surroundings to help readers understand her.

WRITING WORKSHOP **325**

Analyzing a Student Model

"Grandma Andrea"

The student model is a character sketch of the writer's grandmother, who greatly influenced his life with the lessons she taught him and the way she lived her life. He includes her words and his favorite image of her to bring her to life on the page and in his memory.

Have students think of someone in their lives that they associate with a favorite saying. Help students to see how a person's words reveal his or her character. Then point out the key words and phrases in the student model that correspond to the elements mentioned in the Rubric in Action.

1. Ask students what impression of Grandma Andrea they gain from the introduction.
   Possible Response: She was unique and holds a special place in the writer's heart.

2. Have students read this paragraph without the dialogue. Ask them how the omission of the question in Spanish affects the sketch.
   Possible Responses: Grandma Andrea's voice isn't heard as clearly; the point about her insistence on both languages is weakened.

3. The number of examples reinforces her generosity. Although her life was busy, she always found time to help others.

4. Ask students why the writer did not begin with the physical description of Grandma Andrea.
   Possible Response: He wanted to emphasize her character.

5. Ask students what other settings the writer could have placed Grandma Andrea in.
   Possible Response: kitchen, dining room

 Mini Lesson

Viewing and Representing

 TEKS 10E, 10L    **TAAS** Reading Obj. 2, 4

PICTURING TEXT STRUCTURE

Instruction While word choice and ideas play key roles in good writing, the structure of a text—the way in which ideas are organized and events unfold—also contributes to the effectiveness of the work.

Activity Have students analyze the organization of the student model by constructing a diagram or other graphic organizer. The following flow chart is an example.

 Use **Reading and Critical Thinking Transparencies**, p. 24, for additional support.

Unique role of Grandma Andrea is established.	Dialogue and anecdote show lessons she taught him.
Background develops: impression of strength.	Setting and physical details create a verbal snapshot of Grandma Andrea.
Advice reveals her personality and values.	The saying reinforces dominant impression of Grandma Andrea.

6. Ask students what Grandma Andrea's words of advice and warning reveal about her values and concerns.

Possible Response: She believes that being busy is a good way to stay out of trouble; she wants her grandson to be independent but wise in his decision making.

7. Ask students how the effect of the character sketch would be different if the essay ended after "photographs."

Possible Response: The emphasis would be on the writer's attempt to remember her physical appearance instead of the way her character shaped his attitude towards life.

Guiding Student Writing

Prewriting
Choosing a Subject

If after reading the Idea Bank students have difficulty choosing a subject for their character sketches, suggest that they try the following:

• List the five most influential people in your life so far and briefly describe how you have been influenced by each one. Choose one of the five to sketch.

• Imagine that your pen pal is coming to visit you, and you have been sending character sketches of your family and friends to prepare him or her for the visit. Decide on the subject for this week's sketch.

Use **Writing Transparencies,** p. 1, for additional support.

always remember this moment when she looked like a very dignified, elegant, and sophisticated lady.

Grandma Andrea was very strict about how I behaved in public. She encouraged me not to get in trouble in the neighborhood. "Don't hang around with nothing to do," she'd say. "I have plenty of things at home that will keep you out of trouble." She didn't stand for any nonsense. But she never tried to stop me from exploring and being a kid. If I wanted to go by myself to the store a few blocks away, she'd let me. She'd only say, "Watch for cars," or "Be on time for dinner." She made me feel safe. I respected her because she respected me.

Grandma Andrea was not only sweet, she was a good friend and teacher. She died in 1995 after a very full life. There is nothing I can do to bring her back but remember her. When my memories of her seem to be fading, I look at old photographs. If I shut my eyes and concentrate, I can hear her voice in Spanish. *"Trabaja mucho y vive bien."* "Work hard and live well." This is the way I will honor her.

❻ Dialogue and details present a vivid picture of the person's personality.

❼ The writer uses a quote to create a powerful conclusion that reinforces the meaning of the subject in the writer's life.

Writing Your Character Sketch

❶ Prewriting
Whom do you want to write about? Start by thinking about your favorite people—teachers, neighbors, coaches, or relatives you know and admire. **Jot down** as many details about these people as you can. See the **Idea Bank** in the margin for more suggestions. Once you've chosen your subject, follow the steps at the top of the next page.

▶ **1. Explore your feelings.** How do you feel about the person? What details or incidents can you describe that show why he or she is important to you?

▶ **2. Create mental images of the person.** Try picturing your subject in his or her usual surroundings. How does your subject act, speak, and look? Make a chart like this one to record details.

Personality Characteristics			
Physical	What subject says	What subject does	How others react

▶ **3. Place your character in a setting.** Describe the person in a time and place that will reveal his or her personality. If your subject is a historical or famous figure, do research using library resources or the Internet. To get information about someone you don't know well, you may choose to interview the person.

▶ **4. Decide on your main impression.** What impression do you want your readers to have about the person? Which details from your chart best create this impression?

❷ Drafting

As you write your first draft, try to visualize the person. Focus on the main impression you want to create. Get your ideas down on paper. You can go back and revise your work later.

Show, Don't Tell

Good character sketches include plenty of details that help readers visualize. Instead of telling readers everything about your subject, use examples and dialogue that show what your subject is like. For example, in *A Christmas Carol* Scrooge refuses to give Christmas tips to his servants or his employee. Readers can see for themselves that Scrooge is stingy.

Organizing Your Draft

There are many ways to begin your draft. One way is to grab your audience's attention with a curious detail or quote. Develop your subject's personality in the **body** of the essay. Your **ending** should leave readers with a clear picture of your subject and how you feel about him or her.

Ask Your Peer Reader

- How do you think I feel about my subject?
- How would you describe my subject's personality?
- What details help you picture my subject?
- What more would you like to know about my subject?

IDEA Bank

1. Your Working Portfolio
Look for ideas in the Writing Options that you completed earlier in this unit.

- **Letter of Recommendation,** p. 285
- **Definition,** p. 297

2. Celebrity Sketch
Look for character sketches in magazines. Notice how they create vivid portraits of subjects. Choose to write a sketch of a leader in your school, town, or city.

3. Word Play
Jot down descriptive words like *brave*, *funny*, *serious*, and *athletic*. Then think of a person you know who has one of those qualities.

Have a question?

See the **Writing Handbook**
Sensory Details, p. R30
Elaboration with Anecdotes, p. R29

Planning Your Personality Profile

1. Encourage students to brainstorm feelings, incidents, and other details. Then have them group ideas that convey a similar impression.

2. Suggest that students look through old photographs, review family videotapes, or keep a notebook handy over the next couple of days to collect concrete details about their subject.

3. Have students describe to a partner the setting that comes immediately to mind when they think of their subject.

4. Have students review all of their groups of details to see which impression predominates.

Drafting

Show, Don't Tell. Have volunteers share incidents and dialogue. Ask students to discuss the traits that are revealed through these examples.

Organizing Your Draft. Ask students what image or saying first comes to mind when they think of their subject. This might be a good way to begin their essay.

Use **Writing Transparencies**, p. 11, 22, for additional support.

Ask Your Peer Reader

Remind students to use the peer reviewer's feedback when revising their drafts.

Revising
VIVID VERBS AND ADJECTIVES

Review the changes in the sample with students. To help students practice choosing vivid verbs and adjectives, ask volunteers to share sentences from their drafts. Have the rest of the class suggest vivid verbs and adjectives that would help to create a livelier and more precise description.

 Use **Writing Transparencies**, p. 15, for additional support.

Editing and Proofreading
PRONOUN ANTECEDENT AGREEMENT

Remind students that a lack of agreement between pronouns and their antecedents creates confusion in the reader. Have the students explain the change in the sample. For more practice, see the Grammar Mini Lesson at the bottom of the page.

Reflecting

As they write their reflections, have students consider what they will be more aware of as they encounter other people.

Option
Managing the Paper Load

When reviewing the first draft, highlight areas of weakness or segments that need more development. Allow students time to react to the highlighted passages and write down how they think they can improve them. Then meet with students individually in a short conference to discuss their ideas.

Need revising help?

Review the **Rubric,** p. 324

Consider **peer reader** comments

Check **Revision Guidelines,** p. R23

SPELLING
From Writing

As you revise your work, look back at the words you misspelled and determine why you made the errors you did. For additional help, refer to the strategies and generalizations in the **Spelling Handbook** on page R86.

Perplexed by pronoun-antecedent agreement?

See the **Grammar Handbook,** p. R66

Publishing
IDEAS

- Exchange character sketches with a classmate. Draw a sketch of the person described. Hang your sketch and the essay in the classroom.

- Prepare a biography talk show. The host will interview you about the subject of your character sketch. Videotape the interviews so that they can be played back for the class.

More Online:
Publishing Options
www.mcdougallittell.com

---

❸ Revising

TARGET SKILL ▶ VIVID VERBS AND ADJECTIVES Carefully chosen verbs and adjectives can bring a character to life. For example, instead of saying *Scrooge walked through the streets,* choose more specific words, as in: *Scrooge shuffled through the crowded streets.* Specific words help to create vivid writing.

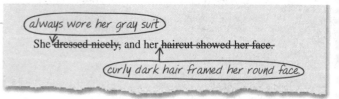

always wore her gray suit
She dressed nicely, and her haircut showed her face.
curly dark hair framed her round face

❹ Editing and Proofreading

TARGET SKILL ▶ PRONOUN-ANTECEDENT AGREEMENT An antecedent usually comes before the pronoun. The antecedent is the noun or pronoun to which the pronoun refers. Pronouns must agree with their antecedents in number, person, and gender. For example, in the sentence *Jane ate because she was hungry,* the pronoun *she* refers back to the antecedent *Jane.* Proofread your character sketch to make sure you catch errors in pronoun-antecedent agreement.

they
My grandmothers took care of me because she wanted to help my mother.

❺ Reflecting

FOR YOUR WORKING PORTFOLIO What did you learn while doing this assignment? How did writing this character sketch change the way you look at people? Attach your reflections to your finished profile. Save your character sketch in your **Working Portfolio.**

Teaching Options

 **Mini Lesson** **Grammar** ▪ **TEKS** 17C ▪ **TAAS** Writing Obj. 6

POSSESSIVE PRONOUN–REFERENT AGREEMENT

For use with Editing and Proofreading, p. 328.
Instruction Tell students that possessive pronouns must agree with their antecedents in number and gender and are not spelled with an apostrophe. Introduce the point that compound subjects joined by *and* will take a plural pronoun. Compound subjects joined by *or* or *nor* in which each part is singular take sin-

gular pronouns. If each part is plural, a plural pronoun is used.
Exercises Have students find the pronoun errors in the following sentences and suggest corrections. Some sentences are correct.
1. The little girl said the toy was her's. *(hers)*
2. Neither the boys nor the girls have turned in their profits from the sale. *(correct)*
3. Jack and his friends ate his lunches outside. *(their)*
4. The dog chewed on it's bone for hours. *(its)*

5. The grandparents spoiled they're grandchildren by giving them money and gifts. *(their)*

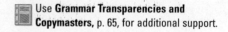 Use **Grammar Transparencies and Copymasters,** p. 65, for additional support.

 Use McDougal Littell's **Language Network,** Chapter 3, for more instruction and practice in pronoun-antecedent agreement.

Read this passage from the first draft of a character sketch. The underlined sections may include the following kinds of errors:

- **pronoun referent agreement**
- **incorrect possessive forms**
- **incorrect verb tense**
- **run-on sentences**

For each underlined section, choose the revision that most improves the writing.

"Waaaaa!" My baby sister's yell shatters the silence of the sleeping house. <u>She is not hurt or scared she is just awake</u> and ready to begin
(1)
her active day. Sophie is like a factory whistle: <u>he</u> begins the day
(2)
shrieking and ends it the same way. After she <u>leap</u> out of bed, she
(3)
demands hugs from everyone. Then she <u>has gone</u> down to the kitchen
(4)
for breakfast. Bath time comes after almost everyone has fled to go to
school or to work. My mother often says that <u>they</u> might as well take
(5)
her bath at the same time because of <u>Sophie's splashing.</u>
(6)

---

1. A. She is not hurt or scared: she is just awake

   B. She is not hurt or scared; she is just awake

   C. She is not hurt, or scared, she is just awake

   D. Correct as is

2. A. she

   B. they

   C. we

   D. Correct as is

3. A. leaped

   B. leaps

   C. leaping

   D. Correct as is

4 A. going

   B. goes

   C. went

   D. Correct as is

5. A. we

   B. she

   C. he

   D. Correct as is

6. A. Sophies' splashing

   B. Sophies splashing

   C. Sophies's splashing

   D. Correct as is

Assessment Practice

Demonstrate how students can eliminate incorrect choices for the first question.

A. The colon is used incorrectly to join two independent clauses.

B. This choice correctly uses a semicolon as punctuation between two independent clauses.

C. This choice incorrectly omits the conjunction that must accompany a comma in a compound sentence.

D. The original sentence is a run-on sentence.

Answers:
1. B; 2. A; 3. B; 4. B; 5. B; 6. D

Need extra help?

See the **Grammar Handbook**

Plural and Possessive Nouns, p. R63

Pronoun-Antecedent Agreement, p. R66

Run-on Sentences, p. R59

Possessives, p. R54

 Grammar **TEKS** 17G **TAAS** Writing Obj. 3, 6, 7

POSSESSIVE PLURALS

For use with Editing and Proofreading, p. 328.

Instruction Remind students that possessive pronouns do not have apostrophes. However, apostrophes must be used to indicate the possessive form of a noun. Add an apostrophe and *s* to form the possessive of a singular noun. To form the possessive of a plural noun that ends in *s,* add an apostrophe after the *s.* For a plural noun that does not end in *s,* add an apostrophe and *s.*

Exercises Have students find the errors in the possessive nouns and pronouns in the following sentences and correct them.

1. Sophie said that the toy was her's. *(hers)*
2. The childrens' bicycles were scattered over the neighbors' driveway. *(children's)*
3. My teachers addresses are listed in the directory. *(teachers')*
4. Their pool is bigger than our's is. *(ours)*
5. His four dog's leashes were on the table. *(dogs')*

6. Someone left yesterdays newspaper on the bus. *(yesterday's)*
7. Henriettas art book was used as the class model. *(Henrietta's)*

 Use **Grammar Transparencies and Copymasters,** p. 64, for additional support.

 Use McDougal Littell's *Language Network,* Chapter 2, for more instruction and practice in using possessive forms.

Objectives

- reflect on unit themes
- review literary analysis skills used in the unit
- paraphrase and summarize text to recall, inform, or organize ideas
- describe mental images that text descriptions evoke
- assess and build portfolios

Reflecting on the Theme

OPTION 1

A successful response will

- isolate and describe messages in the unit about reaching out
- select two or more of the messages that are particularly appropriate for young people
- discuss reasoning for the choices in a brief written form

OPTION 2

A successful response will

- analyze character growth as a result of choices in the selections
- include interaction with classmates in discussion about character growth as a result of choice
- offer observations, make connections, react, speculate, interpret and raise questions in response to texts
- demonstrate effective communications skills that reflect such demands as providing information

OPTION 3

A successful response will

- creatively approach the problem of building self-confidence in the role-playing situation
- clarify and support spoken ideas with evidence, elaborations, and examples
- make reference to personal judgments about the characters in the selection and their qualities

Self Assessment

Clarify the meaning of the quotation with students in a class discussion before they begin writing. Ask students to suggest representative selections that illustrate the quotation.

Relationships

How have your ideas about reaching out to others developed as you read the selections in this unit? Are you more willing now to face obstacles? Choose one or more of the options in each of the following sections to help you explore what you've learned.

Reflecting on the Theme

OPTION 1

Making Connections Jot down the messages about reaching out that you got from the selections you read in this unit. Then choose two or more messages that you think young people should take to heart. Write a paragraph or two, explaining your choices.

OPTION 2

Discussing Which of the characters in Unit Two do you think develops the most as a result of his or her choices? Which characters develop little or not at all? Discuss these questions with a small group of classmates. Support your views with examples from the selections and insights from your own experience.

OPTION 3

Role-Playing Imagine that a friend needs more self-confidence to meet a new challenge. With a partner, role-play a conversation in which you attempt to inspire your friend with the will to overcome the obstacle. To support your points, use examples from several of this unit's selections. Which characters have you found the most inspiring? What qualities help them meet their challenges?

Self ASSESSMENT

📖 READER'S NOTEBOOK

Think about the quotation at the beginning of this unit: page 188. Write a paragraph explaining how reading the selections in the unit has given you a better understanding of the quotation's meaning.

REVIEWING YOUR PERSONAL WORDList

Vocabulary Review the new words you learned in this unit. If necessary, use a dictionary to check the meaning of each word.

Spelling Review your list of spelling words. If you're not sure of the correct spelling, use a dictionary or refer to the *Spelling Handbook* on page R86.

Reviewing Literary Concepts

OPTION 1

Rhyme and Rhythm Rhyme and rhythm are elements of many poems. Rhyme is a similarity of ending sounds in words. Rhythm is the pattern of stressed and unstressed syllables in a poem's lines. Some poems have regular rhythms. Others have irregular rhythms that are more like speech. Look back at the poems in this unit. In which is rhyme used? Which have regular rhythms and which do not? Record your findings in a chart.

Selection	Rhyme?	Regular Rhythm	Rhythm of Spoken Language?

OPTION 2

Visualizing Scenes Stage directions are instructions in a play's script about the settings of scenes and the actions of characters. When reading a play, you can use the stage directions to help you visualize the appearance of the stage and the characters. With a small group of classmates, choose a scene from "The Noble Experiment" and discuss how you would turn it into a play. Write the stage directions for one scene of your proposed play.

Building Your Portfolio

- **Writing Options** Several of the Writing Options in this unit asked you to put yourself in the position of certain characters. Choose the one that you feel best conveys the way a particular character would speak or act. Then write a cover note explaining your choice. Place it in your **Presentation Portfolio.**

- **Writing Workshops** In this unit you wrote an interpretation of a poem and a character sketch. Reread the two pieces and decide which is a stronger piece of writing. Explain your choice and place it in your **Presentation Portfolio.**

- **Additional Activities** Think back to any of the assignments you completed for **Activities & Explorations** and **Inquiry & Research.** Keep a record in your portfolio of any assignments that you especially enjoyed, found helpful, or would like to do further work on in the future.

Self ASSESSMENT

READER'S NOTEBOOK

On a sheet of paper, copy the following literary terms introduced in this unit. Next to each term, jot down a brief definition. If you don't understand a particular concept very well, refer to the **Glossary of Literary Terms** on page R6.

rhyme scheme	dialogue
end rhyme	acts and scenes
imagery	speaker
figurative language	informative nonfiction
simile	fable
metaphor	moral
static and dynamic characters	modern fable
stanza	

Self ASSESSMENT

Review all the writing samples in your **Presentation Portfolio.** Which reflect your strengths as a writer? What skills would you like to improve?

Setting GOALS

Look back through your portfolio, worksheets, and **READER'S NOTEBOOK.** What did you learn from this unit that might help you in your own life? Make a list of ideas that you would like to learn more about.

OPTION 1

Use the Unit Two Resource Book, page 80, to provide students a ready-made chart for recording and analyzing character development.

OPTION 2

A successful response will

- include interaction with classmates about what would be required to convert the story to a play
- extract from the story the information about setting that is necessary to develop stage directions
- demonstrate effective use of writing skills to develop stage directions for one scene

Building Your Portfolio

Students should evaluate the items in their Working Portfolios and choose pieces that represent their highest-quality work for their Presentation Portfolios.

Before students make their choices, ask them to consider what makes a piece of writing successful. Point out that sometimes very well-written pieces do not succeed as well as more poorly written pieces, because they do not say anything interesting or do not serve the purpose for which they were supposedly intended. Ask students to consider what they have written both in terms of the writing quality and intended purpose.

Self Assessment and Setting Goals

Point out to students that one of the difficulties with self assessment is that it is easy to forget the lessons of the past. Explain that making notes about goals is a good way to keep making progress in many areas of life, including writing.

For more information on using portfolios, use *Teacher's Guide to Assessment and Portfolio Use,* beginning on page 53.

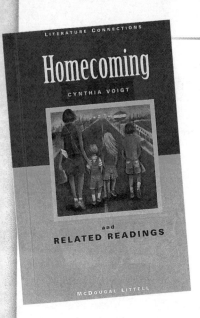

LITERATURE CONNECTIONS
Homecoming

By Cynthia Voigt

In this moving novel by Cynthia Voigt, 13-year-old Dicey is left to care for her two brothers and sister when the Tillerman children are abandoned by their mother in a parking lot. Determined to keep her siblings together, Dicey leads them on a hike across Connecticut to Aunt Cilla's, where the fight for her family begins.

These thematically related readings are provided along with *Homecoming*:

Shells
By Cynthia Rylant

Little Sister
By Nikki Grimes

A Christmas Tree for Lydia
By Elizabeth Enright

The Journey
By Hu Feng

from **The Resilient Child**
By Kevin Bushweller

Train Time
By D'Arcy McNickle

A Celebration of Grandfathers
By Rudolfo A. Anaya

And Even *More* . . .

Bridge to Terabithia

By Katherine Paterson

In this Newbery Award-winning novel, Leslie is an outcast among her peers. She has outrun all the boys, inspired jealousy in most of the girls, and, worst of all, has become the teacher's pet. By escaping to Terabithia, an imaginary land she and her best friend, Jess, create, they grow close despite differences.

Books
Neighborhood Odes
By Gary Soto
From his library to his cat, the poet pays tribute to his community and those in it.

Going Over to Your Place
Edited by Paul Janeczko
From family tributes to poems of first love, a contemporary collection

Midnight Is a Place
By Joan Aiken
England in the Industrial Age is a hard place for a boy.

So Far from the Bamboo Grove

BY YOKO KAWASHIMA WATKINS

Yoko Kawashima, though Japanese, spent most of her childhood in Nanam, Korea, where she attended Japanese schools. Yoko was only seven when Japan entered World War II in 1941. Four years later, Kawashima's family had to flee from its home and begin a trek to Seoul, Korea. In *So Far from the Bamboo Grove,* Kawashima retells her family's struggle to survive.

These thematically related readings are provided along with *So Far from the Bamboo Grove*:

Refugee Mother and Child
BY CHINUA ACHEBE

Old Man at the Bridge
BY ERNEST HEMINGWAY

from **The Endless Steppe:**
Growing Up in Siberia
BY ESTHER HAUTZIG

The First Day of the War
BY MAIA WOJCIECHOWSKA

Generations
BY AMY LOWELL

The Key
BY VŌ PHIÊN

Please Don't Leave
BY MR. LUE LEE

Taking a Stand Against Racism and Racial Discrimination
BY PATRICIA AND FREDRICK MCKISSACK
Discussion of what can be done when one encounters prejudice

Squids Will Be Squids: Fresh Morals, Beastly Fables
BY JON SCIESZKA
A fun look at the modern fable

Other Media

Dickens: A Christmas Carol
Dickens's novel narrated by Patrick Hogan
Cassette Bookshelf Listening Library
(AUDIOCASSETTE)

Casey at the Bat
The struggle for the American dream plays out on the ballfield.
Playhouse Video
(VIDEOCASSETTE)

The Jackie Robinson Story
The first African American in Major League baseball stars as himself.
MGM/UA
(VIDEOCASSETTE)

SimAnt
Control an ant colony to learn the biology and behavior of these social insects.
Maxis
(CD-ROM)

This Reading & Writing for Assessment feature provides more practice in taking standardized tests. As students work through this lesson, they will have an opportunity to practice strategies for reading comprehension questions, multiple choice questions, and essay and short-answer questions. Boxed strategies located alongside the text will help guide students through the activities. These strategies model processes for students to follow when taking standardized tests.

This feature is based on and will help to prepare students for state assessments and the Scholastic Assessment Tests (SAT).

OBJECTIVES

- understand and apply strategies for reading a test selection
- recognize literary techniques in a test selection
- recognize and answer questions about tone in a test selection
- understand and apply strategies for answering multiple-choice questions about a text selection
- respond to a prompt by pulling information from the text and presenting it in a written answer
- understand and apply strategies for revising and proofreading a test response

Reading&Writing for Assessment

Throughout middle school, you will be tested on your ability to read and understand many different kinds of reading selections. The following pages will give you helpful test-taking strategies. Practice applying these strategies by working through the following models.

PART 1 How to Read the Test Selection

In many tests, you will read a passage and then answer multiple-choice questions about it. Applying the basic test-taking strategies that follow can help you focus on the right information.

> **STRATEGIES FOR READING A TEST SELECTION**
>
> ▸ **Before you begin reading, skim the questions that follow the passage.** These can help focus your reading.
>
> ▸ **Use active reading strategies such as analyzing, predicting, and questioning.** Make notes in the margin only if the test directions allow you to mark on the test itself.
>
> ▸ **Think about the title, the message, and the theme.** What does the title suggest about the overall selection? What larger lesson can you draw from the passage?
>
> ▸ **Look for main ideas.** These are often stated at the beginning or end of paragraphs. Sometimes they are implied, not stated. After reading each paragraph, ask, "What was this passage about?"
>
> ▸ **Examine the sequence of ideas.** Are the ideas developed in chronological order, order of importance, or organized in some other way?
>
> ▸ **Evaluate the literary elements and techniques used by the writer.** How does the writer use tone (writer's attitude toward the subject), point of view, figurative language, or other elements to create a certain effect or get the message across?
>
> ▸ **Unlock word meanings.** Use context clues and word parts to help you unlock the meaning of unfamiliar words.

❶ The Power of a Voice

by Danna Ruby

1   "You've got too much going against you. You're black, you're a woman, and you're large." In 1964 a political analyst spoke these words to a young African-American lawyer from Texas after she had lost her first political race. ❷ However, Barbara Charline Jordan refused to give up. She had a mission—to stamp out discrimination and make a difference in people's lives. Eventually she would fulfill this mission and more.

2   Barbara Jordan was born in 1936 in Houston, Texas, the youngest of three daughters. Her family was not well-off, and she grew up in a world of ❸ segregation. The separation of blacks and whites in all areas of life, including in the schools, was enforced by law.

3   Despite ongoing discrimination, Jordan excelled in school and honed her speaking skills on her high school speech team. In the 1954 case of *Brown v. Board of Education of Topeka,* the Supreme Court ruled that segregation kept African-Americans from receiving an education equal to that received by whites. Two years later Jordan graduated with honors from Texas Southern University, where she had been an award-winning member of the previously all-male debate team. In 1959, she received a law degree from Boston University. Although she passed the bar examination in Massachusetts and
4   Texas, politics pulled her away from practicing law.

   ❹ The door to a political career opened by accident. In 1960 she was inspired by the civil-rights platform of Democrat John F. Kennedy, a United States senator running for president. Jordan stuffed envelopes at the headquarters of the Harris County, Texas, Democratic Committee until a twist of fate pushed her into the spotlight. One evening a speaker called in sick. Jordan was asked to fill in and speak to the congregation of a local African-American church. Her deep, booming voice and powerful message impressed her listeners. Before long she began lecturing, asking African Americans to register and vote as Democrats. Soon, the voter turnout was the largest Harris County had ever seen. This, along with Kennedy's presidential victory, propelled Jordan into politics.

❶ Think about the title.

ONE STUDENT'S THOUGHTS

"I wonder what the writer means by *power.*"

❷ Skim the questions that follow the passage.

ONE STUDENT'S THOUGHTS

"One question asks how Jordan's upbringing influenced her success. She grew up with segregation, so how could this help her in politics?"

❸ Use context clues to understand vocabulary.

ONE STUDENT'S THOUGHTS

"It seems that *segregation* means blacks and whites were forced to be separated."

❹ Look for main ideas.

ONE STUDENT'S THOUGHTS

"It's amazing that her speaking skills led her into politics."

YOUR TURN
Find one or two other key ideas in this selection.

Teaching the Lesson

Begin by previewing the text. Then read through the questions and prompts at the end of the test. As you read each question, ask students what they will need to look for as they read.

1   Help students to consider the extended meanings of the words *power* and *voice.* For example, *power* refers not only to physical strength but also to strength of character, influence, or ability. The word *voice* refers not only to actual speech but also to an expressed opinion or point of view.

2   Students should infer that Jordan's early experiences as an African American living in a world of inequality and segregation taught her to work extra hard and to understand the effects of injustice. Her own pain and frustration most likely fueled her drive to be heard and to protect the rights of others.

3   Remind students that sometimes they will encounter words that are unfamiliar. They should evaluate the word's importance in the selection. If the word is not important to the overall meaning of the selection, then they might choose to move on. However, if the word relates to a key event or idea, they should
   • study the meaning of the surrounding sentence and paragraph.
   • take a guess at the meaning of the unknown word and see if that meaning makes sense in the sentence
   The student quoted does not know exactly what segregation means but makes a guess that it must relate to the separating of blacks and whites in a society.

4   To help students understand what a main idea is, read these examples and ask the students if they are main ideas or not:
   Jordan admired John F. Kennedy, who was a senator running for President in 1960 (no);
   Jordan found she had an amazing ability to reach people through her lectures (yes); Jordan started out stuffing envelopes at the Harris County, Texas, Democratic Committee (no).

YOUR TURN Jordan never gave up, even in the face of defeat and discouraging remarks. Even the biggest obstacles do not have to stop people from reaching their goals. Jordan felt firsthand the effects of discrimination and injustice, so she was determined to be a positive influence in government and improve the lives of others.

5 Ask students to formulate other questions based on this particular paragraph. Did most people protest or welcome this change in society? How did Jordan view the passage of the Civil Rights Act? Did her family's wish that she get married and have a family affect Jordan? Why, at the time, was it difficult for a woman to be married and working in politics? Did Jordan ever have any regrets about the path she chose to take? Tell students that questioning can help them to understand the topic, but they should be sure that their questions have relevance to information in the selection.

6 Encourage students to visualize the word *erupted* to get a strong sense of the situation being described. Point out the quoted student's visualization of the word.

YOUR TURN The writer wants to give readers a sense of the frightening, disruptive nature of the scandal. The situation was unexpected, disturbing, and quickly out of control. If the writer had wanted to give a more benign image of the problem, she could have used a neutral word such as *occurred*.

7 Point out that the student quoted does not actually address the issue of tone. Tell students that the writer's tone is her general feeling toward her subject. Point out the following phrases as indicating the writer's tone: " . . . she would fulfill this mission and more. . . . Jordan excelled . . . Her deep, booming voice and powerful message . . . Her speaking skills were praised all over the world. . . . She again impressed the nation. . . . Her life is an example of how neither poverty, race, nor gender should stop us from reaching our goals." These phrases imply the writer's admiration for Jordan's attitude, hard work, talent, and accomplishments.

Check Your Understanding
Have students use the following questions to test their understanding of the selection before they answer the questions in their texts.

- What is the basic topic of the selection?
- What is the writer's attitude toward the girl in the selection?
- In what type of publication might the selection have originally appeared? How can you tell?
- Did the selection answer all your questions about the subject? If not, what questions remain unanswered?

---

5   Jordan ran for the Texas House of Representatives in 1962 but was defeated. She lost again in 1964, the same year ❺ Congress passed the Civil Rights Act, banning segregation in public facilities and guaranteeing equal employment. Jordan relied on her family's support. They wished she would get married and have a family, but Jordan chose to devote her life to politics.

6   In 1966, she finally won a seat in the Texas House of Representatives. She became the first African-American state senator since 1883. Six years later, she won a congressional seat in the U.S. House of Representatives, becoming the first African-American woman from the Deep South to be elected to that body.

7   Soon after, the ❻ Watergate scandal erupted. The nation learned that President Richard Nixon was involved in the cover-up of the 1972 burglary of the headquarters of the Democratic National Committee. Jordan was asked to state her feelings on the issue. On July 25, 1974, she spoke during a televised hearing and asked that President Nixon be impeached for his crime. ❼ "My faith in the Constitution is whole, it is complete, it is total." Her speaking skills were praised all over the world, and she rose in the spotlight. Nixon resigned his office soon after, and Jordan was reelected to another term.

8   In 1976, Jordan was selected by the Democratic Party to deliver the keynote address for the party's national convention. She again impressed the nation with her inspirational words in support of Jimmy Carter, the Democratic presidential candidate. Carter was elected and Jordan served a third term in Congress before retiring from politics. She became a professor at the University of Texas at Austin.

9   In 1990, Barbara Jordan was inducted into the National Women's Hall of Fame. She was awarded the Spingarn Medal by the NAACP for outstanding achievement by an African American in 1992, and in 1994 the Presidential Medal of Freedom, the highest civilian award in the nation. She died of complications of leukemia in 1996. Her life is an example of how neither poverty, racial discrimination, nor gender bias should stop us from reaching our goals.

❺ **Read actively by asking questions.**
"The Civil Rights Act must have changed things for African Americans as well as whites. I wonder how people's lives were affected."

❻ **Note literary elements like use of figurative language.**
"The writer uses the word *erupted* to describe the Watergate scandal. Sounds like it was like a volcano, and that people were unprepared for it."
YOUR TURN
Determine the writer's purpose.

❼ **Look for examples of tone.**
"The writer chooses an interesting quote. It really shows what Barbara Jordan was like."
YOUR TURN
How else does the writer show Jordan's character?

Use the strategies and notes in the side column to help you answer the questions below and on the following pages.

Based on the selection you have just read, choose the best answer for each of the following questions.

1. Why does the writer begin by quoting a person who had tried to discourage Jordan?

   A. because research papers must include quotes

   B. to show how cut-throat political candidates can be

   C. to show the obstacles that Jordan faced

   D. to prove that Jordan really was a Democrat

2. In paragraph 9, what did Jordan mean when she said, "My faith in the Constitution is whole"?

   A. The Constitution should apply to everyone, including the president.

   B. She has lost faith in the Constitution.

   C. She should not be blamed for the president's crimes.

   D. Watergate shook her faith in the Constitution.

3. How did Jordan's upbringing influence her success?

   A. After growing up poor, she was determined to make money through politics.

   B. Because her family did not support her, she did not want her own family.

   C. She had felt the effects of discrimination and was determined to do something about it.

   D. She became suspicious of politicians and therefore never ran for president.

4. How does the title of the article relate to its theme?

   A. It doesn't relate to the theme.

   B. Jordan used her voice to make changes in the world.

   C. Using your voice is the only way to gain power.

   D. One voice is stronger than many voices.

5. What is the writer's tone toward Barbara Jordan?

   A. She believes that Jordan should have listened to her critics and gotten out of politics.

   B. She admires Jordan for her achievements.

   C. She judges Jordan poorly for not getting married.

   D. She pities Jordan for having had a tough life.

STRATEGIES FOR ANSWERING MULTIPLE-CHOICE QUESTIONS

▸ **Ask questions** that help you eliminate some of the choices.

▸ **Pay attention to choices** such as "all of the above" or "none of the above." To eliminate them, all you need to find is one answer that doesn't fit.

▸ **Skim your notes.** Details you noticed as you read may provide answers.

STRATEGIES IN ACTION

Skim your notes.

ONE STUDENT'S THOUGHTS
"The writer doesn't mention Jordan ever wanting to run for president. *So I can eliminate choice D.*"

YOUR TURN
What other choices can you eliminate?

Ask questions. What makes sense in the real world?
"The writer wouldn't use a title that doesn't relate to the theme. Also, using your voice is one way to gain power, but it is not the only way. *So, I can eliminate choices A and C.*"

YOUR TURN
Which other choice doesn't make sense?

Guiding Student Response

Multiple-Choice Questions
1. C
2. A
3. C

YOUR TURN Choice A is incorrect because the essay never implies that Jordan was motivated by a wish for money. There is also no evidence that she made a great deal of money in politics. Choice B can be eliminated because the essay clearly states that Jordan relied on her family's support. The essay does not imply that Jordan devalued family.

4. B

YOUR TURN The other choice that can be eliminated is A, because the theme of a strong voice having the power to make a difference is evident in the selection. Choice B is the only correct option.

5. B

Guiding Student Response

Short-Answer Question

It is clear from the essay that the writer finds Barbara Jordan's story to be inspirational and admirable. The writer feels that Jordan's life is an example of how people can achieve their goals, despite great obstacles. The writer also wants people to understand how experiences and hardships can shape people's convictions and make them stronger.

YOUR TURN The writer gives specific examples of hardships and discouraging moments that Jordan faced on her road to success. The writer also gives specific examples of Jordan's extraordinary accomplishments and impressive awards. The closing line is especially clear in its purpose—it states directly a lesson that can be learned from Jordan's life.

Essay Question

By all accounts, Barbara Jordan's life was full of success. What motivates one person to work so hard and achieve so much? In Jordan's case, personal experiences with racism and gender discrimination may have actually shaped her convictions and given her the determination to succeed.

When Jordan was a child in Texas, she experienced racial segregation first-hand. Laws in place told her and the members of her family where they could walk, shop, sit, and even attend school. Often the services available to African Americans were inferior to those available to whites. This traumatic early experience is reflected in the political path Jordan took. The role models to which she was drawn as a teenager and young adult were people fighting for civil rights. In everything she pursued, her most important mission was always to protect the constitution and the rights of all people.

As an adult, Jordan quickly learned that she needed more than ideals to achieve her goals. Although she was no longer living in the segregated world of her childhood, she found that racism and discrimination were still part of her life. In fact, when she lost her first political race an analyst told her that the fact that she was a black woman worked against her. Jordan was not discouraged by these words, however. Jordan, driven by values shaped by her experiences, made personal sacrifices and finally earned a place in the Texas House of Representatives in 1966. The racism and discrimination that Jordan faced as a child and as an adult was unfortunate,

---

PART 3 ## How to Respond in Writing

You may be asked to write answers to questions about a reading passage. **Short-answer questions** often ask you to answer in a sentence or two. **Essay questions** require a fully developed piece of writing.

Short-Answer Questions

STRATEGIES FOR RESPONDING TO SHORT-ANSWER QUESTIONS

▶ **Identify key words** in the writing prompt that tell you the ideas to discuss. Make sure you know what each word means.
▶ **State your response directly** and to the point.
▶ **Support your ideas** by using evidence from the selection.
▶ **Use correct grammar.**

> **Sample Question**
>
> Answer the following question in one or two sentences.
>
> Explain what you think the writer's purpose was in researching and reporting on Barbara Jordan's life.

Essay Question

STRATEGIES FOR ANSWERING ESSAY QUESTIONS

▶ **Look for direction words** in the writing prompt such as *essay, analyze, describe,* or *compare and contrast.*
▶ **List the points** you want to make before beginning to write.
▶ **Writing an interesting introduction** that presents your main point.
▶ **Develop your ideas** by using evidence from the selection that supports the statements you make. Present the ideas in a logical order.
▶ **Write a conclusion** that summarizes your points.
▶ **Check your work** for correct grammar.

> **Sample Prompt**
>
> Write an essay in which you analyze how early obstacles may have actually contributed to Barbara Jordan's desire to succeed.

Identify key words.

ONE STUDENT'S THOUGHTS

"The key words are *explain* and *purpose*. This means that I'll have to decide why the writer wrote the article and tell why I think that way."

YOUR TURN
What clues to the writer's purpose can you find in the selection?

Look for direction words.

ONE STUDENT'S THOUGHTS

"The important words are *essay* and *analyze*. This means that I'll have to create a fully developed piece of writing that explains the connections between things."

YOUR TURN
What are the main points you will need to cover?

---

but it gave Jordan the strength, determination, hope, and insight she needed to succeed. She knew from experience that equal rights and equal opportunities had value and should be protected. She also knew that the greatest achievements required hard work and determination.

YOUR TURN The main points are the specific challenges that Jordan faced, i.e. discrimination, segregation, sexism, etc., and how these challenges directly influenced the political path she took.

Here is a student's first draft in response to the writing prompt at the bottom of page 338. Read it and answer the multiple-choice questions that follow.

> 1 Some people are spurred on by challenges. Barbara
> 2 Jordan is one such person. She faced many challenges.
> 3 She was determined to make changes in the world.
> 4 Being raised in an era of discrimination; she felt the
> 5 effects on a daily basis. Her early experiences may have
> 6 left her with powerful feelings about fairness and equality.
> 7 She developed a strong desire and to become a powerful
> 8 speaker in order to voice her views.

1. What is the BEST way, if any, to combine the sentences in lines 2 and 3 ("She faced . . . in the world.")?

   A. Because she faced many challenges, she was determined to make changes in the world.

   B. She was determined to make changes in the world, but she faced many challenges.

   C. Because she made changes in the world, she faced many challenges.

   D. Make no change.

2. What is the BEST change, if any, to make to the sentence in lines 4 and 5 ("Being raised . . . daily basis.")?

   A. Remove the semicolon after *discrimination*.

   B. Replace the semicolon after *discrimination* with a colon.

   C. Replace the semicolon after *discrimination* with a comma.

   D. Make no change.

3. What is the BEST way, if any, to change the sentence in lines 7 and 8 ("She developed . . . voice her views.")?

   A. She developed a strong desire to become a powerful speaker in order to voice her views.

   B. She developed a strong desire but became a powerful speaker in order to voice her views.

   C. She developed a strong desire to become a powerful speaker but to voice her views.

   D. Make no change.

STRATEGIES FOR REVISING, EDITING, AND PROOFREADING

▸ **Read the passage carefully.**

▸ **Note the parts that are confusing** or don't make sense. What kinds of errors would that signal?

▸ **Look for errors** in grammar, usage, spelling, and capitalization. Common errors include:
  - run-on sentences
  - sentence fragments
  - lack of subject-verb agreement
  - unclear pronoun antecedents
  - lack of transition words

Guiding Student Response

Answers
1. A
2. C
3. A

Check Your Understanding
Have students reread their own response to the short-answer and essay questions. Then have them use the following questions to guide them as they revise and edit their own work.

- Have I responded directly to the direction words in the writing prompt?
- Have I presented the points I wanted to make?
- Have I begun with an interesting introduction?
- Have I supported my ideas with evidence from the selection?
- Have I presented my ideas in a logical order?
- Have I written a conclusion that summarizes my points?
- Have I used correct grammar?

U.S. Immigration Presentation

OVERVIEW

The United States has seen an extraordinary—and continuous—flow of immigrants since the land was first colonized. Some sought refuge from religious and political strife; others arrived unwillingly, as slaves; but the greatest number came, starting in the early 1800s, for economic reasons. In the century that followed, tens of millions immigrated "yearning to breathe free," little knowing what their new country would yield or how central they would be to its formation.

Research Questions

• Who came to the United States during the great immigration of the 18th and early 19th centuries, and why?

• What was life like in their new country?

Investigation The class will work as a team to produce an oral presentation about U.S. immigration in the century preceding World War I, a time when the United States received more than half the world's immigrants. The presentation will cover information about the experiences of immigrants to the United States as well as reasons so many left their countries of origin. Students will work together to find and summarize literature about the immigrant experience, to research the causes of European immigration to the United States, and to understand the conditions many faced in their new country. They will present this information, with visual aids, to other classes, and use complementary written materials to create a bulletin-board display. This project could be part of a larger unit on U.S. immigration.

Wrap-up Students will present their work to other classes and/or to an audience of family members. They may wish to videotape the event. If possible, have students watch videotapes beforehand that depict immigrant experience through photographs and historical narrative.

Links and Extended Reading
www.mcdougallittell.com

**LaserLinks: Background
Historical Connection**

OBJECTIVES

❑ present oral summaries and carefully chosen quotations from literature about the immigrant experience

❑ research and deliver presentations on primary factors affecting peak European immigration to the United States

❑ understand the health risks faced by many immigrants

❑ create a bar graph representing immigrant populations

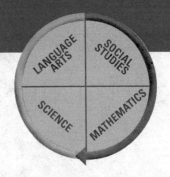

Team Assignments

CONNECT TO **LANGUAGE ARTS**   Immigrants have been a formative voice in American literature, in nonfiction and fiction alike. Each student should find a book that deals with immigrant life in the United States. Possibilities include Ernesto Galarza's *Barrio Boy;* Laurence Yep's *Dragonwings;* Karen Hesse's *Letters from Rifka;* and Myron Levoy's *Alan and Naomi.* Each student should skim their selected memoir or novel to find an anecdote that speaks about life as a U.S. immigrant. Next, they should summarize the anecdote and retell it orally to the class. They can also select and present a few quotes from the work that vividly depict an author's or character's particular perspective. After the presentation, summaries and quotes can be displayed on a bulletin board. *(3–4 class periods)*

YOU WILL NEED:
- novels and memoirs about U.S. immigrant life
- construction paper
- index cards

CONNECT TO **SOCIAL STUDIES**   Until the middle of the twentieth century, more than three quarters of immigrants to the United States came from Europe. Working in small groups, students should research factors that contributed to European immigration in the nineteenth and early twentieth centuries. The primary factors are generally considered to be:

- the population boom in Europe

- the rise of commercial farming and factories, which put individual farmers and craftsmen out of business

- the growth of accessible transportation, mainly steamboats and railroads.

Each group should write a headline about their subject and a few paragraphs that give information about the factor and its significance. Maps, statistics, and images may be shared during the verbal presentation of this research. *(Note: Teachers wishing to expand on this subject could ask students to research the National Origins Act, which in 1924 severely restricted immigration through discriminatory quotas, and to research the legislation that in 1965 abolished those quotas.) (4 class periods)*

YOU WILL NEED:
- encyclopedias
- colored pencils or markers
- construction paper

CONNECT TO **SCIENCE**   For many immigrants, settling in the United States brought serious health risks. Infant mortality was high, and child labor widespread. Factory workers contracted pneumonia from moving between extreme heat indoors and cold outside. In urban areas, tuberculosis spread. Assign small groups of students to research a health topic and make a poster explaining for example, how a particular disease may have spread, or a risk-factor such as conditions in factories. Some students may wish to investigate tenement housing, and how insufficient ventilation contributed to the spread of disease. Others might study the efforts of settlement house workers, such as Jane Addams and Lilian Wald, who sought to relieve health threats in immigrant communities. Students will use their posters as visual aids during an oral presentation. *(4 class periods)*

YOU WILL NEED:
- Web access (optional)
- reference and history books
- posterboard
- colored pens and pencils

CONNECT TO **MATHEMATICS**   The numbers of people who immigrated to the United States in the nineteenth and early twentieth centuries are astounding. Accurate records of these numbers have been kept since 1820. Students should locate statistics on the ten most numerous immigrant groups from the beginning of data collection until World War I. They should list the countries of origin in order of greatest immigrant population (Germany, Italy, Ireland, Austria-Hungary, Canada, etc.), and create a bar graph that represents those numbers. Students should present their graphs to an audience, asking questions that may be answered with the graph. *(To expand this activity tell students that, since 1965, with a new immigration law, the United States has experienced a new wave of immigration. In the 1980s, about 85 percent of all immigrants—some 6.3 million—came either from Asia or from Latin America. Have students make a comparison chart of the ten countries that have been the greatest source of immigrants since 1965: Mexico, Vietnam, Philippines, etc.) (4 class periods)*

YOU WILL NEED:
- almanacs
- graph paper
- rulers
- colored pens or pencils

Civil Rights Exhibit

OVERVIEW

The U.S. civil rights movement had fought for the equal status of black and white Americans since the end of the Civil War. Not until after World War II, however, did it gather momentum on the national stage—particularly after a series of court battles led by the National Association for the Advancement of Colored People (NAACP) culminated in *Brown vs. Board of Education of Topeka* (1954), which declared racial segregation in public facilities unconstitutional. In the ten years that followed, the movement achieved most of its primary goals. The following project could complement a unit of study on the civil rights movement.

Research Questions

• What were the chief goals of the civil rights movement?

• What were its accomplishments during the 1950s and 1960s?

Investigation The class will act as a team to produce an exhibit about civil rights activity in the 1950s and 1960s. The exhibit will include information about organizations at the helm of the movement as well as about key events of the era. Students will work together to create a lively backdrop comprising pictures, captions, quotes, a time line, and a portrait gallery. The time line will run along the bottom of the backdrop, with descriptions of events positioned chronologically above. Information about key organizations will also be posted on the backdrop, with yarn connecting these groups to events in which they were involved. In addition, students will guide visitors through the exhibit.

Wrap-up Students will host visiting classes or other guests, guiding them through the exhibit. A team of guides will offer presentations on their areas of expertise and then take questions. If possible, invite a museum guide or tour guide to speak to the class about presenting information effectively.

Links and Extended Reading
www.mcdougallittell.com

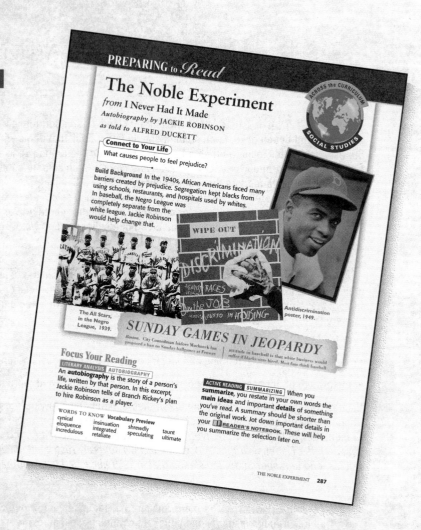

OBJECTIVES

❑ research key organizations of the civil rights movement

❑ explain the significance of the movement's achievements

❑ describe and represent the gains made possible by affirmative action

❑ measure and mark an accurate time line of the civil rights era

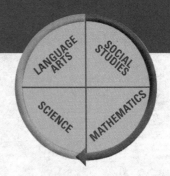

Team Teaching Assignments

CONNECT TO **LANGUAGE ARTS** Because the civil rights movement was a collective effort, it is important to recognize the organizations that mobilized it and laid the groundwork for its success. Such organizations include the National Association for the Advancement of Colored People (NAACP), the Southern Christian Leadership Conference, and the Student Nonviolent Coordinating Committee. For each group, consider the following: When and where did it originate? Who participated in it, and how? What was its focus? Is it still in existence today? Working in small groups, students should read what they can find about their organization. Next, they should make a poster about it, writing paragraph-length summaries and adding images and quotations where appropriate. Lastly, they should practice sharing this information with each other verbally. (*4–5 class periods*)

YOU WILL NEED:
- Web access (optional)
- reference books
- posterboard
- colored pencils

CONNECT TO **SOCIAL STUDIES** The civil rights movement changed the nation. Working in small groups, students should research its most significant events. Key topics include *Brown vs. Board of Education of Topeka;* the integration of Central High School in Little Rock, Arkansas; the Montgomery bus boycott; the Freedom Rides; the march from Selma to Montgomery; the March on Washington; and the legislation of 1964–65, specifically the Civil Rights Act of 1964, the Voting Rights Act, and the Twenty-fourth Amendment. Next, using construction paper, students should write a headline about their subject and a short paragraph that explains what took place and why it is significant. Again, they should practice presenting the information verbally. In addition, students may wish to use construction paper to post definitions of unfamiliar terms they encounter—*segregation, boycott, poll tax,* etc. (*2–3 class periods*)

YOU WILL NEED:
- encyclopedias
- colored pencils or markers
- construction paper

CONNECT TO **SCIENCE** In 1965, President Johnson issued Executive Order 11246. It required groups that did business with the federal government to take "affirmative action" to remedy the past discrimination against African Americans. Later, the policy came to include women and other minorities. Affirmative action is still under debate, but it did lead to increased opportunities for minorities. Students should research and report on the following example of how a federal agency has responded to affirmative action. The National Aeronautical and Space Administration has increased the number of African Americans, women, and other minorities on its staff. Students should create a portrait gallery of African American astronauts. If they wish, they can expand the gallery to include women and other minorities. They should include the scientific qualifications necessary to become an astronaut or a member of NASA's ground staff. (*2–3 class periods*)

YOU WILL NEED:
- Web access (optional)
- reference books
- information from NASA

CONNECT TO **MATHEMATICS** The civil rights era was a time of rapid, sweeping social change. A time line can help students better understand the sequence of the events they research. Students may wish to begin with *Brown* and end with the federal legislation of 1965, or make a time line that extends from World War II through the 1960s. In either case, students should be careful to measure even intervals of space between benchmark years, and to place their descriptions of events accurately along the time line. (*1–2 class periods*)

YOU WILL NEED:
- graph paper or plain paper
- rulers
- colored pencils

Flights of Imagination

The selections in this unit offer readers a surprising or different perspective from which to view people, events, or objects. The unit is divided into two parts: Part 1, "Surprising Turns," and Part 2, "Fantastic Tales." The writers in both parts share their visions of how imagination can transform the ordinary into the extraordinary and expand horizons.

Part 1

Surprising Turns The poetry, nonfiction, and fiction in this part warn readers to "expect the unexpected" and to see life's unpredictability as a gift. Being chased by an adult was the last thing the children were anticipating in the excerpt from *An American Childhood* by Annie Dillard. Yet for the writer, the incident becomes a glorious episode and a highlight of her childhood.

Part 2

Fantastic Tales The varied genres in this part show how imagination allows people to transcend their reality to create a new reality. The new reality may be a fictional colony on Mars as envisioned by Ray Bradbury in "Dark They Were, and Golden-Eyed" or the real life accomplishments of space pioneers, charted by Louis L'Amour in his essay "The Eternal Frontier."

Flights of Imagination

"The man who has no imagination has no wings."

Muhammad Ali   *American prizefighter and world heavyweight title holder*

© Kamil Vojnar/Photonica

340

 Viewing and Representing   TEKS 22A

ART APPRECIATION

Instruction Remind students that the composition of a work of art, or the arrangement of its parts, is carefully planned by the artist. Point out the depth of the foreground of this painting and the distance that the eye must travel to locate the central figure in the work. Moving the figure closer to the front or farther to the right or left would change the effect of the picture completely.

Ask: What is the effect that is achieved by positioning the figure and object where they are?

Possible Responses: The ball intersects the horizon, the point at which the earth meets the sky. Because of this placement, the boy seems to rise into the sky and be poised on the verge of taking off. Instead of having the ground behind him, which would suggest he was earthbound, he instead is liberated by the backdrop of space.

 See the Skills Trace at the beginning of the unit for information on TEKS covered in this lesson.

Features and Selections	Literary Analysis	TEKS	Reading and Critical Thinking	TEKS	Writing Opportunities	TEKS
Flights of Imagination **Surprising Turns**						
Learning the Language of Literature **Plot**	Plot, 343 **TAAS READING OBJ. 2, 4, 5**	12D, F, G, I				
The Active Reader **Skills and Strategies**			Making Inferences, 347 **TAAS READING OBJ. 5**	10A, H, 11A		
SHORT STORY **One Ordinary Day, with Peanuts** Difficulty Level: *Challenging*	Irony, 348, 350, 354, 356, 358	12J	Making Inferences, 348, 350, 352, 356, 358 Connect to Your Life, 348 Standardized Test Practice, 356 **TAAS READING OBJ. 5**	10H, L, 11A 4A 10H, K	Dialogue, 359 Random Act of Kindness, 359 **TAAS WRITING OBJ. 1**	11B, 15A, G 15C
SHORT STORY **Amigo Brothers** Difficulty Level: *Average*	Suspense, 361, 362, 366, 370, 372	12J	Predicting, 361, 362, 364, 368, 370, 372 Standardized Test Practice, 370 **TAAS READING OBJ. 6**	10A, L 10K, 12H	Boxing Profile, 373 Editorial, 373 **TAAS WRITING OBJ. 1**	15C 11B, C, 15B
POETRY **Ode to an Artichoke** Difficulty Level: *Average*	Metaphor, 375, 376, 378, 379 Review: Personification, 379	12J 12J	Visualizing, 375, 376, 378, 379 Standardized Test Practice, 378 **TAAS READING OBJ. 4**	10D, 11B 10H, K	Everyday Ode, 380 War Correspondence, 380 **TAAS WRITING OBJ. 1**	11B, 15D 10L, 15C, 24A
NARRATIVE NONFICTION *from* **An American Childhood** Difficulty Level: *Challenging* Literary Link **Winter Poem**	Narrative Nonfiction, 381, 382, 384, 386, 388 **TAAS READING OBJ. 6**	12A, E	Cause and Effect, 381, 382, 384, 386, 388 Comparing Texts, 388 Standardized Test Practice, 386 **TAAS READING OBJ. 2, 4**	11B, 12I 10I, 11D 10E, K	Adventure Narrative, 389 Letter to the Editor, 389 **TAAS WRITING OBJ. 1**	15A, G 11B, 15B
POETRY **The Bat** **Mooses** Difficulty Level: *Average*	Symbol, 391, 392, 394 Review: Humor, 394	12J 12J	Clarify, 391, 392, 394 Connect to Your Life, 391 Comparing Texts, 394 Informal Assessment, 393 **TAAS READING OBJ. 2, 3, 4** **TAAS WRITING OBJ. 2**	10C, 11A 4A 10I, 11C, D 10F	Animal Poem, 395 Poetry Essay, 395 **TAAS WRITING OBJ. 1**	15D 11A, 15A
Real World Link **They're Well-Suited to Study Moose** Building Vocabulary			Magazine Article: Summarizing, 397 **TAAS READING OBJ. 3**	10G		
Writing Workshop: **Problem-Solution Essay** Assessment Practice			Analyzing a Student Model, 404 **TAAS READING OBJ. 2, 3**	10F, 11C, 19A, D	Problem-Solution Essay, 406 Writing an Introduction, 407 **TAAS WRITING OBJ. 2, 4, 5**	18A, B, D, 19C 18C

Features and Selections	Literary Analysis	TEKS	Reading and Critical Thinking	TEKS	Writing Opportunities	TEKS
Fantastic Tales						
Learning the Language of Literature **Science Fiction and Fantasy**	Science Fiction and Fantasy, 410 **TAAS READING OBJ. 6**	10L, 12B				
The Active Reader **Skills and Strategies**			Author's Purpose, 414 **TAAS READING OBJ. 6**	10C, 12H		

Speaking and Listening Viewing and Representing	TEKS	Inquiry and Research	TEKS	Grammar, Usage, and Mechanics	TEKS	Vocabulary	TEKS
Art Appreciation, 340	22A						
Paired Activity, 358 Dramatic Scene, 359 Comic Strip, 359 Interviews, 353 Art Appreciation, 357	10L, 11B 11B 11B, 24A 11B 23B	Defining Trust, 359 Edgar Allen Poe Award, 360 **TAAS READING OBJ. 1**	6C, 13C 13C	Using Vivid and Precise Adjectives, 360 DLS, 348 Subject-Verb Agreement, 352 Demonstrative Adjectives, 360 **TAAS WRITING OBJ. 3–7**	17D 16B, 17A, H 17C 17D	Assessment Practice, 359 Synonyms, 349 Analogies, 355 Prefixes in-, im-, il-, ir-, 359 **TAAS READING OBJ. 1** **TAAS WRITING OBJ. 3, 7**	6A, 10K 9B, C 9B 16C
Paired Activity, 372 Postfight Interview, 373 Victory Speech, 373 Art Connection, 373 Art Appreciation, 365	4A, 10L, 11B, C 11B 5A, B, 11A, 15A 22A 22A	A Physical Education, 373 Fiction and Real Life, 374	13C	Coordinate Adjectives, 374 DLS, 361 Compound Adjectives, 366 Punctuating Coordinate Adjectives, 374 **TAAS WRITING OBJ. 3, 5, 6, 7**	16B, 17C 16D, 17C 17D 16B, 17A	Meaning Clues, 373 Meaning Clues, 362 Words from French, 367 Using Context Clues, 369 **TAAS READING OBJ. 1**	6A, 9B 9B 16G 6A
Paired Activity, 379 Vegetable Art, 380 Poetry Reading, 380 Memorize and Recite, 377	11B 11B, 24A 3A, 7D 5C, 7D, 11B	Where Do Artichokes Grow?, 380 Neruda's Life Abroad, 380 **TAAS READING OBJ. 4**	13C, 24A 13B	DLS, 375 **TAAS WRITING OBJ. 3, 6, 7**	16B, 17C		
Paired Activity, 388 Comic Strip, 389 Snow Poem, 389 Art Connection, 389 Debate on Equality in Sports, 387 **TAAS READING OBJ. 2, 5**	10L, 11B, 12G 11B, 24A 10L, 15D 22A 5F	Chilly Challenges!, 389 Tales of Childhood, 390	13C 10I	Avoiding Too Many Adjectives, 390 DLS, 381 Strong Verbs, 384 Writing with Adjectives, 390 **TAAS WRITING OBJ. 3–7**	17D 17A, D 17D 17D	Synonyms and Antonyms, 389 Greek Word Parts, 389 Synonyms and Antonyms, 382 Greek Word Parts, 389 **TAAS READING OBJ. 1, 6**	6C, 9C 6B, 9G 9B, F 16G
Paired Activity, 394 Animal Collage, 395	11B 11B, 24A	Animal Behavior, 395	13C	DLS, 391 **TAAS WRITING OBJ. 6**	17C		
		Activity Link: "Mooses," 397 Inquiry & Research, 397 **TAAS READING OBJ. 6**	13C 12C, 12H			Interpreting Analogies, 398 **TAAS READING OBJ. 1**	9B
Picturing Text Structure, 404 **TAAS READING OBJ. 2, 4**	10E, L			Consistent Verb Tense, 407 Revising and Editing, 408 Consistent Verb Tense, 408 **TAAS WRITING OBJ. 1, 3, 5, 6, 7**	17F, 18E, H 16F, 17A, C, F 17F		

Features and Selections	Literary Analysis	TEKS	Reading and Critical Thinking	TEKS	Writing Opportunities	TEKS
DRAMA The Monsters are Due on Maple Street **Difficulty Level:** *Average*	Teleplay, 415, 416, 418, 424, 426, 429 Review: Suspense, 429	12D, E 12D, J	Author's Purpose, 415, 416, 422, 428, 429 Connect to Your Life, 415 Std. Test Practice, 427, 428 **TAAS READING OBJ. 5, 6**	11B, 12H 4A 10F, K, 12H	Stage Directions, 430 Draft a Proposal, 430 **TAAS WRITING OBJ. 1, 2, 4**	11B, 15C 15B
SHORT STORY Key Item **Difficulty Level:** *Easy*	Science Fiction, 432, 434, 436	12B	Predicting, 432, 434, 436 Comparing Texts, 436 Standardized Test Practice, 435 **TAAS READING OBJ. 4**	11A, C 11C, D 10H, K	Radio Commercial, 437 Science Fiction, 437	10L, 11B 15A
SHORT STORY The Serial Garden **Difficulty Level:** *Average*	Fantasy, 438, 440, 442, 448, 452, 454, 455 Review: Humor, 440, 444, 448, 450, 455	12B 12D, J	Predicting, 438, 440, 444, 446, 448, 450, 452, 455 Comparing Texts, 455 Standardized Test Practice, 454 **TAAS READING OBJ. 2, 4, 5**	11A, C 11D 10K, 12G	Escape Plan, 456 Humorous Recipe, 456 **TAAS WRITING OBJ. 1**	11B, 15C 11B, 15D
POETRY Sara Cynthia Sylvia Stout Would Not Take the Garbage Out Jabberwocky **Difficulty Level:** *Challenging*	Sound Devices, 458, 460, 461	12D, J	Clarify, 458, 460, 461 Comparing Texts, 461 Informal Assessment, 462 **TAAS READING OBJ. 4, 6** **TAAS WRITING OBJ. 1**	4A, 10C, L, 11B 10I, L, 11D 12H	Nonsense Poem, 462 Newspaper Article, 462 **TAAS WRITING OBJ. 1**	11B, 15D 11B,15C
ESSAY The Eternal Frontier **Difficulty Level:** *Average*	Persuasive Essay, 463, 464, 466, 467	12E	Evaluating, 463, 464, 466, 467 Standardized Test Practice, 466 Informal Assessment, 468 **TAAS READING OBJ. 2–6** **TAAS WRITING OBJ. 4**	10H, 12H 10H, K 10F	A Different Response, 468 Persuasive Letter, 468 **TAAS WRITING OBJ. 1**	15B 11B, 15B
Real World Link Four Decades in Space **Building Vocabulary**			Newspaper Article: Skimming, Scanning, and Understanding Graphics, 471	10M		

AUTHOR STUDY
Ray Bradbury

Features and Selections	Literary Analysis	TEKS	Reading and Critical Thinking	TEKS	Writing Opportunities	TEKS
SHORT STORY Dark They Were, and Golden-Eyed **Difficulty Level:** *Average*	Circular Plot Structure, 478, 480, 482, 488, 490, 491 **TAAS READING OBJ. 2, 5**	12G, I	Visualizing, 478, 480, 482, 484, 486, 491 Connect to Your Life, 478 Std. Test Practice, 485, 489 **TAAS READING OBJ. 2, 3, 5**	10D, 11C 4A 10F, K		
SHORT STORY The Golden Kite, the Silver Wind **Difficulty Level:** *Average*	Theme, 492, 494, 496, 498	12D	Connect with Other Stories, 492, 494, 496, 498 Standardized Test Practice, 496 **TAAS READING OBJ. 2, 4**	4A, 10A, 11D 12I, K		
INTERVIEW An Interview with Ray Bradbury **The Author's Style** **Author Study Project**	Interview, 500 Key Style Points, 502 **TAAS READING OBJ. 6**	12E 12D, J, K	Active Reading, 502	11B	Writing, 502 Fable, 503 Time Capsule, 503 **TAAS WRITING OBJ. 1**	15C 11B, 15D, 18A 11B
Writing Workshop: Short Story **Assessment Practice**			Analyzing a Student Model, 507 Using Concrete Details, 510 **TAAS READING OBJ. 2, 5, 6** **TAAS WRITING OBJ. 1–5**	12G, H, J 19A, D, 18C, E	Short Story, 509 **TAAS WRITING OBJ. 2, 4**	15D, G, 18A, B, 19C
Reflect and Assess	Experiencing Suspense, 513 Exploring Theme, 513 **TAAS READING OBJ. 2, 3**	12D 10F, G			More Than Meets the Eye, 512 Close to Home, 512 Building your Portfolio, 513	11C, 15A 10A, 15A 19C, E

Speaking and Listening Viewing and Representing	TEKS	Inquiry and Research	TEKS	Grammar, Usage, and Mechanics	TEKS	Vocabulary	TEKS
Paired Activity, 429 Comic Book, 430 Human Sculpture, 430 Art Appreciation, 416 Drama Performance, 425	4A, 11B 11B, 24A 11C, 22A 22A, 23B 5C, E, 11B, 24C	Prejudice and Suspicion, 430 The Twilight Zone, 431	15A	Participles, 431 DLS, 415 Identifying Participles and Their Functions, 426 Present and Past Participles, 431	17A, C 17A 17F 17F	Analogies, 430 Analogies, 419 Word Parts—Affixes, 422 Suffixes -ance/-ant, -ence/-ent, 423 **TAAS READING OBJ. 1**	9B 6A, 9B 6B, 9D 16C
Paired Activity, 436 Computer Cartoon, 437 Talking Computer, 437 Art Appreciation, 433	10L, 12B 11B, 24A 5A, 11B 23A	Artificial Intelligence, 437	13C	DLS, 432 **TAAS WRITING OBJ. 3, 6, 7**	16B, 17G	Using a Dictionary, 434 Words Often Misspelled, 437 **TAAS READING OBJ. 1**	6A, C, 9B, C 6C, 9G, 16G
Paired Activity, 455 Monologue, 456 Dog House Poster, 456 Art Appreciation, 442, 451 Readers Theater, 448	11B, 12B 11B 11B, 24A 22A 3B, 5C, D, E	Garden Plots, 456 The Fate of the Armitages, 457	13C	Placement of Adverbs, 457 DLS, 438 Double Negatives, 450 Using Adverbs, 457 **TAAS WRITING OBJ. 3, 4, 6, 7**	17D 16B 17C 17D	Assessment Practice, 456 Antonyms, 439 Word Meaning, 452 Suffixes -able and -ible, 456 **TAAS READING OBJ. 1** **TAAS WRITING OBJ. 3, 7**	6A, 9B, 10K 9B 6A, C 16C
Paired Activity, 461 Trial Arguments, 462 Favorite Poem Project, 460	7E, 10L, 11B, 12J 11B 3B, 4A, 5C, D, E, 7D	Poetry Performance, 462	11B, 13C	DLS, 458 **TAAS WRITING OBJ. 3, 7**	16B, D		
Paired Activity, 467 Multimedia Presentation, 468 Author Interview, 468 **TAAS READING OBJ. 6**	10J, 11C 11B, 24A, B 5B, 11B	Space Station, 468 The Western Frontier, 469	13F 8C	Precise Adverbs, 469 DLS, 463 Writing with Precise Adverbs, 469 **TAAS WRITING OBJ. 3–7**	17D 17A 17D	Word Meaning, 468 Using Context Clues, 464 **TAAS READING OBJ. 1**	9B 6A
		Activity Link: "The Eternal Frontier," 472 Inquiry & Research, 472	13F 20C			Learning and Remembering New Words, 473 **TAAS READING OBJ. 1**	6A, 9B, C, D
Paired Activity, 491 Art Appreciation, 479, 482, 486	4A, 10L, 11B, C 22A			DLS, 478 Time Order, 484 Transitional Expressions, 488 **TAAS WRITING OBJ. 3, 4, 6, 7**	16B 17D 17C	Synonyms, 480 Word Usage, 487 **TAAS READING OBJ. 1**	6A, C, 9B, C 6B, 9D
Cooperative Learning Activity, 498 Art Appreciation, 493, 494 Persuasion, 497	11B 22A 2B, F, 5A, D, E, 11B, C			Essential and Nonessential Modifiers, 499 DLS, 492 Using Essential and Nonessential Modifiers, 499 **TAAS WRITING OBJ. 3, 5, 6, 7**	16B, 17A, C 16B 17A	Context Clues, 499 Word Meaning, 499 Using Context Clues, 495 **TAAS READING OBJ. 1**	6A, 9B 6A, 9B 6A
Speaking and Listening, 502 Film Review, 503 Creating a Comic Strip, 503	11B, C 4A, 11B, 12C, 23B 11B, 15D, 21A, 24A	To Mars!, 503	13C				
Picturing Text Structure, 507 **TAAS READING OBJ. 2, 4**	10E, L			Parallelism, 510 Revising and Editing, 511 Punctuating Dialogue, 510 Parallelism, 511 **TAAS WRITING OBJ. 5–7**	17C, 18H 17A, C, D 16B 17F		
Guess My Name, 512	11B						

UNIT THREE
RESOURCE MANAGEMENT GUIDE
PART 1

To introduce the theme of this unit, use Fine Art Transparencies T25–T27 in the Communications Transparencies and Copymasters.

	Unit Resource Book	Assessment	Integrated Technology and Media	Additional Support Literary Analysis Transparencies
One Ordinary Day, with Peanuts *pp. 348–360*	• Summary p. 4 • Active Reading p. 5 • Literary Analysis p. 6 • Words to Know p. 7 • Grammar p. 8 • Spelling p. 9 • Selection Quiz p. 10	• Selection Test, Formal Assessment pp. 53–54 Test Generator	Audio Library	• Narrator and Point of View T22 • Irony T27
Amigo Brothers *pp. 361–374*	• Summary p. 11 • Active Reading p. 12 • Literary Analysis p. 13 • Words to Know p. 14 • Grammar p. 15 • Spelling p. 16 • Selection Quiz p. 17	• Selection Test, Formal Assessment pp. 55–56 Test Generator	Audio Library	• Conflict T8
Ode to an Artichoke/ Oda a la alcachofa *pp. 375–380*	• Active Reading p. 18 • Literary Analysis p. 19	• Selection Test, Formal Assessment pp. 57–58 Test Generator	Audio Library	• Poetry: Figurative Language T19
***from* An American Childhood** *pp. 381–390*	• Summary p. 20 • Active Reading p. 21 • Literary Analysis p. 22 • Words to Know p. 23 • Grammar p. 24 • Spelling p. 25 • Selection Quiz p. 26	• Selection Test, Formal Assessment pp. 59–60 Test Generator	Audio Library	• Elements of Storytelling T1 • Plot T5
The Bat **Mooses** *pp. 391–395*	• Active Reading p. 27 • Literary Analysis p. 28	• Selection Test, Formal Assessment pp. 61–62 Test Generator	Audio Library	• Form in Poetry: Rhyme and Meter T17 • Poetry: Figurative Language T19 • Poetry: Sound Devices T20

Writing Workshop: Problem-Solution Essay

		Unit Assessment	Unit Technology	
Unit Three Resource Book • Prewriting p. 30 • Drafting and Elaboration p. 31 • Peer Response Guide pp. 32–33 • Revising, Editing, and Proofreading p. 34 • Student Models pp. 35–37 • Rubric for Evaluation p. 38 Writing Coach	**Writing Transparencies** T1–4, T15, T33 **Reading and Critical Thinking Transparencies** T25, T39 **Grammar Transparencies and Copymasters** C74 **Teacher's Guide to Assessment and Portfolio Use**	• Unit Three Part 1 Test, Formal Assessment pp. 63–64 Test Generator • Unit Three Integrated Test, Integrated Assessment pp. 13–18	ClassZone www.mcdougallittell.com	

UNIT THREE
PART 2

To introduce the theme of this unit, use Fine Art Transparencies T25–27 in the Communications Transparencies and Copymasters.

	Unit Resource Book	Assessment	Integrated Technology and Media	Additional Support Literary Analysis Transparencies
The Monsters Are Due on Maple Street *pp. 415–431*	• Summary p. 39 • Active Reading p. 40 • Literary Analysis p. 41 • Words to Know p. 42 • Grammar p. 43 • Spelling p. 44 • Selection Quiz p. 45	• Selection Test, Formal Assessment pp. 65–66 Test Generator	Audio Library	• Drama: Stage Directions T23

Reading and Critical Thinking Transparencies	Grammar Transparencies and Copymasters	Vocabulary Transparencies and Copymasters	Writing Transparencies	Communications Transparencies and Copymasters
• Making Inferences T5	• Daily Language SkillBuilder T11 • Subject-Verb Agreement C119 • Demonstrative Adjectives C80	• Synonyms C45 • Analogies C46	• Personal Narrative T25 • Effective Language T15	• Interviewing T9 • Impromptu Speaking: Dialogue, Role-Play T13
• Predicting T7	• Daily Language SkillBuilder T11 • Compound Adjectives C83 • Punctuating Coordinate Adjectives C127	• Meaning Clues C47 • Context Clues C48	• Elaboration T13	• Interviewing T9
• Visualizing T10	• Daily Language SkillBuilder T12		• Generating Writing Ideas T1 • Locating Information Using Print References T45	• Reading Aloud T11 • Dramatic Reading T12
• Cause and Effect T3 • Story Map T34	• Daily Language SkillBuilder T12 • Strong Verbs C137 • Writing with Adjectives C138	• Synonyms and Antonyms C49	• Generating Writing Ideas T1 • Organizing Your Writing T11 • Using Periodical Indexes T44 • Locating Information Using the Internet T47–48	• Persuasive Techniques T3 • Dramatic Reading T12
• Strategies for Reading T1	• Daily Language SkillBuilder T12		• Elaboration T13 • Figurative Language and Sound Devices T17	

STUDENTS ACQUIRING ENGLISH

The **Spanish Study Guide,** pp. 67–84, includes language support for the following pages:
• Family and Community Involvement (per unit)

• Selection Summaries and Vocabulary
• Active Reading
• Literary Analysis

Reading and Critical Thinking Transparencies	Grammar Transparencies and Copymasters	Vocabulary Transparencies and Copymasters	Writing Transparencies	Communications Transparencies and Copymasters
• Author's Purpose and Audience T4	• Daily Language SkillBuilder T13 • Identifying Participles and Their Functions, C96 • Present and Past Participles C98	• Analogies C50 • Word Parts: Prefixes and Suffixes C51	• Elaboration T13	• Dramatic Reading T12

UNIT THREE
RESOURCE MANAGEMENT GUIDE
PART 2

To introduce the theme of this unit, use Fine Art Transparencies T25–T27 in the Communications Transparencies and Copymasters.

Additional Support

	Unit Resource Book	Assessment	Integrated Technology and Media	Literary Analysis Transparencies
Key Item *pp. 432–437*	• Summary p. 46 • Active Reading p. 47 • Literary Analysis p. 48 • Words to Know p. 49 • Grammar p. 50 • Spelling p. 51 • Selection Quiz p. 52	• Selection Test, Formal Assessment pp. 67–68 Test Generator	Audio Library Research Starter www.mcdougallittell.com	
The Serial Garden *pp. 438–457*	• Summary p. 53 • Active Reading p. 54 • Literary Analysis p. 55 • Words to Know p. 56 • Grammar p. 57 • Spelling p. 58 • Selection Quiz p. 59	• Selection Test, Formal Assessment pp. 69–70 Test Generator	Audio Library	
Sarah Cynthia Sylvia Stout Would Not Take the Garbage Out Jabberwocky *pp. 458–462*	• Active Reading p. 60 • Literary Analysis p. 61	• Selection Test, Formal Assessment pp. 71–72 Test Generator	Audio Library	• Poetry: Sound Devices T20
The Eternal Frontier *pp. 463–469*	• Summary p. 62 • Active Reading p. 63 • Literary Analysis p. 64 • Words to Know p. 65 • Grammar p. 66 • Spelling p. 67 • Selection Quiz p. 68	• Selection Test, Formal Assessment pp. 73–74 Test Generator	Audio Library LaserLinks, Teacher's SourceBook p. 21 Research Starter www.mcdougallittell.com	• Persuasive Techniques T15
Dark They Were, and Golden-Eyed *pp. 478–491*	• Summary p. 70 • Active Reading p. 71 • Literary Analysis p. 72 • Words to Know p. 73 • Grammar p. 74 • Spelling p. 75 • Selection Quiz p. 76	• Selection Test, Formal Assessment pp. 75–76 Test Generator	Audio Library LaserLinks, Teacher's SourceBook p. 22	• Text Structure T12
The Golden Kite, the Silver Wind *pp. 492–499*	• Summary p. 77 • Active Reading p. 78 • Literary Analysis p. 79 • Words to Know p. 80 • Grammar p. 81 • Spelling p. 82 • Selection Quiz p. 83	• Selection Test, Formal Assessment pp. 77–78 Test Generator	Audio Library	• Theme T7 • Fables/Myths/Tall Tales T30

Writing Workshop: Short Story

		Unit Assessment	*Unit Technology*	
Unit Three Resource Book • Prewriting p. 84 • Drafting and Elaboration p. 85 • Peer Response Guide pp. 86–87 • Revising, Editing, and Proofreading p. 88 • Student Models pp. 89–91 • Rubric for Evaluation p. 92 Writing Coach	**Writing Transparencies** T1–4, T13, T24, T34 **Literary Analysis Transparencies** T28 **Reading and Critical Thinking Transparencies** T24 **Grammar Transparencies and Copymasters** C129, C143 **Teacher's Guide to Assessment and Portfolio Use**	• Unit Three, Part 2 Test, Formal Assessment pp. 79–80 Test Generator • Unit Three Integrated Test, Integrated Assessment pp. 13–18	ClassZone www.mcdougallittell.com	

Reading and Critical Thinking Transparencies	Grammar Transparencies and Copymasters	Vocabulary Transparencies and Copymasters	Writing Transparencies	Communications Transparencies and Copymasters
• Predicting T7	• Daily Language SkillBuilder T13	• Using a Dictionary C52	• Elaboration T13 • Dialogue T24 • Note Taking T49	
• Predicting T7	• Daily Language SkillBuilder T14 • Using Adverbs C85 • Double Negatives C86	• Antonyms C53 • Word Meaning C54	• Generating Writing Ideas T1	• Dramatic Reading T12 • Giving and Using Feedback to Improve Performance T16
	• Daily Language SkillBuilder T14		• Generating Writing Ideas T1	• Persuasive Techniques T3 • Reading Aloud T11
• Evaluating T14	• Daily Language SkillBuilder T15 • Writing with Precise Adverbs C139	• Context Clues C55	• Elaboration T13 • Mulitmedia Presentation T39	• Interviewing T9 • Formal Presentation T10
• Visualizing T10	• Daily Language SkillBuilder T15 • Time Order C94 • Transitional Expressions C95	• Synonyms C56 • Word Usage C57		
• Connecting T2	• Daily Language SkillBuilder T16 • Using Essential and Nonessential Modifiers C87	• Context Clues: Restatement C58	• Generating Writing Ideas T1	• Persuasive Techniques T3 • Evaluation Matrix: Film/Video T7

STUDENTS ACQUIRING ENGLISH

The **Spanish Study Guide,** pp. 85–105, includes language support for the following pages:
• Family and Community Involvement (per unit)

• Selection Summaries and Vocabulary
• Active Reading
• Literary Analysis

Selection	SkillBuilder Sentences	Suggested Answers
One Ordinary Day, with Peanuts	1. When the story opens, him seems to be having an ordinary day. 2. The story mainly describes Mr. Johnsons day.	1. When the story opens, **he** seems to be having an ordinary day. 2. The story mainly describes Mr. **Johnson's** day.
Amigo Brothers	1. Antonio worked out at the Boys Club with Felix on 10th Street. 2. The situation of having to fight each other could of destroy their friendship.	1. Antonio worked out **with Felix at the Boys Club** on 10th Street. 2. The situation of having to fight each other could **have** destroy**ed** their friendship.
Ode to an Artichoke	1. Artichokes grow in California, you can see the fields from the road. 2. The plants are a gray-green, and it has large flower buds.	1. Artichokes grow in California; you can see the fields from the road. 2. The plants are a gray-green, and **they have** large flower buds.
from An American Childhood	1. Dillard recalls this as one of the most happiest times in her life. 2. After six inches of fresh snow fell she and her friends met outside.	1. Dillard recalls this as one of the **happiest** times in her life. 2. After six inches of fresh snow fell, she and her friends met outside.

Selection	SkillBuilder Sentences	Suggested Answers
The Bat Mooses	1. There was many bats in that old barn. 2. I once saw a moose in the woods; in fact, they startled me.	1. There **were** many bats in that old barn. 2. I once saw a moose in the woods; in fact, **it** startled me.
The Monsters Are Due on Maple Street	1. A spacecraft which people at first believe is a meteor causes strange happenings on Maple Street. 2. Confused and frightened the neighbors turn against one another.	1. A spacecraft, which people at first believe is a meteor, causes strange happenings on Maple Street. 2. Confused and frightened, the neighbors turn against one another.
Key Item	1. Can computers become so powerful that people won't need to think anymore. 2. It has'nt happened yet.	1. Can computers become so powerful that people won't need to think anymore? 2. It **hasn't** happened yet.
The Serial Garden	1. Mrs armitage declares that brekkfast brikks look like doormats. 2. Mark says to his father, please, eat some more cereal.	1. Mrs. **A**rmitage declares that **B**rekkfast **B**rikks look like doormats. 2. Mark says to his father, "**P**lease, eat some more cereal."

Selection	SkillBuilder Sentences	Suggested Answers
Jabberwocky Sarah Cynthia Sylvia Stout . . .	1. They're styles are very different, but both poets make there readers feel as if their part of the imaginary world of the poem. 2. Sarah cynthia sylvia stout would Not Take the garbage Out is a long title.	1. **Their** styles are very different, but both poets make **their** readers feel as if **they're** part of the imaginary world of the poem. 2. "Sarah **C**ynthia **S**ylvia **S**tout **W**ould Not Take the **G**arbage Out" is a long title.
The Eternal Frontier	1. The author believes in the power of the pioneer spirit he cites scientific, medical, and technological advances that have resulted from that spirit. 2. Im not sure if I agree with the authors emphasis on space exploration as the key to our future.	1. The author believes in the power of the pioneer spirit. **He** cites scientific, medical, and technological advances that have resulted from that spirit. 2. **I'm** not sure if I agree with the **author's** emphasis on space exploration as the key to our future.
Dark They Were, and Golden-Eyed	1. Harry, as well as other humans, hope to begin a new life on Mars. 2. She says that her eyes haven't never been brown.	1. Harry, as well as other humans, hope**s** to begin a new life on Mars. 2. She says that her eyes haven't **ever** been brown.
The Golden Kite, the Silver Wind	1. The daughter might have gave different advice if she had known what happened. 2. Some people take omens serious.	1. The daughter might have **given** different advice if she had known what **would happen.** 2. Some people take omens **seriously**.

	Unit One	Unit Two	Unit Three	Unit Four	Unit Five	Unit Six
Grammar Focus by Unit	The Sentence and Its Parts	Nouns, Pronouns, and Verbs	Modifiers	Phrases	Compound and Complex Sentences	Review

The Language of Literature offers several options for integrating grammar instruction and literature.

- Each unit has a specific grammar focus. The grammar focus for this unit is highlighted on the planning chart. Categories of grammar skills for this unit are shown in red.

- The Pupil's Edition includes instructive features entitled *Grammar in Context*. The instruction in these features arises from the selections and relates to the grammar focus for each unit.

- The Writing Workshops in the Pupil's Edition include grammar tips that help the students produce error-free drafts.

- Mini Lessons in the Teacher's Edition complement the instruction in the *Grammar in Context* features. Additional Mini Lessons relate to the grammar focus for each unit as well as to the literature.

- Daily Language SkillBuilders in the Teacher's Edition provide students with ongoing proofreading practice and reinforce punctuation, spelling, grammar and usage, and capitalization.

- Grammar Copymasters and Transparencies, which may be used independently or in conjunction with the Mini Lessons in the Teacher's Edition, present grammar in a traditional, systematic sequence.

PE instruction shown in black
TE Mini Lessons shown in green

Part 1

VERBS
Consistent Verb Tense
Writing Workshop, p. 407
Consistent Verb Tense
Assessment Practice, p. 408

ADJECTIVES AND ADVERBS
Demonstrative Adjectives
"One Ordinary Day, with Peanuts," p. 360
Compound Adjectives
"Amigo Brothers," p. 366
Coordinate Adjectives
"Amigo Brothers," p. 374

SUBJECT-VERB AGREEMENT
Subject-Verb Agreement
"One Ordinary Day, with Peanuts," p. 352

PUNCTUATION
Punctuating Coordinate Adjectives
"Amigo Brothers," p. 374

STYLE
Using Vivid and Precise Adjectives
"One Ordinary Day, with Peanuts," p. 360
Strong Verbs
"An American Childhood," p. 384
Avoiding Too Many Adjectives
"An American Childhood," p. 390
Writing with Adjectives
"An American Childhood," p. 390

Part 2

ADJECTIVES AND ADVERBS
Double Negatives
"The Serial Garden," p. 450
Placement of Adverbs
"The Serial Garden," p. 457
Using Adverbs
"The Serial Garden," p. 457
Precise Adverbs
"The Eternal Frontier," p. 469
Essential and Nonessential Modifiers
"The Golden Kite, the Silver Wind," p. 499
Using Essential and Nonessential Modifiers
"The Golden Kite, the Silver Wind," p. 499

PREPOSITIONS, CONJUNCTIONS, INTERJECTIONS
Time Order
"Dark They Were, and Golden-Eyed," p. 484
Transitional Expressions
"Dark They Were, and Golden-Eyed," p. 488

VERBALS AND VERB PHRASES
Identifying Participles and Their Functions
"The Monsters Are Due on Maple Street," p. 426
Participles
"The Monsters Are Due on Maple Street," p. 431
Present and Past Participles
"The Monsters Are Due on Maple Street," p. 431

PUNCTUATION
Punctuating Dialogue
Writing Workshop, p. 510

STYLE
Writing with Precise Adverbs
"The Eternal Frontier," p. 469
Parallelism
Writing Workshop, p. 510
Parallelism
Assessment Practice, p. 511

Students explore imaginative worlds and characters by working in small groups to produce and perform original skits for an audience.

Project at a glance The selections in Unit Three focus on imagination—in particular, on imagined characters and worlds (Part 1 deals with characters who use their imagination to become someone else, and Part 2 deals with futuristic and fantastic worlds). For this project, students will write and act in skits that show a person who uses his or her imagination to solve a problem (either by becoming a different character or by visiting another world). Skits may be humorous or serious. All skits will be performed in front of a live audience and should be complete with costumes, scenery, and props (insofar as they are practical). This project might be coordinated with a schoolwide Talent Show, or the skits might be scheduled for a time when families can be invited to watch.

SCHEDULING

Skits should take no more than 15 minutes each. You may want to schedule the skits over the course of this unit, or at the end of this unit, depending on your purposes.

PROJECT OBJECTIVES

• To demonstrate the speaking and listening skills introduced in the activity
• To explore the theme of imagination through characters in a dramatic script
• To plan, prepare, and present an original skit
• To develop listening and viewing skills by watching and evaluating the performance of others

SUGGESTED GROUP SIZE

4–6 students per group

Getting Started

Explain that students will be working in groups to plan, write, and act out skits that explore the topic of imagination. You might ask students to make a list of TV shows that deal with fantastic characters, worlds, or details.

Use the resources in your school. Invite your school's drama teacher or a volunteer from a local theater group to a few rehearsals. If students will be painting props, make arrangements for materials with your school's art teacher. Also consider borrowing musical instruments from your music department.

If your school has an auditorium, schedule time for each group to hold at least one dress rehearsal. If the skits are to take place in the classroom, arrange for side screens or curtains where students can go "off-stage" during performances.

This project lends itself to everything from a classroom to a schoolwide performance. You may even want to schedule an evening show and sell tickets to give students experience in advertising, sales, and management.

Writing Workshop Connection

As a springboard, students may use the Writing Workshop assignment **Short Story**, p. 506, which they will complete in Part 2.

Directing the Project

Preparing (1 class period) Discuss all that is needed in a theatrical production. Remind students that skits should follow the general format of exposition, conflict, and resolution.

▶ Divide students into groups. Have them create main characters who use their imaginations to solve a problem. Each group should brainstorm ideas about the focus of their skit. When they have developed an idea, individual assignments can be made. Encourage everyone to contribute to the writing and acting, as well as to the behind-the-scenes duties. Students should familiarize themselves with the general format of writing for the theater. Entrances, exits, and other movements should be indicated in the scripts.

Assigning Roles In addition to individual character roles, you may want to choose a director, stage manager, acting coach, costume designer, and prop person (or people).

▶ After students have done the preliminary planning, they should submit a list and description of characters, and a plot summary. Meet with each group to discuss the scenario before students begin writing. Attend two or more rehearsals for the skit to offer advice and note progress and any difficulties.

▶ You should also work with students to create a set of guidelines for evaluation (i.e. What Makes a Good Skit) to be filled out after the final performances.

Practicing (1 class period) Have each group read their parts aloud several times to make sure they understand the words and events of the plot. Then have students do a walk-through, in which they perform their movements, gestures, and facial expressions as they say their lines. Students should do a final rehearsal using the actual props, lighting, and so on.

▶ Tell students that giving and receiving feedback during the rehearsal stage is crucial. Refer to the tips in the Feedback Center.

Presenting (2–3 class periods) This project could culminate in a Talent Show for the entire student body or just for your class.

▶ To begin, have students take a few deep breaths. Make sure props are in place and that there is adequate seating. You might want to have one student introduce the entire show and provide a concluding thought about the theme of the skits (or you may want to do this yourself).

Evaluation Also, have student audience members complete a brief evaluation after each performance, as well as complete evaluations of their own performances. These should be turned in to you at the end of each performance and can be used for later discussion.

Teaching the Speaking and Listening Skills

The student is expected to:

Analyze the use of aesthetic language for its effects

Teaching Suggestions: Discuss with students how language can be used to create certain effects on an audience. Explain how certain words, phrasings, and rhyme patterns are pleasing to the ear, while others create a sense of disharmony. Also discuss how metaphors, similes, and other forms of figurative language can create pictures in an audience's mind. Have students incorporate these elements into their scripts. For more information, have students turn to the Communication Handbook, page R102.

Generate criteria to evaluate presentations of others and generate criteria to evaluate his/her own presentations

Teaching Suggestions: Tell students that before they perform their skits, they must develop a set of guidelines to evaluate their own as well as others' performances. Ask for suggestions about what makes an effective skit—in particular, notes about voice, delivery, pacing, and so on. From this discussion, you can create worksheets for students to use during the final performances. It will also be helpful to have students rate their own performances according to these guidelines.

Compare perceptions with perceptions of others

Teaching Suggestions: After each group has presented and has been evaluated by the class, have students compare their self-evaluations with the evaluations given by others. To do this, you might want to set a list of standards for discussion and explain what is meant by "constructive criticism." This might work best if you act as moderator.

Feedback Center

Students can use the following guidelines when giving and receiving feedback during this project:

Giving Feedback

▶ Provide feedback about the story idea (Does the story make sense?).

▶ Question the characters' tone and motivation (Are they appropriate to the subject?).

▶ Comment on the verbal and nonverbal delivery (pitch, pace, volume, body language) and its impact on the listener.

Receiving Feedback

▶ Listen to constructive criticism with an open mind.

▶ Use audience feedback and modify the presentation to clarify meaning or organization.

▶3 Assessing the Project

The following rubric can be used for group or individual assessment.

3 Full Accomplishment

The group followed directions and produced an engaging skit that involves an imaginative story. Students evaluated their own performance as well as the performance of others and demonstrated thoughtful reflection on strengths and weaknesses. Students demonstrated all three of the Speaking and Listening Skills listed.

2 Substantial Accomplishment

The students produced a skit, but the script is incomplete. It shows some use of futuristic or fantastic elements and some use of aesthetic language. Two out of the three Speaking and Listening Skills were demonstrated.

1 Little Accomplishment

The students' script and skit are incomplete or do not fulfill the requirements of the assignment. Students did not work effectively in a group and demonstrated only one of the Speaking and Listening Skills.

Reflecting on the Theme We usually have expectations about people and situations, and think we can predict what is likely to happen. Life, however, often takes surprising turns. The same is true of stories. We think we know what a character will do or how a situation will turn out, but the writer surprises us with a turn we didn't expect. Being caught off guard is part of the pleasure of reading.

ACTIVITY

Was there a time when you were completely surprised by some event? What happened? What were you expecting? List some of these times, then choose one as the basis for a story. Try to recreate the event so you surprise your readers just as you were surprised. Share your story with a classmate.

Expectation	Surprise
1.	
2.	
3.	
4.	
5.	

Plot

> *A story to me means a plot where there is some surprise. . . . Because that is how life is— full of surprises.*
>
> —Isaac Bashevis Singer

When someone comes to join you as you are watching a television program, what's the first thing he or she asks you? "What happened?" In response, you might give a brief description of the show's **plot.** Plot refers to the **sequence of events** in a story. Every piece of fiction and drama has a plot, as does some nonfiction and poetry. In most cases, a plot moves forward because of some sort of **conflict.** The reader wants to find out what will happen to the **characters** next, how they will **change,** and how they will resolve the conflict. In a good, tight plot, there will be plenty of suspense to keep the reader interested. There may also be a surprise ending. A typical plot contains an **exposition, rising action,** a **climax,** and **falling action** (sometimes called the **resolution**).

PLOT AT A GLANCE

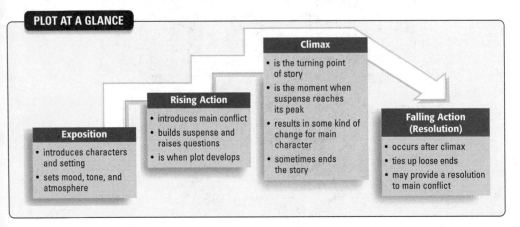

Climax
- is the turning point of story
- is the moment when suspense reaches its peak
- results in some kind of change for main character
- sometimes ends the story

Rising Action
- introduces main conflict
- builds suspense and raises questions
- is when plot develops

Exposition
- introduces characters and setting
- sets mood, tone, and atmosphere

Falling Action (Resolution)
- occurs after climax
- ties up loose ends
- may provide a resolution to main conflict

OVERVIEW

Objectives
- understand and identify the following literary terms:
  - plot
  - conflict
  - exposition
  - rising action
  - climax
  - falling action (resolution)
  - story structure
  - flashback
  - foreshadowing
  - cause-and-effect
  - external conflict
  - internal conflict
  - change
- recognize and interpret literary devices such as foreshadowing and flashback
- recognize and analyze story plot and problem resolution
- analyze characters, including their traits, conflicts, and changes they undergo

Teaching the Lesson

This lesson introduces students to the concept of plot by examining its basic elements in detail using text and visual aids.

Introducing the Concepts
Have students think of a film they have recently seen or a book they have recently read. Using the chart on this page as a model, ask them to summarize the plot of the work and specifically identify its central conflict, its climax, and the resolution of the conflict. Ask volunteers to chart their responses on the chalkboard.

 Use **Literary Analysis Transparencies,** pp. 5, 8, for additional support.

 See the Skills Trace at the beginning of the unit for information on TEKS covered in this lesson.
TEKS

Ask students to think of a film they
have seen or a book they have read
that uses the technique of flashback.
Ask them to think about and discuss
the role that flashback played in the
work. How would the work differ if the
author or filmmaker had not included
flashback scenes? What specific effect
did the flashback have on the reader or
audience? What purpose did it serve in
the work?

YOUR TURN
Possible Response: She had earned
the jacket fairly and deserved it even
though she could not afford to buy it
when the school decided to charge
for it.

Sequence of Events

Every piece of writing with a plot has a **story structure**.
The story makes sense because the reader can see how one
event leads to the next. Two techniques that may affect story
structure are flashbacks and foreshadowing. **Flashbacks**
occur when there is a break in action and the audience is
shown a scene from the past. **Foreshadowing** is a signal that
might hint at events in the future. Both of these techniques
are used widely in films as well as in literature.

When discussing sequence of events, it is also important to
consider cause and effect. A **cause-and-effect** relationship
occurs when one event brings about, or causes, another.
The story wheel below shows the sequence of events
in "The Scholarship Jacket."

YOUR TURN Look at the story wheel.
What do you think caused the
principal to decide to give
the jacket to Martha?

From "The Scholarship Jacket"

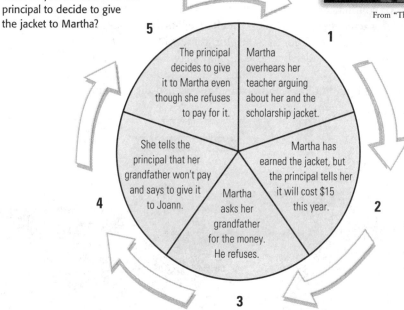

5 The principal decides to give it to Martha even though she refuses to pay for it.

1 Martha overhears her teacher arguing about her and the scholarship jacket.

2 Martha has earned the jacket, but the principal tells her it will cost $15 this year.

3 Martha asks her grandfather for the money. He refuses.

4 She tells the principal that her grandfather won't pay and says to give it to Joann.

Conflict

The conflict in a plot generally has to do with what a character wants and what is stopping him or her from getting it. When a character struggles against another character or an outside force, the conflict is **external**. When the struggle is within the character, the conflict is **internal**.

YOUR TURN What does the boy in this excerpt from "Thank You, M'am" want at this point? What is standing in his way?

> ### CONFLICT
>
> The water dripping from his face, the boy looked at her. There was a long pause. A very long pause. After he had dried his face and not knowing what else to do dried it again, the boy turned around, wondering what next. The door was open. He could make a dash for it down the hall. He could run, run, run, run, *run!*
>
> —Langston Hughes,
> "Thank You, M'am"

Change

Sometimes what happens to a **character** in a story causes him or her to **change.** In "Thank You, M'am," it seems very likely that, as a result of his meeting with Mrs. Jones, Roger will never try to steal another pocketbook. A story of personal change can be just as powerful and absorbing as a story with lots of exciting events.

YOUR TURN How did the characters in "A Retrieved Reformation" change? Remember that Ben Price had been looking for Jimmy Valentine in connection with some robberies. He has just witnessed Jimmy using his tools to save a little girl. Has either character changed? How? What do you think caused the changes?

> ### CHANGE
>
> Jimmy Valentine put on his coat, and walked outside the railings toward the front door. As he went he thought he heard a faraway voice that he once knew call "Ralph!" But he never hesitated. At the door a big man stood somewhat in his way.
>
> "Hello, Ben!" said Jimmy, still with his strange smile. "Got around at last, have you? Well, let's go. I don't know that it makes much difference, now."
>
> And then Ben Price acted rather strangely.
>
> "Guess you're mistaken, Mr. Spencer," he said. "Don't believe I recognize you. Your buggy's waiting for you, ain't it?"
>
> And Ben Price turned and strolled down the street.
>
> —O. Henry,
> "A Retrieved Reformation"

From "A Retrieved Reformation"

Conflict

Ask students to discuss examples from stories they have previously read of characters that face external conflicts and characters that face internal conflicts. Have them explain what these conflicts were and how they affected the character.

YOUR TURN
Possible Response: The boy wants to escape and run through the door and down the hall. His own uncertainty is stopping him.

Change

Have students think about stories they have read as a class in which the main character underwent a dramatic change. Ask them to discuss what this change was and what they think caused it. Have them analyze how the change in this character affected his or her relationship with other characters in the story.

YOUR TURN
Possible Response: Both characters in this story change. Jimmy Valentine uses his talents to save a life instead of to rob a safe and, by doing so, jeopardizes his freedom. Ben Price comes to realize that people can change, and he believes that Jimmy Valentine is a changed man. The changes in these characters are caused by the situation in Jimmy Valentine's case and by Valentine's actions in Ben Price's case. Their relationship changes because Ben Price stops hunting down Jimmy Valentine and recognizes him as a new man, Ralph Spencer.

Endings

Have students think about endings of stories that stand out to them. What makes certain endings more memorable than others? Do they surprise? Shock? Give comfort? Students might also think about endings that have disappointed them. Encourage them to think about specific reasons why these endings were not satisfying. Were they unbelievable or unrelated to the story?

YOUR TURN

Students should think about how the ending completes the story's theme. Ask them what the author probably wanted readers to think or feel on reading this ending. You might invite students to write their own original endings to the story, like the student models featured on this page.

Wrapping Up the Plot . . .

Endings are an important part of a story. Often, they are what we remember most. A good ending may leave us with a strong image, feeling, or realization. Some endings are open-ended, sparking more questions, while others tie all the loose ends together with an action or event. Many people like surprise endings, in which an unexpected event or realization changes the outcome of the story.

YOUR TURN Read the ending from "What Do Fish Have to Do with Anything," by Avi. Willie has just found out his mother has had his homeless friend "removed." Ask yourself how you feel about the ending. Think about whether you would have ended the story differently.

Avi's story is open-ended. The reader wonders whether Willie will ever forgive his mother. Two seventh-graders wrote their own endings to this story. Ending 1 uses a surprise ending—the police have been looking for the man. In Ending 2, Willie and his mother look for the man. Think about how these different endings affect your feelings about the story and characters. Remember the power that endings have to turn a story around.

Willie glared at his mother. "No, you can't [see]. You're a fish. You live in a cave."

"Fish?" retorted Mrs. Markham. "What do fish have to do with anything? Willie, don't talk nonsense."

"My name isn't Willie. It's William. And I know how to keep from being unhappy. I do!" He was yelling now. "What a person needs is always more than they say! Always!"

He turned on his heel and walked back toward the school. At the corner he glanced back. His mother was following. He kept going. She kept following.

—Avi, "What Do Fish Have to Do with Anything?"

From "What Do Fish Have to Do with Anything?"

ENDING 1

"I called the police, and they told me that they've been looking for that man for some time now."

Willie looked at his mother. "It's not true!"

"People like that want to fool you. You shouldn't be so trusting."

Willie thought for a moment and stared off into the distance.

"I've been blind, just like the fish." With that, Willie went into the house and shut off the lights. He would sit in his cave and he didn't know for how long.

ENDING 2

"I want to go and look for him," said Willie.

"Don't be ridiculous," his mother replied.

"Please," Willie said. "He is my friend. He is a kind man."

His mother watched the tear rolling down Willie's cheek just before he brushed it away.

"Okay," she whispered. "We'll go look, but only for a short while."

Have you ever heard the phrase "read between the lines"? It means coming to a logical conclusion or **inference** about something based on evidence. As you read, look for clues in the text and read between the lines. The deeper meaning may not be as hidden as you think!

*M*aking Inferences

How to Apply the Skill

To **make inferences**, an active reader will:
• Pay attention to details and clues
• **Evaluate** based on what he or she knows
• **Visualize** descriptions
• **Connect** personally to the text

Try It Now!

Read and make inferences about the excerpt below.

> Outside [Mr. Johnson] found a beggar staring into the windows of the restaurant he had left and, carefully looking through the money in his pocket, Mr. Johnson approached the beggar and pressed some coins and a couple of bills into his hand.
> —Shirley Jackson, "One Ordinary Day, with Peanuts"

Here's how Leah uses the skill:

*"To **make inferences** I use details and clues from the text. As I read, I **evaluate** the information and develop my own opinions about Mr. Johnson's character. I can imagine how Mr. Johnson looks, and I can see myself acting in a similar way if I were in the same situation. From this excerpt, I can infer that Mr. Johnson is a generous and kind man. He is thoughtful and unselfish."*

Need More Help?

Remember that active readers use the essential reading strategies explained on page 4: • **visualize** • **predict** • **clarify** • **question** • **connect** • **evaluate** • **monitor**.

THE ACTIVE READER **347**

Objectives
• develop effective strategies for making inferences
• draw inferences such as conclusions or generalizations and support them with text evidence and experience

Teaching the Lesson

The strategies on this page will help students understand how to make inferences about characters, plot, and setting in the literature they read.

Presenting the Strategies

Help students understand the strategies by asking for volunteers to read them aloud. Emphasize to students that they will be using these strategies as they read the selections in this book.

• Choose several selections from this unit to read, and divide the class into small groups, assigning a different story to each group. Using the strategies outlined on this page, ask each group to make inferences about the setting or plot of each work.

• Ask each group to list the details and clues that provide crucial information about the setting or plot.

• Next, have them evaluate the information they have gathered, based on their own experiences and their past reading. Remind them to use the descriptions and details given by the author as support for their responses.

• Ask them to consider what they can infer about the setting or the plot in the selection based on the evidence in the text and their own life experience.

• Ask for a volunteer from each group to share with the class the group's conclusions and to explain how they used the strategies to arrive at their inferences.

Try it Now!

Possible Response: Mr. Johnson is compassionate; Mr. Johnson lives in an urban area that has different socioeconomic groups.

Use **Reading and Critical Thinking Transparencies**, p. 5, for additional support.

Objectives

1. understand and appreciate a **short story** (Literary Analysis)
2. understand role of **situational irony** in plot (Literary Analysis)
3. use the skill **making inferences** to understand the characters in the story (Active Reading)

Summary

When Mr. John Philip Johnson leaves his house one bright morning, he seems to radiate well-being. He walks leisurely uptown, stopping often to help people and share the peanuts and candy he purchases. Seeing a woman who is struggling to deal with both movers and a young child, Johnson offers to watch the boy and winds up helping them both. Later, he introduces two young people who are rushing to work and gives them money to enjoy the day together. Mr. Johnson continues his stroll throughout the day, dispensing peanuts and good deeds. At the end of the day, he returns home and greets his wife. She has spent her day quarreling with people, trying to get them arrested or fired from their jobs, and generally creating trouble for everyone around her. Because she is tired, her husband suggests that they change roles the following day. It will be her day to be good and his day to be mean-spirited.

Thematic Link

Readers are led to believe that Mr. Johnson is simply a kind and generous man. At the very end, however, the story takes a surprising turn. Strangely enough, Mr. Johnson's actions are not driven by kindness but by something else.

5-Minute Warm-Up

Daily Language SkillBuilder 🏴 **TEKS** 16B, 17G, 17H

Have students **proofread** the display sentences on page 341i and write them correctly. The sentences also appear on Transparency 11 of **Grammar Transparencies and Copymasters.**

One Ordinary Day, with Peanuts

Short Story by SHIRLEY JACKSON

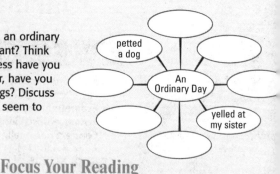

Connect to Your Life

Random Acts of Kindness What do you do on an ordinary day to make other people's lives more pleasant? Think about the past few days. What acts of kindness have you done for people you know? For strangers? Or, have you done something that hurt somebody's feelings? Discuss some positive and negative experiences that seem to take place on a typical day.

Build Background

Shirley Jackson has a distinctive writing style, and readers who have not read her stories before can benefit from knowing what to expect. Jackson's writing is matter-of-fact and unemotional. Her stories often appear to be about normal events, but the reader discovers that behind these apparently ordinary events may hide a twisted reality.

Drawing by Charles Addams. Copyright © 1946, 1974 The New Yorker Magazine, Inc.

WORDS TO KNOW Vocabulary Preview

ambiguous   impertinent   repress
genial   insatiable

Focus Your Reading

LITERARY ANALYSIS IRONY One form of **irony** occurs when there is a difference between what a reader expects to happen in a literary work and what actually happens. Ironic events also occur in life. For example, when you get a high grade on the one test that you were sure you were going to get a low grade on, it is a surprise—and it is **ironic**. Shirley Jackson is known for writing stories with ironic surprises like these. "One Ordinary Day, with Peanuts" is no exception.

ACTIVE READING MAKING INFERENCES While you read a story, you learn details that help you understand what is happening. Using these details and what you know from your own experience, you can figure out more than what the words actually say. A logical guess based on evidence and what you already know is called an **inference**. Every time you use evidence to figure something out, you are making inferences.

📓 **READER'S NOTEBOOK** As you read "One Ordinary Day, with Peanuts," record details on a chart that help you make inferences and the inferences you make.

Detail from Story	What I Can Infer
Mr. Johnson smiled at people he passed on the street.	Mr. Johnson is in a good mood; he likes people.

 See the Skills Trace at the beginning of the unit for information on TEKS covered in this lesson.

LESSON RESOURCES

UNIT THREE RESOURCE BOOK, pp. 4–10

ASSESSMENT
Formal Assessment, pp. 53–54
Teacher's Guide to Assessment and Portfolio Use
Test Generator

SKILLS TRANSPARENCIES AND COPYMASTERS
Literary Analysis
• Irony, TR 27 (for Paired Activity, p. 358)

Reading and Critical Thinking
• Making Inferences, TR 5 (for Thinking Through the Literature, p. 358)
Grammar
• Subject-Verb Agreement, CM 117–119 (for Mini Lesson, p. 352)
• Demonstrative Adjectives, CM 80–81 (for Mini Lesson, p. 360)

Vocabulary
• Synonyms, CM 45 (for Mini Lesson, p. 349)
• Analogies, CM 46 (for Mini Lesson, p. 355)

Communications
• Interviewing, TR 9 (for Mini Lesson, p. 353)

INTEGRATED TECHNOLOGY
Audio Library

Visit our website:
www.mcdougallittell.com

one ordinary day, with peanuts

shirley jackson

Mr. John Philip Johnson shut his front door behind him and went down his front steps into the bright morning with a feeling that all was well with the world on this best of all days, and wasn't the sun warm and good, and didn't his shoes feel comfortable after the resoling, and he knew that he had undoubtedly chosen the very precise tie that belonged with the day and the sun and his comfortable feet, and, after all, wasn't the world just a wonderful place? In spite of the fact that he was a small man, and though the tie was perhaps a shade vivid, Mr. Johnson radiated a feeling of well-being as he went down the steps and onto the dirty sidewalk, and he smiled at people who passed him, and some of them even smiled back. He stopped at the newsstand on the corner and bought his paper, saying, "*Good* morning" with real conviction to the man who sold him the paper and the two or three other people who were lucky enough to be buying papers when Mr. Johnson skipped up.

84 Madison (1982), Philip Reisman. Oil on canvas, 48¼″ × 22″, Edwin A. Ulrich Museum of Art, Wichita (Kansas) State University, Endowment Association Art Collection (84.7.3). **349**

ONE ORDINARY DAY, WITH PEANUTS **349**

Literary Analysis IRONY

Remind students that irony is the difference between what a reader expects and what actually happens. To prepare students for irony in the selection, ask them to try to make judgments and predictions as they read. They should use details in the selection and their own understanding of human nature to try to figure out the main idea of the story. When they reach the end of the story they can compare their expectations concerning Mr. Johnson with what actually happens.

 Use **Unit Three Resource Book,** p. 6 for more practice.

Active Reading MAKING INFERENCES

A Ask students to draw conclusions about the kind of man Mr. Johnson is and to support them with text evidence and experience.

Possible Responses: He is kind; he likes people; he does kind things; people who behave as he does are nice.

 Use **Unit Three Resource Book,** p. 5 for more practice.

ACTIVE READING

B **VISUALIZE** Encourage students to explain what they visualize. Their responses should be based on details in the text.

He remembered to fill his pockets with candy and peanuts, and then he set out to get himself uptown. He stopped in a flower shop and bought a carnation for his buttonhole, and stopped almost immediately afterward to give the carnation to a small child in a carriage, who looked at him dumbly, and then smiled, and Mr. Johnson smiled, and the child's mother looked at Mr. Johnson for a minute and then smiled, too.

When he had gone several blocks uptown, Mr. Johnson cut across the avenue and went along a side street, chosen at random; he did not follow the same route every morning, but preferred to pursue his eventful way in wide detours, more like a puppy than a man intent upon business. It happened this morning that halfway down the block a moving van was parked, and the furniture from an upstairs apartment stood half on the sidewalk, half on the steps, while an amused group of people loitered, examining the scratches on the tables and the worn spots on the chairs, and a harassed woman, trying to watch a young child and the movers and the furniture all at the same time, gave the clear impression of endeavoring to shelter her private life from the people staring at her belongings. Mr. Johnson stopped, and for a moment joined the crowd, then he came forward and, touching his hat civilly, said, "Perhaps I can keep an eye on your little boy for you?"

The woman turned and glared at him distrustfully, and Mr. Johnson added hastily, "We'll sit right here on the steps." He beckoned to the little boy, who hesitated and then responded agreeably to Mr. Johnson's <u>genial</u> smile. Mr. Johnson took out a handful of peanuts from his pocket and sat on the steps with the boy, who at first refused the peanuts on the grounds that his mother did not allow him to accept food from strangers; Mr. Johnson said that probably his mother had not

intended peanuts to be included, since elephants at the circus ate them, and the boy considered, and then agreed solemnly. They sat on the steps cracking peanuts in a comradely fashion, and Mr. Johnson said, "So you're moving?"

"Yep," said the boy.

"Where you going?"

"Vermont."

"Nice place. Plenty of snow there. Maple sugar, too; you like maple sugar?"

"Sure."

"Plenty of maple sugar in Vermont. You going to live on a farm?"

"Going to live with Grandpa."

"Grandpa like peanuts?"

"Sure."

"Ought to take him some," said Mr. Johnson, reaching into his pocket. "Just you and Mommy going?"

"Yep."

"Tell you what," Mr. Johnson said. "You take some peanuts to eat on the train."

The boy's mother, after glancing at them frequently, had seemingly decided that Mr. Johnson was trustworthy, because she had devoted herself wholeheartedly to seeing that the movers did not—what movers rarely do, but every housewife believes they will—crack a leg from her good table, or set a kitchen chair down on a lamp. Most of the furniture was loaded by now, and she was deep in that nervous stage when she knew there was something she had forgotten to pack—hidden away in the back of a closet somewhere, or left at a neighbor's and forgotten, or on the clothesline—and was trying to remember under stress what it was.

"This all, lady?" the chief mover said, completing her dismay.

Uncertainly, she nodded.

"Want to go on the truck with the furniture,

WORDS TO KNOW **genial** (jēn'yəl) *adj.* pleasant; friendly

350

---

onny?" the mover asked the boy, and laughed. The boy laughed, too, and said to Mr. Johnson, "I guess I'll have a good time at Vermont."

"Fine time," said Mr. Johnson, and stood up. "Have one more peanut before you go," he said to the boy.

The boy's mother said to Mr. Johnson, "Thank you so much; it was a great help to me."

"Nothing at all," said Mr. Johnson gallantly. "Where in Vermont are you going?"

The mother looked at the little boy accusingly, as though he had given away a secret of some importance, and said unwillingly, "Greenwich."

"Lovely town," said Mr. Johnson. He took out a card, and wrote a name on the back. "Very good friend of mine lives in Greenwich," he said. "Call on him for anything you need. His wife makes the best doughnuts in town," he added soberly to the little boy.

"Swell," said the little boy.

"Goodbye," said Mr. Johnson.

He went on, stepping happily with his new-shod[1] feet, feeling the warm sun on his back and on the top of his head. Halfway down the block he met a stray dog and fed him a peanut.

At the corner, where another wide avenue faced him, Mr. Johnson decided to go on uptown again. Moving with comparative laziness, he was passed on either side by people hurrying and frowning, and people brushed past him going the other way, clattering along to get somewhere quickly. Mr. Johnson stopped on every corner and waited patiently for the light to change, and he stepped out of the way of anyone who seemed to be in any particular hurry, but one young lady came too fast for him, and crashed wildly into him when he stooped to pat a kitten, which had run out onto the sidewalk from an apartment house and was now unable to get back through the rushing feet.

"Excuse me," said the young lady, trying frantically to pick up Mr. Johnson and hurry on at the same time, "terribly sorry."

The kitten, regardless now of danger, raced back to its home. "Perfectly all right," said Mr. Johnson, adjusting himself carefully. "You seem to be in a hurry."

"Of course I'm in a hurry," said the young lady. "I'm late."

he was extremely cross, and the frown between her eyes seemed well on its way to becoming permanent. She had obviously awakened late, because she had not spent any extra time in making herself look pretty, and her dress was plain and unadorned with collar or brooch, and her lipstick was noticeably crooked. She tried to brush past Mr. Johnson, but, risking her suspicious displeasure, he took her arm and said, "Please wait."

"Look," she said ominously, "I ran into you, and your lawyer can see my lawyer and I will gladly pay all damages and all inconveniences suffered therefrom, but please this minute let me go because *I am late.*"

ACTIVE READING

VISUALIZE If you close your eyes, can you form a picture of the young lady in your mind?

"Late for what?" said Mr. Johnson; he tried his winning smile on her but it did no more than keep her, he suspected, from knocking him down again.

"Late for work," she said between her teeth. "Late for my employment. I have a job, and if I am late I lose exactly so much an hour and I cannot really afford what your pleasant conversation is costing me, be it *ever* so pleasant."

---

1. **new-shod:** wearing new shoes.

Customizing Instruction

Multiple Learning Styles
Linguistic Learners
Encourage students to read the dialogue aloud the way they imagine the characters might say it. Their readings should reveal an understanding of characters and situations.

Less Proficient Readers
Use the following questions to guide students to understand the scene with the movers.

1. What is the woman trying to do and why is it hard?
   Answer: She is trying to watch the movers and the furniture at the same time.

2. What does Mr. Johnson do?
   Answer: He sits down with the boy and talks to him.

3. How does the woman respond at first, and finally?
   Possible Response: At first, she looks at Mr. Johnson distrustfully, but later she thanks him warmly.

Students Acquiring English
1 Help students understand the idiom *keep an eye on,* which means "to watch or take care of."
2 Since so much of this dialogue is in the form of fragments, you may wish to summarize it for students. Explain that Mr. Johnson is asking the boy about his plans for the future and giving the mother the name of someone who could help her in her new home.

Reading and Analyzing

Literary Analysis: POINT OF VIEW

A Ask students whose point of view is expressed here.

Answer: The point of view is that of the woman.

📖 Use **Literary Analysis Transparencies,** p. 22, for additional support.

Reading Skills and Strategies: COMPARING

B To help students compare ideas across texts, ask students to compare this scene with the one in which the woman and her child are moving. What similarities do students see?

Possible Responses: Both women do not trust him at first; Mr. Johnson gets both women to smile and listen to him.

Active Reading | MAKING INFERENCES |

C Ask students to infer why the man initially behaves as he does toward Mr. Johnson and why he continues to listen to him.

Possible Responses: He doesn't know what he wants; he thinks that he's a beggar; he is curious.

| ACTIVE READING |

D QUESTION Students must use their own knowledge to comprehend why people are wary of Mr. Johnson. Many will distrust him because they fear that he wants something or is hiding something.

"I'll pay for it," said Mr. Johnson. Now, these were magic words, not necessarily because they were true, or because she seriously expected Mr. Johnson to pay for anything, but because Mr. Johnson's flat statement, obviously innocent of irony, could not be, coming from Mr. Johnson, anything but the statement of a responsible and truthful and respectable man.

"What *do* you mean?" she asked.

"I said that since I am obviously responsible for your being late, I shall certainly pay for it."

"Don't be silly," she said, and for the first time the frown disappeared. "*I* wouldn't expect you to pay for anything—a few minutes ago I was offering to pay *you*. Anyway," she added, almost smiling, "it *was* my fault."

"What happens if you don't go to work?" She stared. "I don't get paid."

"Precisely," said Mr. Johnson.

"What do you mean, precisely? If I don't show up at the office exactly twenty minutes ago I lose a dollar and twenty cents an hour, or two cents a minute or"—she thought—"almost a dime for the time I've spent talking to you."

Mr. Johnson laughed, and finally she laughed, too. "You're late already," he pointed out. "Will you give me another four cents' worth?"

"I don't understand why."

"You'll see," Mr. Johnson promised. He led her over to the side of the walk, next to the buildings, and said, "Stand here," and went out into the rush of people going both ways. Selecting and considering, as one who must make a choice involving perhaps whole years of lives, he estimated the people going by. Once he almost moved, and then at the last minute thought better of it and drew back. Finally, from half a block away, he saw what he wanted, and moved out into the center of the traffic to intercept a young man, who was hurrying, and dressed as though he had awakened late, and frowning.

"Oof," said the young man, because Mr. Johnson had thought of no better way to

---

Teaching Options

SUBJECT-VERB AGREEMENT

Instruction Remind students that a noun or pronoun that stands for one person, place, thing, or idea is singular, and a noun or pronoun that stands for more than one is plural. A word's number refers to the difference between singular and plural. Tell them that verbs also have singular and plural forms. In a sentence, the verb must always agree in number with its subject. Have students read the highlighted passage on page 352. Point out that *were* is a plural verb that agrees with the

🔵 **Mini Lesson** **Grammar** **TEKS 17C** **TAAS Writing Obj. 6**

plural subjects *these* and *they*. Ask students to replace *these* and *they* with the word *it*. How would they rewrite each verb to agree with the subject *it*? Students should understand that *were* would have to be changed to *was*.

Exercises Have students choose the correct verb to complete each sentence.

1. His unusual behavior (surprise, surprises) many strangers. *(surprises)*

2. Mr. Johnson's actions (are, is) difficult to understand. *(are)*

3. They (sit, sits) at home and compare stories. *(sit)*

4. I (were, was) interested in reading other stories by Shirley Jackson. *(was)*

📖 Use **Grammar Transparencies and Copymasters,** p. 119.

📘 Use McDougal Littell's *Language Network,* Chapter 9, for more instruction and practice in subject-verb agreement.

intercept anyone than the one the young woman had unwittingly used upon him. Where do you think you're going?" the young man demanded from the sidewalk.

"I want to speak to you," said Mr. Johnson ominously.

The young man got up nervously, dusting himself and eyeing Mr. Johnson. "What for?" he said. "What'd I do?"

"That's what bothers me most about people nowadays," Mr. Johnson complained broadly to the people passing. "No matter whether they've done anything or not, they always figure someone's after them. About what you're going to do," he told the young man.

"Listen," said the young man, trying to brush past him, "I'm late, and I don't have any time to listen. Here's a dime, now get going."

"Thank you," said Mr. Johnson, pocketing the dime. "Look," he said, "what happens if you stop running?"

"I'm late," said the young man, still trying to get past Mr. Johnson, who was unexpectedly clinging.

"How much you make an hour?" Mr. Johnson demanded.

"A Communist,[2] are you?" said the young man. "Now will you please let me—"

"No," said Mr. Johnson insistently, "*how* much?"

"Dollar fifty," said the young man. "And *now* will you—"

"You like adventure?"

The young man stared, and, staring, found himself caught and held by Mr. Johnson's genial smile; he almost smiled back and then repressed it and made an effort to tear away. "I got to *hurry*," he said.

"Mystery? You like surprises? Unusual and exciting events?"

"You selling something?"

"Sure," said Mr. Johnson. "You want to take a chance?"

The young man hesitated, looking longingly up the avenue toward what might have been his destination and then, when Mr. Johnson said, "I'll pay for it" with his own peculiar convincing emphasis, turned and said, "Well, okay. But I got to *see* it first, what I'm buying."

Mr. Johnson, breathing hard, led the young man over to the side, where the girl was standing; she had been watching with interest Mr. Johnson's capture of the young man and now, smiling timidly, she looked at Mr. Johnson as though prepared to be surprised at nothing.

Mr. Johnson reached into his pocket and took out his wallet. "Here," he said, and handed a bill to the girl. "This about equals your day's pay."

"But no," she said, surprised in spite of herself. "I mean, I *couldn't*."

"Please do not interrupt," Mr. Johnson told her. "And *here*," he said to the young man, "this will take care of *you*." The young man accepted the bill dazedly, but said, "Probably counterfeit" to the young woman out of the side of his mouth.

ACTIVE READING

QUESTION Why are most people wary of Mr. Johnson?

"Now," Mr. Johnson went on, disregarding the young man, "what is your name, miss?"

"Kent," she said helplessly. "Mildred Kent."

"Fine," said Mr. Johnson. "And you, sir?"

"Arthur Adams," said the young man stiffly.

"Splendid," said Mr. Johnson. "Now, Miss Kent, I would like you to meet Mr. Adams.

---

2. **Communist:** At the time the story was written (1951), Communists—people who believed that workers should own all businesses—were thought to be everywhere, trying to bring down the United States by convincing workers that they were underpaid, oppressed, and should control the government.

WORDS
TO   **repress** (rǐ-prěs') v. to hold something back
KNOW

353

Multiple Learning Styles
Mathematical Learners

1 Ask students how long Mr. Johnson and the woman must have talked, according to her calculations, and how long Mr. Johnson thought he could talk for four cents' worth of time.
Answer: five minutes; two minutes

Kinesthetic Learners

2 Invite students to pantomime this scene, which may help them capture its stop-go quality.

Students Acquiring English

3 Break this scene into three short episodes for students: one, when Mr. Johnson first bumps into the man; two, when the young man keeps trying to leave after giving Mr. Johnson a dime; and three, when the young man listens to Mr. Johnson and walks with him to where the girl waits.

Less Proficient Readers

Help students recognize that the woman is just standing and watching while the action on this page takes place. Explain that the young man wants to leave, but Mr. Johnson keeps stopping him.

Mini Lesson **Speaking and Listening** **TEKS 11B**

INTERVIEWS

Prepare Remind students that an interview is an effective way to gather information. The interviewer should be well prepared with questions that will elicit the kind of information that the interviewer wants or needs. The subject should listen carefully and respond as thoughtfully and completely as possible. Have students work with partners to interpret text ideas through enactment. One should act as the interviewer; the other as one of the characters that Mr. Johnson encounters either in the story or during the next day. The interviewer should prepare a list of questions for the character about what happened and what impressions the person had of Mr. Johnson. From the responses, the interviewer should be able to tell on which day the subject met Mr. Johnson.

Present Students may enjoy developing their interviews in separate teams and then presenting them during a single class.

BLOCK SCHEDULING This activity is particularly well suited for longer class periods.

Use **Communications Transparencies and Copymasters**, p. 9, for additional support.

ACTIVE READING

A **CLARIFY** Possible Response: The couple decides to follow Mr. Johnson's suggestion and use his money to do something fun.

Literary Analysis: SETTING

B Remind students that the setting is the time and place in which a story takes place. Ask students what they can infer about the setting of this story. Have them give reasons for their responses.
Possible Response: The story takes place in a large city. It is set in an earlier era, judging by what things cost and by peoples' willingness to trust strangers.

Literary Analysis IRONY

C Ask students if this is the type of behavior they might expect from Mr. Johnson. Have them give reasons for their responses.
Possible Response: Most students will say yes, because he is always doing kind things and giving things away.

ACTIVE READING

D **MAKE INFERENCES** Possible Responses: He likes to see people happy; he is a good person; he has a son and daughter of his own, and so he likes to treat young people with generosity; he does not place himself before the happiness of others.

Mr. Adams, Miss Kent."

Miss Kent stared, wet her lips nervously, made a gesture as though she might run, and said, "How do you do?"

Mr. Adams straightened his shoulders, scowled at Mr. Johnson, made a gesture as though *he* might run, and said, "How do you do?"

"Now, *this*," said Mr. Johnson, taking several bills from his wallet, "should be enough for the day for both of you. I would suggest, perhaps, Coney Island—although I personally am not fond of the place—or perhaps a nice lunch somewhere, and dancing, or a matinee, or even a movie, although take care to choose a really *good* one; there are *so* many bad movies these days. You might," he said, struck with an inspiration, "visit the Bronx Zoo, or the Planetarium. Anywhere, as a matter of fact," he concluded, "that you would like to go. Have a nice time."

1 As he started to move away, Arthur Adams, breaking from his dumbfounded stare, said, "But see here, mister, you *can't* do this. Why—how do you know—I mean, *we* don't even know—I mean, how do you know we won't just take the money and not do what you said?"

"You've taken the money," Mr. Johnson said. "You don't have to follow any of my suggestions. You may know something you prefer to do—perhaps a museum, or something."

"But suppose I just run away with it and leave her here?"

"I know you won't," said Mr. Johnson gently, "because you remembered to ask *me* that. Goodbye," he added, and went on.

As he stepped up the street, conscious of the sun on his head and his good shoes, he heard from somewhere behind him the young man saying, "Look, you know you don't *have* to if

you don't want to," and the girl saying, "But unless *you* don't want to. . ." Mr. Johnson smiled to himself and then thought that he had better hurry along; when he wanted to he could move very quickly, and before the young woman had gotten around to saying, "Well, *I* will if *you* will," Mr. Johnson was several blocks away and had already stopped twice, once to help a lady lift several large packages into a taxi, and once to hand a peanut to a sea gull. By this time he was in an area of large stores and many more people, and he was buffeted constantly from either side by people hurrying and cross and late and sullen. Once he offered a peanut to a man who asked him for a dime, and once he offered a peanut to a bus driver who had stopped his bus at an intersection and had opened the window next to his seat and put out his head as though longing for fresh air and the comparative quiet of the traffic. The man wanting a dime took the peanut because Mr. Johnson had wrapped a dollar bill around it, but the bus driver took the peanut and asked ironically, "You want a transfer, Jack?"

On a busy corner Mr. Johnson encountered two young people—for one minute he thought they might be Mildred Kent and Arthur Adams—who were eagerly scanning a newspaper, their backs pressed against a storefront to avoid the people passing, their heads bent together. Mr. Johnson, whose curiosity was <u>insatiable</u>, leaned onto the storefront next to them and peeked over the

once He offered a peanut to a man who asked Him for a dime.

Teaching Options

Cross Curricular Link **Science**

PEANUTS Approximately a third of the people with food allergies are allergic to peanuts, and some allergic reactions to peanuts are so severe that they prove fatal. On the other hand, peanuts are also highly nutritious and useful. George Washington Carver (1861?-1943), an African-American scientist, developed about 300 products derived from peanuts when he was the director of agricultural research at Tuskegee Normal and Industrial Institute.

Have one group of students research the nutritional value of peanuts. Have another group research information about Carver and some of the products that he developed. Encourage them to locate information relevant to research questions using multiple sources, including electronic texts and print resources. Reports can be shared orally or by means of posters or bulletin board displays.

man's shoulder; they were scanning the Apartments Vacant columns.

Mr. Johnson remembered the street where the woman and her little boy were going to Vermont and he tapped the man on the shoulder and said amiably, "Try down on West Seventeen. About the middle of the block people moved out this morning."

"Say, what do you—" said the man, and then, seeing Mr. Johnson clearly, "Well, thanks. Where did you say?"

"West Seventeen," said Mr. Johnson. "About the middle of the block." He smiled again and said, "Good luck."

"Thanks," said the man.

"Thanks," said the girl as they moved off.

"Goodbye," said Mr. Johnson.

He lunched alone in a pleasant restaurant, where the food was rich, and only Mr. Johnson's excellent digestion could encompass two of their whipped-cream-and-chocolate-and-rum-cake pastries for dessert. He had three cups of coffee, tipped the waiter largely, and went out into the street again into the wonderful sunlight, his shoes still comfortable and fresh on his feet. Outside he found a beggar staring into the windows of the restaurant he had left and, carefully looking through the money in his pocket, Mr. Johnson approached the beggar and pressed some coins and a couple of bills into his hand. "It's the price of the veal cutlet lunch plus tip," said Mr. Johnson. "Goodbye."

After his lunch he rested; he walked into the nearest park and fed peanuts to the pigeons. It was late afternoon by the time he was ready to start back downtown, and he had refereed two checker games, and watched a small boy and girl whose mother had fallen asleep and awakened with surprise and fear that turned to amusement when she saw Mr. Johnson. He had given away almost all of his candy, and

had fed all the rest of his peanuts to the pigeons, and it was time to go home. Although the late afternoon sun was pleasant, and his shoes were still entirely comfortable, he decided to take a taxi downtown.

 He had a difficult time catching a taxi, because he gave up the first three or four empty ones to people who seemed to need them more; finally, however, he stood alone on the corner and—almost like netting a frisky fish—he hailed desperately until he succeeded in catching a cab that had been proceeding with haste uptown, and seemed to draw in toward Mr. Johnson against its own will.

"Mister," the cabdriver said as Mr. Johnson climbed in, "I figured you was an omen, like. I wasn't going to pick you up at all."

"Kind of you," said Mr. Johnson ambiguously.

"If I'd of let you go it would of cost me ten bucks," said the driver. "Really?" said Mr. Johnson.

"Yeah," said the driver. "Guy just got out of the cab, he turned around and give me ten bucks, said take this and bet it in a hurry on a horse named Vulcan,³ right away."

"Vulcan?" said Mr. Johnson, horrified. "A fire sign on a Wednesday?"

"What?" said the driver. "Anyway, I said to myself, if I got no fare between here and there I'd bet the ten, but if anyone looked like they needed a cab I'd take it as an omen and I'd take the ten home to the wife."

---
3. **Vulcan:** the god of fire in Roman mythology.

ACTIVE READING

MAKE INFERENCES
What inferences can you make about Mr. Johnson's character?

WORDS TO KNOW

insatiable (ĭn-sā′shə-bəl) *adj.* impossible to satisfy (p. 354)
ambiguous (ăm-bĭg′yōō-əs) *adj.* can be understood in more than one way

355

ACTIVE READING

A **PREDICTING** Responses will vary. Students should explain their ideas.

Active Reading | MAKING INFERENCES

B To help students analyze characters, including their relationships, ask students what kind of relationship the Johnsons have and what details show this.

Possible Responses: They seem to get along well. She calls him dear and smiles and kisses him, asking about his day. He remembers the cheesecake.

C Ask students how they would sum up Mrs. Johnson's day. Have them draw inferences such as conclusions or generalizations and support them with text evidence and experience.

Possible Responses: She spent her days doing bad deeds; she created trouble.

Reading Skills and Strategies:
CLARIFYING

D Ask students to interpret the text in these two paragraphs, especially Mr. Johnson's question, "Want to change over tomorrow?" Students should support their responses by referring to relevant aspects of text and to their own experiences.

Possible Response: Mr. Johnson is asking, "Do you want to switch roles?" This is based on what readers know about each person's day, where one was good and the other bad.

Literary Analysis | IRONY

E What is ironic about this ending?

Possible Response: Readers discover that Mr. Johnson is not necessarily a nice man, but merely taking on a role. This is a twist that turns out to be the opposite of what most readers expect.

"You were very right," said Mr. Johnson heartily. "This is Wednesday, you would have lost your money. Monday, yes, or even Saturday. But never never never a fire sign on a Wednesday. Sunday would have been good, now."

"Vulcan don't run on Sunday," said the driver.

"You wait till another day," said Mr. Johnson. "Down this street, please, driver. I'll get off on the next corner."

"He *told* me Vulcan, though," said the driver.

"I'll tell you," said Mr. Johnson, hesitating with the door of the cab half open. "You take that ten dollars and I'll give you another ten dollars to go with it, and you go right ahead and bet that money on any Thursday on any horse that has a name indicating . . . let me see, Thursday . . . well, grain. Or any growing food."

"Grain?" said the driver. "You mean a horse named, like, Wheat or something?"

"Certainly," said Mr. Johnson. "Or, as a matter of fact, to make it even easier, any horse whose name includes the letters C, R, L. Perfectly simple."

"Tall Corn?" said the driver, a light in his eye. "You mean a horse named, like, Tall Corn?"

"Absolutely," said Mr. Johnson. "Here's your money."

"Tall Corn," said the driver. "Thank *you*, mister."

"Goodbye," said Mr. Johnson.

He was on his own corner, and went straight up to his apartment. He let himself in and called, "Hello?" and Mrs. Johnson answered from the kitchen, "Hello, dear, aren't you early?"

"Took a taxi home," Mr. Johnson said. "I remembered the cheesecake, too. What's for dinner?"

Mrs. Johnson came out of the kitchen and kissed him; she was a comfortable woman, and smiling as Mr. Johnson smiled. "Hard day?" she asked.

"Not very," said Mr. Johnson, hanging his coat in the closet. "How about you?"

"So-so," she said. She stood in the kitchen doorway while he settled into his easy chair and took off his good shoes and took out the paper he had bought that morning. "Here and there," she said.

"I didn't do so badly," Mr. Johnson said. "Couple young people."

"Fine," she said. "I had a little nap this afternoon, took it easy most of the day. Went into a department store this morning and accused the woman next to me of shoplifting, and had the store detective pick her up. Sent three dogs to the pound—*you* know, the usual thing. Oh, and listen," she added, remembering.

"What?" asked Mr. Johnson.

"Well," she said, "I got onto a bus and asked the driver for a transfer, and when he helped someone else first I said that he was impertinent, and quarreled with him. And then I said why wasn't he in the army,[4] and I said it loud enough for everyone to hear, and I took his number and I turned in a complaint. Probably got him fired."

"Fine," said Mr. Johnson. "But you do look tired. Want to change over tomorrow?"

"I *would* like to," she said. "I could do with a change."

"Right," said Mr. Johnson. "What's for dinner?"

"Veal cutlet."

"Had it for lunch," said Mr. Johnson. ❖

---

4. **"why wasn't he in the army . . .":** In 1951 the United States was in the middle of the Korean War, and thousands of males volunteered or were drafted for army duty.

WORDS TO KNOW
impertinent (ĭm-pûr′tn-ənt) *adj.* not having good manners; rude

356

Teaching Options

✓ **Assessment** **Standardized Test Practice** TEKS 10H, 10K TAAS Reading Obj. 5

MAKING INFERENCES AND DRAWING CONCLUSIONS In some standardized tests, students are asked to draw inferences such as conclusions or generalizations and support them with text evidence and experience. After students have read this page, write the following question on the board or read it aloud:

Based on information in the story, the reader can tell that:

A. the young man is a responsible and truthful person.

B. the young woman is frequently late.

C. Mr. Johnson is determined to introduce the young man to the young woman.

D. the young man and the woman are both underpaid.

Lead students through the process of choosing the best answer. Help them recognize that no evidence supports answers A, B, or D. However, several details, including Mr. Johnson's verbal insistence, support the third conclusion. Therefore, the best answer is C.

Autobiographical (1954), Moses Soyer. Courtesy of ACA Galleries, New York.

Students Acquiring English

1 If students do not understand these two paragraphs they will not understand the story. Help them understand what it means to accuse someone of shoplifting, send dogs to the pound, and get someone fired.

Less Proficient Readers

2 Help students understand these passages by directing attention to the line "*You* know, the usual thing."

Multiple Learning Styles
Linguistic Learners

Students might enjoy reading Mrs. Johnson's little speech aloud, noting how she goes from her little nap to accusing a woman of shoplifting.

Mini Lesson   Viewing and Representing   TEKS 23B

Autobiographical
by Moses Soyer

ART APPRECIATION Moses Soyer, a Russian-American artist, was influenced by the Ashcan school, a movement that emphasized realistic details of ordinary life and common people.

Instruction To help students compare and contrast print media with a written story, point out that an illustrator recreates story details in pictorial form. However, an original painting may also be used as an illustration if it contains important story details or recreates the mood, setting, or some other literary element.

Application: Have students study the picture, looking for details that are like those in the story and details that are different. Have students jot down their responses and then have a general discussion of the likenesses and differences.

Possible Responses: Likenesses: a husband and wife; urban, comfortable setting; the people seem to be thinking, as if planning what they will do. Differences: figures are static, while the story has action; the contrast between the characters is not obvious; the picture lacks the drama of the story.

GUIDING STUDENT RESPONSE

Connect to the Literature

1. Accept all reasonable responses.

Comprehension Check

• He keeps an eye on her little boy for her.
• He is friendly and helpful to the young couple who are looking for an apartment.
• They alternate the ways in which they treat people, one is kind while the other is mean.

 Use Selection Quiz
Unit Three Resource Book, p. 10.

Think Critically

2. Answers will vary. Students might guess that their behavior gives them a sense of power and control over people and situations. Perhaps they've been hurt or rejected by people in the past, and that's why they play a game that keeps them distanced from people and real life.

 Use **Reading and Critical Thinking Transparencies,** p. 5, for additional support.

3. Possible Response: The story is both serious and humorous. Mr. Johnson's kindnesses seem puzzling to the point of being funny. But the story is serious when it points out the ways in which people don't take seriously the hurt they inflict on others.

4. Responses will vary. Students should explain the perceptions they had of the story when they began reading and how these perceptions did or did not change. Students should explain why they were or were not fooled by Mr. Johnson.

Literary Analysis

Irony Students' charts should reflect the unexpectedness of the ending. Their entries into the right-hand column might include something similar to the following: Mr. Johnson will act unkindly the next day; Mrs. Johnson described her day's unkindnesses to her husband.

 Use **Literary Analysis Transparencies,** p. 27, for additional support.

Connect to the Literature

1. **What Do You Think?**
What was your reaction to the ending of the story? Explain.

Comprehension Check
• How does Mr. Johnson help the woman who is moving?
• What is Mr. Johnson's attitude toward the young couple?
• Why do Mr. and Mrs. Johnson seem to spend most days separately?

Think Critically

2. **ACTIVE READING MAKING INFERENCES** Review the chart you made in your 📖 **READER'S NOTEBOOK.** Why do you think Mr. and Mrs. Johnson spend their days the way they do?

> **THINK ABOUT**
> • the mood each is in at the end of the day
> • what values you think they have
> • what they may gain from their deceptive behavior

3. Would you describe the story as serious or humorous? Explain your answer.

4. Did its ending change your understanding of the story? Why or why not?

Extend Interpretations

5. **Critic's Corner** One of the members of our student advisory board wrote that the story "seemed like a fairy tale until almost the end. Then I thought the irony was great." Do you agree or disagree with this observation? Explain your reasoning.

6. **Connect to Life** Do you feel kind and friendly toward people on certain days? On other days do you feel less sociable and prefer to be alone? Discuss your ideas in class.

358 UNIT THREE PART 1: SURPRISING TURNS

Literary Analysis

IRONY One type of irony is **situational irony,** or the contrast between what a reader or character expects and what actually exists or happens. For example, in "One Ordinary Day, with Peanuts," Mr. Johnson performs acts of kindness for strangers throughout the story, but at the end the reader sees him as he really is: a dishonest person who was just pretending to be nice. This example of situational irony, an unexpected twist at the end of a story, is also an example of a **surprise ending.**

Paired Activity Working with a partner, make a chart to explain examples of situational irony in "One Ordinary Day, with Peanuts." For each character, identify what the reader expects to happen and what actually happens.

Situational Irony	
What I expect to happen	**What actually happens**
Mr. Johnson will repeat his day's kindnesses the next day.	
Mrs. Johnson will describe her day's kindnesses to Mr. Johnson.	

Extend Interpretations

5. **Critic's Corner** This question is well suited for gifted students. If you wish to make this question easier, you can first remind students of the elements of fairy tales, which include flat characters and events that are unlikely to happen in real life. Responses might include Johnson's unrelenting cheerful generosity to strangers, which is seldom seen.

6. **Connect to Life** Most students' answers will reflect the fact that their moods change and that they feel more sociable on some days than on others. A few students may usually feel either sociable or unsociable.

Writing Options

1. Dialogue Toward the end of the story, Mrs. Johnson mentions a few of the mean things she did during the day, such as falsely accusing someone of shoplifting. Write a dialogue that shows what might have been said between Mrs. Johnson and one of her victims. Place your piece in your **Working Portfolio.**

2. Random Act of Kindness Write a description of a random act of kindness you have done for a family member, a neighbor, or a friend. Explain the circumstances of your decision to perform a kind act at random.

Activities & Explorations

1. Dramatic Scene Suppose it is now the end of the next day in the story, a day during which Mr. and Mrs. Johnson have switched their behaviors. With a partner, act out the two of them talking about their day—what they did and how they felt about what they did. ~ **PERFORMING**

2. Comic Strip Choose a scene from the story and present it in the form of a cartoon or comic strip. ~ **ART**

Inquiry & Research

Defining Trust How do you know when someone is trustworthy? Is it the way the person looks? The way the person acts? Sometimes it is hard to explain why we trust one person and not another. Look up the word *trust* in the dictionary. Write down two or three different definitions on a sheet of paper. Show the definitions to three or four people. Do a survey of your findings.

Vocabulary in Action

EXERCISE A: ASSESSMENT PRACTICE On a separate sheet of paper, write the letter of the word that most closely matches the underlined word in meaning.

1. Mr. Johnson had a <u>genial</u> smile on his face as he left the house.
a. cheerful **c.** big
b. intelligent **d.** sarcastic

2. The young man couldn't <u>repress</u> a smile in response to Mr. Johnson.
a. recall **c.** comprehend
b. restrain **d.** reduce

3. Wishing to seem sincere, Mr. Johnson gave the cab driver an <u>ambiguous</u> answer.
a. huge **c.** unclear
b. quick **d.** honest

4. Mr. Johnson always wanted to know things; his curiosity was <u>insatiable</u>.
a. unsatisfiable **c.** unstable
b. unrelaxed **d.** understandable

5. Mrs. Johnson accused the bus driver of having bad manners and being <u>impertinent</u>.
a. important **c.** rude
b. temporary **d.** indignant

EXERCISE B In small groups, tell a "round robin" story. One person starts a story and keeps talking until he or she has spoken one vocabulary word. The next person continues the story, and so on, until all vocabulary words have been used.

Building Vocabulary
For an in-depth study on synonyms, see p. 631.

WORDS TO KNOW					
	ambiguous	genial	impertinent	insatiable	repress

ONE ORDINARY DAY, WITH PEANUTS **359**

---

1. Dialogue Students' dialogue should show that Mrs. Johnson is the person who instigates trouble. To get students started on this assignment, ask them what Mrs. Johnson might have said or done to get someone arrested for shoplifting or to get dogs sent to the pound, for example.

2. Random Act of Kindness If students are unable to think of an event, suggest that they describe one that they would like to perform. Have them explain why they would like to do something nice for this person.

Use **Writing Transparencies,** p. 25, for additional support.

Activities & Explorations

1. Dramatic Scene To help students get started, first have them brainstorm good and bad deeds that Mr. and Mrs. Johnson might have performed. Then have students work in pairs to dramatize their discussion.

Use **Communications Transparencies and Copymasters,** p. 13, for additional support.

2. Comic Strip To make this more challenging, encourage students to make their cartoons similar in style to specific ones that they admire.

Inquiry & Research

Defining Trust Encourage students to collect definitions from a variety of dictionaries, including on-line dictionaries and any that provide word histories. When students finish the survey, they can discuss connotations that different definitions have. They may even find it useful to do a semantic features analysis.

Vocabulary in Action

Exercise A
1. a
2. b
3. c
4. a
5. c

Exercise B
Students should use all vocabulary words correctly, and each student should get a turn.

 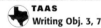

PREFIXES *in-, im-, il-, ir-*
Instruction Tell students that the prefix *in-* means either "not" or "in." In spelling certain words, variations of *in-* are used. For example, before roots or base words beginning with *b*, *m*, or *p*, *in-* becomes *im-*. Before *l*, *in-* usually becomes *il-*, and before *r*, *in-* usually becomes *ir-*.

in + satiable = insatiable
in + pertinent = impertinent

Exercises Have students add the prefix *in-, im-, il-,* or *ir-* to the following roots and base words.

1. responsible
2. logical
3. plant
4. active
5. balance
6. replaceable
7. luminate
8. fect
9. practical
10. rational
11. clude
12. polite

Have students look for more words that fit this pattern and add these words to their personal word lists.

Use **Unit Three Resource Book,** p. 9 for more practice.

ONE ORDINARY DAY, WITH PEANUTS **359**

Grammar in Context

WRITING EXERCISE

Possible Responses:

1. The girl gave Mr. Johnson a <u>suspicious</u> look.
2. The girl carried an <u>enormous</u> purse.
3. Her scowl looked <u>permanent</u>.
4. The <u>impatient</u> taxi driver wanted a <u>swift</u> horse.

CONNECT TO THE LITERATURE

Students' paragraphs should contain three or four sentences describing animals in a zoo. The nouns should be circled and the adjectives underlined.

 Use **Writing Transparencies,** p. 15, for additional support.

Shirley Jackson

This story appeared in the 1956 volume of *The Best American Short Stories.* Shirley Jackson's friends and critics used to describe the reclusive writer as "Madame of Mystery" and "Queen of the Macabre." Some even joked that she wrote with a broomstick, referring to the strangeness of some stories.

Author Activity

Edgar Allan Poe Award Asks students to research the award and the reasons why people win it. They may enjoy learning about other writers who have won it.

Grammar in Context: Using Vivid and Precise Adjectives

Shirley Jackson vividly sets the scene for "One Ordinary Day, with Peanuts" in the first sentence.

> Mr. John Philip Johnson shut his front door behind him and went down his front steps into the bright morning with a feeling that all was well with the world on this best of all days, and wasn't the sun warm and good, and didn't his shoes feel comfortable after the resoling. . . .

An **adjective** is a word that modifies a noun or pronoun; that is, an adjective adds information about the noun or pronoun that makes it more specific and precise. In this excerpt the adjectives not only describe what kind of day it was, they make clear that the main character, Mr. Johnson, is in a very good mood.

WRITING EXERCISE Replace the underlined phrase with one or two precise, vivid adjectives.

Example: *Original* The boy's mother decided Mr. Johnson was <u>somebody she could trust.</u>

Rewritten The boy's mother decided Mr. Johnson was trustworthy.

1. The girl gave Mr. Johnson a look <u>that said she thought she couldn't trust him.</u>
2. The girl carried a purse <u>into which she could fit lots of things.</u>
3. Her scowl looked <u>like it was going to last forever.</u>
4. The taxidriver <u>who was in a hurry</u> wanted a horse <u>that could run fast.</u>

Connect to the Literature Suppose that the young couple take Mr. Johnson's advice and visit a zoo. Using precise, vivid adjectives, write three or four sentences describing the animals they might see. Circle your nouns and underline your adjectives.

Grammar Handbook Using Modifiers Effectively, p. R70

"I will not tolerate having these other worlds called imaginary."

Shirley Jackson
1919–1965

Rebel with a Cause Shirley Jackson was born to a wealthy San Francisco family. From an early age, she rebelled against what she considered her family's selfish lifestyle. Instead of taking part in social events, she would disappear into her journals. Here, she would strike out against the snobbish attitudes she witnessed among the wealthy.

Home in Vermont After she married, Jackson moved to a small town in Vermont, where she raised her family. She continued to write essays, novels, and short stories. She almost never gave interviews but was generous in advising young writers about how to turn experience into writing.

An Early Death For much of her life, Jackson suffered from stress and anxiety. In her later years, her physical and mental health declined. Jackson was only 45 years old when she died.

AUTHOR ACTIVITY

Edgar Allan Poe Award In 1961 Jackson was honored with the Edgar Allan Poe Award for her short story "Louisa, Please." Use an encyclopedia or the Internet to find out more about this award—what it is, why it is significant, and how recipients are chosen.

Teaching Options

 Mini Lesson **Grammar** **TEKS 17D** 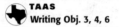 **TAAS Writing Obj. 3, 4, 6**

DEMONSTRATIVE ADJECTIVES

Instruction Explain that students can use demonstrative adjectives—*this, that, these,* and *those*—appropriately to make writing precise. For example, when Mrs. Johnson says that she had a nap "this afternoon," her husband knows which afternoon she means. The demonstrative adjectives *this* and *that* modify singular nouns; *these* and *those* modify plural nouns or pronouns. The words *this, that, these,* and *those* are not always demonstrative adjectives. When they stand alone and do not modify other words, they are demonstrative *pronouns.* Point out that *this* and *these* usually refer to things that are close by whereas *that* and *those* refer to things that are farther away.

Application Have students use each demonstrative adjective in a sentence.

 Use **Unit Three Resource Book,** p. 8.
Use **Grammar Transparencies and Copymasters,** p. 80.

Use McDougal Littell's *Language Network,* Chapter 5, for more instruction and practice in demonstrative adjectives.

Amigo Brothers

Short Story by PIRI THOMAS

"Both fighters had a lot of psyching up to do before the big fight."

 See the Skills Trace at the beginning of the unit for information on TEKS covered in this lesson.

Connect to Your Life

Suppose that you have to compete against a good friend in order to win something you really want. Maybe you and your friend are competing on opposing teams for a championship trophy or are running against each other in a class election. What would it be like to be your friend's rival? Share your ideas with the class.

Build Background

CONNECT TO HISTORY In "Amigo Brothers" two good friends compete against each other in a boxing tournament. Boxing, one of the oldest forms of athletic competition, was popular in Sumeria more than 5,000 years ago. It was later incorporated as an event in the Olympic games of ancient Greece.

For most of the history of the sport, boxers fought without gloves. Then, in the mid-1860s, the marquis of Queensberry, an English nobleman, helped to establish rules to protect boxers from serious injury. The Queensberry Rules called for the use of padded gloves, three-minute rounds separated by one-minute rest periods, and a ten-second count for a knockout.

Today, boxers are classified and matched in different divisions according to their weights. Amateur boxers are not paid for their bouts and compete in tournaments sponsored by local and national organizations. Of all the amateur tournaments, none is more famous than the annual Golden Gloves tournament.

WORDS TO KNOW **Vocabulary Preview**

barrage	evading	improvise	perpetual
bedlam	feint	pensively	unbridled
dispel	game		

Focus Your Reading

LITERARY ANALYSIS SUSPENSE The feeling of growing tension and excitement felt by a reader who wants to know what's going to happen next is called **suspense**. Writers create suspense by raising questions in readers' minds about what might happen. In "Amigo Brothers" the suspense begins to mount shortly after two friends, both amateur boxers, learn they will have to fight each other.

ACTIVE READING PREDICTING A **prediction** is an attempt to answer the question "What will happen next?" Sound predictions are based on both what you read and your own prior knowledge. When reading a suspenseful story, active readers pay attention to details about character, plot, and setting in order to make predictions.

READER'S NOTEBOOK Two questions a reader might expect the story to answer are: Will either Felix or Antonio not hit hard in order not to hurt his friend? Will their friendship survive if they fight their hardest? As you read, look for details that will help you predict the answers to these two questions. Record your answers on a chart.

Question	Details from the Story	Your Prediction
Will they not fight hard?		
Will they remain friends after the fight?		

 This selection is included in the **Grade 7 InterActive Reader**.

This selection appears in Spanish in the **Spanish Study Guide**.

Objectives

1. understand and appreciate **plot** (Literary Analysis)
2. understand the role of **suspense** in a short story (Literary Analysis)
3. understand the **surprise ending** (Literary Analysis)
4. use the strategy of **predicting** outcomes in plot (Active Reading)

Summary

Seventeen-year-olds Antonio Cruz and Felix Varga are best friends who both dream of being lightweight boxing champions. When they are paired against each other in the Boys Club division finals, the *amigo* brothers decide to train separately and fight as if they were strangers. On the day of the match, they square off in the ring, each not knowing quite what to expect. But when the bell sounds, they give their all. Antonio dances gracefully around the ring and jabs. Felix delivers his powerhouse punches. After two rounds, the fight is even. In the third and final round, the boys pound wildly at each other, delivering blows even after the final bell has rung. Once the referee and trainers pry them apart, the friends rush toward each other and hug. Then, before the announcer can name the winner, Antonio and Felix leave the ring arm in arm.

Thematic Link

The *amigo* brothers' approach to their fight leads to some surprising turns in their boxing match.

 5-Minute Warm-Up

Daily Language SkillBuilder TEKS 16D, 17C

Have students **proofread** the display sentences on page 341i and write them correctly. The sentences also appear on Transparency 11 of **Grammar Transparencies and Copymasters**.

 Mini Lesson Preteaching Vocabulary

If you would like to preteach the WORDS TO KNOW for this selection, use the Mini Lesson, p. 362.

LESSON RESOURCES

UNIT THREE RESOURCE BOOK, pp. 11–17

ASSESSMENT
Formal Assessment, pp. 55–56
Teacher's Guide to Assessment and Portfolio Use
Test Generator

SKILLS TRANSPARENCIES AND COPYMASTERS
Reading and Critical Thinking
• Predicting, TR 7 (for Thinking Through the Literature, p. 372)

Grammar
• Compound Adjectives, CM 83 (for Mini Lesson, p. 366)
• Punctuating Coordinate Adjectives, CM 127 (for Mini Lesson, p. 374)

Vocabulary
• Meaning Clues CM 47 (for Mini Lesson, p. 362)
• Context Clues, CM 48 (for Mini Lesson, p. 369)

INTEGRATED TECHNOLOGY
Audio Library

Visit our website:
www.mcdougallittell.com

Reading and Analyzing

Reading Skills and Strategies:
PREVIEW

Briefly describe to students the setting, the two characters, and the way Antonio and Felix are different from other teenagers in their part of the city. Ask students to think about how achieving success in boxing could affect the boys' futures.

Literary Analysis | SUSPENSE |

 Remind students that writers create suspense by hinting at events to come. Ask students how the author begins to create suspense by this early reference to the boys' shared dream.

Possible Response: Because they both want the same thing, the reader wonders if they will come into conflict with each other and which boy might achieve his goal first.

Use **Unit Three Resource Book,** p. 13 for more practice.

Active Reading | PREDICTING |

 Ask students what they would predict about each boy's ability to fight the other from this information.

Possible Response: They are both good boxers and would probably be evenly matched in a bout with each other.

Use **Unit Three Resource Book,** p. 12 for more practice.

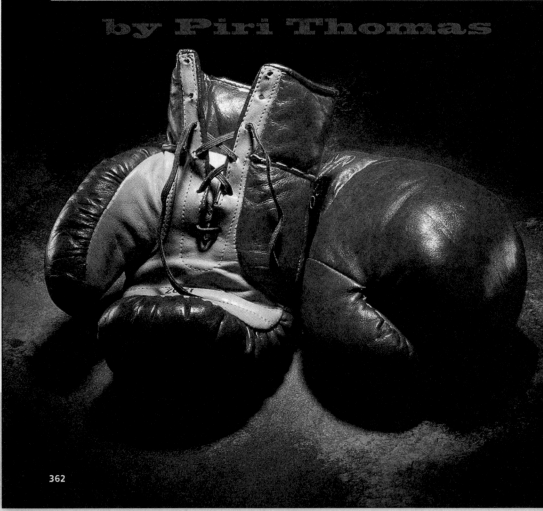

AMIGO BROTHERS

by Piri Thomas

362

Teaching Options

Mini Lesson **Preteaching Vocabulary** TEKS 9B TAAS Reading Obj. 1

MEANING CLUES
Instruction Tell students that their experiences and knowledge can help them to define unfamiliar words. Often, thinking of an image or situation associated with the word can lead to word recognition. For example, stand-up comedians perform improvisational theater. From that example, students might guess that the definition of *improvise* is to do something without preparation.
Exercises Have students replace the underlined part of each sentence with one of the WORDS TO KNOW.

1. The runaway horse galloped with <u>great enthusiasm</u>. *(unbridled)*
2. The young athlete was <u>ready</u> for anything. *(game)*
3. The army will <u>strip him of</u> the illusion that he is important. *(dispel)*
4. The pendulum illustrated the law of <u>never-ceasing</u> motion. *(perpetual)*

 Use **Unit Three Resource Book,** p. 14 for more practice.
Use **Vocabulary Transparencies and Copymasters,** p. 47, for additional support.

Antonio Cruz and **Felix Vargas** were both seventeen years old. They were so together in friendship that they felt themselves to be brothers. They had known each other since childhood, growing up on the lower east side of Manhattan in the same tenement building on Fifth Street between Avenue A and Avenue B.

Antonio was fair, lean, and lanky, while Felix was dark, short, and husky. Antonio's hair was always falling over his eyes, while Felix wore his black hair in a natural Afro style.

Each youngster had a dream of someday becoming lightweight champion of the world. Every chance they had the boys worked out, sometimes at the Boys Club on 10th Street and Avenue A and sometimes at the pro's gym on 14th Street. Early morning sunrises would find them running along the East River Drive, wrapped in sweatshirts, short towels around their necks, and handkerchiefs Apache style around their foreheads.

While some youngsters were into street negatives, Antonio and Felix slept, ate, rapped, and dreamt positive. Between them, they had a collection of *Fight* magazines second to none, plus a scrapbook filled with torn tickets to every boxing match they had ever attended and some

Flight (1988), Douglas Safranek. Egg tempera on panel, 40" × 32", courtesy of Schmidt Bingham Gallery, New York.

clippings of their own. If asked a question about any given fighter, they would immediately zip out from their memory banks divisions,[1] weights, records of fights, knockouts, technical knockouts, and draws or losses.

Each had fought many bouts representing their community and had won two gold-plated medals plus a silver and bronze medallion. The

---

1. **divisions:** weight groups into which boxers are separated.

AMIGO BROTHERS **363**

Customizing Instruction

Less Proficient Readers
To interest students in the story, ask them what qualities they look for in a friend. Explore the interests students share with their friends.

Set a Purpose Have students read to find out how Antonio and Felix are similar and different and how they decide to deal with their upcoming competition.

Students Acquiring English
This selection contains many Spanish words, some of which are slang. If possible, invite Spanish-speaking volunteers to preteach words and expressions such as *panin, cheverote, hermano, suavecito, sabe, señores y señoras*, and *mucho corazón* to the rest of the class.

Use **Spanish Study Guide,** pp. 73–75 for additional support.

Gifted and Talented
As students read "Amigo Brothers," have them discuss how the boys' focus on boxing is a preparation for life. Ask students how Antonio and Felix can use outside of the ring their skills and the qualities that make them good boxers.

BLOCK SCHEDULING: MANAGING TIME

If your schedule requires that you cover the lesson objectives in a shorter time, use . . .
• Preparing to Read, p. 361
• Thinking Through the Literature, p. 372
• Vocabulary in Action, p. 373
• Grammar in Context, p. 374

If you want to take advantage of longer class time, use . . .
• TE Teaching Options: Preteaching Vocabulary, p. 362; Cross-Curricular Links, pp. 364, 368; Viewing and Representing, p. 365; Grammar, pp. 366, 374; Spelling, p. 367; Vocabulary Strategy, p. 369; Standardized Test Practice, p. 370
• Choices & Challenges and Author Activity, pp. 373-374

Active Reading `PREDICTING`

 Have students predict what might happen to the boys' friendship as a result of their fight.

Possible Responses: Their friendship might be shattered; they could emerge as better friends.

Literary Analysis: INTERNAL CONFLICT

B Ask students to describe the source of each boy's inner conflict.

Possible Response: Each boy wants to win but does not want to have to hurt his friend or jeopardize their friendship to achieve victory.

C Invite students to analyze the boys' willingness to discuss the conflict. What does this willingness reveal about their characters and their friendship? Challenge students to explain what the boys' language reveals about their relationship.

Possible Response: They both care about keeping their friendship and are too honest to pretend the situation doesn't exist. Their forms of address reveal mutual respect, admiration, and affection. Using words from their native language shows how relaxed the boys are with each other.

📖 Use **Literary Analysis Transparencies**, p. 8, for additional support.

Reading Skills and Strategies: EVALUATING

D Ask students to explain whether this is the best solution to the boys' problem.

Possible Response: Yes. If each fighter does not do his best, he will have let down himself and his friend. To win against someone who does not try his hardest is a hollow victory.

difference was in their style. Antonio's lean form and long reach made him the better boxer, while Felix's short and muscular frame made him the better slugger. Whenever they had met in the ring for sparring sessions, it had always been hot and heavy.

Now, after a series of elimination bouts,[2] they had been informed that they were to meet each other in the division finals that were scheduled for the seventh of August, two weeks away— the winner to represent the Boys Club in the Golden Gloves Championship Tournament.

The two boys continued to run together along the East River Drive. But even when joking with each other, they both sensed a wall rising between them.

One morning less than a week before their bout, they met as usual for their daily workout. They fooled around with a few jabs at the air, slapped skin, and then took off, running lightly along the dirty East River's edge.

Antonio glanced at Felix, who kept his eyes purposely straight ahead, pausing from time to time to do some fancy leg work while throwing one-twos followed by upper cuts to an imaginary jaw. Antonio then beat the air with a barrage of body blows and short devastating lefts with an overhand, jawbreaking right.

After a mile or so, Felix puffed and said, "Let's stop for awhile, bro. I think we both got something to say to each other."

Antonio nodded. It was not natural to be acting as though nothing unusual was happening when two ace boon buddies were going to be blasting . . . each other within a few short days.

They rested their elbows on the railing separating them from the river. Antonio wiped his face with his short towel. The sunrise was now creating day.

Felix leaned heavily on the river's railing and stared across to the shores of Brooklyn. Finally, he broke the silence.

". . . , man. I don't know how to come out with it."

Antonio helped. "It's about our fight, right?"

"Yeah, right." Felix's eyes squinted at the rising orange sun.

"I've been thinking about it too, *panin*.[3] In fact, since we found out it was going to be me and you, I've been awake at night, pulling punches[4] on you, trying not to hurt you."

"Same here. It ain't natural not to think about the fight. I mean, we both are *cheverote*[5] fighters, and we both want to win. But only one of us can win. There ain't no draws in the eliminations."

Felix tapped Antonio gently on the shoulder. "I don't mean to sound like I'm bragging, bro. But I wanna win, fair and square."

Antonio nodded quietly. "Yeah. We both know that in the ring the better man wins. Friend or no friend, brother or no . . ."

Felix finished it for him. "Brother. Tony, let's promise something right here. Okay?"

"If it's fair, *hermano*,[6] I'm for it." Antonio admired the courage of a tugboat pulling a barge five times its welterweight[7] size.

"It's fair, Tony. When we get into the ring, it's gotta be like we never met. We gotta be like two heavy strangers that want the same

---

2. **elimination bouts:** matches to determine which boxers advance in a competition.
3. *panin* (pä′nēn) *American Spanish:* pal; buddy.
4. **pulling punches:** holding back in delivering blows.
5. *cheverote* (chě-vě-rō′tě) *American Spanish:* really cool.
6. *hermano* (ĕr-mä′nō) *Spanish:* brother.
7. **welterweight:** one of boxing's weight divisions, with a maximum weight of 147 pounds.

WORDS TO KNOW	**barrage** (bə-räzh′) *n.* a rapid, heavy attack

Teaching Options

Cross Curricular Link   **Sports**

BOXING: GOLDEN GLOVES TOURNAMENT This famous amateur competition originated in the mind of a sports editor for the *Chicago Tribune*. Arch Ward thought of the idea, and in 1926 his paper sponsored the first competition. An element of excitement was added the next year, when a New York team was sponsored by the *New York Daily News*. The idea grew in popularity. Other cities started to send teams, and it became a national tournament.

Winning the Golden Gloves tournament has led to other championships for some boxers, including professional world champions Joe Louis, Sugar Ray Robinson, Barney Ross, Floyd Patterson, and Sugar Ray Leonard. Cassius Clay (later known as Muhammad Ali) was the winner of the Golden Gloves title six times.

hing, and only one can have it. You under-
tand, don'tcha?"

"Sí, I know." Tony smiled. "No pulling
punches. We go all the way."

"Yeah, that's right. Listen, Tony. Don't you
think it's a good idea if we don't see each
other until the day of the fight? I'm going to
stay with my Aunt Lucy in the Bronx. I can
use Gleason's Gym for working out. My
manager says he got some sparring partners

with more or less your style."

Tony scratched his nose <u>pensively</u>. "Yeah, it
would be better for our heads." He held out
his hand, palm upward. "Deal?"

"Deal." Felix lightly slapped open skin.

"Ready for some more running?" Tony
asked lamely.

"Naw, bro. Let's cut it here. You go on. I
kinda like to get things together in my head."

"You ain't worried, are you?" Tony asked.

El abrazo [The Hug] (1966), Fletcher Martin. Acrylic on paper, 22" × 17", private collection.

WORDS
TO   **pensively** (pĕn'sĭv-lē) *adv.* in a way that suggests deep thought
KNOW

365

2

Customizing Instruction

Less Proficient Readers
Check students' comprehension by asking the following questions:
• How are Antonio and Felix similar?
  How are they different?
Possible Responses: The boys grew
up in the same neighborhood and are
both successful prizefighters. They have
different fighting styles: Antonio is the
better boxer; Felix is the better slugger.
• How do the boys resolve their
  conflict and deal with the
  upcoming competition?
Answer: They decide to fight their best
and act as if they are strangers in the
ring.
Set a Purpose Have students read to
find out how each boy spends the
night before the fight and how Antonio
decides to deal with Felix once inside
the ring.

Students Acquiring English
1 Point out that the spelling of
don'tcha reflects the way that "don't
you" is often pronounced in informal
spoken English.
2 Guide students to understand
that the word *heads* in the phrase "it
would be better for our heads" is not
used literally. Rather, *heads* refers to
the feelings and attitudes of the two
characters.

Mini Lesson — Viewing and Representing
TEKS 22A

El Abrazo [The Hug]
by Fletcher Martin

ART APPRECIATION Fletcher Martin (1904–1979)
was descended from pioneers; his ancestors were
English, Irish, and French settlers who landed in
America in the 1600s. He grew up in the West,
where his father was a newspaper publisher and
rancher. Largely self-taught, Martin attained promi-
nence in the art world.
Instruction Point out to students that the artist
conveys a sense of the relationship in this painting
without the help of the subjects' facial expres-

sions. Ask students what emotions they think have
prompted this hug and why.
Possible Response: There is a strong feeling of
affection or support or sympathy projected by the
way the arms totally wrap around the figure in the
foreground. Shading suggests strength and force.
This has the appearance of a sincere gesture.
Application Ask students whether they think
Antonio and Felix would express their friendship
in this manner. Why or why not?
Possible Response: Yes. Neither one is afraid of
physical contact. Each feels strong affection for the
other.

AMIGO BROTHERS **365**

Reading Skills and Strategies: EVALUATING

(A) Ask students what the preparations for the fight made by Antonio and Felix reveal about their personalities and friendship.

Possible Response: Antonio and Felix spend the night before the fight alone, thinking about the fight and each other. Both boys need time alone to think. They are both thoughtful, concerned people.

Literary Analysis: INTERNAL CONFLICT

(B) Ask students how Antonio resolves his conflict about facing Felix in the ring the next day.

Possible Responses: He decides that Felix will be just another opponent; he won't think of him as Felix.

Reading Skills and Strategies: SYNTHESIZING

(C) Ask students why they think the fight has generated so much interest in the community.

Possible Responses: because the boys are liked and well respected and each has his own loyal following; because boxing is an important sport in their neighborhood

Literary Analysis | SUSPENSE |

(D) Ask students to explain how the author builds suspense.

Possible Responses: The "beehive" of activity, the move to a larger space, and the boys' internal conflicts all create a sense of anticipation before the fight.

"No way, man." Felix laughed out loud. "I got too much smarts for that. I just think it's cooler if we split right here. After the fight, we can get it together again like nothing ever happened."

The amigo brothers were not ashamed to hug each other tightly.

"Guess you're right. Watch yourself, Felix. I hear there's some pretty heavy dudes up in the Bronx. *Suavecito,*[8] okay?"

"Okay. You watch yourself too, *sabe*[9]?"

Tony jogged away. Felix watched his friend disappear from view, throwing rights and lefts. Both fighters had a lot of psyching up to do before the big fight.

The days in training passed much too slowly. Although they kept out of each other's way, they were aware of each other's progress via the ghetto grapevine.

(A) The evening before the big fight, Tony made his way to the roof of his tenement. In the quiet early dark, he peered over the ledge. Six stories below, the lights of the city blinked, and the sounds of cars mingled with the curses and the laughter of children in the street. He tried not to think of Felix, feeling he had succeeded in psyching his mind. But only in the ring would he really know. To spare Felix hurt, he would have to knock him out, early and quick.

Up in the South Bronx, Felix decided to take in a movie in an effort to keep Antonio's face away from his fists. The flick was *The Champion* with Kirk Douglas, the third time Felix was seeing it.

The champion was getting . . . beat . . . , his face being pounded into raw, wet hamburger. His eyes were cut, jagged, bleeding, one eye swollen, the other almost shut. He was saved only by the sound of the bell.

Felix became the champ and Tony the challenger.

The movie audience was going out of its

head, roaring in blood lust at the butchery going on. The champ hunched his shoulders, grunting and sniffing red blood back into his broken nose. The challenger, confident that he had the championship in the bag, threw a left. The champ countered with a dynamite right that exploded into the challenger's brains.

Felix's right arm felt the shock. Antonio's face, superimposed on the screen, was shattered and split apart by the awesome force of the killer blow. Felix saw himself in the ring, blasting Antonio against the ropes. The champ had to be forcibly restrained. The challenger was allowed to crumble slowly to the canvas, a broken, bloody mess.

When Felix finally left the theatre, he had figured out how to psyche himself for tomorrow's fight. It was Felix the Champion vs. Antonio the Challenger.

He walked up some dark streets, deserted except for small pockets of wary-looking kids wearing gang colors. Despite the fact that he was Puerto Rican like them, they eyed him as a stranger to their turf. Felix did a last shuffle, bobbing and weaving, while letting loose a torrent of blows that would demolish whatever got in its way. It seemed to impress the brothers, who went about their own business.

Finding no takers, Felix decided to split to his aunt's. Walking the streets had not relaxed him, neither had the fight flick. All it had done was to stir him up. He let himself quietly into his Aunt Lucy's apartment and went straight to bed, falling into a fitful sleep with sounds of the gong for Round One.

Antonio was passing some heavy time on his rooftop. How would the fight tomorrow affect his relationship with Felix? After all, fighting was like any other profession. Friendship had nothing to do with it. A gnawing doubt crept

---

8. *Suavecito* (swä-vĕ-sē′tō) *American Spanish:* Take it easy.
9. *sabe?* (sä′bĕ) *Spanish:* you know?

Teaching Options

 Mini Lesson **Grammar**   TEKS 17D   TAAS Writing Obj. 3, 4, 6

COMPOUND ADJECTIVES

Instruction Tell students that a compound adjective consists of two words that work together as one unit to modify the same noun. For example, draw students' attention to the highlighted phrase in the second column of this page: *wary-looking kids.* Other examples in the story include

gold-plated medals
dynamite-packed fists
roped-off path
cold-water sponges

Point out that in each of these examples, two words operate as one adjective. Explain that when compound adjectives come before the words they modify, a hyphen should usually join their parts. Tell students that they should never use a comma to separate the parts of a compound adjective. Have them place commas between the example compound-adjective parts and then explain why commas incorrectly change their meaning. Then have students look at the highlighted words in the first column of this page. Ask them to try to explain the difference between these adjectives and the adjectives in the examples.

Possible Response: The highlighted adjectives in the first column work separately to modify the noun *eyes,* not as a single adjective.

Application Have students work in pairs to write five sentences that contain compound adjectives.

📖 Use **Grammar Transparencies and Copymasters**, p. 83.

Use McDougal Littell's ***Language Network***, Chapter 5, for more instruction and practice in using compound adjectives.

n. He cut negative thinking real quick by doing some speedy fancy dance steps, bobbing and weaving like mercury. The night air was blurred with <u>perpetual</u> motions of left hooks and right crosses. Felix, his *amigo* brother, was not going to be Felix at all in the ring. Just an opponent with another face. Antonio went to sleep, hearing the opening bell for the first round. Like his friend in the South Bronx, he prayed for victory via a quick, clean knockout in the first round.

Large posters plastered all over the walls of local shops announced the fight between Antonio Cruz and Felix Vargas as the main bout.

The fight had created great interest in the neighborhood. Antonio and Felix were well liked and respected. Each had his own loyal following. Betting fever was high and ranged from a bottle of Coke to cold, hard cash on the line.

Antonio's fans bet with <u>unbridled</u> faith in his boxing skills. On the other side, Felix's admirers bet on his dynamite-packed fists.

Felix had returned to his apartment early in the morning of August 7th and stayed there, hoping to avoid seeing Antonio. He turned the radio on to salsa music sounds and then tried to read while waiting for word from his manager.

The fight was scheduled to take place in Tompkins Square Park. It had been decided that the gymnasium of the Boys Club was not large enough to hold all the people who were sure to attend. In Tompkins Square Park, everyone who wanted could view the fight, whether from ringside or window fire escapes or tenement rooftops.

The morning of the fight, Tompkins Square was a beehive of activity with numerous workers setting up the ring, the seats, and the guest speakers' stand. The scheduled bouts began shortly after noon, and the park had begun filling up even earlier.

The local junior high school across from Tompkins Square Park served as the dressing room for all the fighters. Each was given a separate classroom, with desktops, covered with mats, serving as resting tables. Antonio thought he caught a glimpse of Felix waving to him from a room at the far end of the corridor. He waved back just in case it had been him.

The fighters changed from their street clothes into fighting gear. Antonio wore white trunks, black socks, and black shoes. Felix wore sky blue trunks, red socks, and white boxing shoes. Each had dressing gowns to match their fighting trunks with their names neatly stitched on the back.

The loudspeakers blared into the open window of the school. There were speeches by dignitaries, community leaders, and great boxers of yesteryear. Some were well prepared, some <u>improvised</u> on the spot. They all carried the same message of great pleasure and honor at being part of such a historic event. This great day was in the tradition of champions emerging from the streets of the lower east side.

Interwoven with the speeches were the sounds of the other boxing events. After the sixth bout, Felix was much relieved when his trainer, Charlie, said, "Time change. Quick knockout. This is it. We're on."

Waiting time was over. Felix was escorted from the classroom by a dozen fans in white T-shirts with the word FELIX across their fronts.

Antonio was escorted down a different stairwell and guided through a roped-off path.

WORDS TO KNOW	**perpetual** (pər-pĕch′ōō-əl) *adj.* continual; unending
	unbridled (ŭn-brīd′ld) *adj.* lacking in restraint or control
	improvise (ĭm′prə-vīz′) *v.* to speak or perform without preparation

367

 Spelling TEKS 16G

WORDS FROM FRENCH

Instruction Explain to students that English has incorporated words from many languages, including French. To make it easier to remember how to spell these words, point out the following letter combinations.

- *age* (pronounced /äzh/)
- *et* (pronounced /ā/)
- *eur* (pronounced /œr/)

Exercises Ask students to spell the following words as you read them aloud.

1. barrage	6. beret
2. ballet	7. mirage
3. corsage	8. espionage
4. amateur	9. chauffeur
5. buffet	10. grandeur

Have students look for more words that fit this pattern, in their own writing and in things that they read, and then add these words to their personal word lists.

 Use **Unit Three Resource Book**, p. 16 for more practice.

Active Reading PREDICTING

A Have students predict who will win the fight and why.

Possible Responses: Some students will say that because Antonio is a better boxer, he will win. Others may say that if Felix gets himself in the right position, he stands a chance of winning because he is a better slugger.

Reading Skills and Strategies: EVALUATING

B Ask students to evaluate Felix's motive in trying to land the first punch.

Possible Responses: Felix's strength is his punching so he has to begin well; he wants to appear aggressive in front of the crowd; he wants to intimidate Antonio.

Reading Skills and Strategies: MAKING JUDGMENTS

C Point out how the writer uses the word *amigos* in the middle of the fight to remind readers that the boys are very close friends. Ask students if they think that it is easier or harder for the boys to fight each other because they know each other so well.

Possible Responses: It is easier, because they know where to hit to inflict the maximum damage; it is harder, because they do not want to hurt each other, which adds to their internal conflict.

Reading Skills and Strategies: CLARIFYING

D Have students describe the tactics the boys use as they fight.

Possible Responses: They try to trick each other with feints, rush each other, send a barrage of blows, and bob and weave.

As the two climbed into the ring, the crowd exploded with a roar. Antonio and Felix both bowed gracefully and then raised their arms in acknowledgment.

Antonio tried to be cool, but even as the roar was in its first birth, he turned slowly to meet Felix's eyes looking directly into his. Felix nodded his head and Antonio responded. And both as one, just as quickly, turned away to face his own corner.

Bong, bong, bong. The roar turned to stillness.

"Ladies and Gentlemen, *Señores y Señoras.*"

The announcer spoke slowly, pleased at his bilingual efforts.

"Now the moment we have all been waiting for—the main event between two fine young Puerto Rican fighters, products of our lower east side."

"Loisaida,"[10] called out a member of the audience.

A "In this corner, weighing 131 pounds, Felix Vargas. And in this corner, weighing 133 pounds, Antonio Cruz. The winner will represent the Boys Club in the tournament of champions, the Golden Gloves. There will be no draw. May the best man win."

The cheering of the crowd shook the windowpanes of the old buildings surrounding Tompkins Square Park. At the center of the ring, the referee was giving instructions to the youngsters.

"Keep your punches up. No low blows. No punching on the back of the head. Keep your heads up. Understand. Let's have a clean fight. Now shake hands and come out fighting."

Both youngsters touched gloves and nodded.

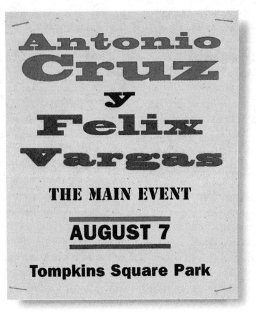

They turned and danced quickly to their corners. Their head towels and dressing gowns were lifted neatly from their shoulders by their trainers' nimble fingers. Antonio crossed himself. Felix did the same. BONG! BONG! ROUND ONE. Felix and Antonio turned and faced each other squarely in a fighting pose. Felix wasted no time. He came in fast, head low, half hunched toward his right shoulder, and lashed out with a straight left.

He missed a right cross as Antonio slipped the punch and countered with one-two-three lefts that snapped Felix's head back, sending a mild shock coursing through him. If Felix had any small doubt about their friendship affecting their fight, it was being neatly <u>dispelled</u>.

---

10. **Loisaida** (lō´-ē-sī´dä): a Hispanic slang pronunciation of *Lower East Side.*

WORDS
TO
KNOW   **dispel** (dĭ-spĕl´) *v.* to scatter; get rid of

368

Cross Curricular Link Social Studies

EL BARRIO El Barrio, as it is familiarly known, is an area of New York City that is also known as East Harlem or Spanish Harlem. Its approximate center is 106th Street and Lexington Avenue. Over the past centuries, East Harlem has been home to many groups of immigrants. The German and the Irish lived there at the turn of the century. Then came Italian and Jewish immigrants who rapidly swelled the population and spurred increased building in the area. By the late 1920s the composition of the area was shifting again as some of the earlier immigrants moved out and Puerto Ricans started to move in. By the late 1990s, the population of East Harlem numbered around 103,000, the majority of whom were Puerto Ricans and African-Americans.

Despite the poverty of the area, the Puerto Rican heritage is rich and visible. Murals, such as a heroic woman wrapped in a Puerto Rican flag, adorn walls and buildings. Mosaics of Caribbean dancers and drummers enliven the subway stations, and cultural centers continue to encourage the efforts of artists to capture the uniqueness of El Barrio and its people.

Right to the Jaw (about 1926), Mahonri Mackintosh Young. Bronze, courtesy of Wood River Gallery, Mill Valley, California.

Antonio danced, a joy to behold. His left hand was like a piston pumping jabs one right after another with seeming ease. Felix bobbed and weaved and never stopped boring in. He knew that at long range he was at a disadvantage. Antonio had too much reach on him. Only by coming in close could Felix hope to achieve the dreamed-of knockout.

Antonio knew the dynamite that was stored in his amigo brother's fist. He ducked a short right and missed a left hook. Felix trapped him against the ropes just long enough to pour some punishing rights and lefts to Antonio's hard midsection. Antonio slipped away from Felix, crashing two lefts to his head, which set Felix's right ear to ringing.

Bong! Both *amigos* froze a punch well on its way, sending up a roar of approval for good sportsmanship.

Felix walked briskly back to his corner. His right ear had not stopped ringing. Antonio gracefully danced his way toward his stool none the worse, except for glowing glove burns, showing angry red against the whiteness of his midribs.

"Watch that right, Tony." His trainer talked into his ear. "Remember Felix always goes to the body. He'll want you to drop your hands for his overhand left or right. Got it?"

Antonio nodded, spraying water out between his teeth. He felt better as his sore midsection was being firmly rubbed.

AMIGO BROTHERS **369**

Customizing Instruction

Less Proficient Readers
Ask students to describe the strengths of each boxer.
Possible Responses: Antonio has a longer reach. Felix has a powerful blow. Point out to students that the fact that there can't be a tie has been emphasized. Ask students what that knowledge adds to their anticipation of the fight.
Possible Response: It makes the fight more suspenseful and more important.
Set a Purpose Have students read to find out what happens in the next two rounds and why boxing is so important to the boys.

Students Acquiring English
1 Explain to students the action of a piston to help them understand the simile.
2 Ask a volunteer to explain the metaphorical use of *dynamite* in this sentence.

 Vocabulary Strategy   TEKS 6A   TAAS Reading Obj. 1

CONTEXT CLUES
Instruction Remind students that when they encounter an unfamiliar word, they should apply knowledge of the context in which the word is used in order to understand the word. The word's meaning might be inferred or guessed from other words or phrases used in the sentence or paragraph. Direct students to the sentence containing the word *nimble* on page 368. The trainers have just neatly lifted off the gowns and towels. Therefore, *nimble* means skillful or adept.
Application Have students divide into pairs and look at how the following words are used in the story. Ask them to pick out the phrases that help them to infer the meanings of the words. Then have students share their definitions with the class.

bilingual (p. 368)
pried (p. 371)
countered (p. 370)
fitful (p. 366)
corridor (p. 367)

 Use **Vocabulary Transparencies and Copymasters**, p. 48.

AMIGO BROTHERS **369**

A Ask students whether they think the brutality shown by each boxer to the other is believable in light of their friendship.

Possible Responses: Yes, because in the fierce competition of sport, everything but the desire to win is forgotten. Yes, because this match could be a turning point in both of their careers. No, because their friendship is too strong for them to ignore.

Literary Analysis SUSPENSE

B Both boys had wished for a first-round knockout. Ask students how the suspense of their prolonged fighting affects the story.

Possible Responses: It makes the outcome more unpredictable; it shows how evenly matched they are and how each one deserves to win.

Active Reading PREDICTING

C Ask students to pause before reading the ending to predict the winner of the match and explain why they would choose that boxer.

Possible Responses: Some might say Felix because he dominated the first part of the second round decisively; others might say Antonio because he showed both the grace of a boxer and the ability to hit hard.

Literary Analysis: SURPRISE ENDING

D Ask students why Felix and Antonio don't wait to hear the name of the winner announced.

Possible Responses: It does not matter to them; they have already both won by fighting their hardest and keeping their friendship intact.

Felix's corner was also busy.

"You gotta get in there, fella." Felix's trainer poured water over his curly Afro locks. "Get in there or he's gonna chop you up from way back."

 Bong! Bong! Round two. Felix was off his stool and rushed Antonio like a bull, sending a hard right to his head. Beads of water exploded from Antonio's long hair.

Antonio, hurt, sent back a blurring barrage of lefts and rights that only meant pain to Felix, who returned with a short left to the head followed by a looping right to the body. Antonio countered with his own flurry, forcing Felix to give ground. But not for long.

Felix bobbed and weaved, bobbed and weaved, occasionally punching his two gloves together.

Antonio waited for the rush that was sure to come. Felix closed in and <u>feinted</u> with his left shoulder and threw his right instead. Lights suddenly exploded inside Felix's head as Antonio slipped the blow and hit him with a pistonlike left, catching him flush on the point of his chin.

A <u>Bedlam</u> broke loose as Felix's legs momentarily buckled. He fought off a series of rights and lefts and came back with a strong right that taught Antonio respect.

Antonio danced in carefully. He knew Felix had the habit of playing possum when hurt, to sucker an opponent within reach of the powerful bombs he carried in each fist.

A right to the head slowed Antonio's pretty dancing. He answered with his own left at Felix's right eye that began puffing up within three seconds.

Antonio, a bit too eager, moved in too close, and Felix had him entangled into a rip-roaring, punching toe-to-toe slugfest that brought the whole Tompkins Square Park screaming to its feet.

Rights to the body. Lefts to the head. Neither fighter was giving an inch. Suddenly a short right caught Antonio squarely on the chin. His long legs turned to jelly, and his arms flailed out desperately. Felix, grunting like a bull, threw wild punches from every direction. Antonio, groggy, bobbed and weaved, <u>evading</u> most of the blows. Suddenly his head cleared. His left flashed out hard and straight catching Felix on the bridge of his nose.

Felix lashed back with a haymaker, right off the ghetto streets. At the same instant, his eye caught another left hook from Antonio. Felix swung out, trying to clear the pain. Only the frenzied screaming of those along ringside let him know that he had dropped Antonio. Fighting off the growing haze, Antonio struggled to his feet, got up, ducked, and threw a smashing right that dropped Felix flat on his back.

Felix got up as fast as he could in his own corner, groggy but still <u>game</u>. He didn't even hear the count. In a fog, he heard the roaring of the crowd, who seemed to have gone insane. His head cleared to hear the bell sound at the end of the round. He was damned glad. His trainer sat him down on the stool.

In his corner, Antonio was doing what all fighters do when they are hurt. They sit and smile at everyone.

The referee signaled the ring doctor to check the fighters out. He did so and then gave his okay. The cold-water sponges brought clarity to both *amigo* brothers. They were rubbed until their circulation ran free.

Bong! Round three—the final round. Up to

WORDS TO KNOW	**feint** (fānt) *v.* to make a pretended attack in order to draw attention away from one's real purpose or target **bedlam** (bĕd'ləm) *n.* a noisy confusion **evading** (ĭ-vā'dĭng) *adj.* avoiding; escaping **evade** *v.* **game** (gām) *adj.* ready and willing to proceed

370

Teaching Options

✓ Assessment **Standardized Test Practice** **TEKS** 10K, 12H  **TAAS** Reading Obj. 6

RECOGNIZING THE AUTHOR'S PURPOSE In some standardized tests, students are asked to identify the author's purpose. Write the following statement and choices on the board or read them aloud.

The author does not reveal the winner of the fight because:

A. he wants an ending that will surprise the reader.

B. each boy has loyal supporters who feel that his boxer has won.

C. the ending must reveal the idea that by fighting their hardest, both boys are champions.

D. there will be other matches between them that they will take turns winning and losing.

Guide students through the process of selecting C as the right answer. Although A, B, and D are or may be true, they could have been accomplished without the specific ending. However, the theme could not have been revealed effectively, if at all, without the omission of an announced winner.

now it had been tick-tack-toe, pretty much even. But everyone knew there could be no draw and that this round would decide the winner.

This time, to Felix's surprise, it was Antonio who came out fast, charging across the ring. Felix braced himself but couldn't ward off the barrage of punches. Antonio drove Felix hard against the ropes.

The crowd ate it up. Thus far the two had fought with *mucho corazón*.[11] Felix tapped his gloves and commenced his attack anew. Antonio, throwing boxer's caution to the winds, jumped in to meet him.

Both pounded away. Neither gave an inch, and neither fell to the canvas. Felix's left eye was tightly closed. Claret red blood poured from Antonio's nose. They fought toe-to-toe.

The sounds of their blows were loud in contrast to the silence of a crowd gone completely mute. The referee was stunned by their savagery.

Bong! Bong! Bong! The bell sounded over and over again. Felix and Antonio were past hearing. Their blows continued to pound on each other like hailstones.

Finally the referee and the two trainers pried Felix and Antonio apart. Cold water was poured over them to bring them back to their senses.

They looked around and then rushed toward each other. A cry of alarm surged through Tompkins Square Park. Was this a fight to the death instead of a boxing match?

The fear soon gave way to wave upon wave of cheering as the two amigos embraced.

No matter what the decision, they knew they would always be champions to each other.

Bong! Bong! Bong! "Ladies and Gentlemen. *Señores* and *Señoras*. The winner and representative to the Golden Gloves Tournament of Champions is . . ."

The announcer turned to point to the winner and found himself alone. Arm in arm, the champions had already left the ring.

---

11. *mucho corazón* (mōō′chô kō-rä-sōn′) *Spanish:* a lot of heart; great courage.

Customizing Instruction

Less Proficient Readers
Ask students the following questions to make sure they understand the story. Who won the fight? Explain.
Possible Responses: Both boys won, because each fought his hardest and so emerged with his pride, self-respect, and friendship intact; readers don't know who actually won, because the author chose not to include this information.
Why is boxing so important to the boys?
Possible Responses: It helps them to achieve recognition in their neighborhood; it may give them a way to achieve a better life.

Multiple Learning Styles
Auditory Learners
1 Have students select background music for this scene that reflects its excitement and suspense.

Students Acquiring English
2 Point out that the expression "giving an inch" is a common English idiom meaning "yielding to another person in an argument or fight."

Gifted and Talented
Have students explain what Antonio and Felix learn from this experience and debate whether it is likely that a real-life friendship would survive in a similar situation.

GUIDING STUDENT RESPONSE

Connect to the Literature

1. Responses will vary. Some students may think the author let them down; others might think that telling the winner would have weakened the theme of the story.

Comprehension Check
- since childhood
- Both have made it through the elimination rounds to the division final, and both are in the same weight class.
- The boys leave the ring before the winner is announced.

 Use Selection Quiz **Unit Three Resource Book,** p. 17.

Think Critically

2. Possible Response: The outcome is not important to them because they feel they have already won by fighting their hardest and staying friends. The author might have chosen this ending to show that a winner is true to his principles and does his or her best in every situation.

3. Possible Responses: They act admirably, since they do not let their inner conflicts disrupt their friendship; they are foolish, because they don't work through their conflicts.

4. Possible Response: Antonio has grace and a long reach. Felix has a powerful punch and tenacity. Each has a style that suits his physique and temperament. Felix plunges into situations headlong; Antonio observes and evades.

5. Possible Responses: They will respect and admire the boys for an intense, clean fight; they will wonder why the boys did not stay in the ring to see who won.

Literary Analysis

Suspense Most students were probably surprised by the omission of the name of the winner. The ending might have been predicted by the emphasis on the friendship more than the outcome of the fight throughout the story and the approach that each boy independently adopts on the day of the fight. Suspense is created by sensory details that describe the fight and the evenness of the boys' matchup.

 Use **Reading and Critical Thinking Transparencies,** p. 7, for additional support.

Connect to the Literature

1. **What Do You Think?** What do you think about the ending of the story?

Comprehension Check
- How long have the two friends known each other?
- Why do they have to fight each other?
- What happens at the end of the fight?

Think Critically

2. Why do you think the two boys leave the ring together before the victor is announced? Why might the author have ended the story this way?

3. What is your opinion of the way Antonio and Felix handle their inner conflicts as two good friends competing for the same prize?

 THINK ABOUT
- the promise they exchange while training for the fight
- how each of them gets psyched up for the fight
- their conduct in the ring

4. How do Antonio's and Felix's fighting styles differ? What does this tell you about each boy?

5. How do you think the community will regard Antonio and Felix after the fight? Explain.

Extend Interpretations

6. **What If?** Imagine that one of the boys had won the boxing match by a knockout. What effect do you think that might have had on their friendship?

7. **Connect to Life** How would you compare your ideas about friendship and competition with those expressed in this story?

Literary Analysis

SUSPENSE The tension or excitement that readers feel as they are drawn into a story is called **suspense.** A writer creates suspense when he or she purposely leaves readers uncertain or excited about what will happen. Sometimes a story builds suspense and then has a **surprise ending.** A surprise ending is an outcome that is different from what readers expect. Did the ending of "Amigo Brothers" surprise you?

Paired Activity Compare the chart you created in your 📖 **READER'S NOTEBOOK** with that of a classmate who made predictions that were different from yours. Discuss with each other the reasons and details you used for your predictions. Do you find clues to the ending you didn't notice when you read the story for the first time? In what ways does Piri Thomas create suspense in the story?

Question	Details from the Story	Your Prediction
Will they not fight hard?	• Each dreamed of becoming lightweight champion of the world.	They will fight hard.
Will they remain friends after the fight?	• They had each already won several medals.	

Extend Interpretations

6. **What If?** Possible Responses: It would probably have harmed the relationship. One would have been seen as decisively better than the other; the boxer who knocked his friend out may have felt guilty and avoided the other.

7. **Connect to Life** Possible Responses: Some may agree that friendship is more important than competition and that by doing their best in fighting each other, the boys were showing their respect for each other. Others may believe that true friends would not have gone through with the event.

Choices & Challenges

Writing Options

1. Boxing Profile Using details from the story, write a profile of either Antonio or Felix for a boxing magazine. Place the profile in your **Working Portfolio.**

2. Editorial Although many people are opposed to boxing because of its violence, some people—like the writer Joyce Carol Oates—are boxing fans. According to Oates, "Boxing, like any sport, or art, or vocation in life, is about character." Write an editorial in favor of or against boxing. Support your opinion with details from the story, and comment on Oates's opinion.

Writing Handbook
See p. R39: Persuasive Writing.

Activities & Explorations

1. Postfight Interview Work with two classmates to role-play a sportscaster's postfight interview with the two boxers. Have Antonio and Felix express their ideas about competition between good friends. Perform the interview for the class. ~ **SPEAKING AND LISTENING**

2. Victory Speech Write a victory speech for the winner. Think about what he would want to say to the crowd, the community, and his friend and opponent. Present the speech to the class. ~ **PERFORMING**

Art Connection

Look at Fletcher Martin's painting *El abrazo* on page 365. Do you think it catches the spirit of Felix and Antonio's friendship? Explain your response.

Inquiry & Research

A Physical Education Research the conditioning programs that boxers must follow to prepare for their bouts. If possible, interview a boxer or a physical education instructor as part of your research. Then present your findings to the rest of the class.

Vocabulary in Action

EXERCISE: MEANING CLUES Match each vocabulary word on the left with the italicized word or phrase on the right that suggests its meaning.

1. unbridled
2. pensively
3. bedlam
4. perpetual
5. game
6. barrage
7. improvise
8. dispel
9. evading
10. feint

  a. Felix was in *continual* motion on his feet.
  b. Antonio's fans had an *uncontrolled* belief in him.
  c. Antonio and Felix were *ready* for the match to begin.
  d. *The crowd was so loud,* Felix couldn't hear himself think.
  e. The trainer sat *deep in thought.*
  f. Felix *pretended to make* a left jab.
  g. Antonio was *dodging* Felix's punches.
  h. Felix threw a *series* of rapid punches.
  i. The community leaders *made up* speeches *on the spot.*
  j. Felix and Antonio *got rid of* any doubts about their friendship.

Building Vocabulary
For an in-depth study of learning and remembering new words, see p. 473.

Writing Options

1. Boxing Profile To get students started on this assignment, provide sample profiles of boxing champions from sports magazines.

2. Editorial Remind students that an editorial attempts to change people's minds about an issue. Students should carefully support their opinions with specific, detailed examples. To extend this assignment, have students debate the issue with a panel of judges ruling on the effectiveness of each side's argument.

 Use **Writing Transparencies,** p. 13, for additional support.

Activities & Explorations

1. Postfight Interview To get students started on this assignment, have them discuss what ideas about competition can be taken from the story and possible ways that each boy would express those thoughts. Remind students to develop interview questions that require elaboration.

  Use **Communications Transparencies and Copymasters,** p. 9, for additional support.

2. Victory Speech To get students started on this assignment, have them brainstorm ideas of what to include in their speech. Then encourage students to put their thoughts in order of importance.

Art Connection

Possible Response: Yes, because the hug is wholehearted and strong. Both Felix and Antonio are wholehearted about their friendship, and both boys are strong enough to be worthy opponents for each other.

Inquiry & Research

A Physical Education Suggest that students work in pairs to complete their research. One partner might investigate the Internet or conduct an interview with a boxer through e-mail; the other partner might interview a physical education teacher and research articles found in periodicals. They then can combine and edit their notes to assemble the final report.

Vocabulary in Action

EXERCISE

1. b
2. e
3. d
4. a
5. c

6. h
7. i
8. j
9. g
10. f

Grammar in Context

WRITING EXERCISE

Possible Responses:

1. In the ring, they acted like fierce, real opponents.
2. The day before the long, difficult fight, both boys were tense.
3. Felix let fly a series of low, quick jabs.
4. Antonio displayed his famous, fancy footwork.

CONNECT TO THE LITERATURE

Possible Responses:

. . . his face being pounded into raw, wet hamburger

. . . eyes cut, jagged, bleeding

. . . crumble slowly to the canvas, a broken, bloody mess

Author Activity

Fiction and Real Life Encourage students to use several subject headings to find information on El Museo del Barrio. If they are using an on-line periodical index, suggest that they give two or three identifying phrases, including Barrio, New York City.

Grammar in Context: Coordinate Adjectives

Piri Thomas uses several adjectives to contrast the appearances of Antonio and Felix in the first sentence of "Amigo Brothers."

> **Antonio was fair, lean, and lanky, while Felix was dark, short, and husky.**

Sometimes, to make their descriptions clear and effective, writers need to use more than one adjective to modify a noun or pronoun. When this happens, the adjectives are called **coordinate adjectives.**

Punctuation Tip: When more than one adjective modifies a noun or pronoun, the adjectives are separated by a comma. "Felix walked the **dark, quiet** streets." But, when the first adjective modifies the second adjective and not the noun or pronoun, the two adjectives are not separated. "Felix wore **dark red** socks."

WRITING EXERCISE Insert coordinate adjectives to modify the underlined nouns. Choose adjectives that would fit the descriptions in "Amigo Brothers."

Example: Original Antonio and Felix were <u>friends</u>.

Rewritten Antonio and Felix were good, close friends.

1. In the ring, they acted like <u>opponents</u>.
2. The day before the <u>fight</u>, both boys were tense.
3. Felix let fly a series of <u>jabs</u>.
4. Antonio displayed his <u>footwork</u>.

Connect to the Literature Look on page 366 for two or three examples of coordinate adjectives. How do these help create the mood of the story?

Grammar Handbook Elements in a Series, p. R77

"I believe every child is born a poet and every poet is born a child."

Piri Thomas
born 1928

An About-Face While serving a prison sentence, Piri Thomas decided to turn his life around. He began writing his autobiography as a step toward accomplishing this goal. For him, writing became a tool to discover his real nature and to depict honestly his Puerto Rican and African-American heritage. After his release from prison, Thomas suffered a severe setback—the manuscript he had labored over for four years was accidentally destroyed. Choosing to begin writing his autobiography anew, he spent more

than five years in completing the work. When *Down These Mean Streets* was finally published in 1967, critics praised its power and honesty as well as its creative use of language and imagery.

Spanish Harlem Thomas's autobiography and his stories are all set in "El Barrio," the Puerto Rican community in New York City where Thomas grew up. His writing, which draws upon his memories of his experiences in Spanish Harlem, celebrates the vitality, strength, and determination of the people in his community.

AUTHOR ACTIVITY

Fiction and Real Life Find out more about the arts in the Puerto Rican community of New York City by researching El Museo del Barrio. What other artists have been inspired by Spanish Harlem?

Teaching Options

Mini Lesson **Grammar** **TEKS** 16B, 17A 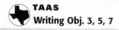 **TAAS** Writing Obj. 3, 5, 7

PUNCTUATING COORDINATE ADJECTIVES

Instruction Remind students that coordinate adjectives are two or more adjectives that modify the same noun. Coordinate adjectives should be separated by commas. Unlike compound adjectives, which depend on each other and work together as one unit, coordinate adjectives are distinctly separate and have equal weight. Display the following examples.

Coordinate Adjectives: His eyes were cut, jagged, bleeding . . . (Adjectives are separate and interchangeable; commas are necessary.)

Compound Adjectives: well-timed entrance; sky blue trunks (*well* modifies *timed; sky* modifies *blue*. Words in each pair are not interchangeable, and commas would change their meaning.)

Tell students that if they can use the word *and* between adjectives in a series and can reverse their order without changing their meaning, then the words are coordinate adjectives.

Exercises Have students rewrite the following sentences using the correct punctuation.

1. Felix listened to fast loud music before the fight. (*fast, loud music*)
2. The crowd grew silent serious and concerned. (*silent, serious, and concerned*)

Use **Unit Three Resource Book,** p. 15.
Use **Grammar Transparencies and Copymasters,** p. 127.

 Use McDougal Littell's *Language Network,* Chapter 11, for more instruction and practice in punctuation.

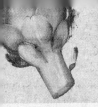

Ode to an Artichoke

Poetry by PABLO NERUDA

Connect to Your Life

Your Dream Job Did you know that it's good to daydream about what you want to do in life? There are many interesting and challenging occupations available to you, but you have to think ahead. What do you dream of becoming one day? Discuss with your classmates what it would take to get the job of your dreams.

Build Background

CONNECT TO GEOGRAPHY In "Ode to an Artichoke," Chilean poet Pablo Neruda celebrates the characteristics of a rugged plant whose immature flowers are cooked and eaten as a vegetable. While artichokes are growing, they look anything but edible. Their large flower buds are each about the size of a man's fist and are covered with hard green petals whose tips end in sharp stickers. In fact, the artichoke is a kind of thistle. It is native to the Mediterranean region of Europe, where it is a delicacy. When people from Spain, Italy, and Portugal settled in the New World, they brought the artichoke with them. Now artichokes are grown in many parts of the New World, such as Chile and California.

Chile is a long, narrow country on the Pacific Ocean coast of South America. Like California, it has a long coastline and sandy, fertile valleys inland that provide a long, cool growing season.

Artichoke plants.

Kevin Schafer/Corbis.

Focus Your Reading

LITERARY ANALYSIS METAPHOR Some **metaphors** are implied comparisons, or comparisons that aren't directly stated. For example, you may have heard on the news that a hurricane "steamrolled" across the Gulf Coast of Texas. The verb *steamrolled* is an implied metaphor that compares the storm and its power to a steamroller. A more direct metaphor, on the other hand, would link the two things more plainly: "The hurricane was a steamroller." As you read "Ode to an Artichoke," notice both the implied and direct metaphors used to describe the artichoke and other vegetables.

ACTIVE READING VISUALIZING When you form mental pictures of things you read about, you are **visualizing**. Good readers use the details supplied by writers to visualize characters, settings, and events in their minds.

READER'S NOTEBOOK As you read, visualize something that Neruda describes. Sketch your mental picture in your notebook. Above the sketch, write the key words or phrase that helped you visualize your picture.

TEKS See the Skills Trace at the beginning of the unit for information on TEKS covered in this lesson.

ODE TO AN ARTICHOKE **375**

Reading and Analyzing

Literary Analysis `METAPHOR`

 Ask students what comparison is being made in the first sentence. To what is the artichoke compared? What do the two things have in common?

Possible Responses: A soldier; someone going into battle. Both are protected by armor.

Use **Unit Three Resource Book,** p. 19, for more practice.

Active Reading `VISUALIZING`

Ask students to describe the mental images that the text descriptions evoke in the first page. Ask how these images contribute to a reader's view of the plants.

Possible Response: Students may describe the plants in human terms. They may think that the imagery helps them see how alive the plants are.

Use **Unit Three Resource Book,** p. 18, for more practice.

Literary Analysis: PERSONIFICATION

Have students point out human qualities that are given to the artichoke and other plants.

Possible Responses: The artichoke dressed in armor and stood at attention; it had a dream; the carrot slept; the cabbage tried on skirts.

Ode to an Artichoke

Oda a la alcachofa

BY

PABLO NERUDA

1 The soft-hearted
artichoke
put on armor,
stood at attention, raised
 a small turret[1]
and kept itself
watertight
under
its scales.
Beside it,
the fertile plants
tangled,
turned into
tendrils, cattails,
moving bulbs.
In the subsoil
the red-whiskered
carrot slept,
the grapevine
parched[2] the shoots
that wine climbs up,
the cabbage
busied itself
with trying on skirts,
the marjoram[3]
with making the world smell sweet,
and the gentle
artichoke
in the kitchen garden,

La alcachofa
de tierno corazón
se vistió de guerrero,
erecta, construyó
una pequeña cúpula,
se mantuvo
impermeable
bajo
sus escamas,
a su lado
los vegetales locos
se encresparon,
se hicieron
zarcillos, espadañas,
bulbos conmovedores,
en el subsuelo
durmió la zanahoria
de bigotes rojos
la viña
resecó los sarmientos
por donde sube el vino,
la col
se dedicó
a probarse faldas,
el orégano
a perfumar el mundo,
y la dulce
alcachofa
allí en el huerto,

---

1. **turret:** a small tower.
2. **parched:** dried out.
3. **marjoram:** a sweet herb used in cooking.

Teaching Options

BLOCK SCHEDULING: MANAGING TIME

If your schedule requires that you cover the lesson objectives in a shorter time, use. . .
- Preparing to Read, p. 375
- Thinking Through the Literature, p. 379

If you would like to take advantage of longer class time, use. . .
- TE Teaching Options: Speaking and Listening, p. 377, Standardized Test Practice, 378
- Choices & Challenges and Author Activity, p. 380

Illustration, © Jeff Venier/
Landry Designs

2 equipped like a soldier,
burnished[4]
like a grenade,
was full of itself.
And one day,
packed with others,
in big willow
baskets, it marched
through the market
to act out its dream—
the militia.[5]
It was never as martial[6]
in rows
as at the fair.
Among the vegetables,
men in white shirts
were
the artichokes'
marshals,
closed ranks,
commands,
the explosion

vestida de guerrero,
bruñida
como una granada,
orgullosa,
y un día
una con otra
en grandes cestos
de mimbre, caminó
por el mercado
a realizar su sueño:
la milicia.
En hileras
nunca fue tan marcial
como en la feria,
los hombres
entre las legumbres
con sus camisas blancas
eran
mariscales
de las alcachofas,
las filas apretadas,
las voces de comando,
y la detonación

4. **burnished:** polished.

5. **militia:** an irregular military force.

6. **martial:** relating to the armed forces.

Reading Skills and Strategies: CLARIFYING

A Ask students why the speaker says that Maria "fearlessly" chooses an artichoke.

Possible Responses: It is tough; it is fierce.

Literary Analysis: PERSONIFICATION

B Ask students what the word *drowns* adds to the comparison between an artichoke and a military person. What is Maria doing?

Possible Responses: A person can be drowned by being submerged in water. Maria is cooking the artichoke.

Active Reading | VISUALIZING

Ask students which images on this page paint the most vivid pictures in their minds.

Possible Responses: Students may mention Maria's holding up the artichoke; the artichoke in the bag; the artichoke's being drowned or being stripped scale by scale.

Literary Analysis | METAPHOR

Ask students how the speaker manages to extend the metaphor from the beginning of the poem to the end.

Possible Responses: The poem begins and ends with a mention of the artichoke's heart; the artichoke is described in human terms throughout the poem.

---

of a falling crate;
but
then
Maria
A shows up
with her basket,
fearlessly
chooses
an artichoke,
studies it, squints at it
against the light like an egg,
buys it,
dumps it
into her bag
with a pair of shoes,
a white cabbage and
a bottle
of vinegar
till
she enters the kitchen
B and drowns it
in the pot.
And so
this armored vegetable
men call an artichoke
ends its career
in peace.
Later,
scale by scale,
we strip
this delight
and dine on
the peaceful pulp
of its green heart.

Translation by Cheli Durán

de una caja que cae,
pero
entonces
viene
María
con su cesto,
escoge
una alcachofa,
no le teme,
la examina, la observa
contra la luz como si fuera un huevo,
la compra,
la confunde
en su bolsa
con un par de zapatos,
con un repollo y una
botella
de vinagre
hasta
que entrando a la cocina
la sumerge en la olla.
Así termina
en paz
esta carrera
del vegetal armado
que se llama alcachofa,
luego
escama por escama
desvestimos
la delicia
y comemos
la pacífica pasta
de su corazón verde.

Teaching Options

 Assessment ## Standardized Test Practice   TEKS 10H, 10K  TAAS Reading Obj. 5

EVALUATING AND MAKING JUDGMENTS In some standardized tests, students are asked to answer different types and levels of questions, such as interpretive. After students have read the poem, write the following question on the board or read it aloud:

Based on information in the poem, the reader can tell that—

A. Maria spends too much on food.

B. Maria is a careful shopper.

C. Maria is a messy person.

D. Maria is a gentle person.

Lead students through the process of choosing the best answer. Help them recognize that no evidence supports answers A, C, or D. However, from Maria's scrutiny of the artichoke, students can determine that she shops carefully. Therefore, the best answer is B.

Connect to the Literature

1. **What Do You Think?** What is your impression of the poem? Did you find it funny? Serious? Difficult? Explain.

Comprehension Check
- Why does the artichoke dream of becoming a warrior?
- Who buys the artichoke at the fair?
- What eventually happens to the artichoke?

Think Critically

2. Neruda wrote odes to many everyday things, such as salt, tomatoes, onions. Why do you think he chose to write this particular one?

 THINK ABOUT
- the artichoke's dream
- how he describes the vegetables
- the artichoke's fate

3. What details does Neruda use to describe the garden? What is it like?

4. How is the artichoke different from the other vegetables?

5. **ACTIVE READING VISUALIZING** In small groups, share the drawings in your 📖 **READER'S NOTEBOOK**. Invite each group's members to explain why they drew the picture as they did. Did anybody choose the same words or phrase to sketch?

6. Does the artichoke end "its career in peace"? Explain.

Extend Interpretations

7. **Critic's Corner** A traditional ode is a complex poem that develops a serious, dignified theme and often celebrates an element of nature. How is "Ode to an Artichoke" like a traditional ode? How is it different? What do you think the poet's intent was in writing an ode to a garden vegetable?

8. **Connect to Life** How are you like the artichoke that Neruda describes in this poem? How are you different? Explain.

Literary Analysis

METAPHOR The most frequent figure of speech in "Ode to an Artichoke" is the **metaphor.** Remember that a metaphor—either implied or directly stated—compares two things that are basically unlike but that have something in common. For example, Neruda describes carrots as sleeping men with whiskers. When the two things are compared at some length and in several ways, the figure of speech is called an **extended metaphor.** The description of the artichoke plant as an armored warrior is an extended metaphor.

Paired Activity Working with a partner, reread "Ode to an Artichoke" and write down as many metaphors as you can find. When you are done, discuss these questions with a group of your classmates.
- Which metaphor do you think is the most vivid? Why?
- What is the effect of the metaphors? Are they serious? Humorous?

Metaphors in "Ode to an Artichoke"

artichoke petals = armor

carrots growing in the ground = sleeping men with red whiskers

REVIEW PERSONIFICATION
Personification is a special kind of metaphor in which the writer gives human qualities to an animal, object, or idea.

Connect to the Literature

1. Response will vary. Students should give reasons for their reactions.

Comprehension Check
- Possible Response: It is soft-hearted but since it is equipped like a soldier, it has always had the dream.
- A woman named Maria buys it.
- It is cooked and eaten.

Think Critically

2. Responses may vary. Students might decide that he looked at the vegetable and thought of its scales as armor.

3. He describes the action of the vegetables, showing that the garden is teeming with life.

4. Possible Responses: It is armored; it is full of itself; it has dreams.

5. Responses will vary. Students may have illustrated any number of words or phrases.

📖 Use **Reading and Critical Thinking Transparencies,** p. 10, for additional support.

6. Responses will vary. Some students may answer yes, because the meal itself is peaceful; others may say no, because the artichoke itself was taken apart.

Literary Analysis

Metaphor Students will probably pick different images, but they should explain why they chose them. Many of the metaphors are humorous, such as the red-whiskered carrot or the cabbage trying on skirts.

Review: Personification Students should mention specific human characteristics that Neruda gives the vegetables, such as emotions (soft-hearted), intention (to act out its dream), or actions (the sleeping carrot).

📖 Use **Literary Analysis Transparencies,** p. 19, for additional support.

Extend Interpretations

7. **Critics Corner** Possible Responses: It is traditional in that it celebrates nature and has a serious tone. It is untraditional in its use of humor and in its use of the ridiculous. If you wish to make this question easier, provide the titles of some classic odes: *Ode to a Nightingale; Ode on a Grecian Urn; Ode to the Confederate Dead; Ode to Evening.* Ask students to speculate about the tone of these odes. Then have them respond to the question.

8. **Connect to Life** Responses may vary. Students might say that like the artichoke they have armored exteriors covering soft hearts or that they, too, have dreams. The differences include what those dreams are

Writing Options

1. Everyday Ode Students' odes should contain their feelings or thoughts about the poem's subject. To get students started on this assignment, have them make lists of common objects that they use during the day.

 Use **Writing Transparencies**, p. 1, for additional support.

2. War Correspondence Students might begin by writing the opening and closing events of the poem. Then they can go back and fill in the other events.

Activities & Explorations

1. Vegetable Art For inspiration, you might have students recall animated objects that they have seen in films and cartoons.

2. Poetry Reading If no students are native Spanish speakers, invite volunteers to take turns reading the poem aloud. Allow students time to read the poem silently several times before reading it aloud.

 Use **Communications Transparencies and Copymasters**, p. 12, for additional support.

Inquiry & Research

Where Do Artichokes Grow? Students might work in teams or pairs, with one group checking out cookbooks, another looking at gardening books, and a third looking at encyclopedias. Then they could share the information and use it to write their brochure. Suggest that they begin the brochure by imagining the questions that grocers would want to ask.

 Use **Writing Transparencies**, p. 45, for additional support.

Pablo Neruda

Pablo Neruda's given name was Neftalí Ricardo Reyes Basoalto. His father was a railroad worker who did not want his son to become a writer. Rather than giving up that dream, the boy gave up his family name. He took the name of Czech writer Jan Neruda.

Author Activity

Neruda's Life Abroad Students might begin by listing the places that Neruda lived and the times that he lived there. Then they could transfer this information onto a map that they create.

Choices & CHALLENGES

Writing Options

1. Everyday Ode An ode is usually a ceremonious poem full of personal emotion and reflection. Neruda's odes are unusual in that they celebrate everyday, ordinary objects, like onions, tomatoes, and salt. Write your own ode celebrating an everyday object.

2. War Correspondence Describe the market and kitchen scenes in the poem as if you were describing a play-by-play account of a "battle" from the artichoke's point of view. Create a time line of the artichoke's day as described in the poem to help organize your writing.
Writing Handbook
See p. R28: Transitions.

Activities & Explorations

1. Vegetable Art Create a sculpture, drawing, or painting highlighting one of the metaphors from the poem. If you wish, you may use your sketch from your **READER'S NOTEBOOK** as a starting point. ~ **ART**

2. Poetry Reading "Ode to an Artichoke" was written in Spanish and then translated into English. If you know Spanish, read the original version of the poem aloud for the class. Afterward, share the line or lines that you enjoyed most. ~ **PERFORMING**

Inquiry & Research

Where Do Artichokes Grow? Using cookbooks, gardening books, or encyclopedias, find out where artichokes grow, how they grow, and what kinds are available where you live. Learn how they are prepared and eaten. After you have done your research, imagine that you are an artichoke farmer. Working in small groups, create an informational brochure that you could hand out to grocers.

"The soft-hearted artichoke put on armor, . . ."

Pablo Neruda
1904–1973

A Young Chilean Poet When Pablo Neruda was ten, his family moved to the southern part of Chile, a region where it rains much of the year, and vegetation is green and lush. Neruda was immediately inspired. "Nature there went to my head," he said. "I was barely ten at the time, but already a poet." By the time Neruda was 20, he had published his first book of poetry.

World Traveler Neruda was appointed to the Chilean diplomatic service and spent time in Burma, Ceylon, the Dutch East Indies, Argentina, Mexico, Spain, and France. His travels influenced his poetry, but nothing was more influential to him than the landscape and culture of Latin America. Neruda received many awards for his poetry, including the Nobel Prize in literature.

AUTHOR ACTIVITY

Neruda's Life Abroad Neruda spent much of his life living in places other than his native Chile. Find out more about Neruda's life abroad. In small groups, create a map that shows places Neruda lived. Be sure to list the years he spent at each location.

PREPARING to *Read*

from An American Childhood

Nonfiction by ANNIE DILLARD

I wanted the glory to last forever."

Connect to Your Life

Harmless Pranks Have you ever been involved in an innocent prank or a prank that *seemed* innocent to you but that caused a different reaction in someone else? What happened? Did you change your mind when you heard the other person's point of view? Share your experiences with the class.

Build Background

CONNECT TO SOCIAL STUDIES

The selection you are about to read takes place in a suburban neighborhood of Pittsburgh, Pennsylvania. Pittsburgh is the largest city in western Pennsylvania. It sprawls over the hilly area where the Allegheny and Monongahela rivers come together to form the Ohio River.

A residential neighborhood of Pittsburgh, Pennsylvania.

WORDS TO KNOW Vocabulary Preview
redundant righteous   translucent
revert   spherical

 See the Skills Trace at the beginning of the unit for information on TEKS covered in this lesson.

Focus Your Reading

LITERARY ANALYSIS **NARRATIVE NONFICTION** The selection you are about to read is a work of **narrative nonfiction.** Like other nonfiction, it describes people, places, and events that are real, not fictional. As a narrative, however, it shares many of the characteristics of fiction, such as **plot, character, setting,** and **dialogue.** Writers of narrative nonfiction use the techniques of fiction to present factual matter in a lively way that draws readers into the action. As you read, notice the fiction techniques the author uses.

ACTIVE READING **CAUSE AND EFFECT** Good readers try to understand relationships of cause and effect when they read. Two events are related as **cause and effect** when one event brings about the other. The event that happens first in time is the cause; the one that follows is the effect. Often an event that is the effect of one cause in turn becomes the cause of another effect, forming a chain of cause and effect. As you read, jot down in your 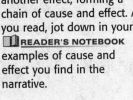 **READER'S NOTEBOOK** examples of cause and effect you find in the narrative.

> Heavy snow covers the ground.
>
> It's not possible to play baseball or football.
>
> Boys and girls look for other things to do outdoors.

OVERVIEW

Objectives
1. understand and identify **narrative nonfiction** (Literary Analysis)
2. understand **suspense, complication** and **climax** as elements of **plot** in narrative nonfiction (Literary Analysis)
3. understand **cause and effect** in plot (Active Reading)

Summary
Annie Dillard knew how to play both football and baseball, but in winter neither was available, so she and the boys threw snowballs at cars. One snowy morning when she was seven, she and five boys managed to hit a slow-moving car. Surprisingly, it stopped and the driver got out and chased the children. They ran away, but he pursued. The group split up, and the man followed Dillard and Mike Fahey. Block after block they raced, and Dillard joyfully realized that this adult knew something that she thought only children trained in football understood: "You have to fling yourself at what you're doing." Finally, he caught up with them and scolded them. Dillard didn't care. She loved the glory of being part of that chase and realized later that there was nothing that the man could have done to prolong the drama.

Thematic Link
Not only is Dillard surprised when the car stops after being pelted by snowballs, but the reader may also be surprised by her reaction to the chase that followed.

Reading and Analyzing

Literary Analysis
NARRATIVE NONFICTION

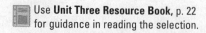

A Ask students how they know in the first sentence that the narrator is a character in this piece.

Answer: She uses the pronoun *me*.

B Review with students, if necessary, three major elements of fiction: plot, character, and setting. Then ask students what they learn in this nonfiction piece about the characters and setting. What clue does the narrator give about the plot?

Possible Responses: It is winter; snow is on the ground. The narrator was seven and there were five boys. She says that she got in trouble throwing snowballs.

Use **Unit Three Resource Book**, p. 22 for guidance in reading the selection.

Active Reading   CAUSE AND EFFECT

C Ask students what caused the driver to stop the car and jump out.

Possible Responses: He was angry; he was frightened; he wanted to scold the kids.

Use **Unit Three Resource Book**, p. 21 for guidance in reading the selection.

Literary Analysis
NARRATIVE NONFICTION

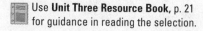

Ask students to explain what they learn about the narrator on this page.

Possible Responses: She likes football; she can throw well; she got in trouble and was happy; she was seven; she thought throwing ice balls was unfair.

from

An American Childhood

BY ANNIE DILLARD

Backyards, Greenwich Village (1914), John Sloan. Oil on canvas, 26" x 32". Photograph by Geoffrey Clements. © 1999: Whitney Museum of American Art.

382   UNIT THREE   PART 1: SURPRISING TURNS

Teaching Options

Mini Lesson   **Preteaching Vocabulary**   TEKS 9B, 9F   TAAS Reading Obj. 1, 6

SYNONYMS AND ANTONYMS

Instruction Call students' attention to the list of WORDS TO KNOW on page 381. Remind them that when they learn new words, they must learn to distinguish denotative and connotative meanings. Even though two words may be synonyms, with similar denotative meanings, they may have different connotations. For example, *big* and *bulky* are synonyms, but *bulky* suggests weight. Antonyms may also have different connotations. Both *wild* and *untamed* are antonyms of *tame*, yet *wild* suggests some element of danger.

Application Have students look through the selection to find the meaning of each word in the list of WORDS TO KNOW. Encourage them to think of synonyms and antonyms for each word before they read. Then, while they read, they should notice if the words that they chose have similar connotations to the words in the selection.

Use **Unit Three Resource Book**, p. 23 for more exercises.

Use **Vocabulary Transparencies and Copymasters**, p. 49, for additional support.

Some boys taught me to play football.
This was fine sport. You thought up a new strategy for every play and whispered it to the others. You went out for a pass, fooling everyone. Best, you got to throw yourself mightily at someone's running legs. Either you brought him down or you hit the ground flat out on your chin, with your arms empty before you. It was all or nothing. If you hesitated in fear, you would miss and get hurt: you would take a hard fall while the kid got away, or you would get kicked in the face while the kid got away. But if you flung yourself wholeheartedly at the back of his knees—if you gathered and joined body and soul and pointed them diving fearlessly—then you likely wouldn't get hurt, and you'd stop the ball. Your fate, and your team's score, depended on your concentration and courage. Nothing girls did could compare with it.

Boys welcomed me at baseball, too, for I had, through enthusiastic practice, what was weirdly known as a boy's arm. In winter, in the snow, there was neither baseball nor football, so the boys and I threw snowballs at passing cars. I got in trouble throwing snowballs, and have seldom been happier since.

On one weekday morning after Christmas, six inches of new snow had just fallen. We were standing up to our boot tops in snow on a front yard on trafficked Reynolds Street, waiting for cars. The cars traveled Reynolds Street slowly and evenly; they were targets all but wrapped in red ribbons, cream puffs. We couldn't miss.

I was seven; the boys were eight, nine, and ten. The oldest two Fahey boys were there—Mikey and Peter—polite blond boys who lived near me on Lloyd Street, and who already had four brothers and sisters. My parents approved

Mikey and Peter Fahey. Chickie McBride was there, a tough kid, and Billy Paul and Mackie Kean, too, from across Reynolds, where the boys grew up dark and furious, grew up skinny, knowing, and skilled. We had all drifted from our houses that morning looking for action, and had found it here on Reynolds Street.

It was cloudy but cold. The cars' tires laid behind them on the snowy street a complex trail of beige chunks like crenellated castle walls. I had stepped on some earlier; they squeaked. We could have wished for more traffic. When a car came, we all popped it one. In the intervals between cars we <u>reverted</u> to the natural solitude of children.

I started making an iceball—a perfect iceball, from perfectly white snow, perfectly <u>spherical</u>, and squeezed perfectly <u>translucent</u> so no snow remained all the way through. (The Fahey boys and I considered it unfair actually to throw an iceball at somebody, but it had been known to happen.)

I had just embarked on the iceball project when we heard tire chains come clanking from afar. A black Buick was moving toward us down the street. We all spread out, banged together some regular snowballs, took aim, and, when the Buick drew nigh, fired.

A soft snowball hit the driver's windshield right before the driver's face. It made a smashed star with a hump in the middle.

Often, of course, we hit our target, but this time, the only time in all of life, the car pulled over and stopped. Its wide black door opened; a man got out of it, running. He didn't even close the car door.

He ran after us, and we ran away from him, up the snowy Reynolds sidewalk. At the corner, I looked back; incredibly, he was still after us. He was in city clothes: a suit and tie,

3
4
C

WORDS	**revert** (rǐ-vûrt') v. to return to a former condition
TO	**spherical** (sfîr'ĭ-kəl) adj. having the shape of a round ball
KNOW	**translucent** (trăns-lōō'sənt) adj. allowing light to pass through

383

Customizing Instruction

Less Proficient Readers
Explain to students that the first paragraph is an introduction. The story begins in the second paragraph.
Set a Purpose Invite students to read to find out why the beginning paragraph about football is important to understanding the story.

Students Acquiring English
Before students read the essay, discuss and explain the following idioms:
1 *a boy's arm:* an arm that was as strong and accurate as a boy's arm
2 *cream puffs:* easy targets
3 *looking for action:* looking for something to do
4 *popped it one:* threw a snowball at it

Use **Spanish Study Guide**, pp. 79–81 for additional support.

Multiple Learning Styles
Visual Learners
Students may find it easier to "see" the story if they create simple story maps such as the following:

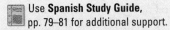

Characters:		
Setting:		
Event 1:		
Event 2:		
Event 3:		
Ending:		

Use **Reading and Critical Thinking Transparencies**, p. 34, for additional support.

Gifted and Talented
Have students consider how a different type of person might have responded to the events of this narrative.

Possible Responses: Some would have felt frightened or angry or unhappy.

BLOCK SCHEDULING: MANAGING TIME

If your schedule requires that you cover the lesson objectives in a shorter time, use. . .
• Preparing to Read, p. 381
• Thinking Through the Literature, p. 388
• Vocabulary and Spelling, p. 389
• Grammar in Context, p. 390

If you would like to take advantage of longer class time, use. . .
• TE Teaching Options: Preteaching Vocabulary, p. 382; Grammar, pp. 384, 390; Multicultural Link, p. 385; Standardized Test Practice, p. 386; Speaking and Listening, p. 387; Spelling, p. 389
• Choices & Challenges and Author Activity, pp. 389–390

Reading and Analyzing

Literary Analysis

NARRATIVE NONFICTION

A Ask students how this paragraph adds to the suspense.

Possible Responses: The narrator expected to run away from the man, but he keeps chasing them. Since he looks active, he might actually catch them, so they are running for their lives.

Active Reading CAUSE AND EFFECT

B Ask what caused the running children to split up.

Answer: They thought they could lose themselves in the neighborhood; it was everyone for himself.

Literary Analysis

NARRATIVE NONFICTION

C Point out that plot complications often come in a series or chain. Ask students to identify various complications that the narrator includes.

Possible Responses: Students might mention where the children ran, or how the narrator kept glancing back.

D Ask students to identify the climax and tell why it is a turning point.

Possible Responses: The climax is when the man catches them; now readers will find out what happened.

384

Teaching Options

 Grammar 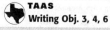 TEKS 17D TAAS Writing Obj. 3, 4, 6

STRONG VERBS

Instruction Just as the right adjective can replace several less-precise ones, so can a strong verb replace a weaker verb and an adverb.

Weak verb: I <u>went</u> into the room <u>quietly</u>.

Stronger: I <u>tiptoed</u> into the room.

Exercises Replace the underlined verbs and adverbs with stronger verbs.

Possible answers are given.

1. Annie <u>threw</u> the snowball <u>hard</u>. *(heaved)*
2. The children <u>ran quickly</u> out of sight. *(raced)*
3. The car <u>came noisily</u> down the street. *(clanked)*
4. The man <u>spoke loudly</u>, but I barely listened. *(yelled)*

 Use **Grammar Transparencies and Copymasters**, p. 137.

 Use McDougal Littell's *Language Network*, Chapter 19, for more instruction and practice in using strong verbs.

street shoes. Any normal adult would have quit, having sprung us into flight and made his point. This man was gaining on us. He was a thin man, all action. All of a sudden, we were running for our lives.

Wordless, we split up. We were on our turf; we could lose ourselves in the neighborhood backyards, everyone for himself. I paused and considered. Everyone had vanished except Mikey Fahey, who was just rounding the corner of a yellow brick house. Poor Mikey—I trailed him. The driver of the Buick sensibly picked the two of us to follow. The man apparently had all day.

He chased Mikey and me around the yellow house and up a backyard path we knew by heart: under a low tree, up a bank, through a hedge, down some snowy steps, and across the grocery store's delivery driveway. We smashed through a gap in another hedge, entered a scruffy backyard, and ran around its back porch and tight between houses to Edgerton Avenue; we ran across Edgerton to an alley and up our own sliding woodpile to the Halls' front yard; he kept coming. We ran up Lloyd Street and wound through mazy backyards toward the steep hilltop at Willard and Lang.

He chased us silently, block after block. He chased us silently over picket fences, through thorny hedges, between houses, around garbage cans, and across streets. Every time I glanced back, choking for breath, I expected he would have quit. He must have been as breathless as we were. His jacket strained over his body. It was an immense discovery, pounding into my hot head with every sliding, joyous step, that this ordinary adult evidently knew what I thought only children who trained at football knew: that you have to fling yourself at what you're doing, you have to point yourself, forget yourself, aim, dive.

Mikey and I had nowhere to go, in our own neighborhood or out of it, but away from this man who was chasing us. He impelled us forward; we compelled him to follow our route. The air was cold; every breath tore my throat. We kept running, block after block; we kept improvising, backyard after backyard, running a frantic course and choosing it simultaneously, failing always to find small places or hard places to slow him down, and discovering always, exhilarated, dismayed, that only bare speed could save us—for he would never give up, this man—and we were losing speed.

He chased us through the backyard labyrinths of ten blocks before he caught us by our jackets. He caught us and we all stopped.

We three stood staggering, half blinded, coughing, in an obscure hilltop backyard: a man in his twenties, a boy, a girl. He had released our jackets, our pursuer, our captor, our hero: he knew we weren't going anywhere. We all played by the rules. Mikey and I unzipped our jackets. I pulled off my sopping mittens. Our tracks multiplied in the backyard's new snow. We had been breaking new snow all morning. We didn't look at each other. I was cherishing my excitement. The man's lower pant legs were wet; his cuffs were full of snow, and there was a prow of snow beneath them on his shoes and socks. Some trees bordered the little flat backyard, some messy winter trees. There was no one around: a clearing in a grove, and we the only players.

Snow (1967), Alice Neel. Oil on canvas, 80″ × 60″, © The Estate of Alice Neel, courtesy of Robert Miller Gallery, New York, NY. Collection Katherine Cole. (page 384)

AN AMERICAN CHILDHOOD **385**

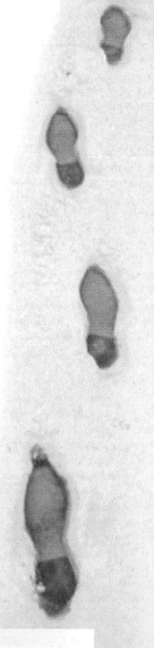

Reading and Analyzing

Active Reading | CAUSE AND EFFECT

A Ask students why the man couldn't speak at first and why the narrator couldn't remember why they were there.

Answer: They were all exhausted from the chase.

Literary Analysis
NARRATIVE NONFICTION

B Ask students how the plot actually resolves itself. What happened at the end of the chase?

Answer: He just said "You stupid kids," and lectured them.

Reading Skills and Strategies:
RECOGNIZING AUTHOR'S PURPOSE

C Ask students why the writer might have ended the narrative this way. Why didn't she just end it with the sentence, "I wanted the glory to last forever"?

Possible Responses: She wanted to reflect on the experience as an adult; she wanted to point out that what the man did was not important, but what she did—giving her all—was what stayed in her mind.

Active Reading | CAUSE AND EFFECT

What caused the narrator to see the race as glorious and the man as "sainted"?

Answer: He had chased them passionately without giving up, and they had run as hard as they could.

A It was a long time before he could speak. I had some difficulty at first recalling why we were there. My lips felt swollen; I couldn't see out of the sides of my eyes; I kept coughing.

"You stupid kids," he began perfunctorily.

B
1 We listened perfunctorily indeed, if we listened at all, for the chewing out was <u>redundant</u>, a mere formality, and beside the point. The point was that he had chased us passionately without giving up, and so he had caught us. Now he came down to earth. I wanted the glory to last forever.

But how could the glory have lasted forever?
We could have run through every backyard in North America until we got to Panama. But when he trapped us at the lip of the Panama Canal, what precisely could he have done to prolong the drama of the chase and cap its glory? I brooded about this for the next few

2 years. He could only have fried Mikey Fahey and me in boiling oil, say, or dismembered us piecemeal, or staked us to anthills. None of which I really wanted, and none of which any adult was likely to do, even in the spirit of fun. He could only chew us out there in the Panamanian jungle, after months or years of exalting pursuit. He could only begin, "You stupid kids," and

C continue in his ordinary Pittsburgh accent with his normal <u>righteous</u> anger and the usual common sense.

If in that snowy backyard the driver of the black Buick had cut off our heads, Mikey's and mine, I would have died happy, for nothing has required so much of me since as being chased all over Pittsburgh in the middle of winter—running terrified, exhausted—by this sainted, skinny, furious redheaded man who wished to have a word with us. I don't know how he found his way back to his car. ❖

WORDS
TO
KNOW

redundant (rĭ-dŭn′dənt) *adj.* more than what is necessary
righteous (rī′chəs) *adj.* caused by an insult to one's sense of right

386

Teaching Options

 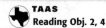

CAUSE AND EFFECT In some standardized tests, students are asked to use and analyze the text's progression of ideas, such as cause and effect. After students have read the story, write the following question on the board or read it aloud: Why did the man decide to chase Annie and Mikey instead of the others?

A. Annie and Mikey looked slow.

B. They all played by the rules.

C. The others had disappeared.

D. The man was in city clothes.

Lead students through the process of choosing the best answer. Help them recognize that there is no cause and effect link between the question and answers A, B, or D. No evidence supports A, and B and D are not causally related to the man's decision to chase those two instead of the others. Therefore, the best answer is C.

Winter Poem

BY NIKKI GIOVANNI

once a snowflake fell
on my brow and i loved
it so much and i kissed
it and it was happy and called its cousins
and brothers and a web
of snow engulfed me then
i reached to love them all
and i squeezed them and they became
a spring rain and i stood perfectly
still and was a flower

Snowflakes Photomicrographs by Wilson A. Bentley (1865–1931). Courtesy Jericho (Vermont) Historical Society.

Customizing Instruction

Students Acquiring English
1 You may want to point out that the idiom *chewing out* means "scolding."

Less Proficient Readers
2 If students have trouble understanding the ending, direct their attention to the following sentences: "The point was that he had chased us"; "But when he trapped us at the lip of the Panama Canal"; "If in that snowy backyard the driver . . .".

LITERARY LINK

This piece reflects some of the ideas in the main selection and is suggested for students' independent reading. Optional discussion questions follow.

1. How is the setting of this poem like that of the narrative?
   Answer: Both take place in snow.
2. In what way are the narrators' feelings alike?
   Answer: Both are delighted.
3. What causes the speaker's delight here, and how is it different from what caused Dillard's?
   Possible Response: This speaker is thrilled by the snow; Dillard was thrilled by the passion of the moment.

Nikki Giovanni

Coming of age in Tennessee during the civil rights movement of the 1960s, Nikki Giovanni (b. 1943) began her career by writing poems about the black experience. Her first two books were *Black Feeling, Black Talk* and *Black Judgment.* Later, she expanded her work to include other kinds of poetry, children's literature, personal essays, and even recordings.

 Assessment **Speaking and Listening**   TEKS 5F

DEBATE ON EQUALITY IN SPORTS
Prepare At the beginning of the story, the narrator mentions that girls' sports lacked the all-or-nothing quality of football. Have students form two teams to debate the question. Explain that debates require participants to clarify and support spoken ideas with evidence, elaborations, and examples. In a debate, each team must
- state its position clearly
- support its position with reasons, facts, statistics, and examples
- use persuasive language
- respond to the other team's arguments

Present Allow time for students to do preliminary research on the subject of women's sports. Then have students set the ground rules for a debate, allowing only a certain amount of time for each speaker. Have students argue the question in front of an audience, who then votes on the winner.

You may wish to link this activity to Connect to Life on page 388.

BLOCK SCHEDULING This activity is particularly well suited for longer class periods.

Use **Communications Transparencies and Copymasters,** p. 3, for additional support.

GUIDING STUDENT RESPONSE

Connect to the Literature

1. Response will vary. Students may say that Dillard seems adventurous, detail-oriented, fun, nostalgic, biased against girls/girls' abilities, self-righteous, proud.

Comprehension Check

- They threw snowballs at his windshield.
- Possible Responses: skinny, wearing a suit, furious, redhaired, determined.
- He yelled at them and scolded them.

 Use Selection Quiz **Unit Three Resource Book**, p. 26

Think Critically

2. Possible Response: It was such a glorious moment. She said that she had "seldom been happier since."
3. Possible Responses: She describes him only in broad outlines. Students may point out the description in the next-to-last sentence.
4. Possible Responses: Students will probably mention the snowball throwing causing the chase and the narrator's love of football as the cause of her delight in the chase.

 Use **Reading and Critical Thinking Transparencies**, p. 3, for additional support.

Literary Analysis

Narrative Nonfiction Students' charts may vary, but might include: car approaching, throwing the snowball, getting chased, being caught, waiting for the man's reaction after the chase. Students who consider Dillard successful may point out that they wanted to keep reading to see what happened, that they never thought the man would last so long, or that he would yell the standard adult yell; students who disagree may point out that they knew all along what was going to happen.

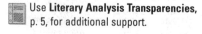 Use **Literary Analysis Transparencies**, p. 5, for additional support.

Connect to the Literature

1. **What Do You Think?**
   Do you think Dillard would make an interesting friend? Explain your response.

   Comprehension Check
   - Why did the man chase Dillard and her friends?
   - What was he like?
   - What happened when he caught up to them?

Think Critically

2. Why do you think Dillard choose to write about this particular childhood memory?

   THINK ABOUT {
   - her reaction when she got caught
   - the chase scene
   - what the man said

3. How well does Dillard describe the man in the story? Find a passage that helps you imagine what kind of person he was.

4. **ACTIVE READING** **CAUSE AND EFFECT** Look over the list you made in your **READER'S NOTEBOOK**. Using your notes, discuss with classmates what you think are the major cause-and-effect events in the story.

Extend Interpretations

5. **COMPARING TEXTS** Read "Winter Poem" on page 387. Compare and contrast how Nikki Giovanni and Annie Dillard describe winter.

6. **What If?** How do you think the telling of the story would have changed if the man had given up before he caught Dillard and her friend?

7. **Connect to Life** Dillard says that when she was growing up, nothing girls did could compare to playing football. Do you think there is still a difference between girls' and boys' athletic activities? Explain your answer.

Literary Analysis

NARRATIVE NONFICTION

Writing that deals with real people, places, and events is called nonfiction. *An American Childhood* is an example of **narrative nonfiction.** It uses elements usually found in fiction, such as **plot, character, setting,** and **dialogue,** to present factual information and bring the events to life for the reader.

Dillard's fast-paced description of the chase reads like one you might find in a short story:

Under a low tree, up a bank, through a hedge, down some snowy steps, and across the grocery store's delivery driveway.

Paired Activity Suspense, complication, and climax are three elements of plot that you can find in this nonfiction narrative from *An American Childhood*. With a partner, go back through the story and find examples of each. Do you think Dillard was successful in creating these three elements of plot? Discuss your opinion with your partner.

Suspense	Complication	Climax
A black car moves forward as the group with snowballs waits.	The group throws snowballs and the driver stops his car and chases.	

Extend Interpretations

5. **Comparing Texts** Possible Responses: Both poets seem to love snow, but Dillard focuses on action—on what happened in snow—while Giovanni's poem is more about feelings and images. **To adapt this assignment to Logical/Mathematical Learners,** suggest that students begin by creating a comparison-contrast chart, like the following:

Dillard	Giovanni

6. **What If?** Possible Responses: The story would have had less suspense; the narrator might have felt disappointed; she might not have told the story at all; she might have stressed how perseverance allows people to win.

7. **Connect to Life** Responses may vary. Some students may point out how much emphasis and money is given to men's sports, such as football and baseball; others will mention the growing popularity of women's sports, including soccer and basketball.

Choices & CHALLENGES

Writing Options

1. Adventure Narrative Write about a real-life adventure you have experienced or heard about. Use elements of narrative nonfiction, such as plot, characters, and setting, to bring your story to life. Place the narrative in your **Working Portfolio.**

2. Letter to the Editor Suppose the man in the black car wanted to warn young people about the dangers of throwing snowballs at moving vehicles. Write the letter you think he might write to a local newspaper about the incident.

Writing Handbook
See p. R39: Persuasive Writing.

Activities & Explorations

1. Comic Strip Review the stages in Dillard's description of the chase. Depict the chase in the form of an action comic strip. ~ **ART**

2. Snow Poem Write a poem about snow. Before beginning the poem, use a cluster diagram to explore your thoughts and expressions. Share your completed poem with your classmates.
~ **SPEAKING AND LISTENING**

Art Connection

Look at the painting by John Sloan on page 382. Describe your feelings as you look at it. Does it capture the mood of the selection? Why or why not?

Inquiry & Research

Chilly Challenges! Using the Internet, an encyclopedia, or other resources, find out more about winter activities and sports. Choose one that especially interests you and prepare a report on it to share with your class.

Vocabulary and Spelling

EXERCISE A: SYNONYMS AND ANTONYMS On a separate sheet of paper, write *S* if the word pairs are synonyms and *A* if they are antonyms. You may use a dictionary to help you.

1. **revert**—return
2. **spherical**—round
3. **translucent**—opaque
4. **redundant**—superfluous
5. **righteous**—immoral

EXERCISE B: GREEK COMBINING FORMS Many English words contain elements derived from Greek words. Recognizing these elements and knowing their meanings can help you spell and understand English words that contain them. Some common Greek combining forms are *astro* (star); *bio* (life); *ge* (earth); *hemi* (half, partial); *logo, logy* (study of);

phys (nature); *psych, psycho* (spirit); *therapy* (medical treatment); *spher, sphere* (sphere).

sphere	spherical	hemisphere
biohazard	antibiotic	biosphere
astrology	biology	geology
psychic	psychology	psychotherapy
physics	physician	astrophysics

1. Which Greek word elements make up the word *psychology*?
2. Which spelling words in Exercise B contain the Greek word element meaning "life"?
3. Write three complete sentences using three or more of the spelling words in Exercise B.

Spelling Handbook p. R86

---

1. Adventure Narrative Students' narratives should be told as if they were stories. They should have distinct characters, a recognizable setting, and a plot. To get students started on this assignment, suggest that they begin by recalling times when they felt a strong emotion, such as fear, delight, or anger.

Use **Writing Transparencies,** p. 1, for additional support.

2. Letter to the Editor Briefly review the elements of a persuasive letter, including reasons that are arranged in some logical order, such as order of importance.

Use **Writing Transparencies,** p. 11, for additional support.

Activities & Explorations

1. Comic Strip Students may enjoy working in teams, as many professionals do. One artist draws while the second inks and colors.

2. Snow Poem To inspire students, especially those who live in warm climates, display pictures of snow. These might be found in magazines, catalogs, and books.

Use **Communications Transparencies and Copymasters,** p. 12, for additional support.

Art Connection

Encourage students to include specific details from the art when they give the reasons for their answers.

Inquiry & Research

Chilly Challenges! To help students begin, you may wish to have a brainstorming session to generate names of various activities and sports. Encourage students to consider ones that they've seen on television, as well as those in which they have participated.

Use **Writing Transparencies,** pp. 44, 47–48, for additional support.

Vocabulary and Spelling

Exercise A	Exercise B
1. S	1. *psych* and *logy*
2. S	2. biohazard, biosphere, biology
3. A	
4. S	3. Sentences will differ.
5. A	

GREEK WORD PARTS

To help students understand the influence of other languages on the spelling of English words, explain that a knowledge of Greek word parts can help them spell any words that contain these parts.

Example: graph   telegraph   photograph
Words with Greek parts from the selection:
   spherical
Other words with Greek parts

bio	biography	biology
logi, logy	logic	apology
phon	telephone	symphony

phys	physical	physics
psych	psychotherapy	psychic

Exercises Choose the spelling word that best completes the sentence.

1. I am sorry; I hope you will accept my _____.
2. The _____ is ringing. Can you get it?
3. The Earth is almost _____ in shape.
4. Were you tired out from _____ or mental work?
5. A _____ is the story of someone's life.

Use **Unit Three Resource Book,** p. 25 for more practice.

Choices & CHALLENGES

Grammar in Context: Avoiding Too Many Adjectives

Annie Dillard uses carefully chosen **adjectives** to make her writing lively and effective.

> We . . . entered a scruffy backyard . . .

> I pulled off my sopping mittens.

A less careful writer might try to make his or her writing vivid by using several adjectives where one, well-chosen adjective would do the job better. What if Dillard had written, "We entered a messy, untidy, and cluttered backyard" or "I pulled off my sopping, wet mittens"? Would that give you a clearer idea of the condition of the yard or the mittens? Do these adjectives add more information than Dillard's original words?

WRITING EXERCISE Replace the underlined adjectives with a single, more precise adjective. You may keep one of the original adjectives if it seems adequate.

Example: *Original* I had, through long, eager practice, developed a mighty strong pitching arm.

Rewritten I had, through enthusiastic practice, developed a strong pitching arm.

1. The owner of the dark, black car was a slender, thin, agile man who seemed to have time on his hands.
2. He was wearing a heavy, warm, lined jacket.
3. Mikey and I ran through the old, familiar, local playground.
4. When he finally caught us, Mikey and I were panting, tired and weary from the chase.

Grammar Handbook Using Modifiers Effectively, p. R70

"I'll go anywhere that beauty leads me."

Annie Dillard
born 1945

Nature Lover Annie Doak Dillard, the eldest of three daughters, was born in Pittsburgh. Her parents encouraged her love of reading and the outdoors. One of Dillard's favorite books while she was growing up was *The Field Book of Ponds and Streams*. With a microscope and a jar of pond water, she would spend many hours observing daphnia, planaria, and other small pond creatures. While in high school, Dillard rebelled against her privileged upbringing and began reading and writing poetry. She particularly admired Ralph Waldo Emerson, who spoke to her love of the natural world.

Inspirational Writer Dillard's 1968 master's thesis, on Henry David Thoreau's *Walden*, pointed to her continued interest in nature. Then frail health led her to spend a year in meditation and closer observation of the natural world. The result was the 1975 Pulitzer Prize-winning *Pilgrim at Tinker Creek*. This work earned Dillard a reputation as an inspirational writer who worked religious teachings and the role of the artist in society into her celebrations of the natural world.

AUTHOR ACTIVITY

Tales of Childhood The story you just read is a chapter from Dillard's book *An American Childhood*. Read one of the other chapters in the book. How is it similar to and how does it differ from the selection you just read? Present an oral report on your chosen selection to your classmates.

Grammar in Context

WRITING EXERCISE
Possible Responses:

1. The owner of the underlined black car was a skinny man who seemed to have time on his hands.
2. He was wearing a winter jacket.
3. Mikey and I ran through the neighborhood playground.
4. When he finally caught us, Mikey and I were panting, exhausted from the chase.

Annie Dillard

When Dillard first went to live near Tinker Creek, she spent most of her indoor time reading. Only after the first year did she begin to spend that time writing. It took her less than a year to turn her notes into a book. However, at the end of that time, she was writing more than 12 hours a day.

Author Activity

Tales of Childhood Students' responses might mention similarities and differences in setting, plot, characters, and feelings.

Teaching Options

 Mini Lesson **Grammar** 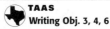 **TEKS 17D** **TAAS Writing Obj. 3, 4, 6**

WRITING WITH ADJECTIVES

Instruction Remind students that a writer must learn to strike a balance between using too few adjectives and using too many. Well-placed, carefully chosen adjectives can bring sentences alive and help readers to visualize a scene or a feeling. Too many adjectives, however, can actually make writing boring and less effective.

Read to students the following examples:

- She stood in the wind and made an ice ball out of snow. Snow soaked into her mittens as she worked.

- She stood in the icy, frigid, cold wind and made a hard, solid, firm ice ball out of damp, wet, snow. Snow soaked into her thick, heavy mittens as she worked.

- She stood in the frigid wind and made an ice ball out of wet snow. Snow soaked into her thick mittens as she worked.

Ask students which passage is most clear and vivid. Students are likely to choose the third passage. Ask them to explain their reasons behind their choices.

Application Ask students to write a descriptive paragraph about an outdoor experience. When they have completed their paragraphs, they should exchange them with a partner. Each student editor should give suggestions on where adjectives could be removed or added.

Use **Unit Three Resource Book**, p. 24.
Use **Grammar Transparencies and Copymasters**, p. 138.

 Use McDougal Littell's *Language Network*, Chapter 19, for more instruction and practice in writing with adjectives.

The Bat

Poetry by THEODORE ROETHKE

Mooses

Poetry by TED HUGHES

Connect to Your Life

Creature Features Has anyone ever told you that you are as wise as an owl? stubborn as a mule? fast as a rabbit? Or, you may have noticed that a favorite pet or zoo animal sometimes behaves in a way that reminds you of someone you know. With your classmates, brainstorm a list of the human features or characteristics that are sometimes applied to animals.

Human characteristic	Animal
loyal, happy	dog
clumsy	hippopotamus
humorous	monkey
	bat
	moose

Build Background

CONNECT TO BIOLOGY The poems in this lesson feature two mammals—bats and moose. Mammals are warm-blooded animals that feed their young with milk. Bats and moose are very different from each other. The bat is small and agile. It is the only mammal capable of flying. The moose, on the other hand, is the largest member of the deer family and lumbers along on the ground, bearing antlers that can weigh up to 85 pounds.

Although many frightening myths have been invented about them, bats are actually helpful to humans. They eat enormous quantities of insect pests. A bat can eat up to 600 mosquitoes in an hour! Today, many bat species are endangered. Scientists and concerned citizens around the world are taking measures to protect bats.

Moose have been more fortunate. Though they have disappeared from large portions of their former range because of hunting and destruction of the forests where they lived, moose are now making a significant comeback in protected areas and are in no danger of extinction.

The poems that follow are as different from each other as are the two mammals they feature, but they have one thread in common. They are inspired by the natural world and they in turn inspire readers to take a second look at themselves as members of that world.

See the Skills Trace at the beginning of the unit for information on TEKS covered in this lesson.

Focus Your Reading

LITERARY ANALYSIS SYMBOL A person, place, object, or action that stands for something beyond itself is a **symbol**. The bald eagle, for example, is a symbol of the United States. Some symbols, such as the dove, which represents peace, are traditional. Others acquire meaning as symbols only in particular literary works. As you read "The Bat" and "Mooses," look for clues that tell you what the bat and the moose in these poems might symbolize.

ACTIVE READING CLARIFY The process of pausing while reading to check your understanding is called **clarifying**. Good readers stop to reflect on what they know in order to better understand what they are reading. One good way to clarify poetry is to read it aloud. After you read the two poems silently to yourself, practice reading them aloud.

READER'S NOTEBOOK As you read each poem silently, write down details, images, and ideas that you notice. Then read the poems aloud and jot down anything interesting that you missed while you read silently.

Objectives

1. understand and appreciate **symbol** in poetry. **(Literary Analysis)**
2. understand and appreciate **humor** **(Literary Analysis)**
3. pause while reading to **clarify** understanding of text **(Active Reading)**

Summary

These two poems both describe animals in unexpected ways. "The Bat," by Theodore Roethke, compares this nocturnal flier to the mouse, by day, and to a loopy flier at night. People fear it only because it is an animal with a human face. The other poem, "Mooses," by Ted Hughes, humorously describes these giants as huge, dopey bumblers, crashing through the woods, bemoaning their lives and their looks. When they meet, they mistake each other for mirrors, and just stand there, "Two dopes of the deep woods."

Thematic Link

People often react in predictable ways to certain animals, but these two poets offer uncommon views of some common creatures.

5-Minute Warm-Up

Daily Language SkillBuilder **TEKS 17C**

Have students **proofread** the display sentences on page 341j and write them correctly. The sentences also appear on Transparency 12 of **Grammar Transparencies and Copymasters.**

LESSON RESOURCES

UNIT THREE RESOURCE BOOK, pp. 27–28

ASSESSMENT
Formal Assessment, pp. 61–62
Teacher's Guide to Assessment and Portfolio Use
Test Generator

SKILLS TRANSPARENCIES AND COPYMASTERS
Literary Analysis
• Poetry: Figurative Language, TR 19 (for Paired Activity, p. 394)
Reading and Critical Thinking
• Strategies for Reading, TR 1 (for Thinking Through the Literature, p. 394)

INTEGRATED TECHNOLOGY
Audio Library

Visit our website:
www.mcdougallittell.com

Reading and Analyzing

Active Reading CLARIFY

Students can monitor their comprehension and make modifications when their understanding breaks down by rereading a portion aloud. After students have read the poems, ask which parts might be easier to understand if they were read aloud.

Possible Responses: Students' responses might include lines 5 and 10 of "The Bat," or the second or final stanza of "Mooses."

 Use **Unit Three Resource Book**, p. 27, for guidance in reading the selection.

Literary Analysis SYMBOL

A What feeling does the speaker describe here, and what characteristics of the bat contribute to that feeling? What quality might the bat symbolize?
Possible Responses: unease; the oddness of a mouse having wings and a human face; the unknown.

B To help students recognize and interpret symbolism, ask: What might these mooses symbolize?
Possible Response: They might symbolize people who are confused.

 Use **Unit Three Resource Book**, p. 28, for guidance in reading the selection.

Thinking Through the Literature

1. Responses will vary.
2. Responses will vary. Students might mention fears that bats attack people or spread diseases.

The Bat
by Theodore Roethke

By day the bat is cousin to the mouse.
He likes the attic of an aging house.

His fingers make a hat about his head.
His pulse beat is so slow we think him dead.

5 He loops in crazy figures half the night
Among the trees that face the corner light.

But when he brushes up against a screen,
We are afraid of what our eyes have seen:

For something is amiss or out of place
10 When mice with wings can wear a human face.

Thinking Through the Literature

1. **What Do You Think?** Did the poem change your opinion about bats? Support your answer.
2. In your opinion, what is it about bats that many people are afraid of? Explain.

Teaching Options

BLOCK SCHEDULING: MANAGING TIME

If your schedule requires that you cover the lesson objectives in a shorter time, use. . .
• Preparing to Read, p. 391
• Thinking Through the Literature, p. 394

If you would like to take advantage of longer class time, use. . .
• TE Teaching Options: Informal Assessment, p. 393
• Choices & Challenges, p. 395
• Real World Link, p. 396

Mooses

by Ted Hughes

Moose Horn State Park (1975), Alex Katz. Oil on canvas, 78″ × 144″. © Alex Katz/Licensed by VAGA, New York, NY./Marlborough Gallery, NY.

The goofy Moose, the walking house-frame,
Is lost
In the forest. He bumps, he blunders, he stands.

With massy bony thoughts sticking out near his ears—
5   Reaching out palm upwards, to catch whatever might be
         falling from heaven—
He tries to think,
Leaning their huge weight
On the lectern of his front legs.

He can't find the world!
10   Where did it go? What does a world look like?
The Moose
Crashes on, and crashes into a lake, and stares at the
         mountain, and cries
"Where do I belong? This is no place!"

He turns and drags half the lake out after him
15   And charges the cackling underbrush—

He meets another Moose.
He stares, he thinks "It's only a mirror!"

"Where is the world?" he groans, "O my lost world!
And why am I so ugly?
20   And why am I so far away from my feet?"

 He weeps.
Hopeless drops drip from his droopy lips.

The other Moose just stands there doing the same.

Two dopes of the deep woods.

Less Proficient Readers
Encourage students to read each poem stanza by stanza. Use the following questions to guide their understanding.
- What does a bat do at night?
  Possible Responses: It flies around; it brushes against a screen.
- Why does the sight of a bat against a screen scare the speaker?
  Possible Response: Something is wrong about a mouse with wings and a face.
- What word or phrase would you use to describe these mooses?
  Possible Responses: foolish; silly.

Students Acquiring English
Discuss the art with students, asking what they know about bats and mooses. Help them understand the meaning of such terms as the following:
- *cousin to the mouse* (related)
- *goofy* (silly)
- *charges the cackling underbrush* (attacks bushes in which he hears noises)
- *dopes* (stupid creatures)

Use **Spanish Study Guide,** pp. 82–84 for additional support.

Gifted and Talented Students
Invite students to compare the two poems. Ask what is similar about the form, the imagery, and the speakers' attitudes.
Possible Responses: Both use stanzas and make important points in the last lines; both use personification; both are involved with the subjects and somewhat—but not entirely—sympathetic.

IDENTIFYING THE MAIN IDEA You can informally assess whether students can paraphrase and summarize text to recall ideas by offering two paraphrases of "The Bat" and asking them to select the better. Begin by asking volunteers to pick the statement that tells what each poem is about. Then have them locate details in each poem that prove, or support, their statements.
1. Bats are strange because they have slow pulses and fly into screens.
2. A daytime bat just sleeps in an attic, but at night a bat can be a little scary.

RUBRIC
3 Full Accomplishment Response reflects a full understanding of the main idea of the poem and of details that support it.
2 Substantial Accomplishment Response shows only that students can distinguish a correct from an incorrect paraphrase.
1 Little or Partial Accomplishment Response shows that students do not understand the poem as a whole but only specific words or phrases.

GUIDING STUDENT RESPONSE

Connect to the Literature

1. **Response will vary.** Students should use details from the poem to support their reactions.

Comprehension Check
- Possible Responses: It is big, with bony antlers; heavy; has droopy lips.
- He can't find the world.
- "Where do I belong?" and "Where is the world? . . . And why am I so ugly? And why am I so far away from my feet?"

Think Critically

2. Response may vary. Students may suggest that the moose is lost in confusion, lost in the woods, lost in questions, lost in self-absorption.

3. Responses will vary. Most students will answer that reading the poem aloud helped clarify the meaning, the words, or the symbols.

Use **Reading and Critical Thinking Transparencies,** p. 1, for additional support.

4. Possible Responses: It stands for anyone who is confused or who questions his place in the universe. Support might include the questions that the moose keeps asking.

Literary Analysis

Symbol Symbols might include the lectern, the questions; the references to homes (house-frame, looking for a home); bony thoughts, suggesting thick-headedness; the deep woods, suggesting confusion.

Review: Humor Responses will vary. Students might mention any of the following: the bat's crazy antics or the fact that he wears a human face; the moose's confusion; his bumping and blundering and charging the underbrush; or the poem's last line.

Use **Literary Analysis Transparencies,** p. 19, for additional support.

Connect to the Literature

1. **What Do You Think?**
What was your reaction to the moose in this poem? Did you find it humorous? sad? Explain.

Comprehension Check
- What does the moose look like?
- What is the moose's problem?
- What questions does the moose ask in the third stanza? in the sixth stanza?

Think Critically

2. What is happening to the moose in this poem? Explain your answer.

3. 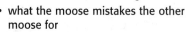 **ACTIVE READING** **CLARIFY** Review the notes you made for "The Bat" and "Mooses" in your **READER'S NOTEBOOK.** How did reading the poems aloud help clarify the things that you missed when you read them silently the first time?

THINK ABOUT
- what the moose is looking for
- what the moose mistakes the other moose for
- what the two moose are called at the end of the poem

4. What do you think the moose symbolizes? Give examples to support your answer.

Extend Interpretations

5. **COMPARING TEXTS** How do the poets differ in their attitude toward the animal each describes in his poem? Do you think the bat and the moose are presented accurately? Give examples to support your answer.

6. **Connect to Life** Do you think it is important that animals are protected? Discuss with classmates.

Literary Analysis

SYMBOL A person, place, object, or action that stands for something beyond itself is called a **symbol.** Some symbols are traditional. A dark forest, for example, has often been used as a symbol of being lost and confused in life. What might the large, awkward moose described by Ted Hughes symbolize? You may find an answer by looking for the ways in which the moose feels lost and confused.

Paired Activity With a partner, reread "Mooses" to look for clues to symbols in the poems. Use the lists you made in your **READER'S NOTEBOOK.**

> *Clues to what the moose may symbolize*
> - *The moose bumps into things, blunders, stands still.*
> - *He tries to think*
> - *He crashes through the forest undergrowth.*

HUMOR What makes readers laugh or smile is difficult to define. Often they find **humor** in descriptions of things that are surprising or very out of place. Think of the moose who discovers another moose in the forest. "He stares, he thinks 'It's only a mirror!'" What other examples of humor can you find in "The Bat" and "Mooses"?

Extend Interpretations

5. **Comparing Texts** Possible Responses: Roethke seems a little in awe of the bat, whereas Hughes pokes fun at the moose. The bat poem provides an accurate picture of bats because of the true characteristics Roethke includes: loops figures during the night, sleeps during the day, likes attics, etc.; the moose poem is more fanciful, since the moose talks and thinks in words.

6. **Connect to Life** Responses may vary. Students should tell why they think animals should be protected. Reasons might include their vulnerability to environmental damage or to hunters.

Writing Options

1. Animal Poem Write a short poem about an encounter you have had with an animal in the wild or in a zoo. Share your finished poem with your classmates.

2. Poetry Essay Hughes and Roethke have very different poetic styles. Choose one of the poems and discuss in an essay what you like and dislike about that poem or poet.

Writing Handbook
See p. R37: Analysis.

Activities & Explorations

Animal Collage Using photos, drawings, and other pictures, create a collage to illustrate one of the poems from this selection. Display your work in class. ~ **ART**

Inquiry & Research

Animal Behavior Each of these poems describes an animal that is not well understood by most humans. In an effort to learn more about moose, for example, some scientists have created and worn moose costumes! Find out more about how scientists go about studying animal behavior. To locate information, use an encyclopedia, a science textbook, a nature guide, or the World Wide Web. Report back to your classmates.

 Real-World Link Before you begin your project, read the article on page 396 about scientists in moose disguise.

"Deep in their roots, all flowers keep the light."

Theodore Roethke
1908–1963

Roots Theodore Roethke was raised in a German immigrant family in Saginaw, Michigan, and helped in a family-run greenhouse and market garden. In high school, he began a lifelong interest in writing.

Work and Play Roethke's early experiences in the family business had a major effect on the developing poet. Through poetry, Roethke explored his love of nature and the challenges of growing up a very shy young man. Although haunted by bouts of depression, he was a popular teacher at a number of universities. Roethke won many awards for his verse, including the Pulitzer Prize.

"We think we're writing something to amuse, but we're actually saying something we desperately need to share."

Ted Hughes
1930–1998

Early Fame Ted Hughes was born in Yorkshire, England. He graduated from Cambridge University in 1954. In 1956, he married the American poet and novelist Sylvia Plath. Both Hughes and Plath became well-known writers in their twenties.

Love of Nature From the beginning, Ted Hughes included the natural world in his poetry. Many of the voices in his first book of poems, *The Hawk in the Rain* (1957), are animals. Ten years later, Hughes introduced the character Crow, a keen observer of human nature. Crow appears in several volumes of Hughes's poetry, including *Crow Wakes* and *Eat Crow.*

THE BAT / MOOSES **395**

Writing Options

1. Animal Poem Students' poems should contain at least some of the elements of poetry: sound devices, such as rhythm or repetition; figurative language; imagery. To get students started on this assignment, have them make word webs surrounding the names of the animals that they selected.

Use **Literary Analysis Transparencies,** pp. 17, 19, 20, for additional support.
Use **Writing Transparencies,** p. 15, for additional support.

2. Poetry Essay Students' essays should include examples from the poem that support the writer's responses.

Use **Writing Transparencies,** p. 13, for additional support.

Activities & Explorations

Animal Collage Remind students that a collage does not have to depict an animal realistically; students can create images that capture the feeling of a poem or focus on details about one of the animals or its environment.

Inquiry & Research

Animal Behavior To make this assignment more challenging, suggest that students read books or articles by or about Konrad Lorenz, Jane Goodall, George B. Schaller, or Dian Fossey.

Theodore Roethke

Roethke was a big man, who was given to big and memorable gestures. He liked to send flowers to friends, but instead of sending a single bouquet, he sent many bouquets at the same time.

Ted Hughes

After Sylvia Plath died in 1963, Hughes remained silent about her for over 30 years. Then, in 1998, he published *Birthday Letters,* a series of poems about his feelings for his late wife.

Source: *National Wildlife*

Real WORLD Link

Magazine Article

Objectives

- read to be informed
- determine a text's main ideas and how those ideas are supported with details
- paraphrase and summarize text to inform
- connect, compare, and contrast ideas across text

Connecting to the Literature

This magazine article connects well to "Mooses" because its subject is the same animal. However, the article approaches the moose from the scientific point of view, as opposed to the poetic point of view that Hughes uses in his poem. The article provides details about the moose's environment and about how scientists can study these animals and get close to them. Students will probably enjoy the image of scientists wearing a moose suit that was designed by a *Star Wars* designer.

They're Well-Suited for Studying **Moose**

by **Steve Mirsky**

If you can't beat 'em, join 'em. That was the conclusion wildlife biologist Joel Berger came to before starting fieldwork studying moose—*Alces alces*—in Wyoming's Grand Teton National Park and in parts of Alaska.

Along with wife and colleague Carol Cunningham, Berger is interested in learning how moose behavior may have been altered by humanity's century-old experiment of removing grizzlies, wolves and other predators from the habitat. "Our research is concerned with what happens to prey in systems where large carnivores[1] are absent," Berger explains. "We feel this is an important issue because in most of the world more systems are going to be losing large carnivores, rather than gaining them. What are the direct consequences of such losses?"

In the course of doing this research, Berger realized that the only way to get the information he was looking for was to perform a variation of the old "wolf in sheep's clothing" routine. He decided to become a "scientist in moose clothing."

He was aware of a wildlife photographer who wore a zebra skin like a poncho to wander among herds in Africa. He has also seen paintings of Native Americans wearing wolf heads and capes to sneak up on bison. He thus enlisted Debra Markert, who was a designer for the *Star Wars* movies, to create a moose suit.

"I thought he was kind of loony to be considering it, to be frank, until I saw the suit in action," recalls Steve Cain, a senior wildlife biologist. "It became clear that the thing might actually have some utility, that it would probably let him approach moose closer than he would be able to on foot."

A big part of the success of the suit, according to Cain, is that Berger and Cunningham do a pretty good moose impression. "They've got their movement to mimic[2] that of a feeding moose," he notes, "one that's calm and basically going about its business. So I don't think the costume drew as much attention, or perhaps fright, from other moose as it would have had less experienced people been in it."

---

1. **carnivore:** a meat-eating animal.
2. **mimic:** to imitate.

Even given their talent for mimicry, traipsing around in the moose suit can be a risky enterprise. A large moose in the lower 48 states weighs as much as 1,000 pounds, so getting charged by one would be highly dangerous.

Berger carries a whistle and pepper spray, but he found a far better defense when a moose suddenly took umbrage as he and Cunningham came too close. "Carol and I were in deep snow and a moose lowered its ears, dropped its head and the hair on its nape stood up," Berger recalls. "Think of a dog, when it gets nervous and its hackles stand up. That's basically what a moose does. And we were only about 15 yards away from it. And because we were in deep snow, it was like, uh oh. So we took the suit off. And the moose was very confused. Its demeanor changed. We went in opposite directions."

Berger will again attempt to approach moose, while trying to put more distance between himself and park visitors. "The typical tourist response when they see us," Berger says, "is they just roar and they want to get pictures." Clearly, some scientists must go to great lengths to get into the animals they study.

Reading for Information

Sometimes as you research a specific topic, you will be asked to present to the class what you have found. To do this, you will want to provide a **summary** of an article.

SUMMARIZING To summarize you need to provide a shortened version of a text in your own words. First find the main idea of the whole article. Then include other important supporting ideas.

YOUR TURN *Use the questions below to help you learn how to summarize.*

❶ As you read, watch for facts and information that might express, or help you find, the main idea of the article. Which of the details in this paragraph do you think are important to the main idea?

❷ Sometimes you have to leave interesting details out of a summary if they are not part of the main idea. What details in these paragraphs are interesting but not necessary for a summary of the article?

Summarizing Now write a summary of the article. Remember not to copy information directly. Use your own words when talking about the main idea and supporting details.

Inquiry & Research

Activity Link: "Mooses," p. 395 Find out more about the moose's feeding habits and environment by consulting reference sources and the Internet. How accurate is the portrayal of the moose's habitat in Ted Hughes's poem?

Reading for Information

Tell students that this article describes the intersection of art and science, since it explains how a film designer helps a scientist. As you go through the article with students, have them use the material in the right-hand column as a guide to summarizing information contained in an informative article. The following are **possible responses** to the two questions and activities.

1 Joel Berger and his wife Carol Cunningham want to learn what happens to prey when people remove large predators from their habitats.

2 Steve Cain thought the idea was "kind of loony"; the scientists mimic a feeding moose.

Summarizing Summaries should include the names of the researchers, their goal, why they decided to use a moose suit, the fact that this can be dangerous, and what they do when confronted by an angry moose.

 Use **Writing Transparencies,** p. 52, for additional support.

The Inquiry & Research activity on this page can be linked to the Animal Collage activity of Choices & Challenges on page 395, following the poems "The Bat" and "Mooses."

Instruction To help student compare communication in different forms, such as contrasting a poem with a nonfiction article, encourage them to first identify the features of a moose that Hughes describes, such as its size and droopy lips. Then have students consult their reference sources. To get students started, remind them that a moose is a mammal that is a member of the deer family. Students may find information by using the search terms *moose, mammal,* or *deer.*

Practice Suggest that students work independently to gather information. Then they can work in pairs to compare what they learned through their research with what they read in Hughes's poem. Have them describe how the author's perspective affects the text of the poem.

Building Vocabulary

Objectives

- identify the relation of word meanings in analogies
- recognize a variety of types of word relationships
- draw on experiences to bring meanings to words in analogies

VOCABULARY EXERCISE

1. chaos—synonyms
2. genial—antonyms
3. brush—worker and tool
4. book—part to whole
5. pensive—synonyms

Use **Unit Three Resource Book**, p. 29, for more practice. Use **Vocabulary Transparencies and Copymasters**, p. 14, for additional support.

Kinds of Comparisons

An **analogy** is a type of comparison. In "Amigo Brothers," an analogy occurs to Felix as he watches the fight film *The Champion* the night before he must fight Antonio. The challenger puts up a good fight, but the champion wins.

You can express the analogy like this:

Felix is to a champion as Antonio is to a challenger.

In abbreviated form, this analogy is:

FELIX : CHAMPION :: Antonio : challenger

When Felix finally left the theatre, he had figured out how to psyche himself for tomorrow's fight. It was Felix the Champion vs. Antonio the Challenger.

—Piri Thomas, "Amigo Brothers"

| Felix compares himself to the champion in the film. | He compares Antonio to the challenger. |

Strategies for Building Vocabulary

You may find analogies in tests as well as in literature. Test analogies involve relationships between pairs of words and ideas. Some analogy problems are expressed like this.

Determine the relationship between the capitalized words. Then decide which of the choices best completes the analogy.

LOVE : HATE :: war : _____

a. soldier b. peace c. battle d. argument

You might express this problem as *Love* is to *hate* as *war* is to _____. Here are some strategies for solving analogy problems.

❶ **Determine Word Relationships** To complete an analogy, you need to figure out the relationship between the first pair of words. In this example *love* and *hate* are antonyms—words with opposite meanings. Therefore, you must find a word that is an antonym to *war*. The best answer is *peace*.

❷ **Learn Relationship Types** The word pairs in analogy problems express various kinds of relationships. Learning these relationships will help you solve analogy problems. The chart above contains some common types.

Common Types of Analogies

Type	Example	Relationship
Part to Whole	LETTER : ALPHABET	is a part of
Synonyms	SERENE : CALM	same meaning
Antonyms	LOUD : QUIET	opposite meaning
Cause-Effect	FIRE : SMOKE	results in or leads to
Worker to Tool	FARMER : PLOW	works with
Grammar	RUN : RAN	grammatically related to
Degree of Intensity	WARM : HOT	is less or more intense than
Item to Category	MARS : PLANET	is a type or example of

EXERCISE Choose the word that best completes each analogy. Identify the type of analogy.

book	contorted	genial	optimistic
brush	dispel	legitimate	serious
chaos	famished	pensive	

1. FUNNY : HUMOROUS :: bedlam : _____
2. SIMPLE : COMPLEX :: _____ : disagreeable
3. PLUMBER : WRENCH :: painter : _____
4. HOUSE : NEIGHBORHOOD :: page : _____
5. WORRIED : TERRIFIED :: _____ : thoughtful

The Night the Bed Fell

by James Thurber

I suppose that the high-water mark of my youth in Columbus, Ohio, was the night the bed fell on my father. It makes a better recitation (unless, as some friends of mine have said, one has heard it five or six times) than it does a piece of writing, for it is almost necessary to throw furniture around, shake doors, and bark like a dog, to lend the proper atmosphere and verisimilitude[1] to what is admittedly a somewhat incredible tale. Still, it did take place.

It happened, then, that my father had decided to sleep in the attic one night, to be away where he could think. My mother opposed the notion strongly because, she said, the old wooden bed up there was unsafe; it was wobbly, and the heavy headboard would crash down on father's head in case the bed fell, and kill him. There was no dissuading him, however, and at a quarter past ten he closed the attic door behind him and went up the narrow twisting stairs. We later heard ominous creakings as he crawled into bed. Grandfather, who usually slept in the attic bed when he was with us, had disappeared some days before. (On these occasions he was usually gone six or eight days and returned growling and out of temper, with the news that the federal Union was run by a passel of blockheads and that the Army of the Potomac[2] didn't have any more chance than a fiddler's dog.)

We had visiting us at this time a nervous first cousin of mine named Briggs Beall, who believed that he was likely to cease breathing when he was asleep. It was his feeling that if he were not awakened every hour during the night, he might die of suffocation. He had been accustomed to setting an alarm clock to ring at intervals until morning, but I persuaded him to abandon this. He slept in my room,

---

1. **verisimilitude** (věr′ə-sĭ-mĭl′ĭ-tōōd′): appearance of truth.
2. **federal Union . . . Army of the Potomac** (pə-tō′mək): references to the government and army of the North during the Civil War.

Possible Objectives
You can use this selection to achieve one or more of the following objectives:
- enjoy silent sustained reading (Option One)
- read and analyze literature with a group (Option Two)
- use the Reader's Notebook to write in response to literature (Option Three)

Summary
This humorous story, told in the first-person, recounts one night during the narrator's youth in Columbus, Ohio. His father decided to sleep in the attic that night, which worried Thurber's mother. She feared that the wobbly old bed would collapse. On the second floor slept the rest of the family. Thurber was sharing a room with a nervous first cousin, Briggs. Because Briggs feared that he might stop breathing in his sleep, he kept spirits of camphor nearby that he could use to revive himself. Thurber's mother was in the adjoining room with his little brother, Herman. Another brother, Roy, slept across the hall, and the dog slept in the hall. Thurber was sleeping on an army cot, which collapsed and tipped during the night. Thurber awoke only partially, but the noise alarmed his mother, who shouted in fear. Her shouting woke Herman, and the ensuing noise woke Briggs, who doused himself with camphor and then broke a window when he rushed to get some air. Now the narrator awoke, found himself under his cot, and joined the shouting. The noise woke Thurber's father, who came downstairs to find utter confusion. The chaos finally ended; the only bad result of the evening was that Thurber's father caught a cold from walking around with bare feet.

Option One
Silent Sustained Reading

You might set aside time each week for independent reading. During this time, you and your students would read for enjoyment. "The Night the Bed Fell" will appeal to many students and can be read independently in 20 minutes or so. To encourage students to read for pleasure, consider making no assignments related to this selection. However, Options Two and Three below offer suggestions in case you do want to make assignments.

Option Two
Shared Reading Groups

You may assign students to groups or allow them to choose their own. Students can read the selection together, alternately reading sections aloud, or they can read independently and meet to cooperate in a project that portrays some element of the story.

Possible Projects

• Pairs of students can role-play an interview between one of the story participants and a police officer, who was called when neighbors complained about the noise.

• Have groups of students write a folk song commemorating "The Night the Bed Fell."

• Have students create a large cartoon depicting the climactic scene. As in newspaper cartoons, they can include the characters' words inside speech balloons.

---

and I told him that I was such a light sleeper that if anybody quit breathing in the same room with me, I would wake instantly. He tested me the first night—which I had suspected he would—by holding his breath after my regular breathing had convinced him I was asleep. I was not asleep, however, and called to him. This seemed to allay his fears a little, but he took the precaution of putting a glass of spirits of camphor[3] on a little table at the head of his bed. In case I didn't arouse him until he was almost gone, he said, he would sniff the camphor, a powerful reviver. Briggs was not the only member of his family who had his crotchets.[4] Old Aunt Melissa Beall (who could whistle like a man, with two fingers in her mouth) suffered under the premonition that she was destined to die on South High Street, because she had been born on South High Street and married on South High Street. Then there was Aunt Sarah Shoaf, who never went to bed at night without the fear that a burglar was going to get in and blow chloroform[5] under her door through a tube. To avert this calamity—for she was in greater dread of anesthetics than of losing her household goods—she always piled her money, silverware, and other valuables in a neat stack just outside her bedroom, with a note reading, "This is all I have. Please take it and do not use your chloroform, as this is all I have." Aunt Gracie Shoaf also had a burglar phobia, but she met it with more fortitude. She was confident that burglars had been getting into her house every night for forty years. The fact that she never missed anything was to her no proof to the contrary. She always claimed that she scared them off before they could take anything, by throwing shoes down the hallway. When she went to bed she piled, where she could get at them handily, all the shoes there were about her house. Five minutes after she had turned off the light, she would sit

up in bed and say "Hark!" Her husband, who had learned to ignore the whole situation as long ago as 1903 would either be sound asleep or pretend to be sound asleep. In either case he would not respond to her tugging and pulling, so that presently she would arise, tiptoe to the door, open it slightly and heave a shoe down the hall in one direction, and its mate down the hall in the other direction. Some nights she threw them all, some nights only a couple of pairs.

But I am straying from the remarkable incidents that took place during the night that the bed fell on father. By midnight we were all in bed. The layout of the rooms and the disposition[6] of their occupants is important to an understanding of what later occurred. In the front room upstairs (just under father's attic bedroom) were my mother and my brother Herman, who sometimes sang in his sleep, usually "Marching Through Georgia" or "Onward, Christian Soldiers." Briggs Beall and myself were in a room adjoining this one. My brother Roy was in a room across the hall from ours. Our bull terrier, Rex, slept in the hall.

My bed was an army cot, one of those affairs that are made wide enough to sleep on comfortably only by putting up, flat with the middle section, the two sides which ordinarily hang down like the sideboards of a drop-leaf table. When these sides are up, it is perilous to roll too far toward the edge, for then the cot is likely to tip completely over, bringing the whole bed down on top of one, with a tremendous banging crash. This, in fact, is precisely what happened, about two o'clock

---

3. **spirits of camphor** (kăm'fər): a liquid with a sharp odor, formerly used to relieve faintness.

4. **crotchets:** peculiar notions.

5. **chloroform** (klôr'ə-fôrm'): a liquid formerly used to put patients into a deep sleep while surgery was performed on them.

6. **disposition:** arrangement.

n the morning. (It was my mother who, in recalling the scene later, first referred to it as 'the night the bed fell on your father.")

Always a deep sleeper, slow to arouse (I had tied to Briggs), I was at first unconscious of what had happened when the iron cot rolled me onto the floor and toppled over on me. It left me still warmly bundled up and unhurt, for the bed rested above me like a canopy. Hence I did not wake up, only reached the edge of consciousness and went back. The racket, however, instantly awakened my mother, in the next room, who came to the immediate conclusion that her worst dread was realized: the big wooden bed upstairs had fallen on father. She therefore screamed, "Let's go to your poor father!" It was his shout, rather than the noise of my cot falling, that awakened Herman, in the same room with her. He thought that mother had become, for no apparent reason, hysterical. "You're all right, Mamma!" he shouted, trying to calm her. They exchanged shout for shout for perhaps ten seconds: "Let's go to your poor father!" and "You're all right!" That woke up Briggs. By this time I was conscious of what was going on, in a vague way, but did not yet realize that I was under my bed instead of on it. Briggs, awakening in the midst of loud shouts of fear and apprehension, came to the quick conclusion that he was suffocating and that we were all trying to "bring him out."

With a low moan, he grasped the glass of camphor at the head of his bed and instead of sniffing it, poured it over himself. The room reeked of camphor. "Ugf, ahfg," choked Briggs, like a drowning man, for he had almost succeeded in stopping his breath under the deluge of pungent spirits. He leaped out of bed and groped toward the open window, but he came up against one that was closed. With his hand, he beat out the glass, and I could hear it crash and tinkle on the alleyway below. It was at this juncture that I, in trying to get up, had the uncanny sensation of feeling my bed above me! Foggy with sleep, I now suspected, in my turn, that the whole uproar was being made in a frantic endeavor to extricate me from what must be an unheard-of and perilous[7] situation. "Get me out of this!" I bawled. "Get me out!" I think I had the nightmarish belief that I was entombed in a mine. "Gugh," gasped Briggs, floundering in his camphor.

By this time my mother, still shouting, pursued by Herman, still shouting, was trying to open the door to the attic, in order to go up and get my father's body out of the wreckage. The door was stuck, however, and wouldn't yield. Her frantic pulls on it only added to the general banging and confusion. Roy and the dog were now up, the one shouting questions, the other barking.

_____

7. **perilous:** dangerous.

Option Three
Reader's Notebook

Provide the following direction to students before they read:

Discuss the concept of humor, and some of the elements that most humorous stories have: surprise (an unexpected turn of events, for instance), exaggeration, characters with odd names or quirks, amusing descriptions, and often a series of absurd or foolish actions or events.

Ask students to read to the end of page 400. Have them record notes in their Reader's Notebooks about the elements of humor that Thurber uses and their responses to each element. Then have them predict what is likely to happen next.

After students have finished the story, have them check their predictions against what actually happened. Have them also write whether they found the story as a whole funny, and why.

After Reading

Possible Activities
Independent Activities

• Ask gifted and talented students to review the story and note how carefully the plot elements link together, "like a gigantic jig-saw puzzle." Have them jot down in their Reader's Notebooks a simple cause-effect chain. Then have them identify those elements that might have been exaggerated or polished to make the story better.

• Have students try to create humorous stories or anecdotes of their own based on real life situations. Encourage them to fictionalize and embellish the true facts, adding what might have happened to what did happen.

© 1999 James Thurber from the cartoonbank.com. All Rights Reserved.

"I suppose the high-water mark of my youth . . . was the night the bed fell on my father."

James Thurber
1894–1961

Father, farthest away and soundest sleeper of all, had by this time been awakened by the battering on the attic door. He decided that the house was on fire. "I'm coming, I'm coming!" he wailed in a slow, sleepy voice—it took him many minutes to regain full consciousness. My mother, still believing he was caught under the bed, detected in his "I'm coming!" the mournful, resigned note of one who is preparing to meet his Maker. "He's dying!" she shouted.

"I'm all right!" Briggs yelled to reassure her. "I'm all right!" He still believed that it was his own closeness to death that was worrying mother. I found at last the light switch in my room, unlocked the door, and Briggs and I joined the others at the attic door. The dog, who never did like Briggs, jumped for him—assuming that he was the culprit in whatever was going on—and Roy had to throw Rex and hold him. We could hear father crawling out of bed upstairs. Roy pulled the attic door open, with a mighty jerk, and father came down the stairs, sleepy and irritable but safe and sound. My mother began to weep when she saw him. Rex began to howl. "What in the name of Pete is going on here?" asked father.

The situation was finally put together like a gigantic jig-saw puzzle. Father caught a cold from prowling around in his bare feet, but there were no other bad results. "I'm glad," said mother, who always looked on the bright side of things, "that your grandfather wasn't here." ❖

Early Years When James Thurber was a child, he was hit in the eye with an arrow. He lost his sight in that eye, and was troubled with vision problems the rest of his life. Despite this setback, Thurber attended Ohio State University for five years. From 1918 to 1920, Thurber worked as a code clerk at the State Department in Washington and later in Paris. He then turned to journalism, working for the *Chicago Tribune* in Paris.

The *New Yorker* Years In 1927 the *New Yorker* magazine published one of Thurber's stories. Shortly thereafter, Thurber was given a full-time job as managing editor and staff writer. Although Thurber left the *New Yorker* after six years, he continued to contribute stories, essays, poems, and cartoons to the magazine for the rest of his life. In addition to writings, Thurber also provided illustrations for many of his works, and, although he did not consider himself an artist, his cartoons had a distinctive style and became as popular as his stories.

Near Blindness By the age of 57, Thurber's childhood eye injury had resulted in almost total blindness. When his vision began to fail completely, Thurber started dictating his stories to a secretary. His memory was so sharp that he could easily compose a 2,000-word story in his mind, remember it overnight, and dictate it to his secretary the next day.

James Thurber

Thurber's distinctive illustrations might never have appeared in *The New Yorker* if it weren't for the writer E. B. White (contributor to *The Elements of Style* and author of such children's classics as *Charlotte's Web, Stuart Little,* and *The Trumpet of the Swan*). White, like Thurber, wrote for *The New Yorker.* One day White discovered some of Thurber's drawings in the wastebasket and submitted them to the magazine. Thurber went on to become a major illustrator as well as writer for *The New Yorker.*

SPEAKING OPPORTUNITY
See the Communication Handbook, p. R100 for speaking and presenting tips.

Writing Workshop

Problem-Solution Essay

Solving a problem . . .

From Reading to Writing Some problems have simple solutions. Others are more complicated. In "Amigo Brothers," Antonio and Felix have a problem that could ruin their friendship and put their futures in jeopardy. They solve their problem by talking honestly and agreeing on a strategy. You, too, can solve problems in your own life. Writing a **problem-solution essay** forces you to explore possible solutions and to choose the best one.

For Your Portfolio

WRITING PROMPT Write a problem-solution essay that helps you to solve an actual problem or conflict.

Purpose: To inform and persuade
Audience: Anyone who is affected by the problem you are addressing

---

Basics in a Box

Problem-Solution Essay at a Glance

Introduction

presents and describes the problem

Body

presents and explains possible solutions

Conclusion

restates the problem and the benefits of the solution

RUBRIC STANDARDS FOR WRITING

A successful problem-solution essay should

- have an introduction that catches readers' attention
- give a clear picture of the problem
- explore all aspects of the problem, including its causes and effects
- offer a reasonable solution and explain how to put it into effect
- use facts, statistics, examples, opinions, or other details to support the solution
- use logical reasoning to convince the reader
- have a strong conclusion

Writing Workshop
Problem-Solution Essay

Objectives

- write a problem-solution essay
- use a written text as a model for writing
- revise a draft to include a provocative introduction
- use consistent verb tense

Introducing the Workshop

Problem-Solution Essay Discuss with students the kinds of problems or conflicts that they encounter every day. Have each student think about one specific conflict or problem, and ask for volunteers to explain how they would present that problem so that all of its elements are clearly understood.

Basics in a Box

Using the Graphic The graphic on this page illustrates the process of writing a problem-solution essay. Point out that each stage of the process contains specific information that students should include in their essays.

Presenting the Rubric To better understand the assignment, students can refer to the Standards for Writing a Successful Problem-Solution Essay. You may also want to share with them the complete rubric, which describes several levels of proficiency.

 Use McDougal Littell's *Language Network*, Chapters 12–19, for more instruction on essential writing skills.

 Power Presentation

To engage students visually, use **Power Presentation** 1, Problem-Solution Essay.

LESSON RESOURCES

USING PRINT RESOURCES
Unit Three Resource Book
- Prewriting, p. 30
- Drafting, p. 31
- Peer Response, pp. 32-33
- Revising, Editing, and Proofreading, p. 34
- Student Models, pp. 35-37
- Rubric, p. 38

LESSON SUPPORT
Writing Transparencies
- Writing Process

Transparencies, TR 1–4
- Writing Style Transparencies: Effective Language, TR 15
- Writing Template Transparencies: Problem-Solution Essay, TR 33

Reading and Critical Thinking Transparencies
- Main Idea and Supporting Details, TR 25
- Sequence Chain, TR 39 (for Mini Lesson, p. 404)

Grammar Transparencies and Copymasters
- Consistent Verb Tense, CM 74 (for Mini Lesson, p. 408)

INTEGRATED TECHNOLOGY
LaserLinks
Writing Springboards
See **Teacher's SourceBook** p. 36 for bar codes.

Writing Coach CD-ROM
Visit our website:
www.mcdougallittell.com

 TEKS See the Skills Trace at the beginning of the unit for information on TEKS covered in this lesson.

Analyzing a Student Model

"Bringing Our Community Together"

The student model describes ethnic barriers that the writer feels keep town residents from acting as one community. In this essay, the writer supports his assertion that these barriers are a problem with a quote from another resident as well as details. The writer supports possible solutions with facts and gives responses to probable opposition. Have students consider the problem they discussed on the previous page. Help them to see how facts and details lend credibility to an argument. Then point out key words and phrases in the student model that correspond to elements mentioned in the Rubric in Action.

1 Ask students why they think asking a question at the beginning of the essay is effective.
Possible Response: Asking a question as an introduction immediately involves the reader in the essay by inviting a response. In this case, it also asks the reader to visualize a vivid mental image.

2 The writer sets out the main problem and then describes the elements that make up that main problem.

3 Ask students what impression they get of the writer's town from the details and descriptions in the essay.
Possible Response: The town could be an interesting place to live if the people acted as one community, but the lack of unity is making life more dangerous and difficult.

4 Ask students what effect the direct quote has on the reader.
Possible Response: The quote lends credibility to the writer's argument that this is an important community problem.

5 The writer of the essay states the solution and supports it with facts.

Use **Reading and Critical Thinking Transparencies,** p. 25, for additional support.

Analyzing a Student Model

**J. Anderson
Foster Middle School**

RUBRIC
IN ACTION

Bringing Our Community Together

Did you ever see a patchwork quilt before it is sewn together? The quilter usually has hundreds and hundreds of squares in separate piles, organized by color and pattern. That is what my community is like—a quilt before it is stitched together. The fact is that my town is very diverse, but people aren't united. The members of different ethnic groups keep to themselves so that instead of one big community working together, there are many small ones looking after their own concerns. People don't trust each other. This is because they don't really know each other.

Such a lack of trust causes many difficulties in my town. Because people cannot work together or agree on issues, many problems, such as the crime rate or the care of town property, are not solved. The town is beginning to look run-down. Some people have even moved rather than live here. And it's not just adults who don't get along. It's teenagers, too. Lately, there have been fights between teenagers of separate ethnic groups. Last week, two teenagers were hurt. Luckily, they will both be okay—this time. We need to do something soon. One resident said, "We have all the problems of a big city without any of the benefits."

I think it doesn't have to be this way. I believe I have a solution to the problems. In my opinion, the only way to solve this lack of trust is for people to get to know each other. I believe that an international community center needs to be created. This center will be a place where people can come together to celebrate their backgrounds and share their culture with others. Some people, of

❶ Catches readers' attention with a question

❷ Introduces the problem

❸ Describes the effects of the problem and explains why it needs to be solved

❹ Supports main idea with a direct quotation

❺ Presents the solution to the problem

404 UNIT THREE PART 1: SURPRISING TURNS

 Mini Lesson ## Viewing and Representing

 TEKS 10E, 10L 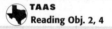 **TAAS** Reading Obj. 2, 4

PICTURING TEXT STRUCTURE

Instruction While facts and details lend strength and credibility to an argument, the structure of the text—the way in which ideas are organized and the order in which they are presented—also contributes to the effectiveness of the work.

Activity Have students analyze the organization of the student model by constructing a diagram or other graphic organizer. The flow chart on the right is an example.

Use **Reading and Critical Thinking Transparencies,** p. 39, for additional support.

Problem of lack of unity is explained
↓
Details and facts illustrate significance of problem
↓
Solution—the creation of an international community center—is proposed
↓
Supports this idea with examples, and answers opposition and criticism
↓
Closing statements reinforce the positive nature of the solution

course, will say that the center will cost too much and that taxes will go up. I have an idea to solve this problem too. The ground floor of the town hall, which has been empty ever since the police department moved to its new building, would be a perfect location for the center. It is completely separate from the town offices on the upper floors and has its own entrance and kitchen. It's also big enough so that all sorts of events could take place there. The center could sponsor activities such as potluck dinners. People could bring food that represents their heritage, and they could decorate their tables with items from their culture. For example, people of Japanese background might bring samples of Japanese art or wear traditional Japanese clothing. After dinner, people could entertain each other with ethnic dances or music and invite everyone to join in. The center might also host an International Day parade with floats from all the cultures.

All of these activities would have the goal of breaking down the barriers that separate people. Once this happens, it will be easier for people to work together to clean up neighborhoods, make the streets safe, and teach their children how to be friends with everyone. Creating an international community center in my town is one way to build trust among members of the community and to get rid of many of the other problems that result from this lack of trust. By learning about one another, community members would begin to discover the beauty that everyone can bring to the patchwork quilt.

RUBRIC
IN ACTION

❻ Answers arguments of the opposition

❼ Gives examples that show the strengths of the solution

Other Options:
- Present facts.
- Use statistics.

❽ Conclusion restates the benefits of the solution.

6 Ask students why they think the writer answers possible objections to the solution before they are voiced. **Possible Response:** By doing so, the writer can prove that all aspects of the solution have been considered and investigated thoroughly.

7 Ask students why including examples rather than statistics in this essay may have been a good idea. **Possible Response:** It makes the writer's solution to the problem seem fun and creative, rather than bureaucratic.

8 Ask students what effect the writer's restatement of his or her solution at the conclusion of the essay has on the reader. **Possible Response:** It ends the essay on a positive note and leaves the reader with the idea that the solution suggested by the writer is positive, fun, creative, and effective.

Prewriting

Choosing a Subject

If after reading the Idea Bank students have difficulty choosing a subject for their problem-solution essay, offer these suggestions:

- Imagine that you had the ability to change anything in the world you wanted. What five things would be on the top of your list to change? Pick one of these things to write about.

- Think back over your favorite works of literature. Make a list of the issues they deal with and choose one to focus on in your essay.

Planning Your Problem-Solution Essay

1. Point out to students that in order to understand their chosen problem fully, they should consider all sides of the issue or argument.

2. Suggest students gather information through magazine and newspaper articles and through discussion with friends and family members in which opinions and arguments are noted.

3. Once they have brainstormed, encourage students to group similar solution ideas together.

4. Have students create a chart listing the pros and cons of each solution.

Drafting

Identify the Problem Have volunteers explain their subjects to the class. Ask students to discuss the issues that are raised by the explanation.

Support Your Explanation Ask students to think about what kind of evidence would have the most impact on their readers and would best illustrate both the seriousness of the problem and the effectiveness of the proposed solution.

Think Ahead Have students think about who their potential readers are and how, as a group, they may react to both the issue and the solution.

Conclude Point out to students that they can conclude their essay by calling for action on the issue.

IDEABank

1. Your Working Portfolio
Look for ideas in the **Writing Options** that you completed earlier in this unit:
- **Editorial**, p. 373
- **Letter to the Editor**, p. 389

2. Global Solutions
With a group of your peers, watch the news or look through the newspaper in search of problems that affect not only you but the world at large. Get together and brainstorm possible solutions to these problems.

3. Target Group
Focus on the problems of one group in society, such as the elderly or teenagers. Interview members of that group to find out what problems they would like to see solved.

Have a question?

See the **Writing Handbook**
Conclusions, p. R29
Organizing Problem-Solution Writing, p. R37

Writing Your Problem-Solution Essay

❶ Prewriting

"Every problem has a gift for you in its hands."
Richard Bach, American write

Think about the word *problem*. **Brainstorm** ideas that come to mind. **Recall** conversations you have had about problems that affect your friends or family. Watch the evening news and **write down** serious problems that might affect you, your town, or your city. See the **Idea Bank** in the margin for more suggestions. After choosing a problem you want to solve, follow the steps below.

Planning Your Problem-Solution Essay

➤ 1. **Define your problem.** Whom does it affect? What will happen if it is not solved? How does the problem affect you? What do you already know about it? What more do you need to find out?

➤ 2. **Research necessary supporting facts.** What kind of information will support your argument? Will you use quotes or examples? Are statistics available? Find out about others who have had this problem.

➤ 3. **Brainstorm possible solutions.** List ideas that you have for solving the problem. Find more information if necessary.

➤ 4. **Choose the best solution.** Review your research. Discuss possible solutions with friends, family members, and others. Choose the solution that seems the most workable.

❷ Drafting

As you begin drafting, keep in mind the general direction of your essay. You should move from problem to solution.

- **Identify** the problem and explain why it must be solved.

- **Support** your explanation of the problem and solution with facts, statistics, and other evidence.

- **Think ahead** about possible concerns of your readers. Address them in your essay.

- **Conclude** by restating the importance of solving the problem.

Ask Your Peer Reader

- What is the problem I am describing?

- Are you convinced that my solution is the best one? Why or why not?

- Where do I need to add more evidence to support my ideas?

❸ Revising

TARGET SKILL ▶ WRITING AN INTRODUCTION Try to catch readers' attention in your introduction. You want the importance of this problem to be obvious from the beginning. Ask a question, or use a quote, statistic, or other creative way to present the problem. Reread your introduction and see what you can do to catch your readers' attention.

> Did you ever see a patchwork quilt before it is ⸍
> ~~My town is made up of people from many different~~
> sewn together?
> ~~cultures. These groups often don't get along.~~ ⸍

❹ Editing and Proofreading

TARGET SKILL ▶ CONSISTENT VERB TENSE When two or more actions or states of being occur at the same time or in sequence, you need to use the same verb tense to describe the actions. Proofread to make sure that all of your verbs are consistent. You may find that present tense serves your purpose best in this problem-solution essay.

> Because people cannot work together or agree on issues, many problems, such as crime rate or the care of
>   *are* ⸍
> town property, ~~were~~ not solved. The town is beginning to look run-down.

❺ Reflecting

FOR YOUR WORKING PORTFOLIO How did writing your essay help you to find a solution to your problem? What other problems would you like to address? What was most difficult about writing your essay? Attach your answers to your finished work. Save your problem-solution essay in your Working Portfolio.

Need revising help?

Review the **Rubric**, p. 403

Consider **peer reader** comments

Check **Revision Guidelines**, p. R23

SPELLING from Writing

As you revise your work, look back at the words you misspelled and determine why you made the errors you did. For additional help, refer to the strategies and generalizations in the **Spelling Handbook** on page R86.

Challenged by verb tense?

See the **Grammar Handbook**, p. R68

Publishing IDEAS

- Create a Web site and post your problem and solution. Ask for reactions to your solution.

- Find a classmate who wrote about a similar problem. Hold an informal debate on your solutions. Ask members of the class to vote on which solution is more convincing.

More Online: Publishing Options
www.mcdougallittell.com

Revising
WRITING AN INTRODUCTION

Review the changes made in the sample with students. To help students practice catching their readers' attention, ask volunteers to share the opening lines of their introductions. Have the rest of the class suggest ways to turn the sentences into questions or other attention-grabbing openers.

Ask Your Peer Reader
Remind students to use the peer reviewer's feedback when revising their drafts.

Editing and Proofreading
CONSISTENT VERB TENSE

Remind students that switching verb tenses throughout the essay creates confusion and will make the argument less effective. Have students explain the change in the sample. For more practice, see the Grammar Mini Lesson at the bottom of the next page.

Reflecting

As they write their reflections, have students consider how writing this essay changed the way they will approach everyday problems and solutions.

Option
Teaching Tip

When reviewing the first draft, check for the logic of the argument, in both the presentation of the problem and the presentation of the solution. Highlight areas that do not follow logical organization or seem confusing. Allow students time to react to the highlighted passages and write down how they think they can clarify the argument. Meet with students individually to discuss their ideas.

Assessment Practice — Revising & Editing

Read this passage from the first draft of a problem-solution essay. The underlined sections may include the following kinds of errors:

- **spelling errors**
- **lack of subject-verb agreement**
- **verb tense errors**
- **correctly written sentences that should be combined**

For each underlined section, choose the revision that most improves the writing.

> Have you tasted water from the Fountain of Youth? If not, one day you, too, <u>would experience</u> old age. Unfortunately, senior citizens in America <u>are</u> a forgotten part of the population. One of the worst problems facing the older generation <u>are</u> loneliness. In many cases, their children <u>lives</u> out of the area. <u>Their friends die. Their friends become too old to drive or walk.</u> Then they have no one to visit them or to take them out. Years ago, neighbors <u>would take care</u> of each other. Now people move too often to get to know their neighbors. Most people have a list of activities <u>witch</u> doesn't include checking up on the older people in their neighborhood.
>
> (1) would experience (2) are (3) lives (4) Their friends die. Their friends become too old to drive or walk. (5) would take care (6) witch

1.
- **A.** would have experienced
- **B.** would be experiencing
- **C.** will experience
- **D.** Correct as is

2.
- **A.** were
- **B.** is
- **C.** have been
- **D.** Correct as is

3.
- **A.** living
- **B.** live
- **C.** would live
- **D.** Correct as is

4.
- **A.** Their friends die, too old to drive or walk.
- **B.** Their friends die or become too old to drive or walk.
- **C.** Their friends die but become too old to drive or walk.
- **D.** Correct as is

5.
- **A.** would have took care
- **B.** would have taken care
- **C.** take care
- **D.** Correct as is

6.
- **A.** which
- **B.** wich
- **C.** whitch
- **D.** Correct as is

Need extra help?

See the **Grammar Handbook**

Quick Reference: Capitalization, p. R58

Quick Reference: Punctuation, p. R56

Verb Tense, p. R68

Subject-Verb Agreement, p. R60

Spelling, p. R86

Teaching Options

Mini Lesson **Grammar**   TEKS 17F   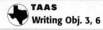 TAAS Writing Obj. 3, 6

CONSISTENT VERB TENSE For use with Editing and Proofreading, p. 407.

Instruction Tell students that each verb has three simple tenses (past, present, and future), and three perfect tenses. Perfect tenses indicate that an action was completed or that a condition existed before a given time. The perfect tenses are formed by using *has*, *have*, or *had* before the past participle.

Exercises Have students find the errors in verb tense in the following sentences and suggest corrections. Some sentences are correct.

1. They exercised to build strength, develop speed, and feeling good about themselves. *(feel good)*
2. In the 1890s, most people will be traveling by train or boat. *(traveled)*
3. Her friends eat all their french fries already. *(have eaten)*

4. My dog has been gone for three days. *(correct)*
5. For ten years, Lucy writes in her diary every day. *(has written)*

 Use **Grammar Transparencies and Copymasters**, p. 74.

 Use McDougal Littell's ***Language Network***, Chapter 4, for more instruction and practice in verb tense.

Reflecting on the Theme Have you ever dreamed of living on another planet or visiting a magical world? Fantasy and science fiction are types of literature that allow us to explore places where the impossible can happen. Often stories about people in strange, fantastic worlds are interesting for what they tell us about ourselves. The unfamiliar setting can make our own characteristics and tendencies more apparent.

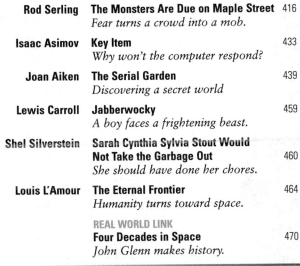
With a partner, design a magical world. Let your imagination take over. What would people look like? How would nature be different? Would gravity still exist? Jot down your ideas on a chart like the one below. Try to describe as many things as possible about your new world.

Magical World

409

Objectives

- understand and identify the following literary terms:
  science fiction
  fantasy
  theme
- understand and appreciate science fiction and fantasy
- determine a text's main or major ideas and how those ideas are supported with details

Teaching the Lesson

This lesson introduces students to the basic elements of science fiction and fantasy and examines the similarities and differences between these two genres.

Introducing the Concepts

Ask students to think of a movie they have seen recently or a book they have recently read that contains unreal elements and that they would consider an example of fantasy. Ask them to discuss the specific details and elements of the work that make it a fantasy in their opinion.

Use **Literary Analysis Transparencies,** p. 6, 7 for additional support.

Science Fiction and Fantasy

"... Science fiction is the art of the possible, not the art of the impossible. As soon as you deal with things that can't happen, you are writing fantasy."
—Ray Bradbury

What if the cure for all of earth's diseases was found in the DNA of an insect? How would it be to live on the moon? What if trees talked and walked and people grew into the earth? Answers to these questions may be found in **science fiction** and **fantasy.** Both types of literature can carry you to new worlds, introduce you to imaginary creatures, and tell you about strange events. In science fiction, imaginary objects and events are based on real or possible science or technology. While **science fiction** is usually set in the future, the characters may face problems similar to those people face today.

Fantasy, on the other hand, is literature that includes at least one completely unreal or fantastic element. A fantasy story may include imaginary creatures—such as elves or talking plants and animals—strange settings, and impossible events. Writers of both of these types of fiction create fantastic characters, settings, and events not only to entertain but also to comment on the present-day real world.

From "Dark They Were, and Golden-Eyed"

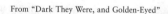

410

See the Skills Trace at the beginning of the unit for information on TEKS covered in this lesson.

Science Fiction

Science fiction is a type of writing that involves scientific data, theories, and technology. Science fiction writers like to imagine what effects scientific theories will have when they are carried out, so they often set their stories in the future. In most science fiction stories, vivid details describe futuristic settings, characters, and events.

Sometimes the ideas of science fiction writers come true. For example, when writer Jules Verne wrote *Twenty-thousand Leagues Under the Sea* in 1870, submarines were very crude vessels that could stay under water only for short periods of time. In his story, Verne described a submarine that was practically a small city. Today, submarines can stay below the water for months, sustaining large crews.

YOUR TURN Read the text above on the right. Which details show things that happen in everyday life? Which details describe things that don't normally happen, or technology that belongs in the future?

SCIENCE FICTION

(The crowd starts to converge around the mother, who grabs Tommy and starts to run with him. The crowd starts to follow, at first walking fast, and then running after him. Suddenly Charlie's lights go off and the lights in other houses go on, then off.)

Man One *(shouting).* It isn't the kid . . . it's Bob Weaver's house.

Woman. It isn't Bob Weaver's house, it's Don Martin's place.

Charlie. I tell you it's the kid.

Don. It's Charlie. He's the one.

(People shout, accuse, and scream as the lights go on and off. . . .)

(. . . We see the metal side of a spacecraft that sits shrouded in darkness. An open door throws out a beam of light from the illuminated interior. Two figures appear, silhouetted against the bright lights. We get only a vague feeling of form.)

Figure One. Understand the procedure now? Just stop a few of their machines and radios and telephones and lawn mowers. . . . Throw them into darkness for a few hours, and then just sit back and watch the pattern.

—Rod Serling, *The Monsters Are Due on Maple Street*

From *The Monsters Are Due on Maple Street*

Presenting the Concepts
Science Fiction

Divide students into pairs. Ask each pair to write a paragraph describing the setting for a science fiction story they would like to write. Remind them that they should use specific and vivid details, and that any technological or scientific details should be within the realm of possibility sometime in the future. Ask for a volunteer from each pair to read their paragraph to the rest of the class.

YOUR TURN
Possible Response: Realistic details include crowds panicking, turning against one another, and looking for someone to blame for trouble. Futuristic details include the presence of a spaceship and the control of earth's machines and technology by an outside force.

Fantasy

Ask students to think about fantasy stories they have previously read. Using these as models, ask them to write the opening paragraph for a fantasy short story they would like to write. This paragraph should describe the setting and at least one main character. Remind students that they should use vivid and specific details, and that their works of fantasy should contain elements that are unreal. Ask for volunteers to read their paragraphs out loud to the rest of the class.

YOUR TURN

Possible Response: A high stone wall could stretch away into the distance so that the end of it is not visible. A paper ironwork gate and stone wall could not suddenly become life size. A life-size gate and wall could not fit into a playroom.

Fantasy

Writers of **fantasy** often create worlds and characters that can exist only in the imagination. These worlds may be totally whimsical and unreal, like the one described in Lewis Carroll's *Alice's Adventures in Wonderland,* where there are talking rabbits and croquet mallets that are actually flamingos. Other writers of fantasy, such as Joan Aiken in "The Serial Garden," create realistic settings and characters along with impossible events. All fantasy includes at least one fantastic or unreal element. To help you believe in the impossible, a writer might include **imaginative settings, fantastic details, imaginary creatures,** or **impossible events.** For example, an author will use such vivid details to describe a setting that when trees and flowers begin to dance, it seems almost believable.

YOUR TURN In the passage to the right, Mark, the main character, is building a tiny model of a garden in his playroom. After reading the passage, decide which things could really happen and which could not.

FANTASY

"Hullo. That's funny," said Mark.

It was funny. The openwork iron gate he had just stuck in position now suddenly towered above him. On either side, to right and left, ran the high stone wall, stretching away into foggy distance. . . .

"I wonder if the gate will open."

He chuckled as he tried it. . . . The gate did open, and he went through into the garden.

—Joan Aiken, "The Serial Garden"

From "The Serial Garden"

Theme

Stories have both a subject and a theme. The **subject** is what the story is about. The **theme** is the central idea or message that the writer wants to share about the subject. It is a perception about life or human nature shared with the reader. In science fiction, for example, the theme may be about the dangers of technological development. It may also be a commentary on human interaction with the environment.

Clues to a story's theme are sometimes found in the **title,** the **setting,** the **plot,** and the way **characters** are shown and how they change. For example, the title *The Monsters Are Due on Maple Street* suggests the subject of the teleplay. The theme is revealed when we find out who the real monsters are. Use a chart like this one to help you find clues to a theme.

Theme

Choose one of the selections from this unit to read as a class. Copy the chart given on this page onto the chalkboard. After the class has read the selection, use this chart as a model for determining the theme of the selection.

Next, ask students to look back at the settings they wrote for their science fiction stories. Have them think about possible themes that might grow out of these settings. Ask for volunteers to share their ideas with the class.

IDENTIFYING THEMES

Where to look	Questions to answer
Title	• What idea does the title emphasize? *unusual characters ("monsters") in a real setting (Maple Street)*
Setting	• What is the setting? *a quiet, tree-lined street in small-town America* • How does it affect characters? *characters are regular people, not used to anything out of the ordinary* • How does it affect plot? *the action is drawn out, people become fearful and suspicious of their neighbors, their hidden prejudices come to light*
Plot	• How do problems arise? • How are they resolved?
Characters	• How do characters act alone? • How do they act with each other? • What do the characters learn? • What does the narrator say about the characters?

From *The Monsters Are Due on Maple Street*

Objectives
- develop effective strategies for determining the author's purpose
- identify the purposes of different types of text, such as to inform, to entertain, to influence, or to express

Teaching the Lesson

The strategies on this page will help students understand and apply the skill of determining an author's purpose for writing.

Presenting the Strategies
Help students understand the strategies by asking for volunteers to read them aloud. Emphasize to students that they will be using these strategies as they read the selections in this book.

- Choose a selection from this unit to read. Have the students read through the story silently. Ask them to take note of any statements of purpose the author makes, either directly or indirectly.
- Divide the class into small groups. Have each group discuss how they think the author presented the information, including the tone and language of the work, and their reactions to the work.
- Ask each group to determine what they think the author's purpose or purposes for writing the work were and to evaluate how well the author did.
- Ask for a volunteer from each group to share their responses and evaluations with the rest of the class.

Try It Now!

Possible Response: The author's purpose is to instruct or explain.

Use **Literary Analysis Transparencies**, p. 16, for additional support.

Author's Purpose

You and your friend watch the same movie. You think it's a comedy, but your friend thinks the movie has a serious message about society. Who is right? It's possible you both are. The movie's writer may have had more than one purpose—to entertain and to express an opinion. An active reader can recognize the author's purpose in literature by carefully evaluating the language, tone, and the way information is presented. There are four basic author's purposes: to entertain, to inform, to express an opinion, or to persuade.

How to Apply the Skill

To determine an **author's purpose**, an active reader will:
- Look for direct or inferred statements of purpose
- Analyze how the author presents the information
- **Clarify** the language and tone of the work
- **Monitor** his or her reaction
- **Evaluate** how well the purpose is achieved

Try It Now!
Read the excerpt below and state the author's purpose.

> **Narrator.** The tools of conquest do not necessarily come with bombs and explosions and fallout. There are weapons that are simply thoughts, attitudes, prejudices—to be found only in the minds of men. For the record, prejudices can kill and suspicion can destroy. A thoughtless, frightened search for a scapegoat has a fallout all its own for the children . . . and the children yet unborn, (*a pause*) and the pity of it is . . . that these things cannot be confined to . . . The Twilight Zone!
>
> —Rod Serling, *The Monsters Are Due on Maple Street*

Here's how Chase uses the skill:

*"To better understand the **author's purpose,** I look for clues. For example, in* The Monsters Are Due on Maple Street, *I analyze the author's strong language—his serious tone. I **monitor** my reaction to the play and agree with the author that people can become ruled by their prejudices. Finally, I **evaluate** how well the author achieved his purposes—to entertain and to express an opinion. I feel that the author made his point very well. I get the message."*

Need More Help?

Remember that active readers use the essential reading strategies explained on page 4: • **visualize** • **predict** • **clarify** • **question** • **connect** • **evaluate** • **monitor.**

The Monsters Are Due on Maple Street

Drama by ROD SERLING

 TEKS See the Skills Trace at the beginning of the unit for information on TEKS covered in this lesson.

"I don't understand. I swear . . . I don't understand. What's happening?"

Connect to Your Life

Facing the Unknown How do you react to the unknown? What happens to you when you think that danger is near? With a classmate, have a brainstorming session in which you use a chart to list the ways in which you and other people react to fear. Then watch as the characters in this selection deal with their fear of the unknown.

Individuals	Groups
dry mouth	cling together

Build Background

CONNECT TO HISTORY *The Twilight Zone* was a television series created by Rod Serling. Eerie and very suspenseful, the series became one of the most popular shows in television history during its 1959–1964 run. Its stories often involved ordinary people in suburban settings typical of the late 1950s. The events in the stories were far from ordinary, however; they were a window into an imaginary world beyond ours—the twilight zone. As the characters faced the unknown, they reacted in both typical and unexpected ways. *The Monsters Are Due on Maple Street* originally aired on March 4, 1960.

Rod Serling. Culver Pictures.

WORDS TO KNOW **Vocabulary Preview**

antagonism	idiosyncrasy	legitimate
contorted	incriminate	optimistic
defiant	intense	persistent
flustered		

Focus Your Reading

LITERARY ANALYSIS **TELEPLAY** A play written for television is called a **teleplay.** Like all drama scripts, a teleplay includes **stage directions.** Printed in italic type in this selection, the stage directions provide suggestions for the actors and the director, explain the setting, and describe props, lighting, and sound effects. The stage directions in a teleplay, however, also include camera directions. As you read, visualize what a television performance of the drama might look like.

ACTIVE READING **AUTHOR'S PURPOSE** An **author's purpose** is his or her reason for creating a particular work. The purpose may be to entertain, to explain or inform, to express an opinion, or to persuade readers to do or believe something. An active reader always tries to identify the author's purpose for writing.

READER'S NOTEBOOK As you read, record the details that help you identify Rod Serling's purpose for writing this drama.

 This selection is included in the **Grade 7 InterActive Reader.**

Objectives
1. understand and appreciate **science fiction (Literary Analysis)**
2. understand and identify **teleplay (Literary Analysis)**
3. understand the term **theme (Literary Analysis)**
4. use the strategy of **thinking about author's purpose and style (Active Reading)**

Summary
A bright object roars over peaceful Maple Street, and suddenly the power goes off, the phones stop working, and cars will not start. Steve Brand and a neighbor, Charlie, plan to walk downtown for help, but young Tommy insists that aliens have landed and they don't want anyone to leave the block. When Les Goodman's car starts by itself, people suspect that Les is an agent of the aliens. A panic ensues as the residents look for someone to blame for all the strange events. One man, Peter Van Horn, is accidentally shot dead by Charlie. The group of neighbors turns into an angry mob. From a distance, aliens watch with satisfaction, commenting that human beings are their own worst enemies.

Thematic Link
The spacecraft's landing causes power failures and strange events that bring out insecurities and aggressions among the residents of Maple Street.

5-Minute Warm-Up

Daily Language SkillBuilder **TEKS 17A**

Have students **proofread** the display sentences on page 341j and write them correctly. The sentences also appear on Transparency 13 of **Grammar Transparencies and Copymasters.**

 Mini Lesson **Preteaching Vocabulary**

If you would like to preteach the WORDS TO KNOW for this selection, use the Mini Lesson, p. 419.

LESSON RESOURCES

UNIT THREE RESOURCE BOOK, pp. 39–45

ASSESSMENT
Formal Assessment, pp. 65–66
Teacher's Guide to Assessment and Portfolio Use
Test Generator

SKILLS TRANSPARENCIES AND COPYMASTERS
Literary Analysis
• Drama: Stage Directions TR 23 (for Paired Activity, p. 429)

Reading and Critical Thinking
• Author's Purpose and Audience, TR 4 (for Thinking Through the Literature, p. 429)
Grammar
• Identifying Participles and their Functions, CM 96 (for Mini Lesson, p. 426)
• Present and Past Participles, CM98 (for Mini Lesson, p. 431)
Vocabulary
• Analogies CM 50 (for Mini Lesson, p. 419)

• Word Parts: Prefixes and Suffixes CM 51 (for Mini Lesson, p. 422)
Communications
• Dramatic Reading, TR 12 (for Mini Lesson, p. 425)

INTEGRATED TECHNOLOGY
Audio Library

Visit our website:
www.mcdougallittell.com

Literary Analysis TELEPLAY

Ask students to name elements that
identify the work as a teleplay.

Possible Responses: Cast of
Characters, "Act One," script format,
italicized stage directions that include
camera directions: "The camera moves
slowly . . . ."; dialogue

 Use **Unit Three Resource Book,**
p. 41 for more practice.

Active Reading AUTHOR'S PURPOSE

The narrator speaks three lines and
then fades out until the end of the play.
Ask students why Serling uses a narrator to open the play.

Possible Responses: The narrator clarifies key points related to place (Maple
Street, U.S.A.—could be any town), time
(6:43 p.m. roar and flash) and plot or
theme (last calm moment before the
monsters came).

 Use **Unit Three Resource Book,**
p. 40 for more practice.

Literary Analysis: SCIENCE FICTION

Introduce or review the characteristics
of the genre: fiction based on real or
imagined scientific developments. Tell
students to watch for science fiction
aspects in plot, setting, and characters.

Literary Analysis: THEME

Review the definition of theme—message about life or human nature that is
conveyed by a literary work. What does
the opening scene (page 417) reveal
about the people in this play?

Possible Responses: They are middle-
class Americans engaged in neighborly
activities.

Teaching Options

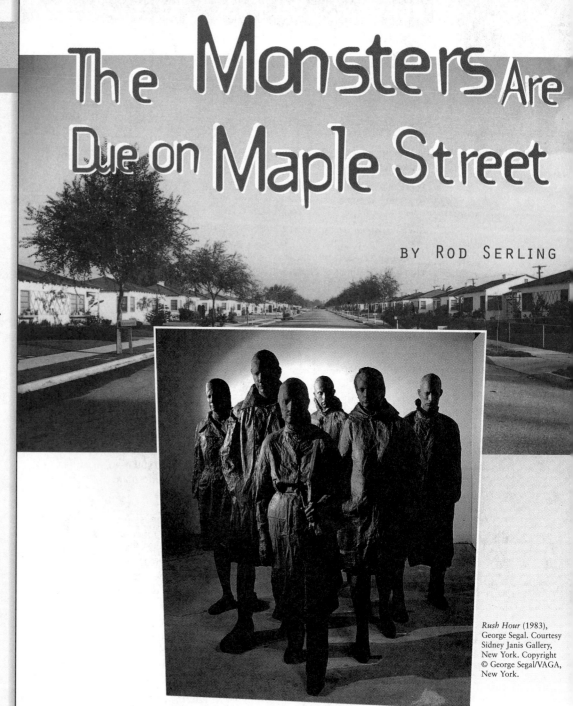

The Monsters Are Due on Maple Street

BY ROD SERLING

Rush Hour (1983),
George Segal. Courtesy
Sidney Janis Gallery,
New York. Copyright
© George Segal/VAGA,
New York.

416   UNIT THREE   PART 2: FANTASTIC TALES

 Viewing and Representing   ◆TEKS 22A, 23B

Rush Hour
by George Segal

ART APPRECIATION George Segal is best known
for his life-size sculptures of real people in real situations. Many of his works are in public areas,
and at first glance his figures are often mistaken
for living people.

Instruction Explain that Segal worked with live
models, wrapping them in strips of plaster-soaked
cheesecloth. In early works, Segal used the plaster
casts as finished products; in later works, such as
Rush Hour, he used the casts as molds, making

the figures more detailed. Ask: What feelings do
the figures in *Rush Hour* convey to you, and why?

Possible Response: Figures seem stark, anonymous, threatening, or like prisoners.

Application Explain that Serling's human characters are much like Segal's figures. As they read,
have students compare the neighbors on Maple
Street with the figures in Segal's art.

Possible Response: Figures and characters are
life-like and could be anyone. At a distance or as a
group they may seem anonymous, less than
human, suspended in time, and disturbing.

CAST OF CHARACTERS

Narrator

Tommy

Steve Brand

Don Martin

Myra Brand, *Steve's wife*

Woman

Voice One

Voice Two

Voice Three

Voice Four

Voice Five

Pete Van Horn

Charlie

Sally, *Tommy's mother*

Man One

Les Goodman

Ethel Goodman, *Les's wife*

Man Two

Figure One

Figure Two

Act One

(Fade in on a shot of the night sky. The various heavenly bodies stand out in sharp, sparkling relief. The camera moves slowly across the heavens until it passes the horizon and stops on a sign that reads "Maple Street." It is daytime. Then we see the street below. It is a quiet, tree-lined, small-town American street. The houses have front porches on which people sit and swing on gliders, talking across from house to house. Steve Brand is polishing his car, which is parked in front of his house. His neighbor, Don Martin, leans against the fender watching him. An ice-cream vendor riding a bicycle is just in the process of stopping to sell some ice cream to a couple of kids. Two women gossip on the front lawn. Another man is watering his lawn with a garden hose. As we see these various activities, we hear the Narrator's *voice.)*

Narrator. Maple Street, U.S.A., late summer. A tree-lined little world of front-porch gliders, hopscotch, the laughter of children, and the bell of an ice-cream vendor.　1

(There is a pause, and the camera moves over to a shot of the ice-cream vendor and two small boys who are standing alongside just buying ice cream.)

THE MONSTERS ARE DUE ON MAPLE STREET **417**

A Note that the dialogue of Voices One, Two, Three, Four, and Five consists of brief, clipped sentences. Ask students how they would describe the effect of these lines.

Possible Response: The short, clipped lines suggest urgency and fear.

Reading Skills and Strategies: MAKING JUDGMENTS

Ask students to evaluate the characters based on their initial responses to the strange happenings on Maple Street.

Possible Response: The characters respond in normal, reasonable ways: They talk to each other, trying to find explanations for why things aren't working. Pete leaves to determine how widespread the problems are.

Reading Skills and Strategies: MAKING INFERENCES

B Ask students why they think Steve and Charlie decide to walk downtown.

Possible Response: They want to find out if anyone else can explain what is happening.

C Ask students what message Steve and Charlie might communicate in the look they exchange.

Possible Response: Whatever is causing the problems is something beyond their understanding and more serious than a meteor.

Narrator. At the sound of the roar and the flash of the light, it will be precisely six-forty-three p.m. on Maple Street.

(*At this moment* Tommy, *one of the two boys buying ice cream from the vendor, looks up to listen to a tremendous screeching roar from overhead. A flash of light plays on the faces of both boys and then moves down the street and disappears. Various people leave their porches or stop what they are doing to stare up at the sky. Steve Brand, the man who has been polishing his car, stands there transfixed, staring upwards. He looks at Don Martin, his neighbor from across the street.*)

Steve. What was that? A meteor?

Don. That's what it looked like. I didn't hear any crash though, did you?

Steve. Nope. I didn't hear anything except a roar.

Myra (*from her porch*). What was that?

Steve (*raising his voice and looking toward the porch*). Guess it was a meteor, honey. Came awful close, didn't it?

Myra. Too close for my money! Much too close.

(*The camera moves slowly across the various porches to people who stand there watching and talking in low conversing tones.*)

Narrator. Maple Street. Six-forty-four p.m. on a late September evening. (*He pauses.*) Maple Street in the last calm and reflective moment (*pause*) before the monsters came!

(*The camera takes us across the porches again. A man is replacing a light bulb on a front porch. He gets off his stool to flick the switch and finds that nothing happens. Another man is working on an electric power mower. He plugs in the plug, flicks the switch of the mower off and on, but nothing happens. Through a window we see a woman pushing her finger up and down on the dial hook of a telephone. Her voice sounds far away.*)

Woman. Operator, operator, something's wrong on the phone, operator! (*Myra Brand comes out on the porch and calls to* Steve.)

Myra (*calling*). Steve, the power's off. I had the soup on the stove, and the stove just stopped working.

Woman. Same thing over here. I can't get anybody on the phone either. The phone seems to be dead.

(*We look down again on the street. Small, mildly disturbed voices are heard coming from below.*)

Voice One. Electricity's off.

Voice Two. Phone won't work.

Voice Three. Can't get a thing on the radio.

Voice Four. My power mower won't move, won't work at all.

Voice Five. Radio's gone dead!

(Pete Van Horn, *a tall, thin man, is seen standing in front of his house.*)

Pete. I'll cut through the back yard to see if the power's still on, on Floral Street. I'll be right back!

(*He walks past the side of his house and disappears into the back yard. The camera pans down slowly until we are looking at ten or eleven people standing around the street and overflowing to the curb and sidewalk. In the background is* Steve Brand's *car.*)

Steve. Doesn't make sense. Why should the power go off all of a sudden and the phone line?

Don. Maybe some kind of an electrical storm or something.

Charlie. That don't seem likely. Sky's just as blue as anything. Not a cloud. No lightning. No thunder. No nothing. How could it be a storm?

Woman. I can't get a thing on the radio. Not even the portable.

Cross Curricular Link **Science**

METEOROIDS Meteoroids are rock fragments traveling through space. Meteoroids that are drawn into Earth's atmosphere by its gravitational field can become visible as glowing streaks in the sky, called meteors. As they enter the atmosphere, they are traveling at speeds of up to 160,000 miles (260,000 kilometers) per hour. The friction produced by their passage through atmospheric gases causes most meteoroids to vaporize before they reach the ground. Those rare meteoroids that reach Earth's surface are called meteorites.

(*The people again begin to murmur softly in wonderment.*)

Charlie. Well, why don't you go downtown and check with the police, though they'll probably think we're crazy or something. A little power failure and right away we get all <u>flustered</u> and everything—

Steve. It isn't just the power failure, Charlie. If it was, we'd still be able to get a broadcast on the portable.

(*There is a murmur of reaction to this. Steve looks from face to face and then at his car.*)

Steve. I'll run downtown. We'll get this all straightened out.

(*He gets in the car and turns the key. Looking through the open car door, we see the crowd watching* Steve *from the other side. He starts the engine. It turns over sluggishly and then stops dead. He tries it again, and this time he can't get it to turn over. Then very slowly he turns the key back to "off" and gets out of the car. The people stare at* Steve. *He stands for a moment by the car and then walks toward them.*)

Steve. I don't understand it. It was working fine before—

Don. Out of gas?

Steve (*shakes his head*). I just had it filled.

Woman. What's it mean?

Charlie. It's just as if (*pause*) as if everything had stopped. (*Then he turns toward* Steve.) We'd better walk downtown.

(*Another murmur of assent to this.*)

Steve. The two of us can go, Charlie. (*He turns to look back at the car.*) It couldn't be the meteor. A meteor couldn't do this.

(*He and* Charlie *exchange a look. Then they start to walk away from the group.* Tommy

Alice Listening to Her Poetry and Music (1970), George Segal. Bayer Staatsgemäldesammlungen–Staatsgalerie Moderner Kunst, Munich, Germany. Copyright © George Segal/VAGA, New York.

comes into view. He is a serious-faced young boy in spectacles. He stands halfway between the group and the two men, who start to walk down the sidewalk.*)

Tommy. Mr. Brand—you'd better not!

Steve. Why not?

Tommy. They don't want you to.

(*Steve and* Charlie *exchange a grin, and* Steve *looks back toward the boy.*)

Steve. Who doesn't want us to?

WORDS TO KNOW **flustered** (flŭs′tərd) *adj.* nervous or confused **fluster** *v.*

419

Customizing Instruction

Less Proficient Readers

1 Ask students to summarize the strange events that have happened on Maple Street up to this point.

Possible Responses: A loud roar is heard, and a blinding flash is seen in the sky; the electricity and phones go out, portable radios don't work, and engines won't start.

Set a Purpose Have students read to find out who Tommy thinks is responsible for the strange events.

Students Acquiring English

2 If necessary, demonstrate the stage direction *shakes his head* and explain that it means "no."

Multiple Learning Styles
Intrapersonal Learners

Ask students to predict how they would respond to the events on Maple Street if they lived there.

 Preteaching Vocabulary 🚩 **TEKS** 6A, 9B 🚩 **TAAS** Reading Obj. 1

ANALOGIES

Instruction Remind students that a word analogy compares two pairs of words. The relationship in the first pair of words is always the same as the relationship in the second pair of words. Display the following examples, which contain words from the list of WORDS TO KNOW:

SADNESS : SORROW :: <u>antagonism</u> : dislike

<u>FLUSTERED</u> : CALM :: charming : rude

Explain that *sadness* and *sorrow* are synonyms, so *antagonism* is a synonym of *dislike;*

rude and charming are opposite in meaning, so flustered is an antonym of *calm*. Tell students that there are many different types of relationships used in analogies. Two other common analogy relationships are cause/effect and type to characteristic.

Exercises Each of the following analogies contains a word from the list of WORDS TO KNOW. Have students figure out the relationship between words in each pair and then define the underlined word.

1. TWISTED : <u>CONTORTED</u> :: solo : alone

2. BOIL : FREEZE :: <u>defiant</u> : cooperative
3. IMPROVEMENT : <u>OPTIMISTIC</u> :: disappointment : hopeless
4. SKYSCRAPER : TALL :: law : <u>legitimate</u>
5. <u>INTENSE</u> : MILD :: prisoner : captor

Answers: 1. synonyms; **2.** antonyms;
3. cause/effect; **4.** type/characteristic;
5. antonyms

 Use **Unit Three Resource Book,** p. 42 for more exercises. Use **Vocabulary Transparencies and Copymasters,** p. 50, for additional support.

ACTIVE READING

A **Clarify** They are frightened because something out of the ordinary is happening.

Reading Skills and Strategies: MAKING JUDGMENTS

B Point out that Tommy is a "young boy," a child. Ask students why they think the adults are willing to listen to Tommy's explanation about what is happening on Maple Street. Have them consider the story situation and personal experience. Then have them decide whether Tommy's role is believable.

Possible Response: Adults don't normally listen to children during a crisis. However, in this situation, the adults have no explanations of their own; they are frightened and willing to listen to any explanation. They may also know Tommy to be worth listening to. Students will have different opinions regarding Tommy's role.

Literary Analysis: THEME

C Ask students what Tommy's comment about what the aliens looked like suggests about the theme.

Response: It supports the idea that the monsters or enemies may be "normal" human beings like the neighbors on Maple Street.

Reading Skills and Strategies: MAKING INFERENCES

D Ask students what they think Steve's "tight grin" suggests about how he feels. When have they felt as he does?

Possible Response: Steve is trying to look calm and amused, but he is actually frightened.

Tommy (*jerks his head in the general direction of the distant horizon*). Them!

Steve. Them?

Charlie. Who are them?

Tommy (*intently*). Whoever was in that thing that came by overhead.

A ▸
> ACTIVE READING
> **CLARIFY** Why are the people of Maple Street so frightened?

(Steve *knits his brows for a moment, cocking his head questioningly. His voice is* _intense_.)

Steve. What?

Tommy. Whoever was in that thing that came over. I don't think they want us to leave here.

(Steve *leaves* Charlie, *walks over to the boy, and puts his hand on the boy's shoulder. He forces his voice to remain gentle.*)

Steve. What do you mean? What are you talking about?

Tommy. They don't want us to leave. That's why they shut everything off.

Steve. What makes you

Detail of *Rush Hour* (1983), George Segal.

say that? Whatever gave you that idea?

Woman (*from the crowd*). Now isn't that the craziest thing you ever heard?

Tommy (_persistent_ *but a little frightened*). It's always that way, in every story I ever read about a ship landing from outer space.

Woman (*to the boy's mother,* Sally, *who stands on the fringe of the crowd*). From outer space yet! Sally, you better get that boy of yours up to bed. He's been reading too many comic books or seeing too many movies or something!

Sally. Tommy, come over here and stop that kind of talk.

Steve. Go ahead, Tommy. We'll be right back. And you'll see. That wasn't any ship or anything like it. That was just a . . . a meteor or something. Likely as not— (*He turns to the group, now trying very hard to sound more* _optimistic_ *than he feels.*) No doubt it did have something to do with all this power failure and the rest of it. Meteors can do some crazy things. Like sunspots.

Don (*picking up the cue*). Sure. That's the kind of thing—like sunspots. They raise Cain[1] with radio reception all over the world. And this thing being so close—why, there's no telling the sort of stuff it can do. (*He wets his lips and smiles nervously.*) Go ahead, Charlie. You and Steve go into town and see if that isn't what's causing it all.

(Steve *and* Charlie *walk away from the group down the sidewalk as the people watch silently.* Tommy *stares at them, biting his lips, and finally calls out again.*)

---

1. **raise Cain:** cause trouble; create a disturbance. (In the Bible, Adam and Eve's son Cain becomes the first murderer when he kills his brother Abel.)

WORDS
TO
KNOW
intense (ĭn-tĕns′) *adj.* showing great concentration or determination
persistent (pər-sĭs′tənt) *adj.* refusing to give up; continuing stubbornly
optimistic (ŏp′tə-mĭs′tĭk) *adj.* hopeful about the future; confident

420

Teaching Options

Ⓒ Cross Curricular Link **Science**

SUNSPOTS Sunspots are dark patches in the photosphere, or surface, of the sun and are caused by variations in the sun's magnetic field. A sunspot can last for only a few hours or for as long as several months. The solar storms associated with sunspots interfere with radio and television reception on Earth.

Tommy. Mr. Brand!

(*The two men stop.* Tommy *takes a step toward them.*)

Tommy. Mr. Brand . . . please don't leave here.

(Steve *and* Charlie *stop once again and turn toward the boy. In the crowd there is a murmur of irritation and concern, as if the boy's words—even though they didn't make sense—were bringing up fears that shouldn't be brought up.* Tommy *is both frightened and* defiant.)

Tommy. You might not even be able to get to town. It was that way in the story. Nobody could leave. Nobody except—

Steve. Except who?

Tommy. Except the people they sent down ahead of them. They looked just like humans. And it wasn't until the ship landed that— (*The boy suddenly stops, conscious of the people staring at him and his mother and of the sudden hush of the crowd.*)

Sally. (*in a whisper, sensing the* antagonism *of the crowd*). Tommy, please son . . . honey, don't talk that way—

Man One. That kid shouldn't talk that way . . . and we shouldn't stand here listening to him. Why this is the craziest thing I ever heard of. The kid tells us a comic book plot, and here we stand listening—

(Steve *walks toward the camera and stops beside the boy.*)

Steve. Go ahead, Tommy. What kind of story was this? What about the people they sent out ahead?

Tommy. That was the way they prepared things for the landing. They sent four people. A mother and a father and two kids who looked just like humans . . . but they weren't.

(*There is another silence as* Steve *looks toward the crowd and then toward* Tommy. *He wears a tight grin.*)

Steve. Well, I guess what we'd better do then is to run a check on the neighborhood and see which ones of us are really human.

(*There is laughter at this, but it's a laughter that comes from a desperate attempt to lighten the atmosphere. The people look at one another in the middle of their laughter.*)

Charlie (*rubs his jaw nervously*). I wonder if Floral Street's got the same deal we got. (*He looks past the houses.*) Where is Pete Van Horn anyway? Isn't he back yet?

(*Suddenly there is the sound of a car's engine starting to turn over. We look across the street toward the driveway of* Les Goodman's *house. He is at the wheel trying to start the car.*)

Sally. Can you get started, Les?

(Les Goodman *gets out of the car, shaking his head.*)

Les. No dice.

(*He walks toward the group. He stops suddenly as, behind him, the car engine starts up all by itself.* Les *whirls around to stare at the car. The car idles roughly, smoke coming from the exhaust, the frame shaking gently.* Les's *eyes go wide, and he runs over to his car. The people stare at the car.*)

Man One. He got the car started somehow. He got *his* car started!

(*The people continue to stare, caught up by this revelation and wildly frightened.*)

Woman. How come his car just up and started like that?

Sally. All by itself. He wasn't anywheres near it.

WORDS TO KNOW

defiant (dĭ-fī'ənt) *adj.* willing to stand up to opposition; bold
antagonism (ăn-tăg'ə-nĭz'əm) *n.* hostility; unfriendliness

421

Cross Curricular Link **Social Studies**

SCIENCE FICTION Science fiction is an extremely popular literary and entertainment genre, as exemplified by the success of the film *Star Wars.* Long before *Star Wars,* however, people enjoyed futuristic worlds created by writers like Jules Verne and H. G. Wells. Verne was a Frenchman; his works include *A Journey to the Center of the Earth* (1864) and *Twenty Thousand Leagues Under the Sea* (1870). H. G. Wells was English; he introduced the now-common themes of time travel (*The Time Machine,* 1895) and alien invasion (*The War of the Worlds,* 1898). Students who want to read classic science fiction might start with the short stories of Ray Bradbury and Isaac Asimov.

One of Rod Serling's models for the plot of this teleplay was *The Crucible* by Arthur Miller. In this 1953 play, a community destroys itself trying to find the source of evil during the Salem witchcraft trials.

Reading and Analyzing

Man Leaning on a Car Door (1963), George Segal. Courtesy Sidney Janis Gallery, New York. Copyright © George Segal/VAGA, New York.

422 UNIT THREE PART 2: FANTASTIC TALES

It started all by itself.

(*Don Martin approaches the group and stops a few feet away to look toward* Les's *car.*)

Don. And he never did come out to look at that thing that flew overhead. He wasn't even interested. (*He turns to the group, his face taut and serious.*) Why? Why didn't he come out with the rest of us to look?

Charlie. He always was an oddball. Him and his whole family. Real odd-ball.

Don. What do you say we ask him?

(*The group starts toward the house. In this brief fraction of a moment, it takes*

ACTIVE READING

MAKE INFERENCES
What does this dialogue tell you about Charlie and Don?

B

the first step toward changing from a group into a mob. The group members begin to head purposefully across the street toward the house. Steve *stands in front of them. For a moment their fear almost turns their walk into a wild stampede, but* Steve's *voice, loud, incisive, and commanding, makes them stop.*)

Steve. Wait a minute . . . wait a minute! Let's not be a mob!

(*The people stop, pause for a moment, and then, much more quietly and slowly, start to walk across the street.* Les *stands alone facing the people.*)

Les. I just don't understand it. I tried to start it, and it wouldn't start. You saw me. All of you saw me.

(*And now, just as suddenly as the engine started, it stops, and there is a long silence that is gradually intruded upon by the*

---

frightened murmuring of the people.)

Les. I don't understand. I swear . . . I don't understand. What's happening?

Don. Maybe you better tell us. Nothing's working on this street. Nothing. No lights, no power, no radio, (*then meaningfully*) nothing except one car—yours!

(*The people's murmuring becomes a loud chant filling the air with accusations and demands for action. Two of the men pass Don and head toward Les, who backs away from them against his car. He is cornered.*)

Les. Wait a minute now. You keep your distance—all of you. So I've got a car that starts by itself—well, that's a freak thing—I admit it. But does that make me a criminal or something? I don't know why the car works— it just does!

(*This stops the crowd momentarily, and Les, still backing away, goes toward his front porch. He goes up the steps and then stops, facing the mob.*)

Les. What's it all about, Steve?

Steve (*quietly*). We're all on a monster kick, Les. Seems that the general impression holds that maybe one family isn't what we think they are. Monsters from outer space or something. Different from us. Aliens from the vast beyond. (*He chuckles.*) You know anybody that might fit that description around here on Maple Street?

Les. What is this, a gag? (*He looks around the group again.*) This a practical joke or something?

(*Suddenly the car engine starts all by itself, runs for a moment, and stops. One woman begins to cry. The eyes of the crowd are cold and accusing.*)

Les. Now that's supposed to <u>incriminate</u> me, huh? The car engine goes on and off, and that

really does it, doesn't it? (*He looks around at the faces of the people.*) I just don't understand it . . . any more than any of you do! (*He wets his lips, looking from face to face.*) Look, you all know me. We've lived here five years. Right in this house. We're no different from any of the rest of you! We're no different at all. . . . Really . . . this whole thing is just . . . just weird—

Woman. Well, if that's the case, Les Goodman, explain why— (*She stops suddenly, clamping her mouth shut.*)

Les (*softly*). Explain what?

Steve (*interjecting*). Look, let's forget this—

Charlie (*overlapping him*). Go ahead, let her talk. What about it? Explain what?

Woman (*a little reluctantly*). Well . . . sometimes I go to bed late at night. A couple of times . . . a couple of times I'd come out here on the porch, and I'd see Mr. Goodman here in the wee hours of the morning standing out in front of his house . . . looking up at the sky. (*She looks around the circle of faces.*) That's right, looking up at the sky as if . . . as if he were waiting for something, (*pauses*) as if he were looking for something.

(*There's a murmur of reaction from the crowd again as Les backs away.*)

Les. She's crazy. Look, I can explain that. Please . . . I can really explain that. . . . She's making it up anyway. (*Then he shouts.*) I tell you she's making it up!

(*He takes a step toward the crowd, and they back away from him. He walks down the steps after them, and they continue to back away. Suddenly he is left completely alone, and he looks like a man caught in the middle of a menacing circle as the scene slowly fades to black.*)

2

WORDS
TO
KNOW

incriminate (ĭn-krĭm′ə-nāt′) *v.* to cause to appear guilty

423

Customizing Instruction

Students Acquiring English

1 Tell students that *we're all on a monster kick* means "all of us are thinking too much about a monster." Help students think of other expressions that use the word *kick* to mean "intense interest." (diet kick, recycling kick, etc.)

Less Proficient Readers

2 Be sure that students understand the main characters of the selection and what is happening among the neighbors. You might ask:

• Why did the neighbors become suspicious of Les?
  Possible Response: His car started itself, he didn't come outside when the flash occurred, and he sometimes looks at the sky at night.

Set a Purpose Have students read to find out why the neighbors suspect Steve.

Gifted and Talented

After students read Act Two, Scene One have them rate the principal characters on a scale of zero (low) to ten (high) in terms of how well they respond to crisis. Near each character's name, students should list the character's strengths and weaknesses, supported by details from the story. Then have them describe the qualities they think would make someone an ideal leader in this crisis. How would that person be different from Les, Charlie, Steve, Sally, or Tommy?

Possible Response: Sally (3) compassionate toward Goodmans, protective of Tommy, weak and hesitant in stating her views

---

 Mini Lesson **Spelling** TEKS 16C 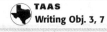 TAAS Writing Obj. 3, 7

SUFFIXES -ance/-ant, -ence/-ent

Instruction Tell students that the suffixes *-ance* and *-ant* are commonly added to complete words. The suffixes *-ence* and *-ent* are commonly added to roots.

Exercises Help them understand that a final *-y* will change to *-i* when a suffix is attached and a final *-e* will disappear when a suffix beginning with a vowel is added.

Have students choose the correct suffix to complete the words in the following sentences.

1. Charlie's consci(<u>ence</u>/ance) didn't seem to bother him.

2. All of the inhabit(ents/<u>ants</u>) of Maple Street were afraid of the unseen danger.

3. All of the appli(ences/<u>ances</u>) stopped working after the blinding flash.

4. Steve offered little guid(ence/<u>ance</u>) to the mob, already wild with fright.

Ask students to look for more words that fit this pattern, in their own writing and in things that they read, and to share these words with the group.

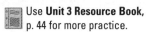 Use **Unit 3 Resource Book,** p. 44 for more practice.

Remind students that in a script dialogue reveals character, shows what characters are thinking and feeling, and helps in explaining what is happening on-scene and off-scene.

(A) What do Sally's lines explain about what is happening at the Goodmans' house?

Possible Response: Neighbors are standing guard over the Goodman house.

• Remember that Sally is Tommy's mother. What do these lines reveal about her character?

Possible Response: She thinks that what is being done to the Goodmans is wrong, but she is too weak and hesitant to change the situation.

(B) Point out that Charlie's dialogue here includes grammatical errors and shortened words. Ask what this dialogue suggests about Charlie.

Possible Response: It suggests that Charlie is not well educated.

ACTIVE READING

(C) AUTHOR'S PURPOSE Responses will vary. Students might guess the author wants people to feel anger or disgust.

Literary Analysis: THEME

(D) Ask students what Steve's words suggest about the theme.

Possible Response: The neighbors are going to destroy each other by their own actions.

Act Two

Scene One

(*Fade in on Maple Street at night. On the sidewalk, little knots of people stand around talking in low voices. At the end of each conversation they look toward* Les Goodman's *house. From the various houses, we can see candlelight but no electricity. The quiet that blankets the whole area is disturbed only by the almost whispered voices of the people standing around. In one group* Charlie *stands staring across at the Goodmans' house. Two men stand across the street from it in almost sentrylike poses.*)

Sally (*in a small, hesitant voice*). It just doesn't seem right, though, keeping watch on them. Why . . . he was right when he said he was one of our neighbors. Why, I've known Ethel Goodman ever since they moved in. We've been good friends—

Charlie. That don't prove a thing. Any guy who'd spend his time lookin' up at the sky early in the morning—well, there's something wrong with that kind of person. There's something that ain't <u>legitimate</u>. Maybe under normal circumstances we could let it go by, but these aren't normal circumstances. Why, look at this street! Nothin' but candles. Why, it's like goin' back into the Dark Ages or somethin'!

(Steve *walks down the steps of his porch, down the street to the Goodmans' house, and then stops at the foot of the steps.* Les *is standing there;* Ethel Goodman *behind him is very frightened.*)

Les. Just stay right where you are, Steve. We don't want any trouble, but this time if anybody sets foot on my porch—that's what they're going to get—trouble!

Steve. Look, Les—

Les. I've already explained to you people. I don't sleep very well at night sometimes. I get up and I take a walk and I look up at the sky. I look at the stars!

Ethel. That's exactly what he does. Why, this whole thing, it's . . . it's some kind of madness or something.

Steve (*nods grimly*). That's exactly what it is—some kind of madness.

Charlie's Voice (*shrill, from across the street*). You best watch who you're seen with, Steve! Until we get this all straightened out, you ain't exactly above suspicion yourself.

Steve (*whirling around toward him*). Or you, Charlie. Or any of us, it seems. From age eight on up!

Woman. What I'd like to know is—what are we gonna do? Just stand around here all night?

Charlie. There's nothin' else we *can* do! (*He turns back, looking toward* Steve *and* Les *again.*) One of 'em'll tip their hand. They got to.

Steve (*raising his voice*). There's something you can do, Charlie. You can go home and keep your mouth shut. You can quit strutting around like a self-appointed judge and climb into bed and forget it.

Charlie. You sound real anxious to have that happen, Steve. I think we better keep our eye on you, too!

ACTIVE READING

AUTHOR'S PURPOSE
How do you think the author wants you to feel toward the people of Maple Street?

Teaching Options

Cross Curricular Link History

THE DARK AGES "Dark Ages" refers to a period in medieval European history, from the fall of the Western Roman Empire in A.D. 476 to about the year 1000. The term was coined as a result of the prejudice that this was a period of limited social progress and unenlightened thought. Historians now believe, however, that the period was in fact an eventful one. Its hallmarks include the navigational and trade advances of the Vikings, who explored and colonized as well as raided, and the rule of Charlemagne, who patronized learning.

During this time, scholars developed a form of standardized writing that simplified the arduous work of copying texts.

A common theme in science fiction is the idea that humanity, as a result of alien attack or man-made environmental or social catastrophe, will actually revert to a primitive lifestyle, such as that imagined to have characterized the Dark Ages, in order to survive in the harsh world of the future.

Don (*as if he were taking the bit in his teeth, takes a hesitant step to the front*). I think everything might as well come out now. (*He turns toward Steve.*) Your wife's done plenty of talking, Steve, about how odd you are!

Charlie (*picking this up, his eyes widening*). Go ahead, tell us what she's said.

(Steve *walks toward them from across the street.*)

Steve. Go ahead, what's my wife said? Let's get it all out. Let's pick out every <u>idiosyncrasy</u> of every single man, woman, and child on the street. And then we might as well set up some kind of citizens' court. How about a firing squad at dawn, Charlie, so we can get rid of all the suspects. Narrow them down. Make it easier for you.

Don. There's no need gettin' so upset, Steve. It's just that . . . well . . . Myra's talked about how there's been plenty of nights you spent hours down in your basement workin' on some kind of radio or something. Well, none of us have ever seen that radio—

(*By this time* Steve *has reached the group. He stands there defiantly.*)

Charlie. Go ahead, Steve. What kind of "radio set" you workin' on? I never seen it. Neither has anyone else. Who do you talk to on that radio set? And who talks to you?

Steve. I'm surprised at you, Charlie. How come you're so dense all of a sudden? (*He pauses.*) Who do I talk to? I talk to monsters from outer space. I talk to three-headed green men who fly over here in what look like meteors.

(Myra Brand *steps down from the porch, bites her lip, calls out.*)

Myra. Steve! Steve, please. (*Then looking around, frightened, she walks toward the group.*) It's just a ham radio set, that's all. I bought him a book on it myself. It's just a ham radio set. A lot of people have them. I can show it to you. It's right down in the basement.

Steve (*whirls around toward her*). Show them nothing! If they want to look inside our house—let them go and get a search warrant.

Charlie. Look, buddy, you can't afford to—

Steve (*interrupting him*). Charlie, don't start telling me who's dangerous and who isn't and who's safe and who's a menace. (*He turns to the group and shouts.*) And you're with him, too—all of you! You're standing here all set to crucify—all set to find a scapegoat—all desperate to point some kind of a finger at a neighbor! Well now, look, friends, the only thing that's gonna happen is that we'll eat each other up alive—

(*He stops abruptly as* Charlie *suddenly grabs his arm.*)

Charlie (*in a hushed voice*). That's not the only thing that can happen to us.

(*Down the street, a figure has suddenly materialized in the gloom. In the silence we hear the clickety-clack of slow, measured footsteps on concrete as the figure walks slowly toward them. One of the women lets out a stifled cry. Sally grabs her boy, as do a couple of other mothers.*)

Tommy (*shouting, frightened*). It's the monster! It's the monster!

(*Another woman lets out a wail, and the people fall back in a group staring toward the darkness and the approaching figure. The people stand in the shadows watching.* Don Martin *joins them, carrying a shotgun. He holds it up.*)

Don. We may need this.

Steve. A shotgun? (*He pulls it out of* Don's *hand.*) No! Will anybody think a thought around here! Will you people wise up. What good would a shotgun do against—

(*The dark figure continues to walk toward them*

D

4

WORDS
TO
KNOW   **idiosyncrasy** (ĭd´ē-ō-sĭng´krə-sē) *n.* a personal way of acting; odd mannerism

425

 Mini Lesson **Speaking and Listening** 🏴 **TEKS** 5C, 5D, 5E, 11B, 24C

DRAMA PERFORMANCE

Prepare Tell students that they can increase their understanding and enjoyment of a teleplay by reading the script aloud. Explain that they should think of themselves as reading in a recording studio. They must use their voices to make a character come alive for the audience. Talk with students about voice qualities that help a character actor reach an audience: for example, rate, pitch, and tone.

Have students form groups and choose an act of the teleplay to present as a Reader's Theater performance. Tell them to pay close attention to stage directions as they practice the rate, pitch, and tone of their lines, so that their delivery will be clear and will convey the character's traits and feelings.

Present Have students read their act for the class. Depending on students' comfort levels, you may wish to have listeners evaluate each reading against criteria established by the group to assess rate, pitch, tone, and other aspects of presentation.

BLOCK SCHEDULING This activity is particularly well suited for longer class periods.

▦ Use **Communications Transparencies and Copymasters**, p. 12, for additional support.

Customizing Instruction

Students Acquiring English

1 Explain to students that "One of 'em'll tip their hand" comes from playing cards. A player tips his or her hand by accidentally holding the cards in such a way that other players can see them. Thus, the other players know what cards are being held and how to play their hands. You might help students think of other terms that come from playing cards: *wild card, not playing with a full deck, fold, call, bluff, poker face, ante up.*

Less Proficient Readers

2 Be sure students recognize the sarcasm in Steve's lines. Why does Steve suggest a firing squad? Why does he say he talks to space creatures?

Possible Response: Steve exaggerates Charlie's attitudes and suspicions to show how ridiculous Charlie is being.

3 Discuss with students the way the neighbors begin to suspect another person each time they learn something new about someone else. Then have students explain why Steve becomes a suspect.

Possible Response: because he works on a ham radio in the basement and no one has ever seen this radio

Set a Purpose Have students read to find out what happens when the neighbors on Maple Street think they see and hear a monster coming.

Multiple Learning Styles
Logical-Mathematical Learners

4 Ask students to use logical reasoning to list several possibilities for who or what might be walking toward the crowd.

Possible Responses: someone from a different part of town; someone who is hurt; the neighbor who went to check on the other street

---

A **Predict** Responses will vary. Students might guess that people will turn on Charlie.

Reading Skills and Strategies: MAKING INFERENCES

B Ask why Charlie now suggests that someone is pulling a gag.
Possible Response: Now his own reputation is at stake.

Reading Skills and Strategies: MAKING JUDGMENTS

C Ask students if they think Charlie really believes that Tommy is the monster.
Possible Response: He probably doesn't think it's Tommy, but he says so to turn the crowd's attention away from himself.

Literary Analysis: THEME

D Have students explain how the view of Maple Street from on high is connected to the theme of the story.
Possible Response: Anyone looking at Maple Street would think—as the reader does at the beginning—that Maple Street is a friendly, American suburb. As the theme suggests, things are not always as they appear.

Literary Analysis `TELEPLAY`

Remind students that in a teleplay character traits are conveyed primarily by dialogue. Have students skim Act Two, Scene One, to identify dialogue that reveals the characters of Steve and Charlie. You might have them chart their findings.

---

as the people stand there, fearful, mothers clutching children, men standing in front of their wives.)

Charlie (*pulling the gun from* Steve's *hands*). No more talk, Steve. You're going to talk us into a grave! You'd let whatever's out there walk right over us, wouldn't yuh? Well, some of us won't!

(Charlie *swings around, raises the gun, and suddenly pulls the trigger. The sound of the shot explodes in the stillness. The figure suddenly lets out a small cry, stumbles forward onto his knees, and then falls forward on his face. Don,* Charlie, *and* Steve *race forward to him.* Steve *is there first and turns the man over. The crowd gathers around them.*)

Steve (*slowly looks up*). It's Pete Van Horn.

Don (*in a hushed voice*). Pete Van Horn! He was just gonna go over to the next block to see if the power was on—

A **PREDICT** What do you think the neighbors will do now?

Woman. You killed him, Charlie. You shot him dead!

Charlie (*looks around at the circle of faces, his eyes frightened, his face* <u>contorted</u>). But . . . but I didn't know who he was. I certainly didn't know who he was. He comes walkin' out of the darkness—how am I supposed to know who he was? (*He grabs* Steve.) Steve— you know why I shot! How was I supposed to know he wasn't a monster or something? (*He grabs* Don.) We're all scared of the same thing. I was just tryin' to . . . tryin' to protect my home, that's all! Look, all of you, that's all I was tryin' to do. (*He looks down wildly at the body.*) I didn't know it was somebody we knew! I didn't know—

(There's a sudden hush and then an intake of breath in the group. Across the street all the

lights go on in one of the houses.)

Woman (*in a hushed voice*). Charlie . . . Charlie . . . the lights just went on in your house. Why did the lights just go on?

Don. What about it, Charlie? How come you're the only one with lights now?

Les. That's what I'd like to know.

(*Pausing, they all stare toward* Charlie.)

Les. You were so quick to kill, Charlie, and you were so quick to tell us who we had to be careful of. Well, maybe you had to kill. Maybe Pete there was trying to tell us something. Maybe he'd found out something and came back to tell us who there was amongst us we should watch out for—

(Charlie *backs away from the group, his eyes wide with fright.*)

Charlie. No . . . no . . . it's nothing of the sort! I don't know why the lights are on. I swear I don't. Somebody's pulling a gag or something.

(*He bumps against* Steve, *who grabs him and whirls him around.*)

Steve. A gag? A gag? Charlie, there's a dead man on the sidewalk, and you killed him! Does this thing look like a gag to you?

(Charlie *breaks away and screams as he runs toward his house.*)

Charlie. No! No! Please!

(A man breaks away from the crowd to chase Charlie. As the man tackles him and lands on top of him, the other people start to run toward them. Charlie gets up, breaks away from the other man's grasp, and lands a couple of desperate punches that push the man aside. Then he forces his way, fighting, through the crowd and jumps up on his front porch. Charlie is on his porch as a rock thrown from the group smashes a window beside him, the broken glass

---

WORDS
TO
KNOW

contorted (kən-tôr'tĭd) *adj.* twisted or pulled out of shape **contort** *v.*

426

 Grammar  TEKS 17F TAAS Writing Obj. 3, 6

IDENTIFYING PARTICIPLES AND THEIR FUNCTIONS
Instruction Remind students that present and past participles can function as modifiers, or adjectives. Help students identify the participle and its function in each sentence.

1. A thoughtless, frightened search for a scapegoat has a fallout all its own. (*frightened, modifies search*)

2. We see Sally holding the boy. (*holding, describes Sally*)

3. The crowd starts to follow, at first walking fast, and then running. (*walking, running describe the crowd*)

Application Have students find participles used as modifiers in the opening scene. Have them write each participle and the noun it modifies. Remind them not to be confused by participles that are part of a sentence's main verb phrase.

Answers: *sparkling* relief; *tree-lined* street; *talking* people; *parked* car; *watching* neighbor; *riding* vendor

 Use **Grammar Transparencies and Copymasters,** p. 96.

 Use McDougal Littell's *Language Network,* Chapter 7, for more instruction and practice in identifying participles and their functions.

flying past him. A couple of pieces cut him. He stands there perspiring, rumpled, blood running down from a cut on the cheek. His wife breaks away from the group to throw herself into his arms. He buries his face against her. We can see the crowd converging on the porch.)

Voice One. It must have been him.

Voice Two. He's the one.

Voice Three. We got to get Charlie.

(Another rock lands on the porch. Charlie pushes his wife behind him, facing the group.)

Charlie. Look, look I swear to you. . . . it isn't me . . . but I do know who it is . . . I swear to you, I do know who it is. I know who the monster is here. I know who it is that doesn't belong. I swear to you I know.

Don *(pushing his way to the front of the crowd).* All right, Charlie, let's hear it!

(Charlie's eyes dart around wildly.)

Charlie. It's . . . it's . . .

Man Two *(screaming).* Go ahead, Charlie.

Charlie. It's . . . it's the kid. It's Tommy. He's the one!

(There's a gasp from the crowd as we see Sally holding the boy. Tommy at first doesn't understand and then, realizing the eyes are all

Detail of *Man Leaning on a Car Door* (1963), George Segal.

on him, buries his face against his mother.)

Sally *(backs away).* That's crazy! He's only a boy.

Woman. But he knew! He was the only one! He told us all about it. Well, how did he know? How could he have known? **1**

(Various people take this up and repeat the question.)

Voice One. How could he know?

Voice Two. Who told him?

Voice Three. Make the kid answer.

(The crowd starts to converge around the mother, who grabs Tommy and starts to run with him. The crowd starts to follow, at first walking fast, and then running after him. Suddenly Charlie's lights go off and the lights in other houses go on, then off.)

Man One *(shouting).* It isn't the kid . . . it's Bob Weaver's house.

Woman. It isn't Bob Weaver's house, it's Don Martin's place.

Charlie. I tell you it's the kid.

Don. It's Charlie. He's the one. **2**

(People shout, accuse, and scream as the lights go on and off. Then, slowly, in the middle of this nightmarish confusion of sight and sound, the camera starts to pull away until, once again, we have reached the opening shot looking at the Maple Street sign from high above.) **D**

Scene Two

(The camera continues to move away while gradually bringing into focus a field. We see the metal side of a spacecraft that sits shrouded in darkness. An open door throws out a beam of light from the illuminated interior. Two figures appear, silhouetted against the bright lights. We get only a vague feeling of form.)

Figure One. Understand the procedure now? Just stop a few of their machines and radios

THE MONSTERS ARE DUE ON MAPLE STREET   **427**

A and telephones and lawn mowers. . . . Throw them into darkness for a few hours, and then just sit back and watch the pattern.

Figure Two. And this pattern is always the same?

B

Figure One. With few variations. They pick the most dangerous enemy they can find . . . and it's themselves. And all we need do is sit back . . . and watch.

Figure Two. Then I take it this place . . . this Maple Street . . . is not unique.

Figure One (*shaking his head*). By no means. Their world is full of Maple Streets. And we'll go from one to the other and let them destroy themselves. One to the other . . . one to the other . . . one to the other—

Scene Three

(*The camera slowly moves up for a shot of the starry sky, and over this we hear the* Narrator's *voice.*)

Narrator. The tools of conquest do not necessarily come with bombs and explosions and fallout.[2] There are weapons that are simply thoughts, attitudes, prejudices—to be found only in the minds of men. For the record, prejudices can kill and suspicion can destroy. A thoughtless, frightened search for a scapegoat has a fallout all its own for the children . . . and the children yet unborn, (a pause) and the pity of it is . . . that these things cannot be confined to . . . The Twilight Zone!

(*Fade to black.*)

---

2. **fallout:** radioactive particles that fall to earth after a nuclear explosion.

Detail of *Rush Hour* (1983), George Segal.

✓ **Assessment** **Standardized Test Practice**   TEKS 10F, 10K   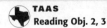 TAAS Reading Obj. 2, 3

RECOGNIZE STATED OR PARAPHRASED MAIN IDEA
In some standardized tests, students are asked to select the best main idea statement about a passage they have read. Write the following question on the chalkboard or read it aloud.
Which statement expresses the main idea of *The Monsters Are Due on Maple Street?*

A. A mysterious flash of light causes the power and phones to go out on Maple Street.

B. A boy convinces people that aliens have invaded their quiet neighborhood.

C. People in a typical American neighborhood turn on each other when they think their street has been invaded by aliens.

D. Aliens are planning to take over Earth by causing trouble in one neighborhood after another.

Guide students through the process of selecting the correct answer. A, B, and D are not correct because each states only a part of the story. C is the best answer because it covers the entire story. A main idea statement does not include all the details in a passage.

Thinking through the LITERATURE

Connect to the Literature

1. What Do You Think?
What is your reaction to the fear and confusion on Maple Street?

.... **Comprehension Check** ....
- When do people first sense something is wrong?
- Why is Pete Van Horn killed?
- Who are the most dangerous enemies of human beings?

Think Critically

2. In your opinion, who are the monsters on Maple Street referred to in the title? Give reasons for your answer.

3. Do you think the aliens are correct in their judgment of human behavior? Explain your answer.

4. After the crowd turns on him, why does Charlie accuse someone else of being the monster? What evidence does he have?

5. Why do you think the author chose Maple Street as the setting of this teleplay?

THINK ABOUT
{
- the children playing along the street
- the peaceful, quiet appearance of the street
- the fact that the houses all look alike

6. **ACTIVE READING** **AUTHOR'S PURPOSE** Have you identified the author's purpose? Compare the list of details in your **READER'S NOTEBOOK** with a classmate's list. Discuss the different purposes that Serling might have had as he wrote.

Extend Interpretations

7. What If? What if the story, instead of being told by someone offstage, were told from the point of view of Charlie? How would the teleplay be different? How would Charlie defend his actions?

8. Connect to Life This teleplay shows what can happen when a crowd becomes a mob. How does being in a crowd change the way people act? What other examples of "mob mentality" have you heard about?

Literary Analysis

 TELEPLAY A play written for television is called a **teleplay.** The **stage directions** in a teleplay are often written in italics, and they include directions for the camera to fade in or out on a shot or to focus on a certain character. Camera directions help readers visualize what the drama might look like on television. They also help the producer of the television program know what details the author wants to emphasize or focus on.

Paired Activity With a partner, go back over the stage directions and find the camera directions. Discuss what the different camera directions lead you to visualize. Do you think that writers ever disagree with filmmakers' interpretations of their camera directions?

REVIEW **SUSPENSE** **Suspense** is the excitement or tension that readers feel as they get involved in a plot and become eager to know what is going to happen next. How does suspense build in this drama?

Extend Interpretations

7. What If? This question is well suited for gifted students. **If you wish to make this question easier,** facilitate a group discussion of how the teleplay would be different if told from Charlie's point of view. Possible Responses: Have someone other than Charlie remark that Van Horn isn't back yet, or play up Charlie's concern; make "monster" look as inhuman and threatening as possible, to excuse his mistake; have another character encourage him to shoot; have others remark that Van Horn seemed suspicious; state his defense more calmly and rationally; give reasons for turning on Tommy.

8. Connect to Life Possible Response: People seem to take less responsibility for their actions when they are in a crowd. An example of "mob mentality" might be a crowd stampede at a sports event.

GUIDING STUDENT RESPONSE

Connect to the Literature

1. What Do You Think?
Responses will vary. Students may express doubt that people would react so violently; they may say they expected such response.

Comprehension Check
- Possible Responses: When they realize nothing is working.
- He is shot by Charlie, who thinks he is a monster coming up the street.
- human beings (themselves)

 Use Selection Quiz **Unit Three Resource Book,** p. 45.

Think Critically

2. Possible Responses: The aliens are the monsters because they started the trouble. The neighbors are the monsters because they turned on one another.

3. Possible Responses: Yes, because people tend to suspect others whom they regard as different. No, since people sometimes show true heroism and concern for others in an emergency.

4. Possible Response: Charlie accuses someone else to turn attention away from himself. He offers no evidence.

5. Possible Response: By using a typical suburban street like Maple Street, the author suggests that this pattern of behavior could happen anywhere.

6. Possible Response: Serling's purpose was to persuade readers that fear, prejudice, and suspicion can overrun common sense and compassion, making people capable of destroying one another.

Use **Reading and Critical Thinking Transparencies,** p. 4, for additional support.

Literary Analysis

Teleplay: Stage Directions Students may say that they think writers and filmmakers talk about camera directions. Sometimes, writers probably do disagree with filmmakers' interpretations.

Review: Suspense Suspense builds as the neighbors realize Tommy may be right, as they become more frightened and panicky, as things begin to work in the homes and cars of accused people, as person after person is accused, and as violence mounts.

 Use **Literary Analysis Transparencies,** p. 23, for additional support.

Choices & CHALLENGES

Writing Options

1. **Stage Directions** Student stage directions will vary but should describe Maple Street in a way that takes into account events suggested at the end of the teleplay. They must include directions for the camera. For example, the camera might at first show a quiet street, then close in to reveal bodies, damaged homes, and children huddled in shock.

2. **Draft a Proposal** Student proposals will vary but might include some of the following changes: Pete Van Horn is not killed but brings back useful information; committees are formed to accomplish various tasks; Maple Street joins with other neighborhoods to face the aliens. Students should give reasons for each change they propose and explain how the change(s) would affect the theme of the play.

Use **Writing Transparencies**, p. 13, for additional support.

Activities & Explorations

Comic Book Art and dialogue should convey key scenes: for example, the opening view of Maple Street, the roar and flash, people's reactions, Pete leaving, Tommy stopping Steve and Charlie, Les's car starting, people accusing each other, the appearance of the gun, Pete's reappearance and death, Charlie's attack on Tommy, the resulting pandemonium, and the aliens.

Art Connection

Human Sculpture Responses will vary, but students may say that the sculptures complement the play's themes. *Rush Hour* can be seen as ordinary people forming an army as a vigilante group forms on Maple Street, turning on and exposing individuals. Sally and Les, for example, seem as alone, ordinary, and vulnerable as the figures in Segal's white sculptures.

Inquiry & Research

Prejudice and Suspicion Student summaries will vary by topic. Student suggestions might include learning from history and literature, learning and role-playing positive responses to frightening situations, and unlearning prejudice and suspicion.

Writing Options

1. **Stage Directions** Write stage directions to describe what a visitor would find on Maple Street the day after the events of this teleplay. Be sure to include directions for the camera.

2. **Draft a Proposal** Think about how you would revise *The Monsters Are Due on Maple Street* to present a more positive perspective on human behavior. Write a proposal for changing the script, describing the reason for each of your changes and the way it would affect the theme of the teleplay. Place the proposal in your **Working Portfolio.**

See p. R39: Persuasive Writing.

Activities & Explorations

Comic Book Create a comic book based on the teleplay. Draw key scenes and write the accompanying dialogue.
~ **ART**

Art Connection

Human Sculpture Pictures of George Segal's sculptures illustrate the teleplay. Do you think they capture an important aspect of the teleplay? Explain your response.

Inquiry & Research

Prejudice and Suspicion How have prejudices and suspicions served to hurt and destroy people throughout history? Find out by looking through books about American and world history. Write a short summary of a tragic situation that was caused by irrational fear and prejudice, such as the Salem witch trials or the "Red scare." Then explain how you think people could avoid repeating such mistakes in the future.

Vocabulary in Action

EXERCISE: ANALOGIES An analogy contains two pairs of words that are related in the same way, as in the example TALL : HIGH :: wild : untamed. The analogy is read *"Tall is to high as wild is to untamed."* In this example, the words are synonyms; that is, they have similar meanings. An analogy may also use antonyms to express a relationship between words. For each item below, decide which Word to Know best completes the second pair of the analogy.

1. QUICK : FAST :: _____ : stubborn
2. DIFFICULT : HARD :: confused : _____
3. SOAKED : DRENCHED :: _____ : peculiarity
4. HIGH : LOW :: _____ : friendship
5. ANGER : RAGE :: twisted : _____
6. CHEERFUL : GENIAL :: accuse : _____
7. FAR : DISTANT :: _____ : lawful
8. ANNOYANCE : PLEASURE :: _____ : gloomy
9. RUNNING : STROLLING :: _____ : weak
10. BORED : INTERESTED :: agreeable : _____

Building Vocabulary
For an in-depth study of interpreting analogies, see p. 398.

WORDS TO KNOW				
antagonism	defiant	idiosyncrasy	intense	optimistic
contorted	flustered	incriminate	legitimate	persistent

Vocabulary in Action

EXERCISE

1. persistent
2. flustered
3. idiosyncrasy
4. antagonism
5. contorted
6. incriminate
7. legitimate
8. optimistic
9. intense
10. defiant

Grammar in Context: Participles

Rod Serling uses **participles** in his stage directions to set the scene in *The Monsters Are Due on Maple Street.*

Tommy stares at them, biting his lips.

Tommy is both frightened and defiant.

Participles are verb forms that function as modifiers. Present participles end in *-ing* and past participles of regular verbs end in *-d* or *-ed.*

Apply to Your Writing A participle has some of the characteristics of a verb, but a participle can never be the main verb in a sentence. A sentence without a main verb is a fragment. Always review your writing to make sure you haven't inadvertently written a sentence with a participle instead of a main verb.

WRITING EXERCISE Rewrite the following sentences to avoid any fragments.

Example: *Original* Small knots of people were watching the sky. Talking in low voices.

Rewritten Small knots of people talking in low voices were watching the sky.

1. Sally stood there. Watching him as he mowed.
2. Walking down the street. A figure suddenly materialized in the gloom.
3. The car idled roughly. Smoke coming from the exhaust.
4. Rumpled and perspiring. Charlie sits there with blood running down his cheek.

Connect to the Literature Look at the stage directions on page 419 that begin *"He gets in the car . . ."* How many participles do you find in that paragraph?

Grammar Handbook Using Modifiers Effectively, p. R70.

". . . I felt a need to write, a kind of compulsion to get some of my thoughts down. . . ."

Rod Serling
1924–1975

Social Issues Rod Serling began his career by writing for radio and television in Cincinnati, Ohio. In 1955, he scored his first big hit with his television drama *Patterns,* which won an Emmy Award. Though the public knew Serling as a creator of exciting television shows, those in the entertainment business knew him as "the angry young man of television." Although Serling wanted to write meaningful plays about important social issues, television sponsors and executives often found his topics too controversial. Thus began his long battle with those who controlled the networks.

Science Fiction Serling turned to writing science fiction and fantasy in series such as *The Twilight Zone* and *Night Gallery.* Because these shows were not realistic, he had more freedom to deal with issues such as prejudice and intolerance. Serling eventually won six Emmy Awards and many other honors for the extraordinary quality of his work.

AUTHOR ACTIVITY

The Twilight Zone Find and watch other episodes of *The Twilight Zone.* Besides the paranoia portrayed in *The Monsters Are Due on Maple Street,* what other social issues did Serling deal with?

THE MONSTERS ARE DUE ON MAPLE STREET **431**

 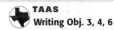

Objectives
1. understand and appreciate **science fiction** (Literary Analysis)
2. understand the **theme** (message) (Literary Analysis)
3. use the strategy of **predicting** (Active Reading)

Summary
Something is wrong in the future. Multivac isn't working. Jack Weaver, Tom Nemerson, and teams of computer specialists can find no technical problems in the complex machine that masterminds the world's economy. Despite Weaver's skepticism—after all, with such complex computers doing their bidding, people don't need to think anymore—Nemerson insists on thinking through the problem. What if, he reasons, Multivac has become so complex that it actually thinks and feels, just like a person? Nemerson listens to Weaver feed information into the Multivac one more time and spots the problem. Multivac won't work until someone says, "please."

Thematic Link
In this view of the future, a computer is so powerful that the world's economy is paralyzed when it stops functioning. As therapy to help deal with their dependence, people are required to talk to Multivac as if it thinks and understands. When it refuses to work until someone says "please," we realize that Multivac has become so complex that it is, in fact, human.

5-Minute Warm-Up

Daily Language SkillBuilder   **TEKS 16B, 17G**

Have students **proofread** the display sentences on page 341j and write them correctly. The sentences also appear on Transparency 13 of **Grammar Transparencies and Copymasters.**

SCIENCE

Key Item
Short Story by ISAAC ASIMOV

(**Connect to Your Life**)
What do you like most about computers?

Build Background Scientists in the field of Artificial Intelligence build machines that perform activities requiring intelligence, such as learning, interacting with human beings, and making decisions. Cog (*below*) is a robot in human form developed in the Artificial Intelligence Laboratory at the Massachusetts Institute of Technology (MIT). Cog represents many of the latest advancements in the field.

The Whole Arm Manipulator (*right*), also developed at MIT, has been designed with complex sensory and motor skills. It is shown here catching a ball.

An MIT researcher plays with Kismet (*above*), a robot capable of a range of expressions and gestures. In Kismet, scientists hope to develop a robot that can interact socially with human beings.

Focus Your Reading

LITERARY ANALYSIS SCIENCE FICTION **Science fiction** is a type of fiction based on real or imagined scientific and technological developments. A science fiction writer generally uses realistic characters but almost always places them in a futuristic setting. Science fiction helps readers imagine what the future might be like.

WORDS TO KNOW **Vocabulary Preview**
accede   circuit   complex   diffidently   neurotic

ACTIVE READING PREDICTING Active readers use information from the work they are reading and from what they already know to make logical **predictions** about plot, character, and setting. As you read the selection, jot down in your **READER'S NOTEBOOK** details that may help you predict what the key item mentioned in the title might be.

 See the Skills Trace at the beginning of the unit for information **TEKS** on TEKS covered in this lesson.

432   UNIT THREE   PART 2: FANTASTIC TALES

LESSON RESOURCES

UNIT THREE RESOURCE BOOK, pp. 46–52

ASSESSMENT
Formal Assessment, pp. 67–68
Teacher's Guide to Assessment and Portfolio Use
Test Generator

SKILLS TRANSPARENCIES AND COPYMASTERS
Reading and Critical Thinking
• Predicting, TR 7 (for Thinking Through the Literature, p. 436)
Vocabulary
• Using a Dictionary, CM 52 (for Mini Lesson 434)

INTEGRATED TECHNOLOGY
Audio Library
Internet: Research Starter

Visit our website:
www.mcdougallittell.com

Key Item

by Isaac Asimov

Illustration by Franco Accornero

Jack Weaver came out of the vitals of Multivac looking utterly worn and disgusted.

From the stool, where the other maintained his own stolid watch, Todd Nemerson said, "Nothing?"

"Nothing," said Weaver. "Nothing, nothing, nothing. No one can find anything wrong with it."

"Except that it won't work, you mean."

"You're no help sitting there!"

"I'm thinking."

"Thinking!" Weaver showed a canine at one side of his mouth.

Nemerson stirred impatiently on his stool. "Why not? There are six teams of computer technologists roaming around in the corridors of Multivac. They haven't come up with anything in three days. Can't you spare one person to think?"

"It's not a matter of thinking. We've got to

TEACHING THE LITERATURE

Customizing Instruction

Less Proficient Readers
- Discuss the term "key item." What is the key item needed to play soccer, for example? What are key items to bring to class?
- **Set a Purpose** Have students read to find out what "key item" is needed to fix a giant machine called Multivac.
- To help students track the speakers, read aloud the opening lines of Nemerson and Weaver. Explain that Nemerson wants to think about the problem, and Weaver believes thinking is a waste of time.
- **1** Explain that *canine* here refers to a tooth. Weaver's expression shows contempt or amusement.

Students Acquiring English
Explain that the word "key" has multiple meanings. In this story, the key item will be an essential item, not a literal key.

Use **Spanish Study Guide,** pp. 88–90 for additional support.

Gifted and Talented
Have students review the term "irony" (a contrast between what a reader or character expects and what actually happens). Then have students identify examples of irony in the story.

Possible Responses:

Page 433—Six teams of computer technologists have examined Multivac for three days, but no one has taken time to *think* about what might be wrong.

Page 434—People built Multivac, but it has become so complex that they can't understand their creation.

Page 434—People have to pretend the machine is a human being so they don't get neurotic over having a machine know more than they do.

Page 435—A simple "please" restarts a complex machine, averting world crisis.

 Viewing and Representing **TEKS 23A**

Illustration by Franc Accornero

ART APPRECIATION In life, most faces are essentially symmetrical: that is, the left side is nearly a mirror image of the right. One way artists convey complexity is by creating asymmetrical features where the viewer expects symmetry.

Instruction Have students compare both facial features and background. How are the left and right sides of the art similar and different?

Possible Responses: Both sides of the face are human in outline. Both backgrounds are solid color. The left side shows clear circuitry, no human features, and a bright background. The right side shows less circuitry, more human features, a piercing blue eye, and an indistinct line between the figure and the dark background.

Application Explain that both art and story deal with the idea of blurring lines between human and machine. Have students compare Asimov's Multivac with Accornero's figure.

Possible Response: Both combine humanoid and mechanical features. The artist's figure has a human outline; Multivac is a huge, complex machine becoming human inside.

Literary Analysis SCIENCE FICTION

Introduce or review the characteristics of the genre: fiction based on real or imagined scientific developments. Discuss the science fiction aspects in plot, setting, and characters.

 Use **Unit Three Resource Book**, p. 48, for more practice.

Active Reading PREDICTING

As students read, encourage them to analyze details that describe Multivac and the people that interact with it. Explain that these details could prove valuable in helping them to predict what the "key item" might be. Students might want to take notes as they read.

A Suggest that students pay close attention to the words of Nemerson as he struggles to solve the problem. Ask students if and when they can predict what his solution might be, based on his ideas.

 Use **Unit Three Resource Book**, p. 47, for more practice.

Literary Analysis: THEME

B Review the definition of theme. When students have finished reading, draw their attention back to this passage. Ask how it relates to the ending, Asimov's ideas on humans and machines, and the story's ultimate theme.

Possible Responses: Machines will become so complex that they will start being human; "Please" is the key item that Multivac needs because it is human now; feelings are the dividing line between humans and machines.

---

look. Somewhere a relay[1] is stuck."

"It's not that simple, Jack!"

"Who says it's simple? You know how many million relays we have there?"

"That doesn't matter. If it were just a relay, Multivac would have alternate <u>circuits</u>, devices for locating the flaw, and facilities to repair or replace the ailing part. The trouble is, Multivac won't only not answer the original question, it won't tell us what's wrong with it. —And meanwhile, there'll be panic in every city if we don't do something. The world's economy depends on Multivac, and everyone knows that."

"I know it, too. But what's there to do?"

"I told you, *think*. There must be something we're missing completely. Look, Jack, there isn't a computer bigwig in a hundred years who hasn't devoted himself to making Multivac more complicated. It can do so much now—it can even talk and listen. It's practically as <u>complex</u> as the human brain. We can't understand the human brain, so why should we understand Multivac?"

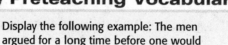

"Aw, come on. Next you'll be saying Multivac is human."

"Why not?" Nemerson grew absorbed and seemed to sink into himself. "Now that you mention it, why not? Could we tell if Multivac passed the thin dividing line where it stopped being a machine and started being human? *Is* there a dividing line, for that matter? If the brain is just more complex than Multivac, and we keep making Multivac more complex, isn't there a point where . . ." He mumbled down into silence.

Weaver said impatiently, "What are you driving at? Suppose Multivac were human. How would that help us find out why it isn't working?"

"For a human reason, maybe. Suppose *you* were asked the most probable price of wheat next summer and didn't answer. Why wouldn't you answer?"

"Because I wouldn't know. But Multivac would know! We've given it all the factors. It can analyze futures in weather, politics, and economics. We know it can. It's done it before."

"All right. Suppose I asked the question and you knew the answer but didn't tell me. Why not?"

Weaver snarled, "Because I had a brain tumor. Because I had been knocked out. Because my machinery was out of order. That's just what we're trying to find out about Multivac. We're looking for the place where its machinery is out of order, for the key item."

"Only you haven't found it." Nemerson got off his stool. "Listen, ask me the question Multivac stalled on."

"How? Shall I run the tape through you?"

"Come on, Jack. Give me the talk that goes along with it. You do talk to Multivac, don't you?"

"I've got to. Therapy."

Nemerson nodded. "Yes, that's the story. Therapy. That's the official story. We talk to it in order to pretend it's a human being so that we don't get <u>neurotic</u> over having a machine know so much more than we do. We turn a frightening metal monster into a protective father image."

---

1. **relay:** a device that responds to a small current or voltage charge by activating switches on an electric circuit.

WORDS TO KNOW
circuit (sûr'kĭt) *n.* the path of an electric current; connected electronic elements
complex (kəm-plĕks') *adj.* consisting of interconnected parts; intricate
neurotic (nŏŏ-rŏt'ĭk) *adj.* having excessive anxiety and emotional upset

434

Teaching Options

Mini Lesson **Preteaching Vocabulary**  TEKS 6A, 6C, 9B, 9C 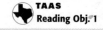 TAAS Reading Obj. 1

USING A DICTIONARY

Instruction When students encounter an unfamiliar word in their reading, they should first look at the context for clues to the word's meaning. If they are still unsure, they can use a dictionary to look up the word. Many words will have more than one meaning listed. Students can use context clues to determine which is the correct meaning for the context.

Display the following example: The men argued for a long time before one would <u>accede</u> to the other's plan. *(agree)*

Exercises Have students use a dictionary to define the underlined words.

1. Household electricity runs on <u>circuits</u> created by wires in the walls. *(closed pathways)*

2. No one could understand the <u>complex</u> directions. *(complicated)*

3. He spoke <u>diffidently</u>, as if worried that he might say something wrong. *(carefully)*

4. Psychological therapy can sometimes help people who have become <u>neurotic</u>. *(suffering excessive anxiety or fear)*

Use **Unit 3 Resource Book**, p. 49 for exercises.
Use **Vocabulary Transparencies and Copymasters**, p. 52, for additional support.

"If you want to put it that way."

"Well, it's wrong and you know it. A computer as complex as Multivac *must* talk and listen to be efficient. Just putting in and taking out coded dots[2] isn't sufficient. At a certain level of complexity, Multivac must be made to seem human because, it *is* human. Come on, Jack, ask me the question. I want to see my reaction to it."

Jack Weaver flushed. "This is silly."

"Come on, will you?"

It was a measure of Weaver's depression and desperation that he <u>acceded</u>. Half sullenly, he pretended to be feeding the program into Multivac, speaking as he did so in his usual manner. He commented on the latest information concerning farm unrest, talked about the new equations describing jet-stream[3] contortions, lectured on the solar constant.[4]

He began stiffly enough, but warmed to this task out of long habit, and when the last of the program was slammed home, he almost closed contact with a physical snap at Todd Nemerson's waist.

He ended briskly, "All right, now. Work that out and give us the answer pronto."

For a moment, having done, Jack Weaver stood there, nostrils flaring, as though he was feeling once more the excitement of throwing into action the most gigantic and glorious machine ever put together by the mind and hands of man.

Then he remembered and muttered, "All right. That's it."

Nemerson said, "At least I know now why *I* wouldn't answer, so let's try that on Multivac. Look, clear Multivac; make sure the investigators have their paws off it. Then run the program into it and let me do the talking. Just once."

Weaver shrugged and turned to Multivac's control wall, filled with its somber, unwinking dials and lights. Slowly he cleared it. One by one he ordered the teams away.

Then, with a deep breath, he began once more feeding the program into Multivac. It was the twelfth time all told, the dozenth time. Somewhere a distant news commentator would spread the word that they were trying again. All over the world a Multivac-dependent people would be holding its collective breath.

He paused and added the key item.

Nemerson talked as Weaver fed the data silently. He talked <u>diffidently</u>, trying to remember what it was that Weaver had said, but waiting for the moment when the key item might be added.

Weaver was done and now a note of tension was in Nemerson's voice. He said, "All right, now, Multivac. Work that out and give us the answer." He paused and added the key item. He said *"Please!"*

And all over Multivac, the valves and relays went joyously to work. After all, a machine has feelings—when it isn't a machine anymore. ❖

---

2. **coded dots:** a reference to an older method of giving a computer directions by inserting a coded instruction card.

3. **jet-stream:** a long, wandering current of high-speed winds, generally blowing from a westerly direction. The winds often exceed 250 miles per hour at altitudes of 10 to 15 miles above Earth.

4. **solar constant:** the average density of solar radiation, measured outside of Earth's atmosphere.

 WORDS TO KNOW
accede (ăk-sēd´) *v.* to consent due to outside influences
diffidently (dĭf´ĭ-dənt-lē) *adv.* reserved or restrained in manner

435

GUIDING STUDENT RESPONSE

Connect to the Literature

1. Accept all reasonable responses.

Comprehension Check

- It won't answer the scientists' questions and it won't tell them what's wrong.
- They talk to it so it will answer them.
- The "key item" is the word "please."

 Use Selection Quiz
Unit Three Resource Book, p. 52.

Think Critically

2. Possible Response: feelings; While machines can process information, they only do so in response to an external command. Feelings are often caused by external situations, but they are internal, wide-ranging, spontaneous impulses that determine how people behave. Multivac, it seems, responds when it feels like it and therefore has crossed the line.

3. Responses will vary.

 Use **Reading and Critical Thinking Transparencies,** p. 7, for additional support.

4. Possible Responses: Some students may feel that the scientists should have been able to answer the question using their own minds. Others may feel that, realistically, computers can process larger amounts of information and the scientists' use of Multivac was simply an efficient way to do their job.

5. Possible Response: Weaver is depressed and desperate from the pressure of the situation. He has been talking to Multivac all along, but only for his own benefit. Nemerson's ideas show that Weaver has not taken Multivac seriously.

Literary Analysis

Science Fiction Technically proficient students may suggest that computers can be programmed to "feel" even as humans are programmed to respond according to certain specific emotions that come from particular life experiences. Other students may find the prospect implausible.

Paired Activity

- Possible Response: the computer's size, its program code of dots, and its control panel of "dials and lights"
- Possible Response: that scientists rely so heavily upon a computer

Connect to the Literature

1. **What Do You Think?** Does it seem possible to you that a computer could have feelings? Share your thoughts with a classmate.

   Comprehension Check
   - What problem is Multivac having as the story begins?
   - Why do the programmers talk to Multivac and pretend it is human?
   - What does the "key item" turn out to be?

Think Critically

2. What do you think the dividing line between being a machine and becoming human might be? Do you think Multivac crossed the line?

3. **ACTIVE READING** **PREDICTING** Review the notes you took in your **READER'S NOTEBOOK.** Did the details you selected help you predict accurately what the key item was? Explain.

4. Do you think the people in the story have become too dependent on the computer? Why or why not?

5. Why do you think Weaver doesn't want to hear Nemerson's ideas about solving the computer problem?

 THINK ABOUT
- the pressure of the situation
- all of the people already working on Multivac
- Nemerson's different way of thinking

Extend Interpretations

6. **COMPARING TEXTS** In both "Key Item" and "An Ordinary Day, with Peanuts," (page 348) there is a surprise ending. In your opinion, which is the better surprise ending? Why?

7. **Connect to Life** Think about other machines, besides computers, that we sometimes give human characteristics. Have you ever talked to or become angry with a machine? Discuss in small groups.

Literary Analysis

SCIENCE FICTION Fiction based on real or imagined scientific and technological advances is called **science fiction.** The characters of science fiction may be either realistic or imaginary, but the plot of a work of science fiction is usually set in the future. Science fiction allows writers and readers to imagine what the unforeseen results of scientific and technological developments might be in the distant future.

In "Key Item," Isaac Asimov suggests that some day computers will be able to think and feel like human beings. Do you think that will happen? What changes would such an occurrence bring about in the the world?

Paired Activity With a partner, reread "Key Item" and look for details that identify it as a work of science fiction. Jot down your findings. Then discuss these questions with your partner:

- What details suggested that this story was written several decades ago?
- What did you find most surprising about Asimov's prediction of the future?

Setting	Scientific Language
• computer of the "future"	• Multivac
	• million relays

Extend Interpretations

6. **Comparing Texts** Possible Responses: Some students may find that the ending of "One Ordinary Day, with Peanuts" is more realistic and more chilling. People are capable of acting in very different ways toward each other and are capable of choosing those ways. With the advances in voice response technology, computers are capable of responding to the word "please," but only as a word. On the other hand, other students may like "Key Item" for its happy ending.

7. **Connect to Life** Accept all reasonable responses. Encourage students to give specific examples and to try to analyze their reactions to various machines.

Choices & CHALLENGES

Writing Options

1. Radio Commercial Using the information in the selection, write a radio commercial for Multivac. Before you begin, it may help to jot down Multivac's characteristics in a web.

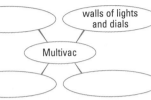

2. Science Fiction Do you have any ideas about technology in the future? Try your hand at science fiction. Write your own story about an important scientific advance that might take place in the future. Place your story in your **Working Portfolio.**

Activities & Explorations

1. Computer Cartoon Computers can do amazing things, but sometimes they break down. Create a cartoon that shows a humorous side to a computer malfunction. **~ART**

2. Talking Computer Imagine that the computer you were working on suddenly began talking to you. What would it say? What would you say back? Write an imaginary dialogue and then read it to the class. If you wish, have a classmate read the computer's lines. **~SPEAKING AND LISTENING**

Inquiry & Research

SCIENCE ARTIFICIAL INTELLIGENCE

Have you ever wished that you could tell the computer what to write, instead of typing the words in yourself? Now scientists have developed technology so you can do just that. Voice-recognition software allows people to instruct their computer simply by speaking to it. Find out more about voice-recognition programs by searching science and computer magazines and the Internet.

"I do not fear computers. I fear the lack of them."

Isaac Asimov
1920–1992

Love at First Sight Isaac Asimov was born in the Soviet Union but left at age three when his parents immigrated to the United States. Once here, his parents opened several candy stores. It was at one of these stores that Asimov first saw a science fiction magazine. He was hooked from the beginning. Soon, Asimov was writing

his own science fiction stories. He submitted his first manuscript to the magazine *Astounding Science* when he was 18.

Popular Writer Although his first stories were rejected by publishers, Asimov was not discouraged and went on to publish hundreds of stories, articles, and books. He has been called "the world's most prolific science writer." In his books, Asimov was able to popularize difficult scientific concepts and introduce new ones. The term *robotics,* for example, is his invention. Asimov wrote not only science fiction but fantasy, mystery, and nonfiction on such topics as astronomy, mathematics, history, and the Bible.

 Mini Lesson **Spelling**  **TEKS** 6C, 9G, 16G **TAAS** Writing Obj. 7

WORDS OFTEN MISSPELLED

Instruction Remind students that English words come from different sources. As a result, they show great variety—and some peculiarities. Some words don't seem to follow conventional spelling rules. For example, point out the word *circuit* in the selection. Ask why its spelling seems unusual. Then ask students to consult a dictionary to learn about its origins. Students should find that *circuit* comes from the Latin word *circuitus,* meaning "a going around." Knowing this origin can help students to commit its spelling to memory.

Exercises Read the following words aloud and have students spell them. Then have them consult a dictionary to check their spellings and learn about the origin of each word. Discuss their findings as a class.

tongue guarantee bough playwright
bureau vacuum business nuisance

 Use **Unit Three Resource Book,** p. 51 for additional practice.

Writing Options

1. **Radio Commercial** Students' commercials may vary in tone and purpose but should be informational or public service messages rather than sales pitches. Students' messages should describe Multivac's appearance, functions, importance, and "humanity" (per reference to therapy and neuroses mentioned on page 434).

2. **Science Fiction** Students' stories will vary but must be based on real or imagined scientific and technological advances. Characters and settings may be realistic or imaginary. The plot should help readers imagine future results of scientific and technological developments.

Activities and Explorations

1. **Computer Cartoon** Cartoons will vary. Art and dialogue should show a humorous side to a computer malfunction.

2. **Talking Computer** Students' dialogues will vary but should be written in script form for two parts: the student and the computer. As students read their lines, they should monitor the pace, pitch, and tone of their voices to achieve desired effects on the audience.

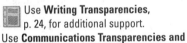 Use **Writing Transparencies,** p. 24, for additional support.
Use **Communications Transparencies and Copymasters,** p. 13, for additional support.

Inquiry and Research

Talking to Computers Students should research voice recognition programs and take notes from various sources. You may want to show them how to credit sources. Students should present their findings—perhaps on a poster or brochure. This activity is particularly suited to gifted and talented students. **To make the activity easier,** help each student identify one source to research. Share findings through a discussion or a group product, such as a bulletin.

Use **Writing Transparencies,** p. 49, for additional support.

Objectives

1. understand and appreciate **fantasy** in a short story (**Literary Analysis**)
2. understand and appreciate **humor** (**Literary Analysis**)
3. use the reading strategy of **predicting (Active Reading)**

Summary

One morning Mark Armitage buys a packet of Brekkfast Brikks cereal from a dingy shop across the street. On the back of the packet is a cutout of a garden, which he eagerly assembles in his playroom. Mark discovers that whenever he sings a special tune, the small cardboard garden changes into a real one. He rushes back to the shop and buys the last five packets of Brekkfast Brikks, each picturing a different section of the garden. When Mark assembles the next-to-last section and enters it, he meets Princess Sophia Maria Louisa. She tells him how she magically slipped inside the pages of the garden book used on the packets over 50 years ago. Ever since, she has been waiting there for her beloved music teacher to play the special tune and join her. Mark questions his own music teacher, Mr. Johansen, about the tune and learns that the elderly musician is Princess Sophia's long-lost love. They go together to Mark's playroom to enter the magic garden—only to find that Mrs. Armitage has tossed the cardboard model in the furnace. Knowing that the original garden book has also been destroyed, Mark's only hope for reuniting the lovers is to advertise for Brekkfast Brikks packets in the newspaper.

Thematic Link

"The Serial Garden" shows that sometimes not even fantastic tales have happy endings.

The Serial Garden

Short Story by JOAN AIKEN

"Why, you foolish boy, it was I who put the spell on the garden . . ."

Connect to Your Life

Fantasies The story you are about to read is a fantasy. Lewis Carroll's *Alice's Adventures in Wonderland* is an example of a well-known fantasy. What other fantasies have you read or seen? Do you have any favorites? Compare your favorites with those of your classmates.

Build Background

CONNECT TO SOCIAL STUDIES "The Serial Garden" is part of a collection of short stories titled *Armitage, Armitage, Fly Away Home,* by Joan Aiken, published in 1968. The story, probably set in the late 1940s or early 1950s in England, portrays the English love of beautiful gardens. Even the smallest English cottage is likely to be adorned with colorful, carefully tended flower gardens.

 See the Skills Trace at the beginning of the unit for information on TEKS covered in this lesson.

Focus Your Reading

LITERARY CONCEPT FANTASY The type of fiction in which impossible and often wondrous events occur is called **fantasy.** Unlike science fiction, which usually involves a future world that is explainable in terms of scientific or technological advances, fantasy involves magic, which cannot be explained. Fantasies can take place in realistic settings or in make-believe ones.

ACTIVE READING PREDICTING Below are ten terms that relate to "The Serial Garden." Use the terms, the story's title, and your knowledge of fantasy to help you predict what might happen in the story.

1. boy
2. corner store
3. cereal box
4. cereal
5. garden
6. princess
7. magic spell
8. teacher
9. shaggy dog
10. spring cleaning

READER'S NOTEBOOK Jot your prediction down in your notebook. As you read, compare your prediction with the actual events. Change your prediction if you uncover new clues. Include the clues that help you change your mind.

WORDS TO KNOW **Vocabulary Preview**				
aggrievedly	convalescing	gaudy	susceptible	vigil
chaos	forage	incalculable	tantalizing	wan

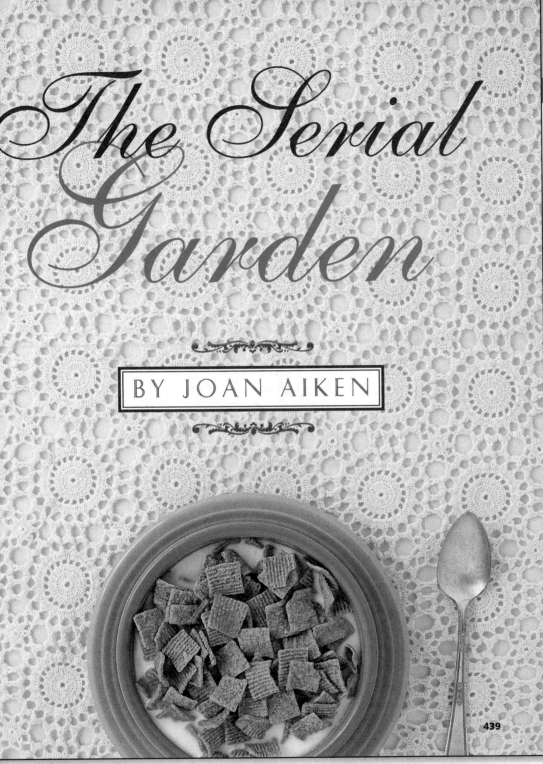

The Serial Garden

BY JOAN AIKEN

439

TEACHING THE LITERATURE

Customizing Instruction

Less Proficient Readers
Interest students in the story by asking them what they like to eat for breakfast. List their favorite foods on the board. Then ask them what they wouldn't eat for breakfast.

Set a Purpose Have students read to find out what Mark does when his mother serves him something he does not like for breakfast.

Students Acquiring English
The story takes place in Great Britain in the late 1940s or early 1950s. The characters speak British English. Help students to understand that although British and American speakers use many of the same words, some expressions will be different. Invite students to "translate"' examples of British usage.

Use **Spanish Study Guide,** pp. 91–93 for additional support.

Gifted and Talented
Challenge students to interpret the symbolism of the garden.
Possible Responses: a perfect world that is impossible to obtain, immortality, ideal love

---

 Preteaching Vocabulary **TEKS 9B** **TAAS Reading Obj. 1**

ANTONYMS

Instruction Remind students that knowing the antonym of an unfamiliar word can help them to define that word. For example, colorless is an antonym for *gaudy*. Therefore, *gaudy* means brightly colored.

Exercises Have students use the antonyms indicated to arrive at a definition for each of the underlined WORDS TO KNOW. Students should then check their definitions against those in the text.

1. <u>wan</u> – robust; healthy
2. <u>susceptible</u> – resistant; unaffected
3. <u>chaos</u> – order; organization
4. <u>tantalizing</u> – fulfilling; satisfying
5. <u>incalculable</u> – exact; certain

Use **Unit Three Resource Book,** p. 56 for more exercises.
Use **Vocabulary Transparencies and Copymasters,** p. 53, for additional support.

"Cold rice pudding for breakfast?" said
Mark, looking at it with disfavor.

"Don't be fussy," said his mother. "You're
the only one who's complaining." This was
unfair, for she and Mark were the only
members of the family at table, Harriet having
developed measles while staying with a school
friend, while Mr. Armitage had somehow
managed to lock himself in the larder.[1] Mrs.
Armitage never had anything but toast and
marmalade for breakfast anyway.

Mark went on scowling at the chilly-looking
pudding. It had come straight out of the
fridge, which was not in the larder.

"If you don't like it," said Mrs. Armitage,
"unless you want Daddy to pass your corn
flakes through the larder ventilator, flake by
flake, you'd better run down to Miss Pride and
get a small packet of cereal. She opens at eight;
Hickmans doesn't open till nine. It's no use
waiting till the blacksmith comes to let your
father out; I'm sure he won't be here for hours
yet."

There came a gloomy banging from the
direction of the larder, just to remind them that
Mr. Armitage was alive and suffering in there.

"*You're* all right," shouted Mark heartlessly
as he passed the larder door. "There's nothing
to stop you having corn flakes. Oh, I forgot,
the milk's in the fridge. Well, have cheese and
pickles then. Or treacle tart."[2]

Even through the zinc grating on the door
he could hear his father shudder at the thought
of treacle tart and pickles for breakfast. Mr.
Armitage's imprisonment was his own fault,
though; he had sworn that he was going to
find out where the mouse got into the larder if
it took him all night, watching and waiting.
He had shut himself in, so that no member of

the family should come bursting in and disturb
his vigil. The larder door had a spring catch
which sometimes jammed; it was bad luck that
this turned out to be one of the times.

Mark ran across the fields to Miss Pride's
shop at Sticks Corner and asked if she had any
corn flakes.

"Oh, I don't think I have any left, dear," Miss
Pride said woefully. "I'll have a look. . . . I think
I sold the last packet a week ago Tuesday."

"What about the one in the window?"

"That's a dummy, dear."

Miss Pride's shop window was full of nasty,
dingy old cardboard cartons with nothing inside
them, and several empty display stands which
had fallen down and never been propped up
again. Inside the shop were a few small, tired-
looking tins and jars, which had a worn and
scratched appearance as if mice had tried them
and given up. Miss Pride herself was small and
wan, with yellowish gray hair; she rooted rather
hopelessly in a pile of empty boxes. Mark's
mother never bought any groceries from Miss
Pride's if she could help it, since the day when
she had found a label inside the foil wrapping
of a cream cheese saying, "This cheese should
be eaten before May 11, 1899."

"No corn flakes I'm afraid, dear."

"Any wheat crispies? Puffed corn? Rice
nuts?"

"No, dear. Nothing left, only Brekkfast
Brikks."

"Never heard of *them*," said Mark
doubtfully.

"Or I've a jar of Ovo here. You spread it on
bread. That's nice for breakfast," said Miss

---

1. **larder:** pantry.
2. **treacle** (trē′kəl) **tart:** a small pastry made with molasses.

WORDS
TO
KNOW
vigil (vĭj′əl) *n.* a time of staying awake in order to keep watch or guard something
wan (wŏn) *adj.* sickly; pale

440

ride, with a sudden burst of salesmanship. Mark thought the Ovo looked beastly, like yellow paint, so he took the packet of Brekkfast Brikks. At least it wasn't very big. . . . On the front of the box was a picture of a fat, repulsive, fair-haired boy, rather like the chubby Augustus, banging on his plate with his spoon.

"They look like tiny doormats," said Mrs. Armitage, as Mark shoveled some Brikks into the bowl.

"They taste like them too. Gosh," said Mark, "I must hurry or I'll be late for school. There's rather a nice cutout garden on the back of the packet though; don't throw it away when it's empty, Mother. Good-by, Daddy," he shouted through the larder door; "hope Mr. Ellis comes soon to let you out." And he dashed off to catch the school bus.

At breakfast next morning Mark had a huge helping of Brekkfast Brikks and persuaded his father to try them.

"They taste just like esparto grass,"[3] said Mr. Armitage fretfully.

"Yes I know, but do take some more, Daddy. I want to cut out the model garden; it's so lovely."

"Rather pleasant, I must say. It looks like an eighteenth-century German engraving," his father agreed. "It certainly was a stroke of genius putting it on the packet. No one would ever buy these things to eat for pleasure. Pass me the sugar, please. And the cream. And the strawberries."

It was the half-term holiday, so after breakfast Mark was able to take the empty packet

"THEY LOOK LIKE TINY DOORMATS" . . . "THEY TASTE LIKE THEM TOO."

away to the playroom and get on with the job of cutting out the stone walls, the row of little trees, the fountain, the yew arch, the two green lawns, and the tiny clumps of brilliant flowers. He knew better than to "stick tabs in slots and secure with paste," as the directions suggested; he had made models from packets before and knew they always fell to pieces unless they were firmly bound together with transparent sticky tape.

It was a long, fiddling, pleasurable job.

Nobody interrupted him. Mrs. Armitage only cleaned the playroom once every six months or so, when she made a ferocious descent on it and tidied up the tape recorders, roller skates, meteorological sets, and dismantled railway engines, and threw away countless old magazines, stringless tennis rackets, abandoned paintings, and unsuccessful models. There were always bitter complaints from Mark and Harriet; then they forgot, and things piled up again till next time.

As Mark worked, his eye was caught by a verse on the outside of the packet:

"Brekkfast Brikks to start the day
Make you fit in every way.
Children bang their plates with glee
At Brekkfast Brikks for lunch and tea!
Brekkfast Brikks for supper too
Give peaceful sleep the whole night through."

2

---

3. **esparto** (ĭ-spär′tō) **grass:** long, coarse grass used in making rope, shoes, and paper.

Less Proficient Readers
Ask students what Mark ate for breakfast, how he got it, and why.
Possible Responses: He went to the store and bought Brekkfast Brikks cereal because he didn't like the rice pudding his mother served him, and his father had accidentally locked himself in the pantry, so Mark couldn't get any cereal from there.

Set a Purpose Have students discover what happens when Mark assembles the cutout garden on the back of the cereal package.

Students Acquiring English
1 Encourage students to use context clues to define *beastly* as horrible or repulsive.
2 Point out that *tea* as used here refers to a British afternoon refreshment that usually includes sandwiches and pastries as well as tea.

Cross Curricular Link Science

GROWING CEREAL GRAINS Many people who enjoy wheat, oat, or corn cereal do not realize the difficulties that can beset farmers and merchants who deal with cereal. Once the field has been prepared, the seed is planted as either a winter or spring crop. It is essential that the grain seed be free from any weed seeds. Weeds rob the developing grain of light, soil nutrients, and water and keep appearing for several years. Even if there are no weeds mixed in with the seeds, they can be carried by birds or wind and affect the crop. Farmers also have to guard against all sorts of insects that can infest young plants. Chemical preparations and other measures such as planting early can help to minimize the damage to the crop. Sometimes, however, the plants may be free from weeds and insects, but develop a fungus, which is equally disastrous.

Even if all of these hurdles are successfully surmounted while the grain is in the field, care has to be taken in transporting and storing it so that other insects and rodents don't take their share. It is far simpler to buy a box of cereal than to grow the grain that is in it!

Reading and Analyzing

Literary Analysis: DIALECT

A Tell students that dialect includes words or expressions particular to a certain group of people or geographical location. Ask students to suggest equivalent expressions to replace Mark's use of "Blimey."
Possible Responses: no way; not on your life

Literary Analysis [FANTASY]

B Ask students how Mark is able to enter the garden.
Possible Response: It magically grows to life size, part of the story's fantasy. Ask if this setting is realistic or make-believe.
Possible Responses: It's make-believe, because cardboard gardens don't grow and become real; it's both—make-believe because it comes to life and realistic because it contains a gate, walls, trees, and fog, like real gardens.

Reading Skills and Strategies: VISUALIZING

C Ask students how the author evokes vivid mental images.
Possible Responses: The author includes details that appeal to sight and touch and organizes the description spatially.

Reading Skills and Strategies: HYPOTHESIZING

D Invite students to hypothesize why Mark has to sing the jingle rather than just say the rhyme to enter and leave the garden.
Possible Response: Music is an important part of the garden's magic.

Portrait of Ari Redon (about 1898), Odilon Redon. Pastel on paper, 44.8 × 30.8 cm, The Art Institute of Chicago, gift of Kate L. Brewster (1950.130). Photo Copyright © 1994 The Art Institute of Chicago, all rights reserved.

442 UNIT THREE PART 2: FANTASTIC TALES

Teaching Options

 Mini Lesson **Viewing and Representing** TEKS 22A

Portrait of Ari Redon
by Odilon Redon

ART APPRECIATION This portrait by French painter Odilon Redon (1840–1916) is typical of the impressionist school of art with its soft and dreamy light and charming poetic quality. Redon departed from the Impressionists, however, in his attempt to portray the realm of mystery that other impressionists avoided.
Instruction Have students look at the painting's composition. Ask students if the subject is centered.

Possible Response: No. The background extends disproportionately above the subject's head.
Ask students why the artist may have painted the portrait in this way.
Possible Response: It might suggest the world within the subject's mind.
Application Ask students if they think the subject of the portrait resembles Mark, and have them give reasons for their answers.
Possible Responses: Yes, because the age seems similar, and the garden is suggestive of his garden. No, this boy seems more solemn.

"Blimey," thought Mark, sticking a cedar tree into the middle of the lawn and then bending a stone wall round at dotted lines A, B, C, and D. "I wouldn't want anything for breakfast, lunch, tea, and supper, not even Christmas pudding. Certainly not Brekkfast Brikks."

He propped a clump of gaudy scarlet flowers against the wall and stuck them in place.

The words of the rhyme kept coming into his head as he worked, and presently he found that they went rather well to a tune that was running through his mind, and he began to hum, and then to sing; Mark often did this when he was alone and busy.

"Brekkfast Brikks to sta-art the day,
Ma-ake you fi-it in every way—

"Blow, where did I put that little bit of sticky tape? Oh, there it is.

"Children bang their pla-ates with glee
At Brekkfast Brikks for lunch and tea

"Slit gate with razor blade, it says, but it'll have to be a penknife.

"Brekkfast Brikks for supper toohoo
Give peaceful sleep the whole night throughoo. . . .

"Hullo. That's funny," said Mark.

It was funny. The openwork iron gate he had just stuck in position now suddenly towered above him. On either side, to right and left, ran the high stone wall, stretching away into foggy distance. Over the top of the wall he could see tall trees, yews and cypresses and others he didn't know.

"Well, that's the neatest trick I ever saw," said Mark. "I wonder if the gate will open."

He chuckled as he tried it, thinking of the larder door. The gate did open, and he went through into the garden.

One of the things that had already struck him as he cut them out was that the flowers were not at all in the right proportions. But they were all the nicer for that. There were huge velvety violets and pansies the size of saucers; the hollyhocks were as big as dinner plates, and the turf was sprinkled with enormous daisies. The roses, on the other hand, were miniature, no bigger than cuff buttons. There were real fish in the fountain, bright pink.

"I made all this," thought Mark, strolling along the mossy path to the yew arch. "Won't Harriet be surprised when she sees it. I wish she could see it now. I wonder what made it come alive like that."

He passed through the yew arch as he said this and discovered that on the other side there was nothing but gray, foggy blankness. This, of course, was where his cardboard garden had ended. He turned back through the archway and gazed with pride at a border of huge scarlet tropical flowers which were perhaps supposed to be geraniums but certainly hadn't turned out that way. "I know! Of course, it was the rhyme, the rhyme on the packet."

He recited it. Nothing happened. "Perhaps you have to sing it," he thought, and (feeling a little foolish) he sang it through to the tune that fitted so well. At once, faster than blowing out a match, the garden drew itself together and shrank into its cardboard again, leaving Mark outside.

"What a marvelous hiding place it'll make when I don't want people to come bothering,"

WORDS TO KNOW   **gaudy** (gô′dē) *adj.* excessively bright and showy

443

he thought. He sang the spell once more, just to make sure that it worked, and there was the high mossy wall, the stately iron gate, and the treetops. He stepped in and looked back. No playroom to be seen, only gray blankness.

At that moment he was startled by a tremendous clanging, the sort of sound the Trump of Doom[4] would make if it was a dinner bell. "Blow," he thought, "I suppose that's lunch." He sang the spell for the fourth time; immediately he was in the playroom, and the garden was on the floor beside him, and Agnes was still ringing the dinner bell outside the door.

"All right, I heard," he shouted. "Just coming."

He glanced hurriedly over the remains of the packet to see if it bore any mention of the fact that the cutout garden had magic properties. It did not. He did, however, learn that this was Section Three of the Beautiful Brekkfast Brikk Garden Series, and that Sections One, Two, Four, Five, and Six would be found on other packets. In case of difficulty in obtaining supplies, please write to Fruhstucksgeschirr-ziegelsteinindustrie (Great Britain), Lily Road, Shepherds Bush.

"Elevenpence a packet," Mark murmured to himself, going to lunch with unwashed hands. "Five elevens are thirty-five. Thirty-five pennies are—no, that's wrong. Fifty-five pence are four-and-sevenpence. Father, if I mow the lawn and carry coal every day for a month, can I have four shillings and sevenpence?"

"You don't want to buy another space gun, do you?" said Mr. Armitage looking at him suspiciously. "Because one is quite enough in this family."

"No, it's not for a space gun, I swear."

"Oh, very well."

"And can I have the four-and-seven now?"

Mr. Armitage gave it reluctantly. "But that lawn has to be like velvet, mind," he said. "And if there's any falling off in the coal supply, I shall demand my money back."

"No, no, there won't be," Mark promised in reply. As soon as lunch was over, he dashed down to Miss Pride's. Was there a chance that she would have Sections One, Two, Four, Five, and Six? He felt certain that no other shop had even heard of Brekkfast Brikks, so she was his only hope, apart from the address in Shepherds Bush.

"Oh, I don't know, I'm sure," Miss Pride said, sounding very doubtful—and more than a little surprised. "There might just be a couple on the bottom shelf—yes, here we are."

They were Sections Four and Five, bent and dusty, but intact, Mark saw with relief. "Don't you suppose you have any more anywhere?" he pleaded.

"I'll look in the cellar, but I can't promise. I haven't had deliveries of any of these for a long time. Made by some foreign firm they were; people didn't seem very keen on them," Miss Pride said aggrievedly. She opened a door revealing a flight of damp stone stairs. Mark followed her down them like a bloodhound on the trail.

*T*he cellar was a fearful confusion of mildewed, tattered, and toppling cartons, some full, some empty. Mark was nearly knocked cold by a shower of pilchards

---

4. **Trump of Doom:** the trumpet that, according to the Bible, will be blown to signal the end of the world.

WORDS TO KNOW — **aggrievedly** (ə-grē'vĭd-lē) *adv.* in a manner suggesting that one has been badly treated

444

Cross Curricular Link **Mathematics**

BRITISH CURRENCY When this story was written, Britain had not yet adopted the decimal currency system that has been in place since the early 1970s. Before the new system of currency was instituted, twenty shillings made up a pound. (A pound was worth anywhere from three to five dollars at that time, depending upon the rate of exchange.) Each shilling was twelve pence or twelve pennies. So when Mark is calculating how much the additional packets will cost him, he adds up the number of pence and divides the total of 55 pence by 12 to arrive at the final amount of four shillings and sevenpence.

After the decimal system was adopted, instead of 240 pence to the pound, only 100 pennies or pence made up a pound. The unit of a shilling was no longer used in speaking of money. Instead, merchandise was labeled with a price in new pence. Often the prices were rounded up to make it easier for shoppers. For example, the price of Brekkfast Brikks would have been a little over four and a half new pence. Miss Pride might have taken the opportunity to charge 5 new pence for the packet.

in tins,[5] which he dislodged onto himself from the top of a heap of boxes. At last Miss Pride, with a cry of triumph, unearthed a little cache of Brekkfast Brikks, three packets which turned out to be the remaining sections, Six, One, and Two.

"There, isn't that a piece of luck now!" she said, looking quite faint with all the excitement. It was indeed rare for Miss Pride to sell as many as five packets of the same thing at one time.

Mark galloped home with his booty and met his father on the porch. Mr. Armitage let out a groan of dismay.

"I'd almost rather you'd bought a space gun," he said. Mark chanted in reply:

"Brekkfast Brikks for supper too
Give peaceful sleep the whole
    night through."

"I don't want peaceful sleep," Mr. Armitage said. "I intend to spend tonight mouse watching again. I'm tired of finding footprints in the Stilton."[6]

During the next few days Mark's parents watched anxiously to see, Mr. Armitage said, whether Mark would start to sprout esparto grass instead of hair. For he doggedly ate Brekkfast Brikks for lunch, with soup, or sprinkled over his pudding; for tea, with jam; and for supper lightly fried in dripping, not to mention, of course, the immense helpings he had for breakfast with sugar and milk.

BREKKFAST BRIKKS FOR SUPPER TOO GIVE PEACEFUL SLEEP THE WHOLE NIGHT THROUGH.

Mr. Armitage for his part soon gave out; he said he wouldn't taste another Brekkfast Brikk even if it were wrapped in an inch-thick layer of *pâté de foie gras*.[7] Mark regretted that Harriet, who was a handy and uncritical eater, was still away, <u>convalescing</u> from her measles with an aunt.

In two days the second packet was finished (sundial, paved garden, and espaliers[8]). Mark cut it out, fastened it together, and joined it onto Section Three with trembling hands. Would the spell work for this section, too? He sang the rhyme in rather a quavering voice, but luckily the playroom door was shut and there was no one to hear him. Yes! The gate grew again above him, and when he opened it and ran across the lawn through the yew arch, he found himself in a flagged garden full of flowers like huge blue cabbages.

Mark stood hugging himself with satisfaction and then began to wander about smelling the flowers, which had a spicy perfume most unlike any flower he could think

----

5. **pilchards** (pĭl′chərdz) **in tins:** cans of sardines.

6. **Stilton:** a rich, crumbly cheese.

7. *pâté de foie gras* (pä-tā′ də fwä grä′) *French:* a food made of chopped goose livers, often eaten spread on crackers.

8. **espaliers** (ĭ-spăl′yərz): trees or shrubs trained to grow flat against a wall.

| WORDS TO KNOW | **convalescing** (kŏn′və-lĕs′ĭng) *adj.* recovering gradually from an illness
convalesce *v.* |

445

Active Reading [PREDICTING]

A Invite students to predict who—or what—is behind the flash of the white-and-gold draperies, using story clues and their prior knowledge.

Possible Responses: The garden is luxurious with many expensive features, such as a sundial, paving, and espaliers. The white-and-gold of the clothing also suggests someone royal, a king, a queen, or a princess.

Literary Analysis: IRONY

B Ask students what is ironic about Mr. Armitage's belief that it's the bad-tasting cereal that is making Mark act so strangely.

Possible Response: It's ironic because it's not what is inside the box that is making Mark act that way; it's what is on the outside of the box—the cutout of the garden.

Literary Analysis: DIALECT

C Several British expressions are used in this dialogue. Mrs. Armitage thinks Mark needs "a dose" or something to perk him up. She decides on a trip to Shinglemud Bay, humorously named by the author. Shingles are small stones so the bay's name suggests a muddy, rocky beach, meant to seem quite unappealing. Ask students what reaction Mrs. Armitage anticipates.

Possible Response: for Mark to be thrilled

Have students rephrase Mark's actual response and why he feels this way.

Possible Response: "Oh, blow" becomes "Oh, bother" or "Oh, no." "Need I go?" becomes "Do I have to go?" He is trying to remember the tune to get into the garden and doesn't want to leave the model.

A of. Suddenly he pricked up his ears. Had he caught a sound? There! It was like somebody crying and seemed to come from the other side of the hedge. He ran to the next opening and looked through. Nothing: only gray mist and emptiness. But, unless he had imagined it, just before he got there, he thought his eye had caught the flash of white-and-gold draperies swishing past the gateway.

"Do you think Mark's all right?" Mrs. Armitage said to her husband next day. "He seems to be in such a dream all the time."

B "Boy's gone clean off his rocker if you ask me," grumbled Mr. Armitage. "It's all these doormats he's eating. Can't be good to stuff your insides with moldy jute.[9] Still I'm bound to say he's cut the lawn very decently and seems to be remembering the coal. I'd better take a day off from the office and drive you over to the shore for a picnic; sea air will do him good."

Mrs. Armitage suggested to Mark that he should slack off on the Brekkfast Brikks, but he was so horrified that she had to abandon the idea. But, she said, he was to run four times round the garden every morning before breakfast. Mark almost said, "Which garden?" but stopped just in time. He had cut out and completed another large lawn, with a lake and weeping willows, and on the far side of the lake had a tantalizing glimpse of a figure dressed in white and gold who moved away and was lost before he could get there.

After munching his way through the fourth packet, he was able to add on a broad grass walk bordered by curiously clipped trees. At the end of the walk he could see the white-and-gold person, but when he ran to the spot, no one was there—the walk

ended in the usual gray mist.

When he had finished and had cut out the fifth packet (an orchard), a terrible thing happened to him. For two days he could not remember the tune that worked the spell. He tried other tunes, but they were no use. He sat in the playroom singing till he was hoarse or silent with despair. Suppose he never remembered it again?

His mother shook her head at him that evening and said he looked as if he needed a dose. "It's lucky we're going to Shinglemud Bay for the day tomorrow," she said. "That ought to do you good."

"Oh, *blow*. I'd forgotten about that," Mark said. "Need I go?"

His mother stared at him in utter astonishment.

But in the middle of the night he remembered the right tune, leaped out of bed in a tremendous hurry, and ran down to the playroom without even waiting to put on his dressing gown and slippers.

The orchard was most wonderful, for instead of mere apples its trees bore oranges, lemons, limes and all sorts of tropical fruits whose names he did not know, and there were melons and pineapples growing, and plantains and avocados. Better still, he saw the lady in her white and gold waiting at the end of an alley and was able to draw near enough to speak to her.

"Who are you?" she asked. She seemed very much astonished at the sight of him.

"My name's Mark Armitage," he said politely. "Is this your garden?"

---

9. **jute:** a strong fiber used for making mats, rope, and sacks.

WORDS TO KNOW

tantalizing (tăn′tə-lī′zĭng) *adj.* arousing interest without satisfying it
tantalize *v.*

Illustration by Ruth Sanderson.

A Have students predict who this character might be, based on what they have read and what they know about characters in fantasies.

Possible Response: This is the figure that Mark caught a glimpse of earlier. She fits the traditional fairy-tale image of a princess.

Literary Analysis: HUMOR

B Ask students why the author gave the princess this name.

Possible Responses: Her name creates humor and prevents the story from being too serious.

Literary Analysis [FANTASY]

C Ask students what elements of fantasy are found in the character of the princess.

Possible Responses: She knows magic and has cast a spell to become perpetually youthful.

Reading Skills and Strategies: CLARIFYING

D Ask students why Mark is eager to speak to his music teacher.

Possible Responses: Mark wants to find out about the tune and the princess's beloved Rudolph; Mark is worried that he will forget the song while he is in the garden and get stuck there for eternity so he wants Mr. Johansen to write it down.

Reading Skills and Strategies: VISUALIZING

E Ask students what details help them to see the garden.

Possible Responses: the description of the wall and gate; the smell of the lime flowers

---

A Close to, he saw that she was really very grand indeed. Her dress was white satin, embroidered with pearls, and swept the ground; she had a gold scarf, and her hair, dressed high and powdered, was confined in a small gold-and-pearl tiara. Her face was rather plain, pink with a long nose, but she had a kind expression and beautiful gray eyes.

"Indeed it is," she announced with hauteur. **B** "I am Princess Sophia Maria Louisa of Saxe-Hoffenpoffen-und-Hamster. What are you doing here, pray?"

"Well," Mark explained cautiously, "it seemed to come about through singing a tune."

"Indeed. That is most interesting. Did the tune, perhaps, go like this?"

The princess hummed a few bars.

"That's it! How did you know?"

"Why, you foolish boy, it was I who put the spell on the garden, to make it come alive when the tune is played or sung."

"I say!" Mark was full of admiration. "Can you do spells as well as being a princess?"

She drew herself up. "Naturally! At the court of Saxe-Hoffenpoffen, where I was educated, all princesses were taught a little magic, not so much as to be vulgar, just enough to get out of social difficulties."

"Jolly useful," Mark said. "How did you work the spell for the garden, then?"

"Why, you see," (the princess was obviously delighted to have somebody to talk to; she sat on a stone seat and patted it, inviting Mark to do likewise) "I had the misfortune to fall in love with Herr Rudolf, the court Kapellmeister,[10] who taught me music. Oh, he was so kind and handsome! And he was most talented, but my father, of course, would not hear of my marrying him because he was only a common person."

"So what did you do?"

"I arranged to vanish, of course. Rudi had given me a beautiful book with many pictures of gardens. My father kept strict watch to see I did not run away, so I used to slip between the pages of the book when I wanted to be alone. Then, when we decided to marry, I asked my maid to take the book to Rudi. And I sent him a note telling him to play the tune when he received the book. But I believe that spiteful Gertrud must have played me false and never taken the book, for more than fifty years have now passed and I have been here all alone, waiting in the garden, and Rudi has never come. Oh, Rudi, Rudi," she exclaimed, wringing her hands and crying a little, "where can you be? It is so long—so long!"

"Fifty years," Mark said kindly, reckoning that must make her nearly seventy. "I must say you don't look it."

"Of course I do not, dumbhead. For me, I make it that time does not touch me. But tell me, how did you know the tune that works the spell? It was taught me by my dear Rudi."

"I'm not sure where I picked it up," Mark confessed. "For all I know it may be one of the Top Ten. I'll ask my music teacher; he's sure to know. Perhaps he'll have heard of your Rudolf too."

Privately Mark feared that Rudolf might very well have died by now, but he did not like to depress Princess Sophia Maria by such a suggestion, so he bade her a polite good night, promising to come back as soon as he could with another section of the garden and any news he could pick up.

---

10. **Kapellmeister** (kə-pĕl′mī′stər): the leader of a choir or orchestra.

Teaching Options

Mini Lesson **Speaking and Listening**

READERS THEATER

Prepare Explain to students that a Readers Theater performance provides an oral interpretation of a work of literature, such as a short story. Different readers interpret the parts of different characters, and a narrator presents the story's exposition and description. Explain that students sit on stools or chairs facing the audience, using effective rate, volume, pitch, and tone to convey their interpretation of the characters and the action.

Present Have students work in small groups to perform passages of "The Serial Garden" as a Readers Theater presentation. Guide students to go over their parts and make notes about characters, motivation, and interpretation. Help listeners to analyze the effects of the oral interpretations by reviewing three steps:

Step 1: They should think about what they already know about the work and establish appropriate guidelines for evaluation. For example, is the

He planned to go and see Mr. Johansen, his music teacher, next morning, but he had forgotten the family trip to the beach. There was just time to scribble a hasty post card to the British office of Fruhstucksgeschirrziegelsteinindustrie, asking them if they could inform him from what source they had obtained the pictures used on the packets of Brekkfast Brikks. Then Mr. Armitage drove his wife and son to Shinglemud Bay, gloomily prophesying wet weather.

In fact, the weather turned out fine, and Mark found it quite restful to swim and play beach cricket and eat ham sandwiches and lie in the sun. For he had been struck by a horrid thought: suppose he should forget the tune again when he was inside the garden—would he be stuck there, like Father in the larder? It was a lovely place to go and wander at will, but somehow he didn't fancy spending the next fifty years there with Princess Sophia Maria. Would she oblige him by singing the spell if he forgot it, or would she be too keen on company to let him go? He was not inclined to take any chances.

It was late when they arrived home, too late, Mark thought, to disturb Mr. Johansen, who was elderly and kept early hours. Mark ate a huge helping of sardines on Brekkfast Brikks for supper—he was dying to finish Section Six—but did not visit the garden that night.

Next morning's breakfast (Brikks with hot milk, for a change) finished the last packet—and just as well, for the larder mouse, which Mr. Armitage still had not caught, was discovered to have nibbled the bottom left-hand corner of the packet, slightly damaging an ornamental grotto[11] in a grove of lime trees. Rather worried about this, Mark decided to make up the last section straightaway, in case the magic had been affected. By now he was becoming very skillful at the tiny fiddling task of cutting out the little tabs and slipping them into the little slots; the job did not take long to finish. Mark attached Section Six to Section Five and then, drawing a deep breath, sang the incantation[12] once more. With immense relief he watched the mossy wall and rusty gate grow out of the playroom floor; all was well.

He raced across the lawn, round the lake, along the avenue, through the orchard, and into the lime grove. The scent of the lime flowers was sweeter than a cake baking.

Princess Sophia Maria came towards him from the grotto, looking slightly put out.

"Good morning!" she greeted Mark. "Do you bring me any news?"

"I haven't been to see my music teacher yet," Mark confessed. "I was a bit anxious because there was a hole—"

"Ach, yes, a hole in the grotto! I have just been looking. Some wild beast must have made its way in, and I am afraid it may come again. See, it has made tracks like those of a big bear." She showed him some enormous footprints in the soft sand of the grotto floor. Mark stopped up the hole with prickly branches and promised to bring a dog when he next came, though he felt fairly sure the mouse would not return.

"I can borrow a dog from my teacher—he has plenty. I'll be back in an hour or so—see you then," he said.

"*Auf Wiedersehen,*[13] my dear young friend." Mark ran along the village street to Mr.

---

11. **grotto:** a structure made to look like a small cave.
12. **incantation** (ῐn'kăn-tā'shən): magic spell.
13. *auf Wiedersehen* (ouf vē'dər-zā'ən) German: goodbye.

Customizing Instruction

Less Proficient Readers
Assess students' comprehension by asking them the following questions:
• Who is the lady?
Possible Response: She is Princess Sophia Maria Louisa of Saxe-Hoffenpoffen-und-Hamster.
• Why is she in the garden?
Possible Response: Her father would not let her marry the man she loved, so she hid in the pages of a book. Her maid was supposed to take the book and the tune to the princess's lover who would then make the garden come alive and be reunited with the princess. Instead her maid sold the book.
Set a Purpose Have students read to find out how Mark learned the special song and what he finds out about the cereal company.

Students Acquiring English
1 Advise students to use context clues and what they know about the personality of the princess to define "slightly put out" as rather annoyed.

Multiple Learning Styles
Kinesthetic Learners
2 Invite students to role-play this scene, suggesting through their actions and gestures the personalities of Mark and the princess.

humor conveyed and a strong sense of character established?
Step 2: They must listen critically to the performers' reading or speaking of the lines to identify both strengths and weaknesses in the interpretation.
Step 3: The audience members should write a brief evaluation, jotting down key ideas and describing their emotional response to the performance.

Students may find it helpful to assess the performances in small groups.

BLOCK SCHEDULING This activity is particularly well suited for longer class periods.

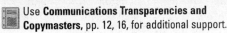 Use **Communications Transparencies and Copymasters,** pp. 12, 16, for additional support.

Reading Skills and Strategies: ANALYZING

A Explain to students that English houses sometimes have names, such as Rose Cottage or Hawthorne House. Ask students to explain how the name of Mr. Johansen's house relates to his life and interests.

Possible Response: The name Houndshaven suggests that his house is a shelter or haven for dogs. This implies that Mr. Johansen likes dogs. Besides teaching, Mr. Johansen boards other people's dogs.

Literary Analysis: HUMOR

B Have students explain the humor in this scene.

Possible Responses: The animals' enjoyment of the music is comic and vivid. Also, readers don't know if the animals are howling in delight or in pain.

Active Reading   PREDICTING

C Ask students what they might guess about Mr. Johansen, based on his reaction to the music and his accent.

Possible Response: that he is Rudi, the princess's lover

Reading Skills and Strategies: CLARIFYING

D Have students explain what information Mark gets from the letter and why it is important.

Possible Responses: He learns that the princess's book was destroyed and its owner, the firm that made the cereal, is out of business. Therefore, unless Mark or someone else can get another complete set of Brekkfast Brikks boxes, Mark has the last remaining model of the garden.

A Johansen's house, Houndshaven Cottage. He knew better than to knock at the door because Mr. Johansen would be either practicing his violin or out in the barn at the back, and in any case the sound of barking was generally loud enough to drown any noise short of gunfire.

Besides giving music lessons at Mark's school, Mr. Johansen kept a guest house for dogs whose owners were abroad or on holiday. He was extremely kind to the guests and did his best to make them feel at home in every way, finding out from their owners what were their favorite foods, and letting them sleep on his own bed, turn about. He spent all his spare time with them, talking to them and playing either his violin or long-playing records of domestic sounds likely to appeal to the canine fancy—such as knives being sharpened, cars starting up, and children playing ball games.

Mark could hear Mr. Johansen playing Brahms's lullaby in the barn, so he went out there; the music was making some of the more <u>susceptible</u> inmates feel homesick: howls, sympathetic moans, and long shuddering sighs came from the numerous comfortably carpeted cubicles all the way down the barn.

B Mr. Johansen reached the end of the piece as Mark entered. He put down his fiddle and smiled welcomingly.

"Ach, how *gut!* It is the young Mark."

"Hullo, sir."

"You know," confided Mr. Johansen, "I play to many audiences in my life all over the world, but never anywhere do I get such a response as from zese dear doggies—it is really remarkable. But come in; come into ze house

and have some coffee cake."

Mr. Johansen was a gentle, white-haired elderly man; he walked slowly with a slight stoop and had a kindly, sad face with large dark eyes. He looked rather like some sort of dog himself, Mark always thought, perhaps a collie or a long-haired dachshund.

"Sir," Mark said, "if I whistle a tune to you can you write it down for me?"

"Why, yes, I shall be most happy," Mr. Johansen said, pouring coffee for both of them.

So Mark whistled his tune once more; as he came to the end, he was surprised to see the music master's eyes fill with tears, which slowly began to trickle down his thin cheeks.

"It recalls my youth, zat piece," he explained, wiping the tears away and rapidly scribbling crotchets and minims on a piece of music paper. "Many times I am whistling it myself—it is wissout doubt from me you learn it—but always it is reminding me of how happy I was long ago when I wrote it."

"You *wrote* that tune?" Mark said, much excited.

"Why yes. What is so strange in zat? Many, many tunes haf I written."

"Well—" Mark said, "I won't tell you just yet in case I'm mistaken—I'll have to see somebody else first. Do you mind if I dash off right away? Oh, and might I borrow a dog—preferably a good ratter?"

"In zat case, better have my dear Lotta—alzough she is so old she is ze best of zem all," Mr. Johansen said proudly. Lotta was his own dog, an enormous shaggy lumbering animal with a tail like a palm tree and feet the size of electric polishers; she was reputed to be of <u>incalculable</u> age; Mr. Johansen called her his

WORDS TO KNOW   **susceptible** (sə-sĕp′tə-bəl) *adj.* easily affected or influenced
incalculable (ĭn-kăl′kyə-lə-bəl) *adj.* too great to be measured or counted

450

 Mini Lesson   **Grammar** **TEKS** 17C   **TAAS** Writing Obj. 6

DOUBLE NEGATIVES

Instruction Remind students that in addition to the adverb *not,* there are other negative words such as *never, nobody, none, no one, nothing,* and *nowhere.* Tell them that *hardly, scarcely,* and *barely* are also considered negatives. Help them understand that two negatives should not be used in the same sentence when one will do.

Exercise Have students rewrite the following sentences to eliminate double negatives.

1. Mr. Johansen did not never get tired of dogs.
2. Mark wouldn't eat nothing but his cereal.

3. No one would never believe his story.
4. The princess couldn't go nowhere else.

SUGGESTED ANSWERS

1. ever
2. would eat nothing   wouldn't eat anything
3. ever
4. anywhere

 Use **Grammar Transparencies and Copymasters,** p. 86.

Use McDougal Littell's *Language Network,* Chapter 5, for more instruction and practice in double negatives.

Le jardin potager, Yerres [The kitchen garden, Yerres] (1875–77), Gustave Caillebotte. Private collection.

strudel-hound. She knew Mark well and came along with him quite biddably, though it was rather like leading a mammoth.

Luckily his mother, refreshed by her day at the sea, was heavily engaged with Agnes the maid in spring cleaning. Furniture was being shoved about, and everyone was too busy to notice Mark and Lotta slip into the playroom.

A letter addressed to Mark lay among the clutter on the table; he opened and read it while Lotta <u>foraged</u> happily among the piles of magazines and tennis nets and cricket bats and rusting electronic equipment, managing to upset several things and increase the general state of huggermugger in the room.

Dear Sir, (the letter said—it was from Messrs. Digit, Digit, & Rule, a firm of chartered accountants)—We are in receipt of your inquiry as to the source of pictures on packets of Brekkfast Brikks. We are pleased to inform you that these were reproduced from the illustrations of a little-known 18th-century German work, *Steinbergen's Gartenbuch.* Unfortunately the only known remaining copy of this book was burnt in the disastrous fire which destroyed the factory and premises of Mssrs.Fruhstucksgeschirrziegelsteinindustrie two months ago. The firm has now gone into liquidation and we are winding up their effects. Yours faithfully, P. J. Zero, Gen. Sec.

D

WORDS TO KNOW   **forage** (fôr′ĭj) *v.* to search for what one wants or needs, especially for food

451

Le jardin potager, Yerres [The kitchen garden, Yerres] **by Gustave Caillebotte**

ART APPRECIATION Gustave Caillebotte (1848-1894) studied to be an engineer but became avidly interested in art. He was a patron to many impressionist artists and painted over 500 works himself.

Instruction Tell students that the impressionists used small brush strokes and unmixed primary colors to reproduce the light and colors of a scene. Ask students what mood is created by the light and colors in this painting.

Possible Response: peaceful and welcoming

Application Ask students which elements of Mark's garden can be seen in the painting.

Possible Responses: the arch, the high stone wall with trees towering in the distance, a path bordered by flowers

Ask students how their mental image of Mark's garden differs from the garden in the painting.

Possible Responses: Mark's garden is more elaborate, with a lake, a fountain, and a grotto. The flowers are vivid and huge. The garden in the painting has muted hues and appears very ordinary.

Reading and Analyzing

Reading Skills and Strategies:
ANALYZING

A Ask students to explain what the burning of the book and closing of the factory means for Mark's model.
Possible Response: It would not be easy to reproduce the garden if anything happened to the model.

Reading Skills and Strategies:
VISUALIZING

B Ask students to pick out the words and phrases that describe the force of Lotta's greeting.
Possible Responses: "hurled herself... like a rocket," "yard of salmon-pink tongue...washing the princess's face," "tail going round faster than a turboprop"

Active Reading PREDICTING

C Ask students to speculate why spring cleaning has been mentioned so frequently.
Possible Responses: to make the story seem more real; to foreshadow that the playroom might be cleaned; to anticipate the possibility that Mrs. Armitage might be in the playroom when the garden is brought to life.

Reading Skills and Strategies:
CLARIFYING

D Ask students why Mr. Johansen doesn't race over to the Armitage house.
Possible Responses: He must feed the dogs first.

Literary Analysis FANTASY

E Ask students why this is the climax of the plot.
Possible Responses: The details lead up to this moment; fantasy meets reality and ceases to exist.

A "Steinbergen's Gartenbuch," Mark thought. "That must have been the book that Princess Sophia Maria used for the spell—probably the same copy. Oh, well, since it's burned, it's lucky the pictures were reproduced on the Brekkfast Brikks packets. Come on, Lotta, let's go and find a nice princess then. Good girl! Rats! Chase 'em!"

He sang the spell, and Lotta, all enthusiasm, followed him into the garden.

They did not have to go far before they saw the princess—she was sitting sunning herself on the rim of the fountain. But what happened then was unexpected. **B** Lotta let out the most extraordinary cry—whine, bark, and howl all in one—and hurled herself towards the princess like a rocket.

"Hey! Look out! Lotta! *Heel!*" Mark shouted in alarm. But Lotta, with her great paws on the princess's shoulders, had about a yard of salmon-pink tongue out, and was washing the princess's face all over with frantic affection.

The princess was just as excited. "Lotta, Lotta! She knows me; it's dear Lotta; it must be! Where did you get her?" she cried to Mark, hugging the enormous dog, whose tail was going round faster than a turboprop.

"Why, she belongs to my music master, Mr. Johansen, and it's he who made up the tune," Mark said.

The princess turned quite white and had to sit down on the fountain's rim again.

IT'S LUCKY THE PICTURES WERE REPRODUCED ON THE BREKKFAST BRIKKS PACKETS.

"*Johansen?* Rudolf Johansen? My Rudi! At last! After all these years! Oh, run, run, and fetch him immediately, please! Immediately!"

Mark hesitated a moment.

"Please make haste!" she besought him. "Why do you wait?"

"It's only—well, you won't be surprised if he's quite *old*, will you? Remember he hasn't been in a garden keeping young like you."

"All that will change," the princess said confidently. "He has only to eat the fruit of the garden. Why, look at Lotta—when she was a puppy, for a joke I gave her a fig from this tree, and you can see she is a puppy still, though she must be older than any other dog in the world! Oh, please hurry to bring Rudi here."

D "Why don't you come with me to his house?"

"That would not be correct etiquette," she said with dignity. "After all, I *am* royal."

"Okay," said Mark. "I'll fetch him. Hope he doesn't think I'm crackers."

E "Give him this." The princess took off a locket on a gold chain. It had a miniature of a romantically handsome young man with dark curling hair. "My Rudi," she explained fondly. Mark could just trace a faint resemblance to Mr. Johansen.

He took the locket and hurried away. At the gate something made him look back: the princess and Lotta were sitting at the edge of the fountain, side by side. The princess had an

---

Teaching Options

Mini Lesson **Vocabulary Strategy** **TEKS** 6A, 6C **TAAS** Reading Obj. 1

WORD MEANING

Instruction Remind students that as they read, they frequently draw upon experience and their own knowledge to determine which definition of a multiple-meaning word is intended. Tell students that common words sometimes may be used in a way that is not familiar to them. Students should rely on context as well as dictionaries or other resources to help them recognize additional meanings of a word. Display the sentence below to illustrate *keen* as it is used to mean a long, wailing funeral song.

From a distance, the dogs' baying resembled a keen.

Exercises Have students define each underlined word as it is used in the sentence. They should consult a dictionary if necessary.

1. The princess wore a <u>brilliant</u> on one of her fingers.
2. The anxiety of the separation will <u>draw</u> Mr. Johansen's strength.
3. She was proud of her illustrious <u>descent</u>.

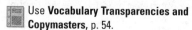 Use **Vocabulary Transparencies and Copymasters**, p. 54.

rm round Lotta's neck; with the other hand
he waved to him, just a little.

"Hurry!" she called again.

Mark made his way out of the house,
through the spring-cleaning chaos,
nd flew down the village to Houndshaven
Cottage. Mr. Johansen was in the house this
ime, boiling up a noisome mass of meat and
ones for the dogs' dinner. Mark said nothing
t all, just handed him the locket. He took one
ook at it and staggered, putting his hand to
is heart; anxiously, Mark led him to a chair.

"Are you all right, sir?"

"Yes, yes! It was only ze shock. Where did
ou get ziss, my boy?"

So Mark told him.

Surprisingly, Mr. Johansen did not find any-
hing odd about the story; he nodded his head
everal times as Mark related the various points.

"Yes, yes, her letter, I have it still—" he pulled
ut a worn little scrap of paper, "but ze *Garten-
uch* it reached me never. Zat wicked Gertrud
must haf sold it to some bookseller who sold it
o Fruhstucksgeschirrziegelsteinindustrie. And so
he has been waiting all ziss time! My poor little
Sophie!"

"Are you strong enough to come to her
now?" Mark asked.

"*Natürlich!* But first we must give ze dogs
their dinner; zey must not go hungry."

So they fed the dogs, which was a long job
as there were at least sixty and each had a
different diet, including some very odd
preferences like Swiss roll spread with Marmite
and yeast pills wrapped in slices of caramel.
Privately, Mark thought the dogs were a bit
spoiled, but Mr. Johansen was very careful to
see that each visitor had just what it fancied.

"After all, zey are not mine! Must I not take
good care of zem?"

At least two hours had gone by before the
last willow-pattern plate was licked clean, and
they were free to go. Mark made rings round
Mr. Johansen all the way up the village; the
music master limped quietly along, smiling a
little; from time to time he said, "Gently, my
friend. We do not run a race. Remember I am
an old man."

That was just what Mark did remember. He
longed to see Mr. Johansen young and happy
once more.

The chaos in the Armitage house had
changed its location: the front hall was now
clean, tidy, and damp; the rumpus of
vacuuming had shifted to the playroom. With
a black hollow of apprehension in his middle,
Mark ran through the open door and stopped,
aghast. All the toys, tools, weapons, boxes,
magazines, and bits of machinery had been
rammed into the cupboards; the floor where
his garden had been laid out was bare. Mrs.
Armitage was in the playroom taking down
the curtains.

"*Mother!* Where's my Brekkfast Brikks
garden?"

"Oh, darling, you didn't want it, did you? It
was all dusty; I thought you'd finished with it.
I'm afraid I've burned it in the furnace. Really
you *must* try not to let this room get into such
a clutter; it's perfectly disgraceful. Why, hullo,
Mr. Johansen," she added in embarrassment.
"I didn't see you; I'm afraid you've called at
the worst possible moment. But I'm sure you'll
understand how it is at spring-cleaning time."

She rolled up her bundle of curtains,
glancing worriedly at Mr. Johansen; he looked
rather odd, she thought. But he gave her his

453

Less Proficient Readers
Have volunteers explain how Mr.
Johansen is connected to the princess.
Answer: He is her lost love, Rudi, of
more than 50 years ago.
Set a Purpose Have students finish the
story to discover if the lovers are reunit-
ed in the garden.

Students Acquiring English
1 Have students figure out the meaning of the colloquialism *crackers* by
thinking how they would react to someone who told them a story like this.

Multiple Learning Styles
Visual Learners
2 Suggest that students design the
locket and miniature portrait of a
youthful Mr. Johansen.

Gifted and Talented
Have students discuss the appeal of
fantasy. Ask them why people enjoy
fantasy stories, even though they know
these stories contain unlikely, and
sometimes, even impossible, events.
Possible Responses: These stories are
entertaining because they are creative
and different from everyday life; they
help us enrich our own dream life.

tired, gentle smile and said, "Why, yes, Mrs. Armitage, I understand; I understand very well. Come, Mark. We have no business here, you can see."

Speechlessly, Mark followed him. What was there to say?

"Never mind," Mrs. Armitage called after Mark. "The Rice Nuts pack has a helicopter on it."

Every week in The Times newspaper you will see this advertisement:

BREKKFAST BRIKKS PACKETS. £100 offered for any in good condition, whether empty or full.

So, if you have any, you know where to send them.

But Mark is growing anxious; none have come in yet, and every day Mr. Johansen seems a little thinner and more elderly. Besides, what will the princess be thinking? ❖

Thinking through the LITERATURE

Connect to Literature

1. What Do You Think?
What were your thoughts as you finished reading this story?

Comprehension Check
- How does Mark get into the magic garden?
- Who does Mark meet in the garden?
- How does Mr. Johansen know the Brekkfast Brikks song?

Think Critically

2. What are some of the things Mark might have done to bring about a different ending to this story? Explain your answer.

3. Do you think Mr. Johansen and Princess Sophia will ever be reunited? Why or why not?

THINK ABOUT
- the princess's knowledge of magic
- Mr. Johansen's age and physical condition
- the advertisement that appears in *The Times* every week

4. If you were in Mark's place, would you go back and forth into the magic garden? Explain your answer.

5. ACTIVE READING PREDICTING Look back at the notes you made in your 📖 READER'S NOTEBOOK. How do the predictions you made compare to the actual events in the story? If you changed any of your predictions as you were reading, what clues led you to do so?

Extend Interpretations

6. COMPARING TEXTS You listed three of your favorite fantasy stories for the Connect to Your Life on page 438. How would you compare "The Serial Garden" with these other stories?

7. Connect to Life People like Mr. Johansen and Princess Sophia are often called star-crossed lovers because they seem prevented by fate from living happily ever after. How do Mr. Johansen and Princess Sophia compare to other star-crossed lovers you have read about?

Literary Analysis

FANTASY A **fantasy** is a story that takes place in an unreal, imaginary world, such as the garden in "The Serial Garden." Fantasies often involve magic, characters with superhuman powers, and impossible events. Sometimes the boundary between fantasy and the real world becomes blurred or hard to recognize, as in this passage from the story:

My father kept strict watch to see I did not run away, so I used to slip between the pages of the book when I wanted to be alone.

Paired Activity With a partner, find three other examples of fantasy in "The Serial Garden."

REVIEW HUMOR Writers often create humor by means of amusing descriptions, witty dialogue, and other devices. What do you find humorous in this story?

Extend Interpretations

6. Comparing Texts Possible Responses: Students might suggest *Alice in Wonderland, Charlotte's Web, The Chocolate Touch, Charlie and the Chocolate Factory, James and the Giant Peach,* and any book in C.S. Lewis's Narnia series, such as *The Lion, the Witch, and the Wardrobe.* Students might say that "The Serial Garden" was sadder, funnier, or more creative.

7. Connect to Life Possible Response: They are different from Romeo and Juliet, because they survive at the end.

Connect to the Literature

1. Possible Responses: Responses will vary. Some students might feel sad for Mr. Johansen and disappointed in the ending. Others might believe that the princess and her Rudi still have a chance to be together.

Comprehension Check
- He sings the Brekkfast Brikks rhyme.
- Mark meets Princess Sophia.
- He wrote it.

 Use Selection Quiz **Unit Three Resource Book,** p. 59.

Think Critically

2. Possible Responses: Mark might have prevented the garden from being destroyed by hiding the model; he might have reunited the lovers by insisting that Mr. Johansen visit the garden before feeding the dogs.

3. Possible Responses: Yes, because the ad will help Mark to get another set of cereal boxes to reconstruct the garden; no, Mr. Johansen will be dead before Mark can gather the pieces that he needs.

4. Possible Responses: Yes, because it would be exciting and fun; no, because I would be afraid of forgetting the melody and being trapped.

5. Possible Responses: Responses will vary. Students may have predicted some of the events, but may not have realized others. The emphasis on certain ideas such as the spring cleaning or the connection between the tune and Mr. Johansen may have led them to change some of their initial predictions.

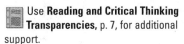 Use **Reading and Critical Thinking Transparencies,** p. 7, for additional support.

Literary Analysis

Fantasy Other examples of fantasy include: the garden becoming real; Mark's ability to enter it; the presence of the princess in the garden; her magical abilities; Lotta's eternal youthfulness.

Review: Humor Possible examples of humor include: Mr. Armitage locking himself in the larder; his description of the taste of Brekkfast Brikks; the description of Mr. Johansen's dogs.

Writing Options

1. **Escape Plan** Suggest that students make a diagram to show possible escape plans. Remind students that they are in the realm of fantasy, so they can include imaginative and even impossible elements in their plan. To make this assignment easier, have students brainstorm possible plans in groups and work together on their diagrams.

Use **Writing Transparencies**, p. 1, for additional support.

2. **Humorous Recipe** To get students started on this assignment, have them review the comments on the cereal found in the story. Encourage them to use cooking terms such as *stir, blend, mix,* and *pour* in their recipe. Guide them to use some of the humorous ingredients that Mr. Armitage suggests. Kinesthetic learners may prefer to stage a cooking show.

Activities & Explorations

1. **Monologue** To get students started on this assignment, have them discuss the characteristics of Princess Sophia that are revealed in the text and her manner of speaking.

2. **Dog House Poster** To get students started on this assignment, have them decide what image they want to project of the guest house and to whom they are trying to appeal. Then suggest that students think of a slogan before designing the graphic elements. This assignment is particularly well suited for visual learners.

Inquiry & Research

Garden Plots Many gardening periodicals include layouts of garden plans. Students may find it helpful to study some of these plans before designing their own. This assignment might also be completed on the computer.

Vocabulary in Action

Exercise A	Exercise B
1. b	1. searching
2. a	2. sleepy
3. c	3. patients
4. d	4. costume party
5. c	5. grains of sand

Choices & CHALLENGES

Writing Options

1. Escape Plan At one point, Mark fears that he might forget the magic tune and that Princess Sophia might keep him in the garden for company. If that happened, how could Mark get back home? Write the escape plan he might design. Place your plan in your **Working Portfolio.**

Writing Handbook
See p. R35: Explanatory Writing.

2. Humorous Recipe Using the descriptions of Brekkfast Brikks as a guide, write a humorous recipe for making the cereal.

Activities & Explorations

1. Monologue Present a monologue that shows how Princess Sophia might react when she finds out that Mark and Mr. Johansen have failed to return. If possible, have a classmate videotape your presentation. ~ **SPEAKING AND LISTENING**

2. Dog House Poster Design a poster that Mr. Johansen could use to advertise his guest house for dogs. Use both art and slogans to make the guest house look appealing. Show your poster to the class. ~ **ART**

Inquiry & Research

Garden Plots Skim the story for details about English gardens. Then check an encyclopedia, a computer database, gardening magazines (a magazine available in some libraries is titled *English Gardens*), or picture books for additional information. Using grid paper to make blueprints, plot a garden of your own.

Vocabulary in Action

EXERCISE A: ASSESSMENT PRACTICE For each sentence below, write the letter of the word that is most nearly opposite in meaning to the underlined Word to Know.

1. Mr. Johansen's music made those dogs that were <u>susceptible</u> howl.
   a. sympathetic   c. friendly
   b. unaffected   d. influenced

2. Miss Pride was a small, <u>wan</u> woman with yellowish hair.
   a. rosy   c. unhealthy
   b. pale   d. depressed

3. Mark had a <u>tantalizing</u> glimpse of someone on the far side of the lake.
   a. pleasing   c. boring
   b. panting   d. interesting

4. Mrs. Pride said <u>aggrievedly</u> that not many people liked Brekkfast Brikks.
   a. resentfully   c. slowly
   b. loudly   d. merrily

5. The house was in spring-cleaning <u>chaos</u> when Mark left.
   a. jumble   c. order
   b. muddle   d. confusion

EXERCISE B Answer the following questions.

1. Is a person who is <u>foraging</u> likely to be arguing, relaxing, or searching?

2. Would a person who has been keeping a <u>vigil</u> be sleepy, happy, or careless?

3. Are the <u>convalescing</u> people in a hospital the doctors, the visitors, or the patients?

4. Would a person be most likely to wear a <u>gaudy</u> outfit to a funeral, a costume party, or a job interview?

5. On a lonely beach, which might you find in <u>incalculable</u> numbers—seals, swimmers, or grains of sand?

Building Vocabulary
For an in-depth lesson on synonyms and antonyms, see p. 631.

Teaching Options

Mini Lesson **Spelling** **TEKS 16C**   **TAAS Writing Obj. 3, 7**

SUFFIXES *-able* and *-ible*
Write change+able=___ on the chalk board, and have students create the resulting word. Repeat the procedure with suscept+ible=___. Explain that the suffix *-able* usually is added to complete words to form adjectives meaning "able to [base word]"; *-ible* usually is added to roots. When either suffix is added to a word or root ending in silent *e,* the *e* is dropped—unless the *e* is preceded by *c* or *g.*

Application Have students add the suffix *-ible* or *-able* to the following roots and words.

1. avail *(available)*
2. aud *(audible)*
3. cred *(credible)*
4. agree *(agreeable)*
5. vis *(visible)*
6. tang *(tangible)*
7. notice *(noticeable)*
8. poss *(possible)*
9. attain *(attainable)*
10. love *(lovable)*

Remind students that when they aren't sure how to spell a word, they should consult a dictionary.

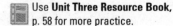 Use **Unit Three Resource Book,** p. 58 for more practice.

Grammar in Context: Placement of Adverbs

Through careful placement of adverbs, writers can emphasize certain words. Notice where Joan Aiken places the **adverbs** in the following sentences.

> Mrs. Armitage only cleaned the playroom once every six months or so, . . .

> Speechlessly, Mark followed him. What was there to say?

In the first sentence, how would the meaning change if *only* appeared before *Mrs. Armitage?* In the second sentence, how would the emphasis change if *speechlessly* were to appear at the end of the sentence rather than the beginning of the sentence?

Apply to Your Writing Changing the position of an adverb in a sentence can vary the meaning and emphasis of the sentence.

WRITING EXERCISE Change the placement of the underlined adverbs. Briefly describe how the change affects the meaning of the sentence.

Example: Original The larder door opened and creaked <u>suddenly</u>.

Rewritten Suddenly the larder door opened and and creaked. [Emphasis shifts from the <u>larder door</u> to <u>suddenly</u>.]

1. <u>Surprisingly</u> Mrs. Pride entered the cellar and found some Brikks.
2. Mark <u>slowly</u> tried to remember the tune.
3. The princess smiled <u>nervously</u> as Mark sneaked into her garden.
4. The princess <u>fondly</u> opened the locket.

Grammar Handbook Using Modifiers Effectively, p. R70

> *"I find short fantasy much easier to manage than long fantasy…. And characters can be much simpler in a short fantasy."*

Joan Aiken
born 1924

Literary Family Joan Aiken, the daughter of American poet Conrad Aiken, was born and raised in England where she still lives. She spent much of her childhood reading and making up stories to amuse herself and her younger stepbrother. She knew at an early age that she wanted to become a writer, having filled notebooks with poems and stories from the time she was five.

Popular Writer Aiken's husband died when their children were young, and she had to work as an editor at a magazine to support her family, supplementing her income by publishing short stories. In 1960 she revised a novel that she had written when she was 17. It became her first published novel, *The Kingdom and the Cave*. Her first big success came soon after, with *The Wolves of Willoughby Chase*. Marketed as a children's book, it was praised and read by adults as well.

AUTHOR ACTIVITY
The Fate of the Armitages Read more about the Armitages in Aiken's book *Armitage, Armitage, Fly Away Home* and present a short report to the class.

Grammar in Context
WRITING EXERCISE
Possible Responses:

1. Miss Pride entered the cellar and <u>surprisingly</u> found some Brikks. [Emphasis shifts from *surprise that Miss Pride entered* to *surprise that she found*.]
2. Mark tried to remember the tune <u>slowly</u>. [Emphasis shifts from *tried* to *remember*.]
3. The princess smiles as Mark <u>nervously</u> sneaks into her garden. [Emphasis shifts from *smiles* to *sneaks* and from the *princess* to *Mark*.]
4. <u>Fondly</u> the princess opened the locket. [Emphasis shifts to *fondly*.]

Joan Aiken
Aiken published her first poems while she was still in school. After her husband's death, she published many stories, but soon decided that she wanted to write longer works that would earn her more money.

Author Activity
The Fate of the Armitages Suggest that students read different stories so that the book is completely reviewed. To make this activity more challenging, ask students to compare and contrast themes or character or plots between stories.

 Grammar **TEKS 17D** 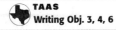 **TAAS Writing Obj. 3, 4, 6**

USING ADVERBS
Instruction Remind students that the careful placement of adverbs can make their writing more interesting and vivid. Read students the following sentences:
Mark followed him.
Speechlessly, Mark followed him.
Point out that in the second sentence, the adverb *speechlessly* allows readers to understand how Mark is feeling as he follows the man.
Exercises Have students rewrite the following sentences, adding adverbs to make them more vivid.

1. Mark searches for more packets of Brekkfast Brikks.
2. Mr. Johansen remembers the love of his life.
3. The boy enters the garden.
4. Mrs. Armitage discards the garden.

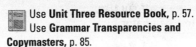 Use **Unit Three Resource Book**, p. 57.
Use **Grammar Transparencies and Copymasters**, p. 85.

 Use McDougal Littell's *Language Network,* Chapter 5, for more instruction and practice in using adverbs.

OVERVIEW

Objectives
1. understand and appreciate **fantasy** (Literary Analysis)
2. understand and identify **sound devices** such as **rhythm, rhyme,** and **repetition**
3. understand the use of **alliteration** and **onomatopoeia** (Literary Analysis)
4. use the active reading strategy of **clarifying**

Summary

"Jabberwocky" tells the story of the boy who slays the dragon, the Jabberwock. His father warns him of the danger of the beast. It bites and has claws that catch. Other creatures, such as the Jubjub bird and the Bandersnatch, might also threaten the boy's quest. Undeterred, the boy takes his sword and seeks the Jabberwock. As he is waiting by the Tumtum tree, the Jabberwock makes his noisy and frightening appearance. The boy cuts off the monster's head and returns to his father, who rejoices in his son's victory.

Sara Cynthia Sylvia Stout is a character who refuses to take the garbage out. She does all her other chores but lets the rotten fruit, coffee grounds, pizza crusts, and other decaying food remnants mount up until the garbage fills her house and reaches to the sky. After all her neighbors move away and none of her friends will come over any more, she agrees to take the garbage out. But it is too late. The trail of garbage stretches from New York to San Francisco and proves to be the end of Sara Cynthia Sylvia Stout.

Thematic Link

These two poems tell fantastic tales about two characters with very different personalities and attitudes toward challenges.

5-Minute Warm-Up

Daily Language SkillBuilder **TEKS 16B, 16D**

Have students **proofread** the display sentences on page 341k and write them correctly. The sentences also appear on Transparency 14 of **Grammar Transparencies and Copymasters.**

Jabberwocky

Sarah Cynthia Sylvia Stout Would Not Take the Garbage Out

Poetry by LEWIS CARROLL

Poetry by SHEL SILVERSTEIN

Connect to Your Life

Challenges Life has many challenges. Some are simple, like making your bed, while others are more risky. Think about a challenge you have had that was either hard to do or that you just didn't want to do. Why was it so hard for you? How did you finally get motivated to do it? Share your experience with your classmates.

 See the Skills Trace at the beginning of the unit for information on TEKS covered in this lesson.

Build Background

CONNECT TO HISTORY The two humorous poems you are about to read were written especially for young people. They have fun-to-read language and elements of fantasy. In "Sarah Cynthia Sylvia Stout Would Not Take the Garbage Out," a pile of garbage keeps getting bigger and bigger until it stretches from New York all the way to California.

"Jabberwocky" tells the story of a boy who slays a dragon. Lewis Carroll wrote the poem to go in his book *Through the Looking Glass.* Carroll's books transformed literature for young adults. Before his work, most people felt that children's books should instruct children in more serious matters. Although some of Carroll's work is serious, most historians agree that his playful attitude toward language and his imaginative settings changed writing for young people. With Carroll's help, books became a playground for the imagination.

Focus Your Reading

LITERARY ANALYSIS SOUND DEVICES Poets use **sound devices** such as **rhyme, rhythm,** and **repetition** to enliven their poems. In **humorous poetry** these devices often are exaggerated for comic effect. Two other sound devices used in the poems you are about to read are alliteration and onomatopoeia. **Alliteration** is the repetition of consonant sounds at the beginnings of words or syllables. *Ten tame tigers* is an example of alliteration. **Onomatopoeia** is the use of sounds that suggest their meaning. *Buzz, whisper,* and *gargle* are common onomatopoetic words. Read a poem aloud to best appreciate its sound devices.

ACTIVE READING CLARIFY Stopping now and then to reread a difficult passage can help you **clarify** a poem's meaning. You can also clarify the meaning of a poem by reading it aloud.

READER'S NOTEBOOK As you read each of the poems aloud, jot down notes about aspects of them that you stop to clarify.

"Jabberwocky"	
A father is telling his son to beware.	The Jabberwock must be dangerous.
The Jabberwock has claws and jaws.	It must be some kind of animal.

LESSON RESOURCES

UNIT THREE RESOURCE BOOK, pp. 60–61

ASSESSMENT

Formal Assessment, pp. 71–72

Teacher's Guide to Assessment and Portfolio Use

Test Generator

SKILLS TRANSPARENCIES AND COPYMASTERS

Literary Analysis
- Poetry: Sound Devices TR 20 (for Paired Activity, p. 461)

Reading and Critical Thinking
- Clarifying, TR 20 (for Thinking Through the Literature, p. 461)

Communications
- Reading Aloud, TR 11 (for Mini Lesson, p. 460)

INTEGRATED TECHNOLOGY
Audio Library

Visit our website:
www.mcdougallittell.com

Jabberwocky

by Lewis Carroll

'Twas brillig, and the slithy toves
    Did gyre and gimble in the wabe:
All mimsy were the borogoves,
    And the mome raths outgrabe.

5 "Beware the Jabberwock, my son!
    The jaws that bite, the claws that catch!
Beware the Jubjub bird, and shun
    The frumious Bandersnatch!"

He took his vorpal sword in hand:
10   Long time the manxome foe he sought—
So rested he by the Tumtum tree,
    And stood awhile in thought.

And, as in uffish thought he stood,
    The Jabberwock, with eyes of flame,
15 Came whiffling through the tulgey wood,
    And burbled as it came!

One, two! One, two! And through and through
    The vorpal blade went snicker-snack!
He left it dead, and with its head
20   He went galumphing back.

"And hast thou slain the Jabberwock?
    Come to my arms, my beamish boy!
O frabjous day! Callooh! Callay!"
    He chortled in his joy.

25 'Twas brillig, and the slithy toves
    Did gyre and gimble in the wabe:
All mimsy were the borogoves,
    And the mome raths outgrabe.

Culver Pictures

Thinking Through the Literature

1. How would you describe the Jabberwock? The boy?

2. What do you think "O frabjous day! Callooh! Callay!" means?

Cross Curricular Link   History

IMPACT OF LEWIS CARROLL ON CHILDREN'S LITERATURE *Alice's Adventures in Wonderland* and *Through the Looking-Glass* (from which "Jabberwocky" is taken) are two of the first children's books to be written to entertain and engage a child's imagination. The Alice books also pioneered the exploration of some of the emotions that pervade a child's psyche. *Alice's Adventures in Wonderland* explores the paradoxical anxiety of wanting to grow up quickly and yet not wanting to leave the world of childhood behind. *Alice's Adventures in Wonderland* also

shows, from a child's perspective, the difficulty of trying to communicate with adults and how meaningless their figurative words seem when the child takes them literally.

The publication of Lewis Carroll's Alice books forced the realization that children inhabit a reality far different from that of adults. The previous emphasis on teaching children through little stories now seemed inadequate. Instead, writers set out to explore the child's world, traveling into magical, idyllic, or nightmarish realms to do so.

Active Reading ‧ CLARIFYING

Ask students what they understand more clearly after rereading the poem.

Possible Responses: who the characters are, the conflict of the poem

> Use **Unit Three Resource Book,** p. 60 for more practice.

Literary Analysis ‧ SOUND DEVICES

A Ask students what the rhyme in "Sarah Stout" contributes to the poem.

Possible Responses: humor; an element of quickness; exaggeration

B Ask students how changing the rhythm of the poem from regular to irregular would affect it.

Possible Responses: lessen the emphasis on the kind and amount of garbage; make it more awkward to read aloud or to read quickly

- Ask students to pick out alliterative phrases that help to evoke vivid mental images of the garbage.

Possible Responses: "gloppy glumps"; "globs of gooey bubble gum"; "brown bananas"

C Ask students to explain the repetition of this phrase.

Possible Response: It is the moral of the poem.

> Use **Unit Three Resource Book,** p. 61 for more practice.

Sarah Cynthia Sylvia Stout Would Not Take the Garbage Out

by Shel Silverstein

A Sarah Cynthia Sylvia Stout
Would not take the garbage out!
She'd scour the pots and scrape the pans,
Candy the yams and spice the hams,
5 And though her daddy would scream
   and shout,
She simply would not take the garbage
   out.
And so it piled up to the ceilings:
Coffee grounds, potato peelings,
Brown bananas, rotten peas,
10 Chunks of sour cottage cheese.
It filled the can, it covered the floor,
B It cracked the window and blocked
   the door
With bacon rinds and chicken bones,
Drippy ends of ice cream cones,
15 Prune pits, peach pits, orange peel,
Gloppy glumps of cold oatmeal,
Pizza crusts and withered greens,
Soggy beans and tangerines,
Crusts of black burned buttered toast,
20 Gristly bits of beefy roasts . . .
The garbage rolled on down the hall,
It raised the roof, it broke the wall . . .
Greasy napkins, cookie crumbs,
Globs of gooey bubble gum,

25 Cellophane from green baloney,
Rubbery blubbery macaroni,
Peanut butter, caked and dry,
Curdled milk and crusts of pie,
Moldy melons, dried-up mustard,
30 Eggshells mixed with lemon custard,
Cold french fries and rancid meat,
Yellow lumps of Cream of Wheat.
At last the garbage reached so high
That finally it touched the sky.
35 And all the neighbors moved away,
And none of her friends would come
   to play.
And finally Sarah Cynthia Stout said,
"OK, I'll take the garbage out!"
But then, of course, it was too late . . .
40 The garbage reached across the state,
From New York to the Golden Gate.
And there, in the garbage she did hate,
Poor Sarah met an awful fate,
That I cannot right now relate
45 Because the hour is much too late.
But children, remember Sarah Stout
And always take the garbage out!

Teaching Options

> Use **Communications Transparencies and Copymasters,** p. 11, for additional support.

 Mini Lesson ‧ **Speaking and Listening**   **TEKS** 3B, 4A, 5C, 5D, 5E, 7D

FAVORITE POEM PROJECT

Prepare Explain to students that when Robert Pinsky was named Poet Laureate in 1997, he created the Favorite Poem Project. This project was designed to record Americans of all ages, races, and economic backgrounds, reading their favorite poems and sharing some personal reflections on them. Have students duplicate the Favorite Poem Project by choosing a poem that they enjoy. Ideas might be taken from the Project's website. Students should prepare a reading copy of the poem by marking significant passages and places to pause.

They should practice using effective rate, volume, pitch, and tone for the audience and setting.

Present Have students present their poems to small groups. Each group should discuss the effect of hearing the poem and their reactions to the poem. Each presenter should add his or her insights on the poem's meaning and appeal. [This activity may be linked with Inquiry & Research project on page 462.]

BLOCK SCHEDULING This activity is particularly well suited for longer class periods.

Connect to the Literature

1. What Do You Think?
What is your reaction to Sarah's predicament?

> **Comprehension Check**
> - What does the garbage do to Sarah's house?
> - How do the neighbors and her friends react?
> - How much garbage is there?

Think Critically

2. How does Silverstein make the garbage so vivid?

3. What do you think Sarah Stout's "awful fate" was?

4. What can you infer about Sarah's parents based on this poem? Explain.

> THINK ABOUT
> - the chores she had to do
> - her stubbornness
> - the fact that they refused to do Sarah's job for her

5. **ACTIVE READING** **CLARIFY** Review the notes you took in your **READER'S NOTEBOOK**. How did reading the poems aloud help you **clarify** their meaning? Compare your notes with those of classmates and discuss differences.

Extend Interpretations

6. **COMPARING TEXTS** How are "Jabberwocky" and "Sarah Cynthia Sylvia Stout Would Not Take the Garbage Out" similar? How are they different? Think about the writers' purposes, the subjects of the poems, and the sound devices the poets use. A Venn diagram may help you organize your ideas.

7. **Connect to Life** How do you react to a challenge? Are you more like Sarah Stout or the boy in "Jabberwocky"? Explain.

Literary Analysis

SOUND DEVICES Poets use **sound devices,** such as alliteration, onomatopoeia, and rhyme to create a unified effect in their poems.

Alliteration is the repetition of consonant sounds at the beginnings of the words and syllables, as in "Tumtum tree" or "moldy melons."

Onomatopoeia is the use of words whose sounds suggest their meaning. The "snicker-snack" of the "vorpal blade," for example, is an onomatopoeia that suggests the blade's rapid movement.

Another important sound device is **rhyme,** the repetition of sounds at the ends of words. Both poems use rhymes at the ends of lines.

Paired Activity With a partner, go through the poems and create a chart to list examples of **sound devices** you find.

"Jabberwocky"		
alliteration	onomatopoeia	rhyme
Callooh! Callay!	Bandersnatch	toves/borogoves
Tumtum tree		wabe/outgrabe

When you finish, take turns reading the poems aloud to one another. Which poem do you think uses sound devices more effectively?

Connect to the Literature

1. Possible Response: Sarah deserves her fate because she brought it on herself.

Comprehension Check
- It raises the roof and breaks the walls.
- The neighbors move away. Her friends no longer come over.
- It reaches from New York to San Francisco.

Think Critically

2. Possible Responses: by listing specific food items; by using alliteration; by including descriptive words and phrases

3. Possible Response: She disappears in a pile of garbage.

4. Possible Responses: Sarah's parents are strict because they assign her chores and won't do them for her. Or her parents might be too lazy to do the work themselves.

5. Possible Responses: Reading "Jabberwocky" aloud made sense of the vocabulary with which Lewis Carroll develops the plot and characters. Reading Shel Silverstein's poem aloud emphasized the enormous amount of garbage.

Use **Reading and Critical Thinking Transparencies,** p. 20, for additional support.

Literary Analysis

Sound Devices Responses will vary. Students should note that each poem uses the different sound devices effectively. Students' charts should reveal a clear understanding of each sound device and a careful reading of each poem.

Use **Literary Analysis Transparencies,** p. 20, for additional support.

Extend Interpretations

6. Comparing Texts Possible Responses: Both poets use sound devices such as rhythm, rhyme, alliteration, onomatopoeia, and repetition. Both poems are entertaining, although Silverstein's has a moral to communicate. One difference is that Lewis Carroll invents many words while Shel Silverstein relies mostly on familiar words to convey his meanings. Also the subject of each differs. "Jabberwocky" tells the story of a heroic deed. "Sarah Cynthia" is about a stubborn girl who is overtaken by the disastrous consequences of her actions.

7. Connect to Life Possible Response: Encourage students to cite instances when they may have behaved one way or the other.

Writing Options

1. **Nonsense Poem** To get students started on this assignment, have them brainstorm ideas for original poems. Then suggest that they list words associated with the subject to see if they can develop rhyming pairs.

 Use **Writing Transparencies,** p. 1, for additional support.

2. **Newspaper Article** Remind students to begin with a lead paragraph that tells *who, what, when,* and *where*. To adapt the assignment for interpersonal learners, have partners conduct mock interviews with Sarah Stout.

Activities & Explorations

Trial Arguments Remind students to support their reasons with details, facts, and examples. They might save the strongest argument for last.

 Use **Communications Transparencies and Copymasters,** p. 3, for additional support.

Inquiry & Research

Poetry Performance Students may wish to find other poems by Lewis Carroll or Shel Silverstein. Encourage them to make reading copies of their poems and practice reading their poems aloud to a partner before performing for the class. Students might wish to give some background before reading their poems. To make this assignment more challenging, have students teach their poems to the class, pointing out the literary devices and the way the devices affect the poem. [This activity can be used in conjunction with the Speaking and Listening Mini Lesson on page 460.]

Lewis Carroll

Charles Lutwidge Dodgson was an avid and talented photographer. He was so serious about photography that he had a glass house built on the roof of his rooms in Christ Church College in Oxford so that he could have enough light to take photographs, year round.

Shel Silverstein

Sheldon Silverstein wanted to be a baseball player when he grew up. As a teenager, he even worked at Comiskey Park selling hot dogs. Instead he became a cartoonist and writer of songs, poems, and books.

Writing Options

1. **Nonsense Poem** Both "Jabberwocky" and "Sarah Cynthia Sylvia Stout Would Not Take the Garbage Out" are humorous poems. Write your own rhymed humorous poem, or if you prefer, write a sequel to either of the selected poems, starting where the poet left off.

2. **Newspaper Article** Imagine that you are a newspaper reporter sent to cover the Sarah Stout story. Write an article about it. If you wish, the article could be in the form of an interview with Sarah Stout. Make sure the article has a beginning, middle, and end.

Activities & Explorations

Trial Arguments Imagine that you are Sarah Stout on trial for excessive littering. The judge calls you to the witness stand and asks: "Why did you do it?" Present your argument to the class. ~ **SPEAKING AND LISTENING**

Inquiry & Research

Poetry Performance Find an anthology of humorous poetry and choose a poem you like. Use an encyclopedia or other resource to learn a little about the author. Memorize the poem and perform it for the class. After you recite the poem, tell the class where you found it and provide information about the author.

"Oh frabjous day! Callooh! Callay!"

Lewis Carroll
1832–1898

Reading, Writing, and Nonsense Lewis Carroll, whose real name was Charles Lutwidge Dodgson, grew up in a family with ten brothers and sisters in rural England. As a child, he read voraciously and made up nonsense stories. At 12, Carroll left for boarding school. His letters home often included sketches and cartoons in the margins.

Mathematician and Children's Writer After Carroll finished school, he became a mathematician at Oxford University. Many of the stories and poems he wrote grew out of tales he told to the children of friends at Oxford. *Alice's Adventures in Wonderland* and *Through the Looking Glass* have become classics.

"Poor Sarah met an awful fate."

Shel Silverstein
1932–1999

City Kid Shel Silverstein was known for his ability to understand and express young people's fears and silliness. It was during his own childhood that Silverstein turned to writing and drawing. Silverstein grew up in Chicago, where he said he "couldn't play ball, couldn't dance. . . . So I started to draw and write." Silverstein himself created all the drawings for his poetry.

Cartoonist, Composer, Poet Silverstein had many books of poetry and prose to his credit, including the very popular *Where the Sidewalk Ends*. He wrote hundreds of poems. Most are silly or comic, though some are more serious. Silverstein was also a distinguished music composer and song writer.

 TEKS 12H    **TAAS Reading Obj. 6**

Teaching Options   **Assessment**   Informal Assessment   **TAAS Writing**

AUTHOR'S PURPOSE

You can informally assess students' understanding of the author's purpose in the selections by having them write a letter to one of the authors explaining their reaction to his poem and why they felt that way. The friendly letter should include specific references to the text and devices of the poem.

RUBRIC

3 Full Accomplishment Letters include a clear statement of reaction such as enjoyment or amusement and explain the reaction through specific references to the author's style and the text.

2 Substantial Accomplishment Responses show understanding of the nature of the poem and give several references to the text in support of the reaction.

1 Little or Partial Accomplishment Responses lack supporting evidence and reveal little understanding of the poem.

PREPARING to *Read*

The Eternal Frontier

Persuasive Essay by LOUIS L'AMOUR

Connect to Your Life

What frontiers would you like to explore?

Build Background Sixteen nations are working together to build the International Space Station. One of the project's goals is the promise of conducting valuable scientific research. Another is to encourage international cooperation.

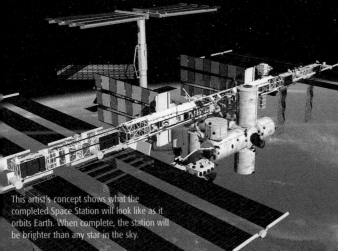

This artist's concept shows what the completed Space Station will look like as it orbits Earth. When complete, the station will be brighter than any star in the sky.

Two astronauts check a module connection during the first stages of construction, December 1998.

Focus Your Reading

LITERARY ANALYSIS | **PERSUASIVE ESSAY**

A **persuasive essay** is a type of nonfiction work that offers an opinion on a subject and tries to sway readers to accept that opinion. A persuasive essay appeals not only to the mind but also to the heart of the reader.

WORDS TO KNOW **Vocabulary Preview**

antidote	impetus	multitude
devastating	incorporate	

 LaserLink: Background for Reading
Science Connection

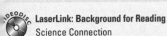 See the Skills Trace at the beginning of the unit for information on TEKS covered in this lesson.

ACTIVE READING | **EVALUATING** | When a reader judges the worth of a work by asking questions and forming opinions about it, that person is **evaluating** the work. A persuasive essay may be evaluated in terms of its believability, originality, or emotional power. Questions you might ask include: Are the reasons the writer provides believable? Is the writer an authority on this subject? What are the writer's biases?

As you read "The Eternal Frontier," evaluate the essay carefully. Record in your **READER'S NOTEBOOK** the questions you ask and the opinions you form.

THE ETERNAL FRONTIER **463**

Literary Analysis: TITLE

A Tell students that a good title may suggest more than one meaning. Ask students what frontier other than space is referred to by the title.

Possible Response: the frontier of the human mind

Literary Analysis | PERSUASIVE ESSAY |

B Remind students that successful persuasion appeals to emotions as well as intellect. Ask students to describe the impact of the simile on the author's persuasiveness.

Possible Responses: Those who don't want to explore space are compared to babies clinging to their mothers. This characterization is negative in its context and would discourage people from taking that view.

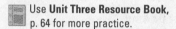 Use **Unit Three Resource Book,** p. 64 for more practice.

Active Reading | EVALUATING |

C Ask students what the author offers in support of this belief.

Possible Response: many examples of people moving on, time after time, just for the sake of exploring

D Ask students if they think L'Amour admires people like pioneers and immigrants who go beyond barriers.

Possible Response: He describes their deeds in positive language, which reveals his admiration for them.

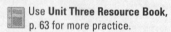 Use **Unit Three Resource Book,** p. 63 for more practice.

THE ETERNAL FRONTIER
by Louis L'Amour

The question I am most often asked is, "Where is the frontier now?"

The answer should be obvious. Our frontier lies in outer space.

The moon, the asteroids, the planets, these are mere stepping stones, where we will test ourselves, learn needful lessons, and grow in knowledge before we attempt those frontiers beyond our solar system. Outer space is a **A** frontier without end, the eternal frontier, an everlasting challenge to explorers not alone of other planets and other solar systems but also of the mind of man.

All that has gone before was preliminary. We have been preparing ourselves mentally for what lies ahead. Many problems remain, but if we can avoid a <u>devastating</u> war we shall move with a rapidity scarcely to be believed. In the past seventy years we have developed the **1** automobile, radio, television, transcontinental and transoceanic flight, and the electrification of the country, among a <u>multitude</u> of other such developments. In 1900 there were 144

miles of surfaced road in the United States. Now there are over 3,000,000. Paved roads and the development of the automobile have gone hand in hand, the automobile being civilized man's <u>antidote</u> to overpopulation.

What is needed now is leaders with perspective; we need leadership on a thousand fronts, but they must be men and women who can take the long view and help to shape the outlines of our future. There will always be the nay-sayers,[1] those who cling to our lovely green planet as a baby clings to its mother, but there will be others like those who have taken us this far along the path to a limitless future.

We are a people born to the frontier. It has been a part of our thinking, waking, and sleeping since men first landed on this continent. The frontier is the line that separates the known from the unknown wherever it may be, and we have a driving

---

1. **nay-sayers:** people who disagree or have negative attitudes.

WORDS TO KNOW

devastating (dĕv′ə-stā′tĭng) *adj.* extremely destructive **devastate** *v.*
multitude (mŭl′tĭ-tōōd′) *n.* a very great number
antidote (ăn′tĭ-dōt′) *n.* something that prevents the evil effects of something else; remedy

464

Teaching Options

Mini Lesson **Preteaching Vocabulary**

CONTEXT CLUES

Instruction Remind students that context clues can help them to recognize a word's meaning. Sometimes a sentence will include a familiar synonym that is used in addition to the unknown word. Write the sentence below to show how the synonym *combine* can be used to define *incorporate:* The countries hope to incorporate their programs in order to combine their efforts in space.

Exercise Have students apply the strategy to define the underlined WORDS TO KNOW.

1. The <u>multitude</u> watching the liftoff on television added up to the biggest crowd ever.

2. The loss of the probe was <u>devastating</u> to the budget but not destructive to the spirits of the scientists.

3. I recommend that remedy as an <u>antidote</u> to motion sickness.

4. The desire to be an astronaut was the <u>impetus</u> that gave him the force to succeed.

 Use **Unit Three Resource Book,** p. 65 for more exercises.

Use **Vocabulary Transparencies and Copymasters,** p. 55, for additional support.

need to see what lies beyond. It was this that brought people to America, no matter what excuses they may have given themselves or others.

Freedom of religion, some said, and the need for land, a better future for their children, the lust for gold, or the desire to escape class restrictions—all these reasons were given. The fact remains that many, suffering from the same needs and restrictions, did not come.

Why then did some cross the ocean to America and not others? Of course, all who felt that urge did not come to America; some went to India, Africa, Australia, New Zealand, or elsewhere. Those who did come to America began almost at once to push inland, challenging the unknown, daring to go beyond the thin line that divides the known and the unknown. Many had, after landing from the old country, developed good farms or successful businesses; they had become people

of standing in their communities. Why then did they move on, leaving all behind?

I believe it to be something buried in their genes, some inherited trait,[2] perhaps something essential to the survival of the species.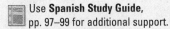

They went to the edge of the mountains; then they crossed the mountains and found their way through impassable forests to the Mississippi. After that the Great Plains, the Rocky Mountains, and on to Oregon and California. They trapped fur, traded with Indians, hunted buffalo, ranched with cattle or sheep, built towns, and farmed. Yet the genes lay buried within them, and after a few months, a few years, they moved on.

Each science has its own frontiers, and the future of our nation and the world lies in research and development, in probing what lies beyond.

---

2. **something buried . . . inherited trait:** a characteristic passed on from ancestors, such as eye color or height.

THE ETERNAL FRONTIER **465**

Customizing Instruction

Less Proficient Readers
To interest students in this selection, ask them how popular television programs or films, such as *Star Trek*, portray space exploration.
Set a Purpose Have students read to find out Louis L'Amour's attitude toward space exploration.

Students Acquiring English
In this selection, the author compares future space exploration with past migrations to the United States.

1 Explain that the prefix *trans-* means "across." Have students infer the meaning of *transcontinental* and *transoceanic flight.*

2 To clarify this sentence, lead students to understand that *this* refers to "a driving need to see what lies beyond" from the previous sentence.

Use **Spanish Study Guide,** pp. 97–99 for additional support.

Gifted and Talented
Explain that not everyone supports L'Amour's belief in the value of space exploration. Some people assert that space exploration wastes precious resources that could better be used to improve the quality of life for the underprivileged. Have students debate the pros and cons of space exploration.
Possible Responses: Space exploration is worthwhile, because it adds to our knowledge of the universe and produces many useful byproducts; the money for space exploration would be better used on medical care, housing, and education.

BLOCK SCHEDULING: MANAGING TIME

If your schedule requires that you cover the objectives in a shorter time, use . . .
- Preparing to Read, p. 463
- Thinking Through the Literature, p. 467
- Vocabulary in Action, p. 468
- Grammar in Context, p. 469

If you want to take advantage of longer class time, use . . .
- TE Teaching Options: Preteaching Vocabulary, p. 464; Standardized Test Practice, p. 466; Informal Assessment, p. 468; Grammar, p. 469
- Choices & Challenges and Author Activity, pp. 468–469
- Real World Link, p. 470

A few years ago we moved into outer space.
We landed men on the moon; we sent a vehicle
beyond the limits of the solar system, a vehicle
still moving farther and farther into that
limitless distance. If our world were to die
tomorrow, that tiny vehicle would go on and
on forever, carrying its mighty message to the
stars. Out there, someone, sometime, would
know that once we existed, that we had the
vision and we made the effort. Mankind is not
bound by its atmospheric envelope or by its
gravitational field, nor is the mind of man
bound by any limits at all.

One might ask—why outer space, when so
much remains to be done here? If that had
been the spirit of man we would still be
hunters and food gatherers, growling over the
bones of carrion[3] in a cave somewhere. It is
our destiny to move out, to accept the
challenge, to dare the unknown. It is our
destiny to achieve.

Yet we must not forget that along the way
to outer space whole industries are springing
into being that did not exist before. The
computer age has arisen in part from the space
effort, which gave great impetus to the
development of computing devices.
Transistors, chips, integrated circuits, Teflon,
new medicines, new ways of treating diseases,
new ways of performing operations, all these
and a multitude of other developments that
enable man to live and to live better are linked
to the space effort. Most of these
developments have been so incorporated into
our day-to-day life that they are taken for
granted, their origin not considered.

If we are content to live in the past, we have
no future. And today is the past. ❖

3. **carrion** (kăr′ē-ən): the flesh of dead animals.

WORDS
TO
KNOW

impetus (ĭm′pĭ-təs) *n.* a force that produces motion or action; impulse
incorporate (ĭn-kôr′pə-rāt′) *v.* to make part of another thing; merge

466

Connect to the Literature

1. What Do You Think?
In what way does the essay make you think about the future? Explain your response.

> **Comprehension Check**
> • According to L'Amour, what is needed now?
> • In L'Amour's opinion, why did Europeans come to America?

Think Critically

2. L'Amour mentions several achievements of 20th-century technology. Which achievement do you consider the most important? Give reasons for your choice.

3. **ACTIVE READING** **EVALUATING** What is your evaluation of L'Amour's persuasiveness? Is the essay convincing? Use the details you recorded in your **READER'S NOTEBOOK** to explain why you agree or disagree with him.

4. In what ways are modern space explorers and the early settlers similar? How are they different?

> **THINK ABOUT**
> • transportation in the 19th century
> • desire for new lands
> • human curiosity

5. What does L'Amour mean when he says, "If we are content to live in the past, we have no future. And today is the past"? What is the effect of closing the essay this way?

6. What does *eternal* mean? How can space be an "eternal" frontier?

Extend Interpretations

7. What If? What if a Native American from the 19th century were to read L'Amour's essay? In what ways might his or her perception of the frontier differ from L'Amour's? Do you think he or she might be persuaded to believe that space exploration is the "eternal" frontier? Explain.

8. Connect to Life What do you think might be the greatest benefit of space exploration to human beings? Support your opinion with reasons.

Literary Analysis

PERSUASIVE ESSAY A **persuasive essay** is a type of writing that presents the writer's opinion on a subject and attempts to convince the reader to accept that opinion. A persuasive essay differs from an informative article in that an informative article—such as a news story—seeks only to provide the facts and does not necessarily provide one particular opinion about them.

The **title** of a persuasive essay is important because it often tells what the writer is trying to persuade the reader of. L'Amour, for example, wants to convince readers that there is an "Eternal Frontier" in space.

Paired Activity With a partner, reread the essay, looking for facts and opinions. A fact is a statement that can be proved; an opinion cannot be proved. List in a chart each fact and opinion that you find. Are there more facts or more opinions? Are the opinions supported by facts? Evaluate the essay for its persuasiveness. Are L'Amour's arguments convincing? Explain your response.

Facts	Opinions
1. In the past 70 years automobiles, radio, television, flight, electrification of the country have occurred.	1.
2.	2.
3.	3.

THE ETERNAL FRONTIER **467**

Extend Interpretations

7. What If? Possible Responses: A 19th century Native American might be hard to convince of the potential that space offers as a frontier. To him or her, the great uncharted lands of the continent might seem to offer enough scope for growth and exploration. Twentieth-century technology has exhausted many of these other avenues little by little, leaving space as the logical next step.

8. Connect to Life Possible Responses: finding new places to live because Earth is getting overcrowded; discovering new species, because they might be able to teach people new skills or how to solve the problems of human existence

Connect to the Literature

1. Possible Responses: Responses will vary. Students should provide specific details to support their answers.

Comprehension Check
• leaders with perspective
• They had a need to explore the unknown.

Use Selection Quiz **Unit Three Resource Book**, p. 68.

Think Critically

2. Possible Response: Medical advances are most important, because they save lives or alleviate suffering.

3. Possible Responses: Students who agree with L'Amour will cite the facts he gives, his appeal to man's noble nature, and his style as convincing factors. Students who disagree with L'Amour may find his essay one-sided. He does not address very many opposing arguments.

Use **Reading and Critical Thinking Transparencies**, p. 14, for additional support.

4. Possible Responses: Some similarities are their courage, their curiosity, and their willingness to endure discomfort. Differences might include their methods of travel and their motives for their exploration.

5. Possible Responses: He means that technology is advancing so rapidly that what seems current is already out of date.

6. Possible Response: *Eternal* means endless. There is no limit to space so the opportunities for exploration are endless.

Literary Analysis

Persuasive Essay Students will find that the opinions are often substantiated by facts, and that generally, the essay is convincing. Facts include: miles of paved road; the reasons for immigration; trail of exploration; space missions already accomplished; technological advances connected with space. Opinions include: space as an eternal frontier; other advancements as preparation for space; need for leaders; our intrinsic desire to explore.

Use **Literary Analysis Transparencies**, p. 15, for additional support.

Writing Options

1. A Different Response Have students define *frontier* and brainstorm possibilities. Remind them that their opinions must be supported by facts and examples. Encourage students to write their draft on the computer.

2. Persuasive Letter Have students do some background reading on the space issue. They should then form a definite opinion and present reasons, backed up with statistics.

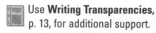 Use **Writing Transparencies,** p. 13, for additional support.

Activities & Explorations

1. Multimedia Presentation Suggest that students carefully plan and rehearse their presentation to make sure that all the media are smoothly integrated. Students may be able to locate historical news broadcasts or political speeches to include in their presentations.

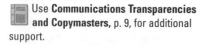 Use **Writing Transparencies,** p. 39, for additional support.
Use **Communications Transparencies and Copymasters,** p. 10, for additional support.

2. Author Interview To get students started on this assignment, have them investigate Louis L'Amour's life, what was happening in space just prior to his writing of this essay, and the themes of his novels. This assignment is well suited for interpersonal learners.

Use **Communications Transparencies and Copymasters,** p. 9, for additional support.

Inquiry & Research

Space Station Students could work in groups on this assignment. Each member could investigate a different source, such as the Internet, periodicals, and the encyclopedia.

Vocabulary in Action

Exercise A
1. e
2. d
3. b
4. a
5. c

Exercise B
Possible Response: Today's *multitude* of *devastating* diseases calls for an *antidote;* fortunately, the *impetus* already exists to *incorporate* new technology with traditional cures.

Choices & CHALLENGES

Writing Options

1. A Different Response At the beginning of the essay, L'Amour poses the question "Where is the frontier now?" Write a draft of a persuasive essay that provides an answer to this question that is different from L'Amour's answer. Place it in your **Working Portfolio.**

2. Persuasive Letter Write a letter to a representative in Congress, supporting or opposing space exploration. Provide facts to back up your opinions.

Writing Handbook
See p. R39: Persuasive Writing.

Activities & Explorations

1. Multimedia Presentation Create a multimedia presentation about one or more "famous firsts" that has taken place either in space or another frontier, such as medicine or communications. If possible, include pictures, slides, and recordings in your presentation. ~ **VIEWING AND REPRESENTING**

2. Author Interview What inspired L'Amour to write this essay? How did he explore frontiers in his own life? What other questions would you ask Louis L'Amour if you could? Get together with a partner, have him or her role-play the part of the author, and conduct an in-depth interview. ~ **SPEAKING AND LISTENING**

Inquiry & Research

SCIENCE | **SPACE STATION**

Search for information about what scientists have learned and are learning currently from space exploration. What new inventions or technologies have resulted from our journeys to space? Organize your research and make a presentation to the class.

Real-World Link As part of your research, read "Four Decades in Space" on p. 470.

Vocabulary in Action

EXERCISE A: WORD MEANING For each phrase in the first column, write the letter of the rhyming phrase in the second column that matches its meaning.

1. add a new quality
2. a guaranteed antidote
3. a multitude of fish
4. an impetus to add salt
5. pausing before putting out a forest fire

a. reason to season
b. masses of bass
c. devastating hesitating
d. sure cure
e. incorporate a trait

EXERCISE B Write a sentence using as many of the vocabulary words as possible. Describe a humorous or unlikely situation if you wish, but be sure to use the words correctly.

Building Vocabulary
For an in-depth lesson on learning and remembering new words, see p. 473.

| WORDS TO KNOW | antidote | devastating | impetus | incorporate | multitude |

 TAAS Writing Obj. 4
 TAAS Reading Obj.

Teaching Options

 Assessment **Informal Assessment**

IDENTIFYING THE MAIN IDEA AND SUPPORTING DETAILS Ask students to distinguish between the main idea and supporting details in the essay by summarizing what they read, as follows:
1. List the important points made by the author.
2. For each point listed, write down at least two supporting details.
3. Using your list of important points and supporting details, write a summary of the main idea.

RUBRIC
3 Full Accomplishment Students follow the directions carefully and distinguish between the main idea and supporting details.
2 Substantial Accomplishment Students summarize the essay but may include extraneous details.
1 Little or Partial Accomplishment Students cannot summarize the essay or distinguish between main ideas and supporting details.

Grammar in Context: Precise Adverbs

Notice how the **adverbs** affect the meaning of the first sentence of "The Eternal Frontier."

> The question I am most often asked is, "Where is the frontier now?"

An **adverb** is a word that modifes a verb, an adjective, or another adverb. Adverbs supply additional information about *when, where, how,* or *how much/to what degree* something happens or is done. They help readers visualize or more clearly understand a scene or character.

Usage Tip: To avoid confusing your readers, place each adverb close to the word that it modifies.

WRITING EXERCISE For each sentence, supply an adverb that gives the reader more detail about *where, how, how much/to what degree,* or *when* each action is performed.

Example: *Original* There will <u>be</u> nay-sayers.

Rewritten There will <u>always</u> be nay-sayers.

1. They will cling to our <u>green</u> planet.
2. Those who came to America <u>began</u> to push inward.
3. What we <u>need</u> is leaders with perspective.
4. There is a vehicle <u>moving</u> into space.

Connect to the Literature Look for the adverbs used to prepare the argument that space is the "eternal" frontier at the beginning of the fourth paragraph of the essay on page 464. What additional information do the adverbs supply?

<u>Grammar Handbook</u> Using Modifiers Effectively, p. R70.

> *"I don't have to imagine what happened in the old West—I know what happened."*

Louis L'Amour
1908–1988

Jack of All Trades When Louis L'Amour left Jamestown, North Dakota, at the age of 15, few would have predicted that he would become one of the most popular writers of the 20th century. L'Amour wandered from place to place, working as a hay shocker, a longshoreman, a lumberjack, a fruit picker, a miner, an elephant handler, an amateur archaeologist, and a professional boxer.

Witness of the West L'Amour was a descendant of pioneers. During his travels, he got to know people who told him stories about the frontier. L'Amour drew on these experiences to make his stories of the frontier seem true to life. Over the years, he wrote some 95 novels and more than 400 short stories. L'Amour received two of the country's highest honors, a Congressional National Gold Medal and the Presidential Medal of Freedom.

AUTHOR ACTIVITY
Read some of L'Amour's western stories, such as "The Gift of Cochise," to find out more about the western frontier.

THE ETERNAL FRONTIER **469**

  Grammar **TEKS 17D**

WRITING WITH PRECISE ADVERBS

Instruction Remind students than an adverb is a word that modifies a verb, an adjective, or another adverb, and that it supplies information such as *when, where, how,* or *how much/to what degree* something happens or is done. Tell students that when they write using descriptive words such as adverbs, they should keep the following points in mind:
- An adverb should be placed close to the word it's modifying.
- Too many adverbs can be just as harmful to

a piece of writing as too few adverbs. Be sure that adverbs are chosen carefully and don't clutter the writing.

Application Have students write a paragraph about a personal exploration. This might be visiting a new place, meeting a new person, or some other life-changing experience. In their paragraphs, students should try to incorporate adverbs to make their writing precise.

When students have finished writing, have them exchange their paragraphs with a partner. Each person should edit his or her partner's

paper, noting where adverbs could be added or removed to make the writing clearer. Partners should discuss their reactions with each other.

Use **Unit Three Resource Book,** p. 66.
Use **Grammar Transparencies and Copymasters,** p. 139.

Use McDougal Littell's *Language Network,* Chapter 19, for more instruction and practice in precise adverbs.

Objectives
- read and analyze news sources
- read to be informed
- use strategies, such as skimming and scanning, to better understand texts
- use visual representations as an aid to comprehension

Connecting to the Literature

This newspaper article presents students with specific facts about the design of the space shuttle, the goal of mission STS-95, and some differences between the Mercury missions in the 1960s and the shuttle missions. With this expanded knowledge of the space program, students can more easily assess the validity of the arguments presented by Louis L'Amour in his persuasive essay "The Eternal Frontier."

Four Decades in Space

By Richard Sanchez and Sean McNaughton / GLOBE STAFF

John Glenn made history in 1962 by becoming the first American to orbit the Earth. In 1998, he made history again, returning to space at the age of 77. This graphic provides a detailed look at Glenn's second trip, mission STS-95. The text that follows the graphic compares the space program at its beginning with developments almost four decades later.

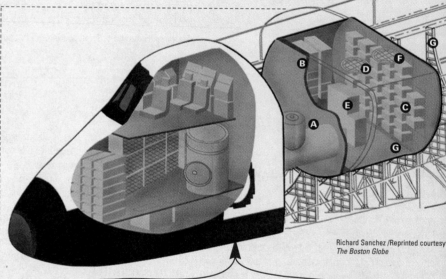

Richard Sanchez /Reprinted courtesy
The Boston Globe

❶

FLIGHT DECK
Flight controls for launch, orbit, and landing; holds the commander, pilot, a mission specialist, and payload specialist during launch.

MID-DECK
Three avionics[1] bays, galley, airlock to access tunnel, waste collection system, sleep accommodations, and storage.

EQUIPMENT DECK
Parts of life support systems and waste disposal.

1. **avionics:** aviation electronics; the science and technology of electronic devices used in air- and spacecrafts.

The Mission

STS-95 marked the 92nd shuttle flight, and the 25th flight for the Discovery. Payloads[2] allowed astronauts to conduct more than three dozen experiments on subjects ranging from solar radiation to the effects of microgravity and equipment tests.

SPACEHAB

10-foot by 13.5-foot removable laboratory module connects to the orbiter mid-deck, and allows the crew to conduct experiments in the cargo bay.

A Access tunnel

B Forward and aft bulkheads

C Lockers and trays: 56-liter volume, 27-kilogram capacity

D Viewport—two windows available

E Racks up to 740 liters volume, 300 kilograms capacity

F External payloads up to 454 kilogram total

G Interior payload 2,177–4,082 kilograms total

Payloads

CRYOTSU
CRYOGENIC THERMAL STORAGE UNIT
Test four thermal control devices for use in future missions.

SEM-4
SPACE EXPERIMENT MODULE 4
Microgravity experiments from eight schools in the U.S., Italy, and Argentina.

BRIC
BIOLOGICAL RESEARCH IN CANNISTERS
Spacehab experiments will examine low gravity's effects on plant growth and cell division.

E-NOSE
ELECTRONIC NOSE
Test new air quality monitor's ability to identify ten airborne toxic chemicals.

2. **payload:** the part of a load that is carried for scientific or commercial purposes.

Reading for Information

Learn how to skim and scan as you view the graphic of mission STS-95 and learn about the history of the space program.

SKIMMING, SCANNING, AND UNDERSTANDING GRAPHICS

To **skim**, you read a passage quickly to get an overview of it. To **scan**, you search through writing and headings for a particular fact or piece of information.

YOUR TURN *Use the questions below to help you learn how to skim and scan.*

❶ Skimming The picture of the shuttle shows the three decks in the spacecraft's nose. *Skim* the information provided about the three decks. Does the nose contain everything the astronauts need? How would you evaluate the arrangement? **Understanding Graphics** Read and study the graphic closely to answer the following questions:

- The payloads are the items in the shuttle's cargo that will be tested while in orbit. The results of the experiments will help scientists develop new technology. In the shuttle, where do the astronauts conduct the tests?

- Which of the payloads involves testing plant growth and cell division?

- Imagine you are on the flight deck and it's your turn to conduct an experiment. How would you get from the flight deck to the Spacehab?

As you go through the article with students, have them use the materials in the right-hand column as a guide to reading news articles. The following are **possible responses** to the two groups of questions:

1 The nose contains all necessities in a compact and efficiently organized arrangement that wastes no room and requires no extra movements.

- They conduct their experiments in the Spacehab.

- The Biological Research in Cannisters or BRIC tests low gravity's effects on plant growth and cell division.

- The astronaut would have to go down to the mid-deck and pass through the airlock to the access tunnel, which leads into the Spacehab.

Use **Reading and Critical Thinking Transparencies,** p. 47, for additional support.

2 The difference is that the left column gives information about the Mercury missions between 1961 and 1963 and the right column tells about the shuttle programs. Mercury-era space suits had a layer of aluminized nylon to keep the astronaut alive if the spacecraft lost pressure.

❷ Mercury *There and back*

The primary goals of the Mercury mission, which made six manned flights between 1961 and 1963, were to orbit the earth, test man's ability to work in space, and recover man and capsule safely.

Shuttles *Working in orbit*

The shuttle program's goal was to create a reusable orbiter for scientific research and commercial payloads, and for satellite deployment, retrieval, and repair.

The Suit

Mercury-era space suits were modified versions of Navy high-altitude jet pilot pressure suits.

An outer layer of aluminized nylon protected an inner layer of Neoprene-coated nylon. Its purpose was to keep the astronaut alive if the spacecraft lost pressure.

Despite fabric breaks at the joints, it was hard to bend the knees and elbows.

John Glenn walks to the Gemini capsule *Friendship 7* before his history-making flight Feb. 20, 1962.

NASA Photo

Better suits let Gemini astronauts make the first U.S. space walks, but Apollo's lunar missions required much greater mobility, comfort, and protection.

Onboard the shuttle, today's astronauts wear cotton T-shirts and pants like you might wear on the street. The suits they use on space walks let astronauts work in the vacuum for hours at a time and maneuver free of the shuttle while protecting them from temperature, radiation, and micro-meteoroids. ■

An astronaut on an untethered space walk in 1994.

NASA Photo

Reading for Information *continued*

❷ Scanning *Scan* the text above to find the answers to these questions: What is the difference between the left and right columns of text? Why did Mercury-era space suits have a layer of aluminized nylon?

Inquiry & Research

Activity Link: "The Eternal Frontier," p. 468
Can human beings handle living in space? Research for information that scientists have gathered about humanity's ability to live in space. What experiments have they conducted? What were the results? Present a one-page report to the class.

 Mini Lesson ## Inquiry & Research   **TEKS 20C**

This activity links to the Inquiry & Research section of Choices & Challenges, page 468, following "The Eternal Frontier."

As they do the Inquiry & Research activity, students will take notes from relevant and authoritative sources such as periodicals and on-line searches.

Instruction This activity provides a good opportunity to help students assess the credibility and usefulness of the information they find. Direct students to check encyclopedia indexes and periodical indexes. If students have access to the

Internet, they should try various searches that include the word NASA, such as "NASA experiments," "NASA research," or they might visit the NASA website.

Practice Have students skim the information they find to see if the material is relevant to the topic. Encourage them to see the relationship between experiments on respiration and gravity and the possibility of long-term human habitation of space.

Unfamiliar Words

How do you figure out the meanings of unfamiliar words you come across in your reading?

Think about words you already know that are related or have similar affixes. You can also look for context clues in the other words around it. These are two good ways of determining the meaning of an unfamiliar word.

> Paved roads and the development of the automobile have gone hand in hand, the automobile being civilized man's **antidote** to overpopulation.
>
> —Louis L'Amour, "The Eternal Frontier"

Related words: **Antidote** might make you think of words like **antibiotic** or **anticlimax,** which share the same prefix *anti-*, meaning "against."

Context: The words around **antidote** describe technological advances.

An antidote is a remedy against something.

Strategies for Building Vocabulary

Consider the following strategies for learning new words. The last strategy suggests a way for you to remember the words you learn.

❶ Use Context Clues You can use context clues to help you understand unfamiliar words like *indomitable.* Read the sentence in box 1. What does the context clue "didn't rest until" suggest about the meaning of the word *indomitable*?

❷ Think of Related Words When you come across a new word, think of words you know that have a similar root or base word. For example, *dominate* ("to rule, to control") is related to *indomitable.* If you know the meanings of related words, you can often figure out the meaning of the new word.

❸ Analyze Word Parts The parts of a word can sometimes reveal its meaning. *Indomitable* has three parts: *in-, -domit-,* and *-able.* If you find out that the Latin prefix *in-* means "not," *domit* comes from the Latin word *domitare,* which means "to tame," and the suffix *-able* means "capable of being," then you can guess a meaning for *indomitable—* "not capable of being tamed."

❹ Use a Dictionary A dictionary lists a word's most common meaning first. When you look up a word, read all the definitions and decide which one best fits the context in which the word appears. Check the **etymology,** or word origin, to help you remember the base word, or root, and connect it to words with similar origins.

❺ Record and Use New Words When you encounter a new word, record the word, its definition, its root, and related words in your 📖 **READER'S NOTEBOOK.** Say it aloud and use it in your writing.

INDOMITABLE	
1 Context Clues	**2 Related Words**
My mother was an <u>indomitable</u> spirit who didn't rest until she made them understand.	dominate, dominant
3 Word Parts	**4 Dictionary**
in- ("not") + *domitare* ("to tame") + *-able* ("capable of being")	**in·dom·i·ta·ble:** incapable of being subdued [from Latin *indomitabilis,* untamable]

ACTIVITY Choose three Words to Know from the selections you have read in this unit. For each word, provide a definition and synonyms for the word.

Objectives

- rely on context to determine the meanings of unfamiliar words
- apply meanings of prefixes and suffixes in order to comprehend unfamiliar words
- apply meanings of root words in order to understand unfamiliar words

VOCABULARY EXERCISE
Possible Responses:

1. genial
Definition: 1. Having a pleasant or friendly disposition or manner; kindly. 2. Conducive to life, growth, or comfort; mild.
Synonyms: kindly, cheerful, pleasant, good natured

2. insatiable
Definition: Incapable of being satiated; never satisfied
Synonyms: gluttonous, greedy

3. impertinent
Definition: 1. Not constrained within proper or established limits, esp. of manners or good taste; insolent. 2. Not pertinent; irrelevant.
Synonyms: insolent, defiant, insulting irrelevant

📑 Use **Unit Three Resource Book,** p. 69 for more practice.
Use **Vocabulary Transparencies and Copymasters,** p. 15, for additional support.

OVERVIEW

Objectives

- read and appreciate the works of one of America's great science fiction and fantasy writers
- understand the influences on Ray Bradbury's work
- realize the impact of Ray Bradbury's writing on other science fiction and fantasy writers and on filmmakers
- learn more about his life and accomplishments

This Author Study offers a unique opportunity for students to focus on the work of one of America's foremost science fiction and fantasy writers. In addition, students will learn about Ray Bradbury's life and what stimulated his imagination and vision of a future world.

Influence

Ⓐ Ray Bradbury's work has appeared in over 800 anthologies. Not only does the reading public enjoy his work; fellow writers have shown their esteem by contributing to an anthology of stories linked to Bradbury's tales and characters, entitled *The Bradbury Chronicles: Stories in Honor of Ray Bradbury.* He has contributed greatly to the emergence of science fiction as a respectable genre.

Author Study RAY BRADBURY

CONTENTS

Master of Fantasy

"What better way is there to become immortal than to write every day of your life?"

born 1920

"In Love with the Future"

Who is Ray Bradbury? Steven Spielberg, director of *Close Encounters of the Third Kind* and *E.T.: the Extra-Terrestrial*, calls him "Papa." Filmmaker Gary Kurtz claims he may never have produced *Star Wars* and *The Empire Strikes Back* if he had not heard Bradbury speak in the 1960s. Who is Ray Bradbury? Perhaps the most influential writer of science fiction and fantasy in generations.

Not only has Bradbury influenced filmmakers, he himself has been deeply influenced by the adventure movies he saw and adored as a child.

Bradbury and Steven Spielberg on the set of *Jurassic Park.*

His LIFE and TIMES

1920 Born August 22 in Waukegan, Illinois

1932 Writes first Martian stories

1950 Publishes *The Martian Chronicles*

1920　　　　1930　　　　1940　　　　195-

1920 Treaty of Versailles takes effect; WW I ends.

1929 Stock market crash

1939 Germany invades Poland; WW II begins.

1945 U.S. drops atomic bombs on Japan; WW II ends.

474

While living in Waukegan, Illinois, his mother took him to his first silent picture—*The Hunchback of Notre Dame*—when he was just three. By the time he was eight, Bradbury had discovered science fiction. "I was in love . . . with monsters and skeletons and circuses and carnivals and dinosaurs and, at last, the red planet Mars," he fondly remembers. At 9, Bradbury started collecting the comic strip Buck Rogers, which he said made him fall "completely in love with the future." Bradbury wrote his first Martian stories when he was 12.

In 1934 Bradbury's family moved to Los Angeles, California. There Bradbury was able to indulge the passion he had felt for movies since early childhood. He would sneak into the film studios and beg the stars for signed photographs—souvenirs that hang in his office today.

"WHEN I WAS 19, I SOLD NEWSPAPERS..."

The world had fallen upon hard times in 1938, the year Bradbury graduated from high school. His family had no money to spare. Bradbury sold newspapers on Los Angeles street corners by day and spent hours reading and writing in the public library at night. Just before his 21st birthday, he sold a story. Soon he was selling about one story a

Did You Know?

- ◆ Ray Bradbury does not know how to drive a car.
- ◆ He refuses to write on a computer and dislikes the Internet.
- ◆ He has published over 500 works, including short stories, plays, novels, television scripts, screenplays, and poetry.
- ◆ *Apollo* astronauts named a crater on the moon *Dandelion Crater* after Bradbury's novel *Dandelion Wine.*

Bradbury, age 14, with comedian George Burns.

Criticism

B Because of Bradbury's lifestyle, some critics have insisted that he is anti-science, a paradox for a science fiction writer. Others say that his way of life, which rejects many of the technological advances, symbolizes the message of his writing. Humans should not let new technology distance them from the qualities and feelings that make them human. Technology is valuable because it adds a dimension to human existence, but it must be used wisely.

Attitudes

C The typewriter has been a significant instrument for Ray Bradbury throughout his life as a writer. He typed out stories and television scripts in his youth on a toy-dial typewriter, saved his lunch money in high school to buy a typewriter for ten dollars, and now uses an IBM Wheelwriter. He boasts that he could out-type anyone using a computer and says that computers are for changes. "I write a short story in three hours, and I don't change it."

Motivations

D One of Ray Bradbury's early motivations to write came from his frustration at the ending of a book he had read. Edgar Rice Burroughs's *The Gods of Mars* concludes with the heroine trapped and waiting for the hero to rescue her. Not wanting to wait until Burroughs's next book was published and knowing that he couldn't afford it anyway, he and a friend wrote the sequel themselves. In Bradbury's version, the heroine is successfully rescued after surviving the year in her sun prison.

Connection to Los Angeles

E Ray Bradbury loved Los Angeles from the moment he moved there. He has lived there ever since. To him it is a city of the future. It is in contrast to his hometown of Waukegan, which represents for him the values of small town America before the Depression.

1953 Publishes *Fahrenheit 451*	1963 Nominated for an Academy Award	1977 Receives World Fantasy Award for Lifetime Achievement	1985 *The Ray Bradbury Theater* debuts on TV	1995 Named Los Angeles Citizen of the Year

	1960	1970	1980	1990	2000

1957 Soviets launch *Sputnik* satellite.	1965–1973 U.S. ground troops in Vietnam War	1969 U.S. astronauts walk on moon.	1975 U.S. *Viking* spacecraft lands on Mars.	1989 Berlin Wall is torn down; German reunification begins.	1998 Construction begins on International Space Station.

RAY BRADBURY **475**

Themes

F The stories within *The Martian Chronicles* are unified by their setting on Mars and their themes. The stories explore the stages in the conquering and colonization of the new frontier, space. Bradbury explores several themes in this story that are revisited in his later works. The colonists, in subduing and taming the wilderness of a new frontier, are themselves changed by their contact with the environment. The promise of the wilderness is lost as it is civilized by the colonists. This work also celebrates simplicity and innocence as epitomized in small town existence.

More on *Fahrenheit 451*

G To Ray Bradbury in his youth, the neighborhood firehouse symbolized the protection of the most precious community institutions—families, schools, libraries. In his novel *Fahrenheit 451*, the firemen become the destroyers. By inverting the symbol of the firemen, Bradbury is making a point that the fundamental American values of prosperity and democracy are at risk to be changed also. Materialism and conformity can lead to spiritual death and a form of totalitarianism, in which the uninformed majority prevails.

month to popular science-fiction and horror magazines. Bradbury quit selling papers and was instead selling his own stories to national magazines, such as *The Saturday Evening Post.* Bradbury's career was off the launchpad.

In 1947, Bradbury, an admirer of Edgar Allan Poe and other masters of fantasy and horror, published a collection of horror tales called *Dark Carnival.* Then came *The Martian Chronicles,* tales of Earth people trying to conquer and settle Mars. These Martian stories reflected fears that many Americans felt during the 1950s—nuclear war, racism, censorship, and a longing to maintain a simpler life against an increasingly technological age.

"I WAS LITERALLY WRITING A DIME NOVEL."

In the early 1950s Bradbury wrote the first draft of the novel that became *Fahrenheit 451* on a coin-operated typewriter in the basement of the library of the University of California, Los Angeles. The typewriters rented for a dime each half hour. Working feverishly, Bradbury spent a total of $9.80 in dimes as he cranked out his novel.

Fahrenheit 451—the temperature at which book paper catches fire—is a novel set in a future when the written word is seen as subversive and forbidden by the authorities. In this world firemen have the job of destroying libraries and burning books. The novel has its roots in Bradbury's revulsion at the Nazi book burnings

that took place before and during World War II, but it is a protest against censorship in general. Bradbury describes a small group of rebels who risk their lives by memorizing entire works of literature in the hope of preserving the accomplishments of the human spirit. In 1967, François Truffaut directed a motion-picture version of *Fahrenheit 451* that was extremely popular.

"Firemen" burning books in *Fahrenheit 451.*

Besides the numerous collections of short stories, poems, and essays Bradbury has authored, he has also written screenplays and scripts for television, including *The Twilight Zone* and *The Ray Bradbury Theater*. And he has shown his creativity not only in his writing. The futuristic U.S. Pavilion at the 1964 New York World's Fair was Bradbury's brainchild. He also designed the Spaceship Earth exhibit at the Epcot Center in Florida. Ray Bradbury's rich imagination has made him a powerful creative force on the American literary scene for more than half a century.

Bradbury in his office, standing behind a desk covered with futuristic toys.

More Online: Author Link
www.mcdougallittell.com

NetActivities: Author Exploration

FUTURE WORLDS, PRESENT REALITY

Science-fiction writers often comment on society and its problems in their works. Even though they may set their stories in the future, these works comment on the real world in which their authors live.

In science fiction, writers are free to imagine worlds in which current trends whose final consequences are still unknown can be seen fully developed. During the Cold War, the period that followed World War II and ended in 1989, many science-fiction writers wrote works that explored the consequences of authoritarian philosophies such as Fascism and Communism. For example, classics such as *Brave New World* (1932), by Aldous Huxley, *Nineteen Eighty-Four* (1949), by George Orwell, *Fahrenheit 451* (1953), by Ray Bradbury, and *Cat's Cradle* (1963), by Kurt Vonnegut, explore worlds in which governments have near total control over the lives, minds, and emotions of ordinary people. These writers were reacting to events of their own day.

When you read science fiction, you should enjoy the fantasy, but you should also pay attention to what the writer may be saying about the world in which you live.

Another Frontier

At sixty, Ray Bradbury decided to channel his energies in another direction and write detective fiction. He had experimented with this genre in the 1940s by writing some crime fiction short stories. He published a collection of those stories and then turned his hand to novels. Although their settings were apparently very different from the futuristic world of science fiction, he found similarities in the way that both detective fiction and science fiction help readers to confront unpleasant realities in a non-threatening form. *Death Is a Lonely Business*, published in 1985, and the sequel were seen by some as his strongest work in many years.

Reflections

Ray Bradbury feels that one of the functions of science fiction is to warn what might happen in the future if care is not taken in the present. Some of his writing has been in reaction to disturbing contemporary trends that have the potential to be very destructive if not arrested. For example, his short story "The Pedestrian" envisions a future in which a man is detained and has to undergo psychological evaluation because he wants to breathe fresh, not air-conditioned, air, and wants to look at reality, not television. Bradbury wrote this story after having been stopped by the police several times for simply taking a walk in his own neighborhood.

OVERVIEW

 This selection is included in the **Grade 7 InterActive Reader.**

Objectives

1. understand and appreciate the **structure** of a short story (**Literary Analysis**)
2. re-examine and appreciate **science fiction** (**Literary Analysis**)
3. use the reading strategy of **visualizing** character, setting, and action (**Active Reading**)

Summary

As soon as Harry Bittering disembarks from the rocket that has brought his family from Earth to Mars, he senses that humans don't belong on Mars. The wind seems to blow away his identity. His wife convinces him to stay. Then the news comes that war has destroyed the rockets on Earth. Now they are cut off from Earth completely. Harry begins to build his own rocket, but none of the men will help him. They are unalarmed by the fact that they are becoming taller, thinner, and golden-eyed. Gradually the building of the rocket seems less important to Harry. He and his family, as well as the other humans, decide to spend the rest of the summer in the mountains where there are many deserted Martian villas. They leave everything behind, promising each other to return in the autumn. Five years later, rescuers from Earth arrive. They find a deserted human settlement and a large Martian colony living in the mountains. As they plot their strategy for settling Mars, the wind sends shivers through them.

Thematic Link

In Bradbury's tale, Harry Bittering struggles to preserve his humanity.

5-Minute Warm-Up

Daily Language SkillBuilder **TEKS 16B**

Have students **proofread** the display sentences on page 341k and write them correctly. The sentences also appear on Transparency 15 of **Grammar Transparencies and Copymasters.**

 Mini Lesson **Preteaching Vocabulary**

If you would like to preteach the WORDS TO KNOW for this selection, use the Mini Lesson, p. 480.

"They stood in the shed and looked at their one cow. It was growing a third horn."

Dark They Were, and Golden-Eyed

Short Story by RAY BRADBURY

Connect to Your Life

Starting a New Life Have you ever been in a situation where you had to adapt to a very different environment from what you were used to? How did you react? What did you do to adapt? What things about yourself did you have to change? Did old habits help or hinder you? Share your thoughts with the class.

I was observant.

What I did to adapt.

Build Background

The Red Planet Named for the Roman god of war because of its "warlike" reddish color, Mars is the fourth planet from the Sun. The first "modern" map of Mars, drawn by astronomer Giovanni Schiaparelli in 1877, showed a planet crisscrossed by channels or canals. Inspired by Schiaparelli's work, astronomer Percival Lowell, in the 1890s, speculated that the "canals" might have been constructed by intelligent beings. This theory is now known to be untrue, but at the time it inspired such writers as H. G. Wells, who wrote *The War of the Worlds* (1898) in which a dying alien race targets Earth for its resources. Mars has been the setting for numerous science-fiction stories, most of which rarely depict the planet realistically.

> **WORDS TO KNOW**
> **Vocabulary Preview**
> amiss   flimsy   recede
> dwindle forlorn

 LaserLink: Background for Reading
Science Connection

 TEKS See the Skills Trace at the beginning of the unit for information on TEKS covered in this lesson.

Focus Your Reading

LITERARY ANALYSIS **CIRCULAR PLOT STRUCTURE**

Plot development is often explained in terms of a triangle, in which the rising action is one side of the triangle, the climax is the apex, and the falling action is the other side (see page 171). Some plots can be explained in terms of a circle because important details and events are repeated at the beginning and end of the story. As you read this story, pay careful attention to the beginning and ending of the story to see what elements make the plot "circular."

ACTIVE READING **VISUALIZE** The process of forming a mental picture based on a written description is called **visualizing,** but visualizing involves all the senses, not just sight. When you read, try to "see" the settings and characters described, but also try to hear, feel, smell, and taste in your imagination everything the writer describes.

READER'S NOTEBOOK As you read "Dark They Were, and Golden-Eyed," jot down a few descriptions that help you visualize the setting, characters, or action.

LESSON RESOURCES

UNIT THREE RESOURCE BOOK, pp. 70–76

ASSESSMENT
Formal Assessment, pp. 75–76
Teacher's Guide to Assessment and Portfolio Use
Test Generator

SKILLS TRANSPARENCIES AND COPYMASTERS
Literary Analysis
• Text Structure, TR 12 (for Paired Activity, p. 491)
Reading and Critical Thinking
• Visualizing TR 10 (for Thinking Through the Literature, p. 491)

Grammar
• Time Order, CM 94 (for Mini Lesson, p. 484)
• Transitional Expressions CM 95 (for Mini Lesson, p. 488)
Vocabulary
• Synonyms, CM 56 (for Mini Lesson, p. 480)
• Word Usage, CM 57 (for Mini Lesson, p. 487)

INTEGRATED TECHNOLOGY
Audio Library
LaserLinks
• Science Connection. See **Teacher's SourceBook,** p. 22
Video: Literature in Performance
• *The Long Years.* See **Video Resource Book,** pp. 23–28

Visit our website:
www.mcdougallittell.com

DARK THEY WERE, AND GOLDEN-EYED

BY RAY BRADBURY

TEACHING THE LITERATURE

Customizing Instruction

Less Proficient Readers
Have students share some of their impressions about outer space and life on other planets. Ask them what they think Martians might look like if they exist.

Set a Purpose Have students read to find out how Harry Bittering feels about living on Mars and what news the Bitterings receive about Earth.

Students Acquiring English
Tell students that the title describes the distinct characteristics of the Martians as Bradbury envisions them.

 Explain the dual meanings of *whispered* as it is used in this sentence. They stepped lightly across the meadow; they softly spoke to each other as they walked across the meadow.

Use **Spanish Study Guide,** pp. 100–102 for additional support.

Gifted and Talented
Tell students that the original title of the story was "The Naming of Names." Ask students to think about which title they would choose and why. They should be prepared to discuss their reasons at the end of the story.

The rocket metal cooled in the meadow winds. Its lid gave a bulging *pop*. From its clock interior stepped a man, a woman, and three children. The other passengers whispered away across the Martian meadow, leaving the man alone among his family.

The man felt his hair flutter and the tissues of his body draw tight as if he were standing at the center of a vacuum. His wife, before him, seemed almost to whirl away in smoke. The children, small seeds, might at any instant be sown to all the Martian climes.

The children looked up at him, as people look to the sun to tell what time of their life it is. His face was cold.

Illustration by Kam Mak (detail).

479

Mini Lesson **Viewing and Representing** ⭐ **TEKS 22A**

Illustration
by Kam Mak

ART APPRECIATION
Instruction Remind students that artists must not only choose their colors carefully but also decide on the intensity of their hues and tones. This artist saturates the picture with dark blue and varying shades of brown and rust. Ask students to describe the effect of the landscape painted in those intense colors.
Possible Response: There is nothing soft or mild or gentle about the landscape. It seems forbidding and harsh.

Ask students to imagine the same illustration in pale blues and light gold. How would the effect be different?
Possible Response: It would seem a friendlier place, which could be adapted to or lived in more easily.
Application Ask students what this illustration might suggest about the humans' attempt to colonize and live on Mars.
Possible Response: It won't be easy for them. The environment is stronger than they are.

Reading and Analyzing

Reading Skills and Strategies:
PREVIEW

Have students discuss the title and look at the illustrations of the story. Explain Harry Bittering's initial conflict and ask them to predict what they think will happen.

Reading Skills and Strategies:
MAKING INFERENCES

A Ask students what emotions Harry is feeling.

Possible Responses: fear, uneasiness, dismay, foreboding

Literary Analysis

CIRCULAR PLOT STRUCTURE

B Remind students that details from the beginning of the story are important to note to recognize circular plot structure. Ask students what Harry says about the goal of the humans.

Possible Response: The goal is to colonize Mars, and the humans seem to be encountering no resistance.

C Ask students what makes David uneasy.

Possible Responses: He associates the wind with the sound of Martians, and he thinks he sees them moving in the mountains.

Use **Unit Three Resource Book,** p. 72 for more practice.

Active Reading VISUALIZING

D Ask students to describe the mental images of the connection between Earth and Mars and the destruction of the rockets that the text evokes.

Possible Responses: "a silver web"; "heaps of molten girders and unsnaked wire"

Use **Unit Three Resource Book,** p. 71 for more practice.

"What's wrong?" asked his wife.

"Let's get back on the rocket."

"Go back to Earth?"

"Yes! Listen!"

The wind blew as if to flake away their identities. At any moment the Martian air might draw his soul from him, as marrow comes from a white bone. He felt submerged in a chemical that could dissolve his intellect and burn away his past.

They looked at Martian hills that time had worn with a crushing pressure of years. They saw the old cities, lost in their meadows, lying like children's delicate bones among the blowing lakes of grass.

"Chin up, Harry," said his wife. "It's too late. We've come over sixty million miles."

The children with their yellow hair hollered at the deep dome of Martian sky. There was no answer but the racing hiss of wind through the stiff grass.

He picked up the luggage in his cold hands. "Here we go," he said—a man standing on the edge of a sea, ready to wade in and be drowned.

They walked into town.

Their name was Bittering. Harry and his wife Cora; Dan, Laura, and David. They built a small white cottage and ate good breakfasts there, but the fear was never gone. It lay with Mr. Bittering and Mrs. Bittering, a third unbidden partner at every midnight talk, at every dawn awakening.

"I feel like a salt crystal," he said, "in a mountain stream, being washed away. We don't belong here. We're Earth people. This is

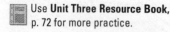

At any moment the Martian air might draw his soul from him, as marrow comes from a white bone.

Mars. It was meant for Martians. For heaven's sake, Cora, let's buy tickets for home!"

But she only shook her head. "One day the atom bomb will fix Earth. Then we'll be safe here."

"Safe and insane!"

Tick-tock, seven o'clock sang the voice-clock; *time to get up.* And they did.

Something made him check everything each morning—warm hearth, potted blood-geraniums—precisely as if he expected something to be amiss. The morning paper was toast-warm from the 6 A.M. Earth rocket. He broke its seal and tilted it at his breakfast place. He forced himself to be convivial.

"Colonial days all over again," he declared. "Why, in ten years there'll be a million Earthmen on Mars. Big cities, everything! They said we'd fail. Said the Martians would resent our invasion. But did we find any Martians? Not a living soul! Oh, we found their empty cities, but no one in them. Right?"

A river of wind submerged the house. When the windows ceased rattling Mr. Bittering swallowed and looked at the children.

"I don't know," said David. "Maybe there're Martians around we don't see. Sometimes nights I think I hear 'em. I hear the wind. The sand hits my window. I get scared. And I see those towns way up in the mountains where the Martians lived a long time ago. And I think I see things moving around those towns, Papa. And I wonder if those Martians *mind* us living here. I wonder if they won't do something to us for coming here."

WORDS
TO
KNOW
amiss (ə-mĭs′) *adj.* out of proper order; wrong

480

Teaching Options

Mini Lesson **Preteaching Vocabulary**

TEKS 6A, 6C, 9B, 9C

TAAS Reading Obj. 1

SYNONYMS

Instruction Remind students that using synonyms, words that share similar meanings, can add variety and clarity to their writing. It is important to choose the accurate synonym for the context of the original word. Using a thesaurus and a dictionary as well as considering the context will lead to the best synonym choice. Display the sentence to demonstrate how *wrong* is the best synonym for *amiss.* The man felt something was *amiss* when he stepped off the rocket.

Exercise Have students replace the underlined WORDS TO KNOW with appropriate synonyms.

1. The <u>flimsy</u> structure toppled in the winds. *(fragile)*

2. He felt his hope <u>dwindle</u> when he heard the news. *(lessen, diminish)*

3. Each day that passed made the thought of the rocket <u>recede</u> further from his mind. *(withdraw)*

4. The <u>forlorn</u> town soon deteriorated. *(deserted, abandoned)*

Use **Unit Three Resource Book,** p. 73 for more exercises.

Use **Vocabulary Transparencies and Copymasters,** p. 56, for additional support.

"Nonsense!" Mr. Bittering looked out the windows. "We're clean, decent people." He looked at his children. "All dead cities have some kind of ghosts in them. Memories, I mean." He stared at the hills. "You see a staircase and you wonder what Martians looked like climbing it. You see Martian paintings and you wonder what the painter was like. You make a little ghost in your mind, a memory. It's quite natural. Imagination." He stopped. "You haven't been prowling up in those ruins, have you?"

"No, Papa." David looked at his shoes.

"See that you stay away from them. Pass the jam."

"Just the same," said little David, "I bet something happens."

Something happened that afternoon.

Laura stumbled through the settlement, crying. She dashed blindly onto the porch.

"Mother, Father—the war, Earth!" she sobbed. "A radio flash just came. Atom bombs hit New York! All the space rockets blown up. No more rockets to Mars, ever!"

"Oh, Harry!" The mother held onto her husband and daughter.

"Are you sure, Laura?" asked the father quietly.

Laura wept. "We're stranded on Mars, forever and ever!"

For a long time there was only the sound of the wind in the late afternoon.

Alone, thought Bittering. Only a thousand of us here. No way back. No way. No way. Sweat poured from his face and his hands and his body; he was drenched in the hotness of his fear. He wanted to strike Laura, cry, "No, you're lying! The rockets will come back!" Instead, he stroked Laura's head against him and said, "The rockets will get through someday."

"Father, what will we do?"

"Go about our business, of course. Raise crops and children. Wait. Keep things going until the war ends and the rockets come again."

The two boys stepped out onto the porch.

"Children," he said, sitting there, looking beyond them, "I've something to tell you."

"We know," they said.

In the following days, Bittering wandered often through the garden to stand alone in his fear. As long as the rockets had spun a silver web across space, he had been able to accept Mars. For he had always told himself: Tomorrow, if I want, I can buy a ticket and go back to Earth.

But now: The web gone, the rockets lying in jigsaw heaps of molten girder and unsnaked wire. Earth people left to the strangeness of Mars, the cinnamon dusts and wine airs, to be baked like gingerbread shapes in Martian summers, put into harvested storage by Martian winters. What would happen to him, the others? This was the moment Mars had waited for. Now it would eat them.

He got down on his knees in the flower bed, a spade in his nervous hands. Work, he thought, work and forget.

He glanced up from the garden to the Martian mountains. He thought of the proud old Martian names that had once been on those peaks. Earthmen, dropping from the sky, had gazed upon hills, rivers, Martian seats left nameless in spite of names. Once Martians had built cities, named cities; climbed mountains, named mountains; sailed seas, named seas. Mountains melted, seas drained, cities tumbled. In spite of this, the Earthmen had felt a silent guilt at putting new names to these ancient hills and valleys.

Nevertheless, man lives by symbol and label. The names were given.

D 3

A Ask students why Harry doesn't want to be seen without his coat and tie.

Possible Responses: He feels like he is underdressed; he feels that he is giving in to his environment, lowering his standards

Literary Analysis
CIRCULAR PLOT STRUCTURE

B Ask students what kinds of names humans gave to landmarks on Mars.

Possible Response: names of famous Americans

Ask students why the humans felt they had to replace Martian names with their own choices.

Possible Response: If the humans named the mountains or valleys, they would feel like they owned them.

Literary Analysis: SYMBOL

C Ask students to interpret the symbolism of the peach tree.

Possible Responses: It is from Massachusetts and represents the settlers themselves.

D Ask students to interpret the significance of the changes in the peach tree for the Bitterings.

Possible Response: It foreshadows that the humans will change too.

Active Reading VISUALIZING

E Ask students how the author helps them to see the unusual environment of Mars.

Possible Responses: The cow is growing a third horn; the grass is purple instead of green.

The Body of a House #1 of 8 (1993), © Robert Beckmann. Oil on canvas, 69″ × 96½″. Photo by Tony Scodwell.

1 Mr. Bittering felt very alone in his garden under the Martian sun, anachronism bent here, planting Earth flowers in a wild soil.

Think. Keep thinking. Different things. Keep your mind free of Earth, the atom war, the lost rockets.

A He perspired. He glanced about. No one watching. He removed his tie. Pretty bold, he thought. First your coat off, now your tie. He hung it neatly on a peach tree he had imported as a sapling from Massachusetts.

He returned to his philosophy of names and mountains. The Earthmen had changed names. **2** Now there were Hormel Valleys, Roosevelt **B** Seas, Ford Hills, Vanderbilt Plateaus, Rockefeller Rivers, on Mars. It wasn't right. The American settlers had shown wisdom, using old Indian prairie names: Wisconsin, Minnesota, Idaho, Ohio, Utah, Milwaukee, Waukegan, Osseo. The old names, the old meanings.

Staring at the mountains wildly, he thought: Are you up there? All the dead ones, you Martians? Well, here we are, alone, cut off! Come down, move us out! We're helpless!

The wind blew a shower of peach blossoms.

He put out his sun-browned hand and gave a small cry. He touched the blossoms and picked them up. He turned them, he touched them again and again. Then he shouted for his wife.

"Cora!"

She appeared at a window. He ran to her. "Cora, these blossoms!"

Teaching Options

Mini Lesson · Viewing and Representing ⚐ TEKS 22A

The Body of a House
by Robert Beckmann

ART APPRECIATION

Instruction Tell students that the mood of a painting is created by various elements including how the objects and space are arranged and the interplay of light and shadow.

Ask students to describe the light that bathes the house.

Possible Responses: eerie, ghostly

Ask students why the house is not in the center.

Possible Response: The space on the right-hand side of the canvas emphasizes the isolation of the house and the deserted landscape that seems to stretch for miles.

Application Ask students to compare the portrayal of this house to the Bitterings' house as it is described in the story.

Possible Responses: The Bitterings' house is a white cottage, not too remote, with cultivated land around it. However, when Harry Bittering is gardening, he feels very alone and isolated from the civilization in which he has found himself. He is standing in the Martian sun, which could cast a similar glow to that seen in the picture.

She handled them.

"Do you see? They're different. They've changed! They're not peach blossoms any more!"

"Look all right to me," she said.

"They're not. They're wrong! I can't tell how. An extra petal, a leaf, something, the color, the smell!"

The children ran out in time to see their father hurrying about the garden, pulling up radishes, onions, and carrots from their beds.

"Cora, come look!"

They handled the onions, the radishes, the carrots among them.

"Do they look like carrots?"

"Yes . . . no." She hesitated. "I don't know."

"They're changed."

"Perhaps."

"You know they have! Onions but not onions, carrots but not carrots. Taste: the same but different. Smell: not like it used to be." He felt his heart pounding, and he was afraid. He dug his fingers into the earth. "Cora, what's happening? What is it? We've got to get away from this." He ran across the garden. Each tree felt his touch. "The roses. The roses. They're turning green!"

And they stood looking at the green roses.

And two days later Dan came running. "Come see the cow. I was milking her and I saw it. Come on!"

They stood in the shed and looked at their one cow.

It was growing a third horn.

And the lawn in front of their house very quietly and slowly was coloring itself like spring violets. Seed from Earth but growing up a soft purple.

"We must get away," said Bittering. "We'll eat this stuff and then we'll change—who knows to what? I can't let it happen. There's only one thing to do. Burn this food!"

"It's not poisoned."

"But it is. Subtly, very subtly. A little bit. A very little bit. We mustn't touch it."

He looked with dismay at their house. "Even the house. The wind's done something to it. The air's burned it. The fog at night. The boards, all warped out of shape. It's not an Earthman's house any more."

"Oh, your imagination!"

He put on his coat and tie. "I'm going into town. We've got to do something now. I'll be back."

"Wait, Harry!" his wife cried. But he was gone.

> "We must get away," said Bittering. "We'll eat this stuff and then we'll change—who knows to what?"

In town, on the shadowy step of the grocery store, the men sat with their hands on their knees, conversing with great leisure and ease. Mr. Bittering wanted to fire a pistol in the air.

What are you doing, you fools! he thought. Sitting here! You've heard the news—we're stranded on this planet. Well, move! Aren't you frightened? Aren't you afraid? What are you going to do?

"Hello, Harry," said everyone.

"Look," he said to them. "You did hear the news, the other day, didn't you?"

They nodded and laughed. "Sure. Sure, Harry."

"What are you going to do about it?"

"Do, Harry, do? What *can* we do?"

"Build a rocket, that's what!"

"A rocket, Harry? To go back to all that trouble? Oh, Harry!"

"But you *must* want to go back. Have you

Cross Curricular Link **Science**

LIFE ON MARS People have speculated about life on Mars for over a hundred years. The seasonal variation in the contrast between light and dark areas and the apparent presence of "canals" sparked the belief that the planet might host life in some form.

By the 1960s, technology made it possible to do more than wonder from a distance. The Mariner missions (1964–1971) closely photographed and studied the planet. The Viking probes in the mid-1970s collected surface samples, studied the composition of the atmosphere, and measured earthquake activity. It was discovered that there were no canals, but there was evidence of surface water. A human mission to Mars is anticipated for 2018.

Meanwhile, the news that a meteorite found in Antarctica in 1984 might contain the remains of Martian microbes has reawakened debate about the possibility of life on Mars. Most scientists agree that the rock came from Mars about 13,000 years ago, but not all are convinced that the meteorite proves the existence of life on Mars.

Reading and Analyzing

Literary Analysis: CONFLICT

(A) Ask students to identify the kinds of conflict Harry is experiencing.
Possible Responses: external–he is struggling to make the men help him; internal–he is fearful about what is happening to him and the others

Literary Analysis: SCIENCE FICTION

(B) Remind students that science fiction takes place in a futuristic world. Ask them what they would infer about the Mars of the future from what they have been told so far about life on the planet.
Possible Responses: It has an atmosphere like Earth's and the capacity to support life; electricity and all the conveniences of home are obtainable; it can be reached easily from Earth by rocket.

Reading Skills and Strategies: ANALYZING

(C) Ask students why Harry won't eat anything that is grown in their garden.
Possible Response: He believes it will contribute to his change.

Active Reading VISUALIZING

(D) Ask students to describe the changes in Harry's family.
Possible Responses: His wife is very dark and has golden eyes. His children are described as *metallic*.

Reading Skills and Strategies: MAKING INFERENCES

(E) Ask students what can be inferred from Harry's action of eating the sandwich.
Possible Responses: Harry would rather change than die; he is starting to accept that he will become different.

---

noticed the peach blossoms, the onions, the grass?"

"Why, yes, Harry, seems we did," said one of the men.

"Doesn't it scare you?"

"Can't recall that it did much, Harry."

"Idiots!"

"Now, Harry."

(A) Bittering wanted to cry. "You've got to work with me. If we stay here, we'll all change. The air. Don't you smell it? Something in the air. A Martian virus, maybe; some seed, or a pollen. Listen to me!"

They stared at him.

"Sam," he said to one of them.

"Yes, Harry?"

"Will you help me build a rocket?"

(B) "Harry, I got a whole load of metal and some blueprints. You want to work in my metal shop on a rocket, you're welcome. I'll sell you that metal for five hundred dollars. You should be able to construct a right pretty rocket, if you work alone, in about thirty years."

Everyone laughed.

"Don't laugh."

Sam looked at him with quiet good humor.

"Sam," Bittering said. "Your eyes—"

"What about them, Harry?"

"Didn't they used to be gray?"

"Well now, I don't remember."

"They were, weren't they?"

"Why do you ask, Harry?"

"Because now they're kind of yellow-colored."

"Is that so, Harry?" Sam said, casually.

"And you're taller and thinner—"

"You might be right, Harry."

"Sam, you shouldn't have yellow eyes."

"Harry, what color eyes have *you* got?" Sam said.

"My eyes? They're blue, of course."

"Here you are, Harry." Sam handed him a pocket mirror. "Take a look at yourself."

Mr. Bittering hesitated, and then raised the mirror to his face.

There were little, very dim flecks of new gold captured in the blue of his eyes.

"Now look what you've done," said Sam a moment later. "You've broken my mirror."

Harry Bittering moved into the metal shop and began to build the rocket. Men stood in the open door and talked and joked without raising their voices. Once in a while they gave him a hand on lifting something. But mostly they just idled and watched him with their yellowing eyes.

"It's suppertime, Harry," they said.

His wife appeared with his supper in a wicker basket.

"I won't touch it," he said. "I'll eat only food from our Deepfreeze. Food that came from Earth. Nothing from our garden."

His wife stood watching him. "You can't build a rocket."

"I worked in a shop once, when I was twenty. I know metal. Once I get it started, the others will help," he said, not looking at her, laying out the blueprints.

"Harry, Harry," she said, helplessly.

"We've *got* to get away, Cora. We've got to!"

The nights were full of wind that blew down the empty moonlit sea meadows past the little white chess cities lying for their twelve-thousandth year in the shallows. In the Earthmen's settlement, the Bittering house shook with a feeling of change.

Lying abed, Mr. Bittering felt his bones shifted, shaped, melted like gold. His wife, lying beside him, was dark from many sunny

---

Teaching Options

   Grammar   ★ TEKS 17D   ★ TAAS Writing Obj. 3, 4, 6

TIME ORDER

Instruction Remind students to use time order transitions to indicate the relationship in time that exists between events. Transitions such as *before, then, after, first,* etc. help to clarify the sequence of events. Point out the highlighted passage and ask students to identify the transitions that link Harry's actions.

Exercise Have students fill in the appropriate time order transitions to complete each sentence.

1. _____ Harry sees himself, he drops the mirror. *(after)*

2. _____ he hears the news about the rockets, he feels that he can leave Mars at any time. *(before)*

3. He sees the plants are changing, and _____ he begins to build a rocket. *(then)*

4. He tries to be cheerful _____ breakfast. *(during)*

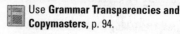 Use **Grammar Transparencies and Copymasters,** p. 94.

 Use McDougal Littell's *Language Network,* Chapter 6, for more instruction and practice in time order transitions.

afternoons. Dark she was, and golden-eyed, burnt almost black by the sun, sleeping, and the children metallic in their beds, and the wind roaring <u>forlorn</u> and changing through the old peach trees, the violet grass, shaking out green rose petals.

The fear would not be stopped. It had his throat and heart. It dripped in a wetness of the arm and the temple and the trembling palm.

A green star rose in the east.

A strange word emerged from Mr. Bittering's lips.

"Iorrt. Iorrt." He repeated it.

It was a Martian word. He knew no Martian.

In the middle of the night he arose and dialed a call through to Simpson, the archaeologist.

"Simpson, what does the word *Iorrt* mean?"

"Why that's the old Martian word for our planet Earth. Why?"

"No special reason."

The telephone slipped from his hand.

"Hello, hello, hello, hello," it kept saying while he sat gazing out at the green star. "Bittering? Harry, are you there?"

The days were full of metal sound. He laid the frame of the rocket with the reluctant help of three indifferent men. He grew very tired in an hour or so and had to sit down.

"The altitude," laughed a man.

"Are you *eating*, Harry?" asked another.

"I'm eating," he said, angrily.

"From your Deepfreeze?"

"Yes!"

"You're getting thinner, Harry."

"I'm not!"

"And taller."

"Liar!"

A strange word emerged from Mr. Bittering's lips. "Iorrt. Iorrt."

His wife took him aside a few days later. "Harry, I've used up all the food in the Deepfreeze. There's nothing left. I'll have to make sandwiches using food grown on Mars."

He sat down heavily.

"You must eat," she said. "You're weak."

"Yes," he said.

He took a sandwich, opened it, looked at it, and began to nibble at it.

"And take the rest of the day off," she said. "It's hot. The children want to swim in the canals and hike. Please come along."

"I can't waste time. This is a crisis!"

"Just for an hour," she urged. "A swim'll do you good."

He rose, sweating. "All right, all right. Leave me alone. I'll come."

"Good for you, Harry."

The sun was hot, the day quiet. There was only an immense staring burn upon the land. They moved along the canal, the father, the mother, the racing children in their swimsuits. They stopped and ate meat sandwiches. He saw their skin baking brown. And he saw the yellow eyes of his wife and his children, their eyes that were never yellow before. A few tremblings shook him, but were carried off in waves of pleasant heat as he lay in the sun. He was too tired to be afraid.

"Cora, how long have your eyes been yellow?"

She was bewildered. "Always, I guess."

"They didn't change from brown in the last three months?"

She bit her lips. "No. Why do you ask?"

"Never mind."

They sat there.

WORDS TO KNOW   **forlorn** (fôr-lôrn') *adj.* a sense of aloneness and sadness

485

 Assessment Standardized Test Practice **TEKS 10H, 10K**  **TAAS Reading Obj. 5**

MAKING INFERENCES For some standardized tests, students will be asked to make inferences, based on the information that has been provided and their own knowledge. To provide students with some help in making inferences, read aloud or write on the board the following statement: Harry Bittering is most fearful of —

A. never seeing Earth again.

B. not getting his rocket built.

C. losing his identity as a human.

D. having gold eyes and dark skin.

Guide students through the process of choosing the correct answer. A, B, and D are incorrect. Harry is fearful that he won't get his rocket built or see Earth again because both are results of the real source of fear, which is that he is becoming Martian and losing his identity. He is not frightened of the physical characteristics of a Martian, just what they represent as a loss of his human nature. Therefore, C is the true source of his fear from which his other anxieties stem.

A Ask students to explain Harry Bittering's comment that he and his wife are children.

Possible Response: The Martian landscape is recreating them as Martians, but the process is not yet complete.

Active Reading | VISUALIZING |

B Have students close their eyes while you read this passage aloud. Ask them what the colorful images suggest about Harry's attitude toward change.

Possible Responses: He is starting to see change as positive; he is no longer as resistant to it; he recognizes that it is natural.

Reading Skills and Strategies:
MAKING INFERENCES

C Ask students what Harry Bittering suddenly realizes.

Possible Response: Not even his family wishes to return home.

Ask students what this realization might do to his urgency to return to Earth.

Possible Responses: He might become more determined before it is too late to save his family or his urgency may decrease.

Reading Skills and Strategies:
COMPARING AND CONTRASTING

D Ask students how the Martian villa compares with the house in the valley.

Possible Response: The villa and its location seem much cooler and more beautiful than the house in town.

Illustration by Tom Curry.

    "The children's eyes," he said. "They're yellow, too."

    "Sometimes growing children's eyes change color."

A   "Maybe *we're* children, too. At least to Mars. That's a thought." He laughed. "Think I'll swim."

    They leaped into the canal water, and he let himself sink down and down to the bottom like a golden statue and lie there in green silence. All was water-quiet and deep, all was peace. He felt the steady, slow current drift him easily.

    If I lie here long enough, he thought, the

Teaching Options

 Viewing and Representing **TEKS 22A**

Illustration
by Tom Curry

ART APPRECIATION

Instruction Tell students that people often study a work of art or look at it more than once to be sure they have seen all of the details. Ask students which details they didn't notice when they first looked at this illustration.

Possible Responses: The ear is on the left side; the nostril is on the left side; there are differences in shading and color between the two sides

Ask students which element of the illustration drew their attention immediately.

Possible Response: the eyes

Ask students to interpret the illustration.

Possible Response: It is showing the gradual process of change that occurs within a person or the fact that one person may have different sides.

Application Ask students how this illustration relates to Harry Bittering's experience.

Possible Response: The life around him, as well as Harry himself, is changing subtly. At a glance, people may look the same, but they are different. The eyes alter most noticeably in the humans as they are transformed into Martians.

ater will work and eat away my flesh until
e bones show like coral. Just my skeleton
ft. And then the water can build on that
keleton—green things, deep water things, red
ings, yellow things. Change. Change. Slow,
eep, silent change. And isn't that what it is
p there?

He saw the sky submerged above him, the
n made Martian by atmosphere and time
nd space.

Up there, a big river, he thought, a Martian
ver; all of us lying deep in it, in our pebble
ouses, in our sunken boulder houses, like
ayfish hidden, and the water washing away
ur old bodies and lengthening the bones
nd—

He let himself drift up through the soft light.

Dan sat on the edge of the canal, regarding
is father seriously.

"*Utha*," he said.

"What?" asked his father.

The boy smiled. "You know. *Utha*'s the
Martian word for 'father.'"

"Where did you learn it?"

"I don't know. Around. *Utha!*"

"What do you want?"

The boy hesitated. "I—I want to change
y name."

"Change it?"

"Yes."

His mother swam over. "What's wrong with
Dan for a name?"

Dan fidgeted. "The other day you called
Dan, Dan, Dan. I didn't even hear. I said to
myself, That's not my name. I've a new name
want to use."

Mr. Bittering held to the side of the canal,
is body cold and his heart pounding slowly.
What is this new name?"

"Linnl. Isn't that a good name? Can I use it?
Can't I, please?"

Mr. Bittering put his hand to his head. He
thought of the silly rocket, himself working
alone, himself alone even among his family,
so alone.

He heard his wife say, "Why not?"

He heard himself say, "Yes, you can use it."

"Yaaa!" screamed the boy. "I'm Linnl,
Linnl!"

Racing down the meadowlands, he danced
and shouted.

Mr. Bittering looked at his wife. "Why did
we do that?"

"I don't know," she said. "It just seemed
like a good idea."

They walked into the hills. They strolled on
old mosaic paths, beside still pumping
fountains. The paths were covered with a thin
film of cool water all summer long. You kept
your bare feet cool all the day, splashing as in
a creek, wading.

They came to a small deserted Martian villa
with a good view of the valley. It was on top
of a hill. Blue marble halls, large murals, a
swimming pool. It was refreshing in this hot
summertime. The Martians hadn't believed
in large cities.

"How nice," said Mrs. Bittering, "if we
could move up here to this villa for the
summer."

"Come on," he said. "We're going back to
town. There's work to be done on the rocket."

But as he worked that night, the thought
of the cool blue marble villa entered his mind.
As the hours passed, the rocket seemed less
important.

In the flow of days and weeks, the rocket
receded and dwindled. The old fever was gone.
It frightened him to think he had let it slip this
way. But somehow the heat, the air, the
working conditions—

WORDS
TO
KNOW

recede (rĭ-sēd′) *v.* to become fainter and more distant
dwindle (dwĭn′dl) *v.* to become less, until little remains

487

Mini Lesson **Vocabulary Strategy**

WORD USAGE

Instruction Tell students that examining the ending or suffix of an unfamiliar word might help them to recognize how it is used in a sentence and what it means. Display the following suffixes and the parts of speech they create:

ous, al, ic, ant   adjectives
ment, ness, ic   nouns
ly   adverbs

Exercises Have students identify the part of speech of each underlined word and define the word, based on its role in the sentence.

Have students check their definitions by consulting a dictionary.

1. They admired the ancient Martian mosaic. *(noun)*
2. The other Martians were convivial and welcomed the newcomers. *(adjective)*
3. He felt himself changing subtly, a little at a time. *(adverb)*
4. The men were reluctant to help Harry. *(adjective)*

Use **Vocabulary Transparencies and Copymasters**, p. 57.

Reading and Analyzing

Literary Analysis: CONFLICT

A Explain the source of Harry's conflict.
Possible Response: Part of him is willing to stop working on the rocket until autumn, but the other part of him resists the idea, knowing that he will never return to it if he leaves it now.

Literary Analysis

CIRCULAR PLOT STRUCTURE

B Ask students to recall what David sees in the mountains soon after their arrival on Mars.
Answer: He sees the Martians moving around in the old villas.
Ask students who had originally changed the old Martian names.
Answer: the human colonists

Literary Analysis: CHARACTER

C Ask students what Harry would have thought about taking the furniture and encyclopedia a few weeks before this.
Possible Response: He would never have left them behind.
What is revealed by his attitude?
Possible Response: He has become less attached to earthly possessions.

Literary Analysis: SYMBOL

D Ask students to interpret the symbolism of the house.
Possible Response: It represents his human identity and life.

Literary Analysis: IRONY

E Ask students to explain the irony of Mr. and Mrs. Bittering's comments.
Possible Responses: They once admired their house and were humans. They used to think Martians were alien; now they think humans are alien.

Skater (1956), Giacomo Manzu. Bronze, 80″ × 17⅛″. Hirshhorn Museum and Sculpture Garden, Smithsonian Institution, gift of Joseph H. Hirshhorn, 1966. Photography by Lee Stalsworth.

488 UNIT THREE **AUTHOR STUDY**

He heard the men murmuring on the porch of his metal shop.

"Everyone's going. You heard?"

"All going. That's right."

Bittering came out. "Going where?" He saw a couple of trucks, loaded with children and furniture, drive down the dusty street.

"Up to the villas," said the man.

"Yeah, Harry. I'm going. So is Sam. Aren't you Sam?"

"That's right, Harry. What about you?"

"I've got work to do here."

"Work! You can finish that rocket in the autumn, when it's cooler."

He took a breath. "I got the frame all set up."

"In the autumn is better." Their voices were lazy in the heat.

"Got to work," he said.

"Autumn," they reasoned. And they sounded so sensible, so right.

"Autumn would be best," he thought. "Plenty of time, then."

No! cried part of himself, deep down, put away, locked tight, suffocating. No! No!

"In the autumn," he said.

"Come on, Harry," they all said.

"Yes," he said, feeling his flesh melt in the hot liquid air. "Yes, in the autumn. I'll begin work again then."

"I got a villa near the Tirra Canal," said someone.

"You mean the Roosevelt Canal, don't you?"

"Tirra. The old Martian name."

"But on the map—"

"Forget the map. It's Tirra now. Now I found a place in the Pillan Mountains—"

"You mean the Rockefeller Range," said Bittering.

"I mean the Pillan Mountains," said Sam.

"Yes," said Bittering, buried in the hot, swarming air. "The Pillan Mountains."

Everyone worked at loading the truck in the hot, still afternoon of the next day.

Teaching Options

TRANSITIONAL EXPRESSIONS

Instruction Tell students to use transitions such as *like, as,* and *similarly* to introduce points of comparison and to use transitions such as *unlike, but,* and *nevertheless* to introduce differences. Display the following example: **Like** the people who arrived five years earlier, the rescuers plan to settle Mars. They thought they would return. **But** they never did. Explain to students that they can show that a cause-and-effect relationship exists between details by using words such as *consequently*

Mini Lesson **Grammar**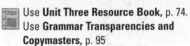

and *as a result.* Display the following example: People did not know what to expect. **Consequently,** they were unprepared.

Exercise Have students fill in the appropriate transitions.

1. The Bittering family traveled to Mars. _____, another family traveled to Mars. *(Similarly)*

2. The war destroyed rockets from Earth. _____, the people on Mars were completely cut off from Earth. *(Consequently, As a result)*

3. _____ the others, Harry is at first interested in building a new rocket. *(Unlike)*

4. They expected to find a human settlement. _____ they found only Martians. *(But, Nevertheless)*

Use **Unit Three Resource Book**, p. 74.
Use **Grammar Transparencies and Copymasters**, p. 95

 Use McDougal Littell's *Language Network,* Chapter 6, for more instruction and practice in transitional expressions.

Laura, Dan, and David carried packages. Or, as they preferred to be known, Ttil, Linnl, and Werr carried packages.

The furniture was abandoned in the little white cottage.

"It looked just fine in Boston," said the mother. "And here in the cottage. But up at the villa? No. We'll get it when we come back in the autumn."

Bittering himself was quiet.

"I've some ideas on furniture for the villa," he said after a time. "Big, lazy furniture."

"What about your encyclopedia? You're taking it along, surely?"

Mr. Bittering glanced away. "I'll come and get it next week."

They turned to their daughter. "What about your New York dresses?"

The bewildered girl stared. "Why, I don't want them any more."

They shut off the gas, the water, they locked the doors and walked away. Father peered into the truck.

"Gosh, we're not taking much," he said. "Considering all we brought to Mars, this is only a handful!"

He started the truck.

Looking at the small white cottage for a long moment, he was filled with a desire to rush to it, touch it, say good-bye to it, for he felt as if he were going away on a long journey, leaving something to which he could never quite return, never understand again.

Just then Sam and his family drove by in another truck.

"Hi, Bittering! Here we go!"

The truck swung down the ancient highway out of town. There were sixty others traveling in the same direction. The town filled with a silent, heavy dust from their passage. The canal waters lay blue in the sun, and a quiet wind moved in the strange trees.

"Good-bye, town!" said Mr. Bittering.

"Good-bye, good-bye," said the family, waving to it.

They did not look back again.

Summer burned the canals dry. Summer moved like flame upon the meadows. In the empty Earth settlement, the painted houses flaked and peeled. Rubber tires upon which children had swung in back yards hung suspended like stopped clock pendulums in the blazing air.

At the metal shop, the rocket frame began to rust.

In the quiet autumn Mr. Bittering stood, very dark now, very golden-eyed, upon the slope above his villa, looking at the valley.

"It's time to go back," said Cora.

"Yes, but we're not going," he said quietly. "There's nothing there any more."

"Your books," she said. "Your fine clothes."

"Your *llles* and your fine *ior uele rre*," she said.

"The town's empty. No one's going back," he said. "There's no reason to, none at all."

The daughter wove tapestries and the sons played songs on ancient flutes and pipes, their laughter echoing in the marble villa.

Mr. Bittering gazed at the Earth settlement far away in the low valley. "Such odd, such ridiculous houses the Earth people built."

 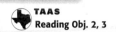

"They didn't know any better," his wife mused. "Such ugly people. I'm glad they've gone."

They both looked at each other, startled by all they had just finished saying. They laughed.

"Such odd, such ridiculous houses the Earth people built."

Customizing Instruction

Less Proficient Readers
Ask students what happens to Harry Bittering's rocket.
Answer: It is unfinished and has been left rusting in the town.
Ask students where the townspeople are.
Answer: They are in the mountains.
Set a Purpose As students finish reading the story, ask them to pay attention to what the rescuers think and do when they arrive on Mars.

Students Acquiring English
1 Point out the use of Martian words in Mrs. Bittering's conversation. She is starting to mix the English and Martian languages as she becomes more and more Martian.

Gifted and Talented
Have students discuss Ray Bradbury's portrayal of life for the Martians in contrast to the lives of humans. Ask students what themes they can take from this contrast.
Possible Responses: Students will see that the Martians' lifestyle is portrayed more positively. Time, material possessions, the need to work, and even their earthly bodies become less important or of no importance. One interpretation might be that humans are too weighed down with the nonessential things of life.

☑ **Assessment Standardized Test Practice** 🏴 **TEKS 10F, 10K** 🏴 **TAAS Reading Obj. 2, 3**

IMPLIED MAIN IDEA For some standardized tests, students will be asked to identify the implied main idea of a passage. To provide students with some help in choosing the main idea, read aloud or write on the board the following question: What is the implied main idea of the conversation on page 489 between Mr. Bittering and his wife as they look down on the valley?
A. It is still too hot to return to the valley.
B. They no longer like the style of their house in the valley.

C. They think that humans are ugly.
D. They have no desire to resume human existence.
Guide students through the process of choosing the best implied main idea. A is incorrect. It is now autumn, not summer. B is incorrect because it is based on one comment. C is incorrect. While it is true that the Bitterings say this about the humans, it does not express the main idea of their entire exchange. D is correct. Their remarks develop the main idea that they are happy in their lives and have no desire to return.

Literary Analysis: SCIENCE FICTION

(A) Ask students to identify realistic and unrealistic elements of the Martians.

Possible Responses: They retain a human appearance with some differences in coloring and stature; they communicate with speech; they enjoy human activities. However, they appear to be ageless, and the transformation is unrealistic.

Literary Analysis: SYMBOL

(B) Ask students to interpret the symbolism of the wind throughout the story.

Possible Response: the force of change

Literary Analysis

CIRCULAR PLOT STRUCTURE

(C) Ask students how the captain's reaction to the wind is similar to the way Harry Bittering reacted.

Answer: They both shivered.

What might this reaction foreshadow?

Answer: The captain will resist change as Harry did.

(D) Ask students what is significant about the captain's desire to rename the Martian landmarks.

Answer: He is trying to establish ownership, just as the other humans did.

(E) Ask students what keeps distracting the lieutenant.

Answer: He keeps looking at the hills.

Reading Skills and Strategies: MAKING INFERENCES

(F) Ask students whether the captain or the lieutenant will give in to the Martian influence first and why.

Possible Response: The lieutenant will give in first. He already admires the Martians.

(A)

"Where did they go?" he wondered. He glanced at his wife. She was golden and slender as his daughter. She looked at him, and he seemed almost as young as their eldest son.

"I don't know," she said.

"We'll go back to town maybe next year, or the year after, or the year after that," he said, calmly. "Now—I'm warm. How about taking a swim?"

They turned their backs to the valley. Arm in arm they walked silently down a path of clear-running spring water.

Five years later a rocket fell out of the sky. It lay steaming in the valley. Men leaped out of it, shouting.

"We won the war on Earth! We're here to rescue you! Hey!"

But the American-built town of cottages, peach trees, and theaters was silent. They found a <u>flimsy</u> rocket frame rusting in an empty shop.

The rocket men searched the hills. The captain established headquarters in an abandoned bar. His lieutenant came back to report.

"The town's empty, but we found native life in the hills, sir. Dark people. Yellow eyes. Martians. Very friendly. We talked a bit, not much. They learn English fast. I'm sure our relations will be most friendly with them, sir."

"Dark, eh?" mused the captain. "How many?"

"Six, eight hundred, I'd say, living in those marble ruins in the hills, sir. Tall, healthy. Beautiful women."

"Did they tell you what became of the men and women who built this Earth settlement, Lieutenant?"

"They hadn't the foggiest notion of what happened to this town or its people."

"Strange. You think those Martians killed them?"

"They look surprisingly peaceful. Chances are a plague did this town in, sir."

"Perhaps. I suppose this is one of those mysteries we'll never solve. One of those mysteries you read about."

The captain looked at the room, the dusty windows, the blue mountains rising beyond, the canals moving in the light, and he heard the soft wind in the air. He shivered. Then, recovering, he tapped a large fresh map he had thumbtacked to the top of an empty table.

"Lots to be done, Lieutenant." His voice droned on and quietly on as the sun sank behind the blue hills. "New settlements. Mining sites, minerals to be looked for. Bacteriological specimens taken. The work, all the work. And the old records were lost. We'll have a job of remapping to do, renaming the mountains and rivers and such. Calls for a little imagination.

"What do you think of naming those mountains the Lincoln Mountains, this canal the Washington Canal, those hills—we can name those hills for you, Lieutenant. Diplomacy. And you, for a favor, might name a town for me. Polishing the apple. And why not make this the Einstein Valley, and farther over . . . are you *listening*, Lieutenant?"

The lieutenant snapped his gaze from the blue color and the quiet mist of the hills far beyond the town.

"What? Oh, *yes,* sir!" ❖

WORDS
TO
KNOW

flimsy (flĭm'zē) *adj.* not solid or strong

490

Thinking through the LITERATURE

Connect to the Literature

1. What Do You Think? What was your reaction to the changes that took place in the colonists from Earth?

Comprehension Check
- Why did the Bitterings settle on Mars?
- Why did the rockets from Earth stop coming to Mars?
- What details tell you that the Bitterings have become more Martian than human?

Think Critically

2. In your opinion, what is the significance of the physical and psychological changes that take place in the Bitterings?

3. What do you think happened to the original inhabitants of Mars? What do you think will happen to the Bitterings?

4. Does the character of Harry Bittering make the story more or less believable?

 THINK ABOUT
- how he deals with his own fears in comparison to Cora's fear of nuclear war
- how he reacts to the children's new names
- how he copes with the changes within himself

5. **ACTIVE READING** **VISUALIZING** Look back at your **READER'S NOTEBOOK**. Which of the descriptions you recorded creates the most vivid picture in your mind? What phrases help you to visualize that scene?

6. The lieutenant likes the Martian landscape. What could you predict from that information?

7. What do you think the relationship between the Bitterings and the newcomers will be? Explain.

Extend Interpretations

8. Critic's Corner One critic said that Bradbury's stories are "of people, real and honest and true in their understanding of human nature. . . ." Do you agree? Cite details from the story to support your answer.

9. Connect to Life How do you think you would react if you were in the Bittering's situation? Explain your answer.

Literary Analysis

 CIRCULAR PLOT STRUCTURE
Some story plots can be called circular because their endings repeat details and events from their beginnings. At the beginning of this selection, the new colonists from Earth, the Bitterings, find themselves in a place they think has been deserted by its former inhabitants. At the end of the story, the Bitterings have retreated to the mountains just as they believe the original Martians had done before them, and a new set of colonists from Earth arrives. Events at the end of the story repeat events at the beginning.

Paired Activity Reread the story, paying attention to the changes that the colonists go through. With a partner, create a circular **story map** to plot the major events. Include as many events as you think important. How are the beginning and the ending of the story similar? What do you predict will happen to the second group of colonists? Why?

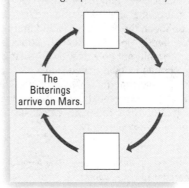

The Bitterings arrive on Mars.

DARK THEY WERE, AND GOLDEN-EYED **491**

Extend Interpretations

8. Critic's Corner Possible Responses: Most students will agree that Harry and his family are very realistic in their behavior, interactions, and reactions. Harry feels fear at the strange circumstances and frustration at the lack of understanding of the other men, and he cares for his family enough to accept their change.

9. Connect to Life Possible Responses: Some might say they would react more violently and insist that their family leave immediately; others might say that they would accept what was happening to them.

Connect to the Literature

1. Possible Responses: Responses will vary. They should have been more dramatic; the gradual changes in the human form were suspenseful and convincing.

Comprehension Check
- to escape predicted atomic war on Earth
- New York and the rockets are destroyed by atomic bombs.
- details about their appearance and the way they talk about humans

Use Selection Quiz **Unit Three Resource Book**, p. 76.

Think Critically

2. Possible Responses: Things of Earth become less important; their earthly qualities and values diminish.

3. Possible Responses: They are still there but no longer visible. The Bitterings will, in time, become one with the landscape and atmosphere.

4. Possible Responses: The character of Harry makes the story more believable because of the way he deals with his family and his own conflict. He gives in when he realizes that he might lose his family.

5. Possible Responses: Responses will vary. Some students may cite the descriptions of the setting or the characters or Harry's thoughts.

Use **Reading and Critical Thinking Transparencies,** p. 10, for additional support.

6. Possible Responses: He won't resist the changes.

7. Possible Responses: The Martians are described as friendly. They will probably have minimal contact with the newcomers because they do not need humans for anything.

Literary Analysis

Circular Plot Structure Some important events are: settlement of the town; changes in earthly life forms; destruction of rockets; Harry's attempt to build one; Bitterings' move to the hills; transformation into Martians.

The new colonists will become Martians. They rename the landmarks, and set up towns.

Use **Literary Analysis Transparencies,** p. 12, for additional support.

OVERVIEW

Objectives
1. understand and appreciate **theme** in a **modern fable** (Literary Analysis)
2. **connect** with other texts (fables) (Active Reading)

Summary
The Mandarin is in despair to hear that the town of Kwan-Si has built a wall in the shape of a pig. His wall is in the shape of an orange, easily devoured by a pig, and he worries that evil will come to his city. His daughter advises him to tell the stonemasons to rebuild the wall in the shape of a club to beat the pig and drive it off. The problem seems solved until Kwan-Si's wall becomes flames to destroy the club. The Mandarin changes the shape of his town's wall in response to each new design of Kwan-Si's. By the middle of the summer, the people of both towns are starving and sick because the harvests and businesses have been neglected. Finally, the daughter weakly whispers to send for the Mandarin of Kwan-Si. She shows both men the kites flying in the wind. The daughter points out that without wind, the kite stays on the ground, and without kites, the sky and wind are not beautiful. She proposes that Kwan-Si's wall become the wind and her father's, a golden kite. Together they will give meaning to the other and restore harmony.

Thematic Link
Out of fantastic tales, such as "The Golden Kite, the Silver Wind," come meaningful lessons.

5-Minute Warm-Up

Daily Language SkillBuilder   **TEKS 16B**

Have students **proofread** the display sentences on page 341k and write them correctly. The sentences also appear on Transparency 16 of Grammar Transparencies and Copymasters.

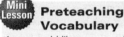 **Preteaching Vocabulary**

If you would like to preteach the WORDS TO KNOW for this selection, use the Mini Lesson, p. 495.

The Golden Kite, the Silver Wind

Short Story by RAY BRADBURY

"I will whisper from behind the silken screen and you will know the words."

Connect to Your Life

Deadlock Have you ever found yourself facing a problem for which there seemed to be no good solution? How did you resolve the problem? Did someone give you helpful advice? With a small group of classmates, discuss your experiences.

Build Background

CONNECT TO HISTORY   The Cold War was a period of strained relations between the Western powers and the communist bloc, following the end of World War II and lasting until 1989. During this time, the West felt threatened by the expansionist policy of the Soviet Union, and the Soviet Union feared incursions by the West.

An aspect of the Cold War was the arms race. Each side tried to protect itself by creating weapons that could match or surpass in destructiveness the weapons created by the other side. The result was that both sides possessed an arsenal of weapons capable of destroying life on Earth several times over. This policy, called "mutually assured destruction," ensured that if either side decided to attack its opponent, the opponent would immediately respond in kind. Therefore, an attack by one side would not only destroy its enemy but guarantee its own destruction.

The fear that the Cold War would turn into a "hot" war was real and was the inspiration for a great number of literary works, including many by Ray Bradbury.

> WORDS TO KNOW **Vocabulary Preview**
> acclaimed   quench   spurn
> pandemonium   ravenous

Focus Your Reading

LITERARY ANALYSIS **THEME**   A **theme** is a central idea or message in a work of literature. "The Golden Kite, the Silver Wind" is a **modern fable**, a type of fiction that usually has a message. One way to discover the theme of a work is to think about what happens to the central characters. The importance of these events, stated in terms that apply to all human beings, is the theme.

ACTIVE READING **CONNECT WITH OTHER STORIES** Active readers seek to **connect** the work they are reading with others they have already read. This enriches their reading and helps them to better understand both the work they are reading and others that they have read. Think of Dorothy West's modern fable "The Richer, the Poorer" (page 316). What characteristics does it have in common with "The Golden Kite, the Silver Wind"?

 READER'S NOTEBOOK As you read, jot down similarities that you find between "The Golden Kite, the Silver Wind" and "The Richer, the Poorer." Think about the characters and the theme of each work.

TEKS   See the Skills Trace at the beginning of the unit for information on TEKS covered in this lesson.

LESSON RESOURCES

UNIT THREE RESOURCE BOOK, pp. 77–83

ASSESSMENT
Formal Assessment, pp. 77–78
Teacher's Guide to Assessment and Portfolio Use
Test Generator

SKILLS TRANSPARENCIES AND COPYMASTERS
Literary Analysis
• Theme, TR 7 (for Cooperative Learning Activity, p. 498)
Reading and Critical Thinking
• Connecting TR 2 (for Thinking Through the Literature, p. 498)

Grammar
• Using Essential and Nonessential Modifiers, CM 87 (for Mini Lesson, p. 499)
Vocabulary
• Context Clues: Restatement, CM 58 (for Mini Lesson, p. 495)

Communications
• Persuasive Techniques, TR3 (for Mini Lesson, p. 497)

INTEGRATED TECHNOLOGY Audio Library

Visit our website:
www.mcdougallittell.com

The Golden Kite, the Silver Wind

by Ray Bradbury

The Yueh-Yang Tower, Hsia Yung (Yuan Dynasty).
Courtesy of the Freer Gallery of Art, Smithsonian
Institution, Washington, D.C. (F1915.36i)

Less Proficient Readers
Tell students that the culture in which Bradbury sets his story relied heavily on interpretation of signs of good and bad luck, prosperity and evil. Ask students for signs that they associate with good or bad luck.

Set a Purpose Have students read to find out why the Mandarin is upset about Kwan-Si's wall and what he does about it.

Gifted and Talented
Ask students to think about what the point of view contributes to the story. Have students discuss how the story would have been affected if the daughter had narrated events in the first person.

Possible Responses: The focus would have shifted to her, making her character more significant, events less important; in turn, the theme would have been altered; the story would have seemed less like a fable.

"In the shape of a pig?" cried the Mandarin.

"In the shape of a pig," said the messenger, and departed.

"Oh, what an evil day in an evil year," cried the Mandarin. "The town of Kwan-Si, beyond the hill, was very small in my childhood. Now it has grown so large that at last they are building a wall."

"But why should a wall two miles away make my good father sad and angry all within the hour?" asked his daughter quietly.

 Viewing and Representing   **TEKS 22A**

The Yueh-Yang Tower, by Hsia Yung
ART APPRECIATION
Instruction Encourage students to notice the wealth of detail executed in fine brushstrokes. Point out to students that the thickness of the lines varies to create dimension and perspective. Ask students what impression of the mountains on the right is given and how this is achieved.
Possible Response: They are quite distant and appear to be rising out of the mist. This effect is created by only painting the tops of the mountains and omitting all detail below.

Ask students what details other than technique would identify this painting as Asian.
Possible Responses: the calligraphy in the top right corner; the shape of the buildings' roofs; the attire of the figures
Application As they read, have students consider how the Mandarin's wall is similar to or different from the wall pictured here.
Possible Response: The wall is around the town. The town is not built on it unlike the town in the painting.

Reading Skills and Strategies:
CAUSE AND EFFECT

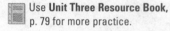 Ask students why the Mandarin fears Kwan-Si's wall.

Possible Response: The wall will attract travelers and merchants, and evil will fall upon the Mandarin's city.

Ask students how the Mandarin responds to Kwan-Si's wall.

Possible Response: He builds a wall shaped like a club.

Literary Analysis THEME

B Remind students that the theme of a modern fable is inferred from its elements. Ask students to interpret the symbolism of the walls.

Possible Responses: power, supremacy

Ask students what theme can be seen in the effort that it takes to build new city walls.

Possible Response: Maintaining a position of power is not easy.

 Use **Unit Three Resource Book,** p. 79 for more practice.

Active Reading CONNECT WITH OTHER STORIES

C Ask students to think back to "The Richer, the Poorer." Ask them what Lottie first thinks she will do with her money and what she actually does. Have them use Lottie's situation to offer observations about the Mandarin's.

Possible Response: Lottie initially saves for specific goals. But she could never save enough. The Mandarin thinks his problem is solved. However, he may find that one wall is not enough.

Use **Unit Three Resource Book,** p. 78 for more practice.

Painting by Nancy Ekholm Burkert (detail

 UNIT THREE AUTHOR STUDY

Teaching Options

 Viewing and Representing TEKS 22A

Painting by Nancy Ekholm Burkert
ART APPRECIATION

Instruction Tell students that the composition of a painting is the way the figures, objects, and space are arranged on the canvas. Ask students why they think the artist placed the flowering tree at the forefront of the picture.

Possible Response: The viewer sees it first and focuses on its details before noticing the figure at the side.

Ask students what idea of the painting is enhanced by this arrangement of elements.

Possible Response: Because the woman initially goes unnoticed, the impression that she is concealing herself or trying to be ignored is reinforced.

Application Ask students how this woman suggests the Mandarin's daughter.

Possible Responses: The Mandarin's daughter is very modest and does not call attention to herself, just as the figure seems to be making herself unobtrusive; the Mandarin's daughter hides behind a screen, and this woman is concealed from the people within by a screen.

"They build their wall," said the Mandarin, [i]n the shape of a pig! Do you see? Our own [ci]ty wall is built in the shape of an orange. [Th]at pig will devour us, greedily!"

"Ah."

They both sat thinking.

Life was full of symbols and omens. Demons [lur]ked everywhere, Death swam in the wetness [of] an eye, the turn of a gull's wing meant rain, [a] fan held so, the tilt of a roof, and, yes, even a [cit]y wall was of immense importance. Travelers [an]d tourists, caravans, musicians, artists, [co]ming upon these two towns, equally judging [th]e portents, would say, "The city shaped like [an] orange? No! I will enter the city shaped like [a] pig and prosper, eating all, growing fat with [go]od luck and prosperity!"

The Mandarin wept. "All is lost! These [sy]mbols and signs terrify. Our city will come [to] evil days."

"Then," said the daughter, "call in your [st]onemasons and temple builders. I will [wh]isper from behind the silken screen and you [wi]ll know the words."

The old man clapped his hands despairingly. [H]o, stonemasons! Ho, builders of towns and [p]alaces!"

The men who knew marble and granite and onyx and quartz came quickly. The Mandarin faced them most uneasily, [hi]mself waiting for a whisper from the silken [sc]reen behind his throne. At last the whisper [ca]me.

"I have called you here," said the whisper.

"I have called you here," said the Mandarin [al]oud, "because our city is shaped like an [or]ange, and the vile city of Kwan-Si has this [d]ay shaped theirs like a _ravenous_ pig—"

Here the stonemasons groaned and wept. Death rattled his cane in the outer courtyard. Poverty made a sound like a wet cough in the shadows of the room.

"And so," said the whisper, said the Mandarin, "you raisers of walls must go bearing trowels and rocks and change the shape of _our_ city!"

The architects and masons gasped. The Mandarin himself gasped at what he had said. The whisper whispered. The Mandarin went on: "And you will change our walls into a club which may beat the pig and drive it off!"

The stonemasons rose up, shouting. Even the Mandarin, delighted at the words from his mouth, applauded, stood down from his throne. "Quick!" he cried. "To work!"

When his men had gone, smiling and bustling, the Mandarin turned with great love to the silken screen. "Daughter," he whispered, "I will embrace you." There was no reply. He stepped around the screen, and she was gone.

Such modesty, he thought. She has slipped away and left me with a triumph, as if it were mine.

The news spread through the city; the Mandarin was acclaimed. Everyone carried stone to the walls. Fireworks were set off and the demons of death and poverty did not linger, as all worked together. At the end of the month the wall had been changed. It was now a mighty bludgeon with which to drive pigs, boars, even lions, far away. The Mandarin slept like a happy fox every night.

"I would like to see the Mandarin of Kwan-Si when the news is learned. Such _pandemonium_ and hysteria; he will likely throw himself from a mountain! A little more of that wine, oh Daughter-who-thinks-like-a-son."

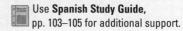

WORDS	**ravenous** (răv'ə-nəs) _adj._ extremely hungry; greedy
TO	**acclaimed** (ə-klāmd') _adj._ to welcome publicly with praise **acclaim** _v._
KNOW	**pandemonium** (păn'də-mō'nē-əm) _n._ a noisy upset; a wild uproar

495

Less Proficient Readers
Ask students why the shape of Kwan-Si's wall upsets the Mandarin.
Possible Response: He sees it as a bad sign for his city. His wall is shaped like an orange. A pig could devour an orange.
• What solution does the Mandarin propose?
 Answer: to rebuild the city wall in the shape of a club
• Who really thinks of the idea?
 Answer: the Mandarin's daughter

Set a Purpose Have students read to find out what happens after the wall is rebuilt to resemble a club.

Students Acquiring English
1 Point out the use of personification in these two sentences. Tell students that giving human characteristics to death and poverty makes them seem more threatening and shows how seriously the townspeople take Kwan-Si's wall.
2 Tell students that sons were revered in the ancient Chinese culture. Therefore, the father is giving his daughter a great compliment.

Use **Spanish Study Guide,** pp. 103–105 for additional support.

Customizing Instruction

 Preteaching Vocabulary   TEKS 6A   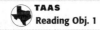 TAAS Reading Obj. 1

CONTEXT CLUES: RESTATEMENT

Instruction Remind students that when they encounter an unfamiliar word, applying knowledge of context clues may help them define it. One type of context clue is restatement. Often in a sentence, the same idea is phrased in different or easier language. Display the sentence to illustrate how the definition of _pandemonium_ is found in the restating of the idea.

The pandemonium of the crowds surprised him; such wild uproar had never been seen.

Exercises Have students define each underlined WORD TO KNOW, using the strategy.

1. Famine made people hungry; they were _ravenous_ for any sort of food.
2. Starvation extinguished his spirit; illness _quenched_ it further.
3. His name was praised all over, and his deed was similarly _acclaimed_.
4. To reject the proposal was to _spurn_ life.

Use **Unit Three Resource Book,** p. 80 for more exercises.
Use **Vocabulary Transparencies and Copymasters,** p. 58, for additional support.

Reading Skills and Strategies:
CAUSE AND EFFECT

A Ask students to identify the immediate and long-term effects of the Mandarin's initial rebuilding of the wall.

Possible Responses: The immediate effect was that Kwan-Si rebuilt its wall. This led to a chain reaction of building and rebuilding. A long-term effect is the neglect of the harvest and businesses, which leads to famine and disease in the towns.

Literary Analysis: IRONY

B Ask students what is ironic about the consequences of the wall rivalry.

Possible Response: It brings about exactly the situation that the Mandarin had feared would result from the wall shaped like a pig.

Active Reading | CONNECT WITH OTHER STORIES

C Ask students to compare the message of the daughter's words with the revelation that Lottie has at the end of "The Richer, the Poorer."

Possible Responses: Lottie realizes that in preparing so diligently for the future and placing so much importance on money, she lost something much more precious, the present. The daughter is saying that in the struggle to appear powerful, they have lost something more valuable, life itself.

Literary Analysis | THEME

D Ask students what important idea is revealed in the resolution to the mandarins' conflict.

Possible Responses: Cooperation will accomplish more than rivalry; people need each other to flourish.

---

*B*ut the pleasure was like a winter flower; it died swiftly. That very afternoon the messenger rushed into the courtroom. "Oh, Mandarin, disease, early sorrow, avalanches, grasshopper plagues, and poisoned well water!"

The Mandarin trembled.

"The town of Kwan-Si," said the messenger, "which was built like a pig and which animal we drove away by changing our walls to a mighty stick, has now turned triumph to winter ashes. They have built their city's walls like a great bonfire to burn our stick!"

The Mandarin's heart sickened within him, like an autumn fruit upon an ancient tree. "Oh, gods! Travelers will <u>spurn</u> us. Tradesmen, reading the symbols, will turn from the stick, so easily destroyed, to the fire, which conquers all!"

"No," said a whisper like a snowflake from behind the silken screen.

"No," said the startled Mandarin.

"Tell my stonemasons," said the whisper that was a falling drop of rain, "to build our walls in the shape of a shining lake."

The Mandarin said this aloud, his heart warmed.

"And with this lake of water," said the whisper and the old man, "we will <u>quench</u> the fire and put it out forever!"

The city turned out in joy to learn that once again they had been saved by the magnificent Emperor of ideas. They ran to the walls and built them nearer to this new vision, singing, not as loudly as before, of course, for they were tired, and not as quickly, for since it had taken a month to build the wall the first time, they had had to neglect business and crops and therefore were somewhat weaker and poorer.

There then followed a succession of horrible and wonderful days, one in another like a nest of frightening boxes.

"Oh, Emperor," cried the messenger, "Kwan-Si has rebuilt their walls to resemble a mouth with which to drink all our lake!"

"Then," said the Emperor, standing very close to his silken screen, "build our walls like a needle to sew up that mouth!"

"Emperor!" screamed the messenger. "They make their walls like a sword to break your needle!"

The Emperor held, trembling, to the silken screen. "Then shift the stones to form a scabbard to sheathe that sword!"

"Mercy," wept the messenger the following morn, "they have worked all night and shaped the walls like lightning which will explode and destroy that sheath!"

Sickness spread in the city like a pack of evil dogs. Shops closed. The population, working now steadily for endless months upon the changing of the walls, resembled Death himself, clattering his white bones like musical instruments in the wind. Funerals began to appear in the streets, though it was the middle of summer, a time when all should be tending and harvesting. The Mandarin fell so ill that he had his bed drawn up by the silken screen and there he lay, miserably giving his architectural orders. The voice behind the screen was weak now, too, and faint, like the wind in the eaves.

"Kwan-Si is an eagle. Then our walls must be a net for that eagle. They are a sun to burn our net. Then we build a moon to eclipse their sun!"

Like a rusted machine, the city ground to a halt.

WORDS TO KNOW
spurn (spûrn) *v.* to reject or turn down scornfully
quench (kwĕnch) *v.* to put out; to extinguish

496

Teaching Options

☑ **Assessment** ## Standardized Test Practice TEKS 10E, 10K  TAAS Reading Obj. 4

CAUSE AND EFFECT For some standardized tests, students will be asked to show their understanding of cause and effect relationships. To provide students with some help in recognizing causes and their effects, read aloud or write on the board the following question:

Why does the daughter of the Mandarin speak directly to both emperors at the end of the story?

A. They have moved outside where there is no silk screen.

B. She is too weak to hide any longer.

C. She is known to all as wise and strong.

D. She wants to convince them by speaking to them face to face.

Guide students through the process of choosing the correct answer. A is correct. Because there is no screen, she must speak directly. There is no screen because they are outside. B is incorrect. She is weak, but that is not the cause of her visible presence. C is also incorrect. It is after she speaks directly to the mandarins that she is acknowledged for her qualities. D is incorrect. The status of women in society would have been a reason to stay hidden.

At last the whisper behind the screen cried out:

"In the name of the gods, send for Kwan-Si!"

Upon the last day of summer the Mandarin Kwan-Si, very ill and withered away, was carried into our Mandarin's courtroom by four starving footmen. The two mandarins were propped up, facing each other. Their breaths fluttered like winter winds in their mouths. A voice said:

"Let us put an end to this."

The old men nodded.

"This cannot go on," said the faint voice. "Our people do nothing but rebuild our cities to a different shape every day, every hour. They have no time to hunt, to fish, to love, to be good to their ancestors and their ancestors' children."

"This I admit," said the mandarins of the towns of the Cage, the Moon, the Spear, the Fire, the Sword and this, that, and other things.

"Carry us into the sunlight," said the voice.

The old men were borne out under the sun and up a little hill. In the late summer breeze a few very thin children were flying dragon kites in all the colors of the sun, and frogs and grass, the color of the sea and the color of coins and wheat.

The first Mandarin's daughter stood by his bed.

"See," she said.

"Those are nothing but kites," said the two old men.

"But what is a kite on the ground?" she said. "It is nothing. What does it need to sustain it and make it beautiful and truly spiritual?"

"The wind, of course!" said the others.

"And what do the sky and the wind need to make *them* beautiful?"

"A kite, of course—many kites, to break the monotony, the sameness of the sky. Colored kites, flying!"

"So," said the Mandarin's daughter. "You, Kwan-Si, will make a last rebuilding of your town to resemble nothing more nor less than the wind. And we shall build like a golden kite. The wind will beautify the kite and carry it to wondrous heights. And the kite will break the sameness of the wind's existence and give it purpose and meaning. One without the other is nothing. Together, all will be beauty and co-operation and a long and enduring life."

Whereupon the two mandarins were so overjoyed that they took their first nourishment in days, momentarily were given strength, embraced, and lavished praise upon each other, called the Mandarin's daughter a boy, a man, a stone pillar, a warrior, and a true and unforgettable son. Almost immediately they parted and hurried to their towns, calling out and singing, weakly but happily.

And so, in time, the towns became the Town of the Golden Kite and the Town of the Silver Wind. And harvestings were harvested and business tended again, and the flesh returned, and disease ran off like a frightened jackal. And on every night of the year the inhabitants in the Town of the Kite could hear the good clear wind sustaining them. And those in the Town of the Wind could hear the kite singing, whispering, rising, and beautifying them.

"So be it," said the Mandarin in front of his silken screen. ❖

Speaking and Listening

PERSUASION

Prepare Have students divide into small groups. One or two groups should take the role of judges while the other groups decide on new shapes for the two towns that will resolve the conflict as effectively as the shapes suggested by the Mandarin's daughter did. Speakers should adapt their vocabulary and diction to the audience and setting and arrange the reasons for the shapes they choose in the most effective order. The groups evaluating the presentations should prepare criteria that will help them analyze the speakers' persuasive techniques.

Present Each group should take turns presenting their recommended shapes for the two towns. The judges should take notes that will help them decide which speakers are most persuasive. At the end of the presentations, the judges should announce their decision and explain their reasons.

BLOCK SCHEDULING This activity is particularly well suited for longer class periods.

Use **Communications Transparencies and Copymasters,** p. 3, for additional support.

Thinking through the LITERATURE

GUIDING STUDENT RESPONSE

Connect to the Literature

1. **Possible Response:** It was a good solution. Neither town appears superior to the other.

Comprehension Check
- to keep intruders out and to show the boundaries of the town
- so that their walls will show their superiority over the other
- The Mandarin's town wall became a golden kite; the wall of the town of Kwan-Si became the silver wind.

 Use Selection Quiz
Unit Three Resource Book, p. 83.

Think Critically

2. **Possible Responses:** She has a great deal of wisdom, and he had no other ideas. Her first suggestions pleased him, and her resolution works well.

3. **Possible Response:** They are representing universal characters, not specific individuals.

4. **Possible Responses:** No, because people would stop before they went to these extremes. Yes, because wars have been fought to prove superiority.

5. **Possible Responses:** People get carried away and don't always think of the consequences. People will risk everything to outdo someone else. In trying to reach a goal, people often lose their perspective.

6. **Possible Responses:** Lottie and the Mandarin come to the same realization. Lottie understands that she will get more out of life if she and Bess travel in the same direction and are friends. The Mandarin appreciates the importance of cooperation with the neighboring town. Both emphasize how focusing completely on a goal can cause someone to lose his or her perspective.

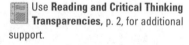 Use **Reading and Critical Thinking Transparencies,** p. 2, for additional support.

Literary Analysis

Theme Possible Responses: People's greed leads them to destroy what is most precious. Cooperation is more beneficial than rivalry. Power struggles can only be resolved through compromise. Through suffering, people gain wisdom.

Use **Literary Analysis Transparencies,** p. 7, for additional support.

498 UNIT THREE   AUTHOR STUDY

Connect to the Literature

1. **What Do You Think?** What was your impression of the solution to the two towns' rivalry? Explain.

Comprehension Check
- Why are both towns surrounded by walls?
- Why do the two towns keep rebuilding these walls?
- How was the towns' rivalry resolved?

Think Critically

2. Why do you think the Mandarin was willing to listen to his daughter's advice?

 THINK ABOUT
- her first question to her father about his anger
- the consequences of her advice
- the compliments of the two mandarins after she solved their problem

3. The characters in this story are described only as the Mandarin, the daughter, the messenger, and so forth. Why do you think none of the characters has a name?

4. Do you think that this story portrays an accurate picture of human behavior? Explain your response.

5. What moral, or lesson about human nature, do you think the author is trying to get across in this tale?

6. **ACTIVE READING   CONNECT WITH OTHER STORIES**
Look back at the notes you made in your **READER'S NOTEBOOK.** What **connections** did you make between "The Golden Kite, the Silver Wind" and "The Richer, the Poorer"? Share your ideas with your classmates.

Extend Interpretations

7. **What If?** What if the two towns had not been able to resolve their rivalry? What might have happened?

8. **Connect to Life** The Mandarin's daughter is praised as "a boy, a man, a stone pillar, a warrior, and a true and unforgettable son." What do you think is meant by this? How would you describe the daughter? Discuss possible descriptions with your classmates.

498   UNIT THREE   **AUTHOR STUDY**

Literary Analysis

THEME A **fable** is a brief story that teaches a lesson about human nature. The lesson, or **moral,** of the fable appears in a statement at the end. Modern fables seldom have stated morals. Instead, they have a **theme,** or message about life or human nature, that the reader must infer. To determine the theme of a work you read, look at the events that happen to the main characters. Restate the significance of these events in terms that apply to all human beings. That is the theme.

Cooperative Learning Activity
With a partner, look at the main events of "The Golden Kite, the Silver Wind." What is their significance to the main characters of the selection? Using your own words, restate this message in more general terms. Share your statement of the theme with other pairs.

Extend Interpretations

7. **What If?** Possible Responses: If the towns had not been able to resolve their rivalry, they would have destroyed themselves and each other, or a third town might have taken advantage of their weakened state.

8. **Connect to Life** Possible Responses: Because males were revered in the Chinese culture at the time the story is set, the daughter is seen to possess the best possible traits. She is courageous, strong, unafraid, and wise, all adjectives that could be used in her description. She also understands her father and wants to help him without diminishing his dignity and status.

Grammar in Context: Essential and Nonessential Modifiers

"The Golden Kite, the Silver Wind," Bradbury [us]es two kinds of modifiers to add important [inf]ormation to his sentences.

> Travelers . . . would say, "The city shaped like an orange? No! I will enter the city shaped like a pig and prosper! . . ."

[An] **essential modifier** is one that is necessary [to] the meaning of a sentence. In the excerpt [ab]ove, "shaped like an orange" and "shaped like [a p]ig" are essential for identifying which city is [ref]erred to. The sentences would not be clear [wi]thout these modifiers.

> "The town of Kwan-Si, beyond the hill, was very small in my childhood. . . ."

[A] **nonessential modifier** is one that adds more [in]formation to a sentence that is already clear [wi]thout the addition. In the sentence above it is [cl]ear which town is referred to without the extra [in]formation "beyond the hill."

[V]ocabulary in Action

[E]XERCISE A: CONTEXT CLUES On a separate [s]heet of paper, write the Word to Know that [b]est completes each sentence.

1. The Mandarin of the city with the wall like an orange was _____ for his wisdom.

2. A neighboring city decided to build its own wall in the shape of a _____ pig.

3. When the neighboring city decided to rebuild its wall in the shape of a bonfire, _____ broke out.

4. The Mandarin feared that travelers would _____ their city if it did not appear powerful.

Punctuation Tip: A nonessential modifier is set off from the rest of the sentence with commas.

WRITING EXERCISE Rewrite each sentence, adding an essential or nonessential modifier to provide more information about the underlined noun or pronoun.

Example: Original The Mandarin feared that the <u>city</u> would devour the city with walls shaped like an orange.

Rewritten The Mandarin feared that the <u>city</u> with walls shaped like a pig would devour the city with walls shaped like an orange.

1. The town of Kwan-Si now had a <u>wall</u>.

2. A <u>voice</u> from behind the screen whispered advice.

3. The Mandarin thought his <u>walls</u> would extinguish the walls built like a fire.

4. The two <u>mandarins</u> decided to stop competing.

Grammar Handbook Punctuation, p. R56

5. Therefore, the Mandarin ordered that the wall be rebuilt in the shape of a lake, to _____ the fire.

EXERCISE B: WORD MEANING For each phrase in the first column, write the letter of the phrase in the second that matches its meaning.

1. hungry streets   **a.** renowned clown

2. acclaimed jester   **b.** spurn a turn

3. great pandemonium   **c.** quench a stench

4. refuse a chance   **d.** ravenous avenues

5. get rid of an odor   **e.** colossal chaos

WORDS TO KNOW	acclaimed	pandemonium	quench	ravenous	spurn

Grammar in Context

Possible Responses:
WRITING EXERCISE

1. The town of Kwan-Si, <u>beyond the hills</u>, now had a wall <u>shaped like a pig</u>.

2. A voice from behind the screen, <u>the Mandarin's daughter</u>, whispered advice.

3. The Mandarin thought his walls <u>built like a shining lake</u> would extinguish the walls built like a fire.

4. The two mandarins, <u>men tired of the struggle</u>, decided to stop competing.

Vocabulary in Action

EXERCISE A
1. acclaimed
2. ravenous
3. pandemonium
4. spurn
5. quench

EXERCISE B
1. d
2. a
3. e
4. b
5. c

Mini Lesson **Grammar** **TEKS 17A**

USING ESSENTIAL AND NONESSENTIAL MODIFIERS

Instruction Remind students that they can add information to an essay or story by using two kinds of modifiers:

- an essential modifier, which adds necessary information to a sentence.
  Example: The daughter of the Mandarin made a suggestion.

- a nonessential modifier, which adds more information to a sentence that is already clear.

Example: The Mandarin, who was a strong leader, wanted to do what was best for his city.

Application Have each student write a short paragraph describing a fable or lesson story that he or she knows well. In the paragraph, they should use at least two essential modifiers and at least two nonessential modifiers punctuated correctly. When students have completed their paragraphs, they should share their papers with a partner.

Use **Unit Three Resource Book**, p. 81.
Use **Grammar Transparencies and Copymasters**, p. 87.

Use McDougal Littell's **Language Network**, Chapter 5, for more instruction and practice in using essential and nonessential modifiers.

Preparing to Read

Focus Your Reading

LITERARY ANALYSIS | **INTERVIEW**

An **interview** is a source of firsthand information about the subject of the interview. Interviews, like letters, stories, essays, poems, and speeches by a writer, are known as **primary sources.**

Illustration by Steve Vance.

Q: YOU DON'T CONSIDER YOURSELF A SCIENCE FICTION WRITER, EVEN THOUGH OTHERS CALL YOU THAT. HOW DO YOU SEE YOURSELF?

A: I am a collector of metaphors. Any idea that strikes me I run with. I've published in the last seven years two murder mysteries, *Death Is a Lonely Business* and *Graveyard for a Lunatic*. I have published two books of essays, *Zen and the Art of Writing*, which I like to think is one of the better books on writing, then *Yestermorrow*, or how to cure current problems and make our society work.

I wrote *The October Country*, which is weird fantasy. There is no science fiction there. And *Halloween Tree*, which is a history of Halloween. And *Dandelion Wine*, which is my childhood in Illinois. *Something Wicked This Way Comes*, which is also my childhood plus fantasy. So when you look at the spread of things, there is only one novel that is science fiction. And that's *Fahrenheit 451*. In other words, science fiction is the art of the possible, not the art of the impossible. As soon as you deal with things that can't happen you are writing fantasy.

Q: I KNOW YOU NEVER HAVE TROUBLE COMING UP WITH IDEAS. WALK ME THROUGH YOUR DAILY INSPIRATION AND WRITING PROCESS.

A: I just wake up with ideas every morning from my subconscious percolating. At 7 in the morning I lie in bed and I watch all the fragments of ideas swarming around in

Illustration by Steve Vance.

y head and these voices
lk to me. And when they
t to a certain point, I
mp out of bed and run
the typewriter. So I'm
ot in control. Two hours
ter I have a new short
ory or an essay or part
f a play.

**Q: WHEN YOU'VE FINISHED TYPING YOUR
SHORT STORIES, DO YOU REVISE?**

A: No. Never. A few words, but that's not
evision. That's just cleaning up.

Q: WHAT ARE YOU PASSIONATE ABOUT?

A: Everything. If you're in love, you're
a love.

**Q: YOU SAID ONCE THAT "THE GREAT
THING ABOUT MY LIFE IS THAT
EVERYTHING I'VE DONE IS A RESULT OF
WHAT I WAS WHEN I WAS 12 OR 13."
WHAT DOES THAT MEAN TO YOU?**

A: Or even younger, when I was 3, when
was 5, when I was 9. All the things that
loved have been part of my writing. *The
Hunchback of Notre Dame* when I was 3
ears old; *The Phantom of the Opera* with
on Chaney when I was 5 in 1925. . . . When
was 9, I collected all the Buck Rogers comic
trips. Edgar Rice Burroughs, the "Tarzan"
ooks, *Warlord of Mars*, I memorized those
ooks. The "Oz" books when I was 9, 10,
1. . . . *King Kong* in 1933 when I was 13,
H. G. Wells, Jules Verne. All those things.
My childhood was packed with metaphors.
Plus the Bible. Plus the hundreds of other
lms during that time.

[*In 1934, the family
moved to Los Angeles.*]
I was a real freak. I hung
around the studios when
I was 14 so I could see
famous people. I intruded
on the life of George Burns
when he and Gracie Allen
were doing their radio
show. I wrote scripts for
the show every week and gave them to
George. They used one routine. I did radio
acting. I read the comic strips to the kiddies
when I was 12 years old. Out of all those
images and metaphors, I became a good
screenwriter, because a good screenwriter is
making storyboards like comic strips. So I am
a natural outgrowth of the impact of all these
wonderful art forms.

**Q: WHAT KIND OF ADVICE WOULD YOU
GIVE BEGINNING WRITERS?**

A: Explode. Don't intellectualize. Get
passionate about ideas. Cram your head full
of images. Stay in the library. Stay off the
Internet. Read all the great books. Read all
the great poetry. See all the great films. Fill
your life with metaphors. And then explode.
And you're bound to do something good.

Thinking Through the Literature

1. What impression do you have of Ray
   Bradbury from this interview?

2. Were you surprised at Bradbury's
   method of writing? Explain.

AN INTERVIEW WITH RAY BRADBURY **501**

The Author's Style

Readers of Ray Bradbury's work enjoy realistic passages of dialogue, vivid imagery, and loosely structured sentences. Students will be made aware of Bradbury's style through the "Key Style Points" and will find examples of the three style points in the excerpts in the right margin.

Key Style Points

Dialogue This passage reveals that the two characters are experiencing a frightening change that neither was expecting.

Imagery Images such as "draw his soul from him," "dissolve his intellect," and "burn away his past" illustrate his fear and helplessness and sense of change.

Loosely Structured Sentences The coordinating conjunction *and* is repeated to give the passage a certain rhythm.

Applications

1. **Active Reading** Students should choose specific passages in a story and explain what these passages reveal or add to the story.
2. **Writing** To help students get started, you might suggest they write about a holiday, a sporting event, a show, or some unusual experience. Remind them to use concrete images and coordinating conjunctions.
3. **Speaking and Listening** Students might try closing their eyes and reading different passages aloud to find out which one helps them to visualize. Invite students to relate images to an item or experience in their own lives.

Ray Bradbury's Poetic Prose

The use of striking images, loosely structured sentences, and long passages of dialogue are important elements of Ray Bradbury's style.

Key Style Points

Dialogue Bradbury often uses dialogue rather than descriptive or explanatory passages to get across his points. What important idea is revealed in the passage to the right?

Imagery Images help readers imagine how things look, feel, sound, smell, and taste. What images does Bradbury use here to create an impression of Mr. Bittering's helplessness and sense of an important change about to happen?

Loosely Structured Sentences Bradbury's prose is characterized by loosely structured poetic sentences connected by coordinating conjunctions. What coordinating conjunction is repeated in the passage below and to the right?

Applications

1. **Active Reading** Working with a small group, look back at the stories and find examples of passages or dialogue that reveal important points of style. Compare your examples with those of other groups.
2. **Writing** Think of an event that has impressed you. Using elements of Bradbury's style, write a description of the event.
3. **Speaking and Listening** With a partner, discuss imagery in one of the selections. Choose a particularly strong passage and write a paragraph about the images that the passage creates in your mind. Point out details that help you imagine how things look, feel, sound, smell, or taste.

502 UNIT THREE **AUTHOR STUDY**

Dialogue

"Sam," Bittering said. "Your eyes—"

"What about them, Harry?"

"Didn't they used to be gray?"

"Well now, I don't remember."

"They were, weren't they?"

"Why do you ask, Harry?"

"Because now they're kind of yellow-colored."

"Is that so, Harry?" Sam said, casually. . . .

"Harry, what color eyes have *you* got?" Sam sa[id]

"My eyes? They're blue, of course."

"Here you are, Harry," Sam handed him a pocket mirror. "Take a look at yourself."

—"Dark They Were, and Golden-Ey[es]

Imagery

The wind blew as if to flake away their identiti[es] At any moment the Martian air might draw [Mr. Bittering's] soul from him, as marrow comes from a white bone. He felt submerged in a chemical that could dissolve his intellect and burn away his past.

—"Dark They Were, and Golden-Eye[s]

Loosely Structured Sentences

And so, in time, the towns became the Town of the Golden Kite and the Town of the Silver Wind. And harvestings were harvested and business tended again, and the flesh return[ed] and disease ran off like a frightened jackal. And on every night of the year the inhabitant[s] in the Town of the Kite could hear the good clear wind sustaining them. And those in the Town of the Wind could hear the kite singing, whispering, rising, and beautifying them.

—"The Golden Kite, the Silver Win[d]

Writing Options

Fable Write a modern fable that contains a lesson about human nature. Before you write, plan your fable. Who will the characters be? What ideas will they stand for? What will the moral be? When you have finished, share your fable with the class. Place the fable in your **Working Portfolio.**

Time Capsule Imagine that you are the last person to leave Earth for Mars. What items would you leave in a time capsule for future scientists and scholars to discover? Make a list. What would the items tell the discoverers about you? Compare your list with that of a classmate.

Activities & Explorations

Film Review View "The Long Years," an episode from *The Ray Bradbury Theater.* Then discuss with classmates similarities and differences between the film's presentation of Mars and the way you visualized it while reading "Dark They Were, and Golden-Eyed."

VIDEO Literature in Performance

Courtesy of Alliance Atlantis
Communications, Inc.

Inquiry and Research

To Mars! Use nonfiction books, the Internet, and other sources to gather information about travel to Mars. Include in your report:

• the distance between Mars and Earth

• the average time a spaceship would take to reach Mars

• the problems of sustaining life on Mars

• the research about Mars that is currently being conducted by NASA or other agencies

Author Study Project
Creating a Comic Strip

Working with a small group, create a comic book version of one of the Bradbury stories you read.

❶ **Choose a Scene** With your group, decide which story and specific scenes you think will work the best. Consider which scenes can be best adapted to a comic book format.

❷ **Draw the Strip** Divide into teams. Have one team write a script for the comic book and a script for a summary of the parts of the story that will not be included. The other team should create the illustrations, making sure they match

the script. For presentation purposes, make your comic book oversized or plan to present it one frame at a time on an overhead projector.

❸ **Share with the Class** Present your comic book and your narration to the rest of the class.

Writing Options

1. Fable To get started, students might try to remember different fables they have heard or brainstorm about issues or ideas that concern them. To make this assignment easier, have students work in pairs to write their fables.

Use **Literary Analysis Transparencies,** p. 30, for additional support. Use **Writing Transparencies,** p. 1, for additional support.

2. Time Capsule Students should focus on items that will be particularly telling to people in the future who are searching for answers to their questions. Students should think about what items symbolize their era or their community.

Activities & Explorations

Film Review Students should compare and contrast specific points in the movie and the story. To make this assignment more challenging, have students write a film review.

Use **Communications Transparencies and Copymasters,** p. 7, for additional support.

Inquiry & Research

To Mars! Suggest that students use a variety of resources to get the most up-to-date, interesting information. Students might also create maps, illustrations, and diagrams.

Author Study Project
Creating a Comic Strip

Encourage students to plot the details of their comic strip before coloring it in. Remind students that comic strips should be easy to read and visually appealing.

You might suggest that students display their comic books in a local library.

Other Works by RAY BRADBURY

Ray Bradbury is commonly given credit for bringing respectability to science fiction and making it a legitimate form of literature. He calls himself a "lover of the whole experience of life" and his sense of expectancy and joy shows in his writing. His stories celebrate the human imagination while exploring serious issues such as racism, censorship, and the impact of technology on morality and values.

The Martian Chronicles 1950

This book tells the story of the first attempts of Earth men and women to colonize Mars during the years 1999–2026 and their encounters with telepathic Martians.

Fahrenheit 451 1953

Awarded the Prometheus Hall of Fame Award for Best Classic Libertarian Science Fiction Novel, 1984

This novel is set in a future in which the written word is forbidden. Firemen do not put out fires. Rather, they are in charge of burning books. Individuals in a group of rebels memorize entire works of literature and philosophy in order to preserve civilization.

Something Wicked This Way Comes   1962

This novel tells the tale of two boys who discover the terrifying mystery behind the carnival that arrives in town during the dark of night.

A Medicine for Melancholy   1960

This fine collection of Bradbury stories contains works of science fiction, fantasy, and realism. Along with "Dark They Were, and Golden-Eyed," it contains favorites such as "All Summer in a Day," "The Pedestrian," and "The Day It Rained Forever."

The Vintage Bradbury   1965

Bradbury's own selection of his best stories, this collection contains "The Veldt" and "The Fog Horn," as well as excerpts from *The Martian Chronicles* and *Dandelion Wine*.

The Toynbee Convector   1988

Awarded the Bram Stoker Award for Superior Achievement in a Fiction Collection

This book, set in the year 2084, tells the story of Craig Bennett Stiles. He is the inventor of the Toynbee Convector, a time machine he last used one hundred years ago in 1984.

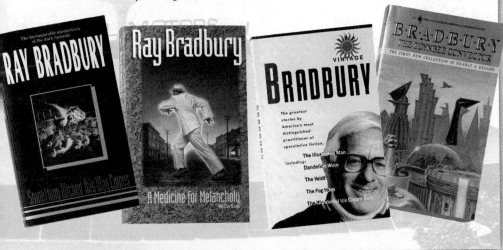

Writing Workshop
Short Story

Objectives
- write a short story
- use a written text as a model for writing
- revise a draft to include concrete details
- use parallel structure

Introducing the Workshop

Short Story Discuss with students suspenseful short stories they have previously read. Have them think about what made the stories especially memorable and the suspense particularly effective.

Basics in a Box
Using the Graphic The graphic on this page shows the three main sections of a short story. Each section performs a function, such as introducing the characters and setting, developing the plot and characters, introducing the conflict, and resolving the conflict.

Presenting the Rubric To better understand the assignment, students can refer to the Standards for Writing a Successful Short Story. You may also want to share with them the complete rubric, which describes several levels of proficiency.

 Use McDougal Littell's *Language Network,* Chapters 12–19, for more instruction on essential writing skills.

 Power Presentation

To engage students visually, use **Power Presentation 2,** Short Story.

 See the Skills Trace at the beginning of the unit for information on TEKS covered in this lesson.

Writing Workshop
Short Story

Weaving a plot . . .

From Reading to Writing Have you ever held your breath in suspense as you read a story? A good suspenseful plot keeps you wondering but also gives enough clues about what *might* happen. For instance, in "The Serial Garden" you may have noticed clues that foreshadowed the fact that Mark's mother would clean the playroom and throw away the magic garden. Writing a suspenseful or mysterious **short story** will help you learn how to keep your readers guessing.

For Your Portfolio

WRITING PROMPT Write a short story with a mysterious or suspenseful plot.

Purpose: To entertain
Audience: Your classmates, family, or general readers

Basics in a Box

Short Story at a Glance

Introduction

Sets the stage by
- introducing the **characters**
- describing the **setting**

Body

Develops the plot by
- introducing the conflict
- telling a sequence of **events**
- developing **characters** through words and actions
- building toward a **climax**

Conclusion

Finishes the story by
- resolving the **conflict**
- telling the **last event**

RUBRIC STANDARDS FOR WRITING

A successful short story should
- have a strong beginning and ending
- use the elements of character, setting, and plot to create a convincing world
- use techniques such as vivid sensory language, concrete details, and dialogue to create believable characters and setting
- have a main conflict, which may or may not be resolved
- present a clear sequence of events
- maintain a consistent point of view

506   UNIT THREE   PART 2: FANTASTIC TALES

LESSON RESOURCES

USING PRINT RESOURCES
Unit Three Resource Book
- Prewriting, p. 84
- Drafting, p. 85
- Peer Response, pp. 86–87
- Revising, Editing, and Proofreading, p. 88
- Student Models, pp. 89–91
- Rubric, p. 92

LESSON SUPPORT
Writing Transparencies
- Writing Process Transparencies, TR 1–4
- Writing Process Transparencies:

Elaboration, TR 13
- Writing Style Transparencies: Dialogue, TR 24
- Writing Template Transparencies: Short Story, TR 34
Literary Analysis Transparencies
- Foreshadowing, TR 28
Reading and Critical Thinking Transparencies
- Text Structure (Organization), TR 24 (for Mini Lesson, p. 507)
Grammar Transparencies and Copymasters
- Punctuating Dialogue, CM 129 (for Mini Lesson, p. 510)

- Parallelism, CM 143 (for Mini Lesson, p. 511)
INTEGRATED TECHNOLOGY
LaserLinks
Writing Springboards
See **Teacher's SourceBook** p. 36 for bar codes.

Writing Coach CD-ROM

Visit our website:
www.mcdougallittell.com

Analyzing a Student Model

SPEAKING OPPORTUNITY

See the Communication Handbook, p. R100 for speaking and presenting tips.

Rachel Leah Granzow
Campbell Junior High

Plan Bee

In the year 3021, Kali trudged down the purple sidewalk on her home planet, Yein. She wiped her tear-stained cheeks and gripped the letter in her shaking hands. *What's wrong with me?* she thought. *Is it the way I look? my clothes? my personality?* She yanked a mirror out of her bag and stared at her reflection. Purple hair, military apparel, grunge boots. . . . She looked like all the other girls on the planet. Then why did her best friend Jareka send a letter stating that their lifelong friendship was over? Kali shoved the mirror back into her bag and read the letter again. "I don't want you to take this the wrong way, but we can't be friends any longer. I'm practically dying when I write this. . . ." Kali read that last sentence over again. *Practically dying?* That didn't make sense. Kali paused a minute and stared off into the distance. From out of nowhere, a group of gray figures surrounded her. "Lanx," she whispered, before a strong blow to the head knocked her out.

"Ow. Oh, *nikum.*" Kali's eyes fluttered open. She found herself in a dark room surrounded by Lanx, the alien species that threatened to take over Yein.

"So, you've awakened," the Lanx said. The smooth, deep voice sent chills up Kali's spine. "You have been brought here to supply us with information we need. You will cooperate. After all, you don't want to end up like your friend over there." It gestured to a bench in the corner of the room. There lay Jareka.

"Why am I here?" Kali stared defiantly at the metal links on their jackets.

"I have not gone to all this trouble to play games. Jareka was the leader of the CDB-99 spy mission. She stole our map with the location of our most powerful missile. We want it back. You are her best friend, so you know where it is. Now, we have a virtual reality recording of a message to you from Jareka."

The Lanx flipped a switch, and a 3D image of Jareka appeared.

"Kali, if you hear this, tell them about the *buzz*, and Plan Bee. The image faded. Kali understood. Jareka had used their special code. It reminded her of the difference between them.

RUBRIC
IN ACTION

❶ The writer sets the stage with specific details about the setting.

❷ The conflict captures readers' attention.

❸ The central conflict is introduced.

❹ Gives concrete technological details

Teaching the Lesson

Analyzing the Model
"Plan Bee"

The student model is a science fiction short story about the friendship between two girls which is threatened when aliens try to take over their planet Yein. The writer includes vivid descriptions of the setting and main character in order to set the mood for the whole story.

Have students consider what kind of setting they would choose for a science fiction short story and what qualities their main character would possess. Help students see how detailed description makes the story more interesting. Then point out the key words and phrases in the student model that correspond to the elements mentioned in the Rubric in Action.

1. Ask students what impression of Yein and Kali they gain from the introduction.

   Possible Response: Purple seems to be the predominant color on Yein, even the sidewalks and Kali's hair. Kali seems like a typical Yein girl.

2. Ask students to describe how Jareka's letter impacts the tone of the story.

   Possible Response: The mysterious tone of the letter changes the story from one of friendship to one of suspense and even danger.

3. Have students discuss why the writer states the conflict so clearly in this story.

   Possible Response: The story centers around the friendship between the two girls so the reason for the attack on them needs to be explained in order for the story to continue.

4. Ask students to explain why the technological details are important to the story.

   Possible Response: The details give the reader a definite image to visualize and give the story a realistic feeling.

Mini Lesson — Viewing and Representing

PICTURING TEXT STRUCTURE

Instruction While word choice and vivid descriptions play key roles in writing a short story, the structure of a text—the way in which ideas are organized and events unfold—also contributes to the effectiveness of the work.

Activity Have students analyze the text structure of the student model by constructing a diagram or other graphic organizer. The following flow chart is an example.

📖 Use **Reading and Critical Thinking Transparencies,** p. 24, for additional support.

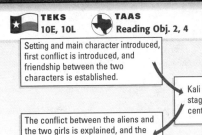

Setting and main character introduced, first conflict is introduced, and friendship between the two characters is established.

Kali is attacked, which sets the stage for the introduction of the central conflict.

The conflict between the aliens and the two girls is explained, and the initial conflict between the girls is resolved.

The actions of Kali and Jareka reveal their characters.

The girls resolve the conflict through action.

5 Background information is needed at this point in the story in order for the action to move forward. Ask students to think of another way this information could be relayed to the reader.

Possible Responses: The information could be given from a first-person point of view with the reader being allowed to read Kali's mind.

6 Ask students if the story would change if the dialogue was removed and narrative was substituted.

Possible Responses: The dialogue reveals more about the characters, and their motives and personalities than narrative does. Dialogue also makes the story more interesting and active.

7 Ask students to describe the effect of the phrases "The hours. . . passed slowly", "Shortly after daybreak".

Possible Responses: These phrases make the order of events easy to follow and they also increase the feeling of suspense that is building.

8 Remind students that giving readers vivid images to visualize makes their writing more interesting and effective.

9 Ask students to think of an alternative way to end the story. Have them explain how a different ending would change the story.

Possible Responses: The story could end abruptly after "The Lanx burst in, armed with lasers." This would allow the reader to imagine different endings and would increase the level of suspense of the story as a whole.

10 Point out to students that the conclusion ties in directly with the opening paragraph of the story, which gives the work as a whole unity and coherence.

Jareka had alien blood, not Lanx but another species called Drone. She was able to turn into a deadly bee in an emergency situation. But the transformation could only take place in the presence of another person who knew the code word "Buzz." Kali was that person. If she could recite the words by Jareka's side, the transformation could take place. However, first she had to make up a story to distract the Lanx.

Kali cleared her throat and began. "Well, since I have no choice, I'll confess."

The creatures smiled.

"What Jareka meant by 'buzz' was the code word to the secret place where your map is hidden. The Yein government headquarters are disguised as bee farms on the far east side of the planet. If you have the code word, they'll let you in."

The leader smiled. "We'll see if you're lying. We'll be back soon. Then you'll be terminated." The Lanx marched out and locked the door behind them.

Kali carefully picked up Jareka's hand and recited the code, "Yuma Kachine Leotie Xanthus Lomasi Cadell Tallulah Niabi Sibyl!"

Slowly, Jareka's chest began to rise and fall. Her eyes flew open. She looked at Kali and smiled quickly. Jareka's human features disappeared as she shrank, turning into a bee. She would remain this way until Kali uttered the code again.

The hours of the night passed slowly. Shortly after daybreak, Kali heard heavy footsteps rushing towards the door. The Lanx burst in, armed with lasers. Unseen, Jareka flew over their heads as they blocked Kali's escape. Suddenly, one Lanx warrior fell. Another thudded to the ground. The rest toppled like dominoes. Soon every Lanx lay on the floor. Kali saw Jareka hovering near her. She recited the code backwards. "Sibyl Niabi Tallulah Cadell Lomasi Xanthus Leotie Kachine Yuma!" Jareka rested on the ground and quickly resumed her human shape. Kali and Jareka smiled at each other in relief.

There would now be peace on Yein, at least for the time being. Kali felt at peace, too. She knew that Jareka had tried to end their friendship to protect her. She also knew that true friendship could conquer all.

❺ Third-person point of view allows the writer to reveal thoughts and feelings of main character as well as the actions and words of other characters.

Another Option:
• Use first-person point of view to narrate the action from the main character's perspective.

❻ Dialogue fits the characters and advances the plot.

❼ Events are ordered chronologically. Transitions make order of events clear.

❽ Uses figurative language to bring the scene to life

❾ The central conflict is resolved.

Another Option:
• Don't resolve the conflict; instead let readers imagine how it might be resolved.

❿ The conclusion ties up all loose ends of the plot and settles the initial conflict of the story.

Writing Your Short Story

❶ Prewriting

Imagination is the highest kite one can fly.
—Lauren Bacall, actress

To find an idea for your short story, **list** possible settings, characters, and plots. Write down mysterious settings in your neighborhood, like abandoned warehouses or houses with creaking shutters and ivy over the windows. **Skim** newspapers for bizarre incidents or unexplained events. See the **Idea Bank** in the margin for more suggestions. After you have an idea for your short story, follow the steps below.

Planning Your Short Story

▶ **1. Consider the elements of character, setting, and point of view.** Who will be your main character? What does he or she look like? Where and when will your story take place? Who will tell your story?

▶ **2. Develop the plot.** What is your central conflict? Try to imagine how your main character will react to the conflict. What events might his or her reaction lead to? How do you want the conflict to be resolved?

▶ **3. Share ideas with other writers.** In a small group, take turns outlining your story line and describing your characters. Take note of suggestions or reactions to your plot or characters. Ask group members to take the part of your main character and speak as they imagine the character would.

❷ Drafting

Set aside a block of time to write your first draft. Try to get all the ideas that are floating in your mind down on paper. You will polish your draft later.

- Write **dialogue** that sounds natural and moves the story along.
- Include **foreshadowing**, or hints of what is to happen, which will increase suspense and keep your readers interested.
- Give your readers **concrete and descriptive details** so that the characters, setting, and action seem real.

IDEABank

1. For Your Working Portfolio
Look for ideas in the **Writing Options** you completed earlier in this unit:
- **Science Fiction**, p. 437
- **Escape Plan**, p. 456
- **Fable**, p. 503

2. Center Stage
Choose three ordinary places that might make interesting story settings, such as a baseball field, a classroom, or a busy supermarket. Imagine what stories could take place in each setting.

3. Strange Matters
Focus on a small but puzzling incident, such as answering the phone and finding no one there or driving into a town that seems completely empty. Brainstorm a list of such incidents with a partner.

Have a question?

See the **Writing Handbook**
Presenting a Description, p. R31
Using Dialogue, p. R33

Ask Your Peer Reader

- How did my story make you feel?
- Where can I add details to make the characters and events more real?
- Did the ending seem realistic and satisfying?

Prewriting
Choosing a Subject
If after reading the Idea Bank students have difficulty choosing a subject for their short story, suggest that they try the following:

- Use someone you know or a person you've noticed whose appearance or demeanor suggests great mystery or tragedy as a model for a main character. Then, develop a plot and setting around the character you have created from a real life model.
- Imagine that you have to tell a different story about the same character to your younger sister every night. Decide what kind of character you would find interesting and what kind of trouble this character could get into.

Planning Your Short Story
1. Encourage students to brainstorm possible characters, plots, and settings.
2. Suggest students think about their own experiences and adventures as starting points for plot development.
3. Encourage students to ask for suggestions from classmates about areas in the story that they may be having difficulty with, such as introducing characters, dialogue, and organization.

Drafting
Dialogue Have volunteers read the dialogue they've written to the class. Ask students to discuss ways to make the dialogue natural and exciting.

Foreshadowing Have students think of ways to include foreshadowing in their introductory paragraph.

Details Remind students that descriptive details help the reader visualize and become more involved in the characters and setting.

Ask Your Peer Reader Remind students to use the peer reviewer's feedback when revising their drafts.

Use **Writing Transparencies**, p. 24, for additional support.
Use **Literary Analysis Transparencies**, p. 28, for additional support.

Revising
USING CONCRETE DETAILS

Review the changes in the sample with students. To help students practice using concrete details, ask volunteers to share sentences from their drafts. Have the rest of the class suggest ways to rewrite the sentences to include concrete details that would help to create a more precise and specific image.

 Use **Writing Transparencies,** p. 13, for additional support.

Editing and Proofreading
PARALLELISM

Remind students that inconsistency in verb tense and form within a sentence creates confusion for the reader. Have the students explain the change in the sample. For more practice, see the Grammar Mini Lesson at the bottom of the next page.

 Use **Grammar Transparencies and Copymasters,** p. 47, for additional support.

Reflecting

As they write their reflections, have students consider how their reading of short stories may have changed.

Option
Managing the Paper Load

Have students choose one major question or area they would like you to address as you review their first drafts. Ask them to write this question on the top of their draft. Some students may want help with organization, others might have difficulty with dialogue or character development. Meet with students individually to discuss your response.

Need revising help?

Review the **Rubric,** p. 507

Consider **peer reader** comments

Check **Revision Guidelines,** p. R23

SPELLING
From Writing

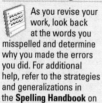 As you revise your work, look back at the words you misspelled and determine why you made the errors you did. For additional help, refer to the strategies and generalizations in the **Spelling Handbook** on page R86.

Panicked about parallelism?

See the **Grammar Handbook,** p. R68

Publishing
IDEAS

- Record your short story on audiotape. Enlist classmates to take the parts of different characters. Plan and create sound effects to go along with the reading.

- Adapt your story for a younger audience. Read it aloud to a group of younger students.

More Online: Publishing Options www.mcdougallittell.com

❸ Revising

TARGET SKILL ▶ USING CONCRETE DETAILS A concrete detail gives a precise and specific image that appeals to the senses. For example, instead of saying that the flowers in a garden were beautiful, which can mean different things to different people, Joan Aiken provides concrete details about the flowers: *"There were huge velvety violets and pansies the size of saucers; the hollyhocks were as big as dinner plates, and the turf was sprinkled with enormous daisies."* Use precise and specific images to involve your readers.

heavy footsteps rushing toward the door
Shortly after daybreak, Kali heard ~~them return.~~

❹ Editing and Proofreading

TARGET SKILL ▶ PARALLELISM One way to avoid awkwardness in your sentences is to make sure they are written in parallel structure. For instance, if you have a compound verb, where appropriate, make sure all of the verbs are in the same tense and form. For example, the verbs in this sentence are not parallel: *Mark sang and was dancing in the garden.* Instead you should write, *Mark sang and danced in the garden.*

locked
The Lanx marched out and ~~were locking~~ the door securely behind them.

❺ Reflecting

FOR YOUR WORKING PORTFOLIO What part of writing the story did you most enjoy? What have you learned about writing a short story? What ideas would you like to remember for your next story? Attach these reflections to your finished story. Save your short story in your **Working Portfolio.**

Teaching Options

 Mini Lesson Grammar ⬤ **TEKS 16B** ⬤ **TAAS Writing Obj. 3, 7**

PUNCTUATING DIALOGUE

Instruction Tell students that it is important to punctuate correctly all dialogue that appears in a short story. Proper punctuation helps readers to clearly understand who is speaking and what is being said. Give students the following guidelines:

- Use quotation marks as you would for all direct quotations.
- Begin a new paragraph each time the speaker changes.
- Place end marks and commas within quotation marks.

Exercises Write the following sentences on the chalkboard. Have students rewrite them correctly. They should think about both paragraph structure and punctuation.

Jackson saw his neighbors Sam and Earl walking to the bus stop. He asked, What are you two doing after school today? Well, I'm going to check out the baseball game at the field, Sam responded. Earl said, I'm going to apply for a job at the library. I like books, and I really need some extra cash.

Answer: Jackson saw his neighbors Sam and Earl walking to the bus stop. He asked, "What

are you two doing after school today?" "Well, I'm going to check out the baseball game at the field," Sam responded. Earl said, "I'm going to apply for a job at the library. I like books, and I really need some extra cash."

 Use **Grammar Transparencies and Copymasters,** p. 129

Language Network Use McDougal Littell's **Language Network,** Chapter 11, for more instruction and practice punctuating dialogue.

Assessment Practice Revising & Editing

Read this paragraph from the first draft of a short story. The underlined sections may include the following kinds of errors:

- **misplaced adverbs**
- **lack of parallel structure**
- **incorrect use of pronouns as direct and indirect objects**
- **double negatives**

For each underlined section, choose the revision that most improves the writing.

> Kali pushed slowly the door open. She had not never seen such thick
> (1)   (2)
> cobwebs as those that formed a gauzy curtain in front of her face. She
> brushed they aside and stepped into the dark attic. She turned on the
> (3)
> light and immediately was seeing the object they're on the windowsill.
>   (4)
> A crash from the stairs warned her of danger. She decided to leave go of
>   (5)
> the bottle and lie it on the nearest piece of furniture so she would not
>   (6)
> be caught with it.

1. **A.** Kali pushed slowly the open door.
   B. Kali pushed the slowly door open.
   C. Slowly, Kali pushed the door open.
   D. Correct as is

2. **A.** She hadn't never seen such thick cobwebs
   B. She didn't never see such thick cobwebs
   C. She had never seen such thick cobwebs
   D. Correct as is

3. **A.** She brushed them aside
   B. She brushed it aside
   C. She brushed their aside
   D. Correct as is

4. **A.** saw
   B. sight
   C. will see
   D. Correct as is

5. **A.** their
   B. there
   C. thier
   D. Correct as is

6. **A.** She decided to let go of the bottle and lay it
   B. She decided to leave go of the bottle lie it
   C. She decided to let go of the bottle and lie it
   D. Correct as is

Need extra help?

See the **Grammar Handbook**

Quick Reference: Capitalization, p. R58

Quick Reference: Punctuation, p. R56

Troublesome Verbs, p. R68

Parallelism, p. R68

WRITING WORKSHOP **511**

 Grammar **TEKS** 17F 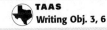 **TAAS** Writing Obj. 3, 6

PARALLELISM For use with Editing and Proofreading, p. 510.

Instruction Tell students that using compound verbs is one way to make their writing more concise and interesting. Remind students that the verb tense and form should remain consistent throughout the sentence.

Exercises Have students find the errors in parallel construction in the following sentences and suggest corrections. Some sentences are correct.

1. The dog sat quietly, looks expectantly at the treats, and wagged her tail. (The *dog sat quietly,* looked *expectantly* at the treats, and *wagged* her tail.)

2. The audience laughed and clapped their hands. (*Correct*)

3. The protesters plan to march and were singing at the same time. (The *protesters plan to march* and sing at the same time.)

4. James looked around, realized he was lost, and shivered with apprehension. (*Correct*)

5. All the wild geese settled near the lake and were drinking the water. (All *the wild* geese settled near the lake and *drank the water.*)

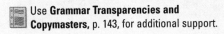 Use **Grammar Transparencies and Copymasters**, p. 143, for additional support.

 Use McDougal Littell's *Language Network*, Chapter 19, for more instruction and practice in parallelism.

Objectives
- reflect on the unit
- review literary analysis skills used in the unit
- paraphrase and summarize text to recall, inform, or organize ideas
- support responses by referring to relevant aspects of text and his/her own experiences
- assess and build portfolios

Reflecting on Theme

OPTION 1

A successful response will
- focus on and describe in detail the characters and people who illustrate this saying.
- describe mental images that text descriptions evoke.
- construct an interpretation of the saying using characters and people as support of the interpretation.

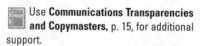
Use **Writing Transparencies,** p. 13, for additional support.

OPTION 2

A successful response will
- analyze characters' situations in selections.
- offer observations, make connections, react, speculate, interpret, and raise questions in response to texts.
- organize similarities and differences into a coherent argument.
- explain how real life and literature differ.

OPTION 3

Have students prepare for the exercise by listing the dominant characteristics of the character they wish to portray, including emotions, identifiable gestures, and memorable actions.

Use **Communications Transparencies and Copymasters,** p. 15, for additional support.

Self Assessment
Clarify the meaning of the quotation with students in a class discussion before they begin writing. Ask students to suggest representative characters who illustrate the quotation.

Flights of Imagination

Through the imagination, we can experience new sights, have adventures, and visit places we have never dreamed of. Whether we seek to experience a distant place or a distant time, stories can take us there. The selections in this unit involve several flights of imagination. Complete one or more of the options below to explore what you have learned.

Reflecting on the Theme

OPTION 1

More Than Meets the Eye When you think about the saying "appearances are deceiving," which characters from this unit come to mind? Which people from your own experience do you think of? Write an essay exploring the meaning of this saying. Use characters from this unit and from real life as examples.

OPTION 2

Close to Home In which of this unit's selections do the characters face situations that remind you of experiences from your own life? For each instance, write two to four paragraphs explaining the similarities and differences between the situation in the story and what happened to you.

OPTION 3

Guess My Name This unit contains a number of memorable characters. With a small group, play a game in which each of you pantomimes a character from the unit for the others to identify. You can use gestures or pantomime emotions to portray the character. Keep playing until each group member has had a chance to pantomime.

Self ASSESSMENT

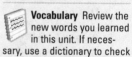
READER'S NOTEBOOK

Think again about the quotation you read at the beginning of the unit: "The man who has no imagination has no wings." Write a paragraph explaining how reading the selections in this unit has helped you to better understand the quotation.

REVIEWING YOUR PERSONAL
WORDList

Vocabulary Review the new words you learned in this unit. If necessary, use a dictionary to check the meaning of each word.

Spelling Review your list of spelling words. If you're not sure of the correct spelling, use a dictionary or refer to the **Spelling Handbook** on page R86.

Reviewing Literary Concepts

OPTION 1

Experiencing Suspense Suspense is the excitement or tension that readers feel as they get involved in a story and become eager to learn the outcome. In this unit, which of the selections do you think generates the most suspense? Which generates the least? Consider the selection that you regard as least suspenseful. How might you change the plot to heighten the suspense?

OPTION 2

Exploring Themes The theme, or message, of a story may be stated directly or only implied. Summarize in a phrase or two the theme of five selections you have read in this unit. Record the themes you have summarized in a chart.

Title	Theme
The Monsters Are Due on Maple Street	
Key Item	

Building Your Portfolio

- **Writing Options** Several of the Writing Options in this unit asked you to respond creatively by writing poems, stories, a boxing profile, and even a radio commercial. From your responses, choose the one that you think is the best. Write a cover note explaining the reasons for your choice. Then attach the note to the assignment and place it in your **Presentation Portfolio.**

- **Writing Workshops** In this unit you wrote an essay in which you identified a problem and proposed a solution. Reread your essay. Then write a note listing several careers in which the skills you learned in writing the essay might be useful. Attach the note to the front of your essay and place it in your **Presentation Portfolio.**

- **Additional Activities** Think back to any assignments you completed under **Activities & Explorations** and **Inquiry & Research.** Keep a record in your portfolio of any assignments that you especially enjoyed, found helpful, or would like to do further work on in the future.

Self ASSESSMENT

READER'S NOTEBOOK

On a sheet of paper, copy the following literary terms introduced in this unit. Next to each term, jot down a brief definition. If you have trouble explaining a particular concept, refer to the **Glossary of Literary and Reading Terms** on page R6.

science fiction	conflict
fantasy	humor
persuasive	surprise
essay	ending
meter	onomatopoeia
scanning	stanza
metaphor	resolution
narrative	teleplay
suspense	irony
symbol	alliteration

Self ASSESSMENT

Now that your **Presentation Portfolio** contains several pieces, determine which kinds of writing show your strongest work. What other kinds of writing do you think you would like to try as the year goes on?

Setting GOALS

As you completed the reading and writing activities in this unit, you might have noticed that you have strengths in certain skills but not in others. Look back through your **READER'S NOTEBOOK.** List one or two skills that you intend to develop in the next unit.

Reviewing Literary Concepts

OPTION 1

Students should support their decisions regarding the degree of suspense with details from each selection. Ask each student to create before-and-after diagrams of the plot, showing the change in events and the heightening of the suspense.

 Use **Literary Analysis Transparencies,** p. 5, for additional support.

OPTION 2

Use the Unit Three Resource Book, page 93, to provide students with a ready-made chart for analyzing themes.

Building Your Portfolio

Students should evaluate the items in their Working Portfolios and choose pieces that represent their highest quality work for their Presentation Portfolios.

Encourage students to include drafts, as well as the final products, in their portfolios, so that they can follow their development at different stages of the writing process.

Self Assessment and Setting Goals

Encourage students to commit to working on skills that they genuinely find difficult and challenging. Ask them to analyze what skills they are good at and to consider if these skills can help them to conquer their difficulties in other areas.

For more information on using Portfolios, use *Teacher's Guide to Assessment and Portfolio Use* beginning on p. 53.

LITERATURE CONNECTIONS
Tuck Everlasting

BY NATALIE BABBITT

This fantasy is about an encounter between a young girl and a family that never ages, near the spring that makes them immortal. A confrontation with a man who plans to market the spring water results in an accident, difficulty with the law, and an exciting rescue.

These thematically related readings are provided along with *Tuck Everlasting*:

Remember
BY CHRISTINA ROSSETTI

Why There Is Death
BY JOHN BIERHORST

from **The Population Explosion**
BY JOHN AND SUE BECKLAKE

The Search for the Magic Lake
BY GENEVIEVE BARLOW

Eastside Chic with Drive
BY ALBERT SPECTOR

Hail and Farewell
BY RAY BRADBURY

Guardian Neighbor
BY LYNDA BARRY

And Even *More* . . .

The Hobbit

BY J. R. R. TOLKEIN

In this award-winning fantasy, a hero struggles to win a dragon's treasure. Find out how Bilbo and his friends battle the forces of evil, fight a dragon, and make personal sacrifices for the good of the community. As you are drawn into their quest you become involved with the characters of a whole new land, called Middle Earth.

Books

The Shadow Guests
BY JOAN AIKEN
Ghosts mysteriously appear to a young boy to ask his help in breaking a curse.

All the Weyrs of Pern
BY ANNE MCCAFFREY
Not all is as it seems as an exciting and dangerous plan develops to end Thread on Pern.

The Hero and the Crown
BY ROBIN MCKINLEY
A girl goes on a quest for the objects that will restore her kingdom. Along the way she battles dragons and an evil magician.

LITERATURE CONNECTIONS
A Wrinkle in Time

BY MADELEINE L'ENGLE

A science fiction novel about the struggle between good and evil, this absorbing story involves supernatural beings, a distant planet, and a daring rescue.

These thematically related readings are provided along with *A Wrinkle in Time:*

Odd Jobs
BY JUDITH GOROG

Reversible
BY OCTAVIO PAZ

Behind Bars
BY FADWA TUQAN

from **World of the Brain**
BY ALVIN AND VIRGINIA SILVERSTEIN

from **It's Our World, Too!**
BY PHILIP HOOSE

The Dark Princess
BY RICHARD KENNEDY

The Sparrow
BY IVAN TURGENEV

Colony
BY RICK WERNLI

Other Media

The Dream Catcher
BY MONICA HUGHES
A 15-year-old girl strives to free people from the control of a giant computer that has taken over their minds.

The Secret Garden
BY FRANCES HODGSON BURNETT
Mary Lennox, orphaned and sent to live with a reclusive uncle, longs for a sense of belonging. A hidden garden and a mysterious young cousin help to transform Mary's sadness.

The Secret Garden
The 1993 version of the classic story is directed by Agnieszka Holland.
WARNER HOME VIDEO
(VIDEOCASSETTE)

A Wrinkle in Time
Read by Madeleine L'Engle
LISTENING LIBRARY
(AUDIOCASSETTE)

Dark They Were, and Golden-Eyed
(AUDIOCASSETTE)

Something Wicked This Way Comes
Ray Bradbury's fantasy told from the point of view of a 13-year-old boy
ANCHOR BAY ENTERTAINMENT
(VIDEOCASSETTE)

Rod Serling's Night Gallery
Collection of Serling classics struck from the original negatives
COLUMBIA HOUSE VIDEO
(VIDEOCASSETTE)

ACROSS the CURRICULUM

Robot Design

OVERVIEW

One subfield within Artificial Intelligence is robotics. Robots are already widely used in scientific research and industries such as manufacturing, but these robots bear little resemblance to the artificial life forms found in science fiction. Today, robots are used to help humans with tasks as varied as building cars, defusing bombs, and exploring archaeological sites.

Research Questions

- What robots and computers have you seen in movies and TV?

- What makes a machine "intelligent"?

- How can robots help people?

Investigation Students will research and discuss what makes a machine "intelligent" and then invent and illustrate a robot intended to perform a specific function. If time allows, students may also write, administer, and analyze results from a survey of feelings about "intelligent" technology. The robot designs and survey results may be presented orally or in the form of a classroom display.

Wrap-up When the robot designs are complete, have students create a flyer or invitations specifying where other students, parents, and community members can view them.

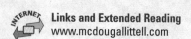

Links and Extended Reading
www.mcdougallittell.com

OBJECTIVES

❏ discuss the portrayal of artificial intelligence in entertainment media and brainstorm a list of tasks that robots could perform

❏ research and respond to the Turing Test

❏ design a robot intended to perform a specific task

❏ write and analyze a survey on attitudes toward artificial intelligence

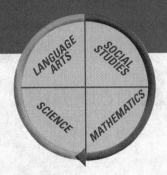

Team Teaching Assignments

CONNECT TO **LANGUAGE ARTS** Lead the class in a discussion about "intelligent" computers and related technology, such as robots. Start by asking volunteer students to look up *computer* and *robot* in a dictionary. Then ask students to name some "intelligent" computers and robots they know about, from literature, television, and movies. Ask the class what makes these characters computers or robots. How do students know that the characters are computers or robots? Tell students that today's robots are used to perform tasks that would be difficult, unsafe, or boring for a person to do. Have the class brainstorm a list of tasks that robots could perform that would be useful to people. You may also wish to have students complete the interdisciplinary assignments below. *(1 class period)*

YOU WILL NEED:
- (no special materials needed)

CONNECT TO **SOCIAL STUDIES** Explain the "Turing Test" to students. (In the 1950s, Dr. Alan Turing said that if a person could ask a computer a question and receive a response that he or she could not differentiate from a human response, then that computer could "think.") Direct students to write a one-page response to the Turing Test, telling whether or not they think it is a good test of a computer's ability to "think," and support their opinion. *(1 class period)*

YOU WILL NEED:
- Web access (optional)
- encyclopedias and other reference books

CONNECT TO **SCIENCE** Direct students, working in small groups, to choose one of the tasks they brainstormed for the Connect to Language Arts activity and design an "intelligent" robot to perform that task. Have students consider the following problems as they develop their robots:

- Appearance: What does the robot look like and why?
- Sensing: How does the robot "know" what is around it?
- Movement: How does the robot move within its environment?
- Manipulation: How does the robot move other objects?
- Energy: How is the robot powered?
- Intelligence: How does the robot "think"?

Each group should create a final sketch of their robot with captions that explain its special features. *(2–3 class periods)*

YOU WILL NEED:
- Web access (optional)
- art materials

CONNECT TO **MATHEMATICS** Guide the class in creating a survey to find out how a group of people feel about the idea of artificial intelligence. A sample question might be, "When do you think intelligent computers will become a reality in everyday life?" with a choice of answers such as *they already exist; in 10 years; in 50 years;* and *in more than 50 years.* Another question might be, "How would you feel about certain jobs being handled by intelligent computers?" with a choice of answers such as *very comfortable, somewhat comfortable,* and *uncomfortable.* Help students administer the survey to another class or to family members. When the surveys are returned, have the class make a display explaining the results, using pie charts and percentages to express the responses to each question. *(2–3 class periods)*

YOU WILL NEED:
- word processing program or paper and pencil
- calculator
- colored pencils
- chart-size paper

Space Station Bulletin Board

OVERVIEW

The International Space Station (ISS) is the next step in humanity's exploration of the frontier of space. The first two pieces of the ISS were launched in 1998. Assembly of the ISS is expected to be completed in 2004, but parts of the space station will be active much sooner. Starting in 2000, the Space Shuttle and two Russian launch vehicles will be used to send astronauts on a series of missions to the ISS. These astronauts will live in part of the station while they attach and assemble the remaining components.

Research Questions

• Why is space exploration important?

• What have we accomplished so far in space travel?

• How and why is the International Space Station being built?

Investigation Students will create a bulletin board about space travel, with an emphasis on space stations. Components of the display may include persuasive essays about space exploration, time lines of achievements in space travel, diagrams and reports about the International Space Station (ISS), and statistics comparing the ISS to Mir.

Wrap-up When the space station bulletin board or boards are complete, invite other students, parents, and community members to view them. You might wish to watch a space-themed movie, such as *Apollo 13* (1995, rated PG), *The Right Stuff* (1983, rated PG), or *October Sky* (1999, rated PG), as a culminating activity.

Links and Extended Reading
www.mcdougallittell.com

LaserLinks: Background
Science Connection

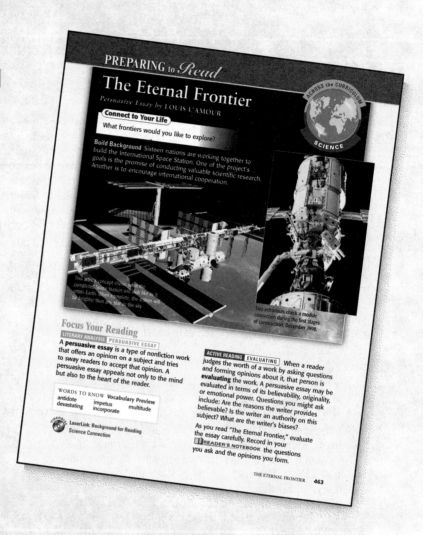

OBJECTIVES

❏ write a persuasive essay

❏ research and create a time line of space exploration

❏ research and describe the International Space Station

❏ compare the International Space Station and Mir using percentages

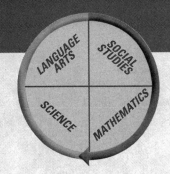

Team Teaching Assignments

CONNECT TO **LANGUAGE ARTS** Have students form small groups and work together to write short persuasive essays similar to Louis L'Amour's "The Eternal Frontier." However, ask students to imagine that they are writing to convince the United States government to participate in the building of the International Space Station. Groups should start by brainstorming a list of points they might want to make in the essays. Then each group can create an outline, write a first draft, revise, and write a final draft. Help students bind the essays into a booklet that can be attached to or displayed near the bulletin board. *(2–3 class periods)*

YOU WILL NEED:
- word processor or paper and pencil
- stapler, tape, or glue

CONNECT TO **SOCIAL STUDIES** The very first space station, called Salyut, was built by the Soviet Union and was launched in 1971. Seven other Salyut stations were launched through 1982. The knowledge and experience gained from the Salyut stations made possible the Russian space station Mir, which in turn has helped to develop the expertise needed to build the International Space Station. Direct students to research milestones in space travel. Have them make a time line of space travel, highlighting developments in space station technology. Display the time lines as part of the bulletin board. *(1–2 class periods)*

YOU WILL NEED:
- Web access (optional)
- encyclopedias and reference books on space exploration
- colored pencils

CONNECT TO **SCIENCE** Have students research the International Space Station. Divide the following research topics among the groups:

- Create a simplified diagram of the International Space Station. Label one part and write a caption explaining its purpose.
- Explain how the station is being constructed. How will it differ from earlier space stations such as Skylab and Mir?
- How will use of the station be divided among different countries, and what research do scientists anticipate using the station to do?

In each group have students divide up roles such as facilitator, recorder, researcher, and artist. Remind students to credit all works cited. Arrange the reports and diagrams on the bulletin board. *(4–5 class periods)*

YOU WILL NEED:
- Web access (optional)
- current reference materials on the ISS and space science
- art materials

CONNECT TO **MATHEMATICS** Upon completion, the ISS will measure approximately 360 feet wide and 290 feet long, and will have a mass of about 460 tons. Space station Mir is about 90 feet wide and 110 feet long, and has a mass of about 100 tons. Have students compare the width, length, and mass of the two space stations. How much wider and longer will the ISS be than Mir? How much greater will its mass be? Students should express their answers in percentages. Post the comparisons on the bulletin board. *(2 class periods)*

YOU WILL NEED:
- calculator

Nothing Stays the Same

The characters in this unit encourage readers to reflect on their constantly changing relationships with themselves, the world, and the people in it. Part 1, "Learning the Hard Way," and Part 2, "Changes of Heart," show that change might be gradual or sudden and may impact the way a person relates to another or sees him or herself.

—————— Part 1 ——————

Learning the Hard Way The selections in this part explore the ways that painful or embarrassing events can lead to growth. The narrator in "The White Umbrella" by Gish Jen suffers the shame of being disloyal to her mother before she is able to accept her mother and herself for who they are.

—————— Part 2 ——————

Changes of Heart In these selections, the impetus for personal change comes from many sources. For example, in the story "Waiting" by Budge Wilson, Henrietta, who has always been in Juliette's shadow, blossoms and eclipses Juliette. Juliette is forced to rethink her relationship with her twin and to view herself differently as a result of this change in Henrietta.

516

 See the Skills Trace at the beginning of the unit for information on TEKS covered in this lesson.
TEKS

 Mini Lesson **Viewing and Representing** **TEKS 22A**

ART APPRECIATION

Instruction Point out to students that details of an illustration or painting that may at first seem unrelated to the central image could have a symbolic significance. The boy's reflection in the mirror is the focal point of this illustration. However, the artist chose to add other details as well instead of setting the mirror against a plain background.

Ask: What is the symbolism of each image and object in this illustration?

Possible Response: The boy's face in the mirror is a person's self-image, which may or may not

be an accurate reflection of the real person. The suspension of the mirror suggests that sometimes people catch a glimpse of themselves unexpectedly and from odd angles or others' perceptions. The suitcase represents exploration of places beyond a person's usual realm of experience. This may lead to a change in his or her self-image. The crumpled envelope and faint old-fashioned writing might symbolize the influence of others or the past on a person.

NOTHING STAYS the SAME

Time
ripens
all
things;
no
one
is
born
wise.

MIGUEL DE CERVANTES SAAVEDRA
Spanish writer,
author of *Don Quixote*

Making Connections

To help students explore the connections between the art, the quotation, and the unit theme, have them consider the following questions:

Ask: Why would the theme of this unit, "Nothing Stays the Same," be important to explore?
Possible Response: to learn what change can teach people; to remind people to fully enjoy the present; to offer hope that present conditions will not stay the same forever; to show the ways in which change can be brought about.

Ask: How would you restate Miguel de Cervantes's quotation in your own words?
Possible Response: Every experience has the potential to teach one something and lead one to become a better person.

Ask: How might the central image of the illustration be interpreted in relation to the theme of this unit?
Possible Response: Not all changes are immediately visible. Some take time to manifest themselves.

Ask: What kinds of stories and experiences might you expect to read about in this unit?
Possible Response: painful events that have had positive effects; unexpected changes; stories about growing up, growing old, or experiencing loss.

Have students share ways that they think they have changed and explain what brought about those changes.
Responses will vary.

Features and Selections	Literary Analysis	TEKS	Reading and Critical Thinking	TEKS	Writing Opportunities	TEKS
Nothing Stays the Same Learning the Hard Way						
Learning the Language of Literature Mood and Tone	Mood and Tone, 519 **TAAS READING OBJ. 6**	**12H, K**				
The Active Reader Skills and Strategies			Predicting, 521 **TAAS READING OBJ. 4**	**10A, 11A**		
SHORT STORY **The White Umbrella** Difficulty Level: *Easy*	Mood and Tone, 522, 524, 526, 528, 530 Review: Symbol, 530 **TAAS READING OBJ. 6**	**12K** **12J**	Predicting, 522, 524, 526, 530 Informal Assessment, 529 **TAAS READING OBJ. 2, 3 TAAS WRITING OBJ. 1**	**10L, 11A, B** **10F, 11B**	Short Story, 531 Opinion Essay, 531 **TAAS WRITING OBJ. 1**	**11B, 15A, C, G** **15A, B**
AUTOBIOGRAPHY *from* Boy: Tales of Childhood Difficulty Level: *Average*	Dialect, 533, 534, 538, 544, 546	**12D**	Connecting, 533, 534, 538, 542, 544, 546 Standardized Test Practice, 542 **TAAS READING OBJ. 6**	**10A, 11B** **10K, 12H**	Opinion Essay, 547 **TAAS WRITING OBJ. 1**	**11C, 15C**
Real World Link A History of Chocolate			Magazine Article: Clarifying, 549	**10C**		
FARCE **A Defenseless Creature** Difficulty Level: *Average*	Farce, 553, 554, 556, 558, 561 Review: Mood, 561 **TAAS READING OBJ. 6**	**12E** **12K**	Visualizing, 553, 554, 558, 560, 561 Informal Assessment, 557 Standardized Test Practice, 560 **TAAS READING OBJ. 2, 4, 5 TAAS WRITING OBJ. 1**	**10D, 11B, C 12I 10K, 12G**	Theater Review, 562 Sequel to the Play, 562 **TAAS WRITING OBJ. 1**	**11B, 15C 11B, 15G**
NARRATIVE POETRY **The Highwayman** Difficulty Level: *Challenging* Building Vocabulary	Word Choice, 564, 566, 568, 570 **TAAS READING OBJ. 6**	**12K**	Responding to the Writer's Style, 564, 566, 568, 570 Standardized Test Practice, 569 **TAAS READING OBJ. 6**	**11B, C, 12K 10K, 12H**	Police Report, 571 **TAAS WRITING OBJ. 1**	**11B, 15A, C, G**
Communication Workshop: Staging a Scene Assessment Practice			Analyzing a Model Script, 580	**12D, 19A, D**		

LEGEND   **DLS – Daily Language SkillBuilder**   **Green type – Teacher's Edition**

Speaking and Listening / Viewing and Representing	TEKS	Inquiry and Research	TEKS	Grammar, Usage, and Mechanics	TEKS	Vocabulary	TEKS
Art Appreciation, 516	22A						
Cooperative Learning Activity, 530 Mother's Day Card, 531 Dramatic Skit, 531 Monologues, 528	10L, 11B 11B, 24A 5C, 11B 3B, 5A, D, E, 11B	Umbrella in China, 531 Mona and Callie, 532 **TAAS READING OBJ. 4**	13C 11C, D	Prepositional Phrases, 532 DLS, 522 Distinguishing Prepositions from Adverbs, 527 Prepositional Phrases, 532 **TAAS WRITING OBJ. 3, 4, 6, 7**	17E 16B, 17D 17E 17E	Word Meaning, 531 Word Meaning, 523 Synonyms, 526 The Suffixes -ible and -able, 531 **TAAS READING OBJ. 1** **TAAS WRITING OBJ. 3, 7**	9B 9C 9B, C 16C
Paired Activity, 546 Dialogue, 547 Portrait of Pratchett, 547 Art Connection, 547 Art Appreciation, 540 Defensive Speeches, 545	10L, 11B, 12D 5C, 11B, 15A, G 11B, 24A 22A 22A 2B, 5A, D, E, 11B	The Origin of Candy, 547 Explore Another Genre, 548	13C 8C	Adjective Phrases, 548 DLS, 533 Compound Sentences, 541 Comparative and Superlative Forms of Adjectives, 544 Adjective Phrases, 548 **TAAS WRITING OBJ. 3–7**	17E 16B, 17C 17A 17D 17E	Antonyms, 547 Silent/Sounded Consonants, 547 Antonyms, 534 Analogies, 538 Silent/Sounded Consonants, 547 **TAAS READING OBJ. 1** **TAAS WRITING OBJ. 3, 7**	9B 16D 6A, 9B 9B 16D
		Activity Link: *Boy: Tales of Childhood*, 552 Inquiry & Research, 552 **TAAS WRITING OBJ. 1**	10L, 15C 13C, 20C, D				
Cooperative Learning Activity, 561 Production of the Play, 562 Theater Poster, 562 Art Connection, 562 Readers' Theater, 558 Art Appreciation, 559	10L, 11B, 12E 5C, 11B 11B, 24A 22A 3B, 5C, E 22A	Classic Comedy, 562 Screenwriter, 563	15A, 23B 23B	Adverb Phrases, 563 DLS, 553 Indirect Objects, 556 Adverb Phrases, 563 **TAAS WRITING OBJ. 4, 6**	17E 17C 17C 17E	Context Clues, 562 Using Context Clues, 554 Synonyms, 562 **TAAS READING OBJ. 1**	9B 6A 9B, F
Cooperative Learning Activity, 570 Choral Reading, 571 Illustrated Map, 571 Art Connection, 571 Art Appreciation, 565 Dramatic Reading, 567	10L, 11B 5E, 7C, 11B 11B, 24A 22A 22A 5C, 11B	Highwaymen, 571 **TAAS WRITING OBJ. 1**	13C, 15C	DLS, 564 Precise Adjectives, 568 Action Verbs, 571 **TAAS WRITING OBJ. 2, 3, 4, 6, 7**	16B, 17C, G 17D 15H	Understanding Denotation and Connotation, 572 **TAAS READING OBJ. 1, 6**	9F
Staging Your Scene, 582 Evaluating the Staging of Your Scene, 583 **TAAS WRITING OBJ. 1**	4A, 15E, 18A, 19C 19C			Revising & Editing, 584 Adverbs and Predicate Adjectives, 584 **TAAS WRITING OBJ. 3, 4, 6, 7**	16F, 17C, E, F 17D		

Features and Selections	Literary Analysis	TEKS	Reading and Critical Thinking	TEKS	Writing Opportunities	TEKS
Changes of Heart						
Learning the Language of Literature Character Development	Character Development, 586 **TAAS READING OBJ. 5**	12F				
The Active Reader Skills and Strategies			Drawing Conclusions, 590 **TAAS READING OBJ. 5**	10A, H, L		
SHORT STORY **An Hour with Abuelo** Difficulty Level: *Average* Literary Link The Old Grandfather and His Little Grandson	First-Person Narrator, 591, 592, 594, 596, 598 **TAAS READING OBJ. 6**	12D, H	Drawing Conclusions, 591, 592, 594, 596, 598 Informal Assessment, 596 **TAAS READING OBJ. 5** **TAAS WRITING OBJ. 1**	10H, L, 11B 10H, 15C	Personal Essay, 599 Diary Entry, 599	15A 11B, 15A
SHORT STORY **Waiting** Difficulty Level: *Challenging*	Unreliable Narrator, 601, 602, 604, 606, 608, 610, 612, 614 Review: Foil, 614 **TAAS READING OBJ. 6**	12H 12D	Making Judgments, 601, 602, 604, 606, 608, 610, 612, 614 Connect to Your Life, 601 Comparing Texts, 614 Standardized Test Practice, 608, 611 **TAAS READING OBJ. 4, 5, 6**	10J, 11A, C 4A 11C, D 10A, H, K	Persuasive Essay, 615 Letter to Henrietta, 615 **TAAS WRITING OBJ. 1**	15B 11B, 15A
Real World Link Face to Face with Twins			Magazine Article: Taking Notes, 617 **TAAS READING OBJ. 3**	10G, 20C		
AUTOBIOGRAPHY *from* **Growing Up** Difficulty Level: *Average* Building Vocabulary	Irony, 621, 622, 624, 626, 628, 629	12J	Recognizing Text Organization, 621, 622, 624, 626, 629 Comparing Texts, 629 Standardized Test Practice, 628 **TAAS READING OBJ. 2, 3, 4**	10E, 11B, C, 12I 11C, D 10F, K	Personal Essay, 630 Autobiographical Paragraph, 630 **TAAS WRITING OBJ. 1**	15A 15A, C
Writing Workshop: Comparison-and-Contrast Essay Assessment Practice			Analyzing a Student Model, 637 **TAAS READING OBJ. 2, 4**	10E, 19A, D	Comparison-and-Contrast Essay, 639 Using Transitions, 640 **TAAS WRITING OBJ. 1–4**	15A, C, H, 18A, 19C 15H
Reflect and Assess	Identifying Mood, 643 Examining Characterization, 643 **TAAS READING OBJ. 5, 6**	12K 10L, 12F			Writing a Dialogue, 642 Portfolio Building, 643	15A, G 19C, E

LEGEND   DLS – Daily Language SkillBuilder   **Green type – Teacher's Edition**

Speaking and Listening Viewing and Representing	TEKS	Inquiry and Research	TEKS	Grammar, Usage, and Mechanics	TEKS	Vocabulary	TEKS
Paired Activity, 598 Personal Interview, 599 Family Maps, 599 Art Appreciation, 595 **TAAS READING OBJ. 5**	10H, L, 11B 5B 11B, 24A 22A	Puerto Rico, 599	13C, 24A	Appositives, 600 DLS, 591 Predicate Adjectives, 594 Identifying Appositives, 600 **TAAS WRITING OBJ. 3, 5, 6, 7**	17C 17A, B 17C 17C	Related Words, 599 Homophones, 599 Related Words, 592 Antonyms, 597 Homophones, 599 **TAAS READING OBJ. 1**	6A, 9B 6A, 9B 6A 9B, C 16D
Cooperative Learning Activity, 614 Play Production, 615 Art Connection, 615 Art Appreciation, 607, 609, 612 Retelling of Story Event, 613	11B, C 5C, 11B 22A 22A 5C, E, 11B	Research About Twins, 615 Letter, 616 Author Activity, 616	15A	Participial Phrases, 616 DLS, 601 Interrupters, 604 Identifying Participial Phrases, 616 **TAAS WRITING OBJ. 3, 5, 6, 7**	17A, C 17C, G 16B 17C	Analogies, 615 Context Clues, 602 Analogies, 610 **TAAS READING OBJ. 1**	9B 6A 9B
		Activity Link: "Waiting," 620 Inquiry & Research, 620	20C 20C, D				
Paired Activity, 629 Oral History, 630 Photography, 624 Dramatic Interpretation, 627	4A, 11B, 12J 5B 22A 5C, 11B	The WPA, 630 Writing a Column, 630	15A	DLS, 621 Avoiding Overuse of Passive Voice of Verbs, 625 Infinitive Phrases, 630 **TAAS WRITING OBJ. 3, 6**	17C, F 17C 17A	Understanding Synonyms and Antonyms, 631 Synonyms, 622 **TAAS READING OBJ. 1**	9B, C 9C
Picturing Text Structure, 637	10E, L			Dangling Modifiers, 640 Revising and Editing, 641 Punctuating Dialogue, 640 Dangling Modifiers, 641 **TAAS WRITING OBJ. 3–7**	17C 16F, 17A, C, F 16B 17D		
Act It Out, 642 Character Change, 642	5C, 11B 4A, 11B						

UNIT FOUR
RESOURCE MANAGEMENT GUIDE
PART 1

To introduce the theme of this unit, use Fine Art Transparencies T28–T30 in the Communications Transparencies and Copymasters.

Additional Support

	Unit Resource Book	Assessment	Integrated Technology and Media	Literary Analysis Transparencies
The White Umbrella *pp. 522–532*	• Summary p. 4 • Active Reading p. 5 • Literary Analysis p. 6 • Words to Know p. 7 • Grammar p. 8 • Spelling p. 9 • Selection Quiz p. 10	• Selection Test, Formal Assessment pp. 89–90 Test Generator	Audio Library	• Tone T25 • Mood T26
from **Boy: Tales of Childhood** *pp. 533–548*	• Summary p. 11 • Active Reading p. 12 • Literary Analysis p. 13 • Words to Know p. 14 • Grammar p. 15 • Spelling p. 16 • Selection Quiz p. 17	• Selection Test, Formal Assessment pp. 91–92 Test Generator	Audio Library LaserLinks, Teacher's SourceBook p. 24	• Dialogue T24
A Defenseless Creature *pp. 553–563*	• Summary p. 18 • Active Reading p. 19 • Literary Analysis p. 20 • Words to Know p. 21 • Grammar p. 22 • Spelling p. 23 • Selection Quiz p. 24	• Selection Test, Formal Assessment pp. 93–94 Test Generator	Audio Library	
The Highwayman *pp. 564–571*	• Active Reading p. 25 • Literary Analysis p. 26	• Selection Test, Formal Assessment pp. 95–96 Test Generator	Audio Library LaserLinks, Teacher's SourceBook p. 25 Research Starter www.mcdougallittell.com	• Author's Style T9 • Poetry: Figurative Language T19 • Poetry: Sound Devices T20

Communication Workshop: Staging a Scene

		Unit Assessment	Unit Technology	
Unit Four Resource Book • Planning and Drafting p. 28 • Practicing and Delivering p. 29 • Peer Response Guide pp. 30–31 • Refining Your Performance p. 32 • Rubric for Evaluation p. 33	**Writing Coach** **Writing Transparencies** T1–4, T38 **Grammar Transparencies and Copymasters** C77 **Communications Transparencies and Copymasters** T16 **Teacher's Guide to Assessment and Portfolio Use**	• Unit Four Part 1 Test, Formal Assessment pp. 97–98 Test Generator • Unit Four Integrated Test, Integrated Assessment pp. 19–24	ClassZone www.mcdougallittell.com Electronic Teacher Tools	

Reading and Critical Thinking Transparencies	Grammar Transparencies and Copymasters	Vocabulary Transparencies and Copymasters	Writing Transparencies	Communications Transparencies and Copymasters
• Predicting T7 • Story Map T34	• Daily Language SkillBuilder T16 • Distinguishing Prepositions from Adverbs C88 • Prepositional Phrases C89	• Word Meaning C59 • Synonyms C60	• Opinion Statement T27 • Short Story T34	• Giving and Using Feedback to Improve Performance T16
• Connecting T2	• Daily Language SkillBuilder T17 • Comparative and Superlative Forms of Adjectives C84 • Adjective Phrases C92 • Compound Sentences C104	• Antonyms C61 • Analogies C62	• Opinion Statement T27	• Persuasive Techniques T3
• Visualizing T10	• Daily Language SkillBuilder T17 • Indirect Objects C55 • Adverb Phrases C93	• Using Context Clues C63 • Synonyms C64	• Elaboration T13	• Dramatic Reading T12
	• Daily Language SkillBuilder T18 • Action Verbs C68 • Precise Adjectives C79		• Levels of Language T14 • Locating Information Using the Internet T47–48	• Reading Aloud T11 • Dramatic Reading T12

STUDENTS ACQUIRING ENGLISH

The **Spanish Study Guide,** pp. 106–120, includes language support for the following pages:
• Family and Community Involvement (per unit)

• Selection Summaries and Vocabulary
• Active Reading
• Literary Analysis

UNIT FOUR
RESOURCE MANAGEMENT GUIDE
PART 2

To introduce the theme of this unit, use Fine Art Transparencies T28–30 in the Communications Transparencies and Copymasters.

Additional Support

	Unit Resource Book	Assessment	Integrated Technology and Media	Literary Analysis Transparencies
An Hour with Abuelo *pp. 591–600*	• Summary p. 34 • Active Reading p. 35 • Literary Analysis p. 36 • Words to Know p. 37 • Grammar p. 38 • Spelling p. 39 • Selection Quiz p. 40	• Selection Test, Formal Assessment pp. 99–100 ⊙ Test Generator	◯ Audio Library ⇗ Research Starter www.mcdougallittell.com	• Narrator and Point of View T22
Waiting *pp. 601–616*	• Summary p. 41 • Active Reading p. 42 • Literary Analysis p. 43 • Words to Know p. 44 • Grammar p. 45 • Spelling p. 46 • Selection Quiz p. 47	• Selection Test, Formal Assessment pp. 101–102 ⊙ Test Generator	◯ Audio Library ⊙ LaserLinks, Teacher's SourceBook p. 26	• Narrator and Point of View T22
***from* Growing Up** *pp. 621–630*	• Summary p. 48 • Active Reading p. 49 • Literary Analysis p. 50 • Words to Know p. 51 • Grammar p. 52 • Spelling p. 53 • Selection Quiz p. 54	• Selection Test, Formal Assessment pp. 103–104 ⊙ Test Generator	◯ Audio Library ⇗ Research Starter www.mcdougallittell.com	• Irony T27

Writing Workshop: Comparison-and Contrast Essay

Unit Four Resource Book
- Prewriting p. 56
- Drafting and Elaboration p. 57
- Peer Response Guide pp. 58–59
- Revising, Editing, and Proofreading p. 60
- Student Models pp. 61–63
- Rubric for Evaluation p. 64

⊙ **Writing Coach**
Writing Transparencies T1–4, T9–10, T28–29
Reading and Critical Thinking Transparencies T24
Grammar Transparencies and Copymasters C115, C130
Teacher's Guide to Assessment and Portfolio Use

Unit Assessment
- Unit Four Part 2 Test, Formal Assessment pp. 105–106
⊙ Test Generator
- Unit Four Integrated Test, Integrated Assessment pp. 19–24

Unit Technology
⇗ ClassZone www.mcdougallittell.com
⊙ Electronic Teacher Tools

Reading and Critical Thinking Transparencies	Grammar Transparencies and Copymasters	Vocabulary Transparencies and Copymasters	Writing Transparencies	Communications Transparencies and Copymasters
• Drawing Conclusions T9	• Daily Language SkillBuilder T18 • Predicate Adjectives C76 • Identifying Appositives C107	• Related Words C65 • Antonyms C66	• Elaboration T13	• Interviewing T9
• Making Judgments T15	• Daily Language SkillBuilder T19 • Interrupters C132 • Identifying Participial Phrases C99	• Context Clues C67 • Analogies C68	• Organizing Your Writing T11	• Dramatic Reading T12
• Text Structure (Organization) T24	• Daily Language SkillBuilder T20 • Avoiding Overuse of Passive Voice C142 • Infinitive Phrases C100	• Synonyms C69	• Locating Information Using the Internet T47–48	• Interviewing T9 • Impromptu Speaking: Dialogue, Role-Play T13

STUDENTS ACQUIRING ENGLISH

The **Spanish Study Guide,** pp. 121–129, includes language support for the following pages:
• Family and Community Involvement (per unit)

• Selection Summaries and Vocabulary
• Active Reading
• Literary Analysis

Selection	SkillBuilder Sentences	Suggested Answers
The White Umbrella	**1.** The narrator plays the piano more good than her sister does. **2.** The narrators mother work's in the afternoons'.	**1.** The narrator plays the piano **better** than her sister does. **2.** The narrator's mother **works** in the **afternoons.**
from Boy: Tales of Childhood	**1.** Neither Roald nor his friends likes Mrs. Pratchett; she don't care for them either. **2.** Their favorite candies were sherbet suckers licorice bootlaces gobstoppers and pear drops.	**1.** Neither Roald nor his friends **like** Mrs. Pratchett; she **doesn't** care for them either. **2.** Their favorite candies were sherbet suckers, licorice bootlaces, gobstoppers, and pear drops.
A Defenseless Creature	**1.** Mr. Kistunov would of been avoiding Mrs. Schukin if he has known what she is like. **2.** A Defenseless Creature is one of my favorite plays she told the class.	**1.** Mr. Kistunov would **have avoided** Mrs. Schukin if he **had** known what she **was** like. **2.** "'A Defenseless Creature' is one of my favorite plays," she told the class.

Selection	SkillBuilder Sentences	Suggested Answers
The Highwayman	1. The highwaymans way of life doesnt lessen Bess love for him. 2. Travel use to be more dangerous before there was state troopers and regulated highway networks.	1. The highwayman**'s** way of life doesn't lessen Bess**'s** love for him. 2. Travel use**d** to be more dangerous before there **were** state troopers and regulated highway networks.
An Hour with Abuelo	1. Grandfather who wanted to be a teacher was ordered to go to war. 2. Arturo thought the visit would be boring, and he was wrong.	1. Grandfather, who wanted to be a teacher, was ordered to go to war. 2. Arturo thought the visit would be boring, **but** he was wrong.
Waiting	1. The two twin's personalities were quite different. 2. Mother was talking about Juliette. She stopped reading to listen.	1. The two **twins'** personalities were quite different. 2. Mother was talking about Juliette. **Juliette** stopped reading to listen.

Selection	SkillBuilder Sentences	Suggested Answers
from Growing Up	1. Russell Baker told how he gets his first job.	1. Russell Baker told how he **got** his first job.
	2. Russell loved lying around reading, his sister liked more action.	2. Russell loved lying around reading, **but** his sister liked more action.

	Unit One	Unit Two	Unit Three	Unit Four	Unit Five	Unit Six
Grammar Focus by Unit	The Sentence and Its Parts	Nouns, Pronouns, and Verbs	Modifiers	Phrases	Compound and Complex Sentences	Review

The Language of Literature offers several options for integrating grammar instruction and literature.

- Each unit has a specific grammar focus. The grammar focus for this unit is highlighted on the planning chart. Categories of grammar skills for this unit are shown in red.

- The Pupil's Edition includes instructive features entitled *Grammar in Context*. The instruction in these features arises from the selections and relates to the grammar focus for each unit.

- The Writing Workshops in the Pupil's Edition include grammar tips that help the students produce error-free drafts.

- Mini Lessons in the Teacher's Edition complement the instruction in the *Grammar in Context* features. Additional Mini Lessons relate to the grammar focus for each unit as well as to the literature.

- Daily Language SkillBuilders in the Teacher's Edition provide students with ongoing proofreading practice and reinforce punctuation, spelling, grammar and usage, and capitalization.

- Grammar Copymasters and Transparencies, which may be used independently or in conjunction with the Mini Lessons in the Teacher's Edition, present grammar in a traditional, systematic sequence.

PE instruction shown in black
TE Mini Lessons shown in green

Part 1

THE SENTENCE AND ITS PARTS
Indirect Objects
"A Defenseless Creature," p. 556

VERBS
Action Verbs
"The Highwayman," p. 571

ADJECTIVES AND ADVERBS
Comparative and Superlative Forms of Adjectives
"Boy: Tales of Childhood," p. 544
Precise Adjectives
"The Highwayman," p. 568
Adverbs and Predicate Adjectives
Assessment Practice, p. 584

PREPOSITIONS, CONJUNCTIONS, INTERJECTIONS
Distinguishing Prepositions from Adverbs
"The White Umbrella," p. 527
Prepositional Phrases
"The White Umbrella," p. 532
Prepositional Phrases
"The White Umbrella," p. 532
Adjective Phrases
"Boy: Tales of Childhood," p. 548
Adjective Phrases
"Boy: Tales of Childhood," p. 548
Adverb Phrases
"A Defenseless Creature," p. 563
Adverb Phrases
"A Defenseless Creature," p. 563

SENTENCE STRUCTURE
Compound Sentences
"Boy: Tales of Childhood," p. 541

Part 2

ADJECTIVES AND ADVERBS
Predicate Adjectives
"An Hour with Abuelo," p. 594

VERBALS AND VERB PHRASES
Participial Phrases
"Waiting," p. 616
Identifying Participial Phrases
"Waiting," p. 616
Infinitive Phrases
"Growing Up," p. 630

SENTENCE STRUCTURE
Appositives
"An Hour with Abuelo," p. 600
Identifying Appositives
"An Hour with Abuelo," p. 600
Dangling Modifiers
Writing Workshop, p. 640
Dangling Modifiers
Assessment Practice, p. 641

PUNCTUATION
Interrupters
"Waiting," p. 604
Punctuating Dialogue
Writing Workshop, p. 640

STYLE
Avoiding Overuse of Passive Voice of Verbs
"Growing Up," p. 625

OVERVIEW

Students conduct research and surveys to analyze the current image of teenagers as portrayed by the media. They present their findings in a Media Panel Discussion.

Project at a glance The selections in Unit Four focus on identity and misperception. They deal with how people and things can appear different from what they truly are. For this project, students will work in small groups to investigate how different forms of the media portray teens, and whether that portrayal is correct. Each group will look at ads in a selected medium (magazines, television, newspaper, and radio). Then each group will conduct a survey to see if others think this image is accurate. They will also interview teens to find how they feel about their own image in the media. Group members will form panels to discuss their findings.

SCHEDULING

Panel discussions should take anywhere from 15 to 20 minutes. You may want to schedule the discussions over the course of this unit, or at the end of this unit, depending on your purposes.

PROJECT OBJECTIVES

- To demonstrate the speaking and listening skills introduced in the activity
- To analyze the various images of teens presented in the media
- To develop media awareness and critical-thinking skills
- To research various media and to interview people about the image presented by the media
- To draw conclusions about the image presented by the media
- To contribute to a panel discussion and present their findings

SUGGESTED GROUP SIZE

5–6 students per group

 Media Panel Discussion

1 Getting Started

Think about the resources available to you and about how you want to structure the project. If you have access to video and audio equipment, students can include television and radio in their investigations and presentations. Since students will be handing out surveys, you may want to make arrangements to use your school's photocopier.

Also decide whether you want to create evaluation forms. If so, have those ready at the end of the project.

Gather a wide selection of magazines and newspapers to get students started. Make sure the collection includes some aimed at teens, some aimed at adults, some hard news, and some gossip papers. Find a few extreme examples that you can discuss later.

You might want to assign each group a bulletin board, or a section of one, on which to display their final projects. They also might be displayed in the main hall or lobby of the school.

If you are including videotaping as part of the project, you will need a television to view parts of the presentation. Make arrangements for one well ahead of time.

2 Directing the Project

Preparing *(2 class periods)* Explain that students will be working in groups to find out how the media portray teens and to draw conclusions about the accuracy of this image. Each group will analyze images of teens in a different form of media (television, radio, print ads, and magazines). Groups will also interview teens and adults to find out whether they think that the teens in the media represent all teens. Groups will draw a conclusion based on the information and present their findings and supporting arguments in panel discussions. Panel members will share, explore, and compare their findings.

Assigning Roles Divide students into groups. Assign these roles for each group (students can have more than one role).
- presenter
- researcher
- surveyor
- interviewer
- materials collector
- writer
- moderator

▶ Have students browse through magazines and find teens in ads. Discuss whether all teens look like the ones in the ads, whether the ads give a negative or positive impression of teens, and whether they represent an accurate picture. Talk about what conclusions might be drawn by people unfamiliar with teens.

▶ Have students research advertising in their group's medium and write a description of the most common type of teenager they find. They will then create and conduct a survey of teens and adults by asking questions such as, "Teens are often portrayed in ____ as ____.

Do you think this is a fair and/or accurate image of teens in general?"

▶ Encourage groups to survey as many types and ages of people as they can and to keep track of the results. You might hold a brief class discussion about the results and conclusions. You should review with students the Speaking and Listening Skills listed on the next page.

Practicing *(1 class period)* Help students break up into panels. Each panel will be composed of one student per medium. Everyone is expected to speak knowledgeably about his or her group's findings. Group members should coach one another before breaking into panels.

▶ During the rehearsal stage, check to make sure all the panels are running smoothly. Tell students that giving and receiving feedback during this stage is crucial. Refer them to the tips in the Feedback Center.

Presenting *(1 class period)* This project could culminate in a schoolwide presentation.

Evaluation

▶ One good way to ensure panelists' participation is to let them know that they will be rating their own performances as well as those of other members after the discussions. After the panel discussion, you may want to bring the whole class together to discuss the findings of each panel, as well as any notable discoveries, issues, or ideas students want to share. You can hand out evaluation sheets at the end of the discussions.

Teaching the Speaking and Listening Skills

The student is expected to:

Monitor and seek clarification as needed

Teaching Suggestions: Tell students that they can take an active role in their own learning. This means monitoring their own understanding and asking for clarification if necessary. Remind them that it is likely that if they don't understand something, others may not understand it either. Tell the panelists that, during the discussion, they will be expected to ask questions of one another, challenge claims made by the speaker(s), and ask for clarification if they don't understand.

Evaluate a spoken message in terms of its content, credibility, and delivery

Teaching Suggestions: Tell students that, whether they are listening to a radio program, watching television, reading a magazine, or listening to a live presentation, they must evaluate the speaker and the message. To do this, they should keep the following questions in mind: Is the delivery effective (loud enough, clear, and so on)? Is the presentation well organized? Is the research up-to-date and from credible sources? Are the main ideas supported by good evidence? Does the speaker present a fair description of the material, or is there a detectable bias that affects the message?

Identify facts, identify opinions, and distinguish the two

Teaching Suggestions: Tell students that they are consumers of information. One way they can become educated consumers is to be on the lookout for opinions presented as facts. Remind students that facts are statements that can be proved while opinions express the judgements or feelings of the speaker and cannot be proved. During the panel discussion, have students try to distinguish facts from opinions. Can they identify judgmental statements or opinions presented as facts? If so, they should seek clarification from the speaker as to the validity of the statement or evidence to support the claim.

Feedback Center

Students can use the following guidelines when giving and receiving feedback during this project:

Giving Feedback

▶ Ask questions concerning content, delivery, purpose, and point of view (for instance, does the speaker have a detectable bias?).

▶ Provide feedback about the coherence and logic of the content, delivery, and overall impact on the listener.

▶ Comment on the verbal and nonverbal delivery (pitch, pace, volume, body language) and its impact on the listener.

▶ Respond to persuasive messages with questions, challenges, or affirmations.

▶ Question the evidence to support the speaker's claims and conclusions.

Receiving Feedback

▶ Listen to constructive criticism with an open mind.

▶ Use audience feedback and modify the presentation to clarify meaning or organization.

 ## Assessing the Project

The following rubric can be used for group or individual assessment.

3 *Full Accomplishment*

The group followed directions to create a coherent description of teens as portrayed by the media and used this successfully as the basis for a survey. Group members drew coherent conclusions and presented their information in an organized fashion in their panel discussion. Statements and claims were well supported by facts. All of the Speaking and Listening Skills were demonstrated.

2 *Substantial Accomplishment*

The group created a description, completed a survey, and drew adequate conclusions based on this information. Most of the information students presented in panel discussions was supported, and speakers were reasonably prepared. Two out of three of the Speaking and Listening Skills were demonstrated.

1 *Little Accomplishment*

The group's description and/or survey was incomplete or did not fulfill the requirements of the assignment. Panelists were unprepared, and their presentation seemed to lack several key elements. Only one of the Speaking and Listening Skills was demonstrated.

Reflecting on the Theme According to an old saying, life is the greatest teacher. Whether you want to or not, you are always learning lessons, both inside and outside the classroom. Some lessons are easy to learn; others are learned with more difficulty and at a greater cost. What lesson have you learned the hard way?

ACTIVITY

Think about a character in a book or movie who has learned a tough lesson. Write a journal entry in which that character expresses his or her views about life before and after the experience. What effect did the lesson have on daily life? How did it change the character? Read the journal entry to your classmates.

Journal Entry

*M*ood and Tone

Fit your figures of speech to the characters and action and to the mood and setting of your story. A city setting could have someone slinking like an alley cat around trash cans, and a country story might have the character moving like a barn cat stalking a field mouse.

—Kathleen C. Phillips

From "After Twenty Years"

Mood is the feeling that the writer creates for the reader. A writer uses details in his or her writing to create this feeling. The **setting,** or time and place of a story, can affect the mood dramatically. For instance, a story that takes place in the jungles of India will have a very different mood from a story that is set on the American frontier in the 1800s.

Tone describes a writer's attitude toward his or her subject. A writer might use a serious tone to write about a subject that he or she feels is very important but a humorous tone to write about a subject that he or she does not take so seriously. Mood and tone differ in that mood is determined by the response of the reader to a piece of writing. Tone, on the other hand, is the writer's attitude about a subject as that attitude comes through in the writing.

LEARNING THE LANGUAGE OF LITERATURE   **519**

OVERVIEW

Objectives
- understand and identify the following literary terms:
  - mood
  - tone
  - foreshadowing
  - author's purpose
- recognize how mood and tone contribute to the effect of the text.

Teaching the Lesson

This lesson helps students understand the elements of mood and tone by defining the terms and analyzing their effect on literary texts.

Introducing the Concepts
Ask students to think of a movie they have seen recently or a book they have recently read in which the mood is dark and scary. Have them discuss how the filmmaker or author created this effect.

Use **Literary Analysis Transparencies,** pp. 25–26, for additional support.

See the Skills Trace at the beginning of the unit for information on TEKS covered in this lesson.

Presenting the Concepts

Mood

Choose a short story that the students have previously read as a class. Ask them to reread it and discuss the setting, details, language, and imagery used by the author. Ask them to describe the mood that the author achieves in this work.

YOUR TURN

Possible Response: The suspenseful mood of the work is created by actions described in the stage directions, short sentences, and exclamations.

Tone

Have students cut out and read an article or editorial from a newspaper or news magazine. Ask them to summarize the content of the item and to determine the author's tone and his or her purpose for writing the piece. Ask for volunteers to share their conclusions with the rest of the class.

YOUR TURN

Possible Response: "Each youngster had a dream"; "Every chance they had the boys worked out".

Mood

A writer has many tools to shape the mood of a piece of writing. He or she carefully selects **details, descriptive words, dialogue, imagery,** and **setting** to create a certain mood and to affect the reader in a particular way. A writer can also use the technique of **foreshadowing**—giving hints about what might happen later in order to create suspense and make the reader feel anxious about what is coming next.

The mood of a work can be anything from silly to terrifying. In the excerpt from *The Monsters Are Due on Maple Street,* notice how the stage directions, setting, and dialogue work together to create a mood. The author uses the ordinary details and frustrations of daily life to help create an extraordinary atmosphere.

YOUR TURN Read the text on the right. Which details create the mood of the teleplay? What is the mood?

Tone

The **tone** of a piece of writing can reflect the author's attitude toward his or her subject. This reflects the **author's purpose.** So, if the author's purpose is to entertain, the tone may be playful. If the author's purpose is to inform, the tone may be serious. Often, a reader will agree with the author's tone, but it is also possible that a reader will disagree. Thinking about the author's tone is one way to help you decide how you feel about a certain subject.

The tone of the passage from "Amigo Brothers" might be described as serious and respectful.

YOUR TURN In the excerpt at the right, which details convey the writer's attitude toward the topic?

MOOD

Les. I just don't understand it. I tried to start it, and it wouldn't start. You saw me. All of you saw me.

(*And now, just as suddenly as the engine started, it stops, and there is a long silence that is gradually intruded upon by the frightened murmuring of the people.*)

Les. I don't understand. I swear . . . I don't understand. What's happening?

Don. Maybe you better tell us. Nothing's working on this street. Nothing. No lights, no power, no radio, (*then meaningfully*) nothing except one car—yours!

(*The people's murmuring becomes a loud chant filling the air with accusations and demands for action. Two of the men pass Don and head toward Les, who backs away from them against his car. He is cornered.*)

—Rod Serling,
The Monsters Are Due on Maple Street

TONE

Each youngster had a dream of someday becoming lightweight champion of the world. Every chance they had the boys worked out, sometimes at the Boys Club on 10th Street and Avenue A and sometimes at the pro's gym on 14th Street. Early morning sunrises would find them running along the East River Drive, wrapped in sweatshirts, short towels around their necks, and handkerchiefs Apache style around their foreheads.

—Piri Thomas, "Amigo Brothers"

The Active Reader: Skills and Strategies

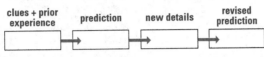

Predicting

How to Apply the Strategy

To **PREDICT**, an active reader will:
• Note clues and details
• Think about outcomes
• **Connect** new information to prior knowledge
• **Evaluate** and revise the prediction
• Use a chart like this one to help make predictions

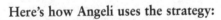

clues + prior experience	prediction	new details	revised prediction

Try It Now!

Read the excerpt below. Predict what will happen next.

> [Narrator] "This is the most beautiful umbrella I have ever seen,"
> I said. "Ever, in my whole life."
> [Miss Crosman] "Do you have an umbrella?"
> [Narrator] "No. But my mother's going to get me one just like this for Christmas."
> [Miss Crosman] "Is she? I tell you what. You don't have to wait until Christmas."
>
> —Gish Jen, "The White Umbrella"

Here's how Angeli uses the strategy:

*"By 'adding up' clues from story events, character clues, illustrations, and my own personal experience, I can **predict** outcomes. From this example, I predict the narrator will be getting an umbrella. At the end of the story, I **evaluate** my predictions to see if I was correct."*

Need More Help?

Remember that active readers use the essential reading strategies explained on page 4: • **visualize** • **predict** • **clarify** • **question** • **connect** • **evaluate** • **monitor**.

THE ACTIVE READER **521**

Have you ever chosen a video just by looking at the cover? Were you able to guess what would happen in the plot? Whenever you use clues to logically infer how something will turn out, it is called predicting. An active reader can also predict when reading a story. A book with a good plot will have you using clues to predict what happens next almost without your thinking about it.

Objective
• develop effective strategies for making predictions

Teaching the Lesson

The strategies on this page will help students understand and apply the strategy of making predictions about the literature they read.

Presenting the Strategies
Help students understand the strategies by asking for volunteers to read them aloud. Emphasize to students that they will be using these strategies as they read the selections in this book.

• Choose a selection from this unit to read. Have the students read through the first page or two silently, then stop.
• Ask them to take note of any details that they think are important so far. Then encourage them to use their personal experiences to make predictions about what might happen next and to predict what the final outcome of the story might be.
• Ask for volunteers to share their predictions with the class.
• As the students continue to read, have them pause and predict what the final outcome of the story might be.
• When the students have finished reading the story, have them discuss how accurate their predictions were.

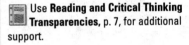 Use **Reading and Critical Thinking Transparencies**, p. 7, for additional support.

Try It Now!

Possible Response: Miss Crosman might give the narrator the umbrella.

OVERVIEW

Objectives

1. understand and appreciate a **short story** (Literary Analysis)
2. understand and appreciate the literary skills of **mood** and **tone** as they relate to the story (Literary Analysis)
3. utilize the reading skill of **making predictions about** outcomes in plot and changes in character (Active Reading)

Summary

Because their mother has to work afternoons, the narrator and her sister must walk to their piano teacher's house after school. One afternoon they are caught in a rainstorm and arrive at the lesson soaking wet. Embarrassed by their condition and Miss Crosman's motherly concern, the narrator spins imaginative lies that make her family sound well-off. During the piano lesson, she plays brilliantly, both to avoid pity and to win praise. Afterward the girls sit on Miss Crosman's steps and wait for their mother, who is often late. As their wait lengthens, Miss Crosman offers more concern and help. The more she offers, the more the narrator resists, until she is left sitting alone in the rain. When Miss Crosman wants to give her a beautiful white umbrella, the narrator's defenses finally break down. She accepts the gift and tells her teacher, "I wish you were my mother." When her mother arrives, the narrator guiltily tucks the umbrella under her skirt. On the trip home, her mother causes a car accident and at first seems hurt. The narrator, ashamed of her own disloyalty, tosses the umbrella down a sewer.

Thematic Link

In moment of panic, the narrator learns a lesson about loyalty and the true feelings she has for her mother.

5-Minute Warm-Up

Daily Language SkillBuilder **TEKS 16B, 17D**

Have students **proofread** the display sentences on page 517i and write them correctly. The sentences also appear on Transparency 16 of **Grammar Transparencies and Copymasters.**

The White Umbrella

Short Story by GISH JEN

"I could not believe that I was actually holding the umbrella."

 TEKS See the Skills Trace at the b[e]ning of the unit for informat[ion] on TEKS covered in this less[on].

Connect to Your Life

Keeping Up Appearances With a small group, discuss the idea of "keeping up appearances." What does the expression mean? How important is keeping up appearances to you? In what ways do you and people you've observed keep up appearances? Share your group's ideas with the class.

Build Background

Like most writers, Gish Jen, the author of "The White Umbrella," draws on many sources for her stories. In any story, she says, there are "lots of different ingredients: some of the ingredients come from your life; some come from things you've read, or from other people's lives; many, many things you've just made up."

The narrator of "The White Umbrella" is a character who tries to "fit in" with American society while holding on to her Chinese heritage. An American-born daughter of immigrant Chinese parents, Jen remembers her family feeling the need to fit in— to be absorbed into the main culture.

WORDS TO KNOW
Vocabulary Preview

audible	illuminate
confirm	maneuver
credibility	resume
discreet	revelation
diverted	stupendous

Focus Your Reading

LITERARY ANALYSIS **MOOD AND TONE** Mood and tone are related but different concepts. **Mood** is the feeling, or atmosphere, that a work conveys to readers. It can be expressed by words such as *peaceful, violent, humorous, serious,* and so forth. **Tone** refers to a writer's attitude and feelings toward a subject. It may be expressed by terms such as *amused, angry,* or *objective.* As you read, note details that help establish mood and tone in "The White Umbrella."

ACTIVE READING **PREDICTING** A logical guess based on information in a story and what you already know is a **prediction.** Active readers make predictions about plot, character, and setting as they read. To be able to predict change or development in a character, you need to pay attention to what that character thinks, feels, and says. Ask yourself how a character with these thoughts and feelings may react when a new event occurs in the plot. As you read "The White Umbrella," pay attention to the thoughts and feelings of the narrator and then try to predict how she will change.

READER'S NOTEBOOK Make a chart with three columns. Jot down the narrator's thoughts and feelings in the first column, important events in the plot in the second column, and your own predictions as to how the narrator will respond to these events in the third. Share your observations with a partner.

Narrator's Thoughts and Feelings	Events in Story	Predictions
The narrator feels jealous of Eugenie Roberts and wants the white umbrella.	Eugenie does not take the umbrella after her piano lesson.	The narrator will try to keep the umbrella for herself.

LESSON RESOURCES

UNIT FOUR RESOURCE BOOK, pp. 4–10

ASSESSMENT
Formal Assessment, pp. 89–90
Teacher's Guide to Assessment and Portfolio Use
Test Generator

SKILLS TRANSPARENCIES AND COPYMASTERS
Literary Analysis
• Mood, TR 26 (for Cooperative Activity, p. 530)
• Tone, TR 25 (for Cooperative Activity, p. 530),

Reading and Critical Thinking
• Predicting, TR 7 (for Thinking Through the Literature, p. 530)
Grammar
• Distinguishing Prepositions from Adverbs, CM 88 (for Mini Lesson, p. 527)
• Prepositional Phrases, CM 89 (for Mini Lesson, p. 532)
Vocabulary
• Word Meaning, CM 59 (for Mini Lesson p. 523)
• Synonyms, CM 60 (for Mini Lesson, p. 526)

Communications
• Giving and Using Feedback t[o] Improve Performance, CM 1[ ] (for Mini Lesson, p. 528)
INTEGRATED TECHNOLOGY
Audio Library

Visit our website:
www.mcdougallittell.com

The White Umbrella

by Gish Jen

When I was twelve, my mother went to work without telling me or my little sister.

"Not that we need the second income." The lilt of her accent drifted from the kitchen up to the top of the stairs, where Mona and I were listening.

"No," said my father, in a barely <u>audible</u> voice. "Not like the Lee family."

The Lees were the only other Chinese family in town. I remembered how sorry my parents had felt for Mrs. Lee when she started waitressing downtown the year before; and so when my mother began coming home late, I didn't say anything and tried to keep Mona from saying anything either.

"But why shouldn't I?" she argued. "Lots of people's mothers work."

"Those are American people," I said.

"So what do you think we are? I can do the pledge of allegiance with my eyes closed."

Nevertheless, she tried to be <u>discreet</u>; and if my mother wasn't home by 5:30, we would

WORDS TO KNOW

audible (ô′də-bəl) *adj.* able to be heard
discreet (dĭ-skrēt′) *adj.* careful about what one says or does

523

Literary Analysis | MOOD AND TONE |

 A Challenge students to identify the author's tone in this passage.

Possible Response: objective

Ask students why the author is not critical of the narrator for her lying.

Possible Response: The narrator is defending her mother from possible criticism.

📖 Use **Unit Four Resource Book,** p. 6 for more practice.

Reading Skills and Strategies: CONNECTING

B Have students explain what the description of Eugenie Roberts reveals about the narrator's self-image. Invite students to describe times when they envied another person.

Possible Response: The narrator is self-conscious about not being a "real" American. She desperately wants to fit in and feels inferior to Eugenie, whom she holds in high regard.

Active Reading | PREDICTING |

 C Ask students to predict the narrator's plan for keeping the umbrella.

Possible Responses: She might ask to borrow it; she might offer to return it to Eugenie.

📖 Use **Unit Four Resource Book,** p. 5 for more practice.

Literary Analysis: SYMBOL

D Have a volunteer read aloud this passage. Ask why the author describes at such length the narrator's fascination with the umbrella.

Possible Response: The umbrella is a symbol of what the narrator wants to be—American like Eugenie.

start cooking by ourselves, to make sure dinner would be on time. Mona would wash the vegetables and put on the rice; I would chop.

For weeks we wondered what kind of work she was doing. I imagined that she was selling perfume, testing dessert recipes for the local newspaper. Or maybe she was working for the florist. Now that she had learned to drive, she might be delivering boxes of roses to people.

"I don't think so," said Mona as we walked to our piano lesson after school. "She would've hit something by now."

A gust of wind littered the street with leaves.

"Maybe we better hurry up," she went on, looking at the sky. "It's going to pour."

"But we're too early." Her lesson didn't begin until 4:00, mine until 4:30, so we usually tried to walk as slowly as we could. "And anyway, those aren't the kind of clouds that rain. Those are cumulus clouds."[1]

We arrived out of breath and wet.

"Oh, you poor, poor dears," said old Miss Crosman. "Why don't you call me the next time it's like this out? If your mother won't drive you, I can come pick you up."

"No, that's okay," I answered. Mona wrung her hair out on Miss Crosman's rug. "We just couldn't get the roof of our car to close, is all. We took it to the beach last summer and got sand in the mechanism." I pronounced this last word carefully, as if the credibility of my lie depended on its middle syllable. "It's never been the same." I thought for a second. "It's a convertible."

"Well then make yourselves at home." She exchanged looks with Eugenie Roberts, whose lesson we were interrupting. Eugenie smiled good-naturedly. "The towels are in the closet across from the bathroom."

Huddling at the end of Miss Crosman's nine-foot leatherette couch, Mona and I watched Eugenie play. She was a grade ahead of me and, according to school rumor, had a boyfriend in high school. I believed it. . . . She had auburn hair, blue eyes, and, I noted with a particular pang,[2] a pure white folding umbrella.

"I can't see," whispered Mona.

"So clean your glasses."

"My glasses *are* clean. You're in the way."

I looked at her. "They look dirty to me."

"That's because *your* glasses are dirty."

Eugenie came bouncing to the end of her piece.

"Oh! Just <u>stupendous</u>!" Miss Crosman hugged her, then looked up as Eugenie's mother walked in. "Stupendous!" she said again. "Oh! Mrs. Roberts! Your daughter has a gift, a real gift. It's an honor to teach her."

Mrs. Roberts, radiant with pride, swept her daughter out of the room as if she were royalty, born to the piano bench. Watching the way Eugenie carried herself, I sat up and concentrated so hard on sucking in my stomach that I did not realize until the Robertses were gone that Eugenie had left her umbrella. As Mona began to play, I jumped up and ran to the window, meaning to call to them—only to see their brake lights flash then fade at the stop sign at the corner. As if to allow them passage, the rain had let up; a quivering sun lit their way.

---

1. **cumulus** (kyŌŌm'yə-ləs) **clouds:** clouds with flat bottoms and fluffy, rounded tops.
2. **pang:** a sudden feeling of longing or distress.

WORDS TO KNOW	**credibility** (krĕd'ə-bĭl'ĭ-tē) *n.* believability
	stupendous (stŌŌ-pĕn'dəs) *adj.* tremendous; amazing

524

BLOCK SCHEDULING: MANAGING TIME

If your schedule requires that you cover the lesson objectives in a shorter time, use . . .
- Preparing to Read, p. 522
- Thinking Through the Literature, p. 530
- Vocabulary in Action, p. 531
- Grammar in Context, p. 532

If you want to take advantage of longer class time, use . . .
- TE Teaching Options: Preteaching Vocabulary, p. 523; Cross-Curricular Link, p. 525; Vocabulary Strategy, p. 526; Grammar, pp. 527, 532; Speaking and Listening, p. 528; Informal Assessment, p. 529; Spelling, 531
- Choices & Challenges and Author Activity, pp. 531–532

Girl at Piano (1966), Will Barnet. Oil on canvas, 64″ × 39″, private collection. Copyright © 1995 Will Barnet/Licensed by VAGA, New York.

The umbrella glowed like a scepter[3] on the blue carpet while Mona, slumping over the keyboard, managed to eke out[4] a fair rendition of a cat fight. At the end of the piece, Miss Crosman asked her to stand up.

"Stay right there," she said, then came back a minute later with a towel to cover the bench. "You must be cold," she continued. "Shall I call your mother and have her bring over some dry clothes?"

"No," answered Mona. "She won't come because she . . ."

"She's too busy," I broke in from the back of the room.

"I see." Miss Crosman sighed and shook her head a little. "Your glasses are filthy, honey," she said to Mona. "Shall I clean them for you?"

Sisterly embarrassment seized me. Why hadn't Mona wiped her lenses when I told her to? As she <u>resumed</u> abuse of the piano, I stared at the umbrella. I wanted to open it, twirl it around by its slender silver handle; I wanted to dangle it from my wrist on the way to school the way the other girls did. I wondered what Miss Crosman would say if I offered to bring it to Eugenie at school tomorrow. She would be impressed with my consideration for others; Eugenie would be pleased to have it back; and I would have possession of the umbrella for an entire night. I looked at it again, toying with the idea of asking for one for Christmas. I knew, however, how my mother would react.

"Things," she would say. "What's the matter with a raincoat? All you want is things, just like an American."

Sitting down for my lesson, I was careful to keep the towel under me and sit up straight.

"I'll bet you can't see a thing either," said Miss Crosman, reaching for my glasses. "And you can relax, you poor dear. . . . This isn't a boot camp."[5]

When Miss Crosman finally allowed me to start playing, I played extra well, as well as I possibly could. See, I told her with my fingers. You don't have to feel sorry for me.

---

3. **scepter** (sĕp′tər): the rod or baton a ruler holds as a sign of authority.

4. **eke out:** to get or produce with great struggle.

5. **boot camp:** a military base where new members of the armed forces receive basic training.

WORDS TO KNOW **resume** (rĭ-zōōm′) *v.* to go on again; continue

525

Cross Curricular Link **Social Studies**

CHINESE AMERICANS The Chinese population in the United States increased dramatically in the 1850s. In 1850 there were only a few hundred Chinese in California; two years later, one out of ten residents was Chinese. Droughts and famines in certain areas of China encouraged many Chinese to emigrate, and opportunities seemed to be abundant in California. Not only were there jobs in the mines and on the railroad-building projects, but the gold rush created a need for many other services, such as laundries for miners' clothes and restaurants to provide good food for hungry workers.

Despite the willingness of the Chinese to contribute on many levels of society, by the 1870s and 1880s a wave of anti-Chinese sentiment was leading to a great deal of harassment for the Chinese and resulted in the enactment of various laws designed to discourage their full participation in society. One such law, the Chinese Exclusion Act, specifically prohibited the Chinese from immigrating to the United States. This act was not repealed until 1943.

A Ask students why Miss Crosman hugs the narrator.

Possible Response: She realizes that the narrator is lying and understands that she is saying this in protection of her mother.

Literary Analysis MOOD AND TONE

B Ask students what contributes to the tension of this scene.

Possible Responses: the narrator's anxiety that Miss Crosman will find out the truth; Mona's desire to tell Miss Crosman that her mother is working; the inquiries of Miss Crosman that become increasingly difficult to fend off

Literary Analysis: CONFLICT

C Ask students to identify the source of the narrator's conflict.

Possible Response: She wants to go inside but does not want to evoke Miss Crosman's pity or show a lack of faith in her mother.

Literary Analysis MOOD AND TONE

D Ask students how the sympathetic tone in this description contributes to the effect of the text.

Possible Response: The narrator is seen as admirable for not wanting to accept Miss Crosman's sympathy.

Active Reading PREDICTING

E Ask students how they think the narrator's mother will react to the umbrella.

Possible Response: She will demand that the narrator return it.

"That was wonderful," said Miss Crosman. "Oh! Just wonderful."

An entire constellation rose in my heart.

"And guess what," I announced proudly. "I have a surprise for you."

Then I played a second piece for her, a much more difficult one that she had not assigned.

"Oh! That was stupendous," she said without hugging me. "Stupendous! You are a genius, young lady. If your mother had started you younger, you'd be playing like Eugenie Roberts by now!"

I looked at the keyboard, wishing that I had still a third, even more difficult piece to play for her. I wanted to tell her that I was the school spelling bee champion, that I wasn't ticklish, that I could do karate.

"My mother is a concert pianist," I said.

A She looked at me for a long moment, then finally, without saying anything, hugged me. I didn't say anything about bringing the umbrella to Eugenie at school.

The steps were dry when Mona and I sat down to wait for my mother.

"Do you want to wait inside?" Miss Crosman looked anxiously at the sky.

"No," I said. "Our mother will be here any minute."

"In a while," said Mona.

"Any minute," I said again, even though my mother had been at least twenty minutes late every week since she started working.

B According to the church clock across the street we had been waiting twenty-five minutes when Miss Crosman came out again.

"Shall I give you ladies a ride home?"

"No," I said. "Our mother is coming any minute."

I could not believe that I was actually holding the umbrella.

"Shall I at least give her a call and remind her you're here? Maybe she forgot about you."

"I don't think she *forgot*," said Mona.

"Shall I give her a call anyway? Just to be safe?"

"I bet she already left," I said. "How could she forget about us?"

Miss Crosman went in to call.

"There's no answer," she said, coming back out.

"See, she's on her way," I said.

"Are you sure you wouldn't like to come in?"

"No," said Mona.

"Yes," I said. I pointed at my sister. "She meant yes too. She meant no, she wouldn't like to go in."

Miss Crosman looked at her watch. "It's 5:30 now, ladies. My pot roast will be coming out in fifteen minutes. Maybe you'd like to come in and have some then?"

"My mother's almost here," I said. "She's on her way."

We watched and watched the street. I tried to imagine what my mother was doing; I tried to imagine her writing messages in the sky, even though I knew she was afraid of planes. I watched as the branches of Miss Crosman's big willow tree started to sway; they had all been trimmed to exactly the same height off the ground, so that they looked beautiful, like hair in the wind.

It started to rain.

"Miss Crosman is coming out again," said Mona.

"Don't let her talk you into going inside," I whispered.

"Why not?"

"Because that would mean Mom isn't really coming any minute."

Mini Lesson **Vocabulary Strategy** ⬛ TEKS 9B, 9C

SYNONYMS

Instruction Remind students that knowing synonyms for words will help them to increase their vocabulary and vary their writing. Using a thesaurus is one way to locate words with similar meanings. Tell students that because not all synonyms are interchangeable, they should use the context of the original word to help them to decide which synonym is the best choice.

Exercise Have students use a thesaurus to locate synonyms for the underlined WORDS TO KNOW in the following sentences.

1. I called my friend to <u>confirm</u> the directions to her home. *(verify)*
2. Everyone agreed that the performance was <u>stupendous.</u> *(exceptional)*
3. Her strong background in politics gave her <u>credibility</u> as a political spokesperson. *(believability)*
4. We were late but tried to be <u>discreet</u> as we entered the room. *(unobtrusive)*

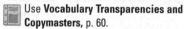 Use **Vocabulary Transparencies and Copymasters,** p. 60.

"But she isn't," said Mona. "She's *working*."

"Shhh! Miss Crosman is going to hear you."

"She's working! She's working! She's working!"

I put my hand over her mouth, but she licked it, and so I was wiping my hand on my wet dress when the front door opened.

"We're getting even *wetter*," said Mona right away. "Wetter and wetter."

"Shall we all go in?" Miss Crosman pulled Mona to her feet. "Before you young ladies catch pneumonia? You've been out here an hour already."

"We're *freezing*." Mona looked up at Miss Crosman. "Do you have any hot chocolate? We're going to catch *pneumonia*."

"I'm not going in," I said. "My mother's coming any minute."

"Come on," said Mona. "Use your *noggin*."[6]

"Any minute."

"Come on, Mona," Miss Crosman opened the door. "Shall we get you inside first?"

"See you in the hospital," said Mona as she went in. "See you in the hospital with *pneumonia*."

I stared out into the empty street. The rain was pricking me all over; I was cold; I wanted to go inside. I wanted to be able to let myself go inside. If Miss Crosman came out again, I decided, I would go in.

She came out with a blanket and the white umbrella.

I could not believe that I was actually holding the umbrella, opening it. It sprang up by itself as if it were alive, as if that were what it wanted to do—as if it belonged in my hands, above my head. I stared up at the network of silver spokes, then spun the umbrella around and around and around. It was so clean and white that it seemed to glow, to <u>illuminate</u> everything around it. "It's beautiful," I said.

Miss Crosman sat down next to me, on one end of the blanket. I moved the umbrella over so that it covered that too. I could feel the rain on my left shoulder and shivered. She put her arm around me.

"You poor, poor dear."

I knew that I was in store for another bolt of sympathy, and braced myself by staring up into the umbrella.

"You know, I very much wanted to have children when I was younger," she continued.

"You did?"

She stared at me a minute. Her face looked dry and crusty, like day-old frosting.

"I did. But then I never got married."

I twirled the umbrella around again.

"This is the most beautiful umbrella I have ever seen," I said. "Ever, in my whole life."

"Do you have an umbrella?"

"No. But my mother's going to get me one just like this for Christmas."

"Is she? I tell you what. You don't have to wait until Christmas. You can have this one."

"But this one belongs to Eugenie Roberts," I protested. "I have to give it back to her tomorrow in school."

"Who told you it belongs to Eugenie? It's not Eugenie's. It's mine. And now I'm giving it to you, so it's yours."

"It is?"

She hugged me tighter. "That's right. It's all yours."

"It's mine?" I didn't know what to say. "Mine?" Suddenly I was jumping up and down in the rain. "It's beautiful! Oh! It's beautiful!" I laughed.

Miss Crosman laughed too, even though she was getting all wet.

---

6. **noggin:** head.

WORDS
TO
KNOW

illuminate (ĭ-lōō′mə-nāt′) *v.* to light up

527

 Grammar **TEKS 17C** **TAAS Writing Obj. 6**

DISTINGUISHING PREPOSITIONS FROM ADVERBS

Instruction Remind students that some words may be used as either adverbs or prepositions. If the word is followed by a noun or pronoun, it is a preposition. An adverb modifies another word and is not followed by an object. Point out that in the first highlighted sentence, *in* is an adverb modifying the verb. In the second sentence, *in* is followed by *hospital* and is a preposition.

Exercises Have students identify each of the underlined words as prepositions or adverbs.

1. The narrator looked <u>up</u> to see if the clouds were thinning. *(adverb)*

2. <u>Up</u> the street, they could see the headlights of a car. *(preposition)*

3. She made up a lie <u>off</u> the top of her head. *(preposition)*

4. She quickly turned the ignition <u>off</u>. *(adverb)*

 Use **Grammar Transparencies and Copymasters**, p. 88.

 Use McDougal Littell's *Language Network*, Chapter 6, for more instruction and practice in prepositions and adverbs.

Reading Skills and Strategies: CONNECTING

A Ask students to use their own experience to comprehend why the narrator feels bad after saying what she does to Miss Crosman. Have volunteers share times when they have said something and immediately wished to take it back.

Possible Responses: She feels disloyal to her mother, as if she has betrayed her. She said it only to please Miss Crosman.

Literary Analysis [MOOD AND TONE]

B Ask students to describe the atmosphere in the car when the narrator's mother tells the girls that she works at the A&P.

Possible Response: The mood is disappointed, strained, or awkward.

Literary Analysis: SETTING

C Ask students to analyze how the setting influences the story.

Possible Responses: Because it is set in a time when few women work, the narrator feels self-conscious about her mother's working outside of the home. There are only two Chinese families in the town, so the narrator feels even more out of place.

Literary Analysis: SYMBOL

D Ask students what event leads the narrator to throw away the umbrella.

Possible Response: the thought that her mother might be dead

Ask students to explain the significance of the narrator's action.

Possible Response: She has come to an acceptance of who she is and who her mother is.

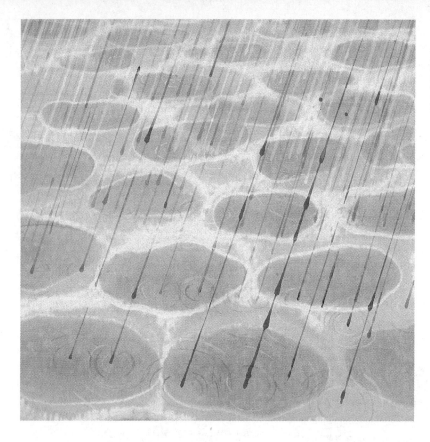

Japanese Rain on Canvas (1972), David Hockney. Acrylic on canvas, 48" × 48". Copyright © David Hockney.

1 "Thank you, Miss Crosman. Thank you very much. Thanks a zillion. It's beautiful. It's *stupendous!*"

"You're quite welcome," she said.

A "Thank you," I said again, but that didn't seem like enough. Suddenly I knew just what she wanted to hear. "I wish you were my mother."

Right away I felt bad.

"You shouldn't say that," she said, but her face was opening into a huge smile as the lights of my mother's car cautiously turned the corner. I quickly collapsed the umbrella and put it up my skirt, holding onto it from the outside, through the material.

"Mona!" I shouted into the house. "Mona! Hurry up! Mom's here! I told you she was coming!"

Then I ran away from Miss Crosman, down to the curb. Mona came tearing up to my side as my mother neared the house. We both backed up a few feet so that in case she went onto the curb, she wouldn't run us over.

"But why didn't you go inside with Mona?" my mother asked on the way home. She had taken off her own coat to put over me and had the heat on high.

"She wasn't using her noggin," said Mona, next to me in the back seat.

Teaching Options

MONOLOGUES

Prepare Have students present a monologue. Remind them that a monologue is a speech by one person from that person's perspective. A monologue may reveal feelings and thoughts or narrate or describe events. Have students decide whether they will present their monologue from the mother's or the narrator's perspective. Then have them review the story to choose the scene they wish to describe or narrate. Students should outline the ideas to be included before writing their monologues and

Mini Lesson **Speaking and Listening**

should be sure that their interpretation of the character is based on evidence from the text. Students should then practice their monologues with a partner to ensure the use of effective language, rate, volume, and pitch for their audience.

Present Audience members should generate criteria to evaluate the monologues. After the monologues have been presented, audience members should discuss how they helped them to appreciate or understand each scene.

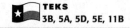 **TEKS** 3B, 5A, 5D, 5E, 11B

BLOCK SCHEDULING This activity is particularly well suited for longer class periods.

Use **Communications Transparencies and Copymasters**, p. 16, for additional support.

should call next time," said my mother. "I just don't like to say where I am."

That was when she finally told us that she was working as a check-out clerk in the A&P. She was supposed to be on the day shift, but the other employees were unreliable, and her boss had promised her a promotion if she would stay until the evening shift filled in.

For a moment no one said anything. Even Mona seemed to find the <u>revelation</u> disappointing.

"A promotion already!" she said, finally.

I listened to the windshield wipers.

"You're so quiet." My mother looked at me in the rear view mirror. "What's the matter?"

"I wish you would quit," I said after a moment.

She sighed. "The Chinese have a saying: one beam cannot hold the roof up."

"But Eugenie Roberts's father supports their family."

She sighed once more. "Eugenie Roberts's father is Eugenie Roberts's father," she said.

As we entered the downtown area, Mona started leaning hard against me every time the car turned right, trying to push me over. Remembering what I had said to Miss Crosman, I tried to <u>maneuver</u> the umbrella under my leg so she wouldn't feel it.

"What's under your skirt?" Mona wanted to know as we came to a traffic light. My mother, watching us in the rear view mirror again, rolled slowly to a stop.

"What's the matter?" she asked.

"There's something under her skirt," said Mona, pulling at me. "Under her skirt."

Meanwhile, a man crossing the street started to yell at us. "Who do you think you are, lady?" he said. "You're blocking the whole crosswalk."

We all froze. Other people walking by stopped to watch.

"Didn't you hear me?" he went on, starting to thump on the hood with his fist. "Don't you speak English?"

My mother began to back up, but the car behind us honked. Luckily, the light turned green right after that. She sighed in relief.

"What were you saying, Mona?" she asked.

We wouldn't have hit the car behind us that hard if he hadn't been moving too but as it was, our car bucked violently, throwing us all first back and then forward.

"Uh oh," said Mona when we stopped. "Another accident."

I was relieved to have attention <u>diverted</u> from the umbrella. Then I noticed my mother's head, tilted back onto the seat. Her eyes were closed.

"Mom!" I screamed. "Mom! Wake up!"

She opened her eyes. "Please don't yell,"she said. "Enough people are going to yell already."

"I thought you were dead," I said, starting to cry. "I thought you were dead."

She turned around, looked at me intently, then put her hand to my forehead.

"Sick," she <u>confirmed</u>. "Some kind of sick is giving you crazy ideas."

As the man from the car behind us started tapping on the window, I moved the umbrella away from my leg. Then Mona and my mother were getting out of the car. I got out after them; and while everyone else was inspecting the damage we'd done, I threw the umbrella down a sewer. ❖

WORDS TO KNOW	**revelation** (rĕv′ə-lā′shən) *n.* something made known to others
	maneuver (mə-nōō′vər) *v.* to guide or direct through a series of movements
	diverted (dĭ-vûr′tĭd) *adj.* turned away **divert** *v.*
	confirm (kən-fûrm′) *v.* to make certain

529

Customizing Instruction

Less Proficient Readers
Ask students what the narrator says to Miss Crosman that makes the narrator feel bad and why it makes her feel guilty.

Possible Response: The narrator says that she wishes Miss Crosman were her mother. Saying this is not only a betrayal of her mother but also a lie. The narrator said this only because she thought it was what Miss Crosman wanted to hear.

Students Acquiring English
1 Explain that although *zillion* has no real numerical meaning, its idiomatic use refers to a very large number, more than a million.

Gifted and Talented
2 Discuss with students the narrator's feelings when the man crossing the street says, "Didn't you hear me? Don't you speak English?" Ask students to discuss the negative attitudes held by some Americans against people who live in the United States but do not speak English fluently.

☑ **Assessment Informal Assessment**   🏴 **TEKS** 10F, 11B   🔺 **TAAS** Reading Obj. 3   🔺 **TAAS** Writing Obj. 1

IDENTIFYING IMPLIED MAIN IDEA
You can informally assess students' understanding of the selection by having them write a diary entry from the narrator's perspective that describes the incident with the man at the crosswalk and then reflects on the main idea of this exchange. Remind students to write in the first person.

RUBRIC

3 Full Accomplishment Response maintains a first-person point of view, records details of the incident accurately, and identifies the implied main idea of the incident, which is that the man judges the narrator and her family on appearances.

2 Substantial Accomplishment Response maintains a first-person point of view, describes the incident quite completely, and assesses the main idea with some accuracy.

1 Little or Partial Accomplishment Response inadequately records the incident and main idea.

GUIDING STUDENT RESPONSE

Connect to the Literature

1. Responses will vary.

Comprehension Check

- They promise not to tell that their mother has a job because she hasn't told them directly, and they feel that it is not something of which to be proud.
- She throws it down the sewer.

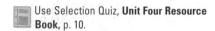 Use Selection Quiz, **Unit Four Resource Book,** p. 10.

Think Critically

2. Possible Response: It represents a way to fit in and to be more American; it becomes for the narrator a sign of her betrayal.

3. Possible Response: Keeping up appearances is very important to the narrator until the end of the story. Mona cares far less about appearances.

4. Possible Response: The narrator says this because Miss Crosman has given her something she longs for and because she thinks Miss Crosman wants to hear it. Her reaction is very natural; she regrets her words as soon as they are spoken.

5. Possible Response: The narrator has realized what her mother means to her and what is more important than appearances.

6. Possible Response: Encourage students to present the clues that help them to predict events. For example, the emphasis on the mother's poor driving leads to the prediction that she will have an accident.

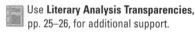 Use **Reading and Critical Thinking Transparencies,** p. 7, for additional support.

Literary Analysis

Mood and Tone Students should note that the mood within the story varies. Encourage students to locate passages in which the tone is critical, objective, or sympathetic.

Use **Literary Analysis Transparencies,** pp. 25–26, for additional support.

Review: Symbol To the narrator the umbrella first symbolizes being an American, then symbolizes betrayal. To the mother it symbolizes superficial values. The use of this symbol shows more clearly the narrator's internal conflict.

Connect to the Literature

1. **What Do You Think?** How did you react to the narrator's behavior at the end of the story? Explain.

Comprehension Check
- What do the sisters promise not to tell at the beginning of the story? Why?
- What does the narrator do with the white umbrella at the end of the story?

Think Critically

2. What does the umbrella really mean to the narrator?

 THINK ABOUT
- why she first wants the umbrella
- her reaction to being given the umbrella
- her reaction to the car accident

3. How important is keeping up appearances to each of the sisters? Explain.

4. Why do you think the narrator says to Miss Crosman, "I wish you were my mother"? How do you feel about the narrator's immediate reaction to her own words?

5. When the narrator says to her mother, "I thought you were dead," how would you describe her feelings toward her mother at that moment? How have those feelings changed throughout the story?

6. **ACTIVE READING** **PREDICTING** With a classmate, compare the predictions you made in your **READER'S NOTEBOOK** with what actually happened.

Extend Interpretations

7. **Critic's Corner** A member of the student board that reviewed the stories in this book said, "I liked how the story was told by the main character. When a story is written like this, I think it makes it more interesting, because you see how the main character feels." How does a first-person narrator help make the story interesting for you? Explain.

8. **Connect to Life** The narrator assumes that Eugenie Roberts "has everything"—looks, talent, and the white umbrella. What assumptions do people make about others based on appearances? When are looks deceptive? Discuss your responses with a partner.

Literary Analysis

MOOD AND TONE **Mood** is the atmosphere that a literary work conveys by various means, including description, setting, and dialogue. The mood of "The White Umbrella," for example, is one of being trapped between conflicting demands—the narrator's desire to keep up appearances and her love of her mother. This mood reaches its most intense point toward the end of the story when the man in the crosswalk demands that the girls' mother back up while a car behind honks at her to move forward.

Tone, on the other hand, is the author's attitude toward his or her subject. In this story, Gish Jen seems both critical and sympathetic toward the narrator.

Cooperative Learning Activity As a class, consider examples from the story that helped set the **mood** at key moments. List them on a chart and discuss the mood they created. Then, look for details that reveal the author's attitude toward her subject—that is, the **tone** of the story. Try to express the tone in words.

REVIEW **SYMBOL** A **symbol** is a person, place, or object that stands for something beyond itself. In literature, objects and images are used to symbolize things that cannot actually be seen, such as an idea or feeling. What do you think the white umbrella symbolizes?

Extend Interpretations

7. **Critic's Corner** Possible Response: Most students will agree that the first-person narrator was necessary to reveal the changes in her character that would not have been observed by someone looking at her from the outside. Her conflicts and the complexity of her feelings convey the themes of the story. A different narrator would change the reader's perception of the events and characters completely.

8. **Connect to Life** Possible Response: Students should note that the white umbrella did not belong to Eugenie. It is easy to make false assumptions. Encourage students to share when they have made false assumptions and to think about the harm that can be done through these assessments, which are based on appearance only.

Choices & CHALLENGES

Writing Options

1. Short Story What do you think finally caused the girls' mother to tell them about her job? Write a story in which you trace the series of events that lead up to her conversation with them in the car. Use details from the story, such as the mother's conversation with the father, but make up details of your own as well, such as what the mother and the store manager might have said to each other. Place the story in your **Working Portfolio.**

2. Opinion Essay At the beginning of the story, the narrator worries that her family is becoming like "American people." Yet, as the story unfolds, she herself wants to be like Eugenie Roberts. How much should someone change in order to fit in? Write an essay that responds to this question.

Writing Handbook
See p. R39: Persuasive Writing.

Activities & Explorations

Mother's Day Card With a group, design a Mother's Day card that you could imagine the narrator giving her mother. Include a message (which could be in poetry or prose) as well as drawings and any artwork you think might express how the narrator feels about her mother. ~ **ART**

Dramatic Skit Imagine what it would have been like for the narrator and Mona to go back to Miss Crosman's for their next piano lesson. With a group, write and rehearse a skit that dramatizes what might take place. Then perform it for the class.
~ **PERFORMING**

Inquiry & Research

In ancient China, the umbrella represented privilege and authority. Find a book on ancient Chinese culture and research how and by whom the umbrella was used. Then write a report and present it to the class.

Vocabulary in Action

EXERCISE: WORD MEANING On a sheet of paper, write the word or phrase that best answers each of the following riddles.

1. A <u>revelation</u> has made me disappear. Was I a city, a secret, or a circle?

2. I <u>confirm</u> the spelling of words. Am I a pen, an eraser, or a dictionary?

3. I <u>illuminate</u> a house. Am I a lamp, a roof, or a sheet of plastic?

4. Rain is <u>diverted</u> by me. Am I a well, an umbrella, or a flower garden?

5. I am very <u>discreet</u>. Do people think me rude, cautious, or bold?

6. I make a very <u>audible</u> sound when eaten. Am I celery, a cupcake, or a hamburger?

7. I am about to <u>resume</u> work. Have I just finished, paused, or kept on working?

8. I am truly a <u>stupendous</u> sight. Do people yawn, giggle, or gasp when they see me?

9. I am well known for my <u>credibility</u>. Am I honest, brave, or sassy?

10. I am trying to <u>maneuver</u> a go-cart. Am I stopping it, steering it, or trying to buy it?

Building Vocabulary
For an in-depth lesson on learning and remembering new words, see p. 473.

THE WHITE UMBRELLA **531**

Writing Options

1. Short Story To get students started on this assignment, have them create a story map, listing events in sequence that lead up to the revelation in the car. Remind students to look back at the story for information about the mother's character that provides clues about why she reacts as she does.

 Use **Writing Transparencies**, p. 34, for additional support. Use **Reading and Critical Thinking Transparencies**, p. 34, for additional support.

2. Opinion Essay To get students started on this assignment, have them brainstorm their qualities and values. Then ask students to think about which of those they would be willing to change or give up and which they would not. Encourage students to make generalizations based on their own feelings and observations. To extend this assignment, have students debate the question of whether someone should have to change to fit in.

Use **Writing Transparencies**, p. 27, for additional support.

Activities & Explorations

Mother's Day Card Encourage students to think about the narrator's mixed feelings for her mother and how these feelings change at the end of the story.

Dramatic Skit To get students started on this assignment, have them think about the character of Miss Crosman and how the narrator feels at the end of the story. Remind students that Mona is not really aware of the narrator's conflict or lies, so she would be able to behave quite naturally.

Inquiry & Research

To make this assignment easier, have students work together to research the umbrella in Chinese culture. Then have students present their report orally. Encourage them to use visual aids such as as charts.

Vocabulary in Action

EXERCISE

1. a secret
2. a dictionary
3. a lamp
4. an umbrella
5. cautious
6. celery
7. paused
8. gasp
9. honest
10. steering it

THE WHITE UMBRELLA **531**

Mini Lesson **Spelling** ★ **TEKS 16C**

THE SUFFIXES *-ible* **AND** *-able*
Instruction Tell students the suffix *-able* is generally, though not always, added to base words, while *-ible* is usually added to roots. Point out that when *-able* is added to base words that end in *y*, the *y* changes to *i*. When *-able* or *-ible* is added to a word ending in a consonant and *e*, the *e* is usually dropped unless the consonant is soft *c* or *g*. Display these examples:

accept<u>able</u>   reli<u>able</u>   believ<u>able</u>
aud<u>ible</u>   elig<u>ible</u>   respons<u>ible</u>

Exercise Have students add *-ible* or *-able* to the following words or roots.

1. break *(breakable)*
2. terr *(terrible)*
3. ed *(edible)*
4. retract *(retractable)*
5. poss *(possible)*
6. permiss *(permissible)*
7. wash *(washable)*
8. amic *(amicable)*
9. compat *(compatible)*
10. applic *(applicable)*

Ask students to look for more words that fit this pattern in their reading and in their own writing. Have them add these words to their personal word lists.

Use **Unit Four Resource Book,** p. 9 for more practice.

Grammar in Context

WRITING EXERCISE
Possible Response:

1. I waited uncomfortably for my lesson.
2. Miss Crosman took my glasses from my head.
3. My pot roast is cooking in the oven.
4. Finally my mother arrived at the house.
5. My mother's head was resting on the seat.

CONNECT TO THE LITERATURE "from the car," "behind us," "on the window," "from my leg," "out of the car," "down a sewer"

Gish Jen

Gish Jen says that the biggest influence on her work has come from Jewish-American writers. She sees a definite sympathy between the Jewish and Chinese cultures.

Author Activity

Mona and Callie Have students chart the changes in the characters and their similarities in the two stories. Students should give examples from each story to support what they are saying.

Grammar in Context: Prepositional Phrases

In "The White Umbrella," Gish Jen uses **prepositional phrases** to add details to her writing.

> The umbrella glowed . . . on the blue carpet . . .

The word *on* is a **preposition**. A preposition shows the relationship between a noun or pronoun—the **object of the preposition**—and some other words in a sentence. A **prepositional phrase** includes the preposition, the noun or pronoun that is the object of the preposition, and all of the words that modify the object.

Common prepositions are *above, across, after, against, at, before, beside, by, for, from, in, inside, into, of, off, on, onto, over, through, to,* and *with*.

WRITING EXERCISE Rewrite the sentences, adding a prepositional phrase to give each sentence more detail.

Example: *Original* Mona continued her abuse.

Rewritten Mona continued her abuse <u>of the piano</u>.

1. I waited uncomfortably.
2. Miss Crosman took my glasses.
3. My pot roast is cooking.
4. Finally my mother arrived.
5. My mother's head was resting.

Connect to the Literature Find three prepositional phrases in the last paragraph of "The White Umbrella."

Grammar Handbook The Sentence and Its Parts, p. R55

"If there is one thing I hope readers come away with, it's to see Asian Americans as 'us' rather than 'other.'"

Gish Jen
born 1956

Growing Up A daughter of immigrant Chinese parents, Gish Jen grew up just north of New York City. "We were almost the only Asian-American family in town," she recalls. "People threw things at us and called us names. We thought it was normal. It was only much later that I realized it had been hard." Jen says these experiences did not make her childhood unhappy. In fact, her writing contains a great deal of humor.

Artistic Beginning Jen's first name is really Lillian. She adopted the name Gish, the last name of the silent-picture actress Lillian Gish, just for fun in high school. After Jen graduated from college, she went to China to teach English and later enrolled at the Writer's Workshop at the University of Iowa. About her writing, Jen says, "If there is one thing I hope readers come away with, it's to see Asian Americans as 'us' rather than 'other.'"

AUTHOR ACTIVITY

Mona and Callie The narrator in "The White Umbrella," along with her sister Mona and their parents, appears in several of Gish Jen's later works. Jen named the narrator Callie and uses her as the narrator for her short story "In the American Country." Read this story and compare it with "The White Umbrella." How have the characters changed, and how have they remained the same?

Teaching Options

Mini Lesson **Grammar** **TEKS 17E** **TAAS Writing Obj. 4**

PREPOSITIONAL PHRASES

Instruction Remind students that a preposition is always followed by an object. The object is either a noun or pronoun. Often, adjectives are found between the preposition and its object. Display the sentence below to illustrate how a prepositional phrase may include modifiers of the noun or pronoun.

When the narrator was sheltered <u>under the clean, white, gleaming umbrella</u>, she felt special.

Exercise Have students pick out the prepositional phrase in each sentence and identify the preposition and its object.

1. <u>After a long, embarrassed silence,</u> the girls mustered the courtesy to congratulate their mother. *(after, silence)*
2. Her mother slowly turned <u>onto the crowded street.</u> *(onto, street)*
3. The narrator played her selections <u>with enthusiastic vigor.</u> *(with, vigor)*

4. The girls quickly ran <u>through the harsh, pelting rain.</u> *(through, rain)*
5. Her fingers gracefully maneuvered their way <u>across the ivory keys.</u> *(across, keys)*

Use **Unit Four Resource Book**, p. 8.
Use **Grammar Transparencies and Copymasters**, p. 89.

 Use McDougal Littell's *Language Network*, Chapter 6, for more instruction and practice in prepositional phrases.

> *I felt like a hero. I was a hero. It was marvelous to be so popular."*

from Boy: Tales of Childhood

Autobiography by ROALD DAHL (rōō′əl däl′)

TEKS See the Skills Trace at the beginning of the unit for information on TEKS covered in this lesson.

Connect to Your Life

Just for Fun Sometimes it is hard to resist the urge to play a prank. Pranks can take many forms—funny or not so funny, harmless or harmful. They may also have unforeseen consequences. Get together with a small group of classmates. Describe some pranks you have played or have heard about. What were their consequences?

Build Background

CONNECT TO SOCIAL STUDIES Roald Dahl, a well-known British author of books for young people, played his share of pranks when he was a schoolboy. In this excerpt from his autobiography, he describes a prank he played as a nine-year-old at Llandaff Cathedral School in Wales. This school was what the British call a preparatory school—an elementary school for students planning to attend a private secondary school. Attending preparatory school is costly, and these schools are known for high standards and challenging academic training. At Dahl's school, the headmaster and teachers were strict, and discipline was rigid.

Schoolchildren in Great Britain. Archive Photos.

Focus Your Reading

LITERARY ANALYSIS DIALECT One of the ways that an author makes a character come alive for the reader is through **dialect**—a type of language spoken by people of a particular class or region. A dialect may differ from standard language in grammar, pronunciation, and vocabulary. As you read the excerpt from *Boy: Tales of Childhood,* pay attention to the dialect of Mrs. Pratchett—not only what she says but how she says it.

ACTIVE READING CONNECTING A reader's process of relating the content of a literary work to his or her own knowledge and experience is called **connecting.** In *Boy: Tales of Childhood* the narrator's description of his schoolboy adventures may lead readers to recall similar events from their own background. Pay attention to how the narrator describes events and characters as well as his own feelings. See if any of these descriptions connect to your own experience.

READER'S NOTEBOOK As you read the selection, note details about actions, characters, thoughts, and emotions from the story that you recognize from your own experience.

The description of the candy sold in the candy store reminds me of candy that I've eaten.

WORDS TO KNOW **Vocabulary Preview**
elaborate   loathsome   saturated
flourishing   malignant

BOY: TALES OF CHILDHOOD **533**

OVERVIEW

Objectives

1. understand and appreciate **autobiography** (Literary Analysis)
2. understand the function and significance of **dialect** in a work of literature (Literary Analysis)
3. utilize the reading skill **connect to personal experience and prior knowledge** (Active Reading)

Summary

Roald Dahl recounts his memories of attending the Llandaff Cathedral School, including an incident at the local sweetshop, run by stingy, untidy Mrs. Pratchett. Playing a prank on Mrs. Pratchett, Dahl puts a dead mouse in a candy jar while his friends distract her. Because the sweetshop is closed the next day, the boys fear that they have caused Mrs. Pratchett to die of a heart attack. Instead, she appears at school and identifies the boys from a lineup of students. Later, each of the boys is punished.

Thematic Link

A young Roald Dahl learns the hard way that not all pranks are seen as good fun by the victims.

5-Minute Warm-Up

Daily Language SkillBuilder **TEKS** 16B, 17C

Have students **proofread** the display sentences on page 517i and write them correctly. The sentences also appear on Transparency 17 of **Grammar Transparencies and Copymasters.**

LESSON RESOURCES

UNIT FOUR RESOURCE BOOK, pp. 11–17

ASSESSMENT
Formal Assessment, pp. 91–92
Teacher's Guide to Assessment and Portfolio Use
Test Generator

SKILLS TRANSPARENCIES AND COPYMASTERS
Reading and Critical Thinking
• Connecting, TR 2 (for Thinking Through the Literature, p. 546)

Grammar
• Compound Sentences, CM 104 (for Mini Lesson, p. 541)
• Comparative and Superlative Forms of Adjectives, CM 84 (for Mini Lesson, p. 544)
• Adjective Phrases, CM 92 (for Mini Lesson, p. 548)
Vocabulary
• Antonyms, CM 61 (for Mini Lesson, p. 534)
• Analogies, CM 62 (for Mini Lesson, pp. 538-539)

Communications
• Persuasive Techniques, TR 3 (for Mini Lesson, p. 545)

INTEGRATED TECHNOLOGY
Audio Library LaserLinks
• Author Background. See **Teacher's SourceBook,** p. 24, for bar codes.

Visit our website:
www.mcdougallittell.com

Mini Lesson **Preteaching Vocabulary**

If you would like to preteach the WORDS TO KNOW for this selection, use the Mini Lesson, p. 534.

PREVIEW

Have students skim the selection, looking at the illustrations and subtitles. Ask them what they think the great mouse plot might be. Then have them read to find out how close they came to guessing the plot.

Literary Analysis | DIALECT |

A Tell students that this selection is set in Wales, a part of Great Britain where many people speak the Welsh language as well as English. Llandaff is a Welsh name. In Welsh, many words start with *ll*. The Anglicized pronunciation is the same as an *l* (lan daff). The correct pronunciation in Welsh, however, is "hlan daff," with a slight, soft *ch* sound. Tell students that, in the speech of the characters of the selection, two distinct dialects of British English can be found, the Standard English of the boys and their teachers, who are members of the middle class, and the working-class dialect of Mrs. Pratchett, the candy-shop owner.

Use **Unit Four Resource Book,** p. 13 for more practice.

Active Reading | CONNECTING |

B Ask students to use their own experience to determine whether Roald Dahl's lack of memory about his two years of school seems realistic. Have students try to recall how much they remember about their experiences in second through fourth grade.

Possible Response: Students will probably find that like the author, they remember certain incidents, but not the day-to-day routine.

Use **Unit Four Resource Book,** p. 12 for more practice.

Teaching Options

from

Mini Lesson **Preteaching Vocabulary**

TEKS 6A | TAAS Reading Obj. 1

ANTONYMS

Instruction Remind students that they can use antonyms to define unfamiliar words. Display the following sentence:

His voice was *reassuring,* but there was something *malignant* in his eyes.

Sentence context should tell students that *reassuring* is an antonym of *malignant*. They can use their understanding of *reassuring* to define *malignant* (threatening).

Exercises Have students define each of the underlined WORDS TO KNOW with the help of the italicized antonym.

1. The *simple* plan became increasingly <u>elaborate</u> as time went by.
2. Far from being *attractive*, the idea was <u>loathsome</u>.
3. The <u>flourishing</u> candy shop stood next to an *unsuccessful* hat shop.
4. The cake, instead of being served *dry*, was <u>saturated</u> with a delicious syrup.

Use **Unit Four Resource Book,** p. 14 for more practice. Use **Vocabulary Transparencies and Copymasters,** p. 61, for additional support.

Y

Tales of
Childhood

by Roald Dahl

The Bicycle and the Sweetshop

When I was seven, my mother decided I should leave kindergarten and go to a proper boys' school. By good fortune, there existed a well-known preparatory school for boys about a mile from our house. It was called Llandaff Cathedral School, and it stood right under the shadow of Llandaff cathedral. Like the cathedral, the school is still there and still <u>flourishing</u>. **A**

But here again, I can remember very little about the two years I attended Llandaff Cathedral School, between the age of seven and nine. Only two moments remain clearly in my mind. The first lasted not more than five seconds, but I will never forget it. **B**

WORDS TO KNOW **flourishing** (flûr′ĭ-shĭng) *adj.* getting along well and successfully; thriving **flourish** *v.*

535

Customizing Instruction

Less Proficient Readers
Ask students to recall an incident from third grade. Discuss why they remember this event.
Set a Purpose Have students read to determine the first memorable event the author describes and what the author's reaction to it reveals.

Students Acquiring English
This story contains British names for a variety of candies. Reassure students acquiring English that their English-speaking classmates are also unfamiliar with these names. As students read, they can use their reading logs to record their guesses about what kinds of candy each name describes. Ask them to note any other names they know for similar candy, such as *licorice stick* for *licorice straw*.

Use **Spanish Study Guide,** pp. 112–114 for additional support.

Gifted and Talented
Ask students to note British slang terms as they read. Have them use context clues to determine the American English equivalents.
Possible Response:
Page 541 – "Hold on a tick . . ." Wait
Page 543 – "Sixth Form over there!" A form is a class.
Page 544 – "Nasty, cheeky lot . . ." *Cheeky* means "fresh, sassy." A lot is a group of people.
Page 544 – "They nick things . . ." They steal things.

BLOCK SCHEDULING: MANAGING TIME

If your schedule requires that you cover the lesson objectives in a shorter time, use . . .
- Preparing to Read, p. 533
- Thinking Through the Literature, p. 546
- Vocabulary in Action, p. 547
- Grammar in Context, p. 548

If you want to take advantage of longer class time, use . . .
- TE Teaching Options: Preteaching Vocabulary, p. 534; Cross-Curricular Link, p. 536; Vocabulary Strategy, pp. 538; Viewing and Representing, p. 540; Grammar, pp. 541, 544, 548; Standardized Test Practice, p. 542; Speaking and Listening, p. 545; Spelling, p. 547
- Choices & Challenges and Author Activity, pp. 547–548
- Real World Link, p. 549

Literary Analysis: CHARACTERIZATION

(A) Ask students what the narrator's admiration for the bicyclist reveals about his own character at that time.

Possible Responses: He wants to appear brave, confident, and admirable. He may feel that he lacks those qualities at this point in his life.

Reading Skills and Strategies: VISUALIZING

(B) Ask students what words and phrases create mental images of the process of making licorice bootlaces.

Possible Responses: "huge, shiny steel cauldron," "bubbling cauldron," "thick, steaming rat stew," "pulpy substance," "shovel the hot rat mash," "gigantic black pancake"

Ask students what impression of the process the text description evokes.

Possible Responses: unpleasant, disgusting, unappealing

Use **Reading and Critical Thinking Transparencies,** p. 10, for additional support.

Reading Skills and Strategies: EVALUATING

(C) Ask students why Dr. Thwaites tells his son this story about licorice bootlaces.

Possible Responses: as a joke; to prevent him from eating too many sweets

Reading Skills and Strategies: CLASSIFYING

(D) Ask students to classify Thwaites and then the other boys as believers or nonbelievers of Dr. Thwaites's description of how licorice bootlaces are made. Have them explain their classification.

Possible Response: Thwaites must have been a believer, since he never ate licorice bootlaces. The boys must have been nonbelievers—since they enjoyed hearing the story over and over but didn't stop eating this candy.

It was my first term, and I was walking home alone across the village green after school when suddenly one of the senior twelve-year-old boys came riding full speed down the road on his bicycle about twenty yards away from me. The road was on a hill, and the boy was going down the slope, and as he flashed by he started back-pedaling very quickly so that the free-wheeling mechanism of his bike made a loud whirring sound. At the same time, he took his hands off the handlebars and folded them casually across his chest. I stopped dead and stared after him. How wonderful he was! How swift and brave and graceful in his long trousers with bicycle clips around them and his scarlet school cap at a jaunty angle on his head! One day, I told myself, one glorious day I will have a bike like that, and I will wear long trousers with bicycle clips, and my school cap will sit jaunty on my head, and I will go whizzing down the hill pedaling backwards with no hands on the handlebars!

I promise you that if somebody had caught me by the shoulder at that moment and said to me, "What is your greatest wish in life, little boy? What is your absolute ambition? To be a doctor? A fine musician? A painter? A writer? Or the Lord Chancellor?"[1] I would have answered without hesitation that my only ambition, my hope, my longing was to have a bike like that and to go whizzing down the hill with no hands on the handlebars. It would be fabulous. It made me tremble just to think about it.

My second and only other memory of Llandaff Cathedral School is extremely bizarre. It happened a little over a year later, when I was just nine. By then I had made some friends, and when I walked to school in the mornings I would start out alone but would pick up four other boys of my own age along the way. After school was over, the same four boys and I would set out together across the village green and through the village itself, heading for home. On the way to school and on the way back we always passed the sweetshop. No we didn't; we never passed it. We always stopped. We lingered outside its rather small window, gazing in at the big glass jars full of bull's-eyes and old-fashioned humbugs and strawberry bonbons and glacier mints and acid drops and pear drops and lemon drops and all the rest of them. Each of us received sixpence[2] a week for pocket money, and whenever there was any money in our pockets, we would all troop in together to buy a pennyworth of this or that. My own favorites were sherbet suckers and licorice bootlaces.

One of the other boys, whose name was Thwaites, told me I should never eat licorice

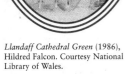

Llandaff Cathedral Green (1986), Hildred Falcon. Courtesy National Library of Wales.

---

1. **Lord Chancellor:** a high-ranking British government official who presides over the House of Lords.
2. **sixpence:** in Great Britain, six pennies.

Cross Curricular Link ## Social Studies

BRITISH PUBLIC SCHOOLS British public schools are what would be known as private schools in the United States. Many evolved from institutions originally founded by benefactors to provide education for boys of poor families. Upper-class families began to take advantage of these schools, and as the reputations of these schools spread, they attracted students from outside the local areas whose parents could afford boarding fees. The schools became public rather than local. They were also intended to prepare students for public life, another reason for the name *public school.*

Enrollment in public schools increased dramatically during the 19th century as more and more children of civil servants and military personnel serving in various parts of the empire were sent back to England to be educated. As a result, many public schools began to limit their acceptance of students to boys 12 and over. Preparatory schools then sprang up to fill the void in educating boys under 12.

In the late 19th century, some public schools for girls were established.

bootlaces. Thwaites's father, who was a doctor, had said that they were made from rats' blood. The father had given his young son a lecture about licorice bootlaces when he had caught him eating one in bed. "Every rat catcher in the country," the father had said, "takes his rats to the Licorice Bootlace Factory, and the manager pays tuppence[3] for each rat. Many a rat catcher has become a millionaire by selling his dead rats to the factory."

"But how do they turn the rats into licorice?" the young Thwaites had asked his father.

"They wait until they've got ten thousand rats," the father had answered, "then they dump them all into a huge, shiny steel cauldron[4] and boil them up for several hours. Two men stir the bubbling cauldron with long poles, and in the end they have a thick, steaming rat stew. After that, a cruncher is lowered into the cauldron to crunch the bones, and what's left is a pulpy substance called rat mash."

"Yes, but how do they turn that into licorice bootlaces, Daddy?" the young Thwaites had asked, and this question, according to Thwaites, had caused his father to pause and think for a few moments before he answered it. At last he had said, "The two men who were doing the stirring with the long poles now put on their Wellington boots[5] and climb into the cauldron and shovel the hot rat mash out onto a concrete floor. Then they run a steamroller over it several times to flatten it out. What is left looks rather like a gigantic black pancake, and all they have to do after that is to wait for it to cool and to harden so they can cut it up into strips to make the bootlaces. Don't ever eat them," the father had said. "If you do, you'll get ratitis."

"What is ratitis, Daddy?" young Thwaites had asked.

"All the rats that the rat catchers catch are poisoned with rat poison," the father had said. "It's the rat poison that gives you ratitis."

"Yes, but what happens to you when you catch it?" young Thwaites had asked.

"Your teeth become very sharp and pointed," the father had answered. "And a short, stumpy tail grows out of your back just above your bottom. There is no cure for ratitis. I ought to know. I'm a doctor."

We all enjoyed Thwaites's story, and we made him tell it to us many times on our walks to and from school. But it didn't stop any of us except Thwaites from buying licorice bootlaces. At two for a penny they were the best value in the shop. A bootlace, in case you haven't had the pleasure of handling one, is not round. It's like a flat black tape about half an inch wide. You buy it rolled up in a coil, and in those days it used to be so long that when you unrolled it and held one end at arm's length above your head, the other end touched the ground.

Sherbet suckers were also two a penny. Each sucker consisted of a yellow cardboard tube filled with sherbet powder, and there was a hollow licorice straw sticking out of it. (Rat's blood again, young Thwaites would warn us, pointing at the licorice straw.) You sucked the sherbet up through the straw, and when it was finished you ate the licorice. They were delicious, those

---

3. **tuppence** (tŭp′əns): in Great Britain, two pennies.
4. **cauldron**: a large kettle.
5. **Wellington boots**: high rubber boots.

Customizing Instruction

Less Proficient Readers
Ask students to describe the author's first vivid memory of his school days.
Answer: The author remembers seeing an older boy riding full speed down the slope on a bicycle with his hands off the handlebars and recalls his wish to do the same.
What does young Roald's reaction to the biker reveal about the author?
Possible Response: He is immature and impressionable.
Set a Purpose Have students read to find out how the boys feel about Mrs. Pratchett and why they feel this way.

Students Acquiring English
1 Point out that the verb *whiz* is an example of onomatopoeia: the sound of the word imitates the sound of a speeding bicycle.

Multiple Learning Styles
Visual Learners
2 Have students create a comic strip showing the sequence of events, as described by Thwaites's father, in making the candy called licorice bootlaces. Encourage them to use creativity and humor in their work. Have students share their comic strips with the class.

A Ask students to think of a place that is very important to them. Ask them what characteristics make it special. Invite students to use their reading logs to draw parallels between the sweetshop and their own special places.

Literary Analysis DIALECT

B Remind students that Mrs. Pratchett's dialect develops the impression of her character. Ask students to identify examples of dialect in her speech.

Possible Response: "watchin'," "yer thievin' fingers," "them chocolates," "Either you forks out or you gets out!"

Reading Skills and Strategies: VISUALIZING

C Have students note the number of physical details that the author includes to help them visualize Mrs. Pratchett. Ask students to summarize the mental image that the description evokes.

Possible Response: Mrs. Pratchett is disgusting—an unattractive, skinny old lady with a moustache, grubby clothes, and dirty hands.

Literary Analysis: CHARACTERIZATION

D Ask students in what way the narrator considers Mrs. Pratchett to be mean.

Possible Response: She is stingy because she never gives bags for small purchases.

Reading Skills and Strategies: EVALUATING

E Ask students if they think the boys' perception is accurate.

Possible Responses: Yes, because the author includes many details that seem to support the description; no, because the description seems exaggerated.

---

sherbet suckers. The sherbet fizzed in your mouth, and if you knew how to do it, you could make white froth come out of your nostrils and pretend you were throwing a fit.

Gobstoppers, costing a penny each, were enormous, hard round balls the size of small tomatoes. One gobstopper would provide about an hour's worth of nonstop sucking, and if you took it out of your mouth and inspected it every five minutes or so, you would find it had changed color. There was something fascinating about the way it went from pink to blue to green to yellow. We used to wonder how in the world the Gobstopper Factory managed to achieve this magic. "How *does* it happen?" we would ask each other. "How *can* they make it keep changing color?"

"It's your spit that does it," young Thwaites proclaimed. As the son of a doctor, he considered himself to be an authority on all things that had to do with the body. He could tell us about scabs and when they were ready to be picked off. He knew why a black eye was blue and why blood was red. "It's your spit that makes a gobstopper change color," he kept insisting. When we asked him to <u>elaborate</u> on this theory, he answered, "You wouldn't understand it if I did tell you."

Pear drops were exciting because they had a dangerous taste. They smelled of nail varnish, and they froze the back of your throat. All of us were warned against eating them, and the result was that we ate them more than ever.

The sweetshop in Llandaff in the year 1923 was the very center of our lives.

Then there was a hard brown lozenge called the tonsil tickler. The tonsil tickler tasted and smelled very strongly of chloroform. We had not the slightest doubt that these things were <u>saturated</u> in the dreaded anesthetic which, as Thwaites had many times pointed out to us, could put you to sleep for hours at a stretch.

"If my father has to saw off somebody's leg," he said, "he pours chloroform onto a pad, and the person sniffs it and goes to sleep, and my father saws his leg off without him even feeling it."

"But why do they put it into sweets and sell them to us?" we asked him.

You might think a question like this would have baffled Thwaites. But Thwaites was never baffled. "My father says tonsil ticklers were invented for dangerous prisoners in jail," he said. "They give them one with each meal, and the chloroform makes them sleepy and stops them rioting."

"Yes," we said, "but why sell them to children?"

"It's a plot," Thwaites said. "A grown-up plot to keep us quiet."

The sweetshop in Llandaff in the year 1923 was the very center of our lives. To us, it was what a bar is to a drunk or a church is to a bishop. Without it, there would have been little to live for. But it had one terrible drawback, this sweetshop. The woman who owned it was a horror. We hated her, and we had good reason for doing so.

WORDS TO KNOW

elaborate (ĭ-lăb′ə-rāt′) *v.* to state at greater length or in greater detail
saturated (săch′ə-rā′tĭd) *adj.* soaked with moisture; drenched

538

Teaching Options

TEKS 9B   TAAS Reading Obj. 1

ANALOGIES

Instruction Tell students that an analogy is a comparison. A word analogy compares two pairs of words. The pairs of words are alike in that the relationship between the two words in the first pair is the same as the relationship between the two words in the second pair. For example, Roald Dahl uses analogies to illustrate the place of the sweetshop in his life. He says that the sweetshop was to the boys as a church was to a bishop. In a word analogy, the comparison might be expressed

as CHURCH : BISHOP :: sweetshop : boys. The two pairs of words express the same kind of relationship: A is a special place to B. Other relationships that might be used in analogies include the following: cause to effect; part to whole; action to consequence; synonyms; antonyms; classification; performer and related object or action; degree of intensity.

To complete a word analogy, state the relationship between the first pair of words in a sentence before trying to complete the second pair.

Her name was Mrs. Pratchett. She was a small, skinny old hag with a moustache on her upper lip and a mouth as sour as a green gooseberry. She never smiled. She never welcomed us when we went in, and the only times she spoke were when she said things like, "I'm watchin' you, so keep yer thievin' fingers off them chocolates!" Or "I don't want you in 'ere just to look around! Either you *forks* out or you *gets* out!"

But by far the most <u>loathsome</u> thing about Mrs. Pratchett was the filth that clung around her. Her apron was grey and greasy. Her blouse had bits of breakfast all over it, toast crumbs and tea stains and splotches of dried egg yolk. It was her hands, however, that disturbed us most. They were disgusting. They were black with dirt and grime. They looked as though they had been putting lumps of coal on the fire all day long. And do not forget, please, that it was these very hands and fingers that she plunged into the sweet jars when we asked for a pennyworth of treacle toffee[6] or wine gums or nut clusters or whatever. There were precious few health laws in those days, and nobody, least of all Mrs. Pratchett, ever thought of using a little shovel for getting out the sweets as they do today. The mere sight of her grimy right hand with its black fingernails digging an ounce of chocolate fudge out of a jar would have caused a starving tramp to go running from the shop. But not us.

Sweets were our lifeblood. We would have put up with far worse than that to get them. So we simply stood and watched in sullen silence while this disgusting old woman stirred around inside the jars with her foul fingers.

The other thing we hated Mrs. Pratchett for was her meanness. Unless you spent a whole sixpence all in one go, she wouldn't give you a bag. Instead you got your sweets twisted up in a small piece of newspaper which she tore off a pile of old *Daily Mirrors* lying on the counter.

So you can well understand that we had it in for Mrs. Pratchett in a big way, but we didn't quite know what to do about it. Many schemes were put forward, but none of them was any good. None of them, that is, until suddenly, one memorable afternoon, we found the dead mouse.

The Great Mouse Plot

My four friends and I had come across a loose floorboard at the back of the classroom, and when we prised it up with the blade of a pocketknife, we discovered a big hollow space underneath. This, we decided, would be our secret hiding place for sweets and other small treasures such as conkers[7] and monkey nuts and birds' eggs. Every afternoon, when the last lesson was over, the five of us would wait until the classroom had emptied; then we would lift up the floorboard and examine our secret hoard, perhaps adding to it or taking something away.

---

6. **treacle toffee:** a hard, chewy candy made from molasses.
7. **conkers:** large brown nuts threaded on strings for use in a children's game.

WORDS
TO
KNOW
loathsome (lōth'səm) *adj.* disgusting

539

D

E

Literary Analysis:
CHARACTERIZATION

A Ask students what they can infer about the author's attitude toward this incident even years later.

Possible Response: He remains proud of the fact that he was the one to have the idea.

Reading Skills and Strategies:
ANALYZING

B Ask students why they think the narrator readily agrees to carry the dead mouse and put it in the candy jar.

Possible Response: He feels he has earned the right, since he came up with the plan; he feels honored to be chosen by his friends.

Literary Analysis: WORD CHOICE

C Emphasize to students how writers choose their words carefully, both for their denotations and connotations. Point out the verb *strutting*. Ask students what that verb conveys.

Possible Response: arrogance, pride, a feeling of confidence or power.
Ask students to compare the author's original sentence with one that has *shuffling* instead of strutting.

Possible Response: An effect of hesitation and uncertainty is created by the different verb.

Reading Skills and Strategies:
MAKE JUDGMENTS

D Ask students if they think the narrator is a hero. Have them consider whether all heroes are popular.

Possible Response: Pulling a prank on someone is mean, not heroic, behavior. While many heroes like astronauts are popular, sometimes being heroic means standing for what is right and not necessarily for what is popular.

Three Boys with a Mouse (1981), Terry Mimnaugh. Bronze, 10½″ × 9″ × 7″, from the series *What Little Boys Are Made Of.*

Teaching Options

Mini Lesson Viewing and Representing ⬤ TEKS 22A

Three Boys with a Mouse
by Terry Mimnaugh

ART APPRECIATION As a child, Mimnaugh (1954 –) was always told that she could succeed at anything she tried. She decided to be a sculptor and wasn't discouraged when she was told that women couldn't be "real" artists. She graduated from art school anyway. Today she spends six months each year planning her next year's work. She has said, "Motivation comes from within. Someone can tell you how to go over a mountain, but the only way to do it is on your own two feet."

Instruction Tell students that a sculptor decides which material will work best for his or her purpose. Ask students what the choice of bronze for this sculpture has allowed the artist to do.

Possible Response: Bronze allows the artist to create textures of hair, skin, and fabric.

Application Ask students how the sculpture of the boys differs from or reinforces their impression of the author and his friends.

Possible Response: There is the same sense of mischief; the boys in the sculpture are more casually dressed and are fewer in number.

One day, when we lifted it up, we found a dead mouse lying among our treasures. It was an exciting discovery. Thwaites took it out by its tail and waved it in front of our faces. "What shall we do with it?" he cried.

"It stinks!" someone shouted. "Throw it out of the window quick!"

"Hold on a tick," I said. "Don't throw it away."

Thwaites hesitated. They all looked at me.

When writing about oneself, one must strive to be truthful. Truth is more important than modesty. I must tell you, therefore, that it was I and I alone who had the idea for the great and daring Mouse Plot. We all have our moments of brilliance and glory, and this was mine.

"Why don't we," I said, "slip it into one of Mrs. Pratchett's jars of sweets? Then when she puts her dirty hand in to grab a handful, she'll grab a stinky dead mouse instead."

The other four stared at me in wonder. Then, as the sheer genius of the plot began to sink in, they all started grinning. They slapped me on the back. They cheered me and danced around the classroom. "We'll do it today!" they cried. "We'll do it on the way home! *You* had the idea," they said to me, "so *you* can be the one to put the mouse in the jar."

Thwaites handed me the mouse. I put it into my trouser pocket. Then the five of us left the school, crossed the village green, and headed for the sweetshop. We were tremendously jazzed up. We felt like a gang of desperados setting out to rob a train or blow up the sheriff's office.

"Make sure you put it into a jar which is used often," somebody said.

"I'm putting it in gobstoppers," I said. "The gobstopper jar is never behind the counter."

"I've got a penny," Thwaites said, "so I'll ask for one sherbet sucker and one bootlace. And while she turns away to get them, you slip the mouse in quickly with the gobstoppers."

Thus everything was arranged. We were strutting a little as we entered the shop. We were the victors now, and Mrs. Pratchett was the victim. She stood behind the counter, and her small, <u>malignant</u> pig-eyes watched us suspiciously as we came forward.

"One sherbet sucker, please," Thwaites said to her, holding out his penny.

I kept to the rear of the group, and when I saw Mrs. Pratchett turn her head away for a couple of seconds to fish a sherbet sucker out of the box, I lifted the heavy glass lid of the gobstopper jar and dropped the mouse in. Then I replaced the lid as silently as possible. My heart was thumping like mad, and my hands had gone all sweaty.

"And one bootlace, please," I heard Thwaites saying. When I turned around, I saw Mrs. Pratchett holding out the bootlace in her filthy fingers.

"I don't want all the lot of you troopin' in 'ere if only one of you is buyin'," she screamed at us. "Now beat it! Go on, get out!"

As soon as we were outside, we broke into a run. "Did you do it?" they shouted at me.

"Of course I did!" I said.

"Well done, you!" they cried. "What a super show!"

I felt like a hero. I *was* a hero. It was marvelous to be so popular.

WORDS
TO
KNOW

malignant (mə-lĭg′nənt) *adj.* filled with evil; threatening

541

Less Proficient Readers
Make sure that students understand the sequence of events that lead up to the narrator's prank.

- What do you think attracted the mouse to the boys' hiding place underneath the floorboards?
  Possible Response: the candy hidden there
- What do the boys do to "get back at" Mrs. Pratchett?
  Possible Response: One of them puts the dead mouse in a candy jar.

Set a Purpose Have students read to find out what the boys see at the sweetshop after they play their prank on Mrs. Pratchett and what conclusions they then draw.

Multiple Learning Styles
Kinesthetic Learners

1 Have students enact this scene to illustrate the split-second timing that would be necessary in order to accomplish this prank successfully.

 Grammar 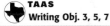 TEKS 17A   TAAS Writing Obj. 3, 5, 7

COMPOUND SENTENCES

Instruction Remind students that a compound sentence is two or more simple sentences joined together. The parts of a compound sentence are joined either by a conjunction and a comma or by a semicolon. The ideas in a compound sentence should be closely related. Draw students' attention to the highlighted sentence on this page to illustrate an effective compound sentence.

Application Have each student write five com-

pound sentences about the story and share them with a classmate, who should check for correct punctuation and coherence.

 Use **Grammar Transparencies and Copymasters**, p. 104.

 Use McDougal Littell's *Language Network*, Chapter 8, for more instruction and practice in compound sentences.

Active Reading | CONNECTING

A Have students discuss the differences between the sweetshop and modern candy stores. Have them use their own knowledge to determine whether the same prank could be played today.
Possible Response: Probably not, because most candy today is packaged, not loose in jars.

Literary Analysis: CHARACTERIZATION

B Ask students what they might infer about Thwaites's position in the group from the way the boys react to him.
Possible Response: Thwaites is a leader and source of information.

Reading Skills and Strategies: VISUALIZING

C Ask students what mental image is evoked by the comparison of Mr. Coombes's face to a ham.
Possible Response: His complexion is pink in color, and his face is broad.

Literary Analysis: FORESHADOWING

D Ask students to describe what Mr. Coombes normally does immediately after finishing the prayers.
Answer: He leads his group out.
Ask what he does on this day and what his actions foreshadow.
Possible Responses: He remains standing. He may be preparing to announce Mrs. Pratchett's death.

Literary Analysis: IRONY

E Have students contrast the narrator's feelings while plotting the prank with his emotions at this point in the excerpt.
Possible Response: Before he felt daring and brilliant; now, he feels scared and ashamed.

Mr. Coombes

The flush of triumph over the dead mouse was carried forward to the next morning as we all met again to walk to school.

"Let's go in and see if it's still in the jar," somebody said as we approached the sweetshop.

"Don't," Thwaites said firmly. "It's too dangerous. Walk past as though nothing has happened."

As we came level with the shop we saw a cardboard notice hanging on the door.

We stopped and stared. We had never known the sweetshop to be closed at this time in the morning, even on Sundays.

"What's happened?" we asked each other. "What's going on?"

We pressed our faces against the window and looked inside. Mrs. Pratchett was nowhere to be seen.

A "Look!" I cried. "The gobstopper jar's gone! It's not on the shelf! There's a gap where it used to be!"

"It's on the floor!" someone said. "It's smashed to bits, and there's gobstoppers everywhere!"

"There's the mouse!" someone else shouted.

We could see it all, the huge glass jar smashed to smithereens with the dead mouse lying in the wreckage and hundreds of many-colored gobstoppers littering the floor.

"She got such a shock when she grabbed hold of the mouse that she dropped everything," somebody was saying.

"But why didn't she sweep it all up and open the shop?" I asked.

Nobody answered me.

We turned away and walked towards the school. All of a sudden we had begun to feel slightly uncomfortable. There was something not quite right about the shop being closed. Even Thwaites was unable to offer a reasonable explanation. We became silent. There was a faint scent of danger in the air now. Each one of us had caught a whiff of it. Alarm bells were beginning to ring faintly in our ears.

After a while, Thwaites broke the silence. "She must have got one heck of a shock," he said. He paused. We all looked at him, wondering what wisdom the great medical authority was going to come out with next.

"After all," he went on, "to catch hold of a dead mouse when you're expecting to catch hold of a gobstopper must be a pretty frightening experience. Don't you agree?"

Nobody answered him.

"Well now," Thwaites went on, "when an old person like Mrs. Pratchett suddenly gets a very big shock, I suppose you know what happens next?"

"What?" we said. "What happens?"

"You ask my father," Thwaites said. "He'll tell you."

"You tell us," we said.

"It gives her a heart attack," Thwaites announced. "Her heart stops beating, and she's dead in five seconds."

For a moment or two my own heart stopped beating. Thwaites pointed a finger at me and said darkly, "I'm afraid you've killed her."

"*Me?*" I cried. "Why just *me?*"

"It was *your* idea," he said. "And what's more, *you* put the mouse in."

All of a sudden, I was a murderer.

At exactly that point, we heard the school bell ringing in the distance, and we had to gallop the rest of the way so as not to be late for prayers.

Prayers were held in the Assembly Hall. We all perched in rows on wooden benches while

Teaching Options

✓ **Assessment** **Standardized Test Practice** 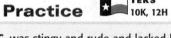 TEKS 10K, 12H  TAAS Reading Obj. 6

RECOGNIZING THE AUTHOR'S POINT OF VIEW AND PURPOSE For some standardized tests, students will be asked to choose the statement that best describes the author's point of view and purpose in a selection. To provide students with some help in choosing the best response, read aloud or write on the board the following:
If the author told someone that he or she was like Mrs. Pratchett, it could be inferred that the person—
A. kept a sweetshop like Mrs. Pratchett.
B. spoke in a similar dialect to Mrs. Pratchett's.

C. was stingy and rude and lacked high standards of personal hygiene.
D. would be affectionately remembered by the author.
Lead students through the process of choosing the best response. A and B do not focus on the traits that distinguish Mrs. Pratchett in the author's memory. D is wrong because she is not remembered with affection. C is correct because the author's purpose was to emphasize these characteristics of Mrs. Pratchett.

he teachers sat up on the platform in armchairs, facing us. The five of us scrambled into our places just as the Headmaster marched in, followed by the rest of the staff.

The Headmaster is the only teacher at Llandaff Cathedral School that I can remember, and for a reason you will soon discover, I can remember him very clearly indeed. His name was Mr. Coombes, and I have a picture in my mind of a giant of a man with a face like a ham and a mass of rusty-colored hair that sprouted in a tangle all over the top of his head. All grown-ups appear as giants to small children. But Headmasters (and policemen) are the biggest giants of all and acquire a marvelously exaggerated stature. It is possible that Mr. Coombes was a perfectly normal being, but in my memory he was a giant, a tweed-suited giant who always wore a black gown over his tweeds and a waistcoat under his jacket.

Mr. Coombes now proceeded to mumble through the same old prayers we had every day; but this morning, when the last amen had been spoken, he did not turn and lead his group rapidly out of the hall as usual. He remained standing before us, and it was clear he had an announcement to make.

"The whole school is to go out and line up around the playground immediately," he said. "Leave your books behind. And no talking."

Mr. Coombes was looking grim. His hammy pink face had taken on that dangerous scowl which only appeared when he was extremely cross and somebody was for the high jump. I

We stopped and stared. We had never known the sweetshop to be closed at this time.

sat there small and frightened among the rows and rows of other boys; and to me at that moment the Headmaster, with his black gown draped over his shoulders, was like a judge at a murder trial.

"He's after the killer," Thwaites whispered to me.

I began to shiver.

"I'll bet the police are here already," Thwaites went on. "And the Black Maria's[8] waiting outside."

As we made our way out to the playground, my whole stomach began to feel as though it was slowly filling up with swirling water. *I am only eight years old*, I told myself. *No little boy of eight has ever murdered anyone. It's not possible.*

Out in the playground on this warm, cloudy September morning, the Deputy Headmaster was shouting, "Line up in forms! Sixth Form over there! Fifth Form next to them! Spread out! Spread out! Get on with it! Stop talking all of you!"

Thwaites and I and my other three friends were in the Second Form, the lowest but one, and we lined up against the red-brick wall of the playground shoulder to shoulder. I can remember that when every boy in the school was in his place, the line stretched right around the four sides of the playground— about one hundred small boys altogether, aged between six and twelve, all of us wearing identical grey shorts and grey blazers and grey stockings and black shoes.

---

8. **Black Maria** (mə-rī′ə): a police patrol wagon.

BOY: TALES OF CHILDHOOD **543**

Reading and Analyzing

"Stop that *talking!*" shouted the Deputy Head. "I want absolute silence!"

But why for heaven's sake were we in the playground at all? I wondered. And why were we lined up like this? It had never happened before.

I half expected to see two policemen come bounding out of the school to grab me by the arms and put handcuffs on my wrists.

A single door led out from the school onto the playground. Suddenly it swung open, and through it, like the angel of death, strode Mr. Coombes, huge and bulky in his tweed suit and black gown; and beside him, believe it or not, right beside him trotted the tiny figure of Mrs. Pratchett herself!

Mrs. Pratchett was alive!

The relief was tremendous.

"She's alive!" I whispered to Thwaites standing next to me. "I didn't kill her!" Thwaites ignored me.

"We'll start over here," Mr. Coombes was saying to Mrs. Pratchett. He grasped her by one of her skinny arms and led her over to where the Sixth Form was standing. Then, still keeping hold of her arm, he proceeded to lead her at a brisk walk down the line of boys. It was like someone inspecting the troops.

"What on earth are they doing?" I whispered.

Thwaites didn't answer me. I glanced at him. He had gone rather pale.

"Too big," I heard Mrs. Pratchett saying.

Wanted Poster from "Mr. Coombes" from *Boy: Tales of Childhood* by Roald Dahl. Copyright © 1984 by Roald Dahl. Reprinted by permission of Farrar, Straus and Giroux, LLC.

"Much too big. It's none of this lot. Let's 'ave a look at some of them titchy ones."

Mr. Coombes increased his pace. "We'd better go all the way round," he said. He seemed in a hurry to get it over with now, and I could see Mrs. Pratchett's skinny goat's legs trotting to keep up with him. They had already inspected one side of the playground where the Sixth Form and half the Fifth Form were standing. We watched them moving down the second side . . . then the third side. "Still too big," I heard Mrs. Pratchett croaking. "Much too big! Smaller than these! Much smaller! Where's them nasty little ones?"

They were coming closer to us now . . . closer and closer.

They were starting on the fourth side . . .

Every boy in our form was watching Mr. Coombes and Mrs. Pratchett as they came walking down the line towards us.

"Nasty, cheeky lot, these little 'uns!" I heard Mrs. Pratchett muttering. "They comes into my shop, and they thinks they can do what they damn well likes!"

Mr. Coombes made no reply to this.

"They nick things when I ain't lookin'," she went on. "They put their grubby 'ands all over everything, and they've got no manners. I don't mind girls. I never 'ave no trouble with girls, but boys is 'ideous and 'orrible! I don't 'ave to tell *you* that, 'Eadmaster, do I?"

"These are the smaller ones," Mr. Coombes said.

Teaching Options

 Grammar 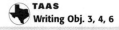 **TEKS 17D** **TAAS Writing Obj. 3, 4, 6**

Exercise Have students give the comparative and superlative forms of the following adjectives.

1. happy   *(happier, happiest)*
2. beautiful   *(more beautiful, most beautiful)*
3. honest   *(more honest, most honest)*
4. grubby   *(grubbier, grubbiest)*
5. bad   *(worse, worst)*

 Use **Grammar Transparencies and Copymasters**, p. 84.

 Use McDougal Littell's *Language Network*, Chapter 5, for more instruction and practice in using the comparative and superlative forms of adjectives.

I could see Mrs. Pratchett's piggy little eyes staring hard at the face of each boy she passed.

Suddenly she let out a high-pitched yell and pointed a dirty finger straight at Thwaites. "That's 'im!" she yelled. "That's one of 'em! I'd know 'im a mile away, the scummy little bounder!"

The entire school turned to look at Thwaites. "W-what have *I* done?" he stuttered, appealing to Mr. Coombes.

"Shut up," Mr. Coombes said.

Mrs. Pratchett's eyes flicked over and settled on my own face. I looked down and studied the black asphalt surface of the playground.

"'Ere's another of 'em!" I heard her yelling. "That one there!" She was pointing at me now.

"You're quite sure?" Mr. Coombes said.

"Of course I'm sure!" she cried. "I never forgets a face, least of all when it's as sly as that! 'Ee's one of 'em all right! There was five altogether! Now where's them other three?"

The other three, as I knew very well, were coming up next.

Mrs. Pratchett's face was glimmering with venom as her eyes traveled beyond me down the line.

"There they are!" she cried out, stabbing the air with her finger. "'*Im* . . . and '*im* . . . and '*im*! That's the five of 'em all right!

We don't need to look no farther than this, 'Eadmaster! They're all 'ere, the nasty, dirty little pigs! You've got their names, 'ave you?"

"I've got their names, Mrs. Pratchett," Mr. Coombes told her. "I'm much obliged to you."

"And I'm much obliged to *you*, 'Eadmaster," she answered.

As Mr. Coombes led her away across the playground, we heard her saying, "Right in the jar of gobstoppers it was! A stinkin' dead mouse which I will never forget as long as I live!"

"You have my deepest sympathy," Mr. Coombes was muttering.

"Talk about shocks!" she went on. "When my fingers caught 'old of that nasty, soggy, stinkin' dead mouse . . ." Her voice trailed away as Mr. Coombes led her quickly through the door into the school building. ❖

Editor's Note: After being identified by Mrs. Pratchett in the schoolyard lineup, Roald and his friends were ordered into the Head-master's office. There they received a caning (beating) from Mr. Coombes, while Mrs. Pratchett watched. When Roald's mother saw her son's bruises, she promised to send him to school in England. The following year, Roald went to boarding school.

Customizing Instruction

Less Proficient Readers
Have students describe the consequences of the prank for the boys.
Possible Response: They had to endure identification in a lineup and a caning.

Students Acquiring English
Work with students to help them understand Mrs. Pratchett's comments as she looks for the culprits.

Gifted and Talented
Have students express opinions about how accurately they think the author has represented the events surrounding the prank. Ask them to discuss the likelihood of the author's exaggerating certain details and to identify the details that may have been exaggerated. Ask them whether or not they think all memoirs of childhood contain exaggeration.

 Mini Lesson ## Speaking and Listening 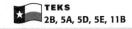 **TEKS** 2B, 5A, 5D, 5E, 11B

DEFENSIVE SPEECHES

Prepare Have students write a speech from the perspective of one of the boys in defense of his actions. Students should choose reasons, explanations, and language that will appeal to the headmaster, to whom they will be presenting their speeches and should organize their ideas logically. Divide the students into pairs so that they can practice using effective rate, volume, pitch, and tone for the audience.

Present Before students present their speeches, have audience members generate criteria that will

analyze the effectiveness of each speaker's persuasive technique and credibility. Audience members should comment orally or in writing after each presentation.

 BLOCK SCHEDULING This activity is particularly well suited for longer class periods.

 Use **Communications Transparencies and Copymasters**, p. 3, for additional support.

GUIDING STUDENT RESPONSE

Connect to the Literature

Connect to the Literature

1. Responses will vary. Encourage students to explain why they chose the part they did.

Comprehension Check
- to have a bike and go whizzing down a hill with no hands on the handlebars
- He assumes that Mrs. Pratchett is dead, and he feels guilt-stricken.

 Use Selection Quiz
Unit Four Resource Book, p. 17.

Think Critically

2. Possible Response: The plot makes him feel brave, clever, and respected by his friends. The plot also helps him to express his anger toward Mrs. Pratchett.

3. Responses will vary. Students might say that Thwaites knowingly distracted Mrs. Pratchett while the narrator placed the mouse in the jar, so he was an equal participant in the prank. Other students might say that he is not as responsible as the narrator because he did not come up with the idea or place the mouse in the jar.

4. Possible Responses: The headmaster was right to punish the boys because the prank was unfair. The headmaster should not have used corporal punishment or the lineup to respond to Mrs. Pratchett's complaints.

5. Responses will vary. Students might say they feel sympathy toward the narrator because he was treated so brutally and that the note adds a touch of seriousness to the tale.

6. Possible Response: Dahl's love of candy; Dahl's closeness to his friends; Dahl's feelings as Mrs. Pratchett draws closer

 Use **Reading and Critical Thinking Transparencies,** p. 2, for additional support.

Literary Analysis

Dialect Possible Responses: dropping the final *g* in words ending in *–ing*; use of unusual word forms, such as *uns* for "ones"; use of odd grammatical forms, such as "They comes into," "they thinks"; use of slang, such as *ain't* and *nick.*

Paired Activity Possible Response: "'I don't want all the lot of you troopin' in 'ere if only one of you is buyin' . . . Now beat it! Go on, get out!'"
I don't want all of you coming in here if only one of you is buying anything. Go! Get out of here!

Connect to the Literature

1. **What Do You Think?** Which part of the selection did you enjoy the most? Share your response with a classmate.

Comprehension Check
- At the beginning of the story, what does the narrator say is his "absolute ambition" in life?
- When the entire school is lined up in the schoolyard, what does the narrator assume has happened? How does he feel?

Think Critically

2. Why do you think the narrator is so proud of "The Great Mouse Plot"?

 THINK ABOUT
- riding a bike with no hands on the handlebars
- his relationship with Thwaites
- his feelings about Mrs. Pratchett

3. How would you describe Thwaites's role in "The Great Mouse Plot"? Do you think he deserved to be punished for that role?

4. How did you feel about the way the headmaster treated the narrator and his friends?

5. Did you feel any differently about the story after you read the Editor's Note at the end? Explain.

6. **ACTIVE READING** **CONNECTING** Read back over your notes in your **READER'S NOTEBOOK**. What details of the story could you relate to the most? Share your reaction with a classmate.

Extend Interpretations

7. **What If?** What if the story had been told from Mrs. Pratchett's point of view? How might she have described the narrator and his friends?

8. **The Writer's Style** How does the author's use of description make the story come alive for you? What words or phrases particularly stand out?

9. **Connect to Life** In your opinion, when does a prank go too far to be acceptable? Explain.

Literary Analysis

DIALECT A **dialect** is a form of language that is spoken in a certain place or by a certain group of people. Dialects of a language may differ from one another in pronunciation, vocabulary, and grammar. Look at this excerpt from *Boy: Tales of Childhood.* The narrator is describing how Mrs. Pratchett speaks to the boys when they come into her shop.

I don't want you in 'ere just to look around! Either you **forks** *out or you* **gets** *out!*

One way Dahl recreates Mrs. Pratchett's British working-class dialect is by dropping the *h* at the beginning of words. What other devices does he use to recreate her dialect?

Paired Activity As a class, make a chart that lists the lines of dialogue spoken by Mrs. Pratchett in either of the scenes in which the boys enter her shop. In a column beside this list, take turns rewriting each sentence from her dialect into standard English.

Mrs. Pratchett's English	Standard English
I don't want you in 'ere just to look around! Either you *forks* out, or you *gets* out!	I don't want you in here just to look around! Either buy something or leave!

Extend Interpretations

7. **What If?** Have students look back at the text to review her reactions to the other characters and her way of expressing herself.

8. **The Writer's Style** Students might refer to words and phrases that describe the sweetshop and Mrs. Pratchett. Encourage students to explain why certain words or phrases stand out in their minds.

9. **Connect to Life** Possible Response: A prank goes too far when the severity of the consequences outweighs the humor of the prank, or when someone is hurt by the prank.

Choices & CHALLENGES

Writing Options

Opinion Essay Do you think that the boys were justified or irresponsible in playing their prank on Mrs. Pratchett? Write an essay that defends one or the other viewpoint. Give reasons to support your defense. Place the essay in your **Working Portfolio.**

Writing Handbook
See page R39: Persuasive Writing.

Activities & Explorations

1. Dialogue With a partner, write a dialogue between the narrator and Thwaites that might have taken place right after their punishment in the headmaster's office for "The Great Mouse Plot." Have them discuss the prank, its conse-quences, their feelings about whether the prank was worth doing, and whether or not they'll go into the sweetshop again. After you have written the dialogue, rehearse and perform it for the whole class. ~ **PERFORMING**

2. Portrait of Pratchett Using the medium of your choice, create a portrait of Mrs. Pratchett based on Dahl's descriptions. Display your portrait in class. ~ **ART**

Art Connection

Look at the photograph of Terry Mimnaugh's sculpture *Three Boys with a Mouse* on page 540. How well do you think the sculpture captures the feelings of the boys as they carry out "The Great Mouse Plot"?

Inquiry & Research

The Origin of Candy Find out about the beginnings of candy. When was it invented? How is today's candy different from candy in the past? in other countries? Has it always been as widely available as it is now? What candies have been around the longest? Research with a partner to find the answers to these questions.

 Real-World Link Before you begin, read "The History of Chocolate" on page 549.

Vocabulary and Spelling

EXERCISE A: ANTONYMS Match each Word to Know on the left with the word or phrase that is most nearly its opposite.

1. _____ elaborate   **a.** attractive
2. _____ flourishing   **b.** dry
3. _____ loathsome   **c.** simplify
4. _____ malignant   **d.** in decline
5. _____ saturated   **e.** well-meaning

EXERCISE B: SILENT/SOUNDED CONSONANTS To spell a word with a silent consonant, think of a similar word in which the consonant is sounded.

mali**gn**	malignant	si**gn**	signal
desi**gn**	designate	de**bt**	debit
colu**mn**	columnist	dou**bt**	dubious

ha**st**en	haste	autu**mn**	autumnal
mu**sc**le	muscular	bo**mb**	bombard

Look at the boldfaced letters in the words above. Which letter is silent in each combination?

1. gn _____   3. mn _____   5. st _____
2. bt _____   4. mb _____   6. sc _____

Write the spelling word that fits each group.

7. winter, summer, spring, _____
8. plan, draw, lay out, _____
9. hurry, rush, run, _____
10. editorial, feature, advice, _____

Spelling Handbook p. R86

Writing Options

Opinion Essay To get students started on this assignment, have them brainstorm reasons for both views and choose the viewpoint that is more strongly supported.

Use **Writing Transparencies,** p. 27, for additional support.

Activities & Explorations

1. Dialogue Have students review the passages that show the interaction between the boys and their reactions to what is happening on the playground. Remind students to keep the language appropriate for nine year olds.

2. Portrait of Pratchett To get students started on this assignment, have them jot down the details of Mrs. Pratchett's appearance. This assignment is particularly well-suited to **visual learners.**

Art Connection

Some students may say that the general impression of intensity and excitement matches the boys' mood. Others may point out that the boys in the story "strutted" into the sweetshop while the boys in the sculpture appear to be sneaking quietly.

Inquiry & Research

The Origin of Candy Have students work in groups with individual members pre-senting different parts of the group's research.

Vocabulary and Spelling

Exercise A
1. c
2. d
3. a
4. e
5. b

Exercise B
1. g
2. b
3. n
4. b
5. t
6. c
7. autumn
8. design
9. hasten
10. column

BOY: TALES OF CHILDHOOD   **547**

  Spelling 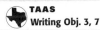 **TEKS** 16D   **TAAS** Writing Obj. 3, 7

SILENT/SOUNDED CONSONANTS

Instruction Tell students that in some pairs of consonants, one of the consonants is silent and the other is sounded. Consonant combinations in which this occurs include *mb, gn, kn, lm, mn, bt, ps,* and *wr.* For instance, in the word *climb,* the *b* is silent but must be included in the correct spelling of the word. Other words that have a silent consonant are *gnaw, know, limb, autumn, psalm, doubt,* and *wretched.*

Exercise Have students find the misspelled word in each of the following sentences and write it correctly.

1. The bootlace didn't have one rinkle in it. *(wrinkle)*
2. He went into det buying candy. *(debt)*
3. Mrs. Pratchett looked as if she had never used a com in her life. *(comb)*
4. He fell off his bicycle and scraped his nee when he tried to ride without holding on. *(knee)*
5. His mother sined the test paper. *(signed)*

 Use **Unit Four Resource Book,** p. 16 for more practice.

Grammar in Context

1. Thwaites was an authority on all things.
2. Tonsil ticklers were invented for dangerous prisoners in jail.
3. We had a hiding place for sweets.
4. Mrs. Pratchett did not die when she found the mouse in the jar.
5. The shopkeeper inspected the boys around the playground.

Roald Dahl

Dahl's memoir *Boy: Tales of Childhood* was selected as one of the Best Books for Young Adults by the Young Adult Library Services Association in 1985. This selection is an excerpt from his memoir.

Author Activity

Explore Another Genre Suggest to students that they discuss plot, character, setting, and theme in their book reports. To make this assignment more challenging, have students compare Dahl's style in nonfiction with his style of writing fiction. To make this assignment easier, have students listen to one of Dahl's works of fiction on tape and work together on their report.

Grammar in Context: Adjective Phrases

Notice how **prepositional phrases** add specific details in *Boy: Tales of Childhood.*

> . . . I will wear long trousers with bicycle clips. . . .

> ". . . only one of you is buyin'."

The **prepositional phrases** in the sentences above are used as adjectives. Adjective phrases are prepositional phrases that modify **nouns** or **pronouns**.

Usage Tip: Adjective phrases nearly always follow the word they modify.

> . . . I lifted the heavy glass lid of the gobstopper jar and dropped the mouse in.

WRITING EXERCISE Rewrite the following sentences, adding a prepositional phrase to modify the underlined words.

Example: *Original* We passed the sweetshop on our <u>walks</u>.

Rewritten We passed the sweetshop on our walks <u>from school</u>.

1. Thwaites was an <u>authority</u>.
2. Tonsil ticklers were invented for dangerous <u>prisoners</u>.
3. We had a hiding <u>place</u>.
4. Mrs. Pratchett did not die when she found the <u>mouse</u>.
5. The shopkeeper inspected the <u>boys</u>.

Grammar Handbook The Sentence and Its Parts, p. R55

> *"I never get any protests from children. All you get are giggles of mirth and squirms of delight."*

Roald Dahl
1916–1990

School Days As a schoolboy, Roald Dahl apparently showed little promise. One report about him included the comments "I have never met a boy who so persistently writes the exact opposite of what he means. He seems incapable of marshaling his thoughts on paper" and "vocabulary negligible, sentences malconstructed. He reminds me of a camel."

Children's Writer Dahl, however, went on to become a writer of best-selling children's books—some of which deal with unpleasant subjects and feature obnoxious characters. For example, in *The Gremlins,* his first book for children, tiny creatures cause mysterious malfunctions in airplanes. In defense of his books, Dahl remarked, "I never get any protests from children. All you get are giggles of mirth and squirms of delight. I know what children like." Dahl also credited his being a parent for his inspiration as a writer. "Had I not had children of my own," he said, "I would have never written books for children, nor would I have been capable of doing so." His other works include *Matilda, James and the Giant Peach,* and *Charlie and the Chocolate Factory.*

AUTHOR ACTIVITY

Explore Another Genre Read one of Roald Dahl's works of fiction. Prepare an oral book report to share with the class.

 LaserLinks: Background for Reading Author Background

Teaching Options

Mini Lesson Grammar **TEKS 17E** **TAAS Writing Obj. 4**

ADJECTIVE PHRASES
Instruction Remind students that an adjective phrase is usually placed next to the noun or pronoun it modifies. Display the following sentence to review adjective phrases.
The *sweetshop* <u>on the corner</u> held a great *attraction* <u>for us</u>.

Exercise Have students pick out the adjective phrases and the nouns or pronouns they modify in the following sentences.
1. The *dirt* <u>under her fingernails</u> looked permanent.
2. The *boy* <u>in the school cap</u> rode a *bicycle* <u>with shiny chrome trim</u>.
3. Thwaites's father probably exaggerated the *dangers* <u>of licorice bootlaces</u>.
4. The *student* <u>next to Thwaites</u> gulped loudly.

 Use **Unit Four Resource Book,** p. 15.
Use **Grammar Transparencies and Copymasters,** p. 92.

Use McDougal Littell's **Language Network,** Chapter 6, for more instruction and practice in adjective phrases.

The History of Chocolate

It's almost impossible to believe it now, but for most of its very long history, chocolate was not something people ate. It was a beverage, and not only was that beverage rarely hot, it was usually not sweet. Read this chronology to see how chocolate developed into its many delicious forms and came to be enjoyed by people all over the world.

1500 B.C. to 400 B.C.
The Olmec Civilization

Colossal stone Olmec head.

Many scholars think that the Olmecs, an ancient civilization that flourished in southern Mexico, were the first to use the cacao bean to make chocolate. But it is not known how they prepared the chocolate. There were great Olmec settlements in the prime cacao-growing areas in the present-day Mexican states of Chiapas and Yucatán and in Guatemala.

Reading for Information

When reading a nonfiction article, do you always understand everything right away? What do you do when you come across unfamiliar words?

CLARIFYING   To **clarify** means to make clear or easier to understand. You may clarify specialized vocabulary or a difficult passage by pausing to check your understanding. Clarifying is one of several reading strategies, such as connecting, predicting, and evaluating.

REAL WORLD LINK   **549**

Objectives
- read to be informed
- read and analyze a magazine article
- use the strategy of clarifying to make the meanings of specialized vocabulary and difficult passages clearer
- monitor comprehension by pausing to reread or adjust reading strategies

Connecting to the Literature
"The History of Chocolate" illustrates the many stages that led from the discovery and first use of the cacao bean by the Olmecs to the development of chocolate as we know it today. Although Roald Dahl delights in other types of candy as a youth, the village sweetshop that he describes would certainly have stocked an ample supply of chocolate as well.

Reading for Information

Suggest that students use the material in the right-hand column as a guide to reading magazine articles.

Use **Reading and Critical Thinking Transparencies,** p. 1, for additional support.

A.D. 250 to 900
Classic Maya Civilization

The Maya, an ancient Central American civilization, used chocolate mainly as a drink. They mixed the roasted, ground cacao beans with water, flavoring it with herbs or spices (chile was common). Then they poured the mixture back and forth from one container to another to make it foamy.

Mayan drinking cup.

14th Century to 1521
The Aztec Empire

The Aztec used the same methods as the Maya to mix their chocolate drink. They, too, used many different flavorings. The Aztecs thought that the beverage was beneficial to warriors. Cacao wafers, intended to be dissolved as needed, were issued to soldiers, in order to fortify them during marches and in battle. The words *cacao* and *chocolate* show traces of Nahuatl, the Aztec language.

1502
Cacao as Currency

The Aztecs used cacao beans as money. An Aztec document containing a list of price equivalents reported that a tomato was worth one cacao bean, an avocado was worth three, and a "good turkey hen" was worth 100 "full" or 120 "shrunken" cacao beans.

1544
First Documented Evidence of Chocolate in Europe

Dominican friars, living in a region of Guatemala occupied by the Maya, accompanied a delegation of Kekchi Maya people to Spain. Among the many gifts they presented to Prince Philip were containers of chocolate, frothed and ready to drink. The Spanish and Portuguese consumed chocolate for nearly a century before the rest of Europe discovered the drink.

European chocolate drinkers in the 18th century.

1753
Food of the Gods

The Swedish botanist Carolus Linnaeus developed a system for classifying living organisms. He assigned the botanical name *Theobroma cacao* to the chocolate tree. *Theobroma*, in Greek, means "food of the gods," while *cacao* is the original word for the plant.

Cacao ready to harves[t]

1828

Invention of Dutch Cocoa

Coenraad Van Houten, in Amsterdam, devised a process for making chocolate powder by using hydraulic pressure to remove almost half of the cocoa butter—the cacao bean's natural fat—from the chocolate. The process produced a hard cake that could be reduced to a powder. The powder could then be mixed with water to make a chocolate drink or added to other foods.

Van Houten cocoa product label.

1847

First Modern Chocolate Bar

Joseph Fry & Son, British chocolate manufacturers, was founded by a Quaker who had been a doctor before opening the business. In 1847, the firm discovered a way to mix the melted cocoa butter back into "Dutched" cocoa powder (along with sugar) to create a paste that could be pressed into a mold. The resulting bar was a huge hit.

Fry's Chocolate advertisement.

Reading for Information continued

YOUR TURN *Practice clarifying and monitoring as you answer the questions below.*

❶ Look in a dictionary or encyclopedia to **clarify** the meaning of *cacao*. How is it different from cocoa?

❷ Clarifying often involves **making inferences**, or figuring something out based on little evidence. Look up *Dominican* and *friar* in the dictionary. From the definitions, what can you infer that the Dominican friars were doing in Guatemala?

❸ Based on what you read in the previous entry (1828), what does the term *Dutched* refer to? What is it? Consult other sources to clarify further. What kind of machine is used in the process?

The following are **possible responses** to the four questions.

1 *Cacao* refers to the original seeds of the tropical tree. The cacao seeds or beans are crushed to make cocoa, which is a powder often mixed with other ingredients.

2 The Dominican friars may have been trying to convert the Mayan people to Christianity.

3 *Dutched* refers to the process developed by Coenraad Van Houten in Amsterdam, in which cocoa powder has half of the cocoa butter removed from it. This process requires the use of a hydraulic-pressure machine that has come to be known as the "cocoa press."

4 *Confections* are mixtures made from sweet things. *D-Rations* are daily rations or allowances of food. *G.I.* is the abbreviation for government or general issue and pertains to the armed forces or servicemen. Although knowing the terms is helpful to full understanding, the main ideas could be comprehended without these definitions.

1875
Invention of Milk Chocolate

During the 1860s, a Swiss chocolate manufacturer, Daniel Peter, tried repeatedly but unsuccessfully to create a chocolate bar flavored with milk. As it happened, in 1867, the chemist Henri Nestlé was working on a concentrated infant food formula and needed to find a way to treat milk so that it would not spoil while in storage. Eventually he developed sweetened condensed milk, which turned out to be perfect for Peter's purposes. The milk's low water content made it possible to mix it with the chocolate into a bar that did not spoil.

1929
Chocolate-Covered Cherries

Celia's Confections (est. 1864) began manufacturing chocolate-covered cherries at their candy factory on West Broadway at Canal Street in New York. In the 19th century this was New York's confectionery district.

WW II
Nourishing the Army

In a move reminiscent of the Aztec practice, the American military decided to include three four-ounce chocolate bars, each with 600 calories, in a soldier's "D-Ration." Although meant to sustain the soldiers, the bars also came to be associated with the return of peace when long-malnourished victims of the Germans found themselves approached by American G.I.'s offering them chocolate. The chocolate is still a standard issue in the military.

Today

Chocolate is a major industry that requires 40% of the world's almonds, 20% of the world's peanuts, and 8% of the world's sugar. About 3.5 million pounds of whole milk are used to make milk chocolate each day. In the United States, Americans consume over 3.1 billion pounds of chocolate a year, or 11.7 pounds per person!

Reading for Information *continued*

4 These two paragraphs contain terms you might not know. Take a moment to find their definitions. What are *confections*? What is a *D-Ration*? What does *G.I.* stand for? Do you need to know what these terms mean to understand the paragraphs?

Inquiry & Research

Activity Link: *Boy: Tales of Childhood,* **p. 547** Now that you have learned about the development of chocolate, what can you predict about the history of other kinds of candy? Choose one and research its past. Write a chronology like the one you have just read. Include a time line with your chronology.

  Inquiry & Research **TEKS** 13C, 20C, 20D

The Inquiry & Research Activity on this page links to the research activity on page 547.

As students do this Inquiry & Research Activity, they will take notes from relevant sources and organize the information in a useful way.

Instruction Have students choose the candy that they would like to research, such as licorice or pear drops. Direct students to try various resources including encyclopedias and the Internet. Books on the history of candy or confectionery may include chapters on the candy of their choice.

Practice Suggest that students take notes on index cards. They should write the date of each development on the top of an index card so that they can easily organize their chronologies and timelines.

A Defenseless Creature

from *The Good Doctor*

Drama by NEIL SIMON

based on a story by ANTON CHEKHOV

I'm skin and bones. I faint at the least provocation . . . Watch."

Connect to Your Life

Some people have a knack for manipulating other people into doing things for them. Maybe you have even done this yourself! With a classmate, discuss a person like this whom you have encountered or know about.

Build Background

The play you are about to read is one scene from a longer play, *The Good Doctor*, by Neil Simon. In *The Good Doctor* Simon takes several early stories by Anton Chekhov and turns them into separate scenes, each of which is complete in itself.

Chekhov was a late-19th-century Russian playwright and short story writer whom Simon admires. Chekhov wrote particularly about ordinary people who have failed or been disappointed in life. His mature stories are considered masterpieces. In them the reader's attention is drawn to the characters and what they learn about themselves and about life.

Anton Chekhov, 1860–1904

See the Skills Trace at the beginning of the unit for information on TEKS covered in this lesson.

Focus Your Reading

LITERARY ANALYSIS **FARCE** A **farce** is an exaggerated comedy with an absurd **plot**, ridiculous situations, and humorous **dialogue.** The main purpose of a farce is to make an audience laugh. Often the characters in a farce are stereotypes with just one exaggerated **character trait** rather than fully developed character traits. As you read "A Defenseless Creature," look for examples of these characteristics.

ACTIVE READING **VISUALIZING** When you read the script of a play, as opposed to watching it being performed on the stage, you should try to **visualize** the characters, set, and action in your imagination. You should also try to hear the dialogue in your head. Visualizing can heighten your understanding and enjoyment of a play that you read.

READER'S NOTEBOOK

Choose one of the characters in "A Defenseless Creature." As you read, jot down some clues that help you visualize that character.

Mrs. Schukin

Detail from Play:	How I Visualize Her:
Poorly dressed, forlorn look (stage direction)	She wears an old hat and a coat with patches on it.
Lets out scream (action)	Her eyes get wide and her face gets red.

Objectives
1. understand and appreciate a **drama** (Literary Analysis)
2. understand the literary skills **farce**, **caricature**, and **plot complications** (Literary Analysis)
3. utilize the reading skill of **visualizing characters**, **actions**, and **setting** as you read (Active Reading)

Summary
Mr. Kistunov, a bank official, arrives at work suffering from a painful case of gout. He cannot even bear to have his clerk speak loudly to him. The clerk asks him if he is well enough to see a woman who wants to talk to the directing manager. Mr. Kistunov says that his work comes before his health. The clerk shows Mrs. Schukin in. She is at the bank to plead the case of her husband, who has been fired from his job after a five month illness. She claims that he is owed money, and she wants the bank to pay her. However, her husband was never employed by the bank. By the time she has cried, screamed, pulled out her hair, fainted, and clutched Mr. Kistunov's bandaged foot, he is willing to give this "defenseless woman," as she calls herself, whatever amount of money she wants. She finally leaves with the promise to return the next day for a letter of recommendation for her husband.

Thematic Link
Mr. Kistunov finds out the hard way what kind of defenses a "defenseless person" has when he encounters Mrs. Schukin.

5-Minute Warm-Up

Daily Language SkillBuilder TEKS 17C

Have students **proofread** the display sentences on page 517i and write them correctly. The sentences also appear on Transparency 17 of **Grammar Transparencies and Copymasters.**

Mini Lesson **Preteaching Vocabulary**

If you would like to preteach the WORDS TO KNOW for this selection, use the Mini Lesson, p. 554.

Reading Skills and Strategies: QUESTIONING

A Ask students how the first appearance of Mrs. Schukin relates to the title.

Possible Response: She seems to be the defenseless person referred to by the title.

Literary Analysis FARCE

B Remind students that an essential component of farce is exaggeration. Ask them what elements of exaggeration the playwright has introduced already.

Possible Responses: Mr. Kistunov's sensitivity to pain; Mrs. Schukin's extreme and surprising reactions

Use **Unit Four Resource Book,** p. 20 for more practice.

Literary Analysis: IRONY

C Tell students that the nature of farce often leads to irony. Ask students what is ironic about Collegiate Assessor Schukin's illness.

Possible Responses: His wife's manner would grate on someone without a nervous disorder and would be doubly painful to someone with one.

Active Reading VISUALIZING

D Ask students to describe how they envision Mr. Kistunov's manner and posture as he says this.

Possible Responses: He is clutching his chair, clenching his teeth, and drawing a deep breath as he tries to respond calmly to Mrs. Schukin.

Use **Unit Four Resource Book,** p. 19 for more practice.

A Defenseless Creature

by Neil Simon

⤫⤬⤫

BASED ON A STORY BY

Anton Chekhov

The lights come up on the office of a bank official, Kistunov. He enters on a crutch; his right foot is heavily encased in bandages, swelling it to three times its normal size. He suffers from the gout[1] and is very careful of any mishap which would only intensify his pain. He makes it to his desk and sits. An Assistant, rather harried, enters.

⤫⤬⤫

Assistant. (*With volume*) Good morning, Mr. Kistunov!

Kistunov. Shhh! Please. . . . Please lower your voice.

Assistant. (*Whispers*) I'm sorry, sir.

Kistunov. It's just that my gout is acting up again and my nerves are like little firecrackers. The least little friction can set them off.

The Reader (1840–1862), Honoré Daumier. Bronze, 6¼″ × 2½″ × 3¼″. Hirshhorn Museum and Sculpture Garden, Smithsonian Institution, gift of Joseph H. Hirshhorn, 1966. Photograph by Lee Stalsworth.

1. **gout:** a condition that causes painful swelling of the joints, especially of the feet and hands.

The Representative Knotting His Tie (1840–1862), Honoré Daumier. Bronze, 7″ × 2¾″ × 2⅛″. Hirshhorn Museum and Sculpture Garden, Smithsonian Institution, gift of Joseph H. Hirshhorn, 1966. Photograph by Lee Stalsworth.

554   UNIT FOUR   PART 1: LEARNING THE HARD WAY

Teaching Options

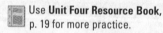

Mini Lesson **Preteaching Vocabulary**   ⬛ TEKS 6A   ⬛ TAAS Reading Obj. 1

CONTEXT CLUES

Instruction Remind students that they can use context clues, such as an implied cause-and-effect relationship, to help them define unfamiliar words. Display the sentence below to illustrate how *petition* can be defined from the cause-and-effect relationship in the sentence.

After she presented her *petition,* she expected him to offer assistance with her problem.

If presenting a petition results in an offer of assistance, petition must mean "a request for help."

Exercise Have students define the underlined

WORDS TO KNOW by determining the cause-and-effect relationship in each sentence.

1. Her loud wailing destroyed his <u>composure</u>.
2. He <u>clenched</u> the paper so tightly that it wrinkled.
3. The <u>provocation</u> of having her hug his painful foot resulted in his screaming aloud.
4. With any sort of leg injury, a person is often <u>incapacitated</u>, even if only temporarily.

 Use **Unit Four Resource Book,** p. 21 for exercises.
Use **Vocabulary Transparencies and Copymasters,** p. 63, for additional support.

Assistant. It must be very painful, sir.

Kistunov. Combing my hair this morning was agony.

Assistant. Mr. Kistunov. . . .

Kistunov. What is it, Pochatkin?

Assistant. There's a woman who insists on seeing you. We can't make head or tail out of her story, but she insists on seeing the directing manager. Perhaps if you're not well—

Kistunov. No, no. The business of the bank comes before my minor physical ailments. Show her in, please . . . quietly. (*The Assistant tiptoes out. A Woman enters. She is in her late forties, poorly dressed. She is of the working class. She crosses to the desk, a forlorn look on her face. She twists her bag nervously*) Good morning, madame. Forgive me for not standing, but I am somewhat <u>incapacitated</u>. Please sit down.

Woman. Thank you.

(*She sits*)

Kistunov. Now, what can I do for you?

Woman. You can help me, sir. I pray to God you can help. No one else in this world seems to care. . . .

(*And she begins to cry, which in turn becomes a wail—the kind of wail that melts the spine of* *strong men*. Kistunov *winces and grits his teeth in pain as he grips the arms of his chair.*)

Kistunov. Calm yourself, madame. I *beg* of you. Please calm yourself.

Woman. I'm sorry.

(*She tries to calm down.*)

Kistunov. I'm sure we can sort it all out if we approach the problem sensibly and quietly. . . . Now, what exactly is the trouble?

Woman. Well, sir. . . . It's my husband. Collegiate Assessor Schukin. He's been sick for five months. . . . Five agonizing months.

Kistunov. I know the horrors of illness and can sympathize with you, madame. What's the nature of his illness?

Woman. It's a nervous disorder. Everything grates on his nerves. If you so much as touch him he'll scream out—

(*And without warning, she screams a loud bloodcurdling scream that sends* Kistunov *almost out of his seat.*)

How or why he got it, nobody knows.

Kistunov. (*Trying to regain his <u>composure</u>*) I have an inkling. . . . Please go on, a little less descriptively, if possible.

Woman. Well, while the poor man was lying in bed—

WORDS
TO
KNOW

incapacitated (ĭn′kə-păs′ĭ-tā′tĭd) *adj.* deprived of the ability to engage in normal activities; disabled

composure (kəm-pō′zhər) *n.* an undisturbed state of mind; calmness

555

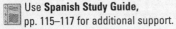

Reading and Analyzing

Literary Analysis [FARCE]

A Have volunteers read this passage aloud. Ask how dialogue contributes to the farce.

Possible Response: Because of its irrelevance, the dialogue increases the confusion of Mr. Kistunov, which, in turn, heightens the absurdity of the situation, resulting in humor.

B Ask students what is absurd about the actions described in these stage directions.

Possible Response: Once hair is removed from the head, it cannot be reattached.

Reading Skills and Strategies: QUESTIONING

C Have students monitor comprehension by asking what Mrs. Schukin wants Mr. Kistunov to do and why he will not do it.

Possible Response: She wants him to give her the money that her husband's employers kept from his pay, but the bank is not his employer.

Literary Analysis: RISING AND FALLING ACTION

D Tell students that complications are problems arising from the central conflict that heighten the tension. Ask students how Mr. Kistunov's refusal to help complicates the situation.

Possible Response: Mrs. Schukin does not accept his answer and changes her tactics.

Literary Analysis: IRONY

E Ask students what is ironic about Mrs. Schukin's portrayal of herself as a "weak, defenseless woman."

Possible Response: She is controlling the interview and has the upper hand.

Kistunov. (*Braces himself*) You're not going to scream again, are you?

Woman. Not that I don't have cause. . . . While he was lying in bed these five months, recuperating, he was dismissed from his job—for no reason at all.

Kistunov. That's a pity, certainly, but I don't quite see the connection with our bank, madame.

Woman. You don't know how I suffered during his illness. I nursed him from morning till night. Doctored him from night till morning. Besides cleaning my house, taking care of my children, feeding our dog, our cat, our goat, my sister's bird, who was sick. . . .

Kistunov. The bird was sick?

Woman. My *sister!* She gets dizzy spells. She's been dizzy a month now. And she's getting dizzier every day. . . .

Kistunov. Extraordinary. However—

Woman. I had to take care of *her* children and *her* house and *her* cat and *her* goat, and then her bird bit one of my children, and so our cat bit her bird, so my oldest daughter, the one with the broken arm, drowned my sister's cat, and now my sister wants my goat in exchange, or else she says she'll either drown my cat or break my oldest daughter's other arm—

Kistunov. Yes, well, you've certainly had your pack of troubles, haven't you? But I don't quite see—

Lithograph with hand coloring (detail), Honoré Daumier. Courtesy of the Boston Public Library, Print Department.

Woman. And then, when I went to get my husband's pay, they deducted twenty-four rubles[2] and thirty-six kopecks.[3] For what? I asked. Because, they said, he borrowed it from the employees' fund. But that's impossible. He could never borrow without my approval. I'd break his arm. . . . Not while he was sick, of course. . . . I don't have the strength. I'm not well myself, sir. I have this racking cough that's a terrible thing to hear—

(*She coughs rackingly*[4]—*so rackingly that* Kistunov *is about to crack.*)

Kistunov. I can well understand why your husband took five months to recuperate. . . . But what is it you want from me, madame?

Woman. What rightfully belongs to my husband—his twenty-four rubles and thirty-six kopecks. They won't give it to me because I'm a woman, weak and defenseless. Some of them have laughed in my face, sir. . . . *Laughed!* (*She laughs loud and painfully.* Kistunov *clenches everything.*) Where's the humor, I wonder, in a poor, defenseless creature like myself?

(*She sobs.*)

Kistunov. None. . . . I see none at all. However, madame, I don't wish to be

---

2. **rubles** (rōō′bəl): units of Russian money.
3. **kopecks** (kō′pĕk): hundredths of a ruble.
4. **rackingly:** with heaves of painful effort.

WORDS TO KNOW   **clench** (klĕnch) *v.* to hold or grip tightly

556

Teaching Options

Mini Lesson   Grammar   TEKS 17C   TAAS Writing Obj. 6

INDIRECT OBJECTS

Instruction Remind students that an indirect object tells for or to whom or what an action is done. It usually appears before a direct object. Point out the highlighted sentence above. If the author had used an indirect object instead of the prepositional phrase *to me*, the sentence would have read, "They won't give me it . . . "

Exercise Have students rewrite the underlined prepositional phrases as indirect objects.

1. Mr. Kistunov offers his help <u>to Mrs. Schukin</u> before she tells her problem <u>to him</u>.
2. She brought his certificate <u>for the bank</u>.

3. He sends an appeal <u>to the guards</u>.

ANSWERS

1. Mr. Kistunov offers Mrs. Schukin his help before she tells him her problem.
2. She brought the bank his certificate.
3. He sends the guards an appeal.

📋 Use **Grammar Transparencies and Copymasters**, p. 55.

Use McDougal Littell's *Language Network*, Chapter 1, for more instruction and practice in indirect objects.

unkind, but I'm afraid you've come to the wrong place. Your petition, no matter how justified, has nothing to do with us. You'll have to go to the agency where your husband was employed.

Woman. *What do you mean?* I've been to *five* agencies already and none of them will even *listen* to my petition. I'm about to lose my mind. The hair is coming out of my head. (*She pulls out a handful.*) Look at my hair. By the fistful. (*She throws a fistful on his desk.*) *Don't tell me to go to another agency!*

Lithograph (detail), Honoré Daumier. Snark/Art Resource, NY.

Kistunov. (*Delicately and disgustedly, he picks up her fistful of hair and hands it back to her. She sticks it back in her hair.*) Please, madame, keep your hair in its proper place. Now listen to me carefully. This-is-a-bank. A bank! We're in the banking business. We bank money. Funds that are brought here are banked by us. Do you understand what I'm saying?

Woman. What are you saying?

Kistunov. I'm saying that I can't help you.

Woman. Are you saying you can't help me?

Kistunov. (*Sighs deeply*) I'm trying. I don't think I'm making headway.

Woman. Are you saying you won't believe my husband is sick? Here! Here is a doctor's certificate. (*She puts it on the desk and pounds it.*) There's the proof. Do you still doubt that my husband is suffering from a nervous disorder?

Kistunov. Not only do I not doubt it, I would *swear* to it.

Woman. *Look at it!* You didn't look at it!

Kistunov. It's really not necessary. I know *full well* how your husband must be suffering.

Woman. *What's the point in a doctor's certificate if you don't look at it?!* LOOK AT IT!

Kistunov. (*Frightened, quickly looks at it*) Oh, yes. . . . I see your husband is sick. It's right here on the doctor's certificate. Well, you certainly have a good case, madame, but I'm afraid *you've still come to the wrong place.* (*Getting perplexed*) I'm getting excited.

Woman. (*Stares at him*) You lied to me. I took you as a man of your word and you lied to me.

Kistunov. I? LIE? WHEN?

Woman. (*Snatches the certificate*) When you said you read the doctor's certificate. You couldn't have. You couldn't have read the description of my husband's illness without seeing he was fired unjustly. (*She puts the certificate back on the desk.*) Don't take advantage of me just because I'm a weak, defenseless woman. Do me the simple courtesy of reading the doctor's certificate. That's all I ask. Read it, and then I'll go.

D

2

E

WORDS TO KNOW

petition (pə-tǐsh′ən) *n.* a formal request

557

Literary Analysis: CARICATURE

A Tell students that a caricature is the representation of a person through the exaggeration of one characteristic. Ask students to analyze the dominant trait of each character.

Possible Responses: Mrs. Schukin is dominating and persistent, despite her claim of being defenseless. Mr. Kistunov is sickly and at Mrs. Schukin's mercy.

Active Reading VISUALIZING

B Ask students what Mr. Kistunov might be doing as he responds to Mrs. Schukin.

Possible Responses: waving the certificate, pointing to the door, leaning forward

Literary Analysis FARCE

C Ask students to pick out the elements of farce in this passage.

Possible Responses: Mrs. Schukin misunderstands Mr. Kistunov's point about getting a haircut in a butcher's; she accuses him of laughing, and he claims that he is hardly breathing; she exaggerates her inability to eat or drink and her capacity for fainting.

Ask students what they think Mr. Kistunov will do in the face of her persistence.

Possible Responses: give her the money; leave his office; have the guards carry her out

---

Kistunov. But I *read* it! What's the point in reading something twice when I've already *read it* once?

Woman. You didn't read it carefully.

Kistunov. I read it *in detail!*

Woman. Then you read it too fast. Read it slower.

Kistunov. *I don't have to read it slower. I'm a fast reader.*

Woman. Maybe you didn't absorb it. Let it sink in this time.

Kistunov. (*Almost apoplectic*[5]) I *absorbed* it! It *sank* in! I could pass a *test* on what's written here, *but it doesn't make any difference because it has nothing to do with our bank!*

Woman. (*She throws herself on him from behind.*) Did you read the part where it says he has a nervous disorder? Read that part again and see if I'm wrong.

Kistunov. THAT PART? OH, YES! I SEE YOUR HUSBAND HAS A NERVOUS DISORDER. MY, MY, HOW TERRIBLE! *ONLY I CAN'T HELP YOU! NOW PLEASE GO!*

(*He falls back into his chair, exhausted.*)

Woman. (*Crosses to where his foot is resting*) I'm sorry, Excellency. I hope I haven't caused you any pain.

Kistunov. (*Trying to stop her*) Please, don't kiss my foot. (*He is too late—she has given his foot a most ardent embrace. He screams in pain.*) Aggghhh! Can't you get this into your balding head? If you would just realize that to come to us with this kind of claim is as strange as your trying to get a haircut in a butcher shop.

Woman. You can't get a haircut in a butcher shop. Why would anyone go to a butcher

shop for a haircut? Are you laughing at me?

Kistunov. *Laughing!* I'm lucky I'm breathing. . . . Pochatkin!

Woman. Did I tell you I'm fasting? I haven't eaten in three days. I want to eat, but nothing stays down. I had the same cup of coffee three times today.

Kistunov. (*With his last burst of energy, screams*) POCHATKIN!

Woman. I'm skin and bones. I faint at the least provocation . . . . Watch. (*She swoons*[6] *to the floor*) Did you see? You saw how I just fainted? Eight times a day that happens.

(*The* Assistant *finally rushes in*)

Assistant. What is it, Mr. Kistunov? What's wrong?

Kistunov. (*Screams*) GET HER OUT OF HERE! Who let her in my office?

Assistant. You did, sir. I asked you and you said, "Show her in."

Kistunov. I thought you meant a human being, not a lunatic with a doctor's certificate.

Woman. (*To* Pochatkin) He wouldn't even read it. I gave it to him, he threw it back in my face. . . . You look like a kind person. Have pity on me. *You* read it and see if my husband is sick or not.

(*She forces the certificate on* Pochatkin.)

Assistant. I *read* it, madame. Twice!

Kistunov. Me too. I had to read it twice too.

Assistant. You just showed it to me outside. You showed it to *everyone*. We *all* read it. Even the doorman.

---

5. **apoplectic** (ăp′ə-plĕk′tĭk): bursting with anger.
6. **swoons:** falls in a faint.

WORDS
TO
KNOW
provocation (prŏv′ə-kā′shən) *n.* something that produces an emotional or physical reaction

---

Teaching Options

Mini Lesson **Speaking and Listening** TEKS 3B, 5C, 5E

READERS THEATER

Prepare Explain to students that a Readers Theater is a presentation of oral interpretations of parts of a play. Meaning must be communicated solely through the tone and expression of the reader's voice and sound effects. Have students divide into small groups and choose the passage they wish to perform. Each student should take the part of a character or narrator or be responsible for sound effects. Students should prepare the passage by examining their characters closely and deciding on their interpretations. They should then

rehearse to achieve effective volume, rate, pitch, tone, and timing.

Present To perform, students should sit on stools facing the audience. After each performance, the audience should analyze the effects of the oral interpretation on their understanding and appreciation of the play.

BLOCK SCHEDULING This activity is particularly well suited for longer class periods.

 Use **Communications Transparencies and Copymasters**, p. 12, for additional support.

Lithograph with hand coloring, Honoré Daumier. Courtesy of the Boston Public Library, Print Department.

Woman. You just looked at it. You didn't read it.

Kistunov. Don't argue. Read it, Pochatkin. For God's sake, read it so we can get her out of here.

Assistant. (*Quickly scans it*) Oh, yes. It says your husband is sick. (*He looks up; gives it back to her.*) Now will you please leave, madame, or I will have to get someone to remove you.

Kistunov. Yes! Yes! Good! Remove her! Get the doorman and two of the guards. Be careful, she's strong as an ox.

Woman. (*To* Kistunov) If you touch me, I'll scream so loud they'll hear it all over the city. You'll lose all your depositors. No one will come to a bank where they beat weak, defenseless women. . . . I think I'm going to faint again. . . .

A DEFENSELESS CREATURE **559**

Customizing Instruction

Less Proficient Readers
- What does Mrs. Schukin do when Mr. Kistunov tells her he has read the certificate but can't help her?
  Possible Responses: She hugs his foot and faints.
- What does Mr. Kistunov want his assistant to do?
  Possible Response: get her out of his office

Set a Purpose Have students read to find out if the conflict between Mrs. Schukin and Mr. Kistunov is resolved.

Multiple Learning Styles
Kinesthetic Learners

1 Have students act out this portion of the scene in order to appreciate the absurdity of these events.

Interpersonal Learners
Have students discuss alternate methods that Mr. Kistunov might have used in dealing with Mrs. Schukin.

Students Acquiring English
2 Explain to the students that Mr. Kistunov uses this analogy to show how ridiculous it is for Mrs. Schukin to think that she will get money from the bank.

3 Explain that the expression "skin and bones" means that she is very thin and frail. Be sure that students understand that this description is probably an exaggeration, just as her frailty is only an illusion.

Gifted and Talented
Have students read another of the vignettes from *The Good Doctor* and compare and contrast characters and style across the texts.

Mini Lesson ## Viewing and Representing **TEKS 22A**

Lithograph
by Honoré Daumier

ART APPRECIATION Honoré Daumier (1808–1879) produced nearly four thousand lithographs and a thousand drawings on wood before he became nearly blind later in his life.

Instruction Explain to students that lithography is the art of printing from treated stone or metal. What is to be printed can be inked, and the remaining area rejects ink. Daumier's lithographs are noted for what they convey through the movement and simplicity of their subjects. Ask students what is expressed by the woman's act of holding the man's wrist while he holds his head.

Possible Responses: She is offering sympathy while he clutches his head in dismay or pain.

Application Ask students to describe the ways in which the man and woman in the lithograph resemble or differ from the characters in the play.

Possible Responses: The man's demeanor expresses Mr. Kistunov's irritation and eagerness to get rid of Mrs. Schukin. He does not have a bandaged foot, however. The woman is more sympathetic than Mrs. Schukin pretends to be.

Reading Skills and Strategies: QUESTIONING

A Ask students what Mr. Kistunov has realized about Mrs. Schukin that causes him to react this way.

Possible Response: She is strong and will get her way. She has the potential to make his life agony.

Active Reading | VISUALIZING |

B Ask students to describe mental images evoked by the stage directions.

Possible Response: The scene in the office is chaotic; Mr. Kistunov is on the floor; Mrs. Schukin is on the desk; there is commotion and movement everywhere.

Literary Analysis: RISING AND FALLING ACTION

C Ask students to identify the climax of the play.

Answer: Mr. Kistunov tells his assistant to give her money.

D Although the action falls after the climax, ask students what event precipitates additional conflict before the end of the play.

Answer: Mrs. Schukin's promise that she will return the next day creates internal conflict within Mr. Kistunov.

Literary Analysis: IRONY

Ask students what is ironic about Mrs. Schukin's departure.

Possible Response: She returns to acting defenseless and weak once she has obtained what she was after; the audience knows that Mrs. Schukin's humility is only an act; Mr. Kistunov has been reduced to a defenseless, weak creature.

A

Kistunov. (*Rising*) WEAK? DEFENSELESS? You are as defenseless as a charging rhinoceros! You are as weak as the King of the Jungle! You are a plague, madame! A plague that wipes out all that crosses your path! You are a raging river that washes out bridges and stately homes! You are a wind that blows villages over mountains! It is women like you who drive men like me to the condition of husbands like yours!

Woman. Are you saying you're not going to help me?

Kistunov. Hit her, Pochatkin! Strike her! I give you permission to knock her down. Beat some sense into her!

Woman. (*To Pochatkin*) You hear? You hear how I'm abused? He would have you hit an orphaned mother. Did you hear me cough? Listen to this cough.

(*She "racks" up another coughing spell.*)

Assistant. Madame, if we can discuss this in my office—

(*He takes her arm.*)

Woman. Get your hands off me. . . . Help! Help! I'm being beaten! Oh, merciful God, they're beating me!

Assistant. I am not beating you. I am just holding your arm.

Kistunov. Beat her, you fool. Kick her while you've got the chance. We'll never get her out of here. Knock her senseless!

(*He tries to kick her, misses and falls to the floor.*)

B

Woman. (*Pointing an evil finger at Kistunov, she jumps on the desk and punctuates each sentence by stepping on his desk bell.*) A curse! A curse on your bank! I put on a curse on you and your depositors! May the money in your vaults turn to potatoes! May the gold in your cellars turn to onions! May your rubles turn to radishes, and your kopecks to pickles. . . .

Kistunov. STOP! Stop it, I beg of you! . . . Pochatkin, give her the money. Give her what she wants. Give her anything—only get her out of here!

Woman. (*To Pochatkin*) Twenty-four rubles and thirty-six kopecks. . . . Not a penny more. That's all that's due me and that's all I want.

Assistant. Come with me, I'll get you your money.

Woman. And another ruble to get me home. I'd walk but I have very weak ankles.

Kistunov. Give her enough for a taxi, anything, only get her out.

Woman. God bless you, sir. You're a kind man. I remove the curse. (*With a gesture*) Curse be gone! Onions to money, potatoes to gold—

Kistunov. (*Pulls on his hair*) REMOVE HERRRR! Oh, God, my hair is falling out!

(*He pulls some hair out.*)

Woman. Oh, there's one other thing, sir. I'll need a letter of recommendation so my husband can get another job. Don't bother yourself about it today. I'll be back in the morning. God, bless you, sir. . . .

(*She leaves.*)

Kistunov. She's coming back. . . . She's coming back. . . . (*He slowly begins to go mad and takes his cane and begins to beat his bandaged leg*) She's coming back. . . . She's coming back. . . .

(*Dim-out*)

Teaching Options

 ✓ **Assessment** **Standardized Test Practice** **TEKS** 10K, 12G 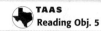 **TAAS** Reading Obj. 5

DESCRIBING PLOT For some standardized tests, students will be asked to choose the best description of the plot. To provide students with some help in choosing the best answer, read aloud or write on the board the following:

Mrs. Schukin walks away with the money after—

A. her emotional narration of her tale moves Mr. Kistunov to have pity for her.

B. she tortures Mr. Kistunov with loud noises and violent gestures and refuses to leave until she obtains what she wants.

C. her logical arguments and rational manner persuade Mr. Kistunov of the truth of her argument.

D. Mr. Kistunov kicks and beats her and then feels guilty about it.

Lead students through the process of choosing the correct answer. *A* is incorrect. He has no pity for her at all. *B* is correct because it describes the events that lead to the climax of the play. *C* is incorrect. She never presents logical arguments. *D* is incorrect. He tries unsuccessfully to kick her and does not beat her.

Connect to the Literature

1. **What Do You Think?**
What were your feelings about the characters at the end of the play? Explain.

Comprehension Check
- What is the matter with Kistunov's foot?
- What does Mrs. Schukin do when she jumps up on Kistunov's desk?
- What does Mrs. Schukin ask for as she leaves?

Think Critically

2. How do you think Kistunov first perceives Mrs. Schukin? How do you think he plans on controlling her?

3. Do you think that the banker should have responded differently in any way to Mrs. Schukin? Explain.

4. By the end of the play, who turns out to be powerful and who is the defenseless creature?

 THINK ABOUT
- ASSISTANT: "Come with me, I'll get your money."
- KISTUNOV: "You are as defenseless as a charging rhinoceros!"
- WOMAN: "I'll be back in the morning."

5. **ACTIVE READING** **VISUALIZING**
Get together with a small group of classmates and compare the notes you took in your **READER'S NOTEBOOK**. Did the members of your group visualize characters and events similarly? Discuss, using examples of dialogue to support your interpretations.

Extend Interpretations

6. **Critic's Corner** One critic writes, "The pain the woman inflicts on Kistunov might be funny if Kistunov were presented as as a figure deserving discomfort." What is your opinion? Does Kistunov "deserve" the treatment the woman gives him? Explain your answer.

7. **Connect to Life** Have you or someone you know ever been in a situation where you had to deal with a particularly difficult person? What was the outcome?

Literary Analysis

FARCE A **farce** is a comedy that exaggerates plot, dialogue, and situation to amuse an audience. For example, the situation of "A Defenseless Creature" centers on Mrs. Schukin's efforts to force Kistunov to pay her money he doesn't owe her. Within that situation, what kind of wild twists and turns do the plot and dialogue take?

Cooperative Learning Activity
What elements of "A Defenseless Creature" fit the characteristics of a farce? Working with a partner, look over the script of "A Defenseless Creature" and jot down aspects of the play that seem exaggerated to really make you laugh.

Twists in the Plot	Lines of Dialogue	Absurd Situations
Mrs. Schukin pulls out a fistful of hair.	After Mrs. Schukin screams and Kistunov says: "You're not going to scream again, are you?"	Mrs. Schukin's relationship with her sister.

REVIEW **MOOD** **Mood** is the feeling, or atmosphere, that a writer creates for the reader. Word choice, dialogue, description, and plot complications are some of the techniques writers use to convey mood. How would you characterize the mood of "A Defenseless Creature"? What techniques does Neil Simon use to convey the mood?

A DEFENSELESS CREATURE **561**

Literary Analysis

Farce Possible Responses:
Twists in the plot:
- Mrs. Schukin's accusations that Mr. Kistunov is beating her
- her promise to return for a letter of recommendation

Lines of dialogue:
- "I had the same cup of coffee three times today."
- "You can't get a haircut in a butcher shop."

Absurd situations:
- Mrs. Schukin's fainting at the slightest provocation
- Mrs. Schukin's jumping onto Mr. Kistunov's desk

Review: Mood Possible Responses: The mood is comical, slapstick, and ironic. Simon achieves this by using caricatures, exaggeration, and plot twists.

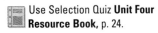

GUIDING STUDENT RESPONSE

Connect to the Literature

1. **What Do You Think?** Responses will vary. Some might feel sympathy for Mr. Kistunov; others might feel that he was weak.

Comprehension Check
- He has gout.
- She starts ringing the bell on his desk.
- She asks for a letter of recommendation.

Use Selection Quiz **Unit Four Resource Book**, p. 24.

Think Critically

2. Possible Response: He sees her as a poor, defenseless, emotional person. At first he feels like he can control the situation by being sensible and forthright.

3. Possible Response: Kistunov probably should have asked her to leave as soon as he realized her story was absurd, but he got caught up in her story and in trying to argue with her.

4. Possible Response: Kistunov is "defenseless," and Mrs. Schukin is powerful in that she has gotten her way. When Mrs. Schukin first comes in, Kistunov prepares to treat her with sympathy; by the end, he is the one needing sympathy.

5. Responses will vary. Students' responses should focus on specific details.

Use **Reading and Critical Thinking Transparencies**, p. 10, for additional support.

Extend Interpretations

6. **Critic's Corner** Responses will vary. Have students think about the source of the humor in the play and how much pain the woman inflicts upon Mr. Kistunov. Encourage students to back up their opinions with evidence from the text.

7. **Connect to Life** Responses will vary. To extend this activity, have students put together a manual of tips for dealing with difficult people.

Writing Options

1. Theater Review To get students started on this assignment, have them formulate a list of criteria for judging the plot and characters of a play. Encourage them to give examples to support their judgments.

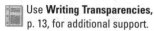 Use **Writing Transparencies,** p. 13, for additional support.

2. Sequel to the Play To get students started on this assignment, have students write down Mr. Kistunov's likely reactions to seeing her again and what his strategy will be for dealing with her. Remind students to keep Mrs. Schukin's character consistent with the way she is presented in the play. To adapt this assignment for kinesthetic learners, have them act out the sequel.

Activities & Explorations

1. Production of the Play To get students started on this assignment, have them assign roles to each member of the group. Each group should then decide on their interpretation and choose costumes and props accordingly. Suggest that they videotape their rehearsals and view the tape to polish their performances.

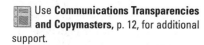 Use **Communications Transparencies and Copymasters,** p. 12, for additional support.

2. About Gout To extend this assignment, have students research the frequency of gout in today's population and how treatment methods vary from those used in the past.

3. Theater Poster To make this assignment more challenging, have students investigate the art of lithography and design a poster using this method.

Art Connection

Divide students into groups and assign each group one of the illustrations that appears in the text.

Inquiry & Research

Classic Comedy Suggest that students use clips from films to support observations in their essays. Students may wish to arrange a film festival with commentary.

Vocabulary in Action

1. incapacitated
2. composure
3. petition
4. clench
5. provocation

Choices & **CHALLENGES**

Writing Options

1. Theatre Review Imagine you are a theater critic and you have just attended opening night of "A Defenseless Creature." Write a review in which you present your reactions to the plot and characters of the play. Save your review in your **Working Portfolio.**

2. Sequel to the Play Continue the play by writing a scene in which Mrs. Schukin returns to the bank the next day. Before you write, plan the arguments Mrs. Schukin will use and how Kistunov will respond. When you have written a draft, ask a classmate to review it. Put your sequel in your **Working Portfolio.**

Writing Handbook
See p. R25: Peer Response.

Activities & Explorations

1. Production of the Play Perform "A Defenseless Creature" with a group of classmates. In addition to the actors, you might have a director, a prop manager, and a costume maker.
~ PERFORMING

2. About Gout Gout used to be known as a rich man's disease. Consult encyclopedias and medical dictionaries to find out why it was called this and what its symptoms are. Give a short report to the class. **~ SCIENCE**

3. Theater Poster Draw or paint a scene from "A Defenseless Creature," using a line of dialogue as a caption. You could paint the characters realistically or as caricatures. **~ ART**

Art Connection

"A Defenseless Creature" is illustrated with engravings by the 19th-century caricaturist, Honoré Daumier. Do you think the engravings capture the spirit of the play? Explain your answer.

Inquiry & Research

Classic Comedy Rent a video of one of the films of Charlie Chaplin, Buster Keaton, or W. C. Fields. As you watch, look for ways in which "A Defenseless Creature" is similar to these classic comedies. Do they use exaggeration, absurd situations, plot complications? Write a short essay on your observations.

Vocabulary in Action

EXERCISE: CONTEXT CLUES On a separate sheet of paper, write the Word to Know that best completes each sentence.

1. The banker has a hard time walking because he is _____ with gout in his legs.

2. The banker tries hard to keep his _____ even though the woman drives him crazy.

3. The woman visits the banker to make a _____ on behalf of her husband, who was dismissed from his job.

4. Whenever the woman shrieked, the banker would _____ the arms of his chair.

5. The woman claims that she will faint from the slightest _____.

Building Vocabulary
For an in-depth lesson on context clues, see p. R67.

WORDS TO KNOW	clench	composure	incapacitated	petition	provocation

---

Teaching Options

Mini Lesson Vocabulary Strategy

SYNONYMS

Instruction Remind students that using synonyms, or words with similar meanings, may help them to convey their meaning more precisely. Although several words might share a common definition, the connotations or ideas associated with a word might make it a better choice than one of its other synonyms. Display the following to illustrate the importance of choosing the best synonym.

Mr. Kistunov is *worn out* after the woman's visit. Synonyms for *worn out* include *tired, drained,* and *exhausted*. Each word conveys a different intensity.

Tired suggests ordinary fatigue. *Drained* indicates total lack of energy; *exhausted* suggests an overall collapse.

Application Have students work in groups to think of or find five synonyms for the word *crying*. Then have students use each word in a sentence that illustrates its connotation and denotation. Students should share their sentences with the class.

Use **Vocabulary Transparencies and Copymasters,** p. 64.

Grammar in Context: Adverb Phrases

Prepositional phrases add important information in these sentences from "A Defenseless Creature."

The business of the bank comes before my minor physical ailments.

He's been sick for five months.

The **prepositional phrases** above are used as adverbs. Adverb phrases modify **verbs**, **adjectives**, or **adverbs**.

Usage Tip: Adverb phrases usually follow the word they modify. However, they also often appear at the beginning of a sentence: *For five months* he's been sick. Notice that in this position the phrase gets more emphasis.

WRITING EXERCISE Rewrite the following sentences. Add a prepositional phrase to modify each underlined word or words.

Example: *Original* The woman <u>is</u> still <u>waiting</u>.

Rewritten The woman <u>is</u> still <u>waiting</u> outside your office.

1. I <u>sympathize</u>.
2. He <u>could</u> never <u>borrow</u>.
3. The woman is <u>offended</u>.
4. <u>Are</u> you <u>laughing</u>?

Connect to the Literature Reread the woman's words beginning "May the money . . ." on page 560. What prepositional phrases do you find? Which are used as adjectives and which as adverbs?

Grammar Handbook The Sentence and Its Parts, p. R55

"To sit in a room alone for six or seven or ten hours, sharing the time with characters that you created, is sheer heaven."

Neil Simon
born 1927

Childhood Marvin Neil Simon was born in the Bronx, New York. During his childhood, Simon's father was frequently absent, so "Do it yourself, Neil" became the future playwright's motto. After graduating from public high school, Simon enlisted in the army and soon began writing for an army camp newspaper. After he was discharged from the service, Simon worked as a mailroom clerk but soon began writing comedy routines with his brother Danny. Before long, Simon was writing for radio and television.

Theatre Success Simon's first play, *Come Blow Your Horn,* opened on Broadway in 1961. He has written almost 30 plays and has more hits in the American theater than any other playwright. Most of Simon's plays deal with life in New York City. He is the only living playwright to have a theatre on Broadway named for him.

On Playwrighting Of his profession Simon says, "For a man who wants to be his own master, to depend on no one else, to make life conform to his own visions rather than to follow the blueprints of others, playwriting is the perfect occupation. To sit in a room alone for six or seven or ten hours, sharing the time with characters that you created, is sheer heaven."

AUTHOR ACTIVITY

Screenwriter Several of Neil Simon's plays have been adapted for film, and he has written a dozen original film comedies. Try to find one of these movies, such as *The Odd Couple,* and watch it. Do you see any resemblances to "A Defenseless Creature"?

Grammar in Context

WRITING EXERCISE

Possible Responses:

1. I can sympathize with you.
2. He could never borrow without my approval.
3. The woman is offended by Kistunov's refusal to help her.
4. Are you laughing at me?

CONNECT TO THE LITERATURE

May the money <u>in your vaults</u> [adjective] turn <u>to potatoes</u> [adverb]! May your rubles turn <u>to radishes</u> [adverb], and your kopecks <u>to pickles</u> [adverb] . . .

Neil Simon

Screenwriter Neil Simon calls doing *The Good Doctor* "a joyous experience." He met his wife during that play, and he says, "Some of the scenes worked; others didn't. The marriage, I'm glad to say, did."

Author Activity

Screenwriter Encourage **logical learners** to create a chart showing the similarities and differences in plot, character, style, theme, and setting.

 Grammar **TEKS** 17E **TAAS** Writing Obj. 4

ADVERB PHRASES

Instruction Remind students that when they see a prepositional phrase, they need to identify the word that is modified to determine whether the phrase is acting as an adverb or an adjective. Adverb phrases modify verbs, adjectives, and adverbs and answer the questions *how, when, where, why,* or *to what extent.* Display the sentence below to illustrate the function of an adverb phrase.
Mr. Kistunov's gout was painful <u>in the night</u>. The adverb phrase answers the question *when* and modifies the adjective *painful.*

Exercises Have students find the adverb phrases in the following sentences. Then have them identify the word or words each modifies and what the phrase tells about the word.

1. Our bank is situated <u>on the corner of the street.</u> (modifies: is situated; tells: where)
2. Mr. Kistunov walks <u>with great effort.</u> (modifies: walks; tells: how)
3. Mrs. Schukin's husband is sensitive <u>to loud noises.</u> (modifies: sensitive; tells: how)
4. Mrs. Schukin arrived at the bank early <u>in the day.</u> (modifies: early; tells: when)

5. <u>After his harrowing experience,</u> Pochatkin went home. (modifies: went; tells: when)

 Use **Unit Four Resource Book,** p. 22.
Use **Grammar Transparencies and Copymasters,** p. 93.

Use McDougal Littell's *Language Network,* Chapter 6, for more instruction and practice in adverb phrases.

This selection is included in the **Grade 7 InterActive Reader.**

Objectives

1. understand and appreciate a **narrative poem (Literary Analysis)**
2. understand the function and significance of **word choice** as it is connected to description **(Literary Analysis)**
3. utilize the reading skill of **responding to the writer's style (Active Reading)**

Summary

The highwayman visits Bess, the land-lord's daughter, before he goes off to rob a stagecoach. He tells her that he will return by midnight of the next night. Their conversation is overheard by Tim, the stablehand. Tim loves Bess and is jealous of the love she shares with the highwayman. He informs the authorities, who send soldiers to take over the inn and wait for the return of the highwayman. They post gunmen at each window, and bind and gag Bess, tying a musket next to her as a jest. After hours of struggling, Bess manages to free one finger so that she can touch the trigger of the gun that is aimed at her heart. She awaits the highwayman, and when he draws close enough to hear, she fires a shot to warn him. The highwayman hears the shot and flees. However, the next day, when he realizes that Bess sacrificed her life to save his, he returns to the inn, enraged. The soldiers shoot him down, but on dark and windy nights, people say that he can be heard riding back to the inn where Bess still awaits him at her window.

Thematic Link

Bess does not hesitate to save the highwayman even though she can only do so the hard way, by sacrificing her own life.

5-Minute Warm-Up

Daily Language SkillBuilder   TEKS 16B, 17C, 17G

Have students **proofread** the display sentences on page 517j and write them correctly. The sentences also appear on Transparency 18 of **Grammar Transparencies and Copymasters.**

SOCIAL STUDIES

The Highwayman

Poetry by ALFRED NOYES

(Connect to Your Life)

Can you name a legendary figure from your family or local community?

Build Background With the cry "Stand and Deliver!" highwaymen halted and robbed the carriages of the upper classes in 17th- and 18th-century England. Highwaymen became legendary in the tradition of such figures as Robin Hood. They were celebrated in song and story by the poor who, exploited by the rich and powerful, felt avenged by the exploits of the highwaymen.

Highwaymen needed to be bold and skillfull riders. Detail of *Turpin's Flight Through Edmonton*, George Cruikshank. Private Collection, Bridgeman Art Library, London/ New York.

Though highwaymen came from all social classes, they often dressed and spoke like their upper-class victims.
From a collection of paste jewelry (18th century), French and English. Cameo Corner, London/ Bridgeman Art Library, London/New York.

The Escort, Robert Alexander Hillingford. John Noott Galleries, Broadway, Worcestershire, U.K./Bridgeman Art Library, London/New York

LITERARY ANALYSIS WORD CHOICE Alfred Noyes uses colorful **images**, vivid and **precise verbs**, and striking **metaphors** and **similes** to create memorable descriptions. For example, by describing the color of the highwayman's coat as "claret," a deep red wine color, Noyes suggests the romantic flashiness of the highwayman's personality in a way that the simple word *red* could not. As you read, pay attention to the author's **word choice** that makes "The Highwayman" come alive.

ACTIVE READING RESPONDING TO THE WRITER'S STYLE An active reader pays attention to the elements that make up an **writer's style**, such as **mood, tone, images,** and **word choice.** A lively, colorful style is meant to entertain; that is, it is meant to capture and hold the reader's interest. As you read, jot down in your

READER'S NOTEBOOK aspects of the writer's style that you notice.

LaserLinks: Build Background Visual Vocabulary Art Gallery

See the Skills Trace at the b[...] ning of the unit for informa[...] on TEKS covered in this les[...]

TEKS

LESSON RESOURCES

UNIT FOUR RESOURCE BOOK, pp. 25–26

ASSESSMENT
Formal Assessment, pp. 95–96

Teacher's Guide to Assessment and Portfolio Use

Test Generator

SKILLS TRANSPARENCIES AND COPYMASTERS
Literary Analysis
• Poetry: Sound Devices, TR 20 (for Mini Lesson, p. 567)
• Author's Style, TR 9 (for Cooperative Learning Activity, p. 570)

Grammar
• Precise Adjectives, CM 79 (for Mini Lesson, p. 568)
• Action Verbs, CM 69 (for Mini Lesson, p. 571)

Communications
• Dramatic Reading, TR 12 (for Mini Lesson, p. 567)

INTEGRATED TECHNOLOGY
Audio Library
LaserLinks
• Visual Vocabulary; Art Gallery. See **Teacher's SourceBook,** p. 25 for bar codes.

Internet: Research Starter

Visit our website:
www.mcdougallittell.com

The Highwayman

BY ALFRED NOYES

Illustrations by Charles Mikolaycak.
Copyright © 1995 Carole Kismaric Mikolaycak.

TEACHING THE LITERATURE

Customizing Instruction

Less Proficient Readers
Ask students to describe what they think a highwayman does. Use information found in the **Build Background** to prompt them.

Set a Purpose Have students read to find out more about the relationship between the highwayman and Boss and what finally happens to them.

Students Acquiring English
Help students to appreciate the appealing rhythms of this narrative poem by reading several stanzas aloud with dramatic emphasis.

 Use **Spanish Study Guide**, pp. 118–120 for additional support.

Gifted and Talented
Encourage students to think about the complexity of the highwayman, who is both a scoundrel (thief) and a devoted lover. Have students find examples in the selection that reflect each of these sides of his personality.

Possible Responses:

Page 566 – "His pistol butts a-twinkle . . . his rapier hilt a-twinkle . . ." (thief)

Page 566 – "One kiss, my bonny sweetheart . . . " (lover)

Page 566 – "I'm after a prize tonight . . ." (thief)

Page 567 – "And he kissed its waves in the moonlight," (lover)

 Mini Lesson ## Viewing and Representing **TEKS 22A**

Illustration by Charles Mikolaycak

ART APPRECIATION

Instruction Students will notice that the only spot of color other than black and white is the red mask worn by the figure. Ask students why the artist may have chosen to use a different color and what the effect is. Direct students to look at the illustrations on pages 567 and 569 for insight.

Possible Response: The use of the color red for the mask draws attention to it. The mask itself suggests the figure's need for mystery or anonymity. The red is carried through to the ribbons in the woman's hair, suggesting the bond between the man and woman. The mask and the ribbons are intertwined in the last illustration, showing the union of the two.

Application Ask students what impression of the highwayman they take from this illustration.

Possible Response: He is well-dressed, as shown by the lace on his shirt and cuffs. He is young and dashing and has a look of determination on his face.

Ask students how the artist suggests movement.

Possible Response: The ribbons on his hat are horizontal, and his hair is streaming in the wind.

A Tell students that to establish mood and setting, the poem opens with a series of metaphors. Ask students what elements of setting are emphasized by these metaphors.

Possible Response: It is a windy night, with the moon showing occasionally through the clouds.

Ask students what mood is created.

Possible Response: It is mysterious, eerie.

Use **Unit Four Resource Book,** p. 26 for more practice.

Reading Skills and Strategies: PREDICTING

B Ask students to predict what role Tim will play in the highwayman's future.

Possible Response: Tim is in love with Bess and probably jealous of the highwayman. He may do something to keep the lovers apart or get the highwayman into trouble.

Active Reading | RESPONDING TO THE WRITER'S STYLE |

C Ask students to paraphrase line 30.

Possible Responses: I'll come to you no matter what; no obstacle will prevent me from returning to you. Have students describe the effect of the poet's version of this sentence.

Possible Response: His phrasing makes the line more forceful and memorable and shows the determination of the highwayman.

D Ask students what idea is conveyed by the poet's use of the simile "His face burned like a brand."

Possible Response: The highwayman is deeply in love with Bess.

Use **Unit Four Resource Book,** p. 25 for more practice.

Part One

A
The wind was a torrent of darkness among the gusty trees.
The moon was a ghostly galleon[1] tossed upon cloudy seas.
The road was a ribbon of moonlight over the purple moor,[2]
And the highwayman came riding—
5   Riding—riding—
The highwayman came riding, up to the old inn-door.

1
He'd a French cocked-hat on his forehead, a bunch of lace at his chin,
A coat of the claret[3] velvet, and breeches of brown doeskin.
They fitted with never a wrinkle. His boots were up to the thigh.
10 And he rode with a jeweled twinkle,
    His pistol butts a-twinkle.
His rapier hilt[4] a-twinkle, under the jeweled sky.

Over the cobbles[5] he clattered and clashed in the dark inn-yard.
He tapped with his whip on the shutters, but all was locked and barred.
15 He whistled a tune to the window, and who should be waiting there
But the landlord's black-eyed daughter,
    Bess, the landlord's daughter,
Plaiting[6] a dark red love-knot into her long black hair.

B
2
And dark in the dark old inn-yard a stable wicket[7] creaked
20 Where Tim the ostler[8] listened. His face was white and peaked.
His eyes were hollows of madness, his hair like moldy hay,
But he loved the landlord's daughter,
    The landlord's red-lipped daughter.
Dumb as a dog he listened, and he heard the robber say—

25 "One kiss, my bonny sweetheart, I'm after a prize tonight,
But I shall be back with the yellow gold before the morning light;
Yet, if they press me sharply, and harry me through the day,

---

1. **galleon** (găl'ē-ən): a large sailing ship.
2. **moor:** an open, rolling wasteland, usually covered with low-growing shrubs.
3. **claret:** dark red, like red wine.
4. **rapier** (rā'pē-ər) **hilt:** sword handle.
5. **cobbles:** rounded stones used for paving roads.
6. **plaiting:** braiding.
7. **wicket:** a small door or gate.
8. **ostler** (ŏs'lər): a worker who takes care of horses at an inn.

Teaching Options

BLOCK SCHEDULING: MANAGING TIME

If your schedule requires that you cover the lesson objectives in a shorter time, use . . .
- Preparing to Read, p. 564
- Thinking Through the Literature, p. 570

If you want to take advantage of longer class time, use . . .
- TE Teaching Options: Viewing and Representing, p. 565; Speaking and Listening, p. 567; Grammar, pp. 568, 571; Standardized Test Practice, 569
- Choices and Challenges, p. 571

Then look for me by moonlight,
    Watch for me by moonlight,
C 30 I'll come to thee by moonlight, though hell should bar the way."

He rose upright in the stirrups. He scarce could reach her hand,
D But she loosened her hair in the casement.[9] His face burnt like a brand
As the black cascade of perfume came tumbling over his breast;
And he kissed its waves in the moonlight,
35   (O, sweet black waves in the moonlight!)
Then he tugged at his rein in the moonlight, and galloped away to the west.

Part Two

He did not come in the dawning. He did not come at noon;
And out of the tawny sunset, before the rise of the moon,
When the road was a gypsy's ribbon, looping the purple moor,
40 A redcoat troop came marching—
    Marching—marching—
King George's men came marching, up to the old inn-door.

They said no word to the landlord. They drank his ale instead.
But they gagged his daughter, and bound her, to the foot of her narrow bed.
45 Two of them knelt at her casement, with muskets at their side!

---

9. **casement:** a window that opens outward on side hinges.

  Speaking and Listening 🏴 **TEKS**
5C, 11B

DRAMATIC READING

Prepare Explain to students that sound devices, such as repetition, are used by poets to create rhythm and to enhance the effect of the poem when it is read aloud. Divide students into pairs. Have them find stanzas that include repetition. Students should read the stanzas silently and then aloud to notice how the repetition creates a strong rhythm and contributes to the effect of the poem. Then have students rewrite the stanzas with synonyms replacing the repeated words. They should analyze the change in rhythm and effect.

Present Each pair should present a dramatic reading of the original stanzas and the modified stanzas. The presenting students should explain what they observed about the impact of repetition and other sound devices on rhythm and dramatic effect. Audience members should contribute their observations.

BLOCK SCHEDULING This activity is particularly well suited for longer class periods.

📖 Use **Communications Transparencies and Copymasters**, p. 12, for additional support. Use **Literary Analysis Transparencies**, p. 20, for additional support.

Reading and Analyzing

Literary Analysis: RHYTHM

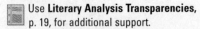 **A** Have students copy these lines and mark the stressed syllables. Ask students to analyze the effect of beginning the lines with a stressed syllable.

Possible Response: The stressed first syllable adds emphasis and urgency to the lines.

Literary Analysis | WORD CHOICE |

B Ask students to pick out the action verbs in these three lines. Have students discuss the impression created by the verbs.

Possible Responses: *twisted, writhed, stretched, strained*; the verbs show Bess's intense effort, painful at times, to free herself from the bonds.

Active Reading | RESPONDING TO THE WRITER'S STYLE |

C Ask students to identify the senses to which this line appeals.

Possible Response: sight, hearing, touch Ask students what they felt upon reading this line.

Possible Response: shock

Literary Analysis: METAPHOR

D Ask students to locate the metaphor and explain its meaning.

Possible Response: The metaphor "the white road smoking behind him" shows the speed of the highwayman's return.

Use **Literary Analysis Transparencies**, p. 19, for additional support.

Reading Skills and Strategies: CLARIFYING

E Have a volunteer read the last two stanzas aloud. Ask students what is different about the verb tense from the first and third stanzas. Have them explain what this difference suggests.

Possible Response: The verbs are in present tense; the change suggests the endurance of the love of Bess and the highwayman beyond life and for eternity.

There was death at every window;
   And hell at one dark window;
For Bess could see, through her casement, the road that *he* would ride.

They had tied her up to attention, with many a sniggering jest.
50 They had bound a musket beside her, with the muzzle beneath her breast!
  "Now, keep good watch!" and they kissed her. She heard the doomed man say—
 *Look for me by moonlight;*
   Watch for me by moonlight;
I'll come to thee by moonlight, though hell should bar the way!

 55 She twisted her hands behind her; but all the knots held good!
She writhed her hands till her fingers were wet with sweat or blood!
They stretched and strained in the darkness, and the hours crawled by like years,
Till, now, on the stroke of midnight,
   Cold, on the stroke of midnight,
60 The tip of one finger touched it! The trigger at least was hers!

The tip of one finger touched it. She strove no more for the rest.
Up, she stood up to attention, with the muzzle beneath her breast.
She would not risk their hearing; she would not strive again;
For the road lay bare in the moonlight;
65   Blank and bare in the moonlight;
And the blood of her veins, in the moonlight, throbbed to her love's refrain.

Tlot-tlot; tlot-tlot! Had they heard it? The horse hoofs ringing clear;
Tlot-tlot, tlot-tlot, in the distance? Were they deaf that they did not hear?
Down the ribbon of moonlight, over the brow of the hill,
70 The highwayman came riding—
   Riding—riding—
The redcoats looked to their priming![10] She stood up, straight and still.

Tlot-tlot, in the frosty silence! *Tlot-tlot,* in the echoing night!
Nearer he came and nearer. Her face was like a light.
75 Her eyes grew wide for a moment; she drew one last deep breath,
Then her finger moved in the moonlight,
    Her musket shattered the moonlight,
 Shattered her breast in the moonlight and warned him—with her death.

---

10. **looked to their priming:** prepared their muskets by pouring in the explosive used to fire them.

Teaching Options   (Mini Lesson) **Grammar**   🚩TEKS 17D

PRECISE ADJECTIVES

Instruction Remind students that adjectives must be chosen carefully to convey the exact meaning of the writer. Point out to students the word *grey* in the highlighted line on the next page. The use of that adjective shows the impact of the news on the highwayman more vividly than an adjective such as *pale* or *colorless*.

Application Divide students into groups. Have them choose two or three lines from the poem and substitute other adjectives for the ones used by the poet. Ask students to share their choices with the class and discuss how the effect of the lines is changed by the substitution of other adjectives.

Use **Grammar Transparencies and Copymasters**, p. 79.

Use McDougal Littell's *Language Network*, Chapter 5, for more instruction and practice in precise adjectives.

He turned. He spurred to the west; he did not know who stood
80 Bowed, with her head o'er the musket, drenched with her own blood!
Not till the dawn he heard it, his face grew grey to hear
    How Bess, the landlord's daughter,
        The landlord's black-eyed daughter,
    Had watched for her love in the moonlight, and died in the darkness there.

 85 Back, he spurred like a madman, shouting a curse to the sky,
With the white road smoking behind him and his rapier brandished high.
Blood-red were his spurs in the golden noon; wine-red was his velvet coat;
    When they shot him down on the highway,
        Down like a dog on the highway,
90 And he lay in his blood on the highway, with a bunch of lace at his throat.

And still of a winter's night, they say, when the wind is in the trees,
When the moon is a ghostly galleon tossed upon cloudy seas,
When the road is a ribbon of moonlight over the purple moor,
A highwayman comes riding—
95 *   Riding—riding—*
A highwayman comes riding, up to the old inn-door.

Over the cobbles he clatters and clangs in the dark inn-yard.
He taps with his whip on the shutters, but all is locked and barred.
He whistles a tune to the window, and who should be waiting there
100 *But the landlord's black-eyed daughter,*
*   Bess, the landlord's daughter,*
Plaiting a dark red love-knot into her long black hair.

THE HIGHWAYMAN   569

Less Proficient Readers
Make sure students understand what sacrifices the landlord's daughter and the highwayman make for each other.
• How does Bess warn the highwayman of the redcoats' trap?
  Answer: She shoots herself, and he hears the sound.
• How does the highwayman die?
  Answer: When he turns and rides at the redcoats, they shoot him down.

Gifted and Talented
Have students discuss whether they think the highwayman can still be called both a scoundrel and a lover at the end of the poem.
Possible Response: He stops being a scoundrel when he knowingly rides toward his death.
Have students debate whether or not they find his actions heroic.
Possible Responses: Yes, he's heroic because he is willing to sacrifice his life to avenge his love. No, his love was dead already, so his sacrifice was a waste. No, it was the fact that he was a thief that put Bess's life in danger.

Multiple Learning Styles
Auditory Learners
Have students choose or compose music that echoes the action and mood of each part of the poem.

✓ **Assessment** **Standardized Test Practice**   🚩 **TEKS** 10K, 12H   **TAAS** Reading Obj. 6

AUTHOR'S PURPOSE For some standardized tests, students will be asked to identify the author's purpose for writing something. To provide students with some help in choosing the best response, read aloud or write on a board the following:
The author's purpose in writing this poem was probably to—
A. show how romantic a life of crime can be.
B. prove that law enforcement officials were cruel.
C. convey the idea that people truly in love should be willing to die for each other.

D. entertain readers with a vividly written and suspenseful narrative.
Lead students through the process of choosing the correct answer. A and B are incorrect. Both offer generalizations that cannot be supported by the instances in the poem. C is incorrect. The poem shows two people who sacrifice their lives for each other, but that is not the reason that the poet wrote his work. D is correct. The poem is a fictional account, which is entertaining to read.

GUIDING STUDENT RESPONSE

Connect to the Literature

1. What Do You Think? Students may mention the highwayman's being shot down, his appearance as he is first described, Bess awaiting him at her window, or Bess tied up and watching for him.

Comprehension Check
• She waits at her window.
• Tim, the ostler, is listening.
• She shoots herself.

Think Critically

2. Possible Responses: Students might say the highwayman is portrayed as handsome, brave, and sure of himself, while Tim is portrayed as small, weak, and mad. Both are scoundrels in their own ways.

3. Possible Responses: They are immoral, cruel, excessive in their actions, and unfair.

4. Possible Response: Students might say Bess's sacrifice is greater, because she knows she has no chance to live if she warns him.

5. Possible Response: No, since these stanzas suggest that the lovers are still together in an afterlife.

6. Responses will vary. Encourage students to explain why they find the images and metaphors they have chosen so memorable.

Literary Analysis

Word Choice Key events include— revelation of his plans to Bess ("I shall be back with the yellow gold," "I'll come to thee by moonlight, though hell should bar the way.")
—takeover of the inn by the redcoats ("A redcoat troop came marching – marching – marching," "There was death at every window; And hell at one dark window;")
—Bess's struggle to reach the gun ("She writhed her hands . . .)
—Bess's firing of the warning shot ("Her musket shattered the moonlight,")
—the highwayman's escape ("He spurred to the west;")
—the highwayman's return and death ("When they shot him down on the highway . . .")

 Use **Literary Analysis Transparencies,** p. 9, for additional support.

Connect to the Literature

1. What Do You Think? What images stayed in your mind after you finished reading the poem? Explain.

Comprehension Check
• In Part One, where does Bess wait for the highwayman?
• As Bess and the highwayman talk, who is secretly listening?
• How does Bess warn the highwayman about the redcoats?

Think Critically

2. Think about how the poet describes Tim the ostler. How is he different from the highwayman? What do they have in common?

3. How do you feel about the conduct of the redcoats?

 THINK ABOUT
{ • their duty to uphold the law
• their treatment of Bess
• how they shoot the highwayman

4. Both Bess and the highwayman make great sacrifices for love. In your opinion, whose sacrifice shows greater courage? Explain your choice.

5. Would you have liked the poem better if the last two stanzas had not been included? Why or why not?

6. **ACTIVE READING** **RESPONDING TO THE WRITER'S STYLE** With a partner, review the notes you took in your **READER'S NOTEBOOK**. What images and metaphors, key aspects of the **writer's style**, stood out for you? Explain your choices.

Extend Interpretations

7. Different Perspectives What if the poem had been told from the point of view of Tim the ostler? What might have been his reaction to the events of the poem?

8. Connect to Life Do you know of a case where someone sacrificed something valuable or meaningful for someone he or she loved? Explain.

Extend Interpretations

7. Different Perspectives Possible Response: Tim the ostler might have seen his actions as virtuous and justified. His reaction to the events may have been a feeling of guilt because he loved Bess or triumph because he was jealous of the highwayman.

8. Connect to Life Responses will vary. Some students might suggest that anyone who donates organs to relatives is making a heroic sacrifice.

Literary Analysis

WORD CHOICE Poets choose their words carefully for the effect they have on the reader. Alfred Noyes quickly establishes the mood of mystery and foreboding in "The Highwayman" with a few carefully chosen images that describe the wind and the moon.

The wind was a torrent of darkness among the gusty trees. The moon was a ghostly galleon tossed upon cloudy seas.

Similarly, the poet's description of Tim the ostler as pale with hair "like moldy hay" establishes his appearance in a much more vivid and memorable way than calling him a *blond* would have. Throughout "The Highwayman," the poet's **word choice** helps create vivid characters and settings and heightens the drama of the poem.

Cooperative Learning Activity As a class, create a sequence diagram that lists the major events in the poem and who is involved in them. Alongside each event, list key words and phrases that made that event come alive for you. As a class, discuss how the language of the poem intensified its sense of drama.

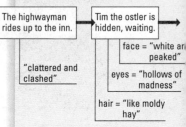

Choices & CHALLENGES

Writing Options

Police Report Imagine that you are the officer in charge of the redcoat brigade that brings down the highwayman. Write a report of the entire incident for your superior officer. Include your reactions to characters like Tim the ostler, the innkeeper, Bess, and the highwayman himself. How do you feel about the actions of your men? Include details from the poem as well as dialogue that you make up.

Writing Handbook
See p. R33: Narrative Writing.

Activities & Explorations

Choral Reading In two groups of four students, read the poem chorally, taking alternating stanzas of the poem. Practice your reading before you present it to the class. Make sure to vary the pitch and volume of your voice, as well as the pace of your reading, to reflect changes in mood. Make a tape of your reading and keep it in your classroom library/listening center.
~ SPEAKING AND LISTENING

Illustrated Map Design an imaginary map of the countryside in which "The Highwayman" is set and illustrate it with episodes from the poem. Try to capture the mood of the poem in your illustrations. **~ ART**

Art Connection

Review Charles Mikolaycak's illustrations that accompany the poem. Do the illustrations match the pictures of Bess and the highwayman that you visualized as you read the poem? Explain.

Research & Inquiry

SOCIAL STUDIES **HIGHWAYMEN**
Using encyclopedias and other reference books, research the problem of highwaymen on the roads of Great Britain during the 18th century. Write a report and present it to the class.

He loved to read and daydream in a "mountain nook."

Alfred Noyes
1880–1958

Early Success Alfred Noyes was born in England and spent much of his childhood on the Welsh coast, where he loved to read and

daydream in a "mountain nook" overlooking the sea. Educated at Oxford University, Noyes wrote most of his poetry before 1942, when glaucoma cost him his eyesight. Noyes's best-known work is "The Highwayman." Generations of students have loved this poem for its driving rhythm and haunting refrain. Noyes wrote the poem in only two days when he was 24 years old.

 LaserLink: Background for Reading Art Gallery

Writing Options

Police Report Have students reread the poem and take notes on the actions of all of the characters. Remind students to keep their tone official and their language formal.

 Use **Writing Transparencies,** p. 14, for additional support.

Activities & Explorations

Choral Reading Prior to reading, have student groups analyze their stanzas and decide on the mood they wish to convey. Review the way pitch, volume, tone, and pace contribute to mood.

Use **Communications Transparencies and Copymasters,** p. 11, for additional support.

Illustrated Map Have students look at pictures of the English moors and inns and imagine how the countryside would have looked a century or two ago. Students with computer proficiency may wish to use a graphics program to design their map and illustrations.

Art Connection

Students can quote lines to show similarities or differences between how they imagine the character and how he or she is illustrated.

Inquiry & Research

Highwaymen Have students try various subject headings such as "Brigands and Robbers" to find information.

 Use **Writing Transparencies,** pp. 47–48, for additional support.

Mini Lesson **Grammar** ⭐ **TEKS 15H**

ACTION VERBS

Instruction Remind students that an action verb tells what the subject of the sentence does. Carefully chosen action verbs strengthen writing and add interest. Contrast the sentences below to show how action verbs enhance meaning and style.

Bess is listening for the first sound.
Bess strains to hear the first sound.

Exercise Have students rewrite each sentence with a more vivid action verb.

1. Her blood is all over the room.
   (Her blood drenches the room.)
2. The horse makes a soft nickering noise.
   (The horse nickers softly.)
3. The soldier goes to her side immediately.
   (The soldier races to her side immediately.)
4. He moves noisily over the cobbles in the dark inn-yard.

(He clatters over the cobbles in the dark inn-yard.)

 Use **Grammar Transparencies and Copymasters,** p. 69.

 Use McDougal Littell's *Language Network,* Chapter 4, for more instruction and practice in action verbs.

Building Vocabulary

Objectives
- distinguish denotative and connotative meanings
- look beyond the literal meanings of words
- understand positive and negative connotations

VOCABULARY EXERCISE
Possible Responses:

Positive Con.	Negative Con.
thin	scrawny
unique	strange
thrifty	cheap

Students' sentences should illustrate the different meanings and emotions expressed by each word.

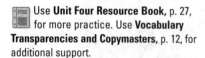 Use **Unit Four Resource Book,** p. 27, for more practice. Use **Vocabulary Transparencies and Copymasters,** p. 12, for additional support.

Choosing Words Carefully

Good writers choose their words carefully. They take into consideration the positive or negative associations and the implied meanings of words.

In the excerpt to the right, Roald Dahl could have used the word *plan* instead of *scheme,* but his choice of *scheme* makes this passage more interesting and dramatic.

> **Many schemes were put forward, but none of them was any good.**
>
> —Roald Dahl,
> from *Boy: Tales of Childhood*

The word **scheme** means "plan" but implies secrecy, dishonesty, or impracticality.

Strategies for Building Vocabulary

A word's **denotation** is its dictionary definition, or literal meaning. A word may also have an implied meaning, an association that suggests a particular emotion. This is its **connotation.** Knowing the connotations of words can help you improve your understanding of literature and enhance your writing.

❶ **Look Beyond the Literal Definition** Writers use words to bring out positive or negative connotations. Consider this sentence, noting Dahl's use of the word *plot:*

> **"It's a plot,"** Thwaites said. **"A grown-up plot to keep us quiet."**

The word *plot*'s negative association with suspicion and distrust fits the situation perfectly.
❷ **Consider Synonyms** Consider the use of the word *loathsome* in the following sentence:

> **But by far the most loathsome thing about Mrs. Pratchett was the filth that clung around her.**

Dahl might have used such synonyms as *unpleasant, disgusting,* and *foul.* Substitute each of these words for *loathsome* and notice

how your impression changes. *Loathsome* conveys the strongest feeling of repulsion.
❸ **Consider Connotations** Think about the connotations of the words you use in your writing. Consider whether particular words have positive associations or negative associations.

Positive Connotations	Negative Connotations
laugh	snicker
multitude	mob

The verbs *laugh* and *snicker* both mean "to express amusement." *Laugh,* however, has a positive connotation of shared enjoyment, whereas *snicker* often connotes making fun of someone or something in an unkind way. In a similar way, *multitude* means a large number of people gathered together, while *mob* has a negative connotation, implying possible danger and disorder.

If you are unsure about a word's connotations, refer to a standard dictionary or thesaurus.

EXERCISE Expand the chart under **Consider Connotations** above with three or four examples of positive and negative connotations. Then write a sentence using each pair of words.

from

KNOTS IN MY YO-YO STRING

by Jerry Spinelli

I was neat.

How neat was I? Say I had to cut a rectangle out of a piece of paper. First I would measure a perfect shape with my ruler, then draw it with a sharp pencil. Then with my scissors I would cut it out. But not just cut it out. I would cut precisely along the right edge of the pencil line, or precisely along the left edge, or I would split

Jerry,
age 12

573

Possible Objectives

You can use this selection to achieve one or more of the following objectives:

- enjoy silent sustained reading (Option One)
- read and analyze literature with a group (Option Two)
- use the Reader's Notebook to write in response to literature (Option Three)

Summary

This autobiographical piece tells what a neat, tidy rule-follower this author was in his youth. "Give me a direction, I followed it," he writes. Once he was unfairly given a detention, which he disregarded. As punishment, he was dropped from every school activity. He then apologized to the teacher and was reinstated. Each summer, he played Ping-Pong at the YMCA, watched Saturday movies, and ate hot dogs. Everything in his life was neat and tidy—except for his yo-yo, which despite his best intentions kept developing knots in the string. Sometimes the boy even fantasized about neatness. Only later does he realize that this quality is not universally useful. Because he was afraid to take risks and fail, he did not excel at some things, such as coloring contests or basketball. On reflection, he realizes that, when he apologized to his teacher after a false accusation, he caved in; he should have fought for what he knew was right. While outwardly conforming, though, he was also developing an interior life. He replayed events in his head that were sometimes better than the real ones. This and his fantasies were the beginnings of developing "an aptitude that thrives on disorder": imagination, a gift that awaited him later.

Option One
Silent Sustained Reading
You might set aside time each week for independent reading. During this time, you and your students would read for enjoyment. The excerpt from *Knots in My Yo-Yo String* will appeal to many students and can be read independently in 15 minutes or so. To encourage students to read for pleasure, consider making no assignments related to this selection. However, Options Two and Three below offer suggestions in case you do want to make assignments.

Option Two
Shared Reading Groups
You may assign students to groups or allow them to choose their own. Students can read the selection together, alternately reading sections aloud, or they can read independently and meet to cooperate in a project that portrays some element of the selection.

Possible Projects
• Have students brainstorm various careers that Jerry Spinelli might have been suited for besides being a writer. Have students begin by listing his characteristics and skills—all of them. These include not only his love of neatness and order, but also his enjoyment of sports and imaginary worlds. Students might mention architecture, computer programming, or carpentry as other possibilities.
• Have students discuss which Jerry Spinelli they would like to meet—the one described in the selection or the older one who is recalling that younger version. Have them give reasons for their responses.

the line in half and cut precisely right down the middle. Consistently, all the way around the rectangle.

In seventh grade at Stewart Junior High, I astonished my shop teacher, Mr. Rohn, with the precision of my mechanical drawings and the perfection of my hand-lettering.

That same year I won numerous Palmer Method penmanship certificates and was declared the outstanding boy penmeister.

Every Eastertime the merchants of the West End shopping district—three blocks on Marshall Street—sponsored a coloring contest. Every day for two weeks line drawings—coloring-book-type pictures—were printed in the *Times Herald*. Each business had its own picture. Kids were invited to cut out the pictures, color them, and deposit their entries in boxes in the stores.

Unlike most kids, I did not use crayons. I used colored pencils. My frequently sharpened points never—never—strayed outside the lines. And my colors were right, too. No green sky or red grass for me.

For me, staying inside the lines was more than a color-the-picture matter.

Give me a direction, I followed it. Put a rule in front of me, I obeyed it. In twelve years I never stayed after school for detention. Once, though, I came close. It happened in the spring of ninth grade. Our homeroom teacher, Miss Busch, announced that our lockers would be reviewed for neatness. Since I kept my locker neat at all times, there was nothing for me to tidy up.

The next morning as the students entered Homeroom 213, we looked to the blackboard for the names of those whose lockers failed to pass muster. Shockingly, my name was among them. The punishment, besides cleaning up the offending locker, was detention.

I told Miss Busch there must be a mistake. She said there wasn't. I said I wouldn't be there for detention. It was the only time I ever talked back to a teacher. She said I'd be sorry.

After school that day, as usual, I went to baseball practice. When I arrived at school the next morning, I discovered I was no longer on the team. Nor was I homeroom president. I was stripped of every office and association.

My locker may have been tidy, but suddenly my life was a mess. One day of watching my backup shortstop was enough. I couldn't stand it. I apologized to Miss Busch, and the picture of my life fell back into place.

I loved routine, repeatedness. To do the same thing twice was to establish a personal tradition. In other words, where there were no lines, I drew my own. I stepped inside and stayed there—cozy, safe.

Summer Saturdays, for example. In the morning I walked a mile from George Street to the YMCA. There I played Ping-Pong in the game room with Lee Holmes, Ralph Cottman, and others. Then a screen and projector were brought out, the lights turned off, and we all settled in to watch a black and white movie, usually a Tarzan adventure.

After the movie I walked down to Main Street, past Block's department store, past the Norris Theater, to Texas Hot Wieners. The best hot dogs in town were sizzling right

> My locker may have been tidy, but suddenly my life was a mess.

ere in the front window, daring each
asserby not to come in. I sat at the counter
nd placed my order, always the same: hot dog
ith mustard and chopped onions, and
hocolate milk. I've had a lot of wimpy hot
ogs since then, hot dogs so soft you can't feel
our teeth go through them, so mushy with fat
nd cereal you could almost drink them with a
traw. Not Texas Hot Wieners. They had
punk. They fought back.

By now it was one o'clock. Across the street
went to the Garrick Theater and the
aturday matinee double feature—cowboy
novies plus a Flash Gordon or Captain
Midnight serial.

Hours later I emerged blinking in the late-
afternoon sun. I walked home along Markley
Street, past the sweet-smelling Wonder Bread
plant, the sidewalk dusty with flour, past the
Times Herald, over the Markley Street bridge
that spanned Stony Creek. I always stopped at
the bridge railing to look for sunfish in the
sparkling water below. Only when I spotted
one would I continue my journey homeward.

Every summer Saturday. The same thing.

Needless to say, I was well acquainted with
perfect attendance in school. Most years went
by without my missing a day.

When I walked, I trained myself to keep my
feet pointed straight ahead, not pigeon-toed or
splayed outward.

Option Three
Reader's Notebook

Provide the following direction to students before they read:

Discuss the difference between biographies and autobiographies. Although both tell the story of people's lives, biographies are more objective and may in fact be written after the subject has died. Autobiographies contain the subject's thoughts, feelings, and detailed experiences.

Ask students as they read to note at least four details that could appear only in fiction or in autobiographies. Have them record those details in their Reader's Notebooks.

After students have finished the selection, have them reread their notes and think about what they learned from them that they could not have learned in a biography written by someone else. Have them summarize their ideas in a few lines explaining either what they like or what they don't like about autobiographies.

After Reading

Possible Activities
Independent Activities

- Ask gifted and talented students to debate the pros and cons of conformity. Have them jot down their ideas in the Reader's Notebooks.
- If Jerry Spinelli were writing a letter today to Miss Busch, what might he say? Have students compose such letters, including details from the selection.
- Have students write a monologue for Miss Busch that describes the detention episode from her point of view.

• Ask students what they think the best way is to deal with unfairness that they might meet in school, at home, or elsewhere. Have them consider the long-term effect of actions as well as the immediate effect.

• Discuss the goal of perfection and whether or not it is a worthy goal that encourages people to try hard or whether it is an obstacle to real success.

• Have students compare and contrast their summers with those of the narrator. What do most kids do today, and how do their activities sound compared with the never-changing routine that the narrator followed on Saturdays?

Assessment Opportunities

• You can assess students comprehension by evaluating what they wrote about autobiographies in their Reader's Notebook.

• You can have students paraphrase what the narrator now thinks of his childhood neatness.

• You can have students explain where the title comes from and what it means.

I even fantasized about neatness. I imagined our house had been selected for a visit by President Eisenhower. I saw myself going from room to room putting everything precisely in its place. On the racks in the bathroom the corners of the towels came together perfectly.

In another fantasy I set out to tidy up the world. Anything I couldn't fix with hedge trimmers and lawn mower I paved over with asphalt. By the time I was finished, the Amazon jungle looked like the flower beds and crewcut lawns of the North End of Norristown.

I spread my peanut butter evenly over my bread.

I never said bad words (unless you count "poop").

I hardly ever laughed out loud.

As I said, I was neat. And though I did not think of it this way, I believe that what I was actually trying to do was to become perfect.

Funny thing: For all my neatness, my sharp pencil points, my devotion to the right side of the line, I never won the West End shopping district coloring contest. Every year I tried harder than before, tried to be even neater, and still I lost. I couldn't figure out why.

Wasn't neatness enough? Wasn't perfection possible?

No, said my yo-yo. Often I had what seemed to be a perfect day—100 on a spelling test, winning touchdown in a pickup game, a new haircut—only to come home and find knots in my yo-yo string. I began to think the string had a mind of its own. I imagined it waiting until I wasn't looking, then rising up like a cobra and looping itself into knots. My paranoia seemed confirmed one morning when I awoke to find knots that I could have sworn

I set out to tidy up the world.

were not there when I went to bed.

When I was eleven and twelve, I played Biddy basketball, the equivalent of Little League baseball. In my final year I made the all-star team, but not because I was a great scorer. The most points I ever scored in a game was twelve, and usually it was half that. I think I made the all-stars as much for what I did not do as for what I did. That is to say, I did not make mistakes.

Playing the guard position, I dribbled a lot and passed a lot. But these were relatively risk-free ventures. Shooting was where the risk was, and I rarely took more than five shots in a game. I wasn't a bad shooter, but each shot I missed discouraged me from taking more. At home after each game, I neatly entered into a

notebook my statistics: assists, shots taken, shots made, fouls. Of course I hardly ever committed a foul. And because I played the game so carefully, I never found out how good a basketball player I might have become. Too late I learned that neatness does not serve all endeavors equally well, that what is good for penmanship is not necessarily good for basketball.

A willingness to take risks, to color outside the lines, was slow in coming to me. Some stubborn idea of perfection deterred me from fully extending myself in simple, pure participation. I was too afraid to fail. I did not appreciate the value of a mess.

Not that I wasn't given the chance. Looking back, I can see now that that's what the

school-locker incident was: an opportunity to grow beyond my own self-imposed limits. And for one day, I did. Falsely accused of having a disorderly locker, I was properly outraged. I defied my teacher. I refused to submit to injustice. I turned my back on detention. I charged across the line. I became a new me.

Then came the consequences—banishment from the baseball team, from all offices. Did I rise up and cry, "Punish me if you will! I don't care! I will never capitulate to this injustice"? Did I finish out the year in noble exile, stripped of all honors? Did I stand up for what I knew was right?

No.

I caved in. I apologized for protesting an unjust verdict. My life was reinstated. Order was restored, the mess was cleaned up. I was back inside the lines. Once again I was the old familiar me.

Yet even as I publicly conformed in word and deed, a contrary tendency was forming within me. It showed briefly in sixth grade when I wrote the unassigned poem on Mexico. It showed in my neatness fantasies—not in the subject matter but in the mere act of fantasizing. It showed in my swooning wonderment over the endlessness of the sky at night.

And it showed most commonly in my own version of the Garrick Theater's double features. When an event in my life—say, a baseball game—was over, it was not really over. For that night in bed I would relive it in my head. I would again see the vivid colors and hear the voices and feel the feelings, and the reliving would be, in its own way, as real to me as the first time around. Sometimes it was even better. Sometimes I couldn't wait for the event to be over and bedtime to arrive so that I could play it back.

As I have said, if you had asked me what I would grow up to be, I would have answered, "A baseball player." But even as I oiled the deep, fragrant pocket of my Marty Marion glove and taped the hickory handle of my thirty-three-ounce bat, I was unknowingly developing the tool of another trade. The urge to write a poem, to daydream, to ruminate, to wonder, even my tolerance of solitude—all became components of a bearing that I would never have guessed would fit me so well, an aptitude that thrives on disorder, that welcomes green sky and red grass, that serves neither master nor homeroom teacher, that

respects no line or limit. I speak, of course, o imagination—a gift that, like my Roadmaster on that Christmas morning, waited in anothe room for my discovery. ❖

"If you had asked me what I would grow up to be, I would have answered, 'A baseball player.'"

Jerry Spinelli
born 1941

Baseball Player Jerry Spinelli never set out to be a writer. During his first 16 years he wanted to be, among other things, a rock skipper, a yo-yo tangler, and above all a baseball player. When he was 12 years old, Spinelli played shortstop in the Connie Mack Knee-Hi League, and his team won the state championship. His favorite book at the time was *The Baseball Encyclopedia*.

Finds Writing In high school, however, things changed. Spinelli's family moved, and he no longer did well in school or in sports. Then, when he was in the tenth grade, he saw his high school's football team score an upset victory. He went home and wrote a poem about the game, which was published by the local newspaper. After that, he was determined to become a writer. He attended Gettysburg College and, later, writing seminars at the Johns Hopkins University. Spinelli published his first novel, *Space Station Seventh Grade,* in 1982. Since then, he has written 19 books, including *Maniac Magee,* a Newbery Medal winner in 1991, and *Wringer,* a Newbery Honor Book in 1998.

JERRY SPINELLI
When young audiences ask Jerry Spinelli where he gets his ideas, he answers, "From you. You're the funny ones." *Knots in My Yo-Yo String* is one of almost two dozen books written by Spinelli. "Nobody wanted the first four," he has said, so not all these books have been published. If students had the opportunity to read just one of his books, Spinelli said he'd recommend *Maniac Magee*" for the message, the story, and the language." In 1991, that book won the Newbery Medal.

See the Communication Handbook, p. R100 for speaking and presenting tips.

SPEAKING OPPORTUNITY

Communication Workshop

Staging a Scene

Bringing a scene to life . . .

From Reading to Staging Have you ever wondered what it would be like to work in a theater or on a movie set? The first step in creating a dramatic production is choosing a script. Neil Simon wrote many scripts for screen and stage. His play *The Good Doctor* is based on short stories by Anton Chekhov. Now you and your classmates can try **staging a scene** from this work. Working together can give you a chance to bring a playwright's words to life.

For Your Portfolio

WRITING PROMPT Create a staged presentation of "A Defenseless Creature" from *The Good Doctor* by Neil Simon.

Purpose: To interpret and perform a scene
Audience: Your classmates and other interested students and adults

---

Basics in a Box

GUIDELINES AND STANDARDS **STAGING A SCENE**

A successful script should

- include an overall description of the set, props, lighting, and costumes
- include specific stage directions about the gestures, movements, and tones of voice the performers should use
- include notes about pacing and stage location

A successful performance should

- show an awareness of the audience—actors' voices must be loud enough, and the audience should have an unblocked view of the actors and actions
- maintain audience interest through strong acting, good pacing, and effective staging
- follow the script

COMMUNICATION WORKSHOP **579**

Communication Workshop

Staging a Scene

Objectives

- stage a scene from a play
- use a written text as a model for writing a script
- practice and present a performance
- evaluate the staging of the scene

Introducing the Workshop

Staging a Scene Discuss with students plays they may have seen on stage or on television. Have them think about what makes a play interesting and memorable.

Basics in a Box
Presenting the Rubric To better understand the assignment, students can refer to the Guidelines and Standards for Staging a Scene. You may also want to share with them the complete rubric, which describes several levels of proficiency.

 Use McDougal Littell's *Language Network,* Chapters 12–19, for more instruction on essential writing skills

 Power Presentation

To engage students visually, use **Power Presentation 1,** Staging a Scene.

 TEKS

See the Skills Trace at the beginning of the unit for information on TEKS covered in this lesson.

LESSON RESOURCES

USING PRINT RESOURCES
Unit Four Resource Book
- Planning and Drafting, p. 28
- Practicing and Delivering, p. 29
- Peer Response Guide, pp. 30–31
- Refining Your Performance, p. 32
- Rubric for Evaluation, p. 33
Writing Transparencies and Copymasters
- Writing Process Transparencies,

TR 1–4
- Writing Template Transparencies: Staging a Scene, TR 38
Grammar Transparencies and Copymasters
- Adverbs and Predicate Adjectives, CM 77 (for Mini Lesson, p. 584)
Communications Transparencies and Copymasters
- Giving and Using Feedback to

Improve Performance, TR 16

INTEGRATED TECHNOLOGY
LaserLinks
Writing Springboards
See **Teacher's SourceBook** p. 36 for bar codes.

Writing Coach CD-ROM
Visit our website:
www.mcdougallittell.com

Analyzing the Model

The Good Doctor, Scene 3, "A Defenseless Creature"

The model script on this page is an excerpt from a director's script, complete with stage directions, set descriptions, character descriptions, and sound and lighting directions. Throughout the script are notes that will help the actors interpret how to act and react at that point in the scene.

Have students think of a play they have seen in which the subject or the mood of the play is apparent just from their first glimpse of the setting and from the list of characters. Help students to see how the setting and scenery in a play can reveal something about the play itself. Then point out the key words and phrases in the model that correspond to the elements mentioned in the Guidelines in Action.

• Ask students what they learn about the play from reading the descriptions of the setting, props, and characters.
Possible Response: The scene takes place in a business office during the day, and, since there is a crutch, one of the characters is hurt or sick.

• Ask students what they learn about Mr. Kistunov and his assistant in the first few lines of this scene.
Possible Responses: Mr. Kistunov seems to be frail, in pain, and cannot stand loud noises. His assistant is a direct contrast and seems to be energetic and loud.

• Ask students to describe their impression of the woman client from her physical description.
Possible Responses: She appears to be shy, nervous, and unsure of herself. The condition of her clothing sets her apart from Mr. Kistunov and his assistant.

Analyzing a Model Script

Excerpts from Director's Script
The Good Doctor, Scene 3, "A Defenseless Creature"

Set, Costumes, Lighting, and Sound
Set is the inside of an office. Costumes are business attire for Kistunov and his assistant and a dress for the woman. Stage is lit brightly. Woman's sound effects are on cassette tape, to be played at maximum volume off-stage.

Characters
Assistant to Kistunov, Kistunov, Woman

Props
Desk; two chairs; footstool; crutch; bandages; woman's handbag

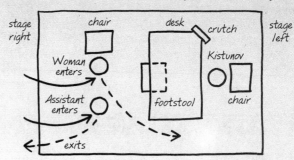

Assistant enters stage right, bounces energetically into office.

Assistant. *(With volume)* Good morning, Mr. Kistunov!
Kistunov. Shhh! Please . . . Please lower your voice.

Kistunov cringes, moving his hands as if to cover his ears.

Assistant. *(Whispers)* I'm sorry, sir.
Kistunov. It's just that my gout is acting up again and my nerves are like little firecrackers. The least little friction can set them off.

Assistant has a sympathetic look on his face.

Assistant. It must be very painful, sir.
Kistunov. Combing my hair this morning was agony.
Assistant. Mr. Kistunov. . . .
Kistunov. What is it, Pochatkin?
Assistant. There's a woman who insists on seeing you. We can't make head or tail out of her story, but she insists on seeing the directing manager. Perhaps if you're not well—

He smiles, is friendly and polite.

Kistunov. No, no. The business of the bank comes before my minor physical ailments. Show her in, please . . . quietly. *(The* Assistant *tiptoes out. A* Woman *enters. She is in her late forties, poorly dressed. She is of the working class. She crosses*

• Director describes set, costumes, lighting, and sound at the beginning of the script.
• A list of performers is given as well as the inventory of props.
• A sketch shows the set-up of the stage and the actors' places.
• Handwritten notes show the pacing, gestures, tones, and movements that the actors should use.

to the desk, a forlorn look on her face. She twists her bag nervously.) Good morning, madame. Forgive me for not standing, but I am somewhat incapacitated. Please sit down.

Woman. Thank you. (*She sits*)

Kistunov. Now, what can I do for you?

Woman. You can help me, sir. I pray to God you can help. No one else in this world seems to care. . . . (*And she begins to cry, which in turn becomes a wail—the kind of wail that melts the spine of strong men.* Kistunov *winces and grits his teeth in pain as he grips the arms of his chair.*)

Kistunov. Calm yourself, madame. I *beg* of you. Please calm yourself.

Woman. I'm sorry. (*She tries to calm down.*)

Kistunov. I'm sure we can sort it all out if we approach the problem sensibly and quietly. . . . Now, what exactly is the trouble?

Woman. Well, sir. . . . It's my husband. Collegiate Assessor Schukin. He's been sick for five months. . . . Five agonizing months.

Kistunov. I know the horrors of illness and can sympathize with you, madame. What's the nature of his illness?

Woman. It's a nervous disorder. Everything grates on his nerves. If you so much as touch him he'll scream out— (*And without warning, she screams a loud bloodcurdling scream that sends* Kistunov *almost out of his seat.*) How or why he got it, nobody knows.

Kistunov. (*Trying to regain his composure*) I have an inkling. . . . Please go on, a little less descriptively, if possible.

Woman. Well, while the poor man was lying in bed—

Kistunov. (*Braces himself*) You're not going to scream again, are you?

Woman. Not that I don't have cause. . . . While he was lying in bed these five months, recuperating, he was dismissed from his job—for no reason at all.

Kistunov. That's a pity, certainly, but I don't quite see the connection with our bank, madame.

Woman. You don't know how I suffered during his illness. I nursed him from morning till night. Doctored him from night till morning. Besides cleaning my house, taking care of my children, feeding our dog, our cat, our goat, my sister's bird, who was sick. . . .

Kistunov. The bird was sick?

Woman. My *sister!*

Woman immediately [lo]ses her shyness, speaks [m]elodramatically. [S]oundtrack of wail echoes [l]oudly with actor's voice.

She opens her mouth wide and looks to the sky while soundtrack of scream is played. He jumps and clutches his leg; his crutch crashes to the ground.

She says last line with great innocence.

He pats his head and loosens his collar.

She walks across the stage, right to left, wringing her hands.

She leans forward and nearly screams her line. He jumps back. Actors hold these positions for several seconds to end the scene.

- Ask students how their initial impression of the woman changes once she begins to speak.
  Possible Response: The woman's dialogue reveals her character as hysterical, loud, and comic which is unexpected based on her physical description.
- Have students read the scene through omitting the handwritten stage notes. Ask them to describe how this omission could change their understanding of the scene.
  Possible Responses: Mr. Kistunov could be interpreted as being grumpy, and the woman's impact on him is lessened. Also, without the physical action and descriptions provided by the notes, the characters are not as easily visualized.
- Ask students to explain what elements make this scene humorous.
  Possible Responses: The humor in this scene comes from the exaggerated gestures and actions of the characters; the juxtaposition of Mr. Kistunov's nervousness and the woman's loud screaming; the woman's innocence as to the cause of her husband's illness.

Planning Your Scene

If, after reading the Idea Bank, students have difficulty choosing a scene to stage, suggest they try the following:

• Choose a scene in which one of the characters must make a momentous decision, face a challenge, or learn an important life lesson.

• Choose the scene that best reveals, through dialogue or actions, the personalities of the main characters of the play.

Steps for Planning Your Scene

1. Suggest that students could double up on roles and crew tasks if the list of cast and crew members is too large for the group.

2. Suggest that students create a chart listing all the possible tasks involved in the production and listing the names of the volunteers next to each task.

3. Have students think about the effect they want the scene to have on the audience. Encourage them to brainstorm ways to achieve that effect through dialogue, scenery, and text structure.

4. Suggest that when students are making their script notes, they should call for gestures and voices which emphasize what a character thinks and feels.

5. Encourage students to improvise if the props they need are not available. Suggest they incorporate the function of the prop into their actions and dialogue.

Developing Your Stage Presentation

Discuss Have students ask a volunteer from outside the group to read through the script to see if the scene is understandable. Encourage students to pay attention to the volunteer's comments.

IDEABank

1. Your Working Portfolio
Look for ideas in the **Writing Options** that you completed earlier in this unit.
• **Theater Review**, p. 562
• **Sequel to the Play**, p. 562

2. Emotional Impact
Choose the scene that is the most humorous or most dramatic.

3. Special Effects
Choose the scene that will allow you to use the most imaginative props, scenery, lighting, and costumes.

Staging Your Scene

❶ Planning Your Scene

With your classmates, choose a part of the scene from "A Defenseless Creature" to present. First **divide** the scene into parts by looking for changes in action or dialogue. If you start in the middle, you could use a narrator to set the scene. See the **Idea Bank** in the margin for more ideas. After selecting a scene, follow the steps below.

Steps for Planning Your Scene

▶ **1. List all cast and crew members.** List the characters in your scene and all the other roles involved in a stage production:

• director	• prompter	• lighting manager
• prop manager	• sound crew	• set designer
• costumer	• acting coach	

▶ **2. Assign responsibilities.** Do you want group members to try out for acting roles or to volunteer as stage hands? What other tasks need to be assigned?

▶ **3. Decide on an interpretation.** Will you try to recreate the playwright's vision, or do you have your own? Think about presenting the scene as a musical or comedy; or creating unusual costumes or backdrops for a desired effect.

▶ **4. Prepare a director's script.** As a group, mark notes on the script about positions of the actors, their gestures and movements, the tones of their voices for certain lines, the type of scenery required, and the lighting, props, and sound effects.

▶ **5. Locate costumes, props, and other items you will need.** Check out attics, basements, and school resources for costumes and props. The simpler your materials, the more smoothly your staging will go. Think about what you will need to create sound effects or background music.

❷ Developing Your Stage Presentation

Discuss the scene in your group to make sure everyone understands it. Then cast members should read through the scene. They should look up any unfamiliar words and make sure they can pronounce them.

Get interpretations on paper. Crew members should mark their scripts with notes on facial expressions, tones of voice, movements, gestures, and stage positions.

Get everyone involved. Stage personnel should mark their scripts with notes on the lighting, sound, props, scenery, and costume requirements. Try to involve everyone in some phase of the production.

❸ Practicing and Presenting

The entire cast should practice the scene several times before presenting it.

- **Do a read-through.** Have the actors read their parts aloud several times to make sure they can say them with the appropriate expression.
- **Have actors do a walk-through.** Reading from their scripts, actors should perform their movements, gestures, and facial expressions.
- **Add the extras.** Set up the stage, have the actors wear costumes and use props, and try out the lighting and sound.
- **Stage a final rehearsal.** Run through the entire scene without stopping. Ask some people to watch the rehearsal and give feedback. Try videotaping the rehearsal for viewing before the performance.

❹ Refining Your Performance

TARGET SKILL ▶ EVALUATING THE STAGING OF YOUR SCENE After your final rehearsal, think about the decisions you and your classmates made in interpreting your scene. Consider your choices in the following areas:

- **Awareness of audience** Could your audience clearly see all of the action on the stage? Was everyone able to hear the actors?
- **Following the script** Did the actors remember their lines? Did the performance stay true to the playwright's script?
- **Creating mood and character** Do all parts of the performance work together to show the emotions of the characters? Did your staging show the action and drama of the scene?

❺ Reflecting

FOR YOUR WORKING PORTFOLIO What did you learn about staging a scene? How did performing your role in the production help you learn more about the scene? Attach your reflections to your script. Save the script in your **Working Portfolio.**

Practicing TIP

Before rehearsing the entire scene, pair up students who have speaking parts with students who are involved backstage. Have the actors practice with their partners in different parts of the room until they feel confident about their pronunciation, volume, and tone and have started to memorize their lines.

Ask Your Peer Reviewers

- What did you like best about the performance?
- What parts were hard to follow? Why?
- How can the acting and staging be improved?
- What actions and emotions seemed most real to you?

Get Interpretations on Paper Have students keep in mind the effect they want the scene to have in order to keep gestures, actions, and tone consistent.

Get Everyone Involved Suggest that students organize a publicity committee to work on posters and programs.

Practicing and Presenting

Do a read-through Encourage students to change dialogue that sounds stilted or unnatural or that does not advance the action in the scene at all.

Have actors do a walk-through Remind students that gestures and facial expressions need to be big enough to be seen without being overly exaggerated—unless that is the desired effect.

Add the extras Have each cast member check to see if the required props and costumes are ready and complete.

Stage a final rehearsal Remind students that this is their last chance to change the setup of the stage if it is awkward for the actors.

Refining Your Performance

EVALUATING THE STAGING OF YOUR SCENE

Awareness of audience Suggest to students that they ask a volunteer audience to sit in various places during rehearsal to ensure that the entire stage is visible and the dialogue is audible even in the back of the room.

Following the script Have students work with a volunteer coach on ways to remember difficult lines and speeches.

Creating mood and character Ask students to describe the effect they want the scene to have, and ask volunteer audience members if that effect was achieved.

Use **Communications Transparencies and Copymasters,** p. 16, for additional support.

Reflecting

 Suggest that students also comment about what they learned about the art of dramatic presentation in general. Was it more difficult than they thought it would be? What frustrations and rewards did they experience?

Option

Teaching Tip

Use the same checklist for evaluating students that they use themselves. Ideally, this checklist should incorporate the Guidelines and Standards from p. 579 and the standards elaborated under Refining Your Performance on p. 583. For your first review, ask each group to highlight three areas that they want detailed feedback on and focus your comments on these areas.

Ask Your Peer Reader Remind students to use the peer reviewer's feedback when evaluating the staging of their scene.

Assessment Practice

Demonstrate how students can eliminate incorrect choices for the first question.

A. This choice is correct because the subject and verb agree.

B. This choice incorrectly places *was* with a plural subject.

C. In this choice, the use of *or* makes the subject single so the verb form is incorrect.

D. The original sentence is incorrect because the plural subject disagrees with *was*.

Answers:

1. A; **2.** C; **3.** A; **4.** A; **5.** D; **6.** D

Assessment Practice Revising & Editing

Read the following passage from the first draft of a student essay. The underlined sections may include the following kinds of errors:

- **lack of subject-verb agreement**
- **incorrect transitive/ intransitive verbs**
- **misplaced prepositional phrases**
- **spelling errors**

For each underlined section, choose the revision that most improves the writing.

> Six students and a teacher was the leading force behind the school's
> (1)
> spring production, senes from *The Good Doctor* by Neil Simon. Earlier
> (2)
> in the year, the students had asked of the teacher about staging a play.
> (3)
> She was open with enthusiasm to the idea and greeted it. The students
> (4)
> put in a great deal of their time. On opening night, the crowd gave us
> (5)
> two standing ovations. All the effort was worth the success.
> (6)

1. **A.** Six students and a teacher were
   B. A teacher and six students was
   C. Six students or a teacher were
   D. Correct as is

2. **A.** seens
   B. sceens
   C. scenes
   D. Correct as is

3. **A.** asked the teacher
   B. asked to the teacher
   C. sought the teacher
   D. Correct as is

4. **A.** She was open to the idea and greeted it with enthusiasm.
   B. She with enthusiasm was open to the idea and greeted it.
   C. With enthusiasm, she was open to the idea and greeted it.
   D. Correct as is

5. **A.** there
   B. thier
   C. they're
   D. Correct as is

6. **A.** sucess
   B. succes
   C. seccess
   D. Correct as is

Need extra help?

See the **Grammar Handbook**

Prepositional Phrases, p. R72

Quick Reference: Capitalization, p. R58

Quick Reference: Punctuation, p. R56

Sentence Fragments, p. R59

Subject-Verb Agreement, p. R60

Transitive and Intransitive Verbs, p. R84

 Mini Lesson Grammar 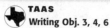 **TEKS** 17D **TAAS** Writing Obj. 3, 4, 6

ADVERBS AND PREDICATE ADJECTIVES

Instruction Before students can decide whether to use an adjective or an adverb, they must first figure out which other word in the sentence is being modified. Display the following examples. This ice cream tastes wonderful. (*Wonderful* is an adjective modifying the noun *ice cream*.) Carlos plays the violin wonderfully. (*Wonderfully* is an adverb modifying the verb *plays*.)

Exercises Have students choose the correct adverb or adjective to complete the sentence and tell what other word it modifies.

1. Roses are very (pretty, prettily). (*pretty; roses*)
2. How did you finish your dessert so (quick, quickly)? (*quickly; finish*)
3. (Slow, Slowly) it vanished. (*Slowly; vanished*)
4. That shirt looks (good, well) on you. (*good; shirt*)

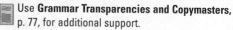 Use **Grammar Transparencies and Copymasters,** p. 77, for additional support.

 Use McDougal Littell's *Language Network,* Chapter 5, for more instruction and practice in adverbs and predicate adjectives.

Reflecting on the Theme Did you ever learn something about a person that made you see him or her in a different light? Perhaps you didn't like someone and then you became good friends. Or perhaps you resisted a certain task, only to enjoy it later. Changes like these are called changes of heart.

ACTIVITY

Write a public-service announcement that encourages students to make positive changes, such as learning a new skill; getting involved in sports, the school band, or other activities; or doing volunteer work. Create a chart to go with your announcement which lists the advantages of different activities.

Positive Changes	
Activities	Advantages

Objectives
- understand and identify the following literary terms:
  - character development
  - major characters
  - minor characters
  - dynamic characters
  - static characters
  - traits
  - characterization
- analyze characters, including their traits, motivations, conflicts, points of view, relationships, changes they undergo

Teaching the Lesson

This lesson helps students understand and appreciate the importance of characters and character development in the literature they read.

Introducing the Concepts

Ask students to think about a movie they have recently seen or a book they have recently read that contained a character that was especially memorable. Have them discuss what made this character special, including personality traits, actions, language, or appearance.

 Use **Literary Analysis Transparencies,** pp. 2–4, for additional support.

Character Development

I have discovered I cannot dream up characters as incredible as the ones I meet in the wilderness.
—Jean Craighead George

Your favorite character in a movie may be a lonesome wolf or a talking snake. Maybe it's a courageous young person about your age. Think about how you learned about this character. How is his or her personality revealed? What about likes and dislikes? Does your character take charge of a scene or remain in the background? By the end of the movie, has your character changed or remained the same?

Character development helps readers recognize which characters in a work are the most important. In literature, just as in movies, **major characters** are the ones who play a large role, while **minor characters** play a small one. Often, main characters undergo changes as the plot unfolds. Such characters are called **dynamic characters**. **Static characters** remain the same throughout the story. Writers help readers learn about characters by emphasizing their **traits,** or qualities. The process by which these traits are revealed is called **characterization.**

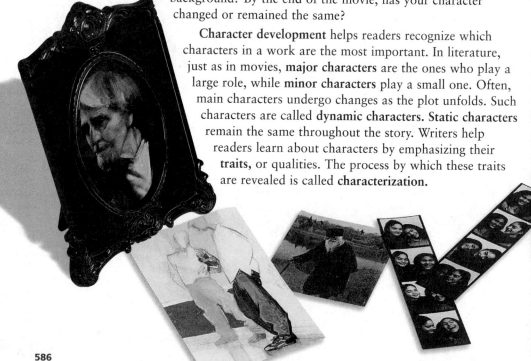

586

 See the Skills Trace at the beginning of the unit for information on TEKS covered in this lesson.

Characterization

Character development is a process by which a writer reveals a character's traits, or qualities. There are four main methods writers use: A writer may describe how a character looks; how a character thinks, speaks, and acts; or what others say or think about the character. The author may also comment directly on the character's behavior or personality. Read below to learn more about the four ways characters are revealed.

- **The Character's Appearance** A person's appearance, or looks, conveys something about what kind of person he or she is. You can form an idea of what a fictional character is like by carefully reading descriptions of the character's face, clothing, and even how the character stands or moves.

- **The Character's Thoughts, Speech, and Actions** What a character thinks, says, and does tells a lot about the kind of person he or she is. The reader can get to know a character far more deeply when the writer reveals the character's thoughts. Notice also the words a character uses in a story. A character who uses simple vocabulary might behave differently than a character who uses very long words.

YOUR TURN Read the excerpt from Shirley Jackson's "One Ordinary Day, with Peanuts." What do Mr. Johnson's actions tell about him?

CHARACTER'S THOUGHTS, SPEECH, AND ACTIONS

When he had gone several blocks uptown, Mr. Johnson cut across the avenue and went along a side street, chosen at random; he did not follow the same route every morning, but preferred to pursue his eventful way in wide detours, more like a puppy than a man intent upon business. . . . Halfway down the block . . . a harassed woman, trying to watch a young child and the movers and the furniture all at the same time, gave the clear impression of endeavoring to shelter her private life from the people staring at her belongings. Mr. Johnson stopped, and for a moment joined the crowd, then he came forward and, touching his hat civilly, said, "Perhaps I can keep an eye on your little boy for you?"

—Shirley Jackson,
"One Ordinary Day, with Peanuts"

From "One Ordinary Day, with Peanuts"

Presenting the Concepts Characterization

Have students to look back over some of the stories they have previously read as a class. Ask them to find an example of a vivid description of a character's appearance and an example of a character being revealed through thoughts, dialogue, or action. Ask them to explain how they visualize the characters they selected and discuss their views as a class.

YOUR TURN
Possible Response: His actions show that he seems to be kind, generous, and observant.

Have students think back over stories they have previously read as a class. Ask them to think of examples of a character being revealed to the reader through the conversations of other characters. How does this affect the reader's perception of that character? Ask them also to discuss what it reveals about the characters doing the talking.

YOUR TURN
Possible Response: He is skilled and efficient at his work.

• **What Others Say about the Character** As in real life, people in fiction talk about each other. When you are reading, notice what characters say about other characters. This will give you another perspective. For example, you might form one impression of a character based on his own thoughts. Then you might read what another character says about him and change your opinion. Note that the narrator of a story sometimes speaks directly about characters.

• **Direct Statements Made by the Writer about the Character** Often in literature, the narrator will make direct comments about a character. The narrator may report that a character is fearful, brave, generous, or stingy. The narrator may also comment on a character's motivations, behavior toward others, or secret longings.

YOUR TURN Read the excerpt on the right. What do Ben Price's words tell you about Jim Valentine?

WHAT OTHERS SAY ABOUT THE CHARACTER

"That's Dandy Jim Valentine's autograph. He's resumed business. Look at that combination knob–jerked out as easy as pulling up a radish in wet weather. He's got the only clamps that can do it. And look how clean those tumblers were punched out! Jimmy never has to drill but one hole. Yes, I guess I want Mr. Valentine. He'll do his bit next time without any short-time or clemency foolishness."

—O. Henry, "A Retrieved Reformation"

From "A Retrieved Reformation"

Dynamic and Static Characters

Think about a time in your life that changed you. Something happened, and as a result you were never the same. This is also true of characters in literature. Often, one or more of a story's main characters change as a result of the events or conflict in the story. A character might grow emotionally, learn a lesson, or change his or her behavior. Such a character is called a dynamic character. A static character, on the other hand, is one who doesn't change.

YOUR TURN In the model passage, do you think Henrietta is a dynamic or a static character? How do you know?

DYNAMIC AND STATIC CHARACTERS

Every once in a while I'd try to figure out what the thing was that made her so different now; and then one day, all of a sudden, I understood. . . . Everything else was the same—the drab white skin; the bony, yes, bony hands; the limp hair. But she had lost her waiting look. Henrietta didn't look as though she were waiting for anything at all anymore.

—Budge Wilson, "Waiting"

From "Waiting"

Dynamic and Static Characters

Ask students to think about a movie they have recently seen or a book they have recently read in which one of the characters underwent a dramatic change. Ask students to describe the character before and after the change occurred and to explain why this character changed. Have them consider how the work would have differed if the character had not changed.

YOUR TURN

Possible Response: Henrietta is a dynamic character because she changes from a girl who looked as though she was always waiting for something to a girl who no longer had that look.

Objectives
- develop effective strategies for drawing conclusions
- draw inferences such as conclusions and support them with text evidence and experience

The strategies on this page will help students understand and apply the skill of drawing conclusions about character, plot, and theme in the literature they read.

Presenting the Strategies

Make sure students understand how to draw a conclusion by using an example from their everyday life or setting up a hypothetical problem from which they can gather information and then draw a conclusion.

Next, help students understand the strategies by asking for volunteers to read them aloud. Emphasize to students that they will be using these strategies as they read the selections in this book.

- Choose a selection from this unit to read. Have the students read through the story silently. Ask them to note the facts and details in the story that describe the main character.

- Divide the class into small groups. Have each group discuss how they view the main character in the story based on their own experiences and discuss how their views relate to the information they've gathered from the story.

- Ask each group to draw conclusions about the main character of the story.

- Ask for a volunteer from each group to share their conclusions and to explain how they arrived at them.

Use **Reading and Critical Thinking Transparencies**, p. 9, for additional support.

Try It Now!

Possible Responses: Facts: He wanted to be a teacher. He always enjoyed books. He used to pay his rent in labor and grow his own vegetables.
Conclusions: This person is a hard worker and has a strong sense of purpose.

If you hear sirens outside your window and notice that smoke is coming from the building across the street, you might reasonably conclude that the building is on fire. You might draw conclusions by combining facts with your own knowledge and experience. An active reader can draw conclusions about a character's motives, or the events or theme of a story. As you read, use the strategies on this page to help you draw conclusions.

Drawing Conclusions

How to Apply the Skill

To **DRAW CONCLUSIONS**, an active reader will:
- Look for facts and details
- Make logical inferences
- **Evaluate** information
- **Connect** to his or her own experience and knowledge
- Use a chart like this one to help draw conclusions

Try It Now!

Read and draw conclusions from the excerpt below.

> I always wanted to be a writer and a teacher. With my heart and my soul I knew that I wanted to be around books all my life. . . . For four years I boarded with a couple [my mother] knew. I paid my rent in labor, and I ate vegetables I grew myself.
>
> —Judith Ortiz Cofer, "An Hour with Abuelo"

Character (or setting or plot)	Inferences	Stated Facts
Conclusions:		

Here's how Rafael uses the skill:

"As I read the facts and details about Arturo's grandfather, I understand his hardships. I can logically guess that Arturo's grandfather was a very motivated person. I **evaluate** this information and conclude that he was very intelligent because he graduated first in his class."

Need More Help?

Remember that active readers use the essential reading strategies explained on page 4: • **visualize** • **predict** • **clarify** • **question** • **connect** • **evaluate** • **monitor.**

An Hour with Abuelo

Short Story by JUDITH ORTIZ COFER

Así es la vida.'
hat's the way
fe is."

TEKS

See the Skills Trace at the beginning of the unit for information
on TEKS covered in this lesson.

Connect to Your Life

Do you know an elderly person, such as a grandparent, who likes to talk about life in the "old days"? With a classmate discuss why a very old person might want to tell a young person about his or her life. What might a young person get out of hearing the stories?

Build Background

CONNECT TO HISTORY In the story you are about o read, the narrator's grandfather talks about eing drafted into the U.S. Army while he was a oung man in Puerto Rico. Puerto Rico, an island bout 1,000 miles southeast of Florida, is a self-overning commonwealth associated with the Jnited States. The island was settled by Span-ards beginning in 1508 and remained under panish control for nearly four centuries. Puerto Rico has developed a rich culture with Spanish, African, and Native American aspects.

At the end of the Spanish-American War, in 898, Puerto Rico became a possession of the Jnited States. In 1917 Puerto Ricans were granted U.S. citizenship. Thousands of Puerto Ricans have served in the U.S. armed forces since World War I. On July 25, 1952, Puerto Rico became a largely self-governing commonwealth where both Spanish and English are official anguages.

WORDS TO KNOW **Vocabulary Preview**

ammunition	orderly	suite
embroidered	parchment	

Focus Your Reading

LITERARY ANALYSIS **FIRST-PERSON NARRATOR**
In a story told from a first-person point of view, the **narrator**—the teller of the story—is also a character. As the narrator tells the story, the words and phrases he or she uses are clues to his or her character. "An Hour with Abuelo" is told by Arturo, a teenager who is the main character. As you read, try to form an idea of Arturo's character as it is revealed by what he says and how he says it.

ACTIVE READING **DRAWING CONCLUSIONS** Active readers often need to **draw conclusions** about aspects of the works they read. To draw conclusions, combine information from what you have read and heard with firsthand knowledge you have gathered from your own experience.

READER'S NOTEBOOK As you read the selection, write down clues you find in the story and combine them with what you know from your own experience to draw conclusions about Arturo and his grandfather.

Clue	My Experience	Conclusion
Arturo keeps a stack of books beside his bed to study for AP English.	To read on your own means you are motivated.	Arturo is a motivated student.

AN HOUR WITH ABUELO **591**

LESSON RESOURCES

UNIT FOUR RESOURCE BOOK,
pp. 34–40

ASSESSMENT
Formal Assessment,
pp. 99–100
Teacher's Guide to Assessment and Portfolio Use
Test Generator

SKILLS TRANSPARENCIES AND COPYMASTERS
Literary Analysis
• Narrator and Point of View, TR 22 (for Paired Activity, p. 598)

Reading and Critical Thinking
• Drawing Conclusions, TR 9 (for Thinking Through the Literature, p. 598)
Grammar
• Predicate Adjectives, CM 76 (for Mini Lesson, p. 594)
• Identifying Appositives, CM 107 (for Mini Lesson, p. 600)
Vocabulary
• Related Words, CM 65 (for Mini Lesson, p. 592)
• Antonyms, CM 66 (for Mini Lesson, pp. 597)

INTEGRATED TECHNOLOGY
Audio Library

Internet: Research Starter

Visit our website:
www.mcdougallittell.com

This selection appears in Spanish in the **Spanish Study Guide**.

Objectives
1. understand and appreciate a **short story (Literary Analysis)**
2. understand characterization through **first-person point of view (Literary Analysis)**
3. utilize the reading skill **drawing conclusions (Active Reading)**

Summary
Teenaged Arturo wants to spend his summer vacation having fun and prepar-ing for the upcoming school year. His mother, however, would like him to spend more time with his aging *abuelo*, or grandfather, who is in a nursing home. To Arturo, the nursing home is an uncomfortable place. He has visited it only on holidays with a crowd of other relatives. Nonetheless, Arturo decides to honor his mother's wish. As he steps out of the car at the nursing home, he makes his mother promise to return for him in exactly one hour—no later. Although Arturo begins the visit by looking at his watch and counting the minutes until he can leave, his attitude soon changes. Arturo walks not into a stale hospital room, but into the interesting world of a man who has lived an admirable life, and who shares Arturo's interest in read-ing and writing. When his time is up, Arturo is not as anxious to leave his grandfather as he thought he would be.

Thematic Link
During a visit he had been dreading, Arturo connects with his grandfather and begins to see the elderly man in a new light.

5-Minute Warm-Up

Daily Language SkillBuilder   TEKS 17A, 17B

Have students **proofread** the display sentences on page 517j and write them correctly. The sentences also appear on Transparency 18 of **Grammar Transparencies and Copymasters.**

Mini Lesson **Preteaching Vocabulary**

If you would like to preteach the WORDS TO KNOW for this selection, use the Mini Lesson, p. 592.

AN HOUR WITH ABUELO **591**

PREVIEW

Tell students that this story is about a teenaged boy's visit with his grandfather. Have them think about what is both rewarding and challenging about spending time with family members who are much older than they are. Then ask them to review the pictures and call-out text and guess what the visit will be like.

ACTIVE READING

 MAKE INFERENCES He would rather read than play games.

Literary Analysis

FIRST-PERSON NARRATOR

 Encourage students to notice details that allow them to understand Arturo as they read. Ask them to describe Arturo's attitude toward visiting the nursing home.

Possible Response: He feels it is a waste of his time.

📋 Use **Unit Four Resource Book**, p. 36 for more practice.

Active Reading

DRAWING CONCLUSIONS

As they read, students should draw conclusions and support them with text evidence and experience. Ask students what conclusions they can draw about Arturo's character, based on details in the selection.

Possible Response: He is stubborn, determined, and a bit self-centered.

📋 Use **Unit Four Resource Book**, p. 35 for more practice.

AN HOUR with *Abuelo*

BY JUDITH ORTIZ COFER

Painting by Jan Wahlin.

"Just one hour, *una hora,*[1] is all I'm asking of you, son." My grandfather is in a nursing home in Brooklyn, and my mother wants me to spend some time with him, since the doctors say that he doesn't have too long to go now. *I don't have much time left of my summer vacation, and there's a stack of books next to my bed I've got to read if I'm going to get into the AP English class I want. I'm going stupid in some of my classes, and Mr. Williams, the principal at Central, said that if I passed some reading tests, he'd let me move up.*

Besides, I hate the place, the old people's home, especially the way it smells like industrial-strength ammonia and other stuff I won't mention, since it turns my stomach. And really the abuelo[2] always has a lot of relatives visiting him, so I've gotten out of going out there except at Christmas, when a whole vanload of grandchildren are herded over there

1

2

to give him gifts and a hug. We all make it quick and spend the rest of the time in the recreation area, where they play checkers and stuff with some of the old people's games, and I catch up on back issues of *Modern Maturity.*[3] I'm not picky, I'll read almost anything.

Anyway, after my mother nags me for about a week, I let her drive me to Golden Years. She drops me off in front. She wants me to go in alone and have a "good time" talking to Abuelo. I tell her to be back in one hour or I'll take the bus back to Paterson. She squeezes

ACTIVE READING

MAKE INFERENCES How is the narrator different from his cousins?

---

1. *una hora* (ōō′nä ō′rä) *Spanish.*
2. **abuelo** (ä-bwĕ′lō): the Spanish word for grandfather.
3. *Modern Maturity:* a magazine for retired people.

Teaching Options

Mini Lesson **Preteaching Vocabulary** TEKS 6A TAAS Reading Obj. 1

RELATED WORDS

Instruction Explain to students that they can sometimes figure out the meaning of a word by looking at words related in meaning that surround it. Have students review the list of WORDS TO KNOW and think about the meaning of each word.

Exercise Have students fill in each blank below with the word from the list of WORDS TO KNOW that is most closely related in meaning.

1. aide, attendant, helper ——— (orderly)
2. paper, notebook, tablet ——— (parchment)
3. decorated, designed, garnished ——— (embroidered)
4. rooms, home, office ——— (suite)
5. weapons, arms, missiles ——— (ammunition)

📋 Use **Unit Four Resource Book**, p. 37 for more practice. Use **Vocabulary Transparencies and Copymasters**, p. 65, for additional support.

I was named after him.

my hand and says, *"Gracias, hijo,"*[4] in a choked-up voice like I'm doing her a big favor.

I get depressed the minute I walk into the place. They line up the old people in wheelchairs in the hallway as if they were about to be raced to the finish line by <u>orderlies</u> who don't even look at them when they push them here and there. I walk fast to room 10, Abuelo's "<u>suite</u>." He is sitting up in his bed writing with a pencil in one of those old-fashioned black hardback notebooks. It has the outline of the island of Puerto Rico on it. I slide into the hard vinyl chair by his bed. He sort of smiles and the lines on his face get deeper, but he doesn't say anything. Since I'm supposed to talk to him, I say, "What are you doing, Abuelo, writing the story of your life?"

It's supposed to be a joke, but he answers, *"Sí,*[5] how did you know, Arturo?"

His name is Arturo too. I was named after him. I don't really know my grandfather. His children, including my mother, came to New York and New Jersey (where I was born) and he stayed on the Island until my grandmother died. Then he got sick, and since nobody could leave their jobs to go take care of him, they brought him to this nursing home in Brooklyn. I see him a couple of times a year, but he's always surrounded by his sons and daughters. My mother tells me that Don[6] Arturo had once been a teacher back in Puerto Rico, but had lost his job after the war. Then he became a farmer. She's always saying in a sad voice, "Ay, bendito![7] What a waste of a fine mind." Then she usually shrugs her shoulders and says, *"Así*

es la vida."[8] That's the way life is. It sometimes makes me mad that the adults I know just accept whatever is thrown at them because "that's the way things are." Not for me. I go after what I want.

Anyway, Abuelo is looking at me like he was trying to see into my head, but he doesn't say anything. Since I like stories, I decide I may as well ask him if he'll read me what he wrote.

I look at my watch: I've already used up twenty minutes of the hour I promised my mother.

Abuelo starts talking in his slow way. He speaks what my mother calls book English. He taught himself from a dictionary, and his words sound stiff, like he's sounding them out in his head before he says them. With his children he speaks Spanish, and that funny book English with us grandchildren. I'm surprised that he's still so sharp, because his body is shrinking like a crumpled-up brown paper sack with some bones in it. But I can see from looking into his eyes that the light is still on in there.

"It is a short story, Arturo. The story of my life. It will not take very much time to read it."

"I have time, Abuelo." I'm a little embarrassed that he saw me looking at my watch.

"Yes, hijo. You have spoken the truth. La verdad. You have much time."

---

4. *Gracias, hijo* (grä′syäs ē′hō) *Spanish:* Thank you, son.

5. **sí** (sē) *Spanish:* yes.

6. **Don:** a Spanish title of respect, used before a man's name.

7. **Ay, bendito!** (ī běn-dē′tō) *Spanish:* Oh, goodness!

8. *Así es la vida* (ä-sē′ ěs lä vē′dä) *Spanish.*

WORDS TO KNOW

orderly (ôr′dər-lē) *n.* an attendant who performs nonmedical tasks in a hospital or similar institution
suite (swēt) *n.* a group of rooms used as a unit

593

Customizing Instruction

Less Proficient Readers
Ask students to stop reading just before Arturo enters the nursing home. During this pause, have them think about how Arturo feels about visiting his grandfather at this point in the story.

Set a Purpose Have students read to find out what young Arturo learns about his grandfather during their visit.

Students Acquiring English
This selection contains some Spanish words and phrases. Spanish-speaking students might instruct others on proper pronunciation.

1 Explain to students that AP English is Advanced Placement English—a more challenging English class that some high school students take, sometimes for college credit.

2 Guide students as they try to understand the following informal slang phrases: *I'm going stupid, turns my stomach,* and *gotten out of.*

Use **Spanish Study Guide,** pp. 121–123 for additional support.

Gifted and Talented
Remind students that this story is told mainly from the point of view of Arturo. Ask students to imagine the story being told from Abuelo's point of view. Invite them to rewrite the scene in which Arturo walks into the room, greets his grandfather, and looks at his watch. How do students think the grandfather views his grandson? How do they think he feels about the nursing home, or about the moment when he sees his grandson look at his watch?

BLOCK SCHEDULING: MANAGING TIME

If your schedule requires that you cover the lesson objectives in a shorter time, use . . .
- Preparing to Read, p. 591
- Thinking Through the Literature, p. 598
- Vocabulary and Spelling, p. 599
- Grammar in Context, p. 600

If you want to take advantage of longer class time, use . . .
- TE Teaching Options: Preteaching Vocabulary, p. 592; Grammar, pp. 594, 600; Viewing and Representing, p. 595; Informal Assessment, p. 596; Vocabulary Strategy, p. 597; Spelling, p. 599
- Choices & Challenges, pp. 599–600

Active Reading

DRAWING CONCLUSIONS

Have students draw conclusions about the character of Abuelo, based on details presented about his youth. How is Abuelo like his grandson?

Possible Response: Like his grandson, he is strong-willed and determined. Also like his grandson, he has an interest in reading and writing.

ACTIVE READING

A CLARIFY He loves books and learning as much as his grandson does.

Literary Analysis

FIRST-PERSON NARRATOR

B Point out to students that during this part of the story, readers get Abuelo's unique perspective. Ask them why teaching was so important to him. Then ask them what Arturo might learn from Abuelo's example.

Possible Response: Teaching was important to him because it was a way to help others. Arturo might learn to think of others, not just himself.

Reading Skills and Strategies:
EVALUATE

Encourage students to think about why the author chooses to present Abuelo's actual speech, rather than have Arturo explain what his grandfather says. Do they believe this is a good technique? Why, or why not?

Possible Responses: Students might say that this technique gives them a better sense of Abuelo. They, like Arturo, can see the grandfather as a well-rounded individual.

Abuelo reads: "'I loved words from the beginning of my life. In the *campo*[9] where I was born one of seven sons, there were few books. My mother read them to us over and over: the Bible, the stories of Spanish conquistadors and of pirates that she had read as a child and brought with her from the city of Mayagüez;[10] that was before she married my father, a coffee bean farmer; and she taught us words from the newspaper that a boy on a horse brought every week to her. She taught each of us how to write on a slate with chalks that she ordered by mail every year. We used those chalks until they were so small that you lost them between your fingers.

"'I always wanted to be a writer and a teacher. With my heart and my soul I knew that I wanted to be around books all of my life. And so against the wishes of my father, who wanted all his sons to help him on the land, she sent me to high school in Mayagüez. For four years I boarded with a couple she knew. I paid my rent in labor, and I ate vegetables I grew myself. I wore my clothes until they were thin as <u>parchment</u>. But I graduated at the top of my class! My whole family came to see me that day. My mother brought me a beautiful *guayabera*,[11] a white shirt made of the finest cotton and <u>embroidered</u> by her own hands. I was a happy young man.

"'In those days you could teach in a country school with a high school diploma. So I went back to my mountain village and got a job teaching all grades in a little classroom built by the parents of my students.

ACTIVE READING

A **CLARIFY** How does Arturo's grandfather feel about books and learning?

"'I had books sent to me by the government. I felt like a rich man although the pay was very small. I had books. All the books I wanted! I taught my students how to read poetry and plays, and how to write them. We made up songs and put on shows for the parents. It was a beautiful time for me.

"'Then the war came, and the American President said that all Puerto Rican men would be drafted. I wrote to our governor and explained that I was the only teacher in the mountain village. I told him that the children would go back to the fields and grow up ignorant if I could not teach them their letters. I said that I thought I was a better teacher than a soldier. The governor did not answer my letter. I went into the U.S. Army.

"'I told my sergeant that I could be a teacher in the army. I could teach all the farm boys their letters so that they could read the instructions on the <u>ammunition</u> boxes and not blow themselves up. The sergeant said I was too smart for my own good, and gave me a job cleaning latrines. He said to me there is reading material for you there, scholar. Read the writing on the walls. I spent the war mopping floors and cleaning toilets.

"'When I came back to the Island, things had changed. You had to have a college degree to teach school, even the lower grades. My parents were sick, two of my brothers had been killed in the war, the others had stayed in Nueva York. I was the only one left to help the old people. I became a farmer. I married a

---

9. ***campo*** (käm′pō) *Spanish:* countryside.
10. **Mayagüez** (mĭ′ə-gwĕz′): a port city on the western coast of Puerto Rico.
11. ***guayabera*** (gwä-yä-bā′rä) *Spanish.*

WORDS TO KNOW	**parchment** (pärch′mənt) *n.* a paperlike writing material made from the skins of sheep or goats	
	embroidered (ĕm-broi′dərd) *adj.* ornamented with stitched designs **embroider** *v.*	
	ammunition (ăm′yə-nĭsh′ən) *n.* the explosive cartridges or shells designed to be used in guns	

594

Teaching Options

 Mini Lesson **Grammar** **TEKS 17C** **TAAS Writing Obj. 6**

PREDICATE ADJECTIVES

Instruction Explain to students that a predicate adjective is an adjective that follows a linking verb. It describes the subject of the sentence. Common linking verbs are *be, look, appear, seem, become, remain, feel, sound, taste, grow,* and *smell.*
Display the following examples:
<u>Abuelo</u> looks *tired.* <u>Arturo</u> is *smart.*
The <u>nursing home</u> was *warm* and *quiet.*
Point out that *tired* modifies *Abuelo, smart* modifies *Arturo,* and *warm* and *quiet* both modify *nursing home.*

Exercises In the following sentences, have students underline the predicate adjectives and the words they modify.

1. <u>Grandfather</u> seems <u>content.</u>
2. <u>Children</u> in the family grow <u>restless.</u>
3. After looking at his watch, <u>Arturo</u> feels <u>guilty.</u>
4. His life <u>story</u> is <u>long</u> and <u>interesting.</u>

 Use **Grammar Transparencies and Copymasters,** p. 76.

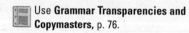 Use McDougal Littell's *Language Network,* Chapter 5, for more instruction and practice in predicate adjectives.

I loved words from the beginning of my life.

Letters (1992), Kim English. Oil, 17″ × 18″. Private Collection.

Less Proficient Readers
Give students the following questions to guide their reading:
- What have been Abuelo's strong interests throughout his life?
  Answer: Reading, writing, and teaching.
- Why was graduating from high school an especially extraordinary achievement for Abuelo?
  Answer: His father wanted him to stay on the farm; he was quite poor and had to work and grow his own food as he attended school.
- Why was Abuelo forced to stop teaching? How did he feel about being forced to stop?
  Answer: He was called to war; he felt terrible about no longer teaching.

Set a Purpose Have students read to learn Arturo's reaction to his grandfather's life story.

Students Acquiring English
1 Tell students that a slate is a small chalkboard that students would use like a notebook.
2 Explain that *latrine* is another word for a bathroom or toilet. Help them to understand the sarcasm in the sergeant's words.

Multiple Learning Styles
Visual Learners
Students who are visual learners might want to map out the major events of Abuelo's life in a kind of timeline.

 Viewing and Representing 📖 TEKS 22A

Letters (1992)
by Kim English

ART APPRECIATION Tell students that artists, just like writers, use small details to build ideas and create characters. Explain that when looking at a painting, they should not only see the piece as a whole but also focus in on small details.
Instruction Encourage students to look closely at the painting on this page. How would they describe the mood, or feeling, of the room? What details give the room a distant mood?
Possible Responses: Students might say the dark shadows, the single bright light, and the rustic-looking floors and furniture give the room a quiet, lonely, or cozy mood.
Have students study the figure in the painting. What ideas do they have about this person?
Possible Responses The person lives alone, has friends far away, is a loner.
Application: How might this painting relate to the story?
Possible Response It focuses on the act of writing, an action important to both Arturo and his grandfather.

Literary Analysis

FIRST-PERSON NARRATOR

A Ask students what Arturo is observing about Abuelo when he says "Maybe he's forgotten that I'm there."

Possible Response: Abuelo seems lost in his own thoughts.

B Have students explain Arturo's first reaction to Abuelo's story.

Possible Response: He is more determined than ever not to let anyone interfere with his dreams.

Reading Skills and Strategies:
EVALUATE

C Encourage students to read to appreciate the writer's craft. For example, ask students why the author includes Mrs. Pink Running Shoes. What does she add to the story?

Possible Response: Students might say she adds some humor and helps readers to see Abuelo as someone who has fun and interesting friends.

Literary Analysis

FIRST-PERSON NARRATOR

D Ask students why Arturo finds the fact that Abuelo has been timing him humorous?

Possible Response: He realizes that Abuelo has his own life and is more on top of things than he originally thought.

ACTIVE READING

E **DRAW CONCLUSIONS** The idea of visiting his grandfather might seem more interesting or important now.

The Yellow Books (1887), Vincent Van Gogh. Oil on canvas, 73 cm × 93 cm. Private Collection, Switzerland/Giraudon, Paris/SuperStock.

good woman who gave me many good children. I taught them all how to read and write before they started school.'"

Abuelo then puts the notebook down on his lap and closes his eyes.

A "*Así es la vida* is the title of my book," he says in a whisper, almost to himself. Maybe he's forgotten that I'm there.

For a long time he doesn't say anything else. I think that he's sleeping, but then I see that he's watching me through half-closed lids, maybe waiting for my opinion of his writing. I'm trying to think of something nice to say. I liked it and all, but not the title. And I think that he could've been a teacher if he had wanted to bad enough. Nobody is going to stop me from doing what I want with my life. I'm not going to let la vida get in my way. I want to discuss this with him, but the words are not coming into my head in Spanish just yet. I'm about to ask him why he didn't keep fighting to make his dream come true, when an old lady in hot-pink running shoes sort of appears at the door.

She is wearing a pink jogging outfit too. The world's oldest marathoner, I say to myself. She calls out to my grandfather in a flirty voice, "Yoo-hoo, Arturo, remember what day this is? It's poetry-reading day in the rec room! You promised us you'd read your new one today."

B

1

2

C

3

I see my abuelo perking up almost immediately. He points to his wheelchair, which is hanging like a huge metal bat in the open closet. He makes it obvious that he wants me to get it. I put it together, and with Mrs. Pink Running Shoes's help, we get him in it. Then he says in a strong deep voice I hardly recognize, "Arturo, get that notebook from the table, please."

I hand him another map-of-the-Island notebook—this one is red. On it in big letters it says, *POEMAS DE ARTURO.*[12]

I start to push him toward the rec room, but he shakes his finger at me.

"Arturo, look at your watch now. I believe your time is over." He gives me a wicked smile.

Then with her pushing the wheelchair—maybe a little too fast—they roll down the hall. He is already reading from his notebook, and she's making bird noises. I look at my watch and the hour is up, to the minute. I can't help but think that my abuelo has been timing me. It cracks me up. I walk slowly down the hall toward the exit sign. I want my mother to have to wait a little. I don't want her to think that I'm in a hurry or anything. ❖

ACTIVE READING

DRAW CONCLUSIONS
How do you think Arturo feels about visiting his grandfather now?

E

---

12. *POEMAS DE ARTURO* (pō-ä′mäs dā är-tōō′rō) *Spanish:* Arturo's poems.

Teaching Options

✓ **Assessment** **Informal Assessment** **TEKS** 10H, 15C   **TAAS** Writing Obj. 1

DRAWING CONCLUSIONS You can informally assess students' understanding of the selection by having them draw conclusions about the importance of young Arturo's hour with Abuelo. Have them imagine that Arturo goes home and writes a paragraph about the significance of his hour with Abuelo. Ask them to describe what he learned from the experience.

RUBRIC

3 **Full Accomplishment** Response shows a complete understanding of Arturo, his relationship with his grandfather, and the significance of their meeting.

2 **Substantial Accomplishment** Response shows a decent but perhaps not complete understanding of Arturo and Arturo's experience.

1 **Little or Partial Accomplishment** Response shows little understanding of Arturo and Arturo's experience.

THE OLD GRANDFATHER AND HIS LITTLE GRANDSON

by LEO TOLSTOY

Hermit (1888), Mikhail Vasilievich Nesterov. Oil on canvas, 91 cm × 84 cm. The State Russian Museum, St. Petersburg, Russia.

The grandfather had become very old. His legs would not carry him, his eyes could not see, his ears could not hear, and he was toothless. When he ate, bits of food sometimes dropped out of his mouth. His son and his son's wife no longer allowed him to eat with them at the table. He had to eat his meals in the corner near the stove.

One day they gave him his food in a bowl. He tried to move the bowl closer; it fell to the floor and broke. His daughter-in-law scolded him. She told him that he spoiled everything in the house and broke their dishes, and she said that from now on he would get his food in a wooden dish. The old man sighed and said nothing.

A few days later, the old man's son and his wife were sitting in their hut, resting and watching their little boy playing on the floor. They saw him putting together something out of small pieces of wood. His father asked him, "What are you making, Misha?"

The little grandson said, "I'm making a wooden bucket. When you and Mamma get old, I'll feed you out of this wooden dish."

The young peasant and his wife looked at each other, and tears filled their eyes. They were ashamed because they had treated the old grandfather so meanly, and from that day they again let the old man eat with them at the table and took better care of him. ❖

Customizing Instruction

Students Acquiring English

1 Explain that hot pink is a very bright shade of pink.

2 Tell students that a "flirty voice" is a teasing voice. You might have another student demonstrate this tone.

3 Inform students that a rec room is a recreation room, where people relax, play games, and talk.

4 Explain that "It cracks me up" means "It makes me laugh" or "It strikes me as funny."

Less Proficient Readers

5 Discuss with students why Arturo does not want his mother to think he is in a hurry.

Possible Response: He has found that he likes and respects his grandfather.

LITERARY LINK

Use the following questions to help students analyze and understand the story.

1. How do the man and his wife treat the grandfather?
   Answer: They treat him with cruelty and coldness.
2. What suddenly forces the man and his wife to put themselves in the grandfather's shoes?
   Answer: the little boy's actions

Leo Tolstoy

Tolstoy (1828–1910) is one of the most famous of Russian writers, known for such classics as *War and Peace* and *Anna Karenina.* He was born into a wealthy family, but later in his life he gave away his worldly possessions and tried to live a simple, moral life as a peasant.

Mini Lesson **Vocabulary Strategy** **TEKS** 9B, 9C   **TAAS** Reading Obj. 1

ANTONYMS

Instruction Remind students that antonyms are words that are opposite in meaning. Tell them that some vocabulary tests will ask them to identify antonyms. Tell them that some reference books feature antonyms.

Application Have students imagine they are creating their own book of antonyms that other students can use as a reference source. Have them work in pairs to think of antonyms for the following common words.

1. dread (*calmness, confidence*)
2. boring (*exciting, interesting*)
3. love (*hate, dislike*)
4. thoughtful (*thoughtless, selfish*)
5. brave (*cowardly, fearful*)
6. enormous (*small, tiny*)
7. kind (*mean, nasty*)
8. compliment (*criticism, punishment*)
9. mild (*severe, strong*)
10. old (*young, new*)

Use **Vocabulary Transparencies and Copymasters,** p. 66.

Connect to the Literature

1. What Do You Think?
Accept all reasonable responses.

Comprehension Check
• He has visited at Christmas.
• He always wanted to be a writer and a teacher.
• "Arturo, look at your watch now. I believe your time is over."

 Use Selection Quiz **Unit Four Resource Book,** p. 40.

Think Critically

2. Possible Response: Arturo finds the nursing home depressing and is more interested in reading for the AP English class he wants to get into. He sees this initiative as being different from the attitude of most adults, an attitude best expressed by a saying of his mother—*Asi es la vida* (That's the way life is). He learns that his grandfather is not someone who has let life defeat him.

3. Ask students to share responses.

 Use **Reading and Critical Thinking Transparencies,** p. 9, for additional support.

4. Possible Response: Abuelo would undoubtedly have made a fine teacher—he is patient, interesting, and a keen observer of young people. But his mind has by no means gone to waste. He is still a writer and a teacher to Arturo.

5. Possible Response: Initially, it is a potential barrier. Arturo wants to get into an AP English class and views a visit with his grandfather as time when he could be preparing for reading tests. But Arturo's attitude is the basis for a bond with Abuelo, who, despite some setbacks, has gone after his goal of being a writer.

6. Possible Response: Arturo says that he felt like his grandfather was "trying to see into my head" and deepen their relationship. The boy discovers how much he shares with his grandfather.

Literary Analysis

First-Person Narrator Students might notice that the two share a keen sense of observation. The grandson observes his grandfather "shrinking like a crumpled-up brown paper sack"

Connect to the Literature

1. What Do You Think?
What especially do you remember after reading "An Hour with Abuelo"? Explain.

Comprehension Check
• When has Arturo visited his grandfather in the past?
• What were Arturo's grandfather's two ambitions?
• What does Abuelo say "with a wicked smile" to Arturo at the end of Arturo's visit?

Think Critically

2. How does Arturo's understanding of his grandfather change during his visit?

THINK ABOUT
• Arturo's plan to visit for exactly one hour
• Arturo's usual feelings about adults
• A surprise visit from "Mrs. Pink Running Shoes"

3. **ACTIVE READING DRAWING CONCLUSIONS** With a partner compare the notes you made in your **READER'S NOTEBOOK.** Did you draw similar conclusions? How did they differ?

4. Arturo's mother feels that her father's life has been "a waste of a fine mind." What do you think?

5. Arturo says, "I go after what I want." How does this attitude affect his relationship with his grandfather?

6. Why do you think the grandfather reads his life story to Arturo? What does Arturo gain from hearing it?

Extend Interpretations

7. **Different Perspectives** Imagine that "Mrs. Pink Running Shoes" had overheard Arturo's visit with his grandfather. How might she describe it to a friend? What kind of a person is the grandfather from her perspective? What kind of person is Arturo?

8. **Connect to Life** Many observers say that elderly people are no longer valued or respected in modern American life. What is your opinion?

Literary Analysis

FIRST-PERSON NARRATOR

A **first-person narrator** in a literary work tells the story in which he or she is a character directly to the reader, using pronouns like *I* and *me.* In "An Hour with Abuelo," the main character, Arturo, is the narrator. The reader learns a great deal about him from the words and expressions he uses and the attitudes he displays. For example, early in the story Arturo mentions how he escapes to the recreation area during earlier visits with his grandfather:

I catch up on back issues of Modern Maturity. I'm not picky, I'll read almost anything.

Arturo's words reveal that he both likes to read and has a sense of humor, two characteristics he shares with his grandfather.

Paired Activity With a partner create a web in which you note things Arturo has in common with his grandfather. Go through the story and find examples that support your observations. When you are finished, see what conclusions you can draw about the similarities of these two characters. Write that conclusion at the center of the web.

Arturo: "I'll read almost anything." Abuelo: "I had books. All the books I wanted."

Arturo: Abuelo "cracks me up." Abuelo gives Arturo "a wicked smile."

?

---

while the grandfather observes his grandson looking at his watch.

 Use **Literary Analysis Transparencies,** p. 22, for additional support.

Extend Interpretations

7. **Different Perspectives** Possible Response: She might initially be threatened by the possibility of Arturo being a rival for Abuelo's attention, but, given her own youthfulness, "Mrs. Pink Running Shoes" may have been impressed by

Abuelo's ability to relate to his young grandson.

8. **Connect to Life** Accept all reasonable responses. Encourage students to support their ideas with examples from everyday life.

Choices & CHALLENGES

Writing Options

1. Personal Essay What does the saying *"Así es la vida"* (That's the way life is) mean to you? Is it sad? Cynical? Could it be humorous? Write a personal essay in which you express your opinion. Draw on your own experiences or those of someone you know.

Writing Handbook
See p. R23: Drafting.

2. Diary Entry Have you ever spent an hour (or a very short time) with someone and had your view of that person completely change? Write a diary entry describing your experience.

Activities & Explorations

1. Personal Interview Interview an elderly person about the connections he or she had as a child with grandparents. Share your findings in a brief oral report to the class.
~ SPEAKING AND LISTENING

2. Family Maps Arturo's relatives live in Puerto Rico, New York, and New Jersey. Make a map that shows where all the members of your extended family live. Or choose the family of someone you know. **~ ART**

Inquiry & Research

Puerto Rico Use encyclopedias, magazines, and Internet databases to learn more about the history, culture, and people of Puerto Rico. When you have finished, put together a travel brochure about the island. Share your brochure with the class.

 More Online: Research Starter
www.mcdougallittell.com

Vocabulary and Spelling

EXERCISE A: RELATED WORDS On a sheet of paper, write the letter of the word that is not related in meaning to the other words in the set.

1. (a) hospital (b) theater (c) nurse (d) orderly
2. (a) suite (b) room (c) apartment (d) park
3. (a) galaxy (b) parchment (c) telescope (d) planet
4. (a) sewn (b) erased (c) knitted (d) embroidered
5. (a) war (b) gun (c) ammunition (d) hammer

EXERCISE B: HOMOPHONES Remember to think about meaning when using **homophones**, words that sound alike but that have different spellings and meanings, such as *suite* and *sweet*.

boarder border   serial   cereal   core   corps
suite   sweet   colonel   kernel

From the list of spelling words, write the homophone that belongs with each set of words below.

1. boundary, rim, outline, _____
2. troop, regiment, division, _____
3. major, general, captain, _____
4. eggs, toast, juice, _____
5. sour, salty, bitter, _____

Spelling Handbook p. R86

Writing Options

1. Personal Essay Students' essays should explain the expression and how it relates to the story and to their own lives and should express an opinion on its tone. To make this assignment more challenging, encourage students to include quotations from other literary works to support their statements.

Use **Writing Transparencies**, p. 13, for additional support.

2. Diary Entry To help students get started, give them several moments to think and jot notes about the topic. Their entries should explain their original view, how this view changed, and why it changed. Students who are visual learners might incorporate sketches that show different views of the same person.

Activities & Explorations

1. Personal Interview Encourage students to prepare their questions before they conduct their interviews. As a class, students might discuss possible questions. To make this assignment easier, you might allow students to work in pairs.

Use **Communications Transparencies and Copymasters**, p. 9, for additional support.

2. Family Maps Students should design their maps to meet their specific needs. For example, if all of their relatives happen to live in a single state, they can create a map of that state. If their relatives happen to be all over the world, they can create a map that includes the relevant countries and continents.

Inquiry & Research

Puerto Rico Encourage students to use their imaginations to create a truly original, eye-catching brochure. Before beginning their research, students should plan what information to include and how to organize it.

Vocabulary and Spelling

EXERCISE A	EXERCISE B
1. b	1. border
2. d	2. corps
3. b	3. colonel
4. b	4. cereal
5. d	5. sweet

 Spelling TEKS 16D  TAAS Writing Obj. 3, 7

HOMOPHONES

Instruction Remind students that homophones are words that sound alike but that have different spellings and meanings.

Exercise From the list of spelling words below, have students choose the homophone that best completes each of the following sentences.

wholly holy soar sore cue queue their there

1. Members of the church tried to teach their children the most sacred, _____ writings. *(holy)*
2. Actors had to wait for an entrance _____. *(cue)*
3. We saw a bird _____ into the clouds. *(soar)*
4. When calling for tickets to the show, they waited in a long phone _____. *(queue)*
5. Jason's feet were _____ after he walked down the driveway barefoot. *(sore)*
6. It was a _____ frightening experience. *(wholly)*
7. I see my books in a pile over _____. *(there)*
8. Did you know that _____ grandfather is a writer? *(their)*

Use **Unit Four Resource Book**, p. 39 for more practice.

Grammar in Context

WRITING EXERCISE
Possible Responses:

1. In the recreation room they play backgammon, a board game.
2. Abuelo starts to read the story, a short one.
3. Abuelo, a talented teacher, was forced to leave his work and join the army.
4. I'm not going to let *la vida,* life, stop me.

CONNECT TO THE LITERATURE
"the principal at Central"

Judith Ortiz Cofer

Ortiz Cofer's stories are a combination of truth and imagination. She says "Many of my story ideas come from my life, but in many cases I use something interesting that has happened to me as a 'trigger' for my imagination." In order to live as a writer and consistently improve her skills, she gets up early and writes for an hour or two each morning, no matter where she is. She also spends a great deal of time reading.

Grammar in Context: Appositives

In "An Hour with Abuelo," appositive phrases add information that make nouns or pronouns more specific and precise.

> . . . I hate the place, the old people's home. . . .

> I walk fast to room 10, Abuelo's "suite."

An **appositive** is a noun or phrase that explains one or more words in a sentence. It is usually placed after a noun or pronoun to explain it. Often the noun or pronoun appositive has **modifiers**. An appositive and its modifiers make up an **appositive phrase.** Appositives giving the Spanish equivalent of English words are a part of this story's style.

> "Just one hour, *una hora,* is all I'm asking of you, son."

WRITING EXERCISE Rewrite each sentence, adding an appositive phrase to explain the underlined word.

Example: *Original* <u>Arturo</u> is the son of farmers.

Rewritten <u>Arturo, my grandfather,</u> is the son of farmers.

1. In the recreation room they play <u>backgammon</u>.
2. Abuelo starts to read the <u>story</u>.
3. <u>Abuelo</u> was forced to leave his work and join the army.
4. I'm not going to let <u>*la vida*</u> stop me.

Connection to the Literature Reread the last sentence in the first paragraph of the story. What appositive phrase do you find there?

Grammar Handbook Appositive, p. R80

"With the stories I tell, . . . I try to get my audience past the particulars of my skin color, my accent, or my clothes."

Judith Ortiz Cofer
born 1952

Living in Two Places Judith Ortiz Cofer was born in Hormigueros, Puerto Rico, and moved to Paterson, New Jersey, as a toddler. She traveled back and forth between Paterson and the island during her childhood. She says her island grandfather taught her poetry, and her island grandmother taught her survival.

Two Languages Ortiz Cofer's family spoke Spanish at home, and she learned English at school. When she was in third grade, a teacher once punished her because she did not understand English. After that she became a dedicated reader. "I had to learn the language of the place where I was living in order to survive."

Latina Wherever I Am Judith Ortiz Cofer describes herself as a Puerto Rican writer whose literary language is English. She writes about both the Puerto Rican and American parts of her experience and identity. She has won recognition for her poetry, essays, and fiction, including the O. Henry Award for her story "Nada" and the 1990 Pushcart Prize for Nonfiction. She teaches writing and literature at the University of Georgia.

600 UNIT FOUR PART 2: CHANGES OF HEART

Teaching Options

Mini Lesson **Grammar** TEKS 17C TAAS Writing Obj. 6

IDENTIFYING APPOSITIVES
Instruction Remind students that an apposi-tive is a noun or phrase that explains the noun that precedes it.
Display the following examples:
My grandson **Arturo** came for a visit. (appositive)
My grandfather, **an interesting man,** has been a teacher and a writer. (appositive phrase)
Application Have students write a paragraph based on some aspect of the story. In their

paragraphs, they should use at least four appos-itives or appositive phrases. When students have completed their paragraphs, have each student exchange paragraphs with a partner. Each partner should underline the appositives in the other's work.
Possible Response: That young boy <u>Arturo</u> is a determined student. One teacher, <u>a teacher of English</u>, said Arturo is the hardest worker he's ever known. This teacher especially enjoyed the story Arturo wrote about his

grandfather. The story, <u>"Abuelo,"</u> was about his grandfather's youth. His grandfather, <u>Arturo,</u> faced many challenges.

Use **Unit Four Resource Book,** p. 38.
Use **Grammar Transparencies and Copymasters,** p. 107.

 Use McDougal Littell's ***Language Network,*** Chapter 8, for more instruction and practice with appositives.

Waiting

Short Story by BUDGE WILSON

See the Skills Trace at the beginning of the unit for information on TEKS covered in this lesson.

But Henrietta was my friend and I ...ers. We were, in fact, best friends."

Connect to Your Life

Best Friends What are the qualities that make somebody a good friend? Working with a small group, create a semantic web listing these qualities. Then share your web with other groups.

honesty

Qualities of a Good Friend

Build Background

CONNECT TO **SOCIAL STUDIES** "Waiting" is set in Nova Scotia, one of Canada's Atlantic provinces. The region's foggy, rocky countryside reminded 18th-century British settlers of Scotland, so they gave it the Latin name meaning "New Scotland." From the 1800s to the middle of the 20th century, Nova Scotia was an important center of shipbuilding.

"Waiting" takes place in the town of Shelburne during World War II, when the threat of German submarines in the waters offshore was real. Halifax, Nova Scotia's capital city, was the center for Allied naval operations in the western Atlantic during the war. Many sailors like those mentioned in the story were stationed in Nova Scotia.

CANADA

UNITED STATES

NOVA SCOTIA · Halifax

Atlantic Ocean

N W E S

Miles 0 100 200

WORDS TO KNOW **Vocabulary Preview**

apathy	flamboyant	saunter	submissive
arresting	infuriatingly	stupefying	vigor
dominant	quarantine		

LaserLinks: Background for Reading
Geographical Connection

Focus Your Reading

LITERARY ANALYSIS **UNRELIABLE NARRATOR**

The narrator of a work of fiction is the character or voice that tells the story. In life, one person's perspective on an event may be very different from another's. The same is true in fiction. A narrator who presents a biased or distorted version of events or of other characters is called an **unreliable narrator.** As you read "Waiting," look for clues that tell you that the main character and narrator, Juliette, may be an unreliable narrator.

ACTIVE READING **MAKING JUDGMENTS**

When you combine information from the work you are reading with what you already know from your own experience in order to evaluate some aspect of the work, you are **making judgments.** In "Waiting," you need to evaluate the things Juliette says to determine which are accurate and which may be distorted.

READER'S NOTEBOOK As you read "Waiting," jot down details and comments that will help you make a judgment as to whether Juliette is a reliable or unreliable narrator.

Is Juliette a Reliable Narrator?

What Juliette Says	Clues from the Story
Juliette says that Henrietta is her best friend.	Juliette yells at Henrietta and calls her "slowpoke".

Objectives
- understand and appreciate a **short story** (Literary Analysis)
- note the significance of and distinction between a **reliable** and **unreliable narrator** (Literary Analysis)
- apply the skill of **making judgments** (Active Reading)

Summary
Juliette, the story's narrator, considers herself talented, smart, lively, and outgoing—the opposite of her pale, quiet twin, Henrietta. When the two girls are almost 13 years old, they and some friends put on a summer play. Juliette has the lead role and a splendid costume. During a key scene, she raises her arm and hears her dress rip down the back. Her sister rescues her from public humiliation by gliding onstage, as if part of the scene, and draping a spread over her, concealing the rip. When the performers take their final bows, Juliette suddenly realizes that Henrietta has become a beautiful, confident young woman who is appealing to boys. The once-reserved twin has lost her "waiting" look. Juliette acknowledges that she will never have Henrietta's quiet power.

Thematic Link
When quiet Henrietta steps out of the background and reaches out to help her sister, the narrator of this story, the lives of both twins change forever.

5-Minute Warm-Up

Daily Language SkillBuilder

TEKS 17C, 17G

Have students **proofread** the display sentences on page 517j and write them correctly. The sentences also appear on Transparency 19 of **Grammar Transparencies and Copymasters.**

Mini Lesson **Preteaching Vocabulary**

If you would like to preteach the WORDS TO KNOW for this selection, use the Mini Lesson, p. 602.

LESSON RESOURCES

UNIT FOUR RESOURCE BOOK, pp. 41-47

ASSESSMENT
Formal Assessment, pp. 101-102
Teacher's Guide to Assessment and Portfolio Use
Test Generator

SKILLS TRANSPARENCIES AND COPYMASTERS
Literary Analysis
- Narrator and Point of View, TR 22 (for Cooperative Learning Activity, p. 614)

Reading and Critical Thinking
- Making Judgments, TR 15 (for Thinking Through the Literature, p. 614)
Grammar
- Interrupters, CM 132 (for Mini Lesson, p. 604)
- Identifying Participial Phrases, CM 99 (for Mini Lesson, p. 616)
Vocabulary
- Context Clues, CM 67 (for Mini Lesson, p. 602)
- Analogies, CM 68 (for Mini Lesson, p. 610)

Communications
- Dramatic Reading, TR 12 (for Mini Lesson, p. 613)

INTEGRATED TECHNOLOGY
Audio Library
LaserLinks
- Geographical Connection; Social Studies Connection. See **Teacher's SourceBook,** p. 26, for bar codes.

Visit our website:
www.mcdougallittell.com

Literary Analysis

UNRELIABLE NARRATOR

A Ask students to identify some of the words that Juliette's mother uses to describe her daughter.

Possible Responses: She calls her complex, many-sided, cute, talented.

B How does Juliette see herself in her daydream?

Possible Responses: as a winner, as humble, as small and attractive

Use **Unit Four Resource Book**, p. 43 for guidance in reading the selection.

Active Reading **MAKING JUDGMENTS**

Juliette's mother says she is not boasting. Ask students to judge whether she is or not. Have them support their responses by referring to relevant aspects of text and to their own experience.

Possible Responses: She is boasting; she calls her daughter cute, charming, talented, and bright, and a leader. Most people who say such things are boasting.

Use **Unit Four Resource Book**, p. 42 for guidance in reading the selection.

Reading Skills and Strategies: CHARACTER

Have students consider why the story opens with the mother's comments about Juliette. What does this opening suggest about Juliette's importance in the story?

Possible Responses: It suggests that she is a main character.

Illustration by Meg Kelleher Aubrey.

Teaching Options

 Mini Lesson **Preteaching Vocabulary**   **TEKS** 6A   **TAAS** Reading Obj. 1

CONTEXT CLUES

Instruction Call students' attention to the list of WORDS TO KNOW on page 601. Explain that they can acquire extensive vocabularies through reading. As they read, they should draw on experiences to bring meanings to words in context. Sometimes they may have to read several sentences to understand a word's meaning. Point out the highlighted section in the second column on page 604. Ask, "What can you tell about the narrator's personality from this passage?" (*She is loud and passionate and shows little restraint.*) Help

students see that these ideas help them understand the meaning of the word *flamboyant.*

Application As students read the selection, encourage them to read the entire paragraph containing each vocabulary word before they read the definition at the bottom of the page. Have them draw conclusions about each word's meaning before they check it against the printed definition.

Use **Unit Four Resource Book**, p. 44 for more practice. Use **Vocabulary Transparencies and Copymasters**, p. 67, for additional support.

Waiting

by Budge Wilson

"You must realize, of course, that Juliette is a very complex child." My mother was talking on the telephone. Shouting, to be more exact. She always spoke on the phone as though the wires had been disconnected, as though she were trying to be heard across the street through an open window. "She's so many-*sided*," she continued. "Being cute, of course, is not enough, although heaven knows she could charm the legs off a table. But you have to have something more than personality."

I was not embarrassed by any of this. Lying on the living room floor on my stomach, I was pretending to read *The Bobbsey Twins at the Seashore.* But after a while I closed the book. Letting her words drop around me, I lay there like a plant enjoying the benefit of a drenching and beneficial rain. My sister sat nearby in the huge wingback chair, legs tucked up under her, reading the funnies.

"I hope you don't regard this as *boasting,* but she really is so very, *very* talented. Bright as a button in school—three prizes, can you believe it, at the last school closing—and an outstanding athlete, even at eight years old."

Resting my head on my folded arms, I smiled quietly. I could see myself eight years from now, receiving my gold medal, while our country's flag rose in front of the Olympic flame. The applause thundered as the flag reached its peak, standing straight out from the pole, firm and strong. As the band broke into a moving rendition of "O Canada," I wept softly. I stood wet and waterlogged from my last race, my tears melding with the chlorine and coursing slowly down my face. People were murmuring, "So young, so small, and so attractive."

"And such a leader!" My mother's voice hammered on. "Even at her age, she seems forever to be president of this and director of that. I feel very blessed indeed to be the mother of such a child." My sister stirred in her chair and coughed slightly, carefully turning a page.

Literary Analysis

UNRELIABLE NARRATOR

A Ask students how Henrietta might describe the relationship between the two sisters and how she might describe her own appearance.

Possible Responses: Rather than using the terms *dominant* and *submissive*, Henrietta might say her sister is bossy or a bully. She might describe herself as being blond and slim.

Active Reading MAKING JUDGMENTS

B From this description, ask students whether they think Henrietta is pretty. Have them support their responses by referring to relevant aspects of text and to their own experience.

Possible Responses: Some students will say no, she appears colorless and bland; others may think she sounds delicate.

ACTIVE READING

C CLARIFY Students might mention that one is loud, while the other is quiet; one is fair while the other is dark; one is bold while the other more timid; or other differences.

Active Reading MAKING JUDGMENTS

D Ask students to judge how good a friend each sister was, based on what they read on these two pages. Have them support their responses.

Possible Responses: Juliette is not a good friend, because she yells at her sister, tries to scare her, blackmails her, and once leaves her tied up for a long time; Henrietta sounds like a friend, since she is willing to try most things and she does not tattle.

It was true. I was president of grade 4 and manager of the Lower Slocum Elementary School Drama Club. I had already starred in two productions, one of them a musical. In an ornate crêpe paper costume composed of giant overlapping yellow petals, I had played Lead Buttercup to a full house. Even Miss Prescott's aggressive piano playing had failed to drown me out, had not prevented me from stealing the show from the Flower Queen. My mother kept the clipping from *The Shelburne Coast Guard* up on the kitchen notice board. It included a blurred newspaper picture of me with extended arms and open mouth. Below it, the caption read, "Juliette Westhaver was the surprise star of the production, with three solos and a most sprightly little dance, performed skillfully and with gusto. Broadway, look out!"

Mama was still talking. "Mm? Oh. Henrietta. Yes, well, she's fine, I guess, just fine. Such a serious, responsible little girl, and so fond of her sister." I looked up at Henrietta, who was surveying me over the top of her comics. There was no expression on her face at all.

But then Henrietta was not often given to expression of any kind. She was my twin, but apart from the accident of our birth, or the coincidence, we had almost nothing in common. It was incredible to me that we had been born to the same parents at almost the same moment, and that we had been reared in the same house.

But Henrietta was my friend and I hers. We were, in fact, best friends, as is so often the case with twins. And as with most close childhood friendships, there was one dominant member, one submissive. There was no doubt in this case as to who played the leading role.

Henrietta even looked submissive. She was thin and pale. She had enormous sky-blue eyes surrounded by a long fringe of totally colorless eyelashes. Her hair was a dim beige color without gradations of light or dark, and it hung straight and lifeless from two barrettes. Her fingers were long and bony, and she kept them folded in her lap, motionless, like a tired old lady. She had a straight little nose and a mouth that seldom smiled—it was serious and still and oddly serene. She often looked as though she were waiting for something.

Untidy and flamboyant, my personality and my person flamed hotly beside her cool apathy. My temper flared, my joys exploded. With fiery red cheeks and a broad snub nose, I grinned and hooted my way through childhood, dragging and pushing Henrietta along as I raced from one adventure to the next. I had a mop of wild black curls that no comb could tame. I was small, compact, sturdy, well-coordinated and extremely healthy. Henrietta had a lot of colds.

ACTIVE READING

C CLARIFY In what ways are Juliette and Henrietta different?

When I start talking about Henrietta and me, I always feel like I'm right back there, a kid again. Sometimes, you know, I got fed up with her. If you have a lot of energy, for instance, it's no fun to go skiing with someone who's got lead in her boots. And for heaven's sake, she kept falling all the time. Scared to death to try the hills, and likely as not going down them on the seat of her pants. "Fraidy-cat! Fraidy-cat!" I'd yell at her from the bottom of the hill where I had landed right-side up, and she would start down the first part of the slope with straight and trembling knees, landing in a snow bank before the hill even got started. There were lots of fields and woods

WORDS TO KNOW	**dominant** (dŏm′ə-nənt) *adj.* ruling or controlling **submissive** (səb-mĭs′ĭv) *adj.* willing to give in to or obey another **flamboyant** (flăm-boi′ənt) *adj.* given to showy display; flashy **apathy** (ăp′ə-thē) *n.* lack of strong feeling or interest

604

Teaching Options

 Mini Lesson **Grammar** 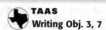 TEKS 16B TAAS Writing Obj. 3, 7

INTERRUPTERS

Instruction Explain to students that interrupters are words or phrases that interrupt, or break, the flow of thought in a sentence. When students write sentences that contain an interrupter, they must punctuate correctly to clarify and enhance meaning. They should place commas before and after the interruption. Point out the highlighted sentence in the first column above and ask a volunteer to identify the interrupter. *(in fact)* Draw attention to the placement of the commas that surround it.

Application Have students read the final paragraph on page 604 and look for two sentences, one right after the other, that both contain interrupters. *(Sometimes, you know, . . . If you have a lot of energy, for instance, . . .)*

 Use **Grammar Transparencies and Copymasters,** p. 132.

 Use McDougal Littell's *Language Network,* Chapter 11, for more instruction and practice in identifying and punctuating interrupters.

round our town, and good high hills if you were looking for thrills. You could see the sea from the top of some of them, and the wild wind up there made me feel like an explorer, a brave Micmac[1] hunter, the queen of the Maritime Provinces. Sometimes I would let out a yell just for the joy of it all—and there, panting and gasping and falling up the hill would be old Henrietta, complaining, forever complaining, about how tired she was, how cold.

But I guess I really loved Henrietta anyway, slowpoke though she was. I had lots and lots of other friends who were more interesting than she was. But it's a funny thing—she was nearly always my first choice for someone to play with.

There was a small woodlot to the east of the village, on land owned by my father. We called it The Grove. It had little natural paths in it, and there were open spaces under the trees like rooms or houses or castles, or whatever you wanted them to be that day. The grove of trees was on the edge of a cliff overhanging some big rocks, and at high tide the sea down there was never still, even when it was flat oil calm. So it could be a spooky kind of place to play in, too. I loved to go there when it was foggy and play spy. It was 1940 and wartime, and by then we were ten, going on eleven. From The Grove we could sometimes see destroyers, and once even a big aircraft carrier. In the fog, it wasn't hard to believe that the Nazis were coming, and that we were going to be blown to bits any minute.

We never told Mama or Papa about going to the cliff when the mist was thick. Henrietta hardly ever wanted to go on those foggy days. She was afraid of falling off the cliff onto the rocks, sure she would drown in the churned-up water, nervous about the ghostly shapes in the thick gray-white air. But she always went. I used to blackmail her. "If you don't go, I'll tell Mama about the time you pretended to be sick and stayed home from school because you didn't have your homework done and were scared of Miss Garrison." Or I would just plain order her around. "I'm *going*, Henrietta, so get a move on and *hurry!*" She'd come padding out of the house in her stupid yellow raincoat, so that she wouldn't get a cold in the wet wind, and off we'd go—me fast and complaining about her slowness, and her slow and complaining about my speed. But she'd be there and we'd be together and we'd have fun. I'd be the spy, and she'd be the poor agonized prisoner of war, tied up to a tree by a bunch of Nazis. Sometimes I'd leave her tethered good and long, so she'd look *really* scared instead of pretend scared, while I prowled around and killed Nazis and searched for hidden weapons. Or we'd play Ghost, and I'd be the ghost—floating along on the edge of the cliff and shrieking in my special death shriek that I saved for ghost games. It started out low like a groan and then rose to a wail, ending in a scream so thin and high that it almost scared *me*. Sometimes, if she was especially wet and tired, Henrietta would start to cry, and that *really* made me mad. Even now, I can't stand crybabies. But you had to have a victim, and this was something she was extra good at. No point in wasting my death shriek on a person who wasn't afraid of ghosts. No fun to have the Nazis tying up someone who was big and strong and brave, particularly when the Nazis weren't actually there and you had to think them up and pretend the whole thing.

One time when we went there with a bunch of kids instead of just us two, I forgot all about her being tied to the tree and got nearly home before I raced back the whole half mile to untie her. She never said a word. It was snowing, and there were big fat snowflakes on those long white lashes of hers, and her eyes looked like they were going to pop right out of her head.

---

1. **Micmac:** a Native American people inhabiting Nova Scotia and other provinces of Canada.

Cross Curricular Link **History**

NOVA SCOTIA HISTORY To help students recognize and analyze setting, explain that the story takes place in Nova Scotia, a province of Canada that comprises a main peninsula and several islands. Thus, there is abundant seacoast, and fishing is both a major industry and a form of recreation. The name *Nova Scotia* means "New Scotland," but the original inhabitants were Abenaki and Micmacs, two Native American tribes; later French and English settlers arrived and struggled for control. Still later, many Irish and Scots arrived. Nova Scotia has a distinguished intellectual history: it was the site of the first Canadian newspaper and one of Canada's first universities.

This story takes place during World War II, when travel was limited and many common items, such as clothes and food, were in short supply. To buy things, people needed government-issued ration stamps.

I said I was real sorry, and next week I even bought her a couple of comic books out of my own allowance money, when she was home sick with bronchitis. Mama said she should have had the sense to wear a scarf and a warm hat, being as she was so prone to colds, and that's certainly true. She never told on me, and I don't know why. She sat up against the pillows and colored in her coloring book or read her funnies, or more often she just lay there on the bed, her hands lying limp on the quilt, with that patient, quiet, waiting look of hers.

ACTIVE READING

A QUESTION Why doesn't Henrietta tell on her sister?

When the spring came, a gang of us would always start going out to The Grove on weekends to start practicing for our summer play. Year after year we did this, and it had nothing to do with those school plays in which I made such a hit. We'd all talk about what stories we liked, and then we'd pick one of them and make a play out of it. I would usually select the play because I was always the one who directed it, so it was only fair that I'd get to do the choosing. If there was a king or a queen, I'd usually be the queen. If you're the director, you can't be something like a page or a minor fairy, because then you don't seem important enough to be giving out instructions and bossing people around, and the kids maybe won't pay attention to all the orders. Besides, as my mother pointed out, I was smart and could learn my lines fast, and you couldn't expect some slow dummy to memorize all that stuff.

1 Henrietta's voice was so soft and quiet that no one could ever hear her unless they were almost sitting on her lap; so of course it would have been stupid to give her a part. She couldn't even be the king's horse or the queen's

milk-white mule because she was so darn scrawny. You can't have the lead animal looking as though it should be picked up by the Humane Society and put in quarantine. But she was really useful to the production, and it must have been very satisfying for her. She got to find all the costume parts and rigged up the stage in the biggest cleared space among the trees, making it look like a ballroom or a throne room or whatever else we needed. She did a truly good job, and if it weren't for the fact that I can't stand conceited people, I probably would even have told her so. I liked Henrietta the way she was. I didn't want her strutting around looking proud of herself and putting on airs. One time one of the kids said, "Hey, Henrietta, that's a really great royal bedroom you made," and right away she started standing and moving around in a way that showed she thought she was a pretty smart stage manager.

I hate that kind of thing, and I knew the others wouldn't like it either. So I said, "Oh, sure! And the king must have just lost his kingdom in the wars. Who ever heard of a king sleeping on a pile of branches or having an old torn dishtowel at the window? Some king!" And everyone laughed. I always think that laughter is very important. It makes everyone happy right away and is a good way to ease tensions.

We had a lot of fun practicing for those plays. No one went away for the summer. No one needed to. The sea was right there alongside the village, with a big sandy beach only a quarter mile away. Some of the fishermen let us use their smaller flats for jigging,[2] and we could always swim or dig for clams or collect mussels. Besides, the war was on; people weren't spending money on cottages or trips. Seems to me that

---

2. **jigging:** boating.

WORDS TO KNOW **quarantine** (kwôr′ən-tēn′) *n.* a place where a diseased animal is kept away from others

Multicultural Link **Performance**

DRAMA To help students articulate and discuss themes and connections that cross cultures, point out that drama, including the types of plays described in this story, is enjoyed throughout the world and has been throughout history.

- Cave paintings from 10,000 B.C. depict masked performers.
- People in ancient Greece enjoyed tragic plays, mime, and comedies.
- Sanskrit drama has been enjoyed at least since the second century A.D., and probably earlier.

- In China, plays produced during the Yuan dynasty entertained audiences with romantic stories and plots from popular novels.
- Japanese No plays are more formal and less story-driven. They combine speech, dance, mime, music, and song, and performers often wear wooden masks.
- The popular Japanese kabuki plays contain a great deal of action and excitement.

Staithes, Yorkshire (about 1900), Dame Laura Knight. Copyright ©
Dame Laura Knight, reproduced by permission of Curtis Brown
Group Ltd., London.

everyone just stuck around home and saved
paper and counted their ration stamps and
listened to the news on the radio. There was a
navy base nearby, and sometimes sailors came to
dinner. They'd tell us about life on the base and
all the dangers they were expecting and hoping
to experience when they started sailing to
Europe. I envied them like anything and couldn't
for the life of me see why you had to be eighteen
before you joined the navy, or why they
wouldn't let girls run the ships or use the guns.
Henrietta said she didn't want to be a sailor
anyway, because she'd be too scared, which of
course is only what you'd expect. Apart from
that, there wasn't much excitement. So the play
practices were our main entertainment during
those years. In the summer, we practiced on
most fine days, and in August we put on the
play in front of all our mothers and fathers and

uncles and aunts, and for the sisters and
brothers too young to take part.

The play we put on in 1942 was
about a rich nobleman called
Alphonse who falls in love with
an exquisitely beautiful but humble country
girl called Genevieve. I played the part of
Genevieve, and it was the nicest part I had
ever played. In the last scene, Genevieve and
the nobleman become engaged, and she gets to
dress up in a very gorgeous gown for a big
court ball. I had a real dress for this scene,
instead of the usual pieced-together scraps of
material dug out of old trunks from our attics.
My mother let me use one of her long dance
dresses from when she was young. It was
covered with sequins and even had some sort
of fluffy feather stuff around the hem; and it
was pale sapphire blue and very romantic
looking. I had trouble getting into it because I
was almost thirteen now and sort of big
through the middle. But my mother put in a
new zipper instead of the buttons, and I was
able to wear it after all. I had to move a little
carefully and not take very deep breaths, but I
was as tall as Mama now, and I felt like a real
woman, a true beauty. The neck was kind of
low, but I was pretty flat, so I didn't need to
worry about being indecent in front of Harold
Boutilier, who played the part of Alphonse.
Mama put a whole lot of makeup on me,
covering up the pimples I was starting to get,
and I thought I looked like a movie star, a **D**
genuine leading lady. The zipper wasn't put
into the dress in time for the dress rehearsal,
but Harold wore a big bow at his neck and his
mother's velvet shorty coat, with a galvanized
chain around his waist that shone like real
silver. He had on his sister's black stockings
and a pair of high rubber boots, and he looked
very handsome. Up until this year he had just
seemed like an okay boy to me, as boys go,

WAITING **607**

 Mini Lesson **Viewing and Representing** 🇺🇸 **TEKS 22A**

Staithes, Yorkshire
by Dame Laura Knight

ART APPRECIATION Tell students that this is a
painting of an English fishing village by Laura
Knight (1877–1970), a leading artist of the 20th
century.
Instruction Point out to students how the
towering cliff and wide ocean contrast with the
sheltered little village. Ask them to find details in
this picture that suggest that the village is safe
and comfortable.

Possible Responses: The houses appear tidy and
sturdy; neighbors are close together; the mountain
gives a sense of security; there are boats, which
suggest that people spend time on the water,
relaxing or fishing for food.
Application Ask students if they believe Juliette
pictures her village this way. Have them explain
their responses.
Possible Responses: Responses will vary.
Students might say Juliette's descriptions in the
book suggest a small, tightly knit village by the
ocean like the one depicted in the painting.

WAITING **607**

A CLARIFY She feels like a real woman, a true beauty; she thinks she looks like a movie star.

Literary Analysis

UNRELIABLE NARRATOR

Ask students how Juliette sees herself here and how she feels about it. Have students support their answers with text evidence and experience.

Possible Responses: She sees herself as beautiful, and she feels good about it. Her mother tells her how pretty she is, and she describes the character as beautiful.

Active Reading **MAKING JUDGMENTS**

Have students make a judgment about which aspect of this play interests Juliette the most.

Possible Responses: how she appears; her part in the play.

---

but this summer I'd spent a lot of time watching him and thinking about him when I went to bed at night. I guess I had a big crush on him. And I was pretty sure that when he saw me in that blue dress, he'd have a crush on me right away, too.

ACTIVE READING

A CLARIFY How does Juliette feel about wearing one of her mother's dresses?

On the day of the play, all our families started arriving at The Grove theater a full hour before we got started. It didn't rain, and there wasn't even one of those noisy Nova Scotian winds that shake the trees and keep you from hearing the lines. My mother was hustling around backstage helping with clothes and makeup. Mostly she was fussing with my face and my first costume and telling me how pretty I looked. We had rigged up eight bedspreads, some torn and holey, some beautiful, depending on the fear or the pride of the mothers who lent them; and behind this strung-out curtain, we prepared ourselves for the two o'clock production. Henrietta was moving quietly about on the stage, straightening furniture, moving props, standing back to look at the effect. Later on, just before the curtain went up, or rather was drawn aside, she went off and sat down against a tree, where she'd have a good view of the performance, but where she'd be out of sight. If any of us needed anything, she could get it for us without the audience seeing what she was doing.

In the first part of the play, the nobleman ignores the beautiful peasant girl, who comes on dressed in rags but heavily made up and therefore beautiful. He is of course looking for a wife, but no one even thinks of her as a possible candidate. She does a lot of sighing and weeping, and Alphonse rides around on his horse (George Cruikshank) looking handsome and tragic. Harold did this very well. Still, I

could hardly wait for the last scene, in which I could get out of those rags and emerge as the radiant court butterfly. But I put all I had into this first scene, because when Alphonse turns down all the eligible and less beautiful women of the land and retires to a corner of the stage to brood (with George Cruikshank standing nearby, munching grass), Genevieve arrives on the scene to a roll of drums (our wooden spoon on Mrs. Eisner's pickling kettle). As Alphonse turns to look at her dazzling beauty, he recognizes her for what she is—not just a poor commoner, but a young woman of great charm and loveliness, worthy of his hand. At this point, she places her hand on her breast and does a deep and graceful curtsy. He stands up, bends to help her rise, and in a tender and significant gesture kisses her outstretched hand.

And that's exactly how we did it, right there on the foxberry patch, which looked like a rich green carpet with a red pattern, if you happened to have the kind of imagination to see it that way. I thought I would faint with the beauty of it all. Then the string of bedspreads was drawn across the scene, curtain hoops squeaking, and the applauding audience awaited the final scene.

I didn't waste any time getting into my other costume. Dressed in my blue gown, I peeked through the hole in Mrs. Powell's bedspread to assess the audience. I had not had time to look until now, but Mama had dressed me first, and she had six other girls to get ready for the ball scene. The crowd outside was large. There must have been forty-five or fifty people of various sizes and ages sitting on the cushions placed on top of the pine needles. The little kids were crawling and squirming around like they always do, and mothers were passing out pacifiers and bags of chips and jelly beans and suckers to keep them quiet during intermission. One little boy—Janet Morash's brother —was crying his head off, and I sure as fire

---

Teaching Options

✓ **Assessment** **Standardized Test Practice**  **TEKS** 10A, 10H, 10K **TAAS** Reading Obj.

MAKING JUDGMENTS In some standardized tests, students are asked to use their own knowledge and experience to comprehend and make judgments. After students have read the story, write the following question on the board or read it aloud:

Which idea is best supported by information in the story?

A. Juliette is actually quite shy.

B. Juliette does not enjoy playing with Henrietta.

C. Juliette is not always kind to Henrietta.

D. Juliette is always kind to Henrietta.

Lead students through the process of choosing the best answer. Help them recognize that there is some evidence to support A, B, or D. There is ample evidence, however, to support C. For example, Henrietta calls her sister a "Fraidy-cat" and blackmails her. Therefore, the best answer is C.

Illustration by Meg Kelleher Aubrey.

Multiple Learning Styles
Visual Learners

1 Encourage students to visualize the production, with the hanging bedspreads and the bustle, and to describe mental images that the text descriptions evoke.

Less Proficient Readers
Use the following questions to guide students.

1. What are the performers using for a curtain?
   Answer: bedspreads.
2. What is Henrietta doing?
   Answer: moving about quietly and then sitting where she can see everything.
3. How is Juliette dressed when the play first begins?
   Answer: in rags
4. What does Juliette change into after the scene ends?
   Answer: the blue gown

 Viewing and Representing 🏴 **TEKS 22A**

Illustration by Meg Kelleher Aubrey

ART APPRECIATION Meg Kelleher Aubrey has illustrated several children's books.
Instruction To help students compare and contrast visual media with a written story, explain that illustrators read a story and select details that they will depict.
Application Ask what details about each character the artist included, and how she showed the relationship of the two characters. Then have

them identify additional story details that the artist included.
Possible Response The artist showed the girls' hair, expressions, and gestures; the artist showed Henrietta in the background and Juliette claiming the limelight; the artist showed the strung-up bedspreads, the blue gown, and the outdoor setting, including the trees.

Reading Skills and Strategies:
MAKING INFERENCES

Ⓐ Ask students to draw inferences about how Juliette feels here and to support their answers with text evidence and experience.
Possible Responses: She is happy and proud; she says that this is her big scene.

Reading Skills and Strategies:
DRAW CONCLUSIONS

Ⓑ Ask students to draw conclusions about why the dress rips.
Answer: It is too tight.

ACTIVE READING

Ⓒ **PREDICT** Students might suggest that she will be too humiliated to complete the play.

Literary Analysis
UNRELIABLE NARRATOR

Ⓓ Juliette says that she has "presence of mind." Who else shows this quality and where?
Possible Response: Her sister Henrietta shows this quality when she grabs the blanket and covers her sister.

Active Reading **MAKING JUDGMENTS**

Ⓔ Ask students whether they agree with Juliette's judgment about her sister. Have them support their responses by referring to relevant aspects of text and to their own experience.
Possible Responses: Most students will agree that Henrietta does have power; the applause and comments show this, as well as the other attention.

---

hoped he'd stop all that racket before the curtain went up. While I watched all this, I looked over to the left and saw three sailors coming through the woods. I knew them. They'd been to our house for supper a couple of times, but I never dreamt we'd be lucky enough to have the navy at our play. My big scene was going to be witnessed by more than just a bunch of parents and kids. There was even a little group of grade 12 boys in the back row.

We were almost ready to begin. Backstage, most of the makeup was done, and Mrs. Elliot was standing by the tree, making up Henrietta just for the heck of it. Henrietta had set up the stage and handed out the costumes, and she was putting in time like some of the rest of us. She just had on that old blue sweatshirt of hers and her dungarees, and it seemed to me that all that makeup was going to look pretty silly on someone who didn't have a costume on; but I didn't really care. If Henrietta wanted to make a fool of herself, it wasn't going to bother *me*.

In the last scene, all the courtiers and aristocrats are milling around in the ballroom, waiting for the nobleman to arrive with his betrothed. The orchestra is playing Strauss waltzes (on Mrs. Corkum's portable wind-up gramophone), and you can see that everyone is itchy footed and dying to dance, but they have to wait around until Alphonse arrives with Genevieve. It is a moment full of suspense, and I had to do a lot of smart and fierce directing to get that bunch of kids to look happy and excited and impatient all at the same time. But they did a really good job that afternoon. You could see that they thought they actually *were* lords and ladies and that it was a real live ball they had come to.

Suddenly there is a sound of trumpets (little Horace Miller's Halloween horn), and Alphonse

comes in, very slowly and stately, with Genevieve on his arm. She is shy and enters with downcast eyes; but he turns around, bows to her, and she raises her head with new pride and confidence, lifting her arms to join him in the dance. We did all this beautifully, if I do say so myself, and as I started to raise my arms, I thought I would burst with the joy and splendor of that moment.

As it turned out, burst is just about exactly what I did. The waltz record was turned off during this intense scene, and there was total silence on the stage and in the audience. As my arms reached shoulder level, a sudden sound of ripping taffeta reached clear to the back of the audience. (Joannie Sherman was sitting in the last row, and she told me about it later.) I knew in one awful, <u>stupefying</u> moment that my dress had ripped up the back, the full length of that long zipper. I can remember standing there on the stage with my arms half raised, unable to think or feel anything beyond a paralyzed horror. After that day, whenever I heard that someone was in a state of shock, I never had to ask the meaning of that term. I knew. Joannie told me later that the whole stageful of people looked like they had been turned to stone and that it really had been a scream to see.

Suddenly, as quiet and quick as a cat, Henrietta glided onstage. She was draped in one of the classier bedspreads from the curtain, and no one would have known that she wasn't supposed to be there. I don't know how anyone as slow-moving as Henrietta could have done so much fast thinking. But she did. She was carrying the very best

ACTIVE READING

PREDICT What will happen to Juliette now that her dress has ripped?

WORDS TO KNOW

stupefying (stoo′pə-fī′ĭng) *adj.* stunning **stupefy** *v.*

610

Mini Lesson **Vocabulary Strategy** **TEKS** 9B **TAAS** Reading Obj. 1

ANALOGIES
Instruction Explain to students that they can draw on experiences to interpret analogies and bring meanings to words in context. Remind them that analogies ask them to think about how words are related. Show this example:
Loud is to *quiet* as *dominant* is to _____.
(This analogy would usually be written as LOUD : QUIET :: dominant: _____.)
Ask students how *loud* and *quiet* are related. Tell them to answer with a sentence.

Possible Response: *Loud* and *quiet* are antonyms. A loud person is not quiet. Explain that the second pair of words will have the same relationship; they could be substituted for *loud* and *quiet* in the sentence. Ask what the antonym of *dominant* is.
Answer: submissive
Exercises Ask students to work in pairs to complete the following analogies. Tell them that each word they choose can be from the list of WORDS TO KNOW.

1. RUN : DASH :: stroll : _____. *(saunter)*
2. INVALID : WEAKNESS :: athlete : _____. *(vigor)*
3. SPEAKING : SHOUTING :: irritating : _____. *(infuriating)*

📖 Use **Vocabulary Transparencies and Copymasters,** p. 68.

---

bedspread—a lovely blue woven one that exactly matched my dress. She stopped in front of me, and lifting the spread with what I have to admit was a lot of ceremony and grace, she placed it gravely over my shoulders. Fastening it carefully with one of the large safety pins that she always kept attached to her sweatshirt during performances, she then moved backward two paces and bowed first to me and then to Harold before moving slowly and with great dignity toward the exit.

Emerging from my shock with the kind of presence of mind for which I was noted, I raised my arms and prepared to start the dance with Alphonse. But Harold, eyes full of amazement, was staring at Henrietta as she floated off the stage. From the back of the audience, I could hear two long, low whistles, followed by a deep male voice exclaiming, "Hubba, *hubba!*" to which I turned and bowed in graceful acknowledgement of what I felt to be a vulgar but nonetheless sincere tribute. The low voice, not familiar to me, spoke again. "Not *you*, pie-face!" he called, and then I saw three or four of the big boys from grade 12 leave the audience and run into the woods.

Somehow or other I got through that scene. Harold pulled his enchanted eyes back onstage, and the gramophone started the first few bars of "The Blue Danube" as we began to dance. Mercifully, the scene was short, and before long we were taking our curtain calls. "Stage manager! Stage manager!" shouted one of the sailors, and after a brief pause, old Henrietta came shyly forward, bedspread gone, dressed once more in her familiar blue sweatshirt and dungarees. The applause from the audience went on and on, and as we all bowed and curtsied, I stole a look at Henrietta. Slender, I thought, throat tight.

Slender, not skinny anymore. All in an instant I saw everything, right in the midst of all that clapping and bowing. It was like one of those long complicated dreams that start and finish within the space of five minutes, just before you wake up in the morning. Henrietta was standing serenely, quietly. As the clapping continued, while the actors and actresses feverishly bobbed up and down to acknowledge the applause, she just once, ever so slightly, inclined her head, gazing at the audience out of her astonishing eyes— enormous, arresting, fringed now with long dark lashes. Mrs. Elliot's makeup job had made us all see what must have been there all the time—a strikingly beautiful face. But there was something else there now that was new. As I continued to bow and smile, the word came to me to describe that strange new thing. *Power.* Henrietta had power. And what's more, she had it without having to *do* a single thing. All she needs to do, I thought, is *be.* The terrible injustice of it all stabbed me. There I was, the lead role, the director, the brains and vigor of our twinship, and suddenly, after all my years in first place, it was she who had the power. Afterwards I looked at them—the boys, the sailors, *Harold*—as they gazed at her. All she was doing was sauntering around the stage picking up props. But they were watching, and I knew, with a stunning accuracy, that there would always be watchers now, wherever she might be, whatever she wore, regardless of what she would be doing. And I also knew in that moment, with the same sureness, that I would never have that kind of power, not ever.

The next day, Mama stationed herself at the telephone, receiving all the tributes that came pouring in. A few moments per call were given over to a brief recognition of my acting talents

E

WORDS
TO
KNOW

arresting (ə-rĕs′tĭng) *adj.* striking
vigor (vĭg′ər) *n.* physical or mental strength, energy, or force
saunter (sôn′tər) *v.* to walk about slowly

611

 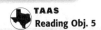

Two Girls on a Cliff (about 1917), Dame Laura Knight. Oil on canvas, 23½″ × 28½″, courtesy of Sotheby's. Copyright © Dame Laura Knight, reproduced by permission of Curtis Brown Group Ltd., London.

and to an uneasy amusement over the split dress. The rest of the time was spent in shouted discussion of Henrietta's startling and surprising beauty. I lay face downward on my bed and let the words hail down upon me. "Yes, indeed. Yes. I quite agree. Simply beautiful. And a real bolt from the blue. She quite astonished all of us. Although of course I recognized this quality in her all along. I've often sat and contemplated her lovely eyes, her milky skin, her delicate hands, and thought, 'Your time will come, my dear! Your time will come!' "

"Delicate hands!" I whispered fiercely into the mattress. "Bony! Bony!"

I suppose, in a way, that nothing changed too drastically for me after that play. I continued to lead groups, direct shows, spark activities with my ideas, my zeal. In school I did well in all my subjects and was good at sports, too. Henrietta's grades were mediocre, and she never even tried out for teams or anything, while I was on the swim team, the baseball team, the basketball team. She still moved slowly, languidly, as though her energy was in short supply, but there was a subtle difference in her that was hard to put your finger on. It wasn't as though she went around covered with all that highly flattering greasepaint that Mrs. Elliot had supplied. In fact, she didn't really start wearing makeup until she was fifteen or sixteen. Apparently she didn't need to. That one dramatic walk-on part with the blanket and the safety pin had done it all, although I'm sure I harbored a hope that we might return to the old Henrietta as soon as she washed her face. Even the sailors started coming to the house more often. They couldn't take her out, of course, or *do* anything with her. But they seemed to enjoy just looking at her, contemplating her. They would sit there on our big brown plush chesterfield under the stern picture of Great-great-grandmother Logan in the big gold frame, smoking cigarette after cigarette and watching Henrietta as she moved about with her <u>infuriatingly</u> slow, lazy grace, her grave confidence. Her serenity

soothed and excited them, all at the same time. Boys from grades 9 and 10 hung around our backyard, our verandah, the nearest street corner. They weren't mean to me. They simply didn't know I was there, not really.

I didn't spend much time with Henrietta anymore, or boss her, or make her go to The Grove in the fog or try to scare her. I just wasn't all that crazy about having her around the entire time, with those eyes looking out at me from under those long lashes, quiet, mysterious, full of power. And of course you had to trip over boys if you so much as wanted to ask her what time it was. Every once in a while I'd try to figure out what the thing was that made her so different now; and then, one day, all of a sudden, I understood. We were down at the beach, and she was just sitting on a rock or something, arms slack and resting on her knees, in a position I had often seen over the years. And in that moment I knew. Everything else was the same—the drab white skin; the bony, yes, bony hands; the limp hair. But she had lost her waiting look. Henrietta didn't look as though she were waiting for anything at all anymore. ❖

WORDS
TO
KNOW
infuriatingly (ĭn-fyōōr'ē-ā'tĭng-lē) *adv.* in a way that makes one very angry **infuriate** *v.*

Multiple Learning Styles
Linguistic Learners

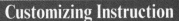 Students may enjoy comparing the author's imagery here, where words "hail down," with that at the beginning of the story, where the words "dropped like drenching rain."

Students Acquiring English

2 You may wish to point out that the words *delicate* and *bony* can both mean "thin," but *delicate* is a word that suggests attractiveness, while *bony* suggests ugliness.

Gifted and Talented

Discuss with students how the story implies that serenity and quiet confidence are more important than physical courage, flamboyance, and a vivacious personality. Invite students to discuss whether the story would work as well if the two main characters were boys, and whether society values the same qualities in both girls and boys.

Assessment **Speaking and Listening** 🏴 TEKS 5C, 5E, 11B

RETELLING OF STORY EVENT

Prepare To provide students with an opportunity to present dramatic interpretations of the story, tell them to retell one story event from Henrietta's point of view. In order to do this, students must prepare by

- selecting one event from the story
- imagining the event from Henrietta's point of view and retelling it using the pronoun *I*.
- determining where the event will begin and end and what details will be included.
- practicing their delivery, using effective rate,

volume, pitch, and tone for the audience and setting.

Present Allow time for students select events and decide how they will retell them. You may wish to encourage students to present their retellings in the same order in which the events occurred in the story.

BLOCK SCHEDULING This activity is particularly well suited for longer class periods.

📋 Use **Communications Transparencies and Copymasters**, p. 12, for additional support.

Connect to the Literature

1. Responses will vary. Students may see either or both sisters differently.

Comprehension Check
- Juliette is more outgoing.
- Henrietta rescues Juliette.
- Henrietta becomes the center of attention.

 Use Selection Quiz, **Unit Four Resource Book,** p. 47.

Think Critically

2. Possible Response: Juliette feels that a best friend is someone who does everything with her. Henrietta may feel the same way.

3. Possible Response: Henrietta becomes the dominant twin; Juliette becomes aware of her sister's beauty, self-assurance, and appeal to boys; Henrietta seems to have come into her own.

4. Possible Response: She has the power to attract attention—what some call charisma.

5. Possible Response: She is no longer waiting to be noticed or to find out who she is.

6. Possible Response: She is not reliable; she always sees her sister in a bad light and herself in a positive light.

 Use **Reading and Critical Thinking Transparencies,** p. 15, for additional support.

Literary Analysis

Unreliable Narrator Many students will answer that Juliette does come to an understanding of herself and her relationship. As evidence, they may point to the fact that Juliette doesn't spend as much time with her twin; or she realizes that nothing has changed except inside Henrietta, i.e. she is no longer waiting for anything.

Review: Foil Students might mention her self-confidence, courage, meanness, selfishness, or intelligence.

 Use **Literary Analysis Transparencies,** p. 22, for additional support.

Connect to the Literature

1. **What Do You Think?** How did your impression of Juliette and Henrietta change as you neared the end of the story?

Comprehension Check
- At first, who is the more outgoing sister?
- Who rescues Juliette onstage?
- Who is the center of attention at the end of the story?

Think Critically

2. In the beginning, Juliette says that she and Henrietta were "best friends." What does friendship mean to Juliette at that point? Do you think Henrietta feels the same way? Explain.

3. How does the relationship between the two girls change after Henrietta's walk-on? Explain.

4. While Juliette takes her bow, she thinks, "Henrietta had power." What does Henrietta's power consist of?

5. At the end of the story, Juliette says that Henrietta had "lost her waiting look." What do you think she means?

 THINK ABOUT
- the games they played in "The Grove"
- the mother's statement that Henrietta was "a serious, responsible little girl."
- Juliette's perception that Henrietta was no longer "skinny," but "slender."

6. **ACTIVE READING** **MAKING JUDGMENTS** Look over the notes you took in your **READER'S NOTEBOOK.** In your judgment, is Juliette reliable as a narrator? What clues from the story helped you decide? Explain.

Extend Interpretations

7. **COMPARING TEXTS** The sisters in "The White Umbrella" (page 522) have a much different relationship from that of Juliette and Henrietta. What differences can you mention? How are the two relationships similar? What judgment could you make about the relationships?

8. **Connect to Life** Think about the people you like to do things with. Which person is a lot like you? How do the qualities you share affect your relationship?

Literary Analysis

UNRELIABLE NARRATOR
Different people often have different perceptions of the same event. Likewise, a narrator of a story who is also a character in the story is likely to have biases or a lack of self-awareness that can distort his or her presentation of the events. A narrator who does not narrate events objectively is called an **unreliable narrator.** Throughout "Waiting," Juliette unintentionally drops hints that her perception of herself and of her sister, Henrietta, is not objective. For example, Juliette daydreams of an audience murmuring, "So young, so small, and so attractive" about her, yet we find that she must hide pimples with makeup before she goes on stage.

Cooperative Learning Activity
Does Juliette ever arrive at an understanding of herself and her relationship with her sister? In small groups, review the story, looking for details that help answer this question. Discuss your answer. Pay careful attention to the final scenes of the story.

REVIEW **FOIL** A foil is a character who provides a contrast to another character. A writer can use a foil to draw attention to characteristics of the main character. In "Waiting" Juliette, the narrator, acknowledges that she and Henrietta are opposites. What qualities in Juliette, admirable and not so admirable, does Henrietta make apparent for the reader?

Extend Interpretations

7. **Comparing Texts** Some students might notice the closeness between both sets of sisters. Others might notice that both sets of sisters are different in how they handle or perceive certain situations.

8. **Connect to Life** Responses may vary. Some students may value people who have different qualities from theirs, while others may like people who have similar ones. Students should explain how the difference or similarity affects the friendship.

Choices & CHALLENGES

Writing Options

1. Persuasive Essay Is competition a positive thing? Is it a negative thing? Write an essay advocating one of these views on competition. Put your essay in your **Working Portfolio**.

Writing Handbook
See p. R39, Persuasive Writing.

2. Letter to Henrietta Imagine that you are Juliette. Write a letter to Henrietta dated the day after the play. What kinds of feelings might you express toward your sister? What have you learned from her about friendship, about competition, and about yourself? Save your letter in your **Working Portfolio**.

Activities & Explorations

Play Production Perform the last scene of the play described in "Waiting," showing Henrietta's rescue of Juliette. The costumes, props, and music used in the scene should reflect the details presented in the story.
~ PERFORMING

Art Connection

Look at Dame Laura Knight's painting *Two Girls on a Cliff*, on page 612. Could this painting illustrate a moment in the lives of Juliette and Henrietta? Explain your answer.

Inquiry & Research

Research About Twins Do some research on the differences and similarities between fraternal and identical twins. Present your information to the class.

 Begin your research by reading the **Real World Link** "Face-to-Face with Twins" on page 617.

Vocabulary in Action

EXERCISE: ANALOGIES An analogy contains two pairs of words that are related in the same way, as in the example TALL : SHORT :: old : young. This analogy is read as "*Tall* is to *short* as *old* is to *young*." In this example, both pairs contain words that are antonyms, that is, words that are opposites. An analogy may also use synonyms to express a relationship between words. For each item below, decide which Word to Know best completes the analogy.

1. LEAD : FOLLOW :: _____ : interest
2. GRACEFUL : CLUMSY :: enlivening : _____

3. HAPPY : GLAD :: confinement : _____
4. QUIET : LOUD :: _____ : overpowering
5. RELUCTANTLY: UNWILLINGLY :: strength : _____
6. HEALTH : ILLNESS :: _____ : pleasingly
7. MISLEAD : INFORM :: rush : _____
8. SAD : UNHAPPY :: _____ : striking
9. FALSIFY : LIE :: _____ : showy
10. LARGE : BIG :: _____ : controlling

Building Vocabulary
For an in-depth lesson on interpreting analogies, see p. 398.

WORDS TO KNOW	apathy	dominant	infuriatingly	saunter	submissive
	arresting	flamboyant	quarantine	stupefying	vigor

Writing Options

1. Persuasive Essay Students' essays should contain clear statements of opinion, followed by reasons. The reasons should be arranged in some logical order.

Use **Writing Transparencies**, p. 11, for additional support.

2. Letter to Henrietta Before students write their letters, have them spend a few moments discussing the mixed emotions that Juliette might feel.

Activities & Explorations

Play Production Encourage **kinesthetic and musical learners** to participate in this activity and to contribute by helping develop staging and music for this scene.

Art Connection

Possible Response: Some students will say yes, since the picture illustrates a similar setting and shows two girls; others will say no, since the art does not reflect the competition between them.

Inquiry & Research

Research About Twins To get students started, you may wish to discuss real twins that students know either from their own experience or from films, literature, myth, and history. At least part of the discussion should focus on why people find twins so interesting.

Vocabulary in Action

1. apathy
2. stupefying
3. quarantine
4. submissive
5. vigor
6. infuriatingly
7. saunter
8. arresting
9. flamboyant
10. dominant

Grammar in Context

Budge Wilson

Budge Wilson taught English and art for a year before working as an artist, librarian, editor, journalist, photographer, and fitness instructor. Her other works include "My Cousin Clarette," "Mr. Manuel Jenkins," and *Breakdown*.

Author Activity

Grammar in Context: Participial Phrases

Descriptions of the characters in "Waiting" are often expressed in **participial phrases.**

> Resting my head on my folded arms, I smiled quietly.

> Soaked to the skin, Henrietta waited patiently.

Participles are verb forms ending in *–ing* or *–ed.* They function as adjectives to modify nouns or pronouns. Participles can also take objects. When they do, the participle, its object, and any words modifying the object are called a **participial phrase.**

WRITING EXERCISE Rewrite each incomplete sentence, adding a participial phrase that uses the participal in parentheses.

Example: *Original* I'd be the ghost, (floating).

Rewritten I'd be the ghost, floating along the edge of the cliff.

1. Henrietta was on the stage, (moving).
2. The zipper broke, (ripping).
3. (Attracted), the boys crowded around Henrietta.
4. I muttered to myself, (complaining).
5. (Having grown up), Henrietta changed my life forever.

Connect to the Literature Find another sentence with a participial phrase in the second paragraph of "Waiting."

Grammar Handbook Participle, p. R83

"A person who loves to write is never lonely; within his or her own head a writer always has a safe and very interesting place to go."

Budge (Marjorie) Wilson
born 1927

Late Start Although Budge Wilson had wanted to be a writer ever since she was a child, she did not begin writing for publication until she was fifty. "It may seem odd for someone my age to be writing for and about children," she said. "But I remember my own youth very vividly, and I've watched my own children and their friends grow up. I don't find it very hard to enter the head of a fictional person who is much younger than I am."

Nova Scotia Writer Wilson, who makes her home in Nova Scotia, Canada, where she grew up, sets many of her stories in that province. These stories reflect her deep curiosity about people and her observations of them. Her fiction for young adults has won several awards. For example, *The Leaving,* a collection of short stories that includes "Waiting," won the Canadian Library Association's Young Adult Book Award for 1991.

AUTHOR ACTIVITY
Budge Wilson has commented on her reasons for writing "Waiting." "I have often been interested in bullies—adult bullies as well as ones who are children. Why do they behave the way they do?" Write a letter to Budge Wilson stating your ideas on bullies.

 LaserLinks: Background for Reading
Social Studies Connection

Teaching Options

 Mini Lesson **Grammar**   **TEKS** 17C   **TAAS** Writing Obj. 6

IDENTIFYING PARTICIPIAL PHRASES
Instruction Tell students that not every verb form ending in *-ing* is a participle. There is another verb form ending in *-ing,* a gerund. Participial phrases are always modifiers. A gerund is used as a noun.

Application Ask students to tell which sentences contain participial phrases. Students should be able to identify the participial phrases in each sentence.

1. <u>Talking on the phone,</u> Mother shouted. *(yes)*
2. <u>Exploding with energy,</u> Juliette skied rapidly. *(yes)*

3. Henrietta, <u>complaining loudly,</u> felt cold. *(yes)*
4. Henrietta feared falling down the hill. *(no)*
5. Performing in public can be fun. *(no)*
6. Juliette, <u>feeling beautiful,</u> came on stage. *(yes)*

 Use **Unit Four Resource Book,** p. 45.
Use **Grammar Transparencies and Copymasters,** p. 99.

Language Network Use McDougal Littell's *Language Network,* Chapter 7, for more instruction and practice in participial phrases.

Face-to-Face with Twins

by Judith E. Rinard

Time to Split!

IDENTICAL TWINS such as Elizabeth and Annie Frazee, 14, of Gettysburg, Pennsylvania, start out in their mother's womb as one egg that splits in two. Here Annie (in the red-flowered dress) and Elizabeth dramatize the split. A set of identical twins consists of either two girls or two boys. They develop with identical genes.

Fraternal, or nonidentical, twins start differently, growing from two separate eggs. Two boys, two girls, or a boy and a girl may make up a set of fraternal twins. They don't always look alike.

In the United States fraternal twins occur once in every 120 births. Identical twins occur only once in every 250 births.

Reading for Information

Knowing which facts to record and how to organize them is a skill that you can use when you research any topic.

TAKING NOTES **Note taking** is a way to collect information from sources. There are three basic techniques:

- **outlining:** arranging main ideas and supporting details in a logical order; using Roman numerals for the main ideas, and capital letters and arabic numerals for the supporting ideas

- **paraphrasing:** using your own words to restate someone else's ideas

- **summarizing:** condensing the text to include only the most important details

YOUR TURN *Use the questions and activities below to help you take notes on twins.*

❶ **Outlining Ideas** Use the format shown here to outline the article. It is not important to copy every word, just the key points.

I. Identical Twins	II. Fraternal Twins
A. one egg that splits in two	A.
B. identical genes	B.
1. two boys	
2. two girls	

Magazine Article

Objectives
- read to be informed
- determine a text's main ideas and how those ideas are supported with details
- paraphrase and summarize text to inform
- use text organizers to locate and organize information, including headings
- connect, compare, and contrast ideas across text

Connecting to the Literature
This magazine article, "Face-to-Face with Twins," is a nonfiction article that can help students gain a greater understanding of the relationship between the two sisters in "Waiting." The article explains how fraternal and identical twins are formed and how they are alike and different after birth. It also discusses the special bond that many twins share, and as examples, it profiles three sets of twins. Like the girls in "Waiting," two twins, Annie and Elizabeth, are described as being "best friends, yet competitive."

Reading for Information

Suggest that students use the material in the right-hand column as a guide to taking notes about informational articles that they read. The following are **possible responses** to the questions and activities.

1 Students should include: Identical twins begin as a single egg; fraternal twins begin as two separate eggs and may not look alike; twins are alike in many ways and different in others; most twins share a strong bond, such as a personal language that only they understand; some sense each other's thoughts or feelings; even twins raised apart are similar in some ways.

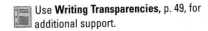 Use **Writing Transparencies,** p. 49, for additional support.

Identical But Not the Same

ANNIE AND ELIZABETH say they're alike in many ways and different in others. That's common among identical twins. Annie and Elizabeth are both right handed. They both wear contact lenses. Their hair looks the same. They lost their baby teeth at about the same time. And they both got their only cavity in the same tooth when they were 9.

2 "But Annie wore braces and I didn't," says Elizabeth, left. "Annie has asthma and I don't. Plus Annie has more freckles." The twins' mother often got confused when the girls were babies. How could she tell them apart? One of Elizabeth's toes was more crooked than Annie's.

About 10 percent of identical twins are "mirror-image" twins: For example, one is right-handed, and the other is left-handed. But all twins have different fingerprints.

Annie and Elizabeth say they're best friends, yet competitive. "We fight over everything, but we do have different tastes in guys," says Annie. Elizabeth adds, "Sometimes being a twin is so weird. It's also fun and kind of cool." Annie agrees.

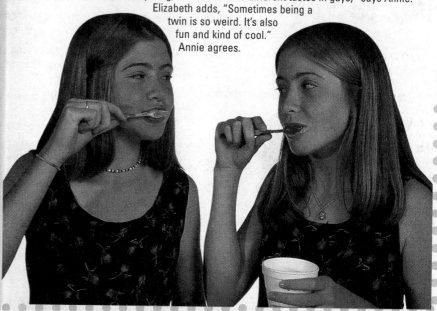

Not Identical...
Yet Alike

We're the only two who know what we meant!

TWIN TALK TWIN TALK

Omari, left, and Jelani shared their own "twin language" when they were toddlers. No one else could understand them.

SURE, OMARI AND JELANI look alike, but they're fraternal, not identical, twins. Like many twins, the boys share a strong bond. When they were very young they communicated with each other using words they invented and only they understood. About 40 percent of twins share such a personal language.

The boys seem to sense each other's thoughts or feelings, something many twins report. Says their mother, "Once at camp one twin was missing. The other twin didn't even know that but said, 'My brother's in trouble.'"

Twins have also told of feeling pain when their twin was hurt. Scientists do not understand how or why this happens.

Reading for Information *continued*

❷ Paraphrasing In this section, the author uses quotations and dialogue to relate the similarities and differences between Annie and Elizabeth. Restate these similarities and differences in your own words.

❸ Would you consider the detail about Omari's and Jelani's personal language a main idea or a supporting detail? Explain.

2 They are both right-handed and they both wear contact lenses. They have the same hair and lost their baby teeth at the same time. There are several differences: Annie wore braces, had asthma, and had more freckles, while Elizabeth had toes that were more crooked.

3 Many students will describe it as a subtopic of the main idea that they share a strong bond; others may see it as a main topic, since supporting details are provided.

4 The Levy twins were separated at birth and raised by different families, yet when they were reunited as adults they recognized many similarities, including their appearance, gestures, and job history.

Lost (and Found) Twins

"**I** ALWAYS FELT THAT there was something missing," says Jerry Levey of Ocean, New Jersey. At age 32, Jerry (below, left) found out what it was. He had an identical twin brother, Mark in Paramus, New Jersey (below, right).

Separated at birth, the brothers had been adopted by different families. When Jerry and Mark were reunited as adults, seeing each other "was like looking in the mirror," Jerry says. They had the same nose, mustache, sideburns, and gestures. The brothers are both volunteer firefighters and bachelors, and both had worked as truckers in forestry.

Other identical twins raised apart have similar stories. Two men, both named Jim by their adoptive parents, married women named Linda, named their dogs "Toy," and developed migraine headaches. A coincidence? No, say researchers. Physical, intelligence, and behavioral tests conducted on twins show amazing similarities.

4

Reading for Information *continued*

4 Summarize in a few sentences the information provided about the Levy twins. What is the main idea? What are the supporting details?

Summarizing Using the notes that you have taken, write a short summary of this article. What is the main idea that relates to each set of twins?

Inquiry & Research

Activity Link: "Waiting," p. 615. Find another article about twins at the library. Use your note-taking skills to create an outline. How do the main ideas differ from those you found in "Face-to-Face with Twins"?

 Mini Lesson ## Inquiry & Research ⛿ **TEKS 20C, 20D**

The Inquiry & Research activity on this page links to the Inquiry & Research activity of Choices & Challenges on page 615, following the story "Waiting."

Instruction Explain that before students begin taking notes on the articles that they found at the library, they should first skim both articles, using text organizers to locate and organize information, including headings. Headings can help them distinguish main ideas from supporting details.

Have students work in pairs. Each pair should read one of the articles that they found in the library and then discuss which ideas are the main ideas and which are subtopics. Then students can create an outline based on their discussion.

PREPARING to *Read*

from Growing Up
Autobiography by RUSSELL BAKER

(**Connect to Your Life**)

What have you heard about the Great Depression?

Building Background Russell Baker grew up during the Great Depression of the 1930s. The stock market collapse in 1929 led to the closing of banks and to business failures. Overnight, people lost their jobs and their life savings. A drought turned farmland into a Dust Bowl. Economic insecurity threatened the majority of Americans and shaped the outlook of a generation.

People wait in relief lines for food and clothing in New York City.

An unemployed man sells apples on the street.

Drought turned farmland into barren deserts.

Focus Your Reading

LITERARY ANALYSIS **IRONY** **Irony** occurs when a writer says one thing but means another. **Exaggeration, understatement,** and **sarcasm** are techniques writers use to express irony. In the very first sentence in the selection you are about to read, the author establishes the ironic tone of his narration through exaggeration. "I began working in journalism when I was eight years old," turns out to mean something entirely different from what the reader expects.

WORDS TO KNOW **Vocabulary Preview**
gumption   maxim   stride   surly   zeal

ACTIVE READING **RECOGNIZING TEXT ORGANIZATION**

One technique writers use to organize information is to **compare and contrast** two characters, events, situations, or other elements. In this selection from *Growing Up*, Russell Baker compares himself to his sister Doris. An active reader notes the details that are being compared and contrasted. As you read, jot down in your **READER'S NOTEBOOK** the ways in which Russell and Doris differ from each other as well as the ways in which they are alike.

 See the Skills Trace at the beginning of the unit for information on TEKS covered in this lesson.
TEKS

GROWING UP   **621**

LESSON RESOURCES

UNIT FOUR RESOURCE BOOK,
pp. 48–54

ASSESSMENT
Formal Assessment,
pp. 103–104
Teacher's Guide to Assessment and Portfolio Use
Test Generator

SKILLS TRANSPARENCIES AND COPYMASTERS
Literary Analysis
• Irony, TR 27 (for Paired Activity, p. 629)

Reading and Critical Thinking
• Text Structure (Organization), TR 24 (for Thinking Through the Literature, p. 629)
Grammar
• Avoiding Overuse of Passive Voice, CM 142 (for Mini Lesson, p. 625)
• Infinitive Phrases, CM 100–101 (for Mini Lesson, p. 630)
Vocabulary
• Synonyms, CM 69 (for Mini Lesson, p. 622)

Communications
• Impromptu Speaking: Dialogue, Role-Play, TR 13 (for Mini Lesson, p. 627)

INTEGRATED TECHNOLOGY
Audio Library
Internet: Research Starter

Visit our website:
www.mcdougallittell.com

OVERVIEW

Objectives
1. understand and appreciate **autobiography** (Literary Analysis)
2. recognize and understand the significance of **irony**; note **understatement, exaggeration,** and **sarcasm** as forms of irony (Literary Analysis)
3. utilize the skill of **recognizing text organization** (Active Reading)

Summary
In this autobiographical piece, Russell Baker explains how his mother wanted him to make something of himself—to have gumption. He lacked this quality, which his sister Doris had in excess. When he was eight, his mother arranged for him to get a job selling magazines on the street. At first, he sold none. Finally, his mother asked Doris to show him how to do it, and she sold them all. Three years later, Russell's mother finally realized that her son needed a different career. When he brought home a school composition that had earned an A, his mother suggested that Russell could be a writer. Right then Baker decided that he'd like to grow up and become a writer—he felt writing would be fun and would not require any gumption at all.

Thematic Link
In this selection, the narrator and his mother each have a change of heart as they weigh young Russell's career options.

5-Minute Warm-Up

Daily Language SkillBuilder   **TEKS 17F, 17C**

Have students **proofread** the display sentences on page 517k and write them correctly. The sentences also appear on Transparency 20 of **Grammar Transparencies and Copymasters**.

Mini Lesson **Preteaching Vocabulary**
If you would like to preteach the WORDS TO KNOW for this selection, use the Mini Lesson, p. 622.

Literary Analysis [IRONY]

(A) Remind students that when writers use irony they say one thing and actually mean another. Ask students for two examples of irony in the first two paragraphs.

Possible Responses: The narrator had a character "flaw"; Doris enjoyed housework; being a girl was a "defect."

📋 Use **Unit Four Resource Book,** p. 50 for guidance in reading the selection.

Active Reading

RECOGNIZING TEXT ORGANIZATION

Help students recognize that the beginning of the story is organized as a comparison of the narrator and his sister Doris. Have students identify the paragraphs that describe the narrator and his sister. What details does he include to emphasize the contrast between them?

Possible Responses: He explains what each likes. He likes lying around reading, while she enjoys action.

📋 Use **Unit Four Resource Book,** p. 49 for guidance in reading the selection.

Literary Analysis: AUTOBIOGRAPHY

(B) Point out that autobiographies contain details that the writer recalls as interesting or important. What insight into the narrator's childhood do readers get here?

Possible Responses: He didn't want to be president; he thought that being a garbage man might be a better job.

from

by RUSSELL BAKER

GROWING UP

I began working in journalism when I was eight years old. It was my mother's idea. She wanted me to "make something" of myself and, after a levelheaded appraisal of my strengths, decided I had better start young if I was to have any chance of keeping up with the competition.

Teaching Options

 Preteaching Vocabulary

 TEKS 9C

SYNONYMS

Instruction Call students' attention to *gumption* in WORDS TO KNOW. Have them read the definition and identify the synonym, *initiative*. Point out the highlighted sentence on page 623. Explain that if students substituted the synonym *initiative* for *gumption* in the passage, it would still make sense. Explain that students can use multiple reference aids to clarify meanings, including a synonym finder. Synonyms for *gumption* include *courage, energy, forcefulness,* and *enterprise.* One way

to select the best synonym is to insert it in the passage and see if the meaning fits.

Application Ask students to find appropriate synonyms for the remaining WORDS TO KNOW. Remind them that their synonyms should fit the meanings of the words as they are used in the story.

1. maxim *(proverb, saying, adage)*
2. stride *(step, walk)*
3. surly *(bad-tempered, grouchy, vicious)*
4. zeal *(enthusiasm, eagerness)*

📋 Use **Unit Four Resource Book,** p. 51 for exercises.
Use **Vocabulary Transparencies and Copymasters,** p. 69, for additional support.

The flaw in my character which she had already spotted was lack of "gumption." My idea of a perfect afternoon was lying in front of the radio rereading my favorite Big Little Book, *Dick Tracy Meets Stooge Viller*. My mother despised inactivity. Seeing me having a good time in repose, she was powerless to hide her disgust. "You've got no more gumption than a bump on a log," she said. "Get out in the kitchen and help Doris do those dirty dishes."

My sister Doris, though two years younger than I, had enough gumption for a dozen people. She positively enjoyed washing dishes, making beds, and cleaning the house. When she was only seven she could carry a piece of short-weighted cheese back to the A&P, threaten the manager with legal action, and come back triumphantly with the full quarter-pound we'd paid for and a few ounces extra thrown in for forgiveness. Doris could have made something of herself if she hadn't been a girl. Because of this defect, however, the best she could hope for was a career as a nurse or schoolteacher, the only work that capable females were considered up to in those days.

This must have saddened my mother, this twist of fate that had allocated all the gumption to the daughter and left her with a son who was content with Dick Tracy and Stooge Viller. If disappointed, though, she wasted no energy on self-pity. She would make me something of myself whether I wanted to or not. "The Lord helps those who help themselves," she said. That was the way her mind worked.

She was realistic about the difficulty. Having sized up the material the Lord had given her to mold, she didn't overestimate what she could do with it. She didn't insist that I grow up to be President of the United States.

Fifty years ago parents still asked boys if they wanted to grow up to be President, and asked it not jokingly but seriously. Many parents who were hardly more than paupers still believed their sons could do it. Abraham Lincoln had done it. We were only sixty-five years from Lincoln. Many a grandfather who walked among us could remember Lincoln's time. Men of grandfatherly age were the worst for asking if you wanted to grow up to be President. A surprising number of little boys said yes and meant it.

I was asked many times myself. No, I would say, I didn't want to grow up to be President. My mother was present during one of these interrogations. An elderly uncle, having posed the usual question and exposed my lack of interest in the Presidency, asked, "Well, what *do* you want to be when you grow up?"

I loved to pick through trash piles and collect empty bottles, tin cans with pretty labels, and discarded magazines. The most desirable job on earth sprang instantly to mind. "I want to be a garbage man," I said.

My uncle smiled, but my mother had seen the first distressing evidence of a bump budding on a log. "Have a little gumption, Russell," she said. Her calling me Russell was a signal of unhappiness. When she approved of me I was always "Buddy."

When I turned eight years old she decided that the job of starting me on the road toward making something of myself could no longer be safely delayed. "Buddy," she said one day, "I want you to come home right after school

> ## "Have a little gumption, Russell."

B

3

WORDS TO KNOW **gumption** (gŭmp'shən) *n.* an ability to think and act without being urged; initiative

623

---

this afternoon. Somebody's coming and I want you to meet him."

When I burst in that afternoon she was in conference in the parlor with an executive of the Curtis Publishing Company. She introduced me. He bent low from the waist and shook my hand. Was it true as my mother had told him, he asked, that I longed for the opportunity to conquer the world of business?

My mother replied that I was blessed with a rare determination to make something of myself.

"That's right," I whispered.

"But have you got the grit, the character, the never-say-quit spirit it takes to succeed in business?"

My mother said I certainly did.

"That's right," I said.

He eyed me silently for a long pause, as though weighing whether I could be trusted to keep his confidence, then spoke man-to-man. Before taking a crucial step, he said, he wanted to advise me that working for the Curtis Publishing Company placed enormous responsibility on a young man. It was one of the great companies of America. Perhaps the greatest publishing house in the world. I had heard, no doubt, of the *Saturday Evening Post*?[1]

Heard of it? My mother said that everyone in our house had heard of the *Saturday Post* and that I, in fact, read it with religious devotion.

Then doubtless, he said, we were also familiar with those two monthly pillars of the magazine world, the *Ladies' Home Journal*[2] and the *Country Gentleman*.[3]

Indeed we were familiar with them, said my mother.

Representing the *Saturday Evening Post* was one of the weightiest honors that could be bestowed in the world of business, he said. He was personally proud of being a part of that great corporation.

My mother said he had every right to be.

Again he studied me as though debating whether I was worthy of a knighthood. Finally: "Are you trustworthy?"

My mother said I was the soul of honesty.

"That's right," I said.

The caller smiled for the first time. He told me I was a lucky young man. He admired my spunk. Too many young men thought life was all play. Those young men would not go far in this world. Only a young man willing to work and save and keep his face washed and his hair neatly combed could hope to come out on top in a world such as ours. Did I truly and sincerely believe that I was such a young man?

> It was 1932, the bleakest year of the Depression.

"He certainly does," said my mother.

"That's right," I said.

He said he had been so impressed by what he had seen of me that he was going to make me a representative of the Curtis Publishing Company. On the following Tuesday, he said, thirty freshly printed copies of the *Saturday Evening Post* would be delivered at our door. I would place these magazines, still damp with the ink of the presses, in a handsome canvas bag, sling it over my shoulder, and set forth through the streets to bring the best in

1. *Saturday Evening Post:* a magazine featuring illustrations, fiction, and essays.
2. *Ladies' Home Journal:* a popular women's magazine.
3. *Country Gentleman:* an agricultural and gardening magazine (not published since 1954).

journalism, fiction, and cartoons to the American public.

He had brought the canvas bag with him. He presented it with reverence fit for a chasuble.[4] He showed me how to drape the sling over my left shoulder and across the chest so that the pouch lay easily accessible to my right hand, allowing the best in journalism, fiction, and cartoons to be swiftly extracted and sold to a citizenry whose happiness and security depended upon us soldiers of the free press.

The following Tuesday I raced home from school, put the canvas bag over my shoulder, dumped the magazines in, and, tilting to the left to balance their weight on my right hip, embarked on the highway of journalism.

We lived in Belleville, New Jersey, a commuter town at the northern fringe of Newark. It was 1932, the bleakest year of the Depression. My father had died two years before, leaving us with a few pieces of Sears, Roebuck furniture and not much else, and my mother had taken Doris and me to live with one of her younger brothers. This was my Uncle Allen. Uncle Allen had made something of himself by 1932. As salesman for a soft-drink bottler in Newark, he had an income of $30 a week; wore pearl-gray spats, detachable collars, and a three-piece suit; was happily married; and took in threadbare relatives.

With my load of magazines I headed toward Belleville Avenue. That's where the people were. There were two filling stations at the

---
4. **chasuble** (chăz′ə-bəl): a long, sleeveless garment worn by a priest during services.

Multiple Learning Styles
Auditory and Linguistic Learners

Students who process knowledge through sounds and words may enjoy reading aloud the scene between the mother, the executive, and the narrator. Encourage them to read aloud in ways that both reflect understanding of the text and engage the listeners.

Students Acquiring English

1 To help students appreciate the exaggerated language that the mother and the executive use here, explain that the executive speaks as if this job were of the utmost importance to society, while the mother speaks as if her son had great drive and ambition. Neither is being completely accurate.

Less Proficient Readers

Ask the following questions to make sure that the students understand the narrative so far.

• What had the narrator's mother told the executive from the publishing company about her son?
  Answer: He wanted an opportunity to conquer the world of business.

• What kinds of questions does the executive ask, and who answers them most fully?
  Answer: He asks about the boy's abilities and traits; the mother answers most fully.

• What is the boy supposed to do?
  Answer: He is supposed to sell magazines to people.

• Who in the family has had great success in sales?
  Answer: the boy's Uncle Allen

Mini Lesson **Grammar**   **TEKS 17C**   **TAAS Writing Obj. 6**

AVOIDING OVERUSE OF PASSIVE VOICE
Instruction To demonstrate active voice, turn students' attention to the highlighted paragraph. Explain that the verbs in this paragraph are in what we call the active voice; in each case, the subject *I* performs the action of the verb. When the subject receives the action, we say the verb is in the passive voice. For example: *The bag was placed over my shoulder, and the magazines were dumped in.*
Writers should not overuse passive voice. It is less lively, direct, and specific.

Exercises Have students rewrite each of the following sentences in the active voice.

1. Magazines were sold by Doris. (*Doris sold magazines.*)
2. The paper was praised. (*The teacher praised the paper.*)
3. His career was chosen. (*He chose his career.*)
4. Money was made. (*He made money.*)

 Use **Grammar Transparencies and Copymasters**, p. 142.

Literary Analysis IRONY

A Ask students why the writer might have made the task sound so simple.

Possible Responses: To be funny, or because his mother made it sound simple.

Active Reading

RECOGNIZING TEXT ORGANIZATION

B Help students recognize the comparison-and-contrast structure here by finding similarities and differences between the father's plain life and the life that the mother envisioned.

Possible Responses: In both kinds of lives, men worked, but in the father's world, work was hard and dirty with little pay. In the mother's vision, work was clean and pay was high.

Literary Analysis: AUTOBIOGRAPHY

C Have students describe how the author's perspective or point of view affects the text. Ask what details they read here that would not appear in a biography written by someone else.

Possible Responses: The narrator was afraid of dogs and timid about ringing strangers' doorbells. He dreaded each Tuesday morning.

Active Reading

RECOGNIZING TEXT ORGANIZATION

D Ask students how Doris's sales method and results differ from the narrator's.

Possible Responses: She is determined and fearless; she pounds on windows and tells people they need the magazine; she sells them all.

> ## "You need this magazine," she piped, "and it only costs a nickel."

intersection with Union Avenue, as well as an A&P, a fruit stand, a bakery, a barber shop, Zuccarelli's drugstore, and a diner shaped like a railroad car. For several hours I made myself highly visible, shifting position now and then from corner to corner, from shop window to shop window, to make sure everyone could see the heavy black lettering on the canvas bag that said *The Saturday Evening Post.* When the angle of the light indicated it was suppertime, I walked back to the house.

"How many did you sell, Buddy?" my mother asked.

"None."

"Where did you go?"

"The corner of Belleville and Union Avenues."

"What did you do?"

"Stood on the corner waiting for somebody to buy a *Saturday Evening Post.*"

"You just stood there?"

"Didn't sell a single one."

"For goodness sake, Russell!"

Uncle Allen intervened. "I've been thinking about it for some time," he said, "and I've about decided to take the *Post* regularly. Put me down as a regular customer." I handed him a magazine and he paid me a nickel. It was the first nickel I earned.

A Afterwards my mother instructed me in salesmanship. I would have to ring doorbells, address adults with charming self-confidence, and break down resistance with a sales talk pointing out that no one, no matter how poor, could afford to be without the *Saturday Evening Post* in the home.

I told my mother I'd changed my mind about wanting to succeed in the magazine business.

"If you think I'm going to raise a good-for-nothing," she replied, "you've got another think coming." She told me to hit the streets with the canvas bag and start ringing doorbells the instant school was out next day. When I objected that I didn't feel any aptitude for salesmanship, she asked how I'd like to lend her my leather belt so she could whack some sense into me. I bowed to superior will and entered journalism with a heavy heart.

My mother and I had fought this battle almost as long as I could remember. It probably started even before memory began, when I was a country child in northern Virginia and my mother, dissatisfied with my father's plain workman's life, determined that I would not grow up like him and his people, with calluses on their hands, overalls on their backs, and fourth-grade educations in their heads. She had fancier ideas of life's possibilities. Introducing me to the *Saturday Evening Post,* she was trying to wean me as early as possible from my father's world where men left with their lunch pails at sunup, worked with their hands until the grime ate into the pores, and died with a few sticks of mail-order furniture as their legacy. In my mother's vision of the better life there were desks and white collars, well-pressed suits, evenings of reading and lively talk, and perhaps—if a man were very, very lucky and hit the jackpot, really made something important of himself—perhaps there might be a fantastic salary of $5,000 a year to support a big house and a Buick with a rumble seat and a vacation in Atlantic City.

And so I set forth with my sack of magazines. I was afraid of the dogs that

---

Cross Curricular Link **Social Studies**

THE YEAR 1932 To help students distinguish fact and opinion in the text, explain that calling 1932 "the bleakest year of the Depression" is an opinion. However, it is an opinion that can be supported with facts. Share with students these facts about 1932:

- The gross national product, a measure of goods and services, was half of what it had been in 1928.

- More than 1400 banks failed.
- Approximately 32,000 businesses failed.
- The average weekly wage was just $21.50.
- 12–15 million people were out of work.
- Almost 21,000 people committed suicide.
- 12,000–15,000 veterans marched on Washington, demanding cash bonuses that had been promised in 1924.

narled behind the doors of potential buyers. I was timid about ringing the doorbells of strangers, relieved when no one came to the door, and scared when someone did. Despite my mother's instructions, I could not deliver an engaging sales pitch. When a door opened I simply asked, "Want to buy a *Saturday Evening Post?*" In Belleville few persons did. It was a town of 30,000 people, and most weeks I rang a fair majority of its doorbells. But I rarely sold my thirty copies. Some weeks I canvassed the entire town for six days and still had four or five unsold magazines on Monday evening; then I dreaded the coming of Tuesday morning, when a batch of thirty fresh *Saturday Evening Posts* was due at the front door.

"Better get out there and sell the rest of those magazines tonight," my mother would say.

I usually posted myself then at a busy intersection where a traffic light controlled commuter flow from Newark. When the light turned red I stood on the curb and shouted my sales pitch at the motorists.

"Want to buy a *Saturday Evening Post?*"

One rainy night when car windows were sealed against me I came back soaked and with not a single sale to report. My mother beckoned to Doris.

"Go back down there with Buddy and show him how to sell these magazines," she said.

Brimming with zest, Doris, who was then seven years old, returned with me to the corner.

She took a magazine from the bag, and when the light turned red she <u>strode</u> to the nearest car and banged her small fist against the closed window. The driver, probably startled at what he took to be a midget assaulting his car, lowered the window to stare, and Doris thrust a *Saturday Evening Post* at him.

"You need this magazine," she piped, "and it only costs a nickel."

Her salesmanship was irresistible. Before the light changed half a dozen times she disposed of the entire batch. I didn't feel humiliated. To the contrary. I was so happy I decided to give her a treat. Leading her to the vegetable store on Belleville Avenue, I bought three apples, which cost a nickel, and gave her one.

"You shouldn't waste money," she said.

"Eat your apple." I bit into mine.

"You shouldn't eat before supper," she said. "It'll spoil your appetite."

Back at the house that evening, she dutifully reported me for wasting a nickel. Instead of a scolding, I was rewarded with a pat on the back for having the good sense to buy fruit instead of candy. My mother reached into her bottomless supply of <u>maxims</u> and told Doris, "An apple a day keeps the doctor away."

By the time I was ten I had learned all my mother's maxims by heart. Asking to stay up past normal bedtime, I knew that a refusal would be explained with, "Early to bed and early to rise, makes a man healthy, wealthy, and wise." If I whimpered about having to get

WORDS TO KNOW

stride (strīd) *v.* to walk with long steps; *past tense*—**strode**
maxim (măkˈsĭm) *n.* a short saying that expresses an accepted truth or rule; proverb

627

Customizing Instruction

Less Proficient Readers

1 Make sure that students recognize and interpret this flashback for what it is—a step back in time. Ask what text clues signal the switch.

Answer: "when I was a country child"

4 Ask students to summarize what happens when Russell tries to sell magazines and what happens when his sister does.

Answer: He sells few or none, but she sells them all.

Multiple Learning Styles
Visual Learners

2 Encourage students to visualize the two kinds of workers and to describe the mental images that the text descriptions evoke. Although the writer mentions lunch pails and pressed suits, what other differences do students visualize?

Possible Responses: The workmen might have shaggy hair, heavy shoes, and careworn faces; the office workers might be well-groomed and relaxed.

Students Acquiring English

3 Before students read, you may wish to summarize what has happened here, explaining that the narrator sells few papers, so his sister tries and succeeds.

Mini Lesson **Speaking and Listening** ★ **TEKS 5C, 11B**

DRAMATIC INTERPRETATION

Instruction Remind students that they can present dramatic interpretations of stories to communicate what they have learned.

Application Have students work together to prepare a dialogue between Russell and the character Juliette in "Waiting" about siblings—brothers and sisters. Assign each half of the group to take notes on one selection. Have students note what the character might say, based on evidence in the story. When students have gathered information, have individual pairs of students select which

notes they wish to incorporate into their dialogues.

Presentation Have pairs of students role-play Russell and Juliette and present the dialogue to their classmates.

You may wish to link this activity to the **Comparing Texts** activity on page 629.

BLOCK SCHEDULING This activity is particularly well suited for longer class periods.

Use **Communications Transparencies and Copymasters**, p. 13, for additional support.

up early in the morning, I could depend on her to say, "The early bird gets the worm."

The one I most despised was, "If at first you don't succeed, try, try again." This was the battle cry with which she constantly sent me back into the hopeless struggle whenever I moaned that I had rung every doorbell in town and knew there wasn't a single potential buyer left in Belleville that week. After listening to my explanation, she handed me the canvas bag and said, "If at first you don't succeed . . ."

Three years in that job, which I would gladly have quit after the first day except for her insistence, produced at least one valuable result. My mother finally concluded that I would never make something of myself by pursuing a life in business and started considering careers that demanded less competitive <u>zeal</u>.

One evening when I was eleven I brought home a short "composition" on my summer vacation which the teacher had graded with an A. Reading it with her own schoolteacher's eye, my mother agreed that it was top-drawer seventh grade prose and complimented me. Nothing more was said

about it immediately, but a new idea had taken life in her mind. Halfway through supper she suddenly interrupted the conversation.

"Buddy," she said, "maybe you could be a writer."

I clasped the idea to my heart. I had never met a writer, had shown no previous urge to write, and hadn't a notion how to become a writer, but I loved stories and thought that making up stories must surely be almost as much fun as reading them. Best of all, though, and what really gladdened my heart, was the ease of the writer's life. Writers did not have to trudge through the town peddling from canvas bags, defending themselves against angry dogs, being rejected by <u>surly</u> strangers. Writers did not have to ring doorbells. So far as I could make out, what writers did couldn't even be classified as work.

I was enchanted. Writers didn't have to have any gumption at all. I did not dare tell anybody for fear of being laughed at in the schoolyard, but secretly I decided that what I'd like to be when I grew up was a writer. ❖

WORDS
TO
KNOW

zeal (zēl) *n.* eagerness; enthusiasm
surly (sûr'lē) *adj.* ill-tempered; gruff

✓ **Assessment** **Standardized Test Practice** TEKS 10F, 10K 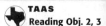 TAAS Reading Obj. 2, 3

MAIN IDEA In some standardized tests, students are asked to recall specific details and facts that support the main idea. To provide students with some help in identifying an implied main idea, have them reread the first complete paragraph on page 628. Then read aloud or write on the chalkboard the following:
Which statement best states the main idea of this paragraph?

A. Russell rang many doorbells.

B. Russell explained his lack of success to his mother.

C. Russell's mother wanted him to keep trying.

D. Russell's mother handed him a canvas bag.

Lead students through the process of choosing the best answer. Help them recognize that answers A, B, and D are only details. The answer C is the main idea that is supported by those details and others. Therefore, the best answer is C.

Thinking through the LITERATURE

Connect to the Literature

1. What Do You Think?
What was your reaction when Russell's mother suggested he might be a writer?

> **Comprehension Check**
> • What did Russell's mother most want for him?
> • How did Russell feel about selling magazines?
> • What was Doris good at?

Think Critically

2. Why is Russell's mother so determined for him to "make something of himself"?

> **THINK ABOUT**
> • her personality
> • Russell's father's life
> • the times they lived in

3. When his mother says he might become a writer, Russell says, "I clasped the idea to my heart" and "I was enchanted." Why do you think Russell is so happy?

4. Russell is not successful when he tries to sell magazines but he doesn't quit. Why?

5. What do you think Russell's mother means by "gumption"? Explain.

6. **ACTIVE READING** **RECOGNIZING TEXT ORGANIZATION** Look back at the chart in your **READER'S NOTEBOOK**. Working with a partner, describe in your own words the differences and similarities between Doris and Russell. Which child has more "gumption"? Explain your answer.

Extend Interpretations

7. **COMPARING TEXTS** Think of the sisters in the story "Waiting" (p. 601). How is Juliette's attitude toward Henrietta similar to Russell's attitude toward Doris? How is it different? How do their attitudes change?

8. **Connect to Life** Do you think it is always possible to have a job that is "right" for you? Explain.

Literary Analysis

 IRONY When a writer says one thing but means another, he or she is said to be using **irony**. Exaggeration, understatement, and sarcasm are techniques writers use to express irony. When using exaggeration, a writer depicts something as being somehow greater than it actually is. Understatement, by contrast, deemphasizes the significance or full impact of something. Sarcasm often uses either exaggeration or understatement but with the intention of upsetting or even offending someone. All three techniques are present in the selection from *Growing Up*.

Paired Learning Activity With a partner, go through the selection and identify examples of irony where the author uses exaggeration or its opposite, understatement. Afterwards, as a class, discuss how Russell Baker's use of irony helped you to appreciate his childhood experiences.

Exaggeration	Understatement
The representative from the Curtis Publishing Company presented the canvas magazine bag with "reverence fit for a chasuble."	"So far as I could make out, what writers did couldn't even be classified as work."

Extend Interpretations

7. Comparing Texts/Possible Responses: Juliette's attitude toward Henrietta is similar to Russell's attitude toward Doris in that both relationships are antagonistic but close in some ways. They are different in that Juliette is in the dominant role while Russell is in the submissive, and that Don's does not seem to bully Russell as Juliette does Henrietta. Juliette changes when she realizes Henrietta is beautiful; Russell changes when he realizes he has a career goal.

8. Connect to Life Responses may vary. Some students may believe that work is just a means to an end, whereas others will think that it should be satisfying as well.

GUIDING STUDENT RESPONSE

Connect to the Literature

1. What Do You Think?
Accept all reasonable responses.

Comprehension Check
• Russell's mother wanted him to "make something of himself."
• He hated selling magazines.
• Doris loved doing chores and was very active and outgoing.

> Use Selection Quiz
> **Unit Four Resource Book**, p. 54.

Think Critically

2. Possible Response: Russell's mother is very determined and has lots of energy and "gumption" herself. The hardships of the Depression were all around them, and there was no "safety net" for families without money.

3. Possible Response: This is a sort of confirmation of who he "really" is and, amazingly, his mother has given an "ok" to something he genuinely likes.

4. Possible Responses: He can't quit because his mother won't let him, and she is dominating.

5. Possible Responses: "Gumption" is "get up and go"; it almost amounts to salesmanship in the story. It means self-assertion, self-motivation, unflagging energy, and never quitting.

6. Possible Responses: Doris is more outgoing and opinionated like her mother. Both children have talent.

> Use **Reading and Critical Thinking Transparencies**, p. 24, for additional support.

Literary Analysis

Irony Students' charts will probably include examples of exaggeration, such as when Baker says that he rang almost every doorbell. During discussion, students might mention that the irony made them laugh or understand the narrator.

> Use **Literary Analysis Transparencies**, p. 27, for additional support.

Choices & CHALLENGES

Writing Options

1. **Personal Essay** Write a short essay on what you think "gumption" means. In your opinion, is gumption necessary in life? Include examples of people you know who either have it or don't. Place your essay in your **Working Portfolio.**

Writing Handbook
See p. R35: Explanatory Writing.

2. **Autobiographical Paragraph** Have you ever had to sell something door-to-door? Write a paragraph describing your experience. Do you think you were successful? Why or why not?

Activities & Explorations

Oral History Almost anyone who lived through the Great Depression has vivid memories of it. Interview such a person about life at the time, the hardships, and what his or her family did to survive. Write your questions in advance and tape-record your interview if possible. Then give an oral report to the class, including some direct quotes. ~ **SPEAKING AND LISTENING**

Inquiry & Research

SOCIAL STUDIES   THE WPA

President Roosevelt's New Deal produced many government-administered relief agencies that created jobs for those left in need by the depression. Among these was the Works Projects Administration (WPA), which sponsored, among other things, countless projects for artists and photographers. Research some of the art and photography produced by the WPA and give a report to the class.

"'Buddy,' she said, 'maybe you could be a writer.' I clasped the idea to my heart."

Russell Baker
born 1925

Rural Infancy Russell Baker was born in Morrisonville, Virginia. His earliest memory is of waking in his crib and "staring into two huge eyes glaring at me from a monstrous skull." It was a cow that had poked its head into his window as it grazed next to the house.

Hard Times Baker's father died when Baker was five, and he and his sister and mother moved to New Jersey to live with an uncle. Baker's mother dominated his childhood. As he puts it, "I would make something of myself, and if I lacked the grit to do it, well, then she would make me make something of myself."

Famous Columnist Baker began as a newspaper reporter in 1947. From 1962 to 1998 he wrote a column called "The Observer" for the *New York Times*. His column was syndicated and appeared in hundreds of newspapers. He has won two Pulitzer Prizes and many other awards and honorary degrees.

AUTHOR ACTIVITY

Writing a Column Russell Baker is known for his humorous columns as well as his political reporting and commentary. He has written about everyday events, such as stopping smoking, trimming a Christmas tree, and having a common cold. Read some of his columns and try writing a column of your own.

Teaching Options

 Mini Lesson **Grammar** **TEKS 17A** 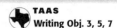 **TAAS Writing Obj. 3, 5, 7**

INFINITIVE PHRASES

Instruction Tell students that an infinitive is a verb form that begins with the word *to: to swim, to laugh, to run.* An infinitive phrase consists of the infinitive, its object, and words modifying the object. An infinitive phrase may function as a noun, adjective, or adverb.

Exercises Rewrite each incomplete sentence, adding an infinitive phrase to complete the meaning.

1. When it comes to the *Saturday Evening Post,* no one can afford to . . .

2. In the 1930s, a salary of $5,000 might allow someone to . . .

3. When Doris knocked, the driver lowered his window to . . .

4. When her brother gave her the apple, Doris did not want to . . .

5. I loved to write, but I hadn't a notion of how to . . .

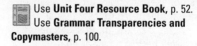 Use **Unit Four Resource Book,** p. 52.
Use **Grammar Transparencies and Copymasters,** p. 100.

 Use McDougal Littell's *Language Network,* Chapter 7, for more instruction and practice in infinitive phrases.

What's the Connection?

Synonyms are words that have almost the same meaning. **Antonyms** have opposite meanings. Look at the pair of antonyms and the pair of synonyms in the excerpt.

Recognizing that *leading* is a synonym of *dominant* helps you guess the meaning of *submissive*, the antonym of *dominant*.

> We were, in fact, best friends, as is so often the case with twins. And as with most close childhood friendships, there was one dominant member, one submissive. There was no doubt in this case as to who played the leading role.
>
> —Budge Wilson, "Waiting"

Did you recognize that *dominant* and *leading* are **synonyms**?

And that *dominant* and *submissive* are **antonyms**?

Strategies for Building Vocabulary

You can use synonyms and antonyms to improve your vocabulary and add variety to your writing. You may also find synonym and antonym questions on tests.

❶ Collect Synonyms If you know many synonyms, you will be better able to choose the most appropriate words to use in your writing. Dictionaries and thesauruses are aids for finding and learning synonyms. In this thesaurus excerpt you can find synonyms for the word *harm*.

> *harm* To spoil the soundness or perfection of: [synonyms] — *blemish, damage, detract from, flaw, hurt, impair, injure, mar, tarnish.*

In synonym test questions you may be asked to indicate words that are similar in meaning. Antonym test questions may ask you to find words that are opposite in meaning.

1. Choose the word most similar in meaning to the underlined word.
   a tardy worker
   a. eager **b.** late **c.** punctual **d.** restless

2. Choose the word opposite in meaning to the underlined word.
   a tense environment
   a. calm **b.** angry **c.** nervous **d.** unhappy

❷ Learn Antonyms Use antonyms when you want to express contrasts. Dictionaries of synonyms and antonyms, as well as some thesauruses, can help you find antonyms of a word.

If you don't have a suitable reference book try adding the prefixes *anti-, in-, un-,* and *ex-* to the word to explore opposites. Also, look up the word's definition in a standard dictionary and then guess what words might have opposite meanings. Check your guesses by looking them up in the dictionary.

EXERCISE Identify each pair as synonyms, antonyms, or unrelated words. Then write sentences using the antonym word pairs.

1. infuriate   pacify   _____
2. genuine   authentic   _____
3. abhor   cherish   _____
4. consolidate consequence   _____
5. prohibit   sanction   _____

Objectives
- identify the relation of word meanings in synonyms and antonyms.
- use reference materials such as a dictionary or thesaurus to determine precise meanings and word usage.

Collect Synonyms
1. b
2. a

EXERCISE
1. antonyms
2. synonyms
3. antonyms
4. unrelated
5. antonyms

Students' sentences should reveal an understanding of the meanings of the following words:

infuriate	pacify
abhor	cherish
prohibit	sanction

Use **Unit Four Resource Book,** p. 55, for more practice. Use **Vocabulary Transparencies and Copymasters,** pp. 10–11, for additional support.

ON YOUR OWN

Possible Objectives

You can use this selection to achieve one or more of the following objectives:

- enjoy silent sustained reading (Option One)
- read and analyze literature with a group (Option Two)
- use the Reader's Notebook to write in response to literature (Option Three)

Summary

In this excerpt from his autobiography, Malcolm X explains how he began his "homemade education." In the past, he had tried reading, but he didn't have the vocabulary to understand what he read. Now, he was also frustrated by his inability to express himself in letters, so he decided to improve both his handwriting and his language skills. He borrowed a dictionary from the Norfolk Prison Colony school and began copying it page by page. For some reason, the word *aardvark* stuck in his memory. When he finished the A section, he went on the B section, and eventually copied the whole book. From that time on, Malcolm X read at every opportunity. The prison library had many books that had been donated by Parkhurst, a man who had been interested in history and religion. The books were plentiful and inmates were encouraged to read. Malcolm X devoured literature, reading mostly in his room. At night, after "lights out," he would read by a dim corridor light. Every hour, when a guard passed, he would jump into bed and pretend to be asleep. When the guard left, he would continue reading for hours.

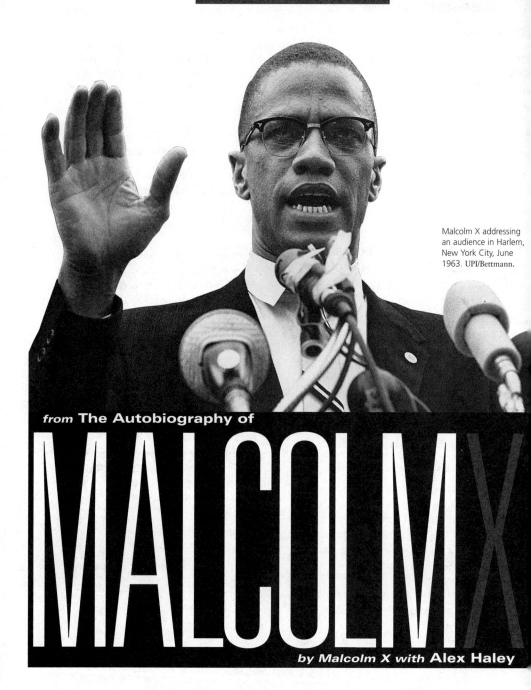

Malcolm X addressing an audience in Harlem, New York City, June 1963. UPI/Bettmann.

from **The Autobiography of**

MALCOLM X

by Malcolm X with **Alex Haley**

632   UNIT FOUR   PART 2: CHANGES OF HEART

t was because of my letters that I happened to stumble upon starting to acquire some kind of a homemade education. I became increasingly frustrated at not being able to express what I wanted to convey in letters that I wrote, especially those to Mr. Elijah Muhammad.[1] In the street, I had been the most articulate hustler out there—I had commanded attention when I said something. But now, trying to write simple English, I not only wasn't articulate, I wasn't even functional. How would I sound writing in slang, the way I would *say* it, something such as, "Look, daddy, let me pull your coat about a cat, Elijah Muhammad—"

Many who today hear me somewhere in person or on television, or those who read something I've said, will think I went to school far beyond the eighth grade. This impression is due entirely to my prison studies.

It had really begun back in the Charlestown Prison, when Bimbi[2] first made me feel envy of his stock of knowledge. Bimbi had always taken charge of any conversations he was in, and I had tried to emulate him. But every book I picked up had few sentences which didn't contain anywhere from one to nearly all of the words that might as well have been in Chinese. When I just skipped those words, of course, I really ended up with little idea of what the book said. So I had come to the Norfolk Prison Colony still going through only book-reading motions. Pretty soon, I would have quit even these motions, unless I had received the motivation that I did.

I saw that the best thing I could do was get hold of a dictionary—to study, to learn some words. I was lucky enough to reason also that I should try to improve my penmanship. It was sad. I couldn't even write in a straight line. It was both ideas together that moved me to request a dictionary along with some tablets

and pencils from the Norfolk Prison Colony school.

I spent two days just riffling uncertainly through the dictionary's pages. I'd never realized so many words existed! I didn't know *which* words I needed to learn. Finally, just to start some kind of action, I began copying.

In my slow, painstaking, ragged handwriting, I copied into my tablet everything printed on that first page, down to the punctuation marks.

I'd never realized so many words existed!

I believe it took me a day. Then, aloud, I read back, to myself, everything I'd written on the tablet. Over and over, aloud, to myself, I read my own handwriting.

I woke up the next morning, thinking about those words—immensely proud to realize that not only had I written so much at one time, but I'd written words that I never knew were in the world. Moreover, with a little effort, I also could remember what many of these words meant. I reviewed the words whose meanings I didn't remember. Funny thing, from the dictionary's first page right now, that *aardvark* springs to my mind. The dictionary had a picture of it, a long-tailed, long-eared, burrowing African mammal, which lives off termites caught by sticking out its tongue as an anteater does for ants.

I was so fascinated that I went on—I copied the dictionary's next page. And the same experience came when I studied that. With every succeeding page, I also learned of people and places and events from history. Actually

---

1. **Elijah Muhammad** (ē-lī′jə mŏŏ-hăm′ĭd): 1897–1975; leader of the Black Muslim movement in the United States.
2. **Bimbi:** a fellow inmate.

THE AUTOBIOGRAPHY OF MALCOLM X **633**

Provide the following direction to students before they read:

Remind students that when they read personal writing, such as autobiographies, they should think about the writer's purpose. Besides wishing to share facts, experiences, and feelings, writers often have additional purposes. For instance, they may want to entertain readers, persuade them, or inform them. Ask students as they read to think about what this author's purpose or purposes might be. Have them record their ideas in their Reader's Notebooks. Encourage them to write down quotations from the selection that helped them infer the writer's purpose.

When students have finished reading, have them think about the writer's theme, the lesson that he learned from the experience. Have them use their notes to write a statement that summarizes this theme.

After Reading

Possible Activities
Independent Activities

- Ask gifted and talented students to consider what part education might play in a person's rehabilitation. Does an education guarantee that someone will turn away from a life of crime? Why or why not? Have them jot down their ideas in their Reader's Notebooks.

- Have students write letters that Malcolm or another prisoner might send to the Parkhurst family about the book collection that had been willed to the library. The letters might contain thanks, or descriptions of how the books are used, or personal responses to them.

---

the dictionary is like a miniature encyclopedia. Finally the dictionary's A section had filled a whole tablet—and I went on into the B's. That was the way I started copying what eventually became the entire dictionary. It went a lot faster after so much practice helped me to pick up handwriting speed. Between what I wrote in my tablet, and writing letters, during the rest of my time in prison I would guess I wrote a million words.

I never had been so truly free in my life.

I suppose it was inevitable that as my word base broadened, I could for the first time pick up a book and read and now begin to understand what the book was saying. Anyone who has read a great deal can imagine the new world that opened. Let me tell you something: from then until I left that prison, in every free moment I had, if I was not reading in the library, I was reading on my bunk. You couldn't have gotten me out of books with a wedge.[3] Between Mr. Muhammad's teachings, my correspondence, my visitors—usually Ella and Reginald[4]—and my reading of books, months passed without my even thinking about being imprisoned. In fact, up to then, I never had been so truly free in my life.

The Norfolk Prison Colony's library was in the school building. A variety of classes was taught there by instructors who came from such places as Harvard and Boston universities. The weekly debates between inmate teams were also held in the school building. You would be astonished to know how worked up convict debaters and audiences would get over subjects like "Should Babies Be Fed Milk?"

Available on the prison library's shelves were books on just about every general subject. Much of the big private collection that Parkhurst[5] had willed to the prison was still in crates and boxes in the back of the library—thousands of old books. Some of them looked ancient: covers faded, old-time parchment-looking binding. Parkhurst, I've mentioned, seemed to have been principally interested in history and religion. He had the money and the special interest to have a lot of books that you wouldn't have in general circulation. Any college library would have been lucky to get that collection.

As you can imagine, especially in a prison where there was heavy emphasis on rehabilitation, an inmate was smiled upon if he demonstrated an unusually intense interest in books. There was a sizable number of well-read inmates, especially the popular debaters. Some were said by many to be practically walking encyclopedias. They were almost celebrities. No university would ask any student to devour literature as I did when this new world opened to me, of being able to read and *understand*.

I read more in my room than in the library itself. An inmate who was known to read a lot could check out more than the permitted maximum number of books. I preferred reading in the total isolation of my own room.

When I had progressed to really serious reading, every night at about ten P.M. I would

---

3. **wedge:** a tapered piece of wood or metal used for splitting wood or rock.
4. **Ella and Reginald:** Malcolm's sister and brother.
5. **Parkhurst:** a millionaire interested in the education and training of prisoners.

outraged with the "lights out." It always seemed to catch me right in the middle of something engrossing.

Fortunately, right outside my door was a corridor light that cast a glow into my room. The glow was enough to read by, once my eyes adjusted to it. So when "lights out" came, I would sit on the floor where I could continue reading in that glow.

At one-hour intervals the night guards paced past every room. Each time I heard the approaching footsteps, I jumped into bed and feigned sleep. And as soon as the guard passed, I got back out of bed onto the floor area of that light-glow, where I would read for another fifty-eight minutes—until the guard approached again. That went on until three or four every morning. Three or four hours of sleep a night was enough for me. Often in the years in the streets, I had slept less than that. ❖

My whole life had been a chronology of—changes.

Malcolm X
1925–1965

Preacher While Malcolm X was in prison he began to follow the teachings of Elijah Muhammad and the Nation of Islam, also known as the Black Muslims. Upon his release from prison, he became a Black Muslim minister and gained a wide reputation as a powerful speaker. Malcolm X preached in favor of black power and black nationalism, opposing white oppression and integration.

Pilgrim Because of a dispute within the faith, Malcolm X was expelled from the Black Muslims. After that, Malcolm X became a follower of traditional Islam. While on a pilgrimage to Mecca, the holy place of the Islamic faith, Malcolm X came to believe in the possibility of brotherhood among all peoples.

Author Upon his return to America Malcolm X began to work on his autobiography with Alex Haley who later wrote *Roots.* On February 21, 1965, Malcolm X was assassinated. His autobiography was published after his death.

 **LaserLink: Background for Reading**
Historical Connection

Discussion Activities

- Have students evaluate Malcolm's method of self-education and compare it with the more traditional classroom methods. Have them make a chart that lists pros and cons of each method.
- Have students discuss possible reasons why Malcolm X changed his life while in prison, whereas many other people do not. Encourage them to explore multiple possibilities, including religious or family influences, the environment of that particular prison, and other causes.

Assessment Opportunities

- You can assess students' comprehension by evaluating the theme statements that they wrote in their Reader's Notebooks.
- You can have students write an essay about the article's theme, using specific details as supporting evidence.

MALCOLM X

Malcolm Little did not have an easy childhood. His father, a Baptist minister, was murdered; his mother was hospitalized for mental illness; and his home was burned by the Ku Klux Klan. Essentially homeless, he moved to Boston at 16 to live with a sister. He also became involved in crime and was sentenced to ten years in jail. It was while he was imprisoned that he converted to the Nation of Islam, the Black Muslim faith, which was then led by Elijah Muhammad. He then followed one of the customs of this faith, which was to drop his last name. Last names were seen as remnants of slavery. Instead of his old name, Little, he used the letter *X*. It was as Malcolm X that he became a minister in the Nation of Islam and eventually one of its most influential and controversial spokespersons.

Writing Workshop
Comparison-and-Contrast Essay

Objectives
- write a comparison-and-contrast essay
- use a written text as a model for writing
- revise a draft to include transitional words and phrases
- use modifiers that relate to a specific word

Introducing the Workshop

Comparison-and-Contrast Essay
Discuss with students comparison-and-contrast essays they may have read in magazines or newspapers. Have them think about what makes a comparison-and-contrast essay effective and informative.

Basics in a Box
Using the Graphic The graphic shows how a comparison-and-contrast essay discusses two subjects both individually and together in order to effectively illustrate similarities and differences. Point out that the graphic suggests elements that students should include when they draft their essays.

Presenting the Rubric To better understand the assignment, students can refer to the Standards for Writing a Successful Comparison-and-Contrast Essay. You may also want to share with them the complete rubric, which describes several levels of proficiency.

 Use McDougal Littell's *Language Network,* Chapters 12–19, for more instruction on essential writing skills.

 Power Presentation
To engage students visually, use **Power Presentation 2,** Comparison-and-Contrast Essay.

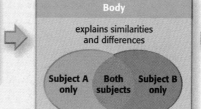

Writing Workshop
Comparison-and-Contrast Essay

Showing differences and similarities . . .

From Reading to Writing Malcolm X and Russell Baker have different writing styles and very different life experiences. If you look closely at their autobiographies, however, you can find similarities. For instance, both felt the need to make important changes in their lives. Comparing two characters—or two other related subjects—helps you to understand each of them better. One way to do this is by writing a **comparison-and-contrast essay.**

For Your Portfolio

WRITING PROMPT Write a comparison-and-contrast essay in which you explore the similarities and differences between two subjects of your choice.

Purpose: To inform, explain, or clarify
Audience: Anyone interested in your subjects

Basics in a Box

Comparison-and-Contrast Essay at a Glance

Introduction
- introduces the **subjects** being compared
- tells the **reason** for the comparison

Body
explains similarities and differences

Subject A only | Both subjects | Subject B only

Conclusion
- summarizes the comparison
- explains new understanding

RUBRIC STANDARDS FOR WRITING

A successful comparison-and-contrast essay should
- introduce the subjects being compared
- state a clear purpose for the comparison
- include both similarities and differences and support each statement with examples and details
- follow a clear organizational pattern
- include transitional words and phrases to make similarities and differences clear
- summarize the comparison in the conclusion

636 UNIT FOUR PART 2: CHANGES OF HEART

LESSON RESOURCES

USING PRINT RESOURCES
Unit Four Resource Book
- Prewriting, p. 56
- Drafting, p. 57
- Peer Response, pp. 58–59
- Revising, Editing, and Proofreading, p. 60
- Student Models, pp. 61–63
- Rubric, p. 64
Writing Transparencies
- Writing Process Transparencies, TR 1–4
- Writing Structure Transparencies: Transitional Words and Phrases, TR 9–10

- Writing Template Transparencies: Comparison-and-Contrast Essay, TR 28–29
Reading and Critical Thinking Transparencies
- Text Structure (Organization), TR 24 (for Mini Lesson, p. 637)
Grammar Transparencies and Copymasters
- Punctuating Dialogue CM 131 (for Mini Lesson, p. 640)

- Dangling Modifiers, CM 115 (for Mini Lesson, p. 641)

INTEGRATED TECHNOLOGY
LaserLinks
Writing Springboards
See **Teacher's SourceBook** p. 36 for bar codes.

Writing Coach CD-ROM
Visit our website:
www.mcdougallittell.com

Analyzing a Student Model

S P E A K I N G
See the Communication Handbook, p. R100 for speaking and presenting tips.
O P P O R T U N I T Y

M. De los Santos
Campbell Junior High

Juliette and Henrietta

When you hear the word *twins*, you probably think of two people who are exactly alike. However, in the story "Waiting" by Budge Wilson, the reader is introduced to Juliette and Henrietta, fraternal twins who seem to be very different. Juliette and Henrietta don't only differ in their physical appearance: their personalities seem to be complete opposites of each other. "She was my twin," Juliette says, "but apart from the accident of our birth, or the coincidence, we had almost nothing in common." Juliette is a brilliant leader, excelling in all of her activities. Henrietta is a follower who seems happiest when she is at home reading or coloring. Through Juliette's first-person point of view, the reader understands the deep differences between the sisters. The story also shows how growing up can reveal the swan that exists inside an ugly duckling.

The first way the twins differ is in their physical appearance. No one looking at Juliette and Henrietta could possibly confuse them. Juliette describes herself as having "fiery red cheeks and a broad snub nose." She has black hair that explodes in curls around her face and that cannot be tamed, like Juliette herself. She is "small, compact, sturdy, well-coordinated and extremely healthy." She is proud of her appearance. In contrast, Henrietta is pale. She is also very thin, with long fingers that Juliette calls bony. Although Henrietta has pretty sky-blue eyes, they are "surrounded by a long fringe of totally colorless eyelashes." According to Juliette, Henrietta's hair is also neutral in color and lifeless. She is serious and still, as if she is waiting for something. While Juliette is healthy, Henrietta is often sick.

Another way they differ is in their attitudes toward life. Juliette is fearless. Henrietta is afraid. Juliette is impossible to overlook. She is the athlete, the actress, the class president, the scholar, and an inventor of games. Juliette loves to ski down the hills and play games in the misty forest that leads to the edge of the cliffs. Juliette is always the hero or the daring spy in games. In the play that she and her friends perform for their parents, Juliette is the

RUBRIC IN ACTION

❶ Introduction identifies the two subjects to be contrasted.

❷ Presents the features that will be compared

❸ Uses feature-by-feature organization (one feature per paragraph: Feature #1–physical appearance, #2–attitudes, #3–relationship with mother).

Another Option:
• Use subject-by-subject organization for overall structure.

❹ Transitional words signal differences.

❺ Provides specific examples to emphasize the contrast between sisters

WRITING WORKSHOP **637**

Teaching the Lesson

Analyzing a Student Model

"Juliette and Henrietta"

The student model is a comparison-and-contrast essay about the twins in the story "Waiting", who are very different in appearance and in personality. The writer contrasts the twins' activities and uses quotations from the story to help readers understand their differences.

Have students think of two people, perhaps members of the same family, who are very different in significant ways. Help students to see how several aspects of these two people can be compared and contrasted so that a mental picture is formed of both of them. Point out the key words and phrases in the student model that correspond to the elements mentioned in the Rubric in Action.

1 Ask students what initial impressions they gain of the twins from the introduction.
   Possible Response: One twin is very outgoing and the other is quiet and reserved; Juliette, at least, sees little or no common ground between them.

2 Point out to students that the writer of the essay sets a main focus.

3 Ask students to evaluate how effective the organization of information is in the second paragraph.
   Possible Response: It is very effective as it makes the physical appearance of the girls easy to visualize because it contrasts complete pictures of them.

4 Have students reread the paragraph, omitting the transitional words. Ask them how these omissions affect meaning.
   Possible Response: The impact of the contrast between the girls is lessened.

5 The examples reinforce the writer's assertion that the girls differ significantly.

Mini Lesson ## Viewing and Representing

 TEKS 10E, 10L    **TAAS** Reading Obj. 2, 4

PICTURING TEXT STRUCTURE

Instruction While details and word choice play key roles in good writing, the structure of a text—the way in which ideas are organized and events unfold—also contributes to the effectiveness of the work.

Activity Have students analyze the organization of the student model by constructing a diagram or other graphic organizer. The following flow chart is an example.

 Use **Reading and Critical Thinking Transparencies**, p. 24, for additional support.

The dissimilarity of the girls is introduced and established.

Their physical appearance is described and contrasted.

Juliette's extrovert nature and Henrietta's introvert nature are analyzed.

The differences in their relationships with their mother are explained and contrasted.

Conclusion reinforces the differences between the girls but explains that Henrietta was not quite as she appeared to be.

leading lady and the director. What she says, the others do. "If you're the director, you can't be something like a page or a minor fairy, because then you don't seem important enough to be giving out instructions and bossing people around. . . ." Henrietta seems content to follow Juliette and let Juliette command the attention. She is afraid to ski, afraid of the cliffs, and afraid of the sea. Henrietta is a natural victim; she is always the prisoner of war left tied to a tree in the forest, sometimes for hours if Juliette forgets her. It is only when Henrietta is confined to bed with an illness that she can finally do what she likes best—color, or read her comics. Working behind the scenes for the annual play makes her happy, and even when Juliette takes praise away from her, she does not seem to resent it.

Another way they differ is in their relationship with their mother. Their mother seems to pay more attention to her talented and outgoing daughter. She tells a friend on the phone, "'I hope you don't regard this as *boasting,* but she really is so very, *very* talented. Bright as a button in school—three prizes, can you believe it, at the last school closing—and an outstanding athlete, even at eight years old.'" A newspaper clipping about Juliette has the place of honor on the kitchen bulletin board, and after Juliette's performances, her mother stations herself at the telephone to receive the complimentary calls. On the other hand, she describes Henrietta very differently. "She's fine, I guess, just fine. Such a serious, responsible little girl, and so fond of her sister."

Henrietta and Juliette are complete opposites in appearance, but it is their different personalities that really set them apart. By the end of the story, Juliette is able to recognize the beauty in her sister. "Henrietta had power," Juliette explains. "And what's more, she had it without having to *do* a single thing. All she needs to do, I thought, is *be.*" Juliette still gets good grades, acts as a leader in school, and shines in sports. However, by the end of the story, she respects Henrietta for the very different kind of person she is.

6 Quotations support the writer's statements about character.
Another Option:
• Provide brief summaries of story events to support statements.

7 Conclusion summarizes the contrast between the two subjects being compared.

8 Explains the new understanding that both the reader and the character achieve

Writing Your Comparison-and-Contrast Essay

❶ Prewriting

Good writers are those who keep the language efficient.
—Ezra Pound, American poet and critic

To gather topics for your essay, **brainstorm** about reasons why you might compare two things. Do you want to see how two subjects are related? Do you want to prove that one idea is better than another? See the **Idea Bank** in the margin for more suggestions. After you choose two subjects to compare, follow the steps below.

Planning Your Comparison-and-Contrast Essay

▶ **1. Explore similarities and differences.** Identify a few of the major features of each subject. For example, if you are comparing two story characters, look at appearance, age, attitude, behavior, and so on. Use a Venn diagram to show how they are similar and different.

▶ **2. Focus on specific features.** What is the point of your essay? Choose the features that will help you make your point.

▶ **3. Organize your thoughts.** There are two ways to organize your essay. You can discuss all the features of subject A before discussing the same features of subject B—this is the **subject-by-subject** pattern. Or, you can discuss how both A and B display one feature, then how A and B display the next feature, and so on—this is the **feature-by-feature** pattern. Choose the pattern that makes the most sense for your subjects.

Subject by Subject	Feature by Feature
Subject A	**Feature 1**
Feature 1	Subject A
Feature 2	Subject B
Subject B	**Feature 2**
Feature 1	Subject A
Feature 2	Subject B

❷ Drafting

It is important to get all your ideas down on paper before you begin to edit your work. You'll make adjustments and corrections later. As you write your first draft, keep the following ideas in mind:

• Make your **purpose** for the comparison clear in the introduction.

IDEABank

1. For Your Working Portfolio 📁
Look for suggestions in the **Writing Options** that you completed earlier in the unit:
• Letter to Henrietta, p. 615
• Personal Essay, p. 630

2. Comparison Shopping
You make decisions about how to spend your money all the time. Think of two products you could compare and contrast, such as two skateboards, computers, pizzas, bicycles, pairs of jeans, or music CDs. Write a comparison-and-contrast essay to help you decide which is the best buy.

3. Critic's Corner
Brainstorm a list of movies or TV shows you have seen recently. Which ones did you especially like or dislike, and why? Pick two to compare and contrast.

Have a question?

See the **Writing Handbook**
Organizing Compare-and-Contrast Writing, p. R35
Paragraphs, p. R27

Ask Your Peer Reader

• Why am I comparing and contrasting these two subjects?

• What is the strongest similarity between my subjects? What is the strongest difference?

• How could I improve the organization of my essay?

Guiding Student Writing

Prewriting

Choosing a Subject

If after reading the Idea Bank students have difficulty choosing a subject for their comparison-and-contrast essay, suggest that they try the following:

• Imagine that you have the ability to travel through time, either into the past or into the future. Write an essay comparing daily life today with the daily life you find in your new era.

• Write an essay comparing and contrasting your most favorite season of the year with your least favorite season of the year. Compare and contrast the significant elements of both seasons.

Planning Your Comparison-and-Contrast Essay

1. Encourage students to brainstorm about the features of each subject that could be compared and contrasted. Advise them to make lists for each subject.

2. Remind students to ask themselves what the purpose of the essay is as they gather their information and decide on focal points.

3. Suggest that students construct a chart for each method of organizing their essay before they decide which method is better.

Drafting

Ask Your Peer Reader Remind students to use the peer reviewer's feedback when revising their drafts.

Purpose Ask students to summarize their purpose for the comparison in one sentence. Have them reread their introduction to make sure their purpose is as clearly stated as it is in the summary sentence.

Organizational Pattern Have students construct an organizational chart for each paragraph of the essay. Ask them to check the charts for consistency in organization.

Transitional Words Have students write a list of transitional words that they might use to show similarities and differences.

Revising
USING TRANSITIONS

Review the changes in the sample with students. To help students use transitional words and phrases, ask volunteers to share sections of their drafts. Have the rest of the class listen for transitional words and phrases, and make suggestions when necessary.

 Use **Writing Transparencies**, pp. 9–10, for additional support.

Editing and Proofreading
DANGLING MODIFIERS

Remind students that dangling modifiers confuse the reader and make their writing less effective. Have the students explain the changes in the sample. For more practice, see the Grammar Mini Lesson at the bottom of the next page.

 Use **Grammar Transparencies and Copymasters**, p. 115, for additional support.

Reflecting

As they write their reflections, ask students to think about other comparisons they might want to investigate.

Option
Managing the Paper Load

Provide students with a checklist of elements and ideas you will focus on in your review of their work.

Need revising help?

Review the **Rubric,** p. 637

Consider **peer reader** comments

Check **Revision Guidelines,** p. R23

Can't get a grip on dangling modifiers?

See the **Grammar Handbook,** p. R70

SPELLING From Writing

As you revise your work, look back at the words you misspelled and determine why you made the errors you did. For additional help, refer to the strategies and generalizations in the **Spelling Handbook** on page R86.

Publishing IDEAS

- Create an oversized chart to illustrate the similarities and differences between your two subjects. Hang your chart in the classroom.
- Videotape a commercial in which you compare and contrast your two items or subjects.

More Online: Publishing Options www.mcdougallittell.com

- Stick to the same **organizational pattern** throughout your essay.
- Include **transitional words** that show similarities and differences between ideas.

❸ Revising
TARGET SKILL ▶ USING TRANSITIONS Transitional words and phrases show the relationship between ideas. To show similarities, use transitions such as *similarly, in the same way, also, like,* or *both.* To point out differences, use words like *however, in contrast, yet, but, on the other hand,* and *while.* Transitions weave your sentences together smoothly, and they show clearly which features are similar or different.

> *While*
> ∧ Juliette is very healthy⁄Henrietta is often sick.

❹ Editing and Proofreading
TARGET SKILL ▶ DANGLING MODIFIERS Few things are more confusing to readers than dangling or misplaced modifiers. Dangling modifiers have no word to modify: *Having studied for six hours, the test was easy.* (Who studied for six hours?) Instead, say: *Having studied for six hours, I found the test easy.* Now the reader knows to whom the sentence refers.

> *you ⤷ think of*
> When you hear the word *twins,* ~~they are~~ probably⤸two
> people who are exactly alike.

❺ Reflecting
FOR YOUR WORKING PORTFOLIO What did you learn about your subjects through writing your comparison-and-contrast essay? How well did your organization work? What was most difficult about writing this essay? Attach your reflections to your finished work. Save your comparison-and-contrast essay in your **Working Portfolio.**

 Mini Lesson **Grammar** **TEKS** 16B **TAAS** Writing Obj. 3, 7

PUNCTUATING DIALOGUE

Instruction Point out to students that the writer of the student model included quotations from the story to reveal similarities and differences between two characters. In this case, the writer usually quoted complete sentences. There might be times, however, when only part of a long quotation is useful in supporting a statement in an essay. Tell students that in this situation, they can use ellipses to replace omitted words or phrases in a sentence. Display the following sentence from

"Waiting," quoted in the student model:
"She was my twin, but . . . we had nothing in common."
Point out that the ellipses indicate that words have been omitted from the sentence.

Application Have students choose two quotations from one of the stories they have read. Have them include only the main idea of the quotation and use ellipses to show where words were omitted.

 Use **Grammar Transparencies and Copymasters**, p. 131, for additional support.

Use McDougal Littell's *Language Network*, Chapter 11, for more instruction and practice in punctuating dialogue.

Assessment Practice Revising & Editing

Read this passage from the first draft of a comparison-and-contrast essay. The underlined sections may include the following kinds of errors:

- **dangling modifiers**
- **incorrect verb tense**
- **spelling errors**
- **incorrect verb forms**

For each underlined section, choose the revision that most improves the writing.

> Before doing some investigating, all dogs seemed to make good family pets. I was interested in many of the new breeds that have sprang up. However, my research showed that two breeds were suited to my family. To decide between those types of dogs, I need to look at similarities and differences in their personalities, exercise demands, and grooming needs. After charting my data, I found that making my decision was easier.
>
> The Labrador retriever and the golden retriever has calm and friendly natures. They enjoy people of all ages; they play with children and are gentle with the elderly.

1. **A.** All dogs, before doing some investigating, seemed
   B. All dogs seemed, before doing some investigating,
   C. Before doing some investigating, I thought all dogs seemed
   D. Correct as is

2. **A.** had sprang
   B. had springed
   C. had sprung
   D. Correct as is

3. **A.** too
   B. to
   C. tew
   D. Correct as is

4. **A.** I had needed
   B. I was needing
   C. I needed
   D. Correct as is

5. **A.** datum
   B. datas
   C. datae
   D. Correct as is

6. **A.** have
   B. having
   C. had
   D. Correct as is

Need extra help?

See the **Grammar Handbook**

Quick Reference: Capitalization, p. R58

Quick Reference: Punctuation, p. R56

Dangling Modifiers, p. R81

Verb Tense, p. R68

Run-On Sentences, p. R59

Transitions, p. R28

Assessment Practice

Demonstrate how students can eliminate incorrect choices for the first question.

A. This choice implies that the dogs did the investigating.

B. This choice incorrectly attributes the investigating to the dogs.

C. This choice correctly associates the investigating with the pronoun I.

D. The original sentence does not say who did the investigating.

Answers:

1. C; **2.** C; **3.** D; **4.** C; **5.** D; **6.** A.

 Grammar **TEKS 17C** **TAAS Writing Obj. 6**

DANGLING MODIFIERS

For use with Editing and Proofreading, p. 640

Instruction Remind students that a modifier "dangles" when its implied subject is different from the subject of the clause that follows it. To avoid using dangling modifiers, give an introductory phrase its own subject, or make the subject of the main clause agree with the implied subject of the introductory phrase.

Application Have students find errors in the use of modifiers in the following sentences and discuss possible corrections. (Possible answers are given. Some sentences are correct.)

1. Having no knowledge of how the machine worked, repairs on it were futile. (*Since I had no knowledge . . . , my repairs . . .*)

2. Realizing the electricity was off, I lit some candles. (*correct*)

3. After making my decision, new information surfaced. (*After I made . . .*)

4. Resuming peace talks after several days, both sides agreed on a compromise. (*corrrect*)

 Use **Grammar Transparencies and Copymasters,** p. 115, for additional support.

 Use McDougal Littell's **Language Network,** Chapter 5, for more instruction and practice in using modifiers.

Objectives

- reflect on the unit, including themes and characters
- recognize how style, tone, and mood contribute to the effect of the text
- paraphrase and summarize text to recall, inform, or organize ideas
- assess and build portfolios

Reflecting on the Theme

OPTION 1

A successful response will
- illustrate the lesson that is learned.
- support ideas with examples from before and after.
- evaluate the relevance of the lesson learned to future experiences.

OPTION 2

A successful response will
- identify characters from Unit Four who changed as a result of their choices.
- support responses by referring to relevant aspects of the text and the student's own experiences.
- demonstrate effective communication skills that reflect such demands as providing information.

OPTION 3

A successful response will
- identify the characters and situations being discussed.
- illustrate a clear understanding of the characters and the differences between them.
- offer observations, make connections, react, speculate, interpret, and raise questions in response to texts.

Self Assessment

In order to help students choose a selection, have them create a chart that lists the ways that each selection shows how things change. Suggest that students consider some situations in which they might apply the insights that they have derived from their chosen selection.

Nothing Stays the Same

Do you agree with the idea that nothing stays the same? That the universe, and everything in it, is forever changing? Look in a mirror. You may look the same as you did yesterday, but in fact you're changing all the time. Each day you grow physically and emotionally. The characters in this unit undergo many changes— the changes of growing up—and learn many lessons.

Reflecting on the Theme

OPTION 1

Act It Out Many of the characters in Unit Four learn from their experiences. With a group of classmates, choose three or more of those characters and prepare, and afterward present, a skit in which the characters discuss the expression "Learning the Hard Way."
THINK ABOUT
- the lesson each character learns
- how the lessons change the characters
- why the lessons are important

OPTION 2

Character Change Which of the characters in Unit Four do you think changes the most as a result of his or her choices? Which of the characters changes little or not at all? Discuss these questions with a small group of classmates, supporting your views with examples from the selections and insights from your own experience.

OPTION 3

Writing a Dialogue Choose a character from a selection in Part 2, and imagine that character in the situation of one of the characters in Part 1. How do you think the character from Part 2 would respond to the situation? What do you think he or she might say about learning the hard way? Write a dialogue between the character from Part 1 and the character from Part 2 to explore your ideas.

Self ASSESSMENT

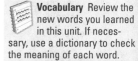READER'S NOTEBOOK

Which of the selections in this unit made you think most deeply about how nothing stays the same? Write a short paragraph in which you explain how the selection has influenced your thinking.

REVIEWING YOUR PERSONAL WORDList

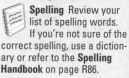**Vocabulary** Review the new words you learned in this unit. If necessary, use a dictionary to check the meaning of each word.

Spelling Review your list of spelling words. If you're not sure of the correct spelling, use a dictionary or refer to the **Spelling Handbook** on page R86.

Reviewing Literary Concepts

Reviewing Literary Concepts

OPTION 1

Suggest that students create a list of the details that they think contribute to the mood of the text they have selected. Next to each detail, have them note how it contributes to the atmosphere or mood.

 Use **Literary Analysis Transparencies,** p. 26, for additional support.

OPTION 2

Use the *Unit Four Resource Book,* page 65, to provide students a ready-made chart for recording and analyzing characterization.

 Use **Literary Analysis Transparencies,** p. 4, for additional support.

Building Your Portfolio

Students should evaluate the items in their Working Portfolios and choose pieces that represent their highest-quality work for their Presentation Portfolios. Before students make their choices, ask them to consider which pieces, put together, would best illustrate not only their writing abilities, but also their understanding of the texts that they read.

Self Assessment and Setting Goals

Students should identify a recent piece that they are proud of and an older piece that they would like to improve. Ask students to look for patterns to their revising processes that might indicate areas in which they have strengthened their writing skills.

For more information on using portfolios, use *Teacher's Guide to Assessment and Portfolio Use,* beginning on p. 53.

OPTION 1

Identifying Mood Mood is the feeling or atmosphere that a literary work conveys to readers, for example, horror, fright, happiness, or tension. Pick a story in this unit other than "The White Umbrella" and describe the mood that it conveys. What details in the story enable you to determine the mood?

OPTION 2

Examining Characterization Characterization includes the techniques that writers use to create and develop characters. Make a chart, listing at the top each main character in the stories you have read. Then rate each technique according to its importance in making the character come alive for you. Use a scale from 1 to 5, with 5 being the most important.

	Steve Brand		
Presenting character's words and actions			
Showing character's thoughts			
Describing character's appearance			
Telling what others think about the character			

Self ASSESSMENT

READER'S NOTEBOOK

Copy the following literary terms introduced in this unit. Next to each term, jot down a brief definition. If you have trouble explaining a particular concept, refer to the **Glossary of Literary Terms on** page R6.

mood	caricature
tone	point of view
dialect	character
foil	development
rhythm	farce
plot	word choice
complications	

Building Your Portfolio

- **Writing Options** Several of the Writing Options in this unit asked you to develop and present your opinions. From your responses, choose the one that you think expresses your ideas most effectively. Explain the reasons for your evaluation in a cover note, attach it to the assignment, and place them together in your **Presentation Portfolio.**

- **Writing Workshops** In your comparison-and-contrast essay, you had the chance to examine and evaluate two different things. Reread your essay. Then write a note listing several careers in which the skills you learned in writing this essay might be useful. Attach the note to your comparison-and-contrast essay.

- **Additional Activities** Review everything you created in your work for this unit, including any pieces you did on your own. Select one piece of writing or one activity that you consider your best work. Write a note explaining how it influenced your ideas about stepping forward. Add the note and the piece of writing to your **Presentation Portfolio.**

Self ASSESSMENT

Your **Presentation Portfolio** probably contains both old and recent pieces of writing. Write a note comparing a recent piece with an earlier one. Identify one strength that only the recent piece reflects.

Setting GOALS

As you completed the activities in this unit, you probably noticed strengths in certain skills but not in others. Look back through your **READER'S NOTEBOOK.** List one or two skills that you intend to develop in the next unit.

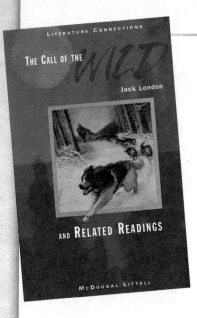

LITERATURE CONNECTIONS
The Call of the Wild

BY JACK LONDON

When the dog Buck is forced into battle for control of his destiny, he responds by following the call of the wild. The story of Buck explores the role environment plays in shaping character. A privileged, dignified dog from southern California is shipped to Alaska during the 1890s Gold Rush. Mistreated, he learns to survive as a member of a dogsled team, where "the law of club and fang" overrides the rules of civilized society.

These thematically related readings are provided along with *The Call of the Wild*:

The Wolf and the Dog
BY MARIE DE FRANCE

***from* The Hidden Life of Dogs**
BY ELIZABETH MARSHALL THOMAS

The Wolf Said to Francis
BY A. G. ROCHELLE

The Man Who Was a Horse
BY JULIUS LESTER

Unsentimental Mother
BY SALLY CARRIGHAR

Long Duel
BY ROBERT MURPHY

And Even *More* . . .

Nothing But the Truth

By AVI

This "documentary novel" is told in the form of school memos, diary entries, letters, radio talk show transcripts, and dialogue. Philip, a high school goof-off, hums along when the National Anthem is played over the school intercom. This gets him caught up in a battle involving patriotism, school policy, the national media . . . and a struggle for justice.

Books

Against the Storm
BY GAYE HIÇYILMAZ
Twelve-year-old Mahmet moves from a Turkish village to a big city. How does he survive?

Dicey's Song
BY CYNTHIA VOIGT
Dicey achieves her goals while learning that nothing stays the same.

The Giver

BY LOIS LOWRY

The Giver is a science fiction story about 12-year-old Jonas, who must choose between a "perfect" world devoid of strife or conflict and one filled with the joys and pains of a life of choices. Jonas begins to realize that his seemingly perfect world has many flaws and must decide where true integrity and loyalty lie.

These thematically related readings are provided along with *The Giver:*

Newbery Award Acceptance Speech
BY LOIS LOWRY

The Role of the Griot
BY D'JIMO KOUYATE

Jeremiah's Song
BY WALTER DEAN MYERS

The Pedestrian
BY RAY BRADBURY

The Forecast
BY DAN JAFFE

Old Glory
BY BRUCE COVILLE

Drawing by Ronnie C., Grade One
BY RUTH LECHLITNER

from **The Landscape of Memory**
BY MILTON MELTZER

Malcolm X: By Any Means Necessary: A Biography
BY WALTER DEAN MYERS
Especially written for young adults

Visions: 19 Short Stories
DONALD R. GALLO (ED.)
Stories on the trials and tribulations of growing-up.

Other Media

Country Life
An updated Australian version of Chekhov's *Uncle Vanya*
MIRAMAX HOME ENTERTAINMENT
(VIDEOCASSETTE)

The Great Depression
Five writers give perspectives on the economic crisis of the 1930s.
BLACKSIDE, INC.
(VIDEOTAPE)

Malcolm X: Make It Plain
from *The American Experience*
MPI HOME VIDEO
(VIDEOCASSETTE)

Malcolm X: Make It Plain
Narrated by David McCullough
(AUDIOCASSETTE)

Maya Angelou
Maya Angelou talks about personal challenges and social progress.
AUDIO SCHOLAR
(AUDIOCASSETTE)

This Reading and Writing for Assessment feature provides more practice in taking standardized tests. Students will have the chance to practice strategies for responding to reading comprehension questions, multiple choice questions, and essay and short-answer questions. Boxed strategies located alongside the text will help guide students through each activity. These strategies model processes for students to follow when taking standardized tests.

This feature should help students to be successful in taking state assessments and the Scholastic Aptitude Test (SAT).

OBJECTIVES

- understand and apply strategies for reading a test selection
- recognize and answer questions about tone in a test selection
- analyze a literary excerpt included in a test selection
- understand and apply strategies for answering multiple-choice questions about a text selection
- respond to a prompt by taking information from the text and presenting it in a written answer
- understand and apply strategies for revising and proofreading a test response

Reading&Writing   for Assessment

When you studied the test-taking strategies on pages 334–339, you learned helpful new techniques. The following pages will give you practice using these strategies and more.

PART 1   How to Read the Test Selection

Listed below are some basic reading strategies. By applying these strategies, and by taking notes, you can identify the information you need in answering test questions.

STRATEGIES FOR READING A TEST SELECTION

▹ **Before you begin reading, skim the questions that follow the passage.** These can help focus your reading.

▹ **Think about the title and message.** What does the title suggest about the overall message or theme of the selection?

▹ **Use active reading strategies such as analyzing, predicting, and questioning.** If the test directions allow you to mark on the test itself, make notes in the margin as you read.

▹ **Look for main ideas.** These are often stated at the beginning or end of paragraphs. Sometimes they are implied, not stated. After reading each paragraph, ask, "What was this passage about?"

▹ **Note the literary elements and techniques used by the writer.** Consider the effects of word choice, figurative language, and mood.

▹ **Evaluate the organization.** For a comparison-and-contrast essay, how well does the use of feature-by-feature or subject-by-subject organization work in the piece?

▹ **Look for expert testimony.** What supporting evidence or sources of information does the writer use? Why are these sources appropriate to the subject?

▹ **Make judgments about the writer's purpose.** Does the writer have a bias or use a particular tone? How does this affect the message and presentation of information?

Teaching the Lesson

❶ A Land of Staggering Proportions

by Brad Darrach and Steve Petranek

1   ❷ Oh, what a fascinating walk you could take near the Martian equator next December, in the middle of a summer day. The weather would be perfect—high 60s and a bright orange Creamsicle-colored sky—but shirtsleeves would be out. You'd be wearing a light space suit to keep your blood from boiling because the "air" on Mars is so thin, about the same density as Earth's at twenty miles above sea level. The space suit would help with two other problems—the deadly ultraviolet light from the Sun, and the unbreathable Martian atmosphere, which is ninety-five percent carbon dioxide, with traces of nitrogen and argon.

2   The physical act of walking would seem effortless; you could endlessly hop, skip, or jump along because gravity is only about a third of what it is on Earth. A hundred-pound woman would feel as if she weighed thirty-eight pounds, and a world-class athlete could run a hundred meters in less than five seconds.

3   The ❸ vista would remind you of the Arizona and California deserts—fine sand littered with rocks and boulders. But the sand would be pink and reddish-brown, turned to rust. Of course, there wouldn't be any cacti or scrub plants like tumbleweed, any darting lizards or rabbits. The terrain would be much drier than any desert on Earth, so dry that an ice cube placed on the ground would quickly disappear, evaporating before it could melt, going straight from solid to vapor. You could walk just about anywhere you wanted on Mars, because the entire surface is land; there are no lakes, rivers, or oceans. Almost all of the water is underground or frozen.

4   ❹ There's as much land on Mars as there is on Earth, even though Mars is only half as big as Earth and weighs only a tenth as much. Because of its weaker gravity, Mars is not as dense as Earth; it's puffed up. If you dig a thousand feet below the surface of Earth, you would probably hit solid rock, but a thousand feet

❶ Think about the title.

ONE STUDENT'S THOUGHTS

"I wonder what kind of land has staggering proportions."

❷ Make judgments about the writers' purpose.

"The subject of the essay is scientific but the tone is conversational. The reader is asked to imagine a familiar scene (a walk) in an unfamiliar setting (Mars)."

YOUR TURN

Why do you think the writers use this tone?

❸ Use context clues to understand vocabulary.

ONE STUDENT'S THOUGHTS

"It seems that *vista* has something to do with the appearance of the land or terrain."

❹ Read actively—analyze.

"If there is as much land on Mars as on Earth, why does Mars weigh only a tenth as much?"

YOUR TURN

Look for evidence to answer this question.

Begin by previewing the text. Point out the title and ask students to identify the subject. Then allow students to read through the questions and prompts at the end of the text. Discuss with students what they should look for as they read the selection.

1 Point out that the title implies that the selection is going to be about a place that has extraordinarily large features. The word *staggering* means "astonishing." The size of this place is evidently going to be the main focus of the piece.

2 Point out that the writer uses words and phrases that will appeal to readers' senses.

YOUR TURN The writers want to make this scientific essay appealing and accessible to the average person who isn't a scientist. If readers can connect to the subject, they are more likely to enjoy and understand the piece.

3 Remind students that they can use sentence context to figure out the meaning of an unfamiliar word. In this case, understanding the word *vista* is important to visualizing the scene being described. The quoted student guesses that *vista* relates to the land. Tell students that this is a good guess given the details, but that the definition could be more specific. Encourage students to use context clues to guess the definition themselves. If they are struggling, tell them the word relates to a view or scene. Then invite them to name the clues in the surrounding sentence or paragraph that support this meaning.

4 Note that evidence explaining why Mars weighs less than Earth is at the bottom of paragraph two.

YOUR TURN The writers explain that Mars is not as dense as Earth. Earth has more solid rock, while Mars has more porous material than Earth does.

READING AND WRITING FOR ASSESSMENT   **647**

5 Explain that the writers also contrast summer on Mars with summer on Earth.

YOUR TURN Comparing each feature of Mars with a feature of Earth helps readers to understand and identify with what is being described.

6 Readers should look for concrete facts that support the idea that the natural wonders of Mars are more impressive than the natural wonders of Earth. Other topics students should note include the meaning of the title, the conversational tone of the piece, and gravity on Mars.

Check Your Understanding

Have students use the following questions to test their understanding of the selection before they answer the questions in their texts.

- What is the meaning of the selection's title?
- What were the main ideas in the selection?
- What is the purpose and tone of the selection?
- What kind of evidence does the writer mention to support his main ideas?
- What structure does the writer use for the selection?

below the crust of Mars you would find porous material, perhaps even a gravely slurry of rock and ice.

5 ⑤ A day's walk on Mars would offer about as much Sun time as on Earth; Mars rotates once every 24 hours, 37 minutes. But the summer would last twice as long because Mars takes 687 Earth days to orbit the Sun.

6 ⑥ A trek to any of Earth's natural wonders would pale by comparison to what can be seen on Mars. Mount Everest, at just over 29,000 feet, would seem a foothill compared to the Tharsis bulge, a broad, raised equatorial plain the size of the United States. On Tharsis sit extraordinary volcanoes, among them Olympus Mons, at almost 90,000 feet the highest known elevation in the solar system. The mighty Colorado River's cut through the Grand Canyon would seem a drainage ditch next to Valles Marineris, a gorge that would stretch from Seattle to Miami. . . .

7 You could spend a lifetime on the surface of Mars and never run out of new formations to see. . . . Just one thing, though. You would want to get back to base before dark. Most nights, even in summer, the temperature drops to about ⁻125°F.

⑤ **Evaluate the writers' use of comparison and contrast.**

ONE STUDENT'S THOUGHTS

"The writers compare one feature in this paragraph, which is the amount of sun time on both planets."

YOUR TURN

How well does feature-by-feature organization work in the essay?

⑥ **Skim the questions that follow the passage.**

ONE STUDENT'S THOUGHTS

"There's a question about natural wonders on both planets. The writers seem to think more highly of Mars, but I wonder how anything could make the Grand Canyon look like a drainage ditch!"

How to Answer Multiple-Choice Questions

Use the strategies in the box and notes in the side column to help you answer the questions below and on the following pages.

Based on the selection you have just read, choose the best answer for each of the following questions.

1. Why do you think the essay is titled "A Land of Staggering Proportions"?
   A. People stagger when they walk on Mars.
   B. Mars has the biggest land mass known to man.
   C. Everything on Mars is in proportion.
   D. Mars has many extreme aspects to it.

2. Why do the writers use a conversational tone?
   A. They don't care about the subject.
   B. They are trying to make the subject seem familiar.
   C. They like to take walks.
   D. Scientific papers should always be casually written.

3. What main idea do the writers support by mentioning that a world-class athlete could run 100 meters in less than five seconds?
   A. It is harder to run on Mars.
   B. There is less gravity on Mars.
   C. Physical movement is easier on Mars and Venus.
   D. There is less gravity on Earth.

4. What do the writers mean when they say that Earth's natural wonders would "pale in comparison" to what can be seen on Mars?
   A. The color of Earth's natural wonders are lighter.
   B. Earth's natural wonders are superior.
   C. Mars' natural wonders are superior.
   D. None of the above.

5. Why do you think the writers include information about how humans would react on Mars?
   A. They think humans will eventually live there.
   B. By putting the information in human terms, they hope to help the reader understand it.
   C. The writers want to show that humans could never live there.
   D. The writers want to show that humans should appreciate Earth.

STRATEGIES FOR ANSWERING MULTIPLE-CHOICE QUESTIONS

▶ **Ask questions** that help you eliminate some of the choices.
▶ **Pay attention to choices** such as "all of the above" or "none of the above." To eliminate them, all you need to find is one answer that does fit.
▶ **Choose the one best answer.** More than one choice may be true, but only one will be true and answer the question completely.

STRATEGIES IN ACTION

Choose the one best answer.

ONE STUDENT'S THOUGHTS
"This essay doesn't deal with other planets, *so I can eliminate choice C.*"

YOUR TURN
What other choices can you eliminate?

Pay attention to choices such as "all of the above."

ONE STUDENT'S THOUGHTS
"I don't think the writers are referring to the color of the planets when they use the word, *pale.* So I can eliminate choice A. That means that choice D—all of the above—can't be right either."

YOUR TURN
Which of the remaining choices makes the most sense?

Guiding Student Response

Multiple-Choice Questions
1. D
2. B
3. B

YOUR TURN Choice A can be eliminated because evidence supports the idea that it would be easier to run on Mars, not harder. Choice D can be eliminated because it contradicts facts presented in the essay.

4. C

YOUR TURN The other choice that can be eliminated is B, because concrete details in the selection support the idea that the natural wonders of Mars are more extraordinary than those on Earth. If something "pales in comparison" to something else, it is not nearly as impressive. Choice C is the only correct option.

5. B

Guiding Student Response

Short-Answer Questions

The writers' purpose is to expand the average reader's knowledge of Mars and to give readers perspective on their own surroundings. The writers want people, even those who are not scientists, to appreciate the extraordinary wonders of our solar system.

YOUR TURN One clue is the structure of the selection and the writers' use of conversational tone. The writers obviously want to draw people in because they use simple, friendly language rather than formal, scientific language. Also, the writers compare each feature of Mars with a feature of Earth. This helps readers to visualize and understand what is being described.

Essay Questions

Most of us are not astronauts, so most of us have experienced only the wonders of Earth. Because of this, we might assume that other planets are like Earth, or that Earth is far superior to other planets in every way. The essay "A Land of Staggering Proportions," however, proves that this is not true. The planet Mars is different from Earth in many ways.

One difference between the two planets is gravitational pull. Gravity on Mars is only about a third of what it is on Earth. Because of this, walking would seem effortless and people would feel lighter and faster.

Another difference is size and density. Mars is half as big as Earth but weighs only a tenth as much. This is because Mars is not as dense—it is made up of more porous material.

Still another difference is the temperature and the length of the seasons. The temperature of Mars can drop to about −225 F. Because Mars takes 687 days to orbit the Sun, summer and other seasons last twice as long.

The most fascinating differences can be observed in natural wonders such as mountains, volcanoes, and gorges. Many of these features on Mars have a great deal more size and magnitude than those on Earth.

You may also be asked to write answers to questions about a reading passage. **Short-answer questions** usually ask you to answer in a sentence or two. **Essay questions** require a fully developed piece of writing.

Short-Answer Questions

STRATEGIES FOR RESPONDING TO SHORT-ANSWER QUESTIONS

▸ **Identify key words** in the writing prompt that tell you the ideas to discuss. Make sure you know what each word means.
▸ **State your response directly** and to the point.
▸ **Support your ideas** by using evidence from the selection.
▸ **Use correct grammar.**

> **Sample Question**
>
> Answer the following question in one or two sentences.
>
> Explain what you think the writer's purpose was in comparing and contrasting Mars and Earth.

Short-Answer Questions

STRATEGIES FOR ANSWERING ESSAY QUESTIONS

▸ **Look for direction words** in the writing prompt that tell you what to write and what to do, such as *essay, analyze, describe,* or *compare and contrast.*
▸ **List the points** you want to make before beginning to write.
▸ **Write a strong introduction** that presents your main point.
▸ **Develop your ideas** by supporting your statements with evidence from the selection. Present the ideas in a logical order.
▸ **Write a conclusion** that summarizes your points.
▸ **Check your work for correct grammar.**

> **Sample Prompt**
>
> The writer of this selection sees Mars as having many outstanding features that make it different from Earth. Write an essay in which you summarize these features.

STRATEGIES IN ACTION

Identify key words.
ONE STUDENT'S THOUGHTS
"The key words are *explain* and *writer's purpose.* This means that I'll have to decide why the writers wrote the article and tell why I think that way."

YOUR TURN
What clues to the writers' purpose can you find in the selection?

Identify direction words.
ONE STUDENT'S THOUGHTS
"The key direction words are *essay* and *summarize.* This means that I'll have to discuss the key features of Mars in a fully developed piece of writing."

YOUR TURN
What important points will you have to include in your essay?

So, you might believe that every planet is like the one that you call home. This essay proves, however, that Mars has many outstanding and unique features that cannot be found on Earth. The next time you run, walk in the cold, or look up at a mountain, think of how different these experiences would be on Mars.

YOUR TURN Points to address include size of the planets, gravity, atmosphere, temperature, and natural wonders.

PART 4

How to Revise, Edit, and Proofread a Test Selection

Here is a student's first draft in response to the writing prompt at the bottom of page 650. Read it and answer the multiple-choice questions that follow.

1	Mars is half as big as Earth: weighing a tenth as much.
2	On Mars, there is less gravity and the air is thinner.
3	Mars is exposed to deadly ultraviolet light and summers
4	twice as long. The terrain is desert-like, containing
5	boulders and rocks littered on sand which varies in color
6	from reddish brown to pink. Mars has huge mountains and
7	gorges, but they have no plants, animals, lakes, rivers, or
8	other bodies of water. All the water is frozen underground.

1. What is the BEST way to revise the sentence in line 1 (Mars is only . . . tenth as much.)?

   A. Mars is half as big as Earth but weighs a tenth as much.

   B. Earth, half as big, weighs a tenth as much as Mars.

   C. Mars is half as big and weighing a tenth as much.

   D. Half as big as Mars, Earth weighs a tenth as much.

2. What is the BEST way to revise the sentence in lines 3–4 (Mars is exposed . . . twice as long.)?

   A. Mars is exposed to deadly ultraviolet light: summers last twice as long as on Earth.

   B. Mars is exposed to deadly ultraviolet light with summers last twice as long as on Earth.

   C. Mars is exposed to deadly ultraviolet light summers last twice as long as on Earth.

   D. Mars is exposed to deadly ultraviolet light; summers last twice as long as on Earth.

3. What is the BEST way to revise the sentence in lines 6–8 (Mars has huge . . . water.)?

   A. Mars has huge mountains and gorges, but no plants, animals, lakes, rivers, or other bodies of water.

   B. Mars has huge mountains and gorges; they have no plants, animals, lakes, rivers, or other bodies of water.

   C. There are huge mountains and gorges; but Mars has no plants, animals, lakes, rivers, or other bodies of water.

   D. Mars has huge mountains and gorges. There is no plants, animals, lakes, rivers, or other bodies of water.

STRATEGIES FOR REVISING, EDITING, AND PROOFREADING

▶ **Read the passage carefully.**

▶ **Notice the parts that are confusing.** What types of errors might cause that confusion?

▶ **Look for errors** in grammar, usage, spelling, and capitalization. Common errors include:
   - sentence fragments
   - lack of subject-verb agreement
   - pronoun-antecedent problems
   - lack of transition words

Answers
1. A
2. D
3. A

Check Your Understanding
Have students reread their own response to the short-answer and essay questions. Then have them use the following questions to guide them as they revise and edit their own work.

- Have I responded directly to the direction words in the writing prompt?
- Have I presented the points I wanted to make?
- Have I begun with an interesting introduction?
- Have I supported my ideas with evidence from the selection?
- Have I presented my ideas in a logical order?
- Have I written a conclusion that summarizes my points?
- Have I used correct grammar?

Dramatic Reading of a Narrative Poem

OVERVIEW

Alfred Noyes's narrative poem "The Highwayman" tells a suspenseful tale with a human lesson. As in short stories or novels, a narrative poem has characters, setting, plot, and theme, and is told from a particular point of view. This makes narrative poetry ideal for dramatic spoken interpretation. A classic form of narrative poetry in ancient Greece and Rome was the epic, which celebrates heroic deeds. Another form of narrative poetry is the ballad.

Research Questions

• In which cultures is narrative poetry found?

• How can you best present a narrative poem using voice and sound?

• What materials make different sound effects?

• What is poetic meter?

Investigation Working in small groups, students research and read selections of narrative poetry, exploring the significance of narrative poetry in several cultures. Together each group chooses a narrative poem for a dramatic reading to be rehearsed and tape recorded with optional music and sound effects. In each group, students work together to decide how to present the poem effectively. As time permits, groups can create sound effects and learn some of the basic principles of how sound is produced. They should also consider questions such as: What type of voice is best for each character? Groups should rehearse their reading to create a smooth final reading. As they practice, students explore their poem's meter, counting beats and feet, and learning descriptive terms. When the groups are ready, they tape record their readings.

Wrap-up The audiotaped readings can be kept in the classroom or school library. Invite other students, families, and community members to listen to them. The teacher or a student may wish to record a brief introduction to the complete recording.

Links and Extended Reading
www.mcdougallittell.com

**LaserLinks: Background
Art Gallery**

ACROSS the CURRICULUM
SOCIAL STUDIES

PREPARING to Read

The Highwayman
Poetry by ALFRED NOYES

Connect to Your Life
Can you name a legendary figure from your family or local community?

Build Background With the cry "Stand and Deliver!" highwaymen halted and robbed the carriages of the upper classes in 17th- and 18th-century England. Highwaymen became legendary in the tradition of such figures as Robin Hood. They were celebrated in song and story by the poor who, exploited by the rich and powerful, felt avenged by the exploits of the highwaymen.

Highwaymen needed to be bold and skillfull riders. *Detail of Turpin's Flight Through Edmonton, George Cruikshank. Private Collection, Bridgeman Art Library, London/ New York.*

Though highwaymen came from all social classes, they often dressed and spoke like their upper-class victims. *From a collection of paste jewelry (18th century), French and English. Cameo Corner, London/ Bridgeman Art Library, London/New York.*

The Escort, Robert Alexander Hillingford. John Noott Galleries, Broadway, Worcestershire, U.K./Bridgeman Art Library, London/New York

LITERARY ANALYSIS WORD CHOICE Alfred Noyes uses colorful **images**, vivid and **precise verbs**, and striking **metaphors** and **similes** to create memorable descriptions. For example, by describing the color of the highwayman's coat as "claret," a deep red wine color, Noyes suggests the romantic flashiness of the highwayman's personality in a way that the simple word *red* could not. As you read, pay attention to the author's **word choice** that makes "The Highwayman" come alive.

ACTIVE READING **RESPONDING TO THE WRITER'S STYLE** An active reader pays attention to the elements that make up an **writer's style**, such as **mood**, **tone**, **images**, and **word choice**. A lively, colorful style is meant to entertain; that is, it is meant to capture and hold the reader's interest. As you read, jot down in your **READER'S NOTEBOOK** aspects of the writer's style that you notice.

564   UNIT FOUR   PART 1: LEARNING THE HARD WAY

LaserLinks: Build Background
Visual Vocabulary
Art Gallery

OBJECTIVES

❏ record a dramatic reading of a narrative poem

❏ research narrative poetry in other cultures

❏ experiment with sound and create sound effects

❏ identify the meter of a poem

Team Teaching Assignments

CONNECT TO LANGUAGE ARTS Have each group skim examples of narrative poems and choose one for performance. One group might choose "The Highwayman." Other possibilities include Lewis Carroll's "The Walrus and the Carpenter" or "Jabberwocky," Ernest Lawrence Thayer's "Casey at the Bat," or well-known poems by Edgar Allan Poe, Edward Lear, or Henry Wadsworth Longfellow. Group members should read their chosen poem carefully, and then discuss it together. The next step is to assign parts and rehearse the reading. Encourage students to strive to express the emotions in the poem through their voices. When each group is ready, they can record their dramatic reading on audiotape. *(2–3 class periods)*

> **YOU WILL NEED:**
> • examples of narrative poems
> • tape recorder and audiotapes

CONNECT TO SOCIAL STUDIES Narrative poetry is written in cultures all over the world, and has been for millennia. Assign groups of students to investigate narrative poetry outside of the English-language tradition. One group can research the Sanskrit poetry of India, and its most famous poetic form, the *Veda*. Another group can investigate the Eddic and skaldic styles of narrative poetry from Norway and Iceland. A third group can look at ancient Greek and Roman epics and other types of narrative poetry. Have each group report to the class on their findings. *(2–3 class periods)*

> **YOU WILL NEED:**
> • Web access (optional)
> • Encyclopedias and reference books

CONNECT TO SCIENCE Students can spend a class period devising sound effects or selecting background music with which they can enhance their dramatic readings. For example, tapping two blocks of wood against a desk could create the sound of horse's hooves. Review with the class how sound waves are formed. Remind students that sound is caused by the vibration of molecules. For example, when a drum is struck, the vibration passes from the drum to surrounding molecules of air, moving from molecule to molecule until the sound reaches our ears. Have students perform a simple experiment in which they strike objects made out of different materials such as metal, stone, wood, and plastic, and compare the qualities of the sounds produced. Ask students to hypothesize about why the sounds produced by striking these materials are different. They might conjecture about which materials conduct sound vibrations with greater or lesser frequency. *(1–2 class periods)*

> **YOU WILL NEED:**
> • samples of metal, stone, wood, plastic, or other materials
> • props for sound effects (such as cups, blocks, gravel, cookie sheets)
> • tape recorder and audiotapes

CONNECT TO MATHEMATICS Help students take a closer look at poetic meter. Explain that poems with a regular rhythm are composed of units of syllables called feet. Each foot includes one heavy beat, or stress, and one or more light beats. The iambic foot is the most common; it consists of one light beat followed by a heavy one. Poetic meter is also classified by the number of feet in a single line. If each line of a poem contains five feet, that poem is written in pentameter. If a poem's lines each contain five iambic feet, it is written in iambic pentameter, one of the most common meters in English-language poetry. Point out to students that the names of the types of meter use Greek number prefixes. The word *pentameter* contains the Greek root *penta-* (five). Have each student copy a line from his or her chosen poem on a sheet of paper, mark the heavy and light stresses of the syllables, and divide the line into feet. Ask them to count the number of feet in the line, and guide them to identify the meter of their poems. *(1 class period)*

> **YOU WILL NEED:**
> • several samples of narrative poetry with regular meter

Illustrated History of the Great Depression

OVERVIEW

The excerpt from Russell Baker's *Growing Up* recounts part of his childhood during the Great Depression, a worldwide economic slump. In the United States, the Great Depression lasted from 1929 until about 1942, shortly after the country entered World War II. The increased production of war materials bolstered the American economy.

Research Questions

• What were the causes of the Great Depression?

• How did it affect Americans?

• What was the Dust Bowl?

Investigation Working as a class or in small groups, students write and illustrate a history of the Great Depression. The history will consist of four main "chapters," addressing basic issues such as the causes and effects of the depression. Students may also add chapters on oral histories of the Great Depression and a more in-depth look at the Dust Bowl. By calculating amounts of money lost in the stock market crash of 1929, students gain a sense for how economically damaging the crash was.

Wrap-up Display the illustrated history of the Great Depression in the classroom. Invite other students, families, and community members to borrow and read it. Students may wish to produce multiple copies of the history so that class members can each have their own copy.

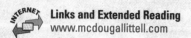

Links and Extended Reading
www.mcdougallittell.com

OBJECTIVES

❑ research and describe the causes of the Great Depression

❑ collect and/or read oral histories of the depression

❑ research and describe the Dust Bowl

❑ calculate percentages representing money lost in the 1929 stock market crash

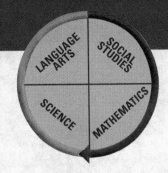

Team Teaching Assignments

CONNECT TO **LANGUAGE ARTS** Divide the class into four groups. Each group will research one aspect of the Great Depression, write a report on it, and find or create illustrations for their report. These essays will form the main "chapters" of the class's illustrated history of the Great Depression. As a class, discuss what students already know about the Great Depression and then brainstorm research questions. Possibilities include the following: Why did the stock market crash in 1929? What caused the Great Depression? How did the depression affect countries outside the United States? What was the New Deal? When the groups have completed their illustrated reports, bind them together in an illustrated cover. *(3–4 class periods)*

YOU WILL NEED:
- reference books
- photocopier (optional)
- art materials

CONNECT TO **SOCIAL STUDIES** Students can add a chapter on oral histories of the Great Depression to their book. A few students may have older relatives who remember the Great Depression. If possible, have students collect oral histories from these family members. Other students can read oral histories in books like *Hard Times* by Studs Terkel and *Making Do: How Women Survived the '30s* by Jeane Westin. Have them create a montage of quotations from published oral histories (being careful to credit their sources) that shows how the depression affected people in all regions of the United States. This section could be illustrated with photocopies of photographs by Dorothea Lange, Walker Evans, and other photographers employed by the Farm Security Administration during the Great Depression. *(3–4 class periods)*

YOU WILL NEED:
- tape recorder and audiotapes
- books of oral histories

CONNECT TO **SCIENCE** In the 1930s, dust storms and drought created the Dust Bowl, a large region of ruined agricultural land in the Midwest and West. Encourage a small group of students to author a chapter on the Dust Bowl that answers the following questions: What caused these natural disasters? How did they contribute to the Great Depression? In addition to nonfiction sources, you may wish to read to students or to provide students copies of selected descriptive passages from John Steinbeck's novel *The Grapes of Wrath*. *(2–3 class periods)*

YOU WILL NEED:
- Web access (optional)
- reference books
- photocopier (optional)

CONNECT TO **MATHEMATICS** While many factors contributed to making the Great Depression as severe as it was, experts agree that the stock market crash of October 24, 1929 precipitated the depression. Within a few months of the crash, major stocks lost as much as 75 percent of their value. Have students make mock stock certificates. They can invent a company name and assign their stock a peak value before the 1929 crash. Have students answer the following questions: Assuming that this stock lost 75 percent of its value, how much would one share have been worth after the crash? How much money would a person have lost if they had bought 10 shares at the stock's peak value before the crash? Make a pocket inside the back cover of the illustrated history in which to store the class's stock certificates. *(2 class periods)*

YOU WILL NEED:
- colored pencils
- calculator

Personal Challenges

The selections in this unit allow readers to see people of different ages, places, and eras confront a variety of personal challenges. The unit is divided into two parts: Part 1, "With Strength and Courage," and Part 2, "Against the Odds." Writers in both parts focus on different combinations of courage, moral strength, and self-knowledge that allow people to face challenges.

—————— **Part 1** ——————

With Strength and Courage In this part, two selections with quite different premises are connected by a common idea—that circumstances can bring out both the best and the worst in people and that people often don't know their own strength and courage until they are tested. In *Exploring the Titanic,* Robert Ballard shows how passengers dealt with the ocean liner's final, tragic night. In "Last Cover," a family must find the courage to overcome personal sorrow and recognize the individuality of each of its members.

—————— **Part 2** ——————

Against the Odds The fiction and non-fiction selections in this part show people striving for excellence and fighting for their beliefs. In "A Crown of Wild Olive," a teenaged boy in ancient Greece works hard to achieve on the athletic field and to cultivate an unlikely friendship. In the selection from *Long Walk to Freedom,* Nelson Mandela explains how he put his own life on hold to resist oppression in his country. The author study of Virginia Hamilton presents views on the struggles of African Americans.

Personal Challenges

taking that powerful energy that you have inside of you and

652

 Viewing and Representing   **TEKS 22A**

ART APPRECIATION

Instruction Remind students that illustrations and photographs often express specific emotions or attitudes. Tell students that as they look at a piece of art, they should notice how the piece's lighting and total composition make them feel. For example, some art might use dark colors, dark shading, heavy objects, and little movement. Others might have bright colors, strong lighting, or subjects that seem to spring off the canvas or page.

Ask: What emotions or attitudes does this piece express? What specific elements express emotion?

Possible Response: Students might say the piece is light, energetic, and optimistic. The bright lighting and the upward leaping movement of the figure express these ideas. There is also movement in the background, and the figure seems to be jumping against this movement. He or she also has outstretched arms, as if fighting for balance or reaching toward a goal.

 See the Skills Trace at the beginning of the unit for information **TEKS** on TEKS covered in this lesson.

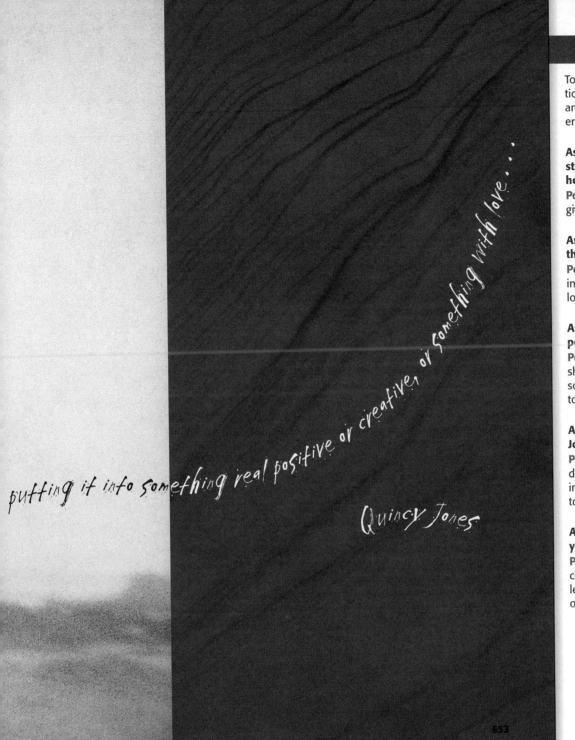

putting it into something real positive or creative or something with love . . . .

Quincy Jones

To help students explore the connections between the art, the quotation, and the unit theme, have them consider the following questions.

Ask: Why might true and fictional stories of personal challenges be helpful to you and your own life?
Possible Response: The selections might give inspiration, comfort, and hope.

Ask: What might the powerful energy that Quincy Jones describes be?
Possible Response: He could be talking about courage, drive, personality, love, and strength.

Ask: For what does Quincy Jones feel people should strive?
Possible Response: He feels they should do something positive, create something, or do something or connect to people with love.

Ask: How does the art relate to Jones's quotation?
Possible Response: The art has a great deal of energy; it shows someone taking a tremendous leap that is not easy to take.

Ask: What kind of selection might you expect to read in this unit?
Possible Response: This unit probably contains adventures, historical pieces, lesson tales, or fictional pieces about ordinary people overcoming great odds.

653

Features and Selections	Literary Analysis	TEKS	Reading and Critical Thinking	TEKS	Writing Opportunities	TEKS
Personal Challenges With Strength and Courage						
Learning the Language of Literature Setting	Setting, 655 TAAS READING OBJ. 2, 5	12G				
The Active Reader Skills and Strategies			Distinguishing Fact from Opinion, 657 TAAS READING OBJ. 6	10J		
INFORMATIVE NONFICTION **Exploring the _Titanic_** Difficulty Level: _Average_	Setting: Time, 658, 660, 662, 664, 668, 672 TAAS READING OBJ. 2, 5	12G	Fact and Opinion, 658, 660, 666, 672 Standardized Test Practice, 663, 668 TAAS READING OBJ. 2, 4, 5, 6	10J, 11A 10J, K, 13D	First-Person Story, 673 TAAS WRITING OBJ. 1	15C, G
Real World Link The Lives of _La Belle_			Newspaper Article: SQ3R, 675	10M		
SHORT STORY **Last Cover** Difficulty Level: _Easy_ **Building Vocabulary**	Setting: Place, 679, 680, 682, 686, 690 Flashback, 690 TAAS READING OBJ. 2, 5	12G 12J	Visualizing, 679, 680, 684, 686, 690 Connect to Your Life, 679 Comparing Texts, 690 Standardized Test Practice, 688 TAAS READING OBJ. 2, 4	10D, 11B 4A 11D 10E, K	Art School Application Essay, 691 Opinion Essay, 691 TAAS WRITING OBJ. 1	11B, 15A, C, 24A 15B
Writing Workshop: Opinion Statement Assessment Practice			Analyzing a Student Model, 700	19A, D	Opinion Statement, 702 Supporting Your Opinion, 703 TAAS WRITING OBJ. 2, 3, 4	15H, 18A, B, 19C 18D

Features and Selections	Literary Analysis	TEKS	Reading and Critical Thinking	TEKS	Writing Opportunities	TEKS
Against the Odds						
Learning the Language of Literature Historical Fiction	Historical Fiction, 706 TAAS READING OBJ. 2, 5	12B, E, F, G				
The Active Reader Skills and Strategies			Recognizing Cause and Effect, 708 TAAS READING OBJ. 2, 4	10E, 12I		
FICTION **A Crown of Wild Olive** Difficulty Level: _Average_	Historical Fiction, 709, 710, 712, 716, 718, 720, 722, 724, 726	12B, E	Cause and Effect, 709, 710, 712, 714, 716, 718, 722, 724, 726 Connect to Your Life, 709 Comparing Texts, 726 Standardized Test Practice, 723, 724 Informal Assessment, 725 TAAS READING OBJ. 2, 4, 5	10E, L, 12I 4A 11D 10E, H, K 10H, 11C	Dramatic Dialogue, 727 Commemorative Poem, 727 Persuasive Essay, 727	11B, 15A, G 11B, 15D 15A, 18A

LEGEND   DLS – Daily Language SkillBuilder   Green type – Teacher's Edition

Speaking and Listening Viewing and Representing	TEKS	Inquiry and Research	TEKS	Grammar, Usage, and Mechanics	TEKS	Vocabulary	TEKS
Art Appreciation, 652	22A						
Cooperative Learning Activity, 672	10L, 11B, 12G	Underwater Exploration, 673		Main Clauses and Compound Sentences, 674	17A	Context Clues, 673	6A, 9B
Titanic Poster, 673	11B, 24A			DLS, 658	17A, H	Context Clues, 659	6A, 9B
Film Critic, 673	12C, 23B			Possessive Plurals, 662	17G	Analogies, 664	9B
Art Appreciation, 661	22B			Coordinating Conjunctions, 666	17B	Words Ending in -ate/-ion, 670	16C
Press Conference, 671	5B, 11B			Independent Clauses and Compound Sentences, 674	17A		
				TAAS WRITING OBJ. 3, 5, 6, 7		**TAAS READING OBJ. 1** **TAAS WRITING OBJ. 3, 7**	
		Activity Link: "Exploring the Titanic," 678	10G, M, 13F				
		Inquiry & Research, 678	10G, 13C				
		TAAS READING OBJ. 3					
Cooperative Learning Activity, 690	11B 5B, C,	Red Fox Facts, 691	13C, 24A	Adverb Clauses of Time, 692	17A	Synonyms, 691	6A, 9B
	11B	Tales of Animals, 692	11D	DLS, 679	17F, H	Multiple-Meaning Words and Homonyms, 693	6C, 9B, C
Talk-Show Interview, 691	11B			Verb Tenses, 683	17F		
Readers Theater, 691	5C, 11B			Adverb Clauses of Time, 692	17A	Synonyms, 680	9B
Art Connection, 691	22A					Different Spellings of Long e, 684	16F
Art Appreciation, 685	22A						
Storytelling, 687	5A, C, D, E					Antonyms, 689	9F
		TAAS READING OBJ. 4		**TAAS WRITING OBJ. 3, 5, 6, 7**		**TAAS READING OBJ. 1** **TAAS WRITING OBJ. 3, 7**	
Picturing Text Structure, 701	10L, 12I	Punctuating Clauses, 703	16B, 17A				
		Revising and Editing, 704	16B, F, 17C, F				
		Verb Tense, 704	17F				
		TAAS WRITING OBJ. 3, 5, 6, 7					
Cooperative Learning Activity, 726	10L, 11B, 12B	The Modern Olympics, 727	13G	DLS, 709	17C, G	Context Clues, 710	6A, 9B
		Other Stories, 727	8C	Subordinate Clauses and Subordinating Conjunctions, 720	17A, B	Homophones, 712	16D
Olympic Medal, 727	11B, 24A					Greek Word Parts, 716	16G
Art Connection, 727	22A			Elaborating with Adjective Clauses, 727	17A, 18C	Base Words, 719	6B, 9D
		TAAS READING OBJ. 5		**TAAS WRITING OBJ. 1–7**		**TAAS READING OBJ. 1** **TAAS WRITING OBJ. 3, 7**	

Features and Selections	Literary Analysis	TEKS	Reading and Critical Thinking	TEKS	Writing Opportunities	TEKS
Real World Link Passing on the Flame			Web Article: Monitor, 729	10C		
MEMOIR Long Walk to Freedom Difficulty Level: *Average*	Memoir, 732, 734, 737	12E	Main Idea and Details, 732, 734, 736, 737 Standardized Test Practice, 736 **TAAS READING OBJ. 2,3**	10F, 11B 10F, K	Personal Essay, 738 **TAAS WRITING OBJ. 1**	15C
POETRY The Elephant The Turtle Difficulty Level: *Challenging* Building Vocabulary	Imagery, 740, 742, 743	12J	Paraphrasing, 740, 742, 743 Standardized Test Practice, 741 **TAAS READING OBJ. 3, 4, 5**	10G, 11B 10H, K, 11A	Editorial About Wild Animals, 744 Animal Poem or Description, 744 **TAAS WRITING OBJ. 1**	15A, C, F

AUTHOR STUDY
Virginia Hamilton

Features and Selections	Literary Analysis	TEKS	Reading and Critical Thinking	TEKS	Writing Opportunities	TEKS
NONFICTION *from* Anthony Burns: The Defeat and Triumph of a Fugitive Slave Difficulty Level: *Average*	Literary Nonfiction, 750, 752, 754, 758, 760, 764, 766	12E	Monitor, 750, 752, 756, 760, 766 Connect to Your Life, 750 Informal Assessment, 760 Standardized Test Practice, 764 **TAAS READING OBJ. 2, 4, 5**	10C, 11B, C 20B 11B, 12G 10E, K		
SLAVE TALE RETELLING The People Could Fly Difficulty Level: *Challenging*	Folktale, 767, 768, 770, 772	12E	Summarizing, 767, 768, 770, 772 Standardized Test Practice, 771 **TAAS READING OBJ. 3**	10G, L, 11B 10G, K		
The Author's Style Author Study Project **TAAS READING OBJ. 6**	Key Style Points, 776	12J, K	Active Reading, 776	11B	Writing, 776 700-Word Summary, 777 **TAAS WRITING OBJ. 1**	15C, G 10G, 15C
Writing Workshop: **Research Report** **Assessment Practice**			Analyze a Student Model, 781	19A, D	Research Report, 783 Presenting Ideas in a Logical Order, 786 **TAAS WRITING OBJ. 2, 3**	13A, C, 15H, 18A, B, 20A, B, C, F, G 18D
Reflect and Assess	Examining Setting, 789 Historical Fiction and Literary Nonfiction, 789 **TAAS READING OBJ. 2, 5**	11B, 12G 10L, 11B, 12E	Making Connections, 788	4A, 14A	Compare and Contrast, 788 Portfolio Building, 789	14A, 15A 19C

LEGEND   DLS – Daily Language SkillBuilder   **Green type – Teacher's Edition**

Speaking and Listening Viewing and Representing	TEKS	Inquiry and Research	TEKS	Grammar, Usage, and Mechanics	TEKS	Vocabulary	TEKS
		Activity Link: "A Crown of Wild Olive," 731 Inquiry & Research, 731 **TAAS READING OBJ. 6**	13F 10J				
Cooperative Learning Activity, 737 South African Music, 738	5F, 13I 10L, 11B	Apartheid, 738	13C, F	Using Adjective Clauses, 739 DLS, 732 Relative Pronouns, 735 Adjective Clauses, 739 **TAAS WRITING OBJ. 3, 4, 6, 7**	17A 16G, 17F 17C 16B, 17A	Antonyms, 738 Suffixes -able and -ible, 738 Antonyms, 733 The Suffixes -able and -ible, 738 **TAAS READING OBJ. 1** **TAAS WRITING OBJ. 3, 7**	6A, 9B 6B, 16C 9B 16C
Cooperative Learning Activity, 743 Poem Illustration, 744 Choral Reading, 744 Nature Video, 744	10L, 11B, 12J 11B, 24A 5C, E, 11B 23B	Elephants and People, 744 "What blazes the trail is not necessarily pretty," 744 **TAAS READING OBJ. 4** **TAAS WRITING OBJ. 1**	13C, F 8C, 11D	DLS, 740 Parallelism, 742 Commas in a Series, 744 **TAAS WRITING OBJ. 3, 4, 6, 7**	17D, G 17C 16B, 17C	Researching Word Origins, 745 **TAAS READING OBJ. 1**	6C, 9G
Cooperative Learning Activity, 766 Art Appreciation, 751 Spirituals, 758 Persuasive Speech, 762	11B, 12D 22A 4A, 5F 2B, 5A, F, 11B			DLS, 750 Phrases and Clauses, 754 Adjective Clauses, 761 **TAAS WRITING OBJ. 3, 5, 7**	 17A 17A	Related Words, 752 Absorbed Prefixes, 756 Latin Roots, 763 **TAAS READING OBJ. 1** **TAAS WRITING OBJ. 3, 7**	6A, B 16C 16C, G
Cooperative Learning Activity, 772 Storytelling, 769 **TAAS READING OBJ. 5**	11B, 12F 5A, C, D			Punctuating Dialogue, 773 DLS, 767 Punctuating Dialogue, 773 **TAAS WRITING OBJ. 3, 7**	16B 16B	Related Words, 773 Word Origins, 773 Word Knowledge, 768 Word Origins, 770 **TAAS READING OBJ. 1**	6A 6C, 9G 6C 6C, 9G
Viewing and Representing, 776 Dramatic Monologue, 777 Storytelling, 777	11B, 24A 5C, 11B 5C, 13C	Fugitive Slave Law, 777					
Picturing Text Structure, 781	10L, 12I, 18A	Supporting Evidence, 784	18D, 20G	Clauses as Fragments, 786 Revising and Editing, 787 Pronoun Case, 787 **TAAS WRITING OBJ. 3, 5, 6, 7**	17A, C 17A, C, D 17H		
Role-Playing, 788	5C, F						

Additional Support

	Unit Resource Book	Assessment	Integrated Technology and Media	Literary Analysis Transparencies
from **Exploring the** *Titanic* *pp. 658–674*	• Summary p. 4 • Active Reading p. 5 • Literary Analysis p. 6 • Words to Know p. 7 • Grammar p. 8 • Spelling p. 9 • Selection Quiz p. 10	• Selection Test, Formal Assessment pp. 107–108 ⊙ Test Generator	⌒ Audio Library ⊙ LaserLinks, Teacher's SourceBook p. 30 ▬ Video: Literature in Performance, Video Resource Book pp. 29–36 ⬌ Research Starter www.mcdougallittell.com	• Setting T6
Last Cover *pp. 679–692*	• Summary p. 11 • Active Reading p. 12 • Literary Analysis p. 13 • Words to Know p. 14 • Grammar p. 15 • Spelling p. 16 • Selection Quiz p. 17	• Selection Test, Formal Assessment pp. 109–110 ⊙ Test Generator	⌒ Audio Library ⊙ LaserLinks, Teacher's SourceBook p. 31 ⬌ Research Starter www.mcdougallittell.com	• Setting T6

Writing Workshop: Opinion Statement

		Unit Assessment	Unit Technology	
Unit Five Resource Book • Prewriting p. 19 • Drafting and Elaboration p. 20 • Peer Response Guide pp. 21–22 • Revising, Editing, and Proofreading p. 23 • Student Models pp. 24–26 • Rubric for Evaluation p. 27	⊙ **Writing Coach** **Writing Transparencies** T1–4, T13, T27 **Reading and Critical Thinking Transparencies** T24 **Grammar Transparencies and Copymasters** C72 **Teacher's Guide to Assessment and Portfolio Use**	• Unit Five, Part 1 Test, Formal Assessment pp. 111–112 ⊙ Test Generator • Unit Five Integrated Test, Integrated Assessment pp. 13–18	⬌ ClassZone www.mcdougallittell.com ⊙ Electronic Teacher Tools	

Additional Support

	Unit Resource Book	Assessment	Integrated Technology and Media	Literary Analysis Transparencies
A Crown of Wild Olive *pp. 709–727*	• Summary p. 28 • Active Reading p. 29 • Literary Analysis p. 30 • Words to Know p. 31 • Grammar p. 32 • Spelling p. 33 • Selection Quiz p. 34	• Selection Test, Formal Assessment pp. 113–114 ⊙ Test Generator	⌒ Audio Library	
from **Long Walk to Freedom** *pp. 732–739*	• Summary p. 35 • Active Reading p. 36 • Literary Analysis p. 37 • Words to Know p. 38 • Grammar p. 39 • Spelling p. 40 • Selection Quiz p. 41	• Selection Test, Formal Assessment pp. 115–116 ⊙ Test Generator	⌒ Audio Library ⊙ LaserLinks, Teacher's SourceBook p. 32 ⬌ Research Starter www.mcdougallittell.com	
The Elephant The Turtle *pp. 740–744*	• Active Reading p. 42 • Literary Analysis p. 43	• Selection Test, Formal Assessment pp. 117–118 ⊙ Test Generator	⌒ Audio Library	• Poetry: Figurative Language T19

Reading and Critical Thinking Transparencies	Grammar Transparencies and Copymasters	Vocabulary Transparencies and Copymasters	Writing Transparencies	Communications Transparencies and Copymasters
• Distinguishing Fact from Opinion T26 • Author's Purpose and Audience T4	• Daily Language SkillBuilder T21 • Possessive Plurals C64 • Coordinating Conjunctions C91 • Independent Clauses and Compound Sentences C105	• Context Clues C70 • Analogies C71	• Locating Information Using Print References T45 • Locating Information Using the Internet T47–48	• Evaluation Matrix: News T4 • Evaluation Matrix: Film/Video T7
• Visualizing T10	• Daily Language SkillBuilder T21 • Verb Tenses C71 • Adverb Clauses of Time C112	• Synonyms C72 • Antonyms C73	• Organizing Your Writing T11 • Opinion Statement T27	• Appreciative Listening T2 • Interviewing T9 • Dramatic Reading T12

STUDENTS ACQUIRING ENGLISH

The **Spanish Study Guide**, pp. 130–138, includes language support for the following pages:
• Family and Community Involvement (per unit)

• Selection Summaries and Vocabulary
• Active Reading
• Literary Analysis

Reading and Critical Thinking Transparencies	Grammar Transparencies and Copymasters	Vocabulary Transparencies and Copymasters	Writing Transparencies	Communications Transparencies and Copymasters
• Cause and Effect T3	• Daily Language SkillBuilder T22 • Combining Sentences to Make Complex Sentences C102 • Elaborating with Adjective Clauses C113 • Subordinate Clauses and Subordinating Conjunctions C114	• Context Clues C74 • Base Words C75	• Opinion Statement T27	• Impromptu Speaking: Dialogue, Role-Play T13
• Main Idea and Details T25	• Daily Language SkillBuilder T22 • Relative Pronouns C108 • Adjective Clauses C109	• Antonyms C76	• Crediting Sources T55	
• Paraphrasing T16	• Daily Language SkillBuilder T23 • Commas in a Series C125 • Parallelism C144		• Elaboration T13	• Reading Aloud T11

	Unit Resource Book	Assessment	Integrated Technology and Media	Additional Support Literary Analysis Transparencies
from **Anthony Burns: The Defeat and Triumph of a Fugitive Slave** pp.750–766	• Summary p. 45 • Active Reading p. 46 • Literary Analysis p. 47 • Words to Know p. 48 • Grammar p. 49 • Spelling p. 50 • Selection Quiz p. 51	• Selection Test, Formal Assessment pp. 119–120 Test Generator	Audio Library Research Starter www.mcdougallittell.com	
The People Could Fly pp. 767–773	• Summary p. 52 • Active Reading p. 53 • Literary Analysis p. 54 • Words to Know p. 55 • Grammar p. 56 • Spelling p. 57 • Selection Quiz p. 58	• Selection Test, Formal Assessment pp. 121–122 Test Generator	Audio Library Research Starter www.mcdougallittell.com	

Writing Workshop: Research Report

		Unit Assessment	*Unit Technology*	
Unit Five Resource Book • Prewriting p. 59 • Drafting and Elaboration p. 60 • Peer Response Guide pp. 61–62 • Revising, Editing, and Proofreading p. 63 • Student Models pp. 64–66 • Rubric for Evaluation p. 67	**Writing Coach** **Writing Transparencies** T1–4, T6, T13, T37 **Reading and Critical Thinking Transparencies** T24 **Grammar Transparencies and Copymasters** C66 **Teacher's Guide to Assessment and Portfolio Use**	• Unit Five, Part 2 Test, Formal Assessment pp. 123–124 Test Generator • Unit Five Integrated Test, Integrated Assessment pp. 13–18	ClassZone www.mcdougallittell.com Electronic Teacher Tools	

Reading and Critical Thinking Transparencies	Grammar Transparencies and Copymasters	Vocabulary Transparencies and Copymasters	Writing Transparencies	Communications Transparencies and Copymasters
	• Daily Language SkillBuilder T23 • Phrases and Clauses C106 • Adjective Clauses C110	• Related Words C77		• Persuasive Techniques T3
• Summarizing T11	• Daily Language SkillBuilder T24 • Punctuating Dialogue C131	• Word Knowledge C78 • Word Origins C79	• How to Summarize T51	• Evaluating Roles in Groups T8 • Verbal Strategies T14 • Giving and Receiving Feedback to Improve Performance T16

STUDENTS ACQUIRING ENGLISH

The **Spanish Study Guide**, pp. 139–153, includes language support for the following pages:
• Family and Community Involvement (per unit)

• Selection Summaries and Vocabulary
• Active Reading
• Literary Analysis

Selection	SkillBuilder Sentences	Suggested Answers
Exploring the *Titanic*	1. Many passengers considered theirselves lucky to be on the maiden voyage of the *Titanic*.	1. Many passengers considered **themselves** lucky to be on the maiden voyage of the *Titanic*.
	2. Harold Bride had little experience as a wireless operator he was willing to work hard and learn.	2. Harold Bride had little experience as a wireless operator, **but** he was willing to work hard and learn.
Last Cover	1. Bandit and him have a special relationship.	1. Bandit and **he** have a special relationship.
	2. The father don't have a lot of sympathy for Bandit because of what the fox has did.	2. The father **doesn't** have a lot of sympathy for Bandit because of what the fox has **done**.
A Crown of Wild Olive	1. When the story begins, Amyntas is just leaving piraeus harbor in Greece.	1. When the story begins, Amyntas is just leaving **P**iraeus **H**arbor in Greece.
	2. Because the other athletes were older, Amyntas felt lonly.	2. Because the other athletes were older, Amyntas felt **lonely**.

Selection	SkillBuilder Sentences	Suggested Answers
Long Walk to Freedom	1. Nelson Mandela was determine to end apartheid in South Africa.	1. Nelson Mandela was determine**d** to end apartheid in South Africa.
	2. He helped to create a new political party, the African national congress.	2. He helped to create a new political party, the African **N**ational **C**ongress.
The Elephant	1. I liked the poem "The Elephant" more better than I liked the other poem about elephants.	1. I liked the poem "The Elephant" **better** than I liked the other poem about elephants.
The Turtle	2. The school is allowing we science students to go to the zoo.	2. The school is allowing **us** science students to go to the zoo.
from Anthony Burns	1. Anthony Burn's hopelessness almost defeats Danas determination.	1. Anthony Burn**s's** hopelessness almost defeats Dana**'s** determination.
	2. Commissioner loring supports the fugitive slave act.	2. Commissioner **L**oring supports the **F**ugitive **S**lave **A**ct.

Selection	SkillBuilder Sentences	Suggested Answers
The People Could Fly	1. Jack said I enjoyed reading that folk tale.	1. Jack said, "I enjoyed reading that folk tale."
	2. Thoughts of freedom could rise the spirits of those left on the plantation.	2. Thoughts of freedom could **raise** the spirits of those left on the plantation.

Grammar Focus by Unit	Unit One	Unit Two	Unit Three	Unit Four	Unit Five	Unit Six
	The Sentence and Its Parts	Nouns, Pronouns, and Verbs	Modifiers	Phrases	Compound and Complex Sentences	Review

The Language of Literature offers several options for integrating grammar instruction and literature.

- Each unit has a specific grammar focus. The grammar focus for this unit is highlighted on the planning chart. Categories of grammar skills for this unit are shown in red.
- The Pupil's Edition includes instructive features entitled *Grammar in Context*. The instruction in these features arises from the selections and relates to the grammar focus for each unit.
- The Writing Workshops in the Pupil's Edition include grammar tips that help the students produce error-free drafts.
- Mini Lessons in the Teacher's Edition complement the instruction in the *Grammar in Context* features. Additional Mini Lessons relate to the grammar focus for each unit as well as to the literature.
- Daily Language SkillBuilders in the Teacher's Edition provide students with ongoing proofreading practice and reinforce punctuation, spelling, grammar and usage, and capitalization.
- Grammar Copymasters and Transparencies, which may be used independently or in conjunction with the Mini Lessons in the Teacher's Edition, present grammar in a traditional, systematic sequence.

PE instruction shown in black
TE Mini Lessons shown in green

Part 1

NOUNS
Possessive Plurals
"Exploring the *Titanic*," p. 662

VERBS
Verb Tenses
"Last Cover," p. 683
Assessment Practice, p. 704

PREPOSITIONS, CONJUNCTIONS, INTERJECTIONS
Coordinating Conjunctions
"Exploring the *Titanic*," p. 666

SENTENCE STRUCTURE
Main Clauses and Compound Sentences
"Exploring the *Titanic*," p. 674
Independent Clauses and Compound Sentences
"Exploring the *Titanic*," p. 674

Adverb Clauses of Time
"Last Cover," p. 692
Adverb Clauses of Time
"Last Cover," p. 692

PUNCTUATION
Punctuating Clauses
Writing Workshop, p. 703
Punctuating Clauses
Writing Workshop, p. 703

Part 2

PRONOUNS
Pronoun Case
Assessment Practice, p. 787

SENTENCE STRUCTURE
Subordinate Clauses and Subordinating Conjunctions
"A Crown of Wild Olive," p. 720
Combining Sentences to Make Complex Sentences
"A Crown of Wild Olive," p. 722
Elaborating with Adjective Clauses
"A Crown of Wild Olive," p. 727
Relative Pronouns
"Long Walk to Freedom," p. 735

Using Adjective Clauses
"Long Walk to Freedom," p. 739
Adjective Clauses
"Long Walk to Freedom," p. 739
"Anthony Burns: The Defeat and Triumph of a Fugitive Slave," p. 761
Phrases and Clauses
"Anthony Burns: The Defeat and Triumph of a Fugitive Slave," p. 754

Clauses as Fragments
Writing Workshop, p. 786

PUNCTUATION
Commas in a Series
"The Elephant/The Turtle," p. 744

Punctuating Dialogue
"The People Could Fly," p. 773
Punctuating Dialogue
"The People Could Fly," p. 773

STYLE
Parallelism
"The Elephant/The Turtle," p. 742

OVERVIEW

Students work with partners to present staged interviews with historical figures.

Project at a glance Many of the selections in Unit Five, Part 2, focus on historical topics or people. For this project, each partnered team will choose a historical figure and deliver a staged interview session. Students will research the life of the historical figure, gather information, and prepare an interview. Both partners will share responsibilities for researching and writing the speech. Students might present the interviews in a "History Day."

SCHEDULING

Partners should take no more than ten minutes to present their interview. You may want to schedule the interviews over the course of 2–3 class periods and/or align them with one of your social studies units, if it is practical.

PROJECT OBJECTIVES

• To demonstrate the speaking and listening skills introduced in the activity
• To research the life and accomplishments of a historical figure
• To play the role of a historical figure
• To demonstrate interviewing skills
• To answer questions from the audience

SUGGESTED GROUP SIZE

Partners

Getting Started

Explain that students will be working with partners to present an interview with a historical figure. For ideas, see the Selections Overview for summaries of the stories in this unit.

Before students begin, do a little research yourself to see if your school library has sufficient information (biographies, autobiographies) on historical figures. If it does not, arrange with a local library for these materials to be available to students.

You might also locate a collection of films or videos on historical figures of your choice. Students should be encouraged to "get into character," which might involve dressing up as the historical figure, with the appropriate costumes, props, makeup, and so on. You should make arrangements for these items to

be available, either from your school's drama department or from some other source.

This project should only require rearranging a bit of furniture in your classroom on the appropriate day. There should be two chairs in the front of the room, as well as seating for audience members. If you think students are ready for a real audience, you might create a History Day and invite other classes, parents, or teachers to act as judges or audience members.

Writing Workshop Connection

As a springboard, students may use the Writing Workshop assignment **Research Report**, p. 780.

Directing the Project

Preparing As a class, briefly discuss the historical topics featured in this unit, as well as any other topics you might be covering in a social studies unit or another related unit.

▶ Divide students into pairs. Tell students that each team will write and present an interview with a historical figure. Have students choose a figure from the unit or another figure. They should decide who will act as the figure and the interviewer.

Assigning Roles Have students divide the work up evenly within each team. Roles might include writer, interviewer, researcher, and so on. You might want to choose one student to write and present an introduction and conclusion for the entire class presentation (or you could fill this position yourself).

▶ After teams have chosen their historical figure, they should begin researching. Meet with them to make sure that there are no duplications. Students should collect information using multiple sources and choose an important event in their subject's life. They should then write an interview script based on that event. Or they may simply choose to focus on their subject's life in general.

▶ Meet with each team to refine the interview, offer help, or make suggestions. Before the presentation, students should check to make

sure all the main points are supported with facts and examples. Review with students the Speaking and Listening Strategies found in the Communication Handbook, page R102.

Practicing Allow time for teams to rehearse their interviews. The interviewer should go over his or her notes, and the historical figure should be well prepared to answer questions.

▶ For this stage, both students may use notes to help prepare; however, this should be discouraged during the final presentation. Remind students to stay in character during the interview, as this is what will make it most convincing.

▶ Tell students that giving and receiving feedback during the rehearsal stage is crucial. Refer to the tips in the Feedback Center.

Presenting This project could culminate in a History Day for the entire student body or just for your class.

▶ To begin, have students take a few deep breaths and focus on what they want to communicate. Students should take their places in front of the audience. After the initial interview, you might open the forum to questions from the audience. The historical figure could then answer in character and provide further insights into his or her life and times.

Teaching the Speaking and Listening Skills

The student is expected to:

Adapt spoken language such as word choice, diction, and usage to the purpose

Teaching Suggestions: Tell students that "getting into character" means learning about the culture and context of their historical figure. This will require research. Perhaps students can watch films set in their speaker's era. Students should adjust their message to fit their audience's knowledge and expectations, and adjust their speech and delivery to fit the occasion (formal vs. informal). Students should also try to match their language to the purpose of their message. For example, if their character is a civil-rights leader, they might choose strong words and deliver them in a deliberate and precise manner. Have students identify their purposes and discuss with them ways in which they might adjust their language to best suit those purposes.

Interpret a speaker's verbal and nonverbal message, purpose, and perspective

Teaching Suggestions: Discuss with students how body language can reflect a speaker's message. Ask students for suggestions as to the types of signals that indicate nonverbal messages (for instance, arms folded across one's chest might mean that the person is not open to new information). During the interview, have student audience members pay particular attention to the historical figure's verbal and nonverbal message. Decide how it reflects their purpose and perspective. Have them take notes during the interviews and discuss nonverbal messages at the end of all of the presentations.

Listen to learn by taking notes, organizing ideas, and summarizing ideas

Teaching Suggestions: Have student audience members take notes during the interviews so that they are prepared to ask questions afterward. Briefly outline note-taking techniques and the use of outline form. Tell students that they don't need to write down everything that is said during an interview or speech—only the major ideas and perhaps a word or phrase that will jog their memory when it is time to ask questions. They should also jot down questions to be asked later.

Feedback Center

Students can use the following guidelines when giving and receiving feedback during this project:

Giving Feedback

▶ Ask questions concerning content, delivery, purpose, and point of view (for instance, is tone appropriate to purpose?).

▶ Provide feedback about the coherence and logic of the content, delivery, and overall impact on the listener.

▶ Comment on the verbal and nonverbal delivery (pitch, pace, volume, body language) and its impact on the listener.

▶ Respond to persuasive messages with questions, challenges, or affirmation.

▶ Question the evidence to support the speaker's claims and conclusions.

Receiving Feedback

▶ Listen to constructive criticism with an open mind.

▶ Use audience feedback and modify the presentation to clarify meaning or organization.

▶ 3 Assessing the Project

The following rubric can be used for group or individual assessment.

3 Full Accomplishment

Students followed directions and presented a coherent interview based on solid research and investigation. The ideas discussed were well supported with evidence and examples. Students worked effectively with partners and demonstrated all of the Speaking and Listening Skills listed.

2 Substantial Accomplishment

Students presented a coherent interview based on adequate research. There was some supporting evidence. Students worked adequately with partners, and the presentation, however lacking in originality or insight, met most of the Speaking and Listening points.

1 Little Accomplishment

Partners' interviews were incomplete or did not fulfill the requirements of the assignment. There was inadequate research, points were not supported with evidence, and the interview lacked a convincing tone.

Reflecting on the Theme Throughout your life, you will be called upon to show courage in many small ways and perhaps in big ways, too. You'll need to accept responsibilities, defend your beliefs, and admit mistakes. You may be afraid or have to overcome great odds. As you read the selections in this unit, imagine how you might react in the situations described.

ACTIVITY

Whom do you consider the most courageous person in your school or community? With a small group, create a list of three names. Discuss what you think makes the people you named so courageous. Create a semantic web to show what your group thinks are the most important elements of courage. Compare your conclusions with other groups.

LEARNING the Language of *Literature*

Setting

> *Setting . . . offers an arena for fantastic adventures, enchantments, heroic exploits, heart-stopping dangers, or comfort, peace, and contentment.*
>
> —*Barbara H. Baskin*

A clean, wide-open neighborhood in 1954, in which every driveway holds two cars, one a shiny new station wagon. An eerie, rain-drenched forest inhabited by fairies and elves. A bustling futuristic city where everyone moves quickly past you and no one looks you in the eye. Each of these describes a particular setting. **Setting** is the time and place where the action of a story, poem, or play occurs. Along with character and plot, setting is a main element in any piece of narrative writing.

Setting includes details about location, historical period, time of year, weather, and time of day. Setting often includes a social background—the beliefs, customs, and activities that make up the background of characters' lives. Readers can learn about what life is like for characters by paying attention to setting. In fact, setting often plays an important role in what happens in a story and why it happens.

Place

Place is an important part of setting. Depending on the story, this might be a specific continent, country, region, city, or neighborhood. It can even be a building, a room, or the inside of a vehicle. Place is usually established through descriptive passages and vivid, concrete details. The excerpt from *Boy: Tales of Childhood*, which you read in Unit Four, for example, is set in a small village in Wales.

LEARNING THE LANGUAGE OF LITERATURE **655**

OVERVIEW

Objectives
• understand and identify the following literary terms:
    setting
    place
    historical period
• recognize and analyze setting
• appreciate a writer's craft

Teaching the Lesson

This lesson analyzes three components of setting in works of literature. It also illustrates how important setting is to the effectiveness of a writer's work.

Introducing the Concepts
Ask each student to think of a story or novel in which the setting is particularly memorable (i.e. scary, peaceful, magical, familiar). Then have the class discuss what makes these settings so vivid and how setting can affect a work of literature.

Presenting the Concepts
Place
Ask students to describe a location they might choose for the setting of a story. Have them explain why the location they choose appeals to them.

Use **Literary Analysis Transparencies,** p. 6, for additional support.

 See the Skills Trace at the beginning of the unit for information on TEKS covered in this lesson.

Historical Period

Invite students to think of a historical period that they might choose for the setting of a short story. Ask them to share some details about that historical period and why they think it would be an interesting period in which to set a story.

YOUR TURN

Possible Responses: Details such as "1932" and "the bleakest year of the Depression" alert the reader to the historical period. The impression left by this passage is of deprivation, hopelessness, and dullness.

Time

Ask students to discuss how a story that is set in the morning might differ from one that takes place in the middle of the afternoon or one that is set during the middle of the night.

Possible Responses: Students should note that characters' activities and the manner in which they go about their activities would change with the times of day. Students might also suggest that the mood, or atmosphere, of a story set in the morning would be different from the mood of a story set in the middle of the night.

YOUR TURN

Possible Responses: The author gives 4:00 and 4:30 as reference times and implies that it is still well before those times. The girls loiter as they walk because they know they have plenty of time.

Historical Period

Another aspect of setting is the **historical period** or era during which the action takes place. Some works are set in the past. Other works, such as science fiction, are set in the future. Everything a character experiences in a story will be affected by the era in which he or she lives. This includes the political, social, and economic conditions of that time.

Short fiction usually takes place in a single time period. Some novels also take place during a single period, but because they are longer, they may also cover years, decades, or even centuries. If the author doesn't establish a specific historical period, the setting is usually the time in which the author wrote the work. Much **contemporary fiction,** that is, fiction written recently, is set in the present.

YOUR TURN What details in the passage to the right and above let you know about its historical period? What impression do you have of the Depression after reading this passage?

Time

A story doesn't happen only in a particular year. It also happens in a specific season or at a particular *time* of day. The weather during a particular season can play a big part in creating the setting, as it may affect the actions of the characters. The passage on the right is taken from "The White Umbrella." The title of the story hints that the weather will play an important role in the story. Keep that in mind as you read the excerpt to the right about two sisters on their way to their piano lessons.

YOUR TURN What details give you a sense of time? In what way does time affect the feelings and actions of the girls in this passage?

HISTORICAL PERIOD

We lived in Belleville, New Jersey, a commuter town at the northern fringe of Newark. It was 1932, the bleakest year of the Depression. My father had died two years before, leaving us with a few pieces of Sears, Roebuck furniture and not much else, and my mother had taken Doris and me to live with one of her younger brothers.

—Russell Baker,
Growing Up

From *Growing Up*

TIME

A gust of wind littered the street with leaves. "Maybe we better hurry up," she went on, looking at the sky. "It's going to pour." "But we're too early." Her lesson didn't begin until 4:00, mine until 4:30, so we usually tried to walk as slowly as we could. "And anyway, those aren't the kind of clouds that rain. Those are cumulus clouds." We arrived out of breath and wet.

—Gish Gen, "The White Umbrella"

Distinguishing Fact from Opinion

How to Apply the Skill

To **distinguish fact from opinion,** an active reader will:
- **Clarify** statements of fact as true or false
- Look for words or phrases that signal opinions
- **Evaluate** the writer's ideas and reasoning
- Look for supporting evidence

Try It Now!

Read and distinguish fact from opinion in the excerpt below.

> On May 31, 1911, the hull of the *Titanic* was launched at the Harland & Wolff shipyards in Belfast, Ireland, before a cheering crowd of 100,000. Bands played, and people came from miles around to see the great wonder of the sea. Twenty-two tons of soap, grease, and train oil were used to slide her into the water. In the words of one eyewitness, she had "a rudder as big as an elm tree . . . propellers as big as a windmill. Everything was on a nightmare scale."
>
> —Robert D. Ballard, *Exploring the* Titanic

Here's how Erlin uses the skill:

*"As I read, I identify whether something can be proved true or false. The first statement is a **fact** and can be proved by verifying the date, time, and place where the* Titanic *was launched. I look for words or phrases that help me recognize **opinions:** always, or never and I believe, and it seems. The second sentence contains an opinion because the word great and the phrase wonder of the sea indicate a judgment and can't be proved."*

Need More Help?

Remember that active readers use the essential reading strategies explained on page 4: • **visualize** • **predict** • **clarify** • **question** • **connect** • **evaluate** • **monitor.**

Objectives
- distinguish fact and opinion in various texts
- support responses by referring to relevant aspects of the text

Teaching the Lesson

The strategies on this page will help students to recognize fact and opinion in written texts.

Presenting the Strategies
Help students understand the strategies by asking for volunteers to read them aloud. Emphasize to students that they will be using these strategies as they read the selections in this book. Ask them to follow the strategies outlined on this page for this project:
- Select an article from a magazine or a newspaper and divide it into sections. Divide the class into small groups and assign one section of the article to each group.
- Have each group use the strategies outlined on this page to identify the facts and opinions in their section.
- Suggest that students construct a chart listing the items under the headings "Fact" and "Opinion" and "Opinion Signal Words."
- Ask a volunteer from each group to copy their chart on the board and to explain their conclusions.

Try It Now!

Possible Response: Students should understand that the date, the location, and concrete details of the launching are based in fact. They should understand that the eyewitness's observations and broad statements such as "miles around" and "great wonder of the sea" are opinion.

Use **Reading and Critical Thinking Transparencies,** p. 26, for additional support.

This selection is included in the **Grade 7 InterActive Reader.**

Objectives

1. to understand and appreciate the genre of **literary nonfiction (Literary Analysis)**
2. to understand the significance of **setting (emphasis: time) (Literary Analysis)**
3. to utilize the skill of distinguishing between **fact and opinion (Active Reading)**

Summary

On April 10, 1912, the "unsinkable" luxury cruise liner *Titanic*, the biggest ship in the world, began its maiden voyage from England to New York. Its passengers, divided among first-class, second-class, and third-class sections of the ship, included 17-year-old Jack Thayer and 12-year-old Ruth Becker. The first three days of the voyage were smooth; on the fourth day, however, the ship collided with an iceberg, and water began pouring into a hole in the bottom half of the ship. The *Titanic's* radio operators signaled for help, but the nearest ship had turned off its radio. The crew began lowering lifeboats into the water at 12:45 A.M. Ruth Becker found a place in a lifeboat, but more than 1500 others remained behind. By 2:05 A.M., the ship was sinking fast. Jack Thayer jumped off the ship as it slid into the icy North Atlantic waters and pulled himself onto an overturned lifeboat. Both he and Ruth witnessed the terrible final sinking of the *Titanic* and were among the survivors rescued at dawn by a ship called the *Carpathia*.

Thematic Link

Many passengers and crew members faced the destruction of the *Titanic* with strength and courage.

5-Minute Warm-Up

Daily Language SkillBuilder   TEKS 17A, 17H

Have students **proofread** the display sentences on page 653i and write them correctly. The sentences also appear on Transparency 21 of **Grammar Transparencies and Copymasters.**

ACROSS the CURRICULUM   SCIENCE

PREPARING to *Read*

from Exploring the *Titanic*

Literary Nonfiction by ROBERT BALLARD

Connect to Your Life

What do you know about exploration beneath the surface of the oceans?

The robot *Jason Junior* exp the interior of the *Titan*

Build Background
Underwater exploration has expanded dramatically since the creation in the 1960s of mini-submarines called submersibles. Submersibles have mapped the ocean floors, discovered ecosystems that exist in total darkness, and explored shipwrecks. In these paintings, the submersible *Alvin* and its attached underwater robot *Jason Junior* explore the wreck of the *Titanic*.

Focus Your Reading

LITERARY ANALYSIS **SETTING: TIME**   The time and place in which a literary work occurs is its **setting.** Time includes both the historical era of the work as well as the season and time of day. This selection narrates the sinking of the ocean liner *Titanic* in the early years of the twentieth century, a time when people were very optimistic about technological and social progress.

WORDS TO KNOW **Vocabulary Preview**

accommodations	feverishly	novelty	toll
dazzled	indefinitely	prophecy	tribute
eerie	list		

ACTIVE READING **FACT AND OPINION**   A fact is a statement that can be proved. An opinion gives personal feelings or beliefs.

Fact: At 7:30 P.M., April 14, 1912, the steamer *Californian* warned the *Titanic* about icebergs.
Opinion: The *Titanic's* crew should have taken those warnings more seriously.

As you read the selection, jot down examples of fact and opinion in your **READER'S NOTEBOOK**.

VIDEODISC   **LaserLink: Background for Reading**
Historical Connection

TEKS   See the Skills Trace at the beginning of the unit for information on TEKS covered in this lesson.

658   UNIT FIVE   PART 1: WITH STRENGTH AND COURAGE

LESSON RESOURCES

WHITE STAR LINE
ROYAL & UNITED STATES MAIL STEAMERS
FIRST SAILING OF THE LATEST ADDITION TO THE WHITE STAR FLEET
The Queen of the Ocean
LENGTH 882½ FT.
TITANIC
OVER 45,000 TONS
TRIPLE-SCREWS
BEAM 92½ FT.
This, the Latest, Largest and Finest Steamer Afloat, will sail from
WHITE STAR LINE, PIER 10, SOUTHAMPTON
WEDNESDAY, APRIL 10TH
AT 12 NOON
calling at Cherbourg & Queenstown, Co. Cork
en route to NEW YORK

FROM • EXPLORING
THE TITANIC

BY ROBERT D. BALLARD

659

EXPLORING THE TITANIC   **659**

Suggest that students skim the selection and look closely at the diagram of the ship. Have them jot down questions that they hope to answer while reading.

Literary Analysis `SETTING: TIME`

 A Remind students to look for details of setting that affect their understanding of what happened and why. Ask students to explain the role of ships in the early 1900s.

Possible Response: Ships were the only way to transport cargo and people across the sea.

 Use **Unit Five Resource Book,** p. 6 for additional practice.

Active Reading `FACT AND OPINION`

B Tell students that opinions often contain judgment words or words expressing personal feelings or beliefs. Ask students to distinguish the opinion in this passage and explain how the writer supports it.

Possible Response: "The final size and richness of this new ship was astounding." He backs it up with facts about the size of the ship

Use **Unit Five Resource Book,** p. 5 for additional practice.

Literary Analysis:
LITERARY NONFICTION

C Tell students that writers of literary nonfiction present facts but use many of the same techniques fiction writers use. Ask students to recognize the distinguishing features of literary nonfiction in this passage.

Possible Response: There are facts about the ship's construction as well as vivid imagery.

The story of the *Titanic* began before anyone had even thought about building the great ship. In 1898, fourteen years before the *Titanic* sank, an American writer named Morgan Robertson wrote a book called *The Wreck of the Titan.*[1] In his story, the *Titan,* a passenger ship almost identical to the *Titanic,* and labeled "unsinkable," sails from England headed for New York. With many rich and famous passengers on board, the *Titan* hits an iceberg in the North Atlantic and sinks. Because there are not enough lifeboats, many lives are lost.

The story of the *Titan* predicted exactly what would happen to the *Titanic* fourteen years later. It was an <u>eerie</u> <u>prophecy</u> of terrible things to come.

In 1907, nearly ten years after *The Wreck of the Titan* was written, two men began making plans to build a real titanic ship. At a London dinner party, as they relaxed over coffee and cigars, J. Bruce Ismay, president of the White Star Line of passenger ships, and Lord Pirrie, chairman of Harland & Wolff shipbuilders, **A** discussed a plan to build three enormous ocean liners. Their goal was to give the White Star Line a competitive edge in the Atlantic passenger trade with several gigantic ships whose <u>accommodations</u> would be the last word in comfort and elegance.

The two men certainly dreamed on a grand scale. When these floating palaces were finally

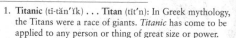

AS HER NAME BOASTED, THE *TITANIC* WAS INDEED THE BIGGEST SHIP IN THE WORLD.

built, they were so much bigger than other ships that new docks had to be built on each side of the Atlantic to service them. Four years after that London dinner party, the first of these huge liners, the *Olympic,* safely completed her maiden voyage.[2]

On May 31, 1911, the hull of the *Titanic* was launched at the Harland & Wolff shipyards in Belfast, Ireland, before a cheering crowd of 100,000. Bands played, and people came from miles around to see this great wonder of the sea. Twenty-two tons of soap, grease, and train oil were used to slide her into the water. In the words of one eyewitness, she had "a rudder as big as an elm tree . . . propellers as big as a windmill. Everything was on a nightmare scale."

For the next ten months the *Titanic* was outfitted and carefully prepared down to the last detail. The final size and richness of this new ship was astounding. She was 882 feet long, almost the length of four city blocks. With nine decks, she was as high as an eleven-story building.

Among her gigantic features, she had four huge funnels, each one big enough to drive

---

1. **Titanic** (tī-tăn′ĭk) . . . **Titan** (tīt′n): In Greek mythology, the Titans were a race of giants. *Titanic* has come to be applied to any person or thing of great size or power.

2. **maiden voyage:** very first trip.

WORDS
TO
KNOW

eerie (îr′ē) *adj.* weird, especially in a frightening way
prophecy (prŏf′ĭ-sē) *n.* a prediction; foretelling of future events
accommodations (ə-kŏm′ə-dā′shənz) *n.* a room and food, especially in hotels or on ships or trains

660

Teaching Options

BLOCK SCHEDULING: MANAGING TIME

If your schedule requires that you cover the lesson objectives in a shorter time, use . . .
- Preparing to Read, p. 658
- Thinking Through the Literature, p. 672
- Vocabulary in Action, p. 673
- Grammar in Context, p. 674

If you want to take advantage of longer class time, use . . .
- TE Teaching Options: Preteaching Vocabulary, p. 659; Viewing and Representing, p. 661; Grammar, pp. 662, 666, 674; Standardized Test Practice, pp. 663, 668; Vocabulary Strategy, p. 664; Cross Curricular Link, p. 667; Spelling, p. 670; Speaking and Listening, p. 671
- Choices & Challenges, pp. 673–674
- Real World Link, p. 675

two trains through. During construction an astonishing three million rivets had been hammered into her hull. Her three enormous anchors weighed a total of thirty-one tons—the weight of twenty cars. And for her maiden voyage, she carried enough food to feed a small town for several months.

As her name boasted, the *Titanic* was indeed the biggest ship in the world. Nicknamed "the Millionaires' Special," she was also called "the Wonder Ship," "the Unsinkable Ship," and "the Last Word in Luxury" by newspapers around the world.

The command of this great ocean liner was given to the senior captain of the White Star Line, Captain Edward J. Smith. This proud, white-bearded man was a natural leader and was popular with both crew members and passengers. Most important, after thirty-eight years' service with the White Star Line, he had an excellent safety record. At the age of fifty-nine, Captain Smith was going to retire after this last trip, a perfect final <u>tribute</u> to a long and successful career.

On Wednesday, April 10, 1912, the *Titanic*'s passengers began to arrive in Southampton for the trip to New York. Ruth Becker was <u>dazzled</u> as she boarded the ship with her mother, her younger sister, and two-year-old brother, Richard. Ruth's father was a missionary in India. The rest of the family was sailing to New York to find medical help for

The *Titanic* had two grand staircases, each five stories high and covered by a glass dome. The staircase shown was named Olympic. Joseph A. Carvalho Collection.

661

Viewing and Representing

 TEKS 22B

ART APPRECIATION
Instruction Tell students that photographs can convey useful information about historical events or time periods. Ask students to examine this photograph and describe what it shows.
Possible Responses: It shows one of the two grand staircases on the *Titanic*. The staircase is wide and sweeping and is decorated with ornate carving and scrollwork.
Application Ask students what impressions of the *Titanic* they gain from this photograph.

Possible Responses: The ship was built on a huge scale. The appearance of the staircase shows the lavishness of the décor for the public areas of the ship.
Have students examine the diagram on pages 662–663. Ask students what a comparison of the first-class areas with the third-class reveals.
Possible Response: The class structure was rigidly upheld. There were many more first-class areas than third. The third-class rooms were in less desirable locations on the ship.

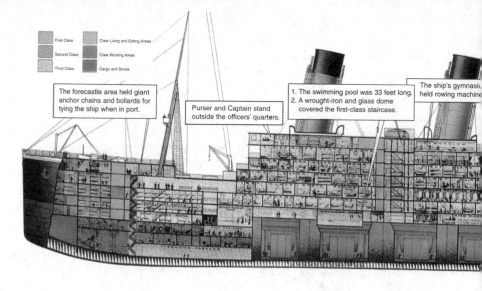

First Class | Crew Living and Eating Areas
Second Class | Crew Working Areas
Third Class | Cargo and Stores

The forecastle area held giant anchor chains and bollards for tying the ship when in port.

Purser and Captain stand outside the officers' quarters.

1. The swimming pool was 33 feet long.
2. A wrought-iron and glass dome covered the first-class staircase.

The ship's gymnasium held rowing machines.

ACTIVE READING

A **FACT AND OPINION** The statement is an opinion, expressing the speaker's personal feelings.

Reading Skills and Strategies:
MAIN IDEAS/DETAILS

B Ask students to determine the main idea of this passage.

Possible Response: The passenger list of the *Titanic* included some of the most influential people of the time.

• Ask students why the author supports his main idea with specific names and details.

Possible Response: Knowing the names and details makes the retelling of the events seem more vivid and real.

Literary Analysis **SETTING: TIME**

C Point out to students that in this passage, the author uses the description of the physical layout of the ship to paint a picture of the event's historical setting. Ask students what inferences they might make about the interaction of the classes in society based on the ship's organization.

Possible Response: In real life as well as on the ship, barriers prevented lower classes from mingling with upper classes; it was difficult to move up in society.

Literary Analysis:
LITERARY NONFICTION

D Remind students that literary nonfiction describes real people, places, and events. Ask them how the writer helps them imagine the launching of the *Titanic*.

Possible Response: by focusing on a single important detail—the size and sound of the ship

---

young Richard, who had developed a serious illness in India. They had booked second-class tickets on the *Titanic*.

Twelve-year-old Ruth was delighted with the ship. As she pushed her little brother about the decks in a stroller, she was impressed with what she saw. "Everything was new. New!" she recalled. "Our cabin was just like a hotel room, it was so big. The dining room was beautiful—the linens, all the bright, polished silver you can imagine."

ACTIVE READING

A **FACT AND OPINION**

Is this statement about the dining room a fact or an opinion?

Meanwhile, seventeen-year-old Jack Thayer from Philadelphia was trying out the soft mattress on the large bed in his cabin. The first-class rooms his family had reserved for themselves and their maid had thick carpets, carved wooden panels on the walls, and marble sinks. As his parents were getting settled in their adjoining stateroom,[3] Jack decided to explore this fantastic ship.

1 On A Deck, he stepped into the Verandah and Palm Court and admired the white wicker furniture and the ivy growing up the trellised walls. On the lower decks, Jack discovered the squash court,[4] the swimming pool, and the Turkish bath[5] decorated like a room in a sultan's palace. In the gymnasium, the instructor was showing passengers the latest in exercise equipment, which included a mechanical camel you could ride on, stationary bicycles, and rowing machines.

Daylight shone through the huge glass dome over the Grand Staircase as Jack went down to join his parents in the first-class reception room.

There, with the ship's band playing in the background, his father pointed out some of the other first-class passengers. "He's supposed to be the world's richest man," said his father of Colonel John Jacob Astor, who was escorting the young Mrs. Astor. He also identified Mr. and Mrs. Straus, founders of Macy's of New York, the world's largest department store. Millionaire Benjamin Guggenheim was aboard, as were Jack's parents' friends from Philadel-

---

3. **stateroom:** a private cabin on a ship.
4. **squash court:** a walled court or room for playing squash, in which a rubber ball is hit off the walls.
5. **Turkish bath:** a steam bath.

Teaching Options

Mini Lesson **Grammar**   TEKS 17G   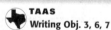 TAAS Writing Obj. 3, 6, 7

POSSESSIVE PLURALS

Instruction Remind students that to form the possessive of any singular noun, they add an apostrophe and *s* (ship's radio). To form the possessive of a plural noun that ends in *s,* add an apostrophe (Millionaires' Special). To form the possessive of a plural noun that does not end in *s,* add an apostrophe and *s* (people's).

Exercise Have students replace the underlined nouns with the correct possessive form.

1. Jack Thayer endured the cold <u>waves</u> pounding until he was rescued. *(waves')*

2. The <u>passengers</u> safety came first. *(passengers')*
3. The <u>childrens</u> belongings were lost when the *Titanic* went down. *(children's)*
4. Survivors talked about the ship's last moments; the <u>survivors</u> stories have impacted people for years. *(survivors')*

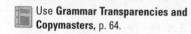 Use **Grammar Transparencies and Copymasters**, p. 64.

 Use McDougal Littell's **Language Network,** Chapter 2, for more instruction and practice in possessive plural nouns.

The boilers were ...er 15 feet high.

Stokers had to shovel coal to power the boilers.

Middle-income people stayed in second-class state rooms.

The first-class promenade deck allowed passengers to walk outside.

Three huge propellers, two of which were 23 feet across, powered the ship.

...phia, Mr. and Mrs. George Widener and their ...on, Harry. Mr. Widener had made a fortune ...building streetcars. Mr. and Mrs. William ...Carter were also friends of the Thayers. Stowed in one of the holds below was a new Renault car that they were bringing back from England.

J. Bruce Ismay, president of the White Star Line, moved about the room saying hello to people. He wanted to make sure that his wealthy passengers were comfortable, that they would feel relaxed and safe aboard his floating palace.

Indeed, when Ruth Becker's mother had asked one of the second-class staff about the safety of the ship, she had been told that there was absolutely nothing to worry about. The ship had watertight compartments that would allow her to float <u>indefinitely</u>. There was much talk among the passengers about the *Titanic* being unsinkable.

In 1912, people were divided into social classes according to background, wealth, and education. Because of these class lines, the

Titanic was rather like a big floating layer cake. The bottom layer consisted of the lowly manual workers sweating away in the heat and grime of the boiler rooms and engine rooms. The next layer was the third-class passengers, people of many nationalities hoping to make a new start in America. After that came the second class—teachers, merchants, and professionals of moderate means like Ruth's family. Then, finally, there was the icing on the cake in first class: the rich and the aristocratic. The differences between these groups were enormous. While the wealthy brought their maids and valets[6] and mountains of luggage, most members of the crew earned such tiny salaries that it would have taken them years to save the money for a single first-class ticket.

At noon on Wednesday, April 10, the *Titanic* cast off. The whistles on her huge funnels were the biggest ever made. As she began her journey to the sea, they were heard for miles around.

---

6. **valets** (vă-lāz'): gentlemen's personal servants.

WORDS TO KNOW   **indefinitely** (ĭn-dĕf'ə-nĭt-lē) *adv.* for an unlimited length of time

663

Literary Analysis [SETTING: TIME]

A Ask students to consider how the setting of the early twentieth century influenced the direction of events.

Possible Responses: The tragedy might have been averted with more sophisticated navigational warning systems and more reliable methods of communication than those available in the early 1900s. The rescue ships were handicapped by the limitations of ships at that time.

Reading Skills and Strategies: AUTHOR'S PURPOSE

B Ask students why they think the author mentions each of the iceberg warnings received in the radio room.

Possible Responses: to keep readers informed of the number of warnings; to build suspense; to emphasize that disaster might have been prevented

Reading Skills and Strategies: INFERRING

C Ask students why they think Jack Thayer's comments about the night's beauty were included.

Possible Responses: to help the reader connect with events on the *Titanic;* to emphasize the contrast between the beauty of the night and the horror of what is about to occur

ACTIVE READING

D QUESTION Possible Response: The message from the *Californian* warned that there were icebergs right ahead of the *Titanic*.

Moving majestically down the River Test, and watched by a crowd that had turned out for the occasion, the *Titanic* slowly passed two ships tied up to a dock. All of a sudden, the mooring ropes holding the passenger liner *New York* snapped with a series of sharp cracks like fireworks going off. The enormous pull created by the *Titanic* moving past her had broken the *New York*'s ropes and was now drawing her stern toward the *Titanic*. Jack Thayer watched in horror as the two ships came closer and closer. "It looked as though there surely would be a collision," he later wrote. "Her stern could not have been more than a yard or two from our side. It almost hit us." At the last moment, some quick action by Captain Smith and a tugboat captain nearby allowed the *Titanic* to slide past with only inches to spare.

It was not a good sign. Did it mean that the *Titanic* might be too big a ship to handle safely? Those who knew about the sea thought that such a close call at the beginning of a maiden voyage was a very bad omen.

Jack Phillips, the first wireless operator on the *Titanic,* quickly jotted down the message coming in over his headphones. "It's another iceberg warning," he said wearily to his young assistant, Harold Bride. "You'd better take it up to the bridge." Both men had been at work for hours in the *Titanic*'s radio room, trying to get caught up in sending out a large number of personal messages. In 1912, passengers on

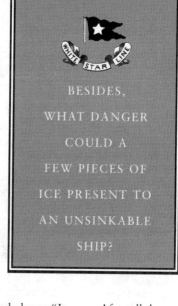

BESIDES, WHAT DANGER COULD A FEW PIECES OF ICE PRESENT TO AN UNSINKABLE SHIP?

ocean liners thought it was a real novelty to send postcard-style messages to friends at home from the middle of the Atlantic.

Bride picked up the iceberg message and stepped out onto the boat deck. It was a sunny but cold Sunday morning, the fourth day of the *Titanic*'s maiden voyage. The ship was steaming at full speed across a calm sea. Harold Bride was quite pleased with himself at having landed a job on such a magnificent new ship. After all, he was only twenty-two years old and had just nine months' experience at operating a "wireless set," as a ship's radio was then called. As he entered the bridge area, he could see one of the crewmen standing behind the ship's wheel steering her course toward New York.

Captain Smith was on duty in the bridge, so Bride handed the message to him. "It's from the *Caronia*, sir. She's reporting icebergs and pack ice ahead." The captain thanked him, read the message, and then posted it on the bulletin board for other officers on watch to read. On his way back to the radio room, Bride thought the captain had seemed quite unconcerned by the message. But then again, he had been told that it was not unusual to have ice floating in the sea lanes during an April crossing. Besides, what danger could a few pieces of ice present to an unsinkable ship?

Elsewhere on board, passengers relaxed on deck chairs, reading or taking naps. Some played cards, some wrote letters, while others chatted with friends. As it was Sunday, church

WORDS TO KNOW **novelty** (nŏv'əl-tē) *n.* something new, original, or unusual

664

 Vocabulary Strategy   **TEKS 9B**   **TAAS Reading Obj. 1**

ANALOGIES

Instruction Remind students that a word analogy compares two pairs of words. The relationship between the second pair of words must be the same as the relationship between the first pair. Give students the example of *sugar : sweet. Sweet* is a characteristic of *sugar.* A similar relationship would be found in the word pair of *hero : brave.* The relationship between word pairs in analogies may be that of synonyms, antonyms, part to a whole, cause and effect, item to category, action to object, or object to purpose.

Application Have students work together to think of a word pair to complete each analogy.

1. ICY : FRIGID ::
2. PANICKY : CALM ::
3. HYPOTHERMIA : DEATH ::
4. COMPASS : NAVIGATION ::

Possible Responses: 1. hot : scorching
2. grouchy : friendly **3.** sleeplessness : exhaustion
4. hammer : construction

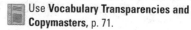 Use **Vocabulary Transparencies and Copymasters,** p. 71.

services had been held in the morning, the first-class service led by Captain Smith. Jack Thayer spent most of the day walking about the decks getting some fresh air with his parents.

Two more ice warnings were received from nearby ships around lunch time. In the chaos of the radio room, Harold Bride only had time to take one of them to the bridge. The rest of the day passed quietly. Then, in the late afternoon, the temperature began to drop rapidly. Darkness approached as the bugle call announced dinner.

Jack Thayer's parents had been invited to a special dinner for Captain Smith, so Jack ate alone in the first-class dining room. After dinner, as he was having a cup of coffee, he was joined by Milton Long, another passenger going home to the States. Long was older than Jack, but in the easy-going atmosphere of shipboard travel, they struck up a conversation and talked together for an hour or so.

At 7:30 P.M., the radio room received three more warnings of ice about fifty miles ahead. One of them was from the steamer *Californian* reporting three large icebergs. Harold Bride took this message up to the bridge, and it was again politely received. Captain Smith was attending the dinner party being held for him when the warning was delivered. He never got to see it. Then, around 9:00 P.M., the captain excused himself and went up to the bridge. He and his officers talked about how difficult it was to spot icebergs on a calm, clear, moonless night like this with no wind to kick up white surf around them. Before going to bed, the captain ordered the lookouts to keep a sharp watch for ice.

After trading travel stories with Milton Long, Jack Thayer put on his coat and walked around the deck. "It had become very much colder," he said later. "It was a brilliant, starry night. There was no moon, and I have never seen the stars shine brighter . . . sparkling like diamonds. . . . It was the kind of night that made one feel glad to be alive." At eleven o'clock, he went below to his cabin, put on his pajamas, and got ready for bed.

In the radio room, Harold Bride was exhausted. The two operators were expected to keep the radio working twenty-four hours a day, and Bride lay down to take a much-needed nap. Phillips was so busy with the passenger messages that he actually brushed off the final ice warning of the night. It was from the *Californian*. Trapped in a field of ice, she had stopped for the night about nineteen miles north of the *Titanic*. She was so close that the message literally blasted in Phillips's ears. Annoyed by the loud interruption, he cut off the *Californian*'s radio operator with the words, "Shut up, shut up. I'm busy."

ACTIVE READING

QUESTION What warning did the *Californian* send the *Titanic*?

The radio room had received a total of seven ice warning messages in one day. It was quite clear that floating icebergs lay ahead of the *Titanic*.

High up in the crow's nest on the forward mast, Fred Fleet had passed a quiet watch. It was now 11:40 P.M., and he and his fellow lookout were waiting to be relieved so they could head below, perhaps for a hot drink before hopping into their warm bunks. The sea was dead calm. The air was bitterly cold.

Suddenly, Fleet saw something. A huge, dark shape loomed out of the night directly ahead of the *Titanic*. An iceberg! He quickly sounded the alarm bell three times and picked up the telephone.

"What did you see?" asked the duty officer.

"Iceberg right ahead," replied Fleet.

Immediately, the officer on the bridge

2

Customizing Instruction

Less Proficient Readers

Have students summarize what happened in the radio room of the *Titanic* early on the fourth night of the ship's voyage.

Possible Response: Warnings were received about icebergs ahead.

- What did the captain do after he received the first message about icebergs ahead?

Possible Response: He posted it on the bulletin board, and later, before going to bed, he ordered the lookouts to watch for icebergs in the ship's path.

Set a Purpose As students read on, have them find out what happened after 11:40 P.M.

Multiple Learning Styles
Kinesthetic Learners

1 Suggest that students role-play the scene in which Bride hands Captain Smith the message about the iceberg warnings.

Students Acquiring English

2 Lead students to understand that Fleet responds with a sentence fragment because he wants to communicate as quickly as possible in an urgent situation. If you wish, invite students to give the corresponding complete sentence. (*There's an iceberg ahead.*)

ordered the wheel turned as far as it would go. The engine room was told to reverse the engines, while a button was pushed to close the doors to the watertight compartments in the bottom of the ship.

The lookouts in the crow's nest braced themselves for a collision. Slowly the ship started to turn. It looked as though they would miss it. But it was too late. They had avoided a head-on crash, but the iceberg had struck a glancing blow along the *Titanic*'s starboard bow. Several tons of ice fell on the ship's decks as the iceberg brushed along the side of the ship and passed into the night. A few minutes later, the *Titanic* came to a stop.

ACTIVE READING

A **CLARIFY** Why had the *Titanic* come to a stop?

Many of the passengers didn't know the ship had hit anything. Because it was so cold, almost everyone was inside, and most people had already gone to bed. Ruth Becker and her mother were awakened by the dead silence.

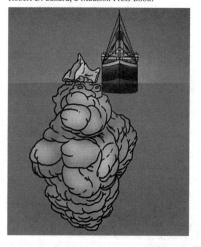

From *Exploring the* Titanic. Copyright © 1988 by Robert D. Ballard, a Madison Press Book.

They could no longer hear the soothing hum of the vibrating engines from below. Jack Thayer was about to step into bed when he felt himself sway ever so slightly. The engines stopped. He was startled by the sudden quiet.

Sensing trouble, Ruth's mother looked out of the door of their second-class cabin and asked a steward[7] what had happened. He told her that nothing was the matter, so Mrs. Becker went back to bed. But as she lay there, she couldn't help feeling that something was very wrong.

Jack heard running feet and voices in the hallway outside his first-class cabin. "I hurried into my heavy overcoat and drew on my slippers. All excited, but not thinking anything serious had occurred, I called in to my father and mother that I was going up on deck to see the fun."

On deck, Jack watched some third-class passengers playing with the ice that had landed on the forward deck as the iceberg had brushed by. Some people were throwing chunks at each other, while a few skidded about playing football with pieces of ice.

Down in the very bottom of the ship, things were very different. When the iceberg had struck, there had been a noise like a big gun going off in one of the boiler rooms. A couple of stokers[8] had been immediately hit by a jet of icy water. The noise and the shock of cold water had sent them running for safety.

Twenty minutes after the crash, things looked very bad indeed to Captain Smith. He and the ship's builder, Thomas Andrews, had made a rapid tour below decks to inspect the damage. The mail room was filling up with water, and sacks of mail were floating about. Water was also pouring into some of the

---

7. **steward:** a worker on a ship who attends to the needs of the passengers.

8. **stokers:** workers who tended the boilers that powered steamships.

Mini Lesson **Grammar** TEKS 17B   TAAS Writing Obj. 3, 6

COORDINATING CONJUNCTIONS
Instruction Remind students that a coordinating conjunction is a word that connects words or groups of words of equal importance. *And, but*, and *or* are common coordinating conjunctions. Substitute *but* or *or* for *and* in the sentence highlighted above to show how conjunctions affect the meaning of a sentence.
Exercise Have students replace the conjunction in each sentence with the correct one.

1. I had heard about the disaster, and I never really knew any details. *(but)*

2. The officers could jump, and they could go down with the ship. *(or)*

3. Were people brave, but were they unaware of the danger? *(or)*

4. They were told to wear coats or bring life jackets. *(and)*

 Use **Grammar Transparencies and Copymasters**, p. 90–91.

 Use McDougal Littell's *Language Network*, Chapter 6, for more instruction and practice in coordinating conjunctions.

forward holds and two of the boiler rooms.

Captain Smith knew that the *Titanic*'s hull was divided into a number of watertight compartments. She had been designed so that she could still float if only the first four compartments were flooded, but not any more than that. But water was pouring into the first five compartments. And when the water filled them, it would spill over into the next compartment. One by one all the remaining compartments would flood, and the ship would eventually sink. Andrews told the captain that the ship could last an hour, an hour and a half at the most.

Harold Bride had just awakened in the radio room when Captain Smith stuck his head in the door. "Send the call for assistance," he ordered.

"What call should I send?" Phillips asked.

"The regulation international call for help. Just that." Then the captain was gone. Phillips began to send the Morse code "CQD" distress call, flashing away and joking as he did it. After all, they knew the ship was unsinkable.

Five minutes later, the captain was back. "What are you sending?" he asked.

"CQD," Phillips answered. Then Bride cut in and suggested that they try the new SOS signal that was just coming into use. They began to send out the new international call for help—it was one of the first SOS calls ever sent out from a ship in distress.

Ruth and her family had stayed in their bunks for a good fifteen minutes or so after the room steward had told them nothing was wrong. But Ruth's mother couldn't stop

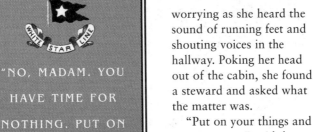

"NO, MADAM. YOU HAVE TIME FOR NOTHING. PUT ON YOUR LIFE JACKETS AND COME UP TO THE TOP DECK."

worrying as she heard the sound of running feet and shouting voices in the hallway. Poking her head out of the cabin, she found a steward and asked what the matter was.

"Put on your things and come at once," said the steward.

"Do we have time to dress?" she asked.

"No, madam. You have time for nothing. Put on your life jackets and come up to the top deck."

Ruth helped her mother dress the children quickly. But they only had time to throw their coats over their nightgowns and put on their shoes and stockings. In their rush, they forgot to put on their life jackets.

Just after midnight, Captain Smith ordered the lifeboats uncovered. The ship's squash court, which was thirty-two feet above the keel, was now completely flooded. Jack Thayer and his father came into the first-class lounge to try to find out exactly what the matter was. When Thomas Andrews, the ship's builder, passed by, Mr. Thayer asked him what was going on. He replied in a low voice that the ship had not much more than an hour to live. Jack and his father couldn't believe their ears.

From the bridge of the *Titanic*, a ship's lights were observed not far away, possibly the *Californian*'s. Captain Smith then ordered white distress rockets fired to get the attention of the nearby ship. They burst high in the air with a loud boom and a shower of stars. But the rockets made no difference. The mystery ship in the distance never answered.

In the radio room, Bride and Phillips now knew how serious the accident was and were

---

Cross Curricular Link Science

MODERN MEANS OF COMMUNICATION IN EARLY 20TH CENTURY Wireless radio, or wireless telegraphy, was invented by the Italian Guglielmo Marconi in the 1890s. Marconi also invented the autoalarm, which signaled transmissions by sounding a loud alarm when the radio operators were off duty. In 1912 not all ships had radios. Eventually, all large ships were required by law to have wireless equipment.

Radiotelegraphy is a means of communication by radio that uses coded signals. A receiver deciphers the code that is sent and converts it into corresponding symbols.

Jack Phillips and Harold Bride used International Morse Code to communicate with other ships. This form of the code was a system of dots and dashes. It was created in 1851, when it was realized that the original Morse code, developed by Samuel Morse in the 1830s, could not accommodate all foreign words. The International Morse Code is simpler than the original and more precise.

Literary Analysis:
LITERARY NONFICTION

A Remind students that some fiction writers try to keep the readers guessing about the outcome of the story. Ask students what the author chooses to do to add suspense to his nonfiction account.
Possible Response: Even though the writer knows whether or not the *Carpathia* arrives in time, he does not reveal that fact to the reader.

Literary Analysis SETTING: TIME

B Ask students to analyze the effect of including the exact time of various events.
Possible Response: The reader becomes aware that time is passing too quickly; it adds to the realism of the account.

Reading Skills and Strategies:
INFERRING

C Ask students to infer why the crew didn't fill the lifeboats.
Possible Responses: They still didn't believe that the ship was in danger; they were inexperienced and not prepared to respond in an emergency.

ACTIVE READING

D **CLARIFY** The captain had said to load the lifeboats with women and children first.

Reading Skills and Strategies:
AUTHOR'S PURPOSE

E Ask students why the author includes the description of this incident.
Possible Response: to show how the confusion and panic were increasing and how people were realizing the enormity of the disaster too late; to create vivid images of the ship's last minutes

---

A feverishly sending out calls for help. A number of ships heard and responded to their calls, but most were too far away to come to the rescue in time. The closest ship they had been able to reach was the *Carpathia*, about fifty-eight miles away. Immediately, the *Carpathia* reported that she was racing full steam to the rescue. But could she get there in time?

Not far away, the radio operator of the *Californian* had gone to bed for the night and turned off his radio. Several officers and crewmen on the deck of the *Californian* saw rockets in the distance and reported them to their captain. The captain told them to try to contact the ship with a Morse lamp. But they received no answer to their flashed calls. No one thought to wake up the radio operator.

1 **B** On board the *Titanic,* almost an hour after the crash, most of the passengers still did not realize the seriousness of the situation. But Captain Smith was a very worried man. He knew that the *Titanic* only carried lifeboats for barely half the estimated twenty-two hundred people on board. He would have to make sure his officers kept order to avoid any panic among the passengers. At 12:30 Captain Smith gave the orders to start loading the lifeboats—women and children first. Even though the *Titanic* was by now quite noticeably down at the bow and <u>listing</u> slightly to one side, many passengers still didn't want to leave the huge, brightly lit ship. The ship's band added to a

THE RADIO SIGNAL GRADUALLY GOT WEAKER AND WEAKER AS THE SHIP'S POWER FADED OUT.

kind of party feeling as the musicians played lively tunes.

About 12:45 the first lifeboat was lowered. It could carry sixty-five people, but left with only twenty-eight aboard. Indeed, many of the first boats to leave were half empty. Ruth Becker noticed that there was no panic among the crowds of passengers milling about on the decks. "Everything was calm, everybody was orderly." But the night air was now biting cold. Ruth's mother told her to go back to their cabin to get some blankets. Ruth hurried down to the cabin and came back with several blankets in her arms. The Beckers walked toward one of the lifeboats, and a sailor picked up Ruth's brother and sister and placed them in the boat.

"That's all for this boat," he called out. "Lower away!"

"Please, those are my children!" cried Ruth's mother. "Let me go with them!"

The sailor allowed Mrs. Becker to step into the lifeboat with her two children. She then called back to Ruth to get into another lifeboat. Ruth went to the next boat and asked the officer if

D ACTIVE READING

CLARIFY Why aren't any men getting in the lifeboats?

she could get in. He said, "Sure," picked her up, and dumped her in.

Boat No. 13 was so crowded that Ruth had to stand up. Foot by foot it was lowered down the steep side of the massive ship. The new

WORDS TO KNOW
feverishly (fē′vər-ĭsh-lē) *adv.* in a highly emotional or nervous way
list (lĭst) *v.* to tilt; lean

668

✓ Assessment **Standardized Test Practice** TEKS 10J, 10K TAAS Reading Obj. 6

DISTINGUISH BETWEEN FACT AND OPINION
For some standardized tests, students will be asked to distinguish between fact and opinion. To help students recognize facts and opinions, read aloud or write on the board the following:
Which facts support the opinion that nothing was too good for first-class passengers on the *Titanic*?
A. There were facilities such as a gymnasium, squash court, swimming pool, and steam bath for them to enjoy.
B. They enjoyed very delicious food at dinner.

C. Their staterooms were decorated with thick carpets, marble sinks, and carved wooden walls.
D. Crew members were really nice to them.
Lead students through the process of distinguishing between fact and opinion. B and D are opinions; they show personal feelings and cannot support the opinion offered in the question. A and C present facts that prove the validity of the opinion that is presented in the question.

pulleys shrieked as the ropes passed through them, creaking under the weight of the boat and its load of sixty-four people. After landing in the water, Ruth's lifeboat began to drift. Suddenly Ruth saw another lifeboat coming down right on top of them! Fearing for their lives, the men in charge of her boat shouted, "Stop!" to the sailors up on the deck. But the noise was so great that nobody noticed. The second lifeboat kept coming down, so close that they could actually touch the bottom of it. All of a sudden, one of the men in Ruth's boat jumped up, pulled out a knife, and cut them free of their lowering ropes. Ruth's boat pushed away from the *Titanic* just as boat No. 15 hit the water inches away from them.

Below, in the third-class decks of the ship, there was much more confusion and alarm. Most of these passengers had not yet been able to get above decks. Some of those who did finally make it out had to break down the barriers between third and first class.

By 1:30 the bow was well down, and people were beginning to notice the slant of the decks. In the radio room, Bride and Phillips were still desperately sending out calls for help: "We are sinking fast . . . women and children in boats."

The last lifeboats pull away from the sinking *Titanic*, leaving approximately 1,500 people on board.
Painting by Ken Marschall from Exploring the *Titanic*. Copyright © 1988 by Robert D. Ballard, a Madison Press Book.

We cannot last much longer." The radio signal gradually got weaker and weaker as the ship's power faded out. Out on the decks, most passengers now began to move toward the stern area, which was slowly lifting out of the water.

By 2:05 there were still over 1,500 people left on the sinking ship. All the lifeboats were now away, and a strange stillness took hold. People stood quietly on the upper decks, bunching together for warmth, trying to keep away from the side of the tilting ship.

A Captain Smith now made his way to the radio room and told Harold Bride and Jack Phillips to save themselves. "Men, you have done your full duty," he told them. "You can do no more. Abandon your cabin. Now it's every man for himself." Phillips kept working the radio, hanging on until the very last moment. Suddenly Bride heard water gurgling up the deck outside the radio room. Phillips heard it, too, and cried, "Come on, let's clear out."

Near the stern, Father Thomas Byles had heard confession and given absolution[9] to over one hundred passengers. Playing to the very end, the members of the ship's brave band finally had to put down their instruments and try to save themselves. In desperation, some of the passengers and crew began to jump overboard as the water crept up the slant of the deck.

> ### ACTIVE READING
> **FACT AND OPINION**
> **B** Is this statement about the band putting down their instruments a fact or an opinion?

A crowded lifeboat from the *Titanic* is hoisted aboard the *Carpathia*. UPI/Bettmann.

Jack Thayer stood with his friend Milton Long at the railing to keep away from the crowds. He had become separated from his father in the confusion on deck. Now Jack and his friend heard muffled thuds and explosions deep within the ship. Suddenly the *Titanic* began to slide into the water. The water rushed up at them. Thayer and Long quickly said goodbye and good luck to each other. Then they both jumped.

As he hit the water, Jack Thayer was sucked down. "The cold was terrific. The shock of the water took the breath out of my lungs. Down and down I went, spinning in all directions." When he finally surfaced, gasping for air and numbed by the water, the ship was about forty feet away from him. His friend Milton Long was nowhere to be seen. Jack would never see him again.

Jack Thayer was lucky. As he struggled in the water, his hand came to rest on an overturned lifeboat. He grabbed hold and hung on, barely managing to pull himself up out of the water. Harold Bride had been washed overboard and now also clung to this same boat.

Both Jack and Harold witnessed the mighty ship's last desperate moments. "We could see groups of . . . people aboard, clinging in clusters or bunches, like swarming bees; only to fall in masses, pairs, or singly, as the great part of the ship . . . rose into the sky. . . ." said Thayer. "I looked upwards—we were

---

9. **heard confession . . . absolution:** Father Byles has conducted a Roman Catholic religious practice in which a priest listens to people confess their sins and then declares them forgiven.

 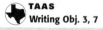

right under the three enormous propellers. For an instant, I thought they were sure to come right down on top of us. Then . . . she slid quietly away from us into the sea."

Out in the safety of her lifeboat, Ruth Becker also witnessed the end of the *Titanic*. "I could look back and see this ship, and the decks were just lined with people looking over. Finally, as the *Titanic* sank faster, the lights died out. You could just see the stern remaining in an upright position for a couple of minutes. Then . . . it disappeared."

Then, as Ruth recalled, "there fell upon the ear the most terrible noise that human beings ever listened to—the cries of hundreds of people struggling in the icy cold water, crying

Aboard the *Carpathia*, the only surviving honeymoon couple, Mr. and Mrs. George Harder, talk to Mrs. Hays, who lost her husband. The Illustrated London News Picture Library.

for help with a cry we knew could not be answered." In Thayer's words, they became "a long continuous wailing chant." Before long this ghastly wailing stopped, as the freezing water took its <u>toll</u>.

Jack Thayer and Harold Bride and a number of other survivors clung to their overturned lifeboat, inches away from an icy death in the North Atlantic. Numb from the cold and not daring to move in case the boat sank under their weight, they prayed and waited for help. Then, as the first light of dawn crept on the horizon, a rocket was seen in the distance. The *Carpathia* had come to their rescue. ❖

| WORDS TO KNOW | **toll** (tōl) *n.* the amount of loss or destruction caused by a disaster |

671

 Mini Lesson **Speaking and Listening** 🏴 **TEKS** 5B, 11B

PRESS CONFERENCE

Prepare Explain to students that at a press conference, one or more speakers usually deliver a statement to an audience of reporters about an event that has occurred. After the statement is read, reporters often ask the speaker questions based on the content of the statement or on their own knowledge of the situation. Have students plan a press conference about the sinking of the *Titanic*. Have some students play the parts of the survivors and possibly a representative of the White Star Line. They should prepare short statements, drawing from the facts in the text.

Present Have the speakers sit at a large table facing the audience. Each one should read his or her prepared statement. Audience members should take turns asking questions of each speaker, who should remain in character. Afterward, the class should discuss what they learned about the need for press conferences in certain situations.

BLOCK SCHEDULING This activity is particularly well suited for longer class periods.

Use **Communications Transparencies and Copymasters**, p. 4, for additional support.

Connect to the Literature

1. Responses will vary. Have students explain their reactions.

Comprehension Check
- He had a long career and a good safety record. This was to be his final reward before retirement.
- They had elaborate rooms, a variety of recreational activities, and fine food.
- The ship *Carpathia* came to their rescue.

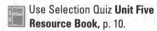 Use Selection Quiz **Unit Five Resource Book,** p. 10.

Think Critically

2. Possible Response: People felt excitement and confidence. They had the feeling they were taking part in a magnificent, once-in-a-lifetime experience.

3. Responses will vary. Some students might feel that the captain should have taken warnings more seriously. Some might say his reaction was understandable, given his confidence in the ship and his own abilities as a captain.

4. Responses will vary. Some students might say ignorance of the situation cost many lives. Lifeboats could have been loaded more efficiently and with more equity. Other students might say that a more efficient response might not have affected the outcome dramatically because nothing could change the fact that there were too few lifeboats.

5. Responses will vary. Students should name specific facts and opinions that made the piece particularly vivid to them.

 Use **Reading and Critical Thinking Transparencies,** p. 26, for additional support.

Literary Analysis

Setting Details that show what was new on the *Titanic* include: a gymnasium with the latest in exercise equipment; biggest whistles ever made.

Details that show what was old on the *Titanic* include: reliance on the lookout to spot icebergs or other obstacles; barriers between first-class and third-class areas; servants.

Use **Literary Analysis Transparencies,** p. 6, for additional support.

Connect to the Literature

1. **What Do You Think?** What was your reaction when you finished the selection?

Comprehension Check
- Why was Captain Smith given command of the *Titanic*?
- What kinds of accommodations did the ship have for wealthy passengers?
- How were the survivors of the *Titanic* finally rescued?

Think Critically

2. How would you describe the mood of the passengers and crew when the *Titanic* first set sail for New York on April 10, 1912?

 THINK ABOUT
- "the Unsinkable Ship"
- "Everything was new. New!"
- the ship's band playing for the wealthiest people in the world

3. Did Captain Smith's response to the first reports of icebergs sent to the *Titanic* by the *Caronia* seem appropriate? Explain.

4. What was your opinion of the behavior of the passengers and crew while the lifeboats were being loaded? Could more lives have been saved if evacuation efforts had been conducted differently?

5. **ACTIVE READING** | **FACT AND OPINION** | Review the notes you took in your **READER'S NOTEBOOK.** How did Ballard's use of fact and opinion influence your reaction to his narration of the disaster?

Extend Interpretations

6. **What If?** *Exploring the* Titanic is a piece of literary nonfiction, that is, it provides you with factual information even as it reads like a piece of fiction. What if Ballard had chosen to write informative nonfiction, providing only the facts of the disaster without such devices as dialogue or characterization? Would the information have been more compelling for you or not? Explain.

7. **Connect to Life** What recent disasters do you know of? How has knowledge of these events affected your life?

Literary Analysis

SETTING: TIME Robert D. Ballard brings to life the first years of the twentieth century by describing what was new and what was old on the *Titanic*. The *Titanic* was perhaps the most modern ship of its time. Because of its watertight compartments, it was called the "Unsinkable Ship." At the same time, the *Titanic* maintained many old social values, such as clearly held class distinctions:

In 1912, people were divided into social classes according to background, wealth, and education. Because of these class lines, the Titanic *was rather like a big floating layer cake.*

Cooperative Learning Activity
With the class, make a chart showing how Robert D. Ballard creates a vivid depiction of 1912 through details that show what was old and what was new on the *Titanic*. Discuss how these details reveal significant opinions and attitudes of the era.

New	Old
Mechanically operated watertight compartments	Working-class families stayed on a low level of the ship.
Passengers liked to send wireless messages to their friends.	First-class passengers had their own promenade deck.

Extend Interpretations

6. **What If?** Responses will vary. Responses should show that students understand the distinguishing features of both types of nonfiction. You might have students rewrite the last part of the excerpt without the recollections of Ruth Becker or Jack Thayer. Have students compare the two versions.

7. **Connect to Life** Responses will vary. Students might name earthquakes, storms, floods, and acts of violence. Encourage students to think of natural and technological disasters around the world. Ask them what they become more aware of as a result of these tragedies.

Choices & CHALLENGES

Writing Options

First-Person Story Expand upon one of the scenes that feature Jack Thayer or Ruth Becker, such as when Ruth pushes her baby brother in a stroller on deck or when Jack must swim for his life as the ship sinks. Describe the scene as if Ruth or Jack were narrating it. Use the details provided and make up any that you think are necessary.

Activities & Explorations

1. Titanic Poster Design a poster showing the *Titanic* in all her original glory. Use details from the text as well as its illustrations to help you capture the ship's elegance and grandeur. ~VIEWING AND REPRESENTING

2. Film Critic Watch the video clip from *A Night to Remember.* How did the clip compare to the way you visualized the night the *Titanic* struck an iceberg and sank? How did it compare to other films of the *Titanic* disaster that you have seen?

 Literature in Performance

Inquiry & Research

 SCIENCE | **UNDERWATER EXPLORATION**

The exploration of the wreckage of the *Titanic* solved many mysteries about the ship's last hours. Find out about other sunken ships that have been explored by archaeologists.

Real World Link Begin your research by reading "The Lives of *La Belle*," page 675, about a sunken ship that is being excavated in Matagorda Bay on the Texas Gulf Coast.

Vocabulary in Action

EXERCISE: CONTEXT CLUES On your paper, write the Word to Know that best completes each sentence.

1. The *Titanic* had _____ for more than 2,000 passengers.
2. The ship had a mechanical camel, a _____ used to entertain the passengers.
3. It is no wonder people were _____ by the ship's size and luxury.
4. The *Titanic* was considered unsinkable, so nobody would have believed a _____ that the ship's name would become a symbol of disaster.
5. The similarities between the fictional sinking of the *Titan* and the real sinking of the *Titanic* are _____.
6. The hull of the *Titanic* was divided into compartments, and even if four were flooded, the ship could stay afloat _____.
7. Water that flooded five compartments made the ship _____ to one side.
8. The crew worked _____ to lower lifeboats, but there wasn't room for every passenger.
9. Would the death _____ have been as high if there had been a law requiring enough lifeboats for all passengers?
10. The passing of this law was more meaningful than any other _____ paid to the memory of the passengers and the crew of the *Titanic*.

Building Vocabulary
For an in-depth study of context clues, see p. 67.

WORDS TO KNOW	accommodations	feverishly	novelty	toll
	dazzled	indefinitely	prophecy	tribute
	eerie	list		

EXPLORING THE *TITANIC* **673**

Writing Options

First-Person Story To get students started on this assignment, have them reread the scene and jot down details that they can use in their own account. Students may wish to write their stories in the form of a letter or memoir about the incident. **To extend this assignment,** have students tell their stories as if they were being interviewed by a reporter.

Activities & Explorations

1. *Titanic* **Poster** Students may wish to include several illustrations of different features of the ship, based on the description in the text. This assignment is particularly well suited for **visual learners. To extend this assignment,** students might check the Internet or library database for additional information on the design and interior of the *Titanic*. Students with an interest in building models might assemble one of the ship.

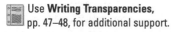 Use **Writing Transparencies,** pp. 47–48, for additional support.

2. **Film Critic** Encourage students to create a chart to organize their comparisons and contrasts. Have students bring in their favorite film versions of the event and explain their choice.

Use **Communications Transparencies and Copymasters,** p. 7, for additional support.

Inquiry & Research

Underwater Exploration Encourage students to use print and online resources in conducting their research. You might also encourage students to contact a representative of the United States Coast Guard to find out how such situations are now handled.

Use **Writing Transparencies,** pp. 45, 47–48, for additional support.

Vocabulary in Action

EXERCISE
1. accommodations
2. novelty
3. dazzled
4. prophecy
5. eerie
6. indefinitely
7. list
8. feverishly
9. toll
10. tribute

Grammar in Context

WRITING EXERCISE
Possible Responses:
1. She was 882 feet long, and her funnels were enormous.
2. Jack heard the explosions inside the ship, and the *Titanic* began to slide into the water.
3. There was no moon, but the stars shone brightly.

CONNECT TO LITERATURE
Possible Response: "A number of ships heard and responded, but most were too far away to come to the rescue in time." "Captain Smith was on duty on the bridge, so Bride handed the message to him."

Robert D. Ballard

As a marine geologist, Ballard helped discover volcanic vents nine thousand feet beneath the Pacific Ocean near the Galápagos Islands. He played a major role in developing the Argo/Jason Junior underwater system that was used to find the *Titanic*.

Grammar in Context: Independent (Main) Clauses and Compound Sentences

To make the relationship between ideas clear, Robert D. Ballard often expresses two closely connected ideas in one compound sentence.

> The mail room was filling up with water, and sacks of mail were floating about.

A **compound sentence** contains two or more independent clauses. A **clause** is a group of words containing a **verb** and its **subject**. An independent clause is one that can stand by itself as a sentence. Independent clauses can be joined to form a compound sentence by using a comma and a **coordinating conjunction** (such as *and, but,* or *or*). When you combine sentences, be sure to choose the coordinating conjunction that expresses the correct relationship between the clauses.

> They had avoided a head-on crash, but the iceberg had struck a glancing blow along the *Titanic*'s starboard bow.

WRITING EXERCISE Rewrite each pair of sentences as a compound sentence.

Example: *Original* The first-class passengers had large cabins. The third-class passengers were packed into small ones.

Rewritten The first-class passengers had large cabins, <u>but</u> the third-class passengers were packed into small ones.

1. She was 882 feet long. Her funnels were enormous.
2. Jack heard explosions inside the ship. The *Titanic* began to slide into the water.
3. There was no moon. The stars shone brightly.

Connect to the Literature Find two other compound sentences in *Exploring the* Titanic. Why did the author link the ideas?

Grammar Handbook Phrases and Clauses, p. R72

"I want to recruit people to study science, just as a coach recruits basketball players."

Robert D. Ballard
born 1942

To the Sea Robert Ballard has been fascinated by the sea since his childhood, when he explored beaches and read about famous sailors such as Captain Cook and Admiral Byrd. As an adult, Ballard helped pay for his education in oceanography by training dolphins at a marine park. Eventually, he joined the staff of the Woods Hole Oceanographic Institute in Massachusetts.

Exploring the *Titanic* Ballard began his search for the *Titanic* using remote-controlled underwater robots. On September 1, 1985, a robotic vessel recorded the first view of the *Titanic* in 73 years.

Recruiting Scientists Ballard, the explorer, has now set his sights on inspiring children to learn. "We need to declare war on ignorance, and the only way is through education," he says. "I want to recruit people to study science, just as a coach recruits basketball players." Ballard's other works include *Exploring Our Living Planet, Discovery of the* Titanic, *The Discovery of the* Bismarck, and *The Lost Wreck of the* Isis.

 LaserLink: Background for Reading Science Connection

Teaching Options

  Grammar 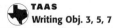 **TEKS 17A** **TAAS Writing Obj. 3, 5, 7**

INDEPENDENT CLAUSES AND COMPOUND SENTENCES

Instruction Tell students that an independent clause has a subject and a verb and can stand by itself as a complete sentence. When two or more independent clauses are combined with a conjunction such as *and, or,* or *but,* they form a compound sentence. Write the following compound sentence to illustrate: Jack Thayer struggled to the surface, but his friend disappeared.

Exercise Have students identify the subject and verb of each independent clause and decide if the sentence is compound.
1. Mrs. Becker jumped into the boat and called to Ruth. *(Mrs. Becker, jumped, called)*
2. Some of the first lifeboats weren't full, but the later boats were too crowded. *(Some, were; boats, were – compound)*
3. The survivors would not forget the sights and sounds of that terrible day. *(survivors, would forget)*
4. The first class passengers could sit on the deck, or they could enjoy other activities. *(passengers, could sit; they, could enjoy – compound)*

Use **Unit Five Resource Book**, p. 8.
Use **Grammar Transparencies and Copymasters**, p. 105.

Use McDougal Littell's *Language Network*, Chapter 8, for more instruction and practice in independent clauses and compound sentences.

Living·Arts

The Lives of La Belle

SPECIAL REPORT

by Bryan Woolley

PALACIOS, Texas— He may have been C. Barange. That's the name engraved on the pewter bowl the archaeologists found beside his skeleton in November.

Near his skeleton the archaeologists found a small wooden cask that once contained wine or brandy, a pair of shoes, some buttons, a ring with a red gemstone setting and a leather wallet containing two wooden combs, one to groom his hair and the other, finer toothed one to remove lice from it.

The dead man and his tiny collection of belongings had lain in the mud since January 1686, when the small frigate they were on sank to the bottom of Matagorda Bay, a site about 80 miles east of what later became Corpus Christi, Texas. The ship was named *La Belle* and was owned by the French explorer René-Robert Cavelier, Sieur de La Salle.

The outline of *La Belle*'s hull begins to emerge from the floor of Matagorda Bay.

Excavating a 300-year-old shipwreck connects the explorers who sailed it and the scientists who found it.

Reading for Information

What does it take to start a town? Scientists are now studying what the French explorer La Salle brought to start a colony in America—thanks to the discovery of one of his ships, *La Belle*, which sank off the coast of Texas in the 17th century.

SQ3R To read nonfiction and remember the information, use the study strategy SQ3R: Scan, Question, Read, Recite, Review.

YOUR TURN *Use SQ3R to answer the questions that follow.*

1 **Scan** the article quickly to find out what it is about. Note the title, subtitles, and photos. What ideas do you find?

Objectives

- read and analyze news sources
- use the study strategy SQ3R to comprehend and remember information
- read to be informed
- find out what archaeologists can learn from shipwrecks

Connecting to the Literature

The article "The Lives of *La Belle*" is an interesting corollary to *Exploring the Titanic* because it shows the process involved in studying a shipwreck to acquire facts about an event or period in history. From their analysis of *La Belle,* archaeologists have learned about life in the 1600s and the way that European colonists approached the settlement of a colony in the New World.

Reading for Information

As you go through the article with students, have them use the material in the right-hand column as a guide to reading newspaper articles. The following are **possible responses** to the five questions.

1 The article tells where the ship was found, gives background on the ship's historical expedition, and explains how the ship is being preserved and studied.

Use **Reading and Critical Thinking Transparencies,** p. 48, for additional support.

The Expedition

2 In 1682, La Salle had explored the entire length of the Mississippi River and claimed its watershed—almost half the present United States—for King Louis XIV of France. He then convinced the king that a colony at the southern end of the great river would protect French lands from France's enemy, the Spanish, whose vast empire lay to the west and south.

King Louis gave La Salle four ships. According to the journal of Henri Joutel, a lieutenant of La Salle's who was eventually one of a handful of survivors, misfortune dogged the expedition from its beginning. First, Spanish pirates captured one of the ships in the Caribbean. Then, because of the primitive navigational methods of his time and even worse maps, La Salle overshot the mouth of the Mississippi, which is near present-day New Orleans. On February 18, 1685, he wound up in Matagorda Bay, halfway between present-day Galveston and Corpus Christi. He thought he had arrived where he wanted to go.

On February 29, *L'Amiable*, the largest of the three remaining ships, which carried many of the supplies needed to found the colony, ran aground and broke apart. Most of the supplies were lost. On March 12, one of the last two ships departed for France with a message to the king that La Salle had arrived at the mouth

Dolphin-shaped handles on a cannon.

of the Mississippi but needed more supplies. The king received La Salle's message but rejected it, complaining that he already had spent more on La Salle than Ferdinand and Isabella had on Columbus.

Meanwhile, back in Texas, the remaining 180 colonists were building a camp they called Fort St. Louis, and La Salle went roaming across the countryside, looking for the Mississippi. On March 15 of the next year, 1686, La Salle returned to learn that *La Belle*, his last ship, had run aground with the remainder of the colony's supplies and trade goods.

Realizing that he was cut off from France and that his dream of building a colony and making a fortune in the New World was doomed, La Salle continued in his searches for the Mississippi. He never found the river. On March 20, 1687, somewhere in East Texas, some of La Salle's own men murdered him.

In 1688, six ragged survivors of the expedition arrived in Canada and eventually returned to France, carrying their journals of the adventure. When they had left Fort St. Louis, only 20 of the colonists were still alive. Some of those died of smallpox. Native Americans killed the rest, except for a few children who were taken captive. They were rescued later by the Spanish.

The Project to Raise La Belle

Archaeologists from all over the country have made their way to the big blue warehouse on the Palacios waterfront on Matagorda Bay that serves as the project headquarters. The ground floor houses the Texas Historical Commission field office and a makeshift lab. There, the recovered artifacts are stabilized and prepared for shipment to Texas A&M, where they're cleaned and preserved for eventual public display.

At 6:30 each morning, about a dozen of the warehouse residents board the Texas Historical Commission's boat *Anomaly* for the hour-long ride to the cofferdam that surrounds the wrecked ship, 15 miles from shore. The cofferdam consists of two concentric circular walls of interlocking iron panels driven deep into the bay floor, 12 feet below the water's surface. The space between the two walls is filled with gravel. The water has been pumped out of the doughnut-shaped dam.

For eight hours a day, seven days a week, the archaeologists labor over the hulk on the muddy bay floor. With great care, they lift objects from

Reading for Information *continued*

❷ After scanning, **question** what you expect to find out when you read. Make a chart like the one below to begin recording your questions. Remember, no question is too simple. For example, you might ask, What else is La Salle known for?

Questions	Answers
What else is La Salle known for?	

❸ **Read** the entire selection carefully. Look for the answers to the questions you formed. Make sure you understand a passage before moving to the next one. What is a cofferdam? You may need to consult a dictionary or reference source.

2 Some questions may include:
What is a watershed?
What would La Salle gain by his explorations?
Who would be the first colonists to come over?
Was his colony successful?
Encourage students to list questions about the other parts of the article.

3 A cofferdam is a watertight case pumped dry in building bridges or for repairing ships. The cofferdam for *La Belle* has been formed by driving two concentric circular walls of interlocking iron panels into the bay floor. The space between the two walls was then filled with gravel to give it stability against the pressure of surrounding sea water. Then the water inside the coffee dam was pumped out.

Stages in the construction of the cofferdam around the sunken remains of *La Belle*.

4 The main ideas are:
- Scientists have found well preserved objects on the sunken ship *La Belle*.
- La Salle intended to colonize the watershed of the Mississippi River for France, but ended up in what is now Texas.
- His supply ships encountered bad luck, the king denied further help, and as a result, La Salle's colony failed and he was murdered by some of his disgruntled crew.
- Extensive archaeological efforts have protected the site of *La Belle* and have recovered many artifacts that reveal significant facts about the colonization process of three centuries ago.

The main idea in this paragraph is that the discovery of *La Belle* is important because it reveals valuable information about the colonizing process.

Supporting details include the items found on the ship, the reason that this information is so significant, and the fact that La Salle's colony failed because the ship did not arrive.

5 Students might say that they could contact Texas A & M University either by mail or e-mail.

the casks in which they were packed more than three centuries ago, mark their location, label them and put them into containers for the trip to shore. About 4:30 P.M. they board the *Anomaly* again, motor back to their dock, and unload the day's finds.

In the lab, Kris Taylor, one of the scientists who have been excavating *La Belle*, shows off some of the rescued artifacts: navigator's dividers, used for plotting courses on charts; buckles from clothing, some of them intricately engraved; a wooden box containing a set of copper cauldrons,

Reading for Information *continued*

4 Recite the main ideas of the entire selection. Then write them down, using your own words. What is the main idea in this paragraph? What are the supporting details?

5 Review the whole article, checking to see how well you remembered the main ideas. Sometimes additional research is necessary. Suppose you want to know if the artifacts are still on display. How would you find the answer to that question?

Inquiry & Research

Activity Link: from *Exploring the* Titanic, p. 673. Research the discovery of a shipwreck other than *La Belle*. Use the study strategy SQ3R to read the articles you find. Then select one article, write a summary of the main ideas, and present your summary to the class.

a ladle, two candlesticks, a colander, and a pot; two seals for impressing wax images onto letters; chess and backgammon pieces; clay pipe stems; a brass writing implement with a screw top, amazingly similar to a modern fountain pen.

Besides such personal items, the archaeologists have recovered tons of lead shot and cannonballs and dozens of barrels and boxes still intact and neatly stacked inside the ship's hull, full of glass beads made in Venice, bronze hewn bells, brass straight pins, bronze finger rings, and iron ax heads, all apparently intended for trade with the Native Americans.

"This ship is a sort of colony kit," says Dr. Jim Bruseth, the project director. "Many colonies were established in the New World, but the stuff the people brought with them is gone. What we have on *La Belle* is a good inventory of what a country in Europe felt was important for establishing a colony in the New World. And the final pivot of LaSalle's dream, the straw that broke the camel's back, was the sinking of the ship which we've found."

"People don't realize how important La Salle was," Dr. Bruseth adds. "If he had been successful, we might be speaking French today in Texas."

Copper pots and a colander: supplies for the colony.

 Mini Lesson **Inquiry & Research** **TEKS** 10G, 13C  **TAAS** Reading Obj. 3

The Inquiry & Research activity on this page links to the Inquiry & Research section of the Choices & Challenges on page 673, following the excerpt from *Exploring the Titanic*.

Instruction Tell students that reference sources, including the Internet and periodicals, will lead them to information on shipwrecks. After students have chosen the article that they wish to summarize, remind them to reread it carefully.

As they read, they may wish to note important words and phrases.

Practice Have students state the main idea of the selection in the first sentence of their summary. Remind students that they should use their own words in writing their summary, but that ideas should be presented in the same order in which they appear in the original article.

PREPARING to *Read*

Last Cover

Short Story by PAUL ANNIXTER

"The fox became Colin's whole life."

Connect to Your Life

Why do you think people develop strong ties with pets? What do pets offer their owners? What qualities does a good pet have? With a small group, make a word web listing them.

Qualities of a good pet

small

Build Background

CONNECT TO SCIENCE The red fox is the most common fox in the United States. Clever, quick, and gifted with keen hearing and a sharp sense of smell, a red fox makes an excellent hunter but a poor pet. A fox and its mate may roam many miles to stake out a territory in which to hunt and raise their young. This territory may be as large as three square miles.

Foxes are often hunted for their fur, for sport, or because their raids on chicken coops are a nuisance to farmers. In some fox hunts, like the one in this story, hunters on horseback use dogs to follow the scent of a fox. The dogs' barking reveals the fox's hiding place.

Fox Hunting, the Find, Currier & Ives. Scala/Art Resource, New York.

WORDS TO KNOW	Vocabulary Preview		
bleak	harried	predestined	wily
confound	invalid	sanction	
essence	passive	sanctuary	

LaserLink: Background for Reading
Science Connection

Focus Your Reading

LITERARY ANALYSIS SETTING: PLACE The time and place in which a literary work occurs are called its **setting.** Just as time includes the historical era, the season, and the time of day, place also has several aspects. To adequately understand a story, it is important to know such things as the region where it takes place; whether it is set in the city or a rural area; whether the geography is mountainous, swampy, dry; and what kind of people live there (farmers, office workers, and so forth).

ACTIVE READING VISUALIZING The process of forming a mental picture based on a written description is called **visualizing.** Good readers use the details writers supply to visualize settings in their minds. As you read, use the details the author gives you to visualize the setting of "Last Cover."

 READER'S NOTEBOOK. Make two columns in your notebook. In the first, jot down some specific details from the story that describe setting. In the second, note the kind of mental picture you formed in your mind after reading these details.

Details From the Story	How I Picture Them
"The leafless woods were bleak and empty....."	I picture a day with a gray sky and no leaves on the trees.

See the Skills Trace at the beginning of the unit for information on TEKS covered in this lesson.

LAST COVER **679**

Objectives
1. to understand and appreciate a **short story (Literary Analysis)**
2. to understand the significance of the **setting (emphasis: place) (Literary Analysis)**
3. to utilize the skill **visualizing (Active Reading)**

Summary
Stan narrates the story of his younger brother, Colin, and their pet fox. The boys' father, a hunter and woodsman, scorns Colin's sensitive, artistic nature. He doesn't know that when Bandit returns to the wild, Colin skillfully tracks and observes his former pet. When neighbors' chickens start disappearing, local hunters plot to kill Bandit. After Bandit is killed, Colin creates a masterful drawing that shows the fox camouflaged in the last hiding place where Colin saw him. Even the best woodsmen had never found this place. The father, seeing that Colin shares his deep affinity for nature, gains new respect for Colin and his art.

Thematic Link
It takes strength and courage for Colin and Stan to remain true to Bandit in the face of their father's disapproval.

5-Minute Warm-Up

Daily Language SkillBuilder **TEKS 17F, 17H**

Have students **proofread** the display sentences on page 653i and write them correctly. The sentences also appear on Transparency 21 of **Grammar Transparencies and Copymasters.**

Mini Lesson **Preteaching Vocabulary**

If you would like to preteach the WORDS TO KNOW for this selection, use the Mini Lesson, p. 680.

LESSON RESOURCES

UNIT FIVE RESOURCE BOOK, pp. 11–17

ASSESSMENT
Formal Assessment, pp. 109–110
Teacher's Guide to Assessment and Portfolio Use
Test Generator

SKILLS TRANSPARENCIES AND COPYMASTERS
Literary Analysis
• Setting, TR 6 (for Cooperative Learning Activity, p. 690)

Reading and Critical Thinking
• Visualizing, TR 10 (for Thinking Through the Literature, p. 690)
Grammar
• Verb Tense, CM 71–73 (for Mini Lesson, p. 683)
• Adverb Clause of Time, CM 112 (for Mini Lesson, p. 692)
Vocabulary
• Synonyms, CM 72 (for Mini Lesson, p. 680)
• Antonyms, CM 73 (for Mini Lesson, p. 689)

Communications
• Appreciative Listening, TR 2 (for Mini Lesson, p. 687)

INTEGRATED TECHNOLOGY
Audio Library
LaserLinks
• Science Connection. See **Teacher's SourceBook,** p. 31, for bar codes.
Internet: Research Starter

Visit our website:
www.mcdougallittell.com

Literary Analysis `SETTING: PLACE`

 Remind students that where a story takes place can have a major influence on the other elements of the work. Ask students what details they learn about the setting from this passage.

Possible Responses: It is winter; the house of the narrator is located near extensive woods and foothills.

Use **Unit Five Resource Book,** p. 13 for more practice.

Active Reading `VISUALIZING`

Ask students to describe mental images evoked by the text description of the woods.

Possible Response: The ground is muddy rather than covered with snow. The trees are bare, and the air is raw.

Use **Unit Five Resource Book,** p. 12 for more practice.

Literary Analysis: CHARACTERIZATION

 Have students analyze the traits of the narrator as revealed through his actions of searching in the woods and trying not to cry.

Possible Responses: He is persistent, determined, observant, patient, and considerate. He is trying to be strong for his brother's sake.

Literary Analysis: CONFLICT

C Remind students that conflict is a struggle between two opposing forces. Ask students to identify the source of the internal conflict felt by the brothers.

Possible Response: They want to believe that their pet fox is all right, but they are worried that he is not.

LAST COVER

by Paul Annixter

I'm not sure I can tell you what you want to know about my brother; but everything about the pet fox is important, so I'll tell all that from the beginning.

A It goes back to a winter afternoon after I'd hunted the woods all day for a sign of our lost pet. I remember the way my mother looked up as I came into the kitchen. Without my speaking, she knew what had happened. For six hours I had walked, reading signs, looking for a delicate print in the damp soil or even a hair that might have told of a red fox passing that way—but I had found nothing.

"Did you go up in the foothills?" Mom asked.

B I nodded. My face was stiff from held-back tears. My brother, Colin, who was going on twelve, got it all from one look at me and went into a heartbroken, almost silent, crying.

C Three weeks before, Bandit, the pet fox Colin and I had raised from a tiny kit, had disappeared, and not even a rumor had been heard of him since.

Teaching Options

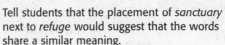

Preteaching Vocabulary

SYNONYMS

Instruction Tell students that writers sometimes use synonyms within the same sentence for emphasis or clarity. Often, synonyms are in a series or are connected by coordinating conjunctions. Recognizing one of the synonyms will help students to define the unfamiliar word. Write the following sentence to demonstrate:

The pool was a *sanctuary* or refuge for Bandit.

Tell students that the placement of *sanctuary* next to *refuge* would suggest that the words share a similar meaning.

Exercises Have students define each of the underlined WORDS TO KNOW.

1. He was a <u>wily</u>, crafty creature, who could <u>confound</u> and confuse with his devious trails.
2. His father felt distressed and <u>harried</u> by the urgency of the hunters.

3. No hunter would ever <u>sanction</u> or approve what we did to rescue the animal.
4. Under the gruff exterior, the woodsman had a kind <u>essence</u> or nature.

Use **Unit Five Resource Book,** p. 14 for exercises.

Use **Vocabulary Transparencies and Copymasters,** p. 72, for additional support.

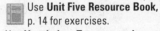

Detail of illustration by Wendell Minor reprinted from *Red Fox Running* by Eve Bunting. Copyright ©1993 by Wendell Minor, published by Clarion Books.

Less Proficient Readers
To interest students in the story, have them share stories about unusual pets—either their own or someone else's.
Set a Purpose Have students read to find out each boy's response to the loss of the fox.

Students Acquiring English
Ask students to name animals from other regions that would be comparable to the red fox in the northern part of the United States.

 Use **Spanish Study Guide**, pp. 136–138 for additional support.

Gifted and Talented
Have students look for clues that reflect the father's feelings about the fox and about Colin and signs of change in those feelings. What makes his feelings change?
Possible Responses:

Page 683: "Ever since you started talking up Colin's art, I've had an invalid for help around the place." (Colin and his art are useless.)

Page 683: "Watch out with all your soft ways,' Father had warned. . . 'You'll make too much of him." (Colin is soft-hearted and spoiled.)

Page 686: "Father, who took pride in all the ritual of the hunt, had refused to be a party to such an affair . . ." (Father can't bear to hunt the fox.)

Page 689: "He sat holding the picture with a sort of tenderness for a long time . . ." (He admires Colin's art.)

Page 689: "When the time came for Colin to go to art school, it was Father who was his solid backer." (Father supports Colin's artistic ability.)

If your schedule requires that you cover the lesson objectives in a shorter time, use . . .
- Preparing to Read, p. 679
- Thinking Through the Literature, p. 690
- Vocabulary in Action, p. 691
- Grammar in Context, p. 692

If you want to take advantage of longer class time, use . . .
- TE Teaching Options: Preteaching Vocabulary, p. 680; Cross Curricular Links, pp. 682, 686; Grammar, pp. 683, 692; Spelling, p. 684; Viewing and Representing, p. 685; Speaking and Listening, p. 687; Standardized Test Practice, p. 688; Vocabulary Strategy, p. 689
- Choices & Challenges and Author Activity, pp. 691–692

Literary Analysis: CONFLICT

A Point out to students the external conflict between Colin and his father over the fox. Ask students what the two opposing opinions are in this conflict.

Possible Response: Father is sure that Bandit is a chicken and egg stealer; Colin loves the fox and thinks his bad habits are due to his being a young fox.

Literary Analysis SETTING: PLACE

B Ask students to recognize and analyze elements of the setting. Have them explain what the setting contributes to the effect of the story.

Possible Response: The harshness of the cold February weather and the bleakness of the woods add to the feeling of anxiety about Bandit and emphasize the uncertainty of whether he can survive in the wild.

Reading Skills and Strategies: EVALUATING

C What does the statement "Father wasn't as hard as he made out, I knew, but he had to hold a balance against all Mom's frothing" indicate about Father's and Stan's relationship with Mom?

Possible Responses: They both see her as the more frivolous member of the family; they "humor" her "frothing" but leave the serious talk to themselves.

Reading Skills and Strategies: CLARIFYING

D Have students discuss the time frame of the events in the story so far.

Possible Responses: The narrator thinks back to the past to remember the winter afternoon that he hunted for Bandit. Then he thinks back even further to the year and a half before, when his brother first found the fox.

"He'd have had to go off soon anyway," Mom comforted. "A big, lolloping fellow like him, he's got to live his life same as us. But he may come back. That fox set a lot of store by you boys in spite of his wild ways."

"He set a lot of store by our food, anyway," Father said. He sat in a chair by the kitchen window mending a piece of harness. "We'll be seeing a lot more of that fellow, never fear. That fox learned to pine for table scraps and young chickens. He was getting to be an egg thief, too, and he's not likely to forget that."

"That was only pranking when he was little," Colin said desperately.

From the first, the tame fox had made tension in the family. It was Father who said we'd better name him Bandit, after he'd made away with his first young chicken.

"Maybe you know," Father said shortly. "But when an animal turns to egg sucking, he's usually incurable. He'd better not come pranking around my chicken run again."

It was late February, and I remember the <u>bleak</u>, dead cold that had set in, cold that was a rare thing for our Carolina hills. Flocks of sparrows and snowbirds had appeared, to peck hungrily at all that the pigs and chickens didn't eat.

"This one's a killer," Father would say of a morning, looking out at the whitened barn roof. "This one will make the shoats[1] squeal."

A fire snapped all day in our cookstove and another in the stone fireplace in the living room, but still the farmhouse was never warm. The leafless woods were bleak and empty, and I spoke of that to Father when I came back from my search.

"It's always a sad time in the woods when the seven sleepers are under cover," he said.

"What sleepers are they?" I asked. Father was full of woods lore.

"Why, all the animals that have got sense enough to hole up and stay hid in weather like this. Let's see, how was it the old rhyme named them?

Surly bear and sooty bat,
Brown chuck and masked coon,
Chippy-munk and sly skunk,
And all the mouses
'Cept in men's houses.

"And man would have joined them and made it eight, Granther Yeary always said, if he'd had a little more sense."

"I was wondering if the red fox mightn't make it eight," Mom said.

Father shook his head. "Late winter's a high time for foxes. Time when they're out deviling, not sleeping."

My chest felt hollow. I wanted to cry like Colin over our lost fox, but at fourteen a boy doesn't cry. Colin had squatted down on the floor and got out his small hammer and nails to start another new frame for a new picture. Maybe then he'd make a drawing for the frame and be able to forget his misery. It had been that way with him since he was five.

I thought of the new dress Mom had brought home a few days before in a heavy cardboard box. That box cover would be fine for Colin to draw on. I spoke of it, and Mom's glance thanked me as she went to get it. She and I worried a lot about Colin. He was small for his age, delicate and blond, his hair much lighter and softer than mine, his eyes deep and wide and blue. He was often sick, and I knew the fear Mom had that he might be

---

1. **shoats** (shōts): young pigs.

WORDS
TO
KNOW **bleak** (blēk) *adj.* harsh and dreary

682

Cross Curricular Link **Science**

HIBERNATION Father recites a rhyme that tells of animals that hibernate or lie dormant through the winter. Although bears are most commonly thought of in connection with hibernation, their winter survival technique is more like a long rest rather than hibernation. Their body temperature rarely goes below 88 degrees Fahrenheit, and they are capable of activity when stimulated. They even give birth to their cubs during the winter, nursing them and keeping them warm until the spring.

True hibernation is a much more risky survival technique. Only certain orders of mammals follow this pattern. Hibernating animals include the hedgehog, ground squirrel, and bat. During hibernation, the animal's body temperature drops to that of its environment, its breathing slows until it is almost undetectable, its internal organs are almost totally inactive, and the animal does not react to being handled. Hibernation is not continuous. However, each alert period consumes energy and heat, so the lower the temperature at which animals hibernate, the fewer the times they will awaken.

redestined. I'm just ordinary, like Father. I'm the sort of stuff that can take it—tough and strong—but Colin was always sort of special.

Mom lighted the lamp. Colin began cutting his white cardboard carefully, fitting it into his frame. Father's sharp glance turned on him now and again.

"There goes the boy making another frame before there's a picture for it," he said. "It's too much like cutting out a man's suit for a fellow that's, say, twelve years old. Who knows whether he'll grow into it?"

Mom was into him then, quick. "Not a single frame of Colin's has ever gone to waste. The boy has real talent, Sumter, and it's time you realized it."

"Of course he has," Father said. "All kids have 'em. But they get over 'em."

"It isn't the pox[2] we're talking of," Mom sniffed.

"In a way it is. Ever since you started talking up Colin's art, I've had an <u>invalid</u> for help around the place."

Father wasn't as hard as he made out, I knew, but he had to hold a balance against all Mom's frothing.[3] For him the thing was the land and all that pertained to it. I was following in Father's footsteps, true to form, but Colin threatened to break the family tradition with his leaning toward art, with Mom "aiding and abetting[4] him," as Father liked to put it. For the past two years she had had dreams of my brother becoming a real artist and going away to the city to study.

It wasn't that Father had no understanding of such things. I could remember, through the years, Colin lying on his stomach in the front room making pencil sketches, and how a good drawing would catch Father's eye halfway across the room, and how he would sometimes gather up two or three of them to study, frowning and muttering, one hand in his beard, while a great pride rose in Colin, and in me too. Most of Colin's drawings were of the woods and wild things, and there Father was a master critic. He made out to scorn what seemed to him a <u>passive</u>, "white-livered" interpretation of nature through brush and pencil instead of rod and rifle.

At supper that night Colin could scarcely eat. Ever since he'd been able to walk, my brother had had a growing love of wild things, but Bandit had been like his very own, a gift of the woods. One afternoon a year and a half before, Father and Laban Small had been running a vixen through the hills with their dogs. With the last of her strength the she-fox had made for her den, not far from our house. The dogs had overtaken her and killed her just before she reached it. When Father and Laban came up, they'd found Colin crouched nearby, holding her cub in his arms.

Father had been for killing the cub, which was still too young to shift for itself, but Colin's grief had brought Mom into it. We'd taken the young fox into the kitchen, all of us, except Father, gone a bit silly over the little thing. Colin had held it in his arms and fed it warm milk from a spoon.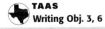

"Watch out with all your soft ways," Father had warned, standing in the doorway. "You'll make too much of him. Remember, you can't make a dog out of a fox. Half of that little critter has to love, but the other half is a wild hunter. You boys will mean a whole lot to him

---

2. **pox:** chickenpox, a contagious disease causing skin eruptions.

3. **frothing** (frôth′ĭng): light, meaningless talking.

4. **aiding and abetting:** helping and encouraging.

WORDS
TO
KNOW

predestined (prē-dĕs′tĭnd) *adj.* having one's fate decided beforehand **predestine** *v.*
invalid (ĭn′və-lĭd) *n.* a sickly or disabled person
passive (păs′ĭv) *adj.* inactive; lacking in energy or willpower

---

 Mini Lesson Grammar 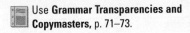 **TEKS** 17F **TAAS** Writing Obj. 3, 6

VERB TENSE

Instruction Tell students that a verb has different forms called tenses. The present tense places an action or condition in the present: Colin <u>attends</u> art school. The past tense places an action or condition in the past: Colin and Stan <u>loved</u> Bandit. The future tense places an action or condition in the future: Colin <u>will draw</u> hundreds of pictures of Bandit.

Exercises Have students read each of the following sentences and tell what tense each verb is in.

1. We <u>fed</u> the fox cub bits of meat. *(past)*
2. Colin <u>makes</u> frames for his pictures. *(present)*
3. Bandit <u>steals</u> chickens during the night. *(present)*
4. The farmers <u>will search</u> for him together. *(future)*
5. The fox <u>hid</u> quietly in the pool. *(past)*

 Use **Grammar Transparencies and Copymasters**, p. 71–73.

Use McDougal Littell's **Language Network**, Chapter 4, for more instruction and practice in verb tenses.

A Ask students to use their own knowledge to comprehend the narrator's feelings.

Reading Skills and Strategies:
CLARIFYING

B Ask students to identify when the events described in this paragraph are taking place.
Possible Response: The narrator is returning to the more recent past after telling how Colin raised Bandit.

Active Reading | VISUALIZING |

C Have students describe the mental images evoked by details of the setting.
Possible Responses: It is a beautiful spring day with blue sky and fluffy clouds and gusts of wind. Bandit's den resembles a pile of leaves by a bush.

Reading Skills and Strategies:
CLARIFYING

D Ask students what the narrator means by the kind of love Bandit gave.
Possible Response: He may mean that Bandit didn't show his affection in the way tame animals do.

Literary Analysis: CONFLICT

E Ask students what conflicts Stan anticipates when he sees the feather.
Possible Response: Bandit in conflict with the farmers; the boys in conflict with their father, who will want to stop Bandit

Reading Skills and Strategies:
PREDICTING

F Have students predict what Colin may be thinking of drawing.
Possible Responses: Bandit, Stan, the woods

---

while he's a kit, but there'll come a day when you won't mean a thing to him and he'll leave you shorn."[5]

For two weeks after that Colin had nursed the cub, weaning it from milk to bits of meat. For a year they were always together. The cub grew fast. It was soon following Colin and me about the barnyard. It turned out to be a patch fox, with a saddle of darker fur across its shoulders.

A I haven't the words to tell you what the fox meant to us. It was far more wonderful owning him than owning any dog. There was something rare and secret like the spirit of the woods about him, and back of his calm, straw-gold eyes was the sense of a brain the equal of a man's. The fox became Colin's whole life.

B Each day, going and coming from school, Colin and I took long side trips through the woods, looking for Bandit. Wild things' memories were short, we knew; we'd have to find him soon, or the old bond would be broken.

Ever since I was ten, I'd been allowed to hunt with Father, so I was good at reading signs. But, in a way, Colin knew more about the woods and wild things than Father or me. What came to me from long observation Colin seemed to know by instinct.

1 It was Colin who felt out, like an Indian, the stretch of woods where Bandit had his den, who found the first slim, small fox-print in the damp earth. And then, on an afternoon in March, we saw him. I remember the day well, the racing clouds, the wind rattling the tops of the pine trees and swaying the Spanish moss. **C** Bandit had just come out of a clump of laurel; in the maze of leaves behind him we caught a glimpse of a slim red vixen, so we knew he had found a mate. She melted from sight like a shadow, but Bandit turned to watch us, his

mouth open, his tongue lolling as he smiled his old foxy smile. On his thin chops, I saw a telltale chicken feather.

Colin moved silently forward, his movements so quiet and casual he seemed to be standing still. He called Bandit's name, and the fox held his ground, drawn to us with all his senses. For a few moments he let Colin actually put an arm about him. It was then I knew that he loved us still, for all of Father's warnings. He really loved us back, with a fierce, secret love no tame thing ever gave. But the urge of his life just then was toward his new mate. Suddenly, he whirled about and disappeared in the laurels.

Colin looked at me with glowing eyes. "We haven't really lost him, Stan. When he gets through with his spring sparking,[6] he may come back. But we've got to show ourselves to him a lot, so he won't forget."

"It's a go," I said.

"Promise not to say a word to Father," Colin said, and I agreed. For I knew by the chicken feather that Bandit had been up to no good.

A week later the woods were budding, and the thickets were rustling with all manner of wild things scurrying on the love scent. Colin managed to get a glimpse of Bandit every few days. He couldn't get close though, for the spring running was a lot more important to a fox than any human beings were.

Every now and then Colin got out his framed box cover and looked at it, but he never drew anything on it; he never even picked up his pencil. I remember wondering if

---

5. **shorn:** cut off, like hair; forsaken.
6. **spring sparking:** the springtime mating period.

Mini Lesson **Spelling** **TEKS 16F** **TAAS Writing Obj. 3, 7**

DIFFERENT SPELLINGS OF LONG e
Instruction Tell students that the long e sound is spelled in a variety of ways. Sometimes it is spelled with two vowels, with the letter y, or with the letter e. Write the following words from the selection on the board to illustrate the various ways that long e might be spelled. Have a volunteer read them aloud.

bl<u>ea</u>k   wil<u>y</u>

harr<u>ie</u>d   sl<u>ee</u>ping

Exercises Have students underline the letters that are pronounced with a long e sound in the following words.

1. n<u>ea</u>t
2. starr<u>y</u>
3. blear<u>y</u>
4. ferr<u>ie</u>d
5. d<u>ee</u>p
6. str<u>ea</u>m
7. worr<u>ie</u>d
8. prett<u>y</u>
9. l<u>ea</u>d
10. bl<u>ee</u>d

Ask students to look for more words that fit this pattern in their own writing and in what they read, and add these words to their personal word list.

 Use **Unit Five Resource Book,** p. 16 for more practice.

Albert's Son (1959), Andrew Wyeth. Tempera on panel, 74 cm × 61.5 cm, Copyright © Andrew Wyeth. The National Museum of Contemporary Art, Oslo, Norway. Photo by Jacques Lathion, Nasjonalgalleriet.

Less Proficient Readers

- Ask students what Colin and Stan do on the way to and from school each day.

Possible Response: They walk in the woods looking for Bandit.

- Ask students what they see one day in March.

Possible Response: They see Bandit emerging from his den, and they catch a glimpse of his mate.

Set a Purpose Have students read to find out what Bandit does to anger the farmers and how he evades them.

Students Acquiring English

1 Students may need help understanding the reference to an Indian, in this case meaning a Native American.

Multiple Learning Styles
Intrapersonal Learners

2 Invite students to imagine what it would be like to be Colin writing a journal about his experiences with Bandit. How would Colin tell the story? Ask students to create a journal entry that describes the day that he rediscovers Bandit in the woods. Then have students form small groups and share their entries.

 Viewing and Representing   **TEKS 22A**

Albert's Son
by Andrew Wyeth

ART APPRECIATION Andrew Wyeth was one of the most popular painters of realistic subjects in the United States. He created this painting with tempera paints in 1959. In it, he shows the personality and character traits of his subject.

Instruction Ask students to identify the elements that make this painting realistic.

Possible Responses: The setting is a realistic barn with rough boards and straw overhanging the loft; the expression on the boy's face seems quite natural and sincere.

Draw students' attention to the use of light and shadow. Ask students how the placement of the subject in the light and the way he gazes into the distance might be interpreted symbolically.

Possible Response: The boy might be looking at a future that is brighter than his past.

Application Colin is described as delicate. Ask students whether they see this boy as sturdy or delicate and why.

Possible Response: He does not seem terribly sturdy. He is thin and has small bone structure.

Literary Analysis: IRONY

A Ask students what is ironic about Father's clear understanding of Bandit's behavior and his understanding of Colin.
Possible Response: Although Father understands that Bandit must live true to his nature, he cannot see that Colin must do the same.

Literary Analysis: CHARACTERIZATION

B Ask students how Father's uneasiness about the hunt is shown in his behavior.
Possible Responses: He refuses to participate, he smiles when he hears that the trail has been broken, and he mopes around the house.

Literary Analysis SETTING: PLACE

C Have students analyze the significance of the setting for the narrator.
Possible Response: It represents memories of happy times and a refuge from his anxiety.

Active Reading VISUALIZING

D Have students explain what the details of the text help them to see.
Possible Response: dappled sunlight casting shadows, branches and leaves floating on the smooth surface of the pool, and two bright eyes peering out of the darkness

Literary Analysis: POINT OF VIEW

E Remind students that the story is told in the first-person point of view. Ask them how this point of view affects the description of the relationship between Stan and Colin.
Possible Response: Stan seems to be telling the story to the reader so that the reader feels like an active participant; Stan's comments about his brother seem direct and truthful.

what Father had said about framing a picture before you had one had spoiled something for him.

I was helping Father with the planting now, but Colin managed to be in the woods every day. By degrees, he learned Bandit's range, where he drank and rested and where he was likely to be according to the time of day. One day he told me how he had petted Bandit again and how they had walked together a long way in the woods. All this time we had kept his secret from Father.

As summer came on, Bandit began to live up to the prediction Father had made. Accustomed to human beings, he moved without fear about the scattered farms of the region, raiding barns and hen runs that other foxes wouldn't have dared go near. And he taught his wild mate to do the same. Almost every night they got into some poultry house, and by late June Bandit was not only killing chickens and ducks but feeding on eggs and young chicks whenever he got the chance.

Stories of his doings came to us from many sources, for he was still easily recognized by the dark patch on his shoulders. Many a farmer took a shot at him as he fled, and some of them set out on his trail with dogs, but they always returned home without even sighting him. Bandit was familiar with all the dogs in the region, and he knew a hundred tricks to confound them. He got a reputation that year beyond that of any fox our hills had known. His confidence grew, and he gave up wild hunting altogether and lived

entirely off the poultry farmers. By September, the hill farmers banded together to hunt him down.

It was Father who brought home that news one night. All time-honored rules of the fox chase were to be broken in this hunt; if the dogs couldn't bring Bandit down, he was to be shot on sight. I was stricken and furious. I remember the misery of Colin's face in the lamplight. Father, who took pride in all the ritual of the hunt, had refused to be a party to such an affair, though in justice he could do nothing but sanction any sort of hunt, for Bandit, as old Sam Wetherwax put it, had been "purely getting in the Lord's hair."

The hunt began next morning, and it was the biggest turnout our hills had known. There were at least twenty mounted men in the party and as many dogs.

Father and I were working in the lower field as they passed along the river road. Most of the hunters carried rifles, and they looked ugly.

Twice during the morning I went up to the house to find Colin, but he was nowhere around. As we worked, Father and I could follow the progress of the hunt by the distant hound music on the breeze. We could tell just where the hunters first caught sight of the fox and where Bandit was leading the dogs during the first hour. We knew as well as if we'd seen it how Bandit roused another fox along Turkey Branch and forced it to run for him and how the dogs swept after it for twenty minutes before they sensed their mistake.

Noon came, and Colin had not come in to eat. After dinner Father didn't go back to the

| WORDS TO KNOW | **confound** (kən-found') *v.* to bewilder; confuse |
| | **sanction** (săngk'shən) *v.* to give approval for |

Cross Curricular Link **Social Studies**

HISTORY OF FOX HUNTING Fox hunting originated in England around the 1600s. It began as a practical measure to save farm animals from being killed by foxes. Modern hunting dates from the 1800s when it became a national pastime of the upper-class. Fox hunters had to observe certain traditions regarding their clothing and the proper way to proceed with a hunt.

The highest members of the hunt wear scarlet coats with white cravats and black velvet caps. On the next level down, the hunters wear scarlet coats with top hats. The rest of the participants wear black coats and top hats.

The hunters and hounds assemble at a central point. Then the hounds are commanded to search out the fox, at which point the hunters follow and the chase begins. Various cries from the hunters and soundings of the horn signal the stages of the hunt.

Fox hunting reached its peak of popularity in England before World War I. Since then, the sport has encountered many obstacles but continues in the British Isles and some parts of the United States between November and April.

eld. He moped about, listening to the hound
alk. He didn't like what was on any more
han I did, and now and again I caught his
mile of satisfaction when we heard the
roken, angry notes of the hunting horn,
elling that the dogs had lost the trail or had
un another fox.

I was restless, and I went up into the hills in
nidafternoon. I ranged the woods for miles,
hinking all the time of Colin. Time lost all
neaning for me, and the short day was nearing
n end when I heard the horn
alking again, telling that the
ox had put over another
rick. All day he had
eviled the dogs and
nocked the hunters.
This new trick and the
coming night would

**The fox had put
over another trick.**

work to save him. I was
wildly glad as I moved
down toward Turkey Branch
and stood listening for a time by
he deep, shaded pool where for years
we boys had gone swimming, sailed boats, and
dreamed summer dreams.

Suddenly, out of the corner of my eye, I saw
the sharp ears and thin, pointed mask of a
fox—in the water almost beneath me. It was
Bandit, craftily submerged there, all but his
head resting in the cool water of the pool and
the shadow of the two big beeches that spread
above it. He must have run forty miles or
more since morning. And he must have hidden
in this place before. His knowing, crafty mask
blended perfectly with the shadows and a mass
of drift and branches that had collected by the
bank of the pool. He was so still that a pair of
thrushes flew up from the spot as I came up,
not knowing he was there.

Bandit's bright, <u>harried</u> eyes were looking
right at me. But I did not look at him direct.
Some woods instinct, swifter than thought,
kept me from it. So he and I met as in another
world, indirectly, with feeling but without sign
or greeting.

Suddenly I saw that Colin was standing
almost beside me. Silently as a water snake, he
had come out of the bushes and stood there.
Our eyes met, and a quick and secret smile
passed between us. It was a rare moment in
which I really "met" my brother,
when something of his <u>essence</u>
flowed into me and I knew
all of him. I've never lost
it since. My eyes still
turned from the fox,
my heart pounding. I
moved quietly away,
and Colin moved with
me. We whistled softly as
we went, pretending to
busy ourselves along the bank
of the stream. There was magic in it,
as if by will we wove a web of protection
about the fox, a ring-pass-not that none might
penetrate. It was so, too, we felt, in the brain
of Bandit, and that doubled the charm. To us
he was still our little pet that we had carried
about in our arms on countless summer
afternoons.

Two hundred yards upstream, we
stopped beside slim, fresh tracks in the
mud where Bandit had entered the
branch. The tracks angled upstream. But in the
water the <u>wily</u> creature had turned down.

We climbed the far bank to wait, and Colin
told me how Bandit's secret had been his secret
ever since an afternoon three months before,

WORDS	**harried** (hăr'ēd) *adj.* worried; distressed **harry** *v.*
TO	**essence** (ĕs'əns) *n.* basic nature or spirit
KNOW	**wily** (wī'lē) *adj.* crafty; sly

687

Customizing Instruction

Less Proficient Readers
• Ask students to summarize what
Bandit does throughout the summer.
Possible Response: He and his mate
raid barns and poultry houses, killing
farm animals.
• Ask students what happens during
the hunt for Bandit.
Possible Response: He tricks the dogs
by sending another fox in his place, he
creates false trails, and he hides in a
shadowy pool, where he is perfectly
camouflaged.
Set a Purpose Have students read to
find out what Colin does with his
framed box cover.

Students Acquiring English
1 Have students note the use of quotation marks around the verb *met.*
Explain that quotation marks are often
used to indicate words whose meanings are not to be understood in their
literal sense.

Mini Lesson **Speaking and Listening** **TEKS** 5A, 5C, 5D, 5E

STORYTELLING
Prepare Explain to students that storytelling is a
very old tradition. People told stories for entertainment and to pass on information about the past.
Storytellers often gathered plot ideas from rumors
and legends of a particular region, so sometimes
story characters included wise or crafty animals
like Bandit. Divide the class into groups of three
or four. Ask them to imagine that they are some
of the hunters who tried to capture Bandit. Have
each group come up with its own "Bandit story,"
in which it describes its hunt for the elusive fox.
Tell students that humor is often a part of story-

telling and remind them to adapt their language
to the audience and purpose.
Present Before students present their stories,
have them write down what they hope to accomplish through their storytelling. Then have groups
gather to tell their stories about Bandit. Students
should use the criteria previously generated to
evaluate their own performances.
BLOCK SCHEDULING This activity is particularly well
suited for longer class periods.

Use **Communications Transparencies and
Copymasters,** p. 2, for additional support.

**Reading Skills and Strategies:
DRAWING CONCLUSIONS**

A Ask students why the writer under-plays Bandit's death.

Possible Response: The understanding and trust between Colin and the fox is the focus of the story; Bandit's death is not.

**Literary Analysis:
CONFLICT**

B Tell students that the resolution of conflicts often comes at the end of a story. Ask students what conflict is resolved when Father looks at the picture.

Possible Response: His opposition to Colin's art ends.

Ask students what the picture proves to Father about Colin.

Possible Response: The picture proves Colin's equality or superiority to his father and Stan in his knowledge of the ways of the woods and wildlife. The father realizes that there are different ways of using that knowledge.

Beech Trees (1903), Gustav Klimt. Österreichische Galerie, Vienna, Austria. Erich Lessing/Art Resource, New York.

Teaching Options

 Assessment **Standardized Test Practice** **TEKS** 10E, 10K **TAAS** Reading Obj. 2

ARRANGING DETAILS IN SEQUENTIAL ORDER For some standardized tests, students will be asked to arrange details or events in the order in which they occurred in the passage. To provide students with practice in placing details in order, read aloud or write on the board the following question:
Which event occurs closest to Bandit's disappearance from the farm?

A. The boys discover he has a mate.

B. Stan spends all day walking in the cold woods to try to find him.

C. Bandit's raids motivate the farmers to organize a hunt.

D. Colin tracks Bandit to his hiding place in the water.

Lead students through the process of choosing the best answer. A is incorrect. It happened second in the sequence of events. B is correct. This action was taken three weeks after Bandit's disappearance. C is incorrect. It is last in this sequence of events. D is incorrect. Colin finds Bandit's hiding place before the hunt takes place.

when he'd watched the fox swim downstream to hide in the deep pool. Today he'd waited on the bank, feeling that Bandit, hard pressed by the dogs, might again seek the pool for sanctuary.

We looked back once as we turned homeward. He still had not moved. We didn't know until later that he was killed that same night by a chance hunter, as he crept out from his hiding place.

That evening Colin worked a long time on his framed box cover that had lain about the house untouched all summer. He kept at it all the next day too. I had never seen him work so hard. I seemed to sense in the air the feeling he was putting into it, how he was believing his picture into being. It was evening before he finished it. Without a word he handed it to Father. Mom and I went and looked over his shoulder.

It was a delicate and intricate pencil drawing of the deep branch pool, and there was Bandit's head and watching, fear-filled

eyes hiding there amid the leaves and shadows, woven craftily into the maze of twigs and branches, as if by nature's art itself. Hardly a fox there at all, but the place where he was—or should have been. I recognized it instantly, but Mom gave a sort of incredulous sniff.

"I'll declare," she said, "it's mazy as a puzzle. It just looks like a lot of sticks and leaves to me."

Long minutes of study passed before Father's eye picked out the picture's secret, as few men's could have done. I laid that to Father's being a born hunter. That was a picture that might have been done especially for him. In fact, I guess it was.

Finally he turned to Colin with his deep, slow smile. "So that's how Bandit fooled them all," he said. He sat holding the picture with a sort of tenderness for a long time, while we glowed in the warmth of the shared secret. That was Colin's moment. Colin's art stopped being a pox to Father right there. And later, when the time came for Colin to go to art school, it was Father who was his solid backer. ❖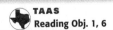

Customizing Instruction

Less Proficient Readers
• Ask students what happens to Bandit after the boys have left him.
Possible Response: He is killed by a random hunter as he leaves his hiding place.
• Ask students what Colin does with his box cover.
Possible Response: He draws a picture of Bandit as he last saw him in the pool.
• What is Father's reaction to the picture?
Possible Response: He is very pleased with it.

Multiple Learning Styles
Visual Learners
1 Have students draw their vision of Colin's picture from the description on page 689. Have students interpret, as they draw, the way Bandit camouflages himself among the branches.

Students Acquiring English
2 Call students' attention to the adjective *mazy.* Point out that the root word *maze* is a noun and the suffix *–y* can be added to many nouns to form adjectives. *Mazy* means "complicated and mysterious; mazelike."

Gifted and Talented
Throughout the story, the writer refers to magic, secrets, and instinct to describe the relationship between Colin and Bandit. What thoughts and emotions do these words evoke in you as a reader?
Possible Response: They evoke a sense of the unknown and of love beyond human teachings or understanding.

WORDS TO KNOW   **sanctuary** (săngk′chōō-ĕr′ē) *n.* shelter; protection

689

Mini Lesson **Vocabulary Strategy**   🚩 **TEKS** 9F   ⬦ **TAAS** Reading Obj. 1, 6

ANTONYMS

Instruction Remind students that antonyms are words that mean the opposite of each other. When choosing an antonym, students must consider both the denotation and connotation of the antonym, as well as the context in which it will be used. For example, antonyms for the word *bleak* would include: *cheerful, comfortable, lush.* A person's expression would be *cheerful*, a room's interior *comfortable*, and a landscape could be described as *lush.*

Exercises Have students choose the best antonym for the underlined word as it is used in the sentence.

1. The <u>tame</u> fox was devoted to Colin. (spirited, <u>wild</u>, violent)

2. His <u>passive</u> temperament irritated his active father. (forceful, <u>energetic</u>, headstrong)

3. The <u>intricate</u> trails confused the dogs. (<u>simple</u>, honest, dull)

4. His father held the drawing <u>tenderly</u>. (mercilessly, <u>roughly</u>, severely)

📖 Use **Vocabulary Transparencies and Copymasters**, p. 73.

GUIDING STUDENT RESPONSE

Connect to the Literature

1. Responses will vary. Have students support their reactions with reasons.

Comprehension Check
- He thinks the fox will steal or kill the local livestock; he thinks that Colin is too emotional in his attachment to the animal.
- He lets Colin put an arm around him and see where he has been hiding.
- He draws Bandit in his hiding place.

 Use Selection Quiz
Unit Five Resource Book, p. 17.

Think Critically

2. Remind students to back up their images with details from the text.

 Use **Reading and Critical Thinking Transparencies,** p. 10, for additional support.

3. Possible Response: Colin might feel that he and Bandit have some things in common: they are both outcasts in a way; they both experience things in an instinctual rather than a direct way.

4. Possible Response: His art tells a story, and he knows that the story of Bandit is unfinished until the end, when the fox is killed.

5. Possible Responses: He realizes how important the fox is to his sons; he is intrigued by the fox's ability to outwit the hunters; he feels that Bandit is only doing what comes naturally; he does not approve of the hunters' breaking the time-honored rules of hunting in their search for Bandit.

6. Responses will vary. Students might say that Stan has gained a new appreciation for Colin. Stan learns more about his feelings and how he fits into his family.

7. Possible Response: The last cover refers to Bandit's hiding place and/or Colin's last box cover.

Literary Analysis

Setting: Place Student choices may include:

Page 682: "A fire snapped all day in our cookstove and another in the stone fireplace in the living room, but still the farmhouse was never warm."

Page 684: "I remember the day well, the racing clouds, the wind rattling the tops of the pine trees and swaying the Spanish moss . . . ."

 Use **Literary Analysis Transparencies,** p. 6, for additional support.

Connect to the Literature

1. **What Do You Think?** How do you feel about the ending of the story? Share your reaction with a partner.

Comprehension Check
- Why does Father disapprove of keeping Bandit as a pet?
- How does Bandit let Colin know that the fox trusts him?
- What picture does Colin draw at the end?

Think Critically

2. **ACTIVE READING** **VISUALIZING** As you read "Last Cover," how did you visualize the setting? Review the notes you took in your **READER'S NOTEBOOK** and compare them with those of a partner.

3. How would you account for Colin's strong attachment to Bandit?

THINK ABOUT
- Colin's first experiences with Bandit
- how Colin feels about nature
- how Colin relates to his family

4. Why do you think Colin leaves the framed box cover blank for the entire summer?

5. Why do you think Father doesn't participate in the hunt?

6. What do you think Stan has learned about Colin by the end of the story? What do you think Stan has learned about himself?

7. What do you think the title of this story means?

Extend Interpretations

8. **Critic's Corner** According to Tai Ling Bloomfield, a seventh-grade member of the student board, "It didn't seem fair that Bandit had to die." Do you agree? Explain.

9. **COMPARING TEXTS** How would you compare Colin and the painter lady in "The War of the Wall"?

10. **Connect to Life** Were you ever particularly inspired to do something because you knew a special person or witnessed a unique event?

Extend Interpretations

8. **Critic's Corner** Possible Responses: Yes, Bandit's death was unfair. It had no effect on the insight that Father gains about Colin. No, Bandit's death was not unfair. One of the themes of the story might be the lesson that in living true to one's nature, there will be hardships and suffering. Also, Bandit's death would have occurred at some point in time, so it is fitting that it happened after the boys had experienced such closeness with him.

9. **Comparing Texts** Possible Responses: Both artists are quiet and introverted; both use their art to express a personal feeling.

10. **Connect to Life** Ask students to explain what they were inspired to do.

Literary Analysis

SETTING: PLACE The time when and place where a story occurs are its **setting.** Place refers to the geographical area, as well as to the customs, values, and beliefs of the people who live in the area. "Last Cover" is set in the woods and hills of the western Carolinas. It is a rural area, and all of the characters in the story live on small farms.

The place where a story is set can have an important influence on a story's plot and characters. Look at how Paul Annixter's description of nature helps to describe how Stan is feeling when Bandit is lost.

It was late February, and I remember the bleak, dead cold that had set in, cold that was a rare thing for our Carolina hills.

Cooperative Learning Activity
With a partner, choose two passages from the story that you find particularly descriptive. Discuss what those passages add to the drama of the story. Present your conclusions to the class.

FLASHBACK An interruption of the action of a story to present a scene that took place at an earlier time is called a flashback. On page 683 a flashback, beginning with the words, "One afternoon a year and a half before . . ." narrates how Colin found Bandit.

Writing Options

1. Art School Application Essay Imagine that you are Colin and you want to use your drawing of Bandit as part of your application to art school. Write an essay describing how you came to make the drawing, as well as what it means to you. Try your hand at recreating Colin's drawing.

2. Opinion Essay When, if ever, is it right to kill an animal? Should certain kinds of killing be illegal, and if so, what kinds? State your opinion in an essay and place it in your **Working Portfolio.**

Writing Handbook
See p. R39: Persuasive Writing.

Activities & Explorations

1. Talk-Show Interview Imagine that Stan from "Last Cover" and Juliette from "Waiting" are guests on a talk show. The topic for discussion is "Relationships with Siblings." With two classmates prepare a sketch. One of you will be the host, and the others will present Stan's and Juliette's opinions. ~ **SPEAKING AND LISTENING**

2. Reader's Theater With a small group, rehearse a Reader's Theater presentation of key episodes from this story. Select background music that is appropriate to the mood of each episode. Present your reading to the class. ~ **PERFORMING**

Art Connection

Look at the painting *Albert's Son* by Andrew Wyeth on page 685. What does Wyeth want you to think about Albert's son? What details give you clues about the boy's personality? Does Albert's son look like your image of either Colin or Stan? Explain.

Inquiry & Research

Red Fox Facts With a small group, create a poster that displays pictures of red foxes and includes interesting facts about them. One member of the group might do library research. Another might visit a zoo or interview a wildlife conservationist. A third might search the Internet for information. A fourth might design the poster.

 **More Online: Research Starter**
www.mcdougallittell.com

Vocabulary in Action

EXERCISE: SYNONYMS Write the Word to Know that is most closely related in meaning to the under-lined word or phrase in each sentence below.

1. Bandit found <u>protection</u> in his hiding place.
2. The boys' father did not <u>support</u> the idea of raising a fox as a pet.
3. Bandit proved himself to be a <u>clever</u> trickster.
4. The winter was <u>cheerless</u> and bitterly cold.
5. Colin's avoidance of chores led his father to compare him to a <u>sick, bedridden person</u>.
6. His mother thought that Colin might be <u>fated, or expected</u>, to die at an early age.
7. The fox was able to <u>confuse</u> the dogs during the hunt.
8. A person who was <u>lacking in spirit and force</u> would not have pleased Colin's father.
9. To understand Colin's <u>true character</u>, his father needed to understand his art.
10. The farmers were <u>irritated</u> by Bandit's constant attacks on their chickens.

WORDS TO KNOW	bleak	essence	invalid	predestined	sanctuary
	confound	harried	passive	sanction	wily

LAST COVER **691**

Inquiry & Research

Red Fox Facts Another option is to have each group research different kinds of foxes and their habits and habitats. In this case, each group can divide up as suggested and present an overall report on their research.

Vocabulary in Action

EXERCISE

1. sanctuary
2. sanction
3. wily
4. bleak
5. (an) invalid
6. predestined
7. confound
8. passive
9. essence
10. harried

Writing Options

1. Art School Application Essay Have students review the details that describe the relationship between Colin and Bandit and the events leading up to the last sighting of Bandit. Remind students to write their essays in first person and to do a preliminary outline of what they wish to include.

 Use **Writing Transparencies,** p. 11, for additional support.

2. Opinion Essay To get students started on this assignment, suggest that they gather some facts about hunting, the euthanasia of animals at shelters, and animal experimen-tation. Remind students that they must support their opinion with facts and examples. **To make this assign-ment more challenging,** have stu-dents debate specific facets of the issue such as animal euthanasia or experimentation.

Use **Writing Transparencies,** p. 27, for additional support.

Activities & Explorations

1. Talk-Show Interview Students may want to choose specific topics as questions, such as sibling rivalry, physical similarities and differences, relationship to mother or father, hobbies, or talents.

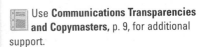 Use **Communications Transparencies and Copymasters,** p. 9, for additional support.

2. Reader's Theater To get students started on this assignment, have them choose the scene they wish to portray and the details they want to include. They may wish to select transitional music that will lead from one episode to the next.

Use **Communications Transparencies and Copymasters,** p. 12, for additional support.

Art Connection

Most students will compare the subject of the painting to Colin because of his coloring and delicate appearance.

Grammar in Context

WRITING EXERCISE
Possible Responses:

1. When we lost our pet, I wanted to cry.
2. After Colin sketched pictures, father would study two or three of them.
3. As soon as they brought the fox home, they crowded around it in the kitchen.
4. While the woods were budding, Bandit found a mate.
5. When noon came, Colin had still not come in to eat.

CONNECT TO LITERATURE
Possible Response: page 686–"As the summer came on, Bandit began to live up to the prediction Father had made."

Paul Annixter

Even as a child, Howard A. Sturtzel was interested in nature and writing. At the age of eight, he wrote a story about the life and death of a cattail and the story of an acorn.

Author Activity

Tales of Animals Suggest that students copy the descriptive passages from each story and discuss the differences in imagery and the effect of each individual passage on the story as a whole.

Grammar in Context: Adverb Clauses of Time

Paul Annixter makes the sequence of events in "Last Cover" clear by using adverb clauses that express time.

> It was Father who said we'd better name him Bandit, after he'd made away with his first young chickens.

> Ever since he had been able to walk, my brother had had a growing love of wild things . . .

An **adverb clause** is a group of words that modifies a verb, adjective, or adverb. A special kind of adverb clause tells when an action occurs. These usually begin with a conjunction such as *after, as, as long as, as soon as, before, during, since, until, when, whenever,* and *while.*

Punctuation Tip: When the adverb clause comes at the beginning of the sentence, use a comma.

WRITING EXERCISE Combine each pair of sentences by making one of them an adverb clause that expresses time.

Example: *Original* Bandit disappeared. The trouble started.

Rewritten When Bandit disappeared, the trouble started.

1. We lost our pet fox. I wanted to cry.
2. Colin sketched pictures. Father would study two or three of them.
3. They brought the fox home. They crowded around it in the kitchen.
4. The woods were budding. Bandit found a mate.
5. Noon came. Colin had still not come in to eat.

Connect to the Literature Find another sentence with an adverb clause of time in "Last Cover."

Grammar Handbook Phrases and Clauses, p. R72

"It was while proving up on the land that I began writing, mostly nature stories about the animals and elements I was up against."

Paul Annixter
1894–1985

Early Training Paul Annixter is the pen name of Howard A. Sturtzel. He was the author of more than 500 short stories. When he was 9, Sturtzel and his mother were left alone to care for themselves and Sturtzel's paralyzed grandmother. To support the family, Sturtzel sold newspapers and candy and later worked as a bellhop. When he was 16, he traveled across the United States and Canada, living the life of a hobo. Eventually, Sturtzel settled on a timber claim in northern Minnesota, where he lived alone for a year and a half and began to write.

Collaboration After attending college, Sturtzel married Jane Comfort, the daughter of his favorite writer and tutor, Will Livington Comfort. Using the pen names Paul and Jane Annixter, Sturtzel and his wife worked together to produce more than 20 novels for young people. "Where one may have a weakness," he said of himself and his wife, "the other is apt to have a strength."

AUTHOR ACTIVITY

Tales of Animals Check out one of Paul Annixter's collections of stories, such as *Pride of Lions,* from your library and read another of his stories. How do his descriptions of nature compare with those you read in "Last Cover"?

Teaching Options Grammar TEKS 17A 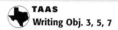 TAAS Writing Obj. 3, 5, 7

ADVERB CLAUSES OF TIME

Instruction Tell students that a subordinate clause is a group of words that contains a subject and a verb but cannot stand alone. An adverb clause is a subordinate clause that modifies a verb, adjective, or another adverb. Sometimes adverb clauses answer the question *when.* An adverb clause of time may begin with *after, before, since, until, when,* or *whenever.* Write the following sentence on the board as an example of a sentence with an adverb clause.

Bandit would be safe <u>after the sun set</u>.

Exercise Have students underline the adverb clauses in the following sentences.

1. <u>When it was time for breakfast</u>, Colin couldn't eat.
2. <u>Until the hunt ended</u>, we could hear the baying of the hounds.

📖 Use **Unit Five Resource Book,** p. 15.
📖 Use **Grammar Transparencies and Copymasters,** p. 112.

 Use McDougal Littell's ***Language Network,*** Chapter 8, for more instruction and practice in adverb clauses.

Mastering Multiple Meanings

Many English words have more than one meaning. Multiple-meaning words are ones that have the same origin but that have acquired additional meanings over time based on the original meaning.

Homonyms are words that are spelled and pronounced alike but that are different in origin and meaning.

> Three weeks before, Bandit, the pet fox Colin and I had raised from a tiny kit, had disappeared, and not even a rumor had been heard of him since.
>
> —Paul Annixter, "Last Cover"

Multiple-meaning word
- an animal kept as a companion
- to pat or caress

Homonym
- a young, furry animal
- a set of implements used for a specific purpose

Strategies for Building Vocabulary

Try the following strategies when you can't tell which meaning of a word is intended.

❶ Use Context Clues When you see a familiar word used in an unfamiliar way, look at the words around it to see if they offer clues to its meaning. What do you think is the meaning of *squash* in the following passage?

> On the lower decks, Jack discovered the squash court, the swimming pool, and the Turkish bath decorated like a room in a sultan's palace.
> —Robert D. Ballard, *Exploring the* Titanic

From the context, it is unlikely that *squash* has anything to do with food. Because a court is mentioned, it probably has to do with sports. *Squash* in this context means a game played with a racket and a rubber ball.

❷ Use a Dictionary If the familiar meaning of a word doesn't make sense and there are no helpful context clues, try looking up the word in a dictionary. Read through the definitions. Try each one in place of the word until you find one that makes sense. Read the following sentence: *They used the scales of the* **bleak** *to make artificial pearls.*

The usual meaning of *bleak* does not fit at all. From context, you could tell that *bleak* is something with scales. The dictionary shows two entries for *bleak*, the first with the expected meaning of "gloomy and somber." The second entry has the meaning "a small European freshwater fish." Because the words have different origins and two separate dictionary entries, we know that *bleak* is a homonym.

EXERCISE Use context clues or a dictionary to find the meaning of each underlined word.

1. The boys began to <u>pine</u> for the fox.
2. Their father did not take part in the hunt, but he did <u>sanction</u> it.
3. The hunters were going to get Bandit, no matter what, and they looked <u>ugly</u>.
4. The fox found <u>sanctuary</u> in a pond.
5. The *Titanic* came within a <u>yard</u> or two of another ship.
6. There were cars in the <u>hold</u>.
7. The lookout on the evening <u>watch</u> hadn't seen anything unusual.
8. As the *Titanic* took on more water, it began to <u>list</u>.
9. The ship's <u>stern</u> rose before the ship sank.
10. The death <u>toll</u> was extremely high.

Objectives
- draw on experiences to bring meanings to multiple-meaning words in context
- identify homonyms
- rely on context to determine the meaning of a homonym
- Use a dictionary to determine the precise usage of a homonym

VOCABULARY EXERCISE
Possible Responses:
1. miss, long for
2. give approval for
3. angry
4. shelter, protection
5. three feet of length
6. cargo area
7. work shift on a ship
8. tilt, lean
9. back end
10. amount of loss caused by a disaster

Use **Unit Five Resource Book,** p. 18.
Use **Vocabulary Transparencies and Copymasters,** p. 13, for additional support.

Possible Objectives

You can use this selection to achieve one or more of the following objectives:

- enjoy silent sustained reading (Option One)
- read and analyze literature with a group (Option Two)
- use the Reader's Notebook to write in response to literature (Option Three)

Summary

In this excerpt from his 1971 autobiography, Ernesto Galarza describes his early weeks in an American elementary school. On the first day, he meets his principal, Miss Hopley, who welcomes him and his mother warmly in a language they don't understand. Then, with the help of a student interpreter, Miss Hopley registers the narrator and delivers him to his first grade teacher, Miss Ryan. Radiant and ever-patient, she helps the boy lose his fears and learn a new language. Miss Ryan works privately with him and with other first-graders who don't understand English. She delights in every success, no matter how small. "Ernesto has learned how to pronounce butterfly!" she announces to the class one day. The school contains children of many ethnicities: Japanese, Italians, Portuguese, Koreans, Yugoslavs, Poles, Irish, and "home-grown Americans." While these children might exchange ethnic insults out of school, such behavior is forbidden in school. There, all the children are taught to be proud Americans, yet no one is ever expected to give up the language or customs of home.

from Barrio Boy

by Ernesto Galarza

Right: Lincoln Grammar School, 4th and P Sts. Sacramento, 1909. *Far right:* McKinley School, Miss Wilcox's class, circa 1914.

My mother and I walked south on Fifth Street one morning to the corner of Q Street and turned right. Half of the block was occupied by the Lincoln School. It was a three-story wooden building, with two wings that gave it the shape of a double-T connected by a central hall. It was a new building, painted yellow, with a shingled roof that was not like the red tile of the school in Mazatlán.[1] I noticed other differences, none of them very reassuring.

We walked up the wide staircase hand in hand and through the door, which closed by itself. A mechanical contraption screwed to the top shut it behind us quietly.

Up to this point the adventure of enrolling me in the school had been carefully rehearsed. Mrs. Dodson had told us how to find it and we had circled it several times on our walks. Friends in the *barrio*[2] explained that the director was called a principal, and that it was a lady and not a man. They assured us that there was always a person at the school who could speak Spanish.

Exactly as we had been told, there was a sign on the door in both Spanish and English: "Principal." We crossed the hall and entered the office of Miss Nettie Hopley.

Miss Hopley was at a roll-top desk to one side, sitting in a swivel chair that moved on wheels. There was a sofa against the opposite

---

1. **Mazatlán** (mä′ sət-län′): A seaport of western Mexico on the Pacific Ocean where Galarza had attended school.

2. **barrio** (bä′ rē-ō′): *Spanish,* an urban neighborhood, especially one where many Latinos live.

694 UNIT FIVE PART 1: WITH STRENGTH AND COURAGE

wall, flanked by two windows and a door that opened on a small balcony. Chairs were set around a table and framed pictures hung on the walls of a man with long white hair and another with a sad face and a black beard.

The principal half turned in the swivel chair to look at us over the pinch glasses crossed on the ridge of her nose. To do this she had to duck her head slightly as if she were about to step through a low doorway.

What Miss Hopley said to us we did not know but we saw in her eyes a warm welcome and when she took off her glasses and straightened up she smiled wholeheartedly, like Mrs. Dodson. We were, of course, saying nothing, only catching the friendliness of her voice and the sparkle in her eyes while she said words we did not understand. She signaled us

to the table. Almost tiptoeing across the office, I maneuvered myself to keep my mother between me and the gringo lady. In a matter of seconds I had to decide whether she was a possible friend or a menace. We sat down.

Then Miss Hopley did a formidable[3] thing. She stood up. Had she been standing when we entered she would have seemed tall. But rising from her chair she soared. And what she carried up and up with her was a buxom superstructure, firm shoulders, a straight sharp nose, full cheeks slightly molded by a curved line along the nostrils, thin lips that moved like steel springs, and a high forehead topped by hair gathered in a bun. Miss Hopley was

---

3. **formidable** (fôr′mĭ-də-bəl): inspiring admiration and wonder.

Option One
Silent Sustained Reading
You might set aside time each week for independent reading. During this time, you and your students would read for enjoyment. Many students will enjoy this excerpt from *Barrio Boy*, especially since it describes such a familiar setting. It can be read independently in 15 minutes or so. To encourage students to read for pleasure, consider making no assignments related to this selection. However, Options Two and Three below offer suggestions in case you do want to make assignments.

Option Two
Shared Reading Groups
You may assign students to groups or allow them to choose their own groups. Students can read the selection together, alternately reading sections aloud, or they can read independently and meet to cooperate in a project that deals with some element of the selection.

Possible Projects
- Students might role-play scenes from the excerpt, such as the one in which the narrator and his mother meet the new principal.
- Students might write advertisements for Lincoln School, encouraging children of many countries to attend and learn.
- For both the narrator and Miss Ryan, students can write diary entries describing various tutoring sessions.

Provide the following direction to students before they read:

Remind students that when they read autobiographies and other kinds of writing, they can draw conclusions about people, places, and events. In other words, they can make logical inferences based on text clues and on their own experience.

While they read, have them draw conclusions about the Lincoln School. Is this a place that the narrator likes or not? Have them record their ideas in their Reader's Notebooks. Encourage them to note quotations or other text details that helped them answer the question.

When students have finished reading, have them write a paragraph telling whether they think the narrator liked the Lincoln School and why.

After Reading

Possible Activities
Independent Activities

• Ask gifted and talented students to think about how they would teach English to students who speak none. What strategies would they try and which would they avoid? Have them jot down their ideas in the Reader's Notebooks.

• Have students imagine or recall what it feels like to be in a school where they don't speak the same language that most students speak. What problems, questions, and feelings would they have? Have students write letters from that point of view to friends or relatives. In these letters, they should describe the first day of school.

not a giant in body but when she mobilized it to a standing position she seemed a match for giants. I decided I liked her.

She strode to a door in the far corner of the office, opened it and called a name. A boy of about ten years appeared in the doorway. He sat down at one end of the table. He was brown like us, a plump kid with shiny black hair combed straight back, neat, cool, and faintly obnoxious.

Miss Hopley joined us with a large book and some papers in her hand. She, too, sat down and the questions and answers began by way of our interpreter. My name was Ernesto. My mother's name was Henriqueta. My birth certificate was in San Blas. Here was my last report card from the Escuela Municipal Numero 3 para Varones of Mazatlán, and so forth. Miss Hopley put things down in the book and my mother signed a card.

As long as the questions continued, Doña Henriqueta could stay and I was secure. Now that they were over, Miss Hopley saw her to the door, dismissed our interpreter and without further ado took me by the hand and strode down the hall to Miss Ryan's first grade.

Miss Ryan took me to a seat at the front of the room, into which I shrank—the better to survey her. She was, to skinny, somewhat runty me, of a withering[4] height when she patrolled the class. And when I least expected it, there she was, crouching by my desk, her blond radiant face level with mine, her voice patiently maneuvering me over the awful idiocies of the English language.

During the next few weeks,

Miss Ryan overcame my fears of tall, energetic teachers as she bent over my desk to help me with a word in the pre-primer. Step by step, she loosened me and my classmates from the safe anchorage of the desks for recitations at the blackboard and consultations at her desk. Frequently she burst into happy announcements to the whole class. "Ito can read a sentence," and small Japanese Ito, squint-eyed and shy, slowly read aloud while the class listened in wonder: "Come, Skipper, come. Come and run." The Korean, Portuguese, Italian, and Polish first graders had similar moments of glory, no less shining than mine the day I conquered "butterfly," which I had been persistently pronouncing in standard Spanish as boo-ter-flee. "Children," Miss Ryan called for attention. "Ernesto has learned how to pronounce butterfly!" And I proved it with a perfect imitation of Miss Ryan. From that celebrated success, I was soon able to match Ito's progress as a sentence reader with "Come, butterfly, come fly with me."

Like Ito and several other first graders who did not know English, I received private lessons from Miss Ryan in the closet, a narrow hall off the classroom with a door at each end. Next to one of these doors Miss Ryan placed a large chair for herself and a small one for me. Keeping an eye on the class through the open door she read with me about sheep in the meadow and a frightened chicken going to see the king, coaching me out of my phonetic ruts in words like *pasture, bow-wow-wow, hay,* and *pretty,* which to my Mexican ear and eye had so many unnecessary sounds and letters. She made me watch her lips and then close my eyes as she repeated words I found hard to read. When we came to know each other better, I tried interrupting to tell Miss Ryan how we said it in Spanish. It didn't work. She only said "oh" and went on with *pasture,*

---

4. **withering** (wĭth′ ər-ĭng): rendering speechless.

> Miss Ryan called for attention. "Ernesto has learned how to pronounce butterfly!"

Classroom (1910).

Discussion Activities

- Point out that modern transportation and technology exposes people to even more cultures than it did during the 1970s, when *Barrio Boy* was originally published. Have students discuss what they think the results of such increased contact between people of different cultures might be. Encourage students to give reasons for their answers.
- Have students discuss the paragraph that begins with the sentence, "Miss Hopley and her teachers never let us forget why we were at Lincoln: for those who were alien, to become good Americans; for those who were so born, to accept the rest of us." Have them consider whether the school's goal then is still worthwhile and whether its strategies, such as private tutoring and prohibiting name-calling, are still useful ways to achieve the goal.

Assessment Opportunities

- You can assess students' comprehension by evaluating the paragraphs that they wrote in their Reader's Notebooks.
- You can have students form pairs or teams and take turns asking and answering questions about the selection.

bow-wow-wow, and *pretty.* It was as if in that closet we were both discovering together the secrets of the English language and grieving together over the tragedies of Bo-Peep. The main reason I was graduated with honors from the first grade was that I had fallen in love with Miss Ryan. Her radiant, no-nonsense character made us either afraid not to love her or love her so we would not be afraid, I am not sure which. It was not only that we sensed she was with it, but also that she was with us.

Like the first grade, the rest of the Lincoln School was a sampling of the lower part of town where many races made their home. My pals in the second grade were Kazushi, whose parents spoke only Japanese; Matti, a skinny Italian boy; and Manuel, a fat Portuguese who would never get into a fight but wrestled you to the ground and just sat on you. Our assortment of nationalities included Koreans, Yugoslavs, Poles, Irish, and home-grown Americans.

Miss Hopley and her teachers never let us forget why we were at Lincoln: for those who were alien, to become good Americans; for those who were so born, to accept the rest of us. Off the school grounds we traded the same insults we heard from our elders. On the playground we were sure to be marched up to the principal's office for calling someone a wop, a chink, a dago, or a greaser.[5] The school was not so much a melting pot as a griddle where Miss Hopley and her helpers warmed knowledge into us and roasted racial hatreds out of us.

At Lincoln, making us into Americans did not mean scrubbing away what made us originally foreign. The teachers called us as our parents did, or as close as they could pronounce our names in Spanish or Japanese. No one was ever scolded or punished for speaking in his native tongue on the playground. Matti told the class about his mother's down quilt, which she had made in Italy with the fine feathers of a thousand geese. Encarnación acted out how boys learned to

fish in the Philippines. I astounded the third grade with the story of my travels on a stagecoach, which nobody else in the class had seen except in the museum at Sutter's Fort. After a visit to the Crocker Art Gallery and its collection of heroic paintings of the golden age of California, someone showed a silk scroll with a Chinese painting. Miss Hopley herself had a way of expressing wonder over these matters before a class, her eyes wide open until they popped slightly. It was easy for me to feel that becoming a proud American, as she said we should, did not mean feeling ashamed of being a Mexican. ❖

---

5. **wop,** etc.: offensive terms for Italians, Chinese, and Mexicans.

"What brought me and my family to the United States from Mexico also brought hundreds of thousands of others like us."

Ernesto Galarza
1905–1984

Planting and Harvesting Ernesto Galarza was born in a village in the mountains of the state of Nayarit, Mexico. Fleeing the upheavals of the Mexican Revolution, his family moved to Sacramento, California, where Galarza attended public school and worked alongside his family in the fields. Galarza, while still a school boy, became concerned about the Mexican agricultural workers' poor living conditions.

When a baby died and many people became sick from drinking polluted water, the workers asked Ernesto, who had learned English in school, to lead a protest. After graduation from

high school Galarza continued his education, becoming the first Mexican American to earn a Ph.D. in Economics from Columbia University.

Teaching and Writing Galarza was the author of numerous books on social and economic topics geared toward the Mexican-American community. He became a labor organizer and, eventually, the executive secretary of the National Farm Labor Union.

In addition, Galarza was deeply committed to the education of young people. He and his wife, Mae, developed a bilingual education program that became a model for other programs. The scarcity of children's literature published in Spanish led Galarza to translate Mother Goose stories and write a series of children's stories called the *Colección Mini Libros*. *Barrio Boy*, published in 1971, grew out of stories he told his daughters. In 1976 Ernesto Galarza became the first Mexican American nominated for the Nobel Prize for Literature.

ERNESTO GALARZA

Born in Mexico in 1905, Ernesto Galarza came to this country during the Mexican Revolution. His early experiences in school and working on farms influenced his attitudes and helped forge a resolve to improve life for working-class Chicanos in this country, both in school and on the job. In a writing career that spanned almost five decades, Galarza wrote more than 100 different pieces, including books, articles, and reports.
Ernesto Galarza was a true groundbreaker. He was the first Mexican-American at Stanford University

and the first to earn a Ph.D in history and political science at Columbia University. A labor organizer and political activist, he also wrote children's books and worked as an educational consultant, helping teachers develop methods that would meet the needs of all students.
Richard Chabran, a UCLA colleague, described him as "a man of stature. He was a man of conviction and action . . . recognized both within the Chicano community and . . . internationally."

SPEAKING OPPORTUNITY

See the Communication Handbook, p. R100 for speaking and presenting tips.

Writing Workshop
Opinion Statement

Stating your beliefs . . .

From Reading to Writing Do you feel strongly about certain issues or events? Perhaps you think there should be better laws to protect wild animals like Bandit in "Last Cover." Or you might have your own ideas about how our natural environment should be preserved. From time to time, such issues will move you to speak out. Writing an **opinion statement** gives you a chance to express a point of view and back it up with reasons and facts.

For Your Portfolio

WRITING PROMPT Write an opinion statement about an issue that strongly interests you.

Purpose: To persuade, help others to understand an opinion

Audience: Your classmates and friends, members of your community

---

Basics in a Box

Opinion Statement at a Glance

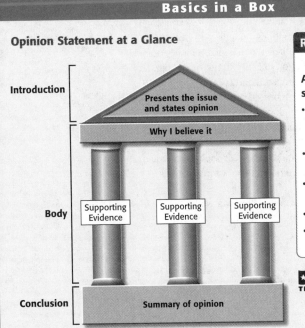

Introduction — Presents the issue and states opinion

Why I believe it

Body — Supporting Evidence | Supporting Evidence | Supporting Evidence

Conclusion — Summary of opinion

RUBRIC STANDARDS FOR WRITING

A successful opinion statement should

- clearly state the issue and your opinion of it in the introduction
- support your opinion with examples, facts, and statistics
- use language and details appropriate for your audience
- show clear reasoning
- sum up your opinion in the conclusion

 TEKS See the Skills Trace at the beginning of the unit for information on TEKS covered in this lesson.

WRITING WORKSHOP **699**

Writing Workshop
Opinion Statement

Objectives

- write an opinion statement that clearly expresses ideas and influences readers
- use a written text as a model for writing
- revise a draft to add supporting details, facts, and examples
- identify and correct comma errors
- recognize and use correctly different verb tenses

Introducing the Workshop

Response to Literature Ask students whether they think that schools should be open year-round. Have them give reasons for their answers. Ask what sorts of reasons might convince them to change their minds. Then point out that issues such as this one are often debated in newspapers, at meetings, and in class. Explain that opinion statements give writers the opportunity to develop strong arguments. Unlike speakers, who may think, "What I should have said was. . . ," writers have the chance to plan what they will say.

Basics in a Box

Using the Graphic Explain that a statement of opinion has a brief introduction that states the issue and the writer's opinion. The main part of the statement, however, is made up of supporting evidence. This evidence is what actually convinces readers.

Presenting the Rubric Review with students the Standards for Writing a Successful Opinion Statement. If necessary, explain the third item by pointing out that a writer might use different language and details if the audience were made up of parents and teachers than if the audience were only classmates. You might also share with them the complete rubric, which describes several levels of proficiency.

 Use McDougal Littell's **Language Network**, Chapters 12–19, for more instruction on essential writing skills.

 Power Presentation

To engage students visually, use **Power Presentation 1**, Opinion Statement.

LESSON RESOURCES

USING PRINT RESOURCES
Unit Five Resource Book
- Prewriting, p. 19
- Drafting, p. 20
- Peer Response, pp. 21-22
- Revising, Editing, and Proofreading, p. 23
- Student Models, pp. 24-26
- Rubric, p. 27

Writing Transparencies
- Writing Process Transparencies TR 1–4

- Writing Structure Transparencies: Elaborating TR 13
- Writing Template Transparencies: Opinion Statement, TR 27

Reading and Critical Thinking Transparencies
- Text Structure (Organization), TR 24 (for Mini Lesson, p. 701)

Grammar Transparencies and Copymasters
- Verb Tense CM 71–73 (for Mini Lesson, p. 704)

INTEGRATED TECHNOLOGY
LaserLinks
Writing Springboards
See **Teacher's SourceBook** p. 36 for bar codes.

Writing Coach CD-ROM

Visit our website:
www.mcdougallittell.com

Analyzing the Model
"Habitat Destruction"

The student model focuses on the destruction of animal habitats by humans, explaining that it is one of the main causes of animal extinction. The writer urges readers to take action and then explains why people destroy habitats. As a response to people who might think this is unimportant, the writer tells why this issue affects everyone. The piece ends with a call for action, with specific recommendations that readers might follow.

After students have read the model, discuss the Rubric in Action with them. Point out the key words and phrases in the student model that correspond to the elements mentioned in the Rubric in Action.

1 Ask what types of questions or quotations would capture readers' attention and would alert them to the problem described here.

   Possible Response: questions or quotations about specific animals, such as the passenger pigeon; questions or quotations about the number of animals that have vanished.

2 Ask students why the writer might have placed the issue and opinion here instead of in the first sentence.

   Possible Response: She wanted to build up to it; she wanted to convince readers that this was important.

3 Ask students how transitions such as *first, second,* and *third* help readers. What transitions show cause and effect?

   Possible Response: They show that these paragraphs are all reasons; they help readers recognize that there are three different reasons; they help readers follow the writer's thinking; other transitions include *this means, because, when,* and *as a result.*

Analyzing a Student Model

Andrea Martinez
La Moille Middle School

Habitat Destruction

   Did you know that over 140 animal species become extinct every day? It's true. In fact, in 1973 there were 109 species on the endangered list for America. As of 1999, that number jumped to 900. Why did this number jump so much in just 26 years? The destruction of natural habitats by humans is one of the main causes of animal extinction. If we don't stop taking away the homes of our nonhuman neighbors, they will be gone.

   There are a few reasons why habitats are destroyed. First, the human population has grown. People are living longer, and more healthy children are being born. More people means more houses and apartments. This means more space is needed. People have moved into animal territory.

   Second, people move more often than they have in the past. Different parts of the country attract large numbers of people because of good jobs or nice weather. When a large number of people move to the popular location, the city limits spread out, and animals' natural habitats are destroyed. Land is often gobbled up by developers who want to make money. Places that were peaceful are turned into huge resorts or condominium complexes. The building process and pollution hurt the ecology of the area. All creatures suffer as a result.

   Third, many businesses use natural resources such as trees and lakes. This takes away habitats from animals. For many years, people didn't know the damaging effects of their actions. Now that we know how much harm we are doing, how can we let the problem continue?

RUBRIC
IN ACTION

❶ Dramatic statistics focus on the seriousness of the situation.

Another Option:
· Use a direct quotation.

❷ States the issue and the writer's opinion clearly

❸ The writer first explains causes of the problem and then describes the effects in each paragraph.

Some people recognize that animal extinction is a problem, but they do nothing because they think it doesn't affect their own lives. They still have birds and squirrels in their back yards, so what's the difference? Well, the problem affects everyone. Imagine a future in which you can only see animals and insects in an encyclopedia. This is not the only negative effect. When a species becomes extinct, it affects the food chain. Several species that do damage to crops or harm other animals have increased in number because they no longer have predators. Eventually, these kinds of changes will affect everyone. Imagine not being able to buy fruit at the grocery store because fruit-eating insects have damaged all the crops.

Many people make the excuse that they don't need to help. They say they haven't done anything wrong. However, if people don't work to make changes, they are adding to the problem. People should get involved in saving the natural habitat of their environment so that animal species can continue to survive. There are many steps that a citizen can take, from contacting his or her senator or representative to joining a local conservation group. If people wait for others to do the job, it will be too late.

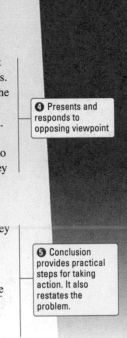

❹ Presents and responds to opposing viewpoint

❺ Conclusion provides practical steps for taking action. It also restates the problem.

4 Point out that the writer addresses people who do nothing because they think that animal extinction doesn't affect their lives. Ask who else might have opposing viewpoints, and what sorts of arguments might convince them to act differently.

Possible Response: Developers, builders, resort operators, and businesses that use resources; arguments that show benefits of protecting animals might persuade them. For example, businesses might be convinced if they think that buyers want to buy from companies that show respect for the environment.

5 Have students compare the last sentence of the conclusion with the last sentence of the first paragraph to see how the writer summarizes the problem.

Mini Lesson **Viewing and Representing**

 TEKS 10L

PICTURING TEXT STRUCTURE

Instruction One way to structure an opinion statement is to provide several good reasons that contain supporting details, such as facts and examples. In addition, the writer of this student model presents opposing viewpoints and reasons that refute them.

Activity Have students analyze the organization of the student model by constructing a diagram, outline or other graphic organizer. The following web is an example.

Use **Reading and Critical Thinking Transparencies**, p. 24, for additional support.

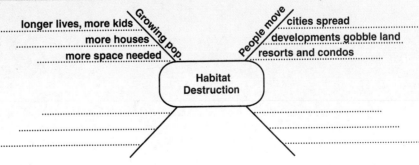

longer lives, more kids
more houses
more space needed
Growing pop.

People move
cities spread
developments gobble land
resorts and condos

Habitat Destruction

Prewriting

Choosing a Subject

If students are still having trouble selecting an issue after reading the suggestions in the Idea Bank, suggest the following:

- Consider a topic that you recently argued with someone about. What was the issue and what was your position?
- What are your opinions on pets? Do you think any one pet is the best?
- What do you think about television or the Internet? Do you think that they make you better informed or waste your time?

Planning Your Opinion Statement

1. Remind students to select a topic that is specific. Writing about school rules would be difficult in a few pages; writing about a particular rule would be easier.
2. Encourage students to try to state their opinions in a single sentence or two.
3. Explain that this is a key step in writing an opinion statement, because the audience will affect not only the amount of background information that a writer must supply, but also the types of reasons that would be most convincing.

Drafting

Students may find it easy to begin if they imagine themselves talking to a specific person whom they are trying to convince. One student might want to start with the opinion and reasons and then go back and improve the introduction and conclusion.

Ask Your Peer Reader

Identifying the strongest and weakest reasons can help students organize them in order of importance.

IDEABank

1. For Your Working Portfolio
Look for ideas in the **Writing Option** you completed earlier in this unit.
- Opinion Essay, p. 691

2. No Stereotypes
Think of groups that you feel are misjudged or treated unfairly. Defend one of them in your opinion statement.

3. Good Neighbors!
Think of a way to improve your neighborhood. Promote your plan in your opinion statement.

Have a question?

See the **Writing Handbook**
Persuasive Writing, p. R39
Elaboration with Facts, p. R29

Writing Your Opinion Statement

❶ Prewriting

Discover your opinions by **listing** your reactions to events in your school or community. **Write down** changes that you think need to be made or things that strike you as unfair. See the **Idea Bank** in the margin for more suggestions. After you have selected an issue, follow the steps below.

> **Planning Your Opinion Statement**
>
> ▶ **1. Explore the issue.** Do you understand the issue completely? What questions do you have about the facts? What are the different sides of the issue?
>
> ▶ **2. Focus your opinion.** Exactly how do you feel about the issue? Why do you feel that way? What facts support your opinion?
>
> ▶ **3. Identify your audience.** How much background do you need to give your audience? What do they already feel about the issue? How might you address their opposing views?
>
> ▶ **4. Gather information.** What additional facts and other evidence do you need to support your opinion? Where will you find that evidence?

❷ Drafting

The most important part of drafting is getting your ideas down in writing. You can revise and polish your work later. Remember, though, that you will need to do each of the following:

- **State your opinion** clearly in your **introduction.**
- **Begin a new paragraph** for each of your **reasons** and include **evidence.** Examples, facts, and statistics will help you support your opinion.
- **Summarize your opinion** in the **conclusion.** Try to leave your audience with a memorable quote, question, or statement.

> **Ask Your Peer Reader Evaluation**
>
> - How well did I explain my opinion?
> - Did I support my statements with adequate evidence?
> - Were my arguments logically organized?

❸ Revising

TARGET SKILL ▶ SUPPORTING YOUR OPINION Your essay should not only express your opinion, it should also persuade others to accept your view. Remember that simply stating your opinion is not enough to convince people. You must provide details, facts, and examples that strengthen your reasons.

> Imagine a future in which you can only see animals and insects in an encyclopedia. This is not the only negative effect. *When a species becomes extinct, it affects the food chain. Several species that do damage to crops or harm other animals have increased in number because they no longer have predators.*

❹ Editing and Proofreading

TARGET SKILL ▶ PUNCTUATING CLAUSES To make your writing flow more smoothly, you might combine two or more clauses into one sentence. Keep your meaning clear by placing a comma after an introductory dependent (subordinate) clause, as shown below.

> When a large number of people move to the popular location the city limits spread out, and animals' natural habitats are destroyed.

❺ Reflecting

FOR YOUR WORKING PORTFOLIO How did your opinion change or develop as you wrote your opinion statement? What did you enjoy most about writing your opinion statement? Attach your answers to your finished essay. Save your opinion statement in your **Working Portfolio.**

Need revising help?

Review the **Rubric,** p. 699

Consider **peer reader** comments

Check **Revision Guidelines,** p. R23

SPELLING From Writing

As you revise your work, look back at the words you misspelled and determine why you made the errors you did. For additional help, refer to the strategies and generalizations in the **Spelling Handbook** on page R86.

Concerned about clause punctuation?

See the **Grammar Handbook,** p. R58

Publishing IDEAS

- Send your opinion statement as a letter to the editor of your local newspaper.
- Present your opinion statement to the class and form an action group to try to bring about a change.

More Online: Publishing Options www.mcdougallittell.com

Revising
SUPPORTING YOUR OPINION

Remind students that they can also support their opinions with quotations and anecdotes. Their support should be selected according to the audience that they are trying to convince. They may need to do research at this point, if they need statistics or additional reasons. Look to Writing Workshop: Research Report pages 784–785 for more information on choosing quotations.

Editing and Proofreading
PUNCTUATING CLAUSES

You may wish to review grammatical terms with students. Remind them that a *clause* is a group of words that contains a subject and a verb. A *subordinate clause* is one that cannot stand by itself as a sentence. Subordinate clauses are introduced by subordinating conjunctions, which include *when, if, since,* and *because. Nonessential clauses* are those that add information to a sentence but that are not necessary for meaning. Readers can still understand the sentence without them.

Reflecting

Encourage students to be specific. For instance, when writing about any changes or developments in their opinions, have them state their initial opinions and tell what changed them. When they tell what they enjoyed most, have them explain why.

Option

Remind students that a picture is worth a thousand words. Students may enjoy illustrating their statements with persuasive drawings, photographs, or before-and-after collages.

704

Assessment Practice

Demonstrate how students can eliminate incorrect choices for the first question.

A. This choice is incorrect, because the phrase *in-line skate* is essential to the sentence and should not have a comma in front of it.

B. This choice is incorrect, because the phrase *I believe* should not be divided by a comma.

C. This choice is correct, because the entire clause that introduces the sentence is set off from the rest of the sentence with a comma.

D. This choice is incorrect, because the comma appears in the middle of the clause *even though I don't in-line skate.*

Answers:

1. C **2.** B **3.** D **4.** C **5.** A **6.** A

Assessment Practice Revising & Editing

Read this passage from the first draft of an opinion statement. The underlined sections include the following kinds of errors:

- **spelling errors**
- **incorrectly used modifiers: adverbs**
- **verb tense errors**
- **comma errors**

For each underlined section, choose the revision that most improves the writing.

> Even though, I don't in-line skate I believe city parks should have
> (1)
> areas set aside for people who do. Having special areas set aside would
> benifit everyone who uses the parks. If a person is taking a quiet stroll,
> (2)   (3)
> he or she doesn't want to be disturbed by in-line skaters going real fast.
>   (4)
> One false move by either person could result in one of them getting hurt
>   (5)
> bad. At the same time, in-line skating is an activity that many people
> enjoy. It was also healthy.
>   (6)

1. **A.** Even though I don't, in-line skate, I believe
    B. Even though I don't in-line skate I, believe
    C. Even though I don't in-line skate, I believe
    D. Correct as is

2. **A.** bennefit
    B. benefit
    C. bennifit
    D. Correct as is

3. **A.** If a person is taking a quiet stroll he or she doesn't want
    B. If a person is taking, a quiet stroll, he or she doesn't want
    C. If a person, is taking a quiet stroll he or she doesn't want
    D. Correct as is

4. **A.** in-line skaters going really quick
    B. in-line skaters going real quickly
    C. in-line skaters going really fast
    D. Correct as is

5. **A.** getting hurt badly
    B. getting hurt really bad
    C. getting hurt very bad
    D. Correct as is

6. **A.** It is also healthy.
    B. It would also be healthy.
    C. It will also be healthy.
    D. Correct as is

Need extra help?

See the **Grammar Handbook**

Quick Reference: Punctuation, p. R56

Spelling, p. R86

Adverbs, p. R70

 Mini Lesson Grammar **TEKS** 17F  **TAAS** Writing Obj. 3, 6

VERB TENSE

Instruction Remind students that verbs have different forms, called tenses, to show whether action takes place in the present, past, or future. Display the following examples:

I *am* here. I *sit* in the front row.

I *was* here. I *sat* in the front row.

I *will be* here. I *will sit* in the front row.

Point out that a writer should always use verbs in the same tense when describing actions that happen at the same time.

Exercises Have students identify the verb in each group that is in a different tense from the other three.

1. break, jump, ride, ran *(ran)*
2. taught, feel, was, slept *(feel)*
3. has used, had seen, will take, have worn *(will take)*
4. had, sees, writes, is *(had)*
5. came, fell, ate, marks *(marks)*
6. will write, will be, was able, will sing *(was able)*

 Use **Grammar Transparencies and Copymasters**, pp. 71–73, for additional support.

 Use McDougal Littell's *Language Network*, Chapter 4, for more instruction and practice in verb tense.

Reflecting on the Theme   It takes strength to bear up when the odds are against you. Sometimes, if the odds are too high, the struggle can break the human spirit. Sometimes the effort to bear up brings out the best in a person's character. In this unit, you will read about the experiences of fictional characters and real people who struggle against the odds.

705

Objectives
- understand and identify the following literary terms:
  - historical fiction
  - real characters
  - imaginary characters
  - setting
  - plot
- appreciate the writer's craft
- recognize the distinguishing features of historical fiction

Teaching the Lesson

This lesson analyzes the elements of historical fiction and shows how the writer combines historical facts with fictional details to create interest and reader involvement.

Introducing the Concepts

Ask students to think of a film they've recently seen or a book they've recently read that was set in an earlier era and that combined historical events with fictitious details (i.e. films such as *Titanic* and *October Sky,* and books such as the *Dear America* series). As a class, discuss what made these works interesting and what students learned from reading or seeing them.

 Use **Literary Analysis Transparencies,** pp. 3, 5, 6 for additional support.

Historical Fiction

I realized when I started doing research for my first book that history wasn't what I'd been taught in school. History is full of gossip; it's real people and emotion.

—Jean Fritz

Have you ever tried to imagine what it was like to live during the American Revolution, or in London at the time Shakespeare was writing his plays? Historical fiction can help make the past come alive.

Historical fiction is fiction set in the past. It contains a rich mixture of fact and fiction. Through novels and short stories, an author may combine factual information about the time, place, events, and real people of the period with fictional characters, dialogue, and details. All of these help you experience what it was like to live during the era when the story takes place.

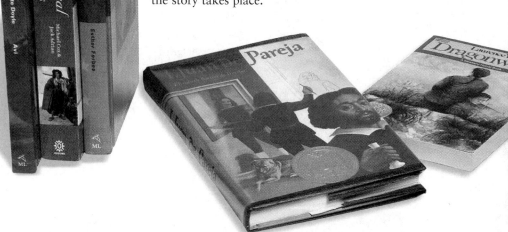

706   UNIT FIVE   PART 2: AGAINST THE ODDS

 See the Skills Trace at the beginning of the unit for information **TEKS** on TEKS covered in this lesson.

Characters: Real and Imaginary

Historical fiction often includes a mix of real people from history as well as invented characters. They may be main characters or they may play only minor roles. The story will contain accurate historical details about them, but it may also include fictional elements such as conversations, thoughts, or feelings that the author creates. This blend of truth and fiction works to make each character come alive.

YOUR TURN "A Crown of Wild Olive" is set at the Olympic Games that took place every four years in Ancient Greece. What details describe the main character, Amyntas?

Setting

Setting is a particularly important element of historical fiction. Writers of historical fiction need to describe a place and time about which a reader may know very little. Before putting the first word on the page, writers do research and become experts on the era in which they set their stories. Some of these details will be real, such as descriptions of the houses people lived in or the kinds of clothes that they wore. Other details will be invented, such as the kind of weather or what people ate for dinner on a particular day.

YOUR TURN Read the passage to the right and think about how the writer created this scene. When and where is the story set?

Plot

In historical fiction, the plot may revolve around an event in history such as a war, a natural disaster, or a famous celebration. As the writer weaves his or her tale, the reader is able to imagine what it was like to participate in or witness that great event. In some cases, the events of the plot are completely made up by the writer, yet the characters and setting may still reflect the time period.

CHARACTER

This was the day of the Sacred Procession; the Priests and Officials, the beasts garlanded for sacrifice, the athletes marching into the waiting Stadium, while the Herald proclaimed the name and state of each one as he passed the rostrum. Amyntas, marching in with the Athenians, heard his own name called, and Leon's, among the names from Samos and Cyrene, Crete and Corinth, and Argos and Megara. And he smelled the incense on the morning air and felt for the first time, under his swelling pride in being Athenian, the thread of his own Greekness interwoven with the Greekness of all those others.

—Rosemary Sutcliff, "A Crown of Wild Olive"

SETTING

Half of Athens, it seemed, had crowded down to the port to watch the *Paralos*, the State Galley, sail for the Isthmus, taking their finest athletes on the first stage on their journey to Olympia.

Every fourth summer it happened; every fourth summer for more than three hundred years. Nothing was allowed to stand in the way, earthquake or pestilence or even war—even the long and weary war which, after a while of uneasy peace, had broken out again last year between Athens and Sparta.

—Rosemary Sutcliff, "A Crown of Wild Olive"

Presenting the Concepts
Characters: Real and Imaginary
Have students choose a historical figure that they would like to center a story around. Ask them to describe what imaginary characters might go along with this central historical character.

YOUR TURN
Possible Responses: The character Amyntas is described through details such as "marching in with the Athenians," "his swelling pride in being Athenian," "the thread of his own Greekness."

Setting
Ask students to describe the historical time period that they find most interesting as the setting for a work of historical fiction. Have them explain their reasons.

YOUR TURN
Possible Responses: The story is set in Athens during the summer, just before the Greek Olympics.

Plot
Ask students to imagine that they had to write a work of historical fiction. Ask them to think about what historical event they would include in the work. What role would the event have in the plot? Ask for volunteers to share their ideas with the rest of the class.

Use **Literary Analysis Transparencies,** p. 1, for additional support.

Objectives
- use the text's structure or progression of ideas, such as cause and effect, to locate and recall information
- analyze ways authors organize and present ideas, such as through cause and effect
- represent text information in different ways, such as with graphic organizers
- use his or her own experience to comprehend

Teaching the Lesson

The strategies on this page will help students recognize and understand cause and effect in written texts.

Presenting the Strategies
Help students understand the strategies by asking for volunteers to read them aloud. Ask them to follow the strategies outlined on this page for the following project:
- Choose a selection from this unit and divide it into sections. Divide students into small groups and assign one section of the story to each group.
- Ask each group to use the strategies outlined on this page to identify cause and effect in their section.
- Suggest that students construct a cause-effect chart identifying their items under the headings "Signal Words," "Cause," and "Effect."
- Ask two volunteers from each group to copy their chart on the board and to explain their conclusions to the rest of the class.
- As a class, discuss cause-effect relationships that happen in daily life.

Try It Now!

Students should understand the cause and effect relationship between the coming of the Herald and the gathering of athletes.

Use **Reading and Critical Thinking Transparencies**, p. 3, for additional support.

What happens when you stay up too late studying or watching television? You're tired the next morning, right? That's an example of a simple cause and effect relationship. Your life is full of them. Events in a story are often related to each other as cause and effect. That is, the first event in time—the cause—is a reason why a later event—the effect—happens. Examining cause-and-effect relationships enables readers better understand how events are connected.

Recognizing Cause and Effect

How to Apply the Skill

To understand **cause and effect**, an active reader will:
- Identify signal words that indicate cause and effect such as *because, therefore, since,* and *so*
- **Question** what happened and why
- **Clarify** the action by making a cause-effect chart
- Use prior knowledge

Try It Now!

Read the exerpt below. Look for cause and effect.

> Back in the spring the Herald had come, proclaiming the Truce of the Games; safe conduct through all lands and across all seas, both for athletes and for those who went to watch them compete. And now, from every Greek state, and from colonies and settlements all around the Mediterranean, the athletes would be gathering. . . .
>
> —Rosemary Sutcliff, "A Crown of Wild Olive"

Here's how Lindsay uses the skill:

"Reading 'A Crown of Wild Olive,' I made a cause-and-effect chart to clarify the plot."

Cause	Effect	Effect
A truce is proclaimed.	Traveling was safe for all the athletes and spectators.	Athletes gathered in Olympia to compete.

Need More Help?

Remember that active readers use the essential reading strategies explained on page 4: • **visualize** • **predict** • **clarify** • **question** • **connect** • **evaluate** • **monitor.**

A Crown of Wild Olive

Historical Fiction by ROSEMARY SUTCLIFF

...et me run the est race that is in ne and think of othing more."

Connect to Your Life

Friendly Competition What are things that can bring together people from conflicting countries, cultures, or groups and help them see each other as human beings? With a small group, make a word map of your ideas. After you have finished, share your map with other groups.

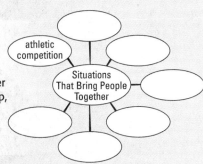

athletic competition

Situations That Bring People Together

Build Background

CONNECT TO **SOCIAL STUDIES** Ancient Greece vas not a united country but a collection of eparate city-states. The two principal city-tates were Athens and Sparta. While Athens valued culture, Sparta valued military trength. In 431 B.C., a war that would last on nd off for many years broke out between Athens and Sparta.

The Olympic Games provided a truce. Part eligious ceremony in honor of Olympian Zeus, he most important god of the Greeks, and part athletic competition, the games took place every four years without interruption between 776 B.C. and about A.D. 393. Events included footraces for men and boys, chariot aces, and the pentathlon, a five-part event hat consisted of the broad jump, discus hurling, javelin throwing, the 200-yard dash, and wrestling. Athletes trained for ten months, he last month near Olympia, the town where he games were held. Each victor's prize was a crown of wild olive taken from a tree that grew within the precinct of the temple of Zeus.

WORDS TO KNOW **Vocabulary Preview**
angular   reel   unaccountably
dappled   substance

Focus Your Reading

LITERARY ANALYSIS **HISTORICAL FICTION** Fiction written in modern times but set in the past is called **historical fiction.** Historical fiction combines facts along with details that come from the author's imagination. Writers of historical fiction sometimes use actual historical figures as characters, but usually the characters are the writer's creations. As you read, notice how the author makes the story come alive for you through factual as well as imaginative detail.

ACTIVE READING **CAUSE AND EFFECT** Two events are related as **cause and effect** when one event brings about the other. The event that happens first in time is the cause; the one that follows is the effect.

📖 **READER'S NOTEBOOK**
In your Reader's Notebook list the examples of cause and effect that you find as you read the story.

Cause	Effect
The offshore wind blew across the water.	It blurs the reflection of the galleys lying at anchor.

Literary Analysis

HISTORICAL FICTION

 A To help students recognize the distinguishing features of genres, including historical fiction, point out that setting is very important in historical fiction. Ask students what they learn about the setting in the first three paragraphs.

Possible Responses: It is summer in Greece; the games have been going on for three hundred years; Athens and Sparta are at war.

Use **Unit Five Resource Book,** p. 30 for guidance in reading the selection.

Active Reading CAUSE AND EFFECT

B Students should be able to use the text's structure or progression of ideas, such as cause and effect, to increase their understanding of the text. Tell them that when they look for causes and effects, they can look within a sentence or paragraph, or they can look at the selection as a whole. To give them practice, explain that much of what happens in the story is the result of the Olympic games. Ask students what effect these games have on the country.

Possible Responses: A truce is declared; people gather from all over to compete.

Use **Unit Five Resource Book,** p. 29 for guidance in reading the selection.

Literary Analysis

HISTORICAL FICTION

 C Ask students to speculate about which details might be historically accurate.

Possible Responses: Boys over twenty having short hair; youthful military service; details about the double stade.

Teaching Options

A Crown of Wild Olive

Detail of black-figure amphora (ca 540 B.C.), Greek, Tampa (Florida) Museum of Art, Joseph Veach Noble Collection, 86.24.

by Rosemary Sutcliff

I t was still early in the day, but already it was growing hot, the white dry heat of the Greek summer; and the faint off-shore wind that made it bearable had begun to feather the water, breaking and blurring the reflections of the galleys lying at anchor in Pireaus Harbor.

A Half of Athens, it seemed, had crowded down to the port to watch the *Paralos*, the State Galley, sail for the Isthmus, taking their finest athletes on the first stage of their journey to Olympia.

Every fourth summer it happened; every fourth summer for more than three hundred years. Nothing was allowed to stand **B** in the way, earthquake or pestilence or even war—even the long and weary war which, after a while of uneasy peace, had broken out again last year between Athens and Sparta.

Back in the spring the Herald[1] had come, proclaiming the Truce of the Games; safe conduct through all lands and across

---

1. **herald:** a person who announces important news.

 Mini Lesson **Preteaching Vocabulary** **TEKS 6A, 9B** **TAAS Reading Obj. 1**

CONTEXT CLUES

Instruction Call students' attention to the list of WORDS TO KNOW. Remind them that they can draw on sentence context to bring meanings to unfamiliar words. Display the following sentence: One man was tall and *angular*, while the other was short and plump.

Explain that they can use comparison and contrast as a context clue to figure out the meaning of the word *angular*. Point out that this sentence contrasts *angular* with *plump*.

Exercises Have students use comparison and contrast clues to define the underlined words in the following sentences. Ask them to explain the clues that lead them to meaning.

1. The <u>dappled</u> fabric resembled the hide of a leopard.
2. Her light windbreaker did not keep her warm enough; she needed a coat with <u>substance.</u>
3. Understandably, he was angry; <u>unaccountably,</u> however, he never punished us.

Use **Unit Five Resource Book,** p. 31 for more practice.

Use **Vocabulary Transparencies and Copymasters,** p. 74, for additional support.

ll seas, both for athletes and for those who
went to watch them compete. And now, from
every Greek state, and from colonies and
settlements all around the Mediterranean, the
athletes would be gathering. . . .

Aboard the *Paralos* was all the ordered
bustle of departure, ropes being cast off,
rowers in their places at the oars. The
Athenian athletes and their trainers with them
had gathered on the afterdeck. Amyntas, son
of Ariston, had drawn a little apart from the
rest. He was the youngest there, still several
months from his eighteenth birthday and
somewhat conscious that he had not yet
sacrificed his boy's long hair to Apollo, while
the rest, even of those entered for the boys'
events—you counted as a boy at Olympia until
you were twenty—were already short-haired
and doing their Military Service. A few of
them even had scars gained in border clashes
with the Spartans, to prove that their real
place, whatever it might be on the race track
or in the wrestling pit, was with the men.
Amyntas envied them. He was proud that he
had been picked so young to run for Athens in
the Boys' Double Stade,[2] the Four Hundred
Yards. But he was lonely. He was bound in
with all the others by their shared training; but
they were bound together by something else,
by another kind of life, other loyalties and
shared experiences and private jokes, from
which he was still shut out.

The last ropes holding ship to shore were
being cast off now. Fathers and brothers and
friends on the jetty were calling last moment
advice and good luck wishes. Nobody called
to Amyntas, but he turned and looked back
to where his father stood among the crowd.
Ariston had been a runner too in his day,
before a Spartan spear wound had stiffened
his left knee and spoiled his own hopes of an
Olympic Olive Crown. Everyone said that he
and Amyntas were very alike, and looking

back now at the slight dark man who still held
himself like a runner, Amyntas hoped with a
warm rush of pride that they were right. He
wished he had said so, before he came aboard.
There were so many things he would have
liked to have said, but he was even more
tongue-tied with his father than he was with
the rest of the world when it came to saying
the things that mattered. Now as the last ropes
fell away, he flung up his hand in salute and
tried to put them all into one wordless
message. "I'll run the best race that's in me,
Father—and if the Gods let me win it, I'll
remember that I'm winning for us both."

Among the waving crowd, his father flung
up an answering hand, as though he had
somehow received the message. The water was
widening between ship and shore. The Bos'n
struck up the rowing time on his flute, and the
rowers bent to their oars, sending the *Paralos*
through the water toward the harbor mouth.
Soon the crowd on shore was only a shingle
of dark and colored and white along the
waterfront. But far off beyond the roofs of the
warehouses and the covered docks, a flake of
light showed where high over Athens the
sunlight flashed back from the upraised spear-
blade of the great Athene of the Citadel,[3] four
miles away.

They were out around the mole now, the
one sail broke out from the mast, and they
headed for the open gulf.

That night they beached the *Paralos* and
made camp on the easternmost point of the
long island of Salamis; and not long past noon
the next day they went ashore at the Isthmus
and took horse for Corinth on the far side,
where a second galley was waiting to take

---

2. **double stade** (dŭb'əl stād): a footrace twice the length of
   a stadium.
3. **Athene . . .** (ə-thē'nə): in Greek mythology, the goddess
   of wisdom and warfare; also spelled Athena.

Customizing Instruction

Less Proficient Readers
Explain to students that they can read
this story in sections, with each section
describing a different time: before
Amyntas arrives at Olympia; before the
race; during the race; and after the race.
Set a Purpose Invite students to find
out what Amyntas is like and what happens on his first day at training camp.

Students Acquiring English
Because this story contains so many
descriptive details, students may have
trouble following the events as they
unfold. You might read part of the story
aloud with them and help them to distinguish necessary details of the plot
from purely descriptive ones.

 Use **Spanish Study Guide**,
pp. 139–141 for additional support.

Gifted and Talented
Have students focus on the ethical
dilemma that confronts the two main
characters: young men from warring
countries who befriend each other.
Have students discuss how they feel
individuals should handle the conflict
between loyalty to country and loyalty
to one's friends.

Multiple Learning Styles
Visual Learner
Encourage students to create sequence
chains to record notes about the major
scenes in the story. Since a causal event
must come before an effect, this type of
graphic organizer is also useful for identifying cause-effect relationships.

BLOCK SCHEDULING: MANAGING TIME

**If your schedule requires that you
cover the lesson objectives in a
shorter time, use. . .**
• Preparing to Read, p. 709
• Thinking Through the Literature,
  p. 726

**If you would like to take advantage
of longer class time, use. . .**
• TE Teaching Options: Preteaching
  Vocabulary, p. 710; Spelling, pp. 712,
  716; Cross-Curricular Link, p. 718;
  Vocabulary Strategy, p. 719;
  Grammar, pp. 720, 722, 727;
  Multicultural Link, p. 721;
  Standardized Test Practice, pp. 723,
  724; Informal Assessment, p. 725;
• Choices & Challenges and Author
  Activity, p. 727
• Real World Link, p. 728

Literary Analysis
HISTORICAL FICTION

Ask students which details on this page they think are historically accurate and which are created within the writer's imagination.

Possible Responses: Many will suggest that the Council of Games greeting, the reading of the rules, and the details about housing are accurate.

Active Reading | **CAUSE AND EFFECT**

A Ask students what caused the scars on the boy's back. Have them draw inferences and support them with text evidence.

Possible Responses: He has been beaten; the text says that there were stories of such beatings.

Reading Skills and Strategies: CONNECTING

B Ask students to recall times when they've met people from different cultures. Have them connect that experience with this scene. Ask what makes the scene realistic.

Possible Responses: Students might mention being careful about what they say around strangers.

Literary Analysis
HISTORICAL FICTION

C Explain that one feature of historical fiction is showing typical problems and experiences that people had in a particular historical setting. Ask what problems these characters faced.

Possible Responses: They trained hard without rest; they had to clear the stadium of weeds.

them down the coast. At evening on the fifth day they rode down into the shallow valley where Olympian Zeus[4] the Father of Gods and men had his sanctuary and where the Sacred Games were celebrated in his honor.

What with the long journey and the strangeness of everything, Amyntas took in very little of that first evening. They were met and greeted by the Council of the Games, whose president made them a speech of welcome, after which the Chief Herald read them the rules. And afterward they ate the evening meal in the athletes' mess; food that seemed to have no more taste nor <u>substance</u> than the food one eats in a dream. Then the dream blended away into a dark nothingness of sleep that took Amyntas almost before he had lain down in the narrow stretcher bed in the athletes' lodging, which would be his for the next month.

He woke to the first <u>dappled</u> fingers of sunlight shafting in through the doorway of his cell. They wavered and danced a little, as though broken by the shadows of tree branches. Somewhere farther down the valley a cuckoo was calling, and the world was real again, and his, and new as though it had been born that morning. He rolled over and lay for a few moments, his hands behind his head, looking up at the bare rafters; then shot off the bed and through the doorway in one swallow-dive of movement, to sluice[5] his head and shoulders in the icy water trickling from the mouth of a stone bull into a basin just outside. He came up for air, spluttering and shaking the water out of his eyes. For a moment he saw the colonnaded[6] court and the plane tree arching over the basin through a splintered brightness of flying droplets. And then suddenly, in the brightness,

there stood a boy of about his own age, who must have come out of the lodging close behind him. A boy with a lean <u>angular</u> body and a dark, bony face under a shock of hair like the crest of an ill-groomed pony. For a long moment they stood looking at each other. Then Amyntas moved aside to let the other come to the conduit.[7]

As the stranger ducked his head and shoulders under the falling water, Amyntas saw his back. From shoulder to flank it was criss-crossed with scars, past the purple stage but not yet faded to the silvery white that they would be in a few years' time; pinkish scars that looked as though the skin was still drawn uncomfortably tight over them.

He must have made some betraying sound or movement, because the other boy ducked out from under the water, thrusting the wet russet hair back out of his eyes, and demanded curtly, "Have you never seen a Spartan back before?"

So that was it. Amyntas, like everyone else, had heard dark stories of Spartan boys flogged, sometimes to death, in a ritual test of courage before the shrine of Artemis Orthia, the Lady of the Beasts.[8]

"No," he said, "I am Athenian." And did not add that he hoped to see plenty of Spartan backs when once he had started his Military Service. It was odd, the cheap jibe came neatly into his head, and yet he did not even want to

---

4. **Zeus** (zoos): in Greek mythology, the principal god, ruler of the heavens, and lord of Olympus, home of the gods.
5. **sluice** (sloos): to wash.
6. **colonnaded** (kŏl'ə-nād'ĕd): having a series of evenly spaced columns.
7. **conduit:** a pipe for transporting fluids.
8. **Artemis . . .** (är'tə-mĭs): in Greek mythology, the goddess of the hunt and the moon.

WORDS TO KNOW	**substance** (sŭb'stəns) *n.* material quality
	dappled (dăp'əld) *adj.* spotted
	angular (ăng'gyə-lər) *adj.* bony and lean

712

 Mini Lesson **Spelling** 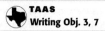 TEKS 16D TAAS Writing Obj. 3, 7

HOMOPHONES
Instruction To help students spell frequently misspelled words correctly, explain that sometimes two or more words may have the same pronunciation but different spellings and meanings. As an example, point to *cell* in the highlighted sentence. Ask what homophone means "offer for sale" (*sell*).
Examples: whether, weather
Homophones in the selection:
to, too; sail, sale
there, their; here, hear

Words in the selection that have homophones:
fourth, would, plane, horse, no, new
Exercise Have students spell words that are homophones for those listed above. Then have them take turns making up sentences for pairs of homophones.
Answers: *forth, wood, plain, hoarse, know, knew*

break it. It was as though here at Olympia, the Truce of the Games was not just a rule of conduct, but something in one's heart. Instead, he added, "And my name is Amyntas."

They seemed to stand confronting each other for a long time. The Spartan boy had the look of a dog sniffing at a stranger's fist and taking his own time to make sure whether it was friendly. Then he smiled; a slow, rather grave smile, but unexpectedly warm. "And mine is Leon."

"And you're a runner." Amyntas was taking in his build and the way he stood.

"I am entered for the Double Stade."

"Then we race against each other."

Leon said in the same curt tone, "May we both run a good race."

"And meanwhile,—when did you arrive, Leon?"

"Last night, the same as you."

Amyntas, who usually found it nearly as difficult to talk to strangers as he did to his own father, was surprised to hear himself saying, "Then you'll have seen no more of Olympia than I have. Shall we go and get some clothes on and have a look around?"

But by that time more men and boys were coming out into the early sunshine, yawning and stretching the sleep out of their muscles. And Amyntas felt a

hand clamp down on his shoulder and heard the voice of Hippias his trainer, "Oh no you don't, my lad! Five days' break in training is long enough, and I've work for you before you do any sightseeing!"

After that, they were kept hard at it, on the practice track and in the wrestling school that had the names of past Olympic victors carved on the colonnade walls. For the last month's training for the Games had to be done at Olympia itself; and the last month's training was hard, in the old style that did not allow for rest days in the modern fashion that most of the Athenian trainers favored. Everything at Olympia had to be done the old way, even to clearing the stadium of its four years' growth of grass and weeds and spreading it with fresh sand. At other Crown Games, the work was done by paid laborers, but here, the contending athletes must do it themselves, to the glory of the Gods, as they had done it in the far-off days when the Games were new. Some of them grumbled a good deal and thought it was time that the Priests of Zeus and the Council of the Games brought their ideas up to date; but to Amyntas there seemed to be a sort of rightness about the thing as it was.

Cloaked Spartan warrior, (sixth century B.C.), Greek. Bronze, red marble base. Wadsworth Atheneum, Hartford (Connecticut). Gift of J. Pierpont Morgan.

A CROWN OF WILD OLIVE **713**

Customizing Instruction

Students Acquiring English
1 Explain that *dark stories of Spartan boys flogged* means "frightening stories of Spartan boys being whipped or beaten."

Less Proficient Readers
Ask the following questions to make sure that the students understand the story so far.

- What happens when Amyntas first arrives at the Olympic site?
  Answer: He is greeted, he hears the rules, he eats and goes to bed.
- Whom does he meet the next morning, and what is this person like?
  Answer: He meets Leon, a boy about his own age. They are at first suspicious but then friendly.
- What is the Double Stade, and why is it important?
  Answer: It is the race in which the two boys will compete.
- Who prepares the stadium and how?
  Answer: The athletes; they pull the grass and weeds and spread fresh sand.

His training time was passed among boys from Corinth and Epidauros, Rhodes and Samos and Macedon. At first they were just figures in outline, like people seen too far off to have faces, whom he watched with interest at track work, at javelin or discus throwing or in the wrestling pit, trying to judge their form as he knew they were trying to judge his and each other's. But gradually as the early days went by, they changed into people with faces, with personal habits, and likes and dislikes, suffering from all the strains and stresses of the last weeks before the Games. But even before those first few days were over, he and the Spartan boy had drifted into a companionable pattern of doing things together. They would sluice each other down, squatting in the stone hip-baths in the washing room after practice, and scrape the mess of rubbing oil and sand off each other's backs—it took Amyntas a little while to learn to scrape the bronze blade of the strigil[9] straight over the scars on Leon's back as though they were not there—and when they took their turn at scraping up the four years' growth of grass and sun-dried herbs from the stadium, they generally worked together, sharing one of the big rush carrying-baskets between them. And in the evenings, after the day's training was over, or in the hot noonday break when most people stretched themselves out in the shade of the plane trees for sleep or quiet talk, they seemed, more often than not, to drift into each other's company.

Once or twice they went to have a look at the town of tents and booths that was beginning to spring up all around the Sacred Enclosure and the Gymnasium buildings—for a Games Festival drew many people besides those who came to compete or to watch: merchants and wine sellers and fortune tellers, poets determined to get poems heard, horse dealers from Corinth and Cyrene, goldsmiths and leather-workers, philosophers gathering for the pleasure of arguing with each other, sword and fire swallowers, and acrobats who could dance on their hands to the soft notes of Phrygian pipes. But Leon did not much like the crowded noisy tent-ground; and most often they wandered down to the river that flung its loop about the south side of Olympia. It had shrunk now in the summer heat, to little more than a chain of pools in the middle of its pale dried-out pebbly bed; but there was shade under the oleander trees, and generally a whisper of moving air. And lying on the bank in the shade was free. It had dawned on Amyntas quite early that the reason Leon did not like the fairground was that he had no money. The Spartans did not use money, or at least, having decided that it was a bad thing, they had no coinage but iron bars so big and heavy that nobody could carry them about or

9. **strigil** (strĭj′əl): an instrument used for scraping the skin after a bath.

Detail of black-figure amphora (about 540–530 B.C.) Swing Painter, Greek. Attic, Tampa (Florida) Museum of Art, Joseph Veach Noble Collection, 86.26. Purchased in part with funds donated by Mr. Frank Duckwall.

Horsemen from the west frieze of the Parthenon. British Museum, London.

en keep a store at home that was worth
 ough to be any use. They were very proud
 their freedom from wealth, but it made life
fficult at a gathering such as this, when they
d to mix with people from other states.
 on covered up by being extremely scornful
 the foolish things for sale in the merchants'
oths and the acrobats who passed the bowl
 ound for contributions after their
 erformance; but he was just that shade too
 ornful to be convincing. And anyway,
 myntas had none too much money himself,
 get him through the month.

So they went to the river. They were down
 ere one hot noontide something over a week
 ter they had first arrived at Olympia; Amyntas
ing on his back, his hands behind his head,
 quinting up into the dark shadow-shapes of
 e oleander branches against the sky; Leon
 tting beside him with his arms around his
 odrawn knees, staring out into the dazzle of
 unlight over the open riverbed. They had been
 lking runners' talk, and suddenly Amyntas
 id, "I was watching the Corinthian making

his practice run this morning. I don't *think* we
have either of us much to fear from him."

"The Rhodian runs well," said Leon, not
bringing back his gaze from the white dance of
sunlight beyond the oleanders.

"But he uses himself up too quickly. He's
the kind that makes all the front running at
first and has nothing left for the home stretch.
Myself, I'd say that red-headed barbarian[10]
from Macedon had the better chance."

"He's well enough for speed; and he knows
how and when to use it. . . . What do you give
for Nikomedes' chances?"

"Nikomedes?—The boy from Megara?
It's hard to say. Not much, from the form
he's shown so far; but we've only seen him
at practice, and he's the sort that sometimes
catches fire when it comes to the real
thing. . . ."

There was a long silence between them, and
they heard the churring of the grasshoppers,

_____
10. **barbarian:** here, a member of a non-Greek people.

A CROWN OF WILD OLIVE   **715**

Reading and Analyzing

Literary Analysis
HISTORICAL FICTION

A Point out that a piece of historical fiction, like any other story, has a plot that centers around a conflict and complications that develop. Ask students what conflict they can identify and what complication develops.

Possible Responses: The conflict is between the two boys; the complication is the wound on Leon's foot.

Reading Skills and Strategies:
EVALUATING

B Ask students to analyze the characters, including their motivations. Have them draw inferences about their behavior. Why does Amyntas clean Leon's wound, and why does Leon say it's only a scratch?

Possible Responses: Amyntas is a good person; he wants to help a friend; Leon does not want to be considered weak; he doesn't think it's serious.

Active Reading   **CAUSE AND EFFECT**

C Ask students what they think causes Amyntas to feel sick.

Possible Responses: He doesn't like the ugly thought that enters his mind.

D When Amyntas spends nearly all of his money buying the little bronze bull, what effect does that action have? What word signals this effect?

Answer: He would not be able to buy the fancy hunting knife; the word *so* signals the effect.

---

like the heat-shimmer turned to sound. And then Amyntas said, "I think you are the one I have most to fear."

And Leon turned his head slowly and looked down at him, and said, "Have you only just woken to that? I knew the same thing of *you*, three days ago."

And they were both silent again and suddenly a little shocked. You might think that kind of thing, but it was best not to put it into words.

Leon made a quick sign with his fingers to avert ill luck; and Amyntas scrambled to his feet. "Come on, it's time we were getting back." They were both laughing, but a little breathlessly. Leon dived to his feet also and shot ahead as they went up through the riverside scrub. But the next instant, between one flying leap and the next, he stumbled slightly and checked, then turned back, stooping to search for something among the dusty root-tangle of dry grass and camomile. Amyntas, swerving just in time to avoid him, checked also.

"What is it?"

"Something sharp. . . ." Leon pulled out from where it had lain half-buried, the broken end of a sickle blade that looked as though it might have lain there since the last Games. "Seems it's not only the Stadium that needs clearing up." He began to walk on, carrying the jagged fragment in his hand. But Amyntas saw the blood on the dry ground where he had been standing.

"You have cut your foot."

"I know," Leon said, and went on walking.

"Yes, I *know* you know. Let me look at it."

"It's only a scratch."

"All the same—show me."

Leon stood on one leg, steadying himself with a hand on Amyntas's shoulder, and turned up the sole of his foot. "Look then. You can hardly see it."

There was a cut on the hard brown sole, n[ ] long, but deep, with the blood welling slowly[ ] Amyntas said in sudden exasperation, "Haven't you *any* sense? Oh we all know about the Spartan boy with the fox under his cloak, and nobody but you Spartans think it's a particularly clever or praiseworthy story; bu[ ] if you get dirt into that cut, you'll like enough have to scratch from the race!"

Leon suddenly grinned. "Nobody but we Spartans understand that story. But about the dirt, you could be right."

"I could. And that bit of iron is dirty enough for a start. Best get the wound cleane[ ] up, in the river before we go back to the Gymnasium. Then your trainer can take over."

So with Leon sitting on a boulder at the edge of the shrunken river, Amyntas set to work with ruthless thoroughness to clean the cut. He pulled it open, the cool water running over his hands, and a thin thread of crimson fronded away downstream. It would help clea[ ] the wound to let it bleed a little; but after a few moments the bleeding almost stopped. N[ ] harm in making sure; he ducked his head to the place, sucked hard and spat crimson into the water. Then he tore a strip from the skirt of his tunic.[11] He would have commandeered Leon's own—after all it was Leon's foot—but he knew that the Spartan boys were allowed t[ ] own only one tunic at a time. If he did that, Leon would be left without a respectable tuni[ ] to wear at the Sacrifices. He lashed the thin brown foot tightly. "Now—put your arm over my shoulder and try to keep your weight off the cut as much as you can."

"Cluck, cluck, cluck!" said Leon, but he di[ ] as Amyntas said.

As they skirted the great open space of the Hippodrome, where the chariot races would b[ ] held on the second day of the Games, they

---

11. **tunic:** a loose-fitting garment extending to the knees.

Teaching Options

GREEK WORD PARTS To help students understand the influence of other languages on the spelling of English words, explain that a knowledge of Greek word parts can help them spell any words that contain these parts.
Example: phon- phonics
Words with Greek parts from the selection:
stadium   philosopher   gymnasium
Other words with Greek parts
arch-   monarch   archenemy
cycl-   bicycle   cyclone

 Spelling  **TEKS 16G**

meter-	diameter	thermometer
photo-	photograph	telephoto
tele-	telephone	televise

Exercise Choose the spelling word that best completes the sentence.

1. A _____ is like a tornado. *(cyclone)*
2. The _____ says it is not yet freezing. *(thermometer)*
3. A _____ might be a king or a queen. *(monarch)*

4. You can order the book my mail or by _____. *(telephone)*
5. The newspaper showed a _____ of the winner crossing the finish line. *(photograph)*

Use **Unit Five Resource Book,** p. 33 for more practice.

me up with a couple of the Athenian
ontingent, strolling under the plane trees.
udorus the wrestler looked around and his
ce quickened with concern, "Run into
ouble?"

"Ran into the remains of a sickle blade
omeone left in the long grass," Amyntas said,
ouching the rusty bit of metal he had taken
om Leon and stuck in his own belt. "It's near
ie tendon, but it's all right, so long as there's
o dirt left in it."

"Near the tendon, eh? Then we'd best be
king no chances." Eudorus looked at Leon.
You are Spartan, I think?—
myntas, go and find the
partan trainer. I'll take over
ere." And then to Leon
gain, "Will you allow me to
arry you up to the lodging?
: seems the simplest way."

Amyntas caught one
arting glimpse of Leon's
igid face as Eudorus lifted
im, lightly as a ten-year-
ld, and set off toward the
ymnasium buildings; and
aughter caught at his
tomach; but mixed with the
aughter was sympathy. He
new he would have been
ust as furious in Leon's
lace. All this fuss and to-do
ver a cut that would have
een nothing in itself—if the Games had not
een only three weeks off.

He set off in search of the trainer.

In the middle of that night, Amyntas
woke up with a thought already shaped
and complete in his mind. It was an ugly
hought, and it sat on his chest and mouthed
t him slyly. "Leon is the one you have most
o fear. If Leon is out of the race. . . ."

He looked at it in the darkness, feeling a
little sick. Then he pushed it away and rolled
over on to his face with his head in his arms,
and after a while he managed to go back to
sleep again.

Next day, as soon as he could slip away
between training sessions, he went out into the
growing town of tents and booths, and found
a seller of images and votive offerings, and
bought a little bronze bull with silvered horns.
It cost nearly all the money that he had to
spare, so that he would not now be able to
buy the hunting knife with silver inlay on the
hilt that had caught his
fancy a day or two since.
With the little figure in his
hand, he went to the Sacred
Enclosure, where, among
altars shaded by plane trees
and statues of Gods and
Olympic heroes, the great
Temple of Zeus faced the
older and darker house of
Hera[12] his wife.

Before the Temple of
Zeus, the ancient wild olive
trees from which the victors'
crowns were made cast
dapple-shade across the
lower steps of the vast
portico. He spoke to the
attendant priest in the deep
threshold shadows beyond.

"I ask leave to enter and make an offering."

"Enter then, and make the offering," the
man said.

And he went through into the vastness of
the Temple itself, where the sunlight sifting
through under the acanthus roof tiles made a
honeycomb glow that hung high in the upper

Minoan bull's head with gold horns, from Knossos,
1600 B.C., Archaeological Museum of Heraklion,
Crete, Greece/Ancient Arts and Architecture
Collection Ltd/Bridgeman Art Library.

---

12. **Hera** (hĭr′ə): in Greek mythology, the wife of Zeus and
goddess of the home.

Customizing Instruction

Students Acquiring English
You may need to define the following
idiomatic phrases for students:
- "Have you only just woken to that?"
  means "Did you only now realize
  that?"
- "I'll take over here" means "I will take
  command now."
- When we say that an item, such as a
  knife, "caught his fancy" we mean
  that it attracted him.

Multiple Learning Styles
Visual Learners

1 Ask students how they picture the
conflict within Amyntas. If they were
illustrating this scene, what visual
images would they select, organize, or
produce to complement meaning?

Possible Responses: They might show
Amyntas with a little devil on one
shoulder and an angel on the other; or
they might show half his face as evil
and the other half as smiling.

Less Proficient Readers

2 Discuss what has happened so far,
making sure that students understand
the story up until this point. Have them
monitor their comprehension and
make modifications when understanding breaks down, such as by searching
for clues and asking questions.

Set a Purpose Have students read to
find out what Amyntas does with the
bronze bull.

A From story details, what do students learn about the part that religion played in the life of the people, especially the athletes?

Possible Responses: It must have been important, since the temple was large; many athletes gave thanks or left offerings large and small.

Active Reading   CAUSE AND EFFECT

B Ask students why Leon has to break training for three days.

Possible Responses: because his foot hurts; because the cut on his foot needs to heal

Reading Skills and Strategies: VISUALIZING

C Ask students to describe the mental images that the text descriptions evoke. What events have they seen that might compare with events in the story?

Possible Responses: Students might mention a royal procession, a film set, or the modern Olympics.

Active Reading   CAUSE AND EFFECT

D What causes Amyntas's excitement on this day?

Possible Responses: This is the day that he is going to run.

---

spaces and flowed down the gigantic columns but scarcely touched the pavement under foot, so that he seemed to wade in cool shadows. At the far end, sheathed in gold and ivory, his feet half lost in shadows, his head gloried with the dim radiance of the upper air, stern and serene above the affairs of mortal men, stood the mighty statue of the God himself. Olympian Zeus, in whose honor the Sacred Games had been held for more than three hundred years. Three hundred years, such a little while; looking up at the heart-stilling face above him, Amyntas wondered if the God had even noticed yet, that they were begun. Everything in the God's House was so huge, even time. . . . For a moment his head swam, and he had no means of judging the size of anything, even himself, here where all the known landmarks of the world of men were left behind. Only one thing, when he looked down at it, remained constant in size; the tiny bronze bull with the silvered horns that he held in his hand.

A   He went forward to the first of the Offering Tables before the feet of the gigantic statue and set it down. Now, the tables were empty and waiting, but by the end of the festival, they would be piled with offerings; small humble ones like his own and silver cups

and tripods of gilded bronze to be taken away and housed in the Temple treasury. On the eve of the Games they would begin to fill up, with votive offerings made for the most part by the athletes themselves, for their own victory or the victory of a friend taking part in a different event. Amyntas was not making the offering for his own victory, nor for Leon's. He was not quite sure why he was making it, but it was for something much more complicated than victory in the Double Stade. With one finger still resting on the back of the little bronze bull, he sent up the best prayer he could sort out from the tangle of thoughts and feelings within himself. "Father of all things, Lord of these Sacred Games, let me keep a clean heart in this; let me run the best race that is in me and think of nothing more."

Outside again, beyond the dapple-shade of the olive trees, the white sunlight fell dazzling across his eyes, and the world of men, in which things had returned to their normal size, received him back; and he knew that Hippias was going to be loudly angry with him for having missed a training session. But unaccountably, everything, including Hippias's anger, seemed surprisingly small.

Bronze figure of Zeus, (ca first century B.C.), Roman. Christie's Images Ltd., 1999.

WORDS TO KNOW   **unaccountably** (ŭn'ə-koun'tə-blē) *adv.* without apparent explanation

718

Teaching Options

Cross Curricular Link   World History

ATHENS AND SPARTA Ancient Athenians and Spartans had very different ideas about what constituted a model citizen. Athenians believed that the upper classes should take care of government, philosophy, and literature, and thus they educated the mind more than the body. Children were taught at home and in neighborhood schools. There they studied reading, mathematics, music, poetry, and physical education. The goal: people who had cultivated minds and good characters. Spartans, however, were primarily raised to be sol-

diers if they were men. (Women were raised to be mothers or wives of soldiers.) Young boys left home at age seven to be schooled communally in *agelas,* or herds, with other boys their age. The goal of a Spartan education was to produce soldiers who were obedient, physically strong, and able to endure pain and other hardships.

Detail of black-figure amphora (sixth century B.C.). A prize for the winner of the hoplite race. Musée Vivenal, Compiegne, France.

...eon had to break training for three days, at least so far as track-work was concerned; and it was several more ...fore he could get back into full training; so ...r a while it was doubtful whether he would ... able to take his place in the race. But with ...ll more than a week to go, both his trainer ...d the Doctor-Priest of Asklepius[13] declared ...m fit, and his name remained on the list of ...trants for the Double Stade.

And then it was the first day of the Festival; ...e day of solemn dedication, when each ...mpetitor must go before the Council to be ...oked over and identified and take the Oath ...f the Games before the great bronze statue of ...eus of the Thunderbolts.

The day passed. And next morning before ...was light, Amyntas woke to hear the ...nmistakable, unforgettable voice of the ...owds gathering in the Stadium. A shapeless ...rf of sound, pricked by the sharper cries of ...e jugglers and acrobats, and the sellers of ...ater and honeycakes, myrtle and victors' ...bbons calling their wares.

This was the day of the Sacred Procession; ...e Priests and Officials, the beasts garlanded for sacrifice, the athletes marching into the waiting Stadium, while the Herald proclaimed the name and state of each one as he passed the rostrum. Amyntas, marching in with the Athenians, heard his own name called, and Leon's, among names from Samos and Cyrene, Crete and Corinth, and Argos and Megara. And he smelled the incense on the morning air and felt for the first time, under his swelling pride in being Athenian, the thread of his own Greekness interwoven with the Greekness of all those others. This must have been, a little, the thing their Great-Grandfathers had felt when they stood together, shield to shield, to hurl back the whole strength of invading Persia so that they might remain free. That had been in a Games year, too. . . .

The rest of that day was given over to the chariot and horse races; and that night Amyntas went to his sleeping cell with the thunder of hooves and wheels still sounding somewhere behind his ears. He seemed to hear

C

D

---

13. **Asklepius** (ə-sklē′pē-əs): in Greek mythology, the god of medicine; also spelled Asclepius.

A CROWN OF WILD OLIVE **719**

 Mini Lesson ## Vocabulary Strategy **TEKS 6B, 9D**  **TAAS Reading Obj. 1**

BASE WORDS

Prepare Tell students that they can understand derivatives by applying the meaning of bases and their affixes—prefixes and suffixes. Point out the highlighted word *unforgettable* and ask students to identify its base, prefix, and suffix. Then ask them to explain how affixes affect the meaning of the word *forget*.

Display these base words and affixes from the selection:

stiffened = base *stiff* + en + ed
upraised = base *raise* + up + ed
unaccountably = base *count* + un + ac + able + y

tightened = base *tight* + en + ed
unmanageable = base *manage* + un + able
onlookers = base *look* + on + er + s

Application Ask students to write a paragraph about an injury that causes an athlete to miss an important game. They should use at least four of the preceding vocabulary words. Then ask them to explain how understanding base words and affixes helped them to understand each word.

📖 Use **Vocabulary Transparencies and Copymasters,** p. 75, for additional support.

A CROWN OF WILD OLIVE **719**

Literary Analysis

HISTORICAL FICTION

A You may want to point out that Greeks allowed and accepted public nudity in situations where clothing would get in the way. These situations included bathing and athletic competitions. Ask students what other details they learn about the games.

Possible Responses: Runners waited outside the Stadium; two other races were the Dolichus and the Stade; a trumpet began the race.

Literary Analysis

HISTORICAL FICTION

B Ask students what they learn about spectators at the events.

Possible Response: There were men only, except for the Priestess of Demeter.

it in his dreams all night, but when he woke in the morning, it had turned into the sound that he had woken to yesterday, the surf-sound of the gathering crowd. But this morning it had a new note for him, for this was the Day, and the crowd that was gathering out there around the Stadium was his crowd, and his belly tightened and the skin prickled at the back of his neck as he heard it.

He lay for a few moments, listening, then got up and went out to the conduit. Leon came out after him as he had done that first morning of all, and they sluiced down as best they could. The water barely dribbled from the mouth of the stone bull now, for with the vast gathering of people and the usual end-of-summer drought, the water shortage was getting desperate, as it always did by the time the Festival days arrived.

"How is the foot?" Amyntas asked.

"I can't remember where the cut was, unless I look for it."

They stood looking at each other, the friendship that they had never put into words trying to find some way to reach across from one to the other.

"We cannot even wish each other luck," Amyntas said at last, helplessly.

And Leon said, almost exactly as he had said it at their first meeting, "May both of us run a good race."

They reached out and touched hands quickly and went their separate ways.

 he next time they saw each other, they were waiting oiled and naked for the track, with the rest of the Double Stade boys just outside the arched way into the Stadium. The Dolichus, the long distance race, and the Stade had been run, each with its boys' race immediately after. Now the trumpet was sounding to start the Double Stade. Amyntas's eyes went to meet Leon's, and

found the Spartan boy's slightly frowning gaze waiting for him. He heard the sudden roar of the crowd, and his belly lifted and tightened. little stir ran through the waiting boys; the next time the starting trumpet sounded, the next time the crowd gave that roar, it would be for them. Hippias was murmuring last-minute advice into Amyntas's ear, but he did not hear a word of it. . . . He was going out there before all those thousands upon thousands of staring eyes and yelling mouths, and he was going to fail. Not just fail to win the race, but *fail*. His belly was churning now, his heart banging away right up in his throat so that it almost choked him. His mouth was dry and the palms of his hands were wet, and the beginnings of panic were whimpering up i him. He looked again at Leon and saw him run the tip of his tongue over his lips as though they were suddenly dry. It was the firs time he had ever known the Spartan boy to betray anything of what was going on inside him, and the sight gave him a sense of companionship that somehow steadied him. He began to take deep quiet breaths, as he ha been taught, and the rising panic quieted and sank away.

The voice of the crowd was rising, rising to a great roar; the Men's Double Stade was over He heard the Herald crying the name of the winner and another roar from the crowd; and then the runners were coming out through the arched entrance; and the boys pressed back to let them past, filthy with sweat and sand and oil. Amyntas looked at the face of the man with the victor's ribbons knotted around his head and arms and saw that it was grey and spent and oddly peaceful.

"Now it's us!" someone said; and the boys were sprinting down the covered way, out into the open sun-drenched space of the Stadium.

The turf banks on either side of the broad track and the lower slopes of the Kronon Hill

---

Teaching Options

 Grammar TEKS 17A, 17B 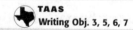TAAS Writing Obj. 3, 5, 6, 7

SUBORDINATE CLAUSES AND SUBORDINATING CONJUNCTIONS

Instruction Explain that a clause is a group of words that contains a subject and a verb. A clause that cannot stand by itself as a complete sentence is a subordinate, or dependent, clause. Point out the highlighted sentence and identify the independent clause (Amyntas felt the scorching heat of the limestone) and subordinate clause (as he braced the ball of his right foot into the shaped groove). Tell students that a subordinate clause is always introduced by a subordinating conjunction. In this

sentence, the subordinating conjunction is *as*. List the following subordinating conjunctions on the board.

after	if	unless
although	in order that	until
because	since	whenever
before	so that	while

Exercises Have students use a subordinating conjunction to introduce a subordinate clause to the beginning or the end of each of the following sentences.

1. Amyntas arrived at Olympia.

2. The boys trained daily.
3. The stadium was cleared.
4. Leon and Amyntas discussed the other runners.
5. Amyntas thought of his father.

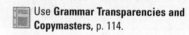 Use **Grammar Transparencies and Copymasters,** p. 114.

Use McDougal Littell's *Language Network,* Chapter 8, for more instruction in subordinating conjunctions.

at looked down upon it were packed with a ast multitude of onlookers. Half-way down on he right-hand side, raised above the tawny grass n which everybody else sat, were the benches or the Council, looking across to the white marble seat opposite, where the Priestess of Demeter, the only woman allowed at the Games, at as still as though she herself were carved rom marble, among all the jostling, swaying, oisy throng. Men were raking over the silver and on the track. The trumpeter stood ready.

They had taken their places now behind the ong white limestone curbs of the starting line. he Umpire was calling: "Runners! Feet to he lines!"

Amyntas felt the scorching heat of the imestone as he braced the ball of his right foot nto the shaped groove. All the panic of a while back had left him; he felt light, and clearheaded, and master of himself. He had drawn the sixth place, with Leon on his left and the boy from Megara on his right. Before him the track stretched white in the sunlight, an infinity of emptiness and distance.

The starting trumpet yelped, and the line of runners sprang forward like a wave of hunting dogs slipped from the leash.

Amyntas was running smoothly and without hurry. Let the green front-runners push on ahead. In this heat they would have burned themselves out before they reached the turning post. He and Leon were running neck and neck with the red-headed Macedonian. The Rhodian had gone ahead now after the front-runners; the rest were still bunched. Then the Corinthian made a sprint and passed the boy from Rhodes, but fell back almost at once. The white track was <u>reeling</u> back underfoot, the

Detail of black-figure stamnos (ca 525–500 B.C.), Group of Louvre, Greek. Tampa (Florida) Museum of Art, Joseph Veach Noble Collection, 86.34.

WORDS
TO   **reel** (rēl) *v.* to go round and round
KNOW

721

Customizing Instruction

Gifted and Talented
1 Ask students what effect seeing the victor from the previous event may have had on Amyntas.

Possible Response: Amyntas, who has been going through a lot of inner turmoil, may have been struck by the "oddly peaceful" look on the victor's face.

Less Proficient Readers
Ask students the following comprehension questions:
- What does Amyntas fear before the race starts?
  Answer: that he will fail
- How does Amyntas feel as he stands with his feet braced to run?
  Answer: calm and clear-headed

Students Acquiring English
To help students follow the race, explain the following expressions:
- *green* means "inexperienced"
- *taken fire* means "begun running as hard as he could"
- *overhaul* means "run up to and by"
- *neck and neck* means "beside each other"

Multiple Learning Styles
Linguistic and Auditory Learners
2 To help students follow the action, ask a facile reader to read aloud the description of the race as if it were a radio broadcast of a sporting event. Listeners may then find the action easier to follow and appreciate.

Multicultural Link

FRIENDLY COMPETITION Point out that the Olympic Games are a form of friendly competition. Many cultures enjoy participating in such competitions. Some were seen as providing practice in skills that were needed for survival, while others were said to predict who would win in a physical struggle. Encourage students to provide examples such as the following:

- Native Americans played *baggataway,* a form of lacrosse.
- *Chess,* an ancient board game, is still played in worldwide competitions.
- The Japanese game of *go,* a board game called *wei-chi* in China, is also played throughout the world.
- Jewish people throughout the world play with a wooden top, called a *dreidel,* to see who will win small prizes.

Active Reading | CAUSE AND EFFECT

A When Leon's cut reopens, what effect do students believe this has on him and on Amyntas?

Possible Responses: Leon slows down; Amyntas begins to wonder what he should do and whether he should let Leon win.

Reading Skills and Strategies: CONNECTING

B Ask students to recall times when they felt conflicted as Amyntas does here. What did they do to resolve the conflict within them?

Active Reading | CAUSE AND EFFECT

C Ask students what causes Amyntas to say, "I shall never be sure whether I won that race."

Possible Responses: He doubts whether he is faster than Leon.

Literary Analysis

HISTORICAL FICTION

Remind students that writers of historical fiction combine factual details with those from the writer's imagination. In what way is the character Leon a combination of both kinds of details?

Possible Responses: The lack of emotion that he shows and his scars reflect factual details about Spartans, while other details about him, such as his hair and what he says, probably come from the writer's imagination.

To help students recognize the distinguishing features of historical fiction, ask them what factual details they learn about the sights and sounds of the last day, the Crowning Day.

Possible Responses: They learn that there are no crowds; that winners receive crowns in the Sacred Enclosure and make sacrifices before the Temples of Zeus and Hera; there are flutes and torches and a feast.

Teaching Options

turning post racing toward them. The bunch had thinned out, the front-runners beginning to drop back already; and as they came up toward the turning post, the first boy from Macedon, and then Nikomedes catching fire at last, slid into the lead, with Amyntas and Leon close behind them. Rounding the post, Amyntas skidded on the loose sand and Leon went ahead; and it was then, seeing the lean scarred back ahead of him, that Amyntas lengthened his stride, knowing that the time had come to run. They were a quarter of the way down the home lap when they passed Nikomedes; the Megaran boy had taken fire too late. They were beginning to overhaul the redhead; and Amyntas knew in his bursting heart that unless something unexpected happened, the race must be between himself and Leon. Spartan and Macedonian were going neck and neck now; the position held for a few paces, and then the redhead gradually fell behind. Amyntas was going all out. There was pain in his breast and belly and in the backs of his legs, and he did not know where his next breath was coming from; but still the thin scarred back was just ahead. And then suddenly Amyntas knew that something was wrong; Leon was laboring a little, beginning to lose the first keen edge of his speed. Snatching a glance downward, he saw a fleck of crimson in the sand. The cut had reopened.

 A is body went on running, but for a sort of splinter of time his head seemed quite apart from the rest of him and filled with an unmanageable swirl of thoughts and feelings. Leon might have passed the top of his speed anyway; it might be nothing to do with his foot—But the cut *had* reopened. . . . To lose the race because of a cut foot. . . . It would be so easy not to make that final desperate effort that his whole body was

crying out against. Then Leon would keep hi lead. . . . And at the same time another part • himself was remembering his father standing on the quayside at Piraeus as the *Paralos* dre away—crying out that he was not running only for himself but for Athens, his City and his people. . . . A crown of wild olive would the greatest thing that anyone could give to h friend. . . . It would insult Leon to let him win . . . you could not do that to your friend. . . . And then, like a clean cold sword of light cutting through the swirling tangle of his thoughts, came the knowledge that greate than any of these things were the Gods. These were the Sacred Games, not some mere struggle between boys in the gymnasium. For one fleeting instant of time, he remembered himself standing in the Temple before the gre statue of Zeus, holding the tiny bronze bull with the silvered horns. "Let me run the best race that is in me and think of nothing more.

He drove himself forward in one last agonizing burst of speed. He was breathing against knives, and the roar of the blood in hi ears drowned the roar of the crowd. He was level with Leon—and then there was nothing ahead of him but the winning post.

The onlookers had crowded right down toward it; even above the howl of the blood i his head he heard them now, roar on solid roa of sound, shouting him in to victory. And then Hippias had caught him as he plunged past th post; and he was bending over the trainer's arm, bending over the pain in his belly, snatching at his breath and trying not to be sick. People were throwing sprigs of myrtle; h felt them flicking and falling on his head and shoulders. The sickness eased a little and his head was clearing; he began to hear friendly voices congratulating him; and Eudorus came shouldering through the crowd with a colored ribbon to tie around his head. But when he looked around for Leon, the Spartan boy had

 Grammar 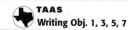 TEKS 17A, 18E | TAAS Writing Obj. 1, 3, 5, 7

COMBINING SENTENCES TO MAKE COMPLEX SENTENCES

Instruction Explain that complex sentences consist of one main clause and one or more subordinate clauses. As students edit drafts, they can combine short sentences to make complex sentences.

Application Have students revise this passage by combining sentence pairs into complex sentences.

Spartans were tough. They tested boys for courage. They whipped them. Scars formed. The scars faded. They became lighter.

 Use **Grammar Transparencies and Copymasters**, p. 102.

 Use McDougal Littell's **Language Network**, Chapter 8, for more instruction and practice in combining sentences.

een swept away by his trainer. And a desolation rose in Amyntas and robbed his moment of its glory.

Afterward in the changing room, some of the other boys came up to congratulate him. Leon did not come; but when they had cleaned off the sand and oil and sweat and sluiced down with the little water that was allowed them, Amyntas hung about, sitting on the well curb outside while the trainer finished seeing to his friend's foot. And when Leon came out at last, he came straight across to the well, as though they had arranged to meet there. His face was as unreadable as usual.

"You will have cooled off enough by now. Do you want to drink?" Amyntas said, mainly because somebody had to say something, and dipped the bronze cup that always stood on the well curb in the pail that he had drawn.

Leon took the cup from him and drank and sat down on the well curb beside him. As Amyntas dipped the cup again and bent his head to drink in his turn, the ends of the victor's ribbon fell forward against his cheek, and he pulled it off impatiently and dropped it beside the well.

"Why did you do that?" Leon said.

"I shall never be sure whether I won that race."

"The judges are not often mistaken, and I never heard yet of folk tying victors' ribbons on the wrong man."

Amyntas flicked a thumb at Leon's bandaged foot. "You know well enough what I mean. I'll never be sure whether I'd have come first past the post, if that hadn't opened up again."

Leon looked at him a moment in silence, then flung up his head and laughed. "Do you really think that could make any difference? It would take more than a cut foot to slow me up, Athenian!—You ran the better race, that's all."

It was said on such a harsh, bragging note that in the first moment Amyntas felt as though he had been struck in the face. Then he wondered if it was the overwhelming Spartan pride talking or simply Leon, hurt and angry and speaking the truth. Either way, he was too tired to be angry back again. And whichever it was it seemed that Leon had shaken it off already. The noon break was over, and the trumpets were sounding for the Pentathlon.

"Up!" Leon said, when Amyntas did not move at once. "Are you going to let it be said that your own event is the only one that interests you?"

They went, quickly and together, while the trainer's eye was off them, for Leon was under orders to keep off his foot. And the people cheered them both when they appeared in the Stadium. They seldom cared much for a good loser, but Leon had come in a close second, and they had seen the blood in the sand.

The next day the heavyweight events were held; and then it was the last day of all, the Crowning Day. Ever after, Amyntas remembered that day as a quietness after great stress and turmoil. It was not, in truth, much less noisy than the days that had gone before. The roaring of the Stadium crowds was gone, but in the town of tents the crowds milled to and fro. The jugglers with knives and the eaters of fire shouted for an audience and the merchants cried their wares, and within the Sacred Enclosure where the winners received their crowns and made their sacrifices before the Temples of Zeus and Hera, there were the flutes and the songs in praise of the victors and the deep-voiced invocations to the Gods.

But in Amyntas himself, there was the quiet. He remembered the Herald crying his name and the light springy coolness of the wild olive crown as it was pressed down on his head; and

---

✓ **Assessment Standardized Test Practice**   ⭐ **TEKS** 10H, 10K   **TAAS** Reading Obj. 5

EVALUATE AND MAKE JUDGMENTS In some standardized tests, students are asked to draw inferences and support them with text evidence and experience. To provide students with some help in evaluating and making judgments, read aloud or write on the chalkboard the following question:
The reader can tell that the Spartans
A. were rich
B. rarely bathed
C. were disciplined
D. did not believe in religion
Lead students through the process of choosing the best answer. Help them recognize that no evidence supports answers A, B, or D. However, several details, including Leon's adherence to training and his control over any display of emotions, show his discipline. Therefore, the best answer is C.

A Ask students what causes the boys to have trouble talking to each other at first.

Possible Response: They realize that the truce created by the Games between Athens and Sparta is over and their homelands will soon be at war again.

B Ask why Amyntas might have wanted to give Leon something.

Possible Responses: as a memento—something to remember him by

Reading Skills and Strategies: CLARIFYING

C Ask students what the narrator means by these two sentences.

Possible Responses: If they did meet after military service, the memory of dead comrades killed by the other's army would drive a wedge between them; one might die; if they ever meet again it will most likely be during some battle.

Literary Analysis

HISTORICAL FICTION

D What does the historical setting contribute to this story? How would the story be different in modern times?

Possible Responses: Leon would not have been cleaning the field in modern times, so he would not have cut his foot; the boys might have had contact by phone after the games.

---

later, the spitting light of pine torches under the plane trees, where the officials and athletes were feasting. And he remembered most, looking up out of the torchlight, and seeing, high and remote above it all, the winged tripods on the roof of the great Temple, outlined against the light of a moon two days past the full.

The boys left before the feasting was over; and in his sleeping cell Amyntas heard the poets sing in praise of some chariot team and the applause, while he gathered his few belongings together, ready for tomorrow's early start, and stowed his olive crown among them. Already the leaves were beginning to wilt after the heat of the day. The room that had seemed so strange the first night was familiar now, part of himself; and after tonight it would not know him anymore.

Next morning in all the hustle of departure, he and Leon contrived to meet and slip off for a little on their own.

The whole valley of Olympia was a chaos of tents and booths being taken down, merchants as well as athletes and onlookers making ready for the road. But the Sacred Enclosure itself was quiet, and the gates stood open. They went through, into the shade of the olive trees before the Temple of Zeus. A priest making the morning offering at a side altar looked at them; but they seemed to be doing no harm and to want nothing, so he let them alone. There was a smell of frankincense[14] in the air and the early morning smell of last night's heavy dew on parched ground. They stood among the twisted trunks and low-hanging branches and looked at each other and did not know what to say. Already they were remembering that there was war between Athens and Sparta, that the Truce of the Games would last them back to their own

states, but no further; and the longer the silence lasted, the more they remembered.

From beyond the quiet of the Enclosure came all the sounds of the great concourse breaking up; voices calling, the stamping of impatient horses. "By this time tomorrow everyone will be gone," Amyntas said at last. "It will be just as it was before we came, for another four years."

"The Corinthians are off already."

"Catching the cool of the morning for those fine chariot horses," Amyntas said, and thought, There's so little time, why do we have to waste it like this?

"One of the charioteers had that hunting knife with the silver inlay. The one you took a fancy to. Why didn't you buy it after all?"

"I spent the money on something else." For a moment Amyntas was afraid that Leon would ask what. But the other boy only nodded and let it go.

He wished suddenly that he could give Leon something, but there was nothing among his few belongings that would make sense in the Spartan's world. It was a world so far off from his own. Too far to reach out, too far to call. Already they seemed to be drifting away from each other, drifting back to a month ago, before they had even met. He put out a hand quickly, as though to hold the other boy back for one more moment, and Leon's hand came to meet it.

"It has been good. All this month it has been good," Leon said.

"It has been good," Amyntas agreed. He wanted to say, "Until the next Games, then." But manhood and Military Service were only a few months away for both of them. If they did meet at another Games, there would be the faces of dead comrades, Spartan or Athenian,

---

14. **frankincense** (frăng′kĭn-sĕns): a sweet-scented resin used as incense.

Teaching Options

✓ **Assessment** **Standardized Test Practice** TEKS 10E, 10K   TAAS Obj. Reading 4

CAUSE AND EFFECT In some standardized tests, students are asked to use the text's structure or progression of ideas such as cause and effect to locate and recall information. To provide students with some help in recognizing cause and effect, read aloud or write on the chalkboard the following question:

Why are the boys training at Olympia instead of at home?

A. A truce is declared during the Games.

B. The last month's training for the Games has to be done there.

C. The names of past victors are carved on the walls.

D. The Stadium needs cleaning.

Lead students through the process of choosing the best answer. Help them recognize that while A, C, and D are true, there is no cause-effect relationship between them and the question. Neither the truce, nor the victors' names, nor the cleaning has anything to do with why the boys are at Olympia. Therefore, the best answer is B.

tween them; and like enough, for one of em or both, there might be no other Games. r more likely, if they ever saw each other gain, it would be over the tops of their shields.

He had noticed before how, despite their fferent worlds, he and Leon sometimes ought the same thing at the same time and nswered each other as though the thought ad been spoken. Leon said in his abrupt, ead-level voice, "The Gods be with you, myntas, and grant that we never meet again."

They put their arms around each other's ecks and strained fiercely close for a moment, ard cheekbone against hard cheekbone.

"The Gods be with you, Leon."

And then Eudorus was calling, "Amyntas! myntas! We're all waiting!"

And Amyntas turned and ran—out through he gateway of the Sacred Enclosure, toward here the Athenian party were ready to start, nd Eudorus was already coming back to look or him.

As they rode up from the Valley of Olympia nd took the tracks toward the coast, Amyntas id not look back. The horses' legs brushed he dry dust-grey scrub beside the track and loosed the hot aromatic scents of wild lavender and camomile and lentisk upon the air. A yellow butterfly hovered past, and watching it out of sight, it came to him suddenly that he and Leon had exchanged gifts of a sort, after all. It was hard to give them a name, but they were real enough. And the outward and visible sign of his gift to Leon was in the little bronze bull with the silvered horns that he had left on the Offering Table before the feet of Olympian Zeus. And Leon's gift to him. . . . That had been made with the Spartan's boast that it would take more than a cut foot to slow him up. He had thought at the time that it was either the harsh Spartan pride or the truth spoken in anger. But he understood now, quite suddenly, that it had been Leon giving up his own private and inward claim to the olive crown, so that he, Amyntas, might believe that he had rightfully won it. Amyntas knew that he would never be sure of that, never in all his life. But it made no difference to the gift.

The track had begun to run downhill, and the pale dust-cloud was rising behind them. He knew that if he looked back now, there would be nothing to see. ❖

Eastern colonnade of the Palaestra, once a public building for athletic training and practice at Olympia.

A CROWN OF WILD OLIVE **725**

 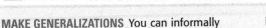

GUIDING STUDENT RESPONSE

Connect to the Literature

1. Accept all reasonable responses.

Comprehension Check
• Leon is hostile when he notices Amyntas looking at his scars.
• Leon cuts his foot on the blade of an old rusty scythe.
• "Let me run the best race that is in me."

Use Selection Quiz
Unit Five Resource Book, p. 34.

Think Critically

2. **Possible Response:** Amyntas wants to win to prove himself because he feels like an outsider among the older Athenian athletes. Also, Amyntas wants to win to try to make up for his father's loss of athletic abilities.

3. **Possible Response:** Leon and Amyntas work together and discover they have much in common. Soon they realize that they are the top athletes among their age group and pose a threat to each other.

4. **Possible Response:** The experience of praying to Zeus allows Amyntas to recover his true commitment to being an athlete. His prayer helps him to realize that not to do his best in the race would be a betrayal to that commitment.

5. **Possible Response:** Many of Amyntas's boyhood ideas about winning and losing and friends and enemies have changed.

6. Important cause and effect relationships are: the summons that begins preparations for the Games; the wound that ends Leon's father's athletic career; Leon stepping on the blade that cuts his foot; Amyntas's prayer to Zeus that helps him to focus on his athletic potential; and the running of the race that causes Leon's wound to reopen.

Use **Reading and Critical Thinking Transparencies**, p. 3, for additional support.

Literary Analysis

Historical Fiction Students' charts will probably include details about coming-of-age-rituals, athletic training, the ancient games, and events surrounding the games. Encourage them also to note details about the religious life of the ancient Greeks.

Connect to the Literature

1. **What Do You Think?** What is your reaction to Amyntas's thoughts as he leaves the valley of Olympia after the games? Explain.

Comprehension Check
• What is Leon's reaction to Amyntas when they first meet?
• How does Leon cut his foot?
• What prayer does Amyntas make to Zeus?

Think Critically

2. As Amyntas sets off for the Games, what do you think winning means to him?

THINK ABOUT
{ • his father's injury
• being the youngest athlete from Athens
• his talk with his father before leaving

3. As they prepare for the Games together, how does Leon become both friend and opponent to Amyntas? How does Leon's injury add to this tension?

4. What do you think Amyntas gains from making his prayer to Zeus? Does he get what he prays for?

5. As Amyntas returns to Athens, how is he different than when he first set sail for the Games? Explain.

6. **ACTIVE READING** **CAUSE AND EFFECT** Review the examples of **cause and effect** you wrote in your **READER'S NOTEBOOK**. How did the examples you found help you to better understand the story?

Extend Interpretations

7. **COMPARING TEXTS** Think of Felix and Antonio from "Amigo Brothers." (page 361) Compare and contrast their situation, friendship, and competition with those of Amyntas and Leon. How are they similar? How do they differ?

8. **Connect to Life** Who are the people who inspire you to do your best? Share some examples with a partner.

Literary Analysis

HISTORICAL FICTION Historical fiction differs from other types of fiction in that its setting and characters have a strong basis in historical fact. **Historical fiction** is always set in a past historical period and may include actual historical personages as characters. "A Crown of Wild Olive" includes details based in the author's research into ancient Greek history. Though there are no actual historical characters in the story, there are many historical details that bring the period to life, such as those describing the wars between Athens and Sparta, the method of raising Spartan boys, and the religious, social, and athletic significance of the Olympic Games.

Cooperative Learning Activity
When you read historical fiction, it is important to distinguish between details based in historical fact and those invented by the author. Divide the class into two groups and have one group chart factual details and imaginative details about Amyntas and the other group do the same regarding Leon. Afterward, as a class, discuss what you learned about ancient Athens and Sparta by reading this story.

AMYNTAS		LEON	
Historical Detail	Imaginative Detail	Historical Detail	Imaginative Detail
Amyntas will cut his hair to mark his entrance into manhood.	He promises his father that he will win the race for both of them.	Leon was beaten to test his courage.	He has a "slow, rather grave" smile.

Extend Interpretations

7. **Comparing Texts** Students should understand that both friendships are driven by common interests and mutual respect, as well as competition. In both situations, the friends must learn how to balance a competitive spirit and individual achievement with their commitment to friendship. Students should also note differences between the two pairs, including the fact that it is unlikely that the friendship between Amyntas and Leon will survive their circumstances. Antonio and Felix, on the other hand, live in an environment that will not necessarily prevent them from remaining friends. "Amigo Brothers" ends on a hopeful note while "A Crown of Wild Olive" brings readers in touch with a rather grim reality.

8. **Connect to Life** Accept all reasonable responses. Responses may include family members, teachers, mentors, coaches, or anyone else who has provided inspiration.

Writing Options

1. Dramatic Dialogue Write a dialogue that might have taken place between Amyntas and his father upon Amyntas's return to Athens. Keep in mind the conversation Amyntas and his father had at the beginning of the story as well as other key events.

2. Commemorative Poem In ancient Greece, poets commemorated the achievements of the athletes at the Olympic Games. Write a poem commemorating the contest between Amyntas and Leon or two other athletes you know. Share your poem with the class.

3. Persuasive Essay How should friends behave toward each other when they compete for the same prize? Brainstorm ideas with a partner and then develop an essay on your own. Place the essay in your **Working Portfolio.**

Writing Handbook
See p. R39: Persuasive Writing.

Activities & Explorations

Olympic Medal Although medals weren't a part of the ancient Olympics, create a design for the Games the story describes. Remember that part of the significance of the Games was that they created a truce between two warring city-states, a truce especially represented by the friendship between Amyntas and Leon. ~ **ART**

Art Connection

Look at the bronze statue of the Spartan warrior on page 713. What impression of Spartans does it and the behavior of the Spartans in "A Crown of Wild Olive" give you? Explain your answer.

Inquiry & Research

The Modern Olympics Choose an Olympics of the past century to research. How were the uniforms different from ones worn today? Were the opening ceremonies different? What country captured the most medals?

 Real-World Link Before you begin, read "Passing on the Flame," p. 728, to learn more about the origin and meaning of an important Olympic tradition.

"To me half the fun of writing a book is the research entailed."

Rosemary Sutcliff
1920–1992

Research and Writing British author Rosemary Sutcliff wrote fiction that enables her readers to imagine the lives of people of long ago. Sutcliff liked to immerse herself in the historical period she depicted in a story. "To me half the fun of writing a book is the research entailed," she said.

Painful Childhood As a child Sutcliff suffered from a form of rheumatoid arthritis and, until the age of ten, was educated at home by her mother, who read to her extensively. Sutcliff said that her mother's reading aloud to her provided examples of good writing that helped her later when she created her own stories.

AUTHOR ACTIVITY

Other Stories "A Crown of Wild Olive" is one of three stories in Sutcliff's *Heather, Oak, and Olive.* Read one of the other stories in the collection. Report back to the class.

A CROWN OF WILD OLIVE   **727**

 Grammar **TEKS** 17A, 18C   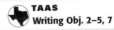 **TAAS** Writing Obj. 2–5, 7

ELABORATING WITH ADJECTIVE CLAUSES
Instruction Tell students that an adjective clause is a subordinate clause that modifies a noun or pronoun. Remind them that they can revise drafts by using adjective clauses to elaborate on existing text. Many adjective clauses begin with *who, which, where,* or *that.*

Exercises Have students revise each sentence by adding an adjective clause:

1. The boys arrived in Olympia.
2. Amyntas missed Ariston.
3. Leon was entered in the Double Stade.
4. Amyntas went to the fairground.
5. In the ground was a sickle blade.
6. Amyntas stood inside the Temple.
7. In his hand was a small bronze bull.
8. The two boys marched into the Stadium.

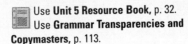 Use **Unit 5 Resource Book**, p. 32.
Use **Grammar Transparencies and Copymasters,** p. 113.

 Use McDougal Littell's *Language Network,* Chapter 8, for more instruction and practice in combining sentences.

Writing Options

1. Dramatic Dialogue To get students started, suggest that they first role-play the meeting between Amyntas and his father.

 Use **Communications Transparencies and Copymasters,** p. 13, for additional support.

2. Commemorative Poem Encourage **auditory learners** to begin by imagining the rhythm of runners' feet or the music that might be played at the event.

3. Persuasive Essay Remind students that a good persuasive essay organizes ideas in some way, often by order of importance. Students might consider either beginning with the strongest idea or else ending with it. Students must also support their ideas with examples and other evidence.

Use **Writing Transparencies,** p. 27, for additional support.

Activities & Explorations

Olympic Medal Encourage **spatial learners** to consider symbols that might depict both the competitive nature of the games and the truce that accompanied them.

Art Connection

Students might mention the emphasis on utility and spareness as opposed to beauty and softness.

Inquiry & Research

The Modern Olympics You may wish to suggest that students begin by researching the Olympic Games of 1928 (first women competed), 1936 (Jesse Owens), 1968 (Black Power salute), 1972 (athletes murdered in Munich), or 1980 (boycott to protest Afghanistan invasion by Soviets).

Rosemary Sutcliff

Students who enjoy Sutcliff's detailed descriptions may enjoy learning that she attended art school, where she specialized in painting miniatures.

Author Activity

Other Stories Since students will read different selections, encourage them to provide brief plot summaries to help listeners understand their reports.

Web Article

Objectives

- read to be informed
- establish and adjust purposes for reading, such as reading to find out
- monitor comprehension and make modifications when understanding breaks down, such as by asking questions
- form and revise questions for investigations, including questions arising from readings
- make connections in response to texts

Connecting to the Literature

The web article "Passing on the Flame" is a strong companion piece to the story "A Crown of Wild Olive." It continues the story by bringing the Olympic Games into the present day. The article explains the origins of two modern Olympic traditions, the torch and the relay. It also explains why the ancient Olympics were abolished for 1500 years and why they were later reinstituted. Finally, the article illustrates how the tradition of peace and unity has been maintained in the modern games by offering as an example the help American Jesse Owens received from a German competitor in 1936.

Back Forward Reload Home Search Images Print Security Stop

Passing on the Flame

No image captures the spirit of the Olympic Games so dramatically. It is the moment during the opening ceremonies when a lone runner, torch raised high, approaches the lamp, salutes the audience and athletes, and dips the torch to light the Olympic flame. The modern Olympic flame harks back to the ancient Greek games, a fire descended directly from the flame kept lit in the temple of Hera at Olympia. Although the torch and relay are inventions of the modern Olympics, they have become a tradition. Every four years, thousands of citizens of the host country participate in a relay that brings the flame from Olympia, Greece, to its new temporary residence.

Few Americans who witnessed the 1996 Summer Olympics in Atlanta, Georgia, will forget the moment Muhammad Ali lit his torch on the flame of the torch carried by Janet Evans and turned to light the Olympic flame. Hands shaking from the effects of Parkinson's disease, Ali was the last member of a torch relay that required more than 10,000 people to run its course. The flame representing spirit, knowledge, and life had arrived in Atlanta after traveling 15,000 miles around the United States. Ali, an Olympic champion himself, stretched with immense effort to light the flame. A similarly powerful scene will transpire at the Summer Olympics in Sydney, Australia, in 2000. Athens, Greece, in 2004 doubtless has the same in store.

The torch has not always been this important, however. The Olympic Games in their present form were reinstituted in

Back Forward Reload Home Search Images Print Security Stop

1896, after being abolished for 1500 years. The Christian Roman emperor Theodosius decreed the end of the ancient Olympic Games in the fourth century A.D., because he felt they glorified the old pagan religion. It took a wealthy baron and a fitness craze in the 19th century to start people thinking about an athletic competition again. The baron was the zealous Pierre de Coubertin, and the new Games featured neither flame nor torch relay. For the idea of the torch, a man in the 1930s named Carl Diem would combine two symbols from the ancient Games.

3 The first record of the ancient Olympics dates back to 776 B.C., at the town of Olympia, Greece. Originally, the event consisted of a simple festival in honor of the god Zeus. It lasted only one day, and visitors spent as much time sacrificing to the gods as competing in foot races. Soon, however, interest in sporting events grew to predominate the festival. Events included short races, long-distance races, boxing, chariot racing, wrestling, and horseback riding, among others.

What is striking about the ancient games is the emphasis the Greeks placed on unity. Since the Greek cities were often at war with each other,

Reading for Information

With nonfiction, what questions do you ask as you read? How do you know you're getting everything out of the article that you should?

MONITOR In the Reading Model (p. 4), you learned the active-reading strategies of **Question, Connect, Predict, Clarify, Visualize,** and **Evaluate.** To be an active reader, you need to **monitor** your use of these strategies as you read. When you have trouble understanding something you are reading, stop and ask yourself: What is the most appropriate active-reading strategy for this piece?

Other questions you might ask include: How can I connect personally to what I'm reading? What part do I need to clarify? What are my opinions of the information in this piece?

YOUR TURN *Use the questions below to monitor your reading of the article.*

1 To get involved in an article, use the Connect strategy to relate information to your own experience: Have you witnessed a dramatic sporting event? How does it compare to this Olympic moment?

2 Would Predicting be an appropriate strategy after reading this passage? Why or why not? What is there to predict?

3 Monitor your understanding of the selection so far. Ask: Have I understood everything? Is there anything I need to clarify? Which strategy might you apply to this paragraph?

Reading for Information

As you go through the article with students, suggest that they use the material in the right-hand column as a guide to using active reading strategies to understand informational articles. The following are **possible responses** to the questions and activities:

1 Students might mention school games, televised events, or events that they have seen in films. Encourage them to consider what made their event dramatic and what made Ali's performance so powerful and moving.

2 Some students will say that prediction is useful, because they can predict that the same relay and torch lighting will happen at the next Olympics; other students will say that it is not useful, because each traditional relay and torch lighting brings its own, unique dramatic moments.

3 Students might mention almost any strategy here. For example, they might question why the event started that year; they might connect the paragraph to the story; they might predict that they will learn more about other Olympic games; they might visualize the simple games.

Use **Reading and Critical Thinking Transparencies**, p. 1, for additional support.

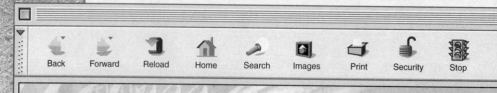

FACKELSTAFFELLAUF OLYMPIA·BERLIN

A German postcard commemorating the first torch relay (1936).

athletes could not always travel safely to and from Olympia. The Greeks solved this problem by declaring a truce for the period of the Games, thus assuring everyone safe passage. To announce the truce, runners swept through the country to herald the time of Olympic peace. The people looked forward to these messengers who ushered in a spirit of unity and a short period of peace.

In addition to the heralds, another symbol associated with the ancient games at Olympia was a flame kept lit in the temple that was dedicated to Hera, the wife of Zeus. For the 1928 Amsterdam Games, Theodore Lewald revived this idea in order to establish a visible connection between the ancient and modern Olympiads. However, it was Carl Diem, a renowned Olympic historian, who brought together both the symbol of the flame and the symbol of the runners when he suggested a modern torch relay for the 1936 Olympics.

In 1936, when the torch relay debuted, 3,075 torchbearers carried the flame from Olympia, Greece, to Berlin, Germany—the site of the Tenth Summer Olympics. For the first time, a flame ignited by the sun in Olympia was faithfully carried by each runner at least a half mile before it was passed to the next. The whole event was carefully choreographed so that the last runner would enter Berlin's 100,000 seat stadium at the scheduled time to commence the Games.

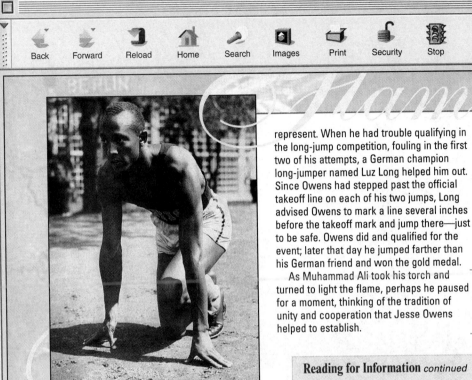

| Back | Forward | Reload | Home | Search | Images | Print | Security | Stop |

represent. When he had trouble qualifying in the long-jump competition, fouling in the first two of his attempts, a German champion long-jumper named Luz Long helped him out. Since Owens had stepped past the official takeoff line on each of his two jumps, Long advised Owens to mark a line several inches before the takeoff mark and jump there—just to be safe. Owens did and qualified for the event; later that day he jumped farther than his German friend and won the gold medal.

As Muhammad Ali took his torch and turned to light the flame, perhaps he paused for a moment, thinking of the tradition of unity and cooperation that Jesse Owens helped to establish. 4

American gold-medalist Jesse Owens (1936).

It was fitting that the birth of the torch relay coincided with African-American runner Jesse Owens's famous Olympic performance. As the German crowd cheered him on, Owens won four gold medals and shattered Hitler's claims that the Aryan race was physically superior. Owens's experience at the Games embodied the spirit of friendly but intense competition that the Olympics were supposed to

Reading for Information *continued*

4 Pause to evaluate: What is your opinion of the use of the Olympic torch relay? What else should you evaluate about the article?

Inquiry & Research

Activity Link: "A Crown of Wild Olive" p. 727. Now that you have learned about the tradition of the torch, find out about the Olympic mascot or another Olympic tradition. With a partner, prepare a fact sheet about the tradition that you choose.

Mini Lesson **Inquiry & Research** TEKS 10J 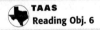 TAAS Reading Obj. 6

The Inquiry & Research activity on this page links to the Inquiry & Research activity of Choices & Challenges on page 727, following the story "A Crown of Wild Olive."

Instruction Tell students that before they can create fact sheets about an Olympic tradition, they must learn to distinguish fact and opinion in various texts. A fact is a statement that can be proved to be correct or incorrect; an opinion

is a statement that tells what someone thinks or believes. Opinions express judgments and feelings, which cannot be proved.

Practice Have students read each statement and tell whether it is a fact or an opinion:

1. The Olympic relay now takes place every four years. (fact)
2. Ali was probably the best-known member of the 1996 relay team. (opinion)

3. Carl Diem made a good suggestion for the 1936 games. (opinion)
4. Berlin's stadium held 10,000 seats. (fact)
5. Owens fouled on his first two long-jump attempts. (fact)
6. Luz Long showed real courage. (opinion)

 Use **Reading and Critical Thinking Transparencies,** p. 26, for additional support.

Objectives

1. understand and appreciate the genre of **autobiography** (Literary Analysis)
2. understand and appreciate the genre of **memoir** (Literary Analysis)
3. use the strategy of **recognizing main idea and supporting details** (Active Reading)

Summary

The oppressions of apartheid in South Africa brought out courage and character in its people. Nelson Mandela explains that courage is not the absence of fear, but the triumph over it. He and his comrades took courage from the belief that if people can be taught to hate, they can be taught to love. Commitment to his people cost Mandela the joys of fulfilling obligations to his family. After an idyllic childhood, he realized that he had no freedom to achieve his potential and that no one, oppressed or oppressor, had freedom in his country. After his release from prison, he continues the "long walk" toward helping South Africans learn that it is not enough to "cast off one's chains," but that to be truly free they must learn to live in "a way that respects and enhances the freedom of others."

Thematic Link

Mandela's words reveal his determination to work for true freedom in South Africa despite the costs to himself and his personal life.

5-Minute Warm-Up

Daily Language SkillBuilder **TEKS 17F, 16G**

Have students **proofread** the display sentences on page 653j and write them correctly. The sentences also appear on Transparency 22 of **Grammar Transparencies and Copymasters.**

from # Long Walk to Freedom

Memoir by NELSON MANDELA

SOCIAL STUDIES

Connect to Your Life

What do you know about the struggle against apartheid?

Build Background In 1948 the white-controlled government of South Africa established apartheid, or racial segregation. The purpose was to maintain white control. Black South Africans had no political rights. The struggle against apartheid intensified in the 1980s. In 1990–1991 apartheid was repealed. In 1994, Nelson Mandela was elected president. In 1999, Thabo Mbeke became the next president.

NON-WHITE SHOP
THIS NOTICE IS DISPLAYED IN ACCORDANCE WITH THE PROVISIONS OF THE SHOP HOURS ORDINANCE. 1959
NIE-BLANKE WINKEL
HIERDIE KENNISGEWING IS VERTOON OOREENKOMSTIG DIE BEPALINGS VAN DIE ORDONANSIE OP WINKELURE.1959

Background: South Africans wait to vote in April 1994. *Above left:* Apartheid was enforced by military and police power. *Above right:* Apartheid-era sign indicating a store where blacks were allowed to shop.

Focus Your Reading

LITERARY ANALYSIS **MEMOIR** A **memoir** is a type of autobiography. In a memoir the author narrates events in his or her own life but also usually describes important events happening in the world. As you read the selection from *Long Walk to Freedom,* notice how Mandela's own story is connected to events in his country.

WORDS TO KNOW **Vocabulary Preview**
curtailed   indivisible   transitory
incomprehensible   resiliency

ACTIVE READING **MAIN IDEA AND DETAILS**
A writer's principal message is called the main idea. The main idea may be the central idea of an entire work or of one paragraph. Details such as facts or additional thoughts clarify, or support, the main idea. As you read this selection, choose a paragraph and jot down the main idea and supporting details in your 📖 READER'S NOTEBOOK.

 LaserLink: Background for Reading Historical Connection

 TEKS See the Skills Trace at the beginning of the unit for information on TEKS covered in this lesson.

732 UNIT FIVE PART 2: AGAINST THE ODDS

LESSON RESOURCES

UNIT FIVE RESOURCE BOOK, pp. 35–41

ASSESSMENT
Formal Assessment, pp. 115–116
Teacher's Guide to Assessment and Portfolio Use
Test Generator

SKILLS TRANSPARENCIES AND COPYMASTERS
Reading and Critical Thinking
• Main Idea and Supporting Details, TR 25 (for Thinking Through the Literature, p. 737)

Grammar
• Relative Pronouns, CM 108 (for Mini Lesson, p. 735)
• Adjective Clauses, CM 110 (for Mini Lesson, p. 739)

Vocabulary
• Antonyms, CM 76 (for Mini Lesson, p. 733)

INTEGRATED TECHNOLOGY
Audio Library
LaserLinks
• Historical Connection See **Teacher's SourceBook,** p. 32
Internet: Research Starter

Visit our website:
www.mcdougallittell.com

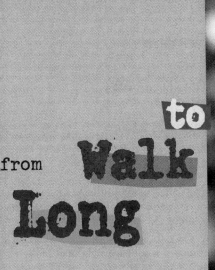

Long Walk to Freedom

from

by
Nelson Mandela

The policy of apartheid created a deep and lasting wound in my country and my people. All of us will spend many years, if not generations, recovering from that profound hurt. But the decades of oppression and brutality had another, unintended effect, and that was that it produced the Oliver Tambos,[1] the Walter Sisulus, the Chief Luthulis, the Yusuf Dadoos, the Bram Fischers, the Robert Sobukwes of our time—men of such extraordinary courage, wisdom, and generosity that their like may never be known

---

1. **Oliver Tambos . . . :** South Africans who, like Mandela, had fought against apartheid.

© Gideon Mendel/Magnum

733

Literary Analysis MEMOIR

Remind students that a memoir is a type of autobiographical writing. Elicit or explain that *auto* means "self," *bio* means "life," and *graphy* means "writing." Ask what word *memoir* sounds like *(memory)*. As students preview the selection, have them identify elements that characterize the work as a memoir. (e.g., first-person POV, history, commentary)

 Use **Unit Five Resource Book**, p. 37 for more practice.

Active Reading | MAIN IDEA AND DETAILS |

A Remind students that a main idea may be stated or implied. Have students read the first paragraph and help them identify the main idea and details.

Possible Response: Main idea: The hardships of apartheid brought out extraordinary qualities in some people. Details: names of heroic people, list of qualities, comparison between natural resources and people.

 Use **Unit Five Resource Book**, p. 36 for more practice.

Literary Analysis: CONFLICT

Review the definition of *conflict* (a struggle between opposing forces). Have students identify the forces in conflict in Mandela's memoir.

Possible Responses: racial conflict, personal conflict (torn between obligations to family and to community), political conflict (resisting unjust laws)

> # I learned that courage
> # was not the absence of fear,
> # but the triumph over it.

again. Perhaps it requires such depth of oppression to create such heights of character. My country is rich in the minerals and gems that lie beneath its soil, but I have always known that its greatest wealth is its people, finer and truer than the purest diamonds.

It is from these comrades in the struggle that I learned the meaning of courage. Time and again, I have seen men and women risk and give their lives for an idea. I have seen men stand up to attacks and torture without breaking, showing a strength and <u>resiliency</u> that defies the imagination. I learned that courage was not the absence of fear, but the triumph over it. I felt fear myself more times than I can remember, but I hid it behind a mask of boldness. The brave man is not he who does not feel afraid, but he who conquers that fear.

I never lost hope that this great transformation would occur. Not only because of the great heroes I have already cited, but because of the courage of the ordinary men and women of my country. I always knew that deep down in every human heart, there is mercy and generosity. No one is born hating another person because of the color of his skin, or his background, or his religion. People must learn to hate, and if they can learn to

hate, they can be taught to love, for love comes more naturally to the human heart than its opposite. Even in the grimmest times in prison, when my comrades and I were pushed to our limits, I would see a glimmer of humanity in one of the guards, perhaps just for a second, but it was enough to reassure me and keep me going. Man's goodness is a flame that can be hidden but never extinguished.

We took up the struggle with our eyes wide open, under no illusion that the path would be an easy one. As a young man, when I joined the African National Congress,[2] I saw the price my comrades paid for their beliefs, and it was high. For myself, I have never regretted my commitment to the struggle, and I was always prepared to face the hardships that affected me personally. But my family paid a terrible price, perhaps too dear a price for my commitment.

In life, every man has twin obligations— obligations to his family, to his parents, to his wife and children; and he has an obligation to his people, his community, his country. In a civil and humane society, each man is able to fulfill those obligations according to his own inclinations and abilities. But in a country like

---

2. **African National Congress:** the political party opposed to apartheid that Mandela helped found.

WORDS TO KNOW
resiliency (rĭ-zĭl′ yən-sē) *n.* the ability to recover quickly from illness, change, or misfortune

734

Teaching Options

BLOCK SCHEDULING: MANAGING TIME

If your schedule requires that you cover the lesson objectives in a shorter time, use . . .
• Preparing to Read, p. 732
• Thinking through the Literature, p. 737
• Vocabulary and Spelling, p. 738
• Grammar in Context, p. 739

If you want to take advantage of longer class time, use . . .
• TE Teaching Options: Preteaching Vocabulary, p. 733; Grammar, pp. 735, 739; Standardized Test Practice, p. 736; Spelling, p. 738
• Choices & Challenges pp. 738–739

South Africa, it was almost impossible for a man of my birth and color to fulfill both of those obligations. In South Africa, a man of color who attempted to live as a human being was punished and isolated. In South Africa, a man who tried to fulfill his duty to his people was inevitably ripped from his family and his home and was forced to live a life apart, a twilight existence of secrecy and rebellion. I did not in the beginning choose to place my people above my family, but in attempting to serve my people, I found that I was prevented from fulfilling my obligations as a son, a brother, a father, and a husband.

In that way, my commitment to my people, to the millions of South Africans I would never know or meet, was at the expense of the people I knew best and loved most. It was as simple and yet as <u>incomprehensible</u> as the moment a small child asks her father, "Why can you not be with us?" And the father must utter the terrible words: "There are other children like you, a great many of them . . ." and then one's voice trails off.

I was not born with a hunger to be free. I was born free—free in every way that I could know. Free to run in the fields near my mother's hut, free to swim in the clear stream that ran through my village, free to roast mealies[3] under the stars and ride the broad backs of slow-moving bulls. As long as I obeyed my father and abided by the customs of my tribe, I was not troubled by the laws of man or God.

It was only when I began to learn that my boyhood freedom was an illusion, when I discovered as a young man that my freedom

had already been taken from me, that I began to hunger for it. At first, as a student, I wanted freedom only for myself, the <u>transitory</u> freedoms of being able to stay out at night, read what I pleased, and go where I chose. Later, as a young man in Johannesburg, I yearned for the basic and honorable freedoms of achieving my potential, of earning my keep, of marrying and having a family—the freedom not to be obstructed in a lawful life.

But then I slowly saw that not only was I not free, but my brothers and sisters were not free. I saw that it was not just my freedom that was <u>curtailed</u>, but the freedom of everyone who looked like I did. That is when I joined the African National Congress, and that is when the hunger for my own freedom became the greater hunger for the freedom of my people. It was this desire for the freedom of my people to live their lives with dignity and self-respect that animated my life, that transformed a frightened young man into a bold one, that drove a law-abiding attorney to become a criminal, that turned a family-loving husband into a man without a home, that forced a life-loving man to live like a monk. I am no more virtuous or self-sacrificing than the next man, but I found that I could not even enjoy the poor and limited freedoms I was allowed when I knew my people were not free. Freedom is <u>indivisible</u>; the chains on any one of my people were the chains on all of them, the chains on all of my people were the chains on me.

It was during those long and lonely years that my hunger for the freedom of my own people became a hunger for the freedom of all

---

3. **mealies** *South African:* corn.

WORDS
TO
KNOW

incomprehensible (ĭn′kŏm-prĭ-hĕn′sə-bəl) *adj.* not understandable
transitory (trăn′sĭ-tôr′ē) *adj.* lasting only a short time; temporary
curtailed (kər-tāld′) *adj.* cut short **curtail** *v.*
indivisible (ĭn′də-vĭz′ə-bəl) *adj.* incapable of being divided

735

Customizing Instruction

Less Proficient Readers
Ask the following questions to make sure that students understand the story.
- What was apartheid?
  Answer: a political system of laws by which black people were denied basic freedoms to work, travel, learn, and live as families
- Why did Mandela join the African National Congress?
  Answer: The ANC was the political party opposed to apartheid; he joined it to work for freedom for people of color.
- Why was Nelson Mandela unable to meet his obligations to his family?
  Answer: His work for the ANC and for freedom for everyone took all his time and attention and led to prison.

Set a Purpose: Have students read to learn what Mandela did after his release, which came when apartheid ended.

Multiple Learning Styles
Intrapersonal Learners
1 Invite students to speculate what they might have done in Mandela's place. How would they have chosen between the obligations to family and country, and why?

Interpersonal Learners
2 Invite students to consider and express for classmates how they think Mandela's family felt about him.

Visual Learners
3 Invite students to chart the changes in Mandela, using arrows to show what he was and what he became.

Gifted and Talented Students
4 Have students explain why they agree or disagree with Mandela's assertion that he is "no more virtuous or self-sacrificing than the next man." Why might he say this?

Mini Lesson **Grammar**    **TEKS 17C**   **TAAS Writing Obj. 6**

RELATIVE PRONOUNS

Instruction Explain that a relative pronoun introduces a subordinate clause that modifies a noun or a pronoun. Display the following sentence:
You gave the answer *that* we expected.
In this case, *that* begins the clause modifying the noun *answer.*
Common relative pronouns include *who, whom, which,* and *that. Who* and *whom* are used for people. *Which* and *that* are used for things.

Note that these words are not always relative pronouns, but this is one of their functions.
Exercises Help students identify relative pronouns and the words they modify in these examples, highlighted in the text:
1. My country is rich in the *minerals* and *gems* **that** lie beneath its soil . . . .
2. The brave man is not *he* **who** does not feel fear, but *he* **who** conquers that fear.
3. A *man* of color **who** attempted to live as a human being was punished and isolated.

4. It was this *desire* for the freedom of my people. . . **that** animated my life, **that** transformed a frightened young man . . . .

 Use **Grammar Transparencies and Copymasters,** p. 108.

Use McDougal Littell's *Language Network,* Chapter 8, for more instruction and practice in relative pronouns.

A Ask students what details support the idea that "the oppressor must be liberated just as surely as the oppressed"?

Possible Response: hunger for freedom of all people, white and black; a man who takes away another's freedom is a prisoner of hatred; bars of prejudice and narrow-mindedness; both robbed of humanity

B Ask what details support the idea that Mandela's walk is not yet ended.

Possible Response: mission not achieved; we are not yet free, but have merely achieved the right not to be oppressed; not the final step but the first step; must live in a way that respects and enhances the freedom of others. Metaphors of walking long road and climbing hill, stopping to look around and back; more hills to climb

Literary Analysis:
AUTHOR'S PURPOSE

Have students think back over the entire selection to answer this question: Why did Mandela write this memoir? List students' ideas.

Possible Response: Students might say he wrote this memoir so that people would appreciate the struggles he and others have endured. He might also want people to know that there is still much to accomplish.

Literary Analysis: CONFLICT

Talk about the degree to which each conflict described by Mandela (racial, personal, political) has been resolved.

---

people, white and black. I knew as well as I knew anything that the oppressor must be liberated just as surely as the oppressed. A man who takes away another man's freedom is a prisoner of hatred, he is locked behind the bars of prejudice and narrow-mindedness. I am not truly free if I am taking away someone else's freedom, just as surely as I am not free when my freedom is taken from me. The oppressed and the oppressor alike are robbed of their humanity.

When I walked out of prison, that was my mission, to liberate the oppressed and the oppressor both. Some say that has now been achieved. But I know that that is not the case. The truth is that we are not yet free; we have merely achieved the freedom to be free, the right not to be oppressed. We have not taken the final step of our journey, but the first step on a longer and even more difficult road. For to be free is not merely to cast off one's chains, but to live in a way that respects and enhances the freedom of others. The true test of our devotion to freedom is just beginning.

I have walked that long road to freedom. I have tried not to falter; I have made missteps along the way. But I have discovered the secret that after climbing a great hill, one only finds that there are many more hills to climb. I have taken a moment here to rest, to steal a view of the glorious vista that surrounds me, to look back on the distance I have come. But I can rest only for a moment, for with freedom come responsibilities, and I dare not linger, for my long walk is not yet ended. ❖

Teaching Options

✓ **Assessment Standardized Test Practice**   TEKS 10F, 10K   TAAS Reading Obj. 3

IDENTIFY MAIN IDEA AND SUPPORTING DETAILS
In some standardized tests, students are asked to identify the main idea in a passage they have read. Write the following question on the chalkboard or read it aloud.

Which statement expresses the main idea of this excerpt from *Long Road to Freedom*?

A. The policy of apartheid created a deep and lasting wound in South Africa.

B. People have twin obligations, one to their families and another to their community.

C. Nelson Mandela made personal sacrifices in his work to end apartheid in South Africa.

D. The struggle for freedom required and continues to require courage and commitment from Mandela and the people of South Africa.

Guide students through the process of selecting the correct answer. A, B, and C are not correct because they are only supporting details (observations, ideas, examples). D is correct because it is the main idea of the excerpt as a whole.

Thinking through the LITERATURE

Connect to the Literature

1. **What Do You Think?**
   What were your thoughts and emotions at the end of this piece?

   > **Comprehension Check**
   > - What does Mandela say are one's "twin obligations"?
   > - What did Mandela realize that he had to do when he walked out of prison?

Think Critically

2. How does Mandela's understanding of freedom change over the course of the selection?

   THINK ABOUT
   - his memories of childhood
   - how his thoughts about freedom changed when he saw the oppression of others "who looked like I did"
   - his mission "to liberate the oppressed and the oppressor both"

3. How would you describe Mandela's goals for himself as a young man in Johannesburg? How do you think he feels about them, looking back over his life?

4. What is your reaction to Mandela's notion of the "twin obligations" of every citizen?

5. What does Mandela mean by "we are not yet free; we have merely achieved the freedom to be free"?

6. **ACTIVE READING** **MAIN IDEA AND DETAILS**
   With a small group, share the notes you took in your **READER'S NOTEBOOK** identifying the main idea and details. Can you observe one idea that runs through all of the paragraphs your group discussed?

Extend Interpretations

7. **Style** Mandela's writing style is very much like a sermon or inspirational speech. With a partner, take turns reading aloud passages from *Long Walk to Freedom*. What makes this piece effective when read aloud?

8. **Connect to Life** From dictators that you might have read about in the newspaper to bullies in the playground, can you think of an example that supports Mandela's notion that the oppressor is as trapped as the oppressed? Explain.

Literary Analysis

MEMOIR In a **memoir** the author recalls significant events in his or her own life. Memoirs are usually told from the first-person point of view and are accounts of real occurrences. The author often establishes connections between his or her life and world events. Besides facts, a memoir may include feelings and opinions that give an idea of the impact of history on people's lives.

Cooperative Learning Activity
As a class, make a chart that lists key events in Mandela's life and what he learned from them. Afterward, discuss how these events, as well as the insights he gained from them, linked Mandela more and more to his country and humanity in general.

Experiences in Mandela's Life	What He Learned from Them
As a child, Mandela likes to swim and roast mealies under the stars.	Looking back, he realizes that he was truly born free.
Mandela experiences hardships in prison.	He learns that even in the guards he can still see a "glimmer of humanity."

Connect to the Literature

1. **What Do You Think?** Accept all reasonable responses.

Comprehension Check
- One has obligations to one's family and to one's community and country.
- He realized that he had to "liberate the oppressed and oppressor both."

Use Selection Quiz **Unit Five Resource Book,** p. 41.

Think Critically

2. Possible Response: Mandela's understanding of freedom changed from a very personal one to a more expansive one. As a child, Mandela believed that he was born free. His entry into young adulthood, however, was marked by the realization that he was not free. As a young lawyer, he realized the extent of oppression in his country. His final transformation came when he realized that the oppressor too was not free.

3. Possible Response: His goals are narrow, relating only to his own life as he lives it from day to day. Given Mandela's later understanding of freedom, he may have thought that his early ideas had more to do with being confined than being free.

4. Accept all reasonable responses.

5. Possible Response: Mandela believes that true freedom is only reached when oppressed and oppressor both are free. The freedom to be free is the freedom to work toward that kind of harmony.

6. Possible Response: The main idea of the selection is Mandela's ongoing search to find freedom; every time Mandela thinks that he has found freedom, he is awakened to the fact that his search must continue.

Use **Reading and Critical Thinking Transparencies,** p. 25, for additional support.

Literary Analysis

Memoir Students might mention joining the African National Congress, living as a young man in Johannesburg, and walking out of prison.

Extend Interpretations

7. **Style** Encourage students to focus on the last paragraph in particular. Draw their attention to how the sentences build in length, going from simple to complex. Taken together, the sentences require the speaker to take breaths so that his or her voice can build in intensity to finish each sentence.

8. **Connect to Life** Accept all reasonable responses. Students might identify specific leaders or notorious people of the past and the present. They should be able to explain their responses.

Writing Options

Personal Essay Students' essays will vary but should 1) discuss the meanings of the terms *fear* and *courage* and 2) describe a time when the student or someone known by the student acted courageously.

Activities & Explorations

South African Music Present-day South African music includes traditional music, jazz, hip-hop, and contemporary popular music. In their reports to the class, students should tell what they like about South African music and play examples.

Inquiry & Research

Apartheid Students' reports should explain what apartheid was, how it was enforced, who opposed it, and how it ended. Resources should include library resources and, if possible, the Internet. You may want to show students how to credit sources. This activity is particularly suited to gifted and talented students. **To make the activity easier,** help each student identify one source to research. Share findings through a discussion or a group product, such as a bulletin board display.

 Use **Writing Transparencies,** p. 55, for additional support.

Vocabulary and Spelling

Exercise A
1. a
2. b
3. c
4. a
5. c

Exercise B
1. The suffix -*able* is added to complete words.
2. The final consonant in a stressed VC syllable is doubled when -*able* is added.
3. Silent *e* is sometimes dropped when -*able* is added.
4. The suffix -*ible* is added to roots.

Writing Options

Personal Essay Mandela says, "The brave man is not he who does not feel afraid, but he who conquers that fear." Write an essay in which you discuss fear and courage and describe a time when you or someone you know acted courageously. Place the essay in your **Working Portfolio.**

Writing Handbook
See p. R35: Explanatory Writing.

Activities & Explorations

South African Music Listen to audiotapes or CDs of present-day South African music. Give a report to the class on what you like about the music, playing examples for everyone to hear. ~ **SPEAKING AND LISTENING**

Inquiry & Research

 SOCIAL STUDIES APARTHEID

Use library resources and the Internet to find out about apartheid. What was it? How was it enforced? Who opposed it, and how did apartheid finally end? Write a brief report on your findings and present it to the class.

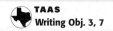 **More Online: Research Starter** www.mcdougallittell.com

Vocabulary and Spelling

EXERCISE A: ANTONYMS On your paper, write the letter of the word that is most opposite in meaning to each boldfaced word.

1. **resiliency:** (a) brittleness (b) strength (c) flexibility
2. **transitory:** (a) lively (b) lasting (c) short
3. **incomprehensible:** (a) companionable (b) spoken (c) understandable
4. **curtailed:** (a) enlarged (b) worried (c) abandoned
5. **indivisible:** (a) invisible (b) understandable (c) divisible

EXERCISE B: SUFFIXES -*able* **AND** -*ible* Study the spelling words. Then, on a sheet of paper, answer the questions.

adapt + able = adaptable	vis + ible = visible
avail + able = available	leg + ible = legible
forget + able = forgettable	divis + ible = divisible
control + able = controllable	indivis + ible = indivisible
advise + able = advisable	cred + ible = credible
excite + able = excitable	tang + ible = tangible
change + able = changeable	ed + ible = edible
notice + able = noticeable	aud + ible = audible

1. Is the suffix -*able* added to complete words or to roots?
2. How do the two words ending with a single vowel plus a single consonant in a stressed syllable change when -*able* is added?
3. Four of the base words end with a silent *e*. What happens to the *e* in the first two examples?
4. Is the suffix -*ible* added to complete words or to roots?

Spelling Handbook, p. R86

Teaching Options

Mini Lesson Spelling   **TEKS 16C**   **TAAS Writing Obj. 3, 7**

THE SUFFIXES -*ABLE* **AND** -*IBLE*

Instruction Tell students that the suffix -*able* is added to complete words. When -*able* is added to a word that ends with a stressed syllable and a vowel-consonant pair, the final consonant is doubled: *regret* + -*able* = *regrettable*. In some cases, the *e* is dropped when -*able* is added to words that end with silent *e*. Final *y* changes to *i* when -*able* is added.

The suffix -*ible* is added to roots. It often requires spelling changes: *sense* + -*ible* = *sensible*

-*able* **and** -*ible* **words from the selection:**
impossible, incomprehensible, terrible, indivisible, honorable

Other -*able* **and** -*ible* **words:**
redeemable, dependable, unforgettable, measurable, excitable, reliable

Exercises Have students use several words from this lesson, or other words ending in -*able* and -*ible,* to write a short profile of Nelson Mandela.

 Use **Unit Five Resource Book,** p. 40 for more practice.

Grammar in Context: Using Adjective Clauses

A writer can add important information to nouns with adjective clauses.

> In South Africa, a man of color **who attempted to live as a human being** was punished and isolated.

An **adjective clause** modifies a noun or pronoun and usually follows the word it modifies. Often it begins with a relative pronoun, such as *that, what, which, who, whom,* or *whose.*

Apply to Your Writing Adjective clauses let you make nouns more precise and help you avoid a series of short, choppy sentences. Compare:

The National Assembly adopted a new constitution. The constitution guarantees equal rights to all.

The National Assembly adopted a new constitution that guarantees equal rights to all.

WRITING EXERCISE Combine these sentences by turning one of them into an adjective clause.

Example: Original I was free to swim in the clear stream. The stream ran through my village.

Rewritten I was free to swim in the clear stream that ran through my village.

1. I never lost my hope. I hoped a great transformation would occur.
2. A father must say no to the child. A father loves the child dearly.
3. I have known men and women. They risked their lives for an idea.
4. Mandela started his walk on the long road. The road led to freedom.
5. The policy of apartheid created a deep wound in my country. The policy ended in 1991.

Grammar Handbook Phrases and Clauses, p. R72

"My long walk is not yet ended."

Nelson Mandela
born 1918

Early Years Nelson Rolihlahla Mandela was born in an African village, the son of a tribal chief. "Rolihlahla" means "pulling the branch of a tree" or "troublemaker." As a boy he herded sheep and cattle and played hunting games with his friends.

Imprisonment After earning a law degree, Mandela and a friend opened the first black law office in South Africa. He joined the African National Congress (ANC) in 1944 and later became its president. The ANC was outlawed by the white government in 1960 because it resisted apartheid, but Mandela continued to lead protests. He was arrested in 1962, convicted of sabotage and treason, and sentenced to life in prison on Robben Island. He spent 27 years in prison and became an international symbol of the fight for racial justice.

Justice Achieved In 1990 Mandela was finally freed to international acclaim. He then worked with white government leaders to end apartheid and give black Africans the right to vote. For their work to end apartheid, Mandela and then–South African president F. W. de Klerk won the Nobel Prize for peace in 1993. In 1994, South Africa held its first election in which all citizens could vote. The ANC party won a majority, and Nelson Mandela became the first black president of South Africa.

Grammar in Context
WRITING EXERCISE
Possible Responses:

1. I never lost my hope that a great transformation would occur.
2. A father must say no to the child whom he loves dearly.
3. I have known men and women who risked their lives for an idea.
4. Mandela started his walk on the long road that led to freedom.
5. The policy of apartheid, which ended in 1991, created a deep wound in my country.

Nelson Mandela

Mandela has established the Nelson Mandela Children's Fund to help South African children who are in need. According to Mandela himself, the reason for the fund is to "help inspire new efforts and strengthen existing ones aimed at repairing the ravaged fabric of our youth's social and economic circumstances." Mandela wants the fund to be something to which people from all walks of life can contribute.

 Mini Lesson **Grammar**  **TEKS 16B, 17A** 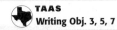 **TAAS Writing Obj. 3, 5, 7**

ADJECTIVE CLAUSES

Instruction Explain that adjective clauses provide details about a person, place, or thing. They often start with relative pronouns such as *who, that,* and *which.* Adjective clauses are set off by commas when they convey information that is not essential to the sentence. Commas are not used with clauses that give essential information. In general, *that* is used for essential information about a place or thing. *Which* is used for nonessential information, set off by commas.

Exercises Have students underline the adjective clause in each sentence and insert commas where needed.

1. Mandela spent his life working for freedom in South Africa, <u>which is a country in Africa</u>.
2. People of color <u>who lived in South Africa</u> long endured a system of oppression.
3. Mandela joined a political party <u>that opposed apartheid</u>.

4. His dedication created hardship for his family, <u>who could not have him present as husband and father</u>.

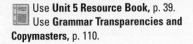 Use **Unit 5 Resource Book,** p. 39.
Use **Grammar Transparencies and Copymasters,** p. 110.

 Use McDougal Littell's *Language Network,* Chapter 8, for more instruction and practice in adjective clauses.

Objectives

1. understand and appreciate **lyric poetry** (Literary Analysis)
2. understand the use and significance of **imagery** (Literary Analysis)
3. utilize the reading skill **paraphrasing** (active reading)

Summary

Both of these poems describe animals who endure despite different hardships. The elephant in Kipling's poem is sick of working for people. It wants to return to its former power and life. At night—perhaps only in its imagination—it returns to the wild. There it forgets its subjugation, and, as a free creature, revisits lost loves and friends. Mary Oliver's subject, a female turtle, struggles up the beach to lay her eggs in the sand. She doesn't think or dream about any goals. She is part of the natural world around her; she is bound to the water and plants and birds "by an unbreakable string."

Thematic Link

The subjects of both poems face formidable opponents. The elephant's foe is human, while the turtle's is nature itself.

5-Minute Warm-Up

Daily Language SkillBuilder **TEKS 17D, 17G**

Have students **proofread** the display sentences on page 653j and write them correctly. The sentences also appear on Transparency 23 of **Grammar Transparencies and Copymasters.**

The Elephant

Poetry by RUDYARD KIPLING

The Turtle

Poetry by MARY OLIVER

(**Connect to Your Life**)

No Choice We don't always have a choice about what happens in life. With a small group of classmates, talk about an experience when you or someone you know had to do something or endure something and had no choice about it. Was it a positive or negative experience?

Build Background

CONNECT TO SCIENCE

Rudyard Kipling was born and lived in India, where elephants were used as work animals. Elephants are still used today in the logging industry in some Asian countries. An elephant can carry a heavy load on its back and can carry a log as heavy as 600 pounds with its trunk.

Mary Oliver's poem describes the egg-laying behavior of a pond turtle. All turtles, even species that live in water, lay their eggs on land. The female crawls to a nesting site, digs a hole with her back feet, and lays her eggs. She covers them with sand or plant material, leaves the nest, and does not return. Baby turtles must dig their way out, find food, and survive entirely on their own.

Focus Your Reading

LITERARY ANALYSIS **IMAGERY** Words and phrases that create vivid sensory experiences for the reader are called **images** or **sensory details.** For example, Pablo Neruda's description of the artichoke as a soldier in "Ode to an Artichoke" is an example of a visual image.

> *The soft-hearted*
> *artichoke*
> *put on armor,*
> *stood at attention . . .*

Many images appeal to the sense of sight, but images may also appeal to hearing, smell, taste, and touch. As you read the poems, pay attention to the imagery.

ACTIVE READING **PARAPHRASING** When you paraphrase something, you restate it in your own words. Paraphrasing can often help you better understand a poem. A paraphrase often uses simpler forms or words than the original, but it is not necessarily shorter, since it is not a summary. A paraphrase is a reshaping of information. To paraphrase, you need to

- find the **main idea** the writer conveys
- notice **details** that indicate what the writer feels or sees
- if possible, think of simpler or more familiar ways of saying what the writer has written

READER'S NOTEBOOK As you read these poems, think of ways you might paraphrase them. This is difficult with poetry; a paraphrase will lack the power and subtlety of the original, but look for main ideas that you could state in your own words and jot them down.

 See the Skills Trace at the beginning of the unit for information on TEKS covered in this lesson.

740 UNIT FIVE PART 2: AGAINST THE ODDS

LESSON RESOURCES

UNIT FIVE RESOURCE BOOK, pp. 42–43

ASSESSMENT
Formal Assessment, pp. 117–118

Teacher's Guide to Assessment and Portfolio Use

Test Generator

SKILLS TRANSPARENCIES AND COPYMASTERS
Literary Analysis
- Poetry: Figurative Language, TR 19 (for Cooperative Activity, p. 743)

Reading and Critical Thinking
- Paraphrasing, TR 16 (for Thinking Through the Literature, p. 743)

Grammar
- Parallelism, CM 143–144 (for Mini Lesson, p. 742)
- Commas in a series, CM 125 (for Mini Lesson, p. 744)

INTEGRATED TECHNOLOGY
Audio Library

Visit our website:
www.mcdougallittell.com

The Elephant

by
RUDYARD KIPLING

I will remember what I was. I am sick of rope and chain—
  I will remember my old strength and all my forest-affairs.
I will not sell my back to man for a bundle of sugar-cane.
  I will go out to my own kind, and the wood-folk in their lairs.

I will go out until the day, until the morning break,
  Out to the winds' untainted kiss, the waters' clean caress.
I will forget my ankle-ring and snap my picket-stake.
  I will revisit my lost loves, and playmates masterless!

National Museum of Khmer Art,
Phnom Penh, Cambodia.

Thinking Through the Literature

- Why does the elephant yearn for its "past life"?
- The elephant says, "I will go out until the day." What does the elephant mean?
- What is the contrast between the elephant's "lost loves, and playmates" and itself?

THE ELEPHANT / THE TURTLE **741**

To help students recognize the distinguishing features of poetry, ask them to identify images in each poem. Ask what aspect of the experience each image emphasizes.

Possible Responses: The rope and chain emphasizes the elephant's bondage; the winds' kiss emphasizes the elephant's affection for it, as well as its sweetness

 Use **Unit Five Resource Book,** p. 43 for guidance in reading the selection.

Active Reading PARAPHRASING

Remind students that paraphrasing, or restating passages in their own words, is a skill that can help them to understand poetry. As students read, encourage them to paraphrase each stanza on paper.

 Use **Unit Five Resource Book,** p. 42 for guidance in reading the selection.

Literary Analysis: STANZA

Each poem is divided into stanzas. Ask students how their stanza patterns are alike and different.

Possible Responses: The stanzas are each about one main idea; in one poem, the pattern is regular, while in the other it is not.

The Turtle

by
MARY
OLIVER

breaks from the blue-black
skin of the water, dragging her shell
with its mossy scutes[1]
across the shallows and through the rushes
and over the mudflats, to the uprise,
to the yellow sand,
to dig with her ungainly[2] feet
a nest, and hunker there spewing
her white eggs down
into the darkness, and you think

of her patience, her fortitude,[3]
her determination to complete
what she was born to do—
and then you realize a greater thing—
she doesn't consider
what she was born to do.
She's only filled
with an old blind wish.
It isn't even hers but came to her
in the rain or the soft wind,
which is a gate through which her life keeps walking.

She can't see
herself apart from the rest of the world
or the world from what she must do
every spring.
Crawling up the high hill,
luminous[4] under the sand that has packed against her skin.
she doesn't dream
she knows
she is a part of the pond she lives in,
the tall trees are her children,
the birds that swim above her
are tied to her by an unbreakable string.

Soup tureen in the form of a turtle (1790s). Sheffield City Museum, South Yorkshire, U.K./Bridgeman Art Library, London/New York.

---

1. **scutes** (sküts): the bottom of the turtle's shell.
2. **ungainly:** clumsy.
3. **fortitude:** strength.
4. **luminous:** glowing.

Teaching Options

 Mini Lesson **Grammar** TEKS 17C TAAS Writing Obj. 6

PARALLELISM

Instruction Explain that when two or more ideas of a sentence have the same importance, those ideas should be expressed using the same parts of speech. Point out the highlighted passages, asking students to identify the four prepositional phrases. Discuss alternatives and how awkward they would sound. Do the same with the highlighted nouns.

Application Have students invent other phrases and nouns that would be parallel to the ones that are highlighted in the poem.

Then have students read this sentence and identify the part that is not parallel. Discuss how they might revise it:

The turtle traveled through blue-black water, dense rushes, sticky mudflats, and sand that was hot.

 Use **Grammar Transparencies and Copymasters,** p. 143–144.

 Use McDougal Littell's **Language Network,** Chapter 8, for more instruction and practice in parallel construction.

Connect to the Literature

1. What Do You Think?
What emotions or thoughts did the last lines of "The Turtle" evoke in you?

Comprehension Check
- What qualities does the turtle need to "complete / what she was born to do"?
- What does the turtle "know" about her relationship to nature?

Think Critically

2. In the first stanza, what would you say impresses the speaker about the turtle's egg laying?

3. In the second stanza, the speaker realizes a "greater thing," namely, that the turtle is filled "with an old blind wish." What do you think this means?

THINK ABOUT
- "she doesn't consider / what she was born to do"
- "She can't see / herself apart from the rest of the world"
- "she knows / she is a part of the pond she lives in"

4. Both the elephant and the turtle have strong relationships to nature. How would you compare and contrast those relationships?

5. **ACTIVE READING** **PARAPHRASING** Select one of the two poems and rewrite it, or a portion of it, in your own words. Look at the notes you took in your ▯READER'S NOTEBOOK for ideas. Your paraphrase should include the important elements of the poem you choose. Share your paraphrase with the class. Compare it with the paraphrases your classmates wrote.

Extend Interpretations

6. Writer's Style Mary Oliver says when reading poetry a reader should, "look for verbs of muscle." How might this apply to each poem?

7. Connect to Life Do you think enough attention is paid to wild animals' need for their environment?

Literary Analysis

IMAGERY Words or phrases that appeal to a reader's senses are called images or sensory details. **Imagery** helps the reader see, hear, taste, smell, or feel what the poet is describing. For example, Mary Oliver writes that the turtle is "luminous under the sand that has packed against her skin." This imagery appealing to the reader's senses of sight and touch makes the description mean more than "the turtle was covered with sand." Similarly, when the elephant says, "I will not sell my back to man for a bundle of sugar-cane," the imagery creates a more powerful picture than saying, "I don't like carrying heavy objects."

Cooperative Learning Activity
With a partner, go back through both poems and use a chart to note images that strike you and their effect in the poems. Then, in a small group, discuss the images you have chosen.

"The Elephant"	"The Turtle"
Image: rope and chain **Effect:** It helped me to imagine how the elephant is being held captive.	**Image:** breaking through "the blue-black skin" of the water **Effect:** It helped me to see the stillness of the water.

Writing Options

1. **Editorial About Wild Animals** Remind students that a good editorial should contain a clear statement of opinion, supported by facts and reasons.

   Use **Writing Transparencies**, p. 13, for additional support.

2. **Animal Poem or Description** Encourage **visual learners** to begin by creating drawings or paintings of the animals. Other students may find word webs or sensory detail charts useful.

Activities & Explorations

1. **Poem Illustration** Remind students that their art might be symbolic instead of representational.

2. **Choral Reading** Point out that speed and rhythm can help students convey meaning.

   Use **Communications Transparencies and Copymasters**, p. 11, for additional support.

3. **Nature Video** Since the poem contains only a few details about turtle egg laying, suggest that students first list those details and then watch the video.

Inquiry & Research

Elephants and People Remind students that many myths were created about elephant behavior in the past, and students should be careful to separate fact from fancy.

Mary Oliver

Other animals that Mary Oliver has written about include the following: egrets, fish, fox, geese, herons, horses, hummingbirds, whales, lambs, moles, owls, sharks, snails, snakes, starfish, toads, and vultures.

Author Activity

"What blazes the trail is not necessarily pretty" Point out that students may need to read several poems before they can form an opinion about Oliver's view of nature.

Writing Options

1. Editorial About Wild Animals Write an editorial about using captive wild animals either as work animals or for entertainment in circuses. Place the editorial in your **Working Portfolio.**

2. Animal Poem or Description Think of an animal that has made a lasting impression on you. What is unique about this animal? Write a poem or a descriptive paragraph about the animal.

Writing Handbook
See p. R31: Description.

Activities & Explorations

1. Poem Illustration Draw or paint an illustration for either "The Turtle" or "The Elephant." Include details suggested by the poem. ~ **ART**

2. Choral Reading With a small group, practice a choral reading of both poems. Practice reading so that the meaning will be clear to a listener. Present your choral reading to the class.
~ **SPEAKING AND LISTENING**

3. Nature Video Find and watch a natural-science video of turtles laying eggs. How accurate is the description in the poem? Report your findings to the class.
~ **SPEAKING AND LISTENING**

Inquiry & Research

Elephants and People
Observers have commented on the many "human" qualities elephants seem to have. Elephants have long memories. Female elephants will care for each other's young. Use library or other resources to investigate elephant behavior and how it resembles human behavior. Present your report to the rest of the class.

"The poem was made not just to exist, but to speak—to be company."

Mary Oliver
born 1935

Solitary Childhood Mary Oliver is known for highly descriptive poems about nature. She grew up in a small Ohio town and knew early on she wanted to write poetry. Her "friends" were the poets she read in books.

Student of Nature As a high school student, Oliver was happier rambling around in the woods than she was in the classroom. She always carried a knapsack filled with books and notebooks in which she recorded her thoughts and observations of nature. The poetry of Walt Whitman was always among the books she carried with her. She later described Whitman as "the brother I did not have."

Writing Poetry Oliver attended Ohio State University and Vassar College. Her first book of poems appeared in 1963. Mary Oliver has written more than 10 books of poetry and won many prizes. Her collection entitled *American Primitive* won the Pulitzer Prize and her *New and Selected Poems* won the National Book Award. She lives in Provincetown, Massachusetts.

AUTHOR ACTIVITY
"What blazes the trail is not necessarily pretty." Oliver's poem "Skunk Cabbage" ends with this line. Read some of her other poems. Does this thought apply to them? What would you say about Oliver's view of nature?

Rudyard Kipling
For a biography, see page 137.

Teaching Options

Mini Lesson Grammar   TEKS 16B, 17C   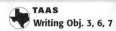TAAS Writing Obj. 3, 6, 7

COMMAS IN A SERIES

Instruction Remind students to place a comma after each item in a series except the last one. Display the following sentence:
We saw a turtle, an African elephant, and many other animals.

Exercises Have students rewrite the following sentences, adding commas where they are necessary. If a sentence is correct, have them write *correct*.
1. He is sick of ropes, chains, ankle-rings and mankind.

2. He craves the winds' untainted kiss, the waters' clean caress, and his other lost loves. *(correct)*
3. The turtle has patience, fortitude and determination.
4. She loves the pond, the tall trees and the birds.

Use **Grammar Transparencies and Copymasters**, p. 125.

Use McDougal Littell's *Language Network,* Chapter 11, for more instruction and practice in using commas in a series.

Thinking Historically

English has absorbed many words from other languages over the centuries. Understanding a word's **etymology**—its history and origin—can help you to make sense of words you don't know and to recognize family relationships between words.

Most English words can be traced back to Old English (the earliest form of the language), Latin, or Greek, but English has borrowed words from other languages as well.

> As they skirted the great open space of the **Hippodrome**, where the chariot races would be held on the second day of the Games, they came up with a couple of the Athenian contingent, strolling under the plane trees.
>
> —Rosemary Sutcliff, "A Crown of Wild Olive"

Greek *hippos:* horse
and *dromos:* racecourse

Latin *carrus:* cart

Old English *trēow:* tree

Strategies for Building Vocabulary

Learning about a word's origins will give you deeper knowledge of the word and will help you remember its meaning. It can also help you understand the meanings of related words. Use the following strategies to figure out etymology.

❶ **Use a Dictionary** An easy way to find a word's etymology is to use a dictionary. This information will usually appear at the beginning or end of the entry. Look at this dictionary entry for *contradict:*

con•tra•dict (kŏn′trə-dĭkt′) *v.* **-dict•ed, -dict•ing, -dicts.** —*tr.* **1.** To assert or express the opposite of (a statement). **2.** To deny the statement of. See synonyms at **deny. 3.** To be contrary to; be inconsistent with. —*intr.* To utter a contradictory statement. [Lat. *contrādīcere, contrādict-,* to speak against : *contrā-,* contra- + *dīcere,* to speak] —**con′tra•dict′a•ble** *adj.* —**con′tra•dict′er, con′tra•dict′or** *n.*

This entry shows that *contradict* came from Latin, with the prefix *contra-,* "against," and *dicere,* "to speak." Its meaning hasn't changed much over time. Some words have gone through a variety of stages. In this situation the

first word listed is the most recent, and the list moves backward in time from there.

❷ **Recognize Word Families** Words with the same origin usually have related meanings. The words in the following chart all come from the Latin word *sistere,* which means "to place, set, stop, or stand." As you can see, all of the words listed have something to do with firmness.

Words Derived from Latin *sistere*	
insist	to be firm in a demand
persist	to be stubbornly insistent or repetitious
resist	to try to fend off

EXERCISE Look up each word in a dictionary. Trace the derivation back to the oldest word listed and its meaning.

1. transitory
2. illustrious
3. resilient
4. seize
5. allege
6. frankfurter
7. footpath
8. honor
9. bottle
10. Olympics

Objectives

- use word origins as an aid to understanding historical influences on English word meanings
- use a dictionary to discover details of a word's etymology
- expand vocabulary by learning to recognize word families, or words connected by origin and meaning

VOCABULARY EXERCISE
Possible Responses:

1. from Latin *transitus* "passage"
2. from Latin *illustrare* "to give glory, to shine upon"
3. from Latin *resilire* "to leap back"
4. from Old French *seisir* "to take possession," of Germanic origin
5. from Latin *ex* (out) + *litigare* "to sue"
6. from Frankfurt, a city in Germany where this sausage was first made
7. combines the words *foot* and *path; foot* is from Old English *fot,* and *path* is from Old English *pæth*
8. Middle English, from Old French, from Latin
9. from Middle English *botel,* from Old French *Botele,* from Medieval Latin *buticula,* from Late Latin *buttis,* "cask"
10. from Olympia, a plain in ancient Greece where ancient Olympic games were first held

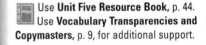 Use **Unit Five Resource Book,** p. 44.
Use **Vocabulary Transparencies and Copymasters,** p. 9, for additional support.

OVERVIEW

Objectives

- read and appreciate the works of one of America's most significant writers of literature for young adults
- understand the contribution of Virginia Hamilton's family to her artistic vision
- trace the influence of her experiences on her writing
- learn her views on writing and reading

This Author Study offers a unique opportunity for students to explore varied genres from a contemporary African-American writer. Students will learn how Virginia Hamilton's family and background have been a catalyst for her writing. Additionally, they will be exposed to the author's own insights about the creative process.

LIFE AND TIMES

Sustaining Tradition

A Virginia Hamilton thinks "in terms of stories," and she describes her creative process as a way to find out how the story ends. She creates the characters, and they tell the stories for her. Just as her relatives bequeathed their knowledge to her through their stories, she wants her books to fill the void that exists in many children's lives. She believes they grow up divorced from their past and ignorant of the history that has contributed to who they are.

Author Study VIRGINIA HAMILTON

CONTENTS

Writer of Past and Present

"The past moves me and with me, although I remove myself from it. Its light often shines on this night traveler: and when it does, I scribble it down."

born 1936

"EXCEPTIONALLY FINE STORYTELLERS"

A Virginia Hamilton grew up with stories. The youngest of five children, she was raised on a 12-acre farm near Yellow Springs, Ohio. In the quiet country evenings, sitting by the fire or on the porch, she loved listening to her parents, aunts, and uncles, who were all storytellers. They were "exceptionally fine storytellers," Hamilton has noted, "and realized, although I don't know how consciously, that they were passing along heritage and culture and a pride in their *history*."

Virginia (*right*) with her uncle and cousin.

Her LIFE and TIMES

1936 Born March 12 in Yellow Springs, Ohio	**1952** Receives scholarship to Antioch College	**1958** Moves to New York City	**1960** Marries Arnold Adoff
1930	**1940**	**1950**	**1960**
	1941 United States enters World War II.	**1942** Congress of Racial Equality (CORE) founded	**1950–1953** Korean War Gen. MacArthur leads UN forces, 1950–1951.

746

See the Skills Trace at the beginning of the unit for information on TEKS covered in this lesson.

TEKS

Fascinated by the stories she heard, Hamilton began to keep a journal in which she wrote things that she thought were interesting or exciting. She loved to read and won prizes in school for reading the most books. At school in the 1940s, Hamilton was the only black child in her class until the seventh grade. Very little was taught in school about black history or accomplishment, but the lively talk and family stories in the Hamilton's home—such as how her maternal grandfather, Levi Perry, escaped from slavery by the Underground Railroad—gave her a deep and lasting pride in her African-American heritage.

"I WANTED WITH ALL MY SOUL TO GET TO MANHATTAN"

After she graduated from high school, Hamilton accepted a scholarship to nearby Antioch College, where she majored in writing. But she yearned for new surroundings. Of that period in her life, Hamilton has written: "I wanted with all my soul to get to Manhattan, but it seemed I was trapped forever." Finally, she found a summer job as a bookkeeper in New York City. Captivated by city life, she left college and moved to New York City.

C

D

Virginia Hamilton in New York City.

Other Firsts

B Virginia Hamilton's professional career has been marked by firsts. In 1992, she became the first American since 1978 to win the Hans Christian Andersen Medal, an honor for writers of children's literature that is comparable to a Nobel Prize. She was the first children's author to be awarded the MacArthur Fellowship. Her achievements have opened a trail for other writers to follow. In her writing too, Virginia Hamilton has fearlessly explored new territory. She was the first to examine interracial dating among teenagers in her book *A White Romance*. *The House of Dies Drear* is the first African-American children's novel to be based on slave history.

Link to Her Past

C Grandpa Levi Perry arrived in Ohio around 1857 as a fugitive slave. His mother did not arrive with him, and some accounts say that she was forced to go back to the plantation by her owner. Virginia's mother told her that every year, her father would sit his ten children down and narrate the story of his escape from slavery. He did this so that they would never allow slavery to happen to them.

Life in the City

D When Virginia Hamilton moved to New York City, she worked part time as a cost accountant at an engineering firm. The rest of the day she reserved for writing. She describes this time as very solitary.

| **1968** Publishes *The House of Dies Drear* | **1975** Wins Newbery Medal and National Book Award | | **1995** Receives Laura Ingalls Wilder Medal for lasting contributions to children's literature | **1999** Publishes *Bluish* |

1970   **1980**   **1990**   **2000**

| **1964** Civil Rights Act passed. | **1965–1973** U.S. ground troops in Vietnam War | **1968** Martin Luther King, Jr., is assassinated. | | **1986** The space shuttle *Challenger* explodes. | **1991** Soviet Union breaks up. |

The Birth of *Zeely*

E One of Virginia Hamilton's classmates from the New School for Social Research encouraged her to turn a college short story into a children's book. *Zeely* was the result. Virginia Hamilton says that *Zeely* is not a "problem book about integration." It is a book about black characters being themselves. The book struck a chord in 1967, a time when black Americans were struggling to be appreciated for who they were.

Importance of Family

F The theme of the family figures prominently in Virginia Hamilton's writing. Living on the family farm has kept her close to the source of her inspiration. Before her mother's death at the age of 97, Virginia Hamilton was able to spend time with her and record stories that her mother remembered in those final years. She wrote *Her Stories*, a collection of female-oriented folktales, as a tribute to her mother.

Wanderers

G Virginia Hamilton describes herself and her family as wanderers. She travels to New York frequently, has taught at Queens College and Ohio State University, and vacations in Puerto Rico and Florida. But she always returns home. Ohio is her base, the source of her nourishment.

In the 1950s, the East Village, the section of New York City where Hamilton lived, was an exciting place to be. It was an active, integrated community of writers, artists, and musicians. The place inspired Hamilton to continue her reading and writing. Among other works of literature, she read the classics and works by Mexican writers. She also worked at different jobs while she continued her study of writing at The New School for Social Research. In 1960 she married Arnold Adoff, a young poet. And, remembering the stories she had heard as a child, Hamilton began to keep a scrapbook about Africa.

"WHAT I SEE IS ANOTHER TIME"

E Hamilton's interest in Africa inspired her first published novel, *Zeely* (1967), the story of a young girl who imagines that a woman in her town is an African queen. Soon after the publication of *Zeely*, Hamilton moved back to Yellow Springs, Ohio. Memories of the stories Hamilton heard as a child continue to nourish her writing. "I choose what I see, and what I see is another time," Hamilton has said. She explains:

Memories of all those years, of summer days, winter nights, storms and sunshine, have given ample food to my imagination all of my life. So has living here in my hometown of Yellow Springs, Ohio. My **F** *husband and I built our house on the last few acres of my family's farm.*

Today, Hamilton and her husband still live and work in Yellow Springs. She continues to write for young people in several genres—including fiction, folktales, fantasy, and nonfiction. Hamilton spends **G** time traveling and making speeches, but her first love is writing. She has published more than 34 books and collected many awards.

Virginia Hamilton and her husband Arnold Adoff, at home in Ohio

TALKING WITH VIRGINIA HAMILTON

In the following interview, Hamilton responds to questions about her life and her writing.

Q: Do you use a computer or word processor to do your writing?

A: When I'm writing, I use a computer with a word processing program.

Q: How do you start writing a novel?

A: That's a funny question. You just start, until a paragraph becomes a page and then you keep going page by page.

Q: Who influenced you to be a writer?

A: I started writing when I was in grade school, so I don't know who influenced me. I heard lots of stories from family.

Q: How do you find a good illustrator for your books?

A: I choose illustrators with my editor. We decide who would be good for a particular book.

Q: Besides yourself, what other authors do you enjoy reading?

A: I read many in my field and other adult writers: Cynthia Voigt, for one. I read extensively in my field.

Q: Do you have any advice for young writers?

A: Young writers should read as much as they can and write for at least 15 minutes a day, and keep a journal.

Q: Would there be any other occupation that you would be interested [in] other than being an author?

A: In my younger days I was a singer. I used to sing in clubs, and I have a daughter who is an opera singer and a son who is a song writer with his own band. So if I weren't a writer, I would be a singer.

Q: Do you visit classrooms and talk with students?

A: I don't do it anymore. I get so many requests, I can't go to schools and get my work done. I do answer a lot of fan mail and email.

Q: What was your favorite book as a child?

A: I loved the Nancy Drew books, because that's what was available. She had her own car and was very independent and solved mysteries.

Q: Did you keep a journal as a young child?

A: I kept a notebook and put everything in it that I thought was exciting. Unfortunately, I lost it when I was 13.

Q: Do you think that books are the future for kids?

A: I think reading is the future for kids whether they read from a computer or books. I think reading leads to books—I think books will continue READING!

More Online: Author Link
www.mcdougallittell.com

NetActivities: Author Exploration

The World at Her Fingertips

Ⓗ Although Virginia Hamilton's husband, poet Arnold Adoff, still uses a Smith Corona for his writing, she not only writes on the computer but has a great enthusiasm for the Internet. She says that she has an awareness of all the people in the world when she "surfs the net." There are no boundaries or geographical limitations to her traveling on the web.

Reason for Writing

Ⓘ Virginia Hamilton disdains the notion that she is trying to accomplish something in each book that she writes. Rather her goal is to tell a good story.

Field of Dreams

Ⓙ Virginia Hamilton says that in her family, they were encouraged to have their own dreams. When Virginia told her older sister that she was going to be a famous writer, her sister greeted the idea with enthusiasm because Virginia's success would make her famous too.

OVERVIEW

 This selection is included in the **Grade 7 InterActive Reader.**

Objectives
1. to understand and appreciate **literary nonfiction (Literary Analysis)**
2. to apply the reading skill **monitor (Active Reading)**

Summary
Anthony Burns, an escaped slave from Virginia, is stunned when slave hunters capture him in Boston. Under the Fugitive Slave Act, he will be returned to his master, Colonel Suttle, after a perfunctory hearing. Knowing he will be punished for any trouble that he causes Colonel Suttle, Anthony hesitates before accepting the help of Richard Henry Dana, a prominent abolitionist lawyer. Dana is determined to scrutinize court proceedings for any hint of impropriety or error while Theodore Parker and other members of the Vigilance Committee, sworn to protect black inhabitants of Boston from bounty hunters, work on publicizing Anthony's case and securing his freedom through other methods. Concerned citizens of Boston see Anthony as a symbol of freedom and take up his cause.

Thematic Link
Dana is determined to defend Anthony Burns's freedom against all odds.

5-Minute Warm-Up

Daily Language SkillBuilder TEKS 16B, 17G

Have students **proofread** the display sentences on page 653K and write them correctly. The sentences also appear on Transparency 23 of **Grammar Transparencies and Copymasters.**

 Preteaching Vocabulary

If you would like to preteach the WORDS TO KNOW for this selection, use the Mini Lesson, p. 752.

"Overnight, without his ever knowing it, Anthony Burns became a symbol of freedom."

from Anthony Burns: The Defeat and Triumph of a Fugitive Slave

Nonfiction by VIRGINIA HAMILTON

Connect to Your Life

Slavery and the Abolitionists What do you know about the institution of slavery in the United States and the abolitionist movement? Make a chart like this one and fill in the first two columns. Complete the third after you read the selection.

What I Know About Slavery and Abolition	What I Want to Know	What I Learned

Build Background

CONNECT TO HISTORY In 1850 Congress enacted the Fugitive Slave Law in an attempt to prevent disputes between the Southern slaveholding states and the free states in the North. Under this law, the federal government claimed jurisdiction over the return of fugitives to slaveholders. Federal marshals were made responsible for helping recapture escaped slaves, and federal court commissioners were appointed to hear fugitive cases. Those who helped slaves to escape would be subject to fines and prison sentences. Some antislavery states—such as Massachusetts—resisted, standing by their personal liberty laws and refusing to accept the federal government's jurisdiction in these matters. Abolitionists, those who fought to abolish slavery, considered the practice of slave-catching to be kidnapping. When Anthony Burns, a fugitive from Virginia, was captured on the streets of Boston in 1854, the abolitionist community stood ready to fight for his freedom.

> **WORDS TO KNOW**
> **Vocabulary Preview**
>
> agitate — mobilize
> alleged — peer
> compliance — petty
> contradict — throb
> illustrious — wretched

Focus Your Reading

LITERARY ANALYSIS · LITERARY NONFICTION Writing that tells about actual people, places, and events is called nonfiction. Informative nonfiction provides information in a straightforward manner. **Literary nonfiction** also conveys information, but it does so by telling a story. Literary nonfiction includes literary elements like setting, character, and conflict. As you read this selection from *Anthony Burns,* notice the literary devices.

ACTIVE READING · MONITOR Good readers actively **monitor** their reading strategies as they read. They stop now and then to review what they've learned and decide whether they need to adjust the reading strategies they are using in order to better understand what they're reading. Monitoring involves questions like: Do I need to ask more questions about what is going on in the selection? Do I need to clarify more in order to better understand the roles of key characters? Do I need to take more notes to remember key details of the selection?

 READER'S NOTEBOOK As you read, use a chart to list the key characters involved in the capture, trial, and defense of Anthony Burns. In a column beside the names, jot down whether that person was trying to free Burns or return him to slavery.

TEKS See the Skills Trace at the beginning of the unit for information on TEKS covered in this lesson.

LESSON RESOURCES

UNIT FIVE RESOURCE BOOK, pp. 45–51

ASSESSMENT
Formal Assessment, pp. 119–120

Teacher's Guide to Assessment and Portfolio Use

Test Generator

SKILLS TRANSPARENCIES AND COPYMASTERS
Grammar
- Phrases and Clauses, CM 106 (for Mini Lesson, p. 754)
- Adjective Clauses, CM 109–111 (for Mini Lesson, p. 761)

Vocabulary
- Related Words, CM 77 (for Mini Lesson, p. 752)

Communications
- Persuasive Techniques TR 3 (for Mini Lesson, p. 762)

INTEGRATED TECHNOLOGY
Internet: Research Starter

Visit our website:
www.mcdougallittell.com

ANTHONY BURNS:
THE DEFEAT AND TRIUMPH OF A FUGITIVE SLAVE

BY
VIRGINIA
HAMILTON

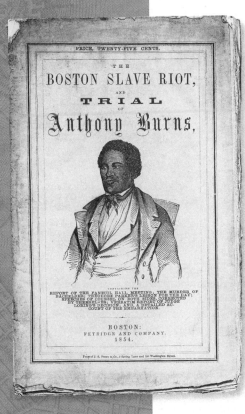

Cover of a pamphlet describing the trial of Anthony Burns and resulting protests, 1854.

Reading Skills and Strategies:
PREVIEW

Have students read the introduction and look at the portraits of the key figures in the text. Identify each man's role in the proceedings: Loring – judge, Reverend Parker – Anthony's supporter, Reverend Grimes – Anthony's friend and supporter, Richard Henry Dana – Anthony's lawyer.

Literary Analysis

LITERARY NONFICTION

Ⓐ Remind students that the writer of literary nonfiction brings the facts to life by using devices often employed by writers of fiction. Ask students to identify the ways in which the author conveys a vivid sense of character and conflict.
Possible Response: The author uses images that reinforce the hopelessness of Anthony's situation, such as "iron bars that seemed to break the day into welts of pain." The author also gives insight into Anthony's inner feelings.
Ⓑ Ask students what details evoke an image of the setting.
Possible Response: "Here I be, like a starved dog in his pen." "The room stank from the odor of stale ale and sweat."

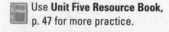 Use **Unit Five Resource Book**, p. 47 for more practice.

Active Reading MONITOR

Ⓒ Remind students to frequently assess the effectiveness of their reading strategies. Ask students what they would predict about Anthony's chances.
Possible Response: Anthony stands little chance of obtaining his freedom.

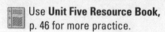 Use **Unit Five Resource Book**, p. 46 for more practice.

Anthony Burns: The Defeat and Triumph of a Fugitive Slave was inspired by real events that took place in Boston in the spring of 1854. Anthony Burns, an escaped slave from Virginia, was arrested on the streets of Boston on the evening of May 24, 1854, while on his way home from work. Under the provisions of the Fugitive Slave Law, a warrant had been issued for Burns's arrest by Colonel Charles F. Suttle, Burns's owner, who had journeyed north hoping to capture Burns and return him to slavery. Burns was brought before the U.S. Commissioner, Edward G. Loring, who, along with Suttle, U.S. District Attorney Benjamin Hallett, and other city officials, wanted to keep Burns's trial quiet. But acquaintances of Burns noticed his absence and by chance saw him being brought in chains into the courthouse, led by U.S. Marshal Freeman and his deputies, John Riley and Asa Butman. Butman was notoriously efficient in catching runaway slaves. Soon, the most prominent abolitionists in the area became involved in Burns's case: Theodore Parker, Richard Henry Dana Jr., and the Reverend Leonard Grimes. Both sides knew that the trial was not just about Anthony Burns; it was about slavery itself.

The excerpt you are about to read describes events on the first day of Burns's trial. It is a scene of internal and external struggle. Throughout his ordeal, Burns thinks back to figures from his childhood: "He Mars" John Suttle, father of Charles Suttle and Burns's owner when he was a child; "Mamaw," his mother; Janety, the sister who raised him; and "Big Walker," "driver," or foreman, of John Suttle's slaves who was rumored to have been Burns's father.

MAY 25, 1854

The weight of the past and the darkness of its night enclosed Anthony until slowly, with the growing light of day, he returned to the present.

Ⓐ The windows of the jury room where he was kept under guard were covered with iron bars that seemed to break the day into welts of pain. If he could somehow keep his eyes from those bright stripes, he might keep his suffering at bay. But it was no use.

Here I be! he despaired. Caught, I am, and no longer a man. Father, protect me!

He tried retreating again into the past, but all that would come to him was the time of sadness in Mamaw's cabin. With him these many years was the same question, born out o that night. "Who am I?" For the thousandth time he asked himself, "Be I the slave owner's own boy or the slave driver's son? He Mars John's or Big Walker's?"

Again, he lifted his good hand, as he had so many times before. Held it close to his eyes to see it better. There was no denying his skin was light brown. Big Walker had been a dark man, his mamaw a very black woman.

It had been whispered about the plantation that Big Walker Burns was once a freeman. That he had been tricked, caught, and brought down South. But Anthony never knew for

---

Teaching Options

 Preteaching Vocabulary TEKS 6A, 6B  TAAS Reading Obj. 1

RELATED WORDS
Instruction Tell students that sometimes they will encounter exercises that ask them to eliminate words unrelated in meaning to the others in the group. If there are unfamiliar words in the group, students should examine their prefixes, suffixes, and roots for clues. Students might also look at how familiar words in the group are related to help them make a decision about which words belong and which don't.
Exercise Have students decide which of the WORDS TO KNOW should be placed with each group.

illustrious   peer   mobilize   petty   agitate
contradict   alleged   wretched   compliance

1. gaze, stare, scrutinize,   *(peer)*
2. unhappy, miserable, sad,   *(wretched)*
3. famous, renowned, prestigious,
   (illustrious)
4. assemble, prepare, marshal,   *(mobilize)*
5. deny, dispute, overthrow,   *(contradict)*

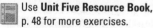 Use **Unit Five Resource Book**, p. 48 for more exercises.
Use **Vocabulary Transparencies and Copymasters**, p. 77, for additional support.

ertain if this was true, nor did any other of Mars John's black folks. Big Walker never said nything about it directly.

What matter any of it now? Anthony thought. Here I be, like a starved dog in his pen.

Anthony's stomach ached him, he was so hungry. He hadn't eaten since sometime in the dayclean before this. The room stank from the odor of stale ale and sweat. Anthony felt dizzy, then sick to his stomach from the stench. He would have to have something to eat and soon, or he would faint dead away.

Presently the heavy door to the jury room swung open. A man entered. He went over to Asa Butman. "Get him ready," he said. "We have to take him down now."

He came over to Anthony. "Deputy Marshal Riley," he said, introducing himself. "You are going to court now, Anthony. Go with Asa here. He will see that you fix yourself up a bit."

Anthony did as he was told. In a small room off to the side he washed his face and smoothed his hair. There was no comb or brush for him. He straightened his clothing. He took a tin cup of cold water that Asa offered him, but that was all he was given. When he and Butman came out again, Deputy Riley ordered irons closed around his wrists.

Anthony went numb into himself. He moved down the steps like a sleepwalker. When he entered the room set aside in this state Court House as a Federal courtroom, he made no response to seeing Colonel Suttle and William Brent there flanked by men he had never seen before—their lawyers. Also present was the one called Marshal Freeman. Some ten of his men, deputies, were with him.

Anthony took the prisoner's seat across from the judge's bench as he was directed by Asa.

"I'm makin' no promises, Tony," Colonel Suttle said to him calmly as he seated himself, "and I'm makin' no threats."

Anthony heard what Suttle said but could give no answer. He was aware of all that went on around him, but it was hard now for him to keep his mind on any one thing for long. His head felt light. He wanted so much just to lie down. The wrist irons and the chain that connected them grew heavier by the minute. Anthony couldn't find the strength or will to lift a finger even to scratch his nose, which itched him. The itching became a dull aching. It in turn spread into a throbbing loneliness throughout his body. He felt miserably hot in his shoulders and deathly cold in his legs.

THE WRIST IRONS AND THE CHAIN THAT CONNECTED THEM GREW HEAVIER BY THE MINUTE.

Anthony bowed his head. For the rest of the time he sat as if hypnotized.

Asa Butman and one of his men took their seats on either side of Anthony. Also present and seated was the U.S. Attorney for the Federal Government, District of Massachusetts, Benjamin Hallett. Hallett was a politician who believed his position as U.S. District Attorney gave him the right to oversee the government's policy of rigidly executing the Fugitive Slave Act. He agreed with that policy, in fact. He and the other officials present hoped that the examination would be completed as soon as possible. There had been no inkling of a fugitive arrest in the morning papers. Reporters knew nothing yet about what was going on.

C

WORDS
TO
KNOW
throb (thrŏb) v. to beat strongly (as though hurting)

753

Customizing Instruction

Less Proficient Readers
• Ask students where Asa Butman and Deputy Marshal Riley take Anthony.
Possible Response: They take him to the courtroom.
• Ask what familiar face does Anthony see in the courtroom?
Possible Response: He sees his former master, Colonel Suttle.
• Ask students how Anthony feels as he sits in the prisoner's seat.
Possible Response: He can't concentrate, he feels lightheaded and wants to lie down, and he is overwhelmed with feelings of loneliness.
Set a Purpose Have students read to find out what Reverend Parker tells Deacon Pitts.

Students Acquiring English
1 Tell students that often slaves did not know who their fathers were. Anthony doesn't know if he is the child of Master John or Big Walker.
Explain to students that *Mars* is the spelling of *Master* as the word is pronounced by Anthony.
2 Explain to students that leaving off the *g* at the end of *makin'* suggests a Southern dialect.

Use **Spanish Study Guide,** pp. 148–150 for additional support.

BLOCK SCHEDULING: MANAGING TIME

If your schedule requires that you cover the lesson objectives in a shorter time, use . . .
• Preparing to Read, p. 750
• Thinking Through the Literature, p. 766

If you want to take advantage of longer class time, use . . .
• TE Teaching Options: Viewing and Representing, pp. 751, 764; Preteaching Vocabulary, p. 752; Grammar, p. 754, 761; Cross-Curricular Links, pp. 755, 757, 759; Spelling, pp. 756, 763; Speaking and Listening, pp. 758, 762; Informal Assessment, p. 760; Standardized Test Practice, p. 764

Reading Skills and Strategies:
CLARIFYING

 Ask students to explain the official procedure for claiming a runaway slave.
Answer: An affidavit of ownership is produced, the slave is arrested, there is a hearing, and the owner is certified to take the prisoner back to the plantation.

Literary Analysis:
MINOR CHARACTERS

B Tell students that in a work of fiction minor characters appear only briefly and play a small role. Deacon Pitts might be considered a minor character in the nonfiction account of Anthony Burns. Ask students what function he fulfills.
Possible Response: Deacon Pitts is the one who notices that Anthony is missing and alerts Reverend Parker.

Literary Analysis

LITERARY NONFICTION

C Tell students that writers of literary nonfiction insert dialogue to inform readers of facts and to build an impression of the person who is speaking. Ask students to analyze Reverend Parker's traits from what he says.
Possible Response: He is sympathetic, generous, hospitable, and active on behalf of the less fortunate.

Literary Analysis: CONFLICT

D Remind students that sometimes one conflict leads to others. Ask students what major conflict is the source of other conflicts in this situation.
Possible Response: The belief of some people that they have a right to keep slaves is in opposition to the view of other people that all individuals have a right to be free.

United States Commissioner Edward G. Loring.

Colonel Suttle and Mr. Brent intended to take the prisoner out of Boston and down South before the dreaded Boston "radicals"[1] knew about his capture. Ben Hallett hoped they would, too. For if the abolitionists found out, they had a hundred ways in which they might come to Burns's defense. They might try to mob Colonel Suttle or even have him prosecuted for kidnapping.

A The prisoner was definitely the slave Anthony Burns. He had admitted as much when he had first faced the Colonel. It was a simple matter, then, of going through the proceeding according to law. Colonel Suttle had provided an affidavit[2] of ownership, and Commissioner Loring had issued a warrant for Burns's arrest. There would be a hearing as

soon as possible, it was hoped—all strictly according to provisions[3] of the Fugitive Slave Act. The Commissioner would then issue the Colonel a certificate allowing him to take the prisoner back to Virginia. But unknown to the Colonel or anyone else in the courtroom, the Boston abolitionists were already informed.

Coffin Pitts, Anthony's employer and landlord, had been looking for him all the previous night.

"Anthony? Anthony!" Coffin Pitts called. When he couldn't find him anywhere in his house, he went out at once in search of him. He looked everywhere in the fugitives' quarter he could think of, but Anthony seemed to have disappeared into thin air. Fearing the worst, he went straight to Exeter Place, the home of the abolitionist Reverend Theodore Parker.

Reverend Parker was the minister of the 28th Congregational Society. He believed, he always said, in an Almighty God and the equality and dignity of all who were God's children. He had gained national attention for the sermons he preached to thousands each Sunday in the enormous music hall called Tremont Temple.

"I know that men urge in argument," Theodore Parker preached, "that the Constitution of the United States is the supreme law of the land, and that it sanctions[4] slavery. There is no supreme law but that

---

1. **Boston "radicals":** local supporters of the abolition of slavery; abolitionists.
2. **affidavit** (ăf ĭ-dā′vĭt): a written declaration made under oath before a notary public or other authorized officer.
3. **provisions:** stipulations of the law.
4. **sanctions:** permits.

Teaching Options

 Grammar TEKS 17A TAAS Writing Obj. 3, 5, 7

PHRASES AND CLAUSES
Instruction Remind students that although phrases and clauses are both groups of words, a clause has a subject and a verb. Subordinate clauses do not express a complete thought; main clauses can stand alone as sentences. Point out that the highlighted sentence above includes a subordinate clause, "When . . . house," and the main clause, "he . . . him." Ask students to pick out the prepositional phrases in the sentence.

Exercises Have students identify the subordinate clauses, main clauses, and prepositional phrases in the following sentences.
1. If the abolitionists found out *(subordinate clause)*, they had a hundred ways to defend Burns. *(main clause)*
2. It made his blood boil *(main clause)* that some men would even think to enslave other men. *(subordinate clause)*
3. As he neared the courthouse *(subordinate clause)*, Parker happened to meet Charles

Mayo Ellis, a member of the Boston Vigilance Committee. *(main clause) (of the Boston Vigilance Committee = prepositional phrase)*

 Use **Grammar Transparencies and Copymasters,** p. 106.

 Use McDougal Littell's **Language Network,** Chapter 8, for more instruction and practice in phrases and clauses.

made by God; if our laws <u>contradict</u> that, the sooner they end or the sooner they are broken, why, the better."

Almost every word that Parker uttered made Coffin Pitts smile in agreement. Yet he couldn't bring himself to awaken Reverend Parker when he got to his home. He waited, nodding and dozing, on Theodore Parker's front steps all night long.

Reverend Parker found him there Thursday morning when he opened the door to let in the morning air. "Good Lord, man, come in, come in!" he said, and ushered Deacon Pitts inside. "You must be chilled through. Here, let us have coffee." Parker proceeded to the kitchen and prepared coffee while Deacon Pitts told him of the missing Anthony Burns.

"I am sorry to have to tell you this," said Parker, "but there are Virginia slavers in town."

"Oh, no!" Deacon Pitts said.

"Yes, I'm afraid so," Parker answered. "Tuesday morning another colored man, a waiter from the Revere House, came to see me. Said he had waited on two Virginia slave hunters at breakfast.

"He gave me useful information," Parker continued. "The slavers are a Colonel Suttle and William Brent. But the man didn't know which slave it was they were after. So for two days I asked everyone I could think of, and nobody knew! Not even Reverend Grimes of your church—and he dared not question his congregation, lest they panic and run away north toward Canada."

Reverend Leonard Grimes had been born in Virginia of free parents who had bought their freedom from a sympathetic owner. As an adult there he ran a livery stable, and he used his horse-drawn carriages to transport fugitives farther north under cover of darkness. Once he went deep into Virginia and carried out an entire slave family; three months later he was caught and sent to prison for two years for the crime of aiding runaways. After his release Reverend Grimes moved to Boston, where he continued his work as a minister and friend to all escaped slaves.

"The slavers have been among us, hunting, and we had no wind of it for two days!" exclaimed Deacon Pitts. "They caught us unawares."

"Yes, and I daresay the slavers are here after your Anthony," replied Reverend Parker. "Well. You may stay as long as you like, Deacon Pitts, but I must be off. Have yourself another of my brew. Get yourself warmed! I'm going to the Court House."

With that, Parker hurried out. He had not let Deacon Pitts see it, but he was seething with anger. That some men would even think to enslave other men made his blood boil. That was why, when the Fugitive Slave Act had become law in 1850, he had slapped a revolver down on his desk and left it there as clear warning to all slave hunters.

He knew that for the South, passage of the Fugitive Slave Act was a signal for an intensive manhunt in the North. And it was not long before Southern authorities sent people North to bring back fugitives and to spy on abolitionist groups. In response to this, Northern blacks and whites took direct action to head off <u>compliance</u> with the law. Theodore Parker found the rising tension and possibility of violence quite unpleasant. He was not a violent man himself. But if forced to, he would without question defend a fugitive with his life.

As he neared the Court House, Parker happened to meet Charles Mayo Ellis, a lawyer and member of the Boston Vigilance Committee. The Vigilance Committee was a large, secret body of abolitionists organized to

© C

© D

755

Customizing Instruction

Less Proficient Readers
• Ask students why Deacon Pitts goes to Reverend Parker's house.
Possible Response: He fears that something bad has happened to Anthony and Reverend Parker may be able to help.
• What does Reverend Parker tell Deacon Pitts?
Possible Response: He knows that there are slave hunters in town, and he thinks they are after Anthony.

Set a Purpose Have students read to find out who learns that Anthony is to appear in court and what they do.

Multiple Learning Styles
Intrapersonal Learners
1 Ask students to imagine the thoughts running through the mind of Coffin Pitts as he waits on the steps of Reverend Parker's house. As Anthony's employer, landlord, and friend, what might he be feeling?

Students Acquiring English
2 Tell students that Reverend Parker's exclamation *Good Lord* shows his concern and surprise and is not used in a profane way.
3 Explain that the title *deacon* as it is used here indicates that Coffin Pitts has a position of responsibility in his church.
4 *Colored* is the word used to describe people of African-American descent at the time this event took place. Explain that it is no longer considered appropriate.

Cross Curricular Link Social Studies

UNDERGROUND RAILROAD The Underground Railroad was a secret cooperative network that helped slaves to escape from the South. Its name came about because it had to shroud its activities in secrecy, and, therefore, railway terms were used as code words to describe the workings of the network. Routes of escape were lines, stopping places along the way were stations, and the people who led slaves along the lines were called conductors. The slaves were referred to as packages or freight.

Men and women of various races and religions cooperated to make the system work. Former slaves, church leaders, and abolitionists took active roles in guiding, hiding, and protecting the people trying to attain freedom. Often black men and women served as the conductors, because slaves might trust them more readily than they would a white person. A legendary conductor was Harriet Tubman, an escaped slave herself. She led more than 300 fugitives to safety in 19 trips without being caught. She had a reputation for being calm and quick-witted, even in crises.

Reading Skills and Strategies: QUESTIONING

A Remind students that active readers ask themselves questions about what has happened or what may happen. Have students raise questions they might have in response to the text.

Possible Responses: What kind of trouble could Reverend Grimes stir up? How would a delay or publicity help Anthony? Why are the armed guards in the courtroom? Is there any way out of the situation for Anthony?

Active Reading MONITOR

B Ask students which participants are abolitionists or friends of Anthony and which are supporters of slavery or the Fugitive Slave Act. Have students monitor their own comprehension and make modifications by rereading the previous portion of the text or taking notes as they read.

Reading Skills and Strategies: FACT AND OPINION

C Ask students what fact explains Dana's motivation to help Anthony Burns.

Possible Response: He accepts slavery in the South but opposes it in new states and territories in the West.

Reading Skills and Strategies: EVALUATING

D Ask students why they think Richard Dana is willing to defend Anthony Burns even after his past experiences.

Possible Response: He continues to hope that justice will prevail; he might be able to find a loophole in the procedure; he will not give up on another man's freedom.

---

operate on a moment's notice. Its main purpose was "to secure the fugitives and colored inhabitants of Boston and vicinity from any invasion of their rights."

Parker quickly explained the situation to Ellis. He then asked Ellis to go to the Court House to observe what was taking place and to keep watch over the fugitive. "I'll go find Richard Dana," Reverend Parker said. Richard Henry Dana was another member of the Vigilance Committee, a well-known novelist as well as an attorney.

But it was Reverend Leonard Grimes of the 12th Baptist Church who was the first of the Vigilance Committee to see Anthony Burns handcuffed in the prisoner's box. Passing by the Court House, he had noticed unusual activity and had gone inside, only to see Anthony surrounded by armed guards. Alarmed, Reverend Grimes approached Anthony.

1 "My son, are you all right?" he asked. "Please, tell me what I may do for you now."

Anthony made no reply, and looked through space at nothing. Sadness and fear, poor soul! the reverend thought. Anthony appeared to be in a trance, unmindful or unknowing of his situation. I can't leave him alone in his condition, the reverend decided.

One of the guards at Anthony's side stood up, menacing the reverend. He put his hand on his gun butt, and Reverend Grimes backed away from the prisoner's dock. He knew it was best to act timidly before such <u>petty</u> officials. Quickly, bowing his head slightly, he took a seat in the rear of the court to wait and see what would happen next.

The Reverend Theodore Parker

The slave catchers watched him sit down. So did District Attorney Ben Hallett. Asa Butman whispered to Hallett, "Sir, might I throw that preacher out? He ain't got any business at all bein' in here."

"No, leave him alone," Hallett said. He knew Reverend Grimes to be a respected colored minister, able enough at fund-raising to have raised ten thousand dollars and built himself a church. "Better to have him in here where we can keep an eye on him than outside where he might make trouble," he explained.

"Yassir, as you wish, then," Asa said. "But give the word and he's out as quick as you please." He winked at Hallett as if they were conspirators.

> WORDS
> TO   **petty** (pĕt′ē) *adj.* of little importance, trivial
> KNOW

756

Teaching Options

Mini Lesson **Spelling** **TEKS** 16C **TAAS** Writing Obj. 3, 7

ABSORBED PREFIXES

Instruction Explain to students that prefixes such as *ad, in,* and *con* change their spelling depending on the first consonant sound of the base word or root. Display the following:

Ad – *ac, af, ag, al, an, ap, ar, as, at*

con – *col, com, cor*

in – *il, im, ir*

Com and *im* are used before words beginning with *b, p,* or *m.*

Exercise Have students add the correct form of the prefix indicated and write the new word.

1. in + legal =   illegal
2. con + menced =   commenced
3. ad + tempt =   attempt
4. ad + fidavit =   affidavit
5. con + respond =   correspond

Ask students to find other words with these prefixes and to write them in their personal word lists.

Ben Hallett looked pained. To think he must depend on the lowest life, such as Butman, to see that the Federal law was enforced! He turned away in distaste and busied himself with his court papers as Asa hurried back to his post beside Anthony.

MAY 25, 1854

Richard Henry Dana was not in his office when Theodore Parker went there looking for him. He had learned early that morning, as had Reverend Grimes, that a fugitive was about to appear in court before Commissioner Edward G. Loring. While passing the Court House on his way to work, Dana had been approached by a stranger and told the bad news.

"Good God!" he had said. "I need a runner!" He soon found a Negro youth he knew well, one of the many among the growing community of free persons and fugitives who lived in Boston.

Without further delay Dana sent the youth to find members of the Boston Vigilance Committee. For it was the Committee's sworn duty to defend, without fee, all black inhabitants of Boston and vicinity against slavers and bounty hunters.

Dana, one of the Committee's most _illustrious_ members, had helped defend the fugitive slave Thomas Sims in court in 1851. As a young man he had withdrawn from Harvard when measles had weakened his eyesight, and had, in 1834, shipped out to California as a sailor to regain his health. After calling at California's ports loading cargo, his ship sailed around Cape Horn and returned home to Boston in 1835.

Dana's travel experiences cured him physically and also taught him sympathy for the less fortunate. He reentered Harvard and was admitted to the Massachusetts bar in 1840. That same year he published _Two Years Before the Mast_, a novel written from diaries he'd kept at sea about "the life of a common sailor as it really is." In it he revealed the awful abuses endured by his fellow seamen at the hands of their superiors. The book made him famous.

When the slavery question moved North with the fugitives, Dana put novel writing aside. His political party was Free Soil, which meant he did not oppose slavery in the South. But he vowed to fight against its spread into the western land tracts, such as Kansas and

> ANTHONY MADE NO REPLY, AND LOOKED THROUGH SPACE AT NOTHING. SADNESS AND FEAR, POOR SOUL!

Nebraska. He lost many of his wealthy, proslavery clients because of this "moderate" view, but he didn't care.

"I am against slavery in the North," he said again and again.

By 1854 Dana no longer put much faith in justice. He had defended two slaves already, Sims and another popularly known as Shadrach, and neither case had ended well. Sims had lost his case and was returned to Georgia, where he died. Shadrach had been "stolen," from the very Court House that now held Anthony Burns, by black abolitionists who managed to get him away to freedom.

Justice and law both had come out scarred and battered, Dana observed grimly at the time. But he believed that gentlemen must

---

WORDS TO KNOW   **illustrious** (ĭ-lŭs′ trē-əs) _adj._ well-known or distinguished

757

Cross Curricular Link **Social Studies**

FUGITIVE SLAVE ACT The first Fugitive Slave Act was passed by Congress in 1793. Under this statute, any federal district judge or state magistrate or circuit court judge could decide the fate of an alleged runaway slave, without a jury trial. Ironically, the passage of this act increased the sympathy for runaway slaves and was a catalyst for the Underground Railroad. The act also stirred up opposition in the Northern states. To obstruct the act, these states enacted personal-liberty laws, which entitled the fugitive to a jury trial if he or she appealed.

Because Southern states were so disgruntled with the lack of success of the first Fugitive Slave Act, the second was passed in 1850. This law prohibited slaves from testifying on their own behalf or having a trial by jury. Federal marshals were penalized for not enforcing the law, and those who helped slaves escape could also expect punishments. But again the adverse reaction outweighed the effectiveness for the slave owners. Abolitionists increased in number, the Underground Railroad helped more slaves than ever, and new personal-liberty laws multiplied in the North.

Literary Analysis

LITERARY NONFICTION

A Remind students that the genre of literary nonfiction allows the author to insert possible thoughts and feelings of historical figures in the account. Ask students to analyze the effect of Richard Dana's mental observations of Anthony.

Possible Responses: His observations add details to the portrait of Anthony and create a picture of slavery. Anthony has been branded as an animal would have been to show who owns him. Dana's assumption that Anthony's deformity is the result of maltreatment emphasizes the generally perceived cruelty of slavery.

Literary Analysis: MINOR CHARACTERS

B Ask students why Colonel Suttle is significant, although he says and does little in this excerpt.

Possible Response: He is the reason that the hearing is taking place; he intimidates Anthony with his presence in the courtroom.

Literary Analysis: CONFLICT

C Ask students to analyze Anthony's internal conflict.

Possible Response: He wants help but is afraid to anger the colonel; he is ashamed that he has been caught.

D How does Anthony's internal conflict lead to conflict for Richard Dana?

Possible Responses: Richard Dana cannot represent him if Anthony does not verbally consent to Dana working on his behalf.

---

behave with justice. And if slave hunters wished to take back a slave, then they would have to proceed at every turn strictly according to the law.

Let them make a single wrong explanation, and I will have them! Richard Dana thought.

Now he braced himself and entered the courtroom.

Dana swiftly took in the scene, observing the armed guards around the prisoner. So that's Burns, he thought. And as pitiful-looking a fugitive as I've ever seen. Not the man Sims was, surely. This one looks lost witted.[5]

> ## "IT'S OF NO USE," ANTHONY RESPONDED, FINALLY. "THEY KNOW ME. MARS CHARLES, THE COLONEL, KNOWS ME. I WILL FARE WORSE IF I RESIST."

The slave had a small scar on his cheek—a brand of some kind, Dana supposed. One hand, his right, was hideously deformed, and Dana assumed at once that Burns had been awfully mistreated by his owner. He glanced over at the man within the bar—the railing that separated the public from the rest of the courtroom—who he rightly guessed was Colonel Charles Suttle, slave owner of Virginia, surrounded by his agent and lawyers.

So then, Dana thought, they mean to have it all their way, and quickly. But not so fast!

He walked over to Anthony, ignoring the guards and Marshal Freeman. "I'm a lawyer," he said to Anthony. "Richard Dana is my name.

Let me help you. And there will be no fee."

Anthony was shocked to hear the learned voice of a white man speaking to him. Who? . . . A buckra[6] again. Seems to care . . . kind voice. But the Colonel, he standing up. Glarin so at me.

Colonel Suttle, hearing what Dana had said, had risen to his feet. His face was red with fury Anthony dared not answer Richard Dana.

"Anthony," Dana persisted, "there are certain papers from Virginia that an owner must have in order. These might have mistakes And you might get off if you have a lawyer."

There was a long silence. Anthony was thinking, Oh, I feel so ashamed. I should have said something to Reverend Grimes first, when Mr. Grimes come to talk to me. Should have said how sorry I was to have got myself captured. How I should've gone to the dedication of Reverend Grimes' church. Then maybe none of this would have happened.

Oh, so many shoulds!

The white man still stood there before him.

"I . . . I . . . ." Anthony began.

"Yes?" Dana said quickly.

"I . . . don't know," Anthony finished, murmuring so low that Dana had to come even closer to hear.

Anthony didn't know what to do. He did know that Mars Charles would make his life miserable if it cost him extra time and money to get Anthony back down South.

"Anthony? Tell me what you want," Dana said.

"It's of no use," Anthony responded, finally. "They know me. Mars Charles, the Colonel, knows me. I will fare worse if I resist."

Dana straightened up. He reasoned that Anthony was frightened out of his wits by the

---

5. **lost witted:** completely bewildered.
6. **buckra:** *old slang,* a white person.

Teaching Options

 Mini Lesson **Speaking and Listening** **TEKS 4A, 5F**

SPIRITUALS

Prepare Give students some background on spirituals. Tell them that spirituals did not exist in written form for many years but were passed down orally. They were religious songs that often had double meanings. On the surface, the words seemed to refer to life after death or Biblical incidents; on a deeper level, the songs expressed feelings or sometimes passed messages about the slaves' present situations. Divide students into small groups. Have them find recordings of spiritu-

als such as "Go Down, Moses" or "Swing Low, Sweet Chariot" and listen to the words carefully. Each group should prepare a short report on their interpretations of the meaning.

Present Have each group play the recording of the spiritual and then explain the meaning. After all of the presentations, have the class discuss the possible effects of the music and the activity of singing on the slaves.

BLOCK SCHEDULING This activity is particularly well suited for longer class periods.

The Reverend Leonard Grimes.

numbers of hostile white men in the room— a dozen guards, all armed, the Marshal, the District Attorney, his owner, and the others. Clearly, Anthony was threatened by them.

I can't defend him unless he wants me to, Dana kept thinking. The fugitive must ask to be represented. Dana could not otherwise take his case. I need time! he was thinking.

At that instant four other abolitionist lawyers, members of the Vigilance Committee, entered the court: Charles Mayo Ellis, Theodore Parker, Wendell Phillips, and a black lawyer, Robert Morriss.

Not two minutes later the Commissioner, Judge Edward Loring, walked briskly in.

Immediately, Marshal Freeman spoke loudly, "The court. All rise."

Anthony was made to stand, as everyone in the courtroom got to his feet. After the judge sat down, Anthony and the rest sat.

Judge Loring looked askance at all the guards in the room. He asked Marshal Freeman why there were so many and was told how difficult were the circumstances surrounding the capture of Burns. Judge Loring then asked whether the defendant was in the prisoner's dock.

"Yes, Your Honor," the Marshal answered.

"Is the claimant[7] here, or his agent?" Loring asked.

"Both of them are here, Judge," Marshal Freeman answered.

"Then we may begin," Judge Loring said.

At that point Richard Dana asked to speak to Loring privately.

Loring agreed, and Dana explained how frightened the prisoner, Anthony Burns, was. "He cannot act even in his own behalf," Dana said. "I suggest that you call him up to the bench instead of addressing him in the prisoner's dock. He will then be out of the way of the gaze of the claimant, Colonel Suttle. And so we might know what he wants to do."

"I intend to do that," Judge Loring said. "But now I must proceed."

"Yes, of course," Dana said, "thank you, Your Honor." And he sat down.

Judge Loring started the proceedings by saying that he was presiding as a U.S. Commissioner, that his duties were executive, and that the hearing was an inquiry. The question before the court, he said, was whether he should award to Charles F. Suttle a certificate authorizing him to take to Virginia the slave Anthony Burns. The claim was that Anthony Burns owed Mr. Suttle service and labor.

---

7. **claimant:** a person who makes a claim in court.

Customizing Instruction

Less Proficient Readers
Ask students to describe how Anthony reacts when Dana approaches him about being his lawyer.

Possible Response: Anthony seems confused and then tells Dana that he will be worse off if he tries to resist the colonel.

• What is Dana's next step after talking to Anthony?

Possible Response: He approaches Commissioner Loring to ask that Anthony be called up to the bench so that he can answer without having to see Colonel Suttle.

Set a Purpose Have students read to find out what is illegal about the proceedings in the courtroom.

Cross Curricular Link Social Studies

RICHARD HENRY DANA To call Richard Henry Dana an abolitionist lawyer and stop at that title is to overlook the many other activities that filled his life. He was a writer, a husband, the father of six children, a sailor, a politician, as well as champion of the oppressed, and an insatiable traveler.

However, it was his work on Anthony Burns's behalf that made him a hero in the eyes of many. Just as Colonel Suttle was about to accept money that had been raised by concerned citizens to buy Anthony's freedom, District Attorney Hallett nullified the sale to force a trial. During the trial, Dana picked holes in the opposing arguments and cleverly used his defense to denounce the Fugitive Slave Act. He could not win but stood for the cause of justice for all.

On the day of the decision, Dana was returning home after finishing some work in the evening. Without warning he was assaulted by a man who had been one of the marshal's guards in the courtroom. Luckily, the blow to Dana's head missed both his temple and his eye. The man was caught and received a jail sentence.

Reading and Analyzing

"There are three facts that are to be proved," Loring said. "And these are: that Anthony Burns escaped from slavery from the state of Virginia; that Anthony Burns was by the law of Virginia the slave of Charles F. Suttle; that the prisoner is indeed Anthony Burns.

"If counsel for Charles Suttle can prove these facts," the judge continued, "I am empowered to issue a certificate stating the proofs; this will allow the rendition of Anthony Burns."

Anthony listened now and understood. He knew what rendition was. Means me, he thought, taken back home by Mars Charles. Means me, a slave again.

He swallowed hard and felt himself retreat within. But there was no comfort now. His loneliness and fear, his <u>wretched</u> hunger, wouldn't permit him to bring the memory of Mamaw into this harsh place. Neither could he bring forth the child he had been. Where was that young Anthony now? he wondered, for he could not summon the image of the boy he had been.

The second counsel for Charles Suttle, Edward G. Parker, now rose, and read from the warrant for Anthony's arrest:

"*In the name of the President of the United States of America, you are hereby commanded forthwith to apprehend Anthony Burns, a negro man, alleged now to be in your District, charged with being a fugitive from labor, and with having escaped from service in the State of Virginia, and have him forthwith before me, Edward G. Loring, one of the Commissioners of the Circuit Court of the United States, there to answer to the complaint of Charles F. Suttle, of Alexandria, alleging under oath that said Burns, on the twenty-fourth day of March last,*

and for a long time prior thereto had owed service and labor to him in the State of Virginia and that, while held to service there by said Suttle, the said Burns escaped into the said State of Massachusetts. . . ."

He next read the record of the Virginia Court as required by the Fugitive Slave Act:

"*In Alexandria Circuit Court, May 16, 1854. On the application of Charles F. Suttle, who this day appeared in Court and made satisfactory proof to the Court that Anthony Burns was held to service and labor by him in the State of Virginia, and service and labor are due to him from the said Anthony, and that the said Anthony has escaped. Anthony is a man of dark complexion, about six feet high, with a scar on one of his cheeks, and also a scar on the back of his right hand, and about twenty-three or four years of age—it is therefore ordered, in pursuance of an act of Congress, 'An Act respecting Fugitives from Justice and Persons escaping from the Service of their masters,' that the matter set forth be entered on the record of this Court.*"

The abolitionist lawyer Charles Mayo Ellis watched the proceedings closely. When he saw Richard Dana speak privately to Judge Loring, he supposed Dana meant to make himself the lawyer for Anthony Burns. But when this did not seem to be his purpose, Mr. Ellis made his way to Dana's side as quietly as he could.

As Edward Parker went on with the Alexandria Circuit Court record, Ellis spoke urgently to Richard Dana. "Loring is sitting as a *judge*, Richard. You must *do* something. Massachusetts law clearly forbids judges sitting on slave cases."

WORDS
TO
KNOW   **wretched** (rĕch′ ĭd) *adj.* miserable

Teaching Options

✓ **Assessment**   **Informal Assessment**   **TEKS** 11B, 12G   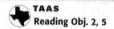 **TAAS** Reading Obj. 2, 5

"There's no jury," Ellis added. "The armed guards sitting illegally in the jury box are plainly petty thieves being used to terrify an already frightened man."

Richard Dana shrugged. "What can I do?" he said. "Anthony Burns would seem to want to go back without trouble to his master. He won't accept my aid."

Reverend Theodore Parker got to his feet. He could stand it no longer. It was clear to him that the poor fugitive was being tried without a lawyer. He marched angrily to the front of the courtroom just as Edward Parker was finishing and before Marshal Freeman could testify.

He strode up to the witness box and <u>peered</u> into it. On seeing that Anthony was handcuffed, he glared indignantly at Judge Loring. Next, he spoke to Anthony.

"I am Theodore Parker," he said. "I am a minister. Surely you want me to help you."

He could see that Anthony was frozen with fear. "Let us give you counsel," Parker said. "Richard Dana there is the best lawyer in Boston. He is on your side! The black man over there is Robert Morriss and a fine lawyer, too. Will you not let us defend you?"

Anthony began to shake all over. Lord, oh, Lord! Tell me what I must do! he thought.

But he couldn't help seeing that Mars Charles Suttle watched him, that Mars Brent watched him. Anthony commenced stammering, "Mars . . . Mars . . . Colonel . . . he know . . . he knows me . . . I shall have to go back. Mars Brent . . . know me."

Richard Henry Dana.

"But it can do you no harm to make a defense," urged Parker.

"I shall have to go back," Anthony said again. "If I must . . . go back, I want ter go back as easy as I can—but—do as you have a mind to."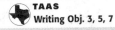

Theodore Parker strode back to his seat. He was thinking that if Charles Suttle's lawyers put a nervous witness on the stand and the witness made a false statement, they might have a case. He gave a nod to Richard Dana, to say that Dana had the prisoner's permission to defend him.

Colonel Suttle's other lawyer, Seth Thomas, now rose. He was upset that Theodore Parker had interrupted, but he did not show it. He at once put William Brent upon the stand as a

WORDS TO KNOW   **peer** (pîr) *v.* to look intently

761

 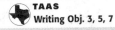

witness to prove the identity of the prisoner with the person named in the arrest warrant. Brent gave his testimony confidently.

He was a merchant from Richmond, Virginia, he said. And he was a close friend of Colonel Suttle.

"Do you know Anthony Burns?" Mr. Thomas asked.

"Yes, I know him well," he said. And he stated that Anthony Burns was the prisoner in the prisoner's box.

"Can you tell us something about Anthony Burns?" Thomas asked.

Brent began speaking as if reciting: "Anthony Burns was owned by the Colonel's mother. Colonel Suttle has owned him for some fourteen years. I paid the Colonel for the services of Anthony Burns in 1846, '47, and '48."

"Good. Now then," the lawyer said, "can you tell me what you know about his escape?"

"In March," said Brent, "Anthony was missing from Richmond. I didn't see him again until last day past, when he spoke to his master."

"Kindly repeat what was said then," said Thomas.

Theodore Parker rose to his feet again. Brent's statements concerning this conversation would be improper testimony. "You've got to defend him now," he told Richard Dana as he stood. "And if you won't, I will!"

Judge Loring struck with his gavel in an effort to quiet Reverend Parker. Before the Marshal and his deputies could think to restrain the pastor, Richard Dana rose to address the court. It was clear to him that the prisoner would have to have his aid at once. Under the Fugitive Slave Act, the testimony of the <u>alleged</u> fugitive could not be admitted as evidence.

Despite this, Anthony's testimony was about to be admitted. Dana had to prevent this.

He presented himself to Judge Loring as *amicus curiae*, or friend of the court—one who is called in to advise the court. "I urge Your Honor that there be a delay so that the prisoner can decide what would be his best course," he said.

"I oppose this motion, Your Honor," responded Seth Thomas. "The prisoner by his own statement has admitted that he is Charles Suttle's slave. He does not want a lawyer, nor does he want a defense."

"The prisoner is in no condition to determine whether he would have counsel or not!" Dana said heatedly. "He does not know what he is saying. He must be given time to recover himself and to talk with a lawyer."

Over the objections of both of Suttle's lawyers, Judge Loring had Anthony Burns brought before him. Marshal Freeman hurriedly unlocked Anthony's wrist irons before leading him to the judge.

Loring spoke to Anthony in a kindly manner, explaining what the claim against him was. "Anthony, do you wish to make a defense to this claim?" he asked. "If you do, you can have counsel to aid you, and you shall have time to make a defense. You have a right to a defense if you wish for one."

Anthony finally dared look around the room slowly. His gaze rested on Richard Dana and then on Robert Morriss, but he made no reply.

Dana thought it was all over then. But Judge Loring said to Anthony reassuringly. "Anthony, do you wish for time to think about this? Do you wish to go away and meet me here tomorrow or next day, and tell me what you will do?"

WORDS
TO   **alleged** (ə-lĕjd') *adj.* supposed
KNOW

762

Speaking and Listening

TEKS
2B, 5A, 5F, 11B

All in the courtroom watched Anthony. He gave a slight twitching of his deformed hand, but no one knew whether he meant yes or no by the movement. He did not know himself.

I will have to go back, he was thinking. I will be whipped unto an inch of my life. I will die a slave.

Judge Loring looked doubtful, but at last he said to Anthony, "I understand you to say that you would."

Very faintly, Anthony said, "I would."

"Then you shall have it," Loring said.

Marshal Freeman whispered to the judge.

> ## HE GAVE A SLIGHT TWITCHING OF HIS DEFORMED HAND, BUT NO ONE KNEW WHETHER HE MEANT YES OR NO BY THE MOVEMENT.

Judge Loring replied out loud, "No sir, he must have the time necessary."

Again the Marshal whispered. Judge Loring replied sternly, "I can't help that, sir—he shall have the proper time."

The day was Thursday. "You shall have until Saturday morning," Judge Loring told Anthony and his defenders, and struck his gavel down.

Anthony was taken back to the jury room high up in the court building. There four men, including Deputy Asa Butman, guarded him.

"Tony, boy," Butman said to him, mimicking words spoken by Charles Suttle, "now we here are curious. Did the Colonel just *raise* you up or did he *buy* you from somebody?"

The other guards nodded encouragement. "Come on, lad, you know us here for your friends."

Anthony knew they thought him a fool. He had figured out that they hoped to get information from him for Mars Charles and Mars Brent. He knew there must be a reward for him. Every runaway slave had a price on his head.

Wonder how much Mars Charles think me worth?

Anthony played dumb; he acted confused, stared off into space, and told his jailers nothing.

THE COURT had emptied, and almost at once news of Anthony's arrest spread throughout Boston. The concerned public learned that slave hunters were in the city, hoping to force another wretched soul back into bondage.

All sympathetic citizens, and there were thousands, felt duty bound to disobey the Fugitive Slave act on behalf of the captured fugitive in their midst. But there was another factor that <u>mobilized</u> them: for months there had been a proposal before Congress that would allow slavery in the Great Plains lands of Kansas and Nebraska. The two tracts were to be territories within the Louisiana Purchase, the enormous parcel of land, stretching from the Gulf of Mexico to Canada, bought from France in 1803. The Missouri Compromise of 1820 had closed the Louisiana Purchase to slavery "forever." But people on the proslavery as well as the antislavery sides had been

---

WORDS
TO
KNOW   **mobilize** (mō′ bə-līz′) *v.* to assemble for a purpose

763

 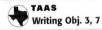

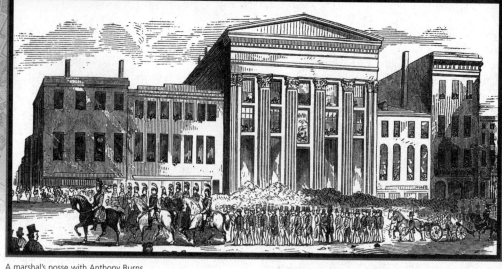

A marshal's posse with Anthony Burns.

sending their settlers into Kansas and Nebraska to agitate and to be in a position to vote for their sides once the territories were divided into states.

On May 25, 1854, the very same day that Anthony appeared in court, the Kansas-Nebraska Bill passed in the United States Senate. It permitted slavery in states that would be carved from the two territories if it was provided for in the state constitutions. So in effect it repealed the Missouri Compromise. After these victories for slavery, the jailing of a poor fugitive in a Boston court house at the bidding of a slave owner was the very last straw for those against slavery. Thus had the slavocracy rocked the cradle of liberty.

By evening the news that Anthony Burns had escaped from the South only to be captured in the free North moved from town to town and newspaper to newspaper across the country.

KIDNAPPING AGAIN! read the first leaflet out of Boston that told the tale:

> **A man was stolen Last Night**
> **By the Fugitive Slave Bill Commissioner**
> **He will have His**
>
> **MOCK TRIAL**
>
> **On Saturday, May 27, in the Kidnapper's Court**
> **Before the Honorable Slave Bill Commissioner**
> **At the Court House in Court Square**
> **SHALL BOSTON STEAL ANOTHER MAN?**
>
> **Thursday, May 25, 1854**

Written by Reverend Parker, the leaflet was printed by the antislavery press and carried across Massachusetts by volunteers who worked on trains, stagecoaches, and trucks. As it was being distributed, Theodore Parker had time to fire off another leaflet:

> **SEE TO IT THAT NO FREE CITIZEN**
> **OF MASSACHUSETTS**
> **IS DRAGGED INTO SLAVERY**

WORDS
TO
KNOW   **agitate** (ăj′ ĭ-tāt′) v. to stir up public interest in a cause

764

Overnight, without his ever knowing it, Anthony Burns became a symbol of freedom. But high up in the Court House he was a tired, miserable prisoner, alone save for his guard of petty criminals.

Anthony felt he had no one to turn to. He had no way of knowing that all through the night men watched the three massive doors of his granite prison Court House. It was a different time from 1851, when Thomas Sims was taken. The watchers made certain the authorities knew of their presence. Their message was clear: Anthony Burns was cared for.

Anthony was unaware that abolitionist ministers and lawyers argued fiercely hour upon hour over their next course of action on his behalf. There was no one to inform him that the slavers, Suttle and Brent, were followed everywhere by black men who never looked at them but were always in their sight. Suttle became so terrified that these blacks would try to lynch him, he and Brent moved to quarters in the Revere House attic and hired bodyguards.

In two short days Anthony had become a symbol to freedom lovers and a devilish token of danger to slavers like Suttle. But the courteous Reverend Leonard Grimes and his deacon, Coffin Pitts, never for an instant confused the man, the fugitive, with his cause. They agreed that Reverend Grimes must try to see Anthony the next morning.

Anthony knew none of this. He wished to shut out the prying questions of guards hoping to trick him. He did what he knew how to do best of all: He retreated within, taking comfort in his unchanging past. ❖

C

Customizing Instruction

Less Proficient Readers
• Ask students to explain the Kansas-Nebraska Bill.

Possible Response: The Kansas-Nebraska Bill permits slavery in the new states formed from the two territories if the state constitutions provide for it.

• How does the passage of that bill affect those working for Anthony Burns?

Possible Response: It is a tremendous defeat for opponents of slavery and makes them more determined to save Anthony Burns.

In the days that followed the initial hearing, several unsuccessful attempts were made to free Anthony Burns. Some of these attempts were peaceful, some of them were not. When the trial resumed, witnesses came forward to testify for both sides, but the final ruling was in the hands of Commissioner Loring. While pretending to be sympathetic to Anthony, Loring made decisions that troubled the defense. These decisions heightened tensions within the courtroom and the crowd that had gathered outside, as well as among a growing number of persons throughout Massachusetts and beyond who had learned of Anthony's plight. Could Anthony Burns resume his life as a free man or would he be returned to Charles Suttle as escaped "property," sure to face punishment and possibly death? The outcome of Loring's decision would prove that both cowardice and courage can be part of the human spirit.

One of the two checks used to purchase Anthony Burns.

Conclusion of *Anthony Burns*

While Anthony Burns awaited trial, abolitionists spread word of his capture throughout Massachusetts and held mass meetings in Boston to rally support for his cause. To the great disappointment of the abolitionists however, Commissioner Loring found in favor of Charles Suttle. Anthony Burns had to return to Virginia to face punishment for running away. Given the notoriety of Burns's case, his jailers in Virginia felt called upon to make the conditions of Burns's imprisonment as harsh and demoralizing as possible. Burns was mistreated and fed poorly. He was daily put on display in a cage in the prison yard where he could be seen and taunted by visitors.

After a four-month confinement in Lumpkin's jail, Burns was sold to a plantation owner from North Carolina. Burns's new master treated him well and within a short time took him to Baltimore where he in turn sold Burns, this time to a Reverend Stockwell and the Reverend Leonard Grimes of Boston. These men brought Burns out of the South and restored his freedom. Burns's case was well known in the North, and for a period of time he gave speeches describing his ordeal. Uncomfortable with the attention, however, Burns soon took the opportunity of attending Oberlin College in Ohio. After two years of college, he left to take charge of a Baptist church in Indianapolis, Indiana. Discriminatory racial laws in Indiana once again forced him to flee, this time to the small community of St. Catharines in Ontario, Canada. It was there that Burns spent his last days as pastor of Zion Baptist Church.

GUIDING STUDENT RESPONSE

Connect to the Literature

1. **What Do You Think?** Accept all reasonable responses.

Comprehension Check
• He escaped from slavery.
• They see him being led to the courthouse.

 Use Selection Quiz **Unit Five Resource Book,** p. 51.

Think Critically

2. Answers will vary. Look for thoughtful responses.
3. Students should try to analyze the abolitionists from Burns's point of view.
4. Responses will vary. Encourage students to back up their responses with reasons.
5. His plight brought slavery close to home for Northerners.

Literary Analysis

Literary Nonfiction Responses will vary. Encourage students to see how the author uses literary devices to strengthen understanding and appreciation of the factual information. For example:

FACT
A vigilance committee had been organized in Boston to protect the rights of fugitives.

LITERARY DEVICE
When Reverend Parker thought about slavery, his "blood boiled." The metaphor emphasizes his humane character and the reason he concerns himself with Anthony Burns.

FACT
Recaptured fugitive slaves were imprisoned until their hearings took place.

LITERARY DEVICE
"The weight of the past and the darkness of its night enclosed Anthony . . ." This description shows the personal suffering of recaptured slaves like Anthony.

Connect to the Literature

1. **What Do You Think?** What were your feelings as you came to the end of this selection? Explain.

Comprehension Check
• Why is Anthony Burns brought before Judge Loring?
• How do the abolitionists find out about Burns's arrest?

Think Critically

2. **ACTIVE READING** **MONITOR** Review the notes you made in your **READER'S NOTEBOOK**. Compare them with those of a classmate to see if you agree on which characters were proslavery and which were antislavery. If you disagree, reread portions of the text and look for details to help you clarify the information.

3. How would you describe the change in the way Anthony Burns felt toward the abolitionists who were trying to help him? Why do you think Burns's feelings changed?

4. What were your feelings about Edward Loring, a judge sworn to uphold the Fugitive Slave Act yet a man who seems to act kindly toward Burns?

5. What do you think the author means when she says, "Anthony Burns became a symbol of freedom"?

THINK ABOUT
• efforts to keep Burns's arrest and trial a secret
• the reaction of Grimes and Dana when they first see Burns
• the pamphlets circulated by Parker

Extend Interpretations

6. **What If?** At one point, Anthony Burns thinks about what would have happened if he had gone to the dedication of Reverend Grimes's church. He thinks that he wouldn't have been arrested because he wouldn't have been on the street where the slave catchers found him. Do you agree? Why or why not?

7. **Connect to Life** Review the chart you created for Connect to Your Life on page 750. Do you have any questions the selection didn't answer? Discuss them with your classmates.

Literary Analysis

LITERARY NONFICTION Writers of both informative nonfiction and **literary nonfiction** describe actual people, places, and events in their works. In informative nonfiction this is done in a straightforward fashion. The writer of literary nonfiction, however, includes elements common to fiction, such as plot, setting, dialogue, and character development, for example, to present the information.

In the excerpt from *Anthony Burns,* Virginia Hamilton presents information about the actual events and participants in the capture and trial of Anthony Burns, but she dramatizes them with fictional elements that bring the events to life for the reader.

Cooperative Learning Activity With a partner, review the selection and jot down what literary elements, such as description or bits of dialogue, you discovered as you read the excerpt from *Anthony Burns.* Afterward, discuss how the selection's literary devices helped you to appreciate the real-life experiences of Anthony Burns.

Literary Elements

Description:
The author's description of the pain Burns felt from his wrist and ankle chains was really powerful.

Extend Interpretations

6. **What If?** Possible Responses: Direct students to look at the manpower dedicated to Anthony's recapture.

7. **Connect to Life** Possible Responses: Encourage students to look for more information on the institution of slavery and individuals' and groups' efforts to abolish it in order to answer their questions.

The People Could Fly

from The People Could Fly
Folk tale retold by VIRGINIA HAMILTON

He said it to their faces. 'We are ones who fly!'"

Connect to Your Life

Pass It On Can you think of an inspiring story that has been passed down to you? What did you learn from this story? Do you think that you could be like the hero or heroes who are a part of it? Share your responses with a partner.

Build Background

CONNECT TO **HISTORY** When Europeans colonized the Western Hemisphere, they brought with them the institution of slavery. A cheap labor supply was needed to support the large-scale farming the colonists established. The trade in people kidnapped in Africa and sent to America as slaves became lucrative. Between the 1500s and the 1800s, some 12 million Africans were sent to the Western Hemisphere. About 2 million of them did not survive the journey across the Atlantic.

Most slaves in the United States worked as field hands, planting and harvesting crops such as indigo, tobacco, rice, and cotton. Their work was long and tedious, usually beginning at sunrise and ending at sunset. Overseers hired by the slave owners enforced strict discipline and made sure no one slacked off. Slaves were clothed, fed, and given shelter by their owners. While conditions varied, they were rarely more than the bare minimum.

Laws in the Southern states prohibited slaves from owning property, getting an education, marrying, and buying their own freedom. Despite these laws, slaves managed to develop a sense of community, a means of communication, a culture, and a tradition. One part of that tradition is the body of stories, myths, and legends that the slaves told. Some of these stories had African origins; some were created in America. "The People Could Fly" is an example of one of these stories.

WORDS TO KNOW **Vocabulary Preview**
glinty   scorn   seize   shuffle   snag

Focus Your Reading

LITERARY ANALYSIS **FOLK TALE** African-American **folk tales** developed among Africans transported to America as slaves. Slaves were not allowed to speak their own language or learn how to read or write English, so they passed down their culture and experience orally. Tales such as "The People Could Fly" provided slaves comfort and hope and preserved their history.

ACTIVE READING **SUMMARIZING** You can check your understanding of what you read, and remember it better, if you **summarize** it. To summarize a story, retell only the **main ideas,** using your own words. Leave out unimportant details.

 READER'S NOTEBOOK. A **story map** is one way to record and remember important details about a selection. A story map can also help you write a summary of a story. As you read, use a story map like this to record details from "The People Could Fly."

Characters: *Toby, Sarah, Driver,*
Conflict:
Time and Place:
Event 1:
Event 2:
Event 3:
Resolution:

Objectives
1. understand and appreciate an **African-American folk tale (Literary Analysis)**
2. understand the significance of **dialect (Literary Analysis)**
3. utilize the reading skill **summarize**

Summary
This poetic folktale tells about Africans who long ago had the power to fly. Captured and sent across the sea on slave ships, they had to leave their wings behind. In their misery, most of them forgot they could fly, although they still had the power. One slave who possessed the magic was an old man named Toby. He worked in the fields alongside Sarah, a woman who once had wings. When an overseer cruelly whipped Sarah and her baby, Toby told her the magic words and she flew to freedom with her child. The next day, Toby spoke the magic words to fellow slaves exhausted by the heat, and they flew away like blackbirds. The master wanted to kill him, but Toby just laughed and flew away with the others, while the slaves who could not fly watched longingly from the ground. Eventually, these slaves escaped to freedom on foot and told their children about the people who could fly, and so the story has been passed down for generations.

Thematic Link
This folktale inspires hope that people will survive against all odds.

5-Minute Warm-Up

Daily Language SkillBuilder   **TEKS 16B**

Have students **proofread** the display sentences on page 653K and write them correctly. The sentences also appear on Transparency 24 of **Grammar Transparencies and Copymasters.**

 Mini Lesson   **Preteaching Vocabulary**

If you would like to preteach the WORDS TO KNOW for this selection, use the Mini Lesson, p. 768.

LESSON RESOURCES

UNIT FIVE RESOURCE BOOK, pp. 52–58

ASSESSMENT
Formal Assessment, pp. 121–122
Teacher's Guide to Assessment and Portfolio Use
Test Generator

SKILLS TRANSPARENCIES AND COPYMASTERS

Reading and Critical Thinking
• Summarizing, TR 11 (for Thinking Through the Literature, p. 772)

Grammar
• Punctuating Dialogue, CM 131 (for Mini Lesson, p. 773)
Vocabulary
• Word Knowledge, CM 78 (for Mini Lesson, p. 768)
• Word Origins, CM 79 (for Mini Lesson, p. 770)

Communications
• Giving and Using Feedback to Improve Performance, TR 16 (for Mini Lesson, p. 769)
Writing
• Elaboration, TR 13 (for Mini Lesson, pp. 784–785)

INTEGRATED TECHNOLOGY
Audio Library
Internet: Research Starter

Visit our website:
www.mcdougallittell.com

TEKS See the Skills Trace at the beginning of the unit for information on TEKS covered in this lesson.

Reading and Analyzing

Literary Analysis
FOLKTALE

A Ask students what the slaves listening to the tale would learn about their history.

Possible Responses: They would learn that they came from Africa and were captured and forced into slavery. Remind students that folktales may include supernatural elements. Ask students what extraordinary ability some of the people originally had.

Possible Response: They knew magic and could fly.

Use **Unit Five Resource Book,** p. 54 for more practice.

Literary Analysis: DIALECT

B Remind students that dialect is a form of language spoken in a certain place or by a particular group of people. Ask students what the use of dialect in this tale contributes to the effect of the text.

Possible Responses: Dialect makes the story sound like it is being told aloud and creates familiarity with the culture of the people whose story it is.

Active Reading   SUMMARIZING

C Tell students that the conflicts must be part of a summary of the story. Ask students what conflict is creating the action in this part of the tale.

Possible Response: Sarah's baby is irritating the Overseer and Driver, and she is not working hard enough to please them.

Use **Unit Five Resource Book,** p. 53 for more practice.

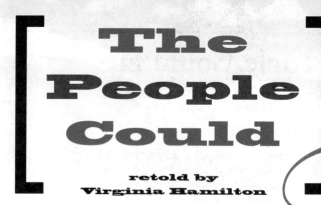

The People Could Fly

retold by
Virginia Hamilton

Illustration by Leo and Diane Dillon, from *The People Could Fly* by Virginia Hamilton. Illustration Copyright © 1985 Leo and Diane Dillon. Reprinted by permission of Alfred A. Knopf, Inc.

768   UNIT FIVE   **AUTHOR STUDY**

Teaching Options

 Mini Lesson **Preteaching Vocabulary**   **TEKS 6C**   **TAAS Reading Obj. 1**

WORD KNOWLEDGE

Instruction Tell students that gaining as much information as possible about unfamiliar words will help them to use the words more precisely. Consulting reference sources will help them to identify the part of speech of the word and introduce them to definitions, synonyms, and the origins of unknown words. For example, knowing that *grab* is a synonym of *seize* clarifies the way that *seize* should be used in a sentence.

Exercises Have students determine whether the underlined WORD TO KNOW in each sentence conveys the correct meaning and is used as the correct part of speech. Have students rewrite sentences in which the word is used inaccurately.

1. The <u>snagged</u> edge of her torn gown almost tripped her.
2. She felt the <u>scorn</u> of the overseer.
3. His eyes glared <u>glinty</u> at her.
4. Toby <u>shuffled</u> over to the fallen slave.
5. The overseer <u>seized</u> her by stepping out of her way and letting her go.

Use **Unit Five Resource Book,** p. 55 for more exercises. Use **Vocabulary Transparencies and Copymasters,** p. 78, for additional support.

They say the people could fly. Say that long ago in Africa, some of the people knew magic. And they would walk up on the air like climbin' up on a gate. And they flew like blackbirds over the fields. Black, shiny wings flappin' against the blue up there.

Then, many of the people were captured for Slavery. The ones that could fly shed their wings. They couldn't take their wings across the water on the slave ships. Too crowded, don't you know.

The folks were full of misery, then. Got sick with the up and down of the sea. So they forgot about flyin' when they could no longer breathe the sweet scent of Africa.

Say the people who could fly kept their power, although they shed their wings. They kept their secret magic in the land of slavery. They looked the same as the other people from Africa who had been coming over, who had dark skin. Say you couldn't tell anymore one who could fly from one who couldn't.

One such who could was an old man, call him Toby. And standin' tall, yet afraid, was a young woman who once had wings. Call her Sarah. Now Sarah carried a babe tied to her back. She trembled to be so hard worked and scorned.

The slaves labored in the fields from sunup to sundown. The owner of the slaves callin' himself their Master. Say he was a hard lump of clay. A hard, glinty coal. A hard rock pile,

wouldn't be moved. His Overseer[1] on horseback pointed out the slaves who were slowin' down. So the one called Driver cracked his whip over the slow ones to make them move faster. That whip was a slice-open cut of pain. So they did move faster. Had to.

Sarah hoed and chopped the row as the babe on her back slept.

Say the child grew hungry. That babe started up bawling too loud. Sarah couldn't stop to feed it. Couldn't stop to soothe and quiet it down. She let it cry. She didn't want to. She had no heart to croon[2] to it.

"Keep that thing quiet," called the Overseer. He pointed his finger at the babe. The woman scrunched low. The Driver cracked his whip across the babe anyhow. The babe hollered like any hurt child, and the woman fell to the earth.

The old man that was there, Toby, came and helped her to her feet.

"I must go soon," she told him.

"Soon," he said.

Sarah couldn't stand up straight any longer. She was too weak. The sun burned her face. The babe cried and cried, "Pity me, oh, pity me," say it sounded like. Sarah was so sad and starvin', she sat down in the row.

---

1. **Overseer:** a person who directs the work of others; a supervisor.
2. **croon:** to sing softly.

WORDS TO KNOW | **scorn** (skôrn) *v.* to treat with contempt
glinty (glĭn' tē) *adj.* sparkling

769

  Speaking and Listening TEKS 5A, 5C, 5D

STORYTELLING

Prepare Explain to students that to be effective storytellers, they should try to
- focus on details that bring characters and scenes to life
- use strong descriptive words that create vivid images
- concentrate (An audience will lose interest if a storyteller's focus begins to wander.)
- slow down and speed up as appropriate
- practice

Divide the class into three groups. Invite each group to choose a familiar fairy tale or legend.

Have group members write down the main points of their story.

Present Have group members take turns telling a part of the story. Each storyteller should end his or her part with "And then . . . " to get the next person started. Students should generate informal criteria based on the suggestions for effective storytelling to evaluate their own presentations and those of others.

BLOCK SCHEDULING This activity is particularly well suited for longer class periods.

Use **Communications Transparencies and Copymasters,** p. 16, for additional support.

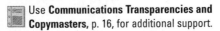

[**There was a great outcryin'. The bent backs straighted up. Old and young who were called slaves and could fly joined hands.**]

A "Get up, you black cow," called the Overseer. He pointed his hand, and the Driver's whip snarled around Sarah's legs. Her sack dress tore into rags. Her legs bled onto the earth. She couldn't get up.

Toby was there where there was no one to help her and the babe.

"Now, before it's too late," panted Sarah. "Now, Father!"

"Yes, Daughter, the time is come," Toby answered. "Go, as you know how to go!"

He raised his arms, holding them out to her. *"Kum . . . yali, kum buba tambe,"* and more magic words, said so quickly, they sounded like whispers and sighs.

1 The young woman lifted one foot on the air. Then the other. She flew clumsily at first, with the child now held tightly in her arms. Then she felt the magic, the African mystery. Say she rose just as free as a bird. As light as a feather.

The Overseer rode after her, hollerin'. Sarah flew over the fences. She flew over the woods. Tall trees could not <u>snag</u> her. Nor could the Overseer. She flew like an eagle now, until she was gone from sight. No one dared speak about it. Couldn't believe it. But it was, because they that was there saw that it was.

Say the next day was dead hot in the fields. A young man slave fell from the heat. The Driver come and whipped him. Toby come over and spoke words to the fallen one. The words of ancient Africa once heard are never remembered completely. The young man forgot them as soon as he heard them. They went way inside him. He got up and rolled over on the air. He rode it awhile. And he flew away.

Another and another fell from the heat. Toby was there. He cried out to the fallen and reached his arms out to them. *"Kum kunka yali, kum . . . tambe!"* Whispers and sighs. And they too rose on the air. They rode the hot breezes. The ones flyin' were black and shinin' sticks, wheelin' above the head of the Overseer. They crossed the rows, the fields, the fences, the streams, and were away.

"<u>Seize</u> the old man!" cried the Overseer. "I heard him say the magic *words*. Seize him!"

| WORDS TO KNOW | **snag** (snăg) *v.* to catch and tear
seize (sēz) *v.* to grab suddenly with force |

770

The one callin' himself Master come runnin'. The Driver got his whip ready to curl around old Toby and tie him up. The slave owner took his hip gun from its place. He meant to kill old black Toby.

But Toby just laughed. Say he threw back his head and said, "Hee, hee! Don't you know who I am? Don't you know some of us in this field?" He said it to their faces. "We are ones who fly!"

And he sighed the ancient words that were a dark promise. He said them all around to the others in the field under the whip, ". . . *buba yali . . . buba tambe . . .*"

There was a great outcryin'. The bent backs straightened up. Old and young who were called slaves and could fly joined hands. Say like they would ring-sing. But they didn't <u>shuffle</u> in a circle. They didn't sing. They rose on the air. They flew in a flock that was black against the heavenly blue. Black crows or black shadows. It didn't matter, they went so high. Way above the plantation, way over the slavery land. Say they flew away to *Free-dom*.

And the old man, old Toby, flew behind them, takin' care of them. He wasn't cryin'. He wasn't laughin'. He was the seer. His gaze fell on the plantation where the slaves who could not fly waited.

"Take us with you!" Their looks spoke it, but they were afraid to shout it. Toby couldn't take them with him. Hadn't the time to teach them to fly. They must wait for a chance to run.

"Goodie-bye!" the old man called Toby spoke to them, poor souls! And he was flyin' gone.

So they say. The Overseer told it. The one called Master said it was a lie, a trick of the light. The Driver kept his mouth shut.

The slaves who could not fly told about the people who could fly to their children. When they were free. When they sat close before the fire in the free land, they told it. They did so love firelight and *Free-dom*, and tellin'.

They say that the children of the ones who could not fly told their children. And now, me, I have told it to you. ❖

WORDS
TO
KNOW

shuffle (shŭf' əl) *v.* to slide the feet along the ground while walking

771

 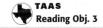

GUIDING STUDENT RESPONSE

Connect to the Literature

1. **What Do You Think?** Responses will vary. Possible Responses: Students might say that they would feel sad or envious or happy for those who escaped.

Comprehension Check
• They had the power to fly.
• He whips them.
• The slaves who could not fly went on to tell the story to their children.

 Use Selection Quiz
Unit Five Resource Book, p. 58.

Think Critically

2. Possible Responses: Student summaries should include the background of the story, the description of the major characters and their roles, the significant conflicts, and the resolution of the conflicts.

Use **Reading and Critical Thinking Transparencies,** p. 11, for additional support.

3. Possible Responses: This tale suggested that although they were enslaved, they still had their identities as Africans and a proud heritage behind them. The story also encouraged them to believe that one day they could rise up and obtain freedom like those who could fly. It might also have served as a reminder of the transitory nature of life and the promise of eternal freedom.

4. Possible Responses: The author uses dialogue and figurative language to bring the characters and action to life. Her description of the flight of the individuals and then of the group includes specific details, such as "lifted one foot on the air" and "flew in a flock that was black against the heavenly blue," to help the reader visualize what is happening.

Connect to the Literature

1. **What Do You Think?** What emotion would you feel if you were one of the people left behind? Discuss your response with a partner.

Comprehension Check
• What special power did some of the people in Africa have?
• What does the Driver do to Sarah and her baby?
• Who went on to tell the story of the people who could fly?

Think Critically

2. **ACTIVE READING SUMMARIZING** Look at the notes that you took in the story map you put in your **📖 READER'S NOTEBOOK**. Summarize the story in your own words. Make your summary as brief as possible, but be sure to include the main ideas. Compare your summary with that of a classmate and discuss how you might improve your summaries.

3. Since people really can't fly, what do you think this story meant to the people who heard it?

> **THINK ABOUT**
> • the way that enslaved people were treated
> • what the people wished for
> • how the people felt about themselves

4. How does Virginia Hamilton make this story and the characters come alive? How does she make it seem almost possible that the people could fly?

Extend Interpretations

5. **Writer's Style** The story retold as "The People Could Fly" was passed on by generations of storytellers before it was written down. In retelling it, Virginia Hamilton chose to have her narrator speak in dialect. The narrator's voice sounds as if it could be that of one of the characters in the story itself. How does this add to the story? How does it affect the reader?

6. **Connect to Life** What kind of power do words hold for you? Look through a book of quotations and choose two that express a feeling or an idea that you think is important. Explain why you think these quotations are powerful.

Literary Analysis

FOLK TALES Stories told by African-American slaves about their real and imaginary experiences are called African-American **folk tales.** These stories combine elements from Africa with American ones. Originally part of the oral tradition—stories told in family or community gatherings—many African-American folk tales were collected and written down by historians to preserve them. Virginia Hamilton wanted to bring them "out of the musty old manuscripts where nobody ever saw them" so that these stories could be read, retold, and understood by new generations. In "The People Could Fly," Hamilton skillfully brings one of them to life for her readers.

Cooperative Learning Activity
The selection mentions a group of unnamed characters known only as "old and young who were called slaves" who joined hands and flew to freedom. As a class, invent some names and ages for these characters, such as "a young man named John" or "an old woman named Rachel."

Record these names and ages on note cards. Then divide into small groups and choose one of the cards. For the character whose name you have chosen, create a story that ends with his or her meeting with Toby. Have someone in your group write the story down. Afterward, share your story by reading it to the class.

Extend Interpretations

5. **Writer's Style** Possible Responses: The choice of narrator makes the story seem more realistic, as if it could have happened. The readers are drawn into the action and sympathize with the plight of the characters. They feel as if they are descended from those who had to stay behind.

6. **Connect to Life** Possible Responses: Responses will vary. Encourage students to connect the feeling or idea to experiences in their own lives that give the quotation particular meaning.

Literary Analysis

Folk Tales Students may wish to begin their stories by relating how the character ended up so far from home and then tell of how the character suffered at the hands of the overseer. Encourage students to bring their characters to life by revealing their thoughts, feelings, and longings.

Grammar in Context: Punctuating Dialogue

Hamilton uses dialogue to capture the unique voices of her characters.

> Toby was there where there was no one to help her and the babe.
> "Now, before it's too late," panted Sarah. "Now, Father!"
> "Yes, Daughter, the time is come," Toby answered. "Go, as you know how to go!"

To avoid confusing the reader, she places quotation marks at the beginning and end of direct speech and begins a new paragraph whenever the speaker changes.

Apply to Your Writing Capitalize the first word in a direct quotation if it is a complete sentence. At the end of a quotation, place periods and commas inside the quotation marks. Place question marks and exclamation points inside if they belong to the quotation; place them outside if they do not belong to the quotation.

WRITING EXERCISE Supply the missing punctuation marks in the sentences.

Example: _Original_ Keep that baby quiet, said the Overseer.

Rewritten "Keep that baby quiet," said the Overseer.

1. I can help you, the old man said to Sarah.
2. Sarah told him, I must go soon.
3. After a while, the Overseer said, Seize the old man!
4. Don't you know who we are? he said to their faces. We are ones who fly!
5. Take us with you! cried those who were left behind.
6. Good-bye, said the ones who could fly.

Grammar Handbook Quotations, p. R79

Vocabulary in Action

EXERCISE A: RELATED WORDS For each Word to Know, create and complete a diagram like the model below.

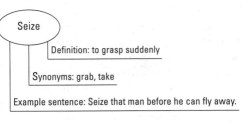

EXERCISE B: WORD ORIGINS Modern scholars believe that many of today's languages have their roots in one common language spoken around 7,000 years ago. English, a member of the Germanic family of languages, contains many words that come from other languages, particularly Greek and Latin. All of the vocabulary words in this selection are descended from Germanic words. Use a dictionary or encyclopedia to find some of the other modern languages in the Germanic family. How might words from a different language have entered English?

Building Vocabulary
For an in-depth study of word origins, see p. 745.

WORDS TO KNOW	glinty	scorn	seize	shuffle	snag

 Grammar 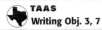 **TEKS** 16B **TAAS** Writing Obj. 3, 7

PUNCTUATING DIALOGUE

Instruction Remind students that direct quotations are set off by quotation marks. Tell students that the first word of a direct quotation is capitalized and that a new paragraph begins each time the speaker changes. Also, end marks that are part of the quotation appear inside the quotation marks, while question marks and exclamation points that are not part of the direct quotation are placed outside the quotation marks.

Exercises Have students rewrite the following dialogue, punctuating it correctly.

I really enjoyed the tale Dina said because there were so many ways to interpret it. Prakash replied for me, the tale brought the horrors of slavery to life and made them seem real. I hope our class reads more folk tales. Don't you, Prakash?

SUGGESTED ANSWER

"I really enjoyed the tale," Dina said, "because there were so many ways to interpret it."

Prakash replied, "For me, the tale brought the horrors of slavery to life and made them seem real."

"I hope our class reads more folk tales. Don't you, Prakash?"

 Use **Unit Five Resource Book,** p. 56.
Use **Grammar Transparencies and Copymasters,** p. 131.

Use McDougal Littell's **_Language Network_,** Chapter 11, for more instruction and practice in punctuating dialogue.

Grammar in Context

Possible Responses:
WRITING EXERCISE

1. "I can help you," the old man said to Sarah.
2. Sarah told him, "I must go soon."
3. After a while, the Overseer said, "Seize the old man!"
4. "Don't you know who we are?" he said to their faces. "We are the ones who fly!"
5. "Take us with you!" cried those who were left behind.
6. "Goodie-bye," said the ones who could fly.

Vocabulary in Action

Exercise A
Sample Response:
Scorn
Definition: treat with anger or dislike
Synonyms: ridicule; disrespect
Sentence: They decided to welcome rather than scorn those who are different from them.

Exercise B
Possible Responses:
languages of the Netherlands; immigration and travel have expanded the English language.

The Cooperative Children's Book Center is located at the University of Wisconsin-Madison. It is a noncirculating library for adults with an interest in examining, studying, and researching children's literature. The Cooperative Children's Book Center has three objectives. The first is to provide a collection of books for children and young adults that includes recent, past, and historical volumes. The second objective is to function as an educational resource for Wisconsin librarians, teachers, and students. The last goal of the center is to support learning, teaching, and research needs for the study of children's literature. The center sponsors a variety of programs related to children's literature including monthly discussions of new books, annual awards discussions, continuing education courses, and a two-day children's and young adult literature conference offered every two years.

**Teaching Nonfiction:
Skills and Strategies**

MAKE INFERENCES
Point out to students that a speaker has some advantages over a writer. A speech is usually prepared for a particular occasion and a specific audience. Knowing this helps the speaker decide what to include and how to phrase his or her thoughts. Ask students why Virginia Hamilton includes the first paragraph in her speech.

Possible Responses: to establish a tone of honesty in her speech; to show that she is willing to share her insights and experiences; to interest her listeners in what she is going to say

Looking for America

**Speech by
Virginia Hamilton**

Preparing to Read

Build Background

In 1993, Virginia Hamilton gave a speech at a banquet in honor of the thirtieth anniversary of the Cooperative Children's Book Center. She spoke of the importance of memory, history, and the telling of stories: "We each have a story. We write it as we live it. We change it, we amend it, we revise it, but we continue telling our tales to ourselves, at least." In the portion of the speech reprinted here, Hamilton expresses how her work continues to grow out of her own life experiences.

I wonder, sometimes, there before the fire in a long winter, how I write certain of my own books. Take *The Planet of Junior Brown*. It's one of the few of my books I never tire of. It still reads well. It still makes me proud. If I could, I'd rewrite *M.C. Higgins, the Great*, but of course, I can't. I'd rewrite *W.E.B. DuBois* and *Paul Robeson*. I love *Anthony Burns* just the way it is—a very hard book to do, but it was good work and it pleases me. I don't know how I wrote the *Justice* trilogy. I like it a lot. I only remember that I was in a state of terror the whole time. There is really good stuff in *A Little Love*, things that I'm proud of—the way Grandmom and Pop talk, their fears, her forgetfulness. Grandmom and Pop seem very human to me. I didn't like Sheema's father when she finds him, but I thought I did a good job of presenting him. He came through as what he was. I think *A White Romance* and *Cousins* are very good books, although very different. They still seem true. *Plain City* seems the truest, but that may be because it's still so close to me. I enjoyed making its degree of difficulty read simply.

This is the way I think about the work I do, and I think about it all the time. I have to do that because when a book is given out to the world, that is, when it is published, it becomes changed by the public who reads it. People have all kinds of ideas about what you have

done. So one needs to be very certain in oneself about what it is you have done.

The books I've mentioned and the rest of them, too, I suppose, come from who I am. I suspect they reflect how I was taught to see when I was very small.

When I was a child, I went looking for America. And looking, it was important that I notice every small thing, every sound, every sight. Things that I learned on our farm in the countryside then stay with me to this day, such as the fact that large birds, like hawks, crows, and owls, live at the tops of tall trees, while smaller birds, such as sparrows, robins, and jays, live lower down on low branches or in the brush trees. A very childish observation; yet, it seems to me I remember, then, that the big heavy birds should live below and the little lighter weight birdies should live atop things. Well, that wasn't the way things were, I observed.

I also noticed that country children like myself rode buses to school, while town children never had to. They could walk all the way, visiting the outdoors, the day, as they went. Sometimes, I wanted so much to be a town child. I often felt outside of things because I came from the countryside, except when it rained and thundered and lightninged, and the town children got caught and got wet. We on the buses laughed and waved at them.

Sometimes, the buses stopped to pick them up if the weather was particularly dangerous, and at those times, we were helpful as they came dripping inside with us.

Every spring, when the rain puddles turned warm from the sun, I would get out my red Elgin balloon-tire bike and pedal to school and back. There was nothing quite like that first day, with my books stacked securely in the wire basket in front, my bike shining from a fresh coat of paint. It's probably a given that I should become a storyteller. I remember vividly the sound of my bike tires over wet blacktop.

I think anyone who is taught to go looking for America will perhaps find it; or, if not, at least they will tell stories about how they went out looking.

Thinking Through the Literature

1. How do you think Virginia Hamilton's background prepared her to be a storyteller?

2. What do you think Hamilton means by the phrase "Looking for America"? Do you think she found it? Discuss.

3. **Connect to Life** Have you gone "Looking for America"? If you have, what have you seen? If you haven't, where would you go? Explain.

VIRGINIA HAMILTON **775**

THE AUTHOR'S STYLE

Readers of Virginia Hamilton's work hear stories—stories told to them in different voices by varied characters. Students will be made aware of Virginia Hamilton's style through the "Key Style Points" and will find examples of the three style points in the excerpts in the right margin.

Key Style Points

Word Choice Point out that the simple language suits sometimes the simplicity of the actions. At other times, this simple language presents complicated events and concepts with a clarity and forthrightness suitable to the book's audience.

Realism Readers can feel the burning sun and the hunger that Sarah is experiencing. Point out that her reaction of just sitting down is a natural one to have under the circumstances.

Imagery The simple metaphor evokes several layers of meaning. Day is usually perceived as bringing with it promise and hope. In this metaphor, that idea is reversed; day viewed through Anthony's prison bars brings only the promise of renewed pain. This pain is equated with that felt by the lashings of the overseer's whip.

Applications

1. **Active Reading** Possible passages include: the description of Anthony's feelings and physical sensations as he waits in the courtroom (page 753); the description of Sarah after the Driver whips her (page 770); the description of the slaves flying away from the plantation (page 771).

2. **Writing** Suggest that students brainstorm events and then physical details of the event before they write their descriptions.

3. **Viewing and Representing** Students may choose to illustrate one of the passages that they picked for the Active Reading exercise. Their sketches should reveal the feelings of the character through the use of physical details.

Hamilton's Descriptive Style

Virginia Hamilton makes her stories come alive for the reader by the way she describes her characters and their experiences. Three elements of her descriptive style include simple language, realistic detail, and imagery.

Key Style Points

Word Choice Hamilton seldom chooses words that send her reader to the dictionary. Read the passage to the right and note how simply but accurately she describes the small details that lead up to Anthony Burns's being brought into the courtroom.

Realism Virginia Hamilton provides realistic descriptions of her characters, not only of how they look and act, but of how they feel and think as well. In this passage from "The People Could Fly," notice how she uses physical details to emphasize Sarah's thoughts and feelings.

Imagery In the excerpt to the right, notice the simple but powerful image that Hamilton uses to suggest Burns's feelings at his imprisonment.

Applications

1. **Active Reading** From either "The People Could Fly" or *Anthony Burns*, find another passage where Hamilton uses physical detail to emphasize a character's thoughts and feelings. Compare your choices with your classmates.

2. **Writing** Write a description of an event from your own experience. Try to include physical details that will help the reader understand how you felt such as, "The old abandoned house made me shiver inside."

3. **Viewing and Representing** Find a passage from either "The People Could Fly" or *Anthony Burns* that is rich in realistic detail and imagery and draw a sketch that illustrates it. Explain how the author's use of realistic details and imagery in that particular scene influenced your drawing.

Word Choice

Anthony did as he was told. In a small room off to the side he washed his face and smoothed his hair. There was no comb or brush for him. He straightened his clothing. He took a tin cup of cold water that Asa offered him, but that was all he was given.

—from *Anthony Burns*

Realism

The sun burned her face. The babe cried and cried, "Pity me, oh, pity me," say it sounded like. Sarah was so sad and starvin', she sat down in the row.

—from "The People Could Fly"

Imagery

The windows of the jury room where he was kept under guard were covered with iron bars that seemed to break the day into welts of pain.

—from *Anthony Burns*

Writing Options

700-Word Summary Write a 700-word summary of the excerpt from *Anthony Burns*. To summarize a work, retell the main ideas in your own words. Leave out unimportant ideas. Check your summary by asking yourself if someone who hasn't read the excerpt could use your summary to understand what happened. Put your summary in your **Working Portfolio**.

Writing Handbook
See p. R46: Summarizing.

Activities & Explorations

Dramatic Monologue Choose one of the passages from *Anthony Burns* in which Burns is thinking about his past or present condition. Expand the passage into a monologue. Perform your monologue for the class. ~ **SPEAKING AND LISTENING**

Inquiry & Research

The Fugitive Slave Law Part of The Compromise of 1850, the Fugitive Slave Law was an attempt to settle the differences between North and South. Research the background of this law, who fought for it, who fought against it, and why it created such hardships for African Americans like Anthony Burns.

 More Online: Research Starter www.mcdougallittell.com

Author Study Project

Storytelling

Events in history are themselves stories that invite us to get to know the people involved. Create a historical retelling of your own.

1 Find Topics As a class, brainstorm a list of historical topics around which you could create stories. Write the topics on slips of paper. Then divide into groups and have a representative of each group draw a topic. As a group, follow the remaining steps and decide which group members will be responsible for research, retelling, and presentation.

2 Gather Information Collect written information related to your topic. Find general historical accounts from an encyclopedia to get the basic facts of the event: *what, where, when, who,* and *why.* Pay special attention to the *people* who were involved in this historical moment. If specific individuals played a key role, check to see if there are any biographies of them in your school library.

3 Create the Retelling Choose a way of retelling the stories of the people you have learned about. A way of doing this could be a story; a dialogue or a monologue in which a character or characters describe a key incident; a poem; or even a ballad or song. One or two members of your group could create a poster to illustrate the retelling.

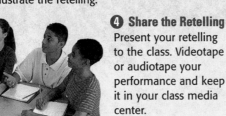

4 Share the Retelling Present your retelling to the class. Videotape or audiotape your performance and keep it in your class media center.

VIRGINIA HAMILTON **777**

Writing Options

700-Word Summary Have students outline the main ideas of the selection before writing their summaries. **To make this assignment easier,** have students share their outlines within a small group and work together on the final summary.

📄 Use **Writing Transparencies,** p. 51, for additional support.

Activities & Explorations

Dramatic Monologue Students should incorporate into their monologues the necessary information about where they are and what is happening as they present their monologues. **To make this assignment more challenging,** have students refer to the complete text of Virginia Hamilton's book to discover other facts about Anthony's life that could help them develop their monologues.

📄 Use **Communications Transparencies and Copymasters,** p. 14, for additional support.

Inquiry & Research

The Fugitive Slave Law Suggest that students try various subject headings, such as the Compromise of 1850 or abolitionist movements, as well as look up information on the people mentioned in *Anthony Burns.*

Author Study Project

Storytelling

After topics have been chosen, encourage all members of the group to research and try to find different perspectives from which to view the event. Suggest that they follow up on some of the less well-known details and people to give their story a unique perspective. Tell students that combining methods of storytelling might be effective. One person could be a narrator while another offers insight into the character's thoughts and feelings through monologues woven throughout the narrative framework. Visual aids, background music, and costumes may enhance their presentations. Finally, have class members listen to or view other taped stories and discuss what they learn.

📄 Use **Communications Transparencies and Copymasters,** p. 8, for additional support.

Creating stories, Virginia Hamilton says, enables her to explore "the known, the remembered, and the imagined, the literary triad of which all stories are made." While Hamilton's stories are set in a variety of times and places, her characters share similar challenges as they make important discoveries about places, people, and themselves.

The House of Dies Drear 1968

Edgar Allan Poe Award

Thomas has mixed feelings about the huge old house that his father has bought. The old house seems to hold a secret, and frightening things begin to happen. Danger and excitement build as Thomas tries to unravel the mystery.

The Planet of Junior Brown 1971

Newbery Honor Book

Two unlikely friends in New York City play hooky from eighth grade for an entire semester. Junior Brown is a 300-pound neurotic musical prodigy who is befriended by Buddy, a tough, homeless, street kid.

M.C. Higgins, the Great 1974

Newbery Medal, Boston Globe-Horn Book Award,
National Book Award

Mayo Cornelius Higgins sits atop a 40-foot steel pole near his home on Sarah's Mountain, surveying the destruction caused by strip mining on the mountain. A huge pile of rubble will soon engulf the family's house, and Higgins is torn between the desire to escape from the destruction and the urge to fight for his home. Two strangers who enter his life may have the solution to his dilemma.

Justice and Her Brothers 1978

Justice has two brothers who are twins: Thomas is mean, and Levi is kind. One summer they discover that they have mysterious powers that allow them to mind-jump a million years into the future. What they find there is both frightening and fascinating. This is the first book of *The Justice Trilogy*. Other titles in the trilogy are *Dustland* and *The Gathering*.

Her Stories 1996

Coretta Scott King Award

Using a variety of voices, dialects, and styles, Hamilton retells trickster tales, folk tales, fairy tales, legends, and autobiographical stories that celebrate African-American women. The information Hamilton provides about the origins of the stories is as colorful and interesting as the stories themselves.

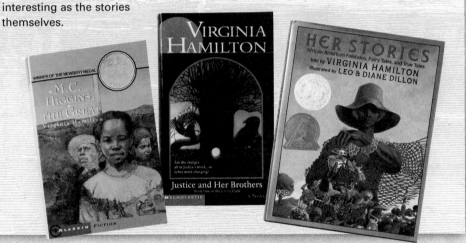

Writing Workshop
Research Report

Objectives

- write a research report
- use a written text as a model for writing
- select and use reference materials and resources as needed for writing
- take notes from relevant and authoritative sources such as periodicals and on-line searches
- develop drafts by organizing ideas into paragraphs
- follow accepted formats for writing research, including documenting sources
- revise a draft to present ideas in a logical order
- identify and correct sentence fragments made from subordinate clauses

Introducing the Workshop

Research Report Ask students whose face is on the Statue of Liberty (the sculptor's mother). Discuss how they might find such information, and ask what other questions someone might ask about the statue. Explain that students can find answers to such questions through research and investigation. Doing research is like solving a mystery, since researchers look for clues that help them answer questions. When questions are answered, students can present their findings in many ways. One way is by writing a research report.

Basics in a Box

Using the Graphic Explain that a research report is actually a series of interlocking parts. The body of the report presents the results of the research. The introduction and conclusion help readers understand this material, and the works cited section presents the sources that the researcher used and allows readers to find additional information if they wish.

Presenting the Rubric To help students understand the assignment, review with them the Standards for Writing a Successful Research Report.

 Use McDougal Littell's *Language Network*, Chapters 12–19, for more instruction on essential writing skills.

 Power Presentation

To engage students visually, use **Power Presentation 2**, Research Report.

Writing Workshop — Research Report

Presenting facts about a topic . . .

From Reading to Writing What would it be like to live in a different place and in a different time period? Nonfiction history writers and writers of historical fiction such as "A Crown of Wild Olive" help readers understand people and societies of the past. They investigate several sources to build complete pictures of their subjects. Writing a **research report** can help you become familiar with sources of information and learn interesting facts about a subject.

Basics in a Box

Research Report at a Glance

Introduction	Body	Conclusion	Works Cited
presents the thesis statement	presents evidence that supports the thesis statement	restates the thesis	lists the sources of information

Research

RUBRIC STANDARDS FOR WRITING

A successful research report should

- include a strong introduction and thesis statement that clearly states the topic and the purpose
- use evidence from primary or secondary sources to develop and support ideas
- credit sources of information
- follow a logical pattern of organization, using transitions between ideas
- use information from multiple sources
- summarize ideas in the conclusion
- include a Works Cited list at the end of the report

 See the Skills Trace at the beginning of the unit for information on TEKS covered in this lesson.

LESSON RESOURCES

USING PRINT RESOURCES
Unit Five Resource Book
- Prewriting, p. 59
- Drafting, p. 60
- Peer Response, pp. 61–62
- Revising, Editing, and Proofreading, p. 63
- Student Models, pp. 64–66
- Rubric, p. 67

Writing Transparencies
- Writing Process Transparencies TR 1–4

- Writing Structure Transparencies: Structuring the Essay, TR 6; Elaboration, TR 13
- Writing Template Transparencies: Research Report, TR 37

Reading and Critical Thinking Transparencies
- Text Structure (Organization), TR 24 (for Mini Lesson, p. 781)

Grammar Transparencies and Copymasters
- Pronoun Case, CM 66 (for Mini Lesson, p. 787)

INTEGRATED TECHNOLOGY
LaserLinks
Writing Springboards
See **Teacher's SourceBook** p. 36 for bar codes.

Writing Coach CD-ROM

Visit our website:
www.mcdougallittell.com

Analyzing a Student Model

SPEAKING OPPORTUNITY
See the Communication Handbook, p. R100, for speaking and presenting tips.

Sager 1

Weston Sager
English 701
Ms. Kilpatrick
May 8

Abe: A Biography

The penny and the five-dollar bill remind us of the 16th president of the United States—a strong, serious-looking man with a beard. President Lincoln didn't always have a beard, however. After he was elected president, a little girl wrote him a letter and suggested that he grow a beard. He followed her suggestion and even thanked her in person for the idea (Whitney 137). This shows his connection to the common people. In addition, the honorable 16th president of the United States abolished slavery, won the Civil War, and tried to hold the United States together during a terrible period in history. President Lincoln's achievements would have been a lot for any president, but they are even more amazing when you consider his background.

Abraham Lincoln's beginnings were humble. His father, Thomas Lincoln, was a farmer who frequently moved the family to different spots in Kentucky, Indiana, and Illinois. His mother, Nancy Hanks Lincoln, died when Abe was nine. However, he loved his stepmother, Sarah Bush Johnston, who encouraged him to try to better himself (Whitney 129). Although Abe was good with an ax and could build log cabins, make fence rails, and clear the forest for farmland, he preferred reading and telling stories to hard physical labor (Armbruster 174–175).

Abraham Lincoln held several jobs that taught him important lessons on his way to the presidency. He hauled cargo on a flatboat down the Mississippi River to New Orleans. This taught him about the horrors of slavery in the South (Whitney 129). He was a clerk and a postmaster general. He was also in the military, became a state legislator, and studied to be a lawyer (Whitney 130). In 1836 he was reelected to the state legislature and received his license to practice law (Whitney 131).

Politics continued to be important to him. In 1858 Abraham Lincoln ran for the Senate against a man named Stephen Douglas. In that

RUBRIC
IN ACTION

❶ Writer begins with an anecdote. The introduction makes the focus of the report clear.

❷ Thesis statement is included here.

❸ Writer chooses chronological order to present information. Specific dates are used.

Another Option:
· Organize by topic.

Teaching the Lesson

Analyzing the Model

The student model is a report about Abraham Lincoln that focuses on his major accomplishments. The thesis is that these accomplishments were particularly amazing considering Lincoln's background. The report traces his early life and jobs, and tells what these experiences taught him. The writer mentions the Lincoln-Douglas Debates and other speaking appearances, which added to Lincoln's popularity. The report then describes Lincoln's role during the Civil War and ends with his assassination.

Have a volunteer read the model aloud, and then discuss the Rubric in Action with students. Point out the key words and phrases in the student model that correspond to the elements mentioned in the Rubric in Action.

1 Explain that an introduction should capture readers' interest and let them know the focus of the report. Ask how the model does this.
Possible Responses: The details in the anecdote are designed to interest readers; the details about Lincoln's accomplishments make the focus of the report clear.

2 Remind students that a thesis statement tells the main idea or purpose of a piece of writing. It prepares readers for what will follow. Ask what kind of information this thesis statement leads them to expect in the body of the report.
Possible Response: information on his achievements and his background

3 Explain that the writer might have chosen order of importance, order of familiarity, or some combination. Ask what advantage chronological order has in a biographical report.
Possible Responses: It is the order in which things happened; it is easy to understand.

 Mini Lesson ## Viewing and Representing  **TEKS 10L, 12I, 18A**

PICTURING TEXT STRUCTURE

Instruction One way to structure a research report is to see it as a series of paragraphs, each giving information about one main idea. The writer in this student model constructed paragraphs this way. He began by stating the main ideas, and then offered evidence to support them.

Activity Have students analyze the text structure of the student model by constructing a diagram to illustrate how the writer organized paragraphs in the research report. The following chart is an example:

Abe: A Biography	
Humble Beginnings	**Jobs Taught Lessons**
father a farmer	
mother died	
stepmother encouraged him	
good with an ax	
preferred reading	

Use **Reading and Critical Thinking Transparencies**, p. 24, for additional support.

4 Point out that writers of research reports must credit sources when they use someone else's ideas or words. They do not need to credit the source of commonly available facts. Ask students what kinds of sources the writer used for this report and what other sources can be used during research.

Response: books, an encyclopedia article, a website; magazine articles, interviews, television programs.

5 Ask students what kinds of facts and details this writer uses to show Lincoln's popularity.

Possible Responses: statistics; reasons, examples of actions

6 Ask students how the source information in the body of the report differs from that given in the listing at the end. Point out conventional punctuation, explaining that students can review this in the Writing Handbook.

Possible Responses: The information in the body of the report is a shorter version that helps readers identify the sources listed at the end.

Sager 2

race, Lincoln had several debates with Douglas. These became known as the Lincoln-Douglas Debates. Big crowds came to listen. Abraham Lincoln was defeated, but the debates helped to make his name known all over the country. His major concern was the growing problem between the North and the South. The issue was whether slavery should be allowed in the land acquired in the Louisiana Purchase. Lincoln was strongly against the spread of slavery. He said, "A house divided against itself cannot stand" (Whitney 134).

By 1859, he was making public speaking appearances and impressed audiences everywhere he went (Whitney 136). In 1860 Abraham Lincoln won the presidential election. In 1864, his share of the votes increased and he won another term ("Lincoln"). His popularity in this election was due to his handling of the Civil War, which was the most important event of Lincoln's presidency. Although Lincoln had never wanted war, he acted shortly after the South broke from the Union and formed the Confederacy. He appointed General Ulysses S. Grant to lead the Union soldiers (Armbruster 182). He also delivered the Emancipation Proclamation. After many difficult battles, the Confederate General Robert E. Lee surrendered to the Union on April 9, 1865. The war ended soon after and the Union was preserved.

However, President Lincoln's leadership of the country was cut short by someone who did not share his opinions ("A. Lincoln"). On April 14, just days after the end of the war, John Wilkes Booth, a Confederate supporter, [...]ey 140). The nation

4 Credits source of each fact or quotation

5 Gives specific facts and other details to support main idea of each paragraph

Sager 4

Works Cited

"A. Lincoln." The History Place. 30 Apr. 2000
<http://www.historyplace.com/lincoln/index.html>.
Armbruster, Maxim E. The Presidents of the United States. New York: Horizon, 1969.
"Lincoln, Abraham." Microsoft Encarta Encyclopedia. CD-ROM. 1998 ed. Redmond: Microsoft, 1998.
Whitney, David C. The American Presidents. Pleasantville: Reader's Digest, 1996.

Works Cited
· Identifies sources of information used
· Presents the entries in alphabetical order
· Gives complete publication information
· Contains correctly punctuated entries
· Follows a preferred style

Need help with Works Cited?

See pages R44–R45 in the **Writing Handbook**

782   UNIT FIVE   PART 2: AGAINST THE ODDS

Writing Your Research Report

❶ Prewriting and Exploring

Find a topic that really interests you by **listing** historical events or people that you want to know more about. Review the nonfiction and historical fiction selections in your book. **Ask** questions about the real people or the cultures that are portrayed. See the **Idea Bank** in the margin for more suggestions. After you have chosen your subject, follow the steps below.

Planning Your Research Report

▶ **1. Find your focus.** Create a cluster diagram of all of the ideas connected to your topic. If there is a lot of information, choose one or two cluster ideas to investigate.

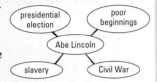

▶ **2. Make a research plan.** Write down questions that you want answered about your topic. Which questions are related? Use your questions to guide your research.

▶ **3. Identify your audience.** Who will read your report? How much background do you need to include about your subject? What will interest your readers most about your subject?

▶ **4. Define your purpose.** What do you want your paper to accomplish? Try writing a **thesis statement**, one sentence that states what you want to emphasize in your report.

❷ Researching

Use the questions that you have written about your topic to guide your research. Add other questions as you find facts that move your investigation farther along.

There are two types of sources—primary and secondary. **Primary sources** offer first-hand information. They include letters, diaries, journals and historical documents. **Secondary sources** explain or comment on material from other sources. Encyclopedias, newspapers, magazines, and many books are examples of secondary sources.

IDEABank

1. Your Working Portfolio
Look for ideas in the **Writing Options** that you completed earlier in this unit.
• Persuasive Essay, p. 727
• Personal Essay, p. 738

2. Local Lore
Find out what historical events or people are connected with your hometown, and research the one that you find most interesting or the one about which you know the least.

3. Objects of Interest
Visit a local museum. Choose an object or artifact that captures your attention. Research the society in which it was used.

Need help with your research report?

See the **Writing Handbook**, p. R41

RESEARCHTip

Secondary sources can help you explain ideas and interpret information. Use primary sources to give examples of the points you make.

More Online: Research Starter
www.mcdougallittel.com

Prewriting and Exploring
Choosing a Topic

If students have trouble selecting a topic after they have read the suggestions in the Idea Bank, have them try the following:

• Find out more about the people whose names appear on public buildings, bridges, or postal stamps.

• Learn the history of a national landmark, such as the Statue of Liberty, the White House, Mount Rushmore, or the Lincoln Memorial.

• Ask and look for answers to new questions about common events, such as "Did any women fight in the Civil War?"

Planning Your Research Report

1. Remind students that a good topic is broad enough to be interesting, yet narrow enough to cover in a short report.

2. Students might begin by writing *who, what, where, when, how,* and *why* questions.

3. Tell students that keeping a specific audience in mind is another way to focus a topic. Remind them that although in school their audience is frequently a teacher or classmates, circumstances might someday require them to adjust their writing for different audiences.

4. Remind students that a good thesis statement identifies the topic and makes a statement about it.

Researching

Point out to students that many primary sources can now be viewed on-line at the Library of Congress, the National Archives, and similar sites. Students who have chosen topics of local interest might also check state and local government sites.

Evaluate Your Sources Point out to students that the Internet contains information from many different sources. Some sources are reliable, but others are not. Students must learn to look at several items to evaluate a Web site. They should ask themselves these questions:

- Who is the sponsor of the site—the group, person, or organization that owns it? That name usually appears on the home page. Students should ask themselves if this is a well-known, reputable organization, such as a school or museum, or if it is just an individual person's Web site.
- Does the part of the URL, or Internet "address," that begins with **www** end with **.gov** (government), **.edu** (educational), **.com** (commercial), or **.org** (nonprofit group)? This provides a clue about the site's sponsor. Educational sites that have a tilde (~) may be created by students, rather than by the institution itself.
- What seems to be the purpose of this site: to entertain, to give information, to persuade, or to sell something?
- Is there a listed author, and is that person qualified in any way?
- How thorough and professional is the content? Is it well organized and written in standard English?
- Is the information current? Many sites tell when they were last updated.

Make Source Cards One fast way to make source cards is to photocopy the front and back of a book's title page and then jot down other information.

Take Notes Remind students that it is important that they remember if information on a note card is a direct quotation or a paraphrase.

Organize Your Material Give students time to review the outline on this page.

Use **Writing Transparencies**, p. 49, for additional support.

RESEARCH Tip

Check the index of the encyclopedia to find related subjects. Use the related subject headings to find other books in the library database.

INTERNET Tip

Try various search engines on the Internet to see if you can find more sources of information.

Evaluate Your Sources

You cannot believe everything that you read. Make sure that each source is reliable—accurate and up to date. Also, make sure the author presents an objective view before you begin to take notes. Check several sources to see if the accounts agree. Ask the following questions about sources found on the Internet.

What are the author's viewpoints and biases? Identify the author's gender, background, and political beliefs. How do they influence the presentation?

What are the qualifications of the author? Is the author from a respected institution? Is he or she a professional? Is the group a recognized organization?

Make Source Cards

Using index cards, create a source card for each source you use. For each, list the publication information in the correct form for that type of source. Then number the source cards sequentially. The cards will help you to create your Works Cited list and to find the source again if neccessary. Follow the formats shown on the right.

Book
Whitney, David C. *The American Presidents.* Pleasantville: Reader's Digest, 1996.
school library
call# 9231 W618

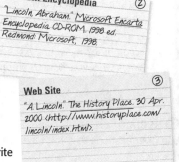

CD-ROM Encyclopedia
"Lincoln, Abraham." *Microsoft Encarta Encyclopedia* CD-ROM. 1998 ed. Redmond: Microsoft, 1998.

Take Notes

Use index cards to record the information in your sources. Write the main idea of the note at the top of each card, along with the number that you assigned the source on the source card and the number of the page on which you found the fact. Write just one piece of information on each card. Paraphrase (rewrite in your own words) the fact or idea.

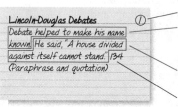

Lincoln-Douglas Debates ①
Debate helped to make his name known. He said, "A house divided against itself cannot stand." 134
(Paraphrase and quotation)

Source Number

Paraphrase Restate ideas in your own words to avoid plagiarism—using someone else's original words or ideas without giving credit.

Quotation Write the quotation exactly as it appears in the source and enclose it in quotation marks.

Page Number

Web Site ③
"A. Lincoln." *The History Place.* 30 Apr. 2000 <http://www.historyplace.com/lincoln/index.html>.

Mini Lesson ## Inquiry and Research

 TEKS 18D, 20G    **TAAS** Writing Obj. 2, 4

SUPPORTING EVIDENCE

Instruction Remind students that when they put together a research report, they need to know the difference between a fact that needs to be credited and a fact that is common knowledge. Tell them that it is also helpful to learn when quoting a source directly will add strength to the report. Tell students that using a direct quotation can be an effective way to make a point if the writer's word choice and phrasing is particularly strong and unique.

Application Read each sentence aloud and ask students how they would treat it. For example, students should decide if the idea or fact expressed is common knowledge, something that needs to be credited, or something that should be quoted directly. Discuss their responses.

1. The Olympics is an athletic event that involves people from all over the world. (common knowledge; no quotes needed)
2. The first record of the ancient Olympics dates back to 776 B.C. (exact date; credit source)

Organize Your Material

Before writing your rough draft, it might be helpful to sort your note cards into groups of similar main ideas. Think about the order in which you want to discuss those main ideas. You might choose **chronological, cause-and-effect, comparison-and-contrast, problem-solution,** or some other method of organizing. Create an outline or a cluster diagram to help you decide on the order of the sections of your report.

Need help organizing your material?

See the **Writing Handbook,** p. R43

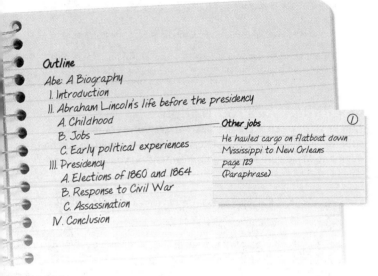

Outline

Abe: A Biography
I. Introduction
II. Abraham Lincoln's life before the presidency
  A. Childhood
  B. Jobs — Other jobs ①
  C. Early political experiences   He hauled cargo on flatboat down
III. Presidency   Mississippi to New Orleans
  A. Elections of 1860 and 1864   page 129
  B. Response to Civil War   (Paraphrase)
  C. Assassination
IV. Conclusion

❸ Drafting

Using your outline as a guide, begin to write your first draft. Your goal is to get your ideas down on paper. You can revise later.

In your **introduction,** start with a question, a quotation, or an intriguing fact. Present your subject and the purpose of your paper in a strong statement of purpose. This will become your thesis statement.

Write a separate body paragraph for each of the main ideas in your outline. Begin with a topic sentence and follow it up with the facts and other details that you've researched. For every fact or idea taken from a source, write the author's name and page number in parentheses at the end of the sentence. Use the title of the source and the page number if no author is named.

Conclude by summarizing the importance of your topic or giving your own interpretation.

DRAFTINGTip

Consider drafting your paper on a computer. Revisions will be easier to make, and the computer's programs can help you in your proofreading.

Ask Your Peer Reader: EVALUATING

- Did I support my statements with facts and examples?
- Was my organization clear and consistent?
- Did I cite sources wherever necessary?

Drafting

Some students find it easier to start drafting with the body and then return to write the introduction. Students who wish to do this, however, should still write a strong statement of purpose before beginning. This will help to keep them on track while they write.

Some students will find it disruptive to break the flow of writing to cite sources. Rather than citing sources while drafting, some students may find it easier to put placeholders, such as empty parentheses, after details that they are quoting or paraphrasing. Then, when they have finished drafting the report, they can insert the correct information at each placeholder. Students who have drafted the paper on a computer can use the find-function to locate each placeholder.

Ask Your Peer Reader

Encourage peer readers to evaluate whether the purpose of the report was clear and how well the work fulfilled that purpose.

3. I have walked that long road to freedom. I have tried not to falter; I have made missteps along the way. But I have discovered the secret that after climbing a great hill, one only finds that there are many more hills to climb. (**Possible Response:** language key to this passage; quote directly and credit source)

4. As a young boy, Nelson Mandela herded sheep and cattle and played hunting games. (not common knowledge; credit source)

5. Johannesburg is a city in the northeast part of South Africa. (general information, no need to credit source)

6. Virginia Hamilton came from a family of story tellers (not common knowledge; credit source)

7. I know that men urge the argument . . . that the constitution of the United States is the supreme law of the land, and that it sanctions slavery. There is no supreme law but that made by God; if our laws contradict that, the sooner they end or the sooner they are broken, why, the better. (**Possible Response:** language key to the passage; quote directly and credit source)

 Use **Writing Transparencies,** p. 13, for additional support.

Revising
PRESENTING IDEAS IN A LOGICAL ORDER

Encourage students to make the order clear by using appropriate transitional words and phrases. For example, if they are using chronological order, transitions might include dates and such phrases as *before she entered, immediately afterwards,* or *when the war began.* You may find it useful to review transitions that show causes and effects, order of importance, and comparison-contrast.

 Use **Writing Transparencies,** p. 9, for additional support.

Editing and Proofreading
CLAUSES AS FRAGMENTS

You may wish to review with students the concept of subordinate clauses. Remind them that a subordinate clause contains both a subject and a verb; however, it frequently begins with a subordinate conjunction, such as *because, since, until,* or *although.* Remind students that there are often several ways to correct or eliminate sentence fragments besides the method shown here.

Making a Works Cited List

Some students may be more familiar with the term *bibliography.*

Reflecting

Students may wish to confer with others afterwards to find out how they solved the problems that they encountered.

Option

Encourage students to include graphics with their reports, such as maps, charts, timelines, photographs, and drawings.

SPELLING
from Writing

As you revise your work, look back at the words you misspelled and determine why you made the errors you did. For additional help, refer to the strategies and generalizations in the **Spelling Handbook** on page R86.

Publishing
IDEAS

- Prepare a slide presentation about your subject. Generate slides on the computer or find them. Use your research report as a script and synchronize your words with the slides. Give your presentation to the class.

- Find a work of fiction or a movie that incorporates the subject of your research report. Develop a prologue for the work or the movie that will add to the reader's or audience's understanding.

More Online:
Publishing Options
www.mcdougallittell.com

---

❹ Revising
TARGET SKILL ▶ PRESENTING IDEAS IN A LOGICAL ORDER
Choose the order for your details that will make your paper most effective. Chronological order shows the relationship of time and events to each other; spatial order shows the physical location of places or things; and least to most important orders the details from weakest to strongest.

> *His mother, Nancy Hanks Lincoln, died when Abe was nine.*
> *However,*
> ∧ ~~H~~e loved his stepmother, Sarah Bush Johnston, who
> encouraged him to try to better himself (Whitney 129).

❺ Editing and Proofreading
TARGET SKILL ▶ CLAUSES AS FRAGMENTS Joining a subordinate clause to a complete sentence can eliminate a sentence fragment. Make sure there are no fragments in your final paper.

> Although Abe was good with an ax and could build log
> cabins, make fence rails, and clear the forest for
>   of the
> farmland ~~He~~ preferred reading and telling stories to hard
> physical labor (Armbruster 174–75).

❻ Making a Works Cited List

When you have finished revising and editing your report, make a **Works Cited** list and attach it to the end of your paper. See pages R44–R45 in the **Writing Handbook** for the correct format.

❼ Reflecting

FOR YOUR WORKING PORTFOLIO What were some problems you faced in doing your research report? What did you learn about doing a research report? Attach your answers to your finished report. Save your research report in your **Working Portfolio.**

Assessment Practice Revising & Editing

Read this passage from the first draft of a research report. The underlined sections may include the following kinds of errors:

- **sentence fragments**
- **incorrect comparative forms: adjectives and adverbs**
- **incorrect pronoun case**
- **double negatives**

For each underlined section, choose the revision that most improves the writing.

> Many people take owning a book for granted. <u>However, before 1450 and the invention of the printing press. Only the very wealthy owned books.</u> (1) Before that time, all books were copied by hand. This meant that books were scarce and <u>much expensiver</u> (2) <u>than us modern readers</u> (3) can imagine. <u>After Johannes Gutenberg invented the</u> (4) first movable-type printing press. <u>People could more easier</u> (5) afford books, and, as a result, more people learned to read. <u>A world without books isn't hardly believable today.</u> (6)

1. **A.** However, before 1450 and the invention of the printing press: Only the very wealthy owned books.
   B. However, before 1450 and the invention of the printing press, only the very wealthy owned books.
   C. However, before 1450 and the invention of the printing press; only the very wealthy owned books.
   D. Correct as is

2. **A.** much more expensive
   B. much expensive
   C. more expensiver
   D. Correct as is

3. **A.** than us
   B. than any of us modern readers
   C. than we modern readers
   D. Correct as is

4. **A.** After Johann Gutenberg invented the first movable-type printing press, people
   B. After Johann Gutenberg invented. The first movable-type printing press, people
   C. After Johann Gutenberg invented the first movable-type printing press; people
   D. Correct as is

5. **A.** could more easy
   B. could more easily
   C. could easilier
   D. Correct as is

6. **A.** A world without books is hardly unbelievable today.
   B. A world without books isn't scarcely believable today.
   C. A world without books is hardly believable today.
   D. Correct as is

Need extra help?

See the **Grammar Handbook**

Quick Reference: Capitalization, p. R58

Quick Reference: Punctuation, p. R56

Double Negatives, p. R71

Sentence Fragments, p. R59

Comparative Adjectives and Adverbs, p. R70

Pronouns, p. R63

Assessment Practice

Demonstrate how students can eliminate incorrect choices for the first question.

A. This choice is incorrect, because two clauses are never connected by a colon; two independent clauses may be joined by a semi-colon, but in this case the first clause is not an independent clause. It is a subordinate clause.

B. This choice is correct, because the subordinate clause has been linked to an independent clause. Since the subordinate clause comes first in the sentence, a comma follows it.

C. This choice is incorrect, because a semi-colon can be used to join only two independent clauses, not a subordinate clause and an independent clause.

D. This choice is incorrect. The first group of words is a fragment, not a complete sentence.

Answers:
1. B 2. A 3. C 4. A 5. B 6. C

 Grammar **TEKS 17H** 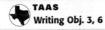 **TAAS Writing Obj. 3, 6**

PRONOUN CASE

Instruction Remind students that pronouns change form according to their use. Pronouns used as subjects are *I, you, she, he, it, we,* and *they.* Pronouns used as objects are *me, you, her, him, it, us,* and *them.* When a pronoun is used with a noun, it uses the same form that it would use if it were used alone.

Exercises Have students complete each sentence with a pronoun.

1. Give the book to _____. *(object)*
2. My sister and _____ have some very old books. *(subject)*
3. One speaker showed Jake and _____ some old schoolbooks. *(object)*
4. They certainly looked difficult to _____. *(object)*
5. _____ had no pictures and very small print. *(subject)*
6. _____ students like newer books. *(you, we)*

 Use **Grammar Transparencies and Copymasters,** p. 66, for additional support.

Use McDougal Littell's *Language Network,* Chapter 3, for more instruction and practice in pronoun case.

Objectives

- reflect on the unit
- review literary concepts introduced in the unit
- represent text information in a graphic organizer
- recognize and analyze setting
- connect, compare and contrast ideas, themes, and issues across texts
- assess and build portfolios

Reflecting on Theme

OPTION 1

A successful response will

- display an understanding of the messages in the selections
- support responses by referring to relevant aspects of the text
- identify similarities and differences between situations in real life and in literature.
- clarify and support spoken ideas with evidence, elaborations, and examples.

OPTION 2

A successful response will

- analyze the situations and the characters' responses in the selection
- react and speculate in response to texts
- support responses by referring to relevant aspects of text and his/her own experience.

OPTION 3

A successful response will

- offer observations, make connections, and react in response to texts.
- demonstrate effective communication skills that reflect such demands as requesting and providing information.
- display an understanding of the problem and demonstrate the ability to arrive at solutions.

Self Assessment

Students should spend time thinking about their personal heroes. Remind students that heroes can be everyday people as well as famous or historical people. Students' paragraphs should reveal an understanding of characters in the unit.

Personal Challenges

In this unit, you read about characters and real people who have a special quality—the strength to stand up and meet challenges. How have your ideas about personal challenges changed or deepened now that you have read the selections in the unit? Use one or more of the options in each of the following sections to help assess the changes.

Reflecting on the Theme

OPTION 1

Making Connections Review the selections in this unit and jot down the message or messages you got from each. Which messages do you think apply to situations encountered by young people? Discuss this question with a small group, supporting your views by relating the messages to situations from real life.

OPTION 2

Compare and Contrast Look back at the situations in selections from this unit that you found especially interesting. How well do the characters handle those situations? Would you react differently or similarly? Write a few paragraphs comparing and contrasting the characters' actions with what you think yours would be.

OPTION 3

Role-Playing Imagine that a friend needs more self-confidence to meet a new challenge. With a partner, role-play a conversation in which you attempt to inspire your friend with the will to overcome the challenge. Use examples from several selections to support your points.

Self ASSESSMENT

📖 READER'S NOTEBOOK

Which of the characters in this unit reminds you the most of your personal heroes? Write a paragraph or two explaining your choice.

REVIEWING YOUR PERSONAL
WORDList

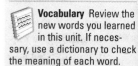 **Vocabulary** Review the new words you learned in this unit. If necessary, use a dictionary to check the meaning of each word.

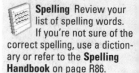 **Spelling** Review your list of spelling words. If you're not sure of the correct spelling, use a dictionary or refer to the **Spelling Handbook** on page R86.

Reviewing Literary Concepts

OPTION 1

Examining Setting Setting is the time and place of the action of a literary work. Review the selections you have read in this unit. Which would be very different if the setting were changed? Which might be almost the same? Discuss these questions with a partner or with a small group of classmates.

OPTION 2

Historical Fiction and Literary Nonfiction How do these two kinds of writing differ? To remember the strengths and weaknesses of each, fill in a chart like the one shown. Then discuss with a partner your ideas about what information can be learned from each form that cannot be learned from the other.

Historical Fiction		Literary Nonfiction	
Strengths	Weaknesses	Strengths	Weaknesses

◻ Building Your Portfolio

- **Writing Options** Select the Writing Option from this unit that you think expresses your ideas most effectively. Explain the reasons for your evaluation in a cover note, attach it to the assignment, and add both to your **Presentation Portfolio.** ◻

- **Writing Workshops** In this unit, you wrote an Opinion Statement and a Research Report. Reread these two pieces and decide which you think is better in showing your strengths as a writer. Explain your choice on a cover page, attach it to the piece you have selected, and place it in your **Presentation Portfolio.** ◻

- **Additional Activities** Think about the assignments you completed for **Activities & Explorations** and **Inquiry & Research.** Which did you find helpful? Which would you like to do more work on in the future? Keep a record of those assignments in your portfolio.

Self ASSESSMENT

▯▯ READER'S NOTEBOOK

Copy the following literary terms onto a sheet of paper. Next to each term, jot down a brief definition. If you have trouble explaining a particular concept, refer to the **Glossary of Literary Terms** on page R6.

historical fiction   setting
literary nonfiction   memoir
folk tale   imagery
sensory detail

Self ASSESSMENT

Look through your **Presentation Portfolio** to find an early draft that shows you learning something important about your subject or about yourself. How might you make it even better? List your suggestions and attach the list to the piece.

Setting GOALS

In the Reflect and Assess for Unit One, you were asked what kinds of writing you would like to become more skilled at. Look again at the list. Circle what you have learned so far. Make a list of the ones that remain and place it in your
▯▯ READER'S NOTEBOOK.

Reviewing Literary Concepts

OPTION 1

Students should support their responses with details from each selection. Ask each group to create a chart noting how much each selection would change and in what specific ways.

OPTION 2

Photocopy the Unit Five Resource Book, page 68, to provide students with a ready-made, full-depth chart for comparing and contrasting fiction and nonfiction.

◻ Building Your Portfolio

Students should evaluate the items in their Working Portfolios and choose pieces that represent their highest quality work for their Presentation Portfolios.

Before students make their choices, ask them to consider which pieces best illustrate not only their writing abilities, but also their understanding of the texts they have read in this unit.

Self Assessment and Setting Goals

Have students create a chart that lists what they consider their strengths and weaknesses as writers. Remind students to set reasonable goals for developing their skills and to list practical suggestions to which they can refer in the future.

▯ For more information on using Portfolios, use *Teacher's Guide to Assessment and Portfolio Use* beginning on page 53.

LITERATURE CONNECTIONS
Where the Red Fern Grows

BY WILSON RAWLS

Told in flashback, this story is about the close relationship between a boy and his hunting dogs on a poor farm in the Ozarks. The boy saves money to buy the dogs and is heartbroken when they die. Dreams, hard work and determination, success and disaster are all featured in the tale.

These thematically related readings are provided along with *Where the Red Fern Grows:*

Lob's Girl
BY JOAN AIKEN

Luke Baldwin's Vow
BY MORLEY CALLAGHAN

Old Dog
BY WILLIAM STAFFORD

The Grip
BY BRENDAN KENNELLY

Friends of the Hunted
BY RYLAND LOOS

Why They Quit: Thoughts from Ex-Hunters
BY DENA JONES JOLMA

Two Dreamers
BY GARY SOTO

And Even *More* . . .

The Flawed Glass

BY IAN STRACHAN

Shona MacLeod's world is so limited that she thinks of herself as being locked in a tower, waiting for a rescuer. Because she is cut off from personal relationships with others, even her own family does not know what Shona can achieve. When a young American boy comes to her Scottish island, Shona learns with joy that he can see past her difficulties and set her free.

Books

Come by Here
BY OLIVIA COOLIDGE
An African-American girl discovers the difference between visiting relatives and living with them.

So Far from the Bamboo Grove
BY YOKO KAWASHA WATKINS
In this historical novel, a Japanese girl and her family flee Korea in the face of war.

Good Night, Mr. Tom
BY MICHAEL MAGORIAN
An abused English boy takes refuge with a kind old man.

Roll of Thunder, Hear My Cry

By MILDRED D. TAYLOR

Set in Mississippi during the early years of the Great Depression, Mildred Taylor's novel describes the members of the African-American Logan family and their relationships with the land, their neighbors, and each other. The Logans must draw together in a fight to keep their 400-acre cotton farm.

These thematically related readings are provided along with *Roll of Thunder, Hear My Cry*:

from **Growing Up in the Great Depression**
By RICHARD WORMSER

Depression
By ISABEL JOSHLIN GLASER

The Stolen Party
By LILIANA HECKER
TRANSLATED BY ALBERTO MANGUEL

from **Black Women in White America**
By GERDA LERNER

Incident
By COUNTEE CULLEN

Equal Opportunity
By JIM WONG-CHU

The Clearing
By JESSE STUART

The Five-Dollar Dive
By YVONNE NELSON-PERRY

Song of the Buffalo Boy
BY SHERRY GARLAND
An Amerasian teenager in Vietnam must decide whether to go to America to find her father.

Other Media

The Jungle Book
Set in the jungles of India, Kipling's classic story tells of Mowgli, a boy raised by wolves.
(AUDIOCASSETTE)

Long Walk to Freedom
TIME WARNER AUDIO BOOKS
(AUDIOCASSETTE)

Race to Freedom: The Story of the Underground Railroad
Learn of the courage and determination of those who escaped from bondage in the American South.
XENON STUDIOS
(VIDEOCASSETTE)

Roll of Thunder, Hear My Cry
ARTISAN ENTERTAINMENT (VIDEOCASSETTE)

Secrets of the *Titanic*
Follow Robert D. Ballard as he explores the remains of the *Titanic* lying on the floor of the North Atlantic.
NATIONAL GEOGRAPHIC SOCIETY
(VIDEOCASSETTE)

Where the Red Fern Grows
FAMILY HOME ENTERTAINMENT
(VIDEOCASSETTE)

Underwater Exploration Diorama

OVERVIEW

The *Titanic* sank about 400 miles south of Newfoundland in 1912. In 1985, underwater explorers first discovered the site of the shipwreck. *Titanic* lay upright in two pieces on the ocean floor, at a depth of about 13,000 feet. The site has been explored several times. With the evidence provided by visual inspection of the hull, scientists reached new conclusions about the reasons that the ship sank. While it previously had been thought that the iceberg opened a long gash in the ship's side, it was found that the collision actually caused a series of thin gashes and fractures and caused seams in nearby hull plates to come apart.

Research Questions

• What are the purposes of underwater exploration?

• Where are sites of underwater archaeology?

• What technology is used in underwater exploration?

Investigation Working in small groups, students research and select one historical example of underwater exploration or a shipwreck salvage operation and research the expedition. Students keep detailed notes as they read and then use these specifics as they create a model or diorama depicting the exploration. The groups will also produce two pieces of writing for use by viewers of the dioramas: a fact sheet giving an overview of the expedition and a museum-style "wall text" explaining the technology used in the expedition. For scale models, students will add to their displays a key identifying the scale used in the diorama.

Wrap-up Have each group share its diorama with the class and give a short oral presentation summarizing the expedition and its significance. Display the dioramas in the classroom. Invite other students, families, and community members to visit the classroom and view them. Two options for a culminating activity include watching a documentary video about underwater exploration or shipwreck salvage, or having a diving instructor visit the class and give a presentation on scuba diving.

 Links and Extended Reading
www.mcdougallittell.com

 LaserLinks: Background
Historical Connection
Science Connection

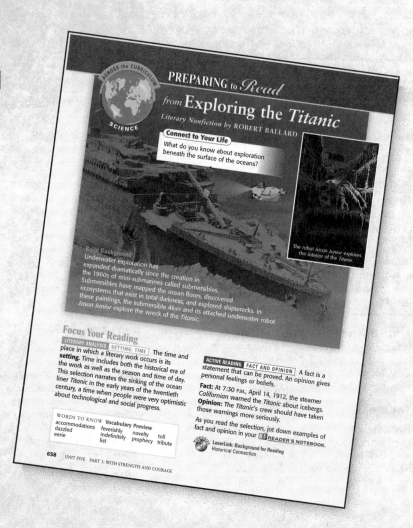

OBJECTIVES

❑ research and write a fact sheet about an underwater exploration

❑ build a diorama accurately depicting an underwater exploration

❑ research current and historical underwater exploration technology

❑ calculate and apply scale measurements to a diorama

Team Teaching Assignments

CONNECT TO **LANGUAGE ARTS** To begin the project, have each group look through books on underwater exploration and choose one shipwreck exploration that interests them. This will be the subject of a fact sheet and a diorama. Direct the groups to research their chosen exploration thoroughly. As students read, they should keep detailed notes to use when they construct their model. First have them write and publish the fact sheet about their chosen exploration. Remind students to try to answer the five W's (who, what, where, when, why). Encourage groups to look for photographs of the exploration that can be scanned or photocopied onto the fact sheets. When the fact sheets are complete, duplicate them so that visitors can read about the explorations as they view the models. *(3–4 class periods)*

YOU WILL NEED:
- reference books about shipwrecks and salvage
- photocopier (optional)

CONNECT TO **SOCIAL STUDIES** Encourage students to increase their understanding of the geographic and/or historical issues involved in their chosen underwater exploration. Have the groups undertake additional research to answer the following questions: In what part of the world did this exploration or salvage take place? Under what conditions did the explorers work? From what culture and time period was the ship or other items that the explorers found? After each group has enough information, group members should create a sketch of their diorama, determine how to divide the work, and, finally, construct the diorama. *(4–5 class periods)*

YOU WILL NEED:
- Web access (optional)
- reference books and an atlas
- diorama materials: boxes, clay, construction paper, scissors, glue, etc.

CONNECT TO **SCIENCE** During a 1996 expedition to the wreck of the *Titanic*, scientists used *Nautile*, a submersible capable of diving to nearly 20,000 feet. This vehicle carries a crew of two plus one additional passenger, and dives at a speed of 100 feet per minute; it takes more than two hours to reach the Titanic. Encourage interested students to find out more about submersibles and the latest advances in underwater exploration technology. Suggest that groups investigate the technology used in the specific expedition they are researching, and depict it as accurately as they can in their models. On index cards, have groups summarize what they learn about the technology used. Post the cards next to each diorama the way wall texts are displayed in museums. *(2–3 class periods)*

YOU WILL NEED:
- Web access (optional)
- reference books about shipwrecks and salvage

CONNECT TO **MATHEMATICS** Discuss the concept of scale measurement with the class. Mention some of the professions in which people must calculate scale measurements, such as architecture and set design. People who build models often work with scale so that the finished models have the proper proportions. Direct groups to decide on a scale for their dioramas, based on the actual size of the main object in their diorama, such as a shipwreck or a submersible, and the size of the box in which they are building the model. For example, in a diorama about the *Titanic*, which is about 880 feet long, in a box that is 10 inches wide, a suitable scale would be 1 inch = 200 feet. If possible, have students apply this scale as they construct their dioramas. They should post a key to the scale on their display. *(1–2 class periods)*

YOU WILL NEED:
- calculator
- ruler

South Africa Conservation Day

OVERVIEW

From 1948 to 1994, when South Africa held its first free elections for all, the country lived under a system called *apartheid*. It made racial separation the official policy in South Africa. The small white minority held all the political and economic power. Nelson Mandela led the struggle against apartheid. He became a leader of the African National Congress (ANC), a political organization for black South African's founded in 1912. In 1994, Nelson Mandela became South Africa's first black president. Now, the country is a popular place to visit. And a recent survey of overseas visitors to South Africa revealed that nine out of ten came primarily to experience its wildlife and unspoiled natural areas.

Research Questions

• What is South African folklore and music like?

• What foods are typical of South African cuisine?

• What sort of habitats support South African wildlife?

• How is South Africa protecting its wildlife?

Investigation Working in small groups, students will plan a "Conservation Day" based on a South African theme. Each group will plan and execute a table display containing part of the research they have done. For their display, the class might play some South African music. One group might retell examples of South African folklore. Others might prepare or display recipes for traditional South African cooking. Students will also prepare a wildlife quiz game, and a map with itinerary for a wildlife safari. A visit from someone who has lived or traveled in South Africa, or from a travel agent might be helpful in answering students' questions.

Wrap-up The project should culminate in a Conservation Day where families, other students, and community members can examine the rich traditions, wildlife, and natural habitats of the country.

Links and Extended Reading
www.mcdougallittell.com

LaserLinks: Background
Historical Connection

OBJECTIVES

❑ research and compile a list of South African folktales

❑ research and report on South African food

❑ research and report on South African wildlife preserves

❑ measure and plan times and distances alotted for a safari through South Africa's largest wildlife park

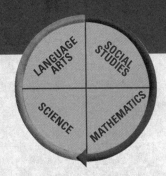

Team Teaching Assignments

CONNECT TO **LANGUAGE ARTS** South African folktales often have strong messages about the power and delicacy of the natural world. Have a small group of students research South African folklore—particularly stories from Zulu or Bantu traditions. Another group might research some of the lyrics from South African music that is well known in the United States. For example, a group from Soweto, Ladysmith Black Mambazo, has recorded many successful albums. Other successful South African artists include Johnny Clegg, Miriam Makeba, Hugh Masekela, and Abdullah Ibrahim. For their display, students should (if possible) play some South African music and illustrate two or three of their own retellings of South African folk tales. (*1–2 class periods*)

YOU WILL NEED:
- Web access (optional)
- books of South African traditional tales
- colored pencils
- South African music and player (optional)

CONNECT TO **SOCIAL STUDIES** Have you ever tasted bobotie, melktert, or sosaties? These South African dishes, influenced by English, Dutch, Malaysian, Xhosa and Zulu cuisine, might be on festival menus. Have pairs of students research South African cooking. Then have them write selected recipes on index cards. The completed recipes should be displayed on a table—preferably accompanied by photos of the dishes or illustrations created by students. A bonus activity would be if some of the students could prepare one or more of the dishes they feature. (*2–3 class periods*)

YOU WILL NEED:
- Web access (optional)
- reference books
- index cards
- poster paper

CONNECT TO **SCIENCE** Wildlife is abundant in South Africa—elephants, lions, rhinos, zebras, and hippos can be seen at close range. Not only is the area exceptionally rich in species but many of these species are found nowhere else (these are called "endemic species"). Have small groups of students research some of the many species of mammal, reptile, amphibian and butterfly that can be found in South Africa's parks. Encourage the groups to draw on this research as they create wildlife quiz cards. Sample topics might include: the animals protected; the number of different species of animals and plants found there. (*2–3 class periods*)

YOU WILL NEED:
- Web access (optional)
- reference books
- graph paper (optional)

CONNECT TO **MATHEMATICS** Have students incorporate mathematics into the scenario of their Conservation Day. Tell them that South Africa's Kruger National Park is the largest protected area in the country. Have students create a schedule and itinerary, based on a a three-day visit to the park. First, they should create an annotated map of the Park. There itinerary might include: the size and location of Kruger National Park; the time allotted for various lengths of travelling each day; the total distances covered each day. (*2–3 class periods*)

YOU WILL NEED:
- Web access (optional)
- travel brochures
- atlas
- rulers, calculators
- graph paper

Across Cultures: The Oral Tradition

In Unit Six, "Across Cultures: The Oral Tradition," Students will read a variety of myths, fables, folktales, and legends from the oral tradition of many cultures. This unit contains five sections, each linked to a previous unit in this book:

Links to Unit One: Learning From Experience
• Prometheus
• Theseus and the Minotaur

Links to Unit Two: Relationships
• Waters of Gold
• Ashputtle

Links to Unit Three: Flights of Imagination
• Narcissus
• Lazy Peter and His Three-cornered Hat

Links to Unit Four: Nothing Stays the Same
• Phaëthon
• The Force of Luck
• Brother Coyote and Brother Cricket

Links to Unit Five: Personal Challenges
• How Odin Lost His Eye
• Pumpkin Seed and the Snake
• Kelfala's Secret Something

You may wish to begin or end Units One through Five with theme-related selections from Unit Six, or you may choose to present the selections from Unit Six as a separate unit.

Discovering the Oral Tradition
Use the following prompts to help students recognize the meaning of the oral tradition.
• What does the term oral tradition mean to you?
  Possible Responses: stories that were originally told orally and later written down; stories passed down from generation to generation

 See the Skills Trace at the beginning of the unit for information on TEKS covered in this lesson.

Across Cultures
THE ORAL TRADITION

"The greatest storyteller in the world is in your family because he's telling the only story you can truly recognize, which is the story of you and your family."

Tim Tingle

Tim Tingle lives in Texas where he keeps the traditions of his family alive through storytelling.

792

 Mini Lesson **Speaking and Listening** **TEKS** 5C

STORYTELLING IN THE CLASSROOM

Prepare Since storytelling is a dramatic experience, you may wish to modify your classroom environment to enhance the speaking, listening, and viewing dimensions of storytelling. Use one or more of the following suggestions:
• Have students sit in a circle rather than in rows.
• Close the shades and dim the lights.
• Provide a box of props and/or costumes that you or your students can use when telling stories.

Present As students tell their stories, they should pay close attention to how they look and sound to their audience. Encourage students to create simple sound effects as they tell the stories. You might tape record the stories so students can listen to themselves performing and can later modify their presentations.

 BLOCK SCHEDULING This activity is particularly well suited for longer class periods.

 Use **Communications Transparencies and Copymasters**, p. 2, for additional support.

- How does the quotation from Texas storyteller Tim Tingle apply to the oral tradition?
  Possible Response: A family is a small community with its own history and traditions. Family members keep their stories, history, and traditions alive by sharing them with their children and grandchildren.
- Tim Tingle is a storyteller. What function do you think he and other storytellers serve today?
  Possible Response: They help preserve and pass on ideals and values of a culture.
- On the basis of the unit title and quotation, what types of selections do you imagine will be in the unit?
  Possible Responses: legends, myths, folklore from a variety of cultures

Introducing Storytelling

To help students understand how stories are embellished and changed as they pass through generations of tellers, invite students to work in small groups to create modern-day endings for traditional fairy tales. Start by having the class brainstorm a list of fairy tales, such as "Snow White," "Cinderella," "Rumpelstiltskin," "Hansel and Gretel," and "Little Red Riding Hood." Then have each group select one of the stories, review the plot, and retell it, changing the ending. After everyone has finished working, invite groups to share their stories with the class. Encourage group members to jump in and revise the story as it is being retold. Discuss how the stories change as different people retell them. Explore how some of the changes make the stories dramatic, rhythmic, and easier to tell. Link this demonstration to the stories that students are about to read in this unit.

793

Features and Selections	Literary Analysis	TEKS	Reading and Critical Thinking	TEKS	Writing Opportunities	TEKS
Across Cultures: The Oral Tradition **Storytellers Past and Present** **Keeping the Past Alive**						20D
Links to Unit 1	Characterization, 800, 802, 808 Create a Graphic, 811 **TAAS READING OBJ. 5**	12F 10L, 11D, 12F	Clarifying, 800, 806, 808 Standardized Test Practice, 803 Informal Assessment, 809 **TAAS READING OBJ. 5** **TAAS WRITING OBJ. 2**	10C 10H, K 10H, 11C		
Links to Unit 2	Figurative Language, 814, 818, 820, 826	12J	Predicting, 816, 818 Make Connections, 829 Standardized Test Practice, 819, 825 **TAAS READING OBJ. 3, 5**	11A 10I, 11D 10H, K, 12G		
Writing Workshop: Cause-and-Effect Essay **Assessment Practice**			Analyze a Student Model, 831 **TAAS READING OBJ. 2, 4**	12I, 19A, D	Writing Your Cause-and-Effect Essay, 833 A Strong Conclusion, 834 **TAAS WRITING OBJ. 1**	15C, H, 17C, 18A, B, C, D, 19C
Links to Unit 3	Irony, 838, 840, 844 Evaluate Characters, 846	12J 11B, 12F	Sequence, 838, 840, 842 Find the "Threes," 847 Informal Assessment, 841, 845 **TAAS READING OBJ. 4, 5** **TAAS WRITING OBJ. 6**	10E 4B, 10L, 11D 10G, 11A, C	Write an Editorial, 846	13C, 15B
Links to Unit 4	Internal Conflict, 850, 856 Compare Characters, 865 **TAAS READING OBJ. 4**	12F 10L, 11D	Connecting, 850, 852, 854, 862 Informal Assessment, 852, 863 Standardized Test Practice, 858 **TAAS READING OBJ. 2, 3, 4** **TAAS WRITING OBJ. 1, 2**	10A, 11A 10E, G 10F, K	Write a Texas Folktale, 864 Write a Persuasive Essay, 865	15D 15B
Links to Unit 5	Plot 868, 874, 876, 880	12G	Evaluating, 868, 874, 878 Informal Assessment, 870, 874 Standardized Test Practice, 881 **TAAS READING OBJ. 4, 5** **TAAS WRITING OBJ. 1**	10H, 11A 10H, 11A 10K, 12G	Write a Poem, 882	15D
Communication Workshop: Multimedia Presentation **Assessment Practice**			Analyzing a Multimedia Presentation, 885	19A, D	Creating a Strong Opening, 888	18C, D
Reflect and Assess			Examining Myths, 890 Evaluating Folktales, 890	10L, 11D, 12E 4A, 11B, 12E	Building Your Portfolio, 890	19C

LEGEND   **DLS – Daily Language SkillBuilder**   **Green type – Teacher's Edition**

Speaking and Listening Viewing and Representing	TEKS	Inquiry and Research	TEKS	Grammar, Usage, and Mechanics	TEKS	Vocabulary	TEKS
Storytelling in the Classroom, 792	5C						
Family Histories, 795	5B						
Dramatize a Tale, 810	5C, 11B	Investigate Fire, 810	13C, I, 24A	DLS, 798	16D, 17B	Context Clues, 811	6A
Create a Greek Gods and Goddesses Bio Board, 810	24A			Past Participles, 804	17F	The Prefix ex-, 801	16C
Compare Approaches, 811	11B, D					Latin Roots, 805	16G
Television Interview, 811	11B						
Role-Playing, 800	5C, 11B						
Art Appreciation, 807	23A, B						
Retelling, 808	2E, 5A, 11B						
TAAS READING OBJ. 4				**TAAS WRITING OBJ. 3, 6**		**TAAS READING OBJ. 1** **TAAS WRITING OBJ. 3, 7**	
Hold a Talk Show, 828	5C, 11B	Make a Sequence Chart, 828	13C, F, 20A, B	DLS, 812	16B, 17G	Assessment Practice, 829	9B
Make a Music Poster, 828	13F, 24A			Who and Whom, 814	17C	Silent Letters, 818	16D
Tell a Story, 829	5C			Adjective Clauses, 824	17A	Doubling Final Consonants, 821	16C
Watch a Video, 829	12C, 23B						
Art Appreciation, 816, 820, 826	22A, 23B						
Storytelling, 817, 827	2D, F, 5C, D, E, 11B						
TAAS READING OBJ. 5				**TAAS WRITING OBJ. 3, 5, 6, 7**		**TAAS WRITING OBJ. 3, 7**	
Picturing Text Structure, 832	10E, L			Combining Sentences, 834	18E		
				Revising & Editing, 835	17A, C, 18E		
				Misplaced Modifiers, 835	17C		
TAAS READING OBJ. 2, 4				**TAAS WRITING OBJ. 3, 5, 6, 7**			
Role-Play a Meeting, 847	11B, D	Compare and Contrast, 846	13C, E	DLS, 836	16B, 17H	Word Meaning, 847	9B
Comic Strips, 847	11B, 24A			Punctuating Compound Sentences, 838	16B, 17A	Words from Spanish, 844	16G
Hold a Contest, 847	15C, 23C			Infinitive Phrases, 843	17C		
Art Appreciation, 839	22A						
Role-Playing, 840	5C, 11B			**TAAS WRITING OBJ. 3, 5, 6, 7**		**TAAS READING OBJ. 1**	
Create a Board Game, 865	11B, 24A	Create a Science Exhibit, 864	13C, I	DLS, 848	17C, G	Related Words, 865	9B
Record a News Report, 865	11B	Complete a Sequence Chart, 864	13E, 20D	Using the Right Verb, 855	17C	Absorbed Prefix ac-, 851	16C
Art Appreciation, 850, 853, 857, 859	22A					Prefixes com- and in-, 860	16C
Retelling, 856	2F, 5A, D, E, 11B						
Comparison of Different Media, 862	12C, 23B, C			**TAAS WRITING OBJ. 6**		**TAAS READING OBJ. 1** **TAAS WRITING OBJ. 3, 7**	
Create Your Own Pa Ndau, 882	11B, 13C, 24A	Create a Phrase Book, 883	4C, 13C	DLS, 866	17D, F	Analogies, 883	9B
Hold a Kikuyu Festival, 882	13C, I	Present a Report, 883	13F	Demonstrative Adjectives, 872	17D	Words with j, ge, and dge, 869	16D
Make an Illustrated Calendar, 883	13C, 24A			Comparison of Adjectives, 879	17D		
Art Appreciation, 868, 871	22A, 23A						
Retelling the Story, 875	2E, 3B, 5A, E, 11B						
Choral Reading, 876	3B, 5C, E, 11B						
Interviews, 880	5B, 20C			**TAAS WRITING OBJ. 3, 4, 6**		**TAAS READING OBJ. 1** **TAAS WRITING OBJ. 3, 7**	
Creating Your Multimedia Presentation, 886	2F, 5A, B, D, E, F, 18A, 24A			Consistent Form, 888	18E		
				Revising & Editing, 889	16B, 17F		
				Verb Tenses, 889	17F		
				TAAS WRITING OBJ. 6			

To introduce the theme of this unit, use Fine Art Transparencies T34–36 in the Communications Transparencies and Copymasters.

Additional Support

	Unit Resource Book	Assessment	Integrated Technology and Media	Literary Analysis Transparencies
Links to Unit 1 *pp. 798–811*	• Summary p. 4 • Active Reading p. 5 • Literary Analysis p. 6 • Words to Know p. 7 • Grammar p. 8 • Spelling p. 9 • Selection Quiz p. 10	• Selection Test, Formal Assessment pp. 125–126 ⊙ Test Generator	⌒ Audio Library	• Fables/Myths/Tall Tales T30 • Greek/Roman Gods Chart T31 • Cross Cultures Comparison T32
Links to Unit 2 *pp. 812–829*	• Summary p. 11 • Active Reading p. 12 • Literary Analysis p. 13 • Words to Know p. 14 • Grammar p. 15 • Spelling p. 16 • Selection Quiz p. 17	• Selection Test, Formal Assessment pp. 127–128 ⊙ Test Generator	⌒ Audio Library	• Fables/Myths/Tall Tales T30 • Cross Cultures Comparison T32

Writing Workshop: Cause and Effect Essay

Unit Six Resource Book
• Prewriting p. 18
• Drafting and Elaboration p. 19
• Peer Response Guide pp. 20–21
• Revising, Editing, and Proofreading p. 22
• Student Models pp. 23–25
• Rubric for Evaluation p. 26

⊙ **Writing Coach**

Writing Transparencies T1–4, T6, T36

Reading and Critical Thinking Transparencies T24

Grammar Transparencies and Copymasters C116

Teacher's Guide to Assessment and Portfolio Use

Additional Support

	Unit Resource Book	Assessment	Integrated Technology and Media	Literary Analysis Transparencies
Links to Unit 3 *pp. 836–847*	• Summary p. 27 • Active Reading p. 28 • Literary Analysis p. 29 • Words to Know p. 30 • Grammar p. 31 • Spelling p. 32 • Selection Quiz p. 33	• Selection Test, Formal Assessment pp. 129–130 ⊙ Test Generator	⌒ Audio Library	• Fables/Myths/Tall Tales T30 • Cross Cultures Comparison T32
Links to Unit 4 *pp. 848–865*	• Summary p. 34 • Active Reading p. 35 • Literary Analysis p. 36 • Words to Know p. 37 • Grammar p. 38 • Spelling p. 39 • Selection Quiz p. 40	• Selection Test, Formal Assessment pp. 131–132 ⊙ Test Generator	⌒ Audio Library ▬ Video: Literature in Performance, Video Resource Book pp. 37–42	• Characterization T4 • Fables/Myths/Tall Tales T30 • Cross Cultures Comparison T32
Links to Unit 5 *pp. 866–883*	• Summary p. 41 • Active Reading p. 42 • Literary Analysis p. 43 • Words to Know p. 44 • Grammar p. 45 • Spelling p. 46 • Selection Quiz p. 47	• Selection Test, Formal Assessment pp. 133–134 ⊙ Test Generator	⌒ Audio Library	• Poetry: Figurative Language T19 • Poetry: Sound Devices T20 • Fables/Myths/Tall Tales T30 • Cross Cultures Comparison T32

Communication Workshop: Multimedia Presentation

Unit Six Resource Book
• Planning and Drafting p. 48
• Practicing and Delivering p. 49
• Peer Response Guide pp. 50–51
• Refining Your Performance p. 52
• Rubric for Evaluation p. 53

⊙ **Writing Coach**

Communications Transparencies and Copymasters T10, T14–15

Writing Transparencies T1–4, T39

Grammar Transparencies and Copymasters C73

Unit Assessment
• Unit Six Test, Formal Assessment pp. 135–136
⊙ Test Generator
• Unit Six Integrated Test, Integrated Assessment pp. 31–36

Unit Technology
⇦ ClassZone www.mcdougallittell.com
⊙ Electronic Teacher Tools

Reading and Critical Thinking Transparencies	Grammar Transparencies and Copymasters	Vocabulary Transparencies and Copymasters	Writing Transparencies	Communications Transparencies and Copymasters
• Venn Diagram T35	• Daily Language Skillbuilder T24 • Past Participles C97			• Evaluating Roles in Groups T8 • Interviewing T9 • Dramatic Reading T12 • Impromptu Speaking: Dialogue, Role-Play T13
• Summarizing T11 • Venn Diagram T35 • Sequence Chain T39	• Daily Language Skillbuilder T25 • *Who* and *Whom* C67 • Adjective Clauses C109–111		• Locating Information Using the Internet T47–48	• Appreciative Listening T2 • Impromptu Speaking: Dialogue, Role-Play T13 • Giving and Using Feedback to Improve Performance T16

STUDENTS ACQUIRING ENGLISH

The **Spanish Study Guide**, pp. 157–162, includes language support for the following pages:
• Family and Community Involvement (per unit)

• Selection Summaries and Vocabulary
• Active Reading
• Literary Analysis

Reading and Critical Thinking Transparencies	Grammar Transparencies and Copymasters	Vocabulary Transparencies and Copymasters	Writing Transparencies	Communications Transparencies and Copymasters
• Questioning T12	• Daily Language Skillbuilder T25 • Punctuating Compound Sentences C126 • Infinitive Phrases C101		• Personal Narrative T25 • Preparing a Works Cited List T56	• Impromptu Speaking: Dialogue, Role-Play T13
• Using Bar Graphs T31 • Sequence Chain T39	• Daily Language Skillbuilder T26 • Using the Right Verb C135		• Generating Research Questions T40	• Verbal Strategies T14 • Nonverbal Strategies T15
• Sequence Chain T39	• Daily Language Skillbuilder T26 • Demonstrative Adjectives C81 • Comparison of Adjectives C82		• Problem-Solution Essay T33	• Interviewing T9 • Dramatic Reading T12 • Verbal Strategies T14 • Nonverbal Strategies T15

STUDENTS ACQUIRING ENGLISH

The **Spanish Study Guide**, pp. 163–171, includes language support for the following pages:
• Family and Community Involvement (per unit)

• Selection Summaries and Vocabulary
• Active Reading
• Literary Analysis

Selection	SkillBuilder Sentences	Suggested Answers
Links to Unit 1	1. Prometheus wanted humans to have fire, but he set out to bring it to them. 2. Theseus questions why the Minotaur should be allowed too threaten there lives.	1. Prometheus wanted humans to have fire, **so** he set out to bring it to them. 2. Theseus questions why the Minotaur should be allowed **to** threaten **their** lives.
Links to Unit 2	1. Ashputtles experience teaches the importance of having hope and treating other's with kindness. 2. We read the story to the group and asked "How far would you go to help a person in need"?	1. Ashputtle**'s** experience teaches the importance of having hope and treating **others** with kindness. 2. We read the story to the group and asked, "How far would you go to help a person in need?"
Links to Unit 3	1. In a trickster tale; a clever person usually shows an ability to outsmart other people. 2. Jamie and me read that Narcissus is a handsome young man who can't stop looking at hisself.	1. In a trickster tale, a clever person usually shows an ability to outsmart other people. 2. Jamie and **I** read that Narcissus is a handsome young man who can't stop looking at **himself**.
Links to Unit 4	1. The wealthy men and the miller is making a deal that might change the miller's life. 2. The boastful coyote didnt' think the crickets strength was any match for his.	1. The wealthy men and the miller **are** making a deal that might change the miller's life. 2. The boastful coyote did**n't** think the cricket**'s** strength was any match for his.
Links to Unit 5	1. Although everything was going good, Odin thought serious about troubles that might be ahead. 2. Kelfala should of knew getting the attention of the quiet young woman would not be easy.	1. Although everything was going **well**, Odin thought **seriously** about troubles that might be ahead. 2. Kelfala **should have known** getting the attention of the quiet young woman would not be easy.

Grammar Focus by Unit	Unit One	Unit Two	Unit Three	Unit Four	Unit Five	Unit Six
	The Sentence and Its Parts	Nouns, Pronouns, and Verbs	Modifiers	Phrases	Compound and Complex Sentences	Review

The Language of Literature offers several options for integrating grammar instruction and literature.

- Each unit has a specific grammar focus. The grammar focus for this unit is highlighted on the planning chart. Categories of grammar skills for this unit are shown in red.

- The Pupil's Edition includes instructive features entitled *Grammar in Context*. The instruction in these features arises from the selections and relates to the grammar focus for each unit.

- The Writing Workshops in the Pupil's Edition include grammar tips that help the students produce error-free drafts.

- Mini Lessons in the Teacher's Edition complement the instruction in the *Grammar in Context* features. Additional Mini Lessons relate to the grammar focus for each unit as well as to the literature.

- Daily Language SkillBuilders in the Teacher's Edition provide students with ongoing proofreading practice and reinforce punctuation, spelling, grammar and usage, and capitalization.

- Grammar Copymasters and Transparencies, which may be used independently or in conjunction with the Mini Lessons in the Teacher's Edition, present grammar in a traditional, systematic sequence.

PE instruction shown in black
TE Mini Lessons shown in green

PRONOUNS
Who and *Whom*
Links to Unit Two, p. 814

VERBS
Verb Tenses
Assessment Practice, p. 889

ADJECTIVES AND ADVERBS
Demonstrative Adjectives
Links to Unit Five, p. 872
Comparison of Adjectives
Links to Unit Five, p. 879

VERBALS AND VERB PHRASES
Past Participles
Links to Unit One, p. 804
Infinitive Phrases
Links to Unit Three, p. 843

SENTENCE STRUCTURE
Adjective Clauses
Links to Unit Two, p. 824

Combining Sentences
Writing Workshop, p. 834
Misplaced Modifiers
Assessment Practice, p. 835

PUNCTUATION
Punctuating Compound Sentences
Links to Unit Three, p. 838

STYLE
Using the Right Verb
Links to Unit Four, p. 855
Consistent Form
Communication Workshop, p. 888

OVERVIEW

Students plan a program of stories to be told during a storytelling festival.

Project at a glance The selections in Unit Six emphasize how storytelling acts as a means of preserving cultural heritage and passes on oral histories and traditions. For this project, students will work in small groups to plan a storytelling festival, in which each member of the group will tell a story that relates to a theme or culture assigned to the group. Groups will collaborate on the selection of stories as well as the props and/or costumes, rehearsing together so others can help with the interpretation of the story and characterization for the narrator. The stories will be told either in a festival or in front of the class.

SCHEDULING

Individual stories should take about five minutes. You may want to schedule the presentations over the course of 2–3 class periods, or at the end of the unit, depending on your purposes.

PROJECT OBJECTIVES

- To demonstrate the speaking and listening skills introduced in the activity
- To learn about the importance and use of folklore and storytelling
- To work collaboratively with a small group to prepare a program of stories
- To develop storytelling skills by recognizing what keeps an audience interested
- To develop listening and speaking skills by participating in a storytelling festival

SUGGESTED GROUP SIZE

5–6 students per group

 Storytelling Festival

1 Getting Started

If you are going to create an actual festival with an invited audience, reserve a date in the auditorium or other appropriate room, as well as some rehearsal time for the groups. If you plan to decorate, start gathering sheets for backdrops that groups can paint. Decide if you will get costumes or if they will be the responsibility of individual groups. Invite not only other students but administrators and families as well.

If you are using your classroom as a stage, consider arranging the audience's seats in a large semicircle, in order to give the storyteller adequate room to move around and, perhaps, to interact with the audience.

If you would like to invite a storyteller to talk to the class, now is the time to locate one and schedule a time. You should also make available different types of books about the cultures students will be focusing on.

You might want to record the storytellers on video to preserve the performances for other classes and for your own review. Arrange for a school media person or volunteer parent to assist with the taping.

Writing Workshop Connection

As a springboard, students may use the Writing Workshop assignments **Cause-and-Effect Essay**, p. 830, and **Multimedia Presentation**, p. 884.

2 Directing the Project

Preparing Divide students into groups. Tell students that they will be working cooperatively to plan and present a program of stories. Each group member will tell a story. Stories should be no longer than five minutes, so group members may have to edit their stories for length.

▶ Select a culture or theme for each group. Have students research the culture before creating their presentation. Groups will decide together which stories will be told and should help one another edit down stories. At this time, explain exactly what you expect in the way of props, costumes, and setting. You might also review with students the Speaking and Listening Skills on the next page.

▶ When groups have finalized their list of stories, meet with them to check for coherency in theme or culture. As groups work to edit the stories, meet again to offer suggestions and help them decide which elements of each story are necessary and which are expendable. Stress that the oral tradition entails personal interpretation each time the tale is retold, so students can add their own touches as long as the basic story and lesson remain intact.

▶ Tell students there is no one "correct" interpretation. Encourage them to imagine how they would feel if they were the actual characters in the situations they are depicting. You should discuss what makes a story interesting to an audience. You might point out that the character of the narrator has a great deal of influence on how the audience responds to the story.

▶ Students should be aware of the guidelines for working in a group, found on page R104 in the Communication Handbook.

Practicing Groups should determine the order in which they would like to tell the stories. They should rehearse as a group, relying on one another to help with interpretation and to give suggestions. Tell students that giving and receiving feedback during the rehearsal stage is crucial. Refer to the tips in the Feedback Center.

▶ If each story is five minutes, give them a cumulative amount of time for the entire group.

Presenting Before the performances, have students focus on the strategies listed in the Communication Handbook on page R100. Share with them this quotation by storyteller Brenda Wong Aoki: ". . . I sculpt a story until I get to the emotional truth, the human truth. It is this truth that makes a bridge of understanding between peoples." Tell them that one of their primary goals is to communicate this truth both verbally and nonverbally.

▶ If you are able to videotape the storytelling, you can share the performance by circulating the tapes around school.

Teaching the Speaking and Listening Skills

The student is expected to:

Identify how language use—for instance, labels (terms) and sayings (idioms)—reflects regions and cultures

Teaching suggestions: Have students explore and discuss the culture from which their story originates. If they are unfamiliar with the culture, have them research the country of origin and relevant points that might affect language, such as history, climate, and so on. Then you might have them read through the story and pick out language that reflects this culture. For example, the idiom "proud as the cotton tree" in the African tale "Kelfala's Secret Something" reflects the farming society of its storyteller.

Compare oral traditions across regions and cultures

Teaching suggestions: After students have a solid basis of understanding about the culture they are focusing on, ask them to discuss the key points of the culture's oral tradition. One way to do this might be to ask, "What values of the society are revealed through the stories?" You may want to bring the class together and create a chart on the board comparing the various cultures they are studying. Ask students to hypothesize:

- Why values and traditions of these cultures may be different
- What factors may have influenced these differences
- How they might have changed over time. For example, in African-American slave tales, animal stories in which a trickster outsmarts a master reflected the fantasies of the storytellers. In Chinese culture, folk tales such as "Waters of Gold" taught listeners how a person was supposed to behave.

Analyze oral interpretations of literature for effects on the listener

Teaching suggestions: Discuss with students how nonverbal gestures, body language, and tone of voice affect the message.

- Does the speaker emphasize the right points?
- Does the speaker use body language to convey the message and create a dramatic affect?
- Is the tone audible, and appropriate to the content?
- Is the audience engaged?

Feedback Center

Students can use the following guidelines when giving and receiving feedback during this project:

Giving Feedback

▶ Ask questions concerning content, purpose, and point of view.

▶ Provide feedback about the interpretation (for instance, the overall impact on the listener).

▶ Comment on the verbal delivery (pitch, pace, volume) and its impact on the listener.

▶ Comment on the nonverbal delivery (body language, including facial expressions and gestures) and its impact on the listener.

▶ Evaluate the credibility of a speaker.

Receiving Feedback

▶ Listen to constructive criticism with an open mind.

▶ Use audience feedback in order to modify the presentation to clarify meaning or organization.

3 ▶ Assessing the Project

The following rubric can be used for group or individual assessment.

3 *Full Accomplishment*

Students followed directions and performed successful oral interpretations that demonstrated an understanding of the content and cultural backdrop of their stories. Students used appropriate body language and tone to enhance the stories, and the audience easily followed their presentations.

2 *Substantial Accomplishment*

Students selected, edited, and performed oral interpretations for an audience, but the selections were unrelated or not easily followed by the audience. The presentations may have lacked a strong delivery and appropriate body language. Some of the Speaking and Listening Skills were demonstrated.

1 *Little Accomplishment*

Students did not fully complete the project to the point of performing, or the performance did not fulfill the requirements of the assignment.

These pages are designed to introduce students to the tradition of storytelling. Students read a transcript of an interview with Tim Tingle, a Texas storyteller. His words give students an opportunity to experience what it is like to feel connected to a family and cultural tradition and to share stories with a modern audience.

Objectives
- understand and appreciate the richness of oral storytelling
- apply and practice skills learned in previous selections

TIM TINGLE:
Tim Tingle performs his original version of the folktale "Brother Coyote and Brother Cricket"

Storyteller Tim Tingle shares with audiences his own interpretation of "The Coyote and the Cricket," a trickster tale known in his home state of Texas. The story is an entertaining look at a clever cricket as well as a lesson about human nature. It is the kind of tale that influenced Tingle most as he was growing up. He says, "I remember my dad . . . his anecdotes were always short but they were always about the character of people. These were the stories that moved me . . ." Although its characters are not human, "The Coyote and the Cricket" focuses on human traits such as arrogance, courage, and resourcefulness.

To make his stories come alive, Tingle uses plenty of concrete details, movement, vocal changes and timed silences that draw attention to important lines. He explains, "The true training of a storyteller is the training of the ear and eye."

STORYTELLERS PAST AND PRESENT

TIM TINGLE

A Present-Day Storyteller Speaks

Tim Tingle is a Texas storyteller whose stories are inspired by the rich cultural background of his family as well as the ethnic diversity of the American Southwest. The stories he admires most are those that celebrate "the specialness of simple people."

I was raised on the Texas Gulf Coast, 45 minutes from the Gulf of Mexico, not far from Galveston Island. The house where I was raised was actually once a bunkhouse where cowboys slept. When my father came back from World War II, he purchased that old bunkhouse, put in indoor plumbing, and moved into it. That's where myself and my four brothers and sisters were raised.

We had a mixture of cultural backgrounds on my father's side. His granddad was Scottish-Irish—that's where the name Tingle comes from. My grandmother was a full-blooded Choctaw. The family moved from Choctaw territory in Oklahoma to Pasadena, Texas, for the jobs that were available there around 1910. I remember just sitting and listening to my dad and his brothers talk about people that they knew. My dad's anecdotes were always short, but they were always about the character of people. The single most important attribute of a good storyteller is to be a good listener and a keen observer.

I first started telling stories when I was in elementary school. Usually they were scary stories that I told around the campfire when I was camping with friends of mine. We'd keep each other up until one or two in the morning. I remember there was an old fellow who lived under a bridge not too far from our house, just kind of an old hermit, and we'd make up stories about how he lived, what prison he escaped from, just wild, imaginary stuff.

794 UNIT SIX: THE ORAL TRADITION

Cross Curricular Link **Social Studies**

Folklore People who study folklore have found startling similarities among the stories told by peoples as diverse as Australian Aborigines, Indian Buddhists, Christians, and Native Americans. Scholars suggest two theories to explain these similarities. One theory is that the themes and concerns of these stories are universal. Almost every culture searches for explanations of natural phenomena, how the world began, how the world will or may end, and how people should act and relate. As storytellers grapple with these concerns, common elements emerge in the tales from diverse cultures: rites of passage, journeys or spiritual quests, earthly or heavenly paradises, and many others. The second theory suggests that as cultures interact through conquest, travel, trade, and intermarriage, stories from different cultures are shared and get changed in the retelling.

Now, I create my stories from several sources. I like to take historical events and put real characters in them. I love to visit places where I've never been before. I just listen and keep my mind open, and what I've found is that people with stories will seek me out. I have a little verse that I open one of my stories with. It goes like this:

I never go looking for stories to tell
But I walk the hallways
And the pathways
And the riverbanks
Where the stories dwell.

After I've performed a story at least a hundred times, then the characters become real to me. And when I tell a story that much, and I know the characters that well, then there will come a time in the telling of the story *when the story comes alive.* And then, before I know it, I look around and magically, the story's over with. We've all been a part of it, and we can all step back and applaud the magic of the story. And that to me is the special thing about live storytelling, that there comes a time, in the story, when the audience dissolves, the storyteller dissolves, and what is left is the *story.*

The key thing for young people of the 21st century is knowing and appreciating storytelling so that they can know *their* story. The films that are made about the lives that people go through in elementary and junior high and high school are never made by people who are experiencing that; they're always made by adults who strive to remember what it was like. The advance of technology doesn't mean that storytelling is dying, it means that it can reach more and more people—but it begins with *your* imagination.

 Literature in Performance

A Traditional Storyteller
Family elders, both men and women, are frequently the ones who are responsible for passing along family tales to their children and grandchildren.

The folklore of the American Southwest is a blend of traditions: Native American, Mexican, African American, and European American influences, as well as many that are unique to the region itself, enrich the vibrant culture of the Southwest.

Raising and lowering the voice can draw listeners into the dramatic tension of a story.

Body language, including hand gestures, brings a tale to life.

STORYTELLERS PAST AND PRESENT **795**

- understand the history and development of oral traditions around the world
- understand and appreciate types of literature in the oral tradition

Reading and Analyzing

Literary Analysis: ORAL TRADITION

To help students distinguish among the types of literature in the oral tradition, ask the following questions:
- Which type concludes with a moral?
  Answer: fable
- How does the main purpose of a myth differ from that of a folk tale?
  Possible Response: Myths offer answers to questions about the world, while folk tales are usually told to entertain.
- How would you best classify a story about a hero of the past who inspires people?
  Possible Response: as a legend

Reading Skills and Strategies: PREDICTING

Point out that the time line stops at A.D. 1876. Ask students to predict what types of stories from the oral tradition might be developed today.
Possible Responses: legends about sports heroes, myths about dramatic events, and fables that teach lessons about 20th-century problems.

Reading Skills and Strategies: INFERRING

After students study the time line, ask them to explain how stories might have been passed across cultures.
Possible Response: when one country colonized another; when a person gained notoriety or traveled

KEEPING THE PAST ALIVE

Storytellers like Tim Tingle represent a tradition that goes back to the dawn of history. In every culture, people told stories. Some of these stories took on a life of their own, outliving their storytellers and passing from one generation to the next. Through them, the past spoke to the present. Through them, the values of a culture stayed alive. These stories make up what is called the **oral tradition**. The chart below lists the types of stories in the oral tradition—**myths, folk tales, oral history, and fables**—together with their distinctive features and their common elements. The time line introduces each culture represented in this unit, listing one or more stories from its oral tradition and an interesting fact from its history.

GREECE

Prometheus. 800
Theseus and the
Minotaur 804
Narcissus. 838
Phaëthon 850

. . .

477–431 B.C. Greek civilization reaches its pinnacle.

KENYA

Kelfala's Secret
Something 876

. . .

about 1000 B.C. People from other parts of Africa begin to settle in Kenya.

MYTHS
- *attempt to answer basic questions about the world*
- *are considered truthful by their originators*

FOLK TALES
- *are told primarily for entertainment*
- *feature humans or humanlike animals*

COMMON ELEMENTS
- **keep the past alive**
- **teach lessons about human behavior**
- **reveal the values of the society**

FABLES
- *are short tales that illustrate morals*
- *have characters that are animals*

ORAL HISTORY
- *is based on real events*
- *is considered factual by the teller*
- *passes along information*

Viewing and Representing

Mini Lesson

TEKS 10L, 20D

USING GRAPHIC ORGANIZERS

Instruction On the board, draw the web shown and then explain that stories from the oral tradition have the following characteristics:
- They are passed down by word of mouth within a culture.
- They reflect such types of literature as legends, folktales, myths, and fables.
- They reveal the values of a particular culture.

Application Invite students to copy the web into their notebooks. As students read the selections in this unit, they can classify each according to the type of literature that it best exemplifies. Suggest that students write the titles directly on the web as examples of each category.

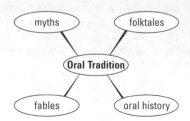

*about **500** B.C. The philosopher Confucius develops a moral system that influences China for more than 2000 years.*

*A.D. **1200s** The Edda—a collection of oral poems based on Scandinavian myths—is written down.*

*A.D. **1508** Spanish colonists begin to settle in Puerto Rico.*

*about A.D. **250–900** Great Native American civilizations flourish in Mexico.*

*A.D. **939** The Vietnamese set up a state that remains independent for more than 900 years.*

*A.D. **1845** Texas becomes the twenty-eighth state of the United States.*

*A.D. **1871** Otto von Bismarck unites Germany under Prussian rule.*

Customizing Instruction

Less Proficient Readers

Because of the intermix of words and pictures, less-proficient readers may have difficulty interpreting the time line. Guide students to read the events in sequence from the earliest to the last. Be sure that students understand the abbreviations A.D. and B.C.

To check students' understanding of the time line, ask the following questions:

• What European countries or regions are included in the time line?

Answer: Germany, Greece, and the Scandinavian countries

• Which events took place in North America?

Answer: Native American Civilizations flourished in Mexico; Puerto Rico was colonized; Texas became a state.

• What Asian countries are included on the timeline?

Answer: China, Vietnam

Gifted and Talented

Encourage students to research several of the cultures represented in this unit and identify other "fascinating facts" to add to the time line. Have them explain why the facts they choose stand out to them or seem to characterize a particular culture.

Mini Lesson **Speaking and Listening** ★ TEKS 5B

TALL TALE

Prepare You might introduce students to the oral tradition by having them find and perform a uniquely American form of folklore, the tall tale. Explain that a tall tale is a humorously exaggerated story about impossible events. Often the main character of a tall tale has extraordinary abilities. The stories of John Henry, Pecos Bill, and Paul Bunyan and Babe the Blue Ox are examples of tall tales. Invite groups of students to find an example of a tall tale that appeals to them. Group members should work cooperatively to create dialogue, actions, and props for each of the characters in the tall tale, and then to perform the tale for the rest of the class.

Present Tape record or videotape the performances. Have members of each group listen to or view their performances and discuss how the performance catches the spirit of the tall tale.

BLOCK SCHEDULING This activity is particularly well suited for longer class periods.

Objectives

1. understand and appreciate a Greek myth

2. appreciate the culture and history of Greece and of the United States

3. extend understanding of the selections through a variety of multimodal and cross-curricular activities

Reading Pathways

• Select one of several students to read each story aloud to the entire class or to small groups of students. Assign this reading in advance so that the readers can incorporate into their presentations some of the techniques used by professional storytellers. Have students listen carefully to the tales without following along in their texts.

• Read each tale aloud to the class, pausing at key points to discuss how elements of the tale inform students about the history or customs of the culture. Have students compare these customs with those of their own culture. Then have them record their observations in their notebooks.

• After students have read the tales once, have them read each tale again to identify such structural elements as main characters, minor characters, conflict, setting, and plot. Then ask students to identify similarities and differences between these tales and the selections in the related unit. For example, they can contrast the boldness of characters such as Prometheus and Theseus in the Greek myths with the caution of the title character in "Zebra" or the uncertainty of Victor in "Seventh Grade."

 See the Skills Trace at the beginning of the unit for information **TEKS** on TEKS covered in this lesson.

LINKS TO UNIT ONE

Learning from Experience

You are making new discoveries all the time—and as you experience new things, you learn more about yourself. You also learn about other people, other places, and other things. In the Greek myths you are about to read, the main characters—Prometheus and Theseus—learn about themselves and the worlds around them as they encounter new situations. These themes and characters link closely with similar themes and characters introduced in Unit One selections.

GREECE

Prometheus

retold by Bernard Evslin

The ancient Greeks believed that the gods controlled people's fates. In many Greek myths, characters overstep bounds or ignore warnings from the gods. Therefore, if someone or something angered the gods, there could be quite a price to pay. The myth "Prometheus" (prə-mē′thē-əs) tells about a Greek Titan who takes a risk to help improve the lives of humans—even though he has been warned not to do so. Prometheus and his brother Epimetheus (ĕp′ə-mē′thē-əs) were the only Titans who sided with Zeus in his battle against his father, Cronus (krō′nəs), to become supreme ruler. Zeus, after his victory, ordered Prometheus to create humans. In this myth, Prometheus disobeys another of Zeus's orders and suffers the consequences.

LESSON RESOURCES

UNIT SIX RESOURCE BOOK,
pp. 4–10

ASSESSMENT
Formal Assessment,
pp. 125–126
Teacher's Guide to Assessment and Portfolio Use
Test Generator

SKILLS TRANSPARENCIES AND COPYMASTERS
Grammar
• Past Participles, CM 97
 (for Mini Lesson, p. 804)
Communications
• Impromptu Speaking:
 Dialogue, Role-Play, TR 13
 (for Mini Lesson, p. 800)

INTEGRATED TECHNOLOGY
Audio Library
Internet: Research Starter

Visit our website:
www.mcdougallittell.com

GREECE

Theseus and the Minotaur

retold by Olivia Coolidge

In "Theseus and the Minotaur" as well as in many Greek myths, keeping one's word was a matter of life and death. A promise was a promise—no excuses. Greek gods were not very forgiving. In this version of the myth, the Greek hero Theseus (thē′sē-əs) kills the hideous Minotaur with the help of the beautiful Ariadne. However, he then leaves Ariadne asleep on the beach to sail back to his father, King Aegeus. Theseus learns what happens when trust is broken and the gods are made angry.

AS YOU READ . . .

Determine the values and customs presented in ancient Greek culture.

Determine which behaviors and traits are rewarded and which are punished.

Consider what the characters learn about themselves and the worlds around them.

LINKS TO UNIT ONE **799**

soned with pride and fancy himself a god, " replies Zeus. This answer does not satisfy Prometheus, so he brings fire to humans in their caves and teaches them how to use it. Soon people are building houses, ships, and chariots; forging metal into tools and weapons; carrying torches and cooking food. Zeus is furious when he discovers what Prometheus has done. He orders that the Titan be chained to a mountain top, where two vultures pluck at his liver. This continues until Heracles rescues him centuries later. Zeus's revenge on humans is to watch them destroy themselves with their new skills.

Reading and Analyzing

Literary Analysis:
CHARACTERIZATION

 To help students analyze characters, including their traits, ask students what this speech reveals about Zeus.
Possible Responses: He's vain and wants people to respect and fear him.

Use **Unit Six Resource Book,** p. 6 for additional practice.

Active Reading: CLARIFYING

 Have students explain Zeus's worry.
Possible Responses: Zeus fears that people will become proud and challenge the gods.

Use **Unit Six Resource Book,** p. 5 for additional practice.

PROMETHEUS

retold by Bernard Evslin

Teaching Options

 Mini Lesson **Speaking and Listening** **TEKS 5C, 11B**

ROLE-PLAYING
Prepare Explain to students that they can present dramatic interpretations of stories to communicate and that role-playing is one technique they can use to better understand characters in a story. Before role-playing a character or scene, they should review the story to look for details or make inferences about a character's personality and motivation. Such information will enhance their performance.

Present Have students work in pairs to role-play a scene from the story, such as when Prometheus and Zeus argue about whether people should have fire. Encourage students to combine quotations from the story with invented dialogue.

BLOCK SCHEDULING This activity is particularly well suited for longer class periods.

Use **Communications Transparencies and Copymasters,** p. 13, for additional support.

Prometheus was a young Titan,[1] no great admirer of Zeus. Although he knew the great lord of the sky hated <u>explicit</u> questions, he did not hesitate to beard[2] him when there was something he wanted to know.

One morning he came to Zeus and said, "O Thunderer, I do not understand your <u>design</u>. You have caused the race of man to appear on earth, but you keep him in ignorance and darkness."

"Perhaps you had better leave the race of man to me," said Zeus. "What you call ignorance is innocence. What you call darkness is the shadow of my decree. Man is happy now. And he is so framed that he will remain happy unless someone persuades him that he is unhappy. Let us not speak of this again."

But Prometheus said, "Look at him. Look below. He crouches in caves. He is at the mercy of beast and weather. He eats his meat raw. If you mean something by this, enlighten me with your wisdom. Tell me why you refuse to give man the gift of fire."

Zeus answered, "Do you not know, Prometheus, that every gift brings a penalty? This is the way the Fates[3] weave destiny—by which gods also must abide. Man does not have fire, true, nor the crafts which fire teaches. On the other hand, he does not know disease, warfare, old age, or that inward pest called worry. He is happy, I say, happy without fire. And so he shall remain."

"Happy as beasts are happy," said Prometheus. "Of what use to make a separate race called man and <u>endow</u> him with little fur, some wit, and a curious charm of unpredictability? If he must live like this, why separate him from the beasts at all?"

"He has another quality," said Zeus, "the capacity for worship. An <u>aptitude</u> for admiring our power, being puzzled by our riddles and amazed by our caprice.[4] That is why he was made."

"Enough, Prometheus! I have been patient with you, but do not try me too far."

"Would not fire, and the graces he can put on with fire, make him more interesting?"

"More interesting, perhaps, but infinitely more dangerous. For there is this in man too: a vaunting pride that needs little sustenance[5] to make it swell to giant size. Improve his lot, and he will forget that which makes him pleasing—his sense of worship, his <u>humility</u>. He will grow big and poisoned with pride and fancy himself a god, and before we know it, we shall see him storming Olympus. Enough, Prometheus! I have been patient with you, but

1. **Titan:** in Greek mythology, one of a family of giants who were overthrown by the family of Zeus.
2. **beard:** to confront.
3. **Fates:** in Greek mythology, the three goddesses who decide the course of people's lives.
4. **caprice** (kə-prēs′): the quality of acting without planning or thinking beforehand.
5. **sustenance** (sŭs′tə-nəns): nourishment; assistance.

Detail of illustration by Robert Baxter from *Prometheus and the Story of Fire* by I. M. Richardson. Copyright © 1983 Troll Associates. Reprinted with permission of the publisher.

WORDS TO KNOW	**explicit** (ĭk-splĭs′ĭt) *adj.* plain; straightforward	
	design (dĭ-zīn′) *n.* a plan	
	endow (ĕn-dou′) *v.* to provide with a quality or a talent	
	aptitude (ăp′tĭ-tōōd) *n.* natural ability	
	humility (hyōō-mĭl′ĭ-tē) *n.* lack of pride	

801

 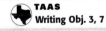

Reading and Analyzing

Literary Analysis: PERSONIFICATION

A Explain to students that personification is the giving of human qualities to an animal, object, or idea. Have students describe the personification here.

Possible Responses: Fire is referred to as a spirit; as a little brother of the sun; as greedy; as a hungry person; as being able to escape.

Reading Skills and Strategies: CONNECTING

B In this tale and in "The Crush," a gift is given. Have students compare the effect that each gift has on its recipient.

Possible Responses: The recipients are changed in both stories. In "The Crush," Dolores acts more feminine after receiving flowers. In "Prometheus," people develop new technologies and change their behavior.

Reading Skills and Strategies: PREDICTING

C Ask students what they think Zeus will do to Prometheus and why.

Possible Responses: He will probably punish him in some way; he will harm him; he is furious, and he has power.

Literary Analysis: CHARACTERIZATION

Ask students to explain whether this piece shows Prometheus to be a hero or not. Have them back their responses with concrete details from the text.

Possible Responses: Yes, because he defies the gods to follow his beliefs; yes, because he is willing to risk his life for people; no, because he disobeyed.

do not try me too far. Go now and trouble me no more with your speculations."

Prometheus was not satisfied. All that night he lay awake making plans. Then he left his couch at dawn and, standing tiptoe on Olympus, stretched his arm to the eastern horizon where the first faint flames of the sun were flickering. In his hand he held a reed filled with a dry fiber; he thrust it into the sunrise until a spark smoldered. Then he put the reed in his tunic and came down from the mountain.

At first men were frightened by the gift. It was so hot, so quick; it bit sharply when you touched it and for pure spite made the shadows dance. They thanked Prometheus and asked him to take it away. But he took the haunch[6] of a newly killed deer and held it over the fire. And when the meat began to sear and sputter, filling the cave with its rich smells, the people felt themselves melting with hunger and flung themselves on the meat and devoured it greedily, burning their tongues.

A "This that I have brought you is called 'fire,'" Prometheus said. "It is an ill-natured spirit, a little brother of the sun, but if you handle it carefully, it can change your whole life. It is very greedy; you must feed it twigs, but only until it becomes a proper size. Then you must stop, or it will eat everything in sight—and you too. If it escapes, use this magic: water. It fears the water spirit, and if you touch it with water, it will fly away until you need it again."

He left the fire burning in the first cave, with children staring at it wide-eyed, and then went to every cave in the land.

B Then one day Zeus looked down from the mountain and was amazed. Everything had changed. Man had come out of his cave. Zeus saw woodmen's huts,

> "Let them destroy themselves with their new skills. This will make a long, twisted game, interesting to watch. . . . My first business is with Prometheus."

farmhouses, villages, walled towns, even a castle or two. He saw men cooking their food, carrying torches to light their way at night. He saw forges[7] blazing, men beating out ploughs, keels, swords, spears. They were making ships and raising white wings of sails and daring to use the fury of the winds for their journeys. They were wearing helmets, riding out in chariots to do battle, like the gods themselves.

Zeus was full of rage. He seized his largest thunderbolt. "So they want fire," he said to himself. "I'll give them fire—more than they can use. I'll turn their miserable little ball of earth into a cinder." But then another thought came to him, and he lowered his arm. "No," he said to himself, "I shall have vengeance— and entertainment too. Let them destroy themselves with their new skills. This will make a long, twisted game, interesting to watch. I'll attend to them later. My first business is with Prometheus."

He called his giant guards and had them seize Prometheus, drag him off to the

---

6. **haunch:** the hip and leg of an animal.
7. **forges:** places where metal is heated and hammered into shape.

WORDS
TO   **vengeance** (vĕn′jəns) *n.* the infliction of punishment in return for an offense
KNOW

802

Teaching Options

Multicultural Link **Fire**

To help students discuss themes and connections that cross cultures, explain that people throughout the world have myths that explain how the world, its people, and its elements came to be. Such myths are called origin myths. Myths that explain the origin of fire are particularly common.
- A Peruvian myth describes how a parrot stole fire from an ogre and brought it to the rest of the world.
- In Ecuador, it was a hummingbird who brought fire to a woman, who shared it with others.

- A Karok tale tells how Coyote stole fire from three sisters. The fire eventually wound up inside a willow, and Coyote taught everyone how to rub the sticks together to make fire.
- In an Apache myth, Fox takes some fire from fireflies and spreads it over the earth. As punishment, he is told that he can never use it himself.

Encourage students to share any other origin myths they know, such as how the world or people were formed.

Caucasus,[8] and there bind him to a mountain peak with great chains specially forged by Hephaestus[9]—chains which even a Titan in agony could not break. And when the friend of man was bound to the mountain, Zeus sent two vultures to hover about him forever, tearing at his belly and eating his liver.

Men knew a terrible thing was happening on the mountain, but they did not know what. But the wind shrieked like a giant in torment and sometimes like fierce birds.

Many centuries he lay there—until another hero was born brave enough to defy the gods. He climbed to the peak in the Caucasus and struck the shackles[10] from Prometheus and killed the vultures. His name was Heracles.[11]

8. **Caucasus** (kô′kə-səs): a mountainous region in southeastern Europe.
9. **Hephaestus** (hǐ-fĕs′təs): in Greek mythology, the god of fire and metalworking.
10. **shackles:** metal bonds for holding the ankles or wrists of a prisoner.
11. **Heracles** (hĕr′ə-klēz): another name for Hercules, a son of Zeus who was famous for his great strength and courage in Greek and Roman mythology.

Illustration by Robert Baxter from *Prometheus and the Story of Fire* by I. M. Richardson. Copyright © 1983 Troll Associates. Reprinted with permission of the publisher.

"Men knew a terrible thing was happening on the mountain."

Bernard Evslin
1922–1993

Multitalented Artist Bernard Evslin was born in Philadelphia, Pennsylvania, and attended Rutgers University. He was an award-winning screenwriter and producer of documentary films before turning to writing in the mid-1960s. Most of his retold stories deal with Greek mythology and history.

Critical Acclaim Evslin wrote more than 30 books for young people, including *The Adventures of Ulysses; The Trojan War; The Greek Gods; Heroes, Gods, and Monsters of the Greek Myths; The Green Hero,* which was nominated for a National Book Award; and *Hercules,* which received the Washington Irving Children's Book Choice Award. More than six million copies of his works are in print.

PROMETHEUS **803**

Summary

Theseus and the Minotaur Theseus arrives in Athens when his father, King Aegeus, is old and frail. Medea, a witch, persuades the king to poison the new arrival, but Theseus saves himself by proving that he is Aegeus's son. Later, Theseus learns that fourteen youths are about to be sent to Crete as a sacrifice to a deadly monster, the Cretan Minotaur. He feels this tribute is unjust and volunteers to go to try to slay the monster. There he tells King Minos of Crete his feelings and is promptly jailed. Ariadne, the king's soft-hearted daughter, releases Theseus and gives him the tools to slay the Minotaur in his labyrinth and to find his way out again. Theseus succeeds, and then he and his men flee with Ariadne. They land on Naxos, where she falls asleep and is left behind by the other sailors. Because the men neglect to put up a white sail, King Aegeus thinks his son is dead and kills himself. Theseus thus takes the throne amidst sorrow rather than joy. He rules heroically for many years.

Reading and Analyzing

Reading Skills and Strategies: INFERRING

A Ask students what they can infer about what has happened in the past, before this story begins.

Possible Responses: Theseus left home years ago and hasn't seen his father since; Theseus had a sword of his father's.

Literary Analysis: PLOT

Based on the title and what they have read so far, ask students what they think the major conflict in this story will be.

Possible Response: whether Theseus will kill the Minotaur

Theseus and the Minotaur

retold by Olivia Coolidge

At Athens the long reign of King Aegeus was coming to an inglorious end. The whole land was split by quarrels between Aegeus' cousins, who considered themselves his heirs, while the old king himself was completely under the sway of the witch, Medea, to whom he had given protection when Corinth drove her out. Even the common people were tired of Aegeus, for he had been defeated in war by Minos of Crete, and the land was forced to pay a dreadful tribute every nine years. Theseus preferred to make no claim on the aged king. He came as a mighty hero who happened to be traveling through Athens and asked the king to receive him as a guest, thinking that his likeness to Aethra would cause the old man to recognize his son.

Aegeus agreed to receive the hero, since he could hardly refuse the request of such a famous man, but Medea, the enchantress, who had learned who Theseus was, had already whispered to him that the young man was a traitor who came to seize his throne. The feeble old king, confused by her dark spells and made suspicious by the constant intrigues around him, believed her. Medea smiled to herself, for she knew that if Theseus were recognized by his father, her reign in Athens would be at an end.

A great crowd of people poured out to meet Theseus at the gates of the city and escorted him with shouts and cheering to the palace of the king. More and more came hurrying from house and dock and workshop, wriggling their way into the crowd to catch sight of him, or standing on tiptoe on the outskirts to get a glimpse of the hero's head as it towered above the rest. Even the palace servants ran out at last, and the old king pressed his thin lips together as he saw them go, while his scanty grey beard quivered with his <u>indignation</u>.

"He is indeed a traitor," he said to Medea. "He steals my very servants from before my eyes."

WORDS TO KNOW

indignation (ĭn'dĭg-nā'shən) *n.* anger that is a reaction to injustice or meanness

804

Teaching Options

 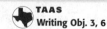 **Grammar** TEKS 17F TAAS Writing Obj. 3, 6

PAST PARTICIPLES

Instruction Tenses are made from the three principal parts of verbs: the present, the past, and the past participle. With regular verbs, such as *drop* and *like*, the past tense is formed by the addition of *-ed* or *-d*, and the past tense and the past participle are spelled the same. In some cases, as with *bring*, the past tense and the past participle are the same. In others, as with *take* and *eat*, the past participle is different from both the present and the past tense. Point out the highlighted clause and ask

students to identify the past participle of *give*.

Present	Past	Past Participle
drop	dropped	(has) dropped
like	liked	(has) liked
bring	brought	(has) brought
take	took	(has) taken
eat	ate	(has) eaten

Exercises Ask students to substitute a helping verb and a past participle for the existing verbs in each of the following sentences.

1. King Aegeus ruled for years. (*had ruled*)

2. Theseus came as a hero. (*had come*)

3. The King spoke to Medea. (*had spoken*)

4. The old man forgot Theseus. (*had forgotten*)

5. Theseus decided to test him. (*had decided*)

Use **Unit Six Resource Book**, p. 8.
Use **Grammar Transparencies and Copymasters**, p. 97.

 Use McDougal Littell's **Language Network**, Chapter 7, for more instruction and practice in using past participles.

Medea smiled at him. "I will deal with him," she said. "Let us go out on the steps to welcome him. We will greet him with honor and bid him come in. When he enters the hall, do you sit him down and call for meat and wine. I myself will pour his wine for him; he shall drink from my golden cup. There are poisons I have brought from Colchis that the witch–goddess helped me brew. Let him take but one sip that I shall pour for him, and he will never claim your throne."

The old king nodded feebly, for he was half crazed by her spells. "Do not fail with the poison," he quavered, "and now help me to the door."

They stood on the steps to greet the hero, the slender, dark-eyed sorceress, and the tottering old man leaning on her arm. Theseus turned from the witch in anger, but he looked his father in the face. The old man had forgotten Aethra; he did not know her son. He bade Theseus welcome formally and invited him within, but he gave no sign of recognition, and the hero followed him wondering.

The traveler was bathed and dressed for feasting. Tables were set up within the hall. Meat was brought in by the servants. Wine and water were mixed in huge bowls. Each guest was brought a wine cup of red earthenware on which a skillful artist had painted some deed of a hero of whom the minstrels sang. Medea would not let Theseus drink from his. "You are our guest of honor," she said. "You shall drink from gold, and a king's daughter shall serve you." With that she fetched him wine in a curious golden cup such as the great artists of Crete had made.

Theseus took the cup and turned to his father, for he had a mind to drink his health in it. The old king was looking at him in a fixed silence, while his fingers drummed nervously

on the table. There was something so unpleasant about his stare that Theseus was startled, and the first hint of <u>treachery</u> came into his mind. He determined to test his father. Therefore he kept his left hand on the winecup, but with his right instead of a knife he drew out his father's sword and made as though he would cut himself a portion of the meat with it. Seeing that sword, the king reached out startled, snatched the winecup from Theseus' hand, and dashed it to the floor. Then he jumped up and flung his arms about the young man, calling him son. For her part, Medea, seeing her treachery was discovered and knowing that her reign was over, vanished from Athens and was seen no more.

Aegeus proudly acknowledged his son and named him as his heir, but the king's cousins, who were not pleased at this, stirred up the common people against King Aegeus. It happened to be the time when the tribute to Minos became due. Seven youths and seven maidens were chosen by lot from among the people to go to Crete as a sacrifice to the dreadful monster, the Cretan Minotaur. What happened to them when they got there no one knew, for no one who once went in had ever come out of the famous labyrinth that Daedalus had made for the beast to dwell in. Men could hear the distant bellowing of the monster in his lair, and it was supposed he ate up his victims, though some said they became priests in his temple. At any rate, because their children were chosen by lot for a dreadful fate, the people were furiously <u>indignant</u>. So too was Theseus when he heard the tale.

"Why has no one dared to slay this Minotaur?" he asked King Aegeus. "This is no way to pay tribute. Let me go to Crete and put an end to it."

"No, my son," said King Aegeus terrified.

WORDS TO KNOW
treachery (trĕch′ə-rē) *n.* willful betrayal of trust or confidence
indignant (ĭn-dĭg′nənt) *adj.* filled with indignation

805

 Mini Lesson **Spelling** **TEKS 16G**

LATIN ROOTS

Instruction Explain to students that a knowledge of common Latin roots can help them spell words that contain these parts. For example, the words *indignation* and *indignant*, which appear in the selection, contain the Latin root *dign-*. This root comes from *dignus*, meaning "worthy." Other words that contain this root include *dignitary*, *dignified*, and *dignity*. Other Latin roots include: **dict**—predict, verdict, dictionary

miss—dismiss, mission, transmission
commun—community, communal, communicate
Exercises Choose the spelling word that best completes the sentence.

1. The jury brought in a _____ of guilty. (*verdict*)

2. The spy was sent on a secret _____. (*mission*)

3. This new park will serve the whole _____. (*community*)

4. The woman carried herself with great _____. (*dignity*)

5. A flag was raised to honor the visiting _____. (*dignitary*)

Use **Unit Six Resource Book**, p. 9 for additional practice.

Literary Analysis: CHARACTER

A Explain, if necessary, that the Minotaur is a monster that has a bull's head on a human body; it is the son of Minos's wife.

Literary Analysis: SETTING

B Explain, if necessary, that the Labyrinth is the palace in which the Minotaur lives. He lives in the center, surrounded by a maze of passages.

Reading Skills and Strategies: INFER

C Ask why the people feel pity when they see Theseus and the others.
Possible Responses: They think he has no chance to live; they think he will suffer.

Active Reading: CLARIFY

D Ask students why the roaring grows suddenly louder.
Possible Responses: It grows louder when the Minotaur spies Theseus and most likely attacks him.

Reading Skills and Strategies: DRAW CONCLUSIONS

E Ask students what they think happens between Theseus and the Minotaur. Have them draw inferences, such as conclusions, and support them with text evidence and experience.
Possible Responses: Theseus kills the beast; he returns and his sword is red with blood.

A "No one can slay the Minotaur, for the young men are not allowed to take any weapons as they go into the labyrinth. **B** Besides, the victims are chosen from the people, and you are not of the people; you are the king's son."

"All the more reason I should go, " said Theseus. "I shall not wait to be chosen. I shall volunteer."

The king implored him with tears in his eyes, but Theseus was determined, and the people idolized him more than ever when they heard what he was to do. The ship made ready for the chosen victims was small and quite unarmed, as the terms of the treaty bade. **1** She had a black sail of mourning, that all might know that she bore the tribute to King Minos and must be allowed to pass. This time Theseus bad them put in a white sail as well. "When we return," he said, "we shall come with open rejoicing as a free people should."

The ship put off from the bay and the weeping people watched it go. King Aegeus sat on the headland looking after it, and there, he told his son, he should watch daily until the ship came home. But the chosen youths and maidens, encouraged by the cheerfulness of Theseus, sang songs to cheer their journey across the sea. When they came to great wharves of the town of Cnossos, they put on a bold face. Even the powerful ships of Minos did not dismay them, or the sight of his huge stone palace, or the crowds of townsfolk who came down to watch the tribute come to land.

C Many a man felt pity as he saw the

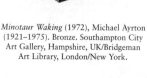

Minotaur Waking (1972), Michael Ayrton (1921–1975). Bronze. Southampton City Art Gallery, Hampshire, UK/Bridgeman Art Library, London/New York.

handsome youth at the head of the little group and heard that he was the king's only son and that he was a volunteer.

There was talk of granting him a weapon that he might have a fair chance against the Minotaur, but King Minos would not hear it. The challenge of Theseus only made him angry.

"How dare you come here in defiance?" he said to the young man. "Tomorrow we will throw you to the monster and we shall see what your boast is worth."

"I dare because the tribute is unjust," replied Theseus firmly. "Armed or unarmed I will fight your hideous bullman. If I prevail, I warn you, O Minos, that we Athenians are a free people and the tribute shall cease. If I die, I die; but the tribute is still unjust."

Some murmured admiration at his boldness, but King Minos stood up from his throne in wrath. "Take his sword," he ordered his guards, "and lock the victims in the dungeons overnight. Tomorrow we will give you to the Minotaur, and after that the tribute will go on. The black-sailed ship shall return to Aegeus to tell him that he has no son. The Athenians need to remember that the sea is mine, and, distant as they are, they must live in dread of my power."

The guards closed in on the Athenians and took them down to cold, dark dungeons. People watched them pityingly, for they knew Theseus had no chance, yet they admired the

WORDS TO KNOW	**implore** (ĭm-plôr') v. to beg

Teaching Options

Multicultural Link **Symbolism of Colors**

The sail on the ship carrying Theseus to Crete was black to signify mourning. To help students determine distinctive and common characteristics of various cultures, point out that black is commonly used to show mourning in some countries. Many countries use colors symbolically, but the symbolism differs around the world.

• In many parts of Asia, the color of mourning is white.

• In China, red and green are colors that signify positive qualities, such as wealth and luck.

• In Western art, blue is a color that often stands for faith and modesty.

• Yellow often has negative connotations in many cultures. Spanish executioners wore yellow, and the Chinese use the color to show that a product is defective.

handsome young man who spoke so boldly before them all. None pitied him so much, however, as the soft-hearted king's daughter, white-footed Ariadne. She had heard Theseus speak in the hall as she stood beside her father, her bright hair about her shoulders and a great crown flashing with jewels upon her head. In the dead of the night she left her chamber and stole on silent feet down the long, stone corridors toward the dungeons, quietly drew the great bolt, and went in.

She stood in the moonlight which fell through a high, little window, and Theseus thought she was some goddess at first, for her white feet were bare on the stone, there was gleaming gold on her scarlet garment, and the bright crown was still on her head. She bade Theseus rise and come with her, making no sound. "I will give you a sword," she whispered softly, "with which you may fight the Minotaur fairly and slay him if you can."

She took his hand to guide him in the long, dark passages, and together they stole down many corridors, past many a darkened door. At last they reached a little room from which ran a passage dimly lighted. From here they heard echoing faintly a low, hoarse bellowing sound.

"Here is the Labyrinth," said Ariadne. "Far off in the center lies the Minotaur. Bend down your ear to listen while I whisper to you the secret clue Daedalus gave my father that he might find the center of the Labyrinth. To return is not so easy. Many doors lead out

from the center; yet only one will bring you here. Take this sword in your right hand and this ball of thread in your left. We will tie the end of it to a pillar and you may unwind it as you go. Then it will be easy to return as you gather the thread."

She gave him the thread and the sword, and watched him out of sight. For a while she heard his footsteps moving round and round within. At times they stopped as though he stood puzzling before the maze of passages, but then they went on again, and presently they died away. She stood there for a long time looking at the shining thread across the floor and hearing the distant roaring which arose from the monster's lair. She heard when he reached the center, because the roar grew suddenly louder and went on and on. Then there fell a dead silence, and for a long while nothing happened. If Theseus were dead or wounded, she might wait till morning and he would never come. It seemed hours that she had been standing, and the stone floor was very cold.

At last she thought she heard footsteps. Someone twitched the line. The sounds came louder and clearer, till Theseus emerged from the passage with the sword red in his hand. She fell upon him eagerly.

"Why were you so long?" she whispered. "It must be nearly dawn."

"It is a dreadful monster," he said in answer. He was still shaken by the sight of the horrible creature whom few living men had seen.

Greek kylix (lip cup), ca. 550 B.C. Inscribed with the potter's name: Tleson. Collection of the Toledo (Ohio) Museum of Art; purchased with funds from the Libbey Endowment. Gift of Edward Drummond Libbey.

 Viewing and Representing **TEKS** 23A, 23B

Minotaur Waking
by Michael Ayrton.
Greek plate by Tleson (*ca.* 550 B.C.)
ART APPRECIATION

Instruction Point out that both pieces of art depict the Minotaur, but one is a contemporary view, while the other is from Ancient Greece. Explain that viewers can draw inferences from art, just as they do from writing. Ask students which piece of art makes the Minotaur appear more dangerous and why.

Possible Responses: Most students will say the plate, which shows the creature actually fighting. However, some may say the statue, which makes the creature appear larger and stronger.

Application Have students compare and contrast the two images of the Minotaur. How are they alike and different?

Possible Response: Students might say that both show the animal qualities of the monster, one through posture and head, the other through its fur. However, the statue is engaged in a private, harmless activity, while the other is shown as a direct threat to a person.

Active Reading: CLARIFYING

A Ask students why the king thought he had nothing to live for.

Answer: He saw the black sail and concluded that his son was dead.

Literary Analysis: MYTH

Ask students what details in this story show that it is a myth and not a historical account.

Possible Responses: Students may mention the Minotaur, the god Dionysus marrying Ariadne, Theseus returning from the dead, or similar details.

Active Reading: CLARIFYING

B Ask students to clarify the meaning of the sentence that begins "Taking these from the bones of Theseus. . . ."

Possible Responses: The Athenians left the bones of Theseus; they brought back the spear and sword and buried them in a tomb.

Literary Analysis: CHARACTERIZATION

Have students compare and contrast the characterization of Prometheus with the characterization of Theseus.

"Quickly, then!" she whispered. "We have not much time." Hand in hand they stole down the long corridors again, roused the group from their dungeon, and sped down to the little ship which was moored beside the wharf. There were urgent explanations in whispers, and then sailors scrambled over one another to hoist the sail. Very quietly they cast her off, and shipped oars as soon as they dared. Then they fled for their lives as the sky grew pale with the first light before dawn.

All day long they raced away in panic fearing pursuit from the great ships of the Cretan fleet. They had put up the black sail in the dark that morning, but when some spoke of it and bade them hoist the white one, the sailors refused to take the time. Frantically they rowed till they were exhausted, landing at last worn out on the island of Naxos, where they lay down to sleep. In the morning there was a false alarm of a sail on the horizon, and tumbling into their ship, they fled again. In vain Theseus called to them that Ariadne had

been left sleeping on the beach. Even though they owed her their lives, they did not care. They were mad to reach Athens and safety.

Ariadne slept without waking till the ship was far out to sea, and then she wandered for a long time up and down, calling vainly for Theseus and the men who had forsaken her. At last the god, Dionysus, found her as he came to Naxos with his train and persuaded her to come up to the heavens and be his bride. To proclaim to all people that she had done so, he took her crown and set it in the heavens, where each jewel became a star, and where it can still be seen.

Theseus' terrified crew still raced toward Athens with no thought in their heads but speed. At last they came within sight of the headland on which King Aegeus sat, looking out over the blue ocean day after day for tidings of his son. Now when he saw the black-sailed ship, he was in despair, for he remembered the white sail they had taken with them and the words of Theseus that he would

Ariadne at Naxos (1877), Evelyn de Morgan (1855–1919). The De Morgan Foundation, London/Bridgeman Art Library, London/New York.

Teaching Options

Mini-Lesson **Speaking and Listening** 🏴 **TEKS** 2E, 5A, 11B

RETELLING

Prepare Explain to students that they can show their understanding of a story by retelling it from different points of view. As an example, ask students to think about what it would be like to tell the story from the point of view of King Aegeus. What language and manner of speaking would they use? What details would they include?

Possible Responses: They might sound confused; they might speak in a quavering voice; they might describe suddenly recognizing Theseus or waiting for his return.

Present Have students retell the story from Ariadne's point of view. To do this, they should review the details and make inferences about her motivations and thoughts. Give students time to prepare and rehearse. Then have them take turns presenting their versions of Ariadne's story. Afterward, have students discuss how the retellings were alike and different.

BLOCK SCHEDULING This activity is particularly well suited for longer class periods.

come back in freedom and rejoicing. The poor old man thought he had nothing to live for and, even while the joyful Theseus looked eagerly at the land, Aegeus threw himself over the cliff to perish in the sea.

Thus Theseus came to his throne with mourning instead of rejoicing. Thereafter he reigned long and his rule was a famous one. The Athenians told many stories of his justice, his kindness to the common people, and of the ways in which he made Athens great. Traditions speak of Theseus offering protection to people who had suffered injustice in other lands. Some even declare that he gave up the title of king, preferring to give power to the people.

There are also tales of his achievements in war; how he fought with the Amazons[1] and won their queen to wife; how he battled with the centaurs;[2] how he even went down to Hades in an unsuccessful attempt to carry off Persephone. There he was caught and imprisoned, and other people came to power in Athens. When he was finally rescued by Heracles, he never regained his power, but was driven out and died on the island of Scyros. Yet in spite of this the Athenians always spoke of him as a great king and patriot. When the mighty king of Persia tried to invade Athens in the year 490 B.C. and was defeated by its little army at the battle of Marathon, one of the famous battles of all times, then the rumor went around and the legend lingered that on that day of crisis the great Theseus, risen from the dead, had appeared to lead the battle.

Later still there was found on the island of Scyros a mighty skeleton, taller than most men and buried with bronze-headed spear and sword. Taking these for the bones of Theseus, the Athenians brought them home and buried them. From that day the tomb of Theseus was a place of refuge for poor men and slaves and all who had suffered wrong. While they were there, no man could harm them. In this way the Athenians honored the memory of the just hero who was kind to the oppressed. ❖

---

1. **Amazon:** a member of a mythical tribe of women warriors.
2. **centaur:** mythical creature with the upper body of a man and the lower body of a horse.

"A young-adult biography is designed for people who want to read straight through it, picking up all the background that they need along the way."

Olivia Coolidge
born 1908

History and the Classics Olivia Coolidge grew up in England and learned to share her family's love of history and the classics. After attending Oxford University, Coolidge came to the United States and taught English and classical languages. She put her wide interests to good use by becoming a successful reteller of Greek and Latin tales and myths.

Fact or Fiction? Coolidge has also written biographies for young people—including accounts of Gandhi and Abraham Lincoln.

Students Acquiring English
Help students understand the following words, which may be confusing:

1 *bade* means "asked them to"

2 *mad* means "insane"

3 *train* means "a group of followers"

Multiple Learning Styles
Intrapersonal Learners

4 Ask students how they would feel if they had been abandoned by people who were in a rush to save themselves.

Possible Responses: angry at being left behind; frightened; sad

Less Proficient Readers
Ask students what happened to Ariadne and Theseus.

Possible Responses: She was left behind on an island and discovered by a god, Dionysus, who married her. Theseus returned to Athens and ruled for many years. He died on Scyros, and was later spoken of as a great man.

✓ **Assessment** **Informal Assessment**   **TEKS 10H**   **TAAS Writing Obj. 2**

MAKE JUDGMENTS You can informally assess students' ability to evaluate and make judgments by asking them which character seemed more heroic, Prometheus or Theseus, and why. Tell them to include details about both characters in their evaluations.

RUBRIC

3 Full Accomplishment Response reflects a detailed understanding of both characters' accomplishments and flaws.

2 Substantial Accomplishment Response shows a general understanding of both characters' main accomplishments.

1 Little or Partial Accomplishment Response shows little understanding either of how the characters differ or of what each has accomplished.

Interdisciplinary Projects

LITERATURE CONNECTION

Dramatize a Tale Explain that students do not need to stage every detail in the story. They should select scenes that will best tell the story.

RUBRIC

3 Full Accomplishment Students work cooperatively to dramatize one of the tales. The presentation is well organized and tells the main story.

2 Substantial Accomplishment Students work cooperatively to present a dramatization, but it is somewhat disorganized or incomplete in its telling of the story.

1 Little or Partial Accomplishment Students have trouble working cooperatively and presenting a coherent dramatization.

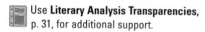 Use **Communications Transparencies and Copymasters**, p. 12, for additional support.

SOCIAL STUDIES CONNECTION

Create a Greek Gods and Goddesses Bio Board Students will find it easier to gather information about the major gods, including the following: Poseidon, Hades, Hera, Ares, Athena, Apollo, Aphrodite, Hermes, and Zeus.

RUBRIC

3 Full Accomplishment The card contains all the requested information, including a picture and information about the name, strengths, weaknesses, and rituals or feasts. It also contains some additional information.

2 Substantial Accomplishment The card contains a picture and a good description of the god or goddess, but some requested information is missing.

1 Little or Partial Accomplishment The card has incomplete information.

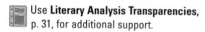 Use **Literary Analysis Transparencies**, p. 31, for additional support.

LITERATURE CONNECTION

Dramatize a Tale Perform as a play one of the tales you just read. Begin by listing the characters, dividing the tale into scenes, and choosing parts. To involve as many students as possible, choose a different cast for each scene. Then form small groups to be in charge of writing the script, props, costumes, music, sets, and publicity.

SOCIAL STUDIES CONNECTION

Create a Greek Gods and Goddesses Bio Board People in Ancient Greece believed in many gods. Find out more about Greek gods and goddesses.

Step 1: Bio Card Choose a god or goddess and create a bio card that includes the following information:

- Name
- Strengths
- Weaknesses
- Rituals/feasts given in his/her honor
- Additional information

Make sure to include a picture of the god or goddess of your choice. You can draw the picture based on what you learn, or you can use a picture that you found in your research.

Step 2: Bio Board When you are done, put your bio card on the class Greek gods and goddesses Bio Board.

More Online: Research Starter www.mcdougallittell.com

SCIENCE CONNECTION

Investigate Fire Myths, such as "Prometheus," attempt to explain the origin of natural forces, such as fire. Ancient people regarded fire as "a gift from the gods" because it was essential for survival. Modern people explain the mystery of fire scientifically. Find out more about fire. What are its elements and properties? How is it produced? What are its by-products? How is it controlled? Conduct research and interviews with people who study or control fire, such as scientists, firefighters, welders, glass blowers, and mill or refinery workers. Construct a display featuring pictures, charts, slides, videos, or other graphics that show the properties, uses, and dangers of fire.

SCIENCE CONNECTION

Investigate Fire Divide the class into three groups. Have one group research the physical aspects of fire, a second group research manufacturing processes that require fire, and a third group interview people who work with fire. After students have completed their research, assign a facilitator to each group to decide how the group will present its findings in a coherent display. Provide needed supplies, such as poster paper, markers, and video playback equipment.

RUBRIC

3 Full Accomplishment Students gather ample information on fire and translate it into a coherent visual display.

2 Substantial Accomplishment Students conduct adequate research but have difficulty determining an effective way to present and display their findings.

1 Little or Partial Accomplishment Students do inadequate research or are unable to translate their research into a coherent presentation or display.

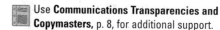 Use **Communications Transparencies and Copymasters**, p. 8, for additional support.

Across Cultures

Create a Graphic
Choose a pair of characters: one character from the tales you've just read and one from Unit One. For example, you might choose Theseus and Jimmy Wells (from "After Twenty Years," page 154), or Prometheus and Victor (from "Seventh Grade," page 20). Compare the two characters' similarities and differences. Draw a Venn diagram like the one shown. In the overlapping area, list the qualities that the characters have in common. Outside this area, list the qualities that are unique to each character.

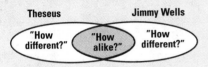

Compare Approaches Choose a character from one of these myths and a character from one of the stories in Unit 1. Think of something you disapprove of in each character's behavior. Working with a partner, discuss how you would explain to each character what you disapprove of. Keeping in mind each character's personality traits, think of what approach might be most effective in getting him or her to change. Compare and contrast approaches.

Television Interview Choose a character from one of these tales to interview. With a partner, come up with a list of questions, such as "Why did you choose to do what you did?" and "Would you do it again, given the outcome?" After you have decided on a list of questions, decide who will be the character from the story and who will be the interviewer. Present a "live" version of the interview to your class.

Vocabulary in Action

EXERCISE: CONTEXT CLUES On a sheet of paper, write the Word to Know that best completes each sentence.

1. The race of men showed an _____ for admiring Zeus's power.

2. Zeus had a grand _____ for humankind.

3. "Why _____ man with a few qualities that separate him from the beasts?" Prometheus asked.

4. Zeus hated _____ questions, preferring indirect ones.

5. When humans displease the gods, they risk that the gods will take _____ on them.

6. _____, rather than pride, was an admirable human quality, in Zeus's opinion.

7. Medea's wicked _____ was discovered and led to her undoing.

8. Aegeus showed _____ when he learned of Medea's betrayal.

9. Aegeus would _____ Theseus not to go to Crete.

10. The unfair tribute makes Theseus very _____.

WORDS TO KNOW	aptitude design	endow explicit	humility implore	indignant indignation	treachery vengeance

Across Cultures
COMPARING TEXTS

Create a Graphic Have the class first compile a list of characters from which students can choose pairs for comparison. Then suggest that students list all the character traits they can for each character in the pair they choose. Have them fit these traits into the graphic.

Use **Reading and Critical Thinking Transparencies**, p. 35, for additional support.

Compare Approaches Remind students that they need to consider what motivates characters before they can persuade them to change. During the discussion, partners should tell why they think one approach would be more or less successful with a given character.

Television Interview Students should work together to come up with both the list of questions and the answers. If the text provides answers to questions, students should use them. However, they should also feel free to ask questions that interest them even if they have to invent the answers. Suggest that students rehearse their interviews before they present them to their classmates.

Use **Communications Transparencies and Copymasters**, p. 9, for additional support.

Vocabulary in Action
EXERCISE
Answers:
1. aptitude
2. design
3. endow
4. explicit
5. vengeance
6. humility
7. treachery
8. indignation
9. implore
10. indignant

Use **Unit Six Resource Book**, p. 7 for additional practice. Use **Unit Six Resource Book**, p. 10 for assessment.

Objectives

1. appreciate and understand a Chinese folktale and a classic European folktale
2. appreciate the values of Chinese and European cultures as revealed through the genre of the folktale
3. extend understanding of the selections through a variety of multimodal and cross-curricular activities

Reading Pathways

- Select one or several students to read each story aloud to the class or to small groups. Assign the presentation in advance to allow readers time to incorporate some of the techniques used by professional storytellers. Have the audience listen to the stories without following along in their texts.

- Read the stories aloud to the class, pausing at key points to discuss how elements of the story inform students about the customs of the cultures. Have students compare these customs with those of their own cultures and regions.

- After students have read the stories once, they can read them again to identify structural elements such as characters, conflict, setting, and plot. Then have students identify similarities and differences between these tales and the selections in Unit Two. For example, have students compare the attitude of Mr. Rickey toward public opinion in "The Noble Experiment" to Auntie Lily's in "Waters of Gold."

5-Minute Warm-Up

Daily Language SkillBuilder   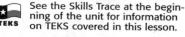 **TEKS 16B, 17G**

Have students **proofread** the display sentences on page 793e and write them correctly. The sentences also appear on Transparency 25 of **Grammar Transparencies and Copymasters.**

TEKS See the Skills Trace at the beginning of the unit for information on TEKS covered in this lesson.

LINKS TO UNIT TWO

Relationships

In Unit Two you read about characters who showed courage or who experienced changes within themselves. The characters had the courage to take risks and—despite their own hardships—succeed in teaching others about forgiveness, kindness, and respect. You are about to read about characters from different cultures who share similar motivations, attitudes, and values.

GERMANY

Ashputtle

retold by Jakob and Wilhelm Grimm

The Grimm brothers started collecting and retelling stories in the early 1800s. Many of their stories, including "Ashputtle," have been retold by other storytellers. You will almost certainly be familiar with at least one other version of "Ashputtle"–probably as "Cinderella." The story probably originated in China, but versions of it are found in many cultures.

The simple message of "Ashputtle" is that goodness is rewarded and evil is punished. In this version of the tale, the Grimm brothers challenge readers to think about what happens when people are forced to reexamine their relationships with others.

812 UNIT SIX   THE ORAL TRADITION

LESSON RESOURCES

UNIT SIX RESOURCE BOOK, pp. 11–17

ASSESSMENT
Formal Assessment, pp. 127–128
Teacher's Guide to Assessment and Portfolio Use
Test Generator

SKILLS TRANSPARENCIES AND COPYMASTERS
Grammar
- *Who* and *Whom*, CM 67 (for Mini Lesson, p. 814)

- Adjective Clauses, CM 111 (for Mini Lesson, p. 824)
Communications
Appreciative Listening TR 2 (for Mini Lesson, p. 817)
Giving and Using Feedback to Improve Performance, TR 16 (for Mini Lesson, p. 827)

INTEGRATED TECHNOLOGY
Audio Library
Internet: Research Starter

Visit our website:
www.mcdougallittell.com

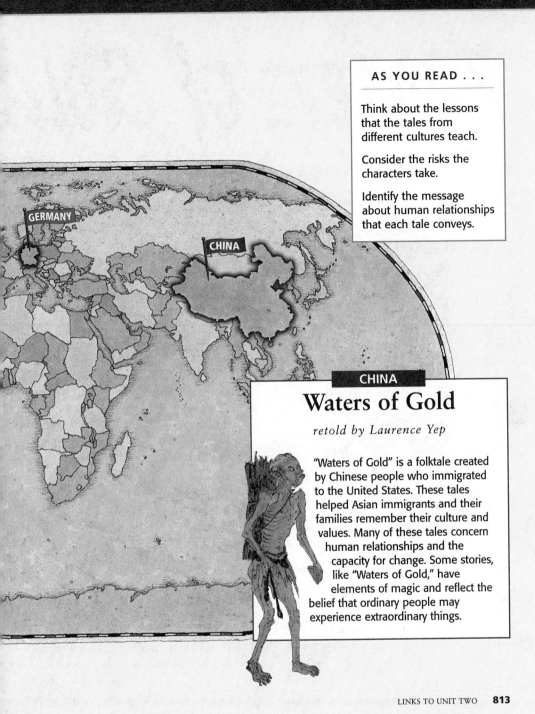

Customizing Instruction

Less Proficient Readers

Before reading the selections, ask students to discuss qualities they most respect and least respect in others.

Set a Purpose Have students read to learn about the qualities of Auntie Lily in the first selection and Ashputtle in the second selection. Students should think about what others can learn from the two women.

Students Acquiring English

Ask students to think about why folktales are a good way to preserve the culture of a group of people. Have students offer examples of traditions in their own culture that are captured in stories and folktales.

Use **Spanish Study Guide,** pp. 160–162 for additional support.

Gifted and Talented

Have students identify the significant values of the culture from which each tale is taken. Discuss with students whether those values are as important in today's society.

Possible Responses: "Waters of Gold"–hospitality, generosity, kindness, compassion, understanding
"Ashputtle"–inner goodness, dignity, humility, sincerity

AS YOU READ . . .

Think about the lessons that the tales from different cultures teach.

Consider the risks the characters take.

Identify the message about human relationships that each tale conveys.

GERMANY

CHINA

CHINA

Waters of Gold

retold by Laurence Yep

"Waters of Gold" is a folktale created by Chinese people who immigrated to the United States. These tales helped Asian immigrants and their families remember their culture and values. Many of these tales concern human relationships and the capacity for change. Some stories, like "Waters of Gold," have elements of magic and reflect the belief that ordinary people may experience extraordinary things.

Summary

Waters of Gold Auntie Lily is famous for her generosity, but this very quality has left her penniless. She is forced to sell her property to her neighbor, a rich woman who charges Lily rent to live in her former house. One day, a filthy beggar enters the village and pleads for water to wash his feet. Everybody refuses him except Auntie Lily. After washing his feet in a bucket, the beggar tells her to keep the used water beside her bed overnight. The next morning, the bucket is filled with gold. As soon as the rich neighbor hears the news, she regrets her own meanness toward the beggar. She drags him to her house when he reappears and forces him to wash his feet. She leaves the bucket of water beside her bed overnight, and, in the morning, she plunges her hand into it—only to be bitten by snakes, lizards, and ants. The woman grows sick, and Auntie Lily nurses her. "Kindness comes with no price, " she teaches the woman. When a leper comes to the village, only Auntie Lily and her neighbor show him hospitality. He cures the neighbor and she remains kind.

Reading and Analyzing

Literary Analysis:
FIGURATIVE LANGUAGE

A Ask students what Auntie Lily means by this statement.
Possible Response: Everybody is special and good in his or her own way.
B Have students identify the metaphors and simile in this passage.
Possible Responses: metaphors: "a trash heap"; "a walking pig wallow." simile: "his hair was as muddy . . ."

Use **Unit Six Resource Book,** p. 13 for additional practice.

Waters of Gold

RETOLD BY LAURENCE YEP

A *Spring Morning at Yen-ling-t'an* (Chekiang) (Qing dynasty, China, 1642–1715), Wang Yuan-ch'i. Handscroll, ink and color on paper, 38 cm × 304.7 cm, courtesy of Museum of Fine Arts, Boston, Keith McLeod Fund (56.10). Photo Copyright © 1995 Museum of Fine Arts, Boston, all rights reserved.

Many years ago, there lived a woman whom everyone called Auntie Lily. She was Auntie by blood to half the county and Auntie to the other half by friendship. As she liked to say, "There's a bit of Heaven in each of us." As a result, she was always helping people out.

Because of her many kind acts, she knew so many people that she couldn't go ten steps without meeting someone who wanted to chat. So it would take her half the day to go to the village well and back to her home.

Eventually, though, she helped so many people that she had no more money. She had

814   UNIT SIX   THE ORAL TRADITION

Teaching Options

  Grammar **TEKS** 17C   **TAAS** Writing Obj. 6

WHO AND WHOM
Instruction Remind students that pronouns, words used to take the place of nouns, have subject (*I*), object (*me*), and possessive (*my, mine*) forms. The pronouns *who* and *whom* are often confused. Explain that *who* is the subject form; *whom* is the object form. Mention that in spoken English, *who* is used in place of *whom* so often that *whom* sounds stilted. Nonetheless, *whom* is still used in formal speaking and writing. Point out the highlighted passage above to illustrate the correct use of *whom*.

Exercises Have students select the correct pronoun in each of the following sentences.
1. (<u>Who</u>, Whom) wouldn't want a bucket of gold?
2. To (who, <u>whom</u>) will the beggar next appeal?
3. (<u>Who</u>, Whom) will be the lucky winner then?
4. (Who, <u>Whom</u>) do you see as the best person in the story?

Use **Grammar Transparencies and Copymasters**, p. 67.

 Use McDougal Littell's *Language Network,* Chapter 3, for more instruction and practice in *who* and *whom*.

to sell her fields and even her house to her neighbor, a rich old woman. "If you'd helped yourself instead of others, you wouldn't have to do this," the neighbor said <u>smugly</u>. "Where are all those other people when you need them?"

"That isn't why I helped them," Auntie Lily said firmly. She wound up having to pay rent for the house she had once owned. She supported herself by her embroidery; but since her eyes were going bad, she could not do very much.

One day an old beggar entered the village. He was a ragbag of a man—a trash heap, a walking pig wallow. It was impossible to tell what color or what shape his clothes had once been, and his hair was as muddy and matted as a bird's nest. As he shuffled through the village gates, he called out, "Water for my feet. Please, water for my feet. One little bowl of water—that's all I ask."

Everyone ignored him, pretending to concentrate on their chores instead. One man went on replacing the shaft of his hoe. A woman swept her courtyard. Another woman fed her hens.

The beggar went to each in turn, but they all showed their backs to him.

After calling out a little while longer, the beggar went to the nearest home, which happened to belong to the rich old woman. When he banged at her door, he left the dirty outline of his knuckles on the clean wood. And when the rich woman opened her door, his smell nearly took her breath away.

Now it so happened that she had been chopping vegetables when the beggar had knocked. When the beggar repeated his request, she raised her cleaver menacingly. "What good would one bowl of water be? You'd need a whole river to wash you clean. Go away."

"A thousand pardons," the old beggar said, and shambled on to the next house.

Though Auntie Lily had to hold her nose, she asked politely, "Yes?"

"I'd like a bowl of water to wash my feet." And the beggar pointed one grimy finger toward them.

Her rich neighbor had stayed in her doorway to watch the beggar. She scolded Auntie Lily now. "It's all your fault those beggars come into the village. They know they can count on a free meal."

It was an old debate between them, so Auntie Lily simply said, "Any of us can have bad luck."

"Garbage," the rich old woman declared, "is garbage. They must have done something bad, or Heaven wouldn't have let them become beggars."

Auntie Lily turned to the beggar. "I may be joining you on the road someday. Wait here."

Much to the neighbor's distress, Auntie Lily went inside and poured water from a large jar in her kitchen into a bucket. Carrying it in both hands, she brought it outside to the beggar and set it down.

The beggar stood on one leg, just like a crane, while he washed one callused, leathery sole over the bucket. "You can put mud on any other part of me, but if my feet are clean, then I feel clean."

As he fussily continued to cleanse his feet, Auntie Lily asked kindly, "Are you hungry? I don't have much, but what I have I'm willing to share."

The beggar shook his head. "I've stayed longer in this village than I have in any other. Heaven is my roof, and the whole world my house."

Auntie Lily stared at him, wondering what she would look like after a few years on the

WORDS TO KNOW

smugly (smŭg′lē) *adv.* in a self-satisfied way

815

Multicultural Link Chinese Literature

CHINESE LITERATURE There are two clear-cut traditions in Chinese literature: the literary and the vernacular, or informal. Both traditions can be traced back more than 2,000 years. The literary tradition began with poetry and grew to include drama, fiction, history, and popular stories. The vernacular tradition includes folk literature. Although as time-honored as works in the literary tradition, these folk stories were long considered beneath literary consideration. The scholar-officials, who were the arbiters of literary standards, had ruled that such colloquial tales as "Waters of Gold" were neither sufficiently polished nor stylized for academic acceptance. It was not until the 20th century that folk literature gained the full acceptance and appreciation of the Chinese literary establishment.

A Remind students that this is a folk-tale, so mysterious and magical things can happen. Then invite students to predict what they think will happen to the bucket of water.

Possible Response: There will be gold in the water.

Use **Unit Six Resource Book,** p. 12 for additional practice.

Literary Analysis: PLOT

B Ask students to explain who the beggar might be and why he has trans-formed the dirty water into a fortune.

Possible Responses: He must be a person who possesses magical powers, perhaps a magician or a holy man. He transforms the water to reward Auntie Lily for her goodness and kindness.

Active Reading: PREDICTING

C Ask students to draw a conclusion about what Auntie Lily will do with the rest of her money, based on the evidence of her character and the way she reacts to her good fortune.

Possible Response: Once she has pur-chased her house and lands back from the rich woman, she will probably use the rest of the money to help others as she has in the past.

road. "Are you very tired? Have you been on the road for very long?"

"No, the road is on me," the beggar said, and held up his hands from his dirty sides. "But thank you. You're the first person to ask. And you're the first person to give me some water. So place the bucket of water by your bed tonight and do not look into it till tomorrow morning."

As the beggar shuffled out of the village again, Auntie Lily stared down doubtfully at the bucket of what was now muddy water. Then, even though she felt foolish, she picked it up again.

"You're not really going to take that scummy water inside?" laughed the rich neighbor. "It'll probably breed mosquitoes."

"It seemed important to him," she answered. "I'll humor him."

"Humoring people," snapped the neighbor, "has got you one step from begging yourself."

However, Auntie Lily carried the bucket inside anyway. Setting it down near her sleeping mat, she covered the mouth of the bucket with an old, cracked plate so she wouldn't peek into it by mistake, and then she got so caught up in embroidering a pair of slippers that she forgot all about the beggar and his bucket of water.

She sewed until twilight, when it was too dark to use her needle. Then, because she had no money for oil or candles, she went to sleep.

The next morning Auntie Lily rose and stretched the aches out of her back. She sighed. "The older I get, the harder it is to get up in the morning."

Detail of *Beggars and Street Characters* (1516), Zhou Chen. Album leaves; ink and colors on paper. Honolulu (Hawaii) Academy of Arts, gift of Mrs. Carter Galt, 1956 (2239.1).

816 UNIT SIX THE ORAL TRADITION

Teaching Options

Mini Lesson **Viewing and Representing** **TEKS** 22A, 23B

Beggars and Street Characters
by Zhou Chen

ART APPRECIATION Zhou Chen painted this depic-tion of a beggar in the early 16th century.

Instruction Point out to students how the misery of the beggar is emphasized by his skeletal appear-ance. Ask students what other details reinforce the impression of the subject's poverty and suffering.

Possible Response: the beggar's empty bowl, which shows how totally dependent upon the generosity of others he is. He is dressed in rags that are tied together. His only other possession is

a bundle of sticks on his back. These sticks would have been collected along the road, and because he has no shelter, they are his source of warmth and might be used to heat up water if he has no other food.

Application Ask students to compare the subject of this painting with their image of the beggar in the story.

Possible Response: The beggar in the story appears dirtier and is described as a "ragbag" so he must be wearing more clothes. Both beggars, however, are suffering.

She was always saying something like that, but she had never stayed on her sleeping mat—even when she was sick. Thinking of all that day's chores, she decided to water the herbs she had growing on one side of her house.

Her eyes fell upon the beggar's bucket with its covering plate. "No sense using fresh water when that will do as well. After all, dirt's dirt to a plant."

Squatting down, she picked up the bucket and was surprised at how heavy it was. "I must have filled it fuller than I thought," she grunted.

She staggered out of the house and over to the side where rows of little green herbs grew. "Here you go," she said to her plants. "Drink deep."

Taking off the plate, she upended the bucket; but instead of muddy brown water, there was a flash of reflected light and a clinking sound as gold coins rained down upon her plants.

Auntie Lily set the bucket down hastily and crouched, not trusting her weak eyes. However, where some of her herbs had been, there was now a small mound of gold coins. She squinted in disbelief and rubbed her aching eyes and stared again; but the gold was still there.

She turned to the bucket. There was even more gold inside. Scooping up coins by the handful, she freed her little plants and made sure that the stalks weren't too bent.

Then she sat gazing at her bucket full of gold until a farmer walked by. "Tell me I'm not dreaming," she called to him.

The farmer yawned and came over with his hoe over his shoulder. "I wish I were dreaming, because that would mean I'm still in bed instead of having to go off to work."

Auntie Lily gathered up a handful of gold coins and let it fall in a tinkling, golden shower back into the bucket. "And this is real?"

The farmer's jaw dropped. He picked up one coin with his free hand and bit into it. He flipped it back in with the other coins. "It's as real as me, Auntie. But where did you ever get that?"

So Auntie Lily told him. And as others woke up and stepped outside, Auntie told them as well, for she still could not believe her luck and wanted them to confirm that the gold was truly gold. In no time at all, there was a small crowd around her.

If the bucket had been filled with ordinary copper cash, that would have been more money than any of them had ever seen. In their wildest dreams, they had never expected to see that much gold. Auntie Lily stared at the bucket uncomfortably. "I keep thinking it's going to disappear the next moment."

The farmer, who had been standing there all this time, shook his head. "If it hasn't disappeared by now, I don't think it will. What are you going to do with it, Auntie?"

Auntie Lily stared at the bucket, and suddenly she came to a decision. Stretching out a hand, she picked up a gold coin. "I'm going to buy back my house, and I'm going to get back my land."

The farmer knew the fields. "Those old things? You could buy a valley full of prime land with half that bucket. And a palace with the other half."

"I want what I sweated for." Asking the farmer to guard her bucket, Auntie Lily closed her hand around the gold coin. Then, as the crowd parted before her, she made her way over to her neighbor.

Now the rich old woman liked to sleep late; but all the noise had woken her up, so she was just getting dressed when Auntie knocked. The old woman yanked her door open as she

  **Speaking and Listening**   **TEKS** 2D, 5C, 5D, 11B

STORYTELLING

Prepare Explain that ancient storytellers not only passed on traditional myths and legends but also relayed current news about births, deaths, big hunts, and celebrations as they walked from village to village. They would also incorporate personal details they knew about people. Arrange students in small groups. Assign each group one of the two stories. Direct each student to pick a different character in the story and to analyze that character's actions so that they can tell the story from the character's perspective. Then have students develop a listening checklist with five items to help them become more active listeners. Remind them that as they listen to the stories, they should think about what they know about the topic, concentrate, and ask questions that use the speaker's words.

Present Have students tell their stories using first-person point of view. Listeners should fill out their checklists for each presentation.

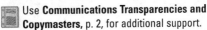 This activity is particularly well suited for longer class periods.

Use **Communications Transparencies and Copymasters**, p. 2, for additional support.

Reading and Analyzing

Active Reading: PREDICTING

A Have students predict what they think might happen next, based on the rich woman's reaction to Auntie Lily's fortune.

Possible Response: The old woman is greedy. She will probably try to get money from the begger.

B Ask students to explain the villagers' actions. Have students predict how the beggar will react.

Possible Responses: They are trying to be nice to the beggar so he will give them a fortune too. He will not give them gold because their actions are based on greed, not kindness.

Literary Analysis: MORAL

C Point out that Auntie Lily's words reflect the story's moral. Have students write a new moral for this story, based on the characters and events.

Possible Response: Goodness is its own reward.

Literary Analysis: FIGURATIVE LANGUAGE

D Have students identify the figurative language used here.

Possible Response: "like an old, discarded cloak."

E Ask students to explain what value the "waters of gold" have, in addition to monetary value.

Possible Response: They help to transform someone into a kinder person.

Reading Skills and Strategies: CONNECTING

Ask students to compare the rich woman with Scrooge in *A Christmas Carol*.

Possible Responses: Both are reluctant to share their wealth; both use their second chances to live better lives.

---

buttoned the last button of her coat. "Who started the riot? Can't a person get a good night's sleep?"

With some satisfaction, Auntie Lily held up the gold coin. "Will this buy back my house and land?"

"Where did you get that?" the old woman demanded.

"Will it buy them back?" Auntie Lily repeated.

The rich old woman snatched the coin out of Auntie Lily's hand and bit into it just as the farmer had. "It's real," the old woman said in astonishment.

"Will it?" Auntie asked again.

"Yes, yes, yes," the old woman said crabbily. "But where did you ever get that much gold?"

A When Auntie Lily told her the story and showed her the bucket of gold, the rich old woman stood moving her mouth like a fish out of water. Clasping her hands together, she shut her eyes and moaned in genuine pain. "And I sent him away. What a fool I am. What a fool." And the old woman beat her head with her fists.

That very afternoon, the beggar—the ragbag, the trash heap, the walking pig wallow—shuffled once more through the village gates with feet as dirty as before. As he went, he croaked, "Water for my feet. Please, water for my feet. One little bowl of water—that's all I ask."

B This time, people dropped whatever they were doing when they heard his plea. Hoes, brooms, and pots were flung down, hens and pigs were kicked out of the way as everyone hurried to fill a bucket with water. There was a small riot by the village well as everyone fought to get water at the same time. Still others rushed out with buckets filled from the jars in their houses.

"Here, use my water," one man shouted, holding up a tub.

A woman shoved in front of him with a bucket in her arms. "No, no, use mine. It's purer."

They surrounded the old beggar, pleading with him to use their water, and in the process of jostling one another, they splashed a good deal of water on one another and came perilously close to drowning the beggar. The rich old woman, Auntie Lily's neighbor, charged to the rescue.

"Out of the way, you vultures," the rich old woman roared. "You're going to trample him." Using her elbows, her feet, and in one case even her teeth, the old woman fought her way through the mob.

No longer caring if she soiled her hands, the old woman seized the beggar by the arm. "This way, you poor, misunderstood creature."

Fighting off her neighbors with one hand and keeping her grip on the beggar with the other, the old woman hauled him inside her house. Barring the door against the rest of the village, she ignored all the fists and feet thumping on her door and all the shouts.

"I really wasn't myself yesterday, because I had been up the night before tending a sick friend. This is what I meant to do." She fetched a fresh new towel and an even newer bucket and forced the beggar to wash his feet.

When he was done, he handed her the now filthy towel. "Dirt's dirt, and garbage is garbage," he said.

However, the greedy old woman didn't recognize her own words. She was too busy trying to remember what else Auntie Lily had done. "Won't you have something to eat? Have you traveled very far? Are you tired?" she asked, all in the same breath.

The old beggar went to the door and waited patiently while she unbarred it. As he shuffled

---

WORDS TO KNOW

jostling (jŏs'lĭng) *n.* roughly bumping, pushing, or shoving **jostle** *v.*
perilously (pĕr'ə-ləs-lē) *adv.* dangerously

818

Teaching Options

 Mini Lesson **Spelling** TEKS 16D 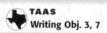 TAAS Writing Obj. 3, 7

SILENT LETTERS

Instruction Write the word *doubtfully* on the board and invite a volunteer to say the word. Underline the *b*, and elicit from the class that the *b* is silent. Then write the word *knuckles* on the board and guide students to see that the *k* is silent in this word. Explain that in certain consonant combinations, one of the consonants may be silent. List the following pairs of consonants in which one of the letters is usually silent: *bt, ps, gn, kn, mb, lm, wh, sw, wr, pb,* and *lk*.

Exercises Have students find the silent letter in each of the following words.

almond	folklore	limbs	sword
answer	foreign	palm	whole
caulk	gnat	psychology	whose
crumbs	knead	sign	wrapped
cupboard	knives	stalk	written

Ask students to look for more words that fit this pattern, in their own writing and in stories and articles they read, and to add these words to their personal word lists.

Use **Unit Six Resource Book,** p. 16 for more practice.

outside, he instructed her to leave the bucket of water by her bed but not to look into it until the morning.

That night, the greedy old woman couldn't sleep as she imagined the heap of shiny gold that would be waiting for her tomorrow. She waited impatiently for the sun to rise and got up as soon as she heard the first rooster crow.

Hurrying to the bucket, she plunged her hands inside expecting to bring up handfuls of gold. Instead, she gave a cry as dozens of little things bit her, for the bucket was filled not with gold but with snakes, lizards, and ants.

The greedy old woman fell sick—some said from her bites, some claimed from sheer frustration. Auntie Lily herself came to nurse her neighbor. "Take this to heart: Kindness comes with no price."

The old woman was so ashamed that she did, indeed, take the lesson to heart. Though she remained sick, she was kind to whoever came to her door.

One day, a leper came into the village. Everyone hid for fear of the terrible disease. Doors slammed and shutters banged down over windows, and soon the village seemed deserted.

Only Auntie Lily and her neighbor stepped out of their houses. "Are you hungry?" Auntie Lily asked.

"Are you thirsty?" the neighbor asked. "I'll make you a cup of tea."

The leper thanked Auntie Lily and then turned to the neighbor as if to express his gratitude as well; but he stopped and studied her. "You're looking poorly, my dear woman. Can I help?"

With a tired smile, the rich old woman explained what had happened. When she was finished, the leper stood thoughtfully for a moment. "You're not the same woman as before: You're as kind as Auntie Lily, and you aren't greedy anymore. So take this humble gift from my brother, the old beggar."

With that, the leper limped out of the village; and as he left, the illness fell away from the old woman like an old, discarded cloak. But though the old woman was healthy again, she stayed as kind as Auntie Lily and used her own money as well and wisely as Auntie Lily used the waters of gold. ❖

 D

 E

2

"I'm always pursuing the theme of being an outsider— an alien—and many teenagers feel they're aliens."

Laurence Yep
born 1948

Young Writer When Laurence Yep was only 25, he published his first book. Two years later, his second book, *Dragonwings,* won a number of

awards, including a Newbery Honor Award. Yep has written 2 plays and some 40 books, many of which reflect his cultural heritage.

Two Cultures Yep is a third-generation Chinese American. Some of his novels—such as *Child of the Owl* and *Sea Glass*—focus on Chinese-American characters who are caught between two cultures.

WATERS OF GOLD **819**

 Assessment **Standardized Test Practice** **TEKS 10H, 10K** 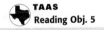 **TAAS Reading Obj. 5**

EVALUATE AND MAKE JUDGMENTS For some standardized tests, students will be asked to evaluate information and choose the best judgment based on that information. To provide students with some help in evaluating and making judgments, read aloud or write on the board the following question: Which idea is best supported by information in the story?

A. Auntie Lily doesn't waste time feeling sorry for herself.

B. The rich old woman has led a good life.

C. The villagers repay all the kindness that Auntie Lily has shown them.

D. The beggar is pleased by the warm reception he receives the second time in the village.

Lead students through the process of choosing the best answer. A is correct. Auntie Lily does the best she can with each day that is given to her. B, C, and D are incorrect. The old woman has been selfish; Auntie Lily wouldn't be poor if the villagers had helped her out; the beggar is aware of why the villagers are nice to him.

Summary
Ashputtle In this version of the Cinderella story, Ashputtle, who is mistreated by her stepmother and stepsisters, is helped by a bird perched in a tree on her mother's grave. One day, an announcement is made that a ball will be held for three nights so that the king's son can pick a wife. Ashputtle's stepmother refuses to allow her to go until she has done several tedious tasks. Although Ashputtle completes them, her stepmother and stepsisters leave without her. Ashputtle turns for help to the bird, who provides her with exquisite clothing so that she can attend the ball. The prince falls in love with her. Each night, however, Ashputtle sneaks home quickly so the prince will not learn of her identity. The last night of the ball, her shoe sticks in the pitch that the prince has had spread on the staircase. Knowing the shoe will fit only the right girl, he uses it to find his bride. He discovers that the shoe fits Ashputtle and promptly marries her.

Reading and Analyzing

Literary Analysis: FORESHADOWING

A Tell students that foreshadowing is a writer's use of clues that hint at events to come. Ask what the mother's words might foreshadow in her little girl's future.
Possible Responses: trying times

Literary Analysis:
FIGURATIVE LANGUAGE

B Have students describe a person with an "ugly and black" heart.
Possible Response: a mean person

Teaching Options

Ashputtle

by
JAKOB GRIMM AND WILHELM GRIMM

Portrait of a Young Woman, Sandro Botticelli, Städelsches Institute of Art, Frankfurt, Germany/SuperStock.

Mini Lesson **Viewing and Representing** **TEKS 22A**

Portrait of a Young Woman
by Sandro Botticelli

ART APPRECIATION Alessandro Botticelli (1445–1510) was born Alessandro di Mariano Filipepi. Botticelli is a nickname that means "little barrel." Although he enjoyed recognition during the earlier part of his career, he worked very little in the last decade of his life and died in obscurity.
Instruction Tell students that one of the adjectives sometimes used to describe Botticelli's style is graceful. Ask students whether the adjective would be aptly applied to this painting and why.

Possible Response: The lines of the painting are flowing and elegant. The woman's appearance is pleasing, and the expression on her face suggests that she is gentle and sweet.
Application Ask students how this portrait resembles the character of Ashputtle.
Possible Responses: The woman in the painting looks wistful and pensive, just as Ashputtle longs for a life that appears out of reach. The woman is young and beautiful; Ashputtle too is lovely in her finery.

A rich man's wife fell sick and, feeling that her end was near, she called her only daughter to her bedside and said: "Dear child, be good and say your prayers; God will help you, and I shall look down on you from heaven and always be with you." With that she closed her eyes and died. Every day the little girl went out to her mother's grave and wept, and she went on being good and saying her prayers. When winter came, the snow spread a white cloth over the grave, and when spring took it off, the man remarried.

His new wife brought two daughters into the house. Their faces were beautiful and lily-white, but their hearts were ugly and black. That was the beginning of a bad time for the poor stepchild. "Why should this silly goose sit in the parlor with us?" they said. "People who want to eat bread must earn it. Get into the kitchen where you belong!" They took away her fine clothes and gave her an old gray dress and wooden shoes to wear. "Look at the haughty princess in her finery!" they cried and, laughing, led her to the kitchen. From then on she had to do all the work, getting up before daybreak, carrying water, lighting fires, cooking and washing. In addition the sisters did everything they could to plague her. They jeered at her and poured peas and lentils into the ashes, so that she had to sit there picking them out. At night, when she was tired out with work, she had no bed to sleep in but had to lie in the ashes by the hearth. And they took to calling her Ashputtle because she always looked dusty and dirty.

One day when her father was going to the fair, he asked his two stepdaughters what he should bring them. "Beautiful dresses," said one. "Diamonds and pearls," said the other. "And you, Ashputtle. What would you like?" "Father," she said, "break off the first branch that brushes against your hat on your way home, and bring it to me." So he bought beautiful dresses, diamonds and pearls for his two stepdaughters, and on the way home, as he was riding through a copse,[1] a hazel branch brushed against him and knocked off his hat. So he broke off the branch and took it home with him. When he got home, he gave the stepdaughters what they had asked for, and gave Ashputtle the branch. After thanking him, she went to her mother's grave and planted the hazel sprig over it and cried so hard that her tears fell on the sprig and watered it. It grew and became a beautiful tree. Three times a day Ashputtle went and sat under it and wept and prayed. Each time a little white bird came and perched on the tree, and when Ashputtle made a wish the little bird threw down what she had wished for.

---

1. **copse** (kŏps): a patch of small trees or shrubs.

WORDS	**haughty** (hô′tē) *adj.* condescendingly proud
TO	**plague** (plāg) *v.* to annoy
KNOW	**jeer** (jîr) *v.* to mock; to taunt

821

Customizing Instruction

Less Proficient Readers
Ask students to describe the stereotypical stepmother in fairy tales. Have students discuss the ways in which Ashputtle's stepmother lives up to this wicked stereotype in the first paragraph.

Set a Purpose Have students read to find out what chores Ashputtle must do before she can go to the ball and what her stepmother says when she finishes them.

Students Acquiring English
1 Be sure students comprehend the cruelty of Ashputtle's stepsisters as revealed through the tasks they invent for Ashputtle to do. Explain how small lentils and peas are and how difficult they would be to find amongst the ashes.

Gifted and Talented
Point out to students that in some other versions of the Cinderella story, the heroine is more fully developed and multifaceted than Ashputtle is. Ask students whether the story of Ashputtle would be enhanced or compromised by more emphasis on her personality. Have students defend their views.

Multiple Learning Styles
Visual Learners
Have students sketch the stepsisters in a way that shows their fundamental evil yet portrays how they are "beautiful and lily-white" on the outside.

 Spelling TEKS 16C 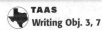 TAAS Writing Obj. 3, 7

DOUBLING FINAL CONSONANTS

Instruction Tell students that the final consonant of a multisyllable word is doubled when adding a suffix only in words that have a single vowel in an accented final syllable with one final consonant. For example, *begin* becomes *beginning*. However, in the word *marvel*, the accent is on the first syllable. Therefore, *marvel* becomes *marveled* with no doubling of the final consonant.

Exercises Have students add –*ed* to the following verbs. Remind them to check the accented syllable in order to determine whether or not to double the final consonant.

1. happen (*happened*)
2. allow (*allowed*)
3. permit (*permitted*)
4. flutter (*fluttered*)
5. prefer (*preferred*)
6. follow (*followed*)
7. differ (*differed*)
8. admit (*admitted*)

Ask students to look for more words that fit this pattern, in their own writing and in things that they read, and to add these words to their personal word lists.

ASHPUTTLE **821**

Reading Skills and Strategies: INFERRING

A Ask students why, in their opinion, the stepmother does not want Ashputtle to come to the ball.

Possible Responses: She does not like Ashputtle and wants her to be unhappy; she is afraid that Ashputtle would appear more attractive than her daughters.

Literary Analysis: FOLKTALE

B Remind students that folktales often contain supernatural elements. Ask students what extraordinary events have occurred so far in this tale.

Possible Response: Ashputtle has a bird that provides her with the things she desires; birds help her to sort lentils from the ashes.

Literary Analysis: CHARACTERIZATION

C Ask students what the stepmother's action of giving Ashputtle this task reveals about her character.

Possible Response: She is vindictive and mean.

Literary Analysis: REPETITION

D Remind students that repetition is a characteristic of oral literature. Ask students what the repetition throughout the tale contributes.

Possible Response: It helps to emphasize important ideas; it shows in this passage the continuing cruelty of the stepmother and the willingness of the birds to keep helping Ashputtle; repetition also helps listeners to remember the story and to anticipate future events.

Now it so happened that the king arranged for a celebration. It was to go on for three days and all the beautiful girls in the kingdom were invited, in order that his son might choose a bride. When the two stepsisters heard they had been asked, they were delighted. They called Ashputtle and said: "Comb our hair, brush our shoes, and fasten our buckles. We're going to the wedding at the king's palace." Ashputtle obeyed, but she wept, for she too would have liked to go dancing, and she begged her stepmother to let her go. "You little sloven!"[2] said the stepmother. "How can you go to a wedding when you're all dusty and dirty? How can you go dancing when you have neither dress nor shoes?" But when **A** Ashputtle begged and begged, the stepmother finally said: "Here, I've dumped a bowlful of lentils in the ashes. If you can pick them out in two hours, you may go." The girl went out the back door to the garden and cried out: "O tame little doves, O turtledoves, and all the birds under heaven, come and help me put

B
     the good ones in the pot,
     the bad ones in your crop."

Two little white doves came flying through the kitchen window, and then came the turtledoves, and finally all the birds under heaven came flapping and fluttering and settled down by the ashes. The doves nodded their little heads and started in, peck peck peck peck, and all the others started in, peck peck peck peck, and they sorted out all the good lentils and put them in the bowl. Hardly an hour had passed before they finished and flew away. Then the girl brought the bowl to her stepmother, and she was happy, for she thought she'd be allowed to go to the wedding. But the stepmother said: "No, Ashputtle. You have nothing to wear and you

don't know how to dance; the people would only laugh at you." When Ashputtle began to cry, the stepmother said: "If you can pick two bowlfuls of lentils out of the ashes in an hour, you may come." And she thought: "She'll never be able to do it." When she had dumped the two bowlfuls of lentils in the ashes, Ashputtle went out the back door to the garden and cried out: "O tame little doves, O turtledoves, and all the birds under heaven, come and help me put

     the good ones in the pot,
     the bad ones in your crop."

Then two little white doves came flying through the kitchen window, and then came the turtledoves, and finally all the birds under heaven came flapping and fluttering and settled down by the ashes. The doves nodded their little heads and started in, peck peck peck peck, and all the others started in, peck peck peck peck, and they sorted out all the good lentils and put them in the bowls. Before half an hour had passed, they had finished and they all flew away. Then the girl brought the bowls to her stepmother, and she was happy, for she thought she'd be allowed to go to the wedding. But her stepmother said: "It's no use. You can't come, because you have nothing to wear and you don't know how to dance. We'd only be ashamed of you." Then she turned her back and hurried away with her two proud daughters.

When they had all gone out, Ashputtle went to her mother's grave. She stood under the hazel tree and cried:

     "Shake your branches, little tree,
     Throw gold and silver down on me."

---

2. **sloven** (slŭv'ən): a person who is careless in appearance.

Teaching Options

 Multicultural Link

Cinderella Stories Across Cultures

The number of versions of the Cinderella story has been estimated to be anywhere from 340 to 1500, including musical and film adaptations. Although the central story line is the same in the majority of the tales, the differences in the magical guardian or helper and the resolution of the conflict often reflect the culture from which the story grew. One of the oldest recorded versions of the tale comes from China. In this tale, Yeh-Shen is helped by a magical fish. After her stepmother kills the fish, Yeh-Shen is aided by its spirit.

The king realizes it is Yeh-Shen who fits the tiny golden shoe lost at a festival, and she is swept away to a life of happiness. Her stepmother and stepsister, however, are left behind in their cave home.

"Yeh-Shen" was written down in the middle of the ninth century, but as was the case in many other cultures, the story had been told orally before it was recorded. However, it is Charles Perrault's written version that imprinted the image of fairy godmothers, pumpkin coaches and glass slippers, and transformed animals upon the

CORBIS/Araldo de Luca

Customizing Instruction

Less Proficient Readers

Ask students what Ashputtle's step-mother tells her to do before she can go to the ball.

Answer: First she tells Ashputtle that she may go to the ball if she sorts one bowl of lentils from the ashes. Then she puts two bowls of lentils in the ashes and tells Ashputtle to sort those as well.

• Ask students to explain the stepmother's response when Ashputtle finishes both tasks.

Answer: She tells Ashputtle that she cannot go because she has nothing to wear and does not know how to dance.

Set a Purpose Have students read to find out who helps Ashputtle get to the ball and what happens after the three-night celebration.

Students Acquiring English

1 Be sure students understand that *crop* as it is used here means a bird's digestive system.

2 Help students to figure out from context that "It's no use" means that Ashputtle should give up hope about going to the ball.

Multiple Learning Styles
Intrapersonal Learners

3 Have students describe the feelings that Ashputtle experiences when her stepmother and stepsisters leave for the ball without her.

popular consciousness. At the time that Charles Perrault wrote "Cinderella, or The Little Glass Slipper" for his collection of stories in 1697, it was the fashion for the French aristocracy to compose and publish fairy tales. To make the peasant folktales fit for aristocratic sensibilities, he eliminated the blood, gore, and cruelty of the original stories. Some sources also believe that he may have confused the French word *vair* (meaning fur) for its homophone *verre* (meaning glass), which may be how Cinderella acquired glass slippers. In Perrault's story, the stepsisters are married off and have their chance to live happily ever after.

The Serbian Cinderella story, "Pepelyouga," does not have a fairy godmother. Instead the natural mother of Pepelyouga has been turned into a cow that helps her daughter with the chores given to her by her cruel stepmother. The cow is killed, but the mother's spirit in the form of birds provides finery for her daughter so that she can attend church, where she attracts the notice of the prince. Rushing home, she loses a shoe, and when the prince realizes it is hers, they are happily married.

Use **Literary Analysis Transparencies,** p. 32, for additional support.

Literary Analysis: THEME

A Ask students to explain what the author is suggesting through the step-mother's failure to appreciate Ashputtle.

Possible Response: People have a certain image of others and often cannot see the real worth of the person.

Literary Analysis: SYMBOL

B Tell students that ashes are a symbol of mourning. Ask students to interpret the significance of Ashputtle's place in the ashes.

Possible Response: She continues to mourn for her mother and her family.

Reading Skills and Strategies: QUESTION

C Ask students to question why Ashputtle hides her identity after each night of the ball.

Possible Response: to test the feelings of the prince; to avoid being found out by her stepmother and punished

Literary Analysis: CHARACTERIZATION

D Ask students to analyze the step-mother's motivation in urging her daughters to mutilate themselves.

Possible Response: She wants to be related to the prince even if it means that her daughters suffer.

Reading Skills and Strategies: EVALUATING

E Ask students why the stepmother and stepsisters turn pale with fear.

Possible Response: They fear punishment for their treatment of Ashputtle. Why do they think this?

Possible Response: They think Ashputtle might behave the way they would.

A Whereupon the bird tossed down a gold and silver dress and slippers embroidered with silk and silver. Ashputtle slipped into the dress as fast as she could and went to the wedding. Her sisters and stepmother didn't recognize her. She was so beautiful in her golden dress that they thought she must be the daughter of some foreign king. They never dreamed it could be Ashputtle, for they thought she was sitting at home in her filthy rags, picking lentils out of the ashes. The king's son came up to her, took her by the hand and danced with her. He wouldn't dance with anyone else and he never let go her hand. When someone else asked for a dance, he said: "She is my partner."

1 She danced until evening, and then she wanted to go home. The king's son said: "I'll go with you, I'll see you home," for he wanted to find out whom the beautiful girl belonged to. But she got away from him and slipped into the dovecote.[3] The king's son waited until her father arrived, and told him the strange girl had slipped into the dovecote. The old man thought: "Could it be Ashputtle?" and he sent for an ax and a pick and broke into the dovecote, but there was no one inside. When they went indoors, Ashputtle was lying in the ashes in her filthy clothes and a dim oil lamp was burning on the chimney piece, for Ashputtle had slipped out the back end of the dovecote and run to the hazel tree. There she had taken off her fine clothes and put them on the grave, and the bird had taken them away. Then she had put her gray dress on again, crept into the kitchen and lain down in the ashes. Next day when the festivities started in again and her parents and stepsisters had gone, Ashputtle went to the hazel tree and said:

B

"Shake your branches, little tree,
Throw gold and silver down on me."

Whereupon the bird threw down a dress that was even more dazzling than the first one. And when she appeared at the wedding, everyone marveled at her beauty. The king's son was waiting for her. He took her by the hand and danced with no one but her. When others came and asked her for a dance, he said: "She is my partner." When evening came, she said she was going home. The king's son followed her, wishing to see which house she went into, but she ran away and disappeared into the garden behind the house, where there was a big beautiful tree with the most wonderful pears growing on it. She climbed among the branches as <u>nimbly</u> as a squirrel and the king's son didn't know what had become of her. He waited until her father arrived and said to him: "The strange girl has got away from me and I think she has climbed up in the pear tree." Her father thought: "Could it be Ashputtle?" He sent for an ax and chopped the tree down, but there was no one in it. When they went into the kitchen, Ashputtle was lying there in the ashes as usual, for she had jumped down on the other side of the tree, brought her fine clothes back to the bird in the hazel tree, and put on her filthy gray dress.

On the third day, after her parents and sisters had gone, Ashputtle went back to her mother's grave and said to the tree:

"Shake your branches, little tree,
Throw gold and silver down on me."

Whereupon the bird threw down a dress that was more radiant than either of the others, and the slippers were all gold. When she appeared at the wedding, the people were too

---

3. **dovecote** (dŭv′kōt′): a structure where tame pigeons are housed.

Mini Lesson **Grammar** **TEKS 17A** 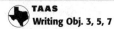 **TAAS Writing Obj. 3, 5, 7**

ADJECTIVE CLAUSES

Instruction Remind students that an adjective clause is a subordinate clause that modifies a noun or pronoun. Adjective clauses often begin with the relative pronouns *who, whom, whose, that,* and *which.* Direct students' attention to the highlighted passage above and ask them to point out the adjective clause modifying *dress.*

Exercises Have students change the second sentence of each pair into an adjective clause, and rewrite the first sentence with the clause.

1. The bird could fulfill her wishes. It perched in the hazel tree. *(The bird that perched in the hazel tree could fulfill her wishes.)*

2. She put on her old dress. It was filthy. *(She put on her old dress, which was filthy.)*

3. Her stepmother mistreated Ashputtle. Her stepmother had two daughters. *(Her stepmother, who had two daughters, mistreated Ashputtle.)*

Use **Unit Six Resource Book,** p. 15.
Use **Grammar Transparencies and Copymasters,** p. 111.

Use McDougal Littell's *Language Network,* Chapter 8, for more instruction and practice in adjective clauses.

amazed to speak. The king's son danced with no one but her, and when someone else asked her for a dance, he said: "She is my partner."

When evening came, Ashputtle wanted to go home, and the king's son said he'd go with her, but she slipped away so quickly that he couldn't follow. But he had thought up a trick. He had arranged to have the whole staircase brushed with pitch, and as she was running down it the pitch pulled her left slipper off. The king's son picked it up, and it was tiny and delicate and all gold. Next morning he went to the father and said: "No girl shall be my wife but the one this golden shoe fits." The sisters were overjoyed, for they had beautiful feet. The eldest took the shoe to her room to try it on and her mother went with her. But the shoe was too small and she couldn't get her big toe in. So her mother handed her a knife and said: "Cut your toe off. Once you're queen you won't have to walk any more." The girl cut her toe off, forced her foot into the shoe, gritted her teeth against the pain, and went out to the king's son. He accepted her as his bride-to-be, lifted her up on his horse, and rode away with her. But they had to pass the grave. The two doves were sitting in the hazel tree and they cried out:

"Roocoo, roocoo,
There's blood in the shoe.
The foot's too long, the foot's too wide,
That's not the proper bride."

He looked down at her foot and saw the blood spurting. At that he turned his horse around and took the false bride home again. "No," he said, "this isn't the right girl; let her sister try the shoe on." The sister went to her room and managed to get her toes into the shoe, but her heel was too big. So her mother handed her a knife and said: "Cut off a chunk of your heel. Once you're queen you won't have to walk any more." The girl cut off a chunk of her heel, forced her foot into the shoe, gritted her teeth against the pain, and went out to the king's son. He accepted her as his bride-to-be, lifted her up on his horse, and rode away with her. As they passed the hazel tree, the two doves were sitting there, and they cried out:

"Roocoo, roocoo,
There's blood in the shoe.
The foot's too long, the foot's too wide,
That's not the proper bride."

He looked down at her foot and saw that blood was spurting from her shoe and staining her white stocking all red. He turned his horse around and took the false bride home again. "This isn't the right girl either," he said. "Haven't you got another daughter?" "No," said the man, "there's only a puny little kitchen drudge that my dead wife left me. She couldn't possibly be the bride." "Send her up," said the king's son, but the mother said: "Oh no, she's much too dirty to be seen." But he insisted and they had to call her. First she washed her face and hands, and when they were clean, she went upstairs and <u>curtseyed</u> to the king's son. He handed her the golden slipper and sat down on a footstool, took her foot out of her heavy wooden shoe, and put it into the slipper. It fitted perfectly. And when she stood up and the king's son looked into her face, he recognized the beautiful girl he had danced with and cried out: "This is my true bride!" The stepmother and the two sisters went pale with fear and rage. But he

3

E
4

WORDS
TO
KNOW

curtsey (kûrt'sē) v. to bend the knees and lower the body as a gesture of respect

825

Customizing Instruction

Less Proficient Readers
- Ask students how Ashputtle is able to go to the ball.
  Answer: The bird in the hazel tree gives her beautiful dresses and shoes each night.
- Have students summarize the events following the third night of the ball.
  Answer: The prince finds the shoe that Ashputtle loses and arrives at her house to find out whose foot fits the shoe. Both daughters try on the shoe and force it to fit, but their tricks are discovered. Finally Ashputtle tries the shoe on, and the prince realizes that she is the one he loves.

Set a Purpose Have students read to find out what happens to the stepsisters.

Students Acquiring English
1 Explain to students that the expression "I'll see you home" means that he will escort Ashputtle to her house.
2 Define *pitch* as "black or dark-brown sticky substance obtained from the distillation of tar."
3 Encourage students to make inferences about the father's attitude toward Ashputtle from his description of her as a "puny little kitchen drudge."

Multiple Learning Styles
Interpersonal Learners

4 Have students role-play the conversation that might have taken place between Ashputtle and her sisters after it is realized that she is the prince's partner.

Literary Analysis:
FIGURATIVE LANGUAGE

A Ask students what sound the words in the first line are meant to suggest.

Possible Response: the cooing of the doves

Reading Skills and Strategies:
INFERRING

B Ask students what the significance of the doves on Ashputtle's shoulders might be.

Possible Response: They are body-guards or guardians.

Literary Analysis: FOLKTALE

C Remind students that traditionally folktales have happy endings. Ask students in what way this story follows tradition.

Possible Response: Ashputtle finds true love and is rewarded for her suffering.

• Ask students what effect the fate of the stepsisters has on the story.

Possible Response: The stepsisters' fate enhances the theme by showing that evil does not go unpunished; they were blind to Ashputtle's value and suffering and now they are literally blind.

Reading Skills and Strategies:
CONNECTING

D Point out that, metaphorically, prejudice is a form of blindness. Ask students what lesson the prejudiced people in "The Noble Experiment" might take from this tale.

Possible Response: Prejudiced people end up suffering from their own distorted vision of others.

Teaching Options

Portrait of a Gentleman, 16th century, Bartolomeo Veneto, Galleria Nazionale d'Arte Antica, Rome/Canali PhotoBank, Milan/Superstock.

 Mini Lesson **Viewing and Representing** **TEKS 22A**

Portrait of a Gentleman
by Bartolomeo Veneto

ART APPRECIATION Bartolomeo Veneto is known to have painted between 1502 and 1531. This portrait was probably painted around 1520.
Instruction Tell students that formal portraits not only capture the likeness of the subject but also preserve a sense of the period in which the subject lived, either through the style of the artist or the details included in the painting. Ask students what inferences they can make about the social status of the subject and the time period from examining the painting.

Possible Response: He is of the upper class, as shown by the luxurious materials of his dress. The indication of his wealth would lead to the inference that his attire was the fashion for men at this time.

Application Ask students whether their mental image of the prince agrees with this portrayal.

Possible Response: yes, because the prince would be elegant; no, because the subject's face wears a hard expression and seems older than the prince.

fted Ashputtle up on his horse and rode away ith her. As they passed the hazel tree, the two hite doves called out:

"Roocoo, roocoo,
No blood in the shoe.
Her foot is neither long nor wide,
This one is the proper bride."

hen they flew down and <u>alighted</u> on shputtle's shoulders, one on the right and one n the left, and there they sat.

On the day of Ashputtle's wedding, the two stepsisters came and tried to <u>ingratiate</u> themselves and share in her happiness. On the way to church the elder was on the right side of the bridal couple and the younger on the left. The doves came along and pecked out one of the elder sister's eyes and one of the younger sister's eyes. Afterward, on the way out, the elder was on the left side and the younger on the right, and the doves pecked out both the remaining eyes. So both sisters were punished with blindness to the end of their days for being so wicked and false. ❖

C

D

"Up to the very end, [Wilhelm and I] worked in two rooms next to each other, always under one roof." —Jakob Grimm

Jakob Grimm
1785–1863

Wilhelm Grimm
1786–1859

Reluctant Lawyers Jakob and Wilhelm Grimm were born in Hanau, Germany, and trained to be lawyers. Their widowed mother struggled to pay for their education. However, the brothers were much more interested in collecting local folktales than they were in practicing law.

The Grimm Legacy Their first book together, *Kinder- und Hausmärchen (*Nursery and household tales*)*, was published in 1812. The book was a scholarly collection of household tales, intended for adult readers, but young people read it anyway. Later editions of the book were made with young people in mind. Illustrations were added, and some of the grisly tales were removed. Today, Grimm fairy tales appear in more than 70 languages. The stories are known and loved throughout the world.

WORDS
TO
KNOW
alight (ə-līt′) *v.* to land lightly, as after flight
ingratiate (ĭn-grā′shē-āt′) *v.* to try to bring oneself into another's favor

827

 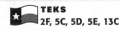 **Mini Lesson** **Speaking and Listening** **TEKS** 2F, 5C, 5D, 5E, 13C

STORYTELLING

Prepare Remind students that ancient storytellers knew that they could convey their messages only if the audience stayed interested in their stories. To sustain the attention of their listeners, storytellers would vary the volume and expression of their voice, incorporate gestures, pause at dramatic moments to increase suspense, and maintain strong eye contact. Have students choose a version of "Cinderella" from a different culture and practice retelling the story with effective gestures, voice expression, and pauses. Students should check the library and on-line resources to find the story they wish to present.

Present Have students tell their stories to the class or small groups. After each presentation, have the audience evaluate the success of the storytelling techniques.

 BLOCK SCHEDULING This activity is particularly well suited for longer class periods.

Use **Communications Transparencies and Copymasters**, p. 16 for additional support.

LITERATURE CONNECTION

Hold a Talk Show Have a volunteer familiar with talk shows summarize a typical talk-show format. As the show progresses, have each character give his or her opinion on the topic and an explanation of the results of his or her interactions. Then invite the audience to challenge the opinions of the characters and to offer their advice and perspective. For example, audience members might remind the stepsisters of the kind of life they might have led after Ashputtle's marriage if they had been nicer to her.

RUBRIC

3 Full Accomplishment Students accurately convey the attitudes of characters in the selection and explain the results of those interactions.

2 Substantial Accomplishment Talk-show format is done well, but characters' attitudes toward others vary somewhat from the actual attitudes revealed in the selection.

1 Little or Partial Accomplishment Students have difficulty with the talk-show format, with portraying the characters, and with their communicating of opinions on the topic.

📋 Use **Communications Transparencies and Copymasters**, p. 13, for additional support.

MUSIC CONNECTION

Make a Music Poster Have students choose a focus for their research before they begin. They may present their information on one poster or one poster per area of research so that text as well as illustrations can be included.

RUBRIC

3 Full Accomplishment Students present information on all aspects of their chosen subject and include accurate illustrations as well as appropriate musical selections.

2 Substantial Accomplishment Students have several facts and some good illustrations. Their presentations are accompanied by music.

1 Little or Partial Accomplishment Student posters have few facts or illustrations and no music.

📋 Use **Writing Transparencies**, pp. 47–48, for additional support.

Interdisciplinary Projects

Hold a Talk Show As a class, hold a talk show on the topic "How people should treat each other."

Step 1: Character List First, list the characters in the selections you have read, how each character interacts with other characters, and the results of their interactions.

Step 2: Volunteers Ask volunteers to role-play the talk show host and the characters who will appear as guests on the show.

Step 3: Performance During the talk show, each character should give his or her opinion on the topic. The rest of the class can portray a TV audience and direct questions to the characters and to the host.

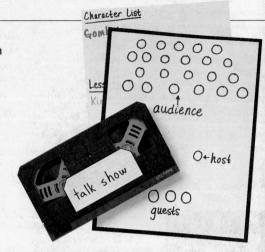

MUSIC **CONNECTION**

Make a Music Poster Folk music, like folk tales, expresses the likes, dislikes, and values of a particular culture or time. Find out more about Chinese folk music or early Germanic folk music. What instruments were used? Why? What types of music were prevalent? If there were lyrics, what do they relate about the culture? Use music encyclopedias, online computer resources, your local music store, and the library to find information. You may also want to ask music teachers at your school to share what they know. Make a poster illustrating your findings. Present your findings to the class; be sure to incorporate some music into your presentation.

SOCIAL STUDIES **CONNECTION**

Make a Sequence Chart "Waters of Gold" is a story that was passed on by Chinese immigrants. The first Chinese newcomers to the United States worked for some of the first railroad companies in California and Texas. With a few classmates, find out more about Chinese immigration to the United States.

First, brainstorm questions about the topic and make a sequence chart like the one shown. Use books, encyclopedias, and computer databases to find out details. Then present your findings in a group report.

🌐 **More Online: Research Starter**
www.mcdougallittell.com

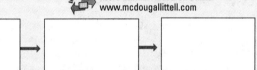

1. Chinese people immigrated to the United States in large numbers starting in about 1848.	→		→		→	

SOCIAL STUDIES CONNECTION

Make a Sequence Chart Have students take notes on index cards that will allow them to easily arrange the facts from various sources. Then suggest that they synthesize what they have read by making a list of key events to include in their charts. In their group report, they may wish to take turns elaborating on various milestones in the history of Chinese immigration.

📋 Use **Reading and Critical Thinking Transparencies**, pp. 11, 39, for additional support.

RUBRIC

3 Full Accomplishment The chart correctly records, in chronological order, the significant events in the history of Chinese immigration. The group report elaborates with accurate facts on these events.

2 Substantial Accomplishment The chart includes most of the important events, and the report elaborates on some significant highlights.

1 Little or Partial Accomplishment The chart does not show the main facts of Chinese immigration in sequence, and the group report is inadequate in its communication of details.

Across Cultures

COMPARING TEXTS **Tell a Story**
Most folktales come from the oral tradition. Tell a story to your class that you've heard told before. It could be a traditional tale or a recent tale from your family's history. You may want to wear a costume to suggest the story's particular time or place. Does your story have elements in common with your classmates' stories? What are they? What are the differences? How do the differences reflect different cultures?

Make Connections Compare a character or a theme from one of the selections in Unit Two with a character or a theme from one of the selections you have just read. For example, you could compare Ashputtle with Martha (from "The Scholarship Jacket," page 278), or you could compare the theme of "Waters of Gold" to that of *A Christmas Carol* (page 250).

Watch a Video View a video version of "Cinderella" and then compare it with "Ashputtle." How are they the same? How are they different? How is the heroine portrayed in each version? Discuss your comparisons with your classmates.

Vocabulary in Action

EXERCISE: ASSESSMENT PRACTICE On your paper, write the Word to Know that is most closely related in meaning to the boldfaced word or phrase in each sentence below.

1. Auntie Lily's neighbor spoke to her **in a self-satisfied way**.
2. Ashputtle's sisters loved to **torment** her with unpleasant tasks.
3. The sisters also liked to **make fun of** Ashputtle.
4. People were **pushing against** each other to reach the beggar.
5. One beggar came **dangerously** close to drowning.
6. Ashputtle was not a bit **proud** like her stepsisters.
7. Squirrels are known to move **quickly**.
8. Women were expected to **bend their knees** before royalty.
9. The doves **land** on a branch.
10. The sisters wanted **to make themselves pleasing** to Ashputtle.

WORDS TO KNOW				
alight	haughty	jeer	nimbly	plague
curtsey	ingratiate	jostling	perilously	smugly

Across Cultures
COMPARING TEXTS

Tell a Story Encourage students to practice telling the story to small groups. To help students compare and contrast elements of the tales, place a chart on the board and after each story is told, have class members list the important ideas of each tale. After all of the tales have been heard, the differences and similarities will be apparent by looking at the chart. **To extend this assignment,** assign students different stories written by the Grimm brothers. Ask students to retell the stories and then discuss the theme which might be taken from each tale.

Make Connections To get students started on this assignment, have them first review characters and themes in Unit Two. Encourage them to see how similar themes could be conveyed by different characters and plots.

Watch a Video Have students use a Venn diagram to help them compare and contrast the video with the story.

Use **Reading and Critical Thinking Transparencies,** p. 35, for additional support.

Vocabulary in Action
EXERCISE
Answers:
1. smugly
2. plague
3. jeer (at)
4. jostling
5. perilously
6. haughty
7. nimbly
8. curtsey
9. alight
10. ingratiate (themselves with)

Use **Unit Six Resource Book,** p. 14 for additional practice.

Use **Unit Six Resource Book,** p. 17 for assessment.

Objectives
- write a cause-and-effect essay
- produce cohesive and coherent written texts by organizing ideas and using effective transitions
- revise a draft to use quotes to show character
- revise selected drafts by combining text

Introducing the Workshop

Cause-and-Effect Point out that since the beginning of time, people have wondered why things happen. They are searching for the causes—the actions and conditions that make other things (the effects) happen. When students write a cause-and-effect essay, they have the opportunity to explore topics that interest them. They can either investigate the causes of events; the effects, or results, of events; or some combination of causes and effects.

Basics in a Box
Using the Graphic Like all essays, a cause-and-effect essay has three main parts. Each part is necessary, and each connects to at least one other part. Explain that the body of the essay may focus primarily on one cause and examine its effects, or it might focus on some effect and examine its causes.

Presenting the Rubric Review with students the Standards for Writing a Successful Cause-and-Effect Essay. You might also share with them the complete rubric, which describes several levels of proficiency.

You may wish to take a few minutes to discuss different types of cause-and-effect explorations. For example, scientists explore the effects of gravity on people in space; economists try to find out what causes prices to rise; police officers want to know what causes crime.

 Use McDougal Littell's *Language Network*, Chapters 12–19, for more instruction on essential writing skills.

 Power Presentation

To engage students visually, use **Power Presentation** 1, Cause-and-Effect Essay.

 TEKS See the Skills Trace at the beginning of the unit for information on TEKS covered in this lesson.

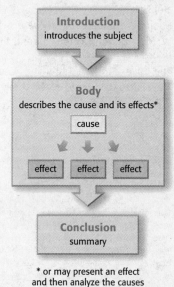

Writing Workshop — Cause-and-Effect Essay

Tracing connections ...

From Reading to Writing Did you ever notice that everything you say and do has an effect? This is true of characters in literature as well. In "Waters of Gold," Auntie Lily's acts of kindness cause wonderful things to happen to her. In "Phaëthon," Apollo's son loses control of the chariot of the sun and scorches the earth in places that become deserts. Writing a **cause-and-effect essay** can help you explore relationships between actions and their effects.

For Your Portfolio

WRITING PROMPT Write a cause-and-effect essay about how a behavior or situation led to a certain effect.

Purpose: To inform and explain
Audience: Your classmates or anyone interested in your subject

Basics in a Box

Cause-and-Effect Essay at a Glance

```
Introduction
introduces the subject
        |
        v
Body
describes the cause and its effects*
      [ cause ]
        |
  +-----+-----+
  v     v     v
[effect][effect][effect]
        |
        v
Conclusion
summary
```

* or may present an effect and then analyze the causes

RUBRIC **STANDARDS FOR WRITING**

A successful cause-and-effect essay should

- clearly state the cause-and-effect relationship
- provide any necessary background information
- make clear the relationship between causes and effects
- arrange details logically and include transitions to show relationships between causes and effects
- summarize the cause-and-effect relationship in the conclusion

---

LESSON RESOURCES

USING PRINT RESOURCES
Unit Six Resource Book
- Prewriting, p. 18
- Drafting, p. 19
- Peer Response, pp. 20–21
- Revising, Editing, and Proofreading, p. 22
- Student Models, pp. 23–25
- Rubric, p. 26

Writing Transparencies
- Writing Process Transparencies, TR 1–4

- Writing Structure Transparencies: Structuring the Essay, TR 6
- Writing Template Transparencies: Cause and Effect Essay, TR 36

Reading and Critical Thinking Transparencies
- Text Structure, TR 24 (for Mini Lesson, p. 832)

Grammar Transparencies and Copymasters
- Misplaced Modifiers, CM 116 (for Mini Lesson, p. 835)

USING MEDIA RESOURCES
LaserLinks
Writing Springboards
See **Teacher's SourceBook** p. 36 for bar codes.

Writing Coach CD-ROM
Visit our website:
www.mcdougallittell.com

Analyzing a Student Model

SPEAKING OPPORTUNITY

See the Communication Handbook, p. R100 for speaking and presenting tips.

Stephen Shimshock
Sunnyvale Middle School

RUBRIC
IN ACTION

A Day at Tiptoe Falls

Trust me—every experience can be worthwhile. Sometimes even the most annoying incident can turn out well. I know this because of an adventure I had while hiking with my family. On one of our favorite paths, we found that a bridge we needed to cross had been broken. This changed the course of our hike. Little did I know it would also change my life at school.

Our hike took place on an ordinary spring Sunday in our state park. After walking for a few minutes, I began running ahead. I almost always do this because I like to be the leader. Soon the trouble began. As I came upon the river I saw cold water rushing by. I saw that the bridge was broken and that park rangers hadn't realized it yet. We were all annoyed. We didn't want to turn back without reaching our goal—seeing the beautiful Tiptoe Falls. We decided to try to walk across the slippery stones. I stepped into the ice-cold water, and then ran to reach the other side as quickly as possible. However, I slipped and fell just a step away from the riverbank. Not only did my sneakers get soaking wet but I also twisted my ankle. "This is going to be a long day," I moaned as I limped away from the river, my feet squishing in my sneakers.

The day wasn't that bad. Because I had to move slowly, I could no longer be the leader. Trailing at the back of the line, I was able to notice things about the woods I had never seen before. I saw interesting trees, different kinds of plants, and oddly colored birds. I asked my mother if I could use the camera to take some pictures. I promised myself that from now on I would try to notice more on our hikes.

We made it to Tiptoe Falls, had lunch, and rested. When it was time to leave, we decided to take another path because my ankle was sore and it would be hard for me to cross the river again. After only a short distance, we came upon five huge trees that had fallen over in a mudslide and were blocking this path. Everyone had to climb over the trees. My father had to carry me on his back to reach the other side. Once everyone was finally across, I stopped to rub my sore ankle. I felt grouchy, cold, and tired. Then I

❶ The writer's conversational tone captures the reader's attention.

The writer presents the subject in the introduction.

❷ Explains the most immediate effects at the beginning of the essay

Another Option:
· Present the effects in order of importance.

Teaching the Lesson

Analyzing the Model
"A Day at Tiptoe Falls"

The student model describes the surprising effects of one misstep on a family hiking trip. Because the narrator hurt his ankle, he trailed at the back of the line of people instead of charging ahead as usual. Forced to slow down, he began noticing things, such as an interesting-looking banana slug. After the trip, he learned that because of his injury he would have to stop playing baseball for three weeks. Since he had a science project due, he spent the time working hard on that, learning more about the banana slug and other animals. As a result of his hard work, he received an A and realized that he was interested in environmental science. A bothersome hiking problem turned out to have a positive effect on his life.

Have a volunteer read the model aloud and then discuss the Rubric in Action with students. Point out the key words and phrases in the student model that correspond to the elements mentioned in the Rubric in Action.

1 Ask students what they learn about the subject of the essay in the introduction.

   Possible Responses: Something happened on the hike; it was annoying; it turned out well; it changed the narrator's life at school.

2 Have students identify some of the causes and effects in this paragraph.

   Possible Responses: Because the bridge was broken, they decided to walk on the slippery stones; because the narrator ran, and because the stones were slippery, he got his sneakers wet and twisted his ankle.

3 Point out that this writer is telling a story as he explains causes and effects. Ask students what other types of cause and effect essays someone might write.

Possible Responses: a persuasive piece; a scientific explanation.

4 Ask students what kinds of details might qualify as *background information*.

Possible Responses: the history of some event; a definition of some sort; an explanation of who someone was or what the person did;

5 Ask students what this adds to the essay and whether every essay would be likely to contain such predictions.

Possible Responses: It adds interest and shows the far-reaching effects of a simple accident; essays that emphasized a single effect that resulted from multiple causes might be less likely to contain predictions.

6 Ask how this conclusion helps tie the whole essay together.

Possible Responses: It clarifies the relationship between all the events in the essay; it shows what the narrator learned from the experience.

remembered the promise I had made to myself earlier—about being more observant. I didn't want the hike to be a waste, so I looked around. There on the muddy ground, I noticed an interesting-looking slug. My mother said it was a banana slug. It was at least 6 inches long and had a huge brown spot on its back. My attitude melted away as I grabbed the camera and took a picture of the slug. I realized that if I had been running ahead as I usually do, I would never have noticed it.

After we returned home, I found that my day of being "thrown off course" in the woods had more effects. First, the doctor said that I should stop playing baseball for three weeks in order to give my ankle a rest. I've always played baseball, so this was terrible news. One afternoon, while I was feeling sorry for myself, my mother showed me the photos from the hike. I saw all the trees, plants, and animals that had caught my eye that day. I was especially interested in the photograph of the funny-looking banana slug. I had an idea. My science project was due in two weeks. Usually during baseball season, I don't give much time to a project. I often do it quickly and get an average grade. This year I had a lot of time and an interest in learning more about the banana slug I had discovered. I also wanted to learn about other creatures like it. So, I did research, created models and charts, and wrote the report. I received my first A on a project! This made me feel good about myself as a student, especially as a science student. This project, along with the photographs from my day in the woods, made me realize I'm interested in environmental science. Who knows? One day I may actually become a scientist who works to save the natural environment. Knowing I have a goal, and knowing I can do well in school, makes me want to work harder.

So, some ordinary hiking problems had a positive effect on my life. Who would have thought that a missing bridge could have caused so much trouble and, at the same time, so much good? My injury helped me notice something about myself I won't forget— that when I slow down and pay attention, I am able to discover a world of amazing things.

❸ The writer cites other effects and explains the connections between all the events and the first cause.

❹ Provides background information

❺ Mentions possible future effects of the cause

❻ The writer concludes by restating the cause-and-effect relationship. He ends by describing an important and permanent effect.

832   UNIT SIX   THE ORAL TRADITION

 Mini Lesson **Viewing and Representing** **TEKS 10E, 10L**

PICTURING TEXT STRUCTURE

Instruction Explain that the organization of cause-and-effect writing is very important. The writer must make the relationship between events clear. Although one event may have multiple causes or multiple effects, often there is one main chain of causes and effects.

Activity Have students analyze the text structure of the student model by constructing a diagram to illustrate the relationship between some of the major events in the model essay. They may

wish to construct a chain like the sample or a similar chart.

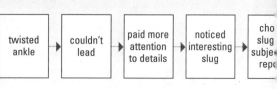

twisted ankle → couldn't lead → paid more attention to details → noticed interesting slug → cho slug subje repo

📖 Use **Reading and Critical Thinking Transparencies**, p. 24, for additional support.

Writing Your Cause-and-Effect Essay

❶ Prewriting

> *Do not write merely to be understood; write so that you cannot possibly be misunderstood.*
> —Robert Louis Stevenson, 19th-century British writer

Brainstorm a list of causes and effects you see in your school or community. List good deeds you have done that have had a positive result. Write down instances when something you did had a negative result. See the **Idea Bank** in the margin for more suggestions. After you have decided on a topic, follow the steps below.

Planning Your Cause-and-Effect Essay

▸ **1. Determine all possible causes and effects.** Does the cause have just one effect? Does the effect have more than one cause? Use a web diagram or flow chart to help you discover all connections.

▸ **2. Identify your audience.** What background information or explanation would your audience need in order to understand the cause-and-effect relationship?

▸ **3. List specific details.** Ask yourself what additional details you need to help you examine the cause-and-effect relationship. Collect facts or note personal experiences or observations.

❷ Drafting

As you write your draft, don't worry about explaining everything perfectly. Just stay focused on fleshing out a cause-and-effect relationship. You will revise and polish your writing later.

• First, identify the cause and effect and state them clearly in the **introduction.**

• In the **body paragraphs,** develop the cause-and-effect relationship with specific details and examples. Also, provide any necessary background information here. Use **transitions**—such as *before, after, therefore, consequently, because,* and *since*— to signal the connections between events.

• **Conclude** by summing up the cause-and-effect relationship.

IDEA Bank

1. Your Working Portfolio
Look for ideas in the projects you completed earlier in the unit.
• Investigate Fire, p. 810
• Make a Sequence Chart, p. 828

2. Surprising Consequences
Watch the news for stories in which a certain cause had surprising or unexpected effects.

3. Root of the Problem
Pick a problem in your community or school and investigate the causes.

Have a question?

See the **Writing Handbook**
Organizing Cause-and-Effect Writing, p. R36
Conclusions, p. R29

Ask Your Peer Reader: EVALUATING

• How well did I explain the cause-and-effect relationship?

• Did I provide enough background information?

• Were my ideas organized in a logical manner?

Guiding Student Writing

Prewriting

Choosing a Subject

If students have trouble selecting a topic after they have read the suggestions in the Idea Bank, have them try the following:

• Think about advice that you have received. Explore the effects of following or not following it.

• Consider actions that caused effects you were not expecting.

• Think about a hobby or activity you enjoy. Explain why you like it or how it affects your life.

Planning Your Cause-and-Effect Essay

1. Remind students not to confuse chronology with causality; merely because one event follows another does not mean that the first caused the second to occur.

2. Explain that a scientific explanation might require background on natural laws, for example.

Drafting

Remind students that an essay's introduction has two functions; besides identifying the cause and effect, it should attract readers' interest or curiosity. It should make them want to continue reading. Discuss different strategies that writers might use to interest readers. These might include beginning with a question, interesting dialogue, or a fascinating fact or observation.

Ask Your Peer Reader

You might ask readers what suggestions they have for improving either your explanation of causes and effects or some other aspect of the essay. You might also ask if your essay provides adequate background material.

Revising
A STRONG CONCLUSION

Remind students that the conclusion should not introduce any new ideas. Instead, it should tie ideas within the piece together. If students want to add new information, they should consider where in the body of the essay it might logically go.

 Use **Writing Transparencies**, p. 6, for additional support.

Editing and Proofreading
COMBINING SENTENCES

Help students recognize that there are numerous ways to combine sentences. You may wish to list various methods: by joining complete sentences or sentence parts using *and, but,* or *or*; by adding single words or groups of words; by using *who, that* and *which*; by using subordinate clauses and conjunctions.

Reflecting

Encourage students to think about how cause-and-effect writing differs from narrative fiction and how it is the same.

Option

Students may wish to take the flowchart or diagram that they created and turn it into a finished piece of computer art to use as illustrations for their completed essays.

Need revising help?

Review the **Rubric,** p. 830

Consider **peer reader** comments

Check **Revision Guidelines,** p. R23

SPELLING
From Writing

As you revise your work, look back at the words you misspelled and determine why you made the errors you did. For additional help, refer to the strategies and generalizations in the **Spelling Handbook** on page R86.

Uncertain about combining sentences?

See the **Grammar Handbook,** p. R59

Publishing
IDEAS

- Represent your cause-and-effect relationship graphically and display both your essay and your graph on the bulletin board.
- Create a dramatic reading of your essay. Have your classmates act out the different parts.

More Online:
Publishing Options
www.mcdougallittell.com

---

❸ Revising
TARGET SKILL ▶ A STRONG CONCLUSION Your concluding paragraph must make a strong final impression on your reader. You could restate the cause-and-effect relationship so the reader is left with no unanswered questions. Or, you could make an observation about the significance of the events or make a prediction. Reread your essay to be sure you finish strongly.

> Who would have thought that a missing bridge could have caused so much trouble and, at the same time, so much good? *My injury helped me notice something about myself I won't forget—that when I slow down and pay attention, I am able to discover a world of amazing things.*

❹ Editing and Proofreading
TARGET SKILL ▶ COMBINING SENTENCES Combining some of your short sentences into longer sentences can create writing that flows smoothly and is interesting to read. You might put two or more short sentences together to form compound or complex sentences.

> I received my first A on a project! This made me feel good about myself as a student*, especially* ~~It made me feel good about myself~~ as a science student.

❺ Reflecting
FOR YOUR WORKING PORTFOLIO What additional causes or effects did you find as you wrote your essay? Which steps were most helpful in writing your essay? Attach your answers to your finished essay. Save your cause-and-effect essay in your **Working Portfolio.**

Read this passage from the first draft of a cause-and-effect essay. The underlined sections may include the following kinds of errors:

- **run-on sentences**
- **misplaced modifiers**
- **lack of subject-verb agreement**
- **correctly written sentences that should be combined**

For each underlined part, choose the revision that most improves the writing.

She won the marathon! <u>Neither her trainer nor her friends were ever in doubt</u>, but she was. <u>She won because of her training. She had begun training sixteen months ago.</u> At first, <u>she only was able to run a mile</u> and had to stop frequently. <u>Then she were able</u> to increase her distance to several miles and added an aerobics workout. A diet high in protein and vitamins <u>reinforced her exercise program the foods she ate</u> made her more resistant to sickness and injury. <u>During the race, she gave up almost once.</u>

(1) (2) (3) (4) (5) (6)

---

1. **A.** Neither her trainer nor her friends was ever in doubt
   B. Neither her trainer nor her friends are ever in doubt
   C. Both her friends and her trainer was never in doubt
   D. Correct as is

2. **A.** She won because of her training, which she had begun sixteen months ago.
   B. She won because of her training, and she had begun it sixteen months ago.
   C. She won because of her training, began sixteen months ago.
   D. Correct as is

3. **A.** At first, only she was able to run a mile
   B. At first, she was able to run only a mile
   C. Only, at first, she was able to run a mile
   D. Correct as is

4. **A.** Then she are able
   B. Then she is able
   C. Then she was able
   D. Correct as is

5. **A.** reinforced her exercise program; the foods she ate
   B. reinforced her exercise program; and the foods she ate
   C. reinforced her exercise program, the foods she ate
   D. Correct as is

6. **A.** Almost during the race, she gave up once.
   B. During the race, she gave up once almost.
   C. During the race, she almost gave up.
   D. Correct as is

Need extra help?

See the **Grammar Handbook**

Quick Reference: Capitalization, p. R58

Quick Reference: Punctuation, p. R56

Run-on Sentences, p. R59

Modifiers, p. R70

Making Subjects and Verbs Agree, p. R60

Assessment Practice

Demonstrate how students can eliminate incorrect choices for the first question.

A. This choice is incorrect, because the sentence has a compound subject joined by *nor*, and in such cases the verb should agree with the subject that is closer to the verb. However, the word *friends* is plural and the verb *was* is singular.

B. This choice is incorrect, because the subject closer to the verb is singular, while the verb is plural.

C. This choice is incorrect, too, because it makes no sense.

D. This choice is correct. The word subject that is closer to the verb is plural, as is the verb.

Answers:
1. D 2. A 3. B 4. C 5. A 6. C

 Mini Lesson **Grammar** **TEKS** 17C **TAAS** Writing Obj. 6

MISPLACED MODIFIERS

Instruction Remind students that modifiers are words or phrases that provide additional information about nouns, pronouns, and verbs. They should be placed as near as possible to the words that they modify. When they are misplaced, they may confuse readers.

Have students write or read the following sentence, inserting the word *only* anywhere they choose:

I placed juice on the table.

Have students compare their sentences and

the different meanings. Help them recognize that the placement of a single modifier, *only*, can affect the meaning of the entire sentence.

Exercises Have students revise each of the following sentences by moving the misplaced phrase or clause closer to the word it modifies.

1. Jordan talked about the math test he took on the way home from school. *(On the way home from school, Jordan talked about the math test he took.)*

2. My sister has a cat who is a veterinarian. *(My sister who is a veterinarian has a cat.)*

3. I made a pie for my guest that has fresh strawberries in it. *(I made a pie that has fresh strawberries in it for my guest.)*

4. Blaring a siren, we heard the fire station. *(We heard the fire station blaring a siren.)*

 Use **Grammar Transparencies and Copymasters,** p. 116, for additional support.

 Use McDougal Littell's *Language Network,* Chapter 8, for more instruction and practice in using modifiers.

Objectives

1. understand and appreciate a Greek Myth and a Puerto Rican folk tale
2. appreciate the culture and history of Puerto Rico and of the United States
3. extend understanding of the selections through a variety of multimodal and cross-curricular activities

Reading Pathways

- Select one of several students to read each story aloud to the entire class or to small groups of students. Assign this reading in advance so that the readers can incorporate into their presentations some of the techniques used by professional storytellers. Have students listen carefully to the tales without following along in their texts.

- Read each tale aloud to the class, pausing at key points to discuss how elements of the tale inform students about the history or customs of the culture. Ask students to compare these customs with those of their own culture. Have them record their observations in their notebooks.

- After students have read the tales once, have them read each tale again to identify such structural elements as main characters, minor characters, conflict, setting, and plot. Then ask students to identify similarities and differences between these tales and the selections in the related unit. For example, have students compare the trickery in "Lazy Peter and His Three-Cornered Hat" with that in "One Ordinary Day with Peanuts."

5-Minute Warm-Up

Daily Language SkillBuilder **TEKS 16B, 17H**

Have students **proofread** the display sentences on page 793e and write them correctly. The sentences also appear on Transparency 25 of **Grammar Transparencies and Copymasters.**

LINKS TO UNIT THREE

Flights of Imagination

In the tales you are about to read, the contrast between appearance and reality is important. A greedy farmer, a selfish nymph, and a self-centered youth learn that things are not always what people imagine them to be. A person or situation that appears one way at first glance may not live up to expectations. These characters and themes are closely linked to similar characters and themes in Unit Three.

PUERTO RICO

PUERTO RICO

Lazy Peter and His Three-Cornered Hat

retold by Ricardo E. Alegría

"Lazy Peter and His Three-Cornered Hat" is a trickster tale that comes from Puerto Rico. The folklore of Puerto Rico has roots in the folklore of Spain, West Africa, and the Taino people of the Caribbean. Although trickster tales reflect an admiration for cleverness, the tricksters themselves are not depicted as heroic but as what they really are—con artists.

LESSON RESOURCES

UNIT SIX RESOURCE BOOK, pp. 27–33

ASSESSMENT
Formal Assessment, pp. 129–130
Teacher's Guide to Assessment and Portfolio Use
Test Generator

SKILLS TRANSPARENCIES AND COPYMASTERS
Grammar
- Punctuating Compound Sentences, CM 126 (for Mini Lesson, p. 838)
- Infinitive Phrases, CM 101 (for Mini Lesson, p. 843)

Communications
- Impromptu Speaking: Dialogue, Role-Play, p. 13 (for Mini Lesson, p. 840)

INTEGRATED TECHNOLOGY
Audio Library
Internet: Research Starter

Visit our website:
www.mcdougallittell.com

TEKS See the Skills Trace at the beginning of the unit for information on TEKS covered in this lesson.

Narcissus

retold by Roger L. Green

Beauty is a key issue in many Greek myths. In many cases, beauty is tied very closely to a character's identity. In the Greek myth "Narcissus," Narcissus, a vain and handsome youth, falls in love with his own reflection. Never having seen his reflection before, he imagines it to be someone else. Echo, a nymph attracted to his good looks, imagines Narcissus' inner beauty to be just as spectacular as his physical appearance. Both characters are deceived and, in typical Greek fashion, taught a lesson.

AS YOU READ . . .

Pay attention to how things appear and how they really are in these tales from different cultures.

Decide what causes some characters to be deceived.

Consider the lessons the characters learn about appearances.

Customizing Instruction

Less Proficient Readers

Explain to students that these two stories originated in different parts of the world, yet both teach lessons about cultural values. As students follow the stories, they should keep these questions in mind:

• Who are the main characters in each tale?
• Who holds the power, humans or some supernatural being?
• What character traits do the main characters have?
• What happens to the main characters as a result of these traits?
• What lesson does each tale teach?

Set a Purpose Have students read to find out which characters are deceived and how.

Students Acquiring English

• Discuss folktales from students' own countries and have students explain the types of lessons they teach.
• Explain that characters in myths and folktales are often simplified so that each shows just one or two main character traits. Encourage students to decide what each character is like and how this affects the story.

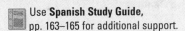 Use **Spanish Study Guide,** pp. 163–165 for additional support.

Gifted and Talented

Have students think about ways in which the characters in both stories are realistic and ways in which they are highly stylized.

Summary

Echo and Narcissus Echo angers Hera, the wife of Zeus, who creates an unusual punishment for the nymph: she will only be able to repeat what others say. Echo later falls in love with handsome Narcissus, but he scorns her and she pines away and dies, leaving only her voice behind. Aphrodite, the goddess of love, is angry at Narcissus and punishes him by making him fall in love with his own reflection in a pool. Unable to tear himself away from it, he too pines away. In the spring, where his body lay, a new flower blossoms.

Reading and Analyzing

Literary Analysis: IRONY

 Remind students that irony is the difference between what is expected and what actually exists or happens. Have students describe the character of Echo. Then have them note the irony in what happens to her.

Possible Response: Students might note that the most beautiful, lively nymph gets the most severe punishment; that her friendliness earns her an enemy.

Use **Unit Six Resource Book,** p. 29 for additional practice.

Active Reading: SEQUENCE

 Ask students what Echo did that caused Hera to punish her in this way. Ask students to notice how Echo's punishment affects the sequence of events in the myth.

Response: She kept Hera talking so that her husband could return to Olympus without being detected.

Use **Unit Six Resource Book,** p. 28 for additional practice.

NARCISSUS

retold by *Roger Lancelyn Green*

U p on the wild, lonely mountains of Greece lived the Oreades, the nymphs or fairies of the hills, and among them one of the most beautiful was called Echo. She was one of the most talkative, too, and once she talked too much and angered Hera, wife of Zeus, king of the gods.

When Zeus grew tired of the golden halls of Mount Olympus, the home of the <u>immortal</u> gods, he would come down to earth and wander with the nymphs on the mountains. Hera, however, was jealous and often came to see what he was doing. It seemed strange at first that she always met Echo, and that Echo kept her listening for hours on end to her stories and her gossip.

But at last Hera realized that Echo was doing this on purpose to detain her while Zeus went quietly back to Olympus as if he had never really been away.

"So nothing can stop you talking?" exclaimed Hera. "Well, Echo, I do not intend to spoil your pleasure. But from this day on, you shall be able only to repeat what other people say—and never speak unless someone else speaks first."

Hera returned to Olympus, well pleased with the punishment she had made for Echo, leaving the poor nymph to weep sadly among the rocks on the mountainside and speak only the words which her sisters and their friends shouted happily to one another.

She grew used to her strange fate after a while, but then a new <u>misfortune</u> befell her.

There was a beautiful youth called Narcissus who was the son of a nymph and the god of a nearby river. He grew up in the plain of Thebes until he was sixteen years old, and then began to hunt on the mountains toward the north where Echo and her sister Oreades lived.

As he wandered through the woods and valleys, many a nymph looked upon him and loved him. But Narcissus laughed at them <u>scornfully</u>, for he loved only himself.

Farther up the mountains Echo saw him. And at once her lonely heart was filled with love for the beautiful youth, so that nothing else in the world mattered but to win him.

Now she wished indeed that she could speak to him words of love. But the curse which Hera had placed upon her tied her tongue, and

WORDS
TO
KNOW

immortal (ĭ-môr′tl) *adj.* undying; not subject to death
misfortune (mĭs-fôr′chən) *n.* a piece of bad luck
scornfully (skôrn′fŏŏl-lē) *adv.* disdainfully

838

Teaching Options

 Grammar TEKS 16B, 17A 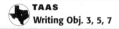 TAAS Writing Obj. 3, 5, 7

PUNCTUATING COMPOUND SENTENCES

Instruction To help students use appropriately punctuated independent clauses, remind them that a compound sentence consists of two or more simple sentences joined together. The parts are joined either by a comma and a coordinating conjunction (*and, but, or, for, so*) or by a semicolon (;). Point to the highlighted sentence as an example.

Application Ask students to tell how they would turn each pair of simple sentences into a compound sentence.

1. Many loved Narcissus. He scorned them all.
2. Echo saw Narcissus. She fell in love.
3. Narcissus called out. Echo answered.
4. Echo was tongue-tied. She could not respond.
5. Aphrodite was angry. She devised an unusual punishment.

Use **Grammar Transparencies and Copymasters,** p. 126.

 Use McDougal Littell's *Language Network,* Chapter 11, for more instruction and practice in punctuating compound sentences.

The Granger Collection, New York

Gifted and Talented

You may want to share with students the related words *narcissist* and *narcissism*—words whose meaning reflects the self-centeredness and vanity of the character Narcissus.

Students Acquiring English

1 You may need to provide some background for students on the Greek myths. For example, explain that the Greeks believed that the gods sometimes appeared on earth and interacted with humans and with lesser gods.

Less Proficient Readers

Ask the following questions to help students follow the story:

- Why did Echo often talk to Hera for long periods of time?
  Response: to give Zeus time to get back to Olympus
- As punishment, what did Hera take away from Echo?
  Response: the ability to talk first; the ability to say what she wanted to say
- What was Echo able to do?
  Response: to repeat what others said
- What was Narcissus like?
  Possible Responses: beautiful; vain; unkind; self-centered

Set a Purpose Have students read to find out whether Narcissus is punished for his vanity and unkindness.

  Viewing and Representing   🏴 **TEKS** 22A

ART APPRECIATION

Instruction Point out that illustrators must make decisions about which aspects of a story to represent and which to omit. As an example, ask which characters and what elements of the setting were omitted from this story illustration.

Possible Responses: Characters might include Echo, Aphrodite; setting might include the Plain of Thebes or Olympus.

Application Have students compare and contrast the portrait of Narcissus with what they learn about him in the story. What elements of his character does this picture show and which does it omit?

Possible Response: Students might say that the picture shows his beauty but not his cruelty; it shows his youth and self-absorption.

she could only follow wherever he went, hiding behind trees and rocks, and feasting her eyes vainly upon him.

One day Narcissus wandered farther up the mountain than usual, and all his friends, the other Theban youths, were left far behind. Only Echo followed him, still hiding among the rocks, her heart heavy with unspoken love.

Presently Narcissus realized that he was lost, and hoping to be heard by his companions, or perhaps by some mountain shepherd, he called out loudly:

"Is there anybody here?"

 "Here!" cried Echo.

Narcissus stood still in amazement, looking all round in vain. Then he shouted, even more loudly:

"Whoever you are, come to me!"

"Come to me!" cried Echo eagerly.

Still no one was visible, so Narcissus called again:

"Why are you avoiding me?"

Echo repeated his words, but with a sob in her breath, and Narcissus called once more:

"Come here, I say, and let us meet!"

"Let us meet!" cried Echo, her heart leaping with joy as she spoke the happiest words that had left her lips since the curse of Hera had fallen on her. And to make good her words, she came running out from behind the rocks and tried to clasp her arms about him.

But Narcissus flung the beautiful nymph away from him in scorn.

"Away with these embraces!" he cried angrily, his voice full of cruel contempt. "I would die before I would have you touch me!"

"I would have you touch me!" repeated poor Echo.

"Never will I let you kiss me!"

"Kiss me! Kiss me!" murmured Echo, sinking down among the rocks, as Narcissus cast her violently from him and sped down the hillside.

"One touch of those lips would kill me!" he called back furiously over his shoulder.

"Kill me!" begged Echo.

> ... NARCISSUS FLUNG HIMSELF DOWN BESIDE THE POOL AND LEANED FORWARD TO DIP HIS FACE IN THE COOL WATER.

And Aphrodite, the goddess of love, heard her and was kind to her, for she had been a true lover. Quietly and painlessly, Echo pined away and died. But her voice lived on, lingering among the rocks and answering faintly whenever Narcissus or another called.

"He shall not go unpunished for this cruelty," said Aphrodite. "By scorning poor Echo like this he scorns love itself. And scorning love, he insults me. He is altogether eaten up with self-love . . . Well, he shall love himself and no one else, and yet shall die of unrequited love!"

It was not long before Aphrodite made good her threat, and in a very strange way. One day, tired after hunting, Narcissus came to a still, clear pool of water away up the mountainside not far from where he had scorned Echo and

WORDS TO KNOW
vainly (vān′lē) *adv.* uselessly; to no avail
contempt (kən-tĕmpt′) *n.* disdain
pine (pīn) *v.* to waste away from longing or grief

840

eft her to die of a broken heart.

With a cry of satisfaction, for the day was ot and cloudless, and he was parched with hirst, Narcissus flung himself down beside the ool and learned forward to dip his face in the ool water.

What was his surprise to see a beautiful face ooking up at him through the still waters of he pool. The moment he saw, he loved—and ove was a madness upon him so that he could hink of nothing else.

"Beautiful water nymph!" he cried. "I love ou! Be mine!"

Desperately he plunged his arms into the vater—but the face vanished and he touched only the pebbles at the bottom of the pool. Drawing out his arms, he gazed intently down, and as the water grew still again, saw once more the face of his beloved.

Poor Narcissus did not know that he was seeing his own reflection: for Aphrodite hid this knowledge from him—and perhaps this was the first time that a pool of water had reflected the face of anyone gazing into it.

Narcissus seemed <u>enchanted</u> by what he saw. He could not leave the pool, but lay by its side day after day looking at the only face in the world which he loved—and could not win; and pining just as Echo had pined.

Slowly Narcissus faded away, and at last his heart broke.

"Woe is me for I loved in vain!" he cried.

"I loved in vain!" sobbed the voice of Echo among the rocks.

"Farewell, my love, farewell," were his last words, and Echo's voice broke and its whisper shivered into silence: "My love . . . farewell!"

So Narcissus died, and the earth covered his bones. But with the spring, a plant pushed its green leaves through the earth where he lay. As the sun shone on it a bud opened and a new flower blossomed for the first time—a white circle of petals round a yellow center. The flowers grew and spread, waving in the gentle breeze which whispered among them like Echo herself come to kiss the blossoms of the first Narcissus flowers. ❖

"Greece has always been my chief inspiration and produced most of my bestsellers."

Roger Lancelyn Green
1918–1987

Ancient Ancestry Roger Lancelyn Green was born in England, where his family has lived in the same ancestral home for more than 900 years. He was often sick as a child and spent long periods confined to his home—devouring Greek myths, medieval romances, and fairy tales.

Lover of Greece Green began a lifelong fascination with Greece and Greek culture when he first visited that country in 1935. He went on to compile and retell many Greek stories, as in his books *Old Greek Fairy Tales,* and *Jason and the Golden Fleece.* Green also wrote a few of his own stories, but he is better known for his adventurous, heroic, and timeless retellings of folktales from around the world.

WORDS TO KNOW **enchanted** (ĕn-chănt′ĭd) *adj.* under a spell; bewitched **enchant** *v.*

841

Students Acquiring English

1 Some students may find Echo's dialogue confusing. Point out the words in Narcissus's dialogue that it copies, and make sure that they understand the punishment that Hera gave Echo.

Gifted and Talented

2 Explain that some accounts of this myth credit Nemesis, the goddess of vengeance, with deciding the fate of Narcissus. Nemesis helped people get even with those who had wronged them, because she was responsible for maintaining the balance of good and evil in the world. Today, the word *nemesis* means "a person or force that torments or defeats someone."

Less Proficient Readers

3 If possible, show students a picture of a narcissus flower.

✓ Assessment **Informal Assessment**   TEKS 10F    TAAS Reading Obj. 5; Writing Obj. 6

SUMMARIZE You can informally assess students' ability to summarize by asking them to tell what they know about the main characters in this story: Hera, Echo, Narcissus, and Aphrodite. Tell them to identify what they know about who the characters are and what they are like.

RUBRIC

3 Full Accomplishment Response reflects an understanding of each character's status and most distinguishing characteristic.

2 Substantial Accomplishment Response shows a general understanding of the differences among the four characters.

1 Little or Partial Accomplishment Response shows confusion about one or more characters or a limited understanding of one of the main characters.

Summary

Lazy Peter and His Three-Cornered Hat Peter is a lazy rascal, who prefers trickery to work. In this story, he visits a village during a country fair and sets up an elaborate scheme. He gives bags of money to the owner of a stand, to a druggist, and to a priest and arranges that they will return the money when he appears with one corner of his hat turned down. Then he targets a rich, greedy farmer, who is also at the fair. He tells him that the hat is magic and that people give him money when he turns down a corner. He "proves" this by going to the owner of the stand, who immediately returns his bag of money. The farmer wants to buy the hat but wants further proof. Peter shows the hat's power twice more and raises the price. Finally, the farmer buys the hat. He immediately tries it out and fails to get money. When he learns that he has been tricked, he furiously tears up the hat and walks home.

Reading and Analyzing

Active Reading: SEQUENCE

A Ask students why Peter might have been handing out bags of money. Encourage students to pay attention to how this action affects events in the story.

Possible Responses: He has some sort of plan; he wants to keep it safe.

Reading Skills and Strategies: CLARIFYING

B Ask students why Peter is so sure that this farmer is his "man."

Possible Responses: He is rich; he is greedy.

Teaching Options

Lazy Peter and His

Carnival in Huejotzingo (1942), Diego Rivera. Watercolor on paper, 5 ¼" × 3 ¼", Courtesy of Sotheby's, New York.

Multicultural Link

Trickster Tales

To help students articulate and discuss themes and connections that cross cultures, point out that Lazy Peter is considered a trickster, a character who fools others. Humorous trickster tales are an important type of folk tales. Sometimes the trickster is in conflict with a bully, sometimes with a fool, and sometimes with a more powerful character. The question of justice and balance of power forms the basis for many such tales, so they often comment on the rights of ordinary people. Readers often side with tricksters because they demonstrate that powerful creatures need not always triumph over weak ones. Other trickster tales are cautionary; the trickster becomes the victim of his or her own cleverness. The trickster is often, but not always, an animal. Well-known tricksters include:

- The Native American Coyote and Raven
- The African hare
- The West African spider, Anansi
- The U.S. Brer Rabbit
- The Japanese fox Kitsune

Three-Cornered Hat

RETOLD BY RICARDO E. ALEGRÍA

This is the story of Lazy Peter, a shameless rascal of a fellow who went from village to village making mischief.

One day Lazy Peter learned that a fair was being held in a certain village. He knew that a large crowd of country people would be there selling horses, cows, and other farm animals and that a large amount of money would change hands. Peter, as usual, needed money, but it was not his custom to work for it. So he set out for the village, wearing a red three-cornered hat.

The first thing he did was to stop at a stand and leave a big bag of money with the owner, asking him to keep it safely until he returned for it. Peter told the man that when he returned for the bag of money, one corner of his hat would be turned down, and that was how the owner of the stand would know him. The man promised to do this, and Peter thanked him. Then he went to the drugstore in the village and gave the druggist another bag of money, asking him to keep it until he returned with one corner of his hat turned up. The druggist agreed, and Peter left. He went to the church and asked the priest to keep another bag of money and to return it to him only when he came back with one corner of his hat twisted to the side. The priest said fine, he would do this.

Having disposed of three bags of money, Peter went to the edge of the village where the farmers were buying and selling horses and cattle. He stood and watched for a while until he decided that one of the farmers must be very rich indeed, for he had sold all of his horses and cows. Moreover, the man seemed to be a miser who was never satisfied but wanted always more and more money. This was Peter's man! He stopped beside him. It was raining; and instead of keeping his hat on to protect his head, he took it off and wrapped it carefully in his cape, as though it were very valuable. It puzzled the farmer to see Peter stand there with the rain falling on his head and his hat wrapped in his cape.

After a while he asked, "Why do you take better care of your hat than of your head?"

Peter saw that the farmer had swallowed the bait, and smiling to himself, he said that the hat was the most valuable thing in all the world and that was why he took care to protect it from the rain. The farmer's curiosity increased at this reply, and he asked Peter what was so valuable about a red three-cornered hat. Peter told him that the hat worked for him; thanks to it, he never had to work for a living because whenever he put the hat on with one of the corners turned over, people just handed him any money he asked for.

  Grammar TEKS 17C TAAS Writing Obj. 6

INFINITIVE PHRASES

Instruction Tell students that an infinitive is a verb form that begins with the word *to*. Examples include *to sing* and *to sleep*. Explain that an infinitive can be used either as a noun, adjective or adverb as in these sentences:

He learned *to sing.* (noun)
They are the people *to see.* (adjective)
I came *to help.* (adverb)

An infinitive phrase contains an infinitive and any modifiers or complements:

I love *to sing in the shower.*
My goal is *to sleep late on Saturday.*

Students may see the word *to* and confuse an infinitive phrase with a prepositional phrase. Remind them that a preposition relates its object to some other word in the sentence. It is followed by a noun or pronoun, not a verb.

Exercises Ask students to identify each underlined phrase as an infinitive or prepositional phrase.

1. Peter did not want <u>to work.</u> *(infinitive)*
2. Peter took the money <u>to a stand.</u> *(prepositional)*
3. A rich farmer had come <u>to the fair.</u> *(prepositional)*
4. <u>To trick him</u> would not be easy. *(infinitive)*
5. The man appeared <u>to be a miser.</u> *(infinitive)*

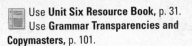 Use **Unit Six Resource Book**, p. 31.
Use **Grammar Transparencies and Copymasters**, p. 101.

 Use McDougal Littell's *Language Network*, Chapter 7, for more instruction and practice in infinitive phrases.

A Ask why the farmer feels that he has to have the hat and why Peter says that he is not interested in selling it.

Possible Responses: The farmer wants the hat because he thinks that it will make him rich; he believes that it is magic; Peter wants to make the farmer want the hat even more.

Literary Analysis: IRONY

B Ask what the farmer's laughter reveals about his character. Have students explain what is ironic about his laughter and his state of mind at this point.

Possible Responses: He wanted to trick Peter; he thinks that he got the better deal. Peter has made a fool of him, despite the fact that he feels superior to Peter.

Reading Skills and Strategies:
INFERRING

C Ask students why the farmer is so angry at the end of the story.

Possible Responses: He feels foolish and embarrassed; he knows that he was tricked.

The farmer was amazed and very interested in what Peter said. As money-getting was his greatest ambition, he told Peter that he couldn't believe a word of it until he saw the hat work with his own eyes. Peter assured him that he could do this, for he, Peter, was hungry, and the hat was about to start working, since he had no money with which to buy food.

With this, Peter took out his three-cornered hat, turned one corner down, put it on his head, and told the farmer to come along and watch the hat work. Peter took the farmer to the stand. The minute the owner looked up, he handed over the bag of money Peter had left with him. The farmer stood with his mouth open in astonishment. He didn't know what to make of it. But of one thing he was sure—he had to have that hat!

A Peter smiled and asked if he was satisfied, and the farmer said yes, he was. Then he asked Peter if he would sell the hat. This was just what Lazy Peter wanted, but he said no, he was not interested in selling the hat because with it, he never had to work and he always had money. The farmer said he thought that was <u>unsound</u> reasoning because thieves could easily steal a hat, and wouldn't it be safer to invest in a farm with cattle? So they talked, and Peter pretended to be impressed with the farmer's arguments. Finally he said yes, that he saw the point, and if the farmer would make him a good offer, he would sell the hat. The farmer, who had made up his mind to have the hat at any price, offered a thousand pesos. Peter laughed aloud and said he could make as much as that by just putting his hat on two or three times.

As they continued <u>haggling</u> over the price, the farmer grew more and more determined to

have that hat, until, finally, he offered all he had realized from the sale of his horses and cows—ten thousand pesos in gold. Peter still pretended not to be interested, but he chuckled to himself, thinking of the trick he was about to play on the farmer. All right, he said, it was a deal. Then the farmer grew cautious and told Peter that before he handed over the ten thousand pesos, he would like to see the hat work again. Peter said that was fair enough. He put on the hat with one of the corners turned up and went with the farmer to the drugstore. The moment the druggist saw the turned-up corner, he handed over the money Peter had left with him. At this the farmer was convinced and very eager to set the hat to work for himself. He took out a bag containing ten thousand pesos in gold and was about to hand it to Peter when he had a change of heart and thought better of it. He asked Peter please to excuse him, but he had to see the hat work just once more before he could part with his gold. Peter said that that was fair enough, but now he would have to ask the farmer to give him the fine horse he was riding as well as the ten thousand pesos in gold. The farmer's interest in the hat revived, and he said it was a bargain!

Lazy Peter put on his hat again, doubled over one of the corners, and told the farmer that since he still seemed to have doubts, this time he could watch the hat work in the church. The farmer was delighted with this, his doubts were stilled, and he fairly beamed thinking of all the money he was going to make once that hat was his.

They entered the church. The priest was hearing confession, but when he saw Peter

---

1. **sacristy** (săk′rĭ-stē): in a church, a room where sacred objects are stored. (page 845)

WORDS
TO
KNOW

unsound (ŭn-sound′) *adj.* not free from fault or weakness; not sensible; inaccurate
haggle (hăg′əl) *v.* to argue about terms or price; bargain
priceless (prīs′lĭs) *adj.* too valuable to be measured by price (page 845)

844

Teaching Options

 Mini Lesson **Spelling** **TEKS 16G**

WORDS FROM SPANISH To help students understand the influence of other languages on the spelling of English words, point to the word *pesos* and explain that it is a Spanish word. Write the singular form, *peso*, and the plural form *pesos*. Explain that English contains many words that came from Spanish and end with *o*. These words form their plurals by adding *-s*. Other words from Spanish that end in *o*:

burro	burros	lasso	lassos
patio	patios	rodeo	rodeos
silo	silos	sombrero	sombreros

Exercises Choose the spelling word that best completes the sentence.
1. Several barns had tall _____ . (silos)
2. These _____ will shade your eyes. (sombreros)
3. Many people use their _____ for summer gatherings. (patios)
4. These small _____ can carry heavy loads. (burros)
5. She won prizes for riding at several _____ . (rodeos)

Use **Unit Six Resource Book,** p. 32 for more practice.

with his hat, he said, "Wait here, my son," and he went to the sacristy[1] and returned with the bag of money Peter had left with him. Peter thanked the priest, then knelt and asked for a blessing before he left. The farmer had seen everything and was fully convinced of the hat's magic powers. As soon as they left the church, he gave Peter the ten thousand pesos in gold and told him to take the horse also. Peter tied the bag of pesos to the saddle, gave the hat to the farmer, begging him to take good care of it, spurred his horse, and galloped out of town.

 As soon as he was alone, the farmer burst out laughing at the thought of the trick he had played on Lazy Peter. A hat such as this was <u>priceless</u>! He couldn't wait to try it. He put it on with one corner turned up and entered the butcher shop. The butcher looked at the hat, which was very handsome indeed, but said nothing. The farmer turned around, then walked up and down until the butcher asked him what he wanted. The farmer said he was waiting for the bag of money. The butcher laughed aloud and asked if he was crazy. The farmer thought that there must be something wrong with the way he had folded the hat. He took it off and doubled another corner down. But this had no

effect on the butcher. So he decided to try it out some other place. He went to the mayor of the town.

The mayor, to be sure, looked at the hat but did nothing. The farmer grew desperate and decided to go to the druggist who had given Peter a bag of money. He entered and stood with the hat on. The druggist looked at him but did nothing.

The farmer became very nervous. He began to suspect that there was something very wrong. He shouted at the druggist, "Stop looking at me and hand over the bag of money!"

The druggist said he owed him nothing, and what bag of money was he talking about, anyway? As the farmer continued to shout about a bag of money and a magic hat, the druggist called the police. When they arrived, he told them that the farmer had gone out of his mind and kept demanding a bag of money. The police questioned the farmer, and he told them about the magic hat he had bought from Lazy Peter. When he heard the story, the druggist explained that Peter had left a bag of money, asking that it be returned when he appeared with a corner of his hat turned up. The owner of the stand and the priest told the same story. And I am telling you the farmer was so angry that he tore the hat to shreds and walked home. ❖

"Culture is the way mankind expresses itself to live and live collectively . . . and it is manifested through popular art . . ."

Ricardo E. Alegría
born 1921

Puerto Rican Patriot Ricardo Enrique Alegría is a leading proponent of Puerto Rican history and culture. He led the movement to save and revitalize Old San Juan—the historic neighborhood of the capital of Puerto Rico. Alegría is director of the Center for Advanced Studies of Puerto Rico and the Caribbean.

Collector of Folktales Alegría is not only an anthropologist and historian but also an avid collector of folktales. He has written many books and articles on the history and folklore of Puerto Rico.

845

Customizing Instruction

Multiple Learning Styles
Logical/Mathematical Learners

1 Students might enjoy figuring out how many dollars ten thousand pesos represents. Students must first determine which country's peso they will use, since several countries use this coin.

Students Acquiring English
2 Explain that a "change of heart" means that the man changed the way he felt about buying the hat.

Less Proficient Readers
Have students summarize how Lazy Peter tricked the farmer.

Answer: He gave money to three different people with instructions to return it when they saw him in his hat. Then he told the farmer that the hat was magic. To prove it, he went back to the three places, where people gave him his money back. However, the farmer thought that people were giving him money because of the hat's powers.

Set a Purpose Have students read to find out what happens to the farmer after he buys the hat.

✓ **Assessment** **Informal Assessment** **TEKS** 11A, 11C  **TAAS** Reading Obj. 4

MAKE PREDICTIONS You can informally assess students' ability to speculate in response to texts by asking whether they think that in the future Lazy Peter and the farmer would do the same thing again. Have them support their responses by referring to relevant aspects of the text and to their own experiences.

RUBRIC

3 Full Accomplishment Response reflects an understanding that Peter is likely to repeat what he did, because he succeeded at his goal, whereas the farmer is not likely to repeat his actions, because he failed to achieve his goals.

2 Substantial Accomplishment Response shows that student understands what at least one character is likely to do and why.

1 Little or Partial Accomplishment Response shows little understanding of how future and past actions are related.

LITERATURE CONNECTION

Evaluate Characters One member of each group should write the ratings as the group determines them. As students debate each character's rating, have them use evidence from the story to support their views. Later, all groups may wish to average their ratings.

RUBRIC

3 Full Accomplishment Students rank the four characters and support each rating with explanations that include story details and a clear value system.

2 Substantial Accomplishment Students rate the level of justice for each character, but the ranking may lack detailed explanations.

1 Little or Partial Accomplishment Students cannot agree on a ranking; the explanations are unclear or illogical; or no evidence supports the rankings.

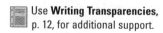 Use **Writing Transparencies,** p. 12, for additional support.

GEOGRAPHY CONNECTION

Compare and Contrast Remind students to note the source of each statistic. You may wish to teach them how to prepare a Works Cited page. If so, consult *Language Network* for guidelines.

RUBRIC

3 Full Accomplishment Students compare and contrast Puerto Rico and Greece in terms of climate, elevation, size, and population. All statistics are current, accurate, and well organized. Sources are clearly noted.

2 Substantial Accomplishment Students compare and contrast Puerto Rico and Greece in terms of climate, elevation, size, and population. Not all statistics are well organized or current.

1 Little or Partial Accomplishment Students do not compare and contrast all aspects of both countries. Information is missing or inaccurate.

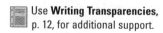 Use **Reading and Critical Thinking Transparencies,** p. 12, for additional support.

ACROSS the CURRICULUM

Interdisciplinary Projects

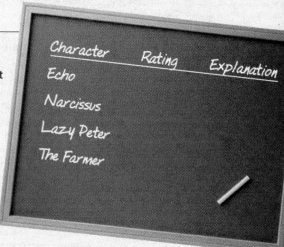

A chalkboard listing:

Character	Rating	Explanation
Echo		
Narcissus		
Lazy Peter		
The Farmer		

LITERATURE CONNECTION

Evaluate Characters Do you think the characters in the tales you have just read get what they deserve in the end? In small groups, rate the level of justice for each important character on a scale of 1 to 5, with 1 representing the most unfair treatment and 5 representing the fairest. Write a brief explanation of why you rated each character the way you did.

GEOGRAPHY CONNECTION

Compare and Contrast The Commonwealth of Puerto Rico consists of a single large island and a number of much smaller islands. Greece is a nation that includes more than 2,000 islands. The sea is an important element in both countries. Compare and contrast Puerto Rico and Greece in terms of climate, elevation, size in square miles, and population. Find out more about the geographical features of each place by referring to encyclopedias, atlases, travel books, other nonfiction books, and Internet databases.

	Puerto Rico	Greece
Climate		
Elevation		
Size		
Population		

SOCIAL STUDIES CONNECTION

Write an Editorial In 1993 Puerto Ricans narrowly voted to remain a U.S. commonwealth, a status given the island in 1952. Today, some Puerto Ricans argue in favor of statehood for Puerto Rico and others support independence. Using encyclopedias, online computer resources, and the Internet, find out about the history of Puerto Rico and what Puerto Rican citizens gain from the island's commonwealth status. What would Puerto Rico lose and what would it gain if it voted for statehood or for independence? Write an article for a news magazine that compares the major advantages and disadvantages of each status.

 **More Online: Research Starter** www.mcdougallittell.com

SOCIAL STUDIES CONNECTION

Write an Editorial Remind students that an editorial states an opinion and provides evidence to support it. The evidence may include reasons, facts, and statistics. Encourage students to research the topic before they decide whether to support statehood, independence, or the status quo. One way to proceed would be to divide the class into teams and ask each team to focus on researching the advantages and disadvantages of one status.

RUBRIC

3 Full Accomplishment Students state an opinion clearly and support it with strong evidence. The evidence is organized in a logical way.

2 Substantial Accomplishment Students state an opinion and support it with some evidence. The evidence may not be well organized or particularly compelling.

1 Little or Partial Accomplishment Students' opinions are not clearly stated or well supported. Little or no factual evidence is included.

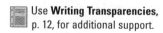 Use **Writing Transparencies,** p. 25, for additional support.

Across Cultures

Find the "Threes" Things often come in threes in folk tales—there may be three tricks, three gifts, three wishes, three visits. Use the diagram to record the things in threes in "Lazy Peter and His Three-Cornered Hat." Then add examples from stories from other cultures—such as "The Three Little Pigs" or "Goldilocks and the Three Bears"—that involve the number three. Share your tables with the rest of the class.

	1st thing	2nd thing	3rd thing
Lazy Peter			
Other tale			
Other tale			

COMPARING TEXTS **Role-Play a Meeting**
Working with a partner, role-play a meeting between Narcissus and the Moose (from "Mooses," page 391), or Lazy Peter and Mr. Johnson (from "One Ordinary Day, with Peanuts,"

page 348). For example, what would Narcissus tell the moose about the importance of appearances? What might Lazy Peter have to say to Mr. Johnson about deception? Drawing upon details from the selections, act out your meeting for the rest of the class.

Comic Strips Turn "Narcissus" or "Lazy Peter and His Three-Cornered Hat" into a comic strip. Add dialogue balloons or captions to your illustrations. Create a cover and share the comic strip with students in other classes.

Hold a Contest See who can find the most advertising logos that contain symbols and names from mythology. Look for them in the yellow pages of telephone books, in newspaper and magazine ads, and on labels for products. Write a brief explanation of why each company would want people to associate the mythological name with its particular product.

Vocabulary in Action

EXERCISE: WORD MEANING On your paper, write *True* if the statement is true. Write *False* if the statement is false.

1. **Immortal** gods have short life spans.
2. A **misfortune** is a lucky break.
3. Treating people **scornfully** means approaching them with respect.
4. If you **vainly** track Narcissus, you will not catch up with him.
5. Kind, polite nymphs treat you with **contempt.**
6. When you see Echo **pine,** you see her laughing.
7. Narcissus was in love with himself and **enchanted** by his own beauty.
8. To spend all you own on a bet probably shows **unsound** reasoning.
9. To **haggle** over the price of an object means to buy it without question.
10. A **priceless** heirloom is worth nothing.

WORDS TO KNOW	contempt	haggle	misfortune	priceless	unsound
	enchanted	immortal	pine	scornfully	vainly

Across Cultures

Find the "Threes" Guide students to consult collections of folk tales from different countries to get the widest and most interesting selection of stories. Explain that they can either read the stories for enjoyment or else skim them for facts.

COMPARING TEXTS

Role-Play a Meeting Suggest that students first discuss what each character's feeling might be and then use that to create the dialogue and actions. Encourage students to use humor in their approaches.

 Use **Communications Transparencies and Copymasters,** p. 13, for additional support.

Comic Strips Suggest that students plan their strips before drawing them. They might begin by listing the major scenes or events that they will picture and then deciding how they will show what happened.

Hold a Contest Students may want to begin by skimming a detailed, illustrated book of Greek myths to familiarize themselves with the names and symbols of the gods and goddesses who appear in the stories.

Vocabulary in Action

EXERCISE
Answers:
1. False
2. False
3. False
4. True
5. False
6. False
7. True
8. True
9. False
10. False

 Use **Unit Six Resource Book,** p. 30 for additional practice.

Use **Unit Six Resource Book,** p. 33 for assessment.

Objectives

1. understand and appreciate a Greek myth, an American trickster tale, and an Hispanic folktale

2. appreciate the cultures of Greece and the Southwestern United States

3. extend understanding of the selections through a variety of multimodal and cross-curricular activities

Reading Pathways

- Select one or several students to read each story aloud to the entire class or to small groups of students. Assign this reading in advance so that the readers can incorporate into their presentations some of the techniques used by professional storytellers. Have students listen carefully to the tales without following along in their texts.

- Read each tale aloud to the class, pausing at key points to discuss how elements of the tale inform students about the customs of the culture. Have students compare these customs with those of their own culture. Have them record their responses and observations in their notebooks.

- After students have read the tales once, have them read each tale again to identify such structural elements as main characters, minor characters, conflict, setting, and plot. Then ask students to identify similarities and differences between these tales and the selections in the related unit. For example, they can contrast the way that Mrs. Schukin resolves to change her financial situation in "A Defenseless Creature" with the miller's approach in "The Force of Luck."

5-Minute Warm-Up

Daily Language SkillBuilder   TEKS 17C, 17G

Have students **proofread** the display sentences on page 793e and write them correctly. The sentences also appear on Transparency 26 of **Grammar Transparencies and Copymasters.**

 See the Skills Trace at the beginning of the unit for information on TEKS covered in this lesson.

848 UNIT SIX THE ORAL TRADITION

LINKS TO UNIT FOUR

Nothing Stays the Same

Everything changes. Nothing ever stays exactly the same. For some people change is difficult, and others take it as it comes. The tales you are about to read show that change is part of life, and we respond to it— whether we like it or not. The themes and characters link closely to similar themes and characters in Unit Four.

UNITED STATES

MEXICO

TEXAS

UNITED STATES

Brother Coyote and Brother Cricket

retold by J. Frank Dobie

"Brother Coyote and Brother Cricket" is a trickster tale that comes from Texas. Many American folktales celebrate using mind over might, brains over brute strength. In "Brother Coyote and Brother Cricket," the cricket's fate is changed because he uses his brain. The coyote learns that not all things change in one's favor.

AS YOU READ . . .

Note and compare how the values and customs of the cultures are presented.

Pay attention to how things are and how things change.

Consider the lessons the characters learn about change.

848 UNIT SIX THE ORAL TRADITION

LESSON RESOURCES

UNIT SIX RESOURCE BOOK, pp. 34–40

ASSESSMENT
Formal Assessment, pp. 131–132
Teacher's Guide to Assessment and Portfolio Use
Test Generator

SKILLS TRANSPARENCIES AND COPYMASTERS
Grammar
- Using the Right Verb, CM 135 (for Mini Lesson, p. 855)
Communications
- Verbal Strategies, TR 14; Nonverbal Strategies, TR 15 (for Mini Lesson, p. 856)

INTEGRATED TECHNOLOGY
Audio Library
Video: Literature in Performance
- "Brother Coyote and Brother Cricket." See **Video Resource Book,** pp. 37–42
Internet: Research Starter

Visit our website:
www.mcdougallittell.com

Phaëthon

retold by Moira Kerr and John Bennett

Greek myths are stories about gods, goddesses, and heroes. These stories attempt to explain natural events or to answer basic questions about the world. In this myth Phaëthon, (fā′ə-thŏn), son of the god Apollo, rides too close to earth in his father's sun chariot, causing the formation of the Libyan desert and a period of drought. This myth explores several issues important to the ancient Greeks, such as the challenges of change and the problem of human limitations.

GREECE

MEXICO

The Force of Luck

retold by Rudolfo A. Anaya

"The Force of Luck" comes from an area of the U.S. Southwest that formerly belonged to Mexico. This area reflects a mixture of cultures that includes Spanish, Mexican, and Native American. In many Hispanic tales, including this one, people explain change as God's will.

Customizing Instruction

Less Proficient Readers
Ask students to think about changes they have experienced in their lives. Discuss ways that people adapt to change. Then encourage students to preview the selections by looking at the illustrations.

Set a Purpose Have students read to find out why Phaëthon wants to drive his father's chariot.

Students Acquiring English
Students may find these selections less challenging in vocabulary and style than some previous works. After students independently read selected passages, ask volunteers to summarize them for the class.

Use **Spanish Study Guide,** pp. 166–168 for additional support.

Gifted and Talented
Have students choose the tale that they feel offers the most valuable lesson and defend their choice to the class.

Summary

Phaëthon Wanting to know if Apollo really is his father, the Greek youth Phaëthon visits the sun god's palace. Apollo replies that he is indeed Phaëthon's parent and promises to give his son anything he wants. When Phaëthon asks to drive the chariot of the sun across the sky, the god–knowing no mortal can survive such a trip–tries to change his mind. But Phaëthon is firm in his desire, and his father cannot break his promise as a god. Full of confidence, Phaëthon leaps into the chariot and takes the reins. The horses immediately race out of control and pull the sun wildly around the sky. To save the world from burning, Zeus hurls a thunderbolt that kills Phaëthon.

Reading and Analyzing

Literary Analysis:
INTERNAL CONFLICT

 Remind students that an external conflict is a struggle between opposing forces, while an internal conflict takes place within a character. Ask students to explain the internal conflict that Apollo faces when he hears his son's request.

Possible Response: He wants to protect his son, but he knows a god cannot break an oath.

Use **Unit Six Resource Book,** p. 36 for additional practice.

Active Reading: CONNECTING

Ask students to compare the narrator's feelings toward her mother in "The White Umbrella" to the feelings of Phaëthon about his father.

Possible Response: Both feel shame. The narrator is ashamed of her mother while Phaëthon is ashamed that he lacks proof of his parentage.

Use **Unit Six Resource Book,** p. 35 for additional practice.

Teaching Options

PHAËTHON

The Fall of Phaëthon (about 1637), Peter Paul Rubens. Oil sketch on wood, The Granger Collection, New York.

850 UNIT SIX THE ORAL TRADITION

 Mini Lesson **Viewing and Representing** **TEKS 22A**

The Fall of Phaëthon
by Peter Paul Rubens

ART APPRECIATION Flemish painter Peter Paul Rubens (1577–1640) was also a diplomat. His travels to Spain and Italy allowed him to study the works of other artists such as Titian, Carracci, and Caravaggio. Rubens's paintings often are scenes depicting religious or mythical events. He is noted for his ability to create rich, sensual surfaces.
Instruction Point out to students that the placement of the figures and the expressions on their faces create a strong sense of movement and emotion. Ask students what feeling the horses convey and how.

Possible Response: They are panicky as shown by their staring eyes and kicking legs.
Ask students to describe Phaëthon's expression.
Possible Response: He is stunned.
Application Ask students what theme of the myth is emphasized by this painting.
Possible Response: Over-confidence and excessive pride may have disastrous results.

RETOLD BY MOIRA KERR AND JOHN BENNETT

One day the fair youth Phaëthon,[1] whose father was the sun god, Apollo, was taunted about his parentage by Epaphus,[2] a youth of the same age whose father was the mighty Zeus.

Stung with shame, Phaëthon reported the insults to his mother, Clymene.[3]

"I am unable to answer them. If my father is really a god, as you have told me, give me proof of my noble birth, and let me take my place in heaven."

Clymene was moved.

"It would not take you long to visit your father's dwelling place. If you wish to do so, go and question the sun himself, for Apollo is indeed your father."

Apollo's abode was a lofty palace of glittering gold and bronze. Its towering columns, supporting a roof of polished ivory, shone like fire. Its double doors reflected the light from their silver surfaces.

After climbing the steep approach, Clymene's son was ushered into the presence of his father, who was dressed in a purple robe and was sitting on a throne of shining emeralds. But Phaëthon could not approach too close, for he could not bear the blinding light.

"What do you want in this citadel,[4] Phaëthon, my son? Son, I call you, for you are one whom any parent would be proud to acknowledge."

"To prove that I am indeed your son, give me evidence."

"To remove any doubt from your mind, Phaëthon, make any request you wish, and you shall have it from me."

Instantly the lad asked to be allowed for one day to drive his father's sun chariot across the sky.

The words were scarcely spoken when Apollo regretted his oath. A mortal may, perhaps, break his word, but not so a god who had sworn by the waters of the Styx.[5] Apollo knew that the request meant death for a mortal, and he used every argument to dissuade his son from a venture that was suicide.

"You cannot possibly keep the horses under control. I, a god, can scarcely manage them. Even Zeus himself couldn't drive the chariot. The heavens are dangerous. You will have to keep to the path, past the horns of the hostile Bull, past the Thracian Archer and the paws of the raging Lion, past the Scorpion's cruel pincers and the clutching claws of the Crab.[6] Release me from my promise. Ask anything else and I shall grant it."

But Phaëthon, full of confidence, would not change his mind, and the reluctant Apollo had the swift Hours[7] yoke his team, lead the four fire-breathing steeds from the stable, and fasten on the jingling harness.

---

1. **Phaëthon** (fā′ə-thŏn′).
2. **Epaphus** (ĕp′ə-fəs): in Greek mythology, the son of Zeus and the mortal woman Io.
3. **Clymene** (klĭm′ə-nē).
4. **citadel:** a fortress.
5. **Styx** (stĭks): in Greek mythology, the river around Hades, which is the kingdom of the dead. When the dead enter Hades, a ferry takes them across the river.
6. **Bull . . . Crab:** the constellations known as Taurus (the Bull), Sagittarius (the Thracian Archer), Leo (the Lion), Scorpio (the Scorpion), and Cancer (the Crab).
7. **Hours:** servants of Apollo.

WORDS TO KNOW
abode (ə-bōd′) *n.* a home
acknowledge (ăk-nŏl′ĭj) *v.* to recognize the status or rights of

851

Customizing Instruction

Less Proficient Readers
Ask students what motivates Phaëthon to visit his father and ask to drive his chariot.

Possible Response: He wants to prove that Apollo is his real father.

Set a Purpose Ask students to read to find out what happens to Phaëthon when he drives his father's chariot.

Gifted and Talented
Ask students to write a persuasive argument that Apollo might have used to convince his son not to drive his chariot across the sky.

Multiple Learning Styles
Visual Learners
1 Have students chart the path that the chariot will take and illustrate the constellations that must be avoided. Students should incorporate into their drawings the details of the constellations from the text.

 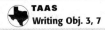 **Spelling** TEKS 16C | TAAS Writing Obj. 3, 7

ABSORBED PREFIX AC-

Instruction Remind students that sometimes a different form of a prefix will be used so that the sound of the prefix is absorbed into the first sound of the word to which it is attached. The prefix *ac* is one form of the prefix *ad*, which means "to or toward." *Ad* changes to *ac* when it is added to words beginning with a *c*. For example, *ad* becomes *ac* when added to the root *cept* to make the word *accept*.

Exercises Have students correct any misspelled words that they find in the following sentences. Some sentences are correct.

1. Phaëthon's estimate of his strength was inacurate. *(inaccurate)*
2. No one could accuse Apollo of breaking his word. *(correct)*
3. Phaëthon was granted immediate acess to his father's presence. *(access)*
4. Unfortunately, Apollo could not acompany his son on the journey. *(accompany)*
5. Instead of slowing down, the horses accelerated toward the earth. *(correct)*

A Ask students what lesson about pride might be taken from Phaëthon's situation as the chariot begins its journey.

Possible Response: Pride sometimes leads people to take foolish risks; pride may blind people to the reality of a situation.

Literary Analysis: PERSONIFICATION

B Ask students to explain the effect of the personification of the constellations in this passage.

Possible Response: Portraying the constellations as monstrous beasts adds to the terror of Phaëthon's journey.

Literary Analysis: MYTH

C Remind students that myths are often used to explain natural events or conditions. Ask students how this story explains the presence of a desert in Libya.

Possible Response: Phaëthon caused all vegetation and sources of water to disappear in the heat.

Active Reading: CONNECTING

Ask students if they have ever taken on more than they could handle or done something against the advice of others, only to regret it later. Have them think about their feelings before and after the situation occured.

A No sooner had the proud youth leaped into the chariot and taken the reins in his hands than the horses knew they had not the firm hands of their master to guide them. Feeling their burden was too light, off they raced, out of control. The lad was panic-stricken. He did not know the path, he did not even know the names of the horses, and he was not able to manage the horses, even had he known. He could only cling helplessly to the sides of the swaying chariot as it plunged hither and thither through the sky.

B For the first time, the cold stars of the Northern Plough grew hot, and the Serpent[8] which lay close to the icy pole was roused to fury as it sweltered in the heat. Phaëthon's terror mounted as he sighted the Scorpion and the other monstrous beasts sprawling over the face of the high heavens. Then the horses went **C** plunging downward towards the earth. The heat of the sun's rays seared[9] the ground, destroying vegetation and drying up rivers and seas. Great cities perished, and whole nations were reduced to ashes. So close did the chariot come to Africa that Libya became a desert. . . .

Everywhere the ground gaped open, and great beams of light descended even to Tartarus,[10] frightening the king of the underworld and his queen. Three times did Poseidon[11] try to emerge above the waters, but the fiery air was too much for him.

It was then that the alarmed Zeus had to interfere, or the whole world would have perished in flame. Mounting to the highest point of heaven, he let fly a powerful thunderbolt against the young charioteer, which dashed the luckless Phaëthon to earth.

His body fell into the Po River, and the Italian nymphs[12] buried it on the bank. On a rock, they set this inscription:

> HERE PHAËTHON LIES: HIS
> FATHER'S CAR HE TRIED—
> THOUGH PROVED TOO WEAK,
> HE GREATLY DARING DIED.

---

8. **Northern Plough** (plou) . . . **Serpent:** the constellations known as the Big Dipper and Draco.
9. **seared:** burned; scorched.
10. **Tartarus** (tär′tər-əs): in Greek mythology, another name for Hades.
11. **Poseidon** (pō-sīd′n): in Greek mythology, the god of the sea.
12. **nymphs** (nĭmfs): beautiful young women

"Much of my interest in life has been exploring the deep wisdom which lies within all of us."

Moira Kerr
born 1938

Canadian Born Moira Kerr grew up in Canada. She taught for several years in Toronto, Ontario. When Kerr's students did not enjoy the versions of the myths they were reading, she began writing her own retellings.

Writer and Psychologist Kerr eventually went on to collaborate with the artist John Bennett on the illustrated book *Myth*. She also moved to Oklahoma to work as a psychologist.

Teaching Options

 Assessment **Informal Assessment** **TEKS** 10E 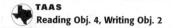 **TAAS** Reading Obj. 4, Writing Obj. 2

UNDERSTANDING CAUSE AND EFFECT You can informally assess students' understanding of the cause-and-effect relationships in the selection by having them prepare an explanation about what happened to Phaëthon that Phaëthon's mother might give to her younger children. The explanation should emphasize the causes of the tragedy. Students may either deliver the speech or submit the text of it.

RUBRIC

3 Full Accomplishment Responses identify all of the causes and accurately show all of the subsequent events.

2 Substantial Accomplishment Responses identify important causes and many of the subsequent events.

1 Little or Partial Accomplishment Responses include few or none of the causes and fail to make a logical connection with the events that follow.

The Force of Luck

Roadside Conference (1953), Archibald J. Motley, Jr. Oil on canvas, 16¾" × 11", Atlanta University Collection of Afro-American Art at Clark Atlanta University.

retold by Rudolfo A. Anaya

Summary

The Force of Luck Two wealthy friends are debating whether a man needs luck or money to be rich. One tries to settle it by giving a poor but honest miller two hundred dollars. Unfortunately, the miller is cursed with bad luck. A hawk flies off with the bag of money. Three months later, the wealthy men return, and the miller tells them what happened to the money. The man who believes in money gives him another two hundred dollars. The miller hides the money in a jar of bran that his wife then unknowingly trades for clay. This time the money man doubts the miller's story. He gives no more cash, but his friend tosses the miller a piece of lead. The miller passes the lead along to a fisherman to weigh down his nets. In return, the miller receives a fish that has a diamond in its stomach, making him rich. Some time later, the wealthy men pass through, and the miller eagerly shows them his new mill and cottage. During the tour, they coincidentally find the money the hawk stole and the money in the bran jar. In this way, the miller proves his honesty, and the friends' original question has an obvious answer.

 This selection appears in Spanish in the **Spanish Study Guide**.

Customizing Instruction

Less Proficient Readers
Interest students in the story by discussing the things or qualities that people need to be successful. Then have students debate what makes a person more successful: luck or money.

Set a Purpose Have students read to find out how the miller gets–and loses–a large amount of money.

 Mini Lesson **Viewing and Representing** 🏴 **TEKS 22A**

Roadside Conference
by Archibald J. Motley, Jr.

ART APPRECIATION This picture was painted in 1953 when Motley, an African-American artist, lived in Mexico. His work often portrayed ordinary people going about everyday activities.

Instruction Point out to students that, although the artist depicts many details in the painting very precisely, he has chosen to blur the facial features of the man in the background. Ask students what is suggested by this lack of definition.

Possible Response: The artist may have wanted to suggest that this figure could be anyone. Also the lack of a particular expression leaves the viewer in doubt about the nature of the conversation between the two men.

Application Ask students how this painting prepares them for the story that they are about to read.

Possible Responses: The painting creates an impression of the setting of the story; it emphasizes that the encounter between the wealthy men and the miller was also a matter of luck.

Literary Analysis: FOLKTALE

A Ask students why the author repeats the argument after explaining it once.

Possible Response: Repetition is part of the style of a folktale. It makes the story easy to remember, which is important for stories that were transmitted through the oral tradition.

Active Reading: CONNECTING

B Ask students how the narrator in "An Hour with Abuelo" would react to this statement by the miller's wife. Have students explain their answers.

Possible Response: He would be annoyed at her acceptance of this bad luck just as he is angry at his mother for saying "That's the way life is." The narrator believes that people should go after what they want.

Literary Analysis: THEME

C Ask students if a contrast is being drawn between the noble poor and the greedy rich in this tale.

Possible Responses: Yes, because the rich men are using the miller as a pawn to settle a petty argument between themselves; no, because the rich men are honest with the miller and he needs the money they give to him.

Reading Skills and Strategies: EVALUATING

D Ask students to evaluate the wisdom in the miller's choice of a hiding place for the money.

Possible Response: His choice of a hiding place is not wise, because food like bran is likely to be used at any time.

Once two wealthy friends got into a heated argument. One said that it was money which made a man prosperous, and the other maintained that it wasn't money, but luck, which made the man. They argued for some time and finally decided that if only they could find an honorable man, then perhaps they could prove their respective points of view.

One day while they were passing through a small village they came upon a miller who was grinding corn and wheat. They paused to ask the man how he ran his business. The miller replied that he worked for a master and that he earned only four bits[1] a day, and with that he had to support a family of five.

The friends were surprised. "Do you mean to tell us you can maintain a family of five on only fifteen dollars a month?" one asked.

"I live modestly to make ends meet," the humble miller replied.

The two friends privately agreed that if they put this man to a test, perhaps they could resolve their argument.

"I am going to make you an offer," one of them said to the miller. "I will give you two hundred dollars, and you may do whatever you want with the money."

"But why would you give me this money when you've just met me?" the miller asked.

"Well, my good man, my friend and I have a long-standing argument. He <u>contends</u> that it is luck which elevates a man to high position, and I say it is money. By giving you this money, perhaps we can settle our argument. Here, take it, and do with it what you want!"

So the poor miller took the money and spent the rest of the day thinking about the strange meeting which had presented him with more money than he had ever seen. What could he possibly do with all this money? Be that as it may, he had the money in his pocket, and he could do with it whatever he wanted.

When the day's work was done, the miller decided the first thing he would do would be to buy food for his family. He took out ten dollars and wrapped the rest of the money in a cloth and put the bundle in his bag. Then he went to the market and bought supplies and a good piece of meat to take home.

On the way home he was attacked by a hawk that had smelled the meat which the miller carried. The miller fought off the bird, but in the struggle he lost the bundle of money. Before the miller knew what was happening the hawk grabbed the bag and flew away with it. When he realized what had happened he fell into deep thought.

"Ah," he moaned, "wouldn't it have been better to let that hungry bird have the meat! I could have bought a lot more meat with the money he took. Alas, now I'm in the same poverty as before! And worse, because now those two men will say I am a thief! I should have thought carefully and bought nothing. Yes, I should have gone straight home, and this wouldn't have happened!"

So he gathered what was left of his provisions and continued home, and when he arrived he told his family the entire story.

When he was finished telling his story his wife said, "It has been our lot to be poor, but have faith in God and maybe someday our luck will change."

The next day the miller got up and went to work as usual. He wondered what the two men would say about his story. But since he had never been a man of money he soon forgot the entire matter.

Three months after he had lost the money to

---

1. **four bits:** a slang term for fifty cents.

WORDS
TO
KNOW

contend (kən-tĕnd') v. to argue

854

Teaching Options

Multicultural Link   ## Southwestern Culture

The area of the American Southwest in which this tale originated was influenced by two cultures with roots in Spain. The older culture is Spanish, primarily found in northern New Mexico and southern Colorado. Centuries ago, settlers from Spain brought their traditions and beliefs to the New World. European communities and culture have been present in this area since the late 1500s with only one interruption.

The more recent influence is that of Mexican Americans. This culture is concentrated mostly along the border between Mexico and the United States. Mexican cultural values are strong in this area, in part because waves of Mexican immigrants have brought Mexican culture back into the lives of third- and fourth- generation Mexican Americans, and in part due to efforts by organizations such as the Mexican Patriotic Committee. This organization works to foster better relations between Mexico and the United States and sponsors celebrations of holidays, parades, and banquets to encourage the appreciation of Mexican culture.

the hawk, it happened that the two wealthy men returned to the village. As soon as they saw the miller they approached him to ask if his luck had changed. When the miller saw them he felt ashamed and afraid that they would think that he had <u>squandered</u> the money on worthless things. But he decided to tell them the truth, and as soon as they had greeted each other he told his story. The men believed him. In fact, the one who insisted that it was money and not luck which made a man prosper took out another two hundred dollars and gave it to the miller.

"Let's try again," he said, "and let's see what happens this time."

The miller didn't know what to think. "Kind sir, maybe it would be better if you put this money in the hands of another man," he said.

"No," the man insisted, "I want to give it to you because you are an honest man, and if we are going to settle our argument you have to take the money!"

The miller thanked them and promised to do his best. Then as soon as the two men left he began to think what to do with the money so that it wouldn't disappear as it had the first time. The thing to do was to take the money straight home. He took out ten dollars, wrapped the rest in a cloth, and headed home.

When he arrived his wife wasn't at home. At first he didn't know what to do with the money. He went to the pantry, where he had stored a large earthenware jar filled with bran. That was as safe a place as any to hide the money, he thought, so he emptied out the grain and put the bundle of money at the bottom of the jar, then covered it up with the grain. Satisfied that the money was safe, he returned to work.

That afternoon when he arrived home from work he was greeted by his wife.

"Look, my husband, today I bought some good clay with which to whitewash[2] the entire house."

"And how did you buy the clay if we don't have any money?" he asked.

"Well, the man who was selling the clay was willing to trade for jewelry, money, or anything of value," she said. "The only thing we had of value was the jar full of bran, so I traded it for the clay. Isn't it wonderful? I think we have enough clay to whitewash these two rooms!"

The man groaned and pulled his hair.

"Oh, you crazy woman! What have you done? We're ruined again!"

"But why?" she asked, unable to understand his <u>anguish</u>.

"Today I met the same two friends who gave me the two hundred dollars three months ago," he explained. "And after I told them how I lost the money they gave me another two hundred. And I, to make sure the money was safe, came home and hid it inside the jar of bran—the same jar you have traded for dirt! Now we're as poor as we were before! And what am I going to tell the two men? They'll think I'm a liar and a thief for sure!"

"Let them think what they want," his wife said calmly. "We will only have in our lives what the good Lord wants us to have. It is our lot to be poor until God wills it otherwise." | 2

So the miller was consoled, and the next day he went to work as usual. Time came and went, and one day the two wealthy friends returned to ask the miller how he had done with the second two hundred dollars. When the poor miller saw them he was afraid they would accuse him of being a liar and a

---

2. **whitewash:** to paint something white.

WORDS TO KNOW

squander (skwŏn′dər) *v.* to spend carelessly
anguish (ăng′gwĭsh) *n.* great physical or mental suffering, as from grief or pain

855

 Grammar

Mini Lesson | **TEKS 17C** | **TAAS Writing Obj. 6**

USING THE RIGHT VERB

Instruction Tell students that some pairs of verbs can cause confusion. These pairs include: *let/leave; lie/lay; sit/set.* Share the following definitions with students:

let means "to allow or permit"; *leave* means "to depart" or "to allow something to remain"
lie means "to recline"; *lay* means "to put or place something"
sit means "to rest"; *set* means "to put something"

Exercises Have students choose the correct verb and use the other in a sentence about the story.

1. The miller (<u>sat</u>, set) down wearily.
2. He did not want to (lie, <u>lay</u>) the money on the counter so he hid it.
3. His wife told him to (leave, <u>let</u>) his regrets go.
4. He could not (<u>leave</u>, let) the bag in the nest.

 Use **Unit Six Resource Book**, p. 38. Use **Grammar Transparencies and Copymasters**, p. 135.

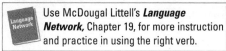 Use McDougal Littell's **Language Network**, Chapter 19, for more instruction and practice in using the right verb.

Literary Analysis: CONFLICT

A Ask students how each man's opinion of the miller reflects his side of the argument about luck and money.
Answer: The "money man" doesn't trust the miller, because according to his argument, the miller should be prospering. The "luck man" wants to trust the miller because the miller's bad luck supports his point– that luck is the key to prosperity.

Literary Analysis: FOLKLORE

B Point out that events often happen in sets of three in folktales. The first two events are similar to set readers up for the third, crucial event. Ask students how this story follows the traditional folklore pattern.
Possible Response: The miller received three gifts from the rich men–two identical sums of money, which he lost, and a worthless lump of lead. According to the pattern, the lead should turn out to be valuable or important to the story's climax and resolution.

Reading Skills and Strategies: PREDICTING

C Invite students to predict what the "piece of glass" might turn out to be.
Possible Responses: a valuable jewel; a magic stone

Reading Skills and Strategies: EVALUATING

D Ask students if they trust the jeweler's wife. Guide students to base their conclusions on the text and the story's theme.
Possible Response: The jeweler's wife contrasts with the poor but honest miller. She seems greedy and thus appears untrustworthy.

---

spendthrift.[3] But he decided to be truthful, and as soon as they had greeted each other he told them what had happened to the money.

"That is why poor men remain honest," the man who had given him the money said. "Because they don't have money they can't get into trouble. But I find your stories hard to believe. I think you gambled and lost the money. That's why you're telling us these wild stories."

A

"Either way," he continued, "I still believe that it is money and not luck which makes a man prosper."

"Well, you certainly didn't prove your point by giving the money to this poor miller," his friend reminded him. "Good evening, you luckless man," he said to the miller.

 "Thank you, friends," the miller said.

B "Oh, by the way, here is a worthless piece of lead I've been carrying around. Maybe you can use it for something," said the man who believed in luck. Then the two men left, still debating their points of view on life.

Since the lead was practically worthless, the miller thought nothing of it and put it in his jacket pocket. He forgot all about it until he arrived home. When he threw his jacket on a chair he heard a thump, and he remembered the piece of lead. He took it out of the pocket and threw it under the table. Later that night after the family had eaten and gone to bed, they heard a knock at the door.

"Who is it? What do you want?" the miller asked.

"It's me, your neighbor," a voice answered. The miller recognized the fisherman's wife. "My husband sent me to ask you if you have any lead you can spare. He is going fishing tomorrow, and he needs the lead to weight down the nets."

The miller remembered the lead he had thrown under the table. He got up, found it, and gave it to the woman.

"Thank you very much, neighbor," the woman said. "I promise you the first fish my husband catches will be yours."

"Think nothing of it," the miller said and returned to bed. The next day he got up and went to work without thinking any more of the incident. But in the afternoon when he returned home he found his wife cooking a big fish for dinner.

"Since when are we so well off we can afford fish for supper?" he asked his wife.

"Don't you remember that our neighbor promised us the first fish her husband caught?" his wife reminded him. "Well, this was the fish he caught the first time he threw his net. So it's ours, and it's a beauty. But you should have been here when I gutted him! I found a large piece of glass in his stomach!"

"And what did you do with it?"

"Oh, I gave it to the children to play with," she shrugged.

When the miller saw the piece of glass he noticed it shone so brightly it appeared to illuminate the room, but because he knew nothing about jewels he didn't realize its value and left it to the children. But the bright glass was such a novelty that the children were soon fighting over it and raising a terrible fuss.

Now it so happened that the miller and his wife had other neighbors who were jewelers. The following morning when the miller had gone to work, the jeweler's wife visited the miller's wife to complain about all the noise her children had made.

"We couldn't get any sleep last night," she moaned.

---

3. **spendthrift:** a person who wastes money.

Mini Lesson **Speaking and Listening**  **TEKS** 2F, 5A, 5D, 5E, 11B

RETELLING

Prepare Tell students that "The Force of Luck" was originally passed down by word of mouth from one generation to the next. Explain that anyone who retells a story interprets it. There are three goals to keep in mind when retelling a story: summarizing it accurately, expressing your interpretation, and entertaining your audience. Discuss these steps in the process:

1. Review the selection beforehand. Summarize the key information.
2. Use your voice to express the story. For example, to emphasize certain words or passages, change the way you say them.

3. Use body language to reinforce your words. Have students work in pairs to retell "The Force of Luck." Encourage the students to apply the steps above and to limit their presentations to three minutes.

Present After students retell the story, have them evaluate each other's success in meeting the three goals.

BLOCK SCHEDULING This activity is particularly well suited for longer class periods.

Use **Communications Transparencies and Copymasters,** p. 14–15, for additional support.

Detail of *Mujer con pescados* [Woman with fish] (1980), Francisco Zúñiga. Lithograph, 21⅞" × 29½", edition of 135. Courtesy of Brewster Gallery, New York.

Customizing Instruction

Less Proficient Readers
Ask students to whom the miller gives his piece of lead.
Answer: He gives it to a fisherman.
• What does the miller receive in return?
Answer: a fish with a piece of glass in its stomach
• What does the glass turn out to be?
Answer: a diamond
Set a Purpose Have students read to find out how the miller becomes successful.

Students Acquiring English
1 If necessary, remind students that the suffix –*less* means "without." Then ask students to find and define two words in these paragraphs that contain this suffix.
Possible Responses: *luckless,* "without luck"; *worthless,* "without worth"

"I know, and I'm sorry, but you know how it is with a large family," the miller's wife explained. "Yesterday we found a beautiful piece of glass, and I gave it to my youngest one to play with, and when the others tried to take it from him he raised a storm."

The jeweler's wife took interest. "Won't you show me that piece of glass?" she asked.

"But of course. Here it is."

"Ah, yes, it's a pretty piece of glass. Where did you find it?"

"Our neighbor gave us a fish yesterday, and when I was cleaning it I found the glass in its stomach."

"Why don't you let me take it home for just a moment. You see, I have one just like it, and I want to compare them."

"Yes, why not? Take it," answered the miller's wife.

So the jeweler's wife ran off with the glass to show it to her husband. When the jeweler saw the glass, he instantly knew it was one of the finest diamonds he had ever seen.

"It's a diamond!" he exclaimed.

"I thought so," his wife nodded eagerly. "What shall we do?"

"Go tell the neighbor we'll give her fifty dollars for it, but don't tell her it's a diamond!"

"No, no," his wife chuckled, "of course not." She ran to her neighbor's house. "Ah,

THE FORCE OF LUCK **857**

Mini Lesson **Viewing and Representing** 🏴 **TEKS 22A**

Mujer con Pescados [Woman with fish]
by Francisco Zúñiga

ART APPRECIATION Born in Costa Rica, artist Francisco Zúñiga (1912–1998) has made his home in Mexico since 1936. This portrayal of a woman with a basket of fish, painted in 1980, is typical of his work and has a startling presence.
Instruction Point out to students that the artist uses muted colors and subtle shadings in this picture. Ask students what impression of the woman is enhanced by the choice of colors.

Possible Response: The woman wears a look of patience and fortitude. The muted colors reinforce the idea that she accepts her life as it is.
Ask students what they think the woman is doing.
Possible Response: She is selling her fish and watching the people go past her table.
Application Ask students what words uttered by the miller's wife would seem to express the attitude of the woman in the painting.
Possible Response: "We will only have in our lives what the good Lord wants us to have. It is our lot to be poor until God wills it otherwise."

A Ask students to analyze the miller's character from this comment.

Possible Responses: He is intelligent and perceptive; he realizes that the neighbor's actions don't make sense.

Reading Skills and Strategies:
ANALYZING

B Ask students to discuss how the miller's previous experience has affected him.

Possible Responses: He has lost money twice and is very cautious about the possibility of another loss; he does not trust his new good fortune.

Literary Analysis: THEME

C Point out the miller's intention to start a business and see how his luck changes. Ask students what theme would be shown if his luck did change.

Possible Response: A person can make his or her own luck with skill, intelligence, and hard work.

Reading Skills and Strategies:
EVALUATING

D Ask students whether they think this folktale is saying that success results from risk-taking or from a cautious approach. Have students explain.

Possible Responses: People should be cautious, as shown by the miller's example; people should take risks, because trying to save money got the miller into trouble.

---

yes, we have one exactly like this," she told the miller's wife. "My husband is willing to buy it for fifty dollars—only so we can have a pair, you understand."

"I can't sell it," the miller's wife answered. "You will have to wait until my husband returns from work."

That evening when the miller came home from work his wife told him about the offer the jeweler had made for the piece of glass.

A "But why would they offer fifty dollars for a worthless piece of glass?" the miller wondered aloud. Before his wife could answer, they were interrupted by the jeweler's wife.

"What do you say, neighbor, will you take fifty dollars for the glass?" she asked.

"No, that's not enough," the miller said cautiously. "Offer more."

"I'll give you fifty thousand!" the jeweler's wife blurted out.

"A little bit more," the miller replied.

"Impossible!" the jeweler's wife cried. "I can't offer any more without consulting my husband." She ran off to tell her husband how the <u>bartering</u> was going, and he told her he was prepared to pay a hundred thousand dollars to acquire the diamond.

He handed her seventy-five thousand dollars and said, "Take this and tell him that tomorrow, as soon as I open my shop, he'll have the rest."

When the miller heard the offer and saw the money he couldn't believe his eyes. He imagined the jeweler's wife was jesting with him, but it was a true offer, and he received the hundred thousand dollars for the diamond. The miller had never seen so much money, but he still didn't quite trust the jeweler.

"I don't know about this money," he confided to his wife. "Maybe the jeweler plans to accuse us of robbing him and thus get it back."

"Oh no," his wife assured him, "the money is ours. We sold the diamond fair and square— we didn't rob anyone."

"I think I'll still go to work tomorrow," the miller said. "Who knows, something might happen and the money will disappear, then we would be without money and work. Then how would we live?"

So he went to work the next day, and all day he thought about how he could use the money. When he returned home that afternoon, his wife asked him what he had decided to do with their new fortune.

"I think I will start my own mill," he answered, "like the one I operate for my master. Once I set up my business we'll see how our luck changes."

The next day he set about buying everything he needed to establish his mill and to build a new home. Soon he had everything going.

Six months had passed, more or less, since he had seen the two men who had given him the four hundred dollars and the piece of lead. He was eager to see them again and to tell them how the piece of lead had changed his luck and made him wealthy.

Time passed and the miller prospered. His business grew, and he even built a summer cottage where he could take his family on vacation. He had many employees who worked for him. One day while he was at his store he saw his two <u>benefactors</u> riding by. He rushed out into the street to greet them and ask them to come in. He was overjoyed to see them, and he was happy to see that they admired his store.

"Tell us the truth," the man who had given him the four hundred dollars said. "You used that money to set up this business."

| WORDS TO KNOW | **bartering** (bär′tər-ing) *n.* arguing over a price; bargaining **barter** *v.* |
| | **benefactor** (bĕn′e-făk′tər) *n.* a person who provides money or help |

858

✓ Assessment **Standardized Test Practice** TEKS 10F, 10K TAAS Reading Obj. 3

IDENTIFYING IMPLIED MAIN IDEA For some standardized tests, students will be asked to identify the implied main idea of a passage. To provide students with some help in choosing the best answer, read aloud or write on the board the following question:
Which of the following statements is the implied main idea of the highlighted paragraphs on page 858?
A. The jeweler and his wife will pay a great deal of money for the diamond.

B. The miller wonders why the glass is so desirable to the jeweler.

C. The jeweler thought he could take advantage of the miller's ignorance.

D. The eagerness of the jeweler's wife encourages the miller to bargain with her.

Lead students through the process of choosing the best answer. A, B, and C are incorrect. They are details from the paragraphs but not the main idea. D is correct. The statement expresses the main idea of all of the paragraphs.

The miller swore he hadn't, and he told them how he had given the piece of lead to his neighbor and how the fisherman had in return given him a fish with a very large diamond in its stomach. And he told them how he had sold the diamond.

"And that's how I acquired this business and many other things I want to show you," he said. "But it's time to eat. Let's eat first, then I'll show you everything I have now."

The men agreed, but one of them still doubted the miller's story. So they ate, and then the miller had three horses saddled, and they rode out to see his summer home. The cabin was on the other side of the river, where the mountains were cool and beautiful. When they arrived the men admired the place very much. It was such a peaceful place that they rode all afternoon through the forest. During their ride they came upon a tall pine tree.

"What is that on top of the tree?" one of them asked.

"That's the nest of a hawk," the miller replied.

"I have never seen one; I would like to take a closer look at it!"

"Of course," the miller said, and he ordered a servant to climb the tree and bring down the nest so his friend could see how it was built. When the hawk's nest was on the ground they examined it carefully. They noticed that there

Cargador al pie de la escalera [Porter at the foot of the stairway] (1956), Diego Rivera. Watercolor on rice paper, 15¼" × 10¾". Photo courtesy of Christie's, New York.

was a cloth bag at the bottom of the nest. When the miller saw the bag he immediately knew that it was the very same bag he had lost to the hawk which fought him for the piece of meat years ago.

"You won't believe me, friends, but this is the very same bag in which I put the first two hundred dollars you gave me," he told them.

THE FORCE OF LUCK **859**

 Viewing and Representing 🏴 **TEKS 22A**

Cargador al pie de la escalera
by Diego Rivera

ART APPRECIATION Diego Rivera (1886–1957) was one of this century's most outstanding Mexican artists, known for his love of common people. He often used his colorful, narrative painting style to express his personal political views, especially in the many murals he painted in the United States and Mexico.
Instruction Remind students that an artist chooses the perspective from which he wants his painting to be viewed. Ask students to identify the focal points in this painting.

Possible Responses: the figure and the staircase
Ask students what meaning is suggested by having the figure at the bottom of the staircase.
Possible Response: The viewer becomes aware of the immensity of the task that is before the porter.
Application Ask students how the painting symbolically represents the story of the miller.
Possible Response: Just as the porter must struggle to reach the top, so the miller had to work hard in order to achieve success.

A Ask students to predict how the story will end.

Possible Response: The miller and the two wealthy men will prove that luck is more important than wealth in achieving success.

Literary Analysis: THEME

B Ask students how the coincidences in the last part of the tale relate to the theme.

Possible Responses: The coincidences are good luck for the miller because he redeems his reputation with the wealthy man. Luck enters into all facets of a person's life. Also, the tale illustrates the real life tendency of people to have a series of fortunate or unfortunate events.

A "If it's the same bag," the man who had doubted him said, "then the money you said the hawk took should be there."

"No doubt about that," the miller said. "Let's see what we find."

The three of them examined the old, weather-beaten bag. Although it was full of holes and crumbling, when they tore it apart they found the money intact. The two men remembered what the miller had told them, and they agreed he was an honest and honorable man. Still, the man who had given him the money wasn't satisfied. He wondered what had really happened to the second two hundred he had given the miller.

They spent the rest of the day riding in the mountains and returned very late to the house.

As he unsaddled their horses, the servant in charge of grooming and feeding the horses suddenly realized that he had no grain for them. He ran to the barn and checked, but there was no grain for the hungry horses. So he ran to the neighbor's granary, and there he was able to buy a large clay jar of bran. He carried the jar home and emptied the bran into a bucket to wet it before he fed it to the horses. When he got to the bottom of the jar he noticed a large lump which turned out to be a rag-covered package. He examined it and felt something inside. He immediately went to give it to his master, who had been eating dinner.

"Master," he said, "look at this package which I found in an earthenware jar of grain which I just bought from our neighbor!"

The three men carefully unraveled the cloth and found the other one hundred and ninety dollars which the miller had told them he had lost. That is how the miller proved to his friends that he was truly an honest man.

And they had to decide for themselves whether it had been luck or money which had made the miller a wealthy man! ❖

"I am an oral storyteller, but now I do it on the printed page."

Rudolfo A. Anaya
born 1937

Rich Cultural Heritage Rudolfo Anaya was born in New Mexico where his family has lived for several generations. He grew up in a Mexican-American community noted for its storytellers. He became fascinated with the oral tradition of Spanish folktales as well as his own cross-cultural background.

Drawn to the Past Anaya is now professor emeritus of English and creative writing at the University of New Mexico. His writings draw on New Mexico's Hispanic past, and he has won many awards for both fiction and nonfiction. The *New York Times* once claimed that Anaya is the most widely read writer in Hispanic communities.

Teaching Options

 Mini Lesson **Spelling** **TEKS** 16C   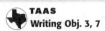 **TAAS** Writing Obj. 3, 7

PREFIXES *COM-* AND *IN-*

Instruction Explain to students that *com-* is the form of the prefix *con-* that is used before roots beginning with *b, m,* and *p. Col-* is a form of *con-* used before words beginning with *l. Con-* is added to all other roots. The prefix *in-* has four forms: *im-* before words beginning with *b, m* or *p; il-* before words beginning with *l; ir-* before words beginning with *r;* and *in-* before all other letters.

Exercises Have students rewrite the new words.

1. com + sole (*console*)
2. com + tend (*contend*)
3. in + tact (*intact*)
4. in + regular (*irregular*)
5. com + mend (*commend*)
6. com + bination (*combination*)
7. com + plicated (*complicated*)
8. in + balance (*imbalance*)
9. in + mature (*immature*)
10. in + logical (*illogical*)

Ask students to look for more words that fit this pattern, in their own writing and in stories and selections that they read, and to add these words to their personal word lists.

 Use **Unit Six Resource Book,** p. 39 for more practice.

Brother Coyote
and
Brother Cricket

by J. Frank Dobie

One summer evening about sundown a coyote trotting across the plain put his foot down on a tuft of grass wherein a cricket was singing *"Sereno en aquellos campos"*—"Serene in those fields."

The cricket jumped out and cried, "But, Brother Coyote, why are you destroying my palace?"

Illustration by Byron Gin.

861

Summary
Brother Coyote and Brother Cricket
In this tale, the coyote provokes a conflict with the cricket by destroying his house. Instead of backing down, the cricket challenges the coyote to a duel. If the cricket wins, he lives. If he loses, he will become a snack for the coyote. At the appointed time, the coyote's forces assemble on the prairie above the water tank. He has called upon all animals with claws and teeth. The cricket waits with his army in the thicket below the tank. He has assembled every creature with a stinger. General Coyote orders the fox to scout out the enemy, who has remained invisible. When the fox draws close to General Cricket's troops, a battalion of black hornets assaults him. The fox escapes by plunging into the water. He cries out to the coyote to retreat as an angry swarm of bumblebees flies overhead. Every member of the coyote's army runs, leaving General Cricket in possession of the field.

Customizing Instruction

Less Proficient Readers
Set a Purpose Have students read to find out who wins the conflict between the coyote and the cricket.

Students Acquiring English
1 Tell students that the use of *wherein* meaning "into which" sets a humorously formal tone for the tale.

Ⓜ **Multicultural Link** **Texas Folklore**

Texas folklore has been shaped by many cultures as various groups over the years have settled or influenced settlers in parts of the state. The Native Americans, Spanish, Mexicans, Anglos, African-Americans, Germans, Cajuns, Dutch, Danes, Polish, and Norwegians have contributed in some way to the body of tales, songs, and customs that comprise the folklore of Texas. This folklore is characterized by five elements, which prove its kinship to the folklore of past cultures. First, it is passed along orally or by demonstration.
For example, the creation myths of the Alabama-Coushatta Indians were communicated by word of mouth from generation to generation. Secondly, much of Texas folklore adheres to fixed forms that keep the cultural integrity. This can be seen in the dress of the cowboys and rituals connected with hunting. The third characteristic is that folklore is variable. The fourth element is the fact that it is changed by successive storytellers who remain anonymous. Lastly, Texas folklore is often set in traditional patterns. For example, events often occur in threes.

A Ask students to analyze traits of the coyote based on his initial actions and words.

Possible Response: He cares little for his fellow creatures. He uses his size to intimidate others.

Literary Analysis: PERSONIFICATION

B Ask students what personification contributes to their appreciation of this tale.

Possible Response: It adds humor and conveys the meaning effectively but in an entertaining way.

Reading Skills and Strategies: CLARIFYING

C Ask students to explain what the coyote means by these comments.

Possible Response: The coyote is confident that his superior size will quickly vanquish the cricket without any challenge.

Literary Analysis: HUMOR

D Have students explain what technique creates the humor in this folktale.

Possible Response: exaggeration

Active Reading: CONNECTING

Ask students how "Brother Coyote and Brother Cricket" might connect to one of the selections from Unit Four.

Possible Response: It could connect with the excerpt from *Boy: Tales of Childhood.* Brother Coyote, like Mrs. Pratchett, never expected to be "attacked" by small, seemingly insignificant creatures.

"I really did not know you lived here until you exposed yourself," the coyote said.

"You are <u>crude</u> and you insult me," the cricket said. He was ready to spring away.

A **1** "Insult you!" the coyote jeered. "Why, you dwarf, I am merely seeking my living, and now that I have you, I am going to eat you up. I had rather have a red watermelon or a fat kid, but I eat a cricket or a grasshopper when it's handy. Maybe you will fill the hollow in one of my molars."

"But, Brother Coyote," the cricket said, now in his soothing way, "it is not fair."

The coyote sat down on the carpet of grass. **B** "Brother Cricket," he said, "you know that when nature offers itself, it is fair for nature to accept."

"But, Brother Coyote, you haven't given me a chance."

"Chance?" exclaimed the coyote. "Why, what sort of chance do you expect?"

"I want to fight a duel."

"You fight a duel with me?" And the coyote laughed.

"Yes, fight a duel with you," the cricket said. "If I win, then my song will go on. If you win, then I'll fill the hollow in one of your respectable teeth."

2 The coyote looked away off across the plain, and saw a crow flying down in play at the waving tail of a striped skunk. "Well," he said, "perhaps the people need a comedy. All right, we'll have your duel, Brother Cricket."

C "Oh, thank you very much, Brother Coyote."

"Now I sit here trembling at the sight of your armor and weapons," the coyote said. "But go on and name your terms."

"It is agreed," said the cricket. "You go and get your army together, and I will go and get my army together. Tomorrow when the sun is straight overhead, you have your army on the prairie just above the water called the Tank of the Seven Coons, and I will have my army in the thicket in the draw just below the dam to this tank. On the hour we shall engage in mortal combat."

"That is clear, General Cricket," said the coyote. "Until tomorrow at high noon, *adiós.*"

"*Adiós,* General Coyote."

That night General Coyote went east and west, north and south, summoning in high voice his forces to gather on the prairie above the Tank of the Seven Coons. He summoned the lobo, the badger, the tiger of the deep canyon, the panther of the rimrock, the wildcat of the chaparral, the coon, the possum, the sharp fox, and all the other people with claws and teeth.

And in a singsong General Cricket summoned his forces—the horseflies, the mosquitoes, the honey bees, the bumblebees, the yellow jackets, the black hornets, and even a colony of red ants—all the people that have stingers and can stick. He told them to gather in the thicket in the draw below the Tank of the Seven Coons.

Long before high noon, the people of fang and claw were assembling on the prairie above the water tank. General Coyote was trotting about, looking this way and that way, smelling and listening. The sun stood straight up, and still he could not see one sign of General Cricket's army.

Finally he called the fox and ordered him to scout out the position of the enemy. With his long nose pointed ahead, his ears alert and his eyes peeled, the fox went trotting down the draw. General Coyote was watching him. When he came to the edge of the thicket, the

WORDS
TO   **crude** (krŏŏd) *adj.* lacking tact or good manners
KNOW

862

 Speaking and Listening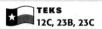

TEKS
12C, 23B, 23C

COMPARISON OF DIFFERENT MEDIA

Prepare Tell students that watching a storyteller perform allows the audience to see gestures and facial expressions and hear changes in the storyteller's voice, which emphasize the importance of details or add to the emotional impact of the words. The effectiveness of the written version of the tale depends upon the ability of the writer to bring the characters and events to life through description and dialogue so that the reader can visualize what is happening. Have students compare the performance video of "Brother Coyote and

Brother Cricket" and J. Frank Dobie's written version. Students should establish areas of comparison such as stylistic devices, character, plot, setting, and theme as well as overall effectiveness. Have students organize their ideas into a presentation.

Present Have students present their comparisons. Audience members should write down points with which they agree or disagree for general discussion after the presentations.

BLOCK SCHEDULING This activity is particularly well suited for longer class periods.

fox flattened to the ground and began twisting into the brush. Just as he was poking his keen snout into a clump of whitebrush to see and smell more closely, General Cricket ordered a battalion[1] of black hornets to <u>assault</u> him.

They did, all at once. They stuck their stingers into his ears, into the corners of his eyes, into his nostrils, into his flanks, into every spot of his body where hair is short and skin is tender. He snapped and pitched, but only for a minute. He turned seventeen somersaults on the ground, and the black hornets came thicker. Then he streaked for the tank of water. He dived to escape his assaulters, and went to the bottom.

But in a minute he had to come back up for air. Then, sticking his long, long mouth out of the water, he cried at the top of his voice, "General Coyote, retreat! The enemy are upon us!"

General Cricket had already ordered the yellow jackets to attack the army of giants on the prairie, and the war cries of the bumblebees were in the air.

"Retreat!" the fox shrieked again.

General Coyote tucked his tail between his legs and retreated and every soldier in the army tucked his tail and retreated also—all except the bobcat. He retreated without tucking his tail. That is how General Cricket won the duel with General Coyote.

Thus a person should avoid being <u>vainglorious</u> and considering himself shrewder than he is. He may be outwitted by his own vanity. ❖

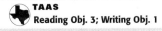
4

---

1. **battalion:** a large body of organized troops.

"One day it came to me that I would collect and tell the legendary tales of Texas . . . "

J. Frank Dobie
1888–1964

Texan by Birth J[ames] Frank Dobie was born on a ranch in Live Oak County, Texas and lived in his native state most of his life. In college, Dobie planned to study law but instead developed a passion for literature and the classics. Dobie was in his forties when his first major novel, *A Vaquero of the Brush Country,*

was published in 1929. His second work, *Coronado's Children*, gained him popular attention.

Texan by Choice Much of Dobie's writing focuses on the folklore of the Southwest, and was inspired by his friendships with cowboys, miners, and other talespinners. In 1939 he began a weekly newspaper column, originally called "My Texas" which ran until his death. He wrote over 25 books—including *A Texan in England*, which was inspired by the year he spent lecturing at Cambridge University. Dobie won numerous awards, including the Boys Club of America Junior Book Award.

WORDS TO KNOW
assault (ə-sôlt') *v.* to attack
vainglorious (vān-glôr'ē-əs) *adj.* vain and boastful

863

Customizing Instruction

Less Proficient Readers
Ask students to describe the members of each army.
Possible Responses: The coyote has assembled animals with teeth and claws such as the badger, lobo, panther, possum, and fox. The cricket has enlisted the help of the creatures who sting such as the hornets, horseflies, mosquitoes, and bees.
• Who wins the duel?
  Answer: the cricket

Students Acquiring English
1 Explain that a *kid* is a baby goat.
2 Be sure that students appreciate the irony of the coyote's remarks. He is making fun of the cricket.
3 Tell students that the saying "eyes peeled" means "to be very observant."
4 Help students to understand that the expression "tail between the legs" indicates a sense of shame. In this situation, the animals tucking their tails between their legs prevents them from being stung on tender parts of their body.

Gifted and Talented
Ask students to analyze the effect of the setting upon the tale.
Possible Responses: The setting emphasizes the harshness of existence and the need for wit and wisdom to ensure survival against those who have more power or strength or influence; it reminds the listener or reader that even the most minute creature has some quality that can be used to advantage; a battlefield configuration enhances the universality of the tale by being interpreted metaphorically as any situation in which someone faces an obstacle or antagonist.

 Assessment **Informal Assessment**   TEKS 10G TAAS Reading Obj. 3; Writing Obj. 1

SUMMARIZING You can informally assess your students' understanding of the selection by having them write a review of the tale for people who have never read it. The first part of their review must include a summary of the main ideas of "Brother Coyote and Brother Cricket." Students may then follow the summary with comments on the plot, character, style, or theme.

RUBRIC

3 Full Accomplishment Responses are written in the students' own words and include all of the main ideas in chronological order.

2 Substantial Accomplishment Responses include most of the main ideas and approximate the order of the original tale. Most ideas are paraphrased.

1 Little or Partial Accomplishment Summaries omit important ideas and lack a logical order.

LITERATURE CONNECTION

Write a Texas Folk Tale Guide students to find information about the topography and animals of the region they choose before they begin to plot their stories. Suggest that they use a story map to help them outline the conflicts, characters, and setting of their stories once they have obtained the necessary information.

RUBRIC

3 Full Accomplishment Responses skillfully weave the details about Texas into the setting, characters, and action of the story. The story is cohesive and entertaining.

2 Substantial Accomplishment Responses include many references to the particular region of Texas and develop the elements of fiction with some conviction.

1 Little or Partial Accomplishment Responses have little information about Texas and lack adequate development.

Use **Reading and Critical Thinking Transparencies** p. 15, for additional support.

SCIENCE CONNECTION

Create a Science Exhibit Suggest that students begin by making a list of questions they want to have answered. Students may want to add music to their audiovisual display. Encourage students to describe aspects of the sun in terms of familiar things–for example, the size of the sun in relation to the size of the earth.

RUBRIC

3 Full Accomplishment Students gather pertinent information and present facts in an original format.

2 Substantial Accomplishment Students find some information about the sun but have difficulty creating an audiovisual display.

1 Little or Partial Accomplishment Students have difficulty gathering facts about the sun and cannot create an audiovisual display.

Use **Writing Transparencies** p. 40, for additional support.

Interdisciplinary Projects

LITERATURE CONNECTION

Write a Texas Folk Tale The story "Brother Coyote and Brother Cricket" names many animals that can be found in Texas. Write a short story set in one of Texas's four major regions: the Coastal Plains, the North-Central Plains, the Great Plains, and the Mountains and Basins region. As you write your story, place yourself as an animal character in the story and include personal observations and questions about traveling in that part of Texas.

More Online: Research Starter
www.mcdougallittell.com

SCIENCE CONNECTION

Create a Science Exhibit In the Greek myth "Phaëthon," four fire-breathing horses gallop across the heavens with Apollo's sun chariot, scorching the earth and endangering life on our planet. Working in pairs or in a small group, compile a list of facts that solar astronomers have discovered about the sun, including its size, distance from the earth, approximate temperatures at the center and at the surface, composition, diameter, and movement. Find out how much closer the sun would need to be to destroy all life on earth. Consult books, magazines, encyclopedias, and CD-ROMs to find information. If possible, visit a planetarium and talk to an astronomer. Then make an audio-visual display to share your sun facts with the rest of the class.

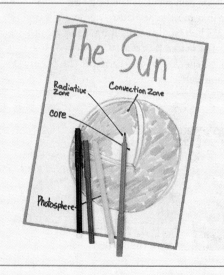

SOCIAL STUDIES CONNECTION

Complete a Sequence Chart A large Hispanic population lives in the southwestern United States, a part of the nation that once belonged to Spain and was a part of Mexico. In 1846, the United States invaded Mexico. The war ended when the Senate ratified the Treaty of Guadalupe Hidalgo in 1848. Find out more about the Mexican-American War. Record the milestones in a sequence chart like the one shown below. Your chart will need more boxes than the one here. End the chart with the Treaty of Guadalupe Hidalgo.

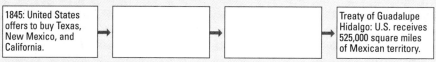

SOCIAL STUDIES CONNECTION

Complete a Sequence Chart Guide students to consult authoritative references on the Mexican-American War, including encyclopedias, history texts, and on-line computer sources. Before they begin to construct their flow charts, suggest that students synthesize what they have read by making a list of key events to include in their charts.

RUBRIC

3 Full Accomplishment The chart correctly records, in chronological order, the key events in the Mexican-American War.

2 Substantial Accomplishment The chart includes most of the events, but some events are missing or out of order.

1 Little or Partial Accomplishment The chart does not show the main events in order.

Use **Reading and Critical Thinking Transparencies** p. 39, for additional support.

Across Cultures

COMPARING TEXTS **Compare Characters**
Compare and contrast the main character in
"The Highwayman," page 564, and Phaëthon,
the main character in "Phaëthon." Like most of
the characters in the stories in this link, they
were obliged to respond to challenge and
change. Begin by listing the qualities of each
character. Then record their similarities and
differences in a chart like the one shown.

The Highwayman and Phaëthon	
Similarities	Differences

Create a Board Game Create a board game
based on one of the tales you just read. Make a
list of rules, including the object of the game and
how many players can play. Design the board
game and the playing pieces. Have a group of
your classmates play your game with you.

Write a Persuasive Essay In "The Force of
Luck" two friends have an argument. One friend
thinks that it is luck that elevates a person to a
high position. The other believes that it is money
that moves a person to a higher status. What do
you think? Write a persuasive essay with
examples that support your opinion.

Record a News Report Suppose you are a
news correspondent sent out to report on the
battle scene in "Brother Coyote and Brother
Cricket." Tape-record a play-by-play account as if
you really witnessed the event.

Vocabulary in Action

EXERCISE: RELATED WORDS Write the letter of the word that is not related
to the other words.

1. (a) agree (b) contend (c) accept (d) confirm
2. (a) protect (b) save (c) squander (d) economize
3. (a) satisfaction (b) pleasure (c) joy (d) anguish
4. (a) bartering (b) ignoring (c) bargaining (d) trading
5. (a) benefactor (b) enemy (c) aide (d) supporter
6. (a) home (b) abode (c) house (d) pathway
7. (a) ignore (b) avoid (c) acknowledge (d) deny
8. (a) refined (b) perfect (c) elegant (d) crude
9. (a) assist (b) assault (c) attack (d) strike
10. (a) humble (b) conceited (c) vainglorious (d) boastful

WORDS TO KNOW	abode acknowledge	anguish assault	bartering benefactor	contend crude	squander vainglorious

---

Across Cultures
COMPARING TEXTS

Compare Characters To get students
started on this assignment, have them
review the poem "The Highwayman"
from Unit Four. Direct students to provide evidence from the text for the
qualities they ascribe to each character
and to make inferences about unstated
motivations of each character.

Use **Literary Analysis Transparencies,**
p. 3, for additional support.

Create a Board Game If students have
the technological expertise, they may
wish to create a computer game for
one of the tales. **To make this assignment easier,** have students adapt an
already existing game, substituting
game pieces, obstacles, and goals but
using the same rules.

Write a Persuasive Essay To get students started on this assignment, have
them brainstorm ideas on both sides of
the question and choose the view for
which they have the most support.
Encourage students to find real life
examples in newspapers or magazines
that back up what they believe. **To
extend this assignment,** have students
poll a number of people and tabulate
their results in bar graphs that they can
use to defend their opinion.

Use **Reading and Critical Thinking
Transparencies** p. 31, for additional
support.

Record a News Report Remind students that a news report must be accurate even while conveying the atmosphere at the scene for the listeners or
viewers. Students may wish to interview participants in the battle, onlookers, or one of the generals.

Vocabulary in Action

EXERCISE
Answers:
1. b
2. c
3. d
4. b
5. b
6. d
7. c
8. d
9. a
10. a

Use **Unit Six Resource Book,**
p. 37, for additional practice. Use **Unit
Six Resource Book,** p. 40 for assessment.

Objectives

1. understand and appreciate a myth and two folktales about characters who take on challenges
2. appreciate the cultures of Scandinavia, Southeast Asia, and Kenya
3. extend understanding of the selections through a variety of multimodal and cross-curricular activities

Reading Pathways

- Select one or several students to read each tale aloud to the entire class or to small groups of students. Assign this reading in advance so that the readers can incorporate into their presentations some of the techniques used by professional storytellers. Have the audience listen carefully to the tales without following along in their texts.

- Read the tales aloud to the class, pausing at key points to discuss how elements of the tale inform students about the customs of the cultures. Have students compare these customs with those of their own culture and region. Have students record their responses and observations in their notebooks.

- After students have read the tales once, they can read them again to identify structural elements such as main characters, minor characters, conflict, setting, and plot. Then have students identify similarities and differences between these tales and the selections in the related unit. For example, have students compare the qualities that the narrator in "Barrio Boy" needs to face his challenges with those that Kelfala possesses in "Kelfala's Secret Something."

5-Minute Warm-Up

Daily Language SkillBuilder **TEKS 17D, 17F**

Have students **proofread** the display sentences on page 793e and write them correctly. The sentences also appear on Transparency 26 of **Grammar Transparencies and Copymasters.**

 See the Skills Trace at the beginning of the unit for information on TEKS covered in this lesson.

LINKS TO UNIT FIVE

Personal Challenges

Often when a personal challenge is great, so too are the rewards for success and the penalties for failure. In the tales you are about to read, characters face personal challenges that test their inner strength. These characters and the challenges they face relate closely to similar characters and challenges in Unit Five.

KENYA

Kelfala's Secret Something

retold by Adjai Robinson

The Kikuyu are the largest ethnic group in Kenya, a nation in east-central Africa. The Kikuyu are predominantly farmers who have a strong work ethic. Among the Kikuyu, the traditions and instructions of parents and elders are binding, almost like laws. Arranged marriages are the custom in this society that forms the backdrop of "Kelfala's Secret Something."

LESSON RESOURCES

UNIT SIX RESOURCE BOOK, pp. 41–47

ASSESSMENT
Formal Assessment, pp. 133–134
Teacher's Guide to Assessment and Portfolio Use
Test Generator

SKILLS TRANSPARENCIES AND COPYMASTERS
Grammar
- Demonstrative Adjectives, CM 81 (for Mini Lesson, p. 872)
- Comparison of Adjectives, CM 82 (for Mini Lesson, p. 879)

Communications
- Verbal Strategies, TR 14; Nonverbal Strategies, TR 15 (for Mini Lesson, p. 875)

- Dramatic Reading, TR 12 (for Mini Lesson, p. 876)
- Interviewing, TR 9 (for Mini Lesson, p. 880)

INTEGRATED TECHNOLOGY
Audio Library
Internet: Research Starter

Visit our website:
www.mcdougallittell.com

How Odin Lost His Eye

retold by Catharine F. Sellew

Scandinavia is the name given to a group of countries in northern Europe that includes Norway, Sweden, and Denmark. In these countries much of the land away from the seas is covered with snow. According to Norse (Scandinavian) mythology, the giant tree that supports all creation has three roots. One of the roots extends to a misty underworld. Another goes to Asgard (ăs'gärd), the heavenly realm where the gods dwell. The third root reaches Jötunheim (yō'tən-hīm'), the icy realm of the frost giants. From his throne in Asgard, Odin, the mightiest Norse god, keeps watch on all the lands of creation.

SCANDINAVIA
NORWAY
SWEDEN
DENMARK

SOUTHEAST ASIA
LAOS
VIETNAM
THAILAND
KENYA

AS YOU READ . . .

Note which behaviors are viewed as virtuous in each culture and how they are rewarded.

Note which behaviors are viewed as negative.

Identify the message about love that each culture conveys.

Decide whether or not the challenge each character faces is worth the end result.

SOUTHEAST ASIA

Pumpkin Seed and the Snake

retold by Norma J. Livo and Dia Cha

The Hmong (hmông) people live in the mountains of Vietnam, Thailand, and Laos. Since they did not develop a written language until the 1950s, they relied on strong oral and artistic traditions—such as pieces of cloth with elaborate needlework—to pass their cultural traditions from generation to generation. After the Vietnam War, many Hmong emigrated to the United States.

LINKS TO UNIT FIVE **867**

Summary

How Odin Lost His Eye This Norse myth tells about Odin, king of gods and creator of the world. Having made men and women, he wants to protect them from evil frost giants. Odin leaves his throne and descends to earth to learn more about the frost giants. He visits a well whose surface reflects images of the past and future–but only to those who have sipped its water. The old man in charge of the well, Mimir, warns Odin that he will have to pay a great price in order to drink the water. Odin resolves to make any sacrifice necessary to save humankind. When the old man asks for one of Odin's eyes, the god plucks it out and hands it over. He then drinks deeply of the water and sees that the future holds sorrow and death, redeemed by promise at the end. As for his eye, it settles at the bottom of Mimir's well as a reminder of Odin's great sacrifice.

Reading and Analyzing

Literary Analysis: PLOT

 Have students explain why frost giants might be central to the plot of a Scandinavian legend. What might they represent in this northern culture?

Possible Response: Frost giants represent the cold–the threat in northern climates.

Use **Unit Six Resource Book,** p. 43 for additional practice.

Active Reading: EVALUATING

 Ask students if they think Odin would be a good leader, based on this passage.

Possible Response: Yes. He is wise, courageous, and farseeing.

Use **Unit Six Resource Book,** p. 42 for additional practice.

Teaching Options

HOW ODIN LOST HIS EYE

RETOLD BY CATHARINE F. SELLEW

Odin astride Sleipnir. Illumination from *Poetic Edda* in a 13th-century Icelandic manuscript, The Granger Collection, New York.

Once when the world was still very young, Odin sat on his throne in the most beautiful palace in Asgard. His throne was so high that he could see over all three parts of the world from where he sat. On his head he wore a helmet shaped like an eagle. On his shoulders perched two black ravens called Memory and Thought. And at his feet crouched two snarling wolves.

The great king gazed thoughtfully down on the earth below him. He had made the green land that stretched out before his eyes. With the help of the other gods he had made men and women who lived on that earth. And he

 Viewing and Representing **TEKS 22A**

Odin Astride Sleipnir

ART APPRECIATION The *Poetic Edda,* or *Elder Edda* as it is also called, is a collection of verses, which originated centuries before they were recorded around A.D. 1270. There are mythological poems, telling of the Norse gods, and heroic poems, celebrating the lives of traditional Germanic heroes.

Instruction Tell students that Sleipnir is Odin's eight-footed horse. According to Norse mythology, a giant was to build the gods a fortress and receive in return Freyja, goddess of love, as well as the sun and the moon. He was helped by his powerful stallion. Just as he was about to complete his task, Loki, who sometimes helped the gods, changed himself into a mare to distract the giant's stallion so the gods would not have to honor their bargain with the giant. Sleipnir was the offspring of the stallion and Loki.

Ask students how the artist has suggested Odin's identity and power in this illustration.

Possible Response: He is without an eye and is carrying a powerful weapon.

felt truly like the All-father he was called.

The fair elves had promised they would help his children of the earth. The elves were the tiny people who lived between heaven and earth. They were so small that they could flit about doing their work unseen. Odin knew that they were the artists who painted the flowers and made the beds for the streams. They took care of all the bees and the butterflies. And it was the elves who brought the gentle rain and sunshine to the earth.

Even the ugly dwarfs, who lived in the heart of the mountains, agreed to help. They <u>forged</u> iron and metals, made tools and weapons. They dug gold and silver and beautiful jewels out of the earth. Sometimes they even cut the grain and ground the flour for the farmers on the earth.

All seemed to be going well. Odin found it hard to think of evil times. But he knew that the frost giants were only waiting for a chance to bring trouble to his children. They were the ones who brought cold and ice to the world and shook the earth in anger. They hated Odin and all the work of the gods.

And from high on his throne Odin looked down beyond the earth deep into the gloomy land of his enemies. He saw dark figures of huge men moving about. They looked like evil shadows. He, the king of the gods, must have more wisdom. It was not enough just to see his enemies. He must know more about them.

So Odin wrapped his tall figure in a blue cloak. Down from his throne he climbed. Down the broad rainbow bridge he strode and across the green earth till he came to one of the roots of the great evergreen tree. There, close by the tree, was a well full of clear water. Its surface was so still it was like a mirror. In it one could see pictures of things that had happened and things that were going to happen.

But beside the well sat an old man. His face was lined with the troubles of the world. His name was Mimir, which means "memory." No one, not even the great Odin, could see the pictures in the well unless he first drank some of its water. Only Mimir could give the magic drink.

"Aged Mimir," Odin said to the old man, "you who hold the knowledge of the past and future in your magic waters, let me have but one sip. Then I can know enough to protect the men and women of the earth from the hate of the giants."

Mimir looked kindly at Odin, but he did not smile. Although he spoke softly, his voice was so deep it reminded Odin of the distant roar of the ocean.

"The price of one drink from this well is not cheap," Mimir said. "And once you have drunk and gazed into the mirror of life, you may wish you had not. For sorrow and death as well as joy are pictured there. Think again before you ask to drink."

But once the king of the gods had made up his mind, nothing could change it. He was not afraid to look upon sorrow and death.

"What is your price, aged Mimir?" Odin asked.

"You are great and good, Odin," answered Mimir. "You have worked hard to make the world. Only those who know hard work may drink from my well. However, that is not enough. What have you given up that is very dear to you? What have you <u>sacrificed</u>? The price of a drink must be a great sacrifice. Are you still willing to pay the price?"

What could the king of the gods sacrifice? What was most dear to him? Odin thought of his handsome son, Balder, whom he loved most in the world. To give up his son would be like giving up life and all that was

WORDS TO KNOW
forge (fôrj) v. to shape metal by heating it and pounding on it with a hammer
sacrifice (săk′rə-fīs′) v. to give up something highly valued for the sake of something or someone more valued

869

 Mini Lesson **Spelling** **TEKS** 16D **TAAS** Writing Obj. 3, 7

WORDS WITH *J*, *GE*, AND *DGE*

Instruction Tell students that the *j* sound can be spelled *j* (as in justice), *ge* (as in urge), and *dge* (as in judge). The letter *j* occurs at the beginning and in the middle of words. The letters *ge* occur at the end of words. The letters *dge* are used only in one-syllable words with short vowels. Point out some of the words that follow this pattern in the selection. (*forged, aged, joy, edge*)

Exercises Have students spell the following words as you dictate them.

1. conjunction
2. rejoice
3. huge
4. bridge
5. jewels
6. courage
7. ledge
8. marriage
9. journal
10. oblige

Ask students to look for more words that fit this pattern, in their own writing and in things that they read, and to add these words to their personal word lists.

 Use **Unit Six Resource Book,** p. 46 for more practice.

Reading Skills and Strategies:
SPECULATING

A Ask students to speculate why Mimir does not request that Odin sacrifice his son.

Possible Response: He knows that Odin would do it in order to save the world so he has no need to force Odin to suffer the loss. Odin's son may have a role to play that is not fulfilled.

Literary Analysis: SYMBOL

B Ask students what Odin gains from the loss of his eye.

Possible Response: Odin gains insight with the sacrifice of his physical ability to see clearly.

Literary Analysis: THEME

C Ask students what warning this myth sends to readers.

Possible Response: Knowledge cannot be gained without sacrifice and struggle.

Reading Skills and Strategies:
CONNECTING

Ask students to connect "How Odin Lost His Eye" with one of the selections from Unit Five.

Possible Response: Odin is comparable to Nelson Mandela in the selection from *Long Walk to Freedom,* in that both characters made profound sacrifices to attain a greater good.

---

wonderful around him. Odin stood silent before Mimir. Indeed that would be a high price!

Then Mimir spoke again. He had read Odin's thoughts.

A "No, I am not asking for your dear son. The Fates[1] say his life must be short, but he has time yet to live and bring happiness to the gods and the world. I ask for one of your eyes."

din put his hands up to his bright blue eyes. Those two eyes had gazed across the world from his high throne in the shining city of the gods. His eyes had taught him what was good and beautiful, what was evil and ugly. But those eyes had also seen his children, the men and women of the earth, struggling against the hate of the giants. One eye was a small sacrifice to win knowledge of how to help them. And without another

thought, Odin plucked out one of his blue eyes and handed it to Mimir.

Then Mimir smiled and gave Odin a horn full of the waters of his well.

"Drink deeply, brave king, so you may see all that you wish in the mirror of life."

Odin lifted the horn to his lips and drank. Then he knelt by the edge of the well and watched the pictures passing across its still and silent surface. When he stood up again, he sighed, for it was as Mimir had said. He had seen sorrow and death as well as joy. It was only the glorious promise at the end that gave him courage to go on.

So Odin, the great king of the gods, became one-eyed. If you can find Mimir's well, you will see Odin's blue eye resting on the bottom. It is there to remind men and women of the great sacrifice he made for them. ❖

---

1. **Fates:** goddesses who decide the course of people's lives.

Catharine F. Sellew
1922–1982

Myth Lover As a child, Catharine Sellew loved to listen as her mother read myths. Sellew later studied mythology and published a collection of

Greek myths, *Adventures with the Gods*. She also retold Norse myths in *Adventures with the Giants* and *Adventures with the Heroes*.

A SKILLED WRITER
Sellew also retold stories from the Old Testament and wrote a novel for teenagers, entitled *Torchlight*.

Teaching Options

 ✓ Assessment **Informal Assessment** 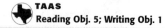 TEKS 10H · TAAS Reading Obj. 5; Writing Obj. 1

MAKE INFERENCES AND DRAW CONCLUSIONS You can informally assess students' ability to make inferences based on textual evidence by having them write the thoughts and reaction that Odin would have had if Mimir had asked him to sacrifice his son for knowledge. Students' responses should maintain the point of view used in the text.

RUBRIC

3 Full Accomplishment Responses show a clear understanding of Odin's character and offer a convincing reaction to the proposal.

2 Substantial Accomplishment Responses reflect some of Odin's traits and show a reaction to the proposal.

1 Little or Partial Accomplishment Inaccurate inferences about Odin's thoughts and feelings are made, and no conclusion is drawn.

PUMPKIN SEED AND THE SNAKE

RETOLD BY NORMA J. LIVO AND DIA CHA

Summary

Pumpkin Seed and the Snake A widow and her daughters, named Pumpkin Vine and Pumpkin Seed, come upon a boulder in their garden. The widow says to herself that if someone can remove the rock, she will let him marry one of her daughters. When the rock disappears the next day, the widow says she was only joking. This happens two more times. After the widow makes her promise a fourth time, a snake says he will remove the rock if she promises not to lie anymore. The widow agrees, and the snake throws the rock into a river and follows her home. When the daughters hear what has happened, they at first refuse to open the door. Finally, when the mother whispers that she will kill the snake when it falls asleep, Pumpkin Seed agrees to marry it. Three times, the widow discovers a handsome young man–instead of a snake–sleeping beside Pumpkin Seed and cannot kill him. Each morning, however, the snake reappears. On the fourth day, Pumpkin Seed must go with the snake to his home. On their way, they come to a stream. The snake tells Pumpkin Seed that she will see colorful bubbles pouring down the stream, and that she should avoid the green ones. While he is gone, she scoops up green bubbles. They turn into twisting snakes that stick to her hands. Moments later, a handsome young man appears and reveals that he is her husband. When he blows on her hands, the snakes fall off.

Customizing Instruction

Less Proficient Readers
Set a Purpose Ask students to read to find out whom Pumpkin Seed marries.

 Viewing and Representing

 TEKS 22B, 23A

Detail from a pa ndau

ART APPRECIATION Pa ndau refers to cloths with intricate needlework created by the Hmong. The use of the cloth determines which symbols adorn it. Because the Hmong have been discouraged by their oppressors throughout the years from developing a written language, it is believed by some that pa ndau artwork may have been used at times to record history and to relay messages in a way that would not be understood by outsiders.
Instruction Have students look at the various colors used by the artist in this pa ndau. Ask students what color represents water.

Answer: white
Ask students how the artist indicates which animals are the same breed.
Possible Response: The same color thread is used for animals of the same breed.
Application Ask students what they can infer about the society of the Hmong from the story and this pa ndau.
Possible Responses: The Hmong are close to the land and use its resources to support their economy. They have a respect for nature.

Literary Analysis: FOLKTALE

 Ask students how the language of the opening shows the influence of the oral tradition.

Possible Response: It is simple, rhythmic, and easy to understand. This would make it easy to remember and retell.

Reading Skills and Strategies: PREDICTING

 Invite students to predict what will happen as a result of the widow's comment.

Possible Response: Someone will come to remove the rock and claim one of her daughters.

Reading Skills and Strategies: CONNECTING

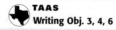 Ask students to use their own experience to comprehend how the daughters feel about their mother's request. Have students discuss how they react when an adult or parent asks them to do something they really don't want to do.

Reading Skills and Strategies: ANALYZING

D Ask students why the widow, who didn't hesitate to break her promise before, now is so anxious to honor her agreement with the snake.

Possible Responses: She realizes that he is no ordinary snake; she is afraid of his power.

Literary Analysis: SUSPENSE

E Ask students to describe the effect of the widow's repeated attempts and failures to kill the snake.

Possible Response: The repetition and delay build excitement and suspense, stimulating readers' interest in finding out what will happen.

"IF SOMEONE COULD REMOVE THIS ROCK FROM THE MIDDLE OF MY GARDEN I WOULD LET HIM MARRY ONE OF MY DAUGHTERS."

A Once long ago, in another time and place, in a small village, there lived a widow and her two daughters. The older daughter was named Pumpkin Vine and the younger one was named Pumpkin Seed.

The family had a garden near the river. They had to work hard to prepare the field for the coming growing season. But they had a problem, because in the middle of the garden was a huge boulder. One day as she was working around the rock, the widow said to herself, B "If someone could remove this rock from the middle of my garden I would let him marry one of my daughters."

At the end of the day, the family went home. The next day, the three women went back to work in the garden and found that the rock was gone! The widow started to laugh and said out loud, "I was only joking. I wouldn't allow either of my daughters to marry whoever removed that rock." The widow thought that was the last of the giant rock. But the next day when the widow and her daughters went back to the field to work, there was the rock, in its original place in the middle of the garden.

Once more the widow said to herself, "If someone would take this rock from the middle of the field I would let him marry one of my daughters."

The next day the rock was gone again, but the widow said, "I did not mean it. I wouldn't allow either of my daughters to marry whoever removed that rock," as she laughed.

The next morning the rock was back in its spot, and the widow again promised one of her daughters in marriage to the person who could remove the rock.

Just like the other times, the rock disappeared from the field and the widow again teased, "I did not mean it. I wouldn't allow either of my daughters to marry the person who moved the rock."

The next morning the widow went to the field alone and found the rock back in its place. Giggling a little, the widow whispered, "If someone would take this rock from the middle of the field I would let him marry one of my daughters."

This time, a snake that was nearby said, "If you promise not to lie anymore I will remove the rock."

The widow was so startled that she promised not to lie anymore. The snake slithered from the edge of the garden, laced his tail around the rock, and threw it into the river. Since the widow's two daughters hadn't come to the field with her, the snake followed the widow home.

When they got home the widow called from outside to her daughters. She told them what had happened and said that one of them would

---

Teaching Options

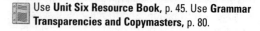 Mini Lesson **Grammar** TEKS 17D TAAS Writing Obj. 3, 4, 6

DEMONSTRATIVE ADJECTIVES

Instruction Write the words *this, that, these,* and *those* on the board. Explain to students that when these words are used as modifiers, they are called demonstrative adjectives. They must agree in number with the noun they modify: *this* and *that* modify singular nouns; *these* and *those* modify plural nouns. Show students the following:

Singular I like this folktale. Did you read that story?

Plural These stories are great! Those stories are better.

Exercises Have students select the correct adjective in the following sentences.

1. We read (<u>this</u>, these) story about a snake.
2. (Those, <u>This</u>) kind of story is a folktale.
3. (<u>These</u>, That) stories involve magic.
4. The storytellers passed (that, <u>these</u>) tales from generation to generation.

Use **Unit Six Resource Book**, p. 45. Use **Grammar Transparencies and Copymasters**, p. 80.

 Use McDougal Littell's *Language Network*, Chapter 5, for more instruction and practice in demonstrative adjectives.

IT WAS NOT AN UGLY SNAKE SLEEPING BESIDE PUMPKIN SEED, BUT THE MOST HANDSOME YOUNG MAN THAT SHE HAD EVER SEEN.

have to marry the snake. Pumpkin Vine and Pumpkin Seed didn't want to marry the snake. They refused to open the door and let the snake into the house.

The snake and the widow waited and waited until it was dark, but the girls wouldn't open the door. Then the mother whispered through the door to her daughters, "I will kill the snake when he falls asleep." Even though her mother had said this would work, Pumpkin Vine, being the older one, still refused to open the door. It was very dark outside by this time. Pumpkin Seed, on the other hand, thought that things would go as easily as her mother said, so she opened the door.

When the snake got into the house, Pumpkin Vine and Pumpkin Seed were frightened by its huge size and ugly shininess. Pumpkin Vine protested bitterly when her mother asked her to marry the snake. The widow finally convinced Pumpkin Seed to marry the snake. The snake followed Pumpkin Seed wherever she went. It curled up beside her feet when she sat down. When she went to bed, the snake slid into her bed and coiled up beside her.

That night, with a sharp knife in one hand and a candle in the other, the widow crept into Pumpkin Seed's bedroom to kill the snake. But she discovered it was not an ugly snake sleeping beside Pumpkin Seed, but the most handsome young man that she had ever seen. She couldn't kill him.

The next day when Pumpkin Seed woke up, the snake was still alive. She cried and demanded to know why her mother hadn't kept her promise and killed it. "I'll kill the snake tonight, Pumpkin Seed. Please trust me," begged the widow.

That night, the snake again slid into Pumpkin Seed's bed and coiled up beside her. The widow came into the room with her sharp knife and the candle and crept up to the bed to kill the snake. Again, though, instead of an ugly snake sleeping beside Pumpkin Seed, it was the handsome young man. Once more, she just couldn't kill him.

The next morning Pumpkin Seed woke up and there the snake was in her bed, still alive. She cried and cried and demanded to know

PUMPKIN SEED AND THE SNAKE **873**

 Multicultural Link

Hmong Culture

"Pumpkin Seed and the Snake" comes from the culture of the Hmong people of Southeast Asia. The Hmong see many animals as possessing symbolic power. The snake, central to this story, is a key symbol. For example, a snake entering the house is a sign that someone in the family may soon die. A bird flying into the house is also an evil portent. Bears and tigers are especially feared. People's souls are thought to be imprisoned in tigers under special circumstances.

A magic soul-tiger is recognized by its five toes; real tigers have only four toes. Elephants are considered a good sign, greatly respected for their strength. The Hmong avoid saying anything bad about these creatures to make sure they do not come and damage the family's property. The rooster is believed to awaken the sun in the morning; the crab shields the opening to the sky that allows floods to cover the earth. Tortoises bring advice from the spirit world to the living.

Literary Analysis: PLOT

A Remind students of the frequency with which events occur in sets of three in folktales. Ask students to predict what will happen after the widow fails to kill the snake for the third time.

Possible Response: There will be a new plot development–the widow may be rewarded or Pumpkin Seed will have to live with the snake forever.

Active Reading: EVALUATING

B Have students evaluate Pumpkin Seed's actions in this passage. Ask students why she disobeys the snake and what the consequences might be.

Possible Responses: She disobeys out of curiosity and excitement. Her actions might prevent the snake's transformation into a man.

Literary Analysis: FOLKTALE

Have students analyze and list the distinguishing features of the folktale genre that this tale shows.

Possible Response: The animal and human characters, long-ago setting, marvelous events, and the happy ending are characteristic elements of folktales.

"WHY SHOULDN'T I HAVE SOME OF THE GREEN BUBBLES?"

why her mother hadn't killed it. "I'll kill the snake tonight, Pumpkin Seed. Please give me one more chance. Please trust me," pleaded the widow.

A When the sun rose the next morning bright and warm, Pumpkin Seed woke up and there was the snake—still alive. Now Pumpkin Seed had no choice. She had to go with the snake to his home. On the way they came to a lovely clear stream. "Pumpkin Seed, I will go take a bath over behind the rocks. You wait here while I am gone." "All right," Pumpkin Seed agreed.

"When I am gone, you will see lots of colorful bubbles pouring down the stream. You must not touch the green bubbles. You can play with the white and yellow ones, but do not touch the green bubbles," warned the snake. Pumpkin Seed nodded in agreement.

The snake had been gone for a while when, sure enough, Pumpkin Seed noticed a variety of colored bubbles floating down the stream. She stood in delighted amazement as the

bright, glittering bubbles traveled smoothly down the clear water. She eagerly pulled out some of the yellow bubbles. To her surprise the bubbles turned into gold jewels in her hands. Then she gathered some white bubbles, and they turned into silver jewels. Pumpkin Seed was so happy. She had never had such beautiful riches. She gaily put them on her neck, her wrists, her ears, and her fingers.

As she was admiring them, she thought, "Why shouldn't I have some of the green bubbles?" So she reached down and scooped up some green bubbles, and before her startled eyes they turned into twisting snakes in her hands. They even stuck all over her hands. She frantically tried to remove the snakes, but they wouldn't come off.

A moment later a young, handsome man came toward her, and she quickly hid her wriggling hands behind her back. "Why are you hiding your hands?" asked the man.

Her voice quivered as she told him, "Oh, my husband is a snake. He went up the stream

Teaching Options

✓ **Assessment** **Informal Assessment**   🏴 **TEKS** 11A   🏴 **TAAS** Reading Obj. 4; Writing Obj. 1

PREDICT PROBABLE FUTURE ACTIONS AND OUTCOMES You can informally assess students' understanding of the selection by having them write a conclusion to the story that might have occurred if Pumpkin Seed had refused to marry the snake. Students should use the evidence from the text to make their predictions.

RUBRIC

3 Full Accomplishment Responses create convincing alternative conclusions based on evidence from the text such as the words of the snake and the character of the mother.

2 Substantial Accomplishment Responses offer a possible conclusion, based on some of the cause and effect relationships in the text.

1 Little or Partial Accomplishment The outcome is improbable and bears little relationship to the evidence in the text.

THE YOUNG MAN SMILED AND SAID, "I AM YOUR HUSBAND...."

to bathe and he told me to keep my hands like this."

The young man smiled and said, "I am your husband. . . ." Pumpkin Seed interrupted him. "No, you can't be!"

The man smiled and said, "Look at this!" He raised his arm and showed her the remaining snakeskin in his armpit. She believed him when she saw the skin and felt ashamed when she showed him her hands. But he simply blew on her hands and the snakes fell off and disappeared like magic. Then they went home and lived happily for the rest of their lives. ❖

"Pumpkin Seed and the Snake" by Norma J. Livo and Dia Cha;
Libraries Unlimited, 800-237-6124; Englewood, CO.
Reprinted with permission.

"No matter what side of the family got together, music and storytelling were important."

Norma J. Livo
born 1929

Family Traditions Raised in Appalachia, Norma Livo says she grew up with her mother's "folklorish" stories and her father's "tall tales, music, and ballads full of mischief." When one of Livo's sons was diagnosed as having a learning disability, she returned to school to learn how to help him. She earned a doctorate in education and began using her own stories to teach her son to read.

Storytelling Scholar Livo introduced storytelling into elementary and secondary classrooms and designed storytelling courses for the University of Colorado, Denver—from where she retired as professor of education in 1992. Livo has also written many books on storytelling and folklore. She worked with Dia Cha, a Hmong immigrant, to retell "Pumpkin Seed and the Snake" and other tales collected in *Folk Stories of the Hmong: People of Laos, Thailand, and Vietnam.*

PUMPKIN SEED AND THE SNAKE **875**

Mini Lesson: Speaking and Listening

⭐ TEKS
2E, 3B, 5A, 5E, 11B

RETELLING THE STORY
Prepare Remind students that the point of view from which a story is told affects the reader's or listener's perception and understanding of the events and characters. For example, Pumpkin Seed's narration of events might make the character of the snake seem more evil than he actually is. Have students reread the story to prepare to tell the tale from the snake's point of view. Students should jot down notes about how the snake would view and narrate the important events in the story.

Encourage students to practice using gestures, tone, facial expressions, and volume to tell their stories effectively.
Present Have students retell the story to small groups. After each student has presented his or her version, have the groups discuss how the difference in point of view affected their perception of the events and characters.

BLOCK SCHEDULING This activity is particularly well suited for longer class periods.

📄 Use **Communications Transparencies and Copymasters**, p. 14–15, for additional support.

Summary

Kelfala's Secret Something Kelfala is the village clown, but he is seriously in love with the local beauty, Wambuna. The much-courted Wambuna does not speak to anyone, for tradition decrees that she must marry the first man outside her family to whom she speaks. Kelfala, trying to coax her into speaking, pulls out every trick in his bag of humor without success. Finally he comes up with a plan. He dresses and paints himself foolishly, then follows Wambuna to her farm. While she is busy weeding, he slips a Gituyu—an animal not even a dog would eat—onto the firestone where her yams are cooking. Then Kelfala laughs so loudly that he unintentionally lures his friends Shortie Bumpie and Longie Tallie out of the bush. As Wambuna joins in their laughter, Kelfala points out the Gituyu roasting in the fire. "A Gituyu! It cannot be!" she cries out, at which Kelfala proclaims her his wife. Immediately his friends point out that Wambuna spoke to all of them—and so all three qualify as husbands. Kelfala begins plotting a new strategy to win Wambuna's hand.

Reading and Analyzing

Literary Analysis: PLOT

Ⓐ Ask students why a storyteller might begin a tale this way.

Possible Responses: to introduce an important idea or theme

Reading Skills and Strategies: ANALYZING

Ⓑ Have students infer what the repetition of the word *tradition* means.

Possible Responses: Traditions are important in the story.

KELFALA'S SECRET SOMETHING

From *Samburu* by Nigel Pavitt.
Copyright © 1992 Nigel Pavitt,
reprinted by permission of
Henry Holt and Co., Inc.

RETOLD BY ADJAI ROBINSON

876

Teaching Options

 Mini Lesson **Speaking and Listening**

★ **TEKS** 3B, 5C, 5E, 11B

CHORAL READING

Prepare Remind students that the stories in this unit are part of the oral tradition. As such, they were first passed on by word of mouth rather than through the written word. Explain to students that storytellers often use body language as well as words to express emotion. The storyteller's hands, face, posture, and movements all help convey the feeling behind the words. For example, a facial expression of a quick double take can convey humor. Arrange students in small groups and have each group prepare a choral reading of a substantial passage from "Kelfala's Secret Something." Direct groups to use body language as well as volume, pitch, and tone in their presentations.

Present Tape record or videotape the choral readings. Have members of each group listen or view their performances and discuss how the group reading contributes to their appreciation of the text.

BLOCK SCHEDULING This activity is particularly well suited for longer class periods.

📋 Use **Communications Transparencies and Copymasters,** p. 12, for additional support.

LISTEN, CHILDREN,

DO YOU KNOW THE

GITUYU? IT IS SUCH

AN ANIMAL THAT IN

KENYA IT IS SAID

THAT EVEN THE DOGS

WILL NOT EAT ITS

MEAT FOR SUPPER,

NOR THE HYENA, NOR

EVEN THE WILDCAT—

AND NEVER THE

POOREST OF PEOPLE.

THAT IS TRADITION.

THIS YOU MUST KNOW.

But the story . . .

On the steep slopes of the Kilimanjaro[1] stood a tiny village of very <u>hardy</u> people. Mountain climbers were they all, and their gardens of tea and pyrethrum[2] and coffee were as dear to their hearts as the cap of snow shielding the head of their father mountain. The men and women had strong hands and great mountain strides. They were a happy people with warm hearts. And they were a people faithful to their traditions. |**B**

The young fellow, Kelfala, was one of these. Kelfala, the clown. People used to say that he was funny from the time he entered his mother's womb. He could make a thousand and one faces with his one fleshy face. His lips, he could twist and curl, and even if you wanted to hiss, your hissing would turn to laughing. If you listened to Kelfala's stories, I tell you, you would see and hear all the animals in the forest in this one Kelfala. And he sprang surprises as fast as he spinned yarns, on everything around.

Kelfala, the clown, was like his grandfather **1** before him. He was funny. He was clever. Oh, he was a charming darling. It seemed that nothing or no one could resist Kelfala.

No one, except the beautiful Wambuna. She would not even turn his way.

Before, as children, these two had played together, laughed together, teased together. But Wambuna had gone into the girl's society, as all girls of the village do. There, the old women had taught her how to wash and care

---

1. **Kilimanjaro** (kĭl′ə-mən-jär′ō): the highest mountain in Africa.
2. **pyrethrum** (pī-rē′thrəm): a showy flowering plant.

| WORDS TO KNOW | **hardy** (här′dē) *adj.* in robust good health |

877

Customizing Instruction

Less Proficient Readers
Discuss some of the modern techniques that a man might use to try to win the attention of a woman.

Set a Purpose Have students read to find out what Kelfala must do to win the woman he wants to marry.

Students Acquiring English
1 Point out that *clown*, as used here, refers to a person who enjoys making other people laugh.

Gifted and Talented
Challenge students to retell this story as if it took place in their own community with local characters and setting.

Multicultural Link   Marriage

An arranged marriage—one in which the parents select a mate for their child—was the accepted form of marriage in many countries for centuries. In pre-revolutionary China, for example, a bride and groom often met for the first time on their wedding day. In some present day societies, in Africa and India for example, in which the large family is the basic unit, marriages are still arranged, often with the idea of securing socioeconomic advantages from the match. Although the family may determine the choice of spouse, an intermediary will often be responsible for setting up the alliance in a way that will be beneficial to both families. Arranged marriages are the custom in the society that forms the backdrop of "Kelfala's Secret Something." That is why some suitors ask Wambuna's father for permission to marry his daughter. Her only other option is to marry the first man outside her own family to whom she speaks.

In societies composed of the nuclear family unit, children usually choose their own mates and less thought is given to the socio-economic benefits of the match.

A Discuss what purposes this tradition might serve.

Possible Responses: It keeps young men and women apart; it lets parents have much more involvement in the choice of their child's mate.

Literary Analysis: NARRATOR

B Ask students how the narrator of this story tries to draw readers in and engage their sympathy for the characters and their problems.

Possible Response: The narrator addresses readers directly and asks them questions, suggests that readers would feel the way the characters do, and alerts readers to what is important.

Literary Analysis: CHARACTER

C Ask students to analyze Kelfala's motives in behaving as he does.

Possible Response: He thinks that this behavior will make Wambuna speak. Ask students what Kelfala's behavior here reveals about his personality.

Possible Responses: He is self-confident; he feels he can charm anyone.

Reading Skills and Strategies: ANALYZING

D Have students explain the effect of the choice of names of Kelfala's friends.

Possible Response: They create humor, which suits the light tone.

Literary Analysis: SUSPENSE

E Ask students to describe how suspense builds in this part of the story.

Possible Responses: The details of Kelfala's plan are revealed slowly, keeping the meaning of Kelfala's actions a secret; it implies that soon Kelfala and Wambuna will be married.

---

for babies, how to prepare leaves and herbs for simple cures, how to sing the village songs, how to cook meats and yams and vegetables. Her roasted peanuts were always brown and tasty. And, if you ate her sauces, you would lick your fingers as if you were going to bite them, too. Her graces were admired even by other young girls. And when she came out,[3] she was given the oath: that from that time on, if she talked to any man outside her family, she was bound to marry him. That was tradition.

Kelfala would sit in the bush and watch this darling Wambuna. Her skin was as smooth as a mirror. Her mahogany-brown arms swayed gracefully by her sides, keeping time with her swaying hips. When she laughed, she showed ivory-white teeth. And just a smile from Wambuna sent warm thrills through clownish Kelfala. Her head, she carried erect, and the rings sat on her neck like rows of diamonds on a crown. The more Kelfala watched, the more he wanted Wambuna for his own.

But she had an endless stream of suitors. (If you could have seen her, you would not mind even being last, as long as you were in line.) Some of these young men went to her father to ask for Wambuna. That was tradition. But many had heard his loud "No-No" and tried to trick Wambuna, instead. But do you think she talked to the young men around? Well! You wait and see.

Always, they paid their visits to her at the garden, always when the elders were having their rest from the hot midday sun.

"Wambuna, let me get you water from the stream."

"Ay'ee, Wambuna, I hit my toe against a stone. It is gushing out blood!"

"Wambuna, your plants are not growing at all. You are so lazy. Yambuyi's plants are better than yours, lazy you!"

"Wambuna, hear your father? He is snoring

From *Samburu* by Nigel Pavitt. Copyright © 1992 Nigel Pavitt, reprinted by permission of Henry Holt and Co., Inc.

so hard under this hot sun, he has driven all the animals away!"

But Wambuna's lips were sealed, and all this teasing and coaxing only kept her lips tighter. She would not even raise her head to smile. She worked in silence, and if she talked at all, she only whispered kind things to her plants.

Now, Kelfala joined the line, too. And—tradition or not—he would not risk the father's "No-No." Why? He, Kelfala, the clown? Kelfala, who could coax words and

---

3. **when . . . out:** when she was officially regarded as having reached adulthood.

Multicultural Link **Polygyny**

Polygyny is the term used to describe the custom of having more than one wife at a time. *Polyandry* refers to the practice of having more than one husband at a time. *Polygamy*, which comes from a Greek word that means "many marriages," can refer to either gender.

Like many other peoples of Africa, the Kikuyu traditionally practiced polygyny. Having more than one wife was a mark of wealth and status. In such circumstances, the children had a *maitu munyinyi,* or "small mother," as well as their *maitu,* or biological mother.

In most countries, polygamy is prohibited by law. For instance, China and Turkey–where polygyny was once customary–now have legislation outlawing this practice. In the United States, Congress passed legislation against polygamy in 1862.

laughter out of trees? He would get Wambuna to speak!

He tried his hippopotamus face, to get her to shout in fear. He turned into a leopard, springing into Wambuna's path when she was alone, so she would cry for help. He hid behind a clump of trees and became Wambuna's mother, asking questions and questions and questions that needed answers.

But Wambuna's lips were sealed.

The stream of suitors grew smaller, like the village stream itself, shrinking and shrinking in the dry season when the rains have stopped. But Kelfala did not give up. Finally, he confided in two friends that he had a something that would win Wambuna for him. A secret something. (He did not tell them what.)

For two weeks Kelfala and his two friends, Shortie Bumpie and Longie Tallie, trailed Wambuna and her family as they went to the farm. Then Kelfala's day came. They spied Wambuna going alone to the farm with her basket balanced on her head. He and Shortie Bumpie and Longie Tallie set out behind her, *kunye, kunye, kunye* as if they were <u>treading</u> on hot coals. They stood behind the trees and bushes, unseen by anyone but themselves, and waited.

On this day, Kelfala had put on his best dress. But if you had seen him, you would think that he was the most unlikely suitor for a young girl. His dress was rags and tatters. He had rubbed grease all over his body, mud on his head, and funny chalk marks on his face. He also had painted his front teeth with red-black clay.

The birds were twitting happily as they caught worms on the dewy grass. Nearby the stream was flowing by, its waters dazzling in the early morning sunlight. From time to time Kelfala opened his sack, touched his something, and smiled to himself.

Wambuna started working hard and fast. Indeed, she was racing the sun. By the time the sun got halfway on its journey, she hoped to have gotten to the end of hers. She only stopped her work for a moment, went to the stream with her calabash[4] for water, then returned and kindled a fire. She took some yams from her little basket, put them on the hot coals, and returned to her plants. She was weeding the new grasses on her tea beds.

Kelfala's opportunity had come. Soon, Kelfala, the clown, Kelfala, the funny one, would be married to the most beautiful, the most gentle, the mildest lady on Kilimanjaro. At least, that is what Kelfala thought.

Kelfala spied here, there, and everywhere from his hiding, stepped out into the open, and hopped and skipped to the fireplace. Out of his sack he pulled his something and placed it on the hot coals beside Wambuna's yams. Then he squatted on the largest firestone and poled the red-hot coals. Shoving Wambuna's yams aside, he uttered a throaty chuckle, which he quickly trapped with his hands. He glanced again at the fireplace, and like a cock ready to peck at the yams, he tittered quietly to himself. But again he quickly stopped himself.

---

4. **calabash** (kăl′ə-băsh′): the dried, hollowed-out shell of a gourd, used as a bowl.

WORDS TO KNOW **tread** (trĕd) *v.* to walk on, in, or along

879

 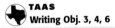

KELFALA'S SECRET SOMETHING **879**

Reading Skills and Strategies: VISUALIZING

A Ask students to describe the mental images that the text description evokes.
Possible Response: The image is of three young men and Wambuna holding their sides and sobbing with laughter as they stagger around the fire. They cannot even straighten themselves up.

Reading Skills and Strategies: CLARIFYING

B To clarify the meaning of a Gituyu, have students review the opening paragraph of the story. Ask students to speculate why they think no person or animal is willing to eat this creature's meat.
Possible Response: It tastes dreadful or smells bad.

Literary Analysis: REPETITION

C Ask students how this repetition affects the tone in this passage of the story.
Possible Responses: It makes the tone very playful.

Literary Analysis: PLOT

D Ask students how Kelfala's final observation changes the end of the story.
Possible Responses: It suggests that the story is not over, that he will try again and maybe win her next time

Reading Skills and Strategies: CONNECTING

E Have students explain how Reverend Parker and Richard Dana in *Anthony Burns: The Defeat and Triumph of a Fugitive Slave* resemble Kelfala.
Possible Response: They share his determination to achieve a goal.

But only for a moment, for suddenly more chuckles escaped, and Kelfala howled like a ruffled owl. He hooted the monkeys out of the treetops. He rolled himself into a ball as he rolled and rolled with laughter. Kelfala, the laughing clown. He laughed and he laughed and he laughed.

 Now, the bush came alive. Shortie Bumpie and Longie Tallie poked their heads out to see what was happening. At first they twitched their faces and cocked their ears. But as Kelfala rolled on and on, and the laughter rolled on and on, it dragged the two young men with it.

Wambuna—who had to poke her fire—tried to sneak past the hooting trio, but the loud roars quickly sank into *her* bones. Oh, how silly those three idle friends! Kelfala, that clown Kelfala! But as she watched them, her grin turned into a broad smile, *her* smile turned into a shy laugh, and without realizing it, she became one of the howling trio. She was all fits of laughter. Oh! How the tears ran down Wambuna's eyes.

All four laughed and laughed, laughed and laughed and laughed.

When all at once Kelfala stood, with arms akimbo[5] and stomach shot forward, and pointed to Wambuna's fireplace.

"A beautiful girl like you," he laughed, "proud as the cotton tree and the greatest cook in the village, you, you roast a Gituyu with your yams!"

Wambuna turned around.

There by the giant firestone, on the ashes, was Kelfala's something. A shrunken, old, burnt Gituyu!

Wambuna caught her breath, looked from Kelfala to his friends, and cried out between tears and laughter. "A Gituyu! It cannot be. It cannot . . ."

AS SHE WATCHED THEM, HER GRIN TURNED INTO A BROAD SMILE, *HER* SMILE TURNED INTO A SHY LAUGH, AND WITHOUT REALIZING IT, SHE BECAME ONE OF THE HOWLING TRIO.

B ut, at that Kelfala threw up his arms. "Aha! You have spoken to Kelfala. Kelfala, the great, Kelfala, the clown! Kelfala, the cunning one. Kelfala, the proud husband of a proud wife!"

"Wait a minute, Kelfala," one of his friends said. "Kelfala, I tell you now, she doesn't belong to you."

---

5. **akimbo** (ə-kĭm′bō): with hands on hips, and elbows bent outward.

Mini Lesson **Speaking and Listening**   **TEKS** 5B, 20C

INTERVIEWS

Prepare Explain to students that when they write articles or reports, they need to gather information from as many sources as possible. One way to gather information is to conduct a personal interview. Present these guidelines:

Before the interview, think carefully about what you want to find out. Define your purpose and prepare your questions in advance.

During the interview, listen carefully and avoid distractions. If possible, tape-record the interview so you can listen to the responses later as often as needed.

After the interview, listen to the recording and make your notes. Identify the main ideas and supporting details.

Have students conduct a personal interview as part of their work on one of the mini-projects on pp. 882–883.

Present Have students take turns summarizing the information they obtained and explaining what they learned about interviewing techniques.

BLOCK SCHEDULING This activity is particularly well suited for longer class periods.

 Use **Communications Transparencies and Copymasters**, p. 9, for additional support.

"Oh, no, you Shortie Bumpie? The trick was mine, see?" and with that, Kelfala hopped.

"The plan was mine, see?" and with that, Kelfala skipped.

"The secret was mine, see?" and with that, he jumped.

"The Gituyu was mine, see? My secret something! And the laughter was mine, see, I started it." And with that, he laughed and laughed and laughed . . .

Wambuna stood, amazed, but she soon found support in Shortie Bumpie and Longie Tallie.

"I know that a man has had three wives, but never on this whole mountain has ever a woman shared three husbands," <u>retorted</u> Shortie Bumpie.

"Yes, Kelfala, this girl either belongs to all of us . . . or none of us," cried the other friend.

You could see Kelfala's heart heaving.

"What did you say? You, Longie Tallie?" Wambuna lifted her eyes.

"Yes," Longie Tallie went on. "Wambuna laughed at you. She cried at you. She mumbled, she grumbled at you. She laughed-cried. She laughed-mumbled-cried at you. But she talked to all three of us!"

Wambuna pressed her lips together in a quiet, sly smile and looked into Kelfala's eyes. Then she walked back to her plants with her head raised up like a large pink rose in early spring.

Kelfala just looked, his head bowed like a weeping willow. But then, he tapped his bag and grinned. "Today is only for today. There is still tomorrow. There will always be another secret."

That was tradition, too. ❖

"Each book that I have written for boys and girls is also a book I have written for myself."

Adjai Robinson
born 1932

Folk Heritage Adjai Robinson was born in Sierra Leone, in West Africa. He grew up listening to local storytellers recount wonderful tales. Years later, Robinson continued the tradition by becoming a storyteller for radio and retelling African folktales.

Back to Africa Robinson came to the United States to lead workshops about African folklore and to attend Columbia University in New York. In 1975, he returned to Africa, where he became the principal education officer at the Nigeria Teachers Institute. Robinson has published a number of children's books.

WORDS TO KNOW   **retort** (rĭ-tôrt') *v.* respond to a comment, such as an insult or argument, with a reply of the same type, often quick, sharp, or witty

881

Less Proficient Readers
Ask students how Kelfala gets Wambuna to speak.
Answer: He places a Gituyu next to the yams she is cooking. This is the animal nobody will eat, so Wambuna is very surprised.
Ask students why Kelfala's plan fails.
Answer: Wambuna speaks to all three men instead of Kelfala alone, so he cannot claim her for himself.

Students Acquiring English
1 Point out that "the bush came alive" is not meant literally; instead, it means that the bush started moving and sounds came from behind it when Kelfala's friends began laughing.

Gifted and Talented
Ask students to describe a prank in which they or someone they know attempted to trick someone into doing something that person really didn't want to do. What was the outcome?

✓ **Assessment Standardized Test Practice** **TEKS** 10K, 12G 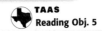 **TAAS** Reading Obj. 5

DESCRIBE PLOT For some standardized tests, students will be asked to choose the best description of the plot of a passage. To provide students with some help in choosing the best answer, read aloud or write on the board the following question: Which of the following statements best describes Kelfala's pursuit of Wambuna?
A. Kelfala formally asks Wambuna's father for her hand in marriage.
B. Kelfala tricks and teases Wambuna in the hope that she will speak to him and have to marry him.
C. He tries to eliminate his competition.
D. Kelfala waits patiently for Wambuna to fall in love with him.
Lead students through the process of choosing the best description. A is incorrect. Kelfala does not approach her father. B correctly describes the strategies that Kelfala employs. C is incorrect. No mention is made of Kelfala's interaction with other suitors. D is incorrect. He is active, not passive, about his courtship.

LITERATURE CONNECTION

Write a poem Have students list the main characters and brainstorm ideas about each before choosing the character for their poem. Encourage students writing a narrative poem to outline important events in sequence before beginning. Students writing a lyric poem might find a word web helpful. Remind students to include sound devices such as rhyme or repetition as well as imagery, similes, metaphors, symbols, or personification.

RUBRIC

3 Full Accomplishment Poems use literary devices to skillfully tell about a character's personal challenge.

2 Substantial Accomplishment Responses portray a clear idea of the challenge and use some poetic devices.

1 Little or Partial Accomplishment Poems fail to communicate ideas about the character's personal challenge.

Use **Writing Transparencies**, p. 33, for additional support.

Use **Literary Analysis Transparencies**, pp. 19 and 20.

ART CONNECTION

Create Your Own Pa Ndau Keep the groups small to make it easier for students to agree on a design and execute it. Suggest that students look for examples of Hmong pa ndau art on the Internet and find out more about traditional stitching techniques from local embroidery guilds, craft books and magazines, and career skills teachers. Suggest that students who wish to try stitching use a large needle and sturdy all-cotton thread. Tell students to create a flow chart for their story before they sketch scenes.

RUBRIC

3 Full Accomplishment Students create a pa ndau story cloth that accurately retells a story in Unit 6.

2 Substantial Accomplishment The pa ndau cloth accurately retells the tale but lacks some drama or visual appeal.

1 Little or Partial Accomplishment The story cloth does not retell the events in sequence.

Use **Reading and Critical Thinking Transparencies**, p. 39, for additional support.

ACROSS the CURRICULUM

Interdisciplinary Projects

LITERATURE CONNECTION

Write a Poem Choose one of the main characters in the stories that you just read. Write a poem about his or her personal challenge. You can write any type of poem you wish: a lyric poem, a narrative poem, a free verse poem, and so on. To review different types of poems, you may want to reread pages 191–194.

ART CONNECTION

Create Your Own Pa ndau The Hmong have depicted their history, folktales, and culture on pa ndau (pǎn-dou'), pieces of cloth with elaborate needlework. Pa ndau art can include appliqué, reverse appliqué, cross-stitches, chain stitches, batik, and embroidery. The stitching or appliqué is traditionally done on a blue background.

Step 1: Research Find pictures or examples of Hmong pa ndau art in art or reference books in your school library.

Step 2: Story Choose a story from Unit Six and create a pa ndau story cloth for it.

Step 3: Sketches Working with your classmates, sketch scenes from the story on paper.

Step 4: Cloth Then use fabric paint or one of the techniques mentioned to make the characters, actions, and scenery come to life on the cloth.

Step 5: Finished Pa ndau Display the pa ndau and use it to retell the story to a younger class.

SOCIAL STUDIES CONNECTION

Hold a Kikuyu Festival Work with your class to put on a Kikuyu Festival that includes art, music, and food from the Kikuyu culture—or any other cultures represented in Unit Six. Choose one of these areas to work on:

Food Find recipes for and prepare dishes from the culture of your choice. Kikuyu recipes may appear in cookbooks from Kenya or other parts of Africa. Compile the recipes into a cookbook to share with your classmates.

Music From your local library, borrow recordings of African music to play during the festival. You also may want to make, draw, or bring in instruments from Africa or the culture of your choice.

Art Draw pictures of the art, architecture, or landscape of East Africa or of the culture of your choice. Bring in examples of arts and crafts from that region.

SOCIAL STUDIES CONNECTION

Hold a Kikuyu Festival Arrange students in small groups to research the food, music, or decorations from the culture the class has chosen. Encourage students to conduct personal interviews with people from that cultural group as well as research print and on-line resources. Students may wish to contact the Parent-Teacher Organization, Chamber of Commerce, local branches of service organizations such as Rotary, and religious groups to find people from these cultures who would like to share their heritage.

RUBRIC

3 Full Accomplishment Students find detailed, accurate, and verifiable information on one area of the country's culture.

2 Substantial Accomplishment Students find information about one aspect of the culture, but the results may lack details.

1 Little or Partial Accomplishment Students have not found accurate, verifiable information about the culture.

Use **Literary Analysis Transparencies**, p. 32, for additional support.

Across Cultures

Make an Illustrated Calendar Find out which days of the week are named for Norse gods and goddesses, which are named for the sun and the moon, and which is named for a Roman god. Use an encyclopedia or other reference books to gather information about Norse and Roman myths. Then paint an accompanying picture or symbol to represent each day of the week.

COMPARING TEXTS **Create a Phrase Book**
Find out more about Swahili, Kenya's national language, or the language of any other culture represented in Unit Five—for example, Greek ("A Crown of Wild Olive," page 709) or Spanish ("Barrio Boy," page 694). Use library resources such as dictionaries, phrase books, and textbooks and, if possible, interview people who speak the language. On your own, or with a few classmates, create a guide book—complete with pronunciations and definitions—for a number of common words and phrases in that language. Teach some of the words and phrases to the class.

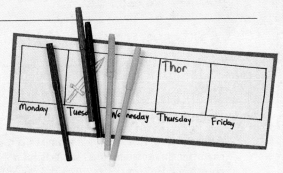

Present a Report The Hmong are some of the most recent immigrants to the United States. Find out about their history and the challenges they face in adjusting to a new culture while trying to preserve their own. Look for stories about the Hmong in magazines and newspapers. Present an oral report on the Hmong to your classmates.

More Online: Research Starter
www.mcdougallittell.com

Vocabulary in Action

EXERCISE: ANALOGIES Look at the first pair of words and decide how they are related. Then write the Word to Know that best completes the second pair.

1. GIFT : PRESENT :: _____ : loss
2. JUMP : LEAP :: _____ : walk
3. YELL : SHOUT :: _____ : reply
4. HOT : COLD :: _____ : frail
5. KNEAD : DOUGH :: _____ : iron

WORDS TO KNOW	forge	hardy	retort	sacrifice	tread

Across Cultures

Make an Illustrated Calendar Suggest that students consult an almanac, encyclopedia, or history of language text for information about the days of the week. Monday comes from the Anglo-Saxon term *Mōnondaeg,* which means moon's day. Tuesday, Wednesday, Thursday, and Friday are named for the Norse gods and goddesses Tyr, Woden/Odin, Thor, and Frigg, respectively. Saturday is named for the Roman god Saturn. Sunday is named for the sun. Students familiar with other languages may know of days of the week named after other gods. For instance, in French, *mardi* and *mercredi*—Tuesday and Wednesday in English—are named after the Roman gods Mars and Mercury, respectively.

COMPARING TEXTS
Create a Language Phrase Book
Caution students that many languages have regional variations or dialects. Tell students to be sure to check each entry in at least two sources to make sure that the spelling, definition, and punctuation are correct. **To extend this assignment,** have students develop language tapes that build in short pauses for the listeners to repeat the phrase or word. **Visual learners** may wish to accompany their pronunciations and definitions with pictures that illustrate the word or phrase.

Present a Report Guide students to sites on the Internet that have information on the Hmong immigrants, and have them consult recent almanacs and government documents for additional facts. Encourage students to find one or more Hmong immigrants who would consent to an interview.

Vocabulary in Action

EXERCISE
Possible Responses:
1. sacrifice
2. tread
3. retort
4. hardy
5. forge

Use **Unit Six Resource Book,** p. **44** for additional practice. Use **Unit Six Resource Book,** p. **47** for assessment.

Objectives

- create a multimedia presentation
- select, organize, or produce visuals to complement and extend meanings
- use media to compare ideas and points of view
- produce communications using technology or appropriate media
- revise to create a strong opening
- revise for consistent form

Introducing the Workshop

Multimedia Presentation Point out that multimedia presentations are a very effective way to communicate messages; most advertisers know this, which is why they create televised ads that combine text, graphics, and sound. Advertisers know that multimedia is very powerful; it strengthens most messages. Students can use this power to communicate their ideas about literature.

Basics in a Box

Content Explain that a good multimedia presentation depends on two elements that must work together. The first part is content. A presentation may be lively and interesting but ultimately unsuccessful if it does not present information in a way that students can understand. Review the bulleted items with students, and have them contrast this list with what is required for a text-only essay.

Delivery Help students recognize that technology can help them, but it must be selected and presented effectively. As students read the list of suggestions for presenters, you may wish to encourage them to visualize speakers who have followed these steps successfully, including speakers they have heard in school, on field trips, and on television programs.

 Use McDougal Littell's **Language Network**, Chapters 12–19, for more instruction on essential writing skills.

 Power Presentation

To engage students visually, use **Power Presentation** 2, Multimedia Presentation

 See the Skills Trace at the beginning of the unit for information on TEKS covered in this lesson.

Communication Workshop — Multimedia Presentation

Bringing your subject to life with media . . .

From Reading to Writing What makes certain characters in literature good subjects for a presentation? Characters such as the clever Brother Cricket ("Brother Coyote and Brother Cricket") or Kelfala, the village clown ("Kelfala's Secret Something"), have human characteristics that make them entertaining. But how a character or a story is presented is equally as important. Creating a **multimedia presentation** is one way to grab an audience's attention. You can bring a character to life through a combination of sounds, visual elements, and text.

For Your Portfolio

WRITING PROMPT Create a multimedia presentation about a favorite fairy-tale character or any other subject that interests you.

Purpose: To inform and entertain
Audience: Classmates, family, friends

Basics in a Box

GUIDELINES AND STANDARDS | MULTIMEDIA PRESENTATION

Content

A successful multimedia presentation should

- use media appropriate to the content
- use media from different sources
- capture the audience's attention with a strong beginning
- clearly, directly, and logically present information
- end by summarizing the topic and the points made

Delivery

An effective presenter should

- have good posture and maintain eye contact with the audience
- vary pacing as well as the pitch, tone, and volume of voice
- use gestures and body language to get the point across
- use visual aids effectively to help the audience understand the topic

---

LESSON RESOURCES

USING PRINT RESOURCES
Unit Six Resource Book
- Planning and Drafting, p. 48
- Practicing and Delivering, p. 49
- Peer Response Guide, pp. 50–51
- Refining Your Performance, p. 52
- Rubric for Evaluation, p. 53

Communications Transparencies and Copymasters
- Formal Presentations, TR 10

- Verbal Strategies, TR 14
- Nonverbal Strategies, TR 15

Writing Transparencies
- Writing Process Transparencies, TR 1–4
- Writing Template Transparencies: Multimedia Presentation, TR 39

Grammar Transparencies and Copymasters
- Verb Tense, CM 73 (for Mini Lesson, p. 889)

INTEGRATED TECHNOLOGY
LaserLinks
Writing Springboards
See Teacher's SourceBook p. 36 for bar codes.

Writing Coach CD-ROM
Visit our website:
www.mcdougallittell.com

Analyzing a Multimedia Presentation

SPEAKING OPPORTUNITY
See the Communication Handbook, p. R100 for speaking and presenting tips.

<show first visual: clip of Cinderella movie>

Does everyone here know the story of Cinderella? OK, but how many of you have heard of Yeh-Shen or Cendrillon? These are Cinderella tales from China and the Caribbean. In each story a poor, mistreated girl is magically given a chance to appear in public wearing beautiful clothes. However, each story emphasizes a different aspect of the main character's personality.

<show second visual: picture of Yeh-Shen>

Yeh-Shen lives in southern China. Her only friend is the spirit that lives in the bones of her pet fish, which her cruel stepmother killed. This spirit gives her fancy clothes so that she can go to a festival. When Yeh-Shen loses one of her golden slippers, however, the fish bones no longer speak to her. Yeh-Shen is heartbroken and tries to get the slipper back, hoping that the spirit will return. Instead she is discovered by a king, who falls in love with her and marries her. The ending of the story is familiar, but Yeh-Shen is unique because she highly values her friendship with the fish.

<show third visual: picture of Cendrillon w/map of Carribean>

Cendrillon lives on a Caribbean island. Despite cruel treatment by her stepmother, she is a generous person. One day her godmother helps her attend a dance where she can meet Paul Thibault, a man who is very wealthy and kind. Cendrillon loses a slipper while leaving. When Paul comes to her house to find the owner of the slipper, the godmother wants to dress Cendrillon in beautiful clothes again.

<play audiotape of story from "She drew a shawl" to "in his eyes">

Cendrillon insists that Paul see her just as she really is.

<show fourth visual: Venn diagram>

Both Yeh-Shen and Cendrillon, like the heroines of most Cinderella tales, are humble and kind. However, each version of the story emphasizes different parts of the main character's personality. Yeh-Shen is memorable for her devoted friendship with the fish spirit, and Cendrillon is special because she insists on honesty in her relationships.

GUIDELINES IN ACTION

❶ Captures viewer's attention with video clip

❷ Introduction asks questions to involve audience; includes a thesis statement.
Another Option:
· Begin with music.

❸ Visual provides concrete image of the subject.

❹ Information is logically arranged in a subject-by-subject order. (First Yeh-Shen, then Cendrillon)
Another Option:
· Use feature-by-feature order.

❺ Audiotape varies the mode of presenting the material.

❻ Sums up similarities and differences between characters

❼ Conclusion reinforces the main idea.

Teaching the Lesson

Analyzing the Multimedia Presentation

The student model is a script for a presentation in which the author explains that there are Cinderella tales in many cultures, including China and the Caribbean. The writer compares the myths and then explains that each story emphasizes different aspects of the main character's personality. The audience then is introduced to Yeh-Shen and her story, and then to Cendrillon and her story. Pictures, a graphic organizer, and an audiotape add interest and information about these characters and the tales in which they appear.

Have a volunteer read the model aloud and then discuss the Guidelines in Action with students. Point out the key words and phrases in the student model that correspond to the elements mentioned in the Guidelines in Action.

1 Ask students how the notes about media elements help the presenter.
Possible Responses: They show what media to use and when to use them; the presenter does not have to make decisions or remember details.

3 Have students name other types of visual media that could be used:
Possible Responses: Students might mention some of these: photographs; posters; diagrams; videos; book jackets; or comic strips.

5 Have students identify other types of sound media that could be used.
Possible Responses: Students might mention any of these: interviews; sound effects; recorded dialogue or stories; excerpts from a speech, radio show, or newscast; songs or other musical compositions

Planning Your Presentation

If subjects have trouble selecting a topic after they have read the suggestions in the Idea Bank, have them try the following:

- Think about characters that you know from comic strips and cartoons.
- Consider characters from science fiction.
- Think about famous animals in stories, myths, and folklore, such as Old Yeller, Rikki-Tikki-Tavi, Zomo, or Pegasus.

Planning Your Multimedia Presentation

Encourage students to consider possible media elements at the same time that they select a character. For example, if they chose characters from another country, they could include pictures of native costumes and tapes of music.

Steps for Planning Your Multimedia Presentation

1. As students do research, they should consider not only the character but the culture in which the character appears.

4. Students might make different types of file cards—information cards and media cards. The information cards could contain brief notes summarizing one type of information; the media cards could contain descriptive notes about various kinds of media. Students could then try arranging the cards in various combinations to see which organization works best.

5. Besides the media elements named, if students have access to the Internet, remind them that they can often download pictures, sound clips, and photos from various sources. Also, they may want to see if a science or social studies teacher has CD-ROMs that contain useful images or sounds.

IDEABank

1. For Your Working Portfolio 📁
Look for ideas in the Writing Options that you completed earlier in the unit.
- **Evaluate Characters,** p. 846
- **Compare Characters,** p. 865

2. Around the World
Explore the fairy tales of a particular country. Pick the character that appears most frequently, the one that reveals some aspect of the culture, or the one you find most interesting.

3. Admirable Aspects
Choose a legendary figure that reveals positive qualities in his or her adventures. Focus on one or two of those qualities in presenting the character.

Have a question?

See the **Multimedia Handbook**
Using Visuals, p. R95
Sound, p. R97

Creating Your Multimedia Presentation

❶ Planning Your Presentation

List the titles of tales that you have read. **Brainstorm** names of characters with supernatural powers, characters that take the form of animals, and characters that resemble real people. See the **Idea Bank** in the margin for more suggestions. After you have chosen your character, follow the steps below.

Steps for Planning Your Multimedia Presentation

▶ **1. Find out everything you can about your character.** Reread the story in which he or she appears and do research to find other information about him or her.

▶ **2. Decide on your focus.** Your presentation can't include everything about your character. Will you show the character through a retelling of a story? Or will you put together ideas from different sources?

▶ **3. Think about your audience.** How much background information do you need to give your audience? How much do they already know about the character?

▶ **4. Organize your information.** What is the best order for presenting your ideas? At what points will media elements be effective?

▶ **5. Plan your media elements.** Choose the best types of media for your presentation. Investigate where to obtain the materials and equipment you'll need. Consider the following options:

- **Audiotapes and compact discs** add sound effects, music, and voices.
- **Charts, posters, photos, slides,** and **graphs** provide visual representations of facts and information.
- **Videos** combine sound and visual effects.
- **Computers** can be used to generate visual aids or to create and project slides.

❷ Developing Your Presentation

You have gathered all the information that you want to include. Now it is time to put together your script and to insert media elements in the best places.

Steps for Developing Your Multimedia Presentation

▶ **1. Write a script.** You want your presentation to go well. Writing out what you want to say will help you be organized. Clearly show where you will use media elements in your script. Introduce and explain the elements if necessary.

▶ **2. Create a strong introduction and conclusion.** Begin your presentation with a vivid visual, a question, or an anecdote. Be sure to finish your presentation in a way that leaves your audience with a strong impression of your subject.

▶ **3. Collect and prepare your media elements.** Are your visuals big enough to be seen from the back of the room? Can your audio and video elements be heard? Have you practiced with the equipment so that you can use it easily?

▶ **4. Think about your media choices.** Are they effective? Do they accomplish what you want them to? Do they support the important points in your presentation? Lists, charts, and graphs will help give key facts and other data.

❸ Practicing and Presenting

You must practice your entire presentation several times so that you can smoothly incorporate the media elements as you speak. Work on the following areas in your rehearsals:

• **Eye contact.** Know your script well enough that you can look at your audience from time to time during your presentation.

• **Facial expressions and gestures.** Practice appropriate expressions in front of a mirror and use gestures to emphasize important points.

• **Voice volume, tone, and pace.** Your voice must reach the back of the room. Vary the tone in which you speak to keep your audience interested. Speak slowly. Remember your audience is hearing your material for the first time.

• **Use of equipment.** Practice using the equipment. Ask for a rehearsal audience after you have practiced on your own. Work on their suggestions.

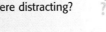

Ask Your Peer Reader

• Where do I need to give more background? Information?

• How can I build a stronger introduction and conclusion?

• Which media elements were effective? Which elements were distracting? Why?

TECHTool

A CD-ROM provides both sound effects and visual images. You might be able to find your tale or legend on a CD-ROM. The text of the story might be accompanied by graphics that would be effective in your presentation. If you need help finding CD-ROMs or using them in a multimedia presentation, ask your school's technology adviser.

Steps for Developing Your Multimedia Presentation

1. One way to write a script is to create two unequal columns, with text in the larger column and media notes in the other. This allows the presenter to see at a glance how much media is used and how it fits in with text. As students write their speeches, encourage them to say them aloud to themselves to be sure that they follow natural speech rhythms.

3. Encourage students to look at their visuals from the back of the room to see if they can be appreciated at that distance.

4. Students who have access to presentation software might try several options before making their final selections. Remind students that media should add to their presentations; they should select what would be most effective, since too many different kinds might confuse the audience.

Practicing and Presenting

Remind students that they can use their voices to enhance meaning. By speaking slowly and clearly, by pausing at appropriate places, and by emphasizing key words, they can make their ideas clearer to the audience.

Use **Communications Transparencies and Copymasters,** pp. 14–15, for additional support.

Ask Your Peer Reader

Students may also wish to have peer readers summarize the main points in their presentations to learn which, if any, are weak or unclear.

Refining Your Presentation:
CREATING A STRONG OPENING

Remind students that anecdotes are not just funny stories; they include any brief story that illustrates or makes a point. Anecdotes might be from the students' experience, from one of the stories, or from current events.

Editing and Proofreading:
CONSISTENT FORM

Discuss why this writer made the changes shown, and what elements might be included in consistent form. Besides capitalization, students should look for parallel verb tense and form; consistent use of either sentences or fragments; consistent punctuation; and consistent use of color or type sizes.

Reflecting

When students note ideas for other multimedia presentations, encourage them to make notes about the media they would like to use, even if they are unavailable. Often, once students know the effects they are trying to create, they can find ways to achieve those effects.

Option

You may want to put together teams of students to make the presentations, just as teams of people create films. Although one student would author each presentation as scriptwriter, others could step in later: artistic students might provide visual direction or props; musical students could select or perform music; mathematical learners could synchronize media; students who might be reserved in presenting their own ideas may enjoy acting as presenters for someone else's script.

Need revising help?
Review the **Guidelines**, p. 884
Consider **peer reviewer** comments
Check **Revision Guidelines**, p. R23

SPELLING
From Writing

As you revise your work, look back at the words you misspelled and determine why you made the errors you did. For additional help, refer to the strategies and generalizations in the **Spelling Handbook** on page R86.

Publishing
IDEAS

- Invite another class to watch your presentation.
- Host a parents' night and do your multimedia presentation.

More Online:
Publishing Options
www.mcdougallittell.com

---

❹ Refining Your Presentation
TARGET SKILL ▶ CREATING A STRONG OPENING When you're surfing the channels on television, a program must grab your attention very quickly. The same is true for the first few seconds of a multimedia presentation. Start off with something that will immediately grab your audience's attention. Elements that work well include questions, humor, audio or video clips, and interesting anecdotes.

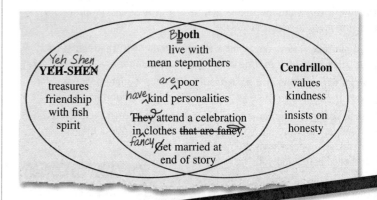

❺ Editing and Proofreading
TARGET SKILL ▶ CONSISTENT FORM A great deal of information is packed into the visuals of a typical presentation. It is important that each visual be easy to read and understand. Remember to use correct and consistent capitalization. Also, always be sure that language is clear, consistent, and to the point.

❻ Reflecting
FOR YOUR WORKING PORTFOLIO What did you learn about your character through doing your multimedia presentation? What did you learn about media while creating your presentation? What ideas do you have for another multimedia presentation? Attach your answers to your presentation script. Save your script in your **Working Portfolio.**

Assessment Practice Revising & Editing

Read this paragraph from the first draft of a student essay. The underlined sections may include the following kinds of errors:

- **verb tense errors**
- **incorrect verb forms**
- **comma errors**
- **capitalization errors**

For each underlined section, choose the revision that improves the writing.

"Cinderella" a classic fairy tale has been told and retold through the
years. Fairy tales were interesting because they tell a great deal about
basic human nature. Most cultures have fairy tales that have been read,
spoken, or sang throughout the years. One of the most famous
collections of fairy tales was published in the early 1800s by the Grimm
brothers, two brothers from Germany. This collection is still popular
today and includes "The Frog Prince," "Rapunzel," and "Hansel and
Gretel." Themes in these famous stories include the following: Things
people fear, Ideas people value, and Dreams people have.

---

1. **A.** "Cinderella," a classic fairy tale has been told
   B. "Cinderella" a classic fairy tale, has been told
   C. "Cinderella," a classic fairy tale, has been told
   D. Correct as is

2. **A.** Fairy tales are interesting
   B. Fairy tales had been interesting
   C. Fairy tales will be interesting
   D. Correct as is

3. **A.** that have been read, spoke, or sung throughout the years.
   B. that have been read, spoke, or sang throughout the years.
   C. that have been read, spoken, or sung throughout the years.
   D. Correct as is

4. **A.** the Grimm brothers two
   brothers from, Germany.
   B. the Grimm brothers two brothers, from Germany.
   C. the Grimm brothers two brothers from Germany.
   D. Correct as is

5. **A.** was still popular today
   B. were still popular today
   C. will still be popular today
   D. Correct as is

6. **A.** things people fear, ideas people value, and dreams people have.
   B. Things people fear, ideas people value, and dreams people have.
   C. Things People Fear, Ideas People Value, and Dreams People Have.
   D. Correct as is

Need Extra Help?

See the **Grammar Handbook**

Quick Reference Capitalization, p. R58

Quick Reference Punctuation, p. R56

Commonly Confused Verbs, p. R69

Assessment Practice

Demonstrate how students can eliminate incorrect choices for the first question.

A. This choice is incorrect, because the phrase "a classic fairy tale" is an appositive that identifies "Cinderella." Therefore, it should be set off with commas and have a comma before and after it. Here no comma follows it.

B. This choice is incorrect, because no comma comes before the appositive.

C. This choice is correct. The appositive phrase is set off with commas.

D. This choice is incorrect, because the words "a classic fairy tale" identify the title that precedes it. Since it is an appositive, it should be set off with commas.

Answers

1. C 2. A 3. C 4. D 5. D 6. A

 Grammar TEKS 17F 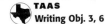 TAAS Writing Obj. 3, 6

VERB TENSES

Instruction Remind students that the present perfect and past perfect tenses of verbs are used to show that one action preceded another. These tenses are formed by using the helping verb *has, have,* or *had* with the past participle of the main verb. Remind students to check if a verb takes a different form in the perfect tense than in the past tense. Point out the word *sung* in the Assessment Practice paragraph above and the word *given* in the

example below. You might want to review other irregular verbs.

Examples: Sal <u>has given</u> her report; I <u>have given</u> my report. (present perfect)
I <u>had given</u> my report before Sal gave hers. (past perfect)

Exercises Have students replace the verb in each sentence with the same verb in the present perfect or past perfect tense.

1. Tony rang the bell. *(has rung)*

2. We ate soup and sandwiches for lunch. *(have eaten)*

3. Arden went home early. *(had gone)*

4. The group chose to meet at noon. *(has chosen)*

 Use **Grammar Transparencies and Copymasters,** p. 73, for additional support.

 Use McDougal Littell's *Language Network,* Chapter 4, for more instruction and practice in present and past perfect tenses.

Objectives
- reflect on the unit
- review literary genres introduced in the unit
- represent text information in a graphic organizer

Reflecting on the Theme

OPTION 1

A successful response will
- display an understanding of the myths in the unit.
- identify basic questions each myth answers about the world and what cultural values are revealed by actions and characters in the story.

Use the Unit 6 Resource Book, page 54 to provide students a ready-made, in-depth chart for examining myths.

Use **Literary Analysis Transparencies,** p. 30, for additional support.

OPTION 2

A successful response will
- distinguish folk tales from other types of literature
- make inferences based on text evidence and experience
- connect the literature they've read to their own lives

Building Your Portfolio

Students should evaluate the items in their Working Portfolios and choose pieces that represent their highest quality work for their Presentation Portfolios. Before students make their choices, ask them to consider which pieces best illustrate not only their writing abilities, but also their understanding of the oral tradition.

For more information on using Portfolios, use **Teacher's Guide to Assessment and Portfolio Use** beginning on page 53.

Across Cultures: The Oral Tradition

In this unit you read stories that reflect many cultures. How have you grown as a reader and a writer because of reading them? Choose one or both of the options below to help assess how your thinking has developed.

Reflecting on the Theme

OPTION 1

Examining Myths Work with a partner to review the myths you have read in this unit. Then in a chart like the one shown, list each myth, the question you think it attempts to answer, and one or more cultural values it reveals to you. Which myth do you think conveys the most important values?

Myth	Question	Cultural Values
"Prometheus"	How did humans obtain fire?	courage, self-sacrifice, endurance

OPTION 2

Evaluating Folk Tales Like myths, folk tales teach important lessons about human behavior. Review the folk tales you read in this unit and jot down a sentence or two about each, describing the lesson the tale teaches. Then decide which tales have the most to say to young people today. Share your evaluations with a group of classmates.

Building Your Portfolio

- **Writing Options** Review all of the projects you completed during this unit. Select the piece that helped you experience a culture most deeply. Write a note explaining what you gained from that writing. Attach the note to the piece of writing, and add both to your **Presentation Portfolio.**

- **Setting Goals** Think about the goals you set for yourself this year. How have you improved as a reader and as a writer? Write a paragraph evaluating your progress over the course of the year and set three more goals for the next year.

LITERATURE CONNECTIONS

Introduction to Mythology

The gods and goddesses, warriors, and heroes of world mythology appear and reappear in literature and films. Here are their origins—presented by scholars and storytellers, from Bullfinch to San Souci. This volume begins with Greek and Roman myths and travels the globe. Maps, diagrams, and time lines add context. Part of the *NexText* series from McDougal Littell, the book comes with online activities at **www.nextext.com**.

LINKS WITH UNIT 1:
Learning from Experience

Greek Myths
OLIVIA COOLIDGE

The Mask of Apollo
MARY RENAULT

Life in Ancient Greece
DON NARDO

Heroes, Gods and Monsters of the Greek Myths
BERNARD EVSLIN
SPOKEN ARTS (AUDIOCASSETTE)

LINKS WITH UNIT 2:
Relationships

Tongues of Jade
LAURENCE YEP

Grimm's Tales for Young and Old: The Complete Stories
RALPH MANHEIM (TRANSLATOR)

LINKS WITH UNIT 3:
Flights of Imagination

Tales of the Greek Heroes
ROGER LANCELYN GREEN

Puerto Rico Mío: Four Decades of Change
JACK DELANO (PHOTOGRAPHER)

Puerto Rico: An Unfinished Story
DENIS J. HAUPTLY

LINKS WITH UNIT 4:
Nothing Stays the Same
D'Aulaires' Book of Greek Myths
INGRI D'AULAIRE AND EDGAR PARIN D'AULAIRE

Cuentos: Tales from the Hispanic Southwest
JOSE GRIEGO Y MAESTAS AND RUDOLFO A. ANAYA

I'll Tell You a Tale: An Anthology
J. FRANK DOBIE

Texas: An Illustrated History
DAVID McCOMB

LINKS WITH UNIT 5:
Personal Challenges

Myths of the Norsemen: Retold from Old Norse Poems and Tales
ROGER LANCELYN GREEN

Anansi the Spider: A Tale of the Ashanti
FILMS INCORPORATED (VIDEOCASSETTE)

Folk Stories of the Hmong: Peoples of Laos, Thailand, and Vietnam
NORMA J. LIVO AND DIA CHA
LIBRARIES UNLIMITED (AUDIOCASSETTE)

EXTEND YOUR READING   **891**

Student *Resource Bank*

Words to Know: Access Guide

A

abode, 851
abundance, 256
accede, 435
acclaimed, 495
accommodations, 660
acknowledge, 851
aggrievedly, 444
agile, 279
agitate, 764
alight, 827
alleged, 762
ambiguous, 355
amiss, 480
ammunition, 594
anguish, 855
angular, 712
anonymous, 256
antagonism, 421
antidote, 464
apathy, 604
aptitude, 801
arresting, 611
assault, 863
assiduously, 165
audible, 523

B

balk, 165
barrage, 364
barren, 33
bartering, 858
beckon, 115
bedlam, 370
benefactor, 858
bleak, 682
bluff, 24
brooding, 93

C

chaos, 453
chaotic, 41
charitable, 266
circuit, 434
clench, 556
coincidence, 281
combatant, 93
compassionate, 104
complex, 434
compliance, 755
composure, 555
compulsory, 165
confirm, 529
confound, 686
consolation, 131
contemplate, 211
contempt, 840
contend, 854
contorted, 426
contradict, 755
convalescing, 445
conviction, 23
convoluted, 41
cower, 125
credibility, 524
crude, 862
crux, 104
cunningly, 131
currency, 264

curtail, 735
curtsey, 825
cynical, 291

D

dappled, 712
dazzled, 661
defiant, 421
design, 801
despair, 279
destitute, 256
devastating, 464
diffidently, 435
din, 226
disciplinarian, 50
discreet, 523
dismally, 158
dismay, 281
dispel, 368
diverted, 529
dominant, 604
drawl, 114
dwindle, 487

E

eerie, 660
elaborate, 538
elective, 21
eloquence, 290
elusive, 166
embroidered, 594
emerge, 257
eminent, 165
enchanted, 841

encrusted, 52
endeavor, 256
endow, 801
enfeebled, 104
enhance, 320
essence, 687
ethnicity, 40
evading, 370
exotic, 41
explicit, 801
exuberantly, 49

F

falsify, 280
feint, 370
ferocity, 22
fervent, 225
feverishly, 668
fidget, 281
finale, 274
flamboyant, 604
flimsy, 490
flourishing, 535
flustered, 419
forage, 451
forge, 869
forlorn, 485
frail, 31
frugally, 318

G

game, 370
gaudy, 443
gaunt, 49

revert, 383
revive, 124
righteous, 386
rummage, 103

S

sacrifice, 869
sanction, 686
sanctuary, 689
saturated, 538
saunter, 611
scheme, 114
scorn, 769
scornfully, 838
scowl, 22
scuttle, 132
seize, 770
self-denial, 319
sentimental, 318
sheepishly, 25
shrewdly, 290
shuffle, 771
simultaneously, 160
smugly, 815
snag, 770
solitude, 254
specify, 41

speculating, 292
spherical, 383
spurn, 496
squander, 855
staunchest, 158
stride, 627
stupefying, 610
stupendous, 524
submissive, 604
substance, 712
suede, 32
suite, 593
summon, 259
surly, 628
surplus, 256
susceptible, 450

T

tantalizing, 446
taunt, 294
teeming, 228
tensing, 58
throb, 753
toll, 671
transform, 253
transitory, 735
translucent, 383

treachery, 805
tread, 879
tribute, 661
trudge, 23

U

ultimate, 294
unaccountably, 718
unbridled, 367
unobtrusively, 168
unperceived, 169
unsound, 844
urgency, 211
usher, 40

V

vainglorious, 863
vainly, 840
valedictorian, 279
vengeance, 802
vicinity, 157
vigil, 440
vigor, 611
vile, 282
virtuous, 165

W

wan, 440
welfare, 260
whim, 318
wily, 687
wince, 50
wretched, 760

Z

zeal, 628

Pronunciation Key

Symbol	Examples	Symbol	Examples	Symbol	Examples
ă	at, gas	m	man, seem	v	van, save
ā	ape, day	n	night, mitten	w	web, twice
ä	father, barn	ng	sing, anger	y	yard, lawyer
âr	fair, dare	ŏ	odd, not	z	zoo, reason
b	bell, table	ō	open, road, grow	zh	treasure, garage
ch	chin, lunch	ô	awful, bought, horse	ə	awake, even, pencil,
d	dig, bored	oi	coin, boy		pilot, focus
ĕ	egg, ten	ŏŏ	look, full	ər	perform, letter
ē	evil, see, meal	ōō	root, glue, through		
f	fall, laugh, phrase	ou	out, cow		**Sounds in Foreign Words**
g	gold, big	p	pig, cap	KH	*German* ich, auch;
h	hit, inhale	r	rose, star		*Scottish* loch
hw	white, everywhere	s	sit, face	N	*French* entre, bon, fin
ĭ	inch, fit	sh	she, mash	œ	*French* feu, cœur;
ī	idle, my, tried	t	tap, hopped		*German* schön
îr	dear, here	th	thing, with	ü	*French* utile, rue;
j	jar, gem, badge	*th*	then, other		*German* grün
k	keep, cat, luck	ŭ	up, nut		
l	load, rattle	ûr	fur, earn, bird, worm		

Stress Marks

′ This mark indicates that the preceding syllable receives the primary stress.
For example, in the word *language,* the first syllable is stressed: lăng′gwĭj.

′ This mark is used only in words in which more than one syllable is stressed.
It indicates that the preceding syllable is stressed, but somewhat more weakly
than the syllable receiving the primary stress. In the word *literature,* for
example, the first syllable receives the primary stress, and the last syllable
receives a weaker stress: lĭt′ər-ə-chŏŏr′.

Adapted from *The American Heritage Dictionary of the English Language,
Third Edition;* Copyright © 1992 by Houghton Mifflin Company. Used with
the permission of Houghton Mifflin Company.

Glossary of Literary and Reading Terms

Act An act is a major section of a play. Each act may be further divided into smaller sections, called scenes. *The Monsters Are Due on Maple Street* has two acts.

African-American Folk Tale African-American folk tales are examples of oral literature. They developed among Africans who had been transported to America as slaves and were passed down orally for generations. "The People Could Fly" is an example of a written retelling of an African-American folk tale.

See also **Oral Literature.**

Alliteration Alliteration is a repetition of a sound or letter at the beginning of words. Writers use alliteration to emphasize particular words and to give their writing a musical quality. Note the repetition of the *c* sound in this line:

> Over the cobbles he clattered and clashed . . .
> —Alfred Noyes, from "The Highwayman"

See pages 193, 461.

Allusion An allusion is a reference to a famous person, place, event, or work of literature. In "A Crown of Wild Olive," the author makes an allusion to the war that broke out between Athens and Sparta in 431 B.C., known by historians as the Peloponnesian War.

Analogy An analogy is a point-by-point comparison between two apparently dissimilar things made to clarify a certain point about one of them. In "Amigo Brothers" Felix draws an analogy between the boxing match he and his friend Antonio must fight and the match in the boxing movie *The Champion* in order to put himself into a competitive frame of mind.

> When Felix finally left the theater, he had figured out how to psyche himself for tomorrow's fight. It was Felix the Champion vs. Antonio the Challenger.
> —Piri Thomas, from "Amigo Brothers"

Analysis Analysis is a process of breaking something down into its elements so that they can be examined individually. When you analyze a literary work, you examine its parts in order to understand how they work together in the piece as a whole.

Anecdote An anecdote is a short, entertaining account about a person or an event. Anecdotes are often included in larger works to entertain or make a point. In the excerpt from *Growing Up*, Russell Baker tells an amusing anecdote about his sister, Doris, returning some cheese to a grocery store.

Antagonist In a story, an antagonist is a force working against the **protagonist,** or main character; an antagonist can be another character, society, or a force within the main character. In "The Scholarship Jacket," Mr. Boone, the math teacher, is an antagonist because he opposes Martha's right to the scholarship jacket.

Mr. Boone's voice sounded calm and quiet. "Look. Joann's father is not only on the Board, he owns the only store in town: we could say it was a close tie and—"

—Marta Salinas, from "The Scholarship Jacket"

See also **Protagonist.**

Author's Perspective An author's perspective is the author's beliefs or attitudes as expressed in his or her work. In "Eleanor Roosevelt," William Jay Jacobs's perspective is that Eleanor Roosevelt was a remarkable woman because she survived a painful childhood and went on to become a great humanitarian. An author usually expresses his or her perspective through voice and tone.

See also **Voice, Tone.**

Author's Purpose An author's purpose is his or her reason for creating a particular work. The purpose may be to entertain, to explain or inform, to express an opinion, or to persuade readers to do or believe something. An author may have more than one purpose for writing, but usually one is the most important.

See pages 101, 414, 415.

Autobiography An autobiography is a form of nonfiction in which a person tells the story of his or her own life. "The Noble Experiment" from Jackie Robinson's *I Never Had It Made* is an example of autobiography.

See pages 83, 296.

Biographer *See* **Biography.**

Biography A biography is the story of a person's life, written by someone else. The subjects of biographies are often famous people, as in William Jay Jacobs's "Eleanor Roosevelt." A biographer is one who writes, composes, or produces a biography.

See pages 83, 98.

Cast of Characters In the script of a play, a cast of characters is a list of all the characters in the play, usually in order of appearance. This list is usually found at the beginning of the script.

See page 247.

Cause and Effect Two events are related as cause and effect when one event brings about the other. The event that happens first is the cause; the one that follows is the effect. This statement shows a cause-and-effect relationship:

He pointed out that I couldn't play for a few days anyhow because of my bum arm.

—Jackie Robinson, from "The Noble Experiment"

See pages 29, 109, 381, 708, 709.

Character A character is a person, an animal, or an imaginary creature that takes part in the action of a literary work. Generally, a work focuses on one or more **main characters,** but it may also include less important characters, called **minor characters.** Characters who change little, if at all, are called **static characters.** Characters who change significantly are called **dynamic characters.**

See pages 17, 62, 161, 216, 275, 589.

Characterization Characterization includes all the techniques writers use to create and develop characters. There are four basic methods of developing a character: (1) presenting the character's words and actions, (2) presenting the character's thoughts, (3) describing the character's appearance, and (4) showing what others think about the character. In "An Hour with Abuelo," Arturo's description of his reading characterizes him as a motivated student.

> *I* don't have much time left of my summer vacation, and there's a stack of books next to my bed I've got to read if I'm going to get into the AP English class I want.
>
> —Judith Ortiz Cofer, from "An Hour with Abuelo"

See pages 62, 586.

Chronological Order Chronological order is the order in which events happen in time. In the biography "Eleanor Roosevelt," the events of Roosevelt's life are told in chronological order, beginning with her birth and ending with her death.

See pages 86, 87.

Clarifying The process of pausing while reading to review previous events in a work and to check one's understanding is called clarifying. Readers stop to reflect on what they know, to make inferences about what is happening, and to better understand what they are reading.

See pages 4, 196, 391, 458.

Climax In the plot of a story or play, the climax (or **turning point**) is the point of maximum interest. At the climax, the conflict is resolved and the outcome of the plot becomes clear. The climax of "The War of the Wall," for example, occurs when the neighborhood kids return and see the finished mural for the first time.

See also **Conflict, Plot.**

Comedy A comedy is a dramatic work that is meant to be light, often humorous in tone, and usually ends happily with a peaceful resolution of the main conflict.

See also **Farce.**

Comparison The process of pointing out what two or more things have in common is called making a comparison. In the excerpt from *Boy: Tales of Childhood*, Roald Dahl compares Mr. Coombes, the headmaster of Llandaff school, as he opens the school door to an avenging angel:

> Suddenly it swung open and, through it, like the angel of death, strode Mr. Coombes. . . .
>
> —Roald Dahl, from *Boy: Tales of Childhood*

See also **Metaphor, Simile.**

Conflict Conflict is a struggle between opposing forces. In an **external conflict,** such as the battle between Rikki and the cobras in "Rikki-tikki-tavi," a character struggles against another character or against some outside force. **Internal conflict,** on the other hand, is a struggle that is within a character. In "Eleanor Roosevelt," for example, the young Eleanor experiences internal conflict after her father's death.

> For many months after her father's death she pretended that he was still alive.
>
> —William Jay Jacobs, from "Eleanor Roosevelt"

See pages 34, 118.

Connecting A reader's process of relating the content of a literary work to his or her own knowledge and experience is called connecting. In "A Day's Wait," for example, Schatz's fever may lead readers to recall their own experiences of being ill.

See pages 19, 278, 533.

Connotation A word's connotations are the ideas and feelings associated with the word, as opposed to its dictionary definition. For example, the word *mother,* in addition to its basic meaning ("a female parent"), has connotations of love, warmth, and security.

Context Clues Unfamiliar words are often surrounded by words or phrases—called context clues—that help readers understand their meaning. A context clue may be a definition, a synonym, an example, a comparison or contrast, or any other expression that enables readers to infer the word's meaning.

Contrast The process of pointing out differences between things is called contrast. In "Last Cover," for example, the narrator contrasts himself with his brother, Colin, when he says,

> I was following in Father's footsteps, true to form, but Colin threatened to break the family tradition. . . .
>
> —Paul Annixter, from "Last Cover"

Couplet A couplet is a rhymed pair of lines in a poem. Shel Silverstein's "Sarah Cynthia Sylvia Stout Would Not Take the Garbage Out" is written almost completely in couplets.

> The garbage reached across the state,
> From New York to the Golden Gate.
>
> —Shel Silverstein, from "Sarah Cynthia Sylvia Stout Would Not Take the Garbage Out"

Deductive Reasoning In nonfiction the structure of a text may be organized using deductive reasoning. Deductive reasoning is the process of logical reasoning from principles to specific instances, or reasoning from whole to part.

See also **Inductive Reasoning, Structure.**

Denotation A word's denotation is its dictionary definition.

See also **Connotation.**

Description Description is the process by which a writer creates a picture in readers' imaginations. A good description includes details that enable readers to visualize a scene, a character, or an object.

Details, Sensory Words and phrases that help readers see, hear, taste, feel, even smell what an author is describing are called sensory details. Note the sensory details in this passage from "The Scholarship Jacket":

> There was a cool breeze blowing and a sweet smell of mesquite fruit in the air, but I didn't appreciate it. I kicked at a dirt clod. I wanted that jacket so much.
>
> —Marta Salinas, from "The Scholarship Jacket"

Dialect A dialect is a form of language that is spoken in a certain place or by a certain class of people. Dialects of a language may differ from one another in pronunciation, vocabulary, and grammar. In the excerpt Mrs. Pratchett speaks a dialect of the British working class:

> "Let's 'ave a look at some of them titchy ones."
>
> —Roald Dahl, from *Boy: Tales of Childhood*

See pages 26, 546, 772.

Dialogue The words that characters speak aloud are called dialogue. In most literary works, dialogue is set off with quotation marks. In play scripts, however, each character's dialogue simply follows his or her name.

See page 248.

Drama A drama, or play, is a form of literature meant to be performed by actors before an audience. In drama, the characters' dialogue and actions tell the story. A playwright, or dramatist, is one who writes plays. Plays are generally performed live on a stage in a theater, or they may be filmed or broadcast.

See also **Prop, Scenery, Script, Stage.**

Drawing Conclusions Combining several pieces of information to make an inference is called drawing a conclusion. A reader's conclusions may be based on the details presented in a literary work, on his or her previous inferences, or on a combination of these.

See pages 206, 590, 591.

Dynamic Character *See* **Character.**

Essay An essay is a short work of nonfiction that deals with a single subject. One type of essay, such as "Homeless," emphasizes personal feelings and is called a **personal essay.** Another, such as "The Eternal Frontier," is written primarily to convey information and persuade the reader. This type is called a **persuasive essay.**

See pages 43, 467.

Evaluating Evaluating is the process of judging the worth of something or someone. A work of literature, or any of its parts, may be evaluated in terms of its entertainment value, its believability, its originality, or its emotional power.

See page 463.

Exaggeration An extreme overstatement of an idea is called an exaggeration, and is often used for purposes of emphasis or humor. Exaggeration is used as a form of irony, along with understatement and sarcasm. In the excerpt from *Growing Up*, Russell Baker uses exaggeration to emphasize the irony in the reverence the representative from the *Saturday Evening Post* has for his product:

> He had brought the canvas bag with him. He presented it with reverence fit for a chasuble.
>
> —Russell Baker, from *Growing Up*

See also Irony, Sarcasm, Understatement.

Exposition Exposition, which is usually found at the beginning of a story or play, serves to introduce the main characters, to describe the setting, and sometimes to establish the conflict. In "The War of the

Wall," for example, the first three paragraph provide most of the exposition.

See also **Plot.**

Extended Metaphor *See* **Metaphor.**

External Conflict *See* **Conflict.**

Fable A fable is a brief story that teaches a lesson about human nature. In many fables animals act and speak, like human beings. Usually, a fable—"Ant and Grasshopper," for example—concludes with a **moral**.

See page 311, 315, 321, 796.

Fact and Opinion A fact is a statement that can be proved, such as "April has 30 days." An opinion, in contrast, is a statement that cannot be proved, such as "April is the nicest month of the year." Opinions usually reflect personal beliefs and are often debatable.

Falling Action *See* **Plot.**

Fantasy A fantasy is a story that takes place in an unreal, imaginary world, such as the garden in "The Serial Garden." Fantasies often involve magic or characters with superhuman powers.

See pages 412, 455.

Farce A farce is a type of exaggerated comedy that contains an absurd plot, ridiculous situations, and humorous dialogue. The main purpose of farce is to keep the audience laughing. Neil Simon's *A Defenseless Creature* is a farce.

> WOMAN. (*Pointing an evil finger at* KISTUNOV, *she jumps on the desk and punctuates each sentence by stepping on his desk bell.*) A curse! A curse on your bank! I put on a curse on you and your depositors! May the money in your vaults turn to potatoes!
>
> —Neil Simon, from *A Defenseless Creature*

Fiction Fiction is prose writing that tells an imaginary story. The writer of a fictional work may invent all the events and characters in it or may base parts of the story on real people or events.

Figurative Language Authors use figurative language to create fresh and original descriptions. Figurative expressions, while not literally true, help readers picture ordinary things in new ways. In many, one thing is described in terms of another—as when this speaker explains:

> an ocean would never laugh
> if clouds weren't there
> to kiss her tears
>
> —Nikki Giovanni, from "The World Is Not A Pleasant Place To Be"

See page 194.
See also **Metaphor, Personification, Simile.**

Flashback In a literary work, a flashback is an interruption of the action to present a scene that took place at an earlier time. In "Last Cover," for example, a flashback is used to show how Colin found Bandit.

> We'd taken the young fox into the kitchen, all of us, except Father, gone a bit silly over the little thing. Colin had held it in his arms and fed it warm milk from a spoon.
>
> —Paul Annixter, from "Last Cover"

Foil A character who provides a striking contrast to a main character is called a foil. The foil helps make the main character's qualities apparent to the reader. For example, Bess acts as a foil for Lottie in "The Richer, the Poorer."

Folklore The traditions, customs, and stories that are passed down within a culture are known as its folklore. Folklore includes various types of literature, such as legends, folk tales, myths, trickster tales, and fables.

Folk Tale A folk tale is a story that has been passed from generation to generation by word of mouth. Folk tales may be set in the distant past and involve supernatural events, and the characters in them may be animals, people, or superhuman beings. "The Force of Luck" is an example of a folk tale.

See page 796.

Foreshadowing Foreshadowing occurs when a writer provides hints that suggest future events in a story. For example, in "Amigo Brothers" the rivalry between the two friends anticipates elements in, and gives readers hints about, the boxing match.

> Felix watched his friend disappear from view, throwing rights and lefts.
>
> —Piri Thomas, from "Amigo Brothers"

Form A literary work's form is its structure or organization. The form of a poem includes the arrangement of words and lines on the page. Some poems follow predictable patterns, with the same number of syllables in each line and the same number of lines in each stanza. Other poems, like Langston Hughes's "To You," have irregular forms.

See page 192.

Free Verse Poetry without regular patterns of rhyme and rhythm is called free verse. Some poets use free verse to capture the sounds and rhythms of ordinary speech. "Mooses" is an example of a poem written in free verse.

> The goofy Moose, the walking house-frame, Is lost
> In the forest. He bumps, he blunders, he stands.
>
> —Ted Hughes, from "Mooses"

See page 204.

Generalization A generalization is a broad statement about an entire group, such as "Novels take longer to read than short stories." Not all generalizations are true. Some are too broad or not supported by sufficient evidence, like the statement "All seventh graders are tall."

Genre A type or category of literature is called a genre. The main literary genres are fiction, nonfiction, poetry, and drama.

Haiku Haiku is a traditional form of Japanese poetry. A haiku normally has three lines and describes a single moment, feeling, or thing. In a traditional haiku, the first and third lines contain five syllables each, and the second line contains seven syllables.

Historical Fiction Historical fiction is fiction that is set in the past. It may contain references to actual people and events of the past. Though based in fact, it also contains fictional elements such as description and dialogue. "A Crown of Wild Olive" is an example of historical fiction.

See pages 706, 726.

Humor Humor is a quality that provokes laughter or amusement. Writers create humor through exaggeration, amusing descriptions, irony, and witty and insightful dialogue. Shel Silverstein's "Sarah Cynthia Sylvia Stout Would Not Take the Garbage Out" is an example of a humorous work.

See pages 394, 455.

Hyperbole An author's use of exaggeration or overstatement for emphasis is called hyperbole. A good example of hyperbole is Ernest Lawrence Thayer's description of the crowd's response to Casey:

> Then from the gladdened multitude went
> up a joyous yell—
> It rumbled in the mountaintops, it rattled
> in the dell;
> It struck upon the hillside and rebounded
> on the flat;
> For Casey, mighty Casey, was advancing
> to the bat.
>
> — Ernest Lawrence Thayer, from
> "Casey at the Bat"

Idiom An idiom is an expression that has a meaning different from the meaning of its individual words. For example, "go to the dogs" is an idiom meaning "go to ruin."

Imagery Imagery consists of words and phrases that appeal to readers' senses. Writers use sensory details to help readers imagine how things look, feel, smell, sound, and taste. Note the imagery in these lines:

> the fertile plants
> tangled,
> turned into
> tendrils, cattails,
> moving bulbs.
>
> —Pablo Neruda, from "Ode to an Artichoke"

See pages 194, 743.

Inductive Reasoning In nonfiction the structure of a text may be organized using inductive reasoning. Inductive reasoning is the process of determining principles, or generalizations, by logic or observation, or reasoning from part to whole.

See also **Deductive Reasoning, Structure.**

Inference An inference is a logical guess or conclusion based on evidence. For example, when Mr. Johnson hands out peanuts to strangers in "One Ordinary Day, with Peanuts," readers can infer that he wants to make new friends.

See pages 46, 347, 348.

Informative Nonfiction *See* **Nonfiction.**

Internal Conflict. See **Conflict.**

Interview An interview is a conversation, such as that conducted by a writer or reporter, in which facts or statements are drawn from another person, recorded, and then broadcast or published.

Irony Irony is a contrast between what is expected and what actually exists or happens. Exaggeration, sarcasm, and understatement are techniques writers use to express irony. The excerpt below turns out to be highly ironic given the kinds of expectations it raises about Russell Baker's early career in journalism and what actually happens:

> I began working in journalism when I was eight years old. It was my mother's idea. She wanted me to "make something" of myself and, after a level-headed appraisal of my strengths, decided I had better start young if I was to have any chance of keeping up with the competition.
>
> —Russell Baker, from *Growing Up*

See also **Exaggeration, Sarcasm, Understatement.**

See pages 358, 629.

Jargon Jargon is a specialized vocabulary used by members of a particular profession.

Legend A legend is a story handed down from the past about a specific person— usually someone of heroic accomplishments. Legends usually have some basis in historical fact.

See page 794.

Limerick A limerick is a short, humorous poem composed of five lines. It usually has the rhyme scheme *aabba*, created by two rhyming couplets followed by a fifth line that rhymes with the first couplet. A limerick typically has a sing-song rhythm.

Literary Nonfiction See **Nonfiction.**

Main Character See **Character**.

Main Idea A main idea is a writer's principal message. It may be the central idea of an entire work or a thought expressed in the topic sentence of a paragraph. (The term *main idea* is usually used in discussions of nonfiction.)

See pages 223, 732.

Memoir A memoir is a form of autobiographical writing in which a person recalls important events in his or her life. Although basically personal, a memoir may deal with events that have significance beyond the writer's individual life. Nelson Mandela's memoir, *Long Walk to Freedom*, for example, describes his growing awareness of the effects of racism in his native country, South Africa.

See page 737.

Metaphor A metaphor is a comparison of two things that have some quality in common. Unlike a simile, a metaphor does not contain the word *like* or *as*; instead, it says that one thing is another. The first lines of Alfred Noyes's "The Highwayman" contain a series of metaphors:

> The wind was a torrent of darkness among the gusty trees.
> The moon was a ghostly galleon tossed upon cloudy seas.
> The road was a ribbon of moonlight over the purple moor, . . .
>
> —Alfred Noyes, from "The Highwayman"

In an **extended metaphor**, two things are compared at some length and in several ways. The poem "Ode to an Artichoke" is based on an extended metaphor in which an artichoke is compared to a soldier.

See pages 194, 379.

Meter In poetry, meter is the pattern of accented and unaccented syllables. The meter in a line of poetry creates its rhythm. Not all poems have regular meter. "The Pasture" is an example of a poem with regular meter.

> I'm going out to clear the pasture spring;
> I'll only stop to rake the leaves away
> (and wait to watch the water clear, I may):
> I shan't be gone long.—You come too.
>
> —Robert Frost, from "The Pasture"

Minor Character See **Character.**

Monitoring Good readers monitor their understanding of what they are reading by stopping occasionally and adjusting their use of the active-reading strategies of visualizing, predicting, clarifying, questioning, connecting, and evaluating.

Mood A mood, or atmosphere, is a feeling that a literary work conveys to readers. Writers use a variety of techniques— including word choice, dialogue, description, and plot complications—to establish moods. In *The Monsters Are Due on Maple Street,* for example, Rod Serling creates a mood of tension and anticipation.

> [Les] *stops suddenly as, behind him, the car engine starts up all by itself. Les whirls around to stare at the car. The car idles roughly, smoke coming from the exhaust, the frame shaking gently. Les's eyes go wide, and he runs over to the car. The people stare at the car.*
>
> —Rod Serling, from *The Monsters Are Due on Maple Street*

See pages 519, 530.

Moral A moral is a lesson that a story teaches. Morals are often stated directly at the end of fables.

Motivation A character's motivation is the reason why he or she acts, feels, or thinks in a certain way. For example, in "Zebra," a desire to help Adam get well is part of John Wilson's motivation. Motivations may be stated directly, or they may be implied.

> She handed him a large brown envelope. It was addressed to Adam Zebrin, Eighth Grade, at the school. The sender was John Wilson with a return address in Virginia.
>
> —Chaim Potok, from "Zebra"

Myth A myth is a traditional story, usually of unknown authorship, that deals with basic questions about the universe. Gods and heroes often figure prominently in myths, which may attempt to explain such things as the origin of the world, mysteries of nature, or social customs. "Phaëthon" is an example of a myth.

See page 796.

Narrative A narrative is writing that tells a story. The events in a narrative may be real, or they may be imaginary. Narratives that deal with real events include biographies and autobiographies. Fictional narratives include myths, short stories, novels, and narrative poems.

See pages 388, 772.

Narrative Poetry Poetry that tells a story is called narrative poetry. Like fiction, narrative poetry contains characters, settings, plots, and themes. It may also contain such elements of poetry as rhyme, rhythm, imagery, and figurative language. "The Highwayman" is an example of a narrative poem.

Narrator The narrator is the teller of a story.

See page 614.
See also **Point of View.**

Nonfiction Writing that tells about real people, places, and events is called nonfiction. Writers of nonfiction often get their information from both **primary sources** (original, firsthand accounts) and **secondary sources** (descriptions based on primary sources). **Informative nonfiction** is written mainly to provide factual information. A work of **literary nonfiction,** on the other hand, reads like a work of fiction—although it too provides factual information.

See pages 82, 230, 766.
See also **Autobiography, Biography, Essay.**

Novel A novel is a work of fiction that is longer and more complex than a short story. A novel's setting, plot, characters, and theme are usually developed in greater detail than a short story's.

Onomatopoeia Onomatopoeia is the use of words whose sound suggests their meaning—like *whir, buzz, pop,* and *sizzle.* In "The Highwayman," the onomatopoeic *tlot-tlot* is used to imitate the clopping of a horse's hoofs on a road.

> *Tlot-tlot; tlot-tlot!* Had they heard it?
>   The horse hoofs ringing clear;
> *Tlot-tlot, tlot-tlot,* in the distance? Were
>   they   deaf that they did not hear?
>
> —Alfred Noyes, from "The Highwayman"

See pages 193, 461.

Oral History Oral histories are stories of people's lives that have been passed down by word of mouth. Oral histories include both factual information and imaginative interpretation. In recent times, many oral histories have been written down.

Oral Literature Oral literature includes different kinds of narratives of unknown authorship that have been passed down by word of mouth from generation to generation. Oral literature includes folk tales, legends, and myths. In recent times,

some oral narratives have been written down, but oral literature remains an important aspect of many cultures throughout the world.

See **African-American Folk Tale, Folk Tale, Myth.**

Parallelism Parallelism is the use of similar grammatical constructions to express ideas that are equal in importance. The parallel elements may be words, phrases, sentences, or paragraphs. Note in the example below how the parallel sentence structures help the reader to see that to Roald Dahl, feeling like a hero was the same as being one.

> I felt like a hero. I *was* a hero. It was marvelous to be so popular.
>
> —Roald Dahl, from *Boy: Tales of Childhood*

Paraphrasing Readers who paraphrase restate information in their own words. Paraphrasing helps readers to clarify meaning.

Personification The giving of human qualities to an animal, object, or idea is known as personification. In "Rikki-tikki-tavi," for example, the mongoose and the cobras are personified, conversing as if they were human.

> Rikki-tikki licked his lips. "This is a splendid hunting ground," he said, and his tail grew bottlebrushy at the thought of it; . . .
>
> —Rudyard Kipling, from "Rikki-tikki-tavi"

See pages 135, 379.

Play *See* **Drama.**

Playwright *See* **Drama.**

Plot A story's plot is the sequence of related events that make up the story. In a typical plot, an **exposition** introduces the characters and establishes the main conflict. **Complications** arise as the characters try to resolve the conflict. Eventually, the plot builds toward a **climax,** the point of greatest interest or suspense. In the **resolution**—the final stage of the plot—loose ends are tied up and the story is brought to a close.

See pages 16, 34, 171, 343, 561.

Poetry Poetry is a type of literature in which ideas and feelings are expressed in compact, imaginative, and musical language. Poets arrange words in ways intended to touch readers' senses, emotions, and minds. Most poems are written in lines, which may contain regular patterns of rhyme and rhythm. These lines may, in turn, be grouped in stanzas.

See page 191.

Point of View Every story is told from a particular point of view, or perspective. When a story is told from the **first-person point of view,** the narrator is a character in the story and uses first-person pronouns, such as *I, me, we,* and *us.* In a story told from a **third-person point of view,** on the other hand, the narrator is not a character; he or she uses third-person pronouns, such as *he, she, it, they,* and *them.*

The **third-person omniscient** (all-knowing) point of view allows the narrator to relate the thoughts and feelings of several, if not all, the story's characters. The narrator of "Rikki-Tikki-Tavi" for example reveals the thoughts and feelings of more than one character. If events are related from a **third-person limited point of view,** as in "Seventh Grade," the narrator tells us what one character thinks, feels, and observes.

See pages 106, 598.

Predicting Using what you know to draw a conclusion about what may happen is called predicting. Good readers gather information as they read and combine that information with prior knowledge to predic upcoming events in a story.

See pages 121, 361, 438, 521, 522.

Primary Sources *See* **Nonfiction.**

Prop The word *prop*, an abbreviation of *property*, refers to any physical object that is used in a drama or play. In Charles Dickens' *A Christmas Carol,* the props include a turkey and a dove.

See also Drama, Scene, Scenery, Script, Stage.

Prose Prose is the ordinary form of spoken and written language—that is, it is language that lacks the special features of poetry.

Protagonist The central character in a story, play, or novel is called the protagonist. The protagonist is involved in the main conflict of the plot and often changes during the course of the work. The character who opposes the protagonist is the **antagonist.** In "A Retrieved Reformation," Jimmy Valentine is the protagonist and his pursuer, Ben Price, is the antagonist.

> Ben Price knew Jimmy's habits. He had learned them while working up the Springfield case. Long jumps, quick getaways, no confederates, and a taste for good society—these ways had helped Mr. Valentine to become noted as a successful dodger of retribution. It was given out that Ben Price had taken up the trail of the elusive cracksman, and other people with burglar-proof safes felt more at ease.
>
> —O. Henry, from "A Retrieved Reformation"

See also Antagonist.

Questioning The process of raising questions while reading is called questioning. Good readers ask questions in an effort to understand characters and events, looking for answers as they continue to read.

See page 299.

Radio Play A radio play is a drama that is written specifically to be broadcast over the radio. Because the audience is not meant to see a radio play, sound effects are often used to help listeners imagine the setting and the action. The stage directions in the play's script indicate the sound effects.

Realism Realism involves the vivid description of characters and the world in which they live. A realistic description emphasizes a character's thoughts and feelings by describing how the character looks and acts. In "The People Could Fly," Virginia Hamilton provides a particularly realistic description of the character of Sarah.

> The sun burned her face. The babe cried and cried, "Pity me, oh, pity me," say it sounded like. Sarah was so sad and starvin', she sat down in the row.
>
> —Virginia Hamilton, from "The People Could Fly"

Repetition Repetition is a use of any element of language—a sound, a word, a phrase, a grammatical structure—more than once. Writers use repetition to stress ideas and to create memorable sound effects, as in these lines:

> He did not come in the dawning. He did not come at noon;
> And out of the tawny sunset, before the rise of the moon, . . .
>
> —Alfred Noyes, from "The Highwayman"

See also **Alliteration, Rhyme.**

Resolution See **Plot.**

Rhyme Rhyme is a repetition of sounds at the end of words. Words rhyme when their accented vowels and all the letters that follow have identical sounds. *Dog* and *log* rhyme, as do *letter* and *better.*

The most common form of rhyme in poetry is **end rhyme,** where the rhyming words occur at the end of lines. Rhyme that occurs within a line is called **internal rhyme.**

See pages 193, 199, 303, 461.

Rhyme Scheme A rhyme scheme is the pattern of rhymes in a poem. A rhyme scheme can be described by using letters to represent the rhyming sounds at the ends of lines. Lines that rhyme are given the same letter. For example, in the following poem, the rhyme scheme is *abab:*

> If I can stop one Heart from breaking   *a*
> I shall not live in vain   *b*
> If I can ease one Life the Aching   *a*
> Or cool one Pain   *b*
>
> —Emily Dickinson, from "If I Can Stop One Heart from Breaking"

Rhythm The rhythm of a line of poetry is the pattern of stressed and unstressed syllables in the line. When this pattern is repeated throughout a poem, the poem is said to have a regular beat. Note the rhythm in these lines (the mark ´ indicates a stressed syllable; the mark ˘, an unstressed syllable):

> The wind was a torrent of darkness among the gusty trees.
> The moon was a ghostly galleon tossed upon cloudy seas.
>
> —Alfred Noyes, from "The Highwayman"

See pages 193, 303, 458.

Rising Action See **Plot.**

Sarcasm Sarcasm is a device writers use to express irony. Sarcasm may use either understatement or exaggeration, but with the purpose of upsetting or even offending someone. When Russell Baker's mother tells him that he has "no more gumption than a bump on a log," she is using exaggeration to the point of sarcasm.

See also **Exaggeration, Irony, Understatement.**

Scanning Scanning is the process of searching through writing for a particular fact or piece of information. When you scan, your eyes sweep across a page, looking for key words that may lead you to the information you want.

Scene In a play, a scene is a section presenting events that occur in one place at one time. Each scene presents an episode of the play's plot. For example, in *A Christmas Carol*, Scene 1 shows what occurs in Scrooge's shop, and Scene 2 shows what occurs at Scrooge's home.

Scenery The painted backdrop or other structures used to create the setting for a play.

See also **Drama, Stage.**

Science Fiction Science fiction is fiction based on real or imagined scientific developments. Science fiction stories are often set in imaginary places and in the future. Ray Bradbury's "Dark They Were, and Golden-Eyed" is an example of science fiction.

See pages 411, 436.

Script The text of a play, motion picture, or broadcast is called a script.

See also **Drama, Stage.**

Secondary Sources See **Nonfiction.**

Sensory Details See **Details.**

Sequence The order in which events occur or ideas are presented is called a sequence. In a narrative, events are usually presented in chronological order—the order in which they happened. A writer may use clue words and phrases—such as *then, until, after a while,* and *finally*—to help readers understand the sequence of events.

See also **Chronological Order.**

Setting The setting of a story, poem, or play is the time and place of the action. Elements of setting may include geographic location, historical period (past, present, or future), the season of the year, the time of day, and the beliefs, customs, and standards of a society. The influence of setting on characters' decisions and actions may vary from work to work.

See pages 18, 26, 43, 655, 672, 690.

Setting a Purpose The process of establishing specific reasons to read a literary work is called setting a purpose. Readers often come to a piece of writing with a purpose in mind, such as reading for entertainment, for information, or to analyze or evaluate a piece of writing. Readers can look at a work's title, headings and subheadings, and illustrations to preview the work and then set a purpose for their reading.

Short Story A short story is a brief work of fiction that can usually be read in a single sitting. A short story generally focuses on one or two main characters and on a single conflict.

Simile A simile is a comparison of two things that have some quality in common. In a simile, the comparison is conveyed by means of the word *like* or *as.* Note the simile in this sentence:

> What is left looks rather like a gigantic, black pancake.
>
> —Roald Dahl, from *Boy: Tales of Childhood*

See page 194.

Skimming Skimming is the process of reading quickly to identify the main idea of, or to get an overview of, a work or passage. It involves reading the title, the headings, the words in special type, and the first sentence of each paragraph, as well as any charts, graphs, and time lines that accompany the writing.

Sound Effects. *See* **Alliteration, Onomatopoeia, Repetition, Rhyme, Rhythm.**

Speaker In a poem, the speaker is the voice that talks to the reader—like the narrator in a work of fiction. Frequently, recognizing the speaker's attitude is a key to understanding a poem's meaning. In some poems, such as "The Bat," by Theodore Roethke, the speaker expresses the feelings of the poet. In others, the speaker's attitude and the poet's may not be the same.

See page 204.

Speech A speech is a prepared talk given in public. Sometimes, speeches are later published. Virginia Hamilton's "Looking For America" is an excerpt from a speech.

Stage The level and raised platform on which entertainers usually perform.

See also **Drama.**

Stage Directions In the script of a play, the instructions to the actors, director, and stage crew are called stage directions. They may suggest scenery, lighting, music, sound effects, and ways for actors to move and speak. In the plays in this book, stage directions appear in italic type and are enclosed in parentheses.

> (*The percussion thunders. Scrooge hurls himself through the descending snowflakes and sends the children scattering.*)
>
> —Frederick Gaines, from *A Christmas Carol*

See pages 246, 275.

Stanza A group of lines within a poem is called a stanza. A stanza is like a paragraph in a work of prose. "The Rider," by Naomi Shihab Nye, for example, contains three stanzas.

See pages 192, 459.

Static Character *See* **Character.**

Stereotype A stereotype is a generalization about a group of people, in which individual differences are disregarded. Stereotypes may lead to unfair judgments of individuals on the basis of race, ethnic background, or physical appearance.

Story Map A story map is a visual organizer that helps a reader understand a work of literature. A story map helps a reader to keep track of setting, characters, events, and conflicts.

Structure The structure of a work of literature is the way in which it is put together. In poetry, structure involves the arrangement of words and lines to produce a desired effect. One structural unit in poetry is the stanza. In prose, structure involves the arrangement of such elements as sentences, paragraphs, and events. "Dark They Were, and Golden-Eyed," for example, has the overall structure of a third-person fictional narrative. It has a circular structure in which the end mirrors the beginning.

See page 491.

Style A style is a manner of writing; it involves how something is said rather than what is said. The excerpt from *Boy: Tales of Childhood,* for example, has a playful style that relies on exaggeration, humor, and colorful words. Many elements contribute to style, including word choice, sentence length, tone, and figurative language.

> I lifted the heavy glass lid of the gobstopper jar and dropped the mouse in. Then I replaced the lid as silently as possible. My heart was thumping like mad, and my hands had gone all sweaty.
>
> —Roald Dahl, from *Boy: Tales of Childhood*

Summarizing Summarizing is telling the main ideas of a piece of writing briefly in one's own words, omitting unimportant details.

See pages 287, 767.

Surprise Ending An unexpected plot twist at the end of a story is called a surprise ending. "A Retrieved Reformation" is an example of a story with a surprise ending.

See page 372.

Suspense Suspense is a feeling of growing tension and excitement felt by a reader. Writers create suspense by raising questions in readers' minds about what might happen. For example, in "A Retrieved Reformation," a suspenseful moment occurs when Agatha is trapped inside the bank vault and readers wonder whether she will suffocate.

See pages 372, 429.

Symbol A symbol is a person, a place, an object, or an action that stands for something beyond itself. In "The White Umbrella," for example, the umbrella mentioned in the story title symbolizes the ambivalence the main character feels toward her mother's having to take a job to help support the family. This ambivalence is resolved at the end of the story when the character throws the umbrella away.

See page 394.

Table of Contents In most nonfiction books or in books arranged by chapter or section, the contents of the book are shown in a table of contents. The table of contents usually appears at the beginning of the book and lists chapter and section titles and the page where each begins. Besides helping you to find specific parts of the book, the table of contents can give you an overview of the material covered by the book.

Tall Tale A tall tale is a humorously exaggerated story about impossible events, often relating the supernatural abilities of the main character. The tales about folk heroes such as Paul Bunyan, Pecos Bill, and Davy Crockett are tall tales.

Teleplay A play written for television is called a teleplay. In a teleplay, the stage directions usually include camera instructions. *The Monsters Are Due on Maple Street* is an example of a teleplay.

See page 429.

Text Organizers Text organizers include headings, tables of contents, and graphic elements such as charts, tables, time lines, boxes, bullets, and captions.

Theme A theme is the message about life or human nature that is conveyed by a literary work. A work may have more than one theme, and in many cases readers must infer the writer's message. One way to infer a fictional work's theme is to decide what general statement could be supported by the experiences of the main character. For example, a theme of "The Scholarship Jacket" is having to stand up for one's beliefs.

See pages 18, 284, 413, 498.

Title The title of a piece of writing is the name that is attached to it. A title often refers to an important aspect of the work to which it is attached. For example, the title "The War of the Wall" refers to Lou and the narrator's conflict with the "painter lady."

See page 467.

Tone The tone of a work is the writer's attitude toward his or her subject. Words such as *amused, objective,* and *angry* can be used to describe different tones. The tone of "Winter Poem," for example, might be described as dreamy or escapist.

> once a snowflake fell
> on my brow and i loved
> it so much and i kissed
> it and it was happy and called its cousins
>
> —Nikki Giovanni, from "Winter Poem"

See pages 519, 530.

Tragedy A tragedy is a dramatic work that presents the downfall of a dignified character or characters who are involved in historically or socially significant events. The events in a tragic plot are set in motion by a decision that is often an error in judgment. Succeeding events are linked in a cause-and-effect relationship and lead to a disastrous conclusion, often death.

Trickster Tale Trickster tales are folktales that reflect an admiration for cleverness. The tricksters themselves are not depicted as heroic but as what they really are—con artists. "Brother Coyote and Brother Cricket" is an example of a trickster tale from Texas.

Turning Point See **Plot.**

Understatement Writers use understatement as a means of expressing irony. Understatement de-emphasizes the significance of something. Writer Russell Baker uses understatement when he comments that, as a child, as far as he could tell, what writers did "couldn't be classified as work."

See also **Exaggeration, Irony, Sarcasm.**

Unreliable Narrator A narrator who does not narrate events objectively is called an unreliable narrator. An unreliable narrator is usually a character in the work whose biases or lack of self-awareness distorts his or her presentation of events. Juliette in "Waiting" is an example of an unreliable

narrator. Note in the quotation below the bias with which she imagines how others will comment about her.

> People were murmuring, "So young, so small, and so attractive."
>
> —Budge Wilson, from "Waiting"

Visualizing The process of forming a mental picture based on a written description is called visualizing. Good readers use the details supplied by writers to picture characters, settings, and events in their minds.

See pages 249, 250, 478, 553.

Voice A writer's or narrator's voice is his or her unique style of expression. Voice can reveal much about the author or narrator's personality, beliefs, and attitudes. The voice in "The Elephant" expresses the pain of imprisonment and longing for freedom.

> I will remember what I was. I am sick
>   of rope and chain—
> I will remember my old strength and
>   all my forest-affairs.
>
> —Rudyard Kipling, from "The Elephant"

See also **Author's Perspective, Tone.**

Word Choice Word choice is an important part of the writing process. Writers carefully select words to give precise descriptions, create a particular mood, and increase the impact of their writing. Notice how the words Gish Jen chooses help to create a mood in "The White Umbrella":

> The umbrella glowed like a scepter on the blue carpet while Mona, slumping over the keyboard, managed to eke out a fair rendition of a cat fight.
>
> —Gish Jen, from "The White Umbrella"

① The Writing Process

The writing process consists of four stages: prewriting, drafting, revising and editing, and publishing and reflecting. As the graphic below shows, these stages are not steps that you must complete in a set order. Rather, you may return to any one at any time in your writing process, using feedback from your readers along the way.

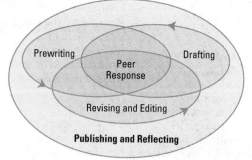

ⓘ Prewriting

In the prewriting stage, you explore your ideas and discover what you want to write about.

Finding Ideas for Writing
Try one or more of the following techniques to help you find a writing topic.

Personal Techniques
- Practice imaging, or trying to remember mainly sensory details about a subject—its look, sound, feel, taste, and smell.
- Complete a knowledge inventory to discover what you already know about a subject.
- Browse through magazines, newspapers, and on-line bulletin boards for ideas.
- Start a clip file of articles that you want to save for future reference. Be sure to label each clip with source information.

Sharing Techniques
- With a group, brainstorm a topic by trying to come up with as many ideas as you can without stopping to critique or examine them.
- Interview someone who knows a great deal about your topic.

Writing Techniques
- After freewriting on a topic, try looping, or choosing your best idea for more freewriting. Repeat the loop at least once.
- Make a list to help you organize ideas, examine them, or identify areas for further research.

Graphic Techniques
- Create a pro-and-con chart to compare the positive and negative aspects of an idea or a course of action.
- Use a cluster map or tree diagram to explore subordinate ideas that relate to your general topic or central idea.

Determining Your Purpose
Your purpose for writing may be to express yourself, to entertain, to describe, to explain, to analyze, or to persuade. To clarify it, ask questions like these:

- Why did I choose to write about my topic?
- What aspects of the topic mean the most to me?
- What do I want others to think or feel after they read my writing?

Identifying Your Audience

Knowing who will read your writing can help you focus your topic and choose relevant details. As you think about your readers, ask yourself questions like these:

- What does my audience already know about my topic?
- What will they be most interested in?
- What language is most appropriate for this audience?

LINK TO LITERATURE Roald Dahl—the author of *Boy: Tales of Childhood,* on page 533—understood the importance of identifying his audience. According to Dahl, "Children are a great discipline because they are highly critical. . . . And if you think a child is getting bored, you must think up something that jolts [the child] back. Something that tickles."

 Drafting

In the drafting stage, you put your ideas on paper and allow them to develop and change as you write.

Two broad approaches in this stage are discovery drafting and planned drafting.

Discovery drafting is a good approach when you are not quite sure what you think about your subject. You just plunge into your draft and let your feelings and ideas lead you where they will. After finishing a discovery draft, you may decide to start another draft, do more prewriting, or revise your first draft.

Planned drafting may work better for research reports, critical reviews, and other kinds of formal writing. Try making a writing plan or a scratch outline before you begin drafting. Then, as you write, you can fill in the details. The changes you make in your writing during this stage usually fall into three categories: revising for content, revising for structure, and proofreading to correct mistakes in mechanics.

Use the questions that follow to assess problems and determine what changes would improve your work.

 Revising, Editing, and Proofreading

Revising for Content

- Does my writing have a main idea or central focus? Is my thesis clear?
- Have I incorporated adequate detail? Where might I include a telling detail, revealing statistic, or vivid example?
- Is any material unnecessary, irrelevant, or confusing?

WRITING TIP Be sure to consider the needs of your audience as you answer the questions under Revising for Content and Revising for Structure. For example, before you can determine whether any of your material is unnecessary or irrelevant, you need to identify what your audience already knows.

Revising for Structure

- Is my writing unified? Do all ideas and supporting details pertain to my main idea or advance my thesis?
- Is my writing clear and coherent? Is the flow of sentences and paragraphs smooth and logical?
- Do I need to add transitional words, phrases, or sentences to make the relationships among ideas clearer?
- Are my sentences well constructed? What sentences might I combine to improve the grace and rhythm of my writing?

Proofreading to Correct Mistakes in Grammar, Usage, and Mechanics

When you are satisfied with your revision, proofread your paper, looking for mistakes in grammar, usage, and mechanics. You may want to do this several times, looking for different types of mistakes each time. The following checklist may help.

Sentence Structure and Agreement

- Are there any run-on sentences or sentence fragments?
- Do all verbs agree with their subjects?

- Do all pronouns agree with their antecedents?
- Are verb tenses correct and consistent?

Forms of Words

- Do adverbs and adjectives modify the appropriate words?
- Are all forms of *be* and other irregular verbs used correctly?
- Are pronouns used correctly?
- Are comparative and superlative forms of adjectives correct?

Capitalization, Punctuation, and Spelling

- Is any punctuation mark missing or not needed?
- Are all words spelled correctly?
- Are all proper nouns and all proper adjectives capitalized?

WRITING TIP For help identifying and correcting problems that are listed in the Proofreading Checklist, see the Grammar Handbook, pages R54–R85.

You might wish to mark changes on your paper by using the proofreading symbols shown in the chart below.

Proofreading Symbols

∧	Add letters or words.	/	Make a capital letter lowercase.
⊙	Add a period.	¶	Begin a new paragraph.
≡	Capitalize a letter.	⌿	Delete letters or words.
⌒	Close up a space.	∿	Switch the positions of letters or words.
∧	Add a comma.		

1.4 Publishing and Reflecting

Always consider sharing your finished writing with a wider audience. Reflecting on your writing is another good way to bring closure to a project.

Creative Publishing Ideas

Following are some ideas for publishing and sharing your writing.

- Post your writing on an electronic bulletin board or send it to others via email.
- Create a multimedia presentation and share it with classmates.
- Publish your writing in a school newspaper or literary magazine.
- Present your work orally in a report, a speech, a reading, or a dramatic performance.
- Submit your writing to a local newspaper or a magazine that publishes student writing.
- Form a writing exchange group with other students.

WRITING TIP You might work with other students to publish an anthology of class writing. Then exchange your anthology with another class or another school. Reading the work of other student writers will help you get ideas for new writing projects and find ways to improve your work.

Reflecting on Your Writing

Think about your writing process and whether you would like to add what you have written to your portfolio. You might attach a note in which you answer questions like these:

- What did I learn about myself and my subject through this writing project?
- Which parts of the writing process did I most enjoy and which did I least enjoy?
- As I wrote, what was my biggest problem? How did I solve it?
- What did I learn that I can use the next time I write?

1.5 Using Peer Response

Peer response consists of the suggestions and comments your peers or classmates make about your writing.

You can ask a peer reader for help at any point in the writing process. For example, your peers can help you develop a topic, narrow your focus, discover confusing passages, or organize your writing.

Questions for Your Peer Readers

You can help your peer readers provide you with the most useful kinds of feedback by following these guidelines:

- Tell readers where you are in the writing process. Are you still trying out ideas, or have you completed a draft?

- Ask questions that will help you get specific information about your writing. Open-ended questions that require more than yes-or-no answers are more likely to give you information you can use as you revise.

- Give your readers plenty of time to respond thoughtfully to your writing.

- Encourage your readers to be honest when they respond to your work. It's OK if you don't agree with them—you always get to decide which changes to make.

Tips for Being a Peer Reader

Follow these guidelines when you respond to someone else's work:

- Respect the writer's feelings.

- Make sure you understand what kind of feedback the writer is looking for, and then respond accordingly.

- Use "I" statements, such as "I like . . . ," "I think . . . ," or "It would help me if . . . ." Remember that your impressions and opinions may not be the same as someone else's.

WRITING TIP Writers are better able to absorb criticism of their work if they first receive positive feedback. When you act as a peer reader, try to start your review by telling something you like about the piece. The chart below explains different peer-response techniques to use when you are ready to share your work.

Peer-Response Techniques

Sharing Use this when you are just exploring ideas or when you want to celebrate the completion of a piece of writing.

- *Will you please read or listen to my writing without criticizing or making suggestions afterward?*

Summarizing Use this when you want to know if your main idea or goals are clear.

- *What do you think I'm saying? What's my main idea or message?*

Replying Use this strategy when you want to make your writing richer by adding new ideas.

- *What are your ideas about my topic? What do you think about what I have said in my piece?*

Responding to Specific Features Use this when you want a quick overview of the strengths and weaknesses of your writing.

- *Are the ideas supported with enough examples? Did I persuade you? Is the organization clear enough for you to follow the ideas?*

Telling Use this to find out which parts of your writing are affecting readers the way you want and which parts are confusing.

- *What did you think or feel as you read my words? Would you show me which passage you were reading when you had that response?*

2 Building Blocks of Good Writing

Whatever your purpose in writing, you need to capture your readers' interest, organize your ideas well, and present your thoughts clearly. Giving special attention to some particular parts of a story or an essay can make your writing more enjoyable and more effective.

2.1 Introductions

When you flip through a magazine trying to decide which articles to read, the opening paragraph is often critical. If it does not grab your attention, you are likely to turn the page.

Kinds of Introductions

Here are some introduction techniques that can capture a reader's interest.

- Make a surprising statement.
- Provide a description.
- Pose a question.
- Relate an anecdote.
- Address the reader directly.
- Begin with a thesis statement.

Make a Surprising Statement Beginning with a startling statement or an interesting fact can capture your reader's curiosity about the subject, as in the model below.

> MODEL
> Bats may seem like a nuisance, but not as much as the 99 pounds of insects a colony of bats can eat in one night. Despite their ugly faces and all the scary stories about them, bats are very important and useful animals.

Provide a Description A vivid description sets a mood and brings a scene to life for your reader. Here, details about wild geese swimming in an unfrozen river during the winter set the tone for an essay about water pollution.

> MODEL
> The temperature is 15 degrees. Drifts of snow hide picnic tables and swings. In the middle of the park, however, steam rises from a lake where Canada geese swim. It sounds beautiful, but the water is warm because it has been heated by a chemical plant upriver. In fact, the geese should have migrated south by now.

Ask a Question Beginning with a question can make your reader want to read on to find out the answer. The following introduction asks what two seemingly different things have in common.

> MODEL
> What do billiard balls and movie film have in common? It was in an effort to find a substitute for ivory billiard balls that John Hyatt created celluloid. This plastic substance was also used to make the first movies.

Relate an Anecdote Beginning with a brief anecdote, or story, can hook readers and help you make a point in a dramatic way. The anecdote below introduces a humorous essay about a childhood experience.

> MODEL
> When I was younger, my friends and I would rub balloons in our hair and make them stick to our clothes. Someone once said, "I get a charge out of this," not knowing that we were really generating static electricity.

Address the Reader Directly Speaking directly to readers establishes a friendly, informal tone and involves them in your topic.

> MODEL
> **Find out how to maintain your cardio-vascular system while enjoying yourself. Come to a free demonstration of Fit for Life at the Community Center Friday night at 7:00 P.M.**

Begin with a Thesis Statement A thesis statement expressing a paper's main idea may be woven into both the beginning and the end of nonfiction writing. The following is a thesis statement that introduces a literary analysis.

> MODEL
> **In "The Great Taos Bank Robbery," Tony Hillerman presents eccentric characters with loving detail. It is clear that he has affection for the hapless criminals as well as for the fascinated, easygoing townspeople.**

WRITING TIP In order to write the best introduction for your paper, you may want to try more than one of the methods and then decide which is the most effective for your purpose and audience.

2.2 Paragraphs

A paragraph is made up of sentences that work together to develop an idea or accomplish a purpose. Whether or not it contains a topic sentence stating the main idea, a good paragraph must have unity and coherence.

Unity

A paragraph has unity when all the sentences support and develop one stated or implied idea. Use the following techniques to create unity in your paragraphs.

Write a Topic Sentence A topic sentence states the main idea of the paragraph; all other sentences in the paragraph provide supporting details. A topic sentence is often the first sentence in a paragraph. However, it may also appear later in the paragraph or at the end, to summarize or reinforce the main idea.

> MODEL
> *Flying a hot-air balloon looks fun, but it requires a good mathematician to fly one safely.* Since a balloon is controlled by heating and cooling the air inside the balloon, the pilot must know the temperature of the air outside it and how high he or she plans to fly in order to calculate the maximum weight the balloon can carry. It the pilot doesn't do the math correctly, the balloon could crash.

LINK TO LITERATURE Notice the use of strong topic sentences in "The Noble Experiment" by Jackie Robinson, as told to Alfred Duckett. For example, on page 290 the first paragraph begins, "Winning his directors' approval was almost insignificant in contrast to the task which now lay ahead of the Dodger president." The rest of the paragraph then explains that task in detail.

Coherence

A paragraph is coherent when all its sentences are related to one another and flow logically from one to the next. The following techniques will help you achieve coherence in paragraphs.

- Present your ideas in the most logical order.
- Use pronouns, synonyms, and repeated words to connect ideas.
- Use transitional devices to show the relationships among ideas.

In the model below, the writer used some of these techniques to create a unified paragraph.

> MODEL
> **Just the name "alligator snapping turtle" brings to mind a ferocious, frightening creature. But this fascinating creature is protected by law. The alligator snapping turtle can grow to more than 200 pounds. In fact, whereas common snapping turtles rarely weigh 30 pounds, alligator snappers have been recorded with weights up to 300 pounds.**

2.3 Transitions

Transitions are words and phrases that show the connections between details. Clear transitions help show how your ideas relate to each other.

Kinds of Transitions

Transitions can help readers understand several kinds of relationships:

- Time or sequence
- Spatial order
- Degree of importance
- Compare and contrast
- Cause and effect

Time or Sequence Some transitions help to clarify the sequence of events over time. When you are telling a story or describing a process, you can connect ideas with such transitional words as *first, second, always, then, next, later, soon, before, finally, after, earlier, afterward,* and *tomorrow.*

> MODEL
> Long *before* mountain bikes were made, bicycles were much less comfortable. The *first* cycle, which actually had four wheels, was made in 1645 and had to be walked. *Later,* two-wheeled cycles with pedals were called boneshakers because of their bumpy ride.

Spatial Order Transitional words and phrases such as *in front, behind, next to, along, nearest, lowest, above, below, underneath, on the left,* and *in the middle* can help readers visualize a scene.

> MODEL
> The audience entered the theater *from the back.* The stage was *in front,* and fire exits were located *to the right and left* of the stage.

Degree of Importance Transitional words such as *mainly, strongest, weakest, first, second, most important, least important, worst,* and *best* may be used to rank ideas or to show degree of importance.

> MODEL
> At *best,* the canoeing trip would mean not hearing my little brother and sister squabbling over the TV. *At the very worst,* I could expect to be living in wet clothes for two weeks.

Compare and Contrast Words and phrases such as *similarly, likewise, also, like, as, neither . . . nor,* and *either . . . or* show similarity between details. However, *by contrast, yet, but, than, unlike, instead, whereas,* and *while* show difference. Note the use of both types of transitions in the model below.

> MODEL
> *While* my local public library is a quieter place to study *than* home, I don't always get much done in the library. I'm so used to the cheerful chatter of my baby brother that, *by contrast,* the stillness of the library makes me sleepy.

WRITING TIP When you begin a sentence with a transition such as *most important, therefore, nevertheless, still,* or *instead,* set the transition off with a comma.

Cause and Effect When you are writing about a cause-and-effect relationship, use transitional words and phrases such as *since, because, thus, therefore, so, due to, for this reason,* and *as a result* to help clarify that relationship and to make your writing coherent.

> MODEL
> *Because* we missed seven days of school as a result of snowstorms, the school year will be extended. *Therefore,* we will be in school until June 17.

2.4 Conclusions

A conclusion should leave readers with a strong final impression. Try any of these approaches.

Kinds of Conclusions

Here are some effective methods for bringing your writing to a conclusion:

- Restate your thesis
- Ask a question
- Make a recommendation
- End with the last event

Restate Your Thesis A good way to conclude an essay is by restating your thesis, or main idea, in different words. If possible, link the beginning of your conclusion with the information you have presented, as the model below shows.

> MODEL
> As these arguments show, planting a tree on Arbor Day is more than just a pleasant symbolic act. It also makes your neighborhood a more attractive place and sets an example for others to follow. Planting one tree will make a difference in the environment that goes well beyond this one day.

Ask a Question Try asking a question that sums up what you have said and gives readers something new to think about. The question below concludes a piece of persuasive writing and suggests a course of action.

> MODEL
> If tutoring a younger student in writing, reading, or math can help you do better in these subjects yourself, shouldn't you take advantage of the opportunities to tutor at Western Elementary School?

Make a Recommendation When you are persuading your audience to take a position on an issue, you can conclude by recommending a specific course of action.

> MODEL
> Since learning a foreign language gives you a chance to expand your world view and make new friends, register for one of the introductory courses that start next fall.

End with the Last Event If you're telling a story, you may end with the last thing that happens. Here, the ending includes an important moment for the narrator.

> MODEL
> As I raced down the basketball court in the final seconds of the game, I felt as lone as I did on all those nights practicing by myself in the driveway. My perfect lay-up drew yells from the crowd, but I was cheering for myself on the inside.

2.5 Elaboration

Elaboration is the process of developing a writing idea by providing specific supporting details so your readers aren't left with unanswered questions.

- **Facts and Statistics** A fact is a statement that can be proved, while a statistic is a fact stated in numbers. Make sure the facts and statistics you supply are from a reliable, up-to-date source. As in the model below, the facts and statistics you use should strongly support the statements you make.

> MODEL
> The Statue of Liberty, one of the most popular monuments in the United States, is expensive to maintain. From 1983 to 1986, it cost $66 million to renovate the copper-covered 151-foot-tall statue.

WRITING TIP Facts and statistics are especially useful in supporting opinions. Be sure that you double-check in your original sources the accuracy of all facts and statistics you cite.

- **Sensory Details** Details that show how something looks, sounds, tastes, smells, or feels can enliven a description, making readers feel they are actually experiencing what you are describing. Which senses does the writer appeal to in this paragraph?

MODEL

I was nervous during my math test last week. Chewing on my pencil left my mouth feeling dry and flaky. My palms were sweating so much, they left stains on the pages. The ticking of the clock seemed like the beating of a drum inside my head.

- **Incidents** From our earliest years, we are interested in hearing stories. One way to illustrate a point powerfully is to relate an incident or tell a story, as shown in the example below.

MODEL

People who are afraid of heights tend to panic even in perfectly safe situations. When my friend Jill and I rode to the top floor of a shopping mall, I enjoyed the view from the glass-enclosed elevator, but Jill's face was pale and her hands trembled.

- **Examples** The model below shows how using an example can help support or clarify an idea. A well-chosen example often can be more effective than a lengthy explanation.

MODEL

The origins of today's professional sporting events can be traced to ancient games from countries all over the world. For example, hockey is believed to have come from an old Dutch game called *kolf*, played on the ice with a ball and crooked sticks.

LINK TO LITERATURE Notice on page 225 the use of examples in the selection from Russell Freedman's *Immigrant Kids.* When the writer states that none of the immigrants forgot his or her first glimpse of the Statue of Liberty, he

elaborates by using the example of immigrant Edward Corsi's first impression.

- **Quotations** Choose quotations that clearly support your points and be sure that you copy each quotation word for word. Remember always to credit the source.

MODEL

Usually, the reader is left to infer the theme of a work, but sometimes the author actually states the theme of his or her work. After the tragic events that come to pass in Rod Serling's teleplay *The Monsters Are Due on Maple Street*, the narrator says to the audience, "The tools of conquest do not necessarily come with bombs and explosions and fallout. There are weapons that are simply thoughts, attitudes, prejudices—to be found only in the minds of men. For the record, prejudices can kill and suspicion can destroy."

2.6 Using Language Effectively

Effective use of language can help readers to recognize the significance of an issue, to visualize a scene, or to understand a character.

- **Specific Nouns** Nouns are specific when they refer to individual or particular things. If you refer to a city, you are being general. If you refer to Dallas, you are being specific. Specific nouns help readers identify the *who, what,* and *where* of your message.

- **Specific Verbs** Verbs are the most powerful words in sentences. They convey the action, the movement, and sometimes the drama of thoughts and observations. Verbs such as *trudged, skipped,* and *sauntered* provide a more vivid picture of the action than the verb *walked.*

- **Specific Modifiers** Use modifiers sparingly, but when you use them, make them count. Is the building *big* or *towering?* Are your poodle's paws *small* or *petite?* Once again, it is the more specific word that carries the greater impact.

③ Descriptive Writing

Descriptive writing appears almost everywhere, from cookbooks to poems. You might use a description to introduce a character in a narrative or to create a strong closing to a persuasive essay. Whatever your purpose and wherever you use description, the following guidelines for good descriptive writing will help you.

3.1 Key Techniques

Consider Your Goals What do you want to accomplish in writing your description? Do you want to show why something is important to you? Do you want to make a person or scene more memorable? Do you want to explain an event?

Identify Your Audience Who will read your description? How familiar are they with your subject? What background information will they need? Which details will they find most interesting?

Gather Sensory Details Which sights, smells, tastes, sounds, and textures make your subject come alive? Which details stick in your mind when you observe or recall your subject? Which senses does it most strongly affect?

MODEL

Red and gold pennants welcomed us to the fairgrounds, where the delicious aroma of popcorn mingled with the pungent odor of the animals. Food vendors hawked their wares, and the tinny music of the carousel filled the air. Munching on roasted peanuts, we took our seats on the rough benches of the judging arena.

You might want to use a chart like the one shown here to collect sensory details about your subject.

Sights	Sounds	Textures	Smells	Tastes

Organize Your Details Details that are presented in a logical order help the reader form a mental picture of the subject. Descriptive details may be organized chronologically, spatially, by order of importance, or by order of impression.

MODEL

As I stepped into my grandmother's front hall, a whirl of sweet and salty odors overwhelmed me. Peeking around the corner, I witnessed a parade of pies, breads, and salads stretching across every inch of counter space.

LINK TO LITERATURE Note on page 440 the organization of details describing Miss Pride's shop in Joan Aiken's "The Serial Garden." The narrator begins with the shop window as seen from the outside, then describes the interior of the store, and finally shows the reader Miss Pride herself.

Show, Don't Tell Instead of just telling about a subject in a general way, provide details and quotations that expand and support what you want to say and that enable your readers to share your experience. The following sentence, for example, just tells and doesn't show: *I was proud of myself when the local paper published my article.* The model below uses descriptive details to show how proud the writer felt:

MODEL

I've delivered newspapers since I was eight, but last Thursday, for the first time, the newspaper printed an article I had written for a contest. I bought a pad of sticky notes and left messages for my customers: "Check out page B7. Enjoy the paper today." I thought about signing the article, but I decided that would be too much.

3.2 Options for Organization

Spatial Order Choose one of these options to show the spatial order of a scene.

EXAMPLE 1

Top → Bottom

EXAMPLE 2

Left → Right

EXAMPLE 3

Outside / Inside

EXAMPLE 4

Far ← Near

MODEL

The room was quiet—too quiet. To my left loomed the big white refrigerator. To my right squatted the gas stove, blue pilots glowing. Straight ahead sat the huge island. Cutting board, knife, and half-chopped carrot lay abandoned upon it now. Stepping cautiously to the right of the island, I came in view of the oven. That's where I froze. The oven door was open. A faint, white light pulsed and flickered high in one corner.

WRITING TIP Some useful transitions for showing spatial relationships are *behind, below, here, in the distance, on the left, over,* and *on top.*

Order of Impression Order of impression is how you notice details.

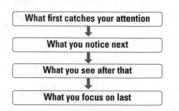

What first catches your attention
↓
What you notice next
↓
What you see after that
↓
What you focus on last

MODEL

As she lost her balance on the slippery pebbles, her first thought was that she was going to sprain her ankle and be swept away by the surf. Her heart beat rapidly, but before she knew it, she was sitting in the sand while the warm surf rolled in, almost covering her. She realized that the water was not going to reach beyond her shoulders and that she was safe. Then, as suddenly, she felt the tug of the water in the other direction as the undertow flowed back, sweeping the sand from under her as it went. As soon as the water had receded she scrambled to her feet.

WRITING TIP Use transitions that help readers understand the order of the impressions you are describing. Some useful transitions are *after, next, during, first, before, finally,* and *then.*

Order of Importance You might use order of importance to organize your description.

Least Important
↓
More Important
↓
Most Important

MODEL

I think our school should offer karate as part of the gym program. There are several reasons this is a good idea. First, karate is fun, and anyone can learn to do it. Many students who want to learn martial arts can't afford to because private lessons are so expensive. Karate is also a great form of exercise. It improves strength, coordination, and grace. The most important reason, though, is that learning karate makes students more confident and gives them skills that can help them throughout life.

WRITING TIP Use transitions that help the reader understand the order of importance. Some useful transitions are *first, second, mainly, more important, less important,* and *least important.*

4 Narrative Writing

Narrative writing tells a story. If you write a story from your imagination, it is a fictional narrative. A true story about actual events is a nonfictional narrative. Narrative writing can be found in short stories, novels, news articles, and biographies.

RUBRIC | STANDARDS FOR WRITING

A successful narrative should

- include descriptive details and dialogue to develop the characters, setting, and plot.
- have a clear beginning, middle, and end.
- have a logical organization with clues and transitions to help the reader understand the order of events.
- maintain a consistent tone and point of view.
- use language that is appropriate for the audience.
- demonstrate the significance of events or ideas.

4.1 Key Techniques

Identify the Main Events What are the most important events in your narrative? Is each event part of the chain of events needed to tell the story? In a fictional narrative, this series of events is the story's plot.

MODEL

Event 1	A kind stranger gives Roger money he doesn't really deserve.
Event 2	Roger goes to buy a fancy new bike with the money.
Event 3	A salesperson accuses him of not having the money to buy the bike.
Event 4	Roger decides not to buy the bike and leaves to find the stranger.

Define the Conflict What is the main problem the character faces? Is the conflict an internal one or an external one?

MODEL

The bikes were lined up in a row, beautiful, shiny, and bright. He ran his hand over the handlebars and felt his face flush with embarrassment. How could he spend all the stranger's money on a fancy bike that he didn't really need?

Depict Characters Vividly What do your characters look like? What do they think and say? How do they act? What vivid details can show readers what the characters are like?

MODEL

The salesperson strolled the show-room carpet like a rich prince walking the halls of his castle. He said nothing, but his pacing made the boy slightly nervous.

WRITING TIP Dialogue is an effective way of developing characters in a narrative. As you write dialogue, choose words that express your characters' personalities and show how the characters feel about one another and about the events in the plot.

MODEL

"Can I help you?" a voice from behind him asked.

Roger turned to see the salesperson looking down at him.

"I was just looking at this 12-speed, super-lightweight bike," Roger said swallowing.

"That's a pretty expensive bike you're touching, young man," the salesperson replied skeptically.

4.2 Options for Organization

Option 1: Chronological Order One way to organize a piece of narrative writing is to arrange the events in chronological order, as shown below.

	MODEL
Introduction *characters and setting*	Roger walked into the store where he had seen the fancy new bikes.
Event 1	"Can I help you?" the salesperson asked, his voice showing interest in a sale. Roger mumbled and pointed toward the bikes against a wall.
Event 2	As his hand glided over the handlebars on the bike, he barely heard the salesperson ask if he even had the money for the new bike.
End *perhaps show the significance of the events*	Roger's hand flashed dollar bills, but he let go of the bike. He ran for the door, knowing he had to find the old woman who had given him the money.

WRITING TIP Try hooking your reader's interest by opening a story with an exciting event or some attention-grabbing dialogue. After your introduction, you may need to go back in time and relate the incidents that led up to the opening event.

Option 2: Character Chronological order is the most common way to organize a narrative. However, you may wish to focus more directly on character.

Introduce the main character.
↓
Describe the conflict the character faces.
↓
Relate the events and the changes the character goes through as a result of the conflict.
↓
Present the final change or new understanding.

Option 3: Focus on Conflict When the telling of a fictional narrative focuses on a central conflict, the story's plot may follow the model shown below.

	MODEL
Describe the main characters and setting	The brothers arrive at the highschool gym long before the rest of the basketball team. Although the twins are physically identical, their personalities couldn't be more different. Mark is outgoing and impulsive, while Matt is thoughtful and shy.
Present the conflict	Matt realizes his brother is missing shots on purpose and believes they will lose the championship.
Relate the events that make the conflict complex and cause the characters to change	• Matt has a chance at a basketball scholarship if they win the championship. • Mark needs money to buy a car. • Matt and Mark have stood by each other no matter what.
Present the resolution or outcome of the conflict	Matt retells a family story in which their grandfather chose honor and integrity over easy money. Mark plays to win.

⑤ Explanatory Writing

Explanatory writing informs and explains. For example, you can use it to explain how to cook spaghetti, to explore the origins of the universe, or to compare two pieces of literature.

5.1 Types of Explanatory Writing

There are many types of explanatory writing. Think about your topic and select the type that presents the information most clearly.

Compare and Contrast How are two or more subjects alike? How are they different?

> MODEL
>
> **While the domestic honeybee has been bred for good honey production and gentleness, the Africanized bee is a "wild" bee that is quick-tempered and uncomfortable around animals and people.**

Cause and Effect How does one event cause something else to happen? Why do certain conditions exist? What are the results of an action or a condition?

> MODEL
>
> **If the Africanized bees drive out or breed into domesticated honeybee colonies, commercial beekeepers in the United States could be forced out of business.**

Analysis/Classification How does something work? How can it be defined? What are its parts? How can it be classified into categories?

> MODEL
>
> **The Africanized honeybee is a new insect nuisance that has the potential to affect agriculture, recreation, and the environment.**

Problem-Solution How can you identify and state a problem? How would you analyze the problem and its causes? How can it be solved?

> MODEL
>
> **The best way to protect yourself against the stings of the Africanized bee is to understand how it behaves and react accordingly.**

5.2 Compare and Contrast

Compare-and-contrast writing examines the similarities and differences between two or more subjects. You might, for example, compare and contrast two short stories, the main characters in a novel, or two movies.

RUBRIC STANDARDS FOR WRITING

Successful compare-and-contrast writing should

- clearly state the subjects that are being compared and contrasted.
- include specific, relevant details.
- be easy to follow, using either feature-by-feature or subject-by-subject organization.
- use transitional words and phrases to signal similarities and differences.
- end with a conclusion that explains the decision made or creates a new understanding of the subjects compared.

Options for Organization

Compare-and-contrast writing can be organized in different ways. The examples that follow demonstrate feature-by-feature organization and subject-by-subject organization.

Option 1: Feature-by-Feature Organization

MODEL

Feature 1 **I. Similarities in Appearance**

Subject A. Domestic honey-bees are about five-eighths of an inch long.

Subject B. Africanized bees, contrary to rumor, are about the same size.

Feature 2 **II. Differences in Temperament**

Subject A. Domestic honey-bees are bred to be gentle.

Subject B. The Africanized bee is a "wild" bee that is quick-tempered around animals and people.

Option 2: Subject-by-Subject Organization

MODEL

Subject A **I. Domestic Honeybees**

Feature 1. Domestic honey-bees are about five-eighths of an inch long.

Feature 2. Domestic honeybees are bred to be gentle.

Subject B **II. Africanized Bees**

Feature 1. Africanized bees are about five-eighths of an inch long.

Feature 2. The Africanized bee is a "wild" bee that is quick-tempered around animals and people.

WRITING TIP Remember your purpose for comparing and contrasting your subjects, and support your purpose with expressive language and specific details.

5.3 Cause and Effect

Cause-and-effect writing explains why something happened, why conditions exist, or what resulted from an action or condition.

RUBRIC STANDARDS FOR WRITING

Successful cause-and-effect writing should

- clearly state the cause-and-effect relationship being examined.
- show clear connections between causes and effects.
- present causes and effects in a logical order and use transitions effectively.
- use facts, examples, and other details to illustrate each cause and effect.
- use language and details appropriate to the audience.

Options for Organization

Your organization will depend on your topic and purpose for writing.

- If you want to explain the causes of an event, such as the threat of Africanized bees to commercial beekeeping, you might first state the effect and then examine its causes.

Option 1: Effect-to-Cause Organization

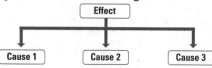

- If your focus is on explaining the effects of an event, such as the appearance of Africanized bees in the United States, you might first state the cause and then explain the effects.

Option 2: Cause-to-Effect Organization

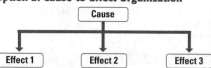

- Sometimes you'll want to describe a chain of cause-and-effect relationships to explore a topic such as the myths about the Africanized honeybee.

Option 3: Cause-and-Effect Chain Organization

WRITING TIP You must test cause-and-effect relationships as you work. First, be sure that the first event you mention comes before the second event in time. Next, be sure that the effect you state could not have happened without the cause you state.

5.4 Problem-Solution

Problem-solution writing clearly states a problem, analyzes the problem, and proposes a solution to the problem. It can be used to identify and solve a conflict between characters, analyze a chemistry experiment, or explain why the home team keeps losing.

RUBRIC STANDARDS FOR WRITING

Successful problem-solution writing should

- give a clear and concise explanation of the problem and its significance.
- present a workable solution and include details that explain and support it.
- conclude by restating the problem.
- use language, tone, and details appropriate to the audience.

Options for Organization

Your organization will depend on the goal of your problem-solution piece, your intended audience, and the specific problem you choose to address. The organizational methods that follow are effective for different kinds of problem-solution writing.

Option 1: Simple Problem-Solution

Option 2: Deciding Between Solutions

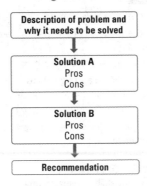

WRITING TIP Have a classmate read and respond to your problem-solution writing. Ask your peer reader: Is the problem clearly stated? Is the organization easy to follow? Do the proposed solutions seem logical?

5.5 Analysis/Classification

In writing an analysis, you explain how something works, how it is defined, or what its parts are. The details you include will depend upon the kind of analysis you write.

Process Analysis What are the major steps or stages in a process? What background information does the reader need to know—such as definitions of terms or a list of needed equipment—to understand the analysis? You might use process analysis to explain how to program a VCR or prepare for a test, or to explain how to replace a window pane.

Definition Analysis What are the most important characteristics of a subject? You might use definition analysis to explain a quality such as proficiency, the characteristics of a sonnet, or the features of a lever.

Parts Analysis What are the parts, groups, or types that make up a subject? Parts analysis could be used to explain the makeup of an organization or the anatomy of an insect.

RUBRIC STANDARDS FOR WRITING

Successful analysis should

- hook the readers' attention with a strong introduction.
- clearly state the subject and its parts.
- use a specific organizing structure to provide a logical flow of information.
- use transitions to connect thoughts.
- use language and details appropriate to the audience.

Options for Organization

Organize your details in a logical order appropriate to the kind of analysis you're writing.

Option 1: Process Analysis A process analysis is usually organized chronologically, with steps or stages in the order they occur.

MODEL

Introduction → **Insect metamorphosis**

Background → **Many insects grow through a four-step cycle.**

Explain Steps → **Step 1 egg**
Step 2 larva
Step 3 pupa
Step 4 adult

Option 2: Definition Analysis You can organize the details in a definition or parts analysis in order of importance or impression.

MODEL

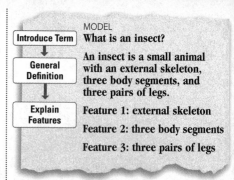

Introduce Term → **What is an insect?**

General Definition → **An insect is a small animal with an external skeleton, three body segments, and three pairs of legs.**

Explain Features → **Feature 1: external skeleton**

Feature 2: three body segments

Feature 3: three pairs of legs

Option 3: Parts Analysis The following parts analysis explains the parts of an insect's body.

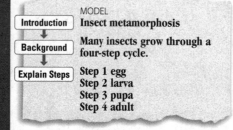

MODEL

Introduce Subject → **An insect's body is divided into three main parts.**

Explain Parts → **Part 1: The head includes eyes, mouth, and antennae.**

Part 2: The thorax has the legs and wings attached to it.

Part 3: The abdomen contains organs for digesting food, eliminating waste, and reproducing.

Option 4: Classification/Division The following classification divides things into groups or categories based on certain characteristics.

MODEL

One way that scientists classify insects is into species that are social insects and those that are not. The vast majority of insects are not social insects. The parents get together simply to mate. The female lays her eggs near a food source and then abandons them. Social insects, on the other hand, live in organized communities in which members depend on one another. Individual insects have specific roles within the community. All termites and ants are social insects. Many bees and some wasps are also social insects.

6 Persuasive Writing

Persuasive writing allows you to use the power of language to inform and influence others. It can take many forms, including speeches, newspaper editorials, billboards, advertisements, and critical reviews.

RUBRIC STANDARDS FOR WRITING

Successful persuasion should

- have a strong introduction.
- clearly state the issue and the writer's position.
- present ideas logically.
- answer opposing viewpoints.
- end with a strong argument or summary or a call for action.

6.1 Key Techniques

State Your Opinion Taking a stand on an issue and clearly stating your opinion are essential to every piece of persuasive writing you do.

> MODEL
> Everyone should read "Waters of Gold." It teaches the importance of helping others and not expecting a reward for your kindness.

Know Your Audience Who will read your writing? What do they already know and believe about the issue? What objections to your position might they have? What additional information might they need? What tone and approach would be most effective?

> MODEL
> Do you ever feel that you could do more to help others? I just read a Chinese folktale about a woman who shared all that she had in order to help others in need.

Support Your Opinion Why do you feel the way you do about the issue? What facts, statistics, examples, quotations, anecdotes, or opinions of authorities support your view? What reasons will convince your readers? What evidence can answer their objections?

> MODEL
> We should all do what we can to help others. Knowing that we have done something worthwhile makes us feel good. Kind deeds are their own reward.

Begin and End with a Bang How can you hook your readers and make a lasting impression? What memorable quotation, anecdote, or statistic will catch their attention at the beginning or stick in their minds at the end? What strong summary or call to action can you conclude with?

Ways to Support Your Argument	
Statistics	Facts that are stated in numbers
Examples	Specific instances that explain your point
Observations	Events or situations you yourself have seen
Anecdotes	Brief stories that illustrate your point
Quotations	Direct statements from authorities

> INTRODUCTION
> If you want to spend an enjoyable evening with your neighbors seeing a live performance, shopping for handmade crafts, or enjoying good food, will you go to the Community Center? Probably not. It's just too hot!

CONCLUSION

Many people have put their time into providing our town with entertainment. Many more have participated in events planned by others. But those numbers are decreasing because the Community Center is uncomfortable on hot summer evenings. Let's purchase an air-conditioning system so people can enjoy the Community Center.

6.2 Options for Organization

In persuasive writing, you need to gather information to support your opinions. Here are some ways you can organize material to convince your audience.

Option 1: Reasons for Your Opinion

MODEL

Your Opinion — Everyone should read "Waters of Gold." It teaches the importance of helping others and not expecting a reward in return.

Reason 1 — It offers a model of behavior in Auntie Lily, who expects nothing for her kindness but is rewarded with a pail full of gold.

Reason 2 — It makes an important moral point when a character is punished for pretending to be kind when she is actually greedy.

Reason 3 — In real life, you probably won't be given gold for doing something kind, but reading the story will remind you of the value of good deeds.

WRITING TIP Effective support for your opinion is often organized from the weakest argument to the strongest.

Depending on the purpose and form of your writing, you may want to show the weaknesses of other opinions as you explain the strength of your own. Two options for organizing writing that includes more than just your side of the issue are shown below.

Option 2: Why Your Opinion Is Stronger

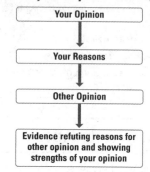

Option 3: Why Another Opinion Is Weaker

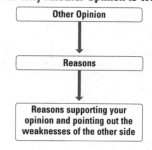

WRITING TIP Start a persuasive piece with a question, a surprising fact, or an anecdote to capture your readers' interest and make them want to keep reading. The ending of a persuasive piece is often the part that sticks in a reader's mind. Your conclusion might summarize the two sides of an issue, restate your position, invite readers to make up their own minds, or call for some action.

❼ Research Report Writing

In research report writing, you can find answers to questions about a topic. You may find new, unanswered questions. Your writing organizes your ideas, questions, and information from various sources and presents it to your readers as a unified and coherent whole.

RUBRIC STANDARDS FOR WRITING

A successful research report should

- clearly state the purpose of the report in a thesis statement.
- use evidence and details from a variety of sources to support the thesis.
- contain only accurate and relevant information.
- document sources correctly.
- develop the topic logically and include appropriate transitions.
- include a properly formatted Works Cited list.

Key Techniques

Formulate Relevant, Interesting, and Researchable Questions Asking thoughtful questions will help you find an interesting, specific topic that you can develop in a research report. Begin by jotting down a list of basic questions about your general topic. Focus on the *who, what, where, when,* and *why* of your topic. If you were researching Eleanor Roosevelt, you might develop questions like these.

> MODEL
> **What were Eleanor Roosevelt's most important accomplishments?**
>
> **What difficulties did she overcome?**
>
> **When did she live? What were the most important events of that time?**

As you become familiar with your topic, narrow your questions down to a single question that will provide a sharp focus that will make your readers think. Your answer to this question will become the thesis statement of your research report.

> MODEL
> **How did Eleanor Roosevelt's activities change the perception of women's roles in society?**

Make sure that there are research sources available that can provide you information to answer your question. If you cannot find sources, you need to revise your question.

Clarify Your Thesis A thesis statement is one or two sentences clearly stating the main idea that you will develop in your report. A thesis may also indicate the organizational pattern you will follow and reflect your tone and point of view.

> MODEL
> **Eleanor Roosevelt's active participation in political and social issues changed the role of future first ladies and offered a new vision for the roles of women in general.**

Document Your Sources You need to document, or credit, the sources where you find your evidence. In the example below, the writer uses and documents information from a magazine article.

> MODEL
> **Eleanor Roosevelt was tireless in her work. A joke in Washington was that President Roosevelt prayed every night, "Dear God, please make Eleanor a little tired" (Goodwin 41).**

Support Your Ideas You should support your ideas with relevant evidence—facts, anecdotes, and statistics—from reliable sources. In the example below, the writer includes a fact about how Eleanor Roosevelt helped women journalists.

MODEL
To encourage newspapers to hire women, Eleanor Roosevelt did not allow men at her White House press conferences (Toor 63).

7.2 Finding and Evaluating Sources

Begin your research by looking for information about your topic in books, magazines, newspapers, and computer databases. In addition to using your library's card or computer catalog, look up your subject in indexes, such as the *Readers' Guide to Periodical Literature* or the *New York Times Index*. The bibliographies in books that you find during your research may also lead to additional sources. The following checklist will help you evaluate the reliability of the sources you find.

Checklist for Evaluating Your Sources	
Authoritative	Someone who has written several books or articles on your subject or whose work has been published in a well-respected newspaper or journal may be considered an authority.
Up-to-date	Check the publication date to see if the source reflects the most current research on your subject.
Respected	In general, tabloid newspapers and popular-interest magazines are not reliable sources. If you have questions about whether you are using a respected source, ask your librarian.

7.3 Making Source Cards

For each source you find, record the bibliographic information on a separate index card. You will need this information to give credit to the sources in your paper. The samples at the right show how to make source cards for encyclopedia entries, magazine articles, and

books. You will use the source number on each card to identify the notes you take during your research.

Encyclopedia Entry

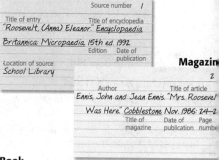

Book

Taking Notes heading with image:

7.4 Taking Notes

As you find material that suits the purpose of your report, record each piece of information on a separate note card. You will probably use all three of the note-taking methods listed below.

- **Paraphrase,** or restate in your own words, the main ideas and supporting details of the passage.

- **Summarize,** or rephrase in fewer words, the original materials, trying to capture the key ideas.

- **Quote,** or copy word for word, the original text, if you think the author's own words best clarify a particular point. Use quotation marks to signal the beginning and the end of the quotation.

For more details on making source cards and taking notes, see the Research Report Workshop on pages 780–786.

Writing a Thesis Statement

A thesis statement in a research report defines the main idea, or overall purpose, of your report. A clear, one-sentence answer to your main question will result in a good thesis statement.

Question What did Eleanor Roosevelt do that made her such an important first lady in American history?

Thesis Statement Eleanor Roosevelt's active participation in political and social issues changed the role of future first ladies and offered a new vision for the roles of women in general.

Making an Outline

To organize your report, group your note cards by main ideas and arrange them in a logical order. Using your notes, make a topic outline, beginning with a shortened version of your thesis statement. Key ideas are listed after Roman numerals, and subpoints are listed after capital letters and Arabic numerals.

MODEL

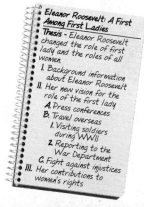

Eleanor Roosevelt: A First Among First Ladies
Thesis - Eleanor Roosevelt changed the role of first lady and the roles of all women.
 I. Background information about Eleanor Roosevelt
 II. Her new vision for the role of the first lady
   A. Press conferences
   B. Travel overseas
     1. Visiting soldiers during WWII
     2. Reporting to the War Department
   C. Fight against injustices
 III. Her contributions to women's rights

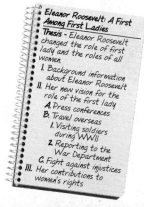 Documenting Your Sources

When you quote one of your sources or rewrite in your own words information you have found in a source, you need to credit that source, using parenthetical documentation.

Guidelines for Parenthetical Documentation

Work by One Author	Put the author's last name and, if appropriate, the page reference in parentheses: **(Toor 29).** If you mention the author's name in the sentence, put only the page reference in parentheses: **(29)**.
Work by Two or Three Authors	Put the last names of the authors and the page reference in parentheses: **(Ennis and Ennis 24)**.
No Author Given	Give the title or a shortened version and the page reference: **("Roosevelt" 172)**.
Works by Same Author	Give the author's last name, the title or a shortened version, and the page reference: **(Roosevelt, This I Remember! 59)**.

WRITING TIP Presenting someone else's writing or ideas as your own is plagiarism. To avoid plagiarism, you need to credit sources as noted. However, if a piece of information is common knowledge—available in several sources—you do not need to credit the source. To see an example of parenthetical documentation, see the report on page 781.

Using Tables of Contents

Some students may not realize that the quickest way of finding information in a reference or nonfiction book is with the table of contents. Point out that a table of contents lists the chapters and sections of a book, giving the page numbers on which each begins. Sometimes a brief chapter summary or bulleted list of main ideas appears with each entry.

Locating Information on a Topic

In any research that students perform it will be helpful to scan tables of contents. For example, ask students to suppose they have begun researching ways in which horses were important to the Sioux. Ask, Through use of a library catalog, you have found 30 books about horses and 30 books on the Sioux; how will you know which books contain information on your topic? If they narrow their catalog searches, they might miss some books. Instead they need to go to the library shelves and begin to check the books' tables of contents. If a table of contents has interesting headings, it might even suggest a new or revised research question.

Organizing Information

As students compile research reports they might wish to organize them into sections with topic headings. This is particularly useful with group projects that combine the focused reports of several students into one broader topic. A table of contents for such a project should list the title and author(s) for each section at the beginning, with page numbers running continuously. You might ask students to save their outlines as they draft their research reports and to consider using their outline headings as section or chapter headings when compiling a work longer than five pages.

7.8 Creating a Works Cited Page

Print Sources

At the end of your research report, you need to include a Works Cited page. Any source that you have cited in your report needs to be listed alphabetically by the author's last name. If no author is given, use the editor's last name on the title of the work. Note the guidelines for spacing and punctuation on the model page.

Electronic Sources

As with print sources, you need to identify the source of information taken from electronic sources, such as CD-ROMs or Internet databases, on your Works Cited page. If you read or print out an article directly off the

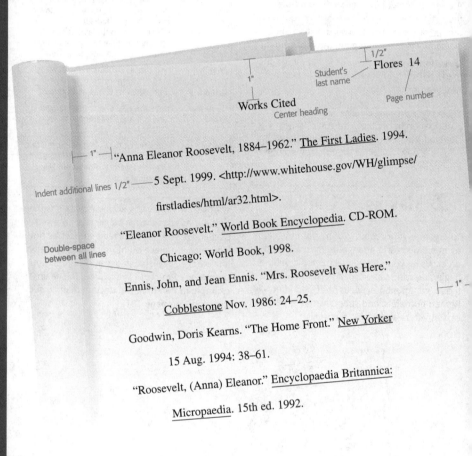

Student's last name — Flores 14
Page number

1"

Works Cited
Center heading

1" — "Anna Eleanor Roosevelt, 1884–1962." The First Ladies. 1994.

Indent additional lines 1/2" —— 5 Sept. 1999. <http://www.whitehouse.gov/WH/glimpse/

firstladies/html/ar32.html>.

"Eleanor Roosevelt." World Book Encyclopedia. CD-ROM.

Chicago: World Book, 1998.

Double-space between all lines

Ennis, John, and Jean Ennis. "Mrs. Roosevelt Was Here."

Cobblestone Nov. 1986: 24–25.

Goodwin, Doris Kearns. "The Home Front." New Yorker

15 Aug. 1994: 38–61.

"Roosevelt, (Anna) Eleanor." Encyclopaedia Britannica:

Micropaedia. 15th ed. 1992.

Internet, document it as shown here. Electronic sources should be included on the Works Cited page with print sources.

Internet Databases Works Cited entries for Internet databases include the same kind of information as entries for print sources. Additionally, you need to include the date you accessed the information and the electronic address of the source. Some of the information about the source may be unavailable. Include as much as you can. For more information on

how to write Works Cited entries for Internet sources, see the MLA guidelines posted on the McDougal Littell Web site.

 **More Online: Style Guidelines**
www.mcdougallittell.com

CD-ROMs Entries for CD-ROMs include the publication medium (CD-ROM), the distributor, and the date of publication. Some of the information shown may not always be available. Include as much as you can.

Flores 15

Roosevelt, Eleanor. The Autobiography of Eleanor Roosevelt.

New York: De Capo, 1992.

Roosevelt, Mrs. Franklin D. (Eleanor). "My Mail." Dear Mrs.

Roosevelt. 7 Feb. 1933 <http://newdeal.feri.org/eleanor/

mymail.htm>.

8 Model Bank

8.1 Summary

BASICS IN A BOX

A successful summary should

❶ accurately restate in your own words the main ideas of the work you are summarizing

❷ begin with your restatement of the main idea of the whole work

❸ contain restatements of the main supporting ideas of the work

❹ omit all unimportant details, no matter how interesting

❺ be shorter than the original work

Model 1: Summary

700-Word Summary of *A Christmas Carol* by Richard Marsden

A Christmas Carol is a play about the change of the wealthy Ebenezer Scrooge from stinginess to generosity. The play begins on the day of Christmas Eve in Victorian London, England, where there is much poverty. Scrooge, however, has no mercy for others and dislikes Christmas. Bob Cratchit, an underpaid clerk working for Scrooge, knows better than to expect any kindness from his employer. Fred, Scrooge's nephew, comes by to give his uncle some Christmas cheer, but Scrooge responds to him with bitterness. He responds the same way when a visitor arrives seeking Christmas donations.

Scrooge continues to complain about Christmas when he returns home that evening. After he goes into his bedroom, he is visited by the spirit of Jacob Marley. Marley was Scrooge's business partner. He died seven years earlier on Christmas Eve. His ghost returns to show Scrooge the heavy chains he must carry. They are the result of the mean ways in which he acted toward people while he was alive. Marley's spirit warns Scrooge that he will have to carry heavier chains than these if he does not change his life.

In order for Scrooge to change, however, he needs more persuasion. After the ghost of Jacob Marley, three more spirits visit Scrooge: the Spirit of Christmas Past, the Spirit of Christmas Present, and the Spirit of Christmas Yet to Come.

The Spirit of Christmas Past arrives as the clock strikes one. He takes Scrooge to a scene at a boarding school, where one by one the boys are leaving for Christmas break. Scrooge sees himself there at an early age, playing with a stuffed bear. The other boys are happy to be going home and celebrating Christmas. But Scrooge is not going home for Christmas. It is possible that this sadness he felt as a young boy is one of the reasons Scrooge grew to hate Christmas.

The spirit then takes Scrooge to a scene where he is a young adult. It is the time that Scrooge rejected his sweetheart because she did not have any money to bring to their marriage. The Spirit of Christmas Past makes it plain that Scrooge might have had a much different and happier life if he hadn't been so worried about money.

The Spirit of Christmas Present arrives next, and takes Scrooge to the Cratchit household. Scrooge thinks their house is not far away, but the spirit informs him that it is an entire world away from Scrooge's house. A funeral procession passes as they descend into the poor section of the city. At the Cratchit's, Scrooge sees Tiny Tim. The boy is his parents' joy. Scrooge also sees that the boy is deathly ill. Scrooge wants to help Tiny Tim, but the spirit repeats the cold, heartless words that Scrooge spoke that afternoon about the deaths decreasing the surplus population. He reminds Scrooge of his opinion that the poor have more than enough help. They can fend for themselves.

When the Spirit of Christmas Yet to Come arrives, Scrooge is not ready for what he sees. He expects this spirit to talk to him like the others did. But the dark form is silent, cloaked, and hidden. His behavior creates a sense of death. First, the spirit takes Scrooge to a time immediately after his own death. Scrooge is shocked at the behavior of his servants. They show no loyalty to him as they plunder his house, stealing anything of value. They never liked their employer and don't respect him after he has died.

Next the spirit takes him to the Cratchit house, where another death has occurred—the death of Tiny Tim. Scrooge watches the Cratchit family struggle to cope with their grief. He is surprised to learn that his nephew, Fred, has offered them his services. It is an act that Scrooge secretly wishes he had done before it was too late.

The four spirits teach Scrooge a hard lesson about charity. He knows that if he does not change his ways, people will not be sorry when he dies. Terrified by that prospect, and now genuinely concerned for others, Scrooge wakes up the next day overjoyed that he still has time to change his life. He realizes that he has another chance to become a better person. Immediately, he begins improving his ways. After buying a Christmas goose for the Cratchits, he sets out to Fred's house brimming with Christmas cheer. Scrooge has changed completely, providing a merry holiday for the Cratchits and everyone else, including himself.

8.2 Book Review

BASICS IN A BOX

A successful book review should

❶ have an introduction that gives the title of the work, its author, and perhaps some information about the author

❷ summarize the work without giving away the ending

❸ if the work is fiction, discuss the plot, setting, and important characters

❹ explain why you admire or dislike the work, supporting your reactions with examples from the work

❺ conclude with a restatement of your opinion of the book or a recommendation to other readers

Model 2: Book Review

The True Confessions of Charlotte Doyle:
Reviewed by Sheila Ashford

Have you ever taken a trip by yourself? Were you excited? Scared? *The True Confessions of Charlotte Doyle* by Avi tells the story of a thirteen-year-old girl who sails aboard a ship called the *Seahawk* from Liverpool, England, to Providence, Rhode Island, in the summer of 1832. As she prepares for the trip, Charlotte looks forward to what she thinks will be a great adventure. But the adventure turns out to be far more exciting—and far more dangerous—than Charlotte ever imagined. *The True Confessions of Charlotte Doyle* tells the gripping story of how a young girl must face mutiny, murder, and the possibility of her own death. ❷

Almost as soon as she boards the *Seahawk*, Charlotte senses that something is wrong. She is befriended by an old, black sailor named Zacharia who tells her that the captain of the *Seahawk*, Captain Jaggery, is a particularly cruel man and not to be trusted. Charlotte goes to Captain Jaggery and tells him that she wants to return to England but the captain flatters Charlotte by telling her that she will be a positive influence on the crew. ❸

As the story continues, the reader learns a lot about what it was like to sail in the early 1800s. The novel describes how the sailors worked, what they ate, as well as what was involved in operating the ship, keeping watch, and making repairs. Charlotte is fascinated by the crew's work and especially impressed with how Captain Jaggery runs things. So impressed, that when she finds out about a plot against him, she tells the captain. Angered by what Charlotte tells him, the captain orders all hands on deck.

From that moment on, Charlotte discovers more and more the true, cruel nature of Captain Jaggery. As an "example," he orders the flogging of Charlotte's friend Zacharia. Shortly thereafter, Charlotte sees a canvas bag that was used to bury sailors in the sea being dumped overboard and she is told that it contains the body of her old friend. Blaming herself, Charlotte joins the crew, asking for no special treatment because she is a girl. Instead, she receives especially cruel treatment from the captain.

Captain Jaggery sails the ship into a hurricane. Avi describes the storm with lots of convincing detail, especially when he shows what the crew had to go through to save the ship. Jaggery drives the crew mercilessly but he saves the worst treatment for Charlotte. When the ship's second in command, a man who helped the captain beat Zacharia, is found dead, Jaggery accuses Charlotte of murder, orders her trial, and finds her guilty. It is only through some unexpected help that Charlotte's story does not end here.

The True Confessions of Charlotte Doyle is a great adventure novel that held my interest from first page to last. It shows how cruel people can be, but it shows how brave people can be too. We might not want to take the kind of trip that Charlotte Doyle did, but we can read her story and feel like we are right on board!

8.3 Friendly Letter

BASICS IN A BOX

A successful friendly letter should

① begin with a heading that contains your street address, town or city, state and ZIP code, and the date you write the letter

② have a salutation that begins with a capital letter and is followed by a comma

③ have a body that is written in an informal, conversational tone

④ have a closing that begins with a capital letter and is followed by a comma

⑤ end with your signature under the closing

Model 3: Friendly Letter

603 Pine Street ①
Alton, Pennsylvania 18406
August 7, 2000

Dear José, ②

    I enjoyed your last letter so much that I had to hurry and answer it. How did you learn to ride a horse so quickly? In the photo you sent me, you look very impressive up there in the saddle. Do you ride in shows or just for fun? Wish me luck when I learn to ride! ③

    Write and tell me more about your wilderness ride. Say "hi" to your family for me.

Your friend, ④

Beth ⑤

8.4 Email

BASICS IN A BOX

A successful email should

① have the exact email address of the person you are writing to in the "To:" line

② state the subject of the email in the "Subject" line

③ have a body that is written in an informal, conversational tone

④ close with your name

⑤ end with your exact email address after your name

Tips on "Netiquette"

- Always end your messages with your name and email address.
- Always include a subject heading.
- Take as much care with spelling and punctuation as you would in a friendly letter.
- Don't write in all capitals because it looks as if you are shouting.

Model 4: Friendly Email

To: Beth_Baldwin@Oneworld.net ①
cc:
bcc:
Subject: Wilderness Rides ②

I'm back from my wilderness ride and it was great. I rode with a guide, seven other kids about my age, and two pack horses. The ride lasted one week. Except for the one afternoon when it rained, the weather was nice. I had such a great time, I would recommend the wilderness ride to anybody who likes to see nature close up. ③

José Salazar ④
joses@infoarrow.net ⑤

8.5 Persuasive Essay

BASICS IN A BOX

A successful persuasive essay should:

❶ open with a dramatic statement of the issue and your opinion

❷ address the audience you are trying to persuade

❸ provide facts, examples, and reasons to support your opinion

❹ answer opposing views

❺ show clear reasoning

❻ include strategies such as summaries to help readers remember your message

❼ end with a strong position statement or call to action

See page R100 for tips on delivering your persuasive presentation orally.

Model 5: Persuasive Essay

Important Hours
by Gina Maraini

"The Golden Years." That is what some people call old age. They think it is a time of peace and relaxation. But many old people spend time alone. Some cannot get out of their homes because of illness. "What can I do?" you ask. More than you think. Even spending an hour a week can mean a lot to an older person who lives alone.

Some kids might say that they can only do good for an older person if they have lots of time and lots of patience. It's easy to talk yourself out of volunteering your time by saying, "I only have an hour a week. What good would that do?" Never underestimate just how much good you can do even in a little bit of time.

Sometimes things happen that seem unimportant to a kid but can really be a problem to an old person. If a small object like a pen or pencil slides under furniture, an older person often is not able to stoop down and pick it up. But they feel embarrassed to ask for help. So, the pen stays there. Sometimes it gets forgotten about and becomes lost. You can help that older person find these things. And by helping, you are reminding that person that he or she is not forgotten about either.

Persuasive Essay at a Glance

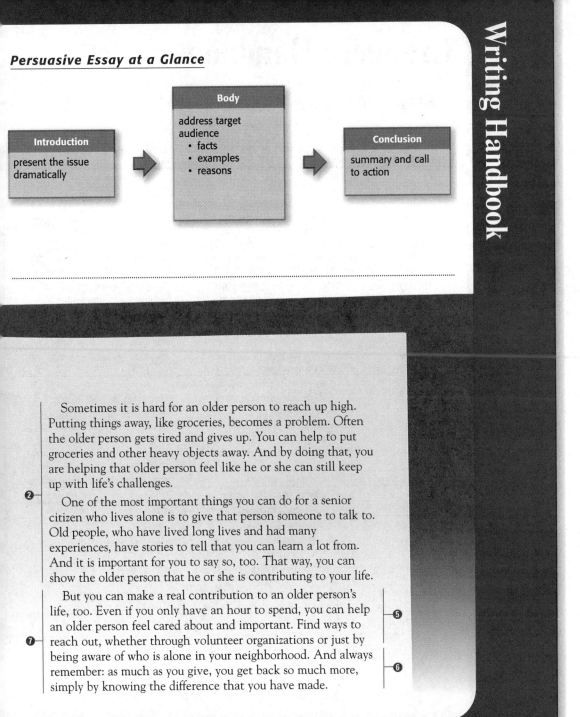

Introduction

present the issue dramatically

Body

address target audience
• facts
• examples
• reasons

Conclusion

summary and call to action

Sometimes it is hard for an older person to reach up high. Putting things away, like groceries, becomes a problem. Often the older person gets tired and gives up. You can help to put groceries and other heavy objects away. And by doing that, you are helping that older person feel like he or she can still keep up with life's challenges.

One of the most important things you can do for a senior citizen who lives alone is to give that person someone to talk to. Old people, who have lived long lives and had many experiences, have stories to tell that you can learn a lot from. And it is important for you to say so, too. That way, you can show the older person that he or she is contributing to your life.

But you can make a real contribution to an older person's life, too. Even if you only have an hour to spend, you can help an older person feel cared about and important. Find ways to reach out, whether through volunteer organizations or just by being aware of who is alone in your neighborhood. And always remember: as much as you give, you get back so much more, simply by knowing the difference that you have made.

Grammar Handbook

❶ Quick Reference: Parts of Speech

Part of Speech	Definition	Examples
Noun	Names a person, place, thing, idea, quality, or action.	Theseus, Greece, boat, freedom, joy, sailing
Pronoun	Takes the place of a noun or another pronoun.	
Personal	Refers to the one speaking, spoken to, or spoken about.	I, me, my, mine, we, us, our, ours, you your, yours, she, he, it, her, him, hers, his, its, they, them, their, theirs
Reflexive	Follows a verb or preposition and refers to a preceding noun or pronoun.	myself, yourself, herself, himself, itself, ourselves, yourselves, themselves
Intensive	Emphasizes a noun or another pronoun.	(Same as reflexives)
Demonstrative	Points to specific persons or things.	this, that, these, those
Interrogative	Signals questions.	who, whom, whose, which, what
Indefinite	Refers to person(s) or thing(s) not specifically mentioned.	both, all, most, many, anyone, everybody, several, none, some
Relative	Introduces subordinate clauses and relates them to words in the main clause.	who, whom, whose, which, that
Verb	Expresses action, condition, or state of being.	
Action	Tells what the subject does or did, physically or mentally.	run, reaches, listened, consider, decides, dreamt
Linking	Connects subjects to that which identifies or describes them.	am, is, are, was, were, sound, taste, appear, feel, become, remain, seem
Auxiliary	Precedes and introduces main verbs.	be, have, do, can, could, will, would, may, might
Adjective	Modifies nouns or pronouns.	**strong** women, **two** epics, **enough** time
Adverb	Modifies verbs, adjectives, or other adverbs.	walked **out**, **really** funny, **far** away
Preposition	Relates one word to another (following) word.	at, by, for, from, in, of, on, to, with
Conjunction	Joins words or word groups.	
Coordinating	Joins words or word groups used the same way.	and, but, or, for, so, yet, nor
Correlative	Join words or word groups used the same way and are used in pairs.	both . . . and, either . . . or, neither . . . nor
Subordinating	Joins word groups not used the same way.	although, after, as, before, because, when, if, unless
Interjection	Expresses emotion.	wow, ouch, hurrah

❷ Quick Reference: The Sentence and Its Parts

The diagrams that follow will give you a brief review of the essentials of the sentence–subjects and predicates–and of some of its parts.

The speaker's **pockets** **bulged** with oranges.

The **complete subject** includes all the words that identify the person, place, thing, or idea that the sentence is about.

pockets

The **complete predicate** includes all the words that tell or ask something about the subject.

bulged

At the drug store, an understanding clerk **had given** the speaker **a chocolate bar.**

A **prepositional phrase** consists of a preposition, its object, and any modifiers of the object. In this phrase, *at* is the preposition and *drug store* is its object.

subject

Verbs often have more than one part. They may be made up of a **main verb,** like *given,* and one or more **auxiliary,** or **helping verbs,** like *had.*

A **direct object** is a word or group of words that tells who or what receives the action of the verb in the sentence.

An **indirect object** is a word or group of words that tells *to whom* or *for whom* or *to what* or *for what* about the verb. A sentence can have an indirect object only if it has a direct object. The indirect object always comes before the direct object in a sentence.

❸ Quick Reference: Punctuation

Punctuation	Function	Examples
End Marks period, question mark, exclamation point	to end sentences	We can start now. When would you like to leave? What a fantastic hit!
	initials and other abbreviations	Mrs. Dorothy Parker, C. P. Cavafy, McDougal Littell Inc., P.M., A.D., lbs., oz., Blvd., Dr.

	items in outlines	I. Volcanoes
		    A. Central-vent
		        1. Shield

	exception: P.O. states	NE (Nebraska), NV (Nevada)
Commas	before conjunction in compound sentence	I have never disliked poetry, but now I really love it.
	items in a series	She is brave, loyal, and kind. The slow, easy route is best.
	words of address	Maria, how can I help you? You must do something, soldier.
	parenthetical expressions	Well, just suppose that we can't? Hard workers, as you know, don't quit. I'm not a quitter, believe me.
	introductory phrases and clauses	In the beginning of the day, I feel fresh. While she was out, I was here. Having finished my chores, I went out.
	nonessential phrases and clauses	Ed Pawn, captain of the chess team, won. Ed Pawn, who is the captain, won.
		The two leading runners, sprinting toward the finish line, ended in a tie.
	in dates and addresses	September 21, 2001. Mail it by May 14, 2000, to Hauptman Company, 321 Market Street, Memphis, Tennessee.
	in letter parts	Dear Jim, Sincerely yours,
	for clarity or to avoid confusion	By noon, time had run out. What the minister does, does matter. While cooking, Jim burned his hand.
Semicolons	in compound sentences that are not joined by coordinators *and*, etc.	The last shall be first; the first shall be last. I read the Bible; however, I have not memorized it.
	with items in series that contain commas	We invited my sister, Jan; her friend, Don; my uncle Jack; and Mary Dodd.
	in compound sentences that contain commas	After I ran out of money, I called my parents; but only my sister was home, unfortunately.

Punctuation	Function	Examples
Colons	to introduce lists	**Correct:** Those we wrote were the following: Dana, John, and Will. **Incorrect:** Those we wrote were: Dana, John, and Will.
	before a long quotation	Abraham Lincoln wrote: "Four score and seven years ago, our fathers brought forth on this continent a new nation. ..."
	after the salutation of a business letter	To Whom It May Concern: Dear Leonard Atole:
	with certain numbers	1:28 P.M., Genesis: 2–5
Dashes	to indicate an abrupt break in thought	I was thinking of my mother—who is arriving tomorrow—just as you walked in.
Parentheses	to enclose less important material	It was so unlike him (John is always on time) that I began to worry. The last World Series game (Did you see it?) was fun.
Hyphens	with a compound adjective before nouns	The not-so-rich taxpayer won't stand for this!
	in compounds with *all-, ex-, self-, -elect*	The ex-firefighter helped rescue him. Our president-elect is self-conscious.
	in compound numbers (to ninety-nine)	Today, I turn twenty-one.
	in fractions used as adjectives	My cup is one-third full.
	between prefixes and words beginning with capital letters	Which pre-Raphaelite painter do you like best? It snowed in mid-October.
	when dividing words at the end of a line	How could you have any reasonable expec- tations of getting a new computer?
Apostrophes	to form possessives of nouns and indefinite pronouns	my friend's book, my friends' book, anyone's guess, somebody else's problem
	for omitted letters in numbers/contractions	don't (omitted **o**); he'd (omitted **woul**) the class of '99 (omitted **19**)
	to form plurals of letters and numbers	I had two A's and no 2's on my report card.
Quotation Marks	to set off a speaker's exact words	Sara said, "I'm finally ready." "I'm ready," Sara said, "finally." Did Sara say, "I'm ready"? Sara said, "I'm ready!"
	for titles of stories, short poems, essays, songs, book chapters	I liked Paulsen's "Dirk the Protector" and Roethke's "The Bat." I like Joplin's "Me and Bobby McGee."
Ellipses	for material omitted from a quotation	"When in the course of human events . . . and to assume among the powers of the earth. . . ."
Italics	for titles of books, plays, magazines, long poems, operas, films, TV series, names of ships	*The House on Mango Street, Hamlet, Newsweek, The Odyssey, Madama Butterfly, Gone with the Wind, Seinfeld, Titanic*

❹ Quick Reference: Capitalization

Category/Rule	Examples
People and Titles	
Names and initials of people	Gish Jen, J. Frank Dobie
Titles with names	Professor Holmes, Senator Long
Deities and members of religious groups	Jesus, Allah, the Buddha, Zeus, Baptists, Roman Catholics
Names of ethnic and national groups	Hispanics, Jews, African Americans
Geographical Names	
Cities, states, countries, continents	Philadelphia, Kansas, Japan, Europe
Regions, bodies of water, mountains	the South, Lake Baykal, Mount McKinley
Geographic features, parks	Great Basin, Yellowstone National Park
Streets and roads, planets	318 East Sutton Drive, Charles Court, Jupiter, Pluto
Organizations and Events	
Companies, organizations, teams	Ford Motor Company, Boy Scouts of America, St. Louis Cardinals
Buildings, bridges, monuments	Empire State Building, Eads Bridge, Washington Monument
Documents, awards	the Declaration of Independence, Stanley Cup
Special named events	Mardi Gras, World Series
Governmental bodies, historical periods and events	U.S. Senate, House of Representatives, Middle Ages, Vietnam War
Days and months, holidays	Thursday, March, Thanksgiving, Labor Day
Specific cars, boats, trains, planes	Porsche, *Mississippi Queen*, Orient Express, Concorde
Proper Adjectives	
Adjectives formed from proper nouns	French cooking, Freudian psychology, Edwardian age, Atlantic coast
First Words and the Pronoun *I*	
The first word in a sentence or quotation	This is it. He said, "Let's go."
Complete sentence in parentheses	(Consult the previous chapter.)
Salutation and closing of letters	Dear Madam, Very truly yours,
First lines of most poetry	Then am I
The personal pronoun *I*	A happy fly If I live Or if I die.
First, last, and all important words in titles	*A Tale of Two Cities*, "The World Is Not a Pleasant Place to Be"

⑤ Writing Complete Sentences

5.1 *Sentence Fragments* A sentence fragment is a group of words that does not express a complete thought. It may be missing a subject, a predicate, or both. A sentence fragment makes you wonder *What is this about?* or *What happened?*

Missing Subject or Predicate You can correct a sentence fragment by adding the missing subject or predicate to complete the thought.

> **INCORRECT:** The Monsters Are Due on Maple Street *is a spooky tale. Tells about ordinary neighbors turning into a mob. Fearful people.*
>
> **CORRECT**: The Monsters Are Due on Maple Street *is a spooky tale <u>that</u> tells about ordinary neighbors turning into a mob <u>of</u> fearful people.*

Phrase and Subordinate-Clause Fragments When the fragment is a phrase or a subordinate clause, you may join the fragment to an existing sentence.

> **INCORRECT:** *Under normal circumstances. The conflicts neighbors have with one another are easy to ignore. However, these unresolved problems can suddenly become huge. When a crisis threatens.*
>
> **CORRECT:** *Under normal circumstances, the conflicts neighbors have are easy to ignore. However, these unresolved problems can suddenly become huge <u>when</u> a crisis threatens.*

GRAMMAR PRACTICE

Rewrite this paragraph, correcting the sentence fragments.

1) In *The Monsters Are Due on Maple Street.* **2)** Normal social bonds were broken. **3)** The small amount of community feeling that existed on Maple Street. **4)** Was quickly destroyed. **5)** A sense of community is necessary. **6)** If people are to live together safely and happily.

7) The earliest human communities came into being. **8)** When the need for safety arose. **9)** Neighbors in a community. **10)** Give one another practical and emotional support. **11)** They work to resolve. **12)** Problems among members rather than ignoring conflict. **13)** Even neighbors who live close together. **14)** Do not necessarily share similar values. **15)** Is essential in building a strong, stable community. **16)** A true community. **17)** Might have been able to stand up to the outside threat posed in this teleplay. **18)** Without community Maple Street.

5.2 *Run-on Sentences* A run-on sentence consists of two or more sentences written incorrectly as one. A run-on sentence occurs because the writer either used no end mark or used a comma instead of a period to end the first complete thought. A run-on sentence may confuse readers because it does not show where one thought ends and the next begins.

Forming Separate Sentences One way to correct a run-on sentence is to form two separate sentences. Use a period or other end punctuation after the first sentence, and capitalize the first letter of the next sentence.

> **INCORRECT:** *In "A Crown of Wild Olive," Amyntas and Leon meet at the Olympic Games they are suspicious of each other because their countries are at war their rooms at Olympia are near each other.*
>
> **CORRECT:** *In "A Crown of Wild Olive," Amyntas and Leon meet at the Olympic Games. They are suspicious of each other because their countries are at war. Their rooms at Olympia are near each other.*

Forming Compound Sentences You can also correct a run-on sentence by rewriting it to form a compound sentence. One way to do this is by using a comma and a coordinating conjunction.

Never join simple sentences with a comma alone, or a run-on sentence will result. You need a comma followed by a conjunction

Grammar Practice Answers

Answers will vary.

In "The Monsters Are Due on Maple Street," normal social bonds were broken. The small amount of community feeling that existed on Maple Street was quickly destroyed. A sense of community is necessary if people are to live together safely and happily. The earliest human communities came into being when the need for safety arose. Neighbors in a community give one another practical and emotional support. They work to resolve problems among members rather than ignoring conflict. Even neighbors who live close together do not necessarily share similar values. Tolerance is essential in building a strong, stable community. A true community might have been able to stand up to the outside threat posed in this teleplay. Without community, Maple Street quickly turned violent.

such as *and, but,* or *or* to hold the sentences together.

> **INCORRECT:** *Leon cut his foot on the sickle, Amyntas helped clean the wound.*
> **CORRECT:** *Leon cut his foot on the sickle, and Amyntas helped clean the wound.*

You may use a semicolon to join two ideas that are closely related.

In addition, you can correct a run-on sentence by using a semicolon and a conjunctive adverb. Commonly used conjunctive adverbs are *however, therefore, nevertheless,* and *besides.*

> **INCORRECT:** *Amyntas spent his money on the bronze bull he left it as an offering. He did not want to be happy that Leon was hurt he still wanted to win.*
> **CORRECT:** *Amyntas spent his money on the bronze bull; he left it as an offering. He did not want to be happy that Leon was hurt; however, he still wanted to win.*

GRAMMAR PRACTICE

Rewrite this paragraph, correcting the run-on sentences.

1) In "A Crown of Wild Olive" Athens and Sparta agree to a truce so they can take part in the Olympic Games many ships from all over Greece sail safely to Olympia. 2) This story reflects an actual tradition from those times. 3) All wars had to stop for many reasons, first, the people wanted the Games to be a time of unity. 4) Often there were battles between the different cities, wars lasted many years. 5) Second, Olympia was a religious center the Games had religious importance. 6) The Greeks worshipped Zeus there people visited from all over the ancient world. 7) In the story, Amyntas spends time in the temple of Zeus he leaves the bronze bull as an offering. 8) Afterward, the Athenians and the Spartans leave Olympia everyone begins thinking about war again.

❻ Making Subjects and Verbs Agree

6.1 Simple and Compound Subjects A verb must agree in number with its subject. **Number** refers to whether a word is singular or plural. When a word refers to one thing, it is singular. When a word refers to more than one thing, it is plural.

Agreement with Simple Subjects Use a singular verb with a singular subject.

When the subject is a singular noun, you use the singular form of the verb. The present-tense singular form of a regular verb usually ends in *-s* or *-es.*

> **INCORRECT:** *In "Seventh Grade" Victor sign up for French class on the first day of school. A girl he like enrolls in the same class.*
> **CORRECT:** *In "Seventh Grade" Victor <u>signs</u> up for French class on the first day of school. A girl he <u>likes</u> enrolls in the same class.*

USAGE TIP To find the subject of a sentence, first find the verb. Then ask *who* or *what* performs the action of the verb. Say the subject and the verb together to see if they agree.

Use a plural verb with a plural subject.

> **INCORRECT:** *Girls pays attention when Victor's friend Michael scowls at them.*
> **CORRECT:** *Girls <u>pay</u> attention when Victor's friend Michael scowls at them.*

Agreement with Compound Subjects Use a plural verb with a compound subject whose parts are joined by *and,* regardless of the number of each part.

> **EXAMPLE:** *Victor and Teresa <u>talk</u> after their French class with Mr. Bueller.*

When the parts of a compound subject are joined by *or* or *nor,* make the verb agree in number with the part that is closer to it.

Usually *or* and *nor* appear with their correlatives *either* and *neither.*

Grammar Practice Answers

1) In "A Crown of Wild Olive" Athens and Sparta agree to a truce so they can take part in the Olympic Games. Many ships from all over Greece sail safely to Olympia. 2) This story reflects an actual tradition from those times. 3) All wars had to stop for many reasons. First, the people wanted the Games to be a time of unity. 4) Often there were battles between the different cities, and wars lasted many years. 5) Second, Olympia was a religious center, and the Games had religious importance. 6) The Greeks worshipped Zeus there, and people visited from all over the ancient world. 7) In the story, Amyntas spends time in the temple of Zeus. He leaves the bronze bull as an offering. 8) Afterward, the Athenians and the Spartans leave Olympia, and everyone begins thinking about war again.

INCORRECT: *Mr. Bueller asks whether Victor or the other students speaks any French. Neither Victor nor Teresa respond at first.*
CORRECT: *Mr. Bueller asks whether Victor or the other students* <u>speak</u> *any French. Neither Victor nor Teresa* <u>responds</u> *at first.*

GRAMMAR PRACTICE

Write the correct form of the verb given in parentheses.

1. In the story "Seventh Grade," Gary Soto (describe, describes) Victor's first day of school.

2. Victor (selects, select) French as his one elective.

3. According to a fashion magazine Michael read, men should (scowls, scowl).

4. Michael's upper lip (quivers, quiver) as he walks down the halls.

5. Neither the girls nor Victor (think, thinks) that Michael's scowl will really work.

6. Fashion magazines (consists, consist) of many advertisements with models in them.

7. In homeroom, Victor and Teresa (sits, sit) two seats away from each other.

8. Some girls (laugh, laughs) when he answers in English class.

9. The math problems in his book (scare, scares) him.

10. In French class, only the teacher (know, knows) that Victor's answer is gibberish.

6.2 *Pronoun Subjects* When a pronoun is used as a subject, the verb must agree with it in number.

Agreement with Personal Pronouns

When the subject is a singular personal pronoun, use a singular verb. When the subject is a plural personal pronoun, use a plural verb.

Even though *I* and *you* are singular, they take the plural form of the verb.

INCORRECT: *In "Zebra" Adam watches as the others play at recess. He are not able to play because of his accident.*
CORRECT: *In "Zebra" Adam watches as the others play at recess. He* <u>is</u> *not able to play because of his accident.*

When *he, she,* or *it* is the part of the subject closer to the verb in a compound subject containing *or* or *nor,* use a singular verb. When a pronoun is a part of a compound subject containing *and,* use a plural verb.

INCORRECT: *When Adam and the other students takes the summer art class, neither they nor he ignore John Wilson as he begins to teach them about art.*
CORRECT: *When Adam and the other students* <u>take</u> *the summer art class, neither they nor he* <u>ignores</u> *John Wilson as he begins to teach them about art.*

Agreement with Indefinite Pronouns

When the subject is a singular indefinite pronoun, use the singular form of the verb.

The following are singular indefinite pronouns: *another, either, nobody, anybody, everybody, somebody, no one, anyone, everyone, someone, one, nothing, anything, everything, something, each,* and *neither.*

EXAMPLE: *In Adam's class with Mrs. English, everybody* <u>listens</u> *to each other's stories.*

When the subject is a plural indefinite pronoun (*both, few, many,* or *several*), use the plural form of the verb.

EXAMPLES: *Few* <u>draw</u> *well at first. Many* <u>need</u> *a lot of practice.*

The indefinite pronouns *some, all, any, none,* and *most* can be either singular or plural. When the pronoun refers to one thing, use a singular verb.

When the pronoun refers to several things, use a plural verb.

EXAMPLES: *Some* <u>believe</u> *that the United States should not have gone to Vietnam, but John Wilson does not give his opinion in the story. All of his energy* <u>goes</u> *into making art.*

Grammar Practice Answers

1. describes
2. selects
3. scowl
4. quivers
5. thinks
6. consist
7. sit
8. laugh
9. scare
10. knows

1. learns
2. tells
3. think
4. go, hang
5. have
6. believe
7. wants
8. take
9. qualifies
10. are
11. seems
12. leaves

Grammar Handbook

GRAMMAR PRACTICE

Write the correct form of the verb given in parentheses.

1. In "Zebra" one (learn, learns) how John Wilson and Adam become friends.

2. John (tell, tells) Adam that he has an idea for a summer art class.

3. Many of Adam's classmates (think, thinks) that the summer art class will be fun.

4. Some (go, goes) to camp during the summer months, while others just (hang, hangs) around.

5. Anybody can learn how to draw, although some (have, has) a special talent for it.

6. Among psychologists, many (believe, believes) that making art is good therapy.

7. Andrea and Adam wonder if anybody else (want, wants) to take the class.

8. Both (take, takes) the summer art class.

9. A broken umbrella, an empty can, a doll—anything (qualify, qualifies) as material for making sculptures.

10. All (are, is) able to be transformed into beautiful objects.

11. In many ways, Adam (seem, seems) to bond with his teacher.

12. Each of the students (leave, leaves) the class having learned something special.

6.3 Common Agreement Problems

Several other situations can cause problems in subject-verb agreement.

Agreement with Irregular Verbs Use the singular forms of the irregular verbs *do, be,* and *have* with singular subjects. Use the plural forms of these verbs with plural subjects.

	Do	Be	Have
Singular Subjects	I do	I am/was	I have
	you do	you are/were	you have
	the dog does	Joe is/was	Pat hasn't
	it does	he isn't/wasn't	she has
	each doesn't	either is/was	anybody has
Plural Subjects	we do	we are/were	we have
	dogs do	boys are/were	girls have
	they do	they are/were	they haven't
	many don't	both are/were	few have

WATCH OUT! Look carefully at words that come before the subject. Remember that the subject may not be the noun or pronoun closest to the verb.

> **INCORRECT:** *The selection "Eleanor Roosevelt" do much to show the struggle of a dynamic first lady, and it have some insights into her success. Eleanor are a splendid achiever; she have qualities that anyone can cultivate.*

> **CORRECT:** *The selection "Eleanor Roosevelt" does much to show the struggle of a dynamic first lady, and it has some insights into her success. Eleanor is a splendid achiever; she has qualities that anyone can cultivate.*

Interrupting Words Be sure the verb agrees with its subject when a word or words come between them.

Sometimes one or more words come between the subject and the verb. The interrupter does not affect the number of the subject.

> **INCORRECT:** *Eleanor, moreover, encourage the hiring of female reporters by closing her press conferences to men.*

> **CORRECT:** *Eleanor, moreover, encourages the hiring of female reporters by closing her press conferences to men.*

Interrupting Phrases Be certain that the verb agrees with its subject when a phrase comes between them.

The subject of a verb is never found in a prepositional phrase, which may follow the subject and come before the verb.

INCORRECT: *Eleanor, in spite of several tragedies in her life, triumph over adversity. This woman of many talents rank high in the list of great Americans.*
CORRECT: *Eleanor, in spite of several tragedies in her life, <u>triumphs</u> over adversity. This woman of many talents <u>ranks</u> high in the list of great Americans.*

Phrases beginning with *including, as well as, along with,* and *in addition to* are not part of the subject.

    EXAMPLE: *Her mother's coldness, as well as her father's alcoholism, <u>creates</u> a challenging situation for a young child. Eleanor's strong will, along with her other outstanding qualities, <u>makes</u> her a wonderful role model.*

The subject of the verb is never found in an appositive, which may follow the subject and come before the verb.

    EXAMPLE: *Eleanor, one of several self-trained diplomats, <u>helps</u> create the United Nations after World War II. Her assistants, a dedicated group, still <u>sing</u> her praises.*

Inverted Sentences When the subject comes after the verb, be sure the verb agrees with the subject in number.

A sentence in which the subject follows the verb is called an inverted sentence. Questions are usually in inverted form, as are sentences beginning with *here, there,* and *where. (Where are the **reporters**? There is a **press conference** today.)*

    EXAMPLE: *Where <u>does</u> Eleanor find the courage to overcome her shyness? How <u>does</u> she grow during her life? <u>Do</u> other first ladies follow her example? There <u>are</u> many more questions we would like answered about the great lady, Eleanor Roosevelt.*

USAGE TIP To check subject verb agreement in inverted sentences, place the subject before the verb. For example, to check agreement, change *There are many people* to *Many people are there.*

Write the correct form of each verb given in parentheses.

1. Readers, while examining "Eleanor Roosevelt," (learn, learns) about the powerful influence that a father can have on his daughter.

2. Eleanor's father, in spite of his faults, (seem, seems) to have helped her feel unconditionally loved.

3. However, Eleanor's mother, in addition to the rest of the family, (was, were) relatively cold to her and filled her with self-doubt.

4. There (was, were) a sort of second mother to Eleanor, who lived near London.

5. How (is, are) Eleanor's early years related to her later achievements?

6. Joseph Lash, one of her biographers, (note, notes) that her childhood loneliness helped her understand people who felt left out.

7. Her heredity, as far as Eleanor was concerned, (appear, appears) to explain her great energy.

8. Looking back, she calmly recalls, "I think I (have, has) a good deal of my uncle Theodore in me. . . ."

9. What do you think (was, were) her greatest achievement?

10. *Presidential Wives,* one of several books by Paul Boller, (remind, reminds) us of the vitality of women like Eleanor.

---

❼ Using Nouns and Pronouns

7.1 *Plural and Possessive Nouns* Nouns refer to people, places, things, and ideas. Nouns are plural when they refer to more than one person, place, thing, or idea. Possessive nouns show who or what owns something.

Grammar Handbook

1. learn
2. seems
3. was
4. was
5. are
6. notes
7. appears
8. have
9. was
10. reminds

Plural Nouns Follow these guidelines to form noun plurals.

Nouns	To Form Plural	Examples
Most nouns	add -s	jaw-jaws
Most nouns that end in *s*, *sh, ch, x,* or *z*	add -es	fox-foxes flash-flashes
Most nouns that end in *ay, ey, oy,* or *uy*	add -s	delay—delays valley—valleys
Most nouns that end in a consonant and *y*	change *y* to *i* and add -es	cavalry—cavalries casualty—casualties
Most nouns that end in *o*	add -s	alto—altos arroyo—arroyos soprano—sopranos
Some nouns that end in a consonant and *o*	add -es	echo—echoes hero—heroes tomato—tomatoes
Most nouns that end in *f* or *fe*	change *f* to *v,* add -es or -s	sheaf—sheaves knife—knives *but* belief-beliefs

WATCH OUT! The plurals of many musical terms that end in *o* preceded by a consonant are formed by adding -s. These nouns include *tempos* and *concertos.*

Some nouns use the same spelling in both singular and plural: *series, fish, sheep, cannon.* Some noun plurals use a form that doesn't follow any rule: *teeth, geese.*

> **INCORRECT:** *In Knotes in My Yo-yo String, Jerry Spinelli writes about his fantasys of perfection. Baseball, yo-yoes, drawing within the lines, and cleaning his locker are a few of the activitys at which he tries to be perfect.*
>
> **CORRECT:** *In* <u>Knots</u> *in My Yo-Yo String, Jerry Spinelli writes about his* <u>fantasies</u> *of perfection. Baseball,* <u>yo-yos</u>*, drawing within the lines, and cleaning his locker are a few of the* <u>activities</u> *at which he tries to be perfect.*

Possessive Nouns Follow these guidelines to form possessive nouns.

Nouns	To Form Possessive	Examples
Singular nouns	add apostrophe and -s	league—league's
Plural nouns ending in *s*	add apostrophe	fields—fields' brigades—brigades'
Plural nouns not ending in *s*	add apostrophe and -s	children—children's oxen—oxen's

> **INCORRECT:** *Jerrys' drawing is never good enough to win the* Times Herald *contest, even though the other childrens' drawings are messier. Neatness, according to the newspapers' judges, isn't the only standard.*
>
> **CORRECT:** *Jerry's drawing is never good enough to win the* Times Herald *contest, even though the other* <u>children's</u> *drawings are messier. Neatness, according to the* <u>newspaper's</u> *judges, isn't the only standard.*

USAGE TIP The dictionary usually lists the plural form of a noun if the plural form is irregular or if there is more than one plural form. Dictionary listings are especially helpful for nouns that end in *o, f,* and, *fe.*

WATCH OUT! Be careful when placing apostrophes in possessive nouns. A misplaced apostrophe changes the meaning. For example, *boy's* refers to possession by one boy, but *boys'* refers to possession by two or more boys.

GRAMMAR PRACTICE

Write the correct noun given in parentheses.

1) This story describes Jerry (Spinelli's, Spinellis') attempts at perfection. **2)** He is a fanatic about making sure his (colores, colors) do not go outside the lines. **3)** He takes few chances when playing (sports, sportes), because he does not want to make an error.

Grammar Practice Answers

1. Spinelli's
2. colors
3. sports
4. plays
5. potatoes
6. boundaries

4) After a game, he goes over the (plaies, plays) in his mind so he can do better next time. **5)** I'll bet if his mom asked him to peel (potatos, potatoes), he would spend a week completing the task. **6)** Fortunately, he realizes that his imagination has no (boundarys, boundaries).

7.2 **Pronoun Forms** A personal pronoun is a pronoun that can be used in the first, second, or third person. A personal pronoun has three forms: the subject form, the object form, and the possessive form.

Subject Pronouns Use the subject form when the pronoun is the subject of a sentence or clause. *I, you, he, she, it, we,* and *they* are subject pronouns.

Using the correct pronoun form is seldom a problem when the sentence has just one pronoun. Problems can arise, however, when a noun and a pronoun or two pronouns are used in a compound subject or compound object. To see if you are using the correct pronoun form, read the sentence, using only one pronoun.

> **INCORRECT:** A Christmas Carol *tells the familiar tale of Scrooge. Him and the three Spirits of Christmas are the main characters.*
> **CORRECT:** A Christmas Carol *tells the familiar tale of Scrooge.* <u>He</u> *and the three Spirits of Christmas are the main characters.*

Use the subject form when the pronoun follows a linking verb.

You often hear the object form used as a predicate pronoun. ("It is him.") For this reason, the subject form may sound awkward to you, though it is preferred in more formal writing.

> **INCORRECT:** *The Spirits showed Scrooge his future, but it was him who decided to change.*
> **CORRECT:** *The Spirits showed Scrooge his future, but it was* <u>he</u> *who decided to change.*

USAGE TIP To check the form of a predicate pronoun, see if the sentence still makes sense when the subject and the predicate pronoun are reversed. *(It was he. He was it.)*

Object Pronouns Use the object form when the pronoun is the object in a clause, sentence, or of a preposition. *Me, you, him, her, it, us,* and *them* are object pronouns.

> **EXAMPLE:** *Scrooge's Christmas Eve changed* <u>him</u>*. His new approach to the Cratchit family worked wonders for* <u>them</u>*.*

Possessive Pronouns Never use an apostrophe in a possessive pronoun. *My, mine, your, yours, his, her, hers, its, our, ours, their,* and *theirs* are possessive pronouns.

Writers may confuse the possessive pronouns *its, your,* and *their* with the contractions *it's, you're,* and *they're.* Remember that the pairs are spelled differently and have different meanings.

> **INCORRECT:** *Scrooge thanked the Spirits for they're help. On Christmas morning, he sent a turkey to the Cratchets. To him, it's price was small for the joy it gave.*
> **CORRECT:** *Scrooge thanked the Spirits for* <u>their</u> *help. On Christmas morning, he sent a turkey to the Cratchits. To him,* <u>its</u> *price was small for the joy it gave.*

GRAMMAR PRACTICE

Write the correct pronoun form given in parentheses.

1) Charles Dickens wrote *A Christmas Carol* in 1843, when (he, him) was 31 years old. **2)** This work of (him, his) was written in only a few weeks. **3)** In 1836 he was a famous writer; that year (he, him) and Catherine Hogarth were married. **4)** (He, Him) was famous enough to tour America in 1842. **5)** Did you know that it was (him, he) who wrote other novels about Christmas? **6)** All of (they're, their) dates of composition are from the 1840s. **7)** (They, Them) include the rest of the books mentioned here, such as *The Chimes,* published in 1844. **8)** The next year saw another Christmas book of (his, him), *The Cricket on the Hearth.* **9)** The year following, *The Battle of Life* took (it's, its)

Grammar Practice Answers

1. he
2. his
3. he
4. He
5. he
6. their
7. They
8. his
9. its
10. his
11. his
12. They
13. its

place among his titles. **10)** Finally, *The Haunted Man,* an 1848 effort, was (him, his). **11)** These books are said to be part of the first phase of (his', his) works. **12)** (Them, They) have rather serious themes mixed with some humor. **13)** When Thackeray, a fellow writer, reviewed *A Christmas Carol,* he said that (its, it's) publication was a national benefit.

7.3 *Pronoun Antecedents* An antecedent is the noun or pronoun to which a personal pronoun refers. The antecedent usually precedes the pronoun.

Pronoun and Antecedent Agreement A pronoun must agree with its antecedent in
> NUMBER—*singular or plural*
> PERSON—*first, second, or third*
> GENDER—*male or female*

Use a singular pronoun to refer to a singular antecedent; use a plural pronoun to refer to a plural antecedent.

Do not allow interrupting words to determine the number of the personal pronoun.
> **INCORRECT:** *In "Dark They Were, and Golden-Eyed," Harry did not let his initial feeling of dread and panic influence him. Instead, he ignored them and settled with his family on Mars.*
> **CORRECT:** *In "Dark They Were, and Golden-Eyed" Harry did not let his initial feeling of dread and panic influence him. Instead, he ignored it and settled with his family on Mars.*

If the antecedent is a noun that could be either male or female, use *he or she (him or her, his or her)* or reword the sentence to avoid the need for a singular pronoun.
> **EXAMPLES:** *Each one of the colonists on Mars began to change, and he or she did not realize that anything odd was happening.*
> **OR**
> *All of the colonists on Mars began to change, and they did not realize that anything odd was happening.*

Be sure that the antecedent of a pronoun is clear.

In most cases, do not use a pronoun to refer to an entire idea or clause. Writing is much clearer when the exact reference is repeated.
> **INCORRECT:** *Harry's worries centered on his fear that he would change like the others. They are hard to ignore because everyone is beginning to look different.*
> **CORRECT:** *Harry's worries centered on his fear that he would change like the others. His worries are hard to ignore because everyone is beginning to look different.*
> **INCORRECT:** *As Sam is talking to Harry outside of the store, he learns that his eyes have changed color to yellow. This is a major turning point in the story. He realizes that he cannot resist change.*
> **CORRECT:** *As Sam is talking to Harry outside of the store, Harry learns that his eyes have changed color to yellow. This is a major turning point in the story. Harry realizes that he cannot resist change.*

USAGE TIP To avoid vague pronoun reference, do not use *this* or *that* alone to start a clause. Instead, include a word that clarifies what *this* or *that* refers to—*this experience, this situation, that concept.*

Indefinite Pronouns as Antecedents
When a singular indefinite pronoun referring to a person is the antecedent, use *he or she (him or her, his or her)* or rewrite the sentence to avoid the need for a singular pronoun.
> **INCORRECT:** *Everyone on Mars was beginning to undergo changes in their appearance without realizing it.*
> **CORRECT:** *Everyone on Mars was beginning to undergo changes in his or her appearance without realizing it.*
> **OR**
> **CORRECT:** *All the colonists on Mars were beginning to undergo changes in their appearance without realizing it.*

Indefinite Pronouns

Singular

another	each	everybody	neither	somebody
anybody	either	everyone	nobody	someone
anyone		everything	no one	something
anything			nothing	
			one	

Plural

both	few	many	several

Singular or Plural

all	any	most	none	some

WATCH OUT! Avoid the indefinite use of *you* and *they*.

INCORRECT: *At home they used Martian words.*

CORRECT: *At home family members used Martian words.*

INCORRECT: *Joe thought you should always thank them.*

CORRECT: *Joe thought a person should always thank his or her friends.*

GRAMMAR PRACTICE

Rewrite this paragraph to make the pronoun reference clear.

1) In "Dark They Were, and Golden-Eyed" a war on Earth eliminates their chance of returning home. 2) When they hear the news, they feel hopeless. 3) Nobody knows what they will do. 4) At first everything is fine, but it changes when Harry sees that the plants are growing differently. 5) People start speaking words they have never heard before, and they sound strange. 6) Each person is changing, but they don't realize it. 7) It is something that only Harry notices. 8) Also, the American names they gave to the land seem strange after a while. 9) They don't sound as natural as the old Martian names. 10) This shows how Mars slowly takes the Earth out of the them and makes them its own.

7.4 **Pronoun Usage** The form that a pronoun takes is always determined by its function within its own clause or sentence.

Who and Whom Use *who* or *whoever* as the subject of a clause or sentence.

INCORRECT: *In "The Night the Bed Fell," whom started all the ruckus?*

CORRECT: *In "The Night the Bed Fell," who started all the ruckus?*

Use *whom* as the direct or indirect object of a verb or verbal and as the object of a preposition.

People often use *who* for *whom* when speaking. In written English the pronouns should be used correctly.

INCORRECT: *Mother wants to rescue who? Who was she worrying about?*

CORRECT: *Mother wants to rescue whom? Whom was she worrying about?*

In trying to determine the correct pronoun form, ignore interrupters that come between the subject and the verb.

INCORRECT: *Whom, in your estimation, was in the most danger during the ordeal?*

EXAMPLE: *Who, in your estimation, was in the most danger during the ordeal?*

Pronouns in Contractions Do not confuse the contractions *it's, they're, who's,* and *you're* with possessive pronouns that sound the same—*its, their, whose,* and *your*.

INCORRECT: *Briggs and the narrator have no idea who's fault the commotion is.*

CORRECT: *Briggs and the narrator have no idea whose fault the commotion is.*

Pronouns with Nouns Determine the correct form of the pronoun in phrases such as *we girls* and *us boys* by dropping the noun and saying the sentence without the noun that follows the pronoun.

INCORRECT: *I believe that a story is most interesting when us readers are confused along with the characters.*

CORRECT: *I believe that a story is most interesting when we readers are confused along with the characters.*

GRAMMAR HANDBOOK **R67**

Grammar Practice Answers

Answers will vary.
1) In "Dark They Were, and Golden-Eyed" a war on Earth eliminates the Bitterings' chance of returning home. 2) When the Bitterings hear the news, they feel hopeless. 3) Nobody knows what he or she will do. 4) At first everything is fine, but that feeling changes when Harry sees that the plants are growing differently. 5) People start speaking words they have never heard before, and the words sound strange. 6) Each person is changing, but he or she doesn't realize it. 7) The change is something that only Harry notices. 8) Also, the American names the townspeople gave to the land seem strange after a while. 9) The American names don't sound as natural as the old Martian names. 10) This shows how Mars slowly takes the Earth out of the Earth people and makes them its own.

Grammar Practice Answers

1. Who
2. whoever
3. who
4. whom
5. whom
6. they're
7. your
8. it's

GRAMMAR PRACTICE

Write the correct pronoun given in parentheses.

1) (Who, Whom) in "The Night the Bed Fell" remains the calmest? **2)** Let (whomever, whoever) thinks he or she would not be scared think again. **3)** Those (who, whom) have a lot of relatives will best understand this story. **4)** To (who, whom) in the class has a similar experience happened? **5)** Heather tells us about a misunderstanding she had with her cousins, (who, whom) she stays with in the summer. **6)** But (their, they're) all still good friends. **7)** What would you do if you heard a crash in the middle of the night in (your, you're) house? **8)** After a scare like that (its, it's) hard to get back to sleep.

8 Using Verbs Correctly

8.1 *Verb Tenses and Forms* Verb tense shows the time of an action or a condition. Writers sometimes cause confusion when they use different verb tenses in describing actions that occur at the same time.

Consistent Use of Tenses When two or more actions occur at the same time or in sequence, use the same verb tense to describe the actions.

> **INCORRECT:** *In "The Eternal Frontier" Louis L'Amour writes about outer space. He considered the effect of space-age technology on our daily lives.*
>
> **CORRECT:** *In "The Eternal Frontier" Louis L'Amour writes about outer space. He considers the effect of space-age technology on our daily lives.*

A shift in tense is necessary when two events occur at different times or out of sequence. The tenses of the verbs should clearly indicate that one action precedes the other.

INCORRECT: *We once have found adventure in the discovery of new lands. Now we will receive transmissions from places that in the past we only imagine.*

CORRECT: *We once found adventure in the discovery of new lands. Now we receive transmissions from places that in the past we only imagined.*

Tense	Verb Form
Present	open/opens
Past	opened
Future	will/shall open
Present perfect	have/has opened
Past perfect	had opened
Future perfect	will/shall have opened

Past Tense and the Past Participle The simple past form of a verb can always stand alone. The past participle of the following irregular verbs should always be used with a helping verb.

Present Tense	Past Tense	Past Participle
be (is/are)	was/were	(have, had) been
begin	began	(have, had) begun
break	broke	(have, had) broken
bring	brought	(have, had) brought
choose	chose	(have, had) chosen
come	came	(have, had) come
do	did	(have, had) done
drink	drank	(have, had) drunk
eat	ate	(have, had) eaten
fall	fell	(have, had) fallen
freeze	froze	(have, had) frozen
give	gave	(have, had) given
go	went	(have, had) gone
lose	lost	(have, had) lost
grow	grew	(have, had) grown

USAGE TIP Some writers use gradual shifts in verb tense (such as from the past to the past participle) to move from the past up through to the present. This can be used to show developments throughout a historical period as in the example above. When using this technique, be careful to use verb tenses that clearly convey your message.

GRAMMAR PRACTICE

Write the correct verb tense for each sentence.

1) "The Eternal Frontier" (deals, dealt, will deal) with the opportunities that the space age offers. 2) Some medical developments (are beginning, began, begun) with the space age—for example, laparoscopy and robotics. 3) Both of these areas (grow, grew, have grown) to advance the field of surgery dramatically. 4) In 1993 a "robotic assistant" (begin, began, has begun) helping in surgery. 5) People also (come, have came, have come) to expect simpler procedures because of these new techniques. 6) Laser surgery (is, have been, will be) another procedure that avoids cutting into tissue. 7) Such techniques (spring, sprang, have sprung) from technology developed for space exploration.

8.2 **Commonly Confused Verbs** The following verb pairs are easily confused.

Let and Leave *Let* means "to allow or permit." *Leave* means "to depart" or "to allow something to remain where it is."

> **INCORRECT:** *Rudyard Kipling, the author of "Rikki-Tikki-Tavi," often leaves animal characters tell his stories.*
> **CORRECT:** *Rudyard Kipling, the author of "Rikki-Tikki-Tavi," often lets animal characters tell his stories.*

Lie and Lay *Lie* means "to rest in a flat position." *Lay* means "to put or place."

> **INCORRECT:** *Rikki-tikki was laying in the middle of the path.*
> **CORRECT:** *Rikki-tikki was lying in the middle of the path.*

Sit and Set *Sit* means "to be in a seated position." *Set* means "to put or place."

> **INCORRECT:** *The mongoose set on the shoulder of the boy who immediately sat a piece of meat before it.*
> **CORRECT:** *The mongoose sat on the shoulder of the boy who immediately set a piece of meat before it.*

Rise and Raise *Rise* means "to move upward." *Raise* means "to move something upward."

> **INCORRECT:** *Nag just raised up, rising his head threateningly.*
> **CORRECT:** *Nag just rose up, raising his head threateningly.*

Learn and Teach *Learn* means "to gain knowledge or skill." *Teach* means "to help someone learn."

> **INCORRECT:** *Rikki-tikki learned Nag to fear something.*
> **CORRECT:** *Rikki-tikki taught Nag to fear something.*

Here are the principal parts of these troublesome verb pairs.

Present Tense	Past Tense	Past Participle
let	let	(have, had) let
leave	left	(have, had) left
lie	lay	(have, had) lain
lay	laid	(have, had) laid
sit	sat	(have, had) sat
set	set	(have, had) set
rise	rose	(have, had) risen
raise	raised	(have, had) raised
learn	learned	(have, had) learned
teach	taught	(have, had) taught

GRAMMAR PRACTICE

Choose the correct verb from each pair of words.

1) Rudyard Kipling's tale "Rikki-tikki-tavi" (learns, teaches) readers many facts about the cobra and its natural enemy, the mongoose.
2) Most snakes (lay, lie) hidden to avoid people

Grammar Practice Answers 8.1

1. deals
2. began
3. have grown
4. began
5. have come
6. is
7. spring

Grammar Practice Answers 8.2

1. teaches
2. lie

Grammar Practice Answers 8.2 (cont.)

3. rises
4. Leaving
5. set
6. rise
7. leaves

Grammar Practice Answers 9.1

1. really
2. respectfully
3. usually
4. valuable
5. deeply
6. perfectly
7. natural

---

and animals much of the time. **3)** The cobra, however, (raises, rises) to seek out its victim. **4)** (Letting, Leaving) a cobra alone is no protection either. **5)** An unintentional disturbance can (set, sit) one against you. **6)** Both male and female, while protecting their eggs, for example, will (raise, rise) up against any approaching intruder. **7)** The venom of the cobra is a deadly nerve- and muscle-paralyzing substance that (lets, leaves) a human being dead in minutes.

❾ Using Modifiers Effectively

9.1 *Adjective or Adverb?* Use an adjective to modify a noun or a pronoun. Use an adverb to modify a verb, an adjective, or another adverb.

> **INCORRECT:** *Traditional Chinese families do not regard a two-income household as high as American families do, so the family in "The White Umbrella" must be real desperate if the mother has to work outside the home.*
>
> **CORRECT:** *Traditional Chinese families do not regard the two-income household as <u>highly</u> as American families do, so the family in "The White Umbrella" must be <u>rather</u> desperate if the mother has to work outside the home.*

Use an adjective after a linking verb to describe the subject.

Remember that in addition to forms of the verb *be,* the following are linking verbs: *become, seem, appear, look, sound, feel, taste, grow,* and *smell.*

> **EXAMPLES:** *The narrator feels <u>bad</u> that her mother is working, although her sister thinks <u>differently</u>, not caring if anybody knows.*

Write the correct modifier in each pair.

1) In "The White Umbrella" the two sisters listen as Eugenie Roberts plays the piano (real, really) well. **2)** They wait (respectful, respectfully) for her lesson to finish. **3)** People (usual, usually) begin piano lessons when they are young. **4)** Children develop (valuable, valuably) skills at the piano, such as the ability to follow rhythm and read music. **5)** Music is something that (deep, deeply) affects all people. **6)** Although musicians come from many different countries, they are able to play together (perfect, perfectly). **7)** Music is a (natural, naturally) human expression.

9.2 *Comparisons and Negatives*

Comparative and Superlative Adjectives
Use the comparative form of an adjective when comparing two things.

Comparative adjectives are formed by adding *-er* to short adjectives *(small-smaller)* or by using the word *more* with longer adjectives *(horrible-more horrible).*

> **INCORRECT:** *Traveling across the Atlantic Ocean in days past was uncomfortabler than flying is today.*
>
> **CORRECT:** *Traveling across the Atlantic Ocean in days past was much <u>more uncomfortable</u> than flying is today.*

Use the superlative form when comparing three or more things.

The superlative is formed by adding *-est* to short adjectives *(tall-tallest)* or by using the word *most* with longer adjectives *(interesting-most interesting).*

> **INCORRECT:** *Obtaining passage, traveling steerage, or passing through customs: which was difficultest?*
>
> **CORRECT:** *Obtaining passage, traveling steerage, or passing through customs: which was <u>most difficult</u>?*

The comparative and superlative forms of some adjectives are irregular.

Adjective	Comparative	Superlative
good	better	best
well	better	best
bad	worse	worst
ill	worse	worst
little	less or lesser	least
much	more	most
many	more	most
far	farther or further	farthest or furthest

Comparative and Superlative Adverbs
When comparing two actions, use the comparative form of an adverb, which is formed by adding -er or the word *more*.

INCORRECT: *European immigrants, frequenter than not, entered the United States frightened and exhausted.*

CORRECT: *European immigrants, <u>more frequently</u> than not, entered the United States frightened and exhausted.*

WATCH OUT! Do not use both *-er* and *more*. Do not use both *-est* and *most*. Remove *more* and *most* from the following sentence: *The ship was more faster than the most fastest winds.* Do you notice the improvement?

When comparing more than two actions, use the superlative form of an adverb, which is formed by adding -est or by using the word *most*.

EXAMPLE: *Of the several ports of entry, European immigrants entered through Ellis Island most often.*

Double Negatives To avoid double negatives, use only one negative word in a clause.

Besides *not* and *no*, the following are negative words: *never, nobody, none, no one, nothing,* and *nowhere.*

EXAMPLE: *Most immigrants <u>didn't ever</u> regret moving to a new country.*

Write the correct modifier in each pair.

1) More than 60 years after Ellis Island opened as the (larger, largest) port of entry to this country, it was abandoned. **2)** In the 1980s the facilities underwent the (greatest, most greatest) restoration ever. **3)** The National Park Service helped supervise but did not try to find (any, no) funding sources. **4)** The Statue of Liberty-Ellis Island Restoration Project (activelier, more actively) solicited contributions. **5)** In 1990 there was a (grand, grandly) reopening of the main building. **6)** The museum and examination rooms remind us that our immigration process used to be (worse, worser). **7)** Which films, objects, and oral histories (more vividly, most vividly) record our past?

9.3 *Special Problems with Modifiers*
The following terms are frequently misused in spoken English, but they should be used correctly in written English.

Them and Those *Them* is always a pronoun and never a modifier for a noun. *Those* is a pronoun when it stands alone. It is an adjective when followed by a noun.

INCORRECT: *In "Growing Up" Baker describes them experiences that led him to become a writer.*

CORRECT: *In "Growing Up" Baker describes <u>those</u> experiences that led him to become a writer.*

Bad and Badly Always use *bad* as an adjective, whether before a noun or after a linking verb. *Badly* should generally be used to modify an action verb.

EXAMPLES: *Knowing that he had done <u>badly</u>, he returned to the house defeated. He felt <u>bad</u> because he did not sell any papers.*

Grammar Practice Answers

1. largest
2. greatest
3. any
4. more actively
5. grand
6. worse
7. most vividly

Grammar Practice Answers

1. those
2. few
3. good
4. This
5. badly
6. little
7. less
8. well

WATCH OUT! Avoid the use of *here* after *this* or *these*. Similarly, avoid using *there* after *that* or *those*. Notice the improvement when *here* and *there* are removed from the following sentence:

> **INCORRECT:** *I was amused by this here story. Russell's attempt to sell that there Saturday Evening Post was funny.*
>
> **CORRECT:** *I was amused by this story. Russell's attempt to sell that Saturday Evening Post was funny.*

This, That, These, and Those Whether used as adjectives or pronouns, *this* and *these* refer to people and things that are nearby, and *that* and *those* refer to people and things that are farther away.

> **EXAMPLES:** *After deciding to concentrate on writing, Baker found* <u>this</u> *work more satisfying than* <u>that</u> *tiresome routine of selling papers.*

Good and Well *Good* is always an adjective, never an adverb. Use *well* as either an adjective or an adverb, depending on the sentence.

When used as an adjective, *well* usually refers to a person's health. As an adverb, *well* modifies an action verb. In the expression "feeling good," *good* refers to being happy or pleased.

> **EXAMPLES:** *Baker's little sister sold papers* <u>well</u>. *Baker felt* <u>good</u> *about her success and bought her an apple.*

Few and Little, Fewer and Less *Few* refers to numbers of things that can be counted; *little* refers to amounts or quantities. *Fewer* is used when comparing numbers of things; *less* is used when comparing amounts or quantities.

> **INCORRECT:** *As a writer, Baker would encounter less angry dogs. He would have few sense of rejection and fewer hardship than he would if he continued trying to sell the Saturday Evening Post.*
>
> **CORRECT:** *As a writer, Baker would encounter* <u>fewer</u> *angry dogs. He would have* <u>less</u> *sense of rejection and* <u>less</u> *hardship than he would if he continued trying to sell the Saturday Evening Post.*

GRAMMAR PRACTICE

Write the modifier from each pair that fits the meaning of the sentence.

1) In "Growing Up," Russell Baker's mother is one of (them, those) mothers who works hard to guide her children. **2)** Times were hard during the Depression and (few, less) people lived in luxury. **3)** Naturally, she was concerned that Russell grow up to have a (good, well) profession. **4)** (This, That) concern motivated her to teach him about character and gumption. **5)** She was disappointed when he sold papers (bad, badly). **6)** Russell had (few, little) interest in selling papers; however, the experience taught him about himself. **7)** He learned that such a profession would give him (few, less) satisfaction than a job collecting garbage. **8)** He needed a job that would accommodate (good, well) his lack of gumption.

⑩ Phrases and Clauses

A phrase is a group of related words that does not have subject and predicate and that functions in a sentence as a single part of speech. Phrases may appear anywhere in a sentence. If a phrase appears at the beginning of a sentence, it is called an introductory phrase. Because phrases can act as a single part of speech, they are classified as prepositional phrases, appositive phrases, infinitive phrases, participial phrases, and gerund phrases.

10.1 *Prepositional Phrases* When a phrase consists of a preposition, its object, and any modifiers of the object, it is called a prepositional phrase. Prepositional phrases that modify nouns or pronouns are called adjective phrases. Prepositional phrases that modify a verb, an adjective, or another adverb are adverb phrases.

> **ADJECTIVE PHRASE:** *In the excerpt from* I Never Had It Made, *Jackie Robinson tells the story* <u>of his integration of the Brooklyn Dodgers</u>.

ADVERT PHRASE: *Jackie Robinson had played for the Montreal Royals.*

10.2 Appositive Phrases An appositive phrase is a group of words that identifies or provides further information about a noun or pronoun that directly precedes the phrase.

EXAMPLE: *Jackie Robinson, an exceptional athlete, was Branch Rickey's pick to be the first African-American player to join the Dodgers.*

10.3 Infinitive Phrases An infinitive phrase consists of an infinitive (*to* + a verb) along with its modifiers and objects.

EXAMPLE: *Branch Rickey wanted to integrate major-league baseball.*

10.4 Participial Phrases A participial phrase is a group of words that includes a participle. There are two kinds of participles: past and present. The past participle is usually formed by adding *-d* or *-ed* to the present tense; however, irregular verbs do not follow this rule. The present participle is formed by adding *-ing* to the present tense of any verb. A participle with its objects and modifiers is called a participial phrase. Participial phrases act as adjectives, modifying a noun or a pronoun.

EXAMPLE: *Having read Robinson's autobiography, I can better imagine the difficulties he faced.*

10.5 Gerund Phrases A gerund is a verb form ending in *-ing* that functions as a noun. A gerund phrase is a group of words that includes a gerund and its modifiers and objects.

EXAMPLE: *Maintaining his self-control was one of Robinson's best defenses.*

GRAMMAR PRACTICE

Identify each underlined phrase as a prepositional phrase, an appositive phrase, an infinitive phrase, a participial phrase, or a gerund phrase.

1. After reading Jackie Robinson's autobiography, I wanted to find out more about Robinson.

2. Searching through the library, I came across several books and articles on the subject.

3. Opposition to Robinson died down after his first year with the Dodgers.

4. Voted the most valuable player in the league in 1949, Robinson went on to be one of the most popular Dodger players.

5. Robinson played his entire major-league career with the same team, the Brooklyn Dodgers.

6. Reading about this period in American sports history was sometimes a painful experience.

7. In 1962 Robinson became the first African American to enter the National Baseball Hall of Fame.

10.6 Independent (Main) and Dependent (Subordinate) Clauses A clause is a group of words that contains a subject and a verb. There are two kinds of clauses: main (independent) clauses and subordinate (dependent) clauses. A main clause can stand alone as a complete sentence. A dependent clause cannot stand alone as a sentence and must be attached to a main clause to form a complex sentence. If a dependent clause is not attached to a main clause, it is considered a sentence fragment.

INDEPENDENT CLAUSE: *I read "Amigo Brothers."*
DEPENDENT CLAUSE: *After I finished dinner*
COMPLEX SENTENCE: *After I finished dinner, I read "Amigo Brothers."*

10.7 Adjective and Adverb Clauses An adjective clause is a dependent clause used as an adjective. Adjective clauses are usually introduced by the relative pronouns *who, whom, whose, which,* and *that.* An adverb clause is a dependent clause that is used as an adverb to modify a verb, an adjective, or another adverb.

ADJECTIVE CLAUSE: *Felix and Antonio are the names of the boys who are the main characters in "Amigo Brothers."*
ADVERB CLAUSE: *The boys had to make a decision before they met in the division final match in August.*

Grammar Practice Answers

1. infinitive phrase
2. participial phrase
3. prepositional phrase
4. participial phrase
5. appositive phrase
6. gerund phrase
7. infinitive phrase

Grammar Practice Answers

1. main clause
2. dependent clause, noun clause
3. dependent clause, adverb clause
4. dependent clause, adjective clause
5. dependent, noun clause

10.8 *Noun Clauses* A noun clause is a dependent clause that is used in a sentence as a noun. A noun clause may be used as a subject, a direct object, an indirect object, a predicate noun, or an object of a preposition.

> **EXAMPLE:** *The division final match would determine* who would represent the Boys Club in the Golden Gloves Championship Tournament.

GRAMMAR PRACTICE

Identify each underlined clause as a main or dependent clause. If the clause is dependent, identify it as an adjective clause, an adverb clause, or a noun clause.

1. Antonio and Felix promised each other not to pull their punches.

2. Each boy wondered what would happen to their friendship after the fight.

3. Felix went to a movie called *The Champion* when he wanted to psych himself for the fight.

4. Antonio went up to the rooftop, where he did some heavy thinking.

5. In the end, Felix and Antonio didn't care which of them won the division final match.

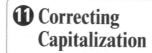

⑪ Correcting Capitalization

11.1 *Proper Nouns and Adjectives*
A common noun names a whole class of persons, places, things, or ideas. A proper noun names a particular person, place, thing, or idea. A proper adjective is an adjective formed from a proper noun. All proper nouns and proper adjectives are capitalized.

Names and Personal Titles Capitalize the name and title of a person.

Also capitalize the initials and abbreviations of titles that stand for those names.

Thomas Alva Edison, T. A. Edison, Governor James Thompson, and *Mr. Aaron Copland* are capitalized correctly.

> **EXAMPLES:** *In* The Autobiography of Malcolm X, Malcolm X *tells how his desire to write letters—to Elijah Muhammad, for example—inspired him to study.*

Capitalize a word referring to a family relationship when it is used as someone's name (Uncle Al) but not when it is used to identify a person (Jill's uncle).

> **EXAMPLES:** *If the people he mentions—Ella and Reginald—had been aunt and uncle instead of* sister *and* brother, *he might have called them* Aunt Ella *and* Uncle Reginald.

WATCH OUT! Do not capitalize personal titles used as common nouns. *(We met the **m**ayor.)*

Languages, Nationalities, Religious Terms Capitalize the names of languages and nationalities as well as religious names and terms.

Capitalize languages and nationalities, such as *French, Gaelic, Chinese,* and *Tagalog.* Capitalize religious names and terms, such as *Allah, Jehovah,* the *Bible,* and the *Koran.*

> **EXAMPLES:** *This famous African American was a Muslim, so he must have read the Koran.*

School Subjects Capitalize the name of a specific school course *(Civics 101, General Science).* Do not capitalize a general reference to a school subject *(social studies, algebra, art).*

> **EXAMPLES:** *Malcolm X read about history and religion, but at first he could have used courses such as Penmanship 101 or Beginning English.*

WATCH OUT! Do not capitalize minor words in a proper noun that is made up of several words *(Field Museum **of** Natural History).*

Organizations, Institutions Capitalize the important words in the official names of organizations and institutions *(Congress, University of Texas).*

Do not capitalize words that refer to kinds of organizations or institutions (*college, hospital, museums*) or words that refer to specific organizations but are not their official names (*to the museum*).

> **EXAMPLES:** *He began reading in Charlestown Prison but really explored in depth the library at Norfolk Prison Colony.*

Geographical Names, Events, Time Periods

Capitalize geographical names, as well as the names of events, historical periods and documents, holidays, and months and days, but not the names of seasons or directions.

WATCH OUT! Do not capitalize a reference that does not use the full name of a place, event, or period. *(The Empire State Building was once the tallest **building** in the world.)*

> **EXAMPLES:** *As Malcolm X studied the dictionary, he learned about the aardvark, a termite-eating mammal from Africa. He read constantly—summer, winter, spring, and fall—in the library and in his cell.*

Names	Examples
Continents	Africa, South America
Bodies of water	Pacific Ocean, Lake Charles, Amazon River
Political units	Maine, Japan, Brasília
Sections of a country	the South, Middle Atlantic States
Public areas	the Loop, the Boston Common
Roads and structures	Park Avenue, Hoover Dam, Chrysler Building
Historical events	the War of 1812, the Emancipation Proclamation
Documents	Magna Carta, the Treaty of Paris
Periods of history	the Middle Ages, Reconstruction
Holidays	Arbor Day, New Year's Day
Months and days	May, Sunday
Seasons	summer, autumn
Directions	north, south

GRAMMAR PRACTICE

Write the correct forms of the words given in parentheses.

1) Like (malcolm X, Malcolm X), Jawaharlal Nehru, first (prime minister, Prime Minister) of India, used prison for serious reading and writing. **2)** While imprisoned, (nehru, Nehru), too, used letter writing to improve his communication skills. **3)** His letters to his daughter, Indira, later (prime minister, Prime Minister) Ghandi, were the basis for a book on (world history, World History). **4)** In prison, too, Nehru completed his (autobiography, Autobiography). **5)** A Brahmin from (kashmir, Kashmir), he was educated at (harrow school, Harrow School) and (cambridge university, Cambridge University) in England. **6)** He was as eloquent in (hindi, Hindi) as in (english, English).

11.2 *Titles of Created Works* Titles need to follow certain capitalization rules.

Poems, Stories, Articles Capitalize the first word, the last word, and all other important words in the title of a poem, a story, or an article. Enclose the title in quotation marks.

> **EXAMPLE:** Walt Whitman's poem "Song of Myself" celebrates his humanity and the joy of living in a glorious world.

Books, Plays, Magazines, Newspapers, Films Capitalize the first word, the last word, and all other important words in the title of a book, play or musical, magazine, newspaper, or film. Underline or italicize the title to set it off.

Within a title, don't capitalize articles, conjunctions, and prepositions of fewer than five letters.

> **EXAMPLE:** It appeared in his book *Leaves of Grass,* whose unconventional form and apparent immodesty shocked readers.

In cases where a title that is ordinarily italicized appears in a sentence that itself is in italics, the title should then appear in ordinary type to set it off from the rest of the sentence.

Grammar Practice Answers

1. Malcolm X, prime minister
2. Nehru
3. Prime Minister, world history
4. autobiography
5. Kashminr, Harrow School, Cambridge University
6. Hindi, English

Grammar Practice Answers 11.2

1) Some of Walt Whitman's first published poems appeared in the small book *Leaves of Grass*. 2) Others—such as those about the Civil War-"Beat! Beat! Drums!," "When Lilacs Last in the Dooryard Bloom'd," and "O Captain! My Captain!"—appeared in the collection *Drumtaps*. 3) Whitman was also a journalist: founder of the *Freeman*, editor-printer of the *Long Islander*, editor of the *Brooklyn Daily Eagle* and the *Brooklyn Times*, and reporter or writer for numerous other newspapers. 4) Some of his short stories were published in popular magazines such as the *Democratic Review*. 5) Others—for example, "The Half-Breed"— appeared in collections. 6) Whitman even wrote a novel: *Franklin Evans*. 7) Some collections of his works include *The Complete Writings of Walt Whitman* and *The Uncollected Poetry and Prose of Walt Whitman*.

Grammar Practice Answers 12.1

1) The boys in the story like the sweetshop, but they dislike Mrs. Pratchett because she is dirty all the time. 2) There were few health codes in 1923, so Mrs. Pratchett could get away with wearing dirty clothes and wrapping up candy in newspaper. 3) There are other reasons the boys don't like her; for example, she often accuses them of stealing. 4) They never steal anything from the shop, but Mrs. Pratchett always yells at them. 5) The mouse prank seems like a good idea, and it is a way to get back at her. 6) Some people, however, cannot take such a scare. 7) The boys think that the prank might have killed Mrs. Pratchett; they are relieved when they see that she is alive.

EXAMPLE: *Madeleine L'Engle's novel* A Wrinkle in Time *is an example of science fiction.*

GRAMMAR PRACTICE

Rewrite this paragraph, correcting punctuation and capitalization of titles.

1) Some of Walt Whitman's first published poems appeared in the small book leaves of grass. 2) Others—such as those about the Civil War—beat! beat! drums!, when lilacs last in the dooryard bloom'd, and o captain! my captain!—appeared in the collection drumtaps. 3) Whitman was also a journalist: founder of the freeman, editor-printer of the long islander, editor of the Brooklyn daily eagle and the Brooklyn times, and reporter or writer for numerous other newspapers. 4) Some of his short stories were published in popular magazines such as the democratic review. 5) Others—for example, the half-breed— appeared in collections. 6) Whitman even wrote a novel: franklin evans. 7) Some collections of his works include the complete writings of walt whitman and the uncollected poetry and prose of walt whitman.

⑫ Punctuation

12.1 Compound Sentences Punctuation helps organize longer sentences that have several clauses.

Commas in Compound Sentences Use a comma before the conjunction that joins the clauses of a compound sentence.

> **EXAMPLE:** *In* Boy: Tales of Childhood *Roald Dahl describes trips to the sweetstore with his friends, and he tells about the prank which got him into trouble.*

Semicolons in Compound Sentences Use a semicolon between the clauses of a compound sentence when no conjunction is used. Use a semicolon before, and a comma after, a conjunctive adverb that joins the clauses of a compound sentence.

Conjunctive adverbs include *therefore, however, then, nevertheless, consequently,* and *besides.*

> **EXAMPLES:** *The boys each received a weekly allowance; they enthusiastically spent their money at the local sweetstore. Licorice was one of their favorite types of candy; however, Thwaites's father told them it was made from rats' blood.*

USAGE TIP Even when clauses are connected by a coordinating conjunction, you should use a semicolon between them if one or both clauses contain a comma.

> *The Great Mouse Plot, a silly little prank, had painful consequences; but the five boys would still say it was fun.*

GRAMMAR PRACTICE

Rewrite these sentences, adding commas and semicolons where necessary.

1) The boys in the story like the sweetshop but they dislike Mrs. Pratchett because she is dirty all the time. 2) There were few health codes in 1923 so Mrs. Pratchett could get away with wearing dirty clothes and wrapping up candy in newspaper. 3) There are other reasons the boys don't like her for example, she often accuses them of stealing. 4) They never steal anything from the shop but Mrs. Pratchett always yells at them. 5) The mouse prank seems like a good idea and it is a way to get back at her. 6) Some people however cannot take such a scare. 7) The boys think that the prank might have killed Mrs. Pratchett they are relieved when they see that she is alive.

12.2 Elements Set Off in a Sentence Most elements that are not essential to a sentence are set off by commas to highlight the main idea of the sentence.

Introductory Words Use a comma to separate an introductory word from the rest of the sentence.

EXAMPLE: *Certainly, "The Old Grandfather and His Little Grandson," by Leo Tolstoy, teaches an important lesson.*

Use a comma to separate an introductory phrase from the rest of the sentence.

Use a comma to set off more than one introductory prepositional phrase but not for a single prepositional phrase in most cases.

EXAMPLE: *In this tale of family life, we see the effect our conduct has. At home our actions are a powerful teacher.*

Interrupters Use commas to set off a word that interrupts the flow of a sentence.

INCORRECT: *The parents fortunately were ashamed when they realized what they were teaching their son. They thought about their behavior therefore and decided to improve their conduct.*

CORRECT: *The parents, fortunately, were ashamed when they realized what they were teaching their son. They thought about their behavior, therefore, and decided to improve their conduct.*

Use commas to set off a group of words that interrupts the flow of a sentence.

EXAMPLE: *Misha noticed his parents treating his grandfather badly and, to his parents' surprise, started to make a wooden bucket for them.*

Nouns of Address Use commas to set off a noun in direct address at the beginning of a sentence.

EXAMPLE: *"Father, your table manners are an embarrassment. Please eat in the corner," the father might have said.*

Use commas to set off a noun in direct address in the middle of a sentence.

EXAMPLE: *The boy's mother asked, "What are you making, Misha, from those pieces of wood?"*

Appositives Set off with commas an appositive phrase that is not necessary to the meaning of the sentence.

The following sentence could be understood without the words set off by commas.

EXAMPLE: *The father, the old man's son, scolded the grandfather.*

Do not set off with commas an appositive phrase that is necessary to the meaning of the sentence.

The following sentence could not be understood without the appositives following Misha:

EXAMPLE: *Misha the child was showing what Misha the man would be like.*

USAGE TIP Sometimes if a comma is missing, a reader may group parts of a sentence in more than one way. A comma separates the parts so they can be read in only one way.

For Clarity Use a comma to prevent misreading or misunderstanding.

EXAMPLE: *While the old man was eating, bits of food that would sometimes drop out of his mouth disgusted the couple.*

GRAMMAR PRACTICE

Rewrite these sentences. Add or delete commas where necessary.

1) In our part of the world aged parents were once expected to live with their children. **2)** Today a variety of lifestyles are available to senior citizens, and the variety is increasing. **3)** Many however still live in familiar surroundings. **4)** They may rent or own senior-citizen housing either house or apartment. **5)** In spite of these options according to the latest census more than 67 percent of seniors still live in family homes. **6)** Some people of course are able to live independently. **7)** These people can get help nursing or housekeeping care. **8)** Would you believe Willard that not even 1 percent live in traditional nursing homes? **9)** People may go in as couples or singly. **10)** In 1992 9,773 more elderly people lived in this country than did in 1980.

12.3 Elements in a Series Commas should be used to separate three or more items in a series and to separate adjectives preceding a noun.

Grammar Practice Answers

1) In our part of the world, aged parents were once expected to live with their children. **2)** Today, a variety of lifestyles are available to senior citizens, and the variety is increasing. **3)** Many, however, still live in familiar surroundings. **4)** They may rent or own senior-citizen housing, either house or apartment. **5)** In spite of these options, according to the latest census, more than 67 percent of seniors still live in family homes. **6)** Some people, of course, are able to live independently. **7)** These people can get help, nursing, or housekeeping care. **8)** Would you believe, Willard, that not even 1 percent live in traditional nursing homes? **9)** People may go in as couples or singly. **10)** In 1992, 9,773 more elderly people lived in this country than did in 1980.

Subjects, Predicates, and Other Elements

Use a comma after every item except the last in a series of three or more items.

Subjects or predicates may occur in series.

EXAMPLE: *In "The Highwayman" the highwayman himself, the landlord's daughter, and the soldiers are the main characters. The soldiers come to the inn, lay a trap there, and tie up the robber's sweetheart.*

Predicate adjectives often occur in series.

EXAMPLE: *The robber's sweetheart is brave, faithful, and self-sacrificing. The entire poem by Alfred Noyes is romantic, atmospheric, and exciting.*

USAGE TIP Note in the example that a comma followed by a conjunction precedes the last element in the series. That comma is always used.

Adverbs and prepositional phrases may also occur in series.

EXAMPLE: *The bold highwayman approaches the inn confidently, eagerly, but quietly. The highwayman came riding at midnight, in the silence, and by moonlight.*

Two or More Adjectives In most sentences, use a comma after each adjective except the last of two or more adjectives that precede a noun.

If you can reverse the order of adjectives without changing the meaning or if you can use *and* between them, separate the two adjectives with a comma.

EXAMPLE: *The beautiful, black-eyed daughter was braiding a dark red loveknot into her lovely long hair.*

GRAMMAR PRACTICE

Rewrite each sentence, inserting commas where they are needed.

1. The poem "The Highwayman" speaks of a time when wagons stagecoaches and carriages were the main means of transportation.

2. The design of these vehicles had changed little from the Middle Ages through the 17th 18th and 19th centuries.

3. Those who preyed on travelers could find wealthy unprotected victims by lying in wait on the roads.

4. The dashing daring dangerous highwaymen held great appeal for many.

5. We often find today's robbers less charming more frightening and often more dangerous.

6. Stagecoaches traveled in stages stopped at scheduled points and changed horses at each stop.

7. Can you visualize the highwayman's big powerful black charger?

12.4 Dates, Addresses, and Letters

Punctuation in dates, addresses, and letters makes information easy to understand.

Dates Use a comma between the day of the month and the year. If the date falls in the middle of a sentence, use another comma after the year.

EXAMPLES: *The sailing recorded in "Exploring the Titanic" took place on April 10, 1912, amidst great fanfare.*

Addresses Use a comma to separate the city and the state in an address or other location. If the city and state fall in the middle of a sentence, use a comma after the state too.

EXAMPLES: *The hull of the ship was launched in Belfast, Ireland, before thousands of spectators and several bands.*

Parts of a Letter Use a comma after the greeting and after the closing in a letter.

EXAMPLE:

Dear Mother,

You cannot imagine how gorgeous the Titanic is. Our stateroom seems straight out of the Grand Hotel!

Affectionately,
Millicent

Grammar Practice Answers

1. The poem "The Highwayman" speaks of a time when wagons, stagecoaches, and carriages were the main means of transportation.

2. The design of these vehicles had changed little from the Middle Ages through the 17th, 18th, and 19th centuries.

3. Those who preyed on travelers could find wealthy, unprotected victims by lying in wait on the roads.

4. The dashing, daring, dangerous highwaymen held great appeal for many.

5. We often find today's robbers less charming, more frightening, and often more dangerous.

6. Stagecoaches traveled in stages, stopped at scheduled points, and changed horses at each stop.

7. Can you visualize the highwayman's big, powerful, black charger?

GRAMMAR PRACTICE

Rewrite the following sentences, correcting the comma errors.

1. Like the wreck of the *Titanic*, the *Hindenburg* disaster of May 6 1937 was the result of a simple accident.

2. The *Hindenburg* was a showpiece in its time, traveling between Germany and Lakehurst New Jersey for a year before it was destroyed.

3. Research at the library in Chicago Illinois revealed that the airship was named for Paul von Hindenburg, a German military leader and president.

4. The hydrogen-filled *Hindenburg* crashed in Lakehurst New Jersey when the gas caught fire.

5. On September 14 1996 I first read about the *Hindenburg* tragedy, in which 35 people met their doom.

12.5 *Quotations* Quotation marks let readers know exactly who said what. Incorrectly placed or missing quotation marks cause confusion.

Quotation Marks Use quotation marks at the beginning and the end of direct quotations and to set off titles of short works.

> **INCORRECT:** *In Langston Hughes's Thank You, M'am, Roger replies simply, Yes'm, to some of the woman's questions. He replies, No'm, to others.*
> **CORRECT:** *In Langston Hughes's "Thank You, M'am," Roger replies simply, "Yes'm," to some of the woman's questions. He replies, "No'm," to others.*

Capitalize the first word of a direct quotation, especially in a piece of dialogue.

> **EXAMPLE:** *The woman replies, "Um-hum," to Roger's apology.*

USAGE TIP If quoted words are from a written source and are not complete sentences, they can begin with a lowercase letter.

> **EXAMPLE:** *Mark Twain said that cauliflower was "nothing but cabbage with a college education."*

End Punctuation Place periods inside quotation marks. Place question marks and exclamation points inside quotation marks if they belong to the quotation; place them outside if they do not belong to the quotation. Place semicolons outside quotation marks.

> **INCORRECT:** *The boy asks, "You gonna take me to jail"?*
> *The woman replies, "Not with that face"!*
> *Offered food, he says, "That will be fine;" then he eats.*
> **CORRECT:** *The boy asks, "You gonna take me to jail?"*
> *The woman replies, "Not with that face!"*
> *Offered food, he says, "That will be fine"; then he eats.*

Use a comma to end a quotation that is a complete sentence but is followed by explanatory words.

> **EXAMPLE:** *"I wanted a pair of blue suede shoes," said the boy.*

Divided Quotations Capitalize the first word of the second part of a direct quotation if it begins a new sentence.

> **EXAMPLE:** *"Well, you didn't have to snatch my pocketbook," Mrs. Jones replied. "You could have asked me."*

GRAMMAR PRACTICE

Rewrite this paragraph, inserting appropriate punctuation and capitalization.

1) Langston Hughes once wrote children should be born without parents. **2)** His difficult childhood may have been the inspiration for one of his best-loved poems, titled dreams. **3)** It begins with the line hold fast to dreams; it is short, so I have memorized it. **4)** You may know it the teacher said. I have seen the first stanza printed on T-shirts. **5)** My soul has grown deep like the rivers Hughes says in The Negro Speaks of Rivers. **6)** How happy he would have been at his memorial service to hear his favorite Ellington song, Do Nothing 'Til You Hear from Me! **7)** Have you read any stories by Hughes other than Thank You, M'am?

Grammar Practice Answers 12.4

1. Like the wreck of the *Titanic*, the *Hindenburg* disaster of May 6, 1937, was the result of a simple accident.
2. The *Hindenburg* was a showpiece in its time, traveling between Germany and Lakehurst, New Jersey, for a year before it was destroyed.
3. Research at the library in Chicago, Illinois, revealed that the airship was named for Paul von *Hindenburg*, a German military leader and president.
4. The hydrogen-filled Hindenburg crashed in Lakehurst, New Jersey, when the gas caught fire.
5. On September 14, 1996, I first read about the *Hindenburg* tragedy, in which 35 people met their doom.

Grammar Practice Answers 12.5

1) Langston Hughes once wrote, "Children should be born without parents." **2)** His difficult childhood may have been the inspiration for one of his best-loved poems, titled "Dreams." **3)** It begins with the line "Hold fast to dreams"; it is short, so I have memorized it. **4)** "You may know it," the teacher said. "I have seen the first stanza printed on T-shirts." **5)** "My soul has grown deep like the rivers," Hughes says in "The Negro Speaks of Rivers." **6)** How happy he would have been at his memorial service to hear his favorite Ellington song, "Do Nothing 'Til You Hear From Me"! **7)** Have you read any stories by Hughes other than "Thank You, M'am"?

Grammar Glossary

This glossary contains various terms you need to understand when you use the Grammar Handbook. Used as a reference source, this glossary will help you explore grammar concepts and the ways they relate to one another.

Abbreviation An abbreviation is a shortened form of a word or word group; it is often made up of initials. (B.C., A.M., *Maj.*)

Active voice. *See* **Voice.**

Adjective An adjective modifies, or describes, a noun or pronoun. (*happy* camper, she is *small*)

A *predicate adjective* follows a linking verb and describes the subject. (The day seemed *long.*)

A *proper adjective* is formed from a proper noun. (*Jewish* temple, *Alaskan* husky)

The *comparative* form of an adjective compares two things. (*more alert, thicker*)

The *superlative* form of an adjective compares more than two things. (*most abundant, weakest*)

What Adjectives Tell	Examples
How many	*some* writers *much* joy
What kind	*grand* plans *wider* streets
Which one(s)	*these* flowers *that* star

Adjective phrase. *See* **Phrase.**

Adverb An adverb modifies a verb, an adjective, or another adverb. (Clare sang *loudly.*)

The *comparative* form of an adverb compares two actions. (*more generously, faster*)

The *superlative* form of an adverb compares more than two actions. (*most sharply, closest*)

What Adverbs Tell	Examples
How	climb *carefully* chuckle *merrily*
When	arrived *late* left *early*
Where	climbed *up* moved *away*
To what extent	*extremely* upset *hardly* visible

Adverb, conjunctive. *See* **Conjunctive adverb.**

Adverb phrase. *See* **Phrase.**

Agreement Sentence parts that correspond with one another are said to be in agreement.

In *pronoun-antecedent agreement*, a pronoun and the word it refers to are the same in number, gender, and person. (*Bill* mailed *his* application. The *students* ate *their* lunches.)

In *subject-verb agreement,* the subject and verb in a sentence are the same in number. (*A child cries* for help. *They cry* aloud.)

Ambiguous reference An ambiguous reference occurs when a pronoun may refer to more than one word. (Bud asked his brother if *he* had any mail.)

Antecedent An antecedent is the noun or pronoun to which a pronoun refers. (If *Adam* forgets *his* raincoat, *he* will be late for school. *She* learned *her* lesson.)

Appositive An appositive is a noun or phrase that explains one or more words in a sentence. (Cary Grant, *an Englishman,* spent most of his adult life in America.)

An *essential appositive* is needed to make the sense of a sentence complete. (A comic strip inspired the musical *Annie.*)

A *nonessential appositive* is one that adds information to a sentence but is not necessary to its sense. (O. Henry, *a short-story write*r, spent time in prison.)

Article Articles are the special adjectives *a, an,* and *the.* (*the* day, *a* fly)

The definite article (the word *the*) is one that refers to a particular thing. (*the* cabin)

An indefinite article is used with a noun that is not unique but refers to one of many of its kind. (*a* dish, *an* otter)

Auxiliary verb. *See* **Verb.**

Clause A clause is a group of words that contains a verb and its subject. (*they slept*)

An *adjective clause* is a subordinate clause that modifies a noun or pronoun. (Hugh bought the sweater *that he had admired.*)

An *adverb clause* is a subordinate clause used to modify a verb, an adjective, or an adverb. (Ring the bell *when it is time for class to begin*.)

A *noun clause* is a subordinate clause that is used as a noun. (*Whatever you say* interests me.)

An *elliptical clause* is a clause from which a word or words have been omitted. (We are not as lucky as *they*.)

A *main (independent) clause* can stand by itself as a sentence. (*the flashlight flickered*)

A *dependent (subordinate) clause* does not express a complete thought and cannot stand by itself. (*while the nation watched*)

Clause	Example
Main (independent)	The hurricane struck
Subordinate (dependent)	while we were preparing to leave.

Collective noun. *See* **Noun.**

Comma splice A comma splice is an error caused when two sentences are separated with a comma instead of an end mark. (*The band played a medley of show tunes, everyone enjoyed the show.*)

Common noun. *See* **Noun.**

Comparative. *See* **Adjective; Adverb.**

Complement A complement is a word or group of words that completes the meaning of a verb. (The kitten finished the *milk*.) *See also* **Direct object; Indirect object.**

An *objective complement* is a word or a group of words that follows a direct object and renames or describes that object. (The parents of the rescued child declared Gus a *hero*.)

A *subject complement* follows a linking verb and renames or describes the subject. (The coach seemed *anxious*.) *See also* **Noun (predicate noun); Adjective (predicate adjective).**

Complete predicate The complete predicate of a sentence consists of the main verb plus any words that modify the verb or complete the verb's meaning. (The student *produces work of high caliber*.)

Complete subject The complete subject of a sentence consists of the simple subject plus any words that modify or describe the simple subject. (*Students of history* believe that wars can be avoided.)

Sentence Part	Example
Complete subject	The man in the ten-gallon hat
Complete predicate	wore a pair of silver spurs.

Compound sentence part A sentence element that consists of two or more subjects, verbs, objects, or other parts is compound. (*Lou* and *Jay* helped. Laura *makes* and *models* scarves. Jill sings *opera* and *popular music*.)

Conjunction A conjunction is a word that links other words or groups of words.

A *coordinating conjunction* connects related words, groups of words, or sentences. (*and, but, or*)

A *correlative conjunction* is one of a pair of conjunctions that work together to connect sentence parts. (*either . . . or, neither . . . nor, not only . . . but also, whether . . . or, both . . . and*)

A *subordinating conjunction* introduces a subordinate clause. (*after, although, as, as if, as long as, as though, because, before, if, in order that, since, so that, than, though, till, unless, until, whatever, when, where, while*)

Conjunctive adverb A conjunctive adverb joins the clauses of a compound sentence. (*however, therefore, yet*)

Contraction A contraction is formed by joining two words and substituting an apostrophe for a letter or letters left out of one of the words. (*didn't, we've*)

Coordinating conjunction. *See* **Conjunction.**

Correlative conjunction. *See* **Conjunction.**

Dangling modifier A dangling modifier is one that does not clearly modify any word in the sentence. (*Dashing for the train, the barriers got in the way.*)

Demonstrative pronoun. *See* **Pronoun.**

Dependent clause. *See* **Clause.**

Direct object A direct object receives the action of a verb. Direct objects follow transitive verbs. (Jude planned the *party*.)

Direct quotation. *See* **Quotation.**

Divided quotation. *See* **Quotation.**

Double negative A double negative is the incorrect use of two negative words when only one is needed. (*Nobody* didn't care.)

Grammar Handbook

End mark An end mark is one of several punctuation marks that can end a sentence. See the punctuation chart on page R56.

Fragment. *See* **Sentence fragment.**

Future tense. *See* **Verb tense.**

G

Gender The gender of a personal pronoun indicates whether the person or thing referred to is male, female, or neuter. (*My cousin plays the tuba; he often performs in school concerts.*)

Gerund A gerund is a verbal that ends in *-ing* and functions as a noun. (*Making pottery takes patience.*)

Helping verb. *See* **Verb (auxiliary verb).**

Illogical comparison An illogical comparison is a comparison that does not make sense because words are missing or illogical. (*My computer is newer than Kay.*)

Indefinite pronoun. *See* **Pronoun.**

Indefinite reference Indefinite reference occurs when a pronoun is used without a clear antecedent. (*My aunt hugged me in front of my friends, and it was embarrassing.*)

Independent clause. *See* **Clause.**

Indirect object An indirect object tells to whom or for whom (sometimes to what or for what) something is done. (*Arthur wrote Kerry a letter.*)

Indirect question An indirect question tells what someone asked without using the person's exact words. (*My friend asked me if I could go with her to the dentist.*)

Indirect quotation. *See* **Quotation.**

Infinitive An infinitive is a verbal beginning with *to* that functions as a noun, an adjective, or an adverb. (*He wanted to go to the play.*)

Intensive pronoun. *See* **Pronoun.**

Interjection An interjection is a word or phrase used to express strong feeling. (*Wow! Good grief!*)

Interrogative pronoun. *See* **Pronoun.**

Intransitive verb. *See* **Verb.**

Inverted sentence An inverted sentence is one in which the subject comes after the verb. (*How was the movie? Here come the clowns.*)

Irregular verb. *See* **Verb.**

Linking verb. *See* **Verb.**

Main clause. *See* **Clause.**

Main verb. *See* **Verb.**

Modifier A modifier makes another word more precise. Modifiers most often are adjectives or adverbs; they may also be phrases, verbals, or clauses that function as adjectives or adverbs. (*small* box, smiled *broadly*, house *by the sea*, dog *barking loudly*)

An *essential modifier* is one that is necessary to the meaning of a sentence. (*Everybody who has a free pass should enter now. None of the passengers got on the train.*)

A *nonessential modifier* is one that merely adds more information to a sentence that is clear without the addition. (*We will use the new dishes, which are stored in the closet.*)

Noun A noun names a person, a place, a thing, or an idea. (*auditor, shelf, book, goodness*)

An *abstract noun* names an idea, a quality, or a feeling. (*joy*)

A *collective noun* names a group of things. (*bevy*)

A *common noun* is a general name of a person, a place, a thing, or an idea. (*valet, hill, bread, amazement*)

A *compound noun* contains two or more words. (*hometown, self-control, screen test*)

A *noun of direct address* is the name of a person being directly spoken to. (*Lee, do you have the package? No, Suki, your letter did not arrive.*)

A *possessive noun* shows who or what owns or is associated with something. (*Lil's* ring, a *day's* pay)

A *predicate noun* follows a linking verb and renames the subject. (*Karen is a writer.*)

A *proper noun* names a particular person, place, or thing. (*John Smith, Ohio, Sears Tower, Congress*)

Number A word is singular in number if it refers to just one person, place, thing, idea, or action and plural in number if it refers to more than one person, place, thing, idea, or action. (The words *he, waiter,* and *is* are singular. The words *they, waiters,* and *are* are plural.)

O

Object of a preposition The object of a preposition is the noun or pronoun that follows a preposition. (The athletes cycled along the *route*. Jane baked a cake for *her*.)

Object of a verb The object of a verb receives the action of the verb. (Sid told *stories*.)

P

Participle A participle is often used as part of a verb phrase. (had *written*) It can also be used as a verbal that functions as an adjective. (the *leaping* deer, the medicine *taken* for a fever)

The **present participle** is formed by adding *-ing* to the present form of a verb. (*Walking* rapidly, we reached the general store.)

The **past participle** of a regular verb is formed by adding *-d* or *-ed* to the present form. The past participles of irregular verbs do not follow this pattern. (*Startled*, they ran from the house. *Spun* glass is delicate. A *broken* cup lay there.)

Passive voice. *See* **Voice.**

Past tense. *See* **Verb tense.**

Perfect tenses. *See* **Verb tense.**

Person Person is a means of classifying pronouns.

A **first-person** pronoun refers to the person speaking. (*We* came.)

A **second-person** pronoun refers to the person spoken to. (*You* ask.)

A **third-person** pronoun refers to some other person(s) or thing(s) being spoken of. (*They* played.)

Personal pronoun. *See* **Pronoun.**

Phrase A phrase is a group of related words that does not contain a verb and its subject. (*noticing everything, under a chair*)

An **adjective phrase** modifies a noun or a pronoun. (The label *on the bottle* has faded.)

An **adverb phrase** modifies a verb, an adjective, or an adverb. (Come *to the fair*.)

An **appositive phrase** explains one or more words in a sentence. (Mary, *a champion gymnast,* won gold medals at the Olympics.)

A **gerund phrase** consists of a gerund and its modifiers and complements. (*Fixing the leak* will take only a few minutes.)

An **infinitive phrase** consists of an infinitive, its modifiers, and its complements. (*To prepare for a test,* study in a quiet place.)

A **participial phrase** consists of a participle and its modifiers and complements. (*Straggling to the finish line,* the last runners arrived.)

A **prepositional phrase** consists of a preposition, its object, and the object's modifiers. (The Saint Bernard does rescue work *in the Swiss Alps*.)

A **verb phrase** consists of a main verb and one or more helping verbs. (*might have ordered*)

Possessive A noun or pronoun that is possessive shows ownership or relationship. (*Dan's* story, *my* doctor)

Possessive noun. *See* **Noun.**

Possessive pronoun. *See* **Pronoun.**

Predicate The predicate of a sentence tells what the subject is or does. (The van *runs well even in winter*. The job seems *too complicated*.) *See also* **Complete predicate; Simple predicate.**

Predicate adjective. *See* **Adjective.**

Predicate nominative A predicate nominative is a noun or pronoun that follows a linking verb and renames or explains the subject. (Joan is a computer *operator*. The winner of the prize was *he*.)

Predicate pronoun. *See* **Pronoun.**

Preposition A preposition is a word that relates its object to another part of the sentence or to the sentence as a whole. (Alfredo leaped *onto* the stage.)

Prepositional phrase. *See* **Phrase.**

Present tense. *See* **Verb tense.**

Pronoun A pronoun replaces a noun or another pronoun. Some pronouns allow a writer or speaker to avoid repeating a proper noun. Other pronouns let a writer refer to an unknown or unidentified person or thing.

A **demonstrative pronoun** singles out one or more persons or things. (*This* is the letter.)

An **indefinite pronoun** refers to an unidentified person or thing. (*Everyone* stayed home. Will you hire *anybody*?)

An **intensive pronoun** emphasizes a noun or pronoun. (The teacher *himself* sold tickets.)

An **interrogative pronoun** asks a question. (*What* happened to you?)

A **personal pronoun** shows a distinction of person. (*I* came. *You* see. *He* knows.)

A **possessive pronoun** shows ownership. (*My* spaghetti is always good. Are *your* parents coming to the play?)

A **predicate pronoun** follows a linking verb and renames the subject. (The owners of the store were *they*.)

Grammar Handbook

GRAMMAR HANDBOOK **R83**

A **reflexive pronoun** reflects an action back on the subject of the sentence. (Joe helped *himself.*)

A **relative pronoun** relates a subordinate clause to the word it modifies. (The draperies, *which* had been made by hand, were ruined in the fire.)

Pronoun-antecedent agreement. *See* **Agreement.**

Pronoun forms

The **subject form** of a pronoun is used when the pronoun is the subject of a sentence or follows a linking verb as a predicate pronoun. (*She* fell. The star was *she.*)

The **object form** of a pronoun is used when the pronoun is the direct or indirect object of a verb or verbal or the object of a preposition. (We sent *him* the bill. We ordered food for *them.*)

Proper adjective. *See* **Adjective.**

Proper noun. *See* **Noun.**

Punctuation Punctuation clarifies the structure of sentences. See the punctuation chart on page R56.

Quotation A quotation consists of words from another speaker or writer.

A **direct quotation** is the exact words of a speaker or writer. (Martin said, "*The homecoming game has been postponed.*")

A **divided quotation** is a quotation separated by words that identify the speaker. ("*The homecoming game,*" said Martin, "*has been postponed.*")

An **indirect quotation** reports what a person said without giving the exact words. (*Martin said that the homecoming game had been postponed.*)

Reflexive pronoun. *See* **Pronoun.**

Regular verb. *See* **Verb.**

Relative pronoun. *See* **Pronoun.**

Run-on sentence A run-on sentence consists of two or more sentences written incorrectly as one. (The sunset was beautiful its brilliant colors lasted only a short time.)

Sentence A sentence expresses a complete thought. The chart below shows the four kinds of sentences.

A **complex sentence** contains one main clause and one or more subordinate clauses. (*Open the windows before you go to bed. If she falls, I'll help her up.*)

A **compound sentence** is made up of two or more independent clauses joined by a conjunction, a colon, or a semicolon. (*The ship finally docked, and the passengers quickly left.*)

A **simple sentence** consists of only one main clause. (*My friend volunteers at a nursing home.*)

Kind of Sentence	Example
Declarative (statement)	Our team won.
Exclamatory (strong feeling)	I had a great time!
Imperative (request, command)	Take the next exit.
Interrogative (question)	Who owns the car?

Sentence fragment A sentence fragment is a group of words that is only part of a sentence. (*When he arrived. Merrily yodeling.*)

Simple predicate A simple predicate is the verb in the predicate. (John *collects* foreign stamps.)

Simple subject A simple subject is the key noun or pronoun in the subject. (The new *house* is empty.)

Split infinitive A split infinitive occurs when a modifier is placed between the word *to* and the verb in an infinitive. (*to quickly speak*)

Subject The subject is the part of a sentence that tells whom or what the sentence is about. (*Lou* swam.) *See* **Complete subject; Simple subject.**

Subject-verb agreement. *See* **Agreement.**

Subordinate clause. *See* **Clause.**

Superlative. *See* **Adjective; Adverb.**

Transitive verb. *See* **Verb.**

Unidentified reference An unidentified reference usually occurs when the word *it, they, this, which,* or *that* is used. (In California *they* have good weather most of the time.)

Verb A verb expresses an action, a condition, or a state of being.

An **action verb** tells what the subject does, has done, or will do. The action may be physical or mental. (Susan *trains* guide dogs.)

An **auxiliary verb** is added to a main verb to express tense, add emphasis, or otherwise affect the meaning of the verb. Together the auxiliary and main verb make up a verb phrase. (*will* intend, *could have* gone)

A **linking verb** expresses a state of being or connects the subject with a word or words that describe the subject. (The ice *feels* cold.) Linking verbs include *appear, be (am, are, is, was, were, been, being),* become, feel, grow, look, remain, seem, smell, sound, and taste.

A **main verb** expresses action or state of being; it appears with one or more auxiliary verbs. (will be *staying*)

The **progressive form** of a verb shows continuing action. (She *is knitting*.)

The past tense and past participle of a **regular verb** are formed by adding *-d* or *-ed*. (open, opened) An **irregular verb** does not follow this pattern. *(throw, threw, thrown; shrink, shrank, shrunk)*

The action of a **transitive verb** is directed toward someone or something, called the object of a verb. (Leo *washed* the windows.) An **intransitive verb** has no object. (The leaves *scattered*.)

Verb phrase. *See* **Phrase.**

Verb tense Verb tense shows the time of an action or the time of a state of being.

The **present tense** places an action or condition in the present. (Jan *takes* piano lessons.)

The **past tense** places an action or condition in the past. (We *came* to the party.)

The **future tense** places an action or condition in the future. (You *will understand*.)

The **present perfect tense** describes an action in an indefinite past time or an action that began in the past and continues in the present. *(has called, have known)*

The **past perfect tense** describes one action that happened before another action in the past. *(had scattered, had mentioned)*

The **future perfect tense** describes an event that will be finished before another future action begins. *(will have taught, shall have appeared)*

Verbal A verbal is formed from a verb and acts as another part of speech, such as a noun, an adjective, or an adverb.

Verbal	Example
Gerund (used as a noun)	Lamont enjoys *swimming*.
Infinitive (used as an adjective, an adverb, or a noun)	Everyone wants *to help*.
Participle (used as an adjective)	The leaves *covering the drive* made it slippery.

Voice The voice of a verb depends on whether the subject performs or receives the action of the verb.

In the **active voice** the subject of the sentence performs the verb's action. (We *knew* the answer.)

In the **passive voice** the subject of the sentence receives the action of the verb. (The team *has been eliminated*.)

Spelling Handbook

Improving Your Spelling

Good spelling is important in all writing, from personal letters to research reports. You can improve your spelling by practicing a few good habits. Read and write as frequently as you can. Keep a personal spelling list of words you are not sure how to spell and review this list regularly. The following tips may also be helpful.

Ways to Improve Your Spelling

1. **Identify your spelling demons and conquer them.** Keep a list of the words you have misspelled in written assignments.

2. **Pronounce words carefully.** Pronouncing words correctly will help you spell them correctly. For example, if you pronounce the word *probably* correctly, you will not misspell it as *probably*.

3. **Get into the habit of seeing the letters in a word.** Look carefully at new or difficult words. For example, look at a word like *picnic*, close your eyes and picture the word in your mind, and spell it to yourself: *p–i–c–n–i–c*.

4. **Create a memory device for a tricky word.** Notice the following examples of memory devices.

bus**i**ness (i)	**I** was involved in a big bus**i**ness.
princi**pal** (pal)	The princi**pal** is my **pal**.
princi**ple** (ple)	Follow this princi**ple**, **ple**ase.
station**er**y (er)	Station**er**y is fine pap**er**.

How to Master the Spelling of Difficult Words

1. Look at the word and say it one syllable at a time.
2. Look at the letters and say each one.
3. Write the word without looking at it.
4. Check to see whether you spelled the word correctly. If you made a mistake, repeat steps 1–3.

One of the best ways to improve your spelling is to learn the following rules.

Words Ending in a Silent e

When a suffix beginning with a vowel is added to a word ending in a silent e, the e is usually dropped.

relate + -ion = relation
create + -ive = creative
amaze + -ing = amazing
fame + -ous = famous

When a suffix beginning with a consonant is added to a word ending in a silent e, the e is usually retained.

hope + -ful = hopeful
noise + -less = noiseless
state + -ment = statement
wide + -ly = widely

The following words are exceptions: *truly, argument, ninth, wholly.*

Words Ending in y

When a suffix is added to a word ending in y preceded by a consonant, the y usually is changed to i.

easy + -ly = easily
sixty + -eth = sixtieth

When *-ing* is added, however, the y does not change.

hurry + -ed = hurried
but hurry + -ing = hurrying
study + -ed = studies
but study + -ing = studying

When a suffix is added to a word ending in *y* preceded by a vowel, the *y* usually does not change.

employ + -er = employer

play + -ing = playing

Words Ending in a Consonant

In words of *one* syllable that end in *one* consonant preceded by one vowel, double the final consonant before adding an ending that begins with a vowel, such as -*ing*, -*ed*, or -*er*. These are sometimes called 1 + 1 + 1 words.

bat + -ed = batted

bed + -ing = bedding

run + -er = runner

grab + -ed = grabbed

The rule does not apply to words of one syllable that end in one consonant preceded by two vowels.

treat + -ing = treating

loot + -ed = looted

near + -er = nearer

feel + -ing = feeling

The Suffixes -ness and -ly

When the suffix -*ly* is added to a word ending in *l*, both *l*'s are retained. When -*ness* is added to a word ending in *n*, retain both of the *n*'s.

actual + -ly = actually

thin + -ness = thinness

Prefixes

When a prefix is added to a word, do not drop a letter from either the prefix or the base word.

mis- + spell = misspell

re- + place = replace

il- + legal = illegal

im- + perfect = imperfect

un- + even = uneven

dis- + approve = disapprove

pre- + view = preview

ir- + regular = irregular

Words with the Seed Sound

Only one English word ends in –*sede*: *supersede.* Three words end in –*ceed*: *exceed, proceed,* and *succeed.* All other verbs ending in the sound *seed* are spelled with –*cede.*

concede   precede   recede   secede

Words with ie and ei

When the sound is long *e* (ē), the word is spelled *ie* except after *c.*

i before *e*		except after *c*	
believe	shield	ceiling	deceive
yield	field	receive	conceive
niece	brief	conceit	receipt

The following words are exceptions: *either, weird, species, neither, seize, leisure.*

Using the Right Word

Like good musicians or good athletes, good writers do the little things well. One of these little things is the correct use of words. It is actually one of the keys to good writing. As you look at the following groups of words, notice how the words' meanings differ. Try to create memory devices to help you associate words and meanings.

accept, except   *Accept* means "to agree to something" or "to receive something." *Except* usually means "not including."

Kay did *accept* the invitation to go camping.

Everyone *except* the reporters dashed onto the field.

all ready, already   *All ready* means "all are ready" or "completely prepared." *Already* means "previously."

The astronauts were *all ready* for the landing.

The other team has *already* started practicing.

all right   *All right* is the correct spelling. *Alright* is nonstandard English and should not be used.

a lot   *A lot* is informal. It should not be used in formal writing. *Alot* is always incorrect.

borrow, lend   *Borrow* means "to receive something on loan." *Lend* means "to give out temporarily."

> Some students *borrow* money to pay for a college education.

> Please *lend* me a pencil.

capital, capitol, the Capitol   *Capital* means "excellent," "most serious," or "most important"; it also means "seat of government." *Capitol* is a "building in which a state legislature meets." *The Capitol* is "the building in Washington, D.C., in which the U.S. Congress meets."

> Murder is a *capital* crime.

> The state senate held hearings at the *capitol*.

> In 1814 British soldiers burned the White House and *the Capitol.*

desert, dessert   *Des′ert* means "a wilderness" or "a dry sandy, barren region." *Desert′* means "to abandon." *Dessert* is a sweet food, such as a cake or pie, served at the end of a meal.

> The Gobi *Desert* is in eastern Asia.

> The soldiers *deserted* their position.

> Strawberry pie is a delicious *dessert.*

good, well   *Good* is always an adjective. *Well* is usually an adverb. *Well* can be an adjective meaning "in good health."

> Juan felt *good* about finishing the marathon.

> Julio plays the drums *well*.

> Marco was not *well* enough to play.

hear, here   *Hear* means "to listen to." *Here* means "in this place."

> Because of the noisy crowd, we couldn't *hear* the candidate.

> After leaving Italy, my grandparents settled *here* in Dallas.

its, it's   *Its* is a possessive pronoun. *It's* is a contraction for it is or it has.

> The city lost *its* electricity.

> *It's* almost time for summer vacation.

Lay, lie   *Lay* is a verb that means "to place." It takes a direct object. *Lie* is a verb that means "to be in a certain place" or "to be in a horizontial position." *Lie* never takes a direct object.

> *Lay* the books on the desk.

> Our land *lies* near the river.

lead, led   *Lead* can be a noun that means "a heavy metal" or a verb that means "to show the way." *Led* is the verb's past tense form.

> A plumb is a weight made of *lead.*

> Maria *leads* the league in home runs.

> She *led* a discussion on ways to help homeless people.

learn, teach   *Learn* means "to gain knowledge." *Teach* means "to instruct."

> Raul is *learning* how to play chess.

> Alicia is *teaching* Spanish.

like, as, as if   Use *as* or *as if,* not *like,* to introduce a clause.

> He walks *as if* his ankle were sore.

loose, lose   *Loose* means "free" or "not fastened." *Lose* means "to mislay or suffer the loss of something."

> The door hinges are *loose*.

> The plane began to *lose* altitude.

of   Use *have*, not *of,* in phrases such as *could have*, *should have*, and *must have*.

> We could *have* won if our leading scorer had not fouled out.

passed, past   *Passed* is the past tense of pass and means "went by." *Past* is an adjective that means "of a former time." *Past* is also a noun that means "the time gone by."

We *passed* through the Grand Tetons during our vacation.

We have learned from our *past* experiences.

Ebenezer Scrooge relives his *past.*

peace, piece　*Peace* means "calm or quiet." *Piece* means a "part of something."

Music can bring a sense of *peace.*

We cut the pizza into *pieces.*

principal, principle　*Principal* means "of chief or central importance" or "the head of a school." *Principle* is a "basic truth," "standard," or "rule of behavior."

The *principal* cities of France include Paris and Marseilles.

The school *principal* presented awards.

In social studies we discussed the *principles* of government.

raise, rise　*Raise* means "to lift" or "to make something go up." It takes a direct object. *Rise* means "to go upward." It does not take a direct object.

Dr. King's speeches *raised* hopes for a more just society.

The sun *rises* in the east.

set, sit　*Set* means "to place." It takes a direct object. *Sit* means "to occupy a seat or a place." It does not take a direct object.

He *set* the papers on the desk.

Let's *sit* here.

stationary, stationery　*Stationary* means "fixed or unmoving." *Stationery* means "fine paper for writing letters."

A *stationary* clock glowed on the wall.

I received a letter written on White House *stationery.*

than, then　*Than* is used to introduce the second part of a comparison. *Then* means "next in order."

The pen is mightier *than* the sword.

The air grew still, and *then* raindrops pattered on the roof.

their, there, they're　*Their* means "belonging to them." *There* means "in that place." *They're* is the contraction for *they are.*

In 1804, Lewis and Clark led *their* expedition from St. Louis.

The explorers built a fort in what is now North Dakota, and they spent the winter *there.*

Lewis and Clark collected valuable information about the geography of the Pacific Northwest; *they're* remembered for their wilderness travels.

to, too, two　*To* means "toward" or "in the direction of." *Too* means "also" or "very." *Two* is the number 2.

We went *to* the Library of Congress in Washington, D. C.

It was *too* cold to play baseball.

Two newspapers sent critics to review the new play.

weather, whether　*Weather* refers to "conditions such as temperature or cloudiness." *Whether* expresses a choice.

Meterologists use computers to forecast the *weather.*

We must decide *whether* to speak out or remain silent.

whose, who's　*Whose* is the possessive form of *who. Who's* is a contraction for *who is* or *who has.*

Whose arguments seem more convincing?

Who's going to volunteer to work at the hospital?

your, you're　*Your* is the possessive form of *you. You're* is a contraction for *you are.*

Please take *your* places at the starting line.

You're going to the library after school, aren't you?

❶ Getting Information Electronically

Electronic resources provide you with a convenient and efficient way to gather information.

⓵⋅¹ Online Resources

When you use your computer to communicate with another computer or with another person using a computer, you are working "online." Online resources include commercial information services and information available on the Internet.

What You'll Need

• To access online resources, you need a computer with a modem to link you to the Internet. Your school computer lab or resource center may be linked to the Internet or to a commercial information service.

• To use CD-ROMs, you need a computer system with a CD-ROM reader.

Commercial Information Services

You can subscribe to various services that offer information such as the following:

• up-to-date news, weather, and sports reports

• access to encyclopedias, magazines, newspapers, dictionaries, almanacs, and databases (collections of information)

• electronic mail (email) to and from other users

• forums, or ongoing electronic conversations among users interested in a particular topic

Internet

The Internet is a vast network of computers. News services, libraries, universities, researchers, organizations, and government agencies use the Internet to communicate and to distribute information. The Internet includes two key features:

• **World Wide Web** provides you with information on particular subjects and links you to related topics and resources (such as the Web pages shown above).

• **Electronic mail** (email), allows you to communicate with other email users worldwide.

⓵⋅² Navigating the Web

With access to the World Wide Web, you can find virtually any piece of information once you know how to look for it. Here are some tips to get you started.

Choose a Search Engine or a Directory

A **search engine** combs through Web sites looking for your topic. A **directory** allows you to search within groups of **databases**, or collections of information arranged for ease of retrieval, which are, in turn, grouped by subject, such as Reference, Sports, or Entertainment.

Enter Key Words

Once you've chosen a starting point, enter the **key word** or words that describe your topic. By using more than one word, you will narrow your search. For example, using the key word "baseball" will find sites with information on baseball. The key words "Dodgers baseball" will help you find sites with information on the specific team.

Investigate Your Options

Once you receive the results of your search, scan the site listings and their summaries to see which ones look promising. If you click on a site and it's not useful, back up and try again. Sites at the top of the list usually will be more relevant than those found farther down.

Tips for Getting the Most out of Your Search

- **Note the source** Because anyone can put information on the Web, it's wise to check where the information comes from. For example, sites produced by government agencies or educational institutions tend to be more reliable than the personal Web pages of individuals.

- **Refine your search** If you're not getting the results you want, search again, using more key words or different key words.

- **Explore other avenues** One search engine may produce different results than another, and the same goes for directories.

- **Link around** Many Web sites have links to other sites with related content that you might not find searching on your own.

 CD-ROM

A CD-ROM (compact–disc–read-only memory) stores data that may include text, sound, photographs, and video.

Almost any kind of information can be found on CD-ROMs, which you can use at the library or purchase, including

- encyclopedias, almanacs, and indexes
- other reference books
- news reports from newspapers, magazines, television, or radio
- museum art collections
- back issues of magazines

 Library Computer Services

Many libraries offer computerized catalogs and a variety of other electronic resources.

Computerized Catalogs

You may search for a book in a library by typing the title, author, subject, or key words into a computer terminal. If you enter the title of a book, the screen will display information such as the book's call number and whether it is on the shelf or checked out of the library.

Other Electronic Resources

In addition to computerized catalogs, many libraries offer electronic versions of books or other reference materials. They may also have a variety of indexes on CD-ROM, which allow you to search for magazine or newspaper articles on topics.

Word Processing

Word-processing programs are a type of software that allow you to draft, revise, edit, and format your writing and to produce neat, professional-looking papers. They also allow you to share your writing with others.

Prewriting and Drafting

A computer makes it easy to experiment with different ways of expressing and organizing your ideas. You can use it to keep an electronic journal or portfolio, to organize your notes in files, or to access templates for special writing formats. It also allows you to store multiple drafts of a paper and even to add graphics to clarify and enhance your message.

WRITING TIP Create a separate file to use as a writing notebook. Keep all of your story starters, ideas to research, and other writing ideas in this file.

2.2 Revising and Editing

The programs that make computer hardware function are called **software**. One type of software is a word-processing program. Improving the quality of your writing becomes easier when you use a word-processing program to revise and edit.

What You'll Need
- Computer
- Word-processing program
- Printer

Revising a Document
Most word-processing programs allow you to make the following kinds of changes:
- add or delete words
- undo a change you have made in the text
- move text from one location in your document to another
- save a document with a new name, allowing you to keep old drafts for reference
- view more than one document at a time, so you can copy text from one document and add it to another

Editing a Document
Many word-processing programs have the following features to help you catch errors and polish your writing:
- The **spell checker** automatically finds misspelled words and suggests possible corrections.
- The **grammar checker** spots possible grammatical errors and suggests ways you might correct them.
- The **thesaurus** suggests synonyms for a word you want to replace.
- The **dictionary** will give you the definitions of words so you can be sure you have used words correctly.
- The **search and replace** feature searches your whole document and corrects every occurrence of something you want to change, such as a misspelled name.

WRITING TIP Even if you use a spell checker, you should still proofread your draft carefully to make sure you've used the right words. For example, you may have used *there* or *they're* when you should have used *their*. A spell checker will not be able to pick up this type of error.

2.3 Formatting Your Work

Format is the layout and appearance of your writing on the page. You may choose your formatting options before or after you write.

Formatting Type

You may want to make changes in the typeface, type size, and type style of the words in your document. For each of these, your word-processing program will most likely have several options to choose from. These options allow you to

- **change the typeface** to create a different look for the words in your document
- **change the type size** of the entire document or of just the headings of sections in the paper
- **change the type style** when necessary; for example, use italics or underline for the titles of books and magazines

Typeface	Size	Style
Geneva	7-point Times	*Italic*
Times	10-point Times	**Bold**
Chicago	12-point Times	Underline
Courier	14-point Times	

Formatting Pages

Not only can you change the way individual words look; you can also change the way they are arranged on the page. Some of the formatting decisions you make will depend either on how you plan to use a printout of a draft or on the guidelines provided for an assignment.

- **Set the line spacing,** or the amount of space you need between lines of text. Double spacing is commonly used for final drafts. Double spacing also allows you room to write changes and corrections as you revise and edit drafts of your writing.

- **Set the margins,** or the amount of white space around the edges of your text. A one-inch margin on all sides is commonly used for final drafts.

- **Create a header** for the top of the page or a footer for the bottom if you want to include such information as your name, the date, or the page number on every page.

- **Determine the alignment** of your text. The screen below shows your options.

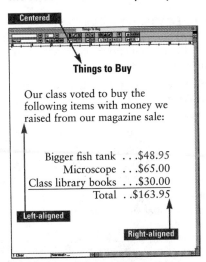

WRITING TIP Keep your format simple. Your goal is to create not only an attractive document but also one that is easy to read. Your readers will have difficulty if you change the type formatting frequently. Formatting that draws attention to itself also draws attention away from what you have to say.

TECHNOLOGY TIP Some word-processing programs or other software packages provide preset templates, or patterns, for writing outlines, memos, letters, newsletters, or invitations. If you use one of these templates, you will not need to adjust the formatting.

Working Collaboratively

Computers allow you to share your writing electronically. Send a copy of your work to someone via email or put it in someone's drop box if your computer is linked to other computers on a network. Then use the feedback of your peers to help you improve your writing.

Peer Editing on a Computer

The writer and the reader can both benefit from the convenience of peer editing on screen, or at the computer.

- Be sure to save your current draft. Then make a copy of it for each of your peer readers.
- You might have your peer readers enter their comments in a different typeface or type style from the one you used for your text, as shown in the the example below.
- Ask each of your readers to include his or her initials in the file name.

- If your computer allows you to open more than one file at a time, open each reviewer's file and refer to the files as you revise your draft.

TECHNOLOGY TIP Some word-processing programs allow you to leave notes for your peer readers in the side column or in a separate text box. If you wish, leave these areas blank so your readers can write comments or questions.

Peer Editing on a Printout

Some peer readers prefer to respond to a draft on paper rather than on the computer.

- Double-space or triple-space your document so that your peer editors can make suggestions between the lines.
- Leave extra-wide margins to give your readers room to note their reactions and questions as they read.
- Print out your draft. Photocopy it if you want to share it with more than one reader.

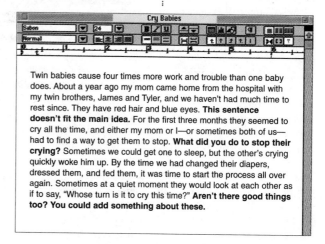

3 Using Visuals

Tables, graphs, diagrams, and pictures often communicate information more effectively than words alone do. Many computer programs allow you to create visuals to use with written text.

3.1 When to Use Visuals

Use visuals when you need a clear, easily understandable way to present complex concepts and processes or large amounts of numerical information such as those that appear in a **technical presentation**. Visuals can also help to make a presentation look more interesting.

Although you should not expect a visual to do all the work of written text, combining words and pictures or graphics can increase a reader's understanding and enjoyment of your writing.

What You'll Need
- A graphics program to create visuals
- Access to clip-art from a CD-ROM, a computer disk, or an online service

A Variety of Programs
Many computer programs allow you to create and insert graphs, tables, time lines, diagrams, and flow charts into your document.

An art program allows you to create border designs for a title page or to draw an unusual character or setting for narrative or descriptive writing.

You may also be able to add clip art, or pre-made pictures, to your document. Clip art can be used to illustrate an idea or concept in your writing or to make your writing more appealing for young readers.

3.2 Kinds of Visuals

Tables
Tables allow you to arrange facts or numbers into rows and columns so that your reader can compare information more easily. In many word-processing programs, you can create a table by choosing the number of vertical columns and horizontal rows you need and then entering information in each box, as the illustration shows. Table-formatting options allow you to change the appearance of your chart in several ways. These options allow you to

- choose the type of border
- vary the size and number of columns and rows
- pick a background color for the chart to set it off from the rest of the presentation

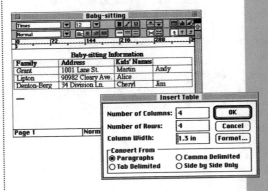

TECHNOLOGY TIP A spreadsheet program provides you with a preset table for your statistics and performs any necessary calculations.

Graphs and Charts

You can sometimes use a graph or chart to help communicate complex information in a clear visual image. For example, you could use a line graph to show how a trend changes over time, a bar graph to compare statistics, or a pie chart, like the one below, to compare percentages. You might want to explore displaying data in more than one visual format before deciding which will work best for you.

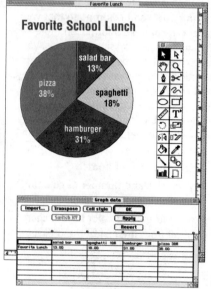

TECHNOLOGY TIP To help your readers easily understand the different parts of a pie chart or bar graph, use a different color or shade of gray for each section.

Other Visuals

Art and design programs allow you to create visuals for your writing. Many programs include the following features:

- **drawing tools** that allow you to draw, color, and shade pictures, such as the drawing below

- **clip art** that you can copy or change with drawing tools

- **page borders** that you can use to decorate title pages, invitations, or brochures

- **text options** that allow you to combine words with your illustrations

- **tools for making geometric shapes** in flow charts, time lines, and diagrams that show a process or sequence of events

④ Creating a Multimedia Presentation

A multimedia presentation is a combination of text, sound, and visuals such as photographs, videos, and animation. Your audience reads, hears, and sees your presentation at a computer, following different "paths" you create to lead the user through the information you have gathered.

4.1 Features of Multimedia Programs

To start planning your multimedia presentation, you need to know what options are available to you. You can combine sound, photos, videos, and animation to enhance any text you write about your topic.

What You'll Need
- Individual programs to create and edit the text, graphics, sound, and videos you will use
- A multimedia authoring program that allows you to combine these elements and create links between screens

Sound
Including sound in your presentation can help your audience understand information in your written text. For example, the user may be able to listen and learn from
- the pronunciation of an unfamiliar or foreign word
- a speech
- a recorded news interview
- a musical selection
- a dramatic reading of a work of literature

Photos and Videos
Photographs and live-action videos can make your subject come alive for the user. Here are some examples:
- videotaped news coverage of a historical event
- videos of music, dance, or theater performances
- charts and diagrams
- photos of an artist's work
- photos or video of a geographical setting that is important to the written text

TECHNOLOGY TIP You can download photos, sound, and video from Internet sources onto your computer. This process allows you to add elements to your multimedia presentation that would usually require complex editing equipment.

Animation

Many graphics programs allow you to add animation, or movement, to the visuals in your presentation. Animated figures add to the user's enjoyment and understanding of what you present. You can use animation to illustrate

- what happens in a story
- the steps in a process
- changes in a chart, graph, or diagram
- how your user can explore information in your presentation

TECHNOLOGY TIP You can now find CD-ROMs with videos of things like wildlife, weather, street scenes, and events, and other CD-ROMs with recordings of famous speeches, musical selections, and dramatic readings.

4.2 Planning Your Presentation

To create a multimedia presentation, first choose your topic and decide what you want to include. Then plan how you want your user to move through your presentation.

Imagine that you are creating a multimedia presentation about the 1980 volcanic eruption of Mount Saint Helens in the state of Washington. You know you want to include the following items:

- text describing the 1980 eruption of Mount Saint Helens
- animated diagram showing what happens when a volcano erupts
- photo of an eruption
- recorded interviews with people affected by the eruption
- video of rescue work and cleanup after the eruption
- photo of Mount Saint Helens today, showing how much vegetation has grown back
- text about current volcano research

You can choose one of the following ways to organize your presentation:

- **step by step** with only one path, or order, in which the user can see and hear the information
- **a branching path** that allows users to make some choices about what they will see and hear, and in what order

A flow chart can help you figure out the path a user can take through your presentation. Each box in the flow chart on the following page represents something about Mount Saint Helens for the user to read, see, or hear. The arrows on the flow chart show a branching path the user can follow.

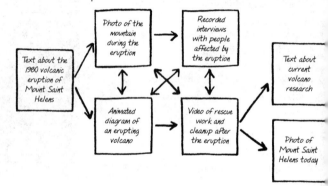

Whenever boxes branch in more than one direction, it means that the user can choose which item to see or hear first.

WRITING TIP You usually need permission from the person or organization that owns the copyright on materials if you want to copy them. You do not need permission, however, if you are not making money from your presentation, if you use it only for educational purposes, and if you use only a small percentage of the original material.

4.3 Guiding Your User

Your user will need directions to follow the path you have planned for your multimedia presentation.

Most multimedia authoring programs allow you to create screens that include text or audio directions that guide the user from one part of your presentation to the next. In the example below, the user can choose between several paths, and directions on the screen explain how to make the choice.

If you need help creating your multimedia presentation, ask your school's technology adviser. You may also be able to get help from your classmates or your software manual.

Navigational buttons take the user back and forth, one screen at a time.

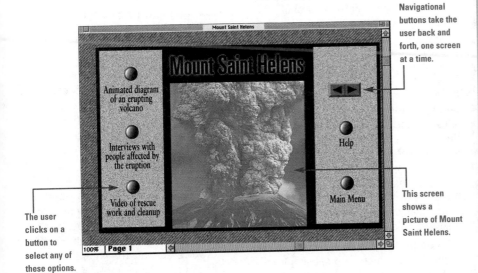

The user clicks on a button to select any of these options.

This screen shows a picture of Mount Saint Helens.

5 Speaking and Listening

Good communicators do more than just talk. They use specific techniques to present their ideas effectively, and they are attentive and critical listeners.

5.1 Speaking and Presenting

In school, in business, and in any community, one of the best ways to present information is to deliver it in person—speaking directly to a live audience.

Audience and Purpose

When preparing and presenting a speech, think about your audience's level of knowledge and interest in your subject. Understanding your audience can help you tailor your speech to your audience's interests. Also, keep in mind your purpose for speaking. Are you trying to persuade the audience to do something? Are you presenting the audience with some of your latest research, or perhaps just entertaining the audience by relating some of your own experiences?

Writing Your Speech

If you are writing your speech beforehand, rather than working from notes, use the following guidelines to help you.

- **Create paragraphs** Make sure that your speech is organized into paragraphs, each of which develops a single main idea.

- **Use appropriate language** Make sure that you use language that is appropriate for the audience, purpose, and occasion.

- **Provide evidence** Include facts, statistics, sensory details, and incidents; quote experts to support your ideas. Elaborate to clarify your ideas.

- **Unify your speech** Just as all the sentences in a paragraph should support the main idea of the paragraph, so all the paragraphs in your speech should support the main idea of the speech.

- **Clarify your ideas** Make sure that you show clear relationships between your ideas. Transitions, or connecting words, can help listeners follow your arguments. (See the Writing Handbook page R28, for a list of transitional expressions.)

- **Use aesthetic language** Effective speakers rely on sound devices such as *onomatopoeia, alliteration,* and *assonance* to help them express their ideas. Onomatopoeia describes words that sound like the thing or action they represent. For example, the word *hiss* sounds very much like the noise of a snake. A speaker might also use a series of words that begin with the same consonant sound to get the audience's attention. This device, which is called alliteration, can be found in a phrase such as "destroy this deadly disease." Finally, assonance allows speakers to emphasize words through the repetition of vowel sounds. The phrase "a campaign of blame" is an example of assonance.

- **Begin your speech** Start with a "hook"—an interesting question or statement to capture people's attention.

- **Finish strong** Restate your main ideas; end your speech with a powerful example or anecdote to reinforce your point.

Prepare/Practice/Present

Confidence is the key to a successful presentation. Use these techniques to help you prepare and present your speech.

Prepare

- **Review your information** Reread your written report and review your background research—you'll feel much more confident during your speech.

- **Organize your notes** Some people prefer to include only a minimum of key points. Others prefer the entire script. Write each main point, or each paragraph, of your speech on a separate index card. Be sure to include your most important evidence and examples. It helps to number your cards.

- **Plan your visual aids** If you are planning on using visual aids, such as slides, posters, charts, graphs, video clips, overhead transparencies, or computer projections, now is the time to design them and decide how to work them.

Practice

- **Rehearse** Rehearse your speech several times, possibly in front of a practice audience. If you are using visual aids, practice handling them. Adapt your rate of speaking, pitch, and tone of voice to your audience and setting. Determine the ideas and words you want to emphasize. Practice putting more **stress** on these as you speak. Your style of performance should express the purpose of your speech.

Purpose	Pace	Pitch	Tone
to persuade	fast but clear	even	urgent
to inform	plenty of pauses	even	authoritative
to entertain	usually builds to a "punch"	varied to create characters or drama	funny or dramatic

TIP: It might also be helpful to time yourself during rehearsals, to ensure that your speech does not run overtime.

- **Evaluate your performance** When you have finished each rehearsal, evaluate your performance. How did you do? Did you slow down for emphasis, pause to let an important point sink in, or use gestures for emphasis? Make a list of aspects of your presentation that you will try to perfect for your next rehearsal.

Present

- **Begin your speech** In order to break the tension of the opening moments, try to look relaxed and remember to smile!

- **Make eye contact** During your speech, try to make eye contact with audience members. This will not only establish the feeling of personal contact, but will help you determine if the audience understands your speech.

- **Remember to pause** A slight pause after important points will provide emphasis and give your audience time to think about what you are saying.

- **Maintain good posture** Stand up straight and avoid nervous movements that may distract the audience's attention from what you are saying.

- **Use expressive body language** A good speaker captures the attention of an audience through body language as well as through speech. Instead of standing motionless in front of an audience, use your entire body to help express your meaning. Lean forward when you make an important point; move your hands and arms for emphasis. Your body language will show that you really believe in what you are saying.

5.2 Oral Interpretation

When you read a poem, a play, or a story aloud, your voice can bring the literature to life.

Oral Reading

An oral reading can be a monologue, during which you assume the voice of a character, the narrator, or the speaker in a poem. Or it may be a dialogue, during which you take on the roles of two or more characters. Reading a poem aloud is another example of an oral reading. Use the following techniques when giving an oral reading.

- **Speak clearly** As you speak, pronounce your words carefully and clearly. Don't mumble.
- **Control your volume** Make sure that you are loud enough to be heard at the back of the room, but do not shout.
- **Pace yourself** Read at a moderate rate, but vary your pace if it seems appropriate to the emotions of the character or to the action you are describing.
- **Vary your voice** Use a different voice for each character. Stress important words or phrases. Use your voice to express different emotions and moods.

Dramatic Reading

When several speakers participate in the reading of a play or other work divided into parts, it is called a dramatic reading. Use the following techniques in your dramatic reading.

- **Prepare** Rehearse your material several times. Become familiar with the humorous and most dramatic parts of your script. Come up with a special voice that fits the personality of your character.

- **Project** As you read your lines, aim your voice toward the very back of the room. This will allow everyone to hear you.
- **Perform** React to the other characters as if you were hearing their lines for the first time. Deliver your own lines with the appropriate emotion. Use your whole body, as well as your hands and face to express your emotions.

5.3 Active Listening for Information

Active listeners listen carefully and think about what they hear—before, during, and after any presentation, whether it's a speech, a class lecture, or even a television program.

Before Listening

Keep an open mind Don't prejudge the speaker. Instead, try to determine the speaker's purpose and main topic. Try to predict what he or she might focus on.

Prepare yourself Review what you already know about the speaker's topic. Then think of some questions you'd like to ask or information you'd like to hear about.

Listen with a purpose Try to match *how* you listen with *why* you're listening.

There are many ways of listening to someone; each way of listening may reflect a different purpose for listening. For example, you would not listen to a friend's joke in the same way that you would listen to a teacher's lesson, because your purpose for listening would be different in each situation. You might listen to a joke for entertainment, while you would listen to a lesson in order to gain information. The following chart will show you how each way of listening reflects a different purpose.

Listening with a Purpose		
Situation	Reason for Listening	How to Listen
Your friend tells a funny story about her pet gerbil.	For enjoyment; to provide your friend with an audience	Maintain eye contact; show you understand; react to the story.
You're listening to a talk and slide show called "Wolves of the Tundra."	For enjoyment; to learn something new	Think about what you already know; listen for ideas that add to your knowledge.
Your mother explains why you can't keep an alligator as a pet.	To understand her point of view; to find opportunities to share your own ideas	Listen carefully; respond positively to valid points; listen for opportunities to state your own reasons.
You and your friends are trying to arrange a trip to a concert.	To solve a problem	Identify goals and problems; listen closely to each other's ideas and build on them.
You are watching a television program about cooking or carpentry.	To follow directions	Listen for words such as *first, second, next,* and *finally;* take notes that you can refer to later.

While Listening

Look for signals of main ideas

- Listen for ideas presented first or last or repeated several times.
- Note statements that begin with phrases such as "My point is . . ." Then listen carefully to what follows.
- Pay attention to ideas presented in a loud voice or with forceful gestures.
- In a multimedia presentation, note the points the speaker has reproduced on a chart or on any other visual aid.
- If the situation permits, ask for clarification of points you do not understand or have questions about.

Block out distractions and focus on the speaker

- Keep your eyes on the speaker.
- Focus your mind if it starts to wander.

Take notes, if appropriate

- Don't worry about writing complete sentences.
- List questions that occur to you as you listen.
- Think about points you would like to explore further.
- Afterward, read over your notes to help you remember what you heard.

Look for relationships between ideas

- Look for comparisons and contrasts. Signal words include: *similarly, but,* and *on the other hand.*
- Pay attention to causes and effects. Signal words include: *because; if . . . , then;* and *as a result.*

After Listening

Ask questions for clarification

- Review any notes that you might have taken.
- Ask for explanations of points that are unclear to you.
- Indicate if you don't agree with something or if you need more information.
- Repeat the speaker's words in your questions, so that you check your understanding as you get answers.

Summarize, paraphrase, and evaluate

- Identify main ideas and details that support them.
- Restate the speaker's ideas in your own words.
- Clarify your reasons for agreeing or disagreeing.

Oral Directions

Active listening to understand oral instructions is a skill that will help you both with your schoolwork and outside of school.

- Listen to understand exactly what you are being asked to do.
- Take notes to refer to as you go about completing the task.
- Ask questions to clarify anything you do not understand.
- Restate the directions in your own words either mentally or in writing.

5.4 Critical Listening

As you listen to a speaker's ideas, you will want to analyze, evaluate, and critique those ideas. Use the following critical listening strategies as you listen to a public speaker:

- **Determine the speaker's purpose** Identify the speaker's purpose in giving the speech. Is the speaker trying to inform, to persuade, to express thoughts or feelings, or to entertain?
- **Listen for the main idea** Try to figure out the speaker's main message; do not get distracted by details of the speech.
- **Distinguish between fact and opinion** Make sure you distinguish between the speaker's opinion and facts that can be verified or proved.

5.5 Group Communication

Group communication can help you in school as you work on group or paired assignments; it can also help prepare you for jobs. Participating in group communication requires all of your listening, speaking, and social skills.

Assigned Roles

A group discussion operates most effectively when each member plays a specific role. A chairperson and a recorder can help group participants stay focused.

Role	Responsibilities
Chairperson	• Introduces the topic for discussion • Explains the goal or purpose of the meeting • Participates in the discussion • Keeps the discussion focused • Helps resolve conflict and maintains fairness
Recorder	• Takes notes on discussion • Participates in discussion • Organizes and writes up notes
Participants	• Contribute facts or ideas to discussion • Respond constructively to others' ideas • Reach agreement or vote on final decision

Guidelines for Discussions

Use these techniques to develop your group communication skills.

- **Listen attentively** Listen carefully and respectfully to each member. Pay attention to important ideas and details. Take notes about issues you want to discuss later.
- **Contribute to the discussion** Join in and share your ideas. Don't be afraid if your ideas are new or different. Share reasons for your ideas. Avoid sarcasm and contribute positive and helpful comments.
- **Compare notes** Everything we see and hear is colored by our own experiences, knowledge, and personality. Because of this, it's always a good idea to compare your perception of a spoken message with the perceptions of others.

5.6 Conducting Interviews

Conducting a personal interview can be an effective way to get information.

Preparing for the interview

- Research any information by or about the person you will interview. The background details will help you get to the point during the interview.

- Prepare a list of questions. Think of more questions than you will need. Include some open-ended questions. Arrange your questions in order of significance, from most important to least important.

Participating in the interview

- Work with a partner. You might choose one note taker and one speaker.
- Ask your questions clearly and listen carefully. Give the person that you are interviewing (the interviewee) plenty of time to answer.
- Listen interactively. Be prepared to follow up on a response you find interesting.

- Avoid arguments. Be tactful and polite.
- Take notes even if you have a recording device. This will help in your write-up of the interview. Jot down main ideas or important statements that can be used as quotes.

Following up on the interview

- Summarize your notes while they are still fresh in your mind.
- Send a thank-you note to the interviewee.

TIP: Remember that as an interviewer, your role is to listen rather than to talk about yourself. Show that you are interested in the person you are interviewing.

6 Critical Thinking

Critical thinking includes the ability to analyze, evaluate, and synthesize ideas and information. Critical thinking goes beyond simply understanding something. It involves making informed judgments based on sound reasoning skills.

6.1 Avoiding Faulty Reasoning

When you write or speak for a persuasive purpose, you must make sure your logic is valid. Avoid these mistakes in reasoning, called **logical fallacies.**

Overgeneralization

Conclusions reached on the basis of too little evidence result in the fallacy called overgeneralization. A person who saw three cyclists riding bicycles without helmets might conclude, "Nobody wears bicycle helmets." That conclusion would be an overgeneralization.

Circular Reasoning

When you support an opinion by simply repeating it in different terms, you are using circular reasoning. For example, "Sport utility vehicles are popular because more people buy them than any other category of new cars." This is an illogical statement because the second part of the sentence simply uses different words to restate the first part of the sentence.

Either-Or Fallacy

Assuming that a complex question has only two possible answers is called the either-or fallacy. "Either we raise the legal driving age or accidents caused by teenage drivers will continue to increase" is an example of the either-or fallacy. The statement ignores other ways of decreasing the automobile accident rate of teenagers.

Cause-and-Effect Fallacy

The cause-and-effect fallacy occurs when you say that event B was caused by event A just because event B occurred after event A. A person might conclude that because a city's air quality worsened two months after a new factory began operation, that new factory caused the air pollution. However, this cause-and-effect relationship would have to be supported by more specific evidence.

 Identifying Modes of Persuasion

Understanding persuasive techniques can help you evaluate information, make informed decisions, and reject persuasive techniques intended to deceive you. Some modes of persuasion appeal to your emotions.

Loaded Language

Loaded language is words or phrases chosen to appeal to the emotions. It is often used in place of facts to shape opinion or to evoke a positive or negative reaction. For example, you might feel positive about a politician who has a *plan*. You might, however, feel negative about a politician who has a *scheme*.

Bandwagon

The bandwagon technique taps into the human desire to belong. It suggests that "everybody" is doing it, or buying it, or believing it. Phrases such as "Don't be the only one . . ." and "Everybody is . . ." signal the bandwagon appeal.

Testimonials

Testimonials offer well-known people or satisfied customers who promote and endorse a product or idea. This technique taps into the appeal of celebrities or into people's need to identify with others.

 Logical Thinking

Persuasive writing and speaking require good reasoning skills. Two means of creating logical arguments are deductive reasoning and inductive reasoning.

Deductive Arguments

A deductive argument begins with a generalization, or premise, and then advances with facts and evidence that lead to a conclusion. The conclusion is a logical outcome of the premise. A false premise leads to a false conclusion; a valid premise leads to a valid conclusion, provided that both the specific facts and the reasoning are correct.

Generalization	We still have much to learn about the healing role of plants.
Specific fact	In some developing countries, many plants are being destroyed as people burn off forests so they can make a living.
Specific conclusion	It is in our best interests to help these developing nations so that they can preserve their plants.

You may use deductive reasoning when writing a persuasive paper or speech. Your conclusion is the thesis of your paper. Facts in your paper supporting your premise should lead logically to that conclusion.

Inductive Arguments

An inductive argument begins with specific evidence that leads to a general conclusion. The conclusion of an inductive argument often includes a qualifying term such as *some, often,* or *most.* This usage helps to avoid the fallacy of overgeneralization.

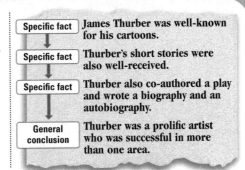

Specific fact	James Thurber was well-known for his cartoons.
Specific fact	Thurber's short stories were also well-received.
Specific fact	Thurber also co-authored a play and wrote a biography and an autobiography.
General conclusion	Thurber was a prolific artist who was successful in more than one area.

⑦ Study Skills and Strategies

As you read an assignment for the first time, review material for a test, or search for information for a research report, you use different methods of reading and studying.

7.1 Skimming

When you run your eyes quickly over a text, paying attention to overviews, headings, topic sentences, highlighted words, and graphic features, you are skimming.

Skimming is a good technique for previewing material in a textbook or other source that you must read for an assignment. It is also useful when you are researching a self-selected topic. Skimming a source helps you determine whether it has pertinent information. For example, suppose you are writing a research report on the detective story. Skimming an essay or a book on Edgar Allan Poe can help you quickly determine whether any part of it deals with your topic.

7.2 Scanning

To find a specific piece of information in a text, use scanning. To scan, place a card under the first line of a page and move it down slowly. Look for key words and phrases that signal the information you are looking for.

Scanning is useful in reviewing for a test or in finding a specific piece of information for a paper. Suppose you are looking for a discussion of hard-boiled private eyes for your research report. You can scan a book chapter or an essay, looking for the names Raymond Chandler and Dashiell Hammett.

7.3 In-Depth Reading

When you must thoroughly understand the material in a text, use in-depth reading.

In-depth reading involves asking questions, taking notes, looking for main ideas, and drawing conclusions as you read slowly and carefully. For example, in researching your report on detective fiction, you may find an article on police procedural stories. Since this is closely related to your topic, you will read it in depth and take notes. You also should use in-depth reading for reading textbooks and literary works.

Index of Fine Art

Index of Fine Art

Index of Skills

Literary Concepts

Free verse. *See* Poetry, free verse.

Genre, 173, R12. *See also* Fiction.

Haiku, R12

Historical fiction, 706–707, 709, 726, 789, R12

Historical period, 656. *See also* Setting.

Humor, 43, 394, 455, R12

Hyperbole, 303, R12

Imagery, 194, 740, 743, 776, R12

Inductive order, R12, R106

Informative nonfiction, 223, 230, R15

Interview, 500, R13

Irony, 348, 358, 621, R13
    situational, 358

Journal, 83

Literary nonfiction, 672, 750, 766, 789, R15

Location, 655. *See also* Setting.

Memoir, 83, 732, 737, R13

Metaphor, 194, 375, 379, 564, R13
    extended, 379, R13

Meter, 193, R14

Modern fable, 311, 316, 321, 492. *See also* Fable.
    characterization in, 321

Mood, 519–520, 522, 530, 643, R14

Moral, of a fable. *See* Fable, moral of.

Motivation. *See* Character.

Myth. *See* Oral tradition.

Narrative nonfiction. *See* Nonfiction, narrative.

Narrative poetry. *See* Poetry, narrative.

Narrator, 247, R14. *See also* Point of view; Speaker, in poetry.
    first-person, 591, 598
    omniscient, R16
    unreliable narrator, 601, 614, R21

Nonfiction, R15. *See also* Essay.
    autobiography, 43, 83, 287, 296
    biography, 83, 87, 98
    informative, 223, 230
    literary, 672, 750, 766, 789
    narrative, 381, 388

Novel, 15, R15. *See also* Fiction.

Ode, 379

Omniscient narrator, R16

Onomatopoeia, R15. *See also* Sound devices.

Oral tradition, 794–796, 890, R15. *See also* Fable.
    folktale, 796, 847, 890, R11
    myth, 796, 798, 890

Organization, 241, R26–R29, R32

Personification, 121, 135, 194, 379, R15

Place. *See* Setting.

Play. *See* Drama.

Plot, 16, 163, 171, 185, 216, 247, 343–346, 707, R15
    cause and effect in, 344
    circular plot structure, 478, 491
    climax, 16, 109, 118, 135, 171, 247, 343
    conflict, 16, 247, 343
    ending, 346
    exposition, 16, 247, 343
    falling action (resolution), 16, 163, 171, 216, 247, 343
    flashback, 344, 690
    foreshadowing, 344, 520
    rising action, 16, 171, 247, 343
    surprise ending, 154, 161, 358, 373

Poetry, 191–195, R16
    alliteration, 193, 458, 461
    form, 192
    free verse, 192, 204, R11
    haiku, R12
    humorous poetry, 458
    imagery, 194, 740, 743
    limerick, R13
    line, 192
    meter, 193, R14
    narrative, 299, R14
    ode, 379
    onomatopoeia, 193, 458, 461
    rhyme, 193, 196, 199, 299, 303, 331, 458, 461, R17
    rhyme scheme, 199, 303, R17
    rhythm, 193, 299, 303, 331, 458, R17
    sound devices, 193, 299, 303, 458, 461
    speaker, 194, 201, 204, R19
    stanza, 192, R19
    word choice, 564, 570, R21

Point of view, R16. *See also* Narrator; Speaker, in poetry.
    first-person, 83, 101, 106, 296, 591, 598, R16
    third-person, R16

Primary sources, 223, 230, R15

Purpose, 520

Realism, 776, R17

Resolution, 16, 247. *See also* Plot, falling action.

Rhyme, 193, 196, 199, 299, 303, 331, 458, 461, R17

end rhyme, 196, 199
    in narrative poetry, 299
Rhyme scheme, 199, 303, R17
Rhythm, 193, 299, 303, 331, 458, R17
Sarcasm, 621, 629, R17
Science fiction, 410–411, 432, 436, R18
Secondary sources, 223, 230, R15
Sensory detail and language, 182
Setting, 18, 20, 26, 43, 413, 519, 520,
    655–656, 658, 672, 679, 690, 707, 789,
    R18
Short story, 15, R18
Simile, 194, 564, R18
Slang, 142. *See also* Dialect.
Sound devices, 193, 299, 303, 458, 461
    alliteration, 193, 458, 461, R6
    onomatopoeia, 193, 458, 461, R15
    repetition, 193, 299, R17
Sources. *See* Primary sources; Secondary
    sources.
Speaker, in poetry, 194, 201, 204, R19. *See
    also* Narrator.
Stanza, 192, R19
Stereotype, 553, R19. *See also* Character
    type.
Story structure, 343–344, 478, 491. *See also*
    Plot.
Storytelling, 795
Style, 43, 175, 199, 284, 303, 502, 743,
    772, 776, R17
Subject, 413
Surprise ending, 154, 161, 358, 372, R20
Suspense, 361, 372, 429, 513, R20
Symbol, 391, 395, 530, R20
Table of contents, R20
Teleplay. *See* Drama, teleplay.
Theme, 14, 18, 81, 184, 185, 190, 244, 278,
    284, 321, 332, 342, 409, 413, 492, 498,
    513, 518, 585, 644, 645, 654, 705, 790,
    791, R20
Third-person narrator, R16
Time (in fiction), 656. *See also* Setting.
Titles, 467, R20
Tone, 519–520, 522, 530, R20
Understatement, 621, 629, R21
Unreliable narrator. *See* Narrator, unreliable
    narrator.
Voice, 194, R21
Word choice, 564, 570, 776, R21

Reading and Critical Thinking Skills

Active reading, strategies for, 4–9. *See also*
    Clarifying; Connecting; Evaluating;
    Predicting; Questioning; Strategies;
    Visualizing.
Analogies, 398, 430, 615, 883, R6
Application, literature to life. *See*
    Connecting, personal connection.
Argument, R106–R107. *See also*
    Generalizing; Inference; Persuasive
    writing *under* Writing Skills, Modes,
    and Formats.
Author's purpose, 37, 101, 106, 388, 414,
    415, 429, R7
Bandwagon, R106
Bias, 139, 141. *See also* Stereotype.
Cause and effect, 109, 118, 381, 708, 709,
    726, R7
Cause-and-effect fallacy, R106
Choices, making. *See* Decision making.
Chronological order, 86, 87, 89, 98, R8
Circular reasoning, R105
Clarifying, 4–9, 19, 86, 195, 391, 394, 414,
    458, 461, 549, 657, 708, R8
Comparing and contrasting, 34, 62, 98, 106,
    118, 162, 204, 311, 316, 321, 388, 394,
    436, 455, 461, 621, 629, 674, 690, 788,
    811, 829, 847
    characters, 64, 171, 185, 271, 726, 811,
        829, 846, 865
    across cultures, 811, 829, 847, 865, 883
    print vs. non-print media, 176, 232,
        271, 276, 285, 379, 503, 547, 562,
        673, 829
Conclusions. *See* Drawing conclusions.
Connecting, R8. *See also* Comparing and
    contrasting, across cultures.
    through art, 35, 109, 217, 285, 373, 389,
        430, 547, 562, 615, 691, 727, 882
    through biology, 312, 391
    through character, 278
    through current events, 101, 206
    through geography, 20, 196, 375, 846
    through history, 154, 163, 250, 361,
        415, 458, 478, 492, 591, 750, 767
    through imagery, 379
    through other stories, 492, 498, 811,
        829, 846, 865, 883

Vocabulary Skills

Grammar, Usage, and Mechanics

Writing Skills, Modes, and Formats

comparison-and-contrast essay, 323, 636–640

definition, 107

escape plan, 456

letter of recommendation, 285

phrase book, 883

police report, 571

problem-solution essay, 403–407, R36

recipe, 200

research report, 780–86, R41–R45

supervisor's report, 176

will, 276

Expressive and personal writing

application essay, 691

autobiography, 630

column, 631

diary, 599

journal writing, 78, 217

letter, 63, 107, 175, 297, 322, 630

letter to editor, 389, 703

opinion essay, 304, 531, 547, 691, 699–703

personal essay, 599, 630, 738

personal response, 75–79

Fact, use of, 406, 700, 703, 782, R29

Formatting, R93. *See also* Word processing.

headers, R93

margins, R93

spacing, R93

text alignment, R93

typeface, R93

Freewriting, 78

Gathering information. *See* Prewriting.

Generalizing, 308

Grammar checker. *See* Word processing.

Graphic aids. *See* Visuals, use of.

Graphic organizers, 223, 323, 585, 617, 767, 783, 811, R95, R96

Hook, R39

Ideas for writing. *See* Prewriting.

Imagery, use of, 502

Informative writing. *See* Expository writing.

Interpretive essay. *See* Writing about literature.

Interview, 85

Introduction, 238–239, 241, 403, 407, 636, 637, 702, 780, 781, 833, 885, R39

Journals, 78, 217

Letter. *See* Expressive and personal writing.

Literary analysis. *See* Writing about literature.

Logical organization. *See* Organization.

Main idea, 78, 223, 330, R27

Narrative and imaginative writing, 506–510, R33–R34

adventure narrative, 389

choosing a narrator, 508

commemorative poem, 727

dialogue, 276, 322, 359, 547, 642, 727

diary and journal, 78, 217, 231

first-person story, 673

folktale, 864

humorous recipe, 456

modern fable, 503

nonsense poem, 462

ode, 380

personal narrative, 44, 63, 119, 178–183

poem, 205, 389, 395, 744, 882

science fiction story, 437

script, 885, 887

sequel, 276, 562

short story, 506–510, 531

song lyrics, 136

stage directions, 331, 430

Note taking, 10, 617, 784, R42

Opinion statement, 699–703

Organization, 179–180, 239–242, 323, 324–328, 403–406, 507–508, 636–640, 699–703, 780–786, 830–834, 885, 886, 888, R26–R45. *See also* Conclusions; Introduction; Paragraphs; Transitions.

cause and effect, 700, 830–834, R28, R36

chronological order, 179–180, 508, 781, R28, R34

cluster diagram, 324

comparing and contrasting, 35, 323, R28

feature by feature, 637, R36

graphic devices, 181, 223, 323, 585, 598, 639, 783, 811, R95, R96

least to most important, 786, R28, R32

main idea, 223, 330

outlining, 223, 323, 617, R43

spatial order, 786, R28, R32

subject by subject, 639, 885, R36

Outlining, 223, 323, 617, R43

Paragraphs, 702, R27

Parallelism, 182, 511

Paraphrasing, 239, 619, 784, R42

Peer editing, R94

Peer review, 78, 181, 241, 407, 509, 702, 785, 833, 887, R25

Personal narrative, 178–183. *See also* Expressive and personal writing.

Persuasive writing, R39–R40
  advice column, 99
  editorial, 119, 373, 744, 846
  letter of recommendation, 285
  persuasive essay, 468, 615, 727, 865
  persuasive letter, 468
  pro-or-con statement, 231
  proposal, 430
  public service announcement, 585
  radio commercial, 437
  speech, 44, 297, 322

Plagiarism, R43

Plotting (in fiction), 506–510, R34

Point of view, 508

Portfolios, 11, 75, 78, 79, 178, 181, 182, 185, 205, 238, 242, 327, 328, 407, 506, 509, 510, 579, 636, 639, 643, 699, 703, 780, 783, 786, 789, 830, 833, 834, 884, 888, 890

Prewriting, 10, 78, 181, 240–241, 326–327, 406, 509, 639, 702, 783, 833, R22–R23
  brainstorming, 181, 406, 509, 639, 833, 886, R22
  choosing a topic, 181, 240, 324, 406, 639, 833, 886, R22, R41
  creating imagery, 327, 509, 885
  freewriting, 78, 326
  gathering information, 240, 406, 702
  setting, 327, 509
  word play, 327

Problem-solution essay, 403–406

Proofreading, 79, 182, 328, 510, 786, 834, R23–R24

Proofreading symbols, R24

Proposal. *See* Persuasive writing, proposal.

Publishing, 79, 182, 242, 328, 510, 640, 703, R25

Quotation, use of, 76, 79, 179, 239, 242, 326, 638, 784, R30

Recording. *See* Note taking.

Report. *See* Expository writing.

Research paper. *See* Expository writing, research report.

Research report, guidelines for writing, 780–786

Restatement, R29

Revising and editing, 79, 182, 242, 323, 328, 329, 407, 510, 640, 703, 786, 834, 888, R23–R24, R92

Rewriting (exercises), 36, 45, 100, 108, 120, 137, 218, 232, 277, 286, 298, 360, 374, 390, 431, 457, 469, 499, 532, 548, 563, 674, 692, 739, 773

Search and replace. *See* Word processing.

Self-assessment. *See* Portfolios; Self-assessment *under* Assessment.

Sensory detail, 182, 325, 507, 510, R30, R31

Sentence structure, 175, 834. *See also* Sentence *under* Grammar, Usage, and Mechanics.
  fragments, R24
  parallel, 510
  run-on, R24
  variation in, 137, 162

Short story, 506–510, 531

Specific language, R30

Spell checking. *See* Word processing.

Spelling, 182, 242, 328, R86–R89

Spelling demons, R86

Statistics, 406, 700, R29

Summarizing, 240, 620, 702, 777, R29, R42. *See also* Paraphrasing.

Supporting ideas, 78, 242, 703, R29–R30, R42

Thesis statement, 65, 78, 780, 781, 885, R27, R41, R43

Time line, 181, 552

Topic sentence, R27

Transitions, 180, 637, 640, R28

Variation in writing. *See* Sentence structure, variation in.

Visuals, use of, R95–R96
  borders, R96
  clip art, R96
  graphs and charts, R96
  tables, R95

Word choice, 218, 328, R30, R87–R89. *See also* Commonly confused words *under* Grammar, Usage, and Mechanics.

Word processing, R92–R94. *See also* Formatting; Visuals, use of; Writing process.
  dictionary, R92
  grammar checker, R92
  search and replace, R92
  spell checking, R92

Inquiry and Research

Viewing and Representing

Index of Titles and Authors

Page numbers that appear in italics refer to biographical information.

Acknowledgments (continued)

Orchard Books: "A Crush," from *A Couple of Kooks and Other Stories About Love* by Cynthia Rylant. Copyright © 1990 by Cynthia Rylant. Reprinted by permission of the publisher, Orchard Books, New York.

Atheneum Books For Young Readers: Excerpt from "Eleanor Roosevelt," from *Great Lives: Human Rights* by William Jay Jacobs. Copyright © 1990 by William Jay Jacobs. Reprinted with the permission of Atheneum Books for Young Readers, an imprint of Simon & Schuster Children's Publishing Division.

Simon & Schuster: Excerpt from *No Ordinary Time* by Doris Kearns Goodwin. Copyright © 1994 by Doris Kearns Goodwin. Reprinted with the permission of Simon & Schuster, Inc.

Random House: Excerpt from *Living Out Loud* by Anna Quindlen. Copyright © 1987 by Anna Quindlen. Reprinted by permission of Random House, Inc.

"Bums in the Attic," from *The House on Mango Street* by Sandra Cisneros, published by Alfred A. Knopf, a division of Random House, Inc., New York in 1994. Copyright © 1984 by Sandra Cisneros. Reprinted by permission of Susan Bergholz Literary Services, New York. All rights reserved.

Pantheon Books: "The War of the Wall," from *Deep Sightings and Rescue Missions* by Toni Cade Bambara. Copyright © 1996 by The Estate of Toni Cade Bambara. Reprinted by permission of Pantheon Books, a division of Random House, Inc.

Life: "Primal Compassion" by Charles Hirshberg, *Life*, November 1996. Copyright © 1996 by Time Inc. Reprinted by permission.

Delacorte Press: Excerpt from *My Life in Dog Years* by Gary Paulsen. Copyright © 1998 by Gary Paulsen. Used by permission of Delacorte Press, a division of Random House, Inc.

Unit Two

Henry Holt and Company: "The Pasture," from *The Poetry of Robert Frost*, edited by Edward Connery Lathem. Copyright 1944, © 1958 by Robert Frost. Copyright © 1967 by Lesley Frost Ballantine. Copyright 1930, 1939, © 1969 by Henry Holt and Company. Reprinted by permission of Henry Holt and Company, Inc.

"A Time to Talk," from *The Poetry of Robert Frost*, edited by Edward Connery Lathem. Copyright 1944, © 1958 by Robert Frost. Copyright © 1967 by Lesley Frost Ballantine. Copyright 1930, 1939, © 1969 by Henry Holt and Company. Reprinted by permission of Henry Holt and Company, Inc.

William Morrow & Company: "The World Is Not a Pleasant Place to Be," from *My House* by Nikki Giovanni. Copyright © 1972 by Nikki Giovanni. Reprinted by permission of William Morrow & Company, Inc.

Alfred A. Knopf: "To You," from *Collected Poems* by Langston Hughes. Copyright © 1994 by the Estate of Langston Hughes. Reprinted by permission of Alfred A. Knopf, Inc.

Candlewick Press: "What Do Fish Have to Do with Anything?" from *What Do Fish Have to Do with Anything?: And Other Stories* by Avi. Copyright © 1997 by Avi Wortis. Reprinted by permission of Candlewick Press, Cambridge, MA.

The Boston Herald: Excerpt from "The Difference a City Year Makes" by Lauren Beckham, *The Boston Herald*, June 10, 1996. Copyright © 1996 by *The Boston Herald*. Reprinted with permission of *The Boston Herald*.

Dutton Children's Books: Excerpt from *Immigrant Kids* by Russell Freedman. Copyright © 1980 by Russell Freedman. Used by permission of Dutton Children's Books, a division of Penguin Putnam Inc.

Susan Bergholz Literary Services: "Good Hot Dogs" / "Buenos hot dogs" from *My Wicked, Wicked Ways* in English, published by Third Woman Press and in hardcover by Alfred A. Knopf, and from *Cool Salsa* in Spanish, published by Henry Holt. Copyright © 1987 by Sandra Cisneros in English. Copyright © 1994 by Sandra Cisneros in Spanish. Reprinted by permission of Susan Bergholz Literary Services, New York. All rights reserved.

Faber and Faber: "Scaffolding," from *Death of a Naturalist* by Seamus Heaney. Copyright © 1966 by Seamus Heaney. Reprinted by permission of Faber and Faber Limited.

University Of Minnesota Press: *A Christmas Carol* by Charles Dickens, adapted by Frederick Gaines, from *Five Plays from the Children's Theatre Company of Minneapolis*, published by the University of Minnesota Press. Copyright © 1975 by Frederick Gaines. All rights reserved.

Bilingual Press/Editorial Bilingüe: "The Scholarship Jacket" by Marta Salinas, from *Nosotras: Latina Literature Today* (1986), edited by María del Carmen Boza, Beverly Silva, and Carmen Valle. By permission of Bilingual Press/Editorial Bilingüe, Arizona State University, Tempe, AZ.

Arte Público Press: "Graduation Morning," from *Chants* by Pat Mora. Reprinted with permission from the publisher of *Chants*, Arte Público Press—University of Houston, 1985.

CMG Worldwide: Excerpt from *I Never Had It Made* by Jackie Robinson, as told to Alfred Duckett. By permission of CMG Worldwide Inc. on behalf of Rachel Robinson.

Laura Cecil Literary Agency: "Ant and Grasshopper," from *Fables from Aesop* retold by James Reeves. Copyright © 1961 by James Reeves. Reprinted by permission of Laura Cecil Literary Agency for the James Reeves Estate.

Ennis Rees: "The Ant and the Grasshopper," from *Fables from Aesop* by Ennis Rees. Copyright © 1964 by Ennis Rees. Reprinted by permission of the author.

Doubleday: "The Richer, the Poorer" by Dorothy West. Copyright © 1995 by Dorothy West. Used by permission of Doubleday, a division of Random House, Inc.

Unit Three

Bantam Books: "One Ordinary Day, with Peanuts," from *Just An Ordinary Day: The Uncollected Stories* by Shirley Jackson. Copyright © 1997 by The Estate of Shirley Jackson. Used by permission of Bantam Books, a division of Random House, Inc.

"The Eternal Frontier" from *Frontier* by Louis L'Amour. Copyright © 1984 by Louis L'Amour Enterprises, Inc. Used by permission of Bantam Books, a division of Random House, Inc.

Piri Thomas: Excerpt from *Stories from El Barrio* by Piri Thomas. Copyright © 1978 by Piri Thomas. Reprinted by permission of the author.

Simon & Schuster Books for Young Readers: "Ode to an Artichoke," translation of the Pablo Neruda poem "Oda a la Alcachofa," from *The Yellow Canary Whose Eye Is so Black* by Cheli Duran. Copyright © 1977 by Cheli Duran Ryan. Reprinted with permission of Simon & Schuster Books for Young Readers, an imprint of Simon & Schuster Children's Publishing Division.

Agencia Literaria: "Oda a la Alcachofa," from *Pablo Neruda Poesía I* by Pablo Neruda. Copyright © 1954 by Pablo Neruda. Reprinted by permission of Agencia Literaria Carmen Balcells.

HarperCollins Publishers: Excerpt from *An American Childhood* by Annie Dillard. Copyright © 1987 by Annie Dillard. Reprinted by permission of HarperCollins Publishers, Inc.

"Sarah Cynthia Sylvia Stout Would Not Take the Garbage Out" from *Where The Sidewalk Ends* by Shel Silverstein. Copyright © 1974 by Evil-Eye Music, Inc. Reprinted by permission of HarperCollins Publishers, Inc.

William Morrow & Company: "Winter Poem," from *My House* by Nikki Giovanni. Copyright © 1972 by Nikki Giovanni. Reprinted by permission of William Morrow & Company, Inc.

Doubleday: "The Bat," from *The Collected Poems of Theodore Roethke* by Theodore Roethke. Copyright © 1938 by Theodore Roethke. Used by permission of Doubleday, a division of Random House, Inc.

Viking Penguin: "Mooses," from *Under the North Star* by Ted Hughes. Copyright © 1981 by Ted Hughes. Used by permission of Viking Penguin, a division of Penguin Putnam Inc.

National Wildlife: "They're Well-Suited for Studying Moose" by Steve Mirsky, *National Wildlife*, June/July 1997. Copyright © 1997 by the National Wildlife Federation. Reprinted with permission from *National Wildlife*.

Barbara Hogenson Agency: "The Night the Bed Fell," from *My Life and Hard Times* by James Thurber. Copyright © 1933 by James Thurber. Copyright © renewed 1961 by Helen Thurber and Rosemary A. Thurber. Reprinted by arrangement with Rosemary A. Thurber and the Barbara Hogenson Agency.

The Rod Serling Trust: "The Monsters Are Due on Maple Street" by Rod Serling. © 1960 by Rod Serling. © 1988 by Carolyn Serling, Jody Serling, and Anne Serling Sutton. Reprinted by permission of The Rod Serling Trust.

"Key Item," from *Buy Jupiter and Other Stories* by Isaac Asimov. Copyright © 1975 by Isaac Asimov. Used by permission of Doubleday, a division of Random House, Inc.

Brandt & Brandt Literary Agents and A. M. Heath: "The Serial Garden," from *Armitage, Armitage, Fly Away Home* by Joan Aiken. Copyright © 1966 by Macmillan & Co., Ltd. Copyright © 1969 by Joan Aiken Enterprises, Ltd. Copyright renewed © 1994 by Joan Aiken Enterprises, Ltd. Reprinted by permission of Brandt & Brandt Literary Agents, Inc., and A. M. Heath & Co., Ltd., on behalf of the author.

The Boston Globe: "Four Decades in Space" by Richard Sanchez and Sean McNaughton, *The Boston Globe*, October 29, 1998. Copyright © 1998 by *The Boston Globe*. Reprinted courtesy of *The Boston Globe*.

Don Congdon Associates: "Dark They Were, and Golden-Eyed" from *Thrilling Wonder Stories* by Ray Bradbury. Copyright © 1949 by Standard Magazines, Inc., renewed 1976 by Ray Bradbury. Reprinted by permission of Don Congdon Associates, Inc.

"The Golden Kite, the Silver Wind" from *Classic Stories I* by Ray Bradbury. Copyright © 1953 by Epoch Associates, renewed 1981 by Ray Bradbury. Reprinted by permission of Don Congdon Associates, Inc.

The Charlotte Observer: Excerpt from "Ray Bradbury, Science Fiction Supernova, Has Little Use for the Internet" by Sandy Hill, *The Charlotte Observer*, October 12, 1997. Copyright © 1997 by *The Charlotte Observer*. Reprinted with permission of *The Charlotte Observer*.

Unit Four

Gish Jen: "The White Umbrella" by Gish Jen, first published in *The Yale Review*. Copyright © 1984 by Gish Jen. Reprinted by permission of the author.

Farrar, Straus & Giroux and David Higham Associates: "The Bicycle and the Sweetshop," "Mr. Coombs," and "The Great Mouse Plot," from *Boy: Tales of Childhood* by Roald Dahl. Copyright © 1984 by Roald Dahl. Reprinted by permission of Farrar, Straus & Giroux, Inc., and David Higham Associates.

CyberPalate: An adaptation of "A Chocolate Timeline," from CuisineNet Diner's Digest, www.cuisinenet.com. Copyright © 1999 by CyberPalate. Reprinted by permission of CyberPalate.

Neil Simon: "A Defenseless Creature," from *The Good Doctor* by Neil Simon. Copyright © 1974 by Neil Simon. Reprinted by permission of Neil Simon.

Hugh Noyes: "The Highwayman," by Alfred Noyes. Reprinted by permission of Hugh Noyes, for the Trustees of the Literary Estate of Alfred Noyes.

Alfred A. Knopf: "Staying in the Lines," from *Knots in My Yo-Yo String: Autobiography of a Kid* by Jerry Spinelli. Copyright © 1998 by Jerry Spinelli. Reprinted by the permission of Alfred A. Knopf, Inc.

Orchard Books: "An Hour with Abuelo," from *An Island Like You: Stories of the Barrio* by Judith Ortiz Cofer. Copyright © 1995 by Judith Ortiz Cofer. Reprinted by permission of Orchard Books, New York.

Philomel Books and Stoddart Publishing Company: "Waiting," from *The Leaving and Other Stories* by Budge Wilson. Copyright © 1990 by Budge Wilson. Used by permission of Philomel Books, a division of Penguin Putnam, Inc., and by permission of Stoddart Publishing Company Ltd., Don Mills, Ontario, Canada.

National Geographic Society: "Face-to-Face with Twins" by Judith Rinard, *National Geographic World*, April 1998. Copyright © 1998 by National Geographic Society. Reprinted by permission of the National Geographic Society.

NTC/Contemporary Publishing, Inc.: Excerpt from *Growing Up* by Russell Baker. Copyright © 1982 by Russell Baker. Used with permission of NTC/Contemporary Publishing Group, Inc.

Random House: Excerpt from *The Autobiography of Malcolm X* by Malcolm X, with the assistance of Alex Haley. Copyright © 1964 by Alex Haley and Malcolm X, renewed © 1965 by Alex Haley and Betty Shabazz. Reprinted by permission of Random House, Inc.

Marian Reiner: "Aardvark," by Julia Fields from *Nine Black Poets*, edited by R. Baird Shuman. Copyright © 1968 by Julia Fields. Used by permission of Marian Reiner for the author.

Unit Five

Scholastic: Excerpt from *Exploring the* Titanic by Robert D. Ballard. Copyright © 1988 by The Madison Press Ltd. Text copyright © 1988 by Robert D. Ballard and Family. Reprinted by permission of Scholastic Inc.

The Dallas Morning News: "The Lives of *La Belle*" by Bryan Woolley, *The Dallas Morning News*, February 9, 1997. Copyright © 1997 by *The Dallas Morning News*. Reprinted with permission of *The Dallas Morning News*.

Hill and Wang: "The Last Cover," from *The Pride of Lions and Other Stories* by Paul Annixter. Copyright © 1960 by Hill and Wang, renewed copyright 1988 by Hill and Wang. Reprinted by permission of Hill and Wang, a division of Farrar, Straus & Giroux, Inc.

University of Notre Dame Press: Excerpt from *Barrio Boy* by Ernesto Galarza. Copyright © 1971 by University of Notre Dame Press. Used by permission of Notre Dame Press.

David Higham Associates: "A Crown of Wild Olive," from *Heather, Oak, and Olive: Three Stories* by Rosemary Sutcliff. Copyright © 1971 by Rosemary Sutcliff. Reprinted by permission of David Higham Associates.

Little, Brown and Company: Excerpt from *Long Walk to Freedom* by Nelson Mandela. Copyright © 1994 by Nelson Rolihlahla Mandela. By permission of Little, Brown and Company.

Grove/Atlantic: "The Turtle," from *Dream Work* by Mary Oliver. Copyright © 1992 by Mary Oliver. Reprinted with permission of Grove/Atlantic, Inc.

The Read-In Foundation: Excerpt from "An Interview with Virginia Hamilton," from The Read-In Foundation, http://www.readin.org. Used by permission of The Read-In Foundation and Virginia Hamilton.

Alfred A. Knopf: Excerpt from *Anthony Burns: The Defeat and Triumph of a Fugitive Slave* by Virginia Hamilton. Copyright © 1988 by Virginia Hamilton. Reprinted by permission of Alfred A. Knopf, Inc.

Excerpt from *The People Could Fly: American Black Folktales* by Virginia Hamilton. Text copyright © 1985 by Virginia Hamilton. Reprinted by permission of Alfred A. Knopf, Inc.

Virginia Hamilton: Excerpt from "Looking for America," a speech given by Virginia Hamilton, 23 October 1993. Originally published by the Friends of the CCBC, Inc. Copyright © 1993 by Virginia Hamilton. Reprinted by permission of Virginia Hamilton.

Unit Six

Scholastic: Excerpt from *The Greek Gods* by Bernard Evslin. Copyright © 1966 by Scholastic Inc. Reprinted by permission of Scholastic Inc.

Houghton Mifflin Company: "Theseus and the Minotaur," from *Greek Myths* by Olivia Coolidge. Copyright © 1949, renewed 1977 by Olivia E. Coolidge. Reprinted by permission of Houghton Mifflin Company. All rights reserved.

Curtis Brown, Ltd.: "Waters of Gold," from *Tongues of Jade* by Laurence Yep, published by HarperCollins. Text copyright © 1991 by Laurence Yep. Reprinted by permission of the author and Curtis Brown, Ltd.

Doubleday: "Ashputtle," from *Grimm's Tales for Young and Old* by Jakob & Wilhelm Grimm. Copyright © 1977 by Ralph Manheim. Used by permission of Doubleday, a division of Random House, Inc.

The Random House Group: "Narcissus," from *Tales the Muses Told: Ancient Greek Myths* selected and related by Roger Lancelyn Green. Text copyright © 1965 by Roger Lancelyn Green. Reprinted by permission of The Random House Group Ltd.

Ricardo E. Alegría: "Lazy Peter and His Three-Cornered Hat," from *The Three Wishes* by Ricardo E. Alegría. Puerto Rican folktale collected and adapted by Ricardo E. Alegría, Ph.D. Reprinted by permission of the author.

Museum of New Mexico Press: "La Suerte: The Force of Luck" by Rudolfo A. Anaya, from *Cuentos: Tales from the Hispanic Southwest* by José Griego y Maestas and Rudolfo Anaya. Copyright © 1980. Reprinted with the permission of the Museum of New Mexico Press.

Little, Brown and Company: "Brother Coyote and Brother Cricket," from *I'll Tell You a Tale* by J. Frank Dobie. Copyright 1928, 1930, 1931, 1935, 1936, 1938, 1939, 1941, 1947, 1949, 1950, 1951, 1952, 1955, © 1960 by J. Frank Dobie. Reprinted by permission of Little, Brown and Company.

"How Odin Lost His Eye," from *Adventures with the Giants* by Catharine Sellew. Copyright © 1950 by Catharine Sellew Hinchman. Reprinted by permission of Little, Brown and Company.

Libraries Unlimited: "Pumpkin Seed and the Snake," from *Folk Stories of the Hmong* by Norma J. Livo and Dia Cha. Copyright © 1991 by Libraries Unlimited, Inc. By permission of Libraries Unlimited, Inc.

G. P. Putnam's Sons: "Kelfala's Secret Something," from *Three African Tales* by Adjai Robinson. Copyright © 1979 by Adjai Robinson. Reprinted by permission of G. P. Putnam's Sons, a division of Penguin Putnam Inc.

Art Credits

Cover

Illustration copyright © 1999 Gary Overacre.

Front Matter

ix School Division, Houghton Mifflin Company; **x** Painting copyright © 1999 Brad Holland; **xii** Illustration by Bernie Fuchs; **xiv** Copyright © Kamil Vojnar/Photonica; **xv** Copyright © Frank Capri/Saga Archive Photos; **xvi** Photography by Laurie Rubin; **xviii** Copyright © 1996 Ann Giordano/Photonica; **xix** Ron Rovtar; **xx, xxi** Larry Cameron.

Unit One

2 *bottom* Science Source/Photo Researchers, Inc./NASA; **2–3** *top* Enzo and Paolo Ragazzi/Corbis; *center* Detail of illustration by Kam Mak; **3** *bottom left* Painting by Ken Marschall from *Exploring the* Titanic. Copyright © 1988 by Robert D. Ballard, The Madison Press Ltd.; *bottom right* RMIP/Richard Haynes; **4–5** Detail of *January Shadows*, Robert Frank; **12–13** *background* Copyright © PhotoDisc; **15** *bottom* Illustration by Robert Ingpen, courtesy of Viking Press; *right* Random House; **17** *center left, Portrait of Prince Eristoff* (1925), Tamara de Lempicka. Private collection, New York. Copyright © 1996 Artists Rights Society (ARS), New York/SPADEM, Paris; *bottom left* Illustration by Hugh Harrison; *bottom center, Mexican Morning* (1942). Private Collection/GG Kopilak/SuperStock; *bottom right, Ada & Vincent* (1967), Alex Katz. Oil on canvas, 94½″ × 71½″. Copyright © Alex Katz/Licensed by VAGA, New York/ Marlborough Gallery, New York; **18** *January's Shadows*, Robert Frank; **19** RMIP/Richard Haynes; **25** Detail of illustration by Pamela Daly; **36** The Granger Collection, New York; **37** *top* Detail of illustration by Rosanne Kaloustian; *bottom* Kiwi Studios; **45** Copyright © Bill Eichner; **46** *background, inset top* UPI/Corbis-Bettmann; *center* DLF Group; *inset bottom* Copyright © Seny Norasingh/Light Sensitive; **49, 55** Details of *Silent Fall*, Nicholas Wilton. Acrylic on wood, 24″ × 14½″; **53** *background* Pat O'Hara/Corbis; **56** Corbis-Bettmann; **63** AP/Wide World Photos; **64** Archive Photos; **65** AP/Wide World Photos; **74** Margaret Miller; **82** *left* Illustration by Ken Marschall from *Exploring the* Titanic by Robert D. Ballard. Copyright © 1988 by Madison Publishing Inc. Used by permission of Scholastic Inc.; *bottom* The *Boston Globe*; *right* Grolier Publishing; **83** *top* Corbis-Bettmann; *bottom* Courtesy of the Franklin D. Roosevelt Library; **85** *left* Brown Brothers; *center* Lewis W. Hine Collection, United States History, Local History, and Genealogy Division, The New York Public Library, Astor, Lenox and Tilden Foundations; **86** RMIP/Richard Haynes; **87** *left to right* Copyright © Archive Photos/PNI; The Granger Collection, New York; Copyright © Archive Photos/PNI; UPI/Corbis-Bettmann; Corbis-Bettmann; **108** Courtesy of The New York Times; **110** Gillian Darley/Corbis; **120** Schomberg Center for Research in Black Culture, The New York Public Library, Astor, Lenox and Tilden Foundations; **121** Copyright © Victoria McCormick/Animals Animals; **122** *montage* Copyright © Victoria McCormick/Animals Animals; Copyright © James H. Carmichael, Jr./The Image Bank; Copyright © Renee Lynn/Photo Researchers, Inc.; **125** E. H. Rao/Photo

Researchers, Inc.; **126** *montage* Copyright © Michael Fogden/DRK Photo; Copyright © Pat Anderson/Visuals Unlimited; **127** Copyright © Sudip D. Bhaumik/Dinodia Picture Agency; **129** *montage* Copyright © Ralph Reinhold/Animals Animals; Copyright © 1999 Ben Klaffke; **130–131** *montage* Copyright © Jim Merli/Visuals Unlimited; D. Cavagnaro/ DRK Photo; **133** *montage* Paolo Koch/Photo Researchers, Inc.; Copyright © Marilyn Silverstone/Magnum Photos, Inc.; **137** Stock Montage; **138, 140** Copyright © 1996 Alon Reininger/Contact Press Images; **150** *center left* Austin History Center, Austin Public Library; *bottom left to right* Austin History Center, Austin Public Library; The Granger Collection, New York; Smithsonian Institution; **151** *center right* Austin History Center, Austin Public Library; *bottom, left to right* Austin History Center, Austin Public Library; National Park Service: Statue of Liberty National Monument; Copyright © Henry Ford Museum & Greenfield Village; **152–153** *bottom* Museum of the City of New York; **152** *center right* O. Henry Memorial Museum; **153** *right* Montana Historical Society; **163** *top* Detail of *Portrait of Prince Eristoff* (1925), Tamara de Lempicka. Private collection, New York. Copyright © 1996 Artists Rights Society (ARS), New York/SPADEM, Paris; *bottom* Austin History Center, Austin Public Library; **173** MGM, William Haines/The Everett Collection; **174** *top* 1935, Warner Brothers/The Kobal Collection; *center left, bottom left* The Everett Collection; **176** *top* *Jimmy Valentine*, Learning Corp. of America. Distributed by Coronet/MTI Films, St. Louis, Missouri; *bottom* RMIP/Richard Haynes; **177** *top* Greensboro Historical Museum, Inc.; *center left* Modern Library/Random House; *bottom left* A Signet Classic/The Penguin Group; **184** Painting Copyright © 1999 Brad Holland; **186, 187** School Division, Houghton Mifflin Company.

Unit Two

191 *left to right* Little, Brown and Company; McFarland & Company, Inc. Publishers; Beacon Press; Penguin Putnam; **195** RMIP/Richard Haynes; **200** The Granger Collection, New York; **205** Copyright © Nancy Crampton; **218** Copyright © Coppelia Kahn; **220, 221** Copyright © City Year, Boston; **223** *top right* Corbis-Bettmann; *bottom left* AP/Wide World Photos; **232** Copyright © 1988 Chicago Tribune Co., all rights reserved; **234, 235** RMIP/Richard Haynes; **236** Copyright © Andrew Onyemere/Photonica; **237** *left* Manuelle Toussaint/Liaison Agency; *right* Georges Merillon/Liaison Agency; **245** *left to right* Heinemann Publishers; Copyright © Plays, Inc.; Movie Still Archives; Copyright © 1997 Playbill Incorporated; **247** Movie Still Archives; **248** Detail of *Rush Hour* (1983), George Segal. Courtesy Sidney Janis Gallery, New York. Copyright © George Segal/Licensed by VAGA, New York; **249** RMIP/Richard Haynes; **250** Photofest; **251** Movie Still Archives; **255** Photofest; **261** Movie Still Archives; **267, 271, 273** Photofest; **277** Culver Pictures; **279** Photo by Sharon Hoogstraten; **285** Detail of *Retrato de muchacha* [Portrait of a girl] (1929), Frida Kahlo. Oil on canvas, 46½″ × 31½″. Collection of the Dolores Olmedo Patiño Foundation, Museo Frida Kahlo, Mexico City; **287** *left* Baseball Hall of Fame Library, Cooperstown, New York; *center, Wipe Out Discrimination* (1949), Milton Ackoff. Offset lithograph, printed in color, 43⅞″ × 32¼″. The Museum of Modern Art, New York, gift of the Congress of Industrial Organizations. Photography copyright © 1998 The Museum of Modern Art, New York; *right* Archive Photos/PNI; **288–289** *background* Photo by Sharon Hoogstraten; **298** Courtesy of The Chicago Defender; **299** *top* Detail of *Baseball Scene of Batter, Catcher, and Umpire* (1915), Joseph Christian Leyendecker. Photo courtesy of the Archives of the American Illustrators

Gallery, New York. Copyright © 1995 ARTShows and Products of Holderness 03245; **304** *left* Harvard University Archives; *right* Courtesy of C.T.I./GLAD Productions, Inc.; **305** Copyright © Peter Roger/Life Magazine; **306, 307, 308** AP/Wide World Photos; **310** *left, The Grasshopper and the Ant*, Charles Henry Bennett (1828–1867). Pen and ink drawing. The Granger Collection, New York; *right, Victorian Parlor II* (1945), Horace Pippin. Oil on canvas, 25¼" × 30". The Metropolitan Museum of Art, Arthur Hoppock Hearn Fund, 1958 (58.26); **311** Copyright © Tony Freeman/PhotoEdit; **314** The Granger Collection, New York; **320** Copyright © Alison Shaw; **322** RMIP International; **330** Illustration by Bernie Fuchs; **332, 333** School Division, Houghton Mifflin Company.

Unit Three

344 *Retrato de muchacha* [Portrait of a girl] (1929), Frida Kahlo. Oil on canvas, 46½" × 31½". Collection of the Dolores Olmedo Patiño Foundation, Museo Frida Kahlo, Mexico City; **345** *Portrait of Prince Eristoff* (1925), Tamara de Lempicka. Private collection, New York. Copyright © 1996 Artists Rights Society (ARS), New York/SPADEM, Paris; **346** *Idle Hands* (1935), Will Barnett. Oil on canvas, 36" × 26". Licensed by VAGA, New York; **347** RMIP/Richard Haynes; **348** *top*, **352** Details of *Autobiographical* (1954), Moses Soyer. Courtesy of ACA Galleries, New York; **360** AP/Wide World Photos; **361, 362** Copyright © G. Bliss/Masterfile; **368, 371** *background* Photos by Sharon Hoogstraten; **371** *inset* Copyright © G. Bliss/Masterfile; **373** *El abrazo* [The hug] (1966), Fletcher Martin. Acrylic on paper, 22" × 17". Private collection; **374** Eugenio Castro; **375, 378** Artichoke. Copyright © Jeff Venier/Landry Design; Illustration Copyright © Jeff Venier/Landry Design; **380** Archive France/Archive Photos; **381** *top* Detail of *Backyards, Greenwich Village* (1914), John Sloan. Oil on canvas, 26" × 32". Photo by Geoffrey Clements. Copyright © 1999 Whitney Museum of American Art; *bottom* Corbis/Nathan Benn; **389** Detail of *Backyards, Greenwich Village* (1914), John Sloan. Oil on canvas, 26" × 32". Photo by Geoffrey Clements. Copyright © 1999 Whitney Museum of American Art; **390** Rollie McKenna; **392** Enzo and Paolo Ragazzi/Corbis; **395** *left* UPI/Bettmann; *right* AP/Wide World Photos; **396, 397** Copyright © Ted Wood Photography; **402** *right* The Granger Collection, New York; **409** Copyright © Frank Capri/Saga/Archive Photos; **410** *left, Skater* (1956), Giacomo Manzu. Bronze, 80" × 23" × 17⅝". Hirshhorn Museum and Sculpture Garden, Smithsonian Institution, Washington, D.C. Gift of Joseph H. Hirshhorn, 1966. Photo by Lee Stalsworth; *bottom* Detail of illustration by Kam Mak; **411** Copyright © Archive Photos; **412** *left, Le jardin potager, Yerres* [The kitchen garden, Yerres] (1875–77), Gustave Caillebotte. Private collection; *right* Illustration by Ruth Sanderson; **413** Illustration by Paul Rátz de Tagyos; **414** RMIP/Richard Haynes; **415** *top, Rush Hour* (1983), George Segal. Courtesy Sidney Janis Gallery, New York. Copyright © George Segal/Licensed by VAGA, New York; **416** *top* Copyright © Archive Photos; **417, 424** Illustration by Paul Rátz de Tagyos; **428** Copyright © Archive Photos; **430** Detail of *Rush Hour* (1983), George Segal. Courtesy Sidney Janis Gallery, New York. Copyright © George Segal/Licensed by VAGA, New York; **431** UPI/Bettmann; **432** *top right* Copyright © 1995 Hank Morgan; *bottom left, bottom center, bottom right* Copyright © Sam Odgen; **437** AP/Wide World Photos; **438** *top* Detail of illustration by Ruth Sanderson; *bottom* Clay Perry/Corbis; **439, 441, 445, 452, 454** Photos by Sharon Hoogstraten; **460** Copyright © Shel Silverstein; **462** *left* Stock Montage; *right* AP/Wide World Photos; **463** NASA; **464–465** Copyright © John Lurner/Tony Stone Images; **466** Science Source/Photo Researchers, Inc./ NASA; **469** AP/Wide World Photos;

470–471 Reprinted courtesy of the Boston Globe; 474–477 *top background* background Kris Coppieters/SuperStock; 474 *top* Copyright © Frank Capri/Saga/Archive Photos; *center left* Copyright © 2001 by Universal City Studio, Inc. Courtesy of Universal Studios Publishing Rights. All rights reserved; *bottom middle* Reprinted by permission of Don Congdon Associates, Inc.; *bottom right* Corbis-Bettmann; 475 *center right* Reprinted by permission of Don Congdon Associates, Inc.; *bottom left* NASA; *bottom right* Courtesy of Alliance Atlantis Communications Inc.; 476–477 *bottom background* Archive Photos; 476 Everett Collection, Inc.; 477 *left* AP/Wide World Photos; *center right, left to right* From *1984* by George Orwell. Reprinted by permission of Penguin Books; From *Brave New World* by Aldous Huxley. Copyright © 1932 by Harper & Brothers. Used by permission of HarperCollins; From *Cat's Cradle* by Kurt Vonnegut, Jr. Reprinted by permission of Dell Publishing, a division of Bantam Doubleday Dell Publishing Group, Inc.; From *Fahrenheit 451* by Ray Bradbury. Reprinted by permission of Ballantine Books, a division of Random House, Inc.; 492 Detail of painting by Nancy Ekholm Burkert; 502–505 *top background* Kris Coppieters/SuperStock; 502 *inset* Copyright © Frank Capri/Saga/Archive Photos; 504 *top* AP/Wide World Photos; *left* From *The Martian Chronicles* by Ray Bradbury. Copyright 1946, 1948, 1950, 1958 by Ray Bradbury. Copyright renewed 1977 by Ray Bradbury. Used by permission of Bantam Books, a division of Random House, Inc.; *right* From *Fahrenheit 451* by Ray Bradbury. Reprinted by permission of Ballantine Books, a division of Random House, Inc.; 505 *bottom, left to right* From *Something Wicked This Way Comes* by Ray Bradbury. Copyright © 1962, 1977 by Ray Bradbury. Used by permission of Avon Books, a division of The Hearst Corporation; From *A Medicine for Melancholy* by Ray Bradbury. Copyright © 1990 by Ray Bradbury. Cover illustration by Tim O'Brien. Used by permission of Avon Books, a division of The Hearst Corporation; From *Vintage Bradbury* by Ray Bradbury. Reprinted by permission of Vintage Books; From *The Toynbee Convector* by Ray Bradbury. Reprinted by permission of Ballantine Books, a division of Random House, Inc.; 512 Copyright © Kamil Vojnar/Photonica; 514, 515 School Division, Houghton Mifflin Company.

Unit Four

516 Photography by Laurie Rubin; 519 Illustration by Stephen Peringer; 521 RMIP/Richard Haynes; 522 Detail of *Girl at Piano* (1966), Will Barnet. Oil on canvas, 64″ × 39″. Private collection. Copyright © 1995 Will Barnet/ Licensed by VAGA, New York; 523 Photo by Sharon Hoogstraten; 532 Copyright © Jerry Bauer; 534, 535, 536–545 *top*, 539, 545 Photos by Sharon Hoogstraten; 548 Copyright © Sophie Baker; 549–552 *top* Copyright © PhotoDisc; 549 *center* Copyright © FoodPix; *bottom* Danny Lehman/Corbis; 550 *top left* North Carolina Museum of Art/Corbis; *center* Historical Picture Archive/Corbis; *bottom right* Alastair Shay, Papilio/Corbis; 551 *center* Gianni Dagli Orti/Corbis; *bottom left* Copyright © David Young-Wolfe/PhotoEdit; *bottom right* Mary Evans Picture Library; 552 *bottom right* Copyright © Richard Hutchings/PhotoEdit; 553 *top* Detail of lithograph with hand coloring, Honoré Daumier. Courtesy of the Boston Public Library, Print Department; *bottom* Sovfoto; 554–555 *border* Copyright © PhotoDisc; 562 Detail of lithograph with hand coloring, Honoré Daumier. Courtesy of the Boston Public Library, Print Department; 563 Bernard Gotfryd/Archive Photos; 564 *background* Copyright © Adam Jones/Natural Selection; *bottom left* From a collection of paste jewelry (18th century), French and English. Cameo Corner, London/Bridgeman Art Library, London/New York; *top right, Turpin's Flight*

Through Edmonton, George Cruikshank. Private collection/Bridgeman Art Library, London/New York; *bottom right, The Escort*, Robert Alexander Hillingford. John Noott Galleries, Broadway, Worcestershire, U.K./Bridgeman Art Library, London/New York; **565, 567, 569** *background* Photo by Sharon Hoogstraten; **571** *top* Detail of illustration by Charles Mikolaycak. Copyright © 1995 Carole Kismaric Mikolaycak; *bottom* The Granger Collection, New York; **573** Courtesy of the author; **575** *left* Photofest; *right* Movie Still Archives; **576–577** UPI/Corbis-Bettmann; **578** Courtesy of the author; **579–581** RMIP/Richard Haynes; **586** *left to right* Detail of painting by Jan Wahlin; Illustration by Hugh Harrison; *Hermit* (1888), Mikhail Vasilievich Nesterov. Oil on canvas, 91 cm × 84 cm. The State Russian Museum, St. Petersburg, Russia; RMIP/Richard Haynes; **587** Details of *Autobiographical* (1954), Moses Soyer. Courtesy of ACA Galleries, New York; **588** Austin History Center, Austin Public Library; **589** Illustrations by Meg Kelleher Aubrey; **590** RMIP/Richard Haynes; **591** *top* Detail of *Letters* (1992), Kim English. Oil, 17″ × 18″. Private collection; *bottom* Kiwi Studios; **600** Courtesy of Arte Público Press; **601** *top* Detail of illustration by Meg Kelleher Aubrey; **602** *background* Cupak/Martius/ H. Armstrong Roberts; **616** Rick Janson; **617–619** Richard Nowitz/National Geographic Society Image Collection; **620** Bob Sacha; **621** *background* UPI/Corbis-Bettmann; *center right* Underwood & Underwood/Corbis; *bottom right* Corbis-Bettmann; **622** Corbis-Bettmann; **625** AP/Wide World Photos; **627** Reprinted by permission of Don Congdon and Associates, Inc. Copyright © 1982 by Russell Baker; **628** Copyright © Archive Photos/PNI; **630** Copyright © Yvonne Hemsey/Liaison Agency; **635** *bottom* The Granger Collection, New York; **642** Photography by Laurie Rubin; **644, 645** School Division, Houghton Mifflin Company.

Unit Five

652 Copyright © 1996 Ann Giordano/ Photonica; **653–654** *background* MicroArt; **654** Frances King Collection/Sacramento (California) Archives and Museum Collection Center; **655** Copyright © Farrell Grehan/Photo Researchers, Inc.; **656** Corbis-Bettmann; **657** RMIP/Richard Haynes; **658** From *Inside the Titanic*, a Loewe/Madison Press Book. Illustrations by Ken Marschall copyright © 1997; **659** Courtesy of The *Titanic* Historical Society, Inc. Photo by Sharon Hoogstraten; **660** Corbis-Bettmann; **662–663** From *Exploring the* Titanic. Copyright © 1988 by Robert D. Ballard, a Madison Press Book; **664** Corbis-Bettmann; **665** Photos by Sharon Hoogstraten; **667, 668** *top middle* Corbis-Bettman; **668** *top right, bottom left,* **669** *top,* **670** Photos by Sharon Hoogstraten; **673** From *A Night to Remember*. Courtesy of Carlton International Media Ltd.; **674** Barbara Nitke; **675–678** Photos courtesy of the Texas Historical Commission; **679** *top,* **686** Detail of illustration by Wendell Minor. Reprinted from *Red Fox Running* by Eve Bunting. Copyright © 1993 by Wendell Minor, published by Clarion Books; **691** Detail of *Albert's Son* (1959), Andrew Wyeth. Tempera on board, 74 cm × 61.5 cm. The National Museum of Contemporary Art, Oslo, Norway. Photo by Jacques Lathion, Nasjonalgalleriet; **692** Farrar, Straus & Giroux; **694–695** *background* Stock Boston; *foreground* Ralph Shaw Collection/ Sacramento (California) Archives and Museum Collection Center; **695** *foreground* Frances King Collection/Sacramento (California) Archives and Museum Collection Center; **697** *background* Stock Boston; *foreground* Brown Brothers; **698** University of Notre Dame Press; **705** Ron Rovtar; **706** *left* Oxford Book of Historical Stories, Oxford University Press; *bottom* From *I, Juan de Pareja*. Used by permission of HarperCollins Canada Ltd.; *right* From *Dragonwings*. Used by permission of Harper & Row;

708 RMIP/Richard Haynes; 709 Detail of black-figure stamnos (about *525–520* B.C.), Group of Louvre, Greek. Tampa (Florida) Museum of Art, Joseph Veach Noble Collection, 86.34; 710 *background*, Photo by Sharon Hoogstraten; 710 *foreground* Photos by Maria Daniels; 712 Photos by Sharon Hoogstraten; 714 Photo by Maria Daniels; 717 *bottom left*, 719, 720 Photo by Sharon Hoogstraten; 721 Photo by Maria Daniels; 722–724 Photo by Sharon Hoogstraten; 725 Michael Bennett. Courtesy of the Perseus Project (www.perseus.tufts.edu); 728 AP/Wide World Photos; 731 Corbis-Bettmann; 732 *background* AP/Wide World Photos; *left* Copyright © Selwyn Tait/Black Star/PNI; *right* Copyright © A. Ramey/Stock Boston/PNI; 739 AP/Wide World Photos; 741 Kevin R. Morris/Corbis; 744 Barbara Savage Cheresh; 746 *top, center left, bottom middle* Photos copyright © 1999. Used by permission of Virginia Hamilton; *bottom right* Corbis-Bettmann; 747 *center right* Photo copyright © 1999. Used by permission of Virginia Hamilton; 748 Jim Callaway Photography; 749 Photo copyright © 1999. Used by permission of Virginia Hamilton; *bottom left* From *The House of Dries Drear*. Used by permission of Simon & Schuster; *bottom middle* UPI/Corbis-Bettmann; 751 *background* Courtesy of The Bostonian Society/Old State House; *foreground*, *The Boston Slave Riot, and Trial of Anthony Burns*. Boston: Fetridge and Company, 1854. Courtesy of the Huntington Library, San Marino, California; 752 Stock Montage; 754 From *History of Harvard Law School*, vol. 2, by Charles Warren; 756 Corbis-Bettmann; 759 From *Men of Mark* by Rev. William J. Simmons; 761, 764 Corbis-Bettmann; 765 Courtesy of the Massachusetts Historical Society; 767 From *The People Could Fly* by Virginia Hamilton. Detail of illustration by Leo and Diane Dillon. Illustrations copyright © 1985 Leo and Diane Dillon. Reprinted by permission of Alfred A. Knopf, Inc.; 774–775 *top background* Earth Scenes/Copyright © Peter Weimann; 774 Photo copyright © 1999. Used by permission of Virginia Hamilton; 775 Copyright © C. Bradley Simmons/Bruce Coleman, Inc.; 776 Photos copyright © 1999. Used by permission of Virginia Hamilton; 777 RMIP/ Richard Haynes; 778 *top* Photo copyright © 1999. Used by permission of Virginia Hamilton; *bottom left* School Division, Houghton Mifflin Company; *bottom right* From *The Planet of Junior Brown*. Used by permission of Simon & Schuster; 779 *bottom left* From *M.C. Higgins, the Great*. Used by permission of Simon & Schuster; *bottom middle* From *Justice and Her Brothers*. Used by permission of Scholastic Inc.; *bottom right* From *Her Stories*. Used by permission of Scholastic Inc.; 788 Copyright © 1996 Ann Giordano/Photonica; 790, 791 School Division, Houghton Mifflin Company.

Unit Six

792–793 *background map* John Sandford; 793,794 Larry Cameron; 795 Richard Waldrep; 796–799 *background maps* John Sandford; 796 *center left* Tleson (potter), Greek (about 550 B.C.). The Toledo (Ohio) Museum of Art. Purchased with funds from the Libbey Endowment. Gift of Edward Drummond Libbey; *center right* The Bettmann Archive; *bottom* Photo by Carl Purcell; 797 *top left* The Granger Collection, New York; *top center* Odyssey/Frerck/ Chicago; *top right* Copyright © Andre Jenny/Stock South/PNI; *middle left* The Bettmann Archive; *center* Copyright © Tom Wagner/Odyssey/Chicago; *middle right* Copyright © Charlotte Kahler; *bottom* La Casa del Libro, San Juan, Puerto Rico; 798 From *Prometheus and the Story of Fire* by I. M. Richardson. Detail of an illustration by Robert Baxter. Copyright © 1983 Troll Associates. Reprinted with permission of the publisher; 799 Detail of *Ariadne at Naxos* (1877), Evelyn de Morgan. The De Morgan Foundation, London/Bridgeman Art

Library, London/New York; **800** *background* Copyright © 1994 Randy Faris/Westlight; *foreground* From *Prometheus and the Story of Fire* by I. M. Richardson. Illustration by Robert Baxter. Copyright © 1983 Troll Associates. Reprinted with permission of the publisher; **804** *page background* Copyright © PhotoDisc; *title background* MicroArt; **812–813** *background map* John Sandford; **812** Detail of *Portrait of a Gentleman* (16th century), Bartolomeo Veneto. Galleria Nazionale d'Arte Antica, Rome/Canali PhotoBank, Milan (Italy)/SuperStock; **813** Detail of *Beggars and Street Characters* (1516), Zhou Chen. Album leaves, ink and colors on paper. Honolulu (Hawaii) Academy of Arts, gift of Mrs. Carter Galt, 1956 (2239.1); **819** Photo by K. Yep; **827** Culver Pictures; **828, 829** Photos by Sharon Hoogstraten; **836–837** *background map* John Sandford; **837** The Granger Collection, New York; **839, 840** *background* MicroArt; **848–849** *background map* John Sandford; **848** Detail of an illustration by Byron Gin; **849** Detail of *Mujer con pescados* [Woman with fish] (1980), Francisco Zúñiga. Lithograph, $21\frac{7}{8}'' \times 29\frac{1}{2}''$, edition of 135. Courtesy of Brewster Gallery, New York; **853** *background* Photo by Sharon Hoogstraten; **860** Mario Longoria; **861** Illustration by Byron Gin; **863** Courtesy of the Barker Texas History Center, University of Texas; **864** Photo by Sharon Hoogstraten; **866–867** *background map* John Sandford; **866** From *Samburu* by Nigel Pavitt. Copyright © 1992 Nigel Pavitt, reprinted by permission of Henry Holt and Co., Inc.; **867** *bottom*, **871, 873, 874** Courtesy of Adrienne McGrath. Photo by Sharon Hoogstraten; **875** Courtesy of Norma J. Livo; **885** RMIP/Richard Haynes.

Sandy Mattox, Coppell Middle School North, Coppell Independent School District

Adrienne Myers, Foster Middle School, Longview Independent School District

Pam Potts, Clute Intermediate School, Brazosport Independent School District

Frank Westermann, Jackson Middle School, North East Independent School District

Bessie Wilson, Greiner Middle School, Dallas Independent School District

CALIFORNIA

Steve Bass, 8th Grade Team Leader, Meadowbrook Middle School, Ponway Unified School District

Cathy Blanchfield, Sequoia Middle School, Fresno Unified School District

Cynthia Brickey, 8th Grade Academic Block Teacher, Kastner Intermediate School, Clovis Unified School District

Karen Buxton, English Department Chairperson, Winston Churchill Middle School, San Juan School District

Sharon Cook, Independent Consultant, Fresno Unified School District

Bonnie Garrett, Davis Middle School, Compton School District

Sally Jackson, Madrona Middle School, Torrance Unified School District

Sharon Kerson, Los Angeles Center for Enriched Studies, Los Angeles Unified School District

Gail Kidd, Center Middle School, Azusa School District

Corey Lay, ESL Department Chairperson, Chester Nimitz Middle School, Los Angeles Unified School District

Myra LeBendig, Forshay Learning Center, Los Angeles Unified School District

Dan Manske, Elmhurst Middle School, Oakland Unified School District

Joe Olague, Language Arts Department Chairperson, Alder Middle School, Fontana School District

Pat Salo, 6th Grade Village Leader, Hidden Valley Middle School, Escondido Elementary School District

FLORIDA

Judi Briant, English Department Chairperson, Armwood High School, Hillsborough County School District

Beth Johnson, Polk County English Supervisor, Polk County School District

Sharon Johnston, Learning Resource Specialist, Evans High School, Orange County School District

Eileen Jones, English Department Chairperson, Spanish River High School, Palm Beach County School District

Jan McClure, Winter Park High School Orange County School District

Wanza Murray, English Department Chairperson (retired), Vero Beach Senior High School, Indian River City School District

Shirley Nichols, Language Arts Curriculum Specialist Supervisor, Marion County School District

Debbie Nostro, Ocoee Middle School, Orange County School District

Barbara Quinaz, Assistant Principal, Horace Mann Middle School, Dade County School District

OHIO

Joseph Bako, English Department Chairperson, Carl Shuler Middle School, Cleveland City School District

Deb Delisle, Language Arts Department Chairperson, Ballard Brady Middle School, Orange School District

Ellen Geisler, English/Language Arts Department Chairperson, Mentor Senior High School, Mentor School District

Dr. Mary Gove, English Department Chairperson, Shaw High School, East Cleveland School District

Loraine Hammack, Executive Teacher of the English Department, Beachwood High School, Beachwood City School District

Sue Nelson, Shaw High School, East Cleveland School District

Mary Jane Reed, English Department Chairperson, Solon High School, Solon City School District

Nancy Strauch, English Department Chairperson, Nordonia High School, Nordonia Hills City School District

Ruth Vukovich, Hubbard High School, Hubbard Exempted Village School District

Manuscript Reviewers *(continued)*

Linda C. Dahl, National Mine Middle School, Ishpeming, Michigan

Shirley Herzog, Reading Department Coordinator, Fairfield Middle School, Fairfield, Ohio

Maryann Lyons, Literacy Specialist, Mentor teacher, San Francisco Unified School District, San Francisco, California

Karis MacDonnell, Ed.D., Dario Middle School, Miami, Florida

Bonnie J. Mansell, Downey Adult School, Downey, California

Martha Mitchell, Memorial Middle School, Orlando, Florida

Nancy Nachman, Landmark High School, Jacksonville, Florida

Karen Williams Perry, English Department Chairperson, Kennedy Jr. High School, Lisle, Illinois

Julia Pferdehirt, free-lance writer, former Special Education teacher, Middleton, Wisconsin

Phyllis Stewart Rude, English Department Head, Mears Jr./Sr. High School, Anchorage, Alaska

Leo Schubert, Bettendorf Middle School, Bettendorf, Iowa

Gertrude H. Vannoy, Curriculum Liaison Specialist, Gifted and Horizon teacher, Meany Middle School, Seattle, Washington

Richard Wagner, Language Arts Curriculum Coordinator, Paradise Valley School District, Phoenix, Arizona

Stephen J. Zadravec, Newmarket Jr./Sr. High School, Newmarket, New Hampshire